ANNIVERSARIO
1967 - 2017

Consorzio del Vino
Brunello di Montalcino®

BRUNELLO

Naviga nei nostri vigneti
Scarica l'applicazione!

consorziobrunellodimontalcino.it

A GUIDE TO THE LEADING OVER 1200 COMPANIES PRODUCING FOODSTUFFS IN ITALY

An indispensable tool for foodies
but even more so for industry insiders
promoting the best of Made-in-Italy worldwide

— TENUTA DI —
LILLIANO

www.lilliano.it

Produttori *Vini* Manduria

MAESTRI IN PRIMITIVO

1932

Gambero Rosso

2018

Italian Wines

VINI D'ITALIA 2018
GAMBERO ROSSO®

Senior Editors
Gianni Fabrizio
Eleonora Guerini
Marco Sabellico

Special Contributors
Antonio Boco
Giuseppe Carrus
Paolo De Cristofaro
Lorenzo Ruggeri
Paolo Zaccaria

Regionali Coordinators
Nino Aiello
Nicola Frasson
Massimo Lanza
Gianni Ottogalli
Nereo Pederzolli
Pierpaolo Rastelli

Technical directors
William Pregentelli

Contributors
Stefania Annese
Francesco Beghi
Sergio Bonanno
Michele Bressan
Pasquale Buffa
Giorgio Buloncelli
Dionisio Castello
Stefano Ghisletta
Giacomo Mojoli
Elena Mozzini
Franco Pallini
William Pregentelli
Leonardo Romanelli
Giulia Sampognaro
Herbert Taschler
Cinzia Tosetti

Other Contributors
Enrico Battistella
Leah Bickford
Lucio Chiesa
Palmiro Ciccarelli
Mario Demattè
Maurizio Fava
Sylvie Franceschini
Michele Muraro
Nicola Piccinini
Alessio Pietrobattista
Andrea Polidoro
Massimo Ponzanelli
Flavia Previtera
Mirko Rainer
Carlo Ravanello
Riccardo Rossetti
Maurizio Rossi
Simona Silvestri
Massimiliano Trenti
Liliana Zanellato
Monia Zanette
Danilo Zannella

Editorial Secretary
Giulia Sciortino

Layout
Marina Proietti

Gambero Rosso S.p.A.
via Ottavio Gasparri, 13/17 - 00152 Roma
tel. 06/551121 - fax 06/55112260
www.gamberorosso.it
email: gambero@gamberorosso.it

Managing Editor Books
Laura Mantovano

Graphics
Chiara Buosi

Commercial Director
Francesco Dammicco

Production
Angelica Sorbara

**Editorial product distribution
and sales manager**
Eugenia Durando

Translation Coordinator and Revisors
Jordan De Maio
Jane Upchurch

Publisher
Gr Usa Corp c/o Csc Services of Nevada Inc
2215-B RENAISSANCE DR
Las Vegas , NV 89119
email: gamberousa@aol.com

Distribution
USA and Canada
by Antique Collector's Club, Eastworks, 116
Pleasant St #18, Easthampton, MA 010207, USA;
UK and Australia by Antique Collector's Club Ltd
Sandy Lane, Old Martlesham, Woodbridge,
Suffolk IP12 4SD - United Kingdom

The final edit of Italian Wines was completed on
5 September 2017

ISBN 9781890142193

Printed in Italy for
Gambero Rosso Holding S.p.A.
in October 2017 by
OMNIMEDIA S.r.l.
Piazza della Ferriera, 1
00015 Monterotondo Scalo (Roma)

SUMMARY

REGIONS

INDEXES

THE GUIDE

Having turned a corner last year with our 30th anniversary edition, here we are back with our 31st. This year, after our tastings had concluded, we asked ourselves a question: why, in the age of apps, smartphones and tablets, do we continue printing a guide? We'll take this opportunity to remind our readers that Gambero Rosso has a digital TV channel, with programs that, today, are also broadcast in Switzerland and China. And as our web TV is translated into English, it's accessible in every corner of the globe. Gambero Rosso's content, Italian Wines included, is also available on social networks and app stores; indeed, the third millennium finds us enthusiastic about our prospects. Though we live in a fluid society, where fluid communication reigns, we continue to make an apparently conservative choice by continuing to print a book that's the size and weight of a small brick. Why? Because there are professionals and wine lovers in Italy and the world who continue to ask for it, demonstrating that where there's quality, paper still has an important role to play, even in the multimedia age. But the real driving force behind this, our 31st edition, lies even deeper. For 30 years we have been telling the stories of Italy's top producers, painstakingly annotating and analyzing the characteristics of their best wines. Our work is a kind of chronology, year after year, of the facts and events in the field. These 31 bricks, in our mind, constitute a single, larger history, that of Italian winemaking going back to the 1980s, an area that has thousands more stories, grapes and wines to be documented. We don't limit ourselves to pure enological journalism, but ask ourselves why certain things are happening, what tendencies, in terms of taste, technology and resources, are driving such an important sector of our agricultural economy. Supported by our three decades of experience, we're trying to intercept those currents driving and influencing the sector, so as to shed light on the future in a way that can be useful to wine lovers and professionals. This is to say, piece by piece, we are telling the history of Italian wine. It's a tale that Italians and the world enjoy hearing, such that the guide is now being successfully translated into German, English, Chinese and Japanese, pointing up the fact that our effort to interpret a phenomenon as complex as Italian wine is credible, authoritative even, for the rest of the planet. And so whoever has the guide in hand knows that it's the result of an experienced, tested, passionate group of tasters who've traveled Italy (as well as Ticino this year) trying more than 45,000 wines, interviewing producers and visiting wineries. The wine lover can focus on the introductions to each region, where we interpret the tendencies of the various territories and their appellations, or on the individual profiles. Italian Wines isn't just a collection of scores and rankings. It is, for us, much more, just as we hope it is for our readers.

Italian wines has become a passport that top Italian wineries can exhibit during the almost 50 events that we organize in 30 capitals around the world. By promoting knowledge of Italy's wines and its top players, these are initiatives that reinforce the image and exportation of Italian wines, both to those countries that are already drinking it and to new markets where we find large populations and growth in consumption. Indeed, these represent opportunities that are increasingly important for the sector.

Our special awards are a condensed version of our vision of the world of wine and a summary of the work carried out by our great team of tasters. The 'Red of the Year' award goes to Ar.Pe.Pe.'s 2017 Valtellina Superiore Sassella Rocce Rosse Riserva, a truly great wine. The 'White of the Year' is I Favati's 2016 Fiano di Avellino Pietramara, a wine of elegance and extraordinary balance. The 'Sparkling Wine of the Year' goes to an artisanal cuvée blend made by a family of passionate winemakers, the Marcalberto Extra Brut Millesimo2mila12, a dense, dynamic, potent and sophisticated Metodo Classico. The 'Sweet Wine of the Year' is Caravaglio's 2016 Malvasia delle Lipari Passito, a deeply Mediterranean wine that's opening up new and modern perspectives for 'meditation wines'. The 'Winery of the Year' for 2018 is the Boscaini family's Masi, which deserves credit for having brought international acclaim (and more) to Amarone and Verona's wines. The 'Best Value for Money' award goes to the delectable 2016 Romagna Sangiovese Superiore Sigismondo, the child of a special project by Le Rocche Malatestiane. The 'Emerging Winery of the Year' award goes to an enthusiastic group of Calabrian producers, Spiriti Ebbri. Our 'Grower of the Year' is Stefano Amerighi, a man who's relationship with the land runs deep. The award for 'Sustainable Viticulture' goes to the Lunelli family's Ferrari, who have for years worked wholeheartedly on behalf of these principles. We close our review by making note of a new initiative, the 'Solidariety Award', which goes to those individuals or wineries who've demonstrated an exceptional social commitment. This year, Elisabetta Fagiuoli, from the Tuscan winery Montenidoli, fully deserves it. She has created a foundation that will provide homes to struggling elderly and young people from varying backgrounds. You'll also find our Tre Bicchieri Verdi in green, those wines made by certified organic or biodynamic producers (there are some 99 this year). Finally, we also make note of those wines awarded that can be bought for €15 or less (there are 110 in all).

We would like to thank the Bolzano EOS Chamber of Commerce, the coordinators of the Strade del Vino e dell'Olio dell'Umbria, the Arezzo Strada dei Vini wine trail, the Istituto Marchigiano di Tutela Vini di Jesi (IMT) and VINEA of Offida, ERSA Friuli Venezia Giulia, Ente vini Bresciani, Carcare (Savona) municipal council, the Comitato Grandi Cru della Costa Toscana, Assovini Sicilia, the E. del Giudice Centro per l'Innovazione in Marsala. Also, the following protection consortiums: Gavi, Barolo, Barbaresco, Alba, Langhe and Roero, Vini dei Colli Tortonesi, Nebbiolo dell'Alto Piemonte, Caluso, Carema and Canavese, Valtellina, Oltrepò Pavese, Franciacorta, Valcalepio, Vini Mantovani, Lugana, Valtenesi, Conegliano Valdobbiadene, Soave, Consorzio Vini Trentini, as well as Bolgheri, Brunello di Montalcino, Chianti Classico, San Gimignano, Montepulciano, Chianti Rufina, Morellino in Scansano, Vini della Maremma Toscana, Montecucco, Carmignano, Orvieto, Montefalco, the Consorzio di Tutela dei Vini Piceni and, finally, the Consorzio di Tutela dei vini DOC Sicilia.

We'd also like to thank the regional wine cellars of Cassino Po in Lombardy, Roero and Nizza Monferrato, Canelli and Astesana, the Cantina Comunale I Söri in Diano d'Alba, the Bottega del Vino in Dogliani, Carpe Diem restaurant in Montaione, the Calidario in Venturina, Tenuta Il Cicalino in Massa Marittima, the Città del Gusto in Rome and Naples, the regional wine cellar of Basilicata in Venosa, Caneva in Mogliano Veneto, Da Nando restaurant in Mortegliano, Casa e Putia restaurant in Messina and, for Ticino, the Atenaeo del Vino in Mendrisio.

Finally, a sincere thanks to all our team, who showed true devotion in helping us realize Italian Wines, from local tastings to drafting the profiles, all the way to the editing of the volume itself, and to all those we've worked with down through the years. A special thanks to Danilo Zannella, director of all our tastings.

Gianni Fabrizio, Eleonora Guerini, Marco Sabellico

TRE BICCHIERI 2018

VALLE D'AOSTA

Valle d'Aosta Chambave Moscato Passito Prieuré '15	La Crotta di Vegneron	27
Valle d'Aosta Chambave Muscat Flétri '15	La Vrille	31
Valle d'Aosta Cornalin '16	Rosset Terroir	31
Valle d'Aosta Nebbiolo Sommet '15	Les Crêtes	27
Valle d'Aosta Petite Arvine '16	Elio Ottin	30
Valle d'Aosta Pinot Gris '16	Lo Triolet	29

PIEDMONT

Alta Langa Brut Zero Nature Sboccatura Tardiva '11	Enrico Serafino	163
Barbaresco Albesani S. Stefano Ris. '12	Castello di Neive	76
Barbaresco Crichët Pajé '08	Roagna	150
Barbaresco Maria di Brün '13	Ca' Rome'	63
Barbaresco Martinenga Camp Gros Ris. '12	Tenute Cisa Asinari dei Marchesi di Grésy	81
Barbaresco Montaribaldi '13	Fiorenzo Nada	126
Barbaresco Nervo '14	Rizzi	149
Barbaresco Ovello '13	Cantina del Pino	65
Barbaresco Ovello '14	Cascina Morassino	73
Barbaresco Pajoré '14	Sottimano	165
Barbaresco Rabajà '13	Bruno Rocca	151
Barbaresco Roncaglie '14	Poderi Colla	83
Barbaresco Serraboella '13	F.lli Cigliuti	81
Barbaresco Sorì Tildìn '14	Gaja	99
Barbaresco Vallegrande '14	Ca' del Baio	62
Barbera d'Asti Bricco dell'Uccellone '15	Braida	54
Barbera d'Asti Sup. Epico '15	Pico Maccario	138
Barbera d'Asti Sup. Nizza Riserva della Famiglia '09	Coppo	87
Barbera d'Asti Sup. Sant' Emiliano '15	Marchesi Incisa della Rocchetta	116
Barbera d'Asti Sup. V. La Mandorla '15	Luigi Spertino	166
Barbera del M.to Giulin '15	Giulio Accornero e Figli	36
Barolo '13	Bartolo Mascarello	118
Barolo Bricco Rocche '13	Ceretto	78
Barolo Brunate '13	Enzo Boglietti	49
Barolo Brunate '13	Giuseppe Rinaldi	148
Barolo Cerretta V. Bricco '11	Elio Altare - Cascina Nuova	39
Barolo del Comune di Barolo Essenze '13	Vite Colte	176
Barolo Falletto V. Le Rocche Ris. '11	Bruno Giacosa	102
Barolo Gabutti '13	Gabutti - Franco Boasso	98
Barolo Ginestra Ris. '09	Paolo Conterno	85
Barolo Lazzarito Ris. '11	Ettore Germano	101
Barolo Monfortino Ris. '10	Giacomo Conterno	85
Barolo Monprivato '12	Giuseppe Mascarello e Figlio	119
Barolo Monvigliero '13	F.lli Alessandria	37
Barolo Ornato '13	Pio Cesare	138
Barolo Paiagallo Casa E. di Mirafiore '13	Fontanafredda	97
Barolo Ravera Bricco Pernice '12	Elvio Cogno	82
Barolo Resa 56 '13	Brandini	54
Barolo Ris. '10	Giacomo Borgogno & Figli	51
Barolo Ris. '11	Paolo Manzone	113
Barolo Rocche dell'Annunziata Ris. '11	Paolo Scavino	160
Barolo Sarmassa V. Bricco Ris. '11	Giacomo Brezza & Figli	56
Barolo Sarmassa V. Merenda '10	Giorgio Scarzello e Figli	160

Barolo Sottocastello di Novello '12	Ca' Viola	64
Barolo V. Lazzairasco '13	Guido Porro	140
Barolo Vigna Rionda '10	Figli Luigi Oddero	130
Barolo Vigna Rionda Ester Canale Rosso '13	Giovanni Rosso	154
Barolo Vigna Rionda Ris. '11	Massolino	119
Barolo Vignarionda Arnaldo Rivera '13	Terre del Barolo	169
Barolo Villero '13	Brovia	60
Barolo Villero Ris. '09	Vietti	173
Boca '12	Le Piane	137
Bramaterra '12	Noah	130
Colli Tortonesi Timorasso Fausto '15	Vigne Marina Coppi	87
Colli Tortonesi Timorasso Ombra di Luna '15	Cascina Salicetti	74
Costa del Vento '15	Vigneti Massa	174
Dogliani Papà Celso '16	Abbona	34
Dolcetto di Ovada '15	Tacchino	168
Erbaluce di Caluso '16	Podere Macellio	111
Erbaluce di Caluso Le Chiusure '16	Benito Favaro	95
Gattinara Osso San Grato '13	Antoniolo	41
Gattinara Ris. '12	Giancarlo Travaglini	170
Gavi del Comune di Gavi GG '15	Cantina Produttori del Gavi	143
Gavi del Comune di Gavi Monterotondo '15	Villa Sparina	175
Gavi V. della Rovere Verde Ris. '15	La Mesma	120
Ghemme V. Pelizzane '11	Torraccia del Piantavigna	170
Grignolino del M.to Casalese '16	Vicara	172
Marcalberto Extra Brut Millesimo2Mila12 M. Cl. '12	Marcalberto	114
Moscato d'Asti '16	Paolo Saracco	158
Moscato d'Asti Canelli Sant'Ilario '16	Ca' d' Gal	62
Moscato d'Asti Casa di Bianca '16	Gianni Doglia	92
Nizza La V. dell'Angelo '14	Cascina La Barbatella	72
Roero Arneis Cecu d'la Biunda '16	Monchiero Carbone	122
Roero Arneis Le Rive del Bricco delle Ciliegie '16	Giovanni Almondo	39
Roero Gepin '13	Stefanino Costa	91
Roero Valmaggiore V. Audinaggio '15	Cascina Ca' Rossa	68
Ruché di Castagnole M.to Laccento '16	Montalbera	123

LIGURIA

Colli di Luni Vermentino Costa Marina '16	Ottaviano Lambruschi	205
Colli di Luni Vermentino Lunae Et. Nera '16	Cantine Lunae Bosoni	206
Colli di Luni Vermentino Sup. Fosso di Corsano '16	Terenzuola	210
Dolceacqua Beragna '16	Ka' Manciné	205
Riviera Ligure di Ponente Pigato Albium '15	Poggio dei Gorleri	209
Riviera Ligure di Ponente Pigato Bon in da Bon '16	BioVio	200
Riviera Ligure di Ponente Pigato U Baccan '15	Bruna	201

LOMBARDY

Brut Rosé	Monsupello	243
Extra Brut Farfalla	Ballabio	220
Franciacorta Nature '61 '10	Guido Berlucchi & C.	222
Franciacorta Brut '12	Lo Sparviere	254
Franciacorta Brut Arcadia '13	Lantieri de Paratico	240
Franciacorta Brut Museum Release '07	Ricci Curbastro	251
Franciacorta Brut Naturae '13	Barone Pizzini	220
Franciacorta Brut Satèn Soul '11	Contadi Castaldi	233

San Pietro di Barbozza Motus Vitae '15	Bortolomiol	352
Valdobbiadene Extra Dry Giustino B. '16	Ruggeri & C.	400
Valdobbiadene Rive di Colbertaldo Asciutto		
Vign. Giardino '16	Adami	345
Valpolicella Cl. Sup. Campo Casal Vegri '15	Ca' La Bionda	356
Valpolicella Sup. '13	Marco Mosconi	390
Valpolicella Sup. Ripasso Campo Ciotoli '15	I Campi	358

FRIULI VENEZIA GIULIA

COF Picolit '12	Livon	465
Collio Bianco '16	Colle Duga	448
Collio Bianco Fosarin '15	Ronco dei Tassi	482
Collio Bianco Giulio Locatelli Ris. '15	Tenuta di Angoris	436
Collio Friulano '16	Russiz Superiore	485
Collio Friulano '16	Schiopetto	487
Collio Pinot Bianco '16	Doro Princic	476
Collio Pinot Bianco '16	Villa Russiz	502
Collio Ribolla Gialla di Oslavia Ris. '13	Primosic	475
Collio Sauvignon '16	Tiare - Roberto Snidarcig	494
Collio Sauvignon Ronco delle Mele '16	Venica & Venica	497
FCO Bianco Identità '15	Leonardo Specogna	491
FCO Friulano Liende '16	La Viarte	497
FCO Malvasia '16	Paolo Rodaro	478
FCO Pinot Bianco Myò '16	Zorzettig	505
FCO Pinot Grigio '16	Torre Rosazza	495
FCO Sauvignon Zuc di Volpe '16	Volpe Pasini	503
Friuli Friulano No Name '16	Le Vigne di Zamò	501
Friuli Grave Pinot Bianco '16	Vigneti Le Monde	464
Friuli Isonzo Friulano I Ferretti '15	Tenuta Luisa	465
Friuli Isonzo Sauvignon Piere '15	Vie di Romans	498
Lis '15	Lis Neris	464
Malvasia '13	Damijan Podversic	474
Ograde '15	Skerk	490
Ribolla Gialla Brut '13	Eugenio Collavini	447
Vintage Tunina '15	Jermann	461

EMILIA ROMAGNA

Colli di Parma Rosso MDV '16	Monte delle Vigne	529
Colli di Rimini Cabernet Sauvignon Montepirolo '13	San Patrignano	537
Lambrusco di Modena Brut Rosé M. Cl. '13	Cantina della Volta	519
Lambrusco di Sorbara del Fondatore '16	Cleto Chiarli Tenute Agricole	522
Lambrusco di Sorbara Leclisse '16	Gianfranco Paltrinieri	532
Lambrusco di Sorbara Secco	Cantina Sociale	
Omaggio a Gino Friedmann '16	di Carpi e Sorbara	520
Lambrusco di Sorbara V. del Cristo '16	Cavicchioli	521
Reggiano Lambrusco Concerto '16	Ermete Medici & Figli	528
Reggiano Lambrusco Secco Marchese Manodori '16	Venturini Baldini	540
Romagna Albana Passito Scacco Matto '13	Fattoria Zerbina	543
Romagna Albana Secco I Croppi '16	Celli	522
Romagna Sangiovese Castrocaro		
e Terra del Sole Crete Azzurre '15	Marta Valpiani	540
Romagna Sangiovese Modigliana		
I Probi di Papiano Ris. '14	Villa Papiano	542

Romagna Sangiovese Sup. Il Sangiovese '16	Noelia Ricci	534
Romagna Sangiovese Sup. Oriolo '16	I Sabbioni	536
Romagna Sangiovese Sup. Sigismondo '16	Le Rocche Malatestiane	535

TUSCANY

Al Passo '14	Tolaini	679
Altrovino '15	Duemani	603
Ameri Governo all'Uso Toscano '15	Podere San Cristoforo	650
Baron'Ugo '13	Monteraponi	634
Bolgheri Sassicaia '14	Tenuta San Guido	666
Bolgheri Sup. Grattamacco '14	Grattamacco	615
Bolgheri Sup. Ornellaia '14	Ornellaia	641
Bolgheri Sup. Paleo '14	Le Macchiole	626
Bolgheri Sup. Sondraia '14	Poggio al Tesoro	651
Brunello di Montalcino '12	Biondi Santi - Tenuta Il Greppo	561
Brunello di Montalcino '12	Brunelli - Le Chiuse di Sotto	564
Brunello di Montalcino '12	Le Chiuse	588
Brunello di Montalcino '12	Corte dei Venti	597
Brunello di Montalcino '12	Poggio di Sotto	653
Brunello di Montalcino '12	Salvioni	664
Brunello di Montalcino Giodo '12	Giodo	613
Brunello di Montalcino Poggio al Vento Ris. '10	Tenuta Col d'Orcia	591
Brunello di Montalcino Ris. '11	Le Macioche	627
Brunello di Montalcino V. Schiena d'Asino '12	Mastrojanni	629
Carmignano Ris. '14	Tenuta Le Farnete/Cantagallo	622
Carmignano Ris. '14	Piaggia	646
Chianti Cl. '15	Badia a Coltibuono	555
Chianti Cl. '15	Borgo Salcetino	561
Chianti Cl. '14	Castello di Albola	580
Chianti Cl. '15	Castello di Monsanto	582
Chianti Cl. '15	Castello di Radda	583
Chianti Cl. '15	Castello di Volpaia	583
Chianti Cl. '14	Le Cinciole	590
Chianti Cl. '15	Le Miccine	630
Chianti Cl. Belcanto '15	Fattoria Nittardi	639
Chianti Cl. Brolio Bettino '15	Barone Ricasoli	559
Chianti Cl. Casavecchia alla Piazza '15	Buondonno Casavecchia alla Piazza	565
Chianti Cl. Gran Sel. '14	Tenuta di Lilliano	624
Chianti Cl. Gran Sel. Riserva di Fizzano '14	Rocca delle Macìe	661
Chianti Cl. Gran Sel. V. del Sorbo '14	Fontodi	608
Chianti Cl. Lamole di Lamole Et. Blu '14	Lamole di Lamole	620
Chianti Cl. Montaperto '15	Fattoria Carpineta Fontalpino	574
Chianti Cl. Novecento Ris. '14	Dievole	601
Chianti Cl. Ris. '14	Bandini - Villa Pomona	557
Chianti Cl. Ris. '14	Brancaia	563
Chianti Cl. Ris. '14	Val delle Corti	681
Chianti Cl. V. Istine '15	Istine	619
Cortona Syrah '14	Stefano Amerighi	552
I Sodi di S. Niccolò '13	Castellare di Castellina	578
Lupicaia '13	Castello del Terriccio	579
Maremma Toscana Alicante Oltreconfine '15	Bruni	564
Maremma Toscana Ciliegiolo V. Vallerana Alta '15	Antonio Camillo	568

Maremma Toscana Rocca di Frassinello '15	Rocca di Frassinello	662
Montecucco Sangiovese Poggio Lombrone Ris. '13	Colle Massari	592
Montevertine '14	Montevertine	635
Morellino di Scansano Madrechiesa Ris. '14	Terenzi	677
Morellino di Scansano Ribeo '15	Roccapesta	663
Nobile di Montepulciano '14	Tenute del Cerro	587
Nobile di Montepulciano '14	Maria Caterina Dei	601
Nobile di Montepulciano '14	Salcheto	664
Nobile di Montepulciano Asinone '14	Poliziano	656
Nobile di Montepulciano Il Nocio '13	Poderi Boscarelli	562
Oreno '15	Tenuta Sette Ponti	673
Orma '14	Orma	640
Petra Rosso '14	Petra	645
Pinot Nero '14	Podere della Civettaja	591
Rosso di Montalcino '15	Baricci	558
Rosso di Montalcino '15	Capanna	572
Rosso di Montalcino '15	Palazzo	643
Rosso di Montalcino '15	Uccelliera	681
Saffredi '14	Fattoria Le Pupille	658
Sapaio '15	Podere Sapaio	668
Siepi '15	Castello di Fonterutoli	582
Terre di Pisa Nambrot '15	Tenuta di Ghizzano	612
Valdarno di Sopra Galatrona '14	Fattoria Petrolo	646
Vermentino '16	San Ferdinando	665
Vernaccia di S. Gimignano Sanice Ris. '14	Vincenzo Cesani	587
Vernaccia di S. Gimignano Tradizionale '15	Montenidoli	632
Vigorello '13	San Felice	665
Vin Santo del Chianti Occhio di Pernice		
Fonti e Lecceta '11	Torre a Cona	680
Vin Santo di Carmignano Ris. '10	Tenuta di Capezzana	573

MARCHE

Castelli di Jesi Verdicchio Cl. Lauro Ris. '15	Poderi Mattioli	730
Castelli di Jesi Verdicchio Cl. Salmariano Ris. '14	Marotti Campi	730
Castelli di Jesi Verdicchio Cl. San Paolo Ris. '15	Pievalta	736
Castelli di Jesi Verdicchio Cl. San Sisto Ris. '15	Fazi Battaglia	726
Castelli di Jesi Verdicchio Cl.		
V. Il Cantico della Figura Ris. '13	Andrea Felici	726
Offida Pecorino '16	Tenuta Santori	741
Offida Pecorino Artemisia '16	Tenuta Spinelli	743
Offida Pecorino Mida '16	Maria Letizia Allevi	714
Offida Rosso Vignagiulia '14	Emanuele Dianetti	725
Piceno Sup. Morellone '12	Le Caniette	718
Rosso Piceno Sup. Roggio del Filare '14	Velenosi	746
Verdicchio dei Castelli di Jesi Cl. Sup. '16	Bucci	717
Verdicchio dei Castelli di Jesi Cl. Sup.		
Insolito del Pozzo Buono '15	Vicari	747
Verdicchio dei Castelli di Jesi Cl. Sup. Misco '16	Tenuta di Tavignano	744
Verdicchio dei Castelli di Jesi Cl. Sup. Podium '15	Gioacchino Garofoli	728
Verdicchio dei Castelli di Jesi Cl. Sup. Qudì '15	Roberto Venturi	747
Verdicchio dei Castelli di Jesi Cl. Sup. V. V. '15	Umani Ronchi	745
Verdicchio di Matelica Cambrugiano Ris. '14	Belisario	715
Verdicchio di Matelica Mirum Ris. '15	La Monacesca	732

| Verdicchio di Matelica Petrara '16 | Borgo Paglianetto | 716 |
| Verdicchio di Matelica Vign. Fogliano '15 | Bisci | 715 |

UMBRIA

05035 Rosso '16	Leonardo Bussoletti	758
Adarmando '15	Giampaolo Tabarrini	773
Cervaro della Sala '15	Castello della Sala	760
Montefalco Sagrantino '13	F.lli Pardi	768
Montefalco Sagrantino Collenottolo '13	Tenuta Bellafonte	757
Montefalco Sagrantino Collepiano '13	Arnaldo Caprai	759
Montefalco Sagrantino Fidenzio '12	Tudernum	775
Orvieto Cl. Sup. Il Bianco '16	Decugnano dei Barbi	763
Torgiano Rosso Rubesco V. Monticchio Ris. '12	Lungarotti	765

LAZIO

Baccarossa '15	Poggio Le Volpi	789
Biancolella Faro della Guardia '16	Casale del Giglio	782
Fiorano Rosso '12	Tenuta di Fiorano	790
Frascati Sup. Eremo Tuscolano '16	Valle Vermiglia	791
Habemus '15	San Giovenale	789
Montiano '15	Falesco - Famiglia Cotarella	785
Poggio della Costa '16	Sergio Mottura	787

ABRUZZO

Cerasuolo d'Abruzzo Fonte Cupa '16	Camillo Montori	806
Cerasuolo d'Abruzzo Myosotis '16	Ciccio Zaccagnini	814
Cerasuolo d'Abruzzo Piè delle Vigne '15	Luigi Cataldi Madonna	800
Montepulciano d'Abruzzo Amorino '13	Castorani	799
Montepulciano d'Abruzzo Mo Ris. '13	Cantina Tollo	811
Montepulciano d'Abruzzo Ursonia '13	Il Feuduccio di Santa Maria D'Orni	804
Pecorino '16	Tiberio	811
Pecorino Casadonna '15	Feudo Antico	804
Trebbiano d'Abruzzo '13	Valentini	813
Trebbiano d'Abruzzo Sup. Notàri '15	Fattoria Nicodemi	807
Trebbiano d'Abruzzo V. del Convento di Capestrano '15	Valle Reale	813

MOLISE

| Molise Aglianico Contado Ris. '14 | Di Majo Norante | 821 |

CAMPANIA

Caiatì '15	Alois	824
Campi Flegrei Falanghina Cruna deLago '15	La Sibilla	847
Campi Flegrei Piedirosso '16	Agnanum	824
Costa d'Amalfi Furore Bianco Fiorduva '16	Marisa Cuomo	831
Falanghina del Sannio Janare Senete '16	La Guardiense	837
Falanghina del Sannio Svelato '16	Terre Stregate	848
Falanghina del Sannio Taburno '16	Fontanavecchia	835
Falanghina del Sannio Taburno '16	Fattoria La Rivolta	842
Fiano di Avellino '16	Colli di Lapio	829
Fiano di Avellino '16	Fonzone	835
Fiano di Avellino Alessandra '12	Di Meo	832
Fiano di Avellino Alimata '15	Villa Raiano	851
Fiano di Avellino Pietramara '16	I Favati	833

Fiano di Avellino V. della Congregazione '16	Villa Diamante	850
Greco di Tufo '16	Cantine Di Marzo	832
Greco di Tufo '16	Donnachiara	833
Greco di Tufo '16	Pietracupa	841
Grecomusc' '15	Contrade di Taurasi	830
Il Fric '16	Casebianche	827
Sabbie di Sopra il Bosco '15	Nanni Copè	839
Sannio Sant'Agata dei Goti Piedirosso Artus '15	Mustilli	838
Taurasi '13	Feudi di San Gregorio	834
Trentenare '16	San Salvatore 1988	844

BASILICATA

Aglianico del Vulture Don Anselmo '13	Paternoster	865
Aglianico del Vulture Il Repertorio '15	Cantine del Notaio	862
Aglianico del Vulture Sup. Cruà '13	Basilisco	862
Aglianico del Vulture Sup. Serpara '12	Re Manfredi	
	Cantina Terre degli Svevi	866
Aglianico del Vulture Titolo '15	Elena Fucci	863

PUGLIA

Castel del Monte Rosso V. Pedale Ris. '14	Torrevento	884
Gioia del Colle Primitivo 17 Vign. Montevella '14	Polvanera	881
Gioia del Colle Primitivo Marpione Ris. '13	Tenuta Viglione	887
Gioia del Colle Primitivo Muro Sant'Angelo		
Contrada Barbatto '14	Tenute Chiaromonte	875
Gioia del Colle Primitivo Ris. '14	Cantine Tre Pini	885
Gioia del Colle Primitivo Senatore '11	Coppi	875
Oltremé '16	Tenute Rubino	882
Orfeo Negroamaro '15	Cantine Paolo Leo	878
Primitivo '15	Carvinea	873
Primitivo di Manduria Raccontami '15	Vespa - Vignaioli per Passione	006
Primitivo di Manduria Sinfarosa Zinfandel '15	Felline	877
Salice Salentino Rosso Per Lui Ris. '15	Leone de Castris	879
Salice Salentino Rosso Selvarossa Ris. '14	Cantine Due Palme	876

CALABRIA

Grisara '16	Roberto Ceraudo	896
Masino '15	iGreco	897
Neostòs Bianco '16	Spiriti Ebbri	901
Terre di Cosenza Pollino Moscato Passito		
Mastro Terenzio '14	Feudo dei Sanseverino	897

SICILY

Astolfo '15	Assuli	909
Cerasuolo di Vittoria Giambattista Valli Paris '15	Feudi del Pisciotto	917
Contrada Sciaranuova '15	Passopisciaro	924
Etna Bianco '16	Planeta	925
Etna Bianco Alta Mora '16	Cusumano	915
Etna Bianco Fondo Filara Contrada Monte Gorna '16	Cantine Nicosia	922
Etna Rosso '15	Tornatore	931
Etna Rosso 'A Rina '15	Girolamo Russo	928
Etna Rosso V. Barbagalli '14	Pietradolce	925
Etna Rosso Zottorinoto Ris. '13	Cottanera	914

Faro '15	Le Casematte	913
Malvasia delle Lipari Passito '16	Caravaglio	913
Mandrarossa Cavadiserpe '16	Cantine Settesoli	929
Passito di Pantelleria Ben Ryé '15	Donnafugata	915
Quater Vitis Rosso '14	Firriato	920
Rosso del Soprano '15	Palari	923
Shymer '14	Baglio di Pianetto	910
Sicilia Bianco Maggiore '16	Rallo	926
Sicilia Catarratto V. di Mandranova '16	Alessandro di Camporeale	908
Sicilia Nerello Mascalese Tascante '14	Tasca d'Almerita	929
Sicilia Saia '15	Feudo Maccari	918
Sicilia Syrah '15	Feudo Principi di Butera	919

SARDINIA

Alghero Torbato Terre Bianche Cuvée 161 '16	Tenute Sella & Mosca	957
Cannonau di Sardegna Barrosu Franzisca Ris. '14	Giovanni Montisci	952
Cannonau di Sardegna Mamuthone '15	Giuseppe Sedilesu	956
Cannonau di Sardegna Senes Ris. '13	Argiolas	944
Cannonau di Sardegna Sincaru Ris. '14	Vigne Surrau	959
Carignano del Sulcis 6Mura '12	Cantina Giba	949
Latinia '11	Cantina di Santadi	955
Vermentino di Gallura Sup. Costarenas '16	Masone Mannu	951
Vermentino di Gallura Sup. Maìa '15	Siddùra	957
Vermentino di Sardegna Stellato '16	Pala	953
Vermentino di Sardegna Tuvaoes '16	Giovanni Maria Cherchi	945
Vernaccia di Oristano Sup. Jughissa '08	Cantina Sociale della Vernaccia	959

GAMBERO ROSSO
AND
BOHEMIA KVĚTNÁ 1794
AWARD

THE BEST

RED OF THE YEAR

VALTELLINA SUP. SASSELLA ROCCE ROSSE RIS. '07 - AR.PE.PE

WHITE OF THE YEAR

FIANO DI AVELLINO PIETRAMARA '16 - I FAVATI

SPARKLER OF THE YEAR

MARCALBERTO EXTRA BRUT MILLESIMO2MILA12 M. CL. '12 - MARCALBERTO

SWEET OF THE YEAR

MALVASIA DELLE LIPARI PASSITO '16 - CARAVAGLIO

KVĚTNÁ 1794
BOHEMIA

WINERY OF THE YEAR

MASI

BEST VALUE FOR MONEY

ROMAGNA SANGIOVESE SUP. SIGISMONDO '16 - LE ROCCHE MALATESTIANE

GROWER OF THE YEAR

STEFANO AMERIGHI

UP-AND-COMING WINERY

SPIRITI EBBRI

AWARD FOR SUSTAINABLE VITICULTURE

FERRARI

SOLIDARITY AWARD

MONTENIDOLI

TRE BICCHIERI VERDI

With our Tre Bicchieri Verdi we make note of those wines that are made through certified organic or biodynamic management (which we indicate in red). This year there are some 99 in all, a number that's growing (last year there were 88), and that constitutes more than 20% of the wines awarded. It's an important figure that testifies to how the trend towards more ecological practices among Italy's best wineries is irreversible. It's a complex issue, no doubt, considering that many wineries who follow such methods never ask for certification. It's also clear that more and more Italian producers are adopting a sustainable approach to agriculture. On those profiles where a producer is committed to such an approach, the reader will find the tag, 'Sustainable Winery'.

Wine	Producer	Region
05035 Rosso '16	Leonardo Bussoletti	Umbria
A. A. Valle Isarco Sylvaner '15	Garlider Christian Kerschbaumer	Alto Adige
Aglianico del Vulture Don Anselmo '13	Paternoster	Basilicata
Aglianico del Vulture Sup. Cruà '13	Basilisco	Basilicata
Altrovino '15	Duemani	Tuscany
Amarone della Valpolicella Vign. Monte Sant'Urbano '13	Viticoltori Speri	Veneto
Ameri Governo all'Uso Toscano '15	Podere San Cristoforo	Toscana
Bardolino Cl. Brol Grande '15	Le Fraghe	Veneto
Barolo Bricco Rocche '13	Ceretto	Piedmont
Barolo Brunate '13	Enzo Boglietti	Piedmont
Barolo del Comune di Barolo Essenze '13	Vite Colte	Piedmont
Barolo Ravera Bricco Pernice '12	Elvio Cogno	Piedmont
Barolo Resa 56 '13	Brandini	Piedmont
Barolo Sarmassa V. Bricco Ris. '11	Giacomo Brezza & Figli	Piedmont
Barolo Vignarionda Arnaldo Rivera '13	Terre del Barolo	Piedmont
Barolo Villero '13	Brovia	Piedmont
Baron'Ugo '13	Monteraponi	Tuscany
Bolgheri Sup. Grattamacco '14	Grattamacco	Tuscany
Brunello di Montalcino '12	Le Chiuse	Tuscany
Brunello di Montalcino '12	Poggio di Sotto	Tuscany
Brunello di Montalcino Poggio al Vento Ris. '10	Tenuta Col d'Orcia	Tuscany
Castelli di Jesi Verdicchio Cl. Lauro Ris. '15	Poderi Mattioli	Marche
Castelli di Jesi Verdicchio Cl. San Paolo Ris. '15	Pievalta	Marche
Chianti Cl. '15	Badia a Coltibuono	Tuscany
Chianti Cl. '15	Castello di Volpaia	Tuscany
Chianti Cl. '14	Le Cinciole	Tuscany
Chianti Cl. '15	Le Miccine	Tuscany
Chianti Cl. Casavecchia alla Piazza '15	Buondonno Casavecchia alla Piazza	Tuscany
Chianti Cl. Gran Sel. V. del Sorbo '14	Fontodi	Tuscany
Chianti Cl. Montaperto '15	Fattoria Carpineta Fontalpino	Tuscany
Chianti Cl. Ris. '14	Bandini - Villa Pomona	Tuscany
Chianti Cl. Ris. '14	Val delle Corti	Tuscany
Colli di Rimini Cabernet Sauvignon Montepirolo '13	San Patrignano	Emilia Romagna
Cortona Syrah '14	Stefano Amerighi	Tuscany
Etna Bianco Fondo Filara Contrada Monte Gorna '16	Cantine Nicosia	Sicily
Etna Rosso 'A Rina '15	Girolamo Russo	Sicily
Falanghina del Sannio Taburno '16	Fattoria La Rivolta	Campania
Faro '15	Le Casematte	Sicily
FCO Bianco Identità '15	Leonardo Specogna	Friuli Venezia Giulia
Fiano di Avellino Alimata '15	Villa Raiano	Campania
Franciacorta Nature '61 '10	Guido Berlucchi & C.	Lombardy
Franciacorta Brut Arcadia '13	Lantieri de Paratico	Lombardy

Franciacorta Brut Naturae '13	Barone Pizzini	Lombardy
Gioia del Colle Primitivo 17 Vign. Montevella '14	Polvanera	Puglia
Gioia del Colle Primitivo Marpione Ris. '13	Tenuta Viglione	Puglia
Gioia del Colle Primitivo Ris. '14	Cantine Tre Pini	Puglia
Gioia del Colle Primitivo Senatore '11	Coppi	Puglia
Grecomusc' '15	Contrade di Taurasi	Campania
Grignolino del M.to Casalese '16	Vicara	Piemonte
Grisara '16	Roberto Ceraudo	Calabria
Habemus '15	San Giovenale	Lazio
Il Fric '16	Casebianche	Campania
Lambrusco di Modena Brut Rosé M. Cl. '13	Cantina della Volta	Emilia Romagna
Malvasia '13	Damijan Podversic	Friuli Venezia Giulia
Malvasia delle Lipari Passito '16	Caravaglio	Sicily
Maremma Toscana Ciliegiolo V. Vallerana Alta '15	Antonio Camillo	Tuscany
Molise Aglianico Contado Ris. '14	Di Majo Norante	Molise
Montecucco Sangiovese Poggio Lombrone Ris. '13	Colle Massari	Tuscany
Montepulciano d'Abruzzo Amorino '13	Castorani	Abruzzo
Nobile di Montepulciano '14	Salcheto	Tuscany
Offida Pecorino '16	Tenuta Santori	Marche
Offida Pecorino Mida '16	Maria Letizia Allevi	Marche
Ograde '15	Skerk	Friuli Venezia Giulia
Pecorino Casadonna '15	Feudo Antico	Abruzzo
Piceno Sup. Morellone '12	Le Caniette	Marche
Pinot Nero '14	Podere della Civettaja	Tuscany
Pinot Nero Arfena '15	Andrea Picchioni	Lombardy
Poggio della Costa '16	Sergio Mottura	Lazio
Primitivo '15	Carvinea	Puglia
Primitivo di Manduria Sinfarosa Zinfandel '15	Felline	Puglia
Quater Vitis Rosso '14	Firriato	Sicily
Reggiano Lambrusco Secco Marchese Manodori '16	Venturini Baldini	Emilia Romagna
Riviera Ligure di Ponente Pigato Bon in da Bon '16	BioVio	Liguria
Roero Valmaggiore V. Audinaggio '15	Cascina Ca' Rossa	Piedmont
Romagna Sangiovese Modigliana I Probi di Papiano Ris. '14	Villa Papiano	Emilia Romagna
Rosso di Montalcino '15	Palazzo	Tuscany
Sicilia Bianco Maggiore '16	Rallo	Sicily
Sicilia Catarratto V. di Mandranova '16	Alessandro di Camporeale	Sicily
Soave Cl. Calvarino '15	Leonildo Pieropan	Veneto
Soave Cl. Contrada Salvarenza V. V. '14	Gini	Veneto
Soave Cl. Staforte '15	Graziano Prà	Veneto
Taurasi '13	Feudi di San Gregorio	Campania
Teroldego Rotaliano Pini '13	Roberto Zeni	Trentino
Terre di Cosenza Pollino Moscato Passito Mastro Terenzio '14	Feudo dei Sanseverino	Calabria
Terre di Pisa Nambrot '15	Tenuta di Ghizzano	Tuscany
Torgiano Rosso Rubesco V. Monticchio Ris. '12	Lungarotti	Umbria
Trebbiano d'Abruzzo Sup. Notàri '15	Fattoria Nicodemi	Abruzzo
Trebbiano d'Abruzzo V. del Convento di Capestrano '15	Valle Reale	Abruzzo
Trentenare '16	San Salvatore 1988	Campania
Trento Dosaggio Zero Ris. '12	Maso Martis	Trentino
Valpolicella Cl. Sup. Campo Casal Vegri '15	Ca' La Bionda	Veneto
Verdicchio dei Castelli di Jesi Cl. Sup. '16	Bucci	Marche
Verdicchio dei Castelli di Jesi Cl. Sup. V. V. '15	Umani Ronchi	Marche
Verdicchio di Matelica Petrara '16	Borgo Paglianetto	Marche
Verdicchio di Matelica Vign. Fogliano '15	Bisci	Marche
Vernaccia di S. Gimignano Sanice Ris. '14	Vincenzo Cesani	Tuscany
Vernaccia di S. Gimignano Tradizionale '15	Montenidoli	Tuscany
Vin Santo di Carmignano Ris. '10	Tenuta di Capezzana	Tuscany

TABLE OF VINTAGES
FROM 1995 TO 2016

The following tables rate vintages by wine type and year. Each bottle symbol represents the quality rating for that vintage.

	BARBARESCO BAROLO	AMARONE	CHIANTI CLASSICO	BRUNELLO DI MONTALCINO	BOLGHERI	TAURASI	MONTEPULCIANO D'ABRUZZO
1995	3	5	4	5	3	3	5
1996	5	3	3	2	4	4	4
1997	4	4	4	5	4	4	4
1999	5	3	5	5	5	5	2
2000	4	3	4	3	4	2	4
2001	5	3	4	5	5	4	4
2004	5	4	4	4	4	3	4
2005	4	3	3	2	3	3	4
2006	4	5	4	5	4	4	4
2007	4	5	4	4	4	4	4
2008	4	4	4	4	5	4	4
2009	4	4	3	2	5	3	3
2010	5	4	4	5	4	4	3
2011	4	4	4	4	4	3	4
2012	4	3	3	3	3	4	4
2013	4	4	5	4	4	4	4
2014	4		3		2		2
2015			4				4

	ALTO ADIGE BIANCO	LUGANA SOAVE	FRIULI BIANCO	VERDICCHIO DEI CASTELLI DI JESI	FIANO DI AVELLINO	GRECO DI TUFO
2006	3	3	5	5	4	5
2007	3	3	5	2	3	3
2008	3	3	3	4	4	3
2009	4	3	4	4	3	4
2010	5	4	2	5	5	5
2011	3	4	3	3	3	2
2012	4	3	4	4	4	4
2013	4	4	3	4	4	4
2014	2	3	3	3	4	4
2015	4	5	4	4	4	3
2016	5	5	5	4	4	3

STARS

★★★★★
55
Gaja (Piedmont)

★★★★
42
Ca' del Bosco (Lombardy)

★★★
38
La Spinetta (Piedmont)

36
Elio Altare - Cascina Nuova
 (Piedmont)

33
Allegrini (Veneto)
Castello di Fonterutoli (Tuscany)
Valentini (Abruzzo)

★★
29
Bellavista (Lombardy)
Giacomo Conterno (Piedmont)
Jermann (Friuli Venezia Giulia)
Tenuta San Guido (Tuscany)
Cantina Produttori San Michele
 Appiano (Alto Adige)

28
Castello della Sala (Umbria)
Fèlsina (Tuscany)
Ferrari (Trentino)
Masciarelli (Abruzzo)
Planeta (Sicily)

27
Tasca d'Almerita (Sicily)

26
Poliziano (Tuscany)
Cantina Tramin (Alto Adige)
Vie di Romans
 (Friuli Venezia Giulia)

25
Marchesi Antinori (Tuscany)
Castello di Ama (Tuscany)
Feudi di San Gregorio
 (Campania)
Bruno Giacosa (Piedmont)
Ornellaia (Tuscany)
Leonildo Pieropan (Veneto)

24
Argiolas (Sardinia)
Livio Felluga (Friuli Venezia Giulia)

Gravner (Friuli Venezia Giulia)
Paolo Scavino (Piedmont)

23
Cantina Bolzano (Alto Adige)
Arnaldo Caprai (Umbria)
Fontodi (Tuscany)
Nino Negri (Lombardy)
Schiopetto (Friuli Venezia Giulia)
Villa Russiz (Friuli Venezia Giulia)

22
Barone Ricasoli (Tuscany)
Domenico Clerico (Piedmont)
Falesco - Famiglia Cotarella (Lazio)
Tenute Sella & Mosca (Sardinia)
Cantina Terlano (Alto Adige)

21
Ca' Viola (Piedmont)
Cascina La Barbatella (Piedmont)
Castello del Terriccio (Tuscany)
Michele Chiarlo (Piedmont)
Cantina Colterenzio (Alto Adige)
Isole e Olena (Tuscany)
Tenuta San Leonardo (Trentino)
Vietti (Piedmont)

20
Cantina di Caldaro (Alto Adige)
Les Crêtes (Valle d'Aosta)
Cusumano (Sicily)
Dorigo (Friuli Venezia Giulia)
Montevetrano (Campania)
Venica & Venica
 (Friuli Venezia Giulia)
Volpe Pasini (Friuli Venezia Giulia)
Elena Walch (Alto Adige)

★
19
Ca' Rugate (Veneto)
Castellare di Castellina
 (Tuscany)
Gioacchino Garofoli (Marche)
Elio Grasso (Piedmont)
Lis Neris (Friuli Venezia Giulia)
Le Macchiole (Tuscany)
Montevertine (Tuscany)
Serafini & Vidotto (Veneto)
Le Vigne di Zamò
 (Friuli Venezia Giulia)

18
Abbazia di Novacella (Alto Adige)
Brancaia (Tuscany)
Castello Banfi (Tuscany)
Luigi Cataldi Madonna
 (Abruzzo)

Conterno Fantino (Piedmont)
Matteo Correggia (Piedmont)
Donnafugata (Sicily)
Massolino (Piedmont)
Mastroberardino (Campania)
Palari (Sicily)
Ruffino (Tuscany)
Luciano Sandrone (Piedmont)
Cantina di Santadi (Sardinia)
Sottimano (Piedmont)
Franco Toros
 (Friuli Venezia Giulia)
Fattoria Zerbina
 (Emilia Romagna)

17
Antoniolo (Piedmont)
Casanova di Neri (Tuscany)
Firriato (Sicily)
Kuenhof - Peter Pliger
 (Alto Adige)
Livon (Friuli Venezia Giulia)
Masi (Veneto)
Monsupello (Lombardy)
Cantina Convento Muri Gries
 (Alto Adige)
Fiorenzo Nada (Piedmont)
Fattoria Petrolo (Tuscany)
Querciabella (Tuscany)
Giuseppe Quintarelli (Veneto)
Bruno Rocca (Piedmont)
Ronco dei Tassi
 (Friuli Venezia Giulia)
San Patrignano (Emilia Romagna)
Umani Ronchi (Marche)

16
Roberto Anselmi (Veneto)
Lorenzo Begali (Veneto)
Bucci (Marche)
Aldo Conterno (Piedmont)
Coppo (Piedmont)
Romano Dal Forno (Veneto)
Miani (Friuli Venezia Giulia)
Doro Princic (Friuli Venezia Giulia)
Albino Rocca (Piedmont)
Velenosi (Marche)

15
Biondi Santi - Tenuta Il Greppo
 (Tuscany)
Cav. G. B. Bertani (Veneto)
Cavit (Trentino)
Tenuta di Ghizzano (Tuscany)
Bartolo Mascarello (Piedmont)
LaMonacesca (Marche)
Pietracupa (Campania)
Tenuta Sant'Antonio (Veneto)
Suavia (Veneto)

Tenuta Unterortl - Castel Juval
(Alto Adige)
Vignalta (Veneto)
Viticoltori Speri (Veneto)
Roberto Voerzio (Piedmont)

14

Abbona (Piedmont)
Avignonesi (Tuscany)
Bricco Rocche - Bricco Asili
(Piedmont)
Di Majo Norante (Molise)
Falkenstein Franz Pratzner
(Alto Adige)
Grattamacco (Tuscany)
Librandi (Calabria)
Lungarotti (Umbria)
Malvirà (Piedmont)
Franco M. Martinetti (Piedmont)
Oasi degli Angeli (Marche)
Graziano Prà (Veneto)
Produttori del Barbaresco
(Piedmont)
Rocca di Frassinello (Tuscany)
Ronco del Gelso
(Friuli Venezia Giulia)
San Felice (Tuscany)
Uberti (Lombardy)
Viviani (Veneto)

13

F.lli Alessandria (Piedmont)
Poderi Boscarelli (Tuscany)
Braida (Piedmont)
Piero Busso (Piedmont)
Cavalleri (Lombardy)
Tenute Cisa Asinari dei Marchesi
di Grésy (Piedmont)
Elvio Cogno (Piedmont)
Tenuta Col d'Orcia (Tuscany)
Le Due Terre
(Friuli Venezia Giulia)
Poderi Luigi Einaudi (Piedmont)
Ferghettina (Lombardy)
Foradori (Trentino)
Gini (Veneto)
Dino Illuminati (Abruzzo)
Edi Keber (Friuli Venezia Giulia)
Leone de Castris (Puglia)
Maculan (Veneto)
Sergio Mottura (Lazio)
Pecchenino (Piedmont)
Piaggia (Tuscany)
Fattoria Le Pupille (Tuscany)
Aldo Rainoldi (Lombardy)
Russiz Superiore
(Friuli Venezia Giulia)
Tormaresca (Puglia)

Tua Rita (Tuscany)
Valle Reale (Abruzzo)
Villa Sparina (Piedmont)

12

Giulio Accornero e Figli
(Piedmont)
Azelia (Piedmont)
Brovia (Piedmont)
Ca' del Baio (Piedmont)
Castello dei Rampolla (Tuscany)
Cavalchina (Veneto)
Eugenio Collavini
(Friuli Venezia Giulia)
Còlpetrone (Umbria)
Cantina Cortaccia (Alto Adige)
Tenute Ambrogio e Giovanni
Folonari (Tuscany)
Marchesi Frescobaldi (Tuscany)
Elena Fucci (Basilicata)
Galardi (Campania)
Ettore Germano (Piedmont)
Köfererhof - Günther Kerschbaumer
(Alto Adige)
Mamete Prevostini (Lombardy)
Marchesi di Barolo (Piedmont)
Monchiero Carbone (Piedmont)
Cantina Nals Margreid
(Alto Adige)
Dario Raccaro
(Friuli Venezia Giulia)
Rocche dei Manzoni (Piedmont)
Salvioni (Tuscany)
Tenuta di Valgiano (Tuscany)
Vigneti Massa (Piedmont)
Villa Medoro (Abruzzo)
Zenato (Veneto)

11

Abate Nero (Trentino)
Gianfranco Alessandria
(Piedmont)
Benanti (Sicily)
Borgo San Daniele
(Friuli Venezia Giulia)
Brigaldara (Veneto)
Cascina Ca' Rossa (Piedmont)
Castello di Albola (Tuscany)
Castello di Volpaia (Tuscany)
F.lli Cigliuti (Piedmont)
Dorigati (Trentino)
Cantine Due Palme (Puglia)
Cantina Girlan (Alto Adige)
Franz Haas (Alto Adige)
LaMassa (Tuscany)
Pio Cesare (Piedmont)
Prunotto (Piedmont)
Torraccia del Piantavigna
(Piedmont)

Torrevento (Puglia)
G. D. Vajra (Piedmont)

10

Alois Lageder (Alto Adige)
Maison Anselmet (Valle d'Aosta)
Enzo Boglietti (Piedmont)
Cà Maiol (Lombardy)
Tenuta di Capezzana (Tuscany)
Cavallotto Tenuta Bricco Boschis
(Piedmont)
Tenute del Cerro (Tuscany)
Colle Massari (Tuscany)
Colli di Lapio (Campania)
Corte Sant'Alda (Veneto)
Marisa Cuomo (Campania)
Fontanafredda (Piedmont)
Guerrieri Rizzardi (Veneto)
Hilberg - Pasquero
(Piedmont)
Tenuta J. Hofstätter
(Alto Adige)
Mastrojanni (Tuscany)
Monte Rossa (Lombardy)
Poderi e Cantine Oddero
(Piedmont)
Poggio Antico (Tuscany)
Poggio di Sotto (Tuscany)
Tenute Rubino (Puglia)
Giampaolo Tabarrini (Umbria)
Tenimenti Luigi d'Alessandro
(Tuscany)
Tenuta delle Terre Nere (Sicily)
Villa Matilde (Campania)
Conti Zecca (Puglia)

HOW TO USE THE GUIDE

WINERY INFORMATION
ANNUAL PRODUCTION
HECTARES UNDER VINE
VITICULTURE METHOD

SYMBOLS
○ WHITE WINE
⊙ ROSÈ
● RED WINE

RATINGS
  MODERATELY GOOD TO GOOD WINES IN THEIR RESPECTIVE CATEGORIES
  VERY GOOD TO EXCELLENT WINES IN THEIR RESPECTIVE CATEGORIES
  VERY GOOD TO EXCELLENT WINES THAT WENT FORWARD TO THE FINAL TASTINGS
  EXCELLENT WINES IN THEIR RESPECTIVE CATEGORIES

WINES RATED IN PREVIOUS EDITIONS OF THE GUIDE ARE INDICATED BY WHITE GLASSES (♀, ♀♀, ♀♀♀),
PROVIDED THEY ARE STILL DRINKING AT THE LEVEL FOR WHICH THE ORIGINAL AWARD WAS MADE.

STAR ★
INDICATES WINERIES THAT HAVE WON TEN TRE BICCHIERI AWARDS FOR EACH STAR

PRICE RANGES
1 up to 5 euro	2 from € 5.01 to € 10.00
3 from € 10.01 to € 15.00	4 from € 15.01 to € 20.00
5 from € 20.01 to € 30.00	6 from € 30.01 to € 40.00
7 from € 40.01 to € 50.00	8 more than € 50.01

PRICES INDICATED REFER TO AVERAGE PRICES IN WINE STORES

ASTERISK *
INDICATES ESPECIALLY GOOD VALUE WINES

ABBREVIATIONS
A. A.	Alto Adige		P.R.	Peduncolo Rosso
C.	Colli			(red bunchstem)
Cl.	Classico		P.	Prosecco
C.S.	Cantina Sociale		Rif. Agr.	Riforma Agraria
	(co-operative winery)			(agrarian reform)
CEV	Colli Etruschi Viterbesi		Ris.	Riserva
Cons.	Consorzio		Sel.	Selezione
Coop.Agr.	Cooperativa Agricola		Sup.	Superiore
	(farming co-operative)		TdF	Terre di Franciacorta
C. B.	Colli Bolognesi		V.	Vigna (vineyard)
C. P.	Colli Piacentini		Vign.	Vigneto (vineyard)
Et.	Etichetta (label)		V. T.	Vendemmia Tardiva
FCO	Friuli Colli Orientali			(late harvest)
M.	Metodo (method)		V. V.	Vecchia Vigna/Vecchie Vigne
M.to	Monferrato			(old vine /old vines)
OP	Oltrepò Pavese			

VALLE D'AOSTA

It's only been recently in the Aosta Valley that the cultivation of grapes and their subsequent vinification and sale have allowed local vine growers to live comfortably. For many years, the only regional wines that were available in wine bars (even in Aosta) were made by the Regional Agricultural Institute's many cooperatives. This center of viticultural research and experimentation is also a school where many local producers were trained. In the long term, of course, cooperation proved to be a necessity. Aosta Valley is a difficult, rugged territory with only 400 hectares of vineyards to its name. And historically, land has been fragmented, making it difficult for individual families to make money out of winemaking. Even today, many small-scale vine growers are only part-time and production volumes cap out at 30,000 bottles (with many wineries not even reaching 15,000). Costantino Charrère himself, owner of Les Crêtes (the largest private producer in the valley, with current volumes of 180,000 bottles per year) was for many years, also a teacher. Many wineries choose not to subject their wines to critical opinion, because when the time comes to taste, there's none left. And yet, despite the small size of its vineyards and wineries, Aosta's wines are getting better by the year. And its best wines are, in their category, at the apex of national excellence. After a few ambiguous years, the region's most important players (with cooperative wineries making up almost half of the the region's production) are back in form with greater conviction and consistence, which has translated to a sharp increase in quality, across the board. Even if La Crotta di Vegneron is back on top, we saw a strong presence of cooperative wineries in our Tre Bicchieri finals. Among the privately owned wineries, the same names are leading the way (it's difficult to discover and develop new talent in a region so limited in size). And so we see well-known wineries but some new wines. Making headlines, for example, is the native grape variety Cornalin. It's still rare, but full of promise. We tasted an excellent version made by the Rosset family. And Costantino Charrère's Nebbiolo, especially, stood out, reminding us that the southern part of the region (in particular Donnas) has something to offer when it comes to this acclaimed cultivar.

★Maison Anselmet

FRAZ. VEREYTAZ, 30
11018 VILLENEUVE [AO]
TEL. +39 0165904851
www.maisonanselmet.it

CELLAR SALES
PRE-BOOKED VISITS
ANNUAL PRODUCTION 100,000 bottles
HECTARES UNDER VINE 11.00

Villeneuve is a town on the outskirts of Aosta, a choice area for the production of Petit Rouge and Torrette. And it's here that we find Anselmet, one of the best producers in the region. Giorgio's wines are many, with a marked focus on native grape varieties, though that hasn't stopped him from taking on the challenge of international varieties as well. New technology is skillfully adapted to tradition, and only a deep knowledge of the territory could bring about such a result. The Pinot Nero Semel Pater once again proves its greatness, with its fruity fragrances calling up blackberries, and hints of cherries fusing with wood and spices. The wine is still young, but it has all it needs to age well over time. The Pinot Gris is notable, a delectable wine in which close-focused fragrances of pear emerge from white fruit. A clean and fresh mouth gives way to a long finish.

Château Feuillet

LOC. CHÂTEAU FEUILLET, 12
11010 SAINT PIERRE
TEL. +39 3287673880
www.chateaufeuillet.vievini.it

CELLAR SALES
ACCOMMODATION AND RESTAURANT SERVICE
ANNUAL PRODUCTION 30,000 bottles
HECTARES UNDER VINE 5.00

Maurizio Fiorano is shy, but when he talks about his wines, all his passion and skill come out. His winery is one of the region's crown jewels, and, year after year, his wines affirm their status as among its most interesting. Situated in the outskirts of the city, the winery is easy to get to, and it's truly worth a visit. Native grape varieties are at the forefront, though Maurizio enjoys taking on the challenge of international varieties as well. The 2016 Fumin has an intense, lively color. On the nose, hints of dark berries emerge from pleasant, vegetal overtones. In the mouth, its structure proves rich, even if its tannins still need to mature. The brilliant ruby red Torrette Supérieur is characterized by aromas of red berries still on the bush. In the mouth it shows good structure, softness and good length, offering up delicate citrus aromas and evocative white flowers on the nose, while in the mouth it's fresh and pleasantly tangy.

○ Valle d'Aosta Chardonnay Élevé en Fût de Chêne '16	♟♟ 5
● Valle d'Aosta Fumin Élevé en Fût de Chêne '15	♟♟ 5
○ Valle d'Aosta Petite Arvine '16	♟♟ 3*
● Valle d'Aosta Pinot Noir Semel Pater '15	♟♟ 7
● Le Prisonnier MMXIII	♟♟ 8
○ Valle d'Aosta Chardonnay '16	♟♟ 3
● Valle d'Aosta Merlot Le Pellerin Élevé en Fût de Chêne '14	♟♟ 6
○ Valle d'Aosta Pinot Gris '16	♟♟ 3
● Valle d'Aosta Pinot Noir Tradition '15	♟♟ 5
○ Valle d'Aosta Chardonnay Élevé en Fût de Chêne '15	♟♟♟ 5
● Valle d'Aosta Pinot Noir Semel Pater '13	♟♟♟ 8

● Valle d'Aosta Cornalin '16	♟♟ 4
● Valle d'Aosta Fumin '16	♟♟ 4
○ Valle d'Aosta Petite Arvine '16	♟♟ 3
● Valle d'Aosta Torrette Sup. '15	♟♟ 3
● Valle d'Aosta Syrah '16	♟ 3
○ Valle d'Aosta Traminer Aromatico '16	♟ 4
○ Valle d'Aosta Petite Arvine '12	♟♟♟ 3*
○ Valle d'Aosta Petite Arvine '11	♟♟♟ 3*
○ Valle d'Aosta Petite Arvine '10	♟♟♟ 3*
● Valle d'Aosta Fumin '15	♟♟ 4
○ Valle d'Aosta Petite Arvine '15	♟♟ 3*

★★Les Crêtes

LOC. VILLETOS, 50
11010 AYMAVILLES [AO]
TEL. +39 0165902274
www.lescretes.it

CELLAR SALES
PRE-BOOKED VISITS
ANNUAL PRODUCTION 180,000 bottles
HECTARES UNDER VINE 20.00
SUSTAINABLE WINERY

At Les Crêtes, the numbers keep growing. Over the past few years, Costantino Charrère has purchased a number of vineyards in some of its more time-honored areas. And today, for example, he's offering a Nebbiolo that only recently became part of their selection. Les Crêtes is undoubtedly the most well-known producer of the region, having developed an international reputation as well. Though, if in recent years we've used words like 'romantic' and 'poetic' to describe the winery, there are changes afoot: the romanticism is giving way to a more modern approach, and to new marketing strategies. The brilliant ruby red 2015 Nebbiolo Sommet offers vibrant, flowery and spicy aromas of licorice and tobacco, with a hint of raspberry. It's powerful in the mouth, but morbid in its tannins, and extremely long. The Cuvée Bois shows admirable consistency. The 2015 has a spicy, complex bouquet featuring vanilla and oak. The mouth is invigorating and fresh. The Petite Arvine has flowery and fruity notes both on the nose and the palate. It proves to be a savory, pervasive wine.

● Valle d'Aosta Nebbiolo Sommet '15	▼▼▼	6
○ Valle d'Aosta Chardonnay Cuvée Bois '15	▼▼	6
○ Valle d'Aosta Neige D'Or '15	▼▼	8
○ Valle d'Aosta Petite Arvine '16	▼▼	3*
○ Valle d'Aosta Chardonnay '16	▼▼	4
● Valle d'Aosta Fumin '15	▼▼	4
● Valle d'Aosta Syrah '15	▼▼	4
○ Valle d'Aosta Chardonnay Cuvée Bois '13	♡♡♡	6
○ Valle d'Aosta Chardonnay Cuvée Bois '10	♡♡♡	6
○ Valle d'Aosta Chardonnay Cuvée Bois '09	♡♡♡	6
○ Valle d'Aosta Petite Arvine '13	♡♡♡	3*
● Valle d'Aosta Syrah Côteau La Tour '14	♡♡♡	4*

La Crotta di Vegneron

P.ZZA RONCAS, 2
11023 CHAMBAVE [AO]
TEL. +39 016646670
www.lacrotta.it

CELLAR SALES
PRE-BOOKED VISITS
RESTAURANT SERVICE
ANNUAL PRODUCTION 300,000 bottles
HECTARES UNDER VINE 39.00

Crotta di Vegneron is situated in Chambave, an area known throughout the world for the production of sweet wine. La Crotta is a cooperative that's highly sensitive to tradition, with many of its wide range of wines made with native grape varieties. The heart of the cooperative is its member-growers who, during the entire year, are followed attentively by in-house and regional technicians. As a result, their quality grapes give rise to elegant wines, perfect for pairing with the region's traditional cuisine, but they're also recognized by some of Italy's best restaurants. Tre Bicchieri for the 2015 Prieuré. It has a beautiful antique gold color, a fantastic bouquet of dried fruit, great structure on the palate and a finish that lingers unendingly. The vibrant ruby red 2015 Fumin offers up a lovely nose of dark fruit and quininc. In the Nus Malvoisie, a straw-yellow Pinot Gris clone, pear emerges from fragrances of white fruit. In the mouth, rich structure balanced by freshness is followed by a long finish. The dry Muscat once again proves interesting.

○ Valle d'Aosta Chambave Moscato Passito Prieuré '15	▼▼▼	5
● Valle d'Aosta Fumin Esprit Follet '15	▼▼	5
○ Valle d'Aosta Nus Malvoisie '16	▼▼	3*
○ Valle d'Aosta Chambave Muscat '16	▼▼	3
● Valle d'Aosta Chambave Sup. Quatre Vignobles '15	▼▼	4
● Valle d'Aosta Syrah Crème '15	▼▼	5
○ Valle d'Aosta Chambave Moscato Passito Prieuré '13	♡♡♡	5
○ Valle d'Aosta Chambave Moscato Passito Prieuré '12	♡♡♡	5
○ Valle d'Aosta Chambave Moscato Passito Prieuré '11	♡♡♡	5
● Valle d'Aosta Fumin Esprit Follet '09	♡♡♡	3
● Valle d'Aosta Syrah Crème '14	♡♡	5

Di Barrò

LOC. CHÂTEAU FEUILLET, 8
11010 SAINT PIERRE
TEL. +39 0165903671
www.dibarro.vievini.it

CELLAR SALES
PRE-BOOKED VISITS
ANNUAL PRODUCTION 20,000 bottles
HECTARES UNDER VINE 2.50

Di Barro is one of Valle d'Aosta's many, small, family-run wineries. The estate is situated in one of the most acclaimed areas of the territory, Saint-Pierre, where the principal grape variety is the Petit Rouge (an integral part of the local, enological tradition). The Di Barrò family, however, haven't hesitated to take on the challenge of international grapes either, like Chardonnay, with superb results. The Syrah Vigne de Conze is noteworthy, with its vibrant ruby red color and its complex, mature nose of red fruit trailing to chocolate. It's a leisurely wine with some body, but it's still looking for the right tannic balance. The straw-yellow Pinot Gris is interesting, intense on the nose with hints of fruit, and full-bodied in the mouth. We also make note of their native-grape monovarietal, Mayolet. The wine offers up charming vegetal fragrances, while its tannins, still a bit austere, make for a finish that's just slightly mouth-drying. Torrette Supérior Clos de Château Feuillet and Fumin are both worth looking into.

○ Valle d'Aosta Pinot Gris '15	♛♛	3
● Valle d'Aosta Syrah V. de Conze '14	♛♛	3
● Valle d'Aosta Fumin '13	♛	4
● Valle d'Aosta Mayolet '15	♛	3
● Valle d'Aosta Torrette Sup. Clos de Château Feuillet '13	♛	3
○ Valle d'Aosta Chardonnay '12	♛♛♛	3*
● Valle d'Aosta Torrette Sup. V. de Torrette '06	♛♛♛	6
○ Valle d'Aosta Chardonnay '14	♛♛	3
● Valle d'Aosta Fumin '11	♛♛	4
● Valle d'Aosta Torrette Sup. Clos de Château Feuillet '12	♛♛	3
● Valle d'Aosta Torrette Sup. Ostro '09	♛♛	5

Caves Cooperatives de Donnas

VIA ROMA, 97
11020 DONNAS [AO]
TEL. +39 0125807096
www.donnasvini.it

CELLAR SALES
PRE-BOOKED VISITS
ANNUAL PRODUCTION 150,000 bottles
HECTARES UNDER VINE 26.00

Donnas is one of the first hamlets you find when you enter Valle d'Aosta, the land of the bassa valle, an area well-suited to the cultivation of Nebbiolo (called Picotendro in the local dialect). La Caves Cooperatives de Donnas is one of the foremost interpreters of this noble cultivar. The red with which it is made is usually only sold after two years of aging in large oak; a wine of superior structure, it's comparable to some of nearby Piedmont's great reds. La Caves also produces early-drinking and white wines, though its crown jewel remains Nebbiolo in all its forms. The same intensity displayed by Donnas Napoléon's ruby red color comes out in its nose, which offers up hints of fruit and slightly bitter, but pleasant, notes, calling up quinine and tar. In the mouth, true Nebbiolo comes out, powerful and fresh, with a significant tanninc presence. The 2014 Donnas exhibits aromas of red fruit and pleasant notes of rhubarb. The power of their Nebbiolo di Bassa Valle comes out in the Donnas Supérieur Vieilles Vignes, as well.

● Valle d'Aosta Donnas Napoléon '14	♛♛	5
● Valle d'Aosta Donnas '14	♛♛	4
● Valle d'Aosta Donnas Sup. V. V. '13	♛♛	5
● Valle d'Aosta Donnas '13	♛♛	4
● Valle d'Aosta Donnas '11	♛♛	2*
● Valle d'Aosta Donnas Napoléon '13	♛♛	5
● Valle d'Aosta Donnas Napoléon '11	♛♛	3
● Valle d'Aosta Donnas Napoléon '10	♛♛	3
● Valle d'Aosta Donnas Napoléon '07	♛♛	3
● Valle d'Aosta Donnas Sup. V. V. '12	♛♛	5
● Valle d'Aosta Donnas Sup. V. V. '07	♛♛	4
● Valle d'Aosta Donnas V. V. '09	♛♛	4

Lo Triolet

Loc. Junod, 7
11010 Introd [AO]
Tel. +39 016595437
www.lotriolet.vievini.it

CELLAR SALES
PRE-BOOKED VISITS
ANNUAL PRODUCTION 42,000 bottles
HECTARES UNDER VINE 5.00

Marco Martin is a perfectionist, and his winery has grown constantly over the years. After the vineyards and cellar took on new life, it was their hospitality residence's turn, while this year they've inaugurated a beautiful tasting area. Lo Triolet is, by now, an established brand, but success has only bolstered their commitment to making wines of outstanding quality. As a specialist in Pinot Gris, Marco Martin is one of it's most reputable interpreters, and not just for Italy. The 2016 Pinot Gris is a wonder. The nose offers up the grape's trademark fruity overtones of pear and ripe white fruit, all expressed with a smooth elegance. In the mouth, extraordinary balance and harmony point up the wine's freshness, and a long, savory finish follows. The Coteau Barrage's ruby red color is lovely and impenetrable, while the nose presents fruity fragrances of dark berries, and nuances of pepper and juniper. The wine is complex in the mouth, and proves to have some character. The Fumin, distinctive in its intense color, is also excellent.

○ Valle d'Aosta Pinot Gris '16	ΨΨΨ 5
● Valle d'Aosta Coteau Barrage '15	ΨΨ 4
● Valle d'Aosta Fumin '15	ΨΨ 5
● Valle d'Aosta Pinot Noir '16	ΨΨ 3
● Valle d'Aosta Rosso Heritage '15	ΨΨ 6
○ Valle d'Aosta Pinot Gris '15	ϒϒϒ 5
○ Valle d'Aosta Pinot Gris '14	ϒϒϒ 3*
○ Valle d'Aosta Pinot Gris '13	ϒϒϒ 3*
○ Valle d'Aosta Pinot Gris '12	ϒϒϒ 3*
○ Valle d'Aosta Pinot Gris Élevé en Barriques '10	ϒϒϒ 5
● Valle d'Aosta Fumin '13	ϒϒ 5
○ Valle d'Aosta Pinot Gris Élevé en Barriques '14	ϒϒ 6
● Valle d'Aosta Rosso Heritage '14	ϒϒ 6

Cave du Mont Blanc de Morgex et La Salle

Fraz. La Ruine
Chemin des Îles, 31
11017 Morgex [AO]
Tel. +39 0165800331
www.caveduvinblanc.com

CELLAR SALES
PRE-BOOKED VISITS
ANNUAL PRODUCTION 140,000 bottles
HECTARES UNDER VINE 19.00

Cultivating and making wine at the foot of Monte Bianco is no easy task. The seasons are extremely short, and March often sees snow. To boot, the plots are extremely small. Regional administration facilitated the founding of this cooperative by making modern enological technology available. Thus the vine growers can produce small quantities of grapes, allowing for a selection that's in line with current market demand for fresh, fragrant wines. The 2014 Glacier is brilliant and fresh, with a pleasant aromatic complexity that brings mineral notes together with overtones of white fruit. In the mouth, it's balanced, with well-integrated sparkle and a fresh, long finish. The Vino Estremi is excellent. It's a pale wine, with close-focused, flowery notes. Then, amidst hints of freshly-cut hay, the fragrance of apple emerges and returns to the palate in a fresh, pleasant finish. The Blanc du Blanc, a sparkling wine, is also original, with its citrusy notes, pleasant mouth and a delicately bitter finish.

○ Valle d'Aosta Blanc de Morgex et de La Salle '16	ΨΨ 2*
○ Valle d'Aosta Blanc de Morgex et de La Salle Brut M. Cl. Blanc du Blanc '14	ΨΨ 4
○ Valle d'Aosta Blanc de Morgex et de La Salle Brut Nature M. Cl. Cuvée du Prince '10	ΨΨ 6
○ Valle d'Aosta Blanc de Morgex et de La Salle Extra Brut M. Cl. Glacier '14	ΨΨ 5
○ Valle d'Aosta Blanc de Morgex et de La Salle Rayon '16	ΨΨ 3
○ Valle d'Aosta Blanc de Morgex et de La Salle Vini Estremi '16	ΨΨ 3

Elio Ottin

FRAZ. POROSSAN NEYVES, 209
11100 AOSTA
TEL. +39 3474071331
www.ottinvini.it

CELLAR SALES
PRE-BOOKED VISITS
ANNUAL PRODUCTION 30,000 bottles
HECTARES UNDER VINE 4.50
SUSTAINABLE WINERY

Elio Ottin is one of Valle d'Aosta's most brilliant vine growers. His beautiful estate can be found just outside the city of Aosta, along the road that goes to Roisan and turns up towards San Bernardo. His strength lies in having inherited the local winemaking tradition, and in knowing how to bring it into the new millennium. It's a mix of artisanal care (in both the vineyard and cellar) and modern enological applications. Since 2007, his wines, made up primarily of native grape varieties, have found an important place in the region. The wine that's most representative of Elio's style is the Petite Arvine, which, with the 2016 vintage, once again earns a Tre Bicchieri. A greenish straw-yellow, the wine's bouquet offers up fruit and fresh vegetal notes embellished by nuances of citrus. It's generous on the palate, deep and polished, extraordinarily fresh and long. The excellent 2015 Fumin is right up there, a wine of wild spirit, as is the 2015 Pinot Nero, with its superb varietal typicity. Once again, the Torrette Supérior also proves up to the task. .

○ Valle d'Aosta Petite Arvine '16	♈♈♈	5
● Valle d'Aosta Fumin '15	♈♈	5
● Valle d'Aosta Pinot Noir '15	♈♈	4
● Valle d'Aosta Torrette Sup. '15	♈♈	5
○ Valle d'Aosta Petite Arvine Nuances '15	♈	5
● Valle d'Aosta Fumin '12	♈♈♈	3*
○ Valle d'Aosta Petite Arvine '15	♈♈♈	5
○ Valle d'Aosta Petite Arvine '14	♈♈♈	4*
○ Valle d'Aosta Petite Arvine '12	♈♈♈	3*
● Valle d'Aosta Fumin '14	♈♈	5
● Valle d'Aosta Pinot Noir '14	♈♈	4
● Valle d'Aosta Torrette Sup. '14	♈♈	5

Ermes Pavese

S.DA PINETA, 26
11017 MORGEX [AO]
TEL. +39 0165800053
www.pavese.vievini.it

CELLAR SALES
PRE-BOOKED VISITS
ANNUAL PRODUCTION 35,000 bottles
HECTARES UNDER VINE 5.00

The pergolas of vines at the foot of Monte Bianco are so low that you're forced to stoop down to work them. But that's not a problem for Ermes Pavese. Despite the difficulties of such extreme viticulture, Ermes continues to establish his reputation as a quality producer. Priè Blanc, the variety used in the Blanc de Morgex et La Salle, is central in the region, and Ermes is a worthy interpreter. The Blanc de Morgex e La Salle once again proved decidedly interesting. The nose is pleasant, and is characterized by fresh scents of apple and white fruit, as well as more distinctive notes of alpine pasture. It's a fresh wine with some body, and comes through long in the mouth. This year, Pavese presents two classic sparklers (aged 24 and 18 months), both undosed. Intense, classic fragrances characterize the former, with a balanced mouth and a full, long finish. Even if it's simpler, the latter is subtle and direct, elegant in the mouth. Wood still dominates in the Nathan, which calls up sweet spices, and offers a rich, buttery mouth.

○ Valle d'Aosta Vin Blanc de Morgex et La Salle '16	♈♈	4
○ Valle d'Aosta Vin Blanc de Morgex et La Salle Nathan '15	♈♈	5
○ Valle d'Aosta Vin Blanc de Morgex et La Salle Pavese Pas Dosé M.Cl. XVIII '14	♈♈	5
○ Valle d'Aosta Vin Blanc de Morgex et La Salle Pavese Pas Dosé M.Cl. XXIV '13	♈♈	5
○ Valle d'Aosta Vin Blanc de Morgex et La Salle Le Sette Scalinate '15	♈	5
○ Valle d'Aosta Vin Blanc de Morgex et La Salle '15	♈♈	4
○ Valle d'Aosta Vin Blanc de Morgex et La Salle Le Sette Scalinate '14	♈♈	5

Rosset Terroir

LOC. TORRENT DE MAILLOD, 4
11020 QUART [AO]
TEL. +39 0165774111
www.rosseterroir.it

CELLAR SALES
PRE-BOOKED VISITS
ANNUAL PRODUCTION 20,000 bottles
HECTARES UNDER VINE 3.00

In just a short time, Niccola Rosset has managed to create a winery that, despite its modest size, has garnered unanimous respect and established itself among the region's top producers. Nicola's entrepreneurial experience and the support of the young, brilliant winemaker, Matteo Moretto, are among the keys to their success. But Rosset isn't one to rest on his laurels. The purchase of new vineyards, in esteemed areas, is in the works, and, for the next few years, an increase in production volume has been assured. Cornalin is becoming a symbol of Valle d'Aosta, and Rosset Terroir knows how to interpret it magnificently. The ruby red 2016 is brilliant and lively in color, with purplish highlights marking its youth. The aromatic profile is vibrant and sophisticated, with notes that range from fresh balsamic nuances of maple bark, to sweeter, darker fragrances of wild berries. In the mouth, the wine is pronounced and full, with velvety tannins.

● Valle d'Aosta Cornalin '16	♟♟♟ 4*
○ Valle d'Aosta Chardonnay '16	♟♟ 4
○ Valle d'Aosta Chambave Muscat '16	♟♟ 4
● Valle d'Aosta Cornalin '15	♟♟♟ 4*
● Valle d'Aosta Syrah '13	♟♟♟ 4*
○ Valle d'Aosta Chardonnay '14	♟♟ 4
○ Valle d'Aosta Chardonnay '13	♟♟ 4
○ Valle d'Aosta Chardonnay '12	♟♟ 4
● Valle d'Aosta Cornalin '14	♟♟ 4
● Valle d'Aosta Cornalin '13	♟♟ 4
● Valle d'Aosta Syrah '15	♟♟ 4
● Valle d'Aosta Syrah '14	♟♟ 4

La Vrille

LOC. GRANGEON, 1
11020 VERRAYES [AO]
TEL. +39 0166543018
www.lavrille-agritourisme.com

CELLAR SALES
PRE-BOOKED VISITS
ACCOMMODATION AND RESTAURANT SERVICE
ANNUAL PRODUCTION 16,000 bottles
HECTARES UNDER VINE 2.40
SUSTAINABLE WINERY

At La Vrille, native grape varieties take center stage. But here, you'll find more than just wine. Indeed, their restaurant deserves a visit, with authentic foods made with their own products and ingredients. You'll also have the chance to meet the owners, Hervé and Luciana Deguillaume, who will proudly tell you their story. Among their selection of organic wines, various versions of Chambave Muscat stand out. The Muscat Flétri di La Vrille is marvelous. It's the color of antique gold, with vibrant, sophisticated fragrances that call up sultana and dried apricots, as well as delicate overtones of honey and crème brulee. The mouth is extraordinarily rich and balanced, with a long finish. The Fumin is an elegant wine, vibrant and impenetrable in its ruby red garnet, with pleasant spicy scents calling up tobacco and licorice; light nuances of wild herbs emerge in the mouth, which proves powerful but well-balanced. The rest of their selection is excellent, from the Cornalin to the Pinot Nero and the Muscat.

○ Valle d'Aosta Chambave Muscat Flétri '15	♟♟♟ 7
● Valle d'Aosta Fumin '13	♟♟ 5
○ Valle d'Aosta Chambave Muscat '15	♟♟ 4
● Valle d'Aosta Cornalin '15	♟♟ 4
● Valle d'Aosta Pinot Noir '14	♟♟ 5
○ Valle d'Aosta Chambave Muscat '12	♟♟♟ 4*
○ Valle d'Aosta Chambave Muscat Flétri '14	♟♟♟ 7
○ Valle d'Aosta Chambave Muscat Flétri '11	♟♟♟ 6
○ Valle d'Aosta Chambave Muscat Flétri '10	♟♟♟ 5
○ Valle d'Aosta Chambave Muscat Flétri '07	♟♟♟ 4*
● Valle d'Aosta Fumin '12	♟♟ 5
● Valle d'Aosta Pinot Noir '13	♟♟ 4

La Crotta de Tanteun e Marietta

VIA VEVEY, 23
11100 AOSTA
TEL. +39 3341822471
www.lacrottadetanteunemarietta.it

CELLAR SALES
PRE-BOOKED VISITS
ANNUAL PRODUCTION 10,000 bottles
HECTARES UNDER VINE 2.50

○ Valle d'Aosta Chambave Muscat '16	♟♟ 5	
● Valle d'Aosta Rouge Farouche '15	♟♟ 5	

Feudo di San Maurizio

FRAZ. MAILLOD, 44
11010 SARRE [AO]
TEL. +39 3383186831
www.vinievino.com

CELLAR SALES
PRE-BOOKED VISITS
ANNUAL PRODUCTION 40,000 bottles
HECTARES UNDER VINE 7.00

○ Valle d'Aosta Petite Arvine '16	♟♟ 3*	
● Saro Djablo	♟♟ 3	
● Saro Djablo Calou	♟♟ 3	
● Valle d'Aosta Mayolet '16	♟♟ 4	

Cave Gargantua

FRAZ. CLOS CHATEL, 1
11020 GRESSAN [AO]
TEL. +39 3299271999
www.cavegargantua.it

ANNUAL PRODUCTION 20,000 bottles
HECTARES UNDER VINE 2.80

● Valle d'Aosta Pinot Noir '16	♟♟ 3*	
● Daphne '15	♟♟ 5	
○ Gargantua Blanc	♟♟ 4	
● Vin de la Fée '16	♟♟ 5	

Grosjean

FRAZ. OLLIGNAN, 1
11020 QUART [AO]
TEL. +39 0165775791
www.grosjean.vievini.it

CELLAR SALES
PRE-BOOKED VISITS
ANNUAL PRODUCTION 90,000 bottles
HECTARES UNDER VINE 10.00
VITICULTURE METHOD Certified Organic

☉ Montmarye Extra Brut Rosé M. Cl.	♟♟ 6	
● Valle d'Aosta Fumin V. Rovettaz '13	♟♟ 6	
○ Valle d'Aosta Petite Arvine V. Rovettaz '16	♟♟ 5	
● Valle d'Aosta Pinot Noir '16	♟♟ 5	

Institut Agricole Régional

LOC. RÉGION LA ROCHÉRE, 1A
11100 AOSTA
TEL. +39 0165215811
www.iaraosta.it

CELLAR SALES
PRE-BOOKED VISITS
ANNUAL PRODUCTION 50,000 bottles
HECTARES UNDER VINE 7.30

● Valle d'Aosta Fumin '14	♟♟ 4	
○ Valle d'Aosta Nus Malvoisie '16	♟♟ 2*	
○ Valle d'Aosta Petite Arvine '16	♟ 4	

La Source

LOC. BUSSAN DESSOUS, 1
11010 SAINT PIERRE
TEL. +39 0165904038
www.lasource.it

CELLAR SALES
PRE-BOOKED VISITS
ANNUAL PRODUCTION 40,000 bottles
HECTARES UNDER VINE 7.00

○ Valle d'Aosta Chardonnay '15	♟♟ 3	
● Valle d'Aosta Cornalin '15	♟♟ 3	
○ Valle d'Aosta Petite Arvine '15	♟♟ 3	

PIEDMONT

2018 finds Piedmont following a trajectory similar
to previous years. Many vineyards and territories
are revolting agains the choke-hold that
Barbaresco and Barolo, especially, have on the
region. A quick glance through this year's results
turns up a surprising figure, the number of whites that
earned Tre Bicchieri. Dry and sweet, still and sparkling, some 15 of the region's 77
awards went to whites (almost 20%). 2016 and 2015 saw excellent results for
almost all the categories tasted, with Timorasso back in the limelight thanks to
Walter Massa (a dissident who's been without an appellation for years) and
Cascina Salicetti's welcome newcomers. Another pleasant surprise comes from
Cortese, an area that gave rise to three top wines, among which are two
neophytes. Moscato, the duke of subalpine whites, duplicates last year's triplet.
Paolo Saracco, whose winery did the most to promote the grape, gets top-honors
for the first time. Canavese kept its decent (and growing) slice of production and
gave rise to two golds. The most inspiring result, however, was a long time
coming. Despite its success among the public, before this year Arneis had never
managed a breakthrough. But with two Tre Bicchieri (from producers long
established for their reds), Roero Arneis has finally reached the heights of national
excellence. Barolo maintains its dominant position with 30 Tre Bicchieri, in part
thanks to some favorable seasons (led by the austere and classic 2013). With the
ill-fated 2014 vintage, Barbaresco reminds us that Nebbiolo has obtained results
that elsewhere and with other varieties would be unimaginable. But the statistic
that should make the region proudest is the number of producers to receive Tre
Bicchieri for the first time. There are new ones and historic ones, small and large,
champions of white or red, from Canavese to Tortona, Gavi and Alto Piemonte.
Among these, Santo Stefano Belbo's Marcalberto deserves a special round of
applause, earning 'Sparkling Wine of the Year' for 2018, thanks to a vintage Pinot
Nero that stands shoulder to shoulder with sparklers from more noted territories.

460 Casina Bric

LOC. CASCINA BRICCO
FRAZ. VERGNE
VIA SORELLO, 1A
12060 BAROLO [CN]
TEL. +39 335283468
www.casinabric-barolo.it

CELLAR SALES
PRE-BOOKED VISITS
ANNUAL PRODUCTION 45,000 bottles
HECTARES UNDER VINE 10.00

460 Casina Bric is situated in an area that is one of the highest in the Barolo DOC zone. In fact, they chose to include the number '460' in their name so as to highlight the estate's altitude. Here, the vineyards enjoy a nice, constant breeze (which helped make Gianluca Viberti's choice to avoid pesticides easier). Nebbiolo is the variety's cultivar 'par excellence', used not only for a respectable Barolo but also for an enlivening Brut Rosé that matures for some 10 months on the lees. The 2013 Barolo Bricco delle Viole sees splendid notes of youthful, dynamic fruit pave the way to a palate in which charming hints of roses and licorice emerge. Good acidity and delicate tannins contribute to making this Langhe red so majestic. The 2013 Barolo is just as pleasant but less complex. Gianluca Viberti is also working on sparkling wines made with Nebbiolo.

● Barolo '13	🍷🍷	6
● Barolo Bricco delle Viole '13	🍷🍷	7
● Ansì '14	🍷🍷	4
☉ Nebbiolo d'Alba Brut Rosé	🍷🍷	4
○ Langhe Arneis Ansì '16	🍷	6
● Ansj '11	🍷🍷	4
● Barolo '12	🍷🍷	6
● Barolo '11	🍷🍷	6
● Barolo '10	🍷🍷	6
● Barolo Bricco delle Viole '11	🍷🍷	7
● Barolo Bricco delle Viole '10	🍷🍷	7
☉ Nebbiolo d'Alba Brut Rosè Prêt-à-Porter Collezione N°8	🍷🍷	4

★Abbona

B.GO SAN LUIGI, 40
12063 DOGLIANI [CN]
TEL. +39 0173721317
www.abbona.com

CELLAR SALES
PRE-BOOKED VISITS
ANNUAL PRODUCTION 350,000 bottles
HECTARES UNDER VINE 50.00

The Abbona family recently expanded their charming underground cellar by building a new structure above it, one which will soon be used as an elegant agritourism. The project is designed to attract wine lovers, who will find true jewels here, made with Dolcetto and Nebbiolo grapes, as well as Barbera, Arneis (a variety from Roero) and Viognier. Their wide-ranging selection has seen the recent addition of Piculin, a passito dried-grape wine made with Moscato cultivated in Dogliani. Their Barolo comes from Monforte d'Alba, Pressenda cru and Novello, where the Cerviano and Ravera vineyards prove more interesting by the year. The 2016 Papà Celso can look forward to aging for many years to come. It's a dynamic wine, with good weight, and thoroughly deserved a Tre Bicchieri once again. The multifaceted 2013 Barolo Pressenda is leisurely and powerful, and moves between citrus peel and licorice, while the modern 2013 Barolo Ravera is already enjoyable and ready to drink. The 2016 Cinerino is a white made with Viognier that has never been so elegant and delicate - very pleasant indeed.

● Dogliani Papà Celso '16	🍷🍷🍷	4*
● Barolo Pressenda '13	🍷🍷	7
○ Langhe Cinerino '16	🍷🍷	5
● Barolo Ravera '13	🍷🍷	7
● Dogliani San Luigi '16	🍷🍷	3
● Nebbiolo d'Alba Bricco Barone '15	🍷🍷	4
● Barolo Cerviano '10	🍷🍷🍷	7
● Barolo Terlo Ravera '08	🍷🍷🍷	6
● Barolo Terlo Ravera '06	🍷🍷🍷	6
● Dogliani Papà Celso '15	🍷🍷🍷	4*
● Dogliani Papà Celso '13	🍷🍷🍷	4*
● Dogliani Papà Celso '11	🍷🍷🍷	3*
● Dogliani Papà Celso '09	🍷🍷🍷	3

Anna Maria Abbona

FRAZ. MONCUCCO, 21
12060 FARIGLIANO [CN]
TEL. +39 0173797228
www.annamariaabbona.it

CELLAR SALES
PRE-BOOKED VISITS
ANNUAL PRODUCTION 75,000 bottles
HECTARES UNDER VINE 14.00

To those wine tourists visiting Langhe we highly recommend a visit to this small, cozy operation run for almost thirty years by Anna Maria Abbona and her husband Franco Schellino. In addition to magnificent panoramas, you can enjoy tales of passion for the land and work of winemaking. Dolcetto is cultivated for their most important wines (with the utmost respect for the territory), with Dogliani San Bernardo and Maioli at the forefront. Though for some years now, their Barolo (cultivated in Monforte) has had notable success as well. The plush 2013 Barolo is already open and eloquent. It may not be particularly powerful, but it shows excellent balance and is rich in herbs and spices. The Dogliani selections are sound, and the Maioli promises to do well after bottle aging. Despite the difficult combination of Dolcetto and Barbera grapes, the 2013 Langhe Cadò delivered. The 2016 Barbera d'Alba wins you over with its approachable pleasantness.

● Barbera d'Alba '16	🍷🍷 2*
● Barolo '13	🍷🍷 6
● Dogliani Sorì dij But '16	🍷🍷 2*
● Dogliani Sup. Maioli '15	🍷🍷 3
● Langhe Nebbiolo '14	🍷🍷 3
○ Langhe Riesling L'Alman '15	🍷🍷 3
● Langhe Rosso Cadò '13	🍷🍷 5
● Langhe Dolcetto '16	🍷 2
○ Langhe Nascetta Netta '15	🍷 3
● Dogliani Sup. San Bernardo '12	🍷🍷🍷 4*
● Dogliani Sup. San Bernardo '11	🍷🍷🍷 4*
● Barolo '12	🍷🍷 6
● Barolo '11	🍷🍷 6
● Barolo '10	🍷🍷 6
● Dogliani Sup. Maioli '14	🍷🍷 3*

Orlando Abrigo

VIA CAPPELLETTO, 5
12050 TREISO [CN]
TEL. +39 0173630533
www.orlandoabrigo.it

CELLAR SALES
PRE-BOOKED VISITS
ACCOMMODATION AND RESTAURANT SERVICE
ANNUAL PRODUCTION 80,000 bottles
HECTARES UNDER VINE 20.00
SUSTAINABLE WINERY

Now that his new, underground cellar is perfectly organized, Giovanni Abrigo can dedicate himself with renewed passion to his vineyards (primarily Nebbiolo). Their Barbaresco, which is cultivated here, possesses good texture and, thanks to the altitude, its able to maintain a nice degree of freshness (even during warmer years). The interesting facility, which is worth visiting (in part for the way it integrates with the landscape) features the panoramic and inviting Foresteria Settevie. The delicate and pure 2012 Barbaresco Rongalio Riserva offers up slight hints of cinchona and sweet wood. The palate sees nice freshness and moderate alcohol, with tannins diluted by a soft fruitiness. The 2014 Meruzzano also put in a strong performance. It features a velvety palate and a particularly fresh nose that calls up aniseed.

● Barbaresco Rongalio Ris. '12	🍷🍷 8
● Barbaresco Meruzzano '14	🍷🍷 5
● Barbaresco Montersino '14	🍷🍷 7
● Barbera d'Alba Mervisano '15	🍷🍷 4
● Barbera d'Alba V. Roreto '15	🍷 2
○ Langhe Très Plus '15	🍷 3
● Barbaresco Meruzzano '13	🍷🍷 5
● Barbaresco Montersino '13	🍷🍷 7
● Barbaresco Rongalio Ris. '11	🍷🍷 8
● Barbera d'Alba Roreto '14	🍷🍷 3
● Langhe Rosso Livraie '13	🍷🍷 4
○ Langhe Très Plus '14	🍷🍷 3

★Giulio Accornero e Figli

Cascina Ca' Cima, 1
15049 Vignale Monferrato [AI]
Tel. +39 0142933317
www.accornerovini.it

CELLAR SALES
PRE-BOOKED VISITS
ACCOMMODATION
ANNUAL PRODUCTION 100,000 bottles
HECTARES UNDER VINE 22.00
SUSTAINABLE WINERY

Elegance and finesse are synonyms, but
only together can they really describe
Ermanno Accornero's wines, wines that are
made possible thanks to a commitment to
terroir, taken together with a strong
territorial bond. Indeed, in this case, the
winery's growth and desire to safeguard
the territory have gone hand in hand,
making for a story that now stands at the
vanguard. Their Grignolino Bricco from
Bosco Vigne Vecchie is probably the most
concrete representation of how the area's
attributes are being brought out through
their wines, in part by combining the
pursuit of originality with the history of
these hills. Practically their whole selection
of wines made it to the finals this year. A
splendid version of the Giulin grabbed a
Tre Bicchieri, ousting the multi-awarded
2015 Bricco Battista, a vintage that
conferred aromatic complexity and power
and length on the palate. The Grignolino
Vigne Vecchie has made it to the finals yet
again, proving it's a thoroughbred, vintage
after vintage. The lovely Grignolino and
Nebbiolo Girotondo also reached the finals.

● Barbera del M.to Giulin '15	▼▼▼ 3*
● Barbera del M.to Sup. Bricco Battista '14	▼▼ 5
● Grignolino del M.to Casalese Bricco del Bosco '16	▼▼ 3*
● Grignolino del M.to Casalese Bricco del Bosco V. V. '12	▼▼ 6
● M.to Girotondo '14	▼▼ 4
● Casorzo Brigantino '16	▼▼ 2*
○ Fonsina '16	▼▼ 3
● Piemonte Barbera Campomoro '15	▼▼ 2*
● Barbera del M.to Sup. Bricco Battista '13	♟♟♟ 5
● Barbera del M.to Sup. Bricco Battista '12	♟♟♟ 5
● Barbera del M.to Sup. Bricco Battista '11	♟♟♟ 5

Marco e Vittorio Adriano

Fraz. San Rocco Seno d'Elvio, 13a
12051 Alda [CN]
Tel. +39 0173362294
www.adrianovini.it

CELLAR SALES
PRE-BOOKED VISITS
ANNUAL PRODUCTION 160,000 bottles
HECTARES UNDER VINE 27.00
SUSTAINABLE WINERY

Marco and Vittorio Adriano's story is
well-known in Italy. Their cellar in San
Rocco Seno d'Elvio was completed after
years of sacrifice and battles, in some
cases involving actual meteorological
disasters. But today things are looking up.
Their Barbarescos, made from grapes
cultivated in their Basarin di Neive, Brico
and Frati crus, have for some time now
been considered a true benchmark for
stylistic continuity and affordability. These
are aged in Slovanian oak barrels and
exhibit a consistency that the winery has
been exploring in greater detail since 2004
with the introduction of their 'Riserva'. The
2012 Barbaresco Basarin Riserva offers up
pleasant fresh aromas of camphor, as well
as more mature fragrances tending toward
tobacco and red fruit. Its palate proves
restrained and austere. The forthright
2014 Barbaresco Basarin has aromas of
ripe grapes and licorice, while its
mouthfilling palate is slightly dried by
tannins at the finish. The 2014 Sanadeive
features herbs, some pleasant vegetal hints
and medium weight.

● Barbaresco Basarin Ris. '12	▼▼ 6
● Barbaresco Basarin '14	▼▼ 5
● Barbaresco Sanadaive '14	▼▼ 5
○ Ardì	♟♟ 2*
● Barbaresco Basarin '13	♟♟ 5
● Barbaresco Basarin '12	♟♟ 4
● Barbaresco Basarin Ris. '11	♟♟ 6
● Barbaresco Sanadaive '13	♟♟ 4
● Barbaresco Sanadaive '12	♟♟ 4
● Barbera d'Alba '15	♟♟ 2*
● Barbera d'Alba Sup. '13	♟♟ 2*
● Dolcetto d'Alba '15	♟♟ 2*
● Langhe Nebbiolo '13	♟♟ 3
○ Langhe Sauvignon Basarico '15	♟♟ 3

Claudio Alario

VIA SANTA CROCE, 23
12055 DIANO D'ALBA [CN]
TEL. +39 0173231808
www.alarioclaudio.it

CELLAR SALES
PRE-BOOKED VISITS
ANNUAL PRODUCTION 46,000 bottles
HECTARES UNDER VINE 10.00

Dolcetto di Diano d'Alba has always been held in high esteem by Langhe's producers. It boasts richness of fruit and commendable vibrance, while the palate is succulent, almost chewy. Claudio Alario was and is one of its greatest interpreters. Their Barolo, first bottled in 1995 and cultivated in Serralunga d'Alba (cru Sorano) and Verduno (Riva Rocca), deserves similar accolades. The winery's stile features frankness, drinkability and pleasantess, with highly guarded use of wood. The 2013 Barolo Sorano is endowed with an exquisite classic style and expressive notes of licorice and cinchona, while its bold and structured palate displays a precise balance. The more delicate 2013 Barolo Riva Rocca is just as well-orchestrated and close-focused. The 2015 Dolcetto di Diano d'Alba Sorì Pradurent exhibits a great tannic structure, while the fruity 2016 Sorì Montagrillo is more caressing and approachable.

● Barolo Sorano '13	▼▼	6
● Barolo Riva Rocca '13	▼▼	5
● Dolcetto di Diano d'Alba Sorì Montagrillo '16	▼▼	2*
● Dolcetto di Diano d'Alba Sup. Sorì Pradurent '15	▼▼	3
● Nebbiolo d'Alba Cascinotto '15	▼▼	4
● Barolo Sorano '05	♟♟♟	7
● Barolo Riva Rocca '12	♟♟	5
● Barolo Sorano '12	♟♟	6
● Barolo Sorano '11	♟♟	6
● Dolcetto di Diano d'Alba Costa Fiore '15	♟♟	2*
● Dolcetto di Diano d'Alba Sorì Montagrillo '15	♟♟	2*
● Dolcetto di Diano d'Alba Sorì Montagrillo '14	♟♟	2*
● Dolcetto di Diano d'Alba Sup. Sorì Pradurent '13	♟♟	3

★F.lli Alessandria

VIA B. VALFRÉ, 59
12060 VERDUNO [CN]
TEL. +39 0172470113
www.fratellialessandria.it

CELLAR SALES
PRE-BOOKED VISITS
ANNUAL PRODUCTION 80,000 bottles
HECTARES UNDER VINE 14.00

Going from being an emerging producer to a star isn't as simple as it might seem, particularly in a territory as competitive as Langhe. The Alessandria family have managed just that in only a few harvests, especially since the youngest, Vittore, joined his father, Gian Battista, and uncle, Alessandro, full-time. It all centers on a multiform selection of Barolo: Gramolere di Monforte d'Alba, Monvigliero and San Lorenzo di Verduno, interpreted through aging in mid-size casks and 2000-3000 litre French oak. Expression that is both precise and seductive simultaneously, found also in their outstanding Pelaverga reds. The 2013 Barolo Monvigliero speaks of elegance and finesse. It's a Tre Bicchieri full of personality that charms the nose with stimulating notes of pepper, licorice and fruity aromas on a base of cherries and raspberries. Its palate proves succulent, fresh and extremely pleasant. The 2013 Barolo San Lorenzo di Verduno comes through slightly more tannic, but just as elegant and charming. The balsamic 2013 Gramolere is complex and firmly structured.

● Barolo Monvigliero '13	▼▼▼	6
● Barolo Gramolere '13	▼▼	6
● Barolo San Lorenzo di Verduno '13	▼▼	6
● Barolo '13	▼▼	5
● Langhe Nebbiolo Prinsiot '15	▼▼	3
● Verduno Pelaverga Speciale '16	▼▼	3
● Barolo Gramolere '11	♟♟♟	6
● Barolo Gramolere '10	♟♟♟	6
● Barolo Monvigliero '12	♟♟♟	6
● Barolo Monvigliero '09	♟♟♟	6
● Barolo Monvigliero '06	♟♟♟	6
● Barolo S. Lorenzo '08	♟♟♟	6
● Barolo '12	♟♟	5
● Barolo Gramolere '12	♟♟	6
● Barolo San Lorenzo di Verduno '12	♟♟	6
● Verduno Pelaverga Speciale '15	♟♟	3

★Gianfranco Alessandria

LOC. MANZONI, 13
12065 MONFORTE D'ALBA [CN]
TEL. +39 0173/8576
www.gianfrancoalessandria.com

CELLAR SALES
PRE-BOOKED VISITS
ANNUAL PRODUCTION 50,000 bottles
HECTARES UNDER VINE 7.00

Gianfranco Alessandria is a classic Langhe
winery: a close-knit couple that's just
celebrated thirty years of business, just a
few hectares of vineyards in outstanding
positions, and a new generation that's
starting to push forward with enthusiasm.
And all of it without too much commotion: a
gradual expansion of the terrain inherited
and a consistent focus on quality. The
result is a selection of modern wines that
are both charming and elegant, as
well-crafted in the cellar as on the vine,
made exclusively with the area's three
historic grape varieties: Nebbiolo (Barolo
mostly), Barbara (their Vittoria line is a
must) and Dolcetto. The fruity, youthful and
slightly licorice 2013 Barolo San Giovanni
presents a remarkably taut mouth.
Moderately assertive tannins provide it with
backbone and a lingering, close-focused,
flavorsome finish. The Barbera d'Alba
Vittoria once again proves elegant, but the
2014 vintage is less caressing than usual.
The fruity 2016 Dolcetto d'Alba,
meanwhile, put in a good performance.

● Barolo '13	▼▼ 6
● Barolo San Giovanni '13	▼▼ 7
● Barbera d'Alba Vittoria '14	▼▼ 5
● Dolcetto d'Alba '16	▼▼ 3
● Barbera d'Alba '16	▼ 3
● Barbera d'Alba Vittoria '11	♛♛♛ 5
● Barolo S. Giovanni '04	♛♛♛ 7
● Barbera d'Alba '14	♛♛ 3
● Barbera d'Alba Vittoria '13	♛♛ 5
● Barolo '12	♛♛ 6
● Barolo '11	♛♛ 6
● Barolo S. Giovanni '12	♛♛ 7
● Dolcetto d'Alba '15	♛♛ 3
● Dolcetto d'Alba '14	♛♛ 2*
● Langhe Nebbiolo '13	♛♛ 3

Marchesi Alfieri

P.ZZA ALFIERI, 28
14010 SAN MARTINO ALFIERI [AT]
TEL. +39 0141976015
www.marchesialfieri.it

CELLAR SALES
PRE-BOOKED VISITS
ACCOMMODATION
ANNUAL PRODUCTION 100,000 bottles
HECTARES UNDER VINE 20.00

As far back as 1337, there are records in
the Alfieri family archives that point to the
presence of vineyards on their terrain.
Today, in some of the most beautiful sorì of
San Marino Alfieri, the San Marino di San
Germano sisters are cultivating mostly
Barbera, according to tradition, and some
hectares of Grignolino, Pinot Nero and
Nebbiolo. Vineyards as old as 80 and
careful attention to quality, both in the field
and in the cellar, make for wines that seek
to bring together elegance, complexity and
territorial identity. The Barbera d'Asti
Superiore Alfiera has proven its top quality,
despite the difficult 2014 vintage. Spicy and
earthy notes merge with hints of black fruit,
accompanied by a long and savory palate
and a finish with elegant herby overtones.
The rest of their wines also proved
well-made, starting with the 2015 Barbera
d'Asti La Tota, a pleasant and approachable
wine. The 2015 Piemonte Pinot Nero San
Germano comes through juicy and gutsy
and the 2013 Terre Alfieri Nebbiolo Costa
Quaglia is intense and austere.

● Barbera d'Asti Sup. Alfiera '14	▼▼ 5
● Barbera d'Asti La Tota '15	▼▼ 3
● Piemonte Pinot Nero San Germano '15	▼▼ 5
● Terre Alfieri Nebbiolo Costa Quaglia '13	▼▼ 4
● M.to Rosso Sostegno '15	▼ 2
● Piemonte Grignolino Sansoero '16	▼ 2
● Barbera d'Asti Sup. Alfiera '07	♛♛♛ 5
● Barbera d'Asti Sup. Alfiera '05	♛♛♛ 5
● Barbera d'Asti Sup. Alfiera '01	♛♛♛ 5
● Barbera d'Asti La Tota '14	♛♛ 3
● Barbera d'Asti Sup. Alfiera '13	♛♛ 5
● Piemonte Grignolino Sansoero '15	♛♛ 2*
● Piemonte Pinot Nero San Germano '12	♛♛ 5

Giovanni Almondo

VIA SAN ROCCO, 26
12046 MONTÀ [CN]
TEL. +39 0173975256
www.giovannialmondo.com

PRE-BOOKED VISITS
ANNUAL PRODUCTION 130,000 bottles
HECTARES UNDER VINE 18.00
SUSTAINABLE WINERY

The Almondo family's winery, managed by Domenico and, increasingly, his two sons, Federico and Stefano, is a leader among Roero's winemakers. They are known mostly for the quality of their Arneis, to which three quarters of their vineyards are dedicated. They follow an organic approach to viticulture that, over time, is moving closer to biodynamic, making for wines of notable character and a varietal stamping that is more and more perceptible. The new 2016 Roero Arneis Le Rive del Bricco delle Ciliegie has earned a Tre Bicchieri. It's made with Arneis grapes grown in the winery's highest vineyards. This charming wine offers up floral and citrusy aromas leading into a fresh, dynamic and savory palate, with notes of chalk and grapefruit. The 2016 Bricco delle Ciliegie is well-made and exhibits similar qualities, though it's more supple. The 2014 Roero Bric Valdiana shows great quality. Aromas of red fruit merge with Mediterranean scrub, while in the mouth the wine proves rich in fruit and succulent.

○ Roero Arneis Le Rive del Bricco delle Ciliegie '16	🍷🍷🍷 4*
● Roero Bric Valdiana '14	🍷🍷 5
○ Roero Arneis Bricco delle Ciliegie '16	🍷🍷 3
● Barbera d'Alba Valbianchéra '15	🍷 3
● Roero '15	🍷 3
● Roero Bric Valdiana '11	🍷🍷🍷 5
● Roero Bric Valdiana '07	🍷🍷🍷 5
● Roero Giovanni Almondo Ris. '13	🍷🍷🍷 5
● Roero Giovanni Almondo Ris. '11	🍷🍷🍷 5
● Roero Giovanni Almondo Ris. '09	🍷🍷🍷 5
○ Roero Arneis Bricco delle Ciliegie '15	🍷🍷 3*
● Roero Bric Valdiana '13	🍷🍷 5

★★★Elio Altare
Cascina Nuova

FRAZ. ANNUNZIATA, 51
12064 LA MORRA [CN]
TEL. +39 017350835
www.elioaltare.com

CELLAR SALES
PRE-BOOKED VISITS
ANNUAL PRODUCTION 70,000 bottles
HECTARES UNDER VINE 11.00

Elio Altare's story continues to be told. Even today, the debate surrounding Nebbiolo is more nuanced than it was 10-20 years ago. Disowned by his father, Giovanni, for having broken too strongly with Langhe's vine growing and winemaking tradition, today Elio finds himself overseeing the passing of the torch to his daughter, Silvia (who is, by now, a fixture at the winery). Their Arborina and Brunate are grown in La Morra, Cannubi in Barolo, Cerretta Vigna Bricco in Serralunga d'Alba: their Barolos are increasingly authoritative. But their Campogrande, which Elio strongly wanted grown in Riomaggiore, is also worth trying. The Cerretta Vigna Bricco is made with grapes from a cru that's proving to be one of the best in this area. It makes for a consistent Barolo that's elegant and complex, as well as structured. This superlative 2011 is the quintessence of refined austerity and earned a Tre Bicchieri. The 2013 Barolo Arborina possesses a wealth sublime aromas. The Langhe Giàrborina, made with Nebbiolo, displays a commendable attention to detail.

● Barolo Cerretta V. Bricco '11	🍷🍷🍷 8
● Barolo Arborina '13	🍷🍷 8
● Langhe Giàrborina '15	🍷🍷 8
● Langhe Larigi '15	🍷🍷 8
● Barolo '13	🍷🍷 8
● Langhe La Villa '15	🍷🍷 8
● Barolo Arborina '09	🍷🍷🍷 8
● Barolo Cerretta V. Bricco '10	🍷🍷🍷 8
● Barolo Cerretta V. Bricco '06	🍷🍷🍷 8
● Barolo Cerretta V. Bricco '05	🍷🍷🍷 8
● Langhe Arborina '08	🍷🍷🍷 8
● Langhe La Villa '06	🍷🍷🍷 8
● Langhe Larigi '13	🍷🍷🍷 8
● Langhe Larigi '12	🍷🍷🍷 8
● Langhe Larigi '07	🍷🍷🍷 7

Amalia Cascina in Langa

LOC. SANT'ANNA, 85
12065 CUNEO
TEL. +39 0173789013
www.cascinaamalia.it

CELLAR SALES
PRE-BOOKED VISITS
ACCOMMODATION
ANNUAL PRODUCTION 60,000 bottles
HECTARES UNDER VINE 14.00
SUSTAINABLE WINERY

Cascina Amalia got its start some 15 years ago. Since then, the Boffa family has found an important and specific focus; create an estate that is not only good for cultivation, but beautiful. And so it is that their cellar, situated in a magnificent panorama, brings together an elegant bed & breakfast and a collection of modern artworks that is as sophisticated as it is elegant. Wine is still at the centre of their commercial interests, thanks in part to the acquisition of Barolo vineyards in the crus of Bussia and Le Coste di Monforte. The very pleasant 2013 Barolo Le Coste di Monforte still hasn't fully expressed its complexity. It displays straightforward aromas of spices and a rich freshness on the palate. The 2013 Barolo Bussia features a lively and complex personality with gutsier tannins. The 2015 Barbera d'Alba Superiore has a modern style and vanilla flavors. Kudos as well to the elegant 2015 Rossese Bianco.

● Barolo Bussia '13		♟♟ 6
● Barolo Le Coste di Monforte '13		♟♟ 6
● Barbera d'Alba Sup. '15		♟♟ 4
● Barolo '13		♟♟ 6
○ Langhe Rossese Bianco '15		♟♟ 4
● Langhe Nebbiolo '16		♟ 4
● Barbera d'Alba '15		♟♟ 4
● Barbera d'Alba '13		♟♟ 4
● Barbera d'Alba Sup. '13		♟♟ 4
● Barolo '11		♟♟ 6
● Barolo Le Coste di Monforte '11		♟♟ 6
● Barolo Le Coste di Monforte '10		♟♟ 5
○ Langhe Rossese Bianco '14		♟♟ 4

Antichi Vigneti di Cantalupo

VIA MICHELANGELO BUONARROTI, 5
28074 GHEMME [NO]
TEL. +39 0163840041
www.cantalupo.net

CELLAR SALES
PRE-BOOKED VISITS
ANNUAL PRODUCTION 200,000 bottles
HECTARES UNDER VINE 35.00

Antichi Vigneti di Cantalupo officially got its start in 1977, thanks to the efforts of Carlo Arlunno. Today, the winery, managed by Carlo's son, Alberto, is without a doubt one of the most well-known and enduring of Ghemme. The historic Novara DOC zone is represented by some four wines: Cantalupo, the crus Collis Breclemae and Collis Carellae, and their Signore di Bayard selection, all reds that are compact and austere. We should add their Nebbiolo Spanna, Vespolina, Uva Rara, Erbaluce, Arneis and Chardonnay. Their estate is comprised of some 35 hectares of vineyards, spread out throughout prized territories like Baraggiola, Rossini, Ai Livelli (Carolus Bianco), Roccolo Maiolo (Abate di Cluny) and Ronco San Pietro. The classic 2010 vintage has created a rather competitive trio of Ghemme wines. Aromas of cinchona, tobacco and rust are present in both the (more powerful) Collis Carellae and the Collis Breclemae (with its stiffer tannins). The Anno Primo, however displays more complexity, saline vigor and delicate extraction.

● Ghemme Cantalupo Anno Primo '10		♟♟ 5
● Ghemme Collis Breclemae '10		♟♟ 6
● Ghemme Collis Carellae '10		♟♟ 6
○ Carolus		♟♟ 2
☉ Colline Novaresi Nebbiolo Il Mimo '16		♟♟ 2*
● Ghemme '05		♟♟♟ 4
● Ghemme Collis Breclemae '00		♟♟♟ 6
● Colline Novaresi Primigenia '13		♟♟ 2*
● Colline Novaresi Vespolina Villa Horta '12		♟♟ 2*
● Ghemme Cantalupo Anno Primo '09		♟♟ 5
● Ghemme Collis Breclemae '06		♟♟ 6
● Ghemme Collis Carellae '09		♟♟ 6
● Ghemme Signore di Bayard '08		♟♟ 6

★Antoniolo

C.SO VALSESIA, 277
13045 GATTINARA [VC]
TEL. +39 0163833612
antoniolovini@bmm.it

CELLAR SALES
PRE-BOOKED VISITS
ANNUAL PRODUCTION 60,000 bottles
HECTARES UNDER VINE 12.00

Pure, crystalline, apparently light but dense in flavor, these are the classic features of Gattinara, made by Antoniolo. Indeed, the Antoniolo family are among those that have best managed to protect the spirit of Alto Piemonte's Nebbiolo, even during periods that have hurt fairer, less full-bodied wines. Alberto and Lorella are the worthy successors to the work begun by their mother, Rosanna. They bring an intimate knowledge of majestic crus like Osso San Grato, San Francesco, Castelle and Borelle to their work, highlighting each's attributes through a traditional, though never passé winemaking style. Wines are aged in large wood. In some cases it's worth waiting decades to uncork them. The Antoniolo family's flagship Gattinara wines seem to have benefited from the fresh and regular 2013 vintage, starting with their elegant base wine. Moving up the selection, the San Francesco and Osso San Grato display increased generosity and depth. The first is sunnier and more together, while the second comes through aromatically more closed, but denser.

● Gattinara Osso San Grato '13	♀♀♀ 8
● Gattinara '13	♀♀ 6
● Gattinara San Francesco '13	♀♀ 8
● Coste della Sesia Nebbiolo Juvenia '15	♀♀ 4
● Gattinara Osso S. Grato '11	♀♀♀ 8
● Gattinara Osso S. Grato '10	♀♀♀ 8
● Gattinara Osso S. Grato '09	♀♀♀ 8
● Gattinara Osso San Grato '12	♀♀♀ 8
● Gattinara S. Francesco '08	♀♀♀ 7
● Gattinara S. Francesco '07	♀♀♀ 5
● Gattinara '12	♀♀ 5
● Gattinara Le Castelle '12	♀♀ 7
● Gattinara S. Francesco '12	♀♀ 8

Odilio Antoniotti

V.LO ANTONIOTTI, 5
13868 SOSTEGNO [BI]
TEL. +39 0163860309
antoniottiodilio@libero.it

CELLAR SALES
PRE-BOOKED VISITS
ANNUAL PRODUCTION 13,000 bottles
HECTARES UNDER VINE 4.50

Among the most recent vigneron to lay claim to the Bramaterra DOC zone are Odilio Antoniotti and his son, Mattia, who attend to their six hectares of vineyards in Sostegno, in the picturesque district of Casa del Bosco. Their flagship red is made with grapes from the Martinazzi cru, and their Pramartello from Costa della Sesia and Pramartel. The addition of a new 'single vineyard' may be on the way, thanks to a new acquisition in Cincignone. Summing up, there may only be a few hectares, but they're good ones. The style is traditional, explored through patient aging in oak, some of which comes from their own property. The 2013 Bramaterra offers up aromas of raspberry, wild strawberries, licorice and herbs. It's irresistibly territorial right from its initial aromatic impact. More time in the bottle should harmonize the luxuriant and pervasive palate even further. The Pramartel proves to be more subtle, but just as recognizable for its fresh fruit.

● Bramaterra '13	♀♀ 4
● Pramartel	♀♀ 3
● Bramaterra '10	♀♀♀ 3*
● Bramaterra '12	♀♀ 4
● Bramaterra '11	♀♀ 3*
● Bramaterra '09	♀♀ 3*
● Bramaterra '08	♀♀ 3*
● Bramaterra '07	♀♀ 3*

PIEDMONT

L'Armangia

FRAZ. SAN GIOVANNI, 122
14053 CANELLI [AT]
TEL. +39 0141824947
www.armangia.it

CELLAR SALES
PRE-BOOKED VISITS
ACCOMMODATION
ANNUAL PRODUCTION 95,000 bottles
HECTARES UNDER VINE 11.00
SUSTAINABLE WINERY

Armangia, managed by Ignazio Giovine and his wife, Giuliana, got its start in the early 1990s, though its core vineyards on the Sant'Antonio a Canelli hills have been in the family since 1850. Today, the winery, in addition to its vineyards in Vanelli (where mostly white grapes are grown) has vineyards in Moasca, San Marzano Oliveto and Castle Boglione. Here their red grapes, most Barbera, are cultivated. Their wines display good structure with characteristics that stay true to the territory. The Nizza Titon once affirms it's status as one of the year's best Barberas. The 2014 highlights aromas of dark fruit, spices and rain-soaked earth, while its palate proves full, fresh and dynamic. The 2016 Moscato d'Asti Canelli features balsamic notes and white chocolate; it's sweet, but not cloying, on the palate. The 2015 Piemonte Chardonnay Robi & Robi offers up rich fruity notes and has good structure and complexity. Both are well-made.

● Nizza Titon '14	▼▼ 3*
○ Lorenzomariasole Extra Brut M. Cl.	▼▼ 4
○ Moscato d'Asti Canelli '16	▼▼ 2*
○ Piemonte Chardonnay Robi & Robi '15	▼▼ 4
● Barbera d'Asti Sopra Berruti '16	▼ 2
○ Mesicaseu	▼ 4
● Barbera d'Asti Sopra Berruti '14	♀♀ 2*
● Barbera d'Asti Sup. Nizza Titon '13	♀♀ 3*
● Barbera d'Asti Sup. Nizza Titon '12	♀♀ 3*
● Barbera d'Asti Sup. Nizza Vignali '11	♀♀ 5
○ M.to Bianco Enneenne '14	♀♀ 2*
○ Moscato d'Asti Canelli '15	♀♀ 2*
○ Moscato d'Asti Canelli '14	♀♀ 2*
○ Piemonte Chardonnay Pratorotondo '14	♀♀ 2*

Paolo Avezza

REG. MONFORTE, 62
14053 CANELLI [AT]
TEL. +39 0141822296
www.paoloavezza.com

CELLAR SALES
PRE-BOOKED VISITS
ANNUAL PRODUCTION 25,000 bottles
HECTARES UNDER VINE 7.00

Since 2001, Paolo Avezza and his family have managed the winery founded by his grandfather Natale 60 years ago. Their estate spans two municipalities: Nizza Monferrato, where their Barbera is cultivated in silty-clay soil and Canelli, where Nebbiolo, Dolcetto, Pino Nero, Chardonnay and Moscato are cultivated in well-exposed, calcareous-marl soil. We should point out their sparkling wine selection, made both with the 'Metodo Classico' and by 'Martinotti'. Their wines display a modern style, putting freshness and aromatic accuracy first. As always, the Nizza Sotto la Muda is their flagship wine. Despite the difficult vintage, the 2014 shows remarkable body and complexity, with notes of cinchona, roots and rain-soaked earth. Despite discernible aging in wood, it still manages to remain dynamic with a lingering and fresh finish. The floral and supple 2016 Moscato d'Asti Canelli La Commenda and the pleasant and approachable 2013 Alta Langa Brut are both well-made.

● Nizza Sotto la Muda '14	▼▼ 4
○ Alta Langa Brut '13	▼▼ 4
○ Moscato d'Asti Canelli La Commenda '16	▼▼ 2*
⊙ Brut Rosé M. Cl.	▼ 3
● Barbera d'Asti Sup. Nizza Sotto la Muda '10	♀♀♀ 4*
● Barbera d'Asti Sup. Nizza Sotto la Muda '07	♀♀♀ 3*
● Barbera d'Asti '15	♀♀ 2*
● Barbera d'Asti '14	♀♀ 2*
● Barbera d'Asti Sup. Nizza Sotto la Muda '13	♀♀ 4
● Barbera d'Asti Sup. Nizza Sotto la Muda '12	♀♀ 4
○ Moscato d'Asti Canelli La Commenda '15	♀♀ 2*
○ Moscato d'Asti La Commenda '14	♀♀ 2*

★Azelia

FRAZ. GARBELLETTO
VIA ALBA BAROLO, 143
12060 CASTIGLIONE FALLETTO [CN]
TEL. +39 017362859
www.azelia.it

CELLAR SALES
PRE-BOOKED VISITS
ANNUAL PRODUCTION 80,000 bottles
HECTARES UNDER VINE 16.00
SUSTAINABLE WINERY

Founded in 1920 by the decorated citizen Lorenzo Scavino, today this beautiful Castiglione Falletto estate is run by his great-grandson, Luigi, wife, Lorella, and son, Lorenzo (the fifth generation to lead). With almost one hundred years of history behind them, Azelia has become a first-rate operation, with more than 15 hectares of vineyards spread out between Montelupo Albese, Castiglione Falletto (Bricco Fiasco) and Serralunga d'Alba (Margheria, San Rocco, Bricco Voghera). Naturally, Nebbiolo comes first, giving life to a variety of Barolos that are made mostly with the help of rotary fermenters, and then aged both in barriques and large barrels. The 2013 Barolos achieved an overall splendid result. Our favorite is the Margheria, which successfully balances raspberry and licorice notes, and features the powerful and caressing palate common to this famous Serralunga d'Alba cru. Their basic Barolo also put in a strong performance, emphasizing what a professional producer Luigi Scavino is. Fresh fruit eases into citrus in the weighty Bricco Fiasco.

● Barolo '13	🍷🍷	6
● Barolo Bricco Fiasco '13	🍷🍷	8
● Barolo Margheria '13	🍷🍷	8
● Barbera d'Alba Punta '13	🍷🍷	5
● Barolo San Rocco '13	🍷🍷	8
● Langhe Nebbiolo '15	🍷🍷	4
● Barolo Bricco Fiasco '12	🍷🍷🍷	8
● Barolo Bricco Fiasco '09	🍷🍷🍷	8
● Barolo Margheria '06	🍷🍷🍷	7
● Barolo S. Rocco '11	🍷🍷🍷	8
● Barolo S. Rocco '08	🍷🍷🍷	8
● Barolo Bricco Voghera Ris. '07	🍷🍷	8
● Barolo Margheria '12	🍷🍷	8
● Barolo S. Rocco '12	🍷🍷	8

Banfi Piemonte

VIA VITTORIO VENETO, 76
15019 STREVI [AL]
TEL. +39 0144362600
www.castellobanfi.com

PRE-BOOKED VISITS
ANNUAL PRODUCTION 2,000,000 bottles
HECTARES UNDER VINE 76.00

Historically, the Mariani family's wine selection is built around their sparkling wines. But, in reality, their wide range is closely tied to the territory: Dolcetto d'Acqui, Albarossa and Brachettto d'Acqui are decidedly local wines. They expand things to the rest of the region with their Gavi, Moscato (both standard cork and sparkling) and their Barbera d'Asti. Their sparkling wines are in great form this year, particularly the very intriguing Cuvée Aurora and the Brut Metodo Classico. Then come their young wines with great character: the impeccably-made Dolcetto d'Acqui L'Ardì, which is exemplary for its wine type, and the Barbera d'Asti L'Altra, which proved to be intense in every tasting stage and possessed of a balanced and well-orchestrated palate. Rosa Regale is a Brachetto Spumante with an excellent nose-palate symmetry, highlighted by a good balance between acidity and residual sweetness.

○ Alta Langa Brut Cuvée Aurora '12	🍷🍷	6
● Barbera d'Asti L'Altra '16	🍷🍷	5
● Bracchetto d'Acqui Rosa Regale '16	🍷🍷	4
○ Brut Banfi M. Cl.	🍷🍷	5
● Dolcetto d'Acqui L'Ardì '16	🍷🍷	3
○ Gavi Principessa Gavia '16	🍷🍷	3
○ Moscato d'Asti Sciandor '16	🍷	3
● Piemonte Albarossa La Lus '14	🍷	5
○ Alta Langa Cuvée Aurora '10	🍷🍷	4
⊙ Alta Langa Cuvée Aurora Rosé '13	🍷🍷	4
● Dolcetto d'Acqui L'Ardì '15	🍷🍷	2*
○ Gavi Principessa Gavia '15	🍷🍷	3
○ Moscato d'Asti Sciandor '15	🍷🍷	2*
● Piemonte La Lus '13	🍷🍷	4

Barbaglia

VIA DANTE, 54
28010 CAVALLIRIO [NO]
TEL. I 39 016380115
www.vinibarbaglia.it

CELLAR SALES
PRE-BOOKED VISITS
ANNUAL PRODUCTION 25,000 bottles
HECTARES UNDER VINE 3.00

This small winery, founded in 1946 by Mario Barbaglia, gets its name from the charming rural hamlet of Cavallirio, an old staging post strategically located by the river Sesia, in the Monte Fenera park. Their Boca DOC is without a doubt the most important of a selection made possible thanks to a collaboration between Sergio and his daughter, Silvia. They don't just make Nebbiolo 'de garde', but also delicious monovarietal wines made with Uva rara, Croatina, Vespolina, Erbaluce. And they don't neglect sparkling wines either, as their Curticella line attests to. Recent tastings have reinforced the hierarchy of Barbaglia's wines. The 2013 Boca offers up characteristic notes of rhubarb and dried flowers, with a clear background of blood-rich meat on a savory and characterful palate. The Curticella Brut is top quality, coming through lemony but not without pulp. The 2013 Croatina proves supple and down-to-earth.

Osvaldo Barberis

B.TA VALDIBÀ, 42
12063 DOGLIANI [CN]
TEL. +39 017370054
www.osvaldobarberis.com

CELLAR SALES
PRE-BOOKED VISITS
ANNUAL PRODUCTION 20,000 bottles
HECTARES UNDER VINE 8.00
VITICULTURE METHOD Certified Organic

Osvaldo Barberis's heart beats primarily for his Dolcetto, cultivated for decades with the utmost respect for the environment. It gives rise to a diverse selection of Doglianis, starting with the Puncin and Valdibà. But this doesn't stop him from working, with growing success, with other varieties. His Nebbiolo d'Alba Muntajà and a new Pinot Nero Ciabot Maifrin are two examples, another is a white that's taking root in Dogliani and Novello (Langhe Nascetta). They're all wines with a strong territorial identity, with cellar work kept to a minimum so as to guarantee purity and drinkability. The high quality of the wines tasted confirms the winery's reliability. The fruity 2016 Dogliani Superiore Puncin still appears a bit tannic. The 2016 Dogliani Valdibà proves more powerful and pleasantly austere. The 2015 Barbera d'Alba Cesca exhibits excellent finesse and barely discernible oak. We enjoyed the lively 2016 Langhe Nascetta Anì, which is delicately aromatic with clear tropical fruit.

● Boca '13	♀♀ 5
● Colline Novaresi Croatina '13	♀♀ 2*
● Colline Novaresi Vespolina Ledi '15	♀♀ 3
○ Curticella Brut M. Cl.	♀♀ 5
○ Colline Novaresi Bianco Lucino '16	♀ 3
● Boca '12	♀♀ 5
● Boca '11	♀♀ 5
● Boca '10	♀♀ 5
○ Colline Novaresi Bianco Biancaluce '14	♀♀ 3
○ Colline Novaresi Bianco Lucino '15	♀♀ 3
● Colline Novaresi Nebbiolo Il Silente '11	♀♀ 3
○ Curticella Caballi Regis Brut M. Cl.	♀♀ 5

● Barbera d'Alba Cesca '15	♀♀ 3
● Dogliani Sup. Puncin '16	♀♀ 3
● Dogliani Valdibà '16	♀♀ 2*
● Langhe Barbera Brichat '16	♀♀ 2*
○ Langhe Nascetta Anì '16	♀♀ 3
● Dogliani Avrì '16	♀ 3
● Nebbiolo d'Alba Muntajà '15	♀ 3
● Barbera d'Alba Castella '12	♀♀ 3*
● Barbera d'Alba Cesca '13	♀♀ 3
● Dogliani Sup. Puncin '13	♀♀ 3*
● Dogliani Valdibà '15	♀♀ 2*
● Dogliani Valdibà '14	♀♀ 2*
● Langhe Pinot Nero Ciabot Maifrin '15	♀♀ 3
● Nebbiolo d'Alba Muntajà '13	♀♀ 3
● Nebbiolo d'Alba Muntajà '11	♀♀ 3*

Batasiolo

Fraz. Annunziata, 87
12064 La Morra [CN]
Tel. +39 017350130
www.batasiolo.com

CELLAR SALES
PRE-BOOKED VISITS
ANNUAL PRODUCTION 2,500,000 bottles
HECTARES UNDER VINE 107.00

10 farmsteads situated in some of the most prized areas of Langhe, 7 Barolo wines, 5 of which lay claim to additional geographic mentions, 140 hectares of property, more than 500 barrels (both small and large), some 30 wines, a resort and a spa: these are just some of the numbers that sum up Beni di Batasiolo. The winery was founded by the Dogliani family with their initial acquisition of Kiola, an old wine cellar. The range of cultivar grown is extremely varied (Chardonnay, Cortese, Arneis, Sauvignon, Pinot Bianco, Moscato, Brachetto, Barbera, Dolcetto), but their Nebbiolo reds, fine-tuned in the cellar for a modern interpretation, serve as their leading selection. They have put forward a series of Barolos with an overall sublime quality, which confirms 2013 as an excellent vintage. The Vigneto Bofani, made with grapes grown in Monforte, and the Boscareto, with grapes from Serralunga, battled it out for first place. Both show a sure charm and rare harmony, but the first is slightly more tannic, while the second is richer in pulp.

● Barolo Boscareto '13	♀♀7	
● Barolo Bussia Vign. Bofani '13	♀♀7	
● Barbaresco '14	♀♀6	
● Barbera d'Alba Sovrana '15	♀♀4	
● Barolo Briccolina '13	♀♀8	
● Barolo Brunate '13	♀♀7	
● Barolo Cerequio '13	♀♀7	
○ Langhe Chardonnay Vign. Morino '15	♀♀5	
○ Gavi del Comune di Gavi Granée '16	♀3	
○ Moscato d'Asti Bosc dla Rei '16	♀3	
○ Roero Arneis '16	♀3	
● Barolo Boscareto '05	♀♀♀7	
● Barolo Boscareto '12	♀♀7	
● Barolo Briccolina '12	♀♀8	

Bava

s.da Monferrato, 2
14023 Cocconato [AT]
Tel. +39 0141907083
www.bava.com

CELLAR SALES
PRE-BOOKED VISITS
ACCOMMODATION
ANNUAL PRODUCTION 490,000 bottles
HECTARES UNDER VINE 55.00

The Bava family's winery is one of the most dynamic in Astigiano. Mostly Barbera is cultivated in their vineyards in Cocconato, Cioccaro di Penango and Agliano Terme (Monferrato), along with Grignolino, Albarossa and international varieties like Chardonnay and Sauvignon. In Castiglione Falletto (Langhe), Nebbiolo and Dolcetto dominate, while their plots in Alta Langa are dedicated to their Giulio Cocchi sparkling wine selection (owned by the Bava family since 1978). The 2012 Alta Langa Brut Bianc 'd Bianc proves to be one of the best monovarietal Chardonnays in the appellation. Subtle notes of fresh herbs, damsons and fresh bread give way to a palate full of harmony and balance, both taut and creamy at the same time. The savory and supple 2014 Nizza PianoAlto stands out with its hints of spices and red fruit. The 2016 Piemonte Chardonnay Thou Bianc features overtones of flint, as well as good acidity and dynamism.

○ Alta Langa Brut Bianc 'd Bianc Giulio Cocchi '12	♀♀6	
● Barbera d'Asti Libera '15	♀♀3	
● Nizza PianoAlto '14	♀♀4	
○ Piemonte Chardonnay Thou Bianc '16	♀♀3	
○ Alta Langa Brut Toto Corde Giulio Cocchi '12	♀5	
○ Alta Langa Pas Dosé Giulio Cocchi '11	♀6	
● Malvasia di Castelnuovo Don Bosco Rosetta '16	♀3	
○ Piemonte Sauvignon Relais Blanc '16	♀3	
● Barbera d'Asti Libera '14	♀♀3	
● Barbera d'Asti Sup. Nizza PianoAlto '12	♀♀4	

Bel Colle

FRAZ. CASTAGNI, 56
12060 VERDUNO [CN]
TEL. +39 0172470196
www.belcolle.eu

CELLAR SALES
PRE-BOOKED VISITS
ANNUAL PRODUCTION 180,000 bottles
HECTARES UNDER VINE 14.00

There are big things on the horizon for Bel Colle. The historic winery managed for almost 40 years by the Pontiglione and Priola families was taken over by Bosio Family Estates in 2015. The group has operated for more than half a century and today their estate comprises more than 350 hectares of vineyards. Bel Colle is going forward with the same brand and identity with a selection of wines whose style, for the moment at least, can only be called classic, though without ignoring modern approaches when it comes to maceration and aging. The Monvigliero vineyard proves to be a great cru again. The 2013 vintage produced a full, serious Barolo that features rich alcohol and structure, with ripe cherries and licorice marking the nose. The 2013 Barolo Simposio, on the other hand, is made with grapes from a combination of different Nebbiolo vineyards. It comes through fresher, more youthful and intensely spicy. The 2015 Barbera d'Alba Superiore Le Masche, a wine delicately aged in wood, displays good character.

● Barbaresco Bosco dei Signori Bosio '14	❧❧ 5
● Barbera d'Alba Sup. Le Masche '15	❧❧ 3*
● Barolo Monvigliero '13	❧❧ 6
● Barbaresco '14	❧❧ 5
● Barolo Bosco dei Signori Bosio '13	❧❧ 5
● Barolo Simposio '13	❧❧ 6
● Nebbiolo d'Alba La Reala '14	❧❧ 3
● Verduno Pelaverga '16	❧❧ 3
● Dolcetto d'Alba '16	❧ 2
○ Roero Arneis '16	❧ 3
● Barbaresco Roncaglie Ris. '08	❧❧❧ 5
● Barolo Monvigliero '09	❧❧❧ 5
● Barolo Monvigliero '07	❧❧❧ 5
● Barbaresco '12	❧❧ 5

Bera

VIA CASTELLERO, 12
12050 NEVIGLIE [CN]
TEL. +39 0173630500
www.bera.it

CELLAR SALES
PRE-BOOKED VISITS
RESTAURANT SERVICE
ANNUAL PRODUCTION 140,000 bottles
HECTARES UNDER VINE 26.00

The Bera family's selection has gradually tended to increase in both quality and quantity. Their classic style comes through in their Moscato whites, which feature aromatic focus and freshness, and their reds, which are characterized by a non-invasive approach to aging. Their commitment to Nebbiolo is also growing, with increasingly impressive results thanks to their two plots, cru Rabajà (Barbaresco) and Basarin (Nieve). The 2016 Moscato d'Asti Su Reimond features seductive aromas, ranging from sage, peach and cat mint to tropical fruit. The palate is both sweet and fresh. The 2013 Barbaresco remains a bit closed for now, but it's already showing some charm. Aromas of red fruit and licorice are followed by a weighty palate with assertive tannins. The Dell'Um.be, a white on its first release, is firmly structured, but also fresh and intensely fragrant.

● Barbaresco '13	❧❧ 5
○ Moscato d'Asti Su Reimond '16	❧❧ 3*
○ Alta Langa Bera Brut '10	❧❧ 3
○ Asti '16	❧❧ 3
○ Dell'Um.be '15	❧❧ 3
● Langhe Nebbiolo Alladio '15	❧❧ 3
○ Moscato d'Asti '16	❧❧ 2*
○ Asti '15	❧❧ 3
● Barbaresco '12	❧❧ 5
● Barbaresco '11	❧❧ 5
● Barbaresco Rabajà Ris. '11	❧❧ 5
● Barbera d'Alba '15	❧❧ 2*
● Barbera d'Alba Sup. La Lena '13	❧❧ 3
● Barbera d'Alba Sup. La Lena '12	❧❧ 3
● Barbera d'Asti Sup. '12	❧❧ 2*
○ Moscato d'Asti Su Reimond '15	❧❧ 3*
○ Moscato d'Asti Su Reimond '14	❧❧ 3*

Cinzia Bergaglio

via Gavi, 29
15060 Tassarolo [AL]
Tel. +39 0143342203
www.vinicinziabergaglio.it

CELLAR SALES
PRE-BOOKED VISITS
ANNUAL PRODUCTION 30,000 bottles
HECTARES UNDER VINE 9.00

Cinzia Bergaglio's story is a tale of two territories, indeed, some of the most varied in Gavi. Their 10 hectares of vineyards, dedicated to the cultivation of Cortese, comprises two areas that in many ways show a kind of symmetry in terms of pedoclimate and expression. Their Grifone delle Roveri is grown on the calcareous, clay hills of Gavi and then fermented in steel after short, cold maceration. La Fornace, instead, is situated in the most iron and tuff-rich area of Tassarolo. In this case the wine is fermented slowly, without skin contact. These stylistic and territorial differences are harmonized in the winery's signature supple, energizing style. The 2016 vintage gave rise to two wines with a very coherent expression. Il Grifone delle Roveri offers up apple, almond and hints of grape skins on the nose, and features a warm, powerful mouth. The La Fornace proves more bashful at first, but overtones of white fruit, dried herbs and tobacco emerge with power and fullness of flavor.

○ Gavi del Comune di Gavi Grifone delle Roveri '16	TT 2*
○ Gavi La Fornace '16	TT 2*
○ Gavi del Comune di Gavi Grifone delle Roveri '15	YY 2*
○ Gavi del Comune di Gavi Grifone delle Roveri '14	YY 2*
○ Gavi del Comune di Gavi Grifone delle Roveri '13	YY 2*
○ Gavi del Comune di Gavi Grifone delle Roveri '12	YY 2*
○ Gavi del Comune di Gavi Grifone delle Roveri '11	YY 2*
○ Gavi La Fornace '15	YY 2*
○ Gavi La Fornace '14	YY 2*
○ Gavi La Fornace '13	YY 2*
○ Gavi La Fornace '12	YY 2*

Nicola Bergaglio

fraz. Rovereto
loc. Pedaggeri, 59
15066 Gavi [AL]
Tel. +39 0143682195
nicolabergaglio@alice.it

CELLAR SALES
PRE-BOOKED VISITS
ANNUAL PRODUCTION 140,000 bottles
HECTARES UNDER VINE 17.00
SUSTAINABLE WINERY

The first bottles authored by Nicola Bergaglio go back to 1970. His name is probably most recognized by those who consider Cortese di Gavi a long-lived wine that is best enjoyed only after some time. Today, Gianluigi is at the rudder, accompanied by his sons Diego and Ilaria. Together, they manage almost 20 hectares of vineyards, with the best plots found along the slopes of Rovereto. Here, the grapes used for their Minaia line are cultivated. Fermented in steel, these are without a doubt the winery's crown jewels. Their selection is rounded out by their Gavi di Gavi, also fermented in Inox tanks. Bergaglio made a wonderful couple of whites for the 2016 vintage. Overtones of greenness detract nothing from their Gavi's brilliant liveliness, which finds its usual aromatic richness and savory power in the Minaia. A dry, lemony finish is a bit edgy, but still sees a clean and close-focused unfolding of flavor.

○ Gavi del Comune di Gavi '16	TT 2*
○ Gavi del comune di Gavi' Minaia' '16	TT 4
○ Gavi del Comune di Gavi Minaia '15	YYY 4*
○ Gavi del Comune di Gavi Minaia '14	YYY 4*
○ Gavi del Comune di Gavi Minaia '11	YYY 4*
○ Gavi del Comune di Gavi Minaia '10	YYY 4
○ Gavi del Comune di Gavi Minaia '09	YYY 4
○ Gavi del Comune di Gavi '15	YY 2*
○ Gavi del Comune di Gavi '13	YY 2*
○ Gavi del Comune di Gavi Et. Bianca '14	YY 3*
○ Gavi del Comune di Gavi Minaia '13	YY 4
○ Gavi del Comune di Gavi Minaia '12	YY 3*

Bersano

P.ZZA DANTE, 21
14049 NIZZA MONFERRATO [AT]
TEL. +39 0141720211
www.bersano.it

CELLAR SALES
PRE-BOOKED VISITS
ANNUAL PRODUCTION 1,500,000 bottles
HECTARES UNDER VINE 230.00

For almost 30 years, Bersano has been in the hands of the Massimelli and Soave families. They have, at their disposal, a large estate, spread out on various plots, from Nizza to Serralunga, Acqui Terme and Castagnole Monferrato. And the varieties cultivated are just as numerous, from Barbera to Nebbiolo, Moscato, Ruché, Grignolino, Branchetto, Pinot Nero and Chardonnary. These are then transformed into a wide range of technically well-crafted wines, including selections that show good territorial expression. The 2014 Nizza La Generale Riserva charms the nose with its wild dark berries, roots, rain-soaked earth and cinchona. A palate rich in pulp and acidity gives way to a finish with marked notes of blackberries, tobacco and forest floor. The 2014 Barbaresco Mantico, on the other hand, offers up floral tones, with notes of licorice and raspberries. Elegant and well-gauged tannins emerge on its rich, savory palate. The Barolos and their sparkling wines are particularly well-made, but the whole selection proves to be of high quality.

● Barbaresco Mantico '14	♟♟6
● Nizza La Generala Ris. '14	♟♟5
○ Arturo Bersano Brut M. Cl. '14	♟♟4
☉ Arturosé Brut M. Cl. '14	♟♟4
● Barbera d'Asti Sup. Cremosina '15	♟♟3
● Barolo Badarina '11	♟♟7
● Barolo Badarina Ris. '10	♟♟7
○ Moscato d'Asti Monteolivo '16	♟♟3
● Ruché di Castagnole M.to San Pietro Realto '16	♟3
● Barbera d'Asti Sup. Generala '97	♟♟♟5
● Barbera d'Asti Sup. Cremosina '14	♟♟3
● Barbera d'Asti Sup. Nizza Generala '13	♟♟5
● Barolo Badarina '10	♟♟7

Guido Berta

LOC. SALINE, 53
14050 SAN MARZANO OLIVETO [AT]
TEL. +39 0141856193
www.guidoberta.com

CELLAR SALES
PRE-BOOKED VISITS
ANNUAL PRODUCTION 50,000 bottles
HECTARES UNDER VINE 20.00

Guido Berta, who was born and raised on the family farmstead in San Marzano Oliveto, founded his winery in 1997. His vineyards, which were planted between 1960 and 1988, are mostly to be found in the same municipality, on calcareous clay soil that is perfect for growing Barbera. His other vineyards are located in Calamandrana and Agliano Terme. In addition to Barbera, he cultivates Chardonnay, Moscato and Nebbiolo. His wines are made with an authentic interpretation of the territory in mind. The 2014 Nizza Canto di Luna is one of the best Barbera's of the vintage. The nose sees aromas of small red fruit (redcurrants and cranberries), with vegetal hints of forest floor. These follow-through onto its full-bodied palate with long and gutsy aromas. The generous 2016 Moscato d'Asti offers up notes of candied fruit and flowers. It's sweet but well-balanced.

● Nizza Canto di Luna '14	♟♟5
○ Moscato d'Asti '16	♟♟3
● Barbera d'Asti '15	♟3
● M.to Rosso '12	♟5
● Barbera d'Asti Le Rondini '15	♟♟3
● Barbera d'Asti Sup. '14	♟♟3
● Barbera d'Asti Sup. '13	♟♟3
● Barbera d'Asti Sup. Nizza Canto di Luna '13	♟♟5
● Barbera d'Asti Sup. Nizza Canto di Luna '12	♟♟5
● Monferrato Rosso '11	♟♟5
○ Moscato d'Asti '14	♟♟3
○ Moscato d'Asti '13	♟♟3

The advanced logistic solution for Wines & Spirits

www.ggori.com

Wine & Spirits Logistic Macrosystem Solution is a logistics package designed specifically for the beverages industry. Giorgio Gori has achieved truly superlative standards in this sector in terms of expertise, partnerships, resources, organization and technology. Secure, modular transport systems, contracts with the most dependable carriers, excellent transport rates and optimum storage conditions will smooth the way for your products, from the bottling line to the consumer's table. Easily accessible web-enabled options combined with effective monitoring and forecasting instruments can provide real time information on the entire logistics process.

WE MOVE PRECIOUS COMMODITIES: YOURS.

GIORGIO GORI
GLOBAL TRANSPORT & LOGISTICS

ARS ITALICA®
CAVIAR

Calvisius GROUP

 @arsitalicacaviar

www. a r s i t a l i c a .it

★Enzo Boglietti

VIA FONTANE, 18A
12064 LA MORRA [CN]
TEL. +39 017350330
www.enzoboglietti.com

CELLAR SALES
PRE-BOOKED VISITS
ACCOMMODATION
ANNUAL PRODUCTION 100,000 bottles
HECTARES UNDER VINE 22.50
VITICULTURE METHOD Certified Organic
SUSTAINABLE WINERY

Enzo and Gianni Boglietti manage their winery's cellar and vineyard, respectively. The brothers, who are known for their richly extracted Barolo, are shifting to organic and overhauling operations in favor of greater freshness. It's worth noting the recent addition of a white to their selection (Langhe Chardonnay), as well as a rosé (the sparkling Brut Rosé Metodo Classico), both youthful and fruity. The core of their selection, however, is still made up of their celebrated Barolos (5 crus and a 'Riserva') and their three Barbera d'Albas. The modern 2013 Barolo Brunate deserves its Tre Bicchieri. It features spices and very assertive tannins that will help it improve over the years. The 2013 Barolo is made with grapes grown in a famous cru, Fossati. Its already complex nose opens with notes of licorice and dried flowers, followed by a full-bodied palate with still discernible tannins. Kudos to the elegant 2013 Barbera d'Alba Vigna dei Romani, which displays rich fruit and freshness.

Bondi - Cascina Banaia

S.DA CAPPELLETTE, 73
15076 OVADA [AL]
TEL. +39 0131299186
www.bondivini.it

CELLAR SALES
PRE-BOOKED VISITS
ANNUAL PRODUCTION 20,000 bottles
HECTARES UNDER VINE 5.00

For some years, the Bondi family has achieved an impressive level of quality. Their wines come to life in a territory known for its viticulture. Their vineyards are situated at significant altitudes, and with excellent exposure to the sun, making for superior grapes. These are then transformed in the cellar using modern methods. Finally, wines are aged in barriques, with care taken to not obscure the the evolution of tertiary aromas, resulting in long-lived wines. The 2015 Barbera del Monferrato Superiore Ruvrin leads the way. It features an intense, almost impenetrable color and aromas of ripe dark berries, cocoa and jam. Its rich and powerful palate is balanced well by acidity, which lengthens into a lingering finish. Nani shows an excellent, though still unexpressed, potential, but continues to grow. Banaiotta, on the other hand, proves a bit less assertive than usual.

● Barolo Brunate '13	▼▼▼ 8
● Barbera d'Alba V. dei Romani '13	▼▼ 6
● Barolo Fossati '13	▼▼ 8
● Barolo Arione '13	▼▼ 8
● Barolo Boiolo '13	▼▼ 6
● Dolcetto d'Alba Tiglineri '15	▼▼ 3
● Barbera d'Alba '15	▼ 3
● Dolcetto d'Alba '15	▼ 3
● Barolo Arione '06	▽▽▽ 8
● Barolo Arione '05	▽▽▽ 8
● Barolo V. Arione '07	▽▽▽ 8
● Barolo Boiolo '12	▽▽ 6
● Barolo Brunate '12	▽▽ 8

● Barbera del M.to Sup. Ruvrin '15	▼▼ 4
● Dolcetto di Ovada Nani '15	▼▼ 2*
● Banaiotta	▼ 4
● Barbera del M.to Banaiotta '10	▽▽ 2*
● Barbera del M.to Ruvrin '10	▽▽ 4
● Dolcetto di Ovada Nani '11	▽▽ 2*
● Dolcetto di Ovada Nani '09	▽▽ 2*
● Dolcetto di Ovada Nani '08	▽▽ 2*
● Dolcetto di Ovada Sup. D'Uien '08	▽▽ 3
● M.to Barbera Banaiotta '09	▽▽ 4
● M.to Rosso Ansensò '11	▽▽ 4
● Ovada D'Uien '13	▽▽ 3
● Ovada D'Uien '11	▽▽ 4
● Ovada D'Uien '09	▽▽ 3

Gilberto Boniperti

VIA VITTORIO EMANUELE, 43/45
28010 BARENGO [NO]
TEL. +39 0321997123
www.bonipertivignaioli.com

CELLAR SALES
ANNUAL PRODUCTION 12,000 bottles
HECTARES UNDER VINE 3.50

Nebbiolo, Vespolina and Barbera are grown on Gilberto Boniperti's three and a half hectares of vineyards. There are three plots, situated at 250 meters above sea level between Barengo and Briona. The project took form in 2003, when the vineyard Bartön, a productive cru in Fara, was planted. Fara is a misunderstood appellation, even if it's capable of producing reds that are original, simultaneously vigorous and relaxed, the result of classic vinification and prolonged maturation in Allier oak of varying sizes (both barriques and 2100 liter oval barrels). Carlin, Favolalunga and Barblin are the monovarietals that, along with Rosadisera, make up the selection. The Boniperti family's solid selection of wines performed extremely well overall. The Vespolina Favolalunga stands out for its marked saltiness and personality, qualities also exhibited by the 2014 Fara Bartön. The 2015 Nebbiolo Carlin sees the addition of aromatic airiness, a spirited palate and velvety tannins.

● Colline Novaresi Nebbiolo Carlin '15	♟♟	4
● Colline Novaresi Vespolina Favolalunga '15	♟♟	2*
● Fara Bartön '14	♟♟	4
● Colline Novaresi Nebbiolo Bartön '10	♟♟	4
● Colline Novaresi Nebbiolo Carlin '14	♟♟	4
● Colline Novaresi Nebbiolo Carlin '13	♟♟	4
● Colline Novaresi Nebbiolo Carlin '12	♟♟	4
● Colline Novaresi Vespolina Favolalunga '12	♟♟	3
● Fara Bartön '13	♟♟	4
● Fara Bartön '12	♟♟	4
⊙ Rosadisera	♟♟	3
⊙ Rosadisera	♟♟	3

Borgo Maragliano

VIA SAN SEBASTIANO, 2
14051 LOAZZOLO [AT]
TEL. +39 014407132
www.borgomaragliano.com

CELLAR SALES
PRE-BOOKED VISITS
ANNUAL PRODUCTION 315,000 bottles
HECTARES UNDER VINE 29.00
SUSTAINABLE WINERY

Carlo and Silvia Galliano's Borgo Maragliano is a symbol of Loazzolo. Situated at 450 meters above sea level, the terrain here is rich in marl and sandstone, and cooled by the Marin, the wind that blows in off the Ligurian sea. The most common variety grown here is the white Moscato Bianco di Canelli, which is used for a number of wines. The other grapes cultivated are Chardonnay and Pinot Nero, which are used both in their 'Metodo Classico' sparklers and still wines. Additionally, they have a small vineyard of Brachetto in Bistagno, Alessandrino. Borgo Maragliano has put forward a splendid series of Metodo Classico wines this year. The two that stand out are the 2013 Giovanni Galliano Brut Rosé and the 2014 Federico Galliano Brut Nature. The first plays on delightful notes of strawberries and redcurrants, with a fresh and elegant palate and a pleasant, lingering finish. The second is more taut and displays great acidity, as well as more richness of aromas, with notes of tropical fruit and confectioner's cream.

○ Federico Galliano Brut Nature '14	♟♟	5
⊙ Giovanni Galliano Brut Rosé '13	♟♟	4
○ Dogma Blanc de Noirs Brut Nature '13	♟♟	5
○ Francesco Galliano Blanc de Blancs '14	♟♟	4
○ Giuseppe Galliano Brut Nature '12	♟♟	4
○ El Calié '16	♟	2
○ Moscato d'Asti La Caliera '16	♟	2
○ Giuseppe Galliano Ris. Brut M. Cl. '01	♟♟♟	4*
○ Dogma Blanc de Noirs M. Cl. '12	♟♟	5
○ Francesco Galliano Blanc de Blancs Brut M. Cl. '13	♟♟	4
⊙ Giovanni Galliano Brut Rosé M. Cl. '12	♟♟	4
○ Giuseppe Galliano Brut M. Cl. '11	♟♟	4

Giacomo Borgogno & Figli

VIA GIOBERTI, 1
12060 BAROLO [CN]
TEL. +39 017356108
www.borgogno.com

CELLAR SALES
PRE-BOOKED VISITS
ANNUAL PRODUCTION 110,000 bottles
HECTARES UNDER VINE 16.00
SUSTAINABLE WINERY

10 years have passed since the Farinetti family bought the centuries-old estate of Borgogno. Today, Andrea is at the helm, a manager who is well-appreciated for his ability to preserve the brand's spirit of the classics, while also implementing a series of innovative projects. Environmental sustainability and a non-invasive approach to winemaking are the key phrases here. But the center of activity is still their 15 hectares of vineyards, half of which grow Nebbiolo. Grapes for their traditionally-styled Barolo are grown in areas spanning Cannubi, Cannubi San Lorenzo, Fossati, Liste, San Pietro delle Viole. Their 'Riserva' line calls for prolonged aging. The far-sighted decision to delay the release of the 2010 Barolo Riserva has paid off and it delivers with a Tre Bicchieri. Multi-faceted and deep aromas range from meadow herbs to incense. Its palate comes through solid and firmly structured, with good tannic texture and length. The 2012 Cannubi shows commendable evolution, with ripe strawberries on the nose and a balanced mouth, as is fitting for this famous cru.

● Barolo Ris. '10	♟♟♟ 8
● Barolo Cannubi '12	♟♟ 8
● Barolo Liste '12	♟♟ 8
● Barolo '10	♟♟ 7
● Langhe Nebbiolo No Name '13	♟♟ 7
○ Langhe Riesling Era Ora '15	♟♟ 5
● Barbera d'Alba '15	♟ 3
● Barolo Fossati '12	♟ 8
● Barolo Liste '11	♟♟♟ 8
● Barolo Liste '10	♟♟♟ 8
● Barolo Liste '08	♟♟♟ 8
● Barolo Liste '07	♟♟♟ 7
● Barolo Cannubi '11	♟♟ 8
● Cesare 04 96 98 82	♟♟ 7

Boroli

VIA PUGNANE, 4
12060 CASTIGLIONE FALLETTO [CN]
TEL. +39 017362927
www.boroli.it

CELLAR SALES
PRE-BOOKED VISITS
ACCOMMODATION AND RESTAURANT SERVICE
ANNUAL PRODUCTION 200,000 bottles
HECTARES UNDER VINE 32.00
SUSTAINABLE WINERY

Today the Boroli family's winery is dedicated exclusively to Barolo (after ceding their cellar and vineyards in Alba to Poderi Colla and Giacomo Borgogno). Their main facility is located at the farmstead La Brunella, in a splendid position just over the celebrated Villero cru. It's definitely worth a visit. Their other famous vineyard is in Barolo, inside the acclaimed Cerequio. Their production approach is centered on research and the elegance of the grape (rather than the use of oak). Of the three Barolos put forward from the fresh 2013 vintage, Cerequio is the most outstanding. It proves elegant, complex and youthful on the nose, with berries and red flowers on a background of meadow herbs. Its palate features length and well-integrated tannins. The Villero is open, already eloquent and slightly rustic. The Brunella displays great structure, complexity on the nose and a very lingering palate.

● Barolo Brunella '13	♟♟ 8
● Barolo Cerequio '13	♟♟ 8
● Barolo Villero '13	♟♟ 8
● Barolo Villero '01	♟♟♟ 6
● Barolo Villero '00	♟♟♟ 4*
● Barolo '12	♟♟ 6
● Barolo '11	♟♟ 6
● Barolo '10	♟♟ 6
● Barolo Cerequio '12	♟♟ 7
● Barolo Villero '12	♟♟ 7
● Barolo Villero '11	♟♟ 7
● Barolo Villero '10	♟♟ 7
● Barolo Villero Ris. '09	♟♟ 8
● Barolo Villero Ris. '06	♟♟ 8

Francesco Boschis

B.TA PIANEZZO, 57
12063 DOGLIANI [CN]
TEL. +39 017370574
www.boschisfrancesco.it

CELLAR SALES
PRE-BOOKED VISITS
ANNUAL PRODUCTION 40,000 bottles
HECTARES UNDER VINE 11.00

The Boschis family's winery is celebrating 50 years. Today, brothers Paolo and Marco (along with their parents) are managing this multifaceted operation. Here, Dolcetto takes center stage, but not exclusively. Barberba, Grignolino, Freisa and Sauvignon are all cultivated, as well as other crops like wheat and hazelnuts. Their work in the vineyard and in the cellar is carried out without the use of chemicals, and the family's pursuit of purity is manifest in their selection, which features their celebrated Dogliani Pianezzo, San Martino and Vigna dei Prey. The whole line achieved commendable results, especially the 2015 Dogliani, which proves it was an excellent vintage for Dolcetto. The Vigne Sorì San Martino exhibits fruity and almost opulent aromas that call up blackberries and cherries, while the mouth comes through with great pulp. The Vigna di Prey displays a more complex nose and is more tannic on the palate.

● Dogliani Sup. V. dei Prey '15	♥♥2*
● Dogliani Sup. V. Sorì San Martino '15	♥♥2*
● Dogliani Sup. V. del Ciliegio '15	♥♥3
● Dogliani V. in Pianezzo '16	♥♥2*
○ Langhe Sauvignon V. dei Garisin '16	♥♥3
● Piemonte Grignolino '16	♥♥2*
● Barbera d'Alba Sup. V. Le Masserie '13	♀♀3
● Dogliani Pianezzo '13	♀♀2*
● Dogliani Sorì San Martino '14	♀♀3
● Dogliani Sup. Sorì San Martino '13	♀♀3
● Dogliani Sup. Sorì San Martino '12	♀♀3*
● Dogliani Sup. V. dei Prey '13	♀♀3
● Dogliani Sup. V. dei Prey '12	♀♀3
● Dogliani V. dei Prey '14	♀♀2*
● Dogliani V. in Pianezzo '15	♀♀2*

Agostino Bosco

VIA FONTANE, 24
12064 LA MORRA [CN]
TEL. +39 0173509466
www.barolobosco.com

CELLAR SALES
PRE-BOOKED VISITS
ANNUAL PRODUCTION 28,000 bottles
HECTARES UNDER VINE 5.50
SUSTAINABLE WINERY

Andrea Bosco's passion has paid off with an excellent selection of wines made with Nebbiolo and Barbera. His delightful cellar (recently renovated and enlarged) is situated in upper La Morra, an area that offers a must-see panorama of Langhe. Both his Barolo crus are valid, the celebrated La Serra as well as the lesser known Neirane (in Verduno). The Barbera d'Alba Volupta, a wine aged at length in French oak, is of constant and commendable quality. The 2013 Barolo Neirane features an absolutely classic style, with clear notes of cinchona and tar on a background of ripe red fruit. Tannins are still discernible on its weighty body. The 2013 Barolo La Serra is more light-bodied and open, with good structure: It's a caressing wine, though without being velvety. The Nebbiolo Rurem proves particularly pleasant, while the Barbera Volupta is bold and well-structured, not to be missed.

● Barolo Neirane '13	♥♥5
● Barbera d'Alba Sup. Volupta '15	♥♥3
● Barolo La Serra '13	♥♥6
● Langhe Nebbiolo Rurem '15	♥♥3
● Dolcetto d'Alba Vantrin '16	♥2
● Barbera d'Alba Sup. Volupta '14	♀♀3
● Barbera d'Alba Sup. Volupta '13	♀♀3
● Barolo La Serra '12	♀♀6
● Barolo La Serra '11	♀♀6
● Barolo La Serra '10	♀♀6
● Barolo Neirane '11	♀♀5
● Barolo Neirane '10	♀♀5
● Dolcetto d'Alba Vantrin '15	♀♀2*
● Dolcetto d'Alba Vantrin '14	♀♀2*

Luigi Boveri

LOC. MONTALE CELLI
VIA XX SETTEMBRE, 6
15050 COSTA VESCOVATO [AL]
TEL. +39 0131838165
www.boveriluigi.com

CELLAR SALES
PRE-BOOKED VISITS
ANNUAL PRODUCTION 80,000 bottles
HECTARES UNDER VINE 15.00

Both the winery and the vineyards are situated in Costa Vescovato, a municipality situated on the stretch of land between the Ossona and Conigliasca rivers (part of the Comunità Montana Valli Curone, Grue and Ossona). The estate comprises 15 hectares, which are divided into nine plots of red grapes and six of white (Barbera, Croatina and Bonarda for the reds and, obviously, Timorasso, Cortese and Moscato for the whites). It's a selection with close ties to the territory that Luigi has been developing since the 1990s. Today it's among the best interpretations in the area. Timorasso has proved particularly gratifying, giving rise to two wines that are in the finals this year. Filari di Timorasso thrills for its aromas of white fruit and citrus on a mineral background of flinty notes. It comes through supple, fresh and powerful on the palate, with a well-orchestrated and lingering finish. Derthona is possessed of an intense suite of aromas, which play on vegetal and mineral notes and lead into a fresh, balanced palate and a heady finish.

○ Colli Tortonesi Timorasso Derthona '15	♥♥ 4
○ Colli Tortonesi Timorasso Derthona Filari di Timorasso '15	♥♥ 5
○ Colli Tortonesi Cortese Terre del Prete '16	♥♥ 2*
● Colli Tortonesi Croatina Sensazioni '15	♥♥ 4
○ Colli Tortonesi Timorasso Derthona '11	♥♥♥ 4*
○ Colli Tortonesi Timorasso Filari di Timorasso '12	♥♥♥ 5
○ Colli Tortonesi Timorasso Filari di Timorasso '07	♥♥♥ 3
● Colli Tortonesi Barbera Boccanera '15	♥♥ 2*
○ Colli Tortonesi Cortese Terre del Prete '15	♥♥ 2*
○ Colli Tortonesi Timorasso Derthona Filari di Timorasso '13	♥♥ 5

Gianfranco Bovio

FRAZ. ANNI INZIATA
B.TA CIOTTO, 63
12064 LA MORRA [CN]
TEL. +39 017350667
www.boviogianfranco.com

CELLAR SALES
PRE-BOOKED VISITS
ANNUAL PRODUCTION 75,000 bottles
HECTARES UNDER VINE 10.00

Alessandro Bovio inherited the winemaking patrimony of his well-known father, Gianfranco. Now he's leading this small winery, which expresses the personality of La Morra Barolo with confidence and classical-style. Their vineyards include plots in the municipalities of Castiglione Falletto and Barolo, but their most elevated terrain is found in Annunziata (La Morra), where Nebbiolo is grown in two crus, Gattera and Arborina. Their selection includes other wines as well. In addition to their Barbera and Dolcetto d'Alba, they make a Langhe Nebbiolo and a Langhe Bianco with Chardonnay and Sauvignon grapes. The 2013 Barolo Arborina, a wine that features aromas of herbs in the sun, isn't particularly fresh but makes up for it with a mouth of notable harmony and grip. The 2013 Barolo Gattera proves fresher and offers up vegetal and fruity notes. The palate shows good body and is rich in tannins and acidity. The Barolo 2013 exhibits small stature and good drinkability, while the 2015 Barbera d'Alba Regiaveja proves flavorsome, clean and approachable.

● Barolo Gattera '13	♥♥ 6
● Barbera d'Alba Regiaveja '15	♥♥ 4
● Barolo '13	♥♥ 6
● Barolo Arborina '13	♥♥ 6
● Barbera d'Alba Il Ciotto '16	♥ 2
● Dolcetto d'Alba Dabbene '16	♥ 2
● Barolo Bricco Parussi Ris. '01	♥♥♥ 6
● Barolo Gattera '11	♥♥♥ 6
● Barolo Rocchettevino '06	♥♥♥ 5*
● Barbera d'Alba Sup. Regiaveja '13	♥♥ 4
● Barolo '12	♥♥ 6
● Barolo Arborina '12	♥♥ 6
● Barolo Gattera '12	♥♥ 6
● Dolcetto d'Alba Dabbene '15	♥♥ 2*

★Braida

LOC. CIAPPELLETTE
S.DA PROVINCIALE 27, 9
14030 ROCCHETTA TANARO [AT]
TEL. +39 0141644113
www.braida.it

CELLAR SALES
PRE-BOOKED VISITS
ACCOMMODATION
ANNUAL PRODUCTION 650,000 bottles
HECTARES UNDER VINE 55.00
SUSTAINABLE WINERY

Founded in 1961 by Giacomo Bologna, today Braida is being run by the third generation, Raffaella and Giuseppe. Over the years they have skillfully managed the prestigious estate, seeing to it that it holds its place as a benchmark for the production of Barbera. Their red grapes are cultivated in Rocchetta Tanaro, with their two most famous vineyards, Costigliole d'Asti and Castelnuovo Calcea, giving rise to their Barbera. White grapes are grown in Trezzo Tinella, and then transformed into their Serra dei Fiori line of wines. Their Moscato is grown in Mango. The 2015 Barbera d'Asti Bricco dell'Uccellone is back on top. It proves balanced and rich in pulp, with notes of spices and black fruit, good roundness and a taut and gutsy finish. The other two 2015 Barbera d'Astis also showed great quality. The Bricco della Bigotta features hints of ripe cherry, while the fresh and approachable Montebruna offers up notes of red fruit, rain-soaked earth and herbs.

● Barbera d'Asti Bricco dell'Uccellone '15	▼▼▼	7
● Barbera d'Asti Bricco della Bigotta '15	▼▼	7
● Barbera d'Asti Montebruna '15	▼▼	3*
● Grignolino d'Asti Limonte '16	▼▼	3
○ Langhe Nascetta La Regina '16	▼▼	3
○ Langhe Riesling Re di Fiori '16	▼▼	3
● Barbera del M.to La Monella '16	▼	3
○ Moscato d'Asti V. Senza Nome '16	▼	3
● Barbera d'Asti Bricco dell'Uccellone '12	♀♀♀	7
● Barbera d'Asti Bricco dell'Uccellone '09	♀♀♀	6
● Barbera d'Asti Montebruna '11	♀♀♀	3*
● Barbera d'Asti Bricco dell'Uccellone '14	♀♀	7
● Barbera d'Asti Montebruna '14	♀♀	3*

Brandini

FRAZ. BRANDINI, 16
12064 LA MORRA [CN]
TEL. +39 017350266
www.agricolabrandini.com

CELLAR SALES
PRE-BOOKED VISITS
ACCOMMODATION AND RESTAURANT SERVICE
ANNUAL PRODUCTION 80,000 bottles
HECTARES UNDER VINE 15.00
VITICULTURE METHOD Certified Organic
SUSTAINABLE WINERY

The Bagnasco family bought this estate with the intention of gradually entering the world of quality wines, quietly but with perserverance. Year after year, something new came out: their first Barolo was followed by the prized Resa 56 selection; then their whites arrived, with the surprising Le Coccinelle, along with two Alta Langhes, in a Brut and a Rosé. And in just a few months we'll see the introduction of their Barolos from the crus of Cerretta (Serralunga d'Alba) and Rocche (Annunziata, La Morra). We should also point out their cozy agritourism. As indicated on the label, the 2013 Barolo Resa 56 is "aged in large barrels", underlining the classic style that inspires this estate's line of wines. Its well-expressed aromas call up bottled fruit and tobacco, then the mouth comes through firm and lingering, with good aging prospects. Tre Bicchieri. The 2013 Barolo del Comune de La Morra features a palate of very tight-knit and mouthfilling tannins. The 2015 Barbera d'Alba offers up commendable candor and typicity, while the 2010 Barolo Riserva is all elegance and complexity.

● Barolo Resa 56 '13	▼▼▼	8
● Barolo del Comune di La Morra '13	▼▼	8
● Barolo Resa 56 Ris. '10	▼▼	8
○ Alta Langa Brut '10	▼▼	8
● Barbera d'Alba Sup. Rocche del Santo '15	▼▼	5
● Langhe Nebbiolo Filari Corti '15	▼▼	5
● Dolcetto d'Alba Filari Lunghi '16	▼	4
○ Langhe Arneis Le Margherite '16	▼	4
● Barolo Resa 56 '12	♀♀♀	8
● Barolo Resa 56 '11	♀♀♀	7
● Barolo Resa 56 '10	♀♀♀	7
● Barolo '12	♀♀	7
● Barolo '11	♀♀	5
● Barolo '10	♀♀	5

Brangero

VIA PROVINCIALE, 26
12055 DIANO D'ALBA [CN]
TEL. +39 017369423
www.brangero.com

PRE-BOOKED VISITS
ANNUAL PRODUCTION 50,000 bottles
HECTARES UNDER VINE 9.00

For almost 20 years Marco Brangero has been managing this interesting operation situated in a charming corner of Langhe (one that's still not too popular, and thus authentic and intact). Their selection features the area's most emblematic wines, with a distinctive style that focuses on the expression of the various cultivar (without too much extraction or excess). The owners also manage a winery in Liguria, the Ginestraia, thus rounding out a unique and appealing selection of wines. Blackberries, red-fleshed fruit and slight hints of spices characterize the excellent 2016 Dolcetto Sorì Cascina Rabino. It comes through elegant, but lively, with a precise and rich palate. The Langhe Nebbiolo Quattro Cloni presents notes of dark berry fruits, tobacco and licorice on the nose. In the mouth, it's clear that its tannins are still integrating, though this takes nothing away from the suppleness its juicy finish.

● Dolcetto di Diano d'Alba Sorì Cascina Rabino '16	♟♟ 2*
● Langhe Nebbiolo Quattro Cloni '15	♟♟ 4
● Langhe Rosso Tremarzo '15	♟♟ 4
● Barbera d'Alba La Soprana '15	♟ 3
○ Langhe Chardonnay Centofile '16	♟ 3
● Barbera d'Alba Langhe Soprana '13	♟♟ 3
● Barolo Monvigliero '12	♟♟ 6
● Barolo Monvigliero '11	♟♟ 6
● Barolo Monvigliero '09	♟♟ 6
● Dolcetto di Diano d'Alba Sorì Rabino Soprano '15	♟♟ 2*
● Dolcetto di Diano d'Alba Sorì Rabino Soprano '11	♟♟ 2*
● Nebbiolo d'Alba Quattro Cloni '14	♟♟ 4

Brema

VIA POZZOMAGNA, 9
14045 INCISA SCAPACCINO [AT]
TEL. +39 014174019
www.vinibrema.com

CELLAR SALES
PRE-BOOKED VISITS
ANNUAL PRODUCTION 150,000 bottles
HECTARES UNDER VINE 25.00
SUSTAINABLE WINERY

Umberto Brema is the fifth generation of family to manage this historic winery, whose roots go back to 1887. In keeping with his father, Ermanno, Umberto is seeing to it that their Barbera is high-quality, and that its character expresses, in the best possible way, the attributes of the territory and the varieties used. Their most important vineyards can be found between Nizza Monferrato and Fontanile d'Asti. These are accompanied by others in various municipalities from Astigiano to San Marzano Oliveto, Incisa Scapaccino and Sessame d'Asti. The 2014 vintage certainly didn't help the Brema family's Barbera, but the results were still good. The Barbera d'Asti Superiore Volpettona features aromas of red fruit and tobacco, with complex notes of well-gauged wood. The palate doesn't see great structure, but it's still good considering the vintage, and fresh, with a long, well-orchestrated finish. The Nizza A Luigi Veronelli, on the other hand, proves less brilliant and close-focused compared to other versions, but it's still well-made.

● Barbera d'Asti Sup. Volpettona '14	♟♟ 5
● Barbera d'Asti Ai Cruss '15	♟♟ 2*
● Nizza A Luigi Veronelli '14	♟♟ 6
● Barbera del M.to Vivace Castagni '16	♟ 2
● Barbera d'Asti Sup. Nizza A Luigi Veronelli '12	♟♟♟ 6
● Barbera d'Asti Sup. Nizza A Luigi Veronelli '06	♟♟♟ 6
● Barbera d'Asti Ai Cruss '14	♟♟ 2*
● Barbera d'Asti Sup. Nizza A Luigi Veronelli '13	♟♟ 6
● Barbera d'Asti Sup. Volpettona '13	♟♟ 5
● M.to Rosso Umberto '13	♟♟ 4

Giacomo Brezza & Figli

VIA LOMONDO, 4
12060 BAROLO [CN]
TEL. +39 0173560921
www.brezza.it

CELLAR SALES
PRE-BOOKED VISITS
ACCOMMODATION AND RESTAURANT SERVICE
ANNUAL PRODUCTION 100,000 bottles
HECTARES UNDER VINE 17.50
VITICULTURE METHOD Certified Organic
SUSTAINABLE WINERY

The Brezza family runs one of Langhe's most historic wineries, one that became officially operational in 1885. Generations of wine lovers have passe by their inn-cellar, enjoying precious hospitality and a selection of wines that is extraordinarily true to tradition, starting with slow aging in medium-large Slovanian oak. Their estate comprises almost 20 hectares of vineyards, most of which are used to grow Nebbiolo for their Barolos (Castellero, Cannubi, Sarmassa and Sarmassa Vigna Bricco, available in a 'Riserva'), with other plots in Monforte d'Alba, Novello, Diano d'Alba and Alba. Barbera, Freisa, Dolcetto and Chardonnay round out the range of varieties cultivated. The 2011 Barolo Sarmassa V. Bricco Riserva opens with notes of leather and licorice on a fruit-driven, balsamic background. It reveals rare precision in the way it balances taste with tight-knit but delicate, enriching tannins. It gets Tre Bicchieri. The magnificent 2013 Barolo Sarmassa runs along the same lines, but proves slightly fresher on the palate.

● Barolo Sarmassa V. Bricco Ris. '11	🍷🍷🍷 7
● Barolo Sarmassa '13	🍷🍷 7
● Barbera d'Alba V. Santa Rosalia '15	🍷🍷 3
● Barolo '13	🍷🍷 5
● Barolo Cannubi '13	🍷🍷 6
● Barolo Castellero '13	🍷🍷 6
○ Langhe Chardonnay '16	🍷 3
● Langhe Freisa '16	🍷 3
● Langhe Nebbiolo '16	🍷 3
● Barolo Bricco Sarmassa '08	🍷🍷🍷 7
● Barolo Bricco Sarmassa '07	🍷🍷🍷 7
● Barolo Sarmassa '11	🍷🍷🍷 6
● Barolo Sarmassa '05	🍷🍷🍷 6
● Barolo Cannubi '12	🍷🍷 6
● Barolo Sarmassa '12	🍷🍷 7

Gallino Domenico Bric Castelvej

MADONNA LORETO, 70
12043 CANALE [CN]
TEL. +39 017398108
www.briccastelvej.com

CELLAR SALES
PRE-BOOKED VISITS
ANNUAL PRODUCTION 100,000 bottles
HECTARES UNDER VINE 12.40

Founded in 1956 by Domenico Gallino, today Bric Castelvej is managed by his son-in-law, Mario Repellino, and his son, Cristiano. All their vineyards are situated in Canale, where they have crus such as Mompissano at their disposal. The soil here is loose, rich in sand, punctuated by loam, clay and limestone. The grapes cultivated are those common to the territory, in particular Arneis, Nebbiolo and Barbera, making for wines that bring together finesse and good structure. Domenico Gallino has presented a lovely selection of wines. The 2016 Barbera d'Alba put in a particularly strong performance. It offers up scents of black cherry and rain-soaked earth, while its dynamic palate is well-supported by acidity and good fruit. The 2016 Barbera d'Alba Superiore Mompissano features spicy, round and generous fragrances. The 2016 Roero Arneis displays aromas of citrus and tropical fruit, as well as a full-bodied palate, while the 2014 Roero Panera Alta Riserva is rich in fruit, with well-integrated tannins.

● Barbera d'Alba '16	🍷🍷 2*
● Barbera d'Alba Sup. Mompissano '16	🍷🍷 2*
○ Roero Arneis '16	🍷🍷 2*
● Roero Panera Alta Ris. '14	🍷🍷 6
● Roero '14	🍷 4
● Roero '13	🏆 4
● Roero '12	🏆 4
○ Roero Arneis '15	🏆 2*
○ Roero Arneis V. Bricco Novara '15	🏆 3*
● Roero Panera Alta Ris. '13	🏆 6
● Roero Panera Alta Ris. '12	🏆 6

Bric Cenciurio

VIA ROMA, 24
12060 BAROLO [CN]
TEL. +39 017356317
www.briccenciurio.com

CELLAR SALES
PRE-BOOKED VISITS
ANNUAL PRODUCTION 50,000 bottles
HECTARES UNDER VINE 15.00

Brothers Alberto and Alessandro Pittatore
are experts in both viticulture and enology.
As a result, they personally manage their
winery's main activities, and only draw on a
trusted consultant for winemaking. Barolo
is their crown jewel, made with grapes
from their crus of Monrobiolo di Bussia and
Coste di Rose. The winery's name comes
from their vineyards in Roero, on the left
bank of the Tanaro, and it's here that they
cultivate the grapes for their two Arneis,
their Langhe Nebbiolo, two Barbera d'Albas
and their aromatic Birbèt. The 2011 Barolo
Coste di Rose Riserva is long and
well-orchestrated, featuring a certain
elegance and pleasant smoky notes. It just
lacks a bit of freshness. The 2013 Barolo
Monrobiolo di Bussia proves more
expansive on the nose (where we find
herbs in the sun, tobacco and wilted
flowers) than on the palate, which is
caressing thanks to its alcohol component.
The succulent 2013 Barolo is a modern
wine with sweet notes of oak. The elegant
2015 Riesling also put in a good
performance.

● Barolo Coste di Rose Ris. '11	♟♟ 7
● Barolo '13	♟♟ 5
● Barolo Monrobiolo di Bussia '13	♟♟ 6
● Langhe Nebbiolo '15	♟♟ 4
○ Langhe Riesling '15	♟♟ 3
● Barbera d'Alba Sup. Naunda '14	♟ 4
○ Roero Arneis Sito dei Fossili '16	♟ 3
● Barbera d'Alba Sup. Naunda '13	♟♟ 4
● Barolo '12	♟♟ 5
● Barolo Coste di Rose '12	♟♟ 6
● Barolo Coste di Rose Ris. '10	♟♟ 7
● Barolo Coste di Rose Ris. '09	♟♟ 7
● Barolo Monrobiolo di Bussia '12	♟♟ 5
● Langhe Nebbiolo '14	♟♟ 4
○ Roero Arneis Sito dei Fossili '14	♟♟ 3

Bricco del Cucù

LOC. BRICCO, 10
12060 BASTIA MONDOVÌ [CN]
TEL. +39 017460153
www.briccocucu.com

CELLAR SALES
PRE-BOOKED VISITS
ANNUAL PRODUCTION 50,000 bottles
HECTARES UNDER VINE 10.00

This family-run winery, headed by Dario
Sciolla and his daughters, Irene and Chiara,
is situated in a unique and almost unknown
corner of Piedmont (between Dogliani and
Langhe Monregalesi). It's a stretch of land
characterized by its altitudes (about 500
meters) and winds, which give rise to the
area's deep and distinctive style of wines,
as well as their sensorial originality
(especially Dolcetto, which has always
thrived here). For many years, the Sciolla
family has proudly and insightfully sought
to represent the territory's quality by
producing original wines that are often
difficult to understand early on, but are
undoubtedly endowed with great character.
The winery's two unique blends
(Superboum and Diavolisanti) didn't appear
in this year's tastings, so various Dolcettos
took the stage. To tell the truth, these
impressed less than in previous editions.
The 2016 Langhe Dolcetto appears to be in
good form, proving succulent and
easy-drinking. The 2013 Bricco San
Bernardo still comes through a bit rough in
its varietal expression.

● Dogliani Sup. Bricco S. Bernardo '13	♟♟ 2*
● Langhe Dolcetto '16	♟♟ 2*
● Dogliani '16	♟ 2
○ Langhe Bianco Livor '16	♟ 2
● Dogliani Sup. Bricco S. Bernardo '09	♟♟♟ 2*
● Dogliani '15	♟♟ 2*
● Dogliani '13	♟♟ 2*
● Dogliani Sup. Bricco S. Bernardo '12	♟♟ 2*
● Dogliani Sup. Bricco S. Bernardo '11	♟♟ 2*
● Dogliani Sup. Bricco S. Bernardo '10	♟♟ 2*
● Langhe Dolcetto '15	♟♟ 2*
● Langhe Rosso Diavolisanti '13	♟♟ 2*
● Langhe Rosso Diavolisanti '12	♟♟ 2*
● Langhe Rosso Superboum '13	♟♟ 2*

Bricco Maiolica

FRAZ. RICCA
VIA BOLANGINO, 7
12055 DIANO D'ALBA [CN]
TEL. +39 0173612049
www.briccomaiolica.it

CELLAR SALES
PRE-BOOKED VISITS
ACCOMMODATION
ANNUAL PRODUCTION 110,000 bottles
HECTARES UNDER VINE 24.00
SUSTAINABLE WINERY

Over more than thirty years of work, Beppe Accomo has earned the appreciation not only of consumers, but also of colleagues, who recognize his Dolcetto as the most representative of Diano d'Alba. In addition to their fruity, dense, full Dolcetto, they offer 11 other wines, with the always-captivating Nebbiolo d'Alba Cumot and the rich Barbera d'Alba Vigna Vigia at the forefront. Their selection of wines made from foreign grape varieties are also commendable, from the sumptuous Langhe Chardonnay Pensiero Infinito to the delicate Pino Nero Perlei. Their wine selection is complemented by a lovely agritourism, Casa Castella, situated just above the town of Alba. The 2013 Barolo Contadin, a vibrant though simple wine endowed with notable weight, did well. It should age well in the bottle (if the primary aromas of juniper detected in its finish are anything to go by). The savory 2014 Nebbiolo Cumot comes through as complex and elegant as ever. The deservedly famous 2014 Barbera d'Alba Vigna Vigia is less powerful and fruity than other vintages.

● Barolo Contadin '13	▼▼ 8
● Nebbiolo d'Alba Sup. Cumot '14	▼▼ 5
● Barbera d'Alba Sup. V. Vigia '14	▼▼ 5
● Diano d'Alba '16	▼▼ 2*
○ Langhe Chardonnay Pensiero Infinito '13	▼▼ 6
● Langhe Merlot Filius '14	▼▼ 5
● Langhe Pinot Nero Perlei '14	▼▼ 5
○ Langhe Sauvignon Castella '16	▼▼ 3
● Diano d'Alba Sup. Sorì Bricco Maiolica '07	▼▼▼ 3*
● Nebbiolo d'Alba Cumot '11	▼▼▼ 5
● Nebbiolo d'Alba Cumot '10	▼▼▼ 4*
● Nebbiolo d'Alba Cumot '09	▼▼▼ 4*
● Nebbiolo d'Alba Sup. Cumot '13	▼▼▼ 5
● Barbera d'Alba Sup. V. Vigia '13	▼▼ 5
○ Langhe Bianco Pensiero Infinito '12	▼▼ 6

Bricco Mondalino

REG. MONDALINO, 5
15049 VIGNALE MONFERRATO [AL]
TEL. +39 0142933204
www.gaudiovini.it

CELLAR SALES
PRE-BOOKED VISITS
ANNUAL PRODUCTION 80,000 bottles
HECTARES UNDER VINE 14.00

Bricco Mondalino is a family-run winery that has distinguished itself in Monferrato Casalese for the quality of its selection and the care shown in realizing it. Moreover, the winery's image is tied to the history of the territory and its native grape varieties, which Mauro Gaudio has skillfully interpreted over the years, thanks to generations of experience and the aid of modern technology. They make Barbera, Grignolino, Freisa, Malvasia di Casorzo and Cortese. The Barbera del Monferrato Superiore stands out with an absolutely brilliant performance. The wine is an intense and almost impenetrable ruby color. Its nose offers up aromas of cherries and ripe plums across tertiary notes of coffee. Good acidity emerges on the palate and leads into an intense and lingering finish. But Mauro Gaudio has more arrows in his quiver. Two classics in his selection are in great form, the Grignolino and the Malvasia di Casorzo

● Barbera del M.to Sup. '15	▼▼ 2*
● Grignolino del M.to Casalese '16	▼▼ 3
● Malvasia di Casorzo Dolce Stil Novo '16	▼▼ 2*
● Barbera del M.to Vivace '16	▼ 2
● Barbera d'Asti Il Bergantino '12	♀♀ 4
● Barbera d'Asti Il Bergantino '10	♀♀ 3
● Barbera del M.to Gaudium Magnum '11	♀♀ 6
● Barbera del M.to Sup. '14	♀♀ 2*
● Grignolino del M.to Casalese Bricco Mondalino '13	♀♀ 2*
● Grignolino del M.to Casalese Bricco Mondalino '11	♀♀ 2*
● Grignolino del M.to Casalese Monte della Sala '13	♀♀ 4
● Malvasia di Casorzo Dolce Stil Novo '15	♀♀ 2*
● Malvasia di Casorzo Dolce Stil Novo '12	♀♀ 2*
● Malvasia di Casorzo Dolce Stil Novo '11	♀♀ 2*

Francesco Brigatti

VIA OLMI, 31
28019 SUNO [NO]
TEL. +39 032285037
www.vinibrigatti.it

CELLAR SALES
PRE-BOOKED VISITS
ANNUAL PRODUCTION 25,000 bottles
HECTARES UNDER VINE 6.50

Francesco Brigatti is the owner, winemaker and agronomist of the winery that bears his name. He is, without a doubt, one of the most notable viticulturists in Novara. His selection has consistently impressed us for its ability to bring together an awareness of the territory and stylistic foresight. It all starts with his seven hectares of terrain located on the Colline Novaresi hills. Nebbiolo makes up the lion's share of the varieties cultivated, as one might expect. Uva Rara, Vespolina, Barbera and Erbaluce complete the puzzle. In terms of aging, he uses wood of various sizes (Slovanian oak for MötZiflon and Ghemme Oltre il Bosco, mid-sized Allier casks for Mötfrei), but there's an austere and uplifting strand that runs throughout. The contest between Brigatti's Nebbiolos is always enthralling. We enjoyed the 2014 MötZiflon for its back-to-basics approach, the 2013 Mötfrei for its citrusy notes and solid mineral support, and the 2012 Ghemme Oltre il Bosco for its racy, hot-blooded trail. But the real surprise proved to be the 2016 Vespolina Maria.

● Colline Novaresi Vespolina Maria '16	♟♟ 3*
● Ghemme Oltre il Bosco '12	♟♟ 4
● Colline Novaresi Barbera Campazzi '16	♟♟ 3
● Colline Novaresi Nebbiolo Mötfrei '13	♟♟ 3
● Colline Novaresi Nebbiolo MötZiflon '14	♟♟ 3
○ Colline Novaresi Bianco Mottobello '16	♟ 3
● Colline Novaresi Uva Rara Selvalunga '16	♟ 2
● Colline Novaresi Nebbiolo MötZiflon '13	♙♙ 3
● Colline Novaresi Nebbiolo MötZiflon '12	♙♙ 3*
● Colline Novaresi Vespolina Maria '15	♙♙ 3
● Colline Novaresi Vespolina Maria '14	♙♙ 2*
● Ghemme Oltre il Bosco '11	♙♙ 4

Broglia - Tenuta La Meirana

LOC. LOMELLINA, 22
15066 GAVI [AL]
TEL. +39 0143642998
www.broglia.it

CELLAR SALES
PRE-BOOKED VISITS
ACCOMMODATION
ANNUAL PRODUCTION 480,000 bottles
HECTARES UNDER VINE 65.00

In 1972, the entrepreneur Bruno Broglia bought one of the most sizable properties in Gavia from the Count Edilio Raggio. Known as the estate of Meirana, today it's being managed by the third generation of Broglia family (Piero's sons, Roberto and Filippo, and Paolo's son, Bruno). The estate comprises about 65 hectares of land, almost all of which are dedicated to Cortese. They produce some six wines, all of which represent different techniques and expressions. The only thing they have in common is fermentation in steel. Doge, La Meirana, Villa Broglia and Bruno Broglia are their dry, still wines, while Roverello and Broglia Brut make up their consistently strong selection of sparkling wines. We saw good signs from the whole of Gavi's selection, starting with a carefree and racy 2016 La Meirana and a seemingly more glycerine-rich 2015 Bruno Broglia. The 2009 Vecchia Annata offers up smoky and balsamic overtones, accompanied by a powerful and lively palate. The Brut Metodo Classico also did well.

○ Gavi del Comune di Gavi Bruno Broglia '15	♟♟ 5
○ Gavi del Comune di Gavi Vecchia Annata '09	♟♟ 3*
○ Broglia Brut M. Cl.	♟♟ 5
○ Gavi del Comune di Gavi La Meirana '16	♟♟ 3
○ Gavi Villa Broglia	♟ 3
○ Gavi del Comune di Gavi Bruno Broglia '12	♙♙♙ 5
○ Gavi del Comune di Gavi Bruno Broglia '08	♙♙♙ 5
○ Gavi del Comune di Gavi Bruno Broglia '07	♙♙♙ 5
○ Gavi del Comune di Gavi Bruno Broglia '14	♙♙ 5
○ Gavi del Comune di Gavi La Meirana '15	♙♙ 3*

★Brovia

via Alba-Barolo, 145
12060 Castiglione Falletto [CN]
Tel. +39 017362852
www.brovia.net

CELLAR SALES
PRE-BOOKED VISITS
ANNUAL PRODUCTION 60,000 bottles
HECTARES UNDER VINE 17.00
VITICULTURE METHOD Certified Organic

Almost 150 years have passed since the Brovia family starting growing grapes and making prized wines in Castiglione Falletto and Serralunga d'Alba. It's only been over the last 30 years, however, that the winery has solidified its position as a benchmark in Langhe, thanks to the work of sisters Cristina and Elena, along with the latter's husband, Alejandro Sanchez Solana. Everything centers on their extraordinary vineyards, and the stylistic lightness of a truly unmistakable selection. Arneis, Barbera, Dolcetto and naturally elegant Barolos are crafted over 15-20 days of fermentation in concrete and three years of aging in large barrels. The 2013 Villero earns a Tre Bicchieri, elbowing out the other crus thanks to its elegance on the nose and a balanced taste expressed through fine tannins. This year, the Garblèt Sue' stood out for its fresh, seductive and joyous drinkability. The balanced and lively Vigna Ca' Mia features lovely fruity pulp, which makes its rich tannins that much more velvety. The enchanting Rocche di Castiglione focuses more on elegance than weight.

● Barolo Villero '13	♟♟♟	8
● Barolo Brea V. Ca' Mia '13	♟♟	8
● Barolo Garblèt Sue' '13	♟♟	8
● Barolo Rocche di Castiglione '13	♟♟	8
● Barbera d'Alba Sorì del Drago '15	♟♟	4
● Barolo '13	♟♟	6
● Dolcetto d'Alba Vignavillej '15	♟♟	3
● Barolo Brea V. Ca' Mia '10	♟♟♟	8
● Barolo Rocche di Castiglione '12	♟♟♟	8
● Barolo Villero '11	♟♟♟	8
● Barolo Villero '10	♟♟♟	8
● Barolo Brea V. Ca' Mia '12	♟♟	8
● Barolo Brea V. Ca' Mia '11	♟♟	8
● Barolo Villero '12	♟♟	8

G. B. Burlotto

via Vittorio Emanuele, 28
12060 Verduno [CN]
Tel. +39 0172470122
www.burlotto.com

CELLAR SALES
PRE-BOOKED VISITS
ACCOMMODATION
ANNUAL PRODUCTION 60,000 bottles
HECTARES UNDER VINE 15.00

Burlotto's past is a glorious one, and the wines added recently by Fabio Alessandria have made for a moment worthy of that history. Indeed, he deserves credit for even having raised the prestige of Langhe's great winery, founded in the mid-1800s by the decorated citizen G.B. Burlotto. Their cellar and delightful family agritourism are here, in Verduno, along with most of their 15 hectares of property: Monvigliero, Neirane, Breri and Rocche dell'Olmo. There are also plots in Cannubi, Barolo. Their most important crus of Nebbiolo are fermented in medium-large barrels, making for wines that shine more and more for their character and classical style. The same can be said for their enticing Pelaverga. The 2013 Barolo Cannubi expresses the excellent harmony that can be obtained from this great cru. Its aromas range from licorice to aniseed, while the mouth exhibits rare balance. The 2013 Barolo Acclivi shows great elegance, with a delicately silky palate. The 2013 Barolo, made with grapes grown in different vineyards, gave a splendid performance. It's enjoyable despite its austere style.

● Barolo '13	♟♟	6
● Barolo Acclivi '13	♟♟	6
● Barolo Cannubi '13	♟♟	7
● Barbera d'Alba Aves '15	♟♟	4
● Barolo Monvigliero '13	♟♟♟	7
○ Langhe Sauvignon Dives '15	♟♟	3
○ Langhe Sauvignon Viridis '16	♟♟	3
● Verduno Pelaverga '16	♟♟	3
● Barolo Acclivi '11	♟♟♟	6
● Barolo Acclivi '07	♟♟♟	6
● Barolo Cannubi '12	♟♟♟	7
● Barolo Monvigliero '10	♟♟♟	7
● Barolo Monvigliero '12	♟♟	7
● Verduno Pelaverga '15	♟♟	3

★Piero Busso

VIA ALBESANI, 8
12052 NEIVE [CN]
TEL. +39 017367156
www.bussopiero.com

CELLAR SALES
PRE-BOOKED VISITS
ANNUAL PRODUCTION 45,000 bottles
HECTARES UNDER VINE 11.50
SUSTAINABLE WINERY

Piero Busso is, without a doubt, one of the most esteemed vine growers in the area of Neive and Treiso. Helped by his wife, Lucia, and their children, Emanuela and Pierguido, he personally manages their dozen or so hectares of vineyards. Almost all of these are dedicated to cultivating the area's time-honored grape varieties, with particular attention to their Barbaresco Nebbiolo. His wines aren't easily categorized, but should be thought of in terms of the personality of each vintage and the various crus. Their reds are solid and eclectic, a commendable balance of sumptuousness and cleanness. The 2014 Barbaresco Mondino offers up fresh and complex aromatic notes, rich in red fruit. Its palate is well-orchestrated, with a pleasant acidity that makes its presence felt without being intrusive, and a very clean finish. The pleasant 2013 Gallina features a different style, more spicy and slightly caressed by oak. The 2011 Albesani Viti Vecchie comes through more rugged and powerful, while the 2013 Vigna Borgese proves brilliant and lively.

● Barbaresco Gallina '13	🍷🍷 8
● Barbaresco Mondino '14	🍷🍷 5
● Barbaresco Albesani V. Borgese '13	🍷🍷 7
● Barbaresco Albesani Viti Vecchie '11	🍷🍷 8
● Barbera d'Alba Majano '15	🍷🍷 3
● Barbera d'Alba S. Stefanetto '15	🍷🍷 5
● Langhe Nebbiolo '15	🍷🍷 4
○ Langhe Bianco '15	🍷 3
● Barbaresco Borgese '09	🍷🍷🍷 6
● Barbaresco Borgese '08	🍷🍷🍷 6
● Barbaresco Gallina '12	🍷🍷🍷 8
● Barbaresco Gallina '11	🍷🍷🍷 8
● Barbaresco Gallina '09	🍷🍷🍷 8
● Barbaresco S. Stunet '11	🍷🍷🍷 7

Ca' Bianca

REG. SPAGNA, 58
15010 ALICE BEL COLLE [AL]
TEL. +39 0144745420
www.cantinacabianca.it

CELLAR SALES
PRE-BOOKED VISITS
ANNUAL PRODUCTION 500,000 bottles
HECTARES UNDER VINE 24.00

Over the last year, Alice Bel Colle's winery has undergone a generational change. Andrea Autino is now at the helm, the young winemaker whose background includes various experiences in Italy and abroad, though we'll only have the chance to taste his first wines next year. In terms of selection, Cà Bianca's wines pursue strong territorial expression, and their wines are generally of an outstanding quality. The selection of wines presented focuses on Barbera d'Asti, with three versions and three different vintages. The 2014 Superiore Chersì has overcome the difficult vintage, coming through fresh and savory, with a palate rich in pulp. Antè still sees wood dominating, but it doesn't spoil the power of its taste profile. Lastly, the 2016 Teis presents good approachable fruit, which lengthens into a fresh and well-orchestrated palate. The complex and firmly structured 2016 Gavi is also worthy of mention.

● Barbera d'Asti Sup. Antè '15	🍷🍷 3
● Barbera d'Asti Sup. Chersì '14	🍷🍷 5
● Barbera d'Asti Teis '16	🍷🍷 3
○ Gavi '16	🍷🍷 3
● Dolcetto d'Acqui '16	🍷 3
● Barbera d'Asti Sup. Antè '13	🍷🍷 3
● Barbera d'Asti Sup. Antè '12	🍷🍷 3
● Barbera d'Asti Sup. Chersì '13	🍷🍷 5
● Barbera d'Asti Sup. Chersì '12	🍷🍷 3
● Barbera d'Asti Teis '14	🍷🍷 2*
● Barbera d'Asti Teis '13	🍷🍷 2*
● Dolcetto d'Acqui '15	🍷🍷 3
● Dolcetto d'Acqui '14	🍷🍷 3
○ Roero Arneis '15	🍷🍷 3

Ca' d' Gal

FRAZ. VALDIVILLA
S.DA VECCHIA DI VALDIVILLA, 1
12058 SANTO STEFANO BELBO [CN]
TEL. +39 0141847103
www.cadgal.it

CELLAR SALES
PRE-BOOKED VISITS
ACCOMMODATION AND RESTAURANT SERVICE
ANNUAL PRODUCTION 95,000 bottles
HECTARES UNDER VINE 12.00

In recent years, Alessandro Boido's Ca' d' Gal has managed to carve out a name for itself in Moscato winemaking, not just for quality, but also for their interpretation of the cultivar and appellation. The result is a Moscato d'Asti that's aged for various years in the bottle. The estate's vineyards, some of which surpass 60 years in age, are situated primarily along the hills of Santo Stefano Belbo, on light terrain that ranges from sandy to calcareous clay. This year the 2016 Moscato d'Asti Canelli Sant'Ilario reached the top level. The nose sees elegant notes of honey, chamomile flowers, verbena and medicinal herbs, while the palate proves rich and opulent, with fruity overtones and a lingering, gutsy finish. The Moscato d'Asti Vite Vecchia is also excellent, managing to remain elegant and complex at the same time (even the 2014). The 2016 Moscato d'Asti Lumine is well-made, with fresh notes of white peach, while the Asti finds the right balance between sweetness and acidity.

○ Moscato d'Asti Canelli Sant'Ilario '16	🍷🍷🍷 4*
○ Moscato d'"Asti Vite Vecchia '14	🍷🍷 7
○ Asti	🍷🍷 3
○ Moscato d'Asti Lumine '16	🍷🍷 3
○ Langhe Bianco '16	🍷 3
○ Moscato d'Asti Canelli Sant'Ilario '15	🍷🍷🍷 3*
○ Moscato d'Asti V. V. '11	🍷🍷🍷 3*
● Barbera d'Asti '12	🍷🍷 3
○ Moscato d'Asti Lumine '15	🍷🍷 3*
○ Moscato d'Asti Lumine '14	🍷🍷 3
○ Moscato d'Asti V. Vecchia '14	🍷🍷 4
○ Moscato d'Asti V. Vecchia '10	🍷🍷 7
○ Moscato d'Asti V. Vecchia '09	🍷🍷 7

★Ca' del Baio

VIA FERRERE SOTTANO, 33
12050 TREISO [CN]
TEL. +39 0173638219
www.cadelbaio.com

CELLAR SALES
PRE-BOOKED VISITS
ANNUAL PRODUCTION 130,000 bottles
HECTARES UNDER VINE 25.00

Ca' del Baio is a classic, family-run business, with parents Giulio and Luciana increasingly accompanied by their three children, Paola, Valentina and Federica Grasso. They are assisted by a first-rate team of winemakers and agronomists, in part because their vineyards are expanding and in part because they now produce 14 different wines (taking into account the very recent addition of their Barbaresco Auitnbej). Their most celebrated and recognized wines are their Barbaresco Asili, Asili Riserva and Pora, but their entire selection, even their more value-oriented wines, are consistently strong. The 2014 Barbaresco Vallegrande is a real gem, with red fruit such as currants and raspberries leading into citrusy notes. Its exemplary tannic weave helps construct a velvety and elegant mouth - a real Tre Bicchieri. Roses, licorice and wild berries distinguish the consistent 2013 Barbaresco Pora, a wine with a fresh, lingering palate. The 2014 Barbaresco Asili is particularly rich and commendably classic.

● Barbaresco Vallegrande '14	🍷🍷🍷 5
● Barbaresco Asili '14	🍷🍷 6
● Barbaresco Asili Ris. '12	🍷🍷 8
● Barbaresco Autinbej '14	🍷🍷 5
● Barbaresco Pora '13	🍷🍷 6
○ Langhe Riesling '15	🍷🍷 3
● Barbaresco Asili '12	🍷🍷🍷 6
● Barbaresco Asili '10	🍷🍷🍷 6
● Barbaresco Asili '09	🍷🍷🍷 5
● Barbaresco Asili Ris. '11	🍷🍷🍷 8
● Barbaresco Pora '10	🍷🍷🍷 5
● Barbaresco Valgrande '08	🍷🍷🍷 5
● Barbaresco Asili '13	🍷🍷 6
● Barbaresco Pora '12	🍷🍷 6
● Barbaresco Vallegrande '13	🍷🍷 5

Ca' Nova

via San Isidoro, 1
28010 Bogogno [NO]
Tel. +39 0322863406
via san isidoro 1

CELLAR SALES
PRE-BOOKED VISITS
ACCOMMODATION
ANNUAL PRODUCTION 45,000 bottles
HECTARES UNDER VINE 10.00

Giada Codecasa's winery can be found along Via San Isidoro, in Bogogno, within the confines of a natural park that also hosts a golf club, a resort, and a solar greenhouse for generating clean energy and organic produce. It also includes a sizable tract of vineyards. All of this has come to pass in just 20 years, the time that Ca' Nova needed to become one of the most ambitious operations of the Colline Novaresi hills, thanks, in part, to their magnificent cru of Vigna San Quirico. Ghemme and Melchiòr round out their selection of top Nebbiolos. Aging takes place in oak of various dimensions, while the rosé, Aurora, and Bocciòlo are worked in steel and designed for early-drinking. We saw a masterful overall performance from Ca' Nova. Their early-drinking wines, such as the 2016 Nebbiolo and the 2015 Vespolina, were just as impressive as the Ghemme wines for laying down. The 2011 expresses more generosity, while the 2012 reveals a firmer texture. Both were made during hot vintages.

● Ghemme '12	♥♥ 5
● Ghemme '11	♥♥ 5
● Colline Novaresi Nebbiolo Bocciòlo '16	♥♥ 2*
● Colline Novaresi Nebbiolo San Quirico '10	♥♥ 4
○ Colline Novaresi Vespolina '15	♥♥ 2*
○ Jad'or Brut M. Cl.	♥♥ 4
○ Colline Novaresi Bianco Rugiada '16	♥ 2
⊙ Colline Novaresi Nebbiolo Aurora '16	♥ 2
● Colline Novaresi Nebbiolo Melchiòr '10	♥ 3
⊙ Jad'Or Extra Brut Rosé M. Cl.	♥ 4
● Colline Novaresi Nebbiolo Melchiòr '09	♀♀ 3*
● Ghemme Ris. '09	♀♀ 5

Ca' Rome'

s.da Rabaja, 86
12050 Barbaresco [CN]
Tel. +39 0173635126
www.carome.com

CELLAR SALES
PRE-BOOKED VISITS
ANNUAL PRODUCTION 30,000 bottles
HECTARES UNDER VINE 5.00

For some years now, Paola and Giuseppe have been a critical factor in carrying forward the legacy of artisan winemaking begun by their father, Romano, in 1994. Here, not only do their Barbarescos shine (Maria di Brun, Sorì Rio Sordo, Chiaramanti), but also Barolo. Indeed, Romano Marengo's mother was born in Serralunga d'Alba, and both their powerful Cerretta and fruity Rapet come from here. Their selection of wines, which includes an important Barbera d'Alba Superiore La Gamberaja, has, for some time, only been sold on international markets. Splendid overtones of raspberries emerge in the earthy 2013 Barbaresco Maria di Brün, a Tre Bicchieri with a consistent, long mouth and balsamic finish. The 2014 Barbaresco Chiaramanti shows a lovely spiciness of wood and red fruit, but proves a bit marked by tannins. The 2014 Rio Sordo comes through more austere and close-knit. The 2013 Barolo Rapet exhibits particular balance and velvetiness, while the more assertive Cerretta of the same vintage still needs to express itself further.

● Barbaresco Maria di Brün '13	♥♥♥ 8
● Barolo del Comune di Serralunga d'Alba Rapet '13	♥♥ 7
● Barbaresco Chiaramanti '14	♥♥ 7
● Barbaresco Chiaramanti Ris. '12	♥♥ 6
● Barbaresco Sorì Rio Sordo '14	♥♥ 6
● Barolo Cerretta '13	♥♥ 7
● Barbaresco Sorì Rio Sordo '06	♀♀♀ 6
● Barolo Rapet '11	♀♀♀ 7
● Barolo Rapet '08	♀♀♀ 7
● Barolo V. Cerretta '09	♀♀♀ 7
● Barbaresco Chiaramanti '13	♀♀ 7
● Barbaresco Rio Sordo '13	♀♀ 7
● Barbaresco Sorì Rio Sordo '13	♀♀ 6
● Barolo Rapet '12	♀♀ 7
● Barolo Rapet Ris. '09	♀♀ 8

★★Ca' Viola

B.TA SAN LUIGI, 11
12063 DOGLIANI [CN]
TEL. +39 017370547
www.caviola.com

CELLAR SALES
PRE-BOOKED VISITS
ACCOMMODATION AND RESTAURANT SERVICE
ANNUAL PRODUCTION 70,000 bottles
HECTARES UNDER VINE 10.00

Ca' Viola got its start in 1991 in Montelupo Albese, in a small cellar carved out beneath the shop of the owner's father (an excellent butcher). Their success was immediate, and so 10 years later Beppe and his wife, Nicoletta, moved to their current, delightful location in Dogliani, where their winemaking facility, cellar, and house all coincide. In addition to the first vineyards, dedicated to Dolcetto and Barbera d'Alba, they now have the important Sottocastello di Novello cru at their disposal. Here their Barolo and Langhe Nebbiolo is cultivated. They also have a plot in Cissone, which gave life to a widely recognized Langhe Riesling in 2014. The lovely 2012 vintage made for excellent, elegant Barolos, as demonstrated by the Sottocastello di Novello. It features very elegant aromas of red fruit, a balanced tannic thrust and a very lingering finish. It thoroughly deserved its Tre Bicchieri. Beppe Caviola does a great job interpreting Riesling, with a 2015 of rare finesse. The rest of the selection is worth noting, starting with the 2015 Dolcetto Barturot and the 2015 Barbera Bric du Luv.

● Barolo Sottocastello di Novello '12	▼▼▼	8
● Barbera d'Alba Bric du Luv '15	▼▼	5
● Dolcetto d'Alba Barturot '15	▼▼	4
○ Langhe Riesling '15	▼▼	5
● Barbera d'Alba Brichet '15	▼▼	4
● Dolcetto d'Alba Vilot '16	▼▼	3
● Langhe Nebbiolo '15	▼▼	5
● Barbera d'Alba Bric du Luv '12	♀♀♀	5
● Barbera d'Alba Bric du Luv '10	♀♀♀	5
● Barolo Sottocastello '06	♀♀♀	7
● Barolo Sottocastello di Novello '11	♀♀♀	8
● Barolo Sottocastello di Novello '10	♀♀♀	7
● Barolo Sottocastello di Novello '08	♀♀♀	7
● Langhe Nebbiolo '08	♀♀♀	5

Cantina del Glicine

VIA GIULIO CESARE, 1
12052 NEIVE [CN]
TEL. +39 017367215
www.cantinadelglicine.it

CELLAR SALES
PRE-BOOKED VISITS
ANNUAL PRODUCTION 37,000 bottles
HECTARES UNDER VINE 6.00

The marvelous, underground bottle cellar that today serves as Adriana Marzi and Roberto Bruno's headquarters goes all the way back to 1582. This house-cellar is in the upper part of Neive, on an area of about five hectares. Their Currà and Marcorino Nebbiolo are made separately, while grapes from different plots give rise to their Barbaresco Vigne Sparse. These are aged mostly in Slovanian oak, and the producers like to point out their traditional style, without being preachy. Their selection is rounded out by wines made of Arneis, Moscato, Dolcetto and Barbera, not to mention their excellent range of grappas and spirits. The wines put forward were very good overall, but without extreme highs or lows, especially the 2014 Barbarescos. Pleasant fresh notes of aniseed and balsam emerge in the Marcorino, while the palate is still marked by slightly green tannins. The Currà offers up refreshing aromas of raspberry and redcurrants, with a return to citrus fruit. It's small in the mouth but has pleasant drinkability. The Vignesparse proves less forthright.

● Barbaresco Currà '14	▼▼	5
● Barbaresco Marcorino '14	▼▼	5
● Barbaresco Vignesparse '14	▼▼	5
● Barbera d'Alba La Dormiosa '15	▼▼	3
● Nebbiolo d'Alba Calcabrume '15	▼▼	3
● Barbera d'Alba La Sconsolata '15	▼	3
● Dolcetto d'Alba '16	▼	2
○ Roero Arneis Il Mandolo '16	▼	3
● Barbaresco Currà '10	♀♀♀	4*
● Barbaresco Marcorino '12	♀♀♀	5
● Barbaresco Currà '13	♀♀	5
● Barbera d'Alba Sup. La Dormiosa '14	♀♀	3
● Dolcetto d'Alba Olmiolo '15	♀♀	2*
● Nebbiolo d'Alba Calcabrume '14	♀♀	3

Cantina del Nebbiolo

VIA TORINO, 17
12050 VEZZA D'ALBA [CN]
TEL. +39 017365040
www.cantinadelnebbiolo.com

CELLAR SALES
PRE-BOOKED VISITS
ANNUAL PRODUCTION 300,000 bottles
HECTARES UNDER VINE 300.00
VITICULTURE METHOD Certified Organic

There aren't many cooperative wineries in Roero. The Cantina del Nebbiolo got its start in 1901 as Cantina Sociale Parrocchiale di Vezza d'Alba, and was then rebuilt in 1959 under its current name. There are 175 member growers, who work vineyards situated in 18 different municipalities in Langhe and Roero. Their various wines are made with native grapes, primarily Nebbiolo (obviously), with a traditional style that's true to the territory, though without eschewing technical precision. The 2013 Barolo del Comune di Serralunga d'Alba features lovely notes of tobacco and licorice, followed by dried herbs and red fruit. The palate shows power, with marked acidity, elegant tannins and a lingcring, vibrant finish. The rest of the selection is well-made, including the 2013 Barbaresco Meruzzano, which has a fruity palate and elegant tannic texture. We enjoyed the 2016 Roero Arneis more than the Arenarium line, with its citrusy tones, freshness and pleasantness.

● Barolo	
del Comune di Serralunga d'Alba '13	🍷🍷 6
● Barbaresco '14	🍷🍷 4
● Barbaresco Meruzzano '13	🍷🍷 5
● Barolo '13	🍷🍷 5
● Nebbiolo d'Alba Valmaggiore '15	🍷🍷 2*
○ Roero Arneis '16	🍷🍷 2*
● Barbera d'Alba '15	🍷 2
○ Roero Arneis Arenarium '16	🍷 2
● Barolo Cannubi Boschis '11	🍷🍷 7
● Barolo	
del Comune di Serralunga d'Alba '12	🍷🍷 6
● Barolo	
del Comune di Serralunga d'Alba '11	🍷🍷 6
● Nebbiolo d'Alba V. Valmaggiore '14	🍷🍷 3

Cantina del Pino

S.DA OVELLO, 31
12050 BARBARESCO [CN]
TEL. +39 0173635147
www.cantinadelpino.com

ANNUAL PRODUCTION 38,000 bottles
HECTARES UNDER VINE 7.00

In many ways, education comes before technique in Renato Vacca's work. His great-grandfather was none other than Domizio Cavazza, the legendary director of the Real Scuola Enologica di Alba during the late 1800s and early 1900s. This heritage was honored by Renato's own work as a director for the association of local Barbaresco producers, which naturally gave way to Cantina del Pino. At the center of everything are his Nebbiolos, made with grapes from two splendid vineyards: Ovello and Albesani. These are then interpreted with long maceration and aged in small wood. Their Barbarescos are 'contemporary' in the best sense of the word, graceful and vigorous simultaneously. Our compliments go to the 2013 Barbaresco, which is definitely one of the best basic versions of the vintage. The lively 2013 Ovello comes through even more elegant, with pulp and alcohol leaving room for a refined and persuasive style that earns it a Tre Bicchieri. The rich and charming 2013 Barbaresco Albesani is slightly marked by wood.

● Barbaresco Ovello '13	🍷🍷🍷 7
● Barbaresco '13	🍷🍷 5
● Barbaresco Albesani '13	🍷🍷 7
● Barbera d'Alba '15	🍷🍷 4
● Langhe Nebbiolo '16	🍷🍷 4
● Dolcetto d'Alba '16	🍷 3
● Barbaresco '04	🍷🍷🍷 5*
● Barbaresco Albesani '05	🍷🍷🍷 6
● Barbaresco Ovello '07	🍷🍷🍷 6
● Barbaresco '12	🍷🍷 5
● Barbaresco Albesani '12	🍷🍷 6
● Barbaresco Ovello '12	🍷🍷 6
● Dolcetto d'Alba '15	🍷🍷 3
● Langhe Nebbiolo '15	🍷🍷 4

La Caplana

VIA CIRCONVALLAZIONE, 4
15060 BOSIO [AL]
TEL. +39 0143684182
www.lacaplana.com

CELLAR SALES
PRE-BOOKED VISITS
ANNUAL PRODUCTION 120,000 bottles
HECTARES UNDER VINE 5.00

Founded by Natalino Guido in the 1990s, La Caplana is a small, family-run affair. The winery is located in Bosio, a small hamlet in the province of Alessandria, just at the foot of the northern Ligurian Apennines and on the left bank of the Ardana river. Here, the terrain is characterized by steep slopes and white clay. It's an area that serves as a dividing line, also in terms of viticulture, between lower Piedmont and the mountain ridge along the coast. Indeed, even their selection is divided in two: on the one hand their Gavi whites, on the other Dolcetto d'Ovada. These are accompanied by Barberas from Astigiano, sparkling wines and Chardonnay. 2016 was certainly a good vintage for La Caplana's classics made with Cortese. The basic Gavi is subtle but vigorous, while the Gavi del Comune di Gavi proves more flavorful and weighty. We are also seeing good signs from their Brut, which features pleasant acidity behind its almost aromatic character, as does the captivating 2014 Dolcetto Narcys.

○ Gavi del Comune di Gavi '16	🍷🍷 2*
○ Caplana Brut	🍷🍷 3
● Dolcetto di Ovada Narcys '14	🍷🍷 3
○ Gavi '16	🍷🍷 2*
○ Gavi Villavecchia '16	🍷🍷 2*
● Barbera d'Asti '15	🍷 2
● Dolcetto di Ovada '16	🍷 2
○ Piemonte Chardonnay '16	🍷 2
● Barbera d'Asti Rubis '12	🍷🍷 3
● Dolcetto di Ovada '15	🍷🍷 2*
● Dolcetto di Ovada Narcys '13	🍷🍷 3*
○ Gavi Villa Vecchia '15	🍷🍷 2*

La Casaccia

VIA D. BARBANO, 10
15034 CELLA MONTE [AL]
TEL. I 39 0142489986
www.lacasaccia.biz

CELLAR SALES
PRE-BOOKED VISITS
ANNUAL PRODUCTION 25,000 bottles
HECTARES UNDER VINE 6.70
VITICULTURE METHOD Certified Organic

La Casaccia is a family-run winery that's marked by respect for local vine growing and winemaking tradition. The Rava couple have renovated a historic factory, situated in an area of rare natural beauty, in Cella Monte. It features a splendid cellar, utilized by generations for making and storing wines. The owners' philosophy brings together respect for tradition with the desire to live a healthy and sustainable life (as manifested in their B&B and agritourism as well). This is a sensational array of wines, with three reaching the finals. When first tasted, the elegant and complex Grignolino Ernesto astonishes for its balance, along with its harmonious structure and long finish. Poggeto has another year of aging under its belt and manages to fully express its complex, vibrant nose across a palate that's full of character. Giuanìn, a Barbera, features impenetrable color and a bouquet of elegant, complex aromas that lead into a classic, well-orchestrated palate.

● Barbera del M.to Giuanìn '15	🍷🍷 2*
● Grignolino del M.to Casalese Ernesto '12	🍷🍷 3*
● Grignolino del M.to Casalese Poggeto '15	🍷🍷 2*
● Barbera del M.to Calichè '14	🍷🍷 3
● M.to Freisa Monfiorenza '15	🍷🍷 3
○ La Casaccia Brut M.Cl. '14	🍷 4
● Barbera del M.to Bricco dei Boschi '13	🍷🍷 3
● Barbera del M.to Calichè '13	🍷🍷 3*
● Barbera del M.to Giuanìn '13	🍷🍷 3
● Grignolino del M.to Casalese Poggeto '14	🍷🍷 2*
● Grignolino del M.to Casalese Poggeto '13	🍷🍷 2*
○ La Casaccia Brut M.Cl. '10	🍷🍷 4
● M.to Freisa Monfiorenza '14	🍷🍷 3
● M.to Freisa Monfiorenza '13	🍷🍷 3

Casalone

VIA MARCONI, 100
15040 LU [AL]
TEL. +39 0131741280
www.casalone.it

CELLAR SALES
PRE-BOOKED VISITS
ANNUAL PRODUCTION 50,000 bottles
HECTARES UNDER VINE 10.00

This historic Lu Monferrato family have passed centuries working in the vineyard and cellar. Today Paolo Casalone manages a dozen of wines, made with both native and international grape varieties. Their wines display good structure, in addition to being long-lived. According to the wine, they may be aged in steel, large barrels or barriques. Their production style is quite modern, but hasn't lost touch with their family's enological heritage, let alone that of the territory. Casalone have chosen a selection from their rich roster of wines that's headed by the Bricco Morlantino. It's a Barbera del Monferrato Superiore with a very youthful appearance and an intense ruby color. Complex tertiary aromas and an intense, rich palate pave the way for its lingering finish. Next we have their Malvasia Grecas, with their lovely, complex, well-orchestrated and elegant Metodo Classico standing out. The still version proves just as pleasant, with clear aromatic characteristics that are followed by a fresh, intense palate.

● Barbera del M.to Sup. Bricco Morlantino '13	▼▼ 2*
○ Monemvasia	▼▼ 2
○ Monemvasia Brut M. Cl.	▼▼ 4
○ Monemvasia Passito	▼ 3
● Barbera d'Asti Rubermillo '13	♀♀ 3
● Barbera del M.to Sup. Bricco Morlantino '11	♀♀ 2*
● Barbera del M.to Sup. Bricco Morlantino '10	♀♀ 2*
● M.to Rosso Fandamat '10	♀♀ 3
● M.to Rosso Rus '12	♀♀ 3
● M.to Rosso Rus '10	♀♀ 3
○ Monemvasia Affinato Barrique	♀♀ 4
○ Monemvasia Passito '10	♀♀ 3
○ Monemvasia Passito '09	♀♀ 3
● Piemonte Grignolino La Caplëtta '15	♀♀ 3*

Cascina Barisél

RFG. SAN GIOVANNI, 30
14053 CANELLI [AT]
TEL. +39 0141824848
www.barisel.it

CELLAR SALES
PRE-BOOKED VISITS
ANNUAL PRODUCTION 35,000 bottles
HECTARES UNDER VINE 4.50

For some years now, the Penna family's winery has been among the most consistent and successful in Astigiano. The vineyards that surround the farmstead host the area's two most important grapes, Barbera and Moscato (except for a small plot of Favorita in San Marzano Oliveto). These are accompanied by small amounts of Chardonnay, Dolcetto and Pinot Nero. Some of their vineyards can range from 40 to more than 60 years old. The 2015 Barbera d'Asti Superiore La Cappelletta is one of the best in the appellation. Its nose sees overtones of dark fruit and Mediterranean scrub, followed by a long, pleasant, succulent palate that plays on fresh fruity notes. The 2016 Moscato d'Asti Canelli is well-made, with notes of candied fruit and gooseberry. It's a wine in which sweetness finds the right balance with acidity. The 2016 Barbera d'Asti is a traditional vintage Barbera, approachable and gutsy.

● Barbera d'Asti Sup. La Cappelletta '15	▼▼ 4
● Barbera d'Asti '16	▼▼ 2*
○ Moscato d'Asti Canelli '16	▼▼ 2*
● Barbera d'Asti Sup. Listoria '15	▼ 2
● Barbera d'Asti '15	♀♀ 2*
● Barbera d'Asti '14	♀♀ 2*
● Barbera d'Asti Sup. La Cappelletta '13	♀♀ 4
● Barbera d'Asti Sup. La Cappelletta '12	♀♀ 4
● Barbera d'Asti Sup. La Cappelletta '11	♀♀ 4
● Barbera d'Asti Sup. Listoria '14	♀♀ 2*
● Barbera d'Asti Sup. Listoria '13	♀♀ 2*
● Barbera d'Asti Sup. Listoria '12	♀♀ 2*
○ Moscato d'Asti Canelli '14	♀♀ 2*
○ Moscato d'Asti Canelli '13	♀♀ 2*

Cascina Bongiovanni

LOC. UCCELLACCIO
VIA ALBA BAROLO, 3
12060 CASTIGLIONE FALLETTO [CN]
TEL. +39 0173262184
www.cascinabongiovanni.com

CELLAR SALES
PRE-BOOKED VISITS
ACCOMMODATION
ANNUAL PRODUCTION 50,000 bottles
HECTARES UNDER VINE 7.20
SUSTAINABLE WINERY

It was winemaker Davide Mozzone's love for
Olga Bongiovanni that brought him to take
over this small and inspiring estate of
splendid vineyards. And for more than 20
years, he's continued to successfully
manage a selection that sees Barolo on
center stage. And he's done it with an
approach that's always been current, but
never too dependent on technology. In his
lovely and recently enlarged cellar we find
wood barrels of various sizes and ages, all
used for the purpose of creating
sophisticated wines. The Langhe Rosso
Faletto, a blend of native and imported
grapes, is the winery's crown jewel. The
2013 Barolo did well, proving to be one of
the most impressive in the vintage. Classic
notes of violets and raspberries merge on a
licorice background that anticipates a dense
and long palate. The notable 2013 Barolo
Pernanno is characterized by aromas of
rain-soaked earth and dark berries, as well
as a potent, alcoholic mouth, with tight-knit,
powerful tannins. The complex, soft and
drinkable 2015 Langhe Rosso Faletto
features aromas of intense black fruit.

● Barolo '13	♀♀	6
● Barolo Pernanno '13	♀♀♀	7
● Langhe Rosso Faletto '15	♀♀	4
● Dolcetto d'Alba '16	♀	3
● Dolcetto di Diano d'Alba '16	♀	3
● Barolo Pernanno '01	♀♀♀	6
● Barbera d'Alba '13	♀♀	3
● Barolo '12	♀♀	6
● Barolo '11	♀♀	5
● Barolo Pernanno '12	♀♀	7
● Dolcetto d'Alba '15	♀♀	3
● Dolcetto di Diano d'Alba '15	♀♀	3*
● Dolcetto di Diano d'Alba '14	♀♀	2*
● Langhe Rosso Faletto '13	♀♀	4

★Cascina Ca' Rossa

LOC. CASCINA CA' ROSSA, 56
12043 CANALE [CN]
TEL. +39 017398348
www.cascinacarossa.com

CELLAR SALES
PRE-BOOKED VISITS
ANNUAL PRODUCTION 90,000 bottles
HECTARES UNDER VINE 16.00
VITICULTURE METHOD Certified Organic

Angelo Ferrio is one of the most famous
and well-respected vine growers in Roero.
Along with his son, Stefano, he works some
of the most important crus of the area,
such as Mompissano (in Canale), where the
terrain is calcareous-clay. He also works
Audinaggio in (Vezza d'Alba), where the
terrain is sandy and where inclines in the
area of Valmaggiore can reach 70%. In
both cases, Nebbiolo is cultivated. For
Barbera, there's Mulassa cru in Canale. The
wines he produces are sophisticated and
elegant and among the most captivating of
Roero. Even with its new name (which
recalls the historic Valmaggiore cru that
gives rise to the wine), the Roero
Valmaggiore Vigna Audinaggio remains one
of the most elegant wines we have tasted.
The 2015 comes through savory and
subtle, fresh and long, with notes of black
fruit, spices and forest floor. It earned a
thoroughly-deserved Tre Bicchieri. The
2015 Barbera d'Alba La Mulassa is
excellent, fruity and earthy, taut and
full-bodied. The 2016 Roero Arneis Merica
also did quite well.

● Roero Valmaggiore V. Audinaggio '15	♀♀♀	5
● Barbera d'Alba Mulassa '15	♀♀	5
● Barbera d'Alba '15	♀♀	3
○ Roero Arneis Merica '16	♀♀	3
● Langhe Nebbiolo Funsu '16	♀	3
● Roero Mompissano Ris. '13	♀♀♀	5
● Roero Mompissano Ris. '12	♀♀♀	5
● Barbera d'Alba '14	♀♀	3
● Langhe Nebbiolo '15	♀♀	3
● Langhe Nebbiolo '12	♀♀	3
○ Roero Arneis Merica '15	♀♀	3
○ Roero Arneis Merica '14	♀♀	3

Cascina Chicco

VIA VALENTINO, 14
12043 CANALE [CN]
TEL. +39 0173979411
www.cascinachicco.com

CELLAR SALES
PRE-BOOKED VISITS
ANNUAL PRODUCTION 435,000 bottles
HECTARES UNDER VINE 48.00
SUSTAINABLE WINERY

The name of the winery comes from a three-generations-old family nickname, 'Chicu'. Today, Cascina Chicco's large estate, founded in the 1950s, comprises vineyards in Roero (in Canale, Vezza d'Alba, Castellinaldo and Castagnito). A few years ago they they also bought a plot of five hectares in Langhe, in one of the most notable Barolo crus, Ginestra (Monforte d'Alba). Their wines always focus on expressing the character of the various territories and their specific attributes. Their wines are always top-level, but this year we particularly appreciated the 2013 Barolo Rocche di Castelletto, with its aromas of red fruit, tobacco and licorice on the nose, and a subtle, fresh, lingering palate. The 2010 Barolo Ginestra Riserva, on the other hand, seemed less brilliant, a bit alcoholic and evolved, with notes of dried herbs. The Cuvée Zero and Cuvèe Zero Rosé, their Metodo Classico sparkling wines, both play on marked freshness and acid grip.

Cascina Corte

FRAZ. SAN LUIGI
B.TA VALDIBERTI, 33
12063 DOGLIANI [CN]
TEL. +39 0173743539
www.cascinacorte.it

CELLAR SALES
PRE-BOOKED VISITS
ACCOMMODATION
ANNUAL PRODUCTION 30,000 bottles
HECTARES UNDER VINE 5.00
VITICULTURE METHOD Certified Organic
SUSTAINABLE WINERY

For 17 years, Sandro Barosi has pursued his dream of living a natural life. From the beginning, he's had the help of his wife, Amalia Battaglia. Today, at organic wine fairs, it's nice to see how he's recognized as the intelligent designer of an estate that blends into and integrates with the environment. It's a small winery that offers local wines, with Dogliani front and center. This is accompanied by small amounts of Langhe Barbera and Nebbiolo, as well as a recent Riesling and Nascetta. Their cozy and relaxing B&B is absolutely delightful. The Barnedòl is made with a blend of Barbera, Nebbiolo and Dolcetto. Pleasant overtones range from sweet tobacco to hay, while the palate is well-balanced and moderately long. The rest of their selection proves interesting, starting with the Pirochetta Vecchie Vigne. But it must remembered that Sandro Barosi's decision to intervene as little as possible in the cellar makes for a lack of elegance.

● Barolo Rocche di Castelletto '13	♥♥ 5
○ Cuvée Zero M. Cl.	♥♥ 4
● Barbera d'Alba Granera Alta '16	♥♥ 3
● Barolo Ginestra Ris. '10	♥♥ 7
☉ Cuvée Zero Rosé M. Cl.	♥♥ 4
● Nebbiolo d'Alba Monpissano '15	♥♥ 3
● Barbera d'Alba Bric Loira '15	♥ 4
○ Roero Arneis Anterisio '16	♥ 3
● Roero Montespinato '15	♥ 3
○ Arcàss Passito '04	♥♥♥ 4
● Roero Valmaggiore Ris. '12	♥♥♥ 4*
● Barolo Ginestra Ris. '09	♀♀ 7
● Roero Valmaggiore Ris. '13	♀♀ 4

● Barnedòl	♥♥ 4
● Dogliani Sup. Pirochetta V. V. '15	♥♥ 3
● Dogliani '16	♥ 3
● Langhe Barbera '15	♥ 3
● Langhe Nebbiolo '15	♥ 4
● Dogliani Vecchie V. Pirochetta '08	♥♥♥ 3*
● Dogliani '15	♀♀ 3*
● Dogliani '14	♀♀ 3
● Dogliani '13	♀♀ 3
● Dogliani Sup. Pirochetta V. V. '13	♀♀ 3
● Dogliani Sup. Pirochetta V. V. '12	♀♀ 3*
● Dogliani Sup. Pirochetta V. V. '11	♀♀ 3*
● Langhe Nebbiolo '14	♀♀ 4
● Langhe Nebbiolo '13	♀♀ 4

Cascina del Monastero

FRAZ. ANNUNZIATA, 112A
CASCINA LUCIANI
12064 LA MORRA [CN]
TEL. +39 01735092450173509245
www.cascinadelmonastero.it

CELLAR SALES
PRE-BOOKED VISITS
ACCOMMODATION
ANNUAL PRODUCTION 40,000 bottles
HECTARES UNDER VINE 12.00
VITICULTURE METHOD Certified Organic
SUSTAINABLE WINERY

Giuseppe Grasso handles all stages of production, from vineyard management to bottling, while his wife, Velda, attends to the particularly spacious and cozy agritourism present on the estate. Following in the stylistic precedent of Alessio, the winery's founder, exclusively red wines are made here. The Barolo Perno, a wine that, according to custom, ages only in Slovenian oak, continues to exhibit traditional personality. Particular attention is paid to the Barolo Riserva Riund, which ages for a year in small wood and two more in mid-sized oak. The Barolo Perno is particularly open and complex, with notes of sweet tobacco and ripe red fruit. It just lacks the freshness that we would expect from a 2013. The 2013 Barolo Bricco Luciani starts off with a pleasant touch of licorice, but loses balance on the palate, due to tannins that are still sensitive and astringent. The 2011 Riserva Riund comes through pleasantly rustic.

Cascina Fonda

VIA SPESSA,29
12052 MANGO [CN]
TEL. +39 0173677877
www.cascinafonda.com

CELLAR SALES
PRE-BOOKED VISITS
ACCOMMODATION
ANNUAL PRODUCTION 110,000 bottles
HECTARES UNDER VINE 12.00

The Barbero brothers began bottling their wines in 1988, managing to grow their winery over the years such that, today, it's considered one of the top producers for Moscato winemaking. Cascina Fonda's estate comprises vineyards along the hills of Mango and Neive, which see the presence of Moscato (ranging from 35 to 60 years old) and other traditional cultivar, such as Arneis, Dolcetto and Nebbiolo. The 2016 La Tardja, a Moscato wine made with grapes grown in the winery's oldest vineyards, impressed us for its elegance, balance and complexity. Aromas of sage and aniseed merge with floral and herbaceous overtones, while the fresh and pleasant palate paves the way for a long, fruity finish. The 2016 Asti Bel Piasì offers up notes of medicinal herbs, apple and apricot, while the palate exhibits great freshness and pleasant drinkability. The 2016 Moscato d'Asti Bel Piano features notes of meadow herbs and flowers, peach and rhubarb preserves. Both are very well-made.

● Barbera d'Alba Sup. Parroco '14	♟♟ 3
● Barolo Bricco Luciani '13	♟♟ 6
● Barolo Bricco Rocca Riund Ris. '11	♟♟ 7
● Barolo Perno '13	♟♟ 5
● Langhe Nebbiolo Monastero '13	♟ 3
● Langhe Rosso Sarset '14	♟ 3
● Barbera d'Alba Parroco '12	♟♟ 3
● Barbera d'Alba Sup. Parroco '13	♟♟ 3
● Barolo Bricco Luciani '12	♟♟ 6
● Barolo Bricco Luciani '11	♟♟ 6
● Barolo Bricco Luciani '10	♟♟ 6
● Barolo Bricco Rocca Riund Ris. '10	♟♟ 6
● Barolo Bricco Rocca Riund Ris. '09	♟♟ 6
● Barolo Perno '12	♟♟ 5
● Langhe Nebbiolo Monastero '12	♟♟ 3

○ La Tardja '16	♟♟ 3*
○ Asti Bel Piasì '16	♟♟ 2*
○ Moscato d'Asti Bel Piano '16	♟♟ 2*
● Piemonte Brachetto Bel Roseto '16	♟ 3
○ Asti Spumante Bel Piasì '15	♟♟ 2*
○ Asti Spumante Bel Piasì '13	♟♟ 2*
● Barbaresco Bertola '12	♟♟ 5
● Barbaresco Bertola '10	♟♟ 5
○ Dolcetto d'Alba Brusalino '14	♟♟ 2*
○ Moscato d'Asti Bel Piano '14	♟♟ 2*
○ Moscato d'Asti Bel Piano '13	♟♟ 2*
○ Moscato Spumante Tardivo '14	♟♟ 3*
○ Moscato Spumante Tardivo '12	♟♟ 3*

Cascina Fontana

LOC. PERNO
P.LO DELLA CHIESA, 2
12065 MONFORTE D'ALBA [CN]
TEL. +39 0173789005
www.cascinafontana.com

CELLAR SALES
PRE-BOOKED VISITS
ANNUAL PRODUCTION 25,000 bottles
HECTARES UNDER VINE 5.00
SUSTAINABLE WINERY

It's not true that only artisans make the best wines. We mean those that, either alone or with occasional help, attend to their vineyards and cellars, from bottling to sales. It is certain, however, that Mario Fontana's wines clearly reflect the grape, the land, the vineyard, the place itself. And what a place, if you think that Barolo started in the world-famous Villero di Castiglione Falletto. Their Barbera, Dolcetto d'Alba and an enticing Langhe Nebbiolo round out their limited selection. The winery's new product, the 2013 Barolo del Comune di Castiglione Falletto Vecchie Vigne, is a classically styled wine. The nose offers up notes of licorice and medicinal herbs, while the palate is rich in fresh fruity pulp. The 2013 Barolo impressed just as much, with its slightly discernible tannins. The 2015 Barbera d'Alba proves invigorating and fruity, with a supple and rich mouth. The frank and fragrant 2015 Langhe Nebbiolo also exhibits tasty drinkability.

● Barolo '13	♟♟ 6
● Barolo del Comune di Castiglione Falletto V. V. '13	♟♟ 7
● Barbera d'Alba '15	♟♟ 3
● Langhe Nebbiolo '15	♟♟ 4
● Barolo '12	♟♟♟ 6
● Barolo '10	♟♟♟ 7
● Barbera d'Alba '14	♟♟ 3
● Barbera d'Alba '13	♟♟ 3
● Barbera d'Alba '12	♟♟ 5
● Barbera d'Alba '11	♟♟ 5
● Barolo '11	♟♟ 6
● Barolo '09	♟♟ 7
● Langhe Nebbiolo '14	♟♟ 4
● Langhe Nebbiolo '13	♟♟ 4

Cascina Gilli

VIA NEVISSANO, 36
14022 CASTELNUOVO DON BOSCO [AT]
TEL. +39 0119876984
www.cascinagilli.it

CELLAR SALES
PRE-BOOKED VISITS
ACCOMMODATION
ANNUAL PRODUCTION 130,000 bottles
HECTARES UNDER VINE 17.00

For years, Gianni Vergnano's work has been directed principally at resuscitating grape varieties native to the hills of Basso Monferrato, from Freisa to Castelnuovo Malvasia to Bonarda. Their vineyards are situated at Castelnuovo Don Bosco, surrounding the farmstead itself, and on the slopes of Cornareto. The terrain is gray-blue marl clay, with Freisa the most common variety. On the hill of Schierano, in Passerano Marmorito, Malvasia, Bonarda and Barbera are cultivated. Nevertheless, their various Freisas serve as the benchmark for the rest of the selection. Cascina Gilli always puts forward solid wines, approachable and pleasant. The 2015 Freisa d'Asti Il Forno offers up spicy notes and cherry. The 2016 Barbera d'Asti Le More plays on wild berry overtones. Lastly, the 2016 Malvasia di Castelnuovo Don Bosco merges aromas and sweetness; it's never cloying, but fresh and easy to drink.

● Barbera d'Asti Le More '16	♟♟ 2*
● Freisa d'Asti Il Forno '15	♟♟ 2*
● Malvasia di Castelnuovo Don Bosco '16	♟♟ 2*
● Barbera d'Asti Sup. Dèdica '14	♟ 3
● Freisa d'Asti Arvelé '14	♟ 3
○ Piemonte Chardonnay Rafé '16	♟ 2
● Barbera d'Asti Le More '15	♟♟ 2*
● Barbera d'Asti Le More '13	♟♟ 2*
● Ulicà	♟♟ 3
● Freisa d'Asti Arvelé '13	♟♟ 3
● Freisa d'Asti Il Forno '14	♟♟ 2*
○ Piemonte Chardonnay Rafé '15	♟♟ 2*

Cascina Giovinale

S.DA SAN NICOLAO, 102
14049 NIZZA MONFERRATO [AT]
TEL. +39 0141793005
www.cascinagiovinale.it

CELLAR SALES
PRE-BOOKED VISITS
ANNUAL PRODUCTION 25,000 bottles
HECTARES UNDER VINE 7.00
SUSTAINABLE WINERY

In the early 1980s, Bruno Ciocca and Anna
Maria Solaini founded Cascina Giovinale on
San Nicolao hill. Since then, this small
operation in Nizza Monferrato has managed
to consistently produce wines of great
typicity. All their vineyards, which were
planted between 1960 and 1970, grow
within Nizza, on sandy calcareous terrain
(with a small percentage of porous clay).
Obviously, Barbera and Moscato are the
principal grape varieties here, with smaller
quantities of Dolcetto, Cortese and
Cabernet Sauvignon. In the absence of the
2014 Nizza Anssèma, the 2013 Barbera
d'Asti Superiore stepped in as the winery's
flagship. It offers up aromas of cinchona
and plums, followed by balsamic notes of
rain-soaked earth. The palate shows good
density, but it's still pleasant and easy to
drink. The 2016 Moscato d'Asti is
well-made, with classic notes of sage and
medicinal herbs. Its palate exhibits good
balance between sugar and acidity.

★★Cascina La Barbatella

S.DA ANNUNZIATA, 55
14049 NIZZA MONFERRATO [AT]
TEL. +39 0141701434
www.labarbatella.com

CELLAR SALES
PRE-BOOKED VISITS
ANNUAL PRODUCTION 25,000 bottles
HECTARES UNDER VINE 4.00

Along Annunziata, up on a hill overlooking
Pizza Monferrato. That's where you'll find
Cascina La Barbatella, where the Perego
family has managed to successfully carry
on the heritage left to them by Angelo
Sonvico. The vineyards, which include two
hectares of terrain planted between 1945
and 1955, are situated on calcareous,
sandy soil, and feature Barbera. Not only is
their selection technically well-crafted, it
also expresses the characteristic attributes
of the territory. The Nizza La Vigna
dell'Angelo remains at the top of the
rankings with its 2014 version. Despite the
difficult vintage, this Barbera shows great
class and typicity, with notes of spices,
black fruit, cherries and rain-soaked earth.
Its palate proves lingering and dynamic.
The 2012 Monferrato Rosso Sonvico is a
historic blend of Barbera and Cabernet
Sauvignon, with good fruit and elegant
tannins. The 2015 Barbera d'Asti La
Barbatella comes through fresh and
pleasant.

● Barbera d'Asti Sup. '13	🍷🍷 2*
○ Moscato d'Asti '16	🍷🍷 3
○ M.to Bianco Naiss '16	🍷 2
● Barbera d'Asti Sup. '12	🏆🏆 2*
● Barbera d'Asti Sup. '11	🏆🏆 2*
● Barbera d'Asti Sup. '10	🏆🏆 2*
● Barbera d'Asti Sup. '09	🏆🏆 2*
● Barbera d'Asti Sup. Nizza Anssèma '13	🏆🏆 3*
● Barbera d'Asti Sup. Nizza Anssèma '12	🏆🏆 4
● Barbera d'Asti Sup. Nizza Anssèma '11	🏆🏆 3
● Barbera d'Asti Sup. Nizza Anssèma '10	🏆🏆 3*
● Barbera d'Asti Sup. Nizza Anssèma '09	🏆🏆 3*
● Barbera d'Asti Sup. Nizza Anssèma '08	🏆🏆 4

● Nizza La V. dell'Angelo '14	🍷🍷🍷 5
● Barbera d'Asti La Barbatella '15	🍷🍷 3
● M.to Rosso Sonvico '12	🍷🍷 6
○ La Badessa Brut M. Cl. '13	🍷 4
○ M.to Bianco Noè '15	🍷 3
● M.to Rosso Ruanera '15	🍷 2
● Barbera d'Asti Sup. Nizza V. dell'Angelo '11	🏆🏆🏆 5
● Barbera d'Asti Sup. Nizza V. dell'Angelo '07	🏆🏆🏆 5
● M.to Rosso Sonvico '09	🏆🏆🏆 6
● M.to Rosso Sonvico '06	🏆🏆🏆 5
● Barbera d'Asti La Barbatella '14	🏆🏆 3
● Barbera d'Asti Sup. Nizza V. dell'Angelo '13	🏆🏆 5
● M.to Rosso Ruanera '13	🏆🏆 2*
● M.to Rosso Sonvico '11	🏆🏆 6

Cascina Montagnola

S.DA MONTAGNOLA, 1
15058 VIGUZZOLO [AL]
TEL. +39 3480742701
www.cascinamontagnola.com

CELLAR SALES
PRE-BOOKED VISITS
ANNUAL PRODUCTION 30,000 bottles
HECTARES UNDER VINE 10.00

Two decades after the founding of her winery, Donatella Giannotti can, all told, be proud of what she's accomplished over the years. Cascina Montagnola carved out an important space for itself during the renaissance of Tortona's wines that began with the rediscovery of Timorasso. Their range of wines includes 12 in all, made with both native and international varieties. The unique, late-harvest Timorasso stands out among them. A splendid Morasso heads the selection of wines this year. It features an intense straw-yellow color, with golden highlights, while the intense and elegant nose offers up aromas of citrus fruit and herbs on a mineral background of camphor. In the mouth it proves abundant, with good structure, alcohol and acidity making for an unending finish. Then come the lovely intense and evolved Barbera Amaranto and the very concentrated and rich Croatina Donaldo.

○ Colli Tortonesi Timorasso Morasso '15	♥♥ 4	
● Colli Tortonesi Barbera Amaranto '13	♥♥ 2*	
● Colli Tortonesi Croatina Donaldo '15	♥♥ 3	
○ Alcesti '16	♥ 3	
○ Colli Tortonesi Cortese Dunin '16	♥ 2	
● Colli Tortonesi Barbera Rodeo '10	♀♀ 5	
○ Colli Tortonesi Cortese Dunin '15	♀♀ 2*	
○ Colli Tortonesi Cortese Dunin '12	♀♀ 2*	
○ Colli Tortonesi Timorasso Morasso '14	♀♀ 4	
○ Colli Tortonesi Timorasso Morasso '13	♀♀ 4	
○ Colli Tortonesi Timorasso Morasso '12	♀♀ 4	

Cascina Morassino

3.DA BERNINO, 10
12050 BARBARESCO [CN]
TEL. +39 0173635149
morassino@gmail.com

CELLAR SALES
PRE-BOOKED VISITS
ANNUAL PRODUCTION 20,000 bottles
HECTARES UNDER VINE 4.50
SUSTAINABLE WINERY

Ovello is one of the most important crus in all of Barbaresco. The vineyard, situated at 260 meters above sea level, with southern and western exposure, is known for giving rise to particularly robust wines with good tannic weave and aging potential. And this is Roberto Bianco's main cru. He's a consistent and serious producer who does his best to confer his own personality on his wines, eschewing frills and exotic touches in favor of aromatic forthrightness and solidity of flavor. His Barbaresco is accompanied by a small, though interesting selection of Langhe Nebbiolo. This Barbaresco Ovello is without a doubt one of 2014's success stories. It exhibits an elegant fruity balance of aroma, as well as a bold structure that features pulp and weight. It's a solid Tre Bicchieri with a rich personality. The very pleasant 2014 Barbaresco Morassino shows exemplary style. It comes through fresh, but not acidic, tannic but not aggressive, with great balance.

● Barbaresco Ovello '14	♥♥♥ 6	
● Barbaresco Morassino '14	♥♥ 5	
● Barbaresco Morassino '09	♀♀♀ 5	
● Barbaresco Morassino '13	♀♀ 5	
● Barbaresco Morassino '12	♀♀ 5	
● Barbaresco Morassino '11	♀♀ 5	
● Barbaresco Morassino '10	♀♀ 5	
● Barbaresco Morassino '08	♀♀ 5	
● Barbaresco Ovello '13	♀♀ 6	
● Barbaresco Ovello '12	♀♀ 6	
● Barbaresco Ovello '11	♀♀ 6	
● Barbaresco Ovello '10	♀♀ 6	
● Barbaresco Ovello '09	♀♀ 6	
● Barbaresco Ovello '08	♀♀ 6	

Cascina Salicetti

VIA CASCINA SALICETTI, 2
15050 MONTEGIOCO [AL]
TEL. +39 01318/5192
www.cascinasalicetti.it

CELLAR SALES
PRE-BOOKED VISITS
ANNUAL PRODUCTION 25,000 bottles
HECTARES UNDER VINE 16.00

Winemaker Anselmo Francosi has inherited a family tradition that spanned the entire last century. With his presence in the winery, a cycle of modernization began, from production processes to management of the supply chain. It's resulted in better use of the grapes, and wines that are structured and long-lived. The style may be a bit modern, but his wines maintain the territory's defining characteristics and are proving to be popular. Ombra di Luna stands out for its power and richness. Timorasso features a palate and aromas characteristic of a true masterpiece and manages to express all its finesse. In the mouth, good acidity supports a palate with very long aromatic length. Il Seguito, a wine made solely with Cabernet Sauvignon grapes, displays intriguing, complex features, with a lovely balanced and well-orchestrated palate. Monteffe is an intense vintage Dolcetto, with crisp fruit and a well-orchestrated palate.

○ Colli Tortonesi Timorasso Ombra di Luna '15	¶¶¶ 4*
● Colli Tortonesi Dolcetto Monteffe '16	¶¶ 2*
● Colli Tortonesi Rosso Il Seguito '15	¶¶ 2*
○ Colli Tortonesi Cortese Montarlino '16	¶ 4
● Colli Tortonesi Barbera Morganti '13	¶¶ 4
○ Colli Tortonesi Cortese Montarlino '14	¶¶ 4
● Colli Tortonesi Croatina Risulò '12	¶¶ 4
● Colli Tortonesi Dolcetto Di Marzi '12	¶¶ 2*
● Colli Tortonesi Rosso Il Seguito '12	¶¶ 2*
○ Colli Tortonesi Timorasso Ombra di Luna '13	¶¶ 4
○ Colli Tortonesi Timorasso Ombra di Luna '12	¶¶ 4

Francesca Castaldi

VIA NOVEMBRE, 6
28072 BRIONA [NO]
TEL. +39 0321826045
www.cantinacastaldi.it

CELLAR SALES
PRE-BOOKED VISITS
ANNUAL PRODUCTION 10,000 bottles
HECTARES UNDER VINE 6.30

Pianazze, Val Ceresole and Belvedere di Briona: these are the areas where Francesca and Giuseppe Castaldi's six hectares of terrain are concentrated. Reviving Fara, the southernmost of the appellations in the morainic strip of Novara, is both a burden and privilege. The Castaldis, descendants of a historic family, started renovating the vineyards in 1997, focusing on traditional grape varieties (mostly Nebbiolo, with occasional patches of of Vespolina and Erbaluce). From these they make a small selection that, from the first vintages, managed to attract attention for their stylistic precision. Their wines continue to improve in terms of aromatic and extractive definition. The 2016 Bianco Lucia's great performance proves its on a winning path. It merges floral and balsamic aromas and strength of taste. Their Nebbiolo reds have shot straight to the top: the 2015 Bigin is austere and dynamic, with very characteristic cinchona and rust, while the 2013 Fara proves more layered and succulent.

● Fara '13	¶¶ 5
○ Colline Novaresi Bianco Lucia '16	¶¶ 3
● Colline Novaresi Nebbiolo Bigin '15	¶¶ 3
● Colline Novaresi Vespolina Nina '16	¶¶ 3
⊙ Colline Novaresi Rosato Rosa Alba '16	¶ 3
● Colline Novaresi Uva Rara Valceresole '16	¶ 3
○ Colline Novaresi Bianco Lucia '15	¶¶ 3
● Colline Novaresi Nebbiolo Bigin '12	¶¶ 3
⊙ Colline Novaresi Rosato Rosa Alba '15	¶¶ 3
⊙ Colline Novaresi Vespolina Nina '15	¶¶ 3
● Fara '12	¶¶ 5
● Fara '11	¶¶ 5
● Fara '10	¶¶ 5

Castellari Bergaglio

Fraz. Rovereto, 136r
15066 Gavi [AL]
Tel. +39 0143644000
www.castelleribergaglio.it

CELLAR SALES
PRE-BOOKED VISITS
ANNUAL PRODUCTION 90,000 bottles
HECTARES UNDER VINE 11.00

According to Castellari Bergaglio's philosophy, traditional roots and a modern attitude can coexist. Today, the winery, an important one in Gavi, is managed by Mario Bergaglio and his son, Marco. Since 2014, they have been converting to organic, with Cortese leading the way by far. The grape is used for seven of their wines: Salluvii can be considered the selection's foundation; Fornaci and Rolona highlight variations in terrain and exposure to sun (in Tassarolo and Gavi); Rovereto focuses on long, temperature-controlled fermentation; and the oldest, Pilin, is aged in barriques after a late harvest. We shouldn't forget their 'Metodo Classico' sparkler, Ardé, and their passito dried-grape wine, Gavium. A varied style makes Castellari Bergaglio's wines more thrilling. They range from the joyous freshness of the 2016 Fornaci to the gutsy temperament of the 2014 Rovereto Vignavecchia, without forgetting the creamy fragrance displayed by the 2011 Ardé Brut. Then there's the 2013 Pilin for those who love more austere Gavis.

○ Gavi Pilin '13	♟♟ 5
○ Gavi Brut Ardé M. Cl. '11	♟♟ 4
○ Gavi del Comune di Gavi Rovereto Vignavecchia '14	♟♟ 3
○ Gavi del Comune di Tassarolo Fornaci '16	♟♟ 2*
○ Gavi del Comune di Gavi Rolona '16	♟ 3
○ Gavium '10	♟ 4
○ Gavi del Comune di Gavi Rovereto Vignavecchia '13	♟♟ 3
○ Gavi del Comune di Tassarolo Fornaci '15	♟♟ 2*
○ Gavi del Comune di Tassarolo Fornaci '14	♟♟ 2*
○ Gavi Fornaci '13	♟♟ 2*
○ Gavi Salluvii '14	♟♟ 2*
○ Gavi Salluvii '13	♟♟ 2*

Castello di Gabiano

via San Defendente, 2
15020 Gabiano [AL]
Tel. +39 0142945004
www.castellodigabiano.com

CELLAR SALES
PRE-BOOKED VISITS
ACCOMMODATION AND RESTAURANT SERVICE
ANNUAL PRODUCTION 120,000 bottles
HECTARES UNDER VINE 21.00

The history of Castello di Gabiano is inextricably linked to Monferrato Casalese's viticulture. It has, since anyone can remember, dominated the Po Valley, surrounded by vineyards whose positions and altitudes represent the ideal microclimate. Little has changed since the castle was built, though they've put down their arms and it's now possible to spend the night in its quarters. The vineyards still enjoy the fresh, nighttime breeze that blows in off the Alps. The 2016 Grignolino del Monferrato Casalese Il Ruvo represented the winery in the finals. It offers up intense floral aromas, with excellent spicy notes anticipating a fresh, intense palate and classic tannins at the finish. The Chardonnay Castello features a nice palate and aromas, but its wood still needs to come into balance. The Adornes is extremely well-made, as are the Rubino di Cantavenna and Il Giardino di Flora, an intense and varietal Malvasia di Casorzo.

● Grignolino del M.to Casalese Il Ruvo '16	♟♟ 2*
● Barbera d'Asti Adornes '12	♟♟ 6
⊙ M.to Chiaretto Castelvere '16	♟♟ 2*
● Malvasia di Casorzo Il Giardino di Flora '16	♟♟ 3
○ Piemonte Chardonnay Castello '15	♟♟ 6
● Rubino di Cantavenna '15	♟♟ 3
● Barbera d'Asti La Braja '15	♟ 2
○ M.to Bianco Corte '16	♟ 3
● Barbera d'Asti La Braja '14	♟♟ 2*
● Gabiano A Matilde Giustiniani Ris. '10	♟♟ 6
● Grignolino del M.to Casalese Il Ruvo '15	♟♟ 2*
● M.to Rosso Gavius '14	♟♟ 3
● M.to Rosso Gavius '12	♟♟ 3*
● Rubino di Cantavenna '14	♟♟ 3

Castello di Neive

c.so Romano Scagliola, 205
12052 Neive [CN]
Tel. +39 017367171
www.castellodineive.it

CELLAR SALES
PRE-BOOKED VISITS
ACCOMMODATION
ANNUAL PRODUCTION 170,000 bottles
HECTARES UNDER VINE 26.00
SUSTAINABLE WINERY

Siblings Anna, Giulio, Italo and Piera
Stupino are the owners of a historic castle
and some 60 hectares of terrain in Neive.
Today, they run the estate started by their
father, Giacomo, in the 1960s. Today,
Castello di Neive is one of the most
important producers in Langhe, cascina
after cascina: Messoirano, Montebertotto,
Basarin, Valtorta, I Cortini, Marcorino. Of
course, we mustn't forget Santo Stefano,
which continues to be the center of their
selection. Also available in a 'Riserva' for
the best vintages, the wine is Barbaresco
to the core both for its temperament and
its capacity to evolve. The dynamic
2012 Barbaresco Albesani Santo Stefano
Riserva shows excellent complexity and
elegance on the nose. Its palate comes
through warm and caressing thanks to
good alcohol and particularly docile tannins.
The Albesani Santo Stefano sees good
freshness and excellent finesse of taste.
The pleasant 2014 Barbaresco Gallina
proves smaller and vegetal, while the lovely
2015 Barbera d'Alba Vigna Santo Stefano
features fresh drinkability.

● Barbaresco Albesani S. Stefano Ris. '12	♥♥♥	8
● Barbaresco Albesani S. Stefano '14	♥♥	6
● Barbaresco Gallina '14	♥♥	7
● Barbera d'Alba Sup. '14	♥♥	5
● Barbera d'Alba V. S. Stefano '15	♥♥	4
○ Langhe Riesling '15	♥♥	5
● Barbaresco '14	♥	6
○ Langhe Arneis Montebertotto '16	♥	3
● Langhe Pinot Nero V. I Cortini '16	♥	5
● Piemonte Albarossa '15	♥	5
○ Piemonte Pinot Nero M. Cl. '13	♥	5
● Barbaresco Albesani S. Stefano '12	♥♥♥	6
● Barbaresco Albesani S. Stefano Ris. '11	♥♥♥	8
● Barbaresco Albesani S. Stefano '13	♥♥	6

Castello di Tassarolo

loc. Alborina, 1
15060 Tassarolo [AL]
Tel. +39 0143342240
www.castelloditassarolo.it

CELLAR SALES
PRE-BOOKED VISITS
ANNUAL PRODUCTION 130,000 bottles
HECTARES UNDER VINE 20.00
VITICULTURE METHOD Certified Organic
SUSTAINABLE WINERY

Flanked by Vincenzo Munì and Henry
Finzi-Constantine, the Bonifacio brothers
and Massimiliana Spinola have presided
over a decisive change in the history of
Castello di Tassarolo. The estate, part of
the noble family's patrimony for more than
seven centuries, has seen a breakthrough
mostly for the conversion to biodynamic of
their some 20 hectares of vineyards
(where primarily Cortese is cultivated). But
they've also undergone a significant
reworking of their selection. For some
years, they've introduced ambitious
experiments without added sulphites, for
example their Monferrato Rosso (a blend of
Barbera and Cabernet Sauvignon) and
their Barbera Titouan. The latest tastings
prove that the selection has no weak
points. The 2016 Il Castello's aromas of
damsons, shrubs and iodine make for a
wine with a complete personality and
flavor. The 2015 Alborina conveys more
exuberant and round fruit, supported by a
solid structure. The 2016 Barbera Titouan
is tops, with its taut, succulent palate.

○ Gavi del Comune di Tassarolo Il Castello '16	♥♥	3*
○ Gavi del Comune di Tassarolo Alborina '15	♥♥	3
○ Gavi del Comune di Tassarolo Titouan '16	♥♥	3
● Piemonte Barbera Titouan '16	♥♥	3
○ Gavi del Comune di Tassarolo Spinola No Solfiti '16	♥	2
○ Gavi Frizzante Sparkling Spinola '16	♥	2
☉ M.to Chiaretto Rosa Spinola '16	♥	3
● M.to Rosso Cuvée '16	♥	2
○ Gavi del Comune di Tassarolo Alborina '13	♥♥	3*
○ Gavi del Comune di Tassarolo Il Castello '14	♥♥	2*
○ Gavi del Comune di Tassarolo Spinola '15	♥♥	2*

Castello di Uviglie

VIA CASTELLO DI UVIGLIE, 73
15030 ROSIGNANO MONFERRATO [AL]
TEL. +39 0142488132
www.castellodiuviglie.com

CELLAR SALES
PRE-BOOKED VISITS
ANNUAL PRODUCTION 90,000 bottles
HECTARES UNDER VINE 25.00

Uviglie's first Tre Bicchieri, awarded in the 2010 guide for their skillfully executed Le Cave '07, was the catalyst for an unstoppable virtuous cycle. 10 years were just enough for Simone Lupano and Mario Ronco, who started working in 1999, to set it all in motion. In the cellar, grapes of outstanding quality meet modern winemaking techniques, which bring together the careful use of wood both in fermentation and aging, allowing for wines that best express their potential. The Pico Gonzaga still manages to express a certain quality despite the difficult vintage. However, the Le Cave emerges and reveals its full potential, thanks to a very good 2015 vintage. The Grignolino San Bastiano is in great form, with striking classic features. The intrinsic quality of Simone's wines highlights the attention he dedicates to them, right across the board.

Castello di Verduno

VIA UMBERTO I, 9
12060 VERDUNO [CN]
TEL. +39 0172470284
www.castellodiverduno.com

CELLAR SALES
PRE-BOOKED VISITS
ACCOMMODATION AND RESTAURANT SERVICE
ANNUAL PRODUCTION 68,000 bottles
HECTARES UNDER VINE 10.00
SUSTAINABLE WINERY

What was once the castle of King Carlo Alberto di Savoia is, today, the perfect space for Gabriella Burlotto and Franco Bianco to carry out their work. The couple, along with their daughters, Marcella and Giovanna, manage some 10 hectares of vineyards, spread out in the areas of Barbaresco and Barolo. All their Nebbiolos are aged in large barrels and sometimes made available in 'Riserva', making for wines of admirable, natural expressivity that are perfect for the table. We find the same character in their impossible-to-imitate Pelavergas: the classic Basadone, the Bellis Perennis, which are fermented without the skins, as is their sparkling S-Ciopèt. The fruity and elegant 2011 Barolo Monvigliero Riserva features an inviting spiciness with notes of pepper and velvety tannins. The 2013 Barolo Massara exhibits a precise classic style and is a touch more austere. The 2013 Barolo, a wine that is simple in theory only, performed splendidly. The 2016 Basadone shows that consumers' growing appreciation for Pelaverga is not just a passing fad.

● Barbera del M.to Sup. Le Cave '15	♟♟ 3*
● Barbera del M.to Sup. Pico Gonzaga '14	♟♟ 5
● Grignolino del M.to Casalese San Bastiano '16	♟♟ 2*
● Barbera del M.to Bricco del Conte '16	♟♟ 2*
○ Bricco del Ciliegio Passito '13	♟♟ 5
○ Le Cave Extra Brut M. Cl. '13	♟♟ 5
○ M.to Bianco San Martino '16	♟♟ 2*
● M.to Rosso 1491 '14	♟♟ 5
● Barbera del M.to Sup. Le Cave '13	♟♟♟ 3*
● Barbera del M.to Sup. Le Cave '09	♟♟♟ 3*
● Barbera del M.to Sup. Le Cave '07	♟♟♟ 3*
● Barbera del M.to Sup. Pico Gonzaga '13	♟♟♟ 5
● Barbera del M.to Sup. Pico Gonzaga '07	♟♟♟ 4*
● Grignolino del M.to Casalese San Bastiano Terre Bianche '12	♟♟ 5

● Barolo '13	♟♟ 5
● Barolo Massara '13	♟♟ 6
● Barolo Monvigliero Ris. '11	♟♟ 7
● Barbaresco '14	♟♟ 5
● Verduno Pelaverga Basadone '16	♟♟ 3
○ S-ciopét Brut Rosé M. Cl. '13	♟ 5
● Barbaresco Rabajà '04	♟♟♟ 6
● Barolo Massara '08	♟♟♟ 6
● Barolo Monvigliero Ris. '08	♟♟♟ 7
● Barolo Monvigliero Ris. '04	♟♟♟ 7
● Barbaresco '13	♟♟ 5
● Barbaresco Rabajà '13	♟♟ 6
● Barbaresco Rabajà Ris. '11	♟♟ 7
● Barolo Monvigliero Ris. '10	♟♟ 7

★Cavallotto
Tenuta Bricco Boschis

LOC. BRICCO BOSCHIS
VIA ALBA-MONFORTE
12060 CASTIGLIONE FALLETTO [CN]
TEL. +39 017362814
www.cavallotto.com

CELLAR SALES
PRE-BOOKED VISITS
ANNUAL PRODUCTION 110,000 bottles
HECTARES UNDER VINE 25.00
VITICULTURE METHOD Certified Organic

The 25 hectares managed by the Cavallotto family for almost a century is essentially a single tract of land. The estate is situated in the heart of the Castiglione Falletto hills. Here, Olivio began producing and selling in 1948. Today it's his children, Alfio, Giuseppe and Laura, who manage the winery according to principles of 'natural' agriculture. In the various plots, we find Barbera, Dolcetto, Freisa, Grignolino, Pinot Nero and Chardonnay. But the best-positioned vineyards are reserved for Nebbiolo, of course. Made with the help of rotary macerators and matured in large barrels, their Barolo Bricco Boschis Vigna San Giuseppe and Vignolo are also available in 'Riserva' versions, for the best vintages. The 2013 Barolo Bricco Boschis exhibits a strictly classic style. Its lovely personality is based on red fruit and licorice, while the palate proves savory and lingering. The 2011 Barolo Vignolo Riserva comes through just as traditional, slightly fruity and open on the nose, warm and powerful on the palate. The still-young 2011 Riserva Vigna San Giuseppe is dryer and purer.

● Barolo Bricco Boschis '13	♀♀	8
● Barolo Bricco Boschis V. S. Giuseppe Ris. '11	♀♀	8
● Barolo Vignolo Ris. '11	♀♀	8
● Barbera d'Alba Sup. V. del Cuculo '15	♀♀	5
● Langhe Freisa '15	♀	4
● Langhe Nebbiolo '15	♀	5
● Barolo Bricco Boschis '12	♀♀♀	8
● Barolo Bricco Boschis V. S. Giuseppe Ris. '05	♀♀♀	8
● Barolo Vignolo Ris. '06	♀♀♀	8
● Barolo Vignolo Ris. '04	♀♀♀	8
● Barbera d'Alba Sup. V. del Cuculo '13	♀♀	5
● Barolo Bricco Boschis V. S. Giuseppe Ris. '10	♀♀	8
● Barolo Vignolo Ris. '10	♀♀	8
● Langhe Nebbiolo '14	♀♀	5

Ceretto

LOC. SAN CASSIANO, 34
12051 ALBA [CN]
TEL. +39 0173282582
www.ceretto.com

CELLAR SALES
PRE-BOOKED VISITS
RESTAURANT SERVICE
ANNUAL PRODUCTION 900,000 bottles
HECTARES UNDER VINE 130.00
VITICULTURE METHOD Certified Organic
SUSTAINABLE WINERY

Federico, Lisa, Alessandro and Roberta Ceretto represent the third generation to lead one of Piedmont's towering producers. The numbers say everything: 160 hectares of certified, organic vineyards (with biodynamic reconversion), 4 cellars (Alba, Castiglione Falletto, Barbaresco, Santo Stefano Belbo), almost 20 wines in their selection, including those distributed in their Terroirs catalog. All this, not to mention their 'side projects' involving hospitality and cultural initiatives, which have become a shared territorial heritage. Indeed, Ceretto is a true macrocosm that allows us to better appreciate the benefits of reworking old and new classics. Cherry, raspberry, licorice and pencil lead are just a few of the aromas offered up by the elegant and solid 2013 Barolo Bricco Rocche. This Tre Bicchieri is as elegant as it is classic and complex. The close-focused, powerful and lingering 2013 Barolo Prapò is a smash hit, displaying impressive character. The fresh 2014 Barbaresco Asili delivered, but remains a bit closed. However, you can still get a glimpse of its clear richness.

● Barolo Bricco Rocche '13	♀♀♀	8
● Barbaresco Asili '14	♀♀	8
● Barolo Prapò '13	♀♀	8
● Barbaresco '14	♀♀	6
● Barbaresco Bernardot '14	♀♀	8
● Barbera d'Alba Piana '16	♀♀	4
● Barolo '13	♀♀	7
● Barolo Brunate '13	♀♀	8
● Nebbiolo d'Alba Bernardina '15	♀♀	5
● Dolcetto d'Alba Rossana '16	♀	3
○ Langhe Arneis Blangè '16	♀	4
○ Langhe Bianco Monsordo '16	♀	4
● Barbaresco Asili '13	♀♀♀	8
● Barolo Bricco Rocche '11	♀♀♀	8
● Barolo Bricco Rocche '09	♀♀♀	8

★★Michele Chiarlo

S.DA NIZZA-CANELLI, 99
14042 CALAMANDRANA [AT]
TEL. +39 0141769030
www.michelechiarlo.it

CELLAR SALES
PRE-BOOKED VISITS
ACCOMMODATION
ANNUAL PRODUCTION 1,100,000 bottles
HECTARES UNDER VINE 120.00
SUSTAINABLE WINERY

Barolo, Barbaresco, Nizza, Gavi, Moscato
d'Asti are just some of the appellations that
the Chiarlo family, a leading regional figure
for more than 50 years, has a hand in. They
have three facilities at their disposal,
situated in Monferrato, Langhe and Gavi,
and divided into 7 different estates. The
20 wines that make up their selection are
of a modern style and demonstrate notable
technical precision, without losing their
individual territorial expression. The
2013 Barolo Cerequio is quite lovely, with
aromas of tobacco and cinchona, and
balsamic hints. Its palate proves rich, juicy
and lingering, with notable tannins. Despite
the absence of the Nizza La Court, which
wasn't produced in 2014, we enjoyed some
very good wines. The 2014 Barbaresco
Faset offers up aromas of spices and dried
flowers and, despite the difficult vintage, it
proves deep, with great extraction. The long
and pleasant 2014 Barbaresco Reyna
shows a notable classic style, with notes of
small red fruit. The rest of the selection
exhibits high quality.

● Barbaresco Faset '14	♟♟ 8
● Barbaresco Reyna '14	♟♟ 6
● Barolo Cannubi '13	♟♟ 8
● Barolo Cerequio '13	♟♟ 8
● Barbaresco Asili '14	♟♟ 8
● Barolo Tortoniano '13	♟♟ 7
○ Gavi del Comune di Gavi Rovereto '16	♟♟ 3
○ Moscato d'Asti Nivole '16	♟♟ 3
● Nizza Cipressi della Court '15	♟♟ 4
● Barbera d'Asti Sup. Nizza La Court '13	♟♟♟ 5
● Barbera d'Asti Sup. Nizza La Court '12	♟♟♟ 5
● Barbera d'Asti Sup. Nizza La Court '09	♟♟♟ 5
● Barolo Cerequio '10	♟♟♟ 7
● Barolo Cerequio '09	♟♟♟ 7

Chionetti

B.TA VALDIBERTI, 44
12063 DOGLIANI [CN]
TEL. +39 017371179
www.chionettiquinto.com

CELLAR SALES
PRE-BOOKED VISITS
ANNUAL PRODUCTION 83,000 bottles
HECTARES UNDER VINE 15.00
VITICULTURE METHOD Certified Organic

Chionetti is an emblem of classic Dolcetto
di Dogliani, thanks to the work of
winemaker Quinto. For many years, there
were just two wines: San Luigi and the
celebrated Briccolero. His nephew, Nicola,
who has managed the cellar for five years
now, continues in the same stylistic vein
that brought international recognition to the
name Chionetti. Though he's also making
his own personal contribution, starting with
organic certification and the small, though
select reintroduction of a long-aged
selection, Dogliani La Costa. We shouldn't
forget about a house Barolo, which will be
coming soon. The 2016 Dogliani Briccolero
opens on the nose with notes of fruit,
tobacco and licorice. The mouth is powerful
and marked by tannins. The 2016 Dogliani
San Luigi reveals multiple facets, ranging
from almonds to blackberries and red
berries. Its palate proves youthful and still a
bit hard, it needs further bottle aging.

● Dogliani Briccolero '16	♟♟ 3
● Dogliani San Luigi '16	♟♟ 3
● Dogliani La Costa '15	♟ 4
● Langhe Nebbiolo La Chiusa '15	♟ 4
● Dolcetto di Dogliani Briccolero '07	♟♟♟ 3*
● Dolcetto di Dogliani Briccolero '04	♟♟♟ 3*
● Dogliani Briccolero '15	♟♟ 3*
● Dogliani Briccolero '14	♟♟ 3
● Dogliani Briccolero '12	♟♟ 3*
● Dogliani Briccolero '11	♟♟ 3*
● Dogliani La Costa '13	♟♟ 4
● Dogliani S. Luigi '11	♟♟ 3*
● Dogliani San Luigi '15	♟♟ 3*
● Langhe Nebbiolo La Chiusa '14	♟♟ 4
● Langhe Nebbiolo La Chiusa '13	♟♟ 4

Ciabot Berton

FRAZ. SANTA MARIA, 1
12064 LA MORRA [CN]
TEL. I 39 017350217
www.ciabotberton.it

CELLAR SALES
PRE-BOOKED VISITS
ANNUAL PRODUCTION 65,000 bottles
HECTARES UNDER VINE 14.00

Under the skillful direction of Marco, the Oberto family's lovely vineyards give rise to first-rate wines, with Nebbiolo taking a leading role. Aromatic freshness is a defining trait of their house Barolos, and fruit is never dominated by wood. It's worth noting that their two most important selections of Barolo, Rocchettevino and Roggeri, see an extra year of aging in the cellar. And the estate's splendid panoramic view makes it a great stop for wine tourists. The 2012 Rocchettevino made it to our tasting finals, thanks to aromas that call up strawberries and raspberries and a great juicy taste that doesn't spoil its generally austere palate. The graceful 2012 Barolo Roggeri comes through slightly more evolved and complex, with a precise classic style. We enjoyed the 2013 Barolo del Comune di La Morra for its balance and richness. The intense 2012 Barolo reveals a pleasant contribution of acidity and tannins on the palate.

● Barolo Rocchettevino '12	🏆🏆 6
● Barolo '12	🏆🏆 5
● Barolo del Comune di La Morra '13	🏆🏆 5
● Barolo Roggeri '12	🏆🏆 6
● Langhe Nebbiolo 3 Utin '15	🏆🏆 3
● Barbera d'Alba Fisetta '16	🏆 3
● Barolo del Comune di La Morra '12	🏆🏆 5
● Barolo del Comune di La Morra '11	🏆🏆 5
● Barolo Rocchettevino '11	🏆🏆 6
● Barolo Rocchettevino '10	🏆🏆 6
● Barolo Rocchettevino Ris. '10	🏆🏆 8
● Barolo Roggeri '10	🏆🏆 6
● Langhe Nebbiolo 3 Utin '11	🏆🏆 2*

Cieck

CASCINA CASTAGNOLA, 2
10090 SAN GIORGIO CANAVESE [TO]
TEL. I 39 0124330522
www.cieck.it

CELLAR SALES
PRE-BOOKED VISITS
ANNUAL PRODUCTION 80,000 bottles
HECTARES UNDER VINE 12.00

Affordability and versatility have always been Cieck's strong points. Intimately familiar with the attributes of Caluso Erbaluce, their wines are among the few in Italy that are capable of credibly expressing sparkling, still and passito versions of the grape. Remo Falconieri and Domenico Caretto have adopted various approaches, according to the wine: only steel for their Erbaluce and Misobolo, large barrels for their 'T' selection, while Calliope and San Giorgio rest on the lees for 36 months. Nebbiolo, Freisa and Barbera, round out their production line. The latest tasting session showed how complete their selection of wines is. The 2015 Nebbiolo, one of the best reds made in Canavese, conveys a rough and earthy pace. The 2013 Erbaluce Nature and the 2014 San Giorgio Spumante are some of the best in their categories, while the 2009 Passito Alladium also provides a thrill.

○ Erbaluce di Caluso Passito Alladium '09	🏆🏆 5
● Canavese Nebbiolo '15	🏆🏆 3
○ Erbaluce di Caluso Cieck Nature '13	🏆🏆 5
○ Erbaluce di Caluso Misobolo '16	🏆🏆 3
○ Erbaluce di Caluso San Giorgio '14	🏆🏆 4
● Canavese Cieck Neretto '16	🏆 3
○ Erbaluce di Caluso '16	🏆 2
○ Erbaluce di Caluso T '15	🏆 3
○ Erbaluce di Caluso Passito Alladium '06	🏆🏆 5
○ Erbaluce di Caluso Brut Calliope M. Cl. '13	🏆🏆 4
○ Erbaluce di Caluso Brut San Giorgio '13	🏆🏆 4

★F.lli Cigliuti

VIA SERRABOELLA, 17
12052 NEIVE [CN]
TEL. +39 0173677185
www.cigliuti.it

CELLAR SALES
PRE-BOOKED VISITS
ANNUAL PRODUCTION 30,000 bottles
HECTARES UNDER VINE 30.00

For almost thirty years, F.lli Cigliuti was the only winery in the area to separately ferment their Serrabeolla grapes (a cru in Neive). Not coincidentally, the cru's name was almost synonymous with the winery, started by Leone and Romualdo Cigliuti after World War II. It's a heritage that Renato is proudly keeping alive, with the help of his wife, Dina and daughters Claudia and Silvia. Grapes for their Vie Erte arrive from Bricco di Neive, thus completing a a pair of Barbarescos that are quite diverse. Mostly aged in Slovenian oak, their wines are often high on the list for those in search of artisanal Nebbiolo (but also Barbera and Dolcetto), in the best sense of the term. When we refer to a palate as "endless", we're obviously exaggerating. However, it's the first word that springs to mind to describe the slow and continual unfolding of this 2013 Barbaresco Serraboella. Incredibly refined and complex aromas convey fruit and fresh herbs. A Tre Bicchieri. The more close-knit and austere 2013 Vie Erte also exhibits good complexity.

● Barbaresco Serraboella '13	🍷🍷🍷
● Barbaresco Vie Erte '13	🍷🍷
● Barbera d'Alba V. Serraboella '14	🍷🍷
● Barbaresco Serraboella '11	🍷🍷🍷
● Barbaresco Serraboella '10	🍷🍷🍷
● Barbaresco Serraboella '09	🍷🍷🍷
● Barbaresco V. Erte '04	🍷🍷🍷
● Barbaresco Serraboella '12	🍷🍷
● Barbaresco Vie Erte '12	🍷🍷
● Barbaresco Vie Erte '11	🍷🍷
● Barbaresco Vie Erte '10	🍷🍷
● Barbaresco Vie Erte '09	🍷🍷
● Barbera d'Alba Campass '13	🍷🍷
● Barbera d'Alba Campass '12	🍷🍷

★Tenute Cisa Asinari dei Marchesi di Grésy

LOC. MARTINENGA
S.DA DELLA STAZIONE, 21
12050 BARBARESCO [CN]
TEL. +39 0173635222
www.marchesidigresy.com

CELLAR SALES
PRE-BOOKED VISITS
ANNUAL PRODUCTION 200,000 bottles
HECTARES UNDER VINE 35.00
SUSTAINABLE WINERY

Theirs is probably the most magnificent contiguous estate in the Barbarersco wine region. Comprised of more than 10 hectares of vineyards for half a century the area has belonged to the Tenute Cisa Asinari dei Marchesi di Grésy. Here, in the heart of the hills, the winery's most celebrated Nebbiolos are forged made through relatively short maceration and maturation that's carried out at least partially in small wood. Their reds are more modern in form than in substance, and particularly well-suited to aging. Other important plots can be found in Cassine, in Monferrato and Monte Aribaldo in Treiso. The 2012 Barbaresco Martinenga Camp Gros Riserva pursues a more delicate elegance. Its seductive notes of incense merge with a background of red fruit, while the mouth proves slow, gradual, pure and harmonious. Tre Bicchieri. The rich and elegant 2013 Barbaresco Martinenga Gaiun remains a bit marked by oak. The complex 2014 Martinenga also did well. They've put forward an overall splendid selection.

● Barbaresco Martinenga Camp Gros Ris. '12	🍷🍷🍷 8
● Barbaresco Martinenga Gaiun '13	🍷🍷 8
● Barbaresco Martinenga '14	🍷🍷 7
● Barbera d'Alba Monte Colombo '12	🍷🍷 5
● Dolcetto d'Alba Monte Aribaldo '16	🍷🍷 3
○ Langhe Chardonnay Grésy '15	🍷🍷 5
○ Langhe Sauvignon '16	🍷🍷 3
● Langhe Virtus '10	🍷🍷 6
○ Langhe Chardonnay '16	🍷 3
● Langhe Nebbiolo '16	🍷 4
○ Langhe Villa Giulia '16	🍷 3
● Barbaresco Camp Gros '06	🍷🍷🍷 8
● Barbaresco Camp Gros Martinenga '09	🍷🍷🍷 8
● Barbaresco Camp Gros Martinenga '08	🍷🍷🍷 8

★★Domenico Clerico

LOC. MANZONI, 67
12065 MONFORTE D'ALBA [CN]
TEL. +39 017378171
www.domenicoclerico.com

PRE-BOOKED VISITS
ANNUAL PRODUCTION 110,000 bottles
HECTARES UNDER VINE 21.00

Among the many websites out there, most of them the same, Domenico Clerico's is absolutely worth checking out. Undoubtedly one of Langhe's most beloved vine growers, on his site he recounts the difficult years in which he decided to go forward with his father's work in Monforte d'Alba, buying a small plot in Briccotto di Bussia. Plots in Ginestra, Pajana, Mosconi followed, and, more recently, Serralunga d'Alba as well (where their Barolo Aeroplanservaj is made). His was among the first winery's to best on small wood. In recent years, the line between traditional and modern seems increasingly burred. But he has left us three lovely interpretations of Barolo. First off the 2013, with its clear red fruit and spices leading into a medium-weighted body. It's a warm wine with good alcohol, thus its substantial tannins are kept at bay. Both of their 2012s impressed: the long and powerful Ciabot Mentin and the spicy Pajana, which is still marked by oak.

● Barolo '13	♀♀ 6
● Barolo Ciabot Mentin '12	♀♀ 8
● Barolo Pajana '12	♀♀ 8
● Barolo Ciabot Mentin '08	♀♀♀ 8
● Barolo Ciabot Mentin Ginestra '05	♀♀♀ 8
● Barolo Ciabot Mentin Ginestra '04	♀♀♀ 8
● Barolo Percristina '01	♀♀♀ 8
● Barolo '12	♀♀ 6
● Barolo '11	♀♀ 6
● Barolo Aeroplanservaj '11	♀♀ 7
● Barolo Ciabot Mentin '11	♀♀ 8
● Barolo Pajana '11	♀♀ 8
● Barolo Percristina '07	♀♀ 8
● Barolo Percristina '06	♀♀ 8

★Elvio Cogno

VIA RAVERA, 2
12060 NOVELLO [CN]
TEL. +39 0173744006
www.elviocogno.com

CELLAR SALES
PRE-BOOKED VISITS
ACCOMMODATION
ANNUAL PRODUCTION 90,000 bottles
HECTARES UNDER VINE 15.00
VITICULTURE METHOD Certified Organic
SUSTAINABLE WINERY

The winery founded by Elvio Cogno, and today managed by his daughter, Nadia, along with her husband Valter Fissore, is situated on the hill of Ravera (probably the most celebrated area in the district of Novello). Here, various plots give rise to the four house Barolos (Vigna Elena, Ravera, Bricco Pernice and Cascina Nuova). These are interpreted with various methods in terms of vinification and aging, with results that can sometimes appear to be in opposition, even if they are bound by power and substance. The same is true for their with Barbera, Dolcetto and Nascetta wines. The exuberant and lively 2012 Barolo Ravera Bricco Pernice offers up fresh aromas. It also proves varied and elegant on the palate, making for a very classy Tre Bicchieri. The 2013 Barolo Ravera comes through just as elegant, with notes of herbs in the sun and tar to add complexity, as well as a particularly long palate. Wilted roses, contrasted by fresh raspberries, dominate the close-focused notes of the 2011 Barolo Ravera Vigna Elena Riserva, which exhibits pleasant acidity.

● Barolo Ravera Bricco Pernice '12	♀♀♀ 8
● Barolo Ravera '13	♀♀ 8
● Barolo Ravera V. Elena Ris. '11	♀♀ 8
● Barbera d'Alba Bricco dei Merli '15	♀♀ 4
● Barolo Cascina Nuova '13	♀♀ 6
○ Langhe Nascetta del Comune di Novello Anas-Cëtta '16	♀♀ 4
● Langhe Nebbiolo Montegrilli '16	♀♀ 4
● Barbaresco Bordini '14	♀ 5
● Dolcetto d'Alba Mandorlo '16	♀ 3
● Barolo Bricco Pernice '11	♀♀♀ 8
● Barolo Bricco Pernice '09	♀♀♀ 8
● Barolo Bricco Pernice '08	♀♀♀ 8
● Barolo Ravera '11	♀♀♀ 7
● Barolo V. Elena Ris. '06	♀♀♀ 8

Poderi Colla

ITAZ. SAN ROCCO SENO D'ELVIO, 82
12051 ALBA [CN]
TEL. +39 0173290148
www.podericolla.it

CELLAR SALES
PRE-BOOKED VISITS
ANNUAL PRODUCTION 150,000 bottles
HECTARES UNDER VINE 26.00

The names Beppe and Tino Colla
immediately evoke the most captivating
years in the viticultural history of Langhe,
mostly because of the prophetic vision
displayed by these pioneers. They were the
first to separately ferment grapes from
various crus. Today their children, Federica
and Pietro, manage their almost 25
hectares of vineyards. Among these are
Roncaglie (where Barbaresco is grown) and
Bussia Dardi Le Rose, along with plots at
Cascina Drago. Their top-of-the-line
Nebbiolos, often capable of bringing
together finesse and substance, are mostly
matured in Slavonian oak. A splendid
interpretation of the 2014 vintage earns the
Barbaresco Roncaglie a Tre Bicchieri. Violets
and raspberries stand out on its complex
nose, while the mouth appears rich, austere
and very long. The 2013 Barolo Bussia
Dardi Le Rose is possessed of a delicately
complex nose and a precise, classic
character. These are confirmed by the
wine's long, powerful palate, which features
tight-knit, gradual tannins.

● Barbaresco Roncaglie '14	♔♔♔ 6
● Barolo Bussia Dardi Le Rose '13	♔♔ 6
● Langhe Bricco del Drago '13	♔♔ 4
● Nebbiolo d'Alba Drago '15	♔♔ 3
● Dolcetto d'Alba Pian Balbo '16	♔ 2
○ Langhe Riesling '15	♔ 3
● Barolo Bussia Dardi Le Rose '09	♔♔♔ 6
● Barolo Bussia Dardi Le Rose '99	♔♔♔ 6
● Barbaresco Roncaglie '13	♔♔ 6
● Barbaresco Roncaglie '12	♔♔ 6
● Barolo Bussia Dardi Le Rose '12	♔♔ 6
● Langhe Bricco del Drago '10	♔♔ 4
● Nebbiolo d'Alba '13	♔♔ 3

Colle Manora

S.DA BOZZOLA, 5
15044 QUARGNENTO [AL]
TEL. +39 0131219252
www.collemanora.it

CELLAR SALES
PRE-BOOKED VISITS
ACCOMMODATION
ANNUAL PRODUCTION 90,000 bottles
HECTARES UNDER VINE 21.00

Colle Manora's selection is mostly focused
on international grapes: Cabernet
Sauvignon, Merlot and Pinot Nero (for the
reds), Chardonnay and Sauvignon Blanc (for
the whites). Yet a territorial bond is
maintained through their Barberas and
Albarossas, both vinified in their
monovarietal form. Their international
varieties, planted at a later moment, are
positioned so that each variety has the best
possible exposure to the sun. In the cellar,
they use the latest equipment and their
surprising barrique cellar completes the
facility, making for a quality selection of
wines. We saw great balance in all the wines
presented, but the splendid 2015 Barbera
d'Asti Superiore Manora achieved
excellence. Its vibrant ruby-red color
foreshadows a sensational nose of fresh
fruit that evolves toward classy tertiary
aromas. Its palate doesn't disappoint,
coming through rich in pulp, with good
acidity supporting a long finish. The Mila
also intrigued.

● Barbera d'Asti Sup. Manora '15	♔♔ 3*
● Barbera del M.to Pais '16	♔♔ 2*
○ M.to Bianco Mila '15	♔♔ 4
○ M.to Bianco Mimosa '16	♔♔ 2*
○ M.to Bianco Mimosa '15	♔♔ 2*
● M.to Rosso Barchetta '14	♔♔ 3
● Barbera d'Asti Sup. Manora '14	♔♔ 3
● Barbera d'Asti Sup. Manora '13	♔♔ 3
○ M.to Bianco Mila '14	♔♔ 4
○ M.to Bianco Mila '13	♔♔ 4
○ M.to Bianco Mimosa '14	♔♔ 2*
● M.to Rosso Paloalto '12	♔♔ 5
● Piemonte Albarossa Ray '14	♔♔ 3
● Piemonte Albarossa Ray '13	♔♔ 3

La Colombera

LOC. VHO
S.DA COMUNALE PER VHO, 7
15057 TORTONA [AL]
TEL. +39 0131867795
www.lacolomberavini.it

CELLAR SALES
PRE-BOOKED VISITS
ANNUAL PRODUCTION 80,000 bottles
HECTARES UNDER VINE 24.00
SUSTAINABLE WINERY

20 years have passed since the Semino family decided to start bottling their own wine (until then they just produced bulk wine). Since then they've produced one wine after another, making for a roster that represents the territory's essence. Traditional, local varieties are the bedrock of their selection: Timorasso, Cortese, Barbera, Croatina, as well as Dolcetto dal Raspo Rosso (or nibiô, as it's known locally). These are worked attentively in a modern cellar, with mid-size casks or barriques reserved for their most important reds. The Montino made it to our finals with its complex nose of mustard and citrus fruit on notes of medicinal herbs. The palate shows good structure with acidity supporting its tangy, long finish. Derthona is just as good, with an intense nose of floral and mineral notes leading into a powerful yet soft palate. The finish comes through fresh and very lingering.

○ Colli Tortonesi Timorasso Derthona '15	♥♥	4
○ Colli Tortonesi Timorasso Il Montino '15	♥♥	5
● Colli Tortonesi Rosso Suciaja '15	♥♥	4
● Colli Tortonesi Barbera Elisa '14	♥	4
○ Colli Tortonesi Cortese Bricco Bartolomeo '16	♥	2
● Colli Tortonesi Croatina Arché '15	♥	4
● Colli Tortonesi Croatina La Romba '16	♥	3
● Colli Tortonesi Rosso Vegia Rampana '16	♥	2
● Colli Tortonesi Barbera Elisa '11	♥♥♥	3*
○ Colli Tortonesi Timorasso Il Montino '13	♥♥♥	5
○ Colli Tortonesi Timorasso Il Montino '09	♥♥♥	5

Diego Conterno

VIA MONTÀ, 27
12065 MONFORTE D'ALBA [CN]
TEL. +39 0173789265
www.diegoconterno.it

CELLAR SALES
PRE-BOOKED VISITS
ANNUAL PRODUCTION 40,000 bottles
HECTARES UNDER VINE 7.50

It didn't take much for Diego Conterno to establish himself among Langhe's top 'emerging' producers. Note the quotation marks; we have to remember his 20 years of prior experience. Today he's accompanied by his son, Stefano, managing some seven hectares of vineyards dedicated to Piedmont's principal varieties, which hold the best positions within the additional geographic mentions (Le Coste and Ginestra di Monforte). His Barolos, which are both vigorous and communicative, elude easy technical categories, in part because of the variety of methods used: concrete, steel, mid-sized casks, large barrels. The 2013 Barolo Ginestra displays marked personality and successfully expresses this magnificent vineyard. It offers up continuous hints of catmint and cinchona, accompanied by rich red fruit. Then the palate comes through powerful but not aggressive. The 2013 Barolo is already open and exhibits a more measured weight, while the close-focused and lightly aromatic Nascetta is worthy of praise.

● Barolo Ginestra '13	♥♥	7
● Barolo '13	♥♥	6
○ Langhe Nascetta '16	♥♥	3
● Nebbiolo d'Alba Baluma '15	♥♥	3
● Barolo Le Coste '09	♥♥♥	6
● Barbera d'Alba Ferrione '12	♥♥	3
● Barbera d'Alba Ferrione '11	♥♥	3
● Barolo '10	♥♥	6
● Barolo Ginestra '12	♥♥	7
● Barolo Ginestra '11	♥♥	6
● Barolo Ginestra '10	♥♥	6
● Barolo Le Coste di Monforte '10	♥♥	6
○ Langhe Nascetta '15	♥♥	3
● Nebbiolo d'Alba Baluma '12	♥♥	3

★★Giacomo Conterno

LOC. ORNATI, 2
12065 MONFORTE D'ALBA [CN]
TEL. +39 017378221
www.conterno.it

PRE-BOOKED VISITS
ANNUAL PRODUCTION 60,000 bottles
HECTARES UNDER VINE 23.00

Started by Giovanni Conterno (in 1908), and inaugurated by his son, Giacomo, today the winery is run by his great-grandson, Roberto. Conterno is undoubtedly one of the most sought after Italian wines in the world. A lot of their success has to do with the almost fabled Monfortino Riserva, a wine capable of evoking the majestic longevity of history's best Barolos. But the present is even more glorious, bolstered even further by the purchase of vineyards like Cerretta and Arione in Serralunga, the perfect companions for Francia. The rest is just obsessive attention to detail and a singular talent for interpreting the moods of the individual vintage, making a description of wine typologies, and production methods, useless. Even today, the robust and long 2010 Barolo Monfortino Riserva exhibits a dream-like palate. The close-focused complexity of its nose is destined to develop for decades. The 2013 Cerretta offers up overflowing fruity aromas. This unmissable Barolo features rich, fresh taste, with a touch of elegant savoriness.

● Barolo Monfortino Ris. '10	♥♥♥	8
● Barbera d'Alba V. Cerretta '15	♥♥	5
● Barolo Cerretta '13	♥♥	8
● Barbera d'Alba V. Francia '15	♥♥	5
● Barolo Cascina Francia '06	♥♥♥	8
● Barolo Cascina Francia '05	♥♥♥	8
● Barolo Cascina Francia '04	♥♥♥	8
● Barolo Francia '12	♥♥♥	8
● Barolo Francia '10	♥♥♥	8
● Barolo Monfortino Ris. '08	♥♥♥	8
● Barolo Monfortino Ris. '06	♥♥♥	8
● Barolo Monfortino Ris. '05	♥♥♥	8
● Barolo Monfortino Ris. '04	♥♥♥	8
● Barolo Monfortino Ris. '02	♥♥♥	8
● Barolo Monfortino Ris. '01	♥♥♥	8

Paolo Conterno

LOC. GINESTRA, 34
12065 MONFORTE D'ALBA [CN]
TEL. +39 017378415
www.paoloconterno.com

CELLAR SALES
PRE-BOOKED VISITS
ACCOMMODATION
ANNUAL PRODUCTION 180,000 bottles
HECTARES UNDER VINE 37.00
SUSTAINABLE WINERY

Paolo Conterno is historically known as Casa della Ginestra, from the name of the celebrated cru of Monforte d'Alba that surrounds it. Today, it's managed by Giorgio and Marisa, great-grandchildren of Paolo (who started making wine back in the late 1800s). The winery has grown exponentially over time, and today it comprises a constellation of estates, some of which are situated in Astigiano and Monferrato (Antico Podere del Sant'Uffizio in Cioccaro di Penango) and Tuscany (Tenuta Ortaglia in Pratolino, near Florence). Their most important wines continue to be their Barolo Riva del Bric and Ginestra (also available as a 'Riserva'), both of which are mostly matured in 3500 liter oak. This 2009 Riserva earns a Tre Bicchieri. It offers up red and black fruit, accompanied by Ginestra cru's signature minty note. And it isn't only about elegance. The wine also features a charming maturity and a bold, caressing mouth, in which tannins form a silky complement to acidity.

● Barolo Ginestra Ris. '09	♥♥♥	8
● Barolo Ginestra '13	♥♥	8
● Barbera d'Alba La Ginestra '15	♥♥	3
● Barolo Riva del Bric '13	♥♥	6
● Langhe Nebbiolo A Mont '15	♥♥	4
● Langhe Nebbiolo Bric Ginestra '15	♥♥	5
● M.to Rosso I Cascinali '15	♥♥	5
○ Piemonte Bianco Föra '15	♥	4
○ Piemonte Chardonnay Divers '15	♥	5
● Barolo Ginestra '10	♥♥♥	8
● Barolo Ginestra Ris. '08	♥♥♥	8
● Barolo Ginestra Ris. '06	♥♥♥	8
● Barolo Ginestra Ris. '05	♥♥♥	8
● Barolo Ginestra '12	♥♥	8

★Conterno Fantino

VIA GINESTRA, 1
12065 MONFORTE D'ALBA [CN]
TEL. +39 017378201
www.conternofantino.it

PRE-BOOKED VISITS
ANNUAL PRODUCTION 150,000 bottles
HECTARES UNDER VINE 25.00
VITICULTURE METHOD Certified Organic
SUSTAINABLE WINERY

Claudio Conterno and Guido Fantino's collaboration is undoubtedly one of the longest and closest in Langhe. Together they crafted some of the most celebrated 'modern' Barolos we have, especially starting in the early 1990s. But they haven't lost sight of their agricultural core, tied to first-rate crus like Sorì Ginestra, Vigna del Gris and Mosconi (in Monforte d'Alba). Increasing attention is paid to conserving energy and to the use of renewable energy sources in their newly enlarged and renovated cellar. The works coincide with a new stylistic approach, one that pursues greater fluidity, naturalness in the mouth and authority to evolve. Of the Barolos put forward from the great 2013 vintage, the best is the Ginestra Vigna del Gris. Hints of spices dominate clean and fair aromas, followed by a palate with good weight and pleasant freshness. The famous Vigna Sorì Ginestra, their flagship wine, remains more woody at the moment, as does the Castelletto Vigna Pressenda. The 2015 Chardonnay is as good as ever.

● Barolo Ginestra V. del Gris '13	♟♟	8
● Barbera d'Alba Vignota '15	♟♟	4
● Barolo Castelletto V. Pressenda '13	♟♟	8
● Barolo Ginestra V. Sorì Ginestra '13	♟♟	8
● Barolo Mosconi V. Ped '13	♟♟	8
● Dolcetto d'Alba Bricco Bastia '16	♟♟	3
○ Langhe Chardonnay Bastia '15	♟♟	5
● Langhe Rosso Monprà '14	♟♟	5
○ Langhe Chardonnay Prinsipi '16	♟	3
● Langhe Nebbiolo Ginestrino '15	♟	4
● Barolo Sorì Ginestra '12	♟♟♟	8
● Barolo Sorì Ginestra '10	♟♟♟	8
● Barolo Sorì Ginestra '07	♟♟♟	8
● Barolo V. del Gris '09	♟♟♟	8

Contratto

VIA G. B. GIULIANI, 56
14053 CANELLI [AT]
TEL. +39 0141823349
www.contratto.it

CELLAR SALES
PRE-BOOKED VISITS
ANNUAL PRODUCTION 140,000 bottles
HECTARES UNDER VINE 21.00

Six years have passed since the winery founded in 1867 by Giuseppe Contratto was purchased by the Rivetti family (who also own La Spinetta). It's a winery with a long and charming history, and the new ownership are revolutionizing the estate, starting with its vineyards. Giorgio Rivetti wants these to conform to regional standards, so as to be suitable for producing DOCG Alta Langa. Their work at Bossolasco, for example, saw 40 hectares of terrain planted with Pinot Nero and Chardonnay. Thus, as of 2011, purchases of grapes from Oltrepò Pavese came to a close. We would like to start by mentioning that in 2011, they went back to producing the already famous Asti De Miranda with the Metodo Classico. The wine ages for four years on the lees and displays incredible finesse and charm in this version. The generous 2013 Alta Langa For England Blanc de Noir Pas Dosé and the sharp 2012 For England Rosé Pas Dosé stand out from among their dry sparkling wines.

○ Alta Langa Pas Dosé		
For England Blanc de Noir '13	♟♟	6
○ Asti De Miranda M. Cl. '11	♟♟	5
⊙ For England Pas Dosé Rosé M. Cl. '12	♟♟	6
○ Blanc de Blancs Pas Dosé '12	♟♟	5
○ Millesimato Pas Dosé M. Cl. '12	♟♟	5
○ Special Cuvée Pas Dosé '09	♟♟	5
○ Asti De Miranda M. Cl. '00	♟♟♟	5
○ Asti De Miranda M. Cl. '97	♟♟♟	5
○ Asti De Miranda M. Cl. '96	♟♟♟	5
● Barolo Cerequio '99	♟♟♟	8
● Barolo Cerequio Tenuta Secolo '97	♟♟♟	8
○ Spumante M. Cl. Brut		
Giuseppe Contratto Ris. '96	♟♟♟	5
○ Spumante M. Cl. Brut		
Giuseppe Contratto Ris. '95	♟♟♟	5

Vigne Marina Coppi

VIA SANT'ANDREA, 5
15051 CASTELLANIA [AL]
TEL. +39 0131837089
www.vignemarinacoppi.com

CELLAR SALES
PRE-BOOKED VISITS
ANNUAL PRODUCTION 25,000 bottles
HECTARES UNDER VINE 4.50

15 years ago, Francesco Bellochio's adventure in the world of winemaking began. He started in a territory rich in history and traditions, a territory whose past was bound up with his own family's. His first season was in 2005, and since then it's been a constant process of growth (both in terms of goals and recognition) that's seen his winery become one of the most representative in the area. In addition to Timorasso, Francesco's vineyards feature Favorita, Barbera, Croatina and Michet Nebbiolo. Fausto has put forward a very complex version, one that features austere aromas, great charm, a powerful palate and an alcoholic finish. Francesca is a young Timorasso presented just within the minimum terms allowed by production regulations (about a year), but this doesn't mean it's any less structured or intense than older wines. The 2013 I Grop proves charming, with an impenetrable color and a complex, rich palate. The Sant'Andrea comes through balanced and well-orchestrated.

○ Colli Tortonesi Timorasso Fausto '15	♟♟♟ 6	
● Colli Tortonesi Barbera Sup. I Grop '13	♟♟ 5	
● Colli Tortonesi Barbera Sant'Andrea '16	♟♟ 3	
○ Colli Tortonesi Timorasso Francesca '16	♟♟ 3	
○ Colli Tortonesi Favorita Marine '15	♟ 5	
● Colli Tortonesi Rosso Lindin '14	♟ 5	
○ Colli Tortonesi Timorasso Fausto '12	♟♟♟ 6	
○ Colli Tortonesi Timorasso Fausto '11	♟♟♟ 6	
○ Colli Tortonesi Timorasso Fausto '10	♟♟♟ 6	
○ Colli Tortonesi Timorasso Fausto '09	♟♟♟ 6	
● Colli Tortonesi Barbera Sant'Andrea '15	♟♟ 3*	

★Coppo

VIA ALBA, 68
14053 CANELLI [AT]
TEL. +39 0141823146
www.coppo.it

CELLAR SALES
PRE-BOOKED VISITS
ANNUAL PRODUCTION 400,000 bottles
HECTARES UNDER VINE 52.00

Coppo is an important benchmark in Asti, not only for its history (it was founded in 1892 and still in the hands of the same family), but also, and especially, for the quality of its wines, from their Barberas to their 'Metodo Classico' sparkling wines to various Chardonnays (which can be considered among the most interesting long-lived whites in Italy). Their vineyards are situated in Canelli, Castelnuovo Calcea and Agliano Terme. Once again, the Coppo family have presented a very high-level selection of wines, starting with their 2009 Barbera d'Asti Superiore Nizza Riserva della Famiglia. It displays great freshness, with notes of rain-soaked earth and red fruit. Its palate proves elegant, balanced and gutsy, with a long finish. The 2014 Barbera d'Asti Pomoross exhibits notes of cherries and redcurrants, with hints of forest floor, while the palate comes through taut and juicy. The 2010 Piemonte Chardonnay Riserva della Famiglia is undoubtedly one of Italy's great Chardonnays, thanks to its complexity and supporting acidity.

● Barbera d'Asti Sup. Nizza Riserva della Famiglia '09	♟♟♟ 8	
● Barbera d'Asti Pomorosso '14	♟♟ 7	
○ Piemonte Chardonnay Riserva della Famiglia '10	♟♟ 8	
○ Piero Coppo Brut Ris. del Fondatore '06	♟♟ 8	
● Barbera d'Asti L'Avvocata '16	♟♟ 2*	
○ Luigi Coppo Brut M. Cl.	♟♟ 4	
○ Moscato d'Asti Moncalvina '16	♟♟ 3	
○ Piemonte Chardonnay Costebianche '15	♟♟ 3	
○ Riserva Coppo Brut M. Cl. '09	♟♟ 5	
○ Gavi La Rocca '16	♟ 3	
● Barbera d'Asti Pomorosso '13	♟♟♟ 7	
● Barbera d'Asti Pomorosso '12	♟♟♟ 7	

Giovanni Corino

FRAZ. ANNUNZIATA, 25B
12064 LA MORRA [CN]
TEL. +39 0173509452
www.corino.it

CELLAR SALES
PRE-BOOKED VISITS
ANNUAL PRODUCTION 45,000 bottles
HECTARES UNDER VINE 8.00

The Corino family arrived in the district of Annunziata, La Morra, in the 1950s as church land tenants, after living as sharecroppers. Gradually, they gave life to what is, today, one of the most intriguing operations in Langhe. In 2005, the family split, with Giuliano maintaining the historic facility and brand founded by his father, while his brother, Renato, founded his own brand. The Barolo cru are still Gachini, Arborina and Vecchie Vigne, which are aged mostly in small, new wood. Even in their richness and toastiness, they mustn't be considered stereotypically 'modern'. There are only 2013 Barolos in our tastings, with results that can only improve over time, when the oak present in all three wines begins to diminish. The Giachini comes through youthful on the nose, with hints of spice that merge into cocoa, and a mouth that's almost savory. The Arborina shows good structure, with a palate slightly dried out by tannins, while the Barolo del Comune di La Morra proves just a bit smaller.

● Barolo Giachini '13	♟♟ 7
● Barolo Arborina '13	♟♟ 7
● Barolo del Comune di La Morra '13	♟♟ 6
● Barolo Giachini '12	♟♟♟ 7
● Barolo Giachini '11	♟♟♟ 7
● Barolo '12	♟♟ 6
● Barolo '10	♟♟ 6
● Barolo Arborina '12	♟♟ 7
● Barolo Arborina '11	♟♟ 7
● Barolo Arborina '10	♟♟ 7
● Barolo Giachini '10	♟♟ 7
● Barolo V. Giachini '09	♟♟ 7
● Barolo V. V. '09	♟♟ 8
● Barolo V. V. '07	♟♟ 8

Renato Corino

FRAZ. ANNUNZIATA
B.TA POZZO, 49A
12064 LA MORRA [CN]
TEL. +39 0173500349
www.renatocorino.it

CELLAR SALES
PRE-BOOKED VISITS
ANNUAL PRODUCTION 50,000 bottles
HECTARES UNDER VINE 7.00

The Rocche, in Annunziata, are among the most celebrated crus in Langhe, and deservedly so. They give rise to a Barolo which, in its first years, stands out for its fresh and balsamic perfumes. Its structure is serious, though never aggressive. Here, Renato Corino, with the critical support of his children, Stefano and Chiara, produces some 4000 bottles of Barolo annually (with the occasional addition of a small 'Riserva'). In addition to the Rocche crus, there is the Arborina vineyard, where their cellar, built in 2005, is also located. Their selection is comprised of two modern wines marked by a polished elegance, whose fruit is always sweet and enticing. This modern and assertive 2013 Barolo is made with grapes grown in the splendid Rocche dell'Annunziata vineyard. Hints of spice and the contribution of wood add elegance to a well-orchestrated and tasty palate. The enjoyable Barolo Arborina features a more restrained structure, while the Barolo del Comune di La Morra of the same vintage is simple and correct. The large and mature 2011 Barolo Riserva lacks a bit of vitality.

● Barolo Rocche dell'Annunziata '13	♟♟ 8
● Barbera d'Alba Pozzo '14	♟♟ 5
● Barolo Arborina '13	♟♟ 7
● Barolo del Comune di La Morra '13	♟♟ 5
● Barolo Ris. '11	♟♟ 8
● Barolo Rocche dell'Annunziata '10	♟♟♟ 7
● Barolo Rocche dell'Annunziata '09	♟♟♟ 7
● Barolo Vign. Rocche '06	♟♟♟ 7
● Barolo Vign. Rocche '04	♟♟♟ 8
● Barolo Vign. Rocche '03	♟♟♟ 8
● Barolo Arborina '12	♟♟ 7
● Barolo Arborina '11	♟♟ 7
● Barolo Arborina '09	♟♟ 7
● Barolo Rocche dell'Annunziata '12	♟♟ 8

Cornarea

VIA VALENTINO, 150
12043 CANALE [CN]
TEL. +39 017365636
www.cornarea.com

CELLAR SALES
PRE-BOOKED VISITS
ACCOMMODATION
ANNUAL PRODUCTION 90,000 bottles
HECTARES UNDER VINE 14.00

The Bovone family are among the principal
figures responsible for the rebirth of Arneis.
In the mid-1960s, they chose to dedicate
the hilltop vineyard surrounding their winery
to this local variety, which had almost
disappeared. Today, their vineyards,
situated on calcareous-clay soil (with a
strong element of magnesium), are a
contiguous plot of Arneis (two-thirds) and
Nebbiolo. Their traditionally-styled selection
are technically well-crafted. The 2016
Roero Arneis is one of the best of its kind.
Citrus, white fruit and hints of spice emerge
on the nose, while the palate shows great
savoriness, guaranteeing structure and
grip, with a characteristic almondy finish.
The 2014 Roero is well-made and pleasant
with elegant tannins, while the 2013 Roero
Arneis Enritard exhibits good structure and
complexity.

○ Roero Arneis '16	♈♈ 3*
● Roero '14	♈♈ 4
○ Roero Arneis Enritard '13	♈♈ 3
● Nebbiolo d'Alba '15	♈ 3
● Roero '13	♈♈ 4
● Roero '12	♈♈ 4
○ Roero Arneis '15	♈♈ 3*
○ Roero Arneis '14	♈♈ 3*
○ Roero Arneis '13	♈♈ 3
○ Tarasco Passito '12	♈♈ 5
○ Tarasco Passito '11	♈♈ 5
○ Tarasco Passito '10	♈♈ 5

★Matteo Correggia

LOC. GARBINETTO
VIA SANTO STEFANO ROERO, 124
12043 CANALE [CN]
TEL. +39 0173978009
www.matteocorreggia.com

CELLAR SALES
PRE-BOOKED VISITS
ANNUAL PRODUCTION 150,000 bottles
HECTARES UNDER VINE 20.00

Ornella Costa Correggia's winery is among
the most notable of Roero. They offer wines
of significant technical precision, though this
takes nothing away from their desire to
experiment so as to best express the
attributes of the territory. Their vineyards are
located in Canale and Santo Stefano Roero,
mostly on Asti's trademark, sandy soil (low in
clay and silt, but rich in mineral salts). Even if
their most famous wine is Roero Ròche
d'Ampsèj Riserva, this is grown in Bric
Pecetto, on soil that is a mix of terrain from
both Asti and Tortona. This year we
particularly enjoyed the fresh and pleasant
2014 Roero La Val dei Preti, with its notes of
wild berries and Mediterranean scrub, and
great drinkability. The rest of the selection
proves well-made, especially the two
Barbera d'Albas. The 2015 is an earthy wine
with good grip, while the 2014 Superiore
Marun is more juicy and dynamic. We
found the 2013 Roero Ròche d'Ampsej
Riserva less glossy than usual, showing
notable density, but hard tannins and a
marked vegetal note.

● Roero La Val dei Preti '14	♈♈ 5
● Barbera d'Alba '15	♈♈ 3
● Barbera d'Alba Sup. Marun '14	♈♈ 5
● Roero '15	♈♈ 3
○ Roero Arneis '16	♈♈ 3
● Roero Ròche d'Ampsèj Ris. '13	♈♈ 6
● Anthos '16	♈ 3
● Roero Ròche d'Ampsèj Ris. '09	♈♈♈ 6
● Roero Ròche d'Ampsèj Ris. '07	♈♈♈ 6
● Roero Ròche d'Ampsèj Ris. '06	♈♈♈ 6
● Langhe Rosso Le Marne Grigie '13	♈♈ 6
● Roero Ròche d'Ampsèj Ris. '12	♈♈ 6

Giuseppe Cortese

S.DA RABAJÀ, 80
12050 BARBARESCO [CN]
TEL. +39 0173035131
www.cortesegiuseppe.it

CELLAR SALES
PRE-BOOKED VISITS
ACCOMMODATION
ANNUAL PRODUCTION 50,000 bottles
HECTARES UNDER VINE 8.00

An authentic, natural amphitheater
connects the hill of Rabajà to Trifolera. Here
you'll find the eight hectares of terrain
managed by siblings Pier Carlo and Tiziana
Cortese, along with Tiziana's husband,
Gabriele. They have the honor and burden
of keeping alive the work of their parents,
Giuseppe and Rossella, who chose to bet
on in the Barbaresco wine region during a
time when few were (the early 1960s).
Their wines are the result of a focus on
lightness and polish, especially their
Nebbiolo reds (aged in oak of various
sizes and types), making for Rabajàs
(vintage and 'Riserva') that are consistently
among the best in the appellation. The
2014 Rabajà is an excellent vintage
Barbaresco. Its color alone gives you an
idea of its youth and brilliance. Aromas of
violets, raspberries and strawberries dictate
its aromatic development, with licorice
emerging only later. We find good weight
on the palate and a finish full of personality,
thanks to well-balanced tannins and acidity.
The rest of the selection performed quite
well, starting with the 2015 Nebbiolo.

● Barbaresco Rabajà '14	♟♟ 6
● Barbera d'Alba '16	♟♟ 3
● Barbera d'Alba Morassina '14	♟♟ 3
○ Langhe Chardonnay '16	♟♟ 2*
● Langhe Nebbiolo '15	♟♟ 3
● Dolcetto d'Alba '16	♟ 2
● Barbaresco Rabajà '11	♟♟♟ 5
● Barbaresco Rabajà '10	♟♟♟ 5
● Barbaresco Rabajà '08	♟♟♟ 5
● Barbaresco Rabajà '13	♟♟ 5
● Barbera d'Alba '15	♟♟ 3
● Dolcetto d'Alba '15	♟♟ 2*
○ Langhe Chardonnay Scapulin '14	♟♟ 3
● Langhe Nebbiolo '14	♟♟ 3*

Clemente Cossetti

VIA GUARDIE, 1
14043 CASTELNUOVO BELBO [AT]
TEL. +39 0141799803
www.cossetti.it

CELLAR SALES
PRE-BOOKED VISITS
ACCOMMODATION AND RESTAURANT SERVICE
ANNUAL PRODUCTION 500,000 bottles
HECTARES UNDER VINE 28.00

For four generations, the Cossetti family
has managed this Montferrat winery
founded in 1891. Their vineyards, all of
which are in Castelnuovo Belbo, grow in
medium-thick clay soil that's rich in
minerals. Barbera and smaller quantities of
Chardonnay, Cortese and Dolcetto are
cultivated. The winery also works as a
négociant, offering an array of wines from
various appellations throughout Piedmont.
The 2015 Nizza truly impressed. It starts off
intense and complex, with notes of cherries
and plums, and a graceful tannic texture
that follows into a fresh, lingering finish.
The 2016 Ruché di Castagnole Monferrato
proves pleasant and glossy, with hints of
wild strawberries and dark fruit, but it also
manages to be caressing and full-bodied.
The 2015 Barbera d'Asti Superiore La
Vigna Vecchia comes through with simpler
aromas, but still shows good structure.

● Nizza '15	♟♟ 4
● Ruché di Castagnole M.to '16	♟♟ 3
● Barbera d'Asti Sup. La Vigna Vecchia '15	♟ 2
● Barbera d'Asti Venti di Marzo '16	♟ 3
○ Moscato d'Asti La Vita '16	♟ 2
● Barbera d'Asti La Vigna Vecchia '13	♟♟ 2*
● Barbera d'Asti La Vigna Vecchia '12	♟♟ 2*
● Barbera d'Asti Sup. Nizza '13	♟♟ 4
● Barbera d'Asti Sup. Nizza '11	♟♟ 4
● Barbera d'Asti Venti di Marzo '14	♟♟ 3
● Grignolino d'Asti '14	♟♟ 2*
○ Moscato d'Asti La Vita '15	♟♟ 2*
● Piemonte Albarossa Amartè '14	♟♟ 3
● Ruché di Castagnole Monferrato '15	♟♟ 3

Stefanino Costa

B.TA BENNA, 5
12046 MONTÀ [CN]
TEL. +39 0173976336
ninocostawine@gmail.com

CELLAR SALES
PRE-BOOKED VISITS
ANNUAL PRODUCTION 50,000 bottles
HECTARES UNDER VINE 9.50

Over the last few years, the Costa family
has managed to position themselves among
the top producers in Roero. It's all thanks to
their consistent effort to bring together
tradition, terroir (and its characteristics),
technical focus and aromatic precision.
Their vineyards are located in Canale,
Montà and Santo Stefano Roero, at altitudes
ranging from 350 to 400 meters, and grow
in mostly sandy terrain. Roero's classic
varieties are all represented, from Nebbiolo
to Arneis, Barbera and Brachetto. The
2013 Roero Gepin proves that it's one of
Italy's best reds thanks to its classic aromas
of red flowers and tobacco, with hints of
cherry and pencil lead. The complex palate
leads into a long finish, with a tight-knit and
gradual tannic texture that remains delicate
and balanced. The 2015 Nebbiolo d'Alba
Cabora proves more approachable with
good fruit, while the 2016 Roero Arneis
Sarun features citrusy notes and a vibrant
tanginess. Both are well-made.

● Roero Gepin '13	▼▼▼ 4*
○ Langhe Bianco Ricordi '16	▼▼ 3
● Nebbiolo d'Alba Cabora '15	▼▼ 4
○ Roero Arneis Sarun '16	▼▼ 3
● Barbera d'Alba Barbot '16	▼ 2
● Roero Gepin '12	♈♈♈ 4*
● Roero Gepin '11	♈♈♈ 4*
● Roero Gepin '10	♈♈♈ 4*
● Barbera d'Alba Cichin '12	♈♈ 2*
● Barbera d'Alba Sup. Genna '13	♈♈ 2*
○ Langhe Bianco Ricordi '13	♈♈ 3
○ Roero Arneis Sarun '15	♈♈ 3*
○ Roero Arneis Sarun '13	♈♈ 3*
● Roero Medic '12	♈♈ 3
● Roero Medic '10	♈♈ 3*

Tenuta Cucco

VIA MAZZINI, 10
12050 SERRALUNGA D'ALBA [CN]
TEL. +39 0173613003
www.tenutacucco.it

CELLAR SALES
PRE-BOOKED VISITS
ACCOMMODATION
ANNUAL PRODUCTION 70,000 bottles
HECTARES UNDER VINE 13.00

Giorgio Rossi Cairo's experience with Gavi a
La Raia convinced him to go a step further.
winemaking. And so it was that in 2015 he
purchased the lovely Cascina Cucco and its
vineyards (which will soon be cultivated
according to organic and biodynamic
principles). Bolstered by a cracking technical
squad, they're finding success with their
Barolos (as well as a selection of local
classics made with Barbera and Dolcetto). A
small but important part is dedicated to
Chardonnay, which give rise to their Langhe
and Brut Metodo Classico. Their wines
exhibit impeccable sophistication and
typicity. We find aromatic complexity and
measured acidity in the elegant and powerful
2013 Barolo Cerrati. The 2013 Barolo del
Comune di Serralunga d'Alba's alcoholic
component tends to slightly soften the wine,
while the 2011 Barolo Cerrati Vigna Cucco
Riserva exhibits clear oak and tight-knit
tannins. The 2015 Langhe Rosso deserves
praise for its pleasant drinkability. It's an
elegant blend of Nebbiolo and Barbera
with small additions of Cabernet Sauvignon
and Merlot.

● Barolo Cerrati '13	▼▼ 7
● Barbera d'Alba Sup. '15	▼▼ 4
● Barolo Cerrati V. Cucco Ris. '11	▼▼ 8
● Barolo del Comune di Serralunga d'Alba '13	▼▼ 6
● Langhe Nebbiolo '16	▼▼ 4
● Langhe Rosso '15	▼▼ 4
● Barbera d'Alba Sup. '13	♈♈ 3
● Barolo Cerrati '12	♈♈ 7
● Barolo Cerrati '11	♈♈ 6
● Barolo Cerrati '10	♈♈ 6
● Barolo Cerrati V. Cucco '11	♈♈ 6
● Barolo Cerrati V. Cucco Ris. '10	♈♈ 8
● Barolo del Comune di Serralunga d'Alba '12	♈♈ 6
● Barolo del Comune di Serralunga d'Alba '11	♈♈ 5

Deltetto

C.SO ALBA, 43
12043 CANALE [CN]
TEL. +39 0173979383
www.deltetto.com

CELLAR SALES
PRE-BOOKED VISITS
ANNUAL PRODUCTION 170,000 bottles
HECTARES UNDER VINE 21.00
VITICULTURE METHOD Certified Organic
SUSTAINABLE WINERY

The Deltetto family winery has, for some years, been a leading figure in Roero's viticulture scene. They are among the few producers in the territory to offer a solid line of sparkling wines. Mostly, these are made with Chardonnay and Pinot Nero, but also Nebbiolo. They offer a selection of wines that ranges from Roero classics, made with Arneis, Nebbiolo or Barbera, to other important appellation like Barolo, Dolcetto d'Alba, Gavi or Moscato d'Asti. The 2016 Roero Arneis San Michele is one of the best expressions of this appellation. Floral aromas feature fruity notes, while the palate proves tangy, chalky, dynamic and long. We were impressed by the two 2015 Barbera d'Alba Superiores, especially the Rocca delle Marasche, with its earthy, gutsy notes rich in fruit, but also the Bramé, which comes through fresh, with notes of cherry and redcurrants. Their various Metodo Classico sparkling wines did well and we particularly enjoyed the citrusy and spicy 2012 Brut.

● Barbera d'Alba Sup.		
Rocca delle Marasche '15	♟♟	5
○ Roero Arneis San Michele '16	♟♟	3*
● Barbera d'Alba Sup. Bramé '15	♟♟	3
● Barolo Bussia '12	♟♟	6
○ Brut M. Cl. '12	♟♟	4
☉ Brut M. Cl. Rosé	♟♟	5
● Roero '14	♟♟	3
○ Roero Arneis Daivej '16	♟♟	2*
● Roero Braja Ris. '09	♟♟♟	4*
● Roero Braja Ris. '08	♟♟♟	4
● Roero Braja Ris. '07	♟♟♟	4
○ Deltetto Extra Brut M. Cl. '10	♟♟	5
● Roero '13	♟♟	3
● Roero Braja Ris. '13	♟♟	4

Gianni Doglia

VIA ANNUNZIATA, 56
14054 CASTAGNOLE DELLE LANZE [AT]
TEL. +39 0141878359
www.giannidoglia.it

CELLAR SALES
PRE-BOOKED VISITS
ANNUAL PRODUCTION 90,000 bottles
HECTARES UNDER VINE 10.00

Gianni Doglia is a wine artisan who, instead of giving interviews, prefers to let is his bottles speak for themselves. His Barbera d'Asti Bosco Donne, aged only in steel, is full but fresh and approachable. His Barbera d'Asti Superiore Genio is a more serious wine that's aged in wood for almost two years. Both his Moscato d'Astis are outstanding. Characterized by tropical fruit and pennyroyal that combine with peach, the award winning Casa di Bianca is a favorite among those who love fullness of taste. His Monferrato Rosso is always enticing, and there are just 1000 bottles of an outstanding Merlot. The 2015 and 2016 vintages produced astonishing results, the first for reds and the second for its sweet whites. The 2016 Moscato d'Asti Casa di Bianca is tops in its category and earns a Tre Bicchieri. Sage, moss and citrus fruit penetrate the nose, while its powerful and rich mouth displays a delicately sweet and enchanting grip. The new 2015 Nizza features elegant hints of spice and fruit and a bold palate. The 2015 Barbera d'Asti Genio shows rare harmony.

○ Moscato d'Asti Casa di Bianca '16	♟♟♟	3*
● Barbera d'Asti Sup. Genio '15	♟♟	4
○ Moscato d'Asti '16	♟♟	2*
● Barbera d'Asti Bosco Donne '16	♟♟	2*
● Nizza '15	♟♟	4
● Grignolino d'Asti '16	♟	2
● Barbera d'Asti Sup. Genio '12	♟♟♟	4*
○ Moscato d'Asti Casa di Bianca '15	♟♟♟	3*
● Barbera d'Asti Bosco Donne '15	♟♟	2
● Barbera d'Asti Sup. Genio '14	♟♟	4
● Barbera d'Asti Sup. Genio '11	♟♟	4
● Grignolino d'Asti '15	♟♟	2*
● M.to Rosso ! '13	♟♟	5
○ Moscato d'Asti Casa di Bianca '14	♟♟	3*
○ Moscato d'Asti Casa di Bianca '13	♟♟	3*

Dosio

Reg. Serradenari, 6
12064 La Morra [CN]
Tel. +39 017350677
www.dosiovigneti.com

CELLAR SALES
PRE-BOOKED VISITS
ACCOMMODATION
ANNUAL PRODUCTION 65,000 bottles
HECTARES UNDER VINE 11.00

Beppe Dosio, known as a great cellarman by his colleagues, left his winery in the hands of the Lenci family. But even at 80 he's giving advice to the technical director, enologist Marco Dotta. Their vineyards are situated in the highest part of Barolo, as is their cellar, at about 500 meters above sea level. Fossati (also available as a 'Riserva') and Serradenari are their Barolo crus, which give rise to the most consistent part of their selection. This includes Barbera and Dolcetto d'Alba, along with two reds from the Langhe appellation. The 2013 Barolo Serradenari closes the tasting with a close-focused and complex finish of rare length. The nose leads with raspberries and sweet tobacco, while the palate features well-orchestrated finesse. The 2011 Barolo Fossati Riserva proves youthful, with hints of licorice and aniseed, while the mouth gradually unfolds, revealing its balance. The warm 2013 Barolo is more approachable, but shows good structure.

● Barolo Fossati Ris. '11	🍷🍷 8
● Barolo Serradenari '13	🍷🍷 6
● Barolo '13	🍷🍷 5
● Langhe Momenti '13	🍷🍷 4
● Langhe Nebbiolo Barilà '14	🍷🍷 5
● Dolcetto d'Alba Sup. Nassone '15	🍷 3
● Barbera d'Alba '13	🍷🍷 2*
● Barolo '12	🍷🍷 5
● Barolo '10	🍷🍷 5
● Barolo Fossati '11	🍷🍷 5
● Barolo Fossati Ris. '08	🍷🍷 8
● Barolo Serradenari '12	🍷🍷 6
● Dolcetto d'Alba '15	🍷🍷 2*
● Langhe Eventi '12	🍷🍷 4
● Langhe Nebbiolo Barilà '13	🍷🍷 5
● Langhe Nebbiolo Barilà '12	🍷🍷 3*
● Langhe Rosso Momenti '11	🍷🍷 5

★Poderi Luigi Einaudi

Loc. Cascina Tecc
B.ta Gombe, 31/32
12063 Dogliani [CN]
Tel. +39 017370191
www.poderieinaudi.com

CELLAR SALES
PRE-BOOKED VISITS
ACCOMMODATION
ANNUAL PRODUCTION 250,000 bottles
HECTARES UNDER VINE 52.00

Bolstered by a decades-old reputation, both in Italy and abroad, Poderi Luigi Einaudi might have rested on its laurels. But instead, Matteo Sardagna continues to aim high, which becomes clear when you enter his splendid underground cellar, where it's easy to get lost among the barrels, vats and casks. In addition to the charming Relais dei Poderi, they've purchased a new vineyard in Bussia, Monforte d'Alba. The move is further proof of their commitment to Barolo. For the moment, it's being grown in their other outstanding crus, Cannubi and Terlo (which also provide the grapes for their Costa Grimaldi selection). The 2013 Barolo Cannubi, a classically styled wine, does an exceptional job of expressing this great cru's qualities. Aromas of tar merge with red fruit, while the palate proves caressing, rich and already enjoyable. The 2013 Terlo is more austere, while the Costa Grimaldi line is showing great potential. The famous 2016 Vigna Tecc is a full-bodied and intense wine, but it's slightly lacking in freshness.

● Barolo Cannubi '13	🍷🍷 8
● Barolo Terlo V. Costa Grimaldi '13	🍷🍷 7
● Barolo Terlo '13	🍷🍷 6
● Dogliani Sup. V. Tecc '16	🍷🍷 3
● Langhe Luigi Einaudi '13	🍷🍷 6
○ Langhe Meira '16	🍷🍷 4
● Langhe Nebbiolo '15	🍷🍷 3
● Piemonte Barbera '16	🍷🍷 3
● Dogliani '16	🍷 3
● Barolo Cannubi '11	🍷🍷🍷 8
● Barolo Cannubi '10	🍷🍷🍷 8
● Barolo Costa Grimaldi '05	🍷🍷🍷 8
● Dogliani Sup. V. Tecc '10	🍷🍷🍷 3*
● Dogliani V. Tecc '06	🍷🍷🍷 4
● Langhe Rosso Luigi Einaudi '04	🍷🍷🍷 5

F.lli Facchino

LOC. VAL DEL PRATO, 210
15078 ROCCA GRIMALDA [AL]
TEL. +39 014385401
www.vinifacchino.it

CELLAR SALES
PRE-BOOKED VISITS
ANNUAL PRODUCTION 80,000 bottles
HECTARES UNDER VINE 30.00

We've been tasting Famiglio Facchino's
wines for years now, and they've always
proved to be sound and well-made. The
breakthrough probably came with the
advent of the new generation, Giorgio and
Diego (their 'enotechnician'), who set in
motion a process of modernizing
production and brought greater attention to
the little details that really matter: it's the
difference between 'good' and 'great'.
Theirs is an essential winery for a territory
that has tremendous and still unrealized
potential. The Facchino brothers presented
a very balanced selection of wines, with the
2015 Dolcetto di Ovada reaching heights of
excellence. This wine is subtle and complex
on the nose, with a powerful and elegant
palate. Then comes the Ovada Carasöi, a
wine characterized by fruity aromas and
vegetal notes. Tannins and acidity make for
a palate that's still tight. The vigorous and
intense Barbera del Monferrato shows
character and personality. The Piemonte
Albarossa and the Cortese Alto Monferrato
both prove well-made.

● Dolcetto di Ovada Poggiobello '15		▼▼2*
● Barbera del M.to '15		▼▼2*
○ Cortese dell'Alto M.to Pacialan '16		▼▼2*
● Ovada Carasöi '15		▼▼3
● Piemonte Albarossa Note d'Autunno '12		▼▼3
● Dolcetto di Ovada Poggiobello '14		♀♀2*
● Dolcetto di Ovada Poggiobello '12		♀♀2*
● M.to Rosso Note d'Autunno '11		♀♀3
● Ovada Carasöi '13		♀♀3

Tenuta Il Falchetto

FRAZ. CIOMBI
VIA VALLE TINELLA, 16
12058 SANTO STEFANO BELBO [CN]
TEL. +39 0141840344
www.ilfalchetto.com

CELLAR SALES
PRE-BOOKED VISITS
ANNUAL PRODUCTION 280,000 bottles
HECTARES UNDER VINE 47.00

The Forno brothers' winery, founded in
1940, was originally dedicated to Moscato,
which was cultivated on the hills of Santo
Stefano Belbo. Today, in addition to these
vineyards, they have various plots at their
disposal throughout Castiglione Tinella,
Agliano Terme and Calosso. This doesn't
mean that their focus isn't on tradition.
Indeed, 80% of their crop is Moscato and
Barbera. All their wines performed well,
starting with the splendid 2016 Moscato
d'Asti Tenuta del Fant. It features aromas of
gingerbread and a citrusy palate, with great
balance between acidity and sweetness,
quite pleasant. The 2016 Moscato d'Asti
Canelli Ciombo is almost on the same level,
displaying aromas of candied citrus fruit
and coming through soft and full. The
2014 Barbera d'Asti Superiore Bricco
Paradiso offers up aromas of black
cherries and forest floor, with a fresh and
fruit-rich palate. But their whole selection
truly impressed.

● Barbera d'Asti Sup. Bricco Paradiso '14		▼▼3*
○ Moscato d'Asti Canelli Ciombo '16		▼▼2*
○ Moscato d'Asti Tenuta del Fant '16		▼▼2*
● Barbera d'Asti Pian Scorrone '16		▼▼3
● Barbera d'Asti Sup. Lurëi '14		▼▼3
● M.to Rosso La Mora '14		▼▼3
○ Piemonte Chardonnay Incompreso '15		▼▼3
○ Moscato d'Asti Ciombo '15		♀♀♀2*
○ Moscato d'Asti Tenuta del Fant '11		♀♀♀2*
○ Moscato d'Asti Tenuta del Fant '09		♀♀♀2*
● Barbera d'Asti Sup. Lurëi '13		♀♀3*
○ Moscato d'Asti Tenuta del Fant '15		♀♀2*
○ Moscato d'Asti Tenuta del Fant '14		♀♀2*

Benito Favaro

DA CHIUSURE, 1 BIS
10010 PIVERONE [TO]
TEL. +39 012572606
www.cantinafavaro.it

CELLAR SALES
PRE-BOOKED VISITS
ANNUAL PRODUCTION 20,000 bottles
HECTARES UNDER VINE 3.50

Benito and Camillo Favaro's multivariate
selection takes shape in the splendid
district of Serra, on the Morainic side of the
hill that faces Piverone Lake. The estate
comprises just over three hectares of
vineyards, where mostly Erbaluce is
cultivated. Syrah, Freisa, Nebbiolo and
Barbara make up the remaining plots,
giving life to jazz-inspired wines like F2,
Easy and Rossomeraviglia. Nevertheless,
the genius loci of the winery is white.
Thanks to its almost 'Germanic' character,
Le Chiusure, which is made in steel, has
been a benchmark for the variety for some
time. But in recent years, their 13 Mesi,
which is fermented and aged partially in
wood, has also grown in stature, The 2015
needs to be tried to be believed. It offers up
white fruit, meadow flowers, hints of
cereals and its long finish holds together
opulence and acidity. The 2016 Erbaluce is
more slim-bodied and biting. It closes on a
young and promising palate of alfalfa and
citrus rind.

Erbaluce di Caluso Le Chiusure '16	♟♟♟ 2*
Erbaluce di Caluso 13 Mesi '15	♟♟ 3*
Rosacherosanonsei '16	♟♟ 3
● Rossomeraviglia '15	♟♟ 5
● Ros '15	♟ 4
Erbaluce di Caluso Le Chiusure '13	♟♟♟ 2*
Erbaluce di Caluso Le Chiusure '12	♟♟♟ 2*
Erbaluce di Caluso Le Chiusure '11	♟♟♟ 2*
Erbaluce di Caluso Le Chiusure '10	♟♟♟ 2*
Erbaluce di Caluso Le Chiusure '15	♟♟ 2*
Rosacherosanonsei '15	♟♟ 3
Sole d'Inverno '13	♟♟ 5

Giacomo Fenocchio

LOC. BUSSIA, 72
12065 MONFORTE D'ALBA [CN]
TEL. +39 017378675
www.giacomofenocchio.com

CELLAR SALES
PRE-BOOKED VISITS
ANNUAL PRODUCTION 90,000 bottles
HECTARES UNDER VINE 15.00
SUSTAINABLE WINERY

That the Fenocchio family produces
enticing, local and affordable wines is
certainly not news. The winery took its first
steps way back in 1860, and yet it's only
been over the last 15 years that it's
received the recognition it deserves. This
thanks to a selection of Nebbiolo that
energetically and accurately expresses
territories as prestigious as Cannubi and
Castellero (in Barolo), Villero di Castiglione
Falletto and Bussia (in Monforte, also
available in the 90 Di Riserva). Long
maceration and aging in 3500-5000 liter
Slovenian oak provide the keys to a style
that is increasingly precise and consistent.
In a vintage that's giving rise to good, but
not sensational, results, the 2013 Barolo
Bussia stands out for its freshness and
liveliness, both on the nose and the palate.
It features a precise classic style, with
flowers and red fruit accompanying spices
and pepper. The mouth proves supple, well-
orchestrated and long. The 2011 Riserva
Bussia 90 Dì comes through more evolved
and tannic. The 2013 Cannubi is a pleasant
expression of this famous vineyard.

● Barolo Bussia '13	♟♟ 6
● Barolo Bussia 90 Dì Ris. '11	♟♟ 6
● Barolo Cannubi '13	♟♟ 6
● Barolo Castellero '13	♟♟ 6
● Barolo Villero '13	♟♟ 6
● Langhe Nebbiolo '15	♟♟ 3
● Barolo Bussia '11	♟♟♟ 6
● Barolo Bussia '09	♟♟♟ 6
● Barolo Bussia 90 Dì Ris. '10	♟♟♟ 8
● Barolo Bussia '12	♟♟ 6
● Barolo Bussia Ris. '09	♟♟ 7
● Barolo Cannubi '12	♟♟ 6
⊙ Barolo Castellero '12	♟♟ 6
● Barolo Castellero '11	♟♟ 6
● Barolo Villero '12	♟♟ 6

Ferrando

VIA TORINO, 599
10015 IVREA [TO]
TEL. +39 0125633550
www.ferrandovini.it

CELLAR SALES
PRE-BOOKED VISITS
ANNUAL PRODUCTION 50,000 bottles
HECTARES UNDER VINE 5.00

The last outpost of Piedmont is practically
in Valle d'Aosta, in a point where the hills of
Carema provide breathtaking views of the
vineyards grafted on the granite rocks and
steep slopes of Alpine ridge. Here, the
Nebbiolo cultivated is chromatically
spartan, yet capable of enduring for
decades. The old vintages kept in Roberto
Ferrando's family's vault have to be tasted
to be believed. The Bianca selection can be
considered their base Carema, while Nera
enjoys longer aging in mid-size oak. Their
Erbaluces, available in two still versions, a
sparkling and two dessert wines, also
deserve attention. A new chapter has been
written in the fabulous epic of mountain
Nebbiolo. With aromas of tobacco, rhubarb
and pencil lead, the 2013 Etichetta Nera
gives us everything we could ask from from
a Carema. It exhibits very tight-knit tannins
and an unending, classy finish. The
Etichetta Bianca of the same vintage proves
leaner and more autumnal.

● Carema Et. Bianca '13	▼▼5
● Carema Et. Nera '13	▼▼7
○ Erbaluce di Caluso Cariola '16	▼▼3
○ Erbaluce di Caluso La Torrazza '16	▼▼3
○ Caluso Passito '10	▼5
● Carema Et. Bianca '12	▼▼▼5
● Carema Et. Nera '11	▼▼▼7
● Carema Et. Nera '09	▼▼▼6
● Carema Et. Nera '08	▼▼▼6
● Carema Et. Nera '07	▼▼▼6
○ Caluso Passito '09	▼▼5
○ Erbaluce di Caluso Brut La Torrazza '09	▼▼4
○ Erbaluce di Caluso Cariola '14	▼▼3
○ Erbaluce di Caluso La Torrazza '14	▼▼3

Roberto Ferraris

REG. DOGLIANO, 33
14041 AGLIANO TERME [AT]
TEL. +39 0141954234
www.robertoferraris.com

CELLAR SALES
PRE-BOOKED VISITS
ANNUAL PRODUCTION 60,000 bottles
HECTARES UNDER VINE 11.00

Roberto represents the third generation of
Ferraris to manage this lovely Asti winery,
which dedicates itself exclusively to
producing Barbera. Indeed, 80% of their
vineyards, cultivated on white, calcareous
terrain (with high silt content and low clay)
host Barbera. Some of the vineyards here
are almost 100 years old, making for wines
that are technically well-crafted and stay
true to the territory. The 2015 Superiore La
Cricca has to be one of the best Barbera
d'Astis presented this year. The nose offers
up aromas of Ferrovia cherry and dark fruit
with hints of rain-soaked earth. Its
succulent, pleasant palate exhibits good
fruit and density. The 2015 Superiore
Bisavolo tends more toward notes of pencil
lead and red fruit. It's a supple and
dynamic wine with good acidity. Then
comes the 2015 Barbera d'Asti Nobbio,
which is lacking in body but still sees
freshness, good pulp and pleasantness.

● Barbera d'Asti Sup. Bisavolo '15	▼▼4
● Barbera d'Asti Sup. La Cricca '15	▼▼5
● Barbera d'Asti Nobbio '15	▼▼3
● Barbera d'Asti Suôrì '16	▼2
● Barbera d'Asti '13	▼▼2
● Barbera d'Asti Nobbio '14	▼▼2
● Barbera d'Asti Nobbio '13	▼▼2
● Barbera d'Asti Suôrì '15	▼▼2
● Barbera d'Asti Sup. Bisavolo '13	▼▼3
● Barbera d'Asti Sup. La Cricca '13	▼▼3
● Barbera d'Asti Sup. La Cricca '12	▼▼3
● M.to Rosso Grixa '12	▼▼3

Carlo Ferro

FRAZ. SALERE, 41
14041 AGLIANO TERME [AT]
TEL. +39 0141954000
www.ferrovini.com

CELLAR SALES
PRE-BOOKED VISITS
ANNUAL PRODUCTION 15,000 bottles
HECTARES UNDER VINE 12.00

Only red grapes are cultivated on the Ferro family's estate, proof of the owners' attention to the territory's natural disposition. Situated in Agliano Terme, the winery has existed since the early 20th century, but has only bottled their own wines for just over two decades. Traditional grapes are grown, primarily Barbera, but also Dolcetto, Grignolino and Nebbiolo (as well as a few plots of Cabernet Sauvignon). The 2015 Barbera d'Asti Giulia performed particularly well. Spicy aromas merge with notes of tobacco and sour cherries. The full-bodied palate finds the right balance between marked acidity and rich pulp, with a long, pleasant finish. The 2013 Monferrato Rosso Paolo, a blend of 40% Barbera, 30% Nebbiolo and Cabernet Sauvignon, is supple, rich in fruit, and features elegant tannins. The 2014 Barbera d'Asti Superiore Notturno proves well-orchestrated, with good complexity, despite the difficult vintage. Both wines are well-made.

● Barbera d'Asti Giulia '15	🍷🍷 2*
● Barbera d'Asti Sup. Notturno '14	🍷🍷 3
● M.to Rosso Paolo '13	🍷🍷 4
● Barbera d'Asti Sup. Roche '14	🍷 3
● Barbera d'Asti '14	🍷🍷 2*
● Barbera d'Asti '13	🍷🍷 1*
● Barbera d'Asti Giulia '14	🍷🍷 2*
● Barbera d'Asti Giulia '13	🍷🍷 2*
● Barbera d'Asti Sup. Notturno '15	🍷🍷 2*
● Barbera d'Asti Sup. Notturno '12	🍷🍷 2*
● Barbera d'Asti Sup. Notturno '11	🍷🍷 2*
● Barbera d'Asti Sup. Roche '13	🍷🍷 3
● Barbera d'Asti Sup. Roche '11	🍷🍷 3

★Fontanafredda

VIA ALBA, 15
12050 SERRALUNGA D'ALBA [CN]
TEL. +39 0173626111
www.fontanafredda.it

CELLAR SALES
PRE-BOOKED VISITS
ACCOMMODATION AND RESTAURANT SERVICE
ANNUAL PRODUCTION 7,500,000 bottles
HECTARES UNDER VINE 100.00
SUSTAINABLE WINERY

It would be impossible to condense Fontanafredda's past and present into just a few lines: Vittorio Emanuele II and Bella Rusìn, hunting grounds and hamlet, their many projects involving sustainability, energy conservation, reducing sulphites, and more. The estate comprises about 100 hectares of terrain, which, along with the contributions of their network of vine- growers, provide the grapes needed for their selection of some 10 wines, which are divided into thematic categories. Plenty of room is given to selections and crus that are, in many ways, 'artisanal'. The 2013 Barolo Paiagallo Casa E. di Mirafiore is a classically styled wine. Aromas range from licorice to incense, while the mouth exhibits a winning, subtle tannic austerity. Tre Bicchieri. The 2013 Barolo del Comune di Serralunga d'Alba also put in a good performance, with spicy aromas and a firmly-structured body. The powerful and worthy 2013 Barolo Casa E. di Mirafiore offers up clean and deep aromas. The whole selection is admirable.

● Barolo Paiagallo Casa E. di Mirafiore '13	🍷🍷🍷 7
● Barolo Casa E. di Mirafiore '13	🍷🍷 6
● Barolo del Comune di Serralunga d'Alba '13	🍷🍷 7
● Barolo Fontanafredda V. La Rosa '13	🍷🍷 7
○ Alta Langa Brut Nature V. Gatinera '08	🍷🍷 5
○ Alta Langa Extra Brut '12	🍷🍷 4
● Barbaresco Coste Rubin '14	🍷🍷 5
● Barolo Casa E. di Mirafiore Ris '10	🍷🍷 8
● Barolo Proprietà in Fontanafredda '13	🍷🍷 8
● Barolo Ris. '10	🍷🍷 8
● Barolo Casa E. di Mirafiore Ris. '04	🍷🍷🍷 8
● Barolo Fontanafredda V. La Rosa '07	🍷🍷🍷 7
● Barolo Paiagallo Casa E. di Mirafiore '12	🍷🍷🍷 7

Fortemasso

LOC. CASTELLETTO, 21
12065 MONFORTE D'ALBA [CN]
TEL. +39 0306527218
www.fortemasso.it

CELLAR SALES
ANNUAL PRODUCTION 27,000 bottles
HECTARES UNDER VINE 5.20

Everything is going according to plan for Agricole Gussalli Beretta, who've landed in Langhe with their purchase of excellent vineyards in Castelletto. Their first Barolos go back to 2013, the year they started producing, and the results are commendable. Credit is due, in part, to collaborations with local experts, proof of the group's commitment to the territory and its traditions. The intense and lively 2013 Barolo Castelletto offers up delicate notes of tobacco, which give way to hints of red fruit and incense. Overall, it proves to be a classic wine with precise finesse and impressive complexity. The palate is well-orchestrated and gradual, with a clean, lingering, characterful finish in which freshness and fruity pulp find the right balance. The lively 2015 Barbera d'Alba is elegant, dense and supple, but also rich. The 2016 Langhe Nebbiolo may still be young, but it possesses pleasant drinkability.

● Barolo Castelletto '13	♟♟ 6
● Barbera d'Alba '15	♟♟ 3
● Langhe Nebbiolo '16	♟♟ 3

Gabutti - Franco Boasso

B.TA GABUTTI, 3A
12050 SERRALUNGA D'ALBA [CN]
TEL. +39 0173613165
www.gabuttiboasso.com

CELLAR SALES
PRE-BOOKED VISITS
ACCOMMODATION
ANNUAL PRODUCTION 25,000 bottles
HECTARES UNDER VINE 7.00

The name alone communicates the inextricable link that binds the Boasso family to one of the greatest crus par excellence of Serralunga d'Alba. Seven hectares of vineyards, which include the geographical mentions of Gabutti, Meriame and Margheria, give rise to a selection that goes back to the 1960s. Theirs are 'traditional' Barolos in the best sense of the word, with recent vintages, especially, proving particularly pleasant in the mouth. To round out their selection, they offer wines made with Barbera, Dolcetto, Moscato and Arneis, all of which are also available in their cozy family agritourism. We have a splendid trio of very good Barolos from the 2013 vintage. First place goes to the Gabutti, which earns a Tre Bicchieri thanks to classic Barolo's signature pure notes, from cinchona to raspberry, blackberry and licorice. The palate displays equal power and harmony. It's a wine that's not to be missed. The Margheria exhibits just a touch of oak. Kudos to the fresh Barolo del Comune di Serralunga d'Alba.

● Barolo Gabutti '13	♟♟♟ 6
● Barolo del Comune di Serralunga d'Alba '13	♟♟ 5
● Barolo Margheria '13	♟♟ 6
● Barbera d'Alba Sup. '14	♟ 2
● Langhe Rosso Grappoli '15	♟ 3
● Barolo Margheria '05	♟♟♟ 5*
● Barbera d'Alba '12	♟♟ 2*
● Barbera d'Alba Sup. '13	♟♟ 2*
● Barolo del Comune di Serralunga d'Alba '11	♟♟ 5
● Barolo Gabutti '12	♟♟ 6
● Barolo Gabutti '11	♟♟ 6
● Barolo Gabutti '10	♟♟ 5
● Barolo Margheria '12	♟♟ 6
● Barolo Margheria '11	♟♟ 6
● Barolo Margheria '10	♟♟ 5

Gaggino

S.DA SANT'EVASIO, 29
15076 OVADA [AL]
TEL. +39 0143822345
www.gaggino.it

CELLAR SALES
PRE-BOOKED VISITS
ANNUAL PRODUCTION 150,000 bottles
HECTARES UNDER VINE 20.00

Gabriele Gaggino is one of the most respected winemakers among those who interpret Dolcetto di Ovada. The variety is difficult to transform into wine, and can only be accomplished through attentive management. His wines have demonstrated an ability to overcome the test of time, and the results in recent years have been superb. For years, Convivio has maintained very high standards, while Sant'Evasio, as of 2013, is no longer aged in wood. And so this potentially great wine can now express its secondary and tertiary aromas more freely. Dolcetto raced into the finals with two wines. This version of Convivio, a Tre Bicchieri veteran, presents mature, complex and elegant aromas, while in the mouth it proves powerful and intense. The basic Dolcetto is intense throughout all the tasting stages, but shows off its youth. Its bold palate underlines the variety's potential. Sant'Evasio has plenty of qualities, but we are waiting for the day when it will realize its full potential.

● Dolcetto di Ovada '16	♟♟ 2*
○ Ovada Convivio '15	♟♟ 3*
● Barbera del M.to La Lazzarina '15	♟♟ 2*
● Ovada Sant'Evasio '13	♟♟ 4
○ Courtesia Brut	♟ 2
○ Piemonte Bianco Pagliuzza '16	♟ 3
● Ovada Convivio '13	♟♟♟ 2*
● Barbera del M.to Lazzarina '14	♟♟ 3
● Barbera del M.to Sup. Il Ticco '11	♟♟ 3*
○ Moscato d'Asti '14	♟♟ 2*
● Ovada Convivio '14	♟♟ 3*
● Ovada S. Evasio '11	♟♟ 2*
● Ovada Sant'Evasio '12	♟♟ 4
○ Piemonte Bianco Pagliuzza '15	♟♟ 3

★★★★★Gaja

VIA TORINO, 18
12050 BARBARESCO [CN]
TEL. +39 0173635158
info@gaja.com

ANNUAL PRODUCTION 350,000 bottles
HECTARES UNDER VINE 92.00

In many ways, it was the top headline of recent months, and not just for Piedmont: Angelo Gaja would once again start offering his super Barbaresco selection. The last time it happened was in 1995, with the Langhe Nebbiolo line, world famous wines like Sorì Tildin, Sorì San Lorenzo, Costa Russi, Sperss and Conteisa. We commend the decision to get the children (Gaia, Rosanna and Giovanni) more involved. It's a step towards a changing of the guard. And, who knows, one day soon we might see the vineyards of origin prominently displayed again, from Secondine to Roncagliette, Marenca and Cerequio. A slight background of oak is still discernible in the 2014 Barbaresco Sorì Tildin. It moves between violets and cherries with grace and finesse, then shows what harmony of taste really means. Tre Bicchieri. The 2014 Barbaresco moves along the same lines, but proves slightly more tannic, while the Costa Russi is more austere. Kudos to the 2013 Barolo Conteisa, which shows how great La Morra's Cerequio cru is.

● Barbaresco Sorì Tildin '14	♟♟♟ 8
● Barbaresco '14	♟♟ 8
● Barbaresco Costa Russi '14	♟♟ 8
● Barolo Conteisa '13	♟♟ 8
● Barolo Sperss '13	♟♟ 8
● Barbaresco '09	♟♟♟ 8
● Barbaresco '08	♟♟♟ 8
● Barbaresco Costa Russi '13	♟♟♟ 8
● Langhe Nebbiolo Costa Russi '10	♟♟♟ 8
● Langhe Nebbiolo Costa Russi '08	♟♟♟ 8
● Langhe Nebbiolo Sorì Tildin '11	♟♟♟ 8
● Langhe Nebbiolo Sperss '11	♟♟♟ 8
● Barbaresco Sorì Tildin '13	♟♟ 8

Filippo Gallino

FRAZ. VALLE DEL POZZO, 63
12043 CANALE [CN]
TEL. +39 017390112
www.filippogallino.com

CELLAR SALES
PRE-BOOKED VISITS
ACCOMMODATION
ANNUAL PRODUCTION 100,000 bottles
HECTARES UNDER VINE 14.00
SUSTAINABLE WINERY

The Gallino family has been producing Barbera and Nebbiolo since the early 20th century. Today, the winery is being led by Filippo Gallino and his son, Gianni. Local grape varieties, like Arneis, Nebbiolo, Barbera and Brachetto, are grown in their vineyards, most of which surround their main facility. All of their vineyards are situated in the municipality of Canale, where the terrain is sandy clay. Their production style is characterized by tradition in the vineyards and a modern approach in the cellar. The 2015 Barbera d'Alba truly impressed. It offers up notes of black fruit and rain-soaked earth on the nose, as well as a full-bodied palate and structure. It's a succulent wine that's rich in fruit. The 2013 Barbera d'Alba Superiore Bonora also put in a good performance, with good fruit, but proves a bit less fresh and dynamic, despite good acidity that makes for a pleasant finish. The 2016 Roero Arneis has a nice tanginess to it, while the 2103 Roero Sorano Riserva comes through rather evolved, with notes of tar and licorice.

● Barbera d'Alba '15	♟♟ 2*
● Barbera d'Alba Sup. Bonora '13	♟♟ 4
○ Roero Arneis '16	♟ 2
● Roero Sorano Ris. '13	♟ 3
● Barbera d'Alba Sup. '05	♟♟♟ 4*
● Barbera d'Alba Sup. '04	♟♟♟ 4*
● Roero '06	♟♟♟ 4*
● Roero Sup. '03	♟♟♟ 3
● Barbera d'Alba Sup. '12	♟♟ 4
● Roero '12	♟♟ 4
○ Roero Arneis '15	♟♟ 2*
○ Roero Arneis '14	♟♟ 2*

Garesio

LOC. SORDO, 1
12050 SERRALUNGA D'ALBA [CN]
TEL. +39 3667076775
www.garesiovini.it

CELLAR SALES
ANNUAL PRODUCTION 35,000 bottles
HECTARES UNDER VINE 5.80
VITICULTURE METHOD Certified Organic

Passion for the land and for the work of their forefathers inspired a family of entrepreneurs, the Garesios (from Turin), to invest in the wine sector. After purchasing a 1 1/2 hectare vineyard of Barbera in the new Nizza appellation (in Incisa Scapaccino), Giovanna Gareso bought a farmstead (destined to become a cozy agritourism) and 10 hectares of terrain (4 1/2 hectares of vineyards) in Cerretta and Gianetto, famous Barolo crus in Serralunga d'Alba. After the first baby steps in Nizza, the 2013 season saw the first wines from Langhe. Garesio's Barolos don't hesitate. The Cerretta and the Barolo del Comune di Serralunga d'Alba (mainly made with grapes from Gianetto) are two 2103s that completely fulfill their promise. The first proves complex and consistent, without any unnecessary hardness, while the basic version sees more tannic austerity.

● Barolo Cerretta '13	♟♟ 7
● Barolo del Comune di Serralunga d'Alba '13	♟♟ 5
○ Geresio Pas Dosé M. Cl.	♟♟ 4
● Langhe Nebbiolo '15	♟♟ 3
● Nizza '14	♟♟ 4
● Barbera d'Asti Superiore Nizza '13	♟♟ 4
● Barbera d'Asti Superiore Nizza '12	♟♟ 4
● Barbera d'Asti Superiore Nizza '11	♟♟ 5

Generaj

ʀ. ᴛᴀ Tᴜᴄᴄɪ, 4
12046 Mᴏɴᴛᴀ̀ [CN]
Tᴇʟ. +39 0173976142
www.generaj.it

CELLAR SALES
PRE-BOOKED VISITS
ANNUAL PRODUCTION 50,000 bottles
HECTARES UNDER VINE 12.00
SUSTAINABLE WINERY

The name Generaj comes from one of Giuseppe Viglione's ancestors. Today, Giuseppe is managing the family's winery, as well its vineyards in Montà, in the northernmost part of the Roero appellation. These grow at altitudes ranging from 350 to 450 meters, in soil that varies from red sand, to calcium-rich to mixed gravel. Arneis, Barbera and Nebbiolo are the principal grapes cultivated, along with smaller quantities of Bonarda and Croatina. The 2013 Roero Bric Aût Riserva performed at truly high levels. Notes of redcurrants and wild strawberries on the nose anticipate a fresh and gutsy palate, with notable length and elegant tannins. Both the 2014 Roero Bric Aût and the 2014 Barbera d'Alba Superiore Ca' d' Pistola see more vegetal notes on the nose. The first displays hints of cinchona and a supple palate with good structure. The second offers up notes of forest floor and a palate that plays more on fruit and freshness.

● Roero Bric Aût Ris. '13	♟♟5
● Barbera d'Alba Sup. Ca' d' Pistola '14	♟♟3
● Roero Bric Aût '14	♟♟4
○ Brut M. Cl. '13	♟5
○ Roero Arneis Bric Varomaldo '16	♟2
○ Roero Arneis Quindicilune '15	♟2
● Barbera d'Alba Sup. Ca' d' Pistola '13	♟♟3*
● Barbera d'Alba Sup. Ca' d' Pistola '12	♟♟3
● Generaj Brut M. Cl. '11	♟♟5
○ Roero Arneis Quindicilune '13	♟♟3
● Roero Bric Aût '13	♟♟4
● Roero Bric Aût '12	♟♟4
● Roero Bric Aût Ris. '12	♟♟5

★Ettore Germano

ʟᴏᴄ. Cᴇʀʀᴇᴛᴛᴀ, 1
12050 Sᴇʀʀᴀʟᴜɴɢᴀ ᴅ'Aʟʙᴀ [CN]
Tᴇʟ. +39 0173613528
www.germanoettore.com

CELLAR SALES
PRE-BOOKED VISITS
ACCOMMODATION
ANNUAL PRODUCTION 90,000 bottles
HECTARES UNDER VINE 16.00

Sergio Germano has pulled off a real hat trick over the last decade, thanks to one of the best selections in Langhe in terms of quantity and variety. The determined Serralunga vine grower shines, both for his Barolos (Cerretta, Prapò, Lazzarito Riserva, and Vignarionda in the wings), and for his sparklers (made with Riesling, Sauvignon, Chardonnay and Pinot Nero), all cultivated on his estate in Aglié, in Alta Langhe. It's an accomplishment that he's managed through admirable humility and a desire to challenge himself, especially in the cellar. Here he works on the quality of extraction and delicacy of fermentation. The 2011 Barolo Lazzarito Riserva's taste progression is enchanting. It exhibits the perfect fusion of structural power and formal style. Aromas of cherry and strawberry open on a veil of oak and spices, with extreme elegance and complexity. Tre Bicchieri. The 2013 Barolo del Comune di Serralunga d'Alba '13 also did well and comes through fresher and slightly more tannic. The 2013 Barbera d'Alba della Madre, meanwhile, deserves praise for its richness.

● Barolo Lazzarito Ris. '11	♟♟♟8
● Barbera d'Alba Sup. V. della Madre '13	♟♟5
● Barolo Cerretta '13	♟♟7
● Barolo del Comune di Serralunga d'Alba '13	♟♟6
○ Langhe Riesling Hérzu '15	♟♟4
○ Alta Langa Brut '13	♟♟5
● Barolo Prapò '13	♟♟7
○ Langhe Bianco Binel '15	♟♟3
○ Langhe Nascetta '15	♟♟3
● Barolo Lazzarito Ris. '10	♟♟♟8
● Barolo Lazzarito Ris. '08	♟♟♟8
● Barolo Prapò '11	♟♟♟7
○ Langhe Bianco Hérzu '11	♟♟♟4*
○ Langhe Bianco Hérzu '10	♟♟♟4*
○ Langhe Bianco Hérzu '09	♟♟♟5

La Ghibellina

FRAZ. MONTEROTONDO, 61
15066 GAVI [AL]
TEL. +39 0143686257
www.laghibellina.it

CELLAR SALES
PRE-BOOKED VISITS
RESTAURANT SERVICE
ANNUAL PRODUCTION 60,000 bottles
HECTARES UNDER VINE 17.00

This small winery, founded in 2000 by Alberto and Marina Ghibellina, can be found in the Monterotondo district of Gavi. The name Monterotondo turns up regularly when it comes to talking about the most prominent crus in the appellation, in terms of force and richness of flavor. Their estate comprises just under eight hectares of vineyards (on a total of 20 hectares of land), where common local varieties are grown. Cortese takes center stage, the variety used for their sparklers ('Metodo Classico' and Cuvée Marina), for their Gavi Mainìn (aged in steel) and for the Altius line, which are partially matured in barriques. Rounding out their selection are their Chiaretto Sandrino and Monferrato Rosso Nero del Montone, two Barbera monovarietals, and Pituj, a blend with Merlot. The favorable 2016 vintage brings us one of the best ever Gavi Mainìns. It's a classic (to say the least). Notes of white fruit, medicinal herbs and fresh almonds unfold on the palate with measure and length, finding further zest and tanginess in its long finish. The 2015 Altius proves larger and more mature.

○ Gavi del Comune di Gavi Mainìn '16	♥♥ 3*
○ Gavi del Comune di Gavi Brut M. Cl. Cuvée Marina '12	♥♥ 5
○ Gavi del Comune di Gavi Altius '15	♥ 5
○ Gavi del Comune di Gavi Brut M. Cl. '14	♥ 4
● M.to Rosso Pituj '15	♥ 4
○ Gavi del Comune di Gavi Altius '14	♀♀ 5
○ Gavi del Comune di Gavi Altius '13	♀♀ 3*
○ Gavi del Comune di Gavi Brut M. Cl. Cuvée Marina '11	♀♀ 7
○ Gavi del Comune di Gavi Mainìn '15	♀♀ 3*
○ Gavi del Comune di Gavi Mainìn '14	♀♀ 3*
● M.to Rosso Pituj '13	♀♀ 3
● M.to Rosso Pituj '12	♀♀ 3

★★Bruno Giacosa

VIA XX SETTEMBRE, 52
12057 NEIVE [CN]
TEL. +39 017367027
www.brunogiacosa.it

ANNUAL PRODUCTION 300,000 bottles
HECTARES UNDER VINE 19.00
SUSTAINABLE WINERY

The Giacosas' choice to highlight the distinction between wines produced using their own grapes, and those made with grapes from local growers, demonstrates a respect for the territory and production roles. After all, the legendary Bruno Giacosa knows better than anyone what it takes to compete with the great figures interpreting Langhe's wines today. Before taking over decades-old plots in Asili (in Barbaresco), Falletto (in Serralunga) and Croera (in La Morra) he was a négociant. His daughter, Bruna, has been at his side for some time, helping produce their white and red wines, with Nebbiolos that are a universal symbol of smoothness and staying power. When talking of Barolo's classic style, a reference to Bruno Giacosa is unavoidable, as this splendid, delicate and charming 2011 Falletto Vigna Le Rocche Riserva demonstrates. Pale in color, it isn't too muscular, with aromas moving discreetly between licorice, raspberries and raisins. It comes through majestic and elegant on a slow palate of silky tannins, with a lively touch of freshness.

● Barolo Falletto V. Le Rocche Ris. '11	♥♥♥ 8
● Barbaresco Rabajà '13	♥♥ 8
● Barolo Falletto V. Le Rocche '13	♥♥ 8
● Nebbiolo d'Alba V. Valmaggiore '15	♥♥ 6
○ Roero Arneis '16	♥♥ 4
● Barbaresco Asili '12	♀♀ 8
● Barbaresco Asili '05	♀♀ 8
● Barbaresco Asili Ris. '11	♀♀ 8
● Barbaresco Asili Ris. '07	♀♀ 8
● Barolo Falletto '07	♀♀ 8
● Barolo Le Rocche del Falletto '05	♀♀ 8
● Barolo Le Rocche del Falletto '04	♀♀ 8
● Barolo Le Rocche del Falletto Ris. '08	♀♀ 8
● Barolo Le Rocche del Falletto Ris. '07	♀♀ 8

Carlo Giacosa

S.DA OVELLO, 9
12050 BARBARESCO [CN]
TEL. +39 0173635116
www.carlogiacosa.it

CELLAR SALES
PRE-BOOKED VISITS
ANNUAL PRODUCTION 42,000 bottles
HECTARES UNDER VINE 5.50

Maria Grazia Giacosa's small winery was founded by her father, Carlo. Today she leads it with passion and skill, finding fame thanks to her simple, clean wines that are never too robust or dominated by wood. In the wake of this success, she offers three Barbarescos: one from their prestigious Montefico cru; the Narin is made from grapes from their Asili, Cole and Ovello vineyards; and, finally, their 'Riserva Luca' (released only on occasion). The rest of their selection is consistently accurate and pleasing, from the simple and fresh Barbera d'Alba Mucin to the fragrant Langhe Nebbiolo Maria Grazia. The Barbaresco is an excellent interpretation of the difficult 2014 vintage. The Montefico offers up lovely fruity notes on the nose, while the palate lacks structure but displays great balance. The very pleasant Narin exhibits more herbaceous notes though the palate remains more biting for the moment. The robust Langhe Nebbiolo Maria Grazia proves delicately fruity, while the 2015 Barbera d'Alba Lina shows great drinkability. Their prices are a big plus.

● Barbaresco Montefico '14	♟♟	5
● Barbaresco Narin '14	♟♟	5
● Barbera d'Alba Mucin '16	♟♟	3
● Barbera d'Alba Sup. Lina '15	♟♟	3
● Langhe Nebbiolo Maria Grazia '15	♟♟	4
○ Dolcetto d'Alba Cuchet '16	♟	3
● Barbaresco Montefico '08	♟♟♟	5*
● Barbaresco Luca Ris. '10	♟♟	6
● Barbaresco Luca Ris. '09	♟♟	6
● Barbaresco Montefico '13	♟♟	5
● Barbaresco Montefico '12	♟♟	5
● Barbaresco Montefico '11	♟♟	5
● Barbaresco Narin '12	♟♟	5
● Barbaresco Narin '11	♟♟	5
● Barbera d'Alba Mucin '15	♟♟	3
● Barbera d'Alba Mucin '14	♟♟	3
● Langhe Nebbiolo Maria Grazia '14	♟♟	3

F.lli Giacosa

VIA XX SETTEMBRE, 64
12052 NEIVE [CN]
TEL. +39 017367013
www.giacosa.it

CELLAR SALES
PRE-BOOKED VISITS
ANNUAL PRODUCTION 500,000 bottles
HECTARES UNDER VINE 50.00
VITICULTURE METHOD Certified Organic
SUSTAINABLE WINERY

The roots of Maurizio and Paolo Giacosa's winery go back to the late 1800s, with the purchase and resale of grapes from Langhe's local growers. Soon enough, their knowledge of the territory gave way to the decision to vinify the best crop. Over the years, the Giacosa family decided to purchase their own vineyards, which today comprise areas in Castiglione Falletto, Monforte and Neive. The winey has adopted an approach centered on energy independence and organic agriculture. The 2014 Barbaresco Basarin Vigna Gianmatè exhibits textbook harmony, with an elegant nose of small fruit and licorice. The mouth proves fresh, caressing and delicate at the same time. Toasty and smoky overtones of wood stand out in the firmly structured 2014 Barbera d'Alba Maria Gioana. The 2012 Barolo Scarrone Vigna Mandorlo features a modern style, with clear sweet spices, tobacco and resin, while an austere palate shows good tannins. The 2013 Barolo Bussia has pleasant notes of tar and medium body.

● Barbaresco Basarin V. Gianmatè '14	♟♟	7
● Barbera d'Alba Maria Gioana '14	♟♟	5
● Barolo Bussia '13	♟♟	7
● Barolo Scarrone V. Mandorlo '12	♟♟	8
● Barbera d'Alba Madonna Como '14	♟	3
○ Langhe Chardonnay Rorea '16	♟	4
● Barbaresco Basarin V. Gianmatè '12	♟♟	6
● Barbaresco Basarin V. Gianmatè '11	♟♟	6
● Barbera d'Alba Maria Gioana '13	♟♟	5
● Barbera d'Alba Maria Gioana '12	♟♟	5
● Barbera d'Alba Maria Gioana '11	♟♟	4
● Barolo Bussia '12	♟♟	7
● Barolo Bussia '11	♟♟	6
● Barolo Scarrone V. Mandorlo '11	♟♟	8
● Barolo Scarrone V. Mandorlo '10	♟♟	7

Giovanni Battista Gillardi

CASCINA CORSALETTO, 69
12060 FARIGLIANO [CN]
TEL. +39 017376306
www.gillardi.it

CELLAR SALES
PRE-BOOKED VISITS
ANNUAL PRODUCTION 35,000 bottles
HECTARES UNDER VINE 7.00

Giovanni Battista Gillardi is one of the great figures to have interpreted Dolcetto di Dogliani, mostly thanks to his skill as a vine grower. He began in 1980, and was soon flanked by his son, Giacolino, who leads Gillardi today and has already left an innovative mark on the winery. First there were the French vineyards, mostly Syrah but also Cabernet Sauvignon, Merlot and a touch of Grenache. Then there was the purchase of a vineyard and a small cellar in Barolo, which has been active since 2011. But Dogliani is still their beating heart, starting with their consistently first-rate Cursalet selection. The 2013 Barolo del Comune di Barolo remains youthful and still a bit woody. The Vignane, on the other hand, displays a classic style and already proves well-orchestrated and elegant. Gillardi's new Barolo wine is named after this cru. The 2016 Dogliani Cursalet is powerful and multi-faceted, with excellent roundness and elegance. The remarkable Maestra comes through more austere and slightly less velvety.

● Barolo Vignane '13	▼▼ 6
● Dogliani Cursalet '16	▼▼ 3*
● Langhe Harys '15	▼▼ 7
● Barolo del Comune di Barolo '13	▼▼ 4
● Dogliani Maestra '16	▼▼ 3
● Dogliani Cursalet '11	▼▼▼ 3*
● Barolo '12	♀♀ 6
● Barolo del Comune di Barolo '11	♀♀ 3*
● Dogliani Cursalet '15	♀♀ 3*
● Dogliani Maestra '15	♀♀ 3
● Langhe Harys '14	♀♀ 7
● Langhe Harys '13	♀♀ 6
● Langhe Ilmerlò '13	♀♀ 8
● Langhe Nebbiolo '14	♀♀ 4
● Langhe Nebbiolo '13	♀♀ 6

La Gironda

S.DA BRICCO, 12
14049 NIZZA MONFERRATO [AT]
TEL. +39 0141701013
www.lagironda.com

CELLAR SALES
PRE-BOOKED VISITS
ANNUAL PRODUCTION 60,000 bottles
HECTARES UNDER VINE 9.00
SUSTAINABLE WINERY

Gironda was founded by Agostino Galandrino, who recently left us. Today the winery is managed by his daughter, Susanna, and her husband, Alberto Adamo. It's situated on the Bricco Cremosina, one of Nizza Monferrato's most well-known crus. Most of their vineyards host Barbera (which is only fitting in an area so well-suited to the grape), but there are lesser quantities of Cortese, Dolcetto, Moscatto, Nebbiolo and international varieties as well. The 2015 Barolo del Comune di Barolo truly won us over. Aromas of ripe wild berries, pepper and Mediterranean scrub pave the way for a palate that's characteristic of a bold red, with good body and a long, well-orchestrated finish. The 2014 Monferrato Rosso Soul, on the other hand, is one of the few high-level Nebbiolos to be found in Asti. Notes of raspberries, tobacco and licorice give way to a palate with good acidity and plenty of pulp to balance its tannins. The rest of the selection presented is well-made.

● Barbera d'Asti La Gena '15	▼▼ 3*
● M.to Rosso Soul '14	▼▼ 5
● Barbera d'Asti La Lippa '16	▼▼ 2*
○ Moscato d'Asti '16	▼▼ 2*
● Nizza La Gironda '14	▼▼ 5
○ Piemonte Sauvignon L'Aquilone '16	▼ 3
● Barbera d'Asti Sup. Nizza Le Nicchie '11	♀♀♀ 5
● Barbera d'Asti La Gena '14	♀♀ 3
● Barbera d'Asti La Lippa '15	♀♀ 2*
● Barbera d'Asti Sup. Nizza Le Nicchie '13	♀♀ 5
● Barbera d'Asti Sup. Nizza Le Nicchie '12	♀♀ 5
● M.to Rosso Soul '12	♀♀ 5
○ Piemonte Sauvignon L'Aquilone '15	♀♀ 2*

Tenuta La Giustiniana

FRAZ. ROVERETO, 5
15066 GAVI [AL]
TEL. +39 0143682132
www.lagiustiniana.it

CELLAR SALES
PRE-BOOKED VISITS
ANNUAL PRODUCTION 200,000 bottles
HECTARES UNDER VINE 39.00

Abbazzia di Rivalta Scrivia is an ex-farmstead that, once upon a time, important Genovese families fought over. It was purchased by the Giustinianis in the early 1600s, and so it is that we have the name by which it is known today. Here, in the district of Rovereto (in Gavi), the Lombardini family have established their base over the years, thanks in part to the help of Enrico Tomalino. Their 40 hectares of organically cultivated vineyards are dedicated principally to Cortese and give rise to a range of white wines. The estate comprises bona fide crus like Lugara (grey marl) and Montessora (red clay). Terre Antiche di Giustiniani and Nostro Gavi (which is also aged in Inox) also form part of their selection. The differences in soil and climate between Gavi's two best areas come out in their 2016s. The Lugarara combines fruity brightness with woodland fullness, then unfolds supple on the palate. The Montessora sees the addition of lively taste, contrasted by lovely earthy touches.

○ Gavi del Comune di Gavi Lugarara '16	♟♟	3*
○ Gavi del Comune di Gavi Montessora '16	♟♟	4
○ Gavi del Comune di Gavi Il Nostro Gavi '07	♟♟♟	4
○ Gavi del Comune di Gavi Il Nostro Gavi '12	♟♟	4
○ Gavi del Comune di Gavi Il Nostro Gavi '10	♟♟	4
○ Gavi del Comune di Gavi Lugarara '15	♟♟	3
○ Gavi del Comune di Gavi Lugarara '14	♟♟	3
○ Gavi del Comune di Gavi Lugarara '13	♟♟	3*
○ Gavi del Comune di Gavi Montessora '15	♟♟	4
○ Gavi del Comune di Gavi Montessora '14	♟♟	4
○ Gavi del Comune di Gavi Montessora '13	♟♟	4

★Elio Grasso

LOC. GINESTRA, 40
12065 MONFORTE D'ALBA [CN]
TEL. +39 017378491
www.eliograsso.it

PRE-BOOKED VISITS
ANNUAL PRODUCTION 90,000 bottles
HECTARES UNDER VINE 18.00
SUSTAINABLE WINERY

Since the late 1960s, Elio Grasso's Nebbiolos have, with good reason, been considered perennial models of style in Langhe's diverse wine scene. His success can be traced back to a vision that goes beyond categorical thinking, even during the most intense periods of debate between tradition and innovation. At the center of it all are his superb vineyards in Monforte d'Alba for his Nebbiolos (Ginestra Case Matè, Gavarini Chiniera, Rüncot). Despite varying approaches to aging (2500 liter Slavonian oak for their vintage Barolos, barriques for their 'Riserva'), these are tied together by their density and verve. Only Barolos were in our tastings this year. The splendid 2011 Riserva Rüncot saw the best fusion, that we can remember, of aging wood and fresh, fruity notes common to this area. In the mouth, its rich pulp is magnificently contrasted by tannins. The elegant 2013 Gavarini Chiniera proves less rich, while the Ginestra Casa Maté exhibits a refined spiciness.

● Barolo Ginestra Casa Maté '13	♟♟	8
● Barolo Rüncot Ris. '11	♟♟	8
● Barolo Gavarini Chiniera '13	♟♟	8
● Barolo Gavarini Chiniera '09	♟♟♟	8
● Barolo Gavarini V. Chiniera '06	♟♟♟	8
● Barolo Ginestra Casa Maté '12	♟♟♟	8
● Barolo Ginestra Casa Maté '07	♟♟♟	8
● Barolo Ginestra V. Casa Maté '05	♟♟♟	8
● Barbera d'Alba V. Martina '13	♟♟	5
● Barbera d'Alba V. Martina '12	♟♟	5
● Barolo Gavarini Chiniera '12	♟♟	8
● Barolo Gavarini Chiniera '11	♟♟	8
● Barolo Ginestra Casa Maté '11	♟♟	8
● Langhe Nebbiolo Gavarini '13	♟♟	3

Silvio Grasso

FRAZ. ANNUNZIATA, 112
12064 LA MORRA [CN]
TEL. +39 017350322
www.silviograsso.com

CELLAR SALES
PRE-BOOKED VISITS
ANNUAL PRODUCTION 90,000 bottles
HECTARES UNDER VINE 14.00

Federico Grasso, his wife, Marilena Pedassa, and their children, Paolo and Silvio have put together a selection of six Barolos. Some of these clearly speak a more 'modern' language, like the noted Bricco Manzoni and Bricco Luciani (both aged in small French wood), while others (especially the Turné), are made with long maceration and aging in Slavonian oak. All their wines, with the small exception of their international wines, L'Insieme and Langhe Rosso, are made with local Langhe grapes: Nebbiolo, Barbera (used for their prized Fontanile) and Dolcetto. The 2013 Barolo Bricco Manzoni features great personality, a precise forthright nose and notable freshness on the palate. The 2013 Barolo Turné displays lively notes of licorice and youthful red fruit, with a rich rather than elegant taste. The 2013 Annunziata Vigna Plicotti cru exhibits noticeable spices, while the 2013 Barolo is good, but a bit mouth-drying, with clearly perceptible oak and catmint.

● Barolo Bricco Manzoni '13	♟♟ 8
● Barolo Turné '13	♟♟ 7
● Barbera d'Alba '15	♟♟ 3
● Barolo '13	♟♟ 5
● Barolo Annunziata V. Plicotti '13	♟♟ 7
● Barolo Bricco Luciani '13	♟ 7
● Barolo Bricco Luciani '04	♟♟♟ 7
● Barolo Bricco Luciani '01	♟♟♟ 6
● Barolo Bricco Luciani '96	♟♟♟ 6
● Barolo Bricco Luciani '95	♟♟♟ 6
● Barolo Bricco Luciani '90	♟♟♟ 6
● Barolo Bricco Manzoni '10	♟♟♟ 7
● Barolo Bricco Luciani '12	♟♟ 7
● Barolo Bricco Luciani '11	♟♟ 7
● Barolo Bricco Manzoni '11	♟♟ 7
● Barolo Turne' '12	♟♟ 7

Bruna Grimaldi

VIA PAREA, 7
12060 GRINZANE CAVOUR [CN]
TEL. +39 0173262094
www.grimaldibruna.it

CELLAR SALES
PRE-BOOKED VISITS
ANNUAL PRODUCTION 70,000 bottles
HECTARES UNDER VINE 14.00

The small vineyard of Badarina can be found in Serralunga d'Alba. At an altitude of 400 meters, the position guarantees cool temperatures and plenty of air for the grapes. Here, Bruna Grimaldi, her husband, Franco Fiorino, and their increasingly helpful son, Simone, forge their crown jewel, Barolo Badarina (during the best vintages, the wine is also available as a 'Riserva'). Their Barolo Camilla and Bricco Ambrogio are certainly interesting wines as well, the former from a vineyard in Grinzane Cavour and the latter from a cheerful plot in Roddi d'Alba. Their wines are expressive and alive, in the classical Langhe tradition. The 2013 Barolo Badarina features a dense and firm structure, with an excellent forthright nose. It remains a bit rigid on the palate and needs further aging, but already offers up stimulating hints of red flowers and licorice. The mature 2011 Riserva is superb, with intense and caressing fruit. The elegant 2015 Nebbiolo d'Alba slightly lacks richness, while the 2014 Barbera d'Alba Scassa shows moderate body and good freshness.

● Barolo Badarina '13	♟♟ 6
● Barolo Badarina Ris. '11	♟♟ 7
● Barbera d'Alba Sup. Scassa '14	♟♟ 3
● Barolo Bricco Ambrogio '13	♟♟ 5
● Barolo Camilla '13	♟♟ 5
● Nebbiolo d'Alba '15	♟♟ 3
● Barbera d'Alba Sup. Scassa '13	♟♟ 3
● Barolo Badarina '12	♟♟ 6
● Barolo Badarina '11	♟♟ 6
● Barolo Badarina '10	♟♟ 6
● Barolo Badarina Ris. '10	♟♟ 7
● Barolo Badarina Ris. '09	♟♟ 6
● Barolo Bricco Ambrogio '12	♟♟ 5
● Barolo Bricco Ambrogio '11	♟♟ 5
● Barolo Bricco Ambrogio '10	♟♟ 5
● Barolo Camilla '12	♟♟ 5
● Barolo Camilla '11	♟♟ 5

Giacomo Grimaldi

VIA LUIGI EINAUDI, 8
12060 BAROLO [CN]
TEL. +39 0173560536
www.giacomogrimaldi.com

CELLAR SALES
PRE-BOOKED VISITS
ANNUAL PRODUCTION 50,000 bottles
HECTARES UNDER VINE 13.00

Ferruccio Grimaldi is an expert both in the vineyard and the cellar. And it's for this reason that, over the years, he alone has managed and developed his selection of wines. The most interesting news concerns the release of the Nebbiolo d'Alba Valmaggiore, from the splendid Roero cru. But just as newsworthy is their completion of an operational underground cellar (perfect for aging). The winery's core production focuses on Barolo, whose grapes are cultivated in their lovely crus of Le Coste and Sotto Castello di Novello, and is available in three versions. There were only two Barolos in the tasting this year, both very high-level. The difference mainly lies in the perception of wood. In the 2013 Le Coste it's more discernible, with rich spices and a touch of vanilla. The 2013 Sotto Castello di Novello, on the other hand, proves more subtle, with fruit dominating. The palate also picks up on this different style: the first enters velvety and charming, with a slightly drying finish, while the lovely balance of the second is characterized by rich and dense pulp.

● Barolo Le Coste '13	♟♟	7
● Barolo Sotto Castello di Novello '13	♟♟	6
● Barolo '13	♟♟	6
● Barolo Sotto Castello di Novello '05	♟♟♟	6
● Barbera d'Alba Fornaci '12	♟♟	4
● Barbera d'Alba Pistin '15	♟♟	3
● Barbera d'Alba Pistin '14	♟♟	3
● Barolo '12	♟♟	6
● Barolo '11	♟♟	6
● Barolo Le Coste '12	♟♟	7
● Barolo Le Coste '11	♟♟	7
● Barolo Le Coste '10	♟♟	6
● Barolo Sotto Castello di Novello '12	♟♟	6
● Barolo Sotto Castello di Novello '11	♟♟	6
● Dolcetto d'Alba '14	♟♟	2*

Sergio Grimaldi
Ca' du Sindic

LOC. SAN GRATO, 15
12058 SANTO STEFANO BELBO [CN]
TEL. +39 0141840341
www.cadusindic.it

CELLAR SALES
PRE-BOOKED VISITS
ANNUAL PRODUCTION 100,000 bottles
HECTARES UNDER VINE 17.00
SUSTAINABLE WINERY

Situated on the hill of San Grato (in Santo Stefano Belbo), amidst some of the most well-known and well-suited terrain for Moscato d'Asti, the Grimaldi family's winery is a benchmark for the wine. In addition to the vineyards surrounding their main facility, the estate spans areas along the hills of San Maurizio, Bauda and Moncucco (all of which fall within the municipality of Santo Stefano Belbo). Their vineyards feature Moscato, which is accompanied by Pinot Nero and Chardonnay (for their sparkling wines), Dolcetto, Barbera and Brachetto. This year we particularly enjoyed the 2016 Moscato d'Asti Vigna Moncucco. Rich fruit merges with floral notes; the wine shows balance and freshness, but also good density and sweetness. The rest of the selection proves well-made, from the gutsy and spicy 2015 Barbera d'Asti San Grato, to the 2016 Moscato d'Asti Capsula Oro Ca' du Sindic, with its hints of mulberries and great generosity on the palate. The 2016 Moscato d'Asti Capsula Argento, meanwhile, comes through more supple, playing more on the aromatic component.

○ Moscato d'Asti V. Moncucco '16	♟♟	3*
● Barbera d'Asti San Grato '15	♟♟	2*
○ Moscato d'Asti Ca' du Sindic Capsula Oro '16	♟♟	3
○ Moscato d'Asti Capsula Argento '16	♟♟	3
○ Ventuno Brut '15	♟	3
⊙ Ventuno Brut Rosé '15	♟	3
● Dolcetto d'Alba '15	♟♟	2*
○ Moscato d'Asti '14	♟♟	2*
○ Moscato d'Asti Ca' du Sindic '15	♟♟	3*
○ Moscato d'Asti Ca' du Sindic '14	♟♟	3
○ Moscato d'Asti Ca' du Sindic '13	♟♟	3
○ Moscato d'Asti V. Moncucco '15	♟♟	3*
○ Ventuno Brut '14	♟♟	3

★Hilberg - Pasquero

VIA BRICCO GATTI, 16
12040 PRIOCCA [CN]
TEL. +39 0173616197
www.hilberg-pasquero.com

CELLAR SALES
PRE-BOOKED VISITS
ANNUAL PRODUCTION 24,000 bottles
HECTARES UNDER VINE 6.50
VITICULTURE METHOD Certified Organic

Miclo Pasquero and Annette Hilberg's more than 20-year partnership led them to realize a winery on Bricco Gatti (a hill overlooking Priocca). They've adopted an approach that's both traditional and alternative, and today the producer is one of Roero's most notable. Their vineyards (in Monteforche and Bricco Stella, in addition to those around their cellar) grow in white, silty and marl terrain, and only local, red grapes are cultivated: Barbera, Brachetto and Nebbiolo. The 2014 Nebbiolo d'Alba Superiore did particularly well. It offers up smoky and vanilla fragrances that marry well with notes of red fruit and licorice. The palate proves balanced without excessive tannins or acidity. The wine closes with a nice long finish. The 2015 Nebbiolo d'Alba Sul Monte is well-made, more structured and juicy, but its tannins display notable elegance. The 2016 Vareij is a blend of Brachetto (70%) and Barbera, featuring signature aromas of roses and a fresh palate with good acidity.

● Nebbiolo d'Alba Sup. '14	♥♥ 5
● Nebbiolo d'Alba Sul Monte '15	♥♥ 5
● Vareij '16	♥♥ 3
● Barbera d'Alba Stella '16	♥ 3
● Barbera d'Alba Sup. '09	♥♥♥ 5
● Nebbiolo d'Alba '06	♥♥♥ 5
● Nebbiolo d'Alba '05	♥♥♥ 5
● Nebbiolo d'Alba '04	♥♥♥ 5
● Nebbiolo d'Alba '03	♥♥♥ 5
● Nebbiolo d'Alba '01	♥♥♥ 5
● Barbera d'Alba '15	♥♥ 3*
● Barbera d'Alba Sup. '14	♥♥ 5
● Vareij Rosso	♥♥ 3

Icardi

LOC. SAN LAZZARO
S.DA COMUNALE BALBI, 30
12053 CASTIGLIONE TINELLA [CN]
TEL. +39 0141855159
www.icardivini.it

CELLAR SALES
PRE-BOOKED VISITS
ANNUAL PRODUCTION 360,000 bottles
HECTARES UNDER VINE 75.00
VITICULTURE METHOD Certified Biodynamic

Claudio Icardi isn't an organic/biodynamic extremist, though he still advocated for these methods. And it's not just about respecting the environment, he believes they result in more lively grapes and wines with more personality. His vast estate, which spans Langhe and Monferrato, gives rise to numerous products that testify well to an approach based on natural, wholesome methods. This doesn't mean that he's not attentive in the cellar or afraid to use wood of various dimensions and types. It's definitely worth a visit. The 2013 Barolo Parej features a modern style. It's refined, slightly balsamic and lightly marked by wood, with a juicy mouth. The 2014 Barbaresco Montubert shows a moderate structure and alcohol component, which are understandable given the lower power of the vintage. It presents an overall forthright and enjoyable drinkability, playing on pleasant fruity scents. A commendable overall result.

● Barbaresco Montubert '14	♥♥ 5
● Barbera d'Alba Surì di Mù '15	♥♥ 5
● Barbera d'Asti Nuj Suj '15	♥♥ 5
● Barolo Parej '13	♥♥ 8
● Langhe Rosso Dadelio Cascina San Lazzaro '15	♥♥ 5
● Langhe Rosso Pafoj '15	♥♥ 6
○ Piemonte Bianco Pafoj '16	♥♥ 4
○ Dadelio Bianco Cascina San Lazzaro '16	♥ 5
● Langhe Nebbiolo Surìsjvan '15	♥ 4
● Barbaresco Montubert '13	♥♥ 5
● Barbaresco Montubert '12	♥♥ 5
● Barbera d'Asti Sup. Nuj Suj '14	♥♥ 5
● Barolo Parej '12	♥♥ 8
● Barolo Parej '11	♥♥ 8

Ioppa

FRAZ. MAULETTA
VIA DELLE PALLOTTE, 10
28078 ROMAGNANO SESIA [NO]
TEL. +39 0163833079
www.viniioppa.it

CELLAR SALES
PRE-BOOKED VISITS
ANNUAL PRODUCTION 140,000 bottles
HECTARES UNDER VINE 20.50

After the tragic death of Gianpiero Ioppa, his brother, Giorgio, is carrying on with the help of the seventh generation of family (Andrea, Marco and Luca). The winery has been working its way up the ladder among the territory's producers, especially in recent seasons, though its roots go all the way back to the mid-1800s. The estate comprises more than 20 hectares of vineyards in Romagnano Sesia and Ghemme, most of them reserved for Nebbiolo. The cultivar finds a clear, modern voice in their three Ghemmes (base, Bricco Balsina and Santa Fè). There are also interesting versions of Erbaluca, Uva Rara and Vespolina, which is also produced as a passito dried-grape wine (their Stransì). We found several options at all different levels in the Ioppa family's selection. For example, the fresh and multi-faceted 2014 Colline Novaresi Nebbiolo or the sweetly spicy 2012 Ghemme Balsina, whose potential hasn't been fully expressed yet. Among their Vespolinas, we came across the tasty 2013 Coda Rossa and the more intense 2012.

● Colline Novaresi Vespolina '12	🍷🍷 3*
● Ghemme Balsina '12	🍷🍷 6
● Colline Novaresi Nebbiolo '14	🍷🍷 2*
⊙ Colline Novaresi Nebbiolo Rusin '16	🍷🍷 2*
● Colline Novaresi Vespolina Coda Rossa '13	🍷🍷 3
● Ghemme '12	🍷🍷 4
● Ghemme Santa Fé '12	🍷🍷 6
○ San Grato Bianco	🍷🍷 2
● Colline Novaresi Vespolina '11	🏆🏆 3*
● Ghemme '11	🏆🏆 4
● Ghemme Bricco Balsina '11	🏆🏆 6
● Ghemme Santa Fé '11	🏆🏆 6

Isolabella della Croce

REG. CAFFI, 3
14051 LOAZZOLO [AT]
TEL. +39 014487166
www.isolabelladellacroce.it

CELLAR SALES
PRE-BOOKED VISITS
ANNUAL PRODUCTION 90,000 bottles
HECTARES UNDER VINE 14.00

In 2001, the Isolabella della Croce family created this small winery in the heart of Alta Langa Astigiana (in the Loazzolo DOC zone). The estate is situated in a splendid natural amphitheater, at more than 500 meters above sea level, and features both native and international grapes (so as to get the most from the territory), from Moscato to Chardonnay and Pinot Nero. The cellar also has plots in Calamandra, in Nizza, where only Barbera is cultivated. The 2013 Piemonte Pinot Nero Bricco del Falco might just be the best version ever. The variety's signature aromas emerge (blueberry and raspberry), accompanied by balsamic hints. Its juicy palate displays great structure and tight-knit fruit. The 2015 Piemonte Chardonnay Solum also proves very interesting, with toasty, spicy and fruity notes. It's elegant and balanced, thanks to a marked acidity that adds unexpected length and freshness.

○ Piemonte Chardonnay Solum '15	🍷🍷 4
● Piemonte Pinot Nero Bricco del Falco '13	🍷🍷 5
● Barbera d'Asti Sup. Nizza Augusta '13	🍷🍷 5
● Barbera d'Asti Sup. Serena '14	🍷🍷 4
○ Piemonte Sauvignon Blanc '16	🍷🍷 3
○ Moscato d'Asti Valdiserre '16	🍷 3
● Barbera d'Asti Sup. Nizza Augusta '12	🏆🏆 5
● Barbera d'Asti Sup. Serena '13	🏆🏆 4
● Barbera d'Asti Sup. Serena '12	🏆🏆 4
○ Moscato d'Asti Valdiserre '15	🏆🏆 3
○ Moscato d'Asti Valdiserre '14	🏆🏆 3
● Piemonte Pinot Nero Bricco del Falco '12	🏆🏆 5
○ Piemonte Sauvignon Blanc '14	🏆🏆 3

Iuli

FRAZ. MONTALDO
VIA CENTRALE, 27
15020 CERKINA MONFERRATO [AL]
TEL. +39 0142946657
www.iuli.it

CELLAR SALES
PRE-BOOKED VISITS
ANNUAL PRODUCTION 50,000 bottles
HECTARES UNDER VINE 13.50
VITICULTURE METHOD Certified Organic

Iuli has reached the heights of excellence, yet every year it continues to surprise us with the force and polish of its wines. Taken in combination with a notable longevity, their entire production is extremely interesting for wine lovers. Moreover, even if they specialize in Barbera, their Nebbiolo (Malidea) is a valid interpretation, as is their Pino Nero (Nino). Barbera is their flagship wine. It's an intense Rossore, with fresh and charming fruit, which lengthens into a fresh, well-orchestrated palate, with a lingering finish. The La Rina is on its first release. It's made with Slarina, a native grape included in Count Nuvolone's census in the late eighteenth century. It's being developed thanks to modern winemaking techniques and Fabrizio Iuli's experiments. This first version features a nice suite of aromas and good drinkability.

Tenuta Langasco

FRAZ. MADONNA DI COMO, 10
12051 ALBA [CN]
TEL. +39 0173286972
www.tenutalangasco.it

CELLAR SALES
PRE-BOOKED VISITS
ANNUAL PRODUCTION 60,000 bottles
HECTARES UNDER VINE 22.00

Ugo Lequio is among Barbaresco's most consistent winemakers. Over 30 years, he has perfected his special feeling with Gallina, one of the most noble crus in Neive. His wines, which are available in both a base and 'Riserva' version, feature long maceration and aging in mid-size oak. But such technical details don't capture the vibrant and almost lush temperament of his wines, which is only favored with age. The selection is rounded out by wines made with Barbera, Dolcetto and Arneis, provided by local vine growers. The 2016 Dolcetto d'Alba Vigna Miclet affirms its status as a benchmark for the category. It reveals notes of ripe cherry and plums, supported by an elegant tannic texture. The Nebbiolo d'Alba Sorì Coppa comes through spicy and slightly balsamic on the nose. It expands into a fresh palate playing on the right balance between tannin and acidity. The Barbera, made with grapes grown in Vigna Madonna di Como, remains a bit withdrawn. It needs further bottle maturation to express its full potential.

● Rossore	♟♟ 5
● La Rina	♟ 3
● Malidea	♟ 7
● Barbera del M.to Sup. Barabba '10	♟♟♟ 6
● Barbera del M.to Sup. Rossore '12	♟♟ 5
● Barbera del M.to Sup. Rossore '10	♟♟ 3*
● M.to Rosso Malidea '11	♟♟ 5
● M.to Rosso Malidea '10	♟♟ 5
● M.to Rosso Nino '12	♟♟ 5
● M.to Rosso Nino '11	♟♟ 5
● M.to Rosso Nino '10	♟♟ 5

● Dolcetto d'Alba Madonna di Como V. Miclet '16	♟♟ 3*
● Dolcetto d'Alba V. Madonna di Como '16	♟♟ 2*
⊙ Gredo Brut Rosé M. Cl.	♟♟ 4
● Nebbiolo d'Alba Sorì Coppa '15	♟♟ 4
● Barbera d'Alba V. Madonna di Como '15	♟ 2
● Barbera d'Alba V. Madonna di Como '13	♟♟ 2*
● Dolcetto d'Alba Madonna di Como V. Miclet '15	♟♟ 3*
● Dolcetto d'Alba V. Madonna di Como '14	♟♟ 2*
● Dolcetto d'Alba V. Miclet '14	♟♟ 3
● Dolcetto d'Alba V. Miclet '13	♟♟ 3*
○ Gredo Brut M. Cl. '12	♟♟ 4
● Nebbiolo d'Alba Sorì Coppa '14	♟♟ 4
● Nebbiolo d'Alba Sorì Coppa '13	♟♟ 4

Ugo Lequio

VIA DEL MOLINO, 10
1205/ NEIVE [CN]
TEL. +39 0173677224
www.ugolequio.it

CELLAR SALES
PRE-BOOKED VISITS
ANNUAL PRODUCTION 30,000 bottles
HECTARES UNDER VINE

Ugo Lequio is among Barbaresco's most consistent interpreters. Over more than 30 years, he's managed to perfect his special bond with the Gallina vineyard, one of Neive's most noble and renowned crus. His selection features both a base and a 'Riserva' version of the wine, and mostly sees long maceration and aging in mid-size oak. But bringing out the wine's lush character also requires that it spend time in the bottle before hitting the market. His solid and affordable selection is rounded out with wines made with Barbera, Dolcetto and Arneis. The 2014 Barbaresco Gallina features a pleasant and balanced combination of fresh notes, such as raspberry and strawberry, and more mature overtones, such as dried herbs and golden-leaf tobacco. The mouth exhibits medium weight, good tight-knit but non-aggressive tannins, and a clean, delicate finish. The 2014 Barbera d'Alba is also very good, not full-bodied, but supple and forthright. The favorable 2015 vintage is on full display in the simple and well-orchestrated Langhe Nebbiolo.

● Barbaresco Gallina '14	♛♛♛ 6
● Barbera d'Alba Sup. V. Gallina '14	♛♛♛ 4
● Langhe Nebbiolo '15	♛♛♛ 4
○ Langhe Arneis '16	♛ 3
● Barbaresco Gallina '13	♛♛ 5
● Barbaresco Gallina '12	♛♛ 5
● Barbaresco Gallina '11	♛♛ 5
● Barbaresco Gallina '10	♛♛ 5
● Barbaresco Gallina Ris. '10	♛♛ 6
● Barbaresco Gallina Ris. '07	♛♛ 6
● Barbera d'Alba Sup. '11	♛♛ 4
● Barbera d'Alba Sup. Gallina '12	♛♛ 4
○ Langhe Arneis '13	♛♛ 3
○ Langhe Arneis '12	♛♛ 3

Podere Macellio

VIA ROMA, 18
10014 CALUSO [TO]
TEL. +39 0119833511
www.erbaluce-bianco.it

CELLAR SALES
PRE-BOOKED VISITS
ANNUAL PRODUCTION 25,000 bottles
HECTARES UNDER VINE 3.50

Podere Macellio, an estate of three and a half hectares of terrain situated on the morainic hill of Caluso, has always been in the hands of the Bianco family. Their first bottles go back to the 1960s and were produced by Signor Renato. Today, Renato is flanked full-time by his son, Daniele, who is also proud to carry on the same tradition. Their selection includes three Erbaluces: a dry-still version, a 'Metodo Classico' sparkler and a passito dried-grape wine that's been aged at length in wood. Their interpretations are austere, to say the least. They are purists, keeping sugary gimmicks at a distance, with a personality as notable as their staying power. The magnificent 2016 Erbaluce personifies its profile to the letter. The nose offers up fresh herbs and white summer fruit, while a balanced palate features rocky hints and a classy finish. It's a magnificent newly-awarded wine. The 2004 Caluso Passito Riserva proves warm and caressing, with characteristic hints of candied citrus fruit and hazelnut.

○ Erbaluce di Caluso '16	♛♛♛ 2*
○ Caluso Passito Ris. '04	♛♛ 5
○ Erbaluce di Caluso Extra Brut	♛♛ 3
○ Caluso Passito '09	♛♛ 5
○ Caluso Passito '08	♛♛ 5
○ Caluso Passito '07	♛♛ 5
○ Caluso Passito '06	♛♛ 5
○ Caluso Passito '05	♛♛ 5
○ Caluso Passito Ris. '03	♛♛ 5
○ Erbaluce di Caluso '15	♛♛ 2*
○ Erbaluce di Caluso '13	♛♛ 2*
○ Erbaluce di Caluso '12	♛♛ 2*
○ Erbaluce di Caluso '11	♛♛ 2*
○ Erbaluce di Caluso '10	♛♛ 2*

Malabaila di Canale

VIA MADONNA DEI CAVALLI, 93
12043 CANALE [CN]
TEL. +39 017398381
www.malabaila.com

CELLAR SALES
PRE-BOOKED VISITS
ANNUAL PRODUCTION 100,000 bottles
HECTARES UNDER VINE 22.00
SUSTAINABLE WINERY

Malabaila di Canale has managed to
successfully take up and relaunch the
Malabaila name, which has been tied to
wine production since the 13th century.
Their vineyards are situated on a 90
hectare estate, on Asti's trademark soil:
loose, sandy marl. The area also features
major slopes (over 50% in some cases)
and plants that go back more than 60
years. Their wines, which display freshness
and richness of fruit, seek to stay true to
the territory. The 2016 Roero Arneis
Pradvaj truly impressed. It earned a place
in our finals, thanks to its floral aromas
and citrusy notes, and a palate with nice
tanginess and generosity. The 2013 Roero
Castelletto Riserva features notes of wild
berries, good length and body, with tannins
and fine elegance. The 2014 Barbera
d'Alba Superiore Mezzavilla is supple
and fresh, while the tangy and pleasant
2016 Roero Arneis Le Tre offers up notes of
peach and apricot. All are very well-made.

○ Roero Arneis Pradvaj '16	♟♟	3*
● Barbera d'Alba Sup. Mezzavilla '14	♟♟	3
○ Roero Arneis Le Tre '16	♟♟	3
● Roero Castelletto Ris. '13	♟♟	4
○ Malabaila 1362 Pas Dosé M. Cl.	♟	3
● Nebbiolo d'Alba Bric Merli '15	♟	3
⊙ Nebbiolo d'Alba Rosé Pas Dosé M. Cl. '10	♟	3
● Roero Bric Volta '14	♟	3
● Barbera d'Alba Giardino '15	♟♟	2*
○ Roero Arneis '15	♟♟	2*
● Roero Bric Volta '13	♟♟	3*
● Roero Bric Volta '12	♟♟	3*
● Roero Castelletto Ris. '12	♟♟	4

★Malvirà

LOC. CANOVA
VIA CASE SPARSE, 144
12043 CANALE [CN]
TEL. +39 0173978145
www.malvira.com

CELLAR SALES
PRE-BOOKED VISITS
ACCOMMODATION AND RESTAURANT SERVICE
ANNUAL PRODUCTION 300,000 bottles
HECTARES UNDER VINE 42.00

The Damonte brothers' winery has been,
for some years, a rock in Roero's wine
scene, both in terms of vine growing and
for its hospitality (thanks to Villa Tiboldi, a
splendid relais situated on Trinità hill). They
also have a vineyards in the municipality of
La Morra, dedicated to the production of
Barolo. Their wines stand out for their local
character and adherence to the territory. Of
the Damonte brothers' various Roeros, we
particularly enjoyed those made with
grapes grown in the Vigna Trinità. The
2016 Roero Arneis offers up rich aromas
of saffron, white pepper and yellow fruit.
The tangy palate shows good body and
grip. The 2013 Roero Riserva features
notes of black fruit, with elegance, good
length and grip. The other 2013 Roero
Riservas are also good. The Vigna
Mombeltramo exhibits gutsy notes of
pepper and redcurrants, while the Renesio
shows balance and well-integrated tannins
The 2014 Barbera d'Alba San Michele is a
pleasant wine, while the 2013 Barolo
Boiolo proves well-made and generous.

○ Roero Arneis V. Trinità '16	♟♟	3*
● Roero V. Trinità Ris. '13	♟♟	5
● Barbera d'Alba S. Michele '14	♟♟	3
● Barolo Boiolo '13	♟♟	7
● Roero V. Mombeltramo Ris. '13	♟♟	5
● Roero V. Renesio Ris. '13	♟♟	5
○ Roero Arneis V. Renesio '16	♟	3
● Roero Mombeltramo Ris. '11	♟♟♟	5
● Roero Mombeltramo Ris. '10	♟♟♟	5
● Roero Renesio Ris. '05	♟♟♟	5
● Roero Trinità Ris. '07	♟♟♟	5
● Roero V. Mombeltramo Ris. '12	♟♟♟	5
● Barolo Boiolo '12	♟♟	7

Giovanni Manzone

VIA CASTELLETTO, 9
12065 MONFORTE D'ALBA [CN]
TEL. +39 017378114
www.manzonegiovanni.com

CELLAR SALES
PRE-BOOKED VISITS
ANNUAL PRODUCTION 45,000 bottles
HECTARES UNDER VINE 7.50
SUSTAINABLE WINERY

Supported full-time by his children, Mauro and Mirella, Giovanni Manzone has definitively established himself as one of the most serious and committed vigneron in Langhe. No gimmicks are needed. His wines, made with grapes from superb plots like Gramolere, Bricat, Castelletto (Monforte d'Alba), circulate thanks to the support of no-frills Barolo lovers. His wines are produced through long maceration and mixed aging in large wood and mid-sized casks. These are stripped-down reds, sometimes austere but often able to deliver over time. Their selection is rounded out with strong local classics, with the intriguing Rossese Bianco being a lone exception. The 2013 Barolo Castelletto offers up particularly complex aromas, ranging from fresh notes of raspberries, strong notes of animal skins and spicy tobacco. The mouth is powerful, bold and almost savory. The 2013 Barolo Bricat features clenched tannins, but comes through close-focused and rich. The 2013 Gramolere is a classically styled wine, while the 2011 Riserva of the same name proves more evolved.

● Barolo Bricat '13	🏆🏆	6
● Barolo Castelletto '13	🏆🏆	6
● Barbera d'Alba Le Ciliegie '15	🏆🏆	3
● Barolo Gramolere '13	🏆🏆	6
● Barolo Gramolere Ris. '11	🏆🏆	8
● Langhe Nebbiolo Il Crutin '15	🏆🏆	3
○ Langhe Rossese Bianco Rosserto '15	🏆🏆	3
● Barolo Bricat '05	🏆🏆🏆	6
● Barolo Castelletto '09	🏆🏆🏆	5
● Barolo Gramolere Ris. '05	🏆🏆🏆	6
● Barolo Le Gramolere '04	🏆🏆🏆	6
● Barolo Le Gramolere Ris. '01	🏆🏆🏆	7
● Barolo Le Gramolere Ris. '00	🏆🏆🏆	7
● Barolo Le Gramolere Ris. '99	🏆🏆🏆	7
● Barolo Bricat '12	🏆🏆	6
● Barolo Gramolere Ris. '09	🏆🏆	8

Paolo Manzone

LOC. MERIAME, 1
12050 SERRALUNGA D'ALBA [CN]
TEL. +39 0173613113
www.barolomeriame.com

CELLAR SALES
PRE-BOOKED VISITS
ACCOMMODATION
ANNUAL PRODUCTION 85,000 bottles
HECTARES UNDER VINE 10.00
SUSTAINABLE WINERY

In a short while the winery owned by Paolo Manzone and his wife, Luisella will be celebrating its 20 year anniversary. It's a period in which experimentation, aimed at bringing out the purity of their Barolo Nebbiolo, has never stopped. Their cellar sees the peaceful coexistence of various wood and steel vats, as well as recently added terra-cotta. Their lovely vineyards, which also host a cozy agritourism, are dominated by the Meriame cru, and give rise to their prized reds, with a small selection of Arneis whites made with grapes from nearby Roero. Spicy and balsamic notes merge in a symphony of fruity aromas in the magnificent 2011 Barolo Riserva. This Tre Bicchieri exhibits a bold taste structure, elegance and great personality. The 2013 Barolo Meriame proves a bit more austere, with pleasant notes of cinchona and similar complexity. The 2013 Barolo del Comune di Serralunga d'Alba is more floral and rich in fruity pulp.

● Barolo Ris. '11	🏆🏆🏆	7
● Barolo Meriame '13	🏆🏆	7
● Barbera d'Alba Sup. Fiorenza '15	🏆🏆	3
● Barolo del Comune di Serralunga d'Alba '13	🏆🏆	6
● Langhe Rosso Luvì '15	🏆🏆	3
● Nebbiolo d'Alba Mirinè '15	🏆🏆	3
● Barbera d'Alba Sup. Fiorenza '14	🏆🏆	3
● Barbera d'Alba Sup. Fiorenza '13	🏆🏆	3
● Barolo del Comune di Serralunga d'Alba '12	🏆🏆	6
● Barolo Meriame '12	🏆🏆	7
● Barolo Meriame '11	🏆🏆	7
● Barolo Meriame '10	🏆🏆	7
● Barolo Ris. '08	🏆🏆	7
● Langhe Rosso Luvì '13	🏆🏆	3
● Nebbiolo d'Alba Miriné '13	🏆🏆	3

Marcalberto

VIA PORTA SOTTANA, 9
12058 SANTO STEFANO BELBO [CN]
TEL. +39 0141844022
www.marcalberto.it

CELLAR SALES
PRE-BOOKED VISITS
ANNUAL PRODUCTION 30,000 bottles
HECTARES UNDER VINE 5.00

Following a well-thought-out program of growth, the Cane family, owners of this small winery, recently purchased a gorgeous piece of terrain on top of Loazzolo, adding it to the vineyards already managed in Calosso, Cossano Belbo and Santo Stefano Belbo. Simultaneously, they've just inaugurated a lovely indoor space dedicated to wine tasting, where you can discover the qualities that distinguish their various Marcalberto Metodo Classico sparkling wines. More than ever, these stand out for their definition and personality. The Blanc de Blancs Pas Dosé proves gutsy, silky, assertive and charming. It's only in its first edition, but we have no doubts as to the extraordinary nature of this wine. The 2012 Millesimato proves dense and supple at the same time, as well as powerful and elegant. It earns not just a Tre Bicchieri, but also a 'Sparkling Wine of the Year' award, crowning the winery's continued and professional work, as well as a vision of style that has adapted over the years. The whole selection is in great form.

○ Marcalberto Extra Brut Millesimo2Mila12 M. Cl. '12	▼▼▼ 5
○ Marcalberto Pas Dosé Blanc de Blancs M. Cl.	▼▼ 4
⊙ Marcalberto Brut Rosé M. Cl.	▼▼ 4
○ Marcalberto Brut Sansannée M. Cl.	▼▼ 4
○ Marcalberto Nature M. Cl. Senza Aggiunta di Solfiti	▼▼ 6
○ Marcalberto Extra Brut Millesimo2Mila10 M. Cl. '10	♼ 5
○ Marcalberto Extra Brut Millesimo2Mila11 M. Cl. '11	♼ 5

Poderi Marcarini

P.ZZA MARTIRI, 2
12064 LA MORRA [CN]
TEL. +39 017350222
www.marcarini.it

CELLAR SALES
PRE-BOOKED VISITS
ACCOMMODATION
ANNUAL PRODUCTION 125,000 bottles
HECTARES UNDER VINE 20.00

With the involvement of siblings Andrea, Chiara and Elisa Marchetti, Poderi Marcarini is now on its sixth generation of leaders. One of the true historic brands of La Morra, the winery's roots go back to the mid-1800s, and are bound up with Brunate and La Serra's collective Barolo tradition. Over the past two decades, the estate has come to include Sargentin (in Neviglie) and Muschiadivino (in Montaldo Roero), bringing their estate to a total of more than 20 hectares, and making room for Dolcetto, Barbera, Moscato and Arneis, not to mention their fortified and aromatized typologies. Only two 2013 Barolos were presented for tasting. We found the classic Brunate rather open with evolved aromas and dried herbs dominating fruit. The palate proves more acidulous, with assertive tannins that tend to clench the palate. The more rustic La Serra exhibits a similar aromatic style, with a lovely, powerful and lingering palate that indicates it will age well.

● Barolo Brunate '13	▼▼ 7
● Barolo La Serra '13	▼▼ 7
● Barolo Brunate '05	♼♼ 6
● Barolo Brunate '03	♼♼ 6
● Barolo Brunate '01	♼♼ 6
● Barolo Brunate '99	♼♼ 6
● Barbera d'Alba Ciabot Camerano '13	♼ 3
● Barolo Brunate '12	♼ 7
● Barolo Brunate '11	♼ 6
● Barolo Brunate '10	♼ 6
● Barolo La Serra '12	♼ 7
● Barolo La Serra '11	♼ 6
○ Moscato d'Asti '15	♼ 2*

Marchese Luca Spinola

FRAZ. ROVERETO DI GAVI
LOC. CASCINA MASSIMILIANA, 97
15066 GAVI [AL]
TEL. +39 0143682514
www.marcheselucaspinola.it

CELLAR SALES
PRE-BOOKED VISITS
ANNUAL PRODUCTION 20,000 bottles
HECTARES UNDER VINE 15.00

Andrea Spinola is only the most recent member of this noble family to inherit their centuries-old tradition of wine production. Here with the supp Vincenzo Munì and Davide Ferrase, Andrea attends to 15 hectares of vineyards, situated, more or less, half in the municipality of Tassarolo and half in Rovereto (in Gavi). Their selection centers on Cortese. Their Gavi di Gavi is worked classically, in steel, while the Tenuta Massimiliana, which serves as their their top-of-the-range wine, is fermented in barriques and aged on the lees in Inox. Their Gavi del Comune di Tassarolo is an unusual semi-sparkling wine. The 2016 Gavi del Comune di Gavi opens with river herbs, almonds and hydrocarbons, and is anything but a simple and easy-drinking white. The Tenuta Massimiliana of the same vintage shows further fruity generosity and tangy grip. It exhibits deeper aromas of aniseed, tobacco and meadow flowers.

○ Gavi del Comune di Gavi '16	♟♟ 2*
○ Gavi del Comune di Gavi Tenuta Massimiliana '16	♟♟ 3*
○ Gavi del Comune di Gavi '15	♟♟ 2*
○ Gavi del Comune di Gavi '12	♟♟ 2*
○ Gavi del Comune di Gavi Et. Blu '14	♟♟ 2*
○ Gavi del Comune di Gavi Tenuta Massimiliana '15	♟♟ 3
○ Gavi del Comune di Gavi Tenuta Massimiliana '14	♟♟ 3
○ Gavi del Comune di Gavi Tenuta Massimiliana '13	♟♟ 3
○ Gavi del Comune di Gavi Tenuta Massimiliana '12	♟♟ 3
○ Gavi del Comune di Tassarolo '13	♟♟ 2*

★Marchesi di Barolo

VIA ROMA, 1
12060 BAROLO [CN]
TEL. +39 0173564400
www.marchesibarolo.com

CELLAR SALES
PRE-BOOKED VISITS
RESTAURANT SERVICE
ANNUAL PRODUCTION 1,500,000 bottles
HECTARES UNDER VINE 201.00

You certainly don't need to underline the competitive advantage that comes with having a heritage as glorious as Anna and Ernesto Abbona's. They are the most recent generation to steer Marchesi di Barolo, the current owner of Castello Falletti, which they took over from the Agenzia della Tenuta Opera Pia. Here, in fact, the myth of Barolo started taking form with Juliette Colbert and many other leading figures of the period. But such fond memories aren't distracting from the present, nor their work tending to 200 hectares of vineyards (taking into account their own plots and their network of growers), spread out on some of the best terrain in Langhe, Roero and Monferrato. The Coste delle Rose cru is well-known for not always producing grapes rich in freshness. The 2013 vintage adds a pleasant vegetal note, which creates a lovely suite of aromas. Its palate is coherent, with pleasant acidity. The 2013 Cannubi proves even more elegant and well-orchestrated. The modern and complex 2010 Barolo Riserva features enchanting spices and power.

● Barolo Cannubi '13	♟♟ 8
● Barolo Coste di Rose '13	♟♟ 8
● Barolo Ris. '10	♟♟ 8
● Barolo Sarmassa '13	♟♟ 8
● Barbaresco '14	♟♟ 5
● Barbaresco Serragrilli '14	♟♟ 6
● Barbera d'Alba Peiragal '15	♟♟ 5
● Barolo del Comune di Barolo '13	♟♟ 8
● Nebbiolo d'Alba Roccheri '15	♟♟ 5
● Dolcetto d'Alba Madonna del Dono '16	♟ 3
○ Langhe Bric Amel '16	♟ 2
● Barolo Cannubi '12	♟♟♟ 8
● Barolo Cannubi '11	♟♟♟ 8
● Barolo Cannubi '10	♟♟♟ 8
● Barolo Sarmassa '09	♟♟♟ 8
● Barolo Sarmassa '08	♟♟♟ 7

Marchesi Incisa della Rocchetta

VIA ROMA, 66
14030 ROCCHETTA TANARO [AT]
TEL. +39 0141644647
www.marchesiincisawines.it

CELLAR SALES
PRE-BOOKED VISITS
ACCOMMODATION AND RESTAURANT SERVICE
ANNUAL PRODUCTION 80,000 bottles
HECTARES UNDER VINE 17.00

The Incisa della Rocchetta family are among Italy's leading producers. Here, in Monferrato, the winery has been operating since the 19th century, even if it only officially came into existence in 1970. Their estate, a part of which is found in the Natural Park of Rocchetta Tanaro, is situated on sandy clay terrain. Barbera is the principal variety cultivated, followed by Grignolino, Pinot Nero and Merlot. The 2015 Barbera d'Asti Superiore Sant'Emiliano is one of the best presented this year. The nose offers up notes of black fruit, rain-soaked earth and spices, while the palate comes through rich in pulp, juicy, lingering and taut. The rest of the selection is excellent. The 2016 Grignolino d'Asti exhibits fresh and pleasant notes of redcurrants. The 2016 Barbera d'Asti Valmorena features the variety's signature notes of red fruit and rain-soaked earth. The 2016 Piemonte Pinot Nero Barbera Rollone proves dynamic with hints of wild berries.

● Barbera d'Asti Sup. Sant' Emiliano '15	▼▼▼5
● Barbera d'Asti Valmorena '16	▼▼3
● Grignolino d'Asti '16	▼▼3
● Piemonte Pinot Nero Barbera Rollone '16	▼▼3
● Barbera d'Asti Sup. Sant'Emiliano '14	♀♀5
● Barbera d'Asti Sup. Sant'Emiliano '12	♀♀5
● Barbera d'Asti Sup. Sant'Emiliano '11	♀♀4
● Barbera d'Asti Valmorena '14	♀♀3*
● Grignolino d'Asti '15	♀♀3
● M.to Rosso Colpo d'Ala '13	♀♀6
● Piemonte Pinot Nero Marchese Leopoldo '14	♀♀5
● Piemonte Pinot Nero Marchese Leopoldo '13	♀♀4

Mario Marengo

LOC. SERRA DENARI, 2A
12064 LA MORRA [CN]
TEL. +39 017350115
marengo1964@libero.it

CELLAR SALES
PRE-BOOKED VISITS
ANNUAL PRODUCTION 35,000 bottles
HECTARES UNDER VINE 7.00

Marco Marengo manages seven hectares of vineyards, but these aren't just any vineyards: Brunate in La Morra and Bricco delle Viole in Barolo, to name the most prestigious. Along with his wife, Eugenia, he represents the fourth generation to lead a winery with deep and well-documented roots (Est. 1899). He's keeping alive the stylistic approach of his father, Mario, who left us in 2001, with the choice to continue to focus on short fermentation in vertical rotary macerators and aging in barriques (for their most important Nebbiolos). The same can be said for his philosophy, which continues to seek to bring together full-bodied force and recognizable expressivity with respect to the various crus. The 2013 Brunate gives us yet another, faithful and charming interpretation of a great vineyard in the Barolo area. Non-wilted violets, licorice and small red fruit anticipate an enchanting juicy palate that's delicately tannic, fresh, lingering and gradual. The other two selections prove a bit less multi-faceted. Kudos to the 2013 Barolo for finesse and structure.

● Barolo '13	▼▼5
● Barolo Bricco delle Viole '13	▼▼6
● Barolo Brunate '13	▼▼▼7
● Barbera d'Alba V. Pugnane '15	▼▼3
● Nebbiolo d'Alba Vign. Valmaggiore '15	▼▼3
● Barolo Brunate '12	♀♀♀7
● Barolo Brunate '11	♀♀♀7
● Barolo Brunate '09	♀♀♀6
● Barolo Brunate '07	♀♀♀6
● Barolo Brunate '06	♀♀♀6
● Barolo '11	♀♀5
● Barolo Bricco delle Viole '12	♀♀6
● Dolcetto d'Alba '15	♀♀2*

Claudio Mariotto

DA PER SAREZZANO, 29
5057 TORTONA [AL]
TEL. +39 0131868500
www.claudiomariotto.it

CELLAR SALES
PRE-BOOKED VISITS
ANNUAL PRODUCTION 100,000 bottles
HECTARES UNDER VINE 32.00

Claudio and Mauro Mariotto are among the producers that have made Timorasso famous. The brothers took over the family winery during the 1990s and, thanks to their hard work and passion, they managed to lead it to the heights of regional excellence. The national (and international) breakthrough coincided with the explosion of Timorasso in the early part of the century. A variety that was once the territory's past, became its future (thanks in part to modern winemaking techniques), and Claudio is one of its best interpreters. The selection of wines presented highlights their skill with Timorasso. Pitasso features a bright, lively color and complex, vibrant aromas and flavors. Cavallina proves balanced and well-orchestrated, with complex aromas, making for a powerful palate and an alcohol-rich finish. Derthona features an incredible palate that's rich and powerful, with exemplary acidity and a long finish.

Marsaglia

VIA MADAMA MUSSONE, 2
12050 CASTELLINALDO [CN]
TEL. +39 0173213048
www.cantinamarsaglia.it

CELLAR SALES
PRE-BOOKED VISITS
ANNUAL PRODUCTION 80,000 bottles
HECTARES UNDER VINE 15.00

Though they started bottling towards the end of the 1980s, the Marsaglia family have been working in the territory since 1900. Their vineyards, which were planted between the 1950s and the year 2000, are all situated in the municipality of Castellinaldo and feature grape varieties local to Roero, from Arneis to Nebbiolo and Barbera. Their wines are characterized by a traditional style and notably consistent quality. Marsaglia has presented a series of excellent wines again this year. Despite the difficult vintage, the 2014 Nebbiolo d'Alba San Pietro presents notes of black cherry on the nose and a medium-structured, pleasant, expansive palate. The 2016 Roero Arneis Serramiana features notes of citron and tangerine on both the nose and palate, good grip and a long, savory finish. The 2016 Barbera d'Alba San Cristoforo exhibits notes of red damsons, followed by a fresh, close-focused palate, driven by fruit and great pleasantness.

○ Colli Tortonesi Timorasso Derthona '15	🍷🍷 5
○ Colli Tortonesi Timorasso Derthona Cavallina '15	🍷🍷 5
○ Colli Tortonesi Timorasso Derthona Pitasso '15	🍷🍷 6
● Colli Tortonesi Barbera Vho '14	🍷🍷 4
● Colli Tortonesi Freisa Braghè '16	🍷🍷 3
○ Colli Tortonesi Timorasso Pitasso '13	🍷🍷🍷 6
○ Colli Tortonesi Timorasso Pitasso '12	🍷🍷🍷 6
○ Colli Tortonesi Timorasso Pitasso '08	🍷🍷🍷 5
○ Colli Tortonesi Timorasso Derthona '14	🍷🍷 5
○ Colli Tortonesi Timorasso Derthona Cavallina '14	🍷🍷 5
○ Colli Tortonesi Timorasso Derthona Pitasso '14	🍷🍷 6

● Barbera d'Alba S. Cristoforo '16	🍷🍷 3
● Nebbiolo d'Alba San Pietro '14	🍷🍷 3
○ Roero Arneis Serramiana '16	🍷🍷 3
● Barbera d'Alba Sup. Castellinaldo '14	🍷 4
● Barbera d'Alba Castellinaldo '11	🍷🍷 4
● Barbera d'Alba Castellinaldo '10	🍷🍷 4
● Barbera d'Alba S. Cristoforo '15	🍷🍷 3
● Barbera d'Alba S. Cristoforo '12	🍷🍷 3
● Nebbiolo d'Alba '12	🍷🍷 3
● Nebbiolo d'Alba San Pietro '11	🍷🍷 3
○ Roero Arneis Serramiana '14	🍷🍷 3
○ Roero Arneis Serramiana '13	🍷🍷 3
● Roero Brich d'America '12	🍷🍷 4
● Roero Brich d'America '11	🍷🍷 4

★Franco M. Martinetti

c.so Turati, 14
10128 Torino
Tel. +39 0118395937
www.francomartinetti.it

PRE-BOOKED VISITS
ANNUAL PRODUCTION 140,000 bottles
HECTARES UNDER VINE 5.00

In talking about Franco Martinetti's international role, it's enough to remember that he's a member of the Académie du vin de France and was once president of the Académie Internationale du Vin. In describing himself, he uses the term 'vinicultore', or 'Franco Senza Terra'. The rest he leaves up to his wines, which he makes in various cellars according to the type. His selection embraces the major appellations of Langhe and Monferrato, with the Barbera d'Asti Montruc and Monferrato Sulbric standing out among the reds and the Timorasso Martin and Gavi Minaia (both of which are superb and long-lived) among his whites. The fragrant and elegant 2016 Gavi Minaia features a charming golden yellow color and fresh, tantalizing palate. The rich and caressing Colli Tortonesi Timorasso Martin once again performs at a high level, with the 2015 proving particularly structured. The 2013 Marasco was a pleasant surprise, Martinetti's best Barolo so far. The 2015 Sul Bric exhibits elegance, structure and enjoyable drinkability.

● Barolo Marasco '13	▼▼ 8
○ Colli Tortonesi Timorasso Martin '15	▼▼ 6
○ Gavi Minaia '16	▼▼ 5
● M.to Rosso Sul Bric '15	▼▼ 6
● Barbera d'Asti Bric dei Banditi '15	▼▼ 4
● Barbera d'Asti Sup. Montruc '15	▼▼ 6
● Barbera d'Asti Sup. Montruc '06	♈♈♈ 5
● Barbera d'Asti Sup. Montruc '01	♈♈♈ 5
● Barolo Marasco '01	♈♈♈ 7
● Barolo Marasco '00	♈♈♈ 7
○ Colli Tortonesi Timorasso Martin '12	♈♈♈ 6
○ Gavi Minaia '14	♈♈♈ 6
● M.to Rosso Sul Bric '10	♈♈♈ 6
● M.to Rosso Sul Bric '09	♈♈♈ 6
● M.to Rosso Sul Bric '00	♈♈♈ 5

★Bartolo Mascarello

via Roma, 15
12060 Barolo [CN]
Tel. +39 01/356125

CELLAR SALES
PRE-BOOKED VISITS
ANNUAL PRODUCTION 30,000 bottles
HECTARES UNDER VINE 5.00

It seems impossible, but there was a time when Barolo was almost given away, especially when it came to the so-called 'traditionals' (those that were aged at length in large barrels, devoid of color but often austere). These were considered 'old-fashioned' with respect to the latest generation of Nebbiolos, made in small wood. As we know, history has, for the most part, put things back in their place. Much of the credit should be given to the militant resistance of the ex-partisan, Bartolo Mascarello, and then his daughter, Maria Teresa, who took over after his death. She further ennobled the expressive identity of the family plots in Cannubi, San Lorenzo, Rué (Barolo) and Rocche (La Morra). The 2013 Barolo expresses brilliance and youth. Vibrant aromas of tobacco and licorice are followed by camphor and, especially, raspberries, making for extreme elegance and complexity. The mouth proves extraordinary for its tight-knit tannic weave and harmonious palate. The finish is long and classy: it's a Tre Bicchieri in pursuit of a purely classical style.

● Barolo '13	▼▼▼ 8
● Barolo '12	♈♈♈ 8
● Barolo '11	♈♈♈ 8
● Barolo '10	♈♈♈ 8
● Barolo '09	♈♈♈ 8
● Barolo '07	♈♈♈ 8
● Barolo '06	♈♈♈ 8
● Barolo '05	♈♈♈ 8
● Barbera d'Alba '07	♈♈ 4
● Barbera d'Alba Vign. S. Lorenzo '06	♈♈ 4
● Barolo '08	♈♈ 8
● Dolcetto d'Alba Monrobiolo e Ruè '07	♈♈ 3
● Langhe Freisa '07	♈♈ 4
● Langhe Freisa '06	♈♈ 3

Giuseppe Mascarello e Figlio

VIA BORGONUOVO, 108
12060 MONCHIERO [CN]
TEL. +39 0173792126
www.mascarello1881.com

CELLAR SALES
PRE-BOOKED VISITS
ANNUAL PRODUCTION 60,000 bottles
HECTARES UNDER VINE 13.50

With their bright and yet rarefied hue, Mauro and Giuseppe Mascarello's wines are, from the first glimpse, impossible to mistake. These are made with grapes from some of the most prestigious crus in Langhe, primarily Monprivato di Castiglione Falletto, which, in the best years, also results in the Cà d' Morissio Riserva (a monovarietal Michèt clone). But there's also Villero, Santo Stefano di Perno (in Monforte d'Alba), as well as plots dedicated to other varieties (Barbera, Dolcetto, Freisa). These are all interpreted with the same delicate and indomitable style that we see in their great Nebbiolo reds, aged in medium and large barrels for at least 36 months. The 2012 Monprivato offers up aromas characteristic of all great Barolos: notes of herbs and wilted roses, with a lively touch of spice culminating in white pepper. It shows great delicacy in the mouth, with excellent pulp and mellow tannins. The 2012 Perno Vigna Santo Stefano displays outstanding finesse, while the Villero is more close-knit and promising.

● Barolo Monprivato '12	▼▼▼ 8	
● Barolo Perno V. Santo Stefano '12	▼▼ 8	
● Barolo Villero '12	▼▼ 8	
● Barolo Monprivato '11	♀♀♀ 8	
● Barolo Monprivato '10	♀♀♀ 8	
● Barolo Monprivato '09	♀♀♀ 8	
● Barolo Monprivato '08	♀♀♀ 8	
● Barolo Perno V. Santo Stefano '11	♀♀ 8	
● Barolo Perno V. Santo Stefano '10	♀♀ 8	
● Barolo Villero '11	♀♀ 8	
● Barolo Villero '10	♀♀ 8	
● Barolo Villero '09	♀♀ 8	
● Barolo Villero '08	♀♀ 8	

★Massolino

P.ZZA CAPPELLANO, 8
12050 SERRALUNGA D'ALBA [CN]
TEL. +39 0173613138
www.massolino.it

CELLAR SALES
PRE-BOOKED VISITS
ANNUAL PRODUCTION 257,000 bottles
HECTARES UNDER VINE 36.00
SUSTAINABLE WINERY

Franco and Roberto Massolino's name has come up for years among Langhe's wine producing elite, and it's not just for the level and consistency of their selection, which interprets Barbera, Dolcetto, Chardonnay and Moscato with superb results. Their success is the consequence of an almost academic adherence to the temperament that many associate with Serralunga d'Alba Barolo: powerful fruit, close-knit tannins, and a full-flavored backbone. These characteristics are explored in a way that is never dogmatic in terms of extraction and aging, thus leaving space for the unique personality of crus like Parafada, Margheria, Vigna Rionda and Parussi to come through. The cellarman's skill has seen to it that the 2011 Barolo Vigna Rionda Riserva maintains its elegant aromatic freshness, with its unbridled fruitiness set on a spicy background. The mouth proves juicy but austere, enough to earn it a Tre Bicchieri. The 2013 Barolo deserves our kudos, with a similar style that's just a bit warmer on the palate. The elegant 2013 exhibits charming balance.

● Barolo Vigna Rionda Ris. '11	▼▼▼ 8	
● Barolo '13	▼▼ 5	
● Barolo Margheria '13	▼▼ 8	
● Barolo Parafada '13	▼▼ 8	
● Barolo Parussi '13	▼▼ 8	
○ Langhe Chardonnay '15	▼▼ 3	
○ Langhe Nebbiolo '15	▼▼ 3	
● Barolo Margheria '05	♀♀♀ 7	
● Barolo Parafada '11	♀♀♀ 8	
● Barolo Vigna Rionda Ris. '10	♀♀♀ 8	
● Barolo Vigna Rionda Ris. '08	♀♀♀ 8	
● Barolo Vigna Rionda Ris. '06	♀♀♀ 8	
● Barolo Vigna Rionda Ris. '05	♀♀♀ 8	
● Barolo Vigna Rionda Ris. '04	♀♀♀ 8	
● Barolo Margheria '12	♀♀ 8	

Tiziano Mazzoni

VIA ROMA, 73
20010 CAVAGLIO D'AGOGNA [NO]
TEL. +39 3488200635
www.vinimazzoni.it

CELLAR SALES
PRE-BOOKED VISITS
ANNUAL PRODUCTION 20,000 bottles
HECTARES UNDER VINE 4.50
SUSTAINABLE WINERY

The winery being managed today by Tiziano Mazzoni, with the crucial support of his wife, Rita, his son, Gilles and the g guidance of Signor Nino, certainly can't be called an 'emerging business'. And yet Mazzoni only started bottling wines again in 1999. Before that only a part of the grapes were kept for the family's production. With the purchase of new vineyards in Ghemme and the re-planting of a Vespolina plot, their estate has come to comprise almost five hectares of land. Nebbiolo dominates the best exposures and is, without a doubt, the strong point of their selection. Their complete range of traditional Novara wines is interpreted with a solid, concrete sensibility. Our latest tasting sees the hierarchy in working order. The 2015 Nebbiolo del Monteregio proves to be one of the wines most in form. Iodine and balsamic hints follow through coherently onto a streamlined palate. The 2013 Ghemme dei Mazzoni is proud and robust, but without giving up floral grace and spontaneity.

● Ghemme dei Mazzoni '13	🍷🍷5
● Colline Novaresi Nebbiolo del Monteregio '15	🍷🍷3
○ Iris	🍷🍷3
● Colline Novaresi Vespolina Il Ricetto '16	🍷3
● Colline Novaresi Nebbiolo del Monteregio '13	🍷🍷2 3
● Colline Novaresi Vespolina Al Ricetto '13	🍷🍷2 2*
● Colline Novaresi Vespolina Il Ricetto '15	🍷🍷2 3
● Colline Novaresi Vespolina Il Ricetto '14	🍷🍷2 3
● Ghemme ai Livelli '11	🍷🍷2 6
● Ghemme ai Livelli '10	🍷🍷2 6
● Ghemme dei Mazzoni '11	🍷🍷2 5
● Ghemme dei Mazzoni '10	🍷🍷2 5

La Mesma

FRAZ. MONTEROTONDO, 7
15066 GAVI [AL]
TEL. +39 0143342012
www.lamesma.it

CELLAR SALES
PRE-BOOKED VISITS
ACCOMMODATION
ANNUAL PRODUCTION 52,000 bottles
HECTARES UNDER VINE 25.00

La Mesma, which debuted in our main section last year, has proved to be one of Gavi's most consistent new producers. The increasing quality of their wines and the heights of excellence reached in the last few years testify to the producer's maturity. Another indicator is the research that went into Indi, a Gavi made with native yeasts that was released only after years of quality and longevity tests. Their great work has been recognized with a Tre Bicchieri. The very young 2015 Riserva is a great wine, with a greenish color. Elegant and complex aromas anticipate a structured palate, where pulp is well-balanced by acidity, making for a very lingering finish. The Etichetta Nera stands up for itself in terms of complexity and finesse. Fresh herbs, white fruit and elegant notes of flint follow through onto a palate with exceptional structure.

○ Gavi V. della Rovere Verde Ris. '15	🍷🍷🍷5
○ Gavi del Comune di Gavi Et. Nera '16	🍷🍷3*
○ Gavi Brut M. Cl. '11	🍷🍷5
○ Gavi del Comune di Gavi Et. Gialla '16	🍷🍷2*
○ Gavi del Comune di Gavi Indi '16	🍷🍷4
○ Gavi Brut M. Cl. '09	🍷🍷2 4
○ Gavi del Comune di Gavi Et. Gialla '15	🍷🍷2 2*
○ Gavi del Comune di Gavi Et. Gialla '14	🍷🍷2 2*
○ Gavi del Comune di Gavi Et. Nera '14	🍷🍷2 3
○ Gavi V. della Rovere Verde Ris. '14	🍷🍷2 5
○ Gavi V. della Rovere Verde Ris. '13	🍷🍷2 3

Moccagatta

S.DA RABAJÀ, 46
12050 BARBARESCO [CN]
TEL. +39 0173635228
www.moccagatta.eu

CELLAR SALES
PRE-BOOKED VISITS
ANNUAL PRODUCTION 65,000 bottles
HECTARES UNDER VINE 12.00
SUSTAINABLE WINERY

Francesco and Sergio Minuto are keeping
alive the historic family business with the
spirit of their predecessors. Indeed, it seems
that they haven't realized how many
changes they've brought about, and how
many more are in the works. With the
increasingly valuable help of the new
generation, Martina and Stefano, they've
decided to shift to organic cultivation and
have enlarged their prominent underground
cellar for both production and aesthetic
purposes. Their three Barbarescos are
rightly celebrated (Basarin, Bric Balin and
Cole). In these parts, being considered one
of the most skilled producers in the area is
no small complement. The 2014 Barbaresco
Bric Balin exhibits lively notes of oak and
fruitiness. The mouth sees rich pulp and
rather docile tannins. Hints of roasted coffee
and vanilla integrate making for good
drinkability. The 2014 Barbaresco Basarin is
still dominated by wood and features a
powerful, pleasant fruity pulp that we didn't
expect from the vintage. The Cole displays
evolved aromas and assertive tannins.

● Barbaresco Basarin '14	♟♟6
● Barbaresco Bric Balin '14	♟♟6
● Barbaresco Cole '14	♟7
● Barbaresco Bric Balin '05	♟♟♟6
● Barbaresco Bric Balin '04	♟♟♟6
● Barbaresco Bric Balin '01	♟♟♟6
● Barbaresco Bric Balin '90	♟♟♟6
● Barbaresco Cole '97	♟♟♟6
● Barbaresco Basarin '11	♟♟6
● Barbaresco Bric Balin '13	♟♟6
● Barbaresco Bric Balin '11	♟♟6
● Barbaresco Bric Balin '10	♟♟6
● Barbaresco Cole '12	♟♟7
● Barbaresco Cole '11	♟♟6

Mauro Molino

FRAZ. ANNUNZIATA GANCIA, 111A
12064 LA MORRA [CN]
TEL. +39 017350814
www.mauromolino.com

CELLAR SALES
PRE-BOOKED VISITS
ANNUAL PRODUCTION 95,000 bottles
HECTARES UNDER VINE 12.00
SUSTAINABLE WINERY

Here, enology is the common language.
Both Mauro and his two children, Martina
and Matteo, are passionate about wine and
graduates from the Enological School of
Alba. Pretty soon, the skilled winemaker
will celebrate 40 years of activity, having
got his start in the vineyards back in 1979,
with his first bottle of Barolo coming out in
1982. The various crus in which his Barolo
is cultivated are all of similar quality, even if
the winery is particularly tied to a small
selection called Conca. The 2013 Barolo
Conca proves the richest in body and will
evolve well over the years. However, it's still
shrouded in notes of oak, with their
corresponding toastiness and spiciness.
The Bricco Luciani offers up rather green
and vegetal tones in a medium-structured
body. The 2013 Barolo La Serra certainly
doesn't lack body, either. It's still a little
overwhelmed by wood and in need of bottle
aging. The Gallinotto comes through
well-developed, with very clear tannins.

● Barolo Bricco Luciani '13	♟♟6
● Barolo Conca '13	♟♟7
● Barolo Gallinotto '13	♟♟6
● Barolo La Serra '13	♟♟7
● Barbera d'Alba V. Gattere '00	♟♟♟5
● Barbera d'Alba V. Gattere '97	♟♟♟7
● Barbera d'Alba V. Gattere '96	♟♟♟7
● Barolo Gallinotto '11	♟♟♟6
● Barolo Gallinotto '03	♟♟♟6
● Barolo Gallinotto '01	♟♟♟6
● Barolo V. Conca '00	♟♟♟7
● Barolo V. Conca '97	♟♟♟7
● Barolo V. Conca '96	♟♟♟7
● Barolo Bricco Luciani '11	♟♟6
● Barolo Conca '12	♟♟7

PIEDMONT

★Monchiero Carbone

VIA SANTO STEFANO ROERO, 2
12043 CANALE [CN]
TEL. +39 017395568
www.monchierocarbone.com

CELLAR SALES
PRE-BOOKED VISITS
ANNUAL PRODUCTION 180,000 bottles
HECTARES UNDER VINE 25.00
SUSTAINABLE WINERY

Francesco and Lucrezia Monchiero's winery has, for some years, been an important benchmark among Roero's wine producers. Most of their vineyards are located in Canale, in crus like Monbirone, Renesio and Frailin, to which we can add vineyards in Vezza d'Alba, Monteu Roero and Priocca. Their wines are characterized by close-focused aromas and richness of fruit, but also age well, thanks to their structure, complexity and balance. Francesco Monchiero is one of the producers who firmly believed in Roero Arneis over the years. This year, his 2016 Roero Arneis Cecu d'la Biunda earns a Tre Bicchieri. It offers up aromas of citrus fruit, almonds and white flowers. The palate features great freshness and grip, good tanginess and a long, mineral finish. The splendid 2013 Roero Printi Riserva exhibits tones of spices and wild berries and comes through savory and elegant. The rest of the selection also proves well-made.

○ Roero Arneis Cecu d'la Biunda '16	♈♈♈ 3*	
● Roero Printi Ris. '13	♈♈ 5	
● Barbera d'Alba Pelisa '15	♈♈ 2*	
○ Roero Arneis Recit '16	♈♈ 2*	
● Roero Srü '14	♈♈ 4	
● Barbera d'Alba MonBirone '10	♈♈♈ 4*	
● Roero Printi Ris. '12	♈♈♈ 5	
● Roero Printi Ris. '11	♈♈♈ 5	
● Roero Printi Ris. '10	♈♈♈ 5	
● Roero Printi Ris. '09	♈♈♈ 5	
● Barbera d'Alba MonBirone '13	♈♈ 5	
○ Roero Arneis Cecu d'la Biunda '15	♈♈ 3*	

Monfalletto Cordero di Montezemolo

FRAZ. ANNUNZIATA, 67
12064 LA MORRA [CN]
TEL. +39 017350344
www.corderodimontezemolo.com

CELLAR SALES
PRE-BOOKED VISITS
ANNUAL PRODUCTION 240,000 bottles
HECTARES UNDER VINE 35.00

One of the most iconic images of Langhe's beauty is the centuries-old cedar (knowns as 'cedro del Libano'), set on Cascina Monfalletto in La Morra. Their 30 hectare estate has been in the hands of the Cordero di Montezemolo family for almost a century. It's divided into subareas dedicated mostly to area's principal varieties, giving life to their Barolo, along with their Gattera, Gorette and Enrico VI (from their Villero cru in Castiglione Falletto). Their approach is mostly characterized by short maceration and aging in small, French oak barrels, making for a somewhat modern styled Nebbiolo. The 2013 Barolo Enrico VI opens with splendid spiciness and delicate notes of sweet oak. Then come classic red fruits, making for an elegant, complex whole. The mouth comes through powerful, lingering and well-orchestrated. The 2013 Monfalletto moves along similar lines, featuring dark berries and golden-leaf tobacco. The 2013 Gattera is slightly more tannic and austere.

● Barolo Enrico VI '13	♈♈ 8	
● Barolo Gattera '13	♈♈ 7	
● Barolo Monfalletto '13	♈♈ 6	
● Barbera d'Alba '16	♈♈ 3	
○ Langhe Chardonnay Elioro '15	♈♈ 5	
● Langhe Nebbiolo '16	♈♈ 3	
● Dolcetto d'Alba '16	♈ 3	
○ Langhe Arneis '16	♈ 2	
● Barolo Enrico VI '04	♈♈♈ 7	
● Barolo Enrico VI '03	♈♈♈ 7	
● Barolo V. Bricco Gattera '99	♈♈♈ 8	
● Barolo V. Enrico VI '00	♈♈♈ 7	
● Barolo Bricco Gattera '11	♈♈ 8	
● Barolo Enrico VI '12	♈♈ 8	
● Barolo Enrico VI '11	♈♈ 8	
● Barolo Gattera '12	♈♈ 7	
● Barolo Monfalletto '12	♈♈ 6	

La Montagnetta

FRAZ. BRICCO CAPPELLO, 4
14018 ROATTO [AT]
TEL. +39 0141938343
www.lamontagnetta.com

CELLAR SALES
PRE-BOOKED VISITS
ANNUAL PRODUCTION 50,000 bottles
HECTARES UNDER VINE 10.00

Montagnetta has made it into the main section of our guide. Guided by Domenico Capello, this small winery's vineyards grow at 250 meters above sea level in the municipalities of Roatto, San Paolo Solbrito and Piovà Massaia, on the northern hills of Val Triversa. Domenico believed strongly in a variety as neglected as Freisa, studying it, experimenting with it and working with it in the vineyard so as to bring out its best. The 2013 Freisa d'Asti Superiore Bugianen is splendid. It offers up notes of pepper, cinchona, herbs and licorice. The palate comes through juicy, rich in fruit and long, with a close-knit and gradual tannic texture. We really liked the two Barbera d'Astis presented. The 2016 Pi-Cit proves a very pleasant vintage Barbera, savory and approachable, juicy, with notes of rain-soaked earth, blackberries and plums. Despite the difficult vintage, the 2014 Superiore Piovà manages to find the right balance between fruit and acidity.

● Freisa d'Asti Sup. Bugianen '13	♟♟ 2*
● Barbera d'Asti Pi-Cit '16	♟♟ 2*
● Barbera d'Asti Sup. Piovà '14	♟♟ 4
● Freisa d'Asti Frizzante i Ronchi '16	♟ 2
● Barbera d'Asti Sup. Piovà '13	♟♟ 4
● Freisa d'Asti Bugianen '15	♟♟ 2*
● Piemonte Bonarda Frizzante Insopita '15	♟♟ 2*

Montalbera

VIA MONTALBERA, 1
14030 CASTAGNOLE MONFERRATO [AT]
TEL. +39 0119433311
www.montalbera.it

CELLAR SALES
PRE-BOOKED VISITS
ANNUAL PRODUCTION 600,000 bottles
HECTARES UNDER VINE 175.00

Over the last decade, the Morando family has managed to make Mantalbera one of Piedmont's top producers, thanks mostly to their insistence on investing in native, though neglected, grape varieties like Ruchè. Today their estate comprises 82 hectares of ruchè in Castagnole Monferrato, accompanied by Grignolino, Barbera and Viognier. Moreover, the winery has also invested in Langhe, in Castiglione Tinella, for their Moscato d'Asti, and in La Morra, Barbaresco and Neive, for their Barolo and Barbaresco. In the 2016 Ruché di Castagnole Monferrato Laccento, floral tones of roses merge with notes of Ferrovia cherries and herbs. The palate proves rich in fruit, long and lingering, with supple tannins. Other wines came in tops in their categories. The 2016 Grignolino d'Asti Grigné, a fresh and approachable wine, features aromas of red fruit and lovely finesse. The 2016 Ruché di Castagnole Monferrato La Tradizione sees overtones of cherries, roses and licorice, and proves juicy and pleasant. The rest of the selection is also well-made.

● Ruché di Castagnole M.to Laccento '16	♟♟♟ 3*
● Grignolino d'Asti Grigné '16	♟♟ 2*
● Ruché di Castagnole M.to La Tradizione '16	♟♟ 3*
● Barbaresco Lintuito '14	♟♟ 5
● Barbera d'Asti Solo Acciaio '16	♟♟ 2*
● Barolo Levoluzione '13	♟♟ 6
● Ruché di Castagnole M.to Vegan '16	♟♟ 3
○ Calypsos Letichettanera '15	♟ 3
○ Calypsos Solo Acciaio '16	♟ 2
● Ruché di Castagnole M.to La Tradizione '15	♟♟♟ 3*
● Barbera d'Asti Sup. Nuda '13	♟♟ 7
● Ruché di Castagnole M.to Laccento '15	♟♟ 3*

Cecilia Monte

VIA SERRACAPELLI, 17
12052 NEIVE [CN]
TEL. +39 017367454
cecilia.monte@libero.it

CELLAR SALES
ANNUAL PRODUCTION 19,000 bottles
HECTARES UNDER VINE 3.50

A visit to this small winery gives you a good idea of what Cecilia Monte has in mind: a product that is simultaneously artistic and artisanal, with no detail overlooked. The result is a captivatingly elegant Barbaresco, built in small steps with the help of prestigious consultants (including her husband, starred chef Maurilio Garola of La Ciau del Tornavento). Their Barbaresco, available in two versions (one of which is dedicated to her father, Paolo), is made with grapes from their Serracapelli cru, a high vineyard with good air circulation. The elegant and layered 2013 Barbaresco Serracapelli features wild berries and a hint of licorice. It displays a classic palate, slightly marked by tannins. The 2015 Barbera d'Alba Maria Teresa proves fresh, complex and deep. It's an excellent example of this wine type. The approachable 2016 Dolcetto d'Alba Montubert comes through richly fruity. The 2013 Barbaresco Dedicato a Paolo will be released next year.

● Barbaresco Serracapelli '13	�♥♥ 5
● Barbera d'Alba Maria Teresa '15	♥♥ 3
● Dolcetto d'Alba Montubert '16	♥♥ 2*
● Barbaresco Serracapelli '11	♀♀ 5
● Barbaresco Serracapelli Dedicato a Paolo '11	♀♀ 6
● Barbaresco Vign. Serracapelli '12	♀♀ 5
● Barbaresco Vign. Serracapelli '09	♀♀ 5
● Langhe Nebbiolo '12	♀♀ 3
● Langhe Nebbiolo '10	♀♀ 3

Tenuta Montemagno

VIA CASCINA VALFOSSATO, 9
14030 MONTEMAGNO [AT]
TEL. +39 014163624
www.tenutamontemagno.it

CELLAR SALES
PRE-BOOKED VISITS
ACCOMMODATION AND RESTAURANT SERVICE
ANNUAL PRODUCTION 140,000 bottles
HECTARES UNDER VINE 15.00
SUSTAINABLE WINERY

Every year, Tenuta Montemagno solidifies its presence. The producer is among Monferrato's foremost, with a selection that, under the guidance of winemaker, Gianfranco Cordero, continues to grow in quality. Their 13 wines (comprising reds, whites, sparklers and dessert wines) seek to highlight the characteristics of the individual vineyards, with a rather modern approach taken to aging and the use of wood. The wine score table speaks for itself. It's solid and dense and highlights the attention the winery pays to their entire selection (as well as its value). This year's newcomer is the Barolo Soranus, a wine that's being tasted for the first time in IW. It proves vibrant and layered, with a complex nose playing on aromas of cinchona and spices, which don't conceal its fruit. The palate comes through powerful and rich in pulp, with a nice, long finish.

● Barbera d'Asti Sup. Mysterium '14	♥♥ 4
● Barolo Soranus '12	♥♥ 6
○ Brut 24 M. Cl.	♥♥ 5
○ M.to Bianco Musae '16	♥♥ 3
○ M.to Bianco Nymphae '16	♥♥ 2*
○ M.to Bianco Solis Vis '15	♥♥ 3
● M.to Rosso Violae '15	♥♥ 2*
● Ruché di Castagnole M.to '16	♥♥ 3
○ TM Brut M. Cl.	♥♥ 5
● Barbera d'Asti Austerum '15	♥ 3
● Grignolino d'Asti Ruber '16	♥ 2
● Malvasia di Casorzo Dulcem '16	♥ 2
● Barbera d'Asti Sup. Mysterium '13	♀♀ 4
● Barbera d'Asti Sup. Mysterium '12	♀♀ 4

Monti

FRAZ. CAMIE
LOC. SAN SEBASTIANO, 39
12065 MONFORTE D'ALBA [CN]
TEL. +39 017378391
www.paolomonti.com

CELLAR SALES
PRE-BOOKED VISITS
ANNUAL PRODUCTION 50,000 bottles
HECTARES UNDER VINE 16.00

Paolo Monti manages to consistently produce wines that are rich in body but also fresh, highly drinkable and polished. The secret lies mostly in the acidity of the grapes used, which grow at particularly high altitudes in Monforte (between 350 and 400 meters). His Barbera d'Alba, which is celebrated throughout the world, is flanked by his Barolo Bussia and an intriguing Langhe L'Aura, made with Chardonnay and Riesling. Merlot plays an important role as the variety is used both in a monovarietal magnum and as a blend (in the charming Langhe Dossi Rossi, made with Sauvignon and Nebbiolo). The 2013 Barolo del Comune di Monforte d'Alba is still a bit marked by oaky spiciness, a reflection of the winery's choice to bottle age their wines for the right balance. Cherries and red flowers emerge on a splendid nose. The palate shows good tannins and a long, clean finish. The wooded 2011 Barolo Bussia Riserva proves more closed and less fruity.

● Barolo del Comune di Monforte d'Alba '13	♟♟ 7
● Barbera d'Alba '14	♟♟ 5
● Barolo Bussia Ris. '11	♟♟ 8
● Nebbiolo d'Alba '14	♟♟ 4
● Barbera d'Alba '13	♟♟ 5
● Barbera d'Alba '12	♟♟ 5
● Barbera d'Alba Sup. '13	♟♟ 7
● Barolo Bussia Ris. '10	♟♟ 8
● Barolo del Comune di Monforte d'Alba '12	♟♟ 7
● Barolo del Comune di Monforte d'Alba '11	♟♟ 7
● Barolo del Comune di Monforte d'Alba '10	♟♟ 7
● Langhe Dossi Rossi '11	♟♟ 5
● Nebbiolo d'Alba '12	♟♟ 4

Stefanino Morra

LOC. SAN PIETRO
VIA CASTAGNITO, 50
12050 CASTELLINALDO [CN]
TEL. +39 0173213489
www.morravini.it

CELLAR SALES
PRE-BOOKED VISITS
ANNUAL PRODUCTION 70,000 bottles
HECTARES UNDER VINE 11.00
SUSTAINABLE WINERY

The Morra family has been producing wines for three generations. Today, the winery, founded in 1925 (and bottling since 1990), is managed by Stefanino. Their vineyards, which span three municipalities in which the soil is mostly sandy and calcareous, feature Roero's most cultivated grapes (Arneis, Favorita, Nebbiolo and Barbera). The wines often display notable structure and pleasantness. It sometimes happens that so-called basic wines turn out to be more interesting than select versions. This is the case for the 2015 Barbera d'Alba. It's rich in fruit, taut and acidulous, in keeping with tradition, with good length. We particularly enjoyed the 2015 Castlè, which comes through pleasant, but lacks the right grip and dynamism on the palate. The rest of the selection proves well-made, though we generally preferred their basic wines. The 2014 Roero shows good body and length, while the 2016 Roero Arneis is pleasant and supple.

● Barbera d'Alba '15	♟♟ 3*
● Roero '14	♟♟ 3
○ Roero Arneis '16	♟♟ 2*
○ Roero Arneis Vign. San Pietro '15	♟♟ 3
● Barbera d'Alba Castlè '15	♟ 5
● Roero Srai Ris. '13	♟ 5
● Barbera d'Alba '14	♟♟ 3
● Barbera d'Alba '13	♟♟ 3*
● Barbera d'Alba Castellinaldo '13	♟♟ 4
● Barbera d'Alba Castlè '12	♟♟ 5
● Roero '13	♟♟ 4
○ Roero Arneis '15	♟♟ 3*
● Roero Srai Ris. '12	♟♟ 5

F.lli Mossio

FRAZ. CASCINA CARAMELLI
VIA MONTÀ, 12
12050 RODELLO [CN]
TEL. +39 0173617149
www.mossio.com

CELLAR SALES
PRE-BOOKED VISITS
ACCOMMODATION
ANNUAL PRODUCTION 50,000 bottles
HECTARES UNDER VINE 10.00
SUSTAINABLE WINERY

Valerio and Remo Mossio's small winery,
one of the most celebrated representatives
of Dolcetto in the area, just toasted 40
years in the business. A visit here gives you
a good idea of their fundamental principle:
it's all about the vineyards. Walking through
these, in addition to the picturesque
panoramas of Alba and Diano, you can see
how important manual work is and how the
use of chemicals has been eschewed. Their
wines are forthright and rich in fruit,
starting with their supremely pleasing
Dolcetto d'Alba Bricco Caramelli and Piano
delli Perdoni The 2016 vintage of Dolcetto
proved gratifying to the Mossio family,
which is why they decided to push back the
release of their two most successful wines:
the Dolcetto d'Alba Piano delli Perdoni and
the famous Bricco Caramelli. We'll come
back to them next year. The approachable
2015 Barbera d'Alba proved pleasant,
while the 2012 Langhe Nebbiolo Luen is a
delicate wine with good harmony.

● Barbera d'Alba '15	▼▼ 4
● Langhe Nebbiolo Luen '12	▼▼ 4
● Dolcetto d'Alba Sup. Gamvs '15	▼ 4
● Le Margherite '13	▼ 5
● Dolcetto d'Alba Bricco Caramelli '00	▼▼▼ 3*
● Barbera d'Alba '14	▼▼ 4
● Barbera d'Alba '13	▼▼ 4
● Dolcetto d'Alba Bricco Caramelli '15	▼▼ 3*
● Dolcetto d'Alba Bricco Caramelli '14	▼▼ 3*
● Dolcetto d'Alba Piano delli Perdoni '15	▼▼ 2*
● Dolcetto d'Alba Piano delli Perdoni '14	▼▼ 2*
● Dolcetto d'Alba Sup. Gamus '13	▼▼ 4
● Langhe Nebbiolo '12	▼▼ 4
● Langhe Rosso '12	▼▼ 4

★Fiorenzo Nada

VIA AUSARIO, 12C
12050 TREISO [CN]
TEL. +39 0173638254
www.nada.it

CELLAR SALES
PRE-BOOKED VISITS
ANNUAL PRODUCTION 45,000 bottles
HECTARES UNDER VINE 10.00
SUSTAINABLE WINERY

Treiso has been part of Barbaresco since
1952, a year after the birth of Bruno Nada.
He decided, at 30, to give up teaching to
start making wine with the family grapes
(under the guidance of his father, Fiorenzo).
Today, the future is taking shape, with his
son, Danilo, coming aboard. Their wines are
fruity, clean, rich in body, and supremely
drinkable. Each of the six wines in their
selection, led by their Barbaresco Rombone
and Langhe Rosso Seifile, stays true to the
variety and the territory. The first vintage
made with grapes from their new
Barbaresco cru, the 2013 Montaribaldi, put
in a particularly strong performance, bringing
home a Tre Bicchieri. It's warm and rich, with
elegant notes of dried flowers and licorice,
followed by a close-focused and long mouth.
The already open 2013 Barbaresco
Rombone shows great personality and
complexity. It proves evolved and elegant on
the nose, and powerful and austere on the
palate. The 2013 Barbaresco Manzola also
did well, displaying excellent freshness,
though it's a less firmly-structured wine.

● Barbaresco Montaribaldi '13	▼▼▼ 7
● Barbaresco Manzola '13	▼▼ 6
● Barbaresco Rombone '13	∧ ▼▼ 7
● Barbera d'Alba '15	▼▼ 4
● Langhe Nebbiolo '15	▼▼ 3
● Langhe Rosso Seifile '13	▼▼ 7
● Barbaresco Manzola '08	▼▼▼ 6
● Barbaresco Manzola '06	▼▼▼ 6
● Barbaresco Rombone '12	▼▼▼ 7
● Barbaresco Rombone '10	▼▼▼ 7
● Barbaresco Rombone '09	▼▼▼ 7
● Barbaresco Rombone '07	▼▼▼ 7
● Barbaresco Rombone '06	▼▼▼ 7
● Barbaresco Rombone '05	▼▼▼ 7
● Barbaresco Rombone '04	▼▼▼ 7

Cantina dei Produttori Nebbiolo di Carema

VIA NAZIONALE, 32
10010 CAREMA [TO]
TEL. +39 0125811160
www.caremadoc.it

CELLAR SALES
PRE-BOOKED VISITS
RESTAURANT SERVICE
ANNUAL PRODUCTION 65,000 bottles
HECTARES UNDER VINE 20.00

The expression 'heroic viticulture' perfectly expresses the enclave of Carema, with its rocky pergolas, its ledges surrounded by the Alpine ridge, its dizzying slopes and temperature ranges, a variety as fussy as Nebbiolo Picotendro and harvests that finish in late Autumn. But the more than 80 member-growers that provide grapes to Cantina dei Produttori Nebbiolo di Carema certainly aren't lacking in courage. We're talking about the largest producer in the appellation, with 17 hectares of vineyards and a selection of wines that stand out for their excellent value. The color of the label identifies the Carema, vintage (black) and 'Riserva' (white), both aged in large barrels for anywhere from 24 to 36 months. We tested two very different wines in terms of expression. The 2014 Carema compensates evolution with a delicately floral, herbal progression of flavor. The complete aromatic suite for which mountain Nebbiolos are known (roots, rust, dried herbs, smoky notes) is on display with the 2013 Riserva, a wine that sees a more vigorous, powerful mouth.

● Carema Ris. '13	♀♀♀ 4
● Carema Et. Nera '14	♀♀♀ 3
● Carema Et. Bianca '07	♀♀♀ 3*
● Carema Et. Bianca Ris. '11	♀♀♀ 3*
● Carema Et. Bianca Ris. '09	♀♀♀ 3*
● Carema Et. Bianca Ris. '08	♀♀♀ 3*
● Carema Et. Bianca Ris. '12	♀♀ 3
● Carema Et. Bianca Ris. '10	♀♀ 3*
● Carema Et. Nera '13	♀♀ 2*
● Carema Et. Nera '12	♀♀ 2*
● Carema Et. Nera '11	♀♀ 2*
● Carema Et. Nera '10	♀♀ 2*
● Carema Et. Nera '08	♀♀ 2*
● Carema Et. Nera '06	♀♀ 2*

Negretti

FRAZ. SANTA MARIA, 53
12064 LA MORRA [CN]
TEL. +39 0173509850
www.negrettivini.com

CELLAR SALES
PRE-BOOKED VISITS
ANNUAL PRODUCTION 40,000 bottles
HECTARES UNDER VINE 13.00

Ezio and Massimo Negretti took over the family's winery about 15 years ago, and have used their studies and their experience to create a producer that aims for quality. Their 13 hectares of vineyards are situated primarily in La Morra, though they also have land in Roddi, in the Bricco Ambrogio cru, whose fame is growing by the year. Their wines have achieved a precise house style, featuring purity of fruit, harmony of flavor and a classic touch with their use of wood. The 2013 Barolo Bricco Ambrogio is a real gem, multi-faceted, with delicate fragrances. The nose offers up aromas of raspberries, licorice, cherries and fresh red flowers. The excellent and non-excessive palate shows great balance. The 2013 Barolo Rive proves equally charming, with more mature hints of dried herbs and golden-leaf tobacco. The palate exhibits a bit more austerity. The 2013 Barolo deserves particular acclaim. Grapes grown in different vineyards make up the blend and it's one of the category's best for the vintage.

● Barolo '13	♀♀ 6
● Barolo Bricco Ambrogio '13	♀♀ 6
● Barolo Rive '13	♀♀ 6
● Barbera d'Alba Sup. '14	♀♀ 3
● Barolo Mirau '13	♀♀ 6
○ Langhe Chardonnay Dadà '15	♀♀ 3
● Nebbiolo d'Alba '14	♀♀ 3
● Barolo '09	♀♀ 6
● Barolo '08	♀♀ 6
● Barolo Bricco Ambrogio '09	♀♀ 6
● Barolo Mirau '09	♀♀ 6
● Barolo Mirau '08	♀♀ 6

Lorenzo Negro

FRAZ. SANT'ANNA, 55
12040 MONTEU ROERO [CN]
TEL. +39 017390645
www.negrolorenzo.com

CELLAR SALES
PRE-BOOKED VISITS
ANNUAL PRODUCTION 35,000 bottles
HECTARES UNDER VINE 8.00
SUSTAINABLE WINERY

The winery founded by Lorenzo Negro in 2006 has carved out a leading role among Roero's producers. Here on the Serra Lupini hill, in the vineyards that surround Lorenzo's cellar, the soil is sandy with smaller amounts of silt and clay. Many of the area's traditional varieties are grown, from Arneis to Nebbiolo and Barbera (as well as a few plots of Bonarda, Dolcetto and Albarossa). Their wines all exhibit qualities true to the territory, and feature nice, focused aromas. The 2013 Roero San Francesco Riserva is back on top. The wine features pleasant aromas of flowers and small red fruit, a juicy palate, with elegant tannins and a lingering and well-orchestrated finish. We also enjoyed the two versions of the Roero Prachirosso. The spicy 2013 exhibits an elegant tannic texture, while the 2014 proves more austere with good grip. The 2016 Roero Arneis is fruity and balsamic. The 2011 Roero Arneis Metodo Classico Brut proves pleasant and dynamic. The 2013 Barbera d'Alba Superiore La Nanda displays good grip and acidity.

Angelo Negro e Figli

FRAZ. SANT'ANNA, 1
12040 MONTEU ROERO [CN]
TEL. +39 017390252
www.negroangelo.it

CELLAR SALES
PRE-BOOKED VISITS
ANNUAL PRODUCTION 350,000 bottles
HECTARES UNDER VINE 60.00
SUSTAINABLE WINERY

The Negro family's winery is, without a doubt, one of the most important and historic producers in Roero, with a selection of wines known for their quality, technical accuracy and ability to express their territory of origin. Their grapes are all native varieties (Arneis, Favorita, Nebbiolo, Barbera, Bonarda, Dolcetto and Brachetto), cultivated in their vineyards in Monteu Roero, Canale, Magliano Alfieri and Santo Stefano Roero. For a few years now, their vineyards in Roero have been flanked by another estate, in Nieve, which they use for their Barbaresco. The 2010 Roero Arneis 7 Anni offers up notes of candied orange and white-fleshed fruit. The palate proves juicy with notable complexity. The 2014 Roero Ciabot San Giorgio Riserva, meanwhile, displays body and structure, with bold tannins and a fruity finish. There's also the traditional and pleasant 2016 Roero Arneis Perdaudin and the charming 2014 Barbaresco Basarin, a long, well-orchestrated wine with notes of blueberries, raspberries and tobacco.

● Roero San Francesco Ris. '13	♥♥ 3*
● Barbera d'Alba Sup. La Nanda '13	♥♥ 3
○ Roero Arneis '16	♥♥ 2*
○ Roero Arneis Brut M. Cl. '11	♥♥ 4
● Roero Prachiosso '14	♥♥ 3
● Roero Prachiosso '13	♥♥ 3
● Barbera d'Alba '14	♥ 2
● Barbera d'Alba '13	♀♀ 2*
● Barbera d'Alba '12	♀♀ 2*
● Barbera d'Alba Sup. La Nanda '12	♀♀ 3
● Langhe Nebbiolo '12	♀♀ 2*
○ Roero Arneis '14	♀♀ 2*
○ Roero Arneis Brut M. Cl. '10	♀♀ 4
● Roero San Francesco Ris. '11	♀♀ 3*
● Roero San Francesco Ris. '10	♀♀ 3

● Barbaresco Basarin '14	♥♥ 5
● Barbaresco Basarin Ris. '12	♥♥ 7
○ Roero Arneis 7 Anni '10	♥♥ 6
● Roero Ciabot San Giorgio Ris. '14	♥♥ 5
● Barolo del Comune di Serralunga d'Alba '13	♥♥ 5
○ Roero Arneis Perdaudin '16	♥♥ 3
○ Roero Arneis Serra Lupini '16	♥♥ 3
● Roero Prachioso '14	♥♥ 4
● Barbera d'Alba Bertu '15	♥ 5
● Roero Sudisfà Ris. '13	♀♀♀ 6
● Roero Sudisfà Ris. '12	♀♀♀ 6
● Roero Sudisfà Ris. '10	♀♀♀ 6
● Roero Sudisfà Ris. '09	♀♀♀ 5
● Roero Sudisfà Ris. '08	♀♀♀ 5

Nervi

c.so Vercelli, 117
13045 Gattinara [VC]
Tel. +39 0163833228
www.nervicantine.it

CELLAR SALES
PRE-BOOKED VISITS
ANNUAL PRODUCTION 120,000 bottles
HECTARES UNDER VINE 24.00

Valferana, Garavoglie, Casacce, Molsino. These are just some of historic places in Gattinara celebrated by Nervi's Nebbiolos. The winery, among the oldest in the area, has, since 2011, belonged to a Scandinavian joint-venture: Erling Astrup and his wife, Kathrine, who are the major shareholders, along with the Wicklund and Skjelbred families. It's a 'new direction' that's solidly anchored by the decades of experience of figures like Ettore Bornate (who's managed Nervi's vineyards since 1973) and Enrico Fileppo (who continues to coordinate production in the cellar). Their top reds confirm their efforts. Their trademark austerity is made possible thanks in part to lengthy aging in mostly large wood. The 2012 Gattinara Vigna Molsino offers up hints of forest floor, topsoil and spices. The palate remains slightly rugged at this stage. The surprising Jefferson 1787 Rosato Dosage Zéro gave an excellent performance. It displays density, grip and creaminess.

● Gattinara V. Molsino '12	🍷🍷 5
● Colline Novaresi Spanna '15	🍷🍷 3
● Gattinara '13	🍷🍷 4
⊙ Jefferson 1787 Rosé Dosage Zéro M. Cl.	🍷🍷 5
○ Erbaluce di Caluso Bianca '16	🍷 4
⊙ Rosa '16	🍷 4
● Gattinara Podere dei Ginepri '01	🍸🍸🍸 5
● Gattinara Vign. Molsino '00	🍸🍸🍸 5
● Gattinara '12	🍸🍸 4
● Gattinara Molsino '11	🍸🍸 5
● Gattinara Molsino '09	🍸🍸 5
● Gattinara Valferana '11	🍸🍸 5
● Gattinara Valferana '09	🍸🍸 5

Cantina Sociale di Nizza

s.da Alessandria, 57
14049 Nizza Monferrato [AT]
Tel. +39 0141721348
www.nizza.it

CELLAR SALES
PRE-BOOKED VISITS
ANNUAL PRODUCTION 200,000 bottles
HECTARES UNDER VINE 560.00
VITICULTURE METHOD Certified Biodynamic
SUSTAINABLE WINERY

The cooperative winery Cantina Sociale di Nizza was founded in 1955 and rapidly became one of the territory's most important producers. Today, 200 members cultivate more than 550 hectares of land, mostly Barbera, though there's also Chardonnay, Cortese, Dolcetto, Freisa and Moscato. Their wines are modern, but also careful to maintain their ties with the territory, as demonstrated by the creation of a new organic line. The 2015 Nizza Ceppi Vecchi made it into our finals thanks to notes of dark fruit, cinchona and rain-soaked earth. The palate features great structure, juiciness, good, vibrant supporting acidity and a long finish. The 2015 Barbera d'Asti Superiore Magister is almost on par, with aromas ranging from pencil lead to blackberries, tobacco and cinchona, velvety tannins and good acidity. The 2016 Piemonte Barbera In Origine proves fresh and approachable. It's an organic wine made from grapes grown with biodynamic viticulture.

● Nizza Ceppi Vecchi '15	🍷🍷 4
● Barbera d'Asti Sup. Magister '15	🍷🍷 2*
● Piemonte Barbera In Origine '16	🍷🍷 2*
○ Bacchebianche '16	🍷 2
● Baccherosse '15	🍷 2
● Barbera d'Asti Le Pole '15	🍸🍸 2*
● Barbera d'Asti Sup. 50 Vendemmie '12	🍸🍸 4
● Barbera d'Asti Sup. Magister '14	🍸🍸 2*
● Barbera d'Asti Sup. Magister '12	🍸🍸 2*
● Barbera d'Asti Sup. Nizza Ceppi Vecchi '14	🍸🍸 4
● Barbera d'Asti Sup. Nizza Ceppi Vecchi '12	🍸🍸 4
● Piemonte Barbera Progetto in Origine '15	🍸🍸 2*
● Piemonte Barbera Progetto in Origine '14	🍸🍸 2*

Noah

c.so Libertà, 59
13862 Brusnengo [BI]
rossonoah@libero.it

CELLAR SALES
PRE-BOOKED VISITS
HECTARES UNDER VINE 4.70

Andrea Mosca and Giovanna Pepe Diaz
founded their winery in 2010, hoping to
change their lives by dedicating themselves
to a new enterprise, one in which nature
would figure prominently. The result, for
now, is an estate of fewer than five
hectares of vineyards. A small section of
volcanic terrain means that a Lessona is
coming soon. But, for the moment, we're
quite happy to make do with a superb
Bramaterra, made with grapes from
Brusnengo. The vines may be young,
but they manage to express the
appellation's strong personality perfectly.
The 2012 Bramaterra exhibits rare and
charming complexity. The nose offers up
aromas ranging from rhubarb and licorice
to hints of iodine. The mouth comes
through austere, seductive, rich in
non-invasive tannins and shrouded by a
delicate fruity pulp. Tre Bicchieri. The very
long 2013 Bramaterra appears more
evolved, with notes of dried herbs and rust.
It features notable acidity and supple
tannins.

● Bramaterra '12	▼▼▼ 5
● Bramaterra '13	▼▼ 5

Figli Luigi Oddero

fraz. Santa Maria
loc. Tenuta Parà, 95
12604 La Morra [CN]
Tel. +39 0173500386
www.figliluigioddero.it

CELLAR SALES
PRE-BOOKED VISITS
ANNUAL PRODUCTION 110,000 bottles
HECTARES UNDER VINE 20.00
SUSTAINABLE WINERY

After Luigi Oddero worked with his brother,
Giacomo, for almost 50 years, he decided
to start his own project in 2006. It was an
adventure that, since his death, his wife
Lena and their children Maria and Giovanni
are keeping alive. Nebbiolo, Dolcetto, Freisa
and Barbera are cultivated on their 20
hectares of vineyards, which include Rive
(Santa Maria in La Morra), Scarrone (in
Castiglione Falletto), Vignarionda
(Serralunga d'Alba), Rombone (in Treiso).
We also shouldn't forget Cascina Fiori in
Trezzo Tinella, where Moscato is cultivated.
Their most important wines are still their
classic Barolos and Barbarescos. Barolo
achieved great results, especially the 2013
with its delicate palate and fresh, pleasant
aromas of raspberries violets and cherries.
The strictly classic 2012 Specola
conveys notes of licorice and aniseed
together with tobacco and refined tar. The
amazing 2010 Vigna Rionda features
aromas of roses and licorice on the nose
and comes through firmly-structured and
well-orchestrated on the palate, with
smooth tannins.

● Barolo Vigna Rionda '10	▼▼▼ 8
● Barbaresco Rombone '14	▼▼ 8
● Barolo '13	▼▼ 8
● Barolo Rocche Ris. '11	▼▼ 8
● Barolo Specola '11	▼▼ 8
● Barbera d'Alba '15	▼▼ 6
● Langhe Nebbiolo '14	▼ 6
● Barbaresco '11	♀♀ 5
● Barbaresco Rombone '13	♀♀ 5
● Barbera d'Alba '13	♀♀ 3
● Barolo '12	♀♀ 6
● Barolo Rocche Rivera '10	♀♀ 6
● Barolo Rocche Rivera '09	♀♀ 8
● Dolcetto d'Alba '15	♀♀ 2*
● Langhe Nebbiolo '12	♀♀ 3
● Langhe Nebbiolo '11	♀♀ 3

★Poderi e Cantine Oddero

FRAZ. SANTA MARIA
VIA TETTI, 28
12064 LA MORRA [CN]
TEL. +39 017350618
www.oddero.it

CELLAR SALES
PRE-BOOKED VISITS
ANNUAL PRODUCTION 150,000 bottles
HECTARES UNDER VINE 35.00
VITICULTURE METHOD Certified Organic
SUSTAINABLE WINERY

Sisters Mariacristina and Mariavittoria
Oddero get a superb roster with every
vintage. It's all made possible thanks to
their 40 hectares of vineyards, mostly
Barolo and Barbaresco Nebbiolo, along with
universally recognized mentions like Villero,
Rocche di Castiglione Falletto, Brunate (La
Morra), Mondoca (Bussia Soprana in
Monforte d'Alba), Vigna Rionda (Serralunga)
and Gallina (Barbaresco). Their reds are
recognizable for their distinct style,
sophisticated and dry, unbound from
mechanical choices concerning maceration
length and container size. Barbera, Dolcetto
and a few international varieties round out
their arsenal. The 2013 Barolo Rocche di
Castiglione is the perfect expression of one
of the most famous crus in the territory.
Aromas range from tar and licorice to dried
herbs, golden-leaf tobacco, ripe fruit and
hints of red fruit. The palate displays good
volume, tannins that are already smooth
and excellent length. The Bussia Vigna
Mondoca exhibits an excellent tannic
weave. The Vignarionda shows great
character and length.

● Barolo Bussia V. Mondoca Ris. '11	♟♟	8
● Barolo Rocche di Castiglione '13	♟♟	8
● Barolo Vignarionda Ris. '07	♟♟	8
● Barbaresco Gallina '14	♟♟	6
● Barolo '13	♟♟	6
● Barolo Villero '13	♟♟	8
○ Langhe Collaretto '15	♟♟	3
● Langhe Nebbiolo '15	♟♟	4
● Barbaresco Gallina '04	♟♟♟	6
● Barolo Bussia V. Mondoca Ris. '10	♟♟♟	8
● Barolo Bussia V. Mondoca Ris. '08	♟♟♟	8
● Barolo Mondoca di Bussia Soprana '04	♟♟♟	7
● Barolo Rocche di Castiglione '09	♟♟♟	7
● Barbaresco Gallina '13	♟♟	6
● Barolo Rocche di Castiglione '12	♟♟	8
● Barolo Vignarionda Ris. '06	♟♟	8

Tenuta Olim Bauda

VIA PRATA, 50
14045 INCISA SCAPACCINO [AT]
TEL. +39 0141702171
www.tenutaolimbauda.it

CELLAR SALES
PRE-BOOKED VISITS
ANNUAL PRODUCTION 180,000 bottles
HECTARES UNDER VINE 30.00
SUSTAINABLE WINERY

The Bertonlino family estate, Tenuta Olim
Bauda, was founded in 1961. Today, the
fourth generation of family, Diana, Dino
and Gianni, are seeing to it that the
producer is a stand-out here in Asti. Their
vineyards, planted between 1950 and
2003, are situated in the municipalities of
Nizza Monferrato, Isola d'Asti, Fontanile,
Castelnuovo Calcea and Gavi. Barbera is
their featured grape, along with Grignolino,
Moscato, Cortese, Chardonnay, and
smaller quantities of Freisa and Nebbiolo.
Olim Bauda's Barberas remain at the top
of their category, even if they didn't get a
gold. The 2014 Nizza exhibits aromas of
red wild berries and a gutsy, full-bodied
palate. It's a juicy wine, with good fruit.
The 2015 Barbera d'Asti Superiore Le
Rocchette features tones of rain-soaked
earth and pencil lead, followed by a
close-knit and concentrated palate. The
2016 Grignolino d'Asti Isolavilla proves
pleasant and fresh with hints of wild
strawberries, while the 2016 Barbera
d'Asti La Villa comes through approachable
and fruity.

● Barbera d'Asti Sup. Le Rocchette '15	♟♟	4
● Nizza '14	♟♟	5
● Barbera d'Asti La Villa '16	♟♟	3
● Grignolino d'Asti Isolavilla '16	♟♟	3
○ Gavi del Comune di Gavi '16	♟	3
○ Moscato d'Asti Centive '16	♟	2
● Barbera d'Asti Sup. Nizza '13	♟♟♟	5
● Barbera d'Asti Sup. Nizza '12	♟♟♟	5
● Barbera d'Asti Sup. Nizza '11	♟♟♟	5
● Barbera d'Asti Sup. Nizza '08	♟♟♟	5
● Barbera d'Asti Sup. Nizza '07	♟♟♟	5
● Barbera d'Asti Sup. Le Rocchette '14	♟♟	4
○ Piemonte Moscato Passito S. Giovanni '06	♟♟	5

Orsolani

VIA MICHELE CHIESA, 12
10090 SAN GIORGIO CANAVESE [TO]
TEL. +39 012432386
www.orsolani.it

CELLAR SALES
PRE-BOOKED VISITS
ANNUAL PRODUCTION 140,000 bottles
HECTARES UNDER VINE 19.00

The Orsolani family's adventure into winemaking began in 1894. It started with an inn and their famed wine shop, followed by a winery in San Giorgio Canavese. But the real breakthrough came in the 1960s, when Gian Francesco had the foresight to specialize in the production of Erbaluce, in every possible form. He gave life to Caluso's first sparkling wines and his choice of crus 'for aging' (Vignot S. Antonio and La Rustia) was newsworthy at the time. We shouldn't forget his passito dried-grape wine, Sulé. Today, his son, Gian Luigi, is by his side, and their vineyards have been enlarged with the addition of the plots of Mazzé and Caluso. Their Erbaluce sparkling wines are generally a good barometer for Orsolani's selection. The 2013 Tradizione Brut is biting and fragrant, while the 2010 Cuvée 1968 proves rounder and more mature. But the La Rustia leads the group once again. The 2016 shines with depth and mineral vigor.

Paitin

FRAZ. BRICCO
VIA SERRABOELLA, 20
12052 NEIVE [CN]
TEL. +39 017367343
www.paitin.it

CELLAR SALES
PRE-BOOKED VISITS
ACCOMMODATION
ANNUAL PRODUCTION 80,000 bottles
HECTARES UNDER VINE 17.00

Giovanni and Silvano inherited a legacy of winemaking from the Pasquero Elia family, which boasts more than a century of experience in bottling wines. At one time they used barriques and short maceration, today they've gone back to large barrels and have adopted a biodynamic approach to cultivation. Obviously, Nebbiolo is front and center, giving rise to their Barbaresco Serraboella Sorì Paitin and their acclaimed Riserva Vecchie Vigne. An elegant, international touch characterizes their Barbera d'Alba Campolive. The young and fruity 2014 Barbaresco Sorì Paitin is a direct wine with firm grip. The 2014 Barbaresco Serraboella shows steady aromas and pace, featuring notes of rhubarb and a palate of medium-weight. The 2013 Barbera d'Alba Superiore Campolive displays generous spicy notes from wood aging, which enrich its fresh and fruity qualities.

○ Erbaluce di Caluso La Rustia '16	♟♟ 3*
○ Caluso Brut Cuvée 1968 '10	♟♟ 5
○ Caluso Brut Cuvée Tradizione '13	♟♟ 4
○ Erbaluce di Caluso Vintage '14	♟♟ 4
○ Caluso Passito Sulé '04	♟♟♟ 5
○ Erbaluce di Caluso La Rustia '15	♟♟♟ 3*
○ Erbaluce di Caluso La Rustia '13	♟♟♟ 3*
○ Erbaluce di Caluso La Rustia '12	♟♟♟ 3*
○ Erbaluce di Caluso La Rustia '11	♟♟♟ 3*
○ Erbaluce di Caluso La Rustia '10	♟♟♟ 2*
○ Erbaluce di Caluso La Rustia '09	♟♟♟ 2*
○ Caluso Brut Cuvée Tradizione M. Cl. '11	♟♟ 5
○ Caluso Passito Sulé '09	♟♟ 5

● Barbaresco Serraboella '14	♟♟ 5
● Barbaresco Serraboella Sorì Paitin '14	♟♟ 6
● Barbera d'Alba Serra '15	♟♟ 4
● Barbera d'Alba Sup. Campolive '13	♟♟ 5
● Langhe Nebbiolo Starda '15	♟♟ 3
● Nebbiolo d'Alba Ca Veja '14	♟♟ 4
● Barbaresco Sorì Paitin '07	♟♟♟ 5
● Barbaresco Sorì Paitin '04	♟♟♟ 5
● Barbaresco Sorì Paitin '97	♟♟♟ 5
● Barbaresco Sorì Paitin '95	♟♟♟ 7
● Barbaresco Sorì Paitin V. V. '04	♟♟♟ 7
● Barbaresco Sorì Paitin V. V. '01	♟♟♟ 7
● Barbaresco Sorì Paitin V. V. '99	♟♟♟ 8
● Langhe Paitin '97	♟♟♟ 5
● Barbaresco Serraboella '13	♟♟ 5
● Barbaresco Sorì Paitin '13	♟♟ 6
● Barbaresco Sorì Paitin '12	♟♟ 6

Palladino

P.ZZA CAPPELLANO, 9
12050 SERRALUNGA D'ALBA [CN]
TEL. +39 0173613108
www.palladinovini.com

CELLAR SALES
ACCOMMODATION
ANNUAL PRODUCTION 200,000 bottles
HECTARES UNDER VINE 11.00

The large Palladino family sees three
generations at work in their winery, all
adept at their specific roles and
responsibilities. And this starts with the
vineyards, both their estate and those
worked by third-party growers, which forms
a complex management puzzle in southern
Piedmont. The core of their production is
set in Serralunga, where the crus of San
Bernardo, Ornato and Parafada are the
principal sources of their Barolo. But every
wine, from their Barbera d'Alba to their
Roero Arneis, expresses its territory well.
The 2013 Barolo Ornato proves quite open,
and the first pleasant notes of aging are
just starting to emerge. Aromas of sweet
tobacco and dried flowers lead into an bold
palate, where tannins are still in control.
The 2013 Barolo Parafada is still a bit
mouth-drying, with significant substance
and impressive austerity. The spicy and
pleasantly supple 2013 Barolo del Comune
di Serralunga d'Alba fared well.

● Barolo Ornato '13	♚♚ 6
● Barolo Parafada '13	♚♚ 6
● Barolo del Comune di Serralunga d'Alba '13	♚♚♚ 5
● Nebbiolo d'Alba '14	♚♚♚ 5
● Barbera d'Alba Sup. Bricco delle Olive '14	♚ 3
● Barolo San Bernardo Ris. '10	♚♚♚ 6
● Barbera d'Alba Sup. Bricco delle Olive '13	♚♚ 2*
● Barolo del Comune di Serralunga d'Alba '12	♚♚ 5
● Barolo Ornato '12	♚♚ 6
● Barolo Parafada '12	♚♚ 6
● Barolo Parafada '11	♚♚ 6

Armando Parusso

LOC. BUSSIA, 55
12065 MONFORTE D'ALBA [CN]
TEL. +39 017378257
www.parusso.com

CELLAR SALES
PRE-BOOKED VISITS
ANNUAL PRODUCTION 125,000 bottles
HECTARES UNDER VINE 23.00

At Armando Parusso they only make wines
rich in personality, ones made from low
yields in vineyards enriched with biodynamic
composts and cultivated without the use of
pesticides. The grapes are only harvested
when sufficiently ripe, so as to obtain the
maximum flavor. Fermentation is carried out
with native yeasts, without added sulphites.
Their Barolo is made with grapes from the
lovely crus of Monforte (in Bussia), Le Coste
and Mariondino, and makes up the lion's
share of production. Their Langhe Bricco
Rovella (from Sauvignon grapes) continues
to stand out, while their new Brut, made with
Nebbiolo, is a poignant addition. The
particularly multifaceted 2013 Barolo
Mariondino displays notes ranging from
leather to spices and red fruit. The palate
comes through well-orchestrated and not
very powerful, but graceful and already
pleasantly drinkable. The other Barolos are a
bit more uniform and marked by wood
aging, with aromas of peach stones and
tannins completing the picture. The
enjoyable 2013 Parusso Brut proves elegant
and rather dry.

● Barolo Mariondino '13	♚♚ 7
● Barolo '13	♚♚ 6
● Barolo Bussia '13	♚♚ 8
○ Parusso Brut M. Cl. '13	♚♚ 6
● Barolo Mosconi '13	♚ 8
● Barbera d'Alba Sup. '00	♚♚♚ 5
● Barolo Bussia V. Munie '99	♚♚♚ 8
● Barolo Bussia V. Munie '97	♚♚♚ 8
● Barolo Bussia V. Munie '96	♚♚♚ 8
● Barolo Le Coste Mosconi '03	♚♚♚ 7
● Barolo V. V. in Mariondino Ris. '99	♚♚♚ 8
● Langhe Rosso Bricco Rovella '96	♚♚♚ 8
● Barolo Bussia '12	♚♚ 8
● Barolo Mariondino '12	♚♚ 7

★Pecchenino

B.TA VALDIBERTI, 59
12063 DOGLIANI [CN]
TEL. +39 017370686
www.pecchenino.com

CELLAR SALES
PRE-BOOKED VISITS
ACCOMMODATION
ANNUAL PRODUCTION 130,000 bottles
HECTARES UNDER VINE 28.00
SUSTAINABLE WINERY

The Pecchenino brother's agricultural business is moving full speed ahead, with Orlando continuing to serve as director of the Consorzio di Tutela del Barolo e del Barbaresco. For 30 years, they have supported clean agriculture, eschewing synthetic products and herbicides in the vineyards, while their work in the cellar sees the use of native yeasts for fermentation. In addition to their selection made with Dolcetto, which features the Dogliani Sirì d'Jermu and Bricco Botti, for a decade now they've offered two Barolos from nearby Monforte d'Alba, the Le Coste and San Giuseppe. Dolcetto achieved great results this year. The Dogliani Superiore Sirì d'Jermu is a classic champion of power and elegance. The 2015 vintage exhibits hints of bitter almonds and warm alcohol. The 2016 Dogliani San Luigi plays more on fruitiness, proving still rather tannic on the palate. The well-made 2103 Barolo San Giuseppe finds the right balance between fruit and wood.

● Dogliani San Luigi '16	🏆🏆 3*
● Dogliani Sup. Sirì d'Jermu '15	🏆🏆 4
● Barbera d'Alba Quass '15	🏆🏆 4
● Barolo San Giuseppe '13	🏆🏆 6
● Dogliani Sup. Bricco Botti '15	🏆🏆 4
○ Langhe Maestro '16	🏆🏆 3
● Langhe Nebbiolo Botti '15	🏆🏆 3
● Langhe Pinot Nero '14	🏆 4
● Barolo Le Coste '05	🏆🏆🏆 8
● Dogliani Bricco Botti '07	🏆🏆🏆 4
● Dogliani Sirì d'Jermu '09	🏆🏆🏆 3*
● Dogliani Sirì d'Jermu '06	🏆🏆🏆 4
● Dogliani Sup. Bricco Botti '10	🏆🏆🏆 4*
● Dolcetto di Dogliani Sup. Bricco Botti '04	🏆🏆🏆 4

Pelassa

B.GO TUCCI, 43
12046 MONTÀ [CN]
TEL. +39 0173971312
www.pelassa.com

CELLAR SALES
ANNUAL PRODUCTION 80,000 bottles
HECTARES UNDER VINE 14.00

Today, the Pelassa family's winery, which was founded in 1960 and began bottling in 1999, sees brothers Davide and Daniele at the helm. The main estate is situated in the northernmost part of Montà d'Alba and benefits from a particularly fresh and woodland environment, while their vineyards in Verduno are dedicated to cultivating grapes for their Barolo. Local classics like Arneis, Barbera, Brachetto, Favorita, Moscato and Nebbiolo are cultivated, along with international grapes, such as Cabernet Sauvignon, Chardonnay and Merlot. The 2013 Roero Antaniolo Riserva is one of the best in the appellation. It features elegant aromas of red wild berries, Mediterranean scrub and spices, with a juicy palate rich in fruit and elegant, relaxed tannins. Their other well-made wines include the fresh, tangy and citrusy 2016 Roero Arneis San Vito, the fruity, pleasant and easy to drink 2015 Barbera d'Alba Superiore San Pancrazio and the expansive 2014 Nebbiolo d'Alba Sot, a wine with good pulp.

● Roero Antaniolo Ris. '13	🏆🏆 4
● Barbera d'Alba Sup. San Pancrazio '15	🏆🏆 3
● Nebbiolo d'Alba Sot '14	🏆🏆 3
○ Roero Arneis San Vito '16	🏆🏆 2*
● Barbera d'Alba Sup. San Pancrazio '13	🏆🏆 3
● Barolo '12	🏆🏆 6
● Barolo '10	🏆🏆 7
● Barolo Bussia '11	🏆🏆 6
● Nebbiolo d'Alba Sot '12	🏆🏆 3
● Roero Antaniolo Ris. '12	🏆🏆 4
● Roero Antaniolo Ris. '10	🏆🏆 4
○ Roero Arneis San Vito '14	🏆🏆 2*
○ Roero Arneis San Vito '13	🏆🏆 2*

Pelissero

VIA FERRERE, 10
12050 TREISO [CN]
TEL. +39 0173638430
www.pelissero.com

CELLAR SALES
PRE-BOOKED VISITS
ANNUAL PRODUCTION 250,000 bottles
HECTARES UNDER VINE 40.00

Wine businessman Giorgio Pelissero has managed to enlarge his terrain over the years and bring to life a selection of wines now featured in restaurants across the five continents. Even his winery's approach in the cellar has been at the vanguard, guaranteeing that its wines exhibit the best of what technology has to offer. Barbaresco takes center stage, but all of Langhe's principal red grapes are represented at Pelissero. Their whites feature the now historic Moscato d'Asti, with a touch of Favorita and the recently added Langhe Riesling Rigadin. The Nubiola set the record for 2014 Barbarescos. It opens with plenty of lively fresh fruit, followed by hints of spices and cocoa. Its nice, enjoyable palate features medium-structure and moderate tannins. The Vanotu proves more marked by oak and shows good length on the palate. The Tulin displays more vegetal aromas and a lightweight body. The 2016 Dolcetto d'Alba Augenta has lovely fruitiness.

Pasquale Pelissero

CASCINA CROSA, 2
12052 NEIVE [CN]
TEL. +39 017367376
www.pasqualepelissero.com

CELLAR SALES
PRE-BOOKED VISITS
ANNUAL PRODUCTION 35,000 bottles
HECTARES UNDER VINE 8.00

Pasquale Pelissero was, foremost, a lovable, skilled, tireless vine grower, who began making wines under his own name in 1971. Over time, he continued to improve his skills as a cellarman. In 2007, his equally passionate daughter, Ornella, took over the winery, with a style that still adheres to classic Barbaresco. The quality of the grapes comes first, with medium-sized barrels used in the cellar. In their vineyards, Nebbiolo dominates, though they've made room for Dolcetto, Barbera and some rows of Pinot Nero and Chardonnay (used for their sparkler, Crosé). The 2014 Barbaresco Bricco San Giuliano exhibits a rich and pleasant nose of red fruit, spices and a touch of licorice. The palate remains a bit austere and its lovely finish shows some savoriness. The 2014 Barbaresco Cascina Crosa is slightly slim-bodied and vegetal, with a firmly-structured mouth and a citrusy finish.

● Barbaresco Nubiola '14	🏆🏆 5
● Barbaresco Vanotu '14	🏆🏆 8
● Barbera d'Alba Piani '15	🏆🏆 3
● Dolcetto d'Alba Augenta '16	🏆🏆 3
Langhe Long Now '14	🏆🏆 5
● Langhe Nebbiolo '15	🏆🏆 3
● Langhe Riesling Rigadin '16	🏆🏆 3
● Barbaresco Tulin '14	🏆 7
● Dolcetto d'Alba Munfrina '16	🏆 2
Barbaresco Vanotu '08	🏆🏆🏆 8
Barbaresco Vanotu '07	🏆🏆🏆 8
Barbaresco Vanotu '06	🏆🏆🏆 8
Barbaresco Vanotu '01	🏆🏆🏆 7
Barbaresco Vanotu '99	🏆🏆🏆 7
Barbaresco Vanotu '97	🏆🏆🏆 6
Barbaresco Vanotu '95	🏆🏆🏆 6

● Barbaresco Bricco San Giuliano '14	🏆🏆 5
● Barbaresco Cascina Crosa '14	🏆🏆 4
● Barbaresco Bricco San Giuliano '12	🏆🏆 5
● Barbaresco Bricco San Giuliano '11	🏆🏆 5
● Barbaresco Bricco San Giuliano '10	🏆🏆 5
● Barbaresco Bricco San Giuliano '09	🏆🏆 5
● Barbaresco Cascina Crosa '13	🏆🏆 4
● Barbaresco Ciabot Ris. '10	🏆🏆 4
● Barbaresco San Giuliano Bricco '13	🏆🏆 5
● Dolcetto d'Alba '11	🏆🏆 2*
● Langhe Nebbiolo Pasqualin '11	🏆🏆 2*

Pertinace

Loc. Pertinace, 2/5
12050 Treiso [CN]
Tel. +39 0173442238
www.pertinace.com

CELLAR SALES
PRE-BOOKED VISITS
ANNUAL PRODUCTION 650,000 bottles
HECTARES UNDER VINE 90.00

This Langhe cooperative, founded under
the leadership of Mario Barbero in 1973,
has developed in an interesting way.
Indeed, recently, steps have been taken to
guarantee solid, sustainable growth for the
winery, with 2014 seeing the completion of
renovations on their facilities. Now, their
17 member growers (who are also
shareholders) can know that the potential
of their crop and 90 hectares of vineyards
is being realized to the maximum. Their
prices are highly competitive in relation to
the quality of their wines, which has
attracted interest both nationally and
abroad. An iconic terroir in Treiso gives rise
to the 2014 Barbaresco Marcarini. It
proves to be very close-focused on the
nose and palate, with balanced tannins
and an elegant, gratifying mouth. The
2014 Barbaresco Castellizzano appears
slightly more rugged on the palate, though
it displays excellent balsamic sensations
and a fresh, lingering finish.

● Barbaresco Marcarini '14	▼▼ 5
● Barbaresco '14	▼▼ 5
● Barbaresco Castellizzano '14	▼▼ 5
● Barbera d'Alba '15	▼▼ 3
● Dolcetto d'Alba '16	▼▼ 2*
● Barbaresco Nervo '14	▼ 5
● Langhe Nebbiolo '16	▼ 3
● Barbaresco '13	♈♈ 5
● Barbaresco '12	♈♈ 5
● Barbaresco Castellizzano '13	♈♈ 5
● Barbaresco Castellizzano '12	♈♈ 5
● Barbaresco Marcarini '13	♈♈ 5
● Barbaresco Nervo '13	♈♈ 5
● Barbaresco Nervo '12	♈♈ 5
● Barbaresco Vign. Castellizzano '11	♈♈ 5
● Barbaresco Vign. Nervo '11	♈♈ 5
● Dolcetto d'Alba '15	♈♈ 2*

Pescaja

Via San Matteo, 59
14010 Cisterna d'Asti [AT]
Tel. +39 0141979711
www.pescaja.com

PRE-BOOKED VISITS
ANNUAL PRODUCTION 200,000 bottles
HECTARES UNDER VINE 23.50

Pescaja, an estate situated between Roero
and Barbera d'Asti, is without a doubt the
most important producer in the Terre Alfieri
appellation. Founded in 1990 by Giuseppe
Guido, it has vineyards in Cisterna d'Asti
and Nizza Moferrato, where, in 1998, it
purchased most of Pescaja Opera Pia's
plots. The more calcareous soil is reserved
for their red grapes (Barbera, Nebbiolo and
Bonarda), while whites are cultivated in
more sandy clay soil (Arneis and
Chardonnay). Giuseppe Guido has put
forward a well-made selection of wines,
starting with the 2014 Nizza Solneri.
Despite the difficult vintage, it highlights
notes of dark fruit and rain-soaked earth.
The palate doesn't demonstrate the same
structure as previous versions, but it comes
through very impressive. The 2016 Barbera
d'Asti Soliter is a classic vintage Barbera,
playing on fruit and an approachable,
easy-drinking palate. The 2016 Terre Alfieri
Arneis is pleasantly floral with good acidity,
while the 2016 Roero Arneis proves tangy
with a classic almondy finish.

● Barbera d'Asti Soliter '16	▼▼ 2
● Nizza Solneri '14	▼▼ 4
○ Roero Arneis '16	▼▼ 2
○ Terre Alfieri Arneis '16	▼▼ 2
● M.to Rosso Solis '14	▼ 3
○ M.to Solo Luna '15	▼ 3
● Barbera d'Asti Soliter '15	♈♈ 2
● Barbera d'Asti Sup. Nizza Solneri '13	♈♈
● Barbera d'Asti Sup. Nizza Solneri '12	♈♈ 4
● M.to Rosso Solis '13	♈♈ 2
○ M.to Solo Luna '14	♈♈ 2
○ Terre Alfieri Arneis '15	♈♈ 2
● Terre Alfieri Nebbiolo Tuké '13	♈♈ 2

Le Piane

.ZZA MATTEOTTI, 1
28010 BOCA [NO]
TEL. +39 3483354185
www.bocapiane.com

CELLAR SALES
PRE-BOOKED VISITS
ANNUAL PRODUCTION 45,000 bottles
HECTARES UNDER VINE 8.00
SUSTAINABLE WINERY

Twenty years ago, Christoph Künzli, an importer, decided to start producing wines as well. Today he is considered, in all respects, the 'father' of modern Boca. After enjoying success, he decided to focus on a small Novara appellation, just a few hectares, taking over the plots of Le Piane from the elderly vine grower, Antonio Cerri. In time he added others, growing his estate to its current eight hectares, where Nebbiolo, Croatina and Vespolina are divided into small terracing, some of which are cultivated with the maggiorina training system. His highest-profile wine is still Boca, aged for three years in 2500-2800 liter Slavonian oak. The latest version is the result of a vintage as unique as 2012. Their Boca sees classic aromas, with clear hints of red fruit, roots and hot spices. The palate proves both exuberant and well-orchestrated at the same time, thanks to salinity and tight-knit tannins.

● Boca '12	▼▼▼	8
● Boca '11	♈♈♈	8
● Boca '10	♈♈♈	7
● Boca '08	♈♈♈	7
● Boca '06	♈♈♈	6
● Boca '05	♈♈♈	6
● Boca '04	♈♈♈	6
● Colline Novaresi Le Piane '09	♈♈	5
● Maggiorina '12	♈♈	3
● Mimmo '11	♈♈	5
● Mimmo '10	♈♈	4
● Piane '12	♈♈	6
● Piane '11	♈♈	5

Le Pianelle

S.DA FORTE, 24
13862 BRUSNENGO [BI]
TEL. +39 3478772726
www.lepianelle.com

PRE-BOOKED VISITS
ANNUAL PRODUCTION 12,000 bottles
HECTARES UNDER VINE 3.00

This original and important winery in Northern Piedmont represents a veritable 'dream come true'. Dieter Heuskel and Peter Dipoli both came from different professional backgrounds, but they shared a passion for this corner of the world, and so they decided to transform their dream into wine. Nebbiolo, Vespolina and Croatina are the principal grape varieties used for a limited, but highly studied selection of wines. Indeed, they're often unable to satisfy the demands of their increasingly large fan base. Despite resulting from a difficult vintage, the 2014 Bramaterra still comes through exuberant on the nose. It's a wine characterized by notes of cinchona, wild berries and eucalyptus. Then comes a bold tannic texture that still need to be integrated. As usual, the 2016 Rosato Al Posto dei Fiori stands out for its personality, suppleness and freshness.

● Bramaterra '14	▼▼	8
⊙ Coste della Sesia Rosato		
Al Posto dei Fiori '16	▼▼	3
● Bramaterra '13	♈♈	8
● Bramaterra '12	♈♈	8
● Bramaterra '11	♈♈	8
⊙ Coste della Sesia Rosato		
Al Posto dei Fiori '15	♈♈	3
⊙ Coste della Sesia Rosato		
Al Posto dei Fiori '14	♈♈	3
⊙ Coste della Sesia Rosato		
Al Posto dei Fiori '13	♈♈	3

Pico Maccario

VIA CORDARA, 87
14046 MOMBARUZZO [AT]
TEL. +39 0141774522
www.picomaccario.com

CELLAR SALES
PRE-BOOKED VISITS
ANNUAL PRODUCTION 650,000 bottles
HECTARES UNDER VINE 70.00

Vitaliano Maccario and the Pico brothers'
estate in Mobaruzzo (in Alto Monferrato) is
a contiguous tract of some 70 hectares.
The terrain here is medium-thick clay and
features Barbera (60 hectares of it) and
smaller parts Merlot, Cabernet Sauvignon,
Chardonnay, Sauvignon, Freisa and
Favorita. Their wines are decidedly modern,
with structure and richness of fruit serving
as their guiding principles. A Tre Bicchieri
for the 2015 Barbera d'Asti Superiore
Epico. It features lovely, close-focused fruit
(cherries and plums), followed by hints of
spices and rain-soaked earth. The fresh
and savory palate shows notable density,
though without being heavy. We also
enjoyed the 2015 Barbera d'Asti Superiore
Tre Roveri, with its notes of dark berries,
cinchona and roots, which lead into a
slightly austere but juicy, full palate. It
closes with a lingering and gutsy finish.
Lastly, we found the Barbera d'Asti
Lavignone and the Villa della Rosa '16 both
well-made.

● Barbera d'Asti Sup. Epico '15	♛♛♛	5
● Barbera d'Asti Sup. Tre Roveri '15	♛♛	4
● Barbera d'Asti Lavignone '16	♛♛	3
● Barbera d'Asti Villa della Rosa '16	♛♛	2*
● Barbera d'Asti Lavignone '15	♛♛	3
● Barbera d'Asti Lavignone '14	♛♛	3
● Barbera d'Asti Sup. Epico '14	♛♛	5
● Barbera d'Asti Sup. Tre Roveri '14	♛♛	4
● Barbera d'Asti Sup. Tre Roveri '13	♛♛	4
○ M.to Bianco Vita '15	♛♛	4

★Pio Cesare

VIA CESARE BALBO, 6
12051 ALBA [CN]
TEL. +39 0173440386
www.piocesare.it

ANNUAL PRODUCTION 400,000 bottles
HECTARES UNDER VINE 70.00

Not everyone knows that Cesare Pio was
the man who, founded one of Piedmont's
most celebrated brands. at the helm, along
with his cousin, Augusto, his nephew,
Cesare Benvenuto, and young daughter,
Federica Rosy. Theirs is a well-oiled team
that spans generations, attending to more
than 70 hectares of vineyards, spread
throughout Barolo and Barbaresco. The
remaining grapes are purchased from
established suppliers, making for a
selection that has shown constancy over
time (apart from some stylistic retouching
of the Nebbiolos, which are modern
though never overdone). The magnificent
2013 Barbaresco Il Bricco opens with red
berries and tobacco on a background of
oak. Then comes a fresh, well-orchestrated
long palate. The 2013 Barolo Ornato, made
with grapes from the magnificent cru of
the same name, proves elegant and
powerful; tannins can still be discerned in
its gradual, firmly-structured mouth.

● Barolo Ornato '13	♛♛♛	8
● Barbaresco '13	♛♛	8
● Barbaresco Il Bricco '13	♛♛	8
● Barolo '13	♛♛	8
● Barbera d'Alba Fides '15	♛♛	5
○ Langhe Chardonnay Piodilei '15	♛♛	6
● Barbaresco Il Bricco '97	♛♛♛	8
● Barolo Ornato '12	♛♛♛	8
● Barolo Ornato '11	♛♛♛	8
● Barolo Ornato '10	♛♛♛	8
● Barolo Ornato '09	♛♛♛	8
● Barolo Ornato '08	♛♛♛	8
● Barolo Ornato '06	♛♛♛	8
● Barolo Ornato '05	♛♛♛	8

Luigi Pira

VIA XX SETTEMBRE, 9
12050 SERRALUNGA D'ALBA [CN]
TEL. +39 0173613106
pira.luigi@alice.it

CELLAR SALES
PRE-BOOKED VISITS
ANNUAL PRODUCTION 50,000 bottles
HECTARES UNDER VINE 12.00

Gianpaolo, Romolo and Claudio Pira have fully embraced the project begun by Luigi Pira in the 1950s. He started out selling grapes, but things changed two decades ago when he began bottling his own wines. After all, their Nebbiolo, almost all of which is cultivated within Serralunga d'Alba, has made a name for itself through the strength of its tannins and full-flavored texture. This eclectic temperament is further shaped by skilled cellar work, which calls for roughly two years of aging in medium-sized oak for their Barolo and Margheria, and mixed aging in barriques, mid-sized casks and 2500 liter barrels for their Marenca and Vignarionda. The 2013 Barolo Vignarionda displays good personality in a strictly classic environment. Aromas of red berries, violets and licorice pave the way for a mouth that plays more on balance than power. The palate is rich but not too weighty, with pleasant acidity that contrasts the warmth of alcohol. The more linear 2013 Barolo Marenca exhibits excellent harmony.

● Barolo Marenca '13	♥♥	7
● Barolo Vignarionda '13	♥♥	8
● Barbera d'Alba '15	♥♥	3
● Barolo del Comune di Serralunga d'Alba '13	♥♥	5
● Barolo Margheria '13	♥♥	6
● Barolo Marenca '11	♥♥♥	7
● Barolo Marenca '09	♥♥♥	7
● Barolo Marenca '08	♥♥♥	7
● Barolo V. Rionda '06	♥♥♥	8
● Barolo Vignarionda '12	♥♥♥	8
● Barolo del Comune di Serralunga '12	♥♥	5
● Barolo Marenca '12	♥♥	7
● Barolo Margheria '12	♥♥	6
● Barolo Margheria '11	♥♥	6
● Barolo V. Rionda '11	♥♥	8

E. Pira & Figli
Chiara Boschis

VIA VITTORIO VENETO, 1
12060 BAROLO [CN]
TEL. +39 017356247
www.pira-chiaraboschis.com

CELLAR SALES
PRE-BOOKED VISITS
ANNUAL PRODUCTION 35,000 bottles
HECTARES UNDER VINE 8.50
VITICULTURE METHOD Certified Organic

A firm believer in modern winemaking styles, Chiara Boschis doesn't stop at short maceration or the use of new wood. Her idea of innovation starts with the vineyards, which are cultivated organically. Her Barolo Cannubi (about 4000 bottles a year) is rich in sweet spices and fruit, and endowed with elegant drinkability. Her Via Nuova is more classic, calling up tar and dried lavender. The first vintages of Barolo Mosconi are even more austere, while the Barbera d'Alba Superiore, made with grapes from Monforte d'Alba, is another compelling wine. In the 2013 Barolo Cannubi, fruit and red flowers anticipate an elegant spicy component stemming from oak. The mouth comes through powerful and dense, rich in pulp and with rare harmony. Despite the fact that the cru isn't well-known, Via Nuova shows it can provide rich grapes which create a velvety taste sensation with excellent balance. The 2015 Barbera d'Alba Superiore displays fine toasting and an austere mouth.

● Barolo Cannubi '13	♥♥	8
● Barolo Via Nuova '13	♥♥	8
● Barbera d'Alba Sup. '15	♥♥	4
● Barolo Mosconi '13	♥♥	8
● Langhe Nebbiolo '15	♥♥	4
● Dolcetto d'Alba '16	♥	2
● Barolo Cannubi '11	♥♥♥	8
● Barolo Cannubi '10	♥♥♥	8
● Barolo Cannubi '06	♥♥♥	8
● Barolo Cannubi '05	♥♥♥	8
● Barbera d'Alba Sup. '14	♥♥	4
● Barolo Cannubi '12	♥♥	8
● Barolo Mosconi '12	♥♥	8
● Barolo Via Nuova '12	♥♥	8

Marco Porello

c.so Alba, 71
12043 Canale [CN]
Tel. +39 0173979324
www.porellovini.it

CELLAR SALES
PRE-BOOKED VISITS
ANNUAL PRODUCTION 130,000 bottles
HECTARES UNDER VINE 15.00

The winery managed by Marco Porello is composed of two structures. Their cellar for winemaking and bottling, as well their main site of operations, is in Canale. They also have a cellar for aging just next to Guarene Castle. Even their vineyards are located in two municipalities. Vezza d'Alba, where Arneis, Favorita and Nebbiolo are grown, features mostly sandy, mineral-rich soil. In Canale the terrain is characterized by medium-density, calcareous clay. Here we find Barbera, Brachetto and Nebbiolo. The Roero Torretta confirms its place among the best in the appellation, even with the difficult 2014 vintage. Notes of small red fruit accompany a mouth with good pulp and balance, elegant tannins and a fresh, pleasant palate. The 2015 Barbera d'Alba Filatura is right up there, with its characteristic notes of rain-soaked earth and cherries, and good body that's supported by a taut, fresh finish. The 2016 Roero Arneis proves to be a pleasant and citrusy wine.

● Barbera d'Alba Filatura '15	▼▼4
● Roero Torretta '14	▼▼4
○ Roero Arneis '16	▼▼2*
● Barbera d'Alba Mommiano '16	▼2
● Nebbiolo d'Alba '15	▼3
○ Roero Arneis Camestri '16	▼3
● Roero Torretta '06	▽▽▽3*
● Roero Torretta '04	▽▽▽3*
● Barbera d'Alba Filatura '14	▽▽3
● Barbera d'Alba Mommiano '15	▽▽2*
○ Langhe Favorita '14	▽▽2*
○ Roero Arneis Camestrì '15	▽▽3
● Roero Torretta '13	▽▽3*

Guido Porro

via Alba, 1
12050 Serralunga d'Alba [CN]
Tel. +39 0173613306
www.guidoporro.com

CELLAR SALES
PRE-BOOKED VISITS
ACCOMMODATION
ANNUAL PRODUCTION 35,000 bottles
HECTARES UNDER VINE 8.00

Guido Porro, a benchmark for the vineyard of Lazzarito (in Serralunga d'Alba), has officially come into his own. Lazzairasco and Santa Caterina are the two plots that perfectly divide the six hectares of terrain here. These are dedicated to two Barolos with very different characters. The first is more intense, in general, while the second is more feminine and graceful. Neither hesitates to declare its classical style, the result of fermentation in steel and concrete, and aging in 2500 liter Slavonian oak. Cru Gianetto was added in 2011, while we're waiting for the first Vignarionda to come from the plots inherited from Tommaso Canale. When the lovely Serralunga d'Alba vineyard comes together with strict respect for the tradition and work of a great artisan, you get a 2013 Barolo Lazzairasco worthy of Tre Bicchieri. Its aromatic elegance and complexity derives from the grapes, not the wood. The palate exhibits an elegant, slow, gradual power, with more pulp than tannins.

● Barolo V. Lazzairasco '13	▼▼▼5
● Barolo Gianetto '13	▼▼5
● Barolo V. Santa Caterina '13	▼▼5
● Barbera d'Alba Sup. V. Santa Caterina '16	▼3
● Barolo V. Lazzairasco '12	▽▽▽5
● Barolo V. Lazzairasco '11	▽▽▽5
● Barolo V. Lazzairasco '09	▽▽▽5
● Barolo V. Lazzairasco '07	▽▽▽5
● Barbera d'Alba V. S. Caterina '15	▽▽3
● Barolo Gianetto '12	▽▽5
● Barolo Gianetto '11	▽▽5
● Barolo V. Santa Caterina '12	▽▽5
● Barolo V. Santa Caterina '11	▽▽5
● Dolcetto d'Alba L'Pari '15	▽▽3
● Lange Nebbiolo Camilu '15	▽▽4

Post dal Vin
Terre del Barbera

FRAZ. POSSAVINA
VIA SALIE, 19
14030 ROCCHETTA TANARO [AT]
TEL. +39 0141644143
www.postdalvin.it

CELLAR SALES
PRE-BOOKED VISITS
ANNUAL PRODUCTION 80,000 bottles
HECTARES UNDER VINE 100.00

La Post dal Vin - Terre del Barbera is a cooperative winery that does an excellent job representing its category. This thanks to their careful work and focus on quality (both for their members and consumers). Most of the terrain cultivated is situated in Rocchetta Tanaro, Cortiglione and Masio, with Barbera dominating (the territory's traditional grape, as evidenced by their name) and giving rise to most of their wines. This cooperative winery always puts forward solid wines. The 2016 Barbera d'Asti Maricca is a perfect vintage Barbera. The nose features rich fruit and characteristic earthy notes, while the palate comes through fresh, juicy and easy-drinking. Other well-made wines include the 2016 Grignolino d'Asti, which is one of the best in the appellation for typicity and aromatic precision. It offers up notes of small red fruit and pepper, elegant tannic texture and a long finish. The 2015 Barbera d'Asti Superiore Briccofiore proves pleasant and spicy.

Giovanni Prandi

FRAZ. CASCINA COLOMBÉ
VIA FARINETTI, 5
12055 DIANO D'ALBA [CN]
TEL. +39 017369248
www.prandigiovanni.it

CELLAR SALES
PRE-BOOKED VISITS
ANNUAL PRODUCTION 20,000 bottles
HECTARES UNDER VINE 5.00
SUSTAINABLE WINERY

It's almost surprising when you walk into a winery where the use of wood is kept to a minimum. But it's normal when you're as firm believers as Alessandro Prandi and his family. The decision to utilize steel and concrete for fermenting and aging their Dolcetto di Diano d'Alba stems from a desire to preserve the wine's characteristic fruity aromas (rather than contaminate them with oak). The grapes are cultivated in two important crus, Sörì Cristina and Sörì Colombé, with small surrounding plots that host Nebbiolo and Barbera (the only grapes that ever see the wood they do use), and Arneis. The 2016 Dolcetto di Diano d'Alba Sörì Cristina focuses on warm pleasantness with a good alcoholic component. The nose features lively red fruit and a clean structure. The well-orchestrated 2015 Nebbiolo d'Alba features a nice, spicy mouth. It's a fresh wine, not too tannic. The elegant 2016 Barbera d'Alba proves close-focused and velvety.

Barbera d'Asti Maricca '16	🍷🍷 2*
Barbera d'Asti Sup. Briccofiore '15	🍷🍷 2*
Grignolino d'Asti '16	🍷🍷 2*
Barbera d'Asti Sup. Castagnassa '15	🍷 3
Barbera d'Asti Castagnassa '13	🍷🍷 2*
Barbera d'Asti Maricca '14	🍷🍷 2*
Barbera d'Asti Sup. Bricco Fiore '13	🍷🍷 2*
Barbera d'Asti Sup. BriccoFiore '12	🍷🍷 2*
Barbera d'Asti Sup. BriccoFiore '12	🍷🍷 2*
Barbera d'Asti Sup. Castagnassa '14	🍷🍷 2*
Barbera d'Asti Sup. Castagnassa '12	🍷🍷 2*
Barbera del M.to La Matutona '15	🍷🍷 2*
Grignolino d'Asti '13	🍷🍷 1*

● Dolcetto di Diano d'Alba Sörì Cristina '16	🍷🍷 2*
● Barbera d'Alba '16	🍷🍷 2*
● Nebbiolo d'Alba '15	🍷🍷 3
● Dolcetto di Diano d'Alba Sörì Colombé '16	🍷🍷 2
● Barbera d'Alba '15	🍷🍷 2*
● Barbera d'Alba '14	🍷🍷 2*
● Dolcetto di Diano d'Alba Sörì Colombè '15	🍷🍷 2*
● Dolcetto di Diano d'Alba Sörì Colombè '14	🍷🍷 2*
● Dolcetto di Diano d'Alba Sörì Cristina '15	🍷🍷 2*
● Dolcetto di Diano d'Alba Sörì Cristina '14	🍷🍷 2*
● Dolcetto di Diano d'Alba Sörì Cristina '13	🍷🍷 2*
● Nebbiolo d'Alba '14	🍷🍷 3
● Nebbiolo d'Alba Colombè '12	🍷🍷 3*

La Prevostura

Cascina Prevostura, 1
13853 I Essona [BI]
Tel. +39 0158853188
www.laprevostura.it

CELLAR SALES
PRE-BOOKED VISITS
RESTAURANT SERVICE
ANNUAL PRODUCTION 15,000 bottles
HECTARES UNDER VINE 4.00

The Bellini brothers' adventure in wine production began in 2003. At first it was just Marco, who took over a historic estate that had belonged to the Marquis La Marmora and Quario families. He was later flanked by Davide, transforming La Prevostura into one of the area's shining contemporary producers. Here, in the heart of the Colline Biellesi, between Lessona and Villa del Bosco, Nebbiolo is grown along with Vespolina and Croatina in the unusual sandy grooves of Bramaterra. Their five hectares are hectares are sufficient to shape a limited but significant selection of vibrant, full-bodied reds, aged at length in barriques and mid-sized casks. The Lessona reinforces its role as the winery's flagship wine with a magnificent 2013. It offers up aromas of ginseng, tobacco, hints of iron and is an overtly territorial wine, also in the vibrant texture of its palate. But their supposed 'second tier' wines are growing as well, such as the graceful and gradual 2013 Rosso Muntacc.

● Coste della Sesia Rosso Muntacc '13	🏆🏆 3*
● Lessona '13	🏆🏆 5
○ Piemonte Rosato Corinna '16	🏆🏆 3
● Lessona '12	🏆🏆🏆 5
● Bramaterra '12	🏆🏆 5
● Bramaterra '11	🏆🏆 5
● Coste della Sesia Rosso Muntacc '12	🏆🏆 3*
● Coste della Sesia Rosso Muntacc '11	🏆🏆 3
● Coste della Sesia Rosso Muntacc '10	🏆🏆 3
● Lessona '11	🏆🏆 5
● Lessona '10	🏆🏆 5
● Lessona '09	🏆🏆 5

Prinsi

via Gaia, 5
12052 Neive [CN]
Tel. +39 017367192
www.prinsi.it

CELLAR SALES
PRE-BOOKED VISITS
ANNUAL PRODUCTION 60,000 bottles
HECTARES UNDER VINE 14.50

For 20 years, Daniele Lequio has been working in his family's winery and by now he's an expert cellarman (in addition to representing his selection on international markets). Daniele, who continues to be helped by his parents, maintains a philosophy in which respect for the grape is central. As a result he uses oak barrels of various sizes for his Barbaresco and Barbera, while all his other wines are aged exclusively in steel. Their lovely facility, which was founded a century ago and deserves a visit, was recently upgraded to include a large bottle cellar. Production focuses on Barbaresco, which is available in three versions. The forthright 2014 Barbaresco Gaia Principe opens with notes of herbs and dried flowers. Its measured and balanced mouth gives way to a clean and medium-weight finish. The more supple 2014 Barbaresco Gallina proves less lively and fresh, unlike what we would expect from the vintage. The 2016 Sauvignon Camp 'd Pietru, a wine that ages solely in steel, put in a particularly strong performance.

● Barbaresco Gaia Principe '14	🏆🏆
● Barbaresco Gallina '14	🏆🏆
○ Camp'd Pietru '16	🏆🏆
● Barbera d'Alba Sup. Il Bosco '15	🏆
● Barbera d'Alba Sup. Much '15	🏆
● Langhe Nebbiolo Sandrina '15	🏆
● Barbaresco Fausone Ris. '08	🏆🏆
● Barbaresco Fausoni Ris. '11	🏆🏆
● Barbaresco Fausoni Ris. '10	🏆🏆
● Barbaresco Gaia Principe '13	🏆🏆
● Barbaresco Gallina '13	🏆🏆
● Barbaresco Gallina '12	🏆🏆
● Barbaresco Gallina '11	🏆🏆
● Barbera d'Alba Sup. Il Bosco '11	🏆🏆

★Produttori del Barbaresco

VIA TORINO, 54
12050 BARBARESCO [CN]
TEL. +39 0173635139
www.produttoridelbarbaresco.com

CELLAR SALES
PRE-BOOKED VISITS
ACCOMMODATION
ANNUAL PRODUCTION 500,000 bottles
HECTARES UNDER VINE 105.00

50 families and more than 100 hectares keep together one of the most important co-operative wineries in Europe. Ferdinando Principiano was founded in 1958, thanks to the efforts of don Fiorino Marengo. The Barbaresco parish wanted to revive the co-operative founded in the late 19th century by the legendary president of the Regia Scuola Enologica di Alba, Domino Cavanna. It stopped operating in the twenties, shortly after his death. The dream came true, as the international success of their wines attests to. Their selection, which centers on Nebbiolo, includes a base Barbaresco and, for the best vintages, nine 'Riserva' crus. All their wines are worked according to tradition, taking into account the essentials, with lengthy aging in Slavonian oak. In the absence of the famous Riserva selections, this year our tasting was necessarily limited to the 2014 Barbaresco. It features a beautiful intense ruby color with a slight garnet rim. The intense and fresh nose sees a slight green note set on a background of oak. The palate isn't huge, slightly tannic, but the finish suggests a potentially nice development in the bottle.

● Barbaresco '14	♈♈	5
● Barbaresco Ovello Ris. '09	♈♈♈	6
● Barbaresco Vign. in Montestefano Ris. '05	♈♈♈	6
● Barbaresco Vign. in Montestefano Ris. '04	♈♈♈	6
● Barbaresco Vign. in Montestefano Ris. '01	♈♈♈	5
● Barbaresco Vign. in Ovello Ris. '08	♈♈♈	6
● Barbaresco Vign. in Pajé Ris. '01	♈♈♈	5*
● Barbaresco Vign. in Pora Ris. '07	♈♈♈	6
● Barbaresco Vign. in Rio Sordo Ris. '01	♈♈♈	5

Cantina Produttori del Gavi

VIA CAVALIERI DI VITTORIO VENETO, 45
15066 GAVI [AL]
TEL. +39 0143642786
www.cantinaproduttoridelgavi.it

CELLAR SALES
PRE-BOOKED VISITS
ANNUAL PRODUCTION 300,000 bottles
HECTARES UNDER VINE 220.00

More than 200 hectares of vineyards and more than 100 member-growers keep alive the ambitions of what is, in all respects, one of the most flourishing co-operatives in Alessandrino. Founded in 1951, and reinaugurated in 1974 as Cantina Produttori del Gavi, the winery is bolstered by its ability to bring together sizable numbers and prices that are affordable, to say the least. And they do it without compromising the character of an extremely diverse range of wines. There are eight Gavi, almost all fermented and aged in steel without the use of malolactic (the only exception being a part of their Aureliana selection, which is aged in barriques). The 2015 GG offers up intense and elegant hints of golden delicious apples and meadow grass set on a mineral background. It reveals a well-orchestrated design that follows through well onto a tangy, long palate. It brings home its first Tre Bicchieri. The G from the same vintage is almost on the same level, while the 2016 Gavi Maddalena and Primo Grappoli play more on easy-drinking and linearity.

○ Gavi del Comune di Gavi GG '15	♈♈♈	3*
○ Gavi G '15	♈♈	3*
○ Gavi Maddalena '16	♈♈	2*
○ Gavi del Comune di Gavi Primi Grappoli '16	♈	2
○ Gavi del Comune di Gavi Et. Nera '15	♈♈	2*
○ Gavi del Comune di Gavi Et. Nera '14	♈♈	2*
○ Gavi del Comune di Gavi La Maddalena '15	♈♈	3*
○ Gavi G '14	♈♈	3*
○ Gavi GG '14	♈♈	3
○ Gavi Il Forte '15	♈♈	2*
○ Gavi Il Forte '14	♈♈	2*
○ Gavi Primi Grappoli '15	♈♈	2*

★Prunotto

c.so Barolo, 14
12051 Alba [CN]
Tel. +39 0173280017
www.prunotto.it

CELLAR SALES
PRE-BOOKED VISITS
ANNUAL PRODUCTION 850,000 bottles
HECTARES UNDER VINE 55.00

Many enthusiasts are surprised to discover that this emblem of the Antinori family in Piedmont got its start more than 100 years ago as 'Cantina Sociale Ai Vini delle Langhe'. The producer was taken over by Alfredo Prunotto, who ran it until 1956, when he handed it over to the Colla brothers, with Carlo Filiberto. Then, in 1994, the celebrated Tuscan group finalized their purchase of the estate. The last two decades have seen it grow to include more than 50 hectares between Langhe and Monferrato, with first-rate vineyards like Bussia (in Monforté), Bric Turot (Barbaresco), Costamiole and Fiulot (Agliano), Mompertone and Bricco Colma (Calliano). The 2011 Barolo Bussia Vigna Colonnello Riserva offers up mature aromas of spices, bottled cherries and oak. In the mouth it proves well-orchestrated and gives way to a finish with a welcome acidulous note. The 2013 Barolo Bussia moves along similar lines, but displays a slightly more austere palate. The 2014 Nebbiolo d'Alba Occhetti did quite well, as did both the Barbarescos.

● Barolo Bussia V. Colonnello Ris. '11	♥♥	8
● Barbaresco '14	♥♥	5
● Barbaresco Bric Turot '14	♥♥	6
● Barolo '13	♥♥	6
● Barolo Bussia '13	♥♥	8
● Nebbiolo d'Alba Occhetti '14	♥♥	4
● M.to Rosso Mompertone '14	♥	3
● Barolo Bussia '01	♥♥♥	8
● Barolo Bussia '99	♥♥♥	8
● Barbaresco '13	♀♀	5
● Barbaresco Bric Turot '12	♀♀	6
● Barbera d'Alba Pian Romualdo '13	♀♀	4
● Barolo Bussia '11	♀♀	8
● Barolo Bussia V. Colonnello Ris. '10	♀♀	8
● Nebbiolo d'Alba Occhetti '13	♀♀	4

La Raia

s.da Monterotondo, 79
15067 Novi Ligure [AL]
Tel. +39 0143743685
www.la-raia.it

CELLAR SALES
PRE-BOOKED VISITS
ACCOMMODATION
ANNUAL PRODUCTION 150,000 bottles
HECTARES UNDER VINE 42.00
VITICULTURE METHOD Certified Biodynamic
SUSTAINABLE WINERY

As of this year, this certified organic winery has enlarged its horizons to include hospitality services. Locanda La Raia is situated in a prominent position, along with their production facility, and has been carefully renovated so as to offer high-end services to its guests. But getting back to their wine: the overall trend in quality has continued to prove positive, such that, today, they figure among the area's leading producers. The Gavis stand out from the crowd, with an excellent performance from the 2015 Riserva. It displays remarkable nose-palate symmetry. Aromas of fresh herbs, on fruity and floral notes, converge on a fresh and well-orchestrated palate with a long finish. The basic Gavi comes through intense and elegant, with overtones of greenness that are coherent with its fresh and tangy palate. The 2016 Barbera's good performance is also worth mentioning. It's a wine that features lovely, forward, crisp fruit.

○ Gavi '16	♥♥	3*
○ Gavi Ris. '15	♥♥	3*
● Piemonte Barbera '16	♥♥	3
● Piemonte Barbera Largé '12	♥	5
○ Gavi '15	♀♀	3*
○ Gavi '13	♀♀	3
○ Gavi Pisé '14	♀♀	4
○ Gavi Pisé '12	♀♀	4
○ Gavi Ris. '12	♀♀	3*
○ Gavi V. della Madonnina Ris. '14	♀♀	3*
○ Gavi V. della Madonnina Ris. '13	♀♀	3*
● Piemonte Barbera '13	♀♀	3
● Piemonte Barbera Largé '10	♀♀	5

...o Ratti

...NZIATA, 7
...LA MORRA [CN]
+39 017350185
...w.renatoratti.com

Ressia

VIA CANOVA, 28
12052 NEIVE [CN]
TEL. +39 0173677305
www.ressia.com

CELLAR SALES
PRE-BOOKED VISITS
ANNUAL PRODUCTION 3,000 bottles
HECTARES UNDER VINE 5.50
SUSTAINABLE WINERY

took over the family ... Renato, was a first-rate winemaker, ... produced written material and the 'Carta del Barolo', a map that's become an indispensable tool for understanding the area. It's a legacy that he's kept alive with commitment and an innovative spirit. And he's done it thanks in part to a long-term collaboration with Massimo Martinelli, who's overseen continued growth in production volumes and brought their selection to international markets. In addition to Barolo and Nebbiolo d'Alba, whose grapes are cultivated in Roero, they feature a selection of wines from Villa Pattono, their historic family estate in Costigliole d'Asti. The solid Rocche dell'Annunziata cru didn't disappoint and gave rise to a 2013 Barolo with a modern style. It features notes of sweet spices on the nose and a plate of rich personality, good continuity and tasty tannins. The 2013 Marcenasco proves even more multifaceted, with forward red fruit and licorice. The solid 2013 Conca is a little more austere on the palate.

view ...a has been working for 20 primarily Nebbiolo is ... ffers a panoramic ...ne. Here, production approach centers on low yields in the vineyards, which is considered fundamental for making wines with personality. Barbaresco Canova is their flagship wine, but in certain years they also produce a small quantity of Barbaresco Riserva Oro. In the cellar, they continue to experiment with vinifying Moscato for a dry white wine, Evien, with only 5000 bottles produced. The only other white offered is made with the fragrant grape Favorita La Miranda. The 2014 Barbaresco Canova's qualities are quite characteristic of the vintage. It displays fresh aromas with vegetal hints, a slim-bodied but well-proportioned structure and a finish of delicate tannins. The 2016 Dolcetto d'Alba Vigna Canova is worth mentioning for its lovely, clean fruitiness.

● Barolo Marcenasco '13	▼▼6
● Barolo Rocche dell'Annunziata '13	▼▼8
● Barolo Conca '13	▼▼8
● M.to Rosso Villa Pattono '15	▼▼5
● Barbera d'Alba Battaglione '16	▼3
● Barbera d'Asti Battaglione '16	▼3
● Dolcetto d'Alba Colombè '16	▼3
● Nebbiolo d'Alba Ochetti '15	▼4
● Barolo Rocche '06	▼▼▼8
● Barolo Rocche Marcenasco '84	▼▼▼6
● Barolo Rocche Marcenasco '83	▼▼▼6
● Barbera d'Alba Battaglione '15	▼▼3
● Barolo Conca '12	▼▼8
● Barolo Rocche dell'Annunziata '12	▼▼8
● Nebbiolo d'Alba Ochetti '14	▼▼4

● Barbaresco Canova '14	▼▼5
● Barbera d'Alba Sup. V. Canova '15	▼▼3
● Dolcetto d'Alba V. Canova '16	▼▼2*
● Langhe Nebbiolo Gepù '14	▼▼4
● Barbera d'Alba Canova '16	▼3
○ Evien	▼2
○ Langhe Favorita La Miranda '16	▼2
● Barbaresco Canova '06	▼▼▼5*
● Barbaresco Canova '13	▼▼5
● Barbaresco Canova '12	▼▼5
● Barbaresco Canova '11	▼▼5
○ Langhe Favorita La Miranda '15	▼▼2*

Réva

LOC. SAN SEBASTIANO, 68
12065 MONFORTE D'ALBA [CN]
TEL. +39 0173789269
www.revamonforte.it

**CELLAR SALES
PRE-BOOKED VISITS
ACCOMMODATION AND RESTAURANT SERV
ANNUAL PRODUCTION 35,000 bottl
HECTARES UNDER VINE 8.00
SUSTAINABLE WINERY**

Réva is a young wi~~~~ boast having
and projects. In restaurant and a golf
excellent wi~~~~
realize~~~~e owner, Miroslav Leke, counts
cou~~~ on the support of a young, skilled team of
exp~~~ts that have quickly caught the
attention of wine lovers. Some of the
vineyards surrounding their cellar are
organic, while their acclaimed Ravera di
Novello vineyard is primarily dedicated to
Barolo. And already they're announcing
wines from crus as prestigious as Lazzarito
(in Serralunga d'Alba) and Cannubi
(Barolo). The solid 2013 Barolo reflects
this fresh vintage quite well and features
balsamic aromas as well as a marked
tannin content. The Ravera of the same
vintage proves rather austere, but shows
excellent fruitiness, with the first hints of
licorice just starting to emerge. The
enjoyable 2015 Nebbiolo d'Alba
appears delicate and floral. We found
both the Barbera d'Alba Superiore and the
2016 Langhe Bianco, made with
Sauvignon, a bit more aggressive.

● Barolo Ravera '13	🍷🍷 7
● Barbera d'Alba Sup. '15	🍷🍷 3
● Barolo '13	🍷🍷 5
● Nebbiolo d'Alba '15	🍷🍷 3
○ Langhe Bianco '16	🍷 3
● Barolo '12	🍷🍷 5
● Barolo Ravera '12	🍷🍷 7

Carlo & Figli Revello

FRAZ. SANTA MARIA
12064 LA MORRA [CN]
TEL. +39 335676~~
www.carlorev~~~~~

Carlo Revello's latest undertaking begins
with a return to the past and a classic style
that doesn't call for major use of wood. And
so mid-sized casks and barriques are
eschewed in favor of Slovenian oak (not to
mention the use of must concentrators,
which are a distant memory in Langhe).
The full potential of the selection will come
with the 2016 vintage, so for now they're
proposing a selection made along with
Carlo's brother, Lorenzo. In the cellar, his
first son, Erik, has already taken on duties,
while the Barolo R.G., a recent addition, is
dedicated to Carlo's father, Giacomo. This
selection is characterized by the casual use
of oak, but the presence of elegant notes of
licorice and raspberries help create a
complex and charming whole. The palate
proves youthful, fresh and moderately
tannic. The 2013 Barolo features distinctive
overtones of herbs in the sun, alcohol and
spices, with a rather soft palate.

● Barolo R.G. '13	🍷🍷 7
● Barolo '13	🍷🍷 5

Elli Revello

FRAZ. ANNUNZIATA, 103
12064 LA MORRA [CN]
TEL. +39 017350276
www.revellofratelli.it

CELLAR SALES
PRE-BOOKED VISITS
ACCOMMODATION
ANNUAL PRODUCTION 45,000 bottles
HECTARES UNDER VINE 8.00
SUSTAINABLE WINERY

Having concluded his work with his brother, Carlo, Lorenzo Revello is carrying on with the same name, but with his own selection of modern, sophisticated wines. He has the help of his wife, Luciana and can now count on the full-time contribution of his daughters, Elena and Simone. This year sees the addition of a new Barolo: 2000 bottles born in the beautiful cru of Cerretta in Serralunga d'Alba. Their Barolos feature an elegant style, and the predominance of small, French wood. The only exception is their Gattera, which is more traditional. Their Barbera d'Alba Ciabot du Re is still superb. They have put forward some splendid 2013 Barolos, starting with a blend of grapes grown in different crus and absolutely one of the best of the vintage. Aromas of cinchona, elegant tar and red fruit come together to exhibit rare elegance. The seductive Gattera proves floral and delicate on the nose, with a juicy and plush palate. The spicy and promising Conca is slightly more marked by wood. The new Cerretta, made with grapes grown in the lovely Serralunga cru, remains a bit tannin-heavy.

● Barolo '13	♟♟5
● Barolo Conca '13	♟♟7
● Barolo Gattera '13	♟♟6
● Barolo Giachini '13	♟♟7
● Barbera d'Alba Ciabot du Re '15	♟♟5
● Barolo Cerretta '13	♟♟7
● Barolo Rocche dell'Annunziata '13	♟♟8
● Barbera d'Alba Ciabot du Re '05	♟♟♟5
● Barbera d'Alba Ciabot du Re '00	♟♟♟5
● Barolo '93	♟♟♟8
● Barolo Rocche dell'Annunziata '01	♟♟♟8
● Barolo Rocche dell'Annunziata '00	♟♟♟8
● Barolo Rocche dell'Annunziata '97	♟♟♟8
● Barolo V. Conca '99	♟♟♟7

Michele Reverdito

FRAZ. RIVALTA
B.TA GARASSINI, 74B
12064 LA MORRA [CN]
TEL. +39 017350336
www.reverdito.it

CELLAR SALES
PRE-BOOKED VISITS
ANNUAL PRODUCTION 70,000 bottles
HECTARES UNDER VINE 16.00

This year, Michele Reverdito's winery is turning 18. Inaugurated in 2000 by Michele, his parents and his sister, Sabina, the idea was to express the best of Langhe's traditional grape varieties (starting with Nebbiolo, of course). And thanks to their continually refined methods, and the occasional new addition (including their Bianco Langhe Nascetta), they've reached their goal. The production style varies according to the selection. As a result, in some cases the presence of oak is more detectable, while in others fruit dominates. The 2013 Barolo Ascheri sees French wood playing its card, with hints of spices calling up vanilla. The palate shows a marked tannin content and good body. The 2013 Barolo Bricco Cogni exhibits slightly blurred aromas, with a close-knit palate. The caressing and rich 2015 Nebbiolo did quite well. The 2016 Nascetta is a simple, slightly aromatic and clean wine.

● Barolo Ascheri '13	♟♟5
● Barolo Bricco Cogni '13	♟♟6
● Langhe Nebbiolo Simane '15	♟♟3
○ Langhe Nascetta '16	♟3
● Barolo Bricco Cogni '04	♟♟♟6
● Barolo 10 Anni Ris. '05	♟♟8
● Barolo Ascheri '12	♟♟5
● Barolo Badarina '12	♟♟6
● Barolo Badarina '11	♟♟5
● Barolo Bricco Cogni '12	♟♟6
● Barolo Bricco Cogni Ris. '09	♟♟6
● Barolo Riva Rocca '12	♟♟5
● Barolo Riva Rocca '11	♟♟5

...inaldi

...CN]
...356156
...di@me.com

...AR SALES
...E-BOOKED VISITS
...NNUAL PRODUCTION 35,000 bottles
HECTARES UNDER VINE 6.50

Francesco Rinaldi & Figli

VIA CROSIA, 30
12060 BAROLO [CN]
TEL. +39 0173440484
www.rinaldifrancesco.it

CELLAR SALES
PRE-BOOKED VISITS
ACCOMMODATION
ANNUAL PRODUCTION 70,000 bottles
HECTARES UNDER VINE 11.00

Every new release unleashes a new, global scavenger hunt. This is just how Beppe Rinaldi is, a vine grower who does things his own way and loved for a Barolo that eludes all categories. And his wines have only grown in precision and charm since daughters, Marta and Carlotta, have come on board full-time. 2010 was, in many ways, the breakthrough year. This is when the Brunate and Tre Tine joined the pair of flagship Nebbiolos. Their philosophy in the cellar hasn't changed. Production is carried out with spontaneous fermentation and aging in large barrels, making for wines that are often unpredictable in their aromas, but of incomparable mineral substance. This 2013 Barolo is a quintessential Brunate. Notes of raspberries and fresh roses are set on a background of golden-leaf tobacco and licorice, making for a truly territorial profile. The palate proves delicate, multi-faceted and velvety. Tre Bicchieri. The Tre Tine also performed well, exhibiting a similar style. Notes of camphor and meadow herbs make for a somewhat fresher wine.

The large barrels of Slavonian oak that you see when visiting Paola and Piera Rinaldi's cellar testify to their desire to follow tradition. This doesn't stop them from paying increased attention to fermentation and aging, with superb results in terms of finesse and harmony of taste. Yet Barolo's trademark tannic weave is never sacrificed, either. The rest of the work happens in the vineyards, in particular the celebrated crus of Cannubi and Brunate, where the Rinaldis have been working since the mid-18th century. The 2013 Barolo Cannubi is well-designed, with a commendably classic style. Notes of dried herbs and spices pave the way to dominating fruit and red flowers. The palate remains a bit austere due to the combination of tannins and significant pulp. The 2013 Barolo Brunate proves just as charming, with aromas tending more toward licorice and tobacco. The palate is slightly richer in acidity.

● Barolo Brunate '13	🏆🏆🏆 7
● Barolo Tre Tine '13	🏆🏆 7
● Barolo Brunate '11	🏆🏆🏆 7
● Barolo Brunate-Le Coste '07	🏆🏆🏆 7
● Barolo Brunate-Le Coste '06	🏆🏆🏆 7
● Barolo Cannubi S. Lorenzo-Ravera '04	🏆🏆🏆 6
● Barolo Brunate '12	🏆🏆 7
● Barolo Brunate '10	🏆🏆 7
● Barolo Cannubi S. Lorenzo-Ravera '09	🏆🏆 7
● Barolo Tre Tine '12	🏆🏆 7
● Barolo Tre Tine '11	🏆🏆 7
● Barolo Tre Tine '10	🏆🏆 7
● Langhe Nebbiolo '13	🏆🏆 4
● Langhe Nebbiolo '11	🏆🏆 4

● Barolo Cannubi '13	🏆🏆 7
● Barbaresco '14	🏆🏆 5
● Barolo Brunate '13	🏆🏆 7
● Barbaresco '13	🏆🏆 5
● Barbera d'Alba '13	🏆🏆 3
● Barbera d'Alba '12	🏆🏆 3
● Barolo '10	🏆🏆 6
● Barolo Brunate '12	🏆🏆 7
● Barolo Brunate '11	🏆🏆 6
● Barolo Brunate '10	🏆🏆 7
● Barolo Cannubi '12	🏆🏆 7
● Barolo Cannubi '11	🏆🏆 7
● Barolo Cannubi '10	🏆🏆 7
● Dolcetto d'Alba Roussot '15	🏆🏆 2

Massimo Rivetti

VIA RIVETTI, 22
12052 NEIVE [CN]
TEL. +39 017367505
www.rivettimassimo.it

CELLAR SALES
PRE-BOOKED VISITS
ANNUAL PRODUCTION 70,000 bottles
HECTARES UNDER VINE 25.00

Massimo Rivetti's winery, situated in the lovely farmstead of Froi, has notched up another good year. Here, quality comes first, and that starts in their vineyards. For years, the producer has eschewed the use of herbicides, and the estate was recently made organic. Their selection focuses on Barbaresco, and among the three versions available, the Serraboella and Froi stand out as particularly well-made. Visiting the winery with Massimo and his three children, you immediately get a sense of the passion that goes into their wines, which are delicious but also express the attributes of their terroir. The 2013 Barbaresco Serraboella displays a splendid youthful pace. We suggest enjoying the wine early on, but also laying down a few bottles for the future. Oak is almost indiscernible on the nose, leaving center stage to fresh red fruit. The palate reveals a structure with excellent weight and harmony. The 2014 Barbaresco Froi proves elegant and delicate.

● Barbaresco Serraboella '13	▼▼▼	7
● Barbaresco '14	▼▼	5
● Barbaresco Froi '14	▼▼	6
● Langhe Nebbiolo Avene '15	▼▼	3
● Barbaresco '13	♀♀	5
● Barbaresco Froi '13	♀♀	5
● Barbaresco Froi '12	♀♀	5
● Barbaresco Froi '11	♀♀	5
● Barbaresco Froi Ris. '09	♀♀	6
● Barbaresco Serraboella '12	♀♀	5
● Barbera d'Alba Sup. V. Serraboella '12	♀♀	4
● Barbera d'Alba V. Serraboella '10	♀♀	4
● Langhe Garasin '13	♀♀	3

Rizzi

VIA RIZZI, 15
12050 TREISO [CN]
TEL. +39 0173638161
www.cantinarizzi.it

CELLAR SALES
PRE-BOOKED VISITS
ACCOMMODATION
ANNUAL PRODUCTION 70,000 bottles
HECTARES UNDER VINE 38.00
SUSTAINABLE WINERY

Rizzi gets its name from the cru surrounding the winery. Here, the Dellapiana family have been working the fields for more than 50 years. As far as producers and wine lovers are concerned, the brand has grown considerably. Yet it has managed to keep its attention squarely focused on the some 30 hectares of vineyards that it cultivates (some of the best in Treiso). Their selection mostly features reds made with Dolcetto, Barbera and Nebbiolo, and shines for its excellent value. But they aren't lacking in top-range wines either. It's difficult to choose from their four Barbarescos (with additional geographic mentions of Rizzi, Pajoré, Nervo and Boito Riserva), all aged in medium-large Slavonian oak. A fresh vegetal note, combined with cinchona and licorice, adds charm to the rich aromas of the 2014 Barbaresco Nervo. The mouth offers up a marked and welcome acidulous note, making for a first-rate palate. The 2014 Barbaresco Pajoré isn't particularly aromatically complex yet, but it is forthright and pleasant. The palate proves slightly astringent with notable body.

● Barbaresco Nervo '14	▼▼▼	6
● Barbaresco Pajorè '14	▼▼	6
● Barbaresco Rizzi '14	▼▼	5
○ Pas Dosé M. Cl.	▼▼	5
○ Langhe Chardonnay '16	▼	3
● Barbaresco Boito Ris. '10	♀♀♀	6
● Barbaresco Boito Ris. '11	♀♀	7
● Barbaresco Nervo '13	♀♀	5
● Barbaresco Pajorè '13	♀♀	6
● Barbaresco Pajorè '11	♀♀	6
● Barbaresco Rizzi '13	♀♀	5
● Barbera d'Alba '13	♀♀	3
● Langhe Nebbiolo '14	♀♀	3

Roagna

LOC. PAJÉ
S.DA PAGLIERI, 7
12050 BARBARESCO [CN]
TEL. +39 0173635109
www.roagna.com

CELLAR SALES
PRE-BOOKED VISITS
ANNUAL PRODUCTION 50,000 bottles
HECTARES UNDER VINE 15.00

Paglieri's story is centuries old, but the presence of young Luca Roagna, who works alongside his father, Alfredo, has brought new life to the producer. Everything centers on the incredible patrimony of old plots (which includes property, partnerships and rents) in some of the most reputable parts of Langhe: Montefico, Pajé (which provides the grapes for their celebrated Crichet Pajé Riserva), Asili and Faset (since 2013) in Barbaresco, Albesani and Gallina (since 2014) in Neive, and Pira in Castiglione Falletto. It's a veritable amusement park for Jazz-inspired Nebbiolo wines, all made through spontaneous fermentation, long maceration and lengthy aging in large barrels. The sumptuous 2008 Crichét Pajé is released ten years after vintage. This classy and exquisite Barbaresco exhibits roses and wilted violets combined with licorice on a very fruity base. The palate is full-bodied and caressing, while its tannic weave proves to be a real masterpiece, dense and graceful as never before. Tre Bicchieri.

● Barbaresco Crichët Pajé '08	♥♥♥	8
● Barbaresco Asili V. V. '12	♥♥	8
● Barbaresco Montefico V. V. '12	♥♥	8
● Barbaresco Pajè V. V. '12	♥♥	8
● Barolo Pira V. V. '12	♥♥	8
● Barbaresco Pajé '12	♥♥	8
● Barolo Pira '12	♥♥	8
● Langhe Rosso '12	♥♥	3
● Barbaresco Asili V. V. '07	♀♀♀	8
● Barbaresco Crichët Pajé '06	♀♀♀	8
● Barbaresco Crichët Pajé '05	♀♀♀	8
● Barbaresco Crichët Pajé '04	♀♀♀	8
● Barbaresco Pajé '11	♀♀♀	8
● Barbaresco Crichët Pajé '07	♀♀	8
● Barbaresco Montefico V. V. '11	♀♀	8

★Albino Rocca

S.DA RONCHI, 18
12050 BARBARESCO [CN]
TEL. +39 0173635145
www.albinorocca.com

CELLAR SALES
PRE-BOOKED VISITS
ANNUAL PRODUCTION 100,000 bottles
HECTARES UNDER VINE 18.00
SUSTAINABLE WINERY

Montersino (in San Rocco Seno d'Elvio), Ovello and Ronchi (in Barbaresco). This is the green line that holds together the past and the present of the charming winery founded by Albino Rocca. Today it is managed by sisters Paola, Monica and Daniela (with the help of Carlo Castellengo), after the premature death of their father, Angelo. Their most recent Barbaresco, made from the three main vineyards' best grapes and then aged in 2000 liter German and Austrian oak for almost two years, is dedicated to him. The same approach has been adopted for their other top-range Nebbiolos (vintage and 'Riserva'), which are neither modern nor retro. Rather, they manage to regularly marry very different stylistic sensibilities. The excellent 2013 Barbaresco Ronchi (mistakenly reviewed last year) opens on classic notes of licorice and ripe red fruit. Its captivating, rich and long palate earns it a place in our finals. Among the 2014 Barbarescos, the Montersino stands out, with its slim, well-orchestrated and gradual body. The Angelo proves more solid and firmly-structured.

● Barbaresco Montersino '14	♥♥	6
● Barbaresco Ronchi '13	♥♥	6
● Barbaresco Angelo '14	♥♥	5
● Barbaresco Ovello V. Loreto '14	♥♥	6
● Barbaresco Angelo '13	♀♀♀	5
● Barbaresco Ovello V. Loreto '11	♀♀♀	6
● Barbaresco Ovello V. Loreto '09	♀♀♀	6
● Barbaresco Ovello V. Loreto '07	♀♀♀	6
● Barbaresco Ronchi '10	♀♀♀	6
● Barbaresco Vign. Brich Ronchi '05	♀♀♀	6
● Barbaresco Vign. Brich Ronchi Ris. '06	♀♀♀	6
● Barbaresco Vign. Brich Ronchi Ris. '04	♀♀♀	6
● Barbaresco Vign. Loreto '04	♀♀♀	6

★Bruno Rocca

.DA RABAJÀ, 60
2050 BARBARESCO [CN]
TEL. +39 0173635112
www.brunorocca.it

CELLAR SALES
PRE-BOOKED VISITS
ANNUAL PRODUCTION 70,000 bottles
HECTARES UNDER VINE 15.00

Bruno Rocca's 15 hectares of land, which he manages personally (with the help of his children, Francesco and Luisa), are situated largely in Rabajà, in the Barbaresco wine region. However, this is only the most preeminent plot of an estate that comprises terrain in Treiso, Neive (Currà) and Vaglio Serra (for their Barbera d'Asti), with the remaining plots reserved for Dolcetto, Cabernet and Chardonnay. Obviously, Nebbiolo leads the way, with four Barbarescos characterized by a modern, though constantly evolving, style. Their base wine and their Coparossa are aged exclusively in barriques. For their Rabajà and Maria Adelaide, they also use large barrels during the second year. The 2013 Barbaresco Rabajà offers up aromas of red fruit, such as raspberries, combined with very stylish spiciness. The fresh and lingering mouth features extraordinary density and complexity, and supple tannins. Tre Bicchieri. The elegant 2014 Barbaresco is even more mature and open, but remains a bit rugged on the palate for the moment due to the strong presence of tannins.

● Barbaresco Rabajà '13	♟♟♟ 8
● Barbaresco '14	♟♟ 7
● Barbera d'Alba '15	♟♟ 5
● Barbera d'Asti '15	♟♟ 4
○ Langhe Chardonnay Cadet '15	♟♟ 4
● Dolcetto d'Alba Trifolè '16	♟ 3
● Langhe Nebbiolo Fralù '15	♟ 4
● Barbaresco Coparossa '04	♟♟♟ 8
● Barbaresco Maria Adelaide '07	♟♟♟ 8
● Barbaresco Maria Adelaide '04	♟♟♟ 8
● Barbaresco Rabajà '12	♟♟♟ 8
● Barbaresco Rabajà '11	♟♟♟ 8
● Barbaresco Rabajà '10	♟♟♟ 8
● Barbaresco Rabajà '09	♟♟♟ 8

Rocche Costamagna

VIA VITTORIO EMANUELE, 8
12064 LA MORRA [CN]
TEL. +39 0173509225
www.rocchecostamagna.it

CELLAR SALES
PRE-BOOKED VISITS
ACCOMMODATION
ANNUAL PRODUCTION 95,000 bottles
HECTARES UNDER VINE 15.80

Alessandro Locatello, son of Giorgio and the painter Claudia Ferraresi, began working in wine some 30 years ago. Over the years, he realized a multi-layered, picturesque and welcoming estate. The heart of production lies in their five hectares of Nebbiolo vineyards, situated in the splendid Rocche del'Annunziata, which give rise to their three Barolos. The grapes are then worked in their lovely cellar, which deserves a visit. Their Riserva Bricco Francesco, a wine aged in large barrels, represents the top of their range. But their entire selection is consistently strong. The 2011 Barolo Rocche dell'Annunziata Riserva Bricco Francesco shows lovely structure, reinforced by a good alcoholic component and aromas of dried herbs. It just lacks a bit of freshness. The 2013 Rocche dell'Annunziata exhibits freshness and complexity, with a still austere finish. The 2013 Barolo proves racier and more youthful, with hints of licorice and tar. The robust and lively Barbera d'Alba Rocche delle Rocche is a lovely interpretation of the 2014 vintage.

● Barolo Rocche dell'Annunziata '13	♟♟ 6
● Barbera d'Alba Sup. Rocche delle Rocche '14	♟♟ 4
● Barolo '13	♟♟ 5
● Barolo Rocche dell'Annunziata Bricco Francesco Ris. '11	♟♟ 8
● Langhe Nebbiolo Roccardo '15	♟♟ 3
○ Langhe Arneis '16	♟ 3
● Barolo Rocche dell'Annunziata '04	♟♟♟ 5
● Barbera d'Alba Sup. Rocche delle Rocche '13	♟♟ 4
● Barolo '12	♟♟ 5
● Barolo Rocche dell'Annunziata '12	♟♟ 6
● Barolo Rocche dell'Annunziata Bricco Francesco Ris. '10	♟♟ 6

★Rocche dei Manzoni

LOC. MANZONI SOPRANI, 3
12065 MONFORTE D'ALBA [CN]
TEL. +39 017378421
www.rocchedeimanzoni.it

CELLAR SALES
PRE-BOOKED VISITS
ANNUAL PRODUCTION 250,000 bottles
HECTARES UNDER VINE 40.00

Rocche dei Manzoni was founded 35 years ago by Valentino Migliorini. Today the winery is managed with commitment and skill by his son, Rodolfo. He's keeping alive their modern and mature selection, which features Barolos from various crus. Out of respect for nature, their large estate has gradually shifted to organic and biodynamic viticulture, while, in their phantasmagoric cellar, various sizes and types of wood take center stage. Rocche dei Manzoni is deservedly famous for their sparkling wines, in particular their Brut Riserva Elena, which ages on the lees for at least four years before disgorgement. Both their sparkling wines put in splendid performances. The 2005 Valentino Brut Zero Riserva shows more complexity with notes of yeast and cake. In the mouth it proves caressing with a particularly complex finish. The 2012 Riserva Elena comes through very elegant and charming, with fresher notes, rich in herbs. It's supple but firmly-structured as never before. The 2007 Barolo Madonna Assunta Riserva proves rich and spicy, as per the winery's style.

● Barolo La Villa V. Madonna Assunta Ris. '07	♥♥8
○ Valentino Brut M. Cl. Elena Ris. '12	♥♥7
○ Valentino Brut Zero Ris. '05	♥♥8
● Barbera d'Alba La Cresta '14	♥♥6
● Barbera d'Alba Sup. S orito Mosconi '11	♥♥7
● Barolo Bricco San Pietro V. d'la Roul '12	♥♥8
○ Langhe Chardonnay L'Angelica '14	♥♥8
● Langhe Rosso Quatr Nas '11	♥♥8
● Barolo V. Big 'd Big '99	♥♥♥8
● Barolo V. Cappella di S. Stefano '01	♥♥♥8
● Barolo V. d'la Roul '07	♥♥♥8
○ Valentino Brut Zero Ris. '98	♥♥♥5
○ Valentino Brut Zero Ris. '93	♥♥♥5
○ Valentino Brut Zerò Ris. '92	♥♥♥5

Il Rocchin

LOC. VALLEMME, 39
15066 GAVI [AL]
TEL. +39 0143642228
www.ilrocchin.it

CELLAR SALES
PRE-BOOKED VISITS
ANNUAL PRODUCTION 50,000 bottles
HECTARES UNDER VINE 20.00

For years, winemaking took a backseat to raising cattle and milk production here at Il Rocchin. Over the years, new blocks and vineyards saw vine growing outpace their other activities. Moreover, a new, fully-equipped cellar was a big step towards even higher quality wines (only a part of which are bottled). This has guaranteed the Zerbo family good margins for growth, in terms of production volumes, for years to come. The Gavi di Gavi Il Bosco leads their selection. The wine features an intense straw-yellow color and a vibrant nose, with aromas of white fruit and citrus turning to elegant mineral notes. The palate proves excellent for its freshness and length. The 2016 Dolcetto di Ovada is also worth mentioning.

○ Gavi del Comune di Gavi Il Bosco '16	♥♥3*
● Dolcetto di Ovada '16	♥♥2*
○ Gavi del Comune di Gavi '16	♥♥2*
● Barbera del M.to '15	♥3
● Dolcetto di Ovada '15	♀♀2*
○ Gavi del Comune di Gavi '15	♀♀2*
○ Gavi del Comune di Gavi '14	♀♀2*
○ Gavi del Comune di Gavi '00	♀♀2*
○ Gavi del Comune di Gavi Il Bosco '15	♀♀3*
○ Gavi del Comune di Gavi V. del Bosco '01	♀♀3

Flavio Roddolo

FRAZ. BRICCO APPIANI
LOC. SANT'ANNA, 5
12065 MONFORTE D'ALBA [CN]
TEL. +39 017378535

CELLAR SALES
PRE-BOOKED VISITS
ANNUAL PRODUCTION 25,000 bottles
HECTARES UNDER VINE 6.00

While we can't call him a 'social' vine grower, Flavio Roddolo, and his cellar-den, continue to represent a fundamental piece of Langhe's modern cultural identity. As authoritative as he is close-mouthed, the producer prefers to let his bottles do the talking. These are only sold when (and if) he feels it's right to do so. It's a rare philosophy in the area, as are his skills for highlighting the attributes of the varieties (tradtional or not) cultivated on his six hectares of property. In any case, it's not just Barolo here. The characters of Ravera and Bricco Appiani (Monforte) let themselves be known, even before Nebbiolo, Barbera, Dolcetto and Cabernet Sauvignon. Anyone who knows this fearless producer, a true artist of the countryside and a wine artisan, knows that the aging times of his wines are extremely long (to say the least). And that he bottles with the August moon, which, unfortunately, doesn't fit in with our tastings. For this reason, we only tasted two wines, which will continue to improve with bottle aging.

● Dolcetto d'Alba Sup. '13	♟♟ 3
● Langhe Rosso Bricco Appiani '08	♟ 6
● Barolo Ravera '08	♟♟♟ 5
● Barolo Ravera '07	♟♟♟ 5
● Barolo Ravera '04	♟♟♟ 5
● Barbera d'Alba '08	♟♟ 3
● Barolo Ravera '10	♟♟ 5
● Barolo Ravera '09	♟♟ 5
● Dolcetto d'Alba Sup. '12	♟♟ 3
● Dolcetto d'Alha Sup. '11	♟♟ 3*
● Dolcetto d'Alba Sup. '10	♟♟ 3*
● Nebbiolo d'Alba '10	♟♟ 4
● Nebbiolo d'Alba '09	♟♟ 4

Ronchi

S.DA RONCHI, 23
12050 BARBARESCO [CN]
TEL. +39 0173635156
www.aziendaagricolaronchi.it

CELLAR SALES
PRE-BOOKED VISITS
ANNUAL PRODUCTION 30,000 bottles
HECTARES UNDER VINE 7.00

Giancarlo Rocca's winery is situated in an enchanting position in the valley of Ronchi (for which both the winery and their most important Barbarescos are named). Production of their wines is carried out with the utmost respect for the environment and the grape, thus herbicides are eschewed in the vineyard and the cellar sees the use of various sized barrels only for slow aging (and never for purposes of altering the wines' aromas). Their prices are good and the winery deserves a visit, both for its beautiful natural landscapes and the people. The fresh and fruity 2013 Barbaresco Ronchi appears quite young despite having aged for an additional year in the bottle before its commercial release. It's a wine that's almost rustic in its pureness of taste. The 2013 Barbaresco comes through simple and forthright, with pleasant notes of hay and red fruit. The palate exhibits good weight and tight-knit tannins.

● Barbaresco '13	♟♟ 5
● Barbaresco Ronchi '13	♟♟ 5
● Barbera d'Alba Terlé '15	♟♟ 3
○ Langhe Chardonnay '15	♟♟ 3
⊙ Rosato Brut M. Cl.	♟♟ 3
○ Langhe Arneis '16	♟ 2
● Barbaresco Ronchi '04	♟♟♟ 6
● Barbaresco '11	♟♟ 5
● Barbaresco '10	♟♟ 5
● Barbaresco Ronchi '12	♟♟ 5
● Barbaresco Ronchi '11	♟♟ 5
○ Langhe Arneis '15	♟♟ 2*
○ Langhe Chardonnay '13	♟♟ 3
○ Langhe Chardonnay Ronchi '12	♟♟ 3*

Giovanni Rosso

Loc. Baudana, 6
12050 Serralunga d'Alba [CN]
Tel. +39 0173613340
www.giovannirosso.com

CELLAR SALES
PRE-BOOKED VISITS
ANNUAL PRODUCTION 130,000 bottles
HECTARES UNDER VINE 18.00

Today, the new winery is managed by the passionate winemaker, Davide Rosso. Here, they're dedicated exclusively to the cultivation and vinification of Nebbiolo grapes from their vineyards in Serralunga d'Alba. Their Barbera d'Alba Donna Margherita, a notable wine that's capable of evolving well over time, is an exception. Barolo dominates, starting with the highly pleasing selection of Vigna Rionda Ester Canale Rosso, and moving on to the potent cru of La Serra, as well as the more elegant Cerretta. Their Barolo del Comune di Serralunga d'Alba continues to prove itself a first-rate wine. The 2013 Barolo Vigna Rionda Ester Canale Rosso displays extraordinary complexity and elegance and proves more charming and pleasant than ever before, a quintessential representative of this famous vineyard. The well-orchestrated 2013 Barolo Serra comes through fresh, elegant and already expressive. It exhibits remarkable pulp and good length, and is still quite youthful. The 2013 Barolo Cerretta remains more clenched and captivating.

● Barolo Vigna Rionda Ester Canale Rosso '13	♟♟♟ 8
● Barolo Cerretta '13	♟♟ 8
● Barolo Serra '13	♟♟ 8
● Barbera d'Alba Donna Margherita '15	♟♟ 3
● Barolo del Comune di Serralunga d'Alba '13	♟♟ 5
● Langhe Nebbiolo '15	♟ 5
● Barolo Cerretta '12	♟♟♟ 8
● Barolo Cerretta '06	♟♟♟ 7
● Barolo La Serra '09	♟♟♟ 7
● Barolo La Serra '08	♟♟♟ 7
● Barolo Serra '10	♟♟♟ 7
● Barolo Vigna Rionda Ester Canale Rosso '11	♟♟♟ 8

Poderi Rosso Giovanni

P.zza Roma, 36/37
14041 Agliano Terme [AT]
Tel. +39 0141954006
www.podorirossogiovanni.it

CELLAR SALES
PRE-BOOKED VISITS
ANNUAL PRODUCTION 50,000 bottles
HECTARES UNDER VINE 12.00

Founded in 1930, today Poderi Rosso Giovanni is managed by Lionello Rosso and is dedicated exclusively to the cultivation and production of Barbera. Their vineyards are situated around two farmsteads, Cascina Perno and Cascina San Sebastiano, in the district of Agliano Terme. Their wines (three Barbera d'Astis and a blend of Barbera and Cabernet Sauvignon, Monferrato Rosso) feature freshness of fruit, approachability and drinkability. The Barbera d'Asti Superiore Carlinet made it to our finals again with the 2015 vintage. It offers up notes of cherries and blackberries, with hints of forest floor. It shows good body, well-balanced softness of fruit and acidity, and lovely length. The 2015 Barbera d'Asti Superiore Cascina Perno moves along the same lines, but it's a spicier wine, gutsy and fruity, with light piquant notes. With a bit more structure it would equal the Carlinet. The 2016 Barbera d'Asti San Bastian is less glossy, but well-managed, playing on suppleness and pleasantness.

● Barbera d'Asti Sup. Carlinet '15	♟♟ 4
● Barbera d'Asti Sup. Cascina Perno '15	♟♟ 3
● Barbera d'Asti San Bastian '16	♟ 2
● Barbera d'Asti Podere San Bastian '14	♟♟ 2*
● Barbera d'Asti San Bastian '15	♟♟ 2*
● Barbera d'Asti San Bastian '13	♟♟ 2*
● Barbera d'Asti Sup. Carlinet '13	♟♟ 4
● Barbera d'Asti Sup. Cascina Perno '14	♟♟ 3
● Barbera d'Asti Sup. Cascina Perno '13	♟♟ 3
● Barbera d'Asti Sup. Cascina Perno '12	♟♟ 4
● Barbera d'Asti Sup. Gioco dell'Oca '13	♟♟ 6
● Barbera d'Asti Sup. Gioco dell'Oca '12	♟♟ 6
● Barbera d'Asti Sup. V. Carlinet '12	♟♟ 3

Rovellotti

Interno Castello, 22
28074 Ghemme [NO]
Tel. +39 0163841781
www.rovellotti.it

CELLAR SALES
ANNUAL PRODUCTION 50,000 bottles
HECTARES UNDER VINE 17.00

Antonello and Paolo Rovellotti's winery is
hidden away in the medieval Ricetto district
of Ghemme, in what is undisputedly one of
the most captivating areas for wine in the
whole of Novara. We expect, and get, wines
that are proudly locked into the area's
tradition, though with some exceptions.
Nebbiolo, Vespolina, Uva Rara and Erbaluce
are at the center of their work in the
vineyards, but they've also experimented
with non-native varieties like Cabernet,
Merlot and Pinot Nero. Size restrictions
make aging difficult, but their most
important reds (like their Ghemme Chioso
dei Pomi and Salmino Riserva) are bottled
after spending a long time in oak. In recent
seasons, the Bianco Criccone Vitigno
Innominabile (Erbaluce) has started to
emerge. The 2016 exhibits a simply
delightful combination of fruity sweetness
and spirited structure. But the winery's
champions remain their two Ghemme. The
Chioso dei Pomi features noble aromas and
an unending palate with a sophisticated
tannic weave.

● Ghemme Chioso dei Pomi '10	♙♙ 4
● Ghemme Costa del Salmino Ris. '09	♙♙ 5
○ Colline Novaresi Bianco Vitigno Innominabile Il Criccone '16	♙♙ 2*
● Colline Novaresi Vespolina Ronco al Maso '16	♙♙ 2*
● Colline Novaresi Nebbiolo Valplazza '13	♙ 2
● Ghemme Chioso dei Pomi '07	♙♙♙ 4*
○ Colline Novaresi Bianco Vitigno Innominabile Il Criccone '14	♗♗ 2*
☉ Colline Novaresi Nebbiolo Rosato Valplazza '13	♗♗ 2*
● Colline Novaresi Nebbiolo Valplazza '12	♗♗ 2*
● Colline Novaresi Nebbiolo Valplazza '10	♗♗ 2*
● Ghemme Chioso dei Pomi '09	♗♗ 4
● Ghemme Chioso dei Pomi '08	♗♗ 4
● Ghemme Costa del Salmino Ris. '07	♗♗ 5

Podere Ruggeri Corsini

Loc. Bussia Bovi 18
12065 Monforte d'Alba [CN]
Tel. +39 017378625
www.ruggericorsini.com

CELLAR SALES
PRE-BOOKED VISITS
ANNUAL PRODUCTION 75,000 bottles
HECTARES UNDER VINE 9.80
SUSTAINABLE WINERY

Loredana Addari and Nicola Agramante are
a couple esteemed in the entire area for
their agronomic skills, such that, at times,
Nicola gets called by other growers to give
his opinion on their vineyard management.
And so their own vineyards are worked with
maximum skill, in addition to the goal of
sustainability, which sees the use of solar
panels and particularly light bottles. Their
main selection centers on their two Barolos
(Bricco San Pietro and Bussia Corsini), but
they've achieved commendable results with
their Barbera d'Alba Superiore Armujan. We
enjoyed an exquisite 2013 Barolo Bussia
Corsini with elegant aromatic complexity
and a powerful palate still marked by
assertive tannins. The 2013 Barbera d'Alba
Superiore Armujan offers up a lovely nose of
red flowers and a rather aggressive palate.
The juicy and refreshing 2016 Rosin, made
with Nebbiolo grapes, is one of Langhe's
best rosés.

● Barolo Bussia Corsini '13	♙♙ 5
● Barbera d'Alba Sup. Armujan '13	♙♙ 3
● Barolo Bricco San Pietro '13	♙♙ 5
○ Langhe Bianco '16	♙♙ 2*
● Langhe Nebbiolo '15	♙♙ 3
● Langhe Pinot Nero Argamakow '14	♙♙ 4
☉ Langhe Rosato Rosin '16	♙♙ 2*
● Barbera d'Alba '13	♗♗ 2*
● Barbera d'Alba Sup. Armujan '12	♗♗ 3*
● Barolo Bricco San Pietro '12	♗♗ 5
● Barolo Bricco San Pietro '11	♗♗ 5
● Barolo Bussia Corsini '12	♗♗ 5
○ Langhe Bianco '15	♗♗ 2*
● Langhe Nebbiolo '13	♗♗ 3

Josetta Saffirio

LOC. CASTELLETTO, 39
12065 MONFORTE D'ALBA [CN]
TEL. +39 0173787270
www.josettasaffirio.com

CELLAR SALES
PRE-BOOKED VISITS
ANNUAL PRODUCTION 30,000 bottles
HECTARES UNDER VINE 5.00
SUSTAINABLE WINERY

Sara Vezza, along with the active support of her parents (professionals in the field, though with different specializations), continues to renovate the family estate. Her efforts are aimed at becoming certified organic and 'off the grid' in terms of energy consumption. Among the their many lovely vineyards in Castelletto, one stands out, the plot planted by her grandfather, Ernesto, in 1948. This gives rise to their Josetta Saffirio and their important Riserva di Barolo. And among their selection of classic wines, based primarily on Nebbiolo and Barbera, the rare Langhe Rossese Bianco is noteworthy. The 2011 Barolo Millenovecento48 Riserva sees rather varied aromas, with tones ranging from cinchona to red flowers and small fresh fruit. The palate proves dense and close-knit, with a seductive harmony. The 2013 Barolo comes though less fresh, despite the vintage, with a relaxed and supple palate. The 2013 Barolo Persiera features complex aromas.

● Barolo Millenovecento48 Ris. '11	♥♥	8
● Barbera d'Alba Sup. '15	♥♥	3
● Barolo '13	♥♥	6
● Barolo Persiera '13	♥♥	8
● Langhe Nebbiolo '15	♥♥	3
○ Langhe Rossese Bianco '15	♥♥	3
⊙ Nebbiolo d'Alba Spumante Brut Rosé M. Cl. '15	♥♥	4
● Barolo '89	♥♥♥	6
● Barolo '88	♥♥♥	6
● Barolo '12	♀♀	5
● Barolo Millenovecento48 Ris. '10	♀♀	7
● Barolo Persiera '12	♀♀	8
● Langhe Nebbiolo '14	♀♀	3

San Bartolomeo

LOC. VALLEGGE
CASCINA SAN BARTOLOMEO, 26
15066 GAVI [AL]
TEL. +39 0143643180
www.sanbartolomeogavi.com

CELLAR SALES
PRE-BOOKED VISITS
ANNUAL PRODUCTION 50,000 bottles
HECTARES UNDER VINE 21.00
SUSTAINABLE WINERY

Giuseppe Bergaglio deserves credit for having purchased a farm manor from the Marquis Orso Serra. The estate had been an ancient convent consecrated in San Bartolomeo, and so the name of the winery becomes clear. Today the estate is managed by Giuseppe's great-grandson, Fulvio. Its more than 20 hectares are situated in the Gavi hills, which enjoy a favorable position and a view of the Lemme river. Cortese is the cornerstone of their selection, which is characterized by a classic approach to production, with temperature-controlled aging in steel, both in their Gavi line and their Pelöia wines. San Bartolomeo's whites put in a remarkable performance, starting with a 2016 Gavi Quinto that features partly compressed aromas, but a lively and assertive taste. The Pelöia of the same vintage raises the bar for vibrance and fullness. White fruit, fern, flint anticipate a rich mid palate and a long, citrusy streak.

○ Gavi del Comune di Gavi Pelöia '16	♥♥	3*
○ Gavi Quinto '16	♥♥	2*
○ Gavi del Comune di Gavi Pelöia '15	♥♥♥	3*
○ Gavi del Comune di Gavi Pelöia '14	♀♀	3*
○ Gavi del Comune di Gavi Pelöia '13	♀♀	3*
○ Gavi del Comune di Gavi Pelöia '12	♀♀	3
○ Gavi del Comune di Gavi Pelöia '11	♀♀	3*
○ Gavi Quinto '15	♀♀	2*
○ Gavi Quinto '14	♀♀	2*
○ Gavi Quinto '13	♀♀	3*
○ Gavi Quinto '12	♀♀	2*
○ Gavi Quinto '11	♀♀	2*

Tenuta San Sebastiano

Cascina San Sebastiano, 41
15040 Lu [AL]
Tel. +39 0131741353
www.dealessi.it

CELLAR SALES
PRE-BOOKED VISITS
ANNUAL PRODUCTION 70,000 bottles
HECTARES UNDER VINE 9.00

Monferrato is farm country. Most of its
terrain is dedicated to vine growing, though
there's a fair amount of hazelnut trees and
arable land, slopes permitting. But
viticulture has always dominated, as
demonstrated by the founding of this
co-operative winery in 1906. In this land of
vine growers, the skill of Roberto De Alessi
stands out. A passionate artisan of vines
and wine, for years he has given us
unforgettable wines that only get better
over time. Mepari has been the winery's
flagship for many years and the 2015
version made it to the finals. This rich and
powerful wine put in an excellent
performance, and it's still evolving. Our
curiosity will be satisfied in a few years,
when we'll be able to enjoy it at its full
potential. The Monfiorato also made it into
the finals. It's a complex and elegant wine
with great character. The Monferrato
Bianco Sperilium appears extremely
well-made while the Passito holds up well
despite a difficult vintage.

● Barbera del M.to Sup. Mepari '15	♀♀ 4
● Piemonte Grignolino Monfiorato '12	♀♀ 4
○ LV Quinquagesimaquinta Mansio Passito '14	♀♀ 4
○ M.to Bianco Sperilium '16	♀♀ 2*
● Piemonte Grignolino '16	♀ 2
● Barbera del M.to '14	♀♀ 2*
● Barbera del M.to '13	♀♀ 2*
● Barbera del M.to Sup. Mepari '11	♀♀ 4
● Barbera del M.to Sup. Mepari '08	♀♀ 4
○ LV Quinquagesimaquinta Mansio Passito '13	♀♀ 4
○ M.to Bianco '14	♀♀ 2*
● Piemonte Grignolino '15	♀♀ 2*
● Piemonte Grignolino Monfiorato '11	♀♀ 4

★Luciano Sandrone

via Pugnane, 4
12060 Barolo [CN]
Tel. +39 0173560023
www.sandroneluciano.com

PRE-BOOKED VISITS
ANNUAL PRODUCTION 110,000 bottles
HECTARES UNDER VINE 27.00
SUSTAINABLE WINERY

The news is that, as of 2013, Aleste has
been reintroduced, in honor of Alessia and
Stefano, the latest generation to work
alongside Luciano Sandrone. Together with
his wife, Mariuccia, his daughter, Barbara,
and his brother, Luca, they constitute none
other than Cannubi Boschis, the winery
that made a name for itself around the
world for producing the first 'Backyard
Barolo'. The wine, a prototype of modern
Nebbiolo in form, and a true classic in
substance, found the perfect companions
in Le Vigne (Merli in Novello, Baudana in
Serralunga d'Alba, Villero in Castiglione
Falletto and Vignane in Barolo) and
Valmaggiore (Vezza d'Alba, Roero). We
shouldn't forget their Barbera and Dolcetto
either. The fledgling 2013 Barolo Aleste
features a fresh mouth marked by still
somewhat solid and lively tannins. The
nose shows a fine, classic style that
ranges from tobacco and sweet spices to
youthful, rich red fruit. The 2013 Barolo Le
Vigne is still simple and close-knit. It needs
bottle aging to evolve its bold structure.

● Barolo Aleste '13	♀♀ 8
● Barolo Le Vigne '13	♀♀ 8
● Nebbiolo d'Alba Valmaggiore '15	♀♀ 5
● Barolo Cannubi Boschis '11	♀♀♀ 8
● Barolo Cannubi Boschis '10	♀♀♀ 8
● Barolo Cannubi Boschis '08	♀♀♀ 8
● Barolo Cannubi Boschis '07	♀♀♀ 8
● Barolo Cannubi Boschis '06	♀♀♀ 8
● Barolo Cannubi Boschis '05	♀♀♀ 8
● Barbera d'Alba '13	♀♀ 5
● Barolo Cannubi Boschis '12	♀♀ 8
● Barolo Le Vigne '12	♀♀ 8
● Barolo Le Vigne '11	♀♀ 8
● Nebbiolo d'Alba Valmaggiore '14	♀♀ 5

Paolo Saracco

VIA CIRCONVALLAZIONE, 6
12053 CASTIGLIONE TINELLA [CN]
TEL. +39 0141855113
www.paolosaracco.it

CELLAR SALES
PRE-BOOKED VISITS
ANNUAL PRODUCTION 600,000 bottles
HECTARES UNDER VINE 46.00

Paolo Saracco has managed the family
winery since 1988, and over the years he's
managed to become one of the area's most
notable producers when it comes to
Moscato. The estate comprises 14
vineyards in the municipalities of Calosso,
Castagnole Lanze, Castiglione Tinella and
Santo Stefano Belbo. These grow at
altitudes ranging from 300 to 500 meters,
in soil made mostly of sand, silt and
limestone. Moscato, along with Pinot Nero,
Chardonnay and Riesling are all cultivated.
The splendid 2016 Moscato d'Asti features
an intense and sophisticated nose, with
lovely notes of fresh herbs and white fruit.
The palate comes through elegant with
sweet notes of candied fruit, and a long,
harmonious finish. The 2016 Piemonte
Moscato d'Autunno proves first-rate, with
classic tones of sage, mint and white fruit,
and a finish with remarkable freshness and
acidity. The 2016 Langhe Chardonnay
Prasué displays good balance between
body and acidity, though it's still awaiting
further evolution.

○ Moscato d'Asti '16	♟♟♟ 3*
○ Piemonte Moscato d'Autunno '16	♟♟ 3*
○ Langhe Chardonnay Prasué '16	♟♟ 3
○ Langhe Riesling '15	♟ 3
● Piemonte Pinot Nero '15	♟ 5
○ Piemonte Moscato d'Autunno '09	♟♟♟ 3*
○ Langhe Riesling '14	♟♟ 3
○ Moscato d'Asti '15	♟♟ 3
○ Moscato d'Asti '14	♟♟ 3
○ Piemonte Moscato d'Autunno '15	♟♟ 3*
○ Piemonte Moscato d'Autunno '14	♟♟ 3*
○ Piemonte Moscato d'Autunno '13	♟♟ 3*
● Piemonte Pinot Nero '13	♟♟ 5
● Piemonte Pinot Nero '12	♟♟ 5
● Piemonte Pinot Nero '11	♟♟ 5

Roberto Sarotto

VIA RONCONUOVO, 13
12050 NEVIGLIE [CN]
TEL +39 0173630228
www.robertosarotto.com

CELLAR SALES
PRE-BOOKED VISITS
ANNUAL PRODUCTION 700,000 bottles
HECTARES UNDER VINE 84.00

Even if his is a sizable winery, rare, even,
considering its regional presence, Roberto
Sarotto has managed to maintain an
artisanal approach to winemaking that's
well-reflected in his selection. His estate's
extensive vineyards, which span the
region's principal appellations, allows him
to work with various cultivar, which are
often characterized by their assertive,
extracted style. It's worth mentioning the
entire selection's reasonable, competitive
pricing model. The two 2016 Gavis we
tasted are an excellent example of their
wine type. They combine the freshness and
expressive liveliness of Cortese with a
firmly-structured and juicy taste profile. As
its name suggests, the 2013 Barolo
Audace proves full-bodied and dense, with
still unresolved tannins and a powerful,
long finish. Their other wines are sound,
standing out for the way they respect the
variety used.

○ Gavi Aurora '16	♟♟ 2*
○ Gavi del Comune di Gavi Bric Sassi Tenuta Manenti '16	♟♟ 2*
● Barbaresco Gaia Principe '14	♟♟ 6
● Barolo Audace '13	♟♟ 6
● Langhe Nebbiolo Nativo '15	♟♟ 3
○ Moscato d'Asti Solatio '16	♟♟ 2
○ Piemonte Chardonnay Puro '15	♟♟ 2
● Barbaresco Currà Ris. '12	♟ 5
● Barbera d'Alba Elena La Luna '14	♟ 5
● Barbaresco Currà Ris. '11	♟♟ 5
● Barbaresco Currà Ris. '10	♟♟ 5
● Barbaresco Gaia Principe '13	♟♟ 6
● Barolo Audace '11	♟♟ 6
○ Gavi del Comune di Gavi Bric Sassi Tenuta Manenti '15	♟♟ 2*

Scagliola

VIA SAN SIRO, 42
14052 CALOSSO [AT]
TEL. +39 0141853183
www.scagliolavini.com

CELLAR SALES
PRE-BOOKED VISITS
ANNUAL PRODUCTION 200,000 bottles
HECTARES UNDER VINE 37.00

In recent years, the Scagliola family have managed to establish themselves not only for their Moscato d'Asti, which is among the appellation's most well-known, but also for a series of highly successful Barberas. The vineyards surrounding their cellar in Calosso, features somewhat compact calcareous clay soil (here mostly Barbera is grown), while their plots in Canelli are sandy marl (mostly Moscato is cultivated here). Their wines are modern, but haven't lost the ability to express the characters of the territory. Once again, the 2015 Barbera d'Asti Superiore Sansì is at the top of its category. The nose reveals notes of plums and toasty hints, while the palate comes through rich and very lingering, with well-balanced acidity and pulp. Their rest of their selection features the 2016 Barbera d'Asti Frem and the 2016 Moscato d'Asti Volo di Farfalle. The first offers up approachable fruity notes on the nose. It's fresh, vibrant and pleasant, as a vintage Barbera should be. The second exhibits tones of candied fruit and fullness supported by good acidity.

● Barbera d'Asti Sup. SanSì '15	♟♟	6
● Barbera d'Asti Frem '16	♟♟	4
○ Moscato d'Asti Volo di Farfalle '16	♟♟	3
● M.to Rosso Azörd '15	♟	5
○ Moscato d'Asti Primo Bacio '16	♟	3
○ Piemonte Chardonnay Casot Dan Vian '16	♟	3
● Barbera d'Asti Sup. SanSì Sel. '01	♟♟♟	6
● Barbera d'Asti Sup. SanSì Sel. '00	♟♟♟	6
● Barbera d'Asti Sup. SanSì Sel. '99	♟♟♟	5
● Barbera d'Asti Sup. SanSì Antologia '13	♟♟	8
● M.to Rosso Azörd '14	♟♟	5
○ Moscato d'Asti Volo di Farfalle '15	♟♟	3*
● Nizza Foravia '14	♟♟	5

Simone Scaletta

LOC. MANZONI, 61
12065 MONFORTE D'ALBA [CN]
TEL. +39 3484912733
www.simonescaletta.it

CELLAR SALES
PRE-BOOKED VISITS
ACCOMMODATION
ANNUAL PRODUCTION 20,000 bottles
HECTARES UNDER VINE 4.75

In 15 years of work in the vineyard and cellar, Simone Scaletta has managed to achieve a balance between eschewing the use of chemicals and bringing out the sensory properties of his wines. Gone are the days when he'd sleep amidst his vineyards in a camper, and today Simone feels ready to expand his selection, making more room for Barolo. His production philosophy calls for minimal intervention, restraining the influence of wood, and leaving space for the grape to express themselves. The 2011 Barolo Riserva achieved a good all-round result. This youthful, glossy and elegant wine still remains very fruity and long, and hinges more on drinkability than power. The 2013 Barolo Chirlet moves along similar lines. We're just now getting a glimpse of its aromatic complexity built around raspberries, tar, licorice and balsamic hints. The mouth is decidedly more fresh than it is tannic. The rich 2015 Barbera Superiore Sarsera is aged in wood and exhibits good acidity.

● Barolo Ris. '11	♟♟	7
● Barbera d'Alba Sup. Sarsera '15	♟♟	4
● Barolo Chirlet '13	♟♟	6
● Langhe Nebbiolo Autin 'd Madama '15	♟♟	4
● Barbera d'Alba Sarsera '11	♟♟	3
● Barolo Bricco San Pietro Chirlet '12	♟♟	6
● Barolo Chirlet '11	♟♟	6
● Barolo Chirlet '10	♟♟	6
● Barolo Chirlet '09	♟♟	6
● Barolo Chirlet '08	♟♟	6
● Dolcetto d'Alba Viglioni '13	♟♟	2*
● Langhe Nebbiolo Autin 'd Madama '13	♟♟	3
● Langhe Nebbiolo Autin 'd Madama '10	♟♟	3

Giorgio Scarzello e Figli

VIA ALBA, 29
12060 BAROLO [CN]
TEL. +39 017356170
www.barolodibarolo.com

CELLAR SALES
PRE-BOOKED VISITS
ANNUAL PRODUCTION 25,000 bottles
HECTARES UNDER VINE 5.50

Federico Scarzello hasn't let himself get distracted by his political activities and continues to propose a selection of wines distinguished for their incomparable class. The small scale of his winery, and the success of his wines, have allowed him to sell these when he believes they're ready. And so it is that, for example, his 2010 Barolos come out in 2017, while 2016 saw the release of his 2011 selection. Sarmassa, one of the area's most well-known and historic crus, gives rise to a Barolo with notable structure and sophisticated complexity that's perfect for lengthy aging in the bottle. The enchanting and youthful 2010 Barolo Sarmassa Vigna Merenda is characterized by aromas of rhubarb, cinchona and raspberries. The palate exhibits bold but delicate tannins, length and good fruit. Tre Bicchieri. The 2010 Barolo del Comune di Barolo opens on slightly more mature notes, with hints of wilted roses and forest floor. The palate comes through lingering and warm with alcohol.

● Barolo Sarmassa V. Merenda '10	▼▼▼	6
● Barolo del Comune di Barolo '10	▼▼	5
● Barbera d'Alba Sup. '15	▼▼	4
● Langhe Nebbiolo '15	▼▼	3
● Barolo V. Merenda '99	♈♈♈	5
● Barbera d'Alba Sup. '10	♈♈	4
● Barolo del Comune di Barolo '11	♈♈	5
● Barolo del Comune di Barolo '09	♈♈	5
● Barolo del Comune di Barolo '08	♈♈	5
● Barolo Sarmassa V. Merenda '11	♈♈	6
● Barolo Sarmassa V. Merenda '09	♈♈	6
● Barolo Sarmassa V. Merenda '08	♈♈	6
● Langhe Nebbiolo '13	♈♈	3
● Langhe Nebbiolo '12	♈♈	3

★★Paolo Scavino

FRAZ. GARBELLETTO
VIA ALBA-BAROLO, 157
12060 CASTIGLIONE FALLETTO [CN]
TEL. +39 017362850
www.paoloscavino.com

CELLAR SALES
PRE-BOOKED VISITS
ANNUAL PRODUCTION 130,000 bottles
HECTARES UNDER VINE 29.00

Enrico Scavino is one of Langhe's true masters. Supported by winemaking experience that goes back to early adolescence, and relationships with prestigious wineries, he's refined his method of cultivating, making and storing wines. The result is a series of Barolos that are appreciated the world over, all without the help of outside consultants. The increasing support of his daughters, Elisa and Enrica, has added security and potential to this great winery. Their Nebbiolo crus are in some of Barolo's best vineyards, starting with the celebrated Bric dël Fiasc and Rocche dell'Annunziata. Tre Bicchieri for the 2011 Rocche dell'Annunziata Riserva. It's a lively and close-focused Barolo, fresh and still slightly marked by oak. The elegant, well-orchestrated palate, rich in pulp, features delicate tannins. The 2013 Barolo Bric dël Fiasc plays more on balance than power. It remains a bit closed but shows great potential. The 2013 Barolo Bricco Ambrogio turned out well, exhibiting cherries and licorice on the nose, with a juicy, lively palate.

● Barolo Rocche dell'Annunziata Ris. '11	▼▼▼	8
● Barolo Bric dël Fiasc '13	▼▼	8
● Barolo Bricco Ambrogio '13	▼▼	8
● Barolo Cannubi '13	▼▼	8
● Barbera d'Alba Affinato in Carati '15	▼▼	4
● Barolo Carobric '13	▼▼	8
● Barolo Enrico Scavino '13	▼▼	7
● Barolo Monvigliero '13	▼▼	8
● Langhe Nebbiolo '15	▼▼	4
○ Langhe Bianco Sorriso '16	▼	3
● Barolo Bric dël Fiasc '12	♈♈♈	8
● Barolo Bric dël Fiasc '11	♈♈♈	8
● Barolo Rocche dell'Annunziata Ris. '08	♈♈♈	8

Schiavenza

VIA MAZZINI, 4
12050 SERRALUNGA D'ALBA [CN]
TEL. +39 0173613115
www.schiavenza.com

CELLAR SALES
PRE-BOOKED VISITS
RESTAURANT SERVICE
ANNUAL PRODUCTION 43,000 bottles
HECTARES UNDER VINE 10.00
SUSTAINABLE WINERY

The Schiavenza family's cellar-inn is a hotspot for Langhe's locals, with its strategic position, just under the majestic castle of Serralunga d'Alba, and vineyard views as far as the eye can see. Everything is peaceful here, at least until Luciano Pira's bottles arrive at the table. With the help of his wife, Maura, and brother-in-law, Walter, he makes wines that display rigor and energy like few others. And these certainly aren't wines that you'd recommend to untrained palates. Prapò, Cerretta, Broglio and Perno (the only plot in Monforte) make for Barolos wedded to tradition, and that are only released after lengthy aging in medium-sized barrels. This small winery with its splendid crus in Serralunga d'Alba only submitted 2013 Barolos for tasting this year. The Prapò comes through warm with alcohol, but remains austere and still hard overall. The fruity Cerretta is less fresh than we would expect from this vintage. The Serralunga d'Alba proves powerful and decidedly tannic.

● Barolo Cerretta '13	♥♥ 6
● Barolo del Comune di Serralunga d'Alba '13	♥♥ 5
● Barolo Prapò '13	♥♥ 6
● Barolo Broglio '13	♥ 6
● Barolo Broglio '11	♥♥♥ 5
● Barolo Broglio '05	♥♥♥ 5
● Barolo Broglio Ris. '08	♥♥♥ 7
● Barolo Broglio Ris. '04	♥♥♥ 5
● Barolo Prapò '08	♥♥♥ 6
● Barbera d'Alba '15	♀♀ 3
● Barolo Broglio '12	♀♀ 6
● Barolo Cerretta '12	♀♀ 6
● Barolo del Comune di Serralunga d'Alba '12	♀♀ 5
● Barolo Prapò '12	♀♀ 6

Mauro Sebaste

FRAZ. GALLO D'ALBA
VIA GARIBALDI, 222BIS
12051 ALBA [CN]
TEL. +39 0173262148
www.maurosebaste.it

CELLAR SALES
PRE-BOOKED VISITS
ANNUAL PRODUCTION 150,000 bottles
HECTARES UNDER VINE 30.00

Mauro Sebaste inherited his passion and skill from his mother, Sylla, deservedly known as the great lady of Langhe's wines. These gifts brought him to found his own winery in 1991, and since then both his vineyards and selection have grown in size, with the latter coming to comprise 13 wines (including 4 whites). His Barolo is available as a blend of various vineyards (the Trèsüri), as a single cru (the Prapò from Serralunga d'Alba) and as a 'Riserva' (the Ghé, from the Cerretta cru in Serralunga). Their entire selection is technically exquisite. The 2011 Barolo Ghè Riserva shows notable pulp and ripeness, and is still marked by oak. The 2013 Barolo Trèsüri features herbs and flowers in the sun, followed by a medium-weight palate and a prominent tannic component. Both of the Centobricchis did well. In addition to the fruity and supple 2015 Barbera d'Alba, we liked the outstanding 2016 Langhe Bianco made with Viognier grapes. It comes through caressing, with a very light aromatic quality. The Moscato d'Asti once again proves pleasant.

● Barbera d'Alba S. Rosalia '15	♥♥ 4
● Barbera d'Alba Sup. Centobricchi '15	♥♥ 5
● Barolo Ghè Ris. '11	♥♥ 8
● Barolo Trèsüri '13	♥♥ 6
○ Gavi '16	♥♥ 3
○ Langhe Bianco Centobricchi '16	♥♥ 5
● Nebbiolo d'Alba Parigi '15	♥♥ 5
○ Roero Arneis '16	♥ 3
● Barbera d'Alba Sup. Centobricchi '13	♀♀ 5
● Barbera d'Asti Valvedani '15	♀♀ 5
● Barolo Ghé Ris. '10	♀♀ 8
● Barolo Ghé Ris. '09	♀♀ 8
● Barolo Prapò '12	♀♀ 8
● Barolo Prapò '11	♀♀ 7
● Barolo Trèsüri '12	♀♀ 6
● Nebbiolo d'Alba Parigi '14	♀♀ 5

F.lli Seghesio

LOC. CASTELLETTO, 19
12065 MONFORTE D'ALBA [CN]
TEL. +39 017378108
www.fratelliseghesio.com

CELLAR SALES
PRE-BOOKED VISITS
ANNUAL PRODUCTION 55,000 bottles
HECTARES UNDER VINE 10.00

The Seghesio brothers' winery was founded during the explosive 1980s, when Langhe was seeing the rise of an enthusiastic generation of vine growers and winemakers. Seghesio immediately set itself apart for its consistently strong selection. Since then, their style as been aimed at elegance and the recognizability of the grapes, with wood used in such a way that it never compromises their integrity. Their sophisticated Barolo La Villa has been awarded repeatedly (also abroad), while their Barbera d'Alba La Chiesa is regularly singled out as among the best of its kind. Today the winery is managed by Riccardo, along with his younger kin, Michela, Sandro and Marco. The 2013 Barolo La Villa exhibits elegant aromas of red and black berries, licorice and dried herbs. It features a powerful mouth with remarkable tannic density and length. It's a wine that you could drink today and for the next thirty years. While waiting for the new La Chiesa, we tasted one of the best vintage Barberas put forward. It's fresh but also very rich in pulp.

● Barolo La Villa '13	♟♟7
● Barbera d'Alba '16	♟♟3
● Barolo '13	♟♟7
● Langhe Rosso Bouquet '14	♟♟4
● Langhe Nebbiolo '16	♟4
● Barbera d'Alba Vign. della Chiesa '00	♟♟♟4*
● Barbera d'Alba Vign. della Chiesa '97	♟♟♟4*
● Barolo La Villa '10	♟♟♟7
● Barolo Vign. La Villa '04	♟♟♟6
● Barolo Vign. La Villa '99	♟♟♟7
● Barolo Vign. La Villa '91	♟♟♟6
● Barbera d'Alba '15	♟♟3

Tenute Sella

VIA IV NOVEMBRE, 130
13060 LESSONA [BI]
TEL. +39 01599455
www.tenutesella.it

CELLAR SALES
PRE-BOOKED VISITS
ANNUAL PRODUCTION 80,000 bottles
HECTARES UNDER VINE 22.00

Lustrous, energetic, delicate in appearance only … the scope of Sella's red wines is pure and deep. Their selection is a benchmark for this corner of Alto Piemonte, and manage to integrate every variation in pedoclimate. The sands of Lessona are represented by a base wine and two others (San Sebastiano allo Zoppo and Omaggio a Quintino Sella), Bramaterra by I Porfidi (meaning porphyry, thus recalling the layout of the terrain). Vespolina, Croatian and Uva Rara accompany the predominant (but never exclusive) Nebbiolo. In the cellar, both large barrels and barriques are to be found (not all of which are new). Tenute Sella's selection doesn't just consist of great reds for laying down. Recent tastings have brought the meticulous, pure character of their whites, the 2016 Piandoro and Doranda, into the spotlight. The 2011 Lessona, on the other hand, proves more austere than usual, with fruit that's just discernible and a vibrant, lingering palate.

● Bramaterra I Porfidi '10	♟♟5
○ Coste della Sesia Bianco Doranda '16	♟♟3
● Coste della Sesia Rosso Orbello '15	♟♟3
● Lessona '11	♟♟5
○ Piemonte Bianco Piandoro '16	♟♟3
⊙ Clementina Brut Rosé	♟3
⊙ Coste della Sesia Rosato Majoli '16	♟3
● Bramaterra I Porfidi '07	♟♟♟5
● Bramaterra I Porfidi '05	♟♟♟5
● Lessona Omaggio a Quintino Sella '06	♟♟♟7
● Lessona Omaggio a Quintino Sella '05	♟♟♟6
● Bramaterra '11	♟♟5
● Lessona '10	♟♟5
● Lessona Omaggio a Quintino Sella '09	♟♟7

Enrico Serafino

C.SO ASTI, 5
12043 CANALE [CN]
TEL. +39 0173979485
www.enricoserafino.it

CELLAR SALES
PRE-BOOKED VISITS
ANNUAL PRODUCTION 500,000 bottles
HECTARES UNDER VINE 12.00

The Krause family has shown great
continuity in managing this historic Roero
winery. Indeed, the purchase of Vietti doesn't
seem to have distracted the owners at all
· from the selection of wines produced in Alta
Langa. They offer three principal lines:
Classici del Piemonte, Spumanti (including
some of Italy's most interesting 'Metodo
Classico' sparklers as of late) and Cantina
Maestra (made with grapes cultivated on
their estate in Canale). Once again, the
Serafino has brought home a Tre Bicchieri,
but this time under the management of the
Krause family. The 2011 Alta Langa Brut
Nature Zero Sboccatura Tardiva offers up
intense aromas of white fruit and crusty
bread. The palate displays great structure,
balanced by a vibrant acidity. Its finish
proves long and well-orchestrated. The
2011 Alta Langa Brut did quite well. It sees
hints of yellow-fleshed fruit and cakes, with
a rich and creamy palate. The 2015 Barbera
d'Alba Superiore San Defendente also put in
a good performance. It's a wine with notes
of spices, rain-soaked earth and licorice, as
well as good freshness and grip.

○ Alta Langa Brut Zero Nature Sboccatura Tardiva '11	♕♕♕	6
○ Alta Langa Brut '11	♕♕	4
● Barbera d'Alba Sup. S. Defendente '15	♕♕	4
● Barbaresco '14	♕♕	5
● Barbera d'Alba '15	♕♕	3
● Barolo '13	♕♕	6
● Nebbiolo d'Alba '14	♕♕	3
○ Roero Arneis '16	♕♕	3
● Roero Oesio '15	♕♕	4
○ Alta Langa Brut Zero Cantina Maestra '09	♕♕♕	6
○ Alta Langa Brut Zero Cantina Maestra '07	♕♕♕	6
○ Alta Langa Brut Zero Cantina Maestra '06	♕♕♕	6
○ Alta Langa Brut Zero Sboccatura Tardiva Cantina Maestra '08	♕♕♕	6

Giovanni Silva

CASCINE ROGGE, 1B
10011 AGLIÈ [TO]
TEL. +39 3473075648
www.silvavini.com

CELLAR SALES
PRE-BOOKED VISITS
ANNUAL PRODUCTION 50,000 bottles
HECTARES UNDER VINE 12.00

We don't think it's a coincidence that the
heart of the Silla family's property in
Cascina Rogge (Agliè) borders the park of
the Ducal Castle, just a stone's throw from
the house of Guido Gozzano. It's a truly
unique position that ties together the works
of the celebrated poet with the most
captivating features of Erbaluce. Their
timeless whites come in a variety of forms,
from the still Dry Ice and Tre Ciochè to
Passito Poetica, not to mention their
charmat and 'Metodo Classico' sparklers.
Nebbiolo, Barbera, Freisa and Bonarda
make up the rest of their 12 hectares of
property, all managed by Giovanni and his
younger kin, Stefano. The Silva family's
Erbaluce wines may have missed out on top
marks, but they remain a style benchmark
for the entire area. The 2016 Dry Ice is
compressed on the nose and has a rather
closed palate. However, it demonstrates
suppleness and naturalness. The youthful
2016 Tre Ciochè proves even more closed
on the nose, but shows an impressive,
vibrant, youthful palate.

○ Erbaluce di Caluso Dry Ice '16	♕♕	2*
○ Erbaluce di Caluso Tre Ciochè '16	♕♕	2*
○ Caluso Passito Poetica '03	♕♕	5
● Canavese Nebbiolo '08	♕♕	2*
○ Erbaluce di Caluso Brut M. Cl. '09	♕♕	5
○ Erbaluce di Caluso Dry Ice '15	♕♕	2*
○ Erbaluce di Caluso Dry Ice '14	♕♕	2*
○ Erbaluce di Caluso Dry Silva '12	♕♕	2*
○ Erbaluce di Caluso Passito Poetica '04	♕♕	5
○ Erbaluce di Caluso Tre Ciochè '15	♕♕	2*
○ Erbaluce di Caluso Tre Ciochè '14	♕♕	2*
○ Erbaluce di Caluso Tre Ciochè '13	♕♕	2*
○ Erbaluce di Caluso Tre Ciochè '12	♕♕	2*

La Smilla

VIA GARIBALDI, 7
15060 BOSIO [AL]
TEL. +39 0143684245
www.lasmilla.it

CELLAR SALES
ANNUAL PRODUCTION 100,000 bottles
HECTARES UNDER VINE 5.00

Bosio may be an outpost of Piedmont but in terms of culture and environment it is basically Liguria. This is part of the reason why it's a great destination for curious travelers. The other reason is to enjoy the wine produced by the Guido family, vine growers for generations in this corner of the region, wedged in between the sea and Apennines. Their six hectares of land are dedicated to various local grapes: Barbera, Dolcetto and Cortese, all recognizable for their gastronomic versatility and natural expressiveness. All their wines are aged in steel with a non-invasive approach to fermentation, the only exceptions are their Gavi I Bergi and Barbera Calicanto, which are aged in barriques. This time the Cortese whites grabbed the limelight. The 2014 Metodo Classico is a clean, pure wine, and made for an impressive prelude to the energy of the 2016 Gavi di Gavi and the 2015 Bergi. The former longer and sharper, while the latter proves more full-bodied and multi-faceted.

○ Gavi I Bergi '15	♟♟	3*
● Dolcetto di Ovada '15	♟♟	2*
○ Gavi Brut M. Cl. '14	♟♟	3
○ Gavi del Comune di Gavi '16	♟♟	2*
● Barbera del M.to '15	♟	2
● M.to Rosso Calicanto '13	♟	3
● Dolcetto di Ovada '13	♟♟	2*
○ Gavi '15	♟♟	2*
○ Gavi '14	♟♟	2*
○ Gavi Brut M. Cl. '13	♟♟	3
○ Gavi del Comune di Gavi '15	♟♟	2*
○ Gavi del Comune di Gavi '14	♟♟	2*
○ Gavi del Comune di Gavi '13	♟♟	2*
● M.to Rosso Calicanto '12	♟♟	3

Socré

S.DA TERZOLO, 7
12050 BARBARESCO [CN]
TEL. +39 3487121685
www.socre.it

CELLAR SALES
PRE-BOOKED VISITS
ANNUAL PRODUCTION 30,000 bottles
HECTARES UNDER VINE 5.50

The cru of Roncaglie di Barbaresco is small and used by very few producers. As a result, it hasn't gotten the attention it deserves. In this vineyard, the architect Marco Piacentino is having notable success, thanks to painstaking care and attention. Today, his work is supported by a lovely, completely renovated cellar, which includes ample space both for fermentation and wood barrels for aging. The estate also includes a plot in Monferrato (Cisterna d'Asti), where, along with Barbera, they are producing solid Croatina. The 2013 Barbaresco Roncaglie offers up a stimulating spiciness on the nose. Tannins and a structure that exhibits good alcohol content pleasantly merge on its balanced palate. The delicate and warm 2014 Barbaresco sees aromas of bottled cherries and red fruit. The clean and fresh 2015 Barbera d'Alba Superiore, a sound wine, proves multi-faceted.

● Barbaresco Roncaglie '13	♟♟	6
● Barbaresco '14	♟♟	5
● Barbera d'Alba Sup. '15	♟♟	3
● Langhe Nebbiolo '15	♟♟	3
● Cisterna d'Asti De Scapin '15	♟	2
● Barbaresco '13	♟♟	5
● Barbaresco '12	♟♟	5
● Barbaresco '11	♟♟	5
● Barbaresco Roncaglie '12	♟♟	6
● Barbaresco Roncaglie '11	♟♟	6
● Barbera d'Alba Sup. '13	♟♟	3
● Cisterna d'Asti De Scapin '13	♟♟	2*
● Cisterna d'Asti De Scapin '12	♟♟	2*
● Langhe Nebbiolo '14	♟♟	3

Giovanni Sordo

FRAZ. GARBELLETTO
VIA ALBA BAROLO, 175
12060 CASTIGLIONE FALLETTO [CN]
TEL. +39 017362853
www.sordogiovanni.it

CELLAR SALES
PRE-BOOKED VISITS
ANNUAL PRODUCTION 350,000 bottles
HECTARES UNDER VINE 53.00

The winery founded by Giuseppe Sordo recently turned 100. Giuseppe's son, Giovanni, and grandson, Giorgio, proceeded to realize an amazing cellar and purchase the vineyards that brought the estate to its present, impressive form. Their efforts come together in their some 15 Barolos. Their crus are widely-known, from Ravera (Novello) to Monprivato, Rocche, Villero di Castiglione Falletto, Perno (Monforte) and Gabutti (Serralunga), along with Monvigliero (Verduno). Their style is marked by accuracy in the classic tradition. The 2013 Barolo Perno, a wine with a splendid personality, proves charming thanks to aromas ranging from cherries to violets set on a background of licorice. Its dense and pleasant tannins are well-integrated into a well-orchestrated and lively body. The 2013 Barolo Parussi features bottled fruit and licorice, while its bold mouth also comes through delicate. Theirs is a high-level selection of Barolos.

● Barolo Monvigliero '13	▼▼6
● Barolo Parussi '13	▼▼7
● Barolo Perno '13	▼▼7
● Barolo Ravera '13	▼▼6
● Barolo Gabutti '13	▼▼7
● Barolo Monprivato '13	▼▼6
● Barolo Perno Ris. '10	▼▼7
● Barolo Rocche di Castiglione '13	▼▼6
● Barolo Villero '13	▼▼6
● Langhe Nebbiolo '15	▼▼3
● Barbera d'Alba Sup. Massucchi '14	▼4
● Dolcetto d'Alba '16	▼2

★Sottimano

LOC. COTTÀ, 21
12052 NEIVE [CN]
TEL. +39 0173635186
www.sottimano.it

CELLAR SALES
PRE-BOOKED VISITS
ANNUAL PRODUCTION 85,000 bottles
HECTARES UNDER VINE 18.00

Rinio and Anna Sottimano's foray into winemaking began in the late 1960s, almost as a bet, in what is one of Langhe's many inspiring success stories. They purchased a farmstead and small plots in Nieve (today almost 20 hectares), with mentions as prestigious as Barbaresco Fausoni, Pajorè, Currà, Basarin, Bric del Salto (Dolcetto) and Paroleiro (Barbera). For some time now, their children, Andrea and Elena, have been on board full-time, but nothing has changed in terms of their modern-leaning selection. They age their wines mostly in small, only partially new, wood. The 2014 Barbaresco Pajoré features fresh red fruit, elegantly contrasted by hints of sweet spices. It earns a Tre Bicchieri with its balance, finesse and drinkability. The 2014 Fausoni is just as charming. It exhibits flowers and sweet tobacco, which follow through onto a palate of subtle freshness and delicate tannins. The 2014 Cottà offers up aromas of roses and licorice and a soft, long palate. The 2013 Currà displays a majestic tannic texture.

● Barbaresco Pajoré '14	▼▼▼7
● Barbaresco Cottà '14	▼▼7
● Barbaresco Currà '13	▼▼8
● Barbaresco Fausoni '14	▼▼7
● Barbaresco Currà '12	♀♀♀8
● Barbaresco Currà '10	♀♀♀8
● Barbaresco Currà '08	♀♀♀7
● Barbaresco Pajoré '10	♀♀♀7
● Barbaresco Pajoré '08	♀♀♀7
● Barbaresco Ris. '10	♀♀♀8
● Barbaresco Ris. '05	♀♀♀8
● Barbaresco Cottà '13	♀♀7
● Barbaresco Pajoré '13	♀♀7
● Maté '15	♀♀3

Luigi Spertino

VIA LEA, 505
14047 MOMBERCELLI [AT]
TEL. +39 0141959090
luigi.spertino@libero.it

CELLAR SALES
PRE-BOOKED VISITS
ANNUAL PRODUCTION 40,000 bottles
HECTARES UNDER VINE 9.00

The Spertino family's historic winery was
founded by Luigi more than 35 years ago.
And thanks to him, it's become a
benchmark for Grignolino. His son, Mauro,
has further elevated the winery, establishing
its reputation as one of the best interpreters
of Asti's Barbera, thanks to his personal
approach to interpreting the terroir and
variety. Their estate features vineyards of
Barbera that are more than 60 years old, as
well as Grignolino, Cortese and Pinot Nero.
The 2015 Barbera d'Asti Superiore Vigna La
Mandorla remains at the top of the
rankings. Aromas of fruit and Mediterranean
scrub emerge on the nose, along with hints
of cinchona and dark chocolate. Then
comes a palate with great density and
tight-knit tannins, but it remains balanced
thanks to remarkable acidity. The first-rate
2015 Barbera d'Asti La Grisa sees a rich
nose of plums and cherries, pepper and
cocoa, and a long, well-orchestrated palate.
The 2016 Grignolino d'Asti exhibits notes of
wild berries and orange rind. It's a fresh,
easy-drinking wine. We're still waiting to
taste their Grignolino.

● Barbera d'Asti Sup. V. La Mandorla '15	🍷🍷🍷 8
● Barbera d'Asti La Grisa '15	🍷🍷 4
● Grignolino d'Asti '16	🍷🍷 3*
● Barbera d'Asti Sup. La Mandorla '13	🍷🍷🍷 8
● Barbera d'Asti Sup. La Mandorla '10	🍷🍷🍷 8
● Barbera d'Asti Sup. La Mandorla '09	🍷🍷🍷 8
● Barbera d'Asti Sup. La Mandorla '07	🍷🍷🍷 7
● Barbera d'Asti Sup. V. La Mandorla '12	🍷🍷🍷 8
● Barbera d'Asti Sup. V. La Mandorla Edizione La Grisa '14	🍷🍷🍷 8
● M.to Rosso La Mandorla '09	🍷🍷🍷 7
● M.to Rosso La Mandorla '07	🍷🍷🍷 5

★★★La Spinetta

VIA ANNUNZIATA, 17
14054 CASTAGNOLE DELLE LANZE [AT]
TEL. +39 0141877396
www.la-spinetta.com

CELLAR SALES
PRE-BOOKED VISITS
ACCOMMODATION
ANNUAL PRODUCTION 500,000 bottles
HECTARES UNDER VINE 100.00
SUSTAINABLE WINERY

The first wine that feature the Dürer
rhinoceros goes back to 1995, the
winery's breakthrough year. Since then,
they've successfully launched a number of
new wines and expanded their market.
However, Giorgio Rivetti and his brothers
haven't abandoned the family tradition,
maintaining undiminished attention for
Moscato and Barbera, the two grapes that
gave the winery its start. Their vineyards
are old, with low yields, and small, new
wood is used in the cellar, making for
Barbarescos, Barolos and Barberas (both
d'Asti and d'Alba) with notable
personalities. The 2014 Barbaresco Gallina
is a modern, spicy, elegant and complex
wine, with well-integrated tannins. It's a
worthy representative of Langhe's great
reds, with moderate notes of oak, packed
with ripe grapes, as per the winery's style.
The 2013 Barolo Campè displays a strong
personality, clearly discernible wood and
an amazing structure, but lacks territorial
identity. The 2016 Bricco Quaglia
confirms its status as one of the best
Moscato d'Astis.

● Barbaresco Gallina '14	🍷🍷 8
● Barbaresco Valeirano '14	🍷🍷 8
● Barolo Campè '13	🍷🍷 8
○ Moscato d'Asti Bricco Quaglia '16	🍷🍷 3*
○ Piemonte Chardonnay Lidia '14	🍷🍷 6
● Barbaresco Bordini '14	🍷🍷 7
● Barbaresco Starderi '14	🍷🍷 8
● Barbera d'Alba Gallina '14	🍷🍷 6
● Barbera d'Asti Ca' di Pian '14	🍷🍷 4
● Barbera d'Asti Sup. Bionzo '14	🍷🍷 6
● Barolo Garretti '13	🍷🍷 7
● M.to Rosso Pin '14	🍷🍷 6
○ Langhe Bianco '14	🍷 6
● Barbaresco Gallina '11	🍷🍷🍷 8
● Barolo Campè '08	🍷🍷🍷 8

Sulin

V.LE PININFARINA, 14
14035 GRAZZANO BADOGLIO [AT]
TEL. +39 0141925136
www.sulin.it

CELLAR SALES
PRE-BOOKED VISITS
ANNUAL PRODUCTION 220,000 bottles
HECTARES UNDER VINE 19.50

As of late, the Fracchia brothers have started to reap the success of a project begun some 20 years ago. Rezoning was required so as to identify the best terrain for their clones and root stocks. Then they moved on to the work of plant spacing and identifying the best pruning systems for high quality yields. It's been long, burdensome work that's bringing excellent results, as demonstrated by the wines themselves. The Barbera del Monferrato and Grignolino led the tasting and gave excellent performances. The former features an impenetrable ruby color, as well as aromas of dark berries and spices on notes of camphor. Its palate proves intense and rich in pulp, with a long finish. The Grignolino exhibits a pale ruby color, with garnet highlights and an intense nose. Lovely notes of pepper and fruit evolve into tobacco and cinchona, then lead into a powerful palate with great character.

● Barbera del M.to '15	♟♟2*
● Grignolino del M.to Casalese '16	♟♟2*
● Casorzo '16	♟♟2*
● M.to Rosso Adriano '15	♟♟3
○ Piemonte Chardonnay '16	♟♟2*
● Barbera del M.to '14	♟♟2*
● Barbera del M.to Sup. Ornella '13	♟♟5
● Grignolino del M.to Casalese '15	♟♟2*
○ Piemonte Chardonnay '15	♟♟2*

Sylla Sebaste

VIA SAN PIETRO, 4
12060 BAROLO [CN]
TEL. +39 017356266
www.syllasebaste.com

CELLAR SALES
PRE-BOOKED VISITS
RESTAURANT SERVICE
ANNUAL PRODUCTION 120,000 bottles
HECTARES UNDER VINE 7.00

Situated in an enchanting position with a view of Langhe's most prestigious hills, today Sylla Sybaste is led by Fabrizio Merlo with the help of Domenico Franco (agronomist) and Luca Caramellino (their wine technician). Gradually, they're carving out an increasingly prominent name for themselves in the area. Their Barolo (and Nebbiolo grapes) form the core of their production, and serve as the winery's calling card. The rest of their selection, however, is just as sound. This year we must point out the excellent 2013 Barolo Bussia, which unfolds with balsamic notes and small red fruit and violets. Then comes a muscular but balanced palate and a fresh, long finish. The 2013 Barolo is slightly less complex, but still managed to exhibit nice varietal definition during tasting. The 2015 Barber d'Alba proves juicy and supple.

● Barbera d'Alba '15	♟♟3
● Barolo '13	♟♟5
● Barolo Bussia '13	♟♟6
● Barolo Bussia '85	♟♟♟6
● Barolo Bussia Ris. '84	♟♟♟6
● Barbera d'Alba '13	♟♟3
● Barolo '12	♟♟5
● Barolo '11	♟♟6
● Barolo '10	♟♟6
● Barolo Bricco delle Viole '12	♟♟5
● Barolo Bussia '12	♟♟6
● Barolo Bussia '11	♟♟6
● Barolo Bussia '10	♟♟6
● Langhe Nebbiolo '13	♟♟3
● Nebbiolo d'Alba '12	♟♟3

Tacchino

VIA MARTIRI DELLA BENEDICTA, 26
15060 CASTELLETTO D'ORBA [AL]
TEL. +39 0143830115
www.luigitacchino.it

CELLAR SALES
PRE-BOOKED VISITS
ANNUAL PRODUCTION 120,000 bottles
HECTARES UNDER VINE 12.00

The continued growth that Tacchino has seen over the past 15 years has forced Romina and Alessio to take on more responsibility in the winery. Then there's the fact that, in an operation of this size, it's necessary to know how to manage everything, from start to finish. Alessio looks after production, while Romina takes care of administration and sales. They've got consultants as well: Alberto Panescchi (agronomist) and Mario Ronco (enologist), both esteemed professionals in the field. Theirs is a finely-tuned machine that's making waves on more than one continent. While waiting to taste the 2014 Du Riva, the Barbera del Monferrato made it into our finals. It comes through complex and intense, with a rich, lingering finish. Tre Bicchieri for the Dolcetto, which proved a bit young at every stage of tasting, but its fresh and tannic palate gave it some character. The basic wines appear to have turned the tables on their more acclaimed companions.

● Dolcetto di Ovada '15	♟♟♟2*
● Barbera del M.to '15	♟♟2*
● Barbera del M.to Albarola '14	♟♟5
○ Piemonte Cortese Marsenca '16	♟♟2*
○ Gavi del Comune di Gavi '16	♟3
● Dolcetto di Ovada Sup. Du Riva '13	♟♟♟4*
● Dolcetto di Ovada Sup. Du Riva '12	♟♟♟5
● Dolcetto di Ovada Sup. Du Riva '11	♟♟♟5
● Dolcetto di Ovada Sup. Du Riva '10	♟♟♟4*
● Dolcetto di Ovada Sup. Du Riva '09	♟♟♟4*
● Dolcetto di Ovada Sup. Du Riva '08	♟♟♟4*
● Barbera del M.to Albarola '13	♟♟5
● Dolcetto di Ovada '14	♟♟2*
○ Gavi del Comune di Gavi '15	♟♟3

Michele Taliano

C.SO A. MANZONI, 24
12046 MONTÀ [CN]
TEL. +39 0173975658
www.talianomichele.com

CELLAR SALES
PRE-BOOKED VISITS
ANNUAL PRODUCTION 60,000 bottles
HECTARES UNDER VINE 12.00

Today, the Taliano family's winery is managed by brothers Alberto and Ezio. They have a series of vineyards in Roero and Langhe. The former, all of them in the municipality of Montà, feature the territory's classic grapes: Arneis, Barbera, Favorita and Nebbiolo. Their Langhe vineyards (in the Barbaresco appellation) host Nebbiolo, Barbera, Dolcetto and Moscato. Taliano gave rise to one of the best vintage Barberas tasted this year. The 2016 Barbera d'Alba A Bon Rendre is rich in fruit, fresh and approachable, with a very pleasant palate. Other notable wines include the 2013 Barbaresco Montersino Ad Altiora and the 2013 Barbera d'Alba Superiore Laboriosa. The former displays good body, with slightly aggressive tannins. It's a long and gutsy wine. The second proves soft and caressing, with good dynamism. The 2013 Roero Ròche dra Bòssora Riserva is usually the winery's flagship Roero, but showed less gloss than usual.

● Barbera d'Alba A Bon Rendre '16	♟♟2*
● Barbaresco Montersino Ad Altiora '13	♟♟5
● Barbera d'Alba Sup. Laboriosa '13	♟♟3
● Barbaresco Tera Mia Ris. '10	♟5
○ Roero Arneis Sernì '16	♟2
● Roero Ròche dra Bòssora Ris. '13	♟3
● Barbaresco Ad Altiora '11	♟♟5
● Barbaresco Ad Altiora Montersino '12	♟♟5
● Barbaresco Tera Mia Ris. '09	♟♟5
● Barbera d'Alba A Bon Rendre '15	♟♟2*
● Nebbiolo d'Alba Blagheur '13	♟♟2*
● Roero Ròche dra Bòssora Ris. '12	♟♟3*
● Roero Ròche dra Bòssora Ris. '11	♟♟3*

Tenuta Tenaglia

S.DA SANTUARIO DI CREA, 5
15020 SERRALUNGA DI CREA [AL]
TEL. +39 0142940252
www.tenutatenaglia.it

CELLAR SALES
PRE-BOOKED VISITS
ACCOMMODATION
ANNUAL PRODUCTION 120,000 bottles
HECTARES UNDER VINE 30.00
SUSTAINABLE WINERY

Tenuta Tenaglia is a leading winery in Monferrato Casalese. The area is known for its natural landscapes, but is also renowned for its viticulture. Its notable elevation (450 meters above sea level), and position/exposure of its vineyards, contribute to the cultivation of quality grapes. In the cellar, their approach is quite modern, with temperature control during fermentation and barriques used for their top-end wines. Of the wines presented, the Barbera del Monferrato Superiore and the Grignolino made it to the finals. The Barbera proved vibrant at every stage of tasting. Evolved aromas on notes of juniper berries pave the way for a well-orchestrated palate with great structure and a long finish. The Grignolino is a classic. Its pale color, floral aromas, notes of pepper and tobacco lead into a powerful palate marked by acidity and elegant tannins.

● Barbera del M.to Sup. 1930 Una Buona Annata '13	🍷🍷 5
● Grignolino del M.to Casalese '16	🍷🍷 2*
● Barbera d'Asti Bricco '16	🍷🍷 2*
● Barbera d'Asti Emozioni '11	🍷🍷 5
● Barbera del M.to Cappella III '16	🍷 2
● M.to Rosso Paradiso '11	🍷 5
○ Piemonte Chardonnay '16	🍷 2
● Barbera d'Asti Bricco '15	YY 2*
● Barbera d'Asti Emozioni '10	YY 5
● Barbera d'Asti Giorgio Tenaglia '10	YY 3*
● Barbera del M.to Cappella III '15	YY 2*
● Barbera del M.to Sup. 1930 Una Buona Annata '11	YY 5
● Grignolino del M.to Casalese '15	YY 2*
● M.to Rosso Paradiso '10	YY 5

Terre del Barolo

VIA ALBA - BAROLO, 8
12060 CASTIGLIONE FALLETTO [CN]
TEL. +39 0173262053
www.arnaldorivera.com

CELLAR SALES
PRE-BOOKED VISITS
ANNUAL PRODUCTION 3,000,000 bottles
HECTARES UNDER VINE 600.00
VITICULTURE METHOD Certified Organic
SUSTAINABLE WINERY

Arnaldo Rivera, the winery's visionary founder, has become an emblem of a selection that's more than just a series of wines. Indeed, his represents a strategy of quality that's beginning to bear fruit. Especially when it comes to his Barolos, which are proving just how good the crus chosen are, from Monforte (Bussia) to Verduno (Monvigliero), Novello (Ravera) and Serralunga (Vignarionda), just to name a few. And the producer's work comes together perfectly in the Undicicomuni, a commendable blend. Tre Bicchieri for the 2013 Barolo Vignarionda Arnaldo Rivera. It's a solid and vibrant wine, with great body and classic aromas of fruit set on a balsamic background. The sensational 2013 Undicicomuni did well, featuring violets and licorice, which enrich its fruity component. Don't miss the enchanting 2013 Rocche di Castiglione, with its slightly spicier notes and herbs. Not all of their wines are at these levels, but they've certainly got off to a great start.

● Barolo Vignarionda Arnaldo Rivera '13	🍷🍷🍷 7
● Barolo Rocche di Castiglione '13	🍷🍷 7
● Barbera d'Alba Valdisera '15	🍷🍷 3
● Barolo Bussia '13	🍷🍷 6
● Barolo Castello '13	🍷🍷 6
● Barolo Monvigliero '13	🍷🍷 6
● Barolo Ravera '13	🍷🍷 6
● Barolo Undicicomuni '13	🍷🍷 5
● Barolo Boiolo '13	🍷 6
● Diano d'Alba Sorì del Cascinotto '16	🍷 2
○ Langhe Nascetta del Comune di Novello '16	🍷 3
● Barolo Monvigliero '10	YY 6
● Barolo Ravera '10	YY 6

★Torraccia del Piantavigna

VIA ROMAGNANO, 20
28074 GHEMME [NO]
TEL. +39 0163840040
www.torracciadelpiantavigna.it

CELLAR SALES
PRE-BOOKED VISITS
ANNUAL PRODUCTION 150,000 bottles
HECTARES UNDER VINE 38.00
SUSTAINABLE WINERY

The 40 hectares of terrain managed by the Francoli family since the 1960s are spread out on at least six different subareas in the provinces of Novara and Vercelli. It all started when the first Nebbiolo vineyard was planted by the current generation's grandfather, a man by the name of Piantavigna, which means 'vineyard planter'! Vespolina and Erbaluce are also cultivated, making for a selection that is complete in all respects. Their Ghemme and Gattinara, aged mostly in oak, are at the top-end. They feature an elegantly dry touch, capable of satisfying less hurried wine drinkers. Their flagship reds have made their mark, even with the enigmatic 2012 vintage. The Gattinara, for instance, sees some alcoholic pungency, but the best versions exhibit a velvety, savory mouth. The real standout remains the Vigna Pelizzane, which brings out the qualities of the 2011 vintage. It's a wine that features complexity on the nose and austere generosity on the palate.

● Ghemme V. Pelizzane '11	▼▼▼6
● Gattinara '12	▼▼6
● Ghemme '12	▼▼6
● Colline Novaresi Nebbiolo Tre Confini '15	▼▼3
● Colline Novaresi Vespolina La Mostella '16	▼▼3
● Colline Novaresi Nebbiolo Ramale '14	▼4
☉ Colline Novaresi Nebbiolo Rosato Barlàn '16	▼3
● Gattinara '09	♈♈♈5
● Ghemme '11	♈♈♈6
● Ghemme '10	♈♈♈5
● Ghemme Ris. '07	♈♈♈5
● Ghemme Ris. '07	♈♈♈5
● Ghemme V. Pelizzane '10	♈♈♈6
● Gattinara '11	♈♈6

Giancarlo Travaglini

VIA DELLE VIGNE, 36
13045 GATTINARA [VC]
TEL. +39 0163833588
www.travaglinigattinara.it

CELLAR SALES
PRE-BOOKED VISITS
ANNUAL PRODUCTION 250,000 bottles
HECTARES UNDER VINE 49.00
SUSTAINABLE WINERY

It's not just the unique, convex, asymmetrical bottles that distinguish Travagliani's wines. For decades they have represented the indomitable, and yet jovial character of Gattinara's best plots. Here, Cinzia Travaglini and Massimo Collauto show determination in looking after their some 50 hectares of land. The terrain here is acid, tending towards porphyry. It's iron-rich mineral content, along with the dry and temperate climate of the nearby Alpine ridge, give life to a Nebbiolo that's more whole than it is powerful. In the cellar their approach changes according to the wine and desired aging (their Tre Vigne or 'Riserva' selection). The glorious epic of Travaglini's Gattinara wines is filled with"instant classics" like the 2012 Riserva. Aromas of mulberries, tobacco and leather are well-integrated with oak and follow through onto a full-bodied palate. It's insistent but quite expansive at the finish. The Il Sogno of the same vintage comes through more mature and expansive.

● Gattinara Ris. '12	▼▼▼7
● Gattinara '13	▼▼6
● Coste della Sesia Nebbiolo '15	▼▼3
● Gattinara Tre Vigne '12	▼▼7
● Il Sogno '12	▼▼8
○ Nebolé Dosaggio Zero M. Cl. '12	▼8
● Gattinara Ris. '06	♈♈♈6
● Gattinara Ris. '04	♈♈♈5
● Gattinara Tre Vigne '04	♈♈♈5
● Coste della Sesia Nebbiolo '13	♈♈3
● Gattinara '12	♈♈6
● Gattinara '11	♈♈4
● Gattinara Ris. '11	♈♈7
● Gattinara Tre Vigne '11	♈♈7
○ Nebolé Dosaggio Zero M. Cl. '11	♈♈8

★G. D. Vajra

LOC. VERGNE
VIA DELLE VIOLE, 25
12060 BAROLO [CN]
TEL. +39 017356257
www.gdvajra.it

PRE-BOOKED VISITS
ACCOMMODATION
ANNUAL PRODUCTION 350,000 bottles
HECTARES UNDER VINE 60.00

It was May of 1968, the period of student
protests in Torino, and Aldo Vajra's father
called him back to Barolo so as to pass the
summer on his grandparents' farm. And so
Aldo, accompanied by his wife, Milena, and
later his children, began his long march to
the heights of regional excellence. He is
often called, 'the most modern of the
traditionalists and the most traditional of the
modernists', as his selection brings together
classic, airy Nebbiolos with brave, innovative
choices, like wines made with Riesling or
Pinot Nero, but also the Freisa 'de garde',
the Claré or their sparkling wines. The rich
2013 Barolo Luigi Baudana is a lively wine,
though a bit unruly. It possesses all the
power we would expect from Serralunga,
with aromas of cinchona and red fruit. The
2013 Albe comes through fresher and
licoricey, with an austere, firmly-structured
palate. The 2013 Bricco delle Viole proves
approachable and still a bit closed, with
medium weight. The 2016 Langhe Riesling
is delicately floral and youthful.

Mauro Veglio

FRAZ. ANNUNZIATA
LOC. CASCINA NUOVA, 50
12064 LA MORRA [CN]
TEL. +39 0173509212
www.mauroveglio.com

CELLAR SALES
PRE-BOOKED VISITS
ANNUAL PRODUCTION 80,000 bottles
HECTARES UNDER VINE 14.00
SUSTAINABLE WINERY

The first vintage bottled by Mauro Veglio,
with the support of his wife, Daniela, was in
1992. It was a rather unfortunate harvest,
but since then things have gone from good
to better. It's all thanks to a Barolo that's
modern and innovative, focusing on
softness and elegance rather than force.
They've been helped by quality vineyards,
from that small but esteemed plot in Rocche
dell'Annunziata to the celebrated Arborina,
in addition to the cru of Castelletto in
Monforte d'Alba. The 2013 Barolo Rocche
dell'Annunziata features a delicate palate
and refined elegance. Supple tannins and
balance mark the mouth, while the nose
offers up elegant hints of oak and lively red
fruit. The powerful and spicy 2013 Barolo
Castelletto shows splendid use of wood and
welcome freshness. The warm 2013 Barolo
Gattera exhibits a bit more wood, sweet
tobacco and red fruit. The 2013 Barolo
Arborina, on the other hand, proves
pleasantly evolved and rich in herbs.

● Barolo Baudana Luigi Baudana '13	♟♟ 6
● Barolo Bricco delle Viole '13	♟♟ 8
● Barbera d'Alba Sup. '14	♟♟ 5
● Barolo Albe '13	♟♟ 6
○ Langhe Riesling '16	♟♟ 5
● Barolo Baudana Luigi Baudana '09	♟♟♟ 6
● Barolo Bricco delle Viole '12	♟♟♟ 8
● Barolo Bricco delle Viole '10	♟♟♟ 8
● Barolo Bricco delle Viole '05	♟♟♟ 8
● Barolo Bricco delle Viole '01	♟♟♟ 8
● Barolo Cerretta Luigi Baudana '08	♟♟♟ 6
● Barolo Albe '11	♟♟ 6
● Barolo Baudana '12	♟♟ 6
● Barolo Ravera '12	♟♟ 7

● Barolo Castelletto '13	♟♟ 7
● Barolo Rocche dell'Annunziata '13	♟♟ 8
● Barbera d'Alba Cascina Nuova '15	♟♟ 5
● Barolo '13	♟♟ 5
● Barolo Arborina '13	♟♟ 7
● Barolo Gattera '13	♟♟ 7
● Barbera d'Alba '16	♟ 3
● Barolo Arborina '10	♟♟♟ 6
● Barolo Rocche dell'Annunziata '12	♟♟♟ 8
● Barolo Vign. Gattera '05	♟♟♟ 6
● Barbera d'Alba Cascina Nuova '14	♟♟ 5
● Barolo '12	♟♟ 5
● Barolo Arborina '12	♟♟ 7
● Barolo Castelletto '12	♟♟ 7
● Barolo Gattera '12	♟♟ 7

Giovanni Viberti

VIA DELLE VIOLE 30
12060 BAROLO [CN]
TEL. +39 017356192
www.viberti-barolo.com

CELLAR SALES
PRE-BOOKED VISITS
RESTAURANT SERVICE
ANNUAL PRODUCTION 80,000 bottles
HECTARES UNDER VINE 18.00

Skilled vine grower and winemaker Claudio Viberti is developing an approach based on low yields in the vineyard, using must with skin contact for short periods and aging in non-toasted vats. It's all done so as to obtain wines with notable structure, wines rich in fresh fruit and not saturated by the presence of wood. Their vineyards are located in Vergne, the district that overlooks Barolo at altitudes ranging from 400 to 500 meters. Barolo takes center stage here and comes in three different reserves. The selection is rounded out by Barbera and Dolcetto d'Alba, Langhe Nebbiolo, Moscato d'Asti and Piemonte Chardonnay. The 2011 Barolo La Volta Riserva is an excellent wine. It clearly expresses Nebbiolo's signature aromas, which range from hints of cinchona to rose petals and blueberries. The palate is still marked by the presence of tannins. The 2011 Barolo San Pietro Riserva features a penetrating nose and a medium-weighted palate. Kudos to the elegant 2016 Chardonnay.

● Barolo La Volta Ris. '11	♟♟8
● Barbera d'Alba Sup. Airoli '13	♟♟4
● Barolo San Pietro Ris. '11	♟♟8
● Langhe Inisj '11	♟♟5
● Langhe Nebbiolo '15	♟♟3
○ Piemonte Chardonnay '16	♟♟3
● Barolo Buon Padre '13	♟6
● Langhe Dolbà '15	♟2
● Barbera d'Alba Sup. Bricco Airoli '11	♟♟4
● Barolo Bricco delle Viole Ris. '10	♟♟7
● Barolo Buon Padre '12	♟♟6
● Barolo Buon Padre '11	♟♟6
● Barolo La Volta Ris. '10	♟♟8
● Barolo San Pietro Ris. '10	♟♟8
● Langhe Nebbiolo '13	♟♟3
● Langhe Nebbiolo '12	♟♟3

Vicara

VIA MADONNA DELLE GRAZIE, 5
15030 ROSIGNANO MONFERRATO [AL]
TEL. +39 0142488054
www.vicara.it

CELLAR SALES
PRE-BOOKED VISITS
ANNUAL PRODUCTION 200,000 bottles
HECTARES UNDER VINE 37.00
VITICULTURE METHOD Certified Biodynamic

The previous edition of Italian Wines saw the first Tre Bicchieri awarded to a Grignolino in the area. It was a recognition of a variety's quality and, above all, its potential. For too long, the grape has been relegated to a predominantly local market. It's difficult to ferment, and results in wines of faded color that are strong aromatically, tannic and rich in acidity. The 2016 Grignolino also brought home a Tre Bicchieri, proving complex and vibrant at every stage of tasting. It exhibits classic qualities and docile tannins, with a long, lingering finish. The Barbera Volpuva is also worth mentioning. It features sensational freshness of fruit, which turns juicy and intense on the palate, and an unending finish.

● Grignolino del M.to Casalese '16	♟♟♟3*
● Barbera del M.to Cascina La Rocca 33 '15	♟♟6
● Barbera del M.to Volpuva '16	♟♟3
● Grignolino del M.to Casalese L'Uccelletta '13	♟♟4
○ M.to Bianco Airales '16	♟♟2*
● M.to Rosso Rubello '13	♟4
● Grignolino del M.to Casalese °G '15	♟♟♟4*
● Barbera del M.to Cascina Rocca 33 '13	♟♟3*
● Barbera del M.to Sup. Cantico della Crosia '13	♟♟4
● Barbera del M.to Sup. Vadmò '12	♟♟4
● Barbera del M.to Volpuva '15	♟♟3
● Grignolino del M.to Casalese L'Uccelletta '12	♟♟4
● M.to Rosso Rubello '11	♟♟4

★★Vietti

P.zza Vittorio Veneto, 5
12060 Castiglione Falletto [CN]
Tel. +39 017362825
www.vietti.com

CELLAR SALES
PRE-BOOKED VISITS
ANNUAL PRODUCTION 250,000 bottles
HECTARES UNDER VINE 37.00

Even after the Krause family took over,
management of the estate and cellar have
remain unchanged. Luca Currado, the
winery's chief, is firm in his decision to
pursue the highest quality for every wine
produced. This is evident even from the
least expensive wines, starting with their
Roero Arneis, which, in 2016, was
presented with a label celebrating 50 years,
and their Langhe Nebbiolo Perbacco, which
was recognized as a prototype in the
category. Barolo remains their crown jewel,
thanks to their six magnificent crus. Luca
Currado is rightly proud of the work done for
the 2013 vintage, having given rise to a
Barolo Ravera that exhibits a rare class and
elegance. Their entire selection is excellent,
though we should point out one of the best
Castigliones ever, as well as the smooth and
complex Brunate. The 2013 Barbaresco
Masseria is a masterpiece. But the austere
2009 Riserva Villero remains unbeatable.
This majestic Tre bicchieri is also adorned
by a label designed by Anton Fuchs.

● Barolo Villero Ris. '09	▼▼▼ 8
● Barbaresco Masseria '13	▼▼ 8
● Barolo Brunate '13	▼▼ 8
● Barolo Castiglione '13	▼▼ 7
● Barolo Lazzarito '13	▼▼ 8
● Barolo Ravera '13	▼▼ 8
● Barbera d'Alba Scarrone V. V. '15	▼▼ 6
● Barbera d'Asti Sup. Nizza La Crena '13	▼▼ 5
● Barolo Rocche di Castiglione '13	▼▼ 8
● Langhe Nebbiolo Perbacco '15	▼▼ 4
● Barolo Ravera '12	♈♈♈ 8
● Barolo Rocche di Castiglione '11	♈♈♈ 8
● Barolo Villero Ris. '07	♈♈♈ 8

I Vignaioli di Santo Stefano

Loc. Marini, 26
12058 Santo Stefano Belbo [CN]
Tel. +39 0141840419
www.ivignaiolidisantostefano.it

CELLAR SALES
PRE-BOOKED VISITS
ANNUAL PRODUCTION 275,000 bottles
HECTARES UNDER VINE 35.00
SUSTAINABLE WINERY

Vignaioli di Santo Stefano was founded in
1976 by the Ceretto and Scavino families.
They hoped to create a model producer for
Moscato winemaking, and 40 years later,
you could say that their mission has been
accomplished. Their vineyards, which host
exclusively Moscato Biano grapes, are
situated in Santo Stefano Belbo, Calosso
and Canelli at altitudes ranging from 320 to
450 meters above sea level. Only two
wines are made: their 'standard cork'
Moscato d'Asti and their Asti. The
extremely well-made 2016 Moscato d'Asti
exhibits a vibrant nose, with notes of peach
and sage followed by candied orange peel.
Its full palate comes through slightly
balsamic, with good grip and freshness,
and an herby finish. The 2016 Asti,
meanwhile, is a rich and generous
sparkling wine, with notes of ripe fruit. Its
medium-structured palate displays good
acidity, while the finish comes through both
creamy and supple.

○ Asti '16	▼▼ 3
○ Moscato d'Asti '16	▼▼ 3
○ Asti '15	♈♈ 3
○ Asti '14	♈♈ 3
○ Asti '13	♈♈ 3
○ Asti '12	♈♈ 3
○ Asti '11	♈♈ 3
○ Asti '10	♈♈ 3
○ Moscato d'Asti '15	♈♈ 3*
○ Moscato d'Asti '14	♈♈ 5
○ Moscato d'Asti '13	♈♈ 4
○ Moscato d'Asti '12	♈♈ 4
○ Moscato d'Asti '11	♈♈ 3
○ Moscato d'Asti '10	♈♈ 3

★Vigneti Massa

P.ZZA G. CAPSONI, 10
15059 MONLEALE [AL]
TEL. +39 013180302
vignetimassa@libero.it

CELLAR SALES
PRE-BOOKED VISITS
ANNUAL PRODUCTION 120,000 bottles
HECTARES UNDER VINE 25.00
SUSTAINABLE WINERY

Winemaker Walter Massa represents the fourth generation to manage the family business. Today they're dedicated mostly to vine growing and winemaking, while in the past they also produced fruit and raised cattle as well. Walter's work has been important in different respects. In addition to being among the first to revive Timorasso, a variety that's central for the territory today, he's one of its foremost advocates and interpreters. Their four Timorassos lead their impressive selection. We tasted one of the best versions ever of Costa Del Vento. Its bright appearance and lively straw-yellow color set the stage for incredibly complex and intense aromas. Then comes the powerful and firmly-structured palate, supported by an explosive acidity, and a long finish. The Montecitorio shows great character.

○ Costa del Vento '15	♟♟♟ 6
○ Montecitorio '15	♟♟ 6
○ Sterpi '15	♟♟ 6
○ Anarchia Costituzionale '16	♟♟ 3
○ Derthona '15	♟♟ 5
● Monleale '13	♟♟ 6
● Pietra del Gallo '16	♟ 2
○ Costa del Vento '12	♟♟♟ 6
○ Derthona '09	♟♟♟ 5
○ Montecitorio '11	♟♟♟ 6
○ Montecitorio '10	♟♟♟ 6
○ Sterpi '13	♟♟♟ 6
○ Derthona '14	♟♟ 5

Vigneti Valle Roncati

VIA NAZIONALE, 10A
28072 BRIONA [NO]
TEL. +39 3355732548
www.vignetivalleroncati.it

CELLAR SALES
PRE-BOOKED VISITS
ANNUAL PRODUCTION 40,000 bottles
HECTARES UNDER VINE 10.00

20 years have passed since Corrado Fassa, along with his wife, Cecilia, decided to follow in the footsteps of Corrado's grandfather, Giuseppe (a vine grower in Briona since the early 1900s). The official first release came some years later, with the 2005 harvest. Today, Valle Roncati spans about 10 hectares of vineyards, where mostly Nebbiolo is cultivated (in addition to Barbera, Vespolina and Uva Rara). The plots in Ghemme and Sizzano, along with the two Faras, provide the grapes necessary for a selection that features Novara's great reds. These are interpreted with a contemporary touch, without preachiness as far as typology and length of aging in oak are concerned. The Vigna di Sopra won its perennial duel with the Fara di Vigneti Valle Roncati. The 2011 stands out for its layered aromas, with clear notes of roots and iodine livening up its long palate. The Ciada Riserva exhibits aromas of confit and sees less dynamic taste.

● Fara V. di Sopra '11	♟♟ 3*
○ Colline Novaresi Bianco Particella 40 '16	♟♟ 2*
● Fara Ciada Ris. '11	♟♟ 3
● Colline Novaresi Barbera V. di Mezzo '15	♟ 2
⊙ Colline Novaresi Nebbiolo Rosato Poderi di Sopra '16	♟ 3
● Colline Novaresi Barbera V. di Mezzo '13	♟♟ 2*
○ Colline Novaresi Bianco Particella 40 '15	♟♟ 2*
● Colline Novaresi Uva Rara '13	♟♟ 2*
● Colline Novaresi Vespolina '13	♟♟ 2*
● Fara Ciada '10	♟♟ 3*
● Ghemme Leblanque '11	♟♟ 5
● Sizzano San Bartolomeo '12	♟♟ 4
● Sizzano San Bartolomeo '11	♟♟ 3*

Villa Giada

REG. CEIROLE, 10
14053 CANELLI [AT]
TEL. +39 0141831100
www.villagiada.wine

CELLAR SALES
PRE-BOOKED VISITS
ACCOMMODATION AND RESTAURANT SERVICE
ANNUAL PRODUCTION 180,000 bottles
HECTARES UNDER VINE 25.00
SUSTAINABLE WINERY

For three generations the Faccio family have been leaders in Canelli. The estate spans three areas. There's their headquarters in Canelli (on the Ceirole hill), where their cellar and seven hectares of Moscato are located. There's Dani (in Agliano Terme), which sees 14 hectares of sandy, clay, mineral-rich soil. And finally, there's La Cascina del Parroco in Calosso, four hectares of mostly Barbera with smaller quantities of other native and international varieties. The Moscato d'Asti Canelli took full advantage of the splendid 2016 vintage. It offers up classic aromas, with lovely notes of panettone, orange peel, mint and sage. The palate displays great complexity and finesse, with generosity and freshness. The 2015 Nizza Bricco Dani is also first-rate, with spicy fragrances and hints of pencil lead. The palate remains a bit veiled by oak, but comes through rich in fruit and with notable acidity. The 2016 Barbera d'Asti Ajan proves fruity and easy to drink.

○ Moscato d'Asti Canelli '16	🏆🏆 2*
● Nizza Bricco Dani '15	🏆🏆 4
● Barbera d'Asti Ajan '16	🏆🏆 2*
● Barbera d'Asti Sup. La Quercia '15	🏆 3
○ Moscato d'Asti Surì '16	🏆 2
● Nizza Dedicato '14	🏆 5
● Barbera d'Asti Sup. La Quercia '13	🏆🏆 3
● Barbera d'Asti Sup. Nizza Bricco Dani '13	🏆🏆 4
● Barbera d'Asti Sup. Nizza Dedicato a... '13	🏆🏆 5
● Barbera d'Asti Surì '15	🏆🏆 2*
○ Moscato d'Asti Canelli '15	🏆🏆 2*
○ Moscato d'Asti Surì '15	🏆🏆 2*

★Villa Sparina

FRAZ. MONTEROTONDO, 56
15066 GAVI [AL]
TEL. +39 0143633835
www.villasparina.it

PRE-BOOKED VISITS
ACCOMMODATION AND RESTAURANT SERVICE
ANNUAL PRODUCTION 550,000 bottles
HECTARES UNDER VINE 65.00

Among the many accomplishments for which siblings Stefano, Massimo and Tiziana Moccagatta are recognized, there is, without a doubt, the fact of having enlarged the potential for hospitality on their splendid estate in Monterotondo di Gavi. This is because Villa Sparina isn't just important for viticulture (with its more than 60 hectares of vineyards). The resort, restaurant and spa make it one of the most vital operations in the entire region. Their entire selection is a snapshot of dynamism. Their wines are known for their density and the longevity of their Cortese whites. Though we shouldn't forget their Spumanti sparkling wines or their reds, made with Dolcetto and Barbera from the vineyards of Cassinelle and Rivalta Bormida. Yet another memorable performance from that true thoroughbred, the Gavi Monterotondo. The 2015 offers up original hints of white flowers, fresh herbs and burnt wheat. The palate displays its usual multidimensional power supported by pulp and backbone. The 2013 Blanc de Blancs proves solid and composed.

○ Gavi del Comune di Gavi Monterotondo '15	🏆🏆🏆 6
○ Gavi del Comune di Gavi '16	🏆🏆 3*
● Barbera del M.to Sup. Rivalta '14	🏆🏆 6
○ Villa Sparina Blanc de Blancs Brut M. Cl. '13	🏆🏆 3
● Barbera del M.to '16	🏆 3
○ Gavi del Comune di Gavi Monterotondo '14	🏆🏆🏆 6
○ Gavi del Comune di Gavi Monterotondo '12	🏆🏆🏆 6
○ Gavi del Comune di Gavi Monterotondo '11	🏆🏆🏆 6
○ Gavi del Comune di Gavi Monterotondo '10	🏆🏆🏆 6
○ Gavi del Comune di Gavi Monterotondo '09	🏆🏆🏆 6
● Barbera del M.to Sup. Rivalta '13	🏆🏆 6

Viticoltori Associati di Vinchio Vaglio Serra

FRAZ. REG. SAN PANCRAZIO, 1
S.DA PROV.LE 40 KM. 3,75
14040 VINCHIO [AT]
TEL. +39 0141950903
www.vinchio.com

CELLAR SALES
PRE-BOOKED VISITS
ANNUAL PRODUCTION 1,600,000 bottles
HECTARES UNDER VINE 472.00

Vinchio Vaglio Serra is a historic co-operative winery made up of 185 member-growers. The total area cultivated, more than 400 hectares, covers plots in the municipalities of Vinchio, Vaglio Serra, Incisa Scapaccino, Cortiglione, Nizza Monferrato, Castelnuovo Belbo, Castelnuovo Calcea and Mombercelli. The terrain here is calcareous and sandy, with the presence of vines that are more than 60 years old. Their wide and varying selection features well-recognized wines with a local character. The Barbera d'Asti Superiore Sei Vigne Insynthesis is back on top. This Barbera is released only after years of aging and this year it's the 2009's turn. It proves expansive and evolved, and rich in notes of ripe red fruit. The 2011 Barbera d'Asti Superiore Vigne Vecchie features a similar style. It's ready to enjoy, without any harshness, but still well-supported by acidity. The 2015 Barbera d'Asti 50° Vigne Vecchie, on the other hand, plays more on tones of fresh red fruit and approachability.

● Barbera d'Asti Sup. Sei Vigne Insynthesis '09	▼▼6
● Barbera d'Asti Sup. Vigne Vecchie '11	▼▼5
● Barbera d'Asti Vigne Vecchie 50° '15	▼▼3*
● Barbera d'Asti Sori dei Mori '16	▼▼2*
● Nizza Laudana '14	▼▼3
● Barbera d'Asti Sup. I Tre Vescovi '15	▼2
● Grignolino d'Asti Le Nocche '16	▼2
● Barbera d'Asti Sup. Sei Vigne Insynthesis '01	▽▽▽6
● Barbera d'Asti Sup. Nizza Laudana '12	▽▽3*
● Grignolino d'Asti Le Nocche '15	▽▽2*
○ Moscato d'Asti Valamasca '15	▽▽2*

Vite Colte

VIA BERGESIA, 6
12060 BAROLO [CN]
TEL. +39 0173564611
www.vitecolte.it

CELLAR SALES
PRE-BOOKED VISITS
ANNUAL PRODUCTION 1,200,000 bottles
HECTARES UNDER VINE 300.00
VITICULTURE METHOD Certified Organic
SUSTAINABLE WINERY

Terre da Vino, founded in 1980, recently decided to modify both their image and their production approach, bringing to life a quality line called 'Vite Colte. Mani. Testa. Cuore'. 180 vine growers, representing 300 hectares of terrain, signed up for the project. It's a rigorous program aimed at guaranteeing the best possible grapes. And so, in their large Barolo cellar, the winery is moving forward with producing and aging their wines, employing French barriques for their Barbera and large barrels for their Barolo. Visitors can observe the different stages of wine production on site. The 2013 Barolo del Comune di Barolo Essenze is what you get when finesse and complexity merge with classic tradition. This Tre Bicchieri offers up aromas ranging from red fruit to aniseed, and displays a palate in which soft pulp, acidity and tannins find their perfect balance. The licoricey 2013 Barolo Paesi Tuoi comes through bit harder on the palate. The 2008 Barbaresco Spezie Riserva exhibits a charming and surprising freshness.

● Barolo del Comune di Barolo Essenze '13	▼▼▼7
● Barbaresco Spezie Ris. '08	▼▼6
● Barbera d'Asti Sup. La Luna e i Falò '15	▼▼4
○ Piemonte Moscato Passito La Bella Estate '15	▼▼5
● Barbera d'Alba Sup. Croere '15	▼▼4
● Barolo Paesi Tuoi '13	▼▼6
● Nizza La Luna e i Falò '15	▼▼5
○ Piemonte Sauvignon Chardonnay Tra Donne Sole '16	▼▼4
● Barolo del Comune di Barolo Essenze '12	▽▽▽6
● Barolo Paesi Tuoi '11	▽▽5
● Nizza La Luna e I Falò '14	▽▽4

F.lli Abrigo

LOC. BERFI
VIA MOGLIA GERLOTTO, 2
12055 DIANO D'ALBA [CN]
TEL. +39 017369104
www.abrigofratelli.com

CELLAR SALES
PRE-BOOKED VISITS
ANNUAL PRODUCTION 100,000 bottles
HECTARES UNDER VINE 27.00

● Barolo Ravera '13	🍷🍷 6
● Diano d'Alba Sorì dei Berfi '16	🍷🍷 3
● Dolcetto di Diano d'Alba Sup. Pietrin '15	🍷🍷 3
● Nebbiolo d'Alba Tardiss '15	🍷🍷 3

Giovanni Abrigo

VIA SANTA CROCE, 9
12055 DIANO D'ALBA [CN]
TEL. +39 017369345
www.abrigo.it

CELLAR SALES
PRE-BOOKED VISITS
ANNUAL PRODUCTION 40,000 bottles
HECTARES UNDER VINE 10.00

● Barbera d'Alba Marminela '15	🍷🍷 2*
● Diano d'Alba Sorì dei Crava '15	🍷🍷 2*
● Diano d'Alba Sup. Garabei '15	🍷🍷 2*
● Nebbiolo d'Alba '15	🍷🍷 3

Annamaria Alemanni

FRAZ. CHERLI INFERIORE, 64
15070 TAGLIOLO MONFERRATO [AL]
TEL. +39 0143896229
doppiaa@libero.it

CELLAR SALES
ACCOMMODATION
ANNUAL PRODUCTION 6,000 bottles
HECTARES UNDER VINE 4.00
SUSTAINABLE WINERY

● Dolcetto di Ovada Arivud '15	🍷🍷 2*
● Dolcetto di Ovada Sup. Ansè '14	🍷🍷 3

Alice Bel Colle

REG. STAZIONE, 9
15010 ALICE BEL COLLE [AL]
TEL. +39 014474413
www.cantinaalicebc.it

CELLAR SALES
PRE-BOOKED VISITS
ANNUAL PRODUCTION 80,000 bottles
HECTARES UNDER VINE 370.00

● Barbera d'Asti Al Casò '16	🍷🍷 2*
● Barbera d'Asti Filari Sociali '16	🍷🍷 2*
● Barbera d'Asti Sup. Alix '14	🍷🍷 3
○ Moscato d'Asti Paié '16	🍷 2

Antica Cascina Conti di Roero

LOC. VAL RUBIAGNO, 2
12040 VEZZA D'ALBA [CN]
TEL. +39 017365459
www.oliveropietro.it

CELLAR SALES
PRE-BOOKED VISITS
ANNUAL PRODUCTION 100,000 bottles
HECTARES UNDER VINE 13.50
SUSTAINABLE WINERY

● Nebbiolo d'Alba '15	🍷🍷 2*
○ Roero Arneis '16	🍷🍷 2*
● Roero V. Sant' Anna '14	🍷 4

Arbiola

LOC. ARBIOLA
REG. SALINE, 67
14050 SAN MARZANO OLIVETO [AT]
TEL. +39 0141856194
www.arbiola.it

CELLAR SALES
PRE-BOOKED VISITS
ACCOMMODATION AND RESTAURANT SERVICE
ANNUAL PRODUCTION 250,000 bottles
HECTARES UNDER VINE 30.00
VITICULTURE METHOD Certified Organic

● Nizza Romilda XIX '14	🍷🍷 4
● Barbera d'Asti Sup. Carlotta '15	🍷 3

L' Astemia Pentita

VIA CROSIA, 40
12060 BAROLO [CN]
TEL. +39 0173560501
www.astemiapentita.it

CELLAR SALES
ANNUAL PRODUCTION 70,000 bottles
HECTARES UNDER VINE 15.00

● Barolo Terlo '13	♟♟ 8
● Barolo Cannubi '13	♟♟ 8
● Barbera d'Alba '15	♟ 3
● Barolo Cannubi Ris. '11	♟ 8

Cantina Sociale Barbera dei Sei Castelli

VIA OPESSINA, 41
14040 CASTELNUOVO CALCEA [AT]
TEL. +39 0141957137
www.barberaseicastelli.it

CELLAR SALES
PRE-BOOKED VISITS
ANNUAL PRODUCTION 80,000 bottles
HECTARES UNDER VINE 620.00

● Barbera d'Asti 50 Anni di Barbera '15	♟♟ 2*
● Grignolino d'Asti '16	♟♟ 2*
● Barbera d'Asti '15	♟ 2
● Nizza '14	♟ 4

Fabrizio Battaglino

LOC. BORGONUOVO
VIA MONTALDO ROERO, 44
12040 VEZZA D'ALBA [CN]
TEL. +39 0173658156
www.battaglino.com

CELLAR SALES
PRE-BOOKED VISITS
ANNUAL PRODUCTION 25,000 bottles
HECTARES UNDER VINE 5.00

○ Roero Arneis '16	♟♟ 2*
● Roero Sergentin Ris. '13	♟♟ 5
● Barbera d'Alba Munbèl '15	♟ 3
● Nebbiolo d'Alba Colla '14	♟ 4

Battaglio

LOC. BORBORE
VIA SALERIO, 15
12040 VEZZA D'ALBA [CN]
TEL. +39 017365423
www.battaglio.com

CELLAR SALES
PRE-BOOKED VISITS
ANNUAL PRODUCTION 35,000 bottles
HECTARES UNDER VINE 5.00

● Barbaresco '14	♟♟ 6
● Barbaresco Serragrilli '14	♟♟ 7
● Nebbiolo d'Alba Valmaggiore '13	♟♟ 3

Bea - Merenda con Corvi

S.DA SANTA CATERINA, 8
10064 PINEROLO [TO]
TEL. +39 3356824880
www.merendaconcorvi.it

CELLAR SALES
PRE-BOOKED VISITS
ACCOMMODATION
ANNUAL PRODUCTION 4,500 bottles
HECTARES UNDER VINE 1.00

● Merenda con Corvi '15	♟♟ 5
● Merlot '15	♟♟ 5
● Bel Ami '15	♟ 7

Antonio Bellicoso

FRAZ. MOLISSO, 5A
14048 MONTEGROSSO D'ASTI [AT]
TEL. +39 0141953233
antonio.bellicoso@alice.it

CELLAR SALES
PRE-BOOKED VISITS
ANNUAL PRODUCTION 10,000 bottles
HECTARES UNDER VINE 4.00
SUSTAINABLE WINERY

● Barbera d'Asti Amormio '16	♟♟ 2*
● Barbera d'Asti Merum '15	♟ 3
● Freisa d'Asti '16	♟ 2

La Bioca

VIA ALBA, 13A
12065 SERRALUNGA D'ALBA [CN]
TEL. +39 0173613022
www.labioca.it

CELLAR SALES
PRE-BOOKED VISITS
ACCOMMODATION
ANNUAL PRODUCTION 50,000 bottles
HECTARES UNDER VINE 9.00

● Barolo Aculei '13	🍷🍷 6
● Barbera d'Alba Sup. Adae '15	🍷🍷 3
● Barolo Bussia '13	🍷🍷 6

Marco Bonfante

S.DA VAGLIO SERRA, 72
14049 NIZZA MONFERRATO [AT]
TEL. +39 0141725012
www.marcobonfante.com

CELLAR SALES
PRE-BOOKED VISITS
ANNUAL PRODUCTION 270,000 bottles
HECTARES UNDER VINE 20.00

● Barbera d'Asti Sup. Menego '14	🍷🍷 4
● Barbera d'Asti Sup. Stella Rossa '15	🍷🍷 2*
● Nizza Bricco Bonfante '14	🍷🍷 5
○ Moscato d'Asti '16	🍷 2

F.lli Serio & Battista Borgogno

LOC. CANNUBI
VIA CROSIA, 12
12060 BAROLO [CN]
TEL. +39 017356107
www.borgognoseriobattista.it

CELLAR SALES
PRE-BOOKED VISITS
ANNUAL PRODUCTION 60,000 bottles
HECTARES UNDER VINE 7.50

● Barolo '13	🍷🍷 5
● Barolo Cannubi '13	🍷🍷 6
● Barolo Cannubi Ris. '11	🍷🍷 7
● Nebbiolo d'Alba '14	🍷 3

Giacomo Boveri

FRAZ. MONTALE CELLI
VIA COSTA VESCOVATO, 15
15050 COSTA VESCOVATO [AL]
TEL. +39 0131838223
www.vignetiboveri.it

CELLAR SALES
PRE-BOOKED VISITS
ANNUAL PRODUCTION 25,000 bottles
HECTARES UNDER VINE 9.00

● Colli Tortonesi Barbera Sup. Bricco della Ginestra '14	🍷🍷 3
○ Colli Tortonesi Timorasso Muntà L'è Ruma '14	🍷🍷 3

Bussia Soprana

LOC. BUSSIA, 88A
12065 MONFORTE D'ALBA [CN]
TEL. +39 039305182
www.bussiasoprana.it

CELLAR SALES
PRE-BOOKED VISITS
ANNUAL PRODUCTION 60,000 bottles
HECTARES UNDER VINE 16.00

● Barolo '12	🍷🍷 7
● Langhe Nebbiolo '13	🍷🍷 3

Oreste Buzio

V. PIAVE, 13
15049 VIGNALE MONFERRATO [AL]
TEL. +39 0142933197
www.orestebuzio.altervista.org

CELLAR SALES
PRE-BOOKED VISITS
ANNUAL PRODUCTION 25,000 bottles
HECTARES UNDER VINE 6.00
VITICULTURE METHOD Certified Organic

● Grignolino del M.to Casalese '16	🍷🍷 3*
● Barbera del M.to '15	🍷🍷 2*
● M.to Freisa '16	🍷🍷 2*
● Barbera del M.to Sup. Riccardo II '13	🍷 4

Marco Canato

FRAZ. FONS SALERA
LOC. CA' BALDEA, 18/2
15049 VIGNALE MONFERRATO [AL]
TEL. +39 0142933653
www.canatovini.it

CELLAR SALES
PRE-BOOKED VISITS
ANNUAL PRODUCTION 30,000 bottles
HECTARES UNDER VINE 11.00

● Grignolino del M.to Casalese Primo '12	♥♥ 4
● Grignolino del M.to Casalese Celio '16	♥♥ 3
● Barbera del M.to Gambaloita '16	♥ 3
● Barbera del M.to Sup. Rupes '08	♥ 3

Pierangelo Careglio

LOC. APRATO, 15
12040 BALDISSERO D'ALBA [CN]
TEL. +39 017240436
www.cantinacareglio.com

CELLAR SALES
PRE-BOOKED VISITS
ANNUAL PRODUCTION 30,000 bottles
HECTARES UNDER VINE 8.00

● Barbera d'Alba '15	♥♥ 2*
○ Roero Arneis '16	♥♥ 2*
● Langhe Nebbiolo '15	♥ 2
● Roero '14	♥ 2

Tenuta Carretta

LOC. CARRETTA, 2
12040 PIOBESI D'ALBA [CN]
TEL. +39 0173619119
www.tenutacarretta.it

CELLAR SALES
PRE-BOOKED VISITS
ACCOMMODATION AND RESTAURANT SERVICE
ANNUAL PRODUCTION 480,000 bottles
HECTARES UNDER VINE 70.00

○ Gavi del Comune di Gavi Poggio Basco '16	♥♥ 2*
● Langhe Nebbiolo Podio '15	♥♥ 3
○ Roero Arneis Cayega '16	♥ 3
● Roero Bric Paradiso Ris. '11	♥ 5

Casavecchia

VIA ROMA, 2
12055 DIANO D'ALBA [CN]
TEL. +39 017369321
www.cantinacasavecchia.com

CELLAR SALES
PRE-BOOKED VISITS
ANNUAL PRODUCTION 40,000 bottles
HECTARES UNDER VINE 8.00

● Barolo del Comune di Castiglione Falletto '11	♥♥ 5
● Diano d'Alba Sörì Bruni '16	♥♥ 2*
● Nebbiolo d'Alba '13	♥♥ 3

Cascina Adelaide

VIA AIE SOTTANE, 14
12060 BAROLO [CN]
TEL. +39 0173560503
www.cascinaadelaide.com

CELLAR SALES
PRE-BOOKED VISITS
ANNUAL PRODUCTION 50,000 bottles
HECTARES UNDER VINE 9.50

● Barolo Cannubi '13	♥♥ 8
● Barolo Baudana '13	♥♥ 7
● Barolo Fossati '13	♥♥ 8

Cascina Alberta

VIA ALBA 5
12050 TREISO [CN]
TEL. +39 335280486
www.calberta.it

CELLAR SALES
PRE-BOOKED VISITS

● Barbaresco Giacone '14	♥♥ 4
● Barbera d'Alba Sup. Tres '15	♥♥ 4
● Dolcetto d'Alba '15	♥♥ 4
● Langhe Nebbiolo '15	♥♥ 4

Cascina Ballarin

FRAZ. ANNUNZIATA, 115
12064 LA MORRA [CN]
TEL. +39 017350365
www.cascinaballarin.it

CELLAR SALES
PRE-BOOKED VISITS
ACCOMMODATION
ANNUAL PRODUCTION 50,000 bottles
HECTARES UNDER VINE 8.00
VITICULTURE METHOD Certified Organic

● Barolo Bricco Rocca Tistot Ris. '10	♟♟ 8
● Barolo Bricco Rocca '13	♟♟ 7
● Barolo Tre Ciabot '13	♟♟ 5
● Barbera d'Alba Pilade '15	♟ 3

Cascina Castlet

S.DA CASTELLETTO, 6
14055 COSTIGLIOLE D'ASTI [AT]
TEL. +39 0141966651
www.cascinacastlet.com

CELLAR SALES
PRE-BOOKED VISITS
ANNUAL PRODUCTION 250,000 bottles
HECTARES UNDER VINE 30.00
SUSTAINABLE WINERY

● Barbera d'Asti '16	♟♟ 2*
● Barbera d'Asti Sup. Passum '15	♟♟ 5
● Barbera d'Asti Sup. Litina '15	♟ 4
○ Moscato d'Asti '16	♟ 2

Cascina Faletta

MANDOLETTA 81
15033 CASALE MONFERRATO [AL]
TEL. +39 0142670068
www.faletta.it

● Piemonte Pinot Nero 3 Fuclll '15	♟♟ 3
○ Piemonte Pinot Nero Brut M. Cl. Marchesa Virginia '14	♟♟ 4
● Rosso di Rosso	♟♟ 3

Cascina Flino

VIA ABELLONI, 7
12055 DIANO D'ALBA [CN]
TEL. +39 017369231
cascinaflino@gmail.com

CELLAR SALES
PRE-BOOKED VISITS
ACCOMMODATION AND RESTAURANT SERVICE
ANNUAL PRODUCTION 10,000 bottles
HECTARES UNDER VINE 4.00

● Barolo Bricco San Pietro '13	♟♟ 5
● Dolcetto di Diano d'Alba Sorì Cascina Flino '16	♟♟ 2*
● Nebbiolo d'Alba Sup. '15	♟ 3

Cascina Galarin
Giuseppe Carosso

VIA CAROSSI, 12
14054 CASTAGNOLE DELLE LANZE [AT]
TEL. +39 0141878586
www.galarin.it

CELLAR SALES
ANNUAL PRODUCTION 30,000 bottles
HECTARES UNDER VINE 6.00
VITICULTURE METHOD Certified Organic

● Barbera d'Asti Le Querce '15	♟♟ 2*
● Barbera d'Asti Sup. Tinella '14	♟♟ 5
○ Moscato d'Asti Prá Dône '16	♟♟ 2*

Cascina Pellerino

LOC. SANT'ANNA, 93
12040 MONTEU ROERO [CN]
TEL. +39 0173978171
www.cascinapellerino.com

CELLAR SALES
PRE-BOOKED VISITS
ANNUAL PRODUCTION 50,000 bottles
HECTARES UNDER VINE 7.00
SUSTAINABLE WINERY

● Barbera d'Alba Eleonora '16	♟♟ 3
● Roero V. del Padre Ris. '13	♟♟ 5
● Barbera d'Alba Gran Madre '15	♟ 4
● Roero Vicot '15	♟ 4

Cascina Val del Prete

S.DA SANTUARIO, 2
12040 PRIOCCA [CN]
TEL. +39 0173616534
www.valdelprete.com

CELLAR SALES
PRE-BOOKED VISITS
ANNUAL PRODUCTION 55,000 bottles
HECTARES UNDER VINE 11.00
VITICULTURE METHOD Certified Organic

● Barbera d'Alba Sup. Carolina '15	♟♟ 5
● Barbera d'Alba Serra de' Gatti '16	♟ 3
● Roero Bricco Medica '14	♟ 3
● Roero V. di Lino '14	♟ 5

Renzo Castella

VIA ALBA, 15
12055 DIANO D'ALBA [CN]
TEL. I 39 017369203
renzocastella@virgilio.it

CELLAR SALES
PRE-BOOKED VISITS
ANNUAL PRODUCTION 20,000 bottles
HECTARES UNDER VINE 8.00

● Barbera d'Alba Sarcat '15	♟♟ 2*
● Dolcetto di Diano d'Alba '16	♟♟ 2*
● Dolcetto di Diano d'Alba V. della Rivolia '16	♟♟ 2*
● Langhe Nebbiolo Madonnina '15	♟ 2

Tenuta Castello di Razzano

FRAZ. CASARELLO
VIA SAN CARLO, 2
15021 ALFIANO NATTA [AL]
TEL. +39 0141922124
www.castellodirazzano.it

CELLAR SALES
PRE-BOOKED VISITS
ACCOMMODATION
ANNUAL PRODUCTION 200,000 bottles
HECTARES UNDER VINE 30.00

● Barbera d'Asti Sup. Del Beneficio '13	♟♟ 4
● Barbera d'Asti Sup. Valentino Caligaris '13	♟♟ 5
● Barbera d'Asti Sup. Campasso '12	♟ 3

Cavalier Bartolomeo

VIA ALBA BAROLO, 55
12060 CASTIGLIONE FALLETTO [CN]
TEL. +39 017362866
www.cavalierbartolomeo.com

ANNUAL PRODUCTION 15,000 bottles
HECTARES UNDER VINE 3.50

● Barolo Altenasso '13	♟♟ 5
● Barolo San Lorenzo '13	♟♟ 5

Le Cecche

VIA MOGLIA GERLOTTO, 10
12055 DIANO D'ALBA [CN]
TEL. +39 017369323
www.lececche.com

CELLAR SALES
PRE-BOOKED VISITS
ANNUAL PRODUCTION 35,000 bottles
HECTARES UNDER VINE 5.00

● Barolo Sorano '13	♟♟ 5
● Diano d'Alba '16	♟♟ 2*
○ Langhe Riesling '15	♟♟ 3
● Langhe Rosso Fiammingo '13	♟♟ 3

Centovigne

VIA CASTELLO, 31
13836 COSSATO [BI]
TEL. +39 3383543101
www.centovigne.it

ANNUAL PRODUCTION 30,000 bottles
HECTARES UNDER VINE 6.50

● Coste della Sesia Nebbiolo Castellengo '13	♟♟ 4
● Rosso della Motta	♟♟ 3
○ Miranda	♟ 3

Cerutti

VIA CANELLI, 205
14050 CASSINASCO [AT]
TEL. +39 0141851286
www.cascinacerutti.it

CELLAR SALES
PRE-BOOKED VISITS
ANNUAL PRODUCTION 20,000 bottles
HECTARES UNDER VINE 7.00
SUSTAINABLE WINERY

● Barbera d'Asti Sup. Foje Russe '12	♟♟ 4
○ Enrico Cerutti Brut M. Cl.	♟♟ 3
○ Moscato d'Asti Canelli Surì Sandrinet '16	♟♟ 2*
○ Piemonte Chardonnay Riva Granda '15	♟♟ 3

Franco e Pierguido Ceste

C.SO ALFIERI, 1
12040 GOVONE [CN]
TEL. +39 017358635
www.cestevini.com

CELLAR SALES
PRE-BOOKED VISITS
ANNUAL PRODUCTION 180,000 bottles
HECTARES UNDER VINE 20.00

● Barbaresco '14	♟♟ 3
● Barolo '13	♟♟ 6
○ Terre Alfieri Arneis Mislet '16	♟♟ 2*
○ Roero Arneis Sanroch '16	♟ 2

Erede di Armando Chiappone

S.DA SAN MICHELE, 51
14049 NIZZA MONFERRATO [AT]
TEL. +39 0141721424
www.erededichiappone.com

CELLAR SALES
PRE-BOOKED VISITS
RESTAURANT SERVICE
ANNUAL PRODUCTION 35,000 bottles
HECTARES UNDER VINE 10.00

● Barbera d'Asti Brentura '14	♟♟ 2*
● Barbera d'Asti Sup. Nizza Ru '12	♟♟ 4

Paride Chiovini

VIA GIUSEPPE GARIBALDI, 20
28070 SIZZANO [NO]
TEL. +39 3394304954
www.paridechiovini.it

CELLAR SALES
PRE-BOOKED VISITS
ANNUAL PRODUCTION 10,000 bottles
HECTARES UNDER VINE 3.00

● Sizzano '12	♟♟ 4
● Ghemme '13	♟♟ 4
● Colline Novaresi Vespolina Afrodite '16	♟ 2

Cantina Clavesana

FRAZ. MADONNA DELLA NEVE, 19
12060 CLAVESANA [CN]
TEL. +39 0173790451
www.inclavesana.it

CELLAR SALES
PRE-BOOKED VISITS
ANNUAL PRODUCTION 3,400,000 bottles
HECTARES UNDER VINE 520.00
SUSTAINABLE WINERY

● Dogliani Sup. Le Clou '15	♟♟ 3
● Langhe Nebbiolo Lan '15	♟♟ 2*
● Dogliani '16	♟ 2
● Dogliani Sup. 587 '13	♟ 3

Aldo Clerico

LOC. MANZONI, 69
12065 MONFORTE D'ALBA [CN]
TEL. +39 017378509
www.aldoclerico.it

CELLAR SALES
PRE-BOOKED VISITS
ANNUAL PRODUCTION 30,000 bottles
HECTARES UNDER VINE 7.00

● Barolo '13	♟♟ 6
● Dogliani '16	♟♟ 2*
● Dolcetto d'Alba '16	♟ 2
● Dolcetto d'Alba '16	♟ 2

Col dei Venti

s.da Comunale Balbi, 25
12053 Castiglione Tinella [CN]
Tel. +39 0141793071
www.coldeiventi.com

PRE-BOOKED VISITS
ANNUAL PRODUCTION 30,000 bottles
HECTARES UNDER VINE 10.00

- ● Barbaresco Túfoblu '14 — 🍷🍷 6
- ● Barbera d'Alba Sopralta '15 — 🍷🍷 3
- ● Barolo Debutto '13 — 🍷🍷 7
- ● Langhe Nebbiolo Lampio '15 — 🍷 4

Collina Serragrilli

via Serragrilli, 30
12052 Neive [CN]
Tel. +39 0173677010
www.serragrilli.it

CELLAR SALES
PRE-BOOKED VISITS
ANNUAL PRODUCTION 100,000 bottles
HECTARES UNDER VINE 15.00

- ● Barbaresco Serragrilli '14 — 🍷🍷 6
- ● Barbera d'Alba Grillaia '14 — 🍷🍷 4
- ● Barbera d'Alba Serraia '15 — 🍷🍷 2*

Colombera & Garella

via Cascina Cottignano, 2
13866 Masserano [BI]
Tel. +39 01596967
colomberaegarella@gmail.com

CELLAR SALES
PRE-BOOKED VISITS
ANNUAL PRODUCTION 30,000 bottles
HECTARES UNDER VINE 9.00

- ● Bramaterra Cascina Cottignano '13 — 🍷🍷 4
- ● Costa della Sesia Rosso Cascina Cottignano '14 — 🍷🍷 4
- ● Lessona Pizzaguerra '13 — 🍷🍷 4

Colombo - Cascina Pastori

reg. Cafra, 172b
14051 Bubbio [AT]
Tel. +39 0144852807
www.colombovino.it

CELLAR SALES
PRE-BOOKED VISITS
ANNUAL PRODUCTION 40,000 bottles
HECTARES UNDER VINE 10.00
SUSTAINABLE WINERY

- ● Piemonte Pinot Nero Apertura '14 — 🍷🍷 3*
- ⊙ Alta Langa Brut Rosé Silvì Ris. '12 — 🍷🍷 5
- ○ Piemonte Chardonnay Spumante Blanc de Blancs Andrè M. Cl. '13 — 🍷🍷 5

Comero

via Giuseppe Corna, 8
28070 Sizzano [NO]
Tel. +39 3332575651
www.cantinacomero.it

CELLAR SALES
ANNUAL PRODUCTION 7,000 bottles
HECTARES UNDER VINE 6.00

- ○ Colline Novaresi Bianco La Grazia del Marchese '16 — 🍷🍷 2*
- ● Colline Novaresi Nebbiolo '15 — 🍷🍷 3
- ● Sizzano '12 — 🍷🍷 4

Crosio

via Roma, 75
10010 Candia Canavese [TO]
Tel. +39 0119836048
www.cantinecrosio.it

CELLAR SALES
PRE-BOOKED VISITS
RESTAURANT SERVICE
ANNUAL PRODUCTION 35,000 bottles
HECTARES UNDER VINE 6.50

- ○ Caluso Passito Eva d'Or '08 — 🍷🍷 4
- ○ Erbaluce di Caluso Brut Incanto '13 — 🍷🍷 5
- ○ Erbaluce di Caluso Costaparadiso '15 — 🍷🍷 3
- ○ Erbaluce di Caluso Primavigna '16 — 🍷🍷 3

Cuvage

Stradale Alessandria, 90
15011 Acqui Terme [AL]
Tel. +39 0144371600
www.cuvage.com

ANNUAL PRODUCTION 80,000 bottles
HECTARES UNDER VINE 200.00

○ Brut Blanc de Blancs M. Cl.	♟♟ 3
⊙ Brut Rosé M. Cl.	♟♟ 3
○ Pas Dosé Cuvage de Cuvage M. Cl.	♟♟ 3

Dacapo

s.da Asti Mare, 4
14041 Agliano Terme [AT]
Tel. +39 0141964921
www.dacapo.it

CELLAR SALES
PRE-BOOKED VISITS
ANNUAL PRODUCTION 50,000 bottles
HECTARES UNDER VINE 8.50
VITICULTURE METHOD Certified Organic

● Barbera d'Asti Sanbastiàn '15	♟♟ 2*
● Barbera d'Asti Sup. Nizza V. Dacapo '13	♟♟ 5
● Ruchè di Castagnole M.to Majoli '16	♟♟ 3

Giovanni Daglio

via Montale Celli, 10
15050 Costa Vescovato [AL]
Tel. +39 0131838262
www.vignetidaglio.io

CELLAR SALES
ANNUAL PRODUCTION 15,000 bottles
HECTARES UNDER VINE 10.00

○ Colli Tortonesi Timorasso Cantico '15	♟♟ 4
○ Colli Tortonesi Timorasso Derthona '15	♟♟ 4

Alessandro e Gian Natale Fantino

via G. Silvano, 18
12065 Monforte d'Alba [CN]
Tel. +39 017378253
www.vinofantino.com

CELLAR SALES
PRE-BOOKED VISITS
ANNUAL PRODUCTION 40,000 bottles
HECTARES UNDER VINE 8.00

● Barolo Bussia Cascina Dardi '13	♟♟ 5
● Barolo Bussia Cascina Dardi Ris. '11	♟♟ 6
● Laboro Disobedient '12	♟♟ 6
● Barbera d'Alba Cascina Dardi '16	♟ 2

Fabio Fidanza

via Rodotiglia, 55
14052 Calosso [AT]
Tel. +39 0141826921
a.a.fidanza@gmail.com

CELLAR SALES
PRE-BOOKED VISITS
ANNUAL PRODUCTION 20,000 bottles
HECTARES UNDER VINE 10.00

● Barbera d'Asti Sup. Sterlino '15	♟♟ 4
● M.to Rosso Que Duàn '15	♟♟ 3
○ Moscato d'Asti Canelli '16	♟♟ 2*
● Barbera d'Asti '15	♟ 2

Fontanabianca

via Bordini, 15
12057 Neive [CN]
Tel. +39 017367195
www.fontanabianca.it

CELLAR SALES
PRE-BOOKED VISITS
ANNUAL PRODUCTION 70,000 bottles
HECTARES UNDER VINE 14.00

● Barbaresco '14	♟♟ 5
● Barbaresco Bordini '14	♟♟ 6
● Barbera d'Alba Sup. '15	♟♟ 3
● Langhe Nebbiolo '15	♟♟ 3

Forteto della Luja

REG. CANDELETTE, 4
14051 LOAZZOLO [AT]
TEL. +39 014487197
www.fortetodellaluja.it

CELLAR SALES
PRE-BOOKED VISITS
ANNUAL PRODUCTION 50,000 bottles
HECTARES UNDER VINE 11.00
VITICULTURE METHOD Certified Organic

● Barbera d'Asti Mon Ross '16	♥♥ 2*
● M.to Rosso Le Grive '15	♥♥ 4
○ Loazzolo V. T. Piasa Rischei '13	♥ 6
○ Moscato d'Asti Piasa Sanmaurizio '16	♥ 3

La Fusina - Luigi Abbona

B.GO SANTA LUCIA, 33
12063 DOGLIANI [CN]
TEL. +39 017370488
www.lafusina.com

CELLAR SALES
PRE-BOOKED VISITS
ANNUAL PRODUCTION 80,000 bottles
HECTARES UNDER VINE 20.00
SUSTAINABLE WINERY

● Barbera d'Alba '16	♥♥ 3
● Barolo '13	♥♥ 5
● Dogliani Gombe '16	♥♥ 2*
○ P.Nero Brut M. Cl.	♥♥ 5

Gagliasso

BORGATA TORRIGLIONE, 7
12064 LA MORRA [CN]
TEL. +39 017350180
www.gagliassovini.it

CELLAR SALES
PRE-BOOKED VISITS
RESTAURANT SERVICE
HECTARES UNDER VINE 12.50

● Barolo Rocche dell'Annunziata '13	♥♥ 6
● Barolo Torriglione '13	♥♥ 6
● Barolo Tre Utin '13	♥♥ 5

Cantine Garrone

VIA SCAPACCIANO, 36
28845 DOMODOSSOLA [VB]
TEL. +39 0324242990
www.cantinegarrone.it

CELLAR SALES
PRE-BOOKED VISITS
ANNUAL PRODUCTION 50,000 bottles
HECTARES UNDER VINE 10.00

● Valli Ossolane Nebbiolo Sup. Prünent '14	♥♥ 4
● Munaloss	♥ 3
● Valli Ossolane Rosso Tarlàp '15	♥ 2

La Giribaldina

FRAZ. SAN VITO, 39
14042 CALAMANDRANA [AT]
TEL. +39 0141718043
www.giribaldina.com

CELLAR SALES
PRE-BOOKED VISITS
ACCOMMODATION
ANNUAL PRODUCTION 70,000 bottles
HECTARES UNDER VINE 11.00

● Barbera d'Asti Monte Del Mare '16	♥♥ 2*
● Barbera d'Asti Sup. Valsarmassa '14	♥♥ 3
● Nizza Cala delle Mandrie '14	♥♥ 4

La Guardia

POD. LA GUARDIA, 74
15010 MORSASCO [AL]
TEL. +39 014473076
www.laguardiavilladelfini.it

CELLAR SALES
PRE-BOOKED VISITS
ANNUAL PRODUCTION 100,000 bottles
HECTARES UNDER VINE 35.00

● Doppio Rosso '14	♥♥ 3
● M.to L'Intrigante '13	♥♥ 3
● M.to Rosso Innominato '13	♥♥ 4
● Anteprima '15	♥ 3

Clemente Guasti

c.so IV Novembre, 80
14049 Nizza Monferrato [AT]
Tel. +39 0141721350
www,clemente.guasti.it

CELLAR SALES
PRE-BOOKED VISITS
ANNUAL PRODUCTION 120,000 bottles
HECTARES UNDER VINE 10.00

● Barbera d'Asti Sup. Severa '12	🍷🍷 3
● Barbera d'Asti Desideria '15	🍷 3
● Barbera d'Asti Sup. Boschetto Vecchio '12	🍷 4
○ Moscato d'Asti Santa Teresa '16	🍷 3

Paride Iaretti

via Pietro Micca, 23b
13045 Gattinara [VC]
Tel. +39 017350119
www.parideiaretti.it

● Coste della Sesia Velut Luna '15	🍷🍷 3
● Gattinara Pietro '13	🍷🍷 4

Lagobava

Ca' Bergantino, 5
15049 Vignale Monferrato [AL]
Tel. +39 3476900656
www.lagobava.it

CELLAR SALES
PRE-BOOKED VISITS
ANNUAL PRODUCTION 12,000 bottles
HECTARES UNDER VINE 5.00
VITICULTURE METHOD Certified Organic

● Barbera del M.to Sup. L'Ago '11	🍷🍷 5
● Monferrato rosso L'Amo '14	🍷🍷 4
● Monferrato rosso Lagobava '10	🍷🍷 6
● Piemonte Barbera '15	🍷🍷 3

Tenuta La Marchesa

via Gavi, 87
15067 Novi Ligure [AL]
Tel. +39 0143743362
www.tenutalamarchesa.it

CELLAR SALES
PRE-BOOKED VISITS
ACCOMMODATION AND RESTAURANT SERVICE
ANNUAL PRODUCTION 250,000 bottles
HECTARES UNDER VINE 56.45

○ Gavi Etichetta Oro '16	🍷🍷 3*
○ Gavi Etichetta Bianca '16	🍷🍷 2*

Marenco

p.zza Vittorio Emanuele II, 10
15019 Strevi [AL]
Tel. +39 0144363133
www.marencovini.com

CELLAR SALES
PRE-BOOKED VISITS
ACCOMMODATION
ANNUAL PRODUCTION 250,000 bottles
HECTARES UNDER VINE 80.00
SUSTAINABLE WINERY

● Brachetto d'Acqui Pineto '16	🍷🍷 3
● Barbera d'Asti Sup. Ciresa '14	🍷 5
○ Moscato d'Asti Scrapona '16	🍷 3
○ Strevi Passri' di Scrapona '12	🍷 6

Le Marie

via San Defendente, 6
12032 Barge [CN]
Tel. +39 0175345159
www.lemarievini.eu

CELLAR SALES
PRE-BOOKED VISITS
RESTAURANT SERVICE
ANNUAL PRODUCTION 24,000 bottles
HECTARES UNDER VINE 8.00

○ Blanc de Lissart '16	🍷🍷 2*
● Pinerolese Dolcetto '16	🍷🍷 2*
● Pinerolese Rosso Debárges '14	🍷🍷 3
● Pinerolese Barbera '14	🍷 3

La Masera

S.DA SAN PIETRO, 32
10010 PIVERONE [TO]
TEL. +39 0113164161
www.lamasera.it

CELLAR SALES
PRE-BOOKED VISITS
ANNUAL PRODUCTION 20,000 bottles
HECTARES UNDER VINE 5.00
SUSTAINABLE WINERY

● Canavese Nebbiolo '13	🍷🍷 3
○ Erbaluce di Caluso Anima '16	🍷🍷 2*
○ Erbaluce di Caluso Brut Masilé '14	🍷🍷 5
○ Erbaluce di Caluso Macaria '15	🍷 3

F.lli Monchiero

VIA ALBA-MONFORTE, 49
12060 CASTIGLIONE FALLETTO [CN]
TEL. +39 017362820
www.monchierovini.it

CELLAR SALES
PRE-BOOKED VISITS
ANNUAL PRODUCTION 40,000 bottles
HECTARES UNDER VINE 12.00

● Barbera d'Alba Sup. '15	🍷🍷 3
● Barolo Rocche di Castiglione '13	🍷🍷 5
● Langhe Nebbiolo '15	🍷 3

Morgassi Superiore

CASE SPARSE SERMORIA, 7
15066 GAVI [AL]
TEL. +39 0143642007
www.morgassisuperiore.it

CELLAR SALES
PRE-BOOKED VISITS
ANNUAL PRODUCTION 130,000 bottles
HECTARES UNDER VINE 20.00

○ Gavi del Comune di Gavi Volo '15	🍷🍷 4
○ Gavi del Comune di Gavi Tuffo '16	🍷 3
○ Monferrato Bianco Timorgasso '14	🍷 4

Diego Morra

VIA CASCINA MOSCA, 37
12060 VERDUNO [CN]
TEL. +39 3284623209
www.morrawines.com

CELLAR SALES
PRE-BOOKED VISITS
ANNUAL PRODUCTION 25,000 bottles
HECTARES UNDER VINE 34.00

● Barolo '12	🍷🍷 6
● Barbera d'Alba '15	🍷🍷 3
● Barolo Monvigliero '12	🍷🍷 6
● Verduno Pelaverga '16	🍷🍷 3

Musso

VIA D. CAVAZZA, 5
12050 BARBARESCO [CN]
TEL. +39 0173635129
www.mussobarbaresco.it

CELLAR SALES
PRE-BOOKED VISITS
ANNUAL PRODUCTION 80,000 bottles
HECTARES UNDER VINE 10.00

● Barbaresco Pora '14	🍷🍷 4
● Barbaresco Rio Sordo '14	🍷🍷 5

Ada Nada

LOC. ROMBONE
VIA AUSARIO, 12
12050 TREISO [CN]
TEL. +39 0173638127
www.adanada.it

CELLAR SALES
PRE-BOOKED VISITS
ACCOMMODATION AND RESTAURANT SERVICE
ANNUAL PRODUCTION 45,000 bottles
HECTARES UNDER VINE 9.00

● Barbaresco Cichin Ris. '12	🍷🍷 6
● Barbaresco Valeirano '14	🍷🍷 5
● Barbera d'Alba Sup. Salgà '15	🍷🍷 3
● Barbaresco Valeirano '13	🍷 5

Giuseppe Negro

VIA GALLINA, 22
12052 NEIVE [CN]
TEL. +39 0173677468
www.negrogiuseppe.com

CELLAR SALES
PRE-BOOKED VISITS
ANNUAL PRODUCTION 52,000 bottles
HECTARES UNDER VINE 9.00

● Barbaresco Gallina '14	♛♛ 6
● Barbera d'Alba Pulin '15	♛♛ 3
● Barbaresco Pian Cavallo '14	♛ 6

Silvano Nizza

FRAZ. BALLA LORA 29A
12040 SANTO STEFANO ROERO [CN]
TEL. +39 017390516
www.nizzasilvano.com

CELLAR SALES
PRE-BOOKED VISITS
ANNUAL PRODUCTION 65,000 bottles
HECTARES UNDER VINE 8.00

● Nebbiolo d'Alba '15	♛♛ 4
○ Roero Arneis '16	♛♛ 3
● Roero Ca' Boscarone Ris. '13	♛♛ 6
● Roero '14	♛ 5

Andrea Oberto

B.TA SIMANE, 11
12064 LA MORRA [CN]
TEL. +39 017350104
www.andreaoberto.com

CELLAR SALES
PRE-BOOKED VISITS
ANNUAL PRODUCTION 100,000 bottles
HECTARES UNDER VINE 16.00

● Barbera d'Alba Glada '15	♛♛ 5
● Barolo Albarella '13	♛♛ 7
● Barolo Rocche dell'Annunziata '13	♛♛ 7
● Barolo '13	♛ 6

Oltretorrente

VIA CINQUE MARTIRI
15050 PADERNA [AL]
TEL. +39 3398195360
www.oltretorrente.com

CELLAR SALES
PRE-BOOKED VISITS
ANNUAL PRODUCTION 20,000 bottles
HECTARES UNDER VINE 7.00
VITICULTURE METHOD Certified Organic

○ Colli Tortonesi Cortese '16	♛♛ 2"
○ Colli Tortonesi Timorasso '15	♛♛ 3
● Colli Tortonesi Barbera Sup. '14	♛ 3

Pace

FRAZ. MADONNA DI LORETO
CASCINA PACE, 52
12043 CANALE [CN]
TEL. +39 0173979544
dinonegropace@gmail.com

CELLAR SALES
PRE-BOOKED VISITS
ANNUAL PRODUCTION 60,000 bottles
HECTARES UNDER VINE 22.00

○ Roero Arneis '16	♛♛ 3
● Roero Ris. '13	♛♛ 5
● Barbera d'Alba '15	♛ 2
○ Langhe Favorita '16	♛ 2

Massimo Pastura
Cascina La Ghersa

VIA CHIARINA, 2
14050 MOASCA [AT]
TEL. +39 0141856012
www.laghersa.it

CELLAR SALES
PRE-BOOKED VISITS
ACCOMMODATION
ANNUAL PRODUCTION 150,000 bottles
HECTARES UNDER VINE 23.00

● Barbera d'Asti Sup. Camparò '15	♛ 2
● Barbera d'Asti Sup. Le Cave '14	♛ 3
● Nizza Muaschae '14	♛ 6
● Nizza Vignassa Ris. '14	♛ 5

Agostino Pavia e Figli

LOC. MOLIZZO, 3
14041 AGLIANO TERME [AT]
TEL. +39 0141954125
www.agostinopavia.it

CELLAR SALES
PRE-BOOKED VISITS
ACCOMMODATION
ANNUAL PRODUCTION 75,000 bottles
HECTARES UNDER VINE 9.00

● Barbera d'Asti Blina '15	♟♟ 2*
● Barbera d'Asti Casareggio '16	♟♟ 2*
● Barbera d'Asti Sup. Moliss '14	♟♟ 3
● Grignolino d'Asti '16	♟♟ 2*

Magda Pedrini

LOC. CA' D'MEO
VIA PRATOLUNGO, 163
15066 GAVI [AL]
TEL. +39 0143667923
www.magdapedrini.it

CELLAR SALES
PRE-BOOKED VISITS
ANNUAL PRODUCTION 90,000 bottles
HECTARES UNDER VINE 10.50
SUSTAINABLE WINERY

○ Gavi del Comune di Gavi E' '16	♟♟ 3*
○ Gavi del Comune di Gavi La Piacentina '16	♟♟ 3
● M.to Rosso Il Pettirosso '14	♟ 4

Elio Perrone

S.DA SAN MARTINO, 3BIS
12053 CASTIGLIONE TINELLA [CN]
TEL. +39 0141855803
www.elioperrone.it

CELLAR SALES
PRE-BOOKED VISITS
ANNUAL PRODUCTION 200,000 bottles
HECTARES UNDER VINE 14.00
SUSTAINABLE WINERY

● Barbera d'Asti Tasmorcan '16	♟♟ 2*
○ Moscato d'Asti Sourgal '16	♟♟ 2*
● Barbera d'Asti Sup. Mongovone '15	♟ 5

Guido Platinetti

VIA ROMA, 60
28074 GHEMME [NO]
TEL. +39 3389945783
platinettivini.com

CELLAR SALES
PRE-BOOKED VISITS
ANNUAL PRODUCTION 15,000 bottles
HECTARES UNDER VINE 5.50

● Ghemme V. Ronco Maso '12	♟♟ 4
● Colline Novaresi Vespolina '16	♟♟ 2*
● Colline Novaresi Nebbiolo '15	♟ 3

I Poderi dei Bricchi Astigiani

FRAZ. REPERGO
VIA BRICCO SAN GIOVANNI, 13
14057 ISOLA D'ASTI [AT]
TEL. +39 0141958974
www.bricchiastigiani.it

CELLAR SALES
PRE-BOOKED VISITS
ANNUAL PRODUCTION 40,000 bottles
HECTARES UNDER VINE 15.00

● Barbera d'Asti '15	♟♟ 2*
● Barbera d'Asti Sup. Bricco del Perg '14	♟♟ 3
● M.to Rosso Bricco San Giovanni '14	♟ 2

Paolo Giuseppe Poggio

VIA ROMA, 67
15050 BRIGNANO FRASCATA [AL]
TEL. +39 0131784929
www.cantinapoggio.com

CELLAR SALES
PRE-BOOKED VISITS
ANNUAL PRODUCTION 18,000 bottles
HECTARES UNDER VINE 3.50

● Colli Tortonesi Barbera Campo La Bà '15	♟♟ 2*
● Colli Tortonesi Barbera Derio '12	♟♟ 3
○ Colli Tortonesi Timorasso Derthona Ronchetto '15	♟ 2

Pomodolce

VIA IV NOVEMBRE, 7
15050 MONTEMARZINO [AL]
TEL. +39 0131878135
www.pomodolce.it

CELLAR SALES
PRE-BOOKED VISITS
RESTAURANT SERVICE
ANNUAL PRODUCTION 14,000 bottles
HECTARES UNDER VINE 4.00
VITICULTURE METHOD Certified Organic

○ Colli Tortonesi Timorasso Diletto '15	♟♟	3*
○ Colli Tortonesi Timorasso Grue '15	♟	5

Diego Pressenda
La Torricella

LOC. SANT'ANNA, 98
12065 MONFORTE D'ALBA [CN]
TEL. +39 017378327
www.latorricella.eu

● Barolo Barbadelchi '13	♟♟	6
● Langhe Nebbiolo '16	♟	3
○ Langhe Riesling '15	♟	3

Pietro Rinaldi

FRAZ. MADONNA DI COMO
12051 ALBA [CN]
TEL. +39 0173360090
www.pietrorinaldi.com

CELLAR SALES
PRE-BOOKED VISITS
ACCOMMODATION
ANNUAL PRODUCTION 70,000 bottles
HECTARES UNDER VINE 10.00

● Barbera d'Alba Sup. Bricco Cichetta '14	♟♟	4
● Barolo '13	♟♟	6
● Barolo Monvigliero '13	♟♟	6
● Langhe Nebbiolo Argante '14	♟♟	4

Maurizio Ponchione

VIA R. SACCO, 9/A
12040 GOVONE [CN]
TEL. +39 017358149
www.ponchionemaurizio.com

CELLAR SALES
PRE-BOOKED VISITS
ANNUAL PRODUCTION 35,000 bottles
HECTARES UNDER VINE 11.00

○ Albazzi Brut M. Cl.	♟♟	3
● Roero Arneis Monfrini '16	♟♟	3
● Roero Arneis Monfrini '15	♟♟	3
● Roero Monfrini '13	♟♟	3

Raineri

LOC. PANEROLE, 24
12060 NOVELLO [CN]
TEL. +39 3396009289
www.rainerivini.com

CELLAR SALES
PRE-BOOKED VISITS
ANNUAL PRODUCTION 20,000 bottles
HECTARES UNDER VINE 3.30
SUSTAINABLE WINERY

● Barbera d'Alba Sagrin '15	♟♟	3
● Barolo '13	♟♟	5
● Barolo Monserra '13	♟♟	7

Silvia Rivella

LOC. MONTESTEFANO, 17
12050 BARBARESCO [CN]
TEL. +39 0173635040
www.agriturismorivella.it

CELLAR SALES
ACCOMMODATION AND RESTAURANT SERVICE
ANNUAL PRODUCTION 7,000 bottles
HECTARES UNDER VINE 1.50

● Barbaresco '14	♟♟	6
● Barbaresco Montestefano '14	♟♟	7

Rivetto

Loc. Lirano, 2
12050 Sinio [CN]
Tel. +39 0173613380
www.rivetto.it

CELLAR SALES
PRE-BOOKED VISITS
ACCOMMODATION
ANNUAL PRODUCTION 100,000 bottles
HECTARES UNDER VINE 20.00

● Barbaresco Marcarini '14	♀♀ 6
● Barolo Leon Ris. '11	♀♀ 8
● Barolo del Comune di Serralunga D'Alba '13	♀ 6

Tenuta Rocca

Loc. Ornati, 19
12065 Monforte d'Alba [CN]
Tel. +39 017378412
www.tenutarocca.com

CELLAR SALES
PRE-BOOKED VISITS
ACCOMMODATION
ANNUAL PRODUCTION 90,000 bottles
HECTARES UNDER VINE 15.00

● Barolo del Comune di Serralunga d'Alba '13	♀♀ 8
● Barolo Bussia '13	♀♀ 6
● Langhe Rosso Or nati '15	♀♀ 5

Roccolo di Mezzomerico

Cascina Roccolo Bellini, 4
28040 Mezzomerico [NO]
Tel. +39 0321920407
www.ilroccolovini.it

CELLAR SALES
PRE-BOOKED VISITS
ANNUAL PRODUCTION 30,000 bottles
HECTARES UNDER VINE 7.00

● Gilgamesh	♀♀ 5
○ Siduri Francesca	♀♀ 5
● Colline Novaresi Nebbiolo Valentina '12	♀ 3

Rossi Contini

s.da San Lorenzo, 20
15076 Ovada [AL]
Tel. +39 0143822530
www.rossicontini.com

CELLAR SALES
PRE-BOOKED VISITS
ANNUAL PRODUCTION 17,000 bottles
HECTARES UNDER VINE 4.50
SUSTAINABLE WINERY

● Barbera del M.to Sup. Cras Tibi '15	♀♀ 3
○ Cortese dell'Alto M.to Cortesia '16	♀♀ 2*
● Dolcetto di Ovada San Lorenzo '16	♀♀ 2*
● Ovada Viign. Ninan '15	♀♀ 4

San Cristoforo

via Pastura, 10
12057 Neive [CN]
Tel. +39 0173677122
www.sassiwines.com

CELLAR SALES
PRE-BOOKED VISITS
ANNUAL PRODUCTION 10,000 bottles
HECTARES UNDER VINE 1.30

● Barbaresco San Cristoforo Ris. '12	♀♀ 6
● Barbaresco Sassi '14	♀♀ 6
● Langhe Nebbiolo '15	♀♀ 3
● Dolcetto d'Alba '15	♀ 2

Tenuta San Pietro

Loc. San Pietro, 2
15060 Tassarolo [AL]
Tel. +39 0143342422
www.tenutasanpietro.it

CELLAR SALES
PRE-BOOKED VISITS
ANNUAL PRODUCTION 250,000 bottles
HECTARES UNDER VINE 30.00
VITICULTURE METHOD Certified Organic
SUSTAINABLE WINERY

○ Gavi del Comune di Tassarolo Il Mandorlo '16	♀♀ 5
○ Gavi del Comune di Tassarolo San Pietro '16	♀♀ 3

Cantine Sant'Agata

REG. MEZZENA, 19
14030 SCURZOLENGO [AT]
TEL. +39 0141203186
www.santagata.com

CELLAR SALES
PRE-BOOKED VISITS
RESTAURANT SERVICE
ANNUAL PRODUCTION 150,000 bottles
HECTARES UNDER VINE 12.00

● Ruché di Castagnole M.to 'Na Vota '16	♥♥ 3
● Barolo Bussia '13	♥ 6
● Langhe Nebbiolo La Fenice '16	♥ 3

Sant'Anna dei Bricchetti

FRAZ. SANT'ANNA
S.DA BRICCHETTI, 11
14055 COSTIGLIOLE D'ASTI [AT]
TEL. +39 01411851012
www.santanna-dei-bricchetti.it

PRE-BOOKED VISITS
ANNUAL PRODUCTION 20,000 bottles
HECTARES UNDER VINE 5.00

● Barbera d'Asti Ricordi '15	♥♥ 3
○ Destino	♥♥ 5
○ Moscato d'Asti '16	♥♥ 3
○ Incanto Brut M. Cl.	♥ 5

Tenuta Santa Caterina

VIA GUGLIELMO MARCONI, 17
14035 GRAZZANO BADOGLIO [AT]
TEL. +39 0141925108
www.tenuta-santa-caterina.it

CELLAR SALES
PRE-BOOKED VISITS
ACCOMMODATION
ANNUAL PRODUCTION 50,000 bottles
HECTARES UNDER VINE 23.00

● Barbera d'Asti Sup. Setecapita '13	♥♥ 5
● Barbera d'Asti Sup. V. Lina '14	♥♥ 3
● Freisa d'Asti Sorì di Giul '13	♥♥ 5
● Grignolino d'Asti Arlandino '15	♥ 3

Santa Clelia

REG. ROSSANA, 7
10035 MAZZÈ [TO]
TEL. +39 0119835187
www.santaclelia.it

○ Caluso Passito Dus '09	♥♥ 4
○ Erbaluce di Caluso Essenthia '16	♥♥ 3
○ Erbaluce di Caluso Ypa '16	♥♥ 3
○ Erbaluce di Caluso Brut Rigore '08	♥ 5

Giacomo Scagliola

REG. SANTA LIBERA, 20
14053 CANELLI [AT]
TEL. +39 0141831146
www.scagliola-canelli.it

CELLAR SALES
ANNUAL PRODUCTION 80,000 bottles
HECTARES UNDER VINE 15.00

● Barbera d'Asti Sup. Bric dei Mandorli '14	♥♥ 3
⊙ Giacomo Scagliola Brut M. Cl.	♥♥ 5
○ Beatrice Scagliola Brut M. Cl.	♥ 5
○ Moscato d'Asti Canelli Sifasol '16	♥ 2

Poderi Sinaglio

FRAZ. RICCA
VIA SINAGLIO, 5
12055 DIANO D'ALBA [CN]
TEL. +39 0173612209
www.poderisinaglio.it

CELLAR SALES
PRE-BOOKED VISITS
ACCOMMODATION
ANNUAL PRODUCTION 35,000 bottles
HECTARES UNDER VINE 13.00

● Dolcetto di Diano d'Alba '16	♥♥ 2*
● Dolcetto di Diano d'Alba Sorì Bric Maiolica '16	♥♥ 2*
○ Moscato d'Asti La Mimosa '16	♥ 2

Francesco Sobrero

VIA PUGNANE, 5
12060 CASTIGLIONE FALLETTO [CN]
TEL. +39 0173/362864
www.sobrerofrancesco.it

CELLAR SALES
PRE-BOOKED VISITS
ACCOMMODATION
ANNUAL PRODUCTION 90,000 bottles
HECTARES UNDER VINE 16.00

● Barolo Ciabot Tanasio '13	♥♥ 6
● Langhe Nebbiolo '15	♥♥ 4
● Barbera d'Alba La Pichetera '15	♥ 3

La Spinosa Alta

C.NE CASCINA SPINOSA ALTA, 8
15038 OTTIGLIO [AL]
TEL. +39 0142921372
www.laspinosaalta.it

CELLAR SALES
PRE-BOOKED VISITS
ACCOMMODATION
ANNUAL PRODUCTION 12,000 bottles
HECTARES UNDER VINE 3.00

● Grignolino del M.to Casalese '15	♥♥ 2*
☉ M.to Chiaretto Vin Rosè '16	♥♥ 2*
● Barbera del M.to Sup. La Punta '13	♥ 3
● M.to Rosso Tenebroso '13	♥ 3

Le Strette

VIA LE STRETTE, 1F
12060 NOVELLO [CN]
TEL. +39 0173744002
www.lestrette.com

CELLAR SALES
PRE-BOOKED VISITS
ANNUAL PRODUCTION 35,000 bottles
HECTARES UNDER VINE 5.00

● Barolo Bergera-Pezzole '13	♥♥ 6
● Barolo Corini-Pallaretta '13	♥♥ 6
○ Langhe Nas-cëtta del Comune di Novello '16	♥♥ 2*

Dario Stroppiana

FRAZ. RIVALTA SAN GIACOMO, 6
12064 LA MORRA [CN]
TEL. +39 0173509419
www.cantinastroppiana.com

CELLAR SALES
PRE-BOOKED VISITS
ANNUAL PRODUCTION 35,000 bottles
HECTARES UNDER VINE 5.00

● Barolo Bussia Ris. '10	♥♥ 6
● Barolo Bussia '12	♥♥ 6
● Barolo Leonardo '13	♥♥ 5

Tenute Rade

FRAZ. SALINE 13/14
14050 SAN MARZANO OLIVETO [AT]
TEL. +39 0141769091
www.cusmano.it

CELLAR SALES
PRE-BOOKED VISITS
HECTARES UNDER VINE 50.00

● Barbera d'Asti La Grissa '15	♥♥ 4
○ Colli Tortonesi Timorasso '16	♥♥ 4
○ M.to Bianco Lunatico '16	♥♥ 2*
● Barbera d'Asti La Pruna '16	♥ 4

Terre Astesane

VIA MARCONI, 42
14047 MOMBERCELLI [AT]
TEL. +39 0141959155
www.terreastesane.it

CELLAR SALES
PRE-BOOKED VISITS
ANNUAL PRODUCTION 100,000 bottles
HECTARES UNDER VINE 240.00

● Barbera d'Asti Anno Domini '15	♥♥ 3*
● Barbera d'Asti Sup. '14	♥♥ 2*
● Barbera d'Asti Sup. Mumbersè '13	♥ 3
● Grignolino d'Asti '16	♥♥ 2*

Tibaldi

S.DA SAN GIACOMO, 49
12060 POCAPAGLIA [CN]
TEL. +39 0172421221
www.cantinatibaldi.com

CELLAR SALES
PRE-BOOKED VISITS
ANNUAL PRODUCTION 35,000 bottles
HECTARES UNDER VINE 7.00

● Barbera d'Alba '16	🍷🍷 3
○ Roero '14	🍷🍷 3
○ Roero Arneis Monic '16	🍷🍷 3
○ Langhe Favorita Danielle '16	🍷 3

La Toledana

LOC. SERMOIRA, 5
15066 GAVI [AL]
TEL. +39 0141837287
www.latoledana.it

CELLAR SALES
PRE-BOOKED VISITS
ANNUAL PRODUCTION 145,000 bottles
HECTARES UNDER VINE 28.00

○ Gavi del Comune di Gavi La Toledana '16	🍷🍷 5
○ Gavi La Doria '16	🍷🍷 3

Trediberri

B.TA TORRIGLIONE, 4
12064 LA MORRA [CN]
TEL. +39 3391605470
www.trediberri.com

CELLAR SALES
PRE-BOOKED VISITS
ANNUAL PRODUCTION 50,000 bottles
HECTARES UNDER VINE 8.00
VITICULTURE METHOD Certified Organic

● Barolo '13	🍷🍷 5
● Barolo Rocche dell'Annunziata '13	🍷🍷 7

Poderi Vaiot

BORGATA LAIONE, 43
12046 MONTÀ [CN]
TEL. +39 0173976283
www.poderivaiot.it

ANNUAL PRODUCTION 25,000 bottles
HECTARES UNDER VINE 4.00

○ Roero Arneis Franco '16	🍷🍷 2*
● Roero Pierin '14	🍷🍷 2*
● Nebbiolo d'Alba Sessantaadì '15	🍷 3

Valfaccenda

FRAZ. MADONNA LORETO
LOC. VAL FACCENDA, 43
12043 CANALE [CN]
TEL. +39 3397303837
www.valfaccenda.it

CELLAR SALES
PRE-BOOKED VISITS
ANNUAL PRODUCTION 16,000 bottles
HECTARES UNDER VINE 3.00
SUSTAINABLE WINERY

● Roero '15	🍷🍷 4
● Roero V. Valmaggiore Ris. '13	🍷🍷 4
○ Roero Arneis '16	🍷 3

Rino Varaldo

VIA SECONDINE, 2
12050 BARBARESCO [CN]
TEL. +39 0173635160
varaldo@varaldo.com

CELLAR SALES
PRE-BOOKED VISITS
ANNUAL PRODUCTION 40,000 bottles
HECTARES UNDER VINE 7.00

● Barbaresco Sorì Loreto '13	🍷🍷 6
● Barbaresco Sorì Loreto Ris. '09	🍷🍷 6
● Langhe Nebbiolo '15	🍷 3

La Vecchia Posta

VIA MONTEBELLO, 2
15050 AVOLASCA [AL]
TEL. +39 0131876254
www.lavecchiaposta-avolasca.com

CELLAR SALES
PRE-BOOKED VISITS
ACCOMMODATION AND RESTAURANT SERVICE
ANNUAL PRODUCTION 10,000 bottles
HECTARES UNDER VINE 2.70
VITICULTURE METHOD Certified Organic

○ Colli Tortonesi Timorasso Il Selvaggio '15	♥♥	3
● Piemonte Rosso Ciliegio '16	♥♥	3
● Colli Tortonesi Barbera Languia '14	♥	3

Giacomo Vico

VIA TORINO, 80/82
12043 CANALE [CN]
TEL. +39 0173970984
www.giacomovico.it

CELLAR SALES
PRE-BOOKED VISITS
ANNUAL PRODUCTION 92,300 bottles
HECTARES UNDER VINE 18.00

● Nebbiolo d'Alba Valmaggiore '13	♥♥	4
○ Roero Arneis '16	♥	3
● Roero Ris. '13	♥	4

Alberto Voerzio

B.GO BRANDINI, 1A
12064 LA MORRA [CN]
TEL. +39 3333927654
www.albertovoerzio.com

CELLAR SALES
ANNUAL PRODUCTION 13,000 bottles
HECTARES UNDER VINE 6.00
SUSTAINABLE WINERY

● Barolo '13	♥♥	6
● Barolo La Serra '13	♥♥	7

Alessandro Veglio

FRAZ. ANNUNZIATA, 53
12064 LA MORRA [CN]
TEL. +39 3385699102
www.risveglioinlanga.it

ANNUAL PRODUCTION 10,000 bottles
HECTARES UNDER VINE 3.00

● Barolo Gattera '13	♥♥	7
● Barbera d'Alba '16	♥♥	3
● Barolo '13	♥♥	5
● Dolcetto d'Alba '16	♥♥	2*

Virna

VIA ALBA, 24
12060 BAROLO [CN]
TEL. +39 017356120
www.virnabarolo.it

CELLAR SALES
PRE-BOOKED VISITS
ANNUAL PRODUCTION 60,000 bottles
HECTARES UNDER VINE 12.00

● Barolo Cannubi Boschis '13	♥♥	6
● Barolo del Comune di Barolo '13	♥♥	6
● Barolo Sarmassa '13	♥	6

Voerzio Martini

S.DA LORETO, 3
12064 LA MORRA [CN]
TEL. +39 0173509194
voerzio.gianni@tiscali.it

CELLAR SALES
PRE-BOOKED VISITS
ANNUAL PRODUCTION 54,000 bottles
HECTARES UNDER VINE 12.00

● Barolo La Serra '13	♥♥	8
● Barbera d'Alba Ciabot della Luna '15	♥♥	4
● Langhe Nebbiolo Ciabot della Luna '15	♥♥	5
○ Moscato d'Asti Vignasergente '16	♥	3

LIGURIA

For many, Liguria is merely sun, sea, relaxing dinners and summer fun. For them it's a little-known fact that Liguria makes excellent wines. And yet it does. This region, wedged in between the sea and the mountains, is capable of offering authentic pearls, even if you have to look for its vineyards, which are often hidden among woods and hills. Even if it's frequently at a enormous personal and economic cost, Ligurian vine growers have managed to revive what little terrain is available so as to cultivate classic native varieties (Vermentino, Pigato, Bianchetta, Bosco, Rossese) and a few nice outsiders (Ormeasco, Granaccia, Syrah), which have done well in its climate. After a few less-than-glorious decades that saw wines unworthy of the region's vine growers and breathtaking beauty, the past 10 years has seen a detectable and constant growth in quality that has allowed Liguria to stand shoulder-to-shoulder with Italy's best. A generational change in management, in some cases, and the founding of new wineries, in others, have given new life to the entire region. Young producers are no longer content with just selling their wines locally. Many have the healthy and stimulating aim of selling nationally and internationally. They've understood that, in the era of globalization, you've got to go beyond your immediate surroundings. But back to current events, the 2016 season was doubtlessly excellent, even if it came in second to the approachable pleasantness of 2015. But together, these two years brought seven Tre Bicchieri to the region. It's an excellent result for a territory that has little more than 1500 hectares of vineyards to its name. As always, the awards are almost equally divided between Levante and Ponente, between Vermentino and Pigato, with the only additional red being Ka' Manciné's Dolceacqua. Such honors faithfully reflect Ligurian viticulture, with regional whites (to the east Vermentino shines while Pigato dominates to the west) making up 70% of the region's production.

Massimo Alessandri

via Costa Parrocchia, 42
18020 Ranzo [IM]
Tel. +39 018253458
www.massimoalessandri.it

CELLAR SALES
PRE-BOOKED VISITS
RESTAURANT SERVICE
ANNUAL PRODUCTION 35,000 bottles
HECTARES UNDER VINE 7.00

Finding new plots to cultivate isn't easy in Liguria, but Massimo Alessandri, a careful and serious vine grower, is continually researching new vineyards for Pigato or Vermentino. Today, the estate spans about seven hectares, even if, starting this year, they officially have a new plot in Ranzo to their name. The land, which is near the producer's cellar and was vacated by a farmworker, already hosts 40-year-old Pigato and will be used for their Vigne Vëggie 'riserva'. The 2015 Granaccia put in a stella performance this year, offering up lovely hints of red fruit - plums, blackberries, blueberries - and spices. Alcohol and sweet tannins combine for a velvety and gracefully contoured mouth, while the finish proves pleasant. The 2015 Pigato Vigne Vëggie is pronounced and multifaceted, with lovely notes of rosemary, iodine and white fruit.

- ● Riviera Ligure di Ponente Granaccia '15 — TT 4
- ○ Riviera Ligure di Ponente Pigato Vigne Vëggie '15 — TT 4
- ● Riviera Ligure di Ponente Rossese Costa de Vigne '16 — TT 4
- ○ Riviera Ligure di Ponente Pigato Costa de Vigne '16 — T 3
- ○ Riviera Ligure di Ponente Vermentino Costa de Vigne '16 — T 3
- ○ Viorus Costa de Vigne '15 — T 5
- ● Ligustico '13 — YY 6
- ● Riviera Ligure di Ponente Granaccia '14 — YY 4
- ○ Riviera Ligure di Ponente Pigato Costa de Vigne '15 — YY 3
- ○ Viorus Costa de Vigne '14 — YY 5

Laura Aschero

p.zza Vittorio Emanuele, 7
18027 Pontedassio [IM]
Tel. +39 0183710307
www.lauraaschero.it

CELLAR SALES
PRE-BOOKED VISITS
ANNUAL PRODUCTION 60,000 bottles
HECTARES UNDER VINE 50.00

Carla and Marco Rizzo's daughter is now a full-blown member of the staff. She's taking care of public relations and hospitality, accompanying the many visitors who come to see this historic cellar built beneath Pontedassio's main square. Today, the winery is structurally equipped for wine tourists, with an itinerary that takes them through the barrels and the tasting room. Even the estate is growing - last year a new, one-hectare vineyard was purchased. It's just been cleaned and will be replanted in 2018. The 2016 Pigato offers up fragrances of sage, thyme and ripe white fruit. In the mouth, it's gracefully-contoured and complex, full and velvety, with good structure and a pleasant richness of flavor. The 2016 Vermentino is also interesting, with its straw-yellow color and greenish highlights. Its Mediterranean fragrances are brought out by an alcohol-dominated body, while a pleasant finish (with some character) is highlighted by a classic touch.

- ○ Riviera Ligure di Ponente Pigato '16 — TT 3
- ○ Riviera Ligure di Ponente Vermentino '16 — TT 3
- ● Riviera Ligure di Ponente Rossese '16 — T 3
- ○ Riviera Ligure di Ponente Vermentino '10 — YYY 3*
- ○ Riviera Ligure di Ponente Pigato '15 — YY 3*
- ○ Riviera Ligure di Ponente Pigato '13 — YY 3*
- ○ Riviera Ligure di Ponente Vermentino '15 — YY 3
- ○ Riviera Ligure di Ponente Vermentino '14 — YY 3
- ○ Riviera Ligure di Ponente Vermentino '12 — YY 3*

La Baia del Sole - Federici

FRAZ. LUNI ANTICA
VIA FORLINO, 3
19034 ORTONOVO [SP]
TEL. +39 0187661821
www.cantinefederici.com

CELLAR SALES
PRE-BOOKED VISITS
ANNUAL PRODUCTION 160,000 bottles
HECTARES UNDER VINE 35.00

La Baia del Sole gets its strength from two young siblings, Luca and Andrea Federici. In the cellar, a notable investment program is being carried out, with new and modern equipment, while their tireless father, Giulio, is replanting two new hectares of land with Vermentino. This recent addition, in Palvotrisia (Castelnuovo Magra), comprises three plots situated at an altitude of about 150 meters above sea level, bringing the estate to a total of 15 hectares in all. Intense fragrances open with notes of thyme and candied lemon … The 2016 Vermentino Sarticola has great character to it, a well-orchestrated body, pleasant richness of flavor and a long finish. The 2016 Vermentino Gladius is pronounced, with lovely notes of candied lemon and dried salt, a fresh structure and a crisp finish.

Maria Donata Bianchi

VIA MEREA, 101
18013 DIANO ARENTINO [IM]
TEL. +39 0183498233
www.aziendaagricolabianchi.it

CELLAR SALES
PRE-BOOKED VISITS
ACCOMMODATION
ANNUAL PRODUCTION 30,000 bottles
HECTARES UNDER VINE 4.00

History changes, new generations push forward and, bolstered by a tried and true cultural heritage, they take the reins. This is what's happening at Maria Donata Bianchi, where she and her husband, Emanuele Trevia, are handing things over to their daughter Marta, and her Portuguese partner, João Ramos. Fresh off their studies in enology and viticulture, as well a months-long experience in New Zealand, they're ready to lead the winery to new frontiers. We should also point out the replanting of their land in Diano Castello with Vermentino and Pigato. The 2016 Pigato offers up vibrant notes of Mediterranean shrub and dried herbs. Its flavor is assertive, with savoriness and character uniting in a long, bold body. The 2016 Vermentino is a fresh, mineral, decidedly pleasant wine of great character. The nose is pronounced, with hints of herbs and Mediterranean pine.

○ Colli di Luni Vermentino Sarticola '16	♟♟	4
● Colli di Luni Eutichiano '16	♟♟	3
○ Colli di Luni Vermentino Gladius '16	♟♟	2*
○ Colli di Luni Vermentino Oro d'Isée '16	♟♟	4
○ Colli di Luni Vermentino Sarticola '15	♟♟♟	4*
● Colli di Luni Eutichiano '15	♟♟	3
○ Colli di Luni Gladius '14	♟♟	2*
● Colli di Luni Terre d'Oriente Ris. '09	♟♟	5
○ Colli di Luni Vermentino Gladius '15	♟♟	2*
○ Colli di Luni Vermentino Oro d'Isée '15	♟♟	4
○ Colli di Luni Vermentino Sarticola '14	♟♟	4
○ Colli di Luni Vermentino Solaris '15	♟♟	3
○ Colli di Luni Vermentino Solaris '14	♟♟	3*
○ Colli di Luni Vermentino Solaris '13	♟♟	2*

○ Riviera Ligure di Ponente Pigato '16	♟♟	3
○ Riviera Ligure di Ponente Vermentino '16	♟♟	3
○ Riviera Ligure di Ponente Pigato '12	♟♟♟	3*
○ Riviera Ligure di Ponente Vermentino '09	♟♟♟	3
○ Riviera Ligure di Ponente Vermentino '07	♟♟♟	3*
○ Riviera Ligure di Ponente Antico Sfizio '15	♟♟	4
○ Riviera Ligure di Ponente Pigato '15	♟♟	3
○ Riviera Ligure di Ponente Pigato '14	♟♟	3*
○ Riviera Ligure di Ponente Vermentino '15	♟♟	3

BioVio

FRAZ. BASTIA
VIA CROCIATA, 24
17031 ALBENGA [SV]
TEL. +39 018220776
www.biovio.it

CELLAR SALES
PRE-BOOKED VISITS
ACCOMMODATION
ANNUAL PRODUCTION 60,000 bottles
HECTARES UNDER VINE 6.00
VITICULTURE METHOD Certified Organic

Not only has this winery benefitted from Aimone Vio's expertise, as well as that of his wife, Chiara. It's also had the management support of the couple's three children. Their personalities are different, and, as a result, so is the winery's vision, though they haven't lost sight of quality as a primary goal. Camilla already takes care of accounting, while Carolina has taken the reins of the agritourism (which will soon open a food service) and Caterina, along with her boyfriend, Vincenzo (both winemakers), are bringing innovation to the production side of things, though without forgetting tradition. The 2016 Pigato Bon in da Bon proved first-rate, with its aromas of rosemary and sage, broom and elderflower, as well as pleasant white fruit. Its quality is indisputable, showing stunning balance and a sublime orchestration of flavor. The 2016 Pigato Ma Renè is close behind, a complex wine with Mediterranean hints, and a pronounced, mineral flavor characterized by pleasant, long freshness.

○ Riviera Ligure di Ponente Pigato Bon in da Bon '16	♟♟♟ 5
○ Riviera Ligure di Ponente Pigato Ma Renè '16	♟♟ 3*
○ Riviera Ligure di Ponente Vermentino Aimone '16	♟♟ 4
○ Riviera Ligure di Ponente Pigato Grand Père '16	♟ 3
● Riviera Ligure di Ponente Rossese U Bastiò '16	♟ 3
○ Riviera Ligure di Ponente Pigato Bon in da Bon '15	♟♟♟ 2*
○ Riviera Ligure di Ponente Vermentino Aimone '11	♟♟♟ 2*
○ Riviera Ligure di Ponente Pigato Ma Renè '15	♟♟ 2*

Samuele Heydi Bonanini

VIA SAN ANTONIO, 72
19017 RIOMAGGIORE [SP]
TEL. +39 0187920959
www.possa.it

CELLAR SALES
PRE-BOOKED VISITS
ANNUAL PRODUCTION 7,000 bottles
HECTARES UNDER VINE 1.50

You need a lot of passion to produce wine in Cinqueterre. The landscape is as difficult as it is spectacular, with its arduous, steep banks lined with dry-stone walls. Samuele works the vineyards using only sulfur and natural products made with seaweed and propolis (there's a honeybee farm on site). But taming these rugged lands is difficult and if the weather is against you too, as happened in June of 2016 when hail damaged 30% of the crop, in addition to passion, you need persistence, determination and character. Their wines show great character, especially their passito dried-grape wines, with Sciacchetrà leading the way. The 2015 Fermentato in Terracotta is a complex, clear amber wine with notes of dried herbs and fruit, nuts and caramel, and a finish that lingers unendingly. The 2012 Riserva is also on the mark, offering up pronounced notes of honey and a nice, long finish.

○ Cinque Terre Sciacchetrà Fermentato in Terracotta '15	♟♟ 8
○ Cinque Terre '16	♟♟ 5
○ Cinque Terre Sciacchetrà Ris. '12	♟♟ 8
● Rinascita Renfursà '16	♟♟ 8
○ Cinque Terre '13	♟♟♟ 5
○ Cinque Terre '12	♟♟♟ 5
○ Cinque Terre '15	♟♟ 5
○ Cinque Terre '14	♟♟ 5
○ Cinque Terre Sciacchetrà '14	♟♟ 8
○ Cinque Terre Sciacchetrà '12	♟♟ 8
○ Cinque Terre Sciacchetrà Ris. '10	♟♟ 8
○ Er Jancu '15	♟♟ 4

Cantine Bregante

VIA UNITÀ D'ITALIA, 47
16039 SESTRI LEVANTE [GE]
TEL. +39 018541388
www.cantinebregante.it

CELLAR SALES
PRE-BOOKED VISITS
ANNUAL PRODUCTION 100,000 bottles
HECTARES UNDER VINE 1.00

As beautiful as Liguria's neatly-organized
plots of land are for tourists, they remain,
for producers, difficult to manage and work.
Sergio Sanguineti divides up his time
between Moneglia, on the coast, and inland
terrain that stretches to Chiavari and
Lavagna, where his small plots of vineyards
(maximum 5000 meters) are situated. It's a
difficult situation to manage, but he's
helped by favorable relationships with small
property owners throughout the area.
Sergio oversees maturation of the grapes,
deciding when and how to harvest. He also
makes the wines themselves. Vibrant on
the palate, with notes of Mediterranean
shrub, dried herbs and white fruit, the
2016 Vermentino is pleasant, with good
richness of flavor and minerality, brought
together in a pronounced body of medium
structure. The 2016 Blanchetta Genovese
may not be complex, but it is subtle and
polished with its hints of ferns and
mountain herbs, chamomile and white fruit.

○ Golfo del Tigullio Portofino Bianchetta Genovese '16	♟♟ 2*
● Golfo del Tigullio Portofino Ciliegiolo '16	♟♟ 2*
● Golfo del Tigullio Portofino Rosso Cà du Diau '16	♟♟ 2*
○ Golfo del Tigullio Portofino Vermentino '16	♟♟ 2*
○ Golfo del Tigullio Baia delle Favole Brut M. Cl.	♟ 5
○ Golfo del Tigullio Portofino Bianco '16	♟ 2
○ Golfo del Tigullio Portofino Moscato '16	♟ 3

Bruna

FRAZ. BORGO
VIA UMBERTO I, 81
18020 RANZO [IM]
TEL. +39 0183318082
www.brunapigato.it

CELLAR SALES
PRE-BOOKED VISITS
ANNUAL PRODUCTION 40,000 bottles
HECTARES UNDER VINE 8.00

Bruna is one of the territory's most
highly-esteemed and important producers.
In fact, its 40,000 bottles are no longer
enough to satisfy markets, such that, in
autumn, only their reserve wines remain.
But, for the moment, Francesca and her
husband, Roberto, aren't looking to grow.
They prefer to focus on quality, with lower
yields and attention to natural cultivation.
The result comes through in the glass, with
wines whose strong territorial bond is easy
to recognize. The 2015 Pigato U Baccan is
wide and vibrant in its aromas, with clear
notes of rosemary and white fruit. The wine
has good balance and a polished, complex
body, and closes in a long, pleasant finish
that's rich in flavor. The 2016 Pigato Majé is
just as afresh, with intense Mediterranean
notes and a well-orchestrated body. The
nose is rich in white fruit and arbutus, which
evolve into peat.

○ Riviera Ligure di Ponente Pigato U Baccan '15	♟♟♟ 5
○ Riviera Ligure di Ponente Pigato Majé '16	♟♟ 3*
● Pulin '15	♟♟ 5
○ Riviera Ligure di Ponente Pigato Le Russeghine '16	♟♟ 4
● Riviera Ligure di Ponente Rossese '16	♟ 3
○ Riviera Ligure di Ponente Pigato U Baccan '13	♟♟♟ 5
○ Riviera Ligure di Ponente Pigato U Baccan '12	♟♟♟ 5
○ Riviera Ligure di Ponente Pigato U Baccan '11	♟♟♟ 5
○ Riviera Ligure di Ponente Pigato U Baccan '07	♟♟♟ 5

Cantine Calleri

LOC. SALEA
REG. FRATTI, 2
17031 ALBENGA [SV]
TEL. +39 018220085
www.cantinecalleri.com

ANNUAL PRODUCTION 55,000 bottles
HECTARES UNDER VINE 6.00

Marcello Calleri, owner of this historic winery, is driven by passion and determination. His wines are made with grapes guaranteed by trusted growers, assuring that the base ingredients are of excellent quality. In the cellar, he personally oversees production, bolstered by his many years of experience by his father, Aldo's, side. His son, Alessio, represents the future. He's already taking his first steps at the Agrarian Institute of Albenga. Marcello Calleri's wines showed a great propensity for quality. The 2016 Vermentino I Müzazzi is a superb wine, intense and sophisticated, with lovely notes of ripe and fresh red fruit that emerge against a backdrop of dried herbs. In the mouth it's rich and full of flavor, perfectly balanced, with a long, savory finish. The 2016 Pigato Saleasco features good minerality and a polished character.

Cheo

VIA BRIGATE PARTIGIANE, 1
19018 VERNAZZA [SP]
TEL. +39 0187821189
bartolocheo@gmail.com

CELLAR SALES
PRE-BOOKED VISITS
ANNUAL PRODUCTION 13,000 bottles
HECTARES UNDER VINE 2.00
SUSTAINABLE WINERY

A new Cinque Terre sets apart Cheo's 2016 vintage. The vineyards are situated in Mavà (Vernazza), along the beautiful, panoramic trail that leads to Monterosso, and connects these two small hamlets, set in the famous Gulf of the Cinque Terre, at just 50 meters from the coast. The vineyard is about half a hectare and features vines from 50 to 80-years-old. The wine is made with only Bosco and Albarola grapes (no Vermentino). The 2016 Cinque Terre Perciò is a young, fresh, vibrant and classic wine, rich in aromas of fresh herbs and white fruit, with notes of Mediterranean shrub. The 2016 Cinque Terre Mavà made its debut, an intense and fresh wine, with notes that are evolved, but also balanced. It's a wine that's still looking for an identity.

○ Riviera Ligure di Ponente Pigato di Albenga Saleasco '16	♀♀ 3*
○ Riviera Ligure di Ponente Vermentino I Müzazzi '16	♀♀ 3*
○ Riviera Ligure di Ponente Vermentino '16	♀♀ 3
○ Riviera Ligure di Ponente Pigato di Albenga '16	♀ 3
○ Riviera Ligure di Ponente Pigato di Albenga '15	♀♀ 3
○ Riviera Ligure di Ponente Pigato di Albenga '14	♀♀ 3*
○ Riviera Ligure di Ponente Pigato di Albenga Saleasco '15	♀♀ 3*

○ Cinque Terre Perciò '16	♀♀ 4
○ Cinque Terre Cheo '16	♀♀ 3
○ Cinque Terre Sciacchetrà '14	♀♀ 8
● Cheo Rosso '15	♀ 4
○ Cinque Terre Mavà '16	♀ 4
○ Cinque Terre Cheo '15	♀♀ 3
○ Cinque Terre Cheo '14	♀♀ 3
○ Cinque Terre Cheo '13	♀♀ 3*
○ Cinque Terre Perciò '15	♀♀ 4
○ Cinque Terre Perciò '14	♀♀ 4
○ Cinque Terre Perciò '13	♀♀ 4
○ Cinque Terre Perciò '12	♀♀ 4
○ Cinque Terre Sciacchetrà '13	♀♀ 8
○ Cinque Terre Sciacchetrà '12	♀♀ 8
○ Cinque Terre Sciacchetrà '11	♀♀ 8

Cantina Cinque Terre

FRAZ. MANAROLA
LOC. GROPPO
19010 RIOMAGGIORE [SP]
TEL. +39 0187920435
www.cantinacinqueterre.com

PRE-BOOKED VISITS
ANNUAL PRODUCTION 200,000 bottles
HECTARES UNDER VINE 45.00

2016 saw a brutal hailstorm that caused
20% of the crop to be lost. Fortunately, the
200 grower-suppliers' plots aren't
concentrated in one area, but are, rather,
spread out on the steep slopes that sharply
descend to the sea, thus the damage was
limited. The producer still has Matteo
Bonanini for its president, Gianfranco Vita
as its winemaker, agronomist and
cellarman, and Ivano Rollandi as
vice-president. The 2016 Cinque Terre
Costa da Posa proved excellent, with a
vibrant aromatic profile featuring
fragrances of thyme, rosemary and citrus.
The palate is enriched by white fruit and
gives way to an almondy finish. The body is
pronounced, pleasant, well-structured. The
2015 Sciacchetrà also deserves a mention.
A wine that is antique gold and amber in
color, it offers up hints of quince and a
bold, rich, long palate.

Fontanacota

FRAZ. PONTI
VIA PROVINCIALE, 137
18100 PORNASSIO [IM]
TEL. +39 3339807442
www.fontanacota.it

CELLAR SALES
PRE-BOOKED VISITS
ANNUAL PRODUCTION 40,000 bottles
HECTARES UNDER VINE 6.00

A new wine has entered Fontanacota's
selection. It's a Vermentino Superiore
Barbazena 2015, made with grapes
cultivated in Fontanacota, in Val Trino, an
area that borders Dolcedo, and rests at
about 100 meters above sea level. After the
harvest, the grapes are fermented in
mid-sized casks and, after racking, they go
back into the barrels, where they stay for
the entire year (per the requisites of the
'Superiore' appellation). It's the first year,
and only 600 bottles were produced.
They hit the market in spring of 2017.
The 2016 Pigato is delicate, with fresh,
Mediterranean notes and white fruit.
The body is soft, intriguing, pleasing.
The 2016 Vermentino was just as satisfying,
with a palate that features strokes of
mineral and iodine, good acidity and a long,
fresh finish. The 2015 Vermentino
Superiore, a wine that's still trying to come
into its own, features balsamic and peaty
notes that give way to imperious wood.

○ Cinque Terre Costa da Posa '16	♙♙	3*
○ Cinque Terre '16	♙♙	2*
○ Cinque Terre Costa de Campu '16	♙♙	3
○ Cinque Terre Pergole Sparse '16	♙♙	3
○ Cinque Terre Sciacchetrà '15	♙♙	6
○ Cinque Terre Costa da Posa '14	♙♙	3
○ Cinque Terre Costa da' Posa '15	♙♙	3
○ Cinque Terre Costa de Sèra '14	♙♙	3
○ Cinque Terre Pergole Sparse '15	♙♙	4
○ Cinque Terre Sciacchetrà '13	♙♙	6
○ Cinque Terre Sciacchetrà '12	♙♙	6
○ Cinque Terre Sciacchetrà '11	♙♙	6

○ Riviera Ligure di Ponente Pigato '16	♙♙	3
○ Riviera Ligure di Ponente Vermentino '16	♙♙	3
● Ormeasco di Pornassio '16	♙	3
○ Ormeasco di Pornassio Sciac-trà '16	♙	3
○ Riviera Ligure di Ponente Vermentino Sup. Barbazenà '15	♙	3
○ Riviera Ligure di Ponente Pigato '11	♙♙♙	3*
● Pornassio '15	♙♙	3
● Pornassio Sup. '12	♙♙	3
○ Riviera Ligure di Ponente Pigato '15	♙♙	3*
○ Riviera Ligure di Ponente Pigato '14	♙♙	3*
○ Riviera Ligure di Ponente Pigato '13	♙♙	3*
○ Riviera Ligure di Ponente Vermentino '15	♙♙	3*
○ Riviera Ligure di Ponente Vermentino '14	♙♙	3

Giacomelli

VIA PALVOTRISIA, 134
19030 CASTELNUOVO MAGRA [SP]
TEL. +39 3496301516
www.azagricolagiacomelli.it

CELLAR SALES
PRE-BOOKED VISITS
ANNUAL PRODUCTION 85,000 bottles
HECTARES UNDER VINE 9.00
SUSTAINABLE WINERY

Starting this year, Roberto Petacchi has a new, young vineyard at his disposal, one that's already started offering up its first fruit. The vineyard grows within the walls of a medieval castle (certified back to 1711) on red terrain. It's been brought back to life and has already seen its first season. Once fermented, these Vermentino grapes will stay in small wood barrels until 2018. A limited number of bottles will then be put on the market, thus giving rise to a new, choice selection. With the new plot, the Giacomelli estate has come to comprise nine hectares. The 2016 Vermentino Pianacce offers up notes of ripe white fruit. In the mouth, we can appreciate all its elegance, conferred by a pleasant warmth, well-orchestrated freshness and great richness of flavor. The 2016 Paduletti is just behind, a fresh wine with vibrant, saline notes and hints of Mediterranean shrub. The body is enticing, succulent, while its finish shows good character.

○ Colli di Luni Vermentino Pianacce '16	🍷🍷 2*
○ Colli di Luni Bianco Paduletti '16	🍷🍷 2*
⊙ Gorgonia Rosato '16	🍷🍷 2*
○ Colli di Luni Vermentino Boboli '15	🍷🍷 4
○ Colli di Luni Vermentino Boboli '13	🍷🍷 4
○ Colli di Luni Vermentino Boboli '11	🍷🍷 4
○ Colli di Luni Vermentino Pianacce '15	🍷🍷 2*
○ Colli di Luni Vermentino Pianacce '14	🍷🍷 2*

La Ginestraia

VIA STERIA
18100 CERVO [IM]
TEL. +39 3272683692
www.laginestraia.com

ANNUAL PRODUCTION 50,000 bottles
HECTARES UNDER VINE 7.00

Through painstaking work and vineyard management, Marco Brangero, and his collaborator, Mauro Leporieri (who deals with sales) have affirmed the quality of their wines. The estate is characterized by two large pieces of land, both in the province of Savona. One is in Arnasco di Albenga, and comprises three hectares, while the other is in Ortovero, and spans four hectares. The latter features three hectares of terrain (around Villa Rolandi Ricci) that give rise to their Riviera Ligure di Ponente Pigato Via Maestra, a wine made from extremely old, head-trained vines, which bestow complexity and structure while still maintaining a pleasant freshness. The 2015 Pigato Via Maestra is intense and brilliant in color, fresh and complex in flavor. It offers us graceful, warm notes of dried herbs and tobacco, with a body that is leisurely and round. The 2016 Pigato Le Marige offers notes of white fruit and aromatic herbs, and a savory, mineral body.

○ Riviera Ligure di Ponente Pigato Via Maestra '15	🍷🍷 3*
○ Riviera Ligure di Ponente Pigato '16	🍷🍷 3
○ Riviera Ligure di Ponente Pigato Le Marige '16	🍷🍷 3
○ Riviera Ligure di Ponente Vermentino '16	🍷🍷 3
○ Riviera Ligure di Ponente Pigato Le Marige '15	🍷🍷🍷 3*
○ Riviera Ligure di Ponente Pigato '15	🍷🍷 3*
○ Riviera Ligure di Ponente Pigato Via Maestra '14	🍷🍷 3*
○ Riviera Ligure di Ponente Vermentino '15	🍷🍷 3
○ Riviera Ligure di Ponente Vermentino '14	🍷🍷 3

Ka' Manciné

FRAZ. SAN MARTINO
VIA MACIURINA, 7
18036 SOLDANO [IM]
TEL. +39 339 3965477
www.kamancine.it

CELLAR SALES
PRE-BOOKED VISITS
ANNUAL PRODUCTION 20,000 bottles
HECTARES UNDER VINE 3.00

While David Casini, a Tuscan with extensive experience in France, has entered the winery as its new enologist, Maurizio Angosso continues to stay true to the territory, pursuing ancient flavors through reduced destemming, and continued quality. The winery is headquartered in Soldano, a small, sheltered hamlet on the bank of the Verbone river, in a landscape that's both picturesque and difficult to cultivate, as is often the case in Liguria. The 2016 Dolceacqua Beragna has a vibrant, high-impact body, with lovely notes of tobacco and spices. These are well-complemented by a rich, soft palate and the development of its tannic weave. The 2016 Dolceacqua Galeae also delivered for its abundance of red fruit and velvety, silky, pleasantly long body.

● Dolceacqua Beragna '16	♟♟♟ 3*
● Dolceacqua Galeae '16	♟♟ 3*
● Dolceacqua Galeae Angè Ris. '15	♟♟ 3
☉ Sciakk '16	♟ 3
○ Tabaka '16	♟ 3
● Dolceacqua Galeae '13	♟♟♟ 3*
● Dolceacqua Beragna '15	♟♟ 3*
● Dolceacqua Beragna '14	♟♟ 3*
● Dolceacqua Beragna '13	♟♟ 3
● Dolceacqua Galeae '15	♟♟ 3
● Dolceacqua Galeae '14	♟♟ 3
● Dolceacqua Galeae Angè Ris. '14	♟♟ 3*
● Dolceacqua Galeae Angè Ris. '13	♟♟ 3*

Ottaviano Lambruschi

VIA OLMARELLO, 28
19030 CASTELNUOVO MAGRA [SP]
TEL. +39 0187674261
www.ottavianolambruschi.com

CELLAR SALES
PRE-BOOKED VISITS
ANNUAL PRODUCTION 36,000 bottles
HECTARES UNDER VINE 10.00

This year, Fabio Lambruschi is presenting a new wine, the Ottaviano, in honor of his father, the winery's founder and current supervisor. It started with a new idea: choose the best grapes from the various plots and harvest them later, towards the end of October, so as to obtain higher sugar concentrations. For some of the grapes, fermentation calls for prolonged maceration, about seven days, in steel tanks. As far as the rest is concerned, everything is proceeding normally, as their high-profile selection once again demonstrates. The 2016 Vermentino Costa Marina is outstanding, with its fresh notes of great complexity and its strong character. It opens with hints of Mediterranean shrub, broom and tobacco. In the mouth, great harmony reigns over a mineral body, and a long, full-flavored finish. Even the 2016 Maggiore, with its Mediterranean notes and hints of white fruit, proves to be a high-quality wine.

○ Colli di Luni Vermentino Costa Marina '16	♟♟♟ 4*
○ Colli di Luni Vermentino Il Maggiore '16	♟♟ 5
○ Colli di Luni Vermentino '16	♟♟ 3
● Colli di Luni Rosso Maniero '16	♟ 2
○ Colli di Luni Vermentino Costa Marina '11	♟♟♟ 4*
○ Colli di Luni Vermentino Costa Marina '09	♟♟♟ 3
○ Colli di Luni Vermentino Il Maggiore '15	♟♟♟ 5
○ Colli di Luni Vermentino Il Maggiore '14	♟♟♟ 5
○ Colli di Luni Vermentino Il Maggiore '13	♟♟♟ 5
○ Colli di Luni Vermentino Il Maggiore '12	♟♟♟ 4*
○ Colli di Luni Vermentino '15	♟♟ 3*
○ Colli di Luni Vermentino '14	♟♟ 3*
○ Colli di Luni Vermentino Costa Marina '15	♟♟ 4

Cantine Lunae Bosoni

FRAZ. ISOLA DI ORTONOVO
VIA BOZZI, 63
19034 ORTONOVO [SP]
TEL. +39 0187669222
www.cantinelunae.com

CELLAR SALES
PRE-BOOKED VISITS
ANNUAL PRODUCTION 550,000 bottles
HECTARES UNDER VINE 80.00

Cantine Lunae Bosoni has a new vineyard to its name. In 2016, it purchased two-hectare tract of land along the hills between Castelnuovo Magra and Luni (known as Ortonovo until 2016). It's a well-suited area, smack in the middle of the Colli di Luni DOC zone, a single, contiguous plot planted with Vermentino in 2017. The winery continues to grow its estate, but it hasn't lost its traditional network of growers, who remain the producer's true source of strength. New investments in production have become necessary, and they're at a good point in terms of upgrading. If everything goes according to plan, their new cellar will be ready for the 2018 harvest. The 2016 Etichetta Nera affirms its status as a high-quality wine, with its vibrant, sophisticated, polished body. The wine is rich in lovely, citrusy notes and ripe white fruit evolving into caramel. In the mouth, we can appreciate its harmony and great pleasantness. The 2016 Etichetta Grigia is extremely well-crafted, with fragrances of jasmine, white fruit and pleasant notes of citrus.

○ Colli di Luni Vermentino Lunae Et. Nera '16	♟♟♟ 4*
○ Colli di Luni Vermentino Et. Grigia '16	♟♟ 3*
○ Colli di Luni Vermentino Numero Chiuso '13	♟♟ 6
○ Colli di Luni Bianco Fior di Luna '16	♟ 3
● Colli di Luni Rosso Niccolò V '13	♟ 4
○ Colli di Luni Vermentino Albarola '16	♟ 4
⊙ Mea Rosa '16	♟ 3
○ Colli di Luni Vermentino Et. Nera '15	♟♟♟ 4*
○ Colli di Luni Vermentino Et. Nera '14	♟♟♟ 4*
○ Colli di Luni Vermentino Et. Nera '13	♟♟♟ 4*
○ Colli di Luni Vermentino Et. Nera '12	♟♟♟ 4*
○ Colli di Luni Vermentino Et. Nera '11	♟♟♟ 4*
○ Colli di Luni Vermentino Et. Nera '10	♟♟♟ 4
○ Colli di Luni Vermentino Albarola '15	♟♟ 4

Maccario Dringenberg

VIA TORRE, 3
18036 SAN BIAGIO DELLA CIMA [IM]
TEL. +39 0184289947
maccariodringenberg@yahoo.it

CELLAR SALES
PRE-BOOKED VISITS
ANNUAL PRODUCTION 23,000 bottles
HECTARES UNDER VINE 4.00

Giovanna Maccario has always paid close attention to quality, and to her not-so-easily cultivated territory. She's investing in a new vineyard that, for some time, has given rise to a white grape known as 'Malaga' in local dialect. It's a piece of land in San Biagio della Cima, a small municipality in upper Vallecrosia, and the grape is harvested earlier than others, so as to preserve its acidity. It's then used to make the white wine, Amiral, a rarity, made up of other, lesser known, local grapes as well, like Massarda and Rossese. Slowly but surely, such grapes are attracting the attention of other producers, and the market as well. As always, Giovanna Maccario's Dolceaquas are of first-rate quality. This year, they presented a highly pleasing 2016, a brilliant, ruby red wine with fruity notes and an elegant, complex, warm body with good tannic thrust. The 2016 Amiral is also very pleasant, with the wine having come into its own.

● Rossese di Dolceacqua '16	♟♟ 3*
● Rossese di Dolceacqua Sup. Luvaira '15	♟♟ 4
● Rossese di Dolceacqua Sup. Posaù Biamonti '15	♟♟ 5
○ L'Amiral '16	♟♟ 3
● Rossese di Dolceacqua Sup. Posaù '15	♟♟ 3
● Dolceacqua Sup. Vign. Posaù '13	♟♟♟ 3*
● Rossese di Dolceacqua Sup. Vign. Luvaira '07	♟♟♟ 4*
● Rossese di Dolceacqua Sup. Vign. Posaù '10	♟♟♟ 3*
● Rossese di Dolceacqua Sup. Vign. Posaù '08	♟♟♟ 3
● Rossese di Dolceacqua '15	♟♟ 3*
● Rossese di Dolceacqua Sup. Luvaira '14	♟♟ 4
● Rossese di Dolceacqua Sup. Posaù '14	♟♟ 3*

...aixei

...c. Porto
...035 Dolceacqua [IM]
... +39 0184205015
...w.maixei.it

CELLAR SALES
PRE-BOOKED VISITS
ANNUAL PRODUCTION 45,000 bottles
HECTARES UNDER VINE 10.00

...e small plots managed by Maixei's
...ppliers are cultivated at altitudes ranging
...m 100 to 400 meters. And one of the
...ost important duties of Fabio Corradi
...inemaker and director) is identifying and
...rvesting the right vineyards. Giancarlo
...ssini still serves as president, while
...squale Restuccio continues in the roles
... agronomist and vice-president. In terms
... style, we should point out the attention
...id to aging, especially when it comes to
...oving the wine into small wood barrels
...d finding the right balance for doing so.
...e 2015 Dolceacqua Superiore, a wine
...at is both elegant and bold, warm and
...ell-orchestrated, features complex
...ertones of red grape on sea salt, and a
...surely, long finish. The 2016 Dolceacqua
...uperiore Barbadirame offers up marvelous
...d fruit with hints of bark and black
...pper, and an extremely rich palate with a
...atifying aftertaste.

Il Monticello

via Groppolo, 7
19038 Sarzana [SP]
Tel. +39 0187621432
www.ilmonticello.it

CELLAR SALES
PRE-BOOKED VISITS
ACCOMMODATION
ANNUAL PRODUCTION 68,000 bottles
HECTARES UNDER VINE 10.00

You'd need to have studied electrical
engineering, like Alessandro Nero, to go in
and understand all the work Il Monticello
does in the vineyards and cellar. The Neri
family have embraced a biodynamic
approach, in addition to pursuing technical
studies and new experimentations. Their
goal isn't just to follow a certain production
philosophy, or reduce the use of heavy
metals (like copper). Their approach has a
wider scope, embracing a precise system of
agriculture made possible through the right
equipment and environmental controls. The
antique gold-colored 2016 Passito dei Neri
offers a vibrant, very clean palate, with
notes of apricot, dried papaya, and
Mediterranean shrub. Rich, complex
overtones are brought together in a classic
body and a finish that lingers unendingly.
The 2015 Vermentino Poggio Paterno is
vibrant and alive with color. Despite its
traditional style, the wine proves pleasant
and leisurely.

Dolceacqua Sup. '15	♟♟ 4
Dolceacqua Sup. Barbadirame '16	♟♟ 4
Dolceacqua '16	♟ 3
Mistral '16	♟ 4
Dolceacqua '15	♟♟ 3
Dolceacqua '14	♟♟ 3*
Dolceacqua '12	♟♟ 3
Dolceacqua Rossese Sup. '10	♟♟ 4
Dolceacqua Sup. '14	♟♟ 4
Dolceacqua Sup. '13	♟♟ 4
Dolceacqua Sup. '12	♟♟ 4
Dolceacqua Sup. Barbadirame '12	♟♟ 4
Mistral '15	♟♟ 4

⊙ Colli di Luni Rosato Serasuolo '16	♟♟ 2*
○ Passito dei Neri '16	♟♟ 4
● Colli di Luni Rosso Poggio dei Magni Ris. '14	♟ 3
○ Colli di Luni Vermentino Poggio Paterno '15	♟ 3
● Colli di Luni Rosso Poggio dei Magni Ris. '11	♟♟ 3
● Colli di Luni Rosso Rupestro '15	♟♟ 2*
○ Colli di Luni Vermentino '12	♟♟ 3*
○ Colli di Luni Vermentino Groppolo '15	♟♟ 3
○ Colli di Luni Vermentino Groppolo '14	♟♟ 3*
○ Colli di Luni Vermentino Poggio Paterno '14	♟♟ 3*
○ Passito dei Neri '12	♟♟ 4

Conte Picedi Benettini

VIA MAZZINI, 57
19038 SARZANA [SP]
TEL. +39 0187625147
www.picedibenettini.it

CELLAR SALES
PRE-BOOKED VISITS
ACCOMMODATION
ANNUAL PRODUCTION 30,000 bottles
HECTARES UNDER VINE 7.00

Villa Il Chioso is situated in Baccano di Arcola, and is surrounded by a vast hill farmstead of 150 hectares (only 7 of which are dedicated to vineyards). In 2016, they started renovating the historic cellar located under the villa, and purchased new steel tanks to work the grapes. The old estate buildings have also been renovated and are now being used for hospitality. Eugenio Picedi Benettini, an esteemed lawyer from Genova, is increasingly present in the cellar, taking the reins of a winery that has not only historical value; it's also the legacy of a great man and producer, Count Papirio Picedi Benettini. The 2016 Vermentino features lovely, classic notes of Mediterranean herbs and juniper flowers, while rich, fresh, mineral notes come through on the palate, and reemerge in an extremely long finish. The 2016 Vermentino Stemma is also vibrant and pleasant, with fruity flavors and a rich, almondy mouth.

○ Colli di Luni Vermentino '16	♥♥	2*
○ Colli di Luni Vermentino Il Chioso '16	♥♥	3
○ Colli di Luni Vermentino Stemma '16	♥♥	3
⊙ Fattoria di Ceserano '16	♥	2
○ Colli di Luni Vermentino Il Chioso '14	♥♥♥	2*
● Colli di Luni Rosso Villa Il Chioso '15	♀♀	3
○ Colli di Luni Vermentino '15	♀♀	2*
○ Colli di Luni Vermentino '13	♀♀	2*
○ Colli di Luni Vermentino Il Chioso '15	♀♀	3*
○ Colli di Luni Vermentino Il Chioso '13	♀♀	2*
○ Colli di Luni Vermentino Stemma '15	♀♀	3
○ Colli di Luni Vermentino Stemma '14	♀♀	3
○ Colli di Luni Vermentino Stemma '13	♀♀	3
○ Colli di Luni Vermentino Stemma '12	♀♀	3
○ Passito del Chioso '14	♀♀	5

La Pietra del Focolare

LOC. ORTONOVO
FRAZ. ISOLA DI ORTONOVO
VIA ISOLA, 76
19034 ORTONOVO [SP]
TEL. +39 0187662129
www.lapietradelfocolare.it

CELLAR SALES
PRE-BOOKED VISITS
ANNUAL PRODUCTION 30,000 bottles
HECTARES UNDER VINE 6.00
SUSTAINABLE WINERY

La Pietra del Focolare is celebrating its 20 anniversary! The endeavor started almost a kind of game, when Augusto proposed to his cousin, Laura, and her husband, Stefano, to purchase an old vineyard from its elderly, and soon-to-be retired owners. The family had a long tradition in the field, and so it was easy to get set up and follow in their parents' footsteps, renovating the cellar (which was in disrepair, but designe for purposes of wine production), enlargin it and making wine with new enological techniques. Their Vermentino Colli di Luni Augusto is dedicated to the couple's cousi A lot's transpired since then, and, today, th estate has come to comprise 13 small vineyards and 6 hectares of terrain. The 2016 Vermentino Villa Linda is a youthful, vibrant, highly sophisticated wine, with notes of rosemary, citrus and white fruit th come together in a body rich in intense flavor. The Vermentino Augusto 2016 features lovely mineral notes and overtone of rosemary, while the body is pronounced soft and very well-balanced.

○ Colli di Luni Vermentino Sup. Villa Linda '16	♥♥	
○ Colli di Luni Vermentino Augusto '16	♥♥	
○ Colli di Luni Vermentino L'Aura di Sarticola '16	♥♥	
● Colli di Luni Rosso La Merla dal Becco '15	♥	
○ Colli di Luni Vermentino Augusto '15	♀♀	
○ Colli di Luni Vermentino L'Aura di Sarticola '14	♀♀	
○ Colli di Luni Vermentino Solarancio '15	♀♀	
○ Colli di Luni Vermentino Sup. Villa Linda '15	♀♀	
○ Colli di Luni Vermentino Villa Linda '14	♀♀	

oggio dei Gorleri

AZ. DIANO GORLERI
SAN LEONARDO
013 DIANO MARINA [IM]
.. +39 0183495207
ww.poggiodeigorleri.com

CELLAR SALES
RE-BOOKED VISITS
CCOMMODATION
NNUAL PRODUCTION 80,000 bottles
ECTARES UNDER VINE 10.50

e Merano Family continues to invest in its
state, whose area, including leased land
d property, now totals 10 hectares (with
rther prospects for expansion in the next
ree months). This year, two new wines are
so being added their selection. Blu di
are is made with grapes from their
operty, and the bottle features a reworked
esign. The new Rebosso is made with
ranaccia grapes from their Gazzellli
neyards, in the Imperia inland. This year
ill also see expansion of their lovely
gritourism, with the addition of four new
ooms. The 2015 Albium is a superb Pigato.
traw-yellow in color and vibrant, its aromas
xplode with notes of dried herbs, white
uit and pleasant almond. In the mouth it
xhibits harmony, presence, warmth and
ood balance. The 2016 Pigato Cycnus is
lso excellent. A complex and elegant
ine, it exhibits minerality and fresh
chness of flavor.

○ Riviera Ligure di Ponente Pigato Albium '15	♥♥♥ 5
○ Riviera Ligure di Ponente Pigato Cycnus '16	♥♥ 3*
○ Riviera Ligure di Ponente Vermentino Blu di Mare '16	♥♥ 3
○ Riviera Ligure di Ponente Vermentino V. Sorì '16	♥♥ 3
● Ormeasco di Pornassio Peinetti '16	♥ 3
● Riviera Ligure di Ponente Granaccia Rebosso '16	♥ 5
○ Riviera Ligure di Ponente Pigato Albium '13	♥♥♥ 5
○ Riviera Ligure di Ponente Pigato Cycnus '13	♥♥♥ 3*
○ Riviera Ligure di Ponente Pigato Cycnus '12	♥♥♥ 3*

Roberto Rondelli

FRAZ. BRUNETTI, 1
18033 CAMPOROSSO [IM]
TEL. +39 3280348055
rondellivini@gmail.com

CELLAR SALES
PRE-BOOKED VISITS
ACCOMMODATION AND RESTAURANT SERVICE
ANNUAL PRODUCTION 22,000 bottles
HECTARES UNDER VINE 3.50

2016 saw a breath of fresh air at Roberto
Rondelli. First, there was their change in
winemaking consultant, then there was
their vineyards' conversion to organic. The
producer has undertaken a commitment to
natural production, with wines production
through spontaneous fermentation
without clarification. In terms of changes in
their selection, their vineyards are in
expansion, thanks to a new block of about
10,000 plants in Dolceacqua. We'll only see
the effect on production, with their
Dolceacqua Migliarina, in the next years.
The 2014 Dolceacqua Migliarina features
notes of red fruit, dried herbs and sweet
wood that evolve into sensations of licorice
and tobacco. In the mouth, tannic structure
and the warmth of its alcohol dominate, and
give way to a clean, lingering finish. The
richly colored 2016 Pigato Vigna Ciotti
offers ripe fruit and a well-structured body.

● Rossese di Dolceacqua Migliarina '14	♥♥ 3*
○ Riviera Ligure di Ponente Pigato V. Ciotti '16	♥♥ 3
○ Riviera Ligure di Ponente Pigato Arcana Bianco '16	♥ 3
● Rossese di Dolceacqua '16	♥ 3
● Dolceacqua '15	♥♥ 3*
● Dolceacqua Migliarina '13	♥♥ 3
● Dolceacqua Migliarina '12	♥♥ 3
○ Riviera Ligure di Ponente Pigato V. Ciotti '15	♥♥ 3
○ Riviera Ligure di Ponente Pigato V. Ciotti '14	♥♥ 3*
○ Riviera Ligure di Ponente Vermentino '14	♥♥ 3

Terenzuola

VIA VERCALDA, 14
54035 FOSDINOVO [MS]
TEL. +39 0187670387
www.terenzuola.it

PRE-BOOKED VISITS
ANNUAL PRODUCTION 180,000 bottles
HECTARES UNDER VINE 18.00

Terenzuola are celebrating their 25th anniversary by introducing two new wines, called Permano, to their range. In the past, more varieties were planted on the small plots of land, leading to 15 different grapes in their Bianco. Winemaking is carried out in concrete, with spontaneous fermentation and temperature control. Their innovation lies in the nearly one-month-long maceration at low temperatures, followed by a further 8-9 months in concrete to stabilize and age the wine before bottling. Finally, Ivan Giuliani hits the marks and presents an extremely well-crafted wine: the 2016 Vermentino Fosso di Corsano. It has brilliant color, and sophisticated overtones of Mediterranean shrub and fruit. It's savory, elegant and complex in the mouth, and its balanced body proves gratifying. The 2016 Vermentino Vigne Base is excellent, rich in pleasant, flowery notes and nice minerality.

○ Colli di Luni Vermentino Sup. Fosso di Corsano '16	♛♛♛ 3*
○ Colli di Luni Vermentino V. Basse '16	♛♛ 3*
○ Cinque Terre '16	♛♛ 4
● Merla della Miniera '14	♛♛ 4
● Permano Rosso '13	♛♛ 5
○ Colli di Luni Vermentino Sup. Fosso di Corsano '11	♔♔♔ 3*
○ Colli di Luni Vermentino Sup. Fosso di Corsano '15	♔♔ 3
○ Colli di Luni Vermentino Sup. Fosso di Corsano '14	♔♔ 3
○ Colli di Luni Vermentino V. Basse '15	♔♔ 3*
● Merla della Miniera '13	♔♔ 4
● Merla della Miniera '12	♔♔ 4

Terre Bianche

LOC. ARCAGNA
18035 DOLCEACQUA [IM]
TEL. ı 39 010431426
www.terrebianche.com

CELLAR SALES
PRE-BOOKED VISITS
ACCOMMODATION
ANNUAL PRODUCTION 55,000 bottles
HECTARES UNDER VINE 8.50
SUSTAINABLE WINERY

Terre Bianche's production volumes have settled around 60,000 bottles, 35,000 of which are whites derived from the Riviera Ligure di Ponente Vermentino e Pigato appellation (the rest to the territory's famous Dolceacqua). The winery has grown significantly in recent years, and has managed to expand into international markets, from Japan to the U.S., by way of Europe. By now, the producer has earned a reputation for quality, with Filippo and Franco, year after year, affirming the importance of their wines through awards and acclaim. The 2016 vintage saw greater, more polished aromatics with respect to the previous year, primarily in their reds. The vibrant 2016 Dolceacqua is ruby red with brilliant, garnet highlights. It offers great complexity, with notes of violet, red fruit and pepper, while the body is bold and the finish both well-orchestrated and long. The 2015 Pigato Arcana is also vibrant and complex. A wine of great finesse, it features a powerful finish.

○ Riviera Ligure di Ponente Pigato Arcana '15	♛♛ 4
○ Riviera Ligure di Ponente Pigato '16	♛♛ 3
● Rossese di Dolceacqua '16	♛♛ 3
● Rossese di Dolceacqua Bricco Arcagna '15	♛♛ 5
○ Riviera Ligure di Ponente Vermentino '16	♛ 3
● Rossese di Dolceacqua Terrabianca '15	♛ 5
● Dolceacqua Bricco Arcagna '14	♔♔♔ 5
● Dolceacqua Bricco Arcagna '12	♔♔♔ 5
● Rossese di Dolceacqua '12	♔♔♔ 3*
● Rossese di Dolceacqua Bricco Arcagna '09	♔♔♔ 4
● Rossese di Dolceacqua Bricco Arcagna '08	♔♔♔ 5

Il Torchio

VIA DELLE COLLINE, 24
19033 CASTELNUOVO MAGRA [SP]
TEL. +39 3318585633
gildamusetti@gmail.com

CELLAR SALES
PRE-BOOKED VISITS
ACCOMMODATION AND RESTAURANT SERVICE
ANNUAL PRODUCTION 60,000 bottles
HECTARES UNDER VINE 12.00

There haven't been any structural changes at Il Torchio. Gilda and Edoardo, the youngest of the family, are gaining experience, and bringing new life. Gilda's husband, Alessandro Chiesi, a Tuscan sommelier who works in tasting and hospitality, is also on board. With their help, the producer has managed to achieve 80% international sales, a figure that's risen thanks in part to a new importer in New York. The 2016 Vermentino stands out for its vibrant color, as well as exhibiting good structure and marked richness of flavor. Rich in aromas of fresh herbs, elderflower, dandelion and light fruity notes, it offers a pleasant, lasting length. The 2016 Nero also needs room to develop. Its energy and graceful tannins bring elegance to a lengthy finish.

○ Colli di Luni Vermentino '16	♟♟	3
● Il Nero '16	♟♟	4
○ Il Bianco '16	♟	3
○ Stralunato '16	♟	3
● Colli di Luni Rosso Il Torchio '13	♙♙	4
○ Colli di Luni Vermentino '15	♙♙	3
○ Colli di Luni Vermentino '14	♙♙	3*
○ Colli di Luni Vermentino '07	♙♙	3*
○ Colli di Luni Vermentino '06	♙♙	3
○ Colli di Luni Vermentino Il Bianco '14	♙♙	3
○ Colli di Luni Vermentino Il Bianco '13	♙♙	3
○ Colli di Luni Vermentino Il Torchio '13	♙♙	3*
○ Stralunato '15	♙♙	3

Vis Amoris

LOC. CARAMAGNA
S.DA MOLINO JAVÈ, 23
18100 IMPERIA
TEL. +39 3483959569
www.visamoris.it

CELLAR SALES
PRE-BOOKED VISITS
ANNUAL PRODUCTION 24,000 bottles
HECTARES UNDER VINE 3.50
VITICULTURE METHOD Certified Organic
SUSTAINABLE WINERY

Vis Amoris continues to produce wines made only with Pigato, the territory's principal grape. Rossana Zappa and Roberto Tozzi are particularly enamored of sparkling winemaking and, despite reduced global production, they dedicate 4500 bottles to it. Thanks to the malleability of their vineyards, their grapes, which are certified organic, are vinified in various ways: from being worked in steel only, to aging that includes the use of barrique, to sparkling wines, to passito dried-grape wines. In the future, they plan to continue to invest in the variety, while, starting this year, they've started experimenting with prolonged maceration of the grapes and must. The 2015 Pigato Sogno got the most attention this year, with its classic aromas of rosemary and iodine and its flowery notes of acacia blossom and elderflower. Its body is elegant and complex, warm and well-structured, with a pleasant and subtle after-taste. The vintage 2010 Zero offers up intense overtones of the sea, while notes of extreme freshness interpenetrate with toasted bread.

○ Riviera Ligure di Ponente Pigato Sogno '15	♟♟	4
○ Riviera Ligure di Ponente Pigato Verum '16	♟♟	3
○ Riviera Ligure di Ponente Pigato Vis Domè '16	♟	3
○ Vis Amoris Brut M. Cl.	♟	5
○ Vis Amoris Zero M. Cl. '10	♟	5
○ Riviera Ligure di Ponente Pigato Sogno '14	♙♙	4
○ Riviera Ligure di Ponente Pigato Sogno '13	♙♙	4
○ Riviera Ligure di Ponente Pigato Verum '15	♙♙	3

Carlo Alessandri

VIA UMBERTO I, 15
18020 RANZO [IM]
TEL. +39 0183318114
az.alessandricarlo@libero.it

CELLAR SALES
PRE-BOOKED VISITS
ANNUAL PRODUCTION 19,100 bottles
HECTARES UNDER VINE 2.13

○ Riviera Ligure di Ponente Pigato '16   🍷🍷 3
● Pornassio '16   🍷 3
○ Riviera Ligure di Ponente
   Vermentino '16   🍷 2

Riccardo Arrigoni

LOC. MIGLIARINA
VIA SARZANA, 224
19126 LA SPEZIA
TEL. +39 0187504060
www.arrigoni1913.it

CELLAR SALES
PRE-BOOKED VISITS
ACCOMMODATION AND RESTAURANT SERVICE
ANNUAL PRODUCTION 150,000 bottles
HECTARES UNDER VINE 18.00
SUSTAINABLE WINERY

○ Cinque Terre Sciacchetrà
   Rosa di Maggio '16   🍷🍷 8
○ Cinque Terre Tramonti '16   🍷🍷 3
○ Colli di Luni Vermentino V. del Prefetto '16   🍷 3

Bisson

C.SO GIANELLI, 28
16043 CHIAVARI [GE]
TEL. +39 0185314462
www.bissonvini.it

CELLAR SALES
PRE-BOOKED VISITS
ANNUAL PRODUCTION 80,000 bottles
HECTARES UNDER VINE 12.00

○ Portofino Cimixà L'Antico '16   🍷🍷 3
○ Portofino Cimixà Villa Fieschi '16   🍷🍷 4
○ Portofino Vermentino Intrigoso '16   🍷🍷 3

Tenuta Anfosso

C.SO VERBONE, 175
18036 SOLDANO [IM]
TEL. +39 0184209900
www.tenutaanfosso.it

CELLAR SALES
ACCOMMODATION
ANNUAL PRODUCTION 23,000 bottles
HECTARES UNDER VINE 5.30

● Dolceacqua Sup. Poggio Pini '15   🍷🍷 4
● Dolceacqua '15   🍷🍷 4

Berry and Berry

VIA MATTEOTTI, 2
17020 BALESTRINO [SV]
TEL. +39 3332805368
www.berryandberry.it

CELLAR SALES
PRE-BOOKED VISITS
ANNUAL PRODUCTION 8,500 bottles
HECTARES UNDER VINE 2.00

○ Baitinin '16   🍷🍷 4
○ Campoulo '15   🍷🍷 5
● Poggi del Santo '14   🍷🍷 5

Cantine Bondonor

VIA ISOLA ALTA, 53
19034 ORTONOVO [SP]
TEL. +39 3488713641
www.cantinebondonor.it

ANNUAL PRODUCTION 15,000 bottles
HECTARES UNDER VINE 3.00

○ Colli di Luni Vermentino Aegidius
   Vintage '16   🍷🍷 3
○ Colli di Luni Vermentino Lunaris '16   🍷🍷 3
● Atrum '11   🍷 3

alvini

SOLARO, 76/78A
38 SANREMO [IM]
+39 0184660242
w.luigicalvini.com

CELLAR SALES
PRE-BOOKED VISITS
ANNUAL PRODUCTION 50,000 bottles
HECTARES UNDER VINE 3.50

Riviera Ligure di Ponente Pigato '16		🍷🍷 3
Riviera Ligure di Ponente Vermentino '16		🍷 3

I Cerri

VIA GARIBOTTI
19012 CARRO [SP]
TEL. +39 3485102780
www.icerrivaldivara.it

ANNUAL PRODUCTION 8,000 bottles
HECTARES UNDER VINE 1.00

○ Campo Grande '16		🍷🍷 3
○ Cian dei Seri '16		🍷🍷 3
● Fonte Dietro il Sole '16		🍷 3

ajaudo
antina del Rossese

BUNDA
A PROV.LE 7
035 ISOLABONA [IM]
+39 0184208095
w.gajaudo.it

CELLAR SALES
PRE-BOOKED VISITS
ANNUAL PRODUCTION 110,000 bottles
HECTARES UNDER VINE 9.00

Dolceacqua Arcagna '15		🍷🍷 3*
Dolceacqua '16		🍷🍷 3

Guglierame

FRAZ. VILLA
VIA VIA CASTELLO, 4
18024 PORNASSIO [IM]
TEL. +39 3475696718
www.ormeasco-guglierame.it

ANNUAL PRODUCTION 16,000 bottles
HECTARES UNDER VINE 2.50

⊙ Ormeasco Sciac-trà '16		🍷🍷 3
● Ormeasco Sup. '14		🍷🍷 3
● Ormeasco '15		🍷 3

enuta La Ghiaia

FALCINELLO, 127
038 SARZANA [SP]
. +39 0187627307
w.tenutalaghiaia.it

CELLAR SALES
ACCOMMODATION
ANNUAL PRODUCTION 45,000 bottles
HECTARES UNDER VINE 5.50

Colli di Luni Vermentino Atys '15		🍷🍷 3
Colli di Luni Vermentino '16		🍷 3

Podere Grecale

LOC. BUSSANA
VIA CIOUSSE
18038 SANREMO [IM]
TEL. +39 01841955158
www.poderegrecale.it

CELLAR SALES
PRE-BOOKED VISITS
ANNUAL PRODUCTION 18,000 bottles
HECTARES UNDER VINE 3.00

○ Riviera Ligure di Ponente Vermentino '16		🍷🍷 3
○ Riviera Ligure di Ponente Vermentino Maèn '16		🍷🍷 3
○ Riviera Ligure di Ponente Pigato '16		🍷 3

Poggi dell'Elmo

C.SO VERBONE, 135
18036 SOLDANO [IM]
TEL. +39 0184289148
www.poggidellelmo.com

CELLAR SALES
PRE-BOOKED VISITS
ACCOMMODATION AND RESTAURANT SERVICE
ANNUAL PRODUCTION 15,000 bottles
HECTARES UNDER VINE 2.50
SUSTAINABLE WINERY

● Dolceacqua Sup. Vign. Pini '15	♟♟	3*
● Dolceacqua '15	♟♟	3

Rossana Ruffini

VIA TIROLO, 58
19020 BOLANO [SP]
TEL. +39 0187939988
g.brandani@libero.it

ANNUAL PRODUCTION 10,000 bottles
HECTARES UNDER VINE 3.00

○ Colli di Luni Vermentino Costa Tirolo '16	♟♟	2*
○ Colli di Luni Vermentino Portolano '16	♟	2

La Vecchia Cantina

FRAZ. SALEA
VIA CORTA, 3
17031 ALBENGA [SV]
TEL. +39 3393733641
www.lavecchiacantinacalleri.it

CELLAR SALES
PRE-BOOKED VISITS
ANNUAL PRODUCTION 15,000 bottles
HECTARES UNDER VINE 4.00

○ Riviera Ligure di Ponente Albenganese Pigato '16	♟♟	3
○ Riviera Ligure di Ponente Albenganese Vermentino '16	♟♟	3

Podere Lavandaro

VIA CASTIGLIONE
54035 FOSDINOVO [MS]
TEL. +39 018768202
www.poderelavandaro.it

CELLAR SALES
PRE-BOOKED VISITS
ANNUAL PRODUCTION 22,000 bottles
HECTARES UNDER VINE 4.00

● Vermentino Nero '16	♟♟
● Vignanera '15	♟♟
○ Colli di Luni Vermentino '16	♟
☉ Merlarosa '16	♟

Natale Sassarini

LOC. PIAN DEL CORSO 1
19016 MONTEROSSO AL MARE [SP]
TEL. +39 0187818063
www.sassarini5terre.it

○ Cinque Terre Bucce '16	♟♟
○ Cinque Terre Sciacchetrà '15	♟♟
○ Cinque Terre '16	♟
○ Cinque Terre Cian du Corsu '16	♟

Zangani

LOC. PONZANO SUPERIORE
VIA GRAMSCI, 46
19037 SANTO STEFANO DI MAGRA [SP]
TEL. +39 0187632406
www.zangani.it

CELLAR SALES
PRE-BOOKED VISITS
ACCOMMODATION AND RESTAURANT SERVICE
ANNUAL PRODUCTION 40,000 bottles
HECTARES UNDER VINE 5.00

○ Marfi Bianco '16	♟♟
○ Boceda '16	♟♟
○ Mortedo '16	♟♟
● Montale '16	♟

LOMBARDY

For most people, Lombardy is more of an industrial region than an agricultural one, and Milan's role as the nation's economic capital surely doesn't help change that image. But Lombardy, with its many terroir, from the Padana plains to the Alps, the river Po and the great lakes of Garda and Iseo, is endowed with an extraordinary agricultural patrimony, especially when it comes to vine growing. Moreover, the region has a knack for transforming small family operations into thriving businesses that grow over time, creating a network around them that lifts the entire territory. This holds for the wine sector as well. The best example is, in this case, probably, Franciacorta. It's an extraordinary territory for wine that, until 1961, was nowhere to be found on maps of Italian winemaking districts. And yet, today, the appellation is among the nation's best. And it's Franciacorta that, for the second year in a row, gave rise to a record number of top wines, with 23 awards going to the territory. Nine of these are cuvée blends, many of which were made by established producers, though we're keen to point out a newcomer, Lantieri de Paratico's excellent 2013 Arcadia Brut. Oltrepò Pavese, another great territory for sparkling wines, follows with its eight wines recognized, especially Pinot Nero. Two excellent rosés, Monsupello's and Calatroni's, are in the mix, as well as five other wines in which red grapes play a leading role, including Bertè & Cordini's pleasant new entry. Andrea Picchioni's excellent Pinot Nero Arfena also made its first appearance in the prestigious club. Lombardy's third large winemaking block is Valtellina. We tasted a number of exciting wines and gave awards to five of them, including none-other-than the 'Red Wine of the Year', Ar.Pe.Pe.'s 2007 Sassella Rocce Rosso Riserva, a sumptuous, captivating wine that will take your breath away. Our list closes with another classic from a successful appellation, Ca' Maiol's 2016 Lugana Molin, a wine of exemplary freshness and cleanness. These were the highest honors, but if you look through these pages you'll find plenty of runners up that will surprise you for their vibrant fragrances and elegance.

Marchese Adorno

VIA GARLASSOLO, 30
27050 RETORBIDO [PV]
TEL. +39 0383374404
www.marcheseadorno-wines.it

CELLAR SALES
PRE-BOOKED VISITS
ANNUAL PRODUCTION 250,000 bottles
HECTARES UNDER VINE 85.00

The winery has been in the Cattaneo Adorno family since 1834. 10 years ago, the the marquis Marcello decided to invest in it, renovating the cellar and their 85 hectares of vineyards (with a focus on Oltrepò Occidentale's most traditional varieties). This year, two of their flagship wines are absent (the Barbera and Pinot Nero) because they've chosen to let them age for another year. Simultaneously, they've launched a new initiative for the production of 'Metodo Classico' sparklers, the fruits of which we'll see in two or three years. It's uncharitable to speak of the 'second rank' here. The 2015 Pinot Nero Brugherio is varietal, with aromas of fruit and a delicately bitter finish. The 2016 Costa del Sole is a fragrant Bonarda, with nice intensity and suppleness. The 2015 Cliviano, a Merlot dear to the marquis, offers up substance and spicy notes. The 2016 Barbera Poggio Marino and Pinot Grigio Dama d'Oro are quite varietal in their respective categories, fresh and drinkable.

● Cliviano '15	♥♥ 3
● OP Bonarda Vivace Costa del Sole '16	♥♥ 2*
● OP Pinot Nero Brugherio '15	♥♥ 2*
● Barbera Poggio Marino '16	♥ 3
○ OP Pinot Grigio Dama d'Oro '16	♥ 3
● Cliviano '14	♥♥ 3
● Cliviano '13	♥♥ 3
● OP Barbera V. del Re '14	♥♥ 4
● OP Barbera V. del Re '12	♥♥ 4
● OP Bonarda Vivace Costa del Sole '15	♥♥ 2*
● OP Pinot Nero Brugherio '14	♥♥ 2*
● OP Pinot Nero Rile Nero '13	♥♥ 5
● OP Pinot Nero Rile Nero Riserva Privata '10	♥♥ 5
○ OP Riesling Sup. Arcolaio '13	♥♥ 3*

F.lli Agnes

VIA CAMPO DEL MONTE, 1
27040 ROVESCALA [PV]
TEL. +39 038575206
www.fratelliagnes.it

CELLAR SALES
PRE-BOOKED VISITS
ANNUAL PRODUCTION 120,000 bottles
HECTARES UNDER VINE 21.00

Passion, knowledge and determination: these are the characteristics that best define the Agnes brothers, Sergio and Cristiano. They may be men of few words, but they have credentials to back them up. They've inherited a family tradition that began with their father, Luigi, and their uncle Albert, who in their day identified the best terrain and Pignola clones. At the same time, Rovescala is wine country for Bonarda and so the Agnes brothers interpret them both in every possible way. Here, native yeasts aren't just some fashion trend, they're used for the purpose of making wines with personality. This year, Fratelli Agnes decided to present only some of their Bonarda Vivaci, feeling that their still wines still weren't ready. The 2016 Bonarda Campo del Monte isn't so far from the one that earned a Tre Bicchieri in 2016: pulp, body, close-focused fruit, balsamic overtones, depth and spot on residual sweetness. The 2016 Cresta del Ghiffi is, as usual, more semi-dry, very heady, with clear, precise fruit. The 2016 Vernietta is a sweet, lively, flavorsome Croatina.

● OP Bonarda Vivace Campo del Monte '16	♥♥ 2*
● OP Bonarda Vivace Cresta del Ghiffi '16	♥♥ 2*
● Croatina Vernietta '16	♥ 2
⊙ Pinot Nero Brut Rosé Martinotti Pindesa	♥ 3
● OP Bonarda Vivace Campo del Monte '15	♥♥♥ 2*
● Loghetto '14	♥♥ 3
● OP Bonarda Millennium '13	♥♥ 4
● OP Bonarda Millennium '11	♥♥ 4
● OP Bonarda Millennium '10	♥♥ 4
● OP Bonarda Vivace Cresta del Ghiffi '15	♥♥ 2*
● Poculum '12	♥♥ 4
● Possessione del Console '15	♥♥ 3

Anteo

LOC. CHIESA
27040 ROCCA DE' GIORGI [PV]
TEL. +39 038599073
www.anteovini.it

CELLAR SALES
PRE-BOOKED VISITS
ANNUAL PRODUCTION 200,000 bottles
HECTARES UNDER VINE 27.00

Ettore Piero and Antonella Cribellati are now managing the winery founded by their father, Trento, in one of the Oltrepò's best-suited areas for winemaking. Here, in Valle Scuropasso (where the river Versa begins), the vineyards can reach up to 400 meters above sea level. It's an area that lends warmth to the Pinot Nero cultivated, giving rise to almost Mediterranean sparkling wines. These age at length in their bottles, which rest on their splendid underground cellar's hand riddling racks. The 2009 Riserva del Poeta is full-flavored and generous, with nice sparkle, balsamic notes, well-sustained acidity, and a clean finish. The 2011 Brut Tradition and the Cruasé have an interesting base, made with Pinot Nerot, that's both full and mineral, even if their respective liqueur isn't particularly balanced. The Martinotti, made with Bonarda and Moscato, is pleasant in its simplicity.

○ OP Pinot Nero Brut Riserva del Poeta '09	♟ 6
○ La Volpe e l'Uva '16	♟ 3
● OP Bonarda Vivace Staffolo '16	♟ 2
⊙ OP Cruasé	♟ 4
○ OP Pinot Nero Brut Martinotti	♟ 2
○ OP Pinot Nero Brut Tradition '11	♟ 3
○ OP Pinot Nero Brut Nature Écru '03	♟♟♟ 4
● OP Bonarda Vivace Staffolo '15	♟♟ 2*
○ OP Pinot Nero Brut Riserva del Poeta '08	♟♟ 6
○ OP Pinot Nero Brut Riserva del Poeta '07	♟♟ 6
○ OP Pinot Nero Nature Écru '10	♟♟ 5
○ OP Spumante Brut Tradition '09	♟♟ 4

Antica Fratta

LOC. MONTICELLI BRUSATI
VIA FONTANA, 11
25040 MONTICELLI BRUSATI [BS]
TEL. +39 030652068
www.anticafratta.it

CELLAR SALES
PRE-BOOKED VISITS
ANNUAL PRODUCTION 350,000 bottles
HECTARES UNDER VINE 4.00

The Monticelli Brusati's Antica Fratta is situated in a lovely 19th century palace, renovated in the late 1960s by the Ziliani family. By virtue of its picturesque underground cellars, which form a Greek cross, it's known as 'the Cantinon' by the locals. Today, the palace, which was once the residence of a wealthy wine merchant, hosts various events and receptions. The winery operates independently of the Guido Berlucchi, and cultivates a small estate of vineyards (in addition to the grapes that it purchases). The 2013 Essence Nature tasted this year affirms the producer's reputation. This blend of Chardonnay and Pinot Nero (30%) has a nice, brilliant color with copper hints, and extremely delicate perlage. A vibrant bouquet offers up red and black fruit, and gives way to a crisp, creamy, zesty and uncompromising palate. The 2013 Brut is also excellent, with its hints of green tea and Japanese medlar.

○ Franciacorta Nature Essence '13	♟♟ 5
○ Franciacorta Brut Essence '13	♟♟ 5
○ Franciacorta Essence '08	♟♟ 5
○ Franciacorta Essence Nature '09	♟♟ 5
○ Franciacorta Extra Brut Quintessence Ris. '07	♟♟ 7
○ Franciacorta Extra Brut Quintessence Ris. '07	♟♟ 7
○ Franciacorta Nature Essence '11	♟♟ 5
○ Franciacorta Rosé Essence '11	♟♟ 5
○ Franciacorta Rosé Essence '10	♟♟ 5
○ Franciacorta Satèn Essence '11	♟♟ 5
○ Franciacorta Satèn Essence '11	♟♟ 5
○ Franciacorta Satèn Essence '10	♟♟ 5

Antica Tesa

LOC. MATTINA
VIA MERANO, 28
25080 BOTTICINO [BS]
TEL. +39 0302691500

CELLAR SALES
PRE-BOOKED VISITS
ANNUAL PRODUCTION 40,000 bottles
HECTARES UNDER VINE 10.00

Pierangelo Noventa and his family have been working their vineyards in Botticino passionately for more than 40 years. They're in the small, but acclaimed appellation of Lombardy, and their vineyards grow at altitudes of 450 meters, with ideal exposures (as well as offering a lovely panoramic view). Botticino is famous for its prestigious marble, but its red wines (made with Sangiovese, Barbera, Marzemino and Schiava Gentile) display character and finesse. This year, Pierangelo and his daughter, Alessandra, are drawing on the agronomic and winemaking expertise of Carlo Ferrini, and the 2015 vintage that we tasted impressed for its expressive finesse. The Gobbio, in particular, distinguished itself for its freshness and nice, spicy character (in part by virtue of the choice to not use dried grapes in the blend). It's one of the best reds in the region.

● Botticino Gobbio '15	♟♟ 5
● Botticino Pià de la Tesa '15	♟♟ 3
● Botticino Colle degli Ulivi '15	♟ 2
● Botticino Pià de la Tesa '12	♟♟ 3
● Botticino Pià de la Tesa '11	♟♟ 3
● Botticino Pià de la Tesa '10	♟♟ 3
● Botticino Pià de la Tesa '09	♟♟ 3
● Botticino Pià de la Tesa '08	♟♟ 3*
● Botticino V. degli Ulivi '07	♟♟ 2*
● Botticino V. del Gobbio '11	♟♟ 5
● Botticino V. del Gobbio '10	♟♟ 5
● Botticino V. del Gobbio '09	♟♟ 5
● Botticino V. del Gobbio '08	♟♟ 5
● Botticino V. del Gobbio 50 '12	♟♟ 5

Antinori - Tenuta Montenisa

FRAZ. CALINO
VIA PAOLO VI, 62
25046 CAZZAGO SAN MARTINO [BS]
TEL. +39 0307750838
www.montenisa.it

PRE-BOOKED VISITS
ANNUAL PRODUCTION 300,000 bottles
HECTARES UNDER VINE 60.00

The Florentine Antinori family have a long tradition in making 'Metodo Classico' sparkling wines, which they've been carrying on successfully since the last century. In 1999 they made an agreement with the Maggi family, in Franciacorta, to purchase the the lovely estate of Calino. After renovation of the vineyards and cellar, Tenuta Montenisa was born, and in just a few years it has established itself as one of the most interesting producers in the appellation. Their selection is constituted of two lines, both labeled 'Machesi Antinori': their classic wines and those only produced during the best years. The 2009 Blanc de Noirs Riserva Conte Aimo testifies to the quality of the producer's wines. It's one of Franciacorta's best Pinot Neros, exhibiting elegance, finesse and fruit, acquired through long fermentation on the lees. Among the non-vintages, the Brut Cuvée Royale deserves attention, with its evocative bouquet of Mediterranean herbs and white fruit, as does the soft and succulent Blanc de Blancs.

○ Franciacorta Brut Conte Aimo Ris. '09	♟♟ 8
○ Franciacorta Brut Blanc de Blancs	♟♟ 5
○ Franciacorta Brut Cuvée Royale	♟♟ 5
⊙ Franciacorta Brut Rosé	♟ 5
○ Franciacorta Brut Conte Aimo '07	♟♟ 8
○ Franciacorta Brut Contessa Camilla Maggi '02	♟♟ 7
○ Franciacorta Brut Contessa Maggi '06	♟♟ 7
○ Franciacorta Brut Contessa Maggi Ris. '07	♟♟ 7
○ Franciacorta Brut Satèn Donna Cora '11	♟♟ 6
○ Franciacorta Satèn '09	♟♟ 6
○ Franciacorta Satèn '06	♟♟ 6
○ Franciacorta Satèn '04	♟♟ 6
○ Franciacorta Satèn '04	♟ 6
○ Franciacorta Satèn '03	♟♟ 6
○ Franciacorta Satèn '02	♟♟ 6

Ar.Pe.Pe.

VIA DEL BUON CONSIGLIO, 4
23100 SONDRIO
TEL. +39 0342214120
www.arpepe.com

CELLAR SALES
PRE-BOOKED VISITS
ANNUAL PRODUCTION 80,000 bottles
HECTARES UNDER VINE 13.00

The Pelizzati Perego family continue to move in the right direction. Their wines display an airy, defined style characteristic of the purity and lightness of the mountains (qualities that are gaining popularity in Italy and the world). Isabella, Guido and Emanuela, the fifth generation of producers, have wisely chosen to focus on innovation to avoid the discrepancies of the past. The two Sassella Riservas are exemplary and elegant. The former is the 2007 Rocce Rosse, a wine of rare complexity with notes of tobacco leaf, ash, and nuances of licorice, tar and ripe plums. It's rich and succulent on the palate, with notable freshness, vibrant acidity and a long, first-rate finish. For us it's the 'Red of the Year'. The latter, the 2009 Ultimi Raggi, is intense, with very elegant aromas, notes of tobacco leaf, rhubarb and dried flowers. The mouth is austere, full, while its lengthy finish is both sophisticated and gently original.

● Valtellina Sup. Sassella Rocce Rosse Ris. '07	▼▼▼	8
● Valtellina Sup. Grumello Rocca De Piro '12	▼▼	5
● Valtellina Sup. Sassella Ultimi Raggi Ris. '09	▼▼	8
● Rosso di Valtellina '15	▼▼	4
● Valtellina Sup. Inferno Fiamme Antiche '12	▼▼	6
● Valtellina Sup. Sassella Stella Retica '12	▼▼	5
● Valtellina Sup. Grumello Buon Consiglio Ris. '07	♈♈♈	6
● Valtellina Sup. Sassella Stella Retica Ris. '10	♈♈♈	5
● Valtellina Sup. Sassella Stella Retica Ris. '06	♈♈♈	4*

Avanzi

VIA TREVISAGO, 19
25080 MANERBA DEL GARDA [BS]
TEL. +39 0365551013
www.avanzi.net

CELLAR SALES
PRE-BOOKED VISITS
ANNUAL PRODUCTION 600,000 bottles
HECTARES UNDER VINE 60.00

Founded in 1931 by Giovanni Avanzi, the winery is now on its third generation of Avanzi family management. It's an inspiring producer that currently has more than 70 hectares of vineyards and olive groves at its disposal (these are divided into four plots, comprising some of the area's most important terrain). In 2007, the winery was completely renovated, with the latest equipment and picturesque underground cellars. They use only their own grapes. Their philosophy embraces each single terroir. Their flagship wines start with the Giovanni Avanzi line, dedicated to the winery's founder. The 2016 Dorobianco is a blend of Riesling, Chardonnay and Pinot Bianco. It's a fresh, flowery wine with notes of chamomile and a linear unfolding of flavor. The 2016 Chiaretto is an explosion of strawberry and raspberry, while the 2016 Lugana di Sirmione sees a nice balance between flowers and white fruit.

○ Dorobianco Avanzi '16	▼▼	2*
○ Lugana di Sirmione Giovanni Avanzi '16	▼▼	2*
⊙ Valtènesi Chiaretto Giovanni Avanzi '16	▼▼	2*
⊙ Garda Brut Rosé Martinotti	▼	2
● Garda Cl. Groppello Predelli Giovanni Avanzi '16	▼	2
● Garda Cl. Groppello '14	♈♈	3
● Garda Cl. Groppello Giovanni Avanzi '13	♈♈	2*
○ Lugana Borghetta Ris. '13	♈♈	3
○ Lugana di Sirmione '15	♈♈	2*
○ Lugana di Sirmione '14	♈♈	2*
● Rebo Montecorno '13	♈♈	3

Ballabio

via San Biagio, 32
27045 Casteggio [PV]
Tel. +39 0383805728
www.ballabio.net

CELLAR SALES
PRE-BOOKED VISITS
ANNUAL PRODUCTION 100,000 bottles
HECTARES UNDER VINE 60.00

Named after its founder, Angelo Ballabio (Est. 1905) is now managed by Filippo Nevelli and situated in one of the loveliest and most efficient winemaking facilities in all of Oltrepò Pavese (especially when it comes to sparklers). The goal is to make a wide range of sparkling wines, gradually eschewing other categories. Their new arrivals, which continue to enjoy the contribution of the skilled expert, Carlo Casavecchia, are a good harbinger of things to come. Once again, the Farfalla gets top marks. This 'Metodo Classico' sparkler is establishing itself as among the best Pinot Neros in the area. It's creamy, close-focused, savory and linear, with accents of red fruit, citrus, aromatic herbs and an elegant, lingering finish. And the 'Metodo Classico' selection is enriched by the Zero Dosage, a drier wine that nevertheless exhibits its own softness, while the aromatic profile is similar to Extra Brut. The Cruasé does more with fruitiness, while the Clastidium proves varietal, offering up substance and personality.

○ Extra Brut Farfalla	▼▼▼ 4*
○ Brut Zero Dosage Farfalla	▼▼ 4
⊙ OP Cruasé Farfalla	▼▼ 4
○ Pinot Grigio Clastidium '16	▼▼ 2*
● Narbusto '15	▼ 3
● OP Bonarda V. delle Cento Pertiche '16	▼ 3
● OP Bonarda V. delle Cento Pertiche '15	▽▽ 3
● OP Bonarda V. delle Cento Pertiche '13	▽▽ 3
● OP Bonarda V. delle Cento Pertiche '11	▽▽ 2*
● OP Bonarda V. delle Cento Pertiche '10	▽▽ 2*
○ OP Pinot Grigio Clastidium '15	▽▽ 3
⊙ OP Pinot Nero Brut Cruasé '07	▽▽ 4

Barone Pizzini

via San Carlo, 14
25050 Provaglio d'Iseo [BS]
Tel. +39 0309848311
www.baronepizzini.it

CELLAR SALES
PRE-BOOKED VISITS
ACCOMMODATION
ANNUAL PRODUCTION 290,000 bottles
HECTARES UNDER VINE 55.00
VITICULTURE METHOD Certified Organic
SUSTAINABLE WINERY

Not only is Barone Pizzini one of Fraciacorta's best wineries. Thanks to the commitment of its owners, and the passionate guidance of Silvano Brescianini, it's also one of Italy's most interesting producers, at the vanguard when it comes to organic and biodynamic cultivation, as well as sustainability. If you need convincing, it's enough to taste their excellent blends or visit their modern cellar (which is exemplary of sustainable architecture and respect for the territory). And these qualities don't only apply to their Franciacorta branch. They're also evident at their satellite facilities in Marche (Pievalta) and Maremma (Ghiaccioforte). A Tre Bicchieri for 2013 Naturae isn't news anymore. It has class, freshness and a soft, elegant finish featuring aromas of fruit and sweet biscotti. The Rosé and Brut Animante are also excellent

○ Franciacorta Brut Naturae '13	▼▼▼ 5
○ Curtefranca Polzina Bianco '16	▼▼ 3
○ Franciacorta Brut Animante	▼▼ 5
⊙ Franciacorta Extra Brut Rosé	▼▼ 5
○ Franciacorta Brut Golf 1927	▼ 5
○ Franciacorta Brut Satèn	▼ 5
○ Franciacorta Brut Naturae '11	▽▽▽ 5
○ Franciacorta Brut Nature '10	▽▽▽ 5
○ Franciacorta Brut Nature '09	▽▽▽ 5
○ Franciacorta Brut Nature '08	▽▽▽ 5
○ Franciacorta Non Dosato Bagnadore Ris. '09	▽▽▽ 6
○ Franciacorta Brut Bagnadore Ris. '08	▽▽ 5
○ Franciacorta Brut Naturae '12	▽▽ 5
○ Franciacorta Satèn '11	▽▽ 5

★★Bellavista

VIA BELLAVISTA, 5
25030 ERBUSCO [BS]
TEL. +39 0307762000
www.bellavistawine.it

CELLAR SALES
PRE-BOOKED VISITS
ANNUAL PRODUCTION 1,400,000 bottles
HECTARES UNDER VINE 190.00
SUSTAINABLE WINERY

Vittorio Moretti's passion for the land and wine has allowed him to reach major goals. 40 years after its founding, Bellavista is one Italy's most prestigious brands, heading the Terra Moretti group that recently purchased important producers like Sella & Mosca in Sardinia, Petra and La Badiola (both in Tuscany), as well as the gem, Teruzzi & Puthod (in San Gimignano, Tuscany). Today, Francesca Moretta (born and raised among the vineyards and winery of Bellavista) is at the helm of this important national winemaker, The Cuvée Meraviglioso isn't on the roster, but it's a wine of extraordinary finesse and complexity. This year, Tre Bicchieri goes to the 2010 Pas Operé, a charming and elegant Franciacorta that enchants for its freshness and for the cleanness of fruity and flowery aromas. The whole selection, however, is first rate.

○ Franciacorta Pas Operé '10	▼▼▼	7
○ Franciacorta Brut Gran Cuvée Alma	▼▼	6
○ Franciacorta Brut Teatro alla Scala '11	▼▼	7
○ Franciacorta Extra Brut Vittorio Moretti '02	▼▼▼	8
○ Franciacorta Extra Brut Vittorio Moretti Ris. '08	▼▼▼	8
○ Franciacorta Extra Brut Vittorio Moretti Ris. '06	▼▼▼	8
○ Franciacorta Gran Cuvée Pas Operé '05	▼▼▼	7
○ Franciacorta Gran Cuvée Pas Operé '04	▼▼▼	7
○ Franciacorta Pas Operé '09	▼▼▼	7
○ Franciacorta Brut Rosé '11	▼▼	7
○ Franciacorta Brut Teatro alla Scala '10	▼▼	7
○ Franciacorta Satèn '11	▼▼	7

F.lli Berlucchi

FRAZ. BORGONATO
VIA BROLETTO, 2
25040 CORTE FRANCA [BS]
TEL. +39 030984451
www.fratelliberlucchi.it

CELLAR SALES
PRE-BOOKED VISITS
ANNUAL PRODUCTION 400,000 bottles
HECTARES UNDER VINE 70.00

The Berlucchi are a historic family here in Franciacorta. Today, this large estate is bolstered by its 70 hectares of lovely vineyards, all managed with passion by Pia Donata (on behalf of her brothers) and her daughter, Tilli Rizzo. Their cellar is situated in the 16th century family villa, Casa Delle Colonne (in Borgonato). The selection is divided into two lines, Casa delle Colonne (dedicated to Franciacorta Riserva) and the vintage Freccia Nera line. The Brut 25 is their base wine and the only non-vintage in the lot. Casa delle Colonne Brut Riserva is a deep and complex Franciacorta made with Chardonnay and 20% Pinot Nero. It has a brilliant straw-yellow color, and a rich, complex bouquet in which overtones of fruit fuse with yeast and oak. The 2013 Freccianera Nature has pressure, freshness and nice, citrusy notes to it, while the 2010 Casa delle Colonne Zero is austere and linear on the palate, soft and intriguing on the nose.

○ Franciacorta Brut Casa delle Colonne Ris. '10	▼▼	8
○ Franciacorta Brut 25	▼▼	4
○ Franciacorta Brut Freccianera '12	▼▼	6
○ Franciacorta Casa delle Colonne Zero Ris. '10	▼▼	8
○ Franciacorta Nature Freccianera '13	▼▼	7
○ Franciacorta Satèn Freccianera '13	▼▼	7
⊙ Franciacorta Freccianera Rosa '13	▼	6
○ Franciacorta Brut Casa delle Colonne Ris. '09	▼▼	7
○ Franciacorta Brut Freccianera '11	▼▼	5
⊙ Franciacorta Freccianera Rosa '12	▼▼	5
○ Franciacorta Nature Freccianera '12	▼▼	5
○ Franciacorta Satèn Freccianera '12	▼▼	5

Guido Berlucchi & C.

LOC. BORGONATO
P.ZZA DURANTI, 4
25040 CORTE FRANCA [BS]
TEL. +39 030984381
www.berlucchi.it

CELLAR SALES
PRE-BOOKED VISITS
ACCOMMODATION
ANNUAL PRODUCTION 4,400,000 bottles
HECTARES UNDER VINE 550.00
VITICULTURE METHOD Certified Organic
SUSTAINABLE WINERY

La Guido Berlucchi & C. is owned by the Ziliani family, and it's one of Italy's most important sparkling winemakers. We have Franco Ziliani, who got his start in the 1960s, to thank for Franciacorta's reputation as 'Metodo Classico' wine country. Today his children make up a close-knit, determined team: Arturo (winemaker), Cristina (marketing) and Paolo (sales). As a leader in the Franciacorta, they also export to a number of other countries. Once again, the 2010 Franciacorta 61 Nature affirms its status as one of the most impressive wines in the DOC zone. It's a zesty, fresh, dynamic and lively Dosaggio Zero with a brilliant, greenish straw-yellow color and fine perlage. It has a charming bouquet that features ripe white fruit and aromatic herbs. On the palate it comes through crisp and assertive, creamy in its sparkle and truly long. The 2008 Satèn Riserva Palazzo Lana also proved excellent.

⊙ Franciacorta Nature '61 '10	▼▼▼ 7
○ Franciacorta Brut Satèn Palazzo Lana Ris. '08	▼▼ 6
○ Franciacorta Brut 61	▼▼ 5
⊙ Franciacorta Rosé 61	▼▼ 5
○ Franciacorta Satèn 61	▼▼ 5
○ Franciacorta Brut Cellarius '08	♈♈♈ 5
○ Franciacorta Brut Cellarius '07	♈♈♈ 5
○ Franciacorta Brut Extrême Palazzo Lana Ris. '06	♈♈♈ 6
○ Franciacorta Extra Brut Extreme Palazzo Lana Ris. '07	♈♈♈ 7
○ Franciacorta Nature 61 '09	♈♈♈ 5
○ Franciacorta Satèn Palazzo Lana '06	♈♈♈ 6

Cantina Bersi Serlini

LOC. CERETO
VIA CERETO, 7
25050 PROVAGLIO D'ISEO [BS]
TEL. +39 0309823338
www.bersiserlini.it

CELLAR SALES
PRE-BOOKED VISITS
ACCOMMODATION AND RESTAURANT SERVICE
ANNUAL PRODUCTION 200,000 bottles
HECTARES UNDER VINE 30.00
VITICULTURE METHOD Certified Organic

The Bersi Serlini family purchased this lovely estate in Provaglio (on the banks of Lake Iseo) in 1886. At one time, it was a piece of farmland for the nearby convent of San Pietro in Lamosa. Today, after recent renovations and additions, the winery is a charming complex in which the modern and historic exist side-by-side (and their extremely well-maintained vineyards offer a lovely view of the lake). They also host important conferences and events for wine tourism. Just a bit more grip would have earned the 2010 Rosé Rosa Rosae a gold. It's one of the best Rosés in the DOC zone, with its coral hints and its generous, complex nose in which wild berries play hide-and-seek with aromas of yeast, vanilla and oak. On the palate it's soft, gentle and creamy. The 2013 Extra Brut proves intriguing in its vegetal hints of sap and nuances of ripe white fruit.

⊙ Franciacorta Brut Rosé Rosa Rosae '10	▼▼ 5
○ Franciacorta Brut Anteprima	▼▼ 5
○ Franciacorta Brut Cuvée n. 4 '13	▼▼ 6
○ Franciacorta Brut Satèn	▼▼ 5
○ Franciacorta Extra Brut '13	▼▼ 6
○ Franciacorta Demi Sec Nuvola	▼ 4
○ Franciacorta Brut Cuvée n. 4 '10	♈♈ 5
○ Franciacorta Brut Vintage Ris. '06	♈♈ 7
○ Franciacorta Extra Brut '12	♈♈ 6
○ Franciacorta Extra Brut '11	♈♈ 6
○ Franciacorta Extra Brut '10	♈♈ 6
○ Franciacorta Satèn '10	♈♈ 5

F.lli Bettini

LOC. SAN GIACOMO
VIA NAZIONALE, 4A
23036 TEGLIO [SO]
TEL. +39 0342786068
www.vinibettini.it

CELLAR SALES
PRE-BOOKED VISITS
ANNUAL PRODUCTION 200,000 bottles
HECTARES UNDER VINE 15.00

Pietro Bettini's winery, which has more than 130 seasons behind it, is bolstered by its reputation as a benchmark for winemaking in Valtellina. Theyr vineyards grow here, in San Giacomo di Teglio, in the heart of Valgella (at 900 meters above sea level). There are 15 hectares total, and they cover Valtellina's main sub zones, making for a solid, varied and well-segmented selection. The producer's style sees fruit-rich, expressive wines, with small wood used for their top range. The 2011 Inferno Prodigio had a good performance. It's deep in its aromas, with slightly ripe fruit, dried herbs and forest floor. The mouth is harmonious, fresh and true to character, with balanced acidity. The 2007 La Botte Ventitrè Riserva is less vibrant, with notes of ripe fruit. On the palate it proves velvety, with nice structure and a lingering finish.

● Sforzato di Valtellina Fruttaio di Spina '13	❷❷ 7
● Valtellina Sup. Inferno Prodigio '11	❷❷ 5
● Valtellina Sup. La Botte Ventitrè Ris. '07	❷❷ 3
● Valtellina Sup. Sant'Andrea '13	❷❷ 5
● Sforzato di Valtellina Vign. di Spina '11	♈♈ 7
● Sforzato di Valtellina Vign. di Spina '10	♈♈ 6
● Valtellina Sup. Inferno Prodigio '10	♈♈ 4
● Valtellina Sup. Inferno Prodigio '09	♈♈ 3
● Valtellina Sup. Sant'Andrea '11	♈♈ 5
● Valtellina Sup. Sassella Reale '11	♈♈ 5
● Valtellina Sup. Sassella Reale '10	♈♈ 4
● Valtellina Sup. Valgella V. La Cornella '11	♈♈ 5
● Valtellina Sup. Valgella V. La Cornella '10	♈♈ 4

Bisi

LOC. CASCINA SAN MICHELE
FRAZ. VILLA MARONE, 70
27040 SAN DAMIANO AL COLLE [PV]
TEL. +39 038575037
www.aziendagricolabisi.it

CELLAR SALES
PRE-BOOKED VISITS
ANNUAL PRODUCTION 90,000 bottles
HECTARES UNDER VINE 30.00

When we speak about Claudio Bisi we risk having to repeat ourselves: in our mind, he's among the best winegrowers in Oltrepò Pavese (and beyond). We're not just talking about passion for his work, but also about his deep knowledge of each plot (Claudio buys new terrain whenever he can, even small areas where he thinks he can get good results) and soil. In a nutshell, the terroir. This makes for wines that are austere and generous at the same time, with notable personality. And they're often best appreciated years after they've been put on the market. Once again, the 2016 Bonarda Vivace La Peccatrice proves to be an excellent wine for those who like a dry, potent style. The 2014 Barbera Roncolongo, as always, needs some time for its powerful body to integrate with the spices of wood. Its little sister, the 2015 Barbera Pezzabianca, also had a good day, offering up vibrant, fruity notes of cherry and chocolate. The 2016 Riesling LaGrà is flowery, clean, close-focused and savory, as usual, while the 2014 Villa Marone, a Malvasia dried grape wine, shows vigor, force and substance.

● Barbera Roncolongo '14	❷❷ 5
● OP Bonarda Vivace La Peccatrice '16	❷❷ 2*
● Barbera Pezzabianca '15	❷❷ 3
○ Bianco Passito Villa Marone '14	❷❷ 5
○ Riesling LaGrà '16	❷❷ 2*
● Barbera Roncolongo '12	♈♈ 3
● Barbera Roncolongo '11	♈♈ 4
○ Bianco Passito Villa Marone '12	♈♈ 4
○ LaGrà '14	♈♈ 3
● OP Bonarda Vivace La Peccatrice '15	♈♈ 2*
○ OP Pinot Nero Calonga '13	♈♈ 3
○ OP Riesling LaGrà '15	♈♈ 2*
● Pramattone '13	♈♈ 3

Castello Bonomi

VIA SAN PIETRO, 46
25030 COCCAGLIO [BS]
TEL. +39 0307721015
www.castellobonomi.it

CELLAR SALES
PRE-BOOKED VISITS
ANNUAL PRODUCTION 100,000 bottles
HECTARES UNDER VINE 20.00

Siblings Carlo, Lucia and Roberto Paladin have passion for wine in their blood. Their main site is the Venetian Paladin, but the family also owns Bosco del Merlo in Friuli, Castelvecchi a Radda in Chianti, and, some years ago, purchased Castello Bonomi in Coccaglio (at the foot of Monte Orfano). Castello Bonomi boasts an important estate, 20 hectares in all (mostly benchlands), at the food of the mountain (and on the territory's oldest soil). Castello Bonomi's blends exhibit notable longevity. The vintage Cruperdu is one of the winery's flagships. The Pinot Nero used in this elegant Chardonnay blend are cultivated on old estate vineyards and then aged for more than seven years on the lees before dégorgement. It has a very fine perlage, and on the nose it features delicate hints of cakes, vanilla and white fruit. The palate proves zesty and harmonic, with close-woven fruit emerging at the end. The 2010 Dosage Zero is a complex, well-orchestrated wine.

○ Franciacorta Brut Cru Perdu Ris. '08	♼♼	7
○ Franciacorta Brut Satèn	♼♼	7
○ Franciacorta Dosage Zero '10	♼♼	8
○ Franciacorta Brut Cru Perdu '04	♼♼♼	7
○ Franciacorta Extra Brut Lucrezia Et. Nera '04	♼♼♼	8
● Curtefranca Rosso Cordelio '11	♼♼	7
● Curtefranca Rosso Cordelio '10	♼♼	7
● Curtefranca Rosso Cordelio '09	♼♼	7
● Curtefranca Rosso Cordelio '07	♼♼	5
○ Franciacorta Brut '06	♼♼	6
○ Franciacorta Dosage Zero '09	♼♼	8
○ Franciacorta Dosage Zero '07	♼♼	8
○ Franciacorta Extra Brut Cuvée Lucrezia Et. Nera '06	♼♼	8
⊙ Franciacorta Rosé Lucrezia Ris. '06	♼♼	8

Bosio

FRAZ. TIMOLINE
VIA M. GATTI, 4
25040 CORTE FRANCA [BS]
TEL. +39 0309826224
www.bosiofranciacorta.it

CELLAR SALES
PRE-BOOKED VISITS
ANNUAL PRODUCTION 100,000 bottles
HECTARES UNDER VINE 30.00
SUSTAINABLE WINERY

Cesare (agronomist and winemaker) and Laura (a graduate in economic science) put their skills together and took over the family winery. They've enlarged the estate to 30 hectares and built a new, modern cellar in Corte Franca. The level of their Franciacortas and wines is excellent, thanks to the quality of their vineyards (which are managed with the utmost respect for the environment) and, obviously, Cesare's skills. While waiting for the latest version of the Riserva Girolamo Bosio, the house blend, we tasted, and were impressed by the 2011 Boschedòr, a fresh and succulent Extra Brut made with equal parts Chardonnay and Pinot Nero. Its structure is full, fruity and creamy, with nice expressive finesse. The 2012 Nature proves elegant and well-rounded, in keeping with the house style, crisp and fresh on the palate, with a nose that intrigues for its round overtones of ripe white fruit and vanilla.

○ Franciacorta Extra Brut Boschedòr '11	♼♼	5
○ Franciacorta Brut	♼♼	5
⊙ Franciacorta Brut Rosé '13	♼♼	5
○ Franciacorta Nature '12	♼♼	5
○ Franciacorta Satèn	♼♼	5
○ Franciacorta Pas Dosé Girolamo Bosio Ris. '09	♼♼♼	5
⊙ Franciacorta Brut Rosé '12	♼♼	5
⊙ Franciacorta Brut Rosé '11	♼♼	5
○ Franciacorta Extra Brut Boschedòr '10	♼♼	5
○ Franciacorta Extra Brut Boschedòr '09	♼♼	5
○ Franciacorta Nature '11	♼♼	5
○ Franciacorta Nature '10	♼♼	5
○ Franciacorta Nature '09	♼♼	5
○ Franciacorta Pas Dosé Girolamo Bosio Ris. '07	♼♼	5

Alessio Brandolini

FRAZ. BOFFALORA, 68
27040 SAN DAMIANO AL COLLE [PV]
TEL. +39 038575232
www.alessiobrandolini.com

CELLAR SALES
PRE-BOOKED VISITS
ANNUAL PRODUCTION 70,000 bottles
HECTARES UNDER VINE 11.00
SUSTAINABLE WINERY

Alessio Brandolini is among those young winemakers who, having inherited the family winery, strive to bring new life to the land. In this case, it's Oltrepò Pavese, a territory whose problems are well-known, but not its potential. Having overcome the premature death of his father, Costante (a point of reference at the winery, especially in the vineyard), Alessio is working to give more finesse and elegance to his wines, without compromising their typicity. The 2013 Rosé Note d'Agosto, an onionskin colored, 'Metodo Classico' sparkler, saw a breakthrough in quality. It's a creamy, clean, linear wine, characterized by close-woven fruit on the nose and a butteriness that doesn't interfere with its elegance. The Luogo d'Agosto comes in a step below the white version, it's a bit evolved. The 2013 Beneficio, a robust and rustic wine, offers up wild berries in abundance, as well as tannins and color. The 2016 Malvasia Secca Il Bardughino once again proves fresh and pleasant.

⊙ Brut M. Cl. Rosé Note d'Agosto '13	🍷🍷 3*
○ Il Bardughino '16	🍷🍷 2*
● Il Beneficio '13	🍷🍷 4
● Il Soffio '16	🍷 2
● OP Bonarda Vivace Il Cassino '16	🍷 2
○ Il Bardughino '15	🍷🍷 2*
○ Il Bardughino '14	🍷🍷 2*
● Il Beneficio '12	🍷🍷 2*
● Il Beneficio '11	🍷🍷 2*
● OP Bonarda Vivace Il Cassino '15	🍷🍷 2*
● OP Bonarda Vivace Il Cassino '14	🍷🍷 2*

★Cà Maiol

VIA COLLI STORICI, 119
25015 DESENZANO DEL GARDA [BS]
TEL. +39 0309910006
www.camaiol.it

CELLAR SALES
PRE-BOOKED VISITS
ANNUAL PRODUCTION 1,500,000 bottles
HECTARES UNDER VINE 160.00
SUSTAINABLE WINERY

Cà Maiol, the Contato family's inspiring winery (known as Provenza until a few years ago) has taken another important step forward, becoming part of the large Venetian group, Santa Margherita (owned by the Marzotto family). It's a leader in Lugano, and among the top producers in the appellation, bolstered by its 150 hectares of vineyards (which are divided into four smaller estates). Fabio Contato, the winery's talented, passionate manager, continues to lead it and serve as a partner. A gold for the Lugana Molin is a classic by now. The 2016 affirms its status as a benchmark of the celebrated DOC zone. It's a modern, close-focused and dynamic wine in its richness of fruit and acidic backbone. These make for an extraordinarily pleasant palate, nice expressive depth and, finally, excellent longevity. The rest of the selection is also extremely strong.

○ Lugana Molin '16	🍷🍷🍷 3*
○ Lugana Sup. Sel. Fabio Contato '15	🍷🍷 5
● Garda Rosso Cl. Sup. Fabio Contato '10	🍷🍷 5
○ Lugana Brut M. Cl. 60 Mesi	🍷🍷 5
○ Lugana Molin Bio '16	🍷🍷 5
○ Lugana Prestige '16	🍷🍷 3
⊙ Valtènesi Chiaretto '16	🍷🍷 3
⊙ Valtènesi Chiaretto Roserì	🍷 3
○ Lugana Molin '15	🍷🍷🍷 3*
○ Lugana Molin '14	🍷🍷🍷 3*
○ Lugana Molin '13	🍷🍷🍷 3*
○ Lugana Molin '12	🍷🍷🍷 3*
○ Lugana Sup. Sel. Fabio Contato '11	🍷🍷🍷 5
○ Lugana Sup. Sel. Fabio Contato '10	🍷🍷🍷 5

LOMBARDY

Cà Tessitori

VIA MATTEOTTI, 15
27043 BRONI [PV]
TEL. +39 038551495
www.catessitori.it

CELLAR SALES
PRE-BOOKED VISITS
ANNUAL PRODUCTION 120,000 bottles
HECTARES UNDER VINE 40.00

Luigi Giorgi, the man leading Cà Tessitori, is a classic, old-fashioned farmer. For him, family and winery are one. For years, his sons, Giovanni and Francesco have been more involved in managing and running the winery, but their father's supervision is still key. Their wines haven't changed much, with a focus on tradition and extremely limited use of wood. Today these stand out for their personality and forthrightness. The Brut M.V., a 'Metodo Classico' sparkler made with 100% Pinot Nero, continues to deliver. It's a supple, racy wine with citrus and wild berries, nice sparkle and a vibrant, mineral finish. The 2016 Bonarda also did well, with its well-defined fruit and creamy spakle, as did the 2016 Avita, which undergoes second-fermentation in the bottle and is characterized by darker notes of forest floor and black fruit. The 2016 Rosso Borghesa is among the best ever, a succulent and mature wine that's sustained by a captivating balsamic vein. The 2011 LB9 proved drier than previous versions.

○ OP Pinot Nero Brut M. V. '12	♥♥	4
● OP Bonarda Avita '16	♥♥	3
● OP Bonarda Vivace '16	♥♥	2*
● OP Rosso Borghesa '16	♥♥	2*
● Gnese '15	♥	3
○ OP Pinot Nero Brut LB9 '11	♥	4
○ Agòlo '14	♀♀	2*
● OP Bonarda Avita '15	♀♀	3
● OP Bonarda Vivace '15	♀♀	2*
○ OP Pinot Nero Brut '11	♀♀	4
○ OP Pinot Nero Brut M. V. '11	♀♀	4
○ OP Pinot Nero Brut M. V. '10	♀♀	4
● OP Rosso Borghesa '15	♀♀	2*

★★★★Ca' del Bosco

VIA ALBANO ZANELLA, 13
25030 ERBUSCO [BS]
TEL. +39 030//66111
www.cadelbosco.com

CELLAR SALES
PRE-BOOKED VISITS
ANNUAL PRODUCTION 1,470,000 bottles
HECTARES UNDER VINE 204.00
SUSTAINABLE WINERY

The producer founded by Maurizio Zanella is the Santa Margherita group's crown jewel, and one of the most important brands in Italy. Maurizio manages an exceptional team, led by the extraordinarily talented Stefano Capelli. A visit to their modern facility mustn't be missed. It's a cozy cellar, rich in works of art, immersed in woodlands and vineyards, and endowed with some of the most sophisticated technology available. Their selection of wines, starting with their Franciacorta, is vast, varying and of outstanding quality. This year we faced a selection of truly exceptional finalists. In addition to the two 2007 versions of the Cuvée Annamaria Clementi, we tasted an excellent 2013 Curtefranca Chardonnay and, finally, an irresistible 2012 Vintage Collection Dosaggio Zero. The last of these is an outstanding Franciacorta that repeats last year's success. It's a blend of 25 base wines of Chardonnay (65%), Pinot Bianco (13%) and Pinot Nero. It's then aged on the lees for four years, and doesn't call for added liqueur, making for a charming, lively, fresh, deep and extremely long wine.

○ Franciacorta Dosage Zéro Vintage Collection '12	♥♥♥	8
○ Curtefranca Chardonnay '13	♥♥	8
⊙ Franciacorta Extra Brut Cuvée Annamaria Clementi Ris. '07	♥♥	8
⊙ Franciacorta Extra Brut Cuvée Annamaria Clementi Rosé Ris. '07	♥♥	8
● Carmenero '10	♥♥	8
○ Curtefranca Bianco '16	♥♥	5
● Curtefranca Rosso '14	♥♥	5
○ Franciacorta Brut Cuvée Prestige	♥♥	5
○ Franciacorta Brut Vintage Collection '12	♥♥	8
○ Franciacorta Dosage Zéro Noir Vintage Collection '08	♥♥	8
○ Franciacorta Satèn Vintage Collection '12	♥♥	8
● Maurizio Zanella '12	♥♥	8

Ca' del Gè

FRAZ. CA' DEL GÈ, 3
27040 MONTALTO PAVESE [PV]
TEL. +39 0383870179
www.cadelge.com

CELLAR SALES
PRE-BOOKED VISITS
ANNUAL PRODUCTION 160,000 bottles
HECTARES UNDER VINE 45.00

Enzo, who founded the winery in 1985 and left us a few years back, would have to be proud of his children, Carlo, Stefania and Sara. With humility, thoughtfulness and dedication, they've kept the family's legacy alive, dividing up the responsibilities and working to bring out the best of their 36 hectares of terrain (all managed so as to reduce environmental impact to a minimum). The estate is divided between Montalto Pavese, where Riesling and Pinot Nero thrive in the white terrain, and Cigognola, where their traditional red grapes are cultivated. Excellent performance and a deserved award for the Padroggi family. The 2013 Brut offers up nice fragrances of candied fruit, while in the mouth it proves supple, with perfectly dosed prickle and a lingering, zesty finish. Among the stills we highlight the 2016 Riesling Brinà, with its hints of citron, citrus and wild flowers, and a mouth that's close-woven but clean and fresh. The other Riesling and Moscato both proved sound.

○ OP Brut Cà del Gé '13	♥♥ 3*
○ OP Riesling Brinà '16	♥♥ 2*
○ OP Moscato '16	♥ 2
○ OP Riesling Filagn Long '16	♥ 2
○ Il Marinoni '15	♥♥ 3
● OP Bonarda Vivace '13	♥♥ 2*
○ OP Moscato Frizzante '13	♥♥ 2*
○ OP Pinot Nero Brut '09	♥♥ 3
○ OP Pinot Nero Brut M. Cl. '11	♥♥ 3
○ OP Pinot Nero Brut M. Cl. '10	♥♥ 3*
○ OP Riesling Brinà '15	♥♥ 2*
○ OP Riesling Brinà '14	♥♥ 2*

Ca' di Frara

VIA CASA FERRARI, 1
27040 MORNICO LOSANA [PV]
TEL. +39 0383892299
www.cadifrara.com

CELLAR SALES
PRE-BOOKED VISITS
ANNUAL PRODUCTION 400,000 bottles
HECTARES UNDER VINE 46.00

Luca Bellani took over the reins of the family winery while still quite young, though he's been helped by his explosive mother, Daniela, and experienced father, Tullio. Even when tasting older vintages, you understand that the terrain here is quite well-suited, and why Tullio is considered one of Oltrepò Pavese's pioneers. Over the years, his style, and the selection have undergone changes, and Luca has been working to bring out the elegance and potency of his wines. Part of this effort has meant launching a new initiative for 'Metodo Classico' sparklers. Thanks to his work, today they are among the territory's top producers. The 2016 Rieseling was excellent this year as well, with its clear, citrusy scents featuring mandarin orange and then aniseed, mint and white flowers. The mouth is lively, succulent, rich in vigor and pressure. Among the reds, we point out their 2015 Io Rosso with its clear notes of wild berries, and a savory, enfolding, balsamic mouth. The Brut Oltre il Classico features notes of over-ripeness and bolder dosage.

○ Brut Oltre il Classico	♥♥ 4
● Io Rosso '15	♥♥ 5
○ OP Riesling Sup. '16	♥♥ 2*
○ Brut Nature Noir	♥ 4
○ Brut Oltre il Classico	♥ 4
○ OP Riesling Oliva Ris. '15	♥ 4
● OP Bonarda La Casetta '15	♥♥ 3
● OP Bonarda Vivace Monpezzato '15	♥♥ 2*
○ OP Pinot Nero Brut Oltre il Classico Nature Ris. '04	♥♥ 5
○ OP Pinot Nero Brut Oltre il Classico Rosé Ris. '08	♥♥ 5
○ OP Riesling '15	♥♥ 4

Ca' Lojera

LOC. ROVIZZA
VIA 1866, 19
25019 SIRMIONE [BS]
TEL. +39 0457551901
www.calojera.com

CELLAR SALES
PRE-BOOKED VISITS
RESTAURANT SERVICE
ANNUAL PRODUCTION 120,000 bottles
HECTARES UNDER VINE 20.00

Ca' Lojera, ('the house of the wolves')
spans 20 hectares of vineyards in the
flatlands near the lake. Their Lugana is
cultivated on the area's classic white-clay
terrain, while red varieties are cultivated in
hillier zones. Owners Franco and Ambra
Tiraboschi have confirmed their status as
among the most attentive and passionate
figures in the appellation. Their cellar, which
forms part of a complex that includes a
restaurant and agritourism, features
modern equipment. As always, three
versions of Lugana were presented by this
close couple, which believes in the aging
potential of this wine. The 2015 La Riserva
del Lupo, a zesty late-harvest white with a
touch of botrytis, proves rich and deep,
expressing ripe but intact fruit with an
intriguing, tropical nuance. Fresh acidity
gives way to a finish in which aromas of
aniseed and elderflower emerge. The other
two versions also proved excellent.

○ Lugana Riserva del Lupo '15	♟♟ 5
○ Lugana '16	♟♟ 3
○ Lugana Sup. '15	♟♟ 3
○ Lugana '15	♟♟ 3
○ Lugana '14	♟♟ 3
○ Lugana Riserva del Lupo '14	♟♟ 5
○ Lugana Riserva del Lupo '13	♟♟ 5
○ Lugana Riserva del Lupo '12	♟♟ 5
○ Lugana Riserva del Lupo '11	♟♟ 4
○ Lugana Sup. '14	♟♟ 3
○ Lugana Sup. '13	♟♟ 3
○ Lugana Sup. '12	♟♟ 3
○ Lugana Sup. '11	♟♟ 3

Calatroni

LOC. CASA GRANDE, 7
27040 MONTECALVO VERSIGGIA [PV]
TEL. +39 038599013
www.calatronivini.it

CELLAR SALES
PRE-BOOKED VISITS
RESTAURANT SERVICE
ANNUAL PRODUCTION 70,000 bottles
HECTARES UNDER VINE 15.00
SUSTAINABLE WINERY

Cristian and Stefano Calatroni represent the
fourth generation of vine growers to
manage the family winery founded by their
grandfather, Luigi, in 1964. These two
skilled young men have taken over the
vineyards, which until now had been
sharecropped, and are focusing on bringing
out the best of the primarily calcareous soil
here (especially Riesling and Pinot Nero for
their sparkling wines). The winery's growth
(which has seen the addition of an
agritourism) has been rapid. The important
thing now is to stay the course. The
2013 NorEma handily earns a Tre Bicchieri
by virtue of a lovely nose featuring citrus,
small wild berries and field flowers. In the
mouth it offers up substance, richness of
flavor and elegance. The 2016 Sangue di
Giuda is the best in its area, with its
generous, captivating aromas of black fruit
and well-focused residual sweetness. The
2013 Brut 64 also did well, offering up
citrus, fine, long sparkle, finesse and
linearity. The 2014 Rieseling is evolved,
mineral and zesty, with lovely notes of
medicinal herbs.

⊙ OP Pinot Nero Rosé M. Cl. NorEma '13	♟♟♟ 4*
● OP Sangue di Giuda '16	♟♟ 2*
○ OP Riesling Viticoltori in Montecalvo '14	♟♟ 5
○ Pinot Nero Brut 64 '13	♟♟ 4
● OP Bonarda Vivace Vigio '16	♟ 2
○ OP Riesling Campo del Dottore '16	♟ 3
● Pinot Nero Fioravanti '15	♟ 3
○ Pinot Nero Brut 64 '11	♟♟♟ 5
● OP Bonarda Vivace Vigiö '15	♟♟ 2*
○ OP Riesling '13	♟♟ 2*
○ OP Riesling Campo del Dottore '15	♟♟ 2*
○ Pinot Nero Brut 64 '12	♟♟ 5

Il Calepino

VIA SURRIPE, 1
24060 CASTELLI CALEPIO [BG]
TEL. +39 035847178
www.ilcalepino.it

CELLAR SALES
PRE-BOOKED VISITS
ANNUAL PRODUCTION 230,000 bottles
HECTARES UNDER VINE 15.00

The work done by the Plebiani brothers over the years on the Bergamot side of Sebino is commendable, especially in terms of their 'Metodo Classico' sparkling wines. Last year, we saw a transition period, because the new vintages still weren't ready. Today they're here and, in many cases, they prove to be outstanding, both for their distinctive style and their quality. The Fra' Ambrogio Riserva is once again at the top of the producer's roster. With the 2009, it affirms its star status, with its golden color, its fine sparkle and its complex hints of butter, vanilla and bread crust. The 2010 Non Dosato also delivered, proving elegant, linear and mineral, with notes of herbs and tropical fruit. The 2011 Rosé has marked notes of wild berries and increased elegance, while the 2010 Brut features style and a long finish. Among the other wines, we also found the 2011 Cabernet Kalòs to be very good.

○ Brut M. Cl. Fra' Ambrogio Ris. '09	♀♀ 4
○ Brut M. Cl. Non Dosato '10	♀♀ 4
⊙ Brut M. Cl. Rosé '11	♀♀ 3
● Kalòs '11	♀♀ 5
○ TdC Brut M. Cl. BDB	♀ 4
○ Valcalepio Bianco '16	♀ 2
● Valcalepio Rosso Surìe Ris. '12	♀ 3
○ Brut M. Cl. Fra' Ambrogio '07	♀♀ 4
○ Brut M. Cl. Fra' Ambrogio Ris. '08	♀♀ 4
○ Brut M. Cl. Il Calepino '10	♀♀ 3
○ Brut M. Cl. Non Dosato '09	♀♀ 4
⊙ Brut M. Cl. Rosé '08	♀♀ 3
● Kalòs '10	♀♀ 5
● MAS '08	♀♀ 5

Camossi

VIA METELLI, 5
25030 ERBUSCO [BS]
TEL. +39 0307268022
www.camossi.it

CELLAR SALES
PRE-BOOKED VISITS
ANNUAL PRODUCTION 60,000 bottles
HECTARES UNDER VINE 30.00

Dario and Claudio Camossl represent a family with deep roots in Franciacorta and winemaking (even if the winery got its start with their grandfather, Pietro, who's still helping out in the vineyards). In the early 1990s they began making wine, but the breakthrough came in 2005 when winemaker Nico Danesi and Giovanni Arcari came on board. The Camossi family's 30 hectares of vineyards span Erbusco (where the cellar is also situated), Paratico (where their Pinot Nero is cultivated) and Provaglio d'Iseo (especially in the district of Provezze). The 'Riserva' version of the 2009 Extra Brut that we liked so much last year had a big day during our finals. It's a modern, racy Franciacorta, all pressure and freshness, rich in white fruit and integrity, with red fruit nuances that make for a truly intriguing bouquet. The other wines in their selection also did well.

○ Franciacorta Extra Brut Ris. '09	♀♀ 6
○ Franciacorta Brut Satèn '11	♀♀ 6
○ Franciacorta Brut Satèn	♀♀ 5
○ Franciacorta Extra Brut '12	♀♀ 6
○ Franciacorta Extra Brut	♀♀ 6
⊙ Franciacorta Extra Brut Rosé	♀♀ 6
○ Franciacorta Extra Brut '11	♀♀ 6
○ Franciacorta Extra Brut '09	♀♀ 6
○ Franciacorta Extra Brut '08	♀♀ 6
○ Franciacorta Extra Brut '08	♀♀ 6
○ Franciacorta Extra Brut '07	♀♀ 5
○ Franciacorta Extra Brut '07	♀♀ 5
○ Franciacorta Extra Brut '06	♀♀ 5
○ Franciacorta Extra Brut Pietro Camossi Ris. '07	♀♀ 8
○ Franciacorta Extra Brut Ris. '08	♀♀ 6

CastelFaglia - Monogram

FRAZ. CALINO
LOC. BOSCHI, 3
25046 CAZZAGO SAN MARTINO [BS]
TEL. +39 030/751042
www.cavicchioli.it

CELLAR SALES
PRE-BOOKED VISITS
ANNUAL PRODUCTION 350,000 bottles
HECTARES UNDER VINE 22.00

Sandro Cavicchioli makes elegant 'Metodo Classico' blends in a lovely cellar at the foot of the Castello Faglia in Calino (Franciacorta), where the family purchased its estate years ago. The Cavicchioli also make sparkling wine in their facility in Modena (Bellei di Bomporto). CastelFaglia also makes Franciacorta blends for their Monogram line, from grapes cultivated on their 22 hectares of vineyards (some of them benchlands) at the foot of the old castel. We very much like the close-focused, clean and taut style of CastelFaglia's blends. This year, the 2013 Zero made a particularly good impression. It has a brilliant, straw-yellow color with greenish highlights, and a very fine perlage. On the nose it offers up fresh notes of white fruit and citrus, which give way to a crisp, even mouth that bewitches for its cleanness, the creaminess of its mousse and the lovely traces of ripe fruit left by its long finish. The Blanc de Blancs features delicate notes of citron and white fruit.

○ Franciacorta Dosage Zero Monogram '13	♈♈	5
○ Franciacorta Brut Blanc de Blancs Monogram	♈♈	5
○ Franciacorta Brut Monogram '10	♈♈	5
○ Franciacorta Dosage Zéro	♈♈	5
○ Franciacorta Rosé Monogram	♈♈	5
○ Franciacorta Satèn Monogram '12	♈♈	5
○ Franciacorta Extra Brut	♈	4
○ Franciacorta Brut Monogram '09	♉♉	5
○ Franciacorta Brut Monogram '07	♉♉	5
○ Franciacorta Brut Monogram '02	♉♉	7
○ Franciacorta Dosage Zéro '09	♉♉	5
○ Franciacorta Dosage Zero Monogram '12	♉♉	5
○ Franciacorta Dosage Zero Monogram '11	♉♉	5
○ Franciacorta Satèn Monogram '11	♉♉	5

Castello di Cigognola

P.ZZA CASTELLO, 1
27040 CIGOGNOLA [PV]
TEL. +39 0385284828
www.castellodicigognola.com

CELLAR SALES
PRE-BOOKED VISITS
ANNUAL PRODUCTION 75,000 bottles
HECTARES UNDER VINE 30.00

The Castello di Cigonola has ancient roots. It was founded in 1212. Then, after the end of feudalism, it hosted a renaissance court. The early 1800s saw its first use for wine production. Today, this lovely place and splendid estate is owned by Gianmarco Moratti and his wife, Letizia. For some years now, it has been producing quality wines with the help of Riccardo Cotarella and resident winemaker, Emilio Defilippi. Together they've carved out a style and personality for their wines, especially their Metodo Classico. Thanks to a good vintage, the 'tradtional method' sparkler, 'More, gets the gold. This Oltrepò, made solely with Pinot Nero, offers up balsamic, minty hints on the nose, rich in fruit and yellow flowers. The mouth is silky, zesty, well-balanced by its fine and elegant sparkle, with a long finish that goes all in on zest. The Cruasé also did well. It's a more full-bodied and structured wine, with notes of small red fruit. Among the still wines, the 2015 Barbera Dodicidodici stood out.

○ OP Brut Pinot Nero 'More '13	♈♈♈	4*
● OP Barbera Dodicidodici '15	♈♈	3
● OP Barbera La Maga '14	♈♈	4
● OP Barbera Talanca '16	♈♈	3
☉ OP Pinot Cruasé 'More	♈♈	4
● Nebbiolo per Papà '12	♈	5
○ Brut 'More '11	♉♉♉	4*
○ Brut 'More '10	♉♉♉	4*
● OP Barbera Castello di Cigognola '07	♉♉♉	6
● OP Barbera Castello di Cigognola '06	♉♉♉	6
● OP Barbera Dodicidodici '11	♉♉♉	3*
○ OP Brut 'More '12	♉♉♉	4*
○ OP Brut Pinot Nero 'More '08	♉♉♉	4*

Castello di Gussago la Santissima

Manica, 9
5064 Gussago [BS]
Tel. +39 0302525267
www.castellodigussago.it

CELLAR SALES
PRE-BOOKED VISITS
ANNUAL PRODUCTION 120,000 bottles
HECTARES UNDER VINE 15.00
SUSTAINABLE WINERY

Some years ago, the Gozio family renovated an old factory in Gussago surrounded by vineyards so as to realize a modern cellar. The estate comprises various positions throughout the municipality, including Santissima (at the foot of the abbey), at an altitude of 450 meters. These last years have testified to their commitment and continued growth in terms of quality (which includes initiatives on behalf of sustainability). Castello di Gussago's Curtefrancas are among the best in the appellation. The 2012 Pas Dosé is one of the most interesting wines tasted this year. It really delivered during the finals, with its fruit, freshness, zest, creamy effervescence and a long finish in which elegant citrus emerges. We also like the close-focused notes of the Brut, the elegant creaminess of the Blanc de Blancs and the succulence of the 2013 Club Cuvée Satèn.

Franciacorta Pas Dosé '12	♟♟	5
Curtefranca Bianco Malandrino '14	♟♟	5
Curtefranca Rosso Pomaro '13	♟♟	4
Franciacorta Brut	♟♟	5
Franciacorta Brut Blanc de Blancs	♟♟	5
Franciacorta Club Cuvée Satèn	♟♟	5
Franciacorta Extra Brut Rosé '12	♟♟	5
Franciacorta Dosaggio Zero Veritas '09	♟♟	4
Franciacorta Pas Dosé '11	♟♟	5
Franciacorta Satèn '12	♟♟	5

★Cavalleri

Via Provinciale, 96
25030 Erbusco [BS]
Tel. +39 0307760217
www.cavalleri.it

CELLAR SALES
PRE-BOOKED VISITS
ANNUAL PRODUCTION 250,000 bottles
HECTARES UNDER VINE 45.00
VITICULTURE METHOD Certified Organic

The Cavalleri's roots in Franciacorta go way back. Records indicate that in 1450 they held land, though it was 'only' in 1968 that Gian Paolo and his son, Giovanni, began producing wine, and later Franciacorta. Today Giovanni's daughters, Maria and Giulia, and grandchildren, Francesco and Diletta, are managing things, with a staff of skilled collaborators that includes Aldo Pagnoni and winemaker Giampaolo Turra. The winery spans 45 hectares of lovely vineyards on some of Erbusco's best-positioned terrain. Among the Cavalleri's selection this year, the 2012 Pas Dosé made the best impression. It has a brilliant gold, straw-yellow color extremely fine perlage and an elegant, complex bouquet that calls up ripe white fruit, yeast and candied citrus. The mouth is zesty, saline and rich, with creamy effervescence and a pleasantly long, refreshing finish. The 2011 Collezione Grandi Cru, a Brut, also did well, with a nice evocative nose featuring aromatic herbs.

○ Franciacorta Pas Dosé '12	♟♟	6
○ Curtefranca Bianco Rampaneto '15	♟♟	4
○ Franciacorta Brut Collezione Grandi Cru '11	♟♟	7
● Curtefranca Rosso '14	♟	4
○ Franciacorta Brut Blanc de Blancs	♟	5
⊙ Franciacorta Brut Rosé '12	♟	6
○ Franciacorta Brut Satèn '13	♟	5
○ Franciacorta Brut Collezione '05	♟♟♟	6
○ Franciacorta Brut Collezione Esclusiva Giovanni Cavalleri '05	♟♟♟	8
○ Franciacorta Brut Collezione Esclusiva Giovanni Cavalleri '04	♟♟♟	7
○ Franciacorta Pas Dosé '07	♟♟♟	5
○ Franciacorta Pas Dosé R. D. '06	♟♟♟	6
○ Franciacorta Pas Dosé '11	♟♟	6

Citari

FRAZ. SAN MARTINO DELLA BATTAGLIA
LOC. CITARI, 2
25015 DESENZANO DEL GARDA [BS]
TEL. +39 0309910310
www.citari.it

CELLAR SALES
PRE-BOOKED VISITS
ANNUAL PRODUCTION 150,000 bottles
HECTARES UNDER VINE 21.00
SUSTAINABLE WINERY

Francesco Mascini has been carrying on the
work of his grandfather, Francesco Gettuli
(who founded the winery in 1975), with
enthusiasm and skill. The estate comprises
25 hectares of land (21 of which are
vineyards), among the hills that straddle
Lugana and San Martino della Battaglia. The
soil here is morainic, a mix of calcareous
clay rich in mineral salts, which gives rise to
zesty wines with aromatic finesse. The more
calcareous areas make for elegance and
longevity. The approach to cultivation tries
to reduce environmental impact, with
harvests done by hand and a modern
winery to boot. The 2016 Eretico is a highly
pleasant white made with a local variant of
Trebbiano, then fermented and aged in
steel. It has a vibrant, fruit-driven nose with
notes of pineapple and citrus, sage and
other aromatic nuances. The palate comes
through full, fresh, gratifying and long. The
zesty, flowery and rich 2016 Lugana Terre
Bianche also showed excellent consistency,
while the 2016 Lugana Sorgente has a
racier, more spirited style, but also nice,
fruity succulence.

○ Eretico '16	♟♟ 2*
○ Lugana Sorgente '16	♟♟ 3
○ Lugana Terre Bianche '16	♟♟ 3
⊙ Garda Cl. Chiaretto 18 e Quarantacinque '16	♟ 3
● Garda Cl. Rosso Bigoncio '15	♟ 3
● Garda Cl. Rosso Ultimo '15	♟ 3
○ Lugana Conchiglia '16	♟ 4
○ Lugana Torre '16	♟ 2
○ Lugana Conchiglia '15	♟♟ 4
○ Lugana Sorgente '14	♟♟ 3
○ Lugana Torre '15	♟♟ 2*
○ Lugana Vign. La Sorgente '13	♟♟ 2*
○ Mimi' '14	♟♟ 2*
○ San Martino della Battaglia Il Vecchio Vigneto '13	♟♟ 3

Battista Cola

VIA INDIPENDENZA, 3
25030 ADRO [BS]
TEL. +39 0307356195
www.colabattista.it

CELLAR SALES
PRE-BOOKED VISITS
ANNUAL PRODUCTION 70,000 bottles
HECTARES UNDER VINE 10.00
SUSTAINABLE WINERY

Battista and Stefano Cola's well-develope
selection of wines are made with grapes
from the family's vineyards. Their
Franciacorta first appeared in 1985, but t
vineyards on Monte Alto (today 10 hectar
of them) were already cultivated by
Stefano's grandfather, Giovanni. The
selection hovers around 70,000 bottles a
year, but the Franciacortas and the Cola's
wines have maintained their authentic
'récoltant' character, with an artisanal
approach taken both in the vineyards and
the cellar. The Colas continue to work on
behalf of sustainability. Stefano Cola's
2012 Non Dosato is one of the best wines
tasted this year. It's a close-focused,
modern, fresh wine that opens with
enticing fragrances of citrus, mountain
herbs and white fruit. The palate has a
creamy smoothness to it, without losing t
crisp assertiveness of the style. The Satèn
proves just as enjoyable, with its nice, fre
grip, and its flowery, citrusy notes that
follow through well on the palate, then gi
way to hints of bergamot and mint.

○ Franciacorta Non Dosato '12	♟♟
○ Franciacorta Brut Satèn '12	♟♟
○ Franciacorta Extra Brut	♟♟
○ Franciacorta Brut	♟
⊙ Franciacorta Brut Rosé Athena '13	♟
○ Franciacorta Brut '11	♟♟
○ Franciacorta Brut '10	♟♟
○ Franciacorta Brut Ris. '07	♟♟
○ Franciacorta Non Dosato '11	♟♟
○ Franciacorta Non Dosato '10	♟♟
⊙ Franciacorta Rosé Athena '12	♟♟
○ Franciacorta Satèn '11	♟♟
○ Franciacorta Satèn '10	♟♟
○ Franciacorta Satèn '09	♟♟

Contadi Castaldi

c. Fornace Biasca
, Colzano, 32
5030 Adro [BS]
l. +39 0307450126
ww.contadicastaldi.it

CELLAR SALES
PRE-BOOKED VISITS
ANNUAL PRODUCTION 1,000,000 bottles
HECTARES UNDER VINE 150.00
SUSTAINABLE WINERY

he Contadi Castaldi di Adro is
ranciacorta's other side (according to
oretti). If Bellavista represents the
andeur of the tradition, with its collection
great vintages, Contadi Castaldi explores
metaphorically) new territories, and doesn't
e of experimenting. The cellar was carved
ut from renovations of the old ovens of
dro. And, in addition to their estate's
rapes, they have rented land at their
sposal, as well as crop purchased from
elect growers. Winemaker Gian Luca
ccelli, who studied at their main facility,
uides the production side with talent and
assion, The 2011 Satèn Soul gets an
nthusiastic Tre Bicchieri. It's a soft, graceful
end that balances Franciacorta Blanc de
lanc's trademark notes of ripe white and
opical fruit, notes of biscotti and butter
ith a fresh, citrusy acidity, and a creamy
fervescence, making for an enticing,
rinkable wine. The 2011 Pinònero Natura
so did extremely well, with its lovely,
reenish highlights, aromas of flowers,
ed fruit, spicy green pepper, and its
xcellent grip.

Franciacorta Brut Satèn Soul '11	♛♛♛	6
Franciacorta Pinònero Natura '11	♛♛	7
Franciacorta Brut	♛♛	4
Franciacorta Brut Rosé	♛♛	5
Franciacorta Brut Satèn '12	♛♛	6
Franciacorta Zero '13	♛♛	5
Franciacorta Satèn Soul '06	♛♛♛	6
Franciacorta Satèn Soul '05	♛♛♛	6
Franciacorta Zero '12	♛♛♛	5
Franciacorta Zero '09	♛♛♛	5
Franciacorta Rosé Soul '10	♛♛	5
Franciacorta Satèn '11	♛♛	5
Franciacorta Satèn Soul '09	♛♛	6
Franciacorta Soul Satèn '08	♛♛	6

Conte Vistarino

FRAZ. Scorzoletta, 82/84
27040 Pietra de' Giorgi [PV]
Tel. +39 038585117
www.contevistarino.it

CELLAR SALES
PRE-BOOKED VISITS
ANNUAL PRODUCTION 400,000 bottles
HECTARES UNDER VINE 200.00

The estate comprises 800 hectares of
property (200 of them vineyards), almost all
of them in Rocca de' Giorgi, with mostly
Pinot Nero grown (a variety introduced by
Count Gancia, who studied in Champagne,
and Vistarino in 1865). Valle Scuropasso
has proved perfect for producing sparkling
wines and wines made with on-the-skins
fermentation. The arrival of Ottavia Giorgi di
Vistarino gave a strong push in terms of
quality, and the results have been notable,
such as identifying the best crus for making
top Pinot Neros. This year there aren't any
Pinot Nero crus. They weren't used during
the unlucky 2014 vintage. Therefore, the
honor goes to 1865, a sparkling wine that
in the 2012 vintage emerges very mature
and with nice vigor. It's a Pinot Nero with
clear overtones of yellow apple, wild
flowers, hints of cakes and traces of fumé.
In the mouth it's zesty, with good acidity.
The 2016 Alcova is a Bonarda Frizzante
that's pleasant in the mouth, with hints of
wild berries, cherry and red flowers. The
2015 Buttafuoco, a wine with fruity and
flowery aromas, is also excellent.

○ OP Pinot Nero Brut Conte Vistarino 1865 '12	♛♛	5
● OP Bonarda L'Alcova '16	♛♛	3
● OP Buttafuoco '15	♛♛	3
● OP Pinot Nero Costa del Nero '15	♛	2
○ OP Pinot Nero Brut Conte Vistarino 1865 '08	♛♛♛	4*
● OP Pinot Nero Pernice '06	♛♛♛	4*
● Pinot Nero Bertone '13	♛♛♛	5
● OP Bonarda L'Alcova '15	♛♛	2*
○ OP Pinot Nero Brut Conte Vistarino 1865 '09	♛♛	4
● Pinot Nero Pernice '13	♛♛	5
● Pinot Nero Tavernetto '13	♛♛	3

La Costa

FRAZ. COSTA
VIA CURONE, 15
23888 PEREGO [LC]
TEL. +39 0395312218
www.la-costa.it

CELLAR SALES
PRE-BOOKED VISITS
ACCOMMODATION AND RESTAURANT SERVICE
ANNUAL PRODUCTION 30,000 bottles
HECTARES UNDER VINE 12.00
VITICULTURE METHOD Certified Organic

The Crippa family's agricultural project is unique in Brianza's vine growing scene. It's endured for more than 20 years, bolstered by 12 hectares of vineyards (situated in the Montevecchia regional park and Curone valley) and a lovely agritourism. The vineyards, which are entirely surrounded by woodlands and cultivated organically, grow in calcareous terrain rich in bone. Riesling Renano, Merlot, Pinot Nero and Syrah take center stage, for a style that privileges force, with measured extraction and fragrant profiles. Thanks to a good year, strong technique and passion, the 2015 Pinot Nero San Giobbe did very well. It's a vibrant wine, with notes of strawberry, small red fruit, tobacco leaf and pepper. The mouth is succulent, with close-woven tannins and a long, fresh finish. The 2015 Càlido, made with dried red Moscato, was a nice surprise, with a nose featuring nice aromas of rose and red berries, and a mouth that sees balanced sweetness, and an elegant finish.

● San Giobbe '15	♟♟ 4
○ Brigante Bianco '15	♟♟ 3
● Brigante Rosso '15	♟♟ 3
○ Càlido '15	♟♟ 5
● San Giobbe '13	♟♟ 4
● San Giobbe '12	♟♟ 4
● Seriz '12	♟♟ 3
● Serìz '11	♟♟ 3
○ Solesta '14	♟♟ 4
○ Solesta '13	♟♟ 4
○ Solesta '12	♟♟ 3*
● Vino del Quattordici '14	♟♟ 3

La Costaiola

FRAZ. COSTAIOLA
VIA COSTAIOLA, 25
27054 MONTEBELLO DELLA BATTAGLIA [PV]
TEL. +39 038383169
www.lacostaiola.it

CELLAR SALES
ACCOMMODATION
ANNUAL PRODUCTION 80,000 bottles
HECTARES UNDER VINE 13.00

The Rossetti and Scrivani families have created a selection of wines (which bears their name) that's entirely dedicated to 'Metodo Classico' sparklers made with Pinot Nero. And they've done it here, at La Costaiola, an estate situated on the splendid hills of Montebello della Battaglia just a stone's throw from Casteggio. It was an important investment, done with an awareness that Pinot Nero (especially bott fermented) represents the future here in Oltrepò Pavese. We're just now seeing the results, which have had their ups and downs, but that's to be expected for such large undertaking. Among the four wines presented, the Nature made the best impression. It opens with a nice, mineral and citrusy nose, while in the mouth it's close-focused, linear and supple. The Brut offers up notes of citrus, melon and kiwi, while the Nové, as the name suggests, is a 'Metodo Classico' sparkler that spends jus nine months on the lees. It features nice, copper highlights and a simple palate.

○ Brut M. Cl. Nature	♟♟
○ Brut M. Cl.	♟♟
○ Brut M. Cl. Nové	♟
⊙ Rossetti & Scrivani Brut Rosé M. Cl.	♟
● OP Bonarda Vivace Giada '13	♟♟
● Pinot Nero Bricca '15	♟♟

Costaripa

via Costa, 1a
25080 Moniga del Garda [BS]
Tel. +39 0365502010
www.costaripa.it

CELLAR SALES
PRE-BOOKED VISITS
ANNUAL PRODUCTION 400,000 bottles
HECTARES UNDER VINE 40.00

Mattia Vezzola inherited a legacy of winemaking that has deep roots in Valtenesi. He's a well-known winemaker with lots do, but he's supported by the fourth generation of family, Nicole (who handles marketing) and Gherado (who studies winemaking). Their mission is to be Valtenesi's wines (especially Groppello) to the national heights of excellence. Obviously sparkling wines are on the roster. Year after year, the Valtenesi Chiaretto gets more and more interesting. It's dedicated to Pompeo Molmenti, who preached the wine's longevity in the last century. The 2013 Rosé is a brilliant, pale pink wine fermented and aged (for two years) in large wood, making for an aromatic complexity that doesn't compromise freshness or pleasantness, and a delectable, almondy finish. The 2016 RosaMara is a modern, racy wine, while the Mattia Vezzola blends are elegant (which is only proper).

⊙ Valtènesi Chiaretto Molmenti '13	🍷🍷	2*
○ Garda Brut Crémant Mattia Vezzola	🍷🍷	4
○ Mattia Vezzola Brut	🍷🍷	5
⊙ Mattia Vezzola Rosé	🍷🍷	5
⊙ Valtènesi Chiaretto RosaMara '16	🍷🍷	2*
● Valtènesi Rosso Campostarne '14	🍷	3
● Valtènsi Rosso Le Castelline '14	🍷	3
○ Lugana Pievecroce '15	🍸🍸	2*
○ Mattia Vezzola Brut '11	🍸🍸	5
○ Mattia Vezzola Brut '10	🍸🍸	5
⊙ Mattia Vezzola Rosé '10	🍸🍸	5
⊙ Valtènesi Chiaretto Molmenti '12	🍸🍸	2*
⊙ Valtènesi Chiaretto RosaMara '15	🍸🍸	2*

Derbusco Cives

via Provinciale, 83
25030 Erbusco [BS]
Tel. +39 0307731164
www.derbuscocives.com

CELLAR SALES
PRE-BOOKED VISITS
RESTAURANT SERVICE
ANNUAL PRODUCTION 90,000 bottles
HECTARES UNDER VINE 12.00

To highlight the centrality and peculiarlty of Erbusco (capital of Franciacorta), a group of five friends, Dario and Giuseppe Vezzoli, Luigi Dotti, Paolo Brescianini and Vanni Bordiga, founded this winery in 2004, calling it simply 'Citizens of Erbusco'. The estate comprises some 12 hectares of land, which are worked with not-quite-so-conventional methods, like refermentation with Franciacorta must and late dégorgement. And their commitment to sustainability is praiseworthy. The 2011 Crisalis is a Blanc de Noirs with a nice, brilliant, gold color to it. It ages on the less for more than five years before dégorgement. It has complex, charming fragrances ranging from ripe fruit to more complex notes of Cuban cigar. The palate is deep, rich, supported by elegant acidity. The 2011 Brut, a monovarietal Chardonnay, charms for its soft depth, the pleasantness of the palate and its overall harmony.

○ Franciacorta Brut Crisalis '11	🍷🍷	6
○ Franciacorta Brut '11	🍷🍷	6
○ Franciacorta Brut Doppio Erre DV	🍷🍷	5
○ Franciacorta Extra Brut '11	🍷🍷	8
○ Franciacorta Brut Doppio Erre Di	🍷	5
○ Franciacorta Brut '10	🍸🍸	6
○ Franciacorta Brut '09	🍸🍸	6
○ Franciacorta Brut '08	🍸🍸	6
○ Franciacorta Brut '07	🍸🍸	6
○ Franciacorta Extra Brut '10	🍸🍸	8
○ Franciacorta Extra Brut '09	🍸🍸	7
○ Franciacorta Extra Brut '07	🍸🍸	6
○ Franciacorta Extra Brut '06	🍸🍸	7
⊙ Franciacorta Extra Brut Rosé '09	🍸🍸	6

Dirupi

LOC. MADONNA DI CAMPAGNA
VIA GRUMELLO, 1
23020 MONTAGNA IN VALTELLINA [SO]
TEL. +39 3472909779
www.dirupi.com

CELLAR SALES
PRE-BOOKED VISITS
ANNUAL PRODUCTION 15,000 bottles
HECTARES UNDER VINE 4.50

Birba and Faso are the loose cannons of Lombardy's wine scene. They're a close couple who complement one another for character and sensibility. And they've brought enthusiasm and interest back to Valtellina. The linearity of their vineyards is reflected in their wines: fragrant, taut and airy, with a vitality of flavor that's contagious to say the least. Their production volumes, which are slowly growing, are based around four wines, from the highly drinkable Olè to the concentration of the Sforzato della Valtellina Vino Sbagliato. The name of the 2015 Sforzato is just a play on words. It's a vibrant, sophisticated wine with intact, close-focused fruit, fragrances of plums and cherries and nuances of cocoa. The most is bold, with the right fullness, and the finish lingers endlessly. The 2014 Riserva Dirupi is exemplary for its fruity notes, with a background of tobacco leaf and licorice. On the palate it's solid, delicate, with well-balanced acidity and alcohol, and a long finish.

● Valtellina Sup. Dirupi Ris. '14	♟♟♟	6
● Sforzato di Valtellina		
Vino Sbagliato '15	♟♟	6
● Rosso di Valtellina Olè '16	♟♟	3
● Valtellina Sup. Dirupi '15	♟♟	4
● Valtellina Sup. Dirupi Ris. '12	♟♟♟	6
● Valtellina Sup. Dirupi Ris. '11	♟♟♟	6
● Valtellina Sup. Dirupi Ris. '09	♟♟♟	6
● Rosso di Valtellina Olè '14	♟♟	3
● Sforzato di Valtellina		
Vino Sbagliato '14	♟♟	6
● Valtellina Sup. Dirupi '14	♟♟	4
● Valtellina Sup. Dirupi '13	♟♟	4
● Valtellina Sup. Dirupi '12	♟♟	4
● Valtellina Sup. Dirupi Ris. '13	♟♟	6

Sandro Fay

LOC. SAN GIACOMO DI TEGLIO
VIA PILA CASELLI, 1
23030 TEGLIO [SO]
TEL. +39 0342786071
www.vinifay.it

CELLAR SALES
PRE-BOOKED VISITS
ANNUAL PRODUCTION 38,000 bottles
HECTARES UNDER VINE 13.00

Founded in 1973 by Sandro Fay, today, Valgella's flagship winery is managed by Marco Fay, who's brought new life to the producer by adopting an approach centered on sustainability (or as the French prefer, 'durability'). The work aimed at bringing out the best of each single vineyard has proved worth it, giving rise to some of Valtellina's deepest and most complex wines. The 2013 Ronco del Picchio is a Sforzato with its sights set on the future. It's a lively, vibrant wine made with semi-dried grapes that offers up notes of fresh plum, tobacco leaf and quinine. The mouth is bold, tannic but without drying, while the finish is lengthy and elegant, austere even. The 2014 Costa Bassa and 2014 Valgella Cà Moréi are fresh, fine, drinkable wines. The former surprises for its fruity aromas, elegant tannins and overall harmony, while the latter offers up intense, spicy fragrances (with a lovely hint of rust), and a succulent, structured mouth with a long finish.

● Sforzato di Valtellina		
Ronco del Picchio '13	♟♟	6
● Valtellina Sup. Costa Bassa '14	♟♟	4
● Valtellina Sup. Sassella Il Glicine '14	♟♟	5
● Valtellina Sup. Valgella Cà Moréi '14	♟♟	5
● Valtellina Sforzato		
Ronco del Picchio '10	♟♟♟	6
● Valtellina Sforzato		
Ronco del Picchio '09	♟♟♟	6
● Valtellina Sforzato		
Ronco del Picchio '02	♟♟♟	6
● Valtellina Sup. Valgella Cà Moréi '13	♟♟♟	5
● La Faya '13	♟♟	5
● Valtellina Sup. Sassella Il Glicine '13	♟♟	4
● Valtellina Sup. Valgella Carterìa Ris. '13	♟♟	5

Ferghettina

Saline, 11
030 Adro [BS]
+39 0307451212
w.ferghettina.it

LAR SALES
E-BOOKED VISITS
NUAL PRODUCTION 400,000 bottles
CTARES UNDER VINE 160.00
STAINABLE WINERY

ry year, we risk repeating ourselves
en talking about Roberto Gatti and his
ily. But building one of Franciacorta's
wn jewels in just 20 years couldn't have
en an easy feat. Roberto and Andreina
wife) had the intuition and courage to
in with just a few thousand bottles. But
fact that today the estate manages 160
ctares and produces top blends is surely
nks in part to their children, Laura and
tteo, winemakers who've been there
m the beginning. Their cellar is also very
ely. The Pas Dosé Riserva '33 is a
ssic of Franciacorta. The 2010 charms
the complexity of its bouquet, which
s up mountain flower honey, crisp white
t and citrus peel. It has fine perlage and
ves generous, zesty and assertive on the
ate, which sees those same aromas
ered back up with coherence and
rmony. The long and spicy finish features
it. The 2011 Extra Brut deserves
ntions for its freshness and stylistic
us; it's one of the best tasted this year.

ranciacorta Pas Dosé 33 Ris. '10	♙♙♙	6
ranciacorta Extra Brut '11	♙♙	6
ranciacorta Satèn '13	♙♙	5
urtefranca Bianco '16	♙♙	2*
ranciacorta Brut	♙♙	4
ranciacorta Brut Milledì '13	♙♙	5
ranciacorta Rosé	♙♙	5
urtefranca Rosso '15	♙	2
ranciacorta Extra Brut '09	♙♙♙	5
ranciacorta Extra Brut '06	♙♙♙	5
ranciacorta Extra Brut '05	♙♙♙	5
ranciacorta Pas Dosé 33 Ris. '09	♙♙♙	6
ranciacorta Pas Dosé 33 Ris. '07	♙♙♙	6
ranciacorta Pas Dosé 33 Ris. '06	♙♙♙	6

Fiamberti

via Chiesa, 17
27044 Canneto Pavese [PV]
Tel. +39 038588019
www.fiambertivini.it

CELLAR SALES
PRE-BOOKED VISITS
ANNUAL PRODUCTION 140,000 bottles
HECTARES UNDER VINE 18.00

The Fiamberti family, father Ambrogio and
son Giulio, manage this historic winery in
Canneto Pavese. As is common in Oltrepò,
they've been following two tracks, traditional
reds of the so-called 'Sperone di Stradella'
and 'Metodo Classico' Pinot Nero sparklers
(in white and rosé versions). The winery,
however, finds itself in a period of transition,
with an eye on improving quality. The Brut
Metodo Classico offers up medicinal herbs
and lavender, while the mouth proves
supple. The 2012 Buttafuoco Vigna Sacca
del Prete shows substance. It's dark, a bit
edgy, but interesting in its typicity. The
Cruasé gets better by the year; it's only
missing a bit of structure. The 2016 Sangue
di Giuda Lella did very well. It's a fruity,
balsamic wine with clear overtones of
cherry and blackcurrant. In the mouth it
proves lean and dynamic, with a nice,
savory, deep palate. The 2016 Riesling Ida,
a white with clear, citrusy nuances and hints
of yellow fruit, is also interesting.

● OP Buttafuoco Storico V. Sacca del Prete '12	♙♙	4
○ OP Brut Fiamberti	♙♙	3
○ OP Riesling Ida '16	♙♙	2*
● OP Sangue di Giuda Lella '16	♙♙	2*
● OP Buttafuoco Cacciatore '14	♙	3
⊙ OP Cruasé Fiamberti	♙	4
● OP Pinot Nero Nero '15	♙	2
● OP Bonarda Vivace La Briccona '15	♙♙	2*
● OP Buttafuoco Storico V. Sacca del Prete '11	♙♙	4
● OP Buttafuoco Storico V. Sacca del Prete '09	♙♙	4
● OP Pinot Nero Nero '13	♙♙	2*
● OP Sangue di Giuda Lella '15	♙♙	2*

Frecciarossa

VIA VIGORELLI, 141
27045 CASTEGGIO [PV]
TEL. +39 0383804465
www.frecciarossa.com

CELLAR SALES
PRE-BOOKED VISITS
ANNUAL PRODUCTION 80,000 bottles
HECTARES UNDER VINE 34.00

The splendid estate purchased by Mario Odero in 1919 and revolutionized 70 years later by his granddaughter Margherita, absolutely deserves to be visited. Its 19th century villa is a gem, and its historic courtyard has been kept intact. Both the cellar and vineyards, managed by Pierluigi Donna, are also worth seeing. But most of all, you should visit for the wine. Tasting wines made 30 years ago shows you why this is one of Oltrepò's top producers. And over the years, with the arrival of Margherita's daughter, Valeria Radici, as well as a team of skilled young people, elegance, quality and terroir have only increased. It just missed getting top marks, but the selection presented is still one of the best yet. The 2014 Giorgio Odero offers up notes of ripe fruit, balsamic accents and nuances of bark. The overall effect is elegant. The 2015 Carillo is simpler, but subtle in the mouth, with close-focused, crisp fruit. The nose features fragrances of raspberry, while the mouth is fresh with good acidity.

● OP Pinot Nero Carillo '15	♥♥	2*
● OP Pinot Nero Giorgio Odero '14	♥♥	5
○ OP Riesling Gli Orti '15	♥♥	2*
⊙ OP Brut Frecciarosé	♥♥	6
○ OP Brut I Moschettieri '13	♥	6
● OP Pinot Nero Giorgio Odero '12	♥♥♥	5
● OP Pinot Nero Giorgio Odero '11	♥♥♥	5
● OP Pinot Nero Giorgio Odero '10	♥♥♥	5
● OP Pinot Nero Giorgio Odero '08	♥♥♥	5
● OP Pinot Nero Giorgio Odero '07	♥♥♥	5
● OP Pinot Nero Giorgio Odero '05	♥♥♥	5

Enrico Gatti

VIA METELLI, 9
25030 ERBUSCO [BS]
TEL. +39 0307267999
www.enricogatti.it

CELLAR SALES
PRE-BOOKED VISITS
ANNUAL PRODUCTION 120,000 bottles
HECTARES UNDER VINE 17.00

The Gatti siblings, Lorenzo and Paola, are a close-knit team that's rounded out by Enr. Balzarini (Paola's brother). The winery, founded more than 40 years ago by their father, Enrico, has established itself as on of Franciacorta's best producers (thanks this brilliant triad). The Gatti work only the own grapes. The estate comprises 17 hectares, all in Erbrusco, which is a facto in their wines' particular structure, fullnes and richness of fruit, as well as the notabl vigor present in all their blends. The Natu is the wine that best expresses Gatti's st. It exhibits structure, depth, and has a nic acidic, mineral vein to it. In addition to ze it offers smoothness and harmony by virt of the freshness of its aromas (delicate fruit, flowers and citrus). It's because of a somewhat lighter structure than usual tha this excellent 2011 is held back, but the whole selection still proves outstanding.

○ Franciacorta Nature '11	♥
○ Franciacorta Brut	♥♥
○ Franciacorta Brut Rosé	♥♥
○ Franciacorta Brut Satèn '13	♥♥
○ Franciacorta Nature	♥♥
○ Franciacorta Brut '05	♥♥♥
○ Franciacorta Nature '07	♥♥♥
○ Franciacorta Satèn '05	♥♥♥
○ Franciacorta Satèn '03	♥♥♥
○ Franciacorta Satèn '02	♥♥♥
○ Franciacorta Satèn '01	♥♥♥
○ Franciacorta Satèn '00	♥♥♥

I Gessi

FRAZ. FOSSA, 8
27050 OLIVA GESSI [PV]
TEL. +39 0383896606
www.cantineigessi.it

CELLAR SALES
PRE-BOOKED VISITS
ACCOMMODATION
ANNUAL PRODUCTION 160,000 bottles
HECTARES UNDER VINE 41.00

Fabbio Defilippi's winery features more than 40 hectares of vineyards (all cultivated organically, primarily on gypsum-rich, calcareous terrain), an agritourism, and the sure hand of his brother (and winemaker), Emilio. Year after year, it's proving one of the most interesting new producers in the area, especially in terms of their 'Metodo Classico' sparkling wines and their still whites. We particularly liked the undosed versions of their sparkling wines, both the white and the rosé. The former has vigor and grip, with well-expressed wild berry. It's a generous, elegant wine. The second sees an even greater presence of wild berry. It's a close-knit, linear wine with notes of licorice. The 2016 Riesling, with its aromas of broom, chamomile and wild flower is noteworthy. The other wines also show good overall quality.

F.lli Giorgi

FRAZ. CAMPONOCE, 39A
27044 CANNETO PAVESE [PV]
TEL. +39 0385262151
www.giorgi-wines.it

CELLAR SALES
PRE-BOOKED VISITS
ANNUAL PRODUCTION 1,600,000 bottles
HECTARES UNDER VINE 30.00

If it's true, as Fabiano Giorgi says, that the family producer got its start primarily as a commercial enterprise, it's also true that they've always bottled their entire production. Fabiano's uncle, Gianfranco, who died young in 2004, had already laid the groundwork for a breakthrough in quality, especially for the 'Metodo Classico' sparklers. Today, the winery (which produces more than one and a half million bottles a year) has notably increased the number of Pinot Nero sparklers, with a parallel rise in quality. Once again, the Giorgi family offer up a wide ranging selection, with many noteworthy and recommendable wines, especially their sparklers. The TOP Zero is without a doubt the most charming and pleasant 'Metodo Classico' on the roster. It offers up fragrances of white flowers, herbs and citrus, with a touch of cakes as well. The 1870 also did well, as did the 2013 Buttafuoco Storico Casa del Corno, the best in its category.

○ OP Pinot Nero Pas Dosé Maria Cristina '11	♟♟ 5
○ OP Pinot Nero Brut Rosé M. Cl. Maria Cristina Pas Dosé	♟♟ 3
○ OP Riesling I Gessi '16	♟♟ 1*
○ OP Pinot Nero Brut Maria Cristina	♟ 3
● OP Barbera I Gessi '15	♟ 2
● OP Bonarda I Gessi '16	♟ 2
○ OP Pinot Grigio Crocetta '16	♟ 2
○ OP Pinot Nero Brut Rosé M. Cl. Maria Cristina	♟ 3
○ OP Pinot Grigio Crocetta '15	♟♟ 2*
○ OP Pinot Nero Pas Dosé Maria Cristina '10	♟♟ 5

○ OP Brut Top Zero	♟♟♟ 4*
○ OP Pinot Nero Brut 1870 '13	♟♟ 5
○ Moscato '16	♟♟ 2*
● OP Bonarda Vivace La Brughera '16	♟♟ 2*
○ OP Brut Fusion	♟♟ 4
○ OP Brut Gerry Scotti '13	♟♟ 4
⊙ OP Brut Rosé '14	♟♟ 3
● OP Buttafuoco Storico V. Casa del Corno '13	♟♟ 3
○ OP Pinot Nero Brut Gianfranco Giorgi '14	♟♟ 5
⊙ Plumgranin '16	♟ 2
○ OP Pinot Nero Brut 1870 '11	♟♟♟ 5
○ OP Pinot Nero Brut 1870 '10	♟♟♟ 5
○ OP Pinot Nero Brut 1870 '09	♟♟♟ 5
○ OP Pinot Nero Brut 1870 '08	♟♟♟ 5
○ OP Pinot Nero Brut 1870 '07	♟♟♟ 5

Isimbarda

Fraz. Castello
Cascina Isimbarda
27046 Santa Giulietta [PV]
Tel. +39 0383899256
www.isimbarda.com

CELLAR SALES
PRE-BOOKED VISITS
ANNUAL PRODUCTION 130,000 bottles
HECTARES UNDER VINE 40.00

In the 17th century, this splendid hill zone
in Santa Giuletta was part of the Marquis
Isimbardi's estate. Thus the name of the
winery purchased by Luigi Meroni in the
1980s. The fact that it's particularly
well-suited to wine production is testified
to by old documents. For years, the winery
has been managed by the Venetian
winemaker Daniele Zangelmi, who seeks
to bring out the best of the soil and its
grapes, in particular white ones. The
2016 Pinot Nero Vigna dei Giganti offers
up aromas of a blackberry and mulberry.
In the mouth it is mature, elegant, clean
and deep. This year the Cruasé delivers
with its fine, dosed and well-integrated
sparkle, and a close-focused finish with
slightly almondy hints. The 2016 Riesling
Vigna Martina continues to prove
delectable, featuring aromas that are still
flowery, with the addition of tertiary
mineral notes.

Lantieri de Paratico

Loc. Colzano
via Videtti
25031 Capriolo [BS]
Tel. +39 030736151
www.lantierideparatico.it

CELLAR SALES
PRE-BOOKED VISITS
ACCOMMODATION AND RESTAURANT SERVICE
ANNUAL PRODUCTION 140,000 bottles
HECTARES UNDER VINE 18.00
VITICULTURE METHOD Certified Organic

The Lantieri de Paratico are one of the
oldest families in Franciacorta. Their
presence here is certified by documents
going back to 930. In the 1500s they
settled in Capriolo, and even back then
their wine was known and appreciated in
Italy and European courts. Today, Fabio
Lantieri is keeping the tradition alive, and in
the historic family villa he's built a modern
cellar where his excellent blends are made.
The Arcadia is a selection of Chardonnay
and Pinot Nero whose base wine ages for
some months in wood before
refermentation. It's the producer's flagship
wine, and the 2013 version shines. It has a
brilliant, straw-yellow color with gold
highlights, supremely fine perlage and a
complex, harmonious bouquet of fruit,
citrus, and a touch of well-integrated oak.
The mouth is succulent and zesty,
sustained by a vein of acidity that guides it
to its long, gratifying finish. In part, this
well-deserved Tre Bicchieri also recognizes
their consistent quality over the years.

⊙ OP Cruasé	♙♙ 4
● OP Pinot Nero V. dei Giganti '16	♙♙ 3
○ OP Riesling Renano V. Martina '16	♙♙ 2*
○ OP Brut Riserva degli Isimbardi	♙ 3
○ OP Pinot Nero Brut Blanc de Noir	♙ 4
○ OP Pinot Nero Brut Première Cuvée	♙ 4
● OP Rosso Monplò '15	♙ 2
● OP Bonarda Vivace V. delle More '13	♙♙ 2*
● OP Bonarda Vivace V. delle More '15	♙♙ 2*
○ OP Riesling Renano V. Martina '14	♙♙ 2*
○ OP Riesling Renano V. Martina '13	♙♙ 2*
○ OP Riesling V. Martina '15	♙♙ 3
● OP Rosso Monplò '13	♙♙ 3

○ Franciacorta Brut Arcadia '13	♙♙♙ 5
⊙ Franciacorta Brut Rosé Arcadia	♙♙ 5
○ Franciacorta Brut Satèn	♙♙ 5
○ Franciacorta Extra Brut	♙♙ 4
○ Franciacorta Nature	♙♙ 4
○ Franciacorta Nature Origines Ris. '11	♙♙ 7
○ Franciacorta Brut	♙ 4
○ Curtefranca Bianco '12	♙♙ 2
○ Franciacorta Brut Arcadia '12	♙♙ 5
○ Franciacorta Brut Arcadia '11	♙♙ 5
○ Franciacorta Brut Arcadia '10	♙♙ 5
○ Franciacorta Extra Brut Origines Ris. '10	♙♙ 7
○ Franciacorta Extra Brut Origines Ris. '09	♙♙ 7
○ Franciacorta Extra Brut Origines Ris. '08	♙♙ 7

ajolini

VALLE
. MANZONI, 3
50 OME [BS]
+39 0306527378
w.majolini.it

LAR SALES
E-BOOKED VISITS
NUAL PRODUCTION 150,000 bottles
CTARES UNDER VINE 24.00
ICULTURE METHOD Certified Organic
STAINABLE WINERY

e Majolini di Ome family are successful
repreneurs, but they have agricultural
ts in Franciacorta (Ome to be precise)
t go way back to the 15th century. And
it was that in 1981 an inspiring winery
ecialized in the production of
nciacorta was born. Today, it's managed
Simone Majolini, a motivated young
n. The estate comprises 24 well-
sitioned hectares (some of them
nchlands) in the district of Ome. The
nch winemaker Jean Pierre Valade
rves as enological consultant. This year
e Rosé Altera made it to our finals. It has
ice, pale pink color to it, with salmon
ghlights, and a nose that offers up
egant scents of wild berries, white fruit
d vanilla, as well as nuances of
editerranean herbs. The perlage
hibits enchanting finesse, while the
late is generous, full, solid and long,
th a finish featuring herbs and aniseed.
e 2013 Satèn proves elegant, as does
e non-vintage Brut.

Franciacorta Rosé Altera	♟♟ 5
Franciacorta Brut	♟♟ 5
Franciacorta Brut Blanc de Noirs	♟♟ 6
Franciacorta Brut Satèn '13	♟♟ 5
Franciacorta Brut Vintage '09	♟♟ 6
Franciacorta Brut Electo '08	♟ 5
Franciacorta Brut Electo '00	♟♟♟ 6
Franciacorta Brut Electo '99	♟♟♟ 5
Franciacorta Brut Electo '97	♟♟♟ 5
Franciacorta Pas Dosé Aligi Sassu '08	♟♟ 5
Franciacorta Pas Dosé Aligi Sassu '07	♟♟ 5
Franciacorta Satèn '11	♟♟ 5
Franciacorta Satèn '10	♟♟ 5
Franciacorta Satèn '09	♟♟ 5

★Mamete Prevostinl

VIA DON PRIMO LUCCHINETTI, 63
23020 MESE [SO]
TEL. +39 034341522
www.mameteprevostini.com

CELLAR SALES
PRE-BOOKED VISITS
RESTAURANT SERVICE
ANNUAL PRODUCTION 180,000 bottles
HECTARES UNDER VINE 20.00
SUSTAINABLE WINERY

It's full speed ahead for Mamete Prevostini,
who continues to serve as ambassador for
Lombardy's wines throughout the world,
thanks to his second job with the Consorzio
per la Tutela dei Vini di Valtellina e Ascovilo,
a regional consortium that promotes
Lombardy's wines internationally. And his
winery in Valchiavenna confirms its status
as among the best in the region, bolstered
by a model cellar (in terms of equipment
and environmental friendliness) and a solid,
consistent selection of wines. These prove
potent and generous in their subtle,
nuanced, fragranced expressions. The
2015 Sforzato Albareda is stylistically
flawless, austere and elegant. Its oak spice
and fresh, close-focused fruitiness are in
perfect harmony. The palate is charmingly
well-orchestrated and structured, with the
use of partially-dried grapes managed
masterfully. The 2015 Sassella San Lorenzo
is generous and vibrant, offering up aromas
of perfectly fused strawberry and cherry,
and balanced hints of coffee and vanilla.
The palate is subtle, with fresh zest and a
long finish.

● Valtellina Sforzato Albareda '15	♟♟♟ 6
● Valtellina Sforzato Corte di Cama '15	♟♟ 6
● Valtellina Sup. Sassella San Lorenzo '15	♟♟ 6
● Rosso di Valtellina Santarita '15	♟♟ 2*
● Valtellina Sup. Sassella '15	♟♟ 4
● Valtellina Sup. Sassella Sommarovina '15	♟♟ 5
● Valtellina Sforzato Albareda '13	♟♟♟ 6
● Valtellina Sforzato Albareda '09	♟♟♟ 6
● Valtellina Sforzato Albareda '08	♟♟♟ 6
● Valtellina Sforzato Albareda '06	♟♟♟ 6
● Valtellina Sup. Ris. '09	♟♟♟ 5
● Valtellina Sup. Sassella San Lorenzo '10	♟♟♟ 5
● Valtellina Sup. Sassella Sommarovina '13	♟♟♟ 5

Le Marchesine

VIA VALLOSA, 31
25050 PASSIRANO [BS]
TEL. +39 030657005
www.lemarchesine.it

CELLAR SALES
PRE-BOOKED VISITS
ANNUAL PRODUCTION 450,000 bottles
HECTARES UNDER VINE 47.00

Loris Biatta, accompanied by his children, Alice and Andrea, is carrying on the work of his father, Giovanni, with passion and skill. Founded in the 1980s, the winery immediately pursued top quality wines. With 47 hectares of lovely vineyards at its disposal, and production volumes reaching almost half a million bottles, it can feel good about its prospects. Winemaking is entrusted to Jean Pierre Valade, an enologist with international experience in the 'Metodo Classico'. The 2010 Brut Secolo Novo made a good impression for its complex nose, rich in fresh aromas of fruit and nuances of aromatic herbs. The palate is relaxed, silky, rich and deep, with a finish that calls up notes of mountain herbs. The 2009 Versione Riserva is an elegant Dosage Zero made exclusively with Chardonnay, and features lovely notes of orange peel and vanilla on the nose. The rest of the selection is of outstanding quality.

○ Franciacorta Brut Secolo Novo '10	♟♟ 7
○ Franciacorta Brut	♟♟ 4
☉ Franciacorta Brut Rosé '12	♟♟ 5
○ Franciacorta Brut Satèn '13	♟♟ 5
○ Franciacorta Dosage Zero Secolo Novo Ris. '09	♟♟ 8
○ Franciacorta Extra Brut	♟♟ 5
○ Franciacorta Brut '04	♟♟♟ 5
○ Franciacorta Brut Blanc de Noir '09	♟♟♟ 5
○ Franciacorta Brut Secolo Novo '05	♟♟♟ 7
○ Franciacorta Dosage Zero Secolo Novo Ris. '08	♟♟♟ 8
○ Franciacorta Brut Blanc de Noir '12	♟♟ 6
☉ Franciacorta Brut Rosé '11	♟♟ 5
○ Franciacorta Brut Secolo Novo '09	♟♟ 7
○ Franciacorta Satèn '12	♟♟ 5

Tenuta Mazzolino

VIA MAZZOLINO, 34
27050 CORVINO SAN QUIRICO [PV]
TEL. +39 03838/6122
www.tenuta-mazzolino.com

CELLAR SALES
PRE-BOOKED VISITS
ANNUAL PRODUCTION 100,000 bottles
HECTARES UNDER VINE 20.00

Since 1980, the Braggiotti family has owned this lovely oasis situated on the hi of central Oltrepò. And, thanks to Giacom Bologna, Enrico Braggiotti and the suppo of Giancarlo Scaglione, they were among the first in the area to ferment Pinot Nero on the skins. After its two great Piedmont the winery focused on a more Burgundy styled wine, such that their current products (early-drinkers, aged and sparkling wines) are almost all made with Pinot Nero and Chardonnay. In spite of a rather unlucky year, the 2014 Noir deliver for its herbaceous notes and aromas of ri fruit. The mouth is fresh, supple with tannins present, but soft and enfolding. Th Blanc de Blancs also did well. It's a wine made elegant by virtue of its notes of peach and green apple, and defined by its good zest. The Cruasé is another solid wine, featuring notes of licorice and coffee as well as close-focused citrus. The Blanc will have to wait a little longer for its wood to integrate.

● OP Pinot Nero Noir '14	♟♟
○ Brut Mazzolino Blanc de Blancs	♟♟
☉ OP Chardonnay Blanc '15	♟♟
☉ OP Cruasé Mazzolino	♟♟
● OP Pinot Nero Rosso Terrazze '16	♟
● OP Pinot Nero Noir '12	♟♟♟
● OP Pinot Nero Noir '10	♟♟♟
● OP Pinot Nero Noir '09	♟♟♟
● OP Pinot Nero Noir '08	♟♟♟
● OP Pinot Nero Noir '07	♟♟♟
● OP Pinot Nero Noir '06	♟♟♟

★Monsupello

Via San Lazzaro, 5
27050 Torricella Verzate [PV]
Tel. +39 0383896043
www.monsupello.it

CELLAR SALES
PRE-BOOKED VISITS
ANNUAL PRODUCTION 260,000 bottles
HECTARES UNDER VINE 50.00

Monsupello is, without a doubt, among Italy's best sparkling winemakers, when we consider how strong they've been over time, the quality of their wines and their well-defined style. Carlo Boatti laid the groundwork, and now the family (and honorary member, winemaker Marco Bertelegni) keeping his legacy alive in the vineyards and in their sparkling wines. Indeed, their selection includes acclaimed whites, early-drinking and aged reds, and, of course, Oltrepò's classic sparklers. And they're all of a quality that's rarely matched here in Italy. This year the Rosé stands out at Monsupello. It's a sparkling wine made exclusively with Pinot Nero, and it stands out for its fine, complex, multifaceted nose. Notes of pomegranate and blackcurrant alternate with nuances of aromatic herbs, which give way to a pleasant, fresh, zesty mouth. In terms of the rest of the selection, the sparkling wines once again stand out, with a Nature that is, for the first time in many years, a bit low-key.

○ Brut Rosé	♥♥♥ 4*
○ Brut	♥♥ 5
○ Brut Cuvée Ca' del Tava	♥♥ 6
○ Brut Nature	♥♥ 4
● OP Bonarda Vivace Vaiolet '16	♥♥ 2*
● Pinot Nero 3309 '09	♥♥ 3
● Pinot Nero Junior '16	♥♥ 3
○ Brut '11	♥♥♥ 5
○ OP Brut Cl. Cuvée Ca' del Tava	♥♥♥ 6
○ OP Brut Classese '04	♥♥♥ 5
○ OP Pinot Nero Cl. Nature	♥♥♥ 4
● Barbera I Gelsi '13	♥♥ 3
○ Brut '11	♥♥ 5
● Cabernet Sauvignon Aplomb '09	♥♥ 5
○ Chardonnay '15	♥♥ 2*

Francesco Montagna Bertè & Cordini

Via Cairoli, 67
27043 Broni [PV]
Tel. +39 038551028
www.cantinemontagna.it - www.bertecordini.it

CELLAR SALES
PRE-BOOKED VISITS
ACCOMMODATION
ANNUAL PRODUCTION 700,000 bottles
HECTARES UNDER VINE 18.00
SUSTAINABLE WINERY

Founded in 1985, it's a winery with a long tradition. The Bertè and Cordini families purchased it in the 1960s and have since moved in a direction similar to other producers in the area. With all the difficulties involved, they've gone from a focus on quantity (a necessary factor economically) to quality, first with Natale Bertè and now even more with her son, Matteo, a winemaker that's passionate about the 'Metodo Classico'. And this is having the best results, through a varying array of high-quality wines. The Cuvée della Casa is a supremely elegant Oltrepò Pavese with fine, creamy, caressing sparkle that pairs well with its lovely vigor. Together they carry the palate towards a nice, long finish. The Nero d'Oro, made with 100% Pinot Nero, is crisp, undosed and linear, with overtones of small red fruit. The Cruasé also delivers, a citrusy wine with good maturity. The Cuvée Tradizione once again shows structure, while the 2009 Oblio, which spends a lot of time on the lees, has maintained its vigor despite its being very evolved.

○ OP Pinot Nero Brut M. Cl. Cuvée della Casa	♥♥♥ 5
⊙ OP Cruasé Bertè & Cordini	♥♥ 5
○ OP Pinot Nero Brut M. Cl. Cuvée Nero d'Oro	♥♥ 4
○ OP Pinot Nero Dosaggio Zero Oblio '09	♥♥ 5
○ OP Pinot Nero Brut Cuvée Tradizione '13	♥ 4
● OP Pinot Nero Nuval '14	♥ 3
● OP Sangue di Giuda '16	♥ 2
● OP Bonarda Sabion '15	♥♥ 2*
● OP Buttafuoco Bertè & Cordini '13	♥♥ 2*
○ OP Pinot Nero Brut Cuvée Tradizione '12	♥♥ 4
○ OP Pinot Nero Brut Cuvée Tradizione '10	♥♥ 4

★Monte Rossa

FRAZ. BORNATO
VIA MONTE ROSSA, 1
25040 CAZZAGO SAN MARTINO [BS]
TEL. I 39 030725066
www.monterossa.com

CELLAR SALES
PRE-BOOKED VISITS
ANNUAL PRODUCTION 500,000 bottles
HECTARES UNDER VINE 70.00

Today, Emanuele Rabotti is leading Monte Rossa, and doing it with passion, extreme care and creativity (he shares the business with Oscar Farinetti). They're among Franciacorta's most historic and representative wineries, founded in 1972 by Paolo and Paola Rabotti and destined to become an icon of the territory. Bolstered by their 70 hectares of vineyards, in various positions, today they produce about 500,000 bottles a year, all of excellent quality. This year, the Non Dosato Coupé made such a good impression that we decided to include it in the finals, where it performed well in part by virtue of its citrusy, flowery bouquet. In the mouth it proves racy and invigorating, with an elegant effervescence that makes for a fruity, creamy palate. The Satèn Sansevé also did quite well, with its smooth softness and crisp, zesty fruit. The 2011 Extra Brut Salvadék, a lean, fresh and drinkable wine, is also noteworthy.

○ Franciacorta Non Dosato Coupé	♟♟ 5
○ Franciacorta Brut Satèn Sansevé	♟♟ 5
○ Franciacorta Extra Brut Salvadék '11	♟♟ 6
⊙ Franciaocorta Rosé Flamingo	♟♟ 5
○ Franciacorta Brut P. R.	♟ 5
○ Franciacorta Brut Prima Cuvée	♟ 4
○ Franciacorta Brut Cabochon '05	♟♟♟ 6
○ Franciacorta Brut Cabochon '04	♟♟♟ 6
○ Franciacorta Brut Cabochon '03	♟♟♟ 6
○ Franciacorta Brut Cabochon '11	♟♟ 7
○ Franciacorta Brut Cabochon '09	♟♟ 7
○ Franciacorta Brut Cabochon '08	♟♟ 7
○ Franciacorta Extra Brut Salvàdek '10	♟♟ 6
○ Franciacorta Extra Brut Salvadek '09	♟♟ 6

Il Mosnel

LOC. CAMIGNONE
VIA BARBOGLIO, 14
25040 PASSIRANO [RS]
TEL. +39 030653117
www.ilmosnel.com

CELLAR SALES
PRE-BOOKED VISITS
RESTAURANT SERVICE
ANNUAL PRODUCTION 250,000 bottles
HECTARES UNDER VINE 40.00

Giulio and Lucia Barzanò are forging ahead with talent and passion, keeping alive the tradition that began in the 1960s when their mother Emanuela Barboglio converted their farm into a vineyard (they were also among the first to produce sparkling wine in Franciacorta). Headquartered in Camignone di Passirano, theirs is a 16th century hamlet, with an adjacent villa that's been perfectly renovated (and is open to visitors and for events). The complex is at the center of 40 hectares of well-maintained vineyards, which give rise to an elegant selection of Franciacortas and local wines. And once again the Extra Brut EBB (2012 version), dedicated by Giulio and Lucia to their mother, Emanuela, intrigued us most. It's a Franciacorta with some character, featuring close-focused notes of fruit, as well as balance, freshness, good consistency, creaminess and length. The excellent Pas Dosé is also noteworthy, with its hints of citron and aromatic herbs, as is the dynamic Nature, made with organically cultivated grapes.

○ Franciacorta Extra Brut EBB '12	♟♟ 5
○ Franciacorta Pas Dosé	♟♟ 4
○ Franciacorta Brut	♟♟ 4
○ Franciacorta Nature Bio	♟♟ 4
⊙ Franciacorta Pas Dosé Parosé '11	♟♟ 5
○ Franciacorta Satèn '13	♟♟ 5
⊙ Franciacorta Brut Rosé	♟ 5
○ Franciacorta Extra Brut EBB '09	♟♟♟ 5
○ Franciacorta Pas Dosé QdE Ris. '04	♟♟♟ 6
○ Franciacorta Satèn '05	♟♟♟ 5
○ Franciacorta Extra Brut EBB '11	♟♟ 5
⊙ Franciacorta Pas Dosé Parosé '10	♟♟ 5
○ Franciacorta Satèn '12	♟♟ 5
○ Franciacorta Satèn '11	♟♟ 5

★Nino Negri

GHIBELLINI
030 CHIURO [SO]
.. +39 0342485211
w.ninonegri.it

CELLAR SALES
RE-BOOKED VISITS
ESTAURANT SERVICE
NNUAL PRODUCTION 900,000 bottles
ECTARES UNDER VINE 161.00
USTAINABLE WINERY

no Negri is one of the wineries that made
ational viticulture history, bringing
altellina's wines to top international
rums. The best way of understanding the
volution of viticulture in the area is to go
own into their cellars, carved out of rock
the Castello Quadrio. They've been
perational since 1897, and today they're
e of the Gruppo Italiano Vini's crown
wels, bolstered by a unique set of
neyards that span more than 160
ectares and comprise all of Valtellina's
est subzones. Balance, harmony and
ture vision define the 2015 Sfursat Carlo
egri, a wine fragrant with aromas of red
uit, quinine and tobacco leaf. The mouth
s succulent, with close-woven tannins,
ice, long pulp and a lingering finish. The
014 Grumello Sassorosso is a fine,
omplex Nebbiolo with a background of red
ruit, notes of rust and dried flowers. The
nouth is solid, with pleasant, vibrant
cidity, and a long, sophisticated finish.

Valtellina Sfursat Carlo Negri '15	♟♟♟ 6
Valtellina Sup. Grumello Sassorosso '14	♟♟ 4
Valtellina Sup. Inferno Carlo Negri '14	♟♟ 5
Ca' Brione '16	♟♟ 5
Valtellina Sup. Mazer '14	♟♟ 4
Valtellina Sup. Sassella Le Tense '14	♟♟ 4
Valtellina Sup. Valgella Sciùr '13	♟♟ 5
Valtellina Sfursat 5 Stelle '13	♟♟♟ 8
Valtellina Sfursat 5 Stelle '11	♟♟♟ 8
Valtellina Sfursat 5 Stelle '10	♟♟♟ 7
Valtellina Sfursat 5 Stelle '09	♟♟♟ 7
Valtellina Sfursat 5 Stelle '07	♟♟♟ 7
Valtellina Sfursat Carlo Negri '11	♟♟♟ 8
Valtellina Sup. Vign. Fracia '08	♟♟♟ 6

Oltrenero

LOC. BOSCO
27049 ZENEVREDO [PV]
TEL. +39 0385245326
www.ilbosco.com

CELLAR SALES
PRE-BOOKED VISITS
ANNUAL PRODUCTION 1,000,000 bottles
HECTARES UNDER VINE 152.00

Many things have changed since the Zonin
family, thirty years ago, decided to invest in
Oltrepò Pavese by purchasing an estate
that, in medieval times, was part of the
monastery of Santa Maria Teodote. From 30
hectares, the estate has come to comprise
152. Moreover, under the supervision of
director Piernicola Olmo, the winery has
worked to select the best Pinot Nero clones
and started fermenting on the skins, making
for a selection of sparkling wines that sees
quality and production growing by the year.
Casa Zonin made the deliberate choice to
carry Oltrenero and offer only 'Metodo
Classico' sparklers. The Cruasé once again
stands out, even if it doesn't get a gold, it
still proves a very well-crafted, well-
sustained, mineral rosé with fine sparkle,
fragrances of wild berries and a hint of
almond at the finish. The non-vintage white
has vigor, maturity and grip; it's a true Pinot
Nero. The 2011 Nature exhibits good acidity
and notable linearity.

⊙ OP Cruasé Oltrenero	♟♟ 5
○ OP Pinot Nero Brut Oltrenero	♟♟ 5
○ OP Pinot Nero Nature Oltrenero '11	♟ 6
● OP Bonarda '13	♟♟ 2*
● OP Bonarda Vivace '15	♟♟ 2*
● OP Bonarda Vivace '14	♟♟ 2*
⊙ OP Cruasé Oltrenero	♟♟ 5
○ OP Pinot Nero Nature Oltrenero '10	♟♟ 6

Pasini San Giovanni

FRAZ. RAFFA
VIA VIDELLE, 2
25080 PUEGNAGO SUL GARDA [BS]
TEL. +39 0365651419
www.pasinisangiovanni.it

CELLAR SALES
PRE-BOOKED VISITS
RESTAURANT SERVICE
ANNUAL PRODUCTION 300,000 bottles
HECTARES UNDER VINE 36.00
SUSTAINABLE WINERY

The Pasini cousins managed to create a
very interesting winery on Lake Garda,
basing their work on their family's
background in vine growing. Pasini San
Giovanni features organic cultivation,
energy from renewable sources and an
approach that makes for minimum
environmental impact. And year after year,
their wines prove more and more
interesting. It won't be long before the
breakthrough comes. We start with the
2016 Chiaretto, with its pink, onionskin
color, and zesty, flowery, lively character.
The Centopercento is a Brut made with
Groppello, fermented off the skins. As
always, it offers up primary aromas of
raspberry and a lovely, mineral vein. The
two 2016 Luganas are on the mark,
with the Lugana proving more complex,
with a fresh base and a note of fumé. The
Lugana Brut is pleasant and saline, while
the 2012 Lugana Riserva Busocaldo has
highly evolved overtones.

○ Centopercento Brut M. Cl.	🏆🏆	4
○ Lugana '16	🏆🏆	2*
○ Lugana Il Lugana '16	🏆🏆	2*
⊙ Valtènesi Chiaretto '16	🏆🏆	2*
⊙ Valtènesi Il Chiaretto '16	🏆🏆	2*
○ Lugana Brut	🏆	3
○ Lugana Busocaldo Ris. '12	🏆	5
○ Brut M. Cl. Ceppo 326 '08	🏆🏆	5
○ Lugana Il Lugana Bio '15	🏆🏆	2*
● San Gioan Rosso i Carati '10	🏆🏆	4
● Valtènesi Arzane '12	🏆🏆	3
⊙ Valtènesi Il Chiaretto '15	🏆🏆	2*

Perla del Garda

VIA FENIL VECCHIO, 9
25017 LONATO [BS]
TEL. +39 0309103109
www.perladelgarda.it

CELLAR SALES
PRE-BOOKED VISITS
ANNUAL PRODUCTION 120,000 bottles
HECTARES UNDER VINE 30.00
VITICULTURE METHOD Certified Organic
SUSTAINABLE WINERY

Perla del Garda is owned by the Prandini
family, who have been making and selling
their wines since 2006. Giovanna Prandini
(who's also president of Strada del Vino e
dei Sapori del Garda) and her brother,
Ettore, are at the helm. The estate boasts
30 hectares of vineyards, primarily
Turbiana, for a high-quality selection of
wines with good export potential. In
addition to their modern facilities, they're
committed to sustainability and low
environmental impact (through a certified
approach). While waiting for the new
vintages of Lugana's single vineyards
(the Madonna della Scoperta and Madre
Perla), we get the 2016 Lugana Bio. It's a
wine that delivers for compactness,
expressive freshness, richness and the
integrity of its fruit. The 2016 Perla comes
in behind. They may have felt that a softer
wine would do better in international
markets. The 2011 Lugana Brut Nature
Metodo Classico is a creamy, zesty and
fresh wine.

○ Lugana Bio '16	🏆🏆	2*
○ Lugana Brut Nature M. Cl. '11	🏆🏆	7
○ Lugana Perla '16	🏆🏆	3
● Garda Merlot Filo Rosso '13	🏆	3
● Leonatus '09	🏆🏆	4
○ Lugana Madreperla '11	🏆🏆	4
○ Lugana Perla '15	🏆🏆	3
○ Lugana Perla '13	🏆🏆	3
○ Lugana Sup. Madonna della Scoperta '13	🏆🏆	4
○ Lugana V. T. '13	🏆🏆	4
○ Lugana V. T. '11	🏆🏆	4

ndrea Picchioni

17. Camponoce, 4
'044 Canneto Pavese [PV]
L. +39 0385262139
ww.picchioniandrea.it

ELLAR SALES
RE-BOOKED VISITS
CCOMMODATION
NNUAL PRODUCTION 70,000 bottles
ECTARES UNDER VINE 10.00
TICULTURE METHOD Certified Organic
JSTAINABLE WINERY

ndrea Picchioni, unlike many of his peers,
n't the child of vine growers. He
ersonally founded his small winery in
988, at just 21, building the cellar and
viving the old vineyards along the slops of
al Solinga that had been partially
andoned (which stand today at 10
ectares). In 1995 he began collaborating
ith the agronomist and winemaker Beppe
atti. His wines have begun to assume a
ell-defined personality. Their true to
rritory, made with classic grapes like
roatina, Barbera and Ughetta di Canneto.
he 2015 Arfena made a notable impact
iis year. It's a Pinot Nero that offers up
ark fruit and sweet spices on the nose,
hile the mouth proves smooth and
raceful, with gentle tannins and nice
epth. The 2013 Rosso d'Asia, made with
roatina and a lesser quantity of Ughetta,
fers up an expressive nose of plums, a
ose-woven mouth and edgy tannins. The
st of the selection proves well-crafted.
he 2013 Riva Bianca, a Buttafuoco with
reat aging potential, continues to be dark
nd vibrant.

Pinot Nero Arfena '15	♛♛♛ 4*
OP Buttafuoco Bricco Riva Bianca '13	♛♛ 4
OP Sangue di Giuda Fior del Vento '16	♛♛ 2*
Rosso d'Asia '13	♛♛ 4
OP Bonarda Vivace Ipazia '16	♛ 2
OP Buttafuoco Cerasa '16	♛ 2
OP Bonarda Vivace '15	♛♛ 2*
OP Buttafuoco Bricco Riva Bianca '12	♛♛ 4
OP Buttafuoco Bricco Riva Bianca '11	♛♛ 4
OP Buttafuoco Cerasa '14	♛♛ 2*
Rosso d'Asia '12	♛♛ 4
Rosso d'Asia '11	♛♛ 4

Piccolo Bacco dei Quaroni

Fraz. Costamontefedele
27040 Montù Beccaria [PV]
Tel. +39 038560521
www.piccolobaccodeiquaroni.it

CELLAR SALES
PRE-BOOKED VISITS
RESTAURANT SERVICE
ANNUAL PRODUCTION 35,000 bottles
HECTARES UNDER VINE 10.00
VITICULTURE METHOD Certified Organic

Since 2001, Mario Cavalli and Laura
Brazzola's family have owned this small
winery positioned in the district of Montù
Beccaria, in the easternmost part of Oltrepò
Pavese. The estate includes four cru in
various zones, spanning the municipalities
of Montù, Bosnasco and Castana, all with
completely different soils and
microclimates. Today, his parents primarily
handle the agritourism, while their children,
Tommaso (winemaker) and Giulia manage
the cellar (in strict accordance with organic
principles). This year our favorite wine was
the 2015 Pinot Nero Vigneto La Fiocca, a
varietal, fragrant, close-focused and taut
wine that features small fruit and forest
floor, qualities characteristic of this variety
in Oltrepò. The 2012 Riesling Vigneto del
Pozzo, with respect to last year's 2013, is
less explosive, but finds charm in its
forwardness. The 2016 Bonarda Mons
Acutus proves well-crafted in its huskiness.

● OP Bonarda Vivace Mons Acutus '16	♛♛ 2*
○ OP Riesling Vign. del Pozzo '12	♛♛ 3
● Il Moreè '15	♛ 2
● OP Pinot Nero Vign. La Fiocca '15	♛ 2
● OP Buttafuoco Ca' Padroni '13	♛ 3
● OP Bonarda Mons Acutus '15	♛♛ 2*
⊙ OP Cruasé PBQ '10	♛♛ 3
⊙ OP Cruasé PBQ '09	♛♛ 3
○ OP Riesling Vign. del Pozzo '13	♛♛ 3*

Plozza

via Cappuccini, 26
23037 Tirano [SO]
Tel. +39 0342701297
www.plozza.com

CELLAR SALES
PRE-BOOKED VISITS
ANNUAL PRODUCTION 350,000 bottles
HECTARES UNDER VINE 25.00

Tirano, a winery that's well-managed by Andrea Zanolari, is among the most active and dynamic producers in Valtellina. It was founded by Pietro Plaza in 1919, and today has 25 hectares of vineyards at its disposal (spanning the principal sub zones of the area, ranging from 400 to 700 meters above sea level). Their wines are characterized by a modern style, fruit-driven and spicy, and by the use of small wood for their selections. It's an approach that, in recent years, is moving gradually towards more rigorous, measured extraction. The 2013 Sforzato Blackedition offers up lovely finesse. It's a wine dense in fragrance, with clear hints of bottled fruit and jam. The overall balance comes through nicely on the palate. It's rich, with a fine-grained tannic weave and a long, lingering finish. The vibrant 2014 Numero 1 is unmistakable with its pronounced use of dried grapes, notes of ripe plums and nuances of chocolate. The mouth is caressing, with a full, long finish.

● Sforzato di Valtellina Blackedition '13	♥♥ 5
● Numero 1 '14	♥♥ 8
● Valtellina Sup. Inferno Rededition Ris. '13	♥♥ 5
● Valtellina Sup. Sassella Rededition Ris. '13	♥♥ 5
● Valtellina Numero Uno '01	♥♥♥ 7
● Numero 1 '13	♥♥ 7
● Sforzato di Valtellina Blackedition '12	♥♥ 5
● Valtellina Numero 1 '12	♥♥ 7
● Valtellina Sup. Inferno Rededition '12	♥♥ 4
● Valtellina Sup. Sassella Rededition '12	♥♥ 3

Pratello

via Pratello, 26
25080 Padenghe sul Garda [BS]
Tel. +39 0309907005
www.pratello.com

CELLAR SALES
ACCOMMODATION AND RESTAURANT SERVIC
ANNUAL PRODUCTION 600,000 bottles
HECTARES UNDER VINE 70.00
VITICULTURE METHOD Certified Organic

70 hectares of certified organic vineyards and olive groves, a vanguard winery, tourism, a stunning villa near Castello di Padenghe (with a splendid view of Lake Garda and its valley). This is Vincenzo Bertola, an explosive man and great interpreter of Garda's terroir. One of his bets has been the realization of whites for laying down. Excellent performance this year. The 2016 Riesling exhibits richness, complexity, typicity and finesse, earning it a place in our finals. The 2016 Rivale, a drier, zestier and deeper, is among the best. The 2016 Lugana Catulliano offers up a nice aromatic profile accompanied by intriguing notes of fumé. Its residual sweetness is well-balanced by acidity and richness of flavor. The 2016 Chiaretto Sant'Emiliano has color and structure, and lovely, fragrant fruit with saline scents. The reds made with Rebo also prove excellent, with a succulent 2015 Nero per Sempre making a name for itself.

○ Riesling '16	♥♥ 3
○ Lugana Catulliano '16	♥♥ 4
○ Lugana Il Rivale '16	♥♥ 5
● Mille 1 '15	♥♥ 3
● Nero per Sempre '15	♥♥ 5
☉ Valtènesi Chiaretto Sant'Emiliano '16	♥♥ 3
○ Pinot Grigio '16	♥ 3
○ Lieti Conversari '15	♥♥ 4
○ Lieti Conversari '15	♥♥ 4
○ Lugana Catulliano '15	♥♥ 4
○ Lugana Catulliano '14	♥♥ 3
○ Lugana Il Rivale '14	♥♥ 5
○ Riesling '14	♥♥ 3
● Valtènesi Torrazzo '15	♥♥ 3
● Valtènesi Torrazzo '13	♥♥ 3

Quadra

VIA SANT'EUSEBIO, 1
25033 COLOGNE [BS]
TEL. +39 0307157314
www.quadrafranciacorta.it

CELLAR SALES
PRE-BOOKED VISITS
RESTAURANT SERVICE
ANNUAL PRODUCTION 150,000 bottles
HECTARES UNDER VINE 32.00

Mario Falcetti, an enologist with a long career as a researcher, is leading the winery owned by Ugo Ghezzi (a businessman working in the field of renewable energy). In 2003, Ugo, along with his children Cristina and Marco, decided to purchase a small cellar and its surrounding vineyards. Today, Quadra boasts some 32 hectares. In addition to Chardonnay, Ghezzi and Falcetti, they're working with Pinot Bianco and Pinot Nero (planted in some of their hill plots, which are ideal for cultivation). Stylistically, the Satèn proves to be right in Quadra's wheelhouse, as the 2012 QSatèn demonstrates (the wine that we felt best represents the producer). It has an elegant bouquet of white fruit with flowery notes and aromatic herbs like thyme and marjoram. The palate comes through generous, soft and smooth, but with good grip and creamy effervescence. Toasty notes, delicate fumé and a nice saline finish prove to be a winning combination with the 2011 QZero, while the rosé QRosé exhibits softness and richness of fruit, with hints of strawberry and raspberry.

○ Franciacorta QSatèn '12	♟♟ 5
○ Franciacorta Brut QRosé	♟♟ 5
○ Franciacorta Dosaggio Zero QZero '11	♟♟ 5
○ Franciacorta Brut QBlack	♟ 4
○ Franciacorta Brut Q39 '08	♟♟ 5
○ Franciacorta Dosaggio Zero EretiQ '10	♟♟ 6
○ Franciacorta Dosaggio Zero EretiQ '10	♟♟ 6
○ Franciacorta Extra Brut Q Zero '08	♟♟ 5
○ Franciacorta Extra Brut QZero '09	♟♟ 5
○ Franciacorta QSatèn '11	♟♟ 5
○ Franciacorta QSatèn '10	♟♟ 5
○ Franciacorta QSatèn '09	♟♟ 5
○ Franciacorta QSatèn '08	♟♟ 5
○ Franciacorta Quvée 46 '09	♟♟ 5
○ Franciacorta Satèn '07	♟♟ 5

Francesco Quaquarini

LOC. MONTEVENEROSO
VIA CASA ZAMBIANCHI, 26
27044 CANNETO PAVESE [PV]
TEL. +39 038560152
www.quaquarinifrancesco.it

CELLAR SALES
PRE-BOOKED VISITS
ANNUAL PRODUCTION 650,000 bottles
HECTARES UNDER VINE 60.00
VITICULTURE METHOD Certified Organic

Francesco Quaquarini and his children, Umberto (winemaker) and Maria Teresa, offer a consistently strong selection of wine. The numbers are important enough, especially for a territory that's as fragmented as theirs, and their selection features a range of traditional, local wines, from Buttafuoco to Sangue di Giuda, Bonarda and Pinot Nero Metodo Classico. There's potential to aim for a greater breakthrough, in terms of quality, with their top range. The 2016 Riesling is, without a doubt, the best wine presented. It's supple in the mouth, with aromas of sage and citrus peel, while the palate proves succulent, deep and zesty. The 2014 Pinot Nero Blau also did well. It's an earthy wine, with overtones of dark fruit, and a lean mouth. Its tannins are sweet, and it exhibits good acidity. The Classese is quite evolved, while the Sangue di Giuda is once again among the best.

● OP Pinot Nero Blau '14	♟♟ 3
○ OP Riesling '16	♟♟ 2*
● OP Sangue di Giuda '16	♟♟ 2*
● OP Bonarda Riva di Sass '16	♟ 3
○ OP Pinot Nero Brut Classese '10	♟ 4
● OP Barbera Poggio Anna '12	♟♟ 2*
● OP Barbera Poggio Anna '11	♟♟ 3
● OP Bonarda Vivace '15	♟♟ 2*
● OP Buttafuoco Storico V. Pregana '09	♟♟ 5
● OP Pinot Nero Blau '13	♟♟ 3
● OP Sangue di Giuda '15	♟♟ 2*

Cantina Sociale Cooperativa di Quistello

VIA ROMA, 46
46026 QUISTELLO [MN]
TEL. +39 0376618118
www.cantinasocialequistello.it

CELLAR SALES
PRE-BOOKED VISITS
ANNUAL PRODUCTION 1,000,000 bottles
HECTARES UNDER VINE 330.00

Even if it's Lombardy, all you have to do is look at a map to realize how this stretch of land along the Secchia river is wedged in among the provinces of Parma, Reggio Emilia and Modena (that is, in Lambrusco country). Quistello is at the center of the territory, and the Cantina Sociale represents its heart, with its 300 members and five million kilos of grapes crushed per year. The best gets bottled, making for a high-quality selection of wines. We start with the Gran Rosso del Vicariato, a wine that's refermented in the bottle and whose 2016 version delivers for its generous fizziness and rich fruit. The 80 Vendemmie also offers up nice fruit, while the rosé features fragrant, highly pleasant strawberry. The 2016 Lambrusco Mantovano Rosso, with its huskier notes, is a notch below.

★Aldo Rainoldi

FRAZ. CASACCE
VIA STELVIO, 128
23030 CHIURO [SO]
TEL. +39 0342482225
www.rainoldi.com

CELLAR SALES
PRE-BOOKED VISITS
ANNUAL PRODUCTION 180,000 bottles
HECTARES UNDER VINE 9.60

The winery led by Aldo Rainoldi continues to forge ahead. It's been operational since 1925, and today has 10 hectares of vineyards at its disposal (in addition to select purchases from other vine growers), making for a well-segmented selection of wines. This ranges from the territory's classics, to reserve wines with a strong identity, and two Sforzatos (including Fruttaio Ca' Rizzieri, a wine that's capable of extraordinary evolution). It's a wide-ranging selection that Aldo has skillfully managed to get his wines noticed on major international markets. The 2013 Sassella Riserva is outstanding. It's a vibrant, austere wine with nuances of red fruit, spicy notes, tobacco leaf and quinine. The mouth is bold, succulent and tangy, with close-woven tannins, great personality and a long finish. The 2013 Sfursat Ca' Rizzieri is complex and multifaceted, with notes of ripe fruit, quinine, licorice and tobacco leaf. The mouth is well-orchestrated and generous with nice, well-sustained freshness and a long finish.

⊙ 80 Vendemmie Rosato '16	▼▼ 2*
● 80 Vendemmie Rosso '16	▼▼ 2*
● Gran Rosso del Vicariato di Quistello '16	▼▼ 2*
● Lambrusco Mantovano Rosso '16	▼ 1*
● 80 Vendemmie '13	♀♀ 2*
● 80 Vendemmie Rosso '15	♀♀ 2*
● Gran Rosso del Vicariato di Quistello '15	♀♀ 2*
● Gran Rosso del Vicariato di Quistello '13	♀♀ 2*
● Gran Rosso del Vicariato di Quistello '12	♀♀ 1*
● Lambrusco Mantovano Rossissimo '15	♀♀ 2*
● Lambrusco Mantovano Rossissimo '12	♀♀ 2*

● Valtellina Sup. Sassella Ris. '13	▼▼▼ 5
● Valtellina Sfursat Ca' Rizzieri '13	▼▼ 6
● Valtellina Sup. Inferno Ris. '13	▼▼ 5
● Valtellina Sup. Sassella '12	▼▼ 5
● Valtellina Sfursat '08	♀♀♀ 5
● Valtellina Sfursat Fruttaio Ca' Rizzieri '11	♀♀♀ 6
● Valtellina Sfursat Fruttaio Ca' Rizzieri '10	♀♀♀ 6
● Valtellina Sfursat Fruttaio Ca' Rizzieri '09	♀♀♀ 6
● Valtellina Sfursat Fruttaio Ca' Rizzieri '06	♀♀♀ 6
● Valtellina Sfursat Fruttaio Ca' Rizzieri '02	♀♀♀ 6
● Valtellina Sup. Sassella Ris. '12	♀♀♀ 5
● Valtellina Sup. Sassella Ris. '06	♀♀♀ 5

Ricci Curbastro

ADRO, 37
5031 CAPRIOLO [BS]
TEL. +39 030736094
www.riccicurbastro.it

CELLAR SALES
PRE-BOOKED VISITS
ACCOMMODATION
ANNUAL PRODUCTION 200,000 bottles
HECTARES UNDER VINE 27.00
SUSTAINABLE WINERY

Riccardo Ricci Curbastro has left a decisive mark on his inspiring family winery (situated in the historic Villa Evelina in Capriolo). Today they have almost 30 hectares of terrain at their disposal, in some of the best parts of the DOC zone, and have realized a fine selection of Franciacortas and still wines. Riccardo, who has also taken on important responsibilities in the wine and agricultural tourism sectors, has been working for years on behalf of sustainability. He's also president of Equalitas, the company that realized the national laws governing the field. Their selection is wide and varying. Riccardo believes that this corning of Lombardy makes blends with great aging potential. Thus he proposes, during the best vintages, Franciacortas that have spent a long time on the lees. It's his Museum Release line, and the 2007 Brut from this collection gets a Tre Bicchieri this year. It's a complex, linear, deep wine that manages to be elegant, fresh and extraordinarily gratifying on the palate.

○ Franciacorta Brut Museum Release '07	♛♛♛ 6
○ Curtefranca Bianco V. Bosco Alto '13	♛♛ 3
● Curtefranca Rosso V. Santella del Gröm '13	♛♛ 3
○ Franciacorta Extra Brut '13	♛♛ 5
○ Franciacorta Rosé	♛♛ 5
○ Franciacorta Satèn '13	♛♛ 5
○ Zero Trattamenti '16	♛♛ 5
● Curtefranca Rosso '14	♛ 2
○ Franciacorta Brut	♛ 4
○ Franciacorta Demi Sec	♛ 4
○ Pinot Bianco '16	♛ 2
○ Franciacorta Dosaggio Zero Gualberto '06	♛♛♛ 6
○ Franciacorta Extra Brut '12	♛♛♛ 5

Ronco Calino

FRAZ. TORBIATO
VIA FENICE, 45
25030 ADRO [BS]
TEL. +39 0307451073
www.roncocalino.it

CELLAR SALES
PRE-BOOKED VISITS
ANNUAL PRODUCTION 70,000 bottles
HECTARES UNDER VINE 13.00
VITICULTURE METHOD Certified Organic
SUSTAINABLE WINERY

In 1996, Paolo Radici, a successful businessman, decided to purchase the estate of Torbiato di Adro, once owned by the celebrated pianist Arturo Benedetti Michelangeli. The winery began producing a fine selection of Franciacortas, and today is managed passionately by Lara Imberti (Paolo's wife). It's a boutique winery with 10 hectares of vineyards in the spectacular morainic amphitheater. They rely on the support of winemaker Leonardo Valenti (who's accompanied by agronomist Pierluigi Donna) for a select range of Franciacorta's and local wines, all produced in their modern cellar. The Satèn dei Radici tasted this year confirms its status as one of the most interesting in the appellation. It has a nice, brilliant, straw-yellow color, vibrant and lively fragrances of white peach and apricot that hover over notes of vanilla. The mouth comes through crisp and close-woven in its frutiness, with a palate well-supported by acidity (that also lengthens its creamy finish). The 2011 Nature is also first-rate. It's a wine that doesn't skimp on fruit either, and features an austere, zesty, assertive palate.

○ Franciacorta Satèn	♛♛ 5
○ Curtefranca Bianco Lèant '16	♛♛ 3
○ Franciacorta Brut '10	♛♛ 5
○ Franciacorta Brut	♛♛ 4
○ Franciacorta Brut Nature '11	♛♛ 5
⊙ Franciacorta Rosé Radijan	♛♛ 5
○ Curtefranca Bianco Lèant '14	♛♛ 3
● Curtefranca Rosso Ponènt '12	♛♛ 4
● Curtefranca Rosso Ponènt '11	♛♛ 4
● Curtefranca Rosso Ponènt '10	♛♛ 4
○ Franciacorta Brut Nature '10	♛♛ 5
○ Franciacorta Extra Brut Centoventi '04	♛♛ 8
● Pinot Nero L'Arturo '12	♛♛ 5
● Pinot Nero L'Arturo '11	♛♛ 5

San Cristoforo

FRAZ. VILLA D'ERBUSCO
VIA VILLANUOVA, 2
25030 ERBUSCO [BS]
TEL. +39 0307760482
www.sancristoforo.eu

CELLAR SALES
PRE-BOOKED VISITS
ANNUAL PRODUCTION 80,000 bottles
HECTARES UNDER VINE 10.00
SUSTAINABLE WINERY

Bruno Dotti and his wife, Claudia, incarnate the philosophy of the récoltant-manipulant. In 1997 they took over this small winery in Franciacorta, which was already known for the quality of its wines. In 20 years, their passionate work saw an increase in the size of their vineyards (today about 10 hectares) and renovations of the cellar, equipping it with modern technology. Theirs remains a 'less formal' selection, but the quality of their blends and their wines continues to grow. Their daughter, Celeste, is also on board full-time. We saw four Franciacortas with impeccable style this year: a highly fresh, plucky ND Non Dosato that shows a softly intimate tone in its buttery nuances, which give way to notes of fresh citrus; a complex and rich 2009 Celeste, also undosed, with freshness on the palate and nuances of honey and saffron on the nose. The 2012 Pas Dosé and Brut are both worth mentioning as well.

○ Franciacorta Brut	🍷🍷 4
○ Franciacorta ND	🍷🍷 6
○ Franciacorta Pas Dosé '12	🍷🍷 6
○ Franciacorta Pas Dosé Celeste '09	🍷🍷 8
○ Franciacorta Brut '11	🍷🍷 6
○ Franciacorta Brut '09	🍷🍷 6
○ Franciacorta Brut '08	🍷🍷 6
○ Franciacorta Brut '07	🍷🍷 4
○ Franciacorta Dosaggio Zero '11	🍷🍷 6
○ Franciacorta Dosaggio Zero Celeste '08	🍷🍷 8
○ Franciacorta Pas Dosé '10	🍷🍷 6
○ Franciacorta Pas Dosé '09	🍷🍷 6
○ Franciacorta Pas Dosé '08	🍷🍷 6
● San Cristoforo Uno '07	🍷🍷 4

Santa Lucia

VIA VERDI, 6
25030 ERBUSCO [BS]
TEL. +39 0307769814
www.santaluciafranciacorta.it

CELLAR SALES
PRE-BOOKED VISITS
ANNUAL PRODUCTION 100,000 bottles
HECTARES UNDER VINE 27.00
VITICULTURE METHOD Certified Organic

Pierluigi Villa, an agronomist, is one of the key figures in Franciacorta's modern history. He's the author of a number of scientific publications, and has participated in the work of zoning the territory (as well as serving as a consultant for a number of important wineries). He himself is a Franciacorta DOCG (born in Rovato) and couldn't resist the temptation to start work himself. Thus Santa Lucia was born a few years ago, in the historic buildings around Palazzo Longhi (in Erbusco). Along with his children, Gregorio (a winemaker with experience in Borgogna) and Michele (who studied agriculture) he makes popular Franciacortas with grapes from his own terrain, and other plots managed by the winery (all in some of the best terrain in the DOC zone). The Villa family's 2013 Pas Dosé made it to our finals by virtue of its elegant bouquet in which fresh notes of fruit are followed by warmer, sweeter hints that riff on classic pain d'épices. The palate is generous, deep and complex, and supported by nice acidity that adds length to a close-focused finish.

○ Franciacorta Pas Dosé '13	🍷🍷 5
◉ Franciacorta Brut Rosé	🍷🍷 5
○ Franciacorta Brut Satèn	🍷🍷 5
○ Franciacorta Extra Brut Brolo dei Longhi Ris. '08	🍷🍷 8
○ Franciacorta Brut	🍷 5

Scuropasso

FRAZ. SCORZOLETTA, 40/42
27043 PIETRA DE' GIORGI [PV]
TEL. +39 038585143
www.scuropasso.it

CELLAR SALES
PRE-BOOKED VISITS
ANNUAL PRODUCTION 200,000 bottles
HECTARES UNDER VINE 15.00

After a few years without him, we welcome back Fabio Marazzi, now accompanied by his daughter, Flavia. What was once known as the Cantine Scuropasso and worked for third parties, is today a solid winery of its own. And considering Fabio's passion for Champagne, as well as the winery's location, it's no surprise that sparkling wines take center stage. Currently, Scuropasso has 15 hectares of vineyards at its disposal (which are in the process of being converted to organic), and the winery has invested in renewable energy such that they are now completely off the grid. The Cruasé makes it to the finals, with his bright pink color, and its clear, clean aromatic profile dominated by small red fruit. It's a 'Metodo Classico' rosé that's better for meals than as a drink. The two 2010 Roccapietras also did well, both of them exhibiting fine sparkle, with a dosage that offers up citrus and aromatic herbs. The Zero, meanwhile, has a grip that's characteristic of pure Pinot Nero.

⊙ OP Cruasé '11	🍷🍷 4
○ OP Pinot Nero Brut Roccapietra	🍷🍷 4
○ Brut Roccapietra Zero '10	🍷🍷 3
○ Moscato '16	🍷🍷 2*
● OP Buttafuoco '15	🍷🍷 4
○ OP Pinot Nero Brut Roccapietra '10	🍷🍷 4
● OP Buttafuoco Lunapiena '12	🍷 3
● OP Bonarda Vivace Palatinus '07	🍾 2*

Cantine Selva Capuzza

FRAZ. SAN MARTINO DELLA BATTAGLIA
LOC. SELVA CAPUZZA
25010 DESENZANO DEL GARDA [BS]
TEL. +39 0309910381
www.selvacapuzza.it

CELLAR SALES
PRE-BOOKED VISITS
ACCOMMODATION AND RESTAURANT SERVICE
ANNUAL PRODUCTION 300,000 bottles
HECTARES UNDER VINE 25.00

Winemaker Vincenzo Formentini founded this inspiring producer that today spans 50 hectares (25 of which are vineyards). The morainic amphitheater that surrounds Lake Garda to the south comprises the appellations of Lugana, San Marino della Battaglia and Garda, and it's here that, today, Luca Formentini makes his wines with traditional grape varieties. Selva Capuzza also boasts an excellent restaurant and offers rural accommodations. The selection presented for the various appellations once again proved wide ranging and of excellent quality. The 2013 Menasasso Riserva stands out. It's an evolved, enjoyable, complex and overall well-balanced wine. The 2016 Groppello San Biagio has a nice, faded, ruby red color, delicate tannins and a truly enticing bouquet. Finally, 2016 Lugana Selva has an elegant nose featuring fruit and flowery notes, with a mouth that proves savory, taut and fruit-driven.

● Garda Cl. Groppello San Biagio '16	🍷🍷 3
○ Lugana Menasasso Ris. '13	🍷🍷 3
○ Lugana Selva '16	🍷🍷 2*
○ Passito Lume	🍷🍷 5
○ San Martino della Battaglia Campo del Soglio '16	🍷🍷 4
⊙ Garda Brut Rosé Hirundo	🍷 3
⊙ Garda Cl. Chiaretto S. Donino '16	🍷 3
○ Lugana Brut M. Cl. Hirundo	🍷 4
○ Lugana Dosaggio Zero M. Cl. Hirundo	🍷 4
○ Lugana San Vigilio '16	🍷 2
⊙ Garda Cl. Chiaretto San Donino '15	🍾 2*
○ Lugana Menasasso Ris. '12	🍾 3
○ Lugana San Vigilio '15	🍾 2*
○ Lugana Selva '15	🍾 2*

Lo Sparviere

VIA COSTA
25040 MONTICELLI BRUSATI [BS]
TEL. +39 030652382
www.losparviere.com

CELLAR SALES
PRE-BOOKED VISITS
ANNUAL PRODUCTION 120,000 bottles
HECTARES UNDER VINE 30.00

Sparviere is a winery in Franciacorta owned by the Agricole Gussalli Beretta group. Indeed, Ugo Gussalli Beretta is at the helm of one of the oldest producers in the world (with documents testifying to its existence as far back as 1526), along with his wife, Monique, and his son, Piero, with whom he shares a passion for the land and for wine. The group continues to grow. In addition to Castello di Radda (in Chianti Classico), and Orlandi Contucci Ponno (in Abruzzo), he recently added ForteMasso (in Monforte d'Alba) and Steinhauserhof (in Alto Adige). Excellent raw ingredients, experience and Francesco Polastri's talents when it comes to the 'metodo classico' (Metodo Classico) come together to create a high quality selection. It's led by the 2012 Franciacorta Brut, a zesty, fresh and citrusy wine that's creamy on the palate, and rich in notes of white fruit both on the nose and its long mouth. Tre Bicchieri. Among the other blends, we point out the Extra Brut, which offers nice, flowery notes on the nose and proves taut and dynamic on the palate.

○ Franciacorta Brut '12	♟♟♟	5
○ Franciacorta Brut Cuvée N. 7	♟♟	4
○ Franciacorta Dosaggio Zero Ris. '09	♟♟	6
○ Franciacorta Extra Brut	♟♟	5
○ Franciacorta Dosaggio Zero Ris. '08	♟♟♟	6
○ Franciacorta Extra Brut '09	♟♟♟	5
○ Franciacorta Extra Brut '08	♟♟♟	5
○ Franciacorta Extra Brut '07	♟♟♟	5
○ Franciacorta Brut '11	♟♟	5
○ Franciacorta Brut '09	♟♟	5
○ Franciacorta Dosaggio Zero Ris. '07	♟♟	6
○ Franciacorta Dosaggio Zero Ris. '06	♟♟	8
○ Franciacorta Extra Brut '06	♟♟	5
○ Franciacorta Extra Brut '05	♟♟	5

Torrevilla

VIA EMILIA, 4
27050 TORRAZZA COSTE [PV]
TEL. +39 038377003
www.torrevilla.it

CELLAR SALES
PRE-BOOKED VISITS
ANNUAL PRODUCTION 3,000,000 bottles
HECTARES UNDER VINE 650.00

Cantina Sociale di Torrazza Coste was founded in 1907, while 1970 saw a merger with Cantina di Codevilla, thus giving life to a single producer (whose names were also fused): Torrevilla. It's a cooperative that's fundamental for western Oltrepò. In 2008 another step was taken, with substantial investment in economic terms that saw the renovation of its equipment and, simultaneously, the launch of a project aimed at improving the overall quality of the grapes supplied by the cooperative's member-growers. This was made possible in part thanks to the help of the University of Milan and the Riccagioia Research Center. La Genisia is the name chosen for their top wines, and now, with the young winemaker Gabriele Picchi leading the way, they expect equally top results. This year the Cruasé was our favorite, a creamy, well-orchestrated wine. The 2016 Bonarda Vivace, a full, fruity wine, also did well. The other wines presented all proved to be of sound quality.

● OP Barbera La Genisia '15	♟♟	2*
● OP Bonarda Vivace La Genisia '16	♟♟	2*
⊙ OP Cruasè La Genisia	♟♟	4
● Pinot Nero La Genisia '16	♟	2
○ O. P. Pinot Nero Brut La Genisia '07	♟♟	5
● OP Bonarda La Genisia '12	♟♟	3
⊙ OP Cruasé La Genisia '12	♟♟	4
⊙ OP Cruasé La Genisia '10	♟♟	4
⊙ OP Cruasé La Genisia '09	♟♟	3
● OP Ginestro Caprera Ris. '08	♟♟	5
○ OP Pinot Grigio La Genisia '14	♟♟	2*

Pietro Torti

FRAZ. CASTELROTTO, 9
27047 MONTECALVO VERSIGGIA [PV]
TEL. +39 038599763
www.pietrotorti.it

CELLAR SALES
PRE-BOOKED VISITS
ACCOMMODATION
ANNUAL PRODUCTION 40,000 bottles
HECTARES UNDER VINE 18.00
VITICULTURE METHOD Certified Organic

Sandro Torti (son of founder, Pietro) has, for some years now, had the help of his young daughter, Chiara (who also seems set on following in her father's footsteps). Inasmuch as it's a family-run winery, and thus artisan in its approach, the results can vary from one year to the next. But each time, this small winery in Montecalvo comes up with something interesting. This year, for example, the 2013 Metodo Classico performed quite well. It's a slightly citrusy wine, with a nice, captivating nose, fine and elegant sparkle, fruit that's present but never invasive, and a gratifying finish. The 2016 Bonarda Vivace, possibly the wine that sees Sandro at his most sure-footed, is excellent, as usual. The 2016 Fagù is a Chardonnay with multifaceted aromas of citrus, medlar and tropical fruit. The Cruasé proved highly rich in fruit.

○ Fagù '16	♟♟	2*
● OP Bonarda Vivace '16	♟♟	2*
○ OP Pinot Nero Brut M. Cl. Torti '13	♟♟	3
● OP Bonarda Verzello '16	♟	3
⊙ OP Cruasé	♟	4
● OP Barbera Campo Rivera '12	♟♟	4
● OP Barbera Campo Rivera '10	♟♟	3
● OP Bonarda '13	♟♟	2*
● Uva Rara '15	♟♟	3

Travaglino

LOC. TRAVAGLINO, 6A
27040 CALVIGNANO [PV]
TEL. +39 0383872222
www.travaglino.it

CELLAR SALES
PRE-BOOKED VISITS
ACCOMMODATION AND RESTAURANT SERVICE
ANNUAL PRODUCTION 200,000 bottles
HECTARES UNDER VINE 80.00

The results are in (are they ever!) for the new direction taken by young Cristina Cerri (with the help of her equally young winemaker, Achille Bergami). After reorganizing vineyard and cellar management, as well as the selection and communications office, what was once, and is, one of the most inspiring and important wineries in the entire area, seems destined to return to its historic heights. This year the Gran Cuvée is delicious. It's a sparkling wine made only with Pinot Nero. The nose sees hints of lime and mandarin orange accompanied by accents of small wild berries. The mouth is well-orchestrated and lean, while its prickle is balanced by zest and freshness. The 2014 Riesling Campo deal Fojada is also excellent. It's a Riserva whose aroma and palate deliver. The vibrant Monteceresino is a rosé that features overtones of red fruit, while the 2014 Poggio della Buttinera proves well-crafted (which is even more impressive when you consider the difficult year).

○ OP Gran Cuvée Blanc de Noir	♟♟	5
○ OP Riesling Campo della Fojada Ris. '14	♟♟	3*
⊙ OP Cruasé Monteceresino	♟♟	4
● Pinot Nero Poggio della Buttinera '14	♟♟	5
● OP Pinot Nero Vincenzo Comi '09	♟	5
○ Brut Cuvée 59 '13	♟♟	4
○ OP Pinot Grigio Ramato '15	♟♟	4
○ OP Pinot Nero Brut Cuvée 59 '12	♟♟	3
● OP Pinot Nero Pernero '15	♟♟	2*
○ OP Riesling Campo della Fojada '15	♟♟	3
○ OP Riesling Campo della Fojada '14	♟♟	3

★Uberti

LOC. SALEM
VIA E. FERMI, 2
25030 ERBUSCO [BS]
TEL. +39 0307267476
www.ubertivini.it

PRE-BOOKED VISITS
ANNUAL PRODUCTION 180,000 bottles
HECTARES UNDER VINE 25.00
VITICULTURE METHOD Certified Organic

Agostino and Eleonora inherited a
centuries-old legacy working the vineyards
and founded this modern cellar in 1980.
From the beginning, Uberti has earned a
number of accolades for the quality of its
selection. And wines like Magnificentia and
Comarì del Salem are classics by now. In
part, their secret lies in their outstanding
vineyards, 25 hectares of them in Ebrusco.
But it's also in the passion demonstrated
by the family. Silvia, a winemaker, and
Francesca, administrator, are now
accompanying their parents in running this
organically cultivated estate. The
increasingly complex (and evolved) style of
the Franciacortas makes us miss the
blends we got so excited about up to a few
years ago. This explains this year's marks,
which are surely beneath the producer's
potential (as well as that of its vineyards).
The Extra Brut Francesco I stands out for
its aromas of ripe fruit and oak, and for its
crisp, zesty, relaxed mouth, while the
Magnificentia features round creaminess.

○ Franciacorta Extra Brut Francesco I	♟♟ 5
⊙ Franciacorta Rosé Francesco I	♟♟ 5
○ Franciacorta Satèn Magnificentia '13	♟♟ 6
○ Franciacorta Brut Francesco I	♟ 5
○ Franciacorta Extra Brut Comarì del Salem	♟ 6
○ Franciacorta Extra Brut Quinque	♟ 8
○ Franciacorta Extra Brut Comarì del Salem '03	♟♟♟ 6
○ Franciacorta Extra Brut Comarì del Salem '02	♟♟♟ 6
○ Franciacorta Extra Brut Comarì del Salem '01	♟♟♟ 6
○ Franciacorta Extra Brut Comarì del Salem '98	♟♟♟ 6

Vanzini

FRAZ. BARBALEONE, 7
27040 SAN DAMIANO AL COLLE [PV]
TEL. +39 038575019
www.vanzini-wine.com

CELLAR SALES
PRE-BOOKED VISITS
ANNUAL PRODUCTION 600,000 bottles
HECTARES UNDER VINE 27.00

The Vanzini family (Antonio, Michela and
Pierpaolo) have a specific business
philosophy. They achieve major production
figures and know how to work Croatina,
Barbera and Pinot Nero in the regional
tradition. Indeed, Bonarda, Sangue di
Giuda, and Metodo Martinotti sparklers
have continued to improve over the years
and distinguish themselves for their
pleasantness (especially their Bonarda,
which is consistently among the best). The
Pinot Nero used would be perfect for good
'Metodo Classico' sparklers. Who knows,
maybe sooner or later? Rosé Martinotti is
an Extra Dry that proves delicious, as usual,
with great cleanness and a nose that offers
up lovely hints of flowers and white fruit. In
the mouth it proves elegant, deep and
tangy. The 2016 Bonarda Frizzana confirms
its status as one of the best in the category.
It's a juicy, fruity wine with aromas of
strawberry, cherry and sweet spices. The
mouth is lean, dynamic and succulent. The
other Metodo Martinotti, wine made with
Pinot Nero, is also good, while the Sangue
di Giuda proves highly pleasant.

● OP Bonarda '16	♟♟ 2*
⊙ Pinot Nero Extra Dry Martinotti Rosé	♟♟ 3*
● OP Sangue di Giuda '16	♟♟ 3
○ Pinot Nero Brut Martinotti	♟♟ 2*
● OP Barbera '16	♟ 2
○ OP Pinot Grigio '16	♟ 3
○ OP Riesling '16	♟ 2
○ Pinot Nero Extra Dry Martinotti Aedo	♟ 3
● OP Bonarda Vivace '15	♟♟ 2*
● OP Sangue di Giuda '15	♟♟ 3

Bruno Verdi

VIA VERGOMBERRA, 5
27044 CANNETO PAVESE [PV]
TEL. +39 038588023
www.brunoverdi.it

CELLAR SALES
PRE-BOOKED VISITS
ANNUAL PRODUCTION 90,000 bottles
HECTARES UNDER VINE 12.00

The selection of wines offered by Paolo Verdi is consistently among the most complete and interesting of the territory. 30 years ago, he found himself having to manage a winery practically by himself (after the premature death of his father, Bruno). Paolo grew into the role, and managed to reach the heights of excellence, both with his traditional, local reds and with his 'Metodo Classico' sparkling wines. His wines are always clear, distinct, with balsamic nuances that are characteristic of this part of Oltrepò. The Verdi put in a textbook performance this year. Their 2012 Vergomberra is a great Italian sparkler, without a doubt among the best undosed wines of its kind. It stands out for its elegance, grip and depth, as well as its superior aromatic complexity. The Bonarda Vivace, a wine that's succulent and dynamic in the mouth, proved delicious enough to make it to our finals. The vibrant 2013 Cavariola has been in the finals a number of times (and twice awarded). The rest of the selection also did quite well.

○ OP Dosage Zero Vergomberra '12	♟♟♟	4*
● OP Bonarda Vivace Possessione di Vergomberra '16	♟♟	2*
● OP Barbera Campo del Marrone '15	♟♟	3
● OP Buttafuoco '16	♟♟	2*
○ OP Riesling V. Costa '15	♟♟	2*
● OP Rosso Cavariola Ris. '13	♟♟	5
● OP Sangue di Giuda Paradiso '16	♟♟	2*
○ OP Pinot Grigio '16	♟	2
● OP Rosso Cavariola Ris. '10	♟♟♟	5
● OP Rosso Cavariola Ris. '07	♟♟♟	4
● OP Barbera Campo del Marrone '13	♟♟	3
● OP Rosso Cavariola Ris. '12	♟♟	5

Villa Crespia

VIA VALLI, 31
25030 ADRO [BS]
TEL. +39 0307451051
www.villacrespia.it

PRE-BOOKED VISITS
ANNUAL PRODUCTION 360,000 bottles
HECTARES UNDER VINE 60.00
SUSTAINABLE WINERY

With 60 hectares of vineyards and significant production figures (all realized with the utmost respect for the environment), Villa Crespia is one of Franciacorta's most important wineries. The Muratori family has solid roots in agriculture, and over the years they created a high quality group, the Arcipelago Muratori. In addition to Villa Crespia, they manage Rubbia al Colle (in Maremma), Oppida Aminea (in Sannio) and, finally, the Giardini Arimei (on the island of Ischia). Technical direction of the group has been entrusted to winemaker Francesco Iacono, who, with Villa Crespia, proposes a series of blends that express the terroir of Franciacorta. The Brut Novalia is not among the Muratori's vintage blends, yet this year it won our hearts for its vibrance and its close-focused, fresh aromas of fruit, cakes and vanilla (both on the nose and the palate). Among their wide and varying selection, we also point out the 2009 Brut Millè, a creamy and soft wine.

○ Franciacorta Brut Novalia	♟♟	4
○ Franciacorta Brut Millè '09	♟♟	5
○ Franciacorta Dosaggio Zero Numerozero	♟♟	5
⊙ Franciacorta Extra Brut Rosé Brolese	♟♟	5
○ Franciacorta Brut Miolo	♟	5
○ Franciacorta Brut Simbiotico	♟	5
○ Franciacorta Satèn Cesonato	♟	5
○ Franciacorta Dosaggio Zero Francesco Iacono Ris. '04	♟♟♟	7

Villa Franciacorta

LOC. VILLA, 12
25040 MONTICELLI BRUSATI [BS]
TEL. +39 030652329
www.villafranciacorta.it

PRE-BOOKED VISITS
ACCOMMODATION AND RESTAURANT SERVICE
ANNUAL PRODUCTION 300,000 bottles
HECTARES UNDER VINE 37.00

Alessandro Bianchi patiently renovated the old buildings in the 16th century hamlet of Villa (in Monticelli Brusati) and transformed them into a luxurious country relais with a restaurant to boot. He did the same with the surrounding estate, replanting the terraced vineyards on Monte della Madonna della Rosa. Today, the producer has 100 hectares of land (40 of which are vineyards) and a modern, completely underground cellar where a million bottles wait for their rémuage. Today, the winery is managed by Alessandra Bianchi and her husband, Paolo Piziol. We very much appreciated the 2011 Pas Dosé Diamant, with its nice, fruity and lively bouquet, and its fresh, tangy palate. The Satèn is a close-focused, succulent wine whose long and fresh finish features a lovely saline note. The 2011 Extra Blu has a nice breadth and depth to it, but suffers a bit for notes that are too evolved for its age. We found the 2010 Cuvette, with its aromas of orange blossom and its succulent, well-orchestrated palate, to be quite on the mark.

○ Franciacorta Pas Dosé Diamant '11	♈♈ 5
○ Franciacorta Brut Cuvette '10	♈♈ 5
○ Franciacorta Brut Emozione '13	♈♈ 5
⊙ Franciacorta Brut Rosé Boké '13	♈♈ 5
⊙ Franciacorta Brut Rosé Boké Noir '13	♈♈ 7
⊙ Franciacorta Demi Sec Rosé Briolette	♈♈ 5
○ Franciacorta Extra Brut Extra Blu '11	♈♈ 5
○ Franciacorta Mon Satèn '13	♈♈ 5
○ Campei '16	♈ 3
● Querqus Sebino '13	♈ 6
● Sella Collezione Sebino '13	♈ 3
○ Franciacorta Brut Emozione '09	♈♈♈ 5
⊙ Franciacorta Brut Rosé Boké '12	♈♈♈ 5
○ Franciacorta Extra Brut '98	♈♈♈ 4*

Chiara Ziliani

VIA FRANCIACORTA, 7
25050 PROVAGLIO D'ISEO [BS]
TEL. +39 030981661
www.cantinachiaraziliani.it

PRE-BOOKED VISITS
ANNUAL PRODUCTION 350,000 bottles
HECTARES UNDER VINE 22.00
SUSTAINABLE WINERY

Chiara Ziliani founded an inspiring winery situated on a hilltop in the morainic zone of Provaglio, which offers a lovely view of the 22 hectare estate of vineyards. These give rise to a number of Franciacortas and local wines, organized into various lines, and are cultivated according to principles of low environmental impact and higher densities (more than 7000 plants per hectare). The favorable position (at 250 meters above sea level), south by southwest exposure, and care taken in the cellar make for high-quality selection of wines. This year we make note of the Brut from the Conte di Provaglio line. It's a wine with a complex, fresh, well-orchestrated nose and a palate that's tangy, saline and taut. The Satèn Ziliani C offers up nice notes of ripe pear and apple and features a soft, creamy effervescence. The Conte di Provaglio, on the other hand, goes more in on flowery, vanilla aromas. The 2010 Satèn Riserva Gran Cuvée Maria Maddalena Cavalieri is also interesting, with its rich fragrances of vanilla and oak.

○ Franciacorta Brut Conte di Provaglio	♈♈ 3
○ Franciacorta Brut Duca Diseo	♈♈ 3
○ Franciacorta Brut Rosé Conte di Provaglio	♈♈ 3
○ Franciacorta Brut Ziliani C '12	♈♈ 4
○ Franciacorta Brut Ziliani C	♈♈ 3
○ Franciacorta Satèn Conte di Provaglio	♈♈ 3
○ Franciacorta Satèn Duca Diseo	♈♈ 3
○ Franciacorta Satèn Gran Cuvée Maria Maddalena Cavalieri Ris. '10	♈♈ 5
○ Franciacorta Satèn Ziliani C '12	♈♈ 4
○ Franciacorta Satèn Ziliani C	♈♈ 3
⊙ Franciacorta Brut Rosé Ziliani C	♈ 4
○ Franciacorta Pas Dosé Ziliani C '12	♈ 4

Al Rocol

VIA PROVINCIALE, 79
25050 OME [BS]
TEL. +39 0306852542
www.alrocol.com

CELLAR SALES
PRE-BOOKED VISITS
ACCOMMODATION AND RESTAURANT SERVICE
ANNUAL PRODUCTION 60,000 bottles
HECTARES UNDER VINE 13.00

○ Franciacorta Dosaggio Zero Castellini '13	▼▼	6
○ Franciacorta Satèn Martignac '13	▼▼	5
○ Franciacorta Brut Ca' del Luf	▼	5
☉ Franciacorta Rosé Le Rive '09	▼	5

Annibale Alziati

LOC. SCAZZOLINO, 55
27040 ROVESCALA [PV]
TEL. +39 038575261
www.gaggiarone.it

CELLAR SALES
PRE-BOOKED VISITS
ANNUAL PRODUCTION 100,000 bottles
HECTARES UNDER VINE 19.00
VITICULTURE METHOD Certified Organic
SUSTAINABLE WINERY

● OP Bonarda Gaggiarone V. V. '15	▼▼	4
● OP Barbera San Francesco '15	▼	4
● OP Bonarda San Francesco '15	▼	2

Paolo Bagnasco

FRAZ. LOGLIO
27047 SANTA MARIA DELLA VERSA [PV]
TEL. +39 0385262329
www.cantinabagnasco.it

CELLAR SALES
PRE-BOOKED VISITS
ANNUAL PRODUCTION 200,000 bottles
HECTARES UNDER VINE 23.00

● OP Bonarda Trenta Filari '16	▼▼	3
● OP Bonarda V. del Sole '16	▼▼	2*
● OP Sangue di Giuda '16	▼	2

Barbacarlo - Lino Maga

S.DA BRONESE, 3
27043 BRONI [PV]
TEL. +39 038551212
barbacarlodimaga@libero.it

CELLAR SALES
PRE-BOOKED VISITS
ANNUAL PRODUCTION 20,000 bottles
HECTARES UNDER VINE 12.00

● Barbacarlo '15	▼▼	5

Barboglio De Gaioncelli

FRAZ. COLOMBARO
VIA NAZARIO SAURO
25040 CORTE FRANCA [BS]
TEL. +39 0309826831
www.barbogliodegaioncelli.it

CELLAR SALES
PRE-BOOKED VISITS
RESTAURANT SERVICE
ANNUAL PRODUCTION 90,000 bottles
HECTARES UNDER VINE 60.00

○ Franciacorta Brut	▼▼	5
☉ Franciacorta Rosé Donna Alberta '10	▼▼	5
○ Franciacorta Satèn	▼▼	4

Cantina Sociale Bergamasca

VIA BERGAMO, 10
24060 SAN PAOLO D'ARGON [BG]
TEL. +39 035951098
www.cantinabergamasca.it

CELLAR SALES
PRE-BOOKED VISITS
ANNUAL PRODUCTION 650,000 bottles
HECTARES UNDER VINE 90.00

○ TdC Brut M. Cl. Colleoni	▼▼	4
☉ TdC Schiava '16	▼▼	2*
● Valcalepio Moscato Passito Perseo '11	▼▼	4

Bertagna

LOC. BANDE
S.DA MADONNA DELLA PORTA, 14
46040 CAVRIANA [MN]
TEL. +39 037682211
www.cantinabertagna.it

CELLAR SALES
PRE-BOOKED VISITS
ANNUAL PRODUCTION 150,000 bottles
HECTARES UNDER VINE 17.00

○ Lugana '16	♈♈ 2*
● Montevolpe Rosso '13	♈♈ 3
● Rosso del Chino '13	♈ 3

Boccadoro

LOC. BOSCHI 10
25046 CAZZAGO SAN MARTINO [BS]
TEL. +39 3929710853
www.cantinaboccadoro.it

ANNUAL PRODUCTION 30,000 bottles
HECTARES UNDER VINE 7.00

○ Franciacorta Brut	♈♈ 4
⊙ Franciacorta Rosé	♈♈ 4

Bonaldi - Cascina del Bosco

LOC. PETOSINO
VIA GASPAROTTO, 96
24010 SORISOLE [BG]
TEL. +39 035571701
www.cascinadelbosco.it

CELLAR SALES
PRE-BOOKED VISITS
ANNUAL PRODUCTION 25,000 bottles
HECTARES UNDER VINE 4.00

○ Brut M. Cl. 24 Mesi	♈♈ 3
○ Valcalepio Bianco '16	♈♈ 3
○ Brut M. Cl. 36 Mesi	♈ 3

Bonfadini

FRAZ. CLUSANE
VIA L. DI BERNARDO, 85
25049 ISEO [BS]
TEL. +39 0309826721
www.bonfadini.it

CELLAR SALES
PRE-BOOKED VISITS
ANNUAL PRODUCTION 120,000 bottles
HECTARES UNDER VINE 12.00

⊙ Franciacorta Brut Rosé Opera	♈♈ 5
○ Franciacorta Dosaggio Zero Nature	♈♈ 5
○ Franciacorta Brut Nobilium	♈ 5
○ Franciacorta Satèn Carpe Diem	♈ 5

Borgo La Gallinaccia

FRAZ. PADERGNONE
VIA 4 NOVEMBRE, 15
25050 RODENGO SAIANO [BS]
TEL. +39 0306810391
www.borgolagallinaccia.it

CELLAR SALES
PRE-BOOKED VISITS
ANNUAL PRODUCTION 16,000 bottles
HECTARES UNDER VINE 3.40

○ Franciacorta Brut '12	♈♈ 4
○ Franciacorta Satèn '12	♈♈ 4
⊙ Franciacorta Brut Rosé	♈ 4
○ Franciacorta Pas Dosé	♈ 5

La Boscaiola

VIA RICCAFANA, 19
25033 COLOGNE [BS]
TEL. +39 0307156386
www.laboscaiola.com

CELLAR SALES
PRE-BOOKED VISITS
ANNUAL PRODUCTION 50,000 bottles
HECTARES UNDER VINE 7.00

○ Franciacorta Brut Nelson Cenci L'Insolita '11	♈♈ 6
○ Franciacorta Brut Sessanta '10	♈♈ 6
○ Franciacorta Satèn La Via della Seta	♈♈ 5

Bosco Longhino

FRAZ. MOLINO MARCONI
27047 SANTA MARIA DELLA VERSA [PV]
TEL. +39 0385798049
www.bosco-longhino.it

● OP Buttafuoco '11	♥♥ 2*
○ Moscato Nessuno '15	♥ 2
○ Pinot Grigio Nessuno '15	♥ 2
● Pinot Nero Campo dei Graci '15	♥ 3

Brunello

VIA ZAPPAGLIA, 8
25010 POZZOLENGO [BS]
TEL. +39 030918570

CELLAR SALES
PRE-BOOKED VISITS
ANNUAL PRODUCTION 80,000 bottles
HECTARES UNDER VINE 8.00

○ Lugana Et. Nera '16	♥♥ 3
○ Lugana Et. Bianca '16	♥ 2

Bulgarini

LOC. VAIBÒ, 1
25010 POZZOLENGO [BS]
TEL. +39 030918224
www.vini-bulgarini.com

CELLAR SALES
ANNUAL PRODUCTION 750,000 bottles
HECTARES UNDER VINE 40.00

○ Lugana Brut M. Cl. Stella di Lugana '14	♥♥ 3
○ Lugana '16	♥ 2

Ca' del Santo

LOC. CAMPOLUNGO, 4
27040 MONTALTO PAVESE [PV]
TEL. +39 0383870545
www.cadelsanto.it

CELLAR SALES
PRE-BOOKED VISITS
ANNUAL PRODUCTION 25,000 bottles
HECTARES UNDER VINE 6.00

○ Pinot Nero Nature '13	♥♥ 3
● Creatina Rosso Passione '16	♥ 3
◉ OP Pinot Nero Cruasé '10	♥ 4
● Pinot Nero Il Nero '14	♥ 3

Patrizia Cadore

LOC. CAMPAGNA BIANCA
25010 POZZOLENGO [BS]
TEL. +39 0309918138
www.vinicadore.eu

ANNUAL PRODUCTION 25,000 bottles
HECTARES UNDER VINE 8.50

● Garda Cabernet Sauvignon '16	♥♥ 3
○ Lugana '16	♥ 3
○ San Martino della Battaglia '16	♥ 3

Andrea Calvi

FRAZ. VIGALONE, 13
27044 CANNETO PAVESE [PV]
TEL. +39 038560034
www.andreacalvi.it

CELLAR SALES
PRE-BOOKED VISITS
ANNUAL PRODUCTION 100,000 bottles
HECTARES UNDER VINE 26.00

● OP Bonarda '16	♥♥ 2*
● Pinot Nero '16	♥♥ 3

Le Cantorìe

FRAZ. CASAGLIO
VIA CASTELLO DI CASAGLIO, 24/25
25064 GUSSAGO [BS]
TEL. +39 0302523723
www.lecantorie.it

ANNUAL PRODUCTION 75,000 bottles
HECTARES UNDER VINE 12.00

○ Franciacorta Brut Armonia	♟♟ 4
⊙ Franciacorta Rosé Rosi delle Margherite	♟♟ 7
○ Franciacorta Satèn Armonia	♟♟ 4

Cantrina

VIA VIA COLOMBERA, 7
25081 BEDIZZOLE [BS]
TEL. +39 3356362137
www.cantrina.it

CELLAR SALES
ANNUAL PRODUCTION 42,000 bottles
HECTARES UNDER VINE 7.90

● Valtènesi Rosso '16	♟♟ 3
○ Riné '15	♟ 3
⊙ Rosato '16	♟ 2

Cascina Belmonte

FRAZ. MONIGA DEL BOSCO
LOC. TOPPE
25080 MUSCOLINE [BS]
TEL. +39 3335051606
www.cascinabelmonte.it

PRE-BOOKED VISITS
ANNUAL PRODUCTION 15,000 bottles
HECTARES UNDER VINE 6.00

○ Serése '16	♟♟ 3
⊙ Valtenesi Chiaretto Costellazioni '16	♟♟ 3
● Fuochi nella Notte di San Giovanni '15	♟ 3

Cascina Clarabella

VIA ENRICO MATTEI
25040 CORTE FRANCA [BS]
TEL. +39 0309821041
www.cascinaclarabella.it

CELLAR SALES
PRE-BOOKED VISITS
ANNUAL PRODUCTION 70,000 bottles
HECTARES UNDER VINE 11.00
VITICULTURE METHOD Certified Organic

○ Franciacorta Brut	♟♟ 4
○ Franciacorta Pas Dosé E'ssenza	♟♟ 5
○ Franciacorta Satèn	♟♟ 5
⊙ Franciacorta Brut Rosé Annalisa Faifer '12	♟ 5

Cascina Gnocco

FRAZ. LOSANA, 20
27040 MORNICO LOSANA [PV]
TEL. +39 0383892280
www.cascinagnocco.it

CELLAR SALES
PRE-BOOKED VISITS
ANNUAL PRODUCTION 60,000 bottles
HECTARES UNDER VINE 13.00

⊙ Brut Rosé	♟♟ 5
● Orione '10	♟ 4

Cascina Maddalena

FRAZ. LUGANA DI SIRMIONE
VIA MADDALENA, 21
25019 SIRMIONE [BS]
TEL. +39 030 9905139
www.cascinamaddalena.com

ANNUAL PRODUCTION 10,000 bottles
HECTARES UNDER VINE 3.50

○ Lugana Capotesta '16	♟♟ 3

Castello di Luzzano

Loc. Luzzano, 5
27040 Rovescala [PV]
Tel. +39 0523863277
www.castelloluzzano.com

CELLAR SALES
PRE-BOOKED VISITS
ACCOMMODATION AND RESTAURANT SERVICE
ANNUAL PRODUCTION 120,000 bottles
HECTARES UNDER VINE 76.00

○ Pinot Nero Martinotti Magot '16	♥♥ 2*
● OP Pinot Nero Umore Nero '16	♥ 2

Castello di Stefanago

Loc. Castello di Stefanago
27040 Borgo Priolo [PV]
Tel. +39 0383875227
www.castellodistefanago.it

CELLAR SALES
PRE-BOOKED VISITS
ANNUAL PRODUCTION 60,000 bottles
HECTARES UNDER VINE 20.00
VITICULTURE METHOD Certified Organic

○ OP Cruasé Stefanago Ancestrale	♥♥ 4
● Croatina Castello di Stefanago '13	♥ 4

Castelveder

Via Belvedere, 4
25040 Monticelli Brusati [BS]
Tel. +39 030652308
www.castelveder.it

CELLAR SALES
PRE-BOOKED VISITS
ANNUAL PRODUCTION 90,000 bottles
HECTARES UNDER VINE 11.00

○ Franciacorta Brut '11	♥♥ 5
○ Franciacorta Extra Brut	♥♥ 4
○ Franciacorta Pas Dosé	♥♥ 5
○ Franciacorta Brut	♥ 4

Cavalli Faletti

Via Giovanni XXIII, 23
24020 Villa di Serio [BG]
Tel. +39 035663246
www.cavallifaletti.it

○ TdC Chardonnay '16	♥♥ 2*
○ TdC Incrocio Manzoni '16	♥♥ 2*
● Vlacalepio Rosso '13	♥♥ 2*

Il Cipresso

Fraz. Tribulina
Via Cerri, 2
24020 Scanzorosciate [BG]
Tel. +39 0354597005
www.ilcipresso.info

CELLAR SALES
PRE-BOOKED VISITS
ANNUAL PRODUCTION 20,000 bottles
HECTARES UNDER VINE 4.00

● Moscato di Scanzo Serafino '13	♥♥ 6
○ Valcalepio Bianco Melardo '16	♥♥ 2*

Colle del Bricco

Via Torre Sacchetti, 70a
27049 Stradella [PV]
Tel. +39 3280866544
www.colledelbricco.it

ANNUAL PRODUCTION 10,000 bottles
HECTARES UNDER VINE 5.00

● Bonarda Frizzante Makedon '16	♥♥ 2*
○ OP Riesling Khione '16	♥ 2

Conti Ducco

LOC. CAMIGNONE
VIA DEGLI EROI, 70
25040 PASSIRANO [BS]
TEL. +39 0306850566
www.contiducco.it

PRE-BOOKED VISITS
ANNUAL PRODUCTION 400,000 bottles
HECTARES UNDER VINE 92.00

○ Franciacorta Brut '12	♛♛ 5
○ Franciacorta Pas Dosé '11	♛♛ 4
● Curtefranca Rosso Rouge '15	♛ 3

Corte Aura

VIA COLZANO, 13
25030 ADRO [BS]
TEL. +39 030 7357281
www.corteaura.it

CELLAR SALES
PRE-BOOKED VISITS
ANNUAL PRODUCTION 170,000 bottles
HECTARES UNDER VINE 5.00

○ Franciacorta Brut	♛♛ 4
⊙ Franciacorta Rosé	♛♛ 5
○ Franciacorta Satèn	♛♛ 4
○ Franciacorta Pas Dosé	♛ 5

Delai

VIA MORO, 1
25080 PUEGNAGO SUL GARDA [BS]
TEL. +39 0365555527

ANNUAL PRODUCTION 80,000 bottles
HECTARES UNDER VINE 8.00

● Garda Bresciano Groppello Mogrì '16	♛♛ 2*
⊙ Brut Rosé	♛ 3
⊙ Garda Bresciano Chiaretto Notterosa '16	♛ 3
● Merzemino Sovenigo '14	♛ 3

Due Pini

LOC. PICEDO
VIA NOVAGLIO, 16
25080 POLPENAZZE DEL GARDA [BS]
TEL. +39 0365675123

ANNUAL PRODUCTION 35,000 bottles
HECTARES UNDER VINE 6.00

● Garda Cl. Groppello Sara '15	♛♛ 3
● Garda Cl. Sup. Samantha '13	♛♛ 4
○ Garda Riesling Emanuela '16	♛♛ 2*
● Garda Cl. Sup. Michela '13	♛ 4

Feliciana

LOC. FELICIANA
25010 POZZOLENGO [BS]
TEL. +39 030918228
www.feliciana.it

○ Lugana Felugan '16	♛♛ 3
○ Lugana Sercè Ris. '14	♛♛ 4

Il Feudo Nico

VIA SAN ROCCO, 63
27040 MORNICO LOSANA [PV]
TEL. +39 0383892452

ANNUAL PRODUCTION 40,000 bottles
HECTARES UNDER VINE 16.00

○ Brut M. Cl. Maria Antonietta '13	♛♛ 4
● Edoardo '15	♛♛ 4

Finigeto

LOC. CELLA, 27
27040 MONTALTO PAVESE [PV]
TEL. +39 328 7095347
www.finigeto.com

CELLAR SALES
PRE-BOOKED VISITS
ACCOMMODATION
ANNUAL PRODUCTION 80,000 bottles
HECTARES UNDER VINE 42.00

○ Riesling Lo Spavaldo '16	♀♀ 3
○ Chardonnay Il Fermo '15	♀ 3
○ Pinot Nero Extrà '16	♀ 3

La Fiòca

FRAZ. NIGOLINE
VIA VILLA, 13B
25040 CORTE FRANCA [BS]
TEL. +39 0309826313
www.lafioca.com

CELLAR SALES
PRE-BOOKED VISITS
ANNUAL PRODUCTION 40,000 bottles
HECTARES UNDER VINE 4.00

○ Franciacorta Dosaggio Zero '10	♀♀ 6
○ Franciacorta Extra Brut Ris. '09	♀♀ 6
○ Franciacorta Brut	♀ 5
○ Franciacorta Satèn	♀ 5

La Fiorita

VIA MAGLIO, 10
25020 OME [BS]
TEL. +39 030652279
www.lafioritafranciacorta.com

CELLAR SALES
PRE-BOOKED VISITS
ACCOMMODATION AND RESTAURANT SERVICE
ANNUAL PRODUCTION 94,000 bottles
HECTARES UNDER VINE 10.00

○ Franciacorta Dosaggio Zero	♀♀ 4
○ Franciacorta Satèn '12	♀♀ 5
⊙ Franciacorta Brut Rosé	♀ 4
○ Franciacorta Satèn	♀ 4

Le Fracce

FRAZ. MAIRANO
VIA CASTEL DEL LUPO, 5
27045 CASTEGGIO [PV]
TEL. +39 038382526
www.lefracce.com

CELLAR SALES
PRE-BOOKED VISITS
ANNUAL PRODUCTION 180,000 bottles
HECTARES UNDER VINE 40.00

⊙ Bussolera Grand Rosé Brut	♀♀ 5
● OP Bonarda Vivace Rubiosa '16	♀♀ 3
○ OP Riesling Landò '16	♀ 3
● Pinot Nero Moro '16	♀ 2

F.lli Guerci

FRAZ. CROTESI, 20
27045 CASTEGGIO [PV]
TEL. +39 038382725
info@guercivini.it

CELLAR SALES
ANNUAL PRODUCTION 300,000 bottles
HECTARES UNDER VINE 42.00

○ OP Pinot Nero Brut M. Cl. 222 a.C. '12	♀♀ 4
○ Moscato '16	♀ 2
○ OP Cruasé 222 a.C.	♀ 3
○ OP Riesling Fior Fiore '16	♀ 2

Tenuta La Vigna

CASCINA LA VIGNA
25020 CAPRIANO DEL COLLE [BS]
TEL. +39 0309748061
www.tenutalavigna.it

CELLAR SALES
PRE-BOOKED VISITS
ANNUAL PRODUCTION 35,000 bottles
HECTARES UNDER VINE 6.00

● Capriano del Colle Marzemino Lamettino '15	♀♀ 3
○ Brut M. Cl. Nature Ugo Botti	♀ 5
● Capriano del Colle Rosso Rubinera '15	♀ 3

Cantine Lebovitz

Fraz. Governolo
V.le Rimembranze, 4
46037 Roncoferraro [MN]
Tel. +39 0376668115
www.cantinelebovitz.it

CELLAR SALES
PRE-BOOKED VISITS
ANNUAL PRODUCTION 500,000 bottles
HECTARES UNDER VINE

● Al Scagarün '16	♟♟ 1*
● Sedamat '16	♟♟ 1*

Eligio Magri

Via Colle dei Pasta, 8a
24060 Torre de' Roveri [BG]
Tel. +39 0354528868
www.eligiomagri.it

CELLAR SALES
PRE-BOOKED VISITS
ANNUAL PRODUCTION 80,000 bottles
HECTARES UNDER VINE 15.00

● Elogio '11	♟♟ 3
○ Lucelio '16	♟♟ 2*

Malavasi

Loc. Casina Sacco, 1
Fraz. San Giacomo
25010 Pozzolengo [BS]
Tel. +39 0309918759
www.malavasivini.it

ANNUAL PRODUCTION 100,000 bottles
HECTARES UNDER VINE 10.00

○ Lugana Camilla '16	♟♟ 3
○ Lugana '16	♟ 3
○ Lugana San Giacomo '16	♟ 4

Manuelina

Fraz. Ruinello di Sotto, 3a
27047 Santa Maria della Versa [PV]
Tel. +39 0385278247
Fraz. Ruinello di Sotto 3/a

CELLAR SALES
PRE-BOOKED VISITS
ANNUAL PRODUCTION 230,000 bottles
HECTARES UNDER VINE 22.00

◉ OP Cruasé	♟♟ 3
● OP Bonarda Achillius '16	♟ 2
○ OP Pinot Nero M. Cl. '12	♟ 3

Marangona

Loc. Marangona 1
25010 Pozzolengo [BS]
Tel. +39 030919379
www.marangona.com

CELLAR SALES
PRE-BOOKED VISITS
ANNUAL PRODUCTION 30,000 bottles
HECTARES UNDER VINE 27.00

○ Lugana Tre Campane '15	♟♟ 2*
○ Lugana '16	♟ 2

Alberto Marsetti

Via Scarpatetti, 15
23100 Sondrio
Tel. +39 0342216329
www.marsetti.it

ANNUAL PRODUCTION 20,000 bottles
HECTARES UNDER VINE 5.00

● Sforzato di Valtellina '12	♟♟ 6
● Valtellina Sup. Grumello '13	♟♟ 5

Martilde

FRAZ. CROCE, 4A
27040 ROVESCALA [PV]
TEL. +39 0385756280
www.martilde.it

CELLAR SALES
PRE-BOOKED VISITS
ANNUAL PRODUCTION 30,000 bottles
HECTARES UNDER VINE 15.00
VITICULTURE METHOD Certified Organic

○ Malvasia Piume '16	🏆🏆 2*
○ Malvasia Dedica '16	🏆 2
● OP Barbera '15	🏆 2

Medolago Albani

VIA REDONA, 12
24069 TRESCORE BALNEARIO [BG]
TEL. +39 035942022
www.medolagoalbani.it

CELLAR SALES
PRE-BOOKED VISITS
ANNUAL PRODUCTION 200,000 bottles
HECTARES UNDER VINE 23.00

○ Brut M. Cl. Medolago Albani	🏆🏆 3*
● Valcalepio Rosso I due Lauri Ris. '12	🏆🏆 4
● Villa Redona '13	🏆🏆 3

Walter Menegola

VIA E. VANONI, 13C
23012 CASTIONE ANDEVENNO [SO]
TEL. +39 349 6945516
www.cantinamenegola.it

ANNUAL PRODUCTION 25,000 bottles
HECTARES UNDER VINE 2.50

● Valtellina Sforzato '12	🏆🏆 6
● Valtellina Sup. Sassella Ris. '12	🏆🏆 5
● Valtellina Sup. Sassella Rupestre '12	🏆🏆 5

Mirabella

VIA CANTARANE, 2
25050 RODENGO SAIANO [BS]
TEL. +39 030611197
www.mirabellafranciacorta.it

CELLAR SALES
PRE-BOOKED VISITS
ANNUAL PRODUCTION 450,000 bottles
HECTARES UNDER VINE 50.00

○ Franciacorta Brut	🏆🏆 4
⊙ Franciacorta Brut Rosé	🏆🏆 4
○ Franciacorta Brut Satèn	🏆🏆 5
○ Franciacorta Extra Brut	🏆 7

Tenuta Monte Delma

VIA VALENZANO, 23
25050 PASSIRANO [BS]
TEL. +39 0306546161
www.montedelma.it

CELLAR SALES
PRE-BOOKED VISITS
ANNUAL PRODUCTION 100,000 bottles
HECTARES UNDER VINE 20.00

○ Franciacorta Brut	🏆🏆 4
⊙ Franciacorta Brut Rosé	🏆🏆 5
○ Franciacorta Brut Satèn	🏆🏆 5
○ Franciacorta Pas Dosé '11	🏆🏆 5

Montelio

VIA D. MAZZA, 1
27050 CODEVILLA [PV]
TEL. +39 0383373090
montelio.gio@alice.it

CELLAR SALES
PRE-BOOKED VISITS
ACCOMMODATION AND RESTAURANT SERVICE
ANNUAL PRODUCTION 130,000 bottles
HECTARES UNDER VINE 27.00

● OP Barbera '15	🏆🏆 2*
○ OP Riesling Il Nadòt '16	🏆🏆 2*
○ Bianco '16	🏆 2
● Rosso '15	🏆 2

Monterucco

VALLE CIMA, 38
27040 CIGOGNOLA [PV]
TEL. +39 038585151
www.monterucco.it

CELLAR SALES
PRE-BOOKED VISITS
ANNUAL PRODUCTION 100,000 bottles
HECTARES UNDER VINE 20.00

● OP Bonarda V. Il Modello '16	🏆🏆	2*
● OP Buttafuoco Sanluigi '15	🏆🏆	3
● OP Pinot Nero Negar '15	🏆	3

La Montina

VIA BAIANA, 17
25040 MONTICELLI BRUSATI [BS]
TEL. +39 030653278
www.lamontina.it

CELLAR SALES
PRE-BOOKED VISITS
RESTAURANT SERVICE
ANNUAL PRODUCTION 450,000 bottles
HECTARES UNDER VINE 70.00

○ Franciacorta Brut Satèn	🏆🏆	4
○ Franciacorta Extra Brut	🏆🏆	4
○ Franciacorta Brut	🏆	4
○ Franciacorta Pas Dosé Baiana Ris. '08	🏆	5

Montonale

LOC. CONTA, 7
25015 DESENZANO DEL GARDA [BS]
TEL. +39 0309103358
www.montonale.com

ANNUAL PRODUCTION 100,000 bottles
HECTARES UNDER VINE 25.00

⊙ Garda Cl. Chiaretto Rosa di Notte '16	🏆🏆	3
○ Lugana Montunal '16	🏆🏆	3
○ Lugana Orestilla '15	🏆🏆	4

Monzio Compagnoni

VIA NIGOLINE, 98
25030 ADRO [BS]
TEL. +39 0307457803
www.monziocompagnoni.com

CELLAR SALES
PRE-BOOKED VISITS
ANNUAL PRODUCTION 170,000 bottles
HECTARES UNDER VINE 17.00

○ Curtefranca Bianco della Seta '15	🏆🏆	4
○ Franciacorta Brut Cuvée Elementare	🏆🏆	4
● Rosso di Luna '15	🏆	4

Nettare dei Santi

VIA CAPRA, 17
20078 SAN COLOMBANO AL LAMBRO [MI]
TEL. +39 0371200523
www.nettaredeisanti.it

CELLAR SALES
PRE-BOOKED VISITS
ANNUAL PRODUCTION 600,000 bottles
HECTARES UNDER VINE 40.00

○ Brut M. Cl. Domm '13	🏆🏆	3
● Franco Riccardi '12	🏆	4
○ Solitaire	🏆	3

Anna Palvarini

VIA VIGNETO, 10
25019 SIRMIONE [BS]
TEL. +39 030919033
corte.anna@alice.it

○ Lugana Sup. Antico Vigneto '15	🏆🏆	3
○ Lugana '15	🏆	3

Panigada - Banino

VIA DELLA VITTORIA, 13
20078 SAN COLOMBANO AL LAMBRO [MI]
TEL. +39 037189103
www.banino.it

CELLAR SALES
PRE-BOOKED VISITS
ANNUAL PRODUCTION 30,000 bottles
HECTARES UNDER VINE 5.00

○ Aureum '14		♟♟ 4
● San Colombano Rosso V. La Merla Ris. '12	♟♟ 3	
● San Colombano Rosso Banino Giovane '16	♟ 2	

La Perla

LOC. TRESENDA
VIA VALGELLA, 29B
23036 TEGLIO [SO]
TEL. +39 3462878894
www.vini-laperla.com

CELLAR SALES
PRE-BOOKED VISITS
ANNUAL PRODUCTION 20,000 bottles
HECTARES UNDER VINE 3.30

● Valtellina Sup. Elisa Rls. '12	♟♟ 5
● Valtellina Sup. La Mossa '12	♟♟ 4

La Piotta

LOC. PIOTTA, 2
27040 MONTALTO PAVESE [PV]
TEL. +39 0383870178
www.padroggilapiotta.it

CELLAR SALES
PRE-BOOKED VISITS
ANNUAL PRODUCTION 90,000 bottles
HECTARES UNDER VINE 20.00
VITICULTURE METHOD Certified Organic

○ OP M. Cl. Talento '13	♟♟ 4
● OP Bonarda Frizzante '16	♟♟ 2*
● OP Barbera Piota '16	♟ 2

La Pergola

VIA PERGOLA, 21
25080 MONIGA DEL GARDA [BS]
TEL. +39 0365502002
www.cantinelapergola.it

CELLAR SALES
PRE-BOOKED VISITS
ANNUAL PRODUCTION 250,000 bottles
HECTARES UNDER VINE 30.00
VITICULTURE METHOD Certified Organic
SUSTAINABLE WINERY

○ Garda Cl. Bianco Zublì '16	♟ 3
● Garda Cl. Groppello '16	♟ 2
○ Lugana Biocora '16	♟ 3
⊙ Valtènesi Chiaretto Selene Bio '16	♟ 2

Pian del Maggio

VIA ISEO, 108
25030 ERBUSCO [BS]
TEL. +39 3355638610
www.piandelmaggio.it

PRE-BOOKED VISITS
ANNUAL PRODUCTION 25,000 bottles
HECTARES UNDER VINE 2.90

○ Franciacorta Brut Naturo Furente '11	♟♟ 5
○ Franciacorta Brut Proscenio	♟♟ 4
⊙ Franciacorta Rosé...e Anna Sorrise	♟ 5
○ Franciacorta Satèn Capriccio	♟ 5

Plozza Ome

VIA LIZZANA, 13
25050 OME [BS]
TEL. +39 0306527775
www.plozzaome.it

CELLAR SALES
PRE-BOOKED VISITS
ANNUAL PRODUCTION 37,000 bottles
HECTARES UNDER VINE 7.00

⊙ Franciacorta Rosé	♟♟ 5
○ Franciacorta Satèn	♟♟ 5
○ Franciacorta Brut	♟ 5

Prime Alture

VIA MADONNA, 109
27045 CASTEGGIO [PV]
TEL. +39 038383214
www.primealture.it

CELLAR SALES
PRE-BOOKED VISITS
ACCOMMODATION AND RESTAURANT SERVICE
ANNUAL PRODUCTION 40,000 bottles
HECTARES UNDER VINE 8.00

○ Brut M. Cl. Io per Te	♥♥ 5
● Pinot Noir Centopercento '15	♥♥ 5
● Pinot Noir Centopercento '14	♥♥ 5
○ Est Il Bianco '16	♥ 3

Le Quattro Terre

FRAZ. BORGONATO
VIA RISORGIMENTO, 11
25040 CORTE FRANCA [BS]
TEL. +39 030984312
www.quattroterre.it

CELLAR SALES
PRE-BOOKED VISITS
ACCOMMODATION AND RESTAURANT SERVICE
ANNUAL PRODUCTION 50,000 bottles
HECTARES UNDER VINE 7.00

○ Franciacorta Dosaggio Zero '11	♥♥ 6
○ Franciacorta Brut 940 Ris. '09	♥♥ 8
○ Franciacorta Satèn	♥♥ 5
⊙ Franciacorta Rosé '13	♥ 5

Tenuta Quvestra

LOC. CASE NUOVE, 9
27047 SANTA MARIA DELLA VERSA [PV]
TEL. +39 3476014109
www.quvestra.it

○ OP Sinfonia In Bianco '15	♥♥ 2*
○ OP Martinotti Gaudium	♥ 3
⊙ OP Pinot Nero Cruasé Zephiro	♥ 3
● Pinot Nero '14	♥ 3

Rebollini

LOC. SBERCIA
27040 BORGORATTO MORMOROLO [PV]
TEL. +39 0383872295
www.rebollini.it

CELLAR SALES
PRE-BOOKED VISITS
ANNUAL PRODUCTION 100,000 bottles
HECTARES UNDER VINE 35.00
SUSTAINABLE WINERY

○ OP Pinot Nero Brut Nature M. Cl. '12	♥♥ 5
○ OP Riesling '16	♥♥ 2*

La Rifra

LOC. PILANDRO, 2
25010 DESENZANO DEL GARDA [BS]
TEL. +39 0309108023
claudiofraccaroli@virgilio.it

ANNUAL PRODUCTION 90,000 bottles
HECTARES UNDER VINE 14.00

○ Lugana Il Bepi Ris. '14	♥♥ 3
○ Lugana Libiam '16	♥♥ 2*
● Garda Cabernet Sauvignon Tremante '15	♥ 2
○ Lugana Brut	♥ 3

Riva di Franciacorta

LOC. FANTECOLO
VIA CARLO ALBERTO, 19
25050 PROVAGLIO D'ISEO [BS]
TEL. +39 0309823701
www.rivadifranciacorta.it

CELLAR SALES
PRE-BOOKED VISITS
ANNUAL PRODUCTION 280,000 bottles
HECTARES UNDER VINE 32.00
SUSTAINABLE WINERY

○ Franciacorta Pas Dosé Solo Riva	♥♥ 6
○ Franciacorta Satèn	♥♥ 5
○ Franciacorta Brut	♥ 5
○ Franciacorta Pas Dosé Rivalto 75	♥ 5

Romantica

A VALLOSA, 29
25050 PASSIRANO [BS]
TEL. +39 030657362
www.romanticafranciacorta.com

CELLAR SALES
PRE-BOOKED VISITS
ACCOMMODATION AND RESTAURANT SERVICE
ANNUAL PRODUCTION 60,000 bottles
HECTARES UNDER VINE 10.00

○ Franciacorta Brut '13	♛♛ 4
○ Franciacorta Brut	♛♛ 5
○ Franciacorta Satèn	♛♛ 5

La Rotonda

LOC. CALINO
FRAZ. 25046
VIA BOSCHI, 1
25046 CAZZAGO SAN MARTINO [BS]
TEL. +39 0307750909
www.larotondafranciacorta.it

PRE-BOOKED VISITS
ANNUAL PRODUCTION 80,000 bottles
HECTARES UNDER VINE 12.72

○ Franciacorta Dosaggio Zero DiZeta '11	♛♛ 5
○ Franciacorta Saten '13	♛♛ 3
○ Franciacorta Dosaggio Zero Radicale DiZeta Ris.	♛ 5

San Michele

VIA PARROCCHIA, 57
25020 CAPRIANO DEL COLLE [BS]
TEL. +39 0309444091
www.sanmichelevini.it

CELLAR SALES
PRE-BOOKED VISITS
ANNUAL PRODUCTION 70,000 bottles
HECTARES UNDER VINE 16.00
VITICULTURE METHOD Certified Organic

● Capriano del Colle Marzemino '16	♛♛ 2*
● Capriano del Colle Rosso 1884 Ris. '13	♛♛ 3
● Capriano del Colle Rosso Carme '15	♛ 2

Poderi di San Pietro

VIA STEFFENINI 2/6
20078 SAN COLOMBANO AL LAMBRO [MI]
TEL. +39 0371208054
www.poderidisanpietro.it

CELLAR SALES
PRE-BOOKED VISITS
ANNUAL PRODUCTION 300,000 bottles
HECTARES UNDER VINE 80.00

○ Ca' della Signora Brut	♛♛ 4
● San Colombano Rosso di Valbissera '15	♛ 3
● Trianon '11	♛ 6

Santus

VIA BADIA, 68
25060 CELLATICA [BS]
TEL. +39 0308367074
www.santus.it

PRE-BOOKED VISITS
ANNUAL PRODUCTION 50,000 bottles
HECTARES UNDER VINE 9.00

○ Franciacorta Satèn '12	♛♛ 4
○ Franciacorta Brut	♛ 4
⊙ Franciacorta Extra Brut Rosé	♛ 4

Tenuta Scerscé

VIA STELVIO, 18
23037 TIRANO [SO]
TEL. +39 3461542970
www.tenutascersce.it

CELLAR SALES
PRE-BOOKED VISITS
ANNUAL PRODUCTION 22,000 bottles
HECTARES UNDER VINE 2.50
SUSTAINABLE WINERY

● Valtellina Sforzato Infinito '11	♛♛ 6
● Valtellina Sup. Essenza '13	♛♛ 5
● Rosso di Valtellina Nettare '15	♛ 3

Pietro Selva

via Vendola, 32
23012 Castione Andevenno [SO]
Tel. +39 3408129270
selvapietro@gmail.com

ANNUAL PRODUCTION 2,000 bottles
HECTARES UNDER VINE 1.50

● Rosso di Valtellina Dosso del Cuculo '15	♙♙	3
● Valtellina Sup. Sassella Ris. '13	♙♙	4

Sullali

via Costa di Sopra, 22
25030 Erbusco [BS]
Tel. +39 3930206080
info@sullali.com

ANNUAL PRODUCTION 10,000 bottles
HECTARES UNDER VINE 3.50

○ Franciacorta Extra Brut	♙♙	4
○ Franciacorta Extra Brut Blanc de Noir	♙♙	4

Terre d'Oltrepò

via Torino, 96
27045 Casteggio [PV]
Tel. +39 038551505
www.bronis.it

CELLAR SALES
PRE-BOOKED VISITS
ANNUAL PRODUCTION 4,000,000 bottles
HECTARES UNDER VINE 4500.00

○ OP Brut M. Cl. Svic 1907	♙♙	3
☉ OP Cruasé Svic	♙	2

Torre degli Alberi

loc. Torre degli Alberi

27040 Ruino [PV]
Tel. +39 0385955905
www.torredeglialberi.it

ANNUAL PRODUCTION 20,000 bottles
HECTARES UNDER VINE 4.00
VITICULTURE METHOD Certified Organic

○ OP Pinot Nero Brut '14	♙♙	3
☉ OP Cruasé	♙	3
○ OP Pinot Nero Brut Pas Dosé M. Cl.	♙	3

Tosi

via Pianazza, 45
27040 Montescano [PV]
Tel. +39 3384781752
www.vinitosi.com

○ OP Pinot Nero Nirfea '12	♙♙	3
● Pinot Nero Theremin '15	♙♙	3
● OP Bonarda Frizzante Violin '16	♙	3

Cooperativa Agricola Triasso e Sassella

fraz. Triasso, 25
23100 Sondrio
Tel. +39 034221710
www.cooptriasso.it

ANNUAL PRODUCTION 8,600 bottles
HECTARES UNDER VINE 2.00

● Valtellina Sup. Sassella i Ciaz '13	♙♙	5
● Valtellina Sup. Sassella Sassi Solivi '14	♙♙	5

F.lli Turina

VIA PERGOLA, 68
25080 MONIGA DEL GARDA [BS]
TEL. +39 0365502103
www.turinavini.it

CELLAR SALES
PRE-BOOKED VISITS
ANNUAL PRODUCTION 300,000 bottles
HECTARES UNDER VINE 20.00

○ Lugana '16	♟♟ 2*
○ Lugana Fenil Boi '16	♟♟ 2*
○ Lugana Brut	♟ 2

L'Ulif

LOC. PICEDO
VIA MONTEZALTO, 14
25080 POLPENAZZE DEL GARDA [BS]
TEL. +39 0365674969
silvano.delai@tin.it

ANNUAL PRODUCTION 22,000 bottles
HECTARES UNDER VINE 3.50
VITICULTURE METHOD Certified Biodynamic

○ Garda Cl. Bianco Preludio '16	♟♟ 2*
⊙ Garda Cl. Chiaretto Minuetto '16	♟ 2
● Garda Cl. Sup. Hibernum '10	♟ 4

Valdamonte di Fiori

FRAZ. VALDAMONTE, 47
27047 SANTA MARIA DELLA VERSA [PV]
TEL. +39 038579665
www.valdamonte.it

ANNUAL PRODUCTION 17,000 bottles
HECTARES UNDER VINE 16.00
VITICULTURE METHOD Certified Organic
SUSTAINABLE WINERY

● OP Bonarda Frizzante Novecento '16	♟♟ 2*
● 347 slm '16	♟ 2
● OP Bonarda Frizzante '15	♟ 2

Agricola Vallecamonica

VIA XXV APRILE, 11
25040 ARTOGNE [BS]
TEL. +39 3355828410
www.vinivallecamonica.com

CELLAR SALES
PRE-BOOKED VISITS
ANNUAL PRODUCTION 20,000 bottles
HECTARES UNDER VINE 4.50

○ Bianco dell'Annunciata '15	♟♟ 3
● Ciass Negher '09	♟♟ 3
○ Brut M. Cl. Nautilus '12	♟ 5

Vercesi del Castellazzo

VIA AURELIANO, 36
27040 MONTÙ BECCARIA [PV]
TEL. +39 0385262098
www.vercesidelcastellazzo.it

CELLAR SALES
PRE-BOOKED VISITS
ANNUAL PRODUCTION 80,000 bottles
HECTARES UNDER VINE 13.00

● OP Barbera Clà '14	♟♟ 2*
● Vespolino '16	♟♟ 2*
○ OP Pinot Nero in Bianco Gugiarolo '16	♟ 2
○ OP Pinot Nero Luogo dei Monti '13	♟ 3

Giuseppe Vezzoli

VIA COSTA SOPRA, 22
25030 ERBUSCO [BS]
TEL. +39 0307267579
www.vezzolivini.it

CELLAR SALES
PRE-BOOKED VISITS
ANNUAL PRODUCTION 200,000 bottles
HECTARES UNDER VINE 63.00

○ Franciacorta Brut	♟♟ 4
○ Franciacorta Brut Satèn	♟♟ 5
○ Franciacorta Extra Brut Nefertiti DiZeta '11	♟♟ 6
○ Franciacorta Extra Brut Vendemmia Zero	♟♟ 6

Vigna Dorata

Fraz. Calino
via Sala, 80
25046 Cazzago San Martino [BS]
Tel. +39 0307254275
www.vignadorata.it

CELLAR SALES
PRE-BOOKED VISITS
ANNUAL PRODUCTION 70,000 bottles
HECTARES UNDER VINE 6.00

○ Franciacorta Brut	♟♟ 4
⊙ Franciacorta Rosé	♟♟ 5
○ Franciacorta Satèn	♟♟ 5
○ Franciacorta Satèn '11	♟ 6

Vigne Olcru

via Buca, 26
27047 Santa Maria della Versa [PV]
Tel. +39 0385799958
www.vigneolcru.com

PRE-BOOKED VISITS
ANNUAL PRODUCTION 190,000 bottles
HECTARES UNDER VINE 29.00
SUSTAINABLE WINERY

○ Gotha Divino '16	♟ 4
○ Infinito '15	♟ 3

Villa Domizia

via Marconi, 1
24060 Torre de' Roveri [BG]
Tel. +39 035580701
www.villadomizia.it

○ TdC Brut M. Cl. Villa Domizia '12	♟♟ 2*
● Valcalepio Rosso Gaudes '12	♟♟ 2*
● TdC Incrocio Terzi Punto Zero '14	♟ 2

Visconti

Fraz. San Martino della Battaglia
via Selva Capuzza, 1
25010 Desenzano del Garda [BS]
Tel. +39 0309910381
www.viscontiwines.it

CELLAR SALES
PRE-BOOKED VISITS
ANNUAL PRODUCTION 250,000 bottles
HECTARES UNDER VINE 20.00

○ Lugana '16	♟♟ 2*
○ Lugana Collo Lungo '16	♟♟ 2*
○ Lugana Franco Visconti '16	♟ 3

Zamichele

via Roveglia Palazzina, 2
25010 Pozzolengo [BS]
Tel. +39 030918631
cantinazamichele@alice.it

CELLAR SALES
PRE-BOOKED VISITS
ANNUAL PRODUCTION 45,000 bottles
HECTARES UNDER VINE 8.00

○ Lugana Gardè '15	♟♟ 2*
○ Lugana '16	♟ 2

Zatti

via Lanfranchi, 10
25080 Calvagese della Riviera [BS]
Tel. +39 3464273907
www.cantinazatti.it

ANNUAL PRODUCTION 10,000 bottles
HECTARES UNDER VINE 2.00

○ Garda Riesling Gep '12	♟♟ 3
○ Brut Sandrjolé '13	♟ 4

CANTON TICINO

After something of a break, Ticino is back in our guide. The area's territorial and cultural affinity with Italy, as well as the quality of its wines, are such that their inclusion is pretty much a necessity. A quick glance will reveal that most of the wines reviewed are made with Merlot. The cultivar was introduced to Ticino about 100 years ago and adjusted perfectly. Even if they've been making wines in the region for at least 2000 years, we know little about its varieties or the way they were cultivated. One thing is certain: before the phylloxera plague of the late 19th century, various American and hybrid grapes were cultivated, not to mention, in Sopraceneri, the interesting variety, Bondola. Starting in 1907, Merlot made its triumphal entrance and remains today the territory's principal grape. There was a time when the wines produced were rather light. It was only later that the more robust Merlot style was established thanks to lower yields, more sophisticated techniques in the cellar and aging in new wood. Ticino's viticulture can be divided in two subregions: Sopraceneri (north of Monte Ceneri) and Sottoceneri (to the south). The former comprises the districts of Bellinzona, Blenio, Leventina, Locarno, Rivera and Vallemaggia. The Leventina and Blenio Valleys, near the Alps, are especially known for giving rise to lighter, more finely fruity Merlots. The latter, Sottoceneri, comprises Lugano and Mendrisio, and here fuller, more robust Merlots are made. Sopraceneri is rich in granite and sand, while the south sees heavier, more calcareous soils with varying quantities of clay. Across the region, Merlot is interpreted in different styles, as a light, fruit-driven, summery wine or in more full-bodied selections aged in barriques, thus more concentrated and suitable for aging. But Ticino doesn't want to be only Merlot wine country. It's gradually incorporating other interesting varieties, from Chardonnay to Pinot Noir, Gamaret, Sauvignon Blanc, Syrah, Cabernet Sauvignon and Franc, as well as Bondola. Finally, a number of other grapes are cultivated as well, some of these are in an experimental phase and others are already being vinified and seeing interesting results. This year, two of the region's wines earn Tre Bicchieri. One is Fawino's 2014 Merlot Musa, with its relaxed style and savory, intriguing fruit. The other is Vinattieri Ticinesi's Merlot Vinattieri, which embodies the deepest, most structured spirit of this wine. Welcome back, Ticino.

Agriloro

LOC. GENESTRERIO
VIA PRELLA, 14
6852 TICINO
TEL. +41916405454
www.agriloro.ch

CELLAR SALES
PRE-BOOKED VISITS
ANNUAL PRODUCTION 200,000 bottles
HECTARES UNDER VINE 23.00

Meinrad Perler's 23 hectares of vineyards are divided into two estates, Ör (in Arzo) and La Prella (Genestrerio, a district of Mendrisio), and are situated in a hilly area that enjoys perfect exposure to the sun. Agriloro is an atypical producer when it comes to the territory's viticulture, with 20 some varieties cultivated (and a wide selection of wines): Gewürztraminer, Moscato, Viognier, Egiodola, Carmenère, Tannat, Arinarnoa are rarities in Ticino. The estate also features an interesting nursery where more than 600 species of vines are cultivated for experimental purposes. Agriloro's wines are high profile, with the best versions proving capable of complexity over time. Sottobosco (made with Merlot, Cabernet Sauvignon, Gamaret, Cabernet Franc and Petit Verdot) is one of the wines that most contributed to the winery's reputation. It's a blend with excellent structure, complexity and balance. The Merlot Riserva La Prella features a long, elegant contours and distinguishes itself for its lovely aromatic profile.

● Ticino Merlot La Prella Ris. '15	♟♟	6
● Ticino Rosso Sottobosco '15	♟♟	6
○ Ticino Bianco Granito '15	♟	5
● Ticino Merlot Riserva da l'Ör '15	♟	6
○ Ticino Sauvignon Blanc '15	♟	5

Brivio Vini

LOC. MENDRISIO
VIA VIGNOO, 3
6850 TICINO
TEL. +41916460919
www.brivio.ch

CELLAR SALES
PRE-BOOKED VISITS
ANNUAL PRODUCTION 500,000 bottles
HECTARES UNDER VINE 60.00

Even if it became part of the Gialdi group in 2001, Brivio boasts a long tradition in viticulture. In fact, it started in the 1980s, when Guido Brivio decided to leap into Medrisiotto's wine production scene. And so began a long collaboration with Felician Gialdi, with the purposes of establishing common commercial and production strategies. Like its sister company, they enlist the help of trusted collaborators to manage their vineyards in the south of Cantone. Their wide-ranging selection of wines touches on all the styles, from early-drinking wines to more complex ones. Winemaker Alfred Demartin confers a sophisticated style on his wines, one endowed with structure and aromatic elegance. Platinum is their flagship, a mouthfilling yet long and lively wine. Riflessi d'Epoca is a modern-styled and decidedly spicy wine. It comes through even in a year as difficult as 2014. Bianco Rovere is one of the few Merlot whites that expresses pleasantness and elegance.

● Ticino Merlot Platinum '13	♟♟	8
○ Ticino Bianco Rovere '16	♟♟	5
● Ticino Merlot Riflessi d'Epoca '14	♟♟	6
● Ticino Rosso V. d'Antan '13	♟♟	6
● Ticino Rosso Dogaia '14	♟	6

Fawino Vini & Distillati

LOC. MENDRISIO
VIA BORROMINI, 20
6850 TICINO
TEL. +4912258664
www.fawino.ch

PRE-BOOKED VISITS
ANNUAL PRODUCTION 20,000 bottles
HECTARES UNDER VINE 3.00

Cantina Fawino is an inspiring and dynamic winery that sees two young winemakers, Simone Favini and Claudio Widmer, personally working and attending to their vineyards with great care and attention. Their philosophy is that their wines should exhibit character, and winemaking shouldn't overwhelm the natural character of the grapes and terroir. Their vineyards are cultivated on the slopes of Monte Generoso and Monte San Giorgio, ranges situated at the southernmost part of Canton Ticino. Minerality and freshness, as well as favorable positions, make for unique wines. When you uncork one of their bottles, you experience all their commitment, as well as the typicity and characteristics of Medrisiotto's wines. Their skill in interpreting 2014 has been rewarded. Musa is one of the best wines we tasted and offers up captivating fragrances. It's a linear, taut, mineral wine with great personality.

● Ticino Merlot Musa '14	♟♟♟ 5
● Ticino Merlot Cantastorie '16	♟ 4

Gialdi Vini

LOC. MENDRISIO
VIA VIGNOO, 3
6850 TICINO
TEL. +41916403030
www.gialchi.ch

CELLAR SALES
PRE-BOOKED VISITS
ANNUAL PRODUCTION 500,000 bottles
HECTARES UNDER VINE 60.00

Gialdi's roots go back to 1953, when the producer was primarily concerned with bottling and selling wines. It was only in 1985 that they decided to focus on making their own. It was a decision that brought them to the heights of regional excellence. As of 2001, the winemaker Alfred Demartin has been working with about 300 vine growers (primarily located in the valley of Sopraceneri) for a collaboration that has brought together productive skill and high quality wines. Their selection is rich and complete, comprising wines of various characters (some of which display quite a bit of personality) and categories (sparkling wines, whites, reds and sweet wines). Among the reds, the Merlot di Arzo stands out for its elegance and sophistication. Sassi Grossi made history for this winery: first produced in 1984, with every vintage it manages to confirm its virility and capacity to improve over the years. The Trentasei, the result of lengthy aging, and only produced during the best years, is a dense, potent wine.

● Ticino Merlot Arzo '13	♟♟ 5
● Ticino Merlot Sassi Grossi '13	♟♟ 6
● Ticino Merlot Trentasei '10	♟♟ 7
● Estro '13	♟ 5
● Ticino Merlot Giornico Oro '13	♟ 5

Cantina Kopp von der Crone Visini

LOC. BARBENGO
VIA NOGA, 2
6917 TICINO
TEL. +41916829616
www.cantinabarbengo.ch

CELLAR SALES
PRE-BOOKED VISITS
ANNUAL PRODUCTION 35,000 bottles
HECTARES UNDER VINE 7.00

Kopp von Crone Visini was founded in 2006 when Kopp von der Crone came together with Paolo Visini's winery in 1997. Anna Barbara von Der Crone and her husband, Ueli Kopp, came to Ticino in 1994 with the idea of making high quality wines. After the premature death of Ueli Kopp, the collaboration between Anna Barbara and Paolo Visini intensified, resulting in the unification of the wineries and the subsequent building of a new cellar in Barbengo. They offer quite a wide range of wines, with aromatically elegant whites and reds of great depth. For the moment, the 2015 Scala ranks among the best. It features perfect balance, spice and richness of flavor. The class and dynamism of the Balin also came through and are particularly evident after a few years of aging. The always excellent 2013 Irto, a blend of various Bordeauxs, continues to prove a rich, potent wine.

● Balin '15	♟♟ 6
● Scala '15	♟♟ 6
● Irto '13	♟♟ 6

Pelossi

LOC. LUGANO - PAZZALLO
VIA CARONA, 8
6912 TICINO
TEL. +41919945677
s.pelossi@gmail.com

CELLAR SALES
PRE-BOOKED VISITS
ANNUAL PRODUCTION 35,000 bottles
HECTARES UNDER VINE 6.00

Out tastings pointed up the high profile of Sacha Pelossi's wines, a result made possible by the ability to interpret the difficult 2014 vintage. After his studies in enology, Sacha (in the early 1990s) took over his family's winery with the purpose of developing its potential. It was scrupulous work that gradually earned him a place among the region's top producers. With the recent purchase of San Matteo (Cagiallo), the estate has come to comprise six hectares, with vineyards scattered throughout the hills and the valley surrounding Lugano. The 2014 Riserva del Ronco reflects the delicacy of the work carried out in the cellar, exhibiting nice concentration and perfectly integrated tannic finesse. Agra Riserva, Riva del Tasso and Lamone confirm the style, offering up highly pleasant sensations in the mouth. We very much appreciated the Bianco della Piana, a blend of Chardonnay, Sauvignon and Sémillon, that features subtle aromatic complexity and a particular freshness.

● Ticino Rosso Riserva del Ronco '14	♟♟ 6
○ Ticino Bianco della Piana '15	♟♟ 5
● Ticino Merlot Agra Ris. '14	♟♟ 6
● Ticino Merlot Lamone '14	♟♟ 6
● Ticino Rosso Riva del Tasso '14	♟♟ 6
○ Ticino Bianco V. dell'Aspide '16	♟ 4
● Ticino Merlot Sassarei '15	♟ 4

Tamborini Vini

LOC. LAMOLE
VIA SERTA, 18
6814 TICINO
TEL. +4191935747
www.tamborinivini.ch

CELLAR SALES
PRE-BOOKED VISITS
ANNUAL PRODUCTION 60,000 bottles
HECTARES UNDER VINE 30.00

Even if the winery has been operational in the field since 1944, it was only in the 1970s that they started working their own grapes (a decision for which Claudio Tamborini was the catalyst). Since then, the estate has seen continued growth, and today spans 30 hecares on the hills of Lugano, in Malcantone and Bellinzona. Their wide-ranging selection of wines includes various typologies, with the best expressions coming from their Merlot, a variety that, depending on its area of cultivation, is capable of giving rise to more concentrated and elegant wines. The Merlot Comano, made with grapes cultivated in the district of the same name, exhibits an unimposing structure of particular elegance and sophistication. San Zeno Costamagna, on the other hand, proves to be a wine of high maturation, with a dense and full-bodied structure (as evidenced by the 2015). The 2013 Vigna Vecchia, a dense and spicy wine, features a similar profile.

● Ticino Merlot Comano '15	♛♛ 7
● Ticino Merlot San Zeno Costamagna '15	♛♛ 7
○ Ticino Merlot Bianco Terre di Gudo '16	♛ 5
● Ticino Merlot San Zeno '15	♛ 7
● Ticino Merlot V. V. '13	♛ 4
○ Ticino Sauvignon Blanc '15	♛ 5

Tenuta Vitivinicola Trapletti

LOC. COLDRERIO
VIA P. F. MOLA, 34
6877 TICINO
TEL. +41916301150
www.avvt.ch

CELLAR SALES
ANNUAL PRODUCTION 140,000 bottles
HECTARES UNDER VINE 13.60

Enrico Trapletti is the son of the Mendrisiotto's wine tradition. He began making his own in the early 1990s and a few years later he established his skills in the field. He's an explosive figure, always ready with new ideas, and was one of the first to focus on concentrating grapes in the vineyards (a technique that he would abandon a decade later in favor of more balanced, elegant wines). He was also the first to focus on Nebbiolo in Ticino, a variety that's existed since the 19th century (before Merlot). Today, thanks to collaboration with other vine growers, the traditional selection has been expanded to include other districts in the region. Culdrée is a high-profile wine with nice balance, well-defined personality and a sleek structure. Trapletti Rosso is a wine of notable structure but that's made in a tradition way, without the use of wood barrels. The Terra Creda also proves to be a pleasant, well-structured wine.

● Ticino Merlot Culdrée '13	♛♛ 7
● Trapletti Rosso '13	♛♛ 5
● Ticino Merlot Terra Creda '15	♛ 5

F.lli Valsagiacomo

LOC. MENDRISIO
V.LE ALLE CANTINE, 6
6853 TICINO
TEL. +41916836053
www.valswine.ch

CELLAR SALES
PRE-BOOKED VISITS
ANNUAL PRODUCTION 200,000 bottles
HECTARES UNDER VINE 18.00

The winery got its start in 1831 and, starting in the early 1900s, it assumed an important role as a benchmark in Canton Ticino. They're now on their sixth generation of management, and have benefitted from the continuity (as well as their ties to the territory). Uberto Valsangiacomo continues to oversee their work in cellar, enthusiastically following in the footsteps of his father, Cesare. Using the most modern techniques, the winery produces high-quality wines that have been classics in the Swiss territory. Aging takes place in Mendrisio's traditional cellars, which enjoy the perfect conditions in terms of temperature and humidity, and promote favorable aging. The primary cultivar used is Merlot. The 2013 Rubro is a nice surprise. It's a complete wine in all respects, with a delicate, captivating bouquet, a trait that it shares with the Gran Segreto and Piccolo Ronco.

● Ticino Merlot Gran Segreto '13	▼▼ 5
● Ticino Merlot Piccolo Ronco '12	▼▼ 5
● Ticino Merlot Rubro '13	▼▼ 5
● Ticino Merlot Rubro di Rubro '11	▼ 8

Vinattieri Ticinesi

LOC. LIGORNETTO
VIA COMI, 4
6853 TICINO
TEL. +41916472332
www.zanini.ch

CELLAR SALES
PRE-BOOKED VISITS
ANNUAL PRODUCTION 500,000 bottles
HECTARES UNDER VINE 100.00

This winery, owned by the Zanini family, is among the region's top producers. There are two production lines: Vinattieri Ticinesi (founded in 1985) manages a hundred hectares of vineyards scattered throughout various districts in Mendrisiotto, and offers a range of wines that seek to stay true the territory (essentially various types of Merlots); the Castello Luigi appellation comprises two exclusive wines, a blend of Merlot, Cabernet Sauvignon and Franc (with a classic Bordeaux style) and a white made with Chardonnay. It's a selection that looks foremost to national and international markets. The 2013 Merlot Vinattieri has achieved excellence. It has a strong personality, thanks to its succulence, smooth tannins and length. An enthusiastic Tre Bicchieri. In the same style, though less complex, we find the Ligornetto, a wine that features elegance and freshness. The 2014 Roncaia is also pleasant.

● Ticino Merlot Vinattieri '13	▼▼▼ 8
● Ticino Merlot Ligornetto '13	▼▼ 6
● Ticino Merlot Roncaia Ris. '14	▼ 5

Vini Angelo Delea

LOC. LOSONE
VIA ZANDONE
6616 TICINO
TEL. +41917910817
www.delea.ch

CELLAR SALES
ANNUAL PRODUCTION 550,000 bottles
HECTARES UNDER VINE 24.00

Theirs is a veritable story of passion, born out of love for their vocation and traditions (though without ignoring innovation either). It's a story that has its beginnings in 1983 with Angelo Deleo, who continues to manage the producer with the same passion and dedication (along with his sons, David and Cesare). Over the years, Angelo has managed to evolve, though while maintaining his wines' excellent quality. And he's done so with the goal of making every sip a unique, engaging experience. Among their wide selection of wines, the 2015 Carato Riserva stands out. It's a truly noteworthy wine that features lovely fruit on the nose with spicy notes and hints of coffee. In the mouth it gives over its best, proving pervasive, with elegant tannins. The white Merlot, Carato, is very pleasant and delicate. Everything is made 'more precious' by the 2013 Diamante, a rich and well-balanced blend made mostly with Merlot. Its higher cost may make it difficult for some wallets. The Sauvignon also definitely deserves a try.

○ Ticino Carato Bianco '15	▼▼ 4
● Ticino Diamante '13	▼▼ 8
○ Ticino Il Sauvignon '16	▼▼ 3
● Ticino Merlot Carato Ris. '15	▼▼ 6
○ Ticino Apocalisse '16	▼ 3
● Ticino Gudo '16	▼ 3
● Ticino Merlot Carato '15	▼ 5
● Ticino Merlot Chiar di Luna '16	▼ 3
● Ticino Merlot Saleggi '15	▼ 3
● Ticino San Carlo '15	▼ 4

Vini Rovio Ronco Gianfranco Chiesa

LOC. ROVIO
VIA IN BASSO, 21
6921 TICINO
TEL. +41916495831
www.vinirovio.ch

CELLAR SALES
PRE-BOOKED VISITS
ANNUAL PRODUCTION 35,000 bottles
HECTARES UNDER VINE 6.00

Upon arriving in Rovio, in Gianfranco Chiesa's modern cellar, you can't help but be surprised by the beauty of the landscape here, the magnificent panorama of Lugano Lake and the mountains of Monte San Giorgio (a UNESCO world patrimony) that line it. It's here that Gianfranco Chiesa gets inspiration for his wines, which are produced simply, with extreme care taken for the grapes (the aspect he's most concerned with). You can get a glimpse of it while walking among his vineyards of Merlot and Chardonnay, as well as Gamaret and Syrah, in Rovio, Pugerna and Ligornetto. The excellent 2013 San Vigilio is a blend of Gamaret and Syrah (75%/25%). It's bold, extremely soft and caressing, with fruity notes and hints of sweet spices. The mouth is potent yet elegant. The Merlot Riserva is very well-orchestrated. In the mouth, the cultivar offers up the best of what it has to offer.

● San Vigilio 75.25 '13	▼▼ 5
● Ticino Merlot Rovio Ris. '15	▼▼ 5
● Ticino San Giorgio '15	▼ 5

Bianchi

LOC. AROGNO
S.DA DA RÖV, 24
6822 TICINO
TEL. +4176 2732050
www.bianchi.bio

CELLAR SALES
PRE-BOOKED VISITS
ANNUAL PRODUCTION 12,000 bottles
HECTARES UNDER VINE 6.00

● Ticino Merlot Piaz Bio '15	♟♟ 5
○ Bio Alma '16	♟ 5

Cantina CAGI

LOC. GIUBIASCO
VIA LINOLEUM, 12
6512 TICINO
TEL. +41918572531
www.cagivini.ch

PRE-BOOKED VISITS
ANNUAL PRODUCTION 600,000 bottles
HECTARES UNDER VINE
SUSTAINABLE WINERY

● Ticino Merlot Montecarasso '13	♟♟ 6
● Ticino Bondola Tera Negra '16	♟ 3
○ Ticino Chardonnay V. Noverasca '15	♟ 4
○ Ticino Merlot Bianco del Centenario '16	♟ 3

Il Cavaliere

LOC. CONTONE - GAMBAROGNO
VIA CANTONALE, 41
6594 TICINO
TEL. +41918583267
www.ilcavaliere.ch

CELLAR SALES
PRE-BOOKED VISITS
ANNUAL PRODUCTION 100,000 bottles
HECTARES UNDER VINE 10.00

● Ticino Cuvée Prestige '11	♟♟ 7
● Ticino Merlot Barrique Ris. '13	♟ 6

Chiericati

LOC. BELLINZONA
VIA CONVENTO, 10
6500 TICINO
TEL. +41916251307
www.chiericati.ch

● Ticino Merlot Al Mercaa Ris. '12	♟ 5
○ Ticino Merlot Bianco Confessore '16	♟ 4
○ Ticino Merlot Bianco Sinfonia '16	♟ 5
● Ticino Merlot Enoteca Convento '13	♟ 4

Cormano Vini

LOC. MORBIO INFERIORE
VIA MAESTRI COMACINI, 51
6834 TICINO
TEL. +4191 6828940
www.cormanovini.ch

PRE-BOOKED VISITS
ANNUAL PRODUCTION 30,000 bottles
HECTARES UNDER VINE 6.00

● Ticino Merlot Cormano '15	♟♟ 7
● Ticino Merlot Caronte '15	♟ 8
● Ticino Merlot Carrara '15	♟ 5

F.lli Corti

LOC. BALERNA
VIA SOTTOBISIO, 13A
6828 TICINO
TEL. +41916833702
www.fratellicorti.ch

CELLAR SALES
PRE-BOOKED VISITS
ANNUAL PRODUCTION 60,000 bottles
HECTARES UNDER VINE 2.00

○ Ticino Chardonnay Sileno '15	♟♟ 7
● Ticino Merlot Lenéo '14	♟♟ 8
○ Ticino Stria Bianca '16	♟♟ 5
● Ticino Merlot Tre Corti '16	♟ 5

Roberto e Andrea Ferrari

LOC. CAPOLAGO
VIA MUNICIPIO, 6
6825 TICINO
TEL. +41765662255
www.viniferrari.ch

ANNUAL PRODUCTION 50,000 bottles
HECTARES UNDER VINE 9.00

● Ticino Castanar Ris. '10	♟♟	7
● Ticino Syrah Loto '12	♟♟	5
○ Ticino Chardonnay Ibisco '16	♟	4
● Ticino Merlot Bella Cima '13	♟	5

I Fracc

LOC. MONTE CARASSO
I FRACC, 26A
6513 TICINO
TEL. +4179 7723735
www.ifracc.ch

ANNUAL PRODUCTION 30,000 bottles
HECTARES UNDER VINE 2.50

● Ido '15	♟♟	5
● Duetto '15	♟	3

Cantine Ghidossi

LOC. PONTE TRESA-CROGLIO
VIA RONCO REGINA, 2
6988 TICINO
TEL. +4179 6193133
www.cantine-ghidossi.ch

ANNUAL PRODUCTION 10,000 bottles
HECTARES UNDER VINE 5.00

● Ticino Merlot Saetta '13	♟♟	7
○ Ticino Bianco Dialogo '15	♟	6
○ Ticino Bianco Terra del Sole '16	♟	4
● Ticino Merlot Terra del Sole '15	♟	4

Hubervini

LOC. MONTEGGIO
6998 TICINO
TEL. +4191 6081754
www.hubervini.ch

● Ticino Merlot Montagna Magica '15	♟♟	7
● Ticino Merlot Ronco di Persico '15	♟♟	5
● Ticino Rosso Costera Ris. '13	♟♟	5
○ Ticino Bianco Volpe Alata '16	♟	5

Famiglia Klausener

LOC. PURASCA
PURASCA INFERIORE, 24
6989 TICINO
TEL. +4191 6063522
www.klausener.blogspot.com

ANNUAL PRODUCTION 8,000 bottles
HECTARES UNDER VINE 2.00

● Belcantonissimo '14	♟	5
● Rosso di Sera '14	♟	6

Luigina

LOC. STABIO
VIA BRUCIATA, 2
8655 TICINO
TEL. +41916821543
www.tenutaluigina.ch

○ Centoquindici '16	♟♟	8
○ Millepetali '16	♟	7
● Ronco dei Profeti '15	♟	7
● Ticino Gemma dell' Est '13	♟	8

F.lli Matasci

LOC. TENERO
VIA VERBANO
6598 TICINO
TEL. +41917356011
www.matasci.com

CELLAR SALES
PRE-BOOKED VISITS
ANNUAL PRODUCTION 80,000 bottles
HECTARES UNDER VINE
SUSTAINABLE WINERY

● Ticino Merlot Sirio '15	♟♟	6
○ Ticino Bianco Cherubino '16	♟	4
● Ticino Merlot Gaggiole '15	♟	8
● Ticino Merlot Loco Coste '15	♟	5

Moncucchetto

LOC. LUGANO
VIA MARIETTA CRIVELLI TORRICELLI, 27
6900 TICINO
TEL. +41919677060
www.moncucchetto.ch

○ Il Murchì '16	♟	4
○ Ticino Bianco dell'Arco '15	♟	4
● Ticino Collina d'Oro Agra '15	♟	5
● Ticino Moncucchetto '15	♟	5

Mondò

LOC. SEMENTINA
VIA AL MONDÒ
6514 TICINO
TEL. +41918574558
www.aziendamondo.ch

ANNUAL PRODUCTION 40,000 bottles
HECTARES UNDER VINE 6.30

● Ticino Mondò '13	♟♟	7
● Ticino Ronco dei Ciliegi '13	♟♟	6
● Ticino Scintilla '14	♟	4

Tenuta Pian Marnino

LOC. GUDO
AL GAGGIOLETTO, 2
6515 TICINO
TEL. +41918590960
pianmarnino@bluewin.ch

PRE-BOOKED VISITS
ANNUAL PRODUCTION 20,000 bottles
HECTARES UNDER VINE 5.00

● Ticino Oro di Gudo '13	♟♟	5
● Ticino Tre Ori di Gudo '11	♟♟	6
○ Ticino Bianco Barrique '15	♟	5

Cantina Pizzorin di Giancarlo Pestoni

LOC. SEMENTINA
VIA ALLA SERTA, 8A
6514 TICINO
TEL. +4191 8573786
www.pizzorin.ch

PRE-BOOKED VISITS
ANNUAL PRODUCTION 18,000 bottles
HECTARES UNDER VINE 2.70

● Ticino Merlot Pizzorin '13	♟♟	6
● Ticino Merlot Pizzorin '12	♟♟	6
● Ticino Merlot Arcada '13	♟	4

Tenuta Sasso Chierico

LOC. GUDO
VIA CANTONALE, 3
6515 TICINO
TEL. +41918592928
www.sassochierico.ch

● Ticino Sasso Chierico Ris. '13	♟♟	6
○ Ticino Bianco Sasso Chierico '16	♟	4
● Ticino Merlot Sasso Chierico '15	♟	4

TRENTINO

Our annual tasting finds Trentino in good
health. Some 12 wines received Tre Bicchieri,
a record for the region. Evidently, something is
afoot in a territory we once held up to scrutiny
for its unrealized potential and lack of forward
momentum. Sparkling winemaking proved particularly
productive, with TrentoDOC representing the region at the highest levels. These are
led by Giulio Ferrari's spectacular 2006 and the 2010 Graal Riserva, which is also
a perennial classic. Maso Martis, MezzaCorona, Letrari and Balter all confirm their
top-status, and Opera is back in the Tre Bicchieri club with their delectable 2011
Nature. Bossi Fedrigotti shows that he's got plenty of arrows in his quiver, and this
year he hit the bullseye with an excellent 2012 TrentoDoc Conte Federico Riserva.
The reds are led by yet another excellent performance from San Leonardo, with
their 2013 confirming its international caliber. The wine introduces us to the
Rotaliana plains, which, this year, gave rise to the excellent 2013 Teroldego Mini
and the 2015 De Vescovi Ulzbach, the crown jewels of a terroir that continues
to gain momentum (as our tastes, and re-tastes demonstrate). Here, wineries
like Barone De Cles, and others, are putting forward serious candidates for the
near future. We close with another great red, LaVis-Valle's 2013 Ritratto, a wine
that celebrates the region's cooperative winery sector, which is proving more
and more capable of putting forward high-profile wines. Most importantly, it
seems cooperatives and the small growers who constitute them are starting to
reintegrate. Rather than representing two opposing worlds, they are coming to
be viewed as flip sides of the same coin. Special honors go to the Lunelli family's
Ferrari for their work towards 'Sustainable Viticulture', recognizing their years of
commitment to these principles. We close by reminding our readers that space
limitations prevent us from acknowledging many of those small producers who
truly deserve attention.

★Abate Nero

Fraz. Gardolo
s.da Trentina, 45
38121 Trento
Tel. +39 0461246566
www.abatenero.it

CELLAR SALES
PRE-BOOKED VISITS
ANNUAL PRODUCTION 65,000 bottles
HECTARES UNDER VINE 65.00

Consistence in quality sets apart this historic producer (one of the first founded along the banks of the Adige and Avisio). It's a reputation that Luciano Lunelli has fought for, bolstered by his more than 40 years of experience. While he got his start by making Teroldego (when he was director of Rotaliana), he's also always been a great enthusiast of sparkle. In fact, he's making a series of sparkling wines that are decidedly first-rate. Marked by a rich, flavorful flow, these are wines of character that withstand the test of time, evolving and confirming that consistent quality that defines this small (but important) winery. The Domini dominate, with the Nero once again among the most prized Trentos crafted here on the banks of the Avisio. It captivates for its forthright, clean aromas, with a palate that marvels, and that's as elegant as it is well-structured. Overall, its contours are soft, though it maintains that trademark acidity that comes from being made with 100% Pinot Nero. Their other Trentos are just as good.

○ Trento Brut Domini '11	♟♟	5
○ Trento Brut Domini Nero '11	♟♟	5
○ Trento Extra Brut	♟♟	4
○ Trento Brut	♟	4
⊙ Trento Domini Rosé	♟	5
○ Trento Brut Cuvée dell'Abate Ris. '04	♟♟♟	6
○ Trento Brut Cuvée dell'Abate Ris. '03	♟♟♟	5
○ Trento Brut Domini '10	♟♟♟	5
○ Trento Brut Domini '07	♟♟♟	5
○ Trento Brut Domini '05	♟♟♟	5
○ Trento Brut Domini Nero '10	♟♟♟	5
○ Trento Brut Domini Nero '08	♟♟♟	5
○ Trento Domìni Nero '09	♟♟♟	5

Nicola Balter

via Vallunga II, 24
38068 Rovereto [TN]
Tel. +39 0464430101
www.balter.it

CELLAR SALES
PRE-BOOKED VISITS
ANNUAL PRODUCTION 80,000 bottles
HECTARES UNDER VINE 10.00

For the Balter family, cultivating the vineyards means cultivating the beauty of the landscape, and keeping alive its traditions. They can boast the honor of having transformed Rovereto's sunniest hill into a viticultural enclave of rare charm. And beneath the hill, there's plenty of room for their winemaking facilities, along with a rural fort that's been transformed into a simple wine shop (situated right at the entrance into their vineyards). Nicola Balter and his two children, Clementina and Giacomo, personally oversee each stage of production, especially when it comes to their Trento, though their stills aren't neglected either, particularly their reds. Once again, the Riserva proves energetic and extremely sophisticated in its perlage, with an overall creaminess that delivers, and fragrances of apple and plum. A well-structured and very long wine, it proves to be as spirited as it is gentle. Their other two Trentos, a Brut and a Rosé, exhibit similarly blessed sparkle.

○ Trento Pas Dosé Balter Ris. '11	♟♟♟	5
○ Trento Brut	♟♟	4
⊙ Trento Brut Rosé	♟♟	5
● Vallagarina Cabernet Sauvignon '14	♟♟	3
● Lagrein Merlot '16	♟	2
○ Vallagarina Traminer Aromatico '16	♟	2

Barone de Cles

VIA G. MAZZINI, 18
38017 MEZZOLOMBARDO [TN]
TEL. +39 0461601081
www.baronedecles.it

CELLAR SALES
PRE-BOOKED VISITS
ANNUAL PRODUCTION 80,000 bottles
HECTARES UNDER VINE 39.00

Giorgio de Cles, vine grower. That's how this young heir to a dynasty calls himself. It's a dynasty that has, since the 1600s, featured cardinals, bishops, history scholars and wine cultivators. Maso Scari was among the first of these, having grown Teroldego in the early 18th century. It's a commitment that Giorgio, a graduate in agriculture driven by a desire to reestablish the fame of his family's wines, has kept alive since the early 1980s. Teroldego and Lagrein are cultivated in the valley vineyards that surround their cellar, in an area considered extremely well-suited to the varieties. But whites are grown as well (Pinot Bianco foremost), along the banks of Cles Lake, right on the slope leading up to the family's castle (and one of the Alp's most beautiful estates). This viticultural dynasty's most recent Teroldegos are decidedly captivating. The 2013 Cadinale is at the top of its game, proving rich, with a palate that's worthy of the family's blazon.

● Teroldego Rotaliano Sup. Cardinale '13	♟♟	5
● Teroldego Rotaliano '14	♟♟	3
● Trentino Lagrein '14	♟♟	3
○ Bianco de Cles '16	♟	3
○ Trentino Traminer '16	♟	3
● Teroldego Rotaliano Cardinale '12	♙♙	5
● Teroldego Rotaliano Cardinale '10	♙♙	5
● Teroldego Rotaliano Maso Scari '13	♙♙	3
● Teroldego Rotaliano Maso Scari '12	♙♙	3
● Teroldego Rotaliano Sup. Riserva del Cardinale '11	♙♙	5

Bellaveder

LOC. MASO BELVEDERE
38010 FAEDO [TN]
TEL. +39 0461650171
www.bellaveder.it

CELLAR SALES
PRE-BOOKED VISITS
ANNUAL PRODUCTION 70,000 bottles
HECTARES UNDER VINE 12.00
SUSTAINABLE WINERY

Tranquillo Lucchetta has the gift of ubiquity, inasmuch as he manages two neighboring areas at once. He's the wise patron of this entirely organic estate (both the eight hectares in Faedo, a stone's throw from their charming, underground cellar, and the handful of hectares cultivated in Cavedine, in the Valle dei Laghi, on the hills leading to Garda). Trento is their flagship wine, with a series of blends still to come, while a promising Roè Nature is ready for its debut. Meticulous attention is paid to certain field blends, fermented in wood, and experimentations with late harvests. This time it's the best among the Trento Nature selection to truly shine. Skillful winemaking make for a perfect synthesis of spontaneity, luxurious fizziness, overall savoriness, and exquisite suppleness.

○ Trento Brut Nature Ris. '12	♟♟	5
● Trentino Lagrein Mansum '13	♟♟	4
○ Trentino Müller Thurgau San Lorenz '16	♟♟	3
● Trentino Pinot Nero '15	♟♟	5
○ Trentino Sauvignon '16	♟♟	2*
○ Trentino Traminer '16	♟♟	3
● Trentino Lagrein Dunkel Mansum Ris. '10	♙♙	4
● Trentino Lagrein Mansum '12	♙♙	4
● Trentino Lagrein Mansum '11	♙♙	4
○ Trentino Müller Thurgau San Lorenz '13	♙♙	2*
○ Trento Brut Nature Ris. '11	♙♙	5
○ Trento Brut Nature Ris. '10	♙♙	5

Borgo dei Posseri

LOC. POZZO BASSO, 1
38061 ALA [TN]
TEL. +39 0464671899
www.borgodeiposseri.com

CELLAR SALES
PRE-BOOKED VISITS
ANNUAL PRODUCTION 60,000 bottles
HECTARES UNDER VINE 21.00
VITICULTURE METHOD Certified Organic
SUSTAINABLE WINERY

The winery is nestled among the Vallagarina range known as 'the little Dolomites' with vineyards situated between woodlands and walls of rock. But Borgo dei Posseri's estate extends well beyond its vineyards, comprising more than 200 hectares of woodlands, with rural farmsteads and residences scattered throughout. It's a pure, picturesque landscape that the owners protect with great care, offering 'sensorial' walks through the vineyards, with stops for tasting the areas' wines. They are focusing on those varieties that are best-suited to the Alps, without ignoring Trento. They deliver immediately with a white made of aromatic grapes, their Müller Thurgau Malusel, a wine that's as rich in aromas as it is precise in its backbone of flavor. Just a bit over-ripe, it's a wine bursting with potential. The Pinot Nero affirms its status as a strong entry, thanks to a lean harmony. The style of winemaking here is absolutely characteristic of the mountains: there's more fragrance than richness of flavor, and an almost austere balance and behavior.

○ Cuvée Malusel '14	🍷🍷	3
○ Müller Thurgau Quaron '16	🍷🍷	3
● Pinot Nero Paradis '15	🍷🍷	3
○ Sauvignon Furiel '16	🍷🍷	3
○ Trento Brut Tananai '13	🍷🍷	5
● Merlot Rocol '15	🍷	3
● Merlot Rocol '14	🍷🍷	3
● Merlot Rocol '13	🍷🍷	3
○ Müller Thurgau Quaron '15	🍷🍷	3
○ Müller Thurgau Quaron '14	🍷🍷	3
○ Müller Thurgau Quaron '13	🍷🍷	3
● Pinot Nero Paradis '13	🍷🍷	3
○ Traminer Arliz '15	🍷🍷	3
○ Trento Brut Tananai '12	🍷🍷	5
○ Trento Brut Tananai '11	🍷🍷	5

Bossi Fedrigotti

VIA UNIONE, 43
38068 ROVERETO [TN]
TEL. +39 0456832511
www.masi.it

CELLAR SALES
PRE-BOOKED VISITS
ANNUAL PRODUCTION 120,000 bottles
HECTARES UNDER VINE 40.00
SUSTAINABLE WINERY

The Bossi Fedrigotti dynasty has had a presence in Vallagrina as far as back as the 1500s, and has been active in vine cultivation since 1697. The family can boast having assembled one of Italy's first Bordeauxs, the 1961 Fojaneghe, a kind of monument to the country's great wine tradition. For some years now, Bossi Fedrigotti has been accompanied by Masi Agricola in management. The dynamic business from Tre Venezie revived the Fojaneghe blazon and brought in a Trento to further enrich the winery's selection. And our tasting just happened to open with a classic sparkling wine dedicated to the man who led the winery's revival. It handily earned a Tre Bicchieri, offering up a lovely aromatic complexity recalling dried fruit and baked cookie spices. In the mouth, its body proved creamy, with a somewhat citrusy acidity, that draws back in the finish, leaving room for a pleasant length.

○ Trento Brut Conte Federico Ris. '12	🍷🍷🍷	5
● Fojaneghe Rosso '13	🍷🍷	5
○ Vign'Asmara '15	🍷🍷	4
● Fojaneghe Rosso '12	🍷🍷🍷	5
● Fojaneghe Rosso '11	🍷🍷	5
● Fojaneghe Rosso '10	🍷🍷	5
● Mas'est '13	🍷🍷	3
● Mas'est '12	🍷🍷	3
○ Trento Brut Conte Federico '11	🍷🍷	5
○ Vign'Asmara '14	🍷🍷	4
○ Vign'Asmara '13	🍷🍷	4

Cavit

DEL PONTE, 31
6040 TRENTO
L. +39 0461381711
ww.cavit.it

CELLAR SALES
PRE-BOOKED VISITS
ANNUAL PRODUCTION 70,000,000 bottles
HECTARES UNDER VINE 5500.00

wo new treats from Cavit, a Pinot Nero
nd Grigio, both made from carefully
elected grapes, and thanks to a
ommitment to agronomic and enological
xcellence. They show how a giant with
000 member-growers can respect terroir
nd diversity, as well as produce wines
apable of taking on the global market.
avit is a brand used to big numbers: 11
cooperative partners, with entrepreneurial
itiatives that involve zones of viticulture
ar from Trento (in Oltrepò, with Cantina La
ersa, even Germany, with the sparkling
ine producer, Kessler). In all cases,
egional gems are well-supported, starting
ith Trento. Of the 20 wines presented by
avit, both stills and sparklers, they all
roved to be of excellent quality. The Graal
ets a gold, once again. This Trento still has
omething to teach us: concentration and
nesse, with fragrances that slide
racefully through mature overtones, all of
vhich resolve in the austerity of its soft,
ervasive mouth.

Cesarini Sforza

FRAZ. RAVINA
VIA STELLA, 9
38123 TRENTO
TEL. +39 0461382200
www.cesarinisforza.com

CELLAR SALES
PRE-BOOKED VISITS
ANNUAL PRODUCTION 1,300,000 bottles
HECTARES UNDER VINE 800.00

Cesarini Sforza is one of Trento's historic
sparkling wine brands. Founded in 1974,
for some years it has served as the
sparkling wine branch of La Vis, the
cooperative winery from which it purchases
its grapes. Special field blends are made
exclusively with grapes cultivated at higher
altitudes, from areas like Valle di Cembra,
but also from upland vineyards like
Valsugana, and even mountains, like those
that separate Vallagarina from Lake Garda.
They offer a vast range of sparklers, and
not only 'Metodo Classico' versions. In
honor of the noble figures that, in their
time, gave rise to the family lineage, the
winery presented a decidedly interesting
Trento. It's called 1673 (the year in which
the Cesarini and Sforza families wed). It
exhibits rich aromas, hints of honey and
mace spice, with a harmony of great
sensorial depth. The rest of the selection
delivered as well. They've kept its range
limited on purpose, so as to heighten the
sparkling winemaker's prestige.

Trento Brut Altemasi Graal Ris. '10	▼▼▼6
Teroldego Rotaliano Sup. Maso Cervara '14	▼▼4
Trentino Sup. Pinot Nero Brusafer '14	▼▼5
Trentino Rosso Quattro Vicariati '13	▼▼4
Trentino Sup. Müller Thurgau Zeveri '16	▼▼3
Trento Altemasi Pas Dosé '10	▼▼5
Trento Altemasi Graal Brut '01	▼▼▼5
Trento Altemasi Graal Brut Ris. '03	▼▼▼6
Trento Altemasi Graal Brut Ris. '02	▼▼▼6
Trento Altemasi Graal Brut Ris. '00	▼▼▼5
Trento Brut Altemasi Graal Ris. '09	▼▼▼6
Trento Brut Altemasi Graal Ris. '08	▼▼▼6

○ Trento Brut	▼▼4
⊙ Trento Brut Rosé Ris. '11	▼▼4
⊙ Trento Extra Brut 1673 Ris. '10	▼▼5
⊙ Trento Brut Rosé	▼4
⊙ Trento Aquila Reale Ris. '05	▼▼▼7
⊙ Trento Aquila Reale Ris. '02	▼▼▼7
⊙ Trento Extra Brut Tridentum '09	▼▼▼4*
⊙ Trento Aquila Reale Ris. '08	▼▼6
○ Trento Brut Tridentum '12	▼▼4
○ Trento Brut Tridentum '11	▼▼4
⊙ Trento Dosaggio Zero Tridentum '12	▼▼5
⊙ Trento Extra Brut Tridentum Ris. '08	▼▼5
⊙ Trento Tridentum Rosé '10	▼▼4

Corvée

LOC. BEDIN, 1
38034 LISIGNAGO [TN]
TEL. +39 3440260170
www.corvee.wine

CELLAR SALES
PRE-BOOKED VISITS
ANNUAL PRODUCTION 50,000 bottles
HECTARES UNDER VINE 13.60

The name evokes a vassal's duty to his feudal lord, but also the dedication shown by vine growers who believe in their efforts and what they're capable of accomplishing. The joy of cultivating grapes for the purpose of making great wine spurred a group of Cembra's vine growers to join together, to do just that, a corvée. Only a few thousand bottles are produced. These are made from hand-picked grapes, cultivated on the steep porphyritic benchlands, as incredible as they are beautiful, that stretch across the valley that rises along the right bank of the Avisio (an area that neighbors the Corvaia trail, which Albrecht Duerer made note of as early as the 1500s). For now, only white wines are made, but they all exhibit notable personality. And if the Müller Thurgau, in its two version, is a symbol of the local winemaking community, the Pinot Bianco is surely already demonstrating a certain class. Rich in mountain aromas, the wine proves zesty in its crystalline elegance, both in taste and color. You can tell, even just from the label, that these are folks who know what it means to make good wines.

○ Trentino Pinot Bianco Cor '16	♀♀	4
○ Trentino Chardonnay Rorè '16	♀♀	4
○ Trentino Müller Thurgau Portegnàc '16	♀♀	4
○ Trentino Müller Thurgau Viach '16	♀♀	4
○ Trentino Pinot Grigio Corvaia '16	♀♀	4

De Vescovi Ulzbach

P.ZZA GARIBALDI, 12
38016 MEZZOCORONA [TN]
TEL. +39 0461605648
www.devescoviulzbach.it

CELLAR SALES
PRE-BOOKED VISITS
ANNUAL PRODUCTION 20,000 bottles
HECTARES UNDER VINE 3.50

In De Vescovi Ulzbach we find a family wh represent authentic Rotaliano wine. It's a term composed of the prefix 'ro' (flat terrain), followed by the pre-Roman 'tal', which, during the Celtic period, referred to the area where duties on wine sales were paid in the Adige valley (the roads leading north and the Non Valley). As far back as 1147, evidence of the wine trade has beer found. Back then, every land owner boasted having the best terrain, and distinguished one another by their geographic names. Giulio de Vescovi is reviving the wine's peculiarities, making exquisite interpretations of Rotaliano in the family's historic, though modernized, cellar The leanest of their Teroldegos delivers, with a formidable character and vitality tha guarantees ageability, and proves that its one-of-a-kind. The Vigilius is still clenched in its opulent complexity.

● Teroldego Rotaliano '15	♀♀♀	3
○ Empeiria '16	♀♀	5
● Kino Nero '15	♀♀	4
○ Sauvignon '16	♀♀	4
● Teroldego Rotaliano Vigilius '15	♀♀	5
⊙ Teroldego Rotaliano Kretzer '16	♀	3
● Teroldego Rotaliano Vigilius '12	♀♀♀	5
○ Empeiria '15	♀♀	4
○ Sauvignon '15	♀♀	4
● Teroldego Rotaliano '14	♀♀	3
● Teroldego Rotaliano '13	♀♀	3
● Teroldego Rotaliano '12	♀♀	3
● Teroldego Rotaliano '11	♀♀	3
● Teroldego Rotaliano Vigilius '13	♀♀	5
● Teroldego Rotaliano Vigilius '11	♀♀	5

★Dorigati

VIA DANTE, 5
38016 MEZZOCORONA [TN]
TEL. +39 0461605313
www.dorigati.it

CELLAR SALES
PRE-BOOKED VISITS
ANNUAL PRODUCTION 100,000 bottles
HECTARES UNDER VINE 10.00
SUSTAINABLE WINERY

The Dorigati are reviving their past, betting on innovation and new initiatives on behalf of quality. They're doing it by proposing a well-thought-out selection of Teroldego, the core business to which the winery owes its reputation and acclaim. For years, their Methius, a Trento, has found a top spot among Italy's best sparkling wines. This year, however, it's skipping a vintage, for the sake of proper aging. However, a Teroldego called Luigi was presented dedicated to the man who, in 1858, founded this splendid Campo Rotaliano winery). As far as the rest of the selection is concerned, the two young cousins (and enology graduates), Michele and Paolo, are overseeing things, seeking to follow in the Dorigati family's heroic footsteps. The whole selection displays skill and insight. Luigi is a bold wine in its elemental grip. The Grener, made with Cabernet and only during the best vintages, is just as brash. The Lagrein performs in a way that's quintessentially Rotaliano.

● Teroldego Rotaliano Luigi Ris. '12	♥♥	6
● Teroldego Rotaliano '15	♥♥	3
● Trentino Cabernet Grener Ris. '12	♥♥	5
○ Trentino Chardonnay Majerla Ris. '15	♥♥	3
● Trentino Lagrein '15	♥♥	3
○ Trentino Lagrein Kretzer '16	♥	3
○ Trento Brut Methius Ris. '09	♥♥♥	6
○ Trento Brut Methius Ris. '08	♥♥♥	6
○ Trento Brut Methius Ris. '06	♥♥♥	6
○ Trento Brut Methius Ris. '05	♥♥♥	6
○ Trento Brut Methius Ris. '04	♥♥♥	6
○ Trento Brut Methius Ris. '03	♥♥♥	6
○ Trento Brut Methius Ris. '02	♥♥♥	6
○ Trento Brut Methius Ris. '00	♥♥♥	6
○ Trento Brut Methius Ris. '98	♥♥♥	6

Endrizzi

LOC. MASETTO, 2
38010 SAN MICHELE ALL'ADIGE [TN]
TEL. +39 0461650129
www.endrizzi.it

CELLAR SALES
PRE-BOOKED VISITS
ANNUAL PRODUCTION 600,000 bottles
HECTARES UNDER VINE 55.00
SUSTAINABLE WINERY

Ethic and aesthetic are two concepts that Christine and Paolo Endrici's family are constantly applying. Indeed, they are behind every initiative undertaken by this historic producer, whose vineyards rise up from the valley floor towards Faedo and the hills that overlook Campo Rotaliano, between the Adige and Noce rivers. The utmost care is shown in vineyard management, while a biodynamic approach is taken to cultivation. In terms of aesthetics, a curious exhibition of artworks lines the trails that lead to the cellar. Their selection of wines is vast, the result of painstaking care, especially their Trento, which put in a superb performance. The Gran Masetto is a Teroldego made with slightly dried grapes. Its legacy of fragrances delivers, and masterly vinification makes for a well-orchestrated structure. The Trento Pian Castello is another wine whose personality stands out. Dynamic in its perlage, it offers an exemplary expression of this typology, with enchanting, fruity notes recalling apricot and ripening peach.

● Gran Masetto '12	♥♥	8
○ Trento Brut Pian Castello Ris. '12	♥♥	4
○ Masetto Bianco '15	♥♥	3
○ Masetto Dorè '15	♥♥	5
● Masetto Nero '14	♥♥	4
● Masetto Due '15	♥	6
● Masetto Due '14	♀♀	5
● Masetto Nero '13	♀♀	3
● Teroldego Rotaliano '13	♀♀	2*
● Teroldego Rotaliano Sup. '13	♀♀	3
● Teroldego Rotaliano Tradizione '14	♀♀	2*
○ Trentino Traminer Aromatico '15	♀♀	2*
○ Trento Brut Pian di Castello '11	♀♀	4
○ Trento Brut Rosé Pian di Castello '09	♀♀	4

★★Ferrari

VIA PONTE DI RAVINA, 15
38123 TRENTO
TEL. +39 0461972311
www.ferraritrento.it

CELLAR SALES
PRE-BOOKED VISITS
RESTAURANT SERVICE
ANNUAL PRODUCTION 4,450,000 bottles
HECTARES UNDER VINE 120.00
SUSTAINABLE WINERY

Ferrari is one of the most respected businesses in high-end fashion and entertainment, as well as one of its most unmistakable brands. They also represent a dynasty of wine entrepreneurs, whose approach to agriculture is predominantly organic, and who are also involved in the production of Prosecco. This year, we're recognizing their commitment with a 'Sustainable Viticulture' award. They offer a series of wines (not just sparkling) that, once again, hold a place among Italy's best. The outstanding quality of their selection is indisputable. Almost all of their products are major achievements. The Giulio Ferrari has always been one and, once again, the wine leads the club of Trentos that received Tre Bicchieri. This emblem of impeccable winemaking is a symbol of mountain Chardonnay, and is unmatched in many respects. A 10-year-old wine, it's characterized by an unmistakable gold-yellow color, notes that alternate between tropical fruit and the most savory walnutskin. It's a noble wine whose finish will move you to tears.

○ Trento Brut Giulio Ferrari Riserva del Fondatore '06	❦❦❦ 8
○ Trento Brut Perlé '11	❦❦ 6
○ Trento Brut Perlé Bianco Ris. '07	❦❦ 6
○ Trento Extra Brut Lunelli Ris. '09	❦❦ 7
○ Trentino Chardonnay Villa Margon '15	❦❦ 4
⊙ Trento Brut Perlé Rosé Ris. '11	❦❦ 7
○ Trento Brut Giulio Ferrari Riserva del Fondatore '05	♛♛♛ 8
○ Trento Brut Giulio Ferrari Riserva del Fondatore '04	♛♛♛ 8
○ Trento Brut Giulio Ferrari Riserva del Fondatore '01	♛♛♛ 8
○ Trento Brut Giulio Ferrari Riserva del Fondatore '00	♛♛♛ 8
○ Trento Extra Brut Lunelli Ris. '07	♛♛♛ 7
○ Trento Extra Brut Perlé Nero '07	♛♛♛ 8

Fondazione Mach

VIA EDMONDO MACH, 1
38010 SAN MICHELE ALL'ADIGE [TN]
TEL. +39 0461615252
www.ismaa.it

CELLAR SALES
PRE-BOOKED VISITS
ANNUAL PRODUCTION 250,000 bottles
HECTARES UNDER VINE 60.00
VITICULTURE METHOD Certified Organic

It's a bastion of history and wine culture, a centuries-old school, a European wine-growing research center and now a university campus dedicated exclusively to grapes and wine. In the old monastery turned wine cellar, thousands of enologists have learnt how to make wines, and not just Trentino, with teaching and production continuing to work in full synergy. Their wines are extremely well-crafted, worthy of the winery's blazon. It continues to invest in research and innovation, without neglecting its commitment to its selection, notably its field blends and a classic Trento. And it was the sparkling wine dedicated to Mach, the school's founder, that made it to our finals. It features fragrances rich in flowery nuances, in some ways smoky, hints of chalk, and notes of candied fruit. In the mouth, the wine is creamy, full-bodied, with a profile that exhibits accents of ginger. Supple on the palate, it may be penalized by its being recently disgorged.

○ Trento Mach Riserva del Fondatore '12	❦❦ 5
● Cabernet Franc Monastero '15	❦❦ 3
○ Manzoni Bianco '16	❦❦ 4
○ Trentino Traminer Aromatico Monastero '16	❦❦ 3
○ Trento Mach Riserva del Fondatore '09	♛♛♛ 5
○ Trento Mach Riserva del Fondatore '07	♛♛♛ 5
○ Trento Mach Riserva del Fondatore '04	♛♛♛ 5
● Cabernet Franc Monastero '13	♛♛ 3
○ Manzoni Bianco Castel San Michele '15	♛♛ 4
● Trentino Cabernet Franc Monastero '13	♛♛ 3
● Trentino Marzemino '15	♛♛ 3
○ Trentino Nosiola '15	♛♛ 3
○ Trentino Riesling Monastero '15	♛♛ 5
○ Trento Mach Riserva del Fondatore '10	♛♛ 5

Grigoletti

VIA GARIBALDI, 12
38060 NOMI [TN]
TEL. +39 0464834215
www.grigoletti.com

CELLAR SALES
PRE-BOOKED VISITS
ANNUAL PRODUCTION 60,000 bottles
HECTARES UNDER VINE 6.00

Grigoletti and Nomi, a phonetic play of words ties this family of authentic vine growers to the territory of Vallagarina, a territory that has, for centuries, safeguarded the Dolomites' viticultural traditions. The grapes cultivated on their vineyards are then vinified in a kind of 'temple of wine', amidst Dionysian decorations and icons. Their focused selection features forthright, easy-drinking reds, with a couple of versions proving truly first-rate, thanks to painstaking work both in the vineyards and in their delightful cellar. And here we have a treat. It's a blend of Merlot and Cabernet (vinified separately, and of different vintages). Just a few thousand bottles are produced, but the wine puts on an excellent performance, proving it's gained some authority. As usual, the same could be said for their fragrant Marzemino and Gonzalier (another Bordeaux that's once again on the mark).

La Vis - Valle di Cembra

VIA CARMINE, 7
38015 LAVIS [TN]
TEL. +39 0461440111
www.la-vis.com

CELLAR SALES
PRE-BOOKED VISITS
ACCOMMODATION AND RESTAURANT SERVICE
ANNUAL PRODUCTION 1,000,000 bottles
HECTARES UNDER VINE 850.00
SUSTAINABLE WINERY

La-Vis returns to the national winemaking scene even more determined and competitive. With the management crisis behind them, thanks to the commitment of their myriad partners, the skills of their new administrators, and, especially, a series of outstanding wines, we can say that the producer has regained all its strength. Their selection is true to its mountain roots, and is offered at decidedly competitive prices, so as to penetrate wider markets. Though they haven't neglected their highest-end wines, those made with grapes grown in Valle di Cembra, and, especially, certain Trentos. Encomio al Ritratto, made with Teroldego, Lagrein and Merlot, has always been one of the cooperative's favorites. It's being offered in a new design, but the wine boasts the same power, vigorous color, succulent mouth and elegant finish. Among the some 15 wines tasted, the Sauvignon Vich proves to be a model for the typology, in synch with the Chardonnay Diaol and Müller Thurgau Vigna delle Forche.

Gonzalier '16	♥♥ 5
● Grigoletti Top	♥♥ 6
● Trentino Marzemino '16	♥♥ 2*
○ San Martin V. T.	♥ 4
○ Trentino Chardonnay L'Opera '16	♥ 3
● Gonzalier '15	♀♀ 5
● Gonzalier '12	♀♀ 5
● Gonzalier '11	♀♀ 5
○ Retiko '13	♀♀ 3
○ Trentino Chardonnay L'Opera '14	♀♀ 3
○ Trentino Chardonnay L'Opera '13	♀♀ 3
● Trentino Marzemino '15	♀♀ 2*
● Trentino Marzemino '13	♀♀ 2*
● Trentino Merlot Antica Vigna '13	♀♀ 4
● Trentino Merlot Antica Vigna '12	♀♀ 4

● Ritratto Rosso '13	♥♥♥ 4*
○ Trentino Sauvignon Vich '15	♥♥ 3*
● Trentino Cabernet Sauvignon Codros '13	♥♥ 4
○ Trentino Chardonnay Diaol '15	♥♥ 3
○ Trentino Müller Thurgau V. delle Forche '16	♥♥ 3
● Trentino Pinot Nero V. di Saosent '15	♥♥ 5
○ Trentino Müller Thurgau V. delle Forche '14	♀♀♀ 3*
○ Trentino Müller Thurgau V. delle Forche '13	♀♀♀ 3*
○ Trentino Müller Thurgau V. delle Forche '12	♀♀♀ 3*

Letrari

VIA MONTE BALDO, 13/15
38068 ROVERETO [TN]
TEL. +39 0464480200
www.letrari.it

CELLAR SALES
PRE-BOOKED VISITS
ANNUAL PRODUCTION 160,000 bottles
HECTARES UNDER VINE 23.00

Letrari is a 'pink' winery. That is, it's entirely managed by women. Lucia Letrari is constantly on the move, amidst her enological duties and presenting their products (especially Trento). Though her father, Nello (who's over 80 by now), still chips in, firmly advocating for innovation in the field of sparkling winemaking. Indeed, their selection is seeing increased diversification, and a capacity to interpret the tendencies of the younger generation through enticing, first-rate sparklers. The results are exciting, to say the least, especially the Rosé, dedicated to the winery's four women. It earns a Tre Bicchieri, the first for a Trento of its kind. Captivating in appearance, with its subtle pink color and copper highlights, the wine offers up an aromatic profile of candied citrus and cinnamon. Vigorating on the palate, it's also succulent and enchanting. The 976 (or Riserva del Fondatore) is right up there. Just a few thousand bottles are produced, but it's a truly excellent wine.

⊙ Trento Brut Rosé +4 '09	▼▼▼ 6
○ Trento Brut 976 Riserva del Fondatore '07	▼▼ 8
● Ballistarius '11	▼▼ 5
○ Trento Brut '13	▼▼ 5
○ Trento Cuvée Blanche	▼▼ 4
○ Trento Dosaggio Zero '14	▼▼ 5
○ Trento Brut 976 Riserva del Fondatore '05	♈♈♈ 8
○ Trento Brut Letrari Ris. '09	♈♈♈ 5
○ Trento Brut Letrari Ris. '08	♈♈♈ 5
○ Trento Brut Letrari Ris. '07	♈♈♈ 5
○ Trento Brut Letrari Ris. '05	♈♈♈ 5
○ Trento Brut Ris. '10	♈♈♈ 5
○ Trento Brut Ris. '06	♈♈♈ 5

Maso Martis

LOC. MARTIGNANO
VIA DELL'ALBERA, 52
38121 TRENTO
TEL. +39 0461821057
www.masomartis.it

CELLAR SALES
PRE-BOOKED VISITS
ANNUAL PRODUCTION 65,000 bottles
HECTARES UNDER VINE 12.00
VITICULTURE METHOD Certified Organic

The Stelzer family has managed to protect an urban area seriously threatened by concrete by transforming the hilltop estate into a kind of agricultural park for Trento. Set amidst silver-rich rocks, there are still traces of silver mines on Mt. Calisio. Here, the vineyards, which clamber up the hill's steep slopes, are cultivated with the utmost respect for nature, making for vintages that get better by the year. The same can be said of Maso Martis' selection of wines, which are only sold to specific markets, so as to maintain the authenticity of their wines, and the producer itself. The Metodo Classico is available in four versions, starting with one characterized by a specific approach to cultivation: organic. The Dosaggio Zero is among Trento's top wines. It's an icon of the area whose straw-yellow color shines, with fine, lasting perlage, and a mix of close-knit, flowery fragrances, especially fruit and mountain herbs.

○ Trento Dosaggio Zero Ris. '12	▼▼▼ 6
○ Trento Brut Ris. '11	▼▼ 5
○ Trento Brut Bio	▼▼ 5
⊙ Trento Extra Brut Rosé Bio Ris. '13	▼▼ 5
○ Trento Dosaggio Zero Ris. '11	♈♈♈ 5
○ Trento Brut Ris. '08	♈♈ 5
○ Trento Brut Ris. '07	♈♈ 5
⊙ Trento Brut Rosé '11	♈♈ 5
○ Trento Dosaggio Zero '10	♈♈ 5
○ Trento Dosaggio Zero Ris. '10	♈♈ 5
○ Trento Madame Martis '06	♈♈ 6
○ Trento Ris. '08	♈♈ 5
⊙ Trento Rosé Ris. '11	♈♈ 5

aso Poli

c. Masi di Pressano, 33
015 Lavis [TN]
.. +39 0461871519
ww.masopoli.it

CELLAR SALES
RE-BOOKED VISITS
NNUAL PRODUCTION 75,000 bottles
CTARES UNDER VINE 13.00

eirs is one of the most enchanting
eyards on Lavis hill, with rows of vines
red for like a garden, keeping time with
e rhythm of the landscape itself. Luigi
gn's family, a historic dynasty of cellarmen
Roverè della Luna, work to protect the
ritory and maintain their commitment to
emaking, thus keeping this splendid
tate alive. And in doing so, they've
nsformed it into a bastion of wine culture,
anaged personally by daughters Martina,
mina and Valentina, as well as son-in-law,
ffredo Pasolli, president of Enolgi del
entino. They only use grapes from the
eyards around the winery, without forcing
ything, so as to obtain wines that are
presentative of the terroir, and that stand
t in terms of personality. Sorni is a cru
t, unfortunately, few choose to focus on.
armoran is on it, offering a blend of
grein and Teroldego. Intense ruby red
hlights define its appearance. It's an
plosive wine, well-crafted and sure-footed
the palate. Pinot Nero has the burden of
splaying the elegance and power of this
itivar; it's a wine that doesn't compromise.

Trentino Sorni Rosso Marmoram '13	♥♥ 3*
Trentino Nosiola '16	♥♥ 3
Trentino Pinot Grigio '16	♥♥ 3
Trentino Pinot Nero Sup. '14	♥♥ 3
Trentino Riesling '16	♥ 3
Teroldego Rotaliano Gaierhof '12	♥♥ 3
Trentino Lagrein '13	♥♥ 4
Trentino Nosiola '15	♥♥ 3
Trentino Pinot Nero '12	♥♥ 3
Trentino Sorni Rosso Marmoram '12	♥♥ 3
Trentino Sorni Rosso Marmoram '11	♥♥ 3
Trentino Sup. Pinot Nero '13	♥♥ 3
Trentino Traminer '15	♥♥ 3
Trento Brut Ris. '10	♥♥ 5

Mezzacorona

via del Teroldego, 1e
38016 Mezzocorona [TN]
Tel. +39 0461616399
www.mezzacorona.it

CELLAR SALES
PRE-BOOKED VISITS
ACCOMMODATION
ANNUAL PRODUCTION 48,000,000 bottles
HECTARES UNDER VINE 2800.00

The Gruppo Mezzacorona has its sights set
well beyond the Dolomites, as evidenced by
an agreement signed with Jack Ma, the
Chinese magnate, and following initiatives in
the U.S.A., as well as in the rest of Europe.
Their wines are focused on approachability,
and are always ready to satisfy the most
disparate demands and tastes. Yet they've
maintained their towering status as one of
Italy's most representative wine producers,
and they're just as committed to their more
specific selections, especially when it comes
to sparkling Trentos. Conciliare Teroldego
and Metodo Classico are among these, both
of which are equally superb, accomplishing
their task with great ease. The Trento Flavio
is a wonder. Creamy and honeyed in its
austerity, with a style true to the region, it
manages to offer up a dynamic, savory finish
without hesitating. The Teroldego Riserva
Castel Firmian is bold and just as versatile. It
brings together insight into winemaking and
respect for tradition, making for a wine that's
not afraid to stand shoulder-to-shoulder with
global competitors. The other wines
presented proved absolutely valid.

○ Trento Brut Rotari Flavio Ris. '09	♥♥♥ 8
● Teroldego Rotaliano Castel Firmian Ris. '14	♥♥ 2*
● Nerofino '14	♥♥ 5
○ Trentino Pinot Grigio Castel Firmian Ris. '15	♥♥ 5
○ Trento Pas Dosé Rotari AlpeRegis '11	♥♥ 6
○ Trento Talento Cuvée 28°	♥♥ 4
● Teroldego Rotaliano Nos Ris. '04	♥♥♥ 5
○ Trento Brut Rotari Flavio Ris. '08	♥♥♥ 5
○ Trento Brut Rotari Flavio Ris. '07	♥♥♥ 5
○ Trento Brut Rotari Flavio Ris. '06	♥♥♥ 5
● Teroldego Rotaliano '15	♥♥ 4
● Teroldego Rotaliano Castel Firmian Ris. '13	♥♥ 2*
○ Trentino Pinot Grigio Castel Firmian Ris. '14	♥♥ 4

Cantine Monfort

VIA CARLO SETTE, 21
38015 LAVIS [TN]
TEL. +39 0461246353
www.cantinemonfort.it

CELLAR SALES
PRE-BOOKED VISITS
ANNUAL PRODUCTION 170,000 bottles
HECTARES UNDER VINE 40.00
SUSTAINABLE WINERY

For the 100-year-anniversary of the 'Great War', the cellar situated in the 1914 wartime fort hosted a series of exhibitions. And so it was that the Simoni family returned home, to Lavis, though without neglecting the vineyards surrounding the Asburgo fort in Civezzano, between Trento and Valsugana. Every vineyard, and its wine, is carefully attended to by Federico Simoni, the family's young winemaker. And we know he's up to the challenge. Just taste their Trento, or any of their best vineyards' wines (Pinot Nero included). And it's Maso Cantanghel that makes it to our finals, affirming its status as a wine of great complexity, enjoyable and bursting with potential, which age will surely bring out. The Riserva continues to prove valid. A brilliant, clear-gold wine, it offers gentle notes of pear, white tea, and a highly pleasing stroke of woodland.

● Trentino Pinot Nero V. Cantanghel '13	♟♟ 5
○ Blanc de Sers '15	♟♟ 3
○ SotSàs '14	♟♟ 3
○ Trentino Müller Thurgau '16	♟♟ 2*
○ Trento Brut Monfort Ris. '11	♟♟ 5
● Trentino Lagrein '13	♟ 3
○ Blanc de Sers '13	♟♟ 3
● San Lorenzo '14	♟♟ 2*
○ SotSàs '13	♟♟ 3
○ Trentino Gewürztraminer '14	♟♟ 3
☉ Trentino Pinot Grigio Rosé '15	♟♟ 3
● Trentino Pinot Nero V. Cantanghel '12	♟♟ 5
○ Trentino Traminer Aromatico '15	♟♟ 3

Moser

FRAZ. GARDOLO DI MEZZO
VIA CASTEL DI GARDOLO, 5
38121 TRENTO
TEL. +39 0461990786
www.cantinemoser.com

CELLAR SALES
PRE-BOOKED VISITS
ACCOMMODATION
ANNUAL PRODUCTION 120,000 bottles
HECTARES UNDER VINE 17.00

Francesco Moser is a legend of modern cycling, a champion of the pedal who continues to enjoy fame and acclaim. And he's made a name for himself outside the sports world, as well, having become a skilled wine businessman. He's also involved his three children, Francesca, Carlo and Ignazio, as well as their cousin, Matteo, who serves as winemaker. They're a competitive team, ready for whatever challenge, with a series of wines made wi⋯ grapes from the family's personally managed vineyards. Their facility is situate⋯ in an enchanting hill farmstead north of Trento, towards the Cembra Valley, in an area known for its variegated terrain, basa⋯ and porphyritic rock, making for full-flavored, fruity wine. The Nature carrie⋯ the day. This recent addition to their selection wasn't born to lie down. It has thrust and determination in each of its nuances, which makes it one of their best wines. The Brut never disappoints, while, among the stills, we noticed a Riesling tha⋯ features taut, dynamic, iodine overtones.

○ Trento Brut Nature '11	♟♟
○ Riesling '15	♟♟
○ Trento Brut 51,151	♟♟
○ Chardonnay '16	♟
○ Müller Thurgau '16	♟
○ 51,151 '10	♟♟
● Lagrein Dea Mater '09	♟♟
● Lagrein Deamater '05	♟♟
○ Moscato Giallo '14	♟♟
○ Riesling '12	♟♟
○ Riesling '10	♟♟
● Teroldego '13	♟♟
○ Trento 51,151 '09	♟♟
☉ Trento Rosé '12	♟♟

Opera

A 3 Novembre, 8
38030 Giovo [TN]
Tel. +39 0461684302
www.operavaldicembra.it

CELLAR SALES
PRE-BOOKED VISITS
ANNUAL PRODUCTION 60,000 bottles
HECTARES UNDER VINE

Splashes of golden light fall across the vineyards amidst rugged benchlands, supported by porphyritic rocks. That's Cembra Valley, a land of geologic juxtaposition, viticultural landscapes forged by the ingenuity of the vine growers of old. How much work and effort were needed to satisfy the demand for wine and grappa that, for centuries, defined this Alpine community? The winery, whose name deliberately refers to the viticultural 'work' of their forefathers, focuses exclusively on sparkling wine, and produced some of the region's first Trentos. The Trento Nature wine, made with hilltop grapes that undergo an almost obsessive selection process, proved superb, thus the 2011 Nature brought home an enthusiastic Tre Bicchieri. The wine features lean fizziness and aromatic power, as well as a crisp palate that's spirited, though extremely delicate. Very slow second-fermentation conferred power to the Riserva, a wine charged with every possible nuance.

○ Trento Opera Nature '11	▼▼▼ 5
○ Trento Opera Nature Ris. '10	▼▼ 4
○ Trento Opera Nature Blanc de Noir '10	▼▼ 5
○ Trento Opera Noir	▼▼ 5
⊙ Trento Opera Rosé	▼
○ Trento Brut Opera '07	♉ 4

Pojer & Sandri

Loc. Molini, 4
38010 Faedo [TN]
Tel. +39 0461650342
www.pojeresandri.it

CELLAR SALES
PRE-BOOKED VISITS
ACCOMMODATION
ANNUAL PRODUCTION 200,000 bottles
HECTARES UNDER VINE 26.00
VITICULTURE METHOD Certified Organic

For more than 40 years, Pojer & Sandri have moved in time with the evolution of the Dolomite's wine culture. And they've done it without losing any enthusiasm. These true pioneers decided to focus on the vineyards of Faedo, a hill set above San Michele all'Adige that was once unjustly considered of lesser importance. Today, Mario Pojer and Fiorentino Sandri are supported, in winemaking and marketing, by their respective children, and they have no intention of holding back on innovation, continuing to experiment with new varieties (such as interspecies) that don't require chemicals. Their wines exhibit notable personality and truly interpret the enological evolution of the Dolomites. And their Bianco Faye, a mix of Chardonnay and Pinot Bianco, has never been so good. Flowery, rich in golden complexity, it finds the right acidity and flow. The Rosso Faye, a full-bodied wine made with four different types of grapes, exhibits a similar harmony, though it's worth tasting again in a few years.

○ Bianco Faye '13	▼▼ 5
○ Pojer & Sandri Extra Brut	▼▼ 5
● Rosso Faye '12	▼▼ 6
○ Essenzia '13	▼▼ 5
● Merlino	▼▼ 5
○ Müller Thurgau Palai '16	▼▼ 3
● Pinot Nero '16	▼▼ 4
⊙ Vin dei Molini '16	▼▼ 3
○ Bianco Faye '08	♉♉♉ 5
○ Bianco Faye '01	♉♉♉ 5
● Pinot Nero Rodel Pianezzi '09	♉♉♉ 5
● Rosso Faye '05	♉♉♉ 5
⊙ Spumante Rosé Cuvée 11-12	♉♉ 5
● Pinot Nero Rodel Pianezzi '13	♉♉ 5

Pravis

LOC. LE BIOLCHE, 1
38076 LASINO [TN]
TEL. +39 0461564305
www.pravis.it

CELLAR SALES
PRE-BOOKED VISITS
ANNUAL PRODUCTION 200,000 bottles
HECTARES UNDER VINE 32.00

Since 1975, three friends, Domenico, Gianni and Mario, have revolutionized the better part of their vineyards in the Valle dei Laghi, between Trento, Lake Toblino, Lake Garda and the mountains leading to the Brenta Dolomites. Today, they're also making room for their children. The estate comprises many small plots, all situated high in the hills, an area kissed by the benevolent winds that pour in off the lake. There's a wine for every vineyard, which revive ancient varieties (like Negrara), but also feature Solaris and its sisters (so-called 'interspecies'), embodiments of naturalness. The vivacity of their wines has allowed this winery to distinguish itself from the Dolomites' other producers. And the Fratagranda proves an exquisite blend. Intense in its concentrated ruby red color, the wine offers up hints of spice, tobacco, cocoa and vanilla. We're similarly enthusiastic for the Stravino di Stravino, a zesty blend of white grapes, including super-ripeness.

Wine	Rating
● Fratagranda '13	♟♟ 4
○ Stravino di Stravino '13	♟♟ 4
○ l'Ora '13	♟♟ 4
● Madruzzo '15	♟♟ 3
○ Nosiola Le Frate '16	♟♟ 2*
○ Polin '16	♟ 2
● Fratagranda '10	♟♟♟ 4*
● Fratagranda '09	♟♟♟ 4*
● Fratagranda '07	♟♟♟ 4
○ Vino Santo Arèle '06	♟♟♟ 6
● Fratagranda '12	♟♟ 4
○ Kerner '15	♟♟ 2*
○ Müller Thurgau St. Thomà '15	♟♟ 2*
● Syrae '13	♟♟ 4

Agraria Riva del Garda

LOC. SAN NAZZARO, 4
38066 RIVA DEL GARDA [TN]
TEL. +39 0464552133
www.agririva.it

CELLAR SALES
PRE-BOOKED VISITS
ANNUAL PRODUCTION 250,000 bottles
HECTARES UNDER VINE 280.00

When it comes to taste, this cooperative winery has overcome every challenge set before it, and its done it with the help of Garda. This is especially true of their extra-virgin olive oil, with the producer taking advantage of their latitude (the 46th parallel) and Casaliva, a cultivar that grows exclusively along the banks of the lake. However, for some seasons now, they've also managed to distinguish themselves for their well-focused selection of wines. These are made primarily with international grape varieties, but their curious sensory qualities suggest a lacustrine character. Indeed, Garda's pervasive influence is to be discovered and enjoyed here, thanks in part to their attentive, organic approach to cultivation. The decision to cultivate international grapes has forced to winery into a tight position, though they're forging ahead with a strong belief in their resources. And a nice Pinot Nero Elesi is pointing up the wisdom of their strategy. It's a wine that's as lean as it is polished, with an excellent, succulent taste profile.

Wine	Rating
● Trentino Sup. Pinot Nero Elesi '15	♟♟ 4
● Maso Lizzone '15	♟♟ 3
● Trentino Lagrein Sasera '15	♟♟ 4
● Rosso Bio '15	♟ 3
○ Trentino Bianco Bio '16	♟ 3
○ Trentino Chardonnay Loré '15	♟ 4
● Maso Lizzone '14	♟♟ 3
● Rosso Gère '13	♟♟ 3
● Teroldego Rivaldego '15	♟♟ 2*
● Trentino Merlot Crèa '11	♟♟ 4

★★Tenuta San Leonardo

Loc. San Leonardo, 1
38063 Avio [TN]
Tel. +39 0464689004
www.sanleonardo.it

CELLAR SALES
PRE-BOOKED VISITS
ANNUAL PRODUCTION 250,000 bottles
HECTARES UNDER VINE 35.00
SUSTAINABLE WINERY

The charm of wine country thrives here,
among the vineyards of this enchanting
estate. Internationally recognized for its
flagship wine, San Leonardo, the winery is
also praised for its beauty: the blazon of the
villa, the incredible biodiversity of the
enormous, majestic natural park around it.
And then there are its vineyards, some of
them new, some of them almost a century
old, which grow amidst every imaginable
type of woodland plant. The Guerrieri
Gonzaga family, Marquis Carlo and his son,
Anselmo, have further bolstered their
vineyards through organic cultivation
practices. Once again, we can't heap
enough praise on the San Leonardo, which
firmly holds onto its top spot among the
region's wines (and not only), thanks to its
vitality, complexity, elegance and harmony.
The Villa Gresti, made with Merlot and a
touch of Carmenere, also affirms its status
as a decisive wine that's perfectly worthy of
the winery's blazon.

Toblino

Fraz. Sarche
via Longa, 1
38076 Madruzzo [TN]
Tel. +39 0461564168
www.toblino.it

PRE-BOOKED VISITS
RESTAURANT SERVICE
ANNUAL PRODUCTION 400,000 bottles
HECTARES UNDER VINE 700.00
VITICULTURE METHOD Certified Organic
SUSTAINABLE WINERY

This cooperative winery works with smaller
agribusinesses while focusing on cultivar
and experimentation with organic
cultivation. President Bruno Lutterotti (who
is also president of Cavit) has implemented
a dynamic management approach. For a
few seasons, the agronomist Carlo De Biasi
has served as director of the winery (which
also features an eatery), as well as leading
the project, Biodistretto Valle dei Laghi. The
member-growers oversee myriad
micro-vineyards capable of satisfying their
winemaking needs, from sparkling wines to
traditional vinification, and even cultivate
Nosiola, a grape that's reserved for Trento's
rare and exclusive raisin wine, Vino Santo.
It's an emblem of the winery, an enticing
passito that can stand shoulder-to-shoulder
with the best of them. The eLimarò, made
with Rebo and other late-harvest grapes,
also put in a great performance, proving a
unique wine with a natural tendency to
develop in the mouth. The Pinot Nero calls
up blackberries and ripe cherries on the
nose, with accents of pencil lead.

● San Leonardo '13	▼▼▼ 8
● Villa Gresti '13	▼▼ 5
● Terre di San Leonardo '14	▼▼ 3
○ Vette di San Leonardo '16	▼▼ 3
● Carmenère '07	♀♀♀ 8
● San Leonardo '11	♀♀♀ 8
● San Leonardo '10	♀♀♀ 7
● San Leonardo '08	♀♀♀ 7
● San Leonardo '07	♀♀♀ 7
● San Leonardo '06	♀♀♀ 7
● San Leonardo '05	♀♀♀ 7
● Terre di San Leonardo '13	♀♀ 3
○ Vette di San Leonardo '15	♀♀ 3
● Villa Gresti '11	♀♀ 5

● eLimarò '13	▼▼ 3
○ Trentino Nosiola '16	▼▼ 2*
● Trentino Pinot Nero '15	▼▼ 2*
○ Trentino Vino Santo '02	▼▼ 6
○ Trento Brut Antares '12	▼▼ 3
○ Trentino Moscato Giallo '16	▼ 2
○ L'Ora '11	♀♀ 3
○ Largiller '07	♀♀ 3
○ Manzoni Bianco '13	♀♀ 2*
○ Moscato Giallo Bio '14	♀♀ 2*
○ Trentino Chardonnay Bio '15	♀♀ 2*
○ Trentino Traminer Aromatico Bio '15	♀♀ 2*
○ Trento Brut Antares '11	♀♀ 3
○ Trento Brut Antares '10	♀♀ 3

Vallarom

LOC. VO' SINISTRO
FRAZ. MASI, 21
38063 AVIO [TN]
TEL. +39 0464684297
www.vallarom.it

CELLAR SALES
PRE-BOOKED VISITS
ACCOMMODATION AND RESTAURANT SERVICE
ANNUAL PRODUCTION 35,000 bottles
HECTARES UNDER VINE 7.00
VITICULTURE METHOD Certified Organic
SUSTAINABLE WINERY

They cultivate their land with the vine growers customary expression, a kind of scowl that's really a sign that they love their work. It's a lifestyle choice, as well as a professional one, and Barbara and Filipppo Scienza are just as enthusiastic about having involved their son, Riccardo. He's determined to pursue purely organic cultivation practices, with an approach in the cellar that features spontaneity and (in honor of their surname) science. Their wines respect the evolution of the vintage, and the singularity of the terrain, which includes an area in the legendary Campi Sarni, the Lagarino bank of the Adige river, an area that has, for centuries, been renowned for its wines. The Pinot Nero made it to the finals, thanks to its absolute forthrightness. Ruby red in color, it offers up overtones that weave with spices and small wild berries. Savory and intense, it also exhibits balanced acidity, thanks to the grapes' organic cultivation. The Trentatrè, a blend of local grapes, is a playful wine for convivial drinking.

● Vallagarina Pinot Nero '15	▼▼	4
○ Trentatrè '16	▼▼	3
○ Vadum Caesaris '16	▼▼	3
○ Vo' '13	▼▼	4
⊙ Vo' Rosé de Saignée	▼	4
● Cabernet Sauvignon Bio '13	♈♈	3
○ Enantio '15	♈♈	3
● Fufluns '11	♈♈	4
● Fuflus '12	♈♈	4
● Trentino Marzemino Bio '15	♈♈	3
○ Vo'	♈♈	4
○ Vo' Dosaggio Zero '12	♈♈	4

Roberto Zeni

FRAZ. GRUMO
VIA STRETTA, 2
38010 SAN MICHELE ALL'ADIGE [TN]
TEL. +39 0461650456
www.zeni.tn.it

CELLAR SALES
PRE-BOOKED VISITS
ANNUAL PRODUCTION 150,000 bottles
HECTARES UNDER VINE 14.00
VITICULTURE METHOD Certified Organic

Fresh off their enological studies at the nearby agrarian school, brothers Andrea and Roberto Zeni founded this winery in 1975. But now that their children are on board, the producer is seeing a changing of the guard. With great skill, the family has managed to diversify the estate's vineyards, situated on their doorstep along the Adige river. Special attention has been paid to their plots at Maso Nero (12 hectares in all), an enchanting area along the steep hill of Lavis, where the new generation is cultivating organic grapes for Zeni's aromatic wines and Trento. But most of their effort goes into Teroldego. It was a deliberate choice that's proved fruitful, considering that the three Teroldegos submitted are truly one-of-a-kind. Pini gets the most accolades. For some years now, it's gone all in on concentration, making for a dense, intriguing, unforgettable wine. It goes well with the two, simpler versions, starting with the Ternet, whose grapes are cultivated along Schwarzhof's steep slopes.

● Teroldego Rotaliano Pini '13	▼▼▼	6
● Teroldego Ternet Schwarzhof '15	▼▼	5
● Teroldego Rotaliano Lealbere '16	▼▼	3
● Teroldego Rotaliano Pini '12	♈♈♈	6
● Teroldego Rotaliano Pini '09	♈♈♈	6
● Teroldego Ternet Schwarzhof '10	♈♈♈	5
● Teroldego Rotaliano Lealbere '13	♈♈	3
● Teroldego Ternet Schwarzhof '13	♈♈	5
○ Traminer Schwarzhof '15	♈♈	4
○ Trentino Nosiola Palustella '15	♈♈	2*
○ Trentino Pinot Bianco Seipergole '14	♈♈	2*
○ Trentino Traminer Schwarzhof '13	♈♈	2*
○ Trento Brut Nero Maso Ris. '10	♈♈	5
○ Trento Dosaggio Zero Maso Nero '11	♈♈	5

Cantina Aldeno

VIA ROMA, 76
38060 ALDENO [TN]
TEL. +39 0461842511
www.cantinaaldeno.com

CELLAR SALES
PRE-BOOKED VISITS
ANNUAL PRODUCTION 240,000 bottles
HECTARES UNDER VINE 340.00

● Trentino San Zeno Ris. '12	♟♟ 4
○ Trento Brut Blanc de Blancs Altinum	♟♟ 4
○ Trento Extra Brut Altinum '11	♟♟ 5
○ Trento Pas Dosé Altinum '15	♟♟ 5

Bolognani

VIA STAZIONE, 19
38015 LAVIS [TN]
TEL. +39 0461246354
www.bolognani.com

CELLAR SALES
PRE-BOOKED VISITS
ANNUAL PRODUCTION 70,000 bottles
HECTARES UNDER VINE 4.40

● Gabàn '12	♟♟ 5
● Teroldego Armilo '15	♟♟ 3
○ Trentino Traminer Aromatico Sanròc '15	♟♟ 3
○ Sauvignon '16	♟ 3

Cantina Sociale di Trento

VIA DEI VITICOLTORI, 2/4
38123 VOLANO [TN]
TEL. +39 0461920186
www.cantinasocialetrento.it

CELLAR SALES
PRE-BOOKED VISITS
ANNUAL PRODUCTION 250,000 bottles
HECTARES UNDER VINE 50.00
SUSTAINABLE WINERY

○ Santacolomba Solaris '16	♟♟ 3
● Trentino Marzemino Heredia '15	♟♟ 3
○ Trento Brut Zell	♟♟ 5
⊙ Trento Brut Zell Rosé	♟♟ 5

Marco Donati

VIA CESARE BATTISTI, 41
38016 MEZZOCORONA [TN]
TEL. +39 0461604141
www.cantinadonatimarco.it

CELLAR SALES
PRE-BOOKED VISITS
ANNUAL PRODUCTION 100,000 bottles
HECTARES UNDER VINE 20.00
SUSTAINABLE WINERY

● Teroldego Rotaliano Bagolari '15	♟♟ 4
● Teroldego Rotaliano Sangue di Drago '14	♟♟ 5
● Teroldego Rotaliano '16	♟ 3
○ Trentino Traminer AromaticoTramonti '16	♟ 3

Etyssa

LOC. MOIA, 4
38121 TRENTO
TEL. +39 3938922784
www.etyssaspumanti.it

ANNUAL PRODUCTION 3,500 bottles
HECTARES UNDER VINE 14.00

○ Trento Extra Brut Cuvée N. 2 '13	♟♟ 5

Gaierhof

VIA IV NOVEMBRE, 51
38030 ROVERÈ DELLA LUNA [TN]
TEL. +39 0461658514
www.gaierhof.com

CELLAR SALES
PRE-BOOKED VISITS
ANNUAL PRODUCTION 500,000 bottles
HECTARES UNDER VINE 150.00
SUSTAINABLE WINERY

○ Trentino Müller Thurgau dei '700 '16	♟♟ 3
○ Trentino Sauvignon '16	♟♟ 3
⊙ Schiava '16	♟ 2
● Teroldego Rotaliano '15	♟ 2

Cantina d'Isera

VIA AL PONTE, 1
38060 ISERA [TN]
TEL. +39 0464433795
www.cantinaisera.it

CELLAR SALES
PRE-BOOKED VISITS
ANNUAL PRODUCTION 500,000 bottles
HECTARES UNDER VINE 246.00
VITICULTURE METHOD Certified Organic

● Trentino Marzemino '15	♀♀ 2*
● Trentino Marzemino Bio '15	♀♀ 3
● Trentino Marzemino Sup. Et. Verde '15	♀♀ 3
○ Trento Brut Ris. '11	♀ 5

Tenuta Maso Corno

LOC. VALBONA
38061 ALA [TN]
TEL. +39 0464421130
www.tenutamasocorno.it

PRE-BOOKED VISITS
ANNUAL PRODUCTION 10,000 bottles
HECTARES UNDER VINE 5.00

○ Trentino Chardonnay Villanova '14	♀♀ 6
● Trentino Pinot Nero Santa Maria '12	♀♀ 6
○ Trentino Sauvignon Declivi '15	♀ 4

Maso Grener

LOC. MASI DI PRESSANO
38015 LAVIS [TN]
TEL. +39 0461871514
www.masogrener.it

CELLAR SALES
PRE-BOOKED VISITS
ANNUAL PRODUCTION 18,000 bottles
HECTARES UNDER VINE 3.00

○ Maso Grener '16	♀♀ 4
○ Trentino Chardonnay V. Tratta '15	♀♀ 3
● Trentino Pinot Nero V. Bindesi '15	♀♀ 5

Giuliano Micheletti

VIA E. CONCI, 74
38123 TRENTO
TEL. +39 3493306929
gm.limina@gmail.com

ANNUAL PRODUCTION 3,000 bottles
HECTARES UNDER VINE 3.00

● Merlot Limen '14	♀♀ 4
○ Riesling Limen '14	♀♀ 4

Mori - Colli Zugna

VIA DEL GARDA, 35
38065 MORI [TN]
TEL. +39 0464918154
www.cantinamoricollizugna.it

CELLAR SALES
PRE-BOOKED VISITS
ANNUAL PRODUCTION 220,000 bottles
HECTARES UNDER VINE 600.00

● Trentino Sup. Marzemino Terra di San Mauro '15	♀♀ 3
○ Trento Brut Morus Ris. '13	♀♀ 5
○ Victoriae '15	♀♀ 5

Pedrotti Spumanti

VIA ROMA, 2A
38060 NOMI [TN]
TEL. +39 0464835111
www.predottispumanti.it

CELLAR SALES
ANNUAL PRODUCTION 30,000 bottles
HECTARES UNDER VINE 3.00
SUSTAINABLE WINERY

○ Trento Pas Dosé Ris. 111 '10	♀♀ 6
○ Trento Nature Bouquet	♀♀ 4
○ Trento Brut Bouquet	♀ 4

Pisoni

LOC. SARCHE
FRAZ. PERGOLESE DI LASINO
VIA SAN SIRO, 7A
38076 MADRUZZO
TEL. +39 0461564106
www.pisoni.net

CELLAR SALES
PRE-BOOKED VISITS
ANNUAL PRODUCTION 23,500 bottles
HECTARES UNDER VINE 16.00

○ Trento Extra Brut Ris. '09	♀♀ 5
○ Trento Brut '13	♀♀ 4
○ Trento Brut Nature '13	♀♀ 4
⊙ Trento Brut Rosé '13	♀ 5

Revì

VIA FLORIDA, 10
38060 ALDENO [TN]
TEL. +39 0461843155
www.revispumanti.com

CELLAR SALES
PRE-BOOKED VISITS
ANNUAL PRODUCTION 20,000 bottles
HECTARES UNDER VINE 1.70
VITICULTURE METHOD Certified Organic

○ Trento Dosaggio Zero '13	♀♀ 5
○ Trento Brut Rosé '13	♀♀ 5
○ Trento Extra Brut Cavaliere Nero '10	♀♀ 5
○ Trento Extra Brut Paladino Ris. '11	♀♀ 5

Cantina Rotaliana

VIA TRENTO, 65B
38017 MEZZOLOMBARDO [TN]
TEL. +39 0461601010
www.cantinarotaliana.it

CELLAR SALES
PRE-BOOKED VISITS
ANNUAL PRODUCTION 1,000,000 bottles
HECTARES UNDER VINE 330.00
SUSTAINABLE WINERY

● Terldego Rotaliano Clesurae '14	♀♀ 6
● Teroldego Rotaliano Et. Rossa '16	♀♀ 3
● Teroldego Rotaliano Ris. '14	♀♀ 4
○ Trento Redor '09	♀♀ 5

Cantina Sociale Roverè della Luna

VIA IV NOVEMBRE, 9
38030 ROVERÈ DELLA LUNA [TN]
TEL. +39 0461658530
www.csrovere1919.it

CELLAR SALES
ANNUAL PRODUCTION 100,000 bottles
HECTARES UNDER VINE 420.00

● Trentino Pinot Nero V. Feldi '14	♀♀ 5
○ Trento Brut Vervè '13	♀♀ 4
● Trentino Lagrein '14	♀ 2
○ Trentino Pinot Grigio '16	♀ 2

Arcangelo Sandri

VIA VANEGGE, 4A
38010 FAEDO [TN]
TEL. +39 0461650935
www.arcangelosandri.it

CELLAR SALES
PRE-BOOKED VISITS
ANNUAL PRODUCTION 22,000 bottles
HECTARES UNDER VINE 3.00

○ Oro di Bac '16	♀♀ 4
● Lagrein Capòr '13	♀♀ 3
○ Traminer Razer '16	♀ 2

Armando Simoncelli

VIA NAVICELLO, 7
38068 ROVERETO [TN]
TEL. +39 0464432373
www.simoncelli.it

CELLAR SALES
PRE-BOOKED VISITS
ANNUAL PRODUCTION 90,000 bottles
HECTARES UNDER VINE 10.50

● Trentino Marzemino '16	♀♀ 4
● Trentino Rosso Navesel '13	♀♀ 5
○ Trento Brut	♀♀ 4

Enrico Spagnolli

VIA G. B. ROSINA, 4A
38060 ISERA [TN]
TEL. +39 0464409054
www.vinispagnolli.it

CELLAR SALES
PRE-BOOKED VISITS
ANNUAL PRODUCTION 85,000 bottles
HECTARES UNDER VINE 18.00

● Tebro '10	♥♥ 3
● Trentino Marzemino '15	♥♥ 2*
● Trentino Marzemino Don Giovanni '15	♥♥ 3
● Vallagarina Lagrein '15	♥ 2

Marco Tonini

LOC. FOLASO
VIA ROSMINI, 8
38060 ISERA [TN]
TEL. +39 3404991043

CELLAR SALES
PRE-BOOKED VISITS
ANNUAL PRODUCTION 8,000 bottles
HECTARES UNDER VINE 4.00

● Trentino Marzemino '15	♥♥ 4
○ Trento Brut '14	♥♥ 5

Villa Corniole

FRAZ. VERLA
VIA AL GREC', 23
38030 GIOVO [TN]
TEL. +39 0461695067
www.villacorniole.com

CELLAR SALES
PRE-BOOKED VISITS
ANNUAL PRODUCTION 60,000 bottles
HECTARES UNDER VINE 4.00
SUSTAINABLE WINERY

○ Kroz '15	♥♥ 4
○ Trento Brut Salisa '13	♥♥ 5
○ Trento Dosaggio Zero Salisa '13	♥♥ 5

Vin de la Neu

FRAZ. COREDO
VIA SAN ROMEDIO, 8
38012 PREDAIA [TN]
TEL. 3474116854
www.vindelaneu.it

○ Vin de la Neu '13	♥♥ 8

Vivallis

VIA PER BRANCOLINO, 4
38068 NOGAREDO [TN]
TEL. +39 0464834113
www.vivallis.it

CELLAR SALES
PRE-BOOKED VISITS
ANNUAL PRODUCTION 1,000,000 bottles
HECTARES UNDER VINE 730.00
VITICULTURE METHOD Certified Organic

○ Trentino Moscato Giallo Castel Beseno '16	♥♥ 3
○ Trentino Müller Thurgau V. Rio Romini '16	♥♥ 3
● Trentino Sup. Marzemino dei Ziresi '15	♥♥ 4

Zanotelli

V.LE 4 NOVEMBRE, 52
38034 CEMBRA [TN]
TEL. +39 0461683131
www.zanotelliwines.com

CELLAR SALES
PRE-BOOKED VISITS
ANNUAL PRODUCTION 40,000 bottles
HECTARES UNDER VINE 11.00

○ Trento Brut Forneri '13	♥♥ 5
○ Kerner Le Strope '16	♥♥ 4
○ Trentino Müller Thurgau '16	♥♥ 4
○ Trentino Riesling Le Strope '14	♥♥ 4

ALTO ADIGE

When it comes to viticulture, Alto Adige is one of Italy's crown jewels. Here vigneron, terroir and cultivar come together for a range of outstanding wines, from the fresh acidity of Valle Isarco to the opulence of the Bolzano plain, the personality of the Mazzon Pinot Nero and the fragrant grace of Caldaro Lake. In a territory that's so diverse, it's natural that many different types of wineries would emerge. There are the smaller producers who cultivate just a few hectares of their own terrain. There are large cooperative wineries, historic wineries, and the third party growers who supply them with grapes. But the thread that binds them all is the care with which they work their vineyards and produce their wines. It's all in the name of making something that fully expresses the territory's shining potential. The region's cooperatives, in particular, are excelling when it comes to representing Alto Adige. There are the Lagreins produced at Cantina Bolzano and Muri Gries, the Sylvaner made at Valle Isarco, and Tramin and Cortaccia's Gewürztraminers. Other areas don't feature a single, iconic variety, and so it is that Pinot Bianco, Sauvignon and Chardonnay have gained such notoriety. And there's plenty of news from those wineries that are getting a gold for the first time. Peter Zemmer has unveiled a sumptuous Riserva di Pinot Grigio Giatl that exhibits both force and balance. Then there's the achievement of the sparkling winemaker Cantina Kettmeier and their house reserve, the Extra Brut 1919. Speaking of vintages, we should note that Schiava had a great year, with a number of wines making it to the finals. Indeed, three wines from Santa Maddalena and Caldaro Lake were awarded Tre Bicchieri. Isarco Valley continues to be a bastion of character, with its plucky and spicy Riesling della Val Venosta. Pinot Bianco, however, continues to reign supreme in Alto Adige. Despite only three wines getting a gold, the grape expressed its character and splendid obedience to climate across the board, making for wines that are ultimately defined by their depth and finesse.

★Abbazia di Novacella

FRAZ. NOVACELLA
VIA DELL'ABBAZIA, 1
39040 VARNA/VAHRN [BZ]
TEL. +39 0472836189
www.abbazianovacella.it

CELLAR SALES
PRE-BOOKED VISITS
RESTAURANT SERVICE
ANNUAL PRODUCTION 650,000 bottles
HECTARES UNDER VINE 20.00

Abbazia di Novacella is probably the most iconic winery in this small but important winemaking area, the Isarco Valley. The valley stretches northeastward from Bolzano, with vineyards producing mainly aromatic white grapes. Most of the winery's 20 hectares are located in this area, although they also have vineyards in warmer areas at lower altitudes. With an overall selection this good, we're only missing a 'standout'. The Praepositus line is their top-notch range, headed by an amazing Riesling. On the nose, notes of smoke and exotic fruit emerge, which follow through onto a full and powerful palate. The Sylvaner, on the other hand, plays on riper and sweeter fruit, while the palate reveals grip and length. The Grüner Veltliner also did well, with its fresher aromas and supple mouth.

★Alois Lageder

LOC. TOR LÖWENGANG
V.LO DEI CONTI, 9
39040 MAGRÈ/MARGREID [BZ]
TEL. +39 0471809500
www.aloislageder.eu

CELLAR SALES
PRE-BOOKED VISITS
RESTAURANT SERVICE
ANNUAL PRODUCTION 1,200,000 bottles
HECTARES UNDER VINE 150.00
VITICULTURE METHOD Certified Biodynamic
SUSTAINABLE WINERY

The Province of Bolzano has a tight-knit agricultural structure, with small family-run wineries and collaborations between owners and local grape growers. Alois Lageder is in this last category. It has gradually converted to biodynamic viticulture, where it is now ahead of many of its collaborators. In addition to producing a selection of wines expressive of the variety, it also offers more ambitious selections that highlight specific features of the region. The strength of the territory comes out, lustrous and rugged, in the 2013 Cabernet Löwengang, a wine made with grapes from the historic Magrè vineyard, where some plants are over a century old. On the nose, fruit melds with vegetal and herby notes, while spices merge with hints of earth. On the palate, the wine's balance is evidenced by its smooth and pleasantly rough tannins. The 2014 Chardonnay of the same name features deep aromas and a dry, taut palate.

○ A. A. Valle Isarco Grüner Veltliner Praepositus '15	🍷🍷 3*
○ A. A. Valle Isarco Riesling Praepositus '15	🍷🍷 4
○ A. A. Valle Isarco Sylvaner Praepositus '16	🍷🍷 4
○ A. A. Valle Isarco Grüner Veltliner '16	🍷🍷 3
○ A. A. Valle Isarco Kerner '16	🍷🍷 3
○ A. A. Valle Isarco Kerner Praepositus '16	🍷🍷 4
● A. A. Valle Isarco Moscato Rosa Praepositus '15	🍷🍷 5
○ A. A. Valle Isarco Müller Thurgau '16	🍷🍷 3
● A. A. Valle Isarco Pinot Nero Praepositus Ris. '15	🍷🍷 4
○ A. A. Valle Isarco Sylvaner '16	🍷🍷 3
○ A. A. Valle Isarco Gewürztraminer Praepositus '16	🍷 4
○ A. A. Valle Isarco Sylvaner Praepositus '15	🍷🍷🍷 4*

● A. A. Cabernet Löwengang '13	🍷🍷 7
○ A. A. Chardonnay Löwengang '14	🍷🍷 6
● A. A. Cabernet Sauvignon Cor Römigberg '13	🍷🍷 8
○ A. A. Casòn '14	🍷🍷 6
○ A. A. Chardonnay Gaun '15	🍷🍷 4
○ A. A. Gewürztraminer Am Sand '15	🍷🍷 5
● A. A. Lagrein Lindenburg '12	🍷🍷 5
○ A. A. Pinot Grigio Porer '15	🍷🍷 4
● A. A. Pinot Nero Krafuss '13	🍷🍷 6
○ Forra '15	🍷 3
● A. A. Cabernet Löwengang '10	🍷🍷🍷 7
● A. A. Cabernet Sauvignon Cor Römigberg '11	🍷🍷🍷 7
● A. A. Cabernet Sauvignon Cor Römigberg '08	🍷🍷🍷 7
○ A. A. Chardonnay Löwengang '13	🍷🍷🍷 6

Tenuta Baron Di Pauli

VIA CANTINE, 12
39052 CALDARO/KALTERN [BZ]
TEL. +39 0471963696
www.barondipauli.com

CELLAR SALES
PRE-BOOKED VISITS
ANNUAL PRODUCTION 46,000 bottles
HECTARES UNDER VINE 15.00

The Oltradige area extends over the hills surrounding Lake Kaltern on up to Appiano and Magrè. These gently rolling hills offer selections. Baron di Pauli has about 15 hectares divided between two estates: Arzenhof in Caldaro, where they mainly grow Bordeaux and Schiava, and Höfl unterm Stein in Termeno, which is one of the best areas for Gewürztraminer. The starring role goes to a memorable 2016 Lago di Caldaro Kalkofen. The nose features hints of sweet ripe fruit intertwined with notes of spices and dried flowers. The palate expands gracefully and lengthens with grip. The 2013 Exilissi also delivered. It's a Gewürztraminer with a mature and relaxed profile that offers up a complex and mineral suite of aromas. The 2013 Arzio proves rich and powerful.

Bessererhof - Otmar Mair

LOC. NOVALE DI PRESULE, 10
39050 FIÈ ALLO SCILIAR/VÖLS AM SCHLERN [BZ]
TEL. +39 0471601011
www.bessererhof.it

CELLAR SALES
PRE-BOOKED VISITS
ANNUAL PRODUCTION 40,000 bottles
HECTARES UNDER VINE 4.50

The Mair family started making wine in the 1950s but it is only over the last 20 years that they have been bottling their wines. Today, Otmar Mair supervises activities in the cellar, while his son Hannes takes care of the vinegrowing side of things. They have a handful of hectares at the entrance to the Isarco Valley and in the Val di Funes, and produce about 40,000 bottles a year. In recent years, the cellar has been completely renovated, enabling the family to work more efficiently and carefully. Their 2016 Pinot Bianco, aged entirely in steel, offers up aromas of white fruit and flowers, and does a nice job following through onto its solid, dry palate. The 2014 Chardonnay Riserva, on the other hand, finishes off aging in wood and thus expresses warmer, more caressing tones. The 2016 Sauvignon passes up on aromatic drive for more mineral, complex overtones.

● A. A. Lago di Caldaro Cl. Sup. Kalkofen '16	♛♛ 3*
○ A. A. Gewürztraminer Elix '16	♛♛ 4
○ A. A. Gewürztraminer Exilissi '13	♛♛ 6
● A. A. Merlot Cabernet Arzio Ris. '13	♛♛ 6
○ A. A. Sauvignon Kinesis '16	♛♛ 4
○ Enosi '16	♛♛ 3
○ Dynamis '16	♛ 4
○ A. A. Gewürztraminer Exilissi '11	♛♛ 6
● A. A. Lago di Caldaro Cl. Sup. Kalkofen '13	♛♛ 3*
● A. A. Lagrein Carano Ris. '13	♛♛ 5
● A. A. Merlot Cabernet Arzio '12	♛♛ 6
○ A. A. Sauvignon Kinesis '15	♛♛ 3
○ Enosi '14	♛♛ 3
○ Enosi '13	♛♛ 3

○ A. A. Pinot Bianco '16	♛♛ 3*
○ A. A. Chardonnay Ris. '14	♛♛ 3
○ A. A. Sauvignon '16	♛♛ 4
○ A. A. Valle Isarco Kerner '16	♛♛ 4
○ A. A. Gewürztraminer '16	♛ 4
○ A. A. Chardonnay Ris. '13	♛♛ 3
○ A. A. Chardonnay Ris. '11	♛♛ 3
○ A. A. Chardonnay Ris. '10	♛♛ 3
○ A. A. Gewürztraminer '15	♛♛ 4
○ A. A. Pinot Bianco '11	♛♛ 3*
○ A. A. Valle Isarco Kerner '15	♛♛ 4
○ A. A. Valle Isarco Kerner '14	♛♛ 4
○ A. A. Valle Isarco Kerner '12	♛♛ 4

ALTO ADIGE

★★Cantina Bolzano

P.ZZA GRIES, 2
39100 BOLZANO/BOZEN
TEL. +39 0471270909
www.cantinabolzano.com

CELLAR SALES
PRE-BOOKED VISITS
ANNUAL PRODUCTION 3,000,000 bottles
HECTARES UNDER VINE 350.00
SUSTAINABLE WINERY

Bolzano winery is one of the leaders of South Tyrolean winemaking. The 300 hectares of vineyards are cultivated by its members and occupy some of the best exposures around the area. The Anreiter and Taber estates stretch across the Gries plain, Huck am Bach is located on the Santa Maddalena hill, while Kleinstein, Mock and Mumelter are in the hills overlooking the regional capital. Stephan Filippi and his staff exploit the different soils and climates to produce wines with personality. The great 2015 vintage contributed to the Lagrein Taber's brilliant performance. The wine offers up intense aromas of cherry, brambles and licorice on the nose, while the mouth sees force met by precision and grip. The Huck am Back, a Santa Maddalena with great depth and a savory palate, is the complete opposite. The Gewürztraminer Kleinstein, on the other hand, manages to combine generous taste with suppleness and finesse.

Josef Brigl

LOC. SAN MICHELE APPIANO
VIA MADONNA DEL RIPOSO, 3
39057 APPIANO/EPPAN [BZ]
TEL. +39 0471662419
www.brigl.com

CELLAR SALES
PRE-BOOKED VISITS
ANNUAL PRODUCTION 1,000,000 bottles
HECTARES UNDER VINE 50.00
SUSTAINABLE WINERY

The Brigl family's winery is situated in the small town of San Michele Appiano and is a beautiful modern structure set in a amidst vineyards and apple orchards. The strength of this winery lies in the 50 hectares of vineyards that are cultivated either directly or by local vinegrowers. They produce wines with an aromatic and easily recognizable style. Some of their best areas are Kaltenburg and Windegg on Lake Kaltern and Rielerhof on the slopes of the Renon plateau. Their Gewürzatraminer Windegg put in an excellent performance. It's a white with trademark hints of exotic fruit and citrus, and a balanced palate in which richness is well-contrasted by acidity. Of the reds, we particularly enjoyed the Lagrein Kalternburg, a Riserva that's still quite closed on the nose, but reveals richness and grip on the palate, with a dry and pleasantly rugged finish. The Santa Maddalena Rielerhof is long, fruity and features very pleasant taste.

● A. A. Lagrein Taber Ris. '15	♟♟♟ 6
○ A. A. Gewürztraminer Kleinstein '16	♟♟ 5
● A. A. Santa Maddalena Cl. Huck am Bach '16	♟♟ 2*
● A. A. Cabernet Mumelter Ris. '15	♟♟ 6
○ A. A. Chardonnay Ris. '15	♟♟ 5
● A. A. Lagrein Prestige Line Ris. '15	♟♟ 4
● A. A. Merlot Siebeneich '15	♟♟ 5
○ A. A. Moscato Giallo Passito Vinalia '15	♟♟ 3
● A. A. Pinot Nero Ris. '15	♟♟ 5
○ A. A. Sauvignon Mock '16	♟♟ 4
○ A. A. Sauvignon Ris. '15	♟♟ 4
● A. A. Lagrein Taber Ris. '14	♟♟♟ 6
● A. A. Lagrein Taber Ris. '13	♟♟♟ 6
● A. A. Lagrein Taber Ris. '12	♟♟♟ 6

○ A. A. Gewürztraminer V. Windegg '16	♟♟ 3
● A. A. Lagrein Kaltenburg Ris. '14	♟♟ 5
● A. A. Merlot Windegg Ris. '14	♟♟ 3
● A. A. Santa Maddalena V. Rielerhof '16	♟♟ 3
○ A. A. Sauvignon '16	♟♟ 3
● A. A. Lago di Caldaro Cl. Sup. V. Kaltenburg '16	♟ 2
○ A. A. Pinot Bianco V. Haselhof '16	♟ 3
○ A. A. Riesling V. Rielerhof '16	♟ 3
● A. A. Schiava V. Haselhof '16	♟ 2
○ A. A. Pinot Grigio Windegg '11	♟♟♟ 3*
○ A. A. Gewürztraminer Windegg '15	♟♟ 3*
● A. A. Lagrein Briglhof '11	♟♟ 5
● A. A. Lagrein Briglhof Ris. '10	♟♟ 5
○ A. A. Terlano Drei König Hof '10	♟♟ 2*

Brunnenhof
Kurt Rottensteiner

LOC. MAZZON
VIA DEGLI ALPINI, 5
39044 EGNA/NEUMARKT [BZ]
TEL. +39 0471820687
www.brunnenhof-mazzon.it

CELLAR SALES
PRE-BOOKED VISITS
ANNUAL PRODUCTION 35,000 bottles
HECTARES UNDER VINE 5.50
VITICULTURE METHOD Certified Organic

Kurt Rottensteiner's winery is situated in the heart of the great Pinot Nero cru in Alto Adige, Mazzon. There are about five hectares of owned and rented land, which give rise to excellent wines made with just a few varieties. The vineyards are on the eastern slope of the valley, with Monte Prato del Re providing shade in the early hours of the day, while the afternoon the sun shines until evening. The 2014 Pinot Nero Riserva offers up intense notes of wild berries on the nose, refreshed by fines herbes and spices. In the mouth, its impact is sweet and round, spruced up at the end by a lovely silky tannic texture. The Lagrein, made with grapes cultivated in an old vineyard down in the valley, also delivered. Aromas of wild fruit, Parma violets and spices follow through onto a solid palate, which finds pressure thanks to its unexpected acidity. The Eva also came through. It's a Manzoni Bianco aged in steel that combines freshness and density.

★★Cantina di Caldaro

VIA CANTINE, 12
39052 CALDARO/KALTERN [BZ]
TEL. +39 0471963149
www.kellereikaltern.com

CELLAR SALES
PRE-BOOKED VISITS
ANNUAL PRODUCTION 3,400,000 bottles
HECTARES UNDER VINE 480.00

Until last year, the small town of Caldaro had two cooperatives which have since merged to create the new Cantina di Caldaro. Now there are 800 members running about 480 hectares of vineyards located throughout the province. This allows them to maintain a good supply of grapes grown in their ideal vinegrowing area, resulting in a wide range of top-quality wines. The most interesting wine of those tasted this year would have to be a Lago di Caldaro. The Pfarrhof has an intense but discreet appearance. Aromatically, it debuts with an intense note of morello cherry and then veers towards fines herbes and spices, concluding with a nice violet overtone. The palate is dry, savory and remarkably pleasant. The Passito Quintessenz is a Moscato Giallo with a supple and very long profile that plays on elegance and finesse.

● A. A. Lagrein V. V. '15	🍷🍷 3
● A. A. Pinot Nero Ris. '14	🍷🍷 5
○ Eva '16	🍷🍷 4
○ A. A. Gewürztraminer '16	🍷 4
○ A. A. Moscato Giallo V. T. Tilda '16	🍷 5
○ A. A. Gewürztraminer '14	🍷🍷 4
○ A. A. Gewürztraminer '11	🍷🍷 4
● A. A. Lagrein V. V. '12	🍷🍷 5
● A. A. Pinot Nero Ris. '13	🍷🍷 5
● A. A. Pinot Nero Ris. '12	🍷🍷 5
● A. A. Pinot Nero Ris. '11	🍷🍷 5
● A.A. Lagrein '13	🍷🍷 5
○ Eva '15	🍷🍷 4
○ Eva '14	🍷🍷 4

● A. A. Lago di Caldaro Cl. Sup. Pfarrhof '16	🍷🍷🍷 3*
○ A. A. Moscato Giallo Passito Quintessenz '14	🍷🍷 6
○ A. A. Sauvignon Stern '16	🍷🍷 3*
○ A. A. Gewürztraminer Campaner '16	🍷🍷 3
● A. A. Lago di Caldaro Cl. Sup. Leuchtenberg '16	🍷🍷 2*
○ A. A. Pinot Bianco Vial '16	🍷🍷 3
○ A. A. Sauvignon '16	🍷🍷 2*
○ A. A. Kerner Carned '16	🍷 3
● A. A. Lago di Caldaro Scelto Cl. Sup. Pfarrhof '13	🍷🍷🍷 3*
○ A. A. Moscato Giallo Passito Serenade '12	🍷🍷🍷 6
○ A. A. Moscato Giallo Passito Serenade '10	🍷🍷🍷 6

Castel Sallegg

v.lo di Sotto, 15
39052 Caldaro/Kaltern [BZ]
Tel. +39 0471963132
www.castelsallegg.it

CELLAR SALES
PRE-BOOKED VISITS
ANNUAL PRODUCTION 140,000 bottles
HECTARES UNDER VINE 30.00

The winery's cellars are concealed within the castle of the Kuenburg Counts, a stone's throw from the historic district of Caldaro. The vineyards span about 30 hectares in the Oltradige area, in the hills stretching from Caldaro to Appiano. They are divided into three main parts, with altitudes ranging from 250 meters from the lake, to 500 at Leisenhof, and 500 meters at Preyhof. They produce early-drinking wines that maintain the character of the varieties, and are drawn from the best grape selections in the region. The Bischofsleiten vineyard is in an excellent position for Schiava grapes, which are used to make a first-rate Lago di Caldaro. On the nose, we find close-focused red fruit, herbs and a subtle hint of spice. It expands in the mouth with suppleness and grip, making for a savory, succulent and pleasant palate. The Moscato Rosa, a late harvest wine with aromas of wild berries and sponge cake, also did well. Sweetness makes its presence felt, but is elegantly contrasted by acidity.

● A. A. Lago di Caldaro Cl. Sup. Bischofsleiten '16	▼▼ 3*
● A. A. Moscato Rosa V. T. '14	▼▼ 6
○ A. A. Gewürztraminer '16	▼▼ 3
● A. A. Lagrein '14	▼▼ 4
● A. A. Merlot Nussleiten '13	▼▼ 6
○ A. A. Pinot Bianco '16	▼▼ 3
○ A. A. Pinot Grigio '16	▼▼ 3
● A. A. Pinot Nero '15	▼▼ 3
● A. A. Pinot Nero Ris. '13	▼▼ 3
● A. A. Merlot Cabernet Chorus Madrigal '13	▼ 2
○ A. A. Moscato Giallo '16	▼ 3
○ A. A. Sauvignon '16	▼ 3
● A. A. Lago di Caldaro Scelto Sup. Bischofsleiten '15	▽▽▽ 2*
● A. A. Cabernet Sauvignon Ris. '13	▽▽ 3*

Castelfeder

via Portici, 11
39040 Egna/Neumarkt [BZ]
Tel. +39 0471820420
www.castelfeder.it

CELLAR SALES
PRE-BOOKED VISITS
ANNUAL PRODUCTION 400,000 bottles
HECTARES UNDER VINE 20.00

Alfons founded the Giovanett family winery in the South Tyrolean Unterland almost half a century ago. Today he works alongside his son Günter and the latest generation, Ivan and Ines, who handle production and sales, respectively. The vineyards are partly owned and partly cultivated by local vinegrowers. The grapes are delivered to Via Portici in Egna, where they are made into a wide range of wines. The Pinot Bianco Tecum performed well. It's a wine with aromas of white fruit and spices, with a slight hint of oak in the background. It's dry, tangy and long in the mouth, a perfect combination of elegance and power, warmth and precision. A memorable finish tops things off. The Sauvignon Burgum Novum, on the other hand, expresses a more mature and complex profile, while in the mouth it proves spirited with the cultivar's trademark finesse on full display.

○ A. A. Pinot Bianco Tecum '15	▼▼ 3*
○ A. A. Sauvignon Burgum Novum Ris. '14	▼▼ 2*
○ A. A. Chardonnay Burgum Novum Ris. '14	▼▼ 4
○ A. A. Gewürztraminer Vom Lehm '16	▼▼ 3
● A. A. Lagrein Burgum Novum '14	▼▼ 4
○ A. A. Pinot Grigio Glener '16	▼▼ 2*
● A. A. Pinot Nero Burgum Novum Ris. '14	▼▼ 5
○ Sauvignon Raif '16	▼▼ 3
○ A. A. Chardonnay Doss '16	▼ 3
○ A. A. Pinot Bianco Vom Stein '16	▼ 2
○ A. A. Pinot Grigio 15 '16	▼ 2
● A. A. Schiava Alte Reben '16	▼ 2
○ A. A. Pinot Bianco Tecum '10	▽▽▽ 3*
○ A. A. Pinot Bianco Tecum '14	▽▽ 3*

★★Cantina Colterenzio

LOC. CORNAIANO/GIRLAN
S.DA DEL VINO, 8
39057 APPIANO/EPPAN [BZ]
TEL. +39 0471664246
www.colterenzio.it

CELLAR SALES
PRE-BOOKED VISITS
ANNUAL PRODUCTION 1,600,000 bottles
HECTARES UNDER VINE 300.00
SUSTAINABLE WINERY

At the end of the last century, Colterenzio played a decisive role in helping South Tyrol to increase its level of quality. Today president Max Niedermayr and winemaker Martin Lemayr are working closely with staff toward multiple goals. Combining quality with ties to the territory, and at the same time striving for environmental sustainability in the vineyards as well as the cellar is foremost in the minds of everyone concerned. The great Chardonnay Lafóa! Colterenzio didn't miss the chance to produce a first-rate wine for the excellent 2015 vintage. Its intense, fruity notes on the nose are complemented by fresh flowers and a discreet touch of oak. The palate features power, precision and elegance right from the first sip. The Sauvignon of the same name is its usual monovaietal self, while the excellent Gewürztraminer Perelise also gives an admirable performance.

○ A. A. Chardonnay Lafóa '15	♟♟♟	5
○ A. A. Gewürztraminer Perelise '16	♟♟	5
○ A. A. Sauvignon Lafóa '15	♟♟	5
○ A. A. Chardonnay Altkirch '16	♟♟	2*
○ A. A. Gewürztraminer Lafóa '15	♟♟	5
● A. A. Lagrein Sigis Mundus '14	♟♟	5
○ A. A. Pinot Bianco Weisshaus '15	♟♟	3
○ A. A. Pinot Grigio Puiten '15	♟♟	3
● A. A. Pinot Nero Villa Nigra '15	♟♟	5
○ A. A. Sauvignon Prail '16	♟♟	3
● A. A. Schiava Menzen '16	♟	2
● A. A. Cabernet Sauvignon Lafóa '12	♟♟♟	7
● A. A. Cabernet Sauvignon Lafóa '11	♟♟♟	7
○ A. A. Sauvignon Lafóa '14	♟♟♟	5

★Cantina Cortaccia

LOC. BREITBACH
S.DA DEL VINO, 23
39040 CORTACCIA/KURTATSCH [BZ]
TEL. +39 0471880115
www.cantina-cortaccia.it

CELLAR SALES
PRE-BOOKED VISITS
ANNUAL PRODUCTION 1,300,000 bottles
HECTARES UNDER VINE 190.00
SUSTAINABLE WINERY

The Cortaccia winery is situated in a small village overlooking the Adige Valley, a few kilometers outside Bolzano. Kurtatsch's 190 members work mainly in the area surrounding the village, unlike other cooperatives where the members are distributed all over the province. Here they can take advantage of some of the best exposures -- Brenntal, Penon, Graun -- and situate the variety to best advantage for altitude. The result are wines that have an assertive character and remarkable fullness. The Gewürztraminer Brenntal proved exemplary during our tasting. It's a Riserva from the 2015 vintage whose nose sees the cultivar's joyous aromatic bounty on full display. In the mouth, however, the wine's territory of origin takes over, with a solid and powerful taste presided over by tangy acidity, thus keeping it on track for precision and length. The 2016 Müller Thurgau Graun also did well, with its fresh and penetrating aromas and its dry, juicy palate.

○ A. A. Gewürztraminer Brenntal Ris. '15	♟♟♟	5
● A. A. Cabernet Kirchhügel Ris. '14	♟♟	4
○ A. A. Müller Thurgau Graun '16	♟♟	3*
○ Aruna V. T. '15	♟♟	6
○ A. A. Bianco Amos '15	♟♟	5
● A. A. Merlot Brenntal Ris. '14	♟♟	6
● A. A. Merlot Cabernet Soma '14	♟♟	5
○ A. A. Pinot Bianco Hoftatt '16	♟♟	3
○ A. A. Sauvignon Kofl '15	♟♟	4
● A. A. Schiava Grigia Sonntaler '16	♟♟	3
○ A. A. Gewürztraminer Brenntal Ris. '14	♟♟♟	5
○ A. A. Gewürztraminer Brenntal Ris. '12	♟♟♟	5
● A. A. Cabernet Kirchhügel Ris. '13	♟♟	4
● A. A. Merlot Brenntal Ris. '13	♟♟	6

Hartmann Donà

VIA RAFFEIN, 8
39010 CERMES/TSCHERMS [BZ]
TEL. +39 3292610628
hartmann.dona@rolmail.net

ANNUAL PRODUCTION 35,000 bottles
HECTARES UNDER VINE 4.65

Hartman Donà is an innovative producer who created a winery not merely as a follower of winning winemaking models. Instead he lets each wine express its utmost potential by enhancing the attributes that vintage and terroir instill in the grapes, and by revealing a complexity only a long period in the cellar can allow. He accomplishes all this with a handful of hectares that supply the grapes for making consistent and expressive wines. The Donà Blanc is a blend of Pinot Bianco and Chardonnay that ferments and ages in oak for a couple of years before maturing in the bottle (for the length of time). On the nose, the ripeness of its fruit embraces fresh and vibrant flowers. In the mouth, it lengthens with tanginess and concludes with a dry and elegant finish. The Donà Noir is also very good. It's a Pinot Noir made in Cornaiano that highlights aromas of wild fruit and forest floor, with a palate full of character and elegance.

○ Donà Blanc '12	♥♥ 3*
○ A. A. Chardonnay '16	♥♥ 3
○ A. A. Gewürztraminer '16	♥♥ 3
● A. A. Lagrein '15	♥♥ 3
○ A.A. Sauvignon '16	♥♥ 3
○ Blanc de Rouge Extre Brut M. Cl.	♥♥ 3
● Donà Noir '12	♥♥ 3
● Donà Rouge '11	♥♥ 3
○ A.A. Pinot Bianco '16	♥ 3
○ A. A. Chardonnay '15	♥♥ 3
○ A. A. Gewürztraminer '15	♥♥ 3
● A. A. Pinot Nero '14	♥♥ 3
○ A. A. Sauvignon '15	♥♥ 3
● A.A. Pinot Nero Donà Noir '11	♥♥ 3*

Tenuta Donà

FRAZ. RIVA DI SOTTO
39057 APPIANO/EPPAN [BZ]
TEL. +39 0473221866
www.weingut-dona.com

CELLAR SALES
PRE-BOOKED VISITS
ACCOMMODATION
ANNUAL PRODUCTION 30,000 bottles
HECTARES UNDER VINE 6.00

After a long period working as Kellermeister at Burgräffler, Hansjörg Donà has taken over the reins of the family winery. Today, with his wife Martina and sons Josef and Martin, he works full-time on the wines. The winery is located in the Adige valley, just outside Bolzano on the road to Merano. They grow only a few varieties, focusing their wines to combine freshness and richness. The most interesting is 2016 Chardonnay which has intense notes of ripe yellow fruit, flowers and a faint hint of spice on the nose. In the mouth, it is dynamic and weighty, but maintains its suppleness and rigor. The 2016 Schiava is so good you won't want to stop drinking it. It offers up aromas of cherry and rose, while in the mouth richness of flavor adds lightness and grip, making for one of the area's best interpretations. The Lagrein is made with a very precise style. The palate is supported by tannins that are smooth but gutsy at the same time.

○ A. A. Terlano Chardonnay '16	♥♥ 4
● A. A. Lagrein '15	♥♥ 5
○ A. A. Sauvignon '16	♥♥ 5
● A. A. Schiava '16	♥♥ 3
● A. A. Lagrein '14	♥♥ 4
○ A. A. Sauvignon '15	♥♥ 3
● A. A. Schiava '14	♥♥ 2*
● A. A. Schiava '13	♥♥ 3
○ A. A. Terlano Chardonnay '15	♥♥ 3
○ A. A. Terlano Chardonnay '14	♥♥ 3
● A.A. Lagrein '13	♥♥ 4
● A.A. Lagrein '12	♥♥ 4
● A.A. Merlot - Lagrein '12	♥♥ 4

Tenuta Ebner
Florian Unterthiner

FRAZ. CAMPODAZZO, 18
39054 RENON/RITTEN [BZ]
TEL. +39 0471353386
www.weingutebner.it

CELLAR SALES
PRE-BOOKED VISITS
RESTAURANT SERVICE
ANNUAL PRODUCTION 20,000 bottles
HECTARES UNDER VINE 4.50

Florian and Brigitte Unterthiner run the family winery at Campodazzo, with about five hectares of vineyards spread out on the eastern slope of the Renon plateau, overlooking the Isarco Valley. Here, the south-facing vineyards are grown with red grape varieties, while the cooler and breezier ones facing southeast are planted with white grapes. The result are wines that perfectly respect features of each variety, and at the same time pursue richness and elegance. The Sauvignon features aromas of exotic fruit and flowers, with a green note that assertively elbows its way in from the background. It reveals great tanginess in the mouth, with a generous and long palate. The Gewürztraminer, on the other hand, expresses its usual suite of aromas: citrus, yellow fruit and spices, which follow through on the palate where the territorys' cool climate lets acidity make its presence felt. The Pinot Bianco is the complete opposite, opting for more pervasive sensations.

○ A. A. Pinot Bianco '16	🏆🏆 3
● A. A. Pinot Nero '16	🏆🏆 3
○ A. A. Sauvignon '16	🏆🏆 3
○ A. A. Valle Isarco Gewürztraminer '16	🏆🏆 4
○ A. A. Valle Isarco Grüner Veltliner '16	🏆 3
○ A. A. Pinot Bianco '15	🏆🏆 3
● A. A. Pinot Nero '14	🏆🏆 3
○ A. A. Sauvignon '15	🏆🏆 3*
○ A. A. Valle Isarco Gewürztraminer '15	🏆🏆 4
○ A. A. Valle Isarco Grüner Veltliner '15	🏆🏆 3*
○ A.A. Pinot Bianco '14	🏆🏆 3
○ A.A. Sauvignon '14	🏆🏆 3
○ A.A. Valle Isarco Veltliner '14	🏆🏆 3

Erbhof Unterganzner
Josephus Mayr

FRAZ. CARDANO
VIA CAMPIGLIO, 15
39053 BOLZANO/BOZEN
TEL. +39 0471365582
www.mayr-unterganzner.it

CELLAR SALES
PRE-BOOKED VISITS
ANNUAL PRODUCTION 65,000 bottles
HECTARES UNDER VINE 9.00

The Santa Maddalena area nestles between the center of Bolzano and the Isarco Valley, appearing as a cushion of vineyards that separates the heat of the plain from the coolness of the steep northern valley. This is where Josephus Mayr and his wife Barbara work as faithful but innovative interpreters of an old tradition. They run fewer than 10 hectares but with exacting care and attention toward the environment. Their grapes produce powerful Lagrein red wines, as well as white wines with fresh acidity. The 2014 Lagrein Riserva is this year's most impressive wine, with its intense aromas of wild fruit and spice, and a deep smoky note dominating the background. Its impact in the mouth is assertive and powerful, highlighting smooth tannins that are pleasantly rough at the same time. The Cabernet Riserva of the same vintage also performed well. It's rich in fruity and cocoa overtones, while the palate is striking for its grip and length.

● A. A. Cabernet Ris. '14	🏆🏆 5
● A. A. Lagrein Ris. '14	🏆🏆 5
○ A. A. Chardonnay Platt & Pignat '16	🏆🏆 3
● A. A. Santa Maddalena Cl. '16	🏆🏆 3
● Composition Reif '14	🏆🏆 6
● Lamarein '14	🏆🏆 6
○ Marie Josephine Passito '15	🏆🏆 6
● Sauvignon Platt & Pignat '16	🏆🏆 3
○ A. A. Kerner '16	🏆 3
⊙ A. A. Lagrein Kretzer Rosato V. T. '16	🏆 3
● A. A. Lagrein Ris. '13	🏆🏆🏆 5
● A. A. Lagrein Ris. '11	🏆🏆🏆 5
● A. A. Lagrein Scuro Ris. '05	🏆🏆🏆 4
● A. A. Lagrein Scuro Ris. '01	🏆🏆🏆 4
● Lamarein '05	🏆🏆🏆 6

ALTO ADIGE

★Falkenstein Franz Pratzner

VIA CASTELLO, 19
39025 NATURNO/NATURNS [BZ]
TEL. +39 0473666054
www.falkenstein.bz

CELLAR SALES
PRE-BOOKED VISITS
ANNUAL PRODUCTION 90,000 bottles
HECTARES UNDER VINE 12.00

The Val Venosta is by far the least-developed wine region in the province, with barely 100 hectares of vineyards. But area's low rainfall, combined with sunny days and cool nights, serves to produce high-profile wines, especially the aromatic Riesling. Franz Pratzner is one of the best-known producers in the area, recognized for his meticulous work in the vineyards and great sensitivity in the cellar. Once again Pratzner's most interesting wine is the Riesling. It offers up complex aromas, where exotic fruit and flowers let spicy notes and faint nuances of flint come through. In the mouth, it proves assertive and gutsy, and lengthens with grip and personality. The Pinot Bianco also did well, playing on ripe fruit and smoky, sulfurous notes that follow through onto a solid palate full of character.

○ A. A. Val Venosta Riesling '15	♟♟♟	5
○ A. A. Val Venosta Pinot Bianco '15	♟♟	5
● A. A. Val Venosta Pinot Nero '14	♟♟	5
○ A. A. Val Venosta Sauvignon '15	♟♟	4
○ A. A. Val Venosta Riesling '14	♟♟♟	5
○ A. A. Val Venosta Riesling '12	♟♟♟	5
○ A. A. Val Venosta Riesling '11	♟♟♟	5
○ A. A. Val Venosta Riesling '10	♟♟♟	5
○ A. A. Val Venosta Riesling '09	♟♟♟	5
○ A. A. Valle Venosta Riesling '13	♟♟♟	5
○ A. A. Val Venosta Pinot Bianco '14	♟♟	4
● A. A. Val Venosta Pinot Nero '12	♟♟	5
○ A. A. Valle Venosta Pinot Bianco '13	♟♟	4

Garlider
Christian Kerschbaumer

VIA UNTRUM, 20
39040 VELTURNO/FELDTHURNS [BZ]
TEL. +39 0472847296
www.garlider.it

CELLAR SALES
PRE-BOOKED VISITS
ANNUAL PRODUCTION 26,000 bottles
HECTARES UNDER VINE 4.20
VITICULTURE METHOD Certified Organic

The Isarco Valley is a small hotbed for big talent. Over the last few years vine growers have been coming to the area from extended farming backgrounds to make winegrowing the focus of their business Christian Kerschbaumer and his wife Veronika run a handful of hectares in Velturno on the right bank of the Isarco river, at altitudes ranging between 500 and 800 meters. Their organic farming techniques are now being used to produce rich, robust wines that have great personality. They have put forward a faultless range of wines this year, with a memorable version of the 2015 Sylvaner. On the nose, notes of iodine, Mediterranean scrub and flint are discernible. In the mouth, its fruit emerges assertively. But the wine also discloses unusual qualities of character and power that make it unforgettable. The Grüner Veltliner of the same vintage is initially concealed by its smokier notes, but these gradually give way to a whirlwind of aromas that follow through onto a dynamic, taut palate.

○ A. A. Valle Isarco Sylvaner '15	♟♟♟	3*
○ A. A. Valle Isarco Grüner Veltliner '15	♟♟	4
○ A. A. Valle Isarco Müller Thurgau '15	♟♟	3
○ A. A. Valle Isarco Sylvaner '14	♟♟♟	3*
○ A. A. Valle Isarco Sylvaner '13	♟♟♟	3*
○ A. A. Valle Isarco Sylvaner '09	♟♟♟	3*
○ A. A. Valle Isarco Veltliner '08	♟♟♟	3*
● A. A. Pinot Nero '12	♟♟	4
○ A. A. Valle Isarco Grüner Veltliner '14	♟♟	4
○ A. A. Valle Isarco Müller Thurgau '13	♟♟	3
● A. A. Valle Isarco Pinot Nero '10	♟♟	3
○ A. A. Valle Isarco Sylvaner '12	♟♟	3*
○ A. A. Valle Isarco Veltliner '13	♟♟	4
○ Pinot Grigio '13	♟♟	4

★Cantina Girlan

LOC. CORNAIANO/GIRLAN
VIA SAN MARTINO, 24
39057 APPIANO/EPPAN [BZ]
TEL. +39 0471662403
www.girlan.it

CELLAR SALES
PRE-BOOKED VISITS
ANNUAL PRODUCTION 1,500,000 bottles
HECTARES UNDER VINE 220.00

In the northernmost part of the Oltradige area, the Girlan winery has radically reinvented itself in the past 10 years to become one of the leading wineries in the South Tyrol. Gerhard Kofler has managed to bring out the best attributes of the region's historic varieties (Schiava, Pinot Nero, Pinot Bianco and Gewürztraminer) with an aim toward combining richness and elegance. Indeed, nothing is lacking in these wines. The cool 2014 vintage conferred incredible finesse to the winery's flagship, their Pinot Nero Trattmann Mazon. It's a Riserva that expresses aromas of fines herbes and wild fruit, with a supple and juicy palate perfectly supported by acidity. The Schiava Gschleier is an exemplary combination of complexity, approachability and pleasantness. There are a number of top wines here just waiting to be enjoyed.

● A. A. Pinot Nero Trattmann Mazon Ris. '14	🍷🍷🍷	5
○ A. A. Bianco Flora Ris. '14	🍷🍷	4
○ A. A. Pinot Bianco Flora Ris. '15	🍷🍷	2*
● A. A. Schiava Gschleier Alte Reben '15	🍷🍷	3*
○ A. A. Chardonnay Flora '15	🍷🍷	5
○ A. A. Gewürztraminer Flora '16	🍷🍷	6
○ A. A. Gewürztraminer V.T. Pasithea Oro '15	🍷🍷	6
● A. A. Lagrein Sandbichler Ris. H. Lun '14	🍷🍷	5
● A. A. Moscato Rosa V. T. Pasithea Rosa '15	🍷🍷	5
○ A. A. Pinot Bianco Plattenriegl '16	🍷🍷	3
○ A. A. Pinot Bianco Sanbichler H. Lun. '16	🍷🍷	3
● A. A. Pinot Nero Sanbichler Ris. H. Lun '14	🍷🍷	3
○ A. A. Sauvignon Flora '15	🍷🍷	4
● A. A. Schiava Faß N° 9 '16	🍷🍷	2*

Glögglhof - Franz Gojer

FRAZ. SANTA MADDALENA
VIA RIVELLONE, 1
39100 BOLZANO/BOZEN
TEL. +39 0471978775
www.gojer.it

CELLAR SALES
PRE-BOOKED VISITS
ACCOMMODATION
ANNUAL PRODUCTION 55,000 bottles
HECTARES UNDER VINE 7.40

When you leave Bolzano and follow the Isarco river upstream, before entering the long, narrow valley and looking to the left you can see a series of gentle hills that form the historic Santa Maddalena area. The Gojer family has been working here for generations and know well how to get the best from the Bolzano appellation. Through the years they have developed their vineyards and searched upstream all the way to Cornedo to find the most suitable areas for freshness necessary for their white grape varieties. The Santa Maddalena always gets your heart racing, especially with this high-profile 2016 Rondell. The nose sees the wine's classic aromas of wild fruit and spices, but in the mouth it changes gear. Lightness, saltiness and richness meld in a succulent and elegant palate that makes you want to keep drinking. The Lagrein is the complete opposite, offering a close-knit and deep suite of aromas, which develop powerfully and assertively in the mouth.

● A. A. Santa Maddalena Cl. Rondell '16	🍷🍷🍷	3*
● A. A. Lagrein '14	🍷🍷	3*
○ A. A. Kerner Karneid '16	🍷🍷	3
● A. A. Santa Maddalena Cl. '16	🍷🍷	2*
● A. A. Schiava Alte Reben '16	🍷🍷	2*
○ A.A. Pinot Bianco Karneid '16	🍷🍷	3
● Pipa XIV	🍷🍷	3
○ A. A. Sauvignon Karneid '16	🍷	2
● A. A. Lagrein Ris. '12	🍷🍷	4
○ A. A. Pinot Bianco Karneid '15	🍷🍷	3
● A. A. Santa Maddalena Cl. '15	🍷🍷	2*
● A. A. Santa Maddalena Cl. Rondell '14	🍷🍷	3*
● A. A. Vernatsch Alte Reben '15	🍷🍷	2*

Griesbauerhof
Georg Mumelter
VIA RENCIO, 66
39100 BOLZANO/BOZEN
TEL. +39 0471973090
www.griesbauerhof.it

CELLAR SALES
PRE-BOOKED VISITS
ANNUAL PRODUCTION 30,000 bottles
HECTARES UNDER VINE 3.80

For generations, the Mumelter family have been running the Griesbauerhof farm at the foot of the hills that make up the Santa Maddalena area. The estate has been the core of the family business for over two centuries. They developed the vinegrowing side of the business by expanding the vineyards, adding to the main estate with the purchase of small plots of land in the Spitz and Moritzing areas on the edge of the regional capital, as well as Weißhaus in Appiano. There's great focus on Mumelter's Lagrein, where even the simplest version proves pleasant, thanks to the excellent 2016 vintage. An explosion of red fruit and spices on the nose follows through onto a generous and succulent palate. The Riserva, on the other hand, features more closed aromas that need to be sought after. In the mouth, the wine reveals power and grip, with a dynamic palate that's full of character.

Gummerhof - Malojer
VIA WEGGESTEIN, 36
39100 BOLZANO/BOZEN
TEL. +39 0471972885
www.malojer.it

CELLAR SALES
PRE-BOOKED VISITS
ANNUAL PRODUCTION 100,000 bottles
HECTARES UNDER VINE 18.00

The Malojer family winery is in the north of Bolzano, virtually at the entrance to the narrow and winding Val Sarentino where houses give way to vines. The family has run the Gummerhof farm for generations and the wine estate has been around for over 500 years. They produce the wines characteristic of the Bolzano plain, Lagrein and Santa Maddalena, combining fullness with elegance. The 2014 Lagrein Riserva performed quite well. On the nose, it displays its signature aromas of ripe black fruit, spices and fines herbes, with a rich intense note of bitter chocolate lurking in the background. In the mouth, it expresses fullness and power and tenses up with its dense tannic texture. The Gewürztraminer Kui also delivered with its trademark aromas. It's a wine that draws you in when tasting, due to a commendable balance between richness and grip.

● A. A. Cabernet Sauvignon Ris. '14	♟♟ 3
● A. A. Lagrein '16	♟♟ 3
● A. A. Lagrein Ris. '14	♟♟ 5
● A. A. Merlot Spitz '15	♟♟ 3
○ A. A. Pinot Bianco '15	♟♟ 3
○ A. A. Pinot Grigio '16	♟♟ 3
● Schiava Isarcus '15	♟♟ 3
⊙ A. A. Merlot Rosé '16	♟ 3
● A. A. Santa Maddalena Cl. '16	♟ 2
● A. A. Lagrein Ris. '09	♟♟♟ 5
● A. A. Cabernet Sauvignon Ris. '13	♟♟ 3
● A. A. Lagrein '13	♟♟ 3*
● A. A. Lagrein Ris. '13	♟♟ 5
● A. A. Merlot Spitz '14	♟♟ 3

● A. A. Lagrein Ris. '14	♟♟ 4
○ A. A. Bianco Cuvée Bautzanum '16	♟♟ 4
● A. A. Cabernet Lagrein Bautzanum Cuvée Ris. '14	♟♟ 4
● A. A. Cabernet Ris. '14	♟♟ 4
○ A. A. Gewürztraminer Kui '16	♟♟ 3
● A. A. Lagrein Gummerhof zu Gries '15	♟♟ 3
○ A. A. Pinot Bianco Kreiter '16	♟♟ 3
○ A. A. Pinot Grigio Gur zu Sand '16	♟♟ 3
○ A. A. Sauvignon Gur zur Sand '16	♟♟ 3
○ A. A. Chardonnay Justinus '16	♟ 3
● A. A. Pinot Nero Gstrein '16	♟ 3
● A. A. Santa Maddalena Cl. Loamer '16	♟ 2
● A. A. Lagrein Gries '09	♟♟♟ 2*
● A. A. Lagrein Gummerhof zu Gries '14	♟♟ 3*
● A. A. Lagrein Ris. '12	♟♟ 4

Gumphof
Markus Prackwieser

LOC. NOVALE DI PRESULE, 8

39050 FIÈ ALLO SCILIAR/VÖLS AM SCHLERN [BZ]
TEL. +39 0471601190
www.gumphof.it

CELLAR SALES
PRE-BOOKED VISITS
ANNUAL PRODUCTION 45,000 bottles
HECTARES UNDER VINE 5.00

Markus Prackwieser's winery is situated in Novale di Presule, a small village in the Isarco Valley where the river flowing from Brennero makes a sharp turn westward, just before merging with the Adige. The vineyards span a few hectares at an altitude of 500 meters, on the southwest facing slope of the valley. The daytime heat and cool evenings produce perfectly-ripened grapes that maintain their elegance and finesse in the glass. Prackweiser's flagship line, Renaissance, is only reserved for high profile vintages (like 2014 for Markus). The Sauvignon is quite closed on the nose, with sulfurous notes that slowly let gooseberries and flowers emerge. In the mouth, the wine proves to have merged perfectly with oak. The palate is taut and sophisticated. The 2016 Sauvignon Praesulis features a more approachable, energetic aromatic expression, and a supple, racy palate.

★Franz Haas

VIA VILLA, 6
39040 MONTAGNA/MONTAN [BZ]
TEL. +39 0471812280
www.franz-haas.it

CELLAR SALES
PRE-BOOKED VISITS
ANNUAL PRODUCTION 350,000 bottles
HECTARES UNDER VINE 55.00
SUSTAINABLE WINERY

Franz Haas defies the stereotype that people from South Tyrol are quiet and reserved. Rather, a tireless, versatile and visionary producer, Haas doesn't miss a chance to talk about his ambitions and the projects he is working on, whether it is the new cellar or the vineyards planted high up in the mountains. The wide range of wines includes classic varietals, as well as his own personal take on local grape varieties in the South Tyrol territory. Franz's Pinot Nero Schweizer is back on top. Made with a selection of grapes from four different vineyards at altitudes ranging from 350 to 700 meters, the wine offers up intense notes of wild berries and medicinal herbs on the nose, while the mouth features a perfect union between the sweetness of its fruit, acidity and its delicate tannic texture. The Manna, a blend of five grape varieties, also fared well, with its elegant aromas and long, well-balanced palate.

○ A. A. Sauvignon Renaissance '14	♛♛♛ 4*
○ A. A. Sauvignon Praesulis '16	♛♛ 4
○ A. A. Pinot Bianco Mediaevum '16	♛♛ 2*
○ A. A. Pinot Bianco Praesulis '16	♛♛ 3
○ A. A. Pinot Bianco Renaissance '14	♛♛ 6
● A. A. Pinot Nero Praesulis '15	♛♛ 5
● A. A. Pinot Nero Renaissance '13	♛♛ 5
○ A. A. Gewürztraminer Praesulis '16	♛ 4
● A. A. Schlava Mediaevum '16	♛ 3
○ A. A. Pinot Bianco Praesulis '15	♛♛♛ 3*
○ A. A. Pinot Bianco Praesulis '14	♛♛♛ 3*
○ A. A. Sauvignon Praesulis '13	♛♛♛ 4*
○ A. A. Sauvignon Praesulis '09	♛♛♛ 3
○ A. A. Sauvignon Praesulis '07	♛♛♛ 3*

● A. A. Pinot Nero Schweizer '13	♛♛♛ 6
● A. A. Moscato Rosa '15	♛♛ 5
○ Manna '15	♛♛ 5
○ A. A. Gewürztraminer '16	♛♛ 4
○ A. A. Pinot Bianco Lepus '16	♛♛ 3
● A. A. Pinot Nero '15	♛♛ 5
○ A. A. Sauvignon '15	♛♛ 5
○ A. A. Moscato Giallo '16	♛ 5
● A. A. Moscato Rosa '12	♛♛♛ 5
● A. A. Moscato Rosa '11	♛♛♛ 5
○ A. A. Sauvignon '13	♛♛♛ 5
○ Manna '07	♛♛♛ 4
○ Manna '05	♛♛♛ 4
○ A. A. Sauvignon '14	♛♛ 5
○ Manna '14	♛♛ 5

Haderburg

FRAZ. BUCHOLZ
LOC. POCHI, 30
39040 SALORNO/SALURN [BZ]
TEL. +39 0471889097
www.haderburg.it

CELLAR SALES
PRE-BOOKED VISITS
ANNUAL PRODUCTION 100,000 bottles
HECTARES UNDER VINE 12.00
VITICULTURE METHOD Certified Biodynamic

Alois Ochsenreiter's winery is located in
Pochi di Salorno in a dominant position on
the plain between Alto Adige and Trentino.
Half a century has gone by since the first
bottles were laid down in the cellar of the
house, and today Haderburg is one of the
most important sparkling winemaking
producers in the province. The 10 hectares
of vineyards just outside the house are
grown under biodynamic management and
recently the winery purchased additional
vineyards in the cooler Isarco Valley. Their
excellent Brut expresses the brightness of
this territory. Intense aromas of white fruit,
melba toast and dried flowers are
embellished by a subtle mineral note that
follows through onto the wine's dry, gutsy,
taut and very long palate. Of the still wines,
we particularly enjoyed the Pinot Grigio
Hausmannhof, which contrasts aromas of
ripe yellow fruit with a dry, but rich and
powerful palate, just as we would expect
from this variety.

○ A. A. Spumante Brut	♟♟ 5
○ A. A. Gewürztraminer Hausmannhof '16	♟♟ 4
● A. A. Merlot Cabernet Erah '13	♟♟ 5
○ A. A. Pinot Grigio Hausmannhof '16	♟♟ 5
● A. A. Pinot Nero Hausmannhof '15	♟♟ 5
○ A. A. Spumante Pas Dosé '13	♟♟ 4
○ A. A. Spumante Hausmannhof Brut Ris. '07	♟♟ 5
○ A. A. Chardonnay Hausmannhof '16	♟ 3
○ A. A. Valle Isarco Sylvaner Obermairlhof '05	♟♟♟ 3*
● A. A. Merlot - Cabernet Sauvignon Erah Hausmannhof '11	♟♟ 5
● A. A. Merlot-Cabernet Sauvignon Erah Hausmannhof '12	♟♟ 5
● A. A. Pinot Nero Hausmannhof Ris. '13	♟♟ 6
○ A. A. Spumante Hausmannhof Brut Ris. '06	♟♟ 5

Kettmeir

VIA DELLE CANTINE, 4
39052 CALDARO/KALTERN [BZ]
TEL. +39 0471963135
www.kettmeir.com

CELLAR SALES
PRE-BOOKED VISITS
ANNUAL PRODUCTION 330,000 bottles
HECTARES UNDER VINE 41.00

Going up from Lake Kaltern and looking
northward to the right of a small hollow
stands Kettmeir, a large structure perfectly
integrated into the South Tyrol landscape.
Joseph Romen runs it like a conductor in
which each member of the orchestra
carries out his task to perfection. As each
delivers his harvest to the cellar, Kettmeir
earmarks it for the most suitable wine.
Their most ambitious wines come from the
areas of Pochi di Salorno, Caldaro and
Soprabolzano. For some years now, the
winery in Via delle Cantine has been
moving into high gear and today it's
reaping the benefits of their meticulous,
ceaseless work. The 2015 Pinot Bianco
Athesis offers up elegant aromas, in which
oak melds perfectly with notes of ripe white
fruit and flowers. In the mouth, the wine
expands gracefully for a memorable and
long finish. The Spumante Brut 1919
Riserva also performed exceptionally well.
It's a blend of Chardonnay and Pinot Nero,
with great fullness and power, and a tangy,
lustrous finish.

○ A. A. Spumante Brut 1919 M. Cl. Ris. '11	♟♟♟ 6
○ A. A. Pinot Bianco Athesis '15	♟♟ 4
○ A. A. Chardonnay '16	♟♟ 3
○ A. A. Chardonnay Maso Reiner '15	♟♟ 4
○ A. A. Gewürztraminer '16	♟♟ 3
○ A. A. Müller Thurgau '16	♟♟ 3
○ A. A. Pinot Bianco '16	♟♟ 3
● A. A. Pinot Nero Athesis '14	♟♟ 5
○ A. A. Spumante Brut Athesis '14	♟♟ 4
⊙ A. A. Spumante Rosé Brut Athesis '14	♟♟ 5
⊙ A. A. Lagrein Rosé '16	♟ 2
○ A. A. Sauvignon '16	♟ 3
○ A. A. Müller Thurgau Athesis '15	♟♟ 4
○ A. A. Pinot Bianco Athesis '14	♟♟ 3*
○ A. A. Sauvignon '15	♟♟ 3*

Tenuta Klosterhof
Oskar Andergassen

LOC. CLAVENZ, 40
39052 CALDARO/KALTERN [BZ]
TEL. +39 0471961046
www.garni-klosterhof.com

CELLAR SALES
PRE-BOOKED VISITS
ACCOMMODATION AND RESTAURANT SERVICE
ANNUAL PRODUCTION 38,000 bottles
HECTARES UNDER VINE 5.00

The Andergassen family cellar is a stone's throw from the center of Caldaro where the vineyards span five hectares spread among three different areas. In Pianizza di Sopra in the Trifal vineyard, they grow Merlot and the white varieties. In the center of town, in the Panigl vineyard, is found Pinot Nero, and towards the Kaltern lake in the Plataditsch area, Schiava rules the roost. The 2014 Pinot Nero Panigl gave a brilliant performance, expressing all the class of its terroir of origin. Its intense aromas of wild berries are accompanied by a lovely smoky and mineral note in the background. In the mouth, the wine proves full, juicy and elegantly long. The Riserva of the same vintage is richer and more solid, while for the whites, we particularly appreciated the fragrant 2016 Pinot Bianco Acapella. Faint aromas of flowers and white fruit follow through onto a dry palate with good grip.

★Köfererhof
Günther Kerschbaumer

FRAZ. NOVACELLA
VIA PUSTERIA, 3
39040 VARNA/VAHRN [BZ]
TEL. +39 3474778009
www.koefererhof.it

CELLAR SALES
PRE-BOOKED VISITS
RESTAURANT SERVICE
ANNUAL PRODUCTION 80,000 bottles
HECTARES UNDER VINE 10.00

The Kerschbaumer family winery is one of the northernmost in the country. It spans about 10 hectares in Novacella, a few kilometers from the entrance to the Puster Valley in the Alps. Bright days and wide temperature ranges give the grapes natural freshness and finesse, which Günther then transforms into a range of wines having exceptional grip. The full and robust Pinot Grigio stands alongside the more characteristic grapes of the valley. The Sylvaner is in usual form. It's a white wine with aromas of white fruit, a lovely note of Mediterranean scrub and dried flowers (for some depth). The palate is tangy and taut with great length. The Grüner Veltliner also proved impressive, expressing more approachable ripe fruit that follows through on the palate with power and fullness. The Riesling appears to be more youthful on the nose, revealing a juicy suppleness in the mouth.

● A. A. Pinot Nero Panigl '14	♟♟ 5
● A. A. Lago di Caldaro Cl. Sup. Plantaditsch '16	♟♟ 2*
● A. A. Pinot Bianco Acapella '16	♟♟ 3
● A. A. Pinot Nero Ris. '14	♟♟ 4
● A. A. Moscato Giallo Birnbaum '16	♟ 3
● A. A. Merlot Ris. '12	♟♟ 4
● A. A. Pinot Bianco Trifall '15	♟♟ 3
● A. A. Pinot Nero Panigl '13	♟♟ 5
● A. A. Pinot Nero Panigl '12	♟♟ 5
● A. A. Pinot Nero Ris. '13	♟♟ 4
● A. A. Lago di Caldaro Cl. Sup. Plantaditsch '14	♟♟ 2*
● A. A. Lago di Caldaro Cl. Sup. Plantaditsch R '12	♟♟ 3*
● A. A. Pinot Bianco Trifall '13	♟♟ 3*
● A. A. Pinot Bianco V. T. '14	♟♟ 4

○ A. A. Valle Isarco Sylvaner '16	♟♟♟ 3*
○ A. A. Valle Isarco Grüner Veltliner '15	♟♟ 4
○ A. A. Valle Isarco Riesling '15	♟♟ 5
○ A. A. Valle Isarco Gewürztraminer '16	♟♟ 4
○ A. A. Valle Isarco Kerner '16	♟♟ 3
○ A. A. Valle Isarco Müller Thurgau '16	♟♟ 3
○ A. A. Valle Isarco Pinot Grigio '16	♟♟ 3
○ A. A. Valle Isarco Sylvaner R '15	♟♟ 5
○ A. A. Valle Isarco Pinot Grigio '15	♟♟♟ 3*
○ A. A. Valle Isarco Pinot Grigio '13	♟♟♟ 3*
○ A. A. Valle Isarco Pinot Grigio '12	♟♟♟ 3*
○ A. A. Valle Isarco Pinot Grigio '11	♟♟♟ 3*
○ A. A. Valle Isarco Pinot Grigio '09	♟♟♟ 3*
○ A. A. Valle Isarco Riesling '10	♟♟♟ 4
○ A. A. Valle Isarco Sylvaner R '13	♟♟♟ 5
○ A. A. Valle Isarco Sylvaner R '09	♟♟♟ 4

Tenuta Kornell

FRAZ. SETTEQUERCE
VIA COSMA E DAMIANO, 6
39010 TERLANO/TERLAN [BZ]
TEL. +39 0471917507
www.kornell.it

CELLAR SALES
PRE-BOOKED VISITS
ANNUAL PRODUCTION 120,000 bottles
HECTARES UNDER VINE 15.00

Florian Brigl runs the family winery in
Settequerce, a small village on the outskirts
of Bolzano on the way to Terlano. It is a vast
flat area at an altitude of over 250 meters,
skimming the hills and where the vineyards
slowly rise a hundred meters. The daytime
heat is countered by the cool winds coming
down from the Alps, creating an
environment that is at the same time
Mediterranean and Alpine. In all, there are
about fifteen hectares, which are divided up
between the main part, Gries, and Appiano
Monte. Given the location of their vineyards,
only a Lagrein could star here. The Staves
is a Riserva from the 2014 vintage, with
aromas of black fruit, spices and fines
herbes. The mouth is powerful and dense,
but acidity manages to add lightness and
grip. The 2015 Sauvignon Oberberg is also
very good. It's a selection that ages only in
steel, with intense aromas of citrus and
sage on the nose, and a dry palate with
good length.

● A. A. Lagrein Staves Ris. '14	♥♥♥	5
○ A. A. Sauvignon Oberberg '16	♥♥	6
○ A. A. Gewürztraminer Damian '16	♥♥	4
● A. A. Lagrein Greif '16	♥♥	3
● A. A. Merlot Staves Ris. '14	♥♥	5
○ A. A. Pinot Bianco Eich '16	♥♥	4
● A.A. Cabernet Staves Ris. '14	♥♥	5
○ A.A. Pinot Grigio Gris '16	♥♥	4
● Zeder '15	♥♥	3
○ A. A. Sauvignon Cosmas '16	♥	3
● A.A. Pinot Nero Marit '16	♥	4
● A. A. Lagrein Staves Ris. '12	♥♥♥	5
○ A. A. Gewürztraminer Damian '15	♥♥	3
● A. A. Merlot Staves Ris. '13	♥♥	5
○ A. A. Sauvignon Oberberg '15	♥♥	3

★Kuenhof - Peter Pliger

LOC. LA MARA, 110
39042 BRESSANONE/BRIXEN [BZ]
TEL. +39 0472850546
pliger.kuenhof@rolmail.net

CELLAR SALES
PRE-BOOKED VISITS
ANNUAL PRODUCTION 38,000 bottles
HECTARES UNDER VINE 6.00
SUSTAINABLE WINERY

The Kuenhof farm has been around for
more than 800 years, and the Pliger family
have been running it for two centuries.
Peter and his wife Brigitte started bottling
their own wine about thirty years ago.
Today the winery is a benchmark for lovers
of white wines from the Isarco Valley. They
have six hectares of vineyards in Mara on
the outskirts of Bressanone, at altitudes
ranging from 500 to 700 meters. The
wines they are producing stand out for their
grip and richness of flavor. The 2016
vintage, with its light, heat and temperature
swings, enabled the winery to produce a
great version of the Riesling Kaiton. Its
aromas are still quite youthful, with white
fruit giving way to floral and delicately
vegetal notes. In the mouth, however, the
wine shows what it's made of right off the
bat, proving assertive and pure, with acidity
and tanginess taking control right from the
start. The palate proves dry with an
incredible and seemingly endless grip.

○ A. A. Valle Isarco Riesling Kaiton '16	♥♥♥	3
○ A. A. Valle Isarco Sylvaner '16	♥♥	3
○ A. A. Valle Isarco Gewürztraminer '16	♥♥	3
○ A. A. Valle Isarco Grüner Veltliner '16	♥♥	3
○ A. A. Valle Isarco Grüner Veltliner '15	♥♥♥	3
○ A. A. Valle Isarco Riesling Kaiton '12	♥♥♥	4
○ A. A. Valle Isarco Riesling Kaiton '11	♥♥♥	4
○ A. A. Valle Isarco Riesling Kaiton '10	♥♥♥	4
○ A. A. Valle Isarco Sylvaner '14	♥♥♥	3
○ A. A. Valle Isarco Sylvaner '13	♥♥♥	3
○ A. A. Valle Isarco Sylvaner '08	♥♥♥	3
○ A. A. Valle Isarco Veltliner '09	♥♥♥	3

Laimburg

Loc. Laimburg, 6
39040 Vadena/Pfatten [BZ]
Tel. +39 0471969590
www.laimburg.bz.it

CELLAR SALES
PRE-BOOKED VISITS
ANNUAL PRODUCTION 100,000 bottles
HECTARES UNDER VINE 20.00
SUSTAINABLE WINERY

More than just a winery, Laimburg is a
research center dedicated to developing
agriculture throughout the province of
Bolzano where vinegrowing is one of the
main activities in the region. Twenty-five
years ago the winery created a new cellar
dug out of the rock and their 20 hectares of
vineyards are located to great advantage in
the best areas. Products from the winery
range from the Vini del Podere, with
simple varietal wines, to the Selezione del
Maniero ones that are more ambitious.
The 2015 Saphir did quite well. It's a
Sauvignon Passito the color of antique gold.
On the nose, we find aromas of saffron,
candied citrus fruit, spices and licorice,
while in the mouth the wine proves to have
great sweetness and unexpected
tanginess, which lighten and embellish the
palate. The Lago di Caldaro Vernacius
Solemnis benefits from partial overripening
on the vine, which confers aromas of
cherry and spice that follow through onto a
dry and well-balanced palate.

● A. A. Lago di Caldaro Cl. Sup.	
Vernacius Solemnis '16	♟♟ 3*
○ A. A. Sauvignon Passito Saphir '15	♟♟ 6
● A. A. Cabernet Sauvignon	
Sass Roà Ris. '14	♟♟ 5
○ A. A. Gewürztraminer Elyònd Ris. '15	♟♟ 5
● A. A. Lagrein Barbagòl Ris. '14	♟♟ 5
● A. A. Merlot Ris. '15	♟♟ 4
○ A. A. Pinot Bianco '16	♟♟ 2*
○ A. A. Riesling '16	♟♟ 4
○ A. A. Sauvignon Oyèll Ris. '15	♟♟ 4
● Col de Réy '12	♟♟ 6
○ Aurona '14	♟ 5
● A. A. Cabernet Sauvignon	
Sass Roà Ris. '13	♟♟ 5
○ A. A. Sauvignon Oyèll Ris. '14	♟♟ 4
○ A. A. Sauvignon Passito Saphir '14	♟♟ 6

Loacker Schwarhof

Loc. Sanct Justina, 3
39100 Bolzano/Bozen
Tel. +39 0471365125
www.loacker.bio

CELLAR SALES
PRE-BOOKED VISITS
ANNUAL PRODUCTION 60,000 bottles
HECTARES UNDER VINE 7.00
VITICULTURE METHOD Certified Organic
SUSTAINABLE WINERY

At the entrance to the Isarco Valley there is
a series of hills on the left that form the
heart of the Santa Maddalena area. Here in
the Sanct Justina district, you can find the
Loacker family winery, spread over a
handful of hectares and grown under
biodynamic management. The wines get
their undeniable character from the
best-known varieties in the region, Lagrein
and Gewürztraminer stand out. Interesting
expressions from Merlot and Cabernet are
placed as well as part of their offerings. The
2015 Gran Lareyn is a Lagrein-based red
with deep and elegant aromas, where
signature nuances of spice and wild fruit
are discernible, and smoky, mineral notes
lurk in the background. Its impact in the
mouth is powerful, but acidity immediately
adds grip and suppleness, making for a
palate with a long finish. The Merlot Ywain
exhibits a similar style, with aromas
focused on ripe red fruit and floral notes.

● Lagrein Gran Lareyn '15	♟♟ 4
● Merlot Ywain '14	♟♟ 4
● A. A. Santa Maddalena Cl. Morit '16	♟♟ 3
○ Chardonnay Ateyon '15	♟♟ 4
○ Kastlet '14	♟♟ 5
○ Sauvignon Blanc Tasnim '16	♟♟ 4
● A. A. Merlot Ywain '04	♟♟♟ 4*
● A. A. Cabernet Lagrein Kastlet '13	♟♟ 4
● A. A. Lagrein Gran Lareyn Ris. '13	♟♟ 4
○ Chardonnay '14	♟♟ 4
● Kastlet '12	♟♟ 5
● Lagrein Gran Lareyn '14	♟♟ 4
● Merlot Ywain '13	♟♟ 4

Manincor

loc. San Giuseppe al Lago, 4
39052 Caldaro/Kaltern [BZ]
Tel. +39 0471960230
www.manincor.com

CELLAR SALES
PRE-BOOKED VISITS
ANNUAL PRODUCTION 330,000 bottles
HECTARES UNDER VINE 50.00
VITICULTURE METHOD Certified Biodynamic
SUSTAINABLE WINERY

Wending your way up the wine route from the lake to Caldaro, you chance upon the entrance to Manincor, the estate of the Goëss-Enzemberg Counts. Behind the gates stands the old villa, while the new cellar is found entirely underground. Look carefully or you will miss the entrance. The care and attention that went into creating the cellar shows the enormous respect the owners have for the territory. Underlining this high regard is the decision to use only biodynamic viticulture in the estate's vineyards and fruit orchards. The Sauvignon Lieben Aich offers up enticing aromas of flowers and exotic fruit. The palate is characterized by well-integrated oak and great length, but it changes pace here, combining power with elegance, depth with balance. Le Petit is made with spontaneously fermented grapes picked at the end of January. It offers up aromas of candied citrus fruit and botrytis, while in the mouth the wine balance sweetness, acidity and structure virtually perfectly.

○ A. A. Terlano Réserve della Contessa '16	🍷🍷	3*
○ A. A. Terlano Sauvignon Lieben Aich '15	🍷🍷	7
○ Le Petit '15	🍷🍷	8
● A. A. Pinot Nero Mason '15	🍷🍷	5
○ A. A. Terlano Chardonnay Sophie '15	🍷🍷	5
○ A. A. Terlano Sauvignon Tannenberg '15	🍷🍷	5
● Cassiano '15	🍷🍷	6
○ A. A. Terlano Pinot Bianco Eichhorn '15	🍷🍷🍷	5
○ A. A. Terlano Pinot Bianco Eichhorn '13	🍷🍷🍷	5
○ A. A. Terlano Pinot Bianco Eichhorn '12	🍷🍷🍷	5
○ A. A. Terlano Pinot Bianco Eichhorn '10	🍷🍷🍷	4
○ A. A. Terlano Pinot Bianco Eichhorn '09	🍷🍷🍷	4
○ A. A. Terlano Sauvignon '08	🍷🍷🍷	4
○ A. A. Terlano Sauvignon Tannenberg '13	🍷🍷🍷	5

K. Martini & Sohn

loc. Cornaiano
via Lamm, 28
39057 Appiano/Eppan [BZ]
Tel. +39 0471663156
www.martini-sohn.it

CELLAR SALES
PRE-BOOKED VISITS
ANNUAL PRODUCTION 230,000 bottles
HECTARES UNDER VINE 30.00

The Martini family's forty-year-old winery is located in the small village of Cornaiano, in the heart of the Oltradige area. They personally run the thirty hectares of vineyards and produce grapes to make high-end wines. Their range is divided into different lines to draw out the best from the territory. Aromatic and fresh wines that highlight the features of the variety are offered, as well as more ambitious selections that express the quintessential qualities of the territory. The 2016 Sauvignon Palladium made it to our finals with its intense aromas of tropical fruit and sage. In the mouth the wine proves tangy and dry, and offers great length. The 2015 Chardonnay Maturum, on the other hand, is striking for its integrity and liveliness. The palate comes through incredibly well-balanced and pleasant. As for the reds, we particularly appreciated the aromatic scent and elegance of taste of the 2015 Pinot Nero Palladium.

○ A. A. Sauvignon Palladium '16	🍷🍷	3*
○ A. A. Chardonnay Maturum '15	🍷🍷	4
○ A. A. Chardonnay Palladium '16	🍷🍷	3
○ A. A. Pinot Bianco Palladium '16	🍷🍷	2*
● A. A. Pinot Nero Palladium '15	🍷🍷	3
● A. A. Schiava Palladium '16	🍷🍷	2*
● Coldirus Palladium '15	🍷🍷	3
○ A. A. Gewürztraminer Palladium '16	🍷	4
○ A. A. Kerner Palladium '16	🍷	2
⊙ A. A. Lagrein Rosé '16	🍷	2
○ A. A. Moscato Giallo '16	🍷	4
○ A. A. Müller Thurgau Palladium '16	🍷	3
○ A. A. Sauvignon Palladium '04	🍷🍷🍷	2*
○ A. A. Pinot Bianco Palladium '15	🍷🍷	2*

Maso Hemberg Klaus Lentsch

S.DA REINSPERG, 18A
39057 APPIANO/EPPAN [BZ]
TEL. +39 0471967263
www.klauslentsch.eu

CELLAR SALES
PRE-BOOKED VISITS
ANNUAL PRODUCTION 50,000 bottles
HECTARES UNDER VINE 6.00

Klaus Lentsch's vineyards span just a few hectares in some of the best areas of the province. Putting down roots first in Campodazzo in the Isarco Valley, he has now expanded into other parts of Otradige. His production is limited but with excellent quality and full of personality. Klaus follows closely all production stages of his wines in the San Paolo cellar, which is nestled in the heart of his vineyards. The 2015 Lagrein Amperg Riserva, made with grapes cultivated in the South Tyrolean Unterland, offers up aromas of forest floor and rain-soaked earth, with red fruit slowly taking center stage. In the mouth, its richness of flavor and power are striking, but well-governed by rough tannins. From the whites, we enjoyed the Sauvignon Amperg with its intense vegetal aromas and more harmonious, elegant character in the mouth.

○ A. A. Bianco Cuvée Syvi '16	♟♟ 3
○ A. A. Gewürztraminer Amperg '16	♟♟ 2*
● A. A. Lagrein Amperg Ris. '15	♟♟ 4
○ A. A. Pinot Bianco Amperg '16	♟♟ 2*
● A. A. Pinot Nero Bachgart '14	♟♟ 4
● A. A. Pinot Nero Bachgart Ris. '13	♟♟ 3
○ A. A. Sauvignon Amperg '16	♟♟ 2*
○ A. A. Valle Isarco Gewürztraminer Fuchslahn '16	♟♟ 2*
○ A. A. Valle Isarco Grüner Veltliner Eichberg '15	♟♟ 3
○ A. A. Moscato Giallo Amperg '16	♟ 2
○ A. A. Pinot Grigio Amperg '16	♟ 2
● A. A. Pinot Nero Bachgart '13	♟♟♟ 4*
● A. A. Pinot Nero Bachgart Ris. '12	♟♟ 3

Cantina Meran

VIA CANTINA, 9
39020 MARLENGO/MARLING [BZ]
TEL. +39 0473447137
www.cantinamerano.it

CELLAR SALES
PRE-BOOKED VISITS
ANNUAL PRODUCTION 1,600,000 bottles
HECTARES UNDER VINE 265.00

The Meran Burggräfler winery draws its strength from 260 members who cultivate mostly tiny plots individually, but combine for a total of 265 hectares of vineyards. Unlike other cooperatives in the region, the members are located mainly in the hills surrounding the city of Merano, such as Lagundo, Marlengo and Tirolo. A small exception is the handful of members working in nearby Val Venosta. The 2015 Pinot Bianco Tyrol is their standard-bearer, with its aromas of white peach, flowers and spices that let a welcome mineral note emerge from the background. In the mouth, the wine proves quintessentially elegant. Tangy, dry and long, it's a wine that's difficult to forget. Elegance is also on full display with the Sauvignon Mervin. The grape's signature aromas follow through onto a solid palate that integrates perfectly with oak. The close-focused and fragrant Schiava Schickenburg features great drinkability.

○ A. A. Pinot Bianco Tyrol '15	♟♟♟ 4*
○ A. A. Sauvignon Mervin '15	♟♟ 4
● A. A. Schiava Schickenburg Graf von Meran '16	♟♟ 2*
● A. A. Cabernet Graf Von Meran '14	♟♟ 4
○ A. A. Chardonnay Goldegg '15	♟♟ 4
○ A. A. Gewürztraminer Graf von Meran '16	♟♟ 3
● A. A. Lagrein Segen Ris. '14	♟♟ 4
○ A. A. Moscato Giallo Passito Sissi '15	♟♟ 6
○ A. A. Pinot Bianco V Years Gran Ris. '11	♟♟ 5
● A. A. Pinot Nero Zeno Ris. '14	♟♟ 4
○ A. A. Val Venosta Pinot Bianco Sonnenberg '15	♟♟ 3
○ A. A. Muller Thurgau Festival '16	♟ 2
○ A. A. Pinot Bianco Tyrol '13	♟♟♟ 4*
○ A. A. Sauvignon Mervin '14	♟♟♟ 4*

★Cantina Convento Muri Gries

P.zza Gries, 21
39100 Bolzano/Bozen
Tel. +39 0471282287
www.muri-gries.com

CELLAR SALES
ANNUAL PRODUCTION 700,000 bottles
HECTARES UNDER VINE 55.00
SUSTAINABLE WINERY

Many vineyards in the heart of Bolzano are surrounded by walls to integrate them seamlessly into residential areas. This is in keeping with the legacy of a deep-rooted farming culture in the area. The most famous of these is Klosteranger, owned by the Muri-Gries Monastery Winery, which has just under 3 hectares all dedicated to Lagrein, its flagship wine. For his white grapes, however, Kellermeister Christian Werth relies on the Appiano wine region. After passing up on production of their Lagrein Abtei Muri Riserva in 2013, here comes Muri Gries' great 2014. Its characteristic thickness and darkness lends the nose a richly-nuanced suite of aromas in which fruit proves the key player, accompanied by smoky, floral and spicy notes. Its impact in the mouth is powerful and assertive, with the wine gradually gaining in suppleness and grip for a dry, harmonious finish. The Bianco of the same name also did quite well. It's a blend of Pinot Bianco and Grigio with a dash of Gewürztraminer.

● A. A. Lagrein Abtei Muri Ris. '14	♔♔♔	5
○ A. A. Bianco Abtei Muri '15	♔♔	3*
● A. A. Lagrein '16	♔♔	3
☉ A. A. Lagrein Rosato '16	♔♔	3
● A. A. Moscato Rosa V.T. Abtei Muri '15	♔♔	5
○ A. A. Pinot Grigio '16	♔♔	3
● A. A. Pinot Nero '16	♔♔	3
○ A. A. Terlano Pinot Bianco '16	♔	3
● A. A. Lagrein Abtei Muri Ris. '12	♔♔♔	5
● A. A. Lagrein Abtei Muri Ris. '11	♔♔♔	5
● A. A. Lagrein Abtei Muri Ris. '10	♔♔♔	5
● A. A. Lagrein Abtei Muri Ris. '09	♔♔♔	5
● A. A. Lagrein Abtei Ris. '07	♔♔♔	5
● A. A. Lagrein Abtei Ris. '06	♔♔♔	4

★Cantina Nals Margreid

Via Heiligenberg, 2
39010 Nalles/Nals [BZ]
Tel. +39 0471678626
www.kellerei.it

CELLAR SALES
PRE-BOOKED VISITS
ANNUAL PRODUCTION 950,000 bottles
HECTARES UNDER VINE 160.00
SUSTAINABLE WINERY

A merger between two such disparate wineries as Nalles and Magré has given the cellar in Via Heilingberg vineyards access to the most important vinegrowing areas in the province. Here, every variety is grown in the area most suited to it and Harald Schraffl has the job of making best advantage of it. In the cellar the lines of wine are guided by the variety, and territory is key. Sirmian is one of their most important vineyards and the grapes are used to make one of the winery's most interesting wines, the 2016 Pinot Bianco of the same name. On the nose, its aromas suite ranges from pear to lime blossom, while in the mouth the wine exhibits a winning concentration and elegance. The Chardonnay Baron Salvadori, made with grapes cultivated in Magrè and aged in oak for one year, also did well. It proves complex and deep on the nose, while the palate comes through elegant with great length.

○ A. A. Pinot Bianco Sirmian '16	♔♔♔	5
○ A. A. Chardonnay Baron Salvadori Ris. '14	♔♔	6
○ A. A. Pinot Grigio Punggl '16	♔♔	5
○ A. A. Chardonnay Magrè '16	♔♔	4
○ A. A. Gewürztraminer Lyra '16	♔♔	4
● A. A. Lagrein Gries Ris. '14	♔♔	5
● A. A. Merlot - Cabernet Anticus Baron Salvadori Ris. '14	♔♔	5
○ A. A. Moscato Giallo Passito Baronesse Baron Salvadori '14	♔♔	6
○ A. A. Pinot Bianco Penon '16	♔♔	3
○ A. A. Sauvignon Gennen '16	♔♔	3
○ A. A. Sauvignon Mantele '16	♔♔	5
● A. A. Schiava Galea '16	♔♔	3
○ A. A. Pinot Bianco Sirmian '15	♔♔♔	5
○ A. A. Pinot Bianco Sirmian '14	♔♔♔	5

Ignaz Niedrist

LOC. CORNAIANO/GIRLAN
VIA RONCO, 5
39057 APPIANO/EPPAN [BZ]
TEL. +39 0471664494
www.ignazniedrist.com

CELLAR SALES
PRE-BOOKED VISITS
ANNUAL PRODUCTION 45,000 bottles
HECTARES UNDER VINE 10.00
SUSTAINABLE WINERY

The Niedrist family winery draws from three different areas, focusing on varieties best suited to the specific soil and climate attributes of each. In Cornaiano, the vineyards are located at five hundred meters and produce full, ripe fruit. Freshness and aroma come from those grown in the cooler, higher area of Appiano Monte, while the Gries plain is better for growing fine Lagrein grapes. The 2016 Trias is made with Chardonnay and a dash of Manseng, Manzoni Bianco and Pinot Grigio grown at the foot of the Mendola and in the Cornaiano hills. It offers up aromas of ripe white fruit and spices, with a discreet hint of oak in the background, while the mouth proves generous and well-balanced. The 2016 Riesling Berg is also quite good, outlined by very young and floral aromas that follow through onto a rich and tangy palate with great drinkability.

Niklaserhof - Josef Sölva

LOC. SAN NICOLÒ
VIA DELLE FONTANE, 31A
39052 CALDARO/KALTERN [BZ]
TEL. +39 0471963434
www.niklaserhof.it

CELLAR SALES
PRE-BOOKED VISITS
ANNUAL PRODUCTION 50,000 bottles
HECTARES UNDER VINE 6.00

The Sölva family have owned the Niklaserhof since the end of the 1960s. Today, Dieter runs the business with his son Michael, who looks constantly to expand his expertise. The six hectares of vineyards are all within the municipality of Caldaro. The plots range from the cooler and higher Via area, to lower and warmer areas such as Prutznai. The goal is to produce limited quantities of diverse select wines. The grapes that make this magnificent Pinot Bianco Riserva, the 2014 Klaser, are grown in the Kardatsch vineyard, a stone's throw from the center of Caldaro. It ages in mid-sized casks for a year, conferring aromas of citrus fruit and oak, with a background of ripe yellow fruit that provides the wine with the right fullness. The palate displays power and is supported by good acidity. The 2014 Lagrein Cabernet of the same name features aromas of red fruit and spice, with good richness and savoriness in the mouth.

○ A. A. Riesling Berg '16	♥♥ 4
○ Trias '16	♥♥ 4
● A. A. Lagrein Berger Gei Ris. '14	♥♥ 4
○ A. A. Pinot Bianco Berg '16	♥♥ 4
● A. A. Pinot Nero Vom Kalk '13	♥♥ 6
○ A. A. Sauvignon Porphyr & Kalk '16	♥♥ 4
○ A. A. Riesling Berg '11	♥♥♥ 4*
○ A. A. Terlano Pinot Bianco '12	♥♥♥ 3*
○ A. A. Terlano Sauvignon '10	♥♥♥ 3
○ Trias '14	♥♥♥ 4*
● A. A. Lagrein Gries Berger Gei '13	♥♥ 5
● A. A. Pinot Nero '13	♥♥ 5
○ A. A. Terlano Pinot Bianco Berg '15	♥♥ 4
○ A. A. Terlano Sauvignon '15	♥♥ 4

○ A. A. Pinot Bianco Klaser Ris. '14	♥♥ 3*
○ A. A. Kerner Mondevinum Ris. '14	♥♥ 4
● A. A. Lago di Caldaro Cl. Charta '16	♥♥ 2*
● A. A. Lagrein Cabernet Klaser Ris. '14	♥♥ 4
○ A. A. Pinot Bianco '16	♥♥ 2*
○ A. A. Sauvignon '16	♥♥ 3
○ A. A. Kerner '16	♥ 2
○ A. A. Bianco Mondevinum Ris. '13	♥♥ 4
● A. A. Lago di Caldaro Cl. Charta '15	♥♥ 2*
● A. A. Lago di Caldaro Scelto Cl. '15	♥♥ 2*
● A. A. Lagrein Cabernet Klaser Ris. '13	♥♥ 4
○ A. A. Pinot Bianco '14	♥♥ 2*
○ A. A. Pinot Bianco Klaser Ris. '13	♥♥ 3*

Pacherhof - Andreas Huber

FRAZ. NOVACELLA
V.LO PACHER, 1
39040 VARNA/VAHRN [BZ]
TEL. +39 0472835717
www.pacherhof.com

CELLAR SALES
PRE-BOOKED VISITS
ACCOMMODATION AND RESTAURANT SERVICE
ANNUAL PRODUCTION 90,000 bottles
HECTARES UNDER VINE 8.50

The Huber family has owned Pacherhof since it was built almost 900 years ago and they were pioneers of vinegrowing in Isarco Valley in the mid-nineteenth century. Today, Andreas runs the 10 hectares of vineyards in the valley. All are dedicated to white grape varieties. Only steel or large barrels are used In the cellar to enhance the distinctive features of their wines, namely aromatic quality and richness of flavor. The fantastic 2016 Grüner Veltliner is made with grapes grown at over 600 meters of altitude and aged in large barrels before being bottled. As you bring the glass to your nose, smoky notes are discernible, which slowly give way to vegetal and sulfurous overtones. In the mouth, it expands gracefully and supply, highlighting its excellent tanginess. The Sylvaner is more subtle and fragrant, with a buoyant palate that plays on the balance between residual sweetness and acidity.

Pfannenstielhof Johannes Pfeifer

VIA PFANNESTIEL, 9
39100 BOLZANO/BOZEN
TEL. +39 0471970884
www.pfannenstielhof.it

CELLAR SALES
PRE-BOOKED VISITS
ANNUAL PRODUCTION 43,000 bottles
HECTARES UNDER VINE 4.00

When you leave the center of Bolzano in any direction, it is striking how the buildings suddenly disappear and give way to vinegrowing, as the landscape returns to its simple charm. Going eastward, this pleasant transformation coincides with the appearance of the Santa Maddalena hills where Hannes and Margareth Pfeifer's winery is situated. Their winery is one of the most engaging producers of Bolzano red. Pfeifer presented two first-rate wines this year, the 2014 Lagrein Riserva and the 2016 Santa Maddalena Classico. The former expresses intense aromas in which red fruit mingles with smoky and herby notes, and a mouth that's straightforward, powerful and has great personality. The latter features elegant aromas of wild fruit, spices and flowers, for a palate with distinctive richness of taste and suppleness.

○ A. A. Valle Isarco Grüner Veltliner '16	▼▼▼	4*
○ A. A. Valle Isarco Sylvaner '16	▼▼	4
○ A. A. Valle Isarco Kerner '16	▼▼	4
○ A. A. Valle Isarco Pinot Grigio '16	▼▼	4
○ A. A. Valle Isarco Gewürztraminer '16	▼	5
○ A. A. Valle Isarco Riesling '04	♈♈♈	3
○ A. A. Valle Isarco Sylvaner Alte Reben '05	♈♈♈	4
○ A. A. Valle Isarco Grüner Veltliner '15	♈♈	4
○ A. A. Valle Isarco Pinot Grigio '15	♈♈	4
○ A. A. Valle Isarco Riesling '15	♈♈	4
○ A. A. Valle Isarco Riesling '14	♈♈	4
○ A. A. Valle Isarco Sylvaner '15	♈♈	4
○ A. A. Valle Isarco Sylvaner Alte Reben '15	♈♈	5
○ A. A. Valle Isarco Sylvaner Alte Reben '14	♈♈	5

● A. A. Lagrein Ris. '14	▼▼	5
● A. A. Santa Maddalena Cl. '16	▼▼	3*
● A. A. Lagrein vom Boden '16	▼▼	3
☉ Lagrein Rosé '16	▼▼	2*
● A. A. Santa Maddalena Cl. '14	♈♈♈	3*
● A. A. Santa Maddalena Cl. '09	♈♈♈	2*
● A. A. Lagrein Ris. '13	♈♈	5
● A. A. Lagrein Ris. '12	♈♈	5
● A. A. Lagrein vom Boden '15	♈♈	3
● A. A. Lagrein vom Boden '14	♈♈	3
● A. A. Pinot Nero '12	♈♈	4
● A. A. Santa Maddalena Cl. '15	♈♈	3*
☉ Lagrein Rosé '15	♈♈	2*

Tenuta Pfitscher

VIA DOLOMITI, 17
39040 MONTAGNA/MONTAN [BZ]
TEL. +39 04711681317
www.pfitscher.it

CELLAR SALES
PRE-BOOKED VISITS
ANNUAL PRODUCTION 60,000 bottles
HECTARES UNDER VINE 7.00

The Pfitscher family has been working for decades on the eastern slope of the South Tyrolean Unterland. Winemaking started in the mid-nineteenth century, but there has been a distinct change in pace since Klaus joined the winery. Today, his father Alfred still works alongside him, along with his children Daniel, Hannes and Marion. Together they cover the most important roles in the winery, while his wife Monika oversees administration. Most of the vineyards are between Egna, Montagna, Cortaccia and Ora, with additional in Fié allo Sciliar, in the Isarco Valley. There is a wide range of top-quality wines here, including the Pinot Bianco Langefeld, which is made with grapes cultivated in Montagna and aged entirely in steel. The variety's signature notes of flowers and white fruit emerge on the nose, while the palate proves tangy and taut with gutsy drinkability. Of the reds, we enjoyed the Merlot Kotznloater, whose closed and almost introverted aromas are contrasted by grip and length.

○ A. A. Pinot Bianco Langefeld '16	♟♟	3*
○ A. A. Chardonnay Arvum '16	♟♟	3
○ A. A. Gewürztraminer Stoass '16	♟♟	4
● A. A. Lagrein Brenntal Ris. '14	♟♟	5
● A. A. Merlot Kotznloater '15	♟♟	4
○ A. A. Müller Thurgau Dola '16	♟♟	4
● A. A. Pinot Nero Matan '14	♟♟	5
○ A. A. Sauvignon Saxum '16	♟♟	4
● Cortazo '15	♟♟	5
● A. A. Lagrein Rivus '16	♟	5
● A. A. Pinot Nero Fuchsleiten '16	♟	4
○ A. A. Gewürztraminer Stoass '15	♟♟	4
● A. A. Merlot Kotznloater '14	♟♟	4
○ A. A. Sauvignon Saxum '15	♟♟	4

Tenuta Ritterhof

S.DA DEL VINO, 1
39052 CALDARO/KALTERN [BZ]
TEL. +39 0471963298
www.ritterhof.it

CELLAR SALES
PRE-BOOKED VISITS
RESTAURANT SERVICE
ANNUAL PRODUCTION 300,000 bottles
HECTARES UNDER VINE 7.50

The Roner family winery is run with skill and a firm hand from Ludwig Kaneppele. A benchmark for enthusiasts of regional wines, the cellar is just outside Caldaro. The vineyards (some owned by family and some by local vinegrowers) are situated in the best areas of the province to take advantage of the most suitable exposures, altitudes and soils for each variety. Once again, the 2016 Gewürztraminer Auratus proves to be Roner's most interesting wine. It's made with a selected harvest in Ronchi di Termeno and fermented and aged in steel only. Its aromas are intense and call up tropical fruit, citrus and licorice, while its powerful and plush palate is contrasted by acidity. The Sauvignon Paratus, made with grapes cultivated in the Montagna and Renon vineyards, also did well, with its dry and tangy palate.

○ A. A. Gewürztraminer Auratus '16	♟♟♟	4*
○ A. A. Gewürztraminer '16	♟♟	3*
○ A. A. Sauvignon Paratus '16	♟♟	2*
● A. A. Cabernet Merlot Ramus '13	♟♟	4
● A. A. Lago di Caldaro Cl. Sup. Novis '16	♟♟	3
● A. A. Lagrein '16	♟♟	3
○ A. A. Müller Thurgau '16	♟♟	2*
○ A. A. Pinot Bianco '16	♟♟	2*
○ A. A. Pinot Bianco Verus '16	♟♟	3
● A. A. Pinot Nero Dignus '13	♟♟	5
● A. A. Santa Maddalena Perlhof '16	♟♟	2*
○ A. A. Sauvignon '16	♟♟	2*
○ A. A. Gewürztraminer Auratus Crescendo '15	♟♟♟	4*

Röckhof - Konrad Augschöll

VIA SAN VALENTINO, 22
39040 VILLANDRO/VILLANDERS [BZ]
TEL. +39 0472847130
roeck@rolmail.net

CELLAR SALES
PRE-BOOKED VISITS
RESTAURANT SERVICE
ANNUAL PRODUCTION 20,000 bottles
HECTARES UNDER VINE 3.50

On the western slope of the Isarco Valley,
the Augschöll family estate spans a few
hectares near Villandro, at an altitude of
650 meters. Here the grapes ripen more to
light than the heat, giving the berries a
marked aromatic quality with firm acidity.
Alongside the classic grape varieties of the
valley, August grows a few less common
red grapes, such as Zweigelt, Saint
Laurent, and an even rarer Furner Hottler.
The 2016 Grüner Veltliner Gail Fuass is
Augschöll's leading wine. It's made with
grapes cultivated at about 600 meters of
altitude, in soil rich in sand and schist.
Aging occurs in steel, except for a small
amount that rests in wood. On the nose,
exotic vegetal notes bring out a lovely flinty
sensation. On the palate, the wine proves
full, with good richness, supported by a
punchy and gutsy acidity. The 2016 Müller
Thurgau sees simpler aromas and a zesty
palate.

Tenuta Hans Rottensteiner

FRAZ. GRIES
VIA SARENTINO, 1A
39100 BOLZANO/BOZEN
TEL. +39 0471282015
www.rottensteiner-weine.com

CELLAR SALES
PRE-BOOKED VISITS
ANNUAL PRODUCTION 450,000 bottles
HECTARES UNDER VINE 90.00

A large winery with premises in the heart
of the regional capital, Rottensteiner has
a presence throughout the Bolzano
province. The family's involvement spans
all stages, from running the vineyards, to
collaborating with the numerous grape
growers who bring their grapes to the
cellar, to the winemaking, to sales. They
produce just under half a million bottles,
suiting every palate and bringing out the
best features of South Tyrol in their wines.
The 2016 Gewürztraminer Cancenai
performed quite well. It's made with grapes
cultivated in Termeno, which is the cradle
of this variety. The nose offers vibrant
aromas, which call up dog rose, citrus and
tropical fruit, while the palate combines
plushness with good tanginess. The grapes
for their 2016 Sylvaner, on the other hand,
are grown in the Isarco Valley. The wine,
which perfectly reflects the variety's key
traits, features a dynamic, long palate.

○ A. A. Valle Isarco Grüner Veltliner Gail Fuass '16	♟♟ 3
○ A. A. Valle Isarco Müller Thurgau '16	♟♟ 3
○ Caruess '16	♟ 3
○ Viel Anders '15	♟ 3
○ A. A. Valle Isarco Grüner Veltliner Gail Fuass '15	♟♟ 3
○ A. A. Valle Isarco Müller Thurgau '15	♟♟ 3
○ A. A. Valle Isarco Müller Thurgau '14	♟♟ 3
○ A. A. Valle Isarco Müller Thurgau '13	♟♟ 3
○ A. A. Valle Isarco Riesling Viel Anders '14	♟♟ 3*
○ A. A. Valle Isarco Riesling Viel Anders '13	♟♟ 3
○ A. A. Valle Isarco Veltliner Gail Fuass '14	♟♟ 3
○ Caruess Weiß '15	♟♟ 3*
○ Caruess Weiß '14	♟♟ 3

● A. A. Cabernet Select Ris. '14	♟♟ 5
○ A. A. Gewürztraminer Cancenai '16	♟♟ 4
○ A. A. Gewürztraminer Passito Cresta '15	♟♟ 6
● A. A. Lagrein Grieser Select Ris. '14	♟♟ 5
○ A. A. Müller Thurgau '16	♟♟ 3
● A. A. Santa Maddalena Cl. V. Premstallerhof '16	♟♟ 3
○ A. A. Sylvaner '16	♟♟ 3
● A. A. Lagrein Rosato '16	♟ 3
○ A. A. Pinot Bianco Carnol '16	♟ 3
○ A. A. Pinot Grigio '16	♟ 3
● A. A. Pinot Nero Select Ris. '14	♟ 5
● A. A. Sauvignon '16	♟ 3
● A. A. Lagrein Ris. '02	♟♟♟ 2*

★★Cantina Produttori San Michele Appiano

VIA CIRCONVALLAZIONE, 17/19
39057 APPIANO/EPPAN [BZ]
TEL. +39 0471664466
www.stmichael.it

CELLAR SALES
PRE-BOOKED VISITS
ANNUAL PRODUCTION 2,200,000 bottles
HECTARES UNDER VINE 380.00

Of all the high-level South Tyrolean cooperatives, center stage should go to San Michele Appiano. It has managed to combine quality with quantity while maintaining territorial identity. This is the result of 300 families running about 400 hectares of vineyards. The strength of this winery lies in the vineyards, spreading out to the villages around Appiano. The grapes are delivered to Hans Terzer who with his staff then transforms them into a wide range of consistently good wines. The whole Sanct Valentin line won over our commission, with four wines making it to the finals. The excellent 2015 Pinot Bianco offers up hints of ripe white fruit and flowers, with nuances of perfectly integrated oak. The fullness on its palate is pleasantly supported by acidity and tanginess. The 2015 Chardonnay plays more on harmony, the 2015 Pinot Grigio on solidity and the 2015 Sauvignon on aromatic freshness.

Cantina Produttori San Paolo

LOC. SAN PAOLO
VIA CASTEL GUARDIA, 21
39057 APPIANO/EPPAN [BZ]
TEL. +39 0471662183
www.stpauls.wine

CELLAR SALES
PRE-BOOKED VISITS
ANNUAL PRODUCTION 1,200,000 bottles
HECTARES UNDER VINE 175.00
SUSTAINABLE WINERY

In the northern part of the Oltradige area, the gentle slopes become steeper then descend sharply towards the Bolzano plain. Here, just outside the small village of San Paolo, is the Cantina Produttori, a cooperative winery with over 200 members who deliver their grapes to Via Castel Guardia. Kellemeister Wolfgang Tratter takes excellent care of them, turning them into wines that poignantly reflect the different altitudes and exposures of the vineyards. There are two wines that stand out this year, a Schiava and a Pinot Bianco, both from the flagship Punta line. The first is from the 2016 vintage and expresses intense notes of wild fruit and spices, which follow through onto the palate where richness of flavor dominates. The second is a 2015 and features an elegant, deep nose where yellow fruit meets iodine and sea breeze. In the mouth, the wine exhibits a distinctive length and elegance.

○ A. A. Pinot Bianco Sanct Valentin '15	♟♟♟ 6
○ A. A. Chardonnay St. Valentin '15	♟♟ 5
○ A. A. Pinot Grigio St. Valentin '15	♟♟ 5
○ A. A. Sauvignon Sanct Valentin '16	♟♟ 6
● A. A. Cabernet Merlot Sanct Valentin '13	♟♟ 5
○ A. A. Gewürztraminer Sanct Valentin '16	♟♟ 6
○ A. A. Pinot Bianco Schulthauser '16	♟♟ 3
○ A. A. Pinot Grigio Anger '16	♟♟ 4
● A. A. Pinot Nero Sanct Valentin '14	♟♟ 5
○ A. A. Riesling Montiggl '16	♟♟ 5
○ A. A. Sauvignon Lahn '16	♟♟ 5
○ A. A. Pinot Bianco St. Valentin '13	♟♟♟ 5
○ A. A. Pinot Grigio St. Valentin '14	♟♟♟ 5
○ A. A. Sauvignon St. Valentin '13	♟♟♟ 5

○ A. A. Pinot Bianco Passion Ris. '15	♟♟ 5
● A. A. Schiava Passion '16	♟♟ 4
○ A. A. Gewürztraminer Kössler '16	♟♟ 3
○ A. A. Gewürztraminer Passion '16	♟♟ 5
● A. A. Lagrein Kössler '16	♟♟ 3
○ A. A. Pinot Bianco Kössler '16	♟♟ 2*
○ A. A. Pinot Bianco Plötzner '16	♟♟ 3
○ A. A. Pinot Grigio Kössler '16	♟♟ 3
● A. A. Pinot Nero Kössler '16	♟♟ 3
● A. A. Pinot Nero Passion Ris. '15	♟♟ 5
○ A. A. Sauvignon Gfill '16	♟♟ 3
○ A. A. Sauvignon Passion '16	♟♟ 5
○ A. A. Spumante Praeclarus Brut	♟♟ 5
○ Petit Manseng Passion '16	♟♟ 5
● A. A. Lagrein Passion Ris. '15	♟ 5
○ A. A. Riesling '16	♟ 3

Peter Sölva & Söhne

VIA DELL'ORO, 33
39052 CALDARO/KALTERN [BZ]
TEL. +39 0471964650
www.soelva.com

CELLAR SALES
PRE-BOOKED VISITS
ANNUAL PRODUCTION 75,000 bottles
HECTARES UNDER VINE 12.00

The Sölva family's connections with vinegrowing date back almost three centuries, but only in the mid-twentieth century did they begin bottling their own wines. Today their vineyards span about a dozen hectares in Oltradige and the South Tyrolean Unterland. Their grapes are used to make three lines of wines: I Vigneti, a simple wine, De Silva, from the old vineyard, and Amistar, where overripening is key. The Pinot Bianco DeSilva, made with grapes cultivated in Pochi di Salorno and Caldaro, is the star wine here. Its delicate and youthful aromas of white fruit and flowers follow through onto a dry palate that plays on elegance and grip. Of the reds, we appreciated the Amistar Edizione Rossa, a complex blend with deep and ripe aromas of red fruit and spices, and a palate that proves solid and powerful.

○ A. A. Pinot Bianco DeSilva '16	▼▼ 4
○ A. A. Sauvignon DeSilva '16	▼▼ 4
○ Amistar Bianco '15	▼▼ 6
● Amistar Edizione Rossa Serie A6 '13	▼▼ 6
● Amistar Rosso '14	▼▼ 5
● A. A. Lago di Caldaro Cl. Sup. Peterleiten DeSilva '16	▼ 2
○ A. A. Terlano Pinot Bianco DeSilva '10	♈♈♈ 3
○ A. A. Terlano Pinot Bianco DeSilva '09	♈♈♈ 3
● A. A. Lago di Caldaro Cl. Sup. Peterleiten DeSilva '15	♈♈ 4
● A. A. Lago di Caldaro Scelto Cl. Sup. Peterleiten '14	♈♈ 2*
○ A. A. Pinot Bianco DeSilva '14	♈♈ 4
○ Amistar Bianco '14	♈♈ 6
● Amistar Rosso '13	♈♈ 5

Stachlburg - Baron von Kripp

VIA MITTERHOFER, 2
39020 PARCINES/PARTSCHINS [BZ]
TEL. I 39 0473968014
www.stachlburg.com

CELLAR SALES
PRE-BOOKED VISITS
ANNUAL PRODUCTION 30,000 bottles
HECTARES UNDER VINE 7.00
VITICULTURE METHOD Certified Organic

Don't be fooled by the small size of the farm, it's actually a very important producer at the entrance to the Val Venosta. The business is divided between winemaking and apple growing. The vineyards are located in three different areas: immediately around the winery in Parcines, and in Naturno, where the altitude above 600 meters gives freshness and grip to the wines, and Andriano, where at 300 meters the wines are more generous and powerful. The Pinot Nero took advantage of the 2014 vintage find an expression in which aromas of wild fruit infuse with more subtle notes of herbs and spices, while oak keeps to the background. In the mouth, the sweetness of its fruit is lengthened by acidity, making for a juicy and long palate. The Merlot, on the other hand, is more mature on the nose, while in the mouth its power is well-governed by tannins and, once again, by acidity.

○ A. A. Pinot Bianco '16	▼▼ 4
● A.A. Merlot Ris. '14	▼▼ 5
○ A.A. Val Venosta Chardonnay Ris. '14	▼▼ 5
● A.A. Val Venosta Pinot Nero '14	▼▼ 5
○ A. A. Val Venosta Chardonnay '16	▼ 4
○ A. A. Valle Venosta Pinot Bianco '13	♈♈♈ 3*
○ A. A. Valle Venosta Pinot Bianco '10	♈♈♈ 3*
● A. A. Lagrein '13	♈♈ 3
● A. A. Merlot '13	♈♈ 4
○ A. A. Terlano Sauvignon '15	♈♈ 4
○ A. A. Terlano Sauvignon '14	♈♈ 4
○ A. A. Val Venosta Chardonnay '15	♈♈ 3
○ A. A. Valle Venosta Chardonnay '14	♈♈ 3
○ A. A. Valle Venosta Gewürztraminer '12	♈♈ 3
○ A. A. Valle Venosta Pinot Bianco '14	♈♈ 3

Strasserhof
Hannes Baumgartner

FRAZ. NOVACELLA
LOC. UNTERRAIN, 8
39040 VARNA/VAHRN [BZ]
TEL. +39 0472830804
www.strasserhof.info

CELLAR SALES
PRE-BOOKED VISITS
ACCOMMODATION
ANNUAL PRODUCTION 45,000 bottles
HECTARES UNDER VINE 5.50

The Isarco Valley is the least densely-
planted of the seven vinegrowing areas in
the Province of Bolzano. However,
character is equally important as hectares
in valuing territory and personality and this
area is second to none. Hannes
Baumgartner runs the family winery in
Novacella, with a few hectares in the high
hills dedicated entirely to white grape
varieties. Mostly steel is used for
winemaking, with the exception that
certain selections from the old vineyard
age in large barrels. The 2016 Grüner
Veltliner excelled this year. It's a white
aged entirely in steel. The nose offers up
intense notes of flowers and white fruit,
which follow through perfectly onto its
tangy, gradual and lengthy palate. The
2016 Sylvaner, a small amount of which
ages in large barrels, is also quite good.
On the nose, it's still very youthful and
dominated by fresh fruit, while in the
mouth the wine proves gutsy, with sharp,
juicy acidity.

Stroblhof

LOC. SAN MICHELE
VIA PIGANÒ, 25
39057 APPIANO/EPPAN [BZ]
TEL. +39 0471662250
www.stroblhof.it

CELLAR SALES
PRE-BOOKED VISITS
ANNUAL PRODUCTION 40,000 bottles
HECTARES UNDER VINE 5.20

Rosmarie Hanny and Andreas Nicolussi-
Leck's small winery is situated in Appiano,
at an altitude of over 500 meters, and has
a southeastern exposure. The family divide
their work between farming, and hospitality
and catering. All are conducted with the
utmost respect for the unique nature of this
territory and its traditions. They make only
a few wines, using only the most suitable
varieties for this magnificent slope.
Stroblhof's Pinot Nero is a real hit, with
three different versions put forward this
year. The top-notch 2014 Pigeno exploited
the cool vintage for intense and elegant
aromas that see wild red fruit accompanied
by notes of forest floor and violets, rather
than dominating. In the mouth, the wine
proves dry and supple, supported by
burnished tannins and good acidity. The
2013 Riserva, on the other hand, features
more full-expressed fruit and a solid,
close-knit palate.

○ A. A. Valle Isarco Grüner Veltliner '16	♟♟ 3*
○ A. A. Valle Isarco Kerner '16	♟♟ 3
○ A. A. Valle Isarco Müller Thurgau '16	♟♟ 3
○ A. A. Valle Isarco Riesling '16	♟♟ 4
○ A. A. Valle Isarco Sylvaner '16	♟♟ 3
○ A. A. Valle Isarco Riesling '12	♟♟♟ 3*
○ A. A. Valle Isarco Riesling '11	♟♟♟ 3*
○ A. A. Valle Isarco Veltliner '10	♟♟♟ 3*
○ A. A. Valle Isarco Veltliner '09	♟♟♟ 3*
○ A. A. Valle Isarco Grüner Veltliner '15	♟♟ 3*
○ A. A. Valle Isarco Kerner '15	♟♟ 3
○ A. A. Valle Isarco Riesling '15	♟♟ 4
○ A. A. Valle Isarco Riesling '14	♟♟ 4
○ A. A. Valle Isarco Sylvaner '15	♟♟ 3
○ A. A. Valle Isarco Sylvaner Anjo '15	♟♟ 4

● A. A. Pinot Nero Pigeno '14	♟♟ 5
● A.A. Pinot Nero Ris. '13	♟♟ 6
○ A. A. Chardonnay Schwarzhaus '16	♟♟ 4
○ A. A. Sauvignon Nico '16	♟♟ 4
○ A. A. Pinot Bianco Strahler '15	♟ 4
⊙ A.A. Pinot Nero Rosé '16	♟ 4
○ A. A. Pinot Bianco Strahler '09	♟♟♟ 3*
● A. A. Pinot Nero Ris. '05	♟♟♟ 5
○ A. A. Pinot Bianco Strahler '15	♟♟ 3
○ A. A. Pinot Bianco Strahler '14	♟♟ 3
● A. A. Pinot Nero Pigeno '13	♟♟ 5
● A. A. Pinot Nero Pigeno '12	♟♟ 5
● A. A. Pinot Nero Ris. '11	♟♟ 6
○ A. A. Sauvignon Nico '15	♟♟ 4
● Pinot Nero Ris. '12	♟♟ 6

Taschlerhof - Peter Wachtler

LOC. MARA, 107
39042 BRESSANONE/BRIXEN [BZ]
TEL. +39 0472851091
www.taschlerhof.com

CELLAR SALES
PRE-BOOKED VISITS
ANNUAL PRODUCTION 30,000 bottles
HECTARES UNDER VINE 4.20

Peter Wachtler runs his small winery just outside of Bressanone, where he has slightly more than four hectares on these steep, slate, southeast-facing slopes. He grows only four varieties: Riesling, Sylvaner, Gewürztraminer and Kerner, namely the four standard bearers of the Isarco Valley. In the vineyard Peter works with the utmost respect for the environment. At the same time in the cellar he strives to bring out the best qualities of his grapes. His wines are aged in both steel and acacia wood barrels. The 2016 Sylvaner is made by assembling about a third of the mass of wine aged in large barrels with that aged in steel. The result is a white with complex fragrances in which fruit seems to be surrounded by notes of dried flowers and spices. In the mouth, the wine expands with acidity and grip, making for a long and juicy finish. The 2015 Lahner also impressed, with its more mature aromas and a richer, but equally taut, palate.

★★Cantina Terlano

VIA SILBERLEITEN, 7
39018 TERLANO/TERLAN [BZ]
TEL. +39 0471257135
www.cantina-terlano.com

CELLAR SALES
PRE-BOOKED VISITS
ANNUAL PRODUCTION 1,000,000 bottles
HECTARES UNDER VINE 165.00

Such an iconic winery is difficult to address after so much has already been said. Yet it's a simple story, 150 members who enthusiastically cultivate their vineyards located mostly in the best areas, with a Kellermeister, Rudi Kofler, who transforms the grapes into wine with great sensitivity and care. Time, large wooden barrels, and careful attention to every stage of production do the rest. Results are some of the most compelling in the region, year after year. The excellent 2015 vintage helped the Sauvignon Quarz to pull a rabbit out of its hat. Its aromatic suite spans tropical fruit and jasmine flowers, though in the mouth the wine changes gear. Here, a perfect balance between power and elegance emerges, as well as freshness and ripeness, allowing for a classy unfolding of flavor and a long, dry finish. The 2014 Nova Domus Riserva is generous and elegant on the nose and features a tangy, precise palate.

○ A. A. Valle Isarco Sylvaner '16	🍷🍷 3*
○ A. A. Valle Isarco Kerner '16	🍷🍷 4
○ A. A. Valle Isarco Riesling '16	🍷🍷 4
○ A. A. Valle Isarco Sylvaner Lahner '15	🍷🍷 4
○ A. A. Valle Isarco Riesling '14	🍷🍷🍷 4*
○ A. A. Valle Isarco Sylvaner '15	🍷🍷🍷 3*
○ A. A. Valle Isarco Kerner '15	🍷🍷 4
○ A. A. Valle Isarco Kerner '14	🍷🍷 4
○ A. A. Valle Isarco Riesling '15	🍷🍷 4
○ A. A. Valle Isarco Riesling '13	🍷🍷 4
○ A. A. Valle Isarco Sylvaner '14	🍷🍷 3*
○ A. A. Valle Isarco Sylvaner '13	🍷🍷 3*
○ A. A. Valle Isarco Sylvaner Lahner '14	🍷🍷 4
○ A. A. Valle Isarco Sylvaner Lahner '13	🍷🍷 4
○ A. A. Valle Isarco Veltliner '14	🍷🍷 3*

○ A. A. Terlano Sauvignon Quarz '15	🍷🍷🍷 6
○ A. A. Gewürztraminer Movado Andriano '15	🍷🍷 5
○ A. A. Terlano Nova Domus Ris. '14	🍷🍷 6
○ A. A. Terlano Sauvignon Winkl '16	🍷🍷 3*
○ A. A. Gewürztraminer Lunare '15	🍷🍷 6
○ A. A. Gewürztraminer Passito Juvelo Andriano '15	🍷🍷 5
● A. A. Lagrein Porphyr Ris. '14	🍷🍷 6
● A. A. Lagrein Tor di Lupo Andriano Ris. '14	🍷🍷 4
● A. A. Merlot Gant Andriano Ris. '14	🍷🍷 4
○ A. A. Pinot Grigio Andriano '16	🍷🍷 2*
○ A. A. Sauvignon Andrius Andriano '15	🍷🍷 5
○ A. A. Terlano Chardonnay Kreuth '15	🍷🍷 4
○ A. A. Terlano Cl. '16	🍷🍷 2*
○ A. A. Terlano Pinot Bianco Vorberg Ris. '14	🍷🍷 5

Tiefenbrunner

FRAZ. NICLARA
VIA CASTELLO, 4
39040 CORTACCIA/KURTATSCH [BZ]
TEL. +39 0471880122
www.tiefenbrunner.com

CELLAR SALES
PRE-BOOKED VISITS
RESTAURANT SERVICE
ANNUAL PRODUCTION 650,000 bottles
HECTARES UNDER VINE 78.00

The Tiefenbrunner family winery is a benchmark for lovers of Adige wines. The vineyard spans 25 hectares in the Niclara, Cortaccia and Magrè areas, and collaboration with many local vinegrowers adds a further 53 hectares. The best quality vineyards are on Mount Favogna with three hectares set aside for Müller Thurgau grapes, resulting in the estate's most characteristic wines. Once again, Tiefenbrunner's most interesting wine is the Feldmarschall von Fenner. It's a Müller Thurgau that's made with grapes cultivated at 1000 meters of altitude. The wine sees a whirlwind of aromas on the nose, where distinctive notes of gooseberries and dried flowers give way to an assertive mineral note of flint. In the mouth, power and taut acidity meld with a dynamic and very long palate. The 2014 Chardonnay Vigna Au, on the other hand, goes all in on finesse and balance.

○ A. A. Müller Thurgau Feldmarschall von Fenner '15	▼▼▼ 5
○ A.A. Chardonnay Vigna Au Ris. '14	▼▼ 8
○ A. A. Chardonnay Turmhof '16	▼▼ 3
○ A. A. Gewürztraminer Linticlarus V.T. '13	▼▼ 6
● A. A. Lagrein Linticlarus Ris. '14	▼▼ 5
○ A. A. Pinot Grigio Turmhof '16	▼▼ 3
● A. A. Pinot Nero Linticlarus Ris. '14	▼▼ 6
● A.A. Cabernet Merlot Cuvée Linticlarus Ris. '14	▼▼ 5
● A.A. Lagrein Turmhof '13	▼▼ 4
○ A.A. Sauvignon Rachtl Ris. '14	▼ 8
○ A. A. Müller Thurgau Feldmarschall von Fenner zu Fennberg '13	♔♔♔ 5
○ A. A. Müller Thurgau Feldmarschall von Fenner zu Fennberg '12	♔♔♔ 5

★★Cantina Tramin

S.DA DEL VINO, 144
39040 TERMENO/TRAMIN [BZ]
TEL. +39 0471096633
www.cantinatramin.it

CELLAR SALES
PRE-BOOKED VISITS
ANNUAL PRODUCTION 1,500,000 bottles
HECTARES UNDER VINE 250.00

Three hundred members and 250 hectares. With less than a hectare per member such an intimate relationship brings the activity of this large cooperative back to real artisan winemaking. Production at Tramin winery is enthusiastically coordinated by Kellermeister Willi Sturz who is instilled with an in-depth knowledge of his area. All of the vineyards are located in the southern part of the province, particularly in Termeno and Cortaccia, the cradle of Gewürztraminer. If territory is a cradle, then the Tramin winery is the university in which Traminer takes on its unforgettable shape and character. The 2015 Nussbaumer expresses its explosive suite of aromas slowly and with depth, anticipating a rich, powerful and supple palate. The Terminum, on the other hand, explores the more exotic and seductive nature of the variety, which conceals its sweetness on the palate so as to reveal balance and style. We'd also like to point out the character and grip of the 2015 Pinot Grigio Unterebner.

○ A. A. Gewürztraminer Nussbaumer '15	▼▼▼ 5
○ A. A. Pinot Grigio Unterebner '15	▼▼ 5
○ A.A. Gewürztraminer V.T. Terminum '14	▼▼ 7
○ A. A. Bianco Stoan '15	▼▼ 4
○ A.A. Gewürztraminer Roen V. T. '15	▼▼ 5
● A. A. Lagrein Urban Ris. '15	▼▼ 5
● A. A. Pinot Nero Maglen Ris. '14	▼▼ 5
○ A. A. Sauvignon Pepi '16	▼▼ 3
● A. A. Schiava Freisinger '16	▼▼ 3
● A.A. Cabernet Merlot Loam Ris. '15	▼▼ 6
○ A.A. Gewürztraminer Selida '16	▼▼ 3
○ A.A. Pinot Bianco '16	▼▼ 3
○ A. A. Gewürztraminer Nussbaumer '14	♔♔♔ 5
○ A. A. Gewürztraminer Nussbaumer '13	♔♔♔ 5

Untermoserhof
Georg Ramoser

LOC. SANTA MADDALENA
VIA SANTA MADDALENA, 36
39100 BOLZANO/BOZEN
TEL. +39 0471975481
untermoserhof@rolmail.net

CELLAR SALES
PRE-BOOKED VISITS
ACCOMMODATION
ANNUAL PRODUCTION 30,000 bottles
HECTARES UNDER VINE 3.70

Georg Ramoser runs the family winery in
the heart of the Santa Maddalena area. It is
located a few dozen meters below the local
church. The vineyards span a handful of
hectares and nearly all are grown with the
historic local red grapes, Lagrein and
Schiava. Merlot and Chardonnay also make
a small appearance. Their wines look to
fully express the fruit, and achieve a solid
palate. The superb 2015 Lagrein Riserva
made the most of the excellent vintage,
offering up intense notes of ripe black fruit,
spices and minerals on the nose. Its entry
in the mouth proves close-knit and
clamped on the tannins, with the wine
gaining in plushness and suppleness at the
end. The 2015 Merlot also delivered, with
its more complex suite of aromas,
embellished with refreshing, vegetal notes.
In the mouth, it expands assertively and
turns out to be dry with good length.

○ A. A. Chardonnay '15	♟♟ 3	
● A. A. Lagrein Ris. '15	♟♟ 4	
● A. A. Merlot Ris. '15	♟♟ 4	
● A. A. Lagrein '16	♟ 3	
● A. A. Santa Maddalena Cl. '16	♟ 3	
● A. A. Lagrein Scuro Ris. '03	♟♟♟ 4*	
● A. A. Lagrein Scuro Ris. '97	♟♟♟ 4*	
● A. A. Lagrein Ris. '13	♟♟ 5	
● A. A. Lagrein Ris. '12	♟♟ 5	
● A. A. Lagrein Untermoserhof Ris. '11	♟♟ 5	
● A. A. Merlot Ris. '13	♟♟ 5	
● A. A. Merlot Untermoserhof Ris. '11	♟♟ 4	
● A. A. Santa Maddalena Cl. '14	♟♟ 3	
● A. A. Santa Maddalena Cl. '13	♟♟ 2*	
● A. A. Santa Maddalena Cl. '12	♟♟ 2*	

★Tenuta Unterortl
Castel Juval

LOC. JUVAL, 1B
39020 CASTELBELLO CIARDES/KASTELBELL TSCHARS [BZ]
TEL. +39 0473667580
www.unterortl.it

CELLAR SALES
PRE-BOOKED VISITS
ANNUAL PRODUCTION 33,000 bottles
HECTARES UNDER VINE 4.00

Martin and Gisela Aurich run this small
Unterortl estate in the Val Venosta, with
vineyards spanning a few hectares
facing south at altitudes between 600 and
800 meters. The incredibly steep vineyards
are warm and sunny during the day,
while at night the nearby Val Senales
channels cool the air to create a dramatic
temperate swing. Their wines are almost
exclusively whites with interpretations
that feature elegance and grip. Martin
and Gisela produce four Rieslings and the
2015 Windbichel is definitely the best. It's
made with a selection of the best grapes
from vineyards located at over 700
meters of altitude. The wine has incredibly
fresh fragrances, especially its more
tropical notes. The palate is dry and tangy
with a taut acidity that adds length. The
2016 Unterortl also delivered. On the nose
it's more floral and fresher, while the palate
features impressive harmony and grip.

○ A. A. Val Venosta Riesling Windbichel '15	♟♟♟ 5	
○ A. A. Val Venosta Riesling Unterortl '16	♟♟ 4	
○ A. A. Val Venosta Müller Thurgau '16	♟♟ 3	
○ A. A. Val Venosta Pinot Bianco '16	♟♟ 2*	
○ A. A. Val Venosta Riesling Gletscherschliff '16	♟♟ 4	
○ A. A. Val Venosta Riesling Spielerei V. T. '14	♟♟ 6	
○ A. A. Val Venosta Pinot Bianco Castel Juval '12	♟♟♟ 3*	
○ A. A. Val Venosta Riesling '10	♟♟♟ 4	
○ A. A. Val Venosta Riesling Castel Juval '11	♟♟♟ 4*	
○ A. A. Val Venosta Riesling Unterortl '15	♟♟♟ 4*	
○ A. A. Valle Venosta Pinot Bianco Castel Juval '13	♟♟♟ 3*	
○ A. A. Valle Venosta Riesling '14	♟♟♟ 4*	

Cantina Produttori Valle Isarco

Via Coste, 50
39043 Chiusa/Klausen [BZ]
Tel. +39 0472847553
www.cantinavalleisarco.it

CELLAR SALES
PRE-BOOKED VISITS
ANNUAL PRODUCTION 900,000 bottles
HECTARES UNDER VINE 150.00
SUSTAINABLE WINERY

The Isarco Valley is a link between hillside and mountain viticulture with extremely steep, often tiny vineyards, which approach an altitude of 1000 meters. The 130 members of the Cantina Produttori della Valle Isarco are dotted about the valley among castles and monasteries. They deliver their grapes to a modern structure in Chiusa. The winery's selection is almost exclusively local whites, but a few types of red are offered as well. The 2016 Sylvaner Aristos features a rich and multifaceted suite of aromas, with white fruit in the foreground, followed by notes of dried flowers, smoke and flint. In the mouth, it reveals its generosity almost immediately, and this is pleasantly contrasted by tanginess and a vibrant acidity. The same vintage and same line for the Grüner Veltliner, which follows a similar stylistic path, but remains more approachable and simple.

Von Blumen

Fraz. Pochi, 18
39040 Salorno/Salurn [BZ]
Tel. +39 0457230110
www.vonblumenwine.com

CELLAR SALES
PRE-BOOKED VISITS
ANNUAL PRODUCTION 38,000 bottles
HECTARES UNDER VINE 11.00
SUSTAINABLE WINERY

The Fugatti brother and sisters, Roberta, Cristina and Giuseppe, are among the most esteemed producers in Valdadige and recently they have started making wine. Their property here is located in Pochi di Salorno and it spans a dozen hectares dedicated to the region's most characteristic varieties. Each one is grown at different exposures and altitudes to facilitate optimal ripening. Their wines pursue an ideal of close-focused aromas and taste, as highlighted by the 2016 Sauvignon, which expresses intense fragrances of exotic fruit and sage leaves, anticipating a juicy and tangy palate. Their flagship wine, however, is the 2015 Pinot Bianco Flowers Selection, which ages for about a year in mid-sized casks, making for refined aromas of fruit and flowers, with oaky scents in the background. The mouth is taut and gutsy, almost austere, for a palate that will be satisfying for many years to come.

○ A. A. Valle Isarco Sylvaner Aristos '16	♟♟♟ 4*
○ A. A. Valle Isarco Grüner Veltliner Aristos '16	♟♟ 4
○ A. A. Valle Isarco Kerner Aristos '16	♟♟ 4
○ A. A. Valle Isarco Kerner Passito Nectaris '15	♟♟ 6
○ A. A. Valle Isarco Müller Thurgau Aristos '16	♟♟ 4
○ A. A. Valle Isarco Pinot Bianco Aristos '16	♟♟ 2*
○ A. A. Valle Isarco Pinot Grigio Aristos '16	♟♟ 4
○ A. A. Valle Isarco Riesling Aristos '16	♟♟ 4
○ A. A. Valle Isarco Gewürztraminer Aristos '16	♟ 4
○ A. A. Valle Isarco Sauvignon Aristos '16	♟ 4
○ A. A. Valle Isarco Sylvaner Aristos '15	♟♟♟ 4*
○ A. A. Valle Isarco Pinot Grigio Aristos '15	♟♟ 4

○ A. A. Pinot Bianco Flowers Selection '15	♟♟ 5
○ A.A. Gewürztraminer '16	♟♟ 4
● A. A. Pinot Nero '16	♟♟ 4
● A.A. Lagrein '15	♟♟ 4
○ A.A. Pinot Bianco '16	♟♟ 3
○ A.A. Sauvignon '16	♟♟ 3
○ A.A. Sauvignon Flowers Selection '15	♟♟ 5
○ A. A. Gewürztraminer '15	♟♟ 3
○ A. A. Pinot Bianco '15	♟♟ 3
○ A. A. Pinot Bianco Flowers Selection '14	♟♟ 3*
● A. A. Pinot Nero '14	♟♟ 3
○ A.A. Gewurztraminer '13	♟♟ 3
○ A.A. Gewürztraminer '14	♟♟ 3
● A.A. Lagrein '13	♟♟ 3
● A.A. Pinot Nero '13	♟♟ 3

★★Elena Walch

VIA A. HOFER, 1
39040 TERMENO/TRAMIN [BZ]
TEL. +39 0471860172
www.elenawalch.com

CELLAR SALES
PRE-BOOKED VISITS
RESTAURANT SERVICE
ANNUAL PRODUCTION 500,000 bottles
HECTARES UNDER VINE 33.00

Elena Walch's winery is in the heart of Termeno, perfectly concealed inside the property at Via Andreas Hofer. The beating heart of the estate is in the nearby hills where a series of little gems unfold at the foot of the Mendola Massif between Termeno and Caldaro. Here there are two pearls: Kastelaz, where the vineyards span five hectares, and Castel Ringberg, where the area is about twenty hectares. Their most interesting wines are made with grapes cultivated at this cru, including the top-notch 2016 Pinot Grigio Vigna Castel Ringberg. It explores the more elegant and deeper character of category, combining hints of pears, dried flowers and tropical fruit with grip and balance. From Kastelaz, on the other hand, we get the 2016 Gewürztraminer, which features intense fragrances of spices and citrus fruit and a tangy, fleshy, supple palate. The 2014 Pinot Nero Ludwig, made with grapes from vineyards around Termeno, also delivered.

○ A. A. Gewürztraminer V. Kastelaz '16	♥♥	5
○ A. A. Pinot Grigio V. Castel Ringberg '16	♥♥	4
● A. A. Pinot Nero Ludwig '14	♥♥	5
○ A. A. Bianco Beyond the Clouds '15	♥♥	6
● A. A. Cabernet Sauvignon V. Castel Ringberg Ris. '13	♥♥	8
● A. A. Lagrein V. Castel Ringberg Ris. '13	♥♥	5
● A. A. Merlot V. Kastelaz Ris. '14	♥♥	6
○ A. A. Sauvignon V. Castel Ringberg '16	♥♥	4
● Kermesse '13	♥♥	6
○ A. A. Gewürztraminer Kastelaz '13	♥♥♥	5
○ A. A. Gewürztraminer Kastelaz '12	♥♥♥	5
○ A. A. Gewürztraminer Kastelaz '11	♥♥♥	5
● A. A. Lagrein Castel Ringberg Ris. '11	♥♥♥	5

Tenuta Waldgries

LOC. SANTA GIUSTINA, 2
39100 BOLZANO/BOZEN
TEL. +39 0471323603
www.waldgries.it

CELLAR SALES
PRE-BOOKED VISITS
ANNUAL PRODUCTION 65,000 bottles
HECTARES UNDER VINE 8.20

Christian Plattner runs the family estate in Santa Giustina, the heart of the Santa Maddalena area. Passion for vinegrowing, respect for the environment, and attentiveness to tradition make Waldgries one of the most interesting wineries in the area. The vineyards span just under ten hectares in three different areas. Red grapes are planted around the main winery building, Pinot Bianco and Sauvignon in Appiano, and in Ora the key player is Lagrein. The 2016 vintage was a good one for Schiava, which made for a memorable Santa Maddalena Antheos. Its lustrous appearance and ruby-red color anticipate sophisticated aromas in which spices intertwine with wild fruit and fines herbes. The palate sees greater fullness while remaining light and savory. Of the whites, we particularly appreciated the delicate aromas of the 2016 Sauvignon Myra, whose palate wins you over with its balance and length.

● A. A. Santa Maddalena Cl. Antheos '16	♥♥♥	5
● A. A. Lagrein Mirell '14	♥♥	6
○ A. A. Sauvignon Myra '16	♥♥	4
● A. A. Lagrein Ris. '14	♥♥	5
● A. A. Moscato Rosa '14	♥♥	5
○ A. A. Pinot Bianco Isos '15	♥♥	4
● A. A. Santa Maddalena Cl. '16	♥♥	3
● A. A. Cabernet Sauvignon '99	♥♥♥	6
● A. A. Lagrein Mirell '09	♥♥♥	6
● A. A. Lagrein Scuro Mirell '08	♥♥♥	6
● A. A. Lagrein Scuro Mirell '07	♥♥♥	6
● A. A. Lagrein Scuro Mirell '01	♥♥♥	6
● A. A. Santa Maddalena Cl. Antheos '13	♥♥♥	4*
● A. A. Santa Maddalena Cl. Antheos '12	♥♥♥	4*
● A. A. Santa Maddalena Cl. Antheos '11	♥♥♥	4*

osef Weger

c. Cornaiano
 Casa del Gesù, 17
9050 Appiano/Eppan [BZ]
l. +39 0471662416
ww.wegerhof.it

CELLAR SALES
RE-BOOKED VISITS
CCOMMODATION AND RESTAURANT SERVICE
NNUAL PRODUCTION 80,000 bottles
ECTARES UNDER VINE 8.00

he Weger family winery has been working
 the Alto Adige area for about six
enerations. Today Johannes is in the
riving seat. The vineyards span fewer than
n hectares and produce consistent wines,
here the variety is easily recognizable.
he cellar consists of several connected
nderground rooms located below the road
ystem. The wine that most impressed our
ommission was the 2015 Lagrein Stoa,
ade with grapes cultivated on the Bolzano
lain and aged in large wood. On the nose,
s characteristic notes of smoke and black
uit are embellished by hints of medicinal
erbs and spices. In the mouth, its impact
s assertive and powerful and with acidity
wooping in to pare down the palate. The
016 Sauvignon Myron features fresh
xotic and vegetal notes, and a dynamic,
aut palate.

A. A. Gewürztraminer Artyo '16	2*
A. A. Lagrein Stoa '15	3
A. A. Pinot Bianco Lithos '16	3
A. A. Pinot Grigio Ried '16	3
A. A. Pinot Nero Johann '15	3
A. A. Sauvignon Myron '16	2*
A. A. Müller Thurgau Pursgla '16	3
A. A. Chardonnay Leite '16	3
A. A. Lagrein Stoa '14	3
A. A. Merlot Maso delle Rose '13	5
A. A. Pinot Bianco Maso delle Rose '15	4
A. A. Pinot Bianco Maso delle Rose '13	4
A. A. Pinot Grigio Ried '15	3
A. A. Sauvignon Maso delle Rose '15	4

Peter Zemmer

s.da del Vino, 24
39040 Cortina Sulla Strada del Vino/Kurtinig [BZ]
Tel. +39 0471817143
www.peterzemmer.com

CELLAR SALES
PRE-BOOKED VISITS
ANNUAL PRODUCTION 500,000 bottles
HECTARES UNDER VINE 65.00

Peter Zemmer's winery is approaching its
hundredth year of activity. Located in the
heart of the South Tyrolean Unterland, on
the border with the province of Trento, it is
on the wine route in Cortina. The winery
was established between the two World
Wars and today it is a benchmark for
enthusiasts of the region's wines. The
vineyards span over sixty hectares,
combining owned land and that of local
grape growers, and are used to make
consistently good wines that perfectly
reflect the character of the territory. The
Pinot Grigio Giatl is made with grapes
cultivated around Cortina and features
intense aromas that call up ripe pears and
dried flowers. In the mouth, the wine
proves full and fleshy, with oak only making
a cameo appearance. Then, thanks to its
tanginess, the wine lengthens with grip and
suppleness. The Chardonnay Crivelli is
sunnier and riper, with warm expressions of
yellow fruit and toasty notes. The palate is
striking for its balance and delicacy. The
Gewürztraminer R is a rich, powerful and
gutsy wine.

O A. A. Pinot Grigio Giatl Ris. '15	3*
O A. A. Chardonnay Crivelli Ris. '15	4
O A. A. Gewürztraminer Selection R '16	4
● A. A. Lagrein Selection R Ris. '15	3
O A. A. Müller Thurgau Caprile '16	3
O A. A. Pinot Bianco Punggl '16	3
O A. A. Pinot Grigio Peter Zemmer '16	2*
O A. A. Riesling Peter Zemmer '16	3
O A. A. Sauvignon Peter Zemmer '16	3
O A. A. Chardonnay Peter Zemmer '16	3
O A. A. Spumante Brut Peter Zemmer '16	3
O Cortinie Bianco '16	3
O A. A. Chardonnay Selection R Ris. '14	4
● A. A. Lagrein Selection R Ris. '14	3*

Baron Widmann

Endergasse, 3
39040 Cortaccia/Kurtatsch [DZ]
Tel. +39 0471880092
www.baron-widmann.it

CELLAR SALES
PRE-BOOKED VISITS
ANNUAL PRODUCTION 35,000 bottles
HECTARES UNDER VINE 15.00

○ A. A. Pinot Bianco '16	♟♟	3
● A. A. Cabernet Merlot '14	♟	4
○ A. A. Sauvignon '16	♟	3

Ferruccio Carlotto

via Clauser, 19
39040 Ora/Auer [BZ]
Tel. +39 0471810407
michelacarlotto@virgilio.it

CELLAR SALES
PRE-BOOKED VISITS
ANNUAL PRODUCTION 10,500 bottles
HECTARES UNDER VINE 2.00

● A. A. Lagrein Di Ora in Ora '15	♟♟	3
● A. A. Pinot Nero Filari di Mazzon '15	♟♟	4

Eichenstein

Katzensteinstrasse, 34
39012 Merano/Meran [BZ]
Tel. +39 3442820179
www.eichenstein.it

ANNUAL PRODUCTION 25,000 bottles
HECTARES UNDER VINE 4.50
SUSTAINABLE WINERY

○ A. A. Chardonnay '16	♟♟	3
○ A. A. Pinot Bianco '16	♟♟	3
○ A. A. Sauvignon Stein '16	♟♟	3
○ Gloria Dei '16	♟♟	3

Bergmannhof

loc. San Paolo
Riva di Sotto, 46
39050 Appiano/Eppan [BZ]
Tel. +39 0471637082
www.bergmannhof.it

CELLAR SALES
PRE-BOOKED VISITS
ANNUAL PRODUCTION 13,000 bottles
HECTARES UNDER VINE 2.20

○ A. A. Chardonnay '16	♟♟	2
○ A. A. Chardonnay Der Bergmann Ris. '15	♟♟	4
● A.A. Lagrein '16	♟	4
● A.A. Lagrein Der Bergmann Ris. '14	♟	4

Egger-Ramer

via Guncina, 5
39100 Bolzano/Bozen [BZ]
Tel. +39 0471280541
www.egger-ramer.com

CELLAR SALES
PRE-BOOKED VISITS
ANNUAL PRODUCTION 120,000 bottles
HECTARES UNDER VINE 14.00

● A. A. Lagrein Kristan '15	♟♟	3
● A. A. Lagrein Kristan Ris. '14	♟♟	3
○ A. A. Pinot Bianco '16	♟♟	2
○ A. A. Gewürztraminer '16	♟	3

Tenuta Grottner

p.zza Chiesa, 9
39050 Fiè allo Sciliar/Völs am Schlern [BZ]
Tel. +39 0471725014
www.hotelturm.it

○ A. A. Pinot Bianco Pica '14	♟♟	4
● A. A. Pinot Nero Corax '14	♟♟	5
○ A. A. Sauvignon Bubo '15	♟	4

Haidenhof

VIA MONTELEONE, 17
39010 CERMES/TSCHERMS [BZ]
TEL. +39 0473562392
www.haidenhof.it

CELLAR SALES
PRE-BOOKED VISITS
RESTAURANT SERVICE
ANNUAL PRODUCTION 30,000 bottles
HECTARES UNDER VINE 3.50

○ A.A. Pinot Bianco '16	♚♚ 2*
○ A.A. Sauvignon '15	♚♚ 2*
● A.A. Pinot Nero Ofen '15	♚ 2

Hof Gandberg
Thomas Niedermayr

S.DA CASTEL PALÚ, 1
39057 APPIANO/EPPAN [BZ]
TEL. +39 0471664152
www.thomas-niedermayr.com

CELLAR SALES
PRE-BOOKED VISITS
ANNUAL PRODUCTION 10,000 bottles
HECTARES UNDER VINE 1.50
VITICULTURE METHOD Certified Organic

○ Abendrot T. N. 06 '14	♚♚ 4
○ Bronner T.N. 04 '15	♚♚ 3
○ Pinot Bianco T. N. 76 '13	♚♚ 4

Tenuta Kollerhof Mazon

VIA DEGLI ALPINI
39044 EGNA/NEUMARKT [BZ]
TEL. +39 3313334468
www.kellerei-kollerhof.com

● A. A. Pinot Nero Kollerhof '15	♚♚ 5
○ Solaris Cucol '16	♚♚ 2*

Larcherhof - Spögler

VIA RENCIO, 82
39100 BOLZANO/BOZEN
TEL. +39 0471365034
larcherhof@yahoo.de

CELLAR SALES
PRE-BOOKED VISITS
ANNUAL PRODUCTION 30,000 bottles
HECTARES UNDER VINE 5.00

● A. A. Merlot '15	♚♚ 3
● A.A. Santa Maddalena Cl. '16	♚♚ 2*
● A. A. Merlot Lagrein '09	♚ 3
○ A. A. Pinot Grigio '16	♚ 3

Lehengut

VIA DELLE FONTI, 2
39020 COLSANO
TEL. +39 3487562676
www.lehengut.it

● A. A. Val Venosta Pinot Nero '15	♚♚ 3
○ A. A. Val Venosta Riesling '16	♚♚ 3
○ A. A. Val Venosta Pinot Bianco '16	♚ 3

Lieselehof
Werner Morandell

VIA KARDATSCH, 6
39052 CALDARO/KALTERN [BZ]
TEL. +39 3299011593
www.lieselehof.com

CELLAR SALES
PRE-BOOKED VISITS
ACCOMMODATION
ANNUAL PRODUCTION 20,000 bottles
HECTARES UNDER VINE 3.00
VITICULTURE METHOD Certified Organic

● Amadeus '16	♚♚ 3
○ Brenner Passito Sweet Claire '14	♚♚ 6
○ Bronner Julian '16	♚♚ 3
○ Vino del Passo '16	♚ 6

Marinushof - Heinrich Pohl

LOC. MARAGNO
3.DA VECCHIA, 9B
39020 CASTELBELLO CIARDES/KASTELBELL TSCHARS [BZ]
TEL. +39 0473624717
www.marinushof.it

CELLAR SALES
PRE-BOOKED VISITS
ACCOMMODATION
ANNUAL PRODUCTION 8,000 bottles
HECTARES UNDER VINE 1.20

● A.A. Valle Venosta Pinot Nero '15	♎♎	5
○ Riesling '16	♎♎	3
○ A.A. Valle Venosta Pinot Grigio '16	♎	4

Lorenz Martini

LOC. CORNAIANO/GIRLAN
VIA PRANZOL, 2D
39057 APPIANO/EPPAN [BZ]
TEL. +39 0471664136
www.lorenz-martini.it

CELLAR SALES
PRE-BOOKED VISITS
ANNUAL PRODUCTION 15,000 bottles
HECTARES UNDER VINE 2.00

○ A. A. Spumante Brut Comitissa Ris. '12	♎♎	5

Messnerhof
Bernhard Pichler

LOC. SAN PIETRO, 7
39100 BOLZANO/BOZEN
TEL. +39 0471977162
www.messnerhof.net

CELLAR SALES
PRE-BOOKED VISITS
ANNUAL PRODUCTION 15,000 bottles
HECTARES UNDER VINE 2.90

● A. A. Lagrein Ris. '14	♎♎	4
● Belleus '14	♎♎	4
● Mos Maiorum '15	♎♎	3
○ A.A. Terlano Sauvignon '16	♎	3

Obermoser
H. & T. Rottensteiner

FRAZ. RENCIO
VIA SANTA MADDALENA, 35
39100 BOLZANO/BOZEN
TEL. +39 0471973549
www.obermoser.it

CELLAR SALES
PRE-BOOKED VISITS
ANNUAL PRODUCTION 30,000 bottles
HECTARES UNDER VINE 3.80

● A. A. Lagrein '16	♎♎	3
● A. A. Lagrein Grafenleiten Ris. '15	♎♎	5
● A. A. Santa Maddalena Cl. '16	♎	2
○ A. A. Sauvignon '16	♎	3

Weingut Pföstl

S.DA VECCHIA, 14
39017 SCENA/SCHENNA [BZ]
TEL. +39 0473230760
www.weinliab.com

○ A. A. Chardonnay Valpitan '15	♎♎	2*
○ A. A. Gewürztraminer '16	♎♎	2*
○ A. A. Pinot Bianco Valpitan '16	♎♎	2*
○ A. A. Sauvignon '16	♎♎	2*

Thomas Pichler

FRAZ. VILLA DI MEZZO
VIA DELLE VIGNE, 4A
39052 CALDARO/KALTERN [BZ]
TEL. +39 0471963094
www.thomas-pichler.it

CELLAR SALES
PRE-BOOKED VISITS
ANNUAL PRODUCTION 15,000 bottles
HECTARES UNDER VINE 1.50

● A. A. Lago di Caldaro Scelto Cl. Sup. Olte Reben '16	♎♎	3*
● A. A. Lagrein Sond Ris. '15	♎♎	5
● Furioso '15	♎♎	8

Plonerhof - Erhard Tutzer

VIA SANTA MADDALENA SOTTO, 29
39100 MARLENGO/MARLING [BZ]
TEL. +39 0471975559

ANNUAL PRODUCTION 5,000 bottles
HECTARES UNDER VINE 1.30

● A. A. Pinot Nero Exclusiv Ris. '14	▼▼ 3
○ A. A. Sauvignon Exclusiv '15	▼▼ 4

Schloss Englar

LOC. PIGENO, 42
39057 APPIANO/EPPAN [BZ]
TEL. +39 0471662628
www.weingut-englar.com

ANNUAL PRODUCTION 15,000 bottles
HECTARES UNDER VINE 7.00

○ A. A. Chardonnay '15	▼▼ 4
○ A. A. Pinot Bianco '16	▼▼ 3
● A. A. Pinot Nero Ris. '15	▼▼ 3
○ Gewürztraminer Passito '15	▼▼ 4

Tenuta Seeperle

LOC. SAN GIUSEPPE AL LAGO, 28
39052 CALDARO/KALTERN [BZ]
TEL. +39 0471 960158
www.seeperle.it

ANNUAL PRODUCTION 15,000 bottles
HECTARES UNDER VINE 2.00

○ A. A. Gewürztraminer Scharf '16	▼▼ 4
○ A. A. Pinot Bianco Leidenschaft '15	▼▼ 2*
○ A. A. Sauvignon Echt Geil '16	▼▼ 4

Tenuta Spitalerhof Günther Oberpertinger

VIA LEITACH, 46
39043 CHIUSA/KLAUSEN [BZ]
TEL. +39 0472847612
www.spitalerhof.it

ANNUAL PRODUCTION 10,000 bottles
HECTARES UNDER VINE 1.60

○ Grüner Veltliner '16	▼▼ 3
○ Sylvaner Sepp Alte Reben '16	▼▼ 3
○ Gewürztraminer '16	▼ 3

St. Quirinus - Robert Sinn

VIA PIANIZZA DI SOPRA, 4B
39052 CALDARO/KALTERN [BZ]
TEL. +39 329 8085003
www.st-quirinus.it

CELLAR SALES
PRE-BOOKED VISITS
ACCOMMODATION
ANNUAL PRODUCTION 12,000 bottles
HECTARES UNDER VINE 2.50
VITICULTURE METHOD Certified Organic

● A. A. Merlot '15	▼▼ 3
○ A. A. Sauvignon '16	▼▼ 3
○ Planties Weiss '16	▼▼ 3
● A. A. Pinot Nero '15	▼ 3

Thurnhof - Andreas Berger

LOC. ASLAGO
VIA CASTEL FLAVON, 7
39100 BOLZANO/BOZEN
TEL. +39 0471288460
www.thurnhof.com

CELLAR SALES
PRE-BOOKED VISITS
ANNUAL PRODUCTION 25,000 bottles
HECTARES UNDER VINE 3.50

● A. A. Lagrein '16	▼▼ 3
● A. A. Lagrein Ris. '14	▼▼ 4
○ A. A. Sauvignon 800 '16	▼▼ 3
○ A. A. Moscato Giallo '16	▼ 3

Thomas Unterhofer

LOC. PIANIZZA DI SOPRA, 5
39052 CALDARO/KALTERN [BZ]
TEL. +39 0471669133
www.weingut-unterhofer.com

CELLAR SALES
PRE-BOOKED VISITS
ANNUAL PRODUCTION 12,000 bottles
HECTARES UNDER VINE 3.00

○ A. A. Chardonnay '16	♟♟	3
○ A. A. Kerner '15	♟♟	3
○ A. A. Sauvignon '16	♟♟	2*
○ Reitl Weiss '16	♟♟	3

Wilhelm Walch

VIA A. HOFER, 1
39040 TERMENO/TRAMIN [BZ]
TEL. +39 0471860172
www.walch.it

CELLAR SALES
PRE-BOOKED VISITS
ANNUAL PRODUCTION 600,000 bottles
HECTARES UNDER VINE 73.00

● A. A. Cabernet Sauvignon Ris. '14	♟♟	4
○ A. A. Chardonnay Pilat '16	♟♟	2*
○ A. A. Pinot Grigio Marat '16	♟♟	2*

Weinberghof
Christian Bellutti

IN DER AU, 4A
39040 TERMENO/TRAMIN [BZ]
TEL. +39 0471863224
www.weinberg-hof.com

ANNUAL PRODUCTION 20,000 bottles
HECTARES UNDER VINE 2.80

○ A. A. Gewürztraminer '16	♟♟	3
○ A. A. Gewürztraminer Gold Edition '15	♟♟	4
● A. A. Lagrein '16	♟♟	3

Vivaldi - Arunda

VIA JOSEF-SCHWARZ, 18
39010 MELTINA/MÖLTEN [R7]
TEL. +39 0471668033
www.arundavivaldi.it

CELLAR SALES
PRE-BOOKED VISITS
ANNUAL PRODUCTION 90,000 bottles
HECTARES UNDER VINE 12.00

○ A. A. Spumante Blanc de Blancs Arunda Extra Brut	♟♟	5
○ A. A. Spumante Extra Brut Arunda Ris. '11	♟♟	5
○ A. A. Spumante Brut Arunda	♟	5

Wassererhof

LOC. NOVALE DI FIÈ, 21

39050 FIÈ ALLO SCILIAR/VÖLS AM SCHLERN [BZ]
TEL. +39 0471724114
www.wassererhof.com

CELLAR SALES
PRE-BOOKED VISITS
RESTAURANT SERVICE
ANNUAL PRODUCTION 35,000 bottles
HECTARES UNDER VINE 4.00

○ A. A. Pinot Bianco '16	♟♟	3
○ A.A. Sauvignon '16	♟♟	3

Weingut Martin Abraham

VIA MADERNETO, 29
39057 APPIANO/EPPAN [BZ]
TEL. +39 0471664192
www.weingutabraham.it

ANNUAL PRODUCTION 20,000 bottles
HECTARES UNDER VINE 3.00

○ Gewürztraminer Upupa Orange '15	♟♟	4
○ Pinot Bianco In der Lamm '15	♟♟	3
● Pinot Nero '14	♟♟	3
○ Upupa Bianco '16	♟	4

VENETO

The great commercial success that Veneto has been enjoying as of late stems largely from their two great appellations, Prosecco and Amarone della Valpolicella. They would seem to be antithetical, one is fragrant and the other deep, one is light and racy, the other potent and poised. What unites them is a deep bond with their respective territories, with their history and traditions, as well as the work of the vine growers who, for generations, have carried on their backbreaking work both in the vineyard and in the cellar. The international presence of these two emblematic wines is proof of the results achieved. The excellent 2015 and 2016 seasons made for a high-quality series of wines across the board, one that spans all the region's appellations. In the first case, regional producers managed to interpret the vintage's great richness, in the second, pressure and aromatic focus figured centrally, making for wines of great character and pleasantness. Some 41 wines, representing some of the most important appellations in Veneto, earned a gold, offering further proof of the agricultural and entrepreneurial excellence that pervades the region. In many cases, producers eschewed more commercially viable models in favor of expressing that extraordinary bond that exists between terroir, vineyard and vigneron. Amarone, which steals the limelight with a series of award-winning wines, is happy to welcome Marco Speri into the fold, as well as Elena and Enrico Moschetta, who've transformed Biancavigna into one of Conegliano Valdobbiadene's emerging wineries in just a few short years. Soave also made headlines with Gaetano Tobin's extensive work finally bringing success to Cantina di Monteforte, and a Soave that brings together character, weight and identity. The quartet of new entries concludes with the Piona family, whose work with Bardolino has made for a fantastic version that's only released after lengthy aging in the cellar. As for the rest, well, there are so many that it's difficult to choose, from the solid fullness of the region's Valpolicella Superiores to the fragrance and character of its Custozas, from its gutsy Bordeauxs to the grace of its Luganas. In closing, we'd like to point out a superb Riesling dalla Valdadige, the Fugatti brothers' Collezione di Famiglia, which interprets this acclaimed German cultivar with personality and class. And once again, Veneto wins the 'Winery of the Year' award, which goes to Masi, a producer that has contributed to making Italy's wines known throughout the world.

A Mi Manera

FRAZ. LISON
VIA CADUTI PER LA PATRIA, 29
30026 PORTOGRUARO [VE]
TEL. +39 336592660
www.vinicolamimanera.com

CELLAR SALES
PRE-BOOKED VISITS
ANNUAL PRODUCTION 42,000 bottles
HECTARES UNDER VINE 7.00

Lison Pramaggiore subscribes to an idea of wine that is both pleasant and respectful of the variety, without asking for much more. Antonio 'Toni' Bigai has chosen a different route, exploring the intimate relationship that the territory has with its grapes. Rather than highlighting the expression of aromas, he seeks to bring out their character and depth. His selection can seem, at times, minimalist and rustic, but the most discerning wine lovers will discover truly captivating wines. The 2016 Tai tops the bill with its aromas of iodine, Mediterranean scrub, dried flowers and spice. It comes through powerfully and assertively on the palate, leaving length and lightness up to acidity. Among the reds, we particularly enjoyed the A Mi Manera Rosso Decimo, a Bordeaux blend with a dash of Franconia and Refosco that features aromas of plums and herbs. It's round on the palate and reveals a confident and juicy mouthfeel. The 2016 Malvasia is a rich and gutsy wine with great personality.

● A Mi Manera Rosso Decimo	♟♟	3
○ Malvasia '16	♟♟	3
● Merlot '15	♟♟	2*
○ Tai '16	♟♟	3
○ A Mi Manera Bianco Undecimo	♟	3
● Cabernet '15	♟	3
○ Malvasia '15	♟♟	3
○ Malvasia d'Istria '12	♟♟	2*
○ Tai '15	♟♟	3

Stefano Accordini

FRAZ. CAVALO
LOC. CAMPAROL, 10
37022 FUMANE [VR]
TEL. +39 0457760138
www.accordinistefano.it

CELLAR SALES
PRE-BOOKED VISITS
ANNUAL PRODUCTION 120,000 bottles
HECTARES UNDER VINE 13.00

Situated in upper Valpolicella, Tiziano and Daniele Accordini's vineyards have seen significant expansion in recent years, reaching more than 10 hectares, most of which are located in the coolest and highest areas of the DOC zone. The two brothers are also making room for the new generation, Giacomo, Paolo and Marco, who are bringing their enthusiasm and energy to Accordini's operations. Their selection is dedicated almost exclusively to Valpolicella classics, interpreted with fullness and grip. The Il Fornetto performed well. The Accordini family only make this Amarone in exceptional vintages. It features aromas of sweet and overripe fruit, cocoa and spice, with oak just peeping out from the background. The Amarone Acinatico, however, exhibits a more approachable and fresher aromatic framework, while the palate proves energetic and long.

● Amarone della Valpolicella Cl. Vign. Il Fornetto '11	♟♟	8
● Amarone della Valpolicella Cl. Acinatico '13	♟♟	7
● Paxxo '15	♟♟	4
● Recioto della Valpolicella Cl. Acinatico '15	♟♟	5
● Valpolicella Cl. '16	♟♟	2*
● Valpolicella Cl. Sup. Ripasso Acinatico '15	♟♟	3
● Amarone della Valpolicella Cl. Acinatico '12	♟♟	7
● Amarone della Valpolicella Cl. Vign. Il Fornetto '10	♟♟	8

Adami

FRAZ. COLBERTALDO
VIA ROVEDE, 27
31020 VIDOR [TV]
TEL. +39 0423982110
www.adamispumanti.it

CELLAR SALES
PRE-BOOKED VISITS
ANNUAL PRODUCTION 700,000 bottles
HECTARES UNDER VINE 12.00

Armando and Franco Adami's winery is an essential source for anyone wanting to know about Prosecco in its homeland, the strip of hills that connects Valdobbiadene to Conegliano. The estate comprises a dozen hectares spread out on some of the best exposures, starting with their vineyard Giardino (in Colbertaldo) and concluding on the Torri di Credazzo (Farra di Soligo). To round out their production, they rely on a tight network of closely-followed vine growers in the area, allowing Franco and Armando to maintain an outstanding standard of quality. And it's Giardino that gives rise to their most interesting wine, a Valdobbiadene Asciutto with aromas of crisp white fruit refreshed by flowery notes. The excellent 2016 vintage conferred solidity and grip to the wine, while maintaining sweetness. Its finish comes through gutsy and long. The Col Credas is a vibrant, well-orchestrated wine with great elegance.

○ Valdobbiadene Rive di Colbertaldo Asciutto Vign. Giardino '16	♟♟♟ 3*
○ Valdobbiadene Rive di Farra di Soligo Brut Col Credas '16	♟♟ 3*
○ Cartizze	♟♟ 5
○ Valdobbiadene Brut Bosco di Gica	♟♟ 3
○ Valdobbiadene Extra Dry Dei Casel	♟♟ 3
○ Treviso Brut Garbel	♟ 2
○ Valdobbiadene Prosecco Sul Lievito '16	♟ 3
○ Valdobbiadene Rive di Farra di Soligo Brut Col Credas '13	♟♟♟ 3*
○ Valdobbiadene Rive di Farra di Soligo Brut Col Credas '12	♟♟♟ 3*

Ida Agnoletti

LOC. SELVA DEL MONTELLO
VIA SACCARDO, 55
31040 VOLPAGO DEL MONTELLO [TV]
TEL. +39 0423621555
www.agnoletti.it

CELLAR SALES
PRE-BOOKED VISITS
ANNUAL PRODUCTION 50,000 bottles
HECTARES UNDER VINE 7.00

Over recent years, Montello, the historic site of Bordeaux in Veneto, has been leaving more room for Glera, the variety used for that global phenom, Prosecco. Ida Agnoletti is still faithful to her own ideas and the viticultural heritage of the land, dedicating much of her attention to Merlot and Cabernet (while finding time for experimentation). The producer operates in Selva del Montello, and offers a wide variety of wines. Of the wines we tasted, the Vita was the one that impressed us the most this year. It's a red made with Bordeaux varieties, with a nose of ripe red fruit that is refreshed by a subtle and fragrant nuance of medicinal herbs. On the palate, it reveals a full body and the character of the Montello. This means tannins are never too exposed and it has a driving and savory acidity, making for a long and sophisticated finish. The Seneca, on the other hand, is more approachable and exhibits similar taste dynamics.

● Montello e Colli Asolani Cabernet Sauvignon Love Is... '15	♟♟ 2*
● Montello e Colli Asolani Merlot La Ida '15	♟♟ 2*
● Montello e Colli Asolani Recantina '15	♟♟ 2*
● Seneca '13	♟♟ 3
● Vita Life is Red '13	♟♟ 3
○ Manzoni 6.0.13 Follia '15	♟ 2
● Montello e Colli Asolani Merlot '15	♟ 2
○ PSL Always Frizzante	♟ 2
● Montello e Colli Asolani Merlot '14	♟♟ 2*
● Montello e Colli Asolani Merlot '13	♟♟ 2*
● Montello e Colli Asolani Merlot La Ida '15	♟♟ 2*
● Montello e Colli Asolani Merlot La Ida '13	♟♟ 2*
● Vita Life is Red '12	♟♟ 3

★★★Allegrini

VIA GIARE, 5
37022 FUMANE [VR]
TEL. +39 0456832019
www.allegrini.it

CELLAR SALES
PRE-BOOKED VISITS
ACCOMMODATION AND RESTAURANT SERVICE
ANNUAL PRODUCTION 1,000,000 bottles
HECTARES UNDER VINE 120.00
SUSTAINABLE WINERY

Theirs is a decades-long story set in the heart of Valpolicella, a vineyard that spans more than one-hundred hectares, attended to by a family closely-tied to their territory and its rhythms. This is Allegrini, one of the most esteemed brands in the world of Italian wine, with its strong selection that knows how to respect tradition and be modern at the same time. The vineyards, situated in the hills at medium and high altitudes, are managed with passion and skill, making for wines defined by their freshness and focused fruit expressions. Every year the Amarone produced by Allegrini manages to earn praise. It's a wine that brings a new style to this historic appellation, while preserving its most interesting traits, such as power and ripeness of fruit. It also modernizes expressions of integrity and freshness. All of this is accompanied by a palate featuring tannins, acidity and richness of taste. The La Grola also performed well. It's a virtually monovarietal Corvina with great grip and finesse.

● Amarone della Valpolicella Cl. '13	♟♟♟ 8
● La Grola '14	♟♟ 5
● Palazzo della Torre '14	♟♟ 4
○ Soave '16	♟♟ 3
● Valpolicella Cl. '16	♟♟ 3
● Amarone della Valpolicella Cl. '12	♟♟♟ 8
● Amarone della Valpolicella Cl. '11	♟♟♟ 8
● Amarone della Valpolicella Cl. '10	♟♟♟ 8
● Amarone della Valpolicella Cl. '09	♟♟♟ 8
● Amarone della Valpolicella Cl. '08	♟♟♟ 8
● Amarone della Valpolicella Cl. '07	♟♟♟ 8
● Amarone della Valpolicella Cl. '06	♟♟♟ 8
● Amarone della Valpolicella Cl. '05	♟♟♟ 7
● Amarone della Valpolicella Cl. '04	♟♟♟ 7

★Roberto Anselmi

VIA SAN CARLO, 46
37032 MONTEFORTE D'ALPONE [VR]
TEL. +39 0457611488
www.anselmi.eu

CELLAR SALES
PRE-BOOKED VISITS
RESTAURANT SERVICE
ANNUAL PRODUCTION 700,000 bottles
HECTARES UNDER VINE 70.00

Even if he hasn't produced Soave for almost 20 years, Roberto Anselmi remains a benchmark in the area. He is the beating heart of a winery that has managed to recreate itself significantly in recent years, while staying true to its own ideas, as well as the stylistic profile of the DOC zone. He can count on the increasingly important support of his children, Tommaso (in the cellar) and Lisa (who serves as a go-between with the market). Theirs is a selection that delivers, even if it comprises only five wines. The Capitel Croce is a white wine that wins you over with its gentle charm. Its aromas of ripe yellow fruit are intertwined with dried flowers and a hint of minerality. In the mouth it's savory, taut and very long, with a memorable finish. The Capitelli is the exact opposite. This dried-grape wine has an explosive aromatic expression, consisting of dried apricots and candied citrus fruit, with the sweetness of the palate supported by its acidity.

○ Capitel Croce '15	♟♟♟ 3*
○ I Capitelli '15	♟♟ 6
○ Capitel Foscarino '16	♟♟ 3
○ San Vincenzo '16	♟♟ 2*
○ Capitel Croce '09	♟♟♟ 3*
○ Capitel Croce '06	♟♟♟ 3
○ Capitel Croce '05	♟♟♟ 3
○ Capitel Croce '04	♟♟♟ 3
○ Capitel Croce '03	♟♟♟ 3
○ Capitel Croce '02	♟♟♟ 3*
○ Capitel Croce '01	♟♟♟ 3

Antolini

VIA PROGNOL, 22
37020 MARANO DI VALPOLICELLA [VR]
TEL. +39 0457755351
www.antolinivini.it

CELLAR SALES
PRE-BOOKED VISITS
ACCOMMODATION
ANNUAL PRODUCTION 60,000 bottles
HECTARES UNDER VINE 9.00
SUSTAINABLE WINERY

The Marano valley cuts sharply to the north and from there it rises, as if in search of the cool air that keeps grapes healthy and fragrant. It's here that brothers Pier Paolo and Stefano Antolini lead their family-run winery, some 10 hectares that are dedicated exclusively to Valpolicella's time-honored varieties. Their style, which is strongly tied to tradition, seeks to join the fullness brought out by drying and the 'ripasso' with the freshness and the grip that the valley bestows the grapes. The Marano brothers make a limited range of wines, but their quality is never called into question. They made an overall positive impression, but there were no home runs. The Recioto is a sweet dried-grape wine that's produced less often than before, but it's a constant at Antolini. On the nose, hints of dried wild fruit are discernible. These are enriched by nuances of fines herbes and pepper. The sweetness is measured in the mouth and well-contrasted by acidity.

● Amarone della Valpolicella Cl. Moròpio '13	♟♟ 8
● Recioto della Valpolicella Cl. '15	♟♟ 6
● Theobroma '12	♟♟ 4
● Valpolicella Cl. '16	♟♟ 3
● Amarone della Valpolicella Cl. Ca' Coato '12	♟♟ 8
● Amarone della Valpolicella Cl. Moròpio '12	♟♟ 8
● Amarone della Valpolicella Cl. Moròpio '11	♟♟ 6
● Corvina '13	♟♟ 4
● Recioto della Valpolicella Cl. '13	♟♟ 6
● Recioto della Valpolicella Cl. '11	♟♟ 5
● Valpolicella Cl. Sup. Ripasso '14	♟♟ 5
● Valpolicella Cl. Sup. Ripasso '13	♟♟ 4

Albino Armani

VIA CERADELLO, 401
37020 DOLCÈ [VR]
TEL. +39 0457290033
www.albinoarmani.com

CELLAR SALES
PRE-BOOKED VISITS
ANNUAL PRODUCTION 900,000 bottles
HECTARES UNDER VINE 220.00
SUSTAINABLE WINERY

Albino Armani is an eclectic producer who's able to go from Valdadige's fresh wines to the rich and powerful reds of Valpolicella, from the simplicity of Piave to the elegance of Grave del Friuli, and do it all without getting lost. The secret lies in his superior skill and a sensibility that allows him to best interpret the territory. Today, the winery has become a major producer among those operating in the northeastern part of the country, with more then 200 hectares and a consistently strong selection of outstanding quality. After a few years of settling in, Valpolicella wines are beginning to rise up our rankings, led by an excellent version of a 2012 Amarone Classico. It has sophisticated aromas that call up wild berry jam and herbs, while in the mouth it's generous, but contrasted by tight-knit tannins. In terms of the nearby Valdadige, it's worth noting the spontaneous and bold Foja Tonda, a red full of character and substance.

● Amarone della Valpolicella Cl. '12	♟♟ 5
● Amarone della Valpolicella Cl. Cuslanus '12	♟♟ 6
● Valdadige Terra dei Forti Foja Tonda Casetta '13	♟♟ 3
○ Valdadige Terra dei Forti Pinot Grigio Colle Ara '16	♟♟ 2*
● Valpolicella Cl. Sup. Egle '14	♟♟ 2*
● Valpolicella Cl. Sup. Ripasso '15	♟♟ 3
○ Sauvignon Campo Napoleone '16	♟ 2
● Valdadige Foja Tonda Casetta Terra dei Forti '12	♟♟ 3
○ Valdadige Terra dei Forti Pinot Grigio Colle Ara '15	♟♟ 2*

Barollo

VIA RIO SERVA, 4B
35123 PREGANZIOL [TV]
TEL. +39 0422633014
www.barollo.com

CELLAR SALES
PRE-BOOKED VISITS
ANNUAL PRODUCTION 88,000 bottles
HECTARES UNDER VINE 45.00
SUSTAINABLE WINERY

The plains that run north of Venice, towards Treviso and the mountains, don't see much viticulture. Among the few exceptions one finds the estate managed by the Barollo brothers, a young operation that believes strongly in the territory and, for more than a decade, has worked to produce a first-rate selection. The vineyards have come to span almost 50 hectares, and each plot is reserved for the best-suited variety. While in the cellar, the brothers work to bring out the grapes' innate expressivity and elegance. Frank did quite well! It's a monovarietal Cabernet Franc that exploits the excellent 2015 vintage to gain an intense nose, with notes of red fruit and spices, and just a hint of pepper peeping out from among its fragrances of plums and herbs. The palate is firm and juicy, without forgoing the characteristic grip of all Barollo's wines, and leads to a long and close-focused finish. The Chardonnay is also very convincing. This white wine marries well with oak to become elegant and tangy.

● Frank! '15	♟♟ 4
○ Alfredo Barollo M. Cl. Brut Ris. '11	♟♟ 5
○ Manzoni Bianco '16	♟♟ 3
○ Piave Chardonnay '15	♟♟ 4
○ Piave Chardonnay Frater '16	♟ 2
● Piave Merlot Frater '16	♟ 2
○ Pinot Bianco '16	♟ 3
○ Prosecco di Treviso Extra Dry '16	♟ 2
○ Sauvignon '16	♟ 3
● Frank! '14	♟♟ 4
○ Manzoni Bianco '15	♟♟ 3
○ Piave Chardonnay '14	♟♟ 4
○ Sauvignon '15	♟♟ 3

Le Battistelle

FRAZ. BROGNOLIGO
VIA SAMBUCO, 110
37032 MONTEFORTE D'ALPONE [VR]
TEL. +39 0456175621
www.lebattistelle.it

CELLAR SALES
PRE-BOOKED VISITS
ANNUAL PRODUCTION 22,000 bottles
HECTARES UNDER VINE 9.00
SUSTAINABLE WINERY

In an area like Soave, where production hasn't always taken advantage of the area's viticultural patrimony, it's a real pleasure to see operations like Gelmino and Cristina Dal Bosco's. Here, in Brognoligo, one of the hamlets that characterizes the heart of the 'zona classica', they cultivate Garganega (exclusively) on fewer than 10 hectares of various, small plots of land, set on the black, basalt hills. The grapes used to make the Soave Roccolo del Durlo come from their steepest and most beautiful vineyard. It's a wine aged on the lees in steel for months before being presented. On the nose, intense ripe fruit gradually gives way to spices, with a subtle note of dried flowers and flint emerging. The generosity of its aromas is well-contrasted by acidity and adds length to a taut, juicy finish. The two simpler Soaves, Le Battistelli and Montesei, are also fresh and pleasant.

○ Soave Cl. Roccolo del Durlo '15	♟♟ 3*
○ Soave Cl. Le Battistelle '15	♟♟ 3
○ Soave Cl. Montesei '16	♟♟ 2*
○ Soave Cl. Battistelle '14	♟♟ 3
○ Soave Cl. Montesei '10	♟♟ 2*
○ Soave Cl. Roccolo del Durlo '14	♟♟ 3

★Lorenzo Begali

VIA CENGIA, 10
37020 SAN PIETRO IN CARIANO [VR]
TEL. +39 0457725148
www.begaliwine.it

CELLAR SALES
PRE-BOOKED VISITS
ANNUAL PRODUCTION 90,000 bottles
HECTARES UNDER VINE 12.00

In an environment like Valpolicella, where, for the past 10 years, wineries have proliferated (thanks to international attention), the Begali family have endured in their role as a leader. Theirs is a small, family-run operation that has maintained a firm, bond with the territory and its traditions. In interpreting these traditions it shows attention and spirit toward creating wines that are both current and rooted. They have a dozen or so hectares of vineyards at their disposal, among which Monte Ca' Bianca and Masua stand out for their excellence. Once again the Monte Ca' Bianca has asserted the superiority of its terroir, enabling the 2012 Amarone of the same name to express itself at the highest level. Wild fruit is close-focused and crisp on the nose, surrounded by medicinal herbs and hints of forest floor, which magnify their freshness in an endless, dynamic, dry and powerful palate. They also make a great Recioto, a dried-grape wine that strikes up good balance between sweetness and lightness.

● Amarone della Valpolicella Cl. Monte Ca' Bianca '12	♈♈♈ 8
● Amarone della Valpolicella Cl. '13	♈♈ 6
● Recioto della Valpolicella Cl. '12	♈♈ 6
● Tigiolo '13	♈♈ 5
● Valpolicella Cl. Sup. Ripasso Vign. La Cengia '15	♈♈ 3
● Valpolicella Cl. '16	♈ 2
● Amarone della Valpolicella Cl. Monte Ca' Bianca '11	♈♈♈ 8
● Amarone della Valpolicella Cl. Monte Ca' Bianca '10	♈♈♈ 8
● Amarone della Valpolicella Cl. Vign. Monte Ca' Bianca '09	♈♈♈ 8

BiancaVigna

LOC. OGLIANO
VIA MONTE NERO, 8
31015 CONEGLIANO [TV]
TEL. +39 0438788403
www.biancavigna.it

CELLAR SALES
PRE-BOOKED VISITS
ACCOMMODATION
ANNUAL PRODUCTION 600,000 bottles
HECTARES UNDER VINE 30.20
SUSTAINABLE WINERY

In just a few years, Elena and Enrico Moschetta have managed to spark their family business, shaping Biancavigna to become one of the most interesting wineries in Conegliano Valdobbiadene. The vineyards span more than thirty hectares in the DOC zone, as well as its neighbor, and their selection of wines also includes grapes from local growers. Careful controls at every stage of production, from the vineyard to the bottle, results in outstanding wines, characterized by attack and grip on the palate. The Rive di Ogliano did quite well. It's a sparkling wine that, on the occasion of its first release, immediately revealed the gifts of its terroir. This Prosecco with an extremely low sugar content is much-appreciated for the fruity freshness of its aromas, embellished with flowers and a subtle overtone of greenness. The excellent vintage helps the palate to stay supple and elegant, it's dry and supported by a tangy and powerful acidity. The Rive di Soligo is more edgy but has great potential.

○ Conegliano Valdobbiadene Rive di Ogliano Brut Nature '16	♈♈♈ 3*
○ Conegliano Valdobbiadene Rive di Soligo Brut Nature '16	♈♈ 3*
○ Conegliano Valdobbiadene Brut '16	♈♈ 3
○ Conegliano Valdobbiadene Brut Biologico '16	♈♈ 3
○ Conegliano Valdobbiadene Extra Dry '16	♈♈ 3
○ Conegliano Valdobbiadene Rive di Soligo Brut Dosaggio Zero '16	♈♈ 3
○ Prosecco Brut	♈♈ 2*
○ Prosecco Extra Dry	♈ 2
○ Prosecco Frizzante	♈ 2
⊙ Spumante Rosa Cuvée 1931	♈ 2
○ Conegliano Valdobbiadene Brut '15	♈♈ 3
○ Conegliano Valdobbiadene Extra Dry '15	♈♈ 3

Bisol

FRAZ. SANTO STEFANO
VIA FOLLO, 33
31049 VALDOBBIADENE [TV]
TEL. +39 0423900138
www.bisol.it

CELLAR SALES
PRE-BOOKED VISITS
ANNUAL PRODUCTION 1,800,000 bottles
HECTARES UNDER VINE 126.00

Vadobbiadene is one of the most beautiful landscapes of Italy, a dense series of steep slopes, where vineyards often stretch all the way to the hilltops. Here, it's as if they're clasping at the sky. The Bisol family personally attends to their vineyards, spread out on these gorgeous hills. They also cultivate several hectares in the eastern part of the DOC zone, and collaborate with various, local vine growers who provide them with additional grapes. The Cartizze Private is a bottle-fermented Brut released two years after vintage. It explores the deepest and most complex nature of Prosecco, featuring aromas of Mediterranean scrub, dried flowers and apple, while the palate sees a perfect balance between sparkle, acidity and tanginess. The Cartizze, a dry sparkling wine, also had a good day. Its sweet, ripe fruit bring finesse to a palate that sees sweetness perfectly supported by acidity.

○ Cartizze Brut Private Fermentato in Bottiglia '14	🍷🍷 5
○ Cartizze	🍷🍷 5
○ Relio Extra Brut M. Cl. Private '10	🍷🍷 6
○ Valdobbiadene Brut Crede '16	🍷🍷 4
○ Valdobbiadene Extra Dry Molera '16	🍷🍷 3
○ Valdobbiadene Extra Dry Vign. del Fol '16	🍷🍷 4
○ Prosecco Brut Bel Star	🍷 3
○ Valdobbiadene Dry Salis '16	🍷 3
○ Valdobbiadene Extra Dry Colmei Jeio	🍷 2
○ Cartizze '15	🍷🍷 5
○ Cartizze Brut Private '13	🍷🍷 5
○ Valdobbiadene Brut Private Garnei '14	🍷🍷 3*
○ Valdobbiadene Extra Dry Vign. del Fol '15	🍷🍷 4

Bolla

FRAZ. PEDEMONTE
VIA A. BOLLA, 3
37029 SAN PIETRO IN CARIANO [VR]
TEL. +39 0456836555
www.bolla.it

CELLAR SALES
PRE-BOOKED VISITS
ANNUAL PRODUCTION 10,000,000 bottles
HECTARES UNDER VINE 188.00

Bolla is among those wineries that have contributed mightily to the success of Verona's wines in the world. Today, this large producer from Piedmont has taken it upon itself to support its most beautiful plots through a more traditional production line. In addition to its own vineyards, they have at their disposal many hectares managed by historic partner-growers, who are supervised closely, making for a selection of wines that is solid and highly consistent. Their Amarone Le Origini is one of the cornerstones of tradition in this territory. Its aromas slowly unfold, with dried fruit running into notes of tobacco, dried flowers and pepper. Its forceful, though well-orchestrated palate unfolds with grace and richness of flavor right up to the wine's long, warm finish. The Amarone Rhetico, on the other hand, plays on more strongly-expressed fruit, proving dynamic, round and more generous in the mouth.

● Amarone della Valpolicella Cl. Le Origini Ris. '11	🍷🍷 6
● Amarone della Valpolicella Cl. Rhetico '11	🍷🍷 6
⊙ Bardolino Chiaretto Cl. La Canestraia '16	🍷🍷 2*
● Creso '13	🍷🍷 4
● Valpolicella Cl. Sup. Ripasso Le Poiane '15	🍷🍷 4
● Bardolino Cl. La Doria '13	🍷 2
○ Lugana '16	🍷 3
○ Prosecco Extra Dry Biologico	🍷 3
○ Custoza La Real Casa '14	🍷🍷 2*
⊙ Soave Cl. Sup. Tufaie '15	🍷🍷 3
● Valpolicella Cl. Sup. Ripasso Le Poiane '14	🍷🍷 4

orgo Stajnbech

Belfiore, 109
020 Pramaggiore [VE]
.. +39 0421799929
ww.borgostajnbech.com

CLLAR SALES
RE-BOOKED VISITS
NNUAL PRODUCTION 90,000 bottles
CTARES UNDER VINE 15.00

e Valent family's winery is one of the
ore interesting operations in the Venetian
rritory, bolstered by 15 hectares of
neyards situated in the plains running
st of Venice. Here the clay-rich soil and
e nearby Adriatic, combined with skillful
anagement of the vineyards themselves,
akes for a selection of wines whose Tai is
p-of-the-line. The range of wines offered
connected to the expression of each
dividual variety, which are interpreted with
grance and harmony. Their top wine is
e Stajnbech white, a Chardonnay
oduced in Pizzo that exploits oak to bring
t its best features. On the nose, its fruit is
scernible amidst oak and spices, with a
btle but intriguing minerality just waiting
emerge. In the mouth, it proves dry and
t, governed by a tangy and racy acidity.
e 150 is as convincing as ever. It's a
on with full and sunny aromas and a
nerous and gratifying palate.

Lison Cl. 150 '15	♟♟ 3
Malbech '16	♟♟ 2*
Stajnbech Bianco '15	♟♟ 3
Pinot Grigio '16	♟ 2
Pinot Nero '15	♟ 2
Refosco P. R. '15	♟ 2
Sauvignon Bosco della Donna '16	♟ 3
Traminer Aromatico '16	♟ 2
Bianco Stajnbech '13	♟♟ 3
Lison Cl. 150 '14	♟♟ 3
Lison-Pramaggiore Cl. 150 '13	♟♟ 3
Refosco P. R. '14	♟♟ 2*
Rosso Stajnbech '13	♟♟ 3
Stajnbech Rosso '11	♟♟ 3

Borgoluce

loc. Musile, 2
31058 Susegana [TV]
Tel. +39 0438435287
www.borgoluce.it

CELLAR SALES
PRE-BOOKED VISITS
ACCOMMODATION AND RESTAURANT SERVICE
ANNUAL PRODUCTION 250,000 bottles
HECTARES UNDER VINE 70.00

Arriving in Susegana from the south, you'll
find the estate of Borgoluce just before the
residential zone. It's an operation that has,
in just a few years, managed to carve out a
place for itself as a leader in Trevigiano's
complex agricultural sector. The Collalto
and Giustinian families have given life to a
business that deals solely with agriculture,
from livestock to viticulture, with the utmost
respect for nature, and a desire to support
both the territory and its residents. Vine
growing takes on a central role here,
mostly in the hills that stretch a few
hundred meters to the north of their new
cellar. The grapes grown here are used to
make their Rive di Collalto Extra Dry. It's a
wine with generous fruit, an example of
how Prosecco from these hills can express
greater richness of fruit and structure. The
mouth is solid and juicy with a long finish.
Their Brut, made with grapes from the
same Rive subzone, is more gutsy and racy.

○ Valdobbiadene Extra Dry	♟♟ 3
○ Valdobbiadene Rive di Collalto Brut '16	♟♟ 2*
○ Valdobbiadene Rive di Collalto Extra Dry '16	♟♟ 2*
○ Valdobbiadene Brut	♟ 3
○ Valdobbiadene Rive di Collalto Brut '15	♟♟ 2*
○ Valdobbiadene Rive di Collalto Brut '14	♟♟ 2*
○ Valdobbiadene Rive di Collalto Brut '13	♟♟ 2*
○ Valdobbiadene Rive di Collalto Extra Dry '14	♟♟ 2*
○ Valdobbiadene Rive di Collalto Extra Dry '13	♟♟ 2*
○ Valdobbiadene Rive di Collalto Extra Dry '12	♟♟ 2*

Borin Vini & Vigne

FRAZ. MONTICELLI
VIA DEI COLLI, 5
35043 MONSELICE [PD]
TEL. +39 042974384
www.viniborin.it

CELLAR SALES
PRE-BOOKED VISITS
ANNUAL PRODUCTION 105,000 bottles
HECTARES UNDER VINE 28.00

The Colli Euganei constitute one of the most intriguing areas in Italy for producing Bordeaux. The area, a large regional park that features a tight range of hills rising up from the Padana plains, hosts the Borin family. Thanks to their 50 years of experience in the sector, and a 30 hectare estate that spans various exposures, positions and altitudes, they've established themselves, and Borin Vini & Vigne, as leaders in the area. Their flagship wine is the Zuan, a Merlot-heavy Bordeaux blend that expresses the sunny nature of this territory. It's dominated by intense notes of red fruit that let overtones of spices and medicinal herbs shine through. In the mouth it proves powerful, refreshed by its acidity and made gutsier by its tight-knit tannins. As for the whites, we particularly enjoyed the precise style of the Fiore di Gaia and the Passito Sette Chiesette's good handling of sweetness.

● Colli Euganei Rosso Zuan '15	♟♟ 3*
● Colli Euganei Cabernet Sauvignon V. Costa '15	♟♟ 3
○ Colli Euganei Fior d'Arancio Fiore di Gaia '16	♟♟ 2*
○ Colli Euganei Fior d'Arancio Passito Sette Chiesette '14	♟♟ 4
○ Sauvignon '16	♟♟ 3
○ Colli Euganei Chardonnay V. Bianca '15	♟ 3
○ Colli Euganei Pinot Bianco Monte Archino '16	♟ 2
○ Colli Euganei Serprino Frizzante '16	♟ 2
● Colli Euganei Cabernet Sauvignon Mons Silicis Ris. '12	♟♟ 4
○ Colli Euganei Manzoni Bianco Corte Borin '15	♟♟ 3

Bortolomiol

VIA GARIBALDI, 142
31049 VALDOBBIADENE [TV]
TEL. +39 04239749
www.bortolomiol.com

CELLAR SALES
PRE-BOOKED VISITS
RESTAURANT SERVICE
ANNUAL PRODUCTION 1,800,000 bottles
HECTARES UNDER VINE 5.00
SUSTAINABLE WINERY

The success that Conegliano Valdobbiadene has enjoyed over the past decade has led to the founding of many wineries of various size and scope. The Bortolomiol family winery, in this rapidly changing landscape, has served as a benchmark, bolstered by a history that goes back to World War II and a tight network of vine growers who supply the grapes used for their selection. Prosecco their core product. The Motus Vitae was a favorite again this year. This Brut is dedicated to the founder of the winery an highlights intensely fruity aromas with enticing subtle hints of acacia flowers. Its mild prickle is perfectly integrated and caresses the palate, right up to its long finish. The Brut Prior was also impressive It's more lively, with a dynamic and succulent taste.

○ Valdobbiadene Brut Rive San Pietro di Barbozza Motus Vitae '15	♟♟♟
○ Cartizze '16	♟♟
○ Valdobbiadene Brut Ius Naturae '16	♟♟
○ Valdobbiadene Brut Prior '16	♟♟
○ Valdobbiadene Dry Maior '16	♟♟
○ Valdobbiadene Extra Dry Banda Rossa '16	♟♟
○ Valdobbiadene Extra Dry Banda Rossa Special Reserve '16	♟♟
○ Valdobbiadene Extra Dry Senior '16	♟♟
○ Filanda Brut Rosé Ris. '15	♟
○ Riserva del Governatore Extra Brut '15	♟
○ Valdobbiadene Demi Sec Suavis '16	♟

arlo Boscaini

Sengia, 15
015 Sant'Ambrogio di Valpolicella [VR]
+39 0457731412
w.boscainicarlo.it

LLAR SALES
E-BOOKED VISITS
COMMODATION
NUAL PRODUCTION 60,000 bottles
CTARES UNDER VINE 14.00

e Boscaini family's history in the field of
nemaking began 70 years ago. Today the
under's grandchildren are managing
ngs, looking after their some 15 hectares
land, in the area of Sant'Ambrogio (the
sternmost part of the DOC zone). Their
tate was just replanted in the early
90s, so Carlo and Mario have the best
ssible vineyards at their disposal. Only
ditional grapes are cultivated, making for
solid selection of wines that are strongly
d to the DOC zone. The Amarone San
orgio is aging in the cellar for another
ar. And so it was that our attention
ung to the 2015 Ripasso Zane. This
Ilpolicella Superiore has always been one
the most impressive wines in the
pellation, displaying ripe and complex
agrances in which fruit seems to be
used with overtones of spices and fines
rbes that refresh aromatically. It proves
nerous with great pressure in the mouth.
e 2016 Ca' Bussin is pleasantly rustic
th a refreshing palate.

Valpolicella Cl. Ca' Bussin '16	🍷🍷 2*
Valpolicella Cl. Sup. Ripasso Zane '15	🍷🍷 4
Recioto della Valpolicella Cl. La Sengia '15	🍷 4
Amarone della Valpolicella Cl. San Giorgio '12	🍷🍷 6
Amarone della Valpolicella Cl. San Giorgio '11	🍷🍷 5
Amarone della Valpolicella Cl. San Giorgio '10	🍷🍷 5
Valpolicella Cl. Sup. La Preosa '14	🍷🍷 3
Valpolicella Cl. Sup. La Preosa '12	🍷🍷 3
Valpolicella Cl. Sup. Ripasso Zane '13	🍷🍷 4
Valpolicella Cl. Sup. Ripasso Zane '11	🍷🍷 4

Bosco del Merlo

via Postumia, 12
30020 Annone Veneto [VE]
Tel. +39 0422768167
www.boscodelmerlo.it

CELLAR SALES
PRE-BOOKED VISITS
ANNUAL PRODUCTION 240,000 bottles
HECTARES UNDER VINE 84.00

Lucia, Carlo and Roberto Paladin lead this
business, founded by their father Valentino
more than 50 years ago in Annone Veneto,
in the heart of the Venetian plains. Bosco
del Merlo is their most ambitious project to
date, spanning almost one-hundred
hectares of land, dedicated entirely to
growing grapes. The soil here is
overwhelmingly clay. This, in combination
with the sea to the south, and the Pre-Alps
to the north, makes for a solid and
distinctive selection. The grape variety that
expresses itself best in these conditions is
Refosco dal Peduncolo Rosso. It gives rise
to a red with intense aromas of wild fruit
and flowers, with an intriguing and
refreshing hint of spice in the background.
It doesn't strive for fullness and power in
the mouth, but rather elegance and finesse,
which arc the distinctive features of their
wines. Its finish is long and supported by a
juicy acidity. The Vineargenti is a dry and
gutsy blend of Merlot and Refosco, which is
deeper, more layered and slower to release
its aromas.

● Lison-Pramaggiore Refosco P. R. Roggio dei Roveri Ris. '14	🍷🍷 5
● Lison-Pramaggiore Rosso Vineargenti Ris. '14	🍷🍷 6
○ Lison-Pramaggiore Sauvignon Turranio '16	🍷🍷 4
● Malbech Gli Aceri Paladin '14	🍷🍷 6
○ Venezia Chardonnay Nicopeja '16	🍷🍷 3
● Lison-Pramaggiore Merlot Campo Camino Ris. '14	🍷 4
○ Prosecco Extra Dry	🍷 5
○ Venezia Pinot Grigio Tudajo '16	🍷 3
● Lison-Pramaggiore Refosco P. R. Roggio dei Roveri Ris. '13	🍷🍷 5
● Lison-Pramaggiore Rosso Vineargenti Ris. '13	🍷🍷 6

★Brigaldara

FRAZ. SAN FLORIANO
VIA BRIGALDARA, 20
37029 SAN PIETRO IN CARIANO [VR]
TEL. +39 0457701055
www.brigaldara.it

CELLAR SALES
PRE-BOOKED VISITS
ANNUAL PRODUCTION 300,000 bottles
HECTARES UNDER VINE 50.00

For almost one hundred years, the Cesari family have run Brigaldara, but it was Stefano who, in the 1980s, started to develop their winemaking business. The few hectares of terrain that surround their 15th century villa are accompanied by estates in Marano, Grezzana and, finally, Marcellise, for a total of 50 hectares of vineyards. They show great conscientiousness in the cellar, for a selection that features mainly Valpolicella reds, and a Soave. This splendid Amarone from the 2013 vintage comes from the Valpolicella Classica area. It features aromas of overripe fruit and spices, with an intriguing nuance of bitter cocoa in the background. The greatness of the wine lies in its mouth, where it proves powerful and lively but maintaining its grip and elegance. The Valpolicella Superiore Case Vecie was also impressive, with its balance of depth and lightness and its long, juicy palate.

● Amarone della Valpolicella Cl. '13	♥♥♥	6
● Amarone della Valpolicella Case Vecie '12	♥♥	6
● Valpolicella Sup. Case Vecie '15	♥♥	3*
○ Soave '16	♥♥	3
● Valpolicella '16	♥♥	3
● Valpolicella Cl. Sup. Ripasso Il Vegro '15	♥♥	4
● Amarone della Valpolicella Case Vecie '07	♀♀♀	7
● Amarone della Valpolicella Cl. '10	♀♀♀	7
● Amarone della Valpolicella Cl. '06	♀♀♀	6
● Amarone della Valpolicella Cl. '05	♀♀♀	6
● Amarone della Valpolicella Ris. '07	♀♀♀	8

Sorelle Bronca

FRAZ. COLBERTALDO
VIA MARTIRI, 20
31020 VIDOR [TV]
TEL. +39 0423987201
www.sorellebronca.com

CELLAR SALES
PRE-BOOKED VISITS
ACCOMMODATION
ANNUAL PRODUCTION 350,000 bottles
HECTARES UNDER VINE 24.00

Ersiliana and Antonella Bronca's estate features an enchanting panoramic view, steep hills with vineyards stretching all the way up and to the south, towards the Piave river (almost reaching the plains). Sorelle Bronca has managed to take a leading role not only in the world of Prosecco, but also still wines. Their estate comprises just over 20 hectares of land that are cultivated with the utmost respect for the environment. The unfortunate 2014 vintage meant the winery didn't produce their red, the Ser Bele, that year. So we turned our attention to their range of Proseccos, which are always among the most consistent in the appellation. The Particella 68 is top-notch once again. It's a Valdobbiadene with sophisticated aromas of lime blossom and gooseberries whose creamy sparkle wins you over in the mouth. Its tangy, dry taste lengthens to become taut and elegant. The Extra Dry version turned out quite well and is more approachable and succulent.

○ Valdobbiadene Brut Particella 68 '16	♥♥	4
○ Valdobbiadene Brut	♥♥	3
○ Valdobbiadene Extra Dry	♥♥	3
○ Valdobbiadene Frizzante Sui Lieviti Difetto Perfetto	♥	3
● Colli di Conegliano Rosso Ser Bele '09	♀♀♀	5
● Colli di Conegliano Rosso Ser Bele '05	♀♀♀	5
○ Valdobbiadene Brut Particella 68 '15	♀♀♀	4
○ Valdobbiadene Brut Particella 68 '13	♀♀♀	4
○ Colli di Conegliano Bianco Delico '15	♀♀	3
● Colli di Conegliano Rosso Ser Bele '13	♀♀	5
● Colli di Conegliano Rosso Ser Bele '12	♀♀	5

Luigi Brunelli

VIA CARIANO, 10
37029 SAN PIETRO IN CARIANO [VR]
TEL. +39 0457701118
www.brunelliwine.com

CELLAR SALES
PRE-BOOKED VISITS
ACCOMMODATION
ANNUAL PRODUCTION 120,000 bottles
HECTARES UNDER VINE 14.00

Despite the fact that Valpolicella's success has led to growth in the area's wine sector, Brunelli has managed to maintain its family-oriented approach. Their 15 hectares of vineyards are dedicated largely to native varieties. In their cellar on Via Cariano, grapes are transformed into wines capable of joining the fullness brought out by partial-drying with the grip and tendency towards drinkability that distinguish Corvina and Corvinone. The Brunelli family make two great versions of Amarone, plus their flagship wine, the Campo Inferi. This Riserva is only produced in the best vintages and is made with grapes cultivated at over three hundred meters of altitude in the municipality of San Pietro in Cariano. It releases intense notes of blood-rich meat and ripe fruit, refreshed by hints of fines herbes and spices that follow through onto the palate, where the wine reveals its character and power.

● Amarone della Valpolicella Cl. Campo Inferi Ris. '12	▼▼ 8
● Amarone della Valpolicella Cl. '13	▼▼ 8
● Amarone della Valpolicella Cl. Campo del Titari Ris. '12	▼▼ 8
● Corte Cariano '14	▼▼ 2*
● Recioto della Valpolicella Cl. '15	▼▼ 5
● Valpolicella Cl. Sup. Ripasso Pa' Riondo '15	▼▼ 4
● Campo del Maestro '14	▼ 4
● Valpolicella Cl. '16	▼ 2
● Amarone della Valpolicella Cl. Campo del Titari '97	▽▽▽ 8
● Amarone della Valpolicella Cl. Campo del Titari '96	▽▽▽ 8

Buglioni

FRAZ. CORRUBBIO
VIA CAMPAGNOLE, 55
37029 SAN PIETRO IN CARIANO [VR]
TEL. +39 0456760681
www.buglioni.it

CELLAR SALES
PRE-BOOKED VISITS
ACCOMMODATION
ANNUAL PRODUCTION 170,000 bottles
HECTARES UNDER VINE 48.00

The Buglioni family's winery can be found in Corrubbio, a tiny plot of flatland nestled in the hills of Valpolicella. The property is quite extensive, even if the area where Mariano Buglioni and his winemaker Diego Bertoni cultivate their grapes forms only a part (about 50 hectares total). In recent years, their wines have made significant progress, gaining ground in both definition and finesse. This year has seen a clear breakthrough in terms of quality, with an impeccably-made Amarone. It's a wine that offers up a rich suite of aromas underlined by dried fruit, fines herbes and spices. It proves bold in the mouth, gradually increasing in grip and suppleness, right up to its long, dry finish. The Valpolicella Superiore L'Imperfetto also did extremely well. It features fresh aromas of wild berries and thyme, with a striking richness of taste and elegance on the palate.

● Amarone della Valpolicella Cl. Il Lussurioso Ris. '12	▼▼ 7
● Valpolicella Cl. Sup. L'Imperfetto '14	▼▼ 5
● Valpolicella Cl. Sup. Ripasso Il Bugiardo '14	▼▼ 5
● Amarone della Valpolicella Cl. Il Lussurioso Ris. '11	▽▽ 7
● Valpolicella Cl. Sup. L'Imperfetto '13	▽▽ 5
● Valpolicella Cl. Sup. Ripasso Il Bugiardo '13	▽▽ 5

Ca' La Bionda

FRAZ. VALGATARA
VIA RIONDA, 4
37020 MARANO DI VALPOLICELLA [VR]
TEL. +39 0456801198
www.calabionda.it

CELLAR SALES
PRE-BOOKED VISITS
ACCOMMODATION
ANNUAL PRODUCTION 150,000 bottles
HECTARES UNDER VINE 29.00
VITICULTURE METHOD Certified Organic

Alessandro and Nicola Castellani have transformed the small winery founded by their father into one of the most interesting operations in the province of Verona. Today, in Ravazzol, they have 30 hectares of vineyards at their disposal, which are dedicated entirely to native varieties and are cultivated according to organic principles. In the cellar, their approach celebrates both tradition and the varieties used, resulting in wines defined by their finesse and grip. There are two wines in particular that perfectly reflect Alessandro and Nicola's way of thinking. One is the Amarone Riserva, which is released after long aging in the cellar and features a seductive complexity and depth of aroma. It's a wine that's full and succulent in the mouth, as well as long, thanks to its savory acidity. The other is the Valpolicella Superiore Campo Casal Vegri, made with fresh grapes. Its crisp notes of wild berries and spices are brought out in its supple, taut and gutsy palate.

● Valpolicella Cl. Sup. Campo Casal Vegri '15	▼▼▼ 6
● Amarone della Valpolicella Cl. Vign. di Ravazzol Ris. '08	▼▼ 8
● Amarone della Valpolicella Cl. '13	▼▼ 8
● Valpolicella Cl. '16	▼▼ 5
● Amarone della Valpolicella Cl. Vign. di Ravazzol '11	♔♔♔ 8
● Amarone della Valpolicella Cl. Vign. di Ravazzol '07	♔♔♔ 6
● Valpolicella Cl. Sup. Campo Casal Vegri '11	♔♔♔ 5

Ca' Lustra

LOC. FAEDO
VIA SAN PIETRO, 50
35030 CINTO EUGANEO [PD]
TEL. +39 042994128
www.calustra.it

CELLAR SALES
PRE-BOOKED VISITS
ANNUAL PRODUCTION 170,000 bottles
HECTARES UNDER VINE 25.50
VITICULTURE METHOD Certified Organic
SUSTAINABLE WINERY

Franco Zanovello and his son, Marco, are at the head of one of the most beautiful wineries in the Colli Euganei hills. Their estate spans more than 20 hectares, situated in some of the most well-aspected areas of the territory. The hills here are clearly of volcanic origin. They rise up out of the Padana plain like a dream, and, as part of the regional park system, are cared for with particular attention. The vineyards are certified organic. In the cellar, the utmost respect for the grapes is shown through careful, minimally invasive methods. The estate's sunny nature translates into red wines of great substance. They are generally made with Bordeaux varieties, though there is no lack of more original wines, like the succulent Marzemino Belvedere. Their flagship wine is the Moro Polo, a blend of predominantly Merlot. It's intense and dominated by ripe and crisp fruit, thanks to the cool 2014 vintage, and wins you over with its grip. The Cabernet Girapoggio on the other hand, has more depth and ripeness, both on the nose and on the palate.

● Colli Euganei Cabernet Girapoggio '12	▼▼ 3*
● Colli Euganei Moro Polo '14	▼▼ 2*
● Colli Euganei Merlot Sassonero '12	▼▼ 3
○ Colli Euganei Moscato Secco 'A Cengia '15	▼▼ 2*
● Marzemino Belvedere '15	▼▼ 2*
○ Moscato di Retia Passito	▼▼ 3
○ Colli Euganei Bianco Olivetani '15	▼ 2
○ Colli Euganei Manzoni Bianco Pedevenda '15	▼ 3
○ Colli Euganei Serprino Frizzante '16	▼ 2
● Colli Euganei Cabernet Girapoggio '05	♔♔♔ 3
○ Colli Euganei Fior d'Arancio Passito '07	♔♔♔ 4

' Orologio

A' OROLOGIO, 7A
30 BAONE [PD]
+39 042950099
.caorologio.com

LAR SALES
-BOOKED VISITS
OMMODATION
UAL PRODUCTION 24,000 bottles
TARES UNDER VINE 12.00
CULTURE METHOD Certified Organic

Colli Euganei hills have always been
ly valued for their wines. In Ca'
logio, the area has one of its most
resting producers. Mariagioia Rosellini
e to Baone 15 years ago and quickly
naged to earn the favor of the market,
the critics. Her selection is bolstered by
12 hectares of vineyards, spread out in
area that has, more than any other,
ught out the attributes of the territory.
selection, which is limited, features the
Calaóne, and a series of smaller lines
, according to the vintage, may be more
ess available. The Relògio is made with
menere and a dash of Cabernet Franc.
appreciated the wine's rich, taut palate.
Calaòne is more elegant and juicy. It's
ordeaux blend, made predominantly
Merlot, that's appealing for the
hness of its fruit imbued with notes of
st floor and thyme. The solid, tight
ate is supported by a racy acidity.

olli Euganei Rosso Calaóne '15	♟♟	4
elógio '15	♟♟	5
aò '15	♟♟	3
unisóle '15	♟♟	4
alaróla '16	♟♟	3
olli Euganei Rosso Calaóne '05	♟♟♟	3*
elógio '09	♟♟♟	4*
elógio '07	♟♟♟	4
elógio '06	♟♟♟	4
elógio '04	♟♟♟	4*
olli Euganei Rosso Calaóne '12	♟♟	4
alaróla '15	♟♟	3

★Ca' Rugate

VIA PERGOLA, 36
37030 MONTECCHIA DI CROSARA [VR]
TEL. +39 0456176328
www.carugate.it

CELLAR SALES
PRE-BOOKED VISITS
ACCOMMODATION
ANNUAL PRODUCTION 650,000 bottles
HECTARES UNDER VINE 72.00
SUSTAINABLE WINERY

For more than 30 years Ca' Rugate has
operated in Soave, though the ties
between the family, the land and its crops
go much further back. Today, Michele
leads the family business with care and
attention, making it not only a benchmark
for lovers of Verona whites, but also those
preferring the powerful Amarone. Their
more than 60 hectares of hills go into
making sophisticated wines that have no
weak spots. This year the results weren't
long coming, with many wines reaching
our finals. Monte Fiorentine and Monte Alto
highlight the two different characters of
Soave: the first is fresh, taut and gutsy,
while the second is sunnier, more relaxed
and gradual. Both palates excel in
elegance and length. But this year, the lead
role goes to the Studio. This blend of
Trebbiano and Garganega features elegant
aromas and a dry palate that delivers for
harmony and grip.

○ Studio '15	♟♟♟	4*
● Amarone della Valpolicella Punta Tolotti '13	♟♟	7
○ Lessini Durello Pas Dosé M. Cl. Amedeo '12	♟♟	5
○ Recioto di Soave La Perlara '14	♟♟	5
○ Soave Cl. Monte Alto '15	♟♟	3*
○ Soave Cl. Monte Fiorentine '16	♟♟	3*
● Recioto della Valpolicella L'Eremita '13	♟♟	5
○ Soave Cl. San Michele '16	♟♟	2*
○ Valpolicella Rio Albo '16	♟♟	2*
● Valpolicella Sup. Campo Lavei '15	♟♟	4
● Amarone della Valpolicella Punta Tolotti '12	♟♟♟	7
○ Soave Cl. Monte Alto '13	♟♟♟	3*

Giuseppe Campagnola

FRAZ. VALGATARA
VIA AGNELLA, 9
37020 MARANO DI VALPOLICELLA [VR]
TEL. +39 0457703900
www.campagnola.com

CELLAR SALES
PRE-BOOKED VISITS
ANNUAL PRODUCTION 5,000,000 bottles
HECTARES UNDER VINE 155.00

Situated in the heart of the Marano valley, Beppe Campagnola's historic winery is firmly rooted in the area and closely tied to its traditions. The vineyards extend for more that 150 hecatres, but their sizable production also draws on the support of numerous local growers, who are followed closely throughout the year. The grapes are then used to make sincere wines that do an outstanding job of representing their respective typologies. Caterina Zardini is Campagnola's flagship selection of wines, which is headed by an excellent Amarone. On the nose the wine displays intense notes of dried red fruit, with hints of spices and fines herbes. It's full and powerful on the palate and can thrill the most expert of tasters. The Ripasso is also very interesting. It's ripe and embellished with nuances of minerals and pepper, which follow through well onto a juicy, rich palate supported by tannins.

I Campi

LOC. ALLODOLA
FRAZ. CELLORE D'ILLASI
VIA DELLE PEZZOLE, 3
37032 ILLASI [VR]
TEL. +39 0456175915
www.icampi.it

CELLAR SALES
PRE-BOOKED VISITS
ANNUAL PRODUCTION 80,000 bottles
HECTARES UNDER VINE 12.00

Flavio Prà's cellar is in Cellore di Illasi, in the heart of Valpolicella Orientale. His vineyards, however, are scattered throughout various locations, comprising the area known for the territory's reds ar the area of Soave, situated entirely betwe medium and upper hill altitudes. Year aft year their selection grows in definition, privileging the most elegant and fresh expressions rather than sheer force. The Ripasso Campo Ciotoli is a wine that doesn't pursue power and opulence, but rather finesse and grip. On the nose, the fruit is ripe and intact, without showing signs of drying, and refreshed by notes o pepper and thyme. In the mouth, acidity and tannins drive a dynamic and crisp palate. The Soave Campo Vulcano offers even finer and fresher aromas of white fr and flowers, in the mouth, the wine lengthens with tanginess and lightness.

● Amarone della Valpolicella Cl. Caterina Zardini Ris. '12	♥♥ 6
● Valpolicella Cl. Sup. Ripasso '15	♥♥ 3*
● Amarone della Valpolicella Cl. Vign. Vallata di Marano '14	♥♥ 6
● Recioto della Valpolicella Cl. Casotto del Merlo '14	♥♥ 5
● Valpolicella Cl. Sup. Caterina Zardini '15	♥♥ 3
☉ Bardolino Chiaretto Cl. Roccolo del Lago '16	♥ 2
● Bardolino Cl. Roccolo del Lago '16	♥ 2
○ Pinot Grigio Arnaces Vign. Campo dei Gelsi Arnaces '16	♥ 2
○ Prosecco Brut Arnaces	♥ 3
○ Soave Cl. Monte Foscarino Le Bine '16	♥ 2
● Valpolicella Cl. Le Bine '16	♥ 2

● Valpolicella Sup. Ripasso Campo Ciotoli '15	♥♥♥
○ Soave Cl. Campo Vulcano '16	♥♥
● Amarone della Valpolicella Campi Lunghi '14	♥♥
● Amarone della Valpolicella Campo Marna 500 '10	♥♥
○ Soave Campo Base '16	♥♥
● Campo Prognare '11	♥
○ Soave Cl. Campo Vulcano '15	♥♥♥
○ Soave Cl. Campo Vulcano '13	♥♥♥
○ Soave Cl. Campo Vulcano '12	♥♥♥
● Valpolicella Sup. Ripasso Campo Ciotoli '13	♥♥♥

Canevel Spumanti

LOC. SACCOL
VIA ROCCAT E FERRARI, 17
31049 VALDOBBIADENE [TV]
TEL. +39 0423975940
www.canevel.it

PRE-BOOKED VISITS
ANNUAL PRODUCTION 700,000 bottles
HECTARES UNDER VINE 12.00

The winery founded by Mario Caramel and Roberto De Lucchi is approaching its 40-year-anniversary. Moreover, last spring, Canevel Spumanti was acquired by Masi, bringing its dozen hectares of vineyards in Conegliano Valdobbiadene to the table, in addition to its long history in the production of sparkling wines. Their selection hasn't undergone any noticeable changes, remaining firmly wed to a style defined by the fruity fullness of their wines. The Vigneto del Faè did well. It's a Prosecco with a dry and assertive profile and aromas of white fruit and flowers. In the mouth, this lack of dosage further highlights the wine's profile, while the variety's trademark tanginess makes for even greater length. The Il Millesimato also delivered. This historic Extra Dry selection plays on sweet juicy fruit that unfolds well on the palate. Finally, its aromatic encore and sparkle meld perfectly with sweetness and acidity.

○ Cartizze '16		♟♟ 5
○ Valdobbiadene Dosaggio Zero		
Vign. del Faè '16		♟♟ 4
○ Valdobbiadene Extra Dry '16		♟♟ 4
○ Valdobbiadene Extra Dry		
Il Millesimato '16		♟♟ 5
○ Valdobbiadene Brut '16		♟ 4
○ Valdobbiadene Brut '15		♟♟ 4
○ Valdobbiadene Dosaggio Zero		
Vign. del Faè '15		♟♟ 4
○ Valdobbiadene Extra Dry '15		♟♟ 4
○ Valdobbiadene Extra Dry		
Il Millesimato '15		♟♟ 5
○ Valdobbiadene Extra Dry		
Il Millesimato '14		♟♟ 5

Canoso

LOC. MONTEFORTE D'ALPONE
VIA ROMA, 97
37032 VERONA
TEL. +39 0456101981
www.canoso.it

CELLAR SALES
PRE-BOOKED VISITS
ANNUAL PRODUCTION 40,000 bottles
HECTARES UNDER VINE 15.00

The Canoso family has worked in vine growing and winemaking for many decades. After a period marked by swings in production, they are back on the market with an absolutely valid selection of wines, dedicated mostly to Soave (however, wines made with other grapes are also available). Their vineyards, which span some 15 hectares total, are divided into various plots. Boschetti and Ca' del Vento are surely the most interesting. We were most impressed with the Verso, a Soave with an added dash of Trebbiano and Manzoni Bianco (to complement Garganega's trademark fullness). The nose displays extraordinary fresh aromas, with fruit that mingles with floral and citrusy notes. In the mouth, its fullness is perfectly accompanied and supported by a fresh and gutsy acidity. The Fonte, on the other hand, is made exclusively with Garganega grapes and expresses pure fruit on the nose, anticipating a dry, slim-bodied palate.

○ Oltre '15		♟♟ 4
○ Recioto di Soave Passo '09		♟♟ 5
○ Soave Cl. Fonte '16		♟♟ 2*
○ Soave Cl. Sup. Verso '15		♟♟ 3

Cantina del Castello

v.lo Corte Pittora, 5
37038 Soave [VR]
Tel. +39 0457680093
www.cantinacastello.it

CELLAR SALES
PRE-BOOKED VISITS
ANNUAL PRODUCTION 130,000 bottles
HECTARES UNDER VINE 13.00

Situated in the heart of Soave's town center, Arturo Stocchetti's winery is a benchmark for lovers of Verona's white wines. Bolstered by a deep knowledge of the territory and 12-hectare estate, Arturo manages Cantina del Castello with passion, holding firm to the notion that this category of wine can be of high-quality without losing its innate lightness and approachability. Only two wines were presented this year. They may be very different, but they each express the value of this territory and its grapes. The Carniga is a Soave that undergoes long aging in the cellar and exploits the full potential of the Garganega and Trebbiano di Soave combination. The nose displays candied citrus fruit and dried flowers, with a slight hint of botrytis in the background. However, it maintains grip and suppleness in the mouth. The Castello is sunnier and more approachable, with marked lightness and crispness.

○ Soave Cl. Carniga '14	🍷🍷 3
○ Soave Cl. Castello '16	🍷🍷 2*
○ Soave Cl. Sup. Monte Pressoni '01	🍷🍷🍷 3
○ Soave Cl. Carniga '13	🍷🍷 3*
○ Soave Cl. Carniga '11	🍷🍷 3*
○ Soave Cl. Castello '15	🍷🍷 2*
○ Soave Cl. Castello '12	🍷🍷 2*
○ Soave Cl. Pressoni '15	🍷🍷 3*
○ Soave Cl. Pressoni '14	🍷🍷 3
○ Soave Cl. Pressoni '13	🍷🍷 3

La Cappuccina

fraz. Costalunga
via San Brizio, 125
37032 Monteforte d'Alpone [VR]
Tel. +39 0456175036
www.lacappuccina.it

CELLAR SALES
PRE-BOOKED VISITS
RESTAURANT SERVICE
ANNUAL PRODUCTION 310,000 bottles
HECTARES UNDER VINE 42.00
VITICULTURE METHOD Certified Organic

The care that the Tessari family shows for the environment has deep roots, considering that La Cappuccina was one of the first wineries to be certified organic. This was back in the mid-1980s, when the world was suspicious of an approach to agriculture that refused invasive chemicals. Today, Elena, Pietro and Sisto, manage a winery that has 40 hectares of vineyards at its disposal, making for a selection of wines that is both reliable and distinctive. The Soave San Brizio is made with Garganega grapes grown behind the manor house and then aged in mid-size casks. Aromatically, it features a harmonious and inviting fusion of oak, fruit, flowers and mineral notes. Its fullness on the palate contrasts well with a tangy and gutsy acidity. The Recioto Arzimo, on the other hand, offers up hints of hazelnut, Mediterranean scrub and dried flowers. The mouth sees measured sweetness, and unfolds with elegance and grip.

○ Recioto di Soave Arzimo '14	🍷🍷 5
○ Soave San Brizio '15	🍷🍷 3*
○ Soave Fontégo '16	🍷🍷 2*
○ Soave Cl. Monte Stelle '15	🍷🍷 3
● Campo Buri '12	🍷 4
○ Sauvignon Basaltik '16	🍷 2
○ Soave '16	🍷 2
○ Basaltik Sauvignon '15	🍷🍷 2*
● Campo Buri '11	🍷🍷 4
○ Recioto di Soave Arzimo '13	🍷🍷 5
○ Soave '15	🍷🍷 2*
○ Soave Cl. Monte Stelle '14	🍷🍷 3
○ Soave San Brizio '14	🍷🍷 3*
○ Villa Buri Brut M. Cl. '10	🍷🍷 4

Le Carline

VIA CARLINE, 24
30020 PRAMAGGIORE [VE]
TEL. +39 0421799741
www.lecarline.com

CELLAR SALES
PRE-BOOKED VISITS
ANNUAL PRODUCTION 400,000 bottles
HECTARES UNDER VINE 18.00
VITICULTURE METHOD Certified Organic

Daniele Piccinin is one of the most interesting producers in the Lison Pramaggiore DOC zone. A pioneer of organic viticulture in a territory bordered by the Adriatic Sea, he lives for his bright, early-drinking wines. His efforts in the countryside, combined with a respectful, minimally invasive approach in the cellar, allows for a selection that offers character and fullness on the palate, without giving up lightness and freshness. His work on the reduction of sulfites is also noteworthy. The 2016 Merlot is the most impressive red. It has a simple, approachable and fruity richness, but it's also very inviting and close-focused. The mouth comes through pure, gradually giving way to a generous and pleasant palate. The Dogale, a dried-grape wine made with Verduzzo grapes, is always quite good. It offers up hints of dates and Mediterranean scrub on the nose, with a palate where sweetness is always balanced by tanginess. The finish features overtones of bitter almonds.

Carpenè Malvolti

VIA ANTONIO CARPENÈ, 1
31015 CONEGLIANO [TV]
TEL. +39 0438364611
www.carpene-malvolti.com

PRE-BOOKED VISITS
ANNUAL PRODUCTION 5,300,000 bottles
HECTARES UNDER VINE 26.00

Conegliano Veneto, a large producer that rendered the Charmat method the most common in Conegliano Valdobbiadenea, is a landmark in the world of modern Prosecco. The winery owns only a small part of the vineyards necessary to meet their production volumes, but they are still closely tied to the vine growers who deliver the rest of the grapes needed to Via Carpené. This results in a selection of strong quality founded almost entirely on Trevignano's native-style of sparkling wine. The Extra Dry 1868 performed well. This Prosecco's jasmine blossom and apple aromas gradually make room for subtle hints of citrus. The mouth sees a perfect union between sparkle, sweetness and acidity, with the wine gracefully unfolding to a dry finish. The Cartizze was also impressive, with riper fruit and an appealing sweetness that adds creaminess and fullness to the palate.

○ Diana Brut M. Cl. '15	♟♟ 4
○ Dogale Passito	♟♟ 3
● Lison-Pramaggiore Merlot '16	♟♟ 2*
● Lison-Pramaggiore Cabernet '16	♟ 2
● Lison-Pramaggiore Refosco P. R. '16	♟ 2
○ Venezia Pinot Grigio '16	♟ 2
● Carline Rosso '12	♟♟ 3
● Carline Rosso '11	♟♟ 3
○ Diana Brut M. Cl. '15	♟♟ 4
○ Lison Cl. '12	♟♟ 2*
● Lison-Pramaggiore Refosco P.R. senza solfiti aggiunti '13	♟♟ 2*

○ Cartizze 1868	♟♟ 5
○ Conegliano Valdobbiadene Extra Dry 1868	♟♟ 3
○ Conegliano Valdobbiadene Brut 1868	♟ 3

Casa Cecchin

VIA AGUGLIANA, 11
36075 MONTEBELLO VICENTINO [VI]
TEL. +39 0444649610
www.casacecchin.it

CELLAR SALES
PRE-BOOKED VISITS
ANNUAL PRODUCTION 30,000 bottles
HECTARES UNDER VINE 7.00

The small town of Gamberella is nestled in a kind of amphitheater of hills, whose origins are volcanic. Here, the land that's cultivated alternates between woody and grassy areas. Mostly Garganega is grown, as is the case in nearby Soave, along with Durella, a variety that's common in the area. Renato Cecchin and his daughter, Roberta, lead the family winery and estate, which comprises fewer than 10 hectares of vineyards entirely dedicated to these two grapes. Their selection features sparkling wines that are of first-rate quality. The Durello Dosaggio Zero perfectly expresses the character of this evocatively-named grape. It expresses fresh flowers and crusty bread, though in a simple way. In the mouth, the producer brings out acidity and the gutsy, vigorous aspects of the grapes, harnessing them for a refined and harmonious palate of unforgettable character. The Pietralava is also interesting. This still wine ages for a year so that its wonderful mineral notes fully emerge.

○ Il Durello '16	♟♟ 2*
○ Lessini Durello Dosaggio Zero M. Cl. '11	♟♟ 5
○ Pietralava '15	♟♟ 3
○ San Nicolò '16	♟♟ 2*
○ Gambellara San Nicolò '15	♟♟ 2*
○ Lessini Durello Extra Brut Nostrum M. Cl. '12	♟♟ 4
○ Lessini Durello Il Durello '14	♟♟ 2*
○ Lessini Durello Pietralava '14	♟♟ 2*
○ Lessini Durello San Nicolò '14	♟♟ 2*

Casa Roma

VIA ORMELLE, 19
31020 SAN PULU DI PIAVE [TV]
TEL. +39 0422855339
www.casaroma.com

CELLAR SALES
PRE-BOOKED VISITS
ANNUAL PRODUCTION 200,000 bottles
HECTARES UNDER VINE 15.00

Gigi Peruzzetto is a stubborn winemaker who, in his San Polo di Piave winery, has managed to bring together the authentic spirit of the historic Raboso grape, with a more commercial sensibility. The soil of his 15 hectares of vineyards alternates between clay and gravel, giving rise to mostly international varieties, These are then interpreted with an eye towards freshness and early-drinking. His Raboso is reserved for his most ambitious wines, with a selection that goes from sparkling wines to passito dried-grape wines. We can see a clear breakthrough in quality this year, with a wide range of top-notch wines, especially the 2010 Raboso. Notes of cherries and fines herbes are discernible on the nose, with a subtle hint of flowers and spices for added freshness. In the mouth, it proves full and savory and the variety's trademark gutsy acidity adds length and elegance to the palate. Their flagship white is still the harmonious and racy Manzoni Bianco.

● Piave Raboso '10	♟♟ 4
○ Marzemina Bianca '16	♟♟ 2*
● Piave Carmenère '16	♟♟ 2*
● Piave Malanotte '11	♟♟ 6
○ Piave Manzoni Bianco '16	♟♟ 2*
● Pro Fondo Rosso Frizzante	♟♟ 2*
● Raboso Sestier '16	♟ 2
● Venezia Cabernet Sauvignon '16	♟ 2
○ Venezia Chardonnay '16	♟ 2
● Venezia Merlot '16	♟ 2
○ Venezia Pinot Grigio '16	♟ 2
○ Marzemina Bianca '15	♟♟ 2*
● Piave Malanotte '09	♟♟ 6
○ San Dordi '15	♟♟ 3

Case Paolin

VIA MADONNA MERCEDE, 53
31040 VOLPAGO DEL MONTELLO [TV]
TEL. +39 0423871433
www.casepaolin.it

CELLAR SALES
PRE-BOOKED VISITS
ANNUAL PRODUCTION 110,000 bottles
HECTARES UNDER VINE 12.00
VITICULTURE METHOD Certified Organic
SUSTAINABLE WINERY

Observing the northern horizon from Treviso, one clearly sees the silhouette of Montello. This upland, whose altitude reaches 350 meters above sea level, is flanked by plains and the Piave river. The Pozzobon brothers' dozen hectares of vineyards stretch from the bends of the hill to the flatlands bordering it. Here the grapes are cultivated organically and then transformed by the three brothers into a selection of wines that features Prosecco and still wines. The excellent 2013 vintage enabled them to produce a San Carlo where notes of ripe fruit, oak and medicinal herbs meld to perfection. These introduce a harmonious palate in which fullness of fruit is well-supported by tannins, and acidity adds lightness and length. The Asolo Brut was also excellent. It's a sparkling wine that immediately expresses the variety with a captivating grip and assertive palate. The cool 2014 vintage gave the Rosso del Milio lightness and suppleness.

● Montello e Colli Asolani Rosso San Carlo '13	▼▼ 4
○ Asolo Brut	▼▼ 2*
○ Manzoni Bianco Costa degli Angeli '15	▼▼ 3
● Rosso del Milio '14	▼▼ 3
○ Asolo Frizzante Col Fondo	▼ 3
● Cabernet '16	▼ 2
○ Prosecco di Treviso Extra Dry	▼ 2
● Montello e Colli Asolani Rosso San Carlo '12	♈ 4
● Rosso del Milio '13	♈ 3
● Rosso del Milio '12	♈ 3

Michele Castellani

FRAZ. VALGATARA
VIA GRANDA, 1
37020 MARANO DI VALPOLICELLA [VR]
TEL. +39 0457701253
www.castellanimichele.it

CELLAR SALES
PRE-BOOKED VISITS
ANNUAL PRODUCTION 300,000 bottles
HECTARES UNDER VINE 50.00

Thanks to his lifetime of experience, Sergio Catellani has a deep knowledge of Valpolicella and its vineyards. Today, Valgatara's 50 hectares of vineyards provide the grapes necessary for its wines, but as the number of bottles produced is relatively low, only the best get used. Concentration is key to the winery's style, though today they pursue it without going to extremes. The Amarone Cinquestelle is one of the best Sergio has ever made. It's a red that offers up its sweet, ripe fruit slowly, allowing the notes of tobacco, dried flowers and pepper to emerge first. In the mouth, its concentration is impressive, but acidity and tannins bring the wine back into austerity. The Campo Casalin is sunnier and more open; its fruit is more close-focused and juicy, while the soft impact of its mouth tenses up at the finish.

● Amarone della Valpolicella Cl. Campo Casalin I Castei '13	▼▼ 6
● Amarone della Valpolicella Cl. Cinquestelle Collezione Ca' del Pipa '13	▼▼ 7
● Recioto della Valpolicella Cl. Monte Fasenara I Castei '15	▼▼ 5
● Valpolicella Cl. Campo del Biotto I Castei '16	▼ 2
● Valpolicella Cl. Sup. Ripasso Costamaran I Castei '15	▼ 3
● Amarone della Valpolicella Cl. Cinquestelle Collezione Ca' del Pipa '12	♈ 7

★Cav. G. B. Bertani

VIA ASIAGO, 1
37023 GREZZANA [VR]
TEL. +39 0458658444
www.bertani.net

CELLAR SALES
PRE-BOOKED VISITS
ANNUAL PRODUCTION 2,100,000 bottles
HECTARES UNDER VINE 200.00
SUSTAINABLE WINERY

This historic winery in Grezzana has, in recent years, launched an effort to renovate and bolster its large estate of vineyards. There are 200 hectares in all, situated in some of the loveliest and best-suited areas of Valpolicella, often surrounded by woods and in positions of rare natural beauty. In the cellar everything goes slowly, like in the old days, with a selection that is faithful to tradition and that pursues the essence of this land's wines. Once again, the Amarone grabs the limelight. It's a wine that's always new, and yet it continues to be an icon of classic winemaking in the territory. The excellent 2009 vintage gave Bertani's flagship wine an intense and approachable fruity expression, refreshed by notes of medicinal herbs and dried flowers. Its power in the mouth is never an end in itself. Instead, it works toward a seemingly never-ending full, savory and succulent palate. The Secco Vintage, on the other hand, is more intense and approachable, with refreshing mouthfeel.

● Amarone della Valpolicella Cl. '09	♟♟♟	8
● Amarone della Valpolicella Valpantena '14	♟♟	6
● Secco Bertani Vintage '14	♟♟	3
○ Soave Sereole '16	♟♟	3
● Valpolicella '16	♟♟	3
● Valpolicella Cl. Sup. Ognisanti '14	♟♟	4
● Amarone della Valpolicella Cl. '08	♟♟♟	8
● Amarone della Valpolicella Cl. '07	♟♟♟	8
● Amarone della Valpolicella Cl. '06	♟♟♟	8
● Amarone della Valpolicella Cl. '05	♟♟♟	8
● Amarone della Valpolicella Cl. '04	♟♟♟	8
● Amarone della Valpolicella Cl. '03	♟♟♟	8
● Amarone della Valpolicella Cl. '01	♟♟♟	8
● Valpolicella Cl. Sup. Vign. Ognisanti '06	♟♟♟	4*

★Cavalchina

LOC. CAVALCHINA
FRAZ. CUSTOZA
VIA SOMMACAMPAGNA, 7
37066 SOMMACAMPAGNA [VR]
TEL. +39 045516002
www.cavalchina.com

CELLAR SALES
PRE-BOOKED VISITS
ANNUAL PRODUCTION 445,000 bottles
HECTARES UNDER VINE 50.00

The area in the southern part of Lake Garda is seeing a revival thanks to wineries like Cavalchina. Franco and Luciano Piona, who manage the winery, have a large estate at their disposal, resulting in a selection of wines characterized by their lightness, fragrance and richness of flavor. Such qualities perfectly identify Bardolino and Custoza, two wines that pursue a balance between depth, character and fullness. The Piona brothers have put forward quite a wide range, made with grapes cultivated in three different areas. Our favorite continues to be the Amedeo, a Custoza Superiore that gives this historic wine a new identity and depth. It features aromas of rare elegance and clarity, while in the mouth the wine proves dry, tangy and very long. As for the reds, we particularly appreciated the fruity expression of the Amarone, with its winning richness of taste on the palate.

○ Custoza Sup. Amedeo '15	♟♟♟	2*
● Amarone della Valpolicella Torre d'Orti '13	♟♟	6
● Bardolino '16	♟♟	2*
⊙ Bardolino Chiaretto '16	♟♟	2*
● Bardolino Sup. S. Lucia '15	♟♟	3
● Garda Cabernet Prendina '15	♟♟	4
● Garda Merlot Faial '14	♟♟	5
○ Garda Riesling '16	♟♟	2*
○ Lugana 'L Lac '16	♟♟	3
● Valpolicella Sup. Morari Torre d'Orti '14	♟♟	4
● Valpolicella Sup. Ripasso Torre d'Orti '14	♟♟	3
○ Custoza '16	♟	2
● Garda Merlot Prendina '16	♟	2
○ Garda Pinot Bianco Prendina '16	♟	3
○ Pinot Grigio Prendina '16	♟	2

Cavazza

C.DA SELVA, 22
36054 MONTEBELLO VICENTINO [VI]
TEL. +39 0444649166
www.cavazzawine.com

CELLAR SALES
PRE-BOOKED VISITS
ACCOMMODATION
ANNUAL PRODUCTION 860,000 bottles
HECTARES UNDER VINE 150.00
SUSTAINABLE WINERY

The historic winery of Montebello Vicentino divides its attention between the territories of Gambellara and Colli Berici. With vineyards spanning 150 hectares, the Cavazza cousins are able to face each harvest in the best possible way and give life to a selection of products with a strong identity. In Colli Berici, the fullness of flavor pursued in recent years has been abandoned in favor of greater finesse and character, while freshness and grip are the priorities in Gambellara. There are some interesting wines from both appellations, but our particular favorite is the Gambellara La Bocara. It's a wine with sophisticated aromas of white fruit and flowers. Its solid but light palate is presided over by a tangy and racy acidity. The Cabernet Cicogna is deeper and slower in letting its aromas unfold. Notes of herbs and spices echo red fruit and are released in a generous palate supported by tight-knit tannins.

● Colli Berici Cabernet Cicogna '13	♟♟ 4
○ Gambellara Cl. La Bocara '16	♟♟ 2*
○ Recioto di Gambellara Cl. Capitel '15	♟♟ 4
○ Chardonnay Corì '16	♟ 3
● Colli Berici Tai Rosso Corallo '15	♟ 3
● Fornetto '15	♟ 3
● Colli Berici Cabernet Cicogna '12	♟♟ 4
● Colli Berici Cabernet Cicogna '11	♟♟ 4
● Colli Berici Merlot Cicogna '13	♟♟ 5
● Colli Berici Merlot Cicogna '12	♟♟ 4
● Colli Berici Merlot Cicogna '11	♟♟ 4
● Colli Berici Tai Rosso Corallo '13	♟♟ 3
○ Gambellara Cl. La Bocara '15	♟♟ 2*

Giorgio Cecchetto

FRAZ. TEZZE DI PIAVE
VIA PIAVE, 67
31028 VAZZOLA [TV]
TEL. +39 043828598
www.rabosopiave.com

CELLAR SALES
PRE-BOOKED VISITS
ANNUAL PRODUCTION 200,000 bottles
HECTARES UNDER VINE 73.00
SUSTAINABLE WINERY

Giorgio Cecchetto works in Trevignano's plains, on about 70 hectares of vineyards that give rise to a consistent selection of wines. In addition to their still and sparkling wines, which pursue pleasantness and freshness, Giorgio's given an important role to Raboso, the historic variety that grows along the banks of the Piave river. The grape's gutsy, resolute character is explored in various products, including a 'Metodo Classico' sparkler, a passito dried-grape wine and two noteworthy reds. Once again, the Gelsaia tops the bill. It's a Malanotte that has successfully combined the richness of its partially-dried grapes and their trademark freshness. On the nose, notes ranging from overripe plums to pepper emerge. These are released in a full, dynamic palate with good length. The Raboso, on the other hand, expresses fresher aromas dominated by notes of fines herbes and spices, for a supple and pleasantly spirited profile.

● Malanotte Gelsaia '13	♟♟ 5
● Piave Raboso '13	♟♟ 3
● Cabernet Sauvignon '16	♟ 2
○ Manzoni Bianco '16	♟ 2
● Merlot '16	♟ 2
● Sante Rosso '15	♟ 4
○ Manzoni Bianco '15	♟♟ 2*
● Piave Raboso '12	♟♟ 3
● Piave Raboso '11	♟♟ 3
● Sante Rosso '12	♟♟ 3

Gerardo Cesari

Loc. Sorsei, 3
37010 Cavaion Veronese [VR]
Tel. +39 0456260928
www.cesariverona.it

CELLAR SALES
PRE-BOOKED VISITS
ANNUAL PRODUCTION 1,500,000 bottles
HECTARES UNDER VINE 120.00
SUSTAINABLE WINERY

The historic winery managed by the Cesari family has, for a couple of years, been part of the Caviro group, but in their cellars in Cavaion and San Floriano they still work with the same care and passion. The core of their quality selection comes from Valpolicella, with the vineyards of Bosco, Bosan and Jema providing the grapes for their most ambitious wines. The Centofilari DOCs are cultivated in Lugana. The longer time taken to release the new vintages allows their wines to express superior harmony, right from the first sip. We had to wait a whole nine years to taste the Amarone Bosan Riserva, but it was definitely worth it. On the nose, ripe, sweet fruit is imbued with nuances of minerals and marron glacé that let its deep and layered complexity shine through. The fullness of its palate is complemented by tannic weight, while it's down to acidity to add length. This wine is at the height of its maturity and has many more good years in it.

● Amarone della Valpolicella Bosan Ris. '08	♈♈	8
● Amarone della Valpolicella Cl. '13	♈♈	6
● Amarone della Valpolicella Cl. Il Bosco '11	♈♈	7
● Valpolicella Sup. Ripasso Bosan '14	♈♈	5
● Jèma Corvina Veronese '12	♈	5
○ Lugana Cento Filari '16	♈	3
● Valpolicella Sup. Ripasso Mara '15	♈	3
● Amarone della Valpolicella Bosan '06	♈♈	8
● Amarone della Valpolicella Bosan '00	♈♈	7
● Amarone della Valpolicella Cl. '12	♈♈	6
● Amarone della Valpolicella Cl. Il Bosco '10	♈♈	7
● Amarone della Valpolicella Cl. Il Bosco '09	♈♈	7
● Amarone della Valpolicella Cl. Il Bosco '08	♈♈	7

Italo Cescon

Fraz. Roncadelle
p.zza dei Caduti, 3
31024 Ormelle [TV]
Tel. +39 0422851033
www.cesconitalo.it

CELLAR SALES
PRE-BOOKED VISITS
ANNUAL PRODUCTION 800,000 bottles
HECTARES UNDER VINE 115.00
VITICULTURE METHOD Certified Organic
SUSTAINABLE WINERY

You could already see that Gloria, Graziella and Domenico Cescon were making changes at Italo Cescon. Today the winery has established itself as a leader in Veneto Orientale. A certified organic vineyard that has come to span more than one-hundred hectares provides the grapes used in their more ambition wines, while their Tralcetto line relies on local growers, who deliver the grapes to their facility. While we expected a test of character from the Madre, the Choku Rei turned out to be a real surprise. It's the new Pinot Grigio that emphasizes the winery's new direction. They have opted for limited yields in the vineyard and have eschewed the use of SO2 and filtration. The result is a white with deep aromas of pear and Mediterranean scrub and a dynamic, lively palate. However, the Madre is the producer's flagship wine. It's elegant, with a slow, citrusy and floral expression, and striking tanginess on the palate.

○ Madre '15	♈♈	5
○ Manzoni Bianco Svejo '16	♈♈	3
○ Pinot Grigio Choku Rei '15	♈♈	4
○ Sauvignon Mejo '16	♈♈	3
○ Madre '14	♈♈♈	4*
● Amaranto 72 '12	♈♈	5
● Amaranto 72 '11	♈♈	5
● Chieto '13	♈♈	4
● Chieto '12	♈♈	4
● Chieto '11	♈♈	3
○ Manzoni Bianco Svejo '15	♈♈	3
○ Manzoni Bianco Svejo '14	♈♈	3
○ Sauvignon Mejo '15	♈♈	3

Coffele

VIA ROMA, 5
37038 SOAVE [VR]
TEL. +39 0457680007
www.coffele.it

CELLAR SALES
PRE-BOOKED VISITS
ANNUAL PRODUCTION 120,000 bottles
HECTARES UNDER VINE 25.00
VITICULTURE METHOD Certified Organic

If a winery's value is estimated according to its estate, the Coffele family's operation is one of the most intriguing in all of Soave. Their property comprises some 25 hectares of contiguous vineyards that stretch along the southwestern side of the Castelcerino hill, where grapes respond to the higher altitudes by producing sophisticated aromas and grip. Their selection, which is limited in size, focuses on Soave itself, with three wines that highlight the sophisticated and fragrant character of the territory. Aged only in steel, the Ca' Visco is the Coffele winery's thoroughbred, a Soave made with grapes from the five hectares of vineyards that surround their Castelcerino facility. Its aromas of fresh flowers and white damsons are vibrant, while in the mouth it offers both fullness and suppleness, with a long, dry finish. Drawing on the 2015 vintage, the Recioto Le Sponde is sunnier and more pervasive. Its palate is captivating and can satisfy even the most expert taster.

○ Recioto di Soave Cl. Le Sponde '15	🍷🍷 5
○ Soave Cl. Ca' Visco '16	🍷🍷 3*
○ Soave Cl. Alzari '15	🍷🍷 3
○ Soave Cl. Castel Cerino '16	🍷🍷 3
○ Recioto di Soave Cl. Le Sponde '09	🍷🍷🍷 5
○ Soave Cl. Ca' Visco '14	🍷🍷🍷 3*
○ Soave Cl. Ca' Visco '05	🍷🍷🍷 3*
○ Soave Cl. Ca' Visco '04	🍷🍷🍷 2
○ Soave Cl. Ca' Visco '03	🍷🍷🍷 2
○ Recioto di Soave Cl. Le Sponde '14	🍸🍸 5
○ Soave Cl. Alzari '14	🍸🍸 3
○ Soave Cl. Alzari '13	🍸🍸 3
○ Soave Cl. Ca' Visco '15	🍸🍸 3*
○ Soave Cl. Castel Cerino '15	🍸🍸 3

Col Vetoraz

FRAZ. SANTO STEFANO
S.DA DELLE TRESIESE, 1
31040 VALDOBBIADENE [TV]
TEL. +39 0423975291
www.colvetoraz.it

CELLAR SALES
PRE-BOOKED VISITS
ANNUAL PRODUCTION 800,000 bottles
HECTARES UNDER VINE 12.00

Situated in one of the most charming corners of Valdobbiadene, Col Vetoraz is one of the most interesting producers in the territory. They are bolstered by tight partnerships with a close-knit group of local growers who provide their grapes. In order to transform one as delicate as Glera into wine, Loris Dall'Acqua, Francesco Miotto and Paolo De Bortoli decided to move their facility into the town's artisanal quarter, a space that allows them to work with accuracy and composure. Their Valdobbiadene Dosaggio Zero tops the bill. It's a sparkling wine with a fresh profile of flowers and white-fleshed fruit. It's striking for the simplicity of its palate, which is perfectly dry and maintains Prosecco's trademark tanginess and lightness. Their whole selection is made up of memorable Prosecco di Valdobbiadene wines, thanks in part to their refusal to cultivate inferior terrain.

○ Valdobbiadene Dosaggio Zero '16	🍷🍷 3*
○ Cartizze '16	🍷🍷 4
○ Valdobbiadene Brut '16	🍷🍷 3
○ Valdobbiadene Dry '16	🍷🍷 3
○ Valdobbiadene Extra Dry '16	🍷🍷 3
○ Cartizze '14	🍸🍸 4
○ Valdobbiadene Brut Zero '15	🍸🍸 3*
○ Valdobbiadene Brut Zero '14	🍸🍸 3

Le Colture

LOC. SANTO STEFANO
VIA FOLLO, 5
31049 VALDOBBIADENE [TV]
TEL. +39 0423900192
www.lecolture.com

CELLAR SALES
PRE-BOOKED VISITS
ACCOMMODATION
ANNUAL PRODUCTION 750,000 bottles
HECTARES UNDER VINE 40.00

In an agricultural context in which the most representative operations have only a few of their own vineyards, and rely mostly on small growers for their grapes, the Ruggeri family's winery stands out as a welcome anomaly. Their estate, which comprises more than 40 hectares of property between Conegliano Valdobbiadene and nearby Montello, provides most of the grapes they need, with Prosecco serving as the cornerstone of their selection. It's difficult to choose from so many strong candidates. Their sparkling wines are close-focused on the nose, harmonious and pleasant. They also interpret the Glera grape quite well. The Gerardo stands out for its originality and character. It's a dry Brut aged for one year, a Prosecco with a simple but gutsy profile that displays refined aromas of apple and lime blossom. The Brut Fagher, on the other hand, offers a sweeter and more inviting nose, which follows through full and juicy on the palate.

○ Cartizze		🏆🏆 3
○ Valdobbiadene Brut Fagher		🏆🏆 3
○ Valdobbiadene Dry Cruner		🏆🏆 3
○ Valdobbiadene Extra Dry Pianer		🏆🏆 3
○ Valdobbiadene Extra Dry Prime Gemme		🏆🏆 3
○ Valdobbiadene Rive di Santo Stefano Brut Gerardo '15		🏆🏆 3
⊙ Rosé Brut		🏆 2
○ Valdobbiadene Sup. Rive di Santo Stefano Brut Gerardo '14		🏆🏆 3

Vignaioli Contrà Soarda

S.DA SOARDA, 26
36061 BASSANO DEL GRAPPA [VI]
TEL. +39 0424505562
www.contrasoarda.it

CELLAR SALES
PRE-BOOKED VISITS
RESTAURANT SERVICE
ANNUAL PRODUCTION 80,000 bottles
HECTARES UNDER VINE 20.00
VITICULTURE METHOD Certified Organic
SUSTAINABLE WINERY

Mirco Gottardi founded his winery 15 years ago on a handful of hectares of land in Breganze. Today his vineyards have come to span some 20 hectares, all in the hills and cultivated according to organic principles. These provide the grapes for his consistently strong selection, wines that represent his way of thinking. Rather than putting everything into Bordeaux, a grape common throughout the territory, he's focusing on a diverse selection that's exploring new frontiers. In the absence of their flagship wine, the Pinot Nero Vigna Corejo, our attention was grabbed by the Torcolato Sarson. It's a wine that has never been so impressive. On the nose, dried fruit calls up hints of apricots and dates, which gradually give way to overtones of dried flowers and licorice. These follow through perfectly onto the palate, which contrasts sweetness with good tanginess, and makes way for a dry and almost bitter finish. The Vignasilan is also very good. It's a Vespaiolo wine, aged at length in the cellar, that shows good mineral depth.

● Breganze Rosso Terre di Lava Ris. '12		🏆🏆 5
○ Breganze Torcolato Sarson '14		🏆🏆 5
○ Breganze Vespaiolo Vignasilan '14		🏆🏆 5
● 121 b. C. Carmenere '14		🏆 5
○ 121 b.C. Vespaiolo '15		🏆 5
○ Breganze Vespaiolo Soarda '16		🏆 3
● Marzemino Nero Gaggion '14		🏆 3
● Pomèa Musso '12		🏆 4
● Breganze Pinot Nero Vignacorejo '12		🏆🏆 7
● Breganze Rosso Terre di Lava Ris. '11		🏆🏆 4
○ Breganze Torcolato Sarson '13		🏆🏆 5
● Musso Serafino '10		🏆🏆 3
● Pinot Nero Vigna Corejo '13		🏆🏆 7

Corte Adami

VIA CIRCONVALLAZIONE ALDO MORO, 32
37038 SOAVE [VR]
TEL. +39 0456190218
www.corteadami.it

CELLAR SALES
PRE-BOOKED VISITS
ANNUAL PRODUCTION 100,000 bottles
HECTARES UNDER VINE 38.00
SUSTAINABLE WINERY

The Adami family's winery is located at the westernmost edge of Soave, in a land that's flat, although there are hills at just a few kilometers away. The vineyards, which run for almost 40 hectares, are subdivided according to the area's most important appellations: Soave for the whites and Valpolicella for the reds. Only the best grapes make it into the bottle, while leftovers are sold to the territory's cooperative winery. The Adami family's winery has grown by leaps and bounds with their Soave Vigna della Corte, a wine that managed to win over our panel. On the nose, it unfolds very slowly, featuring sulfurous and flinty notes in the foreground. These give way to a dynamic palate that sees the emergence of yellow fruit and dried flowers. As for the reds, we particularly appreciated the classic style of the Ripasso, a Valpolicella Superiore that opts for elegance of palate rather than intensity of fruit.

○ Soave V. della Corte '15	♛♛ 3*
○ Soave '16	♛♛ 2*
○ Soave Cl. Cimalta '16	♛♛ 2*
○ Soave Decennale '15	♛♛ 2*
● Valpolicella Sup. '14	♛♛ 3
● Valpolicella Sup. Ripasso '14	♛♛ 3
● Amarone della Valpolicella '13	♛ 6
○ Recioto di Soave '14	♛ 4
● Amarone della Valpolicella '12	♟♟ 6
● Amarone della Valpolicella '11	♟♟ 6
○ Soave Il Decennale '13	♟♟ 6
○ Soave V. della Corte '14	♟♟ 3
○ Soave V. della Corte '13	♟♟ 3
● Valpolicella Sup. '13	♟♟ 3

Corte Gardoni

LOC. GARDONI, 5
37067 VALEGGIO SUL MINCIO [VR]
TEL. +39 0457950382
www.cortegardoni.it

CELLAR SALES
PRE-BOOKED VISITS
ANNUAL PRODUCTION 180,000 bottles
HECTARES UNDER VINE 25.00

Situated at the south-westernmost edge of the Custoza DOC zone, the Piccoli family's winery is a benchmark for lovers of Garda's fragrant wines. The estate, which is quite extensive, is mostly dedicated to the cultivation of local varieties. Thanks in part to transalpine influences, their wines display finesse, grip on the palate, and evolve with age. The red side of Lake Garda gives rise to excellent wines, two memorable Bardolinos in particular. On the one hand, there's the floral and spicy freshness of Le Fontane, with its pronounced notes of dog rose and pepper that, in the mouth, bring out the Garda appellation's trademark fragrance and richness of flavor. On the other hand, we very much appreciated the depth and poise of the Superiore Pradicà, with its aromas of forest floor and wild fruit, and its long, dry, pleasant palate.

● Bardolino Le Fontane '16	♛♛ 2*
● Bardolino Sup. Pradicà '15	♛♛ 3*
⊙ Bardolino Chiaretto '16	♛♛ 2*
● Becco Rosso '15	♛♛ 3
○ Custoza '16	♛♛ 2*
○ Fenili Passito '15	♛♛ 5
● Rosso di Corte '15	♛♛ 3
○ Bianco di Custoza Mael '09	♛♛♛ 2*
○ Bianco di Custoza Mael '08	♛♛♛ 2*
○ Custoza Mael '13	♛♛♛ 3*
○ Custoza Mael '11	♛♛♛ 3*
⊙ Bardolino Chiaretto '15	♟♟ 2*
● Bardolino Le Fontane '15	♟♟ 2*
○ Custoza Mael '15	♟♟ 3*
○ Fenili Passito '11	♟♟ 5

Corte Moschina

VIA MOSCHINA, 1
37030 RONCÀ [VR]
TEL. +39 0457460788
www.cortemoschina.it

CELLAR SALES
PRE-BOOKED VISITS
ANNUAL PRODUCTION 80,000 bottles
HECTARES UNDER VINE 35.00
SUSTAINABLE WINERY

Ronca is a small town found between the Soave and Gambellara DOC zones. Here, with the Lessinia hills soaring in the background, Patrizia Niero and her sons, Alessandro and Giacomo, have in just a few years made Corte Moschina a noteworthy operation. Soave and Durello serve as the cornerstones of their selection, with a style that focuses on freshness of taste and traction in the mouth. The exception to this style might well be the I Tarai, a Soave made with grapes from older vineyards and partly aged in oak. On the nose, the ripeness of its yellow fruit comes through, just giving way to notes of dried flowers and faint hints of oak. Richness of flavor is not an end in itself. Rather, it's aimed at bringing out Soave's natural pervasiveness. The Evaos is fresher and gutsier, while the Incanto proved to be one of the best Recioto di Soave Incantos.

○ Soave Sup. I Tarai '15	🏆🏆 3*
○ Lessini Durello Brut M. Cl. '12	🏆🏆 4
○ Lessini Durello Brut M. Cl. 60 Mesi Ris. '10	🏆🏆 5
○ Recioto di Soave Incanto '14	🏆🏆 4
○ Soave Evaos '16	🏆🏆 3
○ Soave Roncathe '16	🏆🏆 2*
○ Durello Frizzante Puro Caso Sui Lieviti	🏆 5
● Valpolicella '15	🏆 2
○ Raise '13	🏆 5
○ Soave Evaos '15	🏆 3*
○ Soave Evaos '14	🏆 2*
○ Soave I Tarai '14	🏆 3
○ Soave I Tarai '13	🏆 3
○ Soave Roncathe '15	🏆 2*

Corte Rugolin

FRAZ. VALGATARA
VIA RUGOLIN, 1
37020 MARANO DI VALPOLICELLA [VR]
TEL. +39 0457702153
www.corterugolin.it

CELLAR SALES
PRE-BOOKED VISITS
ANNUAL PRODUCTION 80,000 bottles
HECTARES UNDER VINE 12.00
SUSTAINABLE WINERY

Valgatara, an area situated at the mouth of the Marano valley, hosts several of Valpolicella's wineries. The Coati family, today represented by Elena and Federico, is one of them. The family has worked the land here for many years, attending to a dozen or so hectares of vineyards dedicated almost exclusively to Valpolicella's native varieties. Great care in the countryside and maximum respect in the cellar make for a sophisticated production style that never falls prey to fashion. Coati's entire range proved impressive this year. Their Amarone Crosara de le Strie is at the top of our list. It's a 2012 that undergoes long aging in the cellar. On the nose, it offers up sunny, warm notes of ripe fruit contrasted with fresher overtones of pepper and herbs. Its fullness on the palate is presided over by a fresh, racy acidity that lengthens the wine. Their Recioto is intense, pervasive and enticing and plays on softer, velvety sensations.

● Amarone della Valpolicella Cl. Crosara de le Strie '12	🏆🏆 7
● Recioto della Valpolicella Cl. '15	🏆🏆 5
● Amarone della Valpolicella Cl. Monte Danieli '11	🏆🏆 7
● Valpolicella Cl. Rugolin '16	🏆🏆 3
● Valpolicella Cl. Sup. Ripasso '14	🏆🏆 5
● Amarone della Valpolicella Cl. Crosara de le Strie '11	🏆 7
● Amarone della Valpolicella Cl. Crosara de le Strie '10	🏆 6
● Valpolicella Cl. '14	🏆 2*
● Valpolicella Cl. Sup. Ripasso '13	🏆 5
● Valpolicella Cl. Sup. Ripasso '12	🏆 4
● Valpolicella Cl. Sup. San Giorgio '14	🏆 5

★Corte Sant'Alda

Loc. Fiui
via Capovilla, 28
37030 Mezzane di Sotto [VR]
Tel. +39 0458880006
www.cortesantalda.it

CELLAR SALES
PRE-BOOKED VISITS
ACCOMMODATION
ANNUAL PRODUCTION 90,000 bottles
HECTARES UNDER VINE 19.00
VITICULTURE METHOD Certified Biodynamic

Marinella Camerani's estate comprises 20 or so hectares of land in the heart of Valpolicella Orientale. The vineyards here are dedicated entirely to Valpolicella's native varieties, with the exception of a small plot used for cultivating Soave. Their biodynamic approach highlights the peculiarities of the individual grape varieties, making for a selection of wines that, while limited in range, shows great character. Their wines are even capable of highlighting the differences in climate that have effected a specific vintage, a fact that makes them captivating, and yet traditional at the same time. This year, two wines have beaten the rest: the Ripasso Campi Magri and the Amarone Valmezzane. The former offers intense aromas on the nose, ranging from dog rose to wild fruit, while the mouth is solid but with a boisterous and gutsy palate. The Amarone, on the other hand, sees riper fruit, though without passing up deeper expressions of pepper, forest floor and macerated leaves. Their Molinetto vineyard in Mezzane gives rise to interesting wines, having led to the creation of the Adalia project.

● Amarone della Valpolicella Valmezzane '12	♟♟ 8
● Valpolicella Sup. Ripasso Campi Magri '14	♟♟ 4
● Amarone della Valpolicella Ruvain Adalia '13	♟♟ 8
○ Soave '16	♟♟ 3
● Valpolicella Ca' Fiui '16	♟♟ 3
● Valpolicella Laute Adalia '16	♟♟ 3
● Valpolicella Sup. Ripasso Balt Adalia '15	♟♟ 4
☉ Agathe Rosato '16	♟ 4
○ Soave Singan Adalia '16	♟ 3
● Amarone della Valpolicella '10	♟♟♟ 8
● Amarone della Valpolicella '06	♟♟♟ 7
● Valpolicella Sup. Mithas '12	♟♟♟ 8
● Valpolicella Sup. Mithas '04	♟♟♟ 6

Dal Cero
Tenuta di Corte Giacobbe

via Moschina, 11
37030 Roncà [VR]
Tel. +39 0457460110
www.dalcerofamily.it

CELLAR SALES
PRE-BOOKED VISITS
ANNUAL PRODUCTION 300,000 bottles
HECTARES UNDER VINE 40.00

The Dal Cero family began making wines back in the period between the two great wars, but it's only been over the last decade, with a new generation stepping up, that they've had their breakthrough in terms of quality. Today, the vineyards run some 40 hectares along the slopes of the Crocetta and Calvarina mountains, the two ancient volcanoes that spawned the area. A small part, however, is dedicated to Valpolicella, and is managed through an agricultural network. Their limited range of wines feature a racy, distinctive style. Partly aged in wood and partly in steel, the Soave Superiore Runcata is a wine with close-focused aromas of white fruit and flowers, and an intriguing fresh vegetal note in the background. On the palate, it exhibits a solid and full body, supported by a particularly gutsy acidity (a consequence of the altitude of the vineyards). The Augusto, a Lessini Durello aged in oak prior to bottle fermentation, is also quite good. It features a striking depth of aroma and a harmoniously powerful palate.

○ Lessini Durello Dosaggio Zero M. Cl. Augusto '12	♟♟ 5
○ Soave Sup. Vign. Runcata '15	♟♟ 4
● Amarone della Valpolicella '12	♟♟ 7
○ Brut M. Cl.	♟♟ 3
○ Soave Corte Giacobbe '16	♟♟ 2*
● Valpolicella '15	♟ 3
○ Soave Sup. Vign. Runcata '14	♟♟♟ 2*
● Amarone della Valpolicella '11	♟♟ 7
○ Soave '15	♟♟ 2*
○ Soave '14	♟♟ 2*
○ Soave Sup. Vign. Runcata '15	♟♟ 4
○ Soave Sup. Vign. Runcata '13	♟♟ 2*
● Valpolicella Sup. Ripasso '14	♟♟ 5

Dal Maso

C.DA SELVA, 62
36054 MONTEBELLO VICENTINO [VI]
TEL. +39 0444649104
www.dalmasovini.com

CELLAR SALES
PRE-BOOKED VISITS
ACCOMMODATION AND RESTAURANT SERVICE
ANNUAL PRODUCTION 350,000 bottles
HECTARES UNDER VINE 30.00
SUSTAINABLE WINERY

The Dal Maso family's winery extends
across two areas that complement one
another, Gambellara and Colli Berici. While
they may be separated by just a few
kilometers, they feature very different
climatic conditions. Gambellara (where
Garganega is grown) sees cooler air and
wider temperature ranges, while Colli Berici
(Bordeaux and Red Tai) sees a warmer,
more Mediterranean climate. Nicola, with
the help of his sisters, Anna and Silvia, then
transforms the grapes into a selection of
sophisticated wines. The Gambellara Riva
del Molino performed well. On the nose,
fruit, flowers and oak come together
perfectly, while the palate features a
captivating delicacy. The Montemitorio,
made with Tai Rosso, proves even more
delicate. It manages to bring out the area's
and variety's sunniness in a profile
refreshed by herbs and spices. In the
mouth, the wine expands gracefully and
assertively, leading to a dry finish that
offers up a bit of character.

● Colli Berici Tai Rosso Montemitorio '15	♟♟ 2*
○ Gambellara Riva del Molino '16	♟♟ 3*
● Cabernet Casara Roveri '15	♟♟ 4
● Cabernet Montebelvedere '15	♟♟ 3
○ Gambellara '16	♟♟ 2*
○ Gambellara Ca' Fischele '16	♟♟ 2*
○ Recioto di Gambellara Cl. Riva dei Perari '15	♟♟ 5
● Colli Berici Tai Rosso '16	♟ 2
○ Lessini Durello Brut	♟ 2
○ Gambellara Cl. Riva del Molino '07	♟♟♟ 2*
○ Gambellara Riva del Molino '15	♟♟ 3

De Stefani

VIA CADORNA, 92
30020 FOSSALTA DI PIAVE [VE]
TEL. +39 042167502
www.de-stefani.it

CELLAR SALES
PRE-BOOKED VISITS
ANNUAL PRODUCTION 500,000 bottles
HECTARES UNDER VINE 60.00
SUSTAINABLE WINERY

The De Stefani family have worked for
years in the plains stretching between the
provinces of Venice and Treviso. The estate
comprises some 50 hectares of vineyards,
spread out on two plots of flatland, one in
Monastier and one in Fossalta di Piave, not
to mention their historic hill country estate
in Refrontolo. In recent years their work in
the vineyards has seen the gradual
elimination of the most invasive chemicals,
making for a selection of wines that, year
after year, shows greater integrity and
fidelity to the grape varieties. De Stefani
handled the complicated 2014 vintage with
great attention and skill. The result is a
wine that's noteworthy for its focus and
harmony. The excellent Kreda is made with
Refosco grapes that are slightly dried. The
technique brings maturity to the wine's
aromas and plushness to its dynamic and
racy palate. The Stefen 1624 is rich and
powerful with great personality. We
particularly appreciated the fragrance and
pleasant palate of the Soler, an original
Bordeaux blend enriched with Marzemino
and Refosco.

● Kreda '14	♟♟ 5
● Piave Malanotte '12	♟♟ 3
● Soler '14	♟♟ 4
● Stefen 1624 '12	♟♟ 8
○ Tombola di Pin Brut M. Cl. '08	♟♟ 7
● Merlot Plavis '14	♟ 3
○ Prosecco di Treviso Brut Nature	♟ 2
○ Venezia Pinot Grigio '16	♟ 3
● Cabernet Sauvignon '14	♟♟ 3
● Colli di Conegliano Rosso Stefen 1624 '11	♟♟ 8
● Kreda Refosco '13	♟♟ 5
○ Olmera '15	♟♟ 5
● Piave Raboso Vign. Terre Nobili '11	♟♟ 4

Conte Emo Capodilista
La Montecchia

VIA MONTECCHIA, 16
35030 SELVAZZANO DENTRO [PD]
TEL. +39 049637294
www.lamontecchia.it

CELLAR SALES
PRE-BOOKED VISITS
ACCOMMODATION
ANNUAL PRODUCTION 144,000 bottles
HECTARES UNDER VINE 30.00
SUSTAINABLE WINERY

Giordano Emo Capodilista runs the family business, an estate of some 30 hectares divided up between two areas: one in the north around villa Emo Capodilista, where, in addition to whites, Merlot and Carmenere are cultivated, and in the south, on Monte Castello, where Cabernet Sauvignon makes up the lion's share. In the cellar, their work is focused on bringing out the character of the grapes, which are then aged in this enchanting oasis. Faced with a vintage as complicated as 2014, Giordano chose to forego production of his most ambitious wines. It was a decision that demonstrated foresight and respect for a vine grower's work. As usual, the Donna Daria proved its worth. It's a Fior d'Arancio Passito with seductively full aromas of citrus and candied fruit. These Introduce a palate where unbridled sweetness is kept in check by acidity. The Merlot is full, juicy and very harmonious.

○ Colli Euganei Fior d'Arancio Passito Donna Daria '15	🍷🍷	5
● Ca' Emo '15	🍷🍷	3
● Cabernet Franc Godimondo '16	🍷🍷	2*
○ Colli Euganei Fior d'Arancio Spumante '16	🍷🍷	2*
● Colli Euganei Merlot '15	🍷🍷	5
○ Colli Euganei Pinot Bianco '16	🍷	2
○ Piùchebello '16	🍷	2
● Raboso Forzatè '13	🍷	2
● Colli Euganei Cabernet Sauvignon Ireneo '12	🍷🍷🍷	4*
○ Colli Euganei Fior d'Arancio Passito Donna Daria '06	🍷🍷🍷	5

Farina

LOC. PEDEMONTE
VIA BOLLA, 11
37029 SAN PIETRO IN CARIANO [VR]
TEL. +39 0457701349
www.farinawines.com

CELLAR SALES
PRE-BOOKED VISITS
ANNUAL PRODUCTION 800,000 bottles
HECTARES UNDER VINE 45.00

The Farina family is among the most active of Valpolicella. Today it's Claudio, Elena and Fabio who are carrying on the work that began so many years ago. Their vineyards span some 10 hectares, though local growers provide many of the grapes used in their cellar in Pedemonte. Their selection is subdivided into various lines, all dedicated to Verona's time-honored classics. In the cellar, they work to marry a traditional approach and a modern one, making for wines that are full, but never excessive or ostentatious. They've been doing some great work at 11 Via Bolla, with a new system that enables them virtually perfect control of the drying curve, This is then cross-referenced with temperature and humidity so as to obtain the best possible expression of fruit. The Amarone Montetante performed amazingly well. Today, the wine (which is aged for an additional year in the cellar) is one of the most interesting in the appellation, with its refined and deep aromas and a dynamic, fresh and elegant palate.

● Amarone della Valpolicella Cl. Montefante Ris. '11	🍷🍷	8
● Valpolicella Cl. Sup. '15	🍷🍷	2*
● Valpolicella Cl. Sup. Ripasso '15	🍷🍷	2*
● Valpolicella Cl. Sup. Ripasso Montecorna '15	🍷🍷	3
● Amarone della Valpolicella Cl. '14	🍷	5
● Corte Conti Cavalli '15	🍷	4
● Valpolicella Cl. '16	🍷	2
● Amarone della Valpolicella Cl. '13	🍷🍷	5
● Valpolicella Cl. Sup. '14	🍷🍷	2*

Fattori

FRAZ. TERROSSA
VIA OLMO, 6
37030 RONCÀ [VR]
TEL. +39 0457460041
www.fattoriwines.com

CELLAR SALES
PRE-BOOKED VISITS
ANNUAL PRODUCTION 280,000 bottles
HECTARES UNDER VINE 72.00
SUSTAINABLE WINERY

Antonio Fattori has shrewdly managed his winery, transforming it by limiting the amount produced for others, and focusing on the production of their own brand. Behind it all, there's a deep knowledge of the territory and its historic grape varieties, as well as superior skill in the cellar. The estate, which has come to comprise more than 70 hectares, isn't restricted to just Soave. It extends to nearby Valpolicella and Lessinia, areas that allow Fattori to offer a rich variety of wines. Once again, the Soave Motto Piane proves quite good. It's made exclusively with Garganega grapes left to rest for a few weeks before crushing. Partial aging in oak completes the work, making for a wine with a warm and ripe profile that maintains its vitality and grip. As for the reds made in Col de la Bastia, the Amarone of the same name is worth noting. It's plush and round both in its aromas and on the palate.

● Amarone della Valpolicella '12	♟♟ 8
● Amarone della Valpolicella Col de la Bastia '13	♟♟ 6
○ Lessini Durello Brut M. Cl. 60 Mesi Roncà '11	♟♟ 6
○ Recioto di Soave Motto Piane '15	♟♟ 5
○ Soave Danieli '16	♟♟ 2*
○ Soave Motto Piane '15	♟♟ 4
● Valpolicella Sup. Ripasso Col de la Bastia '15	♟♟ 5
○ Lessini Durello Brut M.Cl. 60 Mesi Roncà Ris. '11	♟ 6
○ Lessini Durello Brut Roncà M.Cl. 36 Mesi '13	♟ 4
○ Pinot Grigio Valparadiso '16	♟ 3
○ Soave Cl. Runcaris '16	♟ 2
● Valpolicella Col de la Bastia '16	♟ 3

Il Filò delle Vigne

VIA TERRALBA, 14
35030 BAONE [PD]
TEL. +39 042956243
www.ilfilodellevigne.it

CELLAR SALES
PRE-BOOKED VISITS
ANNUAL PRODUCTION 50,000 bottles
HECTARES UNDER VINE 22.00

Filò delle Vigne is a splendid estate that stretches along the southeastern side of Monte Cecilia, in the southern part of the Colli Euganei hills. With more than 50 hectares of land at their disposal, 20 of which are vineyards, the Giordani family are able to cultivate their terrain with precision. In the cellar, Matteo Zanaica manages all production stages personally, making for a selection of wines that, while limited in range, shows substance and character. Once again, the star wine is the Borgo delle Casette, a Cabernet Riserva that is consistently one of the region's most interesting wines. Its meaty red fruit is imbued with notes of sweet spices and herbs. These follow through on a palate in which power and suppleness merge perfectly. The Casa del Merlo is only in its second year. It's a Merlot with sunnier and riper aromas that expand into a silky palate with admirable length.

● Colli Euganei Cabernet Borgo delle Casette Ris. '13	♟♟ 5
● Colli Euganei Merlot Casa del Merlo '13	♟♟ 5
● Colli Euganei Cabernet Cecilia di Baone Ris. '14	♟♟ 4
● Volo '15	♟♟ 3
○ Terralba di Baone '15	♟ 3
● Colli Euganei Cabernet Borgo delle Casette Ris. '12	♟♟♟ 5
● Colli Euganei Cabernet Borgo delle Casette Ris. '10	♟♟♟ 5
● Colli Euganei Cabernet Borgo delle Casette Ris. '06	♟♟♟ 5

ilvano Follador

c. Follo
az. Santo Stefano
Callonga, 11
040 Valdobbiadene [TV]
.. +39 0423900295
ww.silvanofollador.it

CELLAR SALES
RE-BOOKED VISITS
ANNUAL PRODUCTION 20,000 bottles
ECTARES UNDER VINE 3.50

w producers have been able to withstand
e impact of the Prosecco phenomenon
thout being marked in some way. That is,
w have been able to stay true to the
ea that wine should represent a territory,
traditions, and respect the environment,
ile also reinterpreting that territory's
es. Alberta and Silvano Follador are
nong the most interesting of
dobbiadene's producers because even
h just a handful of wines, they find
emselves at the top of the DOC zone.
eir selection starts with just a few
ctares of land in Valdobbiadene, where
e hills reach notable altitudes and the
cades-old vineyards are cultivated
cording to principles of natural,
odynamic agriculture. The Valdobbiadene
ut Nature has faint aromas of white fruit
d wild flowers. It's dry and assertive in the
outh, with Glera's trademark zesty acidity
lping to bring out the wine's dynamic and
phisticated palate. Their latest creation,
e Bianco Fermo, is made exclusively with
era grapes. It proves approachable on the
se and exhibits great tanginess.

Valdobbiadene Brut Nature '16	♟♟♟	5
Bianco Fermo '16	♟♟	3
Cartizze Brut '08	♟♟♟	4
Cartizze Brut Nature '13	♟♟	4
Cartizze Brut Nature '11	♟♟	4
Cartizze Nature '12	♟♟	4
Valdobbiadene Brut Nature '15	♟♟	4
Valdobbiadene Brut Nature '14	♟♟	4
Valdobbiadene Brut Nature '13	♟♟	4
Valdobbiadene Brut Nature '12	♟♟	3*
Valdobbiadene Brut Nature '11	♟♟	3*
Valdobbiadene Sup. Brut Dosaggio Zero M. Cl. '12	♟♟	3

Le Fraghe

loc. Colombara, 3
37010 Cavaion Veronese [VR]
Tel. +39 0457236832
www.fraghe.it

CELLAR SALES
PRE-BOOKED VISITS
ACCOMMODATION
ANNUAL PRODUCTION 120,000 bottles
HECTARES UNDER VINE 28.00
VITICULTURE METHOD Certified Organic

In addition to managing her family's winery,
for a couple of years now, Matilde Poggi
has also served as President of FIVI (Italian
Federation of Independent Vine growers), a
testimony to a commitment that goes
beyond just winemaking, to embracing the
entire sector itself. Their estate comprises
30 hectares of vineyards that stretch along
the gravelly, well-ventilated terrain that's
common to the low valley of Adige. Here
they mostly cultivate grapes used for
making Bardolino. Two good vintages, 2015
and 2016, have made for two Bardolinos
with great expressiveness. After aging in
large barrels, the Brol Grande displays a
refined aromatic profile in which wild
berries intertwine with notes of pepper and
dog rose. On the palate it offers richness,
though without losing the wine's trademark
savory grip. The Bardolino 2016 is fresher
and more approachable, playing on crisp
fruit and a refreshing, gutsy palate.

● Bardolino Cl. Brol Grande '15	♟♟♟	3*
● Bardolino '16	♟♟	2*
⊙ Bardolino Chiaretto Rodon '16	♟♟	2*
● Cabernet Quaiare '15	♟♟	4
○ Garganega Camporengo '16	♟♟	2*
● Rondinella Chelidon '15	♟	2
● Bardolino Cl. Brol Grande '12	♟♟♟	3*
● Bardolino Cl. Brol Grande '11	♟♟♟	3*
● Bardolino '15	♟♟	2*
⊙ Bardolino Chiaretto Ròdon '15	♟♟	2*
○ Garganega Camporengo '15	♟♟	2*

Marchesi Fumanelli

FRAZ. SAN FLORIANO
VIA SQUARANO, 1
37029 SAN PIETRO IN CARIANO [VR]
TEL. +39 0457704875
www.squarano.com

CELLAR SALES
PRE-BOOKED VISITS
RESTAURANT SERVICE
ANNUAL PRODUCTION 50,000 bottles
HECTARES UNDER VINE 23.00

Valpolicella is a territory of diverse landscapes where wide valleys alternate in turn with flat valley floors. Thanks to success in recent decades, the area has seen growth and development in the agricultural sector. Yet one has the impression that Marchesi Fumanelli has been the one overseeing the phenomenon, bolstered by a vineyard that spans more than 20 hectares and a limited selection of wines made with only the best grapes. Their wines are zippy, but never excessive or ostentatious. San Floriano's Valpolicella Superiore doesn't follow models of super concentration and power, but looks to bring out the finesse and suppleness of the grapes. On the nose, you find clear notes of ripe cherry, refreshed by a whiff of pepper and herbs. In the mouth, fullness is perfectly supported by acidity, leaving it to the wine's tannins to close cleanly and elegantly. It's a wine with character and identity.

● Valpolicella Cl. Sup. '14	♔♔ 3
● Amarone della Valpolicella Cl. '11	♔♔ 5
● Amarone della Valpolicella Cl. '07	♔♔ 5
● Amarone della Valpolicella Cl. Octavius Ris. '10	♔♔ 8
● Amarone della Valpolicella Cl. Octavius Ris. '07	♔♔ 8
● Amarone della Valpolicella Cl. Octavius Ris. '05	♔♔ 8
● Valpolicella Cl. Sup. '11	♔♔ 3
● Valpolicella Cl. Sup. '09	♔♔ 3
● Valpolicella Cl. Sup. Squarano '14	♔♔ 3
● Valpolicella Cl. Sup. Squarano '10	♔♔ 3
● Valpolicella Cl. Sup. Squarano '06	♔♔ 3

Gamba Gnirega

VIA GNIREGA, 19
37020 MARANO DI VALPOLICELLA [VR]
TEL. +39 0456801714
www.vinigamba.it

CELLAR SALES
PRE-BOOKED VISITS
ANNUAL PRODUCTION 60,000 bottles
HECTARES UNDER VINE 7.00

The Aldrighetti family winery can be found in the valley of Marano, which is less well-known than Valpolicella Classica. It's narrow valley where the vine is still the uncontested queen of the territory. Giovanni, Giuseppe and Martino follow every stage of production, from the vineyard to the bottle, as trusted guardian of an ancient tradition that, still, gets reinterpreted with every vintage. Their selection is divided into two lines: Campedel, which pursues higher concentrations of fruit, and Le Quare, wh is tied to a more classic, agile style. The Amarone Le Quare performed well. It age in large barrels and features a suite of aromas made up of sweet fruit and spice with a fresh note of fines herbes pushing up from below. In the mouth it proves well-orchestrated, with its powerful body held in check by a light hand and good grip. The Ripasso Campedel also did well with slowly unfolding, complex aromas, a captivating grip and length.

● Amarone della Valpolicella Cl. Campedel '13	
● Amarone della Valpolicella Le Quare Cl. '13	
● Valpolicella Cl. Le Quare '16	♔♔
● Valpolicella Cl. Ripasso Campedel '14	♔♔
● Campedel '13	
● Recito della Valpolicella Le Quare '13	
● Valpolicella Cl. Sup. Ripasso Le Quare '14	
● Amarone della Valpolicella Cl. Campedel '12	♔
● Amarone della Valpolicella Cl. Campedel Ris. '10	♔

Gini

Matteotti, 42
·032 Monteforte d'Alpone [VR]
. +39 0457611908
·w.ginivini.com

CELLAR SALES
·RE-BOOKED VISITS
·NNUAL PRODUCTION 200,000 bottles
·ECTARES UNDER VINE 58.00
·TICULTURE METHOD Certified Organic

·ndro and Claudio Gini are among the
·ost esteemed figures interpreting the
·pellation of Soave. In their work, they
·e bolstered by their 50 hectares of
·eyards, which are situated on some of
·e most interesting hills in the area, and a
·nerations-old relationship with this land
·d its bounty. Their wines are aged at
·ngth at their cellar on Via Matteotti, and
·e released only once they've reached full
·rmony. In addition to their Soaves, they
·er a small, but significant, line of wines
·ade from international grape varieties,
·ltivated on the nearby hills. A further
·ar of aging for the La Froscà and
·lvarenza confers a suite of aromas with
·eat depth, where fruity and floral notes
·ve way to the first hints of benzine. In the
·outh, the La Froscà proves solid and
·cy, while the Salvarenza comes through
·l, tangy and refined.

Soave Cl. Contrada Salvarenza V. V. '14	▼▼▼ 5
Soave Cl. La Froscà '15	▼▼ 4
Pinot Nero Campo alle More '13	▼▼ 5
Soave Cl. '16	▼▼ 3
Soave Cl. Contrada Salvarenza V. V. '09	♀♀♀ 5
Soave Cl. Contrada Salvarenza V. V. '08	♀♀♀ 5
Soave Cl. Contrada Salvarenza V. V. '07	♀♀♀ 5
Soave Cl. La Froscà '11	♀♀♀ 4*
Soave Cl. La Froscà '06	♀♀♀ 4*
Soave Cl. La Froscà '05	♀♀♀ 4*
Soave Cl. Sup. Contrada Salvarenza V. V. '00	♀♀♀ 5

Giusti Wine

via del Volante, 4
31040 Nervesa della Battaglia [TV]
Tel. +39 0422720198
www.giustiwine.com

CELLAR SALES
PRE-BOOKED VISITS
ACCOMMODATION
ANNUAL PRODUCTION 200,000 bottles
HECTARES UNDER VINE 75.00
SUSTAINABLE WINERY

Ermenegildo Giusti doesn't slow down.
Today, after renovating his old cellar in Via
Arditi, and after the extraordinary
development of his viticultural operations,
he's got his sights set on the ruins of the
old Abbey of Sant'Eustacchio. His Nervesa
winery, Giusti Wine, has undertaken to
restore an important part of the
community's heritage. Concerning their
production, we point out their constant
growth and their faith in wines that display
elegance while staying true to the grape
variety. Giusti have paid a lot of attention to
their Proseccos, which becomes obvious
when you taste their wines. They are led by
an excellently-made Asolo Brut with
aromas of white fruit and a tangy, dry and
easy-drinking palate. As for the still wines,
we appreciated the fruity fragrance of the
Recantina, a traditional red that's not
produced here often. Alongside fruit, it
offers up appealing spicy and floral
overtones on a savory and racy palate.

● Amarone della Valpolicella Cl. '13	▼▼ 8
○ Asolo Brut	▼▼ 2*
○ Chardonnay Dei Carni '16	▼▼ 3
● Montello e Colli Asolani Recantina '15	▼▼ 5
○ Pinot Grigio Longheri '16	▼▼ 3
○ Asolo Extra Dry	▼ 2
○ Prosecco Rosalia Extra Dry	▼ 3
● Amarone della Valpolicella Cl. '12	♀♀ 8
● Antonio '14	♀♀ 5
○ Chardonnay Dei Carni '15	♀♀ 3
● Umberto I '11	♀♀ 8
● Umberto I '09	♀♀ 8
● Valpolicella Ripasso Sup. '13	♀♀ 5

Gorgo

FRAZ. CUSTOZA
LOC. GORGO
37066 SOMMACAMPAGNA [VR]
TEL. +39 045516063
www.cantinagorgo.com

ANNUAL PRODUCTION 350,000 bottles
HECTARES UNDER VINE 50.00

The southeastern part of inland Garda is made up of a fascinating complex of slightly elevated, morainic hills. Here, vineyards alternate with farmland, and what's left of what was once the forest of the Padana plains. And here, the Bricolo family have been working for more than 40 years. Among the most esteemed figures in the territory, they divide their attention between Bardolino and Custoza, two typologies that are interpreted with close-focus and grip. The San Michelin really delivered. It's their historic Custoza, made with grapes ripened to the limit and then aged in steel, making for a nose with intense overtones of flowers and white-fleshed fruit. In the mouth, it changes pace, highlighting good generosity supported by a powerful acidity and a very pleasant zesty taste. The Bardolino Superiore Monte Maggiore is also very interesting, with its aromas of forest floor and wild fruit, and its dynamic, crisp palate.

○ Custoza San Michelin '16	♔♔ 2*
☉ Bardolino Chiaretto '16	♔♔ 2*
● Bardolino Sup. Monte Maggiore '15	♔♔ 3
● Bardolino '16	♔ 2
☉ Bardolino Chiaretto Brut Perlato Rosa	♔ 2
● Ca' Nova '14	♔ 2
○ Custoza '16	♔ 2
○ Custoza Brut Perlato	♔ 3
○ Custoza San Michelin '15	♕♕ 2*
○ Custoza San Michelin '14	♕♕ 2*
○ Custoza San Michelin '13	♕♕ 2*
○ Custoza Sup. Summa '15	♕♕ 2*
○ Custoza Sup. Summa '14	♕♕ 2*
○ Custoza Sup. Summa '13	♕♕ 2*

Gregoletto

FRAZ. PREMAOR
VIA SAN MARTINO, 83
31050 MIANE [TV]
TEL. +39 0438970463
www.gregoletto.com

CELLAR SALES
PRE-BOOKED VISITS
ANNUAL PRODUCTION 200,000 bottles
HECTARES UNDER VINE 18.00

Few of Conegliano Valdobbiadene's wineries have managed to face the Prosecco phenomenon without being overwhelmed by it. Supported by many years of experience, Luigi Gregoletto was able to stay true to the territory and its traditions, without turning his vineyards upside-down or filling up his cellar with autoclaves. He manages almost 20 hectares of vineyards, making for a selection of outstanding quality that sees still wines at the forefront. Once again, the Prosecco Tranquillo is clearly the best in the appellation, thanks to the excellent 2016 vintage. It's a wine with faint and deep aromas, in which fruit is accompanie by beautiful floral nuances. In the mouth, i gracefully expands with balance and finesse, thus revealing all its tangy strength. The Albio 2016, a Collio di Conegliano Bianco, is also very interesting with its scents of yellow ripe fruit on the nose that embellish the palate with freshness and elegance.

○ Conegliano Valdobbiadene Prosecco Tranquillo '16	♔♔ 2
○ Colli di Conegliano Bianco Albio '16	♔♔ 3
○ Conegliano Valdobbiadene Brut	♔♔ 3
○ Conegliano Valdobbiadene Extra Dry	♔♔ 3
● Merlot '15	♔♔ 2
○ P. di Conegliano Valdobbiadene Tranquillo '16	♔♔ 2
● Cabernet '15	♔ 2
○ Chardonnay '16	♔ 2
○ Verdiso Frizzante Sui Lieviti '16	♔ 3
● Cabernet '14	♕♕ 2
● Colli di Conegliano Rosso '11	♕♕ 5
○ Conegliano Valdobbiadene Prosecco Tranquillo '15	♕♕ 2

★Guerrieri Rizzardi

S.DA CAMPAZZI, 2
37011 BARDOLINO [VR]
TEL. +39 0457210028
www.guerrieri-rizzardi.it

CELLAR SALES
PRE-BOOKED VISITS
ANNUAL PRODUCTION 700,000 bottles
HECTARES UNDER VINE 100.00
SUSTAINABLE WINERY

The Rizzardi family has managed to face Valpolicella's success with the right attitude, taking advantage of the phenomenon to establish a distinctive and elegant style. Kudos to Giuseppe and Agostino who, on their one-hundred hectares of vineyards, situated in Verona's most important DOC zones, cultivate the grapes necessary for a balanced and consistently strong selection of wines. The excellent 2013 vintage enabled them to produce an unforgettable version of the Amarone Calcarole. Its intense fruity notes gradually make room for medicinal herbs, spices and mineral overtones. In the mouth, its full but light body is supported by acidity and smooth, silky tannins. The Ripasso Pojega, on the other hand, is richer and fruitier than usual, due to the generous 2015 vintage.

● Amarone della Valpolicella Cl. Calcarole '13	♛♛♛ 8
● Valpolicella Cl. Sup. Ripasso Pojega '15	♛♛ 3*
● Bardolino Cl. Tacchetto '16	♛♛ 2*
● Clos Roareti '13	♛♛ 5
● Munus '15	♛♛ 3
○ Recioto di Soave Cl. Costeggiola '10	♛♛ 4
○ Soave Cl. '16	♛♛ 2*
○ Soave Cl. Costeggiola '16	♛♛ 2*
● Valpolicella Cl. '16	♛♛ 2*
⊙ Bardolino Chiaretto Cl. '16	♛ 2
● Bardolino Cl. '16	♛ 2
● Amarone della Valpolicella Cl. Calcarole '11	♚♚♚ 8
● Valpolicella Cl. Sup. Ripasso Pojega '13	♚♚♚ 3*

La Giuva

VIA TREZZOLANO, 20C
37141 VERONA
TEL. +39 3421117089
www.lagiuva.com

CELLAR SALES
PRE-BOOKED VISITS
ANNUAL PRODUCTION 20,000 bottles
HECTARES UNDER VINE 9.50
VITICULTURE METHOD Certified Organic

Treozzolano is a small district on upper Val Sqauaranto. The area features a handful of houses and a rather select culture of vine growing, kept alive by the few producers there, and led by La Giuva. The Malesani family's estate comprises some 10 hectares of land, all cultivated with the utmost respect for the environment. Here, at 400 meters above sea level, the grapes enjoy superb exposure, wide temperature ranges (between day and night) and constant air, making for healthy, thick grape skins. The Valpo is always one of the most interesting Valpolicellas in the appellation. This red, with its intense aromas of wild berries, pepper and a hint of dog rose, is made by Giulia and Valentina with the help of their father Alberto. In the mouth, the wine proves dry and savory with a juicy taste. The Rientro, on the other hand, is the Superiore version. It's aged in oak in their new, functional cellar, making for a solid, gutsy and refined expression of the terroir.

● Amarone della Valpolicella '13	♛♛ 7
● Recioto della Valpolicella '15	♛♛ 6
● Valpolicella Il Valpo '16	♛♛ 3
● Valpolicella Sup. Il Rientro '14	♛♛ 5
● Amarone della Valpolicella '12	♚♚ 7
● Recioto della Valpolicella '13	♚♚ 3
● Recioto della Valpolicella '12	♚♚ 3
● Valpolicella '13	♚♚ 2*
● Valpolicella Il Valpo '15	♚♚ 3
● Valpolicella Sup. Il Rientro '13	♚♚ 5
● Valpolicella Sup. Il Rientro '12	♚♚ 3
● Valpolicella Sup. Il Rientro '11	♚♚ 3

Latium

VIA FIENILE, 2
37030 MEZZANE DI SOTTO [VR]
TEL. +39 0457834648
www.latiummorini.it

CELLAR SALES
PRE-BOOKED VISITS
ANNUAL PRODUCTION 150,000 bottles
HECTARES UNDER VINE 40.00
SUSTAINABLE WINERY

Latium's symbol is a flower with seven petals because there are seven partners involved in the winery. These are the Morini siblings and cousins, who've taken over the producer founded by their parents almost 50 years ago. The estate has come to span 40 hectares in eastern Valpolicella, particularly in the valleys of Mezzane, Illasi and Valpantena. Their selection is dedicated mostly to Valpolicella reds, which are interpreted with a special focus on force, and to Soave (Valpolicella's alter ego), all of which do battle for the best exposures. Their top wine is the 2013 Valpolicella Superiore Campo Prognai, a red made from grapes dried for about one month. The nose sees intense and penetrating hints of cherry jam, with balsamic notes and spices for added freshness. Its impact on the palate is warm and powerful, supported by tight-knit tannins. The Soave is a fresh, supple and juicy white with an approachable and pleasant taste.

● Amarone della Valpolicella Campo Leon '12	▼▼ 6
○ Soave '16	▼▼ 2*
● Valpolicella Sup. Campo Prognai '13	▼▼ 4
● Valpolicella Sup. Ripasso Campo dei Ciliegi '13	▼▼ 3
● Amarone della Valpolicella Due Mori Ris. '11	▼ 8
○ Forziello '12	▼ 2
○ Soave Campo Le Calle '16	▼ 2
● Valpolicella '16	▼ 2
● Amarone della Valpolicella Due Mori Ris. '08	♈ 8

Conte Loredan Gasparini

FRAZ. VENEGAZZÙ
VIA MARTIGNAGO ALTO, 23
31040 VOLPAGO DEL MONTELLO [TV]
TEL. +39 0423870024
www.loredangasparini.it

CELLAR SALES
ACCOMMODATION
ANNUAL PRODUCTION 450,000 bottles
HECTARES UNDER VINE 60.00

Situated on the southern side of Montello Hill, the Palla family are principally involved in two activities. On the one hand, there's their reds, wines of superior character that are made using grapes from their vineyards in Venegazzù. Then there's the estate of Giavera, slightly more to the east, where the grapes for their Prosecco are grown. If their reds pursue pressure and fullness, their sparkling wines aren't lacking in captivating experiments in taste. This year, two reds from two completely different vintages get all the attention: the 2012 for more ambitious wines and the 2014 for simpler ones. The Capo di Stato has pulled off one of its best performances in recent years. It offers slow and layered aromas on the nose, starting with red fruit and gradually giving way to spices, medicinal herbs and pencil lead. In the mouth, its full body is supported by tannins, expanding assertively towards an exhilarating finish.

● Montello e Colli Asolani Rosso Capo di Stato '12	▼▼ 7
● Montello e Colli Asolani Cabernet Sauvignon '14	▼▼ 3
● Montello e Colli Asolani Rosso Venegazzù della Casa '12	▼▼ 4
● Merlot Falconera '14	▼ 3
○ Asolo Extra Brut V. Monti '13	♈ 3
○ Asolo Extra Dry Cuvée Indigene '13	♈ 3
● Montello e Colli Asolani Cabernet Sauvignon '13	♈ 3
● Montello e Colli Asolani Venegazzù Sup. Capo di Stato '11	♈ 6

Maculan

ASTELLETTO, 3
42 BREGANZE [VI]
+39 0445873733
w.maculan.net

CLLAR SALES
E-BOOKED VISITS
NUAL PRODUCTION 650,000 bottles
CTARES UNDER VINE 50.00

ganze is a narrow strip of hills that run
n Thiene to the mouth of the Valsugana
ey. The vineyards planted along these
tle slopes are generally exposed to the
th, enjoying daytime heat and the cool
ds of the Asiago plateau. Here, Fausto
culan has been working for decades,
ay with the help of his daughters Angela
Maria Vittoria. Their selection, which
blished itself long ago, centers on the
ess of the reds and the complexity of
passito dried-grape wines. The
nplicated 2014 vintage meant the
culan family couldn't produce their most
ortant wines, so they presented their
sara earlier than expected. It still
formed incredibly well, with intense
mas of red fruit and spices. It exhibits
admirable use of oak, which is
cernible without overpowering. On the
ate, it proves powerful and supple at the
e time. Torcolato also did quite well
, after an extra year aging in the cellar,
splays great harmony and finesse.

reganze Torcolato '12	🍷🍷 6
abernet Sauvignon Palazzotto '14	🍷🍷 2*
rosara '15	🍷🍷 8
reganze Pinot Nero '14	🍷🍷 3
reganze Pinot Nero Altura '13	🍷🍷 5
entino '15	🍷🍷 3
abernet '15	🍷🍷 2*
arzemino Cornorotto '15	🍷🍷 3
beaia '14	🍷🍷 3
dibi '16	🍷 2
reganze Vespaiolo '16	🍷 2
indarello '16	🍷 4
no & Toi '16	🍷 2
auvignon Ferrata '16	🍷 4
e Volti Brut M. Cl.	🍷 5

Manara

LOC. SAN FLORIANO
VIA DON CESARE BIASI, 53
37029 SAN PIETRO IN CARIANO [VR]
TEL. +39 0457701086
www.manaravini.it

CELLAR SALES
PRE-BOOKED VISITS
ANNUAL PRODUCTION 130,000 bottles
HECTARES UNDER VINE 11.00
SUSTAINABLE WINERY

If you're looking for high-impact wines that
are brooding, concentrated and soft, don't
go to Via Don Cesare Biasi. If, instead, you
like subtle wines that reveal themselves
slowly and express a commitment to
tradition, then Manara is the place for you.
Lorenzo, Favio and Giovanni, who today
enjoy the help of their children, lead this
historic, family-run winery. With an estate
that features vineyards in some of the best
parts of Valpolicella Classica, their
selection is as fastidious in its range as it
is restrained in the number of bottles
produced. A great performance by the
Amarone Postera. Its grapes are cultivated
on a hill in the municipality of Marano di
Valpolicella and dried at length before
being made into wine. The nose is striking
for its sweet fruit jam, which quickly gives
way to spicy notes. These follow through
onto a solid, powerful and never-overstated
palate supported by important tannins and
fresh acidity. The Ripasso Le Morete is also
very good, with its simpler aromas and
juicy palate.

● Amarone della Valpolicella Cl.	
Postera '11	🍷🍷 6
● Recioto della Valpolicella Cl.	
Moronalto '14	🍷🍷 5
● Valpolicella Cl. Sup. Ripasso	
Le Morete '15	🍷🍷 3
● Guido Manara '11	🍷 6
● Valpolicella Cl. '16	🍷 2
● Amarone della Valpolicella Cl. '00	🍷🍷🍷 5
● Amarone della Valpolicella Cl.	
Postera '10	🍷🍷 6
● Recioto della Valpolicella Cl.	
El Rocolo '12	🍷🍷 5
● Valpolicella Cl. Sup. Vecio Belo '14	🍷🍷 2*

Masari

LOC. MAGLIO DI SOPRA
VIA BEVILACQUA, 2A
36078 VALDAGNO [VI]
TEL. +39 0445410780
www.masari.it

CELLAR SALES
PRE-BOOKED VISITS
ANNUAL PRODUCTION 30,000 bottles
HECTARES UNDER VINE 4.00

Situated in the high valley of Agno, Massimo Dal Lago and Arianna Tessari's winery is not only one of the most interesting in the region, it's also one of the few that has sought to develop agriculture operations in a valley of such environmental and natural integrity. Their vineyards are spread out across various plots, some of which are mature while others have only recently been planted. Their style is unmistakable, characterized by fullness, aromatic integrity and pressure. The Monte Pulgo is an iconic Merlot only made in exceptional vintages. Its appealing and inviting nose offers up intense notes of red fruit and spices. In the mouth, the roundness of its fruit gives way to a dynamic, taut taste, supported by tight-knit tannins. The San Martino, on the other hand, is a Bordeaux blend of Merlot and Cabernet, with fresh and elegant aromas that add richness of taste and length to the palate.

● Monte Pulgo '11	♟♟	8
● Vicenza Rosso San Martino '13	♟♟	3*
○ AgnoBianco '15	♟♟	2*
○ Antico Pasquale Passito Bianco '08	♟♟	8
○ Doro Passito Bianco 10 Anni '07	♟♟	5
○ Leon Durello Dosaggio Zero M. Cl.	♟♟	4
○ AgnoBianco '14	♟♟	2*
○ Antico Pasquale Passito Bianco '07	♟♟	8
● Masari '13	♟♟	5
● Masari '12	♟♟	5
● Masari '11	♟♟	5
● Monte Pulgo '09	♟♟	8
● Vicenza Rosso San Martino '14	♟♟	3
● Vicenza Rosso San Martino '12	♟♟	3
● Vicenza Rosso San Martino '11	♟♟	3*

★Masi

FRAZ. GARGAGNAGO
VIA MONTELEONE, 26
37015 SANT'AMBROGIO DI VALPOLICELLA [VR]
TEL. +39 0456832511
www.masi.it

CELLAR SALES
PRE-BOOKED VISITS
ACCOMMODATION
ANNUAL PRODUCTION 4,300,000 bottle
HECTARES UNDER VINE 670.00

Thanks to their long experience, and a capacity for reinterpreting tradition year-after-year, the Boscaini family's win has managed to bring Valpolicella, and Amarone, to the entire world. Their vineyards stretch for many hectares, son of which are managed by the family themselves while others are cultivated by local vine growers. Their wide range of wines includes Amarone, the cornerstone of their selection, with its rich and close-knit style. Masi have plenty of arro in their quiver, including a couple of real gems. The Amarone Campolongo di Torb (from the vineyard of the same name in upper Valpolicella) features aromas of overripe fruit and spices freshened by a blast of herbs. Its generous mouth delive with confidence and length. The Amaron Costasera Riserva is more explosive and close-knit, both on the nose and on the palate. It's a very young wine with a promising, bright future. Masi is this edition's 'Winery of the Year'.

● Amarone della Valpolicella Cl. Campolongo di Torbe '11	♟♟♟
● Amarone della Valpolicella Cl. Costasera Ris. '12	♟
● Amarone Valpolicella Cl. Vaio Armaron Serego Alighieri '12	♟♟
● Recioto della Valpolicella Cl. Amandorlato Mezzanella '11	♟
● Valpolicella Cl. Sup. Monte Piazzo Serego Alighieri '13	♟♟
● Amarone della Valpolicella Cl. Campolongo di Torbe '09	♟♟♟
● Amarone della Valpolicella Cl. Vaio Armaron Serègo Alighieri '11	♟♟♟

Masottina

Loc. Castello Roganzuolo
Via Bradolini, 54
31020 San Fior [TV]
Tel. +39 0438400775
www.masottina.it

CELLAR SALES
PRE-BOOKED VISITS
ANNUAL PRODUCTION 1,000,000 bottles
HECTARES UNDER VINE 230.00

Situated at the easternmost part of the
Conegliano Valdobbiadene DOC zone, the
Dal Bianco family have worked in sparkling
wines for 50 years. As a result, theirs is
one of the most reliable and attentive
winemaking operations in the territory,
including when acting on behalf of third
parties. Their vineyards, which stretch for
more than 200 hectares, are mostly used
to cultivate grapes for their Prosecco,
though they also offer a limited, but
impressive, range of still wines. These last
have a subtle and harmonious character.
Their important Proseccos have stolen the
limelight, though they only make a few of
them. The best positions are reserved for
two wines: the Rive di Ogliano Contrada
Granda Brut and the Rive di Ogliano Extra
Dry. They are the Dal Bianco family's
top-quality wines; our particular favorite is
the tangy and racy Brut. As for the still
wines, the Montesco performed well. It's a
Bordeaux blend with a supple and long
profile.

● Colli di Conegliano Rosso Montesco '10	♟♟	5
○ Conegliano Valdobbiadene Extra Dry	♟♟	3
○ Conegliano Valdobbiadene Rive di Ogliano Brut Contrada Granda '16	♟♟	4
○ Conegliano Valdobbiadene Rive di Ogliano Extra Dry '16	♟♟	4
○ Conegliano Valdobbiadene Brut	♟	3
○ Conegliano Valdobbiadene Rive di Ogliano Extra Dry '15	♟♟	4
● Piave Merlot Ai Palazzi Ris. '10	♟♟	3

Roberto Mazzi e Figli

Loc. San Peretto
Via Crosetta, 8
37024 Negrar [VR]
Tel. +39 0457502072
www.robertomazzi.it

CELLAR SALES
PRE-BOOKED VISITS
ACCOMMODATION AND RESTAURANT SERVICE
ANNUAL PRODUCTION 50,000 bottles
HECTARES UNDER VINE 8.00

Antonio and Stefano Mazzi's estate, founded
by their father Roberto, comprises fewer
than 12 hectares of terrain in the heart of
Valpolicella Classica. Their aging casks are
housed in a small, efficient cellar, situated
next to an old farmhouse that used to be a
water-powered mill. Here wines wait
patiently for years before being put on the
market. Only traditional varieties are
cultivated, for a range of wines that
perfectly expresses the character of the
grapes, which are interpreted with an eye
towards elegance. The Amarone Punta Villa
has spent a further year in the cellar and
has gained more aromatic depth and
elegance on the palate. Its aromas are still
dominated by sweet and chewy red fruit,
but Valpolicella's trademark hints of
medicinal herbs and pepper elbow their way
through. On the palate its power is
well-managed, and the wine holds together
thanks to its acidity and smooth tannins.
The Valpolicella Piega is a fresh and supple
Superiore with texture and density.

● Amarone della Valpolicella Cl. Punta di Villa '12	♟♟	7
● Valpolicella Cl. Sup. Sanperetto '15	♟♟	3*
● Valpolicella Cl. Sup. Vign. Poiega '14	♟♟	4
● Valpolicella Cl. '16	♟♟	2*
● Amarone della Valpolicella Cl. Punta di Villa '11	♟♟♟	7
● Valpolicella Cl. Sup. Sanperetto '11	♟♟♟	3*
● Amarone della Valpolicella Cl. Vign. Castel '12	♟♟	7
● Amarone della Valpolicella Cl. Vign. Castel '10	♟♟	7
● Valpolicella Cl. '15	♟♟	2*
● Valpolicella Cl. Sup. Sanperetto '14	♟♟	3*
● Valpolicella Cl. Sup. Vign. Poiega '13	♟♟	4

Menegotti

Loc. Acquaroli, 7
37069 Villafranca di Verona [VR]
Tel. +39 0457902611
www.menegotticantina.com

CELLAR SALES
PRE-BOOKED VISITS
ACCOMMODATION
ANNUAL PRODUCTION 250,000 bottles
HECTARES UNDER VINE 30.00
SUSTAINABLE WINERY

The coasts of Lake Garda are characterized by their wealth of vineyards. Mostly traditional varieties grow here, while the rest were imported some decades ago. The Menegotti brothers managed to find new uses for the territory's red and white grapes, spawning a successful line of sparkling wines. The vineyards that meander through the gentle, boulder clay hills that line the southernmost shore of the basin, give life to a consistently strong selection of wines. The Custoza Superiore Elianto has taken over the role of leading wine, thanks to its complex and layered aromatic expression. Ripe white fruit lets through notes of dried flowers and sweet spices, with a subtle hint of benzine anticipating its later evolution. In the mouth it proves full, with nice follow-through. As for the sparkling wines, we saw a good performance from the Brut, an original blend of Chardonnay and Corvina fermented off the skins with a dry and elegant profile.

○ Brut M. Cl. '13	♟♟ 4
○ Custoza '16	♟♟ 2*
○ Custoza Sup. Elianto '15	♟♟ 3
○ Extra Dry M. Cl.	♟♟ 3
● Mezzacosta '14	♟♟ 3
● Bardolino '16	♟ 2
⊙ Bardolino Chiaretto '16	♟ 2
○ Biancospino M.Cl.	♟ 2
⊙ Biancospino Rosé M.Cl.	♟ 2
● Cabernet Sauvignon Le Bugne '15	♟ 2
● Geodoro '13	♟ 5
○ Lugana '16	♟ 3
○ Brut M. Cl. '12	♟♟ 4
○ Custoza '15	♟♟ 2*
○ Custoza Sup. Elianto '14	♟♟ 3

Merotto

Loc. Col San Martino
via Scandolera, 21
31010 Farra di Soligo [TV]
Tel. +39 0438989000
www.merotto.it

CELLAR SALES
PRE-BOOKED VISITS
ANNUAL PRODUCTION 550,000 bottles
HECTARES UNDER VINE 27.00

The area of Valdobbiadene offers a landscape of rare beauty. Small but steep hills are densely cultivated with vineyards that seem suspended just a few centimeters off the ground. Here, on a land that's as difficult as it is captivating, Graziano Merotto has worked for 40 years. This meticulous wine grower has brought together passion for the countryside with an awareness in the cellar, establishing Merotto as a leader in the Trevignano DOC zone. It's hard to choose their best wine, whether it's the gutsy and biting Graziano Merotto or the more charming and cosseting Castel. The former features fresh aromas of white fruit and flowers, and a palate that's solid, dry, long and exhilarating. The latter plays more on ripe fruit and expands gracefully, with sparkle enduring right to the end. There are no weak points in the rest of their wines, with particular applause for the Extra Brut Le Fare.

○ Valdobbiadene Brut Rive di Col San Martino Cuvée del Fondatore Graziano Merotto '16	♟♟♟ 4*
○ Valdobbiadene Extra Dry Castèl '16	♟♟ 4
○ Cartizze	♟♟ 5
○ Le Fare Extra Brut	♟♟ 3
○ Valdobbiadene Brut Bareta	♟♟ 3
○ Valdobbiadene Dry Rive di Col San Martino La Primavera di Barbara '16	♟♟ 3
○ Valdobbiadene Extra Dry Colbelo	♟♟ 3
⊙ Grani Rosa di Nero Brut	♟ 3
○ Prosecco di Treviso Dry Colmolina '16	♟ 3
● Rosso Dogato '13	♟ 4
○ Valdobbiadene Brut Rive di Col San Martino Cuvée del Fondatore Graziano Merotto '15	♟♟♟ 4*

rnella Molon

ᴀᴢ. Campo di Pietra
Risorgimento, 40
040 Salgareda [TV]
.. +39 0422804807
ww.ornellamolon.it

ELLAR SALES
RE-BOOKED VISITS
ESTAURANT SERVICE
NNUAL PRODUCTION 500,000 bottles
ECTARES UNDER VINE 42.00
USTAINABLE WINERY

wer Piave has in Ornella Molon and
ancarlo Traverso's winery a historic
nchmark, a producer that's been
erating for some time, faithfully
terpreting the wines of the territory. In
cent years, their children have taken on a
ore significant role, as much in the
neyards as in the cellar and sales. The
mily have obstinately resisted investing in
osecco, the star of the moment, opting to
ntinue with a focus on still wines. The
ost impressive wine this year was the
osso di Villa, a monovarietal Merlot that
as abandoned some of its trademark
ncentration in favor a fresh nose of red
uit and spice. In the mouth, its style
oves defined by elegance and grip. The
anco di Ornella also did quite well. It's a
ied-grape wine with a fresh aromatic
xpression of flowers and citrus fruit,
ghlighting an excellent balance between
veetness and suppleness on the palate.

Monte dall'Ora

loc. Castelrotto
via Monte dall'Ora, 5
37029 San Pietro in Cariano [VR]
Tel. +39 0457704462
www.montedallora.com

CELLAR SALES
PRE-BOOKED VISITS
ANNUAL PRODUCTION 35,000 bottles
HECTARES UNDER VINE 6.00
VITICULTURE METHOD Certified Organic

The hill of Castelrotto almost seems like a
terrace looking out on the city of Verona, at
the southern edge of the hills that make up
Valpolicella Classica. Here, Carlo Venturini
and his wife, Alessandra, manage fewer
than 10 hectares of vineyards. Their
first-rate selection of wines seeks to strike
up a balance between richness and
drinkability. Both in the countryside and in
the cellar, their work keeps chemicals to a
minimum, making for a range of wines
entirely dedicated to the area's classics.
Carlo and Alessandra's range of wines has
garnered praise and does a good job of
summing up Valpolicella and its wines. The
Amarone Stropa is being presented after
eight years of aging, with a suite of delicate
aromas ranging from dried fruit to spices.
The generous and juicy palate is lightened
by its richness of taste and tannins. The
Valpolicella Saustò, which is no longer
made with the Ripasso technique, features
smoky notes of dried flowers, while its
palate comes through balanced and long.

Bianco di Ornella '13	♥♥ 4
Piave Merlot Rosso di Villa '12	♥♥ 5
Vite Rossa '13	♥♥ 4
Piave Raboso '11	♥ 5
Prosecco Brut	♥ 2
Prosecco Extra Dry	♥ 2
Traminer '16	♥ 3
Bianco di Ornella '11	♀♀ 4
Piave Merlot Ornella '10	♀♀ 3
Piave Merlot Rosso di Villa '11	♀♀ 5
Piave Raboso Ornella '09	♀♀ 5
Vite Rossa '11	♀♀ 4
Vite Rossa '10	♀♀ 4

● Amarone della Valpolicella Cl. Stropa '09	♥♥ 8
● Valpolicella Cl. Sup. Saustò '13	♥♥ 5
● Valpolicella Cl. Saseti '16	♥♥ 2*
● Valpolicella Cl. Sup. Camporenzo '14	♥♥ 4
● Valpolicella Cl. Sup. Camporenzo '13	♀♀♀ 4*
● Valpolicella Cl. Sup. Camporenzo '11	♀♀♀ 4*
● Valpolicella Cl. Sup. Camporenzo '10	♀♀♀ 4*
● Valpolicella Cl. Sup. Ripasso Saustò '07	♀♀♀ 5
● Amarone della Valpolicella Cl. Stropa '08	♀♀ 8
● Amarone della Valpolicella Cl. Stropa '07	♀♀ 8
● Valpolicella Cl. Saseti '15	♀♀ 2*
● Valpolicella Cl. Sup. Ripasso Saustò '12	♀♀ 5

Monte del Frà

S.DA PER CUSTOZA, 35
37066 SOMMACAMPAGNA [VR]
TEL. +39 045510490
www.montedelfra.it

CELLAR SALES
PRE-BOOKED VISITS
ANNUAL PRODUCTION 1,000,000 bottles
HECTARES UNDER VINE 197.00

Marica and Massimo Bonomo have managed to give a major push to the winery founded by their parents, making the family winery a benchmark in the area. In addition to the many vineyards that run along the morainic hills at the southern bank of lake Garda, they have vineyards in nearby Valpolicella Classica at their disposal, making for a selection that features polish and grip. The 2015 Ca' del Magro is simply magnificent. It's a Custoza that explores all the potential of the Garda appellation, combining freshness and ripeness, power and lightness, balance and personality, thus making for a truly complete wine. As for the reds, their Amarone Scarnocchio has taken another step forward. The slow and layered aromatic expression affords the palate a solid and gutsy profile and drinkability. The Colombara, made with overripe Garganega, is deep and welcoming, with great expressiveness.

○ Custoza Sup. Ca' del Magro '15	♟♟♟ 3*
● Amarone della Valpolicella Cl. Scarnocchio Lena di Mezzo '12	♟♟ 8
○ Colombara '13	♟♟ 3*
● Amarone della Valpolicella Cl. Lena di Mezzo '13	♟♟ 8
● Bardolino '16	♟♟ 2*
⊙ Bardolino Chiaretto '16	♟♟ 2*
○ Custoza '16	♟♟ 2*
● Valpolicella Cl. Lena di Mezzo '16	♟♟ 3
● Valpolicella Cl. Sup. Ripasso Lena di Mezzo '15	♟♟ 3
○ Custoza Sup. Ca' del Magro '14	♟♟♟ 3*
● Amarone della Valpolicella Cl. Scarnocchio Lena di Mezzo '11	♟♟ 7

Monte Santoccio

LOC. SANTOCCIO, 6
37022 FUMANE [VR]
TEL. +39 3496461223
www.montesantoccio.it

CELLAR SALES
PRE-BOOKED VISITS
ANNUAL PRODUCTION 14,000 bottles
HECTARES UNDER VINE 3.00

Nicola Ferrari's winery is situated just over Fumane. Here, his house and cellar integrate with a splendid agricultural landscape, surrounded by a handful of vineyards that Nicola and his wife, Laura, tend to with painstaking care. In the cellar all their work is aimed at bringing out the attributes of Valpolicella's historic varieties, which are carefully interpreted in pursuit of the right balance between richness and lightness, pleasantness and character. The selection is comprised of just a few wines, each of which faithfully reflects the DOC zone. The Ripasso is tops this year. It's a Valpolicella Superiore that plays on a combination of overripe fruit and notes of spices and crushed flowers, with a captivating richness of flavor in the mouth. The 2012 Amarone, on the other hand, offers up classic sweet cherry and pepper on the nose. It changes gear on the palate. Its full and succulent impact is followed by savoriness and acidity, thus making for a juicy, long drink.

● Amarone della Valpolicella Cl. '12	♟♟
● Recioto della Valpolicella Cl. Amandorlarto '14	♟♟
● Valpolicella Cl. Sup. '15	♟♟
● Valpolicella Cl. Sup. Ripasso '15	♟
● Valpolicella Cl. '16	♟
● Amarone della Valpolicella Cl. '11	♟♟
● Amarone della Valpolicella Cl. '09	♟♟
● Amarone della Valpolicella Cl. '08	♟♟
● Valpolicella Cl. Sup. '14	♟♟
● Valpolicella Cl. Sup. Rip. '10	♟♟
● Valpolicella Cl. Sup. Ripasso '13	♟♟
● Valpolicella Cl. Sup. Ripasso '12	♟♟
● Valpolicella Cl. Sup. Ripasso '11	♟♟

Monte Tondo

LOC. MONTE TONDO
VIA SAN LORENZO, 89
37038 SOAVE [VR]
TEL. +39 0457680347
www.montetondo.it

CELLAR SALES
PRE-BOOKED VISITS
ACCOMMODATION
ANNUAL PRODUCTION 200,000 bottles
HECTARES UNDER VINE 32.00

The Magnabosco family's winery extends throughout the heart of Soave Classica. The estate also includes a few hectares in the DOC zone itself, as well as in Campiano. Here, Gino and his sons manage their vineyards, growing the grapes used in their Amarone and Valpolicella. More than 30 hectares of terrain give rise to a selection of outstanding quality, with simple whites characterized by a slim-bodied profile, and richer selections that show great aging potential. The Foscarin Slavinus is made with grapes cultivated on the Monte Foscarino's beautiful slopes. These are picked when fully ripe, and mixed with a small amount of overripe grapes. The nose offers sweet and chewy yellow fruit, which gets through notes of flint and dried flowers. In the mouth, its full and powerful body is well-managed by acidity and salt. The Casette Foscarin, from the same vineyard, offers up fresh aroma and a juicy, racy palate.

○ Soave Cl. Sup. Foscarin Slavinus '15	♟♟ 4	
○ Soave Cl. Casette Foscarin '15	♟♟ 3	
○ Soave Cl. Monte Tondo '16	♟♟ 2*	
● Valpolicella Ripasso Campo Grande '14	♟♟ 4	
● Amarone della Valpolicella '13	♟ 6	
● Valpolicella Sup. San Pietro '15	♟ 2	
○ Soave Cl. Monte Tondo '06	♟♟♟ 2*	
● Amarone della Valpolicella '12	♟♟ 6	
○ Soave Cl. '15	♟♟ 2*	
○ Soave Cl. Casette Foscarin '14	♟♟ 3	
○ Soave Cl. Casette Foscarin '14	♟♟ 3	
○ Soave Cl. Casette Foscarin '13	♟♟ 3*	
○ Soave Cl. Sup. Foscarin Slavinus '14	♟♟ 4	
○ Soave Cl. Sup. Foscarin Slavinus '14	♟♟ 4	

Monte Zovo

LOC. ZOVO, 23A
37013 CAPRINO VERONESE [VR]
TEL. +39 0457281301
www.montezovo.com

CELLAR SALES
PRE-BOOKED VISITS
ACCOMMODATION AND RESTAURANT SERVICE
ANNUAL PRODUCTION 6,000,000 bottles
HECTARES UNDER VINE 167.00
SUSTAINABLE WINERY

Even if he's been in business for fewer than 20 years, Diego Cottini's past is closely tied to Valpolicella and its wines. His vineyards have come to span 150 hectares, mostly concentrated in eastern Valpolicella, while his cellar was built at the northwestern most part of the DOC zone. In addition to his free-style wines, he produces the area's classics, with an interpretation that focuses on richness and rigor. Their Amarone is getting more impressive by the year, and gave a memorable performance with the 2013 vintage. It features intense notes of overripe red fruit infused with hints of sweet spices in which oak is just faintly perceptible. Its impact on the palate is warm and soft, finding more precision and grip at the finish. The Valpolicella Superiore also impressed, it's crisp on the nose, racy and supple on the palate.

● Amarone della Valpolicella '13	♟♟ 7	
○ Sauvignon '16	♟♟ 4	
● Valpolicella Sup. '15	♟♟ 4	
● Valpolicella Sup. Ripasso '15	♟♟ 4	
● Ca' Linverno '13	♟ 4	
● Amarone della Valpolicella '12	♟♟ 6	
● Amarone della Valpolicella '11	♟♟ 6	
● Amarone della Valpolicella '07	♟♟ 8	
● Amarone della Valpolicella Ris. '09	♟♟ 8	
● Amarone della Valpolicella Ris. '08	♟♟ 8	
○ Sauvignon '15	♟♟ 4	
● Valpolicella Sup. Ripasso '14	♟♟ 4	
● Valpolicella Sup. Ripasso '12	♟♟ 4	
● Valpolicella Sup. Ripasso '11	♟♟ 4	

Cantina Sociale di Monteforte d'Alpone

Via XX Settembre, 24
37032 Monteforte d'Alpone [VR]
Tel. +39 0457610110
www.cantinadimonteforte.it

CELLAR SALES
PRE-BOOKED VISITS
ANNUAL PRODUCTION 3,000,000 bottles
HECTARES UNDER VINE 1300.00

Founded more than 60 years ago, the Cantina Sociale di Monteforte continues its work in promoting the territory and its vineyards while providing grapes to many of the area's producers (from its facility on Via XX Settembre). Their vineyards span 1300 hectares, with its in-house production reaching three million bottles. Such numbers highlight the selection process that takes place before production, with partners choosing only the best grapes for their wines. Their Soave Castellaro is always one of the most interesting in the area. It's a white wine made exclusively with Garganega fermented and aged for a year in wood of various sizes. On the nose, ripe fruit meets overtones of flowers and spices, with oak just discernible in the background. In the mouth, it expands with class and rich flavor, giving way to a long, juicy finish. The real star, in terms of value for money, is the Soave Clivus, with its intense aromas, great elegance and balance on the palate.

○ Soave Cl. Sup. Vign. di Castellaro '15	♔♔♔ 2*
○ Recioto di Soave Cl. Il Sigillo '15	♔♔ 3
○ Soave Cl. Clivus '16	♔♔ 2*
○ Soave Cl. Il Vicario '16	♔♔ 2*
● Valpolicella Ripasso '14	♔♔ 2*
● Amarone della Valpolicella Re Teodorico '14	♔ 5
● Cavaliere Cabernet Sauvignon '15	♔ 2
○ Lessini Durello Brut	♔ 2
○ Soave Cl. Clivus '15	♔♔ 1*
○ Soave Cl. Clivus '14	♔♔ 1*
○ Soave Cl. Sup. Vign. di Castellaro '14	♔♔ 2*
○ Soave Cl. Sup. Vign. di Castellaro '13	♔♔ 2*
● Valpolicella Ripasso '14	♔♔ 2*

Montegrande

Via Torre, 2
35030 Rovolon [PD]
Tel. +39 0495226276
www.vinimontegrande.it

CELLAR SALES
PRE-BOOKED VISITS
ANNUAL PRODUCTION 250,000 bottles
HECTARES UNDER VINE 30.00

Raffaele Cristofanon runs his family's winery in the heart of Colli Euganei. After working in the sector for some years, he managed a decisive change of direction. Greater focus on quality, along with important collaborations in the cellar, have made for an overall improvement in the entire selection. Montegrande's interpretations, however, are still true to the characteristics of the varieties, vintages and vineyards. Good concentration and richness are well-balanced by tangy freshness and tannins. Alongside a rich selection of vintage wines, there are two lines that focus on the attributes of the territory. The Cabernet Sereo features rich and ripe expressions of fruit, with oak adding warmth and aromatic pervasiveness. In the mouth, the generosity of the palate is contrasted by healthy and exuberant tannins. The same holds for the Vigna delle Roche, a Merlot-heavy Bordeaux blend with a sunny and approachable profile.

● Colli Euganei Cabernet Sereo '13	♔♔ 3
○ Colli Euganei Fior d'Arancio Spumante '16	♔♔ 2
● Colli Euganei Rosso '16	♔♔ 2
● Colli Euganei Rosso V. delle Roche '13	♔♔ 3
○ Castearo '16	♔ 2
○ Colli Euganei Bianco Erto '16	♔ 2
● Colli Euganei Cabernet '16	♔ 2
○ Colli Euganei Chardonnay S. Giorgio '15	♔ 2
● Colli Euganei Merlot '16	♔ 2
○ Colli Euganei Pinot Bianco Marani '16	♔ 2
○ Colli Euganei Seprino Extra Dry	♔ 2
● Colli Euganei Cabernet Sereo '12	♔♔ 3
○ Colli Euganei Fior d'Arancio Passito '13	♔♔ 3
● Colli Euganei Rosso '15	♔♔ 2

Monteversa

FRAZ. MONTE VERSA, 1024
35030 Vò [PD]
TEL. +39 0499941092
www.monteversa.it

CELLAR SALES
PRE-BOOKED VISITS
ANNUAL PRODUCTION 23,000 bottles
HECTARES UNDER VINE 17.00
VITICULTURE METHOD Certified Organic

The Voltazza family's winery can be found in the Colli Euganei Regional Park, a long tract of land that stretches to the west, through the towns of Vò and Lozzo Atestino, and totaling more than 20 hectares. On the north side of the hill, mostly white grapes are cultivated, with mostly Bordeaux cultivated to the south. Both in the countryside and in the cellar, the environment is treated with the utmost respect. The unfortunate 2014 vintage didn't allow them to produce their flagship wine, the Animaversa Rosso. So we turned our attention to the Versacinto, a Bordeaux blend made primarily with Merlot that expresses dynamic, crisp fruit, and hints of spice and pencil lead. In the mouth, the wine proves full and precise but exhibits superior drinkability as well. The Fior d'Arancio Spumante offers up good aromatic expression, it's a wine in which acidity and tanginess help keep sweetness in check.

Colli Euganei Fior d'Arancio Spumante '16	⚑⚑ 4
Colli Euganei Rosso Versacinto '16	⚑⚑ 3
Biodiversa '16	⚑ 3
Colli Euganei Manzoni Bianco Animaversa '15	⚑ 3
Primaversa Frizzante '16	⚑ 3
Versavò Bianco	⚑ 2
Colli Euganei Cabernet Animaversa '12	⚑⚑ 4
Colli Euganei Rosso Animaversa '13	⚑⚑ 4
Colli Euganei Rosso Versacinto '15	⚑⚑ 3
Colli Euganei Rosso Versacinto '13	⚑⚑ 3
Versavò '15	⚑⚑ 2*

Le Morette

FRAZ. SAN BENEDETTO DI LUGANA
V.LE INDIPENDENZA, 19D
37019 PESCHIERA DEL GARDA [VR]
TEL. +39 0457552724
www.lemorette.it

CELLAR SALES
PRE-BOOKED VISITS
ANNUAL PRODUCTION 380,000 bottles
HECTARES UNDER VINE 32.00
SUSTAINABLE WINERY

The southern part of the basin of Garda has one of the most 'en vogue' appellations at the moment: Lugana. Many wineries have sprung up along the hills that surround Lake Garda, focusing on whites made with Turbiana grapes. Brothers Zenato, Fabio and Paolo have continued to grow the business founded by their father, though they haven't forgotten their family's agricultural roots carrying on their important work as nurserymen. The Lugana Riserva performed quite well. It's a white that explores the Garda appellation's great aging potential and is only released to the public after a long stay in the cellar. It's made with grapes grown in clay-rich soil. These are aged on the lees in steel for a long period and then worked into a small quantity of wine that rests in mid-sized casks. The result is a wine with deep aromas, where fully-expressed fruit meets notes of spices and dried flowers. The palate is full, solid and very balanced.

○ Lugana Ris. '13	⚑⚑ 4
⊙ Bardolino Chiaretto Cl. '16	⚑⚑ 2*
○ Lugana Benedictus '15	⚑⚑ 3
○ Lugana Mandolara '16	⚑⚑ 3
● Bardolino Cl. '16	⚑ 2
○ Accordo Passito Bianco '12	♑♑ 4
● Bardolino Cl. '15	♑♑ 2*
○ Lugana Benedictus '14	♑♑ 3
○ Lugana Mandolara '15	♑♑ 3
○ Lugana Mandolara '14	♑♑ 2*
○ Lugana Mandolara '13	♑♑ 2*
○ Lugana Ris. '12	♑♑ 5
○ Lugana Ris. '11	♑♑ 3
● Perseo '12	♑♑ 5

Marco Mosconi

VIA PARADISO, 5
37031 ILLASI [VR]
TEL. +39 0456529109
www.marcomosconi.it

CELLAR SALES
PRE-BOOKED VISITS
ANNUAL PRODUCTION 25,000 bottles
HECTARES UNDER VINE 10.00

In an agricultural environment like Valpolicella, dense with producers of various sizes and backgrounds, Marco Mosconi has managed to emerge. He's done it by proposing modern interpretations that are, at the same time, true to the tradition of the territory's wines. Ten hectares in the eastern part of the DOC zone provide the grapes for their selection, which features close-focused fruits and crispness. Their solid, succulent wines deserve serious attention. Very few wines are made in Via Paradiso, but the Valpolicella Superiore is the one that stands out. It's a red that plays on ripe fruit, enriched by notes of pepper and thyme. The palate is generous and perfectly accompanied by savory acidity. They also make a good vintage Valpolicella, which explores the simplest and most fragrant nature of these traditional grapes and features a captivatingly pleasant palate.

● Valpolicella Sup. '13	♟♟♟ 5
○ Soave Corte Paradiso '16	♟♟ 2*
○ Soave Rosetta '15	♟♟ 3
● Turan '13	♟♟ 3
● Valpolicella Montecurto '16	♟♟ 3
● Valpolicella Sup. '12	♟♟♟ 5
● Amarone della Valpolicella '12	♟♟ 8
● Amarone della Valpolicella '11	♟♟ 8
● Recioto della Valpolicella '11	♟♟ 6
○ Soave Corte Paradiso '15	♟♟ 2*
○ Soave Corte Paradiso '14	♟♟ 2*
● Valpolicella Montecurto '15	♟♟ 3
● Valpolicella Montecurto '14	♟♟ 3
● Valpolicella Sup. '11	♟♟ 5

Mosole

LOC. CORBOLONE
VIA ANNONE VENETO, 60
30029 SANTO STINO DI LIVENZA [VE]
TEL. +39 0421310404
www.mosole.com

CELLAR SALES
PRE-BOOKED VISITS
ANNUAL PRODUCTION 230,000 bottles
HECTARES UNDER VINE 30.00

Over his decades of experience in Venetian viticulture, Lucio Mosole has managed to gain recognition both from the market and from critics (as well as colleagues). It's all thanks to a continued commitment to the territory, without pursuing easy, commercial shortcuts. Thus he has given life to an outstanding selection of wines that excel when it comes to representing the terroir. The clay that characterizes the soil here is particularly well-suited to cultivating Merlot and Tai. The Hora Prima is the key player here, it's an original blend of Chardonnay aged in wood, Tai, and a dash of Sauvignon aged in steel. It's striking for the finesse of its aromas, notes of white fruit, flowers and citrus. The palate stands out for its elegance and delicacy rather than richness or power. The Eleo, a Lison with texture and elegance, is also quite impressive, as is the passito dried-grape wine Ad Nonam, a sweet wine with rare balance and freshness.

○ Ad Nonam Passito '15	♟♟ 4
○ Hora Prima '15	♟♟ 4
○ Lison Eleo '16	♟♟ 4
○ Sauvignon '16	♟♟ 4
● Venezia Cabernet Franc '16	♟♟ 4
○ Venezia Chardonnay '16	♟♟ 4
○ Venezia Pinot Grigio '16	♟♟ 4
● Lison-Pramaggiore Merlot '16	♟ 4
● Lison-Pramaggiore Refosco P. R. '16	♟ 4
○ Tai '16	♟ 4
○ Hora Prima '14	♟♟ 4
● Lison Pramaggiore Cabernet Hora Sexta '13	♟♟ 4
● Lison-Pramaggiore Merlot Ad Nonam '13	♟♟ 5
○ Venezia Pinot Grigio '15	♟♟ 4

Mottolo

LOC. LE CONTARINE
VIA COMEZZARA, 13
35030 BAONE [PD]
TEL. +39 3479456155
www.ilmottolo.it

CELLAR SALES
PRE-BOOKED VISITS
ANNUAL PRODUCTION 27,000 bottles
HECTARES UNDER VINE 7.00

The Colli Euganei Regional Park
encompasses one of the most interesting
zones for vine growing in the region. The
southern part is particularly of note. Here
Bordeaux, which has grown in the area for
more than a century, finds the right
conditions for ripening regularly. Sergio
Fortin's vineyards and cellar can be found
in the district of Le Contarine. Sergio is a
scientist turned vine grower and has, in just
a few years, managed to earn everyone's
approval. His wines are rich in fruit and
crisp. They are energetic in the mouth and
rewarding. The Serro lives up to
expectations thanks to the careful selection
performed during the 2014 vintage. It's a
blend of Merlot and a smaller part
Cabernet. The nose offers intense notes of
ripe and crisp red fruit imbued with healthy
and refreshing vegetal and spicy overtones.
It's a rich and succulent wine, with good
length. The Vigna del Pozzo is a
harmonious and elegant dried-grape wine
with an intense and lively aromatic profile.

Colli Euganei Rosso Serro '14	🍷🍷 4
Cabernet V. Marè '15	🍷🍷 2*
Colli Euganei Fior d'Arancio Passito V. del Pozzo '15	🍷🍷 3
Le Contarine '16	🍷🍷 2*
Merlot Comezzara '15	🍷🍷 2*
Colli Euganei Rosso Serro '11	🍷🍷🍷 3*
Colli Euganei Rosso Serro '10	🍷🍷🍷 3*
Colli Euganei Rosso Serro '09	🍷🍷🍷 3*
Colli Euganei Rosso Serro '13	🍷🍷 4
Colli Euganei Rosso Serro '12	🍷🍷 3*
Comezzara Merlot '14	🍷🍷 2*
Vingnànima '13	🍷🍷 3*

Mulin di Mezzo

VIA MOLIN DI MEZZO, 16
30020 ANNONE VENETO [VE]
TEL. +39 0422 769398
www.mulindimezzo.com

PRE-BOOKED VISITS
ANNUAL PRODUCTION 40,000 bottles
HECTARES UNDER VINE 6.00

Paolo Lazzarini is the beating heart of Mulin
di Mezzo, an inspiring operation that spans
six hectares in the Venetian plains (flanked
by the Tagliamento and Livenza rivers). As
often happened in this part of Veneto, the
vineyards are mostly dedicated to red
Bordeaux varieties, even if there's also
Chardonnay and Sauvignon. Here, however,
Tai has a special place, the variety that
constitutes the most important appellation
in the territory. The Lison Classico is the
wine that most caught our attention. It's a
white with intense aromas of yellow fruit
and Mediterranean scrub. Thanks to very
low yields and careful work in the cellar, the
wine features a dynamic, powerful palate
with extraordinary tanginess. The Rosso
Molino is also very interesting. It's a
Bordeaux blend whose fruity aromas are
refreshed by vegetal notes and a dry,
pleasantly rustic taste.

● Il Priore '10	🍷🍷 4
○ Lison Cl. '16	🍷🍷 2*
● Rosso Molino '15	🍷🍷 2*
● Merlot '13	🍷 2
○ Sauvignon '16	🍷 2
● Venezia Cabernet Sauvignon '16	🍷 2

Musella

LOC. FERRAZZE
VIA FERRAZZETTE, 2
37036 SAN MARTINO BUON ALBERGO [VR]
TEL. +39 045973385
www.musella.it

CELLAR SALES
PRE-BOOKED VISITS
ACCOMMODATION
ANNUAL PRODUCTION 260,000 bottles
HECTARES UNDER VINE 50.00
VITICULTURE METHOD Certified Biodynamic

Maddalena Pasqua runs her family's winery just outside Verona, within the area of Musella. The property, secured by walls, spans many hectares of terrain, such that Musella's vineyards are found growing along slopes of varying climates and soils. Cultivation takes place according to biodynamic principles. Along with a production approach that shows respect for the grape, this makes for a selection marked by character and grip, that stays true to the characteristics of the territory's grapes. The 2012 Amarone has a lustrous, though not intense, appearance. On the nose, it offers aromas that call up overripe red fruit, cocoa beans and crushed flowers. In the mouth, the wine proves astonishingly well-orchestrated, exuberant yet supple and juicy, and refreshed at the end by gutsy tannins. The Valpolicella Superiore is also very good, with its fresher and more approachable fruity expression and its dynamic, pleasantly crisp palate.

● Amarone della Valpolicella '12	▼▼ 6
● Valpolicella Sup. '15	▼▼ 3*
○ Fibio Pinot Bianco '15	▼▼ 2*
● Valpolicella Sup. Ripasso '14	▼▼ 4
☉ Drago Rosé '16	▼ 3
● Amarone della Valpolicella Ris. '07	▼▼▼ 6
● Valpolicella Sup. '13	▼▼▼ 3*
● Valpolicella Sup. '12	▼▼▼ 2*
● Amarone della Valpolicella '11	♀♀ 6
● Amarone della Valpolicella Ris. '10	♀♀ 6
● Amarone della Valpolicella Senza Titolo '08	♀♀ 8
● Recioto della Valpolicella '12	♀♀ 5
● Valpolicella Sup. '14	♀♀ 3*
● Valpolicella Sup. Ripasso '12	♀♀ 4

Daniele Nardello

VIA IV NOVEMBRE, 56
37032 MONTEFORTE D'ALPONE [VR]
TEL. +39 0457612116
www.nardellovini.it

CELLAR SALES
PRE-BOOKED VISITS
ANNUAL PRODUCTION 75,000 bottles
HECTARES UNDER VINE 16.00

Situated in the southern part of the Soave Classico DOC zone, Federica and Daniele Nardello's winery extends for some 15 hectares, mostly along the slopes of Monte Zoppega. Here, Garganega, Soave's crown jewel, is able to ripen with a particularly soft and welcoming character. At Nardello, the grape finds its perfect complement in the grippy, subtle Trebbiano di Soave, making for wines of impeccable craftsmanship that express the immense value of the territory. The strong 2015 vintage enabled Daniele to make an excellent Monte Zoppega (the name of the mountain where its grapes are cultivated). It's a Soave aged partially in wood and partially in steel. Aromatically, the wine sees an explosion of fruit, with peach and pear taking center stage. These are accompanied by flowers, spices and a background of faint oak. Its palate proves generous and very balanced. The Vigna Turbian, on the other hand, offers more freshness and suppleness. It also benefits from the presence of Trebbiano di Soave, which confers grip to the wine.

○ Soave Cl. Monte Zoppega '15	▼▼ 3
○ Soave Cl. V. Turbian '16	▼▼ 2
○ Aetas Brut	▼ 2
○ Blanc de Fe' '16	▼ 2
○ Soave Cl. Meridis '16	▼ 3
○ Blanc De Fè '14	♀♀ 2
○ Recioto di Soave Suavissimus '11	♀♀ 4
○ Soave Cl. Meridis '15	♀♀ 2
○ Soave Cl. Meridis '14	♀♀ 2
○ Soave Cl. Meridis '13	♀♀ 2
○ Soave Cl. Monte Zoppega '14	♀♀ 2
○ Soave Cl. Monte Zoppega '13	♀♀ 2
○ Soave Cl. V. Turbian '15	♀♀ 2
○ Soave Cl. V. Turbian '14	♀♀ 2
○ Soave Cl. V. Turbian '13	♀♀ 2

Angelo Nicolis e Figli

VIA VILLA GIRARDI, 29
37029 SAN PIETRO IN CARIANO [VR]
TEL. +39 0457701261
www.vininicolis.com

CELLAR SALES
PRE-BOOKED VISITS
ANNUAL PRODUCTION 220,000 bottles
HECTARES UNDER VINE 42.00

The Nicolis Family has worked for generations in Valpolicella Classica and today brothers Giuseppe and Giancarlo are following in their parents' footsteps. Their vineyards span several hectares, yet the fact that their production levels aren't particularly elevated proves the quality of the grapes that are selected for use. Their vines are defined by a style that looks to tradition, interpreted with superior freshness and integrity. The Amarone Classico is only released after long aging in the cellar, so that, today, we get to appreciate its layered aromatic expression. Sweet, dried fruit appears, then spices emerge, followed by herbs and hints of leather. The palate displays good concentration but also suppleness and grip (by virtue of the grapes' characteristic acidity). The Ripasso Seccal is also ripe and pervasive, with its generous aromas and delicate palate.

● Amarone della Valpolicella Cl. '11	▾▾ 6
● Recioto della Valpolicella Cl. '13	▾▾ 5
● Valpolicella Cl. Sup. Ripasso Seccal '15	▾▾ 3
● Valpolicella Cl. '16	▾ 2
● Amarone della Valpolicella Cl. Ambrosan '06	▾▾▾ 7
● Amarone della Valpolicella Cl. Ambrosan '98	▾▾▾ 7
● Amarone della Valpolicella Cl. Ambrosan '93	▾▾▾ 6
● Amarone della Valpolicella Cl. '10	♈▾ 6
● Amarone della Valpolicella Cl. Ambrosan '08	♈▾ 7
● Recioto della Valpolicella Cl. '11	♈▾ 5
● Valpolicella Cl. Sup. Ripasso Seccal '13	♈▾ 3
● Valpolicella Cl. Sup. Ripasso Seccal '12	♈▾ 3

Novaia

VIA NOVAIA, 1
37020 MARANO DI VALPOLICELLA [VR]
TEL. +39 0457755129
www.novaia.it

CELLAR SALES
PRE-BOOKED VISITS
ANNUAL PRODUCTION 45,000 bottles
HECTARES UNDER VINE 7.00
VITICULTURE METHOD Certified Organic
SUSTAINABLE WINERY

Giampaolo and Cesare Vaona's children, Marcello and Cristina, work by their side, and are taking on an ever-greater role in managing the family winery. Their estate comprises fewer than 10 hectares in one of the most interesting of Valpolicella Classica's valleys. Here the soil type alternates between calcareous clay and more unusual volcanic tuff (a small island in Verona's large DOC zone). Grapes are organically cultivated, with a general approach to production that is defined by respect for tradition. It may be lacking a star performer, but nonetheless Novaia has presented a truly impressive selection. The winery's skill lies in their sensitivity to tradition and timing. This is immediately clear when tasting the Amarone Corte Vaona. Aromatically, it calls up sweet, meaty local cherries and herbs, while on the palate it balances light and racy (with powerful body). Hats off to them!

● Amarone della Valpolicella Cl. Corte Vaona '12	▾▾ 6
● Recioto della Valpolicella Cl. Le Novaje '15	▾▾ 4
● Valpolicella Cl. '16	▾▾ 2*
● Valpolicella Cl. Sup. Ripasso '14	▾▾ 3
● Amarone della Valpolicella Cl. Corte Vaona '11	♈▾ 5
● Amarone della Valpolicella Cl. Le Balze '11	♈▾ 8
● Recioto della Valpolicella Cl. Le Novaje '14	♈▾ 4
● Recioto della Valpolicella Cl. Le Novaje '13	♈▾ 4
● Valpolicella Cl. '13	♈▾ 2*
● Valpolicella Cl. Sup. I Cantoni '12	♈▾ 4
● Valpolicella Cl. Sup. Ripasso '13	♈▾ 3
● Valpolicella Cl. Sup. Ripasso '12	♈▾ 3

Ottella

FRAZ. SAN BENEDETTO DI LUGANA
LOC. OTTELLA
37019 PESCHIERA DEL GARDA [VR]
TEL. +39 0457551950
www.ottella.it

CELLAR SALES
PRE-BOOKED VISITS
ANNUAL PRODUCTION 350,000 bottles
HECTARES UNDER VINE 40.00

Along the southern coast of Lake Garda, agriculture has been thriving as of late, thanks in part to the production of Lugana. The Montresor brothers, Francesco and Michele, are among the leaders of this important appellation, bolstered by a vineyard that stretches for many hectares both in the areas adjacent to Frassino lake (where Turbiana reigns supreme) and in the nearby hills (where reds are cultivated). This year's selection put in an excellence performance and was led, as usual, by the Riserva Molceo. It's made exclusively with Turbiana, picked when overripe in October, and then aged primarily in steel (with just a small quantity aged in oak). The result is a white with intense aromas of citrus and flowers, and meaty yellow fruit that peeks through. The cool vintage lends the palate suppleness, grip and lightness.

○ Lugana Molceo Ris. '15	♟♟♟ 4*
○ Lugana Le Creete '16	♟♟ 3*
○ Blanc de Blancs Brut M. Cl.	♟♟ 4
● Campo Sireso '14	♟♟ 4
○ Lugana '16	♟♟ 2*
⊙ Roses Roses '16	♟♟ 2*
● Valpolicella Ripasso '14	♟♟ 4
⊙ Vignenuove '16	♟ 2*
● Gemei Rosso '16	♟ 2
⊙ Roses Roses Brut M. Cl.	♟ 4
○ Lugana Molceo Ris. '14	♟♟♟ 4*
○ Lugana Molceo Ris. '13	♟♟♟ 4*
○ Lugana Molceo Ris. '12	♟♟♟ 4*
○ Lugana Sup. Molceo '11	♟♟♟ 4*
○ Lugana Sup. Molceo '10	♟♟♟ 4*
○ Lugana Sup. Molceo '09	♟♟♟ 4
○ Lugana Sup. Molceo '08	♟♟♟ 4

Pasqua - Cecilia Beretta

LOC. SAN FELICE EXTRA
VIA BELVEDERE, 135
37131 VERONA
TEL. +39 0458432111
www.pasqua.it

CELLAR SALES
PRE-BOOKED VISITS
ANNUAL PRODUCTION 13,000,000 bottles
HECTARES UNDER VINE 300.00

The Pasqua family came here from Apulia almost a century ago, and today theirs is one of the most developed operations in Valpolicella. Today the third generation is pushing forward, with Alessandro, Riccardo Cecilia and Giovanni representing the face of Pasqua. Their estate comprises many hectares of land, some of which surround their modern cellar in San Felice, and some of which are spread out in prized territories like Castello di Montorio, Mizzole and Montevegro, which provide the grapes for their more ambitious wines. This year, the winery based in Via Belvedere presented a very high-level selection, with three of them reaching our finals. All three are Amarones, representing three different and unique expressions of this great traditional wine. The Pasqua family have highlighted the wine's most open and harmonious nature, made possible by savoriness and grip. The Terre di Cariano is the most powerful and close-knit of the three, whereas the new addition, the Mai Dire Mai, explores a more austere and rigid style.

● Amarone della Valpolicella Famiglia Pasqua '13	♟♟♟ 6
● Amarone della Valpolicella Cl. Terre di Cariano Cecilia Beretta '12	♟♟ 8
● Amarone della Valpolicella Mai Dire Mai '10	♟♟ 6
● Amarone della Valpolicella Cl. Villa Borghetti '14	♟♟ 6
● Valpolicella Sup. Ripasso Famiglia Pasqua '15	♟♟ 4
○ Passimento Bianco '16	♟ 3
● Passimento Rosso '15	♟ 3
○ Soave Cl. Brognoligo Cecilia Beretta '16	♟ 1*
● Amarone della Valpolicella Cl. Terre di Cariano '04	♟♟♟ 8

★★Leonildo Pieropan

ᴀ Camuzzoni, 3
7038 Soave [VR]
ᴇʟ. +39 0456190171
www.pieropan.it

CELLAR SALES
PRE-BOOKED VISITS
ANNUAL PRODUCTION 550,000 bottles
HECTARES UNDER VINE 70.00
VITICULTURE METHOD Certified Organic

ast year Leonildo Pieropan celebrated his
fiftieth harvest. That alone should give you
an idea of his knowledge of Soave, and its
grapes. But Nino's long career is more than
just that. He's been both a pioneer and a
trusted protector of tradition, a farmer and
an ambassador, representing the best of
what this territory has to offer. His wife,
Teresita, is still by his side, and today his
sons Dario and Andrea also join him in his
work. There was no way the two excellent
vintages, the 2015 and 2016, were going
to catch the winery in Via Camuzzoni
unprepared. Rather, they have pulled an
almost perfect range of wines out of their
hat. The Calvarino stands out for the depth
of its aroma, with fruit finding the right
savory grip. The La Rocca, on the other
hand, features an appealing aromatic
expression, the likes of which we haven't
seen for a long time. Its refined and
persistent aromas make for a dynamic and
juicy drinkability.

Albino Piona

Fʀᴀᴢ. Custoza
ᴠɪᴀ Bellavista, 48
37060 Sommacampagna [VR]
Tᴇʟ. +39 045516055
www.albinopiona.it

CELLAR SALES
PRE-BOOKED VISITS
ANNUAL PRODUCTION 350,000 bottles
HECTARES UNDER VINE 77.00

If the two appellations of Garda, Custoza
and Bardolino, are getting a lot of attention,
credit must be given to wineries like the
Piona brothers'. Without giving up on the
trademark lightness and fragrance of these
varieties, the brothers have set the goal of
enhancing their personality, grip and
identity. Their large estate has allowed
them to select only the best grapes. The
2013 Bardolino SP was an amazing taste.
The wine has eschewed its reputation as a
simple, fruity and quaffable wine (all too
common in the appellation) in favor of
sophistication. It's lustrous and clear in
appearance, while the nose offers intense
notes of smoke and wild berries, which give
way to medicinal herbs. On the palate it
proves rich and light, yet also gutsy and
remarkably long. It shouldn't be missed.

○ Soave Cl. Calvarino '15	♛♛♛ 4*	● Bardolino SP '13	♛♛♛ 2*
○ Soave Cl. La Rocca '15	♛♛ 5	○ Custoza '16	♛♛ 2*
Amarone della Valpolicella V. Garzon '13	♛♛ 7	● Bardolino '16	♛♛ 2*
○ Recioto di Soave Cl. Le Colombare '12	♛♛ 5	⊙ Bardolino Chiaretto '16	♛♛ 2*
○ Soave Cl. '16	♛♛ 3	● Campo Massimo Corvina Veronese '13	♛♛ 2*
● Valpolicella Sup. Ruberpan '14	♛♛ 4	○ Gran Cuvée Pas Dosé M. Cl.	♛♛ 4
○ Soave Cl. Calvarino '13	♛♛♛ 4*	○ Estro di Piona Blanc Brut	♛ 4
○ Soave Cl. Calvarino '09	♛♛♛ 4*	○ Verde Piona Frizzante	♛ 2
○ Soave Cl. Calvarino '08	♛♛♛ 4	● Bardolino '15	♕♕ 2*
○ Soave Cl. Calvarino '07	♛♛♛ 4	⊙ Bardolino Chiaretto '15	♕♕ 2*
○ Soave Cl. Calvarino '06	♛♛♛ 4	○ Custoza '15	♕♕ 2*
○ Soave Cl. La Rocca '14	♛♛♛ 5	○ Custoza SP '13	♕♕ 2*
○ Soave Cl. La Rocca '12	♛♛♛ 5	○ Custoza Sup. Campo del Selese '13	♕♕ 2*
○ Soave Cl. La Rocca '11	♛♛♛ 5		
○ Soave Cl. La Rocca '10	♕♕♕ 5		

Piovene Porto Godi

FRAZ. TOARA
VIA VILLA, 14
36020 VILLAGA [VI]
TEL. +39 0444885142
www.piovene.com

CELLAR SALES
PRE-BOOKED VISITS
ANNUAL PRODUCTION 100,000 bottles
HECTARES UNDER VINE 36.00

Tomaso Piovene's cellar can be found in Toara, in the heart of a small, natural amphitheater in the southeastern part of the Colli Berici. Their property spans 200 hectares, 40 of which are vineyards. Here, mostly international varieties are grown, as is customary in this part of Veneto, but much attention is paid to the variety that, more than any other, characterizes the area: Tai Rosso. In the cellar, production is aimed at highlighting the splendor of the territory, combined with fragrance and grip. Their selection is limited this year, as the unfortunate 2014 vintage meant they couldn't produce their more ambitious wines. However, the overall result hasn't suffered in the slightest. The Merlot Fra i Broli offers up intensely fruity aromas, with herbs adding freshness to plums and cherries. On the palate, it betrays its youth, displaying an exuberance that bodes well for the future. The Sauvignon Campigie is rich, mature and all-embracing.

● Colli Berici Merlot Fra i Broli '15	♥♥ 4	
○ Colli Berici Garganega Vign. Riveselle '16	♥♥ 2*	
○ Colli Berici Pinot Bianco Polveriera '16	♥♥ 4	
● Colli Berici Tai Rosso Vign. Riveselle '16	♥♥ 2*	
● Polveriera Rosso '16	♥♥ 2*	
○ Sauvignon Campigie '15	♥♥ 3	
○ Colli Berici Sauvignon Vign. Fostine '16	♥ 2	
● Colli Berici Cabernet Vign. Pozzare '12	♥♥♥ 4*	
● Colli Berici Cabernet Vign. Pozzare '07	♥♥♥ 3	
● Colli Berici Cabernet Vign. Pozzare '13	♥♥ 4	
● Colli Berici Tai Rosso Thovara '13	♥♥ 5	

★Graziano Prà

VIA DELLA FONTANA, 31
37032 MONTEFORTE D'ALPONE [VR]
TEL. +39 045/612125
www.vinipra.it

CELLAR SALES
PRE-BOOKED VISITS
ACCOMMODATION
ANNUAL PRODUCTION 350,000 bottles
HECTARES UNDER VINE 35.00
VITICULTURE METHOD Certified Organic
SUSTAINABLE WINERY

Graziano Prà's winery has come to possess two souls. The white one represents their Soave roots, and keeps them tied to tradition and the territory. The red one is their more passionate side. This soul is aimed at the future. In the middle there's Graziano, a viticulturist who's bridging yesterday and tomorrow, the helmsman of a winery that's forging straight ahead and doing it with all due respect for the environment. With the 2016 vintage, Graziano decided to delay presenting his Soave Monte Grande so as to allow it another year in the cellar. As a result, topping the bill is his Soave Staforte, a wine aged entirely in steel that stands out for its complex aromas, which are just now showing the first hints of benzine. The palate sees generosity well-supported by acidity. The Ripasso, a dynamic red full of character, also performed well.

○ Soave Cl. Staforte '15	♥♥♥ 3*	
● Valpolicella Sup. Ripasso Morandina '15	♥♥ 4	
● Amarone della Valpolicella '11	♥♥ 7	
○ Soave Cl. Colle Sant'Antonio '14	♥♥ 5	
○ Soave Cl. Otto '16	♥♥ 3	
● Valpolicella Morandina '16	♥♥ 3	
○ Soave Cl. Monte Grande '11	♥♥♥ 4*	
○ Soave Cl. Monte Grande '08	♥♥♥ 4*	
○ Soave Cl. Monte Grande '06	♥♥♥ 4*	
○ Soave Cl. Staforte '14	♥♥♥ 4*	
○ Soave Cl. Staforte '13	♥♥♥ 4*	
○ Soave Cl. Staforte '11	♥♥♥ 4*	
○ Soave Cl. Staforte '08	♥♥♥ 4*	
○ Soave Cl. Staforte '06	♥♥♥ 4*	

★Giuseppe Quintarelli

via Cerè, 1
37024 Negrar [VR]
Tel. +39 0457500016
vini@giuseppequintarelli.it

CELLAR SALES
PRE-BOOKED VISITS
ANNUAL PRODUCTION 60,000 bottles
HECTARES UNDER VINE 10.00

Some years after losing its patriarch, the winery on Via Cerè has finished renovating its cellar. Today Fiorenza Quintarelli and children can work with greater attention and ample space in their lovely, entirely underground structure. Even if their selection is comprised of just a few wines, these must wait in oak, and in their bottles, for many years before reaching the market. The Amarone Riserva is being presented today, ten years after harvest. The nose offers intense notes of fruit jam, coffee powder and fines herbes, with a subtle and fresh spicy note pushing up from below. In the mouth the impact is full and succulent, with a soft and caressing profile that's well-supported by savoriness and acidity. It's a great red that interprets Valpolicella, and its traditions, perfectly, but manages to stay current as well.

- Amarone della Valpolicella Cl. Ris. '07 ▼▼▼ 8
- Amarone della Valpolicella Cl. '06 ▽▽▽ 8
- Amarone della Valpolicella Cl. '03 ▽▽▽ 8
- Amarone della Valpolicella Cl. '98 ▽▽▽ 8
- Amarone della Valpolicella Cl. '97 ▽▽▽ 8
- Amarone della Valpolicella Cl. Sup. Monte Cà Paletta '00 ▽▽▽ 8
- Recioto della Valpolicella Cl. '01 ▽▽▽ 8
- Recioto della Valpolicella Cl. '95 ▽▽▽ 5
- Recioto della Valpolicella Cl. Monte Ca' Paletta '97 ▽▽▽ 8
- Valpolicella Cl. Sup. '99 ▽▽▽ 7

Le Ragose

fraz. Arbizzano
via Le Ragose, 1
37024 Negrar [VR]
Tel. +39 0457513241
www.leragose.com

CELLAR SALES
PRE-BOOKED VISITS
ANNUAL PRODUCTION 120,000 bottles
HECTARES UNDER VINE 18.00

Paolo and Marco Galli manage the family winery in a southern part of the Classica DOC zone, practically overlooking the city of Verona. Their vineyards, which are almost exclusively dedicated to traditional grape varieties, are all to be found in the hills, between 250 and 400 meters above sea level. In the cellar, Paolo and Marco show the utmost respect for tradition and for the time needed for their wines to best express their qualities. The result is a selection that offers elegance and harmony. The 2008 Amarone proves iconic. Nine years after harvest, the wine has finally achieved full balance. Its aromas slowly unfold, first dried fruit, then sweet spices and finally a deep mineral note that promises further development. On the palate, its full and caressing impact is spruced up by tannins at the finish. The Recioto was also impressive, with a lively expression of fruit and a long and juicy palate.

- Amarone della Valpolicella Cl. '08 ▼▼ 7
- Recioto della Valpolicella Cl. '14 ▼▼ 5
- Valpolicella Cl. Sup. Ripasso Le Sassine '13 ▼▼ 4
- Amarone della Valpolicella Cl. Caloetto '06 ▽▽▽ 7
- Amarone della Valpolicella Cl. Marta Galli '05 ▽▽▽ 8
- Amarone della Valpolicella Cl. Caloetto '07 ▽▽ 7
- Recioto della Valpolicella Cl. '13 ▽▽ 5
- Rhagos Ammandorlato '07 ▽▽ 8
- Valpolicella Cl. '15 ▽▽ 2*

F.lli Recchia

LOC. JAGO
VIA CA' BERTOLDI, 30
37024 NEGRAR [VR]
TEL. +39 0457500584
www.recchiavini.it

CELLAR SALES
PRE-BOOKED VISITS
ANNUAL PRODUCTION 250,000 bottles
HECTARES UNDER VINE 100.00

The Recchia family's winery can be found in the highest part of Negrar, in the district of Jago, one of the historic cradles of Amarone. Today they have some 100 hectares of terrain at their disposal, in many parts of the DOC zone. The result is a consistently strong selection that largely draws on the area's local grapes. In the cellar, they work to bring out the attributes of Valpolicella's varieties. For their more ambitious wines, they pursue a synergy between the variety and territory. The Amarone Ca' Bertoldi comes under this second category, with its aromas of sweet and overripe red fruit, while in the mouth the wine is supported by an extraordinary richness of flavor. The Ripasso Le Muraie, on the other hand, offers a warm, spicy nose that's brought out in the mouth by its soft and approachable palate. The Masua di Jago line is very interesting. It's a selection deeply tied to tradition whose wines stand out for their lean profile and acidity.

● Amarone della Valpolicella Cl. Ca' Bertoldi '11	♥♥ 5
● Amarone della Valpolicella Cl. Masua di Jago '13	♥♥ 5
● Valpolicella Cl. Masua di Jago '16	♥♥ 2*
● Valpolicella Cl. Sup. Masua di Jago '15	♥♥ 2*
● Valpolicella Cl. Sup. Ripasso Le Muraie '15	♥♥ 3
● Valpolicella Cl. Sup. Ripasso Masua di Jago '15	♥♥ 2*
● Recioto della Valpolicella Cl. Masua di Jago '15	♥ 4
● Amarone della Valpolicella Cl. Ca' Bertoldi '10	♥♥ 5

Roccolo Grassi

VIA SAN GIOVANNI DI DIO, 19
37030 MEZZANE DI SOTTO [VR]
TEL. +39 0458880089
www.roccolograssi.it

PRE-BOOKED VISITS
ANNUAL PRODUCTION 49,000 bottles
HECTARES UNDER VINE 14.00
SUSTAINABLE WINERY

Some 20 years ago, Marco and Francesca Sartori inherited their parents' patrimony … and they completely revolutionized it, making Roccolo Grassi one of the most interesting operations in Valpolicella. Their 14 hectares of vineyards are entirely dedicated to historic varieties (both for Valpolicella and Soave). These are attended to with passion and care, with only the best grapes making it into their wines. Their wines display superior fullness of fruit and solidity, without losing their elegance. This Amarone made the most of the excellent 2012 vintage and gave a luscious performance. The nose opens with the wine's trademark aromas of fruit, which quickly give way to more original notes of minerals and spices, and refreshing pepper. It's defined, however, by its palate, which sees remarkable concentration managed with precision and lightness. The result is a long, charming unfolding of flavor. The Soave, a thoroughbred white that's not easy to forget, features depth and grip.

● Amarone della Valpolicella '12	♥♥ 8
○ Soave Sup. La Broia '15	♥♥ 3*
● Amarone della Valpolicella Roccolo Grassi '07	♥♥♥ 8
● Amarone della Valpolicella Roccolo Grassi '00	♥♥♥ 7
● Amarone della Valpolicella Roccolo Grassi '99	♥♥♥ 7
● Valpolicella Sup. '13	♥♥♥ 5
● Valpolicella Sup. '11	♥♥♥ 5
● Valpolicella Sup. Roccolo Grassi '09	♥♥♥ 5
● Valpolicella Sup. Roccolo Grassi '07	♥♥♥ 5
● Valpolicella Sup. Roccolo Grassi '04	♥♥♥ 5
○ Soave Sup. La Broia '14	♥♥ 3*

Roeno

VIA MAMA, 5
37020 BRENTINO BELLUNO [VR]
TEL. +39 0457230110
www.cantinaroeno.com

CELLAR SALES
PRE-BOOKED VISITS
ACCOMMODATION AND RESTAURANT SERVICE
ANNUAL PRODUCTION 350,000 bottles
HECTARES UNDER VINE 80.00
SUSTAINABLE WINERY

The Fugatti siblings, Roberta, Cristina and
Giuseppe, have successfully embraced the
heritage left to them by their father, and
made Roeno one of the most interesting
wineries in the region. Their vineyards unfold
along the banks of the Adige, from Trentino
all the way to the edges of Lake Garda.
Every plot, every exposition and every
altitude is dedicated to the variety it best
expresses, making for a selection that, today,
ranges from strong reds to passito wines, to
the most sophisticated and determined
whites. Their two top wines this year are the
Cristina, a late harvest blend of Pinot Grigio,
Chardonnay, Gewürztraminer and Sauvignon
with an appealing and harmonious profile,
and, especially, the Collezione di Famiglia
Riesling. This last, from the 2012 vintage, is
a white that's aged for a year and a half in
oak before being bottled (and a further three
years before we had the chance to taste it).
Its intense aromas of exotic fruit, flint and
candied citrus fruit develop into a "German"
palate, where residual sugar is kept in check
by taut acidity and give way to a long and
lingering finish.

○ Riesling Renano Collezione di Famiglia '12	♟♟♟	6
○ Cristina V. T. '14	♟♟	5
● Marzemino La Rua '16	♟♟	2*
○ Praecipuus Riesling Renano '15	♟♟	4
● Roeno Il Vino del Fondatore '13	♟♟	4
○ Valdadige Pinot Grigio Tera Alta '16	♟♟	2*
● Valdadige Terra dei Forti Enantio '13	♟♟	4
○ Cristina V. T. '13	♟♟♟	5
○ Cristina V. T. '12	♟♟♟	5
○ Cristina V. T. '11	♟♟♟	5
○ Cristina V. T. '08	♟♟♟	5

Ronca

VIA VAL DI SONA, 7
37066 SOMMACAMPAGNA [VR]
TEL. +39 0458961641
www.cantinaronca.it

CELLAR SALES
PRE-BOOKED VISITS
ANNUAL PRODUCTION 30,000 bottles
HECTARES UNDER VINE 20.00

About 10 years ago, Massimo Ronca took
over the reins of the family winery, an
estate of 20 rolling hectares of land in the
southern part of Lake Garda's backcountry.
Great attention is shown to the area's local
wines, Bardolino and Custoza. These are
interpreted in such a way as to highlight
their peculiarities without compromising
the lightness and fragrance that have
always characterized these appellations.
The 2016 Bardolino was very good, with its
aromas of wild fruit and forest floor. The
mouth revealed excellent richness of flavor
and grip, making for a wine that's great on
the palate. The new Custoza Superiore,
Ulderico, a wine aged at length in small
oak, proved even more Interesting. Wood is
discernible on the nose, but instead of
spoiling and suffocating the fruit, it lends
integrity and freshness, giving way to a
lovely floral overtone. The dry and powerful
mouth is presided over by marked acidity,
which adds length to the wine.

● Bardolino '16	♟♟	2*
● Corvina '16	♟♟	2*
○ Custoza '16	♟♟	2*
○ Custoza Sup. Ulderico '15	♟♟	3
⊙ Bardolino Chiaretto '16	♟	2
○ Garganega '16	♟	2
○ Pinot Grigio '16	♟	2
● Ulderico Rosso '11	♟	6
● Bardolino '15	♟♟	2*
● Corvina '15	♟♟	2*
○ Custoza '15	♟♟	2*

Rubinelli Vajol

FRAZ. SAN FLORIANO
VIA PALADON, 31
37029 SAN PIETRO IN CARIANO [VR]
TEL. +39 0456839277
www.rubinellivajol.it

CELLAR SALES
PRE-BOOKED VISITS
ACCOMMODATION
ANNUAL PRODUCTION 50,000 bottles
HECTARES UNDER VINE 10.00

Valpolicella Classica is crossed by four valleys that wind northwards through a picturesque landscape. It's here that we find the natural amphitheater that hosts the Rubinelli family's cellar, surrounded by 10 hectares of vineyards situated at 150 and 200 meters above sea level. In the cellar, their selection is dedicated entirely to traditional wines, interpreted with lightness and grip. The Ripasso has a wonderful aromatic expression, with wild berries and brambles enriched by a whiff of herbs that magnify the sensation of freshness. In the mouth, it proves savory and lengthens with lightness and grip. The Recioto is more mature and in keeping with tradition, dominated by hints of dried fruit. Sweetness on the palate is contrasted by assertive and pleasantly rough tannins.

Ruggeri & C.

FRAZ. ZECCHEI
VIA PRÀ FONTANA, 1
31049 VALDOBBIADENE [TV]
TEL. +39 04239092
www.ruggeri.it

CELLAR SALES
PRE-BOOKED VISITS
ANNUAL PRODUCTION 1,000,000 bottles
HECTARES UNDER VINE 17.00
SUSTAINABLE WINERY

If it weren't for the press release that came out in February, we'd say that nothing has changed at Via Prà Fontana. Instead, the Bisol family become part of the Rotkäppchen group. They've maintained management of the cellar, and partnerships with various local growers (an aspect that is particularly important for Paolo and the winery). In terms of production, nothing has changed, both in terms of volume and quality. The time has come to taste the Giustino B, a wine that had one of its best years. Boosted by the excellent 2016 vintage, this sparkler offers up aromas of fresh fruit and flowers that follow through perfectly on a tangy, balanced palate with nice sparkle and acidity. The Vecchie Viti put in its usual, gutsy and assertive performance. Flowers, white fruit and a faint vegetal hint make for a long, pure palate.

● Recioto della Valpolicella Cl. '13	▼▼ 6
● Valpolicella Cl. Sup. Ripasso '14	▼▼ 5
● Valpolicella Cl. '16	▼ 2
● Amarone della Valpolicella Cl. '11	♀♀ 7
● Amarone della Valpolicella Cl. '10	♀♀ 6
● Amarone della Valpolicella Cl. '07	♀♀ 6
● Recioto della Valpolicella Cl. '12	♀♀ 6
● Recioto della Valpolicella Cl. '11	♀♀ 6
● Valpolicella Cl. '13	♀♀ 2*
● Valpolicella Cl. Sup. '12	♀♀ 4
● Valpolicella Cl. Sup. '11	♀♀ 4
● Valpolicella Cl. Sup. '10	♀♀ 4
● Valpolicella Cl. Sup. Ripasso '12	♀♀ 5
● Valpolicella Cl. Sup. Ripasso '11	♀♀ 4

○ Valdobbiadene Extra Dry Giustino B. '16	▼▼▼ 4*
○ Valdobbiadene Brut V. V. '16	▼▼ 5
○ Cartizze	▼▼ 5
○ Valdobbiadene Brut Quartese	▼▼ 3
○ Valdobbiadene Extra Dry Altevigne	▼▼ 4
○ Valdobbiadene Extra Dry Giall'Oro	▼▼ 3
○ Valdobbiadene Dry S. Stefano	▼ 3
○ Valdobbiadene Brut V. V. '14	♀♀♀ 4*
○ Valdobbiadene Brut Vecchie Viti '13	♀♀♀ 4*
○ Valdobbiadene Extra Dry Giustino B. '15	♀♀♀ 4*
○ Valdobbiadene Extra Dry Giustino B. '12	♀♀♀ 3*
○ Valdobbiadene Extra Dry Giustino B. '11	♀♀♀ 3*
○ Valdobbiadene Extra Dry Giustino B. '10	♀♀♀ 3
○ Valdobbiadene Extra Dry Giustino B. '09	♀♀♀ 3

Le Salette

VIA PIO BRUGNOLI, 11C
37022 FUMANE [VR]
TEL. +39 0457701027
www.lesalette.it

CELLAR SALES
PRE-BOOKED VISITS
ANNUAL PRODUCTION 130,000 bottles
HECTARES UNDER VINE 20.00

Franco Scamperle's winery is located in the center of Fumane, a small town in the heart of Valpolicella Classica. His vineyards, however, run for some 20 hectares through some of the most notable and esteemed plots in the DOC zone (for example, four hectares on Masua or four more on the Salette Sanctuary, just over the town). Their selection is dedicated in large part to the area's traditional wines, which are interpreted with a focus on fruit and ripeness. As always, the leading role goes to the Amarone Pergole Vece. It's a red with rich aromas of dried red fruit that gradually give way to notes of minerals and thyme. In the mouth, it proves powerful and close-knit, defined by vibrant tannins and a gratifying richness of flavor. The Recioto Le Traversagne also impressed. It's aged exclusively In concrete and offers an intense nose of stewed small fruit. These follow through well in an enthusiastic and supple palate.

● Amarone della Valpolicella Cl. Pergole Vece '13	💯 8
● Amarone della Valpolicella Cl. La Marega '13	💯 6
● Recioto della Valpolicella Cl. Le Traversagne '14	💯 5
● Valpolicella Cl. Sup. Ripasso I Progni '15	💯 3
● Ca' Carnocchio '14	💯 4
○ Cesare Passito '13	💯 5
● Valpolicella Cl. '16	💯 2
● Amarone della Valpolicella Cl. Pergole Vece '05	💯💯💯 8
● Amarone della Valpolicella Cl. Pergole Vece '95	💯💯💯 8

Tenute SalvaTerra

LOC. CENGIA
VIA CENGIA, 8
37029 SAN PIETRO IN CARIANO [VR]
TEL. +39 0456859025
www.tenutesalvaterra.it

CELLAR SALES
PRE-BOOKED VISITS
ANNUAL PRODUCTION 80,000 bottles
HECTARES UNDER VINE 16.00

SalvaTerra was started a few years ago by the Furia brothers and a group of investors who strongly believe in Valpolicella and its wines. The vineyards are many, scattered throughout both the 'Classica' and eastern parts of the DOC zone. The cellar and offices are located in the splendid Villa Giona (in Cengia). Their selection is made up of only a few wines (mostly traditional), which are interpreted with well-informed grace. The Amarone Cave di Prun is made with grapes cultivated in the high hills and aged at length in the cellar. On the nose, it features delicate and generous aromas, with fruit surrounded by notes of dried flowers and spices, and faint hints of oak in the background. In the mouth, the wine's trademark generosity proves well-orchestrated, expanding with suppleness and length. The Amarone Classico is more approachable, playing on overtones of fruit. It's still quite youthful in taste, but has great aging potential.

● Amarone della Valpolicella Cl. '10	💯 8
● Amarone della Valpolicella Cl. Cave di Prun Ris. '08	💯 8
● Valpolicella Cl. '15	💯 3
● Valpolicella Cl. Sup. '14	💯 3
○ Pinot Grigio '16	💯 5
○ Prosecco Extra Dry	💯 4
● Amarone della Valpolicella Cl. '09	💯 8
● Amarone della Valpolicella Cl. '08	💯 8
● Amarone della Valpolicella Cl. Cave di Prun Ris. '07	💯 8
● Amarone della Valpolicella Cl. Cave di Prun Ris. '04	💯 8
● Valpolicella Cl. Sup. Ripasso '13	💯 5

Marco Sambin

LOC. VALNOGAREDO
VIA FATTORELLE, 20A
35030 CINTO EUGANEO [PD]
TEL. +39 3456812050
www.vinimarcus.com

CELLAR SALES
PRE-BOOKED VISITS
RESTAURANT SERVICE
ANNUAL PRODUCTION 10,000 bottles
HECTARES UNDER VINE 3.00
VITICULTURE METHOD Certified Organic
SUSTAINABLE WINERY

The territory of Colli Euganei is characterized by extraordinarily rich soil and offers an intact landscape with tremendous potential for viticulture. The volcanic origins of these hills, along with the protection they are afforded as part of the Regional Park system, serve as the basis for those producers working to promote and support the area. Marco Shambin's winery is no exception. His few hectares of vineyards face south, and provide the grapes used in a selection of wines defined by their fullness and ripeness. These are the exact features expressed by the Marcus al Quadrato, with its aromas of sweet and open fruit. Its suite of spices are expressed even more clearly in the mouth, where the wine proves warm, caressing and hardened by rough tannins. The latter wine, the Alter, follows much the same aromatic path, though comes through fresher on the nose and more spirited in taste, making for a more supple and gratifying palate.

● Alter '15	♟♟ 4
● Marcus al Quadrato '13	♟♟ 6
● Le Femminelle '16	♟ 3
○ Martha Frizzante '15	♟ 4
○ Sarah '16	♟ 3
● Alter '14	♟♟ 4
● Alter '13	♟♟ 4
● Francisca XI Passito	♟♟ 5
● Marcus '13	♟♟ 5
● Marcus '12	♟♟ 5
● Marcus '11	♟♟ 5
○ Martha Frizzante '14	♟♟ 4

San Cassiano

VIA SAN CASSIANO, 17
37030 MEZZANE DI SOTTO [VR]
TEL. +39 0458880665
www.cantinasancassiano.it

CELLAR SALES
PRE-BOOKED VISITS
ANNUAL PRODUCTION 50,000 bottles
HECTARES UNDER VINE 11.00
SUSTAINABLE WINERY

Mirko Sella manages his family's winery in the heart of Mezzane, one of the the eastern valleys in the DOC zone. Here, he personally looks after the cultivation of some 15 hectares of vineyards, and 10 or so hectares dedicated to olive trees. Over the years, Mirko has built a cellar and installed a press, so as to oversee every phase of production. Based entirely on traditional grapes, his wines are solid and crisp. The 2013 Amarone performed beautifully. It's a wine with aromas of sweet dried fruit, although it finds its forte in the mouth. Full and powerful, its generous flavor is supported by juicy acidity, which is refreshed and lengthened until the finish comes through dry and satisfying. As for the Valpolicella, we particularly appreciated the Ripasso, which also features clearly discernible fruit on the nose, and a palate that reveals grip and remarkable traction.

● Amarone della Valpolicella '13	♟♟ 6
● Valpolicella '15	♟♟ 2*
● Valpolicella Sup. Ripasso '14	♟♟ 3
● Amarone della Valpolicella Ris. '12	♟ 6
● Amarone della Valpolicella '11	♟♟ 6
● Valpolicella '10	♟♟ 2*
● Valpolicella Sup. Ripasso '12	♟♟ 2*

San Rustico

FRAZ. VALGATARA DI VALPOLICELLA
VIA POZZO, 2
37020 MARANO DI VALPOLICELLA [VR]
TEL. +39 0457703348
www.sanrustico.it

CELLAR SALES
PRE-BOOKED VISITS
ANNUAL PRODUCTION 250,000 bottles
HECTARES UNDER VINE 22.00

The name 'Campagnola' is a common one in the area, and it's often connected to winemaking. This Campagnola family's winery can be found at the mouth of the Marano valley, where the vineyards descend from the hilltops all the way down to road level. Their production is strongly wed to tradition, drawing on more than 20 hectares of vineyards in the valley. The grapes are made into solid wines that are well supported by their acidity, just as one would expect from Valpolicella's historic grapes. The most important vineyard, Gaso, gives rise to grapes for both their flagship Amarone and their Ripasso. The former features closed aromas that unfold very slowly, with fruit gradually emerging in a background of medicinal herbs and spices. In the mouth, its impact is soft and the wine tenses up and gains grip at the finish. The Ripasso has a more rustic aromatic expression, with dried fruit coming together with vegetal notes. The palate follows the same style, highlighting the fullness of its good, assertive tannins.

● Amarone della Valpolicella Cl. '12	▼▼ 6
● Amarone della Valpolicella Cl. Gaso '11	▼▼ 8
● Valpolicella Cl. Sup. Ripasso Gaso '14	▼▼ 4
● Valpolicella Cl. '16	▼ 2
● Valpolicella Cl. Sup. '15	▼ 2
● Amarone della Valpolicella Cl. '11	♈♈ 6
● Amarone della Valpolicella Cl. '10	♈♈ 6
● Amarone della Valpolicella Cl. '09	♈♈ 6
● Amarone della Valpolicella Cl. Gaso '10	♈♈ 8
● Amarone della Valpolicella Cl. Gaso '09	♈♈ 8
● Valpolicella Cl. Sup. '14	♈♈ 2*
● Valpolicella Cl. Sup. '12	♈♈ 2*
● Valpolicella Cl. Sup. Ripasso Gaso '12	♈♈ 4
● Valpolicella Cl. Sup. Ripasso Gaso '11	♈♈ 4

La Sansonina

LOC. SANSONINA
37019 PESCHIERA DEL GARDA [VR]
TEL. +39 0457551905
www.sansonina.it

CELLAR SALES
ANNUAL PRODUCTION 35,000 bottles
HECTARES UNDER VINE 13.00

The southern coast of Lake Garda is characterized by the cultivation of Turbiana, the grape that serves as the foundation of one of Italy's most well-establish wines, Lugana. Some twenty years ago, Carla Prospero decided to invest in the territory, dedicating herself to making Lugana. But she didn't neglect Merlot, either, a grape that found the perfect habitat in the clay soil of this patch of land between Verona and Brescia. In recent years, she has adopted an increasingly natural approach to vine growing and winemaking, pursuing methods that have a low environmental impact. The Lugana Vigna del Moraro Verde, made through spontaneous fermentation, offers up complex aromas ranging from dried flowers to apple pips, with a subtle vegetal hint for a touch of liveliness. The palate has a solid body and good roundness, with acidity and an intriguing delicately tannic note that adds character and assertiveness.

○ Lugana V. del Morano Verde '15	▼▼ 3*
● Garda Cabernet Evaluna '15	▼▼ 4
● Sansonina '14	▼▼ 6
● Garda Evaluna '14	♈♈ 4
○ Lugana Sansonina '13	♈♈ 3
○ Lugana Sansonina '12	♈♈ 3
○ Lugana Sansonina '11	♈♈ 3
○ Lugana Sansonina '10	♈♈ 6
○ Lugana Sansonina '09	♈♈ 3*
○ Lugana V. del Morano Verde '14	♈♈ 3
● Sansonina '13	♈♈ 6
● Sansonina '12	♈♈ 6
● Sansonina '10	♈♈ 6
● Sansonina '09	♈♈ 6

Tenuta Sant'Anna

FRAZ. LONCON
VIA MONSIGNOR P. L. ZOVATTO, 71
30020 ANNONE VENETO [VE]
TEL. +39 0422864511
www.tenutasantanna.it

CELLAR SALES
PRE-BOOKED VISITS
ANNUAL PRODUCTION 2,800,000 bottles
HECTARES UNDER VINE 140.00

For many years, the Genagricola group has operated in the territory of Venice, on a long strip of vineyards whose clay soil makes it perfect for the cultivation of Tai and Merlot. The vineyards, which span more than one-hundred hectares, are cared for with precision. The grapes cultivated are used for a wide selection of wines, which focuses on the attributes of each single variety, while maintaining a style that features clarity and fragrance. Loncon have put forward an expansive selection this year, with Prosecco and still wines sharing center stage. The Merlot Poderi proved impressive, playing on inviting expressions of fruit, and making for a generous palate with juicy drinkability. As for the Proseccos, we particularly appreciated the Valdobbiadene Extra Dry, a harmonious sparkling wine that features a perfect balance between sparkle, sweetness and acidity.

● Lison-Pramaggiore Merlot Poderi '16	▼▼	2*
○ Valdobbiadene Extra Dry	▼▼	3
○ Venezia Pinot Grigio '16	▼▼	2*
○ Brut di Pinot	▼	2
○ Cartizze	▼	5
○ Cuvée Blanche Extra Dry	▼	2
○ Cuvée Maudit Brut	▼	2
○ Lison Cl. Goccia '16	▼	2
○ Lison-Pramaggiore Chardonnay Goccia '16	▼	2
● Lison-Pramaggiore Refosco P. R. Poderi '16	▼	2
○ Lison-Pramaggiore Savignon Goccia '16	▼	2
○ Prosecco Brut	▼	3
○ Prosecco Extra Dry	▼	3
○ Traminer Goccia '16	▼	2

★Tenuta Sant'Antonio

LOC. SAN ZENO
VIA CERIANI, 23
37030 COLOGNOLA AI COLLI [VR]
TEL. +39 0457650383
www.tenutasantantonio.it

CELLAR SALES
PRE-BOOKED VISITS
ANNUAL PRODUCTION 700,000 bottles
HECTARES UNDER VINE 100.00

Situated in Valpolicella Orientale, the Castagnedi brothers' winery has established itself as a leader in the territory. When they started twenty years ago, they had 50 hectares of terrain at their disposal. Today, Armando, Tiziano, Paolo and Massimo manage more than 100 hectares, most of them dedicated to Valpolicella's red grapes (though without neglecting Garganega, which has to compete for room). Their wines, aged slowly, are characterized by a solid, crisp style. Choosing the best of San Zeno's wines proves a difficult task, especially with their great Amarone Campo dei Gigli leading the pack. Intense aromas of fresh fruit introduce a wine with a dynamic and long palate. The La Bandina, on the other hand, features a mature, multifaceted nose, set against a palate with great grip and elegance. Lastly, the Soave Monte Ceriani is deep, tangy and long.

● Amarone della Valpolicella Campo dei Gigli '13	▼▼▼	8
○ Soave Monte Ceriani '15	▼▼	3*
● Valpolicella Sup. La Bandina '13	▼▼	5
● Amarone della Valpolicella Télos '12	▼▼	6
○ Soave V. V. '15	▼▼	3
● Valpolicella Sup. Ripasso Monti Garbi '15	▼▼	3
● Valpolicella Sup. Tèlos '15	▼	3
● Amarone della Valpolicella Campo dei Gigli '12	♔♔♔	8
● Amarone della Valpolicella Campo dei Gigli '11	♔♔♔	8
● Amarone della Valpolicella Campo dei Gigli '10	♔♔♔	8

Santa Margherita

VIA ITA MARZOTTO, 8
30025 FOSSALTA DI PORTOGRUARO [VE]
TEL. +39 0421246111
www.santamargherita.com

CELLAR SALES
PRE-BOOKED VISITS
ANNUAL PRODUCTION 13,500,000 bottles
HECTARES UNDER VINE 50.00

The approach taken by Santa Margherita is increasingly impressive. The large winery from Fossalta di Portogruaro, which is managed by the Marzotto family, has made important investments in the area of Prosecco, as well as renovating their entire cellar. Today their facility, designed with great care for energy conservation, is a true gem, while while outside the region they have struck up important collaborations for the production of their flagship wine, Pinot Grigio. The Pinot Grigio Impronta del Fondatore is the most successful of Fossalta's wines. It's a white made with grapes grown in some of Alto Adige's best locations and features a suite of aromas consisting of pears and smoky floral notes. These unfold in a full and juicy palate with excellent tanginess. As for the Proseccos, we particularly enjoyed the Rive di Refrontolo Brut and Extra Dry 52, two elegant sparkling wines that win you over from the first sip.

○ A. A. Pinot Grigio Impronta del Fondatore '16	♟♟ 3
○ Cartizze	♟♟ 5
○ Valdobbiadene Brut	♟♟ 3
○ Valdobbiadene Brut Rive di Refrontolo 52 '16	♟♟ 3
○ Valdobbiadene Extra Dry 52	♟♟ 3
● Lison-Pramaggiore Malbech Impronta del Fondatore '15	♟ 3
● Lison-Pramaggiore Refosco P.R. Impronta del Fondatore '15	♟ 3
○ Lison-Pramaggiore Verduzzo Passito Dulcedo '13	♟ 3
○ Valdadige Pinot Grigio '16	♟ 3
○ Valdobbiadene Extra Dry	♟ 3

Santa Sofia

FRAZ. PEDEMONTE DI VALPOLICELLA
VIA CA' DEDÉ, 61
37029 SAN PIETRO IN CARIANO [VR]
TEL. +39 0457701074
www.santasofia.com

CELLAR SALES
PRE-BOOKED VISITS
ANNUAL PRODUCTION 550,000 bottles
HECTARES UNDER VINE 53.00

For many years, Luciano Begnoni has led the family winery, making important changes to its production processes. Significant investments were also made to expand their vineyards and build a new cellar. Their selection continues to look to Verona's classic wines, with particular attention paid to the reds of Valpolicella, the area in which the winery has its roots. The improvements observed last year have been fully confirmed this year, with a top-quality range of wines that represent their respective categories brilliantly. At the top of our ranking is the Valpolicella Superiore Montegradella, with its sweet, ripe fruit and good suppleness and grip on the palate. The Amarone, on the other hand, from the 2012 vintage, offers up fine and penetrating aromas that follow through onto a gutsy and long palate.

● Amarone della Valpolicella Cl. '12	♟♟ 7
● Recioto della Valpolicella Cl. '11	♟♟ 5
● Valpolicella Cl. Sup. Montegradella '14	♟♟ 4
● Valpolicella Sup. Ripasso '14	♟♟ 4
● Valpolicella Cl. '15	♟ 2
● Amarone della Valpolicella Cl. '11	♟♟ 7
● Amarone della Valpolicella Cl. '09	♟♟ 7
● Amarone della Valpolicella Cl. '08	♟♟ 6
● Amarone della Valpolicella Cl. Gioé '07	♟♟ 7
● Valpolicella Cl. '14	♟♟ 2*
● Valpolicella Cl. Sup. Montegradella '11	♟♟ 4
● Valpolicella Sup. Ripasso '13	♟♟ 4
● Valpolicella Sup. Ripasso '12	♟♟ 4
● Valpolicella Sup. Ripasso '10	♟♟ 4

Santi

VIA UNGHERIA, 33
37031 ILLASI [VR]
TEL. +39 0456529068
www.cantinasanti.it

CELLAR SALES
PRE-BOOKED VISITS
ANNUAL PRODUCTION 1,400,000 bottles
HECTARES UNDER VINE 50.00

The historic business, Gruppo Italiano Viti, has reopened its doors. After a decade in which production had been moved to other cellars, Cristian Ridolfi is overseeing a major renovation of the facilities at Via Ungheria. The vineyards are spread out throughout the territory, from Valpolicella Classica to Orientale, providing a selection of wines that look to rigor and respect for the classics as their guiding principles. The new Valpolicella Superiore, the Ventale, is immediately striking. This red is made from grapes grown in the Illasi valley and aren't dried. On the nose, hints of wild fruit intertwine with nuances of fines herbes and pepper, while in the mouth it exhibits very impressive grip and length. The Amarone Proemio is deeper and more austere. Notes of dried fruit go hand in hand with sweet spices and tobacco, which follow through onto its dry and pleasantly rugged palate.

Casa Vinicola Sartori

FRAZ. SANTA MARIA
VIA CASETTE, 4
37024 NEGRAR [VR]
TEL. +39 0456028011
www.sartorinet.com

CELLAR SALES
PRE-BOOKED VISITS
ANNUAL PRODUCTION 16,000,000 bottles
HECTARES UNDER VINE 120.00
SUSTAINABLE WINERY

The Sartori family have worked in the heart of Valpolicella since the winery's founding at the end of the 19th century. Today, Casa Vinicola Sartori is a major operation that's firmly rooted in the territory and that draws on the support of its important partners, for a selection that features, at its core, Verona's principal wines. Their clean, fruity style applies both to their early-drinking wines as well as those aged with patience in their cellar in Santa Maria di Negrar. The Amarone Reius is made with grapes cultivated in Valpolicella Classica and aged for at least four years in the cellar, in medium and large barrels, and then in the bottle. Its suite of aromas range from ripe cherry to pepper, and give way to a palate with good richness and grip. The Valpolicella Superiore I Saltari, on the other hand, is made with grapes from multiple-pass harvesting then aged in various-sized barrels. The result is a wine with great balance and depth.

● Amarone della Valpolicella Cl. Proemio '11	♼♼ 6
● Valpolicella Cl. Sup. Ventale '15	♼♼ 3*
● Amarone della Valpolicella Cl. '12	♼♼ 6
○ Soave Cl. Vign. Monteforte '16	♼♼ 2*
● Valpolicella Cl. Sup. Ripasso Solane '15	♼♼ 4
○ Lugana Melibeo '16	♼ 3
● Amarone della Valpolicella Proemio '05	♼♼♼ 6
● Amarone della Valpolicella Proemio '03	♼♼♼ 6
● Amarone della Valpolicella Proemio '00	♼♼♼ 5
● Valpolicella Cl. Sup. Ripasso Solane '09	♼♼♼ 3*
● Amarone della Valpolicella Cl. '11	♼♼ 6
● Bardolino Cl. Ca' Bordenis '15	♼♼ 2*
○ Lugana Melibeo '14	♼♼ 2*
● Valpolicella Cl. Sup. Ripasso Solane '14	♼♼ 4
● Valpolicella Cl. Sup. Ripasso Solane '13	♼♼ 4

● Amarone della Valpolicella Cl. Reius '11	♼♼ 7
● Valpolicella Sup. I Saltari '12	♼♼ 4
● Amarone della Valpolicella I Saltari '10	♼♼ 8
● Cent'Anni '13	♼♼ 4
● Valpolicella Cl. Sup. Montegradella '13	♼♼ 3
● Valpolicella Sup. Ripasso Regolo '14	♼♼ 4
○ Marani '15	♼ 3
● Amarone della Valpolicella Cl. Corte Brà '09	♼♼ 7
● Amarone della Valpolicella Cl. Reius '10	♼♼ 7
● Amarone della Valpolicella I Saltari '09	♼♼ 8
● Valpolicella Cl. Sup. Montegradella '12	♼♼ 3
● Valpolicella Sup. I Saltari '11	♼♼ 4
● Valpolicella Sup. Ripasso Regolo '13	♼♼ 4

Secondo Marco

VIA CAMPOLONGO, 9
37022 FUMANE [VR]
TEL. +39 0456800954
www.secondomarco.it

CELLAR SALES
PRE-BOOKED VISITS
ACCOMMODATION
ANNUAL PRODUCTION 75,000 bottles
HECTARES UNDER VINE 15.00

Marco Speri, with the help of his father, Benedetto, founded his winery in the heart of Valpolicella Classica just over 10 years ago. Their 15 hectares of vineyards are dedicated exclusively to the territory's classic wines, making for a selection in which 'slowness' is the underlying doctrine. Partial drying and extended maceration give life to wines that are then aged at length in the cellar. Here large oak barrels alternate with concrete, both patiently waiting for time to run its course. They did a great job with the 2011 Amarone. Aromas of sweet cherry are characteristic of this valley, and here these are embellished with nuances of pepper and medicinal herbs. In the mouth, a generous palate is accompanied by acidity and pleasantly rough tannins, making for a long, captivating wine. The Recioto, on the other hand, plays on more direct and succulent fruit, which is brought out in the mouth where sweetness is clearly discernible and contrasted by a savory acidity.

● Amarone della Valpolicella Cl. '11	♥♥♥ 8
● Recioto della Valpolicella Cl. '13	♥♥ 6
● Valpolicella Cl. '15	♥♥ 3
● Valpolicella Cl. Sup. Ripasso '14	♥♥ 5
● Amarone della Valpolicella Cl. '10	♀♥ 7
● Amarone della Valpolicella Cl. '09	♀♥ 7
● Recioto della Valpolicella Cl. '12	♀♥ 6
● Recioto della Valpolicella Cl. '11	♀♥ 6
● Recioto della Valpolicella Cl. '10	♀♥ 6
● Valpolicella Cl. '14	♀♥ 3
● Valpolicella Cl. '13	♀♥ 3
● Valpolicella Cl. '12	♀♥ 2*
● Valpolicella Cl. Sup. Ripasso '13	♀♥ 5
● Valpolicella Cl. Sup. Ripasso '12	♀♥ 5
● Valpolicella Cl. Sup. Ripasso '11	♀♥ 4

★Serafini & Vidotto

VIA LUIGI CARRER, 8
31040 NERVESA DELLA BATTAGLIA [TV]
TEL. +39 0422773281
www.serafinividotto.it

CELLAR SALES
PRE-BOOKED VISITS
ANNUAL PRODUCTION 250,000 bottles
HECTARES UNDER VINE 23.00
SUSTAINABLE WINERY

Francesco Serafini and Antonello Vidotto are among those best known for interpreting Italian Bordeaux blends. The adventure began at the end of the 1980s, along the slopes of Montello. Today the Nervesa winery attends to its more than 20 hectares of vineyards with painstaking care and respect for the environment, with a selection of wines that has Rosso dell'Abazia as its warhorse. Elegance is at the core of their style, accomplished through great care in the cellar and the knowing use of oak. We have always found their second wine, the Phigaia, very elegant. With the 2014 season they made a special version to celebrate the 20th vintage. It's not just a restyling of the label, but a real special edition that drew on all the grapes usually destined for the Rosso dell'Abbazia. Intense aromas of fruit meet with herbs and notes of forest floor, for a seemingly endless, exhilarating, savory and juicy palate.

● Montello e Colli Asolani Rosso Phi 20 '14	♥♥ 6
○ Asolo Extra Dry Bollicine di Prosecco	♥♥ 3
○ Montello e Colli Asolani Manzoni Bianco '16	♥♥ 2*
● Montello e Colli Asolani Recantina '16	♥♥ 4
○ Prosecco di Treviso Extra Dry Bollicine di Prosecco	♥ 2
● Montello e Colli Asolani Il Rosso dell'Abazia '13	♀♀♥ 6
● Montello e Colli Asolani Il Rosso dell'Abazia '12	♀♀♥ 5
● Montello e Colli Asolani Il Rosso dell'Abazia '11	♀♀♥ 6
● Montello e Colli Asolani Il Rosso dell'Abazia '10	♀♀♥ 5

I Stefanini

VIA CROSARA, 21
37032 MONTEFORTE D'ALPONE [VR]
TEL. +39 0456175249
www.istefanini.it

CELLAR SALES
PRE-BOOKED VISITS
ANNUAL PRODUCTION 100,000 bottles
HECTARES UNDER VINE 17.00

Francesco Tessari has transformed what was once a small, family-run producer dedicated to farming grapes into one of the most interesting operations in Soave. Their estate comprises more than 15 hectares of vineyards on Monte Tenda and, in part, the surrounding plains. The area concentrated on the hill is dedicated to two different wines, Monte di Fice and Monte de Toni, two nearby plots separated by a few rows of olive trees. The vineyards are dedicated entirely to Garganega, the crown jewel of this territory. The highest part of the hill is dedicated to the Monte di Fice, a white wine with intense aromas of ripe yellow fruit and floral scents that seem to appear from nowhere. In the mouth, it makes a full and powerful impact but the wine gradually regains grip and lightness by means of its marked acidity. The Monte de Toni, on the other hand, expresses a similar suite of aromas, but the palate is more supple and racy.

○ Soave Cl. Sup. Monte di Fice '16	♟♟ 3*
○ Soave Cl. Monte de Toni '16	♟♟ 2*
○ Soave Il Selese '16	♟♟ 1*
○ Soave Cl. Monte de Toni '12	♟♟♟ 2*
○ Soave Cl. Sup. Monte di Fice '07	♟♟♟ 2*
○ Soave Cl. Monte de Toni '15	♟♟ 2*
○ Soave Cl. Monte de Toni '14	♟♟ 2*
○ Soave Cl. Monte de Toni '13	♟♟ 2*
○ Soave Cl. Monte di Fice '14	♟♟ 3
○ Soave Cl. Sup. Monte di Fice '15	♟♟ 3
○ Soave Cl. Sup. Monte di Fice '13	♟♟ 3*
○ Soave Cl. Sup. Monte di Fice '12	♟♟ 3*
○ Soave Il Selese '14	♟♟ 1*
○ Soave Il Selese '12	♟♟ 1*

David Sterza

VIA CASTERNA, 37
37022 FUMANE [VR]
TEL. +39 0457704201
www.davidsterza.it

CELLAR SALES
PRE-BOOKED VISITS
ANNUAL PRODUCTION 30,000 bottles
HECTARES UNDER VINE 4.50

This small winery in Casterna is one of the most interesting in Vallata di Fumane. The estate comprises just a few hectares of land, which give life to a selection of wines that focuses on local classics. David and his cousin, Paolo, don't limit themselves to a single, time-honored approach, however. They've reinterpreted Amarone and Valpolicella by following a more current profile in which guaranteeing the integrity of fruit is a cardinal rule. Their wines are solid and crisp, but never overdone. Their pressure and attack will win you over. Upon tasting, the 2013 Amarone proved exemplary. It's a red with intense fruity, fresh and inviting aromas that let the most subtle nuances of fine herbs and pepper shine through. It's solid, dry and powerful in the mouth, lightened by the presence of Verona's trademark acidity. Aromas of the Recioto seem to want to remain hidden, but reveal themselves in the mouth, where we find a perfect balance between sweetness, acidity and tannins.

● Amarone della Valpolicella Cl. '13	♟♟♟ 6
● Recioto della Valpolicella Cl. '15	♟♟ 5
● Valpolicella Cl. Sup. Ripasso '15	♟♟ 3
● Valpolicella Cl. '16	♟ 2
● Amarone della Valpolicella Cl. '12	♟♟♟ 6
● Amarone della Valpolicella Cl. '11	♟♟ 6
● Amarone della Valpolicella Cl. '10	♟♟ 6
● Recioto della Valpolicella Cl. '14	♟♟ 5
● Recioto della Valpolicella Cl. '13	♟♟ 5
● Recioto della Valpolicella Cl. '12	♟♟ 5
● Valpolicella Cl. '14	♟♟ 2*
● Valpolicella Cl. '13	♟♟ 2*
● Valpolicella Cl. Sup. Ripasso '14	♟♟ 3
● Valpolicella Cl. Sup. Ripasso '13	♟♟ 3*

★Suavia

FRAZ. FITTÀ DI SOAVE
VIA CENTRO, 14
37038 SOAVE [VR]
TEL. +39 0457675089
www.suavia.it

CELLAR SALES
PRE-BOOKED VISITS
ANNUAL PRODUCTION 100,000 bottles
HECTARES UNDER VINE 12.00

Situated in the small village of Fittà, the Tessari sisters' winery is a benchmark for lovers of Verona's whites. Their vineyards are mostly dedicated to Garganega, which acquires unusual depth and character thanks to the black soil of these hills, making for a selection of solid, sophisticated wines. They haven't forgotten the territory's other historic variety, Trebbiano di Soave, which is used for a still white and a sparkling version. The Monte Carbonare excels as usual. This Soave is aged exclusively in steel, thus highlighting its intense aromas. Fruit shares center stage with flowers and early, faint sulfurous and smoky notes. In the mouth, it starts out delicate but suddenly unleashes its personality and attack. Massafitti is a monovarietal Trebbiano di Soave that sees more delicate aromas and flavors, for an elegant and supple palate.

○ Soave Cl. Monte Carbonare '15	♧♧♧ 3*
○ Massifitti '14	♧♧ 3*
○ Le Rive '13	♧♧ 4
○ Recioto di Soave Acinatium '12	♧♧ 5
○ Soave Cl. '16	♧♧ 2*
○ Opera Semplice Dosaggio Zero M. Cl.	♧ 4
○ Soave Cl. Monte Carbonare '14	♕♕♕ 3*
○ Soave Cl. Monte Carbonare '12	♕♕♕ 3*
○ Soave Cl. Monte Carbonare '11	♕♕♕ 3*
○ Soave Cl. Monte Carbonare '10	♕♕♕ 3*
○ Soave Cl. Monte Carbonare '09	♕♕♕ 3*
○ Soave Cl. Monte Carbonare '08	♕♕♕ 3*
○ Soave Cl. Monte Carbonare '07	♕♕♕ 3*
○ Soave Cl. Monte Carbonare '06	♕♕♕ 3*

Sutto

LOC. CAMPO DI PIETRA
VIA ARZERI, 34/1
31040 SALGAREDA [TV]
TEL. +39 0422744063
www.sutto.it

CELLAR SALES
PRE-BOOKED VISITS
ACCOMMODATION AND RESTAURANT SERVICE
ANNUAL PRODUCTION 397,000 bottles
HECTARES UNDER VINE 75.00

The Sutto brothers' winery is one of the most interesting in the area. Here, in the flatlands that stretch through the provinces of Venice and Treviso, where vineyards have sprouted since time immemorial, clay soil alternates with deep pockets of gravel. And here, Stefano and Luigi, without ignoring Prosecco's success, have gone in pursuit of solidity and elegance with their selection of still wines. Their approach seeks out a balance between the heat of the plains and the coolness of the northern hills. The winery's process of expansion has enabled Stefano and Luisa to produce an excellent Campo Sella, despite the complicated 2014 vintage. On the nose, notes of sweet ripe fruit emerge, with a subtle vegetal note of fines herbes that provides for just the right touch of freshness. The mouth is full and creamy, supported by smooth tannins and a crisp acidity. Among the whites, we enjoyed the fullness of the Pinot Grigio, and our favorite Prosecco proved to be the Extra Dry.

● Merlot Campo Sella '14	♧♧ 5
○ Bianco di Sutto '16	♧♧ 2*
● Cabernet '16	♧♧ 2*
○ Chardonnay '16	♧♧ 2*
● Dogma Rosso '15	♧♧ 4
● Ferruccio Secondo '15	♧♧ 4
○ Pinot Grigio '16	♧♧ 2*
○ Ultimo Passito '15	♧♧ 4
○ Valdobbiadene Extra Dry Batiso '16	♧♧ 3
● Merlot '16	♧ 2
● Piave Raboso '12	♧ 4
○ Prosecco Brut	♧ 2
○ Prosecco Extra Dry	♧ 3
● Cabernet '15	♕♕ 2*
○ Chardonnay '15	♕♕ 2*
● Dogma Rosso '14	♕♕ 4
○ Ultimo Passito '14	♕♕ 4

T.E.S.S.A.R.I.

LOC. BROGNOLIGO
VIA FONTANA NUOVA, 86
37032 MONTEFORTE D'ALPONE [VR]
TEL. +39 0456176041
www.cantinatessari.com

CELLAR SALES
PRE-BOOKED VISITS
ANNUAL PRODUCTION 40,000 bottles
HECTARES UNDER VINE 17.00

After passing the center of Monteforte d'Alpone and proceeding north, the road winds through a densely cultivated patch of land. Here, the vineyards on the valley floor co-mingle with those climbing the slopes in search of cooler air. The black soil in which they grow betrays the area's volcanic origins. This is Borgnoligo, where the Tessari family carry out their painstaking work on almost 20 hectares of land, with equal care shown in the cellar. The Le Bine Longhe is a Soave made from overripe Garganega grapes grown in the Costalta area and aged for long periods in steel before being bottled. The ripeness of its fruit is clearly discernible on the nose, together with notes of dried flowers and flint. The fullness of the palate is contrasted by a fresh and racy acidity. The Soave Grisela, on the other hand, plays more with balance and elegance.

Tamellini

FRAZ. COSTEGGIOLA
VIA TAMELLINI, 4
37038 SOAVE [VR]
TEL. +39 0457675328
piofrancesco.tamellini@tin.it

CELLAR SALES
PRE-BOOKED VISITS
ANNUAL PRODUCTION 250,000 bottles
HECTARES UNDER VINE 27.00

The Tamellini brothers' winery was founded just over twenty years ago, almost as a kind of dare. Today, theirs is a splendid estate, 30 hectares of vineyards set on highly prized terrain. Gateano and Pio Francesco are bolstered by a longstanding relationship with viticulture, with generations of family having worked in the sector and on this very land. Their wines manage to bring together the freshness and lightness of Soave with the depth and elegance of the classic whites. The Tamellini brothers have limited their production and there are only two Soaves, but they sum up the work of an entire year. Le Bine de Costìola is made exclusively with Garganega grapes aged in the cellar for a year. The nose offers up notes of inviting ripe yellow fruit, which lets through smoky and flinty nuances. In the mouth, it proves virtually perfect, tangy, harmonious and long, making for a great wine to drink and to store. The Soave Classico is also excellent, proving fresh, juicy and very pleasant.

○ Soave Cl. Grisela '16	♟♟ 2*
○ Soave Cl. Le Bine Longhe '15	♟♟ 5
○ Garganega Brut Arcerus	♟ 3
○ Garganega Frizzante Sur Lie Avus	♟ 3
○ Recioto di Soave Tre Colli '13	♟♟ 5
○ Soave Cl. Bine Longhe '13	♟♟ 3*
○ Soave Cl. Grisela '15	♟♟ 2*
○ Soave Cl. Grisela '14	♟♟ 2*
○ Soave Cl. Grisela '13	♟♟ 2*
○ Soave Cl. Grisela '12	♟♟ 2*
○ Soave Cl. Grisela '11	♟♟ 2*
○ Soave Cl. Le Bine Longhe di Costalta '12	♟♟ 3
○ Soave Cl. Le Bine Longhe di Costalta '11	♟♟ 3

○ Soave Cl. Le Bine de Costiola '15	♟♟ 3*
○ Soave Cl. '16	♟♟ 2*
○ Soave Cl. Le Bine '04	♟♟♟ 3*
○ Soave Cl. Le Bine de Costiola '14	♟♟♟ 3*
○ Soave Cl. Le Bine de Costiola '13	♟♟♟ 3*
○ Soave Cl. Le Bine de Costiola '11	♟♟♟ 3*
○ Soave Cl. Le Bine de Costiola '06	♟♟♟ 3*
○ Soave Cl. Le Bine de Costiola '05	♟♟♟ 3*
○ Soave '15	♟♟ 2*
○ Soave '14	♟♟ 2*
○ Soave Cl. '12	♟♟ 2*
○ Soave Cl. Le Bine de Costiola '12	♟♟ 3*
○ Soave Cl. Le Bine de Costiola '10	♟♟ 3*

Giovanna Tantini

FRAZ. OLIOSI
LOC. I MISCHI
37014 CASTELNUOVO DEL GARDA [VR]
TEL. +39 3488717577
www.giovannatantini.it

CELLAR SALES
PRE-BOOKED VISITS
ACCOMMODATION
ANNUAL PRODUCTION 30,000 bottles
HECTARES UNDER VINE 11.50

Giovanna Tantini's winery can be found in the southern backcountry of Lake Garda, between the municipalities of Sona and Castelnuovo. Here, along the rolling hills of morainic origins, the area's classic grapes of Bardolino and Custom have grown for centuries. Tantini's estate spans 20 hectares, with just over half dedicated to vine growing. In realizing his selection, even the simplest wines are aged before being released on the market. The 2015 Bardolino delivered. It features intense notes of ripe cherry and pepper on the nose, with a fresh and intriguing floral note in the background. In the mouth it proves quite savory and supple, making for a succulent and gratifying palate. Ettore, a blend of slightly dried Corvina, Cabernet Sauvignon and Merlot, offers up intense notes of sweet and meaty fruit. These follow through well onto the palate, where the wine displays its grip and length.

● Bardolino '15	🍷🍷 2*
☉ Bardolino Chiaretto '16	🍷🍷 2*
● Ettore '11	🍷🍷 4
○ Custoza '16	🍷 2
● Garda Corvina Ma.Gi.Co. '16	🍷 2
● Greta '12	🍷 5
● Bardolino '14	🍷🍷 2*
● Bardolino '12	🍷🍷 2*
● Bardolino '11	🍷🍷 2*
● Bardolino '10	🍷🍷 2*
☉ Bardolino Chiaretto '15	🍷🍷 2*
● Ettore '09	🍷🍷 4
● Greta '09	🍷🍷 5

F.lli Tedeschi

FRAZ. PEDEMONTE
VIA G. VERDI, 4
37029 SAN PIETRO IN CARIANO [VR]
TEL. +39 0457701487
www.tedeschiwines.com

CELLAR SALES
PRE-BOOKED VISITS
ANNUAL PRODUCTION 500,000 bottles
HECTARES UNDER VINE 46.00
SUSTAINABLE WINERY

Antonietta, Sabrina and Riccardo Tedeschi manage their family winery in Pedemonte, bolstered by tradition and a bond with the territory that goes back generations. In addition to their historic vineyards, Monte Olmi and Fabriseria, set in Valpolicella Classica, they manage the increasingly important Maternigo estate. Theirs is a splendid winery, situated high in the hills, in an area of rare natural integrity. In the cellar, they make wines that reflect tradition, and express both character and vigor. Their flagship wine is the Amarone Capitel Monte Olmi, a red that is second to none when it comes to personality. On the nose, simpler notes of overripe fruit are accompanied by a whirlwind of more original fragrances, including olives in brine, thyme, sweet spices and Mediterranean scrub, which follow through onto a rich and powerful palate. The Maternigo features finer aromas. It's a Valpolicella Superiore that is initially plush but gains precision and grip at the finish.

● Amarone della Valpolicella Cl. Capitel Monte Olmi '11	🍷🍷🍷 8
● Valpolicella Cl. Sup. La Fabriseria '13	🍷🍷 5
● Valpolicella Sup. Maternigo '14	🍷🍷 4
● Amarone della Valpolicella '13	🍷🍷 6
● Valpolicella Sup. Capitel Nicolò '15	🍷🍷 3
● Valpolicella Sup. Ripasso San Rocco '15	🍷🍷 4
● Valpolicella Cl. Lucchine '16	🍷 2
● Amarone della Valpolicella Cl. Capitel Monte Olmi '07	🍷🍷🍷 8
● Amarone della Valpolicella Cl. La Fabriseria Ris. '11	🍷🍷🍷 8
● Valpolicella Sup. Maternigo '11	🍷🍷🍷 4*

Le Tende

VIA TENDE, 35
37017 LAZISE [VR]
TEL. +39 0457590748
www.letende.it

CELLAR SALES
PRE-BOOKED VISITS
ANNUAL PRODUCTION 100,000 bottles
HECTARES UNDER VINE 12.50
VITICULTURE METHOD Certified Organic

Even when the market seemed solely interested in wines of high concentration, La Tende never betrayed its roots, continuing to interpret Garda's historic wines with an eye towards finesse and lightness. Mauro Fortuna manages some 10 hectares of vineyards where mostly traditional grape varieties are grown. Their balanced selection of wines strives to stay true to the territory and the characteristics of its grapes. They have a nice touch when it comes to Verona's historic cultivar, Corvina. Mauro's interpretations highlight the grape's spicy and dynamic character, both the monovarietal and the Bardolino Superiore. The former features notes of pepper, dog rose and cherry, which give way to a savory, taut and very pleasant palate. The latter starts out with fruity notes enriched by hints of iris and forest floor, while the palate proves slim-bodied and gutsy.

● Bardolino Cl. Sup. '15	♟♟ 3
● Corvina '16	♟♟ 3
○ Custoza '16	♟♟ 2*
⊙ Bardolino Chiaretto Brut Voluttà	♟ 3
⊙ Bardolino Chiaretto Cl. '16	♟ 2
● Bardolino Cl. '16	♟ 2
○ Lucillini '16	♟ 3
● Bardolino Cl. '14	♟♟ 2*
● Bardolino Cl. Sup. '14	♟♟ 3
● Cicisbeo '13	♟♟ 4
● Cicisbeo '12	♟♟ 3
● Corvina '15	♟♟ 3
○ Custoza '15	♟♟ 2*
○ Custoza '14	♟♟ 2*

Gianni Tessari

VIA PRANDI, 10
37030 RONCÀ [VR]
TEL. +39 0457460070
www.giannitessari.wine

CELLAR SALES
PRE-BOOKED VISITS
ANNUAL PRODUCTION 450,000 bottles
HECTARES UNDER VINE 55.00

This historic winery in Roncà represents one of the most interesting operations in the area spanning Soave and Lessinia. Bolstered by a vineyard that extends for more than 50 hectares, the estate is rounded out by an important plot on Colli Berici. The selection is divided into three sections, each of which is devoted to a specific project. Lessinia is entirely dedicated to sparkling wines, Soave is their Scaligero white, while Colli Berici is dedicated mostly to their reds. Their most impressive wine is the 2015 Soave Pigno, made with 100% Garganega aged in barrels of various sizes. The nose features intense aromas of ripe yellow fruit, with oak just peeking out from the background. In the mouth, its fullness is perfectly supported by a tangy and juicy acidity. The Durello 60 Mesi also did well. It's an Extra Brut with aromas of dried flowers and ripe fruit, and an assertive palate characterized by the acidity of the cultivar.

○ Soave Cl. Pigno '15	♟♟ 3*
● Colli Berici Tocai Rosso '15	♟♟ 2*
○ Lessini Durello Extra Brut M. Cl. Ris. 60 Mesi '10	♟♟ 5
○ Soave Cl. Monte Tenda '16	♟♟ 3
● Colli Berici Rosso Pianalto '13	♟ 5
● Due '14	♟ 2
○ Lessini Durello Extra Brut M. Cl. 36 Mesi	♟ 5
○ Soave Cl. Pigno Gianni Tessari '13	♟♟♟ 3*
○ Lessini Durello Extra Brut M. Cl. 60 Mesi '08	♟♟ 5

Tezza

FRAZ. POIANO DI VALPANTENA
VIA STRADELLA MAIOLI, 4
37142 VERONA
TEL. +39 045550267
www.tezzawines.it

CELLAR SALES
PRE-BOOKED VISITS
ANNUAL PRODUCTION 200,000 bottles
HECTARES UNDER VINE 28.00

The winery of the Tezza cousins, Flavio, Vanio and Federico, is situated in Valpantena, a large valley that rises to the north and that, historically, constitutes the only subzone in Valpolicella. The area doesn't reach particularly high altitudes. But its heavily gravel soil, combined with the cool air that flows through the valley and temperature variance between day and night, guarantee that their grapes ripen in the best possible way. Their selection is divided into two lines, with the Brolo delle Giare line representing their top-range. It's from this line that we get their most interesting wine, the Riserva di Amarone. This 'Riserva' is the result of a 2009 vintage that, today, offers up an intense hint of sweet, dried fruit on the nose, rounded out by a solid and weighty palate. Their Ripasso displays more intricate aromas embellished by subtle herb hints, which give it a refreshing touch.

● Amarone della Valpolicella Valpantena Brolo delle Giare Ris. '09	▼▼ 7
● Valpolicella Valpantena Sup. Ripasso '14	▼▼ 3
● Valpolicella Valpantena Sup. Ripasso Brolo delle Giare '13	▼▼ 4
● Valpolicella Sup. Ripasso Corte Majoli '15	▼ 3
● Valpolicella Sup. Ripasso Ma Roat '14	▼ 2
● Amarone della Valpolicella Valpantena Brolo delle Giare Ris. '06	♀♀ 7
● Recioto della Valpolicella Valpantena '09	♀♀ 5
● Valpolicella Valpantena Ripasso Brolo delle Giare '09	♀♀ 4
● Valpolicella Valpantena Sup. Ripasso Brolo delle Giare '11	♀♀ 4

Tommasi Viticoltori

LOC. PEDEMONTE
VIA RONCHETTO, 4
37029 SAN PIETRO IN CARIANO [VR]
TEL. +39 0457701266
www.tommasi.com

CELLAR SALES
PRE-BOOKED VISITS
ACCOMMODATION AND RESTAURANT SERVICE
ANNUAL PRODUCTION 1,500,000 bottles
HECTARES UNDER VINE 205.00
SUSTAINABLE WINERY

The giant Tommasi continues to expand, with wineries spread throughout all of Italy's most important DOC zones. Their core remains solidly grounded in Valpolicella and the province of Verona, where the family manages almost 200 hectares. Giancarlo is in the driver's seat, overseeing all stages of production, seeking to transmit a personal style to his wines without losing traditional values. Their wines display a clearly fruit-rich expression but are never pushed into unwanted levels of concentration. The Amarone Classico went extremely well. Following a very stylistic path, we appreciated the generosity of its red fruit, refreshed by spicy hints and subtle herbs. In the mouth, a soft impact finds the right support in acidity, which gently gives way to a long and dry finish. The Ripasso also delivers. Dominated by balsamic hints and small wild berries, these offer up richness and harmony to the palate, with a finish highlighting its tannins' sweetness.

● Amarone della Valpolicella Cl. '13	▼▼ 7
● Valpolicella '16	▼▼ 2*
● Valpolicella Cl. Sup. Rafael '15	▼▼ 4
● Valpolicella Cl. Sup. Ripasso '15	▼▼ 4
● Arele '15	▼ 3
○ Lugana Le Fornaci '16	▼ 2
○ Soave Cl. Le Volpare '16	▼ 3
● Amarone della Valpolicella Cl. '12	♀♀ 7
● Amarone della Valpolicella Cl. Ca' Florian Ris. '09	♀♀ 7
● Amarone della Valpolicella Cl. Ca' Florian Ris. '08	♀♀ 7
● Valpolicella Cl. Sup. Rafael '14	♀♀ 4
● Valpolicella Cl. Sup. Ripasso '14	♀♀ 4

La Tordera

VIA ALNÈ BOSCO, 23
31020 VIDOR [TV]
TEL. +39 0423985362
www.latordera.it

CELLAR SALES
PRE-BOOKED VISITS
ANNUAL PRODUCTION 450,000 bottles
HECTARES UNDER VINE 33.00
VITICULTURE METHOD Certified Organic
SUSTAINABLE WINERY

The Vettoretti family winery is located in Guida di Valdobbiadene, where the vineyards seem to join the earth with the sky and defy the laws of gravity. Year after year, they've shown tremendous attention to the environmental impact of their work, both in the countryside and in the cellar. The cellar, built in the area of Vidor, is certified 'Casa Clima Wine'. Their most impressive wine comes right from Rive di Guida, l'Otreval. This Valdobbiadene Brut doesn't go looking for help in sugars. On the nose, it offers up intense, fresh hints of flowers and white fruit. In the mouth it strikes you immediately for the creaminess and endurance of its sparkle. The Extra Dry Serrai displays sweeter fruit that is also expressed to a greater degree. In the mouth, we discover a lean body and a succulent, full-flavored palate. The Cartizze is even more well-rounded and pervasive.

○ Cartizze	⚑⚑ 4
○ Valdobbiadene Extra Dry Serrai '16	⚑⚑ 3
○ Valdobbiadene Rive di Guida Brut Otreval '16	⚑⚑ 3
⊙ Gabry Brut Rosé	⚑ 2
○ Valdobbiadene Brut Brunei	⚑ 3
○ Valdobbiadene Rive di Vidor Dry Tittoni '16	⚑ 3

Trabucchi d'Illasi

LOC. MONTE TENDA
37031 ILLASI [VR]
TEL. +39 0457833233
www.trabucchidillasi.it

CELLAR SALES
PRE-BOOKED VISITS
ANNUAL PRODUCTION 120,000 bottles
HECTARES UNDER VINE 25.00
VITICULTURE METHOD Certified Organic

The Trabucchi family's estate is one of the most beautiful in Valpolicella Orientale, featuring a vineyard set on the hillsides that divide Valpolicella and Soave. Their cultivation techniques have been certified organic for years, and their wines are released only when time has bestowed on them the correct proportions of harmony and depth. Their reds display a solid, gutsy character, in which fruit concentration is contrasted by the historic grapes' customary acidity. Trabucchi's Amarone is released only after lengthy aging. Today, eight years after the vintage, it displays an extraordinarily fresh suite of aromas. Crisp fruit leaves room for balsamic hints and spices, while oak turns up only later. Its force in the mouth is notable and the wine elongates with decisiveness and grip. In terms of aromas, the Terre di San Colombano goes all in on fruit and spices. Dynamic in the mouth, its tannins hold up in the finish.

● Amarone della Valpolicella '09	⚑⚑ 8
● Valpolicella Sup. Terre di S. Colombano '10	⚑⚑ 3*
● Valpolicella Sup. Terre del Cereolo '09	⚑⚑ 5
● Amarone della Valpolicella '06	⚑⚑⚑ 8
● Amarone della Valpolicella '04	⚑⚑⚑ 8
● Recioto della Valpolicella Cereolo '05	⚑⚑⚑ 8
● Valpolicella Sup. Terre di S. Colombano '03	⚑⚑⚑ 4*
● Amarone della Valpolicella '08	⚑⚑ 8
● Amarone della Valpolicella Alberto Trabucchi Ris. '08	⚑⚑ 8
● Recioto della Valpolicella '07	⚑⚑ 7
● Valpolicella Sup. Terre del Cereolo '08	⚑⚑ 5
● Valpolicella Sup. Terre di S. Colombano '09	⚑⚑ 3
● Valpolicella Un Anno '15	⚑⚑ 2*

Spumanti Valdo

VIA FORO BOARIO, 20
31049 VALDOBBIADENE [TV]
TEL. +39 04239090
www.valdo.com

CELLAR SALES
PRE-BOOKED VISITS
ANNUAL PRODUCTION 9,000,000 bottles
HECTARES UNDER VINE 155.00

Decades ago, the Bolla family left its native land in Verona to come to Valdobbiadene. Today Valdo is one of Conegliano Valdobbiadene's most internationally well-established brands. As always, they use grapes from their own vineyards, as well as large quantities from local suppliers, who deliver the fruit to their cellar in Via Foro Boario. Their selection is entirely dedicated to sparkling wines, with Prosecco playing a leading part, as you might have guessed. Numero 10 takes on the role of leader at Valdo. This Valdobbiadene, made with the traditional 'Metodo Classico', explores the deepest, most sophisticated elements of the appellation. Pleasantly dry, it also shows superior grip. Cuvée di Boj also delivered. This Brut displays faint aromatic hints of apple and wisteria, and we greatly appreciated the way its sparkle manages to perfectly accompany the palate.

○ Valdobbiadene Brut M. Cl. Numero 10 '14	🍷🍷 4
○ Valdobbiadene Brut Cuvée di Boj	🍷🍷 2*
○ Valdobbiadene Cuvée del Fondatore	🍷🍷 3
○ Cartizze Cuvée Viviana	🍷 5
○ Valdobbiadene Extra Dry	🍷 2
○ Valdobbiadene Extra Dry Cuvée 1926	🍷 2
○ Valdobbiadene Brut Cuvée del Fondatore '14	🍷🍷 3
○ Valdobbiadene Cuvée del Fondatore '13	🍷🍷 3

Cantina Valpantena Verona

LOC. QUINTO
VIA COLONIA ORFANI DI GUERRA, 5B
37142 VERONA
TEL. +39 045550032
www.cantinavalpantena.it

CELLAR SALES
PRE-BOOKED VISITS
ANNUAL PRODUCTION 9,000,000 bottles
HECTARES UNDER VINE 750.00

Valpantena is a wide valley that stretches out from the eastern outskirts of Verona and curves north for some 30 kilometers before giving way to the hills of Lessinia. It's here that you'll find Cantina Valpantena Verona, the large cooperative winery from Quinto that, thanks to its large membership, cultivates more than 600 hectares and gives rise to a selection that's getting more impressive by the year. Valpantena Verona seeks to bring tradition to wines for early-drinking, with an eye towards highlighting fruit and fragrance. Quinto offers a number of wines, many of which proved first-rate during our tasting. Their Valpolicella, Ripasso Torre del Falasco, is part of their more ambitious line. We appreciated the harmony of its palate, which brings out the fruity hints that characterize its nose. Their outstanding 2013 Amarone is from the same line. This red, with its intense, cherry and thyme aromas, features a well-orchestrated palate and superior drinkability.

● Amarone della Valpolicella Torre del Falasco '13	🍷🍷 6
● Amarone della Valpolicella '14	🍷🍷 5
● Recioto della Valpolicella Tesauro '14	🍷🍷 5
● Valpolicella Sup. Ripasso Torre del Falasco '15	🍷🍷 3
● Valpolicella Sup. Torre del Falasco '15	🍷🍷 2*
● Valpolicella Valpantena Ripasso Ritocco '15	🍷🍷 3
○ Chardonnay Baroncino '16	🍷 2
○ Garganega Torre del Falasco '16	🍷 1*
○ Lugana Torre del Falasco '16	🍷 3
● Recioto della Valpolicella Tesauro '12	🍷🍷 5
● Valpolicella Valpantena Ritocco '14	🍷🍷 3

Cantina Valpolicella Negrar

VIA CA' SALGARI, 2
37024 NEGRAR [VR]
TEL. +39 0456014300
www.cantinanegrar.it

CELLAR SALES
PRE-BOOKED VISITS
RESTAURANT SERVICE
ANNUAL PRODUCTION 7,000,000 bottles
HECTARES UNDER VINE 700.00

Thanks to the work of more than 200 members cultivating 700 hectares of vineyards, Cantina Valpolicella Negrar has established itself as one of the most important cooperative wineries in the area of Valpolicella Classica. Mostly grapes tied to Verona's winemaking tradition are grown. Then, in their large facility on Via Ca' Salgari, these are transformed into a selection based on the territory's classic wines. Their core brand is Domini Veneti, dedicated to forceful, precise reds. When an exceptional vintage allows for it, the winery offers Amarone in their Expressioni line. The selection features a wine for every oneh of the valleys in the 'Classica' zone, each aimed at bringing out the attributes of the territory. And so we have Mazzurega, a high-altitude (460 meters) Amarone from the valley of Fumane. Its smoky aromas are characterized by red fruit and spices. In the mouth it proves strong with rugged tannins. The Mater offers up sweeter, riper fruit while, in the mouth, it demonstrates grace under pressure.

● Amarone della Valpolicella Cl. Mater Domini Veneti Ris. '11	🍷🍷 8
● Amarone della Valpolicella Cl. Mazzurega Domini Veneti '11	🍷🍷 5
● Amarone della Valpolicella Cl. Castelrotto Domini Veneti '11	🍷🍷 7
● Amarone della Valpolicella Cl. Monte Domini Veneti '11	🍷🍷 6
● Amarone della Valpolicella Cl. S. Rocco Domini Veneti '11	🍷🍷 8
● Amarone della Valpolicella Cl. Villa Domini Veneti '11	🍷🍷 5
● Recioto della Valpolicella Cl. Vign. di Moron Domini Veneti '13	🍷🍷 4
● Valpolicella Cl. Sup. Ripasso La Casetta Domini Veneti '15	🍷🍷 4
● Valpolicella Cl. Sup. Vign. di Torbe Domini Veneti '15	🍷🍷 2*

Odino Vaona

LOC. VALGATARA
VIA PAVERNO, 41
37020 MARANO DI VALPOLICELLA [VR]
TEL. +39 0457703710
www.vaona.it

CELLAR SALES
PRE-BOOKED VISITS
ANNUAL PRODUCTION 70,000 bottles
HECTARES UNDER VINE 10.00
SUSTAINABLE WINERY

Alberto Vaona manages his family's winery in the heart of the Marano valley, one of the most interesting areas in Valpolicella. The vineyards here extend for 10 hectares. The oldest are still grown with the pergola method, while the most recent follow Guyot. The final goal, in any case, is the same: a selection that stays true to tradition, and that exhibits lightness and fragrance. The Riserva di Amarone Pegrandi is made with grapes grown at 250 meters above sea level; the wine is then aged for three years in 1000 liter barrels. Today it displays an aromatic profile in which fruit is followed by medicinal herbs. In the mouth it reveals its youth, arriving full and juicy, and then receding until finding its rightful harmony. The pleasantness of the Amarone Paverno derives from its more open notes, which anticipate a dry, long, grippy palate.

● Amarone della Valpolicella Cl. Paverno '13	🍷🍷 5
● Amarone della Valpolicella Cl. Pegrandi Ris. '11	🍷🍷 8
● Valpolicella Cl. '16	🍷🍷 2*
● Valpolicella Sup. '14	🍷🍷 2*
● Castaroto '13	🍷 4
● Valpolicella Cl. Sup. Ripasso Pegrandi '15	🍷 3
● Amarone della Valpolicella Cl. Pegrandi '09	🍷🍷🍷 5
● Amarone della Valpolicella Cl. Pegrandi '08	🍷🍷🍷 5
● Valpolicella Cl. Sup. Ripasso Pegrandi '13	🍷🍷 3

Venturini

FRAZ. SAN FLORIANO
VIA SEMONTE, 20
37029 SAN PIETRO IN CARIANO [VR]
TEL. +39 0457701331
www.viniventurini.com

CELLAR SALES
PRE-BOOKED VISITS
ANNUAL PRODUCTION 100,000 bottles
HECTARES UNDER VINE 12.00

The Venturini family, Giuseppina, Daniele and Mirco, manage their family's estate in San Floriano, some dozen hectares of hillside vineyards dedicated entirely to local grape varieties. A couple of years ago, they moved to a new cellar, built at the foot of the hill that divides the Negrar and Marano valleys. Their wines are strongly tied to tradition, expressing fruity richness and a character that enfolds delicately. The Amarone Campo Masua is Venturini's star, a red that's allowed to mature in large barrels and mid-sized casks before being bottled. The nose finds extraordinary ripe cherry. Meaty and enticing, it offers up a blast of freshness in its spices and mineral notes. In the mouth it proves full and potent, but its body is managed with lightness and richness of flavor. In the Amarone Classic, on the other hand, fruit takes on a more prominent role, with a rich and generous palate.

● Amarone della Valpolicella Cl. '12	▼▼ 6
● Amarone della Valpolicella Cl. Campo Masua '11	▼▼ 7
● Valpolicella Cl. Sup. '14	▼▼ 3
● Valpolicella Cl. Sup. Ripasso Semonte Alto '13	▼▼ 4
● Massimino '11	▼ 5
● Valpolicella Cl. '16	▼ 2
● Amarone della Valpolicella Cl. Campomasua '07	▽▽▽ 6
● Amarone della Valpolicella Cl. Campomasua '05	▽▽▽ 6
● Recioto della Valpolicella Cl. Le Brugnine '97	▽▽▽ 5

Agostino Vicentini

FRAZ. SAN ZENO
VIA C. BATTISTI, 62C
37030 COLOGNOLA AI COLLI [VR]
TEL. +39 0457650539
www.vinivicentini.com

CELLAR SALES
PRE-BOOKED VISITS
ANNUAL PRODUCTION 100,000 bottles
HECTARES UNDER VINE 20.00

San Zeno is a small winery set at the mouth of the d'Illasi valley, in an area where vineyards dominate the agricultural sector. Agostino Vicentini, along with his wife, Teresa, and children, Manuele and Francesca, is a leader among Soave's producers. His vineyard is managed with an almost obsessive care, making for wines that display superior character and presence. In their cellar on Via Battisti, they also produce a small but sophisticated selection of Valpolicella reds. The star of the show is, however, still Il Casale, a Soave Superiore aged in steel that leads a style defined by character and fullness. Made only with Garganega that's harvested when perfectly ripe, it's then aged slowly in the cellar. The result is a wine that, even when tasted shortly after being bottled, earned the consensus of our panel. White fruit, flowers and a plucky vegetal note followed through to a richly, decisive palate of superior continuity.

○ Soave Sup. Il Casale '16	▼▼▼ 3*
○ Soave Vign. Terre Lunghe '16	▼▼ 2*
● Valpolicella Boccascalucce '15	▼ 3
● Valpolicella Sup. Idea Bacco '13	▼▼ 5
● Valpolicella Sup. '14	▼ 3
○ Soave Sup. Il Casale '15	▽▽▽ 3*
○ Soave Sup. Il Casale '14	▽▽▽ 3*
○ Soave Sup. Il Casale '13	▽▽▽ 3*
○ Soave Sup. Il Casale '12	▽▽▽ 3*
○ Soave Sup. Il Casale '09	▽▽▽ 3*
○ Soave Sup. Il Casale '08	▽▽▽ 3*
○ Soave Sup. Il Casale '07	▽▽▽ 3*
○ Soave Vign. Terre Lunghe '15	▽▽ 2*
● Valpolicella Sup. Idea Bacco '12	▽▽ 5
● Valpolicella Sup. Palazzo di Campiano '12	▽▽ 5

Vigna Roda

LOC. CORTELÀ
VIA MONTE VEHSA, 1569
35030 VO [PD]
TEL. +39 0499940228
www.vignaroda.com

CELLAR SALES
PRE-BOOKED VISITS
ANNUAL PRODUCTION 52,000 bottles
HECTARES UNDER VINE 17.00

Gianni Strazzacappa took over the reins of his family's winery 20 years ago, transforming what had been an ordinary producer into one of the area's most interesting. Today, along with his wife, Elena, he manages some 20 hectares of land, cultivating mostly the red Bordeaux varieties that have grown here for almost two centuries. His wines are full and generous in their early stages, but they know how to age with harmony. This year's tasting highlighted the progress the winery has made in terms of finesse, with the Cabernet Espero offering a more defined, lengthy palate (while maintaining its trademark energetic, eager profile). The result is one of the more intriguing vintages in the appellation. The Scarlatto proved fresh in its aromas and highly drinkable - it's a top interpretation of the 2014 vintage. We should also mention their pleasant Colli Euganei Rosso.

Vignale di Cecilia

LOC. FORNACI
VIA CROCI, 14
35030 BAONE [PD]
TEL. +39 042951420
www.vignaledicecilia.it

PRE-BOOKED VISITS
ANNUAL PRODUCTION 20,000 bottles
HECTARES UNDER VINE 8.00
VITICULTURE METHOD Certified Organic

The heart of Paolo Brunello's estate (in the southern part of the Colli Euganei) is made up of a natural amphitheater that opens towards the west. From these beginnings, over time, four more hectares were rented and used to cultivate white grapes. In the fields they've adopted a low-impact environmental approach that includes organic certification, while in their small but efficient cellar on Via Croci they're constantly experimenting, thus giving life to wines defined by expression of character. The outstanding 2015 vintage made for the best Covolo yet. This red was fated to play a supporting role to the more important Passacaglia, but today it has taken the lead. Intense fruit aromas are the prelude to a rich, juicy palate that endures. The Passacaglia expresses greater depth and complexity on the nose, while in the mouth it is lean and harmonious.

● Colli Euganei Cabernet Espero '16	▾▾ 2*
● Colli Euganei Rosso '16	▾▾ 2*
● Colli Euganei Rosso Scarlatto '14	▾▾ 3
● Merlot Il Damerino '16	▾▾ 2*
○ Aroma 2.0 '16	▾ 2
○ Colli Euganei Fior d'Arancio Spumante '16	▾ 2
○ Colli Euganei Serprino Frizzante '16	▾ 2
● Colli Euganei Cabernet Espero '15	♈ 2*
● Colli Euganei Cabernet Espero '14	♈ 2*
● Colli Euganei Rosso Scarlatto '13	♈ 3
● Colli Euganei Rosso Scarlatto '12	♈ 3*

○ Benavides '15	▾▾ 2*
● Colli Euganei Rosso Covolo '15	▾▾ 3
● Colli Euganei Rosso Passacaglia '13	▾▾ 4
○ Cocài '15	▾ 3
● Colli Euganei Rosso Covolo '14	♈ 3
● Colli Euganei Rosso Covolo '13	♈ 3
● Colli Euganei Rosso Covolo '10	♈ 3
● Colli Euganei Rosso Passacaglia '12	♈ 4
● Colli Euganei Rosso Passacaglia '11	♈ 4
● Colli Euganei Rosso Passacaglia '09	♈ 4
● El Moro '10	♈ 3

★Vignalta

VIA SCALETTE, 23
35032 ARQUÀ PETRARCA [PD]
TEL. +39 0429777305
www.vignalta.it

CELLAR SALES
PRE-BOOKED VISITS
ANNUAL PRODUCTION 230,000 bottles
HECTARES UNDER VINE 35.00
SUSTAINABLE WINERY

The Colli Euganei are among the first areas where Merlot and Cabernet flourished. This hill area, protected under the regional park system, offers a dry, warm climate and soils that alternate between volcanic trachyte and calcareous 'scaglia bianca', a mix that confers personality and character to the grapes. More than any other, Vignalta represents this DOC zone, nurtured by 30 years of experience and prized vineyards. Gemola and Arquà contend for first place at the winery located at Via Scalette. These two Bordeaux are predominantly made of Merlot, and are characterized by two different expressions. The first offers up extraordinary richness of fruit and, in the mouth, it is full, generous and approachably pleasant, certainly deserving Tre Bicchieri. The second is more hidden. It lets its spicy, Cabernet Franc core emerge. In the mouth it is drier and firmer. Of note also is Alpianae's excellent performance. It proved itself a sunny, juicy passito.

● Colli Euganei Rosso Gemola '13	♛♛♛	6
○ Colli Euganei Fior d'Arancio Passito Alpianae '14	♛♛	6
● Colli Euganei Rosso Arquà '11	♛♛	6
○ Brut Vintage M. Cl. '10	♛♛	5
○ Colli Euganei Chardonnay '15	♛♛	4
○ Colli Euganei Manzoni Bianco Agno Casto '16	♛♛	4
○ Colli Euganei Moscato Secco Sirio '16	♛♛	3
● Colli Euganei Rosso Ris. '12	♛♛	3
● Marrano '10	♛♛	5
○ Colli Euganei Pinot Bianco '16	♛	3
● Colli Euganei Rosso Venda '14	♛	3
● Colli Euganei Rosso Gemola '09	♛♛♛	5
● Colli Euganei Rosso Gemola '08	♛♛♛	5

Le Vigne di San Pietro

VIA SAN PIETRO, 23
37066 SOMMACAMPAGNA [VR]
TEL. +39 045510016
www.levignedisanpietro.it

CELLAR SALES
PRE-BOOKED VISITS
ANNUAL PRODUCTION 70,000 bottles
HECTARES UNDER VINE 10.00

Carlo Nerozzi's winery runs along an upland separating Sommacampagna from the highway. It's a small hill that, on its peak, hosts a splendid cellar, surrounded by a handful of hectares of vineyards. Situated in a position of rare natural beauty, these are cultivated with the utmost respect for the environment. Their other vineyards can be found not far from the spot, with 10 or so hectares in all. Elegance and the ability to evolve with age are the focus of the selection made from the grapes that are grown here. This year, Carlo's selection proved exemplary, with a Custoza Sanpietro that deserves to be framed. The nose sees a whirlwind of fragrances, yellow fruit and dried flowers, flint and white pepper. The palate manages to stay solid and stylish at the same time. Most impressive. In terms of their reds, we were struck by their Bardolino Superiore. Aromas of wild berries and wild rose give way to an energetic palate that is grippy and highly pleasant.

● Bardolino Sup. '15	♛♛	3*
○ Custoza Sup. Sanpietro '15	♛♛	3*
● Bardolino '16	♛♛	2*
⊙ Bardolino Chiaretto CorDeRosa '16	♛♛	2*
○ Custoza '16	♛♛	2*
● Bardolino '14	♛♛♛	2*
● Bardolino '11	♛♛♛	2*
● Refolà Cabernet Sauvignon '04	♛♛♛	6
● Bardolino '15	♛♛	2*
● Bardolino '15	♛♛	2*
⊙ Bardolino Chiaretto CorDeRosa '15	♛♛	2*
● Bardolino Sup. '13	♛♛	3
○ Custoza '15	♛♛	2*

Vigneto Due Santi

V.LE Asiago, 174
36061 Bassano del Grappa [VI]
Tel. +39 0424502074
www.vignetoduesanti.it

CELLAR SALES
PRE-BOOKED VISITS
ANNUAL PRODUCTION 100,000 bottles
HECTARES UNDER VINE 18.00
SUSTAINABLE WINERY

Vigneto Due Santi is set on the side of a hill range that rises up towards the Asiago plateau and overlooks the plains below. Here, in an area cooled by winds from nearby Valsugana, cousins Stefano and Adriano Zonta are cultivate almost exclusively Bordeaux grape varieties. Their work is carried out with passion and skill, making for a highly valued and consistently strong selection of wines. Their choice wines are characterised by a style that brings together force and elegance. Cabernet Due Santi, the winery's top wine, took great focus to produce. Confronted with a truly fresh vintage, the winery chose not to fight with nature but, instead, they decided to work more accommodatingly. The result is a superb red wine, fresh in its expression of wild fruit and fine herbs. With strong delivery it paves the way to a long finish.

● Breganze Cabernet Due Santi '14	♟♟♟	4*
○ Breganze Bianco Rivana '16	♟♟	2*
● Breganze Cabernet '13	♟♟	2*
● Breganze Merlot '14	♟♟	2*
○ Breganze Torcolato '13	♟♟	5
○ Malvasia Campo di Fiori '16	♟♟	2*
○ Prosecco Extra Dry	♟	2
● Breganze Cabernet Vign. Due Santi '12	♟♟♟	4*
● Breganze Cabernet Vign. Due Santi '08	♟♟♟	4*
● Breganze Cabernet Vign. Due Santi '07	♟♟♟	4
● Breganze Cabernet Vign. Due Santi '05	♟♟♟	4
● Breganze Cabernet Vign. Due Santi '04	♟♟♟	4
● Breganze Cabernet Vign. Due Santi '03	♟♟♟	4*
● Breganze Cabernet Vign. Due Santi '00	♟♟♟	4

Villa Sandi

via Erizzo, 112
31035 Crocetta del Montello [TV]
Tel. +39 04238607
www.villasandi.it

CELLAR SALES
PRE-BOOKED VISITS
ACCOMMODATION AND RESTAURANT SERVICE
ANNUAL PRODUCTION 5,300,000 bottles
HECTARES UNDER VINE 560.00

The Moretti Polegato family's winery is assuming an ever greater role in the area of Prosecco. Their estate, which now encompasses hundreds of hectares, manages to achieve large volume while staying true to the territory. At the center of their effort is most surely the area of Conegliano Valdobbiadene, which extends into the nearby Asolano hills. The result is a selection that has sparkling wines as its core business. The Vigna la Rivetta performed superbly. This Cartizze was interpreted in a Brut. It managed to bring together two polar opposites: on the one hand, the lightness, freshness and approachability that's common to Trevignano's sparklers; on the other hand, the depth, poise and pressure that characterize a great sparkling wine. In terms of their still wines, the Corpore performed extremely well, having faced the complicated 2014 vintage with style and finesse.

○ Cartizze Brut V. La Rivetta	♟♟♟	6
○ Amalia Moretti Brut M. Cl.		
Opere Trevigiane Ris.	♟♟	8
● Còrpore '14	♟♟	5
○ Valdobbiadene Dry Cuvée Oris	♟♟	3
○ Asolo Brut	♟	3
● Cabernet Filio '14	♟	4
○ Montello e Colli Asolani		
Manzoni Bianco Marinali '16	♟	3
○ Cartizze Brut V. La Rivetta '11	♟♟♟	4*
○ Cartizze Brut V. La Rivetta '10	♟♟♟	4
○ Cartizze Brut V. La Rivetta '09	♟♟♟	4

Villa Spinosa

LOC. JAGO
VIA JAGO DALL'ORA, 16
37024 NEGRAR [VR]
TEL. +39 0457500093
www.villaspinosa.it

CELLAR SALES
PRE-BOOKED VISITS
ACCOMMODATION
ANNUAL PRODUCTION 45,000 bottles
HECTARES UNDER VINE 20.00
SUSTAINABLE WINERY

In the late 20th century, the Negrar valley, an area known for its vineyards, was thrown into disarray by the real estate market. Going from the town centre towards the hamlet of Jago, viticulture is restoring to the landscape a rare harmony. It is here that Enrico Cascella manages his Villa Spinosa, a winery that has managed to face the changes with great composure and calm, establishing itself as a true jewel of Valpolicella. The same calm we find in the performance of their wines. These are released only after lengthy aging in the cellar. The Amarone Albasini, whose grapes are cultivated in the district of the same name, gives off stratified, complex aromas that, in addition to super-ripe fruit, offer up spicy notes of dried flowers and autumn leaves. In the mouth, its potent body proceeds slowly and delicately, impressive for its harmony and length. There's even more complexity in the Guglielmi di Jago 10 Anni, with its sophisticated, well-balanced palate.

● Amarone della Valpolicella Cl. Albasini '10	♟♟♟ 7
● Amarone della Valpolicella Cl. Guglielmi di Jago 10 Anni '07	♟♟ 8
● Amarone della Valpolicella Cl. '12	♟♟ 6
● Valpolicella Cl. '15	♟♟ 2*
● Valpolicella Cl. Sup. Ripasso Jago '12	♟♟ 3
● Amarone della Valpolicella Cl. '08	♟♟♟ 7
● Valpolicella Cl. Sup. Ripasso Jago '11	♟♟♟ 3*
● Amarone della Valpolicella Cl. '06	♟♟ 7
● Recioto della Valpolicella Cl. Francesca Finato Spinosa '11	♟♟ 5
● Valpolicella Cl. '14	♟♟ 2*
● Valpolicella Cl. '13	♟♟ 2*
● Valpolicella Cl. Sup. Figari '12	♟♟ 3

Vigneti Villabella

FRAZ. CALMASINO DI BARDOLINO
LOC. CANOVA, 2
37011 BARDOLINO [VR]
TEL. +39 0457236448
www.vignetivillabella.com

CELLAR SALES
PRE-BOOKED VISITS
ACCOMMODATION
ANNUAL PRODUCTION 500,000 bottles
HECTARES UNDER VINE 220.00

The Cristoforetti and Delibori families' large operation has worked in Garda for decades, overseeing a vast area of vineyards that are partially used for their wine production. Their crown jewel is most certainly the plot surrounding Villa Cordevigo, which is managed with the utmost respect for the environment and provides the grapes used for their most ambitious wines, wines that feature clarity of fruit and elegance in the mouth. The new Bardolino, whose grapes are cultivated on this estate, brings out these very characteristics. Scents of small, wild fruit and forest floor are complemented by a delicate flowery note. This gives way to a dry, spirited palate that delivers for its richness of flavor and length. The Amarone Fracastoro is also very interesting. More than power, it pursues aromatic complexity and harmony of the palate. Thanks to its polished tannins and notable richness, it delivers.

● Bardolino Villa Cordevigo '15	♟ 5
● Amarone della Valpolicella Cl. Fracastoro Ris. '07	♟♟ 6
⊙ Bardolino Chiaretto Cl. '16	♟♟ 2*
⊙ Bardolino Chiaretto Cl. Villa Cordevigo '16	♟♟ 2*
● Bardolino Cl. V. Morlongo '15	♟♟ 2*
○ Fiordilej Passito Codervigo '12	♟♟ 3
● Montemazzano '13	♟♟ 3
● Valpolicella Cl. Sup. Ripasso '15	♟♟ 3
○ Villa Cordevigo Bianco '13	♟♟ 4
○ Custoza '16	♟ 2
○ Garda Chardonnay '16	♟ 2
○ Lugana '16	♟ 3
● Valpolicella Cl. '16	♟ 2
● Villa Cordevigo Rosso '10	♟ 5

★Viticoltori Speri

Loc. Pedemonte
via Fontana, 14
37029 San Pietro in Cariano [VR]
Tel. +39 0457701154
www.speri.com

CELLAR SALES
PRE-BOOKED VISITS
ANNUAL PRODUCTION 350,000 bottles
HECTARES UNDER VINE 60.00
VITICULTURE METHOD Certified Organic
SUSTAINABLE WINERY

Bolstered by a large vineyard that spans many hectares and a deep knowledge of the area and its grapes, the Speri family winery is also one of Valpolicella's most historic. Today the winery has begun expanding its most beautiful plot, Monte Sant'Urbano, where, like the others, only local grapes will be grown according to organic principles of cultivation. Their wines display solidity, stay true to tradition, and age with great elegance. The outstanding 2013 vintage made for a memorable Amarone Sant'Urbano. Its intense, luminous ruby red color prepares us for its compelling aromas, ranging from ripe cherry to pepper, while sprinkling in hints of flowers, thyme and sweet spices. In the mouth it is full and juicy while holding on to its style and grip, thanks to fresh acidity and solid, plucky tannic texture. Their Valpolicella Superiore (of the same name) is a quintessential red characterized by finesse and pressure. The wine is exemplary for highlighting the appellation's more subtle core.

● Amarone della Valpolicella Vign. Monte Sant'Urbano '13	▼▼▼ 7
● Valpolicella Cl. Sup. Sant'Urbano '14	▼▼ 4
● Valpolicella Cl. Sup. Ripasso '15	▼▼ 4
● Valpolicella Cl. '16	▼ 3
● Amarone della Valpolicella Cl. Vign. Monte Sant'Urbano '12	♀♀♀ 7
● Amarone della Valpolicella Cl. Vign. Monte Sant'Urbano '09	♀♀♀ 7
● Amarone della Valpolicella Cl. Vign. Monte Sant'Urbano '08	♀♀♀ 7
● Amarone della Valpolicella Cl. Vign. Monte Sant'Urbano '07	♀♀♀ 7
● Amarone della Valpolicella Cl. Vign. Sant'Urbano '11	♀♀♀ 7

★Viviani

via Mazzano, 8
37020 Negrar [VR]
Tel. +39 0457500286
www.cantinaviviani.com

CELLAR SALES
PRE-BOOKED VISITS
ANNUAL PRODUCTION 80,000 bottles
HECTARES UNDER VINE 10.00
SUSTAINABLE WINERY

In Alta Valpolicella, to be precise in the small village of Mazzano, Claudio Viviani manages the family winery, Viviani, a true benchmark for lovers of Verona's wines. On their estate, the old pergolas alternate with more modern vineyards, while in the cellar, different containers are used for different wines, according to their characteristics and scope. This mix results in a limited selection of wines that perfectly expresses the territory's attributes. Their Amarone Casa dei Bepi didn't make the roster, as it was considered too young to be bottled. And so we focused on a splendid version of Recioto, a passito whose nose offers extraordinary floral freshness, with scents of wild fruit that alternate with spices. In the mouth, sweetness is accompanied by a fresh and tangy acidity, which provide lightness and length. The Amarone Classico was also much appreciated, with its fragrance and dry, plucky palate.

● Amarone della Valpolicella Cl. '12	▼▼ 6
● Recioto della Valpolicella Cl. '11	▼▼ 6
● Valpolicella Cl. '16	▼▼ 2*
● Amarone della Valpolicella Cl. Casa dei Bepi '11	♀♀♀ 8
● Amarone della Valpolicella Cl. Casa dei Bepi '10	♀♀♀ 8
● Amarone della Valpolicella Cl. Casa dei Bepi '09	♀♀♀ 8
● Amarone della Valpolicella Cl. Casa dei Bepi '05	♀♀♀ 8
● Amarone della Valpolicella Cl. Casa dei Bepi '04	♀♀♀ 8
● Valpolicella Cl. Sup. Campo Morar '09	♀♀♀ 5
● Valpolicella Cl. Sup. Campo Morar '05	♀♀♀ 5

Pietro Zanoni

FRAZ. QUINZANO
VIA ARE ZOVO, 16D
37125 VERONA
TEL. +39 0458343977
www.pietrozanoni.it

CELLAR SALES
PRE-BOOKED VISITS
ANNUAL PRODUCTION 25,000 bottles
HECTARES UNDER VINE 6.50

The Quinzano valley slopes down from the hills, extending to Verona's outer limits. It's a valley that, in the past, was exploited for its quarries. Today it is still used and recognized for vine cultivation by winemakers like Pietro Zanoni. Pietro has managed to infuse his selection with vigor and character, seeking out the most interesting clones among the territory's viticultural patrimony and working to bring out their maximum expressivity. His wines display a decisive and crisp character, as well as a capacity for aging slowly and gracefully. The Valpolicella Superiore was simply superb. The wine expresses intense, close-focused, crisp aromas of red fruit, with a side of dried flowers and pepper. In the mouth it is full, juicy and endowed with an outstanding vitality, while its finish is long and dry. The Ripasso, however, goes after sweeter, riper fruit. On the palate it highlights richness without breaching the Amarone's flavor profile. The result is a well-balanced and savory wine.

● Valpolicella Sup. '15	♟♟ 2*
● Amarone della Valpolicella Zovo '12	♟♟ 7
● Valpolicella Sup. Ripasso '15	♟♟ 4
● Amarone della Valpolicella Zovo '11	♟♟ 7
● Amarone della Valpolicella Zovo '10	♟♟ 6
● Amarone della Valpolicella Zovo '09	♟♟ 6
● Amarone della Valpolicella Zovo '07	♟♟ 6
● Recioto della Valpolicella '11	♟♟ 5
● Recioto della Valpolicella '09	♟♟ 4
● Valpolicella Sup. '14	♟♟ 2*
● Valpolicella Sup. '13	♟♟ 2*
● Valpolicella Sup. Campo Denari '11	♟♟ 4
● Valpolicella Sup. Campo Denari '10	♟♟ 4
● Valpolicella Sup. Ripasso '13	♟♟ 4

Pietro Zardini

VIA DON P. FANTONI, 3
37029 SAN PIETRO IN CARIANO [VR]
TEL. +39 0456800989
www.pietrozardini.it

CELLAR SALES
PRE-BOOKED VISITS
ANNUAL PRODUCTION 20,000 bottles
HECTARES UNDER VINE 7.00

After dedicating most of his life to collaborating with local wineries, today Pietro Zardini manages his own in the heart of Valpolicella Classica. The vineyards span just a few hectares, but his long experience has allowed Pietro to realize a selection that finds the right balance between tradition and modern sensibilities, force and elegance, making his one of the most interesting wineries in recent memory. His wines are mostly dedicated to Valpolicella, although there's the occasional creative interpretation of the area's historic grapes. The Amarone Leone Zardini is a wide-ranging 'Riserva' that slowly gives up its aromas of dried cherry and thyme, pepper and forest floor. Yet it manages to engage the palate with a balanced fullness, where alcohol, tannins, and acidity fuse and support one another perfectly. The Amarone Classico was also much appreciated. More approachable in its expression of fruit, it's also endowed with a leaner, more stylish palate, making for a long wine of pleasant drinkability.

● Amarone della Valpolicella Cl. Leone Zardini Ris. '10	♟♟ 6
● Amarone della Valpolicella Cl. '12	♟♟ 6
● Recioto della Valpolicella Cl. '15	♟♟ 4
● Valpolicella Cl. Sup. Ripasso '13	♟♟ 3
● 70 30 Corvina Cabernet '13	♟ 2
● Amarone della Valpolicella '11	♟♟ 6
● Amarone della Valpolicella '10	♟♟ 6
● Amarone della Valpolicella Cl. Leone Zardini Ris. '08	♟♟ 6
● Amarone della Valpolicella Leone Zardini Ris. '09	♟♟ 6
● Valpolicella Sup. Ripasso Austero '12	♟♟ 4
● Valpolicella Sup. Ripasso Austero '11	♟♟ 4

★Zenato

fraz. San Benedetto di Lugana
via San Benedetto, 8
37019 Peschiera del Garda [VR]
Tel. +39 0457550300
www.zenato.it

CELLAR SALES
PRE-BOOKED VISITS
ANNUAL PRODUCTION 2,000,000 bottles
HECTARES UNDER VINE 95.00

The Zenato family's large winery is known throughout the world for the quality of its wines, two in particular, Amarone and Lugana, which are the most representative of Veneto Orientale. Their terrain spans many hectares, though they also have partnerships with local vine growers. Their consistently strong, high-quality selection includes round, boisterous reds and whites whose fruity fragrance has been brought forth. The superb 2011 vintage allowed for production of the winery's flagship wine, Amarone Sergio Zenato. This 'Riserva' offers up aromas of jammy fruit, spices and dark chocolate, while in the mouth, a bold fullness is still well-controlled by acidity and tannins, giving way to a warm, dry finish. The Lugana (of the same name) faced the 2014 vintage by going after aromatic sophistication and a stylish palate - a grippy wine of succulent drinkability.

● Amarone della Valpolicella Cl. Sergio Zenato Ris. '11	🍷🍷🍷	8
○ Lugana Sergio Zenato Ris. '14	🍷🍷	5
● Amarone della Valpolicella Cl. '12	🍷🍷	7
● Cresasso '11	🍷🍷	5
○ Lugana Massoni S. Cristina '16	🍷🍷	3
● Recioto della Valpolicella Cl. '14	🍷🍷	6
● Valpolicella Sup. Ripasso Ripassa '13	🍷🍷	4
● Amarone della Valpolicella Cl. Sergio Zenato Ris. '10	🍷🍷🍷	8
● Amarone della Valpolicella Cl. Sergio Zenato Ris. '09	🍷🍷🍷	8
○ Lugana Sergio Zenato '08	🍷🍷🍷	4

Zeni 1870

via Costabella, 9
37011 Bardolino [VR]
Tel. +39 0457210022
www.zeni.it

CELLAR SALES
PRE-BOOKED VISITS
ANNUAL PRODUCTION 1,000,000 bottles
HECTARES UNDER VINE 25.00

The Zeni family, Fausto, Elena and Federica manage their winery in Bardolino, a winery that over the decades has established itself as a benchmark for those who love the fresh wines of Verona's riviera. Their vineyards extend for some two-dozen hectares, though partnerships with numerous local vine growers are fundamental. Grapes are delivered to their new, operational cellar situated on the hills that overlook Lake Garda. Even if the winery's heart beats in Bardolino, the wine that persuaded our panel more than any other came from nearby Valpolicella. This is their Amarone, dedicated to their father, Nino. This red, released only after lengthy aging, offers up hints of cherry jam and tanned leather, aromatic herbs and pepper, making for a mouth-filling wine that highlights this type of wine's warmer, more enticing core. The Bardolino Vigne Alte is fresh and full. Its richness of flavor and grip are common characteristics of Lake Garda.

● Amarone della Valpolicella Cl. Nino Zeni '10	🍷🍷	8
● Amarone della Valpolicella Cl. '14	🍷🍷	6
● Amarone della Valpolicella Cl. Barrique '12	🍷🍷	7
⊙ Bardolino Chiaretto Cl. Vigne Alte '16	🍷🍷	2*
● Bardolino Cl. Sup. '15	🍷🍷	3
● Bardolino Cl. Vigne Alte '16	🍷🍷	2*
● Costalago Rosso '15	🍷🍷	3
● Valpolicella Sup. Vigne Alte '15	🍷🍷	2*
⊙ Bardolino Chiaretto Brut	🍷	2
● Bardolino Cl. Filari del Nino '16	🍷	5
○ Costalago Bianco '16	🍷	3
● Cruino Rosso '12	🍷	6
○ Lugana Marogne '16	🍷	3
○ Lugana Vigne Alte '16	🍷	2
● Valpolicella Sup. Ripasso Marogne '15	🍷	3

Zonin 1821

VIA BORGOLECCO, 9
36053 GAMBELLARA [VI]
TEL. +39 0444640111
www.zonin.it

CELLAR SALES
PRE-BOOKED VISITS
ANNUAL PRODUCTION 38,000,000 bottles
HECTARES UNDER VINE 2000.00

Founded in Gambellara almost two centuries ago, the Zonin family's winery is one of the largest private operations in Italy, bolstered by two thousand hectares of vineyards situated in some of the most important DOC zones in the country. Their affinity for Veneto shows, with particular attention for those wines that have come to represent the territory throughout the world, Amarone and Prosecco. Its deepest roots, however, are still firmly set in its native soil of Gambellara. And Gambellara Il Giangio is the wine that performed the best. This white doesn't settle for aromatic simplicity and acidity. Rather, it offers up flowery, apple scents with a faintly mineral backdrop that waits before completely revealing itself. In the mouth, its acidity provides the right amount of pressure and grip to complement its leanness. In terms of reds, the typicity of the Ripasso was much appreciated. The wine proved itself to be endowed with an energetic and pleasantly rugged palate.

○ Friuli Aquileia Pinot Grigio '16	♈♈ 2*
○ Gambellara Cl. Il Giangio '16	♈♈ 2*
● Valpolicella Sup. Ripasso '15	♈♈ 3
○ Friuli Aquileia Chardonnay '16	♈ 2
○ Prosecco Brut Cuvée 1821	♈ 2
○ Recioto di Gambellara Cl. Il Giangio '14	♈ 4
○ Recioto di Gambellara Spumante	♈ 3
○ Soave Cl. '16	♈ 2
● Valpolicella Cl. '16	♈ 2
● Amarone della Valpolicella '13	♈♈ 6
● Amarone della Valpolicella '12	♈♈ 5
● Amarone della Valpolicella '11	♈♈ 6
○ Recioto di Gambellara Il Giangio '11	♈♈ 5
● Valpolicella Sup. Ripasso '13	♈♈ 3

Zymè

LOC. SAN FLORIANO
VIA CA' DEL PIPA, 1
37029 SAN PIETRO IN CARIANO [VR]
TEL. +39 0457701108
www.zyme.it

CELLAR SALES
PRE-BOOKED VISITS
ANNUAL PRODUCTION 80,000 bottles
HECTARES UNDER VINE 30.00
SUSTAINABLE WINERY

Over the course of his life, Celestino Gaspari has played many different roles in the world of wine, from a young cellar manager to a consultant. Finally, he decided to dedicate himself completely to his pride and joy, Zymè, a winery whose estate comprises some 30 hectares of vineyards situated in some of the most interesting DOC zones of the region. In his modern, charming cellar, carved out next to an old stone cave, his wines are aged at length, making for a selection of great solidity and character. Celestino's Amarone takes great awareness to produce, as demonstrated by our tasting of the winery's two stars, Classico and Riserva La Mattonara. The former proved to be a veritable explosion of fruit aromas, which entice once in the mouth. Here the wine delivers for fullness and grip. Despite the latter's extraordinary freshness, it seems to hide itself before giving up its perfectly fused richness, style and rigor to the palate.

● Amarone della Valpolicella Cl. '09	♈♈ 8
● Amarone della Valpolicella Cl. La Mattonara Ris. '06	♈♈ 8
○ Il Bianco From Black to White '16	♈♈ 3
● Kairos '12	♈♈ 8
● Oseleta '10	♈♈ 6
● Valpolicella Cl. Sup. '13	♈♈ 5
● Valpolicella Reverie '16	♈♈ 3
● Amarone della Valpolicella Cl. '06	♈♈♈ 8
● Amarone della Valpolicella Cl. La Mattonara Ris. '03	♈♈♈ 8
● Amarone della Valpolicella Cl. La Mattonara Ris. '01	♈♈♈ 8

Ai Galli

VIA LOREDAN, 28
30020 PRAMAGGIORE [VE]
TEL. +39 0421799314
www.aigalli.it

CELLAR SALES
PRE-BOOKED VISITS
ACCOMMODATION AND RESTAURANT SERVICE
ANNUAL PRODUCTION 600,000 bottles
HECTARES UNDER VINE 60.00

○ Lison-Pramaggiore Verduzzo Passito '12	🍷🍷 3
○ Lison-Pramaggiore Chardonnay '15	🍷 3
○ Lison-Pramaggiore Sauvignon Sel. '16	🍷 3

Aldegheri

VIA A. VOLTA, 9
37015 SANT'AMBROGIO DI VALPOLICELLA [VR]
TEL. +30 0456861356
www.cantinealdegheri.it

CELLAR SALES
PRE-BOOKED VISITS
ANNUAL PRODUCTION 800,000 bottles
HECTARES UNDER VINE 52.00

● Amarone della Valpolicella Cl. '12	🍷🍷 6
● Amarone della Valpolicella Cl. Ris. '07	🍷🍷 8
● Amarone della Valpolicella Cl. Santambrogio '12	🍷🍷 6

Andreola

FRAZ. COL SAN MARTINO
VIA CAVRE,19
31010 FARRA DI SOLIGO [TV]
TEL. +39 0438989379
www.andreola.eu

CELLAR SALES
PRE-BOOKED VISITS
ANNUAL PRODUCTION 900,000 bottles
HECTARES UNDER VINE 77.00
SUSTAINABLE WINERY

○ Valdobbiadene Rive Di Refrontolo Brut Col Del Forno '16	🍷🍷 3
○ Valdobbiadene Brut Vign. Dirupo	🍷 3
○ Valdobbiadene Dry '16	🍷 3

Astoria Vini

VIA CREVADA, 12
31020 REFRONTOLO [TV]
TEL. +39 04236699
www.astoria.it

CELLAR SALES
PRE-BOOKED VISITS
ANNUAL PRODUCTION 15,000,000 bottles
HECTARES UNDER VINE 40.00
SUSTAINABLE WINERY

○ Conegliano Valdobbiadene Rive di Refrontolo Sup. Casa Vittorino '16	🍷🍷 3
○ Valdobbiadene Extra Dry '16	🍷🍷 4
○ Cartizze Arzanà	🍷 4

Balestri Valda

VIA MONTI, 44
37038 SOAVE [VR]
TEL. +39 0457675393
www.vinibalestrivalda.com

CELLAR SALES
PRE-BOOKED VISITS
ANNUAL PRODUCTION 65,000 bottles
HECTARES UNDER VINE 13.00
VITICULTURE METHOD Certified Organic
SUSTAINABLE WINERY

○ Soave Cl. '16	🍷🍷 2*
○ Recioto di Soave Cl. '15	🍷 5

Beato Bartolomeo da Breganze

VIA ROMA, 100
36042 BREGANZE [VI]
TEL. +39 0445873112
www.cantinabreganze.it

CELLAR SALES
ANNUAL PRODUCTION 2,500,000 bottles
HECTARES UNDER VINE 700.00

● Breganze Cabernet Sup. Savardo '15	🍷🍷 2*
○ Breganze Torcolato '13	🍷🍷 5
● Breganze Merlot Sup. Savardo '15	🍷 2
○ Breganze Vespaiolo Sup. Savardo '16	🍷 2

Bellussi Spumanti

VIA ERIZZO, 215
31049 VALDOBBIADENE [TV]
TEL. +39 0423983411
www.bellussi.com

CELLAR SALES
PRE-BOOKED VISITS
ANNUAL PRODUCTION 1,300,000 bottles
HECTARES UNDER VINE

○ Valdobbiadene Brut Belcanto	♟♟	3
○ Valdobbiadene Extra Dry Belcanto	♟♟	3
○ Valdobbiadene Brut	♟	3
○ Valdobbiadene Extra Dry	♟	3

Bergamini

LOC. COLÀ
VIA CÀ NOVA, 3
37017 LAZISE [VR]
TEL. +39 0456490407
www.bergaminivini.it

CELLAR SALES
PRE-BOOKED VISITS
ANNUAL PRODUCTION 65,000 bottles
HECTARES UNDER VINE 13.00

● Bardolino '16	♟♟	2*
○ Custoza '16	♟♟	2*
● Bardolino Chiaretto '16	♟	2
○ Custoza Sup. '15	♟	2

Bonotto delle Tezze

FRAZ. TEZZE DI PIAVE
VIA DUCA D'AOSTA, 36
31028 VAZZOLA [TV]
TEL. +39 0438488323
www.bonottodelletezze.it

CELLAR SALES
PRE-BOOKED VISITS
ANNUAL PRODUCTION 150,000 bottles
HECTARES UNDER VINE 48.00

● Piave Malanotte '13	♟♟	G
● Raboso Passito '14	♟♟	5
● Piave Carmenere Barabane '15	♟	3
● Piave Merlot Spezza '15	♟	3

F.lli Bortolin

FRAZ. SANTO STEFANO
VIA MENEGAZZI, 5
31049 VALDOBBIADENE [TV]
TEL. +39 0423900135
www.bortolin.com

CELLAR SALES
PRE-BOOKED VISITS
ANNUAL PRODUCTION 300,000 bottles
HECTARES UNDER VINE 20.00

○ Valdobbiadene Brut	♟♟	2*
○ Valdobbiadene Dry	♟♟	2*
○ Valdobbiadene Extra Dry	♟♟	2*
○ Valdobbiadene Brut Zan	♟	3

Cà Rovere

VIA BOCARA
36045 ALONTE [VI]
TEL. +39 0444436234
www.carovere.it

CELLAR SALES
PRE-BOOKED VISITS
ANNUAL PRODUCTION 50,000 bottles
HECTARES UNDER VINE 30.00
SUSTAINABLE WINERY

○ Blanc de Blanc Brut M. Cl. '12	♟♟	4
○ Brut M. Cl. '12	♟	4
○ Demi Sec M. Cl. '11	♟	4
○ Rosé Extra Dry M. Cl. '11	♟	4

Ca' Corner

VIA CA CORNER SUD, 55
30020 MEOLO [VE]
TEL. +39 042161191
www.vinicacorner.com

CELLAR SALES
PRE-BOOKED VISITS
ANNUAL PRODUCTION 100,000 bottles
HECTARES UNDER VINE 20.00

● Petalo Rosso '13	♟	3
● Piave Merlot '15	♟	2
○ Prosecco Extra Dry	♟	2
● Raboso '15	♟	2

Ca' Ferri

VIA CA' FERRI, 43
35020 CASALSERUGO [PD]
TEL. +39 049655518
www.vinicaferri.com

CELLAR SALES
PRE-BOOKED VISITS
ANNUAL PRODUCTION 10,000 bottles
HECTARES UNDER VINE 8.00

● Colli Euganei Rosso Taurilio '15	♀♀ 2*
● Rubro dei Colli '14	♀ 2

Conte Collalto

VIA XXIV MAGGIO, 1
31058 SUSEGANA [TV]
TEL. +39 0438435811
www.cantine-collalto.it

CELLAR SALES
PRE-BOOKED VISITS
ANNUAL PRODUCTION 850,000 bottles
HECTARES UNDER VINE 164.00
SUSTAINABLE WINERY

○ Conegliano Valdobbiadene Brut	♀♀ 3
● Piave Cabernet Torrai Ris. '11	♀♀ 5
○ Rosabianco '16	♀ 2
○ Valdobbiadene Extra Dry	♀ 3

Corte Figaretto

FRAZ. POIANO
VIA CLOCEGO, 48A
37142 VERONA
TEL. +39 0458700753
www.cortefigaretto.it

CELLAR SALES
PRE-BOOKED VISITS
ANNUAL PRODUCTION 49,500 bottles
HECTARES UNDER VINE 7.50

● Amarone della Valpolicella Valpantena Brolo del Figaretto '13	♀♀ 5
● Amarone della Valpolicella Valpantena Graal '13	♀♀ 6

Corte Mainente

V.LE DELLA VITTORIA, 45
37038 SOAVE [VR]
TEL. +39 0457680303
www.cantinamainente.com

CELLAR SALES
PRE-BOOKED VISITS
ANNUAL PRODUCTION 20,000 bottles
HECTARES UNDER VINE 12.00
SUSTAINABLE WINERY

○ Soave Cl. Tovo al Pigno '16	♀♀ 2*
○ Soave Netrroir '15	♀♀ 3
○ Recioto di Soave Luna Nova '15	♀ 3
○ Soave Cengelle '16	♀ 2

Costa Arente

LOC. COSTA, 86
37023 GREZZANA [VR]
TEL. +39 0422864511
www.arente.it

PRE-BOOKED VISITS
ANNUAL PRODUCTION 50,000 bottles
HECTARES UNDER VINE 17.00
SUSTAINABLE WINERY

● Amarone della Valpolicella '13	♀♀ 7
● Valpolicella Sup. Ripasso '15	♀ 4
● Valpolicella Valpantena '16	♀ 3

Paolo Cottini

FRAZ. CASTELROTTO
VIA BELVEDERE, 29
37029 VERONA
TEL. +39 0456837293
www.paolocottini.it

CELLAR SALES
PRE-BOOKED VISITS
ANNUAL PRODUCTION 40,000 bottles
HECTARES UNDER VINE 3.50

● Amarone della Valpolicella '13	♀♀ 6
● PaCo '14	♀ 3
● Valpolicella Cl. '16	♀ 2
● Valpolicella Cl. Sup. Ripasso '14	♀ 4

Cantina di Custoza

LOC. CUSTOZA
VIA STAFFALO, 1
37066 SOMMACAMPAGNA [VR]
TEL. +39 045516200
www.cantinadicustoza.it

CELLAR SALES
PRE-BOOKED VISITS
ANNUAL PRODUCTION 4,000,000 bottles
HECTARES UNDER VINE 1000.00
VITICULTURE METHOD Certified Organic

● Amarone della Valpolicella Cl. Custodia '11	♟♟ 5
○ Custoza Sup. Custodia '15	♟♟ 3
● Cuordisasso Custodia '13	♟ 3
○ Custoza Val dei Molini '16	♟ 2

F.lli Degani

FRAZ. VALGATARA
VIA TOBELE, 3A
37020 MARANO DI VALPOLICELLA [VR]
TEL. +39 0457703360
www.deganivini.it

CELLAR SALES
PRE-BOOKED VISITS
ANNUAL PRODUCTION 100,000 bottles
HECTARES UNDER VINE 9.00

● Amarone della Valpolicella Cl. '13	♟♟ 5
● Amarone della Valpolicella Cl. La Rosta '13	♟♟ 5
● Valpolicella Cl. Sup. Cicilio Ripasso '14	♟♟ 3
● Valpolicella Cl. '16	♟ 2

La Farra

VIA SAN FRANCESCO, 44
31010 FARRA DI SOLIGO [TV]
TEL. +39 0438801242
www.lafarra.it

CELLAR SALES
PRE-BOOKED VISITS
ANNUAL PRODUCTION 200,000 bottles
HECTARES UNDER VINE 20.00

○ Valdobbiadene Extra Dry	♟♟ 2*
○ Valdobbiadene Rive di Farra di Soligo Extra Dry '16	♟♟ 3

Dal Din

VIA MONTEGRAPPA, 29
31020 VIDOR [TV]
TEL. +39 0423987295
www.daldin.it

CELLAR SALES
PRE-BOOKED VISITS
ANNUAL PRODUCTION 400,000 bottles
HECTARES UNDER VINE 12.00
SUSTAINABLE WINERY

○ Valdobbiadene Brut	♟♟ 3
○ Valdobbiadene Brut Dosaggio Zero Ry	♟♟ 3
○ Valdobbiadene Extra Dry	♟♟ 3
○ Valdobbiadene Dry Vidoro Mill. '16	♟ 3

Francesco Drusian

FRAZ. BIGOLINO
VIA ANCHE, 1
31030 VALDOBBIADENE [TV]
TEL. +39 0423982151
www.drusian.it

CELLAR SALES
PRE-BOOKED VISITS
ANNUAL PRODUCTION 1,200,000 bottles
HECTARES UNDER VINE 80.00
SUSTAINABLE WINERY

○ Cartizze	♟♟ 4
○ Valdobbiadene Dry Mill. '16	♟♟ 3
○ Valdobbiadene Brut	♟ 3
○ Valdobbiadene Extra Dry	♟ 3

Lenotti

VIA SANTA CRISTINA, 1
37011 BARDOLINO [VR]
TEL. +39 0457210484
www.lenotti.com

CELLAR SALES
PRE-BOOKED VISITS
ANNUAL PRODUCTION 1,400,000 bottles
HECTARES UNDER VINE 105.00

○ Bardolino Chiaretto Cl. Decus '16	♟♟ 3
○ Custoza '16	♟♟ 2*
● Valpolicella Cl. Sup.Ripasso Le Crosare '14	♟♟ 5

Giuseppe Lonardi

VIA DELLE POSTE, 2
37020 MARANO DI VALPOLICELLA [VR]
TEL. +39 0457/55154
www.lonardivini.it

CELLAR SALES
PRE-BOOKED VISITS
ACCOMMODATION
ANNUAL PRODUCTION 51,000 bottles
HECTARES UNDER VINE 7.00

● Amarone della Valpolicella Cl. '13	♟♟ 8
● Recioto della Valpolicella Cl. Le Arele '14	♟♟ 6
● Valpolicella Cl. Sup. Ripasso '15	♟♟ 4
● Valpolicella Cl. '15	♟ 2

Maeli

VIA DIETRO CERO, 1c
35031 BAONE [PD]
TEL. +39 0429538144
www.maeliwine.it

CELLAR SALES
PRE-BOOKED VISITS
ANNUAL PRODUCTION 4 bottles
HECTARES UNDER VINE 130.00

● Colli Euganei Rosso Infinito '15	♟♟ 5
○ Colli Euganei Fior d'Arancio Bianco Infinto '15	♟♟ 5
○ Colli Euganei Fior d'Arancio Spumante '15	♟ 5

Le Mandolare

LOC. BROGNOLIGO
VIA SAMBUCO, 180
37032 MONTEFORTE D'ALPONE [VR]
TEL. +39 0456175083
www.cantinalemandolare.com

CELLAR SALES
PRE-BOOKED VISITS
ANNUAL PRODUCTION 65,000 bottles
HECTARES UNDER VINE 20.00

○ Recioto di Soave Le Schiavette '15	♟♟ 5
○ Soave Il Roccolo '16	♟♟ 2*
○ Soave Monte Sella '14	♟♟ 3
○ Soave Corte Menini '16	♟ 2

Le Manzane

LOC. BAGNOLO
VIA MASET, 3
31020 SAN PIETRO DI FELETTO [TV]
TEL. +39 0438486606
www.lemanzane.it

CELLAR SALES
PRE-BOOKED VISITS
ANNUAL PRODUCTION 700,000 bottles
HECTARES UNDER VINE 40.00

○ Conegliano Valdobbiadene Brut	♟♟ 3
○ Conegliano Valdobbiadene Extra Dry	♟ 3
○ Conegliano Valdobbiadene Extra Dry 20.10 '16	♟ 3

Marsuret

LOC. GUIA DI VALDOBBIADENE
VIA BARCH, 17
31049 VALDOBBIADENE [TV]
TEL. +39 0423900139
www.marsuret.it

CELLAR SALES
PRE-BOOKED VISITS
ANNUAL PRODUCTION 600,000 bottles
HECTARES UNDER VINE 50.00

○ Conegliano Valdobbiadene Cartizze	♟♟ 5
○ Valdobbiadene Brut Rive di Guia '16	♟♟ 3
○ Valdobbiadene Brut San Boldo '16	♟ 3
○ Valdobbiadene Extra Dry Il Soller	♟ 3

Firmino Miotti

VIA BROGLIATI CONTRO, 53
36042 BREGANZE [VI]
TEL. +39 0445873006
www.firminomiotti.it

CELLAR SALES
PRE-BOOKED VISITS
ANNUAL PRODUCTION 25,000 bottles
HECTARES UNDER VINE 5.00

● Breganze Cabernet '13	♟♟ 3
○ Breganze Torcolato '08	♟♟ 5
○ Sampagna Frizzante '16	♟♟ 2*
● Gruajo	♟ 3

Monte Cillario

VIA SANTA CRISTINA, 1B
37124 VERONA
TEL. +39 045941387
www.montecillariovini.com

CELLAR SALES
PRE-BOOKED VISITS
ANNUAL PRODUCTION 22,000 bottles
HECTARES UNDER VINE 30.00
SUSTAINABLE WINERY

- Amarone della Valpolicella Casa Erbisti '13   ♟♟ 6
- Amarone della Valpolicella
  Rinaldo Marchesini Ris. '12   ♟♟ 7
- Valpolicella Sup. Ripasso I Berari '14   ♟ 4

Montecariano

VIA VALENA, 3
37029 SAN PIETRO IN CARIANO [VR]
TEL. +39 0456838335
www.montecariano.it

CELLAR SALES
PRE-BOOKED VISITS
ANNUAL PRODUCTION 20,000 bottles
HECTARES UNDER VINE 21.00

- Amarone della Valpolicella Cl. '12   ♟♟ 7
- Valpolicella Cl. Sup. Corte Monte '14   ♟♟ 3

Monteci

VIA SAN MICHELE, 34
37026 PESCANTINA [VR]
TEL. +39 0457151188
www.monteci.it

CELLAR SALES
PRE-BOOKED VISITS
ANNUAL PRODUCTION 500,000 bottles
HECTARES UNDER VINE 190.00
VITICULTURE METHOD Certified Organic
SUSTAINABLE WINERY

- Valpolicella Cl. '16   ♟♟ 2*
- Valpolicella Cl. Sup. Ripasso '13   ♟♟ 3
- Amarone della Valpolicella Cl. '12   ♟ 6
- Bardolino '16   ♟ 2

Walter Nardin

LOC. RONCADELLE
VIA FONTANE, 5
31024 ORMELLE [TV]
TEL. +39 0422851622
www.vinwalternardin.it

PRE-BOOKED VISITS
ANNUAL PRODUCTION 350,000 bottles
HECTARES UNDER VINE 30.00

- Rosso della Ghiaia La Zerbaia '13   ♟♟ 4
- Tai La Zerbaia '15   ♟♟ 2*
- Lison-Pramaggiore Lison Chardonnay '16   ♟ 2
- Rosso del Nane La Zerbaia '15   ♟ 2

Orto di Venezia

LOC. ISOLA DI SANT'ERASMO
VIA DELLE MOTTE, 1
30141 VENEZIA
TEL. +39 0415237410
www.ortodivenezia.com

ANNUAL PRODUCTION 15,000 bottles
HECTARES UNDER VINE 4.50

- Orto '15   ♟♟ 5

Pegoraro

VIA CALBIN, 24
36024 MOSSANO [VI]
TEL. +39 0444886461
www.cantinapegoraro.it

ANNUAL PRODUCTION 30,000 bottles
HECTARES UNDER VINE 7.00

- Colli Berici Tai Rosso '16   ♟♟ 2*
- Colli Berici Tai '16   ♟ 2

Il Pignetto

LOC. PIGNETTO, 108B
37012 BUSSOLENGO [VR]
TEL. +39 0457151232
www.cantinailpignetto.com

CELLAR SALES
PRE-BOOKED VISITS
ACCOMMODATION
ANNUAL PRODUCTION 50,000 bottles
HECTARES UNDER VINE 8.00
SUSTAINABLE WINERY

⊙ Bardolino Chiaretto '16	♀♀ 2*
○ Custoza 218 '15	♀♀ 3
○ Custoza '16	♀ 2

Tenuta Polvaro

VIA POLVARO, 35
30020 ANNONE VENETO [VE]
TEL. +39 0421281023
www.tenutapolvaro.it

CELLAR SALES
PRE-BOOKED VISITS
ANNUAL PRODUCTION 300,000 bottles
HECTARES UNDER VINE 60.00

○ Polvaro Oro '16	♀♀ 2*
● Venezia Cabernet Sauvignon '15	♀ 2
● Venezia Merlot '15	♀ 1*
○ Venezia Pinot Grigio '16	♀ 2

Umberto Portinari

LOC. BROGNOLIGO
VIA SANTO STEFANO, 2
37032 MONTEFORTE D'ALPONE [VR]
TEL. +39 0456175087
portinarivini@libero.it

CELLAR SALES
PRE-BOOKED VISITS
ANNUAL PRODUCTION 30,000 bottles
HECTARES UNDER VINE 4.00

○ Soave Albare '15	♀♀ 2*
○ Soave Cl. Ronchetto '15	♀♀ 2*
○ Soave U. P. '15	♀♀ 3
○ Soave Cl. Santo Stefano '14	♀ 3

Punto Zero

VIA MONTE PALÙ, 1
36045 LONIGO [VI]
TEL. +39 049659881
www.puntozerowine.it

CELLAR SALES
PRE-BOOKED VISITS
ANNUAL PRODUCTION 16,000 bottles
HECTARES UNDER VINE 11.00

● Dimezzo '13	♀♀ 5
○ Trasparenza '16	♀♀ 3
● Idea '16	♀ 3

Quota 101

VIA MALTERRENO, 12
35038 TORREGLIA [PD]
TEL. +39 0425410922
www.quota101.com

ANNUAL PRODUCTION 35,000 bottles
HECTARES UNDER VINE 7.50

○ Colli Euganei Fior d'Arancio '16	♀♀ 3
○ Colli Euganei Fior d'Arancio Passito Il Gelso di Lapo '14	♀♀ 5
● Colli Euganei Rosso Ortone '14	♀ 3

Raval

VIA RAVAL, 1
37011 BARDOLINO [VR]
TEL. +39 045 7236569

ANNUAL PRODUCTION 95,000 bottles
HECTARES UNDER VINE 12.00

● Bardolino Cl. '16	♀♀ 2*
● Bardolino Cl. Sup. '15	♀♀ 2*
⊙ Bardolino Chiaretto '16	♀ 2

Rechsteiner

FRAZ. PIAVON
VIA FRASSENÈ, 2
31046 ODERZO [TV]
TEL. +39 0422752074
www.rechsteiner.it

CELLAR SALES
PRE-BOOKED VISITS
ACCOMMODATION AND RESTAURANT SERVICE
ANNUAL PRODUCTION 150,000 bottles
HECTARES UNDER VINE 48.00
SUSTAINABLE WINERY

● Piave Carmenere '15	🍷🍷 2*
○ Manzoni Bianco '16	🍷 2
○ Rosato Dry '16	🍷 3
○ Venezia Pinot Grigio '16	🍷 3

San Nazario

LOC. CORTELÀ
VIA MONTE VERSA, 1519
35030 Vò [PD]
TEL. +39 0499940194
www.vinisannazario.it

CELLAR SALES
PRE-BOOKED VISITS
ANNUAL PRODUCTION 50,000 bottles
HECTARES UNDER VINE 10.00
VITICULTURE METHOD Certified Organic

○ Colli Euganei Fior d'Arancio Spumante '16	🍷🍷 4
● Colli Euganei Rosso Brolo delle Femmine '15	🍷🍷 2*
● Prà dei Mistri '15	🍷🍷 3

Savian

LE VITTORIA, 22
30020 ANNONE VENETO [VE]
TEL. +39 0422864068
www.savianvini.it

HECTARES UNDER VINE
VITICULTURE METHOD Certified Organic
SUSTAINABLE WINERY

○ Venezia Cabernet Franc '16	🍷🍷 2*
○ Lison Cl. '16	🍷 2
● Lison-Pramaggiore Refosco P.R. '16	🍷 2
○ Venezia Pinot Grigio '16	🍷 2

Tenuta Solar

VIA DANTE, 125
37032 MONTEFORTE D'ALPONE [VR]
TEL. +39 0456100550

○ Recioto di Soave Cl. El Re '10	🍷🍷 5
○ Soave Cl. Le Bancole '16	🍷🍷 3
○ Soave Cl. Sup. Le Caselle '16	🍷 3

Spagnol - Col del Sas

VIA SCANDOLERA, 51
31020 VIDOR [TV]
TEL. +39 0423987177
www.coldelsas.it

CELLAR SALES
PRE-BOOKED VISITS
ANNUAL PRODUCTION 450,000 bottles
HECTARES UNDER VINE 32.00

● Valdobbiadene Brut Col del Sas '16	🍷🍷 2*
● Valdobbiadene Brut Rive di Solighetto '15	🍷🍷 3
● Valdobbiadene Extra Dry Col del Sas '16	🍷 2

Tanoré

FRAZ. SAN PIETRO DI BARBOZZA
VIA MONT DI CARTIZZE, 3
31040 VALDOBBIADENE [TV]
TEL. +39 0423975770
www.tanore.it

CELLAR SALES
PRE-BOOKED VISITS
ANNUAL PRODUCTION 90,000 bottles
HECTARES UNDER VINE 10.00

○ Cartizze	🍷🍷 4
○ Valdobbiadene Brut Rive di Guia '14	🍷🍷 3
○ Valdobbiadene Extra Dry	🍷🍷 2*
○ Valdobbiadene Brut	🍷 3

Terra Felice

VIA MARLUNGHE, 19
35032 ARQUÀ PETRARCA [PD]
TEL. +39 0429718143
agri.terrafelice@gmail.com

ANNUAL PRODUCTION 50,000 bottles
HECTARES UNDER VINE 10.00

● Cabernet '12	♟♟ 5
● Pianoro '13	♟♟ 2*
○ Chardonnay '15	♟ 2
○ Sereno '15	♟ 2

Tenute Ugolini

S.DA DI BONAMICO, 11
37029 SAN PIETRO IN CARIANO [VR]
TEL. +39 0457703830
www.tenuteugolini.it

ANNUAL PRODUCTION 50,000 bottles
HECTARES UNDER VINE 22.00

● Valpolicella Cl. Sup. San Michele '13	♟♟ 4
● Amarone della Valpolicella Cl. Valle Alta '12	♟ 7
● Recioto della Valpolicella Cl. Valle Lena '15	♟ 5

Villa Angarano

FRAZ. SANT'EUSEBIO
VIA CONTRÀ CORTE, 15
36061 BASSANO DEL GRAPPA [VI]
TEL. +39 0424503086
www.villaangarano.com

CELLAR SALES
PRE-BOOKED VISITS
ANNUAL PRODUCTION 30,000 bottles
HECTARES UNDER VINE 8.00

● Breganze Rosso Angarano '14	♟♟ 3
○ Ca' Michiel '14	♟♟ 4
● Quare di Angarano '13	♟♟ 5
○ Breganze Vesapiolo Bianco Angarano '16	♟ 2

Villa Canestrari

VIA DANTE BROGLIO, 2
37030 COLOGNOLA AI COLLI [VR]
TEL. +39 0457650074
www.villacanestrari.com

CELLAR SALES
PRE-BOOKED VISITS
ANNUAL PRODUCTION 150,000 bottles
HECTARES UNDER VINE 20.00

● Amarone della Valpolicella 1888 Ris. '10	♟♟ 8
● Amarone della Valpolicella Plenum '10	♟♟ 7
○ Soave Sup. Ris. '14	♟♟ 3
○ Soave V. di Sande '16	♟ 2

Villa Minelli

VIA POSTIOMA, 66
31020 VILLORBA [TV]
TEL. +39 0422912355
www.villaminelli.it

CELLAR SALES
PRE-BOOKED VISITS
ANNUAL PRODUCTION 40,000 bottles
HECTARES UNDER VINE 9.50

○ Passito '13	♟♟ 3
○ Pinot Grigio '14	♟♟ 2*
○ Chardonnay '16	♟ 2
○ Malvasia '16	♟ 3

Zardetto

VIA MARTIRI DELLE FOIBE, 18
31015 CONEGLIANO [TV]
TEL. +39 0438394969
www.zardettoprosecco.com

CELLAR SALES
ANNUAL PRODUCTION 2,000,000 bottles
HECTARES UNDER VINE 40.00
VITICULTURE METHOD Certified Organic

○ Conegliano Valdobbiadene Brut	
Rive di Ogliano Treventi '16	♟♟ 3
○ Conegliano Valdobbiadene	
Rive di Cozzuolo Viti di San Mor '15	♟♟ 3

FRIULI VENEZIA GIULIA

Friuli's wines are getting 'whiter' by the year. The eastern Alps see an immense natural amphitheater slope down towards the Adriatic Sea. Its eastern winds and southern sea breeze guarantee that just the right amount of rain reaches Collio and Colli Orientali. These alternate with the cooler air that comes in off the Alps; it's a circumstance that makes for excellent air circulation and a healthy range of temperatures. When it comes to the region's soil, its hills are characterized by porous marl limestone, or 'ponca', while the plains see terrain rich in gravel. Once you understand these basic features, it's easy to see why whites dominated this year. Reds are made, some of them excellent, and often with native grapes (such as Refosco dal Penduncolo Rosso or Schioppettino). But Friuli's whites are simply irresistible. We usually open with Collio, and this year is no different, with some 11 wines recognized. Among these we'd like to point out the felicitous return of Venica with their outstanding 2016 Sauvignon Ronco delle Mele, and Villa Russiz, with their excellent 2016 Pinot Bianco. This last is an important winery in terms of quality, but also because it supports a foundation that helps troubled youth. Even if it's not designated, Jermann's 2015 Vintage Tunina is a full-blooded Collio, and this year it's celebrating its 40th vintage. It's a historic wine for Friuli and beyond. Colli Orientali is a rich and complex appellation whose excellence spans white blends, Malvasia, Picolit, Pinot Bianco and Sauvignon, as well as Friulano, of course, a cultivar that does well in all the region's territories. Specogna is welcomed into the Tre Bicchieri club with its white blend, the 2015 Identità. This year sees another important anniversary, the 30th vintage of Colli Orientali's sparkler, the 2013 Ribolla Gialla. It's a wine made by Eugenio Collavini, the man who deserves credit for having first identified the potential of the cultivar (which is enjoying extraordinary success). Isonzo, an area where regional classics like Sauvignon and Friuliano express their structure and vigor, saw four wines recognized, thus affirming its importance. Karst, a land of great, macerated whites, brought us two wines that can't be missed, Podversic's 2013 Malvasia and Skerk's 2015 Ograde. Le Monde's elegant, fruit-driven 2016 Pinot Bianco, the wine that best expresses the potential of this favorable terroir, closes out our regional overview.

Tenuta di Angoris

LOC. ANGORIS, 7
34071 CORMÒNS [GO]
TEL. +39 048160923
www.angoris.it

CELLAR SALES
PRE-BOOKED VISITS
RESTAURANT SERVICE
ANNUAL PRODUCTION 650,000 bottles
HECTARES UNDER VINE 90.00
SUSTAINABLE WINERY

With 110 hectares of vineyards that stretch across some of the best terrain of the region, Tenuta di Angoris can feel good about their prospects. Though the estate's roots go way back to 1648, the Locatelli family took over the winery in 1968. They were able to take full advantage of Angoris's potential, achieving strong production figures while maintaining high quality, and establishing Angoris as a leader in the region. Credit must be given to the entrepreneurial skills of Marta Locatelli. Along with her winemaker, Alessandro Dal Zovo, and a dynamic, close-knit team, she has been able to catapult the winery into a new phase of quality and growth. A well-known Italian proverb says "all good things come in threes" and this is the third time in a row that an Angoris wine has earned a Tre Bicchieri. It's the 2015 Collio Bianco Riserva, a splendid mix of Friulano and Sauvignon with a dash of Malvasia.

Antonutti

FRAZ. COLLOREDO DI PRATO
VIA D'ANTONI, 21
33037 PASIAN DI PRATO [UD]
TEL. +39 0432662001
www.antonuttivini.it

CELLAR SALES
PRE-BOOKED VISITS
ANNUAL PRODUCTION 780,000 bottles
HECTARES UNDER VINE 51.00
SUSTAINABLE WINERY

Despite their sizable production volumes, Antonutti has managed to remain a family-run winery that is deeply rooted in the territory. And while they are open to innovation, they are also respectful of tradition. They have the persistence and skill of Adriana Antonutti to thank for their success, along with her husband Lino and their children Caterina and Nicola. It was Adriana's grandfather, Ignazio, who was inspired by the rocky terrain of Grave del Friuli to start growing wine - in time, other generations followed. Their rich selection of wines includes something for everyone. Their constant and ingrained quality has been confirmed by unanimous acclaim from our tasting panel. The 2016 Friulano and the 2016 Pinot Grigio Ramato are ambassadors of a great vintage and stand out for their fragrance and consistency. The vigorous and concentrated 2014 Ros di Murì is also excellent.

○ Collio Bianco Giulio Locatelli Ris. '15	♟♟♟ 4*
○ FCO Chardonnay Spiule Giulio Locatelli Ris. '15	♟♟ 4
○ 16 48 Brut '13	♟♟ 5
○ COF Picolit '11	♟♟ 6
○ Collio Pinot Grigio '16	♟♟ 3
○ FCO Friulano '16	♟♟ 3
● FCO Merlot Ravost Giulio Locatelli Ris. '14	♟♟ 4
● FCO Pignolo Giulio Locatelli Ris. '12	♟♟ 5
● FCO Schioppettino '15	♟♟ 3
○ Friuli Isonzo Friulano '16	♟ 2
○ Friuli Isonzo Pinot Bianco '16	♟ 2
○ FCO Chardonnay Spiule '13	♟♟♟ 4*
○ FCO Friulano '15	♟♟♟ 3*
○ Collio Bianco '12	♟♟ 3*
○ FCO Chardonnay Spiule '14	♟♟ 4

○ Ant Brut M. Cl. '12	♟♟
○ Friuli Grave Friulano '16	♟♟
○ Friuli Grave Pinot Grigio Ramato '16	♟♟
● Ros di Murì '14	♟♟
○ Friuli Grave Chardonnay '16	♟
● Friuli Grave Merlot '15	♟
○ Friuli Grave Pinot Grigio '16	♟
● Friuli Grave Pinot Nero '16	♟
● Friuli Grave Refosco P. R. '15	♟
○ Ribolla Gialla '16	♟
○ Ant Brut M. Cl. '11	♟♟
● Friuli Grave Cabernet Sauvignon '14	♟♟
● Friuli Grave Cabernet Sauvignon '13	♟♟
● Friuli Grave Merlot '14	♟♟
● Friuli Grave Refosco P. R. '14	♟♟
○ Friuli Grave Sauvignon '14	♟♟

Bastianich

LOC. GAGLIANO
VIA DAHNAZZACCO, 44/2
33043 CIVIDALE DEL FRIULI [UD]
TEL. +39 0432700943
www.bastianich.com

CELLAR SALES
PRE-BOOKED VISITS
ACCOMMODATION AND RESTAURANT SERVICE
ANNUAL PRODUCTION 270,000 bottles
HECTARES UNDER VINE 35.00

Joe Bastianich and his mother Lidia, both
owners of a number of restaurants abroad,
deserve credit for being true ambassadors
of the 'Made in Italy' brand. For years they
have exported and promoted Italy's
gastronomic excellence throughout the
world, especially its wine. In 1997, Joe,
aware of Friuli's potential for white wine,
decided to found Bastianich, a winery that
he personally manages. He still makes
frequent visits to the facility in Gagliano,
near Cividale, where his close-knit team
works under the expert guidance of
winemaker Emilio Del Medico and with the
precious support of Maurizio Castelli. The
2015 Vespa Bianco has proved it belongs at
the top with the best vintages. It thoroughly
deserved to reach the finals for its aromatic
impact and especially the creaminess of its
palate. The 2016 Sauvignon also gave a
great performance. It's fresh, crisp and
particularly fruity, but also resinous and
minty.

FCO Sauvignon '16	♟♟ 3*
Vespa Bianco '15	♟♟ 5
FCO Friulano '16	♟♟ 3
FCO Pinot Grigio '16	♟♟ 3
FCO Ribolla Gialla '16	♟ 3
COF Tocai Friulano Plus '02	♟♟♟ 3*
Vespa Bianco '03	♟♟♟ 4
Vespa Bianco '01	♟♟♟ 4
Vespa Bianco '00	♟♟♟ 3
Vespa Bianco '99	♟♟♟ 3*
Plus '13	♟♟ 6
Plus '09	♟♟ 6
Vespa Bianco '13	♟♟ 5
Vespa Bianco '12	♟♟ 5
Vespa Rosso '11	♟♟ 5
Vespa Rosso '10	♟♟ 5

Tenuta Beltrame

FRAZ. PRIVANO
LOC. ANTONINI, 4
33050 BAGNARIA ARSA [UD]
TEL. +39 0432923670
www.tenutabeltrame.it

CELLAR SALES
PRE-BOOKED VISITS
ANNUAL PRODUCTION 80,000 bottles
HECTARES UNDER VINE 25.00

In 1991, the Beltrame family bought an
estate that had been the property of the
Antoninis, an aristocratic family of counts,
near the old fortress of Palmanova. The
area includes the original Antonini family
residence (which goes back to the 1400s)
and 40 hectares of land, 25 of which are
vineyards. The then young Cristian
Beltrame proceeded to renovate the
buildings and the old wine cellars. With
impressive foresight, he replanted the
vineyards, prioritizing native grapes,
especially reds, which are famous for best
representing the distinctive clay soil of the
Friuli Aquileia DOC zone. Today his
vineyards are ready and Cristian is reaping
the fruit of his brave choices. Recent
innovations in the wines, plus the restyling
of the bottles and labels, meant we weren't
able to taste enough samples to get a
precise idea about the winery's new style.
However, we did like the aromas and
consistency of their wines.

○ Pinot Grigio '16	♟♟ 3
● Pinot Nero '14	♟♟ 3
○ Friuli Chardonnay '16	♟ 3
○ Friuli Friulano '16	♟ 3
○ Friuli Sauvignon '16	♟ 3
● Friuli Aquileia Cabernet Franc '14	♟♟ 3
● Friuli Aquileia Cabernet Sauvignon '14	♟♟ 3
● Friuli Aquileia Cabernet Sauvignon Ris. '12	♟♟ 3
○ Friuli Aquileia Chardonnay Pribus '13	♟♟ 3
● Friuli Aquileia Merlot Ris. '13	♟♟ 4
● Friuli Aquileia Refosco P.R. '14	♟♟ 3
○ Pinot Grigio '15	♟♟ 3
● Rebus '12	♟♟ 3

Borgo delle Oche

VIA BORGO ALPI, 5
33098 VALVASONE ARZENE [PN]
TEL. +39 0434840640
www.borgodelleoche.it

CELLAR SALES
PRE-BOOKED VISITS
ACCOMMODATION
ANNUAL PRODUCTION 35,000 bottles
HECTARES UNDER VINE 7.00
SUSTAINABLE WINERY

The city of Valvasone, in Pordenone, features a medieval town center that's divided into smaller hamlets. And it was here, in in one of these, the Borgo delle Oche, that Luisa Menini and Nicola Pittini founded their winery in 2004. Rather than calling it a family-run winery, we might want to use the word 'couple', with Luisa in the countryside and Nicola working on the production end. Together they have, in just a few years, established themselves as a model, an example of how even in the plains, with lower yield per hectare and painstaking care, you can make extremely solid, distinct wines that can keep up with any highland variety. Not many wines were put forward, but the range is extensive and all the wine types received unanimous consensus: white, red, sweet and sparkling. The excellent vintage is expressed particularly well in the 2016 Friulano, which stands out for aroma and density, embellished with pleasant notes of exotic fruit and white chocolate.

○ Friuli Friulano '16	♥♥ 2*
○ Malvasia '15	♥♥ 2*
● Merlot '14	♥♥ 2*
○ Pinot Grigio '16	♥♥ 2*
○ Terra e Cielo Brut '13	♥♥ 4
○ Traminer Passito Alba '15	♥♥ 5
○ Sauvignon '16	♥ 2
○ Traminer Aromatico '16	♥ 2
○ Lupi Terrae '14	♥♥ 3
○ Lupi Terrae '13	♥♥ 3
● Merlot '13	♥♥ 2*
● Merlòt '12	♥♥ 2*
● Refosco P. R. '13	♥♥ 2*
● Refosco P. R. '12	♥♥ 2*
● Rosso Svual '11	♥♥ 3
○ Traminer Aromatico '15	♥♥ 2*

★Borgo San Daniele

VIA SAN DANIELE, 28
34071 CORMÒNS [GO]
TEL. +39 048160552
www.borgosandaniele.it

CELLAR SALES
PRE-BOOKED VISITS
ACCOMMODATION
ANNUAL PRODUCTION 6,000 bottles
HECTARES UNDER VINE 19.00
VITICULTURE METHOD Certified Organic
SUSTAINABLE WINERY

In 1990 two young siblings, Mauro and Alessandra Mauri, inherited some vineyards from their grandfather. Showing initiative (and maybe just a hint of foolhardiness), they decided to run things themselves. And so it was that Borgo San Daniele was founded (it's named after the hamlet of Cormòns where they're located). In just a few years they've been able to transform that small estate into a producer known for its top-quality wines. Their selection is small but absolutely outstanding, the result of painstaking care of their vineyards and oversight of the winemaking process itself. The logical next step is a full conversion to organic wine, which will happen shortly. The 2009 Gortmarin makes for yet another thrilling year from Mauro and Alessandro. It's only produced in exceptional vintages, from vines that are over forty years old. The 2015 Friulano and the 2015 Arbis Bianco are also magnificent.

○ Arbis Blanc '15	♥♥ 5
○ Friuli Isonzo Friulano '15	♥♥ 4
● Gortmarin '09	♥♥ 2
● Arbis Ròs '12	♥♥ 5
○ Friuli Isonzo Malvasia '15	♥♥ 4
○ Friuli Isonzo Pinot Grigio '15	♥♥ 4
○ Arbis Blanc '10	♥♥♥ 4
○ Arbis Blanc '09	♥♥♥ 4
○ Arbis Blanc '05	♥♥♥ 4
○ Friuli Isonzo Friulano '08	♥♥♥ 4
○ Friuli Isonzo Friulano '07	♥♥♥ 4
○ Friuli Isonzo Pinot Grigio '04	♥♥♥ 4
○ Friuli Isonzo Tocai Friulano '03	♥♥♥ 4
● Gortmarin '03	♥♥♥ 5

Borgo Savaian

VIA SAVAIAN, 36
34071 CORMONS [GO]
TEL. +39 048160725
stefanobastiani@libero.it

CELLAR SALES
PRE-BOOKED VISITS
ANNUAL PRODUCTION 100,000 bottles
HECTARES UNDER VINE 18.00

Since 2001, Stefano and Rosanna Bastiani have managed this family-run winery, located at the foot of Mount Quarin, the famous hill that protects Cormòns from the cold winds blowing in off Valle del Vipacco, near Slovenia. The two young siblings, fresh off their studies but already seasoned experts, have calmly faced the problems of growing and making wine, creating and gradually refining a system that has allowed them to reach respectable quality standards. Their wines set themselves apart for their unabashed forthrightness and local character. The wines made in the Isonzo area enjoy the influence of the nearby Adriatic sea and effuse salty and iodine aromas, but the 2016 Sauvignon made in Collio has that 'something else'. It made the finals because of its pleasant aromas and caressing palate.

Collio Sauvignon '16	♟♟ 3*
Collio Friulano '16	♟♟ 3
Collio Pinot Grigio '16	♟♟ 3
Friuli Isonzo Merlot '15	♟♟ 3
Collio Ribolla Gialla '16	♟ 3
Friuli Isonzo Malvasia '16	♟ 3
Collio Friulano '15	♟♟ 3*
Collio Merlot Tolrem '09	♟♟ 3
Collio Pinot Grigio '15	♟♟ 3
Collio Ribolla Gialla '14	♟♟ 3
Collio Sauvignon '15	♟♟ 3
Friuli Isonzo Cabernet Franc '14	♟♟ 3
Friuli Isonzo Cabernet Franc '13	♟♟ 3
Friuli Isonzo Cabernet Franc '12	♟♟ 3*
Friuli Isonzo Malvasia '14	♟♟ 3

Cav. Emiro Bortolusso

VIA OLTREGORGO, 10
33050 CARLINO [UD]
TEL. +39 043167596
www.bortolusso.it

CELLAR SALES
PRE-BOOKED VISITS
ACCOMMODATION
ANNUAL PRODUCTION 120,000 bottles
HECTARES UNDER VINE 40.00

For some years already, Sergio and Clara Bortolusso have managed the most thriving and representative winery in the Friuli Annia DOC zone, an area known for its natural beauty, situated just next to the reserve of Marano Lagunare. And thanks to their proximity to the Adriatic, the vineyards here enjoy a sea breeze that aids in both ripening the grapes and bestowing the aromas for which they are known. Thanks also to the teaching and experience of their father, Emiro, Sergio and Clara offer a wide selection of high-quality wines at prices that reflect their quality but are most certainly also competitive. Their wines get unanimous acclaim each year, which underlines the attention paid to each and every grape variety. The 2016 Malvasia, in particular, is tangy and charming, while the 2016 Chardonnay stands out for its lovely combination of fruity notes, both on the nose and in the mouth.

O Chardonnay '16	♟♟ 2*
O Malvasia '16	♟♟ 2*
O Pinot Grigio '16	♟♟ 2*
O Sauvignon '16	♟♟ 2*
O Friuli Annia Friulano '16	♟ 2
O Traminer Aromatico '16	♟ 2
O Chardonnay '15	♟♟ 2*
O Friuli Annia Friulano '15	♟♟ 2*
O Friuli Annia Friulano '14	♟♟ 2*
O Malvasia '15	♟♟ 2*
O Malvasia '14	♟♟ 2*
O Pinot Grigio '15	♟♟ 2*
O Pinot Grigio '14	♟♟ 2*
O Sauvignon '15	♟♟ 2*
O Sauvignon '14	♟♟ 2*
O Traminer Aromatico '15	♟♟ 2*

Branko

LOC. ZEGLA, 20
34071 CORMÒNS [GO]
TEL. +39 0481639826
www.brankowines.com

CELLAR SALES
PRE-BOOKED VISITS
ANNUAL PRODUCTION 45,000 bottles
HECTARES UNDER VINE 9.00

In 1950, Branko Erzetic formalized the documents that made a generations-old, family winemaking tradition official. Here, in the heart of Collio and just along the Slovenian border, Igor is carrying on his father's love for his land and vineyards. Most of them are in Zegla, near Cormòns, gently sloping from the surrounding hills. Given its limited size, Igor is able to manage his winery with extreme care and skill. His wines are always a shining example of cleanness and soundness. A particularly refined and exuberant 2016 Chardonnay wins over the nose, while freshness and tanginess enhance the pleasant palate. It also did very well in the final selections, where it was joined by a fragrant 2016 Sauvignon, which was so close to excellence.

○ Collio Chardonnay '16	🏆🏆 4
○ Collio Sauvignon '16	🏆🏆 4
○ Capo Branko '16	🏆🏆 4
○ Collio Friulano '16	🏆🏆 4
○ Collio Pinot Grigio '16	🏆🏆 4
● Red Branko '14	🏆🏆 4
○ Collio Pinot Grigio '14	🏆🏆🏆 4*
○ Collio Pinot Grigio '08	🏆🏆🏆 3*
○ Collio Pinot Grigio '07	🏆🏆🏆 3
○ Collio Pinot Grigio '06	🏆🏆🏆 3
○ Collio Pinot Grigio '05	🏆🏆🏆 3
○ Capobranko '13	🏆🏆 4
○ Collio Chardonnay '13	🏆🏆 4
○ Collio Pinot Grigio '15	🏆🏆 4
○ Collio Sauvignon '15	🏆🏆 4
○ Collio Sauvignon '12	🏆🏆 4

Livio e Claudio Buiatti

VIA LIPPE, 25
33042 BUTTRIO [UD]
TEL. +39 0432674317
www.buiattivini.it

CELLAR SALES
PRE-BOOKED VISITS
ANNUAL PRODUCTION 35,000 bottles
HECTARES UNDER VINE 8.00

The Buiatti family already had a relationshi with their estate in the early 1900s. The vineyards here run up along the gentle slopes of the Buttrio, the hills nearest to th Adriatic Sea, which open onto the splendi natural amphitheater exposed to the sea breeze and protected by the Julian Alps. As often happens in family-run wineries, everyone looks after everything. For many years now, Claudio has attended to the precious eight hectares of land he inherite from his father, Livio, though today he's flanked by his son, Matteo, who's bringing new energy, freshness and enthusiasm to their work; and his presence isn't just felt in the vineyard, it's also reflected in their wines. Indeed, Buiatti are aiming high. From here, they haven't got much father to go. A fantastic 2016 Sauvignon has grabbed the limelight and whipped the res of the field (for its category) getting a much-deserved place in the finals. Citrus and peppermint on the nose disclose a fragrance that develops in the mouth with fresh, pleasant and lingering notes of citrine.

○ FCO Sauvignon '16	🏆🏆 3
○ FCO Friulano '16	🏆🏆 3
● FCO Momon Ros Ris. '13	🏆🏆 3
○ FCO Pinot Grigio '16	🏆🏆 3
○ FCO Malvasia '16	🏆 3
● COF Momon Ros Ris. '10	🏆🏆
○ COF Sauvignon '13	🏆🏆
○ FCO Friulano '15	🏆🏆
○ FCO Friulano '14	🏆🏆
○ FCO Malvasia '15	🏆🏆
○ FCO Malvasia '14	🏆🏆
● FCO Merlot '13	🏆🏆
● FCO Momon Ros Ris. '12	🏆🏆
○ FCO Pinot Grigio '14	🏆🏆 3
○ FCO Sauvignon '15	🏆🏆 3

La Buse dal Lôf

VIA RONCHI, 90
33040 PREPOTTO [UD]
TEL. +39 0432701523
www.labusedallof.com

CELLAR SALES
PRE-BOOKED VISITS
ANNUAL PRODUCTION 100,000 bottles
HECTARES UNDER VINE 25.00

For years Michele Pavan has been managing Buse dal Lôf, a thriving regional player whose name means 'the fox's den'. The estate, founded in 1972 by Michele's father Giuseppe, comprises 25 hectares around Prepotto, an area famous for its 'Schioppettino' and that falls in the Colli Orientali del Friuli DOC zone. The area enjoys a favorable microclimate, thanks to its proximity to the Julian Alps and the Adriatic breeze. The rich terrain, which slopes gradually towards the lowlands, goes back to the Eocene period and is mostly composed of marl and sandstone. The 2013 Schioppettino di Prepotto impacts with a pot pourri of spices, tobacco, leather and dried medicinal herbs, while the mouth is plush and flavorsome. The 2016 Ribolla Gialla excels in freshness, with wonderful floral notes of broom. The 2015 Refosco dal Peduncolo Rosso offers a nice portrayal of the variety's austere character.

FCO Refosco P. R. '15	♟♟ 3
FCO Ribolla Gialla '16	♟♟ 3
FCO Schioppettino di Prepotto '13	♟♟ 4
FCO Cabernet Franc '16	♟ 3
FCO Friulano '16	♟ 3
FCO Sauvignon '16	♟ 3
COF Refosco P. R. '11	♟♟ 3
COF Schioppettino di Prepotto '11	♟♟ 4
FCO Cabernet Franc '14	♟♟ 3
FCO Chardonnay '15	♟♟ 3
FCO Friulano '15	♟♟ 3
FCO Pinot Bianco In Bocca al Lupo '15	♟♟ 3
FCO Ribolla Gialla '15	♟♟ 3
FCO Sauvignon '15	♟♟ 3
FCO Schioppettino di Prepotto '12	♟♟ 4

Valentino Butussi

VIA PRÀ DI CORTE, 1
33040 CORNO DI ROSAZZO [UD]
TEL. +39 0432759194
www.butussi.it

CELLAR SALES
PRE-BOOKED VISITS
ACCOMMODATION
ANNUAL PRODUCTION 120,000 bottles
HECTARES UNDER VINE 18.00
VITICULTURE METHOD Certified Organic
SUSTAINABLE WINERY

Generations of experience, knowledge and wine growing secrets go into Butussi wines. Indeed, the roots of this winery run deep in the sandstone and marl soil of Prà di Corte in Corno di Rosazzo, in the Colli Orientali del Friuli DOC zone. The latest generation, Tobia, Filippo, Mattia and Erika, still get help from their parents, providing a classic example of how a family-run winery can achieve excellence through teamwork and the proper division of responsibilities. Their selection of wines is robust, with something for every type of market. And their commitment to quality, carried out through constant dedication and hard work, is getting the recognition it deserves. A splendid 2016 Sauvignon has whipped the competition in this very crowded category and thoroughly deserved to make the finals. It has a distinctive elegant aroma, with an assertive but discreet varietal imprint, while the palate has pleasant and lingering aromatic overtones.

○ FCO Sauvignon '16	♟♟ 2*
● FCO Cabernet Sauvignon '15	♟♟ 3
○ FCO Chardonnay '16	♟♟ 2*
○ FCO Friulano '16	♟♟ 2*
○ Ribolla Gialla Brut	♟♟ 5
● FCO Merlot '15	♟ 3
○ FCO Pinot Grigio Ramato '16	♟ 2
● FCO Refosco P. R. '15	♟ 3
○ FCO Ribolla Gialla '16	♟ 2
○ COF Chardonnay '13	♟♟ 2*
● COF Pignolo '09	♟♟ 5
● FCO Cabernet Sauvignon '13	♟♟ 3
○ FCO Friulano '16	♟♟ 2*
○ FCO Friulano '15	♟♟ 2*
● FCO Merlot '13	♟♟ 3
● FCO Refosco P. R. '12	♟♟ 3*
○ FCO Sauvignon '15	♟♟ 2*

Maurizio Buzzinelli

LOC. PRADIS, 20
34071 CORMÒNS [GO]
TEL. +39 048160902
www.buzzinelli.it

CELLAR SALES
PRE-BOOKED VISITS
ACCOMMODATION
ANNUAL PRODUCTION 120,000 bottles
HECTARES UNDER VINE 35.00

Love for the land, commitment and dedication are the principles that have made Maurizio Buzzinelli's winery a standout in a region crowded with competition. Together with his wife Marzia, he's bringing his family's three generations of experience and accomplishments to the role, personally overseeing care of the vineyards and the winemaking process itself. His task is made easier thanks to the fortuitous position of his vineyards in the Pradis hills, in Cormòns, which enjoy a favorable microclimate and offer an enchanting view of the plains below, reaching all the way to the Adriatic. The quality standard reached and maintained over time confirms Maurizio's winemaking skills. He interprets the potential of Collio really well, albeit without great exploits, but there are sporadic moments of great satisfaction. An example is the case of the 2016 Friulano, which earned a place in the finals for its typicity and pleasantness.

○ Collio Friulano '16	♀♀	3*
○ Collio Malvasia '16	♀♀	2*
○ Collio Sauvignon '16	♀♀	3
○ Collio Ribolla Gialla '16	♀	3
○ Collio Chardonnay '15	♀♀	3
○ Collio Chardonnay '14	♀♀	3
○ Collio Friulano '15	♀♀	3
○ Collio Malvasia '15	♀♀	2*
○ Collio Pinot Grigio '13	♀♀	3*
○ Collio Ribolla Gialla '15	♀♀	3
○ Collio Ribolla Gialla '14	♀♀	3
○ Collio Sauvignon '15	♀♀	3
○ Collio Sauvignon '14	♀♀	3*

Ca' Bolani

VIA CA' BOLANI, 2
33052 CERVIGNANO DEL FRIULI [UD]
TEL. +39 043132670
www.cabolani.it

CELLAR SALES
PRE-BOOKED VISITS
ANNUAL PRODUCTION 2,700,000 bottles
HECTARES UNDER VINE 550.00

Tenuta Ca' Bolani spans the heart of the Friuli Aquileia DOC zone. Formerly owned by the noble Bolani family, the estate was bought by the Zonins in 1970. Today it includes the vineyards of Cà Vescovo and Molin di Ponte, purchased, respectively, in 1980 and 1998. Overall, its 550 hectares of vineyards make it the largest grower in the region. Along with expert management, it has benefitted from the knowledge and experience of winegrower Marco Rabino, who guarantees that their entire selection meet quality standards, from their already established line of whites to their finely crafted reds, especially their Refosco dal Peduncolo Rosso. Both versions of the Pinot Bianco gave an excellent performance. The vintage wine excelled for its floral aromas of lily of the valley and hawthorn, as well as the freshness and crispness of the palate. The Opimio, on the other hand, is more aristocratic, with a light aromatic quality and a full, lingering palate.

○ Friuli Aquileia Pinot Bianco '16	♀♀	4
● Friuli Aquileia Merlot '15	♀♀	4
○ Friuli Aquileia Pinot Bianco Opimio '15	♀♀	6
○ Friuli Aquileia Pinot Grigio '16	♀♀	4
○ Friuli Aquileia Sauvignon Aquilis '15	♀♀	5
● Friuli Aquileia Cabernet '15	♀	4
○ Friuli Aquileia Friulano '16	♀	4
● Friuli Aquileia Refosco P. R. '15	♀	4
○ Friuli Aquileia Sauvignon '16	♀	4
○ Friuli Aquileia Traminer Aromatico '16	♀	4
○ Prosecco Brut	♀	3
○ Friuli Aquileia Pinot Bianco '09	♀♀♀	2
● Friuli Aquileia Refosco P. R. Alturio '09	♀♀	4
○ Friuli Aquileia Sauvignon Aquilis '14	♀♀	2
○ Friuli Aquileia Sauvignon Aquilis '11	♀♀	2

Ca' Tullio

VIA BELIGNA, 41
33051 AQUILEIA [UD]
TEL. +39 0431919700
www.catullio.it

CELLAR SALES
PRE-BOOKED VISITS
ANNUAL PRODUCTION 200,000 bottles
HECTARES UNDER VINE 100.00

Ca' Tullio brings together two separate and distinct territories under a single name. About half of their vineyards surround their main facility in Aquileia, while the other half can be found on the gently slopping hills of the Colli Orientali del Friuli DOC zone (in Manzano). The different types of terrains and microclimates allow the winery to best express the attributes and potential of the area, highlighting the conditions that are specific to each one. For years Paolo Calligaris, the owner, has entrusted Ca'Tulio's selection of wines to winemaker Francesco Visintin. Both of the production areas are expressed in the wines through very distinct features. Iodine and sea salt notes mark those produced in proximity to the Adriatic, while wines made with grapes cultivated on the hills are denser, with more aromatic complexity, length and pleasantness on the palate.

○ FCO Chardonnay '16	♥♥ 2*
● FCO Merlot '16	♥♥ 2*
● FCO Pignolo '13	♥♥ 3
○ FCO Pinot Grigio '16	♥♥ 2*
● FCO Schioppettino '14	♥♥ 3
● FCO Cabernet Franc '16	♥ 2
○ FCO Ribolla Gialla '16	♥ 3
○ FCO Sauvignon '16	♥ 2
○ Friuli Aquileia Müller Thurgau '16	♥ 2
● Friuli Aquileia Refosco P. R. '15	♥ 2
○ Friuli Aquileia Traminer Viola '16	♥ 2
● FCO Pignolo '12	♥♥ 3
○ FCO Sauvignon '15	♥♥ 3
● FCO Schioppettino '13	♥♥ 3
○ Friuli Aquileia Pinot Grigio '15	♥♥ 2*
○ Friuli Aquileia Traminer Viola '15	♥♥ 2*

Cadibon

VIA CASALI GALLO, 1
33040 CORNO DI ROSAZZO [UD]
TEL. +39 0432759316
www.cadibon.com

CELLAR SALES
PRE-BOOKED VISITS
RESTAURANT SERVICE
ANNUAL PRODUCTION 55,000 bottles
HECTARES UNDER VINE 14.00
VITICULTURE METHOD Certified Organic

Cadibon officially got its start in 1977, in Corno di Rosazzo (Casali Gallo), after generations of Bon family had dedicated themselves to growing wine in the area. For some years, the Cadibon has been in the hands of Luca and Francesca, who've managed the winery with enthusiasm and unquestionable skill. Luca is a committed supporter of the biodynamic approach, which he has been employing for some time already. Last year they also received certification for being organic. Widespread recognition has gained the producer attention from international markets as well. We saw an excellent performance by the two versions of the 2016 Sauvignon. The first deservedly got through to the finals for its intriguing nose and plush palate. The second version, called Lavoron, shows their enormous commitment to producing a forthright varietal wine.

○ Collio Sauvignon '16	♥♥ 3*
○ Collio Chardonnay '16	♥♥ 3
○ Collio Pinot Grigio '16	♥♥ 3
○ Collio Sauvignon Lavoron '16	♥♥ 3
○ FCO Friulano Bontaj '16	♥♥ 3
○ Friuli Bianco Ronco del Nonno '16	♥♥ 3
○ Verduzzo Friulano '15	♥♥ 3
○ FCO Ribolla Gialla '16	♥♥ 3
○ Collio Sauvignon '15	♥♥ 3
● FCO Cabernet Franc '15	♥♥ 3
○ FCO Friulano Bontaj '15	♥♥ 3
○ FCO Pinot Grigio '15	♥♥ 3
● FCO Refosco P. R. '14	♥♥ 3
○ FCO Ribolla Gialla '15	♥♥ 3
● FCO Schioppettino '14	♥♥ 3
○ Ronco del Nonno '15	♥♥ 3

Canus

LOC. CASALI GALLO
VIA GRAMOGLIANO, 21
33040 CORNO DI ROSAZZO [UD]
TEL. +39 0432759427
www.canus.it

CELLAR SALES
PRE-BOOKED VISITS
ANNUAL PRODUCTION 50,000 bottles
HECTARES UNDER VINE 11.00

Otto Casonato is Canus's new owner. The winery, situated on the hill of Gramogliano, in Corno di Rosazzo, has roots that go far back, but it got its name only in 2004 (after a previous change of owners). The Latin word, 'canus', refers to the wisdom and benefits that come with age. Otto wrote 'I left the countryside as a young man so as to follow my dreams. Now that I'm a white-haired 'canuto', I'm closing the circle and going back to my origins, to the land - an incredibly exciting land that's full of potential.' And so it's a new beginning for the winery, with a solid foundation that comprises 11 hectares of vineyards, which enjoy the perfect exposure for wines that have matured to the maximum of their potential. If this is the beginning, it's a very reassuring one and bodes well for the future. The skilled hand that went into the selection is immediately discernible. They are all excellent quality, fragrant and juicy, with clear references to the different characteristics of the varieties.

○ COF Pinot Grigio '15	♟♟ 3
○ FCO Bianco Gramogliano '15	♟♟ 4
○ FCO Friulano '15	♟♟ 3
● FCO Merlot '11	♟♟ 4
● FCO Pignolo '15	♟♟ 5
● FCO Refosco P. R. '11	♟♟ 4
○ FCO Ribolla Gialla '15	♟♟ 3
● FCO Rosso Mezzo Secolo '10	♟♟ 5
○ FCO Chardonnay '15	♟ 3
○ Chardonnay Ronco del Gris '14	♟♟ 2*
● FCO Refosco P. R. '10	♟♟ 4
○ Malvasia Ronco del Gris '14	♟♟ 2*

Fernanda Cappello

S.DA DI SEQUALS, 15
33090 SEQUALS [PN]
TEL. +39 042793291
www.fernandacappello.it

CELLAR SALES
PRE-BOOKED VISITS
RESTAURANT SERVICE
ANNUAL PRODUCTION 100,000 bottles
HECTARES UNDER VINE 126.00
SUSTAINABLE WINERY

In 1988, the architect Fernanda Cappello decided to abandon her previous job and dedicate herself full-time to making wine. Driven by a passion for the field, she leapt into what she herself calls 'an exciting adventure'. The estate spans 135 hectares, 126 of which are vineyards, between the Cellina and Meduna rivers, just beneath the Sequals hills, in Pordenone. The terrain here is alluvial, and composed of calcareous, Dolomite stone. Fernanda's increasingly ambitious goals brought her to enlist the help of winemaker, Fabio Coser, resulting in a breakthrough in quality that has made Cappello one of western Friuli's top producers. The varied range of wines shows a remarkable level of quality, especially from the point of view of value for money. Its sensory properties are very distinctive and respect to the peculiarities of each and every variety. Both the still wines and sparkling wines guarantee freshness and fragrance.

● Friuli Grave Cabernet Franc '15	♟♟ 2*
○ Friuli Grave Chardonnay '16	♟♟ 2*
○ Friuli Grave Pinot Grigio '16	♟♟ 2*
● Friuli Grave Refosco P. R. '13	♟♟ 2*
○ Friuli Grave Ribolla Gialla '16	♟♟ 2*
○ Friuli Grave Friulano '16	♟ 2
○ Friuli Grave Sauvignon '16	♟ 2
○ Friuli Grave Traminer Aromatico '16	♟ 2
○ Prosecco Extra Dry	♟ 2
○ Ribolla Gialla Brut	♟ 2
● Friuli Grave Cabernet Sauvignon '14	♟♟ 2*
○ Friuli Grave Chardonnay Perla dei Sassi '14	♟♟ 3

Il Carpino

LOC. SOVENZA, 14A
34070 SAN FLORIANO DEL COLLIO [GO]
TEL. +39 0481884097
www.ilcarpino.com

CELLAR SALES
PRE-BOOKED VISITS
ANNUAL PRODUCTION 70,000 bottles
HECTARES UNDER VINE 16.00

In 1987 Anna and Franco Solo founded Il
Carpino, choosing to name their winery
after the area, as is often the case. Borgo
del Carpino can be found in Sovenza, along
the road running from Oslavia to San
Floriano del Collio. Here the old and the
new meet in a welcome synergy. While
grapes from the youngest vineyards are
worked in steel, there's still a strong
impulse towards the past and, as is the
case with many local producers,
1500/2000 liter oak barrels are coming
back in style. Grapes are worked according
to tradition, macerated on the skins for
several days so as to obtain complex,
powerful wines. Their wines are very
concentrated and require long aging, first
in barrels and then in the bottle, which is
why the 2012 Chardonnay is being sold
five years after the vintage. The wine secs
gratifying aromas of roasted barley and
crème caramel, with an intense and
lingering palate.

○ Chardonnay '12	♟♟ 5
○ Exordium '13	♟♟ 5
○ Collio Chardonnay V. Runc '15	♟♟ 3
○ Collio Malvasia V. Runc '15	♟♟ 3
○ Friuli Isonzo Friulano V. Runc '15	♟♟ 3
○ Vis Uvae '13	♟♟ 5
○ Collio Bianco V. Runc '10	♟♟♟ 2*
○ Collio Malvasia V. Runc '11	♟♟♟ 3*
○ Malvasia '11	♟♟♟ 5
● Rubrum '99	♟♟♟ 3*
○ Bianco Runc '12	♟♟ 3*
○ Collio Malvasia V. Runc '14	♟♟ 3*
○ Collio Malvasia V. Runc '12	♟♟ 3*
○ Collio Ribolla Gialla V. Runc '12	♟♟ 5
○ Exordium '12	♟♟ 5
○ Malvasia '12	♟♟ 5

Castello di Buttrio

VIA DEL POZZO, 5
33042 BUTTRIO [UD]
TEL. +39 0432673015
www.castellodibuttrio.it

CELLAR SALES
PRE-BOOKED VISITS
ACCOMMODATION AND RESTAURANT SERVICE
ANNUAL PRODUCTION 60,000 bottles
HECTARES UNDER VINE 25.00

Marco Felluga bought Tenuta del Castello di
Buttrio in 1994, later entrusting it to his
daughter, Alessandra, who brought her
entrepreneurial skills to the winery. She also
patiently restored the walls of the castle,
which both houses the wine cellar and
serves as a reception area. Buttrio is
situated just a few kilometers from Udine,
where the hills of the Colli Orientali del Friuli
DOC zone begin and go on to look out over
the Adriatic Sea. Now that Hartman Donà,
the winemaker from Trentino, is with the
winery, their entire selection has seen a new
emphasis on consistency and pleasantness.
Most of the wines put forward for tasting
come from vintages prior to the last. The top
prize goes to the 2013 Bianco Torre Butria
Riserva (a great mix of Chardonnay, Friulano
and Sauvignon), which is assertive and
complex on the nose, tangy and captivating
on the palate.

○ FCO Bianco Torre Butria Ris. '13	♟♟ 5
○ FCO Bianco Mon Blanc '15	♟♟ 3
● FCO Merlot '13	♟♟ 4
● FCO Pignolo '11	♟♟ 5
○ FCO Sauvignon '15	♟♟ 3
○ FCO Friulano '16	♟ 4
○ COF Bianco Mon Blanc '13	♟♟ 3
○ FCO Bianco Mon Blanc '14	♟♟ 3
○ FCO Friulano '15	♟♟ 4
○ FCO Friulano '14	♟♟ 3
● FCO Merlot '12	♟♟ 4
● FCO Pignolo '10	♟♟ 5
● FCO Rosso Mon Rouge '13	♟♟ 3
○ FCO Sauvignon '14	♟♟ 3
○ FCO Sauvignon Ettaro Ris. '13	♟♟ 6
○ FCO Torre Butria Ris. '11	♟♟ 5

Castello di Spessa

VIA SPESSA, 1
34070 CAPRIVA DEL FRIULI [GO]
TEL. +39 048160445
www.castellodispessa.it

CELLAR SALES
PRE-BOOKED VISITS
ACCOMMODATION AND RESTAURANT SERVICE
ANNUAL PRODUCTION 300,000 bottles
HECTARES UNDER VINE 83.00

As with all old estates, Castello di Spessa holds a certain charm, though not only for the sophistication of its buildings, the beauty of its historic park and Italian garden. Castello di Spessa also has centuries of history, rich in events and historic figures. In 1987, the current owner, Loretto Pali, created the winery, reviving the adjacent vineyards and launching an initiative to promote the castle as a historic monument. Here a bunker built in 1939 (and used by soldiers during the second world war) houses vintage wines, where temperature and humidity are naturally maintained. The large number of wines tasted gave us an overall idea of the winery's range. The unanimous consensus and acclaim for the entire selection confirms their leading position in regional winemaking. But the Collio wines definitely have an edge.

Castello Sant'Anna

LOC. SPESSA
VIA SANT'ANNA, 9
33043 CIVIDALE DEL FRIULI [UD]
TEL. +39 0432716289
www.castellosantanna.it

CELLAR SALES
PRE-BOOKED VISITS
ANNUAL PRODUCTION 25,000 bottles
HECTARES UNDER VINE 7.00
VITICULTURE METHOD Certified Organic

In 1966, Giuseppe Giaiotti decided to give up a thriving role in industry to return to the simple life that was nearer to his heart. He purchased the estate Castello Sant'Anna, once a summer retreat for the area's noble families, and established the winery. Today Castello Sant'Anna is managed by Giuseppe's grandson, Andrea, who has adopted an approach of bringing together modern techniques and the slower ways of nature and tradition. The charm of the estate has only been enhanced by his additions, including a marvelous underground cellar. We couldn't taste the white wines, because they still hadn't been bottled at the time of tasting. We had to settle for just three reds, all excellently made and with marked personality. They were enough to confirm Andrea's winemaking skills.

○ Collio Pinot Bianco Santarosa '16	▼▼ 3*
○ Collio Friulano '16	▼▼ 3
● Collio Merlot V. Rosaris '15	▼▼ 4
○ Collio Pinot Grigio '16	▼▼ 3
● Collio Pinot Nero Grand '15	▼▼ 3
○ Collio Sauvignon '16	▼▼ 3
○ Collio Sauvignon Segrè '16	▼▼ 5
● Friuli Isonzo Cabernet Sauvignon '15	▼▼ 3
○ Friuli Isonzo Friulano '16	▼▼ 3
○ Ribolla Gialla Brut Perté '16	▼▼ 3
○ Collio Pinot Bianco '14	▼▼▼ 3*
○ Collio Pinot Bianco '13	▼▼▼ 3*
○ Collio Pinot Bianco '11	▼▼▼ 3*
○ Collio Pinot Bianco '06	▼▼▼ 3*
○ Collio Tocai Friulano '05	▼▼▼ 3*

● FCO Pignolo '09	▼▼ 5
● FCO Refosco P. R. '13	▼▼ 4
● FCO Schioppettino '12	▼▼ 5
○ COF Pinot Grigio '12	♀♀ 3*
○ COF Ribolla Gialla '12	♀♀ 3*
● FCO Cabernet Franc '13	♀♀ 4
● FCO Cabernet Franc '12	♀♀ 4
○ FCO Friulano '15	♀♀ 3
○ FCO Friulano '13	♀♀ 3
● FCO Merlot '12	♀♀ 4
○ FCO Pinot Grigio '15	♀♀ 3*
○ FCO Pinot Grigio '13	♀♀ 3
○ FCO Ribolla Gialla '15	♀♀ 3
○ FCO Sauvignon '15	♀♀ 3
○ FCO Sauvignon '13	♀♀ 3
● FCO Schioppettino '11	♀♀ 5

Castelvecchio

VIA CASTELNUOVO, 2
34078 SAGRADO [GO]
TEL. +39 048199742
www.castelvecchio.com

CELLAR SALES
PRE-BOOKED VISITS
ACCOMMODATION AND RESTAURANT SERVICE
ANNUAL PRODUCTION 180,000 bottles
HECTARES UNDER VINE 35.00
SUSTAINABLE WINERY

The Terraneo family have for years entrusted their wine to Gianni Menotti, and the results speak for themselves. Among the leading producers of the region, Castelvecchio is the crown jewel of Carso Goriziano. The area offers beautiful landscapes fused with an ancient, noble history, as evidenced by its renaissance villas and centuries-old oaks. The soil is rocky, rich in iron and limestone but short on organic material with only a slight layer of red earth on the surface. This, together with the area's windiness and late harvests make for a unique, albeit limited, selection of wines. The 2016 Malvasia Dileo deserved to make the finals, standing out for its fragrance, crispness and a perfect nose-palate harmony.

★Eugenio Collavini

LOC. GRAMOGLIANO
VIA DELLA RIBOLLA GIALLA, 2
33040 CORNO DI ROSAZZO [UD]
TEL. +39 0432753222
www.collavini.it

CELLAR SALES
PRE-BOOKED VISITS
RESTAURANT SERVICE
ANNUAL PRODUCTION 1,200,000 bottles
HECTARES UNDER VINE 140.00
SUSTAINABLE WINERY

Eugenio Collavini got its name from the man who founded this historic winery in 1896. In the 1960s the estate was enlarged thanks to Manlio Collavini, who bought a 16th century manner in Corno di Rosazzov, using it both as a residence and as the producer's wine cellar. Collavini were the first to believe in Ribolla Gialla, and take advantage of the grape's potential, well before it had achieved its current success and popularity. And while they have always put up impressive numbers, their wines set themselves apart for their consistency and affordability, when it comes to both their top and middle-range wines. For the first time, 2013 Ribolla Gialla Brut has earned a Tre Bicchieri. The credit is all Manlio's, who, after plenty of experimenting, has finely tuned a tried and tested method for making sparkling wine from the famous native grape. He has been using it for thirty years and it involves long periods resting on the lees in horizontal pressure tanks.

○ Carso Malvasia Dileo '16	♈♈ 4
○ Carso Malvasia '16	♈♈ 3
● Carso Merlot Dileo '11	♈♈ 5
○ Carso Pinot Grigio '16	♈♈ 3
● Carso Refosco P. R. '14	♈♈ 3
○ Carso Sauvignon '16	♈♈ 3
○ Carso Vitovska '16	♈♈ 3
● Sagrado Rosso '11	♈♈ 5
● Carso Cabernet Sauvignon Dileo '12	♈ 5
○ Carso Traminer Aromatico '16	♈ 3
○ Carso Malvasia Dileo '15	♈♈♈ 4*
● Carso Cabernet Franc '11	♈♈ 4
○ Carso Malvasia Dileo '14	♈♈ 4
● Carso Merlot '06	♈♈ 5
○ Carso Sauvignon '12	♈♈ 3*
● Sagrado Rosso '05	♈♈ 5

○ Ribolla Gialla Brut '13	♈♈♈ 5
○ Collio Bianco Broy '16	♈♈ 5
○ Collio Friulano '16	♈♈ 3
● Collio Merlot dal Pic '12	♈♈ 5
○ Collio Sauvignon '16	♈♈ 3
● FCO Pignolo '09	♈♈ 6
○ Collio Bianco Broy '15	♈♈♈ 5
○ Collio Bianco Broy '14	♈♈♈ 5
○ Collio Bianco Broy '13	♈♈♈ 5
○ Collio Bianco Broy '11	♈♈♈ 4*
○ Collio Bianco Broy '10	♈♈♈ 4
○ Collio Bianco Broy '09	♈♈♈ 4*
○ Collio Bianco Broy '08	♈♈♈ 4*
○ Collio Bianco Broy '07	♈♈♈ 4

Colle Duga

LOC. ZEGLA, 10
34071 CORMÒNS [GO]
TEL. +39 048161177
www.colleduga.com

CELLAR SALES
PRE-BOOKED VISITS
ANNUAL PRODUCTION 50,000 bottles
HECTARES UNDER VINE 9.00

When Damijan Princic took over as heir to Colle Duga in 1991, he immediately followed his heart, lowering yields and reducing production volumes for this already small winery. Naturally, at first, he butt heads with his predecessors, but they came around to supporting his choice once they saw the improvement in quality. Without exception, the few wines Colle Duga do produce are of outstanding quality. In just a short time Damijan has conquered even the most discriminating palates, making his winery a leader in the market and perfectly representing the potential of the Collio DOC zone. It was in the air. After many placings and awards, the 2016 Collio Bianco has made a comeback and earned a Tre Bicchieri once again. It's a well-deserved recognition for a wine and a winery that have kept up a commendable level of excellence for many years, without overdoing it.

○ Collio Bianco '16	▼▼▼	4*
○ Collio Chardonnay '16	▼▼	3*
○ Collio Friulano '16	▼▼	3
● Collio Merlot '15	▼▼	4
○ Collio Pinot Grigio '16	▼	3
○ Collio Sauvignon '16	▼▼	3
○ Collio Bianco '11	♈♈♈	4*
○ Collio Bianco '08	♈♈♈	3*
○ Collio Bianco '07	♈♈♈	3
○ Collio Friulano '09	♈♈♈	3*
○ Collio Tocai Friulano '06	♈♈♈	3*
○ Collio Tocai Friulano '05	♈♈♈	3*

Colli di Poianis

VIA POIANIS, 23
33040 PREPOTTO [UD]
TEL. +39 0432713185
www.collidipoianis.it

CELLAR SALES
PRE-BOOKED VISITS
ACCOMMODATION
ANNUAL PRODUCTION 65,000 bottles
HECTARES UNDER VINE 11.00
SUSTAINABLE WINERY

Many wineries are a dream-come-true for their owners. This is the case with Colli di Pioanis. It's a dream that Paolino Marinig followed for 77 years, and that became a reality in 1991, thanks to his son, Gabriele. Today it's one of the most inspiring producers in Prepotto, in the Friuli Colli Orientali DOC zone. And not only did Gabriele work to revive the area's native grape varieties, he also showed great care in safeguarding the territory by maintaining its original, historic layout. He took pains to protect the natural balance that existed between the slopes, trails and vineyards, and that, over time, had promoted biodiversity. In past editions, we always highlighted the performance of the Schioppettino di Prepotto, which is the most representative wine of the area. However, all the wines we tasted this year are white and from the last vintage. The table below speaks for itself, they are all excellently made.

○ FCO Chardonnay '16	▼▼	4
○ FCO Friulano '16	▼▼	4
○ FCO Malvasia '16	▼▼	4
○ FCO Ribolla Gialla '16	▼▼	4
○ FCO Sauvignon '16	▼▼	4
○ FCO Pinot Grigio '16	▼	3
○ COF Chardonnay '13	♈♈	3
○ COF Friulano '13	♈♈	3
● COF Rosso Ronco della Poiana '11	♈♈	4
● COF Schioppettino di Prepotto '11	♈♈	5
○ FCO Friulano '15	♈♈	3
○ FCO Malvasia '15	♈♈	3
○ FCO Pinot Grigio '15	♈♈	3
○ FCO Pinot Grigio '14	♈♈	3
● FCO Schioppettino di Prepotto '13	♈♈	5

Colmello di Grotta

LOC. GROTTA
VIA GORIZIA, 133
34072 FARRA D'ISONZO [GO]
TEL. +39 0481888445
www.colmello.it

CELLAR SALES
PRE-BOOKED VISITS
ANNUAL PRODUCTION 75,000 bottles
HECTARES UNDER VINE 15.00

The two plots of land that make up the estate of Colmello di Grotta are very different, even if they lie in close proximity to one another. About half of their vineyards are in the gravelly, calcium-rich Friuli Isonzo DOC zone, leading to sophisticated, fragrant wines, while the other half are in the marl and sandstone terrain of the Collio hills, resulting in aromatically complex wines of muscular structure. Francesca Bortolotto has been managing this lively winery with entrepreneurial skill for some time now, showing that she's open to change and knows how to use it to positive ends. With mixed results, the wines produced in the two different appellations had the consensus of our tasting panel, confirming their long-standing quality standard. The gap between wines from the hills and those from the plains has been bridged, all in favor of drinkability.

○ Collio Pinot Grigio '16	♟♟	3
○ Collio Sauvignon '16	♟♟	3
○ Friuli Isonzo Bianco Sanfilip '16	♟♟	4
○ Friuli Isonzo Sauvignon '16	♟♟	3
○ Collio Ribolla Gialla '16	♟	3
○ Friuli Isonzo Brut '16	♟	5
○ Friuli Isonzo Friulano '16	♟	3
○ Collio Bianco Sanfilip '15	♟♟	3
○ Collio Chardonnay '15	♟♟	3
○ Collio Friulano '15	♟♟	3
○ Collio Pinot Grigio '15	♟♟	3
○ Collio Pinot Grigio '14	♟♟	3
○ Collio Sauvignon '15	♟♟	3
○ Friuli Isonzo Chardonnay '15	♟♟	3
● Rondon '13	♟♟	5

Gianpaolo Colutta

VIA ORSARIA, 32A
33044 MANZANO [UD]
TEL. +39 0432510654
www.coluttagianpaolo.com

CELLAR SALES
PRE-BOOKED VISITS
ANNUAL PRODUCTION 150,000 bottles
HECTARES UNDER VINE 30.00

Elisabetta Colutta is the driving force behind this winery, which is named after her father Gianpaolo even if it was on her mother's side, through the Countess Anna di Prampero, that she inherited a millennium's worth of experience in agriculture. The noble family seal is stamped on every bottle, promoting the territorial attributes that Elisabetta wanted to highlight in her wines, which prioritize native grapes. Her vineyards span about thirty hectares, reaching across the gentle slopes of the Colli Orientali del Friuli DOC zone. Hers are the first hills on the northeast, the ones with the best exposure to the Adriatic breeze and that form part of a natural amphitheater that is deeply appreciated by local winegrowers. A well-structured combination of the liveliness of Ribolla Gialla and the elegance of Chardonnay goes into the 2016 Bianco Prariòn, which expresses a perfect balance between the features of the two grape varieties. The 2016 Friulano and the 2016 Pinot Grigio are also excellent and rich in varietal overtones.

○ FCO Bianco Prariòn '16	♟♟	4
○ FCO Friulano '16	♟♟	3
○ FCO Pinot Grigio '16	♟♟	3
● FCO Cabernet '13	♟	3
○ FCO Riesling '16	♟	4
○ FCO Sauvignon '16	♟	3
● COF Schioppettino '12	♟♟	5
○ FCO Chardonnay '15	♟♟	3
○ FCO Chardonnay '14	♟♟	3
○ FCO Friulano '15	♟♟	3
○ FCO Pinot Grigio '15	♟♟	3
○ FCO Pinot Grigio '14	♟♟	3
● FCO Rosso Frassinolo '12	♟♟	5
○ FCO Verduzzo Friulano '14	♟♟	4
○ FCO Verduzzo Friulano '14	♟♟	4

Giorgio Colutta

VIA ORSARIA, 32
33044 MANZANO [UD]
TEL. +39 0432740315
www.colutta.it

CELLAR SALES
PRE-BOOKED VISITS
ACCOMMODATION
ANNUAL PRODUCTION 140,000 bottles
HECTARES UNDER VINE 21.00

Giorgio Colutta's winery is situated in
Manzano, in an old 18th century residence
bought by Antonio Colutta in the early
1900s. The estate's vineyards, all managed
by the master winegrower Antonio Maggio,
span Buttrio, Manzano and Rosazzo, and
fall within the prestigious Parco della Vite e
del Vino as well as the Colli Orientali del
Friuli DOC zone. From the vineyard to the
cellar, all their winemaking is carried out
according to principles of environmental
sustainability and compatibility. They pay
particular attention to native varieties of
grapes, especially those that have been, or
are being rediscovered. They have
identified crus for just these, and they are
considered the crown jewel of the winery.
It's interesting to note that all the wines,
both whites and reds, nearly got the same
score. This is a sure sign that the same
attention is paid to each and every grape
variety. The vintage whites are crisp and
even, while the reds express the aromatic
complexity of bottle aging.

○ FCO Friulano '16	♟♟ 3
● FCO Merlot '13	♟♟ 3
● FCO Pignolo '11	♟♟ 7
○ FCO Pinot Grigio '16	♟♟ 3
● FCO Refosco P. R. '14	♟♟ 3
○ FCO Sauvignon '16	♟♟ 3
● FCO Schioppettino '13	♟♟ 5
○ FCO Ribolla Gialla '16	♟ 4
○ Prosecco Brut	♟ 2
○ FCO Friulano '15	♟♟ 3
● FCO Pignolo '10	♟♟ 7
○ FCO Pinot Grigio '15	♟♟ 3
○ FCO Pinot Grigio '14	♟♟ 3
○ FCO Ribolla Gialla '15	♟♟ 4
○ FCO Sauvignon '15	♟♟ 3
● FCO Schioppettino '12	♟♟ 5

Paolino Comelli

CASE COLLOREDO, 8
33040 FAEDIS [UD]
TEL. +39 0432711226
www.comelli.it

CELLAR SALES
PRE-BOOKED VISITS
ACCOMMODATION AND RESTAURANT SERVICE
ANNUAL PRODUCTION 60,000 bottles
HECTARES UNDER VINE 12.50
SUSTAINABLE WINERY

The Paolino Comelli winery, named after its
founder, has for years demonstrated an
ability to stay in step with new techniques
and markets and to consistently guarantee
high quality across its whole product line.
Pierluigi Comelli, his wife Daniela and their
children Nicola and Filippo are now
managing this producer, which has been
family-run since Paolino purchased an old,
abandoned hamlet in 1946 and with great
foresight transformed it into an facility for
winemaking. The old farm residences, now
equipped with modern comforts, serve as a
charming agritourism, It's interesting that a
different wine heads the ranking each year,
but it's also a clear sign that the same
attention is given to each and every grape
variety. The 2016 Sauvignon sets the pace
for an array of wines that are carefully
looked after in every respect, regardless of
the type of wine.

○ FCO Sauvignon '16	♟♟ 3*
○ Amplius Pinot Grigio '16	♟♟ 2*
○ COF Picolit '14	♟♟ 5
○ FCO Malvasia '15	♟♟ 3
● Soffumbergo '15	♟♟ 4
○ FCO Friulano '16	♟ 3
● Esprimo Red '13	♟♟ 2*
○ Esprimo White '13	♟♟ 2*
○ FCO Friulano '15	♟♟ 3
○ FCO Malvasia '14	♟♟ 3*
○ FCO Malvasia Locum Nostrum '13	♟♟ 3
○ FCO Pinot Grigio Amplius '15	♟♟ 3
○ FCO Pinot Grigio Amplius '14	♟♟ 3
○ Soffumbergo Bianco '13	♟♟ 4
● Soffumbergo Rosso '13	♟♟ 4

Dario Coos

VIA RAMANDOLO, 5
33045 NIMIS [UD]
TEL. +39 0432790320
www.dariocoos.it

CELLAR SALES
PRE-BOOKED VISITS
ANNUAL PRODUCTION 65,000 bottles
HECTARES UNDER VINE 10.00

Dario Coos represents the fifth generation of expert vigneron that have grown and made wine on the steep slopes of Ramandolo since the end of the 1800s. Here, in the extreme northern part of the Colli Orientali del Friuli, where the hills are almost mountainous, the nights are cold, the days are hot and it rains more than usual. And here, as long as anyone can remember, they've cultivated yellow Verduzzo, a variety of grape that comes in small bunches with thick, hearty skin that's perfect for raisining. And it's the grape from which they make Ramandolo, a sweet wine that has managed to conquer even the most discriminating palates. In recent years the winery has evolved and is now able to offer a variety of commendable dry wines, both white and red. We are in the land of Ramandolo, but it's a different sweet wine that whipped the fierce competition to reach the finals: the 2015 Picolit dei Colli Orientali del Friuli. It has a light golden color and thrills the nose with notes of honey, peach and almond. Its sweetness on the palate is unforgettable.

○ COF Picolit '15	🏆🏆 6
○ Friuli Chardonnay '16	🏆🏆 4
○ Friuli Friulano '16	🏆🏆 3
○ Friuli Malvasia '16	🏆🏆 3
○ Friuli Pinot Grigio '15	🏆🏆 3
○ Friuli Sauvignon '16	🏆🏆 3
● Pignolo '12	🏆🏆 4
○ Ramandolo V.T. '15	🏆🏆 4
○ Ramandolo Il Longhino '15	🏆 4
○ Ribolla Gialla '16	🏆 3
● Schioppettino '15	🏆 4
○ FCO Friulano '15	🏆🏆 3*
○ FCO Picolit '13	🏆🏆 6
○ Malvasia '15	🏆🏆 4
○ Ramandolo V.T. '14	🏆🏆 4
● Refosco P.R. '13	🏆🏆 4

Cantina Produttori Cormòns

VIA VINO DELLA PACE, 31
34071 CORMÒNS [GO]
TEL. +39 048162471
www.cormons.com

CELLAR SALES
PRE-BOOKED VISITS
ACCOMMODATION AND RESTAURANT SERVICE
ANNUAL PRODUCTION 2,250,000 bottles
HECTARES UNDER VINE 430.00
SUSTAINABLE WINERY

'I drink Cormòns' is the slogan chosen by the Cantina Produttori di Cormòns to promote their wines. It's a winning slogan that highlights the relationship between this town and the wines it produces. This charming story began in the 1960s when a group of local winegrowers decided to join forces so as to draw attention to their territory's attributes and potential, something they couldn't have managed on their own. Today they can count more than two hundred members among their ranks, all of whom provide grapes from the five most common regional DOC zones: Collio, Colli Orientali del Friuli, Carso, Friuli Isonzo and Friuli Aquileia. Not many wines were put forward for tasting, but there are enough of them to confirm the winery's very high quality standard. The Collio wines definitely have the edge over the others, but the superb performance by the 201 Malvasia shows that even on the plains there is the potential to aspire to excellence.

○ Collio Chardonnay '16	🏆🏆 2*
○ Collio Friulano '16	🏆🏆 3
○ Friuli Isonzo Malvasia '16	🏆🏆 2*
○ Collio Bianco Collio & Collio '16	🏆 3
● Friuli Isonzo Cabernet Sauvignon '15	🏆 2
○ Collio Bianco Collio & Collio '15	🏆🏆 3
○ Collio Bianco Collio & Collio '14	🏆🏆 3
○ Collio Friuliano '15	🏆🏆 3
○ Collio Friuliano '13	🏆🏆 3
○ Collio Friuliano '12	🏆🏆 2*
○ Collio Pinot Bianco '14	🏆🏆 3
○ Collio Pinot Bianco '13	🏆🏆 3
○ Collio Pinot Grigio '13	🏆🏆 3
○ Friuli Isonzo Malvasia '15	🏆🏆 2*
○ Vino della Pace '09	🏆🏆 5
○ Vino della Pace '87	🏆🏆 5

Crastin

LOC. RUTTARS, 33
34070 DOLEGNA DEL COLLIO [GO]
TEL. +39 0481630310
www.vinicrastin.it

CELLAR SALES
PRE-BOOKED VISITS
ANNUAL PRODUCTION 35,000 bottles
HECTARES UNDER VINE 6.00

Back in the 1950s, two landholders, Olivo and Cornelia Collarig, founded a farm comprising two and a half hectares of land on the hills of Ruttars in Collio Goriziano, not far form the Slovenian border. In 1980 their son Sergio took over and, sensing an opportunity, dedicated himself to growing wine grapes, eventually extending the estate to include a further six hectares of specialized vineyards. The high quality of their entire selection immediately drew the attention of serious wine lovers. And their competitive prices haven't hurt either. Intensity of aroma is the element that distinguishes all the wines and enhances the aromatic nuances of each and every variety. The 2016 Pinot Grigio was particularly appreciated for its crisp fruity notes and pervasive palate. The lively and captivating 2015 Cabernet Franc is also excellent.

● Collio Cabernet Franc '15	♥♥ 3
○ Collio Friulano '16	♥♥ 3
○ Collio Pinot Grigio '16	♥♥ 3
○ Collio Sauvignon '16	♥♥ 3
○ Collio Ribolla Gialla '16	♥ 3
● Collio Cabernet Franc '14	♀♀ 3
○ Collio Friulano '15	♀♀ 3*
○ Collio Friulano '14	♀♀ 2*
● Collio Merlot '13	♀♀ 4
● Collio Merlot '12	♀♀ 2*
○ Collio Pinot Grigio '15	♀♀ 3
○ Collio Pinot Grigio '14	♀♀ 3
○ Collio Ribolla Gialla '15	♀♀ 3
○ Collio Ribolla Gialla '14	♀♀ 2*
○ Collio Sauvignon '15	♀♀ 3
○ Collio Sauvignon '14	♀♀ 3

di Lenardo

FRAZ. ONTAGNANO
P.ZZA BATTISTI, 1
33050 GONARS [UD]
TEL. +39 0432928633
www.dilenardo.it

CELLAR SALES
PRE-BOOKED VISITS
ANNUAL PRODUCTION 750,000 bottles
HECTARES UNDER VINE 55.00
SUSTAINABLE WINERY

Di Lenardo's roots go back to 1878, making it one of the area's more historic wineries. Di Lenardo has made a name for itself by successfully bringing out the characteristics of the lean and sun-soaked terrain of the Friuli plains, but the best chapters of their history are being written by the current owner, Massimo di Lenardo. Massimo inherited his predecessors' love for the land, adding his own, inherent entrepreneurial skills, which he's passing down to his young son, Vittorio. He's been able to make waves abroad, in part because he treats all his wines with the same respect and dignity. Indeed, his wide selection of wines are all exemplary both for their simplicity and the integrity of the grape varieties used. The 2016 Thanks is the winery's future top wine and made it to the finals. However, it's important to point out the good overall performance of the rest of the large line-up we tasted, especially the 2016 Chardonnay and the 2016 Pinot Grigio, which stood out for their aromas, and the 2016 Merlot with its pleasant taste.

○ Thanks '16	♥♥ 4
○ Chardonnay '16	♥♥ 2*
○ Friuli Friulano Toh! '16	♥♥ 2*
○ Friuli Pinot Grigio '16	♥♥ 2*
● Merlot '16	♥♥ 2*
● Merlot Just Me '14	♥♥ 4
● Refosco P.R. '16	♥♥ 2*
● Cabernet '16	♥ 2
○ Chardonnay Father's Eyes '16	♥ 3
○ Pass The Cookies! '16	♥ 3
○ Pinot Grigio Ramato Gossip '16	♥ 2
○ Ribolla Gialla Comemivuoi '16	♥ 2
○ Sarà Brut	♥ 3
○ Sauvignon '16	♥ 2
○ Chardonnay '15	♀♀♀ 2*

★★Dorigo

S.DA PROV.LE 79
33040 Premariacco [UD]
Tel. +39 0432634161
www.dorigowines.com

CELLAR SALES
PRE-BOOKED VISITS
ANNUAL PRODUCTION 120,000 bottles
HECTARES UNDER VINE 20.00
SUSTAINABLE WINERY

Dorgio. A brand that has for more than half a century written important chapters in the history of the region's winemaking culture. In 2012, Girolamo Dorigo passed the torch to his son Alessio. The coming of a new generation coincided with a series of changes that's breathed new life into the winery's staff. The main facility has permanently moved to a new, elegant building equipped with spaces that serve their current needs, while also leaving room for growth. Alessio's winemaking skills have also ensured that their products have in no way suffered. Rather, he has enhanced them, bringing new balance and identity to Dorigo's selection of wines. Having two wines in the finals without obtaining excellence may be cause for regret, but it shows they are on the right track. The reds and the sparkling wines (all strictly Metodo Classico) are also excellent, which confirms the winery's knack for these categories.

○ FCO Friulano '16	♈♈ 3*
○ FCO Ribolla Gialla '16	♈♈ 3*
○ Blanc de Blancs Pas Dosé	♈♈ 5
○ Blanc de Noir Dosage Zéro	♈♈ 5
○ COF Picolit '15	♈♈ 8
○ Dorigo Brut Cuvée	♈♈ 5
○ FCO Chardonnay Ronc di Juri '15	♈♈ 5
● FCO Pignolo '13	♈♈ 8
● FCO Rosso Montsclapade '13	♈♈ 6
○ FCO Sauvignon '16	♈♈ 3
● COF Rosso Montsclapade '06	♈♈♈ 6
● COF Rosso Montsclapade '04	♈♈♈ 6
● COF Rosso Montsclapade '98	♈♈♈ 6

Draga - Miklus

LOC. Scedina, 8
34070 San Floriano del Collio [GO]
Tel. +39 0481884182
www.draga-miklus.com

CELLAR SALES
PRE-BOOKED VISITS
ANNUAL PRODUCTION 40,000 bottles
HECTARES UNDER VINE 14.00
SUSTAINABLE WINERY

Draga (from a local word meaning 'precious') are among the classic, family-run wineries working the slopes of San Floriano del Collio, in Scendina. Milan Miklus represents the third generation of tenant winemakers here, with family roots that go back to the late 19th century. When he took over the estate in 1982, it had just one hectare of vineyards. He immediately began expanding them and, ten years later, he was bottling his wines and having surprising success doing it. Both in the vineyard and in the cellar, his methods are both modern and traditional, and always geared towards sustainability. This year the 2015 Sacrisassi Bianco has turned the tables on the reds and ranks first in score and acclaim. Made of only native grapes (Tocai Friulano and Ribolla Gialla), it has aromas of white peach, citron, orange cream and almonds. The palate is caressing with a tangy finish.

○ Ribolla Gialla Miklus '12	♈♈ 6
○ Collio Friulano '16	♈♈ 3
○ Collio Malvasia Miklus '14	♈♈ 4
○ Collio Pinot Grigio '16	♈♈ 3
● Collio Rosso Miklus Negro di Collina '13	♈♈ 4
○ Collio Ribolla Gialla '16	♈ 3
○ Collio Sauvignon '16	♈ 3
○ Collio Malvasia Miklus '10	♈♈♈ 7
○ Collio Friulano '15	♈♈ 3
○ Collio Malvasia Miklus '13	♈♈ 4
○ Collio Malvasia Miklus '12	♈♈ 4
○ Collio Pinot Grigio Miklus '11	♈♈ 4
○ Collio Ribolla Gialla Miklus Natural Art '09	♈♈ 5
○ Collio Sauvignon '15	♈♈ 3

Drius

VIA FILANDA, 100
34071 CORMÒNS [GO]
TEL. +39 048160998
www.drius.it

CELLAR SALES
PRE-BOOKED VISITS
ANNUAL PRODUCTION 50,000 bottles
HECTARES UNDER VINE 15.00
SUSTAINABLE WINERY

The history of the Drius family is similar to
dozens of other families that have, for
generations, worked the land in Cormòns.
Mauro Drius's winery is a classic, intimate
and authentic kind of operation. He is
among those small producers that are
proud of their craft and love the land with a
certain faith that, in good times and bad, it
will always pay you back. And Mauro is a
true artisan when it comes to wine, with an
instinct for bringing out the best of his
territory's attributes. His prized vineyards
run along the high plains of the Friuli Isonzo
DOC zone and on the slopes of Monte
Quarin, in the heart of Collio. The
umpteenth excellent performance in the
tasting highlights how equal status is given
to all the wines, regardless of the
production area. Aroma and drinkability
are the elements they all have in common
and make them seem simple, but in reality
they feature aromatic varietal overtones of
rare elegance.

○ Collio Friulano '16	▼▼ 3
○ Collio Sauvignon '16	▼▼ 3
○ Friuli Isonzo Bianco Vignis di Siris '15	▼▼ 3
● Friuli Isonzo Cabernet Sauvignon '15	▼▼ 4
○ Friuli Isonzo Malvasia '16	▼▼ 3
○ Friuli Isonzo Pinot Bianco '16	▼▼ 3
○ Friuli Isonzo Pinot Grigio '16	▼▼ 3
○ Friuli Isonzo Chardonnay '16	▼ 3
○ Friuli Isonzo Friulano '16	▼ 3
○ Collio Tocai Friulano '05	▼▼▼ 3*
○ Collio Tocai Friulano '02	▼▼▼ 2*
○ Friuli Isonzo Bianco Vignis di Siris '02	▼▼▼ 3*
○ Friuli Isonzo Friulano '07	▼▼▼ 3
○ Friuli Isonzo Malvasia '08	▼▼▼ 3*
○ Friuli Isonzo Pinot Bianco '00	▼▼▼ 3*

★Le Due Terre

VIA ROMA, 68B
33040 PREPOTTO [UD]
TEL. +39 0432713189
fortesilvana@libero.it

CELLAR SALES
PRE-BOOKED VISITS
ANNUAL PRODUCTION 18,000 bottles
HECTARES UNDER VINE 5.00

Le Due Terre is a small winery, but a true
gem for the municipality of Prepotto.
Managed harmoniously by a lovely couple,
Flavio Basilicata and Silvana Forte, the
estate is perched on a hill that, on one side
is made up of marl and on the other red
earth (thus the name, Le Due Terre). Flavio
spends the bulk of his time pouring over
his five hectares of vineyards here, seeing
to it that every detail is painstakingly
managed. And with only five hectares
there are only four varieties of wine. The
choice to go organic is a natural one. In
the cellar they only use native yeasts,
spontaneous fermentation, aging in oak
casks and absolutely no racking. This year
the 2015 Sacrisassi Bianco has turned the
tables on the reds and ranks first in score
and appreciation. Made of only native
grapes (Tocai Friulano and Ribolla Gialla), it
has aromas of white peach, citron, orange
cream and almonds. The palate is
caressing with a tangy finish.

○ FCO Bianco Sacrisassi '15	▼▼ 5
● FCO Merlot '15	▼▼ 5
● FCO Pinot Nero '15	▼▼ 5
● FCO Rosso Sacrisassi '15	▼▼ 5
○ COF Bianco Sacrisassi '05	▼▼▼ 5
● COF Merlot '03	▼▼▼ 5
● COF Merlot '02	▼▼▼ 5
● COF Merlot '00	▼▼▼ 5
● COF Rosso Sacrisassi '12	▼▼▼ 5
● COF Rosso Sacrisassi '11	▼▼▼ 5
● COF Rosso Sacrisassi '10	▼▼▼ 5
● COF Rosso Sacrisassi '09	▼▼▼ 5
● COF Rosso Sacrisassi '08	▼▼▼ 5
● COF Rosso Sacrisassi '07	▼▼▼ 5
● FCO Rosso Sacrisassi '13	▼▼▼ 5

Ermacora

FRAZ. IPPLIS
VIA SOLZAREDO, 9
33040 PREMARIACCO [UD]
TEL. +39 0432716250
www.ermacora.it

CELLAR SALES
PRE-BOOKED VISITS
ANNUAL PRODUCTION 180,000 bottles
HECTARES UNDER VINE 47.00
SUSTAINABLE WINERY

When the Ermacora family decided on the
hills of Ipplis for their vineyards, in 1922, they
set the stage for the production of
outstanding varieties of wine. Brothers Dario
and Luciano have been managing their
winery for years already, pushing it to the
forefront and establishing its reputation as
solid and reliable. Their vineyards stretch
across the marl, sandstone soil for which the
Colli Orientali del Friuli DOC zone is known.
The terrain, which is composed of
calcium-rich clay that goes back to the
Eocene, isn't particularly fertile but is bursting
with mineral salts. Working with perfect
synergy and professionalism, they have been
able to make wines that are unique but that
haven't lost their distinctive local character,
and that set themselves apart for their
authenticity, balance and personality. The
very sweet and captivating 2014 Picolit dei
Colli Orientali del Friuli has managed to win
the highest accolades and access to the final
selections. But this is just the tip of the
iceberg of a range of excellently-made wines
that have, over time, established the brand
on an international level.

○ COF Picolit '14	🍷🍷 6
○ FCO Friulano '16	🍷🍷 2
● FCO Pignolo '11	🍷🍷 5
○ FCO Pinot Grigio '16	🍷🍷 3
○ FCO Ribolla Gialla '16	🍷🍷 3
○ FCO Sauvignon '16	🍷🍷 3
● FCO Schioppettino '15	🍷🍷 3
○ FCO Pinot Bianco '16	🍷 3
● FCO Rosso Rîul '15	🍷 4
● COF Pignolo '00	🍷🍷🍷 5
○ FCO Friulano '15	🍷🍷 3*
○ FCO Picolit '13	🍷🍷 6
○ FCO Pinot Bianco '15	🍷🍷 3
○ FCO Pinot Grigio '15	🍷🍷 3
○ FCO Ribolla Gialla '15	🍷🍷 3
○ FCO Sauvignon '15	🍷🍷 3

Fantinel

FRAZ. TAURIANO
VIA TESIS, 8
33097 SPILIMBERGO [PN]
TEL. +39 0427591511
www.fantinel.com

CELLAR SALES
PRE-BOOKED VISITS
RESTAURANT SERVICE
ANNUAL PRODUCTION 5,000,000 bottles
HECTARES UNDER VINE 300.00
SUSTAINABLE WINERY

This family-run winery got its start when
Mario Fantinel purchased some vineyards in
Dolegna del Collio, in 1969, with the aim of
providing wine to the clients of his hotel in
Carnia. The generations after him followed
suit, continuing to enlarge the estate so that
today it counts some 300 hectares of
vineyards spread across three distinct
locations: Sant'Helena a Vencò (in Collio), La
Roncaia a Nimis (Colli Orientali) and Borgo
Tesis a Tauriano di Spilimbergo, in the vast
plains of the Friuli Grave DOC zone, where
you'll find their elegant facility, with offices
and a cellar, tucked away among the green
vineyards. This year, Fantinel wines have
earned praise for their Collio wines. The
2016 Prosecco Brut One&Only also
deserves to be mentioned, having beat the
rest of its category. It offers fruity notes,
spruced up by a subtle perlage.

○ Collio Bianco Frontiere Sant'Helena '15	🍷🍷 4
○ Collio Friulano Sant'Helena '16	🍷🍷 3
○ Collio Pinot Grigio Sant'Helena '16	🍷🍷 3
● Collio Rosso Venko Sant'Helena '11	🍷🍷 4
○ Collio Sauvignon Sant'Helena '16	🍷🍷 3
○ Prosecco Brut One&Only '16	🍷🍷 3
● Refosco P.R. Sant'Helena '12	🍷🍷 3
● Cabernet Sauvignon Sant'Helena '13	🍷 3
○ Ribolla Gialla Brut	🍷 3
○ Ribolla Gialla Sant'Helena '16	🍷 3
● Cabernet Sauvignon Sant'Helena '12	🍷🍷 3
○ Collio Bianco Frontiere Sant'Helena '14	🍷🍷 4
○ Collio Pinot Grigio Sant'Helena '15	🍷🍷 3
○ Collio Pinot Grigio Sant'Helena '14	🍷🍷 3
● Collio Rosso Venko Sant'Helena '10	🍷🍷 4
○ Collio Sauvignon Sant'Helena '15	🍷🍷 3

★★Livio Felluga

FRAZ. BRAZZANO
VIA RISORGIMENTO, 1
34071 CORMÒNS [GO]
TEL. +39 048160203
www.liviofelluga.it

PRE-BOOKED VISITS
ANNUAL PRODUCTION 800,000 bottles
HECTARES UNDER VINE 170.00
SUSTAINABLE WINERY

Livio Felluga, who was rightfully known as the 'the patriarch of Friuli wine culture', left us. But over the 102 years of his long life he was a point of reference for everyone, and left an important heritage to his four children. It's a heritage made of tradition, love for the land and daily challenges. The history of the Felluga family spans the Austro-Hungarian empire and the early days of the Italian Kingdom. They moved from the rocky coast of the Istria peninsula and Grado lagoon to settle on the hills of Friuli, the very hills which Livio chose to feature on his bottles of wine, the famous 'map' that you can see on the shelves of wine sellers across the world. Their vineyards in the famous Rosazzo subzone are part of the Friuli Colli Orientali appellation. They are the winery's jewel in the crown and it's no coincidence that this year the 2015 Rosazzo Terre Alte and the 2014 Rosazzo Abbazia di Rosazzo reached our finals.

Marco Felluga

VIA GORIZIA, 121
34072 GRADISCA D'ISONZO [GO]
TEL. +39 048109164
www.marcofelluga.it

CELLAR SALES
PRE-BOOKED VISITS
RESTAURANT SERVICE
ANNUAL PRODUCTION 600,000 bottles
HECTARES UNDER VINE 100.00
SUSTAINABLE WINERY

Roberto Felluga represents the fifth generation of a dynasty of Istrian vine-growers that goes back to the second half of the 1800s. After the 'great war' they moved to the other part of the gulf, first Grado and then Friuli. Marco Felluga, who settled in the Collio Goriziano, founded the winery that bears his name in 1956, dedicating himself full time to promoting the attributes of the territory that made him famous and that he owes so much. Roberto, with just as much grit and determination, manages this thriving winery and has for some years overseen an initiative towards improving the longevity of Collio's white wines, choosing vintages that enter the market long after harvest. Felluga's wines are always a guarantee and this year they have once again proved outstanding. We really enjoyed the 2016 Friulano, which reached the finals. The two versions of the Pinot Grigio Mongis, the vintage and the Riserva, were also judged excellent. Both are elegant and rich in flavor.

○ Rosazzo Abbazia di Rosazzo '14	♥♥	7
○ Rosazzo Terre Alte '15	♥♥	7
○ FCO Bianco Illivio '15	♥♥	5
○ FCO Chardonnay '16	♥♥	4
○ FCO Friulano '16	♥♥	4
○ FCO Pinot Grigio '16	♥♥	4
● FCO Refosco P. R. '14	♥♥	5
● FCO Rosso Sossò Ris. '14	♥♥	7
○ FCO Sauvignon '16	♥♥	4
○ COF Bianco Illivio '10	♥♥♥	5
○ COF Rosazzo Bianco Terre Alte '09	♥♥♥	7
○ COF Rosazzo Bianco Terre Alte '08	♥♥♥	7
○ FCO Bianco Illivio '14	♥♥♥	5
○ Rosazzo Terre Alte '12	♥♥♥	7
○ Rosazzo Terre Alte '11	♥♥♥	7

○ Collio Friulano '16	♥♥	3*
○ Collio Chardonnay '16	♥♥	5
○ Collio Pinot Grigio Mongris '16	♥♥	5
○ Collio Pinot Grigio Mongris Ris. '15	♥♥	5
● Collio Rosso Carantan '10	♥♥	7
● Refosco P.R. Ronco dei Moreri '13	♥♥	3
○ Collio Bianco Molamatta '14	♥	5
○ Collio Ribolla Gialla '16	♥	3
○ Collio Bianco Molamatta '13	♥♥	5
○ Collio Chardonnay '15	♥♥	5
○ Collio Friulano '15	♥♥	3
○ Collio Pinot Grigio '14	♥♥	5
○ Collio Pinot Grigio Mongris Ris. '13	♥♥	5
○ Collio Sauvignon '15	♥♥	3

I Feudi di Romans

FRAZ. PIERIS
VIA CÀ DEL BOSCO, 16
34075 SAN CANZIAN D'ISONZO [GO]
TEL. +39 048176445
www.ifeudidiromans.it

CELLAR SALES
ANNUAL PRODUCTION 500,000 bottles
HECTARES UNDER VINE 90.00

In 1974, Enzo Lorenzon, who had five hectares of vineyards and a farmstead at the time, founded the winery that bears his name. With great passion and rare determination, he purchased other vineyards and began carving out a position for himself at the forefront of wine production. The breakthrough came in 1991, when he purchased I Feudi di Romans, with his children, Davide and Nicola, coming on board the following year. Today, they manage 90 hectares in all, in the heart of the Friuli Isonzo DOC zone, and represent one of the most important producers in the area. Production management is entrusted to Davide, who has the precious advice of Fabio Coser to help him. I Feudi di Romans is a winery which produces large quantities and exports to 25 countries. However, over the course of their growth they haven't lost of their wine as an expression of the territory. This year we noticed a clear improvement across the board. Hats off to them.

○ Friuli Isonzo Friulano '16	🏆🏆 3
○ Friuli Isonzo Malvasia '16	🏆🏆 3
● Friuli Isonzo Merlot '15	🏆🏆 3
○ Friuli Isonzo Pinot Bianco '16	🏆🏆 3
● Friuli Isonzo Pinot Nero '15	🏆🏆 3
○ Ribolla Gialla '16	🏆🏆 3
○ Friuli Isonzo Pinot Grigio '16	🏆 3
○ Friuli Isonzo Sauvignon Blanc '16	🏆 3
○ Traminer Aromatico '16	🏆 3
● Friuli Isonzo Cabernet Franc '14	🏆🏆 3
○ Friuli Isonzo Chardonnay '14	🏆🏆 2*
○ Friuli Isonzo Friulano '15	🏆🏆 3
○ Friuli Isonzo Pinot Bianco '14	🏆🏆 2*
● Friuli Isonzo Refosco P.R. '14	🏆🏆 3

Fiegl

FRAZ. OSLAVIA
LOC. LENZUOLO BIANCO, 1
34170 GORIZIA
TEL. +39 0481547103
www.fieglvini.com

CELLAR SALES
PRE-BOOKED VISITS
ANNUAL PRODUCTION 160,000 bottles
HECTARES UNDER VINE 30.00
SUSTAINABLE WINERY

The history of the Fiegls is the history of a compact and close-knit family that has for two centuries maintained and promoted the values of the farming way of life. It is a history that has, in this borderland, seen its share of tragedy, and put to the test the determination of a population while also shaping its character. And it's with determination and drive that the new generation, Martin, Robert and Matej, are steering this winery towards the heights of regional excellence. Out of respect for nature they are following the principles of low yields, under-sowing the vineyards and the use of eco-friendly products, so as to reduce to a minimum their environmental impact. The 2016 Friulano is once again the key player in the final selections and nearly repeated last year's success. However, all the vintage whites stood out for their aroma and territoriality. The Leopold Cuvée also had a good day, both the 2015 Blanc and the 2010 Rouge, which proved complex and layered.

○ Collio Friulano '16	🏆🏆 3*
○ Collio Bianco Leopold Cuvée Blanc '15	🏆🏆 4
○ Collio Chardonnay '16	🏆🏆 3
○ Collio Malvasia '16	🏆🏆 3
○ Collio Pinot Grigio '16	🏆🏆 3
● Collio Rosso Leopold Cuvée Rouge '10	🏆🏆 5
⊙ Fiegl Rosé Brut M. Cl.	🏆🏆 4
○ Meja '01	🏆🏆 5
○ Collio Ribolla Gialla '16	🏆 3
○ Collio Sauvignon '16	🏆 3
○ Collio Friulano '15	🏆🏆🏆 3*
○ Collio Pinot Grigio '04	🏆🏆🏆 2*
○ Collio Ribolla Gialla Oslavia '14	🏆🏆 5
● Collio Rosso Leopold Cuvée Rouge '09	🏆🏆 5

Gigante

VIA ROCCA BERNARDA, 3
33040 CORNO DI ROSAZZO [UD]
TEL. +39 0432755835
www.adrianogigante.it

CELLAR SALES
PRE-BOOKED VISITS
ACCOMMODATION
ANNUAL PRODUCTION 100,000 bottles
HECTARES UNDER VINE 25.00

Among the many vine-growers that have
made the hills around Corno di Rosazzo
famous, the name Adriano Gigante is
undoubtedly at the top. He has managed
his success by drawing on the attributes of
his vineyards of tocai friulano grapes,
Storico DOC, and pushing the quality of his
wines to ever greater heights. His winery is
among the most exemplary in the region. It
is a benchmark, a source of pride, a
guarantee. Thanks to a play on words,
which is both accidental and meaningful,
we can assure you that Adriano is truly
'gigantic' in his role as a wine artisan. We
find a couple of wines in the finals every
year, but they are hardly ever the same
ones. This year we were thrilled by an
excellent 2009 Picolit dei Colli Orientali del
Friuli, with aromas of ripe yellow peach and
caramelized orange peel. The slightly
tropical 2016 Sauvignon is just as good.

○ COF Picolit '09	♙♙ 6
○ FCO Sauvignon '16	♙♙ 3*
○ FCO Friulano '16	♙♙ 3
○ FCO Friulano Vign. Storico '16	♙♙ 4
● FCO Merlot '15	♙♙ 3
○ FCO Pinot Grigio '16	♙♙ 3
○ FCO Ribolla Gialla '16	♙♙ 3
● FCO Schioppettino '12	♙♙ 3
○ Friuli Bianco Storico & Friends '16	♙♙ 4
○ Friuli Isonzo Malvasia '16	♙♙ 3
○ FCO Chardonnay '16	♙ 3
⊙ Prima Nera Brut Rosé	♙ 3
○ Ribolla Gialla Brut	♙ 3
○ COF Tocai Friulano Vign. Storico '06	♙♙♙ 4
○ COF Tocai Friulano Vign. Storico '05	♙♙♙ 4
○ FCO Picolit '08	♙♙♙ 6

Gori

VIA G.B. GORI, 14
33045 NIMIS [UD]
TEL. +39 0432878475
www.goriagricola.it

PRE-BOOKED VISITS
ANNUAL PRODUCTION 50,000 bottles
HECTARES UNDER VINE 18.00

Gori was inspired by Gianpiero Gori's desire
to return to his origins, by a love for his
homeland, which, in 2009, led to the
successful entrepreneur deciding to
radically change sectors and dedicate
himself full-time to winemaking. To crown
his dream-come-true, Gianpiero (known
only as Piero to his friends) build a
gorgeous cellar in the westernmost (and
coldest) part of Nimis, in the Friuli Colli
Orientali DOC zone. It's an architecturally
modern and well-studied facility,
constituted of three underground floors,
which allows production to take full
advantage of gravity in making wine. The
wood area, for their reds, is made up of
mid-sized casks and large, French oak
barrels. Piero personalizes his wines by
combining strange names, often from local
sayings, with the name of the variety. For
instance, Bonblanc, meaning "a good glass
of white wine", and the 2015 Friulano
Bonblanc really is a good wine, so much so
that it made the final selections.

○ FCO Friulano Bonblanc '15	♙♙ 3*
○ FCO Chardonnay Giugiù '15	♙♙ 3
○ FCO Sauvignon Busseben '15	♙♙ 3
● FCO Schioppettino TitaG '15	♙♙ 3
○ Ramandolo OrodiNemas '14	♙ 4
○ Chardonnay Giugiù '13	♉♉ 4
● FCO Merlot Toni Vasùt '14	♉♉ 3
○ FCO Sauvignon Busseben '14	♉♉ 3
● Refosco P. R. Redelbosco '13	♉♉ 3*
● Refosco P. R. Redelbosco '12	♉♉ 4
● Rosso Meni Vasùt '13	♉♉ 3
● Rosso Meni Vasùt '12	♉♉ 4

Gradis'ciutta

Loc. Giasbana, 10
34070 San Floriano del Collio [GO]
Tel. +39 0481390237
www.gradisciutta.eu

CELLAR SALES
PRE-BOOKED VISITS
ANNUAL PRODUCTION 100,000 bottles
HECTARES UNDER VINE 20.00

In 1997 Robert Princic founded
Gradis'ciutta, taking the name from a small
hamlet in Giasbana, San Floriano del
Collio. The hamlet used to be called
Monvinoso, which tells you something
about the long tradition of wine making in
these hills. By now, 'Collio' means wine,
white wine to be exact. It is a wine made
of three native varieties of grape: tocai
friulano, Malvasia istriana and ribolla gialla.
And Robert, who treats them each with
equal respect, uses them in equal parts to
make his Bratinis, an ambassador of
Collio wines throughout the world. The fact
that some vineyards are more than
80-years-old is further proof that this
estate is worth safekeeping. With great
continuity, we found the 2016 Friulano
and the 2015 Bratinis in the finals again
this year. Both wines are the best
expression of the features of the native
grapes. The 2016 Sauvignon debuted this
year, proving Collio's great potential for this
international variety.

○ Collio Bianco Bratinis '15	♈♈ 3*
○ Collio Friulano '16	♈♈ 3*
○ Collio Sauvignon '16	♈♈ 3*
○ Collio Chardonnay '16	♈♈ 3
○ Collio Pinot Grigio '16	♈♈ 3
○ Collio Ribolla Gialla '16	♈♈ 3
○ Collio Bianco Bratinis '14	♈♈ 3*
○ Collio Bianco Bratinis '13	♈♈ 3*
○ Collio Bianco Ris. '09	♈♈ 3
○ Collio Chardonnay '15	♈♈ 3
○ Collio Friulano '15	♈♈ 3*
○ Collio Pinot Grigio '15	♈♈ 3
○ Collio Ribolla Gialla '15	♈♈ 3
○ Collio Sauvignon '15	♈♈ 3

★★Gravner

Fraz. Oslavia
Loc. Lenzuolo Bianco, 9
34070 Gorizia
Tel. +39 048130882
www.gravner.it

CELLAR SALES
PRE-BOOKED VISITS
ANNUAL PRODUCTION 30,000 bottles
HECTARES UNDER VINE 18.00

Everything you can imagine has already
been written or said about Josko Gravner.
And yet every time you taste his wines it
ignites your senses, inspires a new vision,
incites new emotions that are, for their
bare authenticity and originality, difficult to
describe. And yet they are simply wines, as
he's said, made by respecting the land and
the seasons, with ancient techniques that
don't disrupt nature's normal rhythms. It's
well known, by now, that his vineyards only
contain ribolla gialla grapes, a variety
that's seeing popularity across the entire
region. But Josko's Ribolla is in a league of
its own, just take the fact that harvest
occurs in November, when the leaves are
all gone. The rest is just artistry. This year,
the 2009 Ribolla, the 2009 Bianco Breg
and the 2005 Rosso Breg have been put
forward for tasting. The latter is a
monovarietal Pignolo, which is the only red
grape variety left in Josko's vineyards. It's
a firmly structured wine and took about a
dozen years to soften the tannins, but it
has really paid off.

○ Bianco Breg '09	♈♈ 7
○ Ribolla Gialla '09	♈♈ 5
● Rosso Breg '05	♈♈ 7
○ Breg '00	♈♈♈ 8
○ Breg Anfora '06	♈♈♈ 7
○ Breg Anfora '03	♈♈♈ 7
○ Breg Anfora '02	♈♈♈ 7
○ Chardonnay '87	♈♈♈ 7
○ Chardonnay '83	♈♈♈ 7
○ Ribolla Anfora '05	♈♈♈ 7
○ Ribolla Anfora '04	♈♈♈ 7
○ Ribolla Anfora '02	♈♈♈ 7
○ Ribolla Anfora '01	♈♈♈ 7
○ Ribolla Gialla '08	♈♈♈ 5
○ Ribolla Gialla '07	♈♈♈ 5
● Rosso Gravner '04	♈♈♈ 7

Iole Grillo

VIA ALBANA, 60
33040 PREPOTTO [UD]
TEL. +39 0432713201
www.vinigrillo.it

CELLAR SALES
PRE-BOOKED VISITS
ACCOMMODATION
ANNUAL PRODUCTION 40,000 bottles
HECTARES UNDER VINE 9.00

Iole Grillo is a lovely winery situated in Albana di Prepotto, a small town set at the mouth of a splendid valley, in the southern part of the Friuli Colli Orientali DOC zone. It's managed with determination and indisputable entrepreneurial skill by Anna Muzzolini, as well as her husband, Andrea. They're keeping alive the legacy of Anna's father, Sergio, who founded the winery in the 1960s and dedicated it to his wife, Iole Grillo. The winery's entranced is marked by a beautiful gate from an 18th century villa, and a chapel dedicated to St. Justine. The basement of the villa, which is characterized by enchanting stone walls, hosts the cellar. Here, their wines age in wood of various sizes. Once again, the whole range gave an excellent performance, but the two different versions of the Sauvignon were particularly good. The vintage wine stands out for its aroma and lovely mouth, while the 2015 Sauvignon Blanc is more complex and refined, making it to the finals.

○ FCO Sauvignon Blanc '15	🍷🍷 3*
● FCO Merlot Ris. '13	🍷🍷 3
● FCO Refosco P. R. '13	🍷🍷 3
○ FCO Ribolla Gialla '16	🍷🍷 3
○ FCO Sauvignon '16	🍷🍷 3
● FCO Schioppettino di Prepotto '14	🍷🍷 3
● Rosso Duedonne	🍷🍷 3
○ FCO Friulano '16	🍷 3
● COF Schioppettino di Prepotto '11	🍷🍷 3
○ FCO Friulano '15	🍷🍷 3
● FCO Merlot Ris. '12	🍷🍷 3
● FCO Merlot Ris. '11	🍷🍷 3
● FCO Refosco P. R. '12	🍷🍷 3
○ FCO Sauvignon '15	🍷🍷 3
● FCO Schioppettino di Prepotto '13	🍷🍷 3

Albano Guerra

LOC. MONTINA
V.LE KENNEDY, 39A
33040 TORREANO [UD]
TEL. +39 0432715479
www.guerraalbano.it

CELLAR SALES
PRE-BOOKED VISITS
ANNUAL PRODUCTION 60,000 bottles
HECTARES UNDER VINE 10.00

The winery was formalized in 1931 by Albano Guerra, but its deeper origins are lost in time. As long as anyone can remember, the Guerra family have cultivated the hill terrain of Montana di Torreano, in the southern part of what is today the Friuli Colli Orientali DOC zone. Since 1997, its been managed by Dario Guerra, a true wine artisan. He loves reminding us that, in these parts, a vine-grower isn't just a professional title, it's a way of being, something that you carry within you from your brith and then pass on to the next generation, along with your culture and territory's history. Their goal here is to make wines while involved the environment, following the needs of the grapes, grassing the terrain, and intervening only when needed. The white grape varieties undergo light maceration on the skins, without oxygen or temperature control. This enables more extraction of aromatic substances, which help to distinguish the marked and recognizable sensory properties of the varieties.

● COF Rosso Gritul Ris. '09	🍷🍷 4
○ FCO Malvasia '16	🍷🍷 2*
○ FCO Pinot Grigio '16	🍷🍷 2*
○ FCO Sauvignon '16	🍷🍷 2*
○ Ribolla Gialla Brut Giuliet '14	🍷🍷 3
○ COF Ribolla Gialla '16	🍷 2
○ FCO Friulano '16	🍷 2
● FCO Merlot '15	🍷 2
● COF Merlot '10	🍷🍷 2*
○ COF Passion Bianco Guerra Albano '12	🍷🍷 2*
○ FCO Friulano '15	🍷🍷 2*
○ FCO Malvasia '15	🍷🍷 2*
○ FCO Malvasia Istriana '14	🍷🍷 2*
● FCO Merlot '11	🍷🍷 2*
○ FCO Sauvignon '15	🍷🍷 2*

Jacùss

FRAZ. MONTINA
V.LE KENNEDY, 35A
33040 TORREANO [UD]
TEL. +39 0432715147
www.jacuss.it

CELLAR SALES
PRE-BOOKED VISITS
ANNUAL PRODUCTION 50,000 bottles
HECTARES UNDER VINE 11.00

The name Jacùss is a version of the last name Iacuzzi in local dialect. It was the Iacuzzi brothers, Sandro and Andrea, who founded this winery in 1990, embracing the tendency of the time to shift from mixed varieties to specialized ones. Working in perfect synergy, with constance and dedication, they proceeded to substantially modernize the vineyards. They didn't have to wait long to see the results, and the improvement in quality helped them stand out in the crowded Colli Orientali del Friuli DOC zone. They deserve credit for their ability to preserve the specific qualities of each variety of grape, whether white, red, sweet or otherwise, in perfect artisanal style. The novelty this year is the Forment, a white made with Tocai Friulano grapes from the 2015 vintage, which ferments on selected yeasts while in experimentation. As it's unfiltered, It could appear hazy, but the nose is excellent and the palate is coherent and elegant.

○ Bianco Forment '15	🍷🍷 3*
○ COF Picolit '11	🍷🍷 6
● FCO Merlot '13	🍷🍷 3
○ FCO Pinot Bianco '16	🍷🍷 3
● FCO Schioppettino Fucs e Flamis '15	🍷🍷 3
● FCO Tazzelenghe '12	🍷🍷 3
○ FCO Verduzzo Friulano '15	🍷🍷 3
● FCO Cabernet Sauvignon '14	🍷 3
○ FCO Friulano '16	🍷 3
○ FCO Sauvignon '16	🍷 3
● FCO Cabernet Sauvignon '12	🍷🍷 3
● FCO Merlot '12	🍷🍷 3
○ FCO Picolit '10	🍷🍷 6
● FCO Schioppettino Fucs e Flamis '14	🍷🍷 3

★★Jermann

FRAZ. RUTTARS
LOC. TRUSSIO, 11
34072 DOLEGNA DEL COLLIO [GO]
TEL. +39 0481888080
www.jermann.it

CELLAR SALES
PRE-BOOKED VISITS
ANNUAL PRODUCTION 900,000 bottles
HECTARES UNDER VINE 160.00

Silvio Jermann's winery is not only a jewel of the region, it's also one of Italy's most internationally recognized producers. It was 1975 when young Silvio put his Vintage Tunina on the market, an outstanding blend that still serves as their flagship wine. Other, just as prestigious, wines followed, establishing Jermann's reputation for quality, tradition and being representative of regional excellence. Silvio is a free spirit and his wines reflect his personality, unchained from the restrictions of production imposed by DOC certification. After a pause last year, when it was the Pinot Grigio who took the highest accolade, it's once again the 2015 Vintage Tunina that steps up the podium. It's stunning and so lively that this is one of the best vintages we can remember. Time will prove us right.

○ Vintage Tunina '15	🍷🍷🍷 7
○ Capo Martino '15	🍷🍷 7
● Pinot Nero Red Angel '14	🍷🍷 4
○ W.... Dreams.... '15	🍷🍷 8
○ Chardonnay '16	🍷🍷 4
○ Collio Picolit '12	🍷🍷 4
○ Pinot Grigio '16	🍷🍷 4
○ Ribolla Gialla Vinnae '16	🍷🍷 4
○ Sauvignon '16	🍷🍷 4
○ Capo Martino '10	🍷🍷🍷 8
○ Pinot Grigio '15	🍷🍷🍷 4*
○ Vintage Tunina '13	🍷🍷🍷 6
○ Vintage Tunina '12	🍷🍷🍷 6
○ Vintage Tunina '11	🍷🍷🍷 6
○ W... Dreams... ... ... '12	🍷🍷🍷 8

FRIULI VENEZIA GIULIA

Kante

Fraz. San Pelagio
Loc. Prepotto, 1a
34011 Duino Aurisina [TS]
Tel. +39 040200255
www.kante.it

ANNUAL PRODUCTION 45,000 bottles
HECTARES UNDER VINE 13.00

Known for its brilliant landscapes, winemaking in Karst can be considered 'heroic'. The vineyards enjoy favorable exposure to the sun and benefit from an influx of sea air and north winds, but planting them means digging trenches in the hard rocks, often with dynamite, and refilling them with fertile soil. And so it was that Edi Kante, in 1980, began to experiment and innovate, blazing a trail that brought in ranks of disciples. His wines are surprising. They have that little something, both his newer vintages and his 'Riserve'. The data sheet this year looks like a photocopy of last year's. The same wines, the same scores, only the vintages have changed. The same three wines are in the finals, underlining the consistency that Edi manages to skillfully maintain, even in different and particularly difficult vintages like 2014.

○ Chardonnay La Bora di Kante '11	♛♛ 4
○ Malvasia '14	♛♛ 4
○ Vitovska '14	♛♛ 4
○ Chardonnay '14	♛♛ 4
○ Sauvignon '14	♛♛ 5
○ Carso Malvasia '07	♛♛♛ 5
○ Carso Malvasia '06	♛♛♛ 5
○ Carso Malvasia '05	♛♛♛ 5
○ Malvasia '12	♛♛♛ 4*
○ Chardonnay '13	♕♕ 4
○ Chardonnay La Bora di Kante '08	♕♕ 4
○ Malvasia '13	♕♕ 4
○ Vitovska '13	♕♕ 4

★Edi Keber

Loc. Zegla, 17
34071 Cormòns [GO]
Tel. +39 048161184
www.edikeber.it

CELLAR SALES
PRE-BOOKED VISITS
ACCOMMODATION
ANNUAL PRODUCTION 50,000 bottles
HECTARES UNDER VINE 12.00

The name of the Keber family is connected to Zegla and Medana. These are borderlands that have known various flags, either because of fortune or political events. At times they were in Austria, then Italy, then Slovenia and then Italy again, all without having to leave home. We've known for years that Edi chose to produce only one wine, Collio, which has always been a symbol of outstanding white wine. There was a time when it wasn't a common practice to produce wines from the same monovarietal, and so this is none other than a return to tradition. His Collio is a mix of tocai friulano, malvasia istriana and ribolla gialla, considered the three white grape varieties 'par excellence' The 2016 Collio expresses the potential of the territory, the characteristics of the varieties and Edi's winemaking philosophy, all at the same time. Aromatic notes of rare pleasantness anticipate overtones that expand on the palate in a gradual, soft and appealing finish.

○ Collio '16	♛♛ 3*
○ Collio Bianco '10	♛♛♛ 3*
○ Collio Bianco '09	♛♛♛ 3
○ Collio Bianco '08	♛♛♛ 3*
○ Collio Bianco '04	♛♛♛ 3*
○ Collio Bianco '02	♛♛♛ 3
○ Collio Tocai Friulano '07	♛♛♛ 3
○ Collio Tocai Friulano '06	♛♛♛ 3
○ Collio Tocai Friulano '05	♛♛♛ 3
○ Collio Tocai Friulano '03	♛♛♛ 3*
○ Collio Tocai Friulano '01	♛♛♛ 3

Alessio Komjanc

Loc. Giasbana, 35
34070 San Floriano del Collio [GO]
Tel. +39 0481391228
www.komjancalessio.com

CELLAR SALES
PRE-BOOKED VISITS
ANNUAL PRODUCTION 70,000 bottles
HECTARES UNDER VINE 24.00
SUSTAINABLE WINERY

The Komjanc family call themselves 'a family joined by the values of tradition, looking enthusiastically to the future with the aim of producing top-quality oils and wines'. This was a goal that Alessio Komjanc gave himself back in 1973 when he founded the winery, and that has incited his four children, Beniamin, Roberto, Patrik and Ivani to work towards excellence with persistence and dedication. Recent vintages have already shown significant progress in terms of quality, probably thanks in part to the precious counsel of Gianni Menotti. Once again, a Komjanc wine made it to the finals, adding prestige to the already qualified potential of the territory around San Floriano del Collio. The 2016 Friulano combines aromas of meadow flowers and crisp fruit with a marked softness and tangy juiciness.

○ Collio Friulano '16	♟♟ 3*
○ Bianco Bratje '15	♟♟ 3
○ Collio Chardonnay '16	♟♟ 3
○ Collio Picolit '15	♟♟ 6
○ Collio Pinot Grigio '16	♟♟ 3
○ Collio Sauvignon '16	♟♟ 3
○ Malvasia '16	♟♟ 3
○ Collio Ribolla Gialla '16	♟ 2
○ Collio Traminer Aromatico '17	♟ 3
○ Collio Chardonnay '15	♟♟ 2*
○ Collio Friulano '15	♟♟ 2*
○ Collio Sauvignon '15	♟♟ 2*
○ Malvasia Istriana '15	♟♟ 3*

Anita Vogric Kurtin

Loc. Novali, 9
34071 Cormòns [GO]
Tel. +39 048160685
www.winekurtin.it

CELLAR SALES
PRE-BOOKED VISITS
ANNUAL PRODUCTION 60,000 bottles
HECTARES UNDER VINE 10.00

The Kurtin family winery was founded in 1906, in Novali (Cormòns). Even back then, the natural amphitheater that faces Slovenia (from Collio) was considered perfect for producing quality white wines. Today, it's owned by Anita Vogric, widow of recently-deceased Albino Kurtin. But it's their son, Alessio, the fourth generation of family, who's been overseeing management since 2009, and taken on the responsibility of winemaking. Gradually, he's trying to grow the winery, and recently added a new vineyard through the rooting of Ribolla Gialla, a native grape variety that offers up freshness and that, in recent years, has seen an exponential growth in popularity. Once again we were only able to taste four wines, all whites. However, they were enough to confirm Alessio's skill in keeping the sensory characteristics of each variety intact. These are enhanced by the territorial features of Collio's magical subsoil.

○ Collio Friulano '16	♟♟ 3
○ Collio Pinot Grigio '16	♟♟ 3
○ Collio Ribolla Gialla '16	♟♟ 3
○ Collio Sauvignon '16	♟♟ 3
○ Collio Chardonnay '15	♟♟ 3
○ Collio Friulano '15	♟♟ 3
○ Collio Sauvignon '14	♟♟ 3
○ Opera Prima Bianco '15	♟♟ 3
○ Opera Prima Bianco '14	♟♟ 3
○ Opera Prima Bianco '13	♟♟ 4

Vigneti Le Monde

LOC. LE MONDE
VIA GARIBALDI, 2
33080 PRATA DI PORDENONE [PN]
TEL. +39 0434622087
www.lemondewine.com

CELLAR SALES
PRE-BOOKED VISITS
ANNUAL PRODUCTION 400,000 bottles
HECTARES UNDER VINE 80.00
SUSTAINABLE WINERY

In all respects, Le Monde represents a model of success for Pordenone. There's no doubt that this is thanks to the skill of Alex Maccan who, in 2008, took over a thriving winery and ably steered it towards the highest peaks of regional excellence. Their secret lies in the low yields (something rare in plains viticulture), in the age of their vineyards (some of which are well older than 30), but especially in the makeup of the clay and calcium-rich soil that characterizes the area. This is the reason why Le Monde is considered to be in a favorable subzone for growing wine. A modern, dynamic, robust winery that is well-guided and continually expanding, Le Monde has its sights set on the future. The 'right price' is this selection's main feature, and when compared to its quality and scores, their prices seem even better. The 2016 Pinot Bianco stands out once again, winning a Tre Bicchieri for the fifth time in a row and confirming its role as the producer's flagship wine.

○ Friuli Grave Pinot Bianco '16	♟♟♟ 2*
● Friuli Grave Cabernet Sauvignon '15	♟♟ 2*
○ Friuli Grave Chardonnay '16	♟♟ 2*
● Friuli Grave Merlot '15	♟♟ 2*
● Friuli Grave Refosco P. R. '15	♟♟ 2*
⊙ Pinot Nero Rosé Brut	♟♟ 2*
○ Pratum Ris. '14	♟♟ 4
○ Ribolla Gialla '16	♟♟ 3
○ Ribolla Gialla Brut	♟♟ 3
● Friuli Grave Cabernet Franc '15	♟ 2
○ Friuli Grave Pinot Grigio '16	♟ 2
● Friuli Grave Refosco P. R. Inaco Ris. '13	♟ 4
○ Friuli Grave Sauvignon '16	♟ 2
○ Friuli Grave Pinot Bianco '15	♟♟♟ 2*
○ Friuli Grave Pinot Bianco '14	♟♟♟ 2*

★Lis Neris

VIA GAVINANA, 5
34070 SAN LORENZO ISONTINO [GO]
TEL. +39 048180105
www.lisneris.it

CELLAR SALES
PRE-BOOKED VISITS
ACCOMMODATION
ANNUAL PRODUCTION 400,000 bottles
HECTARES UNDER VINE 70.00
SUSTAINABLE WINERY

What more is there to say about Alvaro Pecorari, the man who knew how to put his winemaking style into practice and create a line of products that stand as a model of excellence? This is the man who made his Pinot Grigio a towering, crown jewel, recognized as among the best wines in all of Italy. Lis Neris is, by now, an international brand, a stalwart, a guarantee stamped on almost half a million bottles, with an attention to detail that sees to it that each individual bottle has its own integrity. And in talking about his success, rather than take the credit himself, Alvaro has always pointed to the attributes of the territory. His modesty speaks to true class. It's usually the Pinot Grigio that best represents the winery, but this year the Gris was outdone in the finals by the 2015 Lis. It's the winery's own blend of Pinot Grigio, Chardonnay and Sauvignon Blanc, which thoroughly deserved to win back a Tre Bicchieri after many years.

○ Lis '15	♟♟♟ 5
○ Friuli Isonzo Pinot Grigio Gris '15	♟♟ 5
○ Friuli Isonzo Sauvignon Picòl '15	♟♟ 4
○ Fiore di Campo '16	♟♟ 3
○ Friuli Isonzo Chardonnay Jurosa '15	♟♟ 4
○ Fiore di Campo '06	♟♟♟ 3
○ Friuli Isonzo Pinot Grigio Gris '13	♟♟♟ 4*
○ Friuli Isonzo Pinot Grigio Gris '12	♟♟♟ 4*
○ Friuli Isonzo Pinot Grigio Gris '11	♟♟♟ 4*
○ Friuli Isonzo Pinot Grigio Gris '10	♟♟♟ 4*
○ Friuli Isonzo Pinot Grigio Gris '09	♟♟♟ 4*
○ Pinot Grigio Gris '08	♟♟♟ 4*
○ Sauvignon Picòl '06	♟♟♟ 3*
○ Tal Lùc Cuvée Speciale	♟♟♟ 8

★Livon

FRAZ. DOLEGNANO
VIA MONTAREZZA, 33
33048 SAN GIOVANNI AL NATISONE [UD]
TEL. +39 0432757173
www.livon.it

CELLAR SALES
PRE-BOOKED VISITS
ACCOMMODATION
ANNUAL PRODUCTION 850,000 bottles
HECTARES UNDER VINE 180.00

The name Dorino Livon appears in the brief list of brave and forward-looking men who, in the 1960s, sensed the potential of the region for producing high-quality wines. Like a true pioneer, he started down a path now being tread by his children Valneo and Tonino who, in perfect union, have overseen the continued growth of the winery. Livon is among the giants of the Italian peninsula. We can add their prestigious wines, which highlight the character of the surrounding DOC zones, to the list of Collio's famous whites. Once again, it was difficult to choose the best of this stunning selection of wines. An excellent 2012 Picolit dei Colli Orientali del Friuli was a surprise and earned a Tre Bicchieri, a trophy that was missing from Livon's rich showcase.

Tenuta Luisa

FRAZ. CORONA
VIA CAMPO SPORTIVO, 13
34070 MARIANO DEL FRIULI [GO]
TEL. +39 048169680
www.tenutaluisa.it

CELLAR SALES
PRE-BOOKED VISITS
ACCOMMODATION
ANNUAL PRODUCTION 350,000 bottles
HECTARES UNDER VINE 100.00
SUSTAINABLE WINERY

Tenuta Luisa has solidly established itself as among the best producers in the region and, especially, the Friuli Isonzo DOC zone. As with any family-run producer, it thinks on its simple origins with pride and fond memories. It was 1927 when Francesco Luisa, a 37-year-old widower with six children, had the chance to buy a few hectares of land. On those few hectares Eddi Luisa began building his future, going from mixed-cultivation to specialized vineyards. Today there are 100 hectares and Michele and Davide are continuing the tradition, united through a strength made possible by their heritage and close family ties. The I Ferretti line is the result of a careful selection of the best grapes and serve as the winery's crown jewels. In the last edition, Desiderium collected the highest accolade (for the second time), while this year Tre Bicchieri goes to the 2015 Friulano I Ferretti.

○ COF Picolit '12	♥♥♥ 6
○ Braide Alte '15	♥♥ 5
○ Collio Bianco Solarco '16	♥♥ 3*
○ Collio Friulano Manditocai '15	♥♥ 5
○ Collio Pinot Bianco Cavezzo '16	♥♥ 2*
○ Collio Ribolla Gialla RoncAlto '16	♥♥ 3
● TiareBlù '14	♥♥ 5
○ Braide Alte '13	♥♥♥ 5
○ Braide Alte '11	♥♥♥ 5
○ Braide Alte '09	♥♥♥ 5
○ Braide Alte '07	♥♥♥ 5
○ Collio Bianco Solarco '15	♥♥♥ 3*
○ Collio Braide Alte '08	♥♥♥ 3
○ Collio Friulano Manditocai '12	♥♥♥ 5
○ Collio Friulano Manditocai '10	♥♥♥ 5

○ Friuli Isonzo Friulano I Ferretti '15	♥♥♥ 3*
○ Desiderium I Ferretti '15	♥♥ 4
● Cabernet Sauvignon '13	♥♥ 4
○ Friuli Isonzo Friulano '16	♥♥ 3
○ Friuli Isonzo Pinot Bianco '16	♥♥ 3
○ Friuli Isonzo Sauvignon '16	♥♥ 3
● Rol '13	♥♥ 4
○ Friuli Isonzo Chardonnay '16	♥ 3
○ Ribolla Gialla '16	♥ 3
○ Desiderium I Ferretti '13	♥♥♥ 4*
○ Desiderium Sel. I Ferretti '09	♥♥♥ 4*
○ Friuli Isonzo Tocai Friulano '03	♥♥♥ 2*

Magnàs

LOC. BOATINA
VIA CORONA, 47
34071 CORMÒNS [GO]
TEL. +39 048160991
www.magnas.it

CELLAR SALES
PRE-BOOKED VISITS
ACCOMMODATION AND RESTAURANT SERVICE
ANNUAL PRODUCTION 25,000 bottles
HECTARES UNDER VINE 10.00

Magnàs is a classic operation 'by the people'. Indeed, thanks to its small scale, it can be managed 'in first person', at every stage of production. It all started in the early 1960s when a young Luciano Visintin had the urge to start a different kind of winery with a personal touch, drawing on his family's background in agriculture. Firmly rooted in his principles, he never let himself be influenced by fashion and stubbornly maintained the winery's original, small size, as well as its roots in tradition and craftsmanship. He passed these principles to his son, Andrea, who's now completely responsible for the winery. The wines enjoy an exemplary cleanness, without frills or artifice, and in their simplicity they express the best characteristics of each variety. The supple and caressing palate favors drinkability, especially in the Chardonnay, which makes you want to come back for more.

○ Chardonnay '16	♥♥ 3*
● Cabernet Franc '15	♥♥ 3
○ Malvasia '16	♥♥ 3
○ Pinot Grigio '16	♥♥ 3
○ Sauvignon '16	♥♥ 3
○ Collio Friulano '16	♥ 3
○ Collio Bianco '15	♀♀ 3
○ Collio Bianco '13	♀♀ 3*
○ Friuli Isonzo Friulano '15	♀♀ 3
○ Malvasia '15	♀♀ 3
● Merlot '13	♀♀ 3
○ Pinot Grigio '15	♀♀ 3*
○ Pinot Grigio '14	♀♀ 3
○ Sauvignon '14	♀♀ 3

Valerio Marinig

VIA BROLO, 41
33040 PREPOTTO [UD]
TEL. +39 0432713012
www.marinig.it

CELLAR SALES
PRE-BOOKED VISITS
ANNUAL PRODUCTION 25,000 bottles
HECTARES UNDER VINE 9.00

In 1921, Luigi Marinig, great-grandfather of Valerio, owned a small farming operation and would soon add a second. There were only a few hectares at the time, but it was enough to get started. Generations after him knew how to use the land, gradually establishing the winery's reputation for quality and presence in the region. Their vineyards are spread out across the hills of Prepotto, including the Friuli Colli Orientati DOC zone, known as the homeland of Schioppettino. The unique microclimates of the Judrio river valley create the conditions for growing quality grapes, which is reflected in the local character of their wines. The 2013 Schioppettino di Prepotto, the 2015 Refosco dal Peduncolo Rosso and the 2013 Pignolo make up the trio of well-made and pleasant native red wines that heads the rankings. But we mustn't overlook the performance of the vintage wines, which we really liked for their aroma and drinkability.

○ FCO Friulano '16	♥♥ 2*
● FCO Pignolo '13	♥♥ 4
● FCO Refosco P. R. '15	♥♥ 3
○ FCO Sauvignon '16	♥♥ 3
● FCO Schioppettino di Prepotto '13	♥♥ 4
○ FCO Verduzzo Friulano '16	♥ 3
● FCO Biel Cûr Rosso '13	♀♀ 4
○ FCO Friulano '15	♀♀ 2*
● FCO Refosco P. R. '14	♀♀ 3
○ FCO Sauvignon '15	♀♀ 3
● FCO Schioppettino di Prepotto '12	♀♀ 4

Masùt da Rive

VIA MANZONI, 82
34070 MARIANO DEL FRIULI [GO]
TEL. +39 048169200
www.masutdarive.com

CELLAR SALES
PRE-BOOKED VISITS
ANNUAL PRODUCTION 80,000 bottles
HECTARES UNDER VINE 22.00
SUSTAINABLE WINERY

The work undertaken by Fabrizio and Marco Gallo has propelled Masùt da Rive into the category of exemplary regional producers. In fact, they've been forced to rethink the design of their bottles and selection, which is now divided into three distinct lines: 'Gli Scudi' are their traditional reds and whites; 'White Label' are wines that are left to ripen for a longer time and aged in wood; 'Black Label' are their top wines, vintages from the best years. The results lived up to expectations and two wines deservedly made it to the finals. An excellent 2016 Pinot Grigio placed itself right at the top of its category, accompanied by the 2015 Chardonnay Maurus, which won over the palate with its finesse and elegance.

○ Friuli Isonzo Chardonnay Maurus '15	♟♟	5
○ Friuli Isonzo Pinot Grigio '16	♟♟	3*
○ Friuli Isonzo Friulano '16	♟♟	3
● Friuli Isonzo Pinot Nero '15	♟♟	5
● Friuli Isonzo Rosso Sassi Rossi '15	♟♟	5
○ Friuli Isonzo Sauvignon '16	♟♟	3
● Friuli Isonzo Cabernet Franc '16	♟	3
○ Friuli Isonzo Chardonnay '16	♟	3
○ Friuli Isonzo Tocai Friulano '04	♟♟♟	3*
● Friuli Isonzo Cabernet Sauvignon '14	♟♟	3
● Friuli Isonzo Pinot Nero '14	♟♟	5
○ Pinot Grigio '15	♟♟	3

Davino Meroi

VIA STRETTA, 7B
33042 BUTTRIO [UD]
TEL. +39 0432673369
www.meroi.wine

CELLAR SALES
PRE-BOOKED VISITS
RESTAURANT SERVICE
ANNUAL PRODUCTION 45,000 bottles
HECTARES UNDER VINE 19.00
SUSTAINABLE WINERY

Davino Meroi is the founder and man who gave his name to the winery now owned and run by Paolo. The latter has made the producer among the best in the region by drawing out the unique character of his vineyards, which go back to his grandfather Domenico and he himself inherited. These run along the hills of Buttrio, located at the beginning of the natural amphitheater of hills that are part of the Colli Orientali del Friuli DOC zone. Both in the vineyard and in the cellar, Paolo counts on the precious help of his collaborator Mirko Degan. Together they make uplifting, rich, concentrated wines, the result of age-old, fine-tuned techniques in the use of wood. A magical 2015 Sauvignon headed the rankings and took part in the final selections, along with the 2013 Merlot Vigna Dominin. Consensus and acclaim is raining down on both of them and, though they may not have earned top marks, they are still on the list of wines that make the territory great.

● FCO Merlot V. Dominin '13	♟♟	8
○ FCO Sauvignon '15	♟♟	4
● FCO Refosco P. R. V. Dominin '13	♟♟	8
○ FCO Chardonnay '15	♟♟	5
○ FCO Friulano '15	♟♟	5
○ COF Friulano '11	♟♟♟	5
○ COF Friulano '10	♟♟♟	5
○ COF Verduzzo Friulano '08	♟♟♟	5
○ COF Friulano '13	♟♟	5
○ FCO Chardonnay '14	♟♟	5
● FCO Merlot Ros di Buri '13	♟♟	5
○ FCO Sauvignon '14	♟♟	4
○ FCO Verduzzo Friulano '13	♟♟	5

Moschioni

LOC. GAGLIANO
VIA DORIA, 30
33043 CIVIDALE DEL FRIULI [UD]
TEL. +39 0432730210
www.michelemoschioni.it

CELLAR SALES
PRE-BOOKED VISITS
ANNUAL PRODUCTION 38,000 bottles
HECTARES UNDER VINE 14.00
SUSTAINABLE WINERY

Making only red wine in a region like Friuli, which is known the world over as white wine country, might seem like a paradox. But it's not for Michele Moschioni, who has always believed that Friuli Colli Orientali has great territorial potential for reds. His vineyards features vines that are over 50 years old. These are ungrafted, which results in full, juicy grapes that are rich in aromas and strong tannins. Fermentation takes place in truncated cone vats. The wine is then aged for a year in French oak, and for three more in large Slavonian oak. But that's not enough. They then spend another year in the same vats in which they were fermented. The winemaking process sometimes leads to high concentrations of aromas and alcohol, but these are very well-balanced with other components. Further aging in the bottle will temper impetuous tannins and harmony will be ensured by soft, caressing juiciness.

● FCO Schioppettino Ris. '11	🍷🍷 7
● FCO Pignolo Ris. '11	🍷🍷 7
● FCO Refosco P. R. Ris. '11	🍷🍷 4
● FCO Rosso Celtico Ris. '11	🍷🍷 5
● FCO Rosso Reâl Ris. '11	🍷🍷 5
● COF Rosso Celtico '04	🍷🍷🍷 5
● COF Schioppettino '06	🍷🍷🍷 6
● COF Pignolo '09	🍷🍷 7
● COF Refosco P. R. '09	🍷🍷 4
● COF Rosso Celtico '09	🍷🍷 5
● COF Rosso Reâl '09	🍷🍷 5
● COF Schioppettino '09	🍷🍷 7
● FCO Rosso Bisest '10	🍷🍷 5

Murva - Renata Pizzulin

VIA CELSO MACOR, 1
34070 MORARO [GO]
TEL. +39 0432713027
www.murva.it

CELLAR SALES
PRE-BOOKED VISITS
ANNUAL PRODUCTION 15,000 bottles
HECTARES UNDER VINE 4.00
SUSTAINABLE WINERY

Thanks to the energy and determination of a young couple, Alberto Pelos and Renata Pizzulin, this small winery came into being along the right bank of the Isonzo river. Murva - Renata Pizzulin immediately established itself as being at the forefront in terms of quality, as demonstrated by their wines. Its smaller scale has also allowed the producer to practice sustainable cultivation. Its vineyards are set in distinct sites, each chosen because it best fits with the characteristics of the cultivar, and each wine is identified by the grapes' vineyard of origin. There is no real difference between the 2015 Chardonnay Monuments and the 2015 Chardonnay Paladis. Both enjoy a fresh aroma and flavorsome drinkability, but there are several nuances which distinguish the production areas. It's a sophistication that enhances the characteristics of the territory.

○ Friuli Isonzo Bianco Teolis '15	🍷🍷 4
○ Friuli Isonzo Chardonnay Monuments '15	🍷🍷 3
○ Friuli Isonzo Chardonnay Paladis '15	🍷🍷 4
○ Friuli Isonzo Malvasia Melaris '15	🍷🍷 4
○ Friuli Isonzo Sauvignon Corvatis '15	🍷 3
○ Friuli Isonzo Bianco Teolis '14	🍷🍷 4
○ Friuli Isonzo Bianco Teolis '13	🍷🍷 3
○ Friuli Isonzo Chardonnay Paladis '14	🍷🍷 3
○ Friuli Isonzo Chardonnay Paladis '13	🍷🍷 3
○ Friuli Isonzo Malvasia Melaris '13	🍷🍷 3
● Refosco P. R. Murellis '13	🍷🍷 4

Muzic

loc. Bivio, 4
34070 San Floriano del Collio [GO]
Tel. +39 0481884201
www.cantinamuzic.it

CELLAR SALES
PRE-BOOKED VISITS
ANNUAL PRODUCTION 90,000 bottles
HECTARES UNDER VINE 21.00
SUSTAINABLE WINERY

In the early 1960s, when everyone had
decided to stop working the land, the Muzic
family had the opportunity to buy five
hectares of vineyards that they had been
working as tenant farmers. Today the
winery has grown, but it's stayed small
enough to be family-run. The current
owner, Giovanni Muzic (better known as
Ivan, though we're not sure why), is a true
wine artisan who loves the land and works
in the open air. His children Elija and
Fabijan, who already contribute to
managing the estate, will guarantee that
the winery stays in the family. Their
underground cellar goes back to the 16th
century and is a true gem, with stone walls
and a vaulted ceiling. The 2016 Friulano
Vigna Valeris affirms its status for the
umpteenth time, making it to the finals for
yet another year. It has never managed to
get the highest marks but this doesn't
detract from a wine with sensory properties
that make it a perfect interpretation of the
variety and the territory.

○ Collio Friulano V. Valeris '16	♟♟ 3*
○ Collio Bianco Stare Brajde '15	♟♟ 3
○ Collio Chardonnay '16	♟♟ 3
○ Collio Malvasia '16	♟♟ 3
○ Collio Pinot Grigio '16	♟♟ 3
○ Collio Ribolla Gialla '16	♟♟ 3
○ Collio Sauvignon V. Pàjze '16	♟♟ 3
● Friuli Isonzo Merlot '15	♟♟ 3
○ Collio Bianco '15	♟♟ 3
○ Collio Chardonnay '15	♟♟ 3
○ Collio Friulano V. Valeris '15	♟♟ 3*
○ Collio Malvasia '15	♟♟ 3*
○ Collio Pinot Grigio '15	♟♟ 3
○ Collio Ribolla Gialla '15	♟♟ 3

Alessandro Pascolo

loc. Ruttars, 1
34070 Dolegna del Collio [GO]
Tel. +39 048161144
www.vinipascolo.com

CELLAR SALES
PRE-BOOKED VISITS
ANNUAL PRODUCTION 25,000 bottles
HECTARES UNDER VINE 7.00
SUSTAINABLE WINERY

Alessandro Pascolo's winery is tiny, a true
pearl set up in the hills of Ruttàrs, in the
territory of Dolegna del Collio. His
grandfather, Angelo, who was a successful
entrepreneur, bought a beautiful
farmhouse surrounded by vineyards in the
1960s with the aim of pursuing his true
passion, the countryside. Today that
farmhouse is the base of operations for
Alessandro, who officially took over
management of the winery in 2006. The
small scale and the limited number of
wines mean that he can be involved
firsthand in every stage of production, from
the vineyard to the cellar, with truly
excellent results. The 2016 Sauvignon is
one of our favorites for its elegance and
complexity of aromas. It gives us hints of
yellow peach, passion fruit and
peppermint, while in the mouth it's juicy
and refreshing. The 2016 Malvasia and the
very spicy and dense 2014 Merlot
Selezione are also excellent.

○ Collio Friulano '16	♟♟ 3
○ Collio Malvasia '16	♟♟ 3
● Collio Merlot Sel. '14	♟♟ 5
○ Collio Sauvignon '16	♟♟ 3
○ Collio Bianco Agnul '15	♟ 4
○ Collio Pinot Bianco '16	♟ 3
○ Collio Bianco Agnul '14	♟♟ 4
○ Collio Bianco Agnul '13	♟♟ 4
○ Collio Friulano '15	♟♟ 3
○ Collio Malvasia '15	♟♟ 3*
● Collio Merlot Sel. '13	♟♟ 5
○ Collio Sauvignon '15	♟♟ 3

Pierpaolo Pecorari

VIA TOMMASEO, 56
34070 SAN LORENZO ISONTINO [GO]
TEL. +39 0481808775
www.pierpaolopecorari.it

CELLAR SALES
PRE-BOOKED VISITS
ANNUAL PRODUCTION 150,000 bottles
HECTARES UNDER VINE 30.00

The Pecorari family's ties with the land and wine may have diminished over time, but it was Pierpaolo who, in the 1960s, took them to new heights of quality. This pioneer still manages the vineyards, which run along the left bank of the Isonzo where the nitrate-rich soil is kissed by the sun and fanned by the Adriatic breeze. His selection is divided into three lines: one for wines produced in wood, which take the name of the vineyards where they are grown (Olivers, Kolaus and Soris); one line called 'Altis', which is made up of wines aged in steel with yeast; and a third line dedicated to young, crisp wines. Though with mixed results, once again we see how the winery seeks to satisfy market demand while staying true to typicity. The elegance of the 2016 Chardonnay stands out, as do the sophisticated 2016 Traminer Aromatico and the 2015 Chardonnay Sorjs, a wine that features tropical overtones.

○ Chardonnay '16	♥♥	3
○ Chardonnay Sorjs '15	♥♥	5
● Merlot Baolar '13	♥♥	5
○ Traminer Aromatico '16	♥♥	4
○ Malvasia '16	♥	3
○ Pinot Grigio '16	♥	3
○ Pinot Grigio Olivers '15	♥	5
○ Sauvignon Kolàus '96	♥♥♥	3*
○ Malvasia '15	♀♀	3*
○ Pinot Grigio Olivers '14	♀♀	5
● Refosco P. R. Tao '12	♀♀	5
○ Sauvignon Kolaus '14	♀♀	5

Perusini

LOC. GRAMOGLIANO
VIA DEL TORRIONE, 13
33040 CORNO DI ROSAZZO [UD]
TEL. +39 0432759151
www.perusini.com

CELLAR SALES
PRE-BOOKED VISITS
ACCOMMODATION AND RESTAURANT SERVICE
ANNUAL PRODUCTION 100,000 bottles
HECTARES UNDER VINE 15.00
VITICULTURE METHOD Certified Organic
SUSTAINABLE WINERY

The Perusini family, a family of aristocratic origins, have produced a number of important political and historical figures over the years. One of these was Giacomo Perusini, who, at the end of the 19th century, began working with local, native grape varieties. He is still credited with having rehabilitated the picolit, a local gem, which found the perfect growing conditions on the Rocca Bernada. His successors also made important contributions to wine and vine-growing culture, safeguarding and passing the winery down through the generations and to its current owner, Teresa Perusini. Along with her sons Carlo, Tomasso and Michele, she has taken on the responsibility of seeing to it that their prestigious brand is appreciated throughout the world. The generational handover is reflected in the entire range of wines, which excels for freshness and vitality. The reds are still exuberant with powerful and vibrant tannins that promise a long future. The very sweet 2014 Picolit is their flagship wine, it's a real gem and a guarantee.

○ COF Picolit '14	♥♥	8
● FCO Cabernet Franc '14	♥♥	3
○ FCO Friulano '16	♥♥	3
● FCO Rosso del Postiglione '14	♥♥	3
○ FCO Sauvignon '16	♥♥	3
○ FCO Ribolla Gialla '16	♥	3
● FCO Cabernet Franc '13	♀♀	3
● FCO Merlot '13	♀♀	3
○ FCO Picolit '13	♀♀	8
○ FCO Pinot Grigio '15	♀♀	3*
● FCO Refosco P.R. '13	♀♀	3
● FCO Rosso del Postiglione '13	♀♀	3
○ FCO Sauvignon '15	♀♀	3

Petrucco

VIA MORPURGO, 12
33042 BUTTRIO [UD]
TEL. +39 0432674387
www.vinipetrucco.it

CELLAR SALES
PRE-BOOKED VISITS
ANNUAL PRODUCTION 80,000 bottles
HECTARES UNDER VINE 25.00

Winemaking at Petrucco, founded by Lina and Paolo Petrucco in 1981, is entrusted to Flavio Cabas. Over time, the enological and agronomic skills of this expert have allowed the winery to maintain a standard of excellence in the region. Indeed, when a new wine was introduced last year, the owners decided to call it Bianco Cabas, in his honor. The wine forms part of their prestigious Ronco del Balba line, which already included a series of concentrated reds made with grapes from World War II era vineyards. An interesting side note is that these were planted by Italo Balbo, the renowned politician and aviator. This year the 2012 Pignolo is the only representative of the Ronco del Balbo line, however it's enough to confirm the acclaim that this prestigious line of wines always receives. All the vintage wines enjoy an exemplary consistency. The particularly elegant and captivating 2016 Pinot Bianco is also worth noting.

○ COF Picolit '13	♟♟	6
○ FCO Friulano '16	♟♟	3
● FCO Pignolo Ronco del Balbo '12	♟♟	5
○ FCO Pinot Bianco '16	♟♟	3
○ FCO Pinot Grigio '16	♟♟	3
○ FCO Sauvignon '16	♟♟	3
○ FCO Malvasia '16	♟	3
○ FCO Ribolla Gialla '16	♟	3
○ FCO Malvasia '15	♀♀	3
● FCO Merlot Ronco del Balbo '13	♀♀	4
● FCO Pignolo Ronco del Balbo '11	♀♀	5
○ FCO Pinot Bianco '15	♀♀	3
○ FCO Sauvignon '15	♀♀	3

Petrussa

VIA ALBANA, 49
33040 PREPOTTO [UD]
TEL. +39 0432713192
www.petrussa.it

CELLAR SALES
PRE-BOOKED VISITS
ACCOMMODATION
ANNUAL PRODUCTION 40,000 bottles
HECTARES UNDER VINE 10.00

Gianni and Paolo Petrussa are firm advocates of a simple and purist's approach to winemaking, based on the farming values of their forefathers. In 1986, they took over the winery from their parents and to this day they are united in the way they manage their estate in Albana di Prepotto, an area that borders Slovenia on the one side and Collio Goriziano on the other. Both for the composition of its soil and its particular microclimate, it's an area that's particularly well-suited to reds, especially Schioppettino, though Gianni and Paolo have shown that even with a few hectares of land, they can cover all the bases, producing top-quality whites and an outstanding dessert wine, Pensiero. The 2014 Schioppettino di Prepotto really pays homage to its place of origin and deserved to get to the final selections. Its impact on the nose is particularly appealing with peppery and resinous notes, followed by cherry jam, undergrowth and peppermint tea. It's plush on the palate and enjoys a vigorous freshness.

● FCO Schioppettino di Prepotto '14	♟♟	5
○ FCO Chardonnay S. Elena '15	♟♟	4
○ FCO Friulano '16	♟♟	3
○ FCO Pinot Bianco '16	♟♟	3
○ FCO Sauvignon '16	♟♟	3
○ Pensiero '14	♟♟	5
○ FCO Ribolla Gialla '16	♟	3
○ FCO Friulano '15	♀♀	3
● FCO Merlot Rosso Petrussa '13	♀♀	5
○ FCO Pinot Bianco '15	♀♀	3
○ FCO Ribolla Gialla '15	♀♀	3
○ FCO Sauvignon '15	♀♀	3
● FCO Schioppettino di Prepotto '13	♀♀	5
○ Pensiero '13	♀♀	5

Norina Pez

VIA ZORUTTI, 4
34070 DOLEGNA DEL COLLIO [GO]
TEL. +39 0481639951
www.norinapez.it

CELLAR SALES
PRE-BOOKED VISITS
ANNUAL PRODUCTION 40,000 bottles
HECTARES UNDER VINE 7.00

The Bernardis family boasts decades of experience in the sector, having worked the hills of Dolegna del Collio (in the northernmost part of Gorizia) for as long as anyone can remember. The breakthrough came in the early 1980s, when Giuseppe and his wife, Norina, formalized the business in her name. For some years now, it's been led by their son, Stefano Bernardis, first a wine technician and now a winemaker. He's been pursuing an ambitious program to establish the producer in the field, while overseeing every stage of production at the winery. All their wines are made with grapes cultivated on their seven hectares of property, making for a production volume of about 40,000 bottles annually. For many years we have been monitoring this winery, which has always wanted to keep a well-defined profile. With remarkable constancy, they have put out consistent, forthright wines that respect the characteristics of the varieties, are easy to drink and feature very competitive prices.

○ Collio Chardonnay '16	🍷🍷 2*
○ Collio Pinot Grigio '16	🍷🍷 2*
○ Collio Sauvignon '16	🍷🍷 2*
● El Neri di Norina '12	🍷🍷 5
● Schioppettino '14	🍷🍷 3
○ Collio Friulano '16	🍷 2
○ Collio Ribolla Gialla '16	🍷 3
○ Verduzzo Friulano '15	🍷 2
○ Aurea Divina '09	🍷🍷 4
● Collio Cabernet Franc '13	🍷🍷 2*
○ Collio Friulano '15	🍷🍷 2*
● Collio Merlot '13	🍷🍷 2*
● Collio Merlot '12	🍷🍷 2*
● Rosso El Neri di Norina '11	🍷🍷 5
● Schioppettino '13	🍷🍷 3

Roberto Picéch

LOC. PRADIS, 11
34071 CORMÒNS [GO]
TEL. +39 048160347
www.picech.com

CELLAR SALES
PRE-BOOKED VISITS
ACCOMMODATION
ANNUAL PRODUCTION 30,000 bottles
HECTARES UNDER VINE 8.00
VITICULTURE METHOD Certified Organic

Roberto Picéch is one of the top vine-growers in the region. An undisputed lead-player and true artisan of wine, he is an icon in Collio. His father Egidio, known by locals as 'the rebel', left him a few hectares of vineyards, as well as a legacy of forthrightness and hardheadedness that allowed him to produce wines with their own unique personality and attributes. Both open to innovation and suspicious of fashion, his style of winemaking calls for long maceration, sometimes for days, as well as white grapes so as to bring out the aromatic qualities of each variety. Both the 2016 Pinot Bianco and the 2016 Malvasia made it to the finals and, oddly enough, the sensory properties of both are virtually the same. Though they have marked and very distinct varietal notes, they are both elegant and appealing on the nose and supple and flavorful on the palate.

○ Collio Malvasia '16	🍷🍷 3*
○ Collio Pinot Bianco '16	🍷🍷 3*
○ Collio Bianco Athena Magnum '15	🍷🍷 7
○ Collio Friulano '16	🍷🍷 3
● Collio Rosso '15	🍷🍷 3
○ Collio Bianco Athena '05	🍷🍷🍷 7
○ Collio Bianco Jelka '11	🍷🍷🍷 4*
○ Collio Bianco Jelka '99	🍷🍷🍷 7
○ Collio Pinot Bianco '13	🍷🍷🍷 3*
○ Collio Friulano '15	🍷🍷 3
○ Collio Malvasia '15	🍷🍷 3
○ Collio Malvasia '14	🍷🍷 3*
○ Collio Pinot Bianco '15	🍷🍷 3
● Collio Rosso '14	🍷🍷 3*

Vigneti Pittaro

VIA UDINE, 67
33033 CODROIPO [UD]
TEL. +39 0432904726
www.vignetipittaro.com

CELLAR SALES
PRE-BOOKED VISITS
ACCOMMODATION
ANNUAL PRODUCTION 300,000 bottles
HECTARES UNDER VINE 90.00
SUSTAINABLE WINERY

Piero Pittaro stands out in the field of winemaking. Over his long working-life he has covered a number of international institutional roles without every losing tough with the demands of his winery, which he still manages personally. For decades he's had the help of Stefano Trinco, a true jack-of-all-trades, and together, well before their time, they launched production of the sparkling wine 'Metodo Classico' that today is the winery's crown jewel. Most of their vineyards can be found around their longstanding facility in Codroipo, while five others are spread across the lovely, steep hills of Ramandolo, where the native grapes of their Ronco Vieri line are grown. The sparkling wines are all strictly 'Metodo Classico' and much-appreciated for their fine perlage and the citrusy freshness of the finish. This year the 2010 Pittaro Brut Etichetta Oro and the 2009 Pittaro Brut Etichetta Oro without dosage were submitted for tasting, and both proved excellent.

○ Pittaro Brut Et. Oro '10	♟♟ 5
○ Pittaro Brut Et. Oro Pas Dosé '09	♟♟ 6
○ FCO Friulano Ronco Vieri '16	♟♟ 3
● FCO Refosco P. R. Ronco Vieri '15	♟♟ 3
○ Manzoni Bianco '16	♟♟ 3
○ Pittaro Brut Et. Argento	♟♟ 4
○ Pittaro Brut Rosé Pink	♟♟ 5
○ Ribolla Gialla Brut	♟♟ 5
○ Friuli Grave Chardonnay Mousquè '16	♟ 3
◎ Moscato Rosa Valzer in Rosa '16	♟ 3
○ Passito Apicio	♟ 3
○ FCO Friulano Ronco Vieri '15	♟♟ 3
○ Friuli Grave Chardonnay Mousquè '15	♟♟ 3
○ Pittaro Brut Et. Oro '09	♟♟ 5

Denis Pizzulin

VIA BROLO, 43
33040 PREPOTTO [UD]
TEL. +39 0432713425
www.pizzulin.com

CELLAR SALES
PRE-BOOKED VISITS
ANNUAL PRODUCTION 30,000 bottles
HECTARES UNDER VINE 11.00

Denis Pizzulin is a young vine-grower who personally oversees his own vineyards in the hills of Prepotto, part of the Colli Orientali del Friuli DOC zone, on land with hundreds of years of winemaking history. The terrain here, situated in a sunny valley and protected from the cold northern winds by the Julian Alps, is a mix of sandstone and marl, making it perfect for vine growing. It's a small estate, just a few hectares of vineyards divided up into sections, and their selection is just as small. But its small scale means that it can be personally managed with care and attention at all stages of production. Our tastings confirmed the producer's long history of outstanding quality. The 2013 Schioppettino di Prepotto offers up particularly captivating spicy notes and an elegant, intense and lingering palate.

● FCO Schioppettino di Prepotto '13	♟♟ 4
○ FCO Bianco Rarisolchi '15	♟♟ 3
○ FCO Friulano '16	♟♟ 3
○ FCO Pinot Bianco '13	♟♟ 3
○ FCO Pinot Grigio '16	♟♟ 3
● FCO Refosco P. R. Ris. '13	♟♟ 4
○ FCO Sauvignon '13	♟♟ 3
● COF Rosso Rarisolchi Ris. '09	♟♟ 4
● COF Schioppettino di Prepotto '12	♟♟ 3
○ FCO Friulano '15	♟♟ 3
● FCO Merlot Scaglia Rossa Ris. '13	♟♟ 4
● FCO Pignolo '11	♟♟ 6
○ FCO Pinot Grigio '15	♟♟ 3
○ FCO Sauvignon '15	♟♟ 3

Damijan Podversic

VIA BRIGATA PAVIA, 61
34170 GORIZIA
TEL. +39 040178217
www.damijanpodversic.com

CELLAR SALES
PRE-BOOKED VISITS
ANNUAL PRODUCTION 24,000 bottles
HECTARES UNDER VINE 10.00
VITICULTURE METHOD Certified Organic
SUSTAINABLE WINERY

Damijan Podversic's philosophy comes
from his life as a farmhand, respecting
nature's rhythms and challenges. His
vineyards run along the beautiful slopes of
Monte Calvario, in Collio. Since he was a
child, he's had to make brave decisions
and over time, he's gotten better at it:
extremely low yields, fermentation with skin
contact that can last for months, no
selected yeasts, no filtration, no clarification
and no temperature control. These are old
techniques that seem outdated but that
make perfect sense when we take nature
into account. By now, Damijan has
accustomed us to excellence and this year
they had three wines in the finals. The
splendid 2013 Malavasia was awarded a
Tre Bicchieri for the thrill it gave us during
tasting and for the exceptional finish.

○ Malvasia '13	♀♀♀	8
○ Nekaj '13	♀♀	6
○ Ribolla Gialla '13	♀♀	8
○ Kaplja '13	♀♀	6
● Prelit '16	♀♀	6
○ Kaplja '08	♀♀♀	6
○ Malvasia '10	♀♀♀	6
○ Malvasia '09	♀♀♀	6
○ Ribolla Gialla '12	♀♀♀	8
○ Malvasia '12	♀♀	8
○ Nekaj '12	♀♀	6
● Rosso Prelit '12	♀♀	6

Isidoro Polencic

LOC. PLESSIVA, 12
34071 CORMÒNS [GO]
TEL. +39 048160655
www.polencic.com

CELLAR SALES
PRE-BOOKED VISITS
ACCOMMODATION
ANNUAL PRODUCTION 120,000 bottles
HECTARES UNDER VINE 28.00

It's time for the new generation, Elisabetta,
Michele and Alex Polencic, to take over a
winery founded by their father Isidoro and
continue a family tradition that, according
to records, goes back to the second half of
the 19th century. They divided the
responsibilities and work together with skill
and perseverance, showing a calm
detachment that is rare for their age. Most
of their vineyards circle their facility in
Plessiva, in Cormòns, straddling Italy and
Slovenia, while others are scattered around
Ruttars, Novali, Mossa and Castelletto. The
variety of terrain and microclimates allow
them to take full advantage of Collio. The
great vintage is represented by white wines
with great freshness and aroma. However,
the 2013 Oblin Blanc (a mix of Chardonnay,
Sauvignon and Ribolla Gialla) wins over the
nose with buttery notes of brioche and
hints of spices, then caresses the palate to
accompany a long finish in the mouth.

○ Oblin Blanc '13	♀♀	4
○ Collio Chardonnay '16	♀♀	3
○ Collio Friulano '16	♀♀	3
○ Collio Friulano Fisc '15	♀♀	4
○ Collio Pinot Grigio '16	♀♀	3
○ Collio Pinot Bianco '16	♀	3
○ Collio Friulano Fisc '07	♀♀♀	3*
○ Collio Pinot Bianco '07	♀♀♀	3
○ Collio Pinot Grigio '98	♀♀♀	3*
○ Collio Tocai Friulano '04	♀♀♀	3*

Pradio

FRAZ. FELETTIS
VIA UDINE, 17
33050 BICINICCO [UD]
TEL. +39 0432990123
www.pradio.it

CELLAR SALES
PRE-BOOKED VISITS
ANNUAL PRODUCTION 300,000 bottles
HECTARES UNDER VINE 33.00

Pradio is a thriving operation, ennobling the stony, dry, sun-baked land that characterizes the Friuli Grave DOC zone. The winery was founded in 1974, by the Cielo brothers, who've benefitted from their family's more than 100 years of experience in the sector. For more than a decade, cousins Luca and Pierpaolo Cielo (the fourth generation of family), have been leading the winery, driven by the same passion for the land and wine. They are firm advocates of the territory's potential, and are oriented towards quality production. Since 2012, they've had the valuable support of Gianni Menotti, an enology consultant, with agronomic management handled by director Enrico Della Mora. Constant improvement in the range of wines has led to more than pleasing results - and we didn't have to wait for long. Two grape blends called Starz, a Bianco and a Rosso, have been added to their selection of monovarietal wines and form the winery's jewel in the crown.

○ Friuli Grave Friulano Gaiare '16	♥♥	2*
● Friuli Grave Merlot Roncomoro '16	♥♥	2*
○ Friuli Grave Pinot Grigio Priara '16	♥♥	2*
● Friuli Grave Refosco P. R. Tuaro '15	♥♥	2*
○ Friuli Grave Starz Bianco '16	♥♥	2*
● Friuli Grave Starz Rosso '13	♥♥	2*
● Friuli Grave Cabernet Sauvignon Crearo '13	♥	2
○ Friuli Grave Chardonnay Teraje '16	♥	2
○ Friuli Grave Sauvignon Sobaja '16	♥	2
○ Friuli Grave Friulano Gaiare '15	♈♈	2*
○ Friuli Grave Pinot Grigio Priara '15	♈♈	2*
● Friuli Grave Refosco P. R. Tuaro '14	♈♈	2*
○ Friuli Grave Sauvignon Sobaja '15	♈♈	2*

Primosic

FRAZ. OSLAVIA
LOC. MADONNINA DI OSLAVIA, 3
34070 GORIZIA
TEL. +39 0481535153
www.primosic.com

CELLAR SALES
PRE-BOOKED VISITS
ANNUAL PRODUCTION 210,000 bottles
HECTARES UNDER VINE 30.00

Historic records demonstrate that the Primosic family, since the 1800s, supplied wines to merchants, who transported the precious drink from the southern hills of the Austro-Hungarian Empire to Vienna. It's a tale of family and vine-growing that's seeing a renewal thanks to the work of brothers Marko and Boris, who gathered their father's stories. Here in Oslavia, the bulwark of Collio that borders Slovenia, where the hills form a kind of amphitheater protected from the cold northern winds by the Julian Alps, the microclimate is perfect for its Adriatic breeze, exposure to the sun and temperature range. As with the last edition, we found the 2013 Ribolla Gialla di Oslavia Riserva and the 2012 Klin in the finals, an indication of the excellent quality of these two wines. Once again the Ribolla Gialla earned a Tre Bicchieri, for the third year in a row. Hats off to them.

○ Collio Ribolla Gialla di Oslavia Ris. '13	♥♥♥	5
○ Collio Bianco Klin '12	♥♥	5
○ Collio Friulano '16	♥♥	3
○ Collio Pinot Grigio '15	♥♥	5
● Collio Rosso Metamorfosis '11	♥♥	4
○ Ribolla Gialla '16	♥♥	3
○ Collio Chardonnay Gmajne '11	♈♈♈	4*
○ Collio Ribolla Gialla di Oslavia Ris. '12	♈♈♈	5
○ Collio Ribolla Gialla di Oslavia Ris. '11	♈♈♈	5
○ Collio Bianco Klin '11	♈♈	5
○ Collio Chardonnay Gmajne '13	♈♈	5
○ Collio Pinot Grigio Ris. '12	♈♈	4
○ Collio Sauvignon Gmajne '15	♈♈	5

★Doro Princic

Loc. Pradis, 5
34071 Cormòns [GO]
Tel. +39 048160723
doroprincic@virgilio.it

CELLAR SALES
PRE-BOOKED VISITS
ANNUAL PRODUCTION 60,000 bottles
HECTARES UNDER VINE 10.00

For Collio, Doro Princic was a forefather, a symbol, a charismatic point of reference. Now the winery he founded in Pradis, in 1950, is managed by his son Alessandro and Alessandro's wife Mariagrazia, who share the same vision, putting into practice the skills inherited from Doro, with the help of their young son Carlo. Together they are able to transmit this character to all their wines, which are exclusively monovarietal, respecting and bringing out the qualities of each one. After seven years of domination by Malvasia and an interlude of Friulano, the 2016 Pinot Bianco (a former mainstay) has reappeared. The wine combines elegance and substance, with a lively, flavorsome and appealing palate, thoroughly deserving of a Tre Bicchieri.

Puiatti - Bertani Domains

Loc. Zuccole, 4
34076 Romans d'Isonzo [GO]
Tel. +39 0481909608
www.puiatti.com

CELLAR SALES
PRE-BOOKED VISITS
ANNUAL PRODUCTION 450,000 bottles
HECTARES UNDER VINE 50.00
SUSTAINABLE WINERY

Vittorio Puiatti is remembered as one of the leading figures to bring the wines of Friuli Venezia Giulia, especially the whites, to the forefront of national excellence in the 1960s. A true forerunner, a firm advocate of steel, he left his unmistakable style on each wine, while respecting their original and natural character, opting for a moderate alcoholic content that also facilitated drinkability. The same philosophy is guiding the winery today, though it's also finding ways to adapt. And adapting hasn't required compromise, if anything, it's meant reinforcing the indestructible bond between humankind and nature. The three versions and three different vintages of Ribolla Gialla presented for tasting enhance the versatility of this native grape (which continues to increase in popularity). In the 2015 Archetipi, it reaches its utmost expressivity for its complexity on the nose and plushness in the mouth.

○ Collio Pinot Bianco '16	▼▼▼ 5
○ Collio Friulano '16	▼▼ 5
○ Collio Malvasia '16	▼▼ 5
● Collio Merlot '13	▼▼ 5
○ Collio Pinot Grigio '16	▼▼ 5
○ Collio Friulano '15	♈♈♈ 5
○ Collio Malvasia '14	♈♈♈ 5
○ Collio Malvasia '13	♈♈♈ 5
○ Collio Malvasia '12	♈♈♈ 5
○ Collio Malvasia '11	♈♈♈ 5
○ Collio Malvasia '10	♈♈♈ 4
○ Collio Malvasia '09	♈♈♈ 4*
○ Collio Malvasia '08	♈♈♈ 4
○ Collio Pinot Bianco '07	♈♈♈ 3
○ Collio Tocai Friulano '06	♈♈♈ 3*

○ Friuli Isonzo Friulano Vuj '16	▼▼ 3
○ Ribolla Gialla Archetipi '15	▼▼ 5
○ Ribolla Gialla Extra Brut M. Cl.	▼▼ 4
○ Ribolla Gialla Lus '16	▼ 3
○ Sauvignon Fun '16	▼ 3
○ Friuli Isonzo Friulano Vuj '15	♈♈ 3
○ Friuli Isonzo Friulano Vuj '14	♈♈ 3
○ Ribolla Gialla Archetipi '14	♈♈ 5
○ Ribolla Gialla Archetipi '13	♈♈ 5
○ Ribolla Gialla Lus '14	♈♈ 3
○ Sauvignon Fun '15	♈♈ 3

La Rajade

LOC. PETRUS, 2
34070 DOLEGNA DEL COLLIO [GO]
TEL. +39 0481639273
www.larajade.it

CELLAR SALES
PRE-BOOKED VISITS
ANNUAL PRODUCTION 50,000 bottles
HECTARES UNDER VINE 6.50

La Rajade is one of the most celebrated wineries in the region, a crown jewel of Dolegna del Collio. The exposure of its vineyards to the sun, which run along the higher hills and are protected by the Julian Alps, inspired their name. 'La Rajade' means 'ray of sun'. The thermal contrast between the sunny daytime and low nighttime temperatures contributes to their grapes' particular range of aromas. For some time now, management has been entrusted to Diego Zanin, a seasoned expert who has helped the winery reach, and maintain, absolutely respectable heights. In past editions, red wines were always at the top of our rankings, but this year they have been outdone by the 2014 Bianco Caprizi Riserva, made mainly from Malvasia, with a dash of Friulano and Chardonnay. It's intense and heady on the nose, rich in flavor and lingering on the palate.

○ Collio Bianco Caprizi Ris. '14	♥♥ 3*
● Collio Cabernet Sauvignon Ris. '14	♥♥ 5
○ Collio Friulano '16	♥♥ 3
● Collio Merlot Ris. '14	♥♥ 5
○ Collio Sauvignon '16	♥♥ 3
● Schioppettino '15	♥♥ 3
○ Collio Ribolla Gialla '16	♥ 3
● Collio Cabernet Sauvignon Ris. '13	♀♀ 4
○ Collio Friulano '15	♀♀ 3
● Collio Merlot Ris. '13	♀♀ 4
○ Collio Pinot Grigio '15	♀♀ 3
○ Collio Ribolla Gialla '15	♀♀ 3
○ Collio Sauvignon '15	♀♀ 3
○ Collio Sauvignon '14	♀♀ 3

Rocca Bernarda

FRAZ. IPPLIS
VIA ROCCA BERNARDA, 27
33040 PREMARIACCO [UD]
TEL. +39 0432716914
www.sagrivit.it

CELLAR SALES
PRE-BOOKED VISITS
ANNUAL PRODUCTION 100,000 bottles
HECTARES UNDER VINE 38.50

Founded in 1559, Rocca Bernarda is certifiably one of Friuli Venezia Giulia's most historic producers. It has for its headquarters a splendid country residence built by the Count Valsason Maniago family way back in 1567 (the site testifies to the existence of the cellars before the villa was built). The tradition of winemaking has endured over the centuries thanks to the Count Perusini family, whose last representative handed over the property to the Sovereign Military Order of Malta in 1977. As of 2006, Rocca Bernarda has been managed by the Società Agricola Vitivinicola Italiana, who've entrusted Maurilio Chioccia with winemaking. Rocca Bernarda's iconic wine has always been the Picolit, however it hasn't been presented for some years. It's a real shame. We still had the chance to taste some of their wines, both whites and reds, and we found them to be well-made, compact, with good nose-palate symmetry and particularly respectful of their varietal characteristics.

○ FCO Friulano '16	♥♥ 3
● FCO Pignolo Novecento 1113-2013 '11	♥♥ 5
● FCO Refosco P. R. '15	♥♥ 3
○ Novecento 1113-2013 '16	♥♥ 3
● FCO Cabernet Franc '16	♥ 3
○ FCO Ribolla Gialla '16	♥ 3
● COF Merlot Centis '99	♀♀♀ 7
○ COF Picolit '03	♀♀♀ 7
● COF Merlot Centis '09	♀♀ 4
○ COF Pinot Grigio '13	♀♀ 3
● COF Refosco P. R. '13	♀♀ 3
○ FCO Sauvignon '15	♀♀ 3
○ Novecento 1113-2013 '13	♀♀ 3

Paolo Rodaro

LOC. SPESSA
VIA CORMONS, 60
33043 CIVIDALE DEL FRIULI [UD]
TEL. +39 00390432716066
www.rodaropaolo.it

CELLAR SALES
PRE-BOOKED VISITS
ANNUAL PRODUCTION 250,000 bottles
HECTARES UNDER VINE 57.00
SUSTAINABLE WINERY

Paolo Rodaro manages a winery that boasts almost two centuries of history in regional winemaking and vine-growing. He says he's proud, in the third millennium, to call himself a farmworker. Curious, motivated and dynamic, he also inherited a love for the land that, despite his accomplishments, is pushing him to continue to seek out new frontiers. Rodaro's selection of wines is robust and varied. The famous and celebrated Romain line, which comprises various noteworthy reds, has been enriched by a couple of 'Metodo Classico' sparklers, a white and a rosé, all of which have found immediate success. The vintage whites' aromas comes out in the 2016 Friulano and the 2016 Malvasia, which both highlight the characteristics of the grape varieties used.

○ FCO Malvasia '16	⟐⟐⟐ 2*
○ FCO Pinot Grigio '16	⟐⟐ 3*
● FCO Schioppettino Romain '12	⟐⟐ 5
○ FCO Friulano '16	⟐⟐ 4
○ FCO Ribolla Gialla '16	⟐⟐ 3
○ FCO Sauvignon '16	⟐⟐ 2*
○ FCO Verduzzo Friulano Pra Zenâr '15	⟐⟐ 5
○ L'Evoluto '12	⟐⟐ 3
● FCO Refosco P. R. Romain '11	⟐ 6
● COF Refosco P. R. Romain '03	⟑⟑⟑ 6
○ Ronc '00	⟑⟑⟑ 3
● FCO Rosso Romain di Romain '09	⟑⟑ 6
● FCO Schioppettino Romain '11	⟑⟑ 5

Ronc di Vico

FRAZ. BELLAZOIA
VIA CENTRALE, 5
33040 POVOLETTO [UD]
TEL. +39 3208822002
roncdivicobellazoia@libero.it

CELLAR SALES
PRE-BOOKED VISITS
ANNUAL PRODUCTION 12,000 bottles
HECTARES UNDER VINE 7.00

Ronc di Vico is situated in Bellazoia, in the municipality of Povoletto, and is dedicated to Gianni Del Fabbro's paternal grandfather, with whom Gianni shared a close bond. It was he who left Gianni some hectares of old, unused vineyards that, in the first years of the 21st century, served as a starting point for his winery. He decided to rent more and, with great enthusiasm and an instinct for quality, in just a few years he earned the accolades of regional experts. His son, Lodovico, after accompanying him for years, is now able to manage the whole process himself, from start to finish. Their small scale and decision to focus on a few varieties has allowed for a level of care and attention that has decidedly worked in their favor. As with previous editions, the 2015 Refosco dal Peduncolo Rosso has the edge over the other wines, although they proved to be on a par with the best performances. It features aromas of ripe red fruit, vanilla and chocolate, while the palate is fresh and plush, with an overtone of greenness.

● FCO Refosco P. R. '15	⟐⟐ 6
○ FCO Il Friulano '16	⟐⟐ 4
○ FCO Sauvignon '16	⟐⟐ 4
● FCO Titit Ros '15	⟐⟐ 6
● FCO Vicorosso '15	⟐⟐ 4
● COF Refosco P. R. '11	⟑⟑ 6
● COF Titit Ros '11	⟑⟑ 6
● COF Vicorosso '11	⟑⟑ 4
○ FCO Il Friulano '15	⟑⟑ 4
● FCO Refosco P. R. '13	⟑⟑ 6
○ FCO Sauvignon '15	⟑⟑ 4
● FCO Titit Ros '12	⟑⟑ 6
● FCO Vicorosso '13	⟑⟑ 4
● FCO Vicorosso '12	⟑⟑ 4

Ronc Soreli

LOC. NOVACUZZO, 46
33040 PREPOTTO [UD]
TEL. +39 0432713005
www.roncsoreli.com

CELLAR SALES
ANNUAL PRODUCTION 100,000 bottles
HECTARES UNDER VINE 42.00

Ronc Soreli got its start in 2008 under Flavio Schiratti, a successful businessman and wine lover who decided to revive the old village of Novacuzzo, where wine has been made for centuries. He launched an ambitious renovation project of the main villa, the cellar and its 42 hectares of vineyards situated between Prepotto, Cividale del Friuli and Corno di Rosazzo. Enlisting the valuable support of experts, he immediately earned a place among Friuli Colli Orientali's already formidable class of top producers. Ronc Soreli is committed to protecting the environmental integrity of the entire estate through sustainable production practices. The entire selection is on a par with the best vintages. We were presented with two versions of the 2016 Sauvignon Vigna dei Peschi, one normal and one organic, both pleasant and impressive. The first is more marked and fragrant, while the second is more appealing, though a bit predictable.

○ FCO Friulano V. delle Robinie '16	🍷🍷	3
○ FCO Pinot Grigio V. dei Melograni '16	🍷🍷	3
○ FCO Ribolla Gialla V. dei Nespoli '16	🍷🍷	3
○ FCO Sauvignon V. dei Peschi '16	🍷🍷	3
○ FCO Sauvignon V. dei Peschi Bio '16	🍷🍷	3
○ FCO Bianco ABC Albarè '16	🍷	3
● FCO Rosso ABC RossoDiSera '16	🍷	3
○ Traminer ABC '16	🍷	3
○ COF Friulano V. delle Robinie '11	🍸🍸🍸	3*
○ FCO Friulano V. delle Robinie '15	🍸🍸	3*
○ FCO Picolit '10	🍸🍸	5
○ FCO Pinot Grigio Ramato '15	🍸🍸	3
● FCO Schioppettino di Prepotto '10	🍸🍸	5

La Roncaia

FRAZ. CERGNEU
VIA VERDI, 26
33045 NIMIS [UD]
TEL. +39 0432790280
www.laroncaia.it

CELLAR SALES
PRE-BOOKED VISITS
ANNUAL PRODUCTION 60,000 bottles
HECTARES UNDER VINE 25.00

La Roncaia is a true gem of a winery. Through research and the use of particular techniques, they've set themselves apart for their selection of outstanding wines. They were acquired by the Fantinel family in 1998, with the aim of carrying on a flourishing, thirty-year tradition of winemaking. Some of their vineyards may have been conceived in more modern times, with international grape varieties, but there are also much older ones with highly-esteemed native grape varieties, making the estate a veritable patrimony worth protecting. The Hungarian enologist Tibor Gal launched an initiative that is getting help from the young Friuli native Gabriele Tami. The 2015 Friulano and the 2015 Bianco Eclisse have the edge over the rest and made it to the top of the rankings, thanks to very clean and precise aromas on the nose, and tanginess and intensity in the mouth.

○ Bianco Eclisse '15	🍷🍷	5
○ FCO Friulano '15	🍷🍷	4
○ COF Picolit '13	🍷🍷	5
● FCO Cabernet Franc '15	🍷🍷	3
● FCO Merlot Fusco '13	🍷🍷	5
○ Ramandolo '13	🍷🍷	5
○ Eclisse '12	🍸🍸🍸	4*
○ Bianco Eclisse '14	🍸🍸	5
○ FCO Friulano '13	🍸🍸	4
● FCO Merlot '12	🍸🍸	5
○ FCO Picolit '11	🍸🍸	5
● FCO Refosco P.R. '12	🍸🍸	5
○ Ramandolo '11	🍸🍸	5

Il Roncal

FRAZ. COLLE MONTEBELLO
VIA FORNALIS, 148
33043 CIVIDALE DEL FRIULI [UD]
TEL. +39 0432730138
www.ilroncal.it

CELLAR SALES
PRE-BOOKED VISITS
ACCOMMODATION AND RESTAURANT SERVICE
ANNUAL PRODUCTION 130,000 bottles
HECTARES UNDER VINE 20.00

Il Roncal is, by now, a well-established brand, a guarantee of quality, a thriving winery that brings eminence to the Colli Orientali del Friuli DOC zone. The winery, headquartered in a lovely country villa looking out on the hills of Montebello (the name says it all), was founded in 1986 thanks to the foresight of Roberto Zorzettig. For more than 10 years it's been in the hands of Martina Moreale, the current owner, who's brought personality and undeniable skill to the job. Martina has managed to realized the dream of her husband, imbuing the wines, and especially the native grape varieties, with a unique, local character. The constant rise in quality we have noticed in recent editions is reaching the heights of excellence and two wines got a much-deserved place in the finals. The 2015 Bianco Ploe di Stelis received acclaim for its continuity, while the 2016 Pinot Grigio's success proved a pleasant surprise.

○ FCO Bianco Ploe di Stelis '15	♥♥ 4
○ FCO Pinot Grigio '16	♥♥ 3*
○ FCO Friulano '16	♥♥ 3
○ FCO Ribolla Gialla '16	♥♥ 3
● FCO Rosso Civon '11	♥♥ 5
○ FCO Sauvignon '16	♥♥ 3
● FCO Schioppettino '13	♥♥ 4
○ FCO Bianco Ploe di Stelis '14	♀♀ 4
● FCO Merlot '13	♀♀ 3
● FCO Pignolo '10	♀♀ 5
○ FCO Ribolla Gialla '15	♀♀ 3
○ FCO Ribolla Gialla '14	♀♀ 3
○ FCO Sauvignon '14	♀♀ 3*

Il Roncat - Giovanni Dri

FRAZ. RAMANDOLO
VIA PESCIA, 7
33045 NIMIS [UD]
TEL. +39 0432790260
www.drironcat.com

CELLAR SALES
PRE-BOOKED VISITS
ANNUAL PRODUCTION 40,000 bottles
HECTARES UNDER VINE 10.00

When Giovanni Dri founded his winery in 1968 at the extreme northern edge of the Colli Orientali del Friuli DOC zone, he chose the name Il Roncat, which means 'steep hill' in the local dialect, after the precipitous and almost uncultivable terrain he'd chosen for his vineyards. Up here, where wine growing is a demanding task, even heroic, the yellow Verduzzo has always been the grape of choice, a variety that risked extinction because of its poor yield but gave life to Ramandolo. Giovanni, who was ahead of his time, sensed the wine's potential. Today his daughter, Stefania runs the winery and has managed to convince even the most discriminating palates. The specialties of the house are, of course, its sweet wines. In fact, both the 2013 Ramandolo and the 2013 Picolit received acclaim, although our favorite was the 2013 Schioppettino Monte dei Carpini, for its lovely spiciness, which thrills the nose, and its gutsy taste.

● FCO Refosco P. R. '13	♥♥ 3
● FCO Rosso Il Roncat '11	♥♥ 5
● FCO Schioppettino Monte dei Carpin '13	♥♥ 4
○ Picolit Il Roncat '13	♥♥ 7
● FCO Cabernet '13	♥ 3
○ Ramandolo '13	♥ 4
● FCO Merlot '12	♀♀ 3
● FCO Refosco P.R. '12	♀♀ 3
● FCO Schioppettino Monte dei Carpin '12	♀♀ 4
○ Ramandolo Uve Decembrine '11	♀♀ 5

Ronchi di Manzano

VIA OHSARIA, 42
33044 MANZANO [UD]
TEL. +39 0432740718
www.ronchidimanzano.com

CELLAR SALES
PRE-BOOKED VISITS
ANNUAL PRODUCTION 200,000 bottles
HECTARES UNDER VINE 60.00

Ronchi di Manzano, a jewel of the Colli Orientali del Friuli DOC zone, is managed with considerable skill by Roberta Borghese, who's now being supported by her daughters, Lisa and Nicole. Their presence is a breath of fresh air that is rubbing of on their wines, which are fresher and more fragrant than ever. Their 60 hectares of vineyards are spread across three distinct areas: Ronc di Scossai and Ronc di Subule surround their two-floor, underground cellar in Manzana, and Ronc di Rosazzo, their crown jewel, is found towards the east. Rosazzo, a famous cru, is situated in a particularly esteemed subzone. With nice variation, one or more wines get to the final selections every year. This proves the constant quality and absolute excellence that exists throughout their whole range. This year the highest accolade went to the 2016 Friulano, which stood out among the crowded category.

Ronchi San Giuseppe

VIA STRADA DI SPESSA, 8
33043 CIVIDALE DEL FRIULI [UD]
TEL. +39 0432716172
www.ronchisangiuseppe.com

CELLAR SALES
PRE-BOOKED VISITS
ANNUAL PRODUCTION 400,000 bottles
HECTARES UNDER VINE 70.00
SUSTAINABLE WINERY

Ronchi San Giuseppe is one of the most important producers in the region. The brand is deeply tied to the territory and is a symbol of the ideal balance between tradition and innovation. Franco Zorzettig, its founder and forefather, is in his nineties, but the winery is being led by the next generations. The message they've been using to promote Ronchi San Giuseppe is clear and meaningful: 'From parents to children, we pass on our passion for vine growing and wine, as well as our values, our language and our identity as part of a great farm working community. It is a heritage that we are proud of'. The selection's value for money is decidedly in the consumer's favor. This has always marked out the winery's philosophy, which is based on simplicity, linearity, good drinkability and preserving the varietal characteristics of each individual grape.

○ FCO Friulano '16	♥♥ 3*
○ FCO Chardonnay '16	♥♥ 3
● FCO Merlot Ronc di Subule '13	♥♥ 3
○ FCO Pinot Grigio '16	♥♥ 3
● FCO Rosso Brauros '13	♥♥ 4
○ FCO Sauvignon '16	♥♥ 3
○ Rosazzo Bianco '15	♥♥ 3
FCO Refosco P. R. '13	♥ 3
○ FCO Ribolla Gialla di Rosazzo '16	♥ 3
○ COF Ellegri '13	♥♥♥ 3*
○ COF Friulano '10	♥♥♥ 3
○ COF Friulano '09	♥♥♥ 3*
○ COF Rosazzo Bianco Ellégri '11	♥♥♥ 3*
○ Rosazzo Bianco '13	♥♥♥ 3*

○ FCO Pinot Grigio '16	♥♥ 2*
● FCO Pinot Nero '16	♥♥ 2*
● FCO Refosco P. R. '15	♥♥ 2*
○ FCO Sauvignon '16	♥♥ 2*
● FCO Schioppettino '15	♥♥ 2*
● FCO Cabernet Franc '16	♥ 2
○ FCO Ribolla Gialla '16	♥ 2
○ FCO Traminer Aromatico '16	♥ 2
○ FCO Friulano '15	♀♀ 2*
○ FCO Pinot Grigio '14	♀♀ 2*
● FCO Refosco P. R. '14	♀♀ 2*
○ FCO Ribolla Gialla '15	♀♀ 2*
○ FCO Sauvignon '15	♀♀ 2*

Ronco Blanchis

VIA BLANCHIS, 70
34070 MOSSA [GO]
TEL. +39 048180519
www.roncoblanchis.it

PRE-BOOKED VISITS
ANNUAL PRODUCTION 60,000 bottles
HECTARES UNDER VINE 14.00
SUSTAINABLE WINERY

Blanchis hill, one of the highest of the Collio range, is particularly well-suited to growing and making white wine. Historical records verify that as far back as two centuries ago, on this hill, noble families stocked up on the wines that would go on to accompany royal feasts. Credit for Ronco Blanchis' current success goes to Lorenzo Palla, who has firmly established it as one of the best wineries in a region that is teeming with them. Along with the support of his trusted winemaker, Gianni Menotti, he has managed few wines, all extremely high-quality whites, of distinct sensory qualities: unabashedly forthright, enticing and intriguing. By now, we are used to the excellent performance of the whole range. Two wines made it to the finals this year (as usual). The 2016 Blanc di Blanchis repeated last year's success and just missed out on the highest accolade, while the 2016 Sauvignon made its debut and excellent in its fragrances.

○ Collio Blanc de Blanchis '16	♟♟ 3*
○ Collio Sauvignon '16	♟♟ 4
○ Collio Chardonnay Particella 3 '16	♟♟ 3
○ Collio Friulano '16	♟♟ 4
○ Collio '13	♟♟♟ 3*
○ Collio '12	♟♟♟ 3*
○ Collio '15	♟♟ 5
○ Collio Blanc de Blanchis '15	♟♟ 3*
○ Collio Blanc de Blanchis '14	♟♟ 3
○ Collio Friulano '15	♟♟ 4
○ Collio Friulano '14	♟♟ 3*
○ Collio Pinot Grigio '14	♟♟ 3
○ Collio Pinot Grigio '13	♟♟ 3
○ Collio Sauvignon '15	♟♟ 4

★Ronco dei Tassi

LOC. MONTONA, 19
34071 CORMÒNS [GO]
TEL. +39 048160155
www.roncodeitassi.it

CELLAR SALES
PRE-BOOKED VISITS
ANNUAL PRODUCTION 110,000 bottles
HECTARES UNDER VINE 18.00

The wine industry in Collio Goriziano is thriving and Ronco Dei Tassi is proving to be one of its most celebrated wineries. After working for a number of other wineries, in 1989 Fabio Coser decided to found his own. He purchased an estate at the outer perimeter of a particularly charming park in Cormòns, Montona, on the side of Monte Quarin that faces Slovenia. His enology expertise allowed him to work as a consultant, as well, without getting distracted from his own production. His hard work paid off, and now his wines are at the top of their class in the region. His sons Matteo and Enrico now have the responsibility of taking over and safeguarding their reputable family name. The Malvasia earned a Tre Bicchieri five years in a row. But this year the highest award has gone to the 2015 Fosarin. It's the winery's own complex and flavorsome grape blend of Pinot Bianco, Tocai Friulano and Malvasia. We also saw an excellent performance by the 2016 Pinot Grigio.

○ Collio Bianco Fosarin '15	♟♟♟ 3
○ Collio Malvasia '16	♟♟ 3
○ Collio Pinot Grigio '16	♟♟ 3
○ Collio Friulano '16	♟♟ 3
● Collio Rosso Cjarandon Ris. '13	♟♟ 5
○ Collio Sauvignon '16	♟♟ 3
○ Collio Ribolla Gialla '16	♟ 3
○ Collio Bianco Fosarin '10	♟♟♟ 3
○ Collio Bianco Fosarin '09	♟♟♟ 3
○ Collio Bianco Fosarin '08	♟♟♟ 3
○ Collio Malvasia '15	♟♟♟ 3
○ Collio Malvasia '14	♟♟♟ 3
○ Collio Malvasia '13	♟♟♟ 3
○ Collio Malvasia '12	♟♟♟ 3
○ Collio Malvasia '11	♟♟♟ 3

Ronco delle Betulle

ʟᴏᴄ. Rosazzᴜ
ᴀ Aʙᴀᴛᴇ Coʟᴏɴɴᴀ, 24
3044 Mᴀɴᴢᴀɴo [UD]
ᴇʟ. +39 0432740547
ww.roncodellebetulle.it

ELLAR SALES
RE-BOOKED VISITS
NNUAL PRODUCTION 60,000 bottles
ECTARES UNDER VINE 12.00
USTAINABLE WINERY

ne Rosazzo hills are the crown jewel of
olli Orientali del Friuli. The area, which
atures a famous 11th century monastery
rrounded by vineyards, is a treasure that
eeds to be protected, both for its cultural
alue and vine-growing heritage. It is here
at Ivana Adams and his son Simone
anage Ronco Delle Betulle, an
xemplary winery that has embraced a
mple philosophy: make high-quality
nes while focusing on bringing out the
herent, natural characteristics of the
ative grape varieties being used. The
015 Rosazzo Bianco made it to the finals
nd had an excellent performance. It's
ade with Friulano and smaller parts
auvignon, Pinot Bianco, Chardonnay and
bolla Gialla. It's a well-put-together mix
at offers elegance, but also structure and
easantness.

Ronco Scagnet

ʟᴏᴄ. Cɪᴍᴇ ᴅɪ Doʟᴇɢɴᴀ, 7
34070 Doʟᴇɢɴᴀ ᴅᴇʟ Coʟʟɪᴏ [GO]
Tᴇʟ. +39 0481639870
www.roncoscagnet.it

CELLAR SALES
PRE-BOOKED VISITS
ANNUAL PRODUCTION 80,000 bottles
HECTARES UNDER VINE 12.50

Valter Cozzarolo and his son, Dimitri, are
authentic wine artisans who lavish their 12
hectares of vineyards with attention.
Situated in Dolegna del Collio, a
municipality that hosts acclaimed
producers (mostly family-run), the estate
runs along the benchlands of the gentle
Lonzano hills. Collio Goriziano is
well-known for its excellent hill exposure,
overlooking the lower plains that stretch all
the way to the sparkling Adriatic Sea. The
particular subsoil, which the locals call
'ponca', is composed of marl and
sandstone. It's a type common to the
pedoclimatic conditions of the area, and
allows for the production of well-structured
wines, with fruity, intense, varietal
fragrances. In the last edition, we saw
Ronco Scagnet's first appearance in the
guide. It was the first time they had
presented their wines for tasting and we
were amazed by their quality. This year, not
only have they repeated the feat, but they
have completely surpassed themselves.
Then if we take a look at their prices,
everything just gets better.

Rosazzo Bianco '15	♟♟ 4
FCO Friulano '16	♟♟ 3
FCO Pignolo Rosazzo '12	♟♟ 6
FCO Pinot Grigio '16	♟♟ 3
FCO Refosco P. R. '14	♟♟ 3
FCO Rosazzo Rosso Narciso '13	♟♟ 5
FCO Sauvignon '16	♟♟ 3
FCO Cabernet Franc '14	♟ 3
FCO Ribolla Gialla '16	♟♟ 3
Franconia '13	♟ 3
Narciso Rosso '94	♟♟♟ 4*
FCO Friulano '15	♟♟ 3
FCO Ribolla Gialla '15	♟♟ 3
FCO Sauvignon '15	♟♟ 3

○ Collio Bianco Folie Blanc '13	♟♟ 2*
○ Collio Chardonnay '15	♟♟ 2*
○ Collio Friulano '16	♟♟ 2*
○ Collio Pinot Grigio '16	♟♟ 2*
○ Collio Ribolla Gialla '16	♟♟ 2*
● Collio Rosso Vignis Rossis '12	♟♟ 2*
○ Collio Sauvignon '16	♟♟ 2*
○ Raggio di Sole '16	♟♟ 2*
○ Collio Pinot Grigio '15	♟♟ 2*
○ Collio Ribolla Gialla '15	♟♟ 2*
○ Collio Sauvignon '15	♟♟ 2*
○ Raggio di Sole '15	♟♟ 2*

Ronco Severo

VIA RONCHI, 93
33040 PREPOTTO [UD]
TEL. +39 04337133440
www.roncosevero.it

CELLAR SALES
PRE-BOOKED VISITS
ANNUAL PRODUCTION 22,000 bottles
HECTARES UNDER VINE 8.00
VITICULTURE METHOD Certified Organic

Stefano Novello is a true wine artisan. He is the heart and soul of this small winery, named after his father, Severo, who started working in the 1960s, after buying a few hectares of land.Here, in Prepotto, an area known as the cradle of Schioppettino, where a shimmering valley crossed by the river Judrio, the microclimate is particularly well suited to vine growing. Taking advantage of the latest technology and drawing on an experience that includes work done abroad, Stefano is also a lover of tradition. He practices long maceration and doesn't use chemical products, selected yeasts, enzymes or sulphur dioxide. By now, we are used to Stefano's wines. They are unusual, juicy, concentrated and sometimes difficult to read. They may seem like complicated wines, yet they have a surprising simplicity. Take the 2015 Friulano Riserva, a wine that gives us hints of iodine on the nose, which then follow through onto the palate.

Roncùs

VIA MAZZINI, 26
34076 CAPRIVA DEL FRIULI [GO]
TEL. +39 0481809349
www.roncus.it

CELLAR SALES
PRE-BOOKED VISITS
ACCOMMODATION
ANNUAL PRODUCTION 40,000 bottles
HECTARES UNDER VINE 10.00

As an expert vigneron, Marco Perco has been able to transmit his personal style to his wines. The secret lies in not being in a rush, bringing together age-old techniques with the best of modern practice. The must spends many months on the (strictly) native yeasts, thus enriching its content of natural preservatives, which makes for extraordinary aging potential. Indeed, his wines possess longevity and express all the character of Capriva del Friuli, an area that is the pride and joy of Collio. Many of their vineyards are more than 50-years-old, and it's well-known that older vineyards are a true heritage. They may produce fewer bunches, but the ones they do produce are rich, with a pleasing concentration of aromas and flavors. This year, a splendid performance follows the thoroughly-deserved Tre Bicchieri (awarded a posteriori to the 2008 Collio Bianco Vecchie Vigne). has been a great display all around, featuring complex, balanced, well-orchestrated, consistent and gradual wine

○ FCO Friulano Ris. '15	♟♟	4
● FCO Refosco P.R. '15	♟♟	4
● FCO Schioppettino di Prepotto '15	♟♟	4
○ Pinot Grigio '15	♟♟	4
○ Ribolla Gialla '15	♟♟	4
○ Severo Bianco '12	♟♟♟	4*
○ FCO Friulano Severo Bianco '08	♟♟	4
● FCO Merlot Artiûl Ris. '13	♟♟	5
● FCO Refosco P.R. '13	♟♟	5
● FCO Schioppettino di Prepotto '13	♟♟	4
○ Pinot Grigio '14	♟♟	4
○ Ribolla Gialla '14	♟♟	4
○ Severo Bianco '14	♟♟	4

○ Collio Bianco '15	♟♟
○ Collio Bianco V. V. '13	♟♟
○ Pinot Bianco '15	♟♟
● Val di Miez '14	♟♟
○ Collio Bianco V. V. '08	♟♟♟
○ Roncùs Bianco V. V. '01	♟♟♟
○ Collio Bianco '14	♟♟
○ Collio Bianco V. V. '12	♟♟
○ Collio Friulano '15	♟♟
○ Collio Friulano '13	♟♟
○ Pinot Bianco '14	♟♟
○ Pinot Bianco '13	♟♟
○ Ribolla Gialla '15	♟♟
● Val di Miez '12	♟♟

★Russiz Superiore

ᴠɪᴀ Russiz, 7
4070 Capriva del Friuli [GO]
ᴛᴇʟ. +39 048180328
www.marcofelluga.it

CELLAR SALES
PRE-BOOKED VISITS
ACCOMMODATION
ANNUAL PRODUCTION 180,000 bottles
HECTARES UNDER VINE 50.00
SUSTAINABLE WINERY

The estate of Russiz Superiore, founded in 1966 by Marco Felluga, dominates the hills of Capriva del Friuli. Unanimously considered a pioneer in the field of regional winemaking/vine-growing, Marco was a true innovator 'par excellence', a man with a gift for foresight, who knew how to bring out Collio's potential. And so it was that he created a brand of outstanding quality. Today Russiz Superiore is being managed by Marco's son, Roberto, who, in addition to maintaining the winery's reputation for regional and national excellence, has launched a courageous initiative to draw consumer attention to aged white wines. He offers his white Riserves after aging them in bottles for some years. Repeated success is always an index of consistency and the 2016 Friulano has beaten the fierce competition to win our Tre Bicchieri for the third year in a row. There was also an excellent performance from the 2012 Sauvignon Riserva, which confirms the producer's decision to put forward wines that are already mature and more complex.

Sant'Elena

ᴠɪᴀ Gasparini, 1
34072 Gradisca d'Isonzo [GO]
ᴛᴇʟ. +39 048192388
www.sant-elena.com

CELLAR SALES
PRE-BOOKED VISITS
ANNUAL PRODUCTION 130,000 bottles
HECTARES UNDER VINE 30.00

The foundation of Sant'Elena goes back to the late 1800s. The property changed hands various times, leading to periods of use and disuse. Finally, in the 1960s, when its potential was fully appreciated, the area was converted into vineyards. In 1997, on behalf of Vinifera Imports, Dominic Nocerino, a noted importer of wines in the U.S., purchased the estate with the aim of making wines that both fully represented the Friuli Isonzo DOC zone and that could be sold at the right price. He built a cellar and entrusted winemaking to the proven experience of Maurizio Drascek. Once again, we didn't see any red wines, a clear sign that they need long bottle aging. We had to make do with examining the whites, but it was enough to confirm last year's accolades.

Collio Friulano '16	♟♟♟	4*
Collio Sauvignon Ris. '12	♟♟	5
Collio Bianco Col Disôre '15	♟♟	5
Collio Cabernet Franc '14	♟♟	4
Collio Merlot '13	♟♟	4
Collio Pinot Bianco '16	♟♟	4
Collio Pinot Grigio '16	♟♟	4
Collio Sauvignon '16	♟♟	4
Collio Friulano '15	♟♟♟	4*
Collio Friulano '14	♟♟♟	4*
Collio Pinot Bianco '07	♟♟♟	4
Collio Pinot Grigio '11	♟♟♟	4*
Collio Sauvignon '05	♟♟♟	3
Collio Sauvignon '04	♟♟♟	5

○ Friuli Isonzo Chardonnay Rive Alte '16	♟♟	3
○ Friuli Isonzo Friulano Rive Alte '16	♟♟	3
○ Friuli Isonzo Pinot Grigio Rive Alte '16	♟♟	3
○ Friuli Isonzo Sauvignon Rive Alte '16	♟	4
○ Friuli Isonzo Traminer Aromatico '16	♟	4
○ Mil Rosis '15	♟	5
○ Friuli Isonzo Friulano Rive Alte '15	♟♟	3
○ Friuli Isonzo Pinot Grigio Rive Alte '15	♟♟	3
● Merlot '11	♟♟	4

Marco Sara

FRAZ. SAVORGNANO DEL TORRE
VIA DEI MONTI, 3A
33040 POVOLETTO [UD]
TEL. +39 0432666066
www.marcosara.com

CELLAR SALES
PRE-BOOKED VISITS
ANNUAL PRODUCTION 25,000 bottles
HECTARES UNDER VINE 8.00
VITICULTURE METHOD Certified Organic

Since 2000, Marco Sara has been running this small winery, which has already managed star-status in a region bursting at the seams with outstanding producers. The winery is situated in Savorgnano del Torre, in the easternmost part (and the coolest) of the Colli Orientali del Friuli DOC zone. The vineyards span just eight hectares and are divided into dozens of smaller sections spread out around various areas. This allows for a greater, more representative, range of possibilities. Since 2005 all their agricultural practices have been organic (they officially received certification in 2011). All their vineyards are native grape varieties, except for an old vineyard of cabernet franc. For the third year in a row, Marco's 2015 Picolit dei Colli Orientali del Friuli has deservedly won a place in the final selections. This confirms his well-established individual style.

○ COF Picolit '15	♥♥ 6
○ FCO Bianco Erba Alta '15	♥♥ 5
○ FCO Friulano '15	♥♥ 3
● FCO Schioppettino '15	♥♥ 4
○ FCO Verduzzo Friulano '15	♥♥ 4
● COF Cabernet Franc Frank '15	♥ 3
○ COF Erba Alta '13	♥♥ 4
○ COF Picolit '13	♥♥ 5
● COF Refosco P. R. El Re '13	♥♥ 3
● COF Schioppettino '13	♥♥ 3
○ FCO Friulano '14	♥♥ 3
○ FCO Friulano '13	♥♥ 2*
○ FCO Picolit '14	♥♥ 5
○ FCO Verduzzo '14	♥♥ 3

Sara & Sara

LOC. SAVORGNANO DEL TORRE
VIA DEI MONTI, 5
33040 POVOLETTO [UD]
TEL. +39 04323859042
www.saraesara.com

CELLAR SALES
PRE-BOOKED VISITS
ANNUAL PRODUCTION 25,000 bottles
HECTARES UNDER VINE 7.50
SUSTAINABLE WINERY

Sara & Sara' translates to 'Alessandro & Manuele', two young brothers who have created a standout brand for Savorgnano del Torre. Here the area is rich in water, perennial woods, and steep, clay hills of marl and sandstone. The cold north winds guarantee a temperature range that is useful for instilling aromas, but that also leads to violent storms, necessitating the use of safety-nets to protect the vineyards. Here Verduzzo and Picolit have found the perfect habitat. These are grown and used to make celebrated dessert wines that are all the more intriguing for the presence of botrytis. This year the winery's flagship wine, the Verduzzo Friulano Crei, wasn't submitted. However, the 2012 Picolit dei Colli Orientali del Friuli managed to fill the gap, giving us fruity notes of peaches in syrup and apricots and gratifying the palate with a juicy and unforgettable sweetness.

○ COF Picolit '12	♥♥ 5
○ FCO Friulano '16	♥♥ 6
○ COF Verduzzo Friulano Crei '10	♥♥♥ 5
○ COF Friulano '12	♥♥ 3
○ COF Friulano '10	♥♥ 3
○ COF Picolit '10	♥♥ 5
○ COF Picolit '09	♥♥ 5
● COF Refosco P. R. '10	♥♥ 3
○ COF Verduzzo Friulano Crei '11	♥♥ 5
○ FCO Picolit '11	♥♥ 6
○ FCO Verduzzo Friulano Crei '13	♥♥ 5
○ FCO Verduzzo Friulano Crei '12	♥♥ 5
○ Sauvignon '12	♥♥ 2

★Schiopetto

Palazzo Arcivescovile, 1
070 Capriva del Friuli [GO]
. +39 048180332
w.schiopetto.it

LLAR SALES
E-BOOKED VISITS
NUAL PRODUCTION 190,000 bottles
CTARES UNDER VINE 30.00
STAINABLE WINERY

...vas the mid-1960s when Mario
hiopetto first began to experiment in
king white wines in Capriva. He used
-the-skins vinification, soft pressing and
nperature controlled must fermentation.
immediately gained a following among
young producers of the area, and
hing was ever the same. The Friuli wine
aissance had begun! Today new
estments underway, in particular
ncerning sustainability and preserving
aromas of the grapes. The 2016
tage was excellent (thanks in part to an
erage vine age of about forty years) and
2016 Friulano won back its Tre
chieri. But the 2016 Pinot Bianco was
t as good, with aromas of hawthorn and
gamot orange and a very good taste.

ollio Friulano '16	♥♥♥	4*
ollio Pinot Bianco '16	♥♥	4
ollio Sauvignon '16	♥♥	4
lanc des Rosis '16	♥♥	4
ollio Malvasia '16	♥♥	4
ollio Pinot Grigio '16	♥♥	4
odere dei Blumeri Rosso '15	♥♥	5
ivarossa '15	♥♥	4
lanc des Rosis '07	♀♀♀	4
ollio Friulano '15	♀♀♀	4*
ollio Friulano '14	♀♀♀	4*
ollio Friulano '13	♀♀♀	4*
lario Schiopetto Bianco '08	♀♀♀	5
lario Schiopetto Bianco '07	♀♀♀	5

La Sclusa

loc. Spessa
via Strada di Sant'Anna, 7/2
33043 Cividale del Friuli [UD]
Tel. +39 0432716259
www.lasclusa.it

CELLAR SALES
PRE-BOOKED VISITS
ACCOMMODATION
ANNUAL PRODUCTION 160,000 bottles
HECTARES UNDER VINE 30.00

The Zorzettig family has tied itself to the
Spessa brand, a name that is, by now,
synonymous with vineyards and wine.
Generations of viticulturists have followed
in the footsteps of founder Giobatta, some
of whom have gone on to found their own
wineries. One of these is La Sclusa,
managed for more than 40 years by
Giobatta's son Gino, who still helps out but
has largely left the winery in the hands of
his own three sons: Germano, Maurizio and
Luciano. Since the beginning, their
philosophy has been inspired by tradition,
working in tandem with the rhythms of
nature and trying to bring out the best of
what the land has to offer, without ever
forcing or exploiting it. The results are
fresh, fragrant whites and full, velvety reds.
Great satisfaction and a place in the finals
for the 2016 Friulano, whose aromas and
tanginess are second to none. It's a high
point of excellence that rubs off on rest of
their selection. The wine benefited from a
decidedly favorable vintage and pays
homage to the territory.

○ FCO Friulano '16	♥♥	3*
○ FCO Chardonnay '16	♥♥	3
○ FCO Pinot Grigio '16	♥♥	3
○ FCO Sauvignon '16	♥♥	3
● FCO Merlot '16	♥	3
○ FCO Ribolla Gialla '16	♥	3
○ FCO Chardonnay '15	♀♀	3
○ FCO Chardonnay '14	♀♀	3
○ FCO Friulano '15	♀♀	3
○ FCO Friulano '14	♀♀	3
○ FCO Picolit '12	♀♀	7
○ FCO Pinot Grigio '14	♀♀	2*
○ FCO Ribolla Gialla '15	♀♀	3
○ FCO Sauvignon '15	♀♀	3

Roberto Scubla

FRAZ. IPPLIS
VIA ROCCA BERNARDA, 22
33040 PREMARIACCO [UD]
TEL. +39 0432716258
www.scubla.com

CELLAR SALES
PRE-BOOKED VISITS
ANNUAL PRODUCTION 50,000 bottles
HECTARES UNDER VINE 11.00

In 1991, Roberto Scubla had the chance to take over a thriving winery on the slopes of the Rocca Bernarda. At the time it was called I Moros and it belonged to the Tavagnacco family. He gave it his own name and, drawing on the winemaking skills of his friend Gianni Menotti, a world-famous consultant, he was able to establish it at the heights of regional excellence, garnering recognition for his entire selection. An old, renovated farmhouse serves as their headquarters. The facility is equipped with cozy rooms and is surrounded by a rustic landscape. The cantina, on the other hand, was integrated into a room for wood. As the space is completely underground, it enjoys consistently cool temperatures. Once again, all their wines proved to be of the highest quality, with four making it to the final selections. The only downside is that they didn't achieve top marks, but such a rich participation confirms their status as one of the best wineries in the region.

Renzo Sgubin

VIA FAET, 15/1
34071 CORMÒNS [GO]
TEL. +39 0481630297
www.renzosgubin.it

CELLAR SALES
PRE-BOOKED VISITS
ANNUAL PRODUCTION 28,000 bottles
HECTARES UNDER VINE 12.00
SUSTAINABLE WINERY

Founded in 1997, Renzo Sgubin's winery can be considered relatively new, though reality this was only the year in which its existence was formalized. Renzo's father, Bruno, an expert vine-grower, had been working since the 1960s, when he managed to acquire some of the terrain that he'd been on as a sharecropper. He' always produced and sold his wine in jug then in 2003 the first bottles came out. T vineyards' core nucleus can be found in Cormòns, Pradis, straddling Collio and th Friuli Isonzo DOC zone. Once we had finished the tastings, we saw that all the wines had received a similar score. This confirmed Renzo's great expertise in getting the best out of every variety (both terms of sensory qualities and territory). There were no particular high points, but real weaknesses, either.

○ FCO Bianco Pomèdes '15	♥♥ 5
○ FCO Friulano '16	♥♥ 3*
○ FCO Pinot Bianco '16	♥♥ 3*
○ FCO Verduzzo Friulano Passito Cràtis '14	♥♥ 6
○ FCO Malvasia Lo Speziale '16	♥♥ 3
● FCO Merlot '15	♥♥ 3
● FCO Rosso Revisus '14	♥♥ 3
○ FCO Sauvignon '16	♥♥ 3
○ Riesling Passito al Vento '15	♥♥ 5
○ COF Bianco Pomèdes '04	♥♥♥ 4
○ COF Verduzzo Friulano Cràtis '09	♥♥♥ 5
○ COF Verduzzo Friulano Cràtis '06	♥♥♥ 5
○ COF Verduzzo Friulano Cràtis '04	♥♥♥ 5

○ Friuli Isonzo Chardonnay '16	♥♥
○ Friuli Isonzo Friulano '16	♥♥
○ Friuli Isonzo Malvasia '16	♥♥
○ Friuli Isonzo Pinot Grigio '16	♥♥
○ Friuli Isonzo Sauvignon '16	♥♥
○ 3, 4, 3 '15	♀
○ 3, 4, 3 '13	♀
● Collio Merlot '13	♀
○ Friuli Isonzo Chardonnay '15	♀
○ Friuli Isonzo Malvasia '15	♀
○ Friuli Isonzo Malvasia '14	♀
○ Friuli Isonzo Pinot Grigio '15	♀
○ Friuli Isonzo Pinot Grigio '14	♀
● Plagnis '11	♀

imon di Brazzan

IZ. BRAZZANO
SAN ROCCO, 17
I070 CORMÒNS [GO]
L. +39 048161182
ww.simondibrazzan.com

ELLAR SALES
RE-BOOKED VISITS
NNUAL PRODUCTION 70,000 bottles
ECTARES UNDER VINE 13.00
TICULTURE METHOD Certified Organic

or more than twenty years Daniele Drius
as managed, independently, Simon di
razzan. The winery is still in the name of
er grandfather, Enrico Veliscig, who, at the
enerable age of 99, still helps out in the
neyards. A firm advocate of biodynamic
ticulture, Daniele gave up the use of
emicals some time ago, opting for
atural methods instead. In the spaces
etween the rows of vines, the land is
eated with a mix of planted herbs on a
tating basis, an approach called green
anure. At the end of May, after flowering,
ey're cut and uprooted. The plant
ructures themselves are sprayed with a
ixture of horsetail and nettle. Repeating
st year's incredible performance would
ave been a great enough feat, but this
ear Daniele has gone even further. The
xcellent grape blend, the 2015 Rinè Blanc,
ad the 2016 Friulano Blanc di Simon were
at the top of our rankings.

Sirch

VIA FORNALIS, 277/1
33043 CIVIDALE DEL FRIULI [UD]
TEL. +39 0432709835
www.sirchwine.com

CELLAR SALES
PRE-BOOKED VISITS
ANNUAL PRODUCTION 150,000 bottles
HECTARES UNDER VINE 25.00

There's a lot on the horizon for Sirch. The
winery, which is already one of the most
important in the region, is on the verge of a
major expansion. It's an ambitious project,
set off by the interest of a large-scale
importer located abroad and made possible
by a partnership with Feudi di San
Gregorio, the winery from Campania that
deals in distributing wines produced in
Friuli by Luca Sirch. The 2015 Bianco
Cladrecis repeated the feat that we defined
as a good omen last year, and deservedly
made the final selections again. It's
basically a Friulano with a small amount of
Riesling, just enough to make it more
aromatic and gratifying.

Friuli Friulano Blanc di Simon '16	¶¶ 3*
Ri.nè Blanc '15	¶¶ 3*
Cabernet Franc '15	¶¶ 3
Malvasia '16	¶¶ 3
Pinot Grigio '16	¶¶ 3
Sauvignon '16	¶¶ 3
Tradizion '11	¶¶ 5
Blanc di Simon '15	¶¶ 3*
Blanc di Simon Tradizion '10	¶¶ 5
Cabernet Franc '14	¶¶ 3
Pinot Grigio '15	¶¶ 3
Pinot Grigio Tradizion '14	¶¶ 5
Ri.nè Blanc '14	¶¶ 3*
Sauvignon '15	¶¶ 3

○ FCO Bianco Cladrecis '15	¶¶ 3*
○ FCO Chardonnay '16	¶¶ 3
○ FCO Friulano '16	¶¶ 3
● FCO Refosco P. R. '15	¶¶ 3
○ FCO Ribolla Gialla '16	¶¶ 3
○ FCO Sauvignon '16	¶ 3
● FCO Schioppettino '16	¶ 3
○ COF Friulano '07	¶¶¶ 2*
○ FCO Bianco Cladrecis '14	¶¶ 3*
○ FCO Chardonnay '15	¶¶ 3
○ FCO Friulano '15	¶¶ 3
○ FCO Pinot Grigio '15	¶¶ 3
● FCO Schioppettino '14	¶¶ 3

Skerk

FRAZ. SAN PELAGIO
LOC. PREPOTTO, 20
34011 DUINO AURISINA [TS]
TEL. +39 040200156
www.skerk.com

CELLAR SALES
PRE-BOOKED VISITS
RESTAURANT SERVICE
ANNUAL PRODUCTION 22,000 bottles
HECTARES UNDER VINE 7.00
VITICULTURE METHOD Certified Organic

Even if he's young, Sandi Skerk is already an icon, one of the most skilled viticulturists in Carso Triestino. He works in an environment that is unique for its restricted spaces and for its terrain, the latter of which is dry, stark and rocky but also rich in calcium and iron. Sandi has been able to take advantage of its peculiarities and, thanks in part to the presence of the sea, produce wines of notable character. In his lovely cellar, completely carved out of rock, wines are worked naturally. They are never clarified or filtered, they undergo maceration on the skin that at times goes on for weeks, and racking only happens during the first days of the waning moon. This year we witnessed the comeback of the 2015 Ograde, a splendid cuvée of Vitovska, Malvasia Istriana, Sauvignon and Pinot Grigio, which won back a Tre Bicchieri. It features aromas of blood orange and citron, while the palate is accomplished, deep, intense and caressing, though not without grip and acidity.

Edi Skok

LOC. GIASBANA, 15
34070 SAN FLORIANO DEL COLLIO [GO]
TEL. +39 3408034045
www.skok.it

CELLAR SALES
PRE-BOOKED VISITS
ANNUAL PRODUCTION 38,000 bottles
HECTARES UNDER VINE 11.00

Brothers Edi and Orietta Skok are classic examples of vigneron who are openly proud of the simple, country origins of their family which ties them deeply to local culture and tradition. They've been working in a new cellar for a few years now. This modern structure is perfectly integrated into the landscape, taking nothing away from the charm of the old 16th century villa that has always stood here. Their 11 hectares of vineyards are spread out along the hills of Giasbana, near San Floriano del Collio, and just in front of the Slovenian border. Edi has shown he can stay in step with the times while respecting tradition, infusing his wines with liveliness and character. The 2015 Bianco Pe Ar is particularly inviting. It's made of Chardonnay, Pinot Grigio and Sauvignon and releases pleasant notes of tropical fruit and sweet spices, followed by hints of broom, lemon cream, honey and citrus confit. On the palate it's creamy and caressing, but also fresh and slightly salty.

○ Ograde '15	♙♙♙ 5
○ Malvasia '15	♙♙ 5
○ Vitovska '15	♙♙ 5
● Terrano '15	♙♙ 5
○ Carso Malvasia '08	♟♟♟ 4
○ Malvasia '13	♟♟♟ 5
○ Ograde '12	♟♟♟ 5
○ Ograde '11	♟♟♟ 5
○ Ograde '10	♟♟♟ 4
○ Ograde '09	♟♟♟ 4*
○ Ograde '13	♟♟ 5
● Terrano '12	♟♟ 5
● Terrano Ris. '06	♟♟ 5
● Terrano Sel. '11	♟♟ 5
○ Vitovska '13	♟♟ 5

○ Collio Bianco Pe Ar '15	♙♙
○ Collio Chardonnay '16	♙♙
● Collio Merlot '15	♙♙
○ Collio Pinot Grigio '16	♙♙
○ Collio Sauvignon '16	♙♙
○ Collio Friulano Zabura '16	♙
○ Collio Bianco Pe Ar '13	♟♟
○ Collio Friulano Zabura '15	♟♟
○ Collio Friulano Zabura '14	♟♟
● Collio Merlot '13	♟♟
● Collio Merlot Villa Jasbinae '11	♟♟
● Collio Merlot Villa Jasbinae '09	♟♟
○ Collio Pinot Grigio '15	♟♟
○ Collio Sauvignon '15	♟♟

Leonardo Specogna

VIA ROCCA BERNARDA, 4
33040 CORNO DI ROSAZZO [UD]
TEL. +39 0432755840
www.specogna.it

CELLAR SALES
PRE-BOOKED VISITS
ANNUAL PRODUCTION 120,000 bottles
HECTARES UNDER VINE 18.00
VITICULTURE METHOD Certified Organic

Michele and Cristian Specogna are two explosive brothers who have been able to to steer the winery founded by their grandfather Leonardo to the heights of regional excellence thanks to their enological and entrepreneurial skills. Credit for their international success must be attributed to the quality of their wines and their gift for communication. Because of their work, a territory as small as Friuli Venezia Giulia, and as unique as Rocca Bernarda, has made it to the front pages of some of the most important magazines in the sector. And the whole region is benefitting. Both their baseline selection and their 'Riserve' prove, year after year, the outstanding quality of this winery. The praise bestowed in past editions has given way to winery's first Tre Bicchieri (for its splendid 2015 Identità). It's the wine that best represents the territory, and is made only from native grapes: Tocai Friulano, Malvasia Istriana and Ribolla Gialla.

○ FCO Bianco Identità '15	♈♈♈ 7
● FCO Rosso Oltre '13	♈♈ 6
○ FCO Sauvignon Blanc Duality '15	♈♈ 3*
○ FCO Chardonnay '16	♈♈ 3
● FCO Pignolo '12	♈♈ 6
○ FCO Pinot Grigio '16	♈♈ 3
○ FCO Sauvignon '16	♈♈ 3
○ Pinot Grigio Ramato	♈♈ 6
○ COF Picolit '13	♈ 6
● FCO Cabernet Franc '15	♈ 3
○ FCO Friulano '16	♈ 3
○ FCO Identità '13	♈♈ 6
● FCO Oltre '11	♈♈ 6
● FCO Pignolo '11	♈♈ 6

Tenuta Stella

LOC. SCRIÒ
VIA SDENCINA, 1
34070 DOLEGNA DEL COLLIO [GO]
TEL. +39 0481639895
www.tenutastellacollio.it

CELLAR SALES
PRE-BOOKED VISITS
ANNUAL PRODUCTION 32,000 bottles
HECTARES UNDER VINE 8.00
VITICULTURE METHOD Certified Organic
SUSTAINABLE WINERY

Founded in 2010 by the decorated businessman Servio Stevanato, Tenuta Stella found immediate success and is now one of the most exemplary wineries of the region. Utilizing the rare virtues of old vineyards, their selection has focused on whites, exclusively native varieties, and they've kept the same philosophy for their newer lines. Erika Barbieri and Alberto Faggiani oversee the estate, which is certified organic, managing the cellar and vineyards with the aim of best highlighting the attributes of their territory. Perfect grapes give life to wines of great structure, while their younger, Yellow Ribolla, are used to produce a highly pleasing 'Metodo Classico'. This year, all the wines received acclaim, which is nothing new in itself. However, the 2015 Friulano managed to cross the threshold into the finals. It beat the competition in its crowded category, with intense and very elegant aromas and fragrant and lingering iodine overtones.

○ Collio Friulano '15	♈♈ 3*
○ Collio Malvasia '15	♈♈ 4
○ Collio Ribolla Gialla '15	♈♈ 4
○ Cuvée Tanni Brut	♈♈ 5
○ Ribolla Gialla Brut	♈♈ 4
○ Collio Bianco '12	♈♈ 3
○ Collio Friulano Scriò '14	♈♈ 3
○ Collio Friulano Scriò '13	♈♈ 3
○ Collio Friulano Scriò '12	♈♈ 3*
○ Collio Malvasia '14	♈♈ 4
○ Collio Malvasia '13	♈♈ 4
○ Collio Malvasia '12	♈♈ 4
○ Collio Ribolla Gialla '14	♈♈ 4
○ Collio Ribolla Gialla '13	♈♈ 4
○ Collio Ribolla Gialla '12	♈♈ 4

Stocco

VIA CASALI STOCCO, 12
33050 BICINICCO [UD]
TEL. +39 0432934906
www.vinistocco.it

CELLAR SALES
PRE-BOOKED VISITS
RESTAURANT SERVICE
ANNUAL PRODUCTION 250,000 bottles
HECTARES UNDER VINE 49.00

In 1910, Francesco Stocco settled in the vast plains of Bicinicco, in an area that would later be called be called Casali Stocco. The breakthrough from traditional farming to viticulture began in the 1960s. Today, the fourth generation (Andrea, Daniela and Paola) are keeping the family's legacy alive. Through commitment and hard work, they've demonstrated, and are demonstrating, that even in the plains, with gravel and red earth, you can make wines of outstanding quality. Their 49 hectares of terrain produce about 250,000 bottles a year. Harvesting is done both manually and mechanically so as to maximize the speed with which the grapes get delivered. Their wide range of wines enables them to satisfy all kinds of customers. Both the whites and the reds are made in steel and wood, especially large barrels. Great attention is paid to their Prosecco and Ribolla Gialla, which spend six months in pressure tanks.

● Cabernet Franc '15	♟♟ 2*
○ Friuli Grave Friulano '16	♟♟ 2*
● Merlot Roos dai Lens '13	♟♟ 4
○ Pinot Bianco '16	♟♟ 2*
○ Pinot Grigio '16	♟♟ 2*
○ Pinot Grigio Ramato '16	♟♟ 2*
○ Sericus '15	♟ 3
● Cabernet Sauvignon '15	♟ 2
○ Chardonnay '16	♟ 5
○ Malvasia '16	♟ 2
○ Prosecco Extra Dry '16	♟ 2
○ Ribolla Gialla Brut	♟ 3
● Cabernet Franc '14	♟♟ 2*
○ Pinot Grigio '15	♟♟ 2*

Subida di Monte

LOC. SUBIDA
VIA SUBIDA, 6
34071 CORMÒNS [GO]
TEL. +39 048161011
www.subidadimonte.it

CELLAR SALES
PRE-BOOKED VISITS
ACCOMMODATION
ANNUAL PRODUCTION 45,000 bottles
HECTARES UNDER VINE 9.00

Cristian and Andrea, the current owners of Subida di Monte, are the children of the legendary Luigi Antonutti, a man of great foresight and vision, a lover of the beautiful and the exquisite. Their lovely estate, which occupies a slope of the Collio Gorizano, stretches from the Isonzo to the Judrio river, there where the sun-kissed vineyards enjoy the protection of the Alps and the salty breeze of the Adriatic. In addition to the unquestionably favorable microclimate, they are grateful for their 'ponca', a local word that refers to the clay, calcium-rich and just a tad bit sandy soil of the Collio. Out of respect for their territory, Cristian and Andrea have adopted sustainable practices, choosing to all but eliminate the use of anti-parasite treatments. Once again, the whole range of wines got high scores, confirming their consistent quality over time. As with the last edition, the highest accolades go to the 2016 Malvasia and the 2015 Cabernet Franc, both of which proved to have that edge.

● Collio Cabernet Franc '15	♟♟ 3
○ Collio Friulano '16	♟♟ 3
○ Collio Malvasia '16	♟♟ 3
● Collio Merlot '15	♟♟ 3
○ Collio Pinot Grigio '16	♟♟ 3
● Collio Rosso Poncaia '13	♟♟ 4
○ Collio Sauvignon '16	♟ 3
● Collio Cabernet Franc '14	♟♟ 3
○ Collio Friulano '15	♟♟ 3
○ Collio Friulano '14	♟♟ 3
○ Collio Malvasia '15	♟♟ 3
○ Collio Malvasia '14	♟♟ 3
○ Collio Sauvignon '15	♟♟ 3

Tenimenti Civa

FRAZ. BELLAZOIA POVOLETTO
VIA SUBIDA 16
33040 UDINE
TEL. +39 04321770380
www.tenimenticiva.com

ANNUAL PRODUCTION 280,000 bottles
HECTARES UNDER VINE 40.00

The guide welcomes this new addition to
the region's winemaking scene! In 2016,
Parma native Valerio Civa decided to put
his extensive experience in the world of
wine to work and found Tenimenti Civa, a
winery headquartered in Bellazoia di
Povoletto, in the Friuli Colli Orientali DOC
zone. Their wines are made with grapes
from the estate, and from constantly
monitored, local suppliers. The philosophy
is summed up by the 85/15 logo displayed
on their labels, meaning 85% of the
grapes are from the appellation, while
15% are from the 40-hectare estate's best
crop. The first season saw 280,000 bottles
produced. If their aim is to produce
medium-high quality wines, we can say
that they've hit the nail right on the head.
The 2016 Sauvignon made the final
selections and came close to achieving
excellence. Indeed, the winery's future is
looking rosy, thanks in part to their
excellent prices.

○ FCO Sauvignon '16		♟♟ 3*
○ FCO Friulano '16		♟♟ 3
○ FCO Ribolla Gialla '16		♟♟ 3

Matijaz Tercic

LOC. BUCUIE, 4A
34070 SAN FLORIANO DEL COLLIO [GO]
TEL. +39 0481884920
www.tercic.com

CELLAR SALES
PRE-BOOKED VISITS
ANNUAL PRODUCTION 30,000 bottles
HECTARES UNDER VINE 9.50

San Floriano del Collio's is bristling with
celebrated, family-run wineries that have,
over time, shifted from farming to
vine-growing. It's a heaven-on-earth for
winemaking, universally recognized as the
best in the DOC zone, thanks to its
exposure to the sun and, in particular, its
microclimate, with the cool winds of the
Vipacco valley mitigated by the breeze of
the nearby Adriatic. It is here that Matijaz
Tercic tends to his precious vineyards with
the care of a true wine artisan, making his
wines available only when he's decided
that they've properly aged. Some of the
best wines are missing this year, maybe
because they aren't ready. But the winery's
roster hasn't particularly suffered for it. The
2015 Sauvignon found a place among the
finalists. It offers up a fragrant varietal
aroma and won over our palates with its
caressing mouth.

○ Collio Sauvignon '15		♟♟ 3*
○ Collio Pinot Grigio '15		♟♟ 3
○ Collio Ribolla Gialla '15		♟♟ 3
○ Friuli Isonzo Friulano '15		♟ 3
○ Collio Pinot Grigio '07		♟♟♟ 3*
○ Collio Bianco Planta '12		♟♟ 4
● Collio Merlot Seme '11		♟♟ 5
○ Collio Pinot Grigio '13		♟♟ 3
○ Collio Pinot Grigio Dar '12		♟♟ 4
○ Collio Sauvignon '14		♟♟ 3
○ Collio Sauvignon '13		♟♟ 3
○ Friuli Isonzo Friulano '14		♟♟ 3
○ Vino degli Orti '13		♟♟ 3*

Tiare - Roberto Snidarcig

FRAZ. VENCÒ
LOC. SANT'ELENA, 3A
34070 DOLEGNA DEL COLLIO [GO]
TEL. +39 048162491
www.tiaredoc.com

CELLAR SALES
PRE-BOOKED VISITS
RESTAURANT SERVICE
ANNUAL PRODUCTION 90,000 bottles
HECTARES UNDER VINE 10.00
SUSTAINABLE WINERY

Year after year we commend the ongoing
progress of this winery that, despite their
already having reached heights of
excellence, continues to blow us away for
the sophisticated fragrance of their wines.
Important international recognition has
awarded the skill and persistence of
Roberto Snidarcig - and that can only be a
source of encouragement. We like to think
about how, in 1985, he began with just
one hectare of land on Monte Quarin, the
hill that protects Cormòns from the cold
eastern winds. Over the following years,
the number of vineyards grew
exponentially. He's since created a new
cellar in Dolegna del Collio and a brand
that has brought prestige to the territory.
In the local dialect, 'tiare' means 'on the
land'. This year we witnessed a splendid
performance from all the wines, three of
which made it into the finals. It was the
first time for the 2015 Pinot Nero Pinòir
and the 2015 Rosemblanc, while the
2016 Sauvignon confirmed its place at
the heights of excellence, winning a Tre
Bicchieri for the fourth time.

○ Collio Sauvignon '16	♛♛♛ 5
○ Collio Bianco Rosemblanc '15	♛♛ 5
● Pinot Nero Pinòir '15	♛♛ 5
○ Collio Chardonnay '16	♛♛ 3
○ Collio Friulano '16	♛♛ 4
○ Collio Malvasia '16	♛♛ 3
○ Collio Pinot Grigio '16	♛♛ 4
○ Collio Ribolla Gialla '16	♛♛ 4
○ Collio Sauvignon Empìre '15	♛♛ 3
○ Il Tiare '16	♛♛ 3
○ Collio Sauvignon '15	♛♛♛ 5
○ Collio Sauvignon '14	♛♛♛ 5
○ Collio Sauvignon '13	♛♛♛ 3*
○ Collio Friulano '15	♛♛ 4
○ Collio Malvasia '15	♛♛ 3

★Franco Toros

LOC. NOVALI, 12
34071 CORMÒNS [GO]
TEL. +39 048161327
www.vinitoros.com

CELLAR SALES
PRE-BOOKED VISITS
ANNUAL PRODUCTION 60,000 bottles
HECTARES UNDER VINE 11.00

For Collio Goriziano, and Cormòns in
particular, Franco Toros is a legend, an
icon, one of the best in the field. He comes
from a long line of farmers who, in the
early 1900s, settled in Novali, not far from
the Plessiva Pass that leads to Slovenia. It
doesn't take much to see that the area
here is particularly well-suited to
vine-growing. Franco loves the outdoors,
and his vineyards. He looks after them with
painstaking care; at times it seems that he
whispers to the vines and grapes. In the
pursuit of excellence, he transforms his
grapes into true works of art, led on by
ancient knowledge, passed down from his
ancestors. This is the umpteenth test of
character for Franco's wines, which almost
perfectly replicated last year's
performance. The 2016 Pinot Bianco and
2016 Friulano are still leading the way and
received top marks.

○ Collio Friulano '16	♛♛ 4
○ Collio Pinot Bianco '16	♛♛ 4
○ Collio Chardonnay '16	♛♛ 4
○ Collio Pinot Grigio '16	♛♛ 4
○ Collio Friulano '12	♛♛♛ 4*
○ Collio Friulano '11	♛♛♛ 4*
○ Collio Friulano '10	♛♛♛ 4
○ Collio Friulano '09	♛♛♛ 4*
○ Collio Friulano '08	♛♛♛ 4*
○ Collio Pinot Bianco '14	♛♛♛ 4*
○ Collio Pinot Bianco '13	♛♛♛ 4*
○ Collio Friulano '15	♛♛ 4
○ Collio Friulano '13	♛♛ 4
○ Collio Pinot Bianco '15	♛♛ 4
○ Collio Pinot Grigio '14	♛♛ 4

Torre Rosazza

FRAZ. OLEIS
LOC. POGGIOBELLO, 12
33044 MANZANO [UD]
TEL. +39 0422864511
www.torrerosazza.com

CELLAR SALES
PRE-BOOKED VISITS
ANNUAL PRODUCTION 200,000 bottles
HECTARES UNDER VINE 90.00
SUSTAINABLE WINERY

In the 1960s, Genagricola, an established group that has brought together a number of celebrated brands from across Italy, had the chance to acquire Torre Rosazza, a historic winery on the hills of Manzano that's housed in the 18th century Palazzo De Marchi. Sensing an opportunity, they accepted and immediately began researching the 90 hectares of vineyards so as to identify the characteristics and composition of each plot of land. They then divided it up according to exposure to the sun and geologic properties so as to best bring out the attributes of each grape variety. With a closely-knit staff that are masterfully orchestrated by Enrico Raddi, they have, for some time now, operated at the heights of excellence. Torre Rosazza's magical moment continues with their 2016 Pinot Grigio, which has whipped strong competition to win a Tre Bicchieri once again. This year it made it the finals together with an excellent 2016 Friulano (they clearly form a solid and winning duo).

○ FCO Pinot Grigio '16	🍷🍷🍷 3*
○ FCO Friulano '16	🍷🍷 3*
○ COF Picolit '13	🍷🍷 5
● FCO Altromerlot '13	🍷🍷 5
● FCO Pignolo '13	🍷🍷 5
○ FCO Pinot Bianco '16	🍷🍷 3
● FCO Pinot Nero Ronco del Palazzo '13	🍷🍷 3
○ FCO Ribolla Gialla '16	🍷🍷 3
○ FCO Sauvignon '16	🍷 3
○ FCO Verduzzo Friulano '14	🍷 3
○ COF Pinot Grigio '13	🍷🍷🍷 3*
○ COF Pinot Grigio '12	🍷🍷🍷 3*
○ FCO Pinot Bianco '14	🍷🍷🍷 3*
○ FCO Pinot Grigio '15	🍷🍷🍷 3*

La Tunella

FRAZ. IPPLIS
VIA DEL COLLIO, 14
33040 PREMARIACCO [UD]
TEL. +39 0432716030
www.latunella.it

CELLAR SALES
PRE-BOOKED VISITS
ANNUAL PRODUCTION 390,000 bottles
HECTARES UNDER VINE 70.00
SUSTAINABLE WINERY

The La Tunella brand, created by Massimo and Marco Zorzettig, has for years operated at the heights of regional excellence, proud of the Colli Orientali del Friuli DOC zone and of representing it. Ever since they were young men, Massimo and Marco have assumed responsibility for managing the winery, drawing on three generations of experience in viticulture. They have, since the beginning, drawn on the winemaking skills of Luigino Zamparo for their selection. The pluck, youth and dynamic quality of the winery is reflected in their wines, which display approachability both in their fragrance and flavor. The variety of their selection, which strives for quality, is capable of satisfying every need. Once again, a splendid range of white, red and sweet wines are on display. As usual, we found more than one wine in the finals, with top awards going to those from the 2015 vintage, which proved more austere, flavorful and mature.

○ FCO BiancoSesto '15	🍷🍷 4
○ FCO Friulano Col Livius '15	🍷🍷 4
○ FCO Sauvignon Col Matiss '15	🍷🍷 4
○ FCO Dolce Noans '15	🍷🍷 5
○ FCO Pinot Grigio '16	🍷🍷 3
○ FCO Ribolla Gialla Col de Bliss '15	🍷🍷 4
○ FCO Ribolla Gialla Rjgialla '16	🍷🍷 3
● L'Arcione '12	🍷🍷 5
● Pignolo '11	🍷🍷 5
● Schioppettino '13	🍷🍷 4
○ FCO Friulano '16	🍷 3
○ COF BiancoSesto '11	🍷🍷🍷 4*
○ COF BiancoSesto '07	🍷🍷🍷 3
○ FCO Bianco LaLinda '14	🍷🍷🍷 4*
○ Noans '12	🍷🍷🍷 5

Valchiarò

FRAZ. TOGLIANO
VIA DEI LAGHI, 1C
33040 TORREANO [UD]
TEL. +39 0432715502
www.valchiaro.it

CELLAR SALES
PRE-BOOKED VISITS
ANNUAL PRODUCTION 45,000 bottles
HECTARES UNDER VINE 14.00
SUSTAINABLE WINERY

Valchiaro is a classic example of how unity leads to strength. At the end of the 20th century, a group of friends, each an owner of a tiny vineyard, decided to create a partnership thus bringing together a number of small operations under one brand: Valchiarò. The name of the winery comes from the river Chiarò, which crosses the valley of Torreano di Cividale, one of the coolest parts of the Colli Orientali. It's an area where the Adriatic Sea winds leave room for the continental northeastern winds, and it's known that the wide range of temperatures contributes to the aromas of the grapes grown here. To best bring these out, they've entrusted their winemaking to the skills of Gianni Menotti. The 2016 Friulano Nexus was a particular success and took its place among a packed group of finalists. Compared to other white wines, it definitely has the edge, both for its complexity and the elegant aromas of the nose, as well as the perfect balance that enraptures the taste buds.

○ FCO Friulano Nexus '16	♟♟	3*
● FCO Merlot '13	♟♟	3
○ FCO Pinot Grigio '16	♟♟	3
● FCO Refosco P. R. Ris. '13	♟♟	3
● FCO Rosso Torre Qual Ris. '13	♟♟	3
○ FCO Sauvignon '16	♟♟	3
○ FCO Verduzzo Friulano '15	♟♟	4
○ FCO Friulano '16	♟	3
○ FCO Friulano Nexus '15	♟♟	3
○ FCO Picolit '11	♟♟	6
○ FCO Pinot Grigio '15	♟♟	3
● FCO Refosco P. R. Ris. '12	♟♟	3
○ FCO Sauvignon '15	♟♟	3
○ FCO Verduzzo Friulano '12	♟♟	4

Valpanera

VIA TRIESTE, 5A
33059 VILLA VICENTINA [UD]
TEL. +39 0431970395
www.valpanera.it

CELLAR SALES
PRE-BOOKED VISITS
ANNUAL PRODUCTION 450,000 bottles
HECTARES UNDER VINE 55.00

Valpanera is a well-established winery and one of the most representative of Friuli Aquileia's potential. Founded by Giampietro Dal Vecchio, who continues to manage it with his son Giovanni, the winery has taken on the responsibility of supporting the Refosco dal Peduncolo Rosso, the native red grape that best displays the region's attributes. This was a brave decision, brought about by research and study into centuries of farming throughout the area, an area where the clay terrain is fanned by the northern winds and the grapes are made ripe thanks to the warm breeze of the nearby Adriatic. Some wines are still aging, so we were only able to taste a few. We liked the Alsatian character of the 2015 Chardonnay Carato, with its aromas of acacia honey and peaches in syrup. However, both the 2012 Refosco dal Peduncolo Rosso Riserva and the 2013 Rosso Alma were by far superior.

● Friuli Aquileia Refosco P. R. Ris. '12	♟♟	5
● Friuli Aquileia Rosso Alma '13	♟♟	5
○ Friuli Aquileia Chardonnay Carato '15	♟	3
● Friuli Aquileia Refosco P. R. '14	♟♟	2*
● Friuli Aquileia Refosco P. R. '13	♟♟	2*
● Friuli Aquileia Refosco P. R. '12	♟♟	2*
● Friuli Aquileia Refosco P. R. Ris. '11	♟♟	5
● Friuli Aquileia Refosco P. R. Sup. '13	♟♟	3
● Friuli Aquileia Refosco P. R. Sup. '12	♟♟	3
● Friuli Aquileia Refosco P. R. Sup. '10	♟♟	3
● Friuli Aquileia Rosso Alma '11	♟♟	5
● Friuli Aquileia Rosso Alma '08	♟♟	5
○ Friuli Aquileia Verduzzo Friulano '13	♟♟	4
● Rosso di Valpanera '12	♟♟	2*

★★Venica & Venica

LOC. CERÒ, 8
34070 DOLEGNA DEL COLLIO [GO]
TEL. +39 048161264
www.venica.it

CELLAR SALES
PRE-BOOKED VISITS
ACCOMMODATION
ANNUAL PRODUCTION 305,000 bottles
HECTARES UNDER VINE 39.00
SUSTAINABLE WINERY

Serena and Marta, the daughters of Gianni and Giorgio Venica, are both fresh off their studies. They're part of a team that's working to promote the celebrated brand Venica & Venica, bringing their youthful spirit to a family-run group that has, for more than half a century, been transforming a small agricultural operation into a full-blown business. And they're writing one of the best chapters in their region's history. Venica & Venica has tied its name to Collio, and its wines have contributed to making the area's attributes known throughout the world. Once again, three splendid wines made it to our finals and the 2016 Sauvignon Ronco delle Mele earned a Tre Bicchieri. After a brief period of oblivion, one of the most representative wines of Collio's potential has returned to the top.

○ Collio Sauvignon Ronco delle Mele '16	�♛♛	6
○ Collio Friulano Ronco delle Cime '16	♛♛	5
○ Collio Pinot Grigio Jesera '16	♛♛	4
○ Collio Malvasia Pètris '16	♛♛	4
○ Collio Pinot Bianco Tàlis '16	♛♛	4
○ Collio Ribolla Gialla L'Adelchi '16	♛♛	4
○ Collio Sauvignon Ronco del Cerò '16	♛♛	5
○ Collio Traminer Aromatico '16	♛♛	4
○ Collio Sauvignon Ronco delle Mele '13	♛♛♛	6
○ Collio Sauvignon Ronco delle Mele '12	♛♛♛	6
○ Collio Sauvignon Ronco delle Mele '11	♛♛♛	6
○ Collio Sauvignon Ronco delle Mele '10	♛♛♛	5
○ Collio Sauvignon Ronco delle Mele '09	♛♛♛	5
○ Collio Sauvignon Ronco delle Mele '08	♛♛♛	5

La Viarte

VIA NOVACUZZO, 51
33040 PREPOTTO [UD]
TEL. +39 0432759458
www.laviarte.it

CELLAR SALES
PRE-BOOKED VISITS
ACCOMMODATION
ANNUAL PRODUCTION 100,000 bottles
HECTARES UNDER VINE 27.00
SUSTAINABLE WINERY

In the local dialect, 'la viarte' means 'spring'. And this splendid winery situated on the Prepotto hills is going through just that, a spring, a breath of fresh air that the current owner, Alberto Piovan, deeply desired. It's been made possible thanks, in part, to the world-renowned winemaker, Gianni Menotti. With his help, the entire selection has flourished, including their 'Liende' line (from the word meaning 'legend'), which comprises their top wines. These are wines that have convinced every tasting panel that's tried them, but that mostly impressed for their fragrance, crispness, continuity and persistence, paying tribute to each vineyard. It's no coincidence that the Liende line of wines grabbed the top two places and both made it to the finals. The 2016 Friulano Liende headed the line and got its first Tre Bicchieri. The white grape blends, the 2016 Arteus, and the 2007 Pignolo, are also excellent, with their winning structure and aging potential.

○ FCO Friulano Liende '16	♛♛♛	5
○ Arteus '16	♛♛	4
● FCO Pignolo '07	♛♛	8
○ FCO Sauvignon Liende '16	♛♛	5
○ Dolce Sium '08	♛♛	4
○ FCO Friulano '16	♛♛	4
○ FCO Pinot Bianco '16	♛♛	3
○ FCO Sauvignon '16	♛♛	5
● FCO Tazzelenghe '11	♛♛	5
○ FCO Sauvignon Liende '15	♛♛♛	5
○ Arteus '15	♛♛	3
○ FCO Friulano '15	♛♛	3
○ FCO Friulano Liende '15	♛♛	5
● FCO Merlot '12	♛♛	4
○ FCO Ribolla Gialla '15	♛♛	3

Vidussi

VIA SPESSA, 18
34071 CAPRIVA DEL FRIULI [GO]
TEL. +39 048180072
www.vinimontresor.it

CELLAR SALES
PRE-BOOKED VISITS
ANNUAL PRODUCTION 500,000 bottles
HECTARES UNDER VINE 30.00

For some years now, the Vidussi family has operated as part of the Montresor di Verona group, who contributed to bolstering their production line, especially their white wines and native grape varieties. In order to enlarge their selection and best cover the market (both nationally and internationally), they have added new vineyards. In addition to the winery's original estate around Collio (in Capriva del Friuli), they now count plots in Colli Orientali del Friuli and Friuli Isonzo as part of the estate. Winemaking, from start to finish, is entrusted to the proven experience of Luigino De Giuseppe. Once again, an excellent performance, and their prices only make this high quality selection of wines even more appealing. Their varietal characteristics are well-defined and the flowing palate favors drinkability. We are spoilt for choice.

★★Vie di Romans

LOC. VIE DI ROMANS, 1
34070 MARIANO DEL FRIULI [GO]
TEL. +39 040169600
www.viediromans.it

CELLAR SALES
PRE-BOOKED VISITS
ANNUAL PRODUCTION 280,000 bottles
HECTARES UNDER VINE 60.00
SUSTAINABLE WINERY

Vie di Romans is a celebrated brand, a model winery, a true jewel in the world of regional viticulture. Gianfranco Gallo, who has a gift for discriminating decision-making and a meticulous approach to winemaking, is the author of this splendid masterpiece. His wines, especially his whites, express the character of the territory, as well as being supported by an impressive structure. His vineyards stretch throughout the Friuli Isonzo DOC zone, just a few kilometers from Triste, where the continental climate fuses with the Mediterranean. The terrain is flat but the microclimate is perfect and the subsoil is rich in minerals. Such high scores could only mean one thing. It was the 2015 Sauvignon Piere's turn to adorn itself with our Tre Bicchieri. But it was a truly hard decision, given the potential displayed by the rest of the selection.

○ Collio Chardonnay '16	🏆🏆 2*
○ Collio Friulano '16	🏆🏆 3
○ Collio Malvasia '16	🏆🏆 2*
○ Collio Ribolla Gialla '16	🏆🏆 2*
○ Collio Sauvignon '16	🏆🏆 2*
● Ribolla Nera o Schioppettino '16	🏆🏆 3
○ Collio Pinot Grigio '16	🏆 2
○ Collio Traminer Aromatico '16	🏆 2
○ Collio Chardonnay '15	🏆🏆 2*
○ Collio Friulano '15	🏆🏆 3
○ Collio Malvasia '15	🏆🏆 2*
○ Collio Pinot Grigio '15	🏆🏆 2*
○ Collio Sauvignon '15	🏆🏆 2*
○ Collio Traminer Aromatico '15	🏆🏆 2*

○ Friuli Isonzo Sauvignon Piere '15	🏆🏆🏆 5
○ Dut'un '14	🏆🏆 6
○ Friuli Isonzo Friulano Dolée '15	🏆🏆 5
○ Friuli Isonzo Pinot Grigio Dessimis '15	🏆🏆 6
○ Friuli Isonzo Sauvignon Vieris '15	🏆🏆 5
○ Friuli Isonzo Bianco Flors di Uis '15	🏆🏆 4
○ Friuli Isonzo Chardonnay Vie di Romans '15	🏆🏆 5
○ Friuli Isonzo Malvasia Dis Cumieris '15	🏆🏆 5
○ Friuli Isonzo Bianco Flors di Uis '09	🏆🏆🏆 4*
○ Friuli Isonzo Chardonnay Ciampagnis Vieris '13	🏆🏆🏆 4*
○ Friuli Isonzo Friulano Dolée '12	🏆🏆🏆 5
○ Friuli Isonzo Friulano Dolée '11	🏆🏆🏆 4*
○ Friuli Isonzo Sauvignon Piere '10	🏆🏆🏆 4*
○ Friuli Isonzo Sauvignon Piere '08	🏆🏆🏆 4*

Vigna del Lauro

LOC. MONTONA, 19
34071 CORMÒNS [GO]
TEL. +39 0481629549
www.vignadellauro.it

CELLAR SALES
PRE-BOOKED VISITS
ANNUAL PRODUCTION 60,000 bottles
HECTARES UNDER VINE 10.00

Vigna del Lauro is a family-run winery that's managed by Fabio Coser (already the owner of Ronco Dei Tassi), his wife Daniela and his children Matteo and Enrico. It was founded in 1994, spawned by a collaboration with the German importer Eberhard Spangenberg, which had made it necessary to differentiate production so as to satisfy the needs of a major slice of the market on the other side of the Alps. The winery follows a philosophy based on care and respect for the grapes, which, they believe, should bring out each's unique varietal characteristics as well as represent the attributes of their territory. The result is sound, coherent, simple wines that are highly drinkable and available at decidedly affordable prices. New this year is the 2013 Pinot Nero Novaj. It has a great appearance, just the right shade for this grape variety. The same goes for its aromas, thanks to hints of spices, which embellish its fruity and balsamic background. In the mouth there's a slight trace of tannins which spruces up the palate and contrasts with its softness.

○ Collio Friulano '16	▼▼ 3
○ Collio Pinot Grigio '16	▼▼ 3
○ Collio Sauvignon '16	▼▼ 3
● Friuli Isonzo Merlot '15	▼▼ 2*
○ Friuli Isonzo Traminer Aromatico '16	▼▼ 2*
● Pinot Nero Novaj '13	▼▼ 3
○ Ribolla Gialla '16	▼▼ 3
○ Friuli Isonzo Chardonnay '16	▼ 2
○ Collio Friulano '15	♈▼ 3
○ Collio Pinot Grigio '15	♈♈ 3
○ Collio Ribolla Gialla '15	♈♈ 3
○ Collio Sauvignon '15	♈♈ 3
● Friuli Isonzo Merlot '14	♈♈ 2*

Vigna Petrussa

VIA ALBANA, 47
33040 PREPOTTO [UD]
TEL. +39 0432713021
www.vignapetrussa.it

CELLAR SALES
PRE-BOOKED VISITS
ANNUAL PRODUCTION 30,000 bottles
HECTARES UNDER VINE 7.00

In 1995, Hilde Petrussa decided to take up the family estate, which had fallen into disrepair after its peak in the early 1900s. She's found herself having to replant the vineyards, giving priority to native varieties and choosing to cultivate according to the Guyot system, which calls for an increase in the number of vines per hectare and completely grassing the vineyard's surface. Naturally, most of her effort goes to the Ribolla Nera, the grape from which Schioppettino is made (the wine would seem to have originated in this valley). Together with a tight group of local vine-growers, she has fought for years for recognition of Schioppettino di Prepotto as a subzone. The 2015 Richenza has made a comeback. It's the winery's own grape blend, made up of Tocai Friulano, Riesling Renano, Malvasia Istriana and Picolit. The wine proves generous on the nose, calling up lemon jelly, meadow flowers, honey and lavender. The palate is creamy, caressing, mouthfilling and soft, but also fresh and tangy.

○ Richenza '15	▼▼ 4
○ COF Picolit '13	▼▼ 6
○ FCO Friulano '16	▼▼ 3
● FCO Schioppettino di Prepotto '13	▼▼ 5
● Refosco P. R. '15	▼▼ 4
● FCO Cabernet Franc '13	▼ 3
● COF Cabernet Franc '12	♈♈ 3
● COF Schioppettino di Prepotto '11	♈♈ 4
○ FCO Friulano '15	♈♈ 3*
○ FCO Picolit '12	♈♈ 5
● FCO Schioppettino di Prepotto '12	♈♈ 4
○ Richenza '13	♈♈ 4
○ Richenza '12	♈♈ 4

Vigna Traverso

VIA RONCHI, 73
33040 PREPOTTO [UD]
TEL. +39 0422804807
www.vignatraverso.it

CELLAR SALES
PRE-BOOKED VISITS
RESTAURANT SERVICE
ANNUAL PRODUCTION 100,000 bottles
HECTARES UNDER VINE 22.00
SUSTAINABLE WINERY

Purchased in 1998, for many years, Vigna Traverso was considered a secondary branch of the famous Venetian producer, Ornella Molon Traverso. Today, however, it's an efficient operation, managed autonomously by Stefano Traverso, who, despite his young age, already boasts extensive experience in the sector. He immediate began reviving the old vineyards in Prepotto, enlisting the support of the vine physiologist, Stefano Zaninotti. When it came to building the new cellar, which is perfectly integrated on the hill's steep slope, Stefano proved both an innovator and a traditionalist. He insisted the old, concrete vats be accompanied by the latest technology. Once again, Stefano has shown he knows what he's doing by presenting an array of wines with enviable quality. Two made it to the finals: the 2013 Refosco da Peduncolo Rosso, which repeated last year's feat, and the 2016 Sauvgnon, which debuted this year.

● FCO Refosco P.R. '13	♥♥	3*
○ FCO Sauvignon '16	♥♥	3*
○ FCO Bianco Sottocastello '14	♥♥	4
● FCO Cabernet Franc '13	♥♥	3
● FCO Merlot '12	♥♥	3
○ FCO Pinot Grigio '16	♥♥	3
○ FCO Ribolla Gialla '16	♥♥	3
● FCO Rosso Troj '13	♥♥	3
● FCO Schioppettino di Prepotto '13	♥♥	4
○ FCO Friulano '16	♥	3
○ FCO Bianco Sottocastello '13	♀♀	4
○ FCO Friulano '15	♀♀	3
○ FCO Ribolla Gialla '15	♀♀	3
○ FCO Sauvignon '15	♀♀	3

Vigne del Malina

FRAZ. ORZANO
VIA PASINI VIANELLI, 9
33047 REMANZACCO [UD]
TEL. +39 0432649258
www.vignedelmalina.com

CELLAR SALES
PRE-BOOKED VISITS
ANNUAL PRODUCTION 45,000 bottles
HECTARES UNDER VINE 10.00
VITICULTURE METHOD Certified Organic

Vigne del Malina is a small producer, but it's a classic example of how you don't need to be on a hill to produce wines of excellent quality. Here, in Orzano di Remanzacco, a bit east of Udine, the flat terrain is crossed by two rivers, the Malina and the Ellero, whose paths, curiously, trace out the form of a glass. In 2007, Roberto Bacchetti and Maria Luisa Trevisan, owners of the vast estate and and 19th century villa at its center, decided to develop a few hectares of terrain, and focus immediately on excellence. All their wines (even whites) undergo long aging in their bottles and are sold only after three years, at least. We knew we would have to wait to taste the wines from the 2013 vintage, but it was well worth it. They are excellent, both for their complexity and their structure. The 2013 Pinot Grigio is particularly good, with its aromas of saffron, crème brûlée, acacia honey and hazelnuts, and a flavorful, tangy, caressing and gradual palate.

○ Pinot Grigio '13	♥♥	3*
○ Chardonnay '13	♥♥	3
○ Sauvignon '13	♥♥	3
● Cabernet Franc '11	♀♀	3
○ Chardonnay '12	♀♀	3
○ Pinot Grigio '12	♀♀	3
○ Pinot Grigio '11	♀♀	3
○ Pinot Grigio '10	♀♀	3
○ Pinot Grigio Ram '09	♀♀	4
● Refosco P.R. '09	♀♀	4
○ Sauvignon '12	♀♀	3
○ Sauvignon '11	♀♀	3
○ Sauvignon Aur '09	♀♀	5

★Le Vigne di Zamò

LOC. ROSAZZO
VIA ABATE CORRADO, 4
33044 MANZANO [UD]
TEL. +39 0432759693
www.levignedizamo.com

CELLAR SALES
PRE-BOOKED VISITS
ANNUAL PRODUCTION 280,000 bottles
HECTARES UNDER VINE 67.00
SUSTAINABLE WINERY

Le Vigne di Zamò, the prestigious brand that's now part of the Farinetti group, is tied to the name Tullio Zamò, the legendary pioneer of quality Friuli wine. In 1978, he founded Vigne dal Leon on the slopes of Rocca Bernarda, creating Abbazia di Rosazzo some years later. Then, in 1996, after purchasing 15 more vineyards in the area of Rosazzo (just in front of the Abbazia), he founded Le Vigne di Zamò along with his sons, Pierluigi and Silvano. Over the last 20 years, the producer has exported regional excellence, earning acclaim from some of the globe's most important markets. Ownership has changed, but everything else has remained the same. Zamò is a legend, a guarantee. The Tocai Friulano has always been the best-loved native grape in the region. Its name may have been cut down, but the quality of the wine is generally excellent. The 2016 Friulano No Name has most-deservedly won back a Tre Bicchieri and the 2015 Friulano V. Cinquant'Anni just missed out one itself.

○ Friuli Friulano No Name '16	♟♟♟ 4*
● FCO Merlot V. Cinquant' Anni '15	♟♟ 5
● FCO Merlot V. Cinquant'Anni '13	♟♟ 5
○ FCO Pinot Grigio '16	♟♟ 3
○ FCO Ribolla Gialla '16	♟♟ 3
○ FCO Sauvignon '16	♟♟ 3
● FCO Schioppettino '13	♟♟ 5
○ COF Friulano V. Cinquant'Anni '09	♟♟♟ 5
○ COF Friulano V. Cinquant'Anni '08	♟♟♟ 5
● COF Merlot V. Cinquant'Anni '09	♟♟♟ 5
● COF Merlot V. Cinquant'Anni '06	♟♟♟ 5
○ COF Tocai Friulano V. Cinquant'Anni '06	♟♟♟ 5
○ FCO Friulano No Name '15	♟♟♟ 5

Villa de Puppi

VIA ROMA, 5
33040 MOIMACCO [UD]
TEL. +39 0432722461
www.depuppi.it

CELLAR SALES
PRE-BOOKED VISITS
ANNUAL PRODUCTION 70,000 bottles
HECTARES UNDER VINE 25.00
SUSTAINABLE WINERY

The de Puppi family are originally from Tuscany, descendants of the celebrated Count Guidi family, lords of Poppi, in Casentino. They were landholders and soldiers of fortune that, in 1200, settled in Cividale del Friuli. For Friuli, they were a high-profile family who distinguished themselves in politics, justice and the ecclesiastic hierarchy. Count Luigi de Puppi's winery, founded in 1991 and managed by his children, Caterina and Valfredo, is headquartered in the main villa of Moimacco, surrounded by the estate's vineyards. 10 more hectares stretch along the splendid hills of Rosazzo, a celebrated subzone of Friuli Colli Orientali. The wines from their Rosa Bosco selection represent their crown jewels. The 2015 Taj Blanc is excellent value for money. The wine, which is made of 100% Tocai Friulano grapes, has perfect balance and intense aromas, with notes of icing sugar and fruit salad. The Rosa Bosco line, with their well-measured use of wood, is also noteworthy.

○ Chardonnay '15	♟♟ 3
○ Ribolla Gialla di Rosa Bosco '15	♟♟ 4
○ Sauvignon Blanc di Rosa Bosco '14	♟♟ 5
○ Taj Blanc '15	♟♟ 3
○ Chardonnay '14	♟♟ 3
● Merlot Il Boscorosso di Rosa Bosco '11	♟♟ 6
○ Pinot Grigio '14	♟♟ 3
○ Ribolla Gialla di Rosa Bosco '14	♟♟ 4
○ Sauvignon Blanc di Rosa Bosco '13	♟♟ 5
○ Taj Blanc '14	♟♟ 3
○ Taj Blanc '13	♟♟ 2*

★★Villa Russiz

LOC. ITALIA
VIA RUSSIZ, 4/6
34070 CAPRIVA DEL FRIULI [GO]
TEL. +39 048180047
www.villarussiz.it

CELLAR SALES
PRE-BOOKED VISITS
ANNUAL PRODUCTION 220,000 bottles
HECTARES UNDER VINE 45.00
SUSTAINABLE WINERY

Villa Russiz is certifiably one of Friuli
Venezia Giulia's most historic wineries. Its
roots go back to 1867, when the French
count, Teodoro de La Tour, decided to follow
his instinct and choose the hills of Capriva
for a home with his Austrian wife, Elvine
Ritter. He deserves credit for having
introduced new Goriziano vineyards to
Collio, as well as modern techniques that
were, at the time, already commonplace in
France. For many years now, the brand has
been synonymous with great wines, and is
known the world over for its consistently
outstanding quality, thus confirming the
commitment of the Fondazione Villa Russiz,
a charitable organization that provides
support for disadvantaged children. In past
editions, we often expressed our regret at
never being able to award a gold to a wine
from this amazing winery. However, Tre
Bicchieri are back again (after a few years
of absence). The excellent 2016 Pinot
Bianco thoroughly deserves it.

Tenuta Villanova

VIA CONTESSA BERETTA, 29
34072 FARRA D'ISONZO [GO]
TEL. +39 0481889311
www.tenutavillanova.com

CELLAR SALES
PRE-BOOKED VISITS
ANNUAL PRODUCTION 600,000 bottles
HECTARES UNDER VINE 105.00

With its more than five centuries of history,
Tenuta Villanova is undoubtedly one of the
bedrocks of Friuli's wine culture. In 1932, it
was purchased by the forward-thinking
entrepreneur, Arnaldo Bennati, and to this
day managed by his wife, Giuseppina
Grossi Bennati, along with her grandson,
Alberto Grossi, who serves as general
director. It's one of the so-called 'Collio
Island's' historic producers, the island
being a small hill area surrounded by the
Isontino plains, where Collio Goriziano's
characteristic soil magically re-emerges.
The vineyards span both territories,
meaning that the wines produced with the
hill's grapes bear the Collio name, while the
others fall within the Friuli Isonzo DOC
zone. The Ronco Cucco line includes all the
Collio wines and is their jewel in the crown.
The 2016 Friulano Ronco Cucco repeated
last year's feat and made it into the finals.
Floral aromas open the nose, followed by
herbs and salt on the palate.

○ Collio Pinot Bianco '16	♟♟♟ 4*
○ Collio Sauvignon de La Tour '16	♟♟ 6
● Collio Cabernet Sauvignon Défi de La Tour '12	♟♟ 6
○ Collio Chardonnay Gräfin de La Tour '13	♟♟ 7
○ Collio Friulano '16	♟♟ 4
○ Collio Malvasia '16	♟♟ 4
○ Collio Pinot Grigio '16	♟♟ 4
○ Collio Friulano '09	♟♟♟ 4*
○ Collio Pinot Bianco '07	♟♟♟ 3
○ Collio Sauvignon de La Tour '08	♟♟♟ 5
○ Collio Tocai Friulano '04	♟♟♟ 3

○ Collio Friulano Ronco Cucco '16	♟♟ 4
○ Collio Chardonnay Ronco Cucco '16	♟♟ 4
○ Collio Picolit Ronco Cucco '15	♟♟ 5
○ Collio Sauvignon Ronco Cucco '16	♟♟ 4
● Friuli Isonzo Cabernet '15	♟ 2
○ Friuli Isonzo Malvasia '16	♟ 2
○ Collio Chardonnay Monte Cucco '97	♟♟♟ 3*
○ Collio Friulano Ronco Cucco '15	♟♟ 4
○ Collio Ribolla Gialla Ronco Cucco '15	♟♟ 3
○ Collio Sauvignon Ronco Cucco '15	♟♟ 4
● Fraja '10	♟♟ 5
● Friuli Isonzo Refosco P. R. '13	♟♟ 2*

Andrea Visintini

VIA GRAMOGLIANO, 27
33040 CORNO DI ROSAZZO [UD]
TEL. +39 0432755813
www.vinivisintini.com

CELLAR SALES
PRE-BOOKED VISITS
ANNUAL PRODUCTION 110,000 bottles
HECTARES UNDER VINE 32.00
VITICULTURE METHOD Certified Organic
SUSTAINABLE WINERY

Visintini is headquartered in a rustic farmstead adorned by a splendid, 16th century tower - it's all that's left of the ancient, feudal castel of Gramogliano that once extended, towers and all, for hundreds of meters around. Over the centuries, it had many owners, until 1884, when the Count Zucco di Cuccagna family handed over to the Vistintini. In 1973, Andrea took the reins, giving the winery its name. Now his children, Oliviero, Cinzia and Palmira are carrying management forward with a new enthusiasm. Oliviero practices a form of viticulture that respects the environment, and for some time now, their wines boast organic certification. Every year, pointing out their excellent prices just comes naturally, especially when you consider the quality of their wines. This year, there is the added satisfaction of having a wine in the finals, the 2016 Sauvignon, which thrills the nose and combines softness of extraction with liveliness.

○ FCO Sauvignon '16	🍷🍷 2*
○ FCO Friulano Toriòn '15	🍷🍷 2*
○ FCO Pinot Bianco '16	🍷🍷 2*
○ FCO Pinot Grigio '16	🍷🍷 2*
● FCO Refosco P. R. '15	🍷🍷 2*
○ FCO Ribolla Gialla '16	🍷🍷 2*
○ Malvasia '16	🍷🍷 2*
● FCO Cabernet '15	🍷 2
○ FCO Friulano '16	🍷 2
○ FCO Riesling '16	🍷 2
○ FCO Friulano '15	🍷🍷 2*
● FCO Pignolo '09	🍷🍷 4
○ FCO Pinot Bianco '15	🍷🍷 2*
○ FCO Sauvignon '15	🍷🍷 2*
○ Malvasia '15	🍷🍷 2*

★★Volpe Pasini

FRAZ. TOGLIANO
VIA CIVIDALE, 16
33040 TORREANO [UD]
TEL. +39 0432715151
www.volpepasini.it

CELLAR SALES
PRE-BOOKED VISITS
ACCOMMODATION
ANNUAL PRODUCTION 400,000 bottles
HECTARES UNDER VINE 52.00
SUSTAINABLE WINERY

Last year, we wrote about the rare beauty of the splendid Venetian villa, whose magnificent stone walls enclose a centuries-old park, and a small vineyard of Ribolla Gialla grapes. The villa is also surrounded by late 17th-century cellars, which today are equipped with the latest technology for winemaking. Indeed, Volte Pasini doesn't only offer up history and culture; it's also a hub of innovation and experimentation. The themes of sustainability and the precision of new technological tools are of particular interest here, with the goal of achieving increasingly higher quality wines. And there's plenty of proof it's working: even after an excellent 2015 vintage, their 2016 wines managed to astonish us. The 2016 Sauvignon Zuc di Volpe has won our Tre Bicchieri for the eighth year in a row and this is a recognition of its continuity. But as with previous years, other wines shined as well, thus confirming the excellent quality of the entire Zuc di Volpe line.

○ FCO Sauvignon Zuc di Volpe '16	🍷🍷🍷 5
● FCO Merlot Focus '13	🍷🍷 6
○ FCO Pinot Bianco Zuc di Volpe '16	🍷🍷 5
○ FCO Pinot Grigio Zuc di Volpe '16	🍷🍷 4
○ FCO Chardonnay Volpe Pasini '16	🍷🍷 3
○ FCO Pinot Grigio Grivò Volpe Pasini '16	🍷🍷 3
○ FCO Ribolla Gialla Zuc di Volpe '16	🍷🍷 4
○ COF Pinot Bianco Zuc di Volpe '12	🍷🍷🍷 4*
○ COF Sauvignon Zuc di Volpe '13	🍷🍷🍷 4*
○ COF Sauvignon Zuc di Volpe '12	🍷🍷🍷 4*
○ COF Sauvignon Zuc di Volpe '11	🍷🍷🍷 4*
○ COF Sauvignon Zuc di Volpe '10	🍷🍷🍷 3*
○ FCO Sauvignon Zuc di Volpe '15	🍷🍷🍷 5
○ FCO Sauvignon Zuc di Volpe '14	🍷🍷🍷 5

Francesco Vosca

FRAZ. BRAZZANO
VIA SOTTOMONTE, 19
34071 CORMÒNS [GO]
TEL. +39 048162135
www.voscavini.it

CELLAR SALES
PRE-BOOKED VISITS
ANNUAL PRODUCTION 60,000 bottles
HECTARES UNDER VINE 10.00
SUSTAINABLE WINERY

Francesco Vosca's winery is one of Cormòns' most inspiring family-run wineries. It has vineyards both on the hill of Collio and the Isonzo plains, allowing their wines to express both territories. Today, we associate Collio with great wines, flourishing nature and widespread wellness. But Francesco loves to remember how, in the 1960s, misery reigned here. In fact, many were forced to leave; Francesco was still a child, and was forced to hoe the fields. Today, his is a thriving winery that's benefitted from the recent addition of his son, Gabriele, to the staff. The table below appears to be a photocopy of last year's. It may just be a coincidence, but, more likely than not, it actually confirms the potential of every grape variety (in relation to the territory the grapes come from). In any case, consistency is always a sign of dedication and professionalism.

○ Collio Friulano '16	♟♟	3
○ Collio Malvasia '16	♟♟	3
○ Collio Ribolla Gialla '16	♟♟	3
○ Friuli Isonzo Chardonnay '16	♟♟	3
○ Friuli Isonzo Pinot Grigio '16	♟♟	3
○ Friuli Isonzo Sauvignon '16	♟	3
○ Collio Friulano '15	♟♟	3
○ Collio Malvasia '15	♟♟	3
○ Collio Ribolla Gialla '15	♟♟	3
○ Collio Ribolla Gialla '14	♟♟	3
○ Friuli Isonzo Chardonnay '15	♟♟	3
○ Friuli Isonzo Pinot Grigio '15	♟♟	3
○ Friuli Isonzo Pinot Grigio '14	♟♟	3
○ Friuli Isonzo Sauvignon '14	♟♟	3

Zidarich

LOC. PREPOTTO, 23
34011 DUINO AURISINA [TS]
TEL. +39 040201223
www.zidarich.it

CELLAR SALES
PRE-BOOKED VISITS
ANNUAL PRODUCTION 28,000 bottles
HECTARES UNDER VINE 8.00

Benjamin Zidarich is a true wine artisan, and one of Karst's best producers. His gorgeous, five-story cellar was carved out of hard rock, and extends downwards for 20 meters, where temperature and humidity remain constant year round. This means that his wines age for years, first in barrels and then in bottles, without being effected by seasonal climates and temperature changes. And, in keeping with local wine tradition (even for whites), must is fermented on the skins. Benjamin had master stonecutters carve a vat out of Karst stone, which he uses to ferment his Vitovska Kamen. Both versions of the Vitovska highlight the potential of this grape variety, which resists the cold lashing Bora wind and manages to give its best only in a limited area of the Trieste part of the Karst plateau. The 2014 Vitovska Kamen features iodine aromas and marine tanginess.

○ Malvasia '15	♟♟	5
○ Vitovska '15	♟♟	5
○ Vitovska Kamen '14	♟♟♟	7
○ Prulke '15	♟♟	5
● Terrano '15	♟♟	5
○ Carso Malvasia '09	♟♟♟	5
○ Carso Malvasia '06	♟♟♟	5
○ Carso Vitovska V. Collezione '09	♟♟♟	8
○ Prulke '10	♟♟♟	5
○ Prulke '08	♟♟♟	5
○ Malvasia '13	♟♟	5
○ Prulke '13	♟♟	5
● Terrano '13	♟♟	5
○ Vitovska '13	♟♟	5

Zorzettig

FRAZ. SPESSA
S.DA SANT'ANNA, 37
33043 CIVIDALE DEL FRIULI [UD]
TEL. +39 0432716156
www.zorzettigvini.it

CELLAR SALES
PRE-BOOKED VISITS
ACCOMMODATION AND RESTAURANT SERVICE
ANNUAL PRODUCTION 800,000 bottles
HECTARES UNDER VINE 110.00
SUSTAINABLE WINERY

Many of the region's top producers, and especially those in the Friuli Collli Orientali DOC zone, are descendants of the Zorzettig family, though they've mostly been renamed to avoid confusion. The only one to have proudly kept it, was the decorated citizen, Giuseppe Zorzettig. Today, management of the winery has been entrusted to his children, Annalisa and Alessandro, who, with commendable commitment and constancy, have managed to aim high while maintaining the low-profile of humble farmworkers. They've enlisted winemaker, Fabio Coser, for their work in the cellar. The decision to devote their best grapes to the Myò selection has proved wise, as today it represents their crown jewel. The 2016 Pinot Bianco Myò confirms its role as the producer's flagship wine and has earned a Tre Bicchieri for the third year in a row. What until recently may have seemed a dream, is now reality. It's the tip of the iceberg of a range of spot-on wines, both for quality and price.

○ FCO Pinot Bianco Myò '16	♈♈♈ 4*
● FCO Refosco P. R. Myò' '14	♈♈ 5
○ FCO Chardonnay '16	♈♈ 3
● FCO Pignolo Myò '13	♈♈ 6
○ FCO Sauvignon '16	♈♈ 3
○ FCO Sauvignon Myò '16	♈♈ 4
● FCO Schioppettino Myò '14	♈♈ 5
○ Ribolla Gialla Brut Optimum '16	♈♈ 3
○ FCO Pinot Grigio '16	♈ 3
○ FCO Pinot Bianco Myò '15	♈♈♈ 4*
○ FCO Pinot Bianco Myò '14	♈♈♈ 4*
○ COF Friulano Myò '13	♈♈ 4
● COF Refosco P.R. Myò '12	♈♈ 4
○ FCO Friulano Myò '15	♈♈ 4
○ FCO Sauvignon Myò '15	♈♈ 4
● FCO Schioppettino Myò '13	♈♈ 5

Zuani

LOC. GIASBANA, 12
34070 SAN FLORIANO DEL COLLIO [GO]
TEL. +39 0481391432
www.zuanivini.it

CELLAR SALES
PRE-BOOKED VISITS
ACCOMMODATION
ANNUAL PRODUCTION 75,000 bottles
HECTARES UNDER VINE 15.00

Zuani is the original name of an old vineyard that climbs up the splendid slopes of San Floriano del Collio, in Giasbana, an area that gets exposure to the sun from dawn to dusk. For many years, Patrizia Felluga had managed her father's winery. Then, in 2001, she was so inspired by the vineyard that she decided to start producing her own wine, getting her young children, Antonio and Caterina, involved as well. Being deeply linked to the traditions of Collio, she decided to utilize multiple grape varieties to produce one wine, just like they used to. The result is a wine, available in two versions, that represents an authentic expression of the territory. And for more than 15 years it has also occupied a position at the top of the region. The 2016 Zuani Vigne, made in steel, wins over the nose with fresh notes of mango, yellow damsons, gentian and peppermint and has surprisingly good drinkability despite its imposing structure. The 2014 Zuani Riserva, aged in small wood, calls up tropical fruit, toasted hazelnuts and star anise.

○ Collio Bianco Zuani Vigne '16	♈♈ 4
○ Collio Bianco Zuani Ris. '14	♈♈ 5
○ Collio Bianco Zuani Vigne '10	♈♈♈ 3
○ Collio Bianco Zuani Vigne '07	♈♈♈ 3
○ Collio Bianco Zuani Ris. '13	♈♈ 5
○ Collio Bianco Zuani Ris. '12	♈♈ 5
○ Collio Bianco Zuani Ris. '11	♈♈ 5
○ Collio Bianco Zuani Ris. '10	♈♈ 5
○ Collio Bianco Zuani Ris. '09	♈♈ 5
○ Collio Bianco Zuani Vigne '15	♈♈ 4
○ Collio Bianco Zuani Vigne '14	♈♈ 4
○ Collio Bianco Zuani Vigne '13	♈♈ 4
○ Collio Bianco Zuani Vigne '12	♈♈ 3*
○ Collio Bianco Zuani Vigne '11	♈♈ 3

Amandum

VIA F. PETRARCA, 40
34070 MORARO [GO]
TEL. +39 335242566
www.amandum.it

ANNUAL PRODUCTION 27,000 bottles
HECTARES UNDER VINE 2.00

○ Friuli Isonzo Friulano '15	♈♈	4
○ Friuli Isonzo Friulano '14	♈♈	4
○ Friuli Isonzo Friulano '13	♈♈	4

Anzelin

VIA PLESSIVA, 4
34071 CORMÒNS [GO]
TEL. +39 0481639821
www.anzelin.it

CELLAR SALES
PRE-BOOKED VISITS
ANNUAL PRODUCTION 24,000 bottles
HECTARES UNDER VINE 9.00

○ Collio Friulano '16	♈♈	3
○ Collio Pinot Bianco '16	♈♈	3
○ Collio Pinot Grigio '16	♈♈	3
○ Collio Sauvignon '16	♈♈	3

Attems

FRAZ. CAPRIVA DEL FRIULI
VIA AQUILEIA, 30
34070 GORIZIA
TEL. +39 0481806098
www.attems.it

CELLAR SALES
PRE-BOOKED VISITS
ANNUAL PRODUCTION 420,000 bottles
HECTARES UNDER VINE 44.00

○ Pinot Grigio Ramato '16	♈♈	3*
○ Collio Friulano '16	♈♈	3
○ Collio Picolit '12	♈♈	5
○ Collio Sauvignon Blanc Cicinis '15	♈♈	5

Bajta

VIA SALES, 108
34010 SGONICO [TS]
TEL. +39 0402296090
www.bajta.it

ANNUAL PRODUCTION 18,000 bottles
HECTARES UNDER VINE 4.00

○ Malvasia '16	♈♈	3
● Terrano '15	♈♈	3
○ Vitovska '16	♈♈	3

Tenuta di Blasig

VIA ROMA, 63
34077 RONCHI DEI LEGIONARI [GO]
TEL. +39 0481475480
www.tenutadiblasig.it

CELLAR SALES
PRE-BOOKED VISITS
RESTAURANT SERVICE
ANNUAL PRODUCTION 80,000 bottles
HECTARES UNDER VINE 12.00

○ Friuli Isonzo Malvasia '16	♈♈	3
● Friuli Isonzo Rosso Affreschi '13	♈♈	4
○ Friuli Isonzo Pinot Grigio '16	♈	3
○ Friuli Isonzo Pinot Grigio Sarcinelli '16	♈	3

Blason

LOC. BRUMA
VIA ROMA, 32
34072 GRADISCA D'ISONZO [GO]
TEL. +39 048192414
www.blasonwines.com

CELLAR SALES
PRE-BOOKED VISITS
ANNUAL PRODUCTION 60,000 bottles
HECTARES UNDER VINE 18.00

○ Friuli Isonzo Friulano '16	♈♈	2*
○ Friuli Isonzo Pinot Grigio '16	♈♈	3
○ Malvasia '16	♈♈	3
○ Ribolla Gialla '16	♈♈	2*

Blazic

LOC. ZEGLA, 16
34071 CORMÒNS [GO]
TEL. +39 048161720
www.blazic.it

CELLAR SALES
PRE-BOOKED VISITS
ANNUAL PRODUCTION 20,000 bottles
HECTARES UNDER VINE 6.50

○ Collio Friulano '16	🍷🍷 3
○ Collio Malvasia '16	🍷🍷 3
○ Collio Pinot Grigio '16	🍷🍷 3
○ Collio Ribolla Gialla '16	🍷 3

Tenuta Borgo Conventi

S.DA DELLA COLOMBARA, 13
24070 FARRA D'ISONZO [GO]
TEL. +39 0481888004
www.borgoconventi.it

CELLAR SALES
PRE-BOOKED VISITS
ANNUAL PRODUCTION 350,000 bottles
HECTARES UNDER VINE 40.00

○ Collio Chardonnay '16	🍷🍷 3
○ Collio Pinot Grigio '16	🍷🍷 3
○ Collio Sauvignon '16	🍷🍷 3
● Schioppettino '11	🍷🍷 3

Borgo Magredo

LOC. TAURIANO
VIA BASALDELLA, 5
33090 SPILIMBERGO [PN]
TEL. +39 0422864511
www.borgomagredo.it

CELLAR SALES
PRE-BOOKED VISITS
ANNUAL PRODUCTION 450,000 bottles
HECTARES UNDER VINE 105.00
SUSTAINABLE WINERY

● Friuli Grave Merlot '16	🍷🍷 2*
○ Friuli Grave Friulano '16	🍷 2
○ Friuli Grave Pinot Grigio '16	🍷 2
○ Friuli Grave Sauvignon '16	🍷 2

Bracco 1881

FRAZ. BRAZZANO
VIA XXIV MAGGIO, 28
34070 CORMÒNS [GO]
TEL. +39 048160002
www.braccovini.it

CELLAR SALES
PRE-BOOKED VISITS
ANNUAL PRODUCTION 30,000 bottles
HECTARES UNDER VINE 6.00

○ Collio Bianco La Mont-Drach '16	🍷🍷 3
○ Collio Malvasia La Mont-Brach '16	🍷🍷 3
○ Friuli Isonzo Friulano Ultimo '15	🍷🍷 3
● Friuli Isonzo Refosco P. R. '13	🍷 3

Braidot

LOC. VERSA
VIA PALMANOVA, 20 B
34076 ROMANS D'ISONZO [GO]
TEL. +39 0481908970
www.braidotwines.it

CELLAR SALES
PRE-BOOKED VISITS
ANNUAL PRODUCTION 400,000 bottles
HECTARES UNDER VINE 60.00

○ Friuli Friulano '16	🍷🍷 3
○ Friuli Friulano 1870 '16	🍷🍷 3
○ Friuli Pinot Grigio 1870 '16	🍷🍷 3
○ Friuli Sauvignon Blanc 1870 '16	🍷🍷 3

Marco Cecchini

LOC. CASALI DE LUCA
VIA COLOMBANI
33040 FAEDIS [UD]
TEL. +39 0432720563
www.cecchinimarco.com

CELLAR SALES
PRE-BOOKED VISITS
ACCOMMODATION
ANNUAL PRODUCTION 35,000 bottles
HECTARES UNDER VINE 8.00

○ FCO Friulano Tovè 1867 '15	🍷🍷 3
○ FCO Verduzzo Friulano Verlit '15	🍷🍷 5
○ Chardonnay '15	🍷 3
● FCO Refosco P. R. '12	🍷 3

I Clivi

LOC. GRAMOGLIANO, 20
33040 CORNO DI ROSAZZO [UD]
TEL. +39 3287269979
www.clivi.it

CELLAR SALES
PRE-BOOKED VISITS
ANNUAL PRODUCTION 50,000 bottles
HECTARES UNDER VINE 12.00
VITICULTURE METHOD Certified Organic

○ FCO Bianco Clivi Galea '15	♀♀ 4
○ FCO Friulano San Pietro '16	♀♀ 3
○ Ribolla Gialla San Pietro '16	♀♀ 8

Tenuta Conte Romano

VIA DELLE PRIMULE, 12
33044 MANZANO [UD]
TEL. +39 0432755339
www.tenutaconteromano.it

CELLAR SALES
PRE-BOOKED VISITS
ACCOMMODATION AND RESTAURANT SERVICE
ANNUAL PRODUCTION 40,000 bottles
HECTARES UNDER VINE 17.00

○ FCO Friulano '16	♀♀ 3
○ FCO Malvasia '16	♀♀ 3
○ FCO Sauvignon '16	♀♀ 2*
● FCO Rosso '15	♀ 3

Cornium

VIA AQUILEIA, 79
33040 CORNO DI ROSAZZO [UD]
TEL. +39 0432755896
info@viniborgojudrio.it

CELLAR SALES
PRE-BOOKED VISITS
ANNUAL PRODUCTION 20,000 bottles
HECTARES UNDER VINE 12.00

○ FCO Friulano '16	♀♀ 2*
● FCO Refosco P. R. '15	♀♀ 2*
○ FCO Sauvignon '16	♀♀ 2*
● FCO Cabernet Franc '15	♀ 2

Viticoltori Friulani La Delizia

VIA UDINE, 24
33072 CASARSA DELLA DELIZIA [PN]
TEL. +39 0434869564
www.ladelizia.com

CELLAR SALES
PRE-BOOKED VISITS
ANNUAL PRODUCTION 16,000,000 bottles
HECTARES UNDER VINE 1950.00

○ Jadèr Cuvée Brut	♀♀ 2*
○ Prosecco Extra Dry Naonis '16	♀♀ 2*
○ Ribolla Gialla Brut Naonis	♀♀ 2*
● Friuli Grave Friulano Sass Ter' '16	♀ 2

Le Due Torri

LOC. VICINALE DEL JUDRIO
VIA SAN MARTINO, 19
33040 CORNO DI ROSAZZO [UD]
TEL. +39 0432759150
www.le2torri.com

CELLAR SALES
PRE-BOOKED VISITS
ANNUAL PRODUCTION 36,000 bottles
HECTARES UNDER VINE 7.60

○ Friuli Grave Friulano Antica Tenuta Sbroiavacca '13	♀♀ 2*
○ Friuli Grave Pinot Grigio '16	♀♀ 2*
● Torri Rosse '11	♀♀ 2*

Fantin Nodar

LOC. ORSARIA
VIA CASALI OTTELIO, 4
33040 PREMARIACCO [UD]
TEL. +39 043428735
www.fantinnodar.it

CELLAR SALES
PRE-BOOKED VISITS
ANNUAL PRODUCTION 40,000 bottles
HECTARES UNDER VINE 22.00

○ FCO Friulano '15	♀♀ 2*
● FCO Merlot '15	♀♀ 2*
○ FCO Pinot Grigio '15	♀♀ 2*
○ FCO Sauvignon '15	♀♀ 2*

Le Favole

LOC. TERRA ROSSA
VIA DIETRO CASTELLO, 7
33070 CANEVA [PN]
TEL. +39 0434735604
www.lefavole-wines.com

CELLAR SALES
PRE-BOOKED VISITS
ACCOMMODATION
ANNUAL PRODUCTION 70,000 bottles
HECTARES UNDER VINE 20.00

○ Friuli Annia Friulano '16	♟♟ 2*
○ Friuli Annia Malvasia '16	♟♟ 2*
● Friuli Annia Merlot '15	♟♟ 3
○ Giallo di Roccia Brut	♟♟ 4

Flaibani

VIA CASALI COSTA, 7
33043 CIVIDALE DEL FRIULI [UD]
TEL. +39 0432730943
www.flaibani.it

CELLAR SALES
PRE-BOOKED VISITS
ANNUAL PRODUCTION 10,000 bottles
HECTARES UNDER VINE 3.50
VITICULTURE METHOD Certified Organic
SUSTAINABLE WINERY

○ FCO Bianco Riviere '16	♟♟ 3
● Schioppettino '14	♟♟ 5
○ FCO Pinot Grigio Ramato '16	♟ 3
● Merlot '14	♟ 4

Foffani

FRAZ. CLAUIANO
P.ZZA GIULIA, 13
33050 TRIVIGNANO UDINESE [UD]
TEL. +39 0432999584
www.foffani.com

CELLAR SALES
PRE-BOOKED VISITS
ACCOMMODATION AND RESTAURANT SERVICE
ANNUAL PRODUCTION 80,000 bottles
HECTARES UNDER VINE 10.00
SUSTAINABLE WINERY

○ Friuli Aquileia Sauvignon Sup. '16	♟♟ 2*
○ Friuli Friulano TerVinum '13	♟♟ 3
○ Merlot Bianco '16	♟ 3
● Refosco P. R. TerVinum '16	♟ 3

Forchir

LOC. CASALI BIANCHINI, 2
33030 CAMINO AL TAGLIAMENTO [UD]
TEL. +39 042796037
www.forchir.it

CELLAR SALES
PRE-BOOKED VISITS
ANNUAL PRODUCTION 1,200,000 bottles
HECTARES UNDER VINE 240.00
VITICULTURE METHOD Certified Organic
SUSTAINABLE WINERY

○ Friuli Friulano Lusor '16	♟♟ 2*
○ Friuli Grave Sauvignon '16	♟♟ 2*
○ Friuli Grave Pinot Bianco Maraveis '16	♟ 3
○ Friuli Grave Traminer Aromatico Glère '16	♟ 2

Fossa Mala

VIA BASSI, 81
33080 FIUME VENETO [PN]
TEL. +39 0434957997
www.fossamala.it

CELLAR SALES
PRE-BOOKED VISITS
ACCOMMODATION AND RESTAURANT SERVICE
ANNUAL PRODUCTION 130,000 bottles
HECTARES UNDER VINE 37.00

○ Friuli Grave Chardonnay '16	♟♟ 2*
● Friuli Grave Merlot '14	♟♟ 2*
○ Friuli Grave Traminer Aromatico '16	♟♟ 2*
○ Friuli Grave Friulano '16	♟ 2

Graunar

VIA SCEDINA
34070 SAN FLORIANO DEL COLLIO [GO]
TEL. +39 0481884115
graunarwines@libero.it

CELLAR SALES
PRE-BOOKED VISITS
ANNUAL PRODUCTION 10,000 bottles
HECTARES UNDER VINE 6.00

○ Collio Bianco '13	♟♟ 3
○ Collio Friulano '13	♟♟ 3
○ Collio Pinot Grigio '15	♟♟ 3
○ Malvasia Istriana '16	♟♟ 3

Humar

LOC. VALERISCE, 20
34070 SAN FLORIANO DEL COLLIO [GO]
TEL. +39 0481884197
www.humar.it

CELLAR SALES
PRE-BOOKED VISITS
ANNUAL PRODUCTION 60,000 bottles
HECTARES UNDER VINE 12.00

○ Collio Pinot Grigio '16		♟♟ 3*
○ Collio Friulano '16		♟♟ 3
○ Collio Sauvignon '16		♟♟ 2*
○ Collio Ribolla Gialla '16		♟ 3

Isola Augusta

CASALI ISOLA AUGUSTA, 4
33056 PALAZZOLO DELLO STELLA [UD]
TEL. +39 043150046
www.isolaugusta.com

CELLAR SALES
PRE-BOOKED VISITS
ACCOMMODATION AND RESTAURANT SERVICE
ANNUAL PRODUCTION 270,000 bottles
HECTARES UNDER VINE 65.00
SUSTAINABLE WINERY

○ Friuli Latisana Friulano '16		♟♟ 2*
● Schioppettino '16		♟♟ 2*
○ Friuli Latisana Pinot Grigio '16		♟ 2
○ Friuli Latisana Ribolla Gialla '16		♟ 2

Rado Kocjancic

FRAZ. DOLINA
VIA DOLINA, 528
34018 SAN DORLIGO DELLA VALLE [TS]
TEL. +39 3483063298
www.radokocjancic.eu

CELLAR SALES
PRE-BOOKED VISITS
ANNUAL PRODUCTION 15,000 bottles
HECTARES UNDER VINE 5.00

○ Brejanka '13		♟♟ 5
○ Muskat '13		♟♟ 4

Vigna Lenuzza

VIA BROLO, 51
33040 PREPOTTO [UD]
TEL. +39 0432713236
www.vignalenuzza.it

ACCOMMODATION
ANNUAL PRODUCTION 30,000 bottles

● FCO Merlot '13		♟♟ 3
○ FCO Ribolla Gialla '16		♟♟ 3
○ FCO Sauvignon '16		♟♟ 3
● FCO Schioppettino di Prepotto '13		♟♟ 3

Magis

VIA FORNALIS, 277/ 1
33043 CIVIDALE DEL FRIULI [UD]
TEL. +39 0421319600
www.neromagis.com

PRE-BOOKED VISITS
ANNUAL PRODUCTION 10,000 bottles
HECTARES UNDER VINE 5.00

● FCO Nero Magis '14		♟♟ 7

Modeano

VIA CASALI MODEANO, 1
33056 PALAZZOLO DELLO STELLA [UD]
TEL. +39 043158244
www.modeano.it

CELLAR SALES
PRE-BOOKED VISITS
ANNUAL PRODUCTION 40,000 bottles
HECTARES UNDER VINE 31.00

● Friuli Latisana Cabernet Sauvignon '15		♟♟ 2*
○ Friuli Malvasia '16		♟♟ 2*
○ Friuli Latisana Friulano '16		♟ 2
○ Friuli Pinot Grigio '16		♟ 2

Mulino delle Tolle

FRAZ. SEVEGLIANO
V. MULINO DELLE TOLLE, 15
33050 BAGNARIA ARSA [UD]
TEL. +39 0432924723
www.mulinodelletolle.it

CELLAR SALES
PRE-BOOKED VISITS
ACCOMMODATION AND RESTAURANT SERVICE
ANNUAL PRODUCTION 100,000 bottles
HECTARES UNDER VINE 22.00

Friuli Aquileia Friulano '16	▼▼ 3
Friuli Aquileia Malvasia '16	▼▼ 3
Friuli Aquileia Rosso Sabellius '14	▼▼ 3
Friuli Aquileia Cabernet Franc '16	▼ 2

Obiz

B.GO GORTANI, 2
33052 CERVIGNANO DEL FRIULI [UD]
TEL. +39 043131900
www.obiz.it

CELLAR SALES
ANNUAL PRODUCTION 100,000 bottles
HECTARES UNDER VINE 25.00

○ Friuli Aquileia Friulano Tampia '16	▼▼ 2*
● Friuli Aquileia Rosso Natissa '15	▼▼ 3
● Friuli Aquileia Refosco P.R. Teodoro '15	▼ 2
○ Ribolla Gialla Bassilla '16	▼ 2

Ostrouska

LOC. SAGRADO, 1
34010 SGONICO [TS]
TEL. +39 0402296672
www.ostrouska.it

ANNUAL PRODUCTION 5,000 bottles
HECTARES UNDER VINE 1.50

Malvasia '15	▼▼ 5
Vitovska '15	▼▼ 5
Terrano '15	▼ 5

Parovel

LOC. CARESANA, 81
34018 SAN DORLIGO DELLA VALLE [TS]
TEL. +39 040227050
www.parovel.com

ANNUAL PRODUCTION 35,000 bottles
HECTARES UNDER VINE 11.00
SUSTAINABLE WINERY

○ Carso Vitovska Onavè '14	▼▼ 5
● Refosco P. R. Imà '11	▼▼ 5

Pighin

FRAZ. RISANO
V.LE GRADO, 11/1
33050 PAVIA DI UDINE [UD]
TEL. +39 0432675444
www.pighin.com

CELLAR SALES
PRE-BOOKED VISITS
ANNUAL PRODUCTION 1,000,000 bottles
HECTARES UNDER VINE 180.00

Collio Chardonnay '16	▼▼ 5
Collio Pinot Grigio '16	▼▼ 5
Collio Sauvignon '16	▼▼ 5
Friuli Grave Friulano '16	▼▼ 4

Pitars

VIA TONELLO, 10
33098 SAN MARTINO AL TAGLIAMENTO [PN]
TEL. +39 043488078
www.pitars.it

CELLAR SALES
PRE-BOOKED VISITS
ANNUAL PRODUCTION 250,000 bottles
HECTARES UNDER VINE 125.00
SUSTAINABLE WINERY

○ Friuli Grave Pinot Grigio '16	▼▼ 2*
● Friuli Grave Rosso Brumal '15	▼▼ 3
○ Malvasia '16	▼▼ 2*
○ Tureis '13	▼▼ 5

Plozner

FRAZ. BARBEANO
VIA DELLE PRESE, 17
33097 SPILIMBERGO [PN]
TEL. +39 3488009670
www.plozner.eu

CELLAR SALES
PRE-BOOKED VISITS
ANNUAL PRODUCTION 200,000 bottles
HECTARES UNDER VINE 43.00

○ Friuli Grave Friulano '15	♛♛ 2*
● Friuli Grave Merlot Peeecoranera '14	♛♛ 3
○ Friuli Grave Sauvignon '15	♛ 2
○ Prosecco Brut	♛ 2

Polje

LOC. NOVALI, 11
34071 CORMÒNS [GO]
TEL. I 39 047160660
www.polje.com

CELLAR SALES
PRE-BOOKED VISITS
ANNUAL PRODUCTION 30,900 bottles
HECTARES UNDER VINE 12.00

○ Collio Sauvignon '16	♛♛
○ Collio Friulano '16	♛♛
○ Collio Pinot Grigio '16	♛♛
○ Collio Ribolla Gialla '16	♛♛

Reguta

VIA BASSI, 16
33050 POCENIA [UD]
TEL. +39 0432779157
www.giuseppeeluigivini.it

CELLAR SALES
PRE-BOOKED VISITS
ANNUAL PRODUCTION 2,000,000 bottles
HECTARES UNDER VINE 240.00

● Altropasso '15	♛♛ 3
● Collio Cabernet Franc '15	♛♛ 3
○ Pinot Grigio '16	♛♛ 1*
○ Ribolla Gialla '16	♛ 1*

Ronco dei Pini

VIA RONCHI, 93
33040 PREPOTTO [UD]
TEL. +39 0432713239
www.roncodeipini.it

CELLAR SALES
PRE-BOOKED VISITS
ANNUAL PRODUCTION 90,000 bottles
HECTARES UNDER VINE 15.00

● FCO Cabernet Sauvignon '15	♛♛
○ FCO Friulano '16	♛♛
○ FCO Sauvignon '16	♛♛
● FCO Schioppettino di Prepotto '13	♛♛

Ronco Margherita

VIA XX SETTEMBRE, 106A
33094 PINZANO AL TAGLIAMENTO [PN]
TEL. +39 0432950845
www.roncomargherita.it

CELLAR SALES
PRE-BOOKED VISITS
ANNUAL PRODUCTION 100,000 bottles
HECTARES UNDER VINE 50.00
SUSTAINABLE WINERY

○ FCO Pinot Grigio '15	♛♛ 2*
● Merlot '15	♛♛ 3
● Ovalis '15	♛♛ 4
● Parvus '15	♛♛ 4

Valter Scarbolo

FRAZ. LAUZACCO
V.LE GRADO, 4
33050 PAVIA DI UDINE [UD]
TEL. +39 0432675612
www.scarbolo.com

CELLAR SALES
PRE-BOOKED VISITS
RESTAURANT SERVICE
ANNUAL PRODUCTION 210,000 bottles
HECTARES UNDER VINE 28.00
SUSTAINABLE WINERY

● Campo del Viotto Merlot '13	♛♛
○ Friuli Friulano '16	♛♛
○ Friuli Grave Pinot Grigio '16	♛♛
● Refosco dal P. R. '13	♛♛

Scolaris

A Boschetto, 4
4070 San Lorenzo Isontino [GO]
Tel. +39 0481809920
www.scolaris.it

CELLAR SALES
PRE-BOOKED VISITS
ANNUAL PRODUCTION 600,000 bottles
HECTARES UNDER VINE 20.00
SUSTAINABLE WINERY

○ Collio Malvasia '15	♈♈ 3
● Collio Pinot Grigio '16	♈♈ 3
○ Collio Sauvignon '16	♈♈ 3
● Collio Cabernet Sauvignon '15	♈ 3

Ferruccio Sgubin

via Mernico, 8
34070 Dolegna del Collio [GO]
Tel. +39 048160452
www.ferrucciosgubin.it

CELLAR SALES
PRE-BOOKED VISITS
ANNUAL PRODUCTION 100,000 bottles
HECTARES UNDER VINE 20.00

○ Collio Pinot Bianco '16	♈♈ 3
○ Collio Sauvignon '16	♈♈ 3
● Schioppettino '13	♈♈ 2*
○ Collio Friulano '16	♈ 3

Skerlj

A Sales, 44
4010 Sgonico [TS]
Tel. +39 040229253
www.skerlj.it

CELLAR SALES
PRE-BOOKED VISITS
ACCOMMODATION AND RESTAURANT SERVICE
ANNUAL PRODUCTION 5,000 bottles
HECTARES UNDER VINE 2.00
VITICULTURE METHOD Certified Organic

○ Malvasia '14	♈♈ 5
○ Vitovska '14	♈♈ 5
● Terrano '14	♈ 5

F.lli Stanig

via Albana, 44
33040 Prepotto [UD]
Tel. +39 0432713234
www.stanig.it

CELLAR SALES
ACCOMMODATION AND RESTAURANT SERVICE
ANNUAL PRODUCTION 45,000 bottles
HECTARES UNDER VINE 9.00

○ FCO Malvasia '16	♈♈ 3
● FCO Merlot '15	♈♈ 3
○ FCO Friulano '16	♈ 3
○ FCO Sauvignon '16	♈ 3

Tarlao

via San Zili, 41
33051 Aquileia [UD]
Tel. +39 043191417
www.tarlao.eu

CELLAR SALES
PRE-BOOKED VISITS
ANNUAL PRODUCTION 18,000 bottles
HECTARES UNDER VINE 5.00

○ Friuli Aquileia Malvasia '16	♈♈ 3
○ Friuli Aquileia Pinot Bianco Poc ma Bon '16	♈♈ 3
○ Friuli Aquileia Traminer Aromatico '16	♈♈ 3

Terre del Faet

v.le Roma, 82
34071 Cormòns [GO]
Tel. +39 3470103325
www.terredelfaet.it

CELLAR SALES
PRE-BOOKED VISITS
ANNUAL PRODUCTION 18,000 bottles
HECTARES UNDER VINE 4.00

○ Collio Bianco del Faet '15	♈♈ 3
○ Collio Friulano '16	♈♈ 3
○ Collio Malvasia '16	♈♈ 3
○ Collio Pinot Bianco '16	♈♈ 3

Terre di Ger

FRAZ. FRATTINA
S.DA DELLA MEDUNA, 17
33076 PRAVISDOMINI [PN]
TEL. +39 0434644452
www.terrediger.it

CELLAR SALES
PRE-BOOKED VISITS
ANNUAL PRODUCTION 100,000 bottles
HECTARES UNDER VINE 50.00

○ Friuli Grave Chardonnay '16	🏆🏆 2*
○ Limine '16	🏆🏆 3
● Friuli Grave Merlot '15	🏆 2
○ Sauvignon Blanc '16	🏆 3

Toblâr

LOC. RAMANDOLO, 17
33045 NIMIS [UD]
TEL. +39 0432755840
www.toblar.it

ANNUAL PRODUCTION 130,000 bottles
HECTARES UNDER VINE 5.00

● Caberbet Franc Toblâr Ros '16	🏆🏆
○ Chardonnay Toblâr Blanc '16	🏆🏆
○ Ramandolo '11	🏆🏆
○ Pinot Grigio Toblâr Blanc '16	🏆

Toniatti Giacometti

VIA ROCCA, 29
33053 LATISANA [UD]
TEL. +39 043150331
www.cantinetoniatti.com

CELLAR SALES
ACCOMMODATION
ANNUAL PRODUCTION 50,000 bottles
HECTARES UNDER VINE 40.00

○ Chardonnay '16	🏆🏆 3
● Merlot '16	🏆🏆 3
○ Sharif '16	🏆🏆 3
● Super Grill '16	🏆🏆 3

Vicentini Orgnani

LOC. VALERIANO
VIA SOTTOPLOVIA, 4A
33094 PINZANO AL TAGLIAMENTO [PN]
TEL. +39 0432950107
www.vicentiniorgnani.it

CELLAR SALES
PRE-BOOKED VISITS
ANNUAL PRODUCTION 50,000 bottles
HECTARES UNDER VINE 18.00
SUSTAINABLE WINERY

○ Friuli Grave Friulano '15	🏆🏆 3
○ Pinot Grigio '15	🏆🏆 2
○ Ucelùt '09	🏆🏆 6
○ Sauvignon '15	🏆 3

Villa Parens

VIA DANTE, 69
34072 FARRA D'ISONZO [GO]
TEL. +39 0481888198
www.villaparens.com

CELLAR SALES
PRE-BOOKED VISITS
ANNUAL PRODUCTION 50,000 bottles
HECTARES UNDER VINE 6.00

○ Blanc de Blancs Extra Brut	🏆🏆 5
⊙ Rosé de Noirs Dosaggio Zero '14	🏆🏆 6
● Pinot Nero '16	🏆 3
○ Ribolla Gialla '16	🏆 3

Zaglia

LOC. FRASSINUTTI
VIA CRESCENZIA, 10
33050 PRECENICCO [UD]
TEL. +39 0431510320
www.zaglia.com

CELLAR SALES
PRE-BOOKED VISITS
ANNUAL PRODUCTION 100,000 bottles
HECTARES UNDER VINE 15.00

● FCO Cabernet Franc Amanti Ris. '14	🏆🏆 2
○ Friuli Chardonnay '16	🏆🏆 2
○ Friuli Friulano '16	🏆🏆 2
● Friuli Merlot '16	🏆🏆 2

EMILIA ROMAGNA

'Lambrusco, Lambrusco and more Lambrusco,' we wanted to say during the last round of tasting. It's the regional wine that's got us the most excited of late, and that's pretty astonishing if you think about it. Lambrusco, in its various appellations, was never among the national elite, where we find Metodo Classico sparklers, strong and fragrant whites, long living reds. It's a bit like Barbera. Lambrusco has always been relegated to that class of wines for everyday drinking, a wine that you buy without thinking too much about it, almost instinctively, and for its lower cost. But it's a wine that everybody likes. So, having said that, it's important to stress that there's Lambrusco and then there's Lambrusco. After the years of the great flood tide of sales, with millions of cases being sold throughout the world, after the subsequent financial crisis, we're at a point where, thanks to the patient work of vine growers and producers, a complex and multi-layered regional fabric is emerging and it's demonstrating that an early-drinker endowed with liveliness and freshness (rather than structure) can be a great wine. This year, seven received Tre Bicchieri, with representatives from Modena, Reggio and especially Sorbara. They are wines that enchant for their finesse, richness of flavor, balance and pleasantness. Sangiovese is hot on its heels with a style that's become popular in the region: not too concentrated, nor worn out by aging in new wood, which suffocates fruit and expressivity. Romagna is offering more and more and at prices that are more than reasonable. It's no coincidence that one of these, Le Rocche Malatestiane's 2016 Sigismondo, won this year's award for 'Best Value for the Money'. Two Albanas also took home honors, Celli's fresh, vibrant and modern 2016 Croppi and the great classic of passito dried-grape wines, La Zerbina's 2013 Scacco Matto. In terms of fresh, relaxed, enjoyable wines, we're seeing encouraging signs from Colli di Parma, which gave rise to Monte delle Vigne's excellent 2016 Rosso MDV, another Tre Bicchieri. Colli Piacentini and Colli Bolognesi continue to exhibit great potential, though it's still not fully realized.

Agrintesa

via G. Galilei, 15
48018 Faenza [RA]
Tel. +39 0546941195
www.cantineintesa.it

CELLAR SALES
PRE-BOOKED VISITS
ANNUAL PRODUCTION 350,000 bottles
HECTARES UNDER VINE 44.00

In recent years, this cooperative winery has managed to set in motion an interesting and innovative stylistic program focused on surprising (if you consider the category) local wines. The nucleus of the project is represented by a group of partners with vineyards in the area of Modigliana. Even the winemaking takes place in the area, in the Marzeno Valley, guaranteeing ideal production times. Their wines are consistently strong and stylistically focused, making it a producer that's certainly worth watching closely. The 2016 Sangiovese Superiore is quite good. It features fruit that call up ripe cherries and an inviting iodine background. The mouth is juicy, mature and pervasive. The 2016 Poderi delle Rose is also outstanding, with its pale yellow color, and juicy but racy palate dominated by flowers and ripe fruit.

○ Romagna Albana Secco Poderi delle Rose '16		🏆🏆 2*
● Romagna Sangiovese Sup. Poderi delle Rose '16		🏆🏆 2*
● Romagna Sangiovese Poderi delle Rose '16		🏆 2
○ Albana di Romagna Secco I Calanchi Loveria '12		🍷🍷 2*
○ Albana di Romagna Secco I Calanchi Spighea '14		🍷🍷 2*
○ Albana di Romagna Secco Poderi delle Rose '15		🍷🍷 2*
● Romagna Sangiovese Poderi delle Rose '15		🍷🍷 2*
● Romagna Sangiovese Poderi delle Rose '15		🍷🍷 2*
● Romagna Sangiovese Sup. Poderi delle Rose '15		🍷🍷 2*

Ancarani

via San Biagio Antico, 14
48018 Faenza [RA]
Tel. +39 3338314188
www.viniancarani.it

CELLAR SALES
PRE-BOOKED VISITS
RESTAURANT SERVICE
ANNUAL PRODUCTION 30,000 bottles
HECTARES UNDER VINE 14.00

Claudio Ancarani and his wife, Rita Babini, show great care when it comes to their vineyards, and their wines certainly deserve recognition. Here, in Torre di Oriolo, they're showing an undeniable knack for producing Albana (when it comes to whites) and the intriguing native grape Centesimino (among reds). Ancarani's selection exhibit a classic style that eschews gimmicks and over-extraction for wines that are more close-knit and relaxed. The 2016 Sangiovese Superiore is a red with a relaxed profile, a wine that's a far cry from being just another 'run-of-the-mill' wine. Its aromas are pervasive, calling up small fruits. These are imbued with an almost resinous trail that's decidedly balsamic and refreshing. It's reminiscent of certain Beaujolais, if you'll excuse the comparison, with a clenched palate and slightly fuzzy tannins.

○ Romagna Albana Secco Santa Lusa '15		🏆🏆 3
● Romagna Sangiovese Sup. Biagio Antico '15		🏆🏆 2*
● Centesimino '16		🏆 3
○ Perlagioia '16		🏆 2
○ Albana di Romagna Santa Lusa '12		🍷🍷 3*
○ Albana di Romagna Santa Lusa '11		🍷🍷 3
○ Romagna Albana Secco Santa Lusa '14		🍷🍷 3
○ Romagna Albana Secco Santa Lusa '13		🍷🍷 3
● Sangiovese di Romagna Oriolo '15		🍷🍷 2*
● Sangiovese di Romagna Oriolo '12		🍷🍷 2*
● Sâvignon Rosso Centesimino '15		🍷🍷 2*
● Sâvignon Rosso Centesimino '12		🍷🍷 3
○ Signore '15		🍷🍷 2*
● Uvappesa '11		🍷🍷 4
● Uvappesa '10		🍷🍷 4
● Uvappesa Centesimino '12		🍷🍷 4

Balìa di Zola

VIA CASALE, 11
47015 MODIGLIANA [FC]
TEL. +39 0546940577
www.baliadizola.com

CELLAR SALES
PRE-BOOKED VISITS
ANNUAL PRODUCTION 30,000 bottles
HECTARES UNDER VINE 5.00

Claudio Fiore and Veruska Eluci's winery got its start in 2003, when the couple decided to leave Tuscany and invest in one of Emilia Romagna's more interesting terroir. Valle dell'Acerrata (Modigliana) is a subzone renowned for its elegant, fine wines, and Balìa di Zola are making a name for themselves by interpreting them with purpose and personality. The house style includes surefooted tannins and a backbone capable of withstanding the tests of time. This is how the 2014 Sangiovese di Romagna Riserva Modigliana Redinoce seemed to us: darker than the average wine from this area, playing on mature and toasty notes, with a certain roundness of taste. The pleasant finish offers contrasting aromas and bitterness. The 2016 Albana Secco Isola calls up aromas of apples. It's a wine of average density and length.

● Romagna Sangiovese Sup. Redinoce Ris. '14	♟♟ 4
○ Romagna Albana Secco Isola '16	♟ 3
● Sangiovese di Romagna Redinoce Ris. '09	♟♟♟ 4*
● Sangiovese di Romagna Redinoce Ris. '08	♟♟♟ 4*
● Romagna Sangiovese Modigliana Redinoce Ris. '12	♟♟ 4
● Romagna Sangiovese Sup. Balitore '15	♟♟ 2*
● Romagna Sangiovese Sup. Balitore '14	♟♟ 2*
● Sangiovese di Romagna Balitore '10	♟♟ 2*
● Sangiovese di Romagna Redinoce Ris. '11	♟♟ 4
● Sangiovese di Romagna Redinoce Ris. '10	♟♟ 4
● Sangiovese di Romagna Sup. Redinoce Ris. '13	♟♟ 4

Le Barbaterre

LOC. BERGONZANO
VIA CAVOUR, 2A
42020 QUATTRO CASTELLA [RE]
TEL. +39 0522247573
www.barbaterre.it

CELLAR SALES
PRE-BOOKED VISITS
ACCOMMODATION AND RESTAURANT SERVICE
ANNUAL PRODUCTION 20,000 bottles
HECTARES UNDER VINE 8.00
VITICULTURE METHOD Certified Organic
SUSTAINABLE WINERY

At the turn of the second millennium, the powerful land-holder Matilde di Canossa reigned in the Terre Matilidiche, an area on the Tuscany-Emilia Romagna border, where the Apennines rise to 330 meters. Today, some of the regions most interesting, small producers are taking hold here, like this small winery whose estate comprises eight hectares. Their production volumes are kept to a minimum, with low yields in the vineyards and an approach that emphasizes sustainability (all their energy needs are met by solar panels installed on the roof of their agritourism). The 2012 Blanc de Noirs did well in the tastings. It's made with Pinot Nero and proved savory and elegant, with fine sparkle and close-focused fruity notes. The 2016 Besmein Capolegh, a bottle-fermented Rosé Marzemino with classic notes of small wild berries, also did well. The 2011 Pinot Nero Brut Nature is almost spicy, with citrusy overtones, while the Lambrusco Ancestrale features rustic fragrances of forest floor.

⊙ Besmein Capolegh Marzemino Frizzante Rosé FB '16	♟♟ 3
○ Blanc de Noirs M. Cl. '12	♟♟ 4
● Lambrusco Metodo Ancestrale '16	♟ 3
○ Pinot Nero Brut Nature M. Cl. '11	♟ 6
⊙ Besmein Capoleg Marzemino Frizzante Rosé '12	♟♟ 2*
○ Blanc de Noirs Brut M. Cl. '10	♟♟ 6
● Lambrusco Rifermentato in Bottiglia '15	♟♟ 3*
○ Oro di Collina '10	♟♟ 5
○ Sauvignon Frizzante Rifermentato in Bottiglia '15	♟♟ 3

Stefano Berti

LOC. RAVALDINO IN MONTE
VIA LA SCAGNA, 18
47121 FORLÌ
TEL. +39 0543488074
www.stefanoberti.it

CELLAR SALES
PRE-BOOKED VISITS
ANNUAL PRODUCTION 40,000 bottles
HECTARES UNDER VINE 7.00

Stefano Berti's roots go back to 1963, with the purchase of two farmsteads on the hills of Forlì. The breakthrough (in terms of vine growing and agriculture) came in the mid-1980s, and continued from there with increased awareness and complexity. At the end of the 1990s, they were focusing on viticulture and winemaking, with results that are, today, very encouraging, having obtained a decidedly elevated standard of quality and a solid style. All in all, the 2015 Romagna Sangiovese Bartimeo features a modern style, a concentrated color and aromas capable of combining fruity and toasty notes. The palate is reliable, with excellent weight and extraction, but is penalized by a rather rigid tannic structure. The powerful and vigorous 2015 Ravaldo, on the other hand, is almost Rhône-like.

Braschi

VIA ROMA, 37
47025 MERCATO SARACENO [FC]
TEL. +39 054791061
www.cantinabraschi.com

CELLAR SALES
PRE-BOOKED VISITS
RESTAURANT SERVICE
ANNUAL PRODUCTION 100,000 bottles
HECTARES UNDER VINE 34.50
VITICULTURE METHOD Certified Organic

Braschi is simultaneously historic and modern. Founded in 1949, this Valle del Savio producer was rethought by winemaker Vincenzo Vernocchi, and commercial manager Davide Moky Castagnoli. As of 2011, they've been steering the winery in a new direction; today, not only are their wines consistently strong, but they're proving they can represent their terroir of origin, starting with Bertinoro and Valle del Savio. The 2015 Sangiovese di Romagna Superiore Il Costone did very well. It opens on the nose with fruity fragrances that are ripe but not excessively, and is gradually refreshed by citrusy and balsamic flashes. The mouth is consistent, calling up blood oranges and closing with well-extracted tannins. It's a warm, flavorsome and generally well-made wine, never redundant or too extracted.

● Romagna Sangiovese Bartimeo '15	▼▼ 2*
● Romagna Sangiovese Predappio Ravaldo '15	▼▼ 2*
● Romagna Sangiovese Sup. Nonà '15	▼▼ 2*
● Romagna Sangiovese Predappio Ravaldo Ris. '12	▼ 3
● Sangiovese di Romagna Sup. Calisto '01	▼▼▼ 4
● Sangiovese di Romagna Sup. Calisto Ris. '09	▼▼ 4
● Sangiovese di Romagna Sup. Calisto Ris. '08	▼▼ 4
● Sangiovese di Romagna Sup. Ravaldo '10	▼▼ 2*

● Romagna Sangiovese Sup. Il Costone '15	▼▼ 3
● Romagna Sangiovese San Vicinio Monte Sasso '15	▼ 3
● Sangiovese di Romagna San Vicinio Monte Sasso '12	▼▼▼ 3*
○ Albana di Romagna Secco Campo Mamante '14	▼▼ 3
● Romagna Sangiovese Bertinoro Il Costone Ris. '12	▼▼ 4
● Romagna Sangiovese San Vicinio Monte Sasso '13	▼▼ 3*
● Sangiovese di Romagna San Vicinio Monte Sasso '14	▼▼ 3
● Sangiovese di Romagna Sup. Il Gelso '13	▼▼ 3

Calonga

LOC. CASTIGLIONE
VIA CASTEL LEONE, 8
47121 FORLÌ
TEL. +39 0543753044
www.calonga.it

CELLAR SALES
PRE-BOOKED VISITS
ANNUAL PRODUCTION 30,000 bottles
HECTARES UNDER VINE 8.00

Founded in 1997 by Maurizio Baravelli, Calonga is still a family-run winery, striving to bring out and promote the attributes of the area's local viticulture, as well as its grapes. Sangiovese, Albana and Pagadebit play central roles in the estate's ampelography. Situated in Monte Poggiolo, on the hills between Forlì and Faenza, the terrain here is predominantly characterized by the area's molasse, sandy soil. The Sangiovese Superiore Leggiolo is an excellent red, and does a good job representing the area's full potential. It features a modern style, with good concentration and clear toasty and spicy overtones. Its fruit comes together so as to confer a supple, flavorful and long mouth.

Cantina della Volta

VIA PER MODENA, 82
41030 BOMPORTO [MO]
TEL. +39 0597473312
www.cantinadellavolta.com

CELLAR SALES
PRE-BOOKED VISITS
ANNUAL PRODUCTION 120,000 bottles
HECTARES UNDER VINE 15.00
VITICULTURE METHOD Certified Organic

Christian Bellei descends from a long line of Lambrusco di Sorbara producers in Bomporto (four generations to be precise), a legacy that goes back to 1920. Bolstered by his experience working in the family winery, he founded his own cellar in 2010 with a group of friends. The goal to make a Lambrusco that receives a second-fermentation in the bottle, as well as exhibiting great personality, has been on the mark, such that, today, we get a selection of products that are, on average, excellent. The 2013 Brut Rosé stands out once again. It's a lightweight wine, but displays a range of captivating floral and citrusy aromas and a slim-bodied, savory and deep palate. The 2013 Trentasei Brut also features citrus (citron, orange peel), as well as wild berries and a remarkable backbone. The 2013 Christian Bellei Brut, made without skin contact, is fresh with notes of citrine.

● Romagna Sangiovese Sup. Leggiolo '15	♟♟♟ 3
● Ordelaffo '16	♟ 2
● Sangiovese di Romagna Sup. Michelangiolo Ris. '07	♟♟♟ 4*
● Sangiovese di Romagna Sup. Michelangiolo Ris. '06	♟♟♟ 4
● Sangiovese di Romagna Sup. Michelangiolo Ris. '05	♟♟♟ 4*
● Sangiovese di Romagna Sup. Michelangiolo Ris. '04	♟♟♟ 4*
● Sangiovese di Romagna Sup. Michelangiolo Ris. '03	♟♟♟ 4
● Ordelaffo '15	♟♟ 2*
● Ordelaffo '14	♟♟ 2*
● Romagna Sangiovese Sup. Michelangiolo Ris. '12	♟♟ 4

⊙ Lambrusco di Modena Brut Rosé M. Cl. '13	♟♟♟ 5
● Lambrusco di Modena Brut M. Cl. Trentasei '13	♟♟ 4
○ Christian Bellei Brut M.Cl. '13	♟ 5
⊙ Lambrusco di Modena Brut Rosé M. Cl. '12	♟♟♟ 5
● Lambrusco di Sorbara Rimosso '13	♟♟♟ 3*
● Lambrusco di Sorbara Rimosso '12	♟♟♟ 3*
⊙ Lambrusco di Modena Brut Rosé M. Cl. '11	♟♟ 5
● Lambrusco di Sorbara Secco Rimosso '15	♟♟ 3*

Tenuta Carbognano

VIA CARBOGNANO, 3
47855 GEMMANO [RN]
TEL. +39 0541984507
www.tenutacarbognano.it

CELLAR SALES
PRE-BOOKED VISITS
ACCOMMODATION
ANNUAL PRODUCTION 10,000 bottles
HECTARES UNDER VINE 3.00
VITICULTURE METHOD Certified Organic

Tenuta Carbognano's estate lies on the slopes of the Valley of Conca, at 250 meters above sea level. Here the vineyards share the land with woods, fields of wheat and olive groves, making for a picturesque and balanced landscape. Even the microclimate is ideal, considering that the valley forms a kind of wind tunnel, flowing from the Carpegna ridges to the sea. The wines we tasted proved excellent, forthright and flavorful, they display notable craftsmanship. We the 2015 Sangiovese Superiore was the best of the lot. Its style intrigued us and it's in line with the idea of a great wine that reflects its region. The nose opens delicately with fine spices, while the mouth has great flavor, finesse and a good weave. Its tannic texture is biting, but precise and full of flavor. It's a fragrant and sharp wine.

● Romagna Sangiovese Sup. '15	♟♟ 2*
● Ali '15	♟ 3
● Ali '13	♟♟ 3
● Ali '12	♟♟ 3
● Ali '10	♟♟ 4
● Sangiovese di Romagna Sup. Amen Ris. '12	♟♟ 3
● Sangiovese di Romagna Sup. Amen Ris. '09	♟♟ 4

Cantina Sociale di Carpi e Sorbara

VIA CAVATA
41012 CARPI [MO]
TEL. +39 059 643071
www.cantinadicarpiesorbara.it

ANNUAL PRODUCTION 2,300,000 bottles
HECTARES UNDER VINE 2300.00

1200 members, 45 million liters of wine per year, 6 facilities (for winemaking and bottling) … These are substantial numbers that demonstrate Carpi e Sorbara's ability to work the main varieties of Lambrusco, from bulk to high-quality bottled wine. The winery got its start in 2012, with the fusion of the two historic producers Cantina di Carpi (Est. 1903) and Sorbara (Est. 1923). The importance of a figure like Gino Friedman, a lawyer who was also an early promoter of cooperation within Modena's agriculture community, is evidenced by their most acclaimed wine, which is dedicated to him. The 2016 Sorbara thoroughly deserved a Tre Bicchieri. It's close-focused, distinctive and fragrant, with well-defined fruit and a pleasant length. The bottle-fermented version has more vegetal notes, a nose of flowers and almonds and a marked tanginess. The 2016 Alfredo Molinari is more rustic, with clear red fruit.

● Lambrusco di Sorbara Secco Omaggio a Gino Friedmann '16	♟♟♟ 3*
● Lambrusco di Sorbara Secco Omaggio a Gino Friedmann FB '16	♟♟ 3
● Lambrusco Salamino di Santa Croce Dedicato ad Alfredo Molinari '16	♟ 3
● Lambrusco di Sorbara Secco Omaggio a Gino Friedmann '13	♟♟♟ 3*
● Lambrusco di Sorbara Secco Omaggio a Gino Friedmann FB '14	♟♟♟ 3*
● Lambrusco di Sorbara Secco Omaggio a Gino Friedmann '15	♟♟ 3*
● Lambrusco di Sorbara Secco Omaggio a Gino Friedmann FB '15	♟♟ 3*

Cavicchioli

VIA CANALETTO, 52
41030 SAN PROSPERO [MO]
TEL. +39 059812412
www.cavicchioli.it

CELLAR SALES
PRE-BOOKED VISITS
ANNUAL PRODUCTION 10,000,000 bottles
HECTARES UNDER VINE 90.00

In 1928, in San Prospero, Umberto Cavicchioli founded a winery whose fame over the years has reached beyond national boundaries. Today it's being managed by his grandchildren, Sandro and Claudio, who most certainly haven't rested on their laurels. Rather, they've given a major push to production, managing to achieve significant results with Sorbara (the most traditional of Modena's Lambrusco grape varieties). They've done it by identifying the best terrain, carefully choosing the grapes used, and relying on techniques such as the 'Metodo Classico' to confer added personality to the final product. The 2016 Vigna del Cristo has confirmed its Tre Bicchieri status: it's savory, mineral and linear, with a wide range of floral aromas. The 2016 Tre Medaglie is also very good, more marked by wild berries and herbs. The 2013 Rosé del Cristo Metodo Classico is taut, spirited and linear, while the Modena Abboccato 1928 is juicy and solidly built.

Caviro

VIA CONVERTITE, 12
48018 FAENZA [RA]
TEL. +39 0546629111
www.caviro.it

CELLAR SALES
ANNUAL PRODUCTION 25,000,000 bottles
HECTARES UNDER VINE 31.00

Caviro is one of Italy's largest and most important cooperative wineries. It brings together 32 smaller cooperatives and 12,000 vine growers from 8 different regions. It's clear that we're talking about immense proportions, both in terms of liters and the number of selections produced. In addition to their more widespread and popular wines, like the acclaimed Tavernello, there are wines that identify more directly with Romagna, which is still the operation's homeland. The 2016 Albana Secco Romio is a solid white wine. It offers up aromas of grape skins and a dense palate, with clear and tasty tannins, just as we would expect from this traditional variety. The 2016 Sangiovese Passito Romio pulls through as well.

● Lambrusco di Sorbara V. del Cristo '16	♟♟♟ 2*
● Lambrusco di Sorbara Tre Medaglie '16	♟♟ 2*
● Lambrusco di Modena Abboccato 1928 '16	♟♟ 2*
☉ Lambrusco di Sorbara Brut Rosé del Cristo M. Cl. '13	♟♟ 4
● Lambrusco di Sorbara V. del Cristo '15	♟♟♟ 2*
● Lambrusco di Sorbara V. del Cristo '14	♟♟♟ 2*
● Lambrusco di Sorbara V. del Cristo '13	♟♟♟ 2*
● Lambrusco di Sorbara V. del Cristo '12	♟♟♟ 2*
● Lambrusco di Sorbara V. del Cristo '11	♟♟♟ 2*
☉ Lambrusco di Sorbara Brut Rosé del Cristo '11	♟♟ 5
☉ Lambrusco di Sorbara Brut Rosé del Cristo M. Cl. '12	♟♟ 4
☉ Rosé del Cristo Brut Rosé '10	♟♟ 5

○ Romagna Albana Secco Romio '16	♟♟ 2*
● Romagna Sangiovese Passito Romio '16	♟ 4
○ Pignoletto Frizzante Romio '15	♟♟ 2*
○ Romagna Albana Secco Romio '15	♟♟ 2*
○ Romagna Albana Secco Romio '14	♟♟ 2*
● Romagna Sangiovese Sup. Terragens Ris. '12	♟♟ 4
○ Romagna Trebbiano Terre Forti '15	♟♟ 1*
● Sangiovese di Romagna Brumale '13	♟♟ 2*
● Sangiovese di Romagna Brumale '12	♟♟ 2*
● Sangiovese di Romagna Terre Forti '13	♟♟ 2*
● Sangiovese di Romagna Terre Forti '12	♟♟ 2*

EMILIA ROMAGNA

Celli

V.LE CARDUCCI, 5
47032 BERTINORO [FC]
TEL. +39 0543445183
www.celli-vini.com

CELLAR SALES
PRE-BOOKED VISITS
ANNUAL PRODUCTION 280,000 bottles
HECTARES UNDER VINE 30.00
SUSTAINABLE WINERY

Celli is a historic winery (we could also say 'pioneering', considering the territory) that has managed to get through more than 50 seasons and assure its place in the industry. Today, the Sirri and Casadei family have 30 hectares of vineyards at their disposal in the terroir of Bertinoro (an area that comprises their own land, as well as property they rent, but manage directly). Here the terrain is calcareous, and rich in seabed tufa. Celli's wines reflect its essence, and the vision of their creators, without ever compromising expressive assuredness and forthrightness. We think the Albana Secco I Croppi is the best interpretation of the vintage for the category. It's a truly wonderful wine, with a dark color and autumnal aromas of rain-soaked earth and chamomile. The notes of grape skins lead into very tasty tannins, accompanied by a dense, vibrant and gratifying palate. It finishes with hints of quince and pineapple.

○ Romagna Albana Secco I Croppi '16	♥♥♥ 2*
○ Romagna Albana Passito Solara '15	♥♥ 4
● Romagna Sangiovese Sup. Le Grillaie Ris. '14	♥♥ 2*
○ Bron & Ruseval '16	♥ 2
○ Pagadebit di Romagna Campi di Fratta '16	♥ 2
● Romagna Sangiovese Sup. Le Grillaie '16	♥ 2
○ Romagna Albana Secco I Croppi '15	♥♥♥ 2*
○ Romagna Albana Dolce Le Querce '15	♥♥ 2*
○ Romagna Albana Secco I Croppi '14	♥♥ 2*
● Romagna Sangiovese Sup. Le Grillaie '15	♥♥ 2*

Cleto Chiarli Tenute Agricole

VIA BELVEDERE, 8
41014 CASTELVETRO DI MODENA [MO]
TEL. I 39 0593163311
www.chiarli.it

CELLAR SALES
PRE-BOOKED VISITS
ANNUAL PRODUCTION 900,000 bottles
HECTARES UNDER VINE 100.00

1860 was an important year for the history of Lambrusco. For 10 years, Cleto Chiarli had been working at the inn he founded, Osteria dell'Artigliere, in the center of Modena. But then, that year, he decided to dedicate himself exclusively to winemaking, a craft that, up until that point, he'd only needed for his inn. Early on, Cleto understood the importance of bottling and selling Lambrusco, and applying the technique of second-fermentation. With the current market's demands for complexity and personality (in addition to the wine's characteristic drinkability), it's a technique that has come back in style. The 2016 Sorbara del Fondatore is superb: dry but not without softness, mineral, elegant, lively and fragrant. The 2016 Vecchia Modena Premium, which plays on floral notes, is also an elegant wine. The 2016 Grasparossa Vigneto Cialdini is fragrant and territorial; the 2016 Villa Cialdini, with its fruity palate, is just as good.

● Lambrusco di Sorbara del Fondatore '16	♥♥♥ 3*
● Lambrusco di Sorbara Vecchia Modena Premium '16	♥♥ 2*
● Lambrusco Grasparossa di Castelvetro Vign. Cialdini '16	♥♥ 2*
● Lambrusco Grasparossa di Castelvetro Villa Cialdini '16	♥♥ 2*
⊙ Rosé de Noir Cuvée Brut	♥♥ 2*
○ Modena Pignoletto Brut Modén Blanc	♥ 2
● Lambrusco di Sorbara del Fondatore '15	♥♥♥ 3*
● Lambrusco di Sorbara del Fondatore '14	♥♥♥ 3*
● Lambrusco di Sorbara del Fondatore '12	♥♥♥ 3*
● Lambrusco di Sorbara del Fondatore '11	♥♥♥ 2*
● Lambrusco di Sorbara Vecchia Modena Premium '13	♥♥♥ 2*

Costa Archi

Loc. Serra
via Rinfosco, 1690
48014 Castel Bolognese [RA]
Tel. +39 3384818346
costaarchi.wordpress.com

CELLAR SALES
PRE-BOOKED VISITS
ANNUAL PRODUCTION 15,000 bottles
HECTARES UNDER VINE 13.00

Gabriele Succi is one of Romagna's most inspired and esteemed vine growers. His winery, founded in the 1960s, comprises 13 hectares of vineyards, in two distinct plots on the Castel Bolognese hills. At 160 meters above sea level, Podere il Beneficio and Monte Brullo feature red and yellow, limestone-rich clay soil. Integrated vineyard management, respect for the terroir, thought-out winemaking and aging that's never invasive make for personal, elegant, flavorsome wines. The Assiolo is a benchmark for Sangiovese in Romagna. The 2015 is an excellent version, although it's still looking for full definition and the right integration, which will come with bottle aging. It's a flavorsome wine, with aromas of raspberries and some toasty hints. The palate is juicy and partly reined in by rather sharp tannins.

Divina Lux

via Caduti di Crivellari, 50
48025 Riolo Terme [RA]
Tel. +39 3286084425
www.divinaluxwinery.com

CELLAR SALES
PRE-BOOKED VISITS
ACCOMMODATION AND RESTAURANT SERVICE
ANNUAL PRODUCTION 25,000 bottles
HECTARES UNDER VINE 7.00

The family of Divina Lux's current owner were originally from the Caucasus region and are well-acquainted with winemaking. An emphasis on naturalness and spiritual values are quite strong here on their estate in the Regional Park of Emilia Romagna (which includes seven hectares of vineyards). We found their wines focused, exhibiting an enticing personality and excellent craftsmanship. Of all the wines tasted, the 2015 Albana Secco Dar is the one that stands out. It's an intense and full-bodied wine, maybe its fruity aromas are a bit sweet, but they're never excessive or exaggerated. The mouth is round, though with verve and balance, and it's easy to drink. The 2015 Trebbiano Hilla, on the other hand, has citrusy notes and an earthy mouth.

● Romagna Sangiovese Serra Assiolo '15	♥♥ 2*
● Romagna Sangiovese Sup. Assiolo '13	♥♥♥ 4*
● GS Sangiovese '13	♥♥ 5
● GS Sangiovese '12	♥♥ 5
● GS Sangiovese '11	♥♥ 3*
● Romagna Sangiovese Serra Monte Brullo Ris. '12	♥♥ 2*
● Romagna Sangiovese Sup. Assiolo '14	♥♥ 2*
● Sangiovese di Romagna Sup. Assiolo '12	♥♥ 2*
● Sangiovese di Romagna Sup. Assiolo '11	♥♥ 2*
● Sangiovese di Romagna Sup. Assiolo '10	♥♥ 2*
● Sangiovese di Romagna Sup. Monte Brullo Ris. '10	♥♥ 2*
● Sangiovese di Romagna Sup. Monte Brullo Ris. '09	♥♥ 2*
● Sangiovese di Romagna Sup. Monte Brullo Ris. '08	♥♥ 2*

○ Romagna Albana Secco Dar '15	♥♥ 4
○ Hilla Trebbiano '15	♥ 4
○ Hilla Trebbiano '14	♥♥ 6
○ Romagna Albana Secco Dar '14	♥♥ 6

Donelli

via Carlo Sigonio, 54
41124 Modena
Tel. +39 0522908715
www.donellivini.it

CELLAR SALES
PRE-BOOKED VISITS
ACCOMMODATION
ANNUAL PRODUCTION 30,000,000 bottles
HECTARES UNDER VINE 120.00
VITICULTURE METHOD Certified Organic

Donelli, founded in 1915 by Adolfo Donelli, is a vast group that exports worldwide. Their ties to the territory are such that their highest-profile wines (made exclusively with their own grapes), are part of the Sergio Scaglietti line. Scaglietti is another of Modena's great historical figures, famous for having designed cars for Ferrari. Friendship and mutual respect for Donelli's current manager, Antonio Giacobazzi, led to the creation of this special selection. The 2016 Lambrusco di Sorbara Sergio Scaglietti is mineral, lively and linear. It expresses fruit and has a vibrant grip, with a well-orchestrated and sustained finish. The 2016 Reggiano Lambrusco Brut Sergio Scaglietti features richness of flavor, notes of citrus fruit and a close-focused finish.

- Lambrusco di Sorbara Secco Sergio Scaglietti '16 — 🍷🍷 2*
- Reggiano Lambrusco Brut Sergio Scaglietti '16 — 🍷 2
- Lambrusco di Sorbara Brut Sergio Scaglietti '15 — 🍷🍷 2*
- Lambrusco di Sorbara Secco Sergio Scaglietti '14 — 🍷🍷 2*
- Lambrusco di Sorbara Secco Sergio Scaglietti '13 — 🍷🍷 2*
- Lambrusco Reggiano Secco Sergio Scaglietti '13 — 🍷🍷 2*
- Reggiano Lambrusco Brut Sergio Scaglietti '15 — 🍷🍷 2*
- Reggiano Lambrusco Secco Sergio Scaglietti '14 — 🍷🍷 2*

Emilia Wine

via 11 Settembre 2001, 3
42019 Scandiano [RE]
Tel. +39 0522989107
www.emiliawine.eu

ANNUAL PRODUCTION 300,000 bottles
HECTARES UNDER VINE 1900.00

Emilia Wine, founded only recently (in 2014), is a cooperative formed by the fusion of three other cooperatives active in the territory: Arceto, Correggio and Prato di Correggio. 726 members work on various types of terrain, from plains (well-suited to Lambrusco) to hills (where mostly white grapes are cultivated in the narrow patch of land between the Enza and Secchia rivers). The philosophy is aimed at obtaining the best from each plot, with honed planting and expert research going into their high-profile selection. The 2016 Rossospino is an expressive and meaty dry Lambrusco, with discernible tannins and an earthy minerality. 1077 is a Brut wine with a fragrant nose of peach and apricot, floral notes and a mouth full of sour cherries and sweet tannins. The 2016 Niveo is a creamy Lambrusco that features aromas of strawberries and red citrus fruit, and a mouth with rather rustic tannins. Darker notes of forest floor, rhubarb, licorice and blackberries for the 2016 Grasparossa Cardinale Pighini, while the 2016 Migliolungo returns to citrusy overtones.

- 1077 Rosso Brut — 🍷🍷 2*
- Colli di Scandiano e di Canossa Lambrusco Rossospino Cantina di Arceto '16 — 🍷🍷 2*
- Colli di Scandiano e Canossa Lambrusco Grasparossa Cardinale Pighini Cantina di Arceto '16 — 🍷 1*
- Migliolungo Lambrusco '16 — 🍷 2
- Reggiano Lambrusco Niveo Cantina di Arceto '16 — 🍷 2
- Colli di Scandiano e di Canossa Lambrusco Rossospino Cantina di Arceto '15 — 🍷🍷 2*
- Reggiano Lambrusco Secco Niveo Cantina di Arceto '15 — 🍷🍷 2*

Stefano Ferrucci

VIA CASOLANA, 3045
48014 CASTEL BOLOGNESE [RA]
TEL. +39 0546651068
www.stefanoferrucci.it

CELLAR SALES
PRE-BOOKED VISITS
ANNUAL PRODUCTION 95,000 bottles
HECTARES UNDER VINE 16.00

Today, sisters Ilaria and Serena manage this historic, family-run winery, founded in the early 1930s. The vineyards are found in the district of Serra, famous for the calcareous clay soil that confers to its grapes (Sangiovese in particular) savory fragrances and surefooted tannins. The house style has evolved over time, having taken shape in the 1980s but remolded in recent years. The best taste, for us, was the 2015 Albana Passito Domus Aurea. It's a classy sweet, aromatic and vibrant wine with aromas of honey, pollen and baked apple, and a deep, meaty and close-knit palate. The 2016 Sangiovese Auriga is a simple and pleasant wine.

○ Romagna Albana Passito Domus Aurea '15	♛♛ 5
○ Colli di Faenza Bianco Chiaro della Serra '16	♛ 2
● Romagna Sangiovese Auriga '16	♛ 2
○ Albana di Romagna Passito Domus Aurea '12	♙♙ 5
○ Romagna Albana Passito Domus Aurea '13	♙♙ 5
● Romagna Sangiovese Auriga '15	♙♙ 2*
● Romagna Sangiovese Sup. Centurione '14	♙♙ 2*
● Romagna Sangiovese Sup. Domus Caia Ris. '13	♙♙ 5
● Romagna Sangiovese Sup. Domus Caia Ris. '12	♙♙ 5
● Sangiovese di Romagna Sup. Domus Caia Ris. '11	♙♙ 5

Paolo Francesconi

LOC. SARNA
VIA TULIERO, 154
48018 FAENZA [RA]
TEL. +39 054643213
www.francesconipaolo.it

CELLAR SALES
PRE-BOOKED VISITS
RESTAURANT SERVICE
ANNUAL PRODUCTION 20,000 bottles
HECTARES UNDER VINE 8.00
VITICULTURE METHOD Certified Biodynamic
SUSTAINABLE WINERY

Paolo Francesconi is a perfect starting point for those looking for authentic, personal, artisanal wines available only in limited quantities. Since the 1990s, they've shown focus in their development, first by embracing organic agriculture and later a biodynamic approach. The results for their Sangiovese, white and 'orange' wines are truly impressive. This year, it was the winery's Sangioveses that most impressed. The Le ladi Riserva features a good citrusy nose, backed up by tasty red fruit, which follows through onto the palate, but stops short a bit at the finish, due to rather mouth-drying tannins. The 2016 Limbecca is decidedly tannic and very fruity.

● Romagna Sangiovese Le ladi Ris. '13	♛♛ 5
● Romagna Sangiovese Sup. Limbecca '16	♛ 3
● Romagna Sangiovese Sup. Limbecca '14	♙♙♙ 3*
● Sangiovese di Romagna Sup. Limbecca '11	♙♙♙ 3*
● Sangiovese di Romagna Sup. Limbecca '10	♙♙♙ 3*
○ Arcaica '15	♙♙ 3
○ Arcaica '14	♙♙ 3
● Romagna Sangiovese Sup. Le ladi Ris. '12	♙♙ 5
● Romagna Sangiovese Sup. Le ladi Ris. '11	♙♙ 5
● Vite in Fiore '15	♙♙ 3

Gruppo Cevico

VIA FIUMAZZO, 72
48022 LUGO [RA]
TEL. +39 054528471 I I
www.gruppocevico.com

CELLAR SALES
PRE-BOOKED VISITS
ANNUAL PRODUCTION 50,000,000 bottles
HECTARES UNDER VINE 7000.00

With 4500 vine growers covering 7000
hectares of vineyards, Gruppo Cevico is a
large operation, both for the region and for
Italy. Such numbers say a lot, but not
everything, considering that in addition to
their size (with is impressive enough), a
number of details and nuances allow this
modern producer to stay up to date with
market demands. Cevico's wines are as
popular as they are capable of exhibiting a
certain identity, at least when it comes to
Terre Cevico, Vigneti Galassi, Sancrispino,
Ronco, Romandiola and Bernardi. The two
Sangioveses that we tasted this year pull
through. The 2016 Vigna Galassi is more
convincing and fruity, with good density.
The 2013 Il Pavone d'Oro della
Romandiola Riserva is obviously more
evolved and spicy.

Lini 910

FRAZ. CANOLO
VIA VECCHIA CANOLO, 7
42015 CORREGGIO [RE]
TEL. +39 0522690162
www.lini910.it

CELLAR SALES
PRE-BOOKED VISITS
ANNUAL PRODUCTION 400,000 bottles
HECTARES UNDER VINE 25.00

The producer's history goes back to 1910,
as its name suggests. For four generations,
the Lini family have run this winery,
dedicating themselves primarily to
Lambrusco, which undergoes second-
fermentation in the bottle, as well as
vinegar (with 1000 barrels in their
Correggio facility). Of the two Metodo
Classico Lambruscos, the 2016 Rosé
stands out for its floral bouquet, fine
sparkle, the lovely suppleness of its fine
tannins and an open, generous finish.
The 2016 Gran Cuvée di Lambrusco sees
plenty of fruity pulp, well discernible
tannins and a roasted almondy finish. The
2016 Lambrusco Scuro is firmly pleasant,
with clear wild berries, generous aromas
and marked tannins that come together in
a rather rustic style of wine.

● Romagna Sangiovese Sup. Vign. Galassi '16	♥♥ 2*
● Romagna Sangiovese I Il Pavone d'Oro Romandiola Ris. '13	♥ 2
○ Albana di Romagna Secco Romandiola '15	♀♀ 3
● Bosco Eliceo Merlot Terre Cevico '14	♀♀ 1*
○ Colli di Imola Pignoletto Frizzante Romandiola '15	♀♀ 2*
● Romagna Sangiovese Sup. Romandiola Novilunio '14	♀♀ 2*
● Romagna Sangiovese Sup. Terre Cevico '14	♀♀ 2*
● Romagna Sangiovese Sup. Vign. Galassi '15	♀♀ 2*
● Romagna Sangiovese Sup. Vign. Galassi '14	♀♀ 2*

⊙ In Correggio Brut Rosé M. Cl. '14	♥♥ 4
● In Correggio Lambrusco Scuro '16	♥♥ 2*
● In Correggio Gran Cuvée di Lambrusco Brut M. Cl.	♥ 4
● Gran Cuvée di Lambrusco M. Cl. '12	♀♀ 4
● In Correggio Lambrusco Scuro '15	♀♀ 2*
● In Correggio Lambrusco Scuro '14	♀♀ 2*
● In Correggio Lambrusco Scuro '13	♀♀ 2*

Cantine Lombardini

VIA CAVOUR, 15
42017 NOVELLARA [RE]
TEL. +39 0522654224
www.lombardinivini.it

CELLAR SALES
PRE-BOOKED VISITS
ANNUAL PRODUCTION 800,000 bottles

Since it was founded by Angelo, in 1925, four generations of family have managed Cantine Lombardini. During this time, it has never left its original headquarters in the historic center of Novellara. In 1970, the decision was made to turn away from the estate's vineyards, focusing exclusively on selecting grapes and must, an activity that's well-suited to small-time operations, especially with such generous terrain. The 2016 Signor Campanone is a blend of Salamino and Sorbara. It offers up nice, deep, close-focused fruit with notes of plums and forest floor, precise tannins and a slightly bitterish finish. The 2016 Lambrusco della Dama, made with Salamino, Marani and Maestri, is fresh and mineral, with hints of citrus fruit and a lovely clean and fragrant finish. The 2016 Reggiano Lambrusco is a pleasantly rustic interpretation, while the 2016 Sorbara goes more in on fruit.

● Lambrusco della Dama '16	🏆 1*
● Reggiano Lambrusco Il Signor Campanone '16	🏆 2*
● Lambrusco di Sorbara C'era Una Volta '16	🏆 2
● Reggiano Lambrusco C'era Una Volta '16	🏆 2

Luretta

LOC. CASTELLO DI MOMELIANO
29010 GAZZOLA [PC]
TEL. +39 0523971070
www.luretta.com

CELLAR SALES
PRE-BOOKED VISITS
ANNUAL PRODUCTION 300,000 bottles
HECTARES UNDER VINE 50.00
VITICULTURE METHOD Certified Organic

Felice Salamini was a farmer, but in 1988, after traveling around France and tasting wine, he came to Val Luretta and took over an old, abandoned vineyard, thus starting a new life. With the support of his family, he purchased 50 hectares of land. It's a period of experimentation, he plants international varieties, enologists around the world get involved, while his son, Lucio, helps his father lead the winery. 2002 saw the definitive move to Castello di Momeliano. The wine that stood out the most was the 2016 Sauvignon I Nani e le Ballerine, with its signature tropical aromas of passion fruit and lime, sustained by a lovely touch of tartness. The 2015 Selín dl'Armari is a juicy Chardonnay with a well-orchestrated finish. The 2011 Cabernet Corbeau has character and backbone, while the 2014 Gutturnio Superiore sees good structure, despite the unfortunate vintage.

○ C. P. Chardonnay Selín dl'Armari '15	🏆🏆 4
○ C. P. Sauvignon I Nani e le Ballerine '16	🏆🏆 3
● C. P. Cabernet Sauvignon Corbeau '11	🏆 6
● C. P. Gutturnio Sup. '14	🏆 3
● C. P. Barbera Carabas '11	🍷🍷 3
⊙ C. P. Brut Rosé On Attend les Invités '11	🍷🍷 4
○ C. P. Chardonnay Selín dl'Armari '11	🍷🍷 4
○ C. P. Malvasia Boccadirosa '11	🍷🍷 2*
○ C. P. Malvasia Dolce le Rane '10	🍷🍷 6
○ C. P. Sauvignon I Nani e le Ballerine '11	🍷🍷 3
● Gutturnio Sup. '12	🍷🍷 3
○ Principessa Pas Dosé Brut M. Cl. '09	🍷🍷 4
○ Principessa Pas Dosé M. Cl. '10	🍷🍷 4

Giovanna Madonia

LOC. VILLA MADONIA
VIA DE' CAPPUCCINI, 130
47032 BERTINORO [FC]
TEL. +39 0543444361
www.giovannamadonia.it

CELLAR SALES
PRE-BOOKED VISITS
RESTAURANT SERVICE
ANNUAL PRODUCTION 60,000 bottles
HECTARES UNDER VINE 13.00

The winery started in the 1990s in Monte Maggio, the coldest part of Bertinoro, and since then it has worked to interpret the peculiarities of the area in the best possible way. Its soil is rich in active limestone that, together with its particular climate, makes for a slow ripening of the grapes and long-lived wines. Madonia's style is characterized by a certain extractive richness, mature fruit and solid tannins. The 2013 Ombroso is a Sangiovese with tertiary and spicy aromas that call up dried leaves and flowers. It's consistent in the mouth, rather full and ready to drink. The 2015 Fermavento is dark but juicy, while the 2016 Tenentino is grapey and well-rounded.

Ermete Medici & Figli

LOC. GAIDA
VIA I. NEWTON, 13A
42040 REGGIO EMILIA
TEL. +39 0522942135
www.medici.it

CELLAR SALES
PRE-BOOKED VISITS
ANNUAL PRODUCTION 800,000 bottles
HECTARES UNDER VINE 75.00
SUSTAINABLE WINERY

The history of this winery follows that of many similar, family-run producers. Founded by Remigio in the late 1800s, it was enlarged and promoted by his son, Ermete. Today, it's on the fourth generation with Alberto, who, through hard work and passion, has made Ermete Medici & Figli one of Lambrusco Reggiano's ambassadors in Italy and the world. One of its strengths has been being able to identify and take advantage of the best crus, drastically lowering yields in the vineyards. The 2016 Concerto won us over with its open and generous fruit; it's dynamic in the mouth and fragrant on the nose. The 2016 Assolo is more floral, while in the mouth citrus fruit and wild berries complete its full and captivating suite of aromas. The rosé version of the 2016 Quercioli offers a bouquet of meadow flowers, where a marked minerality emerges. This sweet version offers up the same, with wild strawberries filling the palate. The 2016 Dolce Grasparossa Bocciolo is even fruitier, with more rustic fragrances.

● Romagna Sangiovese Bertinoro Ombroso Ris. '13	♟5
● Romagna Sangiovese Sup. Fermavento '15	♟3
● Tenentino '16	♟2
○ Romagna Albana Secco Neblina '14	♟♟♟2*
● Sangiovese di Romagna Sup. Ombroso Ris. '06	♟♟♟5
● Sangiovese di Romagna Sup. Ombroso Ris. '01	♟♟♟5
○ Romagna Albana Secco Neblina '15	♟♟2*
● Romagna Sangiovese Bertinoro Ombroso Ris. '12	♟♟5
● Romagna Sangiovese Sup. Fermavento '13	♟♟3

● Reggiano Lambrusco Concerto '16	♟♟♟2*
● Reggiano Lambrusco Assolo '16	♟♟2*
⊙ Reggiano Lambrusco Rosato I Quercioli '16	♟♟2*
● Colli di Scandiano e di Canossa Lambrusco Grasparossa Dolce Bocciolo '16	♟2
● Reggiano Lambrusco Dolce I Quercioli '16	♟2
● Reggiano Lambrusco Concerto '15	♟♟♟2*
● Reggiano Lambrusco Concerto '14	♟♟♟2*
● Reggiano Lambrusco Concerto '13	♟♟♟2*
● Reggiano Lambrusco Concerto '12	♟♟♟2*
● Reggiano Lambrusco Concerto '11	♟♟♟2*
● Reggiano Lambrusco Concerto '10	♟♟♟2*

Monte delle Vigne

Loc. Ozzano Taro
via Monticello, 22
43046 Collecchio [PR]
Tel. +39 0521309704
www.montedellevigne.it

CELLAR SALES
PRE-BOOKED VISITS
ACCOMMODATION
ANNUAL PRODUCTION 350,000 bottles
HECTARES UNDER VINE 60.00

Andrea Ferrari founded the winery in 1983, starting with seven hectares and a desire to produce still wines in an area historically known for its semi-sparklers. 2004 saw an important meeting with Paolo Pizzarotti, owner of a large, neighboring plot; in 2006, this led to the inauguration of a new, underground cellar, powered by solar panels. Today, the certified organic vineyards host a number of traditional and international varieties (according to exposure and position) and, in recent years, an important initiative on behalf of semi-sparkling wines has been launched, starting with the Lambrusco Maestri. The Colli di Parma Rosso duplicated last year's success. It's a blend of Barbera and Bonarda, with aromas of blackberries and plums, while the mouth proves supple, vibrant and fresh. The Nabucco also features Barbera, as well as 30% Merlot: the aromatic bouquet plays on red and black fruit, while the palate is mature, caressing and plush.

● Colli di Parma Rosso MDV '16	▼▼▼	3*
○ Callas Malvasia '14	▼▼	4
● Nabucco '15	▼▼	5
● Lambrusco I Salici '15	▼	4
● Colli di Parma Rosso MDV '14	♈♈♈	2*
○ Callas Malvasia '12	♈♈	2*
○ Callas Malvasia '11	♈♈	4
○ Colli di Parma Malvasia Poem '14	♈♈	2*
○ Colli di Parma Sauvignon '13	♈♈	2*

Fattoria Monticino Rosso

via Montecatone, 7
40026 Imola [BO]
Tel. +39 054240577
www.fattoriadelmonticinorosso.it

CELLAR SALES
PRE-BOOKED VISITS
ANNUAL PRODUCTION 70,000 bottles
HECTARES UNDER VINE 18.00

Fattoria Monticino Rosso is a producer worth following. Over recent years, they have been turning out wines that show increasing focus and originality. Albana takes center stage here. This local, white grape variety has seen a number of interpretations, with extremely encouraging results. Their success is the consequence of careful management by the Zeoli family, and the territory in which their grapes are cultivated, on the Imola hills, right on the border between Emilia and Romagna. The 2016 Albana Secco is a delight. It offers up aromas of apple, pineapple and broom flowers, while the mouth is juicy, fresh and deep. The 2015 Codronchio is more honeyed, with hints of saffron. The simple but tasty 2016 Sangiovese Superiore is one of their best reds.

○ Romagna Albana Secco A '16	▼▼	2*
○ Romagna Albana Secco Codronchio '15	▼▼	3
● Romagna Sangiovese Sup. S '16	▼▼	2*
● Romagna Sangiovese Sup. Le Morine Ris. '12	▼	4
○ Albana di Romagna Secco Codronchio '08	♈♈♈	3*
○ Romagna Albana Passito '11	♈♈	4
○ Romagna Albana Secco A '14	♈♈	2*
○ Romagna Albana Secco Codronchio '14	♈♈	3
○ Romagna Albana Secco Codronchio '13	♈♈	3
● Romagna Sangiovese Sup. Le Morine '11	♈♈	3
● Romagna Sangiovese Sup. S '15	♈♈	2*
● Romagna Sangiovese Sup. S '14	♈♈	2*

Fattoria Moretto

VIA TIBERIA, 13B
41014 CASTELVETRO DI MODENA [MO]
TEL. +39 059790183
www.fattoriamoretto.it

CELLAR SALES
PRE-BOOKED VISITS
ANNUAL PRODUCTION 65,000 bottles
HECTARES UNDER VINE 10.00
VITICULTURE METHOD Certified Organic
SUSTAINABLE WINERY

Founded in 1971, on the hills where
Lambrusco Grasparossa di Castelvetro
thrives, this family-run winery is on their
third generation, with Fausto and Fabio
Altariva at the helm (helped by their father,
Domenico). They've been organic for 10
years now, and today they're aiming to
develop this Lambrusco variety by bringing
out the best of the silt clay that
characterizes the soil here. Their approach
to winemaking has been a bit topsy-turvy if
you look at other producers. They started
with second-fermentation in the bottle, but
the Altariva brothers have since moved to
the autoclave so as to give more coherence
to their wines. The Monovitigno and the
Canova are solid proof. The first expresses
fragrant notes of blackberries and ripe
strawberries, with whiffs of flowers that call
up lavender and a fresh, flavorsome and
pleasantly rustic mouth. The second has an
inviting nose and is delicately earthy, savory
and mineral on the palate.

● Lambrusco Grasparossa di Castelvetro Secco Canova '16		♥♥ 3
● Lambrusco Grasparossa di Castelvetro Secco Monovitigno '16		♥♥ 3
● Lambrusco Grasparossa di Castelvetro Amabile Semprebon '16		♥ 2
● Lambrusco Grasparossa di Castelvetro Secco Tasso '16		♥ 2
● Lambrusco Grasparossa di Castelvetro Secco Canova '15		♀♀ 3
● Lambrusco Grasparossa di Castelvetro Secco Canova '14		♀♀ 3*
● Lambrusco Grasparossa di Castelvetro Secco Monovitigno '15		♀♀ 3*
● Lambrusco Grasparossa di Castelvetro Secco Monovitigno '14		♀♀ 3

Poderi Morini

LOC. ORIOLO DEI FICHI
VIA GESUITA
48018 FAENZA [RA]
TEL. +39 0546634257
www.poderimorini.com

ANNUAL PRODUCTION 100,000 bottles
HECTARES UNDER VINE 26.00
SUSTAINABLE WINERY

Alessandro Morini's is a decidedly
interesting operation, both for its production
philosophy and for its commitment to
reviving and promoting the area's most
common, local grape varieties. This vine
grower cultivates 26 hectares of land in
Oriolo dei Fichi, on the gentle slopes of
Faenza, an area characterized by its classic
travertine geology and a favorable
microclimate (which features a mix of
Adriatic breezes and Apennine winds). Their
wines are artisanal in style, with the
producer on the front line when it comes to
Albana and Centesimino, two varieties that
see a number of interesting interpretations.
The 2016 Sangiovese Superiore Morale is
a well-made red with good intensity. There
are mature aromas of red and black fruit,
while the palate is balanced and consistent,
more plush than sharp, but never tiring or
stagnant. The Albana Sette Note has lively
acidity and aromas centered on flowers and
yellow fruit. The Pignoletto is good, with
overtones of crusty bread.

● Romagna Sangiovese Sup. Morale '16		♥♥ 2
○ Pignoletto Frizzante Morale '16		♥ 2
○ Romagna Albana Secco Sette Note '16		♥ 3
○ Romagna Albana Secco Sette Note '15		♀♀ 2*
● Romagna Sangiovese Sup. Morale '15		♀♀ 3
● Sangiovese di Romagna Sup. Morale '14		♀♀ 3
● Sangiovese di Romagna Sup. Nonno Rico Ris. '10		♀♀ 2*
● Sangiovese di Romagna Sup. Torre di Oriolo '11		♀♀ 3
● Savignone Centesimino '13		♀♀ 2*
● Savignone Centesimo '15		♀♀ 2*

attoria Nicolucci

UMBERTO I, 21
7016 PREDAPPIO [FC]
L. +39 0543922361
ww.vininicolucci.com

CELLAR SALES
RE-BOOKED VISITS
NNUAL PRODUCTION 70,000 bottles
ECTARES UNDER VINE 10.00
USTAINABLE WINERY

attoria Nicolucci is located in Pedappio
ta, an area that, for as long as anyone
an remember, has been known for its
angiovese, and the results it's capable of
roducing. Indeed, the lean, calcareous,
ony terrain gives rise to fruit that the
colucci family are adept at interpreting,
ith wines aged in concrete vats and large
ood barrels. The winery evokes a classic
yle that's relaxed and capable of
aduring over time. They are a benchmark
r the whole of Romagna, and a clear
presentation of the subzone's
mportance. The 2014 Vigna del Generale
a complex and multifaceted red, rich in
picy notes and good tertiary aromas. The
uit is relaxed but intense, well-integrated
nd rich in nuances. The mouth is dense
d meaty. The only shame is its slightly
outh-drying tannins which rein in depth.
s without a doubt a good wine for
airing. The 2016 Tre Rocche is simpler,
t just as good.

Enio Ottaviani

LOC. SANT'ANDREA IN CASALE
VIA PIAN DI VAGLIA, 17
47832 SAN CLEMENTE [RN]
TEL. +39 0541952608
www.enioottaviani.it

CELLAR SALES
PRE-BOOKED VISITS
ANNUAL PRODUCTION 130,000 bottles
HECTARES UNDER VINE 12.00

The winery bears the name of its founder,
a man who managed to launch an
interesting business when few were doing
so. Today, his grandchildren, Davide and
Massimo Lorenzi, along with their cousins,
Marco and Milena, are running Enio
Ottaviani. They're bringing a new attitude
and agricultural program to the estate's 12
hectares of vineyards. These are located in
the southern part of Romagna, at the foot
of the Conca Valley, along the Catholic
hills. The 2016 Sangiovese Superiore
Caciara stands out for its pleasant style
and its fine, delicate range of aromas,
backed up by whiffs of flowers and red
fruit. Hints of cherries, raspberries and
watermelon are enriched with fine spices
and refreshed by balsamic hints. The
palate is slim-bodied but not grassy, linear
without being too edgy. It isn't particularly
deep, but it's quite enjoyable.

Romagna Sangiovese Sup. Predappio di Predappio V. del Generale Ris. '14	♟♟ 5
Romagna Sangiovese Sup. Tre Rocche '16	♟♟ 3
Romagna Sangiovese Sup. V. del Generale Ris. '13	♟♟♟ 5
Romagna Sangiovese Sup. V. del Generale Ris. '12	♟♟♟ 5
Sangiovese di Romagna Predappio di Predappio V. del Generale '11	♟♟♟ 5
Sangiovese di Romagna Sup. V. del Generale Ris. '10	♟♟♟ 5
Sangiovese di Romagna Sup. V. del Generale Ris. '08	♟♟♟ 5
Sangiovese di Romagna V. del Generale Ris. '09	♟♟♟ 5

● Romagna Sangiovese Sup. Caciara '16	♟♟ 3
○ Clemente I '16	♟ 3
● Merlot '14	♟ 5
● Novecento28 '15	♟ 4
○ Romagna Pagadebit Strati '16	♟ 2
○ Clemente Primo '15	♟♟ 2*
○ Clemente Primo '14	♟♟ 2*
● Merlot '13	♟♟ 2*
● Romagna Sangiovese Caciara '15	♟♟ 3
● Romagna Sangiovese Primalba '14	♟♟ 2*
● Romagna Sangiovese Sup. Caciara '14	♟♟ 2*
● Romagna Sangiovese Sup. Primalba '13	♟♟ 2*
● Romagna Sangiovese Sup. Sole Rosso Ris. '13	♟♟ 4
● Romagna Sangiovese Sup. Sole Rosso Ris. '11	♟♟ 3

Gianfranco Paltrinieri

FRAZ. SORBARA
VIA CRISTO, 49
41030 BOMPORTO [MO]
TEL. +39 059902047
www.cantinapaltrinieri.it

CELLAR SALES
PRE-BOOKED VISITS
ANNUAL PRODUCTION 90,000 bottles
HECTARES UNDER VINE 15.00

In the heart of Cristo di Sorbara, in an area flanked by the Secchia and Panaro rivers, Alberto Paltrinieri and his wife, Barbara, are keeping alive the legacy of their father, Gianfranco, and the winery's founder, grandfather Achille. It's a legacy that involves making Lambrusco that is as true to the territory as possible. This requires choosing the right cru, and the appropriate winemaking approach - from second-fermentation in autoclaves to the 'Metodo Classico' - for wines that exhibit notable personality and flavor, and that are always interesting, whatever the interpretation. In a selection that we could almost define as exemplary for Sorbara, our favorite was definitely the Leclisse. Herbs and slightly earthy notes combine with overtones of raspberries; the mouth is dynamic and exhibits fantastic continuity, acid acceleration and a pleasantly fruity and citrusy finish.

Pandolfa

FRAZ. FIUMANA
VIA PANDOLFA, 35
47016 PREDAPPIO [FC]
TEL. +39 0543940073
www.pandolfa.it

CELLAR SALES
ANNUAL PRODUCTION 120,000 bottles
HECTARES UNDER VINE 30.00
SUSTAINABLE WINERY

It's not just Noelia Ricci that deserves attention, its parent company does as well. And so we're dedicating space to Tenuta Pandolfa and its excellent wines. The name derives from Sigismondo Pandolfo Malatesta, the Renaissance lord, while from 1626 to 1941 the Marquis Albicini owned the estate. After that, the torch passed to Knight Commander Giuseppe Ricci and then to his daughter, Noelia. In more recent years, Paola Piscopo and her son, Marco Cirese, have been in a position to take things to the next level. A shining example of the results achieved is the Sangiovese Romagna Superiore Federico. The 2016 is an outstanding version, with its aromas of small ripe red fruits and fresh flowers, and a mouth that captures its fruity sweetness and freshness right up to its lengthy finish.

● Lambrusco di Sorbara Leclisse '16	🍷🍷🍷	2*
● Lambrusco di Sorbara Piria '16	🍷🍷	2*
● Lambrusco di Sorbara Sant'Agata '16	🍷🍷	2*
● Lambrusco di Modena Brut M. Cl. Grosso '14	🍷	4
● Lambrusco di Sorbara Radice '16	🍷	2
● Lambrusco Solco Semisecco '16	🍷	2
● Lambrusco di Sorbara Leclisse '10	🍷🍷🍷	3*
● Lambrusco di Sorbara Radice '13	🍷🍷🍷	2*
● Lambrusco di Sorbara Leclisse '15	🍷🍷	2*
● Lambrusco di Sorbara Leclisse '14	🍷🍷	2*
● Lambrusco di Sorbara Leclisse '13	🍷🍷	2*
● Lambrusco di Sorbara Radice '15	🍷🍷	2*
● Lambrusco di Sorbara Radice '14	🍷🍷	2*
● Lambrusco di Sorbara Sant'Agata '15	🍷🍷	2*
● Radice Tappo a Corona '15	🍷🍷	2*

● Romagna Sangiovese Sup. Federico '16	🍷🍷	
● Romagna Sangiovese Sup. Pandolfo '16	🍷🍷	
○ Battista '16	🍷	
● Romagna Sangiovese Pandolfo Ris. '13	🍷	
● Pezzolo Cabernet Sauvignon '05	🍷🍷	
● Sangiovese di Romagna Sup. Villa degli Spiriti Ris. '05	🍷🍷	
● Sangiovese di Romagna Sup. Villa degli Spiriti Ris. '04	🍷🍷	

Fattoria Paradiso

FRAZ. CAPOCOLLE
VIA PALMEGGIANA, 285
47032 BERTINORO [FC]
TEL. +39 0543445044
www.fattoriaparadiso.com

CELLAR SALES
PRE-BOOKED VISITS
ANNUAL PRODUCTION 130,000 bottles
HECTARES UNDER VINE 50.00

The estate that was once known as Castello Ugarte Lovatelli, and today goes by the name of Fattoria Paradiso, lies on a sunny hilltop next to Bertinoro. There are 50 hectares of vineyards in all, including a desirable patrimony of old vineyards and new, high-density blocks. Sangiovese serves as a foundation, while other native grape varieties (Albana, Pagadebit, Cagnina and Barbarossa) are also cultivated. A small quantity of Cabernet Sauvignon and Merlot complete the puzzle. The best taste for us was the 2016 Sangiovese Superiore Vigna del Molino Maestri di Vigna. It exhibits a darker profile, starting with the color, which leads into a nose playing on black fruit and toasty, almost smoky hints. We particularly enjoyed the young and racy palate, which is never too hemmed in by clenched tannic weight, and features a nice fullness of flavor.

Tenuta Pertinello

S.DA ARPINETO PERTINELLO, 2
47010 GALEATA [FC]
TEL. +39 0543983156
www.tenutapertinello.it

CELLAR SALES
PRE-BOOKED VISITS
ANNUAL PRODUCTION 70,000 bottles
HECTARES UNDER VINE 14.00
VITICULTURE METHOD Certified Organic

Moreno Mancini has revived Valle del Bidente's long tradition of winemaking. The area is characterized by its loose, marl and sandstone soil, noteworthy altitudes and old, head-trained vineyards. His winery, Pertinello, takes advantage of the territory's know-how and potential, managing to produce wines of great finesse and inherent elegance. The tastings this year have given us a contrasting picture. We thought their Sangiovese wines seemed a bit uncertain and slightly blurred, while a delightful 2015 Pinot Nero excelled. It's a red with unmistakable, almost whispered, varietal traits, with very delicate extraction. It's really quite an enjoyable wine.

● Romagna Sangiovese Sup. V. del Molino Maestri di Vigna '16	♥♥ 2*
● Il Dosso '14	♥♥ 4
● Romagna Sangiovese Sup. Bertinoro V. delle Lepri Ris. '12	♥ 4
○ Albana V.T. '15	♀♀ 2*
● Barbarossa Il Dosso '13	♀♀ 4
● Mito '13	♀♀ 6
● Mito '10	♀♀ 6
● Romagna Sangiovese Sup. V. del Molino Maestri di Vigna '15	♀♀ 2*
● Romagna Sangiovese Sup. V. delle Lepri Ris. '13	♀♀ 3
● Sangiovese di Romagna Sup. V. delle Lepri Ris. '12	♀♀ 3
● Sangiovese di Romagna V. Lepri Rina Pezzi Ris. '09	♀♀ 3

● Pinot Nero '15	♥♥ 4
● Colli Romagna Centrale Sangiovese Pertinello '08	♀♀♀ 3
● Colli Romagna Centrale Sangiovese Il Bosco '15	♀♀ 2*
● Colli Romagna Centrale Sangiovese Il Bosco '14	♀♀ 2*
● Colli Romagna Centrale Sangiovese Il Sasso Ris. '11	♀♀ 5
● Colli Romagna Centrale Sangiovese Il Sasso Ris. '10	♀♀ 5
● Colli Romagna Centrale Sangiovese Pertinello '13	♀♀ 3*
● Colli Romagna Centrale Sangiovese Pertinello '12	♀♀ 3
● Colli Romagna Centrale Sangiovese Pertinello '11	♀♀ 3

Quinto Passo

LOC. SOZZIGALLI DI SOLIERA
VIA CANALE, 267
41019 SOLIERA [MO]
TEL. +39 0593163311
www.quintopasso.it

CELLAR SALES
ANNUAL PRODUCTION 40,000 bottles
HECTARES UNDER VINE 12.00

Quinto Passo means 'the fifth step', and, since the mid-1800s, five generations of Chiarli have been making Modena's Lambrusco known throughout the world. The union of this extraordinary family heritage and the still-undiscovered potential of Lambrusco di Sorbara led to the founding of this 'pillar', which is dedicated exclusively to 'Metodo Classico' Sorbara, starting with the process of identifying and selecting the best of their terrain's grapes. The 2014 Rosé is made with 100% Sorbara. It's fresh, close-focused, taut but creamy at the same time, delicately citrusy and pleasantly tangy. The 2014 Cuvée Paradiso is just as good, made with 80% Chardonnay and a smaller part Sorbara. It has a pervasive aromatic profile, while the mouth is sustained by delicately salty vibrations intertwined with hints of cake.

Noelia Ricci

FRAZ. FIUMANA
VIA PANDOLFA, 35
47016 PREDAPPIO [FC]
TEL. +39 0543940073
www.noeliaricci.it

CELLAR SALES
PRE-BOOKED VISITS
ACCOMMODATION
ANNUAL PRODUCTION 58,000 bottles
HECTARES UNDER VINE 9.00
SUSTAINABLE WINERY

Noelia Ricci is, without a doubt, one of Romagna's most brilliant wineries, a producer capable of an extremely precise and contemporary agricultural, enological and stylistic program. To accomplish this, Marco Cirese revolutionized the family's historic estate, utilizing some of the grapes from the historic Tenuta Pandolfa (which has its own profile here in the guide). With fewer wines, those that remain are as elegant and stylish as they are rich in flavor. The 2016 Sangiovese is a delight and without a doubt one of the top tastes in this edition of the guide. The cultivar is brought out in a fine, airy red, with masterful texture. It's a linear wine, but warm as well, with youthful tannins rich in flavor. Hats off to them. The 2015 Godenza is aromatically less precise, with tight-knit and slightly sandy tannins.

○ Cuvée Paradiso Brut M. Cl. '14	�♙ 4
⊙ Modena Brut Rosé M. Cl. '14	♙♙ 4
○ Pas Dosé M. Cl. '14	♙ 5
⊙ Modena Brut Rosé M. Cl. '13	♙♙ 4
⊙ Modena Brut Rosé M. Cl. '12	♙♙ 4
○ Pas Dosé '13	♙♙ 5

● Romagna Sangiovese Sup. Il Sangiovese '16	♙♙♙ 3*
● Romagna Sangiovese Sup. Godenza '15	♙♙ 4
● Romagna Sangiovese Sup. Godenza '14	♙♙♙ 3*
● Romagna Sangiovese Sup. Il Sangiovese '14	♙♙♙ 2*
○ Bro '15	♙♙ 3
○ Bro '14	♙♙ 3
● Romagna Sangiovese Sup. '13	♙♙ 2*
● Romagna Sangiovese Sup. Godenza '13	♙♙ 2*
● Romagna Sangiovese Sup. Il Sangiovese '15	♙♙ 2*

Cantine Riunite & Civ

VIA G. BRODOLINI, 24
42040 CAMPEGINE [RE]
TEL. +39 0522905711
www.riuniteciv.com

CELLAR SALES
ANNUAL PRODUCTION 130,000,000 bottles
HECTARES UNDER VINE 3500.00

Is one of the largest cooperatives in the world, bolstered by 2600 members and 3500 hectares of vineyards, and it's the largest in Italy for semi-sparkling wines. Fortunately, Emilia's economic model is making it possible for large producers and smaller, artisanal winemakers to live side-by-side. Moreover, over the years, thanks to the work of general director, Gianni Lusetti, the group has managed to produce a number of outstanding wines (in addition to their war horses). In keeping with the traditions of the territory, these are made according to the old system of second-fermentation in the bottle. Several wines stand out among the winery's rich selection, such as the supple and racy Sorbara Gaetano Righi, the juicy and tasty Grasparossa Codarossa Albinea Canali, and the expressive and very pleasant Salamino di Santa Croce Secco, with its aromas of dark fruit and flowers. Of the bottle-fermented wines, we enjoyed the Senzatempo, a varietal, close-knit and juicy wine made with Salamino.

Colli di Scandiano e di Canossa Lambrusco Grasparossa Amabile Codarossa Albinea Canali '16	♟♟ 1*
Lambrusco di Sorbara Gaetano Righi '16	♟♟ 2*
Lambrusco di Sorbara Semisecco '16	♟♟ 1*
Lambrusco Grasparossa di Castelvetro §Amabile Il Fojonco '16	♟♟ 2*
Lambrusco Grasparossa di Castelvetro Secco Gaetano Righi '16	♟♟ 1*
Lambrusco Salamino di Santa Croce Secco '16	♟♟ 1*
Lambrusco Senzatempo RF '16	♟♟ 1*
Ottocentorosa Extra Dry Rosé Albinea Canali	♟♟ 2*
Lambrusco di Modena Semisecco Vecchio Ducato '16	♟ 1*
Reggiano Lambrusco Cuvée 1950 '16	♟ 1*

Le Rocche Malatestiane

VIA EMILIA, 104
47900 RIMINI
TEL. +39 0541743079
www.lerocchemalatestiane.it

CELLAR SALES
PRE-BOOKED VISITS
ANNUAL PRODUCTION 700,000 bottles
HECTARES UNDER VINE 800.00

From the 13th to the 15th centuries, the Malatesta were a wealthy and powerful family of patrons in Rimini. Today, their name represents this winery, which brings together 500 vines-growers and 800 hectares of land. The vineyards stretch from the high Val Marecchia to the inland territory of Cattolica, to the border between Romagna and Marche. The breakthrough came in 2011, and was the result of development initiatives centered on Sangiovese and other traditional, local grape varieties. The 2016 Sangiovese Superiore Sigismondo is truly surprising, not just for its level, but also, and especially, for its style. It offers up linear and close-focused aromas, which are finely embellished with notes of wild berries, watermelon and orange; the mouth is slow, juicy and fresh. It may not be the pinnacle of complexity, but it's quite well-made and great to drink. And considering its excellent price, it's earned out award for 'Best Value for Money'. The 2016 Superiore I Diavoli is floral, fascinating and rich in nuances.

● Romagna Sangiovese Sup. Sigismondo '16	♟♟♟ 2*
● Romagna Sangiovese Sup. I Diavoli '16	♟♟ 2*
● Romagna Sangiovese Sup. Tre Miracoli '16	♟♟ 2*
● Colli di Rimini Sangiovese Mons Iovis '15	♟♟ 3
● Romagna Sangiovese Il Mastino Ris. '14	♟ 3
● Romagna Sangiovese Sup. I Diavoli '14	♟♟ 2*
● Romagna Sangiovese Sup. I Tre Miracoli '14	♟♟ 3
● Romagna Sangiovese Sup. Tre Miracoli '15	♟♟ 2*
● Romagna Sangiovese Sup. I Diavoli '15	♟♟ 2*
● Romagna Sangiovese Sup. Sigismondo '15	♟♟ 2*

Cantine Romagnoli

Loc. Villò
via Genova, 20
29020 Vigolzone [PC]
Tel. +39 0523870904
www.cantineromagnoli.it

CELLAR SALES
PRE-BOOKED VISITS
ANNUAL PRODUCTION 300,000 bottles
HECTARES UNDER VINE 45.00
SUSTAINABLE WINERY

Cantine Romagnoli goes back to 1857, when it formed part of the Podestà di Morfasso estate (back then it was used for common agriculture and breeding practices). In 1926 it came into the hands of the Romagnoli family, but winemaking at the site only took hold in 1978. The Ferrari and Perini families have been writing the latest chapter in the producer's history, having taken it over in 2012 (at which point they entrusted Luciana Biondo, an enologist from Piedmont, with winemaking). The estate comprises 45 hectares of vineyards, on primarily red terrain in Val Nure, the cradle of Piacenza's viticulture. The 2016 Gutturnio Superiore Colto Vitato della Bellaria has a nice dark ruby color, and offers up aromas of black wild berries and spices. Its tannins are lively and ripe. The 2016 Barbera Colto Vitato del Cicotto has a purplish-red color and features close-focused notes of sour cherries. The 2016 Caravaggio Bianco plays on floral notes, while the Pigro is a 'Metodo Classico' sparkler made with fruity Pinot Nero.

● C. P. Gutturnio Sup. Colto Vitato della Bellaria '16	▼▼ 2*
● Colto Vitato del Cicotto '16	▼▼ 2*
○ Brut M. Cl. Cuvée Il Pigro	▼ 3
○ Caravaggio Bianco '16	▼ 3
● Michelangelo da Caravaggio '16	▼ 5
● Caravaggio '12	♈♈ 5
● Colto Vitato del Cicotto '15	♈♈ 2*
● Colto Vitato del Cicotto '14	♈♈ 2*
● Gutturnio Frizzante Sasso Nero '13	♈♈ 3
● Gutturnio Sup. Colto Vitato della Bellaria '15	♈♈ 2*
○ Ortrugo Frizzante Sasso Nero Tappo a Corona '13	♈♈ 2*
○ Sasso Nero del Nure Bianco '14	♈♈ 2*
○ Sasso Nero del Nure Malvasia '14	♈♈ 2*
● V. del Cicotto Barbera '13	♈♈ 3

I Sabbioni

Loc. Sabbioni
via dei Sabbioni, 22
47121 Forlì
Tel. +39 0543755711
www.isabbioni.it

CELLAR SALES
ANNUAL PRODUCTION 46,000 bottles
HECTARES UNDER VINE 15.00

I Sabbioni boasts 15 hectares of vineyards in the provinces of Forlì and Faenza. The terrain here features mid-sized slopes, with medium-textured soil characterized by red clay and yellow sand (called 'molasse' by the locals). It's the latter that gives the area and winery, its name ('sabbia' means 'sand'). Their selection is completely dedicated to Sangiovese, which gives rise to a number of different wines and wine types. One of the best tastes of the year is the 2016 Romagna Sangiovese Oriolo. It's a direct, forthright, sanguine, floral and fruity red. The palate is linear, sometimes edgy, but shows great determination and a clear style. We enjoyed it thoroughly. The 2014 Sangiovese Superiore Riserva I Rifiugi is good but not too evolved, slightly blurred and quite spicy.

● Romagna Sangiovese Sup. Oriolo '16	▼▼▼
● Romagna Sangiovese Sup. I Rifugi Ris. '14	▼▼
● Romagna Sangiovese Sup. I Voli dei Gruccioni '16	▼▼
● Romagna Sangiovese Rubrarosa Oriolo Sisto '14	♈♈
● Romagna Sangiovese Sup. Rubrarosa Bonadea '15	♈♈
● Romagna Sangiovese Sup. Rubrarosa Bonadea '14	♈♈
● Romagna Sangiovese Sup. Rubrarosa Elaide Ris. '13	♈♈

★San Patrignano

A San Patrignano, 53
47853 Coriano [RN]
Tel. +39 0541362111
www.spaziosanpa.com

PRE-BOOKED VISITS
RESTAURANT SERVICE
ANNUAL PRODUCTION 500,000 bottles
HECTARES UNDER VINE 110.00
VITICULTURE METHOD Certified Organic

San Patrignano is an acclaimed winery that belongs to, and bears the name of, the drug support center founded by Vincenzo Muccioli in 1978. Situated on the Colli di Rimini hills, the estate features exceptional vineyards spanning some 110 hectares. Enological management is precise and clearly styled, with the estate's grapes giving rise to modern wines. Their Bordeaux grows in an ideal climate, while Sangiovese's trademark edges get softened here, giving way to extractive density and roundness. This year, the top wine in the selection is the 2013 Colli di Rimini Cabernet Sauvignon Montepirolo. It's a dark and concentrated wine, dominated by intense, toasty aromas of black fruit and grass. The mouth follows along the same lines, finding density, body and an assertive tannic texture. As for the whites, it's worth noting the 2016 Aulente, a blend of Chardonnay and Sauvignon with intense aromas.

Cantina Sociale Santa Croce

Fraz. Santa Croce
s.da st.le 468 di Correggio, 35
41012 Carpi [MO]
Tel. +39 059664007
www.cantinasantacroce.it

CELLAR SALES
ANNUAL PRODUCTION 400,000 bottles
HECTARES UNDER VINE 600.00

This cooperative winery got its start in 1907, in the very territory from which Lambrusco Salamino got its name, Santa Croce di Carpi. Even if the physical site of the winery has undergone renovations, it hasn't moved in 110 years. 250 members dedicate themselves primarily to Salamino di Santa Croce, obviously, then to Grasparossa di Castelvetro, Sorbara and Ancellotta. The grapes cultivated on the area's flat, clay terrain are then interpreted by Maurizio Boni, who manages to create authentic, vigorous Salamino that's closely tied to the territory. The Tradizione offers up fresh contrasts of herbs that emerge from a background of ripe red fruit. The mouth proves taut, mineral, close-knit and solid. The basic version is also very pleasant, with aromas of flowers and citrus fruit anticipating a fresh and close-focused palate. The Castello Secco is simpler, but just as enjoyable.

Colli di Rimini Cabernet Sauvignon Montepirolo '13	▼▼▼ 4*
Aulente Bianco '16	▼▼ 2*
Noi '15	▼▼ 3
Romagna Sangiovese Sup. Avi Ris. '14	▼ 4
Colli di Rimini Cabernet Montepirolo '06	♈♈♈ 5
Colli di Rimini Cabernet Montepirolo '04	♈♈♈ 5
Colli di Rimini Cabernet Sauvignon Montepirolo '12	♈♈♈ 4*
Romagna Sangiovese Sup. Avi Ris. '11	♈♈♈ 5
Sangiovese di Romagna Sup. Avi Ris. '08	♈♈♈ 5
Sangiovese di Romagna Sup. Avi Ris. '07	♈♈♈ 5
Sangiovese di Romagna Sup. Avi Ris. '06	♈♈♈ 5
Sangiovese di Romagna Sup. Avi Ris. '05	♈♈♈ 5
Sangiovese di Romagna Sup. Ora '12	♈♈♈ 3*
Sangiovese di Romagna Sup. Ora '11	♈♈♈ 3*

● Il Castello Lambrusco Secco '16	▼▼ 1*
● Lambrusco Salamino di Santa Croce Secco '16	▼▼ 1*
● Lambrusco Salamino di Santa Croce Secco Tradizione '16	▼▼ 1*
☉ 100 Vendemmie Brut Rosé	▼ 2
● Lambrusco di Sorbara '16	▼ 1*
● Lambrusco Salamino di Santa Croce Amabile '16	▼ 1*
● Lancellotta dell'Emilia Filtrato Dolce '16	▼ 1*
● Lambrusco Salamino di S. Croce Secco Linea '15	♈♈ 1*
● Lambrusco Salamino di S. Croce Tradizione '15	♈♈ 1*
● Lambrusco Salamino di S. Croce Tradizione '14	♈♈ 1*

Tenuta Santini

FRAZ. PASSANO
VIA CAMPO, 33
47853 CORIANO [RN]
TEL. +39 0541656527
www.tenutasantini.com

CELLAR SALES
PRE-BOOKED VISITS
ANNUAL PRODUCTION 40,000 bottles
HECTARES UNDER VINE 22.00

Tenuta Santini was founded in the 1960s by brothers Giuseppe and Primo. The estate is situated between San Marino and Val Marecchia, on the gentle, open Coriano hills lying behind Rimini and Riccione. Here, the calcareous clay terrain and mild climate have led to people calling it the 'Adriatic Bolgheri',connecting it with the renowned Tuscan terroir. And so it's an area well-suited to Bordeaux, through they've steadfastly cultivated Sangiovese for their wines as well. Let's start with the 2016 Sangiovese Superiore. It's a wine with lovely fruity aromas and a juicy palate, closed by clear tannins that are slightly bitter, but full-flavored. The 2015 Battarreo is a blend of Sangiovese, Cabernet and Merlot that ages in barriques. Its aromas are dark and toasty, the palate is solid, though not very dynamic.

La Stoppa

LOC. ANCARANO
29029 RIVERGARO [PC]
TEL. +39 0523958159
www.lastoppa.it

CELLAR SALES
PRE-BOOKED VISITS
RESTAURANT SERVICE
ANNUAL PRODUCTION 160,000 bottles
HECTARES UNDER VINE 32.00
VITICULTURE METHOD Certified Organic

The history of La Stoppa goes back many years, when it was founded in the early 20th century by the Genoese lawyer, Ageno, who planted French vineyards here In 1973, it was purchased by the Pantaleoni family, though many chapters o history have been written in recent years, especially since Elena Pantaleoni and Giuli Armani decided to convert the estate entirely to organic, giving their wines a ver different character. The old French vineyards coexist with Val Trebbia's traditional varieties, giving rise to wines with a strong identity. They aren't always approachable. These are wines that need t breathe at length before revealing all their multifaceted charm. In any case, a clean nose is not their strong point. The Trebbiol is a blend of Barbera and Bonarda, with good pulp and a dynamic flavor that works with a certain rusticity. The same goes for the Vigna del Volta, a sweet wine made with Malvasia di Candia.

● Battarreo '15	♀♀ 3
● Romagna Sangiovese Sup. Beato Enrico '16	♀♀ 2*
● Battarreo '14	♀♀ 3*
● Romagna Sangiovese Sup. Beato Enrico '15	♀♀ 2*
● Romagna Sangiovese Sup. Cornelianum Ris. '13	♀♀ 4
● Sangiovese di Romagna Sup. Beato Enrico '11	♀♀ 2*
● Sangiovese di Romagna Sup. Cornelianum Ris. '12	♀♀ 4
● Sangiovese di Romagna Sup. Cornelianum Ris. '10	♀♀ 4
● Sangiovese di Romagna Sup. Cornelianum Ris. '09	♀♀ 4

● Trebbiolo Rosso Fermo '15	♀♀ 3
○ Vigna del Volta	♀♀ 5
○ Ageno '12	♀ 4
● C. P. Cabernet Sauvignon Stoppa '96	♀♀♀ 5
○ C. P. Malvasia Passito V. del Volta '06	♀♀♀ 5
○ C. P. Malvasia Passito V. del Volta '04	♀♀♀ 5
○ C. P. Malvasia Passito V. del Volta '03	♀♀♀ 5
○ C. P. Malvasia Passito V. del Volta '97	♀♀♀ 5
● Macchiona '06	♀♀♀ 5
● Macchiona '05	♀♀♀ 5
○ Vigna del Volta '08	♀♀♀ 5
○ Ageno '10	♀♀ 4
● Barbera della Stoppa '10	♀♀ 4
● Macchiona '11	♀♀ 4
● Trebbiolo Rosso Fermo '14	♀♀ 2

Torre San Martino

VIA SAN MARTINO IN MONTE
47015 MODIGLIANA [FC]
TEL. +39 0689786312
www.torre1922.co

CELLAR SALES
PRE-BOOKED VISITS
ANNUAL PRODUCTION 45,000 bottles
HECTARES UNDER VINE 10.00

This estate boasts having the oldest vineyard in Romagna, dated 1922. It's found in Modigliana, an area noted for its full-flavored, fine and extremely long-lived wines. To be specific, the winery is found in the Acerreta Valley, one of the three on the Apennines, an area characterized by a larger share of clay than the others. Even if their wines are marked by the classic finesse of the district, they lack nothing in terms of matière, density and support. The Sangiovese Riserva Vigna 1922 is made with grapes cultivated on their old vineyard. It features aromas ranging from pomegranate to freshly-picked red fruit, while the mouth has a hardness that's well-sustained by flavor and aromatic consistency. It's a wine that needs to evolve in the bottle to find more balance.

● Romagna Sangiovese Sup. V. 1922 Ris. '14	▼▼ 5
● Colli di Faenza V. Claudia '15	▼ 3
● Romagna Sangiovese Modigliana Sup. V. 1922 Ris. '13	▼▼▼ 6
● Romagna Sangiovese Sup. Gemme '14	▼▼▼ 3*
● Sangiovese di Romagna V. 1922 Ris. '11	▼▼▼ 6
● Colli di Faenza V. Claudia Ris. '13	♀♀ 3
● Colli di Faenza V. Claudia Ris. '12	♀♀ 3
○ Colli di Faenza V. della Signora '13	♀♀ 2*
● Romagna Sangiovese Sup. V. 1922 Ris. '12	♀♀ 6
● Romagna Sangiovese Modigliana Sup. Gemme '15	♀♀ 3*

La Tosa

LOC. LA TOSA
29020 VIGOLZONE [PC]
TEL. +39 0523870727
www.latosa.it

CELLAR SALES
PRE-BOOKED VISITS
ANNUAL PRODUCTION 120,000 bottles
HECTARES UNDER VINE 19.00

Stefano and Ferruccio Pizzamiglio may have been born in Milan, but their hearts are in the hills of Piacenza, thanks to their mother (a native of Vigolzone). Bolstered by their 19 hectares of naturally-grown vineyards and a great passion for their work, they've come a long way since 1985, with the winery establishing itself as one a leader in the area. The 2015 Vignamorello is an intense, fragrant and meaty Gutturnio Superiore. It's already solid, but its wood could integrate further, thus its evolution should be watched closely. The 2016 Riodeltordo is a floral white with marked notes of peach that brings together the aromas of Malvasia di Candia and the minerality of Ortrugo. The 2016 TerredellaTosa is a simpler Gutturnio, approachable, fresh, with sweet tannins and a fragrant, enticing nose. The same holds of the 2015 Cabernet Luna Selvatica as for the Vignamorello: pulp, fruit, varietal vegetal notes and new wood have yet to be absorbed and integrated. The 2016 Sauvignon is very varietal and supple, with good aromatic intensity.

● C. P. Gutturnio Sup. TerredellaTosa '16	▼▼ 2*
● C. P. Gutturnio Sup. Vignamorello '15	▼▼ 4
○ C. P. Valnure Riodeltordo '16	▼▼ 2*
● C. P. Cabernet Sauvignon Luna Selvatica '15	▼ 5
○ C. P. Sauvignon '16	▼ 3
● C. P. Gutturnio Sup. TerredellaTosa '12	♀♀ 2*
● C. P. Gutturnio Sup. Vignamorello '11	♀♀ 4

Marta Valpiani

LOC. CASTROCARO TERME
VIA BAGNOLO, 156/158
47011 FORLÌ
TEL. +39 0543769598
www.vinimartavalpiani.it

CELLAR SALES
PRE-BOOKED VISITS
ANNUAL PRODUCTION 19,000 bottles
HECTARES UNDER VINE 11.50

In Marta Valpiani, we have one of the region's most interesting headlines. The producer's wines impressed us for their purity, balance, innate polish and capacity to forge a style as elegant as it is contemporary. The winery, which got its start in 1999 in Castrocaro Terme, bears the name of its founder, who today is flanked by her daughter, Elisa. They only have a few hectares of vineyards at their disposal, but as we've mentioned, the selection is excellent. It's not hard to imagine a bright future for them The 2015 Sangiovese Crete Azzurre is scintillating. It's slightly closed, but gradually frees itself in the glass to reveal its lovely and pure character. Everything focuses on delicate fragrances, with notes of fresh flowers, small wild berries, orange and licorice. All of this comes through on a linear, juicy and pervasive palate, but one that's also welcoming and tasty. It's a great example of quality and style for this type of wine.

● Romagna Sangiovese Castrocaro e Terra del Sole Crete Azzurre '15	▼▼▼ 3*
● Romagna Sangiovese Sup. '15	▼▼ 2*
○ Bianco '16	▼ 3
○ Bianco '15	♈♈ 2*
● Castrum Castrocari Et. Bianca '11	♈♈ 2*
● Marta Valpiani '12	♈♈ 2*
● Romagna Sangiovese Sup. '14	♈♈ 2*

Venturini Baldini

FRAZ. RONCOLO
VIA TURATI, 42
42020 QUATTRO CASTELLA [RE]
TEL. +39 0522249011
www.venturinibaldini.it

CELLAR SALES
PRE-BOOKED VISITS
RESTAURANT SERVICE
ANNUAL PRODUCTION 90,000 bottles
HECTARES UNDER VINE 35.00
VITICULTURE METHOD Certified Organic

Active since 1975, Venturini Baldini is situated on Roncolo hill, in the territory of Quattro Castella. The estate comprises 150 hectares of terrain, including prairies and woods, with more than 35 hectares dedicated to organically cultivated vineyards. For some years now, the property has been part of an important investment project led by Luxembourg's Iverna Holdings, which believes in the commercial potential of Reggio Emilia and Lambrusco. The results weren't long coming. The first Tre Bicchieri for the winery goes to the Marchese Manodori, a Reggiano Lambrusco. It offers up a striking range of close-focused aromas playing on sour cherries, strawberries and violets and a close-knit, solid and slightly tannic mouth that adds nuances to the palate. The Rubino del Cerro Brut was also very impressive, coming through taut, tangy and fresh, with a slightly citrusy finish in the mouth. The fragrant and full-bodied Quaranta Extra Brut also proved outstanding.

● Reggiano Lambrusco Secco Marchese Manodori '16	▼▼▼ 3*
● Reggiano Lambrusco Spumante Brut Rubino del Cerro	▼▼ 3
● Reggiano Lambrusco Spumante Extra Brut Quaranta	▼▼ 3
○ Colli di Scandiano e di Canossa Malvasia Graniers '16	▼ 2
⊙ Reggiano Lambrusco Rosato Spumante Secco Cadelvento '15	♈♈ 3
● Reggiano Lambrusco Secco '14	♈♈ 2*
● Reggiano Lambrusco Secco Marchese Manodori '15	♈♈ 3*
● Reggiano Lambrusco Secco Spumante Rubino del Cerro '15	♈♈ 3

Francesco Vezzelli

FRAZ. SAN MATTEO
VIA CANALETTO NORD, 878A
41122 MODENA
TEL. +39 059318695
aavezzelli@gmail.com

CELLAR SALES
PRE-BOOKED VISITS
ANNUAL PRODUCTION 120,000 bottles
HECTARES UNDER VINE 15.00

This small producer has been operating since 1958, and is now on its third generation of leaders. The estate is defined by the position of its vineyards, situated along the left bank of the Secchia river, in the municipality of Soliera (just opposite Cristo di Sorbara). These are wet plains, perfect for Sorbara, which offers up its best here, giving rise to linear, mineral, taut wines that have little in common with softer, more endearing Lambruscos. The winery also produces Lambrusco Grasparossa with grapes bought right in Castelvetro. The 2016 version of the Rive dei Ciliegi calls up sour and ripe cherries, with a slightly tannic but juicy mouth. As for the Sorbaras, we enjoyed the Soldino, which is simple, linear, dry and taut, as only a Sorbara can be. The Sorbara Brut II Selezione is slightly subdued compared to other versions.

- Lambrusco di Sorbara Soldino '16 ▼▼ 2*
- Lambrusco Grasparossa di Castelvetro Secco Rive dei Ciliegi '16 ▼▼ 2*
- Lambrusco di Sorbara Spumante Brut II Selezione ▼ 2
- Lambrusco di Sorbara II Selezione '15 ♈ 2*
- Lambrusco di Sorbara Rifermentazione Ancestrale '14 ♈ 2*
- Lambrusco di Sorbara Secco Soldino '15 ♈ 2*
- Lambrusco di Sorbara Spumante Brut MoRosa Rosé '15 ♈ 2*
- Lambrusco Grasparossa di Castelvetro Rive dei Ciliegi '14 ♈ 2*

Villa di Corlo

LOC. BAGGIOVARA
S.DA CAVEZZO, 200
41126 MODENA
TEL. +39 059510736
www.villadicorlo.com

CELLAR SALES
PRE-BOOKED VISITS
ANNUAL PRODUCTION 85,000 bottles
HECTARES UNDER VINE 26.50

Maria Antonietta Munari's winery is just outside Modena, to the southeast of the city, and comprises terrain that's best-suited to Lambrusco Grasparossa. However, on the hillside, with exposure towards the south-southeast, Cabernet Sauvignon, Merlot and Chardonnay are cultivated at 300 meters above sea level, with the last of these giving rise to a 'Metodo Classico' sparkling wine. As is tradition in Modena, the loft of the villa hosts a vinegar cellar, which features an excellent Aceto Balsamico Tradizionale (among others). The 2016 Corleto did quite well, with an expressive nose that offers up ripe strawberries and flowers, and a succulent mouth that's slightly contrasted by a veil of tannins. The Grasparossa Secco also proves very pleasant, with fresh and multifaceted aromas that range from dark flowers to citrus fruit, and a palate that's dry and dynamic. The Sorbara Primevo has a distinctive driving and vibrant acidity.

- Lambrusco Grasparossa di Castelvetro '16 ▼▼ 2*
- Lambrusco Grasparossa di Castelvetro Corleto '16 ▼▼ 2*
- ⊙ Lambrusco di Sorbara Brut Rosé Elettra FB ▼ 3
- Lambrusco di Sorbara Primevo '16 ▼ 2
- ⊙ Lambrusco Grasparossa di Castelvetro Brut Rosé Rosanto ▼ 2
- Lambrusco di Sorbara Primevo '14 ♈ 2*
- Lambrusco Grasparossa di Castelvetro Amabile '13 ♈ 2*
- Lambrusco Grasparossa di Castelvetro Corleto '15 ♈ 2*
- Lambrusco Grasparossa di Castelvetro Corleto '13 ♈ 2*

EMILIA ROMAGNA

Villa Papiano

VIA IBOLA, 24
47015 MODIGLIANA [FC]
TEL. +39 3381041271
www.villapapiano.it

CELLAR SALES
PRE-BOOKED VISITS
ANNUAL PRODUCTION 50,000 bottles
HECTARES UNDER VINE 10.00
VITICULTURE METHOD Certified Organic
SUSTAINABLE WINERY

Villa Papiano does a masterful job interpreting the territory of Modigliana. The estate is situated on the south side of Monte Chioda, where the soil is characterized by marl sandstone, and boasts some of the highest plots in the region (at 450 meters). These characteristics are well-developed by the winery, which manages to produce fine, flavorful, complex wines that are capable of enduring over time. The 2014 Sangiovese Riserva I Probi di Papiano is a scintillating wine. Bottle maturation allows its toasty hints (bark and pencil lead) to come together perfectly with fruit, thus releasing the grape's aromas and flavor. There is no lack of dynamism or purity in the mouth, and the vibrations are decidedly positive. It's one of the region's best.

Villa Venti

LOC. VILLAVENTI DI RONCOFREDDO
VIA DOCCIA, 1442
47020 FORLÌ
TEL. +39 0541949532
www.villaventi.it

CELLAR SALES
PRE-BOOKED VISITS
ACCOMMODATION
ANNUAL PRODUCTION 27,500 bottles
HECTARES UNDER VINE 7.00
VITICULTURE METHOD Certified Organic

Thanks in part to a seasoned set of vineyards, Villa Venti is a veritable benchmark for Romagna's wine. This holds true for the winery's doubted quality, obviously, but also for its production philosophy and the stylistic characteristics of its wines. Mauro Giardini and Davide Castellucci deserve the credit; they're proving themselves increasingly capable of producing authentic, artisanal wines that impeccably reflect and represent the territory. The 2015 Primo Segno is an intriguing red. Captivating, fruity aromas are enriched by an iodine (almost marine) background and enriched by light wafts of fine spices. The mouth is juicy and flavorsome, proving easy to drink without losing complexity. T 2016 Centesimino A, which is fermented in Georgian amphorae, is just as good. It features forthright aromas of red fruit and a supple and spicy mouth.

● Romagna Sangiovese Modigliana I Probi di Papiano Ris. '14	♟♟♟ 4*
○ Le Tresche di Papiano '16	♟♟ 3
● Romagna Sangiovese Sup. Le Papesse di Papiano '16	♟♟ 3
○ Tregenda VT '15	♟ 4
● Romagna Sangiovese I Probi di Papiano Ris. '12	♟♟♟ 3*
● Romagna Sangiovese Modigliana I Probi di Papiano Ris. '13	♟♟♟ 3*
● Sangiovese di Romagna I Probi di Papiano Ris. '11	♟♟♟ 3*
● Sangiovese di Romagna I Probi di Papiano Ris. '10	♟♟♟ 3*

● Centesimino A '16	♟♟ 4
● Sangiovese di Romagna Sup. Primo Segno '15	♟♟ 3
● Sangiovese di Romagna Longiano Primo Segno '11	♟♟♟ 3*
● Sangiovese di Romagna Sup. Primo Segno '09	♟♟♟ 3*
● Sangiovese di Romagna Sup. Primo Segno '08	♟♟♟ 3*
● Romagna Sangiovese Longiano Ris. '12	♟♟ 4
● Sangiovese di Romagna Longiano Ris '11	♟♟ 4
● Sangiovese di Romagna Sup. Primo Segno '13	♟♟ 3*
● Sangiovese di Romagna Sup. Primo Segno '12	♟♟ 3

★Fattoria Zerbina

FRAZ. MARZENO
VIA VICCHIO, 11
48018 FAENZA [RA]
TEL. +39 054640022
www.zerbina.com

CELLAR SALES
PRE-BOOKED VISITS
ANNUAL PRODUCTION 220,000 bottles
HECTARES UNDER VINE 33.00

Cristina Geminiani and her partners have designed, managed and developed one of the region's most important and historic producers. Even their vineyards (many of which are head-trained and grow in Marzeno's customary red clay soil) have reached a certain maturity, giving rise to balanced grapes and wines with a solid, full-flavored backbone. In the cellar, they show precision and knowledge, both for their reds (like Sangiovese) and their wines made with Albana. The sweet version made with this native grape continues to prove outstanding. The 2013 Albana Passito Scacco Matto is simply wonderful. It's bright and lustrous with a golden color, while its aromas are fresh and mature at the same time. Full of contrasts and changes in pace, the wine could stand shoulder-to-shoulder with a top-level Sauternes. After some time, an intriguing note of saffron emerges, while the mouth proves vibrant and quite deep, drawn by a delightful acidity and just the right amount of sweetness.

○ Romagna Albana Passito Scacco Matto '13		♛♛♛ 6
○ Romagna Albana Passito Arrocco '15		♛♛ 5
● Il 500 '16		♛ 2
● Romagna Sangiovese Marzeno Pietramora Ris. '13		♛ 5
⊙ Rosa di Ceparano '16		♛ 2
○ Albana di Romagna Passito AR Ris. '06		♛♛♛ 8
● Marzieno '08		♛♛♛ 4*
● Marzieno '04		♛♛♛ 5
● Marzieno '03		♛♛♛ 5
● Sangiovese di Romagna Sup. Pietramora Ris. '11		♛♛♛ 5
● Sangiovese di Romagna Sup. Pietramora Ris. '08		♛♛♛ 6
● Sangiovese di Romagna Sup. Pietramora Ris. '06		♛♛♛ 6

Zucchi

LOC. SAN LORENZO
VIA VIAZZA, 64
41030 SAN PROSPERO [MO]
TEL. +39 059908934
www.vinizucchi.it

CELLAR SALES
PRE-BOOKED VISITS
ANNUAL PRODUCTION 130,000 bottles
HECTARES UNDER VINE 10.00
SUSTAINABLE WINERY

In the 1950s, Bruno Zucchi began making wine with grapes from his property in San Prospero, one of Sorbara's choice districts. He handed down this passion to his son, Davide, who leads the winery today, along with his wife, Maura. Their daughter, Silvia (the third generation of family), is giving the winery an added push, having graduated in enology in Conegliano, and bolstered by experiences both in Italy and abroad. The producer, which brings together technology and tradition, gives rise to dry, austere wines with a strong personality, and marked territorial identity. The Rito exhibits classic, pure features. It's a lean, angular wine, marked by acidity and richness of flavor. In the 2016 version, these qualities were taken to the extreme, maybe at the expense of flavor. The Marascone is very impressive. Made with 100% Salamino, it's a grapey wine with wafts of small ripe black fruit. In the mouth it proves creamy and well-paced.

● Lambrusco di Modena Marascone '16	♛♛ 2*
● Lambrusco di Sorbara Rito '16	♛♛ 3
● Lambrusco di Sorbara Secco '16	♛ 2
● Lambrusco di Sorbara Rito '14	♛♛♛ 2*
● Lambrusco di Sorbara Secco Rito '15	♛♛♛ 2*
● Lambrusco di Sorbara Dosaggio Zero M. Cl. '13	♛♛ 2*
● Lambrusco di Sorbara Secco '15	♛♛ 2*
● Lambrusco di Sorbara Secco '14	♛♛ 2*
● Lambrusco di Sorbara Secco Rifermentazione in Bottiglia '14	♛♛ 2*
● Modena Lambrusco Marascone '14	♛♛ 2*

Tenuta Bonzara

loc. Sanchierlo
via Sanchierlo, 37a
40050 Monte San Pietro [BO]
Tel. +39 0516768324
www.bonzara.it

CELLAR SALES
PRE-BOOKED VISITS
ACCOMMODATION AND RESTAURANT SERVICE
ANNUAL PRODUCTION 70,000 bottles
HECTARES UNDER VINE 15.00

● #1.0 Negretto '14	🏆🏆 2*
● C. B. Cabernet Sauvignon Bonzarone '14	🏆 5
○ C. B. Pignoletto Frizzante Bonzarino '16	🏆 2

Ca' di Sopra

loc. Marzeno
via Feligara, 15
48013 Brisighella [RA]
Tel. +39 3284927073
www.cadisopra.com

CELLAR SALES
PRE-BOOKED VISITS
ANNUAL PRODUCTION 30,000 bottles
HECTARES UNDER VINE 28.00
SUSTAINABLE WINERY

● Romagna Sangiovese Marzeno '15	🏆🏆 3
● Romagna Sangiovese Sup. Crepe '16	🏆 2

Tenuta Casali

via della Liberazione, 32
47025 Mercato Saraceno [FC]
Tel. +39 0547690334
www.tenutacasali.it

PRE-BOOKED VISITS
HECTARES UNDER VINE 18.00

● Romagna Sangiovese Sup. Baruccia '15	🏆🏆 3*
○ Romagna Albana Secco Valleripa '16	🏆🏆 3
○ Famoso '16	🏆 3

Castelluccio

loc. Poggiolo di Sotto
via Tramonto, 15
47015 Modigliana [FC]
Tel. +39 0546942486
www.ronchidicastelluccio.it

CELLAR SALES
PRE-BOOKED VISITS
ACCOMMODATION
ANNUAL PRODUCTION 85,000 bottles
HECTARES UNDER VINE 16.00

● Romagna Sangiovese Sup. Le More '16	🏆🏆 3

Floriano Cinti

fraz. San Lorenzo
via Gamberi, 48
40037 Sasso Marconi [BO]
Tel. +39 0516751646
www.collibolognesi.com

CELLAR SALES
PRE-BOOKED VISITS
ANNUAL PRODUCTION 95,000 bottles
HECTARES UNDER VINE 24.00

● C.B. Cabernet '15	🏆🏆 2*
● C. B. Barbera '15	🏆 2
● C. B. Cabernet Sauvignon Sassobacco '15	🏆 3
○ C. B. Pignoletto Cl. Sassobacco '15	🏆 2

Podere La Collina

via Paglia, 19
48013 Brisighella [RA]
Tel. +39 054681095
www.poderelacollina.com

CELLAR SALES
PRE-BOOKED VISITS
ANNUAL PRODUCTION 20,000 bottles
HECTARES UNDER VINE 5.00

● Alya '14	🏆🏆 8
● Carranca '14	🏆 6

Condé

LOC. FILIMANA DI PREDAPPIO
VIA LUCCHINA, 27
47016 PREDAPPIO [FC]
TEL. +39 0543940860
www.conde.it

CELLAR SALES
PRE-BOOKED VISITS
ACCOMMODATION AND RESTAURANT SERVICE
ANNUAL PRODUCTION 150,000 bottles
HECTARES UNDER VINE 77.00
SUSTAINABLE WINERY

● Romagna Sangiovese Predappio Ris. '13 ♥♥ 6

Leone Conti

FRAZ. SANTA LUCIA
VIA POZZO, 1
48018 FAENZA [RA]
TEL. +39 0546642149
www.leoneconti.it

CELLAR SALES
PRE-BOOKED VISITS
ANNUAL PRODUCTION 80,000 bottles
HECTARES UNDER VINE 17.00

○ Romagna Albana Secco
La mia Albana Progetto 1 '16 ♥♥ 3

Drei Donà Tenuta La Palazza

LOC. MASSA DI VECCHIAZZANO
VIA DEL TESORO, 23
47121 FORLÌ
TEL. +39 0543769371
www.dreidona.it

CELLAR SALES
PRE-BOOKED VISITS
ANNUAL PRODUCTION 130,000 bottles
HECTARES UNDER VINE 27.00
SUSTAINABLE WINERY

● Le Vigne Nuove '16 ♥ 2
● Romagna Sangiovese Sup. Notturno '15 ♥ 3

La Ferraia - Manara

LOC. VICOMARINO, 140
29010 ZIANO PIACENTINO [PC]
TEL. +39 0523860209
www.robertomanara.it

CELLAR SALES
PRE-BOOKED VISITS
ANNUAL PRODUCTION 130,000 bottles
HECTARES UNDER VINE 40.00

● C.P. Gutturnio Cl. Sup Le Staffe '15 ♥♥ 2*
⊙ Abrakadabra Brut Rosé ♥ 2
○ C.P. Sauvignon Il Grì '16 ♥ 3

Fondo Cà Vecja

LOC. PONTICELLI
VIA MONTANARA, 333
40020 IMOLA [BO]
TEL. +39 0542665194
www.fondocavecja.com

CELLAR SALES
PRE-BOOKED VISITS
ACCOMMODATION
ANNUAL PRODUCTION 40,000 bottles
HECTARES UNDER VINE 19.00
SUSTAINABLE WINERY

○ Rubicone Due Pievi Manzoni Bianco '16 ♥♥ 2*
○ Colli di Imola Pignoletto Frizzante
Le Bornici '16 ♥ 2
○ Rubicone Colvento Sauvignon '16 ♥ 3

Maria Letizia Gaggioli

VIA F. RAIBOLINI IL FRANCIA, 55
40069 ZOLA PREDOSA [BO]
TEL. +39 051753489
www.gaggiolivini.it

CELLAR SALES
PRE-BOOKED VISITS
ACCOMMODATION AND RESTAURANT SERVICE
ANNUAL PRODUCTION 160,000 bottles
HECTARES UNDER VINE 21.00
SUSTAINABLE WINERY

● C.B. Merlot '15 ♥♥ 3
● C. B. Cabernet Sauvignon '14 ♥ 3
○ C. B. Pignoletto Frizzante '16 ♥ 2
● C.B. Rosso Bologna '15 ♥ 3

Maria Galassi

LOC. PADERNO DI CESENA
VIA CASETTA, 688
47023 CESENA [FC]
TEL. +39 054721177
www.galassimaria.it

CELLAR SALES
PRE-BOOKED VISITS
ANNUAL PRODUCTION 18,000 bottles
HECTARES UNDER VINE 18.00
VITICULTURE METHOD Certified Organic

● Romagna Sangiovese Sup. Paternus '15	♟♟ 3
○ Fiaba '16	♟ 3

Gallegati

VIA LUGO, 182
48018 FAENZA [RA]
TEL. +39 0546621149
www.aziendaagricolagallegati.it

CELLAR SALES
PRE-BOOKED VISITS
ACCOMMODATION
ANNUAL PRODUCTION 15,000 bottles
HECTARES UNDER VINE 6.00

○ Colli di Faenza Corallo Bianco '16	♟ 3
○ Romagna Albana Secco Corallo Giallo '16	♟ 3
● Romagna Sangiovese Brisighella Corallo Rosso '15	♟ 2

Gavioli

VIA PROVINCIALE OVEST
41015 NONANTOLA [MO]
TEL. +39 059545462
www.gaviolivini.com

CELLAR SALES
PRE-BOOKED VISITS
ANNUAL PRODUCTION 250,000 bottles
HECTARES UNDER VINE 60.00

● Lambrusco di Sorbara Secco '16	♟♟ 2*
● Lambrusco Emilia Pas Dosé M. Cl. '13	♟ 4
● Modena Lambrusco Rifermentazione Ancestrale '16	♟ 3

Giacobazzi

V.LE CARLO SIGONIO, 50
41124 MODENA
TEL. +39 059222014
www.giacobazzivini.it

CELLAR SALES
PRE-BOOKED VISITS
ANNUAL PRODUCTION 1,200,000 bottles
HECTARES UNDER VINE 70.00

● Lambrusco di Sorbara Secco '16	♟♟ 2*
○ Pignoletto 9 Brut	♟ 2

Gualdora

FRAZ. MONTALBO
LOC. CASE GUALDORA, 196
29010 ZIANO PIACENTINO [PC]
TEL. +39 3923902160
www.gualdora.it

CELLAR SALES
PRE-BOOKED VISITS
ACCOMMODATION
ANNUAL PRODUCTION 12,000 bottles
HECTARES UNDER VINE 3.00
VITICULTURE METHOD Certified Organic
SUSTAINABLE WINERY

● C. P. Gutturnio Sup. Otto '15	♟♟ 2*
○ Dal Tramonto all'Alba Brut M.Cl.	♟ 3
● Na' de Na' '15	♟ 3

Conti Guarini Matteucci

FRAZ. SAN TOMÉ
VIA MINARDA, 2
47122 FORLÌ
TEL. +39 0543476147
www.viniguarini.it

CELLAR SALES
PRE-BOOKED VISITS
ACCOMMODATION
ANNUAL PRODUCTION 40,000 bottles
HECTARES UNDER VINE 15.00
SUSTAINABLE WINERY

● Romagna Sangiovese Sup. Mero Ris. '13	♟♟ 3
● Romagna Sangiovese Sup. Rubbio '16	♟♟ 2*
● Romagna Sangiovese '15	♟ 2

Manicardi

VIA MASSARONI, 1
41014 CASTELVETRO DI MODENA [MO]
TEL. +39 059799000
www.manicardi.it

CELLAR SALES
PRE-BOOKED VISITS
ANNUAL PRODUCTION 100,000 bottles
HECTARES UNDER VINE 16.90

● Ruby Laury '16	🍷🍷 3
● Lambrusco Grasparossa di Castelvetro Enzo '16	🍷 2
○ Pignoletto Frizzante '16	🍷 2

Tenuta Mara

VIA CA' BACCHINO, 1665
47832 SAN CLEMENTE [RN]
TEL. +39 0541988870
www.tenutamara.com

CELLAR SALES
PRE-BOOKED VISITS
ANNUAL PRODUCTION 20,000 bottles
HECTARES UNDER VINE 6.50
VITICULTURE METHOD Certified Organic

● Maramia Sangiovese '15	🍷🍷 7

Tenuta Masselina

LOC. SERRÀ
VIA POZZE, 1030
48014 CASTEL BOLOGNESE [RA]
TEL. +39 0545284711
www.masselina.it

ACCOMMODATION
ANNUAL PRODUCTION 50,000 bottles
HECTARES UNDER VINE 16.00

● Romagna Sangiovese Sup. 138 '16	🍷🍷 2*

Opera 02 di Ca' Montanari

FRAZ. LEVIZZANO RANGONE
VIA MEDUSIA, 32
41014 CASTELVETRO DI MODENA [MO]
TEL. +39 059741019
www.opera02.it

CELLAR SALES
PRE-BOOKED VISITS
ACCOMMODATION AND RESTAURANT SERVICE
ANNUAL PRODUCTION 75,000 bottles
HECTARES UNDER VINE 20.00
VITICULTURE METHOD Certified Organic
SUSTAINABLE WINERY

● Lambrusco di Modena '16	🍷🍷 2*
● Lambrusco di Modena Amabile '16	🍷 2
● Lambrusco Grasparossa di Castelvetro Opera Pura Brut	🍷 2

La Piana

VIA OSSI, 4B
41014 CASTELVETRO DI MODENA [MO]
TEL. +39 059790303
www.lambruscolapiana.it

CELLAR SALES
PRE-BOOKED VISITS
ANNUAL PRODUCTION 60,000 bottles
HECTARES UNDER VINE 7.80
VITICULTURE METHOD Certified Organic
SUSTAINABLE WINERY

☉ Lambrusco Grasparossa di Castelvetro Rosato Noi Due Extra Dry	🍷🍷 2*
● Lambrusco Grasparossa di Castelvetro Lacrime di Bosco '16	🍷 2

Poderi dal Nespoli 1929

LOC. NESPOLI
VILLA ROSSI, 50
47012 CIVITELLA DI ROMAGNA [FC]
TEL. +39 0543989911
www.poderidalnespoli.com

CELLAR SALES
PRE-BOOKED VISITS
ACCOMMODATION
ANNUAL PRODUCTION 1,000,000 bottles
HECTARES UNDER VINE 180.00
SUSTAINABLE WINERY

● Borgo dei Guidi '15	🍷 5
● Romagna Sangiovese Sup. Il Prugneto '16	🍷 2

Rocca Le Caminate

s.da Meldola Rocca delle Caminate, 15a
47014 Meldola [FC]
Tel. +39 0543493482
www.roccalecaminate.it

CELLAR SALES
PRE-BOOKED VISITS
ANNUAL PRODUCTION 20,000 bottles
HECTARES UNDER VINE 6.00
VITICULTURE METHOD Certified Biodynamic

● Romagna Sangiovese Predappio Sbargoleto '15	♼♼ 3
● Romagna Sangiovese Predappio Bramabene '15	♼ 2

Tenuta Saiano

fraz. Montebello di Poggio Torriana
via Casone, 35
47825 Torriana [RN]
Tel. +39 0541675515
www.tenutasaiano.it

CELLAR SALES
PRE-BOOKED VISITS
ACCOMMODATION AND RESTAURANT SERVICE
ANNUAL PRODUCTION 20,000 bottles
HECTARES UNDER VINE 11.00
VITICULTURE METHOD Certified Organic

● Saiano '16	♼♼ 3
● Romagna Sangiovese Montebello Ris. '14	♼ 4

Tenuta Santa Lucia

via Giardino, 1400
47025 Mercato Saraceno [FC]
Tel. +39 054790441
www.santaluciavinery.it

CELLAR SALES PRE-BOOKED VISITS
ACCOMMODATION
ANNUAL PRODUCTION 90,000 bottles
HECTARES UNDER VINE 17.00
VITICULTURE METHOD Certified Biodynamic
SUSTAINABLE WINERY

○ Romagna Albana Secco Albarara '16	♼♼ 3*
○ Romagna Albana Passito Albarara '11	♼♼ 4
● Centuplo Centesimino '15	♼ 3

Tre Monti

loc. Bergullo
via Lola, 3
40026 Imola [BO]
Tel. +39 0542657116
www.tremonti.it

CELLAR SALES
PRE-BOOKED VISITS
ANNUAL PRODUCTION 180,000 bottles
HECTARES UNDER VINE 40.00
VITICULTURE METHOD Certified Organic

○ Romagna Albana Secco '16	♼♼ 2*
● Romagna Sangiovese Sup. Campo di Mezzo '16	♼♼ 2*
● Romagna Sangiovese Sup. Sono '16	♼♼ 2*

Trerè

loc. Monticoralli
via Casale, 19
48018 Faenza [RA]
Tel. +39 054647034
www.trere.com

CELLAR SALES
PRE-BOOKED VISITS
ACCOMMODATION AND RESTAURANT SERVICE
ANNUAL PRODUCTION 150,000 bottles
HECTARES UNDER VINE 30.00

○ Romagna Albana Passito Mrosa '14	♼ 4
● Romagna Sangiovese Lona Bona '16	♼ 2

Consorzio Vini Tipici di San Marino

loc. Borgo Maggiore
fraz. Valdragone - Strada Serrabolino, 89
47893 San Marino
Tel. +39 0549903124
www.consorziovini.sm

CELLAR SALES
PRE-BOOKED VISITS
ANNUAL PRODUCTION 700,000 bottles
HECTARES UNDER VINE 120.00

○ Oro dei Goti di San Marino Passito '12	♼♼ 5
○ Moscato Spumante di San Marino	♼ 2
○ Roncale di San Marino '16	♼ 3

TUSCANY

Tuscany is a region with a long and great history of viticulture, the cradle of appellations prepared to stand shoulder-to-shoulder with the world's best. For centuries it played host to seemingly immutable principles and institutions. It's a past defined by the region's commerce, the ingenuity and shrewdness of its citizens, its conquests and family estates. And it's a past that's given rise to wineries that, today, continue to astonish us, pursuing ideals while proposing new ones. At times they loyally follow tradition, and at times they've adopted a more contemporary approach. At times we see a complete break from the past, when a producer eschews all paradigms and certainties and dares to take the road less travelled. As usual, Chianti Classico enchants. Wild, airy, melancholy, moody and luminous, this magical territory manages to be everything and its opposite. Its wines do the talking, and when they do they never hesitate to touch our deepest selves, literally causing us to fall in love. And so it is that the appellation raked in 21 Tre Bicchieri, 8 of which are from the seemingly ill-fated 2014 vintage and 6 of which apply to local IGTs. Among them are wines being recognized for the first time, like Buondonno and Dievole. Chianti Classico calls and Montalcino answers,14 wines in all and a rousing success for the 2015 Rosso, some 4 in all, thanks to an outstanding season that conferred grace, ease and complexity to the wines. We saw some nice 2012s as well, but we should point out that, contrary to those critics who sang its praises, we found it a bit less interesting than expected. But it still had its share of Tre Bicchieri: Corte dei Venti and Le Macioche with the 2012 Brunello and Palazzo with its 2015 Rosso. The coast suffered, however, up and down the region. Both Bolgheri and Maremma saw their best wines go back to 2014, a year that spared no one. Even those who received the highest marks had to sweat for it, drawing on experience and know how. We close with a recognition of those smaller appellations (in terms of geographic size and production volumes) that proved just as interesting as their larger counterparts: from Montepulciano's Vino Nobile to San Gimignano's Vernaccia, Cortona (who provided our 'Viticulturist of the Year', Stefano Amerighi) Montecucco, Valdarno and Carmignano. A special mention for San Ferdinando's 2016 Vermentino, a precise and racy white from Val di Chiana, as well as Podere San Cristoforo's 2015 Ameri, a Governo all'Uso Toscano that will give you goosebumps. Finally, our Solidarity Award goes to Elisabetta Fagiuoli's Montenidoli.

Acquabona

LOC. ACQUABONA, 1
57037 PORTOFERRAIO [LI]
TEL. +39 0565933013
www.acquabonaelba.it

CELLAR SALES
PRE-BOOKED VISITS
ANNUAL PRODUCTION 90,000 bottles
HECTARES UNDER VINE 18.00

Acquabona is named after the freshwater
spring between Portoferraio and Porto
Azzurro, location of the original part of the
farm that was established early in the
1700s. For the last sixty years vine
growing has been the main activity, and
thirty years ago three agronomist friends
took over the winery and began to reshape
it. Adopting farming methods to safeguard
the environment, their focus is on growing
the most characteristic native grape
varieties. The 2013 Riserva is a pleasant
wine. Its vibrant nose features spicy, fruity
notes of blackberries. The mouth is warm,
compact and flavorsome, with a nice,
lengthy finish. The 2016 Vermentino is
intriguing, offering up fruity hints of peach,
vanilla and aromatic herbs. The body is
solid, full-flavored and soft, with a fresh,
lively finish.

● Elba Rosso Ris. '13	♈♈ 4
○ Elba Vermentino '16	♈♈ 3
● Benvenuto '15	♈ 2
○ Elba Ansonica '16	♈ 3
○ Elba Bianco '16	♈ 2
⊙ Elba Rosato '16	♈ 2
● Elba Rosso '15	♈ 2
○ Elba Ansonica '15	♈♈ 3
○ Elba Bianco '15	♈♈ 2*
● Elba Rosso Ris. '11	♈♈ 4
● Voltraio '12	♈♈ 4
● Voltraio '11	♈♈ 4

Altesino

LOC. ALTESINO, 54
53024 MONTALCINO [SI]
TEL. +39 0577806208
www.altesino.it

CELLAR SALES
PRE-BOOKED VISITS
ACCOMMODATION
ANNUAL PRODUCTION 250,000 bottles
HECTARES UNDER VINE 49.00

The Consonni family created the Altesino
brand in the 1970s, but it was taken over
in 2002 by Elisabetta Gnudi Angelini. The
original vineyards are in Montosoli, a hill on
the northern slope of Montalcino whose
fame as a grand cru is well-deserved.
Eventually they added other prestigious
properties between Castelnuovo dell'Abate
and Pianezzine, reaching a total of 50
hectares. Varieties cultivated include
Merlot, Cabernet, Chardonnay, Vermentino,
Viognier, Trebbiano and Malvasia, although
their range of wines focuses, as always, on
Sangiovese for their mature and austere
Brunello. This year, Altesino's best wines
are from the controversial 2012 vintage.
The Our 40th Harvest, a classic, warm and
luxurious Brunello, features wood berries,
juniper and roots. The Montosoli's character
is even more pronounced. Hints of plums
and morello cherries give way to a crisp,
glycerin-rich mouth. The 2015 Rosso came
across as a bit husky in weight.

● Brunello di Montalcino Montosoli '12	♈♈ 8
● Brunello di Montalcino Our 40th Harvest '12	♈♈ 7
● Rosso di Montalcino '15	♈ 3
● Brunello di Montalcino '11	♈♈ 6
● Brunello di Montalcino '10	♈♈ 6
● Brunello di Montalcino '00	♈♈ 6
● Brunello di Montalcino Montosoli '11	♈♈ 8
● Brunello di Montalcino Montosoli '10	♈♈ 8
● Brunello di Montalcino Ris. '10	♈♈ 8
● Toscana Rosso '14	♈♈ 3

Amantis

FRAZ. MONTENERO D'ORCIA
LOC. COLOMBAIO BIRBE
58040 CASTEL DEL PIANO [GR]
TEL. +39 3461402687
www.agricolaamantis.com

ANNUAL PRODUCTION 40,000 bottles
HECTARES UNDER VINE 5.20
SUSTAINABLE WINERY

Benedetta Angela Tacconi has made her debut as head of this winery located in the Montenero d'Orcia hills in Montecucco. Here on clayish soil there are just over five hectares of vineyards employing a high planting density that provides low yields but superior grape quality. Sangiovese makes up the lion's share, but there's also room for international varieties such as Cabernet Franc. Each plot is vinified separately, then blended according to vintage. Our tastes suggest that the direction is the right one. The 2012 Montecucco Sangiovese has a nice, multifaceted nose that sees ripe red fruit emerging from a flowery and spicy backdrop. The same come through in a taut, well-developing mouth, with a savory undertone that remains fresh until a fruit-driven finish. The 2012 Birbanera is just as good, though softer and more pervasive.

● Montecucco Rosso Birbanera '12	♟♟	3
● Montecucco Sangiovese '12	♟♟	4

Fattoria Ambra

VIA LOMBARDA, 85
59015 CARMIGNANO [PO]
TEL. +39 3358282552
www.fattoriaambra.it

CELLAR SALES
PRE-BOOKED VISITS
ANNUAL PRODUCTION 80,000 bottles
HECTARES UNDER VINE 20.00
VITICULTURE METHOD Certified Organic

Beppe Rigoli is an enologist and agronomist who's worked as a consultant for several wineries in Tuscany and also helps out at his family's estate, which they've owned since the middle of the last century. Managing it all perfectly, he divides the territories into four main crus. Somewhat like a Burgundy where every wine is enhanced and diverse, this kind of microzoning work has enabled him to gain in-depth knowledge of every single vineyard. The 2013 Carmignano Riserva Montalbiolo proves elegant on the nose, with overtones of fruit and faint grass. In the mouth it's pleasant, quite traditional and a bit subtle with good equilibrium. It finishes with a nice, appetizing, full-flavored finish. The 2013 Carmignano Riserva Elzana has an aromatic bouquet in which dark fruit mingle with mineral notes and hints of aromatic herbs. In the mouth it's succulent, stylish, full and close-woven in its tannic weave. The 2009 Vin Santo is intriguing on the nose, with citrusy hints. In the mouth it proves warm and harmonic.

● Carmignano Montalbiolo Ris. '13	♟♟	5
● Carmignano Elzana Ris. '13	♟♟	5
○ Vin Santo di Carmignano '09	♟♟	5
● Barco Reale '16	♟	2
☉ Rosato di Carmignano Vin Ruspo '16	♟	2
○ Trebbiano '16	♟	2
● Carmignano Elzana Ris. '11	♟♟	5
● Carmignano Montalbiolo Ris. '12	♟♟	5
● Carmignano Montalbiolo Ris. '11	♟♟	5
● Carmignano Montefortini '12	♟♟	3
● Carmignano Santa Cristina in Pilli '13	♟♟	3
○ Trebbiano '15	♟♟	2*
○ Vin Santo di Carmignano '08	♟♟	5
○ Vin Santo di Carmignano '07	♟♟	5

Stefano Amerighi

LOC. POGGIOBELLO DI FARNETA
52044 CORTONA [AR]
TEL. +39 0575648340
www.stefanoamerighi.it

CELLAR SALES
PRE-BOOKED VISITS
ANNUAL PRODUCTION 28,000 bottles
HECTARES UNDER VINE 8.50
VITICULTURE METHOD Certified Biodynamic
SUSTAINABLE WINERY

Stefano Amerighi is a champion of
sustainable viticulture and biodynamics,
which means farming according to lunar
phases and planetary cycles. Employing
maceration and natural products protects
the health of his plants and limits their
exposure to copper and sulfur. And his
winemaking is carried out without corrective
actions or chemicals. Initially, his idea was to
produce quality wine from just one variety,
Syrah, which does well here. However, he's
now aiming to turn the winery into a
laboratory devoted to sustainable farming.
His goal is to extend the same principles and
practices to growing cereals, fruit and
vegetables, and even to animal breeding.
For this reason, he's our 'Viticulturist of the
Year'. And his 2014 Cortona Syrah gets Tre
Bicchieri. Its aromatic profile features
fragrances that are just a touch gamey,
leathery, and move on to close-woven fruit,
cherry and plums, and finally iodine, mineral
notes. The mouth is fresh, dynamic, meaty
with good weight and fine-grained,
well-integrated tannins. The finish rises, with
a good aftertaste.

● Cortona Syrah '14	♥♥♥	5
● Cortona Syrah Apice '13	♥♥	6
● Cortona Syrah '11	♀♀♀	5
● Cortona Syrah '10	♀♀♀	5
● Cortona Syrah '09	♀♀♀	5
● Cortona Syrah '13	♀♀	5
● Cortona Syrah '12	♀♀	5
● Cortona Syrah Apice '11	♀♀	6
● Cortona Syrah Apice '10	♀♀	6

★★Marchesi Antinori

P.ZZA DEGLI ANTINORI, 3
50123 FIRENZE
TEL. +39 05523595
www.antinori.it

CELLAR SALES
PRE-BOOKED VISITS
ACCOMMODATION AND RESTAURANT SERVICE
ANNUAL PRODUCTION 2,000,000 bottles
HECTARES UNDER VINE 2350.00

The winery, based in a beautiful structure in
Bargino, is a benchmark for Italian
winemaking. Special attention is paid to
Chianti Classico, where recently Antinori has
taken over yet another estate -- Tenuta
Capraia, in Castellina in Chianti. However, it's
clear that this ancient Florentine family has
chosen the whole of Tuscany as their base of
operations. They currently own the Pian delle
Vigne estate in Montalcino, Le Mortelle and
Aldobrandesca in Maremma, La Braccesca
in Cortona, Guado al Tasso in Bolgheri and
Monteloro in Fiesole. The 2015 Chianti
Classic Pèppoli is decidedly well-crafted,
with an intriguing nose that alternates
between dark fruit and spices. These come
together coherently in a soft and balanced
mouth and a pleasant, savory finish. The
2015 Botrosecco, a Maremmano blend of
Cabernet Sauvignon and Cabernet Franc, is
also quite agreeable, with a vibrant aromatic
profile and a fresh, well-paced unfolding of
flavor. The 2014 Mobile di Montepulciano is
a solid wine that stands out for its
fragrances of violet and sugared almond.

● Chianti Cl. Pèppoli '15	♥♥	3
● Rosso di Montalcino Pian delle Vigne '15	♥♥	4
● Solaia '14	♥♥	8
● Tignanello '14	♥♥	8
● Brunello di Montalcino Pian delle Vigne '12	♥♥	7
● Chianti Cl. Gran Sel. Badia a Passignano '12	♥♥	6
● Chianti Cl. Marchese Antinori Ris. '14	♥♥	5
● Maremma Toscana Botrosecco Le Mortelle '15	♥♥	3
● Nobile di Montepulciano La Braccesca '14	♥♥	4
○ Maremma Viva Le Mortelle '16	♀	4
● Nobile di Montepulciano Santa Pia La Braccesca Ris. '13	♀	5
○ Villa Antinori Bianco '16	♀	2
● Villa Antinori Rosso '14	♀	4

Tenuta di Arceno - Arcanum

LOC. ARCENO
FRAZ. SAN GUSMÉ
53010 CASTELNUOVO BERARDENGA [SI]
TEL. +39 0577359346
www.tenutadiarceno.com

CELLAR SALES
PRE-BOOKED VISITS
ANNUAL PRODUCTION 250,000 bottles
HECTARES UNDER VINE 92.00

Since 1994, Tenuta di Arceno has belonged
to Jess Jackson and Barbara Banke,
owners of the U.S. giant Kendall-Jackson.
Their wines present a modern style, with
forward ripe fruit (not difficult to obtain from
Castelnuovo Berardenga) and a generous
use of aging wood. Power and intensity
are the watchwords, exhibiting an
interpretation that reflects the owners'
taste. The 2015 Chianti Classic is a fruity,
vibrant wine. It proves pervasive in its notes
of ripe fruit, spices and balsamic hints,
making for a well-rounded mouth and a
wide finish. The 2014 Riserva does a good
job of interpreting a difficult vintage,
offering up flavor and definition, as well as
a precise finish that recalls spices and faint
vegetal hints.

Tenuta Argentiera

LOC. I PIANALI
FRAZ. DONORATICO
VIA AURELIA, 412A
57022 CASTAGNETO CARDUCCI [LI]
TEL. +39 0565773176
www.argentiera.eu

CELLAR SALES
PRE-BOOKED VISITS
ANNUAL PRODUCTION 450,000 bottles
HECTARES UNDER VINE 75.00

This is undoubtedly one of the most
beautiful and charming wineries in the
whole of Bolgheri. First, consider the fact
that the vineyard covers something like
seventy hectares in one of the best areas
on stony, clay soil. For the rest, work is
carried out in the cellar with obsessive care
and attention to detail, producing some of
the best and most famous wines in
Bolgheri. The 2014 Bolgheri Superiore
shines less than usual, which isn't
surprising considering the vintage. It shows
discreet extraction and toasty, herbaceous
fragrances,, but its various components
don't come together in ways seen in better
versions. We prefer the 2015 Bolgheri
Rosso Villa Donoratico, a wine that's
aromatically dark, redolent with nuances of
licorice and jazzy herbal hints. Its mouth is
consistent, full of flavor, showing
commendable extraction.

● Chianti Cl. '15	♟♟ 3
● Chianti Cl. Ris. '14	♟♟ 5
● Chianti Cl. Strada al Sasso Ris. '13	♟ 5
● Chianti Cl. '13	♙♙ 3
● Chianti Cl. '12	♙♙ 3
● Chianti Cl. '11	♙♙ 3
● Chianti Cl. Ris. '12	♙♙ 5
● Chianti Cl. Strada al Sasso Ris. '10	♙♙ 5

● Bolgheri Rosso Sup. '14	♟♟ 8
● Bolgheri Rosso Villa Donoratico '15	♟♟ 5
● Bolgheri Rosso Poggio ai Ginepri '15	♟ 3
● Bolgheri Sup. Argentiera '10	♟♟♟ 7
● Bolgheri Sup. Argentiera '06	♟♟♟ 7
● Bolgheri Sup. Argentiera '05	♟♟♟ 7
● Bolgheri Sup. Argentiera '04	♟♟♟ 7
● Bolgheri Rosso Poggio ai Ginepri '13	♙♙ 3
● Bolgheri Rosso Sup. '13	♙♙ 8
● Bolgheri Sup. '12	♙♙ 8
● Bolgheri Villa Donoratico '13	♙♙ 5
● Giorgio Bartholomaus '12	♙♙ 8
● Giorgio Bartholomaus '11	♙♙ 8
● Lavinia Maria '11	♙♙ 8

Artimino

FRAZ. ARTIMINO
V.LE PAPA GIOVANNI XXIII, 1
59015 CARMIGNANO [PO]
TEL. +39 0558751423
www.artimino.com

CELLAR SALES
PRE-BOOKED VISITS
ACCOMMODATION AND RESTAURANT SERVICE
ANNUAL PRODUCTION 420,000 bottles
HECTARES UNDER VINE 88.00

Breathe in deeply the history at this winery, purchased by the Olmo family in the 1980s. Look to the heart of the property and you'll find a sixteenth-century villa that was once owned by the Medicis. But history has not held the Olmo's back. Rather, their investments have led to expanded vineyards, and there is new equipment in the cellar. Steadily increasing quality has been their reward. The 2010 Vin Santo Occhio di Pernice offers up a close-focused, fragrant nose in which chocolate, hazelnut, walnut, tamarind and carob emerge. In the mouth it shows incredible richness, proving wide, sweet, caressing and long. The 2012 Carmignano Grumarello Riserva exhibits a polished, fresh aromatic profile of dark fruit and hints of sage. In the mouth it's rich in pulp, with solid tannins, and a proper (not very long) finish. The 2014 Carmignano Poggilarca is fruity and flowery on the nose, full-flavored and fresh in the mouth.

● Vin Santo di Carmignano Occhio di Pernice '10	▼▼▼ 5
● Carmignano Poggilarca '14	▼▼ 3
● Carmignano V. Grumarello Ris. '12	▼▼ 4
● Artumes '16	▼ 1*
● Barco Reale Ser Biagio '16	▼ 2
⊙ Barco Reale Vin Ruspo '16	▼ 2
● Chianti Montalbano '15	▼ 2
● Carmignano '13	▽▽ 3
● Carmignano '11	▽▽ 3
● Carmignano Ris. '12	▽▽ 4
● Carmignano V. Grumarello Ris. '10	▽▽ 4
○ Vin Santo di Carmignano '12	▽▽ 4
○ Vin Santo di Carmignano '10	▽▽ 4
● Vin Santo di Carmignano Occhio di Pernice '09	▽▽ 5

Assolati

FRAZ. MONTENERO
POD. ASSOLATI, 47
58040 CASTEL DEL PIANO [GR]
TEL. +39 0564954146
www.assolati.it

CELLAR SALES
PRE-BOOKED VISITS
ACCOMMODATION
ANNUAL PRODUCTION 18,000 bottles
HECTARES UNDER VINE 5.00

Sangiovese is undisputed king among Floriano Giannetti's rows of vines. Located in the hills that separate Maremma from Amiataa, he grows five hectares of vineyards, representing only a small portion of the 105-hectare farm that he inherited from his parents and grandparents. This wild, wooded area has been transformed into fertile farming land. As well as wine, Assolati makes oil from local olive varieties, and the old farmhouse has been renovated to form the heart of a dynamic holiday business featuring traditional cuisine. The small winery, once again, shows that it's in excellent health, offering a solid selection of wines. The Montecucco Sangiovese has a nice, fruity nose in which whiffs of spice and pepper emerge. The mouth is taut, well-defined and fresh, making for a good interpretation of the difficult 2014 vintage. The 2015 Montecucco Rosso is truly pleasant, thanks to a nose that offers up hints of small red fruit, and a fluent, precise mouth.

○ Dionysos '16	▼▼ 2*
● Montecucco Rosso '15	▼▼ 2*
● Montecucco Sangiovese '14	▼▼ 3
⊙ Afrodite '16	▼ 2
● Montecucco Rosso '14	▽▽ 2*
● Montecucco Rosso '12	▽▽ 2*
● Montecucco Rosso '11	▽▽ 2*
● Montecucco Rosso '10	▽▽ 2*
● Montecucco Sangiovese '13	▽▽ 3
● Montecucco Sangiovese Ris. '13	▽▽ 4
● Montecucco Sangiovese Ris. '12	▽▽ 3
● Montecucco Sangiovese Ris. '10	▽▽ 3

★Avignonesi

FRAZ. VALIANO DI MONTEPULCIANO
VIA LODOLA, 1
53045 MONTEPULCIANO [SI]
TEL. +39 0578724304
www.avignonesi.it

CELLAR SALES
PRE-BOOKED VISITS
RESTAURANT SERVICE
ANNUAL PRODUCTION 700,000 bottles
HECTARES UNDER VINE 180.00
VITICULTURE METHOD Certified Organic

Virgine Saverys established her majestic and uncompromising winery about five years ago. The ambitiously complex program to convert 200 hectares to certified biodynamic farming is probably the most striking aspect of this estate. Avignonesi continues to be one of the most important in Montepulciano winemaking. Its production of memorable wine types such as Vin Santo perpetuates a treasured local tradition. The 2015 Rosso di Montepulciano is delectable. Its fragrant aromas of violet and fresh cherry introduce a dynamic mouth in which continuity, consistency and pleasantness come together. The 2014 Nobile exhibits good overall balance. Its aromas are clean and its flavors unfold with good weight and pace, though the finish is just a bit grassy. The 2013 Mobile Grandi Annate is more austere but certainly no less interesting, showing a close-woven structure and a pronounced nose.

● Rosso di Montepulciano '15	▼▼	3*
● Nobile di Montepulciano '14	▼▼	5
● Nobile di Montepulciano Grandi Annate '13	▼▼	7
● 50 & 50 Avignonesi e Capannelle '99	▼▼▼	8
● 50 & 50 Avignonesi e Capannelle '97	▼▼▼	8
● Nobile di Montepulciano Ris. '85	▼▼▼	8
○ Vin Santo '98	▼▼▼	8
○ Vin Santo '96	▼▼▼	8
○ Vin Santo '95	▼▼▼	8
○ Vin Santo '93	▼▼▼	8
● Vin Santo Occhio di Pernice '97	▼▼▼	8
● Vin Santo Occhio di Pernice '93	▼▼▼	8
○ Vin Santo Occhio di Pernice '90	▼▼▼	8
● Vin Santo Occhio di Pernice '89	▼▼▼	8

Badia a Coltibuono

LOC. BADIA A COLTIBUONO
53013 GAIOLE IN CHIANTI [SI]
TEL. +39 0577746110
www.coltibuono.com

CELLAR SALES
PRE-BOOKED VISITS
ACCOMMODATION AND RESTAURANT SERVICE
ANNUAL PRODUCTION 240,000 bottles
HECTARES UNDER VINE 62.00
VITICULTURE METHOD Certified Organic
SUSTAINABLE WINERY

This was one of the first wineries in Chianti to move toward organic farming, but at the same time it maintained a traditional approach to winemaking that favored an authentic and coherent expression of Sangiovese. The use of ancient varieties such as Foglia Tonda, Ciliegiolo and Malvasia Nera was a key to success in this balancing act. In terms of respect for both the territory and wine quality, the direction the Stucchi brothers are going in has made their winery one of the most important in the appellation. The 2015 Chianti Classico is delicious and absolutely delightful, and it's not the first time that the wine affirms its status as one of the territory's most representative wines. Its fragrances pass from wild flowers to clearer notes of fresh cherry. In the mouth it exhibits great richness of flavor and contrast, with an uplifting finish. The 2016 Collebello, made with Sangiovese and complementary grapes from older vineyards, is nice, though tends towards simplicity. It offers up graceful fragrances and delicate, balanced taste.

● Chianti Cl. '15	▼▼▼	4*
● Chianti Cetamura '16	▼▼	2*
● Collebello '16	▼▼	2*
● Chianti Cl. Cultus Boni Ris. '13	▼	5
● Sangioveto '13	▼	7
● Chianti Cl. '13	▼▼▼	3*
● Chianti Cl. '12	▼▼▼	3*
● Chianti Cl. '06	▼▼▼	3*
● Chianti Cl. Cultus Boni '09	▼▼▼	4*
● Chianti Cl. Ris. '09	▼▼▼	5
● Chianti Cl. Ris. '07	▼▼▼	5
● Chianti Cl. Ris. '04	▼▼▼	5
● Sangioveto '95	▼▼▼	6
● Chianti Cl. Ris. '12	▼▼	5
● Chianti Cl. RS '13	▼▼	2*

Badia di Morrona

VIA DEL CHIANTI, 6
56030 TERRICCIOLA [PI]
TEL. +39 0587658505
www.badiadimorrona.it

CELLAR SALES
PRE-BOOKED VISITS
ACCOMMODATION AND RESTAURANT SERVICE
ANNUAL PRODUCTION 350,000 bottles
HECTARES UNDER VINE 110.00

Morrona Abbey, most probably a Benedictine convent, dates back to the year 1000. Today this marvel is a hallmark of modern vine growing and winemaking ventures in the Pisa province. Here in Terriciola they own 600 hectares, 100 of which are vineyards. Our opinion is that their wines are becoming increasingly focused and are constantly improving. For example, the 2016 Chianti I Sodi del Paretaio hits surprising levels. Its a close-focused, precise, well-extracted wine with an aromatic profile that's on the mark. It offers up fragrances of ripe red fruit that merge well with spicy notes of pepper. In the mouth it proves succulent and streamlined, as well as precise in its tannins, with a lovely finish to follow. The 2013 VignaAlta is also excellent, more full-bodied but no less racy. The 2011 Vin Santo is at the top of its game.

● Chianti I Sodi del Paretaio '16	♟♟	2*
● VignaAlta '13	♟♟	5
○ Vin Santo del Chianti '11	♟♟	4
● Chianti I Sodi del Paretaio Ris. '14	♟	3
○ Felciaio '16	♟	2
○ La Suvera '11	♟	3
● Taneto '14	♟	3
● Chianti I Sodi del Paretaio '15	♟♟	2*
● N'Antia '13	♟♟	5
● Taneto '13	♟♟	3
● Taneto '12	♟♟	3
● Taneto '11	♟♟	3*

Fattoria di Bagnolo

LOC. BAGNOLO
VIA IMPRUNETANA PER TAVARNUZZE, 36
50023 IMPRUNETA [FI]
TEL. +39 0552313403
www.bartolinibaldelli.it

CELLAR SALES
PRE-BOOKED VISITS
ANNUAL PRODUCTION 25,000 bottles
HECTARES UNDER VINE 10.00

This estate with ten hectares of vineyards in the sunny, breezy hills around Florence is one of three Tuscan properties owned by the Bartolini Baldelli family. The other two are Castello di Montozzi in Pergine Valdarno, Arezzo, and Fattoria di Scaletta in San Miniato, Pisa. Today, Marco Bartolini Baldelli runs this land purchased by his ancestors in the nineteenth century. The soil is mostly clay and limestone, and hosts Sangiovese, Colorino, Canaiolo, Malvasia and Trebbiano, with a few rows of Cabernet Sauvignon and Merlot thrown in for good measure. In addition to wine they produce oil from native Tuscan olive varieties. Even if 2014 was quite a difficult year, the vintage's Riserva can hold its head high. Its boasts an aromatic profile that goes from dark, ripe fruit to oaky notes refreshed by balsamic. The tannic weave is close-knit and dense, while in the mouth it proves well-sustained and dynamic. The 2015 Chianti is also good, bringing together a mature, warm nose and a lean body of good continuity.

● Chianti Colli Fiorentini Ris. '14	♟♟	4
● Chianti Colli Fiorentini '15	♟♟	2*
● Capro Rosso '12	♟♟	5
● Capro Rosso '11	♟♟	5
● Capro Rosso '10	♟♟	5
● Chianti Colli Fiorentini '14	♟♟	2*
● Chianti Colli Fiorentini '13	♟♟	2*
● Chianti Colli Fiorentini Ris. '13	♟♟	4
● Chianti Colli Fiorentini Ris. '12	♟♟	4
● Chianti Colli Fiorentini Ris. '11	♟♟	4
● Chianti Colli Fiorentini Ris. '10	♟♟	4

Bandini - Villa Pomona

LOC. POMONA, 39
S.DA CHIANTIGIANA
53011 CASTELLINA IN CHIANTI [SI]
TEL. +39 0577740473
www.fattoriapomona.it

CELLAR SALES
PRE-BOOKED VISITS
ACCOMMODATION
ANNUAL PRODUCTION 16,000 bottles
HECTARES UNDER VINE 4.70
VITICULTURE METHOD Certified Organic

This winery based in Castellina in Chianti is a good example of the artisan Italian winemaking that has made a lasting mark on our tradition. The strong point of Villa Pomona wines is classic style, featuring aging in large wood, abiding no shortcuts in the cellar, and, above all, working in the vineyards under strict organic management. The results are original wines that express a marked character, and they are one of the strongest links with the territory found in Chianti Classico. Even if the 2014 Chianti Classico Riserva comes out of a complicated vintage (to say the least), it behaves like a major wine. Its aromas are well-delineated and its fruit proves fragrant and well-sustained. The mouth is balanced, and not without contrasts; only the finish is lacking a bit in structure. The 2015 Chianti Classico is pleasant and well-crafted, offering a generous and generally wide mouth, as well as intense, fruity aromas.

● Chianti Cl. Ris. '14	♟♟♟ 4*
● Chianti Cl. '15	♟♟ 3
● Chianti Cl. '13	♟♟♟ 3*
● Chianti Cl. '12	♟♟♟ 3*
● Chianti Cl. '14	♟♟ 3
● Chianti Cl. '11	♟♟ 3
● Chianti Cl. '10	♟♟ 3
● Chianti Cl. Ris. '13	♟♟ 4
● Chianti Cl. Ris. '12	♟♟ 4
● Chianti Cl. Ris. '11	♟♟ 4
● Chianti Cl. Ris. '10	♟♟ 4

Baracchi

LOC. CEGLIOLO, 21
52044 CORTONA [AR]
TEL. +39 0575612679
www.baracchiwinery.com

CELLAR SALES
PRE-BOOKED VISITS
ACCOMMODATION AND RESTAURANT SERVICE
ANNUAL PRODUCTION 140,000 bottles
HECTARES UNDER VINE 32.00
SUSTAINABLE WINERY

Riccardo and his son Benedetto come from a family that has been working in wine since 1860. They favor growing the Syrah variety which has found its ideal habitat here, but they also grow Trebbiano and Sangiovese. The grapes are used to make different types of wine, including a sparkling wine. All are made in their winery. They have also arisen to the challenge of planting Pinot Nero. Nearby the estate there are hotels, restaurants and spas surrounded by some of the vineyards. These are situated in four different areas -- San Martino, Gabbiano, Pietraia and Montanare. The 2014 Cortona Syrah Smeriglio made it to the finals, with its feral and vegetal hints calling up undergrowth, and light sprinkles of pepper. In the mouth it shows pleasing, linear attack, not immense but fresh, with good drinkability. The 2014 Cortona Pinot Nero offers up an aromatic profile linked to wild berries and herbs. The body is lean, balanced in freshness and tannins, with a lingering finish.

● Cortona Syrah Smeriglio '14	♟♟ 4
○ Brut Trebbiano '14	♟♟ 5
● Cortona Cabernet Ris. '13	♟♟ 6
● Cortona Pinot Nero '14	♟♟ 4
⊙ Brut Rosé M. Cl. Sangiovese '14	♟ 5
● Cortona Ardito '12	♟ 6
● Ardito '12	♟♟ 6
● Cortona Smeriglio Syrah '13	♟♟ 4
● Cortona Syrah Ris. '13	♟♟ 6
● Cortona Syrah Ris. '12	♟♟ 6
● O'Lillo '14	♟♟ 2*
● Pinot Nero '13	♟♟ 6

Fattoria dei Barbi

LOC. PODERNOVI, 170
53024 MONTALCINO [SI]
TEL. +39 0577841111
www.fattoriadeibarbi.it

CELLAR SALES
PRE-BOOKED VISITS
ACCOMMODATION AND RESTAURANT SERVICE
ANNUAL PRODUCTION 600,000 bottles
HECTARES UNDER VINE 66.00

When you hear the name Fattoria dei Barbi, Montalcino winemaking springs to mind. On closer look you'll find the story of gambles and innovation that exists behind the Cinelli Colombini family's cellar-cum-museum. Among many firsts, it was first in the area to export to France (1817), to sell Brunello by mail order (1832), to open a hotel for wine tourism (1960s), to create a range of Super Tuscans (Brusco dei Barbi, 1969), to distil spirits from Sangiovese Grosso (1974), and to adopt the use of organic fertilizers. A modern sensitivity is discernible in their three flagship reds - Vigna del Fiore cru, Riserva, and vintage wine. Having put in its usual, impressive performance, the only thing missing from Barbi's selection was a standout. The 2015 Rosso sees vegetal and balsamic hiding on the primary aromas, with an austere suite of fruit to follow. The 2012 Brunello Vigna del Fiore proves wider, all herbs and iodine, just a bit warm and dry at the finish. The 2011 Brunello Riserva is a classic.

● Brunello di Montalcino Ris. '11	♥♥ 7
● Brunello di Montalcino V. del Fiore '12	♥♥ 7
● Morellino di Scansano '15	♥♥ 3
● Rosso di Montalcino '15	♥♥ 3
● Brunello di Montalcino '12	♥ 5
● Brunello di Montalcino '11	♀♀ 5
● Brunello di Montalcino '10	♀♀ 5
● Brunello di Montalcino Ris. '10	♀♀ 7
● Brunello di Montalcino V. del Fiore '11	♀♀ 7
● Brunello di Montalcino V. del Fiore '10	♀♀ 7
● Brunello di Montalcino V. del Fiore '08	♀♀ 7
● Rosso di Montalcino '14	♀♀ 3

Baricci

LOC. COLOMBAIO DI MONTOSOLI, 13
53024 MONTALCINO [SI]
TEL. +39 0577848109
www.baricci.it

CELLAR SALES
PRE-BOOKED VISITS
ANNUAL PRODUCTION 30,000 bottles
HECTARES UNDER VINE 5.00

Producers, professionals and enthusiasts arrived from all over Italy and the world to say their goodbyes to Nello Baricci. He passed away around the time of the 50th anniversary celebrations for the Consorzio Del Vino Brunello di Montalcino, of which he was a founding member and the first signatory. Such a display of affection speaks volumes. We have lost a giant, a man, and a vine grower. Our condolences go to his children Graziano and Graziella, his son-in-law Piero Buffi and his grandsons, Federico and Francesco. For some time now they have been carrying on the extraordinary work he started in 1955, that which made Podere Colombaio's five hectares in Montosoli indeed a unique place. Among Signor Nello's achievements is his having conferred such dignity on the Rosso di Mantalcino. It's not a little Brunello, but, rather, a wine of its own, as the splendid 2015 version demonstrates. Raspberries, petals, balsams, its aromatic brilliance couples perfectly with the harmony of its palate, which goes all in on grace and flavor.

● Rosso di Montalcino '15	♥♥♥ 4*
● Brunello di Montalcino '12	♥♥ 6
● Brunello di Montalcino '10	♀♀♀ 6
● Brunello di Montalcino '09	♀♀♀ 5
● Brunello di Montalcino '07	♀♀♀ 5
● Brunello di Montalcino Nello Ris. '10	♀♀♀ 6
● Brunello di Montalcino '11	♀♀ 6
● Brunello di Montalcino '08	♀♀ 5
● Rosso di Montalcino '14	♀♀ 4
● Rosso di Montalcino '13	♀♀ 4
● Rosso di Montalcino '11	♀♀ 3*
● Rosso di Montalcino '10	♀♀ 3

★★Barone Ricasoli

LOC. MADONNA A BROLIO
53013 GAIOLE IN CHIANTI [SI]
TEL. +39 05777301
www.ricasoli.it

CELLAR SALES
PRE-BOOKED VISITS
ACCOMMODATION
ANNUAL PRODUCTION 2,500,000 bottles
HECTARES UNDER VINE 235.00
SUSTAINABLE WINERY

With 230 hectares of vineyards at altitudes ranging from 500 to 230 meters, Castello di Brolio encompasses all the soil and climate features of Chianti Classico. In fact a study carried out by the winery demonstrated their soil mimics almost perfectly those found in the whole appellation, with the exception of the clay found in the lower area of Castellina in Chianti. These results explain why the current direction of the winery under Francesco Ricasoli's guidance is establishing a benchmark. The 2015 Chianti Classico Bettino is a wine that highlights drinkability, though without being merely "approachable". In fact, its aromas posses complexity and dynamism, ranging from fruit to flower, and are always rounded out by earthy, spicy hints. In the mouth, it proves dynamic, with a sweetness made longer by a well-sustained, spirited verve. We could put the 2015 Chianti Classico Brolio on the same plane, though it's a bit less complex.

Chianti Cl. Brolio Bettino '15	♟♟♟	5
Chianti Cl. Brolio '15	♟♟	3
Chianti Cl. Rocca Guicciarda Ris. '14	♟♟	5
Chianti Cl. Brolio Ris. '14	♟	6
Casalferro '08	♟♟♟	8
Casalferro '05	♟♟♟	8
Casalferro '03	♟♟♟	5
Chianti Cl. Castello di Brolio '07	♟♟♟	8
Chianti Cl. Castello di Brolio '06	♟♟♟	8
Chianti Cl. Castello di Brolio '04	♟♟♟	7
Chianti Cl. Castello di Brolio '03	♟♟♟	5
Chianti Cl. Colledilà '10	♟♟♟	7
Chianti Cl. Gran Sel. Colledilà '13	♟♟♟	8
Chianti Cl. Gran Sel. Colledilà '11	♟♟♟	8
Chianti Cl. Rocca Guicciarda Ris. '12	♟♟♟	5

Basile

POD. MONTE MARIO
58044 CINIGIANO [GR]
TEL. +39 0564993227
www.basilessa.it

CELLAR SALES
PRE-BOOKED VISITS
ANNUAL PRODUCTION 50,000 bottles
HECTARES UNDER VINE 8.00
VITICULTURE METHOD Certified Organic
SUSTAINABLE WINERY

Giovanbattista Basile's estate rests on eight hectares of vineyards in wood-covered hills in Cinigiano, in the heart of Montecucco. In 1999, he and his family set off from Naples to buy a winery in a place that was not well known for winemaking. It was not unknown for long. Working diligently on land that had been uncultivated for decades and running his vineyards with organic farming techniques in order to respect the land, Giovanbattista soon brought it to life. The vineyards are planted on galestro soil at altitudes ranging from 330 to 380 meters. The Riserva Ad Agio doesn't manage to duplicate last year's success, but it still shows that it's a wine of great character. A dark and inky aromatic profile features mineral whiffs, foreshadowing a mouth that's precise in its tannic weave, close-knit, and well-dosed in its management of wood, while fruit lends succulence and flavor. The 2014 Cartacanta is a bit too mature. It continues to be supple, but it's also too simple.

● Montecucco Sangiovese Ad Agio Ris. '13	♟♟	5
○ Artéteca '16	♟	3
● Maremma Toscana Rosso Comandante '14	♟	4
● Montecucco Sangiovese Cartacanta '14	♟	3
● Montecucco Sangiovese Ad Agio Ris. '12	♟♟♟	5
● Montecucco Cartacanta '11	♟♟	3
● Montecucco Sangiovese Ad Agio Ris. '11	♟♟	5
● Montecucco Sangiovese Cartacanta '13	♟♟	3
● Montecucco Sangiovese Cartacanta '12	♟♟	3

Pietro Beconcini

FRAZ. LA SCALA
VIA MONTORZO, 13A
56028 SAN MINIATO [PI]
TEL. +39 0571464785
www.pietrobeconcini.com

CELLAR SALES
PRE-BOOKED VISITS
ANNUAL PRODUCTION 95,000 bottles
HECTARES UNDER VINE 12.00

Leonardo Beconcini has been instrumental in bringing the previously unknown San Miniato winemaking area to the public's attention. Thanks to his and Eva Bellagamba's initiative, other vine growers are following suit and letting the world know about the complexity of their wines. Together they have set up the Consorzio dei Vignaioli di San Miniato. When Leonardo discovered an early 20th century Tempranillo vineyard on his estate, he changed course in his vineyard management and now focuses on grape blends. In addition to the Spanish variety, he also grows Sangiovese, Canaiolo, Colorino and Malvasia, both Bianca and Nera. A good overall performance, starting with the 2013 Reciso, a monovarietal Sangiovese whose nose offers up hints of chocolate, cherry and the occasional assorted spice. The mouth is soft and succulent, with a docile finish. The 2015 IXE, made with Tempranillo, is intriguing, with a nose that features balsamic and aromatic herbs, a dynamic body whose tannins are well-distributed and a long finish.

● IXE '15	▼▼ 3
● Maurleo '15	▼▼ 2*
● Reciso '13	▼▼ 5
● Chianti Ris. '13	♀♀ 2*
● IXE '14	♀♀ 3
● IXE '13	♀♀ 3
● Maurleo '13	♀♀ 2*
● Vigna alle Nicchie '12	♀♀ 6
● Vigna alle Nicchie '11	♀♀ 6
● Vigna alle Nicchie '09	♀♀ 6
○ Vin Santo del Chianti Caratello '08	♀♀ 5
○ Vin Santo del Chianti Caratello '07	♀♀ 5

Bindella

FRAZ. ACQUAVIVA
VIA DELLE TRE BERTE, 10A
53045 MONTEPULCIANO [SI]
TEL. +39 0578767777
www.bindella.it

CELLAR SALES
PRE-BOOKED VISITS
ANNUAL PRODUCTION 160,000 bottles
HECTARES UNDER VINE 36.50

Today, Bindella belongs to a Swiss company that works in the wine and restaurant industry. The cellar, named after the area, is on the Vallocaia estate and it already has several vintages under its belt. This historic Montepulciano winery makes spot-on wines gaining in favor with growing consensus. The selection is missing a star, but it still put in an excellent performance this year. The two Nobile di Montepulcianos in particular, distinguished themselves for finesse and craftsmanship, along with the intriguing 2012 Vin Santo Dolce Sinfonia. But, getting back to the Nobiles, the Vallocaia alternates ripe notes with a hardness of taste that give us a glimpse of the wine's staying power. The 2014 is more delicate and already pleasing.

● Nobile di Montepulciano '14	▼▼ 4
● Nobile di Montepulciano Vallocaia Ris. '13	▼▼ 6
○ Vin Santo di Montepulciano Dolce Sinfonia '12	▼▼ 5
○ Gemella '16	▼ 3
● Rosso di Montepulciano Fossolupaio '15	▼ 2
● Nobile di Montepulciano I Quadri '13	♀♀♀ 5
● Nobile di Montepulciano I Quadri '12	♀♀♀ 5
● Nobile di Montepulciano '13	♀♀ 4
● Nobile di Montepulciano '12	♀♀ 4
● Vin Santo di Montepulciano Occhio di Pernice Dolce Sinfonia '07	♀♀ 7

★Biondi Santi
Tenuta Il Greppo

LOC. VILLA GREPPO, 183
53024 MONTALCINO [SI]
TEL. +39 0577848087
www.biondisanti.it

CELLAR SALES
PRE-BOOKED VISITS
ACCOMMODATION
ANNUAL PRODUCTION 80,000 bottles
HECTARES UNDER VINE 25.00

As mentioned in the last edition, a new era has begun for Biondi Santi. Or more precisely, for the family that in the public imagination virtually 'invented' the recipe for Brunello wines at the end of the 19th century. They went on to set the pace for the history of Montalcino with a long series of legendary Riservas. Franco's son, Jacopo, has been joined by Christopher Descours, CEO of EPI, a French holding for luxury goods. The firm also owns Piper and Charles Heidsieck in Champagne and Château la Verrerie in the Rhône. More developments are in the offing, but in the meantime, Sangiovese wines from the Greppo estate are earning an increasingly prominent position on the world winemaking stage. The most recent tastings proved that their fame is well-deserved, starting with the 2014 Rosso, a wine that displays the contribution of the grapes normally used in their flagship Brunello. And, speaking of the wine, the 2012 is a classic (though deceptive) Biondi Santi, endowed with tremendous saline force, as is the 2011 Riserva.

● Brunello di Montalcino '12	♛♛♛	8
● Brunello di Montalcino Ris. '11	♛♛	8
● Rosso di Montalcino Fascia Rossa '14	♛♛	8
● Brunello di Montalcino '10	♛♛♛	8
● Brunello di Montalcino '09	♛♛♛	8
● Brunello di Montalcino Ris. '10	♛♛♛	8
● Brunello di Montalcino Ris. '07	♛♛♛	8
● Brunello di Montalcino Ris. '06	♛♛♛	8
● Brunello di Montalcino '08	♛♛	8
● Brunello di Montalcino '07	♛♛	8
● Brunello di Montalcino Ris. '08	♛♛	8
● Rosso di Montalcino '10	♛♛	4

Borgo Salcetino

LOC. LUCARELLI
53017 RADDA IN CHIANTI [SI]
TEL. +39 0577733541
www.livon.it

PRE-BOOKED VISITS
ANNUAL PRODUCTION 95,000 bottles
HECTARES UNDER VINE 15.00

The Tuscan estate of Livon, owned by the family of Friuli winemakers since the mid-1990s, produces wines that are faithful to the Chianti Classico tradition and to the area in which Borgo Salcetino is situated: Radda in Chianti. Their wines are the result of targeted decisions such as aging in large wood and respect for the time-tested approaches to local winemaking. Their style is spot-on with a balanced combination of clean execution and territorial expression, making them one of the most interesting wineries in the area. The 2015 Chianti Classico is a wine that, without getting into too much detail, manages to sum the principal characteristics of a great product: in the mouth it shows flavor, elegance and depth; on the nose, its aromatic profile is fragrant, multifaceted and very well-defined. The 2013 Chianti Classico Lucarello Riserva, a wine with an almost linear palate, is also very good, featuring lively acidity, fragrances of fresh cherry and pepper.

● Chianti Cl. '15	♛♛♛	3*
● Chianti Cl. Lucarello Ris. '13	♛♛	4
● Rossole '14	♛	3
● Chianti Cl. '14	♛♛♛	3*
● Chianti Cl. '13	♛♛♛	3*
● Chianti Cl. '11	♛♛♛	3*
● Rossole '12	♛♛♛	3*
● Chianti Cl. '10	♛♛	3
● Chianti Cl. Lucarello Ris. '12	♛♛	4
● Chianti Cl. Lucarello Ris. '10	♛♛	4

Il Borro

FRAZ. SAN GIUSTINO VALDARNO
LOC. IL BORRO, 1
52020 LORO CIUFFENNA [AR]
TEL. +39 055977053
www.ilborro.it

CELLAR SALES
PRE-BOOKED VISITS
ACCOMMODATION AND RESTAURANT SERVICE
ANNUAL PRODUCTION 160,000 bottles
HECTARES UNDER VINE 45.00
VITICULTURE METHOD Certified Organic
SUSTAINABLE WINERY

After coming to this area for years, Ferruccio Ferragamo bought the entire estate in 1993. He then began the recovery and promotion of 700 hectares, village and villas. Taking years to identify the best terrains for new varieties, the first vintage was at last produced in 1999. Over time a new cellar was fitted out and further hectares of vineyards were planted. Now they are in the process of converting to biodynamics using renewable energy, natural fertilizers and banning pesticides. Today, the winery is run by his son, Salvatore. In a year in which their most representative wines are missing, like the Borro or their sparkling wine, the 2014 Petruna made a good debut. The wine, made with Sangiovese matured in amphoras, exhibits a pale color and a delicate, subtle bouquet. In the mouth, it enters elegantly, with completely integrated tannins, a fresh, acidic note and a docile, relaxed finish.

★Poderi Boscarelli

LOC. CERVOGNANO
VIA DI MONTENERO, 28
53045 MONTEPULCIANO [SI]
TEL. +39 0578767277
www.poderiboscarelli.com

CELLAR SALES
PRE-BOOKED VISITS
ANNUAL PRODUCTION 100,000 bottles
HECTARES UNDER VINE 14.00

The De Ferrari family winery has become a perennial benchmark for the appellation. Every wine, from top to bottom of the pyramid retains quality, making them one of the most important producers in Tuscany. With a precise style where nothing is forced, and with a constant search for balance, elegance and character these wines always perform well. It really is difficult to choose the best wine of Boscarelli's selection, they're all that good. The 2016 Rosso di Montepulciano Prugnolo is extraordinarily delicious. Its aromas bring together fresh cherry, herbs and accents of forest floor. In the mouth it's simply perfect, dynamic and supple, with lovely, peppery notes in the finish. The 2013 Nobile Il Nocio is no less good. It's aromatically well-defined, and offers a fresh, succulent mouth with perfectly expressed tannins.

● Petruna '14	♀♀ 7
● Pian di Nova '14	♀ 3
● Polissena '13	♀ 5
● Valdarno di Sopra Borrigiani '15	♀ 3
☉ Brut Bolle di Borro '11	♀♀ 8
● Il Borro '13	♀♀ 7
● Il Borro '09	♀♀ 4
● Pian di Nova '13	♀♀ 3
● Polissena '11	♀♀ 5
● Vin Santo del Chianti Occhio di Pernice '09	♀♀ 7
● Vin Santo del Chianti Occhio di Pernice '08	♀♀ 5
● Vin Santo del Chianti Occhio di Pernice '07	♀♀ 5

● Nobile di Montepulciano Il Nocio '13	♀♀♀ 8
● Rosso di Montepulciano Prugnolo '16	♀♀ 3
● Cortona Merlot '14	♀♀ 4
● De Ferrari '16	♀♀ 3
● Nobile di Montepulciano '14	♀♀ 5
● Nobile di Montepulciano Sottocasa Ris. '12	♀♀ 6
○ Vin Santo di Montepulciano Familiae '05	♀♀ 7
● Nobile di Montepulciano Ris. '12	♀ 5
● Nobile di Montepulciano Il Nocio '12	♀♀♀ 8
● Nobile di Montepulciano Il Nocio '11	♀♀♀ 8
● Nobile di Montepulciano Nocio dei Boscarelli '10	♀♀♀ 8
● Nobile di Montepulciano Nocio dei Boscarelli '09	♀♀♀ 8
● Nobile di Montepulciano Nocio dei Boscarelli '08	♀♀♀ 8

★Brancaia

Loc. Poppi, 42
53017 Radda in Chianti [SI]
Tel. +39 0577742007
www.brancaia.it

CELLAR SALES
PRE-BOOKED VISITS
ACCOMMODATION
ANNUAL PRODUCTION 725,000 bottles
HECTARES UNDER VINE 80.00
SUSTAINABLE WINERY

The history of the Widmer family winery began in the early 1980s. Over thirty years they have become a benchmark for Chianti Classico, as well as for Maremma with the Poggio La Mozza estate. Their wines are consistent, featuring a convergence of fruit and oak that's made possible by aging in barriques. But there is also given aromatic elegance and expansion on the palate. It is a winning combination that combines the soul of the territory with an international character. Despite the vintage's unfavorable climatic conditions, the 2014 Chianti Classico Riserva is still the winery's flagship wine. Aromas of small red fruit cross with elegant, spicy and smoky notes, while in the mouth the wine exhibits depth and dynamism, even if the use of oak makes itself known. The 2015 Chianti Classic is elegant from the outset, offering up flowery accents and a light toastiness.

● Chianti Cl. Ris. '14	♔♔♔	5
● Chianti Cl. '15	♔♔	4
● Cabernet Sauvignon '15	♔♔	4
● Ilatraia '14	♔	6
● Brancaia Il Blu '08	♕♕♕	8
● Brancaia Il Blu '07	♕♕♕	7
● Brancaia Il Blu '06	♕♕♕	6
● Brancaia Il Blu '05	♕♕♕	6
● Brancaia Il Blu '04	♕♕♕	6
● Brancaia Il Blu '03	♕♕♕	6
● Chianti Cl. Brancaia '13	♕♕♕	4*
● Chianti Cl. Ris. '13	♕♕♕	5
● Chianti Cl. Ris. '11	♕♕♕	5
● Chianti Cl. Ris. '10	♕♕♕	4*
● Chianti Cl. Ris. '09	♕♕♕	7

Brancatelli

Loc. Riotorto
Loc. Casa Rossa, 2
57025 Piombino [LI]
Tel. +39 056520655
www.brancatelli.eu

CELLAR SALES
PRE-BOOKED VISITS
ACCOMMODATION AND RESTAURANT SERVICE
ANNUAL PRODUCTION 75,000 bottles
HECTARES UNDER VINE 15.00
VITICULTURE METHOD Certified Organic

This is a small family-run winery where they work respecting the environment, hence the decision to opt for organic cultivation. But the beauty of the place is equally important and, fortunately, you can spend the night in a farmhouse on the property. This is what Giuseppe Brancatelli has been creating since he found the property of his dreams in Val di Cornia, in the 1990s. Situated between the mountains and the sea, it reminded him of his father's Sicilian vineyard, the one that led him to cultivate a passion for wine. The 2013 Syrah Valle del Sogno has a powerful, fruit-driven nose that features cherry, blackcurrant, pepper and vegetal notes. In the mouth it proves solid, austere, with a finish that unfolds in crescendo. The 2015 Questo Dedicato A is made up of equal parts Cabernet Franc and Sauvignon, Petit Verdot and Syrah. It offers up notes of malt, and vibrant blueberry and blackberry. The mouth proves to be well-structured and warm, with a finish that also delivers. The 2012 Re della Valle is captivating on the nose and enticing in the mouth.

● Aleatico Re della Valle '12	♔♔	4
● Questo Dedicato A '15	♔♔	3
● Segreto '13	♔♔	7
● Valle del Sogno '13	♔♔	4
○ Ansonica Splendente '16	♔	3
● Giuseppe Brancatelli '13	♔	4
⊙ Loren '16	♔	2
● Valle delle Stelle '15	♔	3
○ Ansonica Splendente '14	♕♕	3
● Cabernet Sauvignon Segreto '12	♕♕	7
● Cabernet Sauvignon Segreto '11	♕♕	7
● Giuseppe Brancatelli '12	♕♕	4
● Questo Dedicato A '14	♕♕	3
● Valle del Sogno '12	♕♕	4
● Valle delle Stelle '13	♕♕	3

Brunelli - Le Chiuse di Sotto

LOC. PODERNOVONE, 157
53024 MONTALCINO [SI]
TEL. +39 0577849337
www.giannibrunelli.it

CELLAR SALES
PRE-BOOKED VISITS
ACCOMMODATION AND RESTAURANT SERVICE
ANNUAL PRODUCTION 30,000 bottles
HECTARES UNDER VINE 6.50
SUSTAINABLE WINERY

Gianni Brunelli's six hectares of vineyards are divided between two estates, each representing different but complementing terroirs. After Gianni passed away his wife, Maria Laura, took over running the winery. The Le Chiuse di Sotto plots of land unfold to the northeast of Montalcino just before Canalicchi, while Podernovone highlights the character found typically south of the town. Playing on these two distinct slopes, the winery produces Brunello wines that can be defined as classic in the best sense of the word. They age in 2000- to 3000-liter oak barrels, revealing their finer, more polished nature best after long bottle maturation. The word 'elegance' is used rarely when talking about the inconsistent 2012 vintage. But the Le Chiuse di Sotto, a Brunello, represents a splendid exception. Wild berries, balsams and light roots characterize the nose, but the wine delivers especially for its harmony of flavor and its extractive element. We give it Tre Bicchieri.

● Brunello di Montalcino '12	▼▼▼ 6
● Rosso di Montalcino '15	▼ 4
● Amor Costante '05	▼▼▼ 5
● Brunello di Montalcino '10	▼▼▼ 6
● Amor Costante '10	▼▼ 5
● Brunello di Montalcino '11	▼▼ 6
● Brunello di Montalcino '09	▼▼ 6
● Brunello di Montalcino '08	▼▼ 6
● Brunello di Montalcino Ris. '10	▼▼ 8
● Brunello di Montalcino Ris. '07	▼▼ 8
● Brunello di Montalcino Ris. '06	▼▼ 8
● Rosso di Montalcino '13	▼▼ 4
● Rosso di Montalcino '12	▼▼ 4

Bruni

FRAZ. FONTEBLANDA
LOC. LA MARTA, 6
58015 ORBETELLO [GR]
TEL. +39 0564885445
www.aziendabruni.it

CELLAR SALES
ANNUAL PRODUCTION 400,000 bottles
HECTARES UNDER VINE 48.00

Two brothers, Marco and Moreno Bruni, own one of the most dynamic wineries in Maremma. Managing a portfolio of original and impeccably-made wines, they've now embarked on a project to renovate their cellar. They are also in the process of reviewing their general wine style, ranging from more modern wines that age in barriques with generous intensity of taste and aroma, to more balanced ones underlining elegance and which age in large wooden barrels. At Cantina Bruni, the cultivar that in Maremma would be known as 'Uva Spagna' finds its ultimate interpretation. The 2015 Maremma Alicante (Grenache) Oltreconfine brings together finesse, varietal expressivity and aromatic generosity for a mix of absolute excellence, thus establishing a place among the area's top wines. The rest of the selection presented also proved sound.

● Maremma Toscana Alicante Oltreconfine '15	▼▼▼ 6
○ Maremma Toscana Vermentino Plinio '16	▼▼ 2*
● Morellino di Scansano Marteto '16	▼▼ 2*
○ Vermentino Perlaia '16	▼▼ 3
○ Maremma Toscana Vermentino Brut Plinio Cuvée '16	▼ 3
● Grenache Oltreconfine '13	▼▼▼ 2*
● Maremma Toscana Grenache Oltreconfine '14	▼▼ 5
● Morellino di Scansano Laire Ris. '13	▼▼ 4
● Morellino di Scansano Laire Ris. '12	▼▼ 4
● Morellino di Scansano Laire Ris. '10	▼▼ 4
● Morellino di Scansano Marteto '13	▼▼ 2*
● Morellino di Scansano Marteto '12	▼▼ 2*
● Syrah Perlaia '13	▼▼ 3
● Syrah Perlaia '11	▼▼ 3

Tenuta del Buonamico

LOC. CERCATOIA
VIA PROVINCIALE DI MONTECARLO, 43
55015 MONTECARLO [LU]
TEL. +39 058322038
www.buonamico.it

CELLAR SALES
PRE-BOOKED VISITS
ACCOMMODATION
ANNUAL PRODUCTION 300,000 bottles
HECTARES UNDER VINE 43.00

Many changes have been made In the last
few years at Tenuta del Buonamico.
Following decades of history, the winery
has been reshaped since coming into the
hands of the Fontana family. Established
in Cercatoia near Montecarlo, in the
1960s, the winery of today is pursuing a
modern and international style. Their wines
follow faithfully from this idea, and a
technical project is under development. The
2015 Cercatoja, made with Sangiovese,
Syrah and Cabernet Sauvignon, is an
excellent, velvety red that exhibits
impeccable extraction. It offers up aromas
of flowers and wild berries, with herbal
streaks providing aromatic curves and
nuances of flavor. The Il Fortino, made with
100% Syrah, and Etichetta Blu are a bit too
toasty. The 2016 Montecarlo Bianco is
simple but pleasant.

● Cercatoja '15	▼▼5
● Il Fortino '15	▼6
○ Montecarlo Bianco Et. Bianca '16	▼3
● Montecarlo Rosso Et. Blu '15	▼3
● Cercatoja Rosso '11	♈♈5
● Cercatoja Rosso '10	♈♈5
● Il Fortino '12	♈♈6
● Il Fortino Syrah '10	♈♈6
○ Montecarlo Bianco '15	♈♈2*
● Montecarlo Rosso '11	♈♈3
○ Vasario '12	♈♈4

Buondonno
Casavecchia alla Piazza

LOC. LA PIAZZA, 37
53011 CASTELLINA IN CHIANTI [SI]
TEL. +39 0577749754
www.buondonno.com

CELLAR SALES
PRE-BOOKED VISITS
ACCOMMODATION
ANNUAL PRODUCTION 40,000 bottles
HECTARES UNDER VINE 11.00
VITICULTURE METHOD Certified Organic
SUSTAINABLE WINERY

Two Neapolitan agronomists, Gabriele
Buondonno and Valeria Sodano, have run
this small winery in Castellina in Chianti
since 1988. Eleven hectares of vineyard
under organic management, unforced
winemaking, and aging in barriques,
mid-sized casks, and large wood are the
features of their production. This allows for
wines with a clear-cut style, presenting a
strong bond with territory and character.
Though Buondonno wines are still
searching for more consistent quality, they
are an interesting example of artisan
winemaking in Chianti. The 2015 Chianti
Classico Casavecchia alla Piazza is, for
example, simply delicious. The nose brings
together iodine and flowery notes, while the
palate proves precise, savory, dynamic. The
2013 Chianti Classico Riserva sees a bit
less in terms of aromatic profile, but finds
its strong point in the way its flavors unfold
in the mouth, amidst pleasantly spirited
tannins and lively acidity.

● Chianti Cl. Casavecchia alla Piazza '15	▼▼▼3*
● Chianti Cl. Ris. '13	▼▼5
● Lemme Lemme '15	▼2
● Campo ai Ciliegi '07	♈♈5
● Campo ai Ciliegi '03	♈♈5
● Campo ai Ciliegi '00	♈♈5
● Chianti Cl. '09	♈♈3
● Chianti Cl. '08	♈♈3
● Chianti Cl. '01	♈♈4
● Chianti Cl. Ris. '08	♈♈5
● Chianti Cl. Ris. '07	♈♈5

Ca' Marcanda

LOC. SANTA TERESA, 272
57022 CASTAGNETO CARDUCCI [LI]
TEL. +39 0565763809
info@camarcanda.com

CELLAR SALES
PRE-BOOKED VISITS
ANNUAL PRODUCTION 450,000 bottles
HECTARES UNDER VINE 120.00

The Gaja family's Bolgheri winery is pursuing an unstoppable course in expanding into territories neighboring the Bolgheri appellation. Currently their vineyards are extensive. One hundred and twenty hectares host varieties that do well in this corner of Tuscany: Cabernet, Sauvignon and Franc, Merlot and Syrah. These are used in varying amounts for Bolgheri's three blends, which are aged in barriques for the appropriate length of time, thus giving rise to wines bearing all the type's desirable characteristics. This year, they're having to pay the price for two seasons that weren't exactly in the territory's wheelhouse. The 2014 Camarcanda isn't able to express its trademark mature fruit, neither on the nose nor in the mouth, opting for more vegetal notes that come across, in some ways, as unripe. Both the 2015 Bolgheri Magari and the 2015 Promis see clenched tannins. It might be a good idea to wait a while longer.

● Bogheri Magari '15	♔♔ 8	
● Bolgheri Camarcanda '14	♔♔ 8	
● Promis '15	♔ 4	
● Bolgheri Camarcanda '07	♔♔♔ 8	
● Bolgheri Camarcanda '12	♔♔ 8	
● Bolgheri Camarcanda '11	♔♔ 8	
● Bolgheri Camarcanda '10	♔♔ 8	
● Bolgheri Camarcanda '09	♔♔ 8	
● Bolgheri Camarcanda '08	♔♔ 8	

Cacciagrande

FRAZ. TIRLI
LOC. AMPIO
58040 CASTIGLIONE DELLA PESCAIA [GR]
TEL. +39 0564944168
www.cacciagrande.com

CELLAR SALES
PRE-BOOKED VISITS
ANNUAL PRODUCTION 100,000 bottles
HECTARES UNDER VINE 20.00
SUSTAINABLE WINERY

Bruno Tuccio owns eighteen hectares of vineyards, plus a few small rented plots. In 1997, at the age of twenty-two, he took on running the family winery, focusing on production of wine, but also of oil. A few kilometers from Castiglione della Pescaia in the heart of Maremma, Bruno is connecting the Tuscan traditions of Vermentino and Sangiovese, which has four different clones to offer more complexity. Adding a touch of innovation and international style recently, he has also decided to plant Viognier, Syrah and Petit Verdot. The selection presented to our tasters proved solid, with the 2016 Cacciagrande standing out. The wine, made of 70% Sangiovese and a 30% blend of Merlot and Cabernet Sauvignon, features fragrances of plums and ripe blackberries, while the mouth is dense and close-knit, a mix of light earthiness and a close-woven tannic weave. The whites also put in a good performance, with a Vermentino of good consistence and a succulent Viogner.

● Maremma Toscana Rosso Cacciagrande '16	♔♔ 2*	
○ Maremma Toscana Vermentino '16	♔♔ 3	
○ Maremma Toscana Viognier '16	♔♔ 2*	
● Castiglione '15	♔ 4	
● Cortigliano '16	♔ 3	
● Castiglione '11	♔♔ 4	
● Cortigliano '15	♔♔ 3	
○ Maremma Toscana Vermentino '15	♔♔ 3	
● Maremma Tosscana Castiglione '13	♔♔ 4	

Caiarossa

LOC. SERRA ALL'OLIO, 59
56046 RIPARBELLA [PI]
TEL. +39 0586699016
www.caiarossa.com

CELLAR SALES
PRE-BOOKED VISITS
ANNUAL PRODUCTION 120,000 bottles
HECTARES UNDER VINE 32.00
VITICULTURE METHOD Certified Biodynamic

This winery was established in 1998 and
gets its name from the presence of jasper
soil that gives the rocks and land a
distinctive reddish color. From the start,
they adopted biodynamic farming methods
in the vineyards. But it was not until 2004
when Eric Albada Jelgersma took over, that
there was a significant increase in quality,
owing to the experience he gained as
manager of two Bordeaux châteaus. The
2013 Caiarossa, a complex blend of Merlot,
Cabernet Franc, Cabernet Sauvignon,
Syrah, Sangiovese, Petit Verdo and Alicante
made it to our finals. A dynamic nose offers
up hints of tomato leaf, wild berries and
aromatic herbs, while the body is harmonic
and well-calibrated with a balanced
freshness; the finish proves relaxed and
enjoyable. The 2014 Oro, made with 100%
Petit Manseng, is elegant in its sweet
fragrances, with a caressing body and
lengthy flavor. The 2013 Pergolaia, made
with 100% Sangiovese, is delicate and
subtle.

● Caiarossa '13	🏆🏆 6
● Aria di Caiarossa '13	🏆🏆 5
○ Oro di Caiarossa '14	🏆🏆 6
● Pergolaia '13	🏆🏆 3
○ Caiarossa Bianco '15	🏆 5
● Aria di Caiarossa '12	♉♉ 5
● Caiarossa '12	♉♉ 6
● Caiarossa '08	♉♉ 6
● Caiarossa '07	♉♉ 7
● Pergolaia '12	♉♉ 3

Tenuta Le Calcinaie

LOC. SANTA LUCIA, 36
53037 SAN GIMIGNANO [SI]
TEL. +39 0577943007
www.tenutalecalcinaie.it

CELLAR SALES
PRE-BOOKED VISITS
ANNUAL PRODUCTION 60,000 bottles
HECTARES UNDER VINE 9.50
VITICULTURE METHOD Certified Organic

Simone Santini's venture began in 1986.
Passionate and meticulous but grounded in
studies as a wine technician, he decided to
put the theory he had learned at school into
practice. The first wines were made in 1993,
and from the start he opted for organic
management of his ten hectares of
vineyards in Santa Lucia, not far from the
Medieval town walls. The winery appeared
to be in good shape this year, owing to a
precise and clean style sacrificing nothing to
flavor and taste. The 2014 Vernaccia Vigna
ai Sassi Riserva once again put in a good
performance, with notes of chamomile,
white flowers and light fruitiness on the
nose, while in the mouth the wine proves to
be a delight. The 2013 Teodoro, a blend of
Sangiovese, Merlot and Cabernet Sauvignon
is complex and fruity on the nose, rich and
flavorsome in the mouth.

○ Teodoro '13	🏆🏆 4
○ Vernaccia di S. Gimignano	
V. ai Sassi Ris. '14	🏆🏆 3
○ Vernaccia di S. Gimignano '16	🏆 2
● Chianti Colli Senesi '12	♉♉ 2*
● Gabriele '07	♉♉ 4
○ Vernaccia di S. Gimignano '15	♉♉ 2*
○ Vernaccia di S. Gimignano '13	♉♉ 2*
○ Vernaccia di S. Gimignano '12	♉♉ 2*
○ Vernaccia di S. Gimignano	
V. ai Sassi '07	♉♉ 3
○ Vernaccia di S. Gimignano	
V. ai Sassi Ris. '13	♉♉ 3*
○ Vernaccia di S. Gimignano	
V. ai Sassi Ris. '10	♉♉ 3*

Camigliano

LOC. CAMIGLIANO
VIA D'INGRESSO, 2
53024 MONTALCINO [SI]
TEL. +39 0577844068
www.camigliano.it

CELLAR SALES
PRE-BOOKED VISITS
ANNUAL PRODUCTION 350,000 bottles
HECTARES UNDER VINE 92.00
SUSTAINABLE WINERY

Upon arriving in Camigliano a breath-taking view awaits the less-hurried traveler. It is an old town in the westernmost part of Montalcino, set in uncontaminated scrub with Alta Maremma and the Metallifere hills on the horizon. The Ghezzi family took it over at the end of the 1950s and made it the beating heart of their business. Today there are about one hundred hectares of vineyards, planted with a very Mediterranean, captivating, and full-flavored Sangiovese. With the 2012 vintage, a new wine has been added to their range of Brunellos. It is aged in 2500- to 6000- liter French oak barrels. Paesaggio Inatteso had an excellent debut. Dark fruit, licorice and forest floor don't overshadow a caressing, sea-inflected character, with an elegance made possible by delicate extraction. These are qualities that come up again in the Brunello, the 2011 Riserva and the 2015 Rosso, all of which feature sweetness and a dynamism of flavor.

● Brunello di Montalcino '12	♟♟ 6
● Brunello di Montalcino Paesaggio Inatteso '12	♟♟ 7
● Brunello di Montalcino Ris. '11	♟♟ 6
● Rosso di Montalcino '15	♟♟ 3
● Brunello di Montalcino '11	♟♟ 6
● Brunello di Montalcino '10	♟♟ 6
● Brunello di Montalcino '09	♟♟ 6
● Brunello di Montalcino '08	♟♟ 6
● Brunello di Montalcino '08	♟♟ 6
● Brunello di Montalcino Gualto Ris. '10	♟♟ 7
● Brunello di Montalcino Gualto Ris. '09	♟♟ 7
● Brunello di Montalcino Gualto Ris. '07	♟♟ 7
● Rosso di Montalcino '13	♟♟ 3

Antonio Camillo

LOC. PIANETTI DI MONTEMERANO
58014 MANCIANO [GR]
TEL. +39 3391525224
www.antoniocamillo.it

CELLAR SALES
PRE-BOOKED VISITS
ANNUAL PRODUCTION 65,000 bottles
HECTARES UNDER VINE 10.00
VITICULTURE METHOD Certified Organic

Antonio Camillo has given new interpretation to the most intriguing features of Ciliegiolo. This grape is cornerstone of his wines, which have become models for style and craftsmanship. His interpretation follows tradition in the winemaking stage and puts special emphasis on the vineyards so as to capture different expressions of the grape. Like uncommonly few in Maremma, the result is a range of original and accomplished wines to bring to the limelight one of the most common varieties in the area. The Ciliegiolo Vallerana Alta affirms its status as a model wine, with a 2015 version that exhibits first-class aromatic breadth, while in the mouth its stylistic finesse and trademark drinkability are slightly restrained by oak. A bit more time in the bottle will correct this small defect of youth. The rest of the selection is less sure-footed, with a bit too much stylistic flourish leaving room for doubt.

● Maremma Toscana Ciliegiolo V. Vallerana Alta '15	♟♟♟ 6
● Maremma Toscana Ciliegiolo Principio '16	♟ 3
● Tutti I Giorni Rosso '16	♟ 2
○ Vermentino '16	♟ 2
● Maremma Toscana Ciliegiolo V. Vallerana Alta '14	♟♟♟ 3*
● Maremma Toscana Ciliegiolo Principio '15	♟♟ 2*
● Maremma Toscana Ciliegiolo V. Vallerana Alta '13	♟♟ 3*
● Maremma Toscana Ciliegiolo V. Vallerana Alta '12	♟♟ 3*
● Maremma Toscana Ciliegiolo V. Vallerana Alta '11	♟♟ 3*

Camperchi

LOC. LA CORNIA
VIA DEL BURRONE, 38
52040 CIVITELLA IN VAL DI CHIANA [AR]
TEL. +39 0575440281
www.camperchi.com

CELLAR SALES
PRE-BOOKED VISITS
ACCOMMODATION
ANNUAL PRODUCTION 100,000 bottles
HECTARES UNDER VINE 22.00

The property belonging to the Cartellone family has an interesting story. The family once emigrated from Sicily to Argentina where they made a fortune in the building trade. Some time after, one of the descendants decided to return to Italy and invest in the wine sector. His choice was Val di Chiana, where he renovated the property and fitted it out for farmstay holidays. The vineyards were planted with international varieties that adapt well to the local microclimate The 2013 Sangiovese is quite pleasant, with vibrant aromas of wild berries and spices amidst a soft, dynamic body. Tannins are well-integrated, while the finish is polished, fresh. The 2013 Merlot is also agreeable, with cloves, cinnamon, raspberry and fruit emerging, while a pervasive, smooth body shows good length. The 2013 Anno 0, made primarily of Sangiovese, exhibits classic fragrances of cherry and plums, with herbaceous accents and a supple body that's well-distributed across its various components. The finish comes through crisp and clean.

● Anno 0 '13	♟♟ 3
○ Colli Etruria Vin Santo '09	♟♟ 3
● Merlot '13	♟♟ 5
● Sangiovese '13	♟♟ 5
● Chianti Ris. '13	♟ 3
● Chianti Sasso Lupaio '14	♟ 3
● Chianti Sup. Sasso Lupaio '13	♟ 3
● Merlot '07	♟♟ 4
● Merlot '06	♟♟ 4
● Moro '03	♟♟ 4
● Sangiovese '07	♟♟ 4

Campo alla Sughera

LOC. CACCIA AL PIANO
S.DA PROV.LE BOLGHERESE, 280
57020 BOLGHERI [LI]
TEL. +39 0565766936
www.campoallasughera.com

CELLAR SALES
PRE-BOOKED VISITS
ACCOMMODATION
ANNUAL PRODUCTION 110,000 bottles
HECTARES UNDER VINE 16.50

Campo alla Sughera is a relatively new winery in Bolgheri owned by the Knauf family, who are successful entrepreneurs in the modern building industry. The cellar, as you would imagine, was built with modern, cutting-edge techniques and was held to the strictest construction measures. The result is a lovely and efficient facility surrounded by vineyards. Their wines are taking off. Last year we noticed significant progress, and this year's tastes confirm the positive trend. The 2014 Bolgheri Superiore Arnione, in particular, is among the best wines of the vintage. It has a close-woven nose marked by vibrant, dark fruit and a balsamic backdrop. In the mouth it's consistent, decisive, bursting with flavor.

● Bolgheri Sup. Arnione '14	♟♟ 6
○ Bolgheri Bianco Achenio '16	♟♟ 5
● Toscana Rosso '13	♟♟ 4
● Bolgheri Rosso Adeo '15	♟ 5
○ Bolgheri Achenio '12	♟♟ 5
● Bolgheri Adeo '12	♟♟ 4
○ Bolgheri Bianco Achenio '14	♟♟ 5
○ Bolgheri Bianco Achenio '13	♟♟ 5
● Bolgheri Rosso Adeo '14	♟♟ 4
● Bolgheri Rosso Sup. Arnione '09	♟♟ 6
● Bolgheri Sup. Arnione '13	♟♟ 6
● Bolgheri Sup. Arnione '12	♟♟ 6
● Bolgheri Sup. Arnione '11	♟♟ 6
● Campo alla Sughera '08	♟♟ 8

Campo del Monte
Eredi Benito Mantellini

VIA TRAIANA, 53A
52028 TERRANUOVA BRACCIOLINI [AR]
TEL. +39 0554684135
www.campodelmonte.it

CELLAR SALES
PRE-BOOKED VISITS
ACCOMMODATION
HECTARES UNDER VINE 7.50

The farm is located in Valdarno and produces wine and oil, following integrated environmentally-friendly farming methods. Adding to the charm is a holiday farmhouse overlooking the vineyards. With attention to the smallest detail and care in the cellar they have achieved excellent results. The two whites both proved excellent. The 2016 Baltea, made with 100% Chardonnay, features vibrant, decisive overtones of white fruit. In the mouth it comes through chewy and dense. On the nose, the 2016 Malvasia Bianca Lunga calls up notes of tea, then apricot and peach. The palate is soft and full, with an enjoyable finish. The 2016 Chianti is also flavorsome, with meaty notes followed by fruity hints of plums and blackcurrant, and a mouth that's tasty, dense and succulent. We appreciated the 2007 Vin Santo Il Conio for its hints of almond and dried fruit, and a creamy, warm body that features an enjoyable, vibrant sweetness.

● Campo del Monte '15	▼▼ 3
○ Valdarno di Sopra Bianca Lunga '16	▼▼ 3
○ Valdarno di Sopra Pratomagno Baltea '16	▼▼ 4
○ Vin Santo del Chianti Il Conio '07	▼▼ 4
● Chianti Campo del Monte '16	▼ 3
● Chianti Ris. '14	▼ 3
● Valdarno di Sopra Rodos '13	▼ 4

Canalicchio
Franco Pacenti

LOC. CANALICCHIO DI SOPRA, 6
53024 MONTALCINO [SI]
TEL. +39 0577849277
www.canalicchiofrancopacenti.it

CELLAR SALES
PRE-BOOKED VISITS
RESTAURANT SERVICE
ANNUAL PRODUCTION 40,000 bottles
HECTARES UNDER VINE 10.00

The estate was founded in the 1960s by Rosildo Pacenti and was turned into a bottling company by his son Franco in 1988. It gets its name from the Canalicchi area on the northern slope of Montalcino, an excellent area for vine growing. Today, his wife, Carla, is at the helm, aided by members of the third generation, Lisa, Serena and Lorenzo. The ten hectares of vineyards are set at 300 meters above sea level on clayish and stony soil, and are planted only with Sangiovese. The grapes are used to make four classic-style wines, which undergo long maceration and are aged in medium and large Slavonian oak barrels. We're used to seeing more sparkling performances from the Pacenti family's wines. Nevertheless, the 2015 Rosso and 2012 Brunello make a great pair. The former proves true to character, pure with notes of black cherry, spices and tobacco leaf, and tannins that are far from sweet. The latter is even more classic and well-equipped with richness of flavor.

● Brunello di Montalcino '12	▼▼ 5
● Rosso di Montalcino '15	▼▼ 3
● Brunello di Montalcino '04	♈♈♈ 5
● Brunello di Montalcino '11	♈♈ 5
● Brunello di Montalcino '10	♈♈ 5
● Brunello di Montalcino '09	♈♈ 5
● Brunello di Montalcino '08	♈♈ 5
● Brunello di Montalcino '07	♈♈ 5
● Brunello di Montalcino Ris. '10	♈♈ 7
● Brunello di Montalcino Ris. '07	♈♈ 7
● Rosso di Montalcino '13	♈♈ 3
● Rosso di Montalcino '10	♈♈ 3

Canalicchio di Sopra

LOC. CASACCIA, 73
53024 MONTALCINO [SI]
TEL. +39 0577848316
www.canalicchiodisopra.com

CELLAR SALES
PRE-BOOKED VISITS
ACCOMMODATION
ANNUAL PRODUCTION 55,000 bottles
HECTARES UNDER VINE 15.00

Canalicchio di Sopra is a longstanding and key player in Montalcino, and we find a recurring number in its rich history: two. Two branches of the family brought together their respective estates, Pacenti and Ripaccioli, in the 1980s. Both were synonymous with the great winemaking traditions in the area. Two vineyards, Canalicchi and Montosoli, are completely dedicated to Sangiovese and authentic grand crus on the northern slope. Two Brunellos, the vintage and the Riserva, are a permanent fixture in the range and get their vigorous temperament from this territorial symmetry. Enhancing it all is the work in the cellar where nothing is left to chance. Another strong performance by Canalicchio di Sopra was only missing the cherry on top. The 2015 Rosso offers up blackberries, licorice and pepper, while in the mouth the wine is partially bridled by some toasty, rough edges, though its flavors still unfold tautly and pervasively. The 2012 Brunello exhibits similar qualities, though it's a softer, more balsamic wine.

● Brunello di Montalcino '12	▼▼6
● Rosso di Montalcino '15	▼▼3*
● Brunello di Montalcino '10	▼▼▼6
● Brunello di Montalcino '07	▼▼▼6
● Brunello di Montalcino '06	▼▼▼6
● Brunello di Montalcino '04	▼▼▼6
● Brunello di Montalcino Ris. '10	▼▼▼8
● Brunello di Montalcino Ris. '07	▼▼▼8
● Brunello di Montalcino Ris. '04	▼▼▼7
● Brunello di Montalcino Ris. '01	▼▼▼7
● Brunello di Montalcino '11	▼▼6
● Rosso di Montalcino '14	▼▼3
● Rosso di Montalcino '13	▼▼3

Candialle

VIA CHIANTIGIANA, KM 34,00
50020 PANZANO [FI]
TEL. +39 055852201
www.candialle.com

CELLAR SALES
PRE-BOOKED VISITS
ANNUAL PRODUCTION 35,000 bottles
HECTARES UNDER VINE 11.30
SUSTAINABLE WINERY

Like so many foreigners before them, Josephin and Jarkko, German and Finnish, respectively, fell in love with Chianti Classico. Their passion led them to establish Candialle in 2002, starting with the purchase of 35 hectares, a third of which are planted with vines. The rows of vines are in the 'Conca d'Oro' in Panzano, at an altitude between 300 and 360 meters. Organic farming methods and a purist approach to winemaking contribute to their production of pure wines that perform well with flavor and personality. The 2015 Chianti Classico La Misse di Candialle is outstanding. It doesn't reveal too much, too quickly, waiting before opening the way to a sanguine atmosphere in which delectable flowery scents and red fruit emerge. It's graceful on the palate, with good tannic support. The 2013 Gran Selezione, a vibrant, mature wine, is a less on the mark in terms of style.

● Chianti Cl. La Misse di Candialle '15	▼▼3*
● Chianti Cl. Gran Sel. '13	▼4
● Chianti Cl. '12	▼▼4
● Chianti Cl. La Misse di Candialle '12	▼▼3

Capanna

LOC. CAPANNA, 333
53024 MONTALCINO [SI]
TEL. +39 0577848298
www.capannamontalcino.com

CELLAR SALES
PRE-BOOKED VISITS
ANNUAL PRODUCTION 70,000 bottles
HECTARES UNDER VINE 21.00

One of the most distinctive wineries in northern Montalcino is celebrating its 60th anniversary. Founded by Giuseppe Cencioni and helped along by sons Benito and Franco, it has grown to over twenty hectares of vineyards. In addition to Sangiovese, they grow Merlot, Pinot Grigio and other varieties used for making different versions of Moscadello di Montalcino. Today, Patrizio is the face of Capanna and is very keen on this wine type. However, the winery is mainly known for making Brunello wines that are rigid, to say the least. Usually they are aged in 1000 to 3000-liter oak and should be thought of as long living. The enigmatic 2012 vintage made for a stylistically faithful Brunello. Incense and candied citrus come through on the nose, while the mouth is austere, pure. But it was the 2015 Rosso that hit a home run with its foresty, colonial suite of aromas (pine resin, sandalwood and pink pepper), and a perfect follow through to a meaty, well-measured mouth.

● Rosso di Montalcino '15	♟♟♟ 3*
● Brunello di Montalcino '12	♟♟ 6
○ Moscadello di Montalcino V. T. '12	♟♟ 4
● Brunello di Montalcino Ris. '10	♟♟♟ 8
● Brunello di Montalcino Ris. '06	♟♟♟ 7
● Brunello di Montalcino Ris. '04	♟♟♟ 7
● Brunello di Montalcino '11	♟♟ 6
● Brunello di Montalcino '10	♟♟ 6
● Brunello di Montalcino '09	♟♟ 6
● Brunello di Montalcino Ris. '07	♟♟ 7
○ Moscadello di Montalcino '14	♟♟ 3
○ Moscadello di Montalcino '13	♟♟ 3
● Rosso di Montalcino '14	♟♟ 3
● Rosso di Montalcino '13	♟♟ 3

Tenuta Caparzo

LOC. CAPARZO
S.DA PROV.LE DEL BRUNELLO KM 1,700
53024 MONTALCINO [SI]
TEL. +39 0577848390
www.caparzo.com

CELLAR SALES
PRE-BOOKED VISITS
ACCOMMODATION
ANNUAL PRODUCTION 900,000 bottles
HECTARES UNDER VINE 90.00

The Caparzo brand made its debut in the 1960s, but after extensive company reorganization it was taken over in 1998 by Elisabetta Gnudi Angelini. It is named after the former site of the historic building, Ca' del Pazzo, where most of the estate is situated today. There are additional plots in other areas of Montalcino, for a total of almost one hundred hectares of vineyards, which host Chardonnay, Sauvignon Blanc, Traminer, Cabernet Sauvignon and, of course, Sangiovese. In the best vintages they make three Brunellos (vintage, Riserva and Vigna La Casa cru), which are often aged in barriques and large barrels. Our most recent tastes suggest that their selection is in excellent form, starting with a tag-team of a 2014 Rosso, surprising (to say the least) considering the vintage, and the La Caduta, which adds complexity and texture to an austere base. But its the 2012 Brunello Vigna La Casa, a lush, citrusy wine, that once again stands out.

● Brunello di Montalcino V. La Casa '12	♟♟ 8
● Brunello di Montalcino '12	♟♟ 6
● Rosso di Montalcino '14	♟♟ 3
● Rosso di Montalcino La Caduta '14	♟♟ 4
● Brunello di Montalcino '10	♟♟ 6
● Brunello di Montalcino '09	♟♟ 6
● Brunello di Montalcino Ris. '09	♟♟ 7
● Brunello di Montalcino Ris. '07	♟♟ 7
● Brunello di Montalcino V. La Casa '10	♟♟ 8
● Brunello di Montalcino V. La Casa '08	♟♟ 8
● Morellino di Scansano '13	♟♟ 3
● Morellino di Scansano Doga delle Clavure '11	♟♟ 3
● Rosso di Montalcino '13	♟♟ 3
● Rosso di Montalcino La Caduta '10	♟♟ 4

★Tenuta di Capezzana

LOC. SEANO
VIA CAPEZZANA, 100
59015 CARMIGNANO [PO]
TEL. +39 0558706005
www.capezzana.it

CELLAR SALES
PRE-BOOKED VISITS
ACCOMMODATION AND RESTAURANT SERVICE
ANNUAL PRODUCTION 450,000 bottles
HECTARES UNDER VINE 90.00
VITICULTURE METHOD Certified Organic

The winery has belonged to the Contini Bonacossi family since the start of the 1900s, when it was bought by Alessandro, fresh from the antiques trade in Spain. Over the years it expanded with the purchase of two neighboring farms. But it wasn't until after World War II, when Alessandro's grandson Ugo, armed with a degree in agricultural science, took over and transformed the estate into a modern farm with a sharecropping structure. The 2010 Vin Santo Riserva earns itself a Tre Bicchieri. On the nose it offers up bewitching notes of honey, candied citrus and dried fruit, while the body is pervasive, velvety and the finish both sweet and captivating. The 2013 Carmignano Trefiano Riserva also made it to the finals, with its pronounced, pulpy richness, and hints of quinine and licorice. In the mouth it's potent and tannic, rugged and tight as well, though with plenty of body and length. The 2013 Ghiaie della Furba, a blend of Cabernet, Merlot and Syrah, also does well, with its aromas of dark fruit, and its mineral, somewhat herbaceous overtones. In the mouth its comes through mature and long, with good weight.

○ Vin Santo di Carmignano Ris. '10	♟♟♟	6
● Carmignano Trefiano Ris. '13	♟♟	6
● Ghiaie della Furba '13	♟♟	6
● Barco Reale '15	♟	3
⊙ Barco Reale Vin Ruspo '16	♟	2
○ Chardonnay '16	♟	3
● Ugo Contini Bonacossi '13	♟	7
● Carmignano Villa di Capezzana '07	♟♟♟	4
○ Vin Santo di Carmignano Ris. '09	♟♟♟	6
○ Vin Santo di Carmignano Ris. '08	♟♟♟	6
○ Vin Santo di Carmignano Ris. '07	♟♟♟	6
○ Vin Santo di Carmignano Ris. '05	♟♟♟	5

Caprili

FRAZ. TAVERNELLE
LOC. CAPRILI, 268
53024 MONTALCINO [SI]
TEL. +39 0577848566
www.caprili.it

CELLAR SALES
PRE-BOOKED VISITS
ACCOMMODATION
ANNUAL PRODUCTION 75,000 bottles
HECTARES UNDER VINE 21.00
SUSTAINABLE WINERY

The Bartolommei family took over Podere Caprili in 1965 but didn't bottle their first Brunello until 1978. It was the result of expertly combined blends from different plots near Villa Santa Restituta, in the heart of central-southwestern Montalcino. Vigna Madre, Ceppo Nero, Testucchiaia, Quadrucci, Palazzetto, each plot is worked separately and the blend is completed at the end, but only after long aging in large barrels. The Riserva is made only in the best vintages. The Trebbiano, Malvasia del Sant'Antimo and Moscadello are made with grapes from the Vigna della Fornacina, which numbers 15 hectares. Caprili's selection continues to exhibit excellence. Their Rosso once again proves that it's a lively interpretation, with a texture that's just a bit dry in the 2015. The 2012 Brunello is generous and complex, with hints of cola, infused herbs and spiciness that give way to a classic, warm and succulent palate.

● Brunello di Montalcino '12	♟♟	6
● Rosso di Montalcino '15	♟♟	3
● Brunello di Montalcino '10	♟♟♟	6
● Brunello di Montalcino '06	♟♟♟	7
● Brunello di Montalcino AdAlberto Ris. '10	♟♟♟	8
● Brunello di Montalcino Ris. '08	♟♟♟	7
● Brunello di Montalcino Ris. '06	♟♟♟	7
● Brunello di Montalcino Ris. '04	♟♟♟	5
● Brunello di Montalcino '11	♟♟	6
● Brunello di Montalcino '09	♟♟	5
● Brunello di Montalcino '08	♟♟	5
● Rosso di Montalcino '14	♟♟	3
● Rosso di Montalcino '13	♟♟	3

Fattoria Carpineta Fontalpino

FRAZ. MONTAPERTI
LOC. CARPINETA
53019 CASTELNUOVO BERARDENGA [SI]
TEL. +39 0577369219
www.carpinetafontalpino.it

CELLAR SALES
PRE-BOOKED VISITS
ACCOMMODATION
ANNUAL PRODUCTION 100,000 bottles
HECTARES UNDER VINE 23.00
VITICULTURE METHOD Certified Organic

They have been working for only some twenty years but are already one of the most important wineries in Chianti Classico. Since 1994 this brother and sister team, Filippo and Gioia Cresti, haven't wasted their time in pursuing a sound approach and precise production style They are located in the southern part of the appellation, near Montaperti in the Sienese countryside. In the cellar, they skillfully sustain soil and climate features of the area, so as to give their wines fullness and maturation, combined with grip and freshness. Carpineta Fontalpino's latest addition, the 2015 Chianti Classico Montaperto, captivates. A sensual nose features mature red fruit and medicinal herbs, light notes of spice, and vague hints of earth and autumn leaves. The mouth is vibrant, luminous and well-fused, while the finish is clean and crisp - a true Chianti. The wine's other recent addition, the 2015 Chianti Classico Dofana, is no less on the mark, though it's a more introverted wine with plenty left to discover.

● Chianti Cl. Montaperto '15	♟♟♟ 4*
● Chianti Cl. Dofana '15	♟♟ 4
● Chianti Cl. Fontalpino '15	♟♟ 3
● Do ut des '13	♟♟♟ 5
● Do ut des '12	♟♟♟ 5
● Do ut des '11	♟♟♟ 5
● Do ut des '10	♟♟♟ 5
● Dofana '10	♟♟♟ 7
● Chianti Cl. Fontalpino '14	♟♟ 3
● Chianti Cl. Fontalpino '13	♟♟ 3

Casa alle Vacche

FRAZ. PANCOLE
LOC. LUCIGNANO, 73A
53037 SAN GIMIGNANO [SI]
TEL. +39 0577955103
www.casaallevacche.it

CELLAR SALES
PRE-BOOKED VISITS
ACCOMMODATION AND RESTAURANT SERVICE
ANNUAL PRODUCTION 115,000 bottles
HECTARES UNDER VINE 28.00

In the 19th century, the oldest building on the farm was used as a shed for cows that drew carts. Hence the name of the winery, Casa alle Vacche, an ever-present reminder of the Ciappi family's legacy. They have been farming the land for generations to produce wine and oil. For some time now they have adopted integrated farming methods, underscoring the attention they pay to the environment and land. Today, the latest generation, brothers Fernando and Lorenzo, run the farm. The 2014 Vernaccia Crocus Riserva, with its bouquet calling up medicinal herbs, ripe apple, almond and faint spices, proves interesting indeed. Dense and succulent, it shows good pervasiveness of flavor, and finishes in a pleasant crescendo. The 2016 Vernaccia I Macchioni is delicate and polished on the nose, with fruity nuances of apricot and pear, notes of fine aromatic herbs and a few hints of citrus. It's taut and lively in the mouth, with a savory, enticing finish. The 2016 Canaiolo is fruit-driven on the nose, lively and fresh in the mouth.

● Canaiolo '16	♟♟ 2*
○ Vernaccia di S. Gimignano Crocus Ris. '14	♟♟ 3
○ Vernaccia di S. Gimignano I Macchioni '16	♟♟ 2*
● Aglieno '14	♟ 2
● Ciliegiolo '16	♟ 2
○ Sangiovese Bianco '16	♟ 2
○ Vernaccia di S. Gimignano '16	♟ 2
● Aglieno '12	♟♟ 2*
○ Vernaccia di S. Gimignano '13	♟♟ 2*
○ Vernaccia di S. Gimignano Crocus Ris. '13	♟♟ 3
○ Vernaccia di S. Gimignano I Macchioni '15	♟♟ 2*
○ Vernaccia di S. Gimignano I Macchioni '14	♟♟ 2*

Casa Emma

LOC. CORTINE
S.DA PROV.LE DI CASTELLINA IN CHIANTI, 3
50021 BARBERINO VAL D'ELSA [FI]
TEL. +39 0558072239
www.casaemma.com

CELLAR SALES
PRE-BOOKED VISITS
RESTAURANT SERVICE
ANNUAL PRODUCTION 90,000 bottles
HECTARES UNDER VINE 25.00

The Bucalossi family have owned Casa Emma for years. They bought it from the Florentine noblewoman, Emma Bizzarri, and by keeping the name they have preserved a trace of the estate's venerable history. It is located in the heart of Chianti Classico, between the Florentine area of Barberino Val d'Elsa and the Sienese Castellina in Chianti. The wines have an easily-recognizable style: modern, mostly aged in barriques, uncompromising, and expressing a personality that reflects its territory of origin. The 2015 Chianti Classico is a truly lovely wine. It offers up generous, vibrant aromas that go from notes of small red fruit to meadows. In the mouth it expands with traction and breadth, while the finish sees just a bit too much oak. The 2013 Chianti Classico Riserva, with its spicy nose and tasty palate, also put in a good performance. Its tannins may be a bit rough at times.

● Chianti Cl. '15	♟♟ 3*
● Chianti Cl. Ris. '13	♟♟ 5
● Chianti Cl. Vignalparco '13	♟ 3
● Soloìo '13	♟ 6
● Chianti Cl. Ris. '95	♟♟♟ 4*
● Chianti Cl. Ris. '93	♟♟♟ 5
● Soloìo '94	♟♟♟ 4*
● Chianti Cl. '14	♟♟ 3
● Chianti Cl. '13	♟♟ 3
● Chianti Cl. Gran Sel. '12	♟♟ 5
● Chianti Cl. Ris. '13	♟♟ 5
● Chianti Cl. Vignalparco '12	♟♟ 3
● Chianti Cl. Vignalparco '11	♟♟ 3
● Soloìo '12	♟♟ 6

Tenuta Casadei

LOC. SAN ROCCO
57028 SUVERETO [LI]
TEL. +39 0558300411
www.tenutacasadei.it

PRE-BOOKED VISITS
ANNUAL PRODUCTION 80,000 bottles
HECTARES UNDER VINE 17.00
VITICULTURE METHOD Certified Organic
SUSTAINABLE WINERY

This winery in Suvereto was bought by Stefano Casadei in 1997. It fulfilled his desire to produce wines from the Tuscan coast using biodynamic soil management. Later, he added an estate in Castello del Trebbio in the Pontassieve hills, which belonged to his wife, Anna Baj Macario. Then a farm in Olianas in Sardinia, which produces wines from native grapes, was added. And most recently, they were joined by the Cline family, winemakers from Sonoma. The 2015 Sogno Mediterraneano, made with Grenache, Syrah and Mourvèdre, exhibits a clean nose that's fragrant with flowers and herbs, while the mouth is dense and decisive. The 2016 Armonia, a field blend of various cultivar (predominantly Merlot and Syrah), offers up a vibrant, potent, vanilla-rich aromatic profile, while in the mouth it's creamy and well-distributed. The 2015 Filare 18, made with 100% Cabernet Franc, comes through with overtones of grass and dark fruit on the nose. In the mouth it shows succulence and a nice, long finish.

● Armonia '16	♟♟ 3
● Filare 18 '15	♟♟ 6
● Sogno Mediterraneo '15	♟♟ 4
● Filare 41 '15	♟ 6
● Armonia '10	♟♟ 2*
● Filare 18 '14	♟♟ 6
● Filare 18 '13	♟♟ 6
● Filare 22 '08	♟♟ 5
● Filare 41 '14	♟♟ 6
● Filare 41 '13	♟♟ 6
● Filare 41 '11	♟♟ 5
● Filare 41 '09	♟♟ 5
● Sogno Mediterraneo '13	♟♟ 4
● Syrah Le Anfore '14	♟♟ 5

Casale dello Sparviero Fattoria Campoperi

LOC. CASALE, 93
53011 CASTELLINA IN CHIANTI [SI]
TEL. +39 0577743228
www.casaledellosparviero.it

CELLAR SALES
PRE-BOOKED VISITS
ACCOMMODATION
ANNUAL PRODUCTION 127,000 bottles
HECTARES UNDER VINE 88.00

Casale dello Sparviero is located in Castellina in Chianti, in a downhill area that distinguishes itself for its somewhat warmer microclimate. They produce technically impeccable wines, perhaps a little short on personality but of overall solid quality. The reason probably lies in their pursuit of balance rather than power, although in this part of the appellation, power might be a coherent choice. Aging is carried out in barriques and large barrels, a mix that appears to support the winery's style. The 2013 Chianti Classico Gran Selezione Vigna Paronza is full-bodied, though not unnecessarily dense, with clean aromas that sees lush fruit accompanied by smoky notes. In the mouth it's long and well-sustained, with richness of flavor in the foreground. The 2013 Chianti Classico Riserva also put in a nice performance, with its fragrances of red fruit and cut grass. It shows a plucky, lively unfolding of flavor.

● Chianti Cl. Gran Sel. V. Paronza '13	♟♟ 3
● Chianti Cl. Ris. '13	♟♟ 3
● Chianti Cl. '15	♟ 3
● Chianti Cl. Gran Sel. Ada Andrighetti '13	♟ 3
● Chianti Sup. '15	♟ 3
● Rosso dello Sparviero '16	♟ 2
● Chianti Cl. '13	♟♟ 3
● Chianti Cl. '08	♟♟ 3
● Chianti Cl. Gran Sel. V. Paronza '12	♟♟ 3
● Chianti Cl. Ris. '12	♟♟ 3

★Casanova di Neri

POD. FIESOLE
53024 MONTALCINO [SI]
TEL. +39 0577834455
www.casanovadineri.com

PRE-BOOKED VISITS
ACCOMMODATION
ANNUAL PRODUCTION 225,000 bottles
HECTARES UNDER VINE 63.00

Le Cetine, Sesta and Cava dell'Onice are in the south, Podernuovo, Cerretalto and Spereta are on the eastern slope, and Fiesole and Poderuccio are in Torrenieri in the northeast. A broad representation of Montalcino's macro areas is found in these 60 hectares of vineyards belonging to Casanova di Neri. Giacomo, Gianlorenzo and Giovanni Neri run this venture today, and they have achieved worldwide success owing to the unmistakable style of their intense, rich wines. The Tenuta Nuova and Cerretalto selections are aged in small, new wood, alongside the vintage Brunello and other wines, including Vermentino, Grechetto, Colorino and Cabernet. Their 2012 Tenuta Nuova, a wine that's made them world-famous, is extremely faithful to its character, with its aromas of dark fruit confit, burnt wood and chocolate. The wine expands broadly in the mouth, sustained by flavor. We prefer the base Brunello, a wine that features hints of red fruit, spices and roots, when it comes to expressive luster and drinkability

● Brunello di Montalcino '12	♟♟ 6
● Brunello di Montalcino Tenuta Nuova '12	♟♟ 8
● Rosso di Montalcino '15	♟ 5
● Brunello di Montalcino '09	♟♟♟ 6
● Brunello di Montalcino Cerretalto '07	♟♟♟ 8
● Brunello di Montalcino Cerretalto '06	♟♟♟ 8
● Brunello di Montalcino Cerretalto '04	♟♟♟ 8
● Brunello di Montalcino Tenuta Nuova '06	♟♟♟ 8
● Brunello di Montalcino Tenuta Nuova '05	♟♟♟ 7
● Brunello di Montalcino '11	♟♟ 6
● Brunello di Montalcino Tenuta Nuova '11	♟♟ 8
● Brunello di Montalcino Tenuta Nuova '10	♟♟ 8
● Rosso di Montalcino '14	♟♟ 5

Castelfalfi

LOC. CASTELFALFI
50050 MONTAIONE [FI]
TEL. +39 0571891400
www.castelfalfi.it

ANNUAL PRODUCTION 50,000 bottles
HECTARES UNDER VINE 23.00

The estate is part of a large complex that includes hotels, restaurants and villas for farmstays. Situated in an ideal location between the provinces of Florence and Pisa, the renovated town of Castelfalfi -- which had been abandoned for years -- has now been turned into a resort. The farm grows three main crops: vines, olives and arable. All the crops are certified organic, and in winemaking, prominence has been given to Sangiovese. And this is the primary cultivar used in their 2016 San Piero (Colorino makes up the rest). The nose is vibrant, with fruity hints of blackcurrant, cherry and blackberries and accents of grass. The body is well-structured, with fresh notes and a flavorful, long finish. The 2014 Poggionero, a blend of Cabernet, Merlot and Alicante, offers up spicy fragrances of cloves, blackberry, as well as light, toasty notes of coffee. In the mouth the wine is warm, succulent and leisurely, with well-distributed tannins.

● Poggionero '14	♼♼	3
● Rancoli Vermentino '15	♼♼	2*
● San Piero '16	♼♼	2*
● Chianti Cercaia '16	♼	2
● Chianti Cercaia Ris. '14	♼	3
● Poggio alla Fame '14	♼	5
● Poggio I Soli '16	♼	2
● Poggio alla Fame '13	♼♼	5
● Poggionero '11	♼♼	3

Castell'in Villa

LOC. CASTELL'IN VILLA
53019 CASTELNUOVO BERARDENGA [SI]
TEL. +39 0577359074
www.castellinvilla.com

CELLAR SALES
PRE-BOOKED VISITS
ANNUAL PRODUCTION 100,000 bottles
HECTARES UNDER VINE 54.00

With remarkable consistency, Coralia Pignatelli produces wines that are classic (in the best sense of the word). Intense, softly elegant, but with spirit, they could be said to sum up Chianti Classico. Stylishly complex and long-lived like few other wines, they bear the fullness of Tuscany's signature wine, putting forth all of Sangiovese's potential with an inborn naturalness. Paradoxically (though not entirely), the 2011 Chianti Classico Riserva is the wine that most impressed. The nose reminds us of the passage of time, though it does so elegantly, in a way that's intriguing, true to character, with a lovely mix of spices, earth and flowers. In the mouth it exhibits flavor, depth and freshness. The 2013 Chianti Classico is more evolved, with aromas of orange and dried flowers, and an austere, hard mouth. At times the tannins feel a bit edgy.

● Chianti Cl. Ris. '11	♼♼	6
● Chianti Cl. '13	♼♼	5
● Chianti Cl. '11	♼♼♼	5
● Chianti Cl. '09	♼♼♼	5
● Chianti Cl. '08	♼♼♼	5
● Chianti Cl. Ris. '85	♼♼♼	6
● Chianti Cl. '12	♼♼	5
● Chianti Cl. '10	♼♼	5
● Chianti Cl. Poggio delle Rose Ris. '10	♼♼	6
● Chianti Cl. Ris. '10	♼♼	6
● Chianti Cl. Ris. '09	♼♼	6
● Chianti Cl. Ris. '08	♼♼	6

Castellani

FRAZ. SANTA LUCIA
VIA DEL POPOLO, 90E
56025 PONTEDERA [PI]
TEL. +39 0587292900
www.castelwine.com

CELLAR SALES
PRE-BOOKED VISITS
ANNUAL PRODUCTION 25,000,000 bottles
HECTARES UNDER VINE 1000.00

Castellani has a long history. Toward the end of the 1800s, an ancestor named Alfredo decided to bottle the wine he had produced himself. In 1903 he made the activity official and created a winery. In the years since, the winery has accumulated a thousand hectares, in Chianti, Chianti Classico and Maremma, distributing them among six estates. Each estate makes and ages its wines independently, but oversight of the thousand hectares of vineyards is constant and with direct control. The 2015 La Cattura put in a good performance. It's a blend in which Teroldego makes up the lion's share, enticing and pleasant on the nose with notes of wild berries, aromatic herbs and minty notes. The mouth is warm and dense, succulent, while the finish is sweet and long. The 2015 Ciliegiolo is also pleasant, with its clean, well-defined aromas followed by faintly spicy and fragrant notes, and potpourri. The 2015 Grand Noir, made with a rare cultivar (a mix of Aramon and Petit Bouchet), is pleasant, balanced and tasty.

● Ciliegiolo Tenuta di Santa Lucia '15	♟♟ 3
● Grand Noir Tenuta di Poggio al Casone '15	♟♟ 4
● La Cattura Tenuta di Poggio al Casone '15	♟♟ 3
● Casone Tenuta di Poggio al Casone '14	♟ 3
○ Vermentino Tenuta Santa Lucia '16	♟ 3
● Violetta Tenuta di Ceppaiano '13	♟ 3
● Alle Viole Tenuta di Ceppaiano '13	♟♟ 3
● Chianti Cl. Vign. di Campomaggio '10	♟♟ 3
● Ciliegiolo Tenuta di Santa Lucia '14	♟♟ 3
● Travalda Tenuta Santa Lucia '11	♟♟ 3
● Violetta Tenuta di Ceppaiano '12	♟♟ 3

★Castellare di Castellina

LOC. CASTELLARE
53011 CASTELLINA IN CHIANTI [SI]
TEL. +39 0577742903
www.castellare.it

CELLAR SALES
PRE-BOOKED VISITS
ACCOMMODATION
ANNUAL PRODUCTION 200,000 bottles
HECTARES UNDER VINE 28.00

This winery was founded in Castellina in Chianti by Paolo Panerai in 1975. It's most probably the flagship estate for the Domini Castellare di Castellina group, which also includes Rocca di Frassinello in Tuscany and the Feudi del Pisciotto and Gurra di Mare estates in Sicily. Their style of wines is based firmly on the search for balance and the authentic expression of Sangiovese, and it's supported by a careful use of wood for aging. The 2013 I Sodi di S. Niccolò, the winery's historic blend of Sangiovese and Malvasia Nera, gets yet another Tre Bicchieri. The wine features pervasive fragrances and an exemplary unfolding of flavor - it's a winemaking classic (and not just for Tuscany). The 2014 Chianti Classico Il Poggiale Riserva also did well, with its fragrances of flowers earth and cherries, and a dynamic, dense fresh mouth. The 2015 Chianti Classico is consistent and highly enjoyable.

● I Sodi di S. Niccolò '13	♟♟♟ 8
● Chianti Cl. Il Poggiale Ris. '14	♟♟ 5
● Chianti Cl. '15	♟ 3
● I Sodi di S. Niccolò '12	♟♟♟ 8
● I Sodi di S. Niccolò '11	♟♟♟ 8
● I Sodi di S. Niccolò '10	♟♟♟ 8
● I Sodi di S. Niccolò '09	♟♟♟ 8
● I Sodi di S. Niccolò '08	♟♟♟ 7
● I Sodi di S. Niccolò '07	♟♟♟ 7
● I Sodi di S. Niccolò '06	♟♟♟ 7
● I Sodi di S. Niccolò '05	♟♟♟ 7
● I Sodi di S. Niccolò '04	♟♟♟ 7
● I Sodi di S. Niccolò '03	♟♟♟ 7
● I Sodi di S. Niccolò '02	♟♟♟ 7
● I Sodi di San Niccolò '01	♟♟♟ 7

★Castello Banfi

FRAZ. SANT'ANGELO SCALO
B.GO CASTELLO DI POGGIO ALLE MURA
53024 MONTALCINO [SI]
TEL. +39 0577840111
www.castellobanfi.com

CELLAR SALES
PRE-BOOKED VISITS
ACCOMMODATION AND RESTAURANT SERVICE
ANNUAL PRODUCTION 10,000,000 bottles
HECTARES UNDER VINE 850.00
SUSTAINABLE WINERY

We owe the creation of one of the most famous Italian brands in the world to John and Harry Mariani. In 1978 these Italo-American brothers, having grasped the potential of Montalcino and its iconic wine, planned out Castello Banfi, with help from Ezio Rivella. Further purchases in Piedmont, Chianti Classico, and Bolgheri made their venture into a holding, but the hub remains at Poggio alle Mura where most of the 850 hectares of vineyards are cultivated. The range includes about ten wines, but their Sangiovese reds standout for their austere succulent touch. Banfi had a great day, and not just their Brunellos. The 2015 Rosso Poggio alle Mura proves a commendable compromise between fruit-rich pleasantness and extract. But the 2013 Excelsius leads the way. It's an irresistible wine with touches of resin and a subtle, yet dynamic silhouette.

★★Castello del Terriccio

LOC. TERRICCIO
VIA BAGNOLI, 16
56040 CASTELLINA MARITTIMA [PI]
TEL. +39 050699709
www.terriccio.com

CELLAR SALES
PRE-BOOKED VISITS
ANNUAL PRODUCTION 150,000 bottles
HECTARES UNDER VINE 60.00

In the heart of the 1800-hectare estate sits Castello del Terriccio, with its thousand-year-old history. But it wasn't until the end of the 1700s that the Poniatowski princes, émigrés from Poland, turned the castle and land into a farm. They set it up to produce wheat, olives and grapes, and they built a cellar. After the Great War, the estate was taken over by the Serafini Ferri Counts who are connected to the current owner's family. In the 1970s, Gian Annibale Rossi Medelana expanded the vineyards and went on to modernize the winery and improve the quality of the wine. The 2013 Lupicaia, a Cabernet Sauvignon with a bit of Petit Verdot, gets Tre Bicchieri. On the nose it offers up herbaceous overtones, with Mediterranean shrub, green pepper and wild berries. In the mouth it proves soft, sweet and fresh, with a complex finish. The 2013 Tassinaia, made of equal parts Cabernet Sauvignon and Merlot, features notes of cherry and blackcurrant, with elegant spicy hints and a flavorful finish.

● Excelsus '13	♛♛ 8
● Brunello di Montalcino '12	♛♛ 8
Brunello di Montalcino Poggio alle Mura '12	♛♛ 8
Brunello di Montalcino Poggio alle Mura Ris. '11	♛♛ 8
● Rosso di Montalcino Poggio alle Mura '15	♛♛ 5
Summus '13	♛♛ 8
● Rosso di Montalcino '15	♛ 2
● Brunello di Montalcino Poggio all'Oro Ris. '04	♛♛♛ 8
Sant'Antimo Mandrielle '04	♛♛♛ 3
Summus '88	♛♛♛ 7
● Brunello di Montalcino Poggio all'Oro Ris. '10	♛♛ 8
○ Fontanelle Chardonnay '15	♛♛ 4

● Lupicaia '13	♛♛♛ 8
○ Con Vento '16	♛♛ 4
● Tassinaia '13	♛♛ 6
● Castello del Terriccio '11	♛♛♛ 8
● Castello del Terriccio '07	♛♛♛ 8
● Lupicaia '11	♛♛♛ 8
● Lupicaia '10	♛♛♛ 8
● Lupicaia '07	♛♛♛ 8
● Castello del Terriccio '10	♛♛ 8
○ Con Vento '13	♛♛ 4
● Lupicaia '12	♛♛ 8
● Tassinaia '12	♛♛ 6
● Tassinaia '11	♛♛ 6
● Tassinaia '10	♛♛ 6

Castello del Trebbio

VIA SANTA BRIGIDA, 9
50065 PONTASSIEVE [FI]
TEL. +39 0558304900
www.castellodeltrebbio.it

CELLAR SALES
PRE-BOOKED VISITS
ACCOMMODATION AND RESTAURANT SERVICE
ANNUAL PRODUCTION 300,000 bottles
HECTARES UNDER VINE 60.00
SUSTAINABLE WINERY

The Castello del Trebbio estate spans 380
hectares between the Colli Fiorentini and
Chianti Rufina. Winemaking is at the core of
their activity but they also grow spelt, olives
and saffron, as well as offering
accommodation in beautifully renovated
farmhouses, set in a traditional Tuscan
landscape. The vineyards cover 60
hectares, planted mostly with native
varieties such as Sangiovese, Canaiolo,
Ciliegiolo and Trebbiano Toscano. Some
international grapes, especially Merlot,
round out the complement. Aging is carried
out mostly in medium and large barrels,
although they are experimenting with the
use of amphorae. As the Lastricato came in
a bit under par with respect to previous,
delectable versions, it was the Chianti
Superiore to come out on top. Red fruit and
spices fuse perfectly, foreshadowing a
mouth that's soft at first, but then gets
leaner until replaced by young, energetic
tannins. A decadent De' Pazzi also
deserves to be mentioned.

● Chianti Sup. '15	♛♛ 3*
● De' Pazzi '14	♛♛ 4
● Chianti Rufina Lastricato Ris. '13	♛ 5
● Pazzesco '14	♛ 5
● Chianti Rufina Lastricato Ris. '11	♛♛♛ 4*
○ Bianco della Congiura '14	♛♛ 3
● Chianti Rufina Lastricato Ris. '12	♛♛ 5
● Chianti Rufina Lastricato Ris. '10	♛♛ 4
● Chianti Sup. '14	♛♛ 2*
● De' Pazzi '11	♛♛ 4
● Pazzesco '11	♛♛ 5
● Sangiovese '13	♛♛ 5
● Vigneti Trebbio '11	♛♛ 4

★Castello di Albola

LOC. PIAN D'ALBOLA, 31
53017 RADDA IN CHIANTI [SI]
TEL. +39 0577738019
www.albola.it

CELLAR SALES
PRE-BOOKED VISITS
ANNUAL PRODUCTION 800,000 bottles
HECTARES UNDER VINE 140.00

Zonin's Chianti stronghold made production
choices untainted by winemaking trends in
vogue at the end of the millennium. These
proved to be decisive for establishing the
current quality standard of their product
portfolio. Choices emphasizing tradition,
respect for the Radda in Chianti terroir
(probably the most characteristic of Chianti
Classico), unforced winemaking, use of
large wood, and vine growing that
encourages natural expression of the
Sangiovese grapes cultivated on this ridge
are what led to this success. Without a
doubt, the 2014 Chianti Classic made by
the Zonin family in Radda in Chianti is
among the best. Its nose is very nice,
alternating spicy notes and accents of flint,
which accompany a marked florality. In the
mouth it expands gracefully amidst
nuances, crunchy tannins and well-
sustained richness of flavor. The
2014 Acciaiolo also did well. It's made with
Sangiovese and Cabernet Sauvignon,
though sees a predominance of the French
cultivar. The 2013 Chianti Classico Riserva
comes through austere and deep.

● Chianti Cl. '14	♛♛♛ 3
● Acciaiolo '14	♛♛ 6
● Chianti Cl. Ris. '13	♛♛ 4
● Chianti Cl. Gran Sel. '13	♛♛♛ 5
● Chianti Cl. Il Solatio Gran Sel. '11	♛♛♛ 5
● Chianti Cl. Il Solatio Gran Sel. '10	♛♛♛ 5
● Chianti Cl. Le Ellere '08	♛♛♛ 3
● Chianti Cl. Ris. '09	♛♛♛ 4
● Chianti Cl. Ris. '08	♛♛♛ 4
● Acciaiolo '13	♛♛ 6
● Chianti Cl. '13	♛♛ 3
● Chianti Cl. '12	♛♛ 3
● Chianti Cl. Le Ellere '11	♛♛ 3
● Chianti Cl. Ris. '12	♛♛ 4

★Castello di Ama

c. Ama
013 Gaiole in Chianti [SI]
. +39 0577746031
w.castellodiama.com

ELLAR SALES
RE-BOOKED VISITS
NNUAL PRODUCTION 300,000 bottles
ECTARES UNDER VINE 90.00

is winery was established in 1972 and is
ated in the small town of Ama, not far
m Gaiole in Chianti. It released its first
ttles onto the market in the late 1970s.
is was the start of their success, but
ace then they have never lost sight of their
iginal idea to focus on the territory and
pellation. Today, Castello di Ama occupies
important place in Chianti's crowded
oduction scene. The 2014 Chianti
assico Gran Selezione San Lorenzo is the
ild of a difficult vintage. The nose sees
ature aromatic strokes that alternate
tween red and dark fruit, and spicy
cents, all set on a toasty background. In
e mouth it's clenched, and exhibits
nerous flavor. The finish features a
eeting between the occasional hint of
rbs and an abundance of oak. The
15 Chianti Classico Ama is simple but
ell crafted, with subtle fragrances and a
licate, well-sustained palate.

Chianti Cl. Gran Sel. San Lorenzo '14	6
Chianti Cl. Ama '15	4
Chianti Cl. Ama '11	4*
Chianti Cl. Castello di Ama '05	5
Chianti Cl. Gran Sel. San Lorenzo '13	6
Chianti Cl. La Casuccia '04	8
Chianti Cl. Ama '13	6
Chianti Cl. Castello di Ama '08	6
Chianti Cl. Gran Sel. San Lorenzo '11	6
Chianti Cl. Gran Sel. San Lorenzo '10	6
Chianti Cl. Gran Sel. Vign. La Casuccia '11	8
L'Apparita '13	8
L'Apparita '10	8

Castello di Bolgheri

LOC. BOLGHERI
S.DA LAURETTA, 7
57020 CASTAGNETO CARDUCCI [LI]
TEL. +39 0565762110
www.castellodibolgheri.eu

CELLAR SALES
PRE-BOOKED VISITS
ACCOMMODATION
ANNUAL PRODUCTION 80,000 bottles
HECTARES UNDER VINE 50.00

In the mid-1990s the winery began planting
the varieties permitted by the production
regulations for this area: Cabernet
Sauvignon, Cabernet Franc, Merlot, Syrah
and Petit Verdot. All the vineyards are
located near town, where they receive a
dual benefit from southwestern exposure
and sea breezes. The soil is sandy-clay and
rich in stones. Clemente and Federico Zileri
Dal Verme make high-level, stylish wines,
with luxuriant but not overbearing fruit,
subtle tannins and great depth. There's
no 2014 Superiore, so it's up to the
2015 Bolgheri Rosso Varvàra to represent
Castello di Bolgheri. The results are
noteworthy. The wine comes across as
well-defined and well-extracted. It also
proved capable of a nice aromatic display of
sweet spices, starting with cinnamon,
amidst fruity and flowery notes that are as
mature as they are vigorous. The mouth is
flavorsome, with excellent tannic backbone.

● Bolgheri Varvàra '15	4
● Bolgheri Sup. Castello di Bolgheri '12	6
● Bolgheri Sup. Castello di Bolgheri '10	6
● Bolgheri Sup. Castello di Bolgheri '09	6
● Bolgheri Sup. Castello di Bolgheri '07	6
● Bolgheri Rosso Sup. '13	7
● Bolgheri Rosso Varvàra '10	4
● Bolgheri Rosso Varvàra '09	4
● Bolgheri Rosso Varvàra '08	4
● Bolgheri Sup. Castello di Bolgheri '11	6
● Bolgheri Sup. Castello di Bolgheri '06	7
● Bolgheri Varvàra '13	4
● Bolgheri Varvàra '12	4
● Bolgheri Varvàra '07	4

★★★Castello di Fonterutoli

LOC. FONTERUTOLI
VIA OTTONE III DI SASSONIA, 5
53011 CASTELLINA IN CHIANTI [SI]
TEL. +39 057773571
www.mazzei.it

CELLAR SALES
PRE-BOOKED VISITS
ACCOMMODATION AND RESTAURANT SERVICE
ANNUAL PRODUCTION 800,000 bottles
HECTARES UNDER VINE 117.00
SUSTAINABLE WINERY

The Mazzei family have owned the estate in Castellina in Chianti for centuries. It is one of the oldest and most important wineries in the entire appellation and has recently contributed to success of the Chianti Classico area as a whole. Today, Fonteruoli, which also depends on Tenuta Belguardo in Maremma, is finely tuning its style. Showing impressive results, power and concentration are combined with balance and elegance to make a truly intriguing mix. The 2015 Siepi, a blend of Sangiovese and Merlot, has solidly assumed the role of Castellina in Chianti's flagship. It's out a year earlier than usual, but its strong points remain its vibrant, polished aromas and soft, generous, nuanced flavor. The 2014 Chianti Classico Ser Lapo Riserva offers up fresh, complex aromas, with a supple, fragrant mouth. The finish is just a bit held back by the woods used for aging.

● Siepi '15	♛♛♛ 8
● Chianti Cl. Ser Lapo Ris. '14	♛♛ 5
● Chianti Cl. '15	♛♛ 4
● Chianti Cl. Gran Sel. Castello di Fonterutoli '13 ♛♛	7
● Maremma Toscana Il Tirreno '15	♛♛ 4
● Morellino di Scansano Bronzone '14	♛♛ 4
● Serrata di Belguardo Tenuta di Belguardo '15 ♛♛	4
● Mix36 '13	♛ 8
● Mix36 '11	♛♛♛ 8
● Mix36 '08	♛♛♛ 8
● Siepi '13	♛♛♛ 8
● Siepi '11	♛♛♛ 8
● Siepi '10	♛♛♛ 8

Castello di Monsanto

VIA MONSANTO, 8
50021 BARBERINO VAL D'ELSA [FI]
TEL. +39 0558059000
www.castellodimonsanto.it

CELLAR SALES
PRE-BOOKED VISITS
ANNUAL PRODUCTION 450,000 bottles
HECTARES UNDER VINE 72.00

Castello di Monsanto is a historic winery i Chianti Classico, established by Fabrizio Bianchi and currently run by his daughter Laura. The vineyards are now maximized terms of age and production of high-level raw materials. Although the winery has brought new and important innovations to the cellar, winemaking remains consistent and favors aging in large wood. The wines have a clear-cut style that is precise, with depth, although sometimes difficult to rea at the moment of release. The 2015 Chia Classico is a sophisticated, polished wine with aromas that alternate between dark and red fruit. The mouth features generou balanced and deep flavors, with well-crafted tannins. The 2014 Chianti Classico Riserva is more austere, and probably more influenced by the mediocre vintage. The wine makes no secret of the use of wood, which comes through a bit t much at times. The 2012 Chianti Classico Poggio Riserva has one too many evolved notes to it.

● Chianti Cl. '15	♛♛♛
● Chianti Cl. Ris. '14	♛♛
● Chianti Cl. Il Poggio Ris. '12	♛
● Chianti Cl. '11	♛♛♛
● Chianti Cl. Cinquantenario Ris. '08	♛♛♛
● Chianti Cl. Il Poggio Ris. '10	♛♛♛
● Chianti Cl. Ris. '11	♛♛♛
● Sangioveto '10	♛♛♛
● Chianti Cl. '14	♛♛
● Chianti Cl. '13	♛♛
● Chianti Cl. Il Poggio Ris. '11	♛♛
● Chianti Cl. Ris. '13	♛♛
● Chianti Cl. Ris. '12	♛♛

Castello di Radda

C. IL BECCO, 101A
3017 RADDA IN CHIANTI [SI]
L. +39 0577738992
ww.castellodiradda.it

CELLAR SALES
PRE-BOOKED VISITS
ANNUAL PRODUCTION 100,000 bottles
HECTARES UNDER VINE 33.00

he Beretta family have finely tuned the
inery they have owned in Chianti since
003. Their vineyards are in Radda in
hianti, a particularly important Chianti
lassico area where some of the most
aracteristic and consistent wines in the
rritory can be found. It is the aim of
astello di Radda wines to convey this, and
ey stand out for their balanced, unforced
yle, especially when it comes to using
ood which is mostly small. Castello di
adda presents a major 2015 Chianti
lassico. The wine is aromatically superb,
ith fragrances that go from wild herbs to
owers to small red fruit and spices. In the
outh it's juicy, and shows dynamic, lively
avor, finishing on a lovely spicy note. The
014 Chianti Classico Riserva also put in a
ood performance. It's less approachable
n the nose, but endowed with a deep,
ultifaceted mouth. The 2013 Chianti
lassico Gran Selezione exhibits an
xcessive influence of oak, but there's still
enty to like.

Chianti Cl. '15	▼▼▼	3*
Chianti Cl. Ris. '14	▼▼	5
Chianti Cl. Gran Sel. '13	▼▼	3
Guss '14	▼	6
Chianti Cl. Ris. '13	♈♈♈	5
Chianti Cl. Ris. '12	♈♈♈	5
Chianti Cl. Ris. '11	♈♈♈	6
Chianti Cl. Ris. '07	♈♈♈	5
Chianti Cl. '14	♈♈	3
Chianti Cl. Gran Sel. '12	♈♈	3*
Chianti Cl. Gran Sel. '11	♈♈	3
Chianti Cl. Gran Sel. '10	♈♈	3
Guss '11	♈♈	6

★Castello di Volpaia

LOC. VOLPAIA
P.ZZA DELLA CISTERNA, 1
53017 RADDA IN CHIANTI [SI]
TEL. +39 0577738066
www.volpaia.com

CELLAR SALES
PRE-BOOKED VISITS
ACCOMMODATION AND RESTAURANT SERVICE
ANNUAL PRODUCTION 200,000 bottles
HECTARES UNDER VINE 46.00
VITICULTURE METHOD Certified Organic
SUSTAINABLE WINERY

The estate is in one of the best and most
beautiful vine growing areas in the whole of
Chianti Classico. It's partly thanks to the
painstaking work of the Mascheroni family.
Giovanna and her children, Nicolò and
Federica, run the winery unfortunately,
without the genius and humanity of their
father, Carlo, who passed away recently.
His legacy remains a benchmark for the
appellation, and his family continues on the
path he carved out fifty years ago that led
to one of the best expressions of Radda in
Chianti. The 2015 Chianti Classico is a
generous wine with a lovely harmony to it.
It earns Tre Bicchieri for its clear,
well-sustained aromatic profile, in which
red fruit dominates. In the mouth, it shows
dense flavor, well-supported by acidity,
which brings out its freshness and length.
The 2013 Chianti Classico Coltassala
Riserva is very elegant, featuring
particularly lively tannins. The other wines
presented also proved solid, with the
2016 Cabernet Sauvignon Prelius, made in
Maremma, standing out for its pronounced
pleasantness.

● Chianti Cl. '15	▼▼▼	4*
● Chianti Cl. Coltassala Ris. '13	▼▼	7
● Maremma Toscana		
Cabernet Sauvignon Prelius '16	▼▼	3
● Chianti Cl. Gran Sel.		
Il Puro Vign. Casanova '13	▼	8
● Chianti Cl. Ris. '14	▼	5
○ Maremma Toscana		
Vermentino Prelius '16	▼	3
● Chianti Cl. '13	♈♈♈	3*
● Chianti Cl. Il Puro		
Vign. Casanova Ris. '08	♈♈♈	8
● Chianti Cl. Ris. '13	♈♈♈	5
● Chianti Cl. Ris. '10	♈♈♈	5
● Chianti Cl. Ris. '08	♈♈♈	5
● Chianti Cl. Ris. '07	♈♈♈	5
● Chianti Cl. Coltassala Ris. '12	♈♈	7

Castello Romitorio

LOC. ROMITORIO, 279
53024 MONTALCINO [SI]
TEL. +39 0577847212
www.castelloromitorio.com

CELLAR SALES
PRE-BOOKED VISITS
ACCOMMODATION
ANNUAL PRODUCTION 150,000 bottles
HECTARES UNDER VINE 30.00

When Sandro Chia took over Castello Romitorio more than thirty years ago, there was considerable media attention directed toward the unusual story of a world-famous artist turned Brunello producer. Recently, however, there's been much more room for farming and winemaking. There are 15 hectares located in different areas of Montalcino (Romitorio, Poggio di Sopra), as well as other plots in Chianti Colli Senesi and 11 hectares on the Ghiaccio Forte estate in Scansano. Techniques in maceration, extraction and aging make his benchmark Sangiovese wines 'modern,' but only in theory, not in taste. Their new approach is having results even for their simplest wines. The 2015 Rosso is an example, a wine that secured a top spot thanks to its fresh, multifaceted profile featuring pomegranate, watermelon and bran, all confirmed by a graceful, succulent mouth that integrates well with its tannins. The Brunello and 2012 Filo di Seta are both just as good.

● Rosso di Montalcino '15	♟♟ 5
● Brunello di Montalcino '12	♟♟ 8
● Brunello di Montalcino Filo di Seta '12	♟♟ 8
● Brunello di Montalcino '10	♟♟♟ 8
● Brunello di Montalcino '05	♟♟♟ 8
● Brunello di Montalcino '11	♟♟ 8
● Brunello di Montalcino '08	♟♟ 7
● Brunello di Montalcino Filo di Seta '11	♟♟ 8
● Brunello di Montalcino Filo di Seta '10	♟♟ 8
● Brunello di Montalcino Ris. '10	♟♟ 8
● Brunello di Montalcino Ris. '07	♟♟ 8
○ Costanza '13	♟♟ 3
● Morellino di Scansano '13	♟♟ 3
● Rosso di Montalcino '12	♟♟ 5

Castello Vicchiomaggio

LOC. LE BOLLE
VIA VICCHIOMAGGIO, 4
50022 GREVE IN CHIANTI [FI]
TEL. I 39 055854079
www.vicchiomaggio.it

CELLAR SALES
PRE-BOOKED VISITS
ACCOMMODATION AND RESTAURANT SERVIC
ANNUAL PRODUCTION 300,000 bottles
HECTARES UNDER VINE 38.00
SUSTAINABLE WINERY

Castello di Vicchiomaggio, in Greve in Chianti, has belonged to the Matta family since 1964. Shifting toward quality wine production in 1982, today their wines occupy a top position on the Florentine sid of Chianti Classico winemaking. The wines have a modern style but are never overdone. They age in both large wood an barriques producing a comfortingly consistent quality. The winery also owns another estate, Villa Vallemaggiore, in Maremma. The 2015 Chianti Classico San Jacopo has a nose in which wood is certainly not secondary, nevertheless, the mouth is very pleasant: full and juicy, with good freshness. The 2013 Chianti Classico Gran Selezione Vigneto La Prima also exhibits a greater oak toastiness, but its aromas manage to emerge in all their fruitiness. Flavors are close-woven and layered. The 2016 Governo Campostella, truly pleasant wine made in Maremma, proves fragrant and savory.

● Chianti Cl. Gran Sel. Vign. La Prima '13	♟♟
● Chianti Cl. San Jacopo da Vicchiomaggio '15	♟♟
● Governo Campostella Villa Vallemaggiore '16	♟♟
● Maremma Poggio Re Villa Vallemaggiore '15	♟♟
● Chianti Cl. Agostino Petri da Vicchiomaggio Ris. '14	♟
● Maremma Toscana Colle Alto Villa Vallemaggiore '15	♟
● Chianti Cl. Gran Sel. Vigna La Prima '10	♟♟♟
● FSM '07	♟♟♟
● FSM '04	♟♟♟
● Chianti Cl. Gran Sel. V. La Prima '12	♟♟
● Ripa delle More '13	♟♟

Castelvecchio

loc. San Pancrazio
a Certaldese, 30
0026 San Casciano in Val di Pesa [FI]
el. +39 0558248032
ww.castelvecchio.it

CELLAR SALES
PRE-BOOKED VISITS
ACCOMMODATION
ANNUAL PRODUCTION 120,000 bottles
HECTARES UNDER VINE 24.00
SUSTAINABLE WINERY

Castelvecchio's recent history began in
962, when Renzo Rocchi built the cellar
and planted the first vineyards. When
Renzo's son, Carlo, and grandchildren,
Filippo and Stefania, joined the winery,
Castelvecchio turned towards quality vine
growing and winemaking. Alberese and
limestone soil lend themselves well to grape
growing and the vineyards are situated on
the best slopes offering excellent ripening
conditions. The sunny southeastern areas
are reserved for Sangiovese, Cabernet
Sauvignon and Petit Verdot, while Merlot,
Canaiolo Nero and Malvasia enjoy a fresh
northwestern exposure. For this edition,
the winery presented a more limited
selection (with respect to previous years).
The 2015 Chianti Santa Caterina, made
with Sangiovese and a small quantity of
Canaiolo Nero, stands out among those
presented. It offers a fresh, close-focused
nose that calls up red cherry, and a linear,
close-knit mouth that's rich in fruit. A truly
pleasant experience.

Chianti S. Caterina '15	♈♈ 2*
● Chianti Colli Fiorentini Il Castelvecchio '15	♈ 2
● Numero Otto Canaiolo '15	♈ 4
○ San Lorenzo '16	♈ 2
● Il Brecciolino '11	♈♈♈ 5
● Chianti Colli Fiorentini Il Castelvecchio '13	♈♈ 2*
● Chianti Colli Fiorentini V. La Quercia Ris. '13	♈♈ 4
● Il Brecciolino '13	♈♈ 5
● Il Brecciolino '12	♈♈ 5
● Numero Otto '13	♈♈ 3
● Orme in Rosso '11	♈♈ 3
● Solo Uno '11	♈♈ 7
○ Vin Santo del Chianti Chiacchierata Notturna '04	♈♈ 6

Castiglion del Bosco

loc. Castiglion del Bosco
53024 Montalcino [SI]
Tel. +39 05771913750
www.castigliondelbosco.com

CELLAR SALES
PRE-BOOKED VISITS
ACCOMMODATION AND RESTAURANT SERVICE
ANNUAL PRODUCTION 250,000 bottles
HECTARES UNDER VINE 62.00
VITICULTURE METHOD Certified Organic

Situated in the northwesternmost part of
Montalcino, the historic Castiglion del
Bosco estate spans over 2,000 hectares.
Sixty hectares host Sangiovese and are
divided into two parts, Gauggiole and
Capanna. The Ferragamo family took over
in 2003 and the town is now the winery's
headquarters. It is also one of the most
popular destinations in the region, with a
marvelous resort, restaurants, spa, and golf
club, it offers great all-round hospitality.
The family has done a great job with recent
vintages of their range of Brunellos, which
have developed over time in definition and
character. It's a direction that's been
certified by the most recent tastes, which
see the warm vigor of the 2012 Brunello
Campo del Drago at the forefront. Plums,
topsoil, cocoa unfold generously without
drying up. In many ways, it's a phased up
version of the 2015 Rosso, a wine that
features mature fruit, woodlands and
extractive sweetness.

● Brunello di Montalcino Campo del Drago '12	♈♈ 8
● Brunello di Montalcino '12	♈♈ 6
● Brunello di Montalcino 1100 Ris. '11	♈♈ 6
● Rosso di Montalcino '15	♈♈ 3
● Brunello di Montalcino '11	♈♈ 6
● Brunello di Montalcino Campo del Drago '11	♈♈ 8
● Brunello di Montalcino Campo del Drago '10	♈♈ 8
● Brunello di Montalcino Campo del Drago '08	♈♈ 8
● Brunello di Montalcino Campo del Drago '07	♈♈ 8
● Brunello di Montalcino Ris. 1100 '10	♈♈ 6
● Rosso di Montalcino '11	♈♈ 3

Famiglia Cecchi

LOC. CASINA DEI PONTI, 56
53011 CASTELLINA IN CHIANTI [SI]
TEL. +39 057754311
www.cecchi.net

CELLAR SALES
PRE-BOOKED VISITS
ANNUAL PRODUCTION 8,000,000 bottles
HECTARES UNDER VINE 330.00
SUSTAINABLE WINERY

Thanks to scrupulous stylistic decision-making, this winery in Castellina in Chianti was one of the first to endow their wines with a marked identity, as well as achieving a solid and reassuringly consistent standard of quality. Thus their selection features expressive wines that are full of character. The Cecchi family doesn't work exclusively in Chianti Classico, however. They also own Castello di Montauto in San Gimignano and the recently renovated Val delle Rose estate in Maremma. The 2015 Chianti Classico Storia di Famiglia is a delightful and well-crafted wine, with an aromatic profile that brings together notes of wild berries, sweet spices and the occasional hint of vanilla. It unfolds in a way that is precise and linear, with a hint of oak that returns in the finish. The 2014 Chianti Classico Villa Cerna Riserva is still evolving, though for now it sees faint aromas of iron, with a generous and layered mouth that's just a bit too hard.

Centolani

LOC. FRIGGIALI
S.DA MAREMMANA
53024 MONTALCINO [SI]
TEL. +39 0577049454
www.tenutafriggialiepietranera.it

CELLAR SALES
PRE-BOOKED VISITS
ACCOMMODATION
ANNUAL PRODUCTION 260,000 bottles
HECTARES UNDER VINE 70.00

The Peluso Centolani family own two estates. Friggiali is to the west, with vineyards at 250 to 400 meters above sea level, on poor, loose soil, rich in galestro. Here there's good air circulation and the grapes give rise to fragrant, ethery and sharp wines. Pietranera, on the other hand, is near the Sant'Antimo Abbey where the soil is more compact and altitudes are lower, thus its wines are more structured and intense. The hot 2012 season sees the Friggiali selection winning out over Pletranera. The Brunello offers mature, fruit a delicate hint of balsamic and spicy accents. The mouth has succulence and length to it, though the finish is a bit bridled by its yet unsettled tannins. The 2011 Riserva is vigorous and flavorsome, generous and layered. Still austere tannins mean that the finish is a bit clenched.

● Chianti Cl. Storia di Famiglia '15	♟♟ 3*
● Chianti Cl. Villa Cerna Ris. '14	♟♟ 5
● Maremma Toscana Aurelio Val delle Rose '16	♟ 4
○ Maremma Toscana Litorale Val delle Rose '16	♟ 3
● Morellino di Scansano Val delle Rose '16	♟ 3
● Chianti Cl. Villa Cerna Ris. '13	♟♟♟ 5
● Chianti Cl. Villa Cerna Ris. '12	♟♟♟ 5
● Chianti Cl. Villa Cerna Ris. '08	♟♟♟ 5
● Coevo '11	♟♟♟ 8
● Coevo '10	♟♟♟ 7
● Chianti Cl. Primo Colle Villa Cerna '14	♟♟ 3
● Merlot La Mora '13	♟♟ 4

● Brunello di Montalcino Tenuta Friggiali '12	♟♟ 6
● Brunello di Montalcino Pietranera '12	♟♟ 5
● Brunello di Montalcino Tenuta Friggiali Ris. '11	♟♟ 6
● Brunello di Montalcino Poggiotondo '12	♟ 6
● Brunello di Montalcino Tenuta Friggiali '04	♟♟♟ 5
● Brunello di Montalcino Pietranera '11	♟♟ 5
● Brunello di Montalcino Pietranera '10	♟♟ 5
● Brunello di Montalcino Pietranera '09	♟♟ 5
● Brunello di Montalcino Pietranera '08	♟♟ 5
● Brunello di Montalcino Poggiotondo '10	♟♟ 5
● Brunello di Montalcino Tenuta Friggiali '11	♟♟ 6
● Brunello di Montalcino Tenuta Friggiali '10	♟♟ 5

Tenute del Cerro

LOC. ACQUAVIVA
VIA GRAZIANELLA, 5
53045 MONTEPULCIANO [SI]
TEL. +39 0578767722
www.fattoriadelcerro.it

CELLAR SALES
PRE-BOOKED VISITS
ACCOMMODATION AND RESTAURANT SERVICE
ANNUAL PRODUCTION 1,300,000 bottles
HECTARES UNDER VINE 181.00

Tenute del Cerro include several properties in top-quality areas: Poderina in Montalcino, Còlpetrone in Montefalco in Umbria, and Monterufoli, where they make Vermentino. Jewel of the crown is Fattoria del Cerro, with 94 hectares of beautiful vineyards, some of the largest in Montalcino. Today, everything is run by the Unipol Group. Their wines possess all of the desirable characteristics, but are modern with rich extraction. The best still come from Montepulciano. The 2014 Nobile offers up toasty, fruity fragrances of excellent maturity. The mouth proves dense and full-bodied, extractive and tannic. The 2013 Riserva proves less close-focused, with tertiary aromas and assertive tannins.

● Nobile di Montepulciano '14	♈♈♈ 3*
● Val di Cornia Rosso Poggio Miniera '11	♈♈ 5
○ Vermentino Pian di Seta '15	♈♈ 4
○ Vin Santo di Montepulciano '13	♈♈ 5
● Nobile di Montepulciano Ris. '13	♈ 5
● Rosso di Montepulciano '15	♈ 3
○ Spumante Cerrus	♈ 3
○ Vermentino '16	♈ 3
● Nobile di Montepulciano '11	♈♈♈ 3*
● Nobile di Montepulciano '10	♈♈♈ 3*
● Nobile di Montepulciano Ris. '12	♈♈♈ 4*
● Nobile di Montepulciano Ris. '11	♈♈♈ 4*
● Nobile di Montepulciano Ris. '06	♈♈♈ 4

Vincenzo Cesani

LOC. PANCOLE, 82D
53037 SAN GIMIGNANO [SI]
TEL. +39 0577955084
www.cesani.it

CELLAR SALES
PRE-BOOKED VISITS
ACCOMMODATION
ANNUAL PRODUCTION 100,000 bottles
HECTARES UNDER VINE 21.00
VITICULTURE METHOD Certified Organic

In the 1950s the Cesani family left Marche and moved to San Gimignano. Straightaway, Vincenzo began working towards twin goals of quality and respect for the environment. After more than sixty years of dedicated work, vine growing and olive growing are both under organic management. Maria Luisa and Letizia have also brought back an ancient but long-forgotten, local product: saffron. On offer as well at the property are farmstays and tastings. Letizia Cesani earns a Tre Bicchieri with the 2014 Vernaccia Sanice Riserva, thanks to a bouquet featuring mineral notes, with hints of forest floor and elements of mature fruit. In the mouth it enters pleasantly, generous and succulent, with excellent richness of flavor. The finish is complex and layered. The 2015 Vernaccia Clamys is also interesting, with its hints of iodine, almond and apple, and an assortment of vegetal notes.

○ Vernaccia di S. Gimignano Sanice Ris. '14	♈♈♈ 3*
○ Vernaccia di S. Gimignano Clamys '15	♈♈ 2*
● Chianti Colli Senesi '16	♈ 2
⊙ Rosta Serarosa '16	♈ 2
○ Vernaccia di S. Gimignano '16	♈ 2
● Luenzo '99	♈♈♈ 4
● Chianti Colli Senesi '15	♈♈ 2*
● Chianti Colli Senesi '13	♈♈ 2*
● Luenzo '12	♈♈ 4
● Luenzo '11	♈♈ 4
● San Gimignano Rosso Cellori '09	♈♈ 4
● Serisè '12	♈♈ 3
○ Vernaccia di S. Gimignano '13	♈♈ 2*
○ Vernaccia di S. Gimignano '12	♈♈ 2*

Giovanni Chiappini

LOC. FELCIAINO
VIA BOLGHERESE, 189C
57020 BOLGHERI [LI]
TEL. +39 0565765201
www.giovannichiappini.it

CELLAR SALES
PRE-BOOKED VISITS
ANNUAL PRODUCTION 70,000 bottles
HECTARES UNDER VINE 23.00
VITICULTURE METHOD Certified Organic
SUSTAINABLE WINERY

In the 1950s several families came to Bolgheri from the Marche to seek their fortune. The Chiappinis are one such family. Today, the well-established winery bearing their name remains anchored to its roots and maintains its proud artisan nature. The vineyards are divided into different plots and are run under organic management. The wines have an aromatic and flavor density, and offer up the best attributes of the variety. The 2015 Bolgheri Rosso Felciaino put in a good performance. It's vibrant and fruit-drive on the nose, with mature cherries and blackberries, and lush in the mouth. It's a wine that has good support and tannins for staying power, but it doesn't lack the approachability that you'd expect from the typology, either. The 2014 Superiore Guado de Gemoli is, honestly, under par, made blurry by its toastiness and caged in by its tannins.

● Bolgheri Rosso Felciaino '15	♥♥ 3
● Bolgheri Sup. Guado de' Gemoli '14	♥ 8
● Bolgheri Felciaino '13	♥♥ 4
● Bolgheri Rosso Felciaino '12	♥♥ 3
● Bolgheri Rosso Ferrugini '11	♥♥ 3
● Bolgheri Sup. Gaudo de' Gemoli '09	♥♥ 6
● Bolgheri Sup. Guado de' Gemoli '13	♥♥ 8
● Bolgheri Sup. Guado de' Gemoli '12	♥♥ 8
● Lienà Cabernet Franc '13	♥♥ 8
● Lienà Cabernet Franc '12	♥♥ 8
● Lienà Cabernet Franc '11	♥♥ 7
● Lienà Cabernet Franc '10	♥♥ 7
● Lienà Cabernet Franc '08	♥♥ 7
● Lienà Cabernet Sauvignon '11	♥♥ 7
● Lienà Cabernet Sauvignon '10	♥♥ 7
● Lienà Cabernet Sauvignon '08	♥♥ 7

Le Chiuse

LOC. PULLERA, 228
53024 MONTALCINO [SI]
TEL. +39 055597052
www.lechiuse.com

CELLAR SALES
PRE-BOOKED VISITS
ACCOMMODATION
ANNUAL PRODUCTION 30,000 bottles
HECTARES UNDER VINE 8.00
VITICULTURE METHOD Certified Organic

The estate's eight hectares are situated together and are surrounded by the best vine growing areas in northern Montalcino from Montosoli to Canalicchi. Simonetta Valiani inherited Le Chiuse when Fiorella Biondi Santi passed away. Here, she, with the help of her husband, Nicolò Magnelli, make Sangiovese wines. In the past thirty years her wines have been synonymous with elegance and vigor, owing to her talent for producing wines in keeping with only the very best of her family's traditions. They have adopted a biocompatible approach to winemaking, with spontaneous fermentation, long maceration and aging in 2000-, 3000- and 5000-liter oak barrels. Le Chiuse put in yet another excellent performance. The 2015 Rosso is already first-rate, with its nuances of raspberry, rosolio and roots, which follow through in a gentle, tasty mouth. But the 2012 Brunello electrifies thanks to its woodland grace and taut, velvety, lingering mouth.

● Brunello di Montalcino '12	♥♥♥ 7
● Rosso di Montalcino '15	♥♥ 4
● Brunello di Montalcino '11	♥♥♥ 7
● Brunello di Montalcino '10	♥♥♥ 7
● Brunello di Montalcino '07	♥♥♥ 7
● Brunello di Montalcino Ris. '07	♥♥♥ 8
● Brunello di Montalcino '09	♥♥ 7
● Brunello di Montalcino '08	♥♥ 7
● Brunello di Montalcino Ris. '09	♥♥ 8
● Rosso di Montalcino '14	♥♥ 4
● Rosso di Montalcino '13	♥♥ 4
● Rosso di Montalcino '12	♥♥ 4
● Rosso di Montalcino '11	♥♥ 4
● Rosso di Montalcino '10	♥♥ 3

Cigliano

VIA CIGLIANO, 17
50026 San Casciano in Val di Pesa [FI]
Tel. +39 055820033
www.villadelcigliano.it

CELLAR SALES
PRE-BOOKED VISITS
ANNUAL PRODUCTION 40,000 bottles
HECTARES UNDER VINE 25.00

The Maccaferri Montecchi family, desandants of a branch of the Antinoris, own this estate on the Chianti Classico slope, near Florence. Their aim has always been for a direct link to the territory and today it is one of the most interesting wineries in the appellation. Currently they are searching for a way to achieve consistent quality. But their wines are elegant, slim-bodied and with a very classic style. Aging is carried out in concrete vats and large wood. Cigliano's 2014 Chianti Classico sees a beautifully classic aromatic profile. The fragrances are fruit-rich, merging with notes of wet earth and herbs. In the mouth, its tannins are spirited, with lively acidity. Even if the wine doesn't exhibit great depth, the palate is supple and pleasantly fresh. The 2013 Chianti Classico Riserva sees a well-sustained and tight-knit tannic weave, though it may be just a bit too hard. The nose, which displays good complexity, moves from flowers to spices.

Cima

HAZ. ROMAGNANO
VIA DEL FAGIANO, 1
54100 Massa
Tel. +39 0585831617
www.aziendagricolacima.it

CELLAR SALES
ANNUAL PRODUCTION 100,000 bottles
HECTARES UNDER VINE 27.00

Lunigiana is not an easy territory, it is full of demanding and difficult situations to handle. Never daunted, the Cima family have been vine growers here for generations, when at the start of the nineteenth century they began farming. Credit for developing and modernizing their winemaking is due to Giovanni and his son, Aurelio, the current owner. While promoting local native varieties such as Vermentino Nero and Massaretta, they also set a focus on more meticulous and consistent wine production. The 2015 Massaretta, made with the cultivar of the same name, has a flowery, fruity and elegant nose. The mouth is succulent and solid, caressing, with a rising finish. The 2015 Chiave di Volta exhibits an aromatic profile in which overtones of fur are followed by aromatic herbs and dark fruit. The body is well-structured and rich with well-integrated tannins and a nice, lingering finish. The 2015 Sangiovese Anchigi offers up balsamic hints and wild berries on the nose. The wine features an elegant structure, a palate rich in taste and balanced freshness.

● Chianti Cl. '14	♟♟ 3
● Chianti Cl. Villa Cigliano Ris. '13	♟♟ 4
● Chianti Cl. Cigliano '13	♟♟♟ 3*
● Chianti Cl. '10	♟♟ 2*
● Chianti Cl. '07	♟♟ 2*
● Chianti Cl. Cigliano '12	♟♟ 3*
● Chianti Cl. Cigliano '11	♟♟ 3
● Chianti Cl. Ris. '99	♟♟ 3
● Chianti Cl. Villa Cigliano Ris. '11	♟♟ 4
● Chianti Cl. Villa Cigliano Ris. '09	♟♟ 4
● Suganella '06	♟♟ 4

● Anchigi '15	♟♟ 3
● Candia dei Colli Apuani Chiave di Volta '15	♟♟ 2*
● Candia dei Colli Apuani Massaretta '15	♟♟ 5
○ Candia dei Colli Apuani Vign. Alto '16	♟♟ 3
○ Candia dei Colli Apuani Vermentino Chiave di Volta '16	♟ 2
● Candia dei Colli Apuani Vermentino Nero '15	♟ 5
○ Candia dei Colli Apuani Vign. Candia Alto '08	♟♟ 3
● Gamo '06	♟♟ 8
● Montervo '08	♟♟ 5
● Romalbo '09	♟♟ 5
● Romalbo '06	♟♟ 5
● Vermentino Nero '06	♟♟ 5

Fattoria di Cinciano

LOC. CINCIANO, 2
53036 POGGIBONSI [SI]
TEL. +39 0577936588
www.cinciano.it

ANNUAL PRODUCTION 70,000 bottles
HECTARES UNDER VINE 25.00

Fattoria di Cinciano is located in a superb winemaking area of Chianti Classico, not far from Barberino Val d'Elsa. Contrary to expectations, the winery hasn't yet achieved constant quality. However, it seems to have taken a correct path, especially in terms of consistency and links with the territory of origin. Very high level raw materials, unforced winemaking, and aging in large wood give the winery a clean style with personality. Even if the use of oak comes through, the 2015 Chianti Classico possesses good matière, which comes through in a well-paced, fresh palate. Its fragrances are vibrant, with fruit prevailing over a spicy, earthy backdrop. The 2014 Chianti Classico Riserva sees a similar presence of oak, but it seems more justified here, considering the complicated vintage. The mouth is well-sustained and its aromas feature fragrant, dark fruit.

Le Cinciole

VIA CASE SPARSE, 83
50020 PANZANO [FI]
TEL. +39 055852636
www.lecinciole.it

CELLAR SALES
PRE-BOOKED VISITS
ANNUAL PRODUCTION 45,000 bottles
HECTARES UNDER VINE 11.00
VITICULTURE METHOD Certified Organic
SUSTAINABLE WINERY

We could sum up Luca and Valeria Orsini's winery as follows: organic viticulture, vineyards over 400 meters above sea level and aging in large and small wood. It is a small but interesting winery, whose importance includes its location in one of the most charming Chianti Classico subzones, Panzano. Their style is defined by fresh wines that often feature a pleasant hardness and good aging potential. Cinciole definitely puts forward one of the best 2014 Chianti Classicos. It's a complicated vintage, but the wine recovered quickly, presenting a first-rate aromatic profile. It moves from hints of watermelon to notes of raspberry and iodine. In the mouth the wine is decadent, well-paced and savory, without wavering. The 2013 Petresco, made with 100% Sangiovese, sees a more austere nose, but certainly no less charming. In the mouth, the wine proves full and layered.

● Chianti Cl. '15	🏆🏆 3
● Chianti Cl. Ris. '14	🏆🏆 3
● Chianti Cl. '12	🏆🏆 3
● Chianti Cl. '11	🏆🏆 3
● Chianti Cl. '06	🏆🏆 3
● Chianti Cl. Gran Sel. '12	🏆🏆 5
● Chianti Cl. Gran Sel. '11	🏆🏆 5
● Chianti Cl. Ris. '13	🏆🏆 3*
● Chianti Cl. Ris. '12	🏆🏆 3*
● Chianti Cl. Ris. '11	🏆🏆 3
● Chianti Cl. Ris. '10	🏆🏆 3*
● Chianti Cl. Ris. '06	🏆🏆 4
● Chianti Cl. Ris. '05	🏆🏆 4
● Pietraforte '11	🏆🏆 2*
● Pietraforte '07	🏆🏆 4

● Chianti Cl. '14	🏆🏆🏆 3*
● Petresco '13	🏆🏆 5
● Camalaione '04	🏆🏆🏆 7
● Chianti Cl. '12	🏆🏆🏆 3*
● Chianti Cl. Petresco Ris. '01	🏆🏆🏆 5
● Petresco '12	🏆🏆🏆 5
● Chianti Cl. '13	🏆🏆 3
● Chianti Cl. '11	🏆🏆 3
● Chianti Cl. '10	🏆🏆 3
● Chianti Cl. A Luigi Ris. '12	🏆🏆 3
● Cinciorosso '13	🏆🏆 3
● Cinciorosso '12	🏆🏆 3
● Petresco '10	🏆🏆 5
⊙ Rosato '13	🏆🏆 2*

Podere della Civettaja

VIA DI CASINA ROSSA, 5A
52100 AREZZO
TEL. +39 3397098418
www.civettaja.it

CELLAR SALES
PRE-BOOKED VISITS
ANNUAL PRODUCTION 7,000 bottles
HECTARES UNDER VINE 3.00
VITICULTURE METHOD Certified Organic

Sometimes places have a meaning that goes beyond what you can see. Vincenzo Tommasi's winery is such a place. It's situated in Casentino, near the Romena church, which is a place of worship open the world. He was brave enough to make difficult decisions like planting Pinot Nero in a territory that had never been good for vines. Results proved him right but instead of resting on his laurels, he began gathering together other keen producers like himself, forming an association of Pinot Nero producers in the Tuscan Apennines. In the meantime, their 2014 behaves smashingly, while, for the second year in a row, they get a Tre Bicchieri. A nice, limpid color, vibrant, fresh, assertive aromas of aromatic herbs (mint included) and fruit, such as blackcurrant and blueberries. Its entry in the mouth is soft, elegant, enticing - it's an extraordinarily drinkable wine. Tannins are fine-grained and well-placed, and the aftertaste offers up spicy hints of cloves.

● Pinot Nero '14	♛♛♛ 6
● Pinot Nero '13	♕♕♕ 6
● Pinot Nero '12	♕♕ 3
● Pinot Nero '11	♕♕ 3

★Tenuta Col d'Orcia

VIA GIUNCHETI
53024 MONTALCINO [SI]
TEL. +39 057780891
www.coldorcia.it

CELLAR SALES
PRE-BOOKED VISITS
ANNUAL PRODUCTION 800,000 bottles
HECTARES UNDER VINE 142.00
VITICULTURE METHOD Certified Organic
SUSTAINABLE WINERY

Col d'Orcia, an estate in southern Montalcino, boasts a centuries-old history. Bought in 1973 by the Marone Cinzano family, it is run today by Count Francesco. One hundred and fifty hectares of vineyards are concentrated between the Sant'Angelo in Colle district and the Orcia river. It is a sun-soaked area, but cooled by air currents coming down from nearby Monte Amiata. With the 2011 vintage, a new Brunello named Nastagio was added to the range. The flagship wine remains the Poggio al Vento Cru, aged for almost four years in 2500- and 7500-liter Allier and Slavonian oak barrels. Not to be forgotten are the Super Tuscans from international grapes, with Nearco and Olmaia at the top of the range. Without a doubt, this has been one of Col d'Orcia's best performances. Sweet fruit, root and topsoil - the 2011 Nastagio is already a credible, complete Brunello. But the 2010 Poggio al Vento Riserva goes even further, bringing together force and dynamism, with an aromatic profile that features mulberry, medicinal herbs and cumin.

● Brunello di Montalcino Poggio al Vento Ris. '10	♛♛♛ 8
● Brunello di Montalcino Nastagio '11	♛♛ 8
● Brunello di Montalcino '12	♛♛ 7
● Rosso di Montalcino '15	♛♛ 5
● Rosso di Montalcino Banditella '14	♛♛ 5
● Sant'Antimo Cabernet Olmaia '13	♛♛ 6
● Sant'Antimo Nearco '14	♛ 5
● Brunello di Montalcino Poggio al Vento Ris. '06	♕♕♕ 8
● Brunello di Montalcino Poggio al Vento Ris. '04	♕♕♕ 8
● Brunello di Montalcino '11	♕♕ 7
● Brunello di Montalcino '10	♕♕ 7
● Rosso di Montalcino Banditella '12	♕♕ 5
● Sant'Antimo Cabernet Olmaia '12	♕♕ 6

Col di Bacche

FRAZ. MONTIANO
S.DA DI CUPI
58051 MAGLIANO IN TOSCANA [GR]
TEL. +39 0564589538
www.coldibacche.com

CELLAR SALES
PRE-BOOKED VISITS
ANNUAL PRODUCTION 80,000 bottles
HECTARES UNDER VINE 13.50

This winery based in Magliano in Tuscany is an excellent example of how to imbue wines with the qualities that define Maremma winemaking. The result is a range of very readable wines with a clear-cut style. As the vineyards get older, complexity and character are coming more to the forefront. In a style that has been generally modern until now, Alberto Carnasciali is currently introducing more traditional elements such as a greater focus on Sangiovese. Good feelings about Col di Bacche's newest wine. The 2014 Sangiovese Poggio all Viole offers up precise, vibrant fragrances that alternate between small red fruit and spices. In the mouth the wine is docile and balanced, with good freshness (though the weakness of the vintage needs to be taken into account). The Morellino di Scansano never disappoints. The 2016 proves absolutely delightful.

● Poggio alle Viole '14	♟♟ 5
● Morellino di Scansano '16	♟♟ 3
● Morellino di Scansano Rovente Ris. '14	♟ 5
○ Vermentino '16	♟ 3
● Cupinero '09	♟♟♟ 5
● Morellino di Scansano Rovente '05	♟♟♟ 4
● Cupinero '13	♟♟ 5
● Cupinero '12	♟♟ 5
● Cupinero '11	♟♟ 5
● Morellino di Scansano '15	♟♟ 3*
● Morellino di Scansano '11	♟♟ 3
● Morellino di Scansano Rovente Ris. '13	♟♟ 5
● Morellino di Scansano Rovente Ris. '12	♟♟ 5
● Morellino di Scansano Rovente Ris. '11	♟♟ 5
● Morellino di Scansano Rovente Ris. '10	♟♟ 5

★Colle Massari

LOC. POGGI DEL SASSO
58044 CINIGIANO [GR]
TEL. +39 0564900406
www.collemassari.it

CELLAR SALES
PRE-BOOKED VISITS
ACCOMMODATION
ANNUAL PRODUCTION 500,000 bottles
HECTARES UNDER VINE 110.00
VITICULTURE METHOD Certified Organic
SUSTAINABLE WINERY

For Claudio Tipa and his sister Maria Iris, Colle Massari was the starting point for establishing a series of wineries in the most prestigious Tuscan terroir. Starting off in Montecucco, they moved on to Montalcino, with Poggio di Sotto and then Bolgheri, with Grattamacco. Colle Massari is on the Tyrrhenian side of Monte Amiata and includes 1200 hectares of woods, arable land and olive groves. There are 110 hectares of vineyards, which primarily host Sangiovese, with small amounts of Ciliegiolo and Cabernet Sauvignon for the reds, and Vermentino for the whites. Colle Massari adds another feather to its already full cap of Tre Bicchieri. Once again, the Poggio Lombrone delivers by virtue of its vibrant nose, which brings together classic overtones of ripe red fruit and spicy, balsamic whiffs. The mouth is solid, its tannins still fresh and lively, with a savory, mineral background that lends extreme elegance to the palate.

● Montecucco Sangiovese Poggio Lombrone Ris. '13	♟♟♟ 6
● Montecucco Vin Santo Occhio di Pernice Scosciamonaca '11	♟♟ 7
● Montecucco Rosso Rigoleto '15	♟♟ 3
● Montecucco Rosso Ris. '14	♟♟ 4
● Canaiolo Tenuta di Montecucco '16	♟ 2
○ Montecucco Vermentino Irisse '15	♟ 3
○ Montecucco Vermentino Melacce '16	♟ 3
● Montecucco Rosso Ris. '13	♟♟♟ 3*
● Montecucco Sangiovese Lombrone Ris. '11	♟♟♟ 6
● Montecucco Sangiovese Lombrone Ris. '10	♟♟♟ 6

Colle Santa Mustiola

VIA DELLE TORRI, 86A
53043 CHIUSI [SI]
TEL. +39 057820525
www.poggioaichiari.it

CELLAR SALES
PRE-BOOKED VISITS
ANNUAL PRODUCTION 18,000 bottles
HECTARES UNDER VINE 5.00
SUSTAINABLE WINERY

Fabio Cenni's winery enjoys constant fame.
Even though his cellar and vineyards are
not in one of the classic Tuscan
appellations, his wines are a benchmark for
enthusiasts of authentic and genuine
Sangiovese. Here near Chiusi, in a border
area between what used to be the Gran
Duchy and the Papal States (respectively,
Tuscany and Umbria), the soil is sandy,
stony and full of clay. The Poggio ai Chiari
is Colle Santa Mustiola's most important
and long-lived wine. It's a wine capable of
intriguing aromatic curves and a rare
length of flavor. Tertiary, but vigorous, as
earthy as it is elegant, the 2010 offers up
an array of relaxed fruit accompanied by its
trademark dried flowers, and revived by
mineral brilliance. Its the palate, in any
case, that makes the difference. The
texture is polished, while its length proves
noteworthy indeed. The 2015 Rosato
Kernos also does well.

Fattoria Colle Verde

FRAZ. MATRAIA
LOC. CASTELLO
55010 LUCCA
TEL. +39 0583402310
www.colleverde.it

CELLAR SALES
PRE-BOOKED VISITS
ANNUAL PRODUCTION 30,000 bottles
HECTARES UNDER VINE 7.00

Piero Tartagni and Francesca Pardini
founded Fattoria Colle Verde years ago,
following their decision to move to the
countryside. They couldn't have chosen a
more beautiful place for their farm: the
Matraia hills around Lucca. In line with the
philosophical and farming choices of many
of the wineries in the area they have
adopted biodynamics as well. The result is
very personal and authentic wines. The
overall impression was excellent, pointing
to a hat trick of flawless, highly
recommendable wines. The Syrah Nero
della Spinosa has dark fragrances and a
solid mouth, despite the not-so-easy
vintage; the 2013 Cabernet Franc Sinòpia
is racy and aromatically coherent with the
cultivar. The 2014 Brania delle Ghiandaie
confirms its outstanding reputation, while
the 2016 Terre di Matraja Rosso surprises.

● Poggio ai Chiari '10	♔♔ 6
☉ Kernos '15	♔♔ 4
● Poggio ai Chiari '07	♔♔♔ 6
● Poggio ai Chiari '06	♔♔♔ 6
● Poggio ai Chiari '09	♔♔ 6
● Poggio ai Chiari '08	♔♔ 6
● Vigna Flavia '12	♔♔ 5
● Vigna Flavia '11	♔♔ 5
● Vigna Flavia '10	♔♔ 5

● Nero della Spinosa '14	♔♔ 5
● Brania delle Ghiandaie '14	♔♔ 5
● Sinòpia '13	♔♔ 8
● Terre di Matraja Rosso '16	♔♔ 3
○ Terre di Matraja Bianco '16	♔ 3
● Colline Lucchesi Rosso Brania delle Ghiandaie '13	♔♔ 5
● Colline Lucchesi Rosso Brania delle Ghiandaie '12	♔♔ 5
● Colline Lucchesi Rosso Brania delle Ghiandaie '11	♔♔ 5
● Colline Lucchesi Rosso Terre di Matraja '12	♔♔ 2*
● Colline Lucchesi Rosso Terre di Matraja '11	♔♔ 2*
● Nero della Spinosa '13	♔♔ 5

Tenuta di Collosorbo

FRAZ. CASTELNUOVO DELL'ABATE
LOC. VILLA A SESTA, 25
53024 MONTALCINO [SI]
TEL. +39 0577835534
www.collosorbo.com

CELLAR SALES
PRE-BOOKED VISITS
ANNUAL PRODUCTION 100,000 bottles
HECTARES UNDER VINE 27.00

After the Tenuta di Sesta inheritance was
divided up, Collosorbo was established in
1995. Situated on the southern slope of
Montalcino between Sant'Angelo in Colle
and Castelnuovo dell'Abate, it is run by
Giovanni Ciacci with help from his
daughters Laura (winemaker) and Lucia
(agronomist). Together they run 27 hectares
of vineyards, mainly Sangiovese, though
there's also Syrah, Cabernet, Merlot and
Petit Verdot. Brunello is there flagship, and
they're aged in 1200- and 5400-liter
French and Slavonian oak barrels. The best
versions are powerful and summery with
nuances of citrus fruit and grape skins. This
time, there's not a specific standout, but
still an excellent performance for the
selection as a whole, starting with the long
2015 Rosso. The 2011 Brunello Riserva is
aromatically darker, and sees an
abundance of tannins and alcohol, while
the 2012 Brunello, a wine with a bit of
spiciness to it, sees a return to airier, more
convivial atmospheres.

● Brunello di Montalcino '12	♥♥ 6
● Brunello di Montalcino Ris. '11	♥♥ 8
● Rosso di Montalcino '15	♥♥ 4
● Brunello di Montalcino '11	♀♀ 6
● Brunello di Montalcino '10	♀♀ 6
● Brunello di Montalcino '07	♀♀ 6
● Brunello di Montalcino '06	♀♀ 6
● Brunello di Montalcino '05	♀♀ 6
● Brunello di Montalcino Ris. '10	♀♀ 8
● Brunello di Montalcino Ris. '07	♀♀ 8
● Brunello di Montalcino Ris. '04	♀♀ 8
● Rosso di Montalcino '08	♀♀ 4
● Sant'Antimo '09	♀♀ 3

Colognole

LOC. COLOGNOLE
VIA DEL PALAGIO, 15
50065 PONTASSIEVE [FI]
TEL. +39 0558319870
www.colognole.it

CELLAR SALES
PRE-BOOKED VISITS
ACCOMMODATION AND RESTAURANT SERVICE
ANNUAL PRODUCTION 90,000 bottles
HECTARES UNDER VINE 27.00

The Spalletti family have owned the estate
since the end of the 19th century. They
have 27 hectares of vineyards in the hills
running along the right bank of the Sieve. In
the early 1990s Gabriella Spalletti Trivelli
began running the farm with her sons,
Cesare and Mario, giving a new lease on
life to their wine (and olive) production.
Sangiovese reigns, but it's supplemented
with Colorino, Merlot and Chardonnay
cultivated in rows so as to form a backdrop
for a perfectly-restored village. Villas,
apartments and farmhouses with swimming
pools complete this flourishing farmstay
business. The Riserva del Don makes it to
our finals. The 2012 presents a complex
nose, going all on in ripe cherry refreshed
by balsamic whiffs, with an intriguing, spicy
atmosphere made possible by the use of
wood. The mouth maintains its freshness
and drinkability amidst a well-defined
tannic weave. The 2015 Le Lastre also put
in a good performance. It's a bit imprecise
on the nose, but still dense and succulent.

● Chianti Rufina Riserva del Don '12	♥♥ 5
● Le Lastre '15	♥♥ 4
● Chianti Rufina '14	♥ 3
● Chianti Sinopie '16	♥ 2
○ Sinopie Bianco '16	♥ 2
● Chianti Rufina '12	♀♀ 2*
● Chianti Rufina Ris. del Don '09	♀♀ 5
● Chianti Rufina Riserva del Don '11	♀♀ 5
● Chianti Sinopie '15	♀♀ 2*

Il Colombaio di Santa Chiara

LOC. RACCIANO
VIA SAN DONATO, 1
53037 SAN GIMIGNANO [SI]
TEL. +39 0577942004
www.colombaiosantachiara.it

CELLAR SALES
PRE-BOOKED VISITS
ACCOMMODATION
ANNUAL PRODUCTION 90,000 bottles
HECTARES UNDER VINE 12.00
VITICULTURE METHOD Certified Organic

Mario Logi's sons, Alessio, Stefano and Giampiero, are at the helm of this winery. Their work is defined by a deep respect for the environment, and is carried out with pesticide-free treatments, attentive care to the vineyards, and careful selection during harvest (which is performed strictly by hand). These important choices result in wines with strong links to the territory. The building used for farmhouse accommodations dates from the 19th century, and the old cellars dug out of tuff remain. On the estate you'll also find the Pieve di San Donato, a picturesque 12th-century Romanesque church. The 2014 Vernaccia Riserva 'Albereta' is excellent, with captivating notes of white fruit, like peach and lychee, and accents of sweet spice. In the mouth it proves to have a succulent body, full and lively, with an uplifting, well-structured finish. The 2016 Vernaccia Selvabianca also did well, with its fresh, almost citrusy notes of lime, then aromatic herbs. It shows good structure, with a savory, enjoyable finish.

○ Vernaccia di S. Gimignano Albereta Ris. '14		♟♟ 3*
○ Vernaccia di S. Gimignano Selvabianca '16		♟♟ 3
● Chianti Colli Senesi Il Priore Ris. '13		♟ 4
☉ Cremisi Rosato '16		♟ 3
● S. Gimignano Rosso Colombaio Ris. '13		♟ 5
○ Vernaccia di S. Gimignano Albereta Ris. '13		♟♟♟ 3*
○ Vernaccia di S. Gimignano Albereta Ris. '12		♟♟♟ 5
○ Vernaccia di S. Gimignano Albereta Ris. '11		♟♟♟ 4*
○ Vernaccia di S. Gimignano Campo della Pieve '11		♟♟♟ 3*
○ Vernaccia di S. Gimignano Selvabianca '15		♟♟ 3

Conte Guicciardini

LOC. POPPIANO
VIA FEZZANA, 45/49
50025 MONTESPERTOLI [FI]
TEL. +39 05582315
www.conteguicciardini.it

CELLAR SALES
PRE-BOOKED VISITS
ANNUAL PRODUCTION 270,000 bottles
HECTARES UNDER VINE 130.00
SUSTAINABLE WINERY

Castello di Poppiano is an imposing building owned by the Guicciardini family, who were already growing vines back in the Middle Ages. Today, Ferdinando Guicciardini is at the helm, helped by his grandson Bernardo. They run the 250 hectares of farming land together, 130 of which are vineyards. There is an additional 56 hectares at Massi di Mandorlaia, the family's Maremma estate in Morellino di Scansano, and nine hectares at Belvedere Campoli in Chianti Classico, on the ridge between Mercatale and Montefiridolfi. This last purchase, made a few years ago, aims to complete their vast range of wines. The selection impressed, starting with the 2015 Chianti Il Cortile, which offers up aromas of black and morello cherry, and features a succulent, juicy mouth. The 2014 Riserva proved more mature, boasting a nice tannic structure. We also had positive feelings about the Scansano line, with the 2015 Morellino I Massi characterized by spicy aromas and a full, succulent mouth.

● Chianti Colli Fiorentini Castello di Poppiano Ris. '14		♟♟ 4
● Chianti Colli Fiorentini Il Cortile Castello di Poppiano '15		♟♟ 3
● Morellino di Scansano I Massi Massi di Mandorlaia '15		♟♟ 3
● Chianti Cl. Belvedere Campoli '15		♟ 4
● La Historia Castello di Poppiano '14		♟ 5
● Morellino di Scansano Massi di Mandorlaia Ris. '14		♟ 4
● Syrah Castello di Poppiano '15		♟ 4
● Toscoforte Castello di Poppiano '15		♟ 4
○ Vermentino Massi di Mandorlaia '16		♟ 2
● Chianti Colli Fiorentini Castello di Poppiano Ris. '12		♟♟ 4

Contucci

VIA DEL TEATRO, 1
53045 MONTEPULCIANO [SI]
TEL. +39 0578757006
www.contucci.it

CELLAR SALES
PRE-BOOKED VISITS
ACCOMMODATION
ANNUAL PRODUCTION 100,000 bottles
HECTARES UNDER VINE 21.00

Although the historic Contucci family cellar
in the center of Montalcino is striking, their
vineyards are no less important. Situated
on the Mulinaccio estate, this portion of
great wine growing land is at the foot of the
hill where the Bravìo barrel race is held.
The style of wines they produce has been
reinforced by a timeless tradition that
bypasses trends, leaving them with a very
austere character, incomparable to most
wines in the area. The 2014 Nobile di
Montepulciano Pietra Rossa is both austere
and delicate at the same time. Its aromas
go all in on fruity fragrance, which follows
through well to a solid, flavorsome palate.
The 2013 Nobile di Montepulciano shows
the occasional evolved accent, with an
aromatic profile featuring spice and vibrant
fruit. In the mouth it's polished, savory, with
slightly spirited tannins and an uplifting
finish.

● Nobile di Montepulciano Pietra Rossa '14	♥♥ 5
● Nobile di Montepulciano Ris. '13	♥♥ 5
● Nobile di Montepulciano Mulinvecchio '14	♥ 5
● Nobile di Montepulciano Mulinvecchio '12	♀♀ 5
● Nobile di Montepulciano Pietra Rossa '13	♀♀ 5
● Nobile di Montepulciano Pietra Rossa '10	♀♀ 4
● Nobile di Montepulciano Ris. '12	♀♀ 5
● Rosso di Montepulciano '14	♀♀ 2*

Il Conventino

FRAZ. GRACCIANO
VIA DELLA CIARLIANA, 25B
53040 MONTEPULCIANO [SI]
TEL. +39 0578715371
www.ilconventino.it

CELLAR SALES
PRE-BOOKED VISITS
ANNUAL PRODUCTION 55,000 bottles
HECTARES UNDER VINE 12.00
VITICULTURE METHOD Certified Organic

Although the Brini brothers have been
running Ciarlana since 1988, it's only
recently had an impact in the appellation.
The vineyards are planted mostly with local
varieties, and are worked under organic
management. At the same time, in the
cellar, winemaking is unforced and their
wines for the most part rest in large wood.
The result is a well-made range of wines,
distinctive for their clean nose and fresh
palate, tweaked with a good dose of
character. The 2013 Nobile di
Montepulciano Riserva is a sound wine,
starting with an aromatic profile that sees
lush fruit merging with an abundances of
spice and balsamic accents. In the mouth it
expands well, and spirited tannins
characterize a finish that has some
welcome personality. The 2014 Nobile di
Montepulciano is more clenched, having
suffered for the difficult vintage. It's quite
simple, but still maintains its pleasantness.

● Nobile di Montepulciano Ris. '13	♥♥ 5
● Nobile di Montepulciano '14	♥ 4
● Nobile di Montepulciano '10	♀♀♀ 4*
● Nobile di Montepulciano '13	♀♀ 4
● Nobile di Montepulciano '12	♀♀ 4
● Nobile di Montepulciano '11	♀♀ 4
● Nobile di Montepulciano '09	♀♀ 4
● Nobile di Montepulciano Ris. '12	♀♀ 5
● Nobile di Montepulciano Ris. '11	♀♀ 5
● Nobile di Montepulciano Ris. '10	♀♀ 5
● Nobile di Montepulciano Ris. '09	♀♀ 5
● Nobile di Montepulciano Ris. '08	♀♀ 5
● Nobile di Montepulciano Ris. '06	♀♀ 5
● Rosso di Montepulciano '12	♀♀ 2*

Tenuta Il Corno

FRAZ. SAN PANCRAZIO
VIA MALAFRASCA, 64
50026 SAN CASCIANO IN VAL DI PESA [FI]
TEL. +39 0558248009
www.tenutailcorno.com

CELLAR SALES
PRE-BOOKED VISITS
ANNUAL PRODUCTION 200,000 bottles
HECTARES UNDER VINE 67.00

Tenuta Il Corno has a long tradition. Built in the 12th century for the noble Florentine Del Corno family, it passed into the hands of the Strozzis in the 1500s. Today it belongs to the Frova family, who have given new verve to its winemaking and farm holiday business. The estate spans over two hundred hectares, about seventy of which are vineyards. Here some ungrafted vines still can be found, and these are used to make rootlings. Sangiovese may be the undisputed king, but there is also an earnest effort to bring Colorino back into play. The selection presented saw its ups and downs. The 2013 San Camillo Riserva, made with 100% Sangiovese, came through well. It's a wine characterized by a flowery, spicy aromatic profile, a relaxed, solid mouth, tannins that merge well with its alcohol, a nice richness of flavor and the right freshness. The 2016 Iris, a fresh, supple, drinkable blend of red grapes, is no less interesting.

● Chianti Colli Fiorentini San Camillo Ris. '13	♟♟ 2*
● Iris '16	♟♟ 2*
● Chianti Colli Fiorentini Foss'a Spina '14	♟ 2
● Colorino del Corno '10	♟ 5
● Minna e Moro '13	♟ 3
● Chianti Colli Fiorentini Foss'a Spina '12	♟♟ 2*
● Chianti Colli Fiorentini San Camillo Ris. '12	♟♟ 2*
● Chianti Colli Fiorentini San Camillo Ris. '10	♟♟ 2*

Corte dei Venti

LOC. PIANCORNELLO, 35
53024 MONTALCINO [SI]
TEL. +39 3473653718
www.lacortedeiventi.it

CELLAR SALES
PRE-BOOKED VISITS
ANNUAL PRODUCTION 20,000 bottles
HECTARES UNDER VINE 5.00

Corte dei Venti was founded in 1990 by a branch of the Pieri family, major players in vine growing in Piancornello. This southern part of Montalcino is marked by good air circulation and is well known for its reddish soil and altitudes skimming 300 meters. Clara Monaci and Maurizio Machetti run their five hectares here, producing wines that have returned to the limelight in recent years. They grow Sangiovese for their Brunellos and others, with wines distinguished by their graceful structure -- the result of delicate extraction and patient aging in medium-sized oak. These qualities emerge perfectly in the 2012 Brunello. Almond peel, bouquet garni, and sulphur come through airy and ethereal, both on the nose and the mouth. It's a wine that's seemingly gentle, yet endowed with force and tannic contrast. The 2015 Rosso is along the same lines, only more subtle.

● Brunello di Montalcino '12	♟♟♟ 8
● Rosso di Montalcino '15	♟♟ 5
● Brunello di Montalcino '11	♟♟ 8
● Brunello di Montalcino Donna Elena Ris. '10	♟♟ 8
● Sant'Antimo Poggio dei Lecci '14	♟♟ 3

Villa Le Corti

LOC. LE CORTI
VIA SAN PIERO DI SOTTO, 1
50026 SAN CASCIANO IN VAL DI PESA [FI]
TEL. +39 055829301
www.principecorsini.com

CELLAR SALES
PRE-BOOKED VISITS
ACCOMMODATION
ANNUAL PRODUCTION 150,000 bottles
HECTARES UNDER VINE 50.00
VITICULTURE METHOD Certified Organic

Duccio Corsini runs one of the oldest wineries in Chianti Classico, located in the San Casciano Val di Pesa hills. Their production style looks to the Chianti tradition, especially, for liveliness and drinkability. The vineyards are worked with precision and under organic management. Winemaking in the cellar is unforced, with alternate use of concrete vats, large wood and barriques for aging. It's a spot-on combination which makes for consistently well-crafted wines, but with a good dose of personality. The 2014 Chianti Classico Cortevecchia Riserva is a pleasantly savory wine. It features a nice unfolding of flavor, with crunchy tannins and a lively acidity. Its aromas are also on the mark, not too complex but distinguished by a nice note of fresh orange. The fragrant 2014 Chianti Classico comes through lean and fluent. It's a wine that's geared towards approachability, and is endowed with an aromatic, balanced palate.

● Chianti Cl. Cortevecchia Ris. '14	▼▼ 4
● Chianti Cl. '14	▼▼ 3
● Chianti Cl. '12	▼▼▼ 3*
● Chianti Cl. Cortevecchia Ris. '05	▼▼▼ 4
● Chianti Cl. Le Corti '10	▼▼▼ 3*
● Birillo Tenuta Marsiliana '13	▼▼ 3
● Chianti Cl. '13	▼▼ 3*
● Chianti Cl. Cortevecchia Ris. '13	▼▼ 4
● Chianti Cl. Cortevecchia Ris. '11	▼▼ 4
● Chianti Cl. Don Tommaso Gran Sel. '11	▼▼ 5
● Chianti Cl. Don Tommaso Gran Sel. '10	▼▼ 5
● Chianti Cl. Le Corti '11	▼▼ 3
● Marsiliana '12	▼▼ 5

Cortonesi

LOC. LA MANNELLA, 322
53024 MONTALCINO [SI]
TEL. +39 0577848268
www.lamannella.it

PRE-BOOKED VISITS
ANNUAL PRODUCTION 35,000 bottles
HECTARES UNDER VINE 8.00

The winds of change are blowing in La Mannella, the name under which our guide, until last year, included the Cortonesi family's excellent wines. It's not simply a change in brand. A generational handover has now been announced and Tommaso is working alongside his father, Marco. This reshaping also involves their two Brunellos: La Manella is the selection made with grapes cultivated near the winery on the northern slope of Montalcino, and aged in 3000-liter Slavonian oak. Poggiarelli is made with grapes from the estate bearing the same name, in Castelnuovo dell'Abate. It's slightly more modern and ages in 500-liter French barrels. It's all reflected perfectly in the line of 2012 Brunellos. La Mannella is multifaceted on the nose, though it's lacking a bit in density and length. I Poggiarelli appears a bit bridled by oak, but it still displays nice grip. Among the lot, an excellent Rosso emerges. The 2015 is the most well-crafted and credible version yet.

● Rosso di Montalcino '15	▼▼ 3*
● Brunello di Montalcino I Poggiarelli '12	▼▼ 5
● Brunello di Montalcino La Mannella '12	▼▼ 5
● Brunello di Montalcino '10	▼▼ 5
● Brunello di Montalcino '09	▼▼ 5
● Brunello di Montalcino '08	▼▼ 5
● Brunello di Montalcino Ris. '10	▼▼ 6
● Brunello di Montalcino I Poggiarelli '11	▼▼ 5
● Brunello di Montalcino I Poggiarelli '10	▼▼ 5
● Brunello di Montalcino I Poggiarelli '09	▼▼ 5
● Brunello di Montalcino I Poggiarelli '08	▼▼ 5
● Rosso di Montalcino '14	▼▼ 3
● Rosso di Montalcino '13	▼▼ 3

Fattoria Corzano e Paterno

LOC. CORZANO
FRAZ. SAN PANCRAZIO
VIA SAN VITO DI SOPRA
50020 SAN CASCIANO IN VAL DI PESA [FI]
TEL. +39 0558248179
www.corzanoepaterno.com

CELLAR SALES
PRE-BOOKED VISITS
ACCOMMODATION
ANNUAL PRODUCTION 85,000 bottles
HECTARES UNDER VINE 19.00
VITICULTURE METHOD Certified Organic

Theirs is a modern estate run under organic management. It produces high-quality wine, oil and cheese, as well as fodder for sheep breeding. The venture started in 1969 with Wendelin Gelpke, but came to involve the entire family. They still carry on his ideals today. His wife, Susan, has organized a farmstay business; his son, Til, looks after the sheep breeding and delivers the cheese; his daughter, Arianna, is a winemaker and oversees work in the cellar. Meanwhile, grandson Aljoscha is a vine grower and agronomist who runs the farm, and his wife, Antonia, manages the dairy. It's a true family business. Once again, the Chianti I Tre Borri leads the way among the estate's wines. Classic notes of cherry and light vegetal nuances emerge on a background that's oakier in the 2014 than with other versions. The mouth is dominated by close-knit tannins. They're still a bit edgy, but display great prospects.

● Chianti I Tre Borri Ris. '14	♥♥ 5
● Chianti Terre di Corzano '15	♥ 2
○ Il Corzanello '16	♥ 2
● Il Corzano '14	♥ 5
● Chianti I Tre Borri Ris. '07	♥♥♥ 5
● Il Corzano '05	♥♥♥ 5
● Il Corzano '97	♥♥♥ 6
● Chianti I Tre Borri Ris. '13	♥♥ 5
● Chianti I Tre Borri Ris. '12	♥♥ 5
● Chianti I Tre Borri Ris. '11	♥♥ 5
● Chianti Terre di Corzano '14	♥♥ 2*
● Il Corzano '13	♥♥ 5
● Il Corzano '11	♥♥ 5
● Il Corzano '10	♥♥ 5
○ Passito di Corzano '11	♥♥ 6

Andrea Costanti

LOC. COLLE AL MATRICHESE
53024 MONTALCINO [SI]
TEL. +39 0577848195
www.costanti.it

CELLAR SALES
PRE-BOOKED VISITS
ANNUAL PRODUCTION 60,000 bottles
HECTARES UNDER VINE 12.00

Casottino and Calbello are the two main vineyards here. They span 10 hectares in Colle al Matrichese and have been run by Andrea Costanti since 1983. The easternmost part of the Montalcino hill, at 310 to 440 meters above sea level, features galestro-rich soil. Primarily Sangiovese is cultivated, but there are also small amounts of Merlot and Cabernet. The grapes are used to make a couple of Brunello wines (a vintage and a Riserva, aged in 900-liter casks and 3000-liter oak) which confidently stand the test of time, offering texture, solidity and vigor in exchange for expressivity. The Costanti style comes through in the triad tested in this last round. The 2015 Rosso is vibrant and unyielding, maybe just a bit compressed. The 2014 Vermiglio exhibits a rawer texture, but better aromatic definition. The 2012 Brunello is, in many ways, a synthesis of the two.

● Brunello di Montalcino '12	♥♥ 6
● Rosso di Montalcino '15	♥♥ 4
● Rosso di Montalcino Vermiglio '14	♥♥ 5
● Brunello di Montalcino '06	♥♥♥ 6
● Brunello di Montalcino '11	♥♥ 6
● Brunello di Montalcino '10	♥♥ 6
● Brunello di Montalcino '09	♥♥ 6
● Brunello di Montalcino '08	♥♥ 6
● Brunello di Montalcino '07	♥♥ 6
● Brunello di Montalcino Ris. '10	♥♥ 8
● Brunello di Montalcino Ris. '07	♥♥ 8
● Brunello di Montalcino Ris. '06	♥♥ 8
● Brunello di Montalcino Ris. '01	♥♥ 8
● Rosso di Montalcino '11	♥♥ 4

La Cura

LOC. CURA NUOVA, 12
58024 MASSA MARITTIMA [GR]
TEL. +39 0566918094
www.cantinalacura.it

CELLAR SALES
PRE-BOOKED VISITS
ANNUAL PRODUCTION 30,000 bottles
HECTARES UNDER VINE 15.00
SUSTAINABLE WINERY

Today Enrico Corsi runs the winery that was bought by his father, Andrea, at the end of the 1960s. Then there were fields of vegetables and cereals in this part of Maremma but Andrea's passion for wine drove him to plant two hectares of vines in the land. Today there are fifteen hectares of vineyards growing international varieties such as Cabernet Sauvignon, Merlot, Syrah Chardonnay, as well as Sangiovese, Vermentino, Ansonica and Malvasia. All of the farm's activities, including vegetable, cereals and fruit growing, are carried out with the utmost respect for the environment and sustainability. And installation of a solar panel system has produced clean electrical power. There's not a standout among the selection, but it's still solid and consistent. All the wines did well, starting with the Cavaliere d'Italia, which is tight in its tannic weave, succulent and dynamic. The Cabernets performed similarly, coming through dense and pervasive. The Merlot proved soft and vibrant.

● Maremma Toscana Cabernet Sauvignon Cabernets '15	♟♟ 5
● Maremma Toscana Merlot '15	♟♟ 5
● Maremma Toscana Sangiovese Cavaliere d'Italia '16	♟♟ 2*
● Monteregio di Massa Marittima Rosso Valdemàr '16	♟♟ 2*
● Predicatore '16	♟ 3
○ Trinus '16	♟ 2
● Maremma Merlot La Cura '12	♟♟ 5
● Maremma Toscana Merlot '13	♟♟ 5
● Monteregio di Massa Marittima Rosso Breccerosse '13	♟♟ 3
● Predicatore '15	♟♟ 3
○ Trinus '15	♟♟ 2*
● Vedetta '13	♟♟ 4

Dal Cero
Tenuta Montecchiesi

LOC. MONTECCHIO

52044 CORTONA [AR]
TEL. +39 0457460110
www.dalcerofamily.it

CELLAR SALES
PRE-BOOKED VISITS
ANNUAL PRODUCTION 300,000 bottles
HECTARES UNDER VINE 65.00

Cortona's Tenuta Montecchiesi has belonged to the Dal Cero family since 1980. Taking after their father, Giuseppe and Dario moved to Tuscany to try their hand at making red wines, planting new varieties in addition to Sangiovese. The estate has grown from 9 to 46 hectares, and comprises plots in Montecchio and Manzano. The former also hosts their cellar, which is housed in a renovated, early 20th century farmstead. The 2013 Klanis delivered. The nose features tones of fur and tanned leather, then cherry and blackcurrant. In the mouth the wine proves balanced, with well-integrated, fresh tannins and a long, savory finish. The 2014 Selverello offers up flowery scents, then fruitier aromas of blackcurrant and light, clove spices. The mouth opens well, docile, with the right acidity. The finish comes through savory and dynamic. The 2014 Verdonnay, a blend of Vermentino and Chardonnay, has a fruity bouquet and a fine-tuned freshness to it.

● Cortona Syrah Klanis '13	♟♟ 5
● Cortona Syrah Selverello '14	♟♟ 3
● Sangiovese '15	♟♟ 2*
○ Verdonnay '14	♟♟ 5
○ Vermentino Chardonnay '16	♟ 2
● Cortona Syrah '13	♟♟ 5
● Cortona Syrah Klanis '12	♟♟ 5
● Cortona Syrah Klanis '11	♟♟ 5
○ Podere Bianchino '14	♟♟ 2*
○ Podere Bianchino '12	♟♟ 2*
● Preziosaterra '13	♟♟ 3
● Sangiovese '14	♟♟ 2*
● Sangiovese '13	♟♟ 2*

Maria Caterina Dei

VIA DI MARTIENA, 35
53045 MONTEPULCIANO [SI]
TEL. +39 0578716878
www.cantinedei.com

CELLAR SALES
PRE-BOOKED VISITS
ACCOMMODATION
ANNUAL PRODUCTION 230,000 bottles
HECTARES UNDER VINE 55.00
SUSTAINABLE WINERY

This winery in Martiena has clocked in almost fifty years of history, and has come a long way since the beginning. A clear-cut, successful style of wines has developed. Based on a solid structure expanded with balance and elegance, their wines are often among the most excellent in the appellation. Maria Caterina Dei runs the winery under a straightforward production philosophy. That is, paying utmost attention to the grapes and a purist approach to winemaking, and accompanying it with aging in small and large wood. Caterina Dei's 2014 Nobile di Montepulciano is unequivocally the best, handily earning a Tre Bicchieri. Its aromatic profile is subtle and complex, with fruit merging with light spices and balsamic accents. In the mouth it gets even better (if that's possible): it's long, well-paced and savory. The 2012 Nobile di Montepulciano Bossona Riserva is just as good, with its flowery aromas and solid structure. It's not lacking in a pleasing hardness either, nor oak.

● Nobile di Montepulciano '14	♔♔♔ 4*
● Nobile di Montepulciano Bossona Ris. '12	♔♔ 6
● Rosso di Montepulciano '16	♔ 3
● Nobile di Montepulciano '13	♔♔♔ 4*
● Nobile di Montepulciano Bossona Ris. '04	♔♔♔ 5
● Nobile di Montepulciano '11	♔♔ 4
● Nobile di Montepulciano '10	♔♔ 4
● Nobile di Montepulciano Bossona Ris. '10	♔♔ 6
● Nobile di Montepulciano Bossona Ris. '09	♔♔ 6
● Nobile di Montepulciano Bossona Ris. '08	♔♔ 5
● Rosso di Montepulciano '12	♔♔ 2*
● Rosso di Montepulciano '11	♔♔ 2*
○ Vin Santo di Montepulciano '07	♔♔ 5

Dievole

FRAZ. VAGLIAGLI
VIA DIEVOLE, 6
53010 CASTELNUOVO BERARDENGA [SI]
TEL. +39 0577322613
www.dievole.it

CELLAR SALES
PRE-BOOKED VISITS
ACCOMMODATION AND RESTAURANT SERVICE
ANNUAL PRODUCTION 350,000 bottles
HECTARES UNDER VINE 80.00

Until a few years ago, this brand was one of the key players in Chianti Classico. After a period of uncertainty they now seem to be back on track. Credit is due to new ownership, the Argentine magnate, Bulgheroni, whose production choices are anything but ordinary. Vineyard management is meticulous, in the cellar fermentation is carried out in concrete, and aging uses only large wood. The result is an impressive range of wines with a clear-cut, focused style centered, without distraction, on excellence. The 2014 Chianti Classico Novecento Riserva is one of the best interpretations of a difficult vintage, highlighting a clean aromatic profile that manages to bring out intriguing hints of flint and iron, and lush, fragrant fruit. In the mouth the wine proves succulent and well-sustained with tannins that are as assertive as they are crunchy. The 2015 Chianti Classico is delightful.

● Chianti Cl. Novecento Ris. '14	♔♔♔ 5
● Chianti Cl. '15	♔♔ 4
● Broccato '08	♔♔ 5
● Chianti Cl. '13	♔♔ 4
● Chianti Cl. Dieulele Ris. '09	♔♔ 7
● Chianti Cl. Dieulele Ris. '06	♔♔ 7
● Chianti Cl. La Vendemmia '12	♔♔ 3
● Chianti Cl. La Vendemmia '07	♔♔ 3
● Chianti Cl. Novecento Ris. '10	♔♔ 5
● Chianti Cl. Novecento Ris. '07	♔♔ 5
● Chianti Cl. Novecento Ris. '06	♔♔ 5
● Chianti Cl. Ris. '13	♔♔ 5

Fabrizio Dionisio

LOC. IL CASTAGNO
FRAZ. OSSAIA, 87
52044 CORTONA [AR]
TEL. +39 063223391
www.fabriziodionisio.it

CELLAR SALES
PRE-BOOKED VISITS
ANNUAL PRODUCTION 45,000 bottles
HECTARES UNDER VINE 15.00
SUSTAINABLE WINERY

In the 1970s Fabrizio Dionisio's father, Sergio, bought this farmhouse, along with seven hectares of vineyards and olive groves, in the hills overlooking Cortona. About twenty years later he bought a new plot of land, bringing the farm to its current size and creating ideal conditions for modern winemaking activity. Fabrizio and his wife, Alessandra, made the decision to replant old vineyards with Syrah, which adapts well to this area. In 2003 they produced their first wine, with optimal results. The 2013 Cuculaia made it to the finals, with its aromatic profile featuring fruit-driven notes of cherry and raspberry, and intriguing spicy hints of cinnamon and pepper. In the mouth it proves full-bodied, with fine-grained, delicate tannins, good acidity and a succulent, long finish. The 2014 Castagno is vibrant on the nose, with aromas of wild berries and pepper. It exhibits good structure, fine-grained tannins and a complex finish. The 2016 Castagnino is polished, subtle, simple and clear on the nose. The body proves well-balanced and racy, with a delicate, pleasing finish.

● Cortona Syrah Cuculaia '13	♟♟ 7
● Cortona Syrah Castagnino '16	♟♟ 3
● Cortona Syrah Il Castagno '14	♟♟ 5
⊙ Rosa del Castagno '16	♟ 3
● Cortona Syrah Il Castagno '12	♟♟♟ 5
● Cortona Syrah Il Castagno '11	♟♟♟ 5
● Cortona Syrah Il Castagno '10	♟♟♟ 5
● Cortona Syrah Castagnino '15	♟♟ 3*
● Cortona Syrah Castagnino '14	♟♟ 3
● Cortona Syrah Cuculaia '10	♟♟ 7
● Cortona Syrah Cuculaia '09	♟♟ 6
● Cortona Syrah Il Castagno '13	♟♟ 5

Donna Olga

LOC. FRIGGIALI
S.DA MAREMMANA
53024 MONTALCINO [SI]
TEL. +39 0577849454
www.tenutedonnaolga.it

CELLAR SALES
PRE-BOOKED VISITS
ACCOMMODATION
ANNUAL PRODUCTION 25,000 bottles
HECTARES UNDER VINE 11.00

Olga Peluso looks after her 10 hectares of vineyards, in addition to the family farm in Centonali. Some of the vineyards are situated on the southwestern slope of Montalcino on volcanic soil. Galestro prevails, but only in the southeast plots, a stone's throw from Castello della Velona where altitudes reach 400 meters. The combination of microclimates and soil produces Brunellos that are modern only in appearance. The wines are partly made in 3000- 5000-liter Slavonian oak , others are made in medium-sized casks. The 2012 vintage made for a varied selection of wines. The base Brunello exhibits a more modern profile than expected, with touches of embers and coffee, but it finds balance in the attack. Mulberry, sandalwood and incense characterize the Favorito, which sees greater stratification, both on the nose and the palate. It's just a bit hurried at the end.

● Brunello di Montalcino '12	♟♟ 7
● Brunello di Montalcino Favorito '12	♟♟ 7
● Brunello di Montalcino '09	♟♟♟ 7
● Brunello di Montalcino '06	♟♟♟ 7
● Brunello di Montalcino '01	♟♟♟ 6
● Brunello di Montalcino Collezione Arte '06	♟♟♟ 7
● Brunello di Montalcino Ris. '01	♟♟♟ 6
● Brunello di Montalcino '11	♟♟ 7
● Brunello di Montalcino '10	♟♟ 7
● Brunello di Montalcino '08	♟♟ 7
● Brunello di Montalcino Favorito '07	♟♟ 7
● Brunello di Montalcino Favorito Collezione Arte '09	♟♟ 7
● Brunello di Montalcino Ris. '10	♟♟ 6
● Brunello di Montalcino Ris. '07	♟♟ 6

Donna Olimpia 1898

FRAZ. BOLGHERI
LOC. MIGLIARINI, 142
57020 CASTAGNETO CARDUCCI [LI]
TEL. +39 0302279601
www.donnaolimpia1898.it

CELLAR SALES
ACCOMMODATION AND RESTAURANT SERVICE
ANNUAL PRODUCTION 250,000 bottles
HECTARES UNDER VINE 45.00
SUSTAINABLE WINERY

Olimpia Alliata, a lady from Biserno,
provided both the inspiration and the name
for Guido Folonori's winery. The vineyards
are sizeable: 45 hectares of Cabernet
Sauvignon, Cabernet Franc, Merlot, Syrah
and Petit Verdot for reds; Vermentino,
Viognier and Petit Manseng for whites. It is
an ambitious and complex project carried
out in collaboration with Professor Attilio
Scienza. The wines are modern in style,
and increasing gradually in definition. We
liked the 2015 Bolgheri Rosso Campo alla
Giostra, a wine that's still a bit undefined in
its toasty accents and hints of pain d'épice.
Considering the strength and brilliance of
fruit, as well as the quality of its extraction,
we have to think that the best is yet to
come. The Bolgheri Rosso 2015 is freer of
wood, maybe a bit less complex, but
perfectly coherent. It's a clean, clear wine,
delicately fragrant, with a mouth that calls
up black cherry and blackberries. It finishes
well, with hints of balsamic.

● Bolgheri Rosso '15	♟♟ 5
● Bolgheri Rosso Campo alla Giostra '15	♟♟ 5
● Millepassi '13	♟♟ 6
○ Bolgheri Bianco '15	♟ 4
○ Obizzo '16	♟ 2
● Bolgheri Rosso Sup. Millepassi '13	♟♟♟ 6
● Bolgheri Rosso Sup. Millepassi '11	♟♟♟ 8
● Bolgheri Rosso '13	♟♟ 5
● Bolgheri Rosso '12	♟♟ 5
● Bolgheri Rosso '10	♟♟ 5
● Bolgheri Rosso '09	♟♟ 5
● Bolgheri Rosso '08	♟♟ 4
● Bolgheri Rosso Sup. Millepassi '12	♟♟ 6
● Bolgheri Rosso Sup. Millepassi '08	♟♟ 6

Duemani

LOC. ORTACAVOLI
56046 RIPARBELLA [PI]
TEL. +39 0583975048
www.duemani.eu

ANNUAL PRODUCTION 40,000 bottles
HECTARES UNDER VINE 10.00
VITICULTURE METHOD Certified Biodynamic
SUSTAINABLE WINERY

Duemani's history began in the year 2000
when winemaker Luca D'Attoma and his
wife, Elena Celli, were looking for a place to
grow their favorite grape varieties: Cabernet
Franc, Syrah and Merlot. Their search came
to an end in the Riparbella hills at a place
overlooking the sea. Elena and Luca
describe it as "an extreme, rugged, wild
and magnetic place, an uncontaminated,
thrilling landscape." They replanted their
vineyards, which are now cultivated under
biodynamic management. Their wines have
a vibrant personality and clear expression
of the territory, bringing out the best of their
grape varieties. The 2015 Altrovino, a blend
of Merlot and Cabernet Franc, earns a Tre
Bicchieri. The nose is intriguing with hints
of mint, and dark fruit like blackcurrants
and blueberry. The body is rich, but
well-distributed, with excellent freshness,
subtle tannins and a succulent, long finish.

● Altrovino '15	♟♟♟ 6
● Duemani '14	♟♟ 8
● Cifra '16	♟♟ 5
⊙ Si '16	♟ 5
● Duemani '13	♟♟♟ 8
● Duemani '12	♟♟♟ 8
● Duemani '09	♟♟♟ 8
● Suisassi '10	♟♟♟ 8
● Cifra '14	♟♟ 5
● Cifra '13	♟♟ 5
● Duemani '11	♟♟ 8
● Suisassi '13	♟♟ 8
● Suisassi '12	♟♟ 8

I Fabbri

LOC. LAMOLE
VIA CASOLE, 52
50022 GREVE IN CHIANTI [FI]
TEL. +39 339412622
www.ifabbrichianticlassico.it

CELLAR SALES
PRE-BOOKED VISITS
ANNUAL PRODUCTION 35,000 bottles
HECTARES UNDER VINE 11.00
VITICULTURE METHOD Certified Organic

The name "I Fabbri" recalls the smith's workshop in the old town overlooking the estate where two sisters, Susanna and Maddalena Grassi, have produced wine since 2000. The winery is in the Lamole subzone and the vineyards are cultivated under organic management at over 500 meters above sea level. Work in the cellar is unforced and aging is carried out in 900-liter casks, steel and concrete. Their wines have a clear-cut style, at times not immediately readable, but are consistent with the Chianti Classico terroir. The 2015 Chianti Classico Olinto features a nice palate that's both succulent and fragrant. The nose, which sees a predominance of toastiness, is less defined. The 2013 Chianti Classico Riserva has an aromatic profile that calls up cellar odors, with the occasional accent of flint and earth, as well as spicy hints. In the mouth it's fresh and well-paced, with a nuanced finish. The 2015 Chianti Classico has fine drinkability to it, though the occasional aromatic impurity comes through.

● Chianti Cl. Olinto '15	♥♥ 4
● Chianti Cl. Ris. '13	♥♥ 4
● Chianti Cl. '15	♥ 4
● Chianti Cl. '13	♥♥ 4
● Chianti Cl. '12	♥♥ 4
● Chianti Cl. '10	♥♥ 4
● Chianti Cl. Gran Sel. '11	♥♥ 6
● Chianti Cl. Lamole '11	♥♥ 2*
● Chianti Cl. Olinto '14	♥♥ 4
● Chianti Cl. Olinto '12	♥♥ 4
● Chianti Cl. Olinto '08	♥♥ 4
● Chianti Cl. Ris. '11	♥♥ 4
● Chianti Cl. Terra di Lamole '13	♥♥ 3*
● Chianti Cl. Terra di Lamole '10	♥♥ 2*

Agricola Fabbriche

VIA FABBRICHE, 2-3A
52046 LUCIGNANO [AR]
TEL. +39 0575836152
www.agricolafabbriche.it

CELLAR SALES
PRE-BOOKED VISITS
ANNUAL PRODUCTION 15,000 bottles
HECTARES UNDER VINE 11.00

This winery has belonged to the Palma family for over fifty years, but only when Caterina joined did it begin to develop professionally. Growing up in Milan and having worked in the events sector, Caterina nonetheless could see the full potential of Valdichiana, an area known for Chianina meat. Currently the winery focuses mostly on international varieties. The 2016 Ninis, a blend of Traminer and Trebbiano, has a fruit-driven nose featuring pear and whitecurrant. The body is solid and well-distributed, with balanced freshness and a long finish. The 2015 Syrah offers up notes of green peppers, black pepper and hints of tobacco leaf on the nose. In the mouth, it proves solid, bold and well-defined, with a savory finish. The 2015 Camargi, a blend of Sangiovese, Merlot and Colorino, is interesting, with an aromatic bouquet featuring vibrant fruity notes of wild berries and spicy hints of cinnamon. The body is balanced, and the tannins well-absorbed, while the finish sees a crescendo of taste.

● Camargi '15	♥♥ 4
○ Ninis '16	♥♥ 2*
● Syrah '15	♥♥ 5
○ Vin Santo del Chianti '12	♥♥ 4
● Chianti Sup. '15	♥ 2
● Merlot '15	♥ 3
● Camargi '08	♥♥ 4
● Merlot Palma '08	♥♥ 4
○ Vin Santo del Chianti Elis '10	♥♥ 3

Tenuta Fanti

FRAZ. CASTELNUOVO DELL'ABATE
PODERE PALAZZO, 14
53020 MONTALCINO [SI]
TEL. +39 0577835795
www.tenutafanti.it

CELLAR SALES
PRE-BOOKED VISITS
ANNUAL PRODUCTION 200,000 bottles
HECTARES UNDER VINE 50.00

Filippo Fanti set up the winery that bears his name in the 1970s and today he runs it with his daughter Elisa. The vineyards span about fifty hectares and constitute some of the best farmland in the ragged territory of southeastern Montalcino around Castelnuovo dell'Abate. This gives rise to their caressing and full-bodied Sangiovese wines. Made with sensitive interpretation, their wines are contemporary rather than modern Brunellos, as they age both in barrels and barriques. Fanti also grows a few international varieties, and some traditional Tuscan white grapes. Our impressions of the Fanti family's most recent selection were decidedly positive. Two wines made it to our finals: the 2015 Rosso is a delectable, Mediterranean wine that's broader than it is deep, but still solid and consistent; the 2012 Brunello is a summery wine (blackberries, bitter orange, bottled cherries) that's also rich in smoky hints and sea salt.

● Brunello di Montalcino '12	♟♟ 6
● Rosso di Montalcino '15	♟♟ 3*
● Brunello di Montalcino V. Le Macchiarelle Ris. '11	♟♟ 6
● Brunello di Montalcino Vallocchio '12	♟ 6
● Brunello di Montalcino '07	♟♟♟ 5
● Brunello di Montalcino '00	♟♟♟ 6
● Brunello di Montalcino '11	♟♟ 6
● Brunello di Montalcino '10	♟♟ 6
● Brunello di Montalcino '08	♟♟ 6
● Brunello di Montalcino V. Le Macchiarelle Ris. '10	♟♟ 6
● Brunello di Montalcino V. Le Macchiarelle Ris. '09	♟♟ 6
● Brunello di Montalcino Vallocchio '11	♟♟ 6
● Brunello di Montalcino Vallocchio '10	♟♟ 6

Fattoi

LOC. SANTA RESTITUTA
POD. CAPANNA, 101
53024 MONTALCINO [SI]
TEL. +39 0577848613
www.fattoi.it

CELLAR SALES
PRE-BOOKED VISITS
ANNUAL PRODUCTION 50,000 bottles
HECTARES UNDER VINE 9.00

The Fattoi family make just three wines, and only when the vintage is good. They have about ten hectares in Santa Restituta, one of the most prestigious names in central-western Montalcino. The venture started almost half a century ago, coasting along before virtually exploding in recent years. Some credit must be given to Ofelio and his children, Leonardo and Lucia, but above all to their current exquisite style. That is great Sangiovese wines for pairing with food, putting drinkability, spontaneity and savoury quality before excessive adherence to expression. These artisan Brunellos and reds are usually aged in 3300- to 4500-liter Slavonian oak barrels. Fattoi's finalists don't quite live up to past performances. Despite some saline verve, the 2015 Rosso feels a bit bridled, both on the nose and on the palate. The 2012 Brunello is more mobile and cohesive. On the nose it offers up aromas characteristic of the Tyrrhenian, while in the mouth it finish with just a touch of warmth.

● Brunello di Montalcino '12	♟♟ 5
● Rosso di Montalcino '15	♟♟ 3
● Brunello di Montalcino '10	♟♟♟ 5
● Brunello di Montalcino '11	♟♟ 5
● Brunello di Montalcino '09	♟♟ 5
● Brunello di Montalcino '07	♟♟ 6
● Brunello di Montalcino Ris. '10	♟♟ 7
● Brunello di Montalcino Ris. '08	♟♟ 7
● Brunello di Montalcino Ris. '07	♟♟ 7
● Brunello di Montalcino Ris. '06	♟♟ 4
● Rosso di Montalcino '14	♟♟ 3
● Rosso di Montalcino '13	♟♟ 3
● Rosso di Montalcino '12	♟♟ 3
● Rosso di Montalcino '10	♟♟ 3

★★Fèlsina

LOC. FÈLSINA
VIA VIA DEL CHIANTI, 101
53019 CASTELNUOVO BERARDENGA [SI]
TEL. +39 0577355117
www.felsina.it

CELLAR SALES
PRE-BOOKED VISITS
ANNUAL PRODUCTION 480,000 bottles
HECTARES UNDER VINE 94.00
VITICULTURE METHOD Certified Organic
SUSTAINABLE WINERY

Felsina is an icon of Tuscan winemaking by virtue of a selection that has made Chianti Classico history. Domenico Poggiali, an entrepreneur from Ravenna, bought the first part of the farm in 1966, laying the foundations for the Felsina winery. In 1981, he took over Castello di Farnetella in Sinalunga, then Pagliarese in Castelnuovo Berardenga in 1995. Recently, their style seems to have taken a less-convincing turn, penalizing Castelnuovo Berardenga's wines and causing them to lose a little of their past magic. The 2015 Chianti Classico sees a clean and somewhat predictable aromatic profile, bringing together red fruit, toastiness and sugared almonds. In the mouth the wine prove soft and well-sustained, with a slightly toasty finish. The two 2015 Chianti Colli Senesi privilege sweetness, both on the nose and the palate. They are simple, but well-crafted wines. The two Metodo Classicos, made with Sangiovese, Chardonnay and Pinot Nero, are pleasant, though still not very layered.

● Chianti Cl. Berardenga '15	♈♈	4
● Chianti Colli Senesi Berardenga '15	♈	2
● Chianti Colli Senesi Castello della Farnetella '15	♈	2
○ Fèlsina Spumante Brut	♈	4
⊙ Fèlsina Spumante Brut Rosé	♈	4
● Lucilla Castello di Farnetella '15	♈	2
● Chianti Cl. Rancia Ris. '07	♈♈♈	6
● Fontalloro '10	♈♈♈	6
● Fontalloro '07	♈♈♈	6
● Fontalloro '06	♈♈♈	6
● Maestro Raro '08	♈♈♈	6
● Fontalloro '12	♈♈	6
● Maestro Raro '13	♈♈	6

Fattoria Fibbiano

VIA FIBBIANO, 2
56030 TERRICCIOLA [PI]
TEL. +39 0587635677
www.fattoria-fibbiano.it

CELLAR SALES
PRE-BOOKED VISITS
ACCOMMODATION AND RESTAURANT SERVICE
ANNUAL PRODUCTION 129,000 bottles
HECTARES UNDER VINE 16.00

The winery's origins date back to the 1300s when it belonged to the Gherardi de Testa Barasaglia family. It spans area that used to be an Etruscan settlement. In 1997, Giuseppe Cantoni returned to Italy and, along with his wife and two sons, founded Fibbiano in Tuscany. After its purchase he established a farmstay business and rejuvenated the old vineyards which are cultivated strictly with native grapes. His wines did well, overall. The 2015 Le Pianette, made with Sangiovese and Colorino, impresses on the nose for its fresh notes of aromatic herbs, its clear fruity hints of cherry and its spicy nuances. It shows good attack in the mouth and balance: it's long in taste, though not too aggressive. The 2015 Ciliegiolo is an intriguing wine with variegated fruit fragrances and small spicy hints. It possesses a body that's solid, though balanced; it has a nice freshness to it and features a relaxed finish. The 2015 Chianti Superiore Casalini is flowery and fruity with hints of blackcurrant. In the mouth it proves full-bodied, harmonic and tasty.

● Chianti Sup. Casalini '15	♈♈	2
● Ciliegiolo '15	♈♈	3
● Le Pianette '15	♈♈	2
● Terre di Pisa Ceppatella '13	♈♈	6
○ Fonte delle Donne '16	♈	2
● L'Aspetto '14	♈	4
○ Sofia Rosato '16	♈	2
● Ceppatella '10	♈♈	5
○ Fonte Delle Donne '15	♈♈	3
○ Fonte delle Donne '14	♈♈	2
● L'Aspetto '13	♈♈	4
● L'Aspetto '11	♈♈	3
● L'Aspetto '10	♈♈	3
● Le Pianette '11	♈♈	2
● Terre di Pisa Ceppatella '12	♈♈	6

Il Fitto

Fraz. Cignano
Loc. Chianacce, 126
52042 Cortona [AR]
Tel. +39 0575648988
www.podereilfitto.com

CELLAR SALES
PRE-BOOKED VISITS
ACCOMMODATION
ANNUAL PRODUCTION 30,000 bottles
HECTARES UNDER VINE 8.00

The Fierli family have owned the winery since the early 1900s and adopted mixed farming for many years. They started making wine in the 1970s, but it wasn't until 2000 that it became an important business. New vineyards were planted with suitable varieties for the territory and the new cellar was built, which enabled them to work and manage their wine aging better. The 2015 Syrah is excellent: a fruity, vibrant nose offers up hints of cherry and wild berries, as well as the occasional spicy hints. The mouth is warm, dense and succulent, while the finish comes through long and appetizing. First, gamey scents come through on the 2015 Sangiovese, then cherry and aromatic herbs. The body is well-structured, balanced and fresh, with a nice fruity aftertaste. The 2015 Ampelos, made with Sangiovese and a lesser quantity of Merlot, has a fresh bouquet that offers up hints of tomato leaf and aromatic herbs. The body is lean, dynamic, with a nice, long flavorsome acidity to it.

● Ampelos '15	▼▼ 4
● Cortona Sangiovese '15	▼▼ 5
● Cortona Syrah '15	▼▼ 5
○ Cortona Vin Santo '12	▼▼ 7
● Cortona Sangiovese Il Fitto '14	♈♈ 2*
● Cortona Syrah '12	♈♈ 2*
● Cortona Syrah Il Fitto '14	♈♈ 3

★Tenute Ambrogio e Giovanni Folonari

Loc. Passo dei Pecorai
via di Nozzole, 12
50022 Greve in Chianti [FI]
Tel. +39 055859811
www.tenutefolonari.com

CELLAR SALES
PRE-BOOKED VISITS
ACCOMMODATION
ANNUAL PRODUCTION 1,400,000 bottles
HECTARES UNDER VINE 200.00

Tenuta di Nozzole is located in Greve in Chianti, on the Florentine slope of Chianti Classico. Their wines have a modern style, where the search for maximum grape ripeness, important structure, use of small wood and impeccable technical execution are clearly discernible. There is no lack of personality in Ambrogio and Giovanni Folonari's wines, which often achieve excellence. The family has multiple facilities in the best Tuscan terroirs, from Campo al Mare in Bolgheri to La Fuga in Montalcino. The 2015 Chianti Classico is distinguished by its vibrant, fruity notes, which give way to a succulent, though balanced unfolding of flavor in the mouth. The presence of oak makes for a few, light ripples on the finish. The 2016 B.S.T. Cabernet Sauvignon e Sangiovese is a supple, fragrant wine that shows good overall balance and finesse.

● Chianti Cl. '15	▼▼ 4
● B.S.T. Cabernet Sauvignon e Sangiovese '16	▼▼ 4
● B.S.T. Cabernet Sauvignon e Merlot '16	▼ 4
● Chianti Cl. Gran Sel. La Forra '13	▼ 5
● Chianti Cl. La Forra Ris. '13	▼ 4
● Cabreo Il Borgo '06	♈♈♈ 5
● Il Pareto '09	♈♈♈ 7
● Il Pareto '07	♈♈♈ 7
● Brunello di Montalcino Le Due Sorelle Tenuta La Fuga Ris. '10	♈♈ 7
● Brunello di Montalcino Tenuta La Fuga '11	♈♈ 6
● Cabreo Il Borgo '13	♈♈ 6
● Cabreo Il Borgo '12	♈♈ 6
● Chianti Cl. Gran Sel. La Forra '12	♈♈ 5
● Il Pareto '11	♈♈ 7

★★Fontodi

FRAZ. PANZANO IN CHIANTI
VIA SAN LEOLINO, 89
50020 GREVE IN CHIANTI [FI]
TEL. +39 055852005
www.fontodi.com

CELLAR SALES
PRE-BOOKED VISITS
ACCOMMODATION
ANNUAL PRODUCTION 300,000 bottles
HECTARES UNDER VINE 80.00
VITICULTURE METHOD Certified Organic

If the famous Conca d'Oro in Panzano is universally recognized as one of the best Chianti Classico subzones, credit must go in large part to the Manetti family winery, which they've owned since 1968. They give a truly authentic interpretation to Sangiovese from this territory. Today, Fontodi continues to improve their quality with organic vine growing and increased focus on the character and personality of their wines. Flying in the face of a tough vintage, the 2014 Chianti Classico Gran Selezione performs superbly. The nose is multifaceted and includes hints of earth, red fruit and light pepper. In the mouth the wine also proves complex, dynamic and rich in flavor, with a long finish that sees the reemergence of fruit. The 2014 Chianti Classico is simpler, naturally, but still offers fragrant aromas and a pleasantly fluent and fresh unfolding of flavor in the mouth.

Fortulla - Agrilandia

LOC. CASTIGLIONCELLO
S.DA VICINALE DELLE SPIANATE
57016 ROSIGNANO MARITTIMO [LI]
TEL. +39 3404524453
www.fortulla.it

CELLAR SALES
PRE-BOOKED VISITS
ACCOMMODATION AND RESTAURANT SERVICE
ANNUAL PRODUCTION 50,000 bottles
HECTARES UNDER VINE 7.00
VITICULTURE METHOD Certified Organic

Fulvio Martini is a Mantuan with a passion for both the sea and for wine. When he set up his farm in 1994 he achieved his dream of giving an abandoned territory a new lease on life. He planted vineyards and olive groves in a place where nothing had grown previously. And while doing so he took great care to safeguard the biodiversity and varied ecosystem that was already present. In addition to wine and oil, the farm produces excellent honey and runs a flourishing farm holiday business. The 2012 Sorpasso, a blend of Cabernet Sauvignon and Franc (with a smattering of Merlot), impresses aromatically for its notes of ripe green peppers and red fruit. In the mouth it's warm, with nice weight and tannins that fuse well with alcohol. The 2015 Pelagico, made with Petit Manseng, features hints of fruit, like apricot and apple, a soft, fresh body and a tasty, saline finish. The 2016 Serpentino, made with Viognier, distinguishes itself for its flowery notes, a subtle body and a nice finish.

● Chianti Cl. Gran Sel. V. del Sorbo '14	▼▼▼ 6
● Chianti Cl. '14	▼▼ 4
● Chianti Cl. '10	♈♈♈ 4*
● Flaccianello della Pieve '12	♈♈♈ 8
● Flaccianello della Pieve '09	♈♈♈ 8
● Flaccianello della Pieve '08	♈♈♈ 8
● Flaccianello della Pieve '07	♈♈♈ 6
● Flaccianello della Pieve '05	♈♈♈ 6
● Chianti Cl. '12	♈♈ 4
● Chianti Cl. '11	♈♈ 4
● Flaccianello della Pieve '11	♈♈ 8
● Pinot Nero Case Via '14	♈♈ 5
● Pinot Nero Case Via '12	♈♈ 5

○ Pelagico '15	▼▼ 5
○ Serpentino '16	▼▼ 4
● Sorpasso '12	▼▼ 6
● Cabernet Sauvignon '12	▼ 4
○ Bianco Fortulla '14	♈♈ 4
● Fortulla Rosso '13	♈♈ 4
● Fortulla Rosso '12	♈♈ 4
● Sorpasso '11	♈♈ 5
● Sorpasso '10	♈♈ 5

Podere Fortuna

VIA SAN GIUSTO A FORTUNA, 7
50038 SCARPERIA E SAN PIERO [FI]
TEL. +39 0558487214
www.poderefortuna.com

CELLAR SALES
PRE-BOOKED VISITS
ACCOMMODATION
ANNUAL PRODUCTION 25,000 bottles
HECTARES UNDER VINE 6.00
SUSTAINABLE WINERY

At the end of the 1990s, Alessandro Brogi relaunched vine growing at Podere Fortuna, on 31 hectares between the valley floor of the Sieve river and the first hills. Where cereals had been grown previously he planted Chardonnay and Pinot Nero, a variety that at the time wasn't common in Tuscany. The results were his reward, and other vine growers followed suit. Herbicides and pesticides are not used on the farm and the vineyards are fertilized with compost made from pomace, manure from nearby cowsheds and waste from pruning. Energy is supplied by solar panels and the winery gets the water it needs from a well. The 1465 is excellent, with an aromatic profile dedicated to red fruit and aromatic herbs. The body is austere and savory, and the finish is tasty. The 2014 Coldaia is fresher and more subtle.

● 1465 MCDLXV '12	♔♔ 8
● Coldaia '14	♔♔ 5
● 1465 MCDLXV '10	♔♔♔ 8
● 1465 MCDLXV '11	♔♔ 8
● 1465 MCDLXV '09	♔♔ 8
● Coldaia '13	♔♔ 5
● Coldaia '12	♔♔ 5
● Coldaia '11	♔♔ 5
● Fortuni '11	♔♔ 6
○ Greto alla Macchia '12	♔♔ 5
○ Greto alla Macchia '10	♔♔ 5

Tenuta La Fortuna

LOC. LA FORTUNA, 83
53024 MONTALCINO [SI]
TEL. +39 0577848308
www.tenutalafortuna.it

CELLAR SALES
PRE-BOOKED VISITS
ANNUAL PRODUCTION 60,000 bottles
HECTARES UNDER VINE 18.00

This inspiring winery owned by the brother-and-sister team, Angelo and Romina Zannoni, has a recognized place among "owners" in Montalcino. These siblings are the latest generation to run La Fortuna and tend 20 hectares of vineyards with their parents, Gioberto and Felicetta. The property is divided into two parts: the estate where it all began, on the northeastern slope, while the more recently-purchased plots are situated near Castelnuovo dell'Abate. Except for a few rows of Cabernet Sauvignon, the vineyards are mostly planted with Sangiovese for making intense and generous Brunello wines, aged in medium-sized barrels or in barriques for the Riserva. 2012 is surely a favorable year for La Fortuna's reds. The Brunello comes through a bit cloudy in its primary aromas, but in the mouth it settles into fresher, more flowery notes that go well with the wine's lean silhouette. The Giobi line are even more subtle, but they're also airier and more complex.

● Brunello di Montalcino Giobi '12	♔♔ 6
● Brunello di Montalcino '12	♔♔ 6
● Rosso di Montalcino '15	♔ 3
● Brunello di Montalcino '06	♔♔♔ 6
● Brunello di Montalcino '04	♔♔♔ 6
● Brunello di Montalcino '01	♔♔♔ 5
● Brunello di Montalcino '10	♔♔ 6
● Brunello di Montalcino '08	♔♔ 6
● Brunello di Montalcino '07	♔♔ 6
● Brunello di Montalcino Giobi '10	♔♔ 6
● Brunello di Montalcino Ris. '07	♔♔ 7
● Brunello di Montalcino Ris. '06	♔♔ 6
● Brunello di Montalcino Ris. '04	♔♔ 6
● Rosso di Montalcino '11	♔♔ 3

La Fralluca

LOC. BARBICONI, 153
57028 SUVERETO [LI]
TEL. +39 0565829076
www.lafralluca.com

CELLAR SALES
PRE-BOOKED VISITS
ANNUAL PRODUCTION 40,000 bottles
HECTARES UNDER VINE 10.00
SUSTAINABLE WINERY

Luca looks after the vines, olive trees and cellar, which was built almost all underground in the midst of the vineyards. Francesca deals with promotion and sales. The dream began about twenty years ago in Milan, in the world of fashion. It was a dream of moving to Tuscany to make wine in a place they fell in love with. It wasn't far from the coast, on the Suvereto hill, with an abandoned farmhouse and magnificent view of woods and Mediterranean scrub, and counted a total of 45 hectares. This is how the farm began, and ten years ago they planted the vineyards following all principles of sustainability. The 2015 Bauci, made with Viogner, put in a nice performance, with its scents of white peach, lychee and its vegetal hints. On the palate it comes through soft, fine-tuned, tasty and fresh. The 2014 Fillide is also pleasant. It's a blend of Sangiovese, Syrah and Alicante with a pleasant, fruity nose and a gamey nuances. The mouth is solid, flavorsome, with well-distributed tannins and a succulent finish.

○ Bauci '15	♟♟ 3
● Cabernet Franc '14	♟♟ 5
● Fillide '14	♟♟ 3
○ Filemone '16	♟ 3
● Pitis '13	♟ 5
● Suvereto Sangiovese Ciparisso '12	♟♟ 5
○ Bauci '14	♟♟ 3
● Cabernet Franc '13	♟♟ 5
● Cabernet Franc '12	♟♟ 5
● Cabernet Franc '11	♟♟ 6
● Fillide '12	♟♟ 3
● Syrah Pitis '12	♟♟ 5
○ Viognier Bauci '13	♟♟ 3
○ Viognier Bauci '12	♟♟ 3

Frank & Serafico

FRAZ. ALBERESE
S.DA SPERGOLAIA
58100 GROSSETO
TEL. +39 0564418491
www.frankeserafico.com

CELLAR SALES
PRE-BOOKED VISITS
RESTAURANT SERVICE
ANNUAL PRODUCTION 90,000 bottles
HECTARES UNDER VINE 25.00

This winery run by Fabrizio Testa and Pierpaolo Pratesi produces coherent and consistent wines. Their clear-cut style has enabled them to carve out a space in Maremma's rich winemaking scene. Although their wines are not particularly distinctive, they are well-made and, by design, avoid complexity. Rather, the focus for this winery is to bring back the enjoyment, pleasure, and simplicity of simply drinking wine. The 2015 Frank is a blend of Cabernet Franc, Merlot and Sangiovese. It's a red with concentrated, vibrant fragrances. On the palate it comes through dense and solid, though a bit reined in by an abundance of oak, which disturbs its overall balance. The rest of the wines presented are all early-drinking. The well-paced 2015 Morellino Mr stands out, as does the 2016 Maremma Redola Bianco and the 2016 Vermentino, with these last two featuring pleasant sea salt on the nose, as well as during the finish.

● Frank '15	♟♟ 3
○ Maremma Toscana Redola Bianco '16	♟ 2
● Morellino di Scansano Mr '15	♟ 2
○ Vermentino VR '16	♟ 2
● Maremma Toscana Sangiovese '12	♟♟ 4
● Montalzato '13	♟♟ 2*
● Morellino di Scansano Mr '13	♟♟ 2*
● Morellino di Scansano Mr '12	♟♟ 2*
● Sangiovese '11	♟♟ 4
○ Serafico '13	♟♟ 4

Frascole

Loc. Frascole, 27a
50062 Dicomano [FI]
Tel. +39 0558386340
www.frascole.it

CELLAR SALES
PRE-BOOKED VISITS
ACCOMMODATION
ANNUAL PRODUCTION 65,000 bottles
HECTARES UNDER VINE 16.00
VITICULTURE METHOD Certified Organic

The Lippi and Santoni families own an
estate spanning almost 100 hectares. It is
located between the hills and the valley
floor of Dicomano, a small town of
Etruscan and Roman origin between the
Mugello valley and Valdisieve. The lower
areas are dedicated to arable crops, while
the hilly areas, which reach up altitudes of
up to 470 meters, are cultivated with
olives and vines. The vineyards are run
under organic farming methods and give
rise to fresh wines with great minerality. In
addition to olive and vine growing, they
have also set up a thriving farm holiday
business and you can stay the night in
perfectly-restored buildings in the small
town. The 2014 Riserva had a good day.
The wine brings together sweet spices
and dark, ripe fruit in an elegant,
multifaceted aromatic bouquet. The attack
shows great personality, with tannins that
are still racy and lively. The finish is
polished. The 2015 Bitornino, a blend of
Sangiovese and Canaiolo (with a
smattering of white grapes), is rustic but
still pleasant.

● Bitornino '15	▼▼	2*
Chianti Rufina Ris. '14	▼▼	3
● Chianti Rufina '15	▼	2
○ In Albis sullebucce '14	▼	5
Chianti Rufina '14	▼▼	2*
● Chianti Rufina '13	▼▼	2*
Chianti Rufina '11	▼▼	2*
● Chianti Rufina Ris. '12	▼▼	3*
● Chianti Rufina Ris. '11	▼▼	3
○ In Albis '13	▼▼	2*
○ In Albis sullebucce '11	▼▼	2*
● Limine '10	▼▼	2*
○ Passito '02	▼▼	8
○ Vin Santo del Chianti Rufina '05	▼▼	7
○ Vin Santo del Chianti Rufina '04	▼▼	7

★Marchesi Frescobaldi

Via Santo Spirito, 11
50125 Firenze
Tel. +39 05527141
www.frescobaldi.it

CELLAR SALES
PRE-BOOKED VISITS
ANNUAL PRODUCTION 7,000,000 bottles
HECTARES UNDER VINE 923.00

The name Frescobaldi has been
inextricably linked with Tuscan history since
the fourteenth century. The winery we
know today is iconic, both for its long
tradition and for its estates in the best
winegrowing areas. The original property
(the historic nucleus of Rufina and nearby
Pomino) has been expanded with
acquisition of other estates in Montalcino,
Chianti Classico, Maremma, Morellino and
Colli Fiorentini. At the helm is Lamberto
Frescobaldi, who in recent years, has
developed crucial themes such as
sustainability. An excellent overall
performance. The 2014 Rufina Vecchie Viti
Riserva made it to the finals, with its
elegant aromatic profile featuring vibrant
fruit, accents of fresh aromatic herbs and
small hints of spice. On the palate it proves
subtle, delicate and fresh, with fine-grained
tannins and a finish that features a touch
of savoriness. The 2014 Montesodi, made
with 100% Sangiovese, offers up flowery
fragrances of geranium and close-focused
fruit.

● Chianti Rufina V. V. Ris. '14	▼▼	6
● Montesodi '14	▼▼	6
○ Pomino Brut Leonia '13	▼▼	6
● Giramonte '13	▼▼	8
○ Gorgona '16	▼▼	8
● Lamaione '12	▼▼	8
● Maremma Toscana Ammiraglia '13	▼▼	6
● Maremma Toscana Cabernet Sauvignon Terre More '15	▼▼	3
● Morellino di Scansano Pietraregia dell'Ammiraglia '14	▼▼	5
● Mormoreto '14	▼▼	8
○ Pomino Benefizio Ris. '15	▼▼	5
⊙ Pomino Brut Rosé Leonia '12	▼▼	7
○ Pomino Vin Santo '08	▼▼	6
● Chianti Rufina Nipozzano V. V. Ris. '13	▼▼▼	5

Fuligni

VIA SALONI, 33
53024 MONTALCINO [SI]
TEL. +39 0577848710
www.fuligni.it

CELLAR SALES
PRE-BOOKED VISITS
ANNUAL PRODUCTION 52,000 bottles
HECTARES UNDER VINE 12.00

The Fuligni is an old Venetian family who settled in Montalcino in the early twentieth century and started producing wine on their prestigious estates in Maremma. At the helm is Maria Floria, helped by a skilled team that tends ten hectares of vineyards, concentrated mainly in Cottimelli. Here on the easternmost part of the hill the area is dominated by stones and galestro, at altitudes skimming 450 meters. The soil and climate conditions enhance the dense, eager temperament of their Brunellos, which after a period in smaller wood are aged in 3000-liter oak barrels. Fuligni's list of accomplishments gets longer thanks to a southern-styled 2012: aromas of blackcurrant and pepper, meatiness in the mouth, as well as close-woven tannins, though never dry or austere. With just a bit more vigor it would be at the top. The succulent 2015 Rosso Ginestreto features flowery and vegetal notes, as well as hints of balsamic.

● Brunello di Montalcino '12	♟♟	6
● Rosso di Montalcino Ginestreto '15	♟♟	4
● Brunello di Montalcino '10	♟♟♟	6
● Brunello di Montalcino Ris. '01	♟♟♟	8
● Brunello di Montalcino '11	♟♟	6
● Brunello di Montalcino '09	♟♟	6
● Brunello di Montalcino '08	♟♟	6
● Brunello di Montalcino Ris. '07	♟♟	8
● Brunello di Montalcino Ris. '06	♟♟	8
● Rosso di Montalcino Ginestreto '13	♟♟	4
● Rosso di Montalcino Ginestreto '10	♟♟	3
● S. J. '12	♟♟	3

★Tenuta di Ghizzano

FRAZ. GHIZZANO
VIA DELLA CHIESA, 4
56037 PECCIOLI [PI]
TEL. +39 0587630096
www.tenutadighizzano.com

CELLAR SALES
PRE-BOOKED VISITS
ACCOMMODATION
ANNUAL PRODUCTION 80,000 bottles
HECTARES UNDER VINE 20.00
VITICULTURE METHOD Certified Organic

This estate is located in a place of dazzling natural beauty, and approaches 350 hectares of owned land. At the helm is one of the most famous and esteemed women in the Italian wine sector: Ginevra Venerosi Pesciolini. The vine rows are planted on soil of marine origin, rich in sand, clay and minerals. Farming techniques initially followed organic methods but now have turned to biodynamics. The wines have a modern style, with good intensity and balance, and are steadily increasing in flavor. The 2015 Nambrot is still very young. Without a doubt it will have to age longer to find the right combination of qualities and realize its immense potential. In any case, it seems that its stylistic approach is set, and the same could be said for the Veneroso, which just gets better by the year. It exhibits toasty fragrances, just a bit too much, but time will take care of that. The rest of its aromatic profile features fruit of rare finesse, fresh, balsamic, herbal hints. In the mouth it shows good acidity and enticing flashes of minerality.

● Terre di Pisa Nambrot '15	♟♟♟	6
● Terre di Pisa Veneroso '14	♟♟	5
○ San Germano Passito '15	♟♟	5
● Nambrot '09	♟♟♟	6
● Nambrot '08	♟♟♟	6
● Nambrot '06	♟♟♟	6
● Nambrot '05	♟♟♟	6
● Nambrot '04	♟♟♟	6
● Nambrot '03	♟♟♟	6
● Nambrot '01	♟♟♟	8
● Terre di Pisa Nambrot '13	♟♟♟	6
● Terre di Pisa Nambrot '12	♟♟♟	6
● Veneroso '10	♟♟♟	5
● Veneroso '07	♟♟♟	5
● Veneroso '04	♟♟♟	5

Marchesi Ginori Lisci

FRAZ. PONTEGINORI
LOC. QUERCETO
56040 MONTECATINI VAL DI CECINA [PI]
TEL. +39 058837443
www.marchesiginorilisci.it

CELLAR SALES
ACCOMMODATION AND RESTAURANT SERVICE
ANNUAL PRODUCTION 35,000 bottles
HECTARES UNDER VINE 17.00
VITICULTURE METHOD Certified Organic

Castello Ginori's long history in the medieval village of Querceto has been linked to that of the Ginori Lisci Marquises for over two centuries. It is perched on a hill in the heart of a 2000-hectare estate in the Val di Cecina backcountry. In the late 1900s, Lionardo Ginori and his grandson, Luigi Malenchini, began transforming the winery with the planting new vineyards and by building a more modern cellar. Today, in the Montescudaio appellation, their vineyards host with Merlot, Cabernet Sauvignon, Sangiovese, Viognier and Vermentino. The 2014 Macchion del Lupo, made with Cabernet, makes it into our finals, with its notes of green peppers and Mediterranean shrub. In the mouth it proves soft and creamy, with fine-grained, subtle tannins. The 2015 Merlot Campordigno has fruity perfumes, a well-balanced and smooth body, good acidity and length. The 2014 Merlot Castello Ginori surprises for its delicate bouquet of wild berries, and its savory, dynamic mouth.

● Montescudaio Cabernet Macchion del Lupo '14	♟♟ 3*
● Montescudaio Merlot Castello Ginori '14	♟♟ 2*
● Montescudaio Rosso Campordigno '15	♟♟ 2*
○ Virgola '16	♟ 2
● Montescudaio Cabernet Macchion del Lupo '13	♟ 3
● Montescudaio Cabernet Macchion del Lupo '11	♟ 3*
● Montescudaio Merlot '08	♟ 2*
● Montescudaio Merlot Campordigno '12	♟ 2*
● Montescudaio Merlot Castello Ginori '12	♟ 2*
● Montescudaio Merlot Castello Ginori '11	♟ 2*
● Montescudaio Merlot Castello Ginori '09	♟ 4
● Montescudaio Rosso Campordigno '10	♟ 2*

Giodo

LOC. PIAZZINI
53011 MONTALCINO [SI]
carlo.ferrini27@gmail.com

ANNUAL PRODUCTION 8,000 bottles
HECTARES UNDER VINE 2.50
SUSTAINABLE WINERY

Carlo Ferrini chose Montalcino for his winemaking venture at the start of the 2000s, and made his official debut with the 2009 vintage. Ironically, it was a new experience for one of the best-known consultant agronomists and winemakers in the country. He found an ideal platform for his Sangiovese reds at Podere Giodo, however, the style is different from what we would imagine: succulent and velvety, anything but ingratiating, and without unnecessary wood. The wines are expressive of the mood of the plots along the road headed south from Castelnuovo dell'Abate to Sant'Angelo in Colle. We're not surprised by the sure-footedness displayed in such a short time by Giodo's Brunellos. On the nose, the 2012 features hints of wild berries, black pepper and Mediterranean shrub, as well as a touch of confit. And it's lost nothing in terms of brilliance of taste and tannic support. It's a delectable force that we find in the 2015 Giodo as well.

● Brunello di Montalcino Giodo '12	♟♟♟ 8
● Giodo '15	♟♟ 6
● Brunello di Montalcino Giodo '11	♟♟ 8
● Giodo '13	♟ 6

I Giusti & Zanza Vigneti

VIA DEI PUNTONI, 9
56043 FAUGLIA [PI]
TEL. +39 058544354
www.igiustiezanza.it

CELLAR SALES
PRE-BOOKED VISITS
ACCOMMODATION
ANNUAL PRODUCTION 100,000 bottles
HECTARES UNDER VINE 17.00
VITICULTURE METHOD Certified Organic

The Giusti family set up their winery in a place of rare beauty. It began in the 1990s in Fuaglia, in the hills between Pisa and Livorno. Since then the winery's growth and improvement has been unstoppable. The vineyard soil is sandy-clay with gravel and their wines have unique characteristics, making them anything but standardized. The 2015 Belcore is made primarily with Sangiovese and rounded out with Merlot (as well as other varieties). It's a sound red, well-orchestrated with fruity, slightly spicy and balsamic fragrances. The mouth is taut and well-defined. The Perbruno is darker in its aromatic profile and palate, and needs more time in the bottle. The Nemorino Rosso surprises for its brilliance of taste and liveliness.

Tenuta di Gracciano della Seta

FRAZ. GRACCIANO
VIA UMBRIA, 59
53045 MONTEPULCIANO [SI]
TEL. +39 0578708340
www.graccianodellaseta.com

CELLAR SALES
PRE-BOOKED VISITS
ANNUAL PRODUCTION 100,000 bottles
HECTARES UNDER VINE 18.00
SUSTAINABLE WINERY

The property includes 20 hectares of vineyards on hillside soil made up of silty clay. Giorgio della Seta now owns Gracciano, a historic estate that formerly counted 400 hectares and 22 farms. The wines receive widespread praise, and continue to follow a successful path for style. The 2013 Nobile RIserva features nuanced, elegant fragrances, as precise as they are surprising, and the mouth sees good follow-through. It's a solid and deep wine, flavorsome and juicy. The 2014 Nobile may have hit a difficult vintage, but it's well-crafted. Lean, subtle and fragrant, it proves highly drinkable. The 2015 Rosso di Montepulciano is also pleasant.

● Belcore '15	❦❦ 3
● Nemorino Rosso '15	❦❦ 2*
● Perbruno '15	❦❦ 4
● Belcore '13	❦❦ 3
● Belcore '12	❦❦ 3
● Dulcamara '13	❦❦ 5
● Dulcamara '12	❦❦ 5
● Dulcamara '11	❦❦ 5
● Dulcamara '10	❦❦ 5
○ Nemorino Bianco '12	❦❦ 2*
● Perbruno '13	❦❦ 4
● Perbruno '10	❦❦ 4

● Nobile di Montepulciano '14	❦❦ 4
● Nobile di Montepulciano Ris. '13	❦❦ 5
● Rosso di Montepulciano '15	❦ 3
● Nobile di Montepulciano Ris. '12	❦❦❦ 5
● Nobile di Montepulciano '13	❦❦ 4
● Nobile di Montepulciano '11	❦❦ 3
● Nobile di Montepulciano '06	❦❦ 5
● Nobile di Montepulciano Ris. '10	❦❦ 5
● Nobile di Montepulciano Ris. '06	❦❦ 5
● Nobile di Montepulciano Ris. '04	❦❦ 5
● Nobile di Montepulciano Ris. '01	❦❦ 5

Bibi Graetz

VIA DI VINCIGLIATA, 19
50014 FIESOLE [FI]
TEL. +39 055597289
www.bibigraetz.com

PRE-BOOKED VISITS
ANNUAL PRODUCTION 500,000 bottles
HECTARES UNDER VINE 10.00

Bibi Graetz is an interesting character who has set up an unconventional winery. Imaging for his wine is unusual as well. Take for instance the names he gives his wines, and their labels, inspired by his paintings. Deciding to inject life back into some old vineyards in Fiesole -- not known as a great winegrowing area -- he ended up promoting varieties that had been shelved for years. These he managed to render quite palatable to an international public. Capping his originality is his decision to make Ansonica del Giglio. After a trip to the island to choose the grapes he convinced local farmers not to abandon the vineyards and to tend them with care. The 2015 Testamatta, made with Sangiovese, makes it to the finals. Its aromatic bouquet features variegated spices like cinnamon and cloves, as well as vibrant fruity notes of cherry and blackcurrant. The mouth opens well, warm and pervasive. Its tannins prove silky, and there's good acidity to boot. The finish is long and complex.

● Testamatta '15	♈♈ 8
○ Bugia '16	♈♈ 6
● Colore '12	♈♈ 8
○ Scopeto '16	♈♈ 3
● Soffocone di Vincigliata '15	♈♈ 5
○ Testamatta Bianco '15	♈♈ 5
○ Casamatta Bianco '16	♈ 2
● Casamatta Rosso '16	♈ 2
● Chianti Le Cicale di Vincigliata '15	♈ 2
○ Bugia '14	♈♈ 6
● Colore '11	♈♈ 8
● Colore '10	♈♈ 8
● Soffocone di Vincigliata '14	♈♈ 5
● Soffocone di Vincigliata '13	♈♈ 5
● Testamatta '13	♈♈ 8
● Testamatta '12	♈♈ 8

★Grattamacco

LOC. LUNGAGNANO
57022 CASTAGNETO CARDUCCI [LI]
TEL. +39 0565765069
www.collemassari.it

CELLAR SALES
PRE-BOOKED VISITS
ANNUAL PRODUCTION 120,000 bottles
HECTARES UNDER VINE 16.00
VITICULTURE METHOD Certified Organic
SUSTAINABLE WINERY

Grattamacco, famous for its fine wines, was one of the first wineries to be set up in Bolgheri in the 1970s. Today it belongs to the Tipa brother and sister team, who also own Colle Massari and Poggio di Sotto. They have spared no effort in expanding their vineyards and improving production stages. The vine rows lie on mixed soil: sandy, limestone and marl. The wines more than hold their own in this area, standing out for their definition, expressiveness and flavor. The 2014 Bolgheri Superiore Grattamacco manages to triumph over the difficult season. And that's not easy. The wine surprised us for its determination, exuberance and structure - you'd never guess it was a hard year. Its aromas are lush and vibrant, spicy and mature in its fruity embrace. The mouth is, as mentioned, solid and thick, with excellent support and depth. The 2015 Bolgheri proves corpulent and well-crafted.

● Bolgheri Sup. Grattamacco '14	♈♈♈ 8
● Bolgheri Rosso '15	♈♈ 4
● Bolgheri Sup. L'Alberello '14	♈♈ 6
● Bolgheri Sup. Grattamacco '13	♈♈♈ 8
● Bolgheri Sup. Grattamacco '12	♈♈♈ 8
● Bolgheri Sup. Grattamacco '10	♈♈♈ 7
● Bolgheri Sup. Grattamacco '09	♈♈♈ 7
● Bolgheri Sup. Grattamacco '07	♈♈♈ 7
● Bolgheri Sup. Grattamacco '06	♈♈♈ 7
● Bolgheri Sup. L'Alberello '11	♈♈♈ 6
● Bolgheri Rosso '14	♈♈ 4
● Bolgheri Rosso '12	♈♈ 4
● Bolgheri Sup. L'Alberello '13	♈♈ 6
● Bolgheri Sup. L'Alberello '12	♈♈ 6
○ Bolgheri Vermentino Grattamacco '13	♈♈ 5

Fattoria di Grignano

VIA DI GRIGNANO, 22
50065 PONTASSIEVE [FI]
TEL. +39 0558398490
www.fattoriadigrignano.com

CELLAR SALES
PRE-BOOKED VISITS
ANNUAL PRODUCTION 200,000 bottles
HECTARES UNDER VINE 53.00
VITICULTURE METHOD Certified Organic
SUSTAINABLE WINERY

The Inghirami family, one of the most prestigious names in Italian fashion, have owned this winery since 1972. It lies to the east of Florence, where the Sieve and Arno rivers merge in the first Apennine hills. The estate spans 600 hectares, divided into 47 farms, mainly cultivated with olives and vines. The cellars are housed in a fifteenth-century villa. There are 53 hectares of vineyards, planted with traditional varieties such as Sangiovese, Canaiolo Nero, Trebbiano Toscano and Malvasia, which co-exist with thriving international ones like Cabernet Sauvignon, Merlot, Syrah and Chardonnay. Organic certification arrived in 2012. This year we tasted a fantastic Riserva Poggio Gualtieri, a wine that's already elegant in its bouquet, featuring mineral overtones, dried red flowers, cloves and hints of balsamic. The mouth is relaxed and well-sustained by virtue of a tannic weave that's tight, but well-integrated.

● Chianti Rufina Poggio Gualtieri Ris. '13		♟♟ 4
○ Vin Santo del Chianti Rufina '09		♟♟ 4
● Chianti Rufina '14		♟ 2
● Chianti Rufina '13		♟♟ 2*
● Chianti Rufina '12		♟♟ 2*
● Chianti Rufina Poggio Gualtieri Ris. '11		♟♟ 4
○ Vin Santo del Chianti Rufina '08		♟♟ 4

Guado al Melo

LOC. MURROTTO, 130A
57022 CASTAGNETO CARDUCCI [LI]
TEL. +39 0565763238
www.guadoalmelo.it

CELLAR SALES
PRE-BOOKED VISITS
ANNUAL PRODUCTION 80,000 bottles
HECTARES UNDER VINE 15.00
SUSTAINABLE WINERY

Michele Scienza is the son of a famous viticulture professor and expert in the field. His winery has rapidly carved out an important role in Bolgheri winemaking. There are seventeen hectares of vineyards, with the most striking feature being the wide variety of grapes. The estate boasts Mediterranean and Caucasian varieties that resulted from experimentation and they form an important base for their wines. These are precise, well-made and interesting. No crown jewels emerge from the miserable 2014 season. But we're consoled by the excellent Bolgheri Rosso Rute, a wine that's dense in its fruity weave, with noticeable toastiness but still exceptionally well-crafted. The mouth is solid, defined and well-extracted. Age will see to it that the wine is even more harmonious and supple. The 2015 Antillo saw more compressed and mouth-drying tannins.

● Bolgheri Rosso Antillo '15		♟♟ 3
● Bolgheri Rosso Rute '15		♟♟ 4
● Bolgheri Rosso Sup. Atis '12		♟♟♟ 6
● Bolgheri Rosso Rute '13		♟♟ 5
● Bolgheri Rosso Sup. Atis '13		♟♟ 6

Tenuta Guado al Tasso

LOC. BOLGHERI
S.DA BOLGHERESE KM 3,9
57020 CASTAGNETO CARDUCCI [LI]
TEL. +39 0565749735
www.guadoaltasso.it

CELLAR SALES
ANNUAL PRODUCTION 1,500,000 bottles
HECTARES UNDER VINE 300.00

Guado al Tasso is owned by the famous Antinori family and is a remarkable property, approaching a thousand hectares of vineyards, woods and Mediterranean scrub. About a third of the land hosts the grape varieties that have become traditional in Bolgheri: Merlot, Cabernet Sauvignon, Petit Verdot, and, of course, Sangiovese for the reds; Vermentino is among those for the whites. The wines have an accurate, spot-on style that is always focused and excellently put together. Among the reds, the 2015 Il Bruciato impressed the most. It's a wine that has intensity, both in its aromas and on the palate, as well as texture and good length. It's a well-crafted wine, with excellent aging potential. The Rosato Scalabrone proves pleasant, flowery and citrusy. It's an excellent model for the category. The 2014 Bolgheri Superiore was less striking.

Il Guercio

LOC. LA FILANDA
53013 GAIOLE IN CHIANTI [SI]
TEL. +39 335429613
seanilguercio@gmail.com

ANNUAL PRODUCTION 2,000 bottles
HECTARES UNDER VINE 5.00

Sean O'Callaghan is a character. He is a winemaker with clear ideas, sensitivity, an uncommon palate and a lot of experience in the Chianti Classico hills and cellars. We gladly welcome his new venture, which came about from a precise philosophy combining territory with expertise, adding in a passion for Sangiovese and winemaking, and capped off with aging styles that follow new and original paths. We expect his wines to be a fine result of all this know-how and energy. The 2015 Guercio is a hit right out of the gate. We don't like comparing one territory's wines with another, and even less so when it comes to varieties. But it's difficult to hold back here. Sean's wine tends towards Borgogna, inasmuch as it's vibrant aromatically and light in structure, streamlined and airy on the palate. It shows intensity and flavor without the frills, thus avoiding heaviness and offering up the best. In a nutshell, purity and flavor. A better start would be hard to imagine.

⊙ Bolgheri Rosato Scalabrone '16	♟♟ 3
● Bolgheri Rosso Il Bruciato '15	♟♟ 5
● Bolgheri Sup. Guado al Tasso '14	♟ 8
○ Bolgheri Vermentino '16	♟ 3
● Bolgheri Sup. Guado al Tasso '01	♟♟♟ 8
● Bolgheri Sup. Guado al Tasso '90	♟♟♟ 8
● Bolgheri Rosso Il Bruciato '14	♟♟ 5
● Bolgheri Rosso Il Bruciato '13	♟♟ 5
● Bolgheri Rosso Il Bruciato '12	♟♟ 4
● Bolgheri Sup. Guado al Tasso '13	♟♟ 8
● Bolgheri Sup. Guado al Tasso '12	♟♟ 8
● Bolgheri Sup. Guado al Tasso '10	♟♟ 8
○ Bolgheri Vermentino '14	♟♟ 3
○ Bolgheri Vermentino '13	♟♟ 3
○ Bolgheri Vermentino '12	♟♟ 3

● Il Guercio '15	♟♟ 7

Tenute Guicciardini Strozzi

LOC. CUSONA, 5
53037 SAN GIMIGNANO [SI]
TEL. +39 0577950028
www.guicciardinistrozzi.it

CELLAR SALES
PRE-BOOKED VISITS
ANNUAL PRODUCTION 800,000 bottles
HECTARES UNDER VINE 115.00

A lot has transpired on the Cusona estate's 530 hectares around San Gimignano. This noble family boasted ties with the Mona Lisa painted by Leonardo da Vinci. In the early twentieth century, Francesco Guicciardini (Minister of Agriculture and Mayor of Florence) turned the estate into a model winery. As the father of the current owner, Girolamo Strozzi, he first bottled Vernaccia in Bordeaux bottles in 1933. Then in the 1970s he began selling his wines and initiated the winery's growth and expansion, continuing into today. In the absence of their most representative Vernaccia, the Cusona 1933, three other versions stepped up: the 2016 vintage has vibrant vegetal fragrances, forest herbs, with faintly fruity overtones. The mouth shows good complexity and acidity, and the finish is nice and clean. The 2014 Riserva, a savory, fruit-drive wine, is among the best. The 2001 Vermentino Arabesque proves fresh and enjoyable.

○ Vernaccia di S. Gimignano '16	♙♙ 2*
○ Vernaccia di S. Gimignano Ris. '14	♙♙ 3
○ Vernaccia di S. Gimignano Titolato Strozzi '16	♙♙ 2*
○ Arabesque '16	♙ 2
● Chianti Colli Senesi Titolato Strozzi '16	♙ 2
● Millanni '16	♙ 6
● Millanni '99	♙♙♙ 5

★★Isole e Olena

LOC. ISOLE, 1
50021 BARBERINO VAL D'ELSA [FI]
TEL. +39 0558072763
www.isolcolona.it

CELLAR SALES
PRE-BOOKED VISITS
ANNUAL PRODUCTION 200,000 bottles
HECTARES UNDER VINE 56.00

Paolo di Marchi's wines stand out for their textbook consistency in style, based on fully-ripe fruit and expert use of wood aging. The winery is widely recognized as one of the best in Chianti Classico and over the years they have never lost their touch. Faithful interpretation of the territory's characteristics is what distinquishes Isole e Olena wines and sets the standard for the whole appellation. 2014 was a year that tested all of Chianti Classico, and Paolo De Marchi's vineyards were no exception. The 2014 Cepparello, a wine that's sensitive to the characteristics of the vintage, exhibits fragrances of clean, small red fruit, but they're a bit flat, while the mouth is pleasant but lacking in depth and a bit too heavy on oak (which comes out in the finish). The 2013 Cabernet Sauvignon is a highly concentrated wine.

● Cepparello '14	♙♙ 8
● Cabernet Sauvignon Collezione De Marchi '13	♙ 8
● Cepparello '13	♙♙♙ 8
● Cepparello '12	♙♙♙ 8
● Cepparello '09	♙♙♙ 8
● Cepparello '07	♙♙♙ 8
● Cepparello '06	♙♙♙ 8
● Cepparello '05	♙♙♙ 8
● Cabernet Sauvignon Collezione De Marchi '12	♙♙ 8
● Cepparello '11	♙♙ 8
● Chianti Cl. '14	♙♙ 5
● Chianti Cl. '13	♙♙ 5
○ Vin Santo del Chianti Classico '06	♙♙ 7

Istine

VIA ROMA, 11
53017 RADDA IN CHIANTI [SI]
TEL. +39 0577733684
www.istine.it

ANNUAL PRODUCTION 32,000 bottles
HECTARES UNDER VINE 34.00

Angela Fronti has set up a winery that improves with every vintage. There are a few excellent rules that she follows to the letter: organic viticulture, purist and unforced winemaking techniques faithful to tradition, and aging in large wood. Informing it all is the expressiveness of Chianti-grown Sangiovese. The result is a range of wines with liveliness, elegance, balance and complexity. Today they are some of the best in the whole appellation. The 2015 Chianti Classico Vigna Istine is simply delectable (and not at all banal), with its light but fragrant aromas, and a succulent, deep unfolding of flavor in the mouth. It's all savory and clenched tannins, but extremely flavorsome. The 2015 Chianti Classico Vigna Cavarchione also did well. Its nose alternates between whole red and black fruit, with a decadent, complex mouth. It's just a bit woody at the end.

● Chianti Cl. V. Istine '15	♛♛♛ 3*
● Chianti Cl. V. Cavarchione '15	♛♛ 3*
● Chianti Cl. '15	♛♛ 3
● Chianti Cl. LeVigne Ris. '14	♛♛ 3
● Chianti Cl. V. Casanova '14	♛♛ 3
● Chianti Cl. LeVigne Ris. '13	♟♟♟ 3*
● Chianti Cl. '14	♟♟ 3*
● Chianti Cl. '13	♟♟ 3
● Chianti Cl. LeVigne Ris. '12	♟♟ 3*
● Chianti Cl. V. Casanova '12	♟♟ 3
● Chianti Cl. V. Cavarchione '14	♟♟ 3
● Chianti Cl. V. Istine '14	♟♟ 3
● Chianti Cl. V. Istine '13	♟♟ 3
● Chianti Cl. V. Istine '12	♟♟ 3

Fattoria Il Lago

FRAZ. CAMPAGNA, 23
50062 DICOMANO [FI]
TEL. +39 055838047
www.fattoriaillago.com

CELLAR SALES
PRE-BOOKED VISITS
ACCOMMODATION
ANNUAL PRODUCTION 50,000 bottles
HECTARES UNDER VINE 17.00
SUSTAINABLE WINERY

For almost fifty years the Spagnoli family have owned this estate, which once belonged to the Vivai Bartolini Salimbeni Marquises. Over time, they have renovated the buildings divided into two villages, and set up a thriving farm holiday business. They have spared no effort in renewing the vineyards, favoring native varieties such as Sangiovese, but also planting some international ones like Syrah and Pinot Nero. The fact that their wines show authenticity and typicity, and the whole selection performed well, puts the winery among the guide's top players. The 2015 Chianti Rufina has an earthy character on the nose, and a savory, taut mouth that's just a bit citrusy at the end. The 2012 Riserva offers up red fruit and spices. It still has a bit too much wood, but in the mouth it works, thanks to a nice acidity that keeps it young. The Vin Santo, a soft but not cloying wine, also delivered.

● Chianti Rufina '15	♛♛ 2*
● Chianti Rufina Ris. '12	♛♛ 3
○ Vin Santo del Chianti Rufina Ris. '07	♛♛ 5
● Chianti Rufina '12	♟♟ 2*
● Chianti Rufina '11	♟♟ 2*
● Pinot Nero '12	♟♟ 5
● Pinot Nero '10	♟♟ 5
● Syrah '10	♟♟ 3

Maurizio Lambardi

LOC. CANALICCHIO DI SOTTO, 8
53024 MONTALCINO [SI]
TEL. +39 0577848476
www.lambardimontalcino.it

CELLAR SALES
PRE-BOOKED VISITS
ANNUAL PRODUCTION 17,000 bottles
HECTARES UNDER VINE 6.50

Also known as Canalicchio di Sotto, this estate run by Maurizio Lambardi has belonged to his family since the 1960s. Their first Brunello made its debut in 1973. Since then the vineyards have been increased to the current size of six and a half hectares. Mostly Sangiovese is cultivated here on northern Montalcino's clayish tuff soil where altitudes skim 350 meters. We expect and indeed find wines that are more long-limbed than powerful, spirited and biting. The features are enhanced by long maceration and aging in 3000- to 5000-liter Slavonian oak barrels. From the controversial 2012 vintage we get a rather classic Brunello (with respect to what the Lambardis offered in previous seasons). Bouquet garni, spiciness, blood-rich meat all transmit energy and verve. It only softens during the finish, by virtue of the wine's rich tannic armor.

Lamole di Lamole

LOC. LAMOLE
50022 GREVE IN CHIANTI [FI]
TEL. +39 0559331256
www.lamole.com

CELLAR SALES
PRE-BOOKED VISITS
RESTAURANT SERVICE
ANNUAL PRODUCTION 294,000 bottles
HECTARES UNDER VINE 57.00
SUSTAINABLE WINERY

The Santa Margherita group chose Villa Vistarenni in Gaiole in Chianti, Sassoregale in Maremma, and Lamole di Lamole in Greve to produce their wine in Tuscany. The latter is one of the best terroir in Chianti. Their Chianti Classico DOC wines have a spot-on style and stand out for drinkability, balance and elegance. The result of sustainable vine growing and meticulous work in the cellar, an attentive use of small and large wood brings it all to full fruition. The 2014 Chianti Classico Etichetta Blu is truly enjoyable. A fragrant aromatic profile, with clear notes of fresh cherry, give way to a flavorsome, crisp mouth in which tannins are present, but flavor reigns. The 2013 Chianti Classico Riserva is just as good. Exhibiting a more modern style, the wine offers up notes of red fruit and faint hints of coffee grind. In the mouth it's just a bit woody. The 2015 Sangiovese Sassoregale, with its overall pleasantness, also did quite well.

● Brunello di Montalcino '12	♟♟	8
● Brunello di Montalcino '10	♟♟	8
● Brunello di Montalcino '09	♟♟	8
● Brunello di Montalcino '08	♟♟	5
● Brunello di Montalcino '07	♟♟	8
● Brunello di Montalcino '06	♟♟	8
● Brunello di Montalcino '05	♟♟	8
● Brunello di Montalcino '00	♟♟	8
● Brunello di Montalcino '99	♟♟	8
● Brunello di Montalcino '97	♟♟	8
● Brunello di Montalcino '96	♟♟	8

● Chianti Cl. Lamole di Lamole Et. Blu '14	♟♟♟	3*
● Chianti Cl. Ris. '13	♟♟	5
● Maremma Toscana Sangiovese Sassoregale '15	♟♟	2*
● Maremma Toscana Syrah Sassoregale '15	♟♟	2*
● Chianti Cl. Lamole di Lamole Et. Bianca '14	♟	3
○ Maremma Toscana Vermentino Sassoregale '16	♟	2
● Chianti Cl. Gran Sel. Vign. di Campolungo '10	♟♟♟	5
● Chianti Cl. Lamole di Lamole Et. Bianca '13	♟♟♟	3*
● Chianti Cl. Lamole di Lamole Et. Blu '12	♟♟♟	3*
● Chianti Cl. Vign. di Campolungo Ris. '09	♟♟♟	5
● Chianti Cl. Vign. di Campolungo Ris. '08	♟♟♟	5

La Lastra

FRAZ. SANTA LUCIA
VIA R. DE GRADA, 9
53037 SAN GIMIGNANO [SI]
TEL. +39 0577941781
www.lalastra.it

CELLAR SALES
PRE-BOOKED VISITS
ANNUAL PRODUCTION 58,000 bottles
HECTARES UNDER VINE 7.00
SUSTAINABLE WINERY

Nadia Betti and her husband, Renato Spanu, arrived in San Gimignano in the 1980s. After ten years of studying and work as winegrowing consultants, they had reached some firm ideas about protecting the environment, the importance of work and people, and the elevation of substance over form. They established La Lastra along with Nadia's brother, Christian Betti, and their friends, Enrico Paternoster and Valerio Zorzi. Their common aim was to produce high-quality, eco-friendly wine and oil expressive of the territory. In the year 2000 they bought another winery, Marciano, comprised of 23 hectares and location for a new holiday farmhouse. The 2015 Vernaccia di San Gimignano Riserva had a good day. It's an elegant wine, decisive in its bouquet of pear, apple and tropical fruit. The mouth is warm and dense, the body elegant and full. The finish delivers, though it's not particularly long. The 2015 Chianti Colli Senesi proves intriguing, with its fruity hints of cherry and wild berries, nice grip and a savory, appetizing finish.

○ Vernaccia di S. Gimignano Ris. '15	♥♥	3*
● Chianti Colli Senesi '15	♥♥	2*
○ Vernaccia di S. Gimignano '16	♥	2
○ Vernaccia di S. Gimignano Ris. '09	♥♥♥	3*
● Rovaio '11	♥♥	4
● Rovaio '09	♥♥	4
○ Vernaccia di S. Gimignano '13	♥♥	2*
○ Vernaccia di S. Gimignano '12	♥♥	2*
○ Vernaccia di S. Gimignano '11	♥♥	2*
○ Vernaccia di S. Gimignano '10	♥♥	2*
○ Vernaccia di S. Gimignano Ris. '14	♥♥	3*
○ Vernaccia di S. Gimignano Ris. '12	♥♥	3*
○ Vernaccia di S. Gimignano Ris. '11	♥♥	3*
○ Vernaccia di S. Gimignano Ris. '10	♥♥	3*

Fattoria Lavacchio

LOC. LAVACCHIO
VIA DI MONTEFIESOLE, 55
50065 PONTASSIEVE [FI]
TEL. +39 0558317472
www.fattorialavacchio.com

CELLAR SALES
PRE-BOOKED VISITS
ACCOMMODATION AND RESTAURANT SERVICE
ANNUAL PRODUCTION 120,000 bottles
HECTARES UNDER VINE 25.00
VITICULTURE METHOD Certified Organic
SUSTAINABLE WINERY

Fattoria Lavacchio dates back to the eighteenth century when it belonged to the Peruzzi family. After a few changes in ownership the farm was bought by the Lottero family in 1978, and today it is enthusiastically run by Faye. Farmstays, a restaurant, a shop and a windmill are just some of its facilites, in addition to the winemaking, which is carried out under organic management with full respect for the environment. Twenty-two hectares of vineyards extend through the Montefiesole hills, where soil rich in galestro and stones gives rise to wines expressive of the territory. The 2015 Cedro sees aromas of flowers and red fruit moving in counterpoint with intriguing spicy notes. The mouth has good consistency and pervasiveness. The 2013 Cedro Riserva is more austere. It's still bridled by wood and a bit stiff, but it's a pleasant wine, nevertheless.

● Chianti Rufina Cedro '15	♥♥	2*
● Chianti Rufina Cedro Ris. '13	♥♥	3
● Chianti Puro '16	♥	2
○ Oro del Cedro V. T. '14	♥	4
○ Pachàr '16	♥	3
○ Vin Santo del Chianti Rufina Ris. '10	♥	4
● Chianti Rufina Cedro '14	♥♥	2*
● Chianti Rufina Cedro '12	♥♥	2*
● Chianti Rufina Cedro Ris. '10	♥♥	4
● Chianti Rufina Ludié Ris. '10	♥♥	5
● Fontegalli '11	♥♥	4
○ Oro del Cedro V. T. '12	♥♥	5
○ Pachar '13	♥♥	4
○ Vin Santo del Chianti Rufina Ris. '09	♥♥	5
○ Vin Santo del Chianti Rufina Ris. '08	♥♥	5

Tenuta Le Farnete/Cantagallo

FRAZ. COMEANA
VIA MACIA
59100 CARMIGNANO [PO]
TEL. +39 0571910078
www.tenutacantagallo.it

CELLAR SALES
PRE-BOOKED VISITS
ACCOMMODATION AND RESTAURANT SERVICE
ANNUAL PRODUCTION 65,000 bottles
HECTARES UNDER VINE 40.00
SUSTAINABLE WINERY

The Pierazzuoli family started farming in the 1970s in Montalbano, Capraia and Limite. Tenuta Cantagallo is their largest estate and features a holiday farmhouse, a restaurant and over thirty hectares of vineyards. Then they took over Le Farnete in 1990, which counts 11 hectares of vineyards. Winemaking and barrel aging are carried out independently on the two estates. The 2014 Carmignano Riserva gets Tre Bicchieri, with its vibrant aromas calling up dark fruit, its faint balsamic hints and overtones of aromatic herbs, such as mint. The mouth is well-defined, generous, with well-integrated tannins, and good, enticing acidity. The finish is long and complex. The 2014 Gioveto, made primarily with Sangiovese (with smaller parts Merlot and Syrah) focuses on spices (like pepper and cinnamon), red fruit (cherry and blackcurrant), with a lean, well-tuned, juicy mouth, good acidity and a lingering finish.

● Carmignano Ris. '14	♟♟♟ 4*
● Chianti Montalbano Tenuta Cantagallo Ris. '14	♟♟ 3*
● Chianti Montalbano Tenuta Cantagallo '16	♟♟ 2*
● Gioveto '14	♟♟ 4
○ Vin Santo Chianti Montalbano Millarium Ris. '10	♟♟ 5
● Barco Reale '16	♟ 2
● Carmignano '15	♟ 3
● Aleatico '09	♟♟ 4
● Carmignano '08	♟♟ 3
● Carmignano Ris. '07	♟♟ 4
● Chianti Montalbano Tenuta Cantagallo '09	♟♟ 2
○ Vin Santo Chianti Montalbano Millarium Ris. '05	♟♟ 5

La Lecciaia

LOC. VALLAFRICO
53024 MONTALCINO [SI]
TEL. +39 0583928366
www.lecciaia.it

PRE-BOOKED VISITS
ANNUAL PRODUCTION 200,000 bottles
HECTARES UNDER VINE 16.00

Situated in the Vallafrico district and stretching eastwards from Montalcino towards Val d'Orcia, La Lecciaia spans about 15 hectares mostly cultivated with Sangiovese. Mauro Pacini purchased the farm in 1983 and since then has developed the agricultural and technical side to the extent that a finely-tuned range of Brunellos, displaying increasing consistency in recent vintages, is the result. The six wine types are aged mostly in large barrels, and include the vintage and basic Riserva, Collina dei Lecci and Vigna Manapetra, a cru set at 450 meters above sea level on sandstone, clay and stony-rich soil. We find them in form in this latest round of tastings, starting with the 2012 Vigna Manapetra, a gentle and harmonic wine. The 2011 Brunello Riserva sees increased extractive intensity and alcohol, while the Collina dei Lecci (aromas of talcum powder, roots and berries) is deliciously 'old style' and the Manapetra (watermelon, candied orange, medicinal herbs) is more summery.

● Brunello di Montalcino Collina dei Lecci Ris. '11	♟♟ 5
● Brunello di Montalcino V. Manapetra '12	♟♟ 6
● Brunello di Montalcino V. Manapetra Ris. '11	♟♟ 6
● Brunello di Montalcino '12	♟ 5
● Brunello di Montalcino Collina dei Lecci '12	♟ 5
● Brunello di Montalcino Ris. '11	♟ 6
● Brunello di Montalcino V. Manapetra '09	♟♟♟ 6
● Brunello di Montalcino '10	♟♟ 5
● Brunello di Montalcino Ris. '10	♟♟ 6
● Brunello di Montalcino Ris. '09	♟♟ 6
● Brunello di Montalcino V. Manapetra '10	♟♟ 6
● Brunello di Montalcino V. Manapetra Ris. '10	♟♟ 6
● Brunello di Montalcino V. Manapetra Ris. '08	♟♟ 6

Tenuta Lenzini

FRAZ. GRAGNANO
VIA DELLA CHIESA, 44
55012 CAPANNORI [LU]
TEL. +39 0583974037
www.tenutalenzini.it

CELLAR SALES
PRE-BOOKED VISITS
ACCOMMODATION
ANNUAL PRODUCTION 60,000 bottles
HECTARES UNDER VINE 14.00
VITICULTURE METHOD Certified Organic

Tenuta Lenzini is establishing itself as a benchmark for local vine growing. Located in Gragnano, a spectacular part of the Lucca hills where the ancient Francigena pilgrim route is found, and Napoleon's troops passed through. It comes as no surprise that the grape varieties have a distinct French flavor: Merlot, Cabernet Sauvignon, Syrah and Alicante Bouschet. Credit is due to Franco Lenzini and today the winery is run by his granddaughter Benedetta and her husband Michele Guarino. A turning point came in 2007 when they opted first for organic methods and then for biodynamics. The 2013 Poggio de' Paoli left a good impression. It goes for precise, fruity notes and assertive herbs on the nose, while in the mouth it shows good balance. The Syrah of the same year also delivered. Its primary reductive notes effect the overall profile which, nevertheless, needs a few minutes to open but then proves generally satisfactory. The 2016 is vegetal, maybe a bit undefined.

● La Syrah '13	▼▼ 5
● Poggio de' Paoli '13	▼▼ 4
○ Vermignon '16	▼ 3
● Syrah '11	♈♈ 5
○ Vermignon '15	♈♈ 3
○ Vermignon '14	♈♈ 3

Cantine Leonardo da Vinci

VIA PROVINCIALE MERCATALE, 291
50059 VINCI [FI]
TEL. +39 0571902444
www.cantineleonardo.it

CELLAR SALES
PRE-BOOKED VISITS
ACCOMMODATION AND RESTAURANT SERVICE
ANNUAL PRODUCTION 4,500,000 bottles
HECTARES UNDER VINE 750.00

In 2012 this winery was taken over by the Caviro group. Previously, some fifty years ago, thirty small producers from Vinci, owning collectively about seventy hectares of vineyards, joined forces and set up a cooperative. Their first action was to build a single site where they could transform their grapes into local red and white wines. In the years following the combination of good intentions and high-quality wines convinced other growers to join them. In 1990 they took over Cantina di Montalcino, leading an expansion into Siena. Today there are two hundred members with a total of about 750 hectares of vineyards. The 2014 Chianti Da Vinci Riserva put in a good performance, with its aromatic profile of dark fruit (blackcurrant and plums) and accents of aromatic herbs. The body shows good weight, good acidity and fine-tuned tannins, with a nice long finish. The 2012 Brunello proves polished, with a balanced body and tasty finish.

○ Bianco dell'Empolese Vin Santo Da Vinci '10	▼▼ 5
● Brunello di Montalcino Cantina di Montalcino '12	▼▼ 5
● Chianti Da Vinci Ris. '14	▼▼ 3
● Chianti Leonardo '16	▼ 2
○ Bianco dell'Empolese Vin Santo Da Vinci '09	♈♈ 5
● Brunello di Montalcino Cantina di Montalcino '11	♈♈ 5
● Chianti Da Vinci Ris. '13	♈♈ 3*
● Chianti Da Vinci Ris. '12	♈♈ 3*
● Chianti Da Vinci Ris. '11	♈♈ 3*
● Chianti Leonardo '13	♈♈ 2*
● Leonardo '14	♈♈ 2*
● Rosso di Montalcino Cantina di Montalcino '13	♈♈ 2*

Tenuta di Lilliano

LOC. LILLIANO, 8
53011 CASTELLINA IN CHIANTI [SI]
TEL.·+39 0577743070
www.lilliano.com

CELLAR SALES
PRE-BOOKED VISITS
ACCOMMODATION
ANNUAL PRODUCTION 150,000 bottles
HECTARES UNDER VINE 35.00

Tenuta di Lilliano has played an important role in Chianti Classico's recent history. Today they have adopted some key modern elements in their production philosophy, all the while respecting the Chianti tradition. The Ruspoli family make wines with a generally austere style, with highlights from generous fruit. Supporting this is a balanced use of small and large oak; it is the aging that guarantees their wines' character and complexity. The 2014 Chianti Classico Gran Selezione delivers. It's a wine with nice fruit-rich expression on the nose and a generous, succulent palate. Its tannins are smooth and the finish uplifting. The 2015 Chianti Classico is a bit open in its fragrances and distinguishes itself for the palate, with a generous unfolding of flavor and nice sweetness. It's just a bit bridled by some rough tannins. The 2014 Chianti Classico Riserva is generally muted in its aromas; on the palate it shows force but also a bit too much toastiness.

● Chianti Cl. Gran Sel. '14	♟♟♟ 6
● Chianti Cl. '15	♟♟ 3
● Chianti Cl. Ris. '14	♟ 5
● Chianti Cl. '10	♟♟♟ 3*
● Chianti Cl. Gran Sel. '11	♟♟♟ 5
● Chianti Cl. Gran Sel. Ris. '10	♟♟♟ 6
● Chianti Cl. Ris. '13	♟♟♟ 5
● Anagallis '11	♟♟ 5
● Chianti Cl. '13	♟♟ 3
● Chianti Cl. '11	♟♟ 3
● Chianti Cl. Gran Sel. '12	♟♟ 5
● Chianti Cl. Ris. '11	♟♟ 5
● Vignacatena '10	♟♟ 5

Lisini

FRAZ. SANT'ANGELO IN COLLE
POD. CASANOVA
53024 MONTALCINO [SI]
TEL. +39 0577844040
www.lisini.com

CELLAR SALES
PRE-BOOKED VISITS
ANNUAL PRODUCTION 90,000 bottles
HECTARES UNDER VINE 21.00

Since the 16th century the relationship between the Lisini-Clementi family and Montalcino has been widely documented. Take, for example, the incredible caveau that houses the old vintages, including those of the legendary Ellina. Her legacy has been taken up by her grandchildren Carlo, Lorenzo and Ludovica, who now run twenty hectares in the south between Sesta and Sant'Angelo in Colle and entirely cultivated with Sangiovese. These plots are used for the Rosso, vintage and Riserva, while a separate wine is made with grapes from the Ugolaia cru whose iron-rich, tuff soil lends a very different expression. And its Lisini's flagship Brunello to lead the pack this year with a 2011 that's faithful to the vintage. Ripe red fruit, balsamic herbs and wood resin, as well as iron and iodine define the nose, which is captivating (to say the least). The finish is a bit rugged, leaving the palate exposed after a balanced and cohesive attack.

● Brunello di Montalcino Ugolaia '11	♟♟ 8
● Brunello di Montalcino '12	♟♟ 6
● Rosso di Montalcino '15	♟ 4
● Brunello di Montalcino Ugolaia '06	♟♟♟ 8
● Brunello di Montalcino Ugolaia '04	♟♟♟ 8
● Brunello di Montalcino Ugolaia '01	♟♟♟ 8
● Brunello di Montalcino Ugolaia '00	♟♟♟ 7
● Brunello di Montalcino '10	♟♟ 6
● Brunello di Montalcino Ris. '10	♟♟ 7
● Brunello di Montalcino Ris. '09	♟♟ 7
● Brunello di Montalcino Ugolaia '10	♟♟ 8
● Brunello di Montalcino Ugolaia '09	♟♟ 8
● Brunello di Montalcino Ugolaia '08	♟♟ 8

Lunadoro

FRAZ. VALIANO
LOC. TERRAROSSA
53040 MONTEPULCIANO [SI]
TEL. +39 348 2215188
www.nobilelunadoro.it

CELLAR SALES
PRE-BOOKED VISITS
ACCOMMODATION
ANNUAL PRODUCTION 60,000 bottles
HECTARES UNDER VINE 12.00
VITICULTURE METHOD Certified Organic
SUSTAINABLE WINERY

The Swiss giant, Schenk Italian Wineries, did the right thing when it decided not to change Lunadoro's basic approach and philosophy. The wines still have a boutique winery element that features a clear-cut, original style with consistent quality. The number of bottles produced has increased but their attention to the vineyard and cellar is unaltered. This means scrupulous care of the grapes, and winemaking that is enforced with no shortcuts. The 2014 Nobile di Montepulciano Pagliareto is a classic styled wine that does a job interpreting a complicated vintage, showing grace and coherence. The nose proves soft and clean, while the palate is well-sustained. But the wine's crunchy tannins are its forte. The 2015 Rosso di Montepulciano Prugnanello is pleasantly flavorsome, with nice, open fragrances. The 2013 Nobile di Montepulciano Quercione Riserva suffers from its stylistic approach, which is a bit banal.

Nobile di Montepulciano Pagliareto '14	♟♟3
Rosso di Montepulciano Prugnanello '15	♟♟2*
Nobile di Montepulciano Quercione Ris. '13	♟4
Nobile di Montepulciano '11	♟♟4
Nobile di Montepulciano Pagliareto '13	♟♟3
Nobile di Montepulciano Pagliareto '12	♟♟4
Nobile di Montepulciano Quercione '11	♟♟4
Nobile di Montepulciano Quercione '10	♟♟4
Nobile di Montepulciano Quercione Ris. '12	♟♟4
Nobile di Montepulciano Quercione Ris. '09	♟♟5
Orcia Eclisse '11	♟♟2*
Rosso di Montepulciano Primo Senso '11	♟♟3
Rosso di Montepulciano Prugnanello '14	♟♟2*

I Luoghi

LOC. CAMPO AL CAPRIOLO, 201
57022 CASTAGNETO CARDUCCI [LI]
TEL. +39 0565777379
www.iluoghi.it

CELLAR SALES
ANNUAL PRODUCTION 15,000 bottles
HECTARES UNDER VINE 3.80
VITICULTURE METHOD Certified Organic

This is a delightful and unusual winery, certainly for Bolgheri. It is artisanal in the most genuine sense of the word and it produces wines with a rare personality. They have succeeded in carving out for themselves a central role in the appellation, one that is well-known among enthusiasts who seek original and impeccably-made wines. Credit is due to the owners, Stefano Granata and his wife, Paola. Their vineyard plots are proving themselves to be very interesting sources for vine growing. The vintage had a significant impact on the producer's wine (which is a fairly time-honored fact). The 2014 Podere Ritorti exhibits an earthy profile of fava beans, cocoa and spices, which pair well with its hints of fruit and dried flowers. The Campo al Fico of the same year is much weaker, coming across as tired both on the nose and palate.

● Bolgheri Sup. Podere Ritorti '14	♟♟5
● Bolgheri Sup. Campo al Fico '14	♟7
● Bolgheri Sup. Campo al Fico '10	♟♟♟7
● Bolgheri Sup. Campo al Fico '09	♟♟♟7
● Bolgheri Sup. Campo al Fico '08	♟♟♟7
● Bolgheri Sup. Podere Ritorti '13	♟♟♟5
● Bolgheri Sup. Campo al Fico '13	♟♟7
● Bolgheri Sup. Campo al Fico '07	♟♟7
● Bolgheri Sup. Campo al Fico '06	♟♟7
● Bolgheri Sup. Podere Ritorti '12	♟♟5
● Bolgheri Sup. Podere Ritorti '11	♟♟5
● Bolgheri Sup. Podere Ritorti '10	♟♟5
● Bolgheri Sup. Podere Ritorti '09	♟♟5
● Bolgheri Sup. Podere Ritorti '08	♟♟5
● Bolgheri Sup. Podere Ritorti '07	♟♟4

★Le Macchiole

LOC. BOLGHERI
VIA BOLGHERESE, 189A
57022 CASTAGNETO CARDUCCI [LI]
TEL. +39 0565766092
www.lemacchiole.it

PRE-BOOKED VISITS
ANNUAL PRODUCTION 165,000 bottles
HECTARES UNDER VINE 27.00

Established in the early 1980s, Le Macchiole is one of the historic Bolgheri wineries. And it is for certain a benchmark for quality Italian wine. Today the winery is expertly and passionately run by Cinzia Merli and her close-knit staff. Together they make any goal seem achievable. Right now there are some changes. No major shake-ups, but they are searching for a convincing contemporary style. Wines from more recent vintages have less extraction than in the past, but they are undeniably elegant and less conditioned by wood aging. The 2015 Bolgheri is entirely the child of a new project and, considering the results, we can only say that the future is looking quite good. It's a truly super wine, maybe the best in the DOC zone, for the year. It's brilliant in its weave of wild berries accompanied by delicate spices; and it exhibits a velvety texture in the mouth. The 2014 Paleo plays (and wins) the elegance game, abandoning structure in favor of flavor and depth.

Podere Il Macchione

FRAZ. GRACCIANO
VIA PROVINCIALE, 18
53045 MONTEPULCIANO [SI]
TEL. +39 0578 758595
www.podereilmacchione.it

CELLAR SALES
PRE-BOOKED VISITS
ANNUAL PRODUCTION 20,000 bottles
HECTARES UNDER VINE 6.00

This is a small artisan winery that deserves attention and more space in IW. It is located in Caggiole, which has always been famous for making characteristic Montepulciano wines. The grapes are cultivated in hillside clay-loam soil with areas of stone, sandy silt and sandstone. Work in the vineyards and cellar is carried out with full and constant respect for nature. The wines produced are the outcome of synergy between place and human endeavor. The 2015 Rosso di Montepulciano, a fresh and intriguing wine, is, in our opinion, one of the best in the DOC zone for the year. It has a multifaceted nose that's rich in fruit and flowers, bound up with an almost woodland atmosphere of Mediterranean shrub. The mouth doesn't disappoint, rather, it completes the wine with a fine texture that's both well-measured and delicious. The 2013 Nobile is more mature, with spicy notes and assertive tannins.

● Bolgheri Sup. Paleo '14	♟♟♟ 8
● Bolgheri Rosso '15	♟♟ 4
● Messorio '14	♟♟ 8
● Messorio '07	♟♟♟ 8
● Messorio '06	♟♟♟ 8
● Paleo Rosso '13	♟♟♟ 8
● Paleo Rosso '12	♟♟♟ 8
● Paleo Rosso '11	♟♟♟ 8
● Paleo Rosso '10	♟♟♟ 8
● Paleo Rosso '09	♟♟♟ 8
● Scrio '08	♟♟♟ 8
● Messorio '13	♟♟ 8
● Messorio '12	♟♟ 8
● Scrio '13	♟♟ 8

● Nobile di Montepulciano '13	♟♟ 5
● Rosso di Montepulciano '15	♟♟ 4
● Nobile di Montepulciano Ris. '11	♟ 5

e Macioche

DA PROV.LE 55 DI SANT'ANTIMO KM 4,850
3024 MONTALCINO [SI]
L. +39 0577849168
ww.lemacioche.it

ELLAR SALES
RE-BOOKED VISITS
CCOMMODATION
NNUAL PRODUCTION 18,000 bottles
ECTARES UNDER VINE 3.00

ne of the most famous "garagiste"
ineries in the area is located in just three
ectares of vineyards in Sant'Antimo, in
outhern Montalcino. Established by
atilde Zecca and Achille Mazzocchi in
985, it has now passed into the hands of
ccardo Caliari, Stefano Brunetto and
assimo Bronzato. They are a close-knit
oup who openly aspire to the consistent
yle and unmistakable lightness of Le
acioche's Brunellos. They pursue this
al through a purist approach in the cellar
at include spontaneous fermentation in
oden vats and long aging in 4000-liter
rrels. The magnificent 2011 Riserva
ings out their approach to interpretation.
s a wine that's distinguished, to say the
ast, by its aromas of light fruit and
alsams. These are enriched by citrus and
noky hints. The mouth proves close-knit
d tasty, despite a finish that's a bit rich in
cohol and tannins. The 2012 Brunello is a
less expressive and relaxed.

Malenchini

LOC. GRASSINA
VIA LILLIANO E MEOLI, 82
50015 BAGNO A RIPOLI [FI]
TEL. +39 055642602
www.malenchini.it

CELLAR SALES
PRE-BOOKED VISITS
ANNUAL PRODUCTION 120,000 bottles
HECTARES UNDER VINE 17.00

The splendid Medici villa in Lilliano, a few
kilometers south of Florence, was bought
by the Malenchini family in 1850. The villa
is at the core of a seventy-hectare estate in
the Bagno a Ripoli hills, in the heart of
Chianti Colli Fiorentini. Diletta heads the
winery and manages her staff with
enthusiasm and a constant eye to the
environment. The vineyard spans 17
hectares at an altitude of over 200 meters,
and is planted with Sangiovese, Canaiolo,
Merlot, Cabernet Sauvignon, Petit Verdot
and Malvasia. Conversion to organic
farming at the winery began in 2015. The
2015 Chianti is clean and close-woven on
the nose, with its notes of cherry, raspberry
and blackcurrant. The mouth is fresh and
even, not complex but truly pleasant,
relaxed and well-sustained. With regard to
Bruzzico, it's the Cabernet that shines, with
its classic, vegetal scents enriched by
iodine. In the mouth it proves dense and
pervasive, close-knit in its tannins. Alcohol
dominates just a bit too much in the finish.

Brunello di Montalcino Ris. '11	♥♥♥ 8
Brunello di Montalcino '12	♥ 7
Brunello di Montalcino '11	♥♥ 7
Brunello di Montalcino '10	♥♥ 7
Brunello di Montalcino '09	♥♥ 7
Brunello di Montalcino '08	♥♥ 7
Brunello di Montalcino '07	♥♥ 7
Brunello di Montalcino '06	♥♥ 6
Brunello di Montalcino Ris. '06	♥♥ 8
Rosso di Montalcino '13	♥♥ 4
Rosso di Montalcino '11	♥♥ 4
Rosso di Montalcino '10	♥♥ 4
Rosso di Montalcino '09	♥♥ 4

● Bruzzico '14	♥♥ 4
● Chianti '15	♥♥ 1*
⊙ Rosato '16	♥ 2
● Bruzzico '11	♥♥ 4
● Bruzzico '10	♥♥ 4
● Chianti Colli Fiorentini '14	♥♥ 2*
● Chianti Colli Fiorentini '13	♥♥ 2*
● Chianti Colli Fiorentini '10	♥♥ 2*
○ Vin Santo Colli Fiorentini '10	♥♥ 4

Il Marroneto

LOC. MADONNA DELLE GRAZIE, 307
53024 MONTALCINO [SI]
TEL. +39 0577849382
www.ilmarroneto.it

CELLAR SALES
PRE-BOOKED VISITS
ANNUAL PRODUCTION 30,000 bottles
HECTARES UNDER VINE 6.00
SUSTAINABLE WINERY

At the end of the 1970s Giuseppe Mori converted a room for drying chestnuts into headquarters for one of the most charming wineries in Montalcino. This event provided the name for the winery. Today it is run by his son Alessandro and they are best-known for their Madonna delle Grazie Brunello, made with grapes from a spectacular cru in the north overlooking the Montosoli hill. All of their Sangiovese wines are receving increased appreciation for their wild and luxuriant texture. However, it is recommended you wait a while to tone down the powerful tannins that are only slightly softened by the long aging in Slavonian oak barrels of different ages and sizes. And these will prove useful for understanding the 2012 Madonna delle Grazie. For the moment, it's far from airy, and it's difficult to read for its almost violent tannins. The 2015 Ignaccio is not a light, carefree red either. Its density of flavor proves that it's much more than just a little Brunello.

● Rosso di Montalcino Ignaccio '15	♟♟ 3*
● Brunello di Montalcino '12	♟♟ 7
● Brunello di Montalcino Madonna delle Grazie '12	♟♟ 8
● Brunello di Montalcino Madonna delle Grazie '11	♟♟♟ 8
● Brunello di Montalcino Madonna delle Grazie '10	♟♟♟ 8
● Brunello di Montalcino Madonna delle Grazie '08	♟♟♟ 8
● Brunello di Montalcino '11	♟♟ 7
● Brunello di Montalcino '10	♟♟ 7
● Brunello di Montalcino '09	♟♟ 7
● Brunello di Montalcino Madonna delle Grazie '09	♟♟ 8
● Rosso di Montalcino Ignaccio '13	♟♟ 3
● Rosso di Montalcino Ignaccio '11	♟♟ 3*

Cosimo Maria Masini

VIA POGGIO AL PINO, 16
56028 SAN MINIATO [PI]
TEL. +39 0571465032
www.cosimomariamasini.it

CELLAR SALES
PRE-BOOKED VISITS
ANNUAL PRODUCTION 35,000 bottles
HECTARES UNDER VINE 17.00

The Masini's, a family of entrepreneurs from various sectors of the economy, bought this estate in the year 2000. A wonderful location with 40 hectares all in one place, the previous owner, and founder of the Agricultural Science Faculty in Pisa, Cosimo Ridolfi, had set it up nicely for adopting biodynamic farming methods. This was welcomed with open arms by the new owner, and it is being carrried forward enthusiastically by Cosimo, the current owner of the winery. The 2016 Daphné, a blend of Trebbiano Toscano and Malvasia, macerated on the skins, offers up a variegated nose of mature fruit and assorted flowers. The body is balanced with richness of flavor and freshness at the forefront; the finish proves appetizing. The 2016 Annick, made with Sauvignon Blanc and Vermentino, is characterized by its fresh overtones of aromatic herbs and citron. The body is succulent and elegant, with an excellent crescendo for the finish. The 2016 San Forte exhibits intense aromas of aromatic herbs and blueberries, as well as a nice, spirited and stylish structure.

○ Annick '16	♟♟
○ Daphné '16	♟♟
● San Forte Rosso '16	♟♟
○ Vin Santo del Chianti Fedardo '09	♟♟
● Chianti '16	♟
● Nicole '16	♟
● Cosimo '15	♟♟
○ Daphné '15	♟♟
● Nicole '15	♟♟
● Nicole '12	♟♟
● Sincero '13	♟♟
○ Vin Santo del Chianti Fedardo '08	♟♟
○ Vin Santo del Chianti Fedardo '06	♟♟

★Mastrojanni

FRAZ. CASTELNUOVO DELL'ABATE
POD. LORETO E SAN PIO
53024 MONTALCINO [SI]
TEL. +39 0577835681
www.mastrojanni.com

CELLAR SALES
PRE-BOOKED VISITS
ACCOMMODATION
ANNUAL PRODUCTION 110,000 bottles
HECTARES UNDER VINE 33.00

In 1975 Roman lawyer Gabriele Mastrojanni bought the San Pio and Loreto estates in Castelnuovo dell'Abate in southeast Montalcino. After his death, the Illy family took over the estates in 2008, and from the start it was clear they meant to continue down the path that made Vigna Loreto and Vigna Schiena d'Asino collectible Brunellos. Andrea Machetti oversees the technical side of things. The wines are charismatic, austere and well-built without passing up softness or flavor. They are finely-polished at the finish by aging in wood of various sizes and origins. The 2012 Vigna Schiena d'Asino once again proves the best of the Mastrojanni cru. It hesitates to reveal too much in its primary aromas, then unleashes a lovely unfolding of coastal shrub, forest floor and dried flowers. These follow through well to an austere, refreshing palate. The 2012 Vigna Loreta is aromatically similar but more rigid.

● Brunello di Montalcino V. Schiena d'Asino '12	▼▼▼ 8
● Brunello di Montalcino V. Loreto '12	▼▼ 7
● Rosso di Montalcino '15	▼▼ 3
Brunello di Montalcino Schiena d'Asino '08	♀♀♀ 8
Brunello di Montalcino V. Loreto '10	♀♀♀ 7
● Brunello di Montalcino V. Loreto '09	♀♀♀ 7
● Brunello di Montalcino V. Schiena d'Asino '10	♀♀♀ 8
Brunello di Montalcino '11	♀♀ 5
Brunello di Montalcino '10	♀♀ 5
● Brunello di Montalcino '09	♀♀ 5
● Brunello di Montalcino V. Loreto '11	♀♀ 7
● Rosso di Montalcino '14	♀♀ 3*
Rosso di Montalcino '13	♀♀ 3

Melini

LOC. GAGGIANO
53036 POGGIBONSI [SI]
TEL. +39 0577998511
www.cantinemelini.it

CELLAR SALES
PRE-BOOKED VISITS
ANNUAL PRODUCTION 3,000,000 bottles
HECTARES UNDER VINE 136.00

Melini and Macchiavelli are Gruppo Italiano Vini's Chianti wineries. The history of the Poggibonsi-based brand goes hand-in-hand with Chianti Classico's history. In point of fact it was Laborel Melini who in 1860 first adopted the straw flask, which was resistant to the pressure of machine-applied stopper, and this icon contributed mightily to the spread of Chianti worldwide. Today, Black Rooster wines produced by GIV show consistent quality and personality. At times they achieve even absolute greatness. The 2013 Chianti Classico La Selvanella Riserva does well, highlighting aromas of close-woven fruit accompanied by notes of wild flowers and spices. In the mouth it's even and well-sustained, certainly not lacking in flavor, with a long finish that sees a bit too much toastiness. The 2015 Chianti Classico Granaio is enjoyable, with fresh, vibrant fragrances and a generous, pleasantly savory mouth. The 2016 Coltri, a blend of Sangiovese, Merlot and Cabernet Sauvignon, is a well-crafted and balanced wine.

● Chianti Cl. La Selvanella Ris. '13	▼▼ 4
● Chianti Cl. Granaio '15	▼▼ 4
● I Coltri '16	▼▼ 2*
● Chianti '16	▼ 2
● Chianti Governo all'uso Toscano '14	▼ 3
● Chianti San Lorenzo '16	▼ 2
● Chianti Cl. La Selvanella Ris. '06	♀♀♀ 5
● Chianti Cl. La Selvanella Ris. '03	♀♀♀ 4
● Chianti Cl. La Selvanella Ris. '01	♀♀♀ 4
● Chianti Cl. Gran Sel. Terrarossa '12	♀♀ 5
● Chianti Cl. Granaio '13	♀♀ 3
● Chianti Cl. La Selvanella Ris. '12	♀♀ 5
● Chianti Cl. Solatio del Tani F attoria Machiavelli '13	♀♀ 3
● I Coltri '15	♀♀ 2*

Stefania Mezzetti

LOC. VERNAZZANO BASSO
06069 TUORO SUL TRASIMENO [PG]
TEL. 0758254060
www.vinimezzetti.it

CELLAR SALES
PRE-BOOKED VISITS
ACCOMMODATION AND RESTAURANT SERVICE
ANNUAL PRODUCTION 40,000bottles
HECTARES UNDER VINE 10.00
VITICULTURE METHOD Certified Organic

Stefania Mezzetti's winery extends from
Umbria, near Lake Trasimeno, in the
municipality of Tuoro, all the way to Tuscany,
in the territory of Cortona. It was her
grandfather, Pietro, a lifetime farmer, who
instilled in her a passion for wine, and left
management of the winery in her hands, in
1994. In addition to wine production, they
produce extra-virgin olive oil (an activity they
pay particular attention to) and offer
agritourism services. The decision to plant
international cultivar has been rewarded with
good results. The 2015 Selvans, made with
Merlot, proved an interesting wine. It offers a
classic aromatic profile of wild berries and
spices, cinnamon and ginger. The body
caresses, with close-woven, silky tannins, a
fresh acidity and a finish that progresses in
crescendo. The 2014 Dardano, made with
Sangiovese, displays fruity, intense
fragrances, with a succulent, dynamic,
lingering mouth. The 2015 Lucumone, made
with Cabernet Sauvignon, offers balsamic
hints and various aromatic herbs. It exhibits
good structure, with tannins and alcohol
nicely in step, and a full finish.

● Cortona Cabernet Sauvignon	
Lucumone '15	♥♥ 4
● Cortona Merlot Selvans '15	♥♥ 4
● Cortona Sangiovese Dardano '14	♥♥ 4
● Annibale '15	♥ 2
● Cortona Syrah Principe '15	♥ 4
● Annibale '10	♥♥ 2*
● Cortona Syrah Principe '10	♥♥ 6

Le Miccine

LOC. LE MICCINE
S.DA STAT.LE TRAVERSA CHIANTIGIANA, 44
53013 GAIOLE IN CHIANTI [SI]
TEL. I 39 0577749526
www.lemiccine.com

CELLAR SALES
PRE-BOOKED VISITS
ACCOMMODATION
ANNUAL PRODUCTION 30,000 bottles
HECTARES UNDER VINE 7.00
VITICULTURE METHOD Certified Organic

Paula Papini Cook's is one of many
family-run artisan wineries dotted around
Chianti Classico. Here, vine growing is
unforced and the winery works under
organic management. The cellar is
streamlined and aging is carried out in
900-liter barrels or large wood. As for style,
their wines display a clear link to their
territory of origin, the Gaiole in Chianti
subzone, they are straightforward,
slim-bodied, pleasant and full of
personality. The 2015 Chianti Classico
makes elegance its forte, with its
close-woven aromas pointing up a vibrant,
yet graceful flowery atmosphere. In the
mouth the wine is silky, streamlined and
lengthy, with a nice, spirited finish. The
2014 Chianti Classico Riserva is a
well-crafted wine but, considering the
stylistic approach and the year (certainly
not an easy one), it comes across as bit too
subtle in flavor.

● Chianti Cl. '15	♥♥♥ 4*
● Chianti Cl. Ris. '14	♥ 5
● Chianti Cl. Ris. '10	♥♥♥ 5
● Carduus '10	♥♥ 5
● Chianti Cl. '11	♥♥ 2*
● Chianti Cl. '09	♥♥ 2*
● Chianti Cl. '07	♥♥ 2
● Chianti Cl. '06	♥♥ 3*
● Chianti Cl. Don Alberto Ris. '07	♥♥ 4
● Chianti Cl. Don Alberto Ris. '06	♥♥ 4
● Chianti Cl. Ris. '13	♥♥ 5
● Chianti Cl. Ris. '12	♥♥ 5
● Chianti Cl. Ris. '09	♥♥ 2*
● La Pricipessa '06	♥♥ 3

Mocali

c. Mocali
53024 Montalcino [SI]
Tel. +39 0577849485
www.mocali.eu

CELLAR SALES
PRE-BOOKED VISITS
ANNUAL PRODUCTION 120,000 bottles
HECTARES UNDER VINE 9.00
VITICULTURE METHOD Certified Organic
SUSTAINABLE WINERY

Tiziano Ciacci's farm counts about 30 hectares, a third of which are vineyards. He inherited the farm from his grandfather, Mino, and named it after an area forming a ridge between the town of Montalcino and its southwest offshoot, lying almost in Maremma. The vineyards are surrounded by woods and Mediterranean scrub, and are mostly cultivated with Sangiovese, at 350 to 400 meters on alberese and galestro soil. He makes Brunellos that are sometimes austere when young but possessing a rich texture. They are aged mostly in Slavonian oak, but he also uses small wood for certain wines and vintages. As usual, Mocali is a consistent selection across the board. The 2015 Rosso is pervasive and sanguine, while the 2012 Vigna delle Raunate is a bit more restrained, but still endowed with good energy. The 2011 Riserva is a complete wine, gratifying in its southern-styled profile of myrtle, helichrysum and dried flowers. In the mouth it proves confident and forthright.

Brunello di Montalcino Ris. '11	♥♥	7
Brunello di Montalcino V. delle Raunate '12	♥♥	6
Rosso di Montalcino '15	♥♥	2*
Brunello di Montalcino '12	♥	5
Brunello di Montalcino V. delle Raunate '08	♥♥♥	6
Brunello di Montalcino '11	♥♥	5
Brunello di Montalcino '10	♥♥	5
Brunello di Montalcino Ris. '10	♥♥	7
Brunello di Montalcino V. delle Raunate '11	♥♥	6
Brunello di Montalcino V. delle Raunate '10	♥♥	6
Brunello di Montalcino V. delle Raunate '09	♥♥	6
Brunello di Montalcino V. delle Raunate Ris. '10	♥♥	8

Monte Solaio

via di Venturina 15
57021 Campiglia Marittima [LI]
Tel. +39 0565843291
www.montesolaio.com

CELLAR SALES
PRE-BOOKED VISITS
ANNUAL PRODUCTION 40,000 bottles
HECTARES UNDER VINE 8.50

The winery was founded on the site of a former hunting lodge, where Castello Bonaria was built at a later date. The castle, now used for tourist accomdation, is the most iconic part of the structure. In addition to wine, they also produce oil and wheat. They have chosen to grow mostly international grape varieties. The 2015 Re del Castello is a monovarietal Merlot with meaty, lively overtones, fruit-rich hints of cherry and plums, as well as notes of Mediterranean shrub. The mouth is pervasive, soft and warm, with well-balanced tannins and a long, complex finish. The 2015 Sassinoro, made with 100% Syrah, offers gamey scents, then aromatic herbs and well-defined fruit. The palate proves rich, succulent and well-structured, with a long, savory finish. The 2015 Tino Rosso, a Bordeaux blend, is fresh on the nose and potent, rich in the mouth.

● Re del Castello '15	♥♥	7
● Sassinoro '15	♥♥	5
○ Allegro '16	♥	3
○ Boccasanta '16	♥	2
● Collevato '15	♥	5
⊙ Sarosa '16	♥	2
● Tino Rosso '15	♥	3

Fattoria Montellori

VIA PISTOIESE, 1
50054 FUCECCHIO [FI]
TEL. +39 0571260641
www.fattoriamontellori.it

CELLAR SALES
PRE-BOOKED VISITS
ACCOMMODATION AND RESTAURANT SERVICE
ANNUAL PRODUCTION 250,000 bottles
HECTARES UNDER VINE 51.00
VITICULTURE METHOD Certified Organic
SUSTAINABLE WINERY

The farm was founded in the late nineteenth century when Giuseppe Nieri bought the villa and lands that make up the historic part of the estate. During the year the vineyard size has increased and the cellar has been fitted out with the latest equipment to produce noteworthy wines. Historically this area of Tuscany was considered unsuitable for vine growing, but in the last thirty years Alessandra has molded the farm into its current identity and taken critical steps towards turning it into a modern facility. The 2013 sparkler Spumante Pas Dosé made it to the finals. This monovarietal Chardonnay offers up aromas of apple, hints of gunflint, flowery fragrances and small, citrusy notes. The mouth is classic, spirited and succulent, showing good weight, with a nice rising finish. The 2013 Salamartano, made mostly with Cabernet Sauvignon and lesser quantities of Merlot and Cabernet Franc, also did well. The nose features cloves and cinnamon spices, light, flowery hints. The mouth is creamy, generous, with subtle tannins and a freshness that's both bold and well-integrated.

○ Montellori Pas Dosé '13	♟♟ 5
○ Bianco dell'Empolese Vin Santo '11	♟♟ 5
● Chianti Sup. Caselle '15	♟♟ 2*
● Moro '14	♟♟ 3
● Salamartano '13	♟♟ 6
● Chianti '15	♟ 2
○ Trebbiano '16	♟ 4
○ Bianco dell'Empolese Vin Santo '10	♟♟ 5
○ Bianco dell'Empolese Vin Santo '09	♟♟ 5
● Dicatum '13	♟♟ 5
○ Montellori Pas Dosé '12	♟♟ 5
● Salamartano '12	♟♟ 6

Montenidoli

LOC. MONTENIDOLI
53037 SAN GIMIGNANO [SI]
TEL. +39 0577941565
www.montenidoli.com

CELLAR SALES
ACCOMMODATION
ANNUAL PRODUCTION 100,000 bottles
HECTARES UNDER VINE 24.00
VITICULTURE METHOD Certified Organic

Elisabetta Fagiuoli moved here in the mid-1960s with Sergio Muratori, who was her partner for 45 years. It was a life choice dictated not only by her love for the land and its fruits, but by a desire to create a place for disadvantaged elderly and young people to meet, study and work. It has been a long and difficult road, but the results are excellent. The first wine was produced years later, in 1971. Their production philosophy favors native varieties, biodynamic farming, and safeguarding the environment. The 2015 Vernaccia di San Gimignano Tradizionale delivers with a Tre Bicchieri. The nose sees pronounced mineral notes joined with full fruity hints of apple and peach, as well as the occasional medicinal herb. In the mouth it proves meaty, dense, succulent, with a long, savory finish. The 2015 Vernaccia Fiore is also tasty, with its faint balsamic notes, and full fruity hints of apple. Its body is balanced and succulent, and the finish is enticing. The 2015 Chianti Colli Senesi Il Garrulo, a fresh and delicate wine, offers up enjoyable fruity notes.

○ Vernaccia di S. Gimignano Tradizionale '15	♟♟♟
● Triassico '15	♟
○ Vernaccia di S. Gimignano Fiore '15	♟♟
● Chianti Colli Senesi Il Garrulo '15	♟
○ Vernaccia di S. Gimignano Carato '12	♟♟♟
○ Vernaccia di S. Gimignano Carato '11	♟♟♟
○ Vernaccia di S. Gimignano Carato '05	♟♟♟
○ Vernaccia di S. Gimignano Fiore '09	♟♟♟
○ Vernaccia di S. Gimignano Tradizionale '12	♟♟♟
○ Vernaccia di S. Gimignano Fiore '13	♟♟
○ Vernaccia di S. Gimignano Tradizionale '14	♟♟

Montepeloso

LOC. MONTEPELOSO, 82
57028 SUVERETO [LI]
TEL. +39 0565828180
www.montepeloso.it

ANNUAL PRODUCTION 22,000 bottles
HECTARES UNDER VINE 7.00
SUSTAINABLE WINERY

Montepeloso was already famous for producing and selling marble, as well as the production of extra virgin oil from the olive trees around the quarry. Fabio Chiarelotto took over in 1999 when it was only a small winery. He embarked on a path aimed at personal and production growth, beginning with a low profile but over time achieving increasingly impressive results. The 2014 Eneo is a blend of mostly Sangiovese and Montepulciano, with smaller amounts of Marselan and Alicante. The nose sees gamey scents, cinnamon, wild berries and faint grass. The mouth comes through docile, drinkable, with both well-balanced freshness and body, and a succulent finish. The 2014 Gabbro, made with Cabernet Sauvignon, brings together notes of wild berries and mint, which give way to a pervasive mouth with well-integrated tannins and a lengthy finish.

Eneo '14	♟♟ 5
Gabbro '14	♟♟ 8
Nardo '14	♟ 8
Gabbro '02	♟♟♟ 8
Nardo '01	♟♟♟ 8
Nardo '00	♟♟♟ 8
A Quo '13	♟♟ 5
Eneo '13	♟♟ 5
Eneo '12	♟♟ 5
Gabbro '13	♟♟ 8
Gabbro '12	♟♟ 8
Gabbro '08	♟♟ 8
Gabbro '06	♟♟ 8
Nardo '13	♟♟ 8
Nardo '12	♟♟ 8

Montepepe

VIA SFORZA, 76
54038 MONTIGNOSO [MS]
TEL. +39 0585831042
www.montepepe.com

CELLAR SALES
PRE-BOOKED VISITS
ACCOMMODATION
ANNUAL PRODUCTION 25,000 bottles
HECTARES UNDER VINE 6.00

Montepepe is a small hill about five kilometers from the sea between the Apuan Alps and Versilia. The winery is very old and at one time belonged to the Duke of Lucca. In 2003 Alberto Poggi planted new vineyards on the 19th century dry stone-walled terraces that occupy the central part of the hill. As an architect, he also fashioned a new underground barrel room and renovated the villa, which is now used for tourists and includes a historic cellar and citrus tree orchard. The vineyard is planted with white grape varieties (Vermentino and Viognier) and reds (Syrah and Massaretta). It's hard to find whites in Tuscany with this aging potential. The 2012 Bianco Vintage, made with Vermentino and Viognier, has a vibrant nose featuring honey, vanilla, assorted citrus and tropical fruit. The mouth is solid and flavorsome, while the finish comes through savory, intriguing and well-sustained. The 2013 Rosso, made with Syrah and Massaretta, also delivered, with its fresh aromas of fruit, such as blackcurrant and cherry, and its spicy notes of vanilla and pepper.

○ Montepepe Bianco Vintage Magnum '12	♟♟ 8
● Montepepe Rosso '13	♟♟ 4
○ Candia dei Colli Apuani Alberico '15	♟ 3
○ Montepepe Bianco '15	♟ 4
○ Degeres '13	♟♟ 5
○ Degeres '12	♟♟ 6
○ Degeres '10	♟♟ 5
○ Degeres '09	♟♟ 5
○ Montepepe Bianco '14	♟♟ 4
○ Montepepe Bianco '13	♟♟ 4
○ Montepepe Bianco Vintage '10	♟♟ 5
● Montepepe Rosso '11	♟♟ 5
● Montepepe Rosso '06	♟♟ 4

Monteraponi

LOC. MONTERAPONI
53017 RADDA IN CHIANTI [SI]
TEL. +39 0577738208
www.monteraponi.it

CELLAR SALES
PRE-BOOKED VISITS
ACCOMMODATION
ANNUAL PRODUCTION 50,000 bottles
HECTARES UNDER VINE 10.00
VITICULTURE METHOD Certified Organic

Michele Braganti's winery hasn't been around long but it's producing good results. After a short period of adjustment, he has chosen to pursue organic viticulture, with a focus on tradition in the cellar. This begins with concrete vats and aging exclusively in large barrels. His wines have a very readable style in which Sangiovese develops all of its complexity. Elegance, balance, aromatic harmony and pleasant taste are well-stated. The 2013 Baron'Ugo proves that its the winery's crown jewel. This blend of Sangiovese, Canaiolo and Colorino offers up flowery aromas, with hints of earth and stone. In the mouth it unfolds well, with a nice, sweet-acid contrast that boosts its length and pleasantness. The 2014 Chianti Classico Il Campitello Riserva didn't perform quite as well. A difficult vintage made for a predominance of oak (both on the nose and in a somewhat muted mouth).

Monteti

S.DA DELLA SGRILLA, 6
58011 CAPALBIO [GR]
TEL. +39 0564896160
www.tenutamonteti.it

CELLAR SALES
PRE-BOOKED VISITS
ANNUAL PRODUCTION 130,000 bottles
HECTARES UNDER VINE 28.00
SUSTAINABLE WINERY

In 1998 Paolo Baratta purchased a 28-hectares winery in an area of Tuscany at the time unrecognized for vine growing. In Capalbio, about 15 kilometers from the sea, Cabernet Sauvignon, Cabernet Franc, Alicante Bouschet and Merlot are planted on clay soil at 150 meters above sea level divided into 28 different plots. The grapes are vinified separately and assembled only after the first stage of aging. Today, Paolo's daughter, Eva, and her husband, Javier, are at the helm and the winery is at the forefront of environmental sustainability. The Monteti, a blend of Petit Verdot, Cabernet Sauvignon and Franc, and the producer's flagship wine, made it to our finals, but just by a hair's breadth it missed a gold. The 2013 boasts a nice nose that offers up dark, ripe fruit fused well with grassy whiffs. At first it's quite pervasive, then, thanks to an elegant savoriness, it proves more even and close-knit. The Caburnio is fragrant and highly drinkable.

● Baron'Ugo '13	▼▼▼ 5
● Chianti Cl. Il Campitello Ris. '14	▼▼ 5
● Chianti Cl. '15	▼ 3
● Baron'Ugo '12	▽▽▽ 8
● Chianti Cl. Baron'Ugo Ris. '10	▽▽▽ 7
● Chianti Cl. Baron'Ugo Ris. '09	▽▽▽ 7
● Chianti Cl. Baron'Ugo Ris. '07	▽▽▽ 5
● Chianti Cl. '13	▽▽ 3
● Chianti Cl. '12	▽▽ 3
● Chianti Cl. Baron'Ugo Ris. '11	▽▽ 7
● Chianti Cl. Il Campitello Ris. '13	▽▽ 5
● Chianti Cl. Il Campitello Ris. '12	▽▽ 5
● Chianti Cl. Il Campitello Ris. '11	▽▽ 5
● Chianti Cl. Il Campitello Ris. '10	▽▽ 5

● Monteti '13	▼▼
● Caburnio '13	▼▼
☉ TM Rosé '16	▼
● Caburnio '12	▽▽
● Caburnio '11	▽▽
● Monteti '12	▽▽
● Monteti '11	▽▽
☉ TM Rosé '14	▽▽

Monteverro

s.da Aurelia Capalbio, 11
58011 Capalbio [GR]
Tel. +39 0564890721
www.monteverro.com

CELLAR SALES
ANNUAL PRODUCTION 120,000 bottles
HECTARES UNDER VINE 30.00

Julia and Georg Weber own this winery, which was founded in the early 2000s and is situated a few kilometers from Capalbio. After scouring Napa Valley, Bordeaux, and Australia for land to produce their ideal wine, the German couple decided on Maremma, a young terroir with great potential. An all-international team tends the 30 hectares of vineyards, which are cultivated mostly with international varieties. The grapes are used to give rise to wines with an international style, while retaining much of a Mediterranean character. Among their selection, we liked the 2014 Tinata, made with Syrah and Grenache, which offers aromas of juniper, pepper and aromatic herbs. In the mouth we found it a bit too vegetal (the result of a notoriously difficult vintage), but the palate still delivers in terms of flavor and intensity. The Monteverro is contracted and well-extracted, still a bit bridled by the sweetness of its wood. The Terra di Monteverro had a nice day. The wine attacks with some light residual sweetness but it then recedes to a pleasant, savory background.

● Monteverro '14	▼▼ 8
● Terra di Monteverro '14	▼▼ 7
● Tinata '14	▼▼ 8
● Verruzzo di Monteverro '14	▼ 5
○ Chardonnay '13	▽▽ 8
● Monteverro '13	▽▽ 8
● Monteverro '12	▽▽ 8
● Terra di Monteverro '13	▽▽ 7
● Terra di Monteverro '12	▽▽ 7
● Tinata '13	▽▽ 8
● Tinata '12	▽▽ 8
○ Vermentino '13	▽▽ 3

★Montevertine

loc. Montevertine
53017 Radda in Chianti [SI]
Tel. +39 0577738009
www.montevertine.it

PRE-BOOKED VISITS
ANNUAL PRODUCTION 85,000 bottles
HECTARES UNDER VINE 18.00

Martino Manetti continues unperturbed on the path set by his father, Sergio, who founded the winery. Fundamental to him is the identity of Tuscan winemaking and, even more so, the identity of Sangiovese. The wines are a benchmark for how Sangiovese is made not only in Radda, but how this Tuscan variety par excellence should be grown and vinified in the whole of the region. The wines express territorial characteristics as well as Sangiovese's far-reaching complexity. 2014 certainly wasn't an easy year for Montevertine, which, with their focus on subtlety, risks a lot in such complicated circumstances. The Montevertine surprised the most. It's a delicate wine in its aromas of dried flowers, wild strawberry, mace and orange. The mouth is delicate, poised, supple and vibrant, like a breath of fresh air.

● Montevertine '14	▼▼▼ 6
● Le Pergole Torte '14	▼▼ 8
● Pian del Ciampolo '15	▼▼ 4
● Le Pergole Torte '13	▽▽▽ 8
● Le Pergole Torte '12	▽▽▽ 8
● Le Pergole Torte '11	▽▽▽ 8
● Le Pergole Torte '10	▽▽▽ 8
● Le Pergole Torte '09	▽▽▽ 8
● Le Pergole Torte '07	▽▽▽ 8
● Le Pergole Torte '04	▽▽▽ 8
● Le Pergole Torte '03	▽▽▽ 7
● Montevertine '04	▽▽▽ 5
● Montevertine '01	▽▽▽ 5

Vignaioli del Morellino di Scansano

LOC. SARAGIOLO
58054 SCANSANO [GR]
TEL. +39 0564507288
www.cantinadelmorellino.it

CELLAR SALES
PRE-BOOKED VISITS
ANNUAL PRODUCTION 2,500,000 bottles
HECTARES UNDER VINE 600.00
SUSTAINABLE WINERY

Cooperatives don't have an easy time of it in Tuscany but Vignaioli di Scansano, with over thirty years of history under its belt, has never shown signs of weakness. To the contrary, they have recently reassessed their production and placed much-improved wines with consistent quality on the market. We are still waiting for a leap to absolute excellence, which could happen soon. The wines are becoming more interesting with an ability to combine traditional and modern elements with increasingly consistent and clear-cut style. The 2014 Morellino di Scansano Roggiano Riserva finds its forte in its aromas, which feature lush fruit, flowery notes and a hint of spice. In the mouth it unfolds well, with just a bit too much wood at the end. The 2013 Morellino di Scansano Sicomoro Riserva, even if a bit evolved, exhibits a fragrant nose and nice personality. In the mouth it's assertive, well-paced and not lacking in pleasant hardness.

Giacomo Mori

FRAZ. PALAZZONE
P.ZZA SANDRO PERTINI, 8
53040 SAN CASCIANO DEI BAGNI [SI]
TEL. +39 0578227005
www.giacomomori.it

CELLAR SALES
PRE-BOOKED VISITS
ACCOMMODATION
ANNUAL PRODUCTION 40,000 bottles
HECTARES UNDER VINE 11.00
VITICULTURE METHOD Certified Organic

Giacomo Mori's winery in Palazzone has a hundred-year-old history, surviving until 1970 with several ups and downs. The winery finally found its legs in 1995 when it was reorganized into its current structure. There are just over 10 hectares of vineyards and vine growing is unforced. Winemaking has been streamlined and aging is carried out in barriques or large wood. The result is a range of wines with clear-cut style and good personality. By design they reject winemaking fads and look more toward drinkability and balance. The 2015 Chianti is a generous wine, with aromas of fresh cherry and herbs, and a delectable mouth that attacks with some sweetness and proceeds with savoriness. The 2014 Chianti Castelrotto Riserva also delivers, despite the difficult vintage. It highlights well-focused, clean aromas and a well-paced, savory mouth, with a pleasantly sweet finish.

● Morellino di Scansano Roggiano Ris. '14	▼▼ 3*
● Morellino di Scansano Sicomoro Ris. '13	▼▼ 4
● Morellino di Scansano Roggiano '16	▼ 2
● Morellino di Scansano Vignabenefizio '16	▼ 2
● Scantianum Sangiovese '16	▼ 2
○ Vermentino V. Fiorini V. T. '16	▼ 2
● Vin del Fattore Governo all'Uso Toscano '16	▼ 2
● Morellino di Scansano Roggiano '15	♈♈ 2*
● Morellino di Scansano Roggiano '14	♈♈ 2*
● Morellino di Scansano Roggiano Bio '15	♈♈ 2*
● Morellino di Scansano Roggiano Ris. '12	♈♈ 3
● Morellino di Scansano Vignabenefizio '15	♈♈ 2*
○ Vermentino V. Fiorini V.T. '15	♈♈ 2*

● Chianti '15	▼▼ 2*
● Chianti Castelrotto Ris. '14	▼▼ 3
● I 5 Mori '13	▼▼ 4
● Chianti '11	♈♈ 2*
● Chianti '10	♈♈ 2*
● Chianti Castelrotto Ris. '13	♈♈ 3
● Chianti Castelrotto Ris. '11	♈♈ 3
● Chianti Castelrotto Ris. '08	♈♈ 3
● Clanis Shiraz '08	♈♈ 3
○ Vin Santo del Chianti '08	♈♈ 6

Morisfarms

LOC. CURA NUOVA
FATTORIA POGGETTI
58024 MASSA MARITTIMA [GR]
TEL. +39 0566919135
www.morisfarms.it

CELLAR SALES
PRE-BOOKED VISITS
ACCOMMODATION
ANNUAL PRODUCTION 300,000 bottles
HECTARES UNDER VINE 70.00

The Moris family left Spain about two hundred years ago to settle in Maremma, a territory still intact from a naturalistic point of view. They have been producing wine here ever since, and today the tradition is carried forward by Giulio Parentini and Ranieri Luigi Moris. The winery is divided in two: Fattoria I Poggetti numbers 37 hectares of vineyards in Massa Marittima, and Poggio La Mozza adds its 33 hectares of vineyards near Grosseto, in Morellino di Scansano. The vineyards are on calcareous clay at an altitude of 80 to 100 meters. In 1990 they were completely replanted. The wine that most impressed this year came from the Scansano side. It's the 2016 Morellino, a wine that features aromas of cherry and blackberry. In the mouth it's succulent and juicy, with tannins conferring some edge. The 2016 Santa Chiara, a blend of Trebbiano, Malvasia and Ansonica, also did well, with its aromas of flowers and white fruit, and its solid mouth.

Mormoraia

LOC. SANT'ANDREA, 15
53037 SAN GIMIGNANO [SI]
TEL. +39 0577940096
www.mormoraia.it

CELLAR SALES
PRE-BOOKED VISITS
ACCOMMODATION
ANNUAL PRODUCTION 230,000 bottles
HECTARES UNDER VINE 40.00

Pino and Franca Passoni are enthusiastically carrying forward their Tuscan venture, one started many years ago by chance. They love this land and their estate, which they have increased to 100 hectares: 40 of which are vineyards and 10 olive groves. Their holiday farmhouse enjoys one of the best panoramic positions in the region. More importantly, they make excellent wines and successfully export their Vernaccia de la Mormoraia all over the world. Their son, Alessandro, has recently started working at the winery. This year we liked the 2016 Vernaccia Suavis best. It has a nice, brilliant straw-yellow color with green highlights, and a vibrant, fresh, close-focused nose in which fruit, aromatic herbs and aniseed move in turn. On the palate the wine proves supple, fruit-driven and racy. Such qualities are to be found in the nice 2015 Chianti Colli Senesi Haurio, as well, a savory, taut, fluent wine.

○ Monteregio di Massa Marittima Santa Chiara '16	🏆🏆 2*
Morellino di Scansano '16	🏆🏆 2*
● Avvoltore '13	🏆 6
○ Maremma Toscana Mandriolo Rosato '16	🏆 2
● Maremma Toscana Mandriolo Rosso '16	🏆 1*
○ Vermentino '16	🏆 2
● Avvoltore '06	🏆🏆🏆 5
● Avvoltore '04	🏆🏆🏆 5
● Avvoltore '01	🏆🏆🏆 5
● Avvoltore '00	🏆🏆🏆 5
● Avvoltore '99	🏆🏆🏆 5
● Avvoltore '12	🏆🏆 6
● Maremma Toscana Mandriolo '15	🏆🏆 1*

● Chianti Colli Senesi Haurio '15	🏆🏆 2*
● Neitea '14	🏆🏆 3
○ Vernaccia di S. Gimignano Suavis '16	🏆🏆 2*
● Mitylus '14	🏆 4
○ Vernaccia di S. Gimignano Antalis Ris. '15	🏆 3
○ Vernaccia di S. Gimignano E' ReZet Mattia Barzaghi '11	🏆🏆🏆 3*
● Chianti Colli Senesi '14	🏆🏆 2*
● Syrah '12	🏆🏆 3
○ Vernaccia di S. Gimignano '14	🏆🏆 2*
○ Vernaccia di S. Gimignano '13	🏆🏆 2*
○ Vernaccia di S. Gimignano Ostrea '15	🏆🏆 3
○ Vernaccia di S. Gimignano Ostrea '13	🏆🏆 3
○ Vernaccia di S. Gimignano Ris. '14	🏆🏆 3*
○ Vernaccia di S. Gimignano Ris. '11	🏆🏆 3*

Fabio Motta

Vigna al Cavaliere, 61
57022 Castagneto Carducci [LI]
Tel. +39 0565773041
www.mottafabio.lt

CELLAR SALES
PRE-BOOKED VISITS
ANNUAL PRODUCTION 23,000 bottles
HECTARES UNDER VINE 6.50

Fabio Motta is one of Bolgheri's brightest
stars. Their vineyards of red grapes are
located in Le Pievi, on the road entering the
Castagneto Carducci hills.There are four
hectares of them, and the vines here are
over twenty years old. Vermentino, on the
other hand, is cultivated in Fornacelle. Their
wines prove spot-on, with a clear-cut style
and spirited personality. Despite the
absence of their crown jewel, the selection
had an excellent day. The 2015 Bolgheri
Rosso Pievi offers up notes of spice and
licorice, which merge in a creamy mouth
that is generally low-key and relaxed. The
2016 Bianco Nova has aromas of apple
and white fruit, while the palate is
authentic, flavorsome and succulent.

○ Bolgheri Bianco Nova '16	▼▼	4
● Bolgheri Rosso Pievi '15	▼▼	4
● Bolgheri Sup. Le Gonnare '13	▼▼▼	8

Muralia

loc. Il Poggiarello
via del Sughereto
58036 Roccastrada [GR]
Tel. +39 0564577223
www.muralia.it

CELLAR SALES
PRE-BOOKED VISITS
ACCOMMODATION AND RESTAURANT SERVICE
ANNUAL PRODUCTION 65,000 bottles
HECTARES UNDER VINE 14.00
SUSTAINABLE WINERY

Chiara and Stefano Casali fell in love with
Maremma in 1997. Shortly after this coup
di foudre, they left Milan and a successful
career to move to Roccastrada in 2003.
Here they bought a vineyard in the
Grosseto countryside. Today the vineyard
spans fourteen hectares and is divided into
two parts, one on flat land in Poggiarello,
near renovated holiday farmhouses. The
other, purchased later, is in the hills around
Sassofortino. Their modern cellar on the Il
Poggiarello estate is perfectly integrated
into its surrounding environment. The
2015 Altana, made with Sangiovese and
much smaller amounts of Cabernet
Sauvignon and Merlot, is a truly
commendable wine. The nose is true to
character and terroir, featuring aromas of
blackberry, raspberry and mineral notes al
simultaneously. The mouth is potent and
muscular, with weighty tannins, but then it
returns to more elegant atmospheres
thanks to a savory background. The
2015 Manolibera is no less interesting.

● Monteregio di Massa Marittima Altana '15	▼▼	3
● Manolibera '15	▼▼	2
● Muralia '13	▼	4
○ Bianco Chiaraluna '13	▽▽	3
● Manolibera '13	▽▽	2
● Manolibera '11	▽▽	2
● Manolibera '10	▽▽	2
● Monteregio di Massa Marittima Altana '11	▽▽	2
● Muralia '10	▽▽	4

Tenute Silvio Nardi

LOC. CASALE DEL BOSCO
53024 MONTALCINO [SI]
TEL. +39 0577808269
www.tenutenardi.com

CELLAR SALES
PRE-BOOKED VISITS
ANNUAL PRODUCTION 250,000 bottles
HECTARES UNDER VINE 80.00

Silvio Nardi is often mentioned as being one of the first outside investors to come to Montalcino. In the early 1950s he made the decision to focus on growing Sangiovese grapes for making Brunello. It was a different era for farming and the economy, especially when compared to the unprecedented explosion the area witnessed later on. Today, Emilia runs 80 hectares, roughly divided over 30 plots on two estates: Manachiara (eastern side) and Casale del Bosco (northwestern slope). They make a varied range of wines, but of course Sangiovese dominates the flagship reds that are aged in large and medium-sized barrels. The entire selection put in one of their best performances, guided by the 2012 Brunello Vigna Manachiara. Intact fruit and smoky hints lend breadth to the nose, while the mouth displays enough force and succulence to free itself of its tannins, which are still austere at this stage. The 2012 Poggio Doria and the 2015 Rosso both had excellent days as well.

● Brunello di Montalcino V. Manachiara '12	♟♟ 8
● Brunello di Montalcino Poggio Doria '12	♟♟ 8
● Rosso di Montalcino '15	♟♟ 3
● Brunello di Montalcino '12	♟ 6
● Brunello di Montalcino Manachiara '99	♟♟♟ 7
● Brunello di Montalcino Manachiara '97	♟♟♟ 7
● Brunello di Montalcino '11	♟♟ 6
● Brunello di Montalcino '10	♟♟ 5
● Brunello di Montalcino Manachiara '06	♟♟ 8
● Brunello di Montalcino Manachiara '04	♟♟ 8
● Brunello di Montalcino Vign. Manachiara '10	♟♟ 8
● Brunello di Montalcino Vign. Poggio Doria '10	♟♟ 8
● Brunello di Montalcino Vign. Poggio Doria Ris. '10	♟♟ 8

Fattoria Nittardi

LOC. NITTARDI
53011 CASTELLINA IN CHIANTI [SI]
TEL. +39 0577740269
www.nittardi.com

CELLAR SALES
PRE-BOOKED VISITS
ANNUAL PRODUCTION 94,000 bottles
HECTARES UNDER VINE 29.00

This winery in Castellina in Chianti has a modern and clear-cut style, however, their wines retain a marked personality with territorial character. Fattoria Nittardi's reds are pleasant on the palate, displaying intense aromas and invigorating taste. Aging is carried out in small oak, used moderately to produce an impressive result. Fattoria Nittardi also owns 37 hectares of vineyards in Maremma where they produce wines that are often among the best in their category. The 2015 Chianti Classico Belcanto is truly delicious. Aromas of ripe plums and spices give way to a generous and succulent mouth. The Maremmano 2015 Ad Astra, a blend of Sangiovese, Cabernet Sauvignon, Merlot, Syrah and Cabernet Franc, is a pleasantly warm wine, with aromas of Mediterranean shrub and a lively, spicy palate.

● Chianti Cl. Belcanto '15	♟♟♟ 4*
● Ad Astra '15	♟♟ 3
● Ad Astra '08	♟♟♟ 6
● Chianti Cl. Ris. '13	♟♟♟ 6
● Chianti Cl. Ris. '11	♟♟♟ 6
● Chianti Cl. Ris. '10	♟♟♟ 6
● Ad Astra '13	♟♟ 3
● Ad Astra '12	♟♟ 3
● Chianti Cl. Belcanto '13	♟♟ 4
● Chianti Cl. Casanuova di Nittardi '14	♟♟ 4
● Chianti Cl. Casanuova di Nittardi '12	♟♟ 4
● Chianti Cl. Ris. '12	♟♟ 6
● Nectar Dei '12	♟♟ 7

Orma

VIA BOLGHERESE
57022 CASTAGNETO CARDUCCI [LI]
TEL. +39 0575477857
www.ormawine.it

ANNUAL PRODUCTION 30,000 bottles
HECTARES UNDER VINE 5.50
SUSTAINABLE WINERY

Antonio Moretti is a well-known entrepreneur from Arezzo who launched himself into the world of wine with great passion and success. Unable to resist the idea of a Bolgheri estate to complete his group of wineries including Tenuta Setteponti, Poggio al Lupo and Feudo Maccari, he has now added Orma to the list. The red he produces here is not part of the appellation, but it is still one of the best in the area. The vineyard spans 5 hectares on stony, clay soil. Orma once again puts in a stellar performance, despite the difficult year. The nose calls up small, black fruit, with fresh notes of Mediterranean herbs and balsamic, as well as a striking touch of bramble. In the mouth, the international varieties complete one another, offering up complexity and drinkability. And if you needed proof that the winery never misses, look no further than their most recent addition, the 2015 Bolgheri Rosso.

● Orma '14	♟♟♟	8
● Bolgheri Rosso '15	♟♟	8
● Orma '13	♟♟♟	8
● Orma '12	♟♟♟	8
● Orma '11	♟♟♟	8
● Orma '10	♟♟♟	7
● Orma '09	♟♟♟	6
● Orma '08	♟♟♟	6
● Orma '07	♟♟♟	5
● Orma '06	♟♟♟	6
● Orma '05	♟♟	6

Fattoria Ormanni

LOC. ORMANNI, 1
53036 POGGIBONSI [SI]
TEL. +39 0577937212
www.ormanni.it

CELLAR SALES
PRE-BOOKED VISITS
ACCOMMODATION
ANNUAL PRODUCTION 70,000 bottles
HECTARES UNDER VINE 68.00

This winery based in Poggibonsi is one of the established benchmarks in Chianti Classico. Certainly not lacking in history, it is quite the opposite. It's been in existence for two centuries with various ups and downs and their style highlights this legacy. Recent and necessary adjustments in winemaking have served to clean up their wines without affecting their honored relationship with Chianti tradition, Fattoria Ormanni's forte. The 2012 Chianti Classico Gran Selezione finds its greatest expression in its aromatic profile, which brings together fruit, earth and truly intriguing spices. It's less punchy in the mouth, not that it's missing grip or depth, it's just that the tannins are a bit stiff. The 2014 Chianti Classic goes in the opposite direction. Its aromas are a bit hazy, while in the mouth it proves subtle, but also flavorsome and well-sustained.

● Chianti Cl. '14	♟♟	3*
● Chianti Cl. Gran Sel. '12	♟♟	3*
● Chianti Cl. Borro del Diavolo Ris. '13	♟	4
● Chianti Cl. '12	♟♟	3
● Chianti Cl. '10	♟♟	3*
● Chianti Cl. '08	♟♟	3
● Chianti Cl. '04	♟♟	2
● Chianti Cl. Borro del Diavolo Ris. '12	♟♟	4
● Chianti Cl. Borro del Diavolo Ris. '08	♟♟	4
● Chianti Cl. Borro del Diavolo Ris. '06	♟♟	3
● Chianti Cl. Borro del Diavolo Ris. '01	♟♟	3
● Chianti Cl. Gran Sel. '11	♟♟	3
● Julius '12	♟♟	5

★★Ornellaia

FRAZ. BOLGHERI
LOC. ORNELLAIA, 191
57022 CASTAGNETO CARDUCCI [LI]
TEL. +39 056571811
www.ornellaia.it

PRE-BOOKED VISITS
ANNUAL PRODUCTION 930,000 bottles
HECTARES UNDER VINE 112.00

This highly-esteemed Ornellaia winery is famous worldwide, belonging to an elite club of Italy's top producers. Founded in the 1980s it has enjoyed unstoppable success ever since. After a few changes in ownership, it now belongs to the great Tuscan Frescobaldi family, whose fame is not limited to wine. Ornellaia is all in one location with a spectacular cellar and the Bellaria vineyard. The wines are compelling and modern, with a clear international style. If it weren't for the excellent 2014 Ornellaia, a wine whose harmony, reading of the vintage and potential are all outstanding, we might be tempted to start with the two intriguing reds, the 2015 Le Volte and Le Serre Nuove. The former is crisp and flavorsome, while the latter is meaty and surprising. The 2014 Masseto was less to our tastes.

Siro Pacenti

LOC. PELAGRILLI, 1
53024 MONTALCINO [SI]
TEL. +39 0577848662
www.siropacenti.it

CELLAR SALES
PRE-BOOKED VISITS
ANNUAL PRODUCTION 60,000 bottles
HECTARES UNDER VINE 22.00

Giancarlo Pacenti was one of the first winemakers in Montalcino to age his wines in small wood and consequently he is often defined as a modernist. But vintage after vintage, many have realized this definition is only partly responsible for bringing out the many-sided character of Sangiovese, which is so closely linked to the areas where it is cultivated. The northeast vineyards of Pelagrilli, set at about 350 meters above sea level on sand and clay, give rise to a Brunello of the same name and the PS Riserva. At Piancornello in the south, the vineyards with iron-rich, stony soil are used for Vecchie Vigne and the Rosso. Giancarlo Pacenti offers us a nicely varied pair of wines. The 2015 Rosso is rich and mature, and we think it will age well. The same could be said of the 2012 Brunello Pelagrilli, which is more coherent in its spicy and toasty hints. Both wines prove austere on the palate.

● Bolgheri Sup. Ornellaia '14	♥♥♥	8
● Bolgheri Rosso Serre Nuove '15	♥♥	6
● Le Volte '15	♥♥	3
● Masseto '14	♥♥	8
● Bolgheri Sup. Ornellaia '13	♀♀♀	8
● Bolgheri Sup. Ornellaia '12	♀♀♀	8
● Bolgheri Sup. Ornellaia '10	♀♀♀	8
● Bolgheri Sup. Ornellaia '07	♀♀♀	8
● Masseto '11	♀♀♀	8
● Masseto '09	♀♀♀	8
● Masseto '06	♀♀♀	8
● Bolgheri Rosso Le Serre Nuove '13	♀♀	6
● Masseto '13	♀♀	8
● Masseto '12	♀♀	8
○ Poggio alle Gazze '12	♀♀	5

● Brunello di Montalcino Pelagrilli '12	♥♥	6
● Rosso di Montalcino '15	♥♥	5
● Brunello di Montalcino PS Ris. '07	♀♀♀	8
● Brunello di Montalcino V. V. '10	♀♀♀	8
● Brunello di Montalcino '09	♀♀	8
● Brunello di Montalcino '05	♀♀	8
● Brunello di Montalcino Pelagrilli '11	♀♀	6
● Brunello di Montalcino Pelagrilli '10	♀♀	6
● Brunello di Montalcino Pelagrilli '09	♀♀	6
● Brunello di Montalcino Pelagrilli '08	♀♀	6
● Brunello di Montalcino PS Ris. '10	♀♀	8
● Brunello di Montalcino V. V. '11	♀♀	8
● Rosso di Montalcino '10	♀♀	5

Pagani de Marchi

LOC. LA NOCERA
VIA DELLA CAMMINATA, 2
56040 CASALE MARITTIMO [PI]
TEL. +39 0586653016
www.paganidemarchi.com

CELLAR SALES
PRE-BOOKED VISITS
ANNUAL PRODUCTION 35,000 bottles
HECTARES UNDER VINE 6.50

This winery is located in the Casale Marittimo hills near Pisa. After the land's purchase, excavations in the late 1980s led to the discovery of several historic findings that ranged from the end of the seventh to the start of the fourth century BC. In the main tomb they found burial objects for a banquet and wine drinking. These findings may have influenced the owners' decision in 1996 to transform the land surrounding the country house from arable to vineyards. All the vineyards are currently run under organic management to fully maintain an environmental balance. The wines presented all performed extremely well. The 2013 Principe Guerriero offers up notes of red fruit and delicate hints of tobacco, with a neat mouth and a succulent, long finish. The 2013 Casalvecchio, made with Cabernet Sauvignon, is an intriguing wine, with aromas of roasted green pepper, grass and blueberries. On the palate it proves rich and balanced in acidity, with a lingering finish.

● Casa Nocera '13	♙♙ 5	
● Casalvecchio '13	♙♙ 5	
● Montescudaio Principe Guerriero '13	♙♙ 4	
○ Vermentino Blumea '16	♙♙ 3	
● Montescudaio Montaleo '15	♙ 2	
● Olmata '13	♙ 4	
● Casa Nocera '10	♙♙ 5	
● Casa Nocera '01	♙♙ 5	
● Casalvecchio '06	♙♙ 5	
● Casalvecchio '03	♙♙ 5	
● Casalvecchio '01	♙♙ 5	
● Montescudaio Montaleo '12	♙♙ 2*	
● Olmata '09	♙♙ 4	
● Olmata '06	♙♙ 3	

Il Palagione

LOC. PALAGIONE
VIA PER CASTEL SAN GIMIGNANO, 36
53037 SAN GIMIGNANO [SI]
TEL. +39 0577953134
www.ilpalagione.com

CELLAR SALES
PRE-BOOKED VISITS
ACCOMMODATION
ANNUAL PRODUCTION 60,000 bottles
HECTARES UNDER VINE 16.00

Monica Rota and Giorgio Comotti's farm is at the top of a hill near the road to Volterra. The land once belonged to Castel San Gimignano, a hamlet built in the fourteenth century to defend the towered city. Documents in Colle Val d'Elsa's episcopal archives show mentions of the estate dating it back to 1594. Today, Palagione is a well-organized farm. The first vineyards were planted in 1997 but they also grow olives, walnuts and cherries. The rest of the estate is covered with woods and arable land. The 2015 Vernaccia Ori Riserva doesn't disappoint, thanks to an aromatic profile in which fresh, aromatic herbs, basil and mint, prevail, with fruity notes of peach, and hints of damson as well. An enticing, succulent, generous mouth also exhibits good weight, with nice grip at the end. The 2015 Chianti Colli Senesi Caelum is enticing, with a nose featuring fruit and spices, and a mouth held together by a robust, soft body.

● Chianti Colli Senesi Caelum '15	♙♙ 2*	
● Chianti Colli Senesi Drago Ris. '14	♙♙ 3	
○ Vernaccia di S. Gimignano Ori Ris. '15	♙♙ 3	
● San Gimignano Ares '13	♙ 4	
⊙ Sunrosé '16	♙ 2	
● Trevite '16	♙ 2	
○ Vernaccia di S. Gimignano Hydra '16	♙ 2	
● Antajr '09	♙♙ 4	
● Chianti Colli Senesi Caelum '13	♙♙ 2*	
● Chianti Colli Senesi Draco Ris. '11	♙♙ 3	
○ Vernaccia di S. Gimignano Ori Ris. '14	♙♙ 3	
○ Vernaccia di S. Gimignano Ori Ris. '13	♙♙ 3	
○ Vernaccia di S. Gimignano Ori Ris. '11	♙♙ 3	

Palazzo

LOC. PALAZZO, 144
53024 MONTALCINO [SI]
TEL. +39 0577849226
www.aziendapalazzo.it

CELLAR SALES
PRE-BOOKED VISITS
ANNUAL PRODUCTION 21,000 bottles
HECTARES UNDER VINE 4.00
VITICULTURE METHOD Certified Biodynamic

t was only a question of time before the
Loia-Palazzo family's historic winery
returned to the main section of IW. Run by
Cosimo and Antonietta, with their sons
Angelo and Elia, it spans about twelve
hectares in eastern Montalcino, at 300
meters above sea level. It is an area
dominated by extremely stony, poor and
shallow soil. This explains the robust and
often austere texture of their Sangiovese
wines, an attribute enhanced by a fluid
style in the cellar. Fermentation is carried
out in concrete and steel, while aging is
carried out in large barrels, mid-sized
casks and barriques for the two Brunellos,
and 2000- to 2500- liter oak barrels for
the Rosso. A truly fantastic performance
has brought Palazzo's wines to center
stage. The 2012 Brunello is already a star,
going all in on spices and balsams. The
2012 Rosso manages to actually outdo its
predecessor in terms of definition of fruit
and the mobility of its aromatic profile, not
to mention a streamlined, dynamic,
harmonic palate.

Rosso di Montalcino '15	♈♈♈ 3*
Brunello di Montalcino '12	♈ 6
Brunello di Montalcino '10	♈♈ 6
Brunello di Montalcino '09	♈♈ 6
Brunello di Montalcino '08	♈♈ 6
Brunello di Montalcino '07	♈♈ 6
Brunello di Montalcino '06	♈♈ 5
Brunello di Montalcino Ris. '10	♈♈ 7
Brunello di Montalcino Ris. '07	♈♈ 7
Brunello di Montalcino Ris. '06	♈♈ 7
Rosso di Montalcino '11	♈♈ 3
Rosso di Montalcino '10	♈♈ 3

Panizzi

LOC. SANTA MARGHERITA, 34
53037 SAN GIMIGNANO [SI]
TEL. +39 0577941576
www.panizzi.it

CELLAR SALES
PRE-BOOKED VISITS
ACCOMMODATION
ANNUAL PRODUCTION 210,000 bottles
HECTARES UNDER VINE 50.00

Giovanni Panizzi was one of the pioneers of
modern Vernaccia. He came from
Lombardy, but fell in love with Tuscany and
bought the Santa Margherita farm near San
Gimignano at the end of the 1970s. Within
a few years his winery became
instrumental in improving the overall quality
of wines produced in the area. In 2005
Giovanni handed over the ownership of the
estate to Luano Niccolai, but continued to
help out, contributing his enthusiasm and
experience until 2010, the year he died.
Today, Simone Niccolai is at the helm and
is currently expanding the vineyard
hectares and range of wine. The Vernaccia
2013 Riserva makes it to the finals by
virtue of its spicy notes and fruity aromas,
with accents of honey and potpourri. In the
mouth it attacks well, coming through full,
rich, succulent and pervasive, with
well-integrated acidity and a pleasant,
layered persistence. The 2015 Vigna Santa
Margherita selection proves elegant and
sophisticated.

○ Vernaccia di S. Gimignano Ris. '13	♈♈ 5
○ Vernaccia di S. Gimignano '16	♈♈ 2*
○ Vernaccia di San Gimignano V. S. Margherita '15	♈♈ 3
⊙ Ceraso Rosato '16	♈ 2
○ Evoè '15	♈ 4
● San Gimignano Pinot Nero '15	♈ 2
○ Vernaccia di S. Gimignano Ris. '07	♈♈♈ 5
○ Vernaccia di S. Gimignano Ris. '05	♈♈♈ 5
○ Passito '13	♈♈ 4
● Pinot Nero '12	♈♈ 2*
○ Vernaccia di S. Gimignano '13	♈♈ 2*
○ Vernaccia di S. Gimignano Ris. '12	♈♈ 5
○ Vernaccia di San Gimignano V. S. Margherita '14	♈♈ 3*
○ Vernaccia di San Gimignano V. S. Margherita '13	♈♈ 3

Parmoleto

LOC. MONTENERO D'ORCIA
POD. PARMOLETONE, 44
58040 CASTEL DEL PIANO [GR]
TEL. +39 0564954131
www.parmoleto.it

CELLAR SALES
PRE-BOOKED VISITS
ACCOMMODATION AND RESTAURANT SERVICE
ANNUAL PRODUCTION 22,000 bottles
HECTARES UNDER VINE 6.00

Parmoleto started out as a cereal farm, but in 1990 the Sodi family, owners hailing from Montalcino, decided to take up winemaking and planted five hectares of vineyards. The estate is in the hills of Val d'Orcia in Castel del Piano, in the shadow of Monte Amiata. The old country farm has been perfectly restored and it houses the cellar. You can stay the night in the farmhouse right at the heart of the estate, and enjoy the natural beauty of this part of Tuscany. The 2013 Montecucco Sangiovese is a concrete, territorial wine, with aromas of cherry and blackcurrant, as well as delicate nuances of blood oranges. The mouth is close-knit, even, very fresh and characterized by tannins that are still a bit young, chaffing. The 2012 Riserva is a bit stiff, maybe, bridled by wood that has yet to integrate. The rest of the selection proved sound, such as the Syrah, a spicy, peppery wine with a supple, lean mouth.

● Montecucco Sangiovese '13	▼▼ 3
● Montecucco Sangiovese Ris. '12	▼▼ 3
○ Carabatto '16	▼ 2
● Maremma Toscana Syrah '14	▼ 3
● Montecucco Rosso '14	▼ 2
● Sormonno '14	▼ 4
● Montecucco Sangiovese '12	♀♀ 3
● Montecucco Sangiovese '11	♀♀ 3
● Montecucco Sangiovese Ris. '11	♀♀ 3*
● Montecucco Sangiovese Ris. '10	♀♀ 3

Tenuta La Parrina

FRAZ. ALBINIA
S.DA DELLA PARRINA
58010 ORBETELLO [GR]
TEL. +39 0564862636
www.parrina.it

CELLAR SALES
PRE-BOOKED VISITS
ACCOMMODATION AND RESTAURANT SERVICE
ANNUAL PRODUCTION 200,000 bottles
HECTARES UNDER VINE 60.00

Marquise Franca Spinola runs the 200-hectare farm in the municipality of Orbetello, where low hills gently sweep down to the lagoon. This estate was founded in the 1830s by a Florentine banker, Michele Giuntini, who decided to invest in land that had never before been used for farming. The vineyards span 60 hectares and are planted with both native varieties (Sangiovese, Ansonica, Vermentino and Trebbiano) and international ones, which have now become completely acclimatized to Maremma. Winegrowing, however, is only one of the activities at the estate, they also grow cereals and olives and breed livestock, all under organic management. A nice performance for the entire selection, starting with the 2016 Sangiovese, a simple, even wine, but delicious and highly drinkable. The 2015 Merlot Radaia also did well, featuring aromas of medicinal herbs and a mouth with close-woven, thick tannins.

● Parrina Merlot Radaia '15	▼▼ 6
○ Ansonica Costa dell'Argentario '16	▼▼ 3
● Parrina Sangiovese '16	▼▼ 2
○ Parrina Vermentino '16	▼▼ 3
○ Parrina Bianco Vialetto '16	▼ 2
● Parrina Rosso Muraccio '15	▼ 3
○ Poggio della Fata '16	▼ 3
○ Ansonica Costa dell'Argentario '14	♀♀ 3
○ Costa dell'Argentario Ansonica '15	♀♀ 3
● Parrina Radaia '13	♀♀ 6
● Parrina Rosso Muraccio '14	♀♀ 3
● Parrina Rosso Muraccio '13	♀♀ 3
● Parrina Rosso Muraccio '11	♀♀ 3
● Parrina Sangiovese '10	♀♀ 4
○ Poggio della Fata '15	♀♀ 3

Perazzeta

LOC. MONTENERO D'ORCIA
VIA DELLA PIAZZA
58040 CASTEL DEL PIANO [GR]
TEL. +39 3803545477
www.perazzeta.it

CELLAR SALES
PRE-BOOKED VISITS
ACCOMMODATION
ANNUAL PRODUCTION 100,000 bottles
HECTARES UNDER VINE 19.00

Montenero d'Orcia represents a kind of
meeting point between Brunello di
Montalcino and Morellino di Scansano.
However, we are in Montecucco, an area
beginning to emerge in the complex and
varied Tuscan winemaking scene. The
Bocci family have been working here since
1998: Alessandro, the head of the family,
runs twenty-hectares of vineyards with his
wife, Rita, and daughter Sara. Seventy
percent of it hosts Sangiovese and the
remaining part is planted with Cabernet,
Syrah and Merlot. The slopes for the most
part face southwest, at altitudes ranging
between 250 and 380 meters. They
reclaim their place among the top
producers thanks to a solid performance by
the entire selection, starting with the
Licurgo Riserva, which offers up ripe cherry
and red citrus on the nose, joined by an
intriguing weave of spices. The mouth is
complex, taut, compact and austere. The
2015 Alfeno, a wine characterized by its
fresh verve, also proves to be of good
character.

● Montecucco Rosso Alfeno '15	♥♥ 2*
● Montecucco Sangiovese Licurgo Ris. '12	♥♥ 4
○ Montecucco Vermentino '16	♥♥ 2*
● Maremma Toscana Sangiovese Terre dei Bocci '13	♥ 2
● Montecucco Rosso Alfeno '14	♀♥ 2*
● Montecucco Rosso Alfeno '12	♀♥ 2*
● Montecucco Rosso Alfeno '11	♀♥ 2*
● Montecucco Rosso Alfeno '10	♀♥ 2*
● Montecucco Sangiovese Licurgo Ris. '11	♀♥ 4
● Montecucco Sangiovese Licurgo Ris. '09	♀♥ 5

Petra

LOC. SAN LORENZO ALTO, 131
57028 SUVERETO [LI]
TEL. +39 0565845308
www.petrawine.it

CELLAR SALES
PRE-BOOKED VISITS
ANNUAL PRODUCTION 350,000 bottles
HECTARES UNDER VINE 94.00
SUSTAINABLE WINERY

Mario Botta designed and created a
futuristic, iconic, efficient cellar, which is
surrounded by the oldest vineyards and
forms the core of this winery. At the helm is
Francesca Moretti, who pursues her
vocation to make wines that express her
love for this unique territory, with its rich
history of culture, products and trade.
Entrepreneurial curiosity is the force behind
any project and this is what drives her to
honor its combination of territory, everyday
hard work and talent. The 2014 season
saw a significant breakthrough in terms of
quality. Tre Bicchieri go to the 2014 Petra,
a blend of Cabernet Sauvignon and Merlot,
with a complex, layered bouquet in which
vegetal notes and aromatic herbs join
together with fruity notes of plums and
cherries. In the mouth the attack comes
through with good body, well-distributed
tannins, fresh acidity and a polished,
lengthy finish. The 2014 Potenti, a
monovarietal Cabernet, is also excellent.

● Petra Rosso '14	♥♥♥ 8
● Alto '14	♥♥ 6
● Potenti '14	♥♥ 6
○ Belvento Vermentino '16	♥♥ 3
● Hebo '15	♥♥ 3
○ La Balena '15	♥♥ 6
● Maremma Toscana Rosso Acquagiusta Tenuta La Badiola '15	♥♥ 3
● Quercegobbe '14	♥♥ 6
● Belvento Cabernet Sauvignon '15	♥ 3
● Belvento Sangiovese '15	♥ 3
⊙ Belvento Velarosa '16	♥ 3
○ Belvento Viognier '16	♥ 3
⊙ Maremma Toscana Rosato Acquagiusta Tenuta La Badiola '16	♥ 3
○ Maremma Toscana Vermentino Acquagiusta Tenuta La Badiola '16	♥ 3

★Fattoria Petrolo

FRAZ. MERCATALE VALDARNO
VIA PETROLO, 30
52021 BUCINE [AR]
TEL. +39 0559911322
www.petrolo.it

PRE-BOOKED VISITS
ACCOMMODATION
ANNUAL PRODUCTION 85,000 bottles
HECTARES UNDER VINE 31.00

Luca Sanjust's grandfather purchased the estate in 1947. It spans 272 hectares in one of Tuscany's top-quality winemaking areas (according to a 1716 edict by Grand Duke Cosimo III). Towards the mid-1980s the vineyards were replanted and the cellar was modernized. They're now focusing on experiments such as fermenting and aging certain wines in terracotta amphorae. As well as producing wine and extra virgin oil, Petrolo also offers accommodation in a delightfully welcoming environment. The Galatrona gets another Tre Bicchieri, now with the 2014 version. It's a monovarietal Merlot that has become a classic. On the nose, the wine's fruitiness is on full display, with blackcurrant and blueberry dominating, then more herbaceous notes. In the mouth it proves fresh, subtle with a balanced structure and uplifting finish. Their selection in amphoras is also interesting. The 2015 Trebbiano stands out for its aromas of aromatic herbs, vanilla and honey. The palate proves warm, dense, succulent and full, with an intriguing finish.

● Valdarno di Sopra Galatrona '14	♥♥♥ 8
○ Bòggina Bianco '15	♥♥ 7
○ San Petrolo '06	♥♥ 8
● Valdarno di Sopra Bòggina '15	♥♥ 7
● Valdarno di Sopra Bògginanfora '15	♥♥ 7
● Valdarno di Sopra Torrione '15	♥♥ 5
● Galatrona '12	♥♥♥ 8
● Galatrona '11	♥♥♥ 8
● Galatrona '10	♥♥♥ 8
● Galatrona '09	♥♥♥ 8
● Torrione '11	♥♥♥ 5
● Valdarno di Sopra Galatrona '13	♥♥♥ 8

★Piaggia

LOC. POGGETTO
VIA CEGOLI, 47
59016 POGGIO A CAIANO [PO]
TEL. +39 0558705401
www.piaggia.com

CELLAR SALES
PRE-BOOKED VISITS
ANNUAL PRODUCTION 75,000 bottles
HECTARES UNDER VINE 15.00

This winery was founded in the 1970s by Mauro Vannucci, a textiles businessman, who for many years ran it as a country house. At the end of the 1980s he decided to take a more professional approach and the first appellation wines date from the early 1990s. He subsequently bought other vineyards in Carmignano and handed over the reins to his daughter, Silvia, who deals mostly with sales and marketing. Yet another Tre Bicchieri for the 2014 Carmignano Riserva, a wine that's aromatically deep, with notes of medical herbs, blackcurrant, blackberries and spicy hints of cloves. In the mouth it proves close-woven, dense and succulent with smooth tannins, richness of flavor and elegance. The 2015 Carmignano Il Sasso also did well. It's a fruity, balsamic wine on the nose, while the mouth is juicy, meaty and compact, with a nice freshness, and smooth, well-distributed tannins. The 2015 Poggio de' Colli, made with 100% Cabernet Franc, is minty on the nose, savory and flavorsome in the mouth.

● Carmignano Ris. '14	♥♥♥ 6
● Poggio de' Colli '15	♥♥ 8
● Carmignano Il Sasso '15	♥♥ 5
● Carmignano Ris. '13	♥♥♥ 6
● Carmignano Ris. '12	♥♥♥ 6
● Carmignano Ris. '11	♥♥♥ 6
● Carmignano Ris. '08	♥♥♥ 5
● Poggio de' Colli '11	♥♥♥ 7
● Poggio de' Colli '10	♥♥♥ 6
● Carmignano Il Sasso '14	♥♥ 5
● Carmignano Il Sasso '13	♥♥ 5
● Poggio de' Colli '14	♥♥ 7
● Poggio de' Colli '13	♥♥ 7

Piancornello

LOC. PIANCORNELLO
53024 MONTALCINO [SI]
TEL. +39 0577844105
piancornello@libero.it

CELLAR SALES
PRE-BOOKED VISITS
ANNUAL PRODUCTION 50,000 bottles
HECTARES UNDER VINE 10.00

Silvana Pieri and Claudio Monaci bought
their beautiful estate in 1950. It is named
after the famous Piancornello volcanic hill,
on the southern slope of Montalcino, where
they own ten hectares. A unique area
overlooking Monte Amiata on the Orcia and
Asso rivers, it has well-drained steep
slopes and is rich in stone and rock.
Combined with the Mediterranean climate
and the relatively low altitude (about 250
meters), it creates perfect conditions for
gutsy, full-bodied Sangiovese wines, which
are fermented in steel and wood, and aged
in barriques and mid-sized casks.
Piancornello's selection put in a first-rate
performance. The 2015 Rosso is, without a
doubt, the most aromatically captivating,
with its hints of light fruit, mint, pistils and
citrus peel; it's just a bit supple on the
palate. The 2012 Brunello is just as brilliant
in its suite of spices, though more potent
and dry as well.

● Brunello di Montalcino '12	♟♟ 6
● Rosso di Montalcino '15	♟♟ 3
● Brunello di Montalcino '10	♟♟♟ 6
● Brunello di Montalcino '06	♟♟♟ 6
● Brunello di Montalcino '99	♟♟♟ 6
● Brunello di Montalcino '11	♟♟ 6
● Brunello di Montalcino '09	♟♟ 6
● Brunello di Montalcino '08	♟♟ 6
● Brunello di Montalcino '07	♟♟ 6
Brunello di Montalcino Ris. '06	♟♟ 6
Brunello di Montalcino Ris. '04	♟♟ 6
● Rosso di Montalcino '11	♟♟ 3
● Rosso di Montalcino '08	♟♟ 3*

Pianirossi

LOC. PORRONA
POD. SANTA GENOVEFFA, 1
58044 CINIGIANO [GR]
TEL. +39 0564990573
www.pianirossi.it

CELLAR SALES
PRE-BOOKED VISITS
ACCOMMODATION AND RESTAURANT SERVICE
ANNUAL PRODUCTION 50,000 bottles
HECTARES UNDER VINE 14.00

Stefano Sincini is a manager in the fashion
industry, who, about 20 years ago, decided
to invest in his dream: make wine that
could represent his passion for the field. He
identified 14 hectares of terrain on the hills
around Cinigiano and began renovating the
old farmsteads there (according to
eco-friendly architectural principles). He
also planted Sangiovese grapes (the area's
primary cultivar), Montepulciano and a few
international varieties, all with the utmost
respect for the territory and environmental
sustainability. We liked the 2015 Sidus. The
blend of Sangiovese and Montepulciano
makes for a wine whose nose comes
through with dark hints of pencil lead, and
boasts savoriness in the mouth, as well as
incredible grip (maybe to the detriment of
its fruit). Despite the difficult vintage, the
2014 Solus manages to express itself
satisfactorily, thanks to a flowery, fragrant
nose, and a fresh mouth that unfolds nicely.

● Montecucco Rosso Sidus '15	♟♟ 2*
● Solus '14	♟♟ 3
● Pianirossi '14	♟ 6
⊙ Sabine '16	♟ 2
● Montecucco Sidus '14	♟♟ 2*
● Montecucco Sidus '13	♟♟ 2*
● Montecucco Sidus '11	♟♟ 4
● Pianirossi '12	♟♟ 6
● Pianirossi '11	♟♟ 6
● Solus '12	♟♟ 3
● Solus '11	♟♟ 4
● Solus '10	♟♟ 4

Pietroso

LOC. PIETROSO, 257
53024 MONTALCINO [SI]
TEL. +39 0577848573
www.pietroso.it

CELLAR SALES
PRE-BOOKED VISITS
ANNUAL PRODUCTION 30,000 bottles
HECTARES UNDER VINE 5.00

Gianni Pignattai, his wife, Cecilia, and their
children, Andrea and Gloria, run 5 hectares
of Sangiovese vineyards situated in four
different areas. Pietroso surrounds the
winery and is a westward continuation of
the central Montalcino hill, marked by rocky
soil and vertiginous slopes. Fornello is in the
north, with galestro soil, while Colombaiolo's
clay and tuff soil is in the south, a stone's
throw from the Sant'Antimo Abbey. Lastly
and not to be forgotten are the plots of land
used for Villa Montosoli, a monovarietal
Sangiovese from the cru of the same name
in the north. The Pietroso's Sangioveses are
consistently among the best options in
Montalcino for stylistic coherence and
drinkability, as the racy 2015 Rosso
reminds us. The 2012 Brunello sees
increased intensity and stratification. It's just
a bit dark aromatically, and somewhat
brusque in its tannins, but of indisputable
character nevertheless.

● Brunello di Montalcino '12	♟♟♟ 6
● Rosso di Montalcino '15	♟♟ 4
● Villa Montosoli '13	♟ 7
● Brunello di Montalcino '09	♟♟♟ 6
● Brunello di Montalcino '11	♟♟ 6
● Brunello di Montalcino '10	♟♟ 6
● Brunello di Montalcino '08	♟♟ 6
● Brunello di Montalcino '04	♟♟ 5
● Brunello di Montalcino Ris. '10	♟♟ 6
● Rosso di Montalcino '14	♟♟ 4
● Rosso di Montalcino '13	♟♟ 4
● Rosso di Montalcino '12	♟♟ 4
● Rosso di Montalcino '11	♟♟ 3*

Pieve Santo Stefano

LOC. SARDINI
55100 LUCCA
TEL. +39 0583394115
www.plevedlsantostefano.com

CELLAR SALES
PRE-BOOKED VISITS
ACCOMMODATION
ANNUAL PRODUCTION 45,000 bottles
HECTARES UNDER VINE 10.60
SUSTAINABLE WINERY

This estate at the foot of a thirteenth-
century Romanesque church in the hills
overlooking Lucca has been producing wine
since Etruscan times. A large villa was built
in the 1700s by the Sardinis amidst
vineyards, olive groves and Italian gardens,
but it has since disappeared from the
60-hectare winery. The farmhouse and
upper floor of the old cellar remain, as well
as other buildings that have been renovated
for tourist accommodation. The grapes
include native varieties, such as Sangiovese
and Ciliegiolo, together with Merlot,
Cabernet Franc and Syrah, and all tended
with eco-friendly methods. The 2016 Colline
Lucchesi Villa Sardini, a wine that exhibits
finesse and grace, goes all in on fragrance
and pleasantness. It's a simple wine,
naturally, but still light years away from
stereotypes of 'approachable' wines. Small
red fruit meets undergrowth and hints of
iron, while in the mouth it proves
well-paced, and not lacking in depth, either.

● Colline Lucchesi Villa Sardini '16	♟♟ 2*
● Lippo '15	♟♟ 4
● Colline Lucchesi Ludovico Sardini '13	♟♟ 4
● Colline Lucchesi Ludovico Sardini '12	♟♟ 4
● Colline Lucchesi Ludovico Sardini '11	♟♟ 2
● Colline Lucchesi Villa Sardini '15	♟♟ 2
● Colline Lucchesi Villa Sardini '13	♟♟ 2
● Colline Lucchesi Villa Sardini '12	♟♟ 2
● Lippo '14	♟♟ 4
● Lippo '11	♟♟ 3
● Lippo '10	♟♟ 3
● Ludovico Sardini '12	♟♟ 3

Podere 414

FRAZ. MONTIANO
LOC. MAIANO LAVACCHIO, 10
58051 MAGLIANO IN TOSCANA [GR]
TEL. +39 0564507818
www.podere414.it

CELLAR SALES
PRE-BOOKED VISITS
ANNUAL PRODUCTION 150,000 bottles
HECTARES UNDER VINE 22.00
VITICULTURE METHOD Certified Organic

This winery has focused all its work on the Morellino di Scansano appellation. Simone Castelli made this decision twenty years ago and he continues to interpret this type of wine with precision and stubbornness. The wines belong to a style category that is not immediately readable and they tend to be austere, but solid and well-made. He counts on the expressiveness of Sangiovese and Ciliegiolo, aging in small and mid-sized wood and concrete, and organic viticulture to bring out the best in his wines. The 2015 Badilante is interesting. It's a monovarietal Sangiovese worked in concrete and mid-sized casks. The name 'badilante' calls up a local word used to describe the farmhands who worked Maremma's land for more than a century. The aromatic profile is delicately fruity; in the mouth it shows good pace and grip, which culminate in a succulent, fresh finish. The 2016 Morellino is tighter, but still pleasant, with aromas of earthy fruit and the occasional touch of flint.

● Badilante '15	▼▼	3
☉ Flower Power '16	▼	2
● Morellino di Scansano '16	▼	4
● Aleatico Passito '14	♕♕	7
● Aleatico Passito '13	♕♕	7
● Morellino di Scansano '14	♕♕	3
● Morellino di Scansano '13	♕♕	3
● Morellino di Scansano '12	♕♕	3
● Morellino di Scansano '10	♕♕	3

Podere Fabbrica

LOC. PODERE FABBRICA, 62
53026 PIENZA [SI]
TEL. +39 0578810030

CELLAR SALES
PRE-BOOKED VISITS
ANNUAL PRODUCTION 15,000 bottles
HECTARES UNDER VINE 35.00
VITICULTURE METHOD Certified Organic
SUSTAINABLE WINERY

Swiss couple, Antonie and Philippe Bertherat (founder of Pictet Group), decided to start a winemaking venture in Tuscany. This in itself is nothing new, however, the winery they built, counting 35 hectares of vineyards in Pienza, a particularly famous area for vine growing, focuses completely on the most charming, and the most difficult, variety in the region: Sangiovese. Currently their only wine, it has a perfectly designed style, good personality, and unforced. The 2013 Prototipo 470.1, a monovarietal Sangiovese, is distinguished by the freshness of its fruit, even if it sees the occasional dimmer stroke. In the mouth it offers up its best, proving well-paced and layered, all flavor and fragrance. The Prototipo 470.2 (made with the same grape) is more or less in the same stylistic vein; while certainly less complex, it's still supple and subtly fragrant.

● Prototipo 470.1 '13	▼▼	5
● Prototipo 470.2 '14	▼▼	5

Podere Le Bèrne

LOC. CERVOGNANO
VIA POGGIO GOLO, 7
53045 MONTEPULCIANO [SI]
TEL. +39 0578767328
www.leberne.it

CELLAR SALES
ANNUAL PRODUCTION 25,000 bottles
HECTARES UNDER VINE 6.00

Andrea Natalini's winery in Cervognanois is characterized by its fifty-year-old vineyards (in a renowned wine region) and a purist approach to winemaking. Their wines have great aging potential and overall pleasantness, and they are wonderfully consistent with the territory. At times, however, the wood aging is slightly overdone and likewise the concentration, sometimes spoiling the final result. The 2016 Rosso di Montepulciano is an extremely pleasant wine from the outset, with its aromas that see flowery notes, wild berries and cinnamon all meeting with hints of balsamic. In the mouth it's lively, savory and succulent. The 2014 Nobile is also pleasant, fruity on the nosed, lightly spicy, with a simple but tasty palate that sees just a bit too much oak. The 2006 Vin Santo di Montepulciano Occhio di Pernice is doughy but not lacking in complexity.

Podere San Cristoforo

FRAZ. BAGNO
LOC. FORNI
58023 GAVORRANO [GR]
TEL. +39 3358212413
www.poderesancristoforo.it

CELLAR SALES
PRE-BOOKED VISITS
ACCOMMODATION
ANNUAL PRODUCTION 50,000 bottles
HECTARES UNDER VINE 15.00
VITICULTURE METHOD Certified Organic
SUSTAINABLE WINERY

Podere San Cristoforo's vineyard spans 15 hectares in the municipality of Gavorrano, on stony and clay-rich soil. The farm is owned by Lorenzo Zonin, who early on opted for biodynamic management in order to respect fully the environment and all forms of life. Most of the ten hectares of vine rows are dedicated to Sangiovese, but there is ample allotment for Petit Verdot, Syrah, Vermentino and Trebbiano. The wine style focuses on expression of the territory. In addition to wine production, the farm also produces cereals and oil, and the estate houses a flourishing farm holiday business. In the absence of the Carandelle, it's the 2015 Ameri, a Tuscan method 'Governo all'Uso Toscano' that earns a Tre Bicchieri. It's fragrant and limpid on the nose, featuring notes of cherry. The mouth is savory, mineral, well-paced and delectable, with an aftertaste that matches perfectly.

● Rosso di Montepulciano '16	♥♥ 2*
● Nobile di Montepulciano '14	♥♥ 3
○ Vin Santo di Montepulciano Occhio di Pernice '06	♥♥ 7
○ Vin Santo di Montepulciano Ada '08	♥ 6
● Nobile di Montepulciano '11	♥♥♥ 3*
● Nobile di Montepulciano '06	♥♥♥ 3
● Nobile di Montepulciano '13	♥♥ 3
● Nobile di Montepulciano '12	♥♥ 3*
● Nobile di Montepulciano Ris. '12	♥♥ 5
● Nobile di Montepulciano Ris. '11	♥♥ 5
● Rosso di Montepulciano '14	♥♥ 2*
○ Vin Santo di Montepulciano Ada '07	♥♥ 5

● Ameri Governo all'Uso Toscano '15	♥♥♥ 6
● Maremma Toscana Sangiovese Amaranto '16	♥♥ 3*
○ Luminoso Dolce	♥♥ 4
● San Cristoforo Petit Verdot '15	♥♥ 5
○ Maremma Toscana Bianco Luminoso '16	♥ 3
● Maremma Toscana Podere San Cristoforo '13	♥♥♥ 3*
● Maremma Toscana Sangiovese Carandelle '15	♥♥♥ 3*
○ Maremma Toscana Luminoso '15	♥♥ 3
● Maremma Toscana Sangiovese Amaranto '15	♥♥ 3
● San Cristoforo '12	♥♥ 5

Poggerino

Loc. Poggerino, 6
53017 Radda in Chianti [SI]
Tel. +39 0577738958
www.poggerino.com

CELLAR SALES
PRE-BOOKED VISITS
ACCOMMODATION
ANNUAL PRODUCTION 60,000 bottles
HECTARES UNDER VINE 11.30
VITICULTURE METHOD Certified Organic

Poggerino has been a Chianti Classico producer since the 1980s. It is only one of many examples of artisan winemaking that distinguishes production in the appellation. This winery is run by Piero and Benedetta Lanza, who have cultivated their vines under organic management for more than ten years now. Procedures are kept to a minimum in the cellar and aging is carried out in barriques and 900-liter casks. This allows for great expression of Sangiovese, giving the winery a style that is clearly recognizable, and full of personality and character. The 2014 Chianti Classico Bugialla Riserva has a vibrant nose, distinguished by its lush fruity and toasty notes. In the mouth the wine proves generous; at the time of tasting, there was still some wood in the foreground. The 2011 Spumante Metodo Classico Rosé, made with Sangiovese, is an intriguing experiment. It's still a bit lacking in complexity, but its aromas are defined and the mouth is pleasant, with fine prickle and pervasive fragrance overall.

● Chianti Cl. Bugialla Ris. '14	♟♟ 6
☉ Spumante M. Cl. Sangiovese '11	♟♟ 5
● Chianti Cl. (N)Uovo '14	♟ 4
● Chianti Cl. Bugialla Ris. '12	♟♟♟ 5
● Chianti Cl. Bugialla Ris. '09	♟♟♟ 5
● Chianti Cl. Bugialla Ris. '08	♟♟♟ 5
● Chianti Cl. '13	♟♟ 4
● Chianti Cl. '12	♟♟ 3*
● Chianti Cl. '08	♟♟ 3
● Chianti Cl. Bugialla Ris. '10	♟♟ 5
● Primamateria '10	♟♟ 5
● Primamateria '07	♟♟ 5
● Primamateria '06	♟♟ 5

Poggio al Tesoro

Loc. Felciaino
via Bolgherese, 189b
57022 Castagneto Carducci [LI]
Tel. +39 0565773051
www.poggioaltesoro.it

CELLAR SALES
PRE-BOOKED VISITS
ANNUAL PRODUCTION 330,000 bottles
HECTARES UNDER VINE 65.00

Poggio al Tesoro belongs to the Allegrini group and is rapidly growing. The owned lands are made up of mixed soil situated in different areas. Sandy and stony soil is better for Cabernet Sauvignon and Franc, while clayish soil has been chosen for other varieties like Merlot. The wines are successful in expressing the finest attributes of the grape varieties and the areas in which they are cultivated. Their most unique wines have an unmistakable aromatic imprint. The 2014 Bolgheri Superiore Sondraia is wonderful. It intoxicates with its dark aromas of black fruit and licorice, refreshes with its elegant herbaceous whiffs and enchants with its splendid, balsamic verve. It all comes together in a captivating, creamy, sophisticated and lengthy mouth. The 2014 Mediterra also did well; tannins are a bit toasty, but it has great prospects.

● Bolgheri Sup. Sondraia '14	♟♟♟ 5
● Mediterra '14	♟♟ 3*
☉ Bolgheri Rosato Teones '16	♟♟ 3
● Bolgheri Rosso '14	♟♟ 2*
● Bolgheri Sup. Sondraia '13	♟♟♟ 5
● Bolgheri Sup. Sondraia '11	♟♟♟ 5
● Bolgheri Sup. Sondraia '10	♟♟♟ 5
● Dedicato a Walter '12	♟♟♟ 7
● Dedicato a Walter '09	♟♟♟ 7
☉ Bolgheri Rosato Cassiopea '13	♟♟ 2*
● Bolgheri Sup. Dedicato a Walter '13	♟♟ 7
● Bolgheri Sup. Sondraia '12	♟♟ 5
○ Bolgheri Vermentino Solosole '15	♟♟ 3
● Dedicato a Walter '11	♟♟ 7
● Mediterra '13	♟♟ 3
● Mediterra '12	♟♟ 3

★Poggio Antico

LOC. POGGIO ANTICO
53024 MONTALCINO [SI]
TEL. +39 0577848044
www.poggioantico.com

CELLAR SALES
PRE-BOOKED VISITS
RESTAURANT SERVICE
ANNUAL PRODUCTION 120,000 bottles
HECTARES UNDER VINE 32.00

The first documents citing Poggio Antico as a highly-esteemed farm in western Montalcino date back to the early nineteenth century. Husband and wife team, the Gloders, bought it in 1984 and today it is run by their youngest daughter, Paola, and her husband, Alberto Montefiori. The vineyards count about thirty hectares strategically positioned at 450 meters. The altitudes are high for this Mediterranean slope and they significantly influence the spirited nature of the Sangiovese used in making their trio of Brunellos. The vintage and Riserva wines age in medium-large Slavonian oak, while the Altero selection is highlighted with a more modern style with aging in 900-liter casks. The 2015 Rosso stands out for its fresh, spring atmospheres, which we also find in the 2012 Brunello, a more close-woven, mature wine. The 2012 Altero sees more texture and extractive proportion.

Poggio Argentiera

LOC. ALBERESE
S.DA BANDITELLA DUE
58100 GROSSETO
TEL. +39 3484952767
www.poggioargentiera.com

CELLAR SALES
PRE-BOOKED VISITS
ACCOMMODATION
ANNUAL PRODUCTION 200,000 bottles
HECTARES UNDER VINE 22.00
VITICULTURE METHOD Certified Organic

Poggio Argentiera is a recent pioneer in the rebirth of Maremma winemaking. It retains this role today and produces a range of wines with a comfortingly solid quality, although they no longer seem able to achieve a level of excellence. It may be that recent issues in ownership are weighing down choices in style. We would like to see them become more clear-cut and readable. The 2016 Morellino di Scansano Bellamarsilia offers a generous, clean and fragrant aromatic spectrum, which features lush and fresh fruit. In the mouth the wine proves dynamic, and not lacking in depth. The 2016 Maremmante, a blend of Alicante and Syrah, is pleasantly spicy on the nose, well-sustained and relaxed in the mouth. The solid 2015 Morellino Capatosta is a vibrant and long wine; there's just a bit of rawness at the end.

● Brunello di Montalcino Altero '12	♼♼8
● Brunello di Montalcino '12	♼♼8
● Rosso di Montalcino '15	♼♼5
● Brunello di Montalcino '05	♼♼♼7
● Brunello di Montalcino Altero '09	♼♼♼7
● Brunello di Montalcino Altero '07	♼♼♼8
● Brunello di Montalcino Altero '06	♼♼♼8
● Brunello di Montalcino Altero '04	♼♼♼8
● Brunello di Montalcino '11	♼♼7
● Brunello di Montalcino '10	♼♼6
● Brunello di Montalcino Altero '11	♼♼8
● Rosso di Montalcino '13	♼♼4
● Rosso di Montalcino '12	♼♼4

● Morellino di Scansano Bellamarsilia '16	♼♼4
● Maremmante '16	♼♼4
● Morellino di Scansano Capatosta '15	♼♼6
● Finisterre '07	♼♼♼6
● Morellino di Scansano Capatosta '00	♼♼♼5*
○ Guazza '13	♼♼2*
● Maremmante '15	♼♼2*
● Morellino di Scansano Bellamarsilia '15	♼♼3
● Morellino di Scansano Bellamarsilia '13	♼♼3*
● Morellino di Scansano Bellamarsilia '12	♼♼2*
● Morellino di Scansano Capatosta '13	♼♼5
● Morellino di Scansano Capatosta '12	♼♼5
● Morellino di Scansano Capatosta '11	♼♼5

Poggio Bonelli

VIA DELL'ARBIA, 2
53019 CASTELNUOVO BERARDENGA [SI]
TEL. +39 057756661
www.poggiobonelli.it

CELLAR SALES
PRE-BOOKED VISITS
ACCOMMODATION
ANNUAL PRODUCTION 125,000 bottles
HECTARES UNDER VINE 87.00

This winery is part of MPS Tenimenti belonging to Gruppo Montepaschi di Siena, which also owns another winery, Villa Chigi Saracini. The Sienese company took over management from the Landucci and Croci families in 2000, though Poggio Bonelli had been producing wine since the 1950s. The vineyards are located near Castelnuovo Berardenga, from where wines can find unusual fullness and power. The winery has a characteristic style and despite a hefty use of small oak, their wines convey good precision and balance Despite the difficult year, the 2014 Chianti Classico did well. Its aromas are clean, and richness of fruit provides fragrance and intensity. In the mouth it's subtle, but also offers liveliness and dynamism. The 2013 Chianti Classico Riserva also put it a nice performance. It's a solid, layered wine that unfolds generously in the mouth. It has a nice aromatic profile as well: vibrant and not lacking in complexity.

★Poggio di Sotto

FRAZ. CASTELNUOVO DELL'ABATE
LOC. POGGIO DI SOTTO
53024 MONTALCINO [SI]
TEL. +39 0577835502
www.collemassari.it

CELLAR SALES
PRE-BOOKED VISITS
ACCOMMODATION
ANNUAL PRODUCTION 30,000 bottles
HECTARES UNDER VINE 16.00
VITICULTURE METHOD Certified Organic
SUSTAINABLE WINERY

The confidence with which the Tipa family has managed to harmonize Poggio di Sotto's transition to a new era is astonishing. They have maintained, even reinforced, the key features we had become accustomed to over the last twenty years from founder, Piero Palmucci. There are still 15 hectares at Castelnuovo dell'Abate, in the southeasternmost part of Montalcino. The plots of land are located between Monte Amiata and the Orcia river, on clay and galestro soil, at altitudes between 200 and 450 meters. The reds made with Sangiovese have a unique combination of force and flavor and are mostly aged in 3000-liter Slavonian oak. Small nuances made the difference in how we responded to this outstanding selection. we preferred the 2012 Brunello, a wine that's irresistible in its earthy notes and hints of medicinal herbs, while the mouth is spontaneous and consistent. We find the same qualities in the 2011 Riserva, a wine that's just a bit evolved, and in the delicious 2014 Rosso.

● Chianti Cl. '14	♟♟ 3
● Chianti Cl. Ris. '13	♟♟ 5
● Poggiassai '11	♟♟♟ 6
● Poggiassai '10	♟♟♟ 6
● Poggiassai '08	♟♟♟ 5
● Poggiassai '07	♟♟♟ 5
● Tramonto d'Oca '10	♟♟♟ 5
● Chianti Cl. '12	♟♟ 3
● Chianti Cl. '10	♟♟ 3
● Chianti Villa Chigi Saracini '15	♟♟ 3
● Chianti Villa Chigi Saracini '14	♟♟ 3
● Chianti Villa Chigi Saracini '13	♟♟ 3
● Chianti Villa Chigi Saracini '12	♟♟ 3
● Poggiassai '12	♟♟ 6

● Brunello di Montalcino '12	♟♟♟ 8
● Brunello di Montalcino Ris. '11	♟♟ 8
● Rosso di Montalcino '14	♟♟ 8
● Brunello di Montalcino '11	♟♟♟ 8
● Brunello di Montalcino '10	♟♟♟ 8
● Brunello di Montalcino '07	♟♟♟ 8
● Brunello di Montalcino '04	♟♟♟ 8
● Brunello di Montalcino Ris. '07	♟♟♟ 8
● Rosso di Montalcino '07	♟♟♟ 6
● Brunello di Montalcino Ris. '10	♟♟ 8
● Brunello di Montalcino Ris. '08	♟♟ 8
● Rosso di Montalcino '13	♟♟ 8
● Rosso di Montalcino '12	♟♟ 8

Tenuta Poggio Rosso

FRAZ. POPULONIA
LOC. POGGIO ROSSO, 1
57025 PIOMBINO [LI]
TEL. +39 056529553
www.tenutapoggiorosso.it

CELLAR SALES
PRE-BOOKED VISITS
ANNUAL PRODUCTION 35,000 bottles
HECTARES UNDER VINE 6.00

Ivano Monelli and his family purchased Tenuta Poggio Rosso in 2001. It is in the westernmost part of Val di Cornia, in Populonia, one of the largest and most important Etruscan and Roman cities in Tuscany. The estate was left in almost complete abandonment, but it along with the old pine forest was salvaged in a very short time. The first rows of vines were planted with both white and red grapes, and a modern cellar was created in rooms on the villa's ground floor. The 2015 Tages, made with Sangiovese and Merlot, offers minty and balsamic overtones, mineral accents, and vibrant fruit. In the mouth it shows balanced attack, proving tasty and refreshing with a flavorsome finish. The 2015 Fufluna is a blend of Cabernet Sauvignon, Cabernet Franc, Merlot and Syrah. On the nose it comes through spicy and vibrant, with accents of wild berries. It shows stylish, balanced structure, while the finish is savory and appetizing. The 2015 Losna, made with 100% Vermentino that's macerated on the skins, also did well.

● Fufluna '15	♛♛ 3
○ Losna '15	♛♛ 6
● Tages '15	♛♛ 4
○ Feronia '16	♛ 4
○ Phylika '16	♛ 3
○ Feronia '14	♛♛ 4
● Tages '13	♛♛ 3*
● Tages '12	♛♛ 3
● Tages '10	♛♛ 3
○ Veive '13	♛♛ 4
○ Veive '11	♛♛ 4
● Velthune '13	♛♛ 6
● Velthune '12	♛♛ 5
● Velthune '09	♛♛ 5

Podere Poggio Scalette

LOC. RUFFOLI
VIA BARBIANO, 7
50022 GREVE IN CHIANTI [FI]
TEL. +39 0558516108
www.poggioscalette.it

CELLAR SALES
PRE-BOOKED VISITS
ACCOMMODATION
ANNUAL PRODUCTION 60,000 bottles
HECTARES UNDER VINE 22.00

The Fiore family have owned Poggio Scalette on the Ruffoli hill near Greve in Chianti since 1991. It is well-known for being a good vine growing area and the winery put itself on a path to sustainable viticulture with very low environmental impact. Over the years their wines have had a hand in making local winemaking history, but recently there were moments of uncertainty regarding their style, and marked by a backward step in quality. Today they appear to be in the process of overcoming these problems. The 2015 Chianti Classic is well-crafted, with a decidedly modern structure. It offers up a vibrant, focused nose, and a generous, sweet mouth. The 2014 Carbonaione, a monovarietal Sangiovese, also delivered, with its focused aromas and well-paced, fragrant mouth. The 2014 Capogatto, a Bordeaux blend made with Cabernet Sauvignon, Cabernet Franc, Merlot and Petit Verdot, also came through. Aromatically it features spice and fruit, while the palate tends to succulence, with nice suppleness as well.

● Capogatto '14	♛♛ 7
● Chianti Cl. '15	♛♛ 3
● Il Carbonaione '14	♛♛ 7
● Il Carbonaione '08	♛♛♛ 6
● Il Carbonaione '05	♛♛♛ 6
● Il Carbonaione '03	♛♛♛ 7
● Capogatto '08	♛♛ 6
● Capogatto '07	♛♛ 6
● Chianti Cl. '12	♛♛ 3
● Chianti Cl. '10	♛♛ 3
● Il Carbonaione '11	♛♛ 6
● Il Carbonaione '09	♛♛ 6
● Il Carbonaione '06	♛♛ 6

Tenuta Il Poggione

FRAZ. SANT'ANGELO IN COLLE
OC. MONTEANO
53024 MONTALCINO [SI]
TEL. +39 0577844029
www.tenutailpoggione.it

CELLAR SALES
PRE-BOOKED VISITS
ACCOMMODATION
ANNUAL PRODUCTION 600,000 bottles
HECTARES UNDER VINE 127.00

With over a hundred hectares of vineyards, Il Poggione is one of the most important wineries in Montalcino. It is situated in Sant'Angelo in Colle, the southern extremity of the appellation, and it has belonged to the Franceschi family since the second half of the nineteenth century. Fabrizio Bindocci has been running the estate ever since he began working as winemaker and head of production. They make a mixed and varied range of wines: Sangiovese naturally takes center stage with traditional winemaking, maceration lasting about twenty days, and aging in 3000-5000-liter French oak barrels. There are also a few plots of Merlot, Vermentino and Chardonnay. The two Rosso de Il Poggiones are from outstanding years, and thus make a nice pair. The 2015 base is open and integrated, while the 2014 Leopold Franceschi sees more austere tannins. The 2012 Brunello got the best response; it's an earthy, pervasive wine that's a just a bit over-ripe in its fruit.

● Brunello di Montalcino '12	♥♥ 7
● Rosso di Montalcino '15	♥ 4
● Rosso di Montalcino Leopoldo Franceschi '14	♥ 5
● Brunello di Montalcino Ris. '97	♥♥♥ 7
● Brunello di Montalcino '11	♥♥ 7
● Brunello di Montalcino '10	♥♥ 7
● Brunello di Montalcino '09	♥♥ 6
● Brunello di Montalcino V. Paganelli Ris. '10	♥♥ 8
● Brunello di Montalcino V. Paganelli Ris. '07	♥♥ 7
● Rosso di Montalcino '14	♥♥ 4
● Rosso di Montalcino '13	♥♥ 4
● Rosso di Montalcino '12	♥♥ 3
● Rosso di Montalcino '11	♥♥ 3
● Toscana Rosso '13	♥♥ 3

Poggiotondo

VIA TORRIBINA, 83
50050 CERRETO GUIDI [FI]
TEL. +39 0571559167
www.poggiotondowines.com

PRE-BOOKED VISITS
ACCOMMODATION
ANNUAL PRODUCTION 300,000 bottles
HECTARES UNDER VINE 20.00

The estate in Cerreto Guidi, halfway between Florence and Pisa, has been owned by this family for generations. Winemaker, Alberto Antonini, runs the vineyards with his wife, Alessandra, employing organic and biodynamic methods. With his work here he has shown it is possible to work in different continents without giving up his personal idea of wine. Growing alongside the Sangiovese, there are Syrah and Vermentino grapes. Procedures in the cellar are kept to a minimum to ensure wines that are as natural as possible. They also produce Extra Virgin olive oil using the same production philosophy. The 2015 Chianti Superiore proves austere and well-defined, with fresh, almost balsamic notes, then plums. The body is potent, savory at the finish. On the nose it proves pleasantly fresh, fruity and flowery all at the same time. The 2016 Chianti is intriguing in the mouth for its good acidity.

● Chianti Sup. '15	♥♥ 2*
● Chianti Sup. '15	♥♥ 2*
● Chianti '16	♥ 2
○ Vermentino '16	♥ 2
● Chianti V. del 1928 Ris. '13	♥♥ 6
● Chianti V. del 28 Ris. '11	♥♥ 6
● Chianti V. delle Conchiglie '13	♥♥ 6
● Chianti V. delle Conchiglie '10	♥♥ 6
● Marmoreccia '11	♥♥ 7
○ Vermentino '14	♥♥ 2*
○ Vermentino '13	♥♥ 2*
○ Vermentino '12	♥♥ 2*

Tenuta Poggioventoso

S.DA DI TERENZANA, 5
56046 RIPARBELLA [PI]
TEL. +39 3938973677
www.poggioventoso.wine

CELLAR SALES
PRE-BOOKED VISITS
ANNUAL PRODUCTION 25,000 bottles
HECTARES UNDER VINE 6.00

Poggioventoso is a small winery that was set up in 2004 by Maricla Affatato. Its limited size makes it one of the many wineries in Tuscany with an artisan quality. Grape varieties include Sangiovese, Merlot, Petit Verdot, as well as Vermentino, Malvasia and Petit Manseng. These Mediterranean wines are precise and well-made, with balance and drinkability. The most impressive features of their production philosophy are aging in small wood, good quality raw materials, and a purist approach to winemaking Even if its makeup (Merlot, Petit Verdot, Sangiovese and Cabernet Sauvignon) makes you think of a boisterous wine, the 2014 Fuochi is relaxed and succulent on the palate, and doesn't lack aromatic complexity either. The 2016 Assurdino, a blend of Sangiovese and Merlot, is a 'carefree' wine (as the name suggests), distinguished by its approachability.

● Assurdino '16	▼▼ 5
● Fuochi '14	▼▼ 8
○ Poetico '16	▼ 6
● Fuochi '13	♀♀ 6
● Fuochi '12	♀♀ 6
○ Poetico '15	♀♀ 5

★★Poliziano

FRAZ. MONTEPULCIANO STAZIONE
VIA FONTAGO, 1
53045 MONTEPULCIANO [SI]
TEL. +39 0578738171
www.carlettipoliziano.com

CELLAR SALES
PRE-BOOKED VISITS
ANNUAL PRODUCTION 650,000 bottles
HECTARES UNDER VINE 145.00

Federico Carletti's winery has been a benchmark in the Nobile di Montepulciano appellation for many years. It is also one of the most consistent wineries in Italy. Constant quality and a distinctive style are a goal that only the best producers can achieve and maintain. There is clearly no lack of excellence and style. Never complacent, some of their wines have gone from power and concentration to balance and complexity, but without abandoning their initial modern imprint. The 2014 Nobile di Montepulciano Asinone impresses once again for its ability to deliver consistently, even in a complicated year. Of course, the wood used for aging comes out, both in the mouth and on the nose, but the wine still exhibits excellence. Its aromas are clean and vibrant, and in the mouth it unfolds well, without imperfections. As always, the rest of the selection proves exemplary.

● Nobile di Montepulciano Asinone '14	▼▼▼ 7
● Cortona Merlot In Violas '14	▼▼ 4
● Nobile di Montepulciano '14	▼▼ 5
● Rosso di Montepulciano '15	▼▼ 3
● Maremma Toscana Mandrone di Lhosa '13	▼ 5
● Le Stanze '03	♀♀♀ 6
● Nobile di Montepulciano '09	♀♀♀ 4*
● Nobile di Montepulciano Asinone '12	♀♀♀ 7
● Nobile di Montepulciano Asinone '11	♀♀♀ 7
● Nobile di Montepulciano Asinone '07	♀♀♀ 6
● Nobile di Montepulciano Asinone '06	♀♀♀ 6
● Nobile di Montepulciano Asinone '05	♀♀♀ 6
● Nobile di Montepulciano Asinone '04	♀♀♀ 6
● Nobile di Montepulciano Asinone '03	♀♀♀ 6
● Nobile di Montepulciano Asinone '01	♀♀♀ 6

Tenuta Le Potazzine

LOC. LE PRATA, 262
53024 MONTALCINO [SI]
TEL. +39 0577846168
www.lepotazzine.it

CELLAR SALES
PRE-BOOKED VISITS
RESTAURANT SERVICE
ANNUAL PRODUCTION 50,000 bottles
HECTARES UNDER VINE 4.70

In Montalcino, the little passerine birds are known locally as "potazzine," a word Giuseppe Gorelli and Gigliola Giannetti used as a nickname for their daughters, Viola and Sofia, when they were little girls. This family word overlapped with a time which coincided with the purchase of the two main vineyard areas. The one near Le Prata is a unique area in the west, with altitudes skimming 500 meters, a windy microclimate, and iron-rich soil. The other one consists of plots of land in Torre, further south towards Sant'Angelo in Colle. Grapes from these two areas are combined to make graceful Brunellos, rich in texture, and aged in 3000-5000-liter Slavonian oak. This fits perfectly with the 2012 version: citrus peels, ginger, incense emerge from a sweet, welcoming nose, while the mouth deviates a bit with its vigorous tannic support. The 2015 Rosso, an authentic, silky Sangiovese, is more relaxed, but certainly not banal or simple.

● Brunello di Montalcino '12	♟♟ 7
● Rosso di Montalcino '15	♟♟ 4
● Parus '15	♟ 3
● Brunello di Montalcino '10	♟♟♟ 7
● Brunello di Montalcino '08	♟♟♟ 7
● Brunello di Montalcino Ris. '06	♟♟♟ 8
● Brunello di Montalcino '11	♟♟ 7
● Brunello di Montalcino '09	♟♟ 7
● Brunello di Montalcino '07	♟♟ 6
● Rosso di Montalcino '14	♟♟ 4
● Rosso di Montalcino '13	♟♟ 4
● Rosso di Montalcino '12	♟♟ 4
● Rosso di Montalcino '10	♟♟ 4

Fabrizio Pratesi

LOC. SEANO
VIA RIZZELLI, 10
59011 CARMIGNANO [PO]
TEL. +39 0558704108
www.pratesivini.it

CELLAR SALES
PRE-BOOKED VISITS
RESTAURANT SERVICE
ANNUAL PRODUCTION 80,000 bottles
HECTARES UNDER VINE 12.00

Fabrizio Pratesi is president of the Consorzio di Carmignano, where he shows the same enthusiasm that he does for the winery that's been in his family since 1875. His dual role is leading him to rethink his previous commitments. At the estate, Fabrizio deserves credit for modernizing the cellar, which involved expanding the rooms and buying new barrels. But he did his best work in the vineyards, which have been completely replanted with a high vine density. The 2014 Carmignano Circo Rosso Riserva offers up fruity aromas of blackcurrant and cherry, with spicy hints and aromatic herbs as well. In the mouth it proves succulent and meaty, fresh, savory and elegant, with expansive tannins and a relaxed, enjoyable finish. The 2015 Carmignano Carmione sees fragrances of dark fruit, blueberry and plums. The body is well-distributed, with smooth tannins, balanced acidity and a lengthy, saline finish. The 2016 Barca Reale is fresh, lively and balanced.

● Carmignano Circo Rosso Ris. '14	♟♟ 3*
● Barco Reale '16	♟♟ 2*
● Carmignano Carmione '15	♟♟ 4
● Carmignano '13	♟♟ 4
● Carmignano '12	♟♟ 3
● Carmignano Circo Rosso Ris. '10	♟♟ 4
● Carmignano Circo Rosso Ris. '08	♟♟ 5
● Carmignano Il Circo Rosso Ris. '12	♟♟ 6
● Carmione '14	♟♟ 6
● Carmione '10	♟♟ 4
● Carmione '08	♟♟ 5
● Merlot Barche di Bacchereto '12	♟♟ 3
● Merlot Barche di Barchereto '10	♟♟ 3

★Fattoria Le Pupille

S.DA PIAGGE DEL MAIANO
58100 GROSSETO
TEL. +39 0564409517
www.fattorialepupille.it

CELLAR SALES
PRE-BOOKED VISITS
ACCOMMODATION
ANNUAL PRODUCTION 450,000 bottles
HECTARES UNDER VINE 80.00

If Maremma continues to take part in Tuscany's winemaking success, much of the credit is due to Elisabetta Geppetti, a pioneer of Morellino di Scansano. The main feature of her winery in Istia d'Ombrone is an undisputed consistent quality, but there is no lack of excellence and impeccable execution in her wines either. The style is modern, she looks for fully ripe fruit and ages her wines in small wood, while the appellation wines made with local varieties use larger wood for longer periods. The Saffredi, a blend of Cabernet Sauvignon, Merlot and Petit Verdot, keeps its top-spot within the winery's selection. The 2014 finds its forte in its multifaceted aromas and solid, layered palate. The 2014 Poggio Valente offers up nuanced aromas of quite ripe fruit, and intense flavor. The 2016 Morellino di Sacansano also proved enjoyable.

● Saffredi '14	▼▼▼	8
● Poggio Valente '14	▼▼	5
● Morellino di Scansano '16	▼	3
● Morellino di Scansano Ris. '14	▼	4
● Pelofino '16	▼	2
● Morellino di Scansano Poggio Valente '04	♀♀♀	5
● Morellino di Scansano Poggio Valente '99	♀♀♀	5
● Saffredi '13	♀♀♀	8
● Saffredi '05	♀♀♀	8
● Saffredi '04	♀♀♀	8
● Saffredi '03	♀♀♀	8
● Saffredi '02	♀♀♀	7
● Saffredi '01	♀♀♀	7
● Saffredi '00	♀♀♀	7

La Querce

VIA IMPRUNETANA PER TAVARNUZZE, 41
50023 IMPRUNETA [FI]
TEL. +39 0552011380
www.laquerce.com

CELLAR SALES
PRE-BOOKED VISITS
ACCOMMODATION
ANNUAL PRODUCTION 35,000 bottles
HECTARES UNDER VINE 8.00

This farm is named after an enormous oak tree that stood in the villa courtyard until WW II. It remains as the symbol of the winery today. The estate was bought in the 1960s by Gino Marchi and is now run enthusiastically by his son, Massimo, and grandchildren, Donatella, Benedetto and Giulio. The estate spans 42 hectares, eight of which are vineyards, in the hills around Impruneta. The exposures mainly face south towards the Sorrettole valley, guaranteeing perfect ripening and cool breezes during the harvest. As well as winemaking, the Marchi family also grow olives and they run a farmstay business. Obviously, Sangiovese is the dominant grape used in the Sorrettole. On the nose, ripe dark fruit emerge, enriched by pleasant notes of cinnamon and sweet spice. The mouth is slightly bridled by its close-woven tannins, but it still maintains its succulence and pleasantness. A good performance for the M, as well, a monovarietal Merlot that goes all in on pepper and drinkability.

● Belrosso Canaiolo '16	▼▼	2
● Chianti Sorrettole '16	▼▼	2
● M '13	▼▼	6
● Chianti Colli Fiorentini La Torretta '15	▼	2
⊙ Rosa di Maggio '16	▼	1
● La Querce '11	♀♀♀	5
● Belrosso '15	♀♀	2
● Chianti Colli Fiorentini La Torretta '13	♀♀	2
● Chianti Colli Fiorentini La Torretta '12	♀♀	2
● Chianti Sorrettole '15	♀♀	2
● La Querce '12	♀♀	5
● La Querce '10	♀♀	5
● M '09	♀♀	6

Le Ragnaie

LOC. LE RAGNAIE
53024 MONTALCINO [SI]
TEL. +39 0577848639
www.leragnaie.com

CELLAR SALES
PRE-BOOKED VISITS
ACCOMMODATION
ANNUAL PRODUCTION 80,000 bottles
HECTARES UNDER VINE 15.50
VITICULTURE METHOD Certified Organic

Riccardo Campinoti's efforts to carefully select vineyard plots is gradually reaching completion. The range currently includes three crus, originating in areas of Montalcino with very different soils and climates. Vecchie Vigne are made with grapes from Le Ragnaie, surrounding the cellar, at an altitude of almost 600 meters above sea level. Fornace-Loreto is from Castelnuovo dell'Abate, in the southeast and at about 400 meters. Likewise, it is Petroso, which is behind the town towards the historic Scarnacuoia road. In addition to Brunellos, they make Rosso wines that are recognizable for their fruity vitality and savory texture, refined with cellar practices that render them anything but overbearing. The most recent tests seem to shake up the hierarchy of the selection. The Brunello Fornace are more mature, while the Vecchie Vigne are longer, though both do a good job interpreting the 2012 vintage. But it's the 2014 Rosso Ragnaie Vecchie Vigne that stands out for its elegant, subtle profile, which goes all in on dynamism.

● Rosso di Montalcino V. V. Ragnaie '14	♟♟ 5
● Brunello di Montalcino Fornace '12	♟♟ 8
● Brunello di Montalcino V. V. '12	♟♟ 8
● Rosso di Montalcino Petroso '14	♟♟ 5
● Brunello di Montalcino '12	♟ 7
● Rosso di Montalcino '14	♟ 5
● Brunello di Montalcino Fornace '08	♟♟♟ 8
● Brunello di Montalcino V. V. '11	♟♟♟ 8
● Brunello di Montalcino V. V. '10	♟♟♟ 8
● Brunello di Montalcino V. V. '07	♟♟♟ 5
● Brunello di Montalcino '11	♟♟ 7
● Brunello di Montalcino Fornace '11	♟♟ 8
● Chianti Colli Senesi '13	♟♟ 2*
● Rosso di Montalcino '13	♟♟ 5

Podere La Regola

LOC. ALTAGRANDA
S.DA REG.LE 68 KM 6,400
56046 RIPARBELLA [PI]
TEL. +39 0586698145
www.laregola.com

CELLAR SALES
PRE-BOOKED VISITS
ANNUAL PRODUCTION 90,000 bottles
HECTARES UNDER VINE 20.00

Bearing witness to the territory's winemaking culture, remains of an ancient Etruscan settlement and several wine amphorae were found where a new cellar was being built. In view of this history it comes as no surprise then that just over twenty years ago, Luca, after graduating in agricultural science, decided to turn the small family business into a real winery. After a few years he was joined by his brother Flavio, a lawyer who deals with administration, marketing and sales. Today, all the vineyards have been converted to organic management. The 2014 La Regola, a blend made with Cabernet Franc and smaller parts Merlot and Petit Verdot, offers up a complex aromatic profile that features green pepper accompanied by fruity notes of plum and blackcurrant, and various minty hints. In the mouth the wine proves generous, warm, with good depth and refreshing acidity.

● La Regola '14	♟♟ 7
○ Lauro '15	♟♟ 5
● Strido '12	♟♟ 8
☉ Rosegola '16	♟ 4
○ Steccaia '16	♟ 4
● La Regola '13	♟♟ 6
● La Regola '12	♟♟ 6
● La Regola '11	♟♟ 6
● Strido '13	♟♟ 8
● Strido '11	♟♟ 8
● Syrah '13	♟♟ 3
● Syrah La Regola '12	♟♟ 3
● Vallino '13	♟♟ 5
● Vallino '11	♟♟ 5

Riecine

LOC. RIECINE
53013 GAIOLE IN CHIANTI [SI]
TEL. +39 0577749098
www.riecine.com

CELLAR SALES
PRE-BOOKED VISITS
ANNUAL PRODUCTION 60,000 bottles
HECTARES UNDER VINE 11.00
VITICULTURE METHOD Certified Organic

A change in ownership seems to have been an overall benefit to this winery in Gaiole in Chianti. After moments of uncertain quality in their wines, they are back on a track befitting their previous reputation as a leading Chianti Classico winery. Their style has returned to its old splendor and their wines are a good expression of the territory. By maintaining a marked character it serves to win back the prestige that once marked their success. The 2015 Chianti Classico sees airy scents of wild berries, which highlight a well-paced, savory unfolding of flavor in the mouth (with just a bit too much toastiness at the end). The 2013 La Gioia, a compact, well-structured monovarietal Sangiovese, proves interesting, managing to unfold with suppleness in the mouth; though it's still a bit veiled in its aromas, with oak dominating. The 2013 Riecine, another Sangiovese, is still clenched, with a tight, woody palate and clean aromas.

● Chianti Cl. '15	▼▼ 3*
● La Gioia '13	▼▼ 6
● Riecine '13	▼ 3
● La Gioia '04	♀♀♀ 6
● La Gioia '01	♀♀♀ 6
● Chianti Cl. '09	♀♀ 3
● Chianti Cl. '07	♀♀ 3
● Chianti Cl. '06	♀♀ 3
● Chianti Cl. Ris. '07	♀♀ 5
● Chianti Cl. Ris. '06	♀♀ 5
● La Gioia '06	♀♀ 6
● Riecine di Riecine '12	♀♀ 5

Podere Le Ripi

LOC. LE RIPI
53021 MONTALCINO [SI]
TEL. +39 0577835641
www.podereleripi.it

CELLAR SALES
PRE-BOOKED VISITS
ANNUAL PRODUCTION 25,000 bottles
HECTARES UNDER VINE 12.00
VITICULTURE METHOD Certified Biodynamic
SUSTAINABLE WINERY

If you're tired of boring websites, take a long look at Podere Le Ripi's. Francesco Illy tells us about his "psychedelic dream," which materialized in 2005 with the purchase of a dozen hectares in Castelnuovo dell'Abate, in southeastern Montalcino. Then came the turning point with biodynamic management, then construction of the golden cellar, and 60,000 plants per hectare in the so-called bonsai vineyard, which is used to make the Rosso of the same name. It is probably the best-known wine in their varied range, which focuses on Sangiovese grapes for making Brunello, as well as Syrah and other international varieties. This year also saw a single tasting: the 2012 Brunello Lupi e Sirene. It's a decidedly strong performance, given the year, despite the fact that the nose needs some time to come into focus (considering the wine's toastiness). After a bit of exposure to the air, fresher, balsamic notes emerge, accompanied by a flavorsome, dynamic mouth.

● Brunello di Montalcino Lupi e Sirene '12	▼▼ 6
● Brunello di Montalcino Lupi e Sirene Ris. '10	♀♀ 6
● Rosso di Montalcino '11	♀♀ 5

Rocca delle Macìe

LOC. LE MACÌE, 45
53011 CASTELLINA IN CHIANTI [SI]
TEL. +39 0577/321
www.roccadellemacie.com

CELLAR SALES
PRE-BOOKED VISITS
ACCOMMODATION AND RESTAURANT SERVICE
ANNUAL PRODUCTION 2,000,000 bottles
HECTARES UNDER VINE 206.70
SUSTAINABLE WINERY

Sergio Zingarelli, president of the Consorzio Chianti Classico, owns a winery with a solid and reassuring quality that pervades his product portfolio. It goes without saying that he holds his top wines to a stricter standard. The idea is to use only Sangiovese for the winery's crus and to carry out aging in large wood facilitating a more precise and original expressiveness in the more important wines. At the same time he aims to maintain a consistent style in terms of balance and elegance. The 2014 Chianti Classico Gran Selezione Riserva di Fizzano offers up a lovely nose of sweet, fragrant fruit. In the mouth it expands softly, showing some contrast, while the finish is nice and long. The 2013 Chianti Classico Gran Selezione Sergio Zingarelli is right behind. It's a modern wine, with a more predictable aromatic profile, while in the mouth it shows texture and nice complexity. The 2015 Chianti Classico Famiglia Zingarelli hits the mark for its category, with a fresh nose and a sweet, well-paced palate.

● Chianti Cl. Gran Sel. Riserva di Fizzano '14	♛♛♛ 6
● Chianti Cl. Gran Sel. Sergio Zingarelli '13	♛♛ 8
● Chianti Cl. Famiglia Zingarelli '15	♛♛ 3
● Chianti Cl. Famiglia Zingarelli Ris. '14	♛♛ 4
● Morellino di Scansano Campomaccione '16	♛♛ 3
● Chianti Cl. Tenuta S. Alfonso '15	♛ 5
● Chianti Cl. Famiglia Zingarelli Ris. '09	♛♛♛ 3*
● Chianti Cl. Fizzano Ris. '10	♛♛♛ 5
● Chianti Cl. Gran Sel. Riserva di Fizzano '13	♛♛♛ 6
● Chianti Cl. Gran Sel. Sergio Zingarelli '11	♛♛♛ 8
● Chianti Cl. Famiglia Zingarelli Ris. '13	♛♛ 4
● Chianti Cl. Gran Sel. Sergio Zingarelli '12	♛♛ 8
● Roccato '13	♛♛ 6

Rocca di Castagnoli

LOC. CASTAGNOLI
53013 GAIOLE IN CHIANTI [SI]
TEL. +39 0577731004
www.roccadicastagnoli.com

CELLAR SALES
PRE-BOOKED VISITS
ACCOMMODATION AND RESTAURANT SERVICE
ANNUAL PRODUCTION 500,000 bottles
HECTARES UNDER VINE 132.00
SUSTAINABLE WINERY

Despite further recent developments and the sale of Tenuta di Capraia, Rocca di Castagnoli remains one of the most important wineries in Chianti Classico. It also includes Poggio Maestrino Spiaggevole, an estate in Maremma. Their wines maintain a consistent quality over time and often achieve the absolute excellence of the appellation in an unforced manner. Rocca di Castagnoli presents a well-crafted Chianti Classico with the 2015 vintage. Its aromas are well-defined, featuring lush fruit. In the mouth the wine proves succulent and generous; unfortunately its tannins are a bit stiff. Spices and semi-dried flowers distinguish the 2013 Chianti Classico Gran Selezione Stielle, a wine with an even palate and some density to it. The 2016 Morellino di Scansano Spiaggiole Poggio Maestrino is very pleasant, a bit peppery on the nose, fresh and relaxed on the palate.

● Chianti Cl. Gran Sel. Stielle '13	♛♛ 6
● Chianti Cl. Rocca di Castagnoli '15	♛♛ 3
● Morellino di Scansano Spiaggiole Poggio Maestrino '16	♛♛ 3
● Chianti Cl. Poggio ai Frati Ris. '14	♛ 4
● Chianti Cl. Capraia Ris. '07	♛♛♛ 4
● Chianti Cl. Poggio ai Frati Ris. '08	♛♛♛ 4
● Chianti Cl. Poggio ai Frati Ris. '06	♛♛♛ 4*
● Chianti Cl. Tenuta di Capraia Ris. '06	♛♛♛ 4*
● Chianti Cl. Tenuta di Capraia Ris. '05	♛♛♛ 4
● Chianti Cl. Poggio ai Frati Ris. '13	♛♛ 4
● Chianti Cl. Rocca di Castagnoli '14	♛♛ 3
● Chianti Cl. Tenuta di Capraia Ris. '13	♛♛ 5
● Le Pratola '12	♛♛ 6

★Rocca di Frassinello

LOC. GIUNCARICO
58023 GAVORRANO [GR]
TEL. +39 056688400
www.roccadifrassinello.it

CELLAR SALES
PRE-BOOKED VISITS
ACCOMMODATION
ANNUAL PRODUCTION 400,000 bottles
HECTARES UNDER VINE 90.00

The winery is located between of Gavorrano
and Roccastrada, in a part of Maremma that
borders Bolgheri to the north and Morellino
di Scansano to the south. Paolo Panerai
already produces wine in Chianti Classico
and in Sicily. He's the owner of this
520-hectare estate, (90 of which are
vineyards). Rows of Sangiovese and
Vermentino flank international varieties like
Cabernet (Franc and Sauvignon), Merlot,
Petit Verdot and Syrah, which are perfectly
acclimatized to the area. His wines exhibit
great structure and Mediterranean
undertones. The Rocca di Frassinello makes
up ground on the Baffo Nero in the fight for
Tre Bicchieri, bringing it to seven. A blend of
Sangiovese and smaller parts Merlot and
Cabernet Sauvignon, it doesn't stray far
from the producer's trademark style; it's
concentrated and mature aromatically, with
close-woven tannins softened by the use of
small wood for aging. The Baffo Nero, a
potent, Mediterranean Merlot, is cut from
the same cloth.

● Maremma Toscana	
Rocca di Frassinello '15	♟♟♟ 6
● Maremma Toscana Baffo Nero '15	♟♟ 8
○ Maremma Toscana Vermentino	
Son La Pia '16	♟♟ 3
● Maremma Toscana	
Le Sughere di Frassinello '15	♟ 4
● Maremma Toscana Ornello '15	♟ 3
● Baffo Nero '12	♟♟♟ 8
● Baffo Nero '11	♟♟♟ 8
● Baffo Nero '10	♟♟♟ 8
● Maremma Toscana Baffo Nero '14	♟♟♟ 8
● Maremma Toscana Baffo Nero '13	♟♟♟ 8
● Rocca di Frassinello '12	♟♟♟ 6
● Rocca di Frassinello '11	♟♟♟ 6

Rocca di Montemassi

LOC. PIAN DEL BICHI
FRAZ. MONTEMASSI
VIA SANT'ANNA
58036 ROCCASTRADA [GR]
TEL. +39 0564579700
www.roccadimontemassi.it

CELLAR SALES
PRE-BOOKED VISITS
ACCOMMODATION
ANNUAL PRODUCTION 480,000 bottles
HECTARES UNDER VINE 180.00
SUSTAINABLE WINERY

The Zonin group's Maremma estate spans
430 hectares between the Colline
Metallifere and the Tyrrhenian coast. It was
bought in 1999 to complete the group's
Tuscan estates, which also include Castello
d'Albola in Chianti Classico and Abbazia di
Monte Oliveto in San Gimignano. There are
165 hectares of vineyards planted with the
area's two traditional varieties, Sangiovese
and Vermentino, as well as common
international varieties: Cabernet Sauvignon
and Franc, Merlot, Petit Verdot and Viognier.
Much attention was paid to the territory
when they renovated the buildings, they are
set perfectly into their environment and are
completely eco-friendly. The Sassabruna is
a blend of Sangiovese, Syrah and Merlot
with multifaceted, nuanced aromas of red
flowers, pepper, blackberries and plums. In
the mouth the wine is vigorous, compact in
its tannic weave; it's just a bit lacking in
complexity. The Vermentino Calasole is
interesting, with its aromas of white flowers
and its fresh, succulent palate.

● Maremma Toscana Rosso	
Sassabruna '15	♟♟ 5
○ Maremma Toscana Vermentino	
Calasole '16	♟♟ 4
⊙ Maremma Toscana Rosato Syrosa '16	♟ 4
● Maremma Toscana Sangiovese	
Le Focaie '16	♟ 4
● Maremma Toscana	
Rocca di Montemassi '13	♟♟♟ 5
● Rocca di Montemassi '10	♟♟♟ 5
● Rocca di Montemassi '09	♟♟♟ 5
● Maremma Rocca di Montemassi '12	♟♟ 5
● Maremma Toscana Sangiovese	
Le Focaie '15	♟♟ 3
● Maremma Toscana Sassabruna '14	♟♟ 3
● Monteregio di Massa Marittima	
Sassabruna '11	♟♟ 3
● Rocca di Montemassi '11	♟♟ 5

Roccapesta

LOC. MACERETO, 9
50854 SCANSANO [GR]
TEL. +39 0564599252
www.roccapesta.it

CELLAR SALES
PRE-BOOKED VISITS
ANNUAL PRODUCTION 100,000 bottles
HECTARES UNDER VINE 18.50

Alberto Tanzini has built a benchmark winery in the Morellino di Scansano appellation based on simplicity and tradition. The varieties are local ones, their wines exhibit an austere style and good aging potential, with long maceration and aging in large wood. It is a balanced and clearly successful combination that produces wines that are increasingly charming and full of personality, vintage after vintage. The 2015 Morellino di Scansano Ribero went over extremely well, thanks to its charming fragrances, which alternate between fruit, notes of flint and aromatic herbs. In the mouth it expands with balance and elegance. The palate proves well-sustained and succulent, with a rising finish. Both the 2015 Morellino di Scansano and the 2014 Pugnitello hit the mark, with the former proving more pleasant and the latter exhibiting aromatic precision and richness of flavor. The 2013 Morellino di Scansano Calestaia Riserva is very small on the palate.

● Morellino di Scansano Ribeo '15	♥♥♥ 3*
● Morellino di Scansano '15	♥♥ 3
● Pugnitello '14	♥♥ 6
● Masca '15	♥ 2
● Morellino di Scansano Calestaia Ris. '13	♥ 8
● Morellino di Scansano Calestaia Ris. '11	♡♡♡ 5
● Morellino di Scansano Calestaia Ris. '10	♡♡♡ 5
● Morellino di Scansano Calestaia Ris. '09	♡♡♡ 5
● Morellino di Scansano Ris. '13	♡♡♡ 4*
● Morellino di Scansano '13	♡♡ 3*
● Morellino di Scansano Ribeo '14	♡♡ 3*
● Morellino di Scansano Ris. '11	♡♡ 4

★Ruffino

P.LE RUFFINO, 1
50065 PONTASSIEVE [FI]
TEL. +39 05583605
www.ruffino.it

CELLAR SALES
PRE-BOOKED VISITS
ANNUAL PRODUCTION 18,000,000 bottles
HECTARES UNDER VINE 550.00

Despite its American affiliation (Constellation Brands), this is a leading Italian winemaking brand. In Tuscany, it brings together wineries of such caliber as Greppone Mazzi in Montalcino, Santedame, Gretolaio, Montemasso and Poggio Casciano in Chianti Classico and La Solatia in Monteriggioni, in Siena. Their wines exhibit a modern style and are mostly aged in barriques, giving a remarkably consistent quality and in some cases reaching quite respectable heights. The 2012 Chianti Classico Gran Selezione Riserva Ducale Oro comes through with aromas of blackcurrant, blackberry and smoky notes, while the mouth proves generous and multifaceted; it's just a bit strained by oak at the end. The 2014 Chianti Classico Santedame shows nicc aromatic cleanness, and a well-paced, supple mouth. The 2013 Modus, a blend of Sangiovese, Merlot and Cabernet Sauvignon with aromas of vanilla and sugared almonds, is still a bit held back by the woods used for aging.

● Chianti Cl. Gran Sel. Riserva Ducale Oro '12	♥♥ 6
● Chianti Cl. Santedame '14	♥♥ 4
● Modus '13	♥ 5
● Brunello di Montalcino Greppone Mazzi '05	♡♡♡ 6
● Modus '04	♡♡♡ 5
● Brunello di Montalcino Greppone Mazzi '08	♡♡ 7
● Chianti Cl. Gran Sel. Riserva Ducale Oro '11	♡♡ 6
● Modus '12	♡♡ 5
● Modus '11	♡♡ 5
● Nobile di Montepulciano Lodola Nuova '11	♡♡ 4

Salcheto

VIA DI VILLA BIANCA, 15
53045 MONTEPULCIANO [SI]
TEL. +39 0578799031
www.salcheto.it

CELLAR SALES
PRE-BOOKED VISITS
ACCOMMODATION AND RESTAURANT SERVICE
ANNUAL PRODUCTION 300,000 bottles
HECTARES UNDER VINE 50.00
VITICULTURE METHOD Certified Organic
SUSTAINABLE WINERY

Salcheto is one of the best-organized and most successful wineries in Italy when it comes to environmental sustainability. The structure is a model of efficiency and innovation, leaving nothing to chance with even the vineyard run toward safeguarding the environment. A turning point came in the late 1990s under Michele Manelli's management, and he eventually became famous for his innovative ideas. Their style is very personal, making for interesting wines across the board. The 2013 Salco has intensity, energy and support. Its aromas, which are clear, mature and graceful, range from wild berries to pencil lead, tanned leather and exotic spices. The 2014 Nobile is on the same level, despite the difficult year. It's a fragrant wine, with good impact on the palate. We prefer it, though not by much, to the 2013 Riserva.

★Salvioni

P.ZZA CAVOUR, 19
53024 MONTALCINO [SI]
TEL. +39 0577848499
www.aziendasalvioni.com

PRE-BOOKED VISITS
RESTAURANT SERVICE
ANNUAL PRODUCTION 15,000 bottles
HECTARES UNDER VINE 4.00

David and Alessia Salvioni are members of the third generation to work full-time at La Cerbaiola. Established by their grandfather, Umberto, it was carried forward by their parents, Giulio and Mirella. Now it is one of the best-loved brands in Montalcino. From the start, it was inextricably linked to the moods of Sangiovese grapes cultivated on four hectares at Le Cerbaie Alte, on the northeastern slope at 400 meters, on limestone soil rich in stones and galestro. The vineyards, vitually all on one site, give rise to their two wines: the Brunello and the Rosso, classic but not old-fashioned. They are made with spontaneous fermentation and age in 2000-liter Slavonian oak. It's not the first time that the Brunello di Salvioni delights us in vintages that aren't so easy to interpret. The 2012 is emblematic in this sense, with its aromas of red fruit jelly, rose petals and a touch of confit. These also emerge on the palate, though without slowing its spirited pace and savoriness.

● Nobile di Montepulciano '14	♟♟♟ 4*
● Nobile di Montepulciano Salco '13	♟♟ 6
● Chianti Colli Senesi '16	♟♟ 2*
● Nobile di Montepulciano Ris. '13	♟♟ 5
● Rosso di Montepulciano '16	♟♟ 2*
○ Obvius Bianco '16	♟ 3
● Obvius Rosso '16	♟ 3
● Nobile di Montepulciano '10	♟♟♟ 4*
● Nobile di Montepulciano '97	♟♟♟ 3*
● Nobile di Montepulciano Salco '11	♟♟♟ 6
● Nobile di Montepulciano Salco '10	♟♟♟ 5
● Nobile di Montepulciano Salco Evoluzione '06	♟♟♟ 6
● Nobile di Montepulciano Salco Evoluzione '01	♟♟♟ 6

● Brunello di Montalcino '12	♟♟♟ 8
● Brunello di Montalcino '09	♟♟♟ 8
● Brunello di Montalcino '06	♟♟♟ 8
● Brunello di Montalcino '04	♟♟♟ 8
● Brunello di Montalcino '00	♟♟♟ 8
● Brunello di Montalcino '99	♟♟♟ 8
● Brunello di Montalcino '97	♟♟♟ 8
● Brunello di Montalcino '11	♟♟ 8
● Brunello di Montalcino '10	♟♟ 8
● Brunello di Montalcino '08	♟♟ 8
● Brunello di Montalcino '07	♟♟ 8
● Rosso di Montalcino '14	♟♟ 8
● Rosso di Montalcino '08	♟♟ 5

★San Felice

LOC. SAN FELICE
53019 CASTELNUOVO BERARDENGA [SI]
TEL. +39 05773991
www.agricolasanfelice.it

CELLAR SALES
PRE-BOOKED VISITS
ACCOMMODATION AND RESTAURANT SERVICE
ANNUAL PRODUCTION 900,000 bottles
HECTARES UNDER VINE 140.00

San Felice and the Chianti Classico
subzone of Castelnuovo Berardenga have
become inseparable. The winery belongs to
the insurance company, Allianz. Their wines
are strongly influenced by the terroir and
highlight intense, sunny aromas, as well as
a robust, complex structure across the
board. San Felice also owns the
Campogiovanni estate in Montalcino and
Perolla in Maremma. The 2013 Chianti
Classico Gran Selezione Poggio Rosso finds
its forte in the intensity of its aromas and
palate. The nose features assertive,
well-sustained fruit, rounded out by toasty
notes and hints of earth. In the mouth the
wine doesn't lack in flavor and proves
generous, with a tight tannic weave. The
2013 Vigorello is a multi-layered, historic
blend whose origins go back to 1968
(today, it's made with Pugnitello, Cabernet
Sauvignon, Merlot and Petit Verdot). It's a
vibrant and well-structured wine defined by
its bold tannins.

San Ferdinando

LOC. CIGGIANO
VIA DEL GARGAIOLO, 33
52041 CIVITELLA IN VAL DI CHIANA [AR]
TEL. +39 0575440355
www.sanferdinando.eu

CELLAR SALES
PRE-BOOKED VISITS
ACCOMMODATION
ANNUAL PRODUCTION 30,000 bottles
HECTARES UNDER VINE 10.00

There's no denying that in recent years the
territory around Arezzo has brought to light
many wineries. Not only big brands or local
names, small wineries with a strong artisan
nature have also been launched onto a new
path. San Ferdinando is one such winery
and it has become an essential part of Val
di Chiana winemaking. It is run by the
Grifoni family who make authentic wines
with native red and white Tuscan grapes.
The 2016 Vermentino amazes: it's a perfect
example of the cultivar grown in
non-coastal areas. The nose sees citrusy
aromas and sea salt, while the fresh, earthy
mouth shows great mineral character. The
2016 is delectable and young, all fruit and
pepper, while the Rosato is intriguing and
complex in its echoes of cellar.

● Vigorello '13	▼▼▼ 6
● Chianti Cl. Gran Sel. Poggio Rosso '13	▼▼ 5
● Chianti Cl. '13	♀♀♀ 3*
● Chianti Cl. Gran Sel. Il Grigio da San Felice '11	♀♀♀ 5
● Chianti Cl. Gran Sel. Il Grigio da San Felice '10	♀♀♀ 5
● Pugnitello '07	♀♀♀ 6
● Vigorello '10	♀♀♀ 6
● Vigorello '08	♀♀♀ 6
● Brunello di Montalcino Campogiovanni '09	♀♀ 6
● Chianti Cl. Gran Sel. Il Grigio da San Felice '13	♀♀ 5
● Chianti Cl. Il Grigio da San Felice Ris. '11	♀♀ 4
● Chianti Cl. Poggio Rosso Ris. '11	♀♀ 6

○ Vermentino '16	▼▼▼ 3*
● Chianti Podere Gamba '15	▼▼ 3
● Ciliegiolo '16	▼▼ 3
☉ Ciliegiolo Rosato '16	▼▼ 3
● Chianti Podere Gamba '14	♀♀ 2*
● Ciliegiolo '15	♀♀ 2*
● Ciliegiolo '12	♀♀ 2*
● Ciliegiolo '10	♀♀ 2*
● Pugnitello '13	♀♀ 3
● Sangiovese '10	♀♀ 3

★★Tenuta San Guido

FRAZ. BOLGHERI
LOC. LE CAPANNE, 27
57022 CASTAGNETO CARDUCCI [LI]
TEL. +39 0565762003
www.sassicaia.com

PRE-BOOKED VISITS
RESTAURANT SERVICE
ANNUAL PRODUCTION 780,000 bottles
HECTARES UNDER VINE 90.00

It is an undisputed Italian wine legend and one of the most prestigious brands in the wine world. In a nutshell, this is Sassicaia. Without the Incisa della Rocchetta family and Tenuta San Guido, the history of Bolgheri would have taken a much different turn. The vineyards are divided into different areas with mixed soils and exposures; some are near the sea, others are in the hills. They grow Cabernet Sauvignon and Franc, which coincidentally make up the historic Sassicaia grape blend. The 2014 Sassicaia put in one of the best performances of the DOC zone. It took a different approach to the difficult year, choosing not to surrender the qualities that best define it (at the expense of coming across as subtle in certain respects). The result is a red of incomparable beauty, with graceful texture and a penetrating palate that unfolds in flavor as if it were weightless. A true delight.

San Polo

LOC. PODERNOVI, 161
53024 MONTALCINO [SI]
TEL. +39 0577835101
www.poggiosanpolo.com

CELLAR SALES
PRE-BOOKED VISITS
ANNUAL PRODUCTION 150,000 bottles
HECTARES UNDER VINE 17.00

San Polo's 17 hectares in Podernovi lie on a kind of natural terrace overlooking the Sant'Antimo valley. This area forms the cornerstone of the winery, which was set up in Montalcino by the Allegrini family. Located in the southeast, it is an extremely steep area featuring a long winemaking tradition and calcareous-clay soil at altitudes skimming 450 meters. It is the perfect place for producing engaging and aromatic Sangiovese wines, whose style is refined with fermentation in concrete, and combination aging in barriques and 3000-liter Slavonia and Allier oak. San Polo's Sangioveses shine once again, especially the 2015 Rosso. Aromas of summer fruit, topsoil and fumé define the nose, while the mouth brings together maturity and flavor, making for a decidedly full-bodied palate (for the typology). The 2012 Brunello is still a bit bridled at this point, though just as charming in its woodland overtones.

● Bolgheri Sassicaia '14	♥♥♥ 8
● Guidalberto '15	♥♥ 6
● Le Difese '15	♥♥ 4
● Bolgheri Sassicaia '13	♀♀♀ 8
● Bolgheri Sassicaia '12	♀♀♀ 8
● Bolgheri Sassicaia '11	♀♀♀ 8
● Bolgheri Sassicaia '10	♀♀♀ 8
● Bolgheri Sassicaia '09	♀♀♀ 8
● Bolgheri Sassicaia '08	♀♀♀ 8
● Bolgheri Sassicaia '07	♀♀♀ 8
● Bolgheri Sassicaia '06	♀♀♀ 8
● Guidalberto '08	♀♀♀ 6
● Guidalberto '14	♀♀ 6
● Guidalberto '12	♀♀ 6
● Le Difese '13	♀♀ 4
● Le Difese '12	♀♀ 4

● Rosso di Montalcino '15	♥♥ 3*
● Brunello di Montalcino '12	♥♥ 6
● Brunello di Montalcino '11	♀♀ 6
● Brunello di Montalcino '10	♀♀ 6
● Brunello di Montalcino '09	♀♀ 6
● Brunello di Montalcino '08	♀♀ 6
● Brunello di Montalcino '07	♀♀ 6
● Brunello di Montalcino Ris. '10	♀♀ 7
● Brunello di Montalcino Ris. '06	♀♀ 7
● Rosso di Montalcino '13	♀♀ 3
● Rosso di Montalcino '12	♀♀ 3
● Rosso di Montalcino '11	♀♀ 3
● Rubio '10	♀♀ 2*

Sangervasio

LOC. SAN GERVASIO
VIA DEI CIPRESSI, 13
56036 PALAIA [PI]
TEL. +39 0587483360
www.sangervasio.com

CELLAR SALES
PRE-BOOKED VISITS
ACCOMMODATION AND RESTAURANT SERVICE
ANNUAL PRODUCTION 100,000 bottles
HECTARES UNDER VINE 22.00
VITICULTURE METHOD Certified Organic

San Gervasio is a 16th century town where you can stop the night and be surrounded by 400 hectares of land. In the mid-1990s, Luca Tommasini opted for organic farming management, renovating the old cellars, regrafting the old vineyards and buying new hectares of land. The result was a leap in wine quality. The main red grape varieties he grows are Sangiovese, Merlot and Cabernet Sauvignon, while the white grapes are Chardonnay, Sauvignon Blanc, Vermentino and Trebbiano. The 2013 Villa Le Torri, a monovarietal Cabernet Franc, is an intriguing wine with notes of medicinal herbs, roast peppers, red fruit and forest floor. The body proves solid, soft, fresh, with a long, gratifying finish. The 2013 Renai, made with 100% Merlot, offers up a vibrant aromatic profile featuring primarily cherry and raspberry, then spices. It's soft and streamlined in the mouth, and closes with length and fulfillment. The 2013 A Sirio, a monovarietal Sangiovese, is elegant aromatically, with a balanced, fresh body.

● Colli dell'Etruria Centrale Vin Santo Occhio di Pernice '16	♏♏ 5
○ Colli Etruria Vin Santo Recinaio '06	♏♏ 5
● I Renai '13	♏♏ 5
● Terre di Pisa Sangiovese A Sirio '13	♏♏ 4
● Villa Le Torri '13	♏♏ 4
● Cabernet Sauvignon '13	♏ 5
● Chianti '16	♏ 2
● Cabernet Sauvignon '11	♏♏ 5
○ Colli dell'Etruria Centrale Vin Santo Recinaio '05	♏♏ 5
● I Renai '11	♏♏ 5
● Terre di Pisa Sangervasio '11	♏♏ 4

Podere Sanlorenzo

POD. SANLORENZO, 280
53024 MONTALCINO [SI]
TEL. +39 3396070930
www.poderesanlorenzo.net

CELLAR SALES
PRE-BOOKED VISITS
ANNUAL PRODUCTION 18,000 bottles
HECTARES UNDER VINE 4.50

In 2003 Luciano Ciolfi transformed Podere Sanlorenzo into a bottling plant, thus completing the work carried out by his great-great grandfather, Renzo, grandfather, Bramante, and father, Paolo. He makes small amounts of wine with Sangiovese grapes cultivated on just over four hectares, in southwestern Montalcino at 500 meters, on the hilly ridge leading from the Civitella hill down to the Ombrone river and Maremma. The stony, galestro, and poor soil make for soberly powerful, supple and vigorous Brunellos, which are supported by long maceration and aging in 3000-liter Slavonian oak. Podere Sanlorenzo's compact selection continues to prove strong. The 2015 is a Rosso that's trying to be a Brunello for maturity of fruit and tannic vigor. And the 2012 Bramante is a commendable interpretation of the vintage, with its aromas of small black fruit, watermelon and cinnamon; it's a wine that manages to be both supple and austere.

● Brunello di Montalcino Bramante '12	♏♏ 6
● Rosso di Montalcino '15	♏♏ 3
● Brunello di Montalcino Bramante '07	♏♏♏ 6
● Brunello di Montalcino Bramante '07	♏♏♏ 8
● Brunello di Montalcino Bramante '11	♏♏ 6
● Brunello di Montalcino Bramante '10	♏♏ 6
● Brunello di Montalcino Bramante '09	♏♏ 6
● Brunello di Montalcino Bramante '08	♏♏ 6
● Brunello di Montalcino Bramante '04	♏♏ 6
● Rosso di Montalcino '14	♏♏ 3
● Rosso di Montalcino '13	♏♏ 3
● Rosso di Montalcino '11	♏♏ 3
● Rosso di Montalcino '10	♏♏ 3
● Rosso di Montalcino '09	♏♏ 3

Sant'Agnese

LOC. CAMPO ALLE FAVE, 1
57025 PIOMBINO [LI]
TEL. +39 0565277069
www.santagnesefarm.it

CELLAR SALES
PRE-BOOKED VISITS
ANNUAL PRODUCTION 25,000 bottles
HECTARES UNDER VINE 6.00
SUSTAINABLE WINERY

Paolo Gigli's passion for land and wine is beginning to deliver results, twenty years after his family bought at auction the farm in the hills overlooking the sea between Tuscany and Elba. The estate included abandoned land and buildings in need of renovation. Enthusiasm, research and hard work have led to the creation of a business that today produces quality wines. Truly impressive is how they manage this small, well-organized, family winery, where traditional Tuscan varieties grow happily alongside international ones, after finding their ideal habitat here. The 2010 Lo Spirito, a monovarietal Merlot, offers well-defined herbaceous notes of tomato leaf and grilled green peppers, the dark fruit. In the mouth it proves lively, with good acidity, balanced tannins and a dynamic, flavorsome finish. The 2016 Kalendamaia, made with 100% Vermentino, is pleasant, with citrusy aromas of peach and apricot. The body is balanced, pervasive, with a savory finish that delivers.

○ Kalendamaia '16	♈♈ 2*
● Spirto '10	♈♈ 5
⊙ A Rose is a Rose '16	♈ 2
○ L'Etrange '15	♈ 3
● I Fiori Blu '10	♈♈ 6
● Rubido '13	♈♈ 2*

Podere Sapaio

LOC. LO SCOPAIO, 212
57022 CASTAGNETO CARDUCCI [LI]
TEL. +39 0565765187
www.sapaio.it

CELLAR SALES
PRE-BOOKED VISITS
ANNUAL PRODUCTION 110,000 bottles
HECTARES UNDER VINE 25.00

Podere Sapaio was founded in 1999 by Massimo Piccini and is now one of the most important wineries in Bolgheri. Classic local varieties are cultivated on sandy and calcareous soil, the grapes are then fermented and aged in barriques. Their wines have a modern character; their precision is impeccable and young toasty notes are reabsorbed after some much-needed bottle maturation. The 2015 Sapaio (no longer in the Bolgheri appellation) has come out early, but leaves no doubt about its excellent quality. If anything, we're finding the winery's style to be more and more persuasive, such that, even a young wine like this manages to the avoid toasty abundances of the past in favor of perfect harmony and first-rate balance. In short, a bit more time in the bottle will make for a great red, certainly among the area's best.

● Sapaio '15	♈♈♈ 6
● Bolgheri Volpolo '15	♈♈ 5
● Bolgheri Rosso Sup. '13	♈♈♈ 7
● Bolgheri Rosso Sup. '12	♈♈♈ 7
● Bolgheri Rosso Sup. '11	♈♈♈ 7
● Bolgheri Sup. Sapaio '10	♈♈♈ 6
● Bolgheri Sup. Sapaio '09	♈♈♈ 6
● Bolgheri Sup. Sapaio '08	♈♈♈ 6
● Bolgheri Sup. Sapaio '07	♈♈♈ 6
● Bolgheri Sup. Sapaio '06	♈♈♈ 6
● Bolgheri Volpolo '13	♈♈ 5
● Bolgheri Volpolo '12	♈♈ 4
● Bolgheri Volpolo '11	♈♈ 4
● Bolgheri Volpolo '08	♈♈ 4
● Bolgheri Volpolo '07	♈♈ 4

Fattoria Sardi

FRAZ. MONTE SAN QUIRICO
VIA DELLA MAULINA, 747
55100 LUCCA
TEL. +39 0583341230
www.fattoriasardi.com

CELLAR SALES
PRE-BOOKED VISITS
ACCOMMODATION
ANNUAL PRODUCTION 120,000 bottles
HECTARES UNDER VINE 17.50
VITICULTURE METHOD Certified Organic

Fattoria Sardi is a place of rare beauty near Lucca, between the Apuan Alps, Apennines and Tyrrhenian Sea. The property lies between the Freddana and Serchio rivers. Downstream, the soil is silty, sandy and just a bit stony. As you go up into the hills, the soil becomes more compact and clayish with increased presence of stones. The mitigating effect of the sea is very clear. The owner has a bright, young approach and has opted for organic and biodynamic methods. The rosés have taken on a central role in the effort. The results are encouraging, and the area seems well-suited to the category. The 2016 Rosé is simpler and fresh, while the Le Cicale of the same year is absolutely commendable. It's made with Sangiovese and small quantities of white fermented and aged in wood. It offers up flowery aromas of wild herbs and wet earth. The mouth is clenched, slightly tannic, with excellent future prospects.

● Colline Lucchesi Vallebuia '16	▼▼ 3
⊙ Le Cicale '16	▼▼ 4
○ Pet Nat Frizzante '16	▼▼ 3
● Colline Lucchesi Sebastiano '14	▼ 5
⊙ Rosé '16	▼ 3
● Colline Lucchesi Merlot Sebastiano '12	▽▽ 3
● Colline Lucchesi Merlot Sebastiano '11	▽▽ 3
● Colline Lucchesi Rosso Sebastiano '13	▽▽ 5
● Colline Lucchesi Rosso Villa Sardi '11	▽▽ 2*
● Colline Lucchesi Rosso Villa Sardi '10	▽▽ 3
○ Colline Lucchesi Vermentino '14	▽▽ 3
● Fattoria Sardi Rosso '12	▽▽ 3
● Fattoria Sardi Rosso '11	▽▽ 3

Sator

FRAZ. POMAIA
VIA MACCHIA AL PINO
56040 SANTA LUCE [PI]
TEL. +39 050740529
www.satorwines.com

CELLAR SALES
PRE-BOOKED VISITS
ANNUAL PRODUCTION 50,000 bottles
HECTARES UNDER VINE 9.50

In the early 1900s, the great-grandfather of the current owners (Gianni and Roberta Moscardini) bought the first plots of land in Pomaia. Sator was set up in 2008, four generations and one century later. Here on the property they work in a modern way, in which they have built over the years a culture aimed at making great wines and at the same time respecting the environment. It's an eco-friendly winery: electricity is supplied by solar power and waste water is reused for the garden. The 2015 Ciliegiolo put in a good performance, with its vibrant nose of gamey, then fruity, hints, and scents of tanned leather. The mouth proves succulent, with well-integrated tannins and a pleasant freshness. The 2015 Operaundici comes through succulent, with a savory finish, while the nose sees fruity notes of cherries and aromatic herbs. The 2016 Vermentino is pleasant with good drinkability. Aromatically, the wine offers fruity hints of damson joined with more flowery overtones.

● Montescudaio Operaundici '15	▼▼ 6
● Sileno Ciliegiolo '15	▼▼ 3
○ Vermentino '16	▼▼ 2*
● Montescudaio Merlot Sileno '15	▼ 3
● Montescudaio Rosso '16	▼ 2
● Montescudaio Sangiovese Sileno '15	▼ 3
⊙ Rosato '16	▼ 2
⊙ Rosato '13	▽▽ 2*
● Sileno Merlot '11	▽▽ 4

Michele Satta

Loc. Vigna al Cavaliere, 61b
57022 Castagneto Carducci [LI]
Tel. +39 0565773041
www.michelesatta.com

CELLAR SALES
PRE-BOOKED VISITS
ANNUAL PRODUCTION 150,000 bottles
HECTARES UNDER VINE 20.00

This is undoubtedly one of the most
original wineries in Bolgheri. They make
interesting wines but with a few surprises.
Michele Satta is a great fan of Sangiovese
and took the chance to experiment with
this variety in an area where you wouldn't
normally find it. In addition, his wide range
of grapes includes classic Bolgheri
varieties. The winery was set up in the
1980s and they now have a well-
established wine style. However, it is never
static. The 2014 Bolgheri Superiore
Piastraia is excellent, with its enticing and
precise aromas. It's a surprising wine,
really, proving to be a generally
harmonious, focused red whose elegant
contours manage to gratify even without a
definite weight. The 2015 Bolgheri Rosso
features lush fruit, tannic support and
good body.

● Bolgheri Rosso '15	♥♥ 4
● Bolgheri Sup. Piastraia '14	♥♥ 6
● Bolgheri Rosso Piastraia '02	♥♥♥ 6
● Bolgheri Rosso Piastraia '01	♥♥♥ 6
○ Bolgheri Bianco Costa di Giulia '15	♥♥ 4
⊙ Bolgheri Rosato '13	♥♥ 2*
● Bolgheri Rosso '13	♥♥ 3
● Bolgheri Rosso '12	♥♥ 3
● Bolgheri Rosso '11	♥♥ 3
● Bolgheri Rosso Piastraia '12	♥♥ 5
● Bolgheri Rosso Piastraia '11	♥♥ 5
● Bolgheri Rosso Piastraia '10	♥♥ 5
● Bolgheri Rosso Sup. I Castagni '12	♥♥ 8
● Syrah '12	♥♥ 5

La Selva

Loc. San Donato
s.da prov.le 81 Osa, 7
58015 Orbetello [GR]
Tel. +39 0564884820
www.laselva.bio

CELLAR SALES
PRE-BOOKED VISITS
ACCOMMODATION
ANNUAL PRODUCTION 200,000 bottles
HECTARES UNDER VINE 32.00
VITICULTURE METHOD Certified Organic

From the start, Karl Egger focused on
organic farming, Maremma wines, and
appellations. These choices were made
almost 40 years ago and have led to a
dynamic winery where consistently quality
wines, at times achieving excellence, are
produced. Although their style favors
pleasant wines, they aren't lacking
complexity. The winemaking is unforced
and maintains the integrity of the grapes.
The 2016 Maremma Toscana Privo, a blend
of Sangiovese and Alicante, comes through
pleasantly fruity on the nose, striving for
enjoyability. The mouth is well-sustained,
fresh, and finishes with a nice note of
blackberry. The 2013 Pugnitello is in the
same stylistic vein, though sees more
vibrant aromas and a layered, fragrant
mouth. The Tins'vil is a simple-yet-
interesting sparkling wine made with
Sangiovese, while the rest of the selection
proved well-crafted.

● Maremma Toscana Privo '16	♥♥ 2*
● Pugnitello '13	♥♥ 5
○ Maremma Toscana Vermentino '16	♥ 2
● Morellino di Scansano '16	♥ 2
○ Tins'vil Brut	♥ 3
○ Bianco Toscano '14	♥♥ 2*
● Maremma Toscana Ciliegiolo '13	♥♥ 3
● Maremma Toscana Ciliegiolo '12	♥♥ 3
● Morellino di Scansano '15	♥♥ 2*
● Morellino di Scansano '12	♥♥ 2*
● Morellino di Scansano Colli dell'Uccellina Ris. '13	♥♥ 3
● Nudo Sangiovese '14	♥♥ 2*
● Pugnitello '11	♥♥ 5

Fattoria Selvapiana

Loc. Selvapiana, 43
50068 Rufina [FI]
Tel. +39 0558369848
www.selvapiana.it

CELLAR SALES
PRE-BOOKED VISITS
ANNUAL PRODUCTION 220,000 bottles
HECTARES UNDER VINE 60.00

This winery is owned by the Giuntini family and today it is run by Federico and Silvia. It is one of the most important in Chianti Rufina, thanks to the 60–hectare vineyard and a strong commitment to the territory. The vineyards are located mainly around the villa at the heart of the winery, just before the Apennines whose proximity guarantees cool summers and wide day-night temperature swings. They adopted organic management in 1990 and produce fresh, elegant wines, which in 1992 they began fermenting without selected yeasts. In the absence of the Bucerchiale, it's up to the Chianti Rufina to lead the winery's selection. It managed to land in our finals, but just missed the bullseye, featuring aromas of cherry, Mediterranean shrub, aromatic herbs and earthy nuances. The mouth is austere, savory, with good vigor. The 2013 Villa Petrognano is fragrant and close-focused.

● Chianti Rufina '15	▼▼ 2*
● Pomino Rosso Villa Petrognano '13	▼▼ 2*
● Fornace '13	▼ 5
● Chianti Rufina '14	♈♈ 2*
● Chianti Rufina '13	♈♈ 2*
● Chianti Rufina '12	♈♈ 2*
● Chianti Rufina '11	♈♈ 2*
● Chianti Rufina '10	♈♈ 2*
● Chianti Rufina Bucerchiale Ris. '13	♈♈ 5
● Chianti Rufina Bucerchiale Ris. '12	♈♈ 5
● Chianti Rufina Bucerchiale Ris. '11	♈♈ 5
● Chianti Rufina Bucerchiale Ris. '10	♈♈ 5
● Fornace '11	♈♈ 5
○ Vin Santo del Chianti Rufina '07	♈♈ 2*

Sensi

via Cerbaia, 107
51035 Lamporecchio [PT]
Tel. +39 057382910
www.sensivini.com

CELLAR SALES
PRE-BOOKED VISITS
ANNUAL PRODUCTION 2,000,000 bottles
HECTARES UNDER VINE 100.00

Massimo and Roberta are the fourth generation to work in winegrowing since the end of the 19th century. The new cellars in Lamporecchio are also the new operational headquarters, where wines are stored, prepared, and bottled across a surface area of about 5000 square meters. The grapes are cultivated at Tenuta del Poggio and Fattoria di Calappiano, in Chianti Colli Fiorentini. Both former Medici hunting lodges in the 1500s, they count between them a total of a hundred hectares of vineyards and olive groves. Several wines were presented for tasting. Among them, the 2016 Vinciano stood out, offering up nice aromas of ripe black fruit on the nose, with a mouth that's elegant and well-integrated in its fine-grained tannic weave. The Morellino Pretorio is no less pleasant, with an aromatic bouquet that stutters a bit but gives way to a succulent, dynamic mouth. The 2014 Riserva Dalcampo also did well, with its earthy, herbaceous nose and neat, precise palate.

● Bolgheri Sabbiato '15	▼▼ 5
● Chianti Dalcampo Ris. '14	▼▼ 3
● Chianti Vinciano Fattoria di Calappiano '16	▼▼ 4
● Lungarno Fattoria di Calappiano '15	▼▼ 7
● Morellino di Scansano Pretorio '16	▼▼ 3
● Testardo '15	▼▼ 4
● Brunello di Montalcino Boscoselvo '12	▼ 7
● Chianti Campoluce '16	▼ 2
● Mantello '15	▼ 4
● Ninfato '16	▼ 4
● Chianti Vinciano Fattoria di Calappiano Ris. '13	♈♈ 6
● Chianti Vinciano Fattoria di Calappiano Ris. '12	♈♈ 6

Serpaia

LOC. FONTEBLANDA
VIA GOLDONI, 15
58100 GROSSETO
TEL. +39 0461650129
www.serpaiamaremma.it

ANNUAL PRODUCTION 135,000 bottles
HECTARES UNDER VINE 30.00

With almost twenty years of experience in the area, the Endrizzi family's wines have achieved a reliable quality. Perhaps not unforgettably original, they are consistently well-made and offer up clear-cut and precise aromas and flavors. Aging is carried out in large wood and barriques, making for wines with more balance and finesse, which are characteristics enjoying a rich appreciation right now. The 2015 Morelllino di Scansano did quite well, with its fruity, sweet, vibrant aromatic impact, to which we can add a balanced, succulent mouth and a finish distinguished by a nice touch of iodine. The 2015 Serpaiolo, a blend of Merlot, Cabernet Sauvignon and Sangiovese aged in large barrels, is more layered and just as good. In time we'll see the wine demonstrate greater complexity, character and expressive finesse.

Serraiola

FRAZ. FRASSINE
LOC. SERRAIOLA
58025 MONTEROTONDO MARITTIMO [GR]
TEL. +39 0566910026
www.serraiola.it

CELLAR SALES
PRE-BOOKED VISITS
ANNUAL PRODUCTION 40,000 bottles
HECTARES UNDER VINE 12.00

This winery has belonged to the Lenzi family since the late 1960s and today Fiorella is at the helm. In recent years she has worked hard to achieve her goal of making quality wines. Fiorella runs a 12-hectare vineyard between the provinces of Grosseto and Livorno, in Monterotondo in Massa Marittima. Over time she has replanted it with the most suitable clones for this part of Maremma. Most of the vine rows host red grapes, Sangiovese and Merlot, while the whites include Trebbiano, Malvasia, Vermentino, Chardonnay and Sauvignon. The 2015 Lentisco did well during out tastings. It's made with Sangiovese grapes planted in the 1960s, and offers up aromas of spice and flowery notes on the nose. In the mouth it's flavorsome, close-woven and solid. The Campo Montecristo, a monovarietal Merlot, is no less interesting, proving meaty, pervasive and soft. In terms of their whites, it's worth mentioning their Violina, a wine with good tanginess and freshness.

● Morellino di Scansano '15	♀♀ 3
● Serpaiolo '15	♀♀ 3
● Morellino di Scansano '14	♀♀ 2*
● Morellino di Scansano '13	♀♀ 2*
● Morellino di Scansano '12	♀♀ 2*
● Morellino di Scansano Dono Ris. '11	♀♀ 3
● Serpaiolo '14	♀♀ 2*

● Campo Montecristo '15	♀♀ 5
● Lentisco '15	♀♀ 3
○ Maremma Toscana Bianco Violina '16	♀♀ 3
○ Serrabacio '16	♀ 3
● Shiraz '15	♀ 4
○ Vermentino '16	♀ 3
● Campo Montecristo '14	♀♀ 5
● Campo Montecristo '13	♀♀ 5
● Lentisco '14	♀♀ 3
● Monteregio di Massa Marittima Lentisco '11	♀♀ 3
● Monteregio Massa Marittima Lentisco '13	♀♀ 3
● Shiraz '13	♀♀ 3

Sesti - Castello di Argiano

LAZ. SANT'ANGELO IN COLLE
LOC. CASTELLO DI ARGIANO
53024 MONTALCINO [SI]
TEL. +39 0577843921
www.sestiwine.com

CELLAR SALES
PRE-BOOKED VISITS
ANNUAL PRODUCTION 61,000 bottles
HECTARES UNDER VINE 9.00

An oasis of peace awaits travelers and wine drinkers at Castello di Argiano. Giuseppe and Elisa Sesti set up their sanctuary and laboratory here on this ancient Etruscan settlement surrounded by woods, on the southwestern border of Montalcino. Sea breezes and sandy-tuff soil makes it ideal for producing sunny but graceful Brunellos with a sublime majestic expression. Winemaking procedures reflect the producers' philosophical and humanistic inspiration, and focus on biodynamics, energy flows and astronomical cycles. The Rosso once again stands out as the best of the lot. It is original, to say the least, in its Mediterranean atmosphere of shrubs, chestnut honey and plowed earth. The 2015 unfolds on the palate with breadth and verve, finishing on what almost seem like whiffs of sea salt. The 2012 Brunello is warmer, but also captivating.

Rosso di Montalcino '15	♟♟ 4
Brunello di Montalcino '12	♟♟ 6
Brunello di Montalcino '06	♟♟♟ 6
Brunello di Montalcino Phenomena Ris. '07	♟♟♟ 8
Brunello di Montalcino Phenomena Ris. '01	♟♟♟ 8
Brunello di Montalcino Phenomena Ris. '04	♟♟♟ 8
Brunello di Montalcino '11	♟♟ 6
Brunello di Montalcino '10	♟♟ 6
Brunello di Montalcino Phenomena Ris. '10	♟♟ 8
Rosato '14	♟♟ 2*
Rosso di Montalcino '14	♟♟ 4
Rosso di Montalcino '13	♟♟ 4
Sauvignon '15	♟♟ 3

Tenuta Sette Ponti

VIA SETTE PONTI, 71
52029 CASTIGLION FIBOCCHI [AR]
TEL. +39 0575477857
www.tenutasetteponti.it

CELLAR SALES
PRE-BOOKED VISITS
ACCOMMODATION
ANNUAL PRODUCTION 225,000 bottles
HECTARES UNDER VINE 55.00
SUSTAINABLE WINERY

The current name was given to this historic estate by Antonio Moretti, a businessman in the fashion sector. He wanted to pay homage to the Sette Ponti road that connects the two banks of the river Arno, between Florence and Arezzo. When he began running the winery he focused primarily on the grapes, first transforming the vineyards then modernizing the cellar. Within a few years, Moretti bought other wineries in Bolgheri, Maremma and Sicily. He combines a great passion for the land and wine with respect for the environment and tradition. His wines display great personality. The 2015 Oreno, a blend of Merlot, Cabernet Sauvignon and Petit Verdot, captures a Tre Bicchieri, with its elegant and complex aromatic profile featuring overtones of wood berries and aromatic herbs. Then toasty, chocolatey accents, and in the mouth it shows consistence and force, but also softness. The finish is long and gratifying. The Crognolo, a blend of Sangiovese, Merlot and Cabernet Sauvignon, also came through in spades.

● Oreno '15	♟♟♟ 8
● Crognolo '15	♟♟ 5
● Chianti V. di Pallino Ris. '14	♟♟ 3
● Poggio al Lupo '15	♟♟ 5
● Morellino di Scansano Poggio al Lupo '15	♟ 2
● Oreno '12	♟♟♟ 7
● Oreno '11	♟♟♟ 7
● Oreno '10	♟♟♟ 7
● Oreno '09	♟♟♟ 7
● Oreno '05	♟♟♟ 7
● Valdarno di Sopra V. dell'Impero '13	♟♟♟ 8
● Oreno '13	♟♟ 8

Streda Belvedere

VIA STREDA, 46
50059 VINCI [FI]
TEL. +39 0571729195
www.streda.it

CELLAR SALES
PRE-BOOKED VISITS
ACCOMMODATION
ANNUAL PRODUCTION 10,000 bottles
HECTARES UNDER VINE 45.00

The Lenzi family's winery is now owned by Claudio, who took over from his father, Roberto. Montalbano is a great winemaking region and the estate enjoys a particularly favorable microclimate, thanks to the Streda lake, not far from the thousand-year-old village it was named after. According to historic documents, Leonardo da Vinci's father, Ser Piero, owned a vineyard in this area. A winning decision to use international varieties, alongside Sangiovese, has led to positive results. The 2015 Drufo, a monovarietal Syrah, has an enticing, pleasant nose, offering up black fruit, like blueberries and blackcurrant, as well as light, spicy hints of pepper and cinnamon. The mouth is solid, enticing, full and balanced, with a rising finish. The 2015 Casanova, made with Sangiovese and smaller parts Merlot and Syrah, sees notes of peppers, cherry, herbaceous hints and sage. In the mouth it's rich, showing good weight, fine-grained tannins and appetizing freshness.

● Casanova '15	♟♟ 3
● Drufo '15	♟♟ 6
● Toiano Merlot '16	♟♟ 4
● Chianti '16	♟ 2
○ Collinare Chardonnay '16	♟ 3
● Casanova '04	♙♙ 2
● Casanova '03	♙♙ 2
○ Chardonnay '11	♙♙ 3
● Chianti '04	♙♙ 2
● Chianti '02	♙♙ 2
● Duccio di Streda Rosso '07	♙♙ 2*
● Merlot di Streda Toiano '04	♙♙ 3
● Syrah '07	♙♙ 4
● Syrah '06	♙♙ 5

Talenti

FRAZ. SANT'ANGELO IN COLLE
LOC. PIAN DI CONTE
53020 MONTALCINO [SI]
TEL. +39 0577844064
www.talentimontalcino.it

CELLAR SALES
PRE-BOOKED VISITS
ANNUAL PRODUCTION 100,000 bottles
HECTARES UNDER VINE 21.00

Talenti's broad range of wines is made with grapes cultivated on twenty hectares of vineyards, divided up into at least seven different plots. Pian del Conte, the historic southwestern part of Montalcino, is just a stone's throw from Sant'Angelo in Colle. It a natural terrace on the Orcia river, at altitudes ranging from 200 to 400 meters above sea level, with a mixed soil of clay, limestone and sea sand. Pierluigi came here from Romagna in 1980 to become a Brunello producer. Today, his grandson Riccardo has taken up the challenge of producing stylish wines, which he ages in combination of mid-sized casks and medium-sized oak. The 2015 Rosso is a snapshot of the Talenti family's achievements: multifaceted aromas of damson, swiss chard and spices also colo a light, jolly palate. The 2012 Brunello see added warmth, with its woodland and river atmospheres; the mid-palate seems to be missing a bit of vigor.

● Brunello di Montalcino '12	♙♙
● Rosso di Montalcino '15	♙♙
● Brunello di Montalcino '04	♙♙♙
● Brunello di Montalcino Ris. '99	♙♙♙
● Brunello di Montalcino Trentennale '11	♙♙♙
● Brunello di Montalcino V. del Paretaio Ris. '01	♙♙♙
● Brunello di Montalcino '10	♙♙
● Brunello di Montalcino '09	♙♙
● Brunello di Montalcino '08	♙♙
● Brunello di Montalcino Pian di Conte Ris. '10	♙♙
● Rosso di Montalcino '14	♙♙
● Rosso di Montalcino '12	♙♙
● Rosso di Montalcino '11	♙♙
● Rosso di Montalcino '09	♙♙

Fattoria della Talosa

VIA TALOSA, 8
53045 MONTEPULCIANO [SI]
TEL. +39 0578758277
www.talosa.it

CELLAR SALES
PRE-BOOKED VISITS
ANNUAL PRODUCTION 100,000 bottles
HECTARES UNDER VINE 32.00

This is one of the most important and uncommonly beautiful wineries in Montepulciano, with a long winemaking tradition. The rooms forming the oldest part of the cellar extend underground beneath two historic buildings, right in the center of Montepulciano. This serves to demonstrate just how important this winery and its wines are to the town. Today, Talosa belongs to Angelo Jacorossi, who produces wines with character and excellent aging potential. We found the 2013 Nobile Filai Lunghi to be excellent. It's made with Sangiovese grapes from Pietrose, grown at altitudes up to 400 meters. It's then aged in containers of various sizes, from large barrels to barrique. On the nose it offers marine and iodine scents, as well as delicious red fruit. There are some toasty notes, but those will be reabsorbed over time. The other wines all proved first-rate.

Nobile di Montepulciano Filai Lunghi '13	🏆🏆	5
Nobile di Montepulciano Ris. '13	🏆🏆	4
● Rosso di Montepulciano '16	🏆🏆	2*
Nobile di Montepulciano '14	🏆	4
Nobile di Montepulciano '13	🏆🏆	4
Nobile di Montepulciano '11	🏆🏆	4
Nobile di Montepulciano '10	🏆🏆	3
Nobile di Montepulciano '08	🏆🏆	3
Nobile di Montepulciano Filai Lunghi '11	🏆🏆	5
Nobile di Montepulciano Filai Lunghi '07	🏆🏆	5
Nobile di Montepulciano Ris. '10	🏆🏆	4
Nobile di Montepulciano Ris. '07	🏆🏆	4
Vin Santo di Montepulciano Ris. '95	🏆🏆	8

★Tenimenti Luigi d'Alessandro

VIA MANZANO, 15
52042 CORTONA [AR]
TEL. +39 0575618667
www.tenimentidalessandro.it

CELLAR SALES
PRE-BOOKED VISITS
ACCOMMODATION AND RESTAURANT SERVICE
ANNUAL PRODUCTION 130,000 bottles
HECTARES UNDER VINE 37.00
VITICULTURE METHOD Certified Organic

Tenimenti D'Alessandro is many things, a resort and restaurant for enjoying traditional local food, a shop that sells local products, a site for visiting historic buildings. But it's foremost a farm, today run by the Calabresi family. Certified organic in 2016, the first Syrah vineyards were planted in the 1960s and the variety went on to become a characteristic feature in Cortona. Two wines reached the finals, both made with Syrah. The 2012 Vecchie Vigne has close-focused aromas on the nose, with precise, fruity overtones of cherry and blackcurrant, mineral notes and herbaceous accents. The body is well-structured, with fine-grained and well-integrated tannins, as well as good acidity. The finish is succulent and warm. The 2012 Migliara has a spicy bouquet with hints of pepper and juniper, accents of blackberry jam, and fresh, minty notes. In the mouth it shows a lot of body, and isn't easy to read. The 2015 Bosco is fresh and vibrant on the nose, with a pleasant and long palate.

● Cortona Syrah Migliara '12	🏆🏆	8
● Cortona Syrah V. V. '13	🏆🏆	5
● Cortona Syrah Borgo '15	🏆🏆	3
● Cortona Syrah Il Bosco '13	🏆🏆	6
○ Bianco del Borgo '16	🏆	3
○ Fontarca '15	🏆	5
● Cortona Il Bosco '09	🏆🏆🏆	6
● Cortona Il Bosco '06	🏆🏆🏆	6
● Cortona Il Bosco '04	🏆🏆🏆	6
● Cortona Il Bosco '03	🏆🏆🏆	5
● Cortona Il Bosco '01	🏆🏆🏆	6
● Cortona Syrah Il Bosco '12	🏆🏆🏆	6
● Cortona Syrah Migliara '08	🏆🏆🏆	8
● Cortona Syrah Migliara '07	🏆🏆🏆	8

Tenuta di Sesta

FRAZ. CASTELNUOVO DELL'ABATE
LOC. SESTA
53024 MONTALCINO [SI]
TEL. +39 0577835612
www.tenutadisesta.it

CELLAR SALES
PRE-BOOKED VISITS
ANNUAL PRODUCTION 150,000 bottles
HECTARES UNDER VINE 30.00

Not many know that one of the most esteemed crus on the southern slope of Montalcino is named after an old sign on the road from Roselle to Chiusi. The Ciacci family set up their estate in the 1960s and christened it "Sexta". Today it is run by Andrea and Francesca, under expert supervision from their father, Giovanni. Thirty hectares of vineyards lie at 350 meters of altitude, on soil rich in stones and limestone (galestro and alberese), with traces of clay and iron. This varied soil is summed up in the reductive and angular expressivity of their Brunello wines, which are aged for long periods in 3000-liter oak. Tenuta di Sesta's most recent selection demonstrates real growth. The 2011 Riserva affirms its status as the producer's flagship, with its taut, lean body and aromas of yellow fruit, citron and ginger; but the 2015 Rosso also does well, showing confidence and measure with its flowery and earthy atmosphere.

● Brunello di Montalcino Ris. '11	♀♀	7
● Rosso di Montalcino '15	♀♀	3*
● Brunello di Montalcino '12	♀	5
● Brunello di Montalcino Ris. '10	♀♀♀	7
● Brunello di Montalcino '10	♀♀	5
● Brunello di Montalcino '09	♀♀	5
● Brunello di Montalcino '08	♀♀	5
● Brunello di Montalcino Ris. '09	♀♀	7
● Brunello di Montalcino Ris. '07	♀♀	7
● Poggio d'Arna '11	♀♀	2*
● Poggio d'Arna '10	♀♀	2*
● Rosso di Montalcino '13	♀♀	3
● Rosso di Montalcino '11	♀♀	3

Tenute Palagetto

VIA MONTEOLIVETO, 46
53037 SAN GIMIGNANO [SI]
TEL. +39 0577943090
www.palagetto.it

CELLAR SALES
PRE-BOOKED VISITS
ACCOMMODATION
ANNUAL PRODUCTION 250,000 bottles
HECTARES UNDER VINE 44.00

This is the heart of the multiple estates belonging to the Niccolai family, who come from San Gimignano. Luano was an industrialist, but he fell in love with the nature and countryside here. His passion for the land was inherited from his father and father-in-law, who were both cellarmen. Today, his daughter Sabrina continues the work he began those years ago. The Niccolai estates are divided between Podere Bellarina in Montalcino and Pian de' Cerri in Montecucco. The two Vernaccias did quite well. The 2013 Riserva surprised with its citrusy notes and spicy overtones, which give way to a solid, full body with savory and complex flavor. The 2015 Vent'anni also proves pleasant. Aromatic herbs, like sage and basil, prevail, along with light fruit, and the finish delivers with elegant aftertaste. The other wines followed suite, displaying pleasant finesse and an elegant style.

○ Vernaccia di S. Gimignano Ris. '13	♀♀	3
○ Vernaccia di S. Gimignano Vent'anni '15	♀♀	3
● Chianti Colli Senesi '15	♀	2
● Chianti Colli Senesi I'Terzo '15	♀	2
○ Niccolò '16	♀	3
● Sbagliato '16	♀	3
○ Vernaccia di S. Gimignano '16	♀	2
○ Vernaccia di S. Gimignano V. Santa Chiara '16	♀	2
○ Sauvignon '15	♀♀	3
○ Vernaccia di S. Gimignano '15	♀♀	2
○ Vernaccia di S. Gimignano Ris. '14	♀♀	3
○ Vernaccia di S. Gimignano V. Santa Chiara '14	♀♀	2
○ Vernaccia di S. Gimignano V. Santa Chiara '13	♀♀	2

Terenzi

ɪᴄ. Montedonico
3054 Scansano [GR]
ᴛ. +39 0564599601
ww.terenzi.eu

CELLAR SALES
PRE-BOOKED VISITS
ACCOMMODATION
ANNUAL PRODUCTION 350,000 bottles
HECTARES UNDER VINE 60.00

he Terenzi family's winery has a short but
tense history. After only ten years they are
ubbing shoulders with the best producers
Morellino di Scansano, and their wines
re spot-on, vintage after vintage. The wine
uality at the base of their production
yramid is consistent, while their finer
ines have a clear-cut style with balance,
egance, and contemporary interpretation
the territory. It is a successful
ombination that has become a model for
e whole area. Once again, it's the
orellino di Scansano Madrechiesa Riserva
emerge confidently. It's a wine that has
anaged to become a veritable benchmark
r the entire DOC zone, exhibiting a
fined, persuasive style that, even in the
014 version, delivers for its aromatic
ecision, balance of flavor and character.
e 2016 Morellino di Scansano proves
licious; it's certainly among the best of
vintage.

Morellino di Scansano Madrechiesa Ris. '14	♟♟♟ 5
Morellino di Scansano '16	♟♟ 3*
Maremma Toscana Vermentino Balbino '16	♟♟ 3
Morellino di Scansano Purosangue Ris. '14	♟♟ 4
Francesca Romana '14	♟ 5
Maremma Toscana Bramaluce '15	♟ 3
Petit Manseng Passito '14	♟ 5
Morellino di Scansano Madrechiesa Ris. '13	� 5
Morellino di Scansano Madrechiesa Ris. '12	♟♟♟ 5
Morellino di Scansano Madrechiesa Ris. '11	♟♟♟ 5

Terre del Marchesato

Fʀᴀᴢ. Bolgheri
ʟᴏᴄ. Sant'Uberto, 164
57022 Castagneto Carducci [LI]
Tᴇʟ. +39 0565749752
www.terredelmarchesato.com

CELLAR SALES
PRE-BOOKED VISITS
ACCOMMODATION
ANNUAL PRODUCTION 80,000 bottles
HECTARES UNDER VINE 15.00

Emilio Fuselli founded Terre del Marchesato
years back, when he moved to Bolgheri
from the Marche to farm land formerly
belonging to the Incisa della Rocchetta
Marquises. His grandson Maurizio must be
given credit for transforming the estate into
a specialized winery. For some years now,
the wines released under this brand have
found their own style and gained a firm
position in the Bolgheri appellation. The
2014 Marchesale is a wine that needs to
be read while looking to the future, a
consequence of the complicated vintage,
which took away a bit of structure and
maturity; in short, it's still looking to come
into its own. The aromas brought by the
use of wood are still at the foreground, and
crowd out the fruit, which is lovely, by the
way. The mouth has a similar quality to it,
and is most surely in need of greater
integration. The Aldone of the same year is
also dark and toasty.

● Aldone '14	♟♟ 7
● Marchesale '14	♟♟ 6
○ Emilio Primo Bianco '16	♟ 3
● Inedito '16	♟ 2
● Tarabuso '14	♟ 5
● Aldone '13	♟♟ 7
● Bolgheri Rosso Emilio I '13	♟♟ 3
● Marchesale '13	♟♟ 6
● Marchesale '12	♟♟ 7
○ Nobilis '13	♟♟ 5
○ Nobilis '11	♟♟ 5
○ Papeo '15	♟♟ 4
○ Papeo '13	♟♟ 6
● Tarabuso '12	♟♟ 6

Terre Nere

LOC. CASTELNUOVO DELL'ABATE
53024 MONTALCINO [SI]
TEL. +39 3358107743
www.terreneremontalcino.it

CELLAR SALES
PRE-BOOKED VISITS
ACCOMMODATION
ANNUAL PRODUCTION 50,000 bottles
HECTARES UNDER VINE 10.00

When it rains, the stony soil on the southeastern slope of Montalcino, mixed with grayish galestro, turns almost black. This explains the name Pasquale Vallone chose for his winery at the start of the 1990s. He runs the estate with the help of his brother, Gaetano, his wife, Piera, and his children, Francesca and Federico. Ten hectares of vineyards in Castelnuovo dell'Abate overlook the Orcia river, which acts as a thermostat and determines the multi-faceted character of the Sangiovese grapes that go into making Brunello. Their wines mostly age in 3000-5000-liter Slavonian oak, underscoring their traditional but not backward-looking style. This character is well illustrated by the pair of Brunellos that came up for tasting, with aromas of black cherry, licorice and black olives emerging and a finish that's a bit more hurried than expected. The 2012 is distinctive for its general sea saltiness. We also find Mediterranean and woodland charm in the 2011 Riserva.

● Brunello di Montalcino '12	▼▼	5
● Brunello di Montalcino Ris. '11	▼▼	6
● Rosso di Montalcino '15	▼	3
● Brunello di Montalcino '11	♀♀	5
● Brunello di Montalcino '10	♀♀	5
● Brunello di Montalcino '09	♀♀	5
● Brunello di Montalcino Ris. '10	♀♀	6

Teruzzi & Puthod

LOC. CASALE, 19
53037 SAN GIMIGNANO [SI]
TEL. +39 0577940143
www.teruzzieputhod.it

CELLAR SALES
PRE-BOOKED VISITS
ANNUAL PRODUCTION 1,000,000 bottles
HECTARES UNDER VINE 94.00

In 1974, Enrico Teruzzi and his wife, Carmen Puthod, left Milan to move to San Gimignano and take up vine growing. Their passion for wine, along with respect for tradition and the territory, were skillfully combined to produce innovations aimed at improving the winery's quality and image. In 2013 it was taken over by a multinational corporation which invested in vineyard renewal and new purchases. Teruzzi & Puthod became a private winery, with the largest vineyard surface area planted with Vernaccia. At the end of 2016 it was bought by Terra Moretti, a holding company owned by a family from Franciacorta. Vernaccia Sant'Elena's new selection is just extraordinary, with a nose characterized by flowery hints, delicate fruit, Mediterranean shrub and bay leaves. The mouth is defined by its tangy, bright acidity, with a crisp, lustrous finish. The 2015 Terre di Tufi, a blend of Trebbiano and Vernaccia, offers up fragrances of white flowers and fruit, made complex by faintly spicy hints. The mouth is both saline and appetizing.

○ Vernaccia di S. Gimignano Sant'Elena '16	▼▼
○ Terre di Tufi '15	▼▼
○ Vernaccia di S. Gimignano '16	▼▼
○ Carmen Puthod '15	▼
● Peperino '14	▼
○ Vernaccia di S. Gimignano Ris. '15	▼
○ Carmen Puthod '14	♀♀
● Peperino '12	♀♀
○ Vernaccia di S. Gimignano '15	♀♀
○ Vernaccia di S. Gimignano '14	♀♀
○ Vernaccia di S. Gimignano '13	♀♀
○ Vernaccia di S. Gimignano '12	♀♀
○ Vernaccia di S. Gimignano '11	♀♀
○ Vernaccia di S. Gimignano Ris. '11	♀♀
○ Vernaccia di S. Gimignano Ris. '10	♀♀

Tiezzi

LOC. PODERE SOCCORSO
53024 MONTALCINO [SI]
TEL. +39 0577848187
www.tiezzivini.it

CELLAR SALES
PRE-BOOKED VISITS
ACCOMMODATION
ANNUAL PRODUCTION 23,000 bottles
HECTARES UNDER VINE 5.50

Enzo Tiezzi, a respected consultant, agronomist and winemaker in Montalcino, decided to set up his own winery in the 1980s. First he took over the Cerrino and Sigaleta farms in the northeast, then the splendid Vigna Soccorso, which is named after the neighboring sanctuary just outside the historic center. The vineyard is situated at 500 meters above sea level and was the first cru in the appellation to grow bush-trained vines. The cellar contains wooden vats used for fermentation and 3000-4000-liter Slavonian oak for aging Brunellos. The Riserva is made only in the best vintages. With great pleasure, we tasted Tiezzi's most recent creations, starting with two excellent Vigna Soccorsos. The 2012 deceives, going all on in sweetness and salinity. The 2011 Riserva has greater tannic support, and a nice aromatic dynamism. The 2015 Rosso Poggio Corrino is actually superior in terms of energy and personality.

Rosso di Montalcino Poggio Cerrino '15	♥♥ 3*
Brunello di Montalcino V. Soccorso '12	♥♥ 6
Brunello di Montalcino V. Soccorso Ris. '11	♥♥ 6
Brunello di Montalcino Poggio Cerrino '12	♥ 5
Brunello di Montalcino Poggio Cerrino '09	♥♥ 5
Brunello di Montalcino V. del Soccorso '08	♥♥ 6
Brunello di Montalcino V. del Soccorso '06	♥♥ 6
Brunello di Montalcino V. Soccorso '10	♥♥ 6
Brunello di Montalcino V. Soccorso '09	♥♥ 6
Brunello di Montalcino V. Soccorso Ris. '08	♥♥ 6

Tolaini

LOC. VALLENUOVA
S.DA PROV.LE 9 DI PIEVASCIATA, 28
53019 CASTELNUOVO BERARDENGA [SI]
TEL. +39 0577356972
www.tolaini.it

CELLAR SALES
PRE-BOOKED VISITS
ANNUAL PRODUCTION 300,000 bottles
HECTARES UNDER VINE 50.00
SUSTAINABLE WINERY

Pierluigi Tolaini's winery is one of the most unique in Chianti Classico, owing to manic care in high-density vineyards and work in the cellar that leaves nothing to chance. Their wines are well-made, especially those from international varieties. He has also come a long way with his interpretations of Chianti Classico. They are all quality wines with a stylish taste component and an excellent, complex make-up. The 2015 Chianti Classico Valle Nuova shows evenness and fragrance, featuring fruity aromas and the occasional hint of charred oak, while in the mouth it proves succulent, relaxed and not lacking in depth. But it's the Al Passo 2014, a blend of Merlot and Sangiovese, that stands out from the rest by virtue of its fresh and spicy nose, and a generous, soft palate made dynamic by its nuances. The 2014 Valdisanti, a blend of Sangiovese, Cabernet Sauvignon and Cabernet Franc, is a bit more straining in the mouth. The influence of wood dominates aromatically.

● Al Passo '14	♥♥♥ 4*
● Chianti Cl. Valle Nuova '15	♥♥ 5
● Valdisanti '14	♥ 5
● Picconero '10	♥♥♥ 8
● Picconero '09	♥♥♥ 8
● Valdisanti '08	♥♥♥ 8
● Al Passo '12	♥♥ 4
● Al Passo '07	♥♥ 4
● Chianti Cl. Gran Sel. '11	♥♥ 5
● Chianti Cl. Montebello Vign. n.7 Ris. '10	♥♥ 6
● Chianti Cl. Ris. '10	♥♥ 5
● Chianti Cl. Ris. '08	♥♥ 5
● Valdisanti '12	♥♥ 5
● Valdisanti '11	♥♥ 5

Torre a Cona

LOC. SAN DONATO IN COLLINA
50067 RIGNANO SULL'ARNO [FI]
TEL. +39 055699000
www.torreacona.com

CELLAR SALES
PRE-BOOKED VISITS
ACCOMMODATION
ANNUAL PRODUCTION 75,000 bottles
HECTARES UNDER VINE 14.50

The Rossi di Montelera Counts bought the property in 1937 and built their villa on the remains of an old Medieval settlement. Slightly off the beaten track, this is one of the most charming and elegant estates in Tuscany today. In recent years, a new generation has joined the winery and expanded both the accommodation and quality winegrowing businesses. Sangiovese takes up the lion's share of the 14 hectares of vineyards, but there is still room for white grapes such as Vermentino, Trebbiano Toscano, Malvasia del Chianti, as well as Merlot which is used to make a monovarietal wine. The selection presented is more limited than usual, but still of extremely high quality. The 2011 Fonti and Lecceta shine. The latter, a Vin Santo, is vibrant and multifaceted on the nose, while in the mouth it proves generous in its hints of dried fruit, with great length and persistence. The 2015 Chianti is no less interesting. It's a fragrant and fruity wine, both assertive and balanced.

● Vin Santo del Chianti Occhio di Pernice Fonti e Lecceta '11	▼▼▼ 6
● Chianti Colli Fiorentini '15	▼▼ 2*
● Casamaggio Colorino '15	▼▼ 4
● Chianti Colli Fiorentini Badia a Corte Ris. '13	▼▼▼ 4*
● Chianti Colli Fiorentini '14	▼▼ 2*
● Chianti Colli Fiorentini '13	▼▼ 3
● Chianti Colli Fiorentini Badia a Corte Ris. '12	▼▼ 4
● Chianti Colli Fiorentini Badia a Corte Ris. '11	▼▼ 4
● Merlot '13	▼▼ 5
● Terre di Cino '13	▼▼ 3
● Terre di Cino '12	▼▼ 3

★Tua Rita

LOC. NOTRI, 81
57028 SUVERETO [LI]
TEL. +39 0565829237
www.tuarita.it

CELLAR SALES
PRE-BOOKED VISITS
ANNUAL PRODUCTION 250,000 bottles
HECTARES UNDER VINE 41.00

Tua Rita is a modern, efficient, and well-organized winery, run by Stefano Frascolla and Simena Bisti. The original two hectares of vineyards were from the beginning cultivated with precision, and this has made it one of the first successful Italian wineries based on the "vin de garage" model. Within ten years they had expanded to 9 hectares, and eventually reached twenty at the start of the millennium. A couple of years ago, they started renting Poggio Argentiera, in Morellino di Scansano. The 2014 Giusto di Notri, a blend of mostly Cabernet Sauvignon with smaller parts Merlot and Cabernet Franc, made it to our finals. It's fruity and vibrant on the nose, with hints of cherry and blueberry, as well as spicy notes of pepper and cloves. The mouth is rich, savory, elegant and precise. The 2015 Perlato del Bosco, a monovarietal Sangiovese with fresh, enticing fragrances of cherry, and complex, flowery scents, also proved excellent. Its mouth is unique, full, intriguing and fun, with a long, flavorsome finish.

● Giusto di Notri '14	▼▼▼ 8
● Perlato del Bosco Rosso '15	▼▼ 5
○ Perlato del Bosco Vermentino '16	▼▼ 3
● Rosso dei Notri '16	▼▼ 4
● Redigaffi '08	▼▼▼ 8
● Redigaffi '07	▼▼▼ 8
● Redigaffi '06	▼▼▼ 8
● Redigaffi '04	▼▼▼ 8
● Redigaffi '03	▼▼▼ 8
● Redigaffi '02	▼▼▼ 8
● Redigaffi '01	▼▼▼ 8
● Redigaffi '00	▼▼▼ 8
● Redigaffi '99	▼▼▼ 8
● Redigaffi '98	▼▼▼ 8

Uccelliera

IT-HAZ. CASTELNUOVO DELL'ABATE
IPOD. UCCELLIERA, 45
53020 MONTALCINO [SI]
TEL. +39 0577835729
www.uccelliera-montalcino.it

CELLAR SALES
PRE-BOOKED VISITS
ANNUAL PRODUCTION 60,000 bottles
HECTARES UNDER VINE 6.00

Andrea Cortonesi's winery has just celebrated its 30th anniversary with the takeover of Uccelliera in Castelnuovo dell'Abate in southeastern Montalcino. Six hectares are concentrated in a particularly hot area that is known historically for producing powerful and expansive Sangiovese wines, thanks to sandy-clay soil and altitudes below 250 meters. Their Brunello and Rosso wines have a lively character, all the while retaining some savory and tannic contrasts. End use is determined at a later date, after the different plots have been fermented and aged in a mix of barriques and untoasted Slavonian oak. One of the best performances yet for the entire selection, which was already bolstered by its Voliero line. The 2012 Brunello calls up the potent, mature style that we're used to, but once again it's the Rosso to hit a home run, with a 2015 whose citrusy subtlety makes it the Brunello's binary opposite.

● Rosso di Montalcino '15	▼▼▼ 4*
● Brunello di Montalcino '12	▼▼ 6
● Brunello di Montalcino Voliero '12	▼▼ 6
● Rosso di Montalcino Voliero '15	▼▼ 4
● Rapace '14	▼ 5
● Brunello di Montalcino '10	♥♥♥ 6
● Brunello di Montalcino '08	♥♥♥ 7
● Brunello di Montalcino Ris. '97	♥♥♥ 8
● Rosso di Montalcino '14	♥♥♥ 4*
● Brunello di Montalcino '11	♥♥ 6
● Brunello di Montalcino '09	♥♥ 6
● Brunello di Montalcino Ris. '08	♥♥ 8
● Brunello di Montalcino Ris. '07	♥♥ 8

Val delle Corti

LOC. LA CROCE, 141
53017 RADDA IN CHIANTI [SI]
TEL. +39 0577738215
www.valdellecorti.it

CELLAR SALES
PRE-BOOKED VISITS
ACCOMMODATION
ANNUAL PRODUCTION 30,000 bottles
HECTARES UNDER VINE 6.00
VITICULTURE METHOD Certified Organic

Roberto Bianchi serves as current president of the Vignaioli di Radda association and it comes as no surprise that he has been chosen for this role. He is one of the leading producers in the subzone and his wines are some of the best at expressing the area. Not terribly approachable wines, rather they offer up a rare depth of taste and authentic territoriality, perceptible in the unique floral expression. This is a unique quality found in a territory like Chianti Classico. An extraordinary and intriguing 2014 Chianti Classico Riserva from a vintage that was, to put it mildly, complicated. Its aromas are elegant and delicate, calling up fresh flowers, accompanied by accents of iodine and flint. In the mouth it's graceful and silky, fragrant and long with tannins that are both savory and spirited. The 2014 Chianti Classico is no less impressive, with its less complex, but just as pleasant aromatic profile. In the mouth flavor emerges immediately, following through fresh and well-paced.

● Chianti Cl. Ris. '14	▼▼▼ 5
● Chianti Cl. '14	▼▼ 4
● Chianti Cl. '13	♥♥♥ 4*
● Chianti Cl. '12	♥♥♥ 4*
● Chianti Cl. '11	♥♥♥ 3*
● Chianti Cl. '10	♥♥♥ 3*
● Chianti Cl. '09	♥♥♥ 2*
● Chianti Cl. '06	♥♥ 2*
● Chianti Cl. '04	♥♥ 2*
● Chianti Cl. Ris. '13	♥♥ 5
● Chianti Cl. Ris. '11	♥♥ 5
● Chianti Cl. Ris. '09	♥♥ 5
● Chianti Cl. Ris. '07	♥♥ 4
● Il Campino	♥♥ 2*

Tenuta Valdipiatta

VIA DELLA CIARLIANA, 25A
53040 MONTEPULCIANO [SI]
TEL. +39 0578757930
www.valdipiatta.it

CELLAR SALES
PRE-BOOKED VISITS
ACCOMMODATION
ANNUAL PRODUCTION 80,000 bottles
HECTARES UNDER VINE 23.00

Tenuta Valdipiatta is undeniably one of the best areas for producing Nobile di Montepulciano wines. After almost thirty years the Caporali family have finely tuned their production, aiming for balanced wines with good drinkability. As sometimes happens, the aging wood, which is mostly small, slows down the development of aromas and flavors in some wines, and more time is needed to develop in the glass. The 2013 Nobile di Montepulciano Riserva did very well. It's a wine characterized by its assertive, flowery and iodine fragrances, while in the mouth it tends towards linearity and flavor, only disturbed by a bit too much toastiness in its aftertaste. The 2014 Nobile di Montepulciano is also good, with a nose that expresses clean fruitiness, maybe just a bit simple. The mouth is solid, with nice length.

Valentini

LOC. VALPIANA
POD. FIORDALISO, 69
58024 MASSA MARITTIMA [GR]
TEL. +39 0566918058
www.agricolavalontini.it

CELLAR SALES
PRE-BOOKED VISITS
ACCOMMODATION
ANNUAL PRODUCTION 40,000 bottles
HECTARES UNDER VINE 5.50

The Valentini family have looked after this property in the heart of Monteregio in the gentle Massa Marittima hills for five generations. Today, Giovanni heads the winery, supported by his son Luca, fresh from winemaking school, and his daughter Chiara. A few years ago they started on a path toward quality, and thanks to a wise decision to replant vineyards and include some international varieties, which are thriving in this area's mild and sunny climate, they are succeeding. And it's the 2015 Monteregio di Massa Marittima, a blend of Sangiovese with smaller parts Merlot and Cabernet Sauvignon, that stands out among the selection presented to our tasters. Its aromatic profile features fruity notes of raspberry and cherry, and flowery hints of red roses. The mouth opens with faintly sweet overtones that subside amidst acidity and tannins in a palate that is close-focused but unyielding. The 2016 Sangiovese also did well. It's a fresh, flavorsome wine of great drinkability and flavor.

● Nobile di Montepulciano Ris. '13	♥♥ 6
● Chianti Colli Senesi Tosca '15	♥♥ 2*
● Nobile di Montepulciano '14	♥♥ 4
● Nobile di Montepulciano Ris. '90	♥♥♥ 5
● Nobile di Montepulciano V. d'Alfiero '99	♥♥♥ 5
● Nobile di Montepulciano '13	♀♀ 4
● Nobile di Montepulciano '12	♀♀ 4
● Nobile di Montepulciano '11	♀♀ 4
● Nobile di Montepulciano '10	♀♀ 4
● Nobile di Montepulciano V. d'Alfiero '13	♀♀ 6
● Nobile di Montepulciano V. d'Alfiero '12	♀♀ 6
● Nobile di Montepulciano V. d'Alfiero '10	♀♀ 6
● Rosso di Montepulciano '10	♀♀ 3

● Monteregio di Massa Marittima Rosso '15	♥♥ 2
○ Maremma Toscana Vermentino '16	♥♥ 2
● Sangiovese '16	♥♥ 2
● Atunis '12	♀♀ 5
● Atunis '11	♀♀ 5
● Monteregio di Massa Marittima '14	♀♀ 2
● Monteregio di Massa Marittima Vivoli '13	♀♀ 4
● Monteregio di Massa Marittima Vivoli '11	♀♀ 4

★Tenuta di Valgiano

VIA DI VALGIANO, 7
55015 LUCCA
TEL. +39 0583402271
www.valgiano.it

CELLAR SALES
PRE-BOOKED VISITS
ANNUAL PRODUCTION 70,000 bottles
HECTARES UNDER VINE 20.00
VITICULTURE METHOD Certified Biodynamic

Tenuta di Valgiano is a magical place with a recognizable human dimension, immersed in the lush nature of the Lucca hills. Moreno Petrini and Laura di Collobiano run the winery with the help of Saverio Petrilli's farming and winemaking expertise. He is Italy's biodynamics guru. Varieties and grape blends are important, but to fully understand Valgiano, territory and a tenacious style philosophy are what count most. The producer didn't make a Tenuta di Valgiano for the problematic 2014 season, testifying to how seriously they take they work. But to compensate, we see progress being made with their second wine, Palistorti Rosso. The 2015 crop saw nice, fruity weave, embellished by a sophisticated whiff of fine spices. The mouth is streamlined, vibrant, backed up by young, but well-extracted, tannins.

● Colline Lucchesi Palistorti Rosso '15	♥♥	5
○ Palistorti Bianco '16	♥♥	5
● Colline Lucchesi Tenuta di Valgiano '13	♥♥♥	8
● Colline Lucchesi Tenuta di Valgiano '12	♥♥♥	6
● Colline Lucchesi Tenuta di Valgiano '11	♥♥♥	6
● Colline Lucchesi Tenuta di Valgiano '10	♥♥♥	6
● Colline Lucchesi Tenuta di Valgiano '09	♥♥♥	6
● Colline Lucchesi Tenuta di Valgiano '08	♥♥♥	6
● Colline Lucchesi Tenuta di Valgiano '07	♥♥♥	6
● Colline Lucchesi Tenuta di Valgiano '06	♥♥♥	6
Colline Lucchesi Tenuta di Valgiano '05	♥♥♥	6
● Colline Lucchesi Tenuta di Valgiano '04	♥♥♥	6
● Colline Lucchesi Tenuta di Valgiano '03	♥♥♥	6
● Colline Lucchesi Tenuta di Valgiano '01	♥♥♥	8

Vecchia Cantina di Montepulciano

VIA PROVINCIALE, 7
53045 MONTEPULCIANO [SI]
TEL. +39 0578716092
www.vecchiacantina.com

CELLAR SALES
PRE-BOOKED VISITS
ANNUAL PRODUCTION 5,000,000 bottles
HECTARES UNDER VINE 1000.00
VITICULTURE METHOD Certified Organic

This is an important cooperative for the appellation and Montepulciano. It counts about 400 members scattered throughout the territory, but was originally founded by 14 pioneers in 1937. They decided to join forces to add luster and interest to the area's traditional wines. In addition to their classic line of wines, there is the Cantina del Redi selection and organic wines made with grapes cultivated by vine growers on a select 25 hectares. The 2014 Nobile sees fruit-driven aromas with smoky accents. Overall, a nice profile, long and delicate, assertive but never bitter in its tannins. Among the Cantina del Red line, we were surprised by the 2013 Nobile, a brilliant, fragrant wine with delectable hints of raspberry. The 2011 Vin Santo also proved delicious, a classic, enticing wine that's among the best of its kind in the territory.

● Nobile di Montepulciano '14	♥♥	3
● Nobile di Montepulciano Cantina del Redi '13	♥♥	4
○ Vin Santo di Montepulciano Poggio Stella '11	♥♥	6
● Chianti Bio '15	♥	2
● Rosso di Montepulciano '15	♥	2
● Nobile di Montepulciano '11	♀♀	3
● Nobile di Montepulciano Briareo Cantina del Redi Ris. '09	♀♀	5
● Nobile di Montepulciano Ris. '12	♀♀	4

I Veroni

VIA TIFARITI, 5
50065 PONTASSIEVE [FI]
TEL. +39 0558368886
www.iveroni.it

CELLAR SALES
PRE-BOOKED VISITS
ACCOMMODATION
ANNUAL PRODUCTION 110,000 bottles
HECTARES UNDER VINE 20.00
VITICULTURE METHOD Certified Organic

This winery headed by Lorenzo Mariani is
named after the balconies on Tuscan
farmhouses that were used for drying
tobacco leaves. Lorenzo has run this estate
since 1966, but its origins date back to the
twelfth century, when the local lords, the
Guidi Counts, built a series of towers to
control the territory. The vineyards span
twenty hectares and have been completely
replanted since the 1990s. They host
mostly Sangiovese and give rise to fresh,
intense, and territorial Chianti Rufinas. Like
the 2014 Quona Riserva, which, even if it
felt the impact of the tough year, offers up
a mouth with close-woven, though just a bit
awkward, tannins. The 2015 Domi also
turned in a good performance. It's a simpler
wine, fresh and linear. The 2008 Vin Santo,
caressing, soft and leisurely, also delivered.
We also make note of the Rosé, which is
among the best of its kind in the territory.

● Chianti Rufina I Domi '15	♟♟ 3
● Chianti Rufina Quona Ris. '14	♟♟ 5
☉ Iveronirosé '16	♟♟ 3
○ Vin Santo del Chianti Rufina '08	♟♟ 5
● I Veroni Rosso '15	♟ 2
● Chianti Rufina '14	♟♟ 3
● Chianti Rufina '13	♟♟ 2*
● Chianti Rufina '12	♟♟ 2*
● Chianti Rufina '11	♟♟ 2*
● Chianti Rufina Ris. '13	♟♟ 5
● Chianti Rufina Ris. '12	♟♟ 4
● Chianti Rufina Ris. '11	♟♟ 4
○ Vin Santo del Chianti Rufina '07	♟♟ 5
○ Vin Santo del Chianti Rufina '06	♟♟ 5

Vignamaggio

VIA DI PETRIOLO, 5
50022 GREVE IN CHIANTI [FI]
TEL. +39 055854661
www.vignamaggio.com

CELLAR SALES
PRE-BOOKED VISITS
ACCOMMODATION AND RESTAURANT SERVICE
ANNUAL PRODUCTION 350,000 bottles
HECTARES UNDER VINE 62.50
VITICULTURE METHOD Certified Organic

Vignamaggio is headed by the French
architect, Patrice Taravella, who took over
the old property in 2014. It is one of the
most important wineries in the Greve in
Chianti subzone. The winery favors
well-structured wines with rich fruit,
accompanied by a good amount of
small and large oak. This was a smart
choice; in point of fact, elegance is never
absent from their wines and at times
they achieve absolute excellence. The
2015 Chianti Classico Terre di Prenzano
is an elegant, delicate wine with aromas
of flowers and fresh herbs rounded out with
scents of flint and iodine. It proves
flavorsome in the mouth, just a bit small,
but absolutely pleasant, with a rising finish.
The 2013 Chianti Classico Gran Selezione
Riserva di Monna Lisa shows nicer
structure, with well-defined aromas of red
fruit and a generous, expansive mouth; it's
just a bit rough at the finish.

● Chianti Cl. Terre di Prenzano '15	♟♟ 3
● Chianti Cl. Gran Sel. Monna Lisa Ris. '13	♟♟ 6
● Chianti Cl. Gherardino Ris. '14	♟ 3
● Vignamaggio '06	♟♟♟ 7
● Vignamaggio '05	♟♟♟ 7
● Vignamaggio '04	♟♟♟ 6
● Vignamaggio '01	♟♟♟ 6
● Cabernet Franc '13	♟♟ 8
● Chianti Cl. Gherardino '13	♟♟ 3
● Chianti Cl. Gran Sel. Castello di Monna Lisa '10	♟♟ 5
● Chianti Cl. Terre di Prenzano '14	♟♟ 3
● Chianti Cl. Terre di Prenzano '13	♟♟ 3
● Chianti Cl. Terre di Prenzano '12	♟♟ 3

Villa La Ripa

LOC. ANTRIA, 38
52100 AREZZO
TEL. +39 057523330
www.villalaripa.it

CELLAR SALES
PRE-BOOKED VISITS
ANNUAL PRODUCTION 10,000 bottles
HECTARES UNDER VINE 5.00
SUSTAINABLE WINERY

La Ripa is a Renaissance villa standing in the middle of olive trees and rows of Sangiovese, Cabernet Sauvignon, Merlot, Syrah and Chardonnay. Notary deeds from the 1500s described it as surrounded by olives, apples, and vines. Current owners, the Luzzi family, are continuing the previous production philosophy. They have planted new vineyards and are working hard to develop their wine quality and style. Saverio and Adriana's daughter, Claudia Luzzi, has used her pharmacy degree to develop a line of red-grape based cosmetics. The 2015 Peconio, a monovarietal Sangiovese, offers up aromas of vibrant, dark fruit like blackberries and plums, softened by fresher hints of bay leaf and sage. The mouth proves warm, well-structured, with tannins and alcohol also integrating well, and a succulent, long finish. The 2014 Psyco, a blend of equal parts Sangiovese and Cabernet Sauvignon, has a bouquet grounded in wild berries, with slightly minty notes on the side. In the mouth it's close-knit, with good, refreshing acidity and well-defined tannins.

● Peconio '15	♈♈	3
● Psyco '14	♈♈	5
● Tiratari '14	♈♈	5
⊙ Spaziolibero '16	♈	2
● Syrah '13	♈	6
● Peconio '12	♉♈	3
● Peconio '11	♉♈	2*
● Psyco '12	♉♈	5
● Psyco '11	♉♈	5
● Tiratari '10	♉♈	4

Villa Pillo

VIA VOLTERRANA, 24
50050 GAMBASSI TERME [FI]
TEL. +39 0571680212
www.villapillo.com

CELLAR SALES
PRE-BOOKED VISITS
ANNUAL PRODUCTION 350,000 bottles
HECTARES UNDER VINE 40.00

Several documents bear witness to the Medieval origins of this winery, which spans 500 hectares and is set in a magnificent landscape in the Tuscan hills, among woods, old farmhouses and fields cultivated with cereals. The location, soil, and climate have always been ideal for agriculture, but especially for vine growing. Since 1989 the winery has been owned by an American couple, John and Kathe Dyson. Today their 40 hectares have been completely replanted with Sangiovese, Syrah, Merlot and Cabernet Franc. The 2015 Vivaldaia, made with Cabernet Franc, offers up vibrant overtones of peppers, then bay leaves, blueberry and cherry. In the mouth it comes through warm, nicely layered, with well-integrated acidity and a warm, enticing finish. The 2015 Cypresses, made with Sangiovese, brings together fruity notes of cherry and a supple, well-distributed, fresh body, with fine-grained tannins and an appetizing finish. The 2015 Syrah is characterized by fruity fragrances of raspberries, spicy hints of pepper, and a meaty, flavorsome structure.

● Cypresses '15	♈♈	3
● Syrah '15	♈♈	5
● Vivaldaia '15	♈♈	4
● Borgoforte '15	♈	3
● Cingalino '16	♈	2
● Sant'Adele '15	♈	5
● Syrah '97	♉♉♈	5
● Borgoforte '13	♉♈	3
● Borgoforte '12	♉♈	3
● Cypresses '12	♉♈	3
● Merlot Sant'Adele '12	♉♈	5
● Sant'Adele '13	♉♈	5
○ Sauvignon Blanc '14	♉♈	2*
● Syrah '12	♉♈	5
● Vivaldaia '13	♉♈	4

Abbadia Ardenga

FRAZ. TORRENIERI
VIA ROMANA, 139
53028 MONTALCINO [SI]
TEL. +39 0577834150
www.abbadiardengapoggio.it

CELLAR SALES
PRE-BOOKED VISITS
ANNUAL PRODUCTION 40,000 bottles
HECTARES UNDER VINE 10.00

● Brunello di Montalcino V. Piaggia '12		♛♛ 5
● Brunello di Montalcino '12		♛ 5

Fattoria Acquaviva

FRAZ. MONTEMERANO
LOC. ACQUAVIVA, 10
58014 MANCIANO [GR]
TEL. +39 0564602890
www.villacquaviva.com

CELLAR SALES
PRE-BOOKED VISITS
ACCOMMODATION AND RESTAURANT SERVICE
ANNUAL PRODUCTION 90,000 bottles
HECTARES UNDER VINE 16.00

● Maremma Toscana Banco Pian di Giorno '15		♛♛ 2*
● Morellino di Scansano Bracaleta '13		♛ 4
● Morellino di Scansano Nero '14		♛ 2

Agricola Del Nudo

VIA DELLE SANTE MARIA, 52
58100 GROSSETO
TEL. +39 3351304989
www.nudo.bio

CELLAR SALES
PRE-BOOKED VISITS
ACCOMMODATION
ANNUAL PRODUCTION 20,000 bottles
HECTARES UNDER VINE 3.00
VITICULTURE METHOD Certified Organic

● Maremma Toscana Rosso Nudo '15		♛♛ 3*
○ Maremma Toscana Vermentino Nudo '16		♛♛ 3

Agrisole

LOC. LA SERRA, 64
56028 SAN MINIATO [PI]
TEL. +39 0571409825
www.agri-sole.it

CELLAR SALES
PRE-BOOKED VISITS
ANNUAL PRODUCTION 30,000 bottles
HECTARES UNDER VINE 7.00

○ Trebbiano '15		♛♛ 4
○ Vin Santo Pisano Bianco di San Torpè '09		♛♛ 2*
○ Mafefa Bianco '16		♛ 2
⊙ Mafefa Rosato '16		♛ 2

Ampeleia

FRAZ. ROCCATEDERIGHI
LOC. MELETA
58028 ROCCASTRADA [GR]
TEL. +39 0564567155
www.ampeleia.it

CELLAR SALES
PRE-BOOKED VISITS
ANNUAL PRODUCTION 135,000 bottles
HECTARES UNDER VINE 35.00
VITICULTURE METHOD Certified Biodynamic
SUSTAINABLE WINERY

● Kepos '15		♛♛ 4
● Cabernet Franc '16		♛ 5
● Carignano '16		♛ 5
● Unlitro '16		♛ 3

Argiano

FRAZ. SANT'ANGELO IN COLLE
53024 MONTALCINO [SI]
TEL. +39 0577844037
www.argiano.net

PRE-BOOKED VISITS
ACCOMMODATION
ANNUAL PRODUCTION 350,000 bottles
HECTARES UNDER VINE 55.00

● Brunello di Montalcino '12		♛♛ 7
● Rosso di Montalcino '15		♛ 4

Arizzi Wine

LOC. CASCIANO
VIA FONTAZZI, 6
53016 MURLO [SI]
TEL. +39 05771655845
www.arizziwine.it

CELLAR SALES
PRE-BOOKED VISITS
ANNUAL PRODUCTION 60,000 bottles
HECTARES UNDER VINE 12.00

● Chianti Colli Senesi	
Il Lato Intenso del Vivere Ris. '14	♥♥ 3
○ Il Lato Spettacolare del Vivere '13	♥ 3

Armilla

VIA TAVERNELLE, 6
53024 MONTALCINO [SI]
TEL. +39 0577816012
www.armillawine.com

● Rosso di Montalcino '15	♥♥ 4
● Brunello di Montalcino '12	♥ 8

Arrighi

LOC. PIAN DEL MONTE, 1
57036 PORTO AZZURRO [LI]
TEL. +39 3356641793
www.arrighivigneolivi.it

CELLAR SALES
PRE-BOOKED VISITS
ANNUAL PRODUCTION 30,000 bottles
HECTARES UNDER VINE 6.00

● Elba Aleatico Passito Silosò '16	♥♥ 5
○ Elba Ansonica Mattanto '16	♥ 3
● Elba Rosso Centopercento '16	♥ 5
○ V.I.P. Anfora '16	♥ 4

Il Balzo

VIA DEL POGGIOLO, 12
50068 RUFINA [FI]
TEL. +39 0558397556
www.podereilbalzo.it

CELLAR SALES
PRE-BOOKED VISITS
ANNUAL PRODUCTION 9,000 bottles
HECTARES UNDER VINE 7.00

● Chianti Rufina '14	♥♥ 2*
● Chianti Rufina Ris. '12	♥♥ 4
● Addiaccio '15	♥ 2

Erik Banti

LOC. FOSSO DEI MOLINI
58054 SCANSANO [GR]
TEL. +39 0564508006
www.erikbanti.com

CELLAR SALES
PRE-BOOKED VISITS
ACCOMMODATION
ANNUAL PRODUCTION 250,000 bottles
HECTARES UNDER VINE 18.00
VITICULTURE METHOD Certified Organic

● Morellino di Scansano '16	♥♥ 2*
● Morellino di Scansano Ciabatta '15	♥♥ 5

Fattoria di Basciano

V.LE DUCA DELLA VITTORIA, 159
50068 RUFINA [FI]
TEL. +39 0558397034
www.renzomasibasciano.it

CELLAR SALES
PRE-BOOKED VISITS
ANNUAL PRODUCTION 200,000 bottles
HECTARES UNDER VINE 35.00

● I Pini '15	♥♥ 4
● Chianti Renzo Masi Ris. '14	♥ 2
● Vigna Il Corto '15	♥ 3

Berretta

LOC. BANDITELLA
53024 CINIGIANO [GR]
TEL. +39 3395022033
www.viniberretta.it

ANNUAL PRODUCTION 15,000 bottles
HECTARES UNDER VINE 3.50

● Maremma Toscana '14	♟♟ 3*

Le Bertille

VIA DELLE COLOMBELLE, 7
53045 MONTEPULCIANO [SI]
TEL. +39 0578758330
www.lebertille.com

CELLAR SALES
PRE-BOOKED VISITS
ACCOMMODATION
ANNUAL PRODUCTION 65,000 bottles
HECTARES UNDER VINE 14.00
SUSTAINABLE WINERY

● Nobile di Montepulciano Ris. '13	♟♟ 5

Tenuta di Bibbiano

VIA BIBBIANO, 76
53011 CASTELLINA IN CHIANTI [SI]
TEL. +39 0577743065
www.bibbiano.com

CELLAR SALES
PRE-BOOKED VISITS
ACCOMMODATION
ANNUAL PRODUCTION 100,000 bottles
HECTARES UNDER VINE 25.00
VITICULTURE METHOD Certified Organic
SUSTAINABLE WINERY

● Chianti Cl. '15	♟♟ 3
● Chianti Cl. Ris. '14	♟ 4

Tenuta di Biserno

LOC. PALAZZO GARDINI
P.ZZA GRAMSCI, 9
57020 BIBBONA [LI]
TEL. +39 0586671099
www.biserno.it

ANNUAL PRODUCTION 160,000 bottles
HECTARES UNDER VINE 99.00

● Biserno '12	♟♟ 8
● Insoglio del Cinghiale '15	♟♟ 4
⊙ Rosato '16	♟ 2

Buccia Nera

LOC. CAMPRIANO, 9
52100 AREZZO
TEL. +39 0575361613
www.buccianera.it

CELLAR SALES
PRE-BOOKED VISITS
ACCOMMODATION
ANNUAL PRODUCTION 200,000 bottles
HECTARES UNDER VINE 50.00
VITICULTURE METHOD Certified Organic
SUSTAINABLE WINERY

○ Colli dell'Etruria Centrale Vin Santo '09	♟♟ 4
● Merlot '15	♟♟ 2*
● Chianti Sup. Sassocupo '15	♟ 2
● Syrah '15	♟ 2

Caccia al Piano 1868

LOC. BOLGHERI
VIA BOLGHERESE, 279
57022 CASTAGNETO CARDUCCI [LI]
TEL. +39 0565763394
www.berlucchi.it

CELLAR SALES
PRE-BOOKED VISITS
ANNUAL PRODUCTION 127,000 bottles
HECTARES UNDER VINE 18.00
SUSTAINABLE WINERY

● Bolgheri Ruit Hora '15	♟♟ 4

Tenuta Campo al Mare

FRAZ. VALLONE DEI MESSI
VIA BOLGHERESE
57024 CASTAGNETO CARDUCCI [LI]
TEL. +39 055859811
www.tenutefolonari.com

PRE-BOOKED VISITS
ANNUAL PRODUCTION 100,000 bottles
HECTARES UNDER VINE 30.00

● Bolgheri Rosso '15	▼▼ 4
○ Bolgheri Vermentino '16	▼ 3

Campo alle Comete

LOC. SUGHERICCIO
VIA FORNACELLE 249
57022 CASTAGNETO CARDUCCI [LI]
TEL. +39 0565766056
www.campoallecomete.it

CELLAR SALES
ANNUAL PRODUCTION 120,000 bottles
HECTARES UNDER VINE 15.00
VITICULTURE METHOD Certified Organic

● Cabernet Sauvignon '15	▼▼ 4
☉ Bolgheri Rosato '16	▼ 5

Camporignano

FRAZ. MONTEGUIDI
53031 CASOLE D'ELSA [SI]
TEL. +39 0577963915
www.camporignano.com

CELLAR SALES
ANNUAL PRODUCTION 30,000 bottles
HECTARES UNDER VINE 10.00

● Comeunavolta '15	▼▼ 4
● Colori '13	▼▼ 5

Cantina 8380

FRAZ. SATURNIA
LOC. PIAN DEL MOLINO
58014 MANCIANO [GR]
TEL. +39 3892586967
www.cantina8380.com

CELLAR SALES
PRE-BOOKED VISITS
ANNUAL PRODUCTION 10,000 bottles
HECTARES UNDER VINE 2.00

● Morellino di Scansano '15	▼▼ 2*

Tenuta Canto alla Moraia

VIA SETTEPONTI, 53
52029 CASTIGLION FIBOCCHI [AR]
TEL. +39 0575 47666
www.tenutacantoallamoraia.com

CELLAR SALES
PRE-BOOKED VISITS
ACCOMMODATION
ANNUAL PRODUCTION 80,000 bottles
HECTARES UNDER VINE 8.30
VITICULTURE METHOD Certified Organic

● Chianti Bacco Felice '14	▼▼ 3
● Moraia '11	▼▼ 6
● Giannetto '12	▼ 7
● Sansereno '14	▼ 3

Le Capanne
Gabriele Mazzeschi

VIA SANTA LUCIA, 26
52043 CASTIGLION FIORENTINO [AR]
TEL. +39 0575659741
www.gabrielemazzeschi.it

CELLAR SALES
HECTARES UNDER VINE 5.00

● Commendatore '15	▼▼ 3
● Foramacchie '15	▼▼ 3

Capanne Ricci

FRAZ. SANT'ANGELO IN COLLE
LOC. CASELLO
53024 MONTALCINO [SI]
TEL. +39 0564902063
www.tenimentiricci.it

ANNUAL PRODUCTION 40,000 bottles
HECTARES UNDER VINE 12.00

● Brunello di Montalcino '12	♟♟ 5
● Rosso di Montalcino '15	♟♟ 3

Marco Capitoni

POD. SEDIME, 63
53026 PIENZA [SI]
TEL. +39 3388981597
www.capitoni.eu

CELLAR SALES
PRE-BOOKED VISITS
ANNUAL PRODUCTION 20,000 bottles
HECTARES UNDER VINE 5.00

● Orcia Capitoni Ris. '13	♟♟ 3
● Orcia Sangiovese Troccolone '16	♟♟ 2*
● Orcia Sangiovese Frasi Ris. '12	♟ 4

Enzo Carmignani

VIA DI CERCATOIA ALTA, 13B
55015 MONTECARLO [LU]
TEL. +39 058322463
www.fattoriacarmignani.com

PRE-BOOKED VISITS
ACCOMMODATION
ANNUAL PRODUCTION 50,000 bottles
HECTARES UNDER VINE 4.00

● Kapogiro '16	♟♟ 2*
● Montecarlo Rosso '16	♟♟ 2*
○ Urano '16	♟ 3

Podere Il Carnasciale

LOC. IL CARNASCIALE
52020 MERCATALE VALDARNO [AR]
TEL. +39 0559911142
www.caberlot.eu

PRE-BOOKED VISITS
ANNUAL PRODUCTION 10,000 bottles
HECTARES UNDER VINE 4.50
SUSTAINABLE WINERY

● Caberlot '14	♟♟ 8

Casa Lucii

LOC. SANTA MARIA A VILLACASTELLI
53037 SAN GIMIGNANO [SI]
TEL. +39 0577950199
www.casalucii.it

ANNUAL PRODUCTION 120,000 bottles
HECTARES UNDER VINE 100.00

○ Vernaccia di S. Gimignano Mareterra Ris. '14	♟♟ 6
○ Vernaccia di S. Gimignano '16	♟♟ 4
○ Vernaccia di S. Gimignano V. CelIori '15	♟ 4

Casa Sola

S.DA DI CORTINE, 5
50021 BARBERINO VAL D'ELSA [FI]
TEL. +39 0558075028
www.fattoriacasasola.it

CELLAR SALES
PRE-BOOKED VISITS
ACCOMMODATION
ANNUAL PRODUCTION 100,000 bottles
HECTARES UNDER VINE 26.00

● Chianti Cl. '15	♟♟ 4
● Pergliamici '15	♟ 2

Fattoria Casabianca

FRAZ. CASCIANO DI MURLO
LOC. CASABIANCA
53016 MURLO [SI]
TEL. +39 0577811033
www.tenutacasabianca.bio

CELLAR SALES
PRE-BOOKED VISITS
ACCOMMODATION AND RESTAURANT SERVICE
ANNUAL PRODUCTION 250,000 bottles
HECTARES UNDER VINE 70.00
VITICULTURE METHOD Certified Organic
SUSTAINABLE WINERY

- Canaiolo '13 ⬤ 🏆🏆 4
- 15 Staiori '14 ⬤ 🏆 6

Casisano

LOC. CASISANO
53024 MONTALCINO [SI]
TEL. +39 0577835540
www.casisano.it

ANNUAL PRODUCTION 90,000 bottles
HECTARES UNDER VINE 22.00

- Brunello di Montalcino '12 ⬤ 🏆🏆 7
- Brunello di Montalcino
  Colombaiolo Ris. '11 ⬤ 🏆🏆 8
- Rosso di Montalcino '15 ⬤ 🏆🏆 4

Castelgiocondo

LOC. CASTELGIOCONDO
53024 MONTALCINO [SI]
TEL. +39 057784131
www.frescobaldi.it

PRE-BOOKED VISITS
ANNUAL PRODUCTION 600,000 bottles
HECTARES UNDER VINE 235.00

- Brunello di Montalcino '12 ⬤ 🏆🏆 6
- Rosso di Montalcino Campo ai Sassi '15 ⬤ 🏆🏆 3

Castello di Gabbiano

FRAZ. MERCATALE VAL DI PESA
VIA GABBIANO, 22
50020 SAN CASCIANO IN VAL DI PESA [FI]
TEL. +39 055821053
www.castellogabbiano.it

CELLAR SALES
PRE-BOOKED VISITS
ACCOMMODATION AND RESTAURANT SERVICE
ANNUAL PRODUCTION 1,000,000 bottles
HECTARES UNDER VINE 145.00

- Chianti Cl. Gran Sel. Bellezza '13 ⬤ 🏆🏆 5
- Chianti Cl. '15 ⬤ 🏆 3

Castello di Meleto

LOC. MELETO
53013 GAIOLE IN CHIANTI [SI]
TEL. +39 0577749217
www.castellomeleto.it

CELLAR SALES
PRE-BOOKED VISITS
ACCOMMODATION AND RESTAURANT SERVICE
ANNUAL PRODUCTION 700,000 bottles
HECTARES UNDER VINE 144.00
SUSTAINABLE WINERY

- Fiore '13 ⬤ 🏆🏆 5
- Chianti Cl. '15 ⬤ 🏆 3

Castello di Monastero

LOC. SESTANO
53019 CASTELNUOVO BERARDENGA [SI]
TEL. +39 0577355789
www.castellodimonastero.com

CELLAR SALES
PRE-BOOKED VISITS
ANNUAL PRODUCTION 170,000 bottles
HECTARES UNDER VINE 62.00

- Chianti Cl. '15 ⬤ 🏆🏆 3*

Castello di Oliveto

VIA DI MONTE OLIVO, 6
50051 CASTELFIORENTINO [FI]
TEL. +39 057164322
www.castellooliveto.it

CELLAR SALES
PRE-BOOKED VISITS
ACCOMMODATION AND RESTAURANT SERVICE
ANNUAL PRODUCTION 250,000 bottles
HECTARES UNDER VINE 40.00

● Chianti Villa Montorsoli '16	🍷🍷 2*
○ Vin Santo del Chianti Ris. '04	🍷🍷 5
○ Bianco dei Papi '16	🍷 2

Castello di Vicarello

POGGI DEL SASSO
58044 CINIGIANO [GR]
TEL. +39 0564990718
www.it.castellodivicarellovini.com

CELLAR SALES
PRE-BOOKED VISITS
ACCOMMODATION AND RESTAURANT SERVICE
ANNUAL PRODUCTION 70,000 bottles
HECTARES UNDER VINE 10.00
VITICULTURE METHOD Biodynamic/
SUSTAINABLE WINERY

● Castello di Vicarello '12	🍷🍷 5
● Terre di Vico '12	🍷🍷 5
● Merah '15	🍷 5

Castello Sonnino

VIA VOLTERRANA NORD, 6A
50025 MONTESPERTOLI [FI]
TEL. +39 0571609198
www.castellosonnino.it

CELLAR SALES
PRE-BOOKED VISITS
ACCOMMODATION
ANNUAL PRODUCTION 150,000 bottles
HECTARES UNDER VINE 40.00
SUSTAINABLE WINERY

● Leone Rosso '16	🍷🍷 2*
○ Vin Santo del Chianti '11	🍷🍷 5
● Chianti Montespertoli '16	🍷 2
● Chianti Montespertoli Ris. '14	🍷 3

Castelsina

LOC. OSTERIA, 54A
53048 SINALUNGA [SI]
TEL. +39 0577663595
www.castelsina.it

CELLAR SALES
PRE-BOOKED VISITS
ANNUAL PRODUCTION 2,000,000 bottles
HECTARES UNDER VINE 400.00

● Chianti '16	🍷🍷 2*
● Chianti Ris. '14	🍷🍷 2*
● Governo all'Uso Toscano '16	🍷🍷 2*
● Chianti Cl. '14	🍷 3

Castelvecchi

LOC. CASTELVECCHI
53017 RADDA IN CHIANTI [SI]
TEL. +39 0577735612
www.chianticastelvecchi.it

CELLAR SALES
PRE-BOOKED VISITS
ACCOMMODATION AND RESTAURANT SERVICE
ANNUAL PRODUCTION 70,000 bottles
HECTARES UNDER VINE 18.00
SUSTAINABLE WINERY

● Chianti Cl. Capotondo '15	🍷🍷 5

Ceralti

VIA DEI CERALTI, 77
57022 CASTAGNETO CARDUCCI [LI]
TEL. +39 0565763989
www.ceralti.com

CELLAR SALES
PRE-BOOKED VISITS
ACCOMMODATION
ANNUAL PRODUCTION 50,000 bottles
HECTARES UNDER VINE 9.00
VITICULTURE METHOD Certified Organic

○ Bolgheri Vermentino '16	🍷🍷 3
● Bolgheri Scirè '15	🍷 3
● Bolgheri Sup. Alfeo '14	🍷 5

La Cerreta

VIA CAMPAGNA SUD, 143
57020 SASSETTA [LI]
TEL. +39 0565794352
www.lacerreta.it

ANNUAL PRODUCTION 20,000 bottles
HECTARES UNDER VINE 8.00
VITICULTURE METHOD Certified Biodynamic

○ Mathis '15	🏆🏆 3
● Rio de' Messi '13	🏆🏆 3
● Sangiovese '15	🏆 3
● Solatio della Cerreta '14	🏆 3

La Ciarliana

FRAZ. GRACCIANO
VIA CIARLIANA, 31
53040 MONTEPULCIANO [SI]
TEL. +39 0578758423
www.laciarliana.it

CELLAR SALES
PRE-BOOKED VISITS
ANNUAL PRODUCTION 30,000 bottles
HECTARES UNDER VINE 12.00

● Rosso di Montepulciano '15	🏆🏆 3
● Nobile di Montepulciano '14	🏆 4

Donatella Cinelli Colombini

LOC. CASATO,17
53024 MONTALCINO [SI]
TEL. +39 0577662108
www.cinellicolombini.it

CELLAR SALES
PRE-BOOKED VISITS
ACCOMMODATION AND RESTAURANT SERVICE
ANNUAL PRODUCTION 120,000 bottles
HECTARES UNDER VINE 34.00

● Rosso di Montalcino '15	🏆🏆 3
● Brunello di Montalcino '12	🏆 6
● Brunello di Montalcino Prime Donne '12	🏆 7

Citille di Sopra

FRAZ. TORRENIERI
LOC. CITILLE DI SOPRA, 46
53024 MONTALCINO [SI]
TEL. +39 0577832749
www.citille.com

CELLAR SALES
PRE-BOOKED VISITS
ANNUAL PRODUCTION 35,000 bottles
HECTARES UNDER VINE 6.00

● Brunello di Montalcino V. Poggio Ronconi '12	🏆🏆 5
● Brunello di Montalcino '12	🏆 5

Colle di Bordocheo

LOC. SEGROMIGNO IN MONTE
VIA DI PIAGGIORI BASSO, 123
55012 CAPANNORI [LU]
TEL. +39 0583929821
www.colledibordocheo.com

CELLAR SALES
PRE-BOOKED VISITS
ACCOMMODATION
ANNUAL PRODUCTION 30,000 bottles
HECTARES UNDER VINE 10.00

○ Bianco dell'Oca '16	🏆🏆 3
○ Colline Lucchesi Bordocheo Bianco '16	🏆 2
● Colline Lucchesi Sangiovese Picchio Rosso '15	🏆 3

Collelceto

LOC. CAMIGLIANO
POD. LA PISANA
53024 MONTALCINO [SI]
TEL. +39 0577816606
www.collelceto.it

CELLAR SALES
PRE-BOOKED VISITS
ANNUAL PRODUCTION 22,000 bottles
HECTARES UNDER VINE 6.00

● Brunello di Montalcino '12	🏆 5
● Rosso di Montalcino '15	🏆 3

Collemattoni

FRAZ. SANT'ANGELO IN COLLE
LOC. COLLEMATTONI, 100
53024 MONTALCINO [SI]
TEL. +39 0577844127
www.collemattoni.it

CELLAR SALES
PRE-BOOKED VISITS
ANNUAL PRODUCTION 60,000 bottles
HECTARES UNDER VINE 11.00
VITICULTURE METHOD Certified Organic
SUSTAINABLE WINERY

● Rosso di Montalcino '15	♥♥ 4
● Brunello di Montalcino '12	♥ 6

Cantina Sociale Colline del Chianti

LOC. FONTANA 23
53036 POGGIBONSI [SI]
TEL. +39 0577930886
www.cantinasocialechianti.it

ANNUAL PRODUCTION 80,000 bottles
HECTARES UNDER VINE 400.00

● Buca del Merlo '14	♥♥ 3
● Chianti Cl. RBB1961 '13	♥♥ 3
● Chianti Cl. Tufo del Gruccione '16	♥ 3

Colline San Biagio

LOC. BACCHERETO
VIA SAN BIAGIO 6/8
59015 CARMIGNANO [PO]
TEL. +39 0558717143
www.collinesanbiagio.it

CELLAR SALES
PRE-BOOKED VISITS
ACCOMMODATION
ANNUAL PRODUCTION 35,000 bottles
HECTARES UNDER VINE 7.00
SUSTAINABLE WINERY

● Quattordicisei Merlot '13	♥♥ 3
☉ Balè Rosato '16	♥ 3
● Carmignano Sancti Blasii '11	♥ 4
● Donna Mingarda '13	♥ 4

Cupelli Spumanti

V.LE MARCONI, 203
56028 SAN MINIATO [PI]
TEL. +39 057143801
www.cupellivini.com

CELLAR SALES
PRE-BOOKED VISITS
RESTAURANT SERVICE
ANNUAL PRODUCTION 30,000 bottles
HECTARES UNDER VINE 8.00

○ L'Erede M. Cl. '10	♥♥ 4
○ L'Erede M. Cl.	♥♥ 4
○ L'Erede Rosé	♥ 5
○ Vin Santo Amelio '09	♥ 4

Diadema

VIA IMPRUNETANA PER TAVARNUZZE, 19
50023 IMPRUNETA [FI]
TEL. +39 0552311330
www.diadema-wine.com

CELLAR SALES
PRE-BOOKED VISITS
ACCOMMODATION
ANNUAL PRODUCTION 170,000 bottles
HECTARES UNDER VINE 15.00

● D'Amare Rosso '15	♥♥ 4
● Diadema Rosso '15	♥♥ 8
○ D'Amare Bianco '16	♥ 3
☉ D'Amare Rosato '16	♥ 3

Donne Fittipaldi

LOC. BOLGHERI
VIA BOLGHERESE, 198
57022 CASTAGNETO CARDUCCI [LI]
TEL. +39 0565762175
www.donnefittipaldi.it

ANNUAL PRODUCTION 60,000 bottles
HECTARES UNDER VINE 9.50

○ Lady F Orpicchio Bianco '16	♥♥ 4
● Bolgheri Rosso '15	♥ 4

Il Falcone

LOC. FALCONE, 186
57028 SUVERETO [LI]
TEL. +39 0565829331
www.ilfalcone.net

CELLAR SALES
PRE-BOOKED VISITS
ACCOMMODATION
ANNUAL PRODUCTION 40,000 bottles
HECTARES UNDER VINE 10.00

● Suvereto Boccalupo '14 🏆🏆 6
● Vallin dei Ghiri '15 🏆🏆 7
○ Falcobianco '16 🏆 3
● Falcorosso '15 🏆 4

Cantine Faralli

LOC. FASCIANO, 4
52040 CORTONA [AR]
TEL. +39 0575613128
www.cantinefaralli.com

CELLAR SALES
ANNUAL PRODUCTION 25,000 bottles
HECTARES UNDER VINE

● Cortona Cabernet Sauvignon I Viti '14 🏆🏆 4
● Cortona Merlot '13 🏆🏆 4

Fertuna

LOC. GRILLI
VIA AURELIA ANTICA KM 205
58040 GAVORRANO [GR]
TEL. +39 056688138
www.fertuna.it

CELLAR SALES
PRE-BOOKED VISITS
ANNUAL PRODUCTION 300,000 bottles
HECTARES UNDER VINE 50.00

● Maremma Toscana Lodai '15 🏆🏆 3
○ Droppello '16 🏆 4
○ Maremma Toscana Vermentino '16 🏆 3

Fietri

LOC. FIETRI
53010 GAIOLE IN CHIANTI [SI]
TEL. +39 0577734048
www.fietri.com

CELLAR SALES
PRE-BOOKED VISITS
ACCOMMODATION
ANNUAL PRODUCTION 15,000 bottles
HECTARES UNDER VINE 8.00
VITICULTURE METHOD Certified Organic

● Chianti Cl. '15 🏆🏆 3

La Fiorita

FRAZ. CASTELNUOVO DELL'ABATE
PODERE BELLAVISTA
53024 MONTALCINO [SI]
TEL. +39 0577835657
www.lafiorita.com

CELLAR SALES
PRE-BOOKED VISITS
ANNUAL PRODUCTION 35,000 bottles
HECTARES UNDER VINE 7.00

● Rosso di Montalcino '15 🏆🏆 5
● Brunello di Montalcino '12 🏆 6

Poderi Firenze

LOC. L'ABBANDONATO
58031 ARCIDOSSO [GR]
TEL. +39 0564967271
www.poderifirenze.it

CELLAR SALES
PRE-BOOKED VISITS
ACCOMMODATION
ANNUAL PRODUCTION 80,000 bottles
HECTARES UNDER VINE 18.00

● Maremma Toscana Ciliegiolo Sciresa '15 🏆🏆 2*
● Montecucco Sangiovese Sottocasa '13 🏆🏆 2*
○ Sottocasa Vermentino '16 🏆 2

Poderi Fontemorsi

VIA DELLE COLLINE
56040 MONTESCUDAIO [PI]
TEL. +39 3356843438
www.fontemorsi.it

CELLAR SALES
ACCOMMODATION
ANNUAL PRODUCTION 50,000 bottles
HECTARES UNDER VINE 8.50
VITICULTURE METHOD Certified Organic

● Montescudaio Rosso Spazzavento '13	♥♥ 2*
● Volterrano '13	♥♥ 4
○ Tresassi Bianco '16	♥ 2
⊙ Tresassi Rosato '16	♥ 2

Le Fonti

FRAZ. PANZANO IN CHIANTI
LOC. LE FONTI
50022 GREVE IN CHIANTI [FI]
TEL. +39 055852194
www.fattorialefonti.it

CELLAR SALES
PRE-BOOKED VISITS
ANNUAL PRODUCTION 45,000 bottles
HECTARES UNDER VINE 8.81
VITICULTURE METHOD Certified Organic

● Chianti Cl. Ris. '13	♥♥ 4
● Fontissimo '13	♥ 5

Fontuccia

VIA PROVINCIALE, 54
58012 ISOLA DEL GIGLIO [GR]
TEL. +39 0564809576
www.fontuccia.it

ANNUAL PRODUCTION 6,500 bottles
HECTARES UNDER VINE 3.00

○ Capperorosso Senti Oh! '15	♥♥ 4
○ Senti Oh! '16	♥♥ 4

La Fornace

POD. FORNACE, 154A
53024 MONTALCINO [SI]
TEL. +39 0577848465
www.agricola-lafornace.it

CELLAR SALES
PRE-BOOKED VISITS
ANNUAL PRODUCTION 15,000 bottles
HECTARES UNDER VINE 4.50

● Brunello di Montalcino Ris. '11	♥♥ 8
● Brunello di Montalcino Origini '12	♥ 6

Fornacelle

LOC. FORNACELLE, 232A
57022 CASTAGNETO CARDUCCI [LI]
TEL. +39 0565775575
www.fornacelle.it

CELLAR SALES
PRE-BOOKED VISITS
ANNUAL PRODUCTION 35,000 bottles
HECTARES UNDER VINE 15.00

● Bolgheri Sup. Foglio 38 '14	♥♥ 7
○ Bolgheri Bianco Zizzolo '16	♥ 3
● Bolgheri Sup. Guarda Boschi '14	♥ 6

Podere Forte

LOC. PETRUCCI, 13
53023 CASTIGLIONE D'ORCIA [SI]
TEL. +39 05778885100
www.podereforte.it

CELLAR SALES
PRE-BOOKED VISITS
ANNUAL PRODUCTION 12,000 bottles
HECTARES UNDER VINE 15.00
VITICULTURE METHOD Certified Biodynamic
SUSTAINABLE WINERY

● Guardiavigna '13	♥♥ 8
● Orcia Petruccino '14	♥ 6

Fattoria di Fubbiano

LOC. SAN GENNARO
VIA DI TOFORI FUBBIANO
55010 CAPANNORI [LU]
TEL. +39 0583978011
www.fattoriadifubbiano.it

CELLAR SALES
PRE-BOOKED VISITS
ACCOMMODATION
ANNUAL PRODUCTION 100,000 bottles
HECTARES UNDER VINE 20.00

○ Colline Lucchesi Bianco '16	♟♟	2*
○ Colline Lucchesi Vermentino '16	♟	2

Gattavecchi

LOC. SANTA MARIA
VIA DI COLLAZZI, 74
53045 MONTEPULCIANO [SI]
TEL. +39 0578757110
www.gattavecchi.it

CELLAR SALES
PRE-BOOKED VISITS
RESTAURANT SERVICE
ANNUAL PRODUCTION 280,000 bottles
HECTARES UNDER VINE 40.00

● Chianti Colli Senesi '16	♟	2
● Nobile di Montepulciano '14	♟	4
● Nobile di Montepulciano Riserva dei Padri Serviti '13	♟	5

Gentili

FRAZ. PIAZZE
VIA DEL TAMBURINO, 120
53040 CETONA [SI]
TEL. +39 0578244038
www.gentiliwine.com

CELLAR SALES
PRE-BOOKED VISITS
ANNUAL PRODUCTION 130,000 bottles
HECTARES UNDER VINE 15.00

○ Chardonnay '16	♟♟	2*
● Le Favorite '15	♟♟	5
● Chianti Le Cerrine Ris. '14	♟	3
● Matero '16	♟	1*

La Gerla

LOC. CANALICCHIO
POD. COLOMBAIO, 5
53024 MONTALCINO [SI]
TEL. +39 0577848599
www.lagerla.it

CELLAR SALES
PRE-BOOKED VISITS
ANNUAL PRODUCTION 80,000 bottles
HECTARES UNDER VINE 11.50

● Brunello di Montalcino '12	♟♟	6
● Rosso di Montalcino '15	♟♟	3
● Brunello di Montalcino Ris. '11	♟	7

Giannoni Fabbri

LOC. SAN MARCO IN VILLA, 2
52044 CORTONA [AR]
TEL. +39 3475883939
www.giannonifabbri.it

CELLAR SALES
PRE-BOOKED VISITS
ANNUAL PRODUCTION 10,000 bottles
HECTARES UNDER VINE 14.00

● Cortona Syrah Amato '14	♟♟	3
○ Cortona Vin Santo '07	♟♟	6
○ Vinciluna Rosato '16	♟	2

Guidi 1929

VIA LIGURIA
53036 POGGIBONSI [SI]
TEL. +39 0577936356
www.guidi1929.com

CELLAR SALES
PRE-BOOKED VISITS
ANNUAL PRODUCTION 100,000 bottles
HECTARES UNDER VINE 14.00
SUSTAINABLE WINERY

○ Chardonnay Prima Luce '16	♟♟	2*
○ Vernaccia di San Gimignano Ris. '15	♟♟	2*
● Sangiovese Ruggente '16	♟	3
○ Vernaccia di San Gimignano '16	♟	2

Icario

VIA DELLE PIETROSE, 2
53045 MONTEPULCIANO [SI]
TEL. +39 0578758845
www.icarin.it

CELLAR SALES
PRE-BOOKED VISITS
ANNUAL PRODUCTION 110,000 bottles
HECTARES UNDER VINE 20.00

● Rosso di Montepulciano '15	♥♥ 2*

Fattoria Kappa

LOC. LE BADIE
VIA ROMA, 118
56040 CASTELLINA MARITTIMA [PI]
TEL. +39 3346619711
a.dimaio74@virgilio.it

CELLAR SALES
PRE-BOOKED VISITS
ANNUAL PRODUCTION 20,000 bottles
HECTARES UNDER VINE 6.00

○ Etabeta '16	♥♥ 4
● Kappa '15	♥♥ 5

Fattoria La Striscia

VIA DEI CAPPUCCINI, 3
52100 AREZZO
TEL. +39 057526740
www.lastriscia.com

ANNUAL PRODUCTION 7,800 bottles
HECTARES UNDER VINE 14.50

● Chianti Bernardino '15	♥♥ 3
● Occhini Sangiovese '15	♥♥ 3

Le Buche

LOC. LE BUCHE
FRAZ. SARTEANO
S.DA VICINALE DELLE BUCHE, 25
53047 SARTEANO [SI]
TEL. +39 0578274066
www.lebuche.com

CELLAR SALES
PRE-BOOKED VISITS
ACCOMMODATION AND RESTAURANT SERVICE
ANNUAL PRODUCTION 100,000 bottles
HECTARES UNDER VINE 30.00
SUSTAINABLE WINERY

● Primaio '15	♥♥ 2*
⊙ Zelia Brut	♥♥ 5
○ Orhora '16	♥ 3
● Tempore '09	♥ 6

Leuta

VIA PIETRAIA, 21
52044 CORTONA [AR]
TEL. +39 3385033560
www.leuta.it

CELLAR SALES
PRE-BOOKED VISITS
ANNUAL PRODUCTION 25,000 bottles
HECTARES UNDER VINE 12.60

● Cortona Merlot 1,618 '13	♥♥ 5
● Cortona Sangiovese Solitario '13	♥♥ 6
● 2,618 Cabernet Franc '14	♥ 5
● Nautilus '14	♥ 8

Livernano

LOC. LIVERNANO, 67A
53017 RADDA IN CHIANTI [SI]
TEL. +39 0577738353
www.livernano.it

CELLAR SALES
PRE-BOOKED VISITS
ACCOMMODATION AND RESTAURANT SERVICE
ANNUAL PRODUCTION 100,000 bottles
HECTARES UNDER VINE 25.00

● Chianti Cl. Gran Sel. '13	♥♥ 7
● Chianti Cl. Gran Sel. Casalvento '13	♥ 7

Luce della Vite
LOC. CASTEL GIOCONDO
53024 MONTALCINO [SI]
TEL. +39 05527141
www.lucedellavite.com

PRE-BOOKED VISITS
ANNUAL PRODUCTION 470,000 bottles
HECTARES UNDER VINE 77.00
SUSTAINABLE WINERY

- ● Brunello di Montalcino Luce '12   ♟♟ 8
- ● Luce '14   ♟♟ 8
- ● Lucente '15   ♟ 6

Le Maciarine
S.DA PROV.LE DI POGGIOFERRO
58038 SEGGIANO [GR]
TEL. +39 3487155650
www.lemaciarine.it

CELLAR SALES
PRE-BOOKED VISITS
ANNUAL PRODUCTION 10,000 bottles
HECTARES UNDER VINE 3.90
SUSTAINABLE WINERY

- ● Montecucco Rosso '13   ♟♟ 3
- ● Montecucco Rosso '14   ♟ 3

La Magia
LOC. LA MAGIA
53024 MONTALCINO [SI]
TEL. +39 0577835667
www.fattorialamagia.it

ANNUAL PRODUCTION 80,000 bottles
HECTARES UNDER VINE 15.00

- ● Brunello di Montalcino '12   ♟♟ 6

Fattoria Mantellassi
LOC. BANDITACCIA, 26
58051 MAGLIANO IN TOSCANA [GR]
TEL. +39 0564592037
www.fattoriamantellassi.it

CELLAR SALES
PRE-BOOKED VISITS
ANNUAL PRODUCTION 1,000,000 bottles
HECTARES UNDER VINE 99.00
SUSTAINABLE WINERY

- ● Maremma Toscana
  Ciliegiolo Maestrale '16   ♟♟ 2*
- ● Morellino di Scansano Mentore '16   ♟ 2

Podere Marcampo
LOC. SAN CIPRIANO
56048 VOLTERRA [PI]
TEL. +39 058885393
www.poderemarcampo.com

CELLAR SALES
PRE-BOOKED VISITS
ACCOMMODATION AND RESTAURANT SERVICE
ANNUAL PRODUCTION 15,000 bottles
HECTARES UNDER VINE 5.00

- ○ Terrablu '16   ♟♟ 2*
- ● Genuino '15   ♟ 2

Maté
LOC. SANTA RESTITUTA
53024 MONTALCINO [SI]
TEL. +39 0577847215
www.matewine.com

CELLAR SALES
PRE-BOOKED VISITS
ANNUAL PRODUCTION 28,000 bottles
HECTARES UNDER VINE 6.50

- ● Rosso di Montalcino '15   ♟♟ 3
- ● Brunello di Montalcino '12   ♟ 6

Giorgio Meletti Cavallari

VIA CASONE UGOLINO,12
57022 CASTAGNETO CARDUCCI [LI]
TEL. +39 0565775620
www.giorgiomeletticavallari.it

CELLAR SALES
PRE-BOOKED VISITS
ACCOMMODATION
ANNUAL PRODUCTION 40,000 bottles
HECTARES UNDER VINE 10.00

○ Bolgheri Bianco Borgeri '16	♟ 3
● Bolgheri Rosso Borgeri '15	♟ 3
● Bolgheri Sup. Impronte '14	♟ 5

Podere Monastero

LOC. MONASTERO
53011 CASTELLINA IN CHIANTI [SI]
TEL. +39 0577740436
www.poderemonastero.com

CELLAR SALES
PRE-BOOKED VISITS
ACCOMMODATION
ANNUAL PRODUCTION 7,000 bottles
HECTARES UNDER VINE 3.00

● La Pineta '15	♟♟ 6
● Campanaio '15	♟♟ 6

La Montanina

LOC. MONTI IN CHIANTI
53020 GAIOLE IN CHIANTI [SI]
TEL. +39 0577747017
www.chianticlassico.com

● Nebbiano '13	♟♟ 3
● Agosto di Monti '13	♟ 3
● Chianti Cl. '14	♟ 3

Fattoria di Montechiari

VIA MONTECHIARI, 27
55015 MONTECARLO [LU]
TEL. +39 058322189
www.montechiari.com

CELLAR SALES
PRE-BOOKED VISITS
ANNUAL PRODUCTION 30,000 bottles
HECTARES UNDER VINE 10.00

○ Donna Catherine Brut	♟♟ 5
○ Oro '15	♟ 4

Montemercurio

VIA DI TOTONA, 25A
53045 MONTEPULCIANO [SI]
TEL. +39 0578716610
www.montemercurio.com

CELLAR SALES
PRE-BOOKED VISITS
ANNUAL PRODUCTION 40,000 bottles
HECTARES UNDER VINE 10.00
VITICULTURE METHOD Certified Organic

○ Caduceo '16	♟♟ 3
● Rosso di Montepulciano Petaso '14	♟♟ 3

Monterinaldi

LOC. LUCARELLI
53017 RADDA IN CHIANTI [SI]
TEL. +39 0577733533
www.monterinaldi.it

ANNUAL PRODUCTION 400,000 bottles
HECTARES UNDER VINE 65.00

● Chianti Cl. Vign. Boscone '15	♟♟ 4
● Chianti Cl. Ris. '14	♟♟ 4

Podere Morazzano

S.DA MORAZZANO 5
56040 MONTESCUDAIO [PI]
TEL. +39 0445529693
www.poderemorazzano.it

ANNUAL PRODUCTION 20,000 bottles
HECTARES UNDER VINE 5.00

● Eriva '13	♟♟ 5
● Montescudaio Rerosso Ris. '13	♟ 4
● Ribuio '13	♟ 2

Alberto Motta

S.DA BANDITELLA 2, 16
58100 GROSSETO
TEL. +39 0564405105
www.mottavini.com

CELLAR SALES
PRE-BOOKED VISITS
ANNUAL PRODUCTION 40,000 bottles
HECTARES UNDER VINE 10.00
VITICULTURE METHOD Certified Organic

● Maremma Toscana Ciliegiolo '16	♟♟ 3
● Morellino dl Scansano '16	♟ 3
● Morellino di Scansano Ris. '14	♟ 5

Oliviera

S.DA PROV.LE 102 DI VAGLIAGLI, 36
53019 CASTELNUOVO BERARDENGA [SI]
TEL. +39 3498950188
www.oliviera.it

ANNUAL PRODUCTION 30,000 bottles
HECTARES UNDER VINE 9.00

● Chianti Cl. Gran Sel. '13	♟♟ 5
● Chianti Cl. '15	♟ 3

Orciaverde

LOC. MONTENERO D'ORCIA
POD. 369
58033 CASTEL DEL PIANO [GR]
TEL. +39 3471072895
www.orciaverde.it

CELLAR SALES
PRE-BOOKED VISITS
ACCOMMODATION AND RESTAURANT SERVICE
ANNUAL PRODUCTION 30,000 bottles
HECTARES UNDER VINE 6.00
VITICULTURE METHOD Certified Organic

● Montecucco Sangiovese '13	♟♟ 3
● Montecucco Rosso '15	♟ 2
● Montecucco Sangiovese Ris. '12	♟ 4

Orsumella

LOC. MONTEFIRIDOLFI
VIA COLLINA 52
50026 SAN CASCIANO IN VAL DI PESA [FI]
TEL. +39 3343115959
www.orsumella.it

● Chianti Cl. '15	♟♟ 3
● Chianti Cl. '14	♟ 3
● Chianti Cl. Corte Rinieri Ris. '13	♟ 3

Padelletti

VIA PADELLETTI, 9
53024 MONTALCINO [SI]
TEL. +39 0577848314
www.padelletti.it

CELLAR SALES
PRE-BOOKED VISITS
ANNUAL PRODUCTION 30,000 bottles
HECTARES UNDER VINE 6.00

● Brunello di Montalcino '12	♟♟ 8

Fattoria Il Palagio

FRAZ. CASTEL SAN GIMIGNANO
LOC. IL PALAGIO
53030 COLLE DI VAL D'ELSA [SI]
TEL. +39 0577953004
www.ilpalagio.it

CELLAR SALES
PRE-BOOKED VISITS
ANNUAL PRODUCTION 800,000 bottles
HECTARES UNDER VINE 79.00

○ Tabocc '14	♥♥ 4
○ Melaia Sauvignon '16	♥ 3
○ Vernaccia di San Gimignano Le Ginestrelle '16	♥ 3

Tenuta Il Palagio

VIA SANT'ANDREA, 11
50063 FIGLINE E INCISA VALDARNO [FI]
TEL. +39 0559502652
www.palagioproducts.com

CELLAR SALES
ACCOMMODATION AND RESTAURANT SERVICE
HECTARES UNDER VINE 12.00

● Casino delle Vie '14	♥♥ 5
● Sister Moon '13	♥♥ 6
● Chianti When We Dance '15	♥ 5

Tenuta Il Palazzo

LOC. ANTRIA
52100 AREZZO
TEL. +39 0575 361338
www.tenutailpalazzo.it

CELLAR SALES
PRE-BOOKED VISITS
ANNUAL PRODUCTION 300,000 bottles
HECTARES UNDER VINE 40.00

● Chianti Ris. '13	♥♥ 3
○ Vin Santo del Chianti '11	♥♥ 4

Palazzo Vecchio

FRAZ. VALIANO
VIA TERRAROSSA, 5
53040 MONTEPULCIANO [SI]
TEL. +39 0578724170
www.vinonobile.it

CELLAR SALES
PRE-BOOKED VISITS
RESTAURANT SERVICE
ANNUAL PRODUCTION 40,000 bottles
HECTARES UNDER VINE 25.00

● Nobile di Montepulciano Ris. '12	♥♥ 5
● Rosso di Montepulciano Dogana '15	♥ 3

Pian delle Querci

VIA GIACOMO LEOPARDI, 10
53024 MONTALCINO [SI]
TEL. +39 0577834174
www.piandellequerci.it

CELLAR SALES
PRE-BOOKED VISITS
ANNUAL PRODUCTION 53,000 bottles
HECTARES UNDER VINE 8.50

● Brunello di Montalcino Ris. '11	♥♥ 5
● Rosso di Montalcino '15	♥ 3

Pian delle Vigne

LOC. PIAN DELLE VIGNE
53024 MONTALCINO [SI]
TEL. +39 0577816066
www.antinori.it

● Rosso di Montalcino '15	♥♥ 5
● Brunello di Montalcino '12	♥♥ 7

La Piana

VIA ROMA, 25
57032 CAPRAIA ISOLA [LI]
TEL. +39 3920592988
www.lapianacapraia.it

CELLAR SALES
PRE-BOOKED VISITS
ANNUAL PRODUCTION 11,000 bottles
HECTARES UNDER VINE 5.00
VITICULTURE METHOD Certified Organic

● Cristino '16		♟♟ 5
○ Palmazio '16		♟♟ 3
◐ Rosa della Piana '16		♟ 3

Le Pianacce

LOC. PIANACCE, 198
57028 SUVERETO [LI]
TEL. I 30 0565020027

CELLAR SALES
PRE-BOOKED VISITS
ANNUAL PRODUCTION 13,000 bottles
HECTARES UNDER VINE 4.00

● Diavolino Rosso '12		♟♟ 4
● Le Pianacce '14		♟ 3
○ Selico '15		♟ 3

Piandaccoli

VIA DI PIANDACCOLI, 7
50055 LASTRA A SIGNA [FI]
TEL. +39 0550750005
www.piandaccoli.it

CELLAR SALES
PRE-BOOKED VISITS
ACCOMMODATION
ANNUAL PRODUCTION 90,000 bottles
HECTARES UNDER VINE 20.00

● Chianti Cosmus Ris. '14		♟♟ 2*
● In Primis '14		♟ 3

Fattoria di Piazzano

VIA DI PIAZZANO, 5
50053 EMPOLI [FI]
TEL. +39 0571994032
www.fattoriadipiazzano.it

CELLAR SALES
PRE-BOOKED VISITS
ACCOMMODATION AND RESTAURANT SERVICE
ANNUAL PRODUCTION 90,000 bottles
HECTARES UNDER VINE 33.00

● Blend 1 '15		♟♟ 4
● Syrah '15		♟♟ 4
● Blend 2 '15		♟ 4
● Chianti Rio Camerata '15		♟ 3

Tenute Piccini

LOC. PIAZZOLE, 25
53011 CASTELLINA IN CHIANTI [SI]
TEL. +39 057754011
www.tenutepiccini.it

ANNUAL PRODUCTION 16,000,000 bottles
HECTARES UNDER VINE 650.00

● Bolgheri Gattabuia Tenuta Moraia '14		♟♟ 3
○ Calasera Vermentino Tenuta Moraia '16		♟♟ 2*
● Chianti Collezione Oro Ris. '14		♟ 2
● Sasso al Poggio '13		♟ 2

Piemaggio

LOC. FIORAIE
53011 CASTELLINA IN CHIANTI [SI]
TEL. +39 0577740658

CELLAR SALES
PRE-BOOKED VISITS
ANNUAL PRODUCTION 40,000 bottles
HECTARES UNDER VINE 11.50

● Chianti Cl. Le Fioraie '12		♟♟ 4
● Chianti Cl. Le Fioraie Ris. '10		♟ 4

Agostina Pieri

FRAZ. SANT'ANGELO SCALO
LOC. PIANCORNELLO
53024 MONTALCINO [SI]
TEL. +39 0577844163
www.pieriagostina.it

ANNUAL PRODUCTION 45,000 bottles
HECTARES UNDER VINE 10.78

● Brunello di Montalcino '12	🍷🍷 6
● Rosso di Montalcino '15	🍷 3

La Pierotta

LOC. LA PIEROTTA, 19
58020 SCARLINO [GR]
TEL. +39 056637218
www.lapierotta.it

CELLAR SALES
PRE-BOOKED VISITS
ANNUAL PRODUCTION 50,000 bottles
HECTARES UNDER VINE 13.00

● Maremma Toscana Ciliegiolo '15	🍷🍷 3
● Monteregio di Massa Marittima Rosso Selvaneta '16	🍷🍷 2*

Pietranova

LOC. CASA AL PIANO, 68
57022 CASTAGNETO CARDUCCI [LI]
TEL. +39 0565774101
www.pietra-nova.com

CELLAR SALES
PRE-BOOKED VISITS
ACCOMMODATION
ANNUAL PRODUCTION 25,000 bottles
HECTARES UNDER VINE 5.00

● Bolgheri 1698 '14	🍷🍷 4
● Bolgheri Casa al Piano '15	🍷 3
● Bolgheri Sup. Renzo '14	🍷 6

Podere il Castellaccio

LOC. SEGALARI, 102
57022 CASTAGNETO CARDUCCI [LI]
TEL. +39 3358210510
www-podereilcastellaccio.it

● Dinostro '15	🍷🍷 4
● Valente '15	🍷🍷 4
● Somatico '15	🍷 4

Tenuta Podernovo

VIA PODERNUOVO, 13
56030 TERRICCIOLA [PI]
TEL. +39 0587655173
www.tenutapodernovo.it

CELLAR SALES
PRE-BOOKED VISITS
ACCOMMODATION
ANNUAL PRODUCTION 140,000 bottles
HECTARES UNDER VINE 25.00
VITICULTURE METHOD Certified Organic

● Aliotto '15	🍷🍷 3
● Teuto '13	🍷 4

Poggio alla Sala

LOC. POGGIO ALLA SALA
VIA DELLE CHIANE, 3
53045 MONTEPULCIANO [SI]
TEL. +39 0578767224
www.poggioallasala.it

CELLAR SALES
PRE-BOOKED VISITS
ACCOMMODATION AND RESTAURANT SERVICE
ANNUAL PRODUCTION 200,000 bottles
HECTARES UNDER VINE 27.00

● Il Torrino '13	🍷🍷 3
● Nobile di Montepulciano Parceto '13	🍷🍷 6
● Rosso di Montepulciano '16	🍷 3

Poggio Brigante

VIA COLLE DI LUPO, 13
58051 MAGLIANO IN TOSCANA [GR]
TEL. +39 0564592507
www.poggiobrigante.it

CELLAR SALES
PRE-BOOKED VISITS
ANNUAL PRODUCTION 70,000 bottles
HECTARES UNDER VINE 15.00
VITICULTURE METHOD Certified Organic

● Morellino di Scansano '16	ΨΨ 3*
● Morellino di Scansano Arsura '15	Ψ 5

Fattoria Poggio Capponi

LOC. MONTESPERTOLI
VIA MONTELUPO, 184
50025 MONTESPERTOLI [FI]
TEL. +39 0571671914
www.poggiocapponi.it

CELLAR SALES
PRE-BOOKED VISITS
ACCOMMODATION
ANNUAL PRODUCTION 200,000 bottles
HECTARES UNDER VINE 32.00

● Chianti Montespertoli Petriccio '13	ΨΨ 3
○ Sovente '15	ΨΨ 2*
○ Bianco di Binto '16	Ψ 2
● Tinorso '12	Ψ 3

Poggio Grande

LOC. POGGIO GRANDE, 11
53023 CASTIGLIONE D'ORCIA [SI]
TEL. +39 3388677637
www.aziendapoggiogrande.it

CELLAR SALES
PRE-BOOKED VISITS
ANNUAL PRODUCTION 22,000 bottles
HECTARES UNDER VINE 6.50

● Orcia Sangiovese Sesterzo '13	ΨΨ 5
● Syrah '15	ΨΨ 5
● Orcia Scorbutico '15	Ψ 3

Poggio Landi

LOC. PODERE BELVEDERE
FRAZ. TORRENIERI
S.DA PROV.LE 71
53024 MONTALCINO [SI]
TEL. +39 0577042736

● Brunello di Montalcino '12	ΨΨ 7
● Rosso di Montalcino '15	Ψ 4

Poggio Mandorlo

LOC. ANSIDONINA
58038 SEGGIANO [GR]
TEL. +39 05641835170
www.poggiomandorlo.it

CELLAR SALES
ANNUAL PRODUCTION 62,000 bottles
HECTARES UNDER VINE 12.00

● Montecucco La Querce '12	ΨΨ 4
● Il Guardiano '14	Ψ 3
● Poggiomandorlo '10	Ψ 6

Poggio Trevvalle

FRAZ. ARCILLE
S.DA PROV.LE 24 FRONZINA, KM 0,600
58042 CAMPAGNATICO [GR]
TEL. +39 0564998142
www.poggiotrevvalle.it

CELLAR SALES
PRE-BOOKED VISITS
ANNUAL PRODUCTION 80,000 bottles
HECTARES UNDER VINE 13.35
VITICULTURE METHOD Certified Biodynamic
SUSTAINABLE WINERY

● Morellino di Scansano Passera '16	ΨΨ 2*

Tenuta Poggio Verrano

S.DA PROV.LE 9, KM 4
58051 MAGLIANO IN TOSCANA [GR]
TEL. +39 0564589943
www.poggioverrano.it

CELLAR SALES
PRE-BOOKED VISITS
ANNUAL PRODUCTION 80,000 bottles
HECTARES UNDER VINE 27.00

● Dròmos '10	♥♥ 6
● Poggio Verrrano 3 '10	♥♥ 4

Pometti

LOC. LA SELVA
53020 TREQUANDA [SI]
TEL. +39 057747833
www.pometti.it

CELLAR SALES
PRE-BOOKED VISITS
ACCOMMODATION AND RESTAURANT SERVICE
ANNUAL PRODUCTION 40,000 bottles
HECTARES UNDER VINE 11.00

● Orcia Centosei '14	♥♥ 3
● Tinotre '14	♥♥ 4
● Villa Boscarello '13	♥ 4

Priorino

VIA MARTIRI DELLA LIBERTÀ, 16
53045 MONTEPULCIANO [SI]
TEL. +39 0578707841
www.cantinapriorino.com

CELLAR SALES
PRE-BOOKED VISITS
RESTAURANT SERVICE
ANNUAL PRODUCTION 15,000 bottles
HECTARES UNDER VINE 30.00

● Nobile di Montepulciano Viola '14	♥♥ 5
● Fonte al Giunco '15	♥ 3

Provveditore

LOC. SALAIOLO, 174
58054 SCANSANO [GR]
TEL. +39 3487018670
www.aziendaprovveditore.it

CELLAR SALES
PRE-BOOKED VISITS
RESTAURANT SERVICE
ANNUAL PRODUCTION 15,000 bottles
HECTARES UNDER VINE 30.00

● Morellino di Scansano Irio '16	♥♥ 2*
○ Maremma Toscana Sauvignon Il Bargaglino '16	♥ 3
● Morellino di Scansano Primo Ris. '13	♥ 4

La Rasina

LOC. RASINA, 132
53024 MONTALCINO [SI]
TEL. +39 0577848536
www.larasina.it

CELLAR SALES
PRE-BOOKED VISITS
ACCOMMODATION
ANNUAL PRODUCTION 60,000 bottles
HECTARES UNDER VINE 12.50

● Brunello di Montalcino '12	♥♥ 6
● Rosso di Montalcino '15	♥♥ 3

Redi

VIA DI COLLAZZI, 5
53045 MONTEPULCIANO [SI]
TEL. +39 0578716092
www.cantinadelredi.com

CELLAR SALES
PRE-BOOKED VISITS
ANNUAL PRODUCTION 120,000 bottles
HECTARES UNDER VINE

● Nobile di Montepulciano '13	♥♥ 3
○ Vin Santo di Montepulciano '11	♥♥ 6

Rigoli

LOC. CAFAGGIO
VIA DEGLI ULVI, 8
57021 CAMPIGLIA MARITTIMA [LI]
TEL. +39 0565843079
www.rigolivini.com

ANNUAL PRODUCTION 30,000 bottles
HECTARES UNDER VINE 5.00

● Assiolo '13	🍷🍷 2*
● Valdicornia Sangiovese Montepitti '14	🍷🍷 2*
○ Accordo '16	🍷 2
○ Rosato '16	🍷 2

Tenute delle Ripalte

LOC. RIPALTE
57031 CAPOLIVERI [LI]
TEL. +39 056594211
www.tenutadelleripalte.it

CELLAR SALES
PRE-BOOKED VISITS
ACCOMMODATION AND RESTAURANT SERVICE
ANNUAL PRODUCTION 60,000 bottles
HECTARES UNDER VINE 15.00
SUSTAINABLE WINERY

● Aleatico dell' Elba Passito Alea Ludendo '13	🍷🍷 6
● Alicante '15	🍷🍷 3
○ Vermentino '16	🍷🍷 3

Rocca di Montegrossi

FRAZ. MONTI IN CHIANTI
53010 GAIOLE IN CHIANTI [SI]
TEL. +39 0577747977
www.roccadimontegrossi.it

CELLAR SALES
PRE-BOOKED VISITS
ANNUAL PRODUCTION 80,000 bottles
HECTARES UNDER VINE 18.00
VITICULTURE METHOD Certified Organic

● Chianti Cl. '15	🍷🍷 3
● Chianti Cl. Gran Sel. Vign. S. Marcellino '13	🍷 5

San Benedetto

LOC. SAN BENEDETTO, 4A
53037 SAN GIMIGNANO [SI]
TEL. +39 3386958705
www.agrisanbenedetto.com

CELLAR SALES
PRE-BOOKED VISITS
ACCOMMODATION
ANNUAL PRODUCTION 40,000 bottles
HECTARES UNDER VINE 25.00

○ Vernaccia di San Gimignano Ris. '15	🍷🍷 4
● Chianti '15	🍷 2
○ Vernaccia di San Gimignano '16	🍷 2

Fattoria San Donato

LOC. SAN DONATO, 6
53037 SAN GIMIGNANO [SI]
TEL. +39 0577941616
www.sandonato.it

CELLAR SALES
PRE-BOOKED VISITS
ACCOMMODATION AND RESTAURANT SERVICE
ANNUAL PRODUCTION 70,000 bottles
HECTARES UNDER VINE 20.00
VITICULTURE METHOD Certified Organic

○ San Gimignano Vin Santo '11	🍷🍷 5
○ Vernaccia di S. Gimignano Benedetta Ris. '14	🍷🍷 3
○ Vernaccia di S. Gimignano Angelica '16	🍷 3

Fattoria San Felo

LOC. PAGLIATELLI DI SOTTO
58051 MAGLIANO IN TOSCANA [GR]
TEL. +39 0564836727
www.fattoriasanfelo.it

ANNUAL PRODUCTION 200,000 bottles
HECTARES UNDER VINE 25.00

● Morellino di Scansano Lampo '15	🍷🍷 3
● Maremma Toscana Balla La Vecchia '15	🍷 3
● Morellino di Scansano '15	🍷 3

San Michele a Torri

VIA SAN MICHELE, 36
50020 SCANDICCI [FI]
TEL. +39 055769111
www.fattoriasanmichele.it

CELLAR SALES
PRE-BOOKED VISITS
ANNUAL PRODUCTION 200,000 bottles
HECTARES UNDER VINE 55.00
VITICULTURE METHOD Certified Organic

● Chicchirossi '16	♼♼ 3
● Chianti Colli Fiorentin '15	♼ 2

Santa Lucia

FRAZ. FONTEBLANDA
S.DA STAT.LE AURELIA, 264
58015 ORBETELLO [GR]
TEL. +39 3929506975
www.azsantalucia.com

CELLAR SALES
PRE-BOOKED VISITS
ACCOMMODATION
ANNUAL PRODUCTION 150,000 bottles
HECTARES UNDER VINE 40.00
SUSTAINABLE WINERY

● Morellino di Scansano A Luciano '16	♼♼ 2
● Morellino di Scansano Tore del Moro '15	♼ 2

Villa Santo Stefano

FRAZ. PIEVE SANTO STEFANO
VIA DELLA CHIESA XIV, 504
55100 LUCCA
TEL. +39 0583395349
www.villa-santostefano.it

ANNUAL PRODUCTION 30,000 bottles
HECTARES UNDER VINE 7.00

● Colline Lucchesi Sereno '15	♼♼ 3
● Loto '15	♼♼ 5

SassodiSole

FRAZ. TORRENIERI
LOC. SASSODISOLE, 85
53024 MONTALCINO [SI]
TEL. +39 0577834303
www.sassodisole.it

CELLAR SALES
PRE-BOOKED VISITS
ANNUAL PRODUCTION 30,000 bottles
HECTARES UNDER VINE 8.00
SUSTAINABLE WINERY

● Rosso di Montalcino '15	♼♼ 4
● Brunello di Montalcino '12	♼ 5

Fulvio Luigi Serni

LOC. LE LAME, 237
57022 CASTAGNETO CARDUCCI [LI]
TEL. +39 0565763585
www.sernifulvioluigi.it

CELLAR SALES
PRE-BOOKED VISITS
ANNUAL PRODUCTION 20,000 bottles
HECTARES UNDER VINE 3.50

○ Bolgheri Bianco Le Lame '16	♼♼ 2*
● Bolgheri Rosso Tegoleto '15	♼♼ 3
○ Bolgheri Vermentino Radius '16	♼ 2

Tenuta Sette Cieli

FRAZ. LA CALIFORNIA
VIA SANDRO PERTINI
57020 BIBBONA [LI]
TEL. +39 0586677435
www.tenutasettecieli.com

CELLAR SALES
ANNUAL PRODUCTION 45,000 bottles
HECTARES UNDER VINE 10.00
SUSTAINABLE WINERY

● Indaco '13	♼♼ 5
● Scipio '13	♼♼ 8
● Yantra '15	♼♼ 3

Solaria - Cencioni Patrizia

POD. CAPANNA, 102
53024 MONTALCINO [SI]
TEL. +39 0577849426
www.solariacencioni.com

CELLAR SALES
PRE-BOOKED VISITS
ANNUAL PRODUCTION 35,500 bottles
HECTARES UNDER VINE 9.00

● Brunello di Montalcino '12	♟♟ 6
● Rosso di Montalcino '15	♟♟ 3

Emanuela Tamburini

VIA CATIGNANO, 106
50050 GAMBASSI TERME [FI]
TEL. +39 0571680235
www.agricolatamburini.it

CELLAR SALES
PRE-BOOKED VISITS
HECTARES UNDER VINE 30.00

● Brunello di Montalcino Somnio '12	♟♟ 5
○ Il Castelluccio '14	♟♟ 3
● Chianti Italo Ris. '13	♟ 3
● Chianti The Boss '14	♟ 3

Tassi

V.LE P. STROZZI, 1/3
53024 MONTALCINO [SI]
TEL. +39 0577848025
www.tassimontalcino.com

ANNUAL PRODUCTION 20,000 bottles
HECTARES UNDER VINE 5.00

● Brunello di Montalcino Franci '12	♟♟ 8
● Brunello di Montalcino Franci Ris. '11	♟♟ 8
● Rosso di Montalcino Franci '14	♟♟ 4

Tenuta dello Scompiglio

VIA DI VORNO, 67
55012 CAPANNORI [LU]
TEL. +39 0583971438
www.delloscompiglio.org

CELLAR SALES
PRE-BOOKED VISITS
RESTAURANT SERVICE
ANNUAL PRODUCTION 8,000 bottles
HECTARES UNDER VINE 15.00
VITICULTURE METHOD Certified Organic
SUSTAINABLE WINERY

● Lavandaia Bassa '14	♟♟ 3
● Lavandaia Madre '14	♟♟ 5

Tenuta di Trinoro

VIA VAL D'ORCIA, 15
53047 SARTEANO [SI]
TEL. +39 0578267110 0578267110
www.tenutaditrinoro.it

PRE-BOOKED VISITS
ANNUAL PRODUCTION 70,000 bottles
HECTARES UNDER VINE 20.00

● Le Cupole '15	♟♟ 5

Tenuta Di Vaira

S.DA PROV.LE BOLGHERESE, 275B
57022 BOLGHERI [LI]
TEL. +39 0565763581
www.tenutadivaira.com

● Bolgheri Sup. Bolgherese '14	♟♟ 5
● Bolgheri Rosso Caccia al Palazzo '15	♟ 5
● Le Ballerine '15	♟ 4

Tenute di Fraternita

VIA VASARI, 6
52100 AREZZO
TEL. +39 057524694
www.tenutedifraternita.it

PRE-BOOKED VISITS
HECTARES UNDER VINE 50.70

● Chianti Ser Mariotto Ris. '13	🏆🏆 4
● Questua '15	🏆🏆 3
● Chianti Priore '13	🏆 2
● Sangiovese '14	🏆 2

Tollena

VIA SAN GIOVANNI, 69
53037 SAN GIMIGNANO [SI]
TEL. +39 0577907178
www.tollena.it

CELLAR SALES
ACCOMMODATION
ANNUAL PRODUCTION 50,000 bottles
HECTARES UNDER VINE 22.00

○ Vernaccia di San Gimignano Signorina Vittoria Ris. '13	🏆🏆 3
● Chianti Colli Senesi Carmina '15	🏆 3
○ Vernaccia San Gimignano Lunario '16	🏆 2

Torre a Cenaia

LOC. CENAIA - CRESPINA
VIA DELLE COLLINE, 63
56040 CRESPINA LORENZANA [PI]
TEL. +39 050643739
www.torreacenaia.it

CELLAR SALES
PRE-BOOKED VISITS
ANNUAL PRODUCTION 240,000 bottles
HECTARES UNDER VINE 30.00

⊙ Pitti Rosato '16	🏆🏆 2*
● Torre del Vajo '13	🏆🏆 4
○ Dolce Peccato	🏆 3

Le Torri

VIA SAN LORENZO A VIGLIANO, 31
50021 BARBERINO VAL D'ELSA [FI]
TEL. +39 0558076161
www.letorri.net

CELLAR SALES
PRE-BOOKED VISITS
ACCOMMODATION AND RESTAURANT SERVICE
ANNUAL PRODUCTION 170,000 bottles
HECTARES UNDER VINE 28.00
SUSTAINABLE WINERY

● Magliano '13	🏆🏆 5
● Meridius '15	🏆 2
● San Lorenzo '13	🏆 5

Oliviero Toscani

VIA PERETA, 10
56040 CASALE MARITTIMO [PI]
TEL. +39 0586652050
www.otwine.com

PRE-BOOKED VISITS
ANNUAL PRODUCTION 80,000 bottles
HECTARES UNDER VINE 15.00

● OT '13	🏆🏆 6
● Lumeo '15	🏆 5

Tenuta Tre Rose

FRAZ. VALIANO
VIA DELLA STELLA, 3
53040 MONTEPULCIANO [SI]
TEL. +39 0577804101
www.tenutatrerose.it

CELLAR SALES
PRE-BOOKED VISITS
ANNUAL PRODUCTION 650,000 bottles
HECTARES UNDER VINE 102.00

● Nobile di Montepulciano S. Caterina '14	🏆🏆 4
● Nobile di Montepulciano Simposio '12	🏆 6

Tenuta di Trecciano

S.DA PROV.LE 52 DELLA MONTAGNOLA, 16
53018 SOVICILLE [SI]
TEL. +39 0577314357
www.trecciano.it

CELLAR SALES
PRE-BOOKED VISITS
ANNUAL PRODUCTION 80,000 bottles
HECTARES UNDER VINE 15.50

● Chianti Colli Senesi '16	❦❦ 3
● Chianti Colli Senesi Terra Rossa Ris. '14	❦❦ 4

Fattoria Uccelliera

VIA RONCIONE, 9
56042 CRESPINA LORENZANA [PI]
TEL. +39 050662747
www.uccelliera.com

CELLAR SALES
PRE-BOOKED VISITS
ACCOMMODATION
ANNUAL PRODUCTION 100,000 bottles
HECTARES UNDER VINE 16.00

● Castellaccio Rosso '15	❦❦ 5
○ Ginepraia '16	❦❦ 2*
○ Ficaia '16	❦ 2

Usiglian Del Vescovo

VIA USIGLIANO, 26
56036 PALAIA [PI]
TEL. +39 0587622138
www.usigliandelvescovo.it

CELLAR SALES
PRE-BOOKED VISITS
RESTAURANT SERVICE
ANNUAL PRODUCTION 150,000 bottles
HECTARES UNDER VINE 28.00
SUSTAINABLE WINERY

○ Il Ginestraio '16	❦❦ 5
● MilleEottantatre '12	❦❦ 8
● Il Grullaio '16	❦ 3

Val di Suga

LOC. VAL DI CAVA
53024 MONTALCINO [SI]
TEL. +39 0577804101
www.valdisuga.it

CELLAR SALES
PRE-BOOKED VISITS
ANNUAL PRODUCTION 270,000 bottles
HECTARES UNDER VINE 55.00

● Brunello di Montalcino '12	❦❦ 5

Valle di Lazzaro

LOC. VALLE DI LAZZARO, 103
57037 PORTOFERRAIO [LI]
TEL. +39 0565916387
www.valledilazzaro.com

CELLAR SALES
PRE-BOOKED VISITS
ANNUAL PRODUCTION 12,000 bottles
HECTARES UNDER VINE 4.00

○ Chardonnay Lazarus '15	❦❦ 4
○ Elba Ansonica '16	❦❦ 3
○ Elba Vermentino '16	❦❦ 3
● Elba Sangiovese Lazarus '15	❦ 3

Valle Picciola

S.DA PROV.LE 9 DI PIEVASCIATA, 21
53019 CASTELNUOVO BERARDENGA [SI]
TEL. +39 05771698718
www.vallepicciola.com

CELLAR SALES
PRE-BOOKED VISITS
HECTARES UNDER VINE 70.00

● Chianti Cl. '15	❦❦ 3*
● Boscobruno Pinot Nero '15	❦❦ 6
● Quercegrosse Merlot '15	❦❦ 6
⊙ Lugherino Rosato '16	❦ 3

Michele Ventura

FRAZ. SOVANA
LOC. PODERE SOPRA RIPA, 7
58010 SORANO [GR]
TEL. +39 3392009155
www.micheleventuravino.eu

CELLAR SALES
PRE-BOOKED VISITS
ANNUAL PRODUCTION 20,000 bottles
HECTARES UNDER VINE 9.50
VITICULTURE METHOD Certified Organic
SUSTAINABLE WINERY

● Naturae '15	♟♟ 5
● Ripa '15	♟♟ 3

Villa a Sesta

P.ZZA DEL POPOLO, 1
53019 CASTELNUOVO BERARDENGA [SI]
TEL. +39 0577359014
www.villasesta.com

CELLAR SALES
PRE-BOOKED VISITS
ACCOMMODATION AND RESTAURANT SERVICE
ANNUAL PRODUCTION 150,000 bottles
HECTARES UNDER VINE 45.00

● Chianti Cl. Ris. '13	♟♟ 3
● Chianti Cl. Il Palei '14	♟ 2

Villa Calcinaia

FRAZ. GRETI
VIA CITILLE, 84
50022 GREVE IN CHIANTI [FI]
TEL. +39 055853715
www.villacalcinaia.it

CELLAR SALES
PRE-BOOKED VISITS
ACCOMMODATION
ANNUAL PRODUCTION 90,000 bottles
HECTARES UNDER VINE 27.00
VITICULTURE METHOD Certified Organic

● Chianti Cl. Gran Sel. V. Bastignano '14	♟♟ 6
● Chianti Cl. Gran Sel. V. La Fornace '14	♟ 3

Villa Sant'Anna

FRAZ. ABBADIA DI MONTEPULCIANO
VIA DELLA RESISTENZA, 143
53045 MONTEPULCIANO [SI]
TEL. +39 0578708017
www.villasantanna.it

CELLAR SALES
PRE-BOOKED VISITS
ANNUAL PRODUCTION 80,000 bottles
HECTARES UNDER VINE 18.00

● Rosso di Montepulciano '14	♟♟ 2*
● Nobile di Montepulciano Poldo '13	♟ 5
○ Vin Santo di Montepulciano '08	♟ 8

Villanoviana

LOC. SANT'UBERTO
VIA SANTA MADDALENA, 172B
57022 CASTAGNETO CARDUCCI [LI]
TEL. +39 0536807308
www.villanoviana.it

● Bolgheri Rosso Imeneo '15	♟♟ 5
○ Teia '16	♟ 5

Giomi Zannoni

VIA AURELIA NORD, 63
57029 CAMPIGLIA MARITTIMA [LI]
TEL. +39 0565846416
www.giomi-zannoni.com

CELLAR SALES
PRE-BOOKED VISITS
RESTAURANT SERVICE
ANNUAL PRODUCTION 18,000 bottles
HECTARES UNDER VINE 7.00

● Aldò 917 '16	♟♟ 5
○ Val di Cornia Bianco Corniola '16	♟♟ 3
● Val di Cornia Sangiovese Rodantonio '15	♟ 5
○ Vermentino Ninà 910 '16	♟ 3

MARCHE

Our tasting of Marche's wines once again demonstrates the breadth of the myriad varieties and territories that make up the region. It's a fabric that features a strong family dimension and that rarely involves large production volumes. If on the one hand we have the charm of small scale wineries, on the other there's the problem of reduced visibility and lesser-known grapes. Marche's consortiums have done a great deal of work, but moving forward will require the region's many producers to come together and pool their energy, resources and interests (and not only their economic ones). Independent of these structural concerns, the region's wines continue to exhibit a reassuring level of quality, especially when it comes to their whites. Castelli di Jesi and Matelica display their usually agility, giving rise to many leading wines, a host of styles and a standard of quality that's consistently high. It's a circumstance that facilitates dynamism and mobility. Among the region's lead players in these respects are the Vicari family, who were awarded a Tre Bicchieri for the first time. The Bucci's house wine, Verdicchio Classico, also makes the list, thus stealing the limelight from their Riserva Villa Bucci. After a break of a year or two, some names with a certain prestige behind them are back: Garofoli, Borgo Paglianetto and Leo Felici. Roberto Venturi showed that his star was destined to shine more than once. Umani Ronchi delivered with a Verdicchio, after the Conero Riserva's stellar performance last year. Pievalta, Poderi Mattioli, Marotti Campi, Belisario, Tenuta di Tavignano, La Monacesca, Fazi Battaglia and Bisci all delivered, showing a praiseworthy commitment to consistency and personality in their wines. The situation in Piceno, the region's other great productive node, is more complicated. Here Percorino dominates among the whites. Despite its recent founding, Tenuta Spinelli seems like a veteran thanks to its five consecutive Tre Bicchieri. They're accompanied by two newcomers, Maria Letizia Allevi's small artisanal winery and the promising Tenuta Santori, both authentic products of the genius loci. Montepulciano finds glory both on its own (for example Emanuele Dianetti's Offida Rosso) and in traditional blends with Sangiovese, like those made by Le Caniette and Velenosi. Other districts are still unable to break through into the top, but we can testify to the fact that they're working busily on their native grape varieties. The idea is to create a bond between cultivar and territory, the only effective response to globalization's flood tide of international grapes. Though they recognize that plenty of time, investment and commitment will be needed to reach that goal.

Maria Letizia Allevi

VIA P. C. ORAZI, 58
63081 CASTORANO [AP]
TEL. +39 073687646
www.vinimida.it

CELLAR SALES
PRE-BOOKED VISITS
ANNUAL PRODUCTION 8,000 bottles
HECTARES UNDER VINE 3.00
VITICULTURE METHOD Certified Organic

In the district of Pescolla, every house you
meet could have a cellar hiding inside. So,
despite the fact that Maria Letizia Allevi's
house overlooks a charming sea of
vineyards and olives groves, you might not
ever notice it. In Castorano, the locals are
used to giving more weight to substance
than form. And this concept explains the
expressive spontaneity of the wines realized
by Roberto Corradetti (Maria Letizia's
husband and man Friday). Indeed, with
their limited circulation and artisanal
craftsmanship, they're well-known by local
wine lovers. The 2016 Pecorino Mida
surprised us. It brings together citrus
freshness, twists of light herbs and a whiff
of aniseed in a palate that is graceful,
despite its strong, tangy backbone… a true
masterpiece. The 2014 Offida Rosso Mida
is a generous Montepulciano, with a dense
palatal texture and precise, varietal hints of
sour cherry. The 2016 Mida Rosato is
made by drawing off the Offida Rosso. It
offers up sweet hints of cherry and good
drinkability, despite its weight.

○ Offida Pecorino Mida '16	♥♥♥	3*
☉ Mida Rosato '16	♥♥	3
● Offida Rosso Mida '14	♥♥	3
☉ Mida '13	♀♀	3
○ Offida Pecorino Mida '15	♀♀	3
● Offida Rosso Mida '13	♀♀	3
● Offida Rosso Mida '11	♀♀	4

Aurora

LOC. SANTA MARIA IN CARRO
C.DA CIAFONE, 98
63073 OFFIDA [AP]
TEL. +39 0736810007
www.viniaurora.it

CELLAR SALES
PRE-BOOKED VISITS
ACCOMMODATION
ANNUAL PRODUCTION 53,300 bottles
HECTARES UNDER VINE 9.50
VITICULTURE METHOD Certified Organic

In 1979 few would have bet that the work
of five partners, joined by a mutual sense of
solidarity and the desire to reestablish a
new relationship with the countryside,
would have endured for so long. Yet Aurora
has faced and overcome the challenges of
convention and conformity, trusting in the
idea that organic agriculture is unavoidable
and that its territory is unique in the world.
In their cellar, among steel and wood
containers of various sizes, they make
wines that are Piceno to the bone, the
result of an instinctive, passionate
approach, boosted by ongoing experience.
The Barricadiero reacted well to the
difficult, 2014 vintage. On the nose it
presents a seductive mix of morello cherry,
ash and browner notes that approach
licorice. In the mouth it shows energy and
more rustic tannins. The 2015 Fiobbo
rapidly overcomes some aromatic
hesitation, hovering around lemon peel and
aromatic herbs. In the mouth it's horizontal
and flavorful, with excellent structure. The
2016 Rosso Piceno is infused with an
authentic, rural character.

○ Offida Pecorino Fiobbo '15	♥♥	3
● Offida Rosso Barricadiero '14	♥♥	4
○ Falerio '16	♀	2
● Rosso Piceno '16	♀	2
● Rosso Piceno Sup. '15	♀	2
● Barricadiero '10	♀♀♀	4*
● Barricadiero '09	♀♀♀	4
● Barricadiero '06	♀♀♀	4
● Barricadiero '04	♀♀♀	3
● Barricadiero '03	♀♀♀	3*
● Barricadiero '02	♀♀♀	3
● Barricadiero '01	♀♀♀	3*
● Offida Rosso Barricadiero '11	♀♀♀	4*
○ Offida Pecorino Fiobbo '14	♀♀	3*
● Offida Rosso Barricadiero '13	♀♀	4

Belisario

VIA ARISTIDE MERLONI, 12
62024 MATELICA [MC]
TEL. +39 0737787247
www.belisario.it

CELLAR SALES
PRE-BOOKED VISITS
ANNUAL PRODUCTION 1,000,000 bottles
HECTARES UNDER VINE 300.00

This year sees the 50th anniversary of Verdicchio di Matelica. Belisario, founded just four years after the first guidelines were set, has since played the role of leader both in the spread and development of the appellation. Even as a cooperative, the winery hasn't limited itself to just collecting its members grapes. It directly manages its own park of vineyards, generating outstanding raw materials subdivided by cru and stage of ripeness. In their large cellar, and after careful selection of grapes, their Verdicchio is transformed into wines that are icons of Matelica. The cold 2014 season made for a masterly Cambrugiano: a polished nosed reminiscent of citrus, broom and a delicate backdrop of oak is followed by a relaxed, pervasive palate, with a finish of unbridled richness of flavor. The wine Is flanked by the delectable 2016 Del Cerro and a 2016 Valbona whose backbone is particularly well-defined. The 2014 Maridia is another story altogether: austere and saline, it's a lighter wine.

○ Verdicchio di Matelica Cambrugiano Ris. '14	♛♛♛ 3*
○ Verdicchio di Matelica Anfora '16	♛♛ 2*
○ Verdicchio di Matelica Del Cerro '16	♛♛ 2*
○ Verdicchio di Matelica Meridia '14	♛♛ 3
○ Verdicchio di Matelica Terre di Valbona '16	♛♛ 2*
⊙ Brut Rosé Cuvée Nadir	♛ 2
○ Verdicchio di Matelica Brut Cuvée Nadir	♛ 2
○ Verdicchio di Matelica Vign. B. '16	♛ 3
○ Verdicchio di Matelica Cambrugiano Ris. '12	♛♛♛ 3*
○ Verdicchio di Matelica Cambrugiano Ris. '08	♛♛♛ 3*
○ Verdicchio di Matelica Meridia '10	♛♛♛ 3*
○ Verdicchio di Matelica Vign. B. '15	♛♛♛ 3*

Bisci

VIA FOGLIANO, 120
62024 MATELICA [MC]
TEL. I 39 0737787490
www.bisci.it

CELLAR SALES
PRE-BOOKED VISITS
ACCOMMODATION
ANNUAL PRODUCTION 90,000 bottles
HECTARES UNDER VINE 20.00
VITICULTURE METHOD Certified Organic

In recent years, the synergy that has devcloped between Mauro Bisci and the winemaker Aroldo Bellelli has given new life to this historic winery. Working on their estate, situated between Matelica and Cerreto d'Esi, they have established a style that is increasingly focused on the attributes of the territory - and that means Verdicchio, in all its, flavorful, elegant glory, achieved through proper maturation and aging in fibreglass-lined concrete containers. With the same lucidity, they have made their Merlot, Sangiovese and Cabernet less of a priority, as these varieties are less interesting than in the past and are, in part, explanted. The quality of their white grapes has been pleasantly confirmed. Their 2015 Vigneto Fogliano transformed its intimate territorial character into a style that features mineral and aniseed infused citrus. The mouth has a sophisticated grace that's capable of keeping together aromatic complexity and inspiring drinkability. Almond, hawthorn blossom and green apple adorn the aromatic contours of the saline 2016 Verdicchio.

○ Verdicchio di Matelica Vign. Fogliano '15	♛♛♛ 4*
○ Verdicchio di Matelica '16	♛♛ 3*
● Villa Castiglioni '11	♛ 3
○ Verdicchio di Matelica Vign. Fogliano '13	♛♛♛ 3*
○ Verdicchio di Matelica Vign. Fogliano '10	♛♛♛ 3*
○ Verdicchio di Matelica Vign. Fogliano '08	♛♛♛ 3*
○ Verdicchio di Matelica '15	♛♛ 3
○ Verdicchio di Matelica '14	♛♛ 2*
○ Verdicchio di Matelica '13	♛♛ 3
○ Verdicchio di Matelica '12	♛♛ 2*
○ Verdicchio di Matelica '11	♛♛ 3
○ Verdicchio di Matelica Vign. Fogliano '11	♛♛ 3*

Boccadigabbia

LOC. FONTESPINA
C.DA CASTELLETTA, 56
62012 CIVITANOVA MARCHE [MC]
TEL. +39 073370728
www.boccadigabbia.com

CELLAR SALES
PRE-BOOKED VISITS
ANNUAL PRODUCTION 100,000 bottles
HECTARES UNDER VINE 25.00

Boccadigabbia is comprised of two areas. Their beautiful estate in Civitanova Marche has, for years, been used to cultivate French varieties of grapes and also hosts their current, modern cellar. Here, in the underground facility, in a large barrique cellar, their more ambitious reds, like Akronte and Pix, are aged in new wood. Instead, in La Floriana di Montanello, an estate in Macerata, native varieties are grown: Ribona and Verdicchio whites, Sangiovese and Montepulciano reds. The 2013 Akronte (made with Cabernet Sauvignon) put in a good performance, and only just missed receiving the highest score. It impressed for its fruity abundance, softened by a hint of aromatic herbs and delicate, spicy accents. The mouth is close-woven, with a notable structural impact. The 2013 Pix is a dense, well-sustained Merlot, with soft tannins. The 2015 Floriana Bianco, made with Verdicchio, has its own expressive originality, with aromas of Rosemary and generous flavor.

● Akronte '13	♟♟ 8
○ Colli Maceratesi Ribona Le Grane '16	♟♟ 3
● Pix '13	♟♟ 6
○ Tenuta La Floriana Bianco '15	♟♟ 6
○ Garbì '16	♟ 2
☉ Rosèo '16	♟ 2
● Akronte '98	♟♟♟ 7
● Akronte '97	♟♟♟ 7
● Akronte '95	♟♟♟ 7
● Akronte '94	♟♟♟ 7
● Akronte '93	♟♟♟ 7
● Akronte Cabernet '92	♟♟♟ 7
● Akronte '12	♟♟ 8
● Pix '12	♟♟ 6

Borgo Paglianetto

LOC. PAGLIANO, 393
62024 MATELICA [MC]
TEL. +39 073785465
www.borgopaglianetto.it

CELLAR SALES
PRE-BOOKED VISITS
ANNUAL PRODUCTION 60,000 bottles
HECTARES UNDER VINE 25.00
VITICULTURE METHOD Certified Organic

A small revolution has hit Borgo Paglianetto: out of sheer desire, the owners have brought in a new, young but experienced staff, while continuing to put their trust in Aroldo Bellelli for technical guidance. In the vineyards of Pagliano, clear whites of great flavor are born, all with pure Verdicchio at their foundation. The new line, Réwine, comprises two wines called Ergon (a verdicchio and a Marche Rosso blend of Sangiovese, Merlot and Lacrima) and draws on biodynamic-inspired methods. The 2016 Petrara's strong performance came as no surprise. It's always among the best vintage Matelicas. Its clear profile, tenacious zest, and succulent character translate into extraordinary drinkability. Tre Bicchieri. The surprising 2011 Matesis, a Montepulciano, proved to be quite the opposite, having little in common with more traditional wines or its territory. The wine proved intact, fresh in its fruit, with a finish marked by polished flavor. The 2015 Vertis exhibits a full, soft style.

○ Verdicchio di Matelica Petrara '16	♟♟♟ 2*
● Matesis '11	♟♟ 3*
○ Verdicchio di Matelica Brut M. Cl. '13	♟♟ 5
○ Verdicchio di Matelica Ergon '15	♟♟ 3
○ Verdicchio di Matelica Terravignata '16	♟♟ 2*
○ Verdicchio di Matelica Vertis '15	♟♟ 3
● Ergon '15	♟ 3
○ Verdicchio di Matelica Jera Ris. '10	♟♟♟ 4*
○ Verdicchio di Matelica Vertis '09	♟♟♟ 3*
○ Verdicchio di Matelica Jera Ris. '12	♟♟ 4
○ Verdicchio di Matelica Jera Ris. '11	♟♟ 4
○ Verdicchio di Matelica Petrara '15	♟♟ 2*
○ Verdicchio di Matelica Terravignata '15	♟♟ 2*
○ Verdicchio di Matelica Vertis '13	♟♟ 3*
○ Verdicchio di Matelica Vertis '12	♟♟ 3*

Brunori

V.LE DELLA VITTORIA, 103
60035 JESI [AN]
TEL. +39 0731207213
www.brunori.it

CELLAR SALES
PRE-BOOKED VISITS
ANNUAL PRODUCTION 60,000 bottles
HECTARES UNDER VINE 7.00

Brunori belongs to that small circle of
Verdicchio's 'titled surnames'. For three
generations, the family have dedicated
themselves to the vineyards of Jesi with
obstinate persistence. They are proudly wed
to a classic style that, despite its being
somewhat effacing in terms of aroma, is
capable of bringing out the most intimate
details of the cultivar. Moreover, Giorgio
Brunori was one of the first vine growers to
develop a sense of cru, with his splendid
Nicolò, a contiguous plot of seven hectares
whose oldest vines go back 40 years. All
their wines are aged in fibreglass-lined
cement. The 2015 San Nicolò Riserva put in
a superb performance: chamomile, a trace
of thyme, toasted almonds and composite,
flowery fragrances create and elegant
sensory profile, brought out by its dynamic
silhouette in the mouth. Aniseed and white
fruit emerge from the clear accents and soft
drinkability of the 2016 San Nicolò Classico
Superiore, while the 2016 Le Gemme was
market by a forthright, almond typicity.

○ Castelli di Jesi Verdicchio Cl. San Nicolò Ris. '15	♟♟ 3*
○ Verdicchio dei Castelli di Jesi Cl. Le Gemme '16	♟♟ 2*
○ Verdicchio dei Castelli di Jesi Cl. Sup. San Nicolò '16	♟♟ 2*
○ Castelli di Jesi Verdicchio Cl. San Nicolò Ris. '12	♟♟ 3
○ Verdicchio dei Castelli di Jesi Cl. Le Gemme '13	♟♟ 2*
○ Verdicchio dei Castelli di Jesi Cl. San Nicolò Ris. '13	♟♟ 3*
○ Verdicchio dei Castelli di Jesi Cl. Sup. San Nicolò '14	♟♟ 2*
○ Verdicchio dei Castelli di Jesi Cl. Sup. San Nicolò '10	♟♟ 2*

★Bucci

FRAZ. PONGELLI
VIA CONA, 30
60010 OSTRA VETERE [AN]
TEL. +39 071964179
www.villabucci.com

CELLAR SALES
PRE-BOOKED VISITS
ANNUAL PRODUCTION 120,000 bottles
HECTARES UNDER VINE 31.00
VITICULTURE METHOD Certified Organic

The years pass and yet every bottle that
comes out of Bucci, the historic winery
from Pongelli, reinforces the role it plays for
the entire region. Their approach to
production draws on tried-and-true
artisanal roots and in wines that are true
icons of elegance and harmony. Seven
vineyards spread throughout Castelli di Jesi
supply the grapes, which are then aged in
Slovenian oak barrels before being bottled
and sold. Their oldest vineyards are in
Riserva Villa Bucci. It's a strange turn of
events: for the first time, the 2016 Classico
steals the show from the Riserva Villa
Bucci. It steps up with an enchanting
version: delectable hints of chamomile,
aniseed and delicate, almond accents
emerge in a dynamic, streamlined, palate
that's rich in taste nuances. The 2015 Villa
Bucci Riserva loses a bit of its incisiveness
but to the benefit of a softer palate. While
graceful, it lacks the depth found in its best
versions.

○ Verdicchio dei Castelli di Jesi Cl. Sup. '16	♟♟♟ 3*
○ Castelli di Jesi Verdicchio Cl. Villa Bucci Ris. '15	♟♟ 6
● Rosso Piceno Tenuta Pongelli '14	♟ 3
○ Castelli di Jesi Verdicchio Cl. Villa Bucci Ris. '14	♟♟♟ 6
○ Castelli di Jesi Verdicchio Cl. Villa Bucci Ris. '13	♟♟♟ 6
○ Castelli di Jesi Verdicchio Cl. Villa Bucci Ris. '12	♟♟♟ 6
○ Castelli di Jesi Verdicchio Cl. Villa Bucci Ris. '10	♟♟♟ 6
○ Verdicchio dei Castelli di Jesi Cl. Villa Bucci Ris. '09	♟♟♟ 6

La Calcinara

FRAZ. CANDIA
VIA CALCINARA, 102A
60131 ANCONA
TEL. +39 3285552643
www.lacalcinara.it

CELLAR SALES
PRE-BOOKED VISITS
ANNUAL PRODUCTION 42,000 bottles
HECTARES UNDER VINE 13.00
SUSTAINABLE WINERY

Paolo and Eleonora Berluti are outgoing siblings, lovers of art and wine. Both are winemakers, and they're influencing the direction of the entire territory with their compelling versions of traditional, Conero wine. In their small cellar in Candia, they use Montepulciano with particular care towards maintaining its original fruitiness, though without sacrificing its phenolic ripeness either. Their approach is characterized by accuracy, slow maceration and aging in wood of various dimensions, with barrique reserved only for the Riserva Folle. The fruity core of the Terra Calcinara boasts complexity, thanks to whiffs of fumé and spices. The mouth is taut and well-sustained, restrained only by its tannic finish (though it's difficult for a 2014 to do much better). If you prefer stronger wines, and more palate density, then the exuberant 2012 Folle is your wine. The 2016 Mun, made with Montepulciano grapes, is probably the best rosé in Marche in terms of distribution of flavor, thanks to its length.

● Conero Terra Calcinara Ris. '14	▼▼ 3*
● Conero Folle Ris. '12	▼▼ 5
⊙ Mun '16	▼▼ 3*
● Rosso Conero Il Cacciatore di Sogni '15	▼▼ 3*
● Conero Folle Ris. '10	▽▽ 5
● Conero Terra Calcinara Ris. '13	▽▽ 3
⊙ Mun '15	▽▽ 2*
⊙ Mun '14	▽▽ 2*
● Rosso Conero Il Cacciatore di Sogni '13	▽▽ 2*
● Rosso Conero Il Cacciatore di Sogni '12	▽▽ 2*

Le Caniette

C.DA CANALI, 23
63065 RIPATRANSONE [AP]
TEL. +39 07359200
www.lecaniette.it

CELLAR SALES
PRE-BOOKED VISITS
ANNUAL PRODUCTION 60,000 bottles
HECTARES UNDER VINE 16.00
VITICULTURE METHOD Certified Organic

The finely-crafted stylistic approach that the Vagnoni brothers bring to their Montepulciano, the grape used for some of the best reds in Piceno, shouldn't overshadow the care that goes into the cultivation of other varieties in their vineyards: from Pecorino to Passerina to Bordeaux (a clone of Grenache). All their wines show character, symmetry and a rare capacity to elevate the notion of 'drinkability'. The modern cellar of Canali hosts steel containers for their vintage whites and small wood for their more ambitious wines. The 2012 Morellone brings together the tradition of long maturation with a poise and integrity that's rare for Piceno. Smooth tannins give substance to a marvelous, full-flavored finish. The 2010 Nero di Vite isn't far, a wine that's silky and stratified in its bouquet. But don't miss the 2013 Cinabro, either, a Bordeaux (Grenache clone) that's grown in south Rodano for its kaleidoscopic aromas of quinine, orange peel and exotic spices.

● Piceno Sup. Morellone '12	▼▼▼ 4*
● Cinabro '13	▼▼ 8
● Piceno Nero di Vite '10	▼▼ 6
○ Offida Pecorino Iosonogaia non sono Lucrezia '15	▼▼ 4
○ Offida Pecorino Veronica '16	▼▼ 3
○ Lucrezia '16	▼ 2
● Piceno Rosso Bello '15	▼ 2
○ Offida Pecorino Iosonogaia non sono Lucrezia '10	▽▽▽ 4*
● Piceno Morellone '10	▽▽▽ 4*
● Piceno Morellone '08	▽▽▽ 4*
○ Offida Pecorino Iosonogaia non sono Lucrezia '14	▽▽ 4
● Piceno Sup. Morellone '11	▽▽ 4

Cantine di Castignano

C.DA SAN VENANZO, 31
63072 CASTIGNANO [AP]
TEL. +39 0736822216
www.cantinedicastignano.com

CELLAR SALES
PRE-BOOKED VISITS
ANNUAL PRODUCTION 450,000 bottles
HECTARES UNDER VINE 500.00
VITICULTURE METHOD Certified Organic

We'll never get tired of commending those cooperatives that operate in the best interest of their members, providing consistent quality and the possibility of economic support to an entire agricultural sector. If the more inland areas of Piceno maintain a tendency towards vine growing, this is in part thanks to Cantine di Castignano. They also deserve credit for their defense of native varieties, which serve as the backbone of their products. Their selection is characterized by reasonable prices and a wide presence throughout the territory. Pecorino's propensity for freshness is fully evident in the 2016 Montemisio's dynamism. This is marked by citrus fragrances and a palate whose drinkability proves irresistible. The 2016 Passerina has the same grace, but with a simpler, more approachable profile. The 2012 Gran Maestro's intense sensory aspect unfolds in red fruit and balsamic echoes, while evolving pervasively in the mouth. The 2016 Sangiovese Bio is flowery and slightly salty.

○ Offida Pecorino Montemisio '16	🍷🍷	2*
○ Notturno	🍷🍷	2*
● Offida Rosso Gran Maestro '12	🍷🍷	3
○ Passerina '16	🍷🍷	2*
● Rosso Piceno Sup. Destriero '15	🍷🍷	1*
● Sangiovese Bio '16	🍷🍷	1*
○ Falerio Pecorino Destriero '16	🍷	1*
● Templaria '15	🍷	2
○ Terre di Offida Passerina Brut '16	🍷	2
○ Falerio dei Colli Ascolani Pecorino Destriero '14	🍷🍷	1*
○ Gramelot '14	🍷🍷	2*
○ Offida Pecorino Montemisio '14	🍷🍷	2*
○ Offida Pecorino Montemisio '13	🍷🍷	2*
○ Offida Pecorino Montemisio '12	🍷🍷	2*
● Offida Rosso Gran Maestro '09	🍷🍷	3
● Templaria '14	🍷🍷	2*

Carminucci

VIA SAN LEONARDO, 39
63013 GROTTAMMARE [AP]
TEL. +39 0735735869
www.carminucci.com

CELLAR SALES
ANNUAL PRODUCTION 350,000 bottles
HECTARES UNDER VINE 46.00
VITICULTURE METHOD Certified Organic

Even if the winery owns a sizable tract of land in the area of Offida, its beating heart is up on the hills of Grottammare. Here, amidst vineyards and olive groves, we find their cellar, which, since the late 20th century, has operated primarily in the production of wholesale wines. It was Giovanni Carminucci who came up with the idea of bottling their own line. Over the years he's put together a brilliant, modern selection. Their whites are characterized by an approachable pleasantness, regulated by fresh fragrances, and their reds are fruity, with smooth tannins, making for a selection in which enological craftsmanship is measured but never of secondary importance. The 2014 Piceno Superiore Naumakos faithfully reflects these qualities. Its nose is characterized by morello cherries and sweet spices, while the mouth is succulent in its caressing, fruity fullness. The 2016 Pecorino Belato is extremely fresh in its outward, citrus inflections. Between the two 2016 Falerios, we're partial to the supple Grotte Sul Mare.

● Rosso Piceno Sup. Naumakos '14	🍷🍷	2*
● Falerio Grotte sul Mare '16	🍷🍷	1*
○ Falerio Naumachos '16	🍷🍷	2*
○ Offida Pecorino Belato '16	🍷🍷	2*
○ Casta '16	🍷	2
○ Chardonnay Naumachos '15	🍷	2
⊙ Rosato Grotte sul Mare '16	🍷	2
● Rosso Piceno Grotte sul Mare '16	🍷	2
○ Falerio Naumachos '14	🍷🍷	2*
○ Offida Pecorino Belato '15	🍷🍷	2*
○ Offida Pecorino Belato '14	🍷🍷	2*
○ Offida Pecorino Belato '13	🍷🍷	2*
● Rosso Piceno Sup. Naumachos '12	🍷🍷	2*
● Rosso Piceno Sup. Naumachos '11	🍷🍷	2*
● Rosso Piceno Sup. Naumachos '10	🍷🍷	2*
● Rosso Piceno Sup. Naumakos '13	🍷🍷	2*

CasalFarneto

VIA FARNETO, 12
60030 SERRA DE' CONTI [AN]
TEL. +39 0731889001
www.casalfarneto.it

CELLAR SALES
PRE-BOOKED VISITS
ANNUAL PRODUCTION 750,000 bottles
HECTARES UNDER VINE 39.00

If natural beauty could be bottled and sold, Casalfarneto would be on top of the world. But, instead, the Togni family work round the clock to produce wines that have a modern feel to them, even while staying true to the territory and the varieties used. Verdicchio grapes are aged to various degrees and worked separately according to the plot and wine. Thus the grapes of Jesi are transformed into a selection that includes lovable, late-vintage wines (Cimaio) or sweet wines (Ikon). There's no standout, but the selection showed excellent solidity. Both the elegant and measured 2014 Crisio and 2016 Fontevecchia earned a top place thanks to their pervasive flavor. The 2015 Grancasale proved stylish and succulent. The Ikon is an intense passito dried-grape wine that features hints of canned peaches. Cimaio offers a good balance between sweetness and length of flavor.

○ Castelli di Jesi Verdicchio Cl. Crisio Ris. '14	♛♛ 3*
○ Verdicchio dei Castelli di Jesi Cl. Sup. Fontevecchia '16	♛♛ 2*
○ Cimaio '14	♛♛ 4
○ Verdicchio dei Castelli di Jesi Cl. Sup. Grancasale '15	♛♛ 3
○ Verdicchio dei Castelli di Jesi Passito Ikòn '13	♛♛ 5
● Merago '13	♛ 3
○ Verdicchio dei Castelli di Jesi Cl. Sup. Cimaio '03	♛♛ 4*
○ Verdicchio dei Castelli di Jesi Cl. Sup. Fontevecchia '08	♛♛ 2*
○ Verdicchio dei Castelli di Jesi Cl. Sup. Grancasale '14	♛♛ 3*

Castrum Morisci

VIA MOLINO, 16
63826 MORESCO [FM]
TEL. +39 3400820708
www.castrummorisci.it

CELLAR SALES
ANNUAL PRODUCTION 25,000 bottles
HECTARES UNDER VINE 7.00

Brothers-in-law David Pettinari and Luca Renzi's affinity for the territory made itself known in the moment they chose a name for their winery. Castrum Morisci is none other than the historic name of Moresco, the picturesque hamlet that looks out on Val d'Aso. Surrounded by vineyards, the two renovated a farmhouse so as to use it as their cellar. They personally carry out their work in the vineyards and winemaking itself, with the expert support of Giuseppe Camilli. The wines that have numbers in their name are aged in steel, while the others are aged in terra-cotta. Their selection shows good personality, styled with a touch that's never overdone, and independent of trendy influences. The 2016 003 is the best of the lot. Fragrances of lemons and herbs form part of a vigorous, fruity palate. The 2016 Gallicano is a blend of Pecorino and Passerina. Its nose features medlar, broom and yellow plums, while the mouth offers up commendable grip. The 2016 Testamozza features aromas of black cherry. It's a fragrant wine that's pleasant to drink.

○ 102 '16	♛♛ 2*
○ Falerio Pecorino 003 '14	♛♛ 3
○ Gallicano '16	♛♛ 5
● Rosso Piceno Sangiovese Testamozza '16	♛♛ 5
⊙ 326 '16	♛ 2
○ Padreterno '16	♛ 5
● Rosso Piceno Sangiovese 237 '16	♛ 3

Giacomo Centanni

CDA ASO, 159
63062 MONTEFIORE DELL'ASO [AP]
TEL. +39 0734938530
www.vinicentanni.it

CELLAR SALES
PRE-BOOKED VISITS
ACCOMMODATION
ANNUAL PRODUCTION 140,000 bottles
HECTARES UNDER VINE 35.00
VITICULTURE METHOD Certified Organic

After his studies in enology, Giacomo Centanni began overseeing the family winery. Thanks to a well-structured stylistic approach, his presence has led to strong growth, year after year. Together with his collaborator, Vittorio Festa, the producer gives life to brilliant, modern wines that draw on the customary intensity of the vintages, which are slightly protracted so as maximize taste, structure and a certain alcoholic vigor. All their wines highlight the fruit component and the effectiveness of the techniques used, at times to the detriment of expressive spontaneity. These qualities characterize the powerful 2016 Offida Pecorino, a wine with an extremely long finish. The 2016 Passerina might be the best of the appellation, thanks to a gratifying, savory mouth of extraordinary detail. In its debut, the 2015 Pecorino Affinato in Legno came through with aromas of ginger and spices, and a consistent, well-structured mouth. The 2015 Monte Floris is a well-structured Monetpulciano matured in barrique and characterized by a succulent, close-knit tannic weave.

Monte Floris '15	♟♟	3
Offida Passerina '16	♟♟	2*
Offida Pecorino '16	♟♟	3
Offida Pecorino Affinato in Legno '15	♟♟	4
Falerio Il Borgo '16	♟	2
Profumo di Rosa '16	♟	2
Rosso Piceno Rosso di Forca '15	♟	2
Terre di Offida Passerina Brut M. Cl. '15	♟	4
Monte Floris '14	♟♟	2*
Monte Floris '13	♟♟	2*
Monte Floris '12	♟♟	2*
Offida Passerina '14	♟♟	2*
Offida Passerina '13	♟♟	2*
Offida Pecorino '15	♟♟	2*
Offida Pecorino '14	♟♟	2*
Offida Pecorino '12	♟♟	2*

Cherri d'Acquaviva

VIA ROMA, 40
63075 ACQUAVIVA PICENA [AP]
TEL. +39 0735764416
www.vinicherri.it

CELLAR SALES
PRE-BOOKED VISITS
ANNUAL PRODUCTION 160,000 bottles
HECTARES UNDER VINE 33.00

Paolo Cherri works in a warm terroir, characterized by the nearby Adriatic and the presence of clay and limestone in the soil. Yet he's always avoided the abundant structure, alcohol and aroma (bordering on over-ripe) that's so common in the wines of his territory these days. Even if he works according to 'classic' protocols of winemaking, thanks to prudent maturation, he's able to preserve fruit and backbone in his wines. At his cellar in Acquaviva, he works mostly with steel, taking advantage of its unique properties in terms of oxidation, while reserving wood for his long-aged reds. The lovely selection of wines presented finds its star in the 2016 Pecorino Altissimo. A multivariate nose features field herbs, citrus and green olives, while the wine's sophisticated mouth offers up a fascinating stroke of rôti. The 2016 Falerio has flavor and length. Both the Picenos are succulent, redolent of black cherry and sweet spices.

○ Offida Pecorino Altissimo '16	♟♟	3*
○ Falerio '16	♟♟	2*
○ Offida Passerina Radiosa '16	♟♟	3
● Rosso Piceno '16	♟♟	2*
● Rosso Piceno Sup. '15	♟♟	2*
⊙ Ancella '16	♟	2
○ Offida Passerina Radiosa '15	♟♟	3
○ Offida Pecorino Altissimo '15	♟♟	3
○ Offida Pecorino Altissimo '14	♟♟	3
○ Offida Pecorino Altissimo '13	♟♟	3*
● Rosso Piceno '14	♟♟	2*
● Rosso Piceno '13	♟♟	2*
● Rosso Piceno Sup. '14	♟♟	2*
● Rosso Piceno Sup. '13	♟♟	2*
● Rosso Piceno Sup. '12	♟♟	2*

Tenuta Cocci Grifoni

LOC. SAN SAVINO
C.DA MESSIERI, 12
63038 RIPATRANSONE [AP]
TEL. I 39 073590143
www.tenutacoccigrifoni.it

CELLAR SALES
PRE-BOOKED VISITS
ACCOMMODATION
ANNUAL PRODUCTION 380,000 bottles
HECTARES UNDER VINE 50.00
SUSTAINABLE WINERY

Marilena and Paola Cocci Grifoni's winery is moving quickly. For decades, their double surname has been among the most famous of Piceno. Today they're carrying on the work of their father, Guido, whose approach was characterized by a strong emphasis on native grapes, long aging periods in large wood, and wines that know how to endure and acquire complexity over time, even when uncorked long after harvest. Their vintage wines, especially those made with Passerina and Pecorino, display greater approachability, without undermining their style. The 2011 Vigna Messier stays true to its role as guardian of local orthodoxy. The nose alternates between hints of woodlands and more generous notes of balsamic and red fruit. In the mouth it's austere with a close-knit tannic weave. The 2015 Colle Vecchio opens with accents of chamomile, and offers up green olives and field herbs. The palate's onset reveals flavor and character.

○ Offida Pecorino Colle Vecchio '15	♟♟ 3*
● Rosso Piceno Sup. V. Messieri '11	♟♟ 4
● Rosso Piceno Rubinio '16	♟♟ 2*
○ Adamantea '16	♟ 3
○ Falerio Pecorino Le Torri '16	♟ 2
○ Offida Pecorino Guido Cocci Grifoni '13	♟♟♟ 4*
○ Falerio Pecorino Le Torri '15	♟♟ 2*
○ Offida Pecorino Colle Vecchio '14	♟♟ 3
○ Offida Pecorino Colle Vecchio '13	♟♟ 3
● Offida Rosso Il Grifone '10	♟♟ 5
● Rosso Piceno '15	♟♟ 2*
● Rosso Piceno Sup. Le Torri '11	♟♟ 2*
● Rosso Piceno Sup. Le Torri '10	♟♟ 3
● Rosso Piceno Sup. Tenute Messieri '10	♟♟ 4
● Rosso Piceno Sup. V. Messieri '10	♟♟ 4

Col di Corte

VIA SAN PIETRO, 19A
60036 MONTECAROTTO [AN]
TEL. +39 073189435
www.coldicorte.it

CELLAR SALES
PRE-BOOKED VISITS
ANNUAL PRODUCTION 40,000 bottles
HECTARES UNDER VINE 11.50
VITICULTURE METHOD Certified Organic
SUSTAINABLE WINERY

At first glance, it may seem like the organic principles followed by Giacomo Rossi's young winery are just the product of a passing fad. All it takes is a few minutes with winemaker Claudio Caldaroni to see how firmly committed they are to an artisanal approach that rejects the use of chemicals. Their vineyards feature Verdicchio, though they also inherited Montepulciano, Cabernet Sauvignon and Lacrima from the estate's previous owners. Starting in 2016, all their wines are made with spontaneous fermentation carried out at controlled temperatures. The succulent character and precise hints of almond and cedar bark make the 2015 Anno Uno a must among vintage Verdicchios. 2016 Tobia is more complex, structured and fruity, but none of these undermine its superior drinkability. Lancestrale, a Montepulciano rosé, undergoes second-fermentation in the bottle and isn't disgorged, making for a wine that exhibits original, fruity tendencies.

○ Verdicchio dei Castelli di Jesi Cl. Anno Uno '16	♟♟
○ Verdicchio dei Castelli di Jesi Cl. Sup. Vign. di Tobia '16	♟♟
● Esino Rosso '15	♟
⊙ Lancestrale	♟
● Sant'Ansovino '14	♟
○ Castelli di Jesi Verdicchio Cl. Sant'Ansovino Ris. '14	♟♟
● Sant'Ansovino '12	♟♟
○ Verdicchio dei Castelli di Jesi Cl. Anno Uno '14	♟♟
○ Verdicchio dei Castelli di Jesi Cl. Sup. '15	♟♟
○ Verdicchio dei Castelli di Jesi Cl. Sup. Anno Zero '12	♟♟

Collestefano

LOC. COLLE STEFANO, 3
62022 CASTELRAIMONDO [MC]
TEL. +39 0737640439
www.collestefano.com

CELLAR SALES
PRE-BOOKED VISITS
ACCOMMODATION
ANNUAL PRODUCTION 110,000 bottles
HECTARES UNDER VINE 17.50
VITICULTURE METHOD Certified Organic

The cool air of Monte Gemmo descends on Rustano even on the hottest summer evenings, thus mitigating the daytime heat. Sometimes, however, its influence can be too much, especially during periods of seasonal transition. In fact, making a wine that displays the aromatic freshness and mineral consistency of Collesteano is by no means easy here. We have the meticulous care of the Marchionni family to thank for this small masterpiece. It all starts in the vineyards, where only Verdicchio is grown (with the exception of a small quantity of Sangiovese, used for their rosé). In the cellar, whole grapes are soft-crushed. Only select yeasts are used and wine is aged in large steel barrels. The 2016 Collestefano offers up vibrant acidity and exceptional drinkability (even if, at this young age, it's still missing a bit of depth). If you can wait, it will, one day, make for a complex and balanced wine. For now, enjoy the 2014 Extra Brut, with its notes of hazelnut and malt cookies, all in a seamless, saline body.

○ Verdicchio di Matelica Collestefano '16		♀♀ 2*
○ Verdicchio di Matelica		
Extra Brut M. Cl. '14		♀♀ 4
○ Rosa di Elena '16		♀ 2
○ Verdicchio di Matelica Collestefano '15		♀♀♀ 2*
○ Verdicchio di Matelica Collestefano '14		♀♀♀ 2*
○ Verdicchio di Matelica Collestefano '13		♀♀♀ 2*
○ Verdicchio di Matelica Collestefano '12		♀♀♀ 2*
○ Verdicchio di Matelica Collestefano '10		♀♀♀ 2*
○ Verdicchio di Matelica Collestefano '07		♀♀♀ 2*
○ Verdicchio di Matelica Collestefano '06		♀♀♀ 2*
○ Verdicchio di Matelica Collestefano '11		♀♀ 2*
○ Verdicchio di Matelica		
Extra Brut M. Cl. '13		♀♀ 3*

Colonnara

VIA MANDRIOLE, 6
60034 CUPRAMONTANA [AN]
TEL. +39 0731780273
www.colonnara.it

CELLAR SALES
PRE-BOOKED VISITS
ANNUAL PRODUCTION 1,000,000 bottles
HECTARES UNDER VINE 120.00

The large territory of Cupramontana features a wide range of exposures and altitudes, making for an extremely variegated landscape. As a result, Colonnara, a local cooperative operating in the area, produces a unique selection. The highest vineyards, some of which grow at mountain altitudes, provide the acidy grapes that go into making their sparkling wines (to which much of their spacious underground cellar is dedicated). The grapes growing in the warmer patches are used for their still wines, all of which are aged in steel and are well-formed, in addition to being of a consistent quality. The 2010 Ubaldo Rosi offers up aromas of camphor, hazelnut and aniseed, followed by a creamy, bristling mouth of prolonged richness of flavor. It's one of the best versions yet. The Luigi Ghislieri is, as always, well-crafted, flowery on the nose and vigorous on the palate. The Cuvée Tradition is a balsamic Martinotti of commendable poise. The 2015 Cuapro celebrates the trademark almond aromas exhibited by only the most authentic Verdicchios.

○ Verdicchio dei Castelli di Jesi Brut		
M. Cl. Ubaldo Rosi Ris. '10		♀♀ 5
○ Verdicchio dei Castelli di Jesi Brut		
Cuvée Tradition		♀♀ 3
○ Verdicchio dei Castelli di Jesi Brut		
M. Cl. Luigi Ghislieri		♀♀ 4
○ Verdicchio dei Castelli di Jesi Cl. Sup.		
Cuapro '15		♀♀ 3
○ Bianchello del Metauro Il Cigno '16		♀ 2
○ Verdicchio dei Castelli di Jesi Cl.		
Lyricus '16		♀ 2
○ Verdicchio dei Castelli di Jesi Cl. Sup.		
Cuprese '16		♀ 2
○ Verdicchio dei Castelli di Jesi M. Cl.		
Brut Ubaldo Rosi Ris. '06		♀♀♀ 5

Il Conte Villa Prandone

C.DA COLLE NAVICCHIO, 28
63033 MONTEPRANDONE [AP]
TEL. +39 073562593
www.ilcontevini.it

CELLAR SALES
PRE-BOOKED VISITS
ANNUAL PRODUCTION 200,000 bottles
HECTARES UNDER VINE 50.00

Emmanuel De Angelis's winery is situated
on the hills of Monteprandone. In addition to
representing Conte Villa Prandone the world
over, he coordinates the work of the various
family members involved in production and
management. The clay soil, the terrain's
southern exposure and short pruning of the
vineyards make for well-ripened grapes,
which give rise to quite flavorsome whites
and reds saturated in color and fruit
(particularly appealing to those who like
sensations of matière in their wines). For
these wines and the passito dried-grape
wine, L'Estro del Mastro, barrique is used.
The others are aged in steel or concrete.
This year, the second selections steal the
show. The 2016 Trebbia proves a dynamic
Trebbiano, with its trademark aromas of
hazelnut. The 2016 Cavaceppo goes all in
on the softness and grace of its palate.
Despite having to work off some wood, the
2015 Marinus has vivid fruit and good
balance on the palate. The 2016 Donello is
a fragrant, succulent Sangiovese - a wine
for everyday drinking.

● Donello '16	♟♟	3
○ L'Estro del Mastro Passerina Passito '15	♟♟	5
○ Offida Passerina Cavaceppo '16	♟♟	3
● Rosso Piceno Sup. Marinus '15	♟♟	3
○ Trebbià '16	♟♟	2*
○ Emmanuel Maria Passerina Extra Dry	♟	3
○ Falerio Pecorino Aurato '16	♟	2
● IX Prandone '13	♟	8
● Lu Kont '14	♟	6
○ Offida Pecorino Navicchio '16	♟	3
● Rosso Piceno Conte Rosso '16	♟	2
● Zipolo '14	♟	5
● Donello '15	♟♟	2*
● LuKont '13	♟♟	6
● Zipolo '13	♟♟	5

Fattoria Coroncino

C.DA CORONCINO, 7
60039 STAFFOLO [AN]
TEL. +39 0731779494
www.coroncino.it

CELLAR SALES
PRE-BOOKED VISITS
ANNUAL PRODUCTION 45,000 bottles
HECTARES UNDER VINE 9.50

When concepts like 'natural', 'artisanal' and
'native' still hadn't entered the wine lexicon,
Lucio Canestrari brought them together in a
style that was, and still is, unique. His
painstaking approach in the vineyards
allowed him to give up chemicals early
enough. With the family, harvests have
always been long, manually-worked affairs,
in which the ripest grapes are sought out.
Over the years, they never stopped using or
researching the Verdicchio clones,
eventually experimenting with Professor
Bruni's crossed varieties. They've also
preserved some rows of red grapes. Suffice
it to say, Canestrari is a unique producer,
whose wines exhibit great personality. They
may not be in line with what's considered
trendy but this selection is indispensable for
understanding the history of Verdicchio. The
2013 Stragio, matured in mid-size casks,
performed well, with its smoky notes and
fruity redolence. It's a sumptuous wine that
also exhibits excellent structure. The
almondy 2015 Coroncino is full and tasty (in
the best, original sense of the term)

○ Verdicchio dei Castelli di Jesi Cl. Sup. Stragaio '13	♟♟	5
○ Verdicchio dei Castelli di Jesi Cl. Sup. Il Coroncino '15	♟♟	2
○ Verdicchio dei Castelli di Jesi Cl. Sup. Vergaro '15	♟♟	4
○ Verdicchio dei Castelli di Jesi Cl. Sup. Gaiospino '03	♟♟♟	4
○ Verdicchio dei Castelli di Jesi Cl. Sup. Gaiospino '97	♟♟♟	4
○ Verdicchio dei Castelli di Jesi Cl. Sup. Gaiospino '14	♟♟	4
○ Verdicchio dei Castelli di Jesi Cl. Sup. Il Coroncino '13	♟♟	2
○ Verdicchio dei Castelli di Jesi Cl. Sup. Stracacio '14	♟♟	5

‎nuta De Angelis

‎SAN FRANCESCO, 10
‎030 CASTEL DI LAMA [AP]
‎+39 073687429
‎w.tenutadeangelis.it

‎LLAR SALES
‎E-BOOKED VISITS
‎NUAL PRODUCTION 500,000 bottles
‎CTARES UNDER VINE 50.00

‎hiero Fausti's first name is that of his
‎ndfather, the founder of this winery,
‎ch some time ago established itself as a
‎ducer and seller of wines for blending.
‎gets his surname from his father,
‎nto, who, in the mid-1980s, began
‎ducing his own selection. A lot has
‎nged since then, and now it's his turn,
‎third generation, to face ever more
‎cult challenges and carry on the family
‎iness. For the moment, he's focusing on
‎solidating their line of reds, represented
‎obust wines made with Montepulciano.
‎ also finding time for their pleasant,
‎age whites, made with Passerina and
‎orino, and opening the door to organic.
‎find the 2016 Offida Pecorino at the
‎Succulent, yet supple, its finish offers
‎ints of bitter orange. The reds hold
‎ own with the 2013 Oro, a mature,
‎y wine with light traces of meat and
‎ine that's also dynamic on the palate.
‎2015 Superiore's generous character
‎ held back by overtones of greeness
‎an abundance of fruity redolence.

‎fida Pecorino '16	♟♟2*
‎sso Piceno Sup. '15	♟♟2*
‎sso Piceno Sup. Oro '13	♟♟3
‎fida Passerina '16	♟2
‎fida Pecorino Quiete '16	♟3
‎fida Rosso Anghelos '14	♟4
‎sso Piceno '16	♟2
‎ghelos '01	♟♟♟4
‎ghelos '99	♟♟♟4*
‎ghelos '12	♟♟3
‎fida Pecorino Quiote '15	♟♟2*
‎sso Piceno '15	♟♟1*
‎sso Piceno Sup. '14	♟♟2*
‎sso Piceno Sup. '13	♟♟2*
‎sso Piceno Sup. Oro '12	♟♟3
‎sso Piceno Sup. Oro '11	♟♟3

Emanuele Dianetti

C.DA VALLEROSA, 25
63063 CARASSAI [AP]
TEL. +39 3383928439
www.dianettivini.it

CELLAR SALES
PRE-BOOKED VISITS
ANNUAL PRODUCTION 18,000 bottles
HECTARES UNDER VINE 2.00

The Menocchia is a small stream that runs
through a valley dense with vineyards at
the northernmost edge of the Offida DOC
zone. Here temperatures are cooler than
average in Piceno, and grapes can ripen
perfectly. Emanuele Dianetti, with the help
of his mother, Giuliana, and Michele
Quagliarini, transforms these into wines
with strong territorial identity, taking
advantage of his Pecorino's acidity while
preserving its citrus hints in steel barrels or
bringing out the fruity character of
Montepulciano, harmonizing the its
enormous tannins in barrique. And so it is
that Carassai has created its own specific
style, perfectly in line with the spirit of the
times. The 2014 Michelangelo Bordò
debuted with well defined aromas of
raspberry and a sweet tannic weave. The
2016 Pecorino Vignagiulia calls up candied
lemon, with a dynamic, savory mouth. But
the 2014 Offida Rosso Vignagiulia takes
the day. A monovarietal Monetpulciano, the
wine is pristine in its aromatic pattern, with
a pure, reactive, perfectly formed mouth.

● Offida Rosso Vignagiulia '14	♟♟♟5
● Michelangelo Bordò '14	♟♟8
○ Offida Pecorino Vignagiulia '16	♟♟3*
● Offida Rosso Vignagiulia '13	♟♟♟5
○ Offida Pecorino Vignagiulia '15	♟♟3*
○ Offida Pecorino Vignagiulia '14	♟♟3*
○ Offida Pecorino Vignagiulia '13	♟♟3
● Offida Rosso Vignagiulia '12	♟♟4
● Offida Rosso Vignagiulia '11	♟♟4

Fazi Battaglia

VIA ROMA, 117
60031 CASTELPLANIO [AN]
TEL. +39 073181591
www.fazibattaglia.it

CELLAR SALES
PRE-BOOKED VISITS
ANNUAL PRODUCTION 1,000,000 bottles
HECTARES UNDER VINE 130.00

Whoever seeks to recreate the enological
history of Marche will notice that, for
several years, it's gone hand-in-hand with
the history of Fazi Battaglia. The celebrated,
amphora-shaped bottle of Titulus was
probably the first bottle of the territory to
make it to the global marketplace. The
Angelini di Bertani Domains family, the
winery's current owners, are firm believers
in quality Verdicchio, and so great attention
is paid to cultivation and to the cru. Their
sophisticated, eloquent selection of wines
is organized according to the ripeness of
the grapes, which are aged in concrete or
barrique. You can only follow your tastes. If
you love an ounce of elegance, complexity
and poise, go with the 2015 San Sisto. If
you prefer greater power and stratification,
go with the excellent aromatic definition of
the flavorsome Massaccio. Moie and Titulus
will please fans of clear fragrances and a
supple mouth. The 2015 Arkezia is a
graceful passito dried-grape wine with silky
consistence.

○ Castelli di Jesi Verdicchio Cl.
  San Sisto Ris. '15   ♟♟♟ 5
○ Arkezia Muffo di San Sisto '15   ♟♟ 5
○ Verdicchio dei Castelli di Jesi Cl. Sup.
  Massaccio '15   ♟♟ 3*
○ Verdicchio dei Castelli di Jesi Cl.
  Le Moie '16   ♟♟ 2*
○ Verdicchio dei Castrelli Cl. Titulus '16   ♟♟ 2*
○ Castelli di Jesi Verdicchio Cl.
  San Sisto Ris. '14   ♟♟♟ 4*
○ Castelli di Jesi Verdicchio Cl.
  San Sisto Ris. '10   ♟♟♟ 4*
○ Verdicchio dei Castelli di Jesi Cl.
  San Sisto Ris. '09   ♟♟♟ 4*
○ Verdicchio dei Castelli di Jesi Cl.
  San Sisto Ris. '07   ♟♟♟ 4

Andrea Felici

C.DA SANT'ISIDORO, 28
62021 APIRO [MC]
TEL. +39 0733611431
www.andreafelici.it

CELLAR SALES
PRE-BOOKED VISITS
ANNUAL PRODUCTION 53,000 bottles
HECTARES UNDER VINE 10.00

The cultivation of their vineyards is at the
foundation of Apiro's agricultural sector.
Here Verdicchio sprouts up out of the co●
terrain, with the presence of Monte San
Vicino conferring a clearly Apennine nuar
to the grapes. Leo Felici and his
winemaker, Aroldo Bellelli, stand by the
territory, creating wines that draw on the
Matelica Verdicchio's acidity while fusing
with the strength of Jesi's. The result is a
vibrant, delicately salty white that feature
a lovely palate and crystal-clear fragranc
Their Cantico della Figura line is made w
grapes from older vineyards, aged in
concrete barrels. The 2013 is a formidal●
white. Its nose is magnificently calibrate●
amidst notes of citrus, almond, aniseed ●
finessed minerality. These find their echo
a supple, bright palate, of dynamic flavor
A big Tre Bicchieri. Though its performan
shouldn't overshadow an enchanting
2016 Andrea Felici, a wine that's natura●
its aromas and irresistible in the mouth.

○ Castelli di Jesi Verdicchio Cl.
  V. Il Cantico della Figura Ris. '13   ♟♟
○ Verdicchio dei Castelli di Jesi Cl. Sup.
  Andrea Felici '16   ♟
○ Castelli di Jesi Verdicchio Cl.
  Il Cantico della Figura Ris. '12   ♟♟
○ Castelli di Jesi Verdicchio Cl.
  Il Cantico della Figura Ris. '11   ♟♟
○ Castelli di Jesi Verdicchio Cl.
  Il Cantico della Figura Ris. '10   ♟♟
○ Verdicchio dei Castelli di Jesi Cl.
  Il Cantico della Figura Ris. '09   ♟♟
○ Verdicchio dei Castelli di Jesi Cl. Sup.
  Andrea Felici '15   ♟
○ Verdicchio dei Castelli di Jesi Cl. Sup.
  Andrea Felici '14   ♟

ilodivino

Serra, 16
030 San Marcello [AN]
.. +39 0731026139
ww.filodivino.it

CELLAR SALES
CCOMMODATION AND RESTAURANT SERVICE
NNUAL PRODUCTION 52,000 bottles
ECTARES UNDER VINE 15.50

berto Gandolfi explains how he and his
rtners, who were used to the rhythms of
dustry and the city, collided with life in the
untryside. It starts with a corner of land
spended between Jesi and Morro d'Alba,
microcosm of Marche's hills, with olive
oves, wheat and sunflowers as far as the
e can see. Then there are, of course,
eyards, where exclusively Verdicchio and
crima Nera are cultivated. The effort is
arly ready. The guest house and food
rvices are already operational, and the
uristic cellar will be as well, in time for
e 2018 harvest. For the moment, aging is
rried out exclusively in steel, on fine lees,
er times that vary according to the
ucture of the wine. Their wines show
eat personality. The 2015 Filotto proves
ectable: echoes of camphor and almond
ticipate a fresh, progressive, savory
uth. The 2016 Matto offers up peach,
d possesses natural drinkability. The
15 Soara is a Lacrima characterized by a
namic mouth and a captivating, delicately
ty finish with hints of dark fruit and
nerality.

Verdicchio dei Castelli di Jesi Cl. Sup. Filotto '15	🍷🍷 3*
Lacrima di Morro d'Alba Diana '15	🍷🍷 3
Lacrima di Morro d'Alba Sup. Soara '15	🍷🍷 3
Verdicchio dei Castelli di Jesi Cl. Sup. Matto '16	🍷🍷 3
Verdicchio dei Castelli di Jesi Cl. Serra 46 '16	🍷 2
Castelli di Jesi Verdicchio Cl. Dino Ris. '14	🍷🍷 4
Verdicchio dei Castelli di Jesi Filotto '14	🍷🍷 3

Fiorano

c.da Fiorano, 19
63067 Cossignano [AP]
Tel. +39 073598446
www.agrifiorano.it

CELLAR SALES
PRE-BOOKED VISITS
ACCOMMODATION
ANNUAL PRODUCTION 40,000 bottles
HECTARES UNDER VINE 7.50
VITICULTURE METHOD Certified Organic
SUSTAINABLE WINERY

Paolo Beretta hasn't just spent the better
part of his vine growing experience in the
countryside, among his organically cultivated
vineyards. He's also served as a parter and
consultant for FIVI, an association of small,
independent vine growers. He and his wife,
Paola, are staunch believers in environmental
sustainability and in the value of artisanal
craftsmanship. On the estate, he manages
everything in first person, from cultivating the
native grape varieties growing around his
cellar, to making the wine itself. And here
everything is temperature controlled with
particular attention paid to guaranteeing
clean aromas. The 2016 Donna Orgilla is
among this year's best-performing
Pecorinos. It stands out for its lovely nose, in
which aniseed and aromatic herbs meet
against a backdrop of citrus and white
peach; these reemerge in a poised, zestful
mouth. The 2014 Terre di Giobbe lets a touch
of barrique through, with notes of vanilla
encircled by richness and fruitiness. The
palate is austere, with a finish that features
just the slightest presence of tannins.

O Offida Pecorino Donna Orgilla '16	🍷🍷 3*
● Rosso Piceno Sup. Terre di Giobbe '14	🍷🍷 3
● Fiorano Sangiovese '16	🍷 2
O Giulia Erminia '15	🍷 5
O Offida Pecorino Donna Orgilla '14	🍷🍷🍷 3*
● Fiorano '14	🍷🍷 2*
● Fiorano Sangiovese '15	🍷🍷 2*
O Giulia Erminia '14	🍷🍷 2*
O Offida Pecorino Donna Orgilla '15	🍷🍷 3
O Offida Pecorino Donna Orgilla '13	🍷🍷 3*
O Offida Pecorino Donna Orgilla '12	🍷🍷 3
● Rosso Piceno Sup. Terre di Giobbe '13	🍷🍷 3
● Rosso Piceno Sup. Terre di Giobbe '12	🍷🍷 3
● Rosso Piceno Sup. Terre di Giobbe '11	🍷🍷 3
● Rosso Piceno Sup. Terre di Giobbe '10	🍷🍷 3

Cantine Fontezoppa

C.DA SAN DOMENICO, 38
62012 CIVITANOVA MARCHE [MC]
TEL. +39 0733790504
www.cantinefontezoppa.it

CELLAR SALES
PRE-BOOKED VISITS
ACCOMMODATION AND RESTAURANT SERVICE
ANNUAL PRODUCTION 290,000 bottles
HECTARES UNDER VINE 38.00

Fontezoppa's wines are made with grapes grown in two separate parts of Macerata, representing two very different types of terrain. Ribona, Incrocio Bruni and international varieties are cultivated on the hills behind Civitanova. Vineyards in Serrapetrona provide their Vernaccia and Pinot Nero. From these they've created a selection of wines that is complete, varied and never lacking in originality, not even in their cleanest and most classical moments. Mosè Ambrosi, who's been at the rudder for the last couple of years, knows that getting out the message means a lot of work and personal sacrifice. He's prepared to do just that in order to tell the story of a Marche that's less known, but full of talent. Red fruit, spices and a refreshing touch of mint come together in the 2013 Carapetto's sensory spectrum. This Cabernet Sauvignon is thick and expansive on the palate. A good debut for the 2013 Ribona Metodo Classio, a wine endowed with an original aromatic charge and an austere mouth. The 2015 Ribona features sulfur notes wed to nuances of yellow fruit, and a lean, plucky mouth.

● Carapetto '13	♊♊ 5
○ Colli Maceratesi Ribona '15	♊♊ 3
○ Colli Maceratesi Ribona Dosaggio Zero M. Cl. '13	♊♊ 4
⊙ Extra Brut Rosé M. Cl. '13	♊♊ 5
● Serrapetrona Carpignano '14	♊ 2
● Serrapetrona Falcotto '14	♊ 4
● Serrapetrona Morò '14	♊ 5
● Carapetto '12	♊♊ 5
● Carapetto '11	♊♊ 5
● San Marone '12	♊♊ 5
● Serrapetrona Falcotto '12	♊♊ 4
● Serrapetrona Morò '13	♊♊ 5

★Gioacchino Garofoli

VIA CARLO MARX, 123
60022 CASTELFIDARDO [AN]
TEL. +39 0717820162
www.garofolivini.it

CELLAR SALES
PRE-BOOKED VISITS
ANNUAL PRODUCTION 2,000,000 bottles
HECTARES UNDER VINE 42.00

The surname Garofoli has come to mean 'grande classico' in the region, this thanks to decades of history and a style that never caved to the dictates of fashion or the market. The winery focuses on Conero and Verdicchio, expressed in various typologies, from early drinkers to their 'Riserva', which age particularly well. Another strong suit is their sparkling wines: the large and well-equipped cellar in Loreto provides the right amount of space and adequate equipment for slow aging in glass. The 2015 Podium returns to form with Tre Bicchieri. A lustrous wine, its crystal clear aromatic profile features aromatic herbs, balsamic and almond, while the mouth offers an elegant weave that delivers for both integrity and expressiveness. The 2013 Sierra Fiorese soft, stratified in its aromas, offering up a long, tapered finish. Bristling pointedness toasted notes and pervasive flavor mark the 2010 Brut Riserva.

○ Verdicchio dei Castelli di Jesi Cl. Sup. Podium '15	♊♊♊
○ Verdicchio dei Castelli di Jesi Brut M. Cl. Ris. '10	♊♊
● Camerlano '12	♊♊
○ Castelli di Jesi Verdicchio Cl. Serra Fiorese Ris. '13	♊♊
○ Kòmaros '16	♊♊
● Rosso Piceno Colle Ambro '15	♊♊
○ Verdicchio dei Castelli di Jesi Cl. Sup. Macrina '16	♊♊
○ Verdicchio dei Castelli di Jesi Pas Dosé M. Cl. Ris. '09	♊♊
● Rosso Conero Piancarda '14	♊
○ Verdicchio dei Castelli di Jesi Cl. Sup. Podium '13	♊♊♊

Marco Gatti

A LAGUA E SAN MARTINO, 2
0043 CERRETO D'ESI [AN]
EL. +39 0732677012
ww.gattiagri.it

ELLAR SALES
RE-BOOKED VISITS
NNUAL PRODUCTION 10,000 bottles
ECTARES UNDER VINE 6.00

he small scale of his winery doesn't stop
Marco Gatti from showing care and
ttention in his approach to winemaking.
mall, steel barrels are used, with grapes
ept separate according to their plot in
erreto d'Esi, near the northernmost limits
f the Verdicchio di Matelica DOC zone.
Marco, an agronomist and nurseryman,
nows which cru guarantee acidity and
vhich are better-suited to structure and
omplexity. His selection follows this logic,
esulting in a range of lip-smacking whites
nat are well-committed to their varietal
deals. The tasters continue to miss the
iserva Millo. Its absence, however, is
nitigated by two significant vintage
Matelicas. In particular, we were impressed
y the 2016 Casale Venza, with its
xtremely detailed, openly citrus nose,
ollowed by a supple mouth, invigorated by
ne contrast between acidity and fruit pulp.
he 2016 Villa Marilla boasts an openly
ruity style, with a mouth of greater density
f flavor and a palate that is broader than it
s deep.

○ Verdicchio di Matelica Casale Venza '16	♟♟ 2*
○ Verdicchio di Matelica Villa Marilla '16	♟♟ 2*
○ Verdicchio di Matelica '14	♟♟ 2*
○ Verdicchio di Matelica '13	♟♟ 2*
○ Verdicchio di Matelica Aristo '15	♟♟ 2*
○ Verdicchio di Matelica Casale Venza '15	♟♟ 2*
○ Verdicchio di Matelica Millo Ris. '13	♟♟ 3*
○ Verdicchio di Matelica Millo Ris. '12	♟♟ 3
○ Verdicchio di Matelica Villa Marilla '15	♟♟ 2*
○ Verdicchio di Matelica Villa Marilla '14	♟♟ 2*
○ Verdicchio di Matelica Villa Marilla '13	♟♟ 2*

Mancini

FRAZ. MOIE
60030 MAIOLATI SPONTINI [AN]
TEL. +39 0731702975
www.manciniwines.it

CELLAR SALES
PRE-BOOKED VISITS
RESTAURANT SERVICE
ANNUAL PRODUCTION 140,000 bottles
HECTARES UNDER VINE 20.00

Benito Mancini inherited the winery of his
father (who'd worked as a member-grower
for a local cooperative winery since the
economic boom). As was common during
the time, in the 1980s he decided to
produce his own wines and built the cellar
in which his three sons still work today. It's
a close-knit, family operation with a strong
territorial identity. For many, years they've
counted on the commitment of tried and
true Verdicchio experts, like the agronomist
Luca Severini and the winemaker Sergio
Paolucci. Recently, they set in motion a
conversion of their vineyards to organic.
The 2013 Riserva's only weak-point is its
limited availability. The wine shows great
varietal adherence with the added bonus of
complexity (as a result of its age). Its palate
is expansive and polished, with a flavor
profile rich in counterpoint. The 2016 Villa
Talliano has an open, fruity character that's
approachably pleasant. The 2016 Santa
Lucia is a bottle that brings together
youthful fragrance and a natural palate.

○ Castelli di Jesi Verdicchio Cl. Ris. '13	♟♟ 5
○ Verdicchio Castelli di Jesi Cl. S. Lucia '16	♟♟ 2*
○ Verdicchio Castelli di Jesi Cl. Sup. Villa Talliano '16	♟♟ 3
○ Brut	♟ 2
○ Verdicchio Castelli di Jesi Cl. S. Lucia '15	♟♟ 2*
○ Verdicchio Castelli di Jesi Cl. Santa Lucia '10	♟♟ 2*
○ Verdicchio Castelli di Jesi Cl. Sup. Villa Talliano '15	♟♟ 3
○ Verdicchio Castelli di Jesi Cl. Sup. Villa Talliano '13	♟♟ 3*
○ Verdicchio Castelli di Jesi Cl. Sup. Villa Talliano '10	♟♟ 2*

Marotti Campi

VIA SANT'AMICO, 14
60030 MORRO D'ALBA [AN]
TEL. +39 0731618027
www.marotticampi.it

CELLAR SALES
PRE-BOOKED VISITS
ACCOMMODATION
ANNUAL PRODUCTION 240,000 bottles
HECTARES UNDER VINE 71.00

Lorenzo Marotti Campi's winery has two souls, really. On the one hand, there's the beloved Verdicchio, which, in Morro d'Alba, is transformed into modern whites. On the other hand, there's the territory's natural propensity for Lacrima Nera, which is interpreted here with great skill. The right harvesting periods and a wide range of choice, thanks to their many hectares of vineyards, has allowed them to temper the exuberant floral character of the grape, honing it so as to achieve a greater presence of fruit. Steel, which is used just about everywhere, preserves primary aromas, even if a discriminating amount of barrique is used for aging their most important wines. The 2014 Salmariano nabs yet another Tre Bicchieri. Its complex sensory spectrum embraces candied citrus peels and peach, which reemerge in a vibrant, energetic palate and sophisticated flavor profile. The 2015 Orgiolo also hits the mark, a Lacrima of rare complexity and vigor. The 2016 Rubico is close-knit in its aromas, delicate and varietal.

○ Castelli di Jesi Verdicchio Cl. Salmariano Ris. '14	▼▼▼ 3*
● Lacrima di Morro d'Alba Sup. Orgiolo '15	▼▼ 3*
⊙ Brut Rosé	▼▼ 3
● Lacrima di Morro d'Alba Rubico '16	▼▼ 2*
○ Verdicchio dei Castelli di Jesi Cl. Sup. Luzano '16	▼▼ 2*
● Xyris '16	▼▼ 2*
○ Verdicchio dei Castelli di Jesi Cl. Albiano '16	▼ 1*
○ Castelli di Jesi Verdicchio Cl. Salmariano Ris. '13	♀♀♀ 3*
○ Verdicchio dei Castelli di Jesi Cl. Salmariano Ris. '08	♀♀♀ 3*

Poderi Mattioli

VIA FARNETO, 17A
60030 SERRA DE' CONTI [AN]
TEL. +39 0731878676
www.poderimattioli.it

CELLAR SALES
PRE-BOOKED VISITS
ANNUAL PRODUCTION 25,000 bottles
HECTARES UNDER VINE 6.50
VITICULTURE METHOD Certified Organic

In Serra de' Conti, Verdicchio is everywher in the rows of vineyards that line the landscape, in the agricultural history of the area, in the hearts and futures of the businesses operating there. For years, the Mattioli family sold their grapes to various wineries, but then the 'young pups' decide to take the next step and become producers themselves. Today the two brothers have separate roles: Giordano takes care of the various cru, beautiful vineyards set in clay, limestone and sand soil; Giacomo's role unfolds in their moder cellar, among steel barrels (pupitre for thei sparkling wines). The 2015 Lauro is extraordinary. A nose fine-tuned to Verdicchio's most common descriptors gives way to a palate of awesome richness of flavor and dynamic attack. It maintains its cohesion, even as it progresses across the palate, with a finish marked by long, saline strokes. The 2015 Ylice exhibits notes of lemon peel and a voluminous mouth that draws pleasantness from balanced and aromatically well-defined fruit.

○ Castelli di Jesi Verdicchio Cl. Lauro Ris. '15	▼▼▼ 4
○ Verdicchio dei Castelli di Jesi Cl. Sup. Ylice '15	▼▼ 3
○ Castelli di Jesi Verdicchio Cl. Lauro Ris. '13	♀♀♀ 3
○ Verdicchio dei Castelli di Jesi Cl. Sup. Ylice '12	♀♀♀ 2
○ Verdicchio dei Castelli di Jesi Cl. Sup. Lauro '10	♀♀ 3
○ Verdicchio dei Castelli di Jesi Cl. Sup. Ylice '14	♀♀ 3
○ Verdicchio dei Castelli di Jesi Cl. Sup. Ylice '13	♀♀ 3
○ Verdicchio dei Castelli di Jesi Cl. Sup. Ylice '11	♀♀ 2

alter Mattoni

Pescolla, 1
030 Castorano [AP]
.. +39 073687329
ww.valtermattoni.it

ELLAR SALES
RE-BOOKED VISITS
NNUAL PRODUCTION 6,500 bottles
ECTARES UNDER VINE 3.50

lter Mattoni took on the role of vine grower as not to abandon those old vineyards of ontepulciano grapes that his grandfather ed to cultivate with such passion. Back in 000, they had just one barrique, and this ve life to the first Arshura. Today it's been tired and replaced by multiple copies - and e narrow garage has become a true cellar. here's never enough time or space', he's nd of saying, increasingly consumed by the oject (despite his regular job as a corator). His nephew, Andrea Bernabè, lps out, as does Marco Casoletti, whose ggestions hold nothing back. Spontaneous mentation, limited ageing, and native ape varieties make for wines of great aracter. The 2015 Trebbien has a tangy tack that then moves to notes of grain, dlar and hazelnut. Its lift contrasts with dense, alcoholic-dominated palate, aking for dynamic, vibrant flavor. The 14 Rossobordò develops similarly, pported by a profile of flowers, garrigue d spices. The 2016 Cosecose is a ngiovese with high sugar residue, a 'vino if' of delectable, extravagant flavor.

Cosecose '16	♟♟ 3
Rossobordò '14	♟♟ 8
Trebbien '15	♟♟ 4
Arshura '11	♟♟♟ 3*
Arshura '14	♟♟ 5
Arshura '13	♟♟ 5
Arshura '12	♟♟ 5
Arshura '10	♟♟ 3*
Rosso Bordò '10	♟♟ 8
Rossobordò '13	♟♟ 8
Rossobordò '12	♟♟ 8
Rossobordò '11	♟♟ 8
Trebbien '14	♟♟ 3
Trebbien '13	♟♟ 3
Trebbien '12	♟♟ 2*

Federico Mencaroni

via Olmigrandi, 72
60013 Corinaldo [AN]
Tel. +39 0717975625
www.mencaroni.eu

PRE-BOOKED VISITS
ANNUAL PRODUCTION 30,000 bottles
HECTARES UNDER VINE 7.50

Federico Mencaroni is a vine grower with a serious passion for sparkling wines. He works in Corinaldo, on the northern border of Castelli di Jesi, in an area that feels the influence of the Adriatic Sea. His vineyards run along gently sloping hills at limited altitudes. In addition to Verdicchio, which dominates, he also cultivates Montepulciano. His small cellar is a maze of shaking tables and piled cases where various vintages of sparkling wine mature slowly, on the lees. In addition to his two classic wines, which are distinguished according to the presence of liqueur d'expedition (or not), the selection now features a rosé made with 80% Verdicchio and 20% Montepulciano. The 2013 Marcello Federico spends 36 months on the lees, making for a dark orange wine that offers up complex aromas of raspberries and bread crust. Its mouth is austere, disinclined to softness, with an assertive palate. 2012 Contatto offers up evolved notes of dried fruit and malt cookies, with a creamy mouth guided by slightly salty acidity.

○ Verdicchio dei Castelli di Jesi Brut M. Cl. Contatto '12	♟♟ 4
⊙ Marcello Federico Extra Brut Rosé M. Cl. '13	♟♟ 5
○ Verdicchio dei Castelli di Jesi Isola '15	♟♟ 3
○ Verdicchio dei Castelli di Jesi Extra Brut M.Cl. Apollonia '12	♟ 5
○ Verdicchio dei Castelli di Jesi Brut M. Cl. Contatto '11	♟♟ 4
○ Verdicchio dei Castelli di Jesi Brut M. Cl. Contatto '10	♟♟ 4
○ Verdicchio dei Castelli di Jesi Brut Nature M.Cl. Apollonia '11	♟♟ 5
○ Verdicchio dei Castelli di Jesi Brut Nature M.Cl. Apollonia '10	♟♟ 5
○ Verdicchio dei Castelli di Jesi Isola '13	♟♟ 3

★La Monacesca

c.da MONACESCA
62024 MATELICA [MC]
TEL. +39 0733672641
www.monacesca.it

CELLAR SALES
PRE-BOOKED VISITS
ANNUAL PRODUCTION 160,000 bottles
HECTARES UNDER VINE 28.00

Aldo Cifola and his father, Miro (La
Monacesca's founder), played an important
part in building the Verdicchio di Matelica
appellation. Their powerful, long-lived
whites were once considered to be in
opposition to local orthodoxy (which called
for slighter builds and approachability).
Today they are considered icons in the
territory, still modern and vital. Over time,
their youthful, fruity verve and richness of
flavor give way to complex expressions,
without losing an iota of their distinctive
energy. The 2015 Mirum brings an
undisputed Tre Bicchieri to Matelica.
Extremely elegant aromas of yellow plum
and almond, delicate strokes of aniseed,
give way to a solidly-structured palate that
progresses rhythmically and gracefully. The
2015 Matelica has some evolved accents
in its color and hints of toasted almonds,
while the mouth is quite flavorsome and
shaped through a balanced density. The
2012 Camerte, made with Sangiovese
and Merlot, offers mature tannins and a
coherent palate.

○ Verdicchio di Matelica Mirum Ris. '15	▼▼▼	5
● Camerte '12	▼▼	4
○ Verdicchio di Matelica '15	▼▼	3
⊙ Camerte Rosé '16	▼	2
● Camerte '99	♈♈♈	5
○ Verdicchio di Matelica Mirum Ris. '14	♈♈♈	5
○ Verdicchio di Matelica Mirum Ris. '12	♈♈♈	5
○ Verdicchio di Matelica Mirum Ris. '11	♈♈♈	5
○ Verdicchio di Matelica Mirum Ris. '10	♈♈♈	4*
○ Verdicchio di Matelica Mirum Ris. '09	♈♈♈	4
○ Verdicchio di Matelica Mirum Ris. '08	♈♈♈	4
○ Verdicchio di Matelica Mirum Ris. '07	♈♈♈	4*
○ Verdicchio di Matelica Mirum Ris. '06	♈♈♈	4
○ Verdicchio di Matelica Mirum Ris. '04	♈♈♈	4
○ Verdicchio di Matelica Mirum Ris. '02	♈♈♈	3

Montecappone

VIA COLLE OLIVO, 2
60035 JESI [AN]
TEL. +39 0731205761
www.montecappone.com

CELLAR SALES
PRE-BOOKED VISITS
ANNUAL PRODUCTION 150,000 bottles
HECTARES UNDER VINE 70.00

Gianluca Mirizzi has an explosive
personality. He's always ready to throw
himself into new projects and experiment
from a pressure-tank for making Charma'
(a rarity in the region), to the latest trials
using amphora for fermentation. The rece
acquisition of a vineyard in Cupramontan
was, for him, an occasion to give life to a
new line that brings out the inherent
structure and richness of Verdicchio. The
heart of the production emphasizes zesty
citrusy wines, the result of limited
production techniques designed to preser
the grapes' original, primary sensory
properties. The 2014 Utopia comes in jus
beneath the maximum score. The child of
an unblessed vintage, it manages to
communicate the cold and rain of that
summer in a citrus nose, streaked with
mineral hints and the occasional vegetal
flourish; its succulent mouth is supported
by a capable architecture of flavor. The
2016 Verdicchio is defined by its fruitines
and a worthy drinkability, coming in on pa
with a captivatingly fruity Rosso Piceno (c
the same year).

○ Castelli di Jesi Verdicchio Cl. Utopia Ris. '14	▼▼
○ Verdicchio dei Castelli di Jesi Cl. '16	▼▼
○ Offida Pecorino Monsieur Rino '16	▼▼
● Rosso Piceno '16	▼▼
● Tabano Rosso '15	▼▼
○ La Breccia '16	▼
○ Madame Rina '16	▼
⊙ Pergolesi A. D. 1710	▼
● Rosso Piceno Utopia '14	▼
○ Tabano Bianco '16	▼
○ Castelli di Jesi Verdicchio Cl. Utopia Ris. '13	♈♈♈
○ Verdicchio dei Castelli di Jesi Cl. Utopia Ris. '08	♈♈♈
○ Verdicchio dei Castelli di Jesi Cl. Utopia Ris. '07	♈♈♈

Claudio Morelli

V.LE ROMAGNA, 47B
61032 FANO [PU]
TEL. +39 0721823352
www.claudiomorelli.it

CELLAR SALES
PRE-BOOKED VISITS
ANNUAL PRODUCTION 110,000 bottles
HECTARES UNDER VINE 40.00

Claudio Morelli inherited his parents'
vocation and can boast having a formidable
knowledge of the grape Bianchello. In
addition to having participated in numerous
harvests, he has experience with a variety
of soils, vineyard positions and
microclimates. Some of his crus look out on
the Adriatic Sea (Vigna delle Terrazze in
Roncosambaccio) while others are situated
on the hills of Fratterosa, halfway between
the Apennines and the sea. His winemaking
cellar can be found in Sant'Andrea di
Suasa, while bottling, and aging of his reds
take place on his estate in the hills of Fano.
The Borgo Torre boasts a commendable
consistence of quality, and the 2016
vintage is no different, finding a place at
the top of the appellation. Fresh aromas of
flowers and yellow fruit give way to a
caressing mouth which lingers in flavor and
richness through the finish.

● Alius '12	♟♟ 4
○ Bianchello del Metauro Sup. Borgo Torre '16	♟♟ 2*
● Mogliano '12	♟♟ 5
○ Bianchello del Metauro La Vigna delle Terrazze '16	♟ 2
○ Bianchello del Metauro S. Cesareo '16	♟ 2
● Suffragium '15	♟ 3
○ Bianchello del Metauro Borgo Torre '15	♟♟ 2*
○ Bianchello del Metauro Borgo Torre '14	♟♟ 2*
○ Bianchello del Metauro Borgo Torre '13	♟♟ 3
○ Bianchello del Metauro Brut M. Cl. Mòrell '12	♟♟ 5
○ Bianchello del Metauro S. Cesareo '13	♟♟ 2*

Alessandro Moroder

VIA MONTACUTO, 121
60029 ANCONA
TEL. +39 071898232
www.moroder-vini.it

CELLAR SALES
PRE-BOOKED VISITS
ANNUAL PRODUCTION 130,000 bottles
HECTARES UNDER VINE 18.00
VITICULTURE METHOD Certified Organic
SUSTAINABLE WINERY

At the end of the 1980s, Conero broke
regional boundaries, gaining itself a place
among the world's wines. Mostly we have
Alessandro Moroder to thank for the
achievement and, at the appellation's
50-year anniversary, it's only proper that we
give credit where credit is due. Today he's
still at the helm, accompanied by his brother,
Marco. Dialogue with the young winemaker,
Marco Gozzi, has brought new life to the
winery: clearly differentiated wines that grow
in complexity and structure, greater stylistic
cohesion… And it's all within the framework
of a kind of overreaching classicism that
provides for the use of large barrels for the
reds, with the exception of barrique for their
Riserva Dorico. The 2013 Moroder Riserva
exhibits a fané charm amidst echoes of
sweet spices, ash and ripe black cherry. In
the mouth it has tactile consistence, though
never in excess. The close-knit tannic weave
of the 2013 Dorico, which is quite evident in
the back palate, provides greater structure,
but a bit too much hardness. Morello cherry
and smoky strokes give character to the
2015 Rosso Conero.

● Conero Ris. '13	♟♟ 5
● Conero Dorico Ris. '13	♟♟ 5
● Rosso Conero '15	♟♟ 2*
⊙ Rosa di Moroder '16	♟ 2
● Conero Dorico Ris. '05	♟♟♟ 5
● Rosso Conero Dorico '93	♟♟♟ 5
● Rosso Conero Dorico '90	♟♟♟ 5
● Rosso Conero Dorico '88	♟♟♟ 5
● Conero Dorico Ris. '11	♟♟ 5
● Conero Dorico Ris. '09	♟♟ 5
● Conero Ris. '12	♟♟ 5
● Conero Ris. '11	♟♟ 5
● Rosso Conero '12	♟♟ 2*
● Rosso Conero Aiòn '14	♟♟ 2*
● Rosso Conero Aiòn '13	♟♟ 2*

Muròla

C.DA VILLAMAGNA, 9
62010 URBISAGLIA [MC]
TEL. +39 0733506843
www.murola.it

CELLAR SALES
PRE-BOOKED VISITS
ANNUAL PRODUCTION 700,000 bottles
HECTARES UNDER VINE 60.00

A marvelous tasting room that faces a picturesque barrique cellar is only the tip of the iceberg of the investments made by the Mosciewicz family. The large estate has an efficient cellar at its disposal, hecatres of vineyards where native grape varieties are grown, and a wide selection of wines characterized by a vibrant approachability, as well as the occasional flourish of originality, like Jurek, a convincing 'Metodo Classico' sparkler made with Ribona grapes. Sangiovese and Montepulciano, which are at the foundation of their reds, are fermented in their monovarietal form. Even if they've chosen the road less traveled, their interpretation is strong. Upon tasting, the selection proved quite solid. Their Sangiovese Camà (matured in large barrels) and Agello (aged in steel and their bottles) share a graceful, elegant makeup, even if the former can boast greater complexity and depth. The 2016 Agar is a quintessential and pleasant Ribona in its vegetal, flowery inflections. Jurek is a citrusy, creamy 'Metodo Classico' sparkler (disgorged in 2017).

● Agello '15	♟♟ 2*
○ Baccius '16	♟♟ 2*
● Camà '15	♟♟ 2*
○ Colli Maceratesi Ribona Agar '16	♟♟ 2*
○ Jurek Brut M.Cl.	♟♟ 4
⊙ Jole Brut Rosé '15	♟ 3
● Rosso Piceno Orbesallia '15	♟ 2
● Teodoro '15	♟ 3
○ Varà Brut Passerina '16	♟ 2
○ Vore Pecorino '16	♟ 2
● Teodoro '12	♟♟♟ 3*
● Agello '14	♟♟ 2*
● Camà '12	♟♟ 2*
○ Colli Maceratesi Ribona Agar '15	♟♟ 2*
● Teodoro '13	♟♟ 3*

★Oasi degli Angeli

C.DA SANT'EGIDIO, 50
63012 CUPRA MARITTIMA [AP]
TEL. +39 0735778569
www.kurni.it

CELLAR SALES
PRE-BOOKED VISITS
ANNUAL PRODUCTION 5,000 bottles
HECTARES UNDER VINE 16.00

To say that Marco Casolanetti is merely a producer of Kurner and Kupra, outstanding wines built on a keen reading of Montepulciano and Bordeaux (a local biotype of Granache), would be offensive. It would mean ignoring the important work he does towards bringing together themes that matter to small producers, his desire to find a common language to face the market, the advice he gives to other small producers to help their products stand out from the pack (without losing their artisanal quality). In this respect, Marco is one of the most important figures in the region, beyond mere debates over the best systems, the right concentration of fruit, or the types of barrels one should use. The 2014 Kupra has smoky notes to it, as well as an unforeseen trace of woodland that dilutes the purity of fruit exhibited in other vintages. The 2015 Kurni is an inextricable grove of tannins, alcohol and residual sugar that will find the right expansion in a few years.

● Kupra '14	♟♟ 8
● Kurni '15	♟♟ 8
● Kupra '13	♟♟♟ 8
● Kupra '12	♟♟♟ 8
● Kupra '10	♟♟♟ 8
● Kurni '10	♟♟♟ 8
● Kurni '09	♟♟♟ 8
● Kurni '07	♟♟♟ 8
● Kurni '04	♟♟♟ 8
● Kurni '03	♟♟♟ 8
● Kurni '02	♟♟♟ 8
● Kurni '01	♟♟♟ 8
● Kurni '00	♟♟♟ 8
● Kurni '98	♟♟♟ 8
● Kurni '97	♟♟♟ 8

Pantaleone

VIA COLONNATA ALTA, 118
63100 ASCOLI PICENO
TEL. +39 3478757476
www.pantaleonewine.com

PRE-BOOKED VISITS
ANNUAL PRODUCTION 60,000 bottles
HECTARES UNDER VINE 16.00
VITICULTURE METHOD Certified Organic

Even if Pantaleone is officially in Ascoli
Piceno, in reality the estate is situated on a
high hill facing Monte Ascensione (and is
effected by its cooler air). The Pantaloni
sisters, Francesca and Federica, have
distilled the spirit of the territory in their
wines with the help of Fracensca's
husband, Giuseppe Infriccioli. The work
they do in the vineyard is like that of a
tailor, making for whites that are fresh,
contemporary and natural, and reds that
are firm and multi-layered. What's more,
expressivity is guaranteed by native
grapes, cultivated in an uncommon area.
The 2016 Onirocep showed its usual,
'mountain' temperament. Lemon, sage
and a touch of gooseberry make up the
aromatic phase, which emerges coherently
in a palate of bright, saline, refreshing
acidity. The Chicca, made with Passerina
grapes, moves in a similar direction,
drawing on vigor and suppleness. The
2013 La Ribalta, a warm and pervasive
Bordeaux of meaty presence, proved rich
in spice.

○ Falerio Pecorino Onirocep '16	♥♥	3*
● La Ribalta '13	♥♥	8
○ Chicca '16	♥♥	2*
● Atto I '15	♥	2
● Atto I '10	♀♀	2*
● Atto I '09	♀♀	2*
● Boccascena '12	♀♀	3
○ Chicca '13	♀♀	2*
○ Falerio Pecorino Onirocep '15	♀♀	2*
○ Falerio Pecorino Onirocep '14	♀♀	2*
○ Falerio Pecorino Onirocep '13	♀♀	2*
● La Ribalta '10	♀♀	8
○ Onirocep '11	♀♀	2*
● Ribalta '12	♀♀	8
○ Sipario '09	♀♀	2*

Tenute Pieralisi Monte Schiavo

FRAZ. MONTESCHIAVO
VIA VIVAIO
60030 MAIOLATI SPONTINI [AN]
TEL. +39 0731700385
www.monteschiavo.it

CELLAR SALES
PRE-BOOKED VISITS
ANNUAL PRODUCTION 950,000 bottles
HECTARES UNDER VINE 103.00
SUSTAINABLE WINERY

Winds of change are blowing on Monte
Schiavo. After the arrival of Carlo Ferrini, in
2015, and the conversion to organic, the
Pieralisi family decided to give life to a new
selection, Tenute Pieralisi. It will comprise
wines made from the vineyards around
their large cellar in Scorcelletti, while
experimenting new approaches to
winemaking in pursuit of greater
expressivity and territorial cohesiveness. At
their disposal, they'll continue to have their
Verdicchio vineyards, which grow in the
splendid plateau of Tassanare di Rosora.
The 2016 Pallio di San Floriano exhibits a
nice taste profile: fruity, expansive on the
palate, soft and yet capable of lingering on
the right richness of flavor. Notes of almond
paste and aromatic herbs mark the mature
Le Giuncare 2015. If the 2015 Conero
Alberto Serenlli offers up a substantial
palate, the 2013 Piceno Re di Ras aims for
complexity and powerful, plush mouthfeel.

○ Castelli di Jesi Verdicchio Cl. Le Giuncare Ris. '15	♥♥	3
● Rosso Conero Alberto Serenelli '15	♥♥	3
● Rosso Piceno Re di Ras Tenute Pieralisi '13	♥♥	4
○ Verdicchio dei Castelli di Jesi Cl. Sup. Pallio di S. Floriano '16	♥♥	3
● Lacrima di Morro d'Alba Marzaiola '16	♥	2
● Rosso Piceno Caccialepre Tenute Pieralisi '15	♥	3
○ Verdicchio dei Castelli di Jesi Cl. Coste del Molino '16	♥	2
○ Verdicchio dei Castelli di Jesi Cl. Sup. Villaia Tenute Pieralisi '16	♥	3
○ Verdicchio dei Castelli di Jesi Cl. Sup. Pallio di S. Floriano '11	♀♀♀	2*

Pievalta

VIA MONTESCHIAVO, 18
60030 MAIOLATI SPONTINI [AN]
TEL. +39 0731705199
www.baronepizzini.it

CELLAR SALES
PRE-BOOKED VISITS
ANNUAL PRODUCTION 125,000 bottles
HECTARES UNDER VINE 26.50
VITICULTURE METHOD Certified Biodynamic
SUSTAINABLE WINERY

In Pievalta, the biodynamic approach has
always been championed, but without
preachiness. This layman's vision, combined
with the persistence of Alessandro Fenino,
results in wines with great personality,
where the nature of Verdicchio expresses
perfectly the character of the vintage. The
various plots of vineyards correspond to
different periods: first those around the
winery, which grow in clay, then those
around Monte Follonica, in sandstone.
Grapes are pressed whole, fermentation is
spontaneous and wines are aged properly,
resulting in wines of superior vitality and
indomitable vigor. The San Paolo Riserva
2015 put in a performance for the ages. Its
many fragrances, all perfectly in line with
the cultivar's classic profile, are followed by
a mouth of overwhelming dynamism, driven
by a well-defined, saline vigor that is both
spontaneous and deep. Zest is also to be
found in the 2016 Dominè, a wine that
proves quite vigorous on the palate. The
2016 Pievalta offers up fruity flair and a
delectable mouth.

○ Castelli di Jesi Verdicchio Cl. San Paolo Ris. '15	♥♥♥ 3*
○ Perlugo Dosaggio Zero M. Cl.	♥♥ 3
○ Verdicchio dei Castelli di Jesi Cl. Sup. Dominè Chiesa del Pozzo '16	♥♥ 2*
○ Verdicchio dei Castelli di Jesi Cl. Sup. Pievalta '16	♥♥ 2*
○ Verdicchio dei Castelli di Jesi Passito Curina '15	♥♥ 4
○ Castelli di Jesi Verdicchio Cl. San Paolo Ris. '13	♥♥♥ 3*
○ Castelli di Jesi Verdicchio Cl. San Paolo Ris. '10	♀♀♀ 3*
○ Verdicchio dei Castelli di Jesi Cl. Sup. Pievalta '09	♀♀♀ 2*

Podere sul Lago

LOC. BORGIANO
VIA CASTELLO, 20
62020 SERRAPETRONA [MC]
TEL. +39 3333017380
www.poderesullago.it

CELLAR SALES
PRE-BOOKED VISITS
ANNUAL PRODUCTION 10,000 bottles
HECTARES UNDER VINE 4.00
SUSTAINABLE WINERY

The climate of Serrapetrona may be cold,
but Lake Caccamo, which the winery faces,
mitigates its influence. Indeed, here olive
groves line the landscape, proving the fact.
Sandrino Quadraroli planted grape varieties
here that aren't afraid of a little chilliness:
the native Vernaccia Nera, Merlot and some
rows of Pinot Nero. Even if the area was hit
hard by the earthquake, the new cellar
resisted. In their small barrique cellar, their
most important wines are aged, while the
earlier-drinkers are aged in steel. The
2015 Ruggero is a Merlot characterized by
well-expressed, natural red fruit. It's pulpy
on the palate, with a nice, long, fragrant
finish. The 2015 Cercis is a blend of equal
parts Merlot and Vernaccia that's aged in
steel. It offers up pleasant hints of fruit and
orange peel, as well as a taut, racy palate.
The 2015 Torcular is a monovarietal
Vernaccia with openly piquant accents. The
mouth is dynamic and graceful.

● Cercis '15	♥♥ 3
● Il Ruggero '15	♥♥ 5
● Torcular '15	♥♥ 2*
● Lacus '15	♥ 5
● Cercis '13	♀♀ 3
● Il Ruggero '14	♀♀ 5
● Il Ruggero '13	♀♀ 5
● Serrapetrona Lacus '14	♀♀ 5
● Serrapetrona Torcular '14	♀♀ 2
● Serrapetrona Torcular '13	♀♀ 2
● Zio Sergio '14	♀♀ 5

Il Pollenza

C.DA CASONE, 4
62029 TOLENTINO [MC]
TEL. +39 0733961989
www.ilpollenza.it

CELLAR SALES
PRE-BOOKED VISITS
ANNUAL PRODUCTION 300,000 bottles
HECTARES UNDER VINE 80.00
SUSTAINABLE WINERY

The fact that their cellar is housed in a
perfectly-maintained structure from the
1500s is enough to give you an idea of how
unique Conte Aldo Brachetti Peretti is. In
reality, behind the beauty, there's a truly
authentic culture of winemaking, starting
with carefully maintained vineyards,
highly-controlled ripening and selection of
grapes, slow maturation in prized oak or
aging in concrete vats. For the rest, all you
need to do is compare the number of bottles
produced with the total area of vineyards to
realize that only the best grapes end up
being used. The 2014 Pollenza is a
Bordeaux blend, with a nose that features
green pepper, printer's ink and dark fruit.
The wine is consistent in the mouth, and a
bit austere in its tannins. The 2014 Cosmino,
made with Cabernet Sauvignon, has green,
varietal nuances to it and a generally spicy
cadence, with a finish that reveals tempered
tannins. The 2015 Pius IX, on the other
hand, is the best of the region's sweet
wines. Bewitching aromas of apricot and
lychee give way to a long, enticing mouth.

● Cosmino '14	♟♟ 5
● Il Pollenza '14	♟♟ 8
○ Pius IX Mastai '15	♟♟ 6
○ Brianello '16	♟♟ 3
○ Colli Maceratesi Ribona Angera '16	♟♟ 3
⊙ Il Pollenza A. BP M. Cl. '12	♟♟ 8
● Porpora '14	♟♟ 3
⊙ Didì '16	♟ 3
● Il Pollenza '12	♟♟♟ 8
● Il Pollenza '11	♟♟♟ 7
● Il Pollenza '10	♟♟♟ 7
● Il Pollenza '09	♟♟♟ 7
● Il Pollenza '07	♟♟♟ 7
● Cosmino '13	♟♟ 5
○ Pius IX Mastai '14	♟♟ 6

Alberto Quacquarini

VIA COLLI, 1
62020 SERRAPETRONA [MC]
TEL. +39 0733908180
www.quacquarini.it

CELLAR SALES
ANNUAL PRODUCTION 180,000 bottles
HECTARES UNDER VINE 35.00

The large country residence that houses the
cellar (and its pressure tanks), and the loft
where the Vernaccia grapes are slowly dried,
were both badly damaged by the 2016
earthquake. But the Quacquarini family has
already found the strength and resources to
continue producing and once again lay claim
to their leading role in Serrapetrona. The
core of their production remains their
sparkling Vernaccia, even if, in recent years,
the still version is climbing the ladder. The
2015 Serrapetrona put in a good
performance. A still wine made with
Vernaccia grapes, it proves piquant,
succulent and carefree - a picnic wine that
can also be served fresh. The 2012 Petronio,
made with 100% dried-grapes, is spicy and
chocolatey, with a dense, voluminous palate
reminiscent of Amarone. The two Vernaccia
sparkling wines bring out the sweet touch of
grape drying. The Dolce is more on point,
exhibiting a lovable originality. The Secco
(which is still sweetish) lets the more
pronounced herbaceous notes emerge.

● Petronio '12	♟♟ 5
● Serrapetrona '15	♟♟ 3
● Vernaccia di Serrapetrona Dolce '15	♟♟ 3
● Colli della Serra '13	♟ 3
● Vernaccia di Serrapetrona Secco '15	♟ 3
● Colli della Serra '12	♟♟ 2*
● Petronio '10	♟♟ 5
● Serrapetrona '14	♟♟ 2*
● Serrapetrona '10	♟♟ 2*

Rocca di Castiglioni

C.DA CASTIGLIONI, 50
63072 CASTIGNANO [AP]
TEL. +39 0736821876
www.rocca-di-castiglioni.it

CELLAR SALES
PRE-BOOKED VISITS
ACCOMMODATION
ANNUAL PRODUCTION 25,000 bottles
HECTARES UNDER VINE 12.00
VITICULTURE METHOD Certified Organic

Valentino Fioravanti is a young man of few words, who's more used to the pace of the countryside than to the practices of public relations. His pragmatism leads him to personally perform the better part of his work in the vineyards while, in the cellar (recently built not far from the medieval walls of Castignano), it's winemaker Valerio Lucciarini who's in charge. Together they make wines that are detectably territorial, marked by an explicit freshness and vigor, made possible by the higher-than-usual altitudes (for Piceno) and nearby Monte Ascensione. The more rigid microclimate favors the rustic, mountain expression of the 2016 Pecorino Valeo Si Vales with its pure, citrusy, airy profile. Thus, when it comes, the lively mouth, modulated across savory flavors, feels befitting. The same profile emerges in the 2016 Passerina Alba Plena, though shifted onto a leaner body. The 2016 Console Castino expresses the freshness of its terroir through green, rooty strokes.

○ Offida Pecorino Valeo Si Vales '16	♟♟ 3*
○ Offida Passerina Alba Plena '16	♟♟ 3
● Rosso Piceno Console Castino '16	♟ 3
○ Offida Pecorino Valeo Si Vales '15	♟♟ 3*
● Rosso Piceno Console Castino '15	♟♟ 2*

Sabbionare

VIA SABBIONARE, 10
60036 MONTECAROTTO [AN]
TEL. +39 0731889004
www.sabbionare.it

CELLAR SALES
PRE-BOOKED VISITS
ANNUAL PRODUCTION 45,000 bottles
HECTARES UNDER VINE 24.00

A legacy, ambition and desire to keep alive a decades-long tradition of family viticulture - the commitment to a second job that becomes a primary one … Sauro Paolucci and Donatella Paoloni's path is one that's common in Marche. Their intuition and sweat was transformed into an opportunity for their children, who will have to decide whether to continue with a philosophy of more gradual development or change the 'family dimension' of the winery. For now, they rely primarily on Verdicchio and steel to create close-knit, flavorful wines. From the Sabbionare cru we get the wine of the same name. The 2016 didn't obtain last year's top marks, possibly because it's still too young. Exemplary aromas of almond and flowers precede an austere, though energetic palate with a superb crescendo for the finish. It will age smashingly. The 2016 El Filetto is simpler, a blend of all the winery's grapes. Drinkability, typicity and an excellent price are its strong points.

○ Verdicchio dei Castelli di Jesi Cl. Sup. Sabbionare '16	♟♟ 3*
○ Verdicchio dei Castelli di Jesi Cl. El Filetto '16	♟ 1*
○ Verdicchio dei Castelli di Jesi Cl. Sup. Sabbionare '15	♟♟♟ 2*
○ Verdicchio dei Castelli di Jesi Cl. El Filetto '15	♟♟ 1*
○ Verdicchio dei Castelli di Jesi Cl. I Pratelli '11	♟♟ 1*
○ Verdicchio dei Castelli di Jesi Cl. Sup. Sabbionare '13	♟♟ 2*
○ Verdicchio dei Castelli di Jesi Cl. Sup. Sabbionare '12	♟♟ 2*

Saladini Pilastri

via Saladini, 5
63078 Spinetoli [AP]
Tel. +39 0736899534
www.saladinipilastri.it

CELLAR SALES
PRE-BOOKED VISITS
ANNUAL PRODUCTION 800,000 bottles
HECTARES UNDER VINE 150.00
VITICULTURE METHOD Certified Organic
SUSTAINABLE WINERY

The history of Saladino Saladini Pilastri, which goes back centuries, features illustrious ancestors and a central role in the agricultural economy of Piceno. Even though the winery was founded in 1986, the background of its terrain certifies just how well-suited it is to viticulture. Organic from the outset, Saladino has never neglected its vineyards of mostly traditional cultivar. Their reds are matured in barrique, over various stages, while their Trebbiano, Passerina and Pecorino whites are aged in steel, thus bringing out their fruit and freshness. And the soft and succulent impact of the 2016 Pecorino, a wine that moves amidst aromas of peach and yellow citrus fruit, is a particularly effective result. The robust Rosso Picenos, blends of Montepulciano and Sangiovese, are also well-crafted. Among the many wines presented, the 2015 Vigna Montetinello performed well, with its fragrances of morello cherry and sweet spices, its streamlined body and worthy tannic expansion.

○ Offida Pecorino '16	🍷🍷 3*
● Rosso Piceno Piediprato '15	🍷🍷 3
● Rosso Piceno Sup. Montetinello '15	🍷🍷 4
● Rosso Piceno Sup. V. Monteprandone '15	🍷🍷 5
○ Falerio '16	🍷 2
○ Falerio Palazzi '16	🍷 3
○ Offida Passerina '16	🍷 3
● Rosso Piceno '16	🍷 2
● Rosso Piceno Sup. V. Monteprandone '00	🍸🍸🍸 3
○ Offida Pecorino '14	🍸🍸 3
● Rosso Piceno Sup. Montetinello '14	🍸🍸 3
● Rosso Piceno Sup. V. Monteprandone '14	🍸🍸 5

Poderi San Lazzaro

b.go Miriam
c.da San Lazzaro, 88
63073 Offida [AP]
Tel. +39 0736889189
www.poderisanlazzaro.it

CELLAR SALES
PRE-BOOKED VISITS
ANNUAL PRODUCTION 50,000 bottles
HECTARES UNDER VINE 7.50
VITICULTURE METHOD Certified Organic

From the terrace of Paolo Capriotti's modern and efficient cellar you can see some of Piceno's most beautiful vineyards. After all, he is at the center of a densely planted district, where vineyards that once featured Montepulciano and Sangiovese have gradually made space for Passerina and Pecorino, which are grown in the cooler zones. Paolo has grown organically for many years. His enological style is not particularly invasive, with a preference for wines that express the bounty of the territory, never shy in their structure, flavor or alcohol content. These qualities describe the 2013 Bordò, foremost. Made with Grenache grapes, it's a full-bodied wine, rich in fragrances of spice, oak, and fruit. The 2014 Podere 72 has a rustic profile but also a vigorous generosity on the palate, shaped by meaty hints of black cherry and plums. The 2016 Pistillo, a Pecorino, offers up notes of field herbs, with a homogenous mouth and a firm structure of flavor.

● Bordò '13	🍷🍷 7
○ Offida Pecorino Pistillo '16	🍷🍷 2*
● Rosso Piceno Sup. Podere 72 '14	🍷🍷 3
● Offida Rosso Grifola '13	🍷 4
● Polesio '16	🍷 2
● Offida Rosso Grifola '11	🍸🍸🍸 4*
● Bordò '12	🍸🍸 7
● Bordò '11	🍸🍸 7
● Offida Rosso Grifola '12	🍸🍸 4
● Piceno Sup. Podere 72 '13	🍸🍸 2*
● Piceno Sup. Podere 72 '12	🍸🍸 2*
● Piceno Sup. Podere 72 '11	🍸🍸 2*
● Polesio '15	🍸🍸 2*
● Polesio '14	🍸🍸 2*
● Polesio '13	🍸🍸 2*

Fattoria San Lorenzo

VIA SAN LORENZO, 6
60036 MONTECAROTTO [AN]
TEL. +39 073189656
az-crognaletti@libero.it

CELLAR SALES
PRE-BOOKED VISITS
ACCOMMODATION AND RESTAURANT SERVICE
ANNUAL PRODUCTION 100,000 bottles
HECTARES UNDER VINE 30.00
VITICULTURE METHOD Certified Organic

Natalino Crognaletti's wines have a peculiar sunniness to them. It's not just the result of early-harvesting of their Verdicchio, Montepulciano and Lacrima grapes (from various crus, the primary of which overlooks their cellar in Montecarotto). They've taken on his natural easiness, always ready for a smile, a quick joke, an open discussion. A rigorous vine grower, though, he's not afraid to admit that he loves a certain alcoholic vigor, an aspect brought on by long fermentation on the lees. And the complexity bestowed by time comes through in tertiary aromas that are undoubtedly captivating. Such qualities are brought out in the 2004 San Lorenzo. 10 years in concrete vats have made for a stratified wine, marked by complex fragrances of toasted almonds, camphor and medicinal herbs fused into a magnetic, deep palate. Thanks to some lift, the rich 2013 Campo delle Oche exhibited energy and character, while the 2011 Paradiso is a Lacrima of rare grip and originality.

○ Il San Lorenzo '04	▼▼ 6
● Il Solleone '09	▼▼ 5
● Paradiso '11	▼▼ 4
○ Verdicchio dei Castelli di Jesi Cl. Sup. Campo delle Oche '13	▼▼ 4
○ Verdicchio dei Castelli di Jesi Cl. ...le Oche... '15	▼ 3
○ Verdicchio dei Castelli di Jesi Cl. Vign. delle Oche Ris. '01	▼▼▼ 3
○ Il San Lorenzo '02	▼▼ 6
● Paradiso '10	▼▼ 4
● Rosso Piceno Di Gino '13	▼▼ 2*
○ Verdicchio dei Castelli di Jesi Cl. Sup. Campo delle Oche '12	▼▼ 4
○ Verdicchio dei Castelli di Jesi ...di Gino... '13	▼▼ 2*

San Michele a Ripa

C.DA SAN MICHELE, 24
63065 RIPATRANSONE [AP]
TEL. +39 3356833088
www.sanmichelearipa.it

CELLAR SALES
PRE-BOOKED VISITS
ANNUAL PRODUCTION 20,000 bottles
HECTARES UNDER VINE 5.00
VITICULTURE METHOD Certified Organic

Marco Alfonsi aims for quality, not numbers … He's working as quickly as he can. He knows his business, as evidenced by the historic palmento wine cellar found in the oak and Scotch broom forest that separates his plots (the lower, cooler positions are reserved for his white grapes, and the higher for his reds). He knows that years are needed to forge the right style. This means taking into consideration the vintage (slightly earlier harvesting for Pecorino and Passerina, so as to preserve their vigor and fragrances, and maturation of the phenolics for the Montepulciano and Petit Verdot), maceration and the use of various sizes of wood. Their wines already offer personality and clarity. Spirited and saline acidity unite the 2016 Falchetti and 2016 Brancuna, with the former displaying greater structure while the second is more inclined towards citrusy, easy-drinking. The 2013 Rubra has hints of red flowers and raspberry syrup. Its unique palate is marked by a notable richness of flavor and close-woven tannins moving towards resolution.

○ Offida Passerina Brancuna '16	▼▼ 3
○ Offida Pecorino Falchetti '16	▼▼ 3
● Offida Rosso Rubra '13	▼▼ 5
○ Offida Pecorino Falchetti '15	▽▽ 3*
● Periplo '14	▽▽ 3

Santa Barbara

go Mazzini, 35
0010 Barbara [AN]
Tel. +39 0719674249
ww.vinisantabarbara.it

CELLAR SALES
PRE-BOOKED VISITS
ANNUAL PRODUCTION 650,000 bottles
HECTARES UNDER VINE 40.00

Stefano Antonucci doesn't stop at just
following the market. He creates it, thanks
to an agile business structure, the
dedication of a trusted team, and the
ability to communicate Santa Barbara's
style without embellishing. Their wines are
as fresh in their fragrance and compelling
in their drinkability as they say, even their
powerful reds made with Merlot and
Montepulciano. And yet, in their wide and
varied selection, you also find those gems
that, uncorked years later, still surprise you
for their integrity and charm. Especially if
the word 'Verdicchio' is written on the
label. It's hard to choose from the long list
of wines offered by Stefano Antonucci. As
always, the 2016 Verdicchio that bears his
name gets the most attention: clear
citrus fragrances and a dynamic, highly
pleasing palate. The carefree and fruity
2016 Le Vaglie and 2015 Back to Basics
are also excellent, with the latter opting for
a more classic, persistent, almondy style.
The 2016 Tardivo is superb: sophisticated,
progressive, divergent.

○ Castelli di Jesi Verdicchio Cl. Tardivo ma non Tardo Ris. '15		♛♛ 5
● Verdicchio dei Castelli di Jesi Cl. Le Vaglie '16		♛♛ 3*
○ Verdicchio dei Castelli di Jesi Cl. Sup. Back to Basics '15		♛♛ 5
○ Verdicchio dei Castelli di Jesi Cl. Sup. Stefano Antonucci '15		♛♛ 4
Mossone '14		♛♛ 8
Rosso Piceno Il Maschio da Monte '15		♛♛ 5
○ Sensuade '16		♛♛ 3
● Stefano Antonucci Brut Rosé M.Cl.		♛♛ 5
● Stefano Antonucci Rosso '15		♛♛ 4
● Mossi Passito '15		♛ 5
Pathos '15		♛ 6
○ Rosso Piceno Stefano Antonucci '16		♛ 2

Tenuta Santori

c.da Montebove, 14
63065 Ripatransone [AP]
Tel. +39 0735584189
www.tenutasantori.it

CELLAR SALES
ANNUAL PRODUCTION 25,000 bottles
HECTARES UNDER VINE 16.00
VITICULTURE METHOD Certified Organic

Marco Santori comes from a family of
nurserymen. A graduate in enology, in
2012 he made his passion a reality, setting
in motion (with the help of his father) the
expansion of his vineyards, while putting
his faith in the area's local grape varieties.
He proceeded with the building of a
functional cellar (partially underground),
whose green terrace offers a panoramic
view on the hills of Ripatransone, a
municipality with deep viticultural roots.
With the support of winemaker Pierluigi
Lorenzetti, he creates contemporary wines
characterized by crystalline fragrances,
vigor and aromatic depth (highlighted by
the use of steel). All the wines presented
demonstrated a surprising quality, but the
2016 Pecorino gave the knockout punch.
Citrus strokes open the way for an
invigorating, fruity palate, with a radiant
finish displaying great aromatic
persistence. The 2016 Passerina offers up
tones of herbs and white peach fused into
a plucky pleasantness. The 2015 Piceno
Superiore is graceful and polished.

○ Offida Pecorino '16		♛♛♛ 3*
○ Offida Passerina '16		♛♛ 2*
● Rosso Piceno Sup. '15		♛♛ 3

Sartarelli

VIA COSTE DEL MOLINO, 24
60030 POGGIO SAN MARCELLO [AN]
TEL. +39 073189732
www.sartarelli.it

CELLAR SALES
PRE-BOOKED VISITS
ANNUAL PRODUCTION 300,000 bottles
HECTARES UNDER VINE 55.00

In Verdicchio veritas. The motto underlines and explicates the winery's complete dedication to the cultivation and vinification of Jesi's white grape. With it, they've constructed a well-diversified selection where each peculiarity can be traced back to the particular vintage, as well as the estate's 55 hectares of vineyards, comprising some of the best plots on the left back of the Esino river. None of their wines see wood - first they're aged in steel and then in glass. Balciana is one of the winery's historic crus. It features northeast exposure and an intriguing late harvest. The 2015 version is among the best in recent years. An explosive nose offers up hints of honey, aromatic herbs and orange peel, which fuse into a creamy palate that's at once creamy, uplifting and pervasive, while the finish holds firm. As always, the 2016 Classic is consistently strong, with its trademark notes of almond and lime blossom. Canned peaches and saffron mark the luscious 2015 Passito.

○ Verdicchio dei Castelli di Jesi Cl. Sup. Balciana '15	🍷🍷 5
○ Verdicchio dei Castelli di Jesi Cl. '16	🍷🍷 2*
○ Verdicchio dei Castelli di Jesi Passito '15	🍷🍷 5
○ Brut	🍷 3
○ Verdicchio dei Castelli di Jesi Cl. Sup. Tralivio '15	🍷 3
○ Verdicchio dei Castelli di Jesi Cl. Sup. Balciana '09	🍷🍷🍷 5
○ Verdicchio dei Castelli di Jesi Cl. Sup. Balciana '04	🍷🍷🍷 5
○ Verdicchio dei Castelli di Jesi Cl. Sup. Contrada Balciana '98	🍷🍷🍷 5

Sparapani - Frati Bianchi

VIA BARCHIO, 12
60034 CUPRAMONTANA [AN]
TEL. +39 0731781216
www.fratibianchi.it

CELLAR SALES
PRE-BOOKED VISITS
RESTAURANT SERVICE
ANNUAL PRODUCTION 40,000 bottles
HECTARES UNDER VINE 18.00

After inaugurating their new cellar a couple of years ago, a true jewel of efficiency and modern style, the three Sparapani brothers haven't stopped working. They expanded their vineyards and added a 'Metodo Classico' sparkler to their selection. Verdicchio reigns supreme, a legacy that goes back to their father, Settimio, a man who left his mark on the area's recent history. Their vineyards in Poggio Cupro and Contrada Salerna (in Cupramontana) and Casetellaro (in Serra San Quirico) produce grapes of vigor, flavor and structure, making for whites that are considered models to the extent that they stay true to the variety used. The 2015 Priore is an excellent choice when it comes to Verdicchio. The nose features a mix of aniseed, subtle balsamic, almond and a delicious touch of peach. The palate is graceful, expansive in flavor. The 2013 Donna Cloe doesn't hide its use of small wood: vanilla, toasty notes weave together with aromas of ripe fruit. In the mouth a lenthy, creamy wideness prevails.

○ Verdicchio dei Castelli di Jesi Cl. Sup. Il Priore '15	🍷🍷 3
○ Castelli di Jesi Verdicchio Cl. Donna Cloe Ris. '13	🍷🍷 5
○ Verdicchio dei Castelli di Jesi Cl. Sup. Salerna '16	🍷 2
○ Verdicchio dei Castelli di Jesi Cl. Sup. Il Priore '14	🍷🍷🍷 2
○ Verdicchio dei Castelli di Jesi Cl. Sup. Il Priore '13	🍷🍷🍷 2
○ Verdicchio dei Castelli di Jesi Cl. Sup. Il Priore '12	🍷🍷🍷 2
○ Verdicchio dei Castelli di Jesi Cl. Sup. Il Priore '06	🍷🍷🍷 2
○ Castelli di Jesi Verdicchio Cl. Donna Cloe Ris. '12	🍷🍷 5
○ Verdicchio dei Castelli di Jesi Cl. Sup. Il Priore '10	🍷🍷 3

Tenuta Spinelli

VIA LAGO, 2
63032 CASTIGNANO [AP]
TEL. I 39 0736821489
www.tenutaspinelli.it

CELLAR SALES
PRE-BOOKED VISITS
ACCOMMODATION
ANNUAL PRODUCTION 30,000 bottles
HECTARES UNDER VINE 7.00

Simone Spinelli could never have imagined that his life as a young vine grower would have changed so quickly. Soon enough, the small cellar that housed Spinell's steel barrels and a few pupitre (for his 'Metodo Classico' sparklers) proved too small. Indeed, his wines, which feature a honed style that brings together vigor and drinkability, were simply too successful. The necessary space was recently inaugurated, with new systems for Pinot Nero and Pecorino, two grapes that always find a home in the cool terroir of Monte Ascensione. The Artemisia earns its fifth Tre Bicchieri in a row, the result of outstanding interpretations of the vintages and the stylistic choices employed. The 2016 version boasts a pervasive flavor, unleashed by the contrast between fruit pulp and the extremely fresh flavor of its acidity. For the finish, wide, citrusy fragrances reemerge in a flavorful crescendo. The 'Metodo Classico', sparkling Mèroe (made with with Pecorino grapes) features notes of green olives and grain.

○ Offida Pecorino Artemisia '16	♈♈♈ 2*
○ Mèroe Pecorino M. Cl.	♈♈ 4
○ Eden '16	♈ 2
○ Offida Pecorino Artemisia '15	♈♈♈ 2*
○ Offida Pecorino Artemisia '14	♈♈♈ 2*
○ Offida Pecorino Artemisia '13	♈♈♈ 2*
○ Offida Pecorino Artemisia '12	♈♈♈ 2*
○ Eden '15	♈♈ 2*
○ Eden '13	♈♈ 2*
○ Eden '11	♈♈ 2*
○ Mèroe Pecorino M. Cl. '09	♈♈ 3
○ Offida Pecorino Artemisia '11	♈♈ 2*

La Staffa

VIA CASTELLARETTA, 19
60039 STAFFOLO [AN]
TEL. +39 0731779810
www.vinilastaffa.it

CELLAR SALES
PRE-BOOKED VISITS
ANNUAL PRODUCTION 45,000 bottles
HECTARES UNDER VINE 10.00
VITICULTURE METHOD Certified Organic

Riccardo Baldi has a number of seasons under his belt; he may be young, but he's no beginner. His wines crossed into international waters some time ago, and he's well known by wine lovers, but the producer hasn't lost an ounce of that burning enthusiasm that drove him to take up management of his family's vineyards in the first place. In the blink of an eye the fires of passion spread rapidly, leading to the construction of a notably efficient underground cellar and the expansion of the estate through new purchases. Of course, the producer also continues to study and research new crus, spontaneous fermentation, and lengthy aging in steel, concrete and glass. Their 2015 Rincrocca offers a nice nose marked by candied citrus and pear. The palate displays a flavorful, succulent weave characterized by a pleasantness that is wider than it is deep. White fruit and light, flowery echoes define the 2015 La Staffa, which goes all in on drinkability and unmitigated richness of flavor.

○ Castelli di Jesi Verdicchio Cl. Rincrocca Ris. '15	♈♈ 4
○ Verdicchio dei Castelli di Jesi Cl. Sup. La Staffa '16	♈♈ 2*
● Rubinia '11	♈♈ 4
○ Verdicchio dei Castelli di Jesi Cl. '13	♈♈ 2*
○ Verdicchio dei Castelli di Jesi Cl. '12	♈♈ 2*
○ Verdicchio dei Castelli di Jesi Cl. Sup. La Rincrocca '10	♈♈ 3
○ Verdicchio dei Castelli di Jesi Cl. Sup. La Staffa '15	♈♈ 3
○ Verdicchio dei Castelli di Jesi Cl. Sup. La Staffa '14	♈♈ 3

Tenuta di Tavignano

LOC. TAVIGNANO
62011 CINGOLI [MC]
TEL. +39 0733617303
www.tenutaditavignano.it

CELLAR SALES
PRE-BOOKED VISITS
ACCOMMODATION
ANNUAL PRODUCTION 100,000 bottles
HECTARES UNDER VINE 30.00
SUSTAINABLE WINERY

Winning the 'White of the Year Award' with their 2015 Misco certainly brought pride and joy to Tenuta di Tavignano, but the euphoria soon wore off and the desire to go above and beyond kicked in. Indeed, for the winery, the prize was a starting point, not a conclusion, after all, hard work and care in winemaking are constants for the team led by Ondine De La Feld. Verdicchio is cultivated in the amphitheater-shaped vineyards that face the cellar and the valley of Musone. In the vineyards behind the cellar, at the highest point of the hill, Montepulciano and other red varieties are grown. The 2016 Misco doesn't have to do much to affirm its status as one of Marche's best whites. Flowers, aniseed and white peach fuse in a long, balanced, well-sustained palate characterized by an elevated notion of drinkability and pleasantness. The 2016 Villa Torre is a sharper wine, smooth and racy. The 2015 Misco Riserva has a lovely nose characterized by aromatic herbs, but also displays a certain tendency to richness of flavor.

○ Verdicchio dei Castelli di Jesi Cl. Sup. Misco '16	♟♟♟ 3*
○ Verdicchio dei Castelli di Jesi Cl. Villa Torre '16	♟♟ 3*
○ Castelli di Jesi Verdicchio Cl. Misco Ris. '15	♟♟ 4
○ Il Pestifero '16	♟♟ 3
● Rosso Piceno Libenter '15	♟♟ 4
⊙ Rosato '16	♟ 3
● Rosso Piceno Cervidoni '15	♟ 3
○ Verdicchio dei Castelli di Jesi Cl. Sup. Misco '15	♟♟♟ 3*
○ Verdicchio dei Castelli di Jesi Cl. Sup. Misco '14	♟♟♟ 3*
○ Verdicchio dei Castelli di Jesi Cl. Sup. Misco '13	♟♟♟ 3*

Fattoria Le Terrazze

VIA MUSONE, 4
60026 NUMANA [AN]
TEL. +39 0717390352
www.fattorialeterrazze.it

CELLAR SALES
PRE-BOOKED VISITS
ANNUAL PRODUCTION 100,000 bottles
HECTARES UNDER VINE 20.00

Antonio Terni is one of the central figures in the history of Conero. His farm, which sits on a small hill in a southern corner of the DOC zone, has been operating for more than a century (though Antonio himself has only been involved personally since the 1980s). For some years now, this advocate of a modern style has entrusted all the technical work to Federico Curtaz, who arrived at Numana 20 years ago in the role of agronomist. In the cellar, built just by the primary residence and surrounded by vineyards, steel is used for the early-drinkers while barrique is reserved for their long-lived wines. At the top of our list is a revived version of Sassi Neri. The 2013 displays a nice weave of morello cherries and oak notes. These come together in a decisive, consistent palate that proves quite tannic at its close. The 2012 Chaos is half Monetpulciano, a quarter Merlot and quarter Syrah. It boasts dark minerality, black pepper and traces of burnt wood in a palate of solid tannic weave.

● Conero Sassi Neri Ris. '13	♟♟ 5
● Chaos '12	♟♟ 5
● Rosso Conero Praeludium '16	♟♟ 2*
○ Le Cave Chardonnay '16	♟ 2
⊙ Pink Fluid '16	♟ 2
● Chaos '04	♟♟♟ 5
● Chaos '01	♟♟♟ 6
● Chaos '97	♟♟♟ 6
● Conero Sassi Neri Ris. '04	♟♟♟ 5
● Rosso Conero Sassi Neri '02	♟♟♟ 5
● Rosso Conero Sassi Neri '99	♟♟♟ 5
● Rosso Conero Sassi Neri '98	♟♟♟ 5
● Rosso Conero Visions of J '01	♟♟♟ 7
● Rosso Conero Visions of J '97	♟♟♟ 7

Terre Cortesi Moncaro

VIA PIANOLE, 7A
63036 MONTECAROTTO [AN]
TEL. 39 073189245
www.moncaro.com

CELLAR SALES
PRE-BOOKED VISITS
RESTAURANT SERVICE
ANNUAL PRODUCTION 7,500,000 bottles
HECTARES UNDER VINE 1200.00

Montepulciano, Sangiovese, Verdicchio and Pecorino. These are that grapes that, either as monovarietals or in blends, go into creating the best wines of the largest cooperative in Marche. Terre Cortesi Moncaro is a partnership of vine growers from the region's three most important districts: Castelli di Jesi, Conero and Piceno. Their operation is a strong signal of loyalty to the territory, expressed in a style that is modern and aimed at an international market. Consistency, therefore, is a must. The taste profile of their wines is characterized by clearness and corpulence, putting fruit first, in the case of the whites, and smooth tannins in the case of the reds. In the absence of their important Riserva Vigna Novali, the award for the best Verdicchio in their selection goes to their 2016 Verde Ca' Ruptae, by virtue of its clear profile and a palate that is both dynamic and supple. Its twin, the 2016 Fondiglie, is less precise but of good character. The 2016 Ofithe is a Pecorino that delivers, going all in on fruit, while the two Piceno Superiores offer full palates, grippy tannins and a seductive aromatic integrity.

● Conero Cimerio Ris. '14	🏆🏆	3
○ Madreperla Brut M. Cl.	🏆🏆	5
○ Offida Pecorino Ofithe '16	🏆🏆	3
● Rosso Piceno Sup. Campo delle Mura '09	🏆🏆	4
● Rosso Piceno Sup. Roccaviva '14	🏆🏆	2*
○ Verdicchio dei Castelli di Jesi Cl. Sup. Fondiglie '16	🏆🏆	3
○ Verdicchio dei Castelli di Jesi Cl. Sup. Verde Ca' Ruptae '16	🏆🏆	3
○ Castelli di Jesi Verdicchio Cl. V. Novali Ris. '10	🏆🏆🏆	3*
○ Castelli di Jesi Verdicchio Cl. V. Novali Ris. '09	🏆🏆🏆	3*
● Rosso Piceno Sup. Roccaviva '12	🏆🏆🏆	2*
○ Verdicchio dei Castelli di Jesi Cl. V. Novali Ris. '08	🏆🏆🏆	3*

★Umani Ronchi

VIA ADRIATICA, 12
60027 OSIMO [AN]
TEL. +39 0717108019
www.umanironchi.com

CELLAR SALES
PRE-BOOKED VISITS
ANNUAL PRODUCTION 3,000,000 bottles
HECTARES UNDER VINE 240.00
VITICULTURE METHOD Certified Organic
SUSTAINABLE WINERY

Their many hectares of vineyards prove that, for the Bernetti family, a commitment to agriculture is a key factor to quality. Their production model has been well-established: a classical approach to winemaking that gives the right emphasis to native grapes (without completely discounting international varieties), leaning on local appellations so as to create consistent, reliable wines that are capable of expressing their terroir all over the world. And this is the reason that the winery is prepared to make significant investments, and why they've put together a first-rate staff in which the names Beppe Caviola (consultant), Giacomo Mattioli and Luigi Piersanti. Despite infighting between a number of excellent wines, the 2015 Vecchie Vigne once again nabs a Tre Bicchieri, bolstered by its extremely elegant style, its austere, yet decisive palate and a nuanced finish that sees a thousand rivulets of salt and crystal clear aromas. The 2014 Plenio is creamy and well focused, while the 2015 Centovie, a Pecorino of sophisticated aromatic stratification, had a nice debut.

○ Verdicchio dei Castelli di Jesi Cl. Sup. V. V. '15	🏆🏆🏆	4*
○ Castelli di Jesi Verdicchio Cl. Plenio Ris. '14	🏆🏆	4
○ Centovie Pecorino '15	🏆🏆	4
● Conero Campo San Giorgio Ris. '12	🏆🏆	7
● Conero Cumaro Ris. '13	🏆🏆	5
○ La Hoz Brut Nature M.Cl. '11	🏆🏆	5
○ Maximo '14	🏆🏆	4
● Pelago '13	🏆🏆	5
● Rosso Conero Serrano '16	🏆🏆	2*
○ Verdicchio dei Castelli di Jesi Cl. Sup. Casal di Serra '16	🏆🏆	3
● Montepulciano d'Abruzzo Jorio '15	🏆	3
● Rosso Conero San Lorenzo '15	🏆	3
○ Umani Ronchi Extra Brut M. Cl.	🏆	4

La Valle del Sole

via San Lazzaro, 46
63035 Offida [AP]
Tel. +39 0736889658
valledelsoleoffida@gmail.com

PRE-BOOKED VISITS
ANNUAL PRODUCTION 25,000 bottles
HECTARES UNDER VINE 11.00
VITICULTURE METHOD Certified Organic

The Di Nicolò family didn't choose to call
their agritourism and adjacent cellar 'La Valle
del Sole' for merely poetic purposes.
Whoever knows the territory, knows that San
Lazzaro is a warm, sunny, generous terroir.
The rows of Picene are managed by the
tireless Silvano. The cellar is the domain of
his daughter, Alessia, along with the support
of winemaker Valerio Lucciarini. Together
they create intense and express wines, at
times uplifting in their management of
texture, but perfectly true to the territory. The
cellar features large concrete vats and large
wooden barrels (used for aging their reds).
The 2015 Piceno Superiore is characterized
by an overtly fruity style and a palate defined
by sweet tannins that are well integrated
into the wine's overall architecture. The
2014 Offida Rosso is supple, soft and spicy.
Both the whites prove worthy entries, though
we preferred the 2016 Pecorinio, which is
well-defined in its citrus accents and offers
an expansive palate. The 2016 Passerina
proved saline and refreshing.

○ Offida Pecorino '16	♟♟	3
● Offida Rosso '14	♟♟	4
○ Passerina '16	♟♟	2*
● Rosso Piceno Sup. '15	♟♟	3
○ Offida Pecorino '15	♟♟	2*
● Rosso Piceno Sup. '14	♟♟	2*

★Velenosi

loc. Monticelli
via dei Biancospini, 11
63100 Ascoli Piceno
Tel. +39 0736341218
www.velenosivini.com

CELLAR SALES
PRE-BOOKED VISITS
ANNUAL PRODUCTION 2,500,000 bottles
HECTARES UNDER VINE 192.00

Angela Velenosi travels the wold non-stop.
It's a tremendous sacrifice that comes with
having a business model oriented towards
exports. But her reward comes in the form of
strong feedback from clients, distributors
and restaurants. After playing, and winning,
the native grape game, the new challenge is
'organic', and with the 2016 vintage a new
selection is being launched. As for the rest,
they haven't given an inch in terms of
making wines that are true children of
Marche's genius loci, while remaining
enthusiasts for the right modern touch.
Consistency and having the proper number
of bottles on the market are always top
priorities. The 2014 Roggio earns Tre
Bicchieri thanks to the precision with which
it mixes the succulence of morello cherries
and black plums with a sophisticated pattern
of spices. In the mouth it offers a palate of
calibrated density and a neat weave of
smooth tannins. The 2015 Rêve proved
superb, with its captivating hints of candied
citrus and long mouth. The 2006 Cuvée Gold
is an original, complex 'Metodo Classico'
sparkler that's disgorged after 10 years.

● Rosso Piceno Sup. Roggio del Filare '14	♟♟♟	6
○ Offida Pecorino Rêve '15	♟♟	5
○ Velenosi Gran Cuvée Gold Brut M. Cl. '06	♟♟	5
○ Offida Pecorino Villa Angela '16	♟♟	3
● Offida Rosso Ludi '14	♟♟	6
● Rosso Piceno Sup. Brecciarolo '15	♟♟	2*
● Rosso Piceno Sup. Brecciarolo Gold '15	♟♟	4
⊙ The Rose Brut M. Cl. '11	♟♟	5
○ Velenosi Gran Cuvée Brut M. Cl. '11	♟♟	5
○ Offida Pecorino Bio '16	♟	3
○ Passerina Bio '16	♟	3
○ Passerina Villa Angela '16	♟	2
○ Offida Pecorino Rêve '14	♟♟♟	5
● Rosso Piceno Sup. Roggio del Filare '12	♟♟♟	7

Roberto Venturi

VIA CASE NUOVE, 1A
60010 CASTELLEONE DI SUASA [AN]
TEL. +39 3381855566
www.viniventuri.it

CELLAR SALES
PRE-BOOKED VISITS
ANNUAL PRODUCTION 60,000 bottles
HECTARES UNDER VINE 8.00

Roberto 'Robi' Venturi has carved out a
place for himself as guardian vine grower.
That's how he likes to call the work, which
he inherited from his father, of defending
vine culture in the northeast area of the
Castelli di Jesi. In addition to the vineyards
that surround their lovely, new cellar, he
manages a hectare of old Verdicchio in the
district of Busche da Montecarotto, which
is used as the producer's flagship, Qudì.
This year the major piece of news is the
release of the Squarciafico, a red made
with Montepulciano aged in mid-sized
casks. Robi presented a spectacular Qudì,
even better than the 2013, which brought
Castelleone di Suasa its first Tre Bicchieri.
Extremely elegant in its aromatic profile
of herbs, almonds and whiffs of balsamic,
the wine offers a well-developed, supple
and balanced palate. Desiderio, made
with Moscato, is extremely citrusy, easy
to drink and flavorful without resorting
to residual sweetness.

○ Verdicchio dei Castelli di Jesi Cl. Sup. Qudì '15	♟♟♟ 3*
● Balsamino '16	♟♟ 2*
○ Desiderio '16	♟♟ 2*
● Squarciafico '15	♟ 3
○ Verdicchio dei Castelli di Jesi San Martino '16	♟ 2
○ Verdicchio dei Castelli di Jesi Cl. Sup. Qudì '13	♟♟♟ 2*
○ Desiderio '15	♟♟ 2*
○ Desiderio '14	♟♟ 2*
○ Desiderio '13	♟♟ 2*
○ Verdicchio dei Castelli di Jesi Cl. Sup. Qudì '14	♟♟ 2*
○ Verdicchio dei Castelli di Jesi Cl. Sup. Qudì '12	♟♟ 2*
○ Verdicchio dei Castelli di Jesi San Martino '15	♟♟ 2*

Vicari

VIA POZZO BUONO, 3
60030 MORRO D'ALBA [AN]
TEL. +39 073163164
www.vicarivini.it

CELLAR SALES
PRE-BOOKED VISITS
ANNUAL PRODUCTION 120,000 bottles
HECTARES UNDER VINE 25.00

Vico Vicari has a rare, visceral passion for
work. He knows his vineyards inside out and
spends more time in his cellar than in his
house. He never gets tired of testing,
studying, choosing. Thanks to the support
of his father, Nazzareno, an authority on
Lacrima, Vico's learnt the secrets of the
varieties, and has conceived a style all his
own: a fruity integrity that's intense and
structurally rich. Valentina, his sister,
serves as the winery's commercial wing.
Together they manifest the young, dynamic
spirit of the appellation that displays
the name 'Morro d'Alba' on its label. The
2015 Verdicchio Insolito del Pozzo Buono
has the honor of debuting the Vicari family
in the Tre Bicchieri club. Putting the
structural excesses of the past aside, it
boasts magnificent equilibrium: crystalline
perceptions of herbs and citrus combine in
a palate of exhilarating energy, and amplify
in a crackling finish. 2016 Essenza is a
Lacrima of uplifting sensory intensity, with
an explosive palate.

○ Verdicchio dei Castelli di Jesi Cl. Sup. Insolito del Pozzo Buono '15	♟♟♟ 3*
● Lacrima di Morro d'Alba Essenza del Pozzo Buono '16	♟♟ 3*
● Lacrima di Morro d'Alba Passito Amaranto del Pozzo Buono '15	♟♟ 4
○ Verdicchio dei Castelli di Jesi Cl. del Pozzo Buono '16	♟♟ 2*
● Lacrima di Morro d'Alba Dasempre del Pozzo Buono '16	♟ 2
● Lacrima di Morro d'Alba Sup. del Pozzo Buono '15	♟ 3
● Lacrima di Morro d'Alba Essenza del Pozzo Buono '15	♟♟ 3
○ Verdicchio dei Castelli di Jesi Cl. Sup. Insolito del Pozzo Buono '14	♟♟ 3

Vignamato

VIA BATTINEBBIA, 4
60038 SAN PAOLO DI JESI [AN]
TEL. +39 0731779197
www.vignamato.com

CELLAR SALES
PRE-BOOKED VISITS
ANNUAL PRODUCTION 100,000 bottles
HECTARES UNDER VINE 27.00

The hard work of modernizing began two years ago with the hiring of winemaker Pierluigi Lorenzetti. Next they proceeded to lighten the structure and alcoholic energy of their wines, in favor of fresher aromas. Andrea Ceci has always been a firm believer that drinkability and the integrity of fruit flavors are the keys to more ambitious wines. Various plots of vineyards, situated between San Paolo and Castelplanio, provide outstanding raw material that, in their efficient cellar in Battinebbia, will be transformed into full-flavored Verdicchio and fruity, Montepulciano reds. The 2013 Ambrosia is an explosion of summery aromas (peach, yellow melon) with a delectable smoky backdrop. In the mouth, its complexity is underlined by a sustained, persistent dynamism. The 2016 Versiano features an intense nose of lime peel and pineapple, followed by a succulent palate that's quite soft and extremely flavorful. A sense of balance and elegance define the 2016 Eos, a wine whose saline approach on the palate delivers.

○ Castelli di Jesi Verdicchio Cl. Ambrosia Ris. '13	♥♥ 3*
○ Ale Brut	♥♥ 3
○ Verdicchio dei Castelli di Jesi Cl. Sup. Eos '16	♥♥ 2*
○ Verdicchio dei Castelli di Jesi Cl. Sup. Versiano '16	♥♥ 3
○ Verdicchio dei Castelli di Jesi Cl. Valle delle Lame '16	♥♥ 2*
⊙ Ale Rosé Brut	♥ 3
○ Versus '16	♥ 2
○ Verdicchio dei Castelli di Jesi Cl. Sup. Versiano '15	♀♀ 3*
○ Verdicchio dei Castelli di Jesi Passito Antares '11	♀♀ 4

Villa Lazzarini

C.DA COLLEVAGO
62010 TREIA [MC]
TEL. +39 3333553460
www.villalazzarini-vini.it

ANNUAL PRODUCTION 60,000 bottles
HECTARES UNDER VINE 8.00

Cristiano Giuliani and Maurizio Raffaelli began planting in 2009, in the countryside of Macerata and Treia. They took the advice of Giuseppe Camilli, who suggested that, rather than focus on local grape varieties, they experiment with alternative cultivar. And so they began testing a few rows of international grapes, and two of Marche's more common varieties: a mix of Bruni 54 and the almost forgotten Garofanata. The idea is that stainless steel would best bring out the typicity of the cultivar, while small wood would only be used for the Cimarella, a blend of Montepulciano and Petit Verdot. It's a wine that, as of 2013, expresses itself with an abundant presence of fruit and muscular structure. But it was the selection of whites, once again, that made the best impression. The 2015 Vellente, made with Garofanata, is excellent: delicately aromatic, supple and well-paced, it reveals an aftertaste of citrus and sophisticated mineral notes. The 2015 Marì, made with Maceratino, is right up there, with an irresistible drinkability featuring herbs and aniseed.

○ Vellente '15	♥♥ 3*
● Cimarella '13	♥♥ 5
● Giulara '13	♥♥ 3
○ Lazzarino '15	♥♥ 3
○ Marì '15	♥♥ 2*
⊙ Risù Rosé Brut	♥ 3

Angeli di Varano

LOC. VARANO, 228
60131 ANCONA
TEL. +39 0718046019
www.angelidivarano.it

CELLAR SALES
PRE-BOOKED VISITS
ACCOMMODATION
ANNUAL PRODUCTION 25,000 bottles
HECTARES UNDER VINE 3.50

Conero Stile Libero Ris. '12	🏆🏆 4
PinKonero '16	🏆 2
Rosso Conero Primo di Tre '15	🏆 3

Ca' Liptra

VIA SAN MICHELE, 21
60034 CUPRAMONTANA [AN]
TEL. +39 3491321442
www.caliptra.it

CELLAR SALES
PRE-BOOKED VISITS
HECTARES UNDER VINE 2.30
VITICULTURE METHOD Certified Organic
SUSTAINABLE WINERY

○ Castelli di Jesi Verdicchio Cl. S. Michele 21 Ris. '15	🏆🏆 4
○ Verdicchio dei Castelli di Jesi Cl. Sup. Kypra '16	🏆 3

Campo di Maggio

LOC. PAGLIARE
FORMALE, 24
63078 SPINETOLI [AP]
TEL. +39 3493110296
www.cantinacampodimaggio.it

CELLAR SALES
PRE-BOOKED VISITS
ANNUAL PRODUCTION 30,000 bottles
HECTARES UNDER VINE 7.00
VITICULTURE METHOD Certified Organic

Offida Pecorino '16	🏆🏆 3
Rosso Piceno '16	🏆🏆 2*
Offida Passerina '16	🏆 3

Cavalieri

VIA RAFFAELLO, 1
62024 MATELICA [MC]
TEL. +39 073784859
www.cantinacavalieri.it

PRE-BOOKED VISITS
ANNUAL PRODUCTION 15,000 bottles
HECTARES UNDER VINE 8.24

○ Verdicchio di Matelica '16	🏆🏆 2*
○ Verdicchio di Matelica d'Antan '15	🏆🏆 3
● Pinot Nero '16	🏆 4

Cantina dei Colli Ripani

VIA TOSCIANO, 28
63065 RIPATRANSONE [AP]
TEL. +39 07359505
www.colliripani.it

CELLAR SALES
PRE-BOOKED VISITS
ANNUAL PRODUCTION 1,300,000 bottles
HECTARES UNDER VINE 650.00
VITICULTURE METHOD Certified Organic

Offida Rosso Leo Ripanus '11	🏆🏆 3
Offida Pecorino Rugaro Gold '16	🏆 2
Offida Passerina Ninfa Ripana Gold '16	🏆 2

Cantina Cològnola Tenuta Musone

LOC. COLOGNOLA, 22A BIS
62011 CINGOLI [MC]
TEL. +39 0733616438
www.tenutamusone.it

CELLAR SALES
PRE-BOOKED VISITS
ANNUAL PRODUCTION 150,000 bottles
HECTARES UNDER VINE 25.00

○ Verdicchio dei Castelli di Jesi Cl. Sup. Ghiffa '15	🏆🏆 3
○ Verdicchio dei Castelli di Jesi Cl. Via Condotto '16	🏆🏆 2*

Conti degli Azzoni

VIA DON MINZONI, 26
62010 MONTEFANO [MC]
TEL. +39 0733850219
www.degliazzoni.it

CELLAR SALES
PRE-BOOKED VISITS
ACCOMMODATION AND RESTAURANT SERVICE
ANNUAL PRODUCTION 100,000 bottles
HECTARES UNDER VINE 130.00

● Passatempo '14	♛♛ 5
● Rosso Piceno '14	♛♛ 2*
○ Colli Maceratesi Ribona '16	♛ 2
○ Grechetto '16	♛ 2

Conti di Buscareto

FRAZ. PIANELLO
VIA SAN GREGORIO, 66
60010 OSTRA [AN]
TEL. +39 0717988020
www.contidibuscareto.com

CELLAR SALES
PRE-BOOKED VISITS
ANNUAL PRODUCTION 250,000 bottles
HECTARES UNDER VINE 70.00

● Bisaccione di Buscareto '14	♛♛ 5
● Lacrima di Morro d'Alba Sup. Compagnia della Rosa '14	♛♛ 4
● Lacrima di Morro d'Alba '16	♛ 2

Fattoria Dezi

C.DA FONTEMAGGIO, 14
63839 SERVIGLIANO [FM]
TEL. +39 0734710090
fattoriadezi@hotmail.com

CELLAR SALES
PRE-BOOKED VISITS
ACCOMMODATION
ANNUAL PRODUCTION 45,000 bottles
HECTARES UNDER VINE 15.00

● Dezio '15	♛♛ 3
○ Falerio Pecorino Servigliano P. '15	♛♛ 3
○ Solagne '15	♛ 3

Domodimonti

VIA MENOCCHIA, 195
63010 MONTEFIORE DELL'ASO [AP]
TEL. +39 0734930010
www.domodimonti.com

CELLAR SALES
PRE-BOOKED VISITS
ACCOMMODATION AND RESTAURANT SERVIC
ANNUAL PRODUCTION 200,000 bottles
HECTARES UNDER VINE 40.00

● I AM '15	♛♛ 2
● Il Messia '13	♛♛ 3
○ Offida Pecorino LiCoste '16	♛♛ 4

Fiorini

LOC. BARCHI
VIA GIARDINO CAMPIOLI, 5
61040 TERRE ROVERASCHE [PU]
TEL. +39 072197151
www.fioriniwines.it

CELLAR SALES
PRE-BOOKED VISITS
ACCOMMODATION
ANNUAL PRODUCTION 200,000 bottles
HECTARES UNDER VINE 45.00
VITICULTURE METHOD Certified Organic

○ Bianchello del Metauro Sup. Tenuta Campioli '16	♛♛ 2*
○ La Galoppa '16	♛♛ 2*
○ Bianchello del Metauro Sup. Andy '15	♛ 3

Luca Guerrieri

VIA SAN FILIPPO, 24
61030 PIAGGE [PU]
TEL. +39 0721890152
www.aziendaguerrieri.it

CELLAR SALES
PRE-BOOKED VISITS
ACCOMMODATION
ANNUAL PRODUCTION 250,000 bottles
HECTARES UNDER VINE 44.53

● Colli Pesaresi Sangiovese '16	♛♛
● Colli Pesaresi Sangiovese Galileo Ris. '14	♛♛
● Guerriero Nero '15	♛♛

Esther Hauser

L.DA CORONCINO, 1A
60039 STAFFOLO [AN]
TEL. +39 0731770203
www.estherhauser.it

CELLAR SALES
PRE-BOOKED VISITS
ANNUAL PRODUCTION 6,000 bottles
HECTARES UNDER VINE 1.00

● Il Cupo '14	♟♟ 5
● Il Ceppo '14	♟♟ 4

Luciano Landi

VIA GAVIGLIANO, 16
60030 BELVEDERE OSTRENSE [AN]
TEL. +39 073162353
www.aziendalandi.it

CELLAR SALES
PRE-BOOKED VISITS
ACCOMMODATION
ANNUAL PRODUCTION 80,000 bottles
HECTARES UNDER VINE 20.00

● Goliardo '14	♟♟ 4
● Lacrima di Morro d'Alba Sup. Gavigliano '15	♟♟ 3
● Lacrima di Morro d'Alba Passito '15	♟ 5

Conte Leopardi Dittajuti

A MARINA II, 24
60026 NUMANA [AN]
TEL. +39 0717390116
www.conteleopardi.it

CELLAR SALES
PRE-BOOKED VISITS
ANNUAL PRODUCTION 350,000 bottles
HECTARES UNDER VINE 49.00

Verdicchio dei Castelli di Jesi Cl. Castelverde '16	♟♟ 2*
Conero Pigmento Ris. '14	♟ 5
Rosso Conero Fructus '16	♟ 2

Mario Lucchetti

VIA SANTA MARIA DEL FIORE, 17
60030 MORRO D'ALBA [AN]
TEL. +39 073163314
www.mariolucchetti.it

CELLAR SALES
PRE-BOOKED VISITS
ANNUAL PRODUCTION 150,000 bottles
HECTARES UNDER VINE 25.00

● Lacrima di Morro d'Alba '16	♟♟ 2*
● Lacrima di Morro d'Alba Sup. Guardengo '15	♟♟ 3

Ma.Ri.Ca.

A ACQUASANTA, 7
60030 BELVEDERE OSTRENSE [AN]
TEL. +39 0731290091
www.cantinamarica.it

CELLAR SALES
PRE-BOOKED VISITS
ANNUAL PRODUCTION 70,000 bottles
HECTARES UNDER VINE 15.00

Verdicchio dei Castelli di Jesi Cl. Sup. Tosius '15	♟♟ 3
Verdicchio dei Castelli di Jesi Cl. Tregaso '16	♟♟ 2*

La Marca di San Michele

VIA TORRE, 13
60034 CUPRAMONTANA [AN]
TEL. +39 0731781183
www.lamarcadisanmichele.com

CELLAR SALES
PRE-BOOKED VISITS
ACCOMMODATION
ANNUAL PRODUCTION 25,000 bottles
HECTARES UNDER VINE 6.00
VITICULTURE METHOD Certified Organic

○ Castelli di Jesi Verdicchio Cl. Passolento Ris. '15	♟♟ 4

Maurizio Marchetti

FRAZ. PINOCCHIO
VIA DI PONTELUNGO, 166
60131 ANCONA
TEL. +39 071897386
www.marchettiwines.it

CELLAR SALES
PRE-BOOKED VISITS
ANNUAL PRODUCTION 60,000 bottles
HECTARES UNDER VINE 20.00

● Conero Villa Bonomi Ris. '14	♟♟ 5
● Rosso Conero Castro di San Silvestro '16	♟♟ 2*
● Rosso Conero Due Amici '16	♟ 2

Enzo Mecella

VIA DANTE, 112
60044 FABRIANO [AN]
TEL. +39 073221680
www.enzomecella.com

CELLAR SALES
PRE-BOOKED VISITS
ANNUAL PRODUCTION 200,000 bottles
HECTARES UNDER VINE 12.00

○ Verdicchio di Matelica Casa Fosca '16	♟♟ 3
○ Verdicchio di Matelica Saniale '15	♟♟ 3
● Conero Rubelliano Ris. '11	♟ 5

Monte Torto

LOC. CASENUOVE
VIA DI JESI, 343
60027 OSIMO [AN]
TEL. +39 0731205764
www.montetorto.it

CELLAR SALES
ANNUAL PRODUCTION 13,000 bottles
HECTARES UNDER VINE 6.30

● Bartolo '16	♟♟ 2*
● Casone '14	♟♟ 3
● Floriano '15	♟♟ 2*
○ Monticello '16	♟ 2

Fattoria Nannì

C.DA ARSICCI
62021 APIRO [MC]
TEL. +39 3406225930
www.fattoriananni.it

CELLAR SALES
PRE-BOOKED VISITS
ANNUAL PRODUCTION 11,000 bottles
HECTARES UNDER VINE
VITICULTURE METHOD Certified Organic

○ Verdicchio dei Castelli di Jesi Cl. Sup. Origini '16	♟♟ 3

Officina del Sole

C.DA MONTEMILONE, 1
63842 MONTEGIORGIO [FM]
TEL. +39 0734967321
www.officinadelsole.it

ANNUAL PRODUCTION 20,000 bottles
HECTARES UNDER VINE 12.00

○ Falerio Pecorino Franco Franco '15	♟♟ 5
● Tignum '15	♟♟ 6
○ Falerio Pecorino Franco '16	♟ 3
○ Sensi '16	♟ 3

Cantina Offida

VIA DELLA REPUBBLICA , 70
63073 OFFIDA [AP]
TEL. +39 0736880104
www.cantinaoffida.com

CELLAR SALES
PRE-BOOKED VISITS
ANNUAL PRODUCTION 400,000 bottles
HECTARES UNDER VINE 300.00
VITICULTURE METHOD Certified Organic

○ Offida Pecorino '16	♟♟ 2
● Rosso Piceno '16	♟♟ 2
● Rosso Piceno Sup. Il Podestà '13	♟♟ 3

Tenute Recchi Franceschini

C.DA VALLE BIANCA
63068 MONTALTO DELLE MARCHE [AP]
TEL. +39 3662786985
www.riservalamarna.it

CELLAR SALES
PRE-BOOKED VISITS
ACCOMMODATION
ANNUAL PRODUCTION 9,000 bottles
HECTARES UNDER VINE 8.00

○ Offida Pecorino Pietraie '15	♟♟ 3
● Rosso Piceno Donna Eugenia '14	♟♟ 3
○ Offida Passerina Notturno '15	♟ 3

Ripawine

FONTE ABECETO, 34
63065 RIPATRANSONE [AP]
TEL. +39 3331419368
info@ripawine.it

CELLAR SALES
ANNUAL PRODUCTION 10,000 bottles
HECTARES UNDER VINE 30.00
VITICULTURE METHOD Certified Organic

○ Offida Passerina Kreta '16	♟♟ 3
○ Offida Pecorino Geko '16	♟♟ 3
● Offida Rosso Klausura '12	♟ 4
● Rosso Piceno Sup. Trufo '15	♟ 3

San Giovanni

C.DA CIAFONE, 41
63035 OFFIDA [AP]
TEL. +39 0736889032
www.vinisangiovanni.it

PRE-BOOKED VISITS
ANNUAL PRODUCTION 250,000 bottles
HECTARES UNDER VINE 45.00
VITICULTURE METHOD Certified Organic

○ Offida Pecorino Kiara '16	♟♟ 3
● Rosso Piceno Gyo '16	♟♟ 2*
● Offida Rosso Zeii '13	♟ 3
● Rosso Piceno Sup. Leo Guelfus '14	♟ 3

Tenuta San Marcello

VIA MELANO, 30
60030 SAN MARCELLO [AN]
TEL. +39 0731267606
www.tenutasanmarcello.net

CELLAR SALES
ACCOMMODATION AND RESTAURANT SERVICE
ANNUAL PRODUCTION 4,000 bottles
HECTARES UNDER VINE 3.50
SUSTAINABLE WINERY

● Lacrima di Morro d'Alba Sup. Melano '16	♟♟ 3
○ Verdicchio dei Castelli di Jesi Cl. Sup. Cipriani '16	♟♟ 3
● Lacrima di Morro d'Alba Bastaro '16	♟ 2

Alberto Serenelli

LOC. PIETRALACROCE
VIA BARTOLINI, 2
60129 ANCONA
TEL. +39 07135505
www.albertoserenelli.com

CELLAR SALES
PRE-BOOKED VISITS
ANNUAL PRODUCTION 30,000 bottles
HECTARES UNDER VINE 7.00

● Rosso Conero Varano '14	♟♟ 7
○ Verdicchio dei Castelli di Jesi Cl. Sora Elvira '16	♟♟ 4

Terra Fageto

VIA VALDASO, 52
63016 PEDASO [FM]
TEL. +39 0734931784
www.terrafageto.it

CELLAR SALES
PRE-BOOKED VISITS
ANNUAL PRODUCTION 100,000 bottles
HECTARES UNDER VINE 40.00
VITICULTURE METHOD Certified Organic

○ Offida Passerina Letizia '16	♟♟ 2*
○ Offida Pecorino Fenèsia '16	♟♟ 3
● Rosso Piceno Rusus '14	♟♟ 3
● Rosso Piceno Serrone '15	♟ 4

Fulvia Tombolini

c.da Cavalline, 2
60039 Staffolo [AN]
Tel. +39 3483805938
www.fulviatombolini.it

CELLAR SALES
ANNUAL PRODUCTION 200,000 bottles
HECTARES UNDER VINE 27.00
SUSTAINABLE WINERY

○ Castelli di Jesi Verdicchio Ris. '14	🍷🍷	3
○ Verdicchio dei Castelli di Jesi Cl. Sup. '16	🍷🍷	3

Tenuta dell'Ugolino

via Copparoni, 32
60031 Castelplanio [AN]
Tel. +39 07310731 812569
www.tenutaugolino.it

CELLAR SALES
PRE-BOOKED VISITS
ANNUAL PRODUCTION 50,000 bottles
HECTARES UNDER VINE 11.00
SUSTAINABLE WINERY

○ Verdicchio dei Castelli di Jesi Cl. Sup. Vign. del Balluccio '15	🍷🍷	3*
○ Verdicchio dei Castelli di Jesi Cl. Le Piaole '16	🍷🍷	2

Vallerosa Bonci

via Torre, 15
60034 Cupramontana [AN]
Tel. +39 0731789129
www.vallerosa-bonci.com

CELLAR SALES
PRE-BOOKED VISITS
ANNUAL PRODUCTION 250,000 bottles
HECTARES UNDER VINE 26.00

○ Verdicchio dei Castelli di Jesi Brut M. Cl. Michelangelo '10	🍷🍷	5
○ Verdicchio dei Castelli di Jesi Cl. Sup. S. Michele '15	🍷🍷	3

Le Vigne di Clementina Fabi

c.da Franile, 3
63069 Montedinove [AP]
Tel. +39 338 7463441
www.levignediclementinafabi.it

CELLAR SALES
PRE-BOOKED VISITS
ACCOMMODATION
ANNUAL PRODUCTION 20,000 bottles
HECTARES UNDER VINE 10.00
VITICULTURE METHOD Certified Organic

○ Offida Pecorino '16	🍷🍷	2*
○ Offida Pecorino Cerì '16	🍷🍷	3

Volverino

c.da Santa Croce, 11a
62010 Mogliano [MC]
Tel. +39 0733557130
www.cantinavolverino.it

CELLAR SALES
PRE-BOOKED VISITS
ACCOMMODATION
ANNUAL PRODUCTION 5,000 bottles
HECTARES UNDER VINE 2.50

● La Civetta Rossa '15	🍷🍷	4
◐ La Farfalla Verde '15	🍷🍷	2*

Zaccagnini

via Salmagina, 9/10
60039 Staffolo [AN]
Tel. +39 0731779892
www.zaccagnini.it

CELLAR SALES
PRE-BOOKED VISITS
ACCOMMODATION AND RESTAURANT SERVICE
ANNUAL PRODUCTION 250,000 bottles
HECTARES UNDER VINE 35.00

○ Verdicchio dei Castelli di Jesi Cl. Sup. Salmàgina '16	🍷🍷	2*
○ Verdicchio dei Castelli di Jesi Cl. Terratufo '16	🍷🍷	3

UMBRIA

The quality of Umbria's wine has been well-known for years. But what we're seeing, vintage after vintage, is an ever-increasing awareness of what certain territories and cultivar can offer in terms of making the region's wines competitive on a national and global scale. And if until a few years ago the names that stood out were a prestigious few or varieties that had already achieved a degree of fame (including international cultivar), today we're seeing the region's essence come to the fore, with native grape varieties, historic districts and, especially, small artisanal producers now representing Umbria's regional viticulture (along with its more acclaimed producers). Moreover, their white wines are having an impact and in this edition of IW we've tried to highlight wines that may not have reached the top but are certainly in a respectable position when it comes to quality. 2016 was a good year and a balanced once as well (at least until September, after temperature drops and rain made their presence felt, especially on late-harvest grapes). It was certainly cooler than the previous, and the region's wines benefitted. Three whites earned Tre Bicchieri, all of them previous winners: the Cervaro della Sala is a great international white and along with Decugnano dei Bari's international white, the two have helped boost Orvieto's reputation. From Orvieto we move to Montefalco, highlighting Tabarrini's 2015 Adarmando, a potent, summery wine balanced by masterful zest. Turning to the reds, we once again bring up the strong 2016 season. Leonardo Bussoletti, the extremely skilled and well-respected vine grower, gave rise to a great Ciliegiolo di Narni. And Rubesco Vigna Monticchio's Torgiano Rosso by Lungarotti put in an outstanding performance, writing yet another chapter in Umbria's history of quality. Last but not least, we come to Montefalco Sagrantino. Some four wines earned Tre Bicchieri. Tudernum made headlines with the Fidenzio (despite the less than stellar 2012 vintage). The rest were all children of the 2013 season, which saw many wines making it into the finals. Pardi duplicated last year's excellent performance, Caprai didn't disappoint with their Collepiano, and the small producer Bellafonte once again proved capable of presenting one of the region's most charming and elegant reds.

Adanti

VIA BELVEDERE, 2
06031 BEVAGNA [PG]
TEL. +39 0742360295
www.cantineadanti.com

CELLAR SALES
PRE-BOOKED VISITS
ANNUAL PRODUCTION 160,000 bottles
HECTARES UNDER VINE 30.00
SUSTAINABLE WINERY

Adanti's selection has always followed
tradition, with wines that are austere,
authentic, and remarkable well after
vintage. Their 30 hectares of vineyards
surround their cellar, housed in a large villa,
and production volumes hover at just over
150,000 bottles. Here, at Adanti, their job is
to bring out the best of their grape varieties,
starting with Sagrantino. This means the
careful, guarded use of wood, fermentation
with native yeasts and extraction that's
never overdone, all aimed at guaranteeing
easy-drinking. The 2011 Montefalco
Sagrantino is an excellent wine, standing
out for its aromas, which go all in on blood
oranges, tobacco and spices. On the palate
it's tight-knit, with mature, evident tannins,
eased by a nice softness. The Montefalco
Grechetto is well-crafted and true to
tradition, while the Montefalco Rosso
Riserva deserves mentioning for its
complexity and structure. The rest of the
selection proved sound.

● Montefalco Sagrantino '11	♥♥ 5
○ Montefalco Grechetto '16	♥♥ 2*
● Montefalco Rosso Ris. '12	♥♥ 4
● Arquata '16	♥ 4
● Montefalco Rosso '13	♥ 2
● Montefalco Sagrantino Il Domenico '09	♥ 6
● Montefalco Sagrantino Arquata '08	♥♥♥ 6
● Montefalco Sagrantino Arquata '06	♥♥♥ 5
● Montefalco Sagrantino Arquata '05	♥♥♥ 5
○ Montefalco Bianco '15	♀♀ 2*
● Montefalco Rosso '11	♀♀ 2*
● Montefalco Sagrantino '10	♀♀ 5
● Montefalco Sagrantino Passito '08	♀♀ 6

Antonelli - San Marco

LOC. SAN MARCO, 60
06036 MONTEFALCO [PG]
TEL. +39 0742379158
www.antonellisanmarco.it

CELLAR SALES
PRE-BOOKED VISITS
ACCOMMODATION
ANNUAL PRODUCTION 300,000 bottles
HECTARES UNDER VINE 50.00
VITICULTURE METHOD Certified Organic
SUSTAINABLE WINERY

Antonelli is situated in San Marco, in a kind
of subzone that's perfect for the cultivation
Sagrantino. The winery has become a
benchmark for the area. With a total of 170
hectares, 50 of which are vineyards, they
operate as a single entity, run according to
principles of organic agriculture. This means
seeking out, and selecting, the best grapes,
which are then worked carefully, especially
during extraction. Medium and large wood i
used. Even terra-cotta and ceramic have
been explored. The final result is authentic,
high-quality wines that clearly carry the mar
of the territory. The 2010 Chiusa di Pannon
one of Sagrantino's veritable crus, affirms it
status as a great red. Fragrances of forest
floor, aromatic resin, dark fruit and spices
characterize the nose, while in the mouth it
wide, with tannins that are powerful but
never mouth-drying (only in the finish is it a
bit cropped). The other reds also put in stron
performances, from the 2012 Montefalco
Sagrantino to the Contrario. The 2016 white
were interesting, one made with Grechetto
and the other with Trebbiano Spoletino.

● Montefalco Sagrantino Chiusa di Pannone '10	♥♥
● Contrario '12	♥♥
● Montefalco Rosso Ris. '12	♥♥
● Montefalco Sagrantino '12	♥♥
● Montefalco Sagrantino Passito '10	♥♥
○ Montefalco Grechetto '16	♥
● Montefalco Rosso '14	♥
○ Spoleto Trebbiano Spoletino Trebium '16	♥
● Montefalco Sagrantino '09	♥♥♥
● Montefalco Sagrantino '08	♥♥♥
● Montefalco Sagrantino Chiusa di Pannone '04	♥♥♥
○ Spoleto Trebbiano Spoletino Trebium '14	♥♥♥
● Montefalco Sagrantino '11	♀♀

Barberani

LOC. CERRETO
05023 BASCHI [TR]
TEL. +39 0/63341820
www.barberani.it

CELLAR SALES
PRE-BOOKED VISITS
ACCOMMODATION
ANNUAL PRODUCTION 350,000 bottles
HECTARES UNDER VINE 55.00
VITICULTURE METHOD Certified Organic
SUSTAINABLE WINERY

Barberani is an inspiring family story that began many years ago. Today the winery is on its third generation, with brothers Bernardo and Niccolò managing this symbol of Orvieto's wine/vineyard tradition with professionalism and determination. Their estate includes 55 hectares of vineyards (their grandfather began with just eight) spread out on some of the best terrain of the area. Moreover, their focus is on native grape varieties, the leading players in the Orvieto DOC zone. Great care is taken in the cellar, where wood is used sparingly for clean, authentic wines that are capable of finesse, elegance and precision while also staying true to the territory. Finally, Barberani show great skill in managing botrytis, a foremost quality of Orvieto's microclimate for as long as anyone can remember. A great performance for the two wines characterized by botrytis, both from 2014. The Luigi e Giovanno is an Orvieto with complex notes of white fruit, as well as hints of saffron, aniseed, candied orange peel and wild flowers. In the mouth it's luscious, though softened by a subtle, savory vein.

○ Orvieto Cl. Sup. Luigi e Giovanna '14	♟♟	5
○ Orvieto Cl. Sup. V.T. Calcaia '14	♟♟	6
○ Orvieto Cl. Sup. Castagnolo '16	♟♟	3
● Foresco '15	♟	3
● Lago di Corbara Rosso Polvento '12	♟	5
○ Moscato Passito '14	♟	6
● Lago di Corbara Rosso Villa Monticelli '04	♟♟♟	4
○ Orvieto Cl. Sup. Luigi e Giovanna '13	♟♟♟	5
○ Orvieto Cl. Sup. Luigi e Giovanna Villa Monticelli '11	♟♟♟	5
○ Orvieto Cl. Sup. Muffa Nobile Calcaia '10	♟♟♟	5
○ Grechetto '15	♟♟	3
○ Orvieto Cl. Sup. Castagnolo '15	♟♟	3
○ Orvieto Cl. Sup. Muffa Nobile Calcaia '13	♟♟	7

Tenuta Bellafonte

LOC. TORRE DEL COLLE
VIA COLLE NOTTOLO, 2
06031 BEVAGNA [PG]
TEL. +39 0742710019
www.tenutabellafonte.it

CELLAR SALES
PRE-BOOKED VISITS
ACCOMMODATION
ANNUAL PRODUCTION 35,000 bottles
HECTARES UNDER VINE 11.00
SUSTAINABLE WINERY

Bellafonte is one of the most impressive young wineries in Umbria. It all started when Peter Helibron, Bellafonte's manager, decided to bet on agriculture, vineyards specifically, in an area near Bevagna (Montefalco) that's particularly well-suited to Sangrantino. From the the outset, their wines have displayed elegance and superior drinkability, the result of measured extraction and a process of aging that brings out the attributes of the territory - all without compromising aroma. To accompany their Montefalco Sagrantino, there's also a Trebbiano Spoletino, which just keeps getting better. The Collenottolo is one of the most convincing Montefalco Sagrantinos we tasted this year. The 2013 offers complex, variegated fragrances of tobacco, plum and a touch of mushroom. The palate proved excellent for balance and harmony, with a lean, caressing entrance, and tannins that integrate perfectly. Acidity does its part, leading the wine into a deep finish.

● Montefalco Sagrantino Collenottolo '13	♟♟♟	6
○ Arnèto '16	♟	4
● Montefalco Sagrantino '09	♟♟♟	6
● Montefalco Sagrantino Collenottolo '11	♟♟♟	6
● Montefalco Sagrantino Collenottolo '10	♟♟♟	6
○ Arnèto '14	♟♟	5
● Montefalco Sagrantino '08	♟♟	5
● Montefalco Sagrantino Collenottolo '12	♟♟	6

Bocale

LOC. MADONNA DELLA STELLA
VIA FRATTA ALZATURA
06036 MONTEFALCO [PG]
TEL. +39 0742399233
www.bocale.it

CELLAR SALES
PRE-BOOKED VISITS
ANNUAL PRODUCTION 25,000 bottles
HECTARES UNDER VINE 4.20

Bocale is a small but intriguing winery situated in Montefalco and managed by the Valentini family. In recent years especially, their selection has featured wines that are more clear-cut in terms of aroma, with good nose to palate follow-through, but that are, mostly, pleasing and polished in the mouth. The use of large barrels for aging their Sagrantino has surely been a benefit, as has a more careful approach to extraction. In addition to their two reds (Montefalco Rosso and Sagrantino), the winery has started making an interesting Trebbiano Spoletino, a bet that, as of late, many in the territory have been making. Both the reds presented proved interesting. The 2015 Montefalco Rosso is slim-bodied, with aromas of small, red fruit and a mouth marked by vigor, silky tannins and a savory finish. The Montefalco Sagrantino is more structured and full-bodied. The 2014 vintage conferred clear hints of plums and forest floor, while the palate is tight-knit and powerful, with a mature tannic structure.

● Montefalco Rosso '15	♟♟	3
● Montefalco Sagrantino '14	♟♟	5
● Montefalco Rosso '14	♟♟	3
● Montefalco Rosso '13	♟♟	3
● Montefalco Rosso '12	♟♟	2*
● Montefalco Rosso '09	♟♟	4
● Montefalco Sagrantino '13	♟♟	5
● Montefalco Sagrantino '12	♟♟	5
● Montefalco Sagrantino '11	♟♟	5
● Montefalco Sagrantino '10	♟♟	5
● Montefalco Sagrantino '09	♟♟	5
● Montefalco Sagrantino '06	♟♟	5
● Montefalco Sagrantino Passito '09	♟♟	5
○ Trebbiano Spoletino '15	♟♟	3

Leonardo Bussoletti

LOC. MIRIANO
S.DA DELLE PRETARE, 62
05035 NARNI [TR]
TEL. +39 0744715687
www.leonardobussoletti.it

PRE-BOOKED VISITS
ANNUAL PRODUCTION 20,000 bottles
HECTARES UNDER VINE 7.00
VITICULTURE METHOD Certified Organic

Leonardo Bussoletti, a vine grower who works in Narni, has been getting lots of attention as of late. It would seem that his bet on Ciliegiolo, the most representative of the local varieties, has paid off. The estate, made up of a collection of old vineyards, has strong ties with the territory and is showing itself to be increasingly on the mark. Their standard of quality is, by now, truly high, with an approach that sees precise fermentation and measured aging. In addition to Ciliegiolo they grow Grechetto, an interesting grape that's a true ambassador of this corner of the region. Excellent performance for the selection put forward by Leonardo Bussoletti, who proves to be a great vine grower and a true interpreter of the local cultivar. His Rosso 05035 takes the gold, a wine made with grapes from an old vineyard of Ciliegiolo, which conferred aromas of small, red fruit, cherry, flowers and spices. The mouth is lean, elegant, succulent and highly dynamic. The Colle Ozio, a Mediterranean Grechetto also did well.

● 05035 Rosso '16	♟♟♟	2*
○ Colle Ozio '15	♟♟	3*
● Brecciaro '15	♟♟	3
● Ràmici '14	♟	3
● Brecciaro '14	♟♟♟	3*
○ Colle Ozio Grechetto '12	♟♟♟	3*
● 05035 Rosso '15	♟♟	2*
● 05035 Rosso '14	♟♟	2*
● Brecciaro '13	♟♟	3*
● Brecciaro '12	♟♟	3
● Ciliegiolo di Narni V. V. '11	♟♟	7
○ Colle Murello '15	♟♟	3
○ Colle Ozio Grechetto '14	♟♟	3*
● Vigna Vecchia '13	♟♟	7

★★Arnaldo Caprai

LOC. TORRE
06036 MONTEFALCO [PG]
TEL. +39 0742378802
www.arnaldocaprai.it

CELLAR SALES
PRE-BOOKED VISITS
ANNUAL PRODUCTION 800,000 bottles
HECTARES UNDER VINE 136.00
SUSTAINABLE WINERY

There's no doubt that Sagrantino owes much of its reputation to Caprai. Since the 1960s, the winery has focused on this particular variety. Continued experimentation, collaborations with universities and almost obsessive research have made Caprai a true benchmark for Italian enology. The 136-hectare estate gives rise to a total production that reaches 800,000 bottles per year. A welcome piece of news is the involvement of Michel Rolland, a celebrated technician who is guiding their selection towards ever greater drinkability, pleasantness and finesse. Two Montefalco Sagrantinos arrived in the finals. The 2013 Collepiano came across as more elegant and balanced, and exhibited great aromatic complexity, offering up fragrances of bark, resin, tobacco and plum. The mouth is tight-knit and austere, with tannins that are powerful, though never bitter. The finish is long and flavorful. It gets a Tre Bicchieri. The 25 Anni is more structured and full-bodied. In terms of the whites, the 2016 Grecante, a fresh and vibrant Colli Martani Grechetto, once again proved a worthy entry.

● Montefalco Sagrantino Collepiano '13	▼▼▼	7
○ Colli Martani Grechetto Grecante '16	▼▼	4
● Montefalco Sagrantino 25 Anni '13	▼▼	8
● Montefalco Rosso Ris. '13	▼▼	6
● Montefalco Rosso V. Flaminia Maremmana '15	▼▼	4
○ Sauvignon '16	▼▼	5
○ Chardonnay '16	▼	5
● Montefalco Rosso '15	▼	4
● Montefalco Sagrantino 25 Anni '10	▽▽▽	8
● Montefalco Sagrantino 25 Anni '09	▽▽▽	8
● Montefalco Sagrantino 25 Anni '08	▽▽▽	8
● Montefalco Sagrantino Collepiano '12	▽▽▽	7
● Montefalco Sagrantino Collepiano '11	▽▽▽	7
● Montefalco Sagrantino Collepiano '08	▽▽▽	6

La Carraia

LOC. TORDIMONTE, 56
05018 ORVIETO [TR]
TEL. +39 0763304013
www.lacarraia.it

CELLAR SALES
PRE-BOOKED VISITS
ANNUAL PRODUCTION 700,000 bottles
HECTARES UNDER VINE 119.00

La Carraia, with its half million bottles a year and almost 120 hectares of terrain, is an important winery for Orvieto. For years they have relied on Riccardo Cotarella to guarantee quality across their entire selection, which includes Poggio Calvelli (an Orvieto DOC white) and various IGTs made with both native and international grape varieties. Their wines are always aromatically clear-cut and clean, yet they're clearly linked to the territory and never mundane. Primarily the whites stood out during tasting. The Poggio Calvelli is an Orvieto Classico that, in 2016, delivered for its notes of white fruit and wild flowers. In the mouth it shows good richness of flavor and length. Le Basque proved very particular. Made with a blend of Grechetto and Viognier, it offers up hints of pear and chamomile, while the flavor of skin-contact and a close-knit weave define the palate.

○ Le Basque '16	▼▼	3
○ Orvieto Cl. Sup. Poggio Calvelli '16	▼▼	2*
● Sangiovese '16	▼▼	2*
● Cabernet Sauvignon '16	▼	2
● Querciascura '08	▼	4
● Tizzonero '15	▼	3
● Fobiano '03	▽▽▽	4
● Fobiano '12	▽▽	5
● Fobiano '11	▽▽	5
○ Orvieto Cl. Sup. Poggio Calvelli '15	▽▽	2*
○ Orvieto Cl. Sup. Poggio Calvelli '14	▽▽	2*
○ Orvieto Cl. Sup. Poggio Calvelli '13	▽▽	2*
● Sangiovese '15	▽▽	2*
● Tizzonero '14	▽▽	3

Tenuta Castelbuono

LOC. BEVAGNA
VOC. CASTELLACCIO, 9
06031 BEVAGNA [PG]
TEL. +39 0742361670
www.tenutelunelli.it

CELLAR SALES
PRE-BOOKED VISITS
ANNUAL PRODUCTION 110,000 bottles
HECTARES UNDER VINE 32.00
VITICULTURE METHOD Certified Organic
SUSTAINABLE WINERY

The Castelbuono winery took its name from
the area in which it's situated. The Lunelli
family, from Trento, decided to invest here by
acquiring vineyards around Bevagna and
Montefalco and building a cellar (the
Carapace) that is at the vanguard of
technology and modern architecture (it was
designed by Arnaldo Pomodoro). Their early
years were dedicated to establishing their
styles, blends and aging. It would seem that
things are now firmly on course: their wines
are consistently capable of expressing the
area of Montefalco, both with their
Sagrantino (the passito version is also
interesting) and the varieties that make up
their Rosso. The wine that most delivered
was the Lampante, a Montefalco Rosso
Riserva 2013 of great complexity.
Fragrances of cherry, aromatic resin and
tobacco give way to a lean, dynamic mouth
that exhibits excellent structure. The Ziggurat
is a simpler red, while the 2013 Montefalco
Sagrantino Carapace opens well, though is a
bit cropped in the finish.

★★Castello della Sala

LOC. SALA
05016 FICULLE [TR]
TEL. +39 076386127
www.antinori.it

CELLAR SALES
PRE-BOOKED VISITS
ANNUAL PRODUCTION 760,000 bottles
HECTARES UNDER VINE 140.00

Castello della Sala is Marchesi Antinori's
Umbrian brand, founded so as to produce
superior whites (to accompany their
top-quality Tuscan reds). The main facility is
just a stone's throw from Orvieto, on a 500
hectare estate (140 of which are vineyards),
spread out across various altitudes (reaching
400 meters above sea-level). The clay soil
here is rich in organic marine matter. Their
selection is guided by their Cervaro della Sala,
a preeminent Italian white that is fermented
and aged in small wood, and rounded out by
their Muffato, an Orvieto DOC, and other,
simpler wines that are, nevertheless,
representative of the area's particularities. An
excellent year for the Cervaro della Sala that,
with the 2015 vintage, had one of its best
performances in recent memory. This
important Umbrian white exhibits aromas of
great complexity, amidst fruit, flowery notes
and spicy hints. There's also a slight touch of
oak as a result of the wine's youth. In the
mouth it's wide and filling, but thanks to a
nice vigor, it progresses vertically. The wine
gets Tre Bicchieri. The 2016 Orvieto San
Giovanni della Sala also proved excellent.

● Montefalco Rosso Lampante Ris. '13	♀♀♀	5
● Montefalco Rosso Ziggurat '14	♀♀	3
● Montefalco Sagrantino Carapace '13	♀	5
● Montefalco Rosso '10	♀♀	3
● Montefalco Rosso Lampante Ris. '10	♀♀	5
● Montefalco Rosso Ris. '09	♀♀	5
● Montefalco Rosso Ris. '08	♀♀	5
● Montefalco Rosso Ziggurat '11	♀♀	3
● Montefalco Sagrantino '10	♀♀	5
● Montefalco Sagrantino '08	♀♀	5
● Montefalco Sagrantino Carapace '12	♀♀	5
● Montefalco Sagrantino Carapace '09	♀♀	5
● Montefalco Sagrantino Passito '12	♀♀	5
● Montefalco Sagrantino Passito '10	♀♀	5

○ Cervaro della Sala '15	♀♀♀	6
○ Orvieto Cl. Sup. San Giovanni della Sala '16	♀♀	3*
○ Muffato della Sala '13	♀♀	6
○ Bramito della Sala '16	♀	3
○ Conte della Vipera '16	♀	5
● Pinot Nero '15	♀	6
○ Cervaro della Sala '14	♀♀♀	6
○ Cervaro della Sala '13	♀♀♀	6
○ Cervaro della Sala '12	♀♀♀	6
○ Cervaro della Sala '11	♀♀♀	6
○ Cervaro della Sala '10	♀♀♀	6
○ Cervaro della Sala '09	♀♀♀	6
○ Bramito del Cervo '15	♀♀	3
○ Conte della Vipera '15	♀♀	5

Castello di Magione

v.le Cavalieri di Malta, 31
06063 Magione [PG]
Tel. +39 0755057319
www.sagrivit.it

CELLAR SALES
PRE-BOOKED VISITS
ANNUAL PRODUCTION 200,000 bottles
HECTARES UNDER VINE 42.00

Castello di Magione is part of S.Agri.V.It., a company that manages 14 producers throughout Italy. The winery is situated primarily in Colli del Trasimeno, though some of their plots belong to the Torgiano appellation. The estate, which is managed by the Knights of Malta, has 32 hectares of vineyards in Trasimeno, and 10 in Torgiano. All are in the hills, at altitudes ranging between 250 and 400 meters. In addition to traditional grape varieties (both red and white), they also cultivate international varieties historically associated with Umbria. Sustainable cultivation practices give rise to elegant, delectable wines. In recent years, we've also seen an increased focus on quality. A superior performance, this year, for Trasimeno's whites, with the Grechetto holding a top spot. The 2016 Monterone offers fragrances of medlar and dried flowers, while in the mouth the wine is fresh and savory. The base version is also very good. Another wine from the Colli del Trasimeno, the Morcinaia (made with Merlot, Cabernet and Sangiovese), also did well.

○ C. del Trasimeno Grechetto '16	🍷🍷 3
○ C. del Trasimeno Grechetto Monterone '16	🍷🍷 3
● C. del Trasimeno Rosso Scelto Morcinaia '12	🍷🍷 5
○ C. del Trasimeno Vin Santo '09	🍷🍷 5
● Sangiovese '16	🍷 2
⊙ Belfiore '15	🥂🥂 2*
○ C. del Trasimeno Grechetto Monterone '15	🥂🥂 2*
○ C. del Trasimeno Grechetto Monterone '14	🥂🥂 2*
○ Chardonnay '15	🥂🥂 3
○ Colli del Trasimeno Grechetto '14	🥂🥂 2*
● Nerocavalieri '13	🥂🥂 4

Cantina Castello Monte Vibiano Vecchio

loc. Monte Vibiano Vecchio di Mercatello
voc. Palombaro, 22
06072 Marsciano [PG]
Tel. +39 0758783386
www.montevibiano.it

CELLAR SALES
PRE-BOOKED VISITS
ANNUAL PRODUCTION 300,000 bottles
HECTARES UNDER VINE 35.00
SUSTAINABLE WINERY

Castello Monte Vibiano Vecchio was founded 15 years ago by the Fasola Bologna family. Situated in Marsciano, on the Perugini hills, in a beautiful area where vineyards and picturesque landscapes alternate in turn, the project is aimed at sustainability (think that guests are given tours of the estate on electric vehicles). Their wines are modern, clear-cut in terms of aroma with a good nose to palate follow-through, but they haven't lost the charm of their territory either. The varieties used are traditional, with non-native grapes used in their various blends. The winery also produces natural cosmetic products out of olive oil from the groves on their estate. The Monvì, a red from the Colli Perugini made with Sangiovese, Merlot, Cabernet Sauvignon and Cabernet Franc, proved excellent. It has a lean, dynamic drink to it, a good entry and a full-flavored finish. The Andrea, another blend of international varieties, also did well. It's a fragrant and close-focused wine, though a bit clenched in the finish. The 2016 Maria Camilla, a simple but clean wine, also came across as well-crafted.

● Colli Perugini Rosso L'Andrea '13	🍷🍷 5
● Colli Perugini Rosso Monvì '14	🍷🍷 2*
○ Maria Camilla '16	🍷 3
● Colli Perugini Rosso L'Andrea '08	🥂🥂🥂 5
● Colli Perugini Rosso L'Andrea '12	🥂🥂 5
● Colli Perugini Rosso L'Andrea '10	🥂🥂 5
● Colli Perugini Rosso Monvì '12	🥂🥂 2*
● Colli Perugini Rosso Monvì '10	🥂🥂 2*
○ Maria Camilla '15	🥂🥂 3
○ Maria Camilla '14	🥂🥂 3
○ Maria Camilla '13	🥂🥂 3
⊙ Maryam '12	🥂🥂 3
○ Villa Monte Vibiano Bianco '14	🥂🥂 2*
● Villa Monte Vibiano Rosso '15	🥂🥂 1*

Cantina Cenci

FRAZ. SAN BIAGIO DELLA VALLE
VOC. ANTICELLO, 1
06072 MARSCIANO [PG]
TEL. +39 3805198980
www.cantinacenci.it

CELLAR SALES
PRE-BOOKED VISITS
ANNUAL PRODUCTION 25,000 bottles
HECTARES UNDER VINE 6.00
SUSTAINABLE WINERY

In San Biagio, between Perugia and Marsciano, Giovanni Cenci is moving his winery, and its five hectares of vineyards, forward. Four-generations-old, the estate stands as a positive example in the territory, for the varieties used, their soil and, above all, their vintages. Thanks to Giovanni's agricultural experience and his experience in enology, he produces wines that are anchored by their force and weight - wines that are well-balanced by fresh acidity and flavor. Wines are made with different varieties (in some cases only one), both native and international varieties that are well-adjusted to the local climate. A good performance for Cenci, with a white and red standing out. The 2015 Sangiovese Piantata has a nice entry; only in the finish does it come across as a bit tight (the result of slightly dusty tannins). It's still a superb wine, especially if you consider its aromatic complexity. The charming 2016 Anticello (a Grechetto) demonstrates typicity and adherence to terroir, with its aromas of grain and a palate defined by richness and the taste of skin-contact.

○ Anticello '16	♟♟ 2*
● Piantata '15	♟♟ 4
● Ascheria '15	♟ 4
○ Giole '16	♟ 2
● Sanbiagio '15	♟ 3
○ Alago '12	♟♟ 3
○ Alago Stellato '15	♟♟ 2*
○ Anticello '15	♟♟ 2*
○ Anticello '14	♟♟ 2*
○ Anticello '12	♟♟ 2*
○ Giole '15	♟♟ 2*
○ Giole '14	♟♟ 2*
● Piantata '14	♟♟ 4
● Piantata '12	♟♟ 2*

Fattoria Colleallodole

VIA COLLEALLODOLE, 3
06031 BEVAGNA [PG]
TEL. +39 0742361897
www.fattoriacolleallodole.com

CELLAR SALES
PRE-BOOKED VISITS
ANNUAL PRODUCTION 70,000 bottles
HECTARES UNDER VINE 20.00

Without a doubt, Colleallodole is a leading figure in the Montefalco grape and wine scene. Owned and run by the Antano family, the winery stands out for its artisanal approach, which is aimed at bringing out (without overwhelming) the attributes of the area's native grape varieties, as well as the area itself. Their selection focuses on Montefalco DOC varieties (there are five reds), which are accompanied by two Grechetto whites and a Rosato. Their unmistakable wines, which are designed to age well, are pervasive and soft, displaying a charming texture and superior drinkability. Colleallodole had an open-ended year. Two wines most stood out: the Rosso and the Sagrantino. The former offers up notes of ripe fruit, as well as a touch of herbs and bark, while the palate is wide and caressing. The latter is a wine of great complexity and structure, though softness and pervasiveness are held back by rugged tannins and a tangy finish. The rest of the selection, which hail back to the 2014 vintage, also proved less impressive than in past years.

● Montefalco Rosso '15	♟♟ 3
● Montefalco Sagrantino '14	♟♟ 6
● Montefalco Rosso Ris. '14	♟ 5
● Montefalco Sagrantino Colleallodole '14	♟ 8
● Montefalco Sagrantino Passito '14	♟ 7
● Montefalco Rosso Ris. '08	♟♟♟ 5
● Montefalco Sagrantino '12	♟♟♟ 6
● Montefalco Sagrantino Colleallodole '10	♟♟♟ 8
● Montefalco Sagrantino Colleallodole '09	♟♟♟ 8
● Montefalco Sagrantino Colleallodole '06	♟♟♟ 8
● Montefalco Rosso Ris. '13	♟♟ 5
● Montefalco Sagrantino '13	♟♟ 6
● Montefalco Sagrantino Colleallodole '13	♟♟ 8
● Montefalco Sagrantino Passito '12	♟♟ 7

Fattoria Colsanto

LOC. MONTARONE
06031 BEVAGNA [PG]
TEL. +39 0742360412
www.livon.it

CELLAR SALES
PRE-BOOKED VISITS
ACCOMMODATION
ANNUAL PRODUCTION 50,000 bottles
HECTARES UNDER VINE 15.00

After a few trial vintages, this Umbrian winery has found its way. The cellar is situated in Bevagna, in Montefalco, on a small hill surrounded by vineyards. Getting there means walking down a path lined with cypress trees. Here the Lion family (Friuli-natives) produce three wines: Montefalco Rosso, Sagrantino and an IGT made using native grapes and a splash of Merlot. The use of large barrels and focused extraction guarantees that their wines display cleanness and finesse. The Ruris, a particular blend of Sangiovese, Merlot, Sagrantino and Montepulcino proved very nice, with a fluent, deep mouthfeel. Tannins are present but quite mature, and you can detect an acid crispness that carries the palate. The Montefalco Rosso was also excellent, simpler but very pleasant in its aromas of red fruit and spices. The 2013 Montefalco Sagrantino is still very young, slightly clenched by the tannins, which shortens the palate a bit.

● Ruris '14	♟♟ 2*
● Montefalco Rosso '14	♟♟ 3
● Montefalco Sagrantino '13	♟ 5
● Montefalco Rosso '13	♟♟ 3
● Montefalco Rosso '10	♟♟ 3
● Montefalco Rosso '09	♟♟ 3*
● Montefalco Sagrantino '12	♟♟ 5
● Montefalco Sagrantino '11	♟♟ 5
● Montefalco Sagrantino '10	♟♟ 5
● Montefalco Sagrantino '09	♟♟ 5
● Montefalco Sagrantino '08	♟♟ 5
● Montefalco Sagrantino '07	♟♟ 5
● Montefalco Sagrantino '03	♟♟ 5
● Ruris Rosso '13	♟♟ 2*
● Ruris Rosso '12	♟♟ 2*

Decugnano dei Barbi

LOC. FOSSATELLO, 50
05018 ORVIETO [TR]
TEL. +39 0763308255
www.decugnano.it

CELLAR SALES
PRE-BOOKED VISITS
ANNUAL PRODUCTION 130,000 bottles
HECTARES UNDER VINE 32.00

Decugnano is one of the most interesting producers in the region, both for the area in which it operates and for the charming Etruscan tuff caverns where their Metodo Classico sparkling wines are kept. Their 32 hectares of vineyards produces 100,000 bottles per year, mostly Orvieto DOCs. Their wines express the essence of the terrain, whose marine matter and shells are visible even just walking through the vineyards. Their selection is rounded out by an interesting red and, as already mentioned, a sparkler that undergoes secondary fermentation in the bottle, made possible thanks to long aging on the lees. Oriveto Il Bianco takes the gold. The 2016 vintage conferred fragrances of white flowers, chamomile, citrus, and an accent of aromatic herbs. It's fresh and elegant in the mouth. It gets a Tre Bicchieri. Among the reds, the Rosso (made with Sangiovese, Syrah and Montepulciano) proved, aromatically complex and highly drinkable.

○ Orvieto Cl. Sup. Il Bianco '16	♟♟♟ 4*
● Il Rosso '15	♟♟ 4
○ Orvieto Cl. Sup. Muffa Nobile Pourriture Noble '15	♟♟ 5
● Villa Barbi Rosso '15	♟♟ 3
○ Decugnano Dosaggio Zero '11	♟ 4
○ Orvieto Cl. Villa Barbi Bianco '16	♟ 3
○ Orvieto Cl. Sup. "IL" '11	♟♟♟ 3*
○ Orvieto Cl. Sup. Il Bianco '15	♟♟♟ 4*
○ Orvieto Cl. Sup. Il Bianco '12	♟♟♟ 3*
○ Orvieto Cl. Sup. Il Bianco '10	♟♟♟ 3
○ Decugnano Dosaggio Zero '10	♟♟ 4
● Il Rosso '13	♟♟ 3
○ Orvieto Cl. Villa Barbi Bianco '15	♟♟ 3
● Villa Barbi Rosso '13	♟♟ 2*

Di Filippo

VOC. CONVERSINO, 153
06033 CANNARA [PG]
TEL. +39 0742731242
www.vinidifilippo.com

CELLAR SALES
PRE-BOOKED VISITS
ANNUAL PRODUCTION 227,000 bottles
HECTARES UNDER VINE 35.00
VITICULTURE METHOD Certified Organic
SUSTAINABLE WINERY

Di Filippo, whose vineyards fall both in the Colli Martani DOC zone and Montefalco is situated in Cannara. They have practiced organic techniques for some years now and, with the experience, the winery has grown significantly, also in terms of their skills in the cellar. All of this makes for wines that are strongly influenced by the territory and that show respect for the varieties used, terrain and vintages. Over recent years, several wines convinced the tasters, starting with their sunny, deep, full-flavored whites. Their Sagrantino continues to prove itself a concentrated and quite drinkable red. Among the many wines produced and presented this year, we most appreciated the whites. The 2016 vintage made for a lovely Trebbiano and Grechetto. The former, Farandola, is a charming wine in its fragrances of candied lemon, yellow fruit and wild flowers. In the mouth it has good character supported by vigor and tanginess. The latter exhibits well-formed fruity aromas, grainy notes and wild herbs. The palate is fresh, supple, well-developed and deep.

○ Colli Martani Grechetto Sassi d'Arenaria '15	♥♥ 3
○ Farandola '16	♥♥ 3
○ Grechetto '16	♥♥ 2*
● Montefalco Rosso Sallustio '14	♥ 3
● Montefalco Sagrantino '13	♥ 5
● Montefalco Sagrantino Etnico '13	♥ 4
● Montefalco Sagrantino Passito '12	♥ 5
● Sangiovese '15	♥ 3
○ Villa Conversino Bianco '16	♥ 2
○ Colli Martani Grechetto Sassi d'Arenaria '14	♀♀ 3
● Colli Martani Sangiovese Properzio Ris. '13	♀♀ 3
● Colli Martani Vernaccia di Cannara '15	♀♀ 5
● Montefalco Sagrantino '12	♀♀ 5

Duca della Corgna

VIA ROMA, 236
06061 CASTIGLIONE DEL LAGO [PG]
TEL. +39 0759652493
www.ducadellacorgna.it

CELLAR SALES
PRE-BOOKED VISITS
ANNUAL PRODUCTION 280,000 bottles
HECTARES UNDER VINE 55.00

Duca della Corgna is a cooperative winery operating on the hills around Lake Trasimeno, on Umbria's border with Tuscany. It's a good example of a cooperative with strong territorial roots that produces quality wines from Gamay Perugino (as it's known locally, though the grape belongs to the Grenache family). Various wines are produced, from standard-label reds that are fresh and fruity to more muscular wines, to Grechetto whites. There are also other varieties common to the area. Without a doubt, the reds made the best impression, especially those made with Gamay Perugino. The Divina Villa Etichetta Bianca is delectable in its notes of crisp red fruit, spices and fresh flowers. This 2016 Gamay is succulent in the mouth, but never banal, with a vertical, deep palate. Both the 2014 Divina Villa Etichetta Nera and the 2014 Corniolo (both Gamays) proved bolder in structure, while slightly diluted in the mid-palate. Their whites, on the other hand, are pleasant, well-crafted and always clean.

● C. del Trasimeno Gamay Divina Villa Et. Bianca '16	♥♥ 2*
● C. del Trasimeno Divina Villa Et. Nera Ris. '14	♥♥ 3
● C. del Trasimeno Rosso Corniolo Ris. '14	♥♥ 4
○ C. del Trasimeno Baccio del Bianco '16	♥ 2
○ C. del Trasimeno Grechetto Nuricante '16	♥ 2
● C. del Trasimeno Baccio del Rosso '16	♥ 2
○ Ascanio '15	♀♀ 2*
● C. del Trasimeno Baccio del Rosso '15	♀♀ 2*
● C. del Trasimeno Gamay Divina Villa Et. Bianca '15	♀♀ 2*
● C. del Trasimeno Rosso Corniolo Ris. '13	♀♀ 4

Fontesecca

Loc. Fontesecca, 30
06062 Città della Pieve [PG]
Tel. +39 3496180516
www.fontesecca.it

CELLAR SALES
PRE-BOOKED VISITS
ACCOMMODATION
ANNUAL PRODUCTION 10,000 bottles
HECTARES UNDER VINE 6.50
VITICULTURE METHOD Certified Organic

The numbers are small but the results are impressive. Fontesecca is an intriguing winery that got its start not far from Città della Pieve and that uses organically-grown native grape varieties for its entire selection. Their wines are authentic and charming, sticking close to the territory, with the occasional, pleasing imperfection thanks to the artisanal approach taken to production. A detail that mustn't be overlooked is their prices, which are reasonable and spot-on. The 2016 Ciliegiolo is the kind of daily-drinking wine that you'd always want by your side: simple but never banal, succulent and fresh in the mouth, deep, with a palate driven by savoriness. Notes of blackcurrant, flowers and spices also lend it a certain charm. The 2014 Sangiovese Pino proved a bit cropped in the finish, but despite the vintage, it shows good structure. The Rosato and Elso, two whites of sure-fire charm, are both well-crafted.

Ciliegiolo '16	♟♟ 4
Pino '14	♟♟ 4
Elso '16	♟ 3
Rosato '16	♟ 3
Canaiolo '14	♟♟ 3
Canaiolo '13	♟♟ 3
Ciliegiolo '14	♟♟ 3*
Ciliegiolo '13	♟♟ 3
Ciliegiolo '12	♟♟ 3
Ciliegiolo '11	♟♟ 3
Elso '15	♟♟ 2*
Elso '13	♟♟ 2*
Elso '12	♟♟ 2*
Pino Sangiovese '13	♟♟ 3*

★Lungarotti

V.le G. Lungarotti, 2
06089 Torgiano [PG]
Tel. +39 075988661
www.lungarotti.it

CELLAR SALES
PRE-BOOKED VISITS
ACCOMMODATION AND RESTAURANT SERVICE
ANNUAL PRODUCTION 2,400,000 bottles
HECTARES UNDER VINE 250.00
VITICULTURE METHOD Certified Organic
SUSTAINABLE WINERY

Without a doubt, Lungarotti is one of the most notable and important wineries in the region, and beyond. Indeed, their influence reaches throughout all of Italy. Their roots go way back. All it takes is a stroll through their cellar, taking in the history of the first vintages, bottled back in the 1960s, to realize what this winery is made of. Today they produce almost 2.5 million bottles a year, divided into various lines in which native grapes meet with non-native (but acclimated) ones. In addition to Torgiano, they also have plots in Montefalco, where both Rosso and Sagrantino are made. The 2012 vintage was another good year for Torgiano, with the Rubesco Vigna Monticchio taking a gold. Fragrances of red fruit, pencil led, aromatic resin and spices characterize the wine, with a touch of tobacco that foreshadows a close-knit, long palate that never wavers. Crossed by an acidic vigor that is fundamental in such complex and structured wines, it gets a Tre Bicchieri. IlBio, a wine made primarily with Sagrantino, is also superb.

● Torgiano Rosso Rubesco V. Monticchio Ris. '12	♟♟♟ 6
● ilBio '15	♟♟ 3*
○ Bianco di Torgiano Torre di Giano '16	♟♟ 2*
● Montefalco Sagrantino '12	♟♟ 5
● Montefalco Sagrantino Passito '12	♟♟ 6
● Montefalco Rosso '14	♟ 3
● Rosso di Torgiano Rubesco '14	♟ 3
○ Torgiano Aurente '15	♟ 4
● Torgiano Rosso Rubesco V. Monticchio Ris. '11	♟♟♟ 6
● Torgiano Rosso Rubesco V. Monticchio Ris. '07	♟♟♟ 6
● Torgiano Rosso V. Monticchio Ris. '10	♟♟♟ 6
● Torgiano Rosso V. Monticchio Ris. '09	♟♟♟ 6
● Torgiano Rosso V. Monticchio Ris. '08	♟♟♟ 6
● Torgiano Rosso V. Monticchio Ris. '06	♟♟♟ 5

La Madeleine

S.DA MONTINI, 38
05035 NARNI [TR]
TEL. +39 0744040427
www.cantinalamadeleine.it

PRE-BOOKED VISITS
ANNUAL PRODUCTION 25,000 bottles
HECTARES UNDER VINE 6.40

La Madeleine is the brainchild of Linda and Massimo D'Alema, who founded the winery in 2008 when they acquired an old farming estate (of which only the name remains). Today the property is in the hands of the D'Almena children, Giulia and Francesco, who are in charge of its 10 hectares of vineyards. Many varieties are used and not only traditional, local ones; indeed, non-native varieties go into making their most important wines. Their selection has an international quality to it: precise, well-crafted aromatics and overall easy-drinking. Of the various cultivar, Pinot Nero stirred up the most emotions, the Nerosé most of all. This 'Metodo Classico' sparkler, made exclusively from the prestigious red grape, features fragrances of small red fruit, as well as cakes. In the mouth, its prickle is measured, while the palate proves lean and pleasant. The 2015 Pinot Nero offers up hints of spice, tobacco and forest floor, with a palate that is paced and pleasant. The other wines all proved well-crafted.

⊙ Nerosé	♟♟ 5
● Pinot Nero '15	♟♟ 6
● NarnOt '14	♟ 6
● Sfide '15	♟ 3
● NarnOt '11	♟♟ 6
⊙ Nerosé	♟♟ 5
● Pinot Nero '14	♟♟ 6
● Sfide '14	♟♟ 3*
● Sfide '13	♟♟ 3*

Madrevite

LOC. VAIANO
VIA CIMBANO, 36
06061 CASTIGLIONE DEL LAGO [PG]
TEL. +39 0759527220
www.madrevite.com

CELLAR SALES
PRE-BOOKED VISITS
RESTAURANT SERVICE
ANNUAL PRODUCTION 45,000 bottles
HECTARES UNDER VINE 10.00

Madrevite is a small but dynamic winery situated in Vaiano, in the municipality of Castiglion del Lago, that's working to support and promote the viticulture of Trasimeno. Their 20 hectares of property includes about 10 hectares of contiguous vineyards, where a variety of native and non-native grapes are grown. The area is particularly well-suited to vine growing, and not by accident: here the economy of agriculture has existed since the mid-1600s. Their wines are aromatically clean and simple on the palate, but never banal. They're fresh-tasting, with measured extraction and particularly reasonable prices Il Capofoco is a particular blend made with Gamay del Trasimeno (Grenache) and Monetpulciano. It's a well-structured, well-bodied red that proves pleasant in the mouth, offering up fragrances of plums, dried flowers and spices, as well as a certain earthiness. The palate is close-knit, austere and savory. The 2013 Che Syrah Sarà displays aromas of black pepper and small red fruit, while tannins provide rhythm to the mouth. Their other wines also proved well-made.

● Capofoco '13	♟♟ 4
● Che Syrah Sarà '13	♟♟ 4
○ Re Minore '16	♟ 2
● Trasimeno Rosso Glanio '15	♟ 2
● Capofoco '12	♟♟ 4
● Colli del Trasimeno Glanio '12	♟♟ 3
● Colli del Trasimeno Glanio '11	♟♟ 3
● Colli del Trasimeno Glanio '10	♟♟ 3
● Glanio '14	♟♟ 3
○ Il Reminore '15	♟♟ 3*
○ Il Reminore '14	♟♟ 3
○ Il Reminore '13	♟♟ 3
○ La Bisbetica Rosé '13	♟♟ 3
○ Re Minore '12	♟♟ 2
○ Re Minore '11	♟♟ 2

Moretti Omero

LOC. SAN SABINO, 20
06030 GIANO DELL'UMBRIA [PG]
TEL. +39 074290426
www.morettiomero.it

CELLAR SALES
PRE-BOOKED VISITS
ACCOMMODATION AND RESTAURANT SERVICE
ANNUAL PRODUCTION 75,000 bottles
HECTARES UNDER VINE 13.00
VITICULTURE METHOD Certified Organic
SUSTAINABLE WINERY

'Farmer' and 'vine grower' are the right
words for Omero Moretti, the owner of the
winery that bears his name and that's
managed by his family. The estate is made
up of just over 10 hectares of vineyards, in
Giano dell'Umbria, all of which are organically
grown for the purpose of making wine
through artisanal methods. In recent years,
their wines have made their presence felt,
truly expressing the attributes of their
territory: their Montefalcos stand out (Bianco,
Rosso, Sagrantino and Passito), and their
Grechetto delivers year after year. Good news
from the Montefalco Sagrantino. 2013 turned
out to be the right vintage, and has made for
a fantastic red with fragrances of tobacco,
spices, pencil lead, resin and blood oranges.
In the mouth, it's on the mark, tannins are
impeccable, and even the finish delivers for
cleanness. With a bit more length, it would
have earned a gold. The 2012 Vignalunga,
made with Sagrantino, is good, though not on
par with 2013. Tannins dominate the
mouthfeel, and the wine is rather clenched,
but its overall complexity delivers. The other
wines also proved interesting.

● Montefalco Sagrantino '13	♟♟ 5
● Montefalco Sagrantino Vignalunga '12	♟♟ 7
○ Grechetto '16	♟ 2
● Montefalco Rosso '14	♟ 3
● Argo Passito '12	♟♟ 5
○ Grechetto '14	♟♟ 2*
○ Montefalco Bianco '15	♟♟ 3
● Montefalco Rosso '10	♟♟ 3
● Montefalco Sagrantino '12	♟♟ 5
● Montefalco Sagrantino '11	♟♟ 5
● Montefalco Sagrantino '09	♟♟ 5
○ Nessuno '14	♟♟ 2*
○ Nessuno '13	♟♟ 2*
○ Nessuno '12	♟♟ 2*

La Palazzola

LOC. VASCIGLIANO
05039 STRONCONE [TR]
TEL. +39 0744609091
www.lapalazzola.it

CELLAR SALES
ANNUAL PRODUCTION 150,000 bottles
HECTARES UNDER VINE 28.00

La Palazzola is the brainchild of Stefano Grilli,
the creative and inspired producer who has,
from the beginning, pursued the original and
unusual. His sparkling wines define the whole
selection, starting with his Metodo Ancestrale
line, which are the result of mixing native
grapes and particular varieties like Riesling.
These are accompanied by dessert wines
and sipping wines, as well as charming still
whites and reds. And, of course, even during
production there's a bit of experimentation,
which has also allowed him to avoid being
lumped in with a single style. A sparkling
wine, a dry wine and sweet wine stood out
this year. The 'Metodo Classico' sparkler finds
a top spot, with the 2012 offering aromas of
white flowers, cakes and golden apples. The
mouth is fluent and full with perfectly
measured prickle. The Syrah also put in a
good performance, a well-structured,
caressing wine that is never too heavy.
Finally, the Caratelli al Pozzo is a Vin Santo di
Amelia of great complexity in its aromatic
profile: fragrances of incense and spices, in
the mouth, sweetness and savoriness are
well-orchestrated.

○ Amelia Vin Santo Caratelli al Pozzo '11	♟♟ 5
○ Metodo Tradizionale Cl. '12	♟♟ 5
● Syrah '14	♟♟ 4
○ Riesling Brut Metodo Ancestrale '13	♟ 5
● Merlot '97	♟♟♟ 4*
○ Amelia Vin Santo '12	♟♟ 4
● Amelia Vin Santo Occhio di Pernice '12	♟♟ 5
○ Extra Dry '11	♟♟ 4
○ Gran Cuvée Brut '13	♟♟ 4
○ Gran Cuvée Brut '11	♟♟ 4
○ Riesling Brut Metodo Ancestrale '11	♟♟ 3
○ Riesling Brut Metodo Ancestrale '09	♟♟ 3
○ Riesling Extra Dry Metodo Ancestrale '08	♟♟ 4
⊙ Rosé Brut '10	♟♟ 4
● Umbria Passito '09	♟♟ 4

Palazzone

LOC. ROCCA RIPESENA, 68
05019 ORVIETO [TR]
TEL. +39 0763344921
www.palazzone.com

CELLAR SALES
PRE-BOOKED VISITS
ACCOMMODATION AND RESTAURANT SERVICE
ANNUAL PRODUCTION 130,000 bottles
HECTARES UNDER VINE 24.00

Palazzone is a true benchmark for Umbrian white wine production, thanks to its excellent' terrain and approach to vine growing, which is aimed at bringing out the best of Orvieto. Their 20-hectare estate is situated near town, in the area's hills. Giovanni Dubini is the man behind the winery, a meticulous vine grower that has found the perfect balance between work in the cellar and the vineyard. The result is a precise, polished selection of wines that stay true to the qualities that make South Umbria unique. Without a doubt, Campo del Guardiano put in the best performance. This 2015 Orvieto Classico offers up fragrances of citrus, white fruit and wild flowers. A touch of herbs precedes a solid, vibrant and crisp palate. The other whites are just as strong. The 2016 Terre Vineate is another solid Orvieto, featuring a variegated nose and a lovely palate. The 2016 Grek is a dynamic, well-structured Grechetto, while Muffa Nobile exhibits great balance between residual sugar and freshness.

○ Orvieto Cl. Sup. Campo del Guardiano '15	♟♟♟3*
○ Grek '16	♟♟2*
○ Orvieto Cl. Sup. Muffa Nobile '16	♟♟5
○ Orvieto Cl. Sup. Terre Vineate '16	♟♟2*
○ Musco '14	♟6
● Piviere '15	♟3
○ Tixe '16	♟2
○ Orvieto Cl. Sup. Campo del Guardiano '14	♟♟♟3*
○ Orvieto Cl. Sup. Campo del Guardiano '11	♟♟♟2*
○ Orvieto Cl. Sup. Campo del Guardiano '09	♟♟♟3
○ Orvieto Cl. Sup. Muffa Nobile '15	♟♟5
○ Orvieto Cl. Sup. Terre Vineate '15	♟♟2*
○ Viognier '15	♟♟3

F.lli Pardi

VIA G. PASCOLI, 7/9
06036 MONTEFALCO [PG]
TEL. +39 0742379023
www.cantinapardi.it

CELLAR SALES
PRE-BOOKED VISITS
ANNUAL PRODUCTION 56,000 bottles
HECTARES UNDER VINE 11.00

F.lli Pardi is a small estate of just over 10 hectares situated in Montefalco. They've been operational for some time now, though in recent years, Pardi have attracted attention for the quality of their selection, starting with their Sagrantino. The grapes used come from different plots, thus creating a dynamic and multilayered wine, both in terms of nose and palate. Guarded extraction and spot-on aging (both for time and the use of wood) contribute to making wines of great drinkability and pleasantness, wines that are deep and polished. The Montefalco Sagrantino affirms is status after last year's fantastic performance. The 2013 stuns for its multitude of fragrances, from tobacco to pencil lead, spices and ripe red fruit. In the mouth, the wine proves creamy and caressing. Tannins provide rhythm, though without cropping the palate, making for a clean, deep finish. It gets Tre Bicchieri. The 2012 Sacrantino, another Montefalco, is tauter and drier, but still exhibits great character. The 2015 Montefalco Rosso goes all in on the simplicity of the palate.

● Montefalco Sagrantino '13	♟♟♟5
● Montefalco Rosso '15	♟♟3
● Montefalco Sagrantino Sacrantino '12	♟♟6
○ Colli Martani Grechetto '16	♟2
● Montefalco Sagrantino Passito '11	♟5
● Montefalco Sagrantino '12	♟♟♟5
○ Colli Martani Grechetto '15	♟♟2*
○ Colli Martani Grechetto '13	♟♟2*
● Montefalco Rosso '14	♟♟2*
● Montefalco Sagrantino '11	♟♟5
● Montefalco Sagrantino '10	♟♟5
● Montefalco Sagrantino Sacrantino '11	♟♟6
○ Spoleto Trebbiano Spoletino '15	♟♟2*
○ Spoleto Trebbiano Spoletino '14	♟♟2*

Cantina Peppucci

LOC. SANT'ANTIMO
FRAZ. PETRORO, 4
06059 TODI [PG]
TEL. +39 0758947439
www.cantinapeppucci.com

CELLAR SALES
PRE-BOOKED VISITS
ACCOMMODATION
ANNUAL PRODUCTION 70,000 bottles
HECTARES UNDER VINE 12.50

Peppucci was founded in Todi, in an area known for its beautiful landscapes, but mostly for its terrain, which is particularly well-suited to vine growing and winemaking. In recent years, the winery has turned out some impressive products, staying true to the territory with wines that are flavorsome and clean, with elegant aromas. Their two whites are entirely based on Grechetto. One is more simple, made in steel, and the other is made in wood. Their reds have a modern quality to them, and reflect the varieties used, from local grapes (here they use Sagrantino, even if they're outside the DOC zone) to international varieties. Excellent performance for Peppucci's wines. The 2012 Giovanni, a red in the tradition of Bordeaux, is intriguing, landing in the finals thanks to a nose of extreme complexity, which offers up fragrances of dark fruit, herbs and peppery nuances. The mouth Is taut and fresh, both tannic and creamy. Both the Grechettos did well. Their 2015 Rovi sees aromas of aniseeds, cloves and sea herbs.

Giovanni '12	🍷🍷 4
Todi Grechetto I Rovi '15	🍷🍷 3
Todi Grechetto Montorsolo '16	🍷🍷 2*
Todi Rosso Petroro 4 '16	🍷 2
Altro Io '12	🍷🍷 5
Altro Io '11	🍷🍷 5
Altro Io '10	🍷🍷 5
Todi Grechetto Montorsolo '15	🍷🍷 2*
Todi Grechetto Montorsolo '14	🍷🍷 2*
Todi Grechetto Montorsolo '13	🍷🍷 2*
Todi Grechetto Montorsolo '12	🍷🍷 2*
Todi Grechetto Sup. I Rovi '14	🍷🍷 3*
Todi Rosso Petroro 4 '14	🍷🍷 2*
Todi Rosso Petroro 4 '13	🍷🍷 2*

Perticaia

LOC. CASALE
06036 MONTEFALCO [PG]
TEL. +39 0742379014
www.perticaia.it

CELLAR SALES
PRE-BOOKED VISITS
ANNUAL PRODUCTION 120,000 bottles
HECTARES UNDER VINE 15.50
SUSTAINABLE WINERY

One of Montefalco's leading wineries, Perticaia is a solid, established producer that's also bringing repute to the whole of Umbria. Last year, the founder, Guido Guardigli, sold the winery to an Umbrian family located abroad, but nothing seems to have changed in terms of production, seeing as through Guardigli himself remains in charge. Their wines show character and grip, yet everything is balanced by freshness, good richness of flavor and linger. Only a few wines are produced, but they all pay tribute to Montefalco. Their reds proved the most impressive, starting with the 2016 Umbria Rosso, a blend of Sangiovese, with Colorino and Merlot. The wine offers intense notes of cherry and blackcurrant, a succulent mouth and a finish that's tightly-knit and spicy. The 2013 Montefalco Sagrantino is also good, and is penalized only for a tannic weave that dries the mouth in the finish. Despite the less-than-perfect 2014 vintage, the Montefalco Rosso offers good structure and a nose that delivers. The rest of the selection proved sound.

● Montefalco Rosso '14	🍷🍷 3
● Montefalco Sagrantino '13	🍷🍷 5
☉ Umbria Rosato Cos'é '16	🍷🍷 2*
● Umbria Rosso '16	🍷🍷 2*
○ Spoleto Trebbiano Spoletino '16	🍷 2
○ Spoleto Trebbiano Spoletino Del Posto '16	🍷 2
● Montefalco Sagrantino '11	🍷🍷🍷 5
● Montefalco Sagrantino '10	🍷🍷🍷 5
● Montefalco Sagrantino '09	🍷🍷🍷 5
● Montefalco Sagrantino '07	🍷🍷🍷 5
● Montefalco Sagrantino '06	🍷🍷🍷 5
● Montefalco Sagrantino '12	🍷🍷 5
○ Spoleto Trebbiano Spoletino '15	🍷🍷 2*
○ Spoleto Trebbiano Spoletino '14	🍷🍷 2*

Pucciarella

LOC. VILLA DI MAGIONE
VIA CASE SPARSE, 39
06063 MAGIONE [PG]
TEL. +39 0758409147
www.pucciarella.it

CELLAR SALES
PRE-BOOKED VISITS
ACCOMMODATION
ANNUAL PRODUCTION 250,000 bottles
HECTARES UNDER VINE 58.50
SUSTAINABLE WINERY

Pucciarella, located in Magione (just a stone's throw from Lago Trasimeno), is a large farm with over 300 hectares of terrain at its disposal. Of these, fewer than 60 are vineyards, with the rest used for olive groves, crops or woods. The terrain's main attributes are its altitude (300 meters above sea level) and its mineral-rich soil. The wines are always true to the territory and spot-on in terms of production. They make IGTs, whites, reds and dessert wines in the Colli del Trasimeno appellation, all of them notable for their excellent value. The Berlingero (Sangiovese with Cabernet Sauvignon and Merlot) is a young, vintage red, fermented in steel and concrete, which exhibits vinosity thanks to its aromas of cherry, strawberry, rose and orange. The mouth is supple and succulent, consistently clean with good depth. The Empireo, a wine made with Merlot and a small amount of Cabernet Sauvignon, is more complex and structure, with earthy, spicy notes of tobacco and forest floor. The mouth is tightly-knit, with tannins that are edgy but never astringent.

● C. del Trasimeno Rosso Berlingero '16	𝟐𝟐 2*
● Empireo '14	𝟐𝟐 3
○ C. del Trasimeno Bianco Agnolo '16	𝟐 2
○ C. del Trasimeno Bianco Ca de' Sass Brut '13	𝟐 3
● C. del Trasimeno Rosso Sant'Anna di Pucciarella Ris. '14	𝟐 3
○ Arsiccio '15	𝟐𝟐 3
○ Arsiccio '13	𝟐𝟐 3
● C. del Trasimeno Cabernet '13	𝟐𝟐 5
● C. del Trasimeno Rosso Sant'Anna Ris. '09	𝟐𝟐 2*
● Colli del Trasimeno Sant'Anna di Pucciarella '13	𝟐𝟐 3
○ Colli del Trasimeno Vin Santo '13	𝟐𝟐 4
● Empireo '10	𝟐𝟐 3

Raina

LOC. TURRI
VIA CASE SPARSE, 42
06036 MONTEFALCO [PG]
TEL. +39 3476014856
www.raina.it

CELLAR SALES
PRE-BOOKED VISITS
RESTAURANT SERVICE
ANNUAL PRODUCTION 60,000 bottles
HECTARES UNDER VINE 10.00
VITICULTURE METHOD Certified Organic
SUSTAINABLE WINERY

Raina's estate comprises about 10 hectares of certified organic vineyards (and currently working towards biodynamic) that make for production volume of over 50,000 bottles a year. Francesco Mariani, a Montefalco native and devoted viticulturist, is focused on well-crafted wines, while conferring an artisanal flavor and seeing to it that the product reflects its territory. Their reds are fresh and highly drinkable, with a pleasing, caressing texture. Their whites have shown notable improvement over recent years, their Grechetto, but especially their Trebbiano Spoletino, a variety that's perfect to cultivate in the area. Nevertheless, the reds continue to carry the day. We tasted an excellent 2013 Campo di Raina, Montefalco Sagrantino, with notes of pencil lead and bark. Its palate is lovely, thanks to a significant tannic presence that is, however, softened by vigor and richness of flavor. The 2014 Montefalco Rosso is fresh and dynam in the mouth, offering up aromas of ripe red fruit and balsamic notes. Finally, both the 2016 Grechetto and the 2016 Trebbiano Spolentino proved well-crafted.

● Montefalco Sagrantino Campo di Raina '13	𝟐𝟐
● Montefalco Rosso '14	𝟐𝟐
○ Grechetto '16	𝟐
○ Spoleto Trebbiano Spoletino '16	𝟐
○ Grechetto '14	𝟐𝟐
○ La Peschiera di Pacino '15	𝟐𝟐
● Montefalco Rosso '13	𝟐𝟐
● Montefalco Rosso '12	𝟐𝟐
● Montefalco Sagrantino Le Pretelle '10	𝟐𝟐
● Rosso della Gobba '14	𝟐𝟐
● Rosso della Gobba '13	𝟐𝟐
● Rosso della Gobba '12	𝟐𝟐
○ Spoleto Trebbiano Spoletino '15	𝟐𝟐
○ Spoleto Trebbiano Spoletino '14	𝟐𝟐

Roccafiore

FRAZ. CHIOANO
LOC. COLLINA, 110A
06059 TODI [PG]
TEL. +39 0758942416
www.roccafiorewines.com

CELLAR SALES
PRE-BOOKED VISITS
ACCOMMODATION AND RESTAURANT SERVICE
ANNUAL PRODUCTION 120,000 bottles
HECTARES UNDER VINE 15.00
SUSTAINABLE WINERY

To call Roccafiore a winery would be an oversimplification. Roccafiore is a project aimed at environmental sustainability that features a beautiful restaurant and a charming hotel (and spa). On the production side, they have 30 hectares of vineyards, scattered throughout the gentle slopes of Todi. The choice to grow native grape varieties and a careful approach to winemaking are the keys to elegant wines that reflect the territory. In addition to local whites and reds, the winery also produces a Montefalco Rosso and Sagrantino. Roccafiore put in a noteworthy performance, even if it didn't earn the highest mark. Two wines were at the top. The first is the 2014 Roccafiore, a Sangiovese with spellbinding fragrances of wild berries, mint, sweet spices and fumé, and a full palate with even-textured tannins. The second is Fiorfiore, a Grechetto that offers up fragrances of yellow flowers, pear and mountain herbs, with a well-structured mouth and good acidity. The rest of the selection proved very well-crafted, starting with the 2014 red, Prova d'Autore.

Fiorfiore '15	¥¥	4
Il Roccafiore '14	¥¥	3*
Prova d'Autore '14	¥¥	5
Collina d'Oro Passito '16	¥	5
Fiordaliso '16	¥	2
Rosso Melograno '15	¥	2
Todi Grechetto Sup. Fiorfiore '14	¥¥¥	3*
Il Roccafiore '13	¥¥	3
Prova d'Autore '13	¥¥	5
Prova d'Autore '12	¥¥	4
Todi Bianco Fiordaliso '15	¥¥	2*
Todi Grechetto Sup. Fiorfiore '13	¥¥	3*
Todi Rosso Melograno '14	¥¥	2*
Todi Rosso Melograno '12	¥¥	2*
Todi Sangiovese Sup. Il Roccafiore '12	¥¥	3

Romanelli

LOC. COLLE SAN CLEMENTE, 129A
06036 MONTEFALCO [PG]
TEL. +39 0742371245
www.romanelli.se

CELLAR SALES
PRE-BOOKED VISITS
ANNUAL PRODUCTION 40,000 bottles
HECTARES UNDER VINE 7.50

In the Montefalco scene, Romanelli may seem like a small winery. But thanks to the quality of their wines and, especially recently, an impressive consistence in terms of production, they have no problems standing shoulder-to-shoulder with the greats. It all starts in their vineyards, just over seven hectares of clay terrain that sit at notably higher altitudes. In the cellar, they work to produce subtle, fresh and polished wines, with a good flavor and depth. The result can be found in their two Sagrantinos, but also in their Montefalco Rosso, which is simple but never mundane. Their Grechetto dei Colli Martani is a perennially interesting white. The two Montefalco Sagrantinos truly delivered this year, especially the 2013, a wine that's more relaxed in the mouth, thanks to a tannic weave that's close-knit, but also integrates well. The Medeo harkens back to the 2012 vintage. It offers up hints of mint and earthy notes. In the mouth it's more extractive and the finish feels a bit cropped. The 2012 Montefalco Rosso Molinetta Riserva is relaxed in the mouth and delectable on the nose.

● Montefalco Sagrantino '13	¥¥	5
● Montefalco Rosso Molinetta Ris. '12	¥¥	5
● Montefalco Sagrantino Medeo '12	¥¥	8
○ Colli Martani Grechetto '16	¥	2
● Montefalco Rosso '14	¥	3
● Montefalco Sagrantino '11	¥¥¥	5
● Montefalco Sagrantino '10	¥¥¥	5
○ Colli Martani Grechetto '15	¥¥	2*
● Montefalco Rosso '11	¥¥	3
● Montefalco Sagrantino '12	¥¥	5
● Montefalco Sagrantino Medeo '11	¥¥	8

Scacciadiavoli

LOC. CANTINONE, 31
06036 MONTEFALCO [PG]
TEL. +39 0742371210
www.scacciadiavoli.it

CELLAR SALES
PRE-BOOKED VISITS
ANNUAL PRODUCTION 200,000 bottles
HECTARES UNDER VINE 37.00
SUSTAINABLE WINERY

Scacciadiavoli's roots go back to the late 1800s when Prince Boncompagni Ludovisi built the estate. In the mid 1950s, it was bought by Amilcare Panbuffetti and, today, it's his grandchildren who manage the winery. The breakthrough came in the early part of this century, with the renovation of the facilities and the implementation of a new approach geared towards high-quality wines. The estate comprises 35 hectares of vineyards in the hills of Montefalco, Gualdo Cattaneo and Giano dell'Umbria. Here the clay terrain, at an altitude of 400 meters, enjoys a unique microclimate. Without a doubt, the reds come out on top, with the 2015 Montefalco Rosso leading the way, a wine that is as simple as it is pleasant. The Montefalco Sagrantino is complex, close-woven and bold in structure. The passito, dried-grape version of the Sagrantino was also very good this year, with a sweetness softened by tannins, freshness and fullness of flavor. The whites were simpler but also well-made, especially the 2016 Montefalco Grechetto.

● Montefalco Rosso '15	♟♟ 3
● Montefalco Sagrantino '12	♟♟ 5
● Montefalco Sagrantino Passito '12	♟♟ 5
○ Montefalco Bianco '15	♟ 3
○ Montefalco Grechetto '16	♟ 2
● Montefalco Sagrantino '10	♟♟♟ 5
◉ Brut Rosé M. Cl. '11	♟♟ 4
○ Montefalco Bianco '14	♟♟ 3
○ Montefalco Bianco '13	♟♟ 3
● Montefalco Rosso '13	♟♟ 3
● Montefalco Rosso '12	♟♟ 3
● Montefalco Rosso '11	♟♟ 3
● Montefalco Sagrantino '11	♟♟ 5
● Montefalco Sagrantino '09	♟♟ 5

Sportoletti

VIA LOMBARDIA, 1
06038 SPELLO [PG]
TEL. +39 0742651461
www.sportoletti.com

CELLAR SALES
PRE-BOOKED VISITS
ANNUAL PRODUCTION 210,000 bottles
HECTARES UNDER VINE 30.00

Both local and international grape varieties are used at Sportoletti, a family-run winery whose current generation is bringing a new dynamism and the right modern touch to things. The vineyards (about 30 hectares) are situated in the hills of Spello and enjoy a microclimate and soil composition that are particularly well-suited to cultivation. Their wines are well-crafted with clean aromas and an international quality to them. Their prices are spot-on, boosting a consistently strong selection. The two Villa Fidelias put in the best performances this year. The 2015 Bianco (a blend of Grechetto and Chardonnay) offers up fragrances of vanilla, yellow apple and broom, with a soft and caressing mouth that's balanced by its savoriness. The tightly-knit, full-bodied 2015 Rosso is made from Merlot, with Cabernet Sauvignon and Cabernet Franc. The nose goes all in on red fruit, while the palate finds the right pace thanks to a subtle vigor that brings finesse. The rest of the selection presented proved sound, as well.

○ Villa Fidelia Bianco '15	♟♟
● Villa Fidelia Rosso '15	♟♟
○ Assisi Grechetto '16	♟
● Assisi Rosso '16	♟
○ Assisi Grechetto '13	♟♟
● Assisi Rosso '14	♟♟
● Assisi Rosso '13	♟♟
○ Villa Fidelia Bianco '14	♟♟
○ Villa Fidelia Bianco '13	♟♟
○ Villa Fidelia Bianco '12	♟♟
● Villa Fidelia Rosso '13	♟♟
● Villa Fidelia Rosso '12	♟♟
● Villa Fidelia Rosso '11	♟♟
● Villa Fidelia Rosso '10	♟♟

★Giampaolo Tabarrini

FRAZ. TURRITA
06036 MONTEFALCO [PG]
TEL. +39 0742379351
www.tabarrini.com

CELLAR SALES
PRE-BOOKED VISITS
ANNUAL PRODUCTION 70,000 bottles
HECTARES UNDER VINE 18.00
SUSTAINABLE WINERY

Giampaolo Tabarrini's project is surely for
real. Just take a look at his new
underground cellar, designed so as to have
enough space to cover all stages of
production, from fermentation to aging
(only large barrels for their reds) to storage
for the winery's historic stock or those
bottles that are being prepared for
shipment. The rest happens in the vineyard,
with the painstaking work of identifying the
best cru so as to vinify varieties separately
and bring out the true nuances of the area.
In addition to a strong territorial bond, their
wines show polish and character, proving
that they can age well and haven't lost their
artisanal qualities. Even if the three
Montefalco Sagrantinos were absolutely on
the mark, the whites carried the day. The
2015 Adarmando, made with Trebbiano
Spoletino, is a great, Mediterranean wine,
with savory, delicately salty, iodine notes
that are slightly fumé. The nose is a
continual succession of broom, candied
lemon peel and flint. The wine flows across
the palate, with a vibrant, deep weave.

Adarmando '15	▼▼▼ 4*
Montefalco Sagrantino Colle alle Macchie '13	▼▼ 6
Montefalco Sagrantino Campo alla Cerqua '13	▼▼ 6
Montefalco Sagrantino Colle Grimaldesco '13	▼▼ 5
Montefalco Rosso Boccatone '14	▼ 3
Montefalco Sagrantino Campo alla Cerqua '12	▽▽▽ 6
Montefalco Sagrantino Campo alla Cerqua '11	▽▽▽ 6
Montefalco Sagrantino Campo alla Cerqua '10	▽▽▽ 6

Terre de la Custodia

LOC. PALOMBARA
06035 GUALDO CATTANEO [PG]
TEL. +39 0742929586
www.terredelacustodia.it

CELLAR SALES
PRE-BOOKED VISITS
ANNUAL PRODUCTION 1,000,000 bottles
HECTARES UNDER VINE 160.00
SUSTAINABLE WINERY

Terre de La Custodia is managed by the
Farchioni family, entrepreneurs who, in
addition to wine, work in the olive oil, flour
and artisanal beer sectors. Theirs is one of
the most important wineries in the region,
especially in terms of production volume,
which has reached one million. Wines are
made from various vineyards, found both
in the Montefalco zone and Todi, areas
well-suited to whites. Their wines show,
on the whole, good stylistic precision.
They have an international feel, always
clean and close-focused on the nose. The
2014 Rubium, a Riserva di Montefalco
Rosso, features a pleasant, well-balanced
mouth. Despite the less-than-perfect
vintage, the wine stands out for its notes of
tobacco and prunes, along with earthy hints
and mushroom. The mouth shows mature,
though never bitter, tannins, with a
noticeable harmony between softness and
acidity. The Exubera is a 10-year-old
Montefalco Sagrantino that's still alive in its
fruity notes and deep mouth. It's only
missing a touch of grip.

● Montefalco Rosso Rubium Ris. '14	▼▼ 5
○ Colli Martani Spumante Gladius	▼ 4
● Montefalco Sagrantino Exubera '07	▼ 8
○ Brut Glaudius	▽▽ 4
○ Colli Martani Grechetto '14	▽▽ 2*
○ Colli Martani Grechetto '13	▽▽ 2*
○ Colli Martani Grechetto Plentis '14	▽▽ 3
● Colli Martani Rosso Collezione '14	▽▽ 2*
○ Colli Martani Spumante Gladius Sublimis '10	▽▽ 4
● Montefalco Rosso '12	▽▽ 4
● Montefalco Rosso Ris. '13	▽▽ 5
● Montefalco Sagrantino '11	▽▽ 6
● Montefalco Sagrantino '10	▽▽ 6
● Montefalco Sagrantino Passito Melano '11	▽▽ 5
○ Sublimis Gladius Brut M. Cl. '10	▽▽ 4

Terre Margaritelli

FRAZ. CHIUSACCIA
LOC. MIRALDUOLO
06089 TORGIANO [PG]
TEL. +39 0757824668
www.terremargaritelli.com

CELLAR SALES
PRE-BOOKED VISITS
ACCOMMODATION
ANNUAL PRODUCTION 120,000 bottles
HECTARES UNDER VINE 52.00
VITICULTURE METHOD Certified Organic

Margaritelli is an interesting winery from
Torgiano that has more than 50 hectares of
vineyards at its disposal, all cultivated
according to organic principles. It's a
contiguous plot that hosts the most
traditional varieties of the region: Grechetto
and Trebbiano, Sangiovese and Canaiolo.
Even if their wines are modern and draw on
an international style, some of them reflect a
desire to stay true to the territory. This can
be perceived both in the aroma and their
fresh, graceful texture, making for
easy-drinking. Moreover, their perennially
strong vintages are more than reasonably
priced. The 2013 Freccia degli Scacchi is
superb. This Torgiano 'Riserva' stands out for
its charming aromas and for its drinkability.
The nose features fragrances of small red
fruit, but there's also slightly smoky notes of
iron, dried flowers and bark. Thanks to soft,
silky tannins, the wine flows in the mouth,
making for a savory, fresh palate. The
2016 Roccascossa and 2015 Malot both
did well.

● Torgiano Rosso		
Freccia degli Scacchi Ris. '13	♟	5
● Malot '15	♟♟	3
● Roccascossa '16	♟♟	2*
○ Greco di Renabianca '16	♟	3
○ Pietramala '16	♟	2
○ Torgiano Bianco Costellato '16	♟	2
● Torgiano Rosso Mirantico '15	♟	2
○ Greco di Renabianca '15	♟♟	3
● Roccascossa '15	♟♟	2*
○ Torgiano Bianco Costellato '15	♟♟	2*
○ Torgiano Bianco Costellato '14	♟♟	2*
○ Torgiano Costellato '13	♟♟	2*
● Torgiano Rosso		
Freccia degli Scacchi Ris. '12	♟♟	5
● Torgiano Rosso		
Freccia degli Scacchi Ris. '10	♟♟	5

Todini

FRAZ. ROSCETO
VOC. COLLINA 29/1
06059 TODI [PG]
TEL. +39 075887122
www.cantinatodini.com

CELLAR SALES
PRE-BOOKED VISITS
ACCOMMODATION AND RESTAURANT SERVIC
ANNUAL PRODUCTION 220,000 bottles
HECTARES UNDER VINE 55.00

20 of the 120 hectares owned by the Todini
family are used as vineyards. For years their
selection has been of a high-quality, with
wines that consistently stand out for their
aromatic precision and modern flavor. The
use of international varieties, which give rise
to their monovarietal Merlot and Chardonna
or are blended with native varieties
(especially Grechetto and Sangiovese), has
lot to do with their success. In recent years
they have focused on wood aging and their
wines have benefitted in terms of their
expressivity and drinkability. Among their
selection, a white and a red hold the top
spots. The 2016 Bianco del Cavaliere is a
Grechetto di Todi with notes of pear and
yellow apple, chamomile and helichrysum.
the mouth, the wine is soft and pervasive,
with a palate that's broader than it is deep.
The Sangiovese di Todi is a red that's fresh
and well-paced in the mouth. It offers up
fragrances of blueberry and tomato flower,
while the palate is caressed by smooth
tannins. The other wines presented proved
pleasant and sound.

○ Grechetto di Todi		
Bianco del Cavaliere Sup. '16	♟♟	
● Sangiovese di Todi '15	♟♟	
○ Chardonnay '16	♟	
● Merlot '15	♟	
○ Grechetto Riesling '12	♟♟	
● Marte '14	♟♟	
○ Marte Bianco '15	♟♟	
● Marte Rosso '15	♟♟	
● Merlot '14	♟♟	
● Merlot '13	♟♟	
● Relais Rosso '13	♟♟	
○ Todi Grechetto '15	♟♟	
○ Todi Grechetto Sup.		
Bianco del Cavaliere '14	♟♟	
● Todi Rubro '12	♟♟	

udernum

. Pian di Porto, 146
059 Todi [PG]
. +39 0758989403
w.tudernum.it

LLAR SALES
E-BOOKED VISITS
COMMODATION AND RESTAURANT SERVICE
NUAL PRODUCTION 2,000,000 bottles
CTARES UNDER VINE 240.00

dernum is a cooperative winery whose
hectares of vineyards are capable of
ducing millions of bottles of wine. Over
past 10 years their standards have
reased significantly and the winery has
ne from average production quality to
king highly celebrated wines that stand
ulder-to-shoulder with some of the best
he region. The cultivation of local grape
ieties has been part of their success
grantino, but also Sangiovese and
chetto), and they've worked hard at it,
ecially in identifying the best-suited
as. Finally, we have to point out their
sonable prices, which applies to their
ole selection. A stellar performance for
ernum, that brings home a Tre Bicchieri
nks to its Fidenzio, a 2012 Montefalco
rantino of great complexity. The nose is a
ebration of fruit, starting with blackcurrant
blueberry, all the way to plum, blood
nges and peach. Farthier notes also
erge, from autumn leaves to forest floor,
shadowing a lean, relaxed mouth,
pite bolder tannins and freshness.

ontefalco Sagrantino Fidenzio '12	♟♟♟ 4*
rechetto di Todi '16	♟♟ 2*
ontefalco Rosso Fidenzio '15	♟ 3
di Rosso Sup. Rojano '15	♟ 3
ontefalco Sagrantino Fidenzio '11	♟♟ 4
ontefalco Sagrantino Fidenzio '10	♟♟ 4
ontefalco Sagrantino Fidenzio '09	♟♟ 4
di Grechetto '15	♟♟ 2*
di Grechetto '14	♟♟ 2*
di Grechetto Sup. Colle Nobile '13	♟♟ 2*
di Rosso '15	♟♟ 2*
di Rosso '14	♟♟ 2*
di Rosso Sup. Rojano '13	♟♟ 3*
di Rosso Sup. Rojano '12	♟♟ 3
di Rosso Sup. Rojano '11	♟♟ 3*

Tenuta Le Velette

Fraz. Canale di Orvieto
Loc. Le Velette, 23
05019 Orvieto [TR]
Tel. +39 076329090
www.levelette.it

CELLAR SALES
PRE-BOOKED VISITS
ANNUAL PRODUCTION 320,000 bottles
HECTARES UNDER VINE 119.00

Located in Orvieto, Tenuta Le Velette is
notable both for its beauty and its
dimensions, almost 120 hectares of
vineyards situated in an area characterized
by particularly volcanic terrain. The winery
itself is charming, especially for its tuff
caverns, which are ideal for aging wine.
Several varieties are cultivated, from local
grapes (perfect for DOC wines) to
international varieties that, here, seem to
have found the ideal terrain and climate.
Their wines are modern, stylistically
precise, without ever losing touch with the
qualities that define the variety itself. And
international varieties make up the Calanco
(Cabernet and Sangiovese), whose 2013
version delivers. The nose offers a
multitude of aromas amidst fragrances of
red fruit and herbs, while the mouth is as
fluent and dynamic as it is tightly-knit,
thanks to a conspicuous tannic weave. The
finish proved excellent, both clean and
lingering at once. The Gaudio, a
monovarietal made with Merlot of good
extraction, also proved excellent.

● Calanco '13	♟♟ 4
● Gaudio '13	♟♟ 4
● Accordo '12	♟ 2
● Gaudio '03	♟♟♟ 4
● Accordo '10	♟♟ 2*
● Calanco '12	♟♟ 4
● Gaudio '10	♟♟ 4
○ Orvieto Cl. Berganorio '15	♟♟ 2*
○ Orvieto Cl. Berganorio '14	♟♟ 2*
○ Orvieto Cl. Berganorio '13	♟♟ 2*
○ Orvieto Cl. Sup. Lunato '15	♟♟ 2*
○ Orvieto Cl. Sup. Lunato '14	♟♟ 2*
○ Orvieto Cl. Sup. Lunato '11	♟♟ 2*
● Rosso Orvietano Rosso di Spicca '13	♟♟ 2*
○ Sole Uve '13	♟♟ 3

Villa Mongalli

VIA DELLA CIMA, 52
06031 BEVAGNA [PG]
TEL. +39 0742360703
www.villamongalli.com

CELLAR SALES
ACCOMMODATION
ANNUAL PRODUCTION 70,000 bottles
HECTARES UNDER VINE 15.00

Villa Mongalli is situated in Bevagna and has, at its disposal, some of the best terrain in Montefalco. The attributes of its 15 hectares of vineyards come out in their wines, starting with their two Montefalco Sagrantinos, whose style highlights the undersoil, and whose character is never undermined by production. For some years now, the Montefalco Rosso has gotten our attention. It's a wine that focuses on traditional grape varieties and stands out for its drinkability and pleasantness. Their selection is rounded out by a Trebbiano Spoletino, a strong wine itself that expresses true artisanal craftsmanship. The Montefalco Sagrantinos presented are excellent, especially those harkening back to the 2013 vintage. Among the two presented, we preferred Della Cima, a wine of great complexity and structure. Fragrances of red orange and wet earth mingle with balsamic and minty nuances. In the mouth, the wine is close-knit and dense, austere and deep. The Pozzo del Curato, a wine that exhibits some tightness as a result of its conspicuous tannic weave, still delivered. The other wines presented also proved well-crafted.

● Montefalco Sagrantino Della Cima '13	♥♥ 8
● Montefalco Sagrantino Pozzo del Curato '13	♥♥ 7
● Montefalco Rosso Le Grazie '15	♥ 5
● Montefalco Sagrantino Colcimino '14	♥ 8
⊙ Trebbiano Spoletino Calicanto '16	♥ 5
⊙ Umbria Rosato Profano '16	♥ 2
● Montefalco Sagrantino Colcimino '08	♥♥♥ 3*
● Montefalco Sagrantino Della Cima '10	♥♥♥ 8
● Montefalco Sagrantino Della Cima '06	♥♥♥ 6
● Montefalco Sagrantino Pozzo del Curato '09	♥♥♥ 6
● Montefalco Rosso Le Grazie '14	♥♥ 5
● Montefalco Sagrantino Pozzo del Curato '12	♥♥ 7
⊙ Trebbiano Spoletino Calicanto '15	♥♥ 5

Zanchi

S.DA PROV.LE AMELIA-ORTE KM 4,610
05022 AMELIA [TR]
TEL. +39 0744970011
www.cantinezanchi.it

CELLAR SALES
PRE-BOOKED VISITS
ANNUAL PRODUCTION 80,000 bottles
HECTARES UNDER VINE 31.00
SUSTAINABLE WINERY

Zanchi is a family-run producer that has been making wine for about 40 years. Bo the main residence and cellar are situate in Amelia, a small town in southern Umbr Zanchi works according to principles of sustainability, employing agronomic practices that demonstrate a deep respe for nature. In the cellar, their work is characterized by an artisanal approach a minimal intervention, thus leaving space the various vintages to develop in their ow way. The cultivar used are those of the territory: Grechetto, Ciliegiolo, Trebbiano and Aleatico. The 2016 Grechetto Arvore without a doubt, the best of the selection and is, among its cultivar, one of the bes the Amelia appellation. The nose feature fragrances of yellow fruit, candied lemon peel and a touch of wildflowers, helichrysum. In the mouth, the wine has structure, proving pervasive, with a palat accompanied by a great richness of flavo The 2016 Ciliegiolo Carmìno is decadent its aromas of small, red fruit and fresh, succulent palate. The rest of the selectio presented also proved well-crafted.

○ Amelia Grechetto Arvore '16	♥
● Amelia Ciliegiolo Carmino '16	♥♥
● Lu Aleatico '15	
○ Vignavecchia Trebbiano '13	
● Amelia Armané '10	♀
○ Amelia Bianco Pizzale '11	♀
● Amelia Ciliegiolo Carmìno '13	♀
○ Amelia Grechetto Arvore '14	♀
○ Amelia Grechetto Arvore '12	♀
○ Amelia Malvasia Flavo '13	♀
● Amelia Rosso Armané '13	♀
● Amelia Rosso Sciurio Ris. '09	♀
○ Vignavecchia '12	♀
○ Vignavecchia '11	♀

antina Altarocca

. Rocca Ripesena, 62
010 Orvieto [TR]
.. +39 0763344210
ww.cantinaaltarocca.com

CELLAR SALES
RE-BOOKED VISITS
CCOMMODATION AND RESTAURANT SERVICE
NNUAL PRODUCTION 65,000 bottles
ECTARES UNDER VINE 11.00
TICULTURE METHOD Certified Organic

Orvieto Cl. Sup. Albaco '16	♥♥ 3*
Orvieto Cl. Arcosesto '16	♥♥ 2*

Argillae

voc. Pomarro, 45
05010 Allerona [TR]
Tel. +39 0763624604
www.argillae.eu

CELLAR SALES
PRE-BOOKED VISITS
ANNUAL PRODUCTION 65,000 bottles
HECTARES UNDER VINE 70.00

○ Grechetto '16	♥♥ 2*
○ Orvieto '16	♥♥ 2*
○ Orvieto Cl. Sup. Panata '16	♥ 2
● Sinuoso '16	♥ 2

enedetti & Grigi

. La Palzella
036 Montefalco [PG]
. +39 0758011560
w.benedettiegrigi.it

CELLAR SALES
NNUAL PRODUCTION 400,000 bottles
CTARES UNDER VINE 68.00

Montefalco Rosso La Gaita del Falco '15	♥♥ 3
Spoleto Trebbiano Spoletino '16	♥♥ 3
Spoleto Trebbiano Spoletino La Gaita del Falco '16	♥♥ 3

Bigi

loc. Ponte Giulio
05018 Orvieto [TR]
Tel. +39 0763315888
www.cantinebigi.it

PRE-BOOKED VISITS
ANNUAL PRODUCTION 4,000,000 bottles
HECTARES UNDER VINE 248.00

○ Grechetto Strozzavolpe '16	♥♥ 2*
○ Orvieto Cl. '16	♥♥ 2*
● Vipra Rossa '16	♥♥ 2*
● Sartiano '15	♥ 3

ticoltori Broccatelli Galli

degli Olmi, 9
083 Bastia Umbra [PG]
. +39 0758001501
w.broccatelligalli.it

LLAR SALES
E-BOOKED VISITS
COMMODATION AND RESTAURANT SERVICE
NNUAL PRODUCTION 2,000,000 bottles
CTARES UNDER VINE 75.00

Montefalco Sagrantino '12	♥♥ 5
Montefalco Sagrantino Preda del Falco '12	♥♥ 7
Bianco di Torgiano '16	♥ 3

Brunozzi

loc. Colle Arfuso, 2
06036 Montefalco [PG]
Tel. +39 3289549774
www.aziendagrariabrunozzi.it

CELLAR SALES
PRE-BOOKED VISITS
ACCOMMODATION
ANNUAL PRODUCTION 10,000 bottles
HECTARES UNDER VINE 2.00

● Montefalco Sagrantino Carlotto '13	♥♥ 6
● Montefalco Rosso Scimella '14	♥ 3
● Montefalco Sagrantino Passito Plautilla '12	♥ 4

Cantine Monrubio

FRAZ. MONTERUBIAGLIO
LOC. LE PRESE, 22
05014 CASTEL VISCARDO [TR]
TEL. +39 0763626064
www.monrubio.it

CELLAR SALES
PRE-BOOKED VISITS
ANNUAL PRODUCTION 200,000 bottles
HECTARES UNDER VINE 800.00

○ Orvieto Cl. Sup. Soana '16	♀♀ 2*
● Palaia '15	♀ 3

Cardeto

FRAZ. SFERRACAVALLO
LOC. CARDETO
05018 ORVIETO [TR]
TEL. +39 0763341286
www.cardeto.com

CELLAR SALES
PRE-BOOKED VISITS
ANNUAL PRODUCTION 3,000,000 bottles
HECTARES UNDER VINE 600.00

● Nero della Greca '15	♀♀
○ Orvieto Cl. Sup. Donna Armida V. T. '16	♀♀
○ Grechetto '16	♀
○ Viognier '16	♀

Castello delle Regine

LOC. LE REGINE
VIA DI CASTELLUCCIO
05022 AMELIA [TR]
TEL. +39 0744702005
www.castellodelleregine.com

CELLAR SALES
PRE-BOOKED VISITS
ACCOMMODATION AND RESTAURANT SERVICE
ANNUAL PRODUCTION 400,000 bottles
HECTARES UNDER VINE 65.00

● Rosso di Podernovo '14	♀♀ 2*
● Poggio delle Regine '16	♀ 2
● Poggio delle Regine Sangiovese '15	♀ 2

Castello di Corbara

LOC. CORBARA, 7
05018 ORVIETO [TR]
TEL. +39 0763304035
www.castellodicorbara.it

CELLAR SALES
PRE-BOOKED VISITS
ANNUAL PRODUCTION 200,000 bottles
HECTARES UNDER VINE 100.00

○ Grechetto '16	♀♀
● Lago di Corbara Sangiovese Calistri '14	♀♀
○ Orvieto Cl. Sup. '16	♀
○ Orzalume '16	♀

Chiorri

LOC. SANT'ENEA
VIA TODI, 100
06132 PERUGIA
TEL. +39 075607141
www.chiorri.it

CELLAR SALES
PRE-BOOKED VISITS
ACCOMMODATION AND RESTAURANT SERVICE
ANNUAL PRODUCTION 100,000 bottles
HECTARES UNDER VINE 25.00
SUSTAINABLE WINERY

● Colli Perugini Saliato '13	♀♀ 3
○ Titus '16	♀♀ 2*
○ Etesia '16	♀ 2
⊙ Ventorosa '16	♀ 2

Le Cimate

FRAZ. CASALE
LOC. CECAPECORE, 41
06036 MONTEFALCO [PG]
TEL. +39 0742290136
www.lecimate.it

CELLAR SALES
PRE-BOOKED VISITS
ACCOMMODATION AND RESTAURANT SERVI
ANNUAL PRODUCTION 800,000 bottles
HECTARES UNDER VINE 20.00
SUSTAINABLE WINERY

● Montefalco Sagrantino '13	♀♀
○ Spoleto Trebbiano Spoletino Sup. Riserva del Cavalier Bartoloni '15	♀

Cantina Colle Ciocco

VIA PIETRAUTA
06036 MONTEFALCO [PG]
TEL. +39 0742379859
www.colleciocco.it

CELLAR SALES
PRE-BOOKED VISITS
ANNUAL PRODUCTION 45,000 bottles
HECTARES UNDER VINE 15.00

● Montefalco Sagrantino '11	♟♟	5
● Montefalco Rosso '13	♟♟	3

★ Còlpetrone

FRAZ. MARCELLANO
VIA PONTE LA MANDRIA, 8/1
06035 GUALDO CATTANEO [PG]
TEL. +39 074299827
www.colpetrone.it

CELLAR SALES
PRE-BOOKED VISITS
ANNUAL PRODUCTION 350,000 bottles
HECTARES UNDER VINE 63.00

● Montefalco Sagrantino Passito '12	♟♟	5
○ Grechetto '16	♟	2
● Montefalco Sagrantino Sacer '08	♟	8

Cantina Dionigi

LOC. MADONNA DELLA PIA, 92
06031 BEVAGNA [PG]
TEL. +39 0742360395
www.cantinadionigi.it

CELLAR SALES
PRE-BOOKED VISITS
ACCOMMODATION
ANNUAL PRODUCTION 40,000 bottles
HECTARES UNDER VINE 6.00

● Montefalco Sagrantino Passito '12	♟♟	5
○ Colli Martani Grechetto V. del Brillo '16	♟♟	3
○ Colle Sorragani '16	♟	3
● Merlot Passito Civico 92 '12	♟	3

Fongoli

LOC. SAN MARCO DI MONTEFALCO
06036 MONTEFALCO [PG]
TEL. +39 0742378930
www.fongoli.com

CELLAR SALES
PRE-BOOKED VISITS
ACCOMMODATION
ANNUAL PRODUCTION 100,000 bottles
HECTARES UNDER VINE 27.00
VITICULTURE METHOD Certified Organic

○ Colli Martani Grechetto '16	♟♟	2*
○ Maceratum '16	♟♟	2*
○ Biancofongoll '16	♟	2
● Montefalco Rosso Sercullo Ris. '13	♟	4

Cantina La Spina

FRAZ. SPINA
VIA EMILIO ALESSANDRINI, 1
06055 MARSCIANO [PG]
TEL. +39 0758738120
www.cantinalaspina.it

CELLAR SALES
PRE-BOOKED VISITS
ANNUAL PRODUCTION 16,000 bottles
HECTARES UNDER VINE 2.20
SUSTAINABLE WINERY

● Merlato '16	♟♟	2*
● Polimante della Spina '15	♟♟	4
○ Rosato '16	♟	2
● RossoSpina '15	♟	3

Lamborghini

LOC. SODERI, 1
06064 PANICALE [PG]
TEL. +39 0758350029
www.tenutalamborghini.com

CELLAR SALES
PRE-BOOKED VISITS
ACCOMMODATION AND RESTAURANT SERVICE
ANNUAL PRODUCTION 150,000 bottles
HECTARES UNDER VINE 32.00

● Campoleone '13	♟♟	6
● Torami '13	♟♟	5
● Era '15	♟	3
● Trescone '15	♟	2

Morami

FRAZ. PANICAROLA
VOC. MORAMI
06060 CASTIGLIONE DEL LAGO [PG]
TEL. +39 0759589107
www.morami.it

CELLAR SALES
PRE-BOOKED VISITS
ACCOMMODATION
ANNUAL PRODUCTION 20,000 bottles
HECTARES UNDER VINE 11.00

● Podicerri '15	♟♟ 4
○ Pratolungo '16	♟♟ 3
● Renaia '13	♟ 6

Cantine Neri

LOC. BARDANO, 28
05018 ORVIETO [TR]
TEL. +39 0763316196
www.neri-vini.it

ANNUAL PRODUCTION 65,000 bottles
HECTARES UNDER VINE 52.00

● Americo '14	♟♟ 3
○ Poggio Forno '15	♟♟ 5
● Vardano '15	♟♟ 3
○ Bianco dei Neri '16	♟ 2

Cantina Ninni

FRAZ. TERRAIA, 60A
06049 SPOLETO [PG]
TEL. +39 3355450523
www.cantinaninnispoleto.com

CELLAR SALES
PRE-BOOKED VISITS
ANNUAL PRODUCTION 12,000 bottles
HECTARES UNDER VINE 3.00

○ Spoleto Trebbiano Spoletino Poggio del Vescovo '16	♟♟ 2*

La Plani Arche

VOC. CONVERSINO, 160A
06033 CANNARA [PG]
TEL. +39 3356389537
www.planiarche.it

ANNUAL PRODUCTION 15,000 bottles
HECTARES UNDER VINE 6.00
VITICULTURE METHOD Certified Organic
SUSTAINABLE WINERY

● Montefalco Sagrantino Brown Label '12	♟♟ 4
● Montefalco Rosso '13	♟♟ 3
● Montefalco Sagrantino Black Label '11	♟♟ 5
○ Umbria Trebbiano '16	♟♟ 2

Santo Iolo

S.DA MONTINI, 30A
05035 NARNI [TR]
TEL. +39 0744796754
www.santoiolo.it

CELLAR SALES
PRE-BOOKED VISITS
ANNUAL PRODUCTION 15,000 bottles
HECTARES UNDER VINE 3.50
SUSTAINABLE WINERY

● Rossoiolo '15	♟♟ 3
● Santoiolo '13	♟♟ 3
○ Pratalia '16	♟ 2
● Rosso Fossile '14	♟ 2

Tenuta di Titignano

LOC. CIVITELLA DEL LAGO
VOC. SALVIANO, 44
05020 BASCHI [TR]
TEL. +39 0744950459
info@titignano.it

CELLAR SALES
PRE-BOOKED VISITS
ANNUAL PRODUCTION 150,000 bottles
HECTARES UNDER VINE 70.00

○ Orvieto Cl. Sup. Salviano '16	♟ 2
● Lago di Corbara Salviano Turlò '14	♟ 3
○ Orvieto Cl. Sup. Salviano V.T. '16	♟ 2
○ Salviano Rosé '16	♟ 3

LAZIO

A Latin proverb says 'no news is good news'. That might not always be true. Take Lazio, for example. For a couple years now, we haven't seen very much that's new in the way of quality. Surely we're partly to blame, that is, we're simply not looking closely enough. But the problem may also be linked to regional viticulture, which seems unable to find its way. Having said that, it's interesting to note the direction being taking by the region's white wines (about two thirds of its production). The most important number comes from the Castelli Romani, especially Frascati, where, despite a professed desire to improve quality, the results haven't exactly raised the bar. Mario Masini's Eremo Tuscolano is back with a Tre Bicchieri, with the winemaker keeping his promise to serve as a stylistic benchmark for the appellation. For the rest, not only didn't we see new high-quality Frascatis, but more importantly, well-known producers weren't able to demonstrate consistent quality. In the region's south, Ponza returns to the forefront with its Biancolella, a classic in our finals represented by Migliaccio and Casale del Giglio, a winery that once again claimed a Tre Bicchieri with its Faro della Guardia. And even if it didn't earn top honors, Bellone is proving its potential. To the north, Grechetto continues to maintain a top-spot. Even if the only award went to Sergio Mottura's Poggio della Costa (a model producer in the district of Tuscia), more and more wineries are making themselves heard, proposing some superb Grechettos with a strong territorial identity. In terms of the region's reds, we continue to await a hoped-for explosion of Cesanese, whether it's Piglio, Affile or Olevano Romano. This year, the cultivar didn't bring home any Tre Bicchieri for its territories, and those working with the grape remain largely the same as a few years ago. Apparently, the problem is still the same: the difficulty of finding the right balance between authenticity and pleasantness, that is, giving luster to a still mirky reputation and an overall selection that features few interesting wines. We'll see what direction these districts take over the next few years. For the moment, Emanuele Pangrazi has chosen the road less traveled, with his Habemus wines. The Etichetta Bianca, one of the year's few headlines, nabbed a Tre Bicchieri. We close by recognizing those producers that have, year in and year out, confirmed their status as Lazio's elite: La Falesco (now just Falesco); Famiglia Cotarella, with their eternal Montiano; Poggio Le Volpi, whose Baccarossa delivered this year; and Tenuta di Fiorano, which has proven the absolute quality of Fiorano Rosso.

Marco Carpineti

S.DA PROV.LE VELLETRI-ANZIO, 3
04010 CORI [LT]
TEL. +39 069679860
www.marcocarpineti.com

CELLAR SALES
PRE-BOOKED VISITS
ANNUAL PRODUCTION 300,000 bottles
HECTARES UNDER VINE 52.00
VITICULTURE METHOD Certified Organic

Carpineti's certified organic vineyards are
situated in some of the area's most
well-suited parcels of land, such as Cori,
while their cellar, in addition to its beauty, is
at the technological vanguard. And so the
brilliant results that Marco Carpineti (now
flanked by his son, Paolo) has managed to
achieve come as no surprise. The fact that,
in the past, half a dozen of his wines have
arrived in the finals demonstrates the overall
quality of his selection. This year, it's enriched
by the Apolide 2012, a Nero Buono aged for
two years in barrique that is expressive and
pervasive, both on the nose and the palate.
Right alongside it, we find the 2015 Moro, a
wine that features a mix of tropical fruit,
citrusy notes, exuberant alcohol and tangy
freshness. While the 2012 Dithyrambus
proves Marco's skill in handling long aging,
wines like the 2016 Capolemole Bianco or
the 2016 Tufaliccio demonstrate that he's
just as good at bringing out a wine's
approachability and the pleasantness of its
fruit. The two Kius complete the range, with
the Brut a bit more on the mark than the
Rosato.

● Apolide '12	♟♟	5
○ Moro '15	♟♟	3*
○ Capolemole Bianco '16	♟♟	2*
● Dithyrambus '12	♟♟	5
○ Kius Brut '14	♟♟	4
● Tufaliccio '16	♟♟	2*
● Capolemole Rosso '14	♟	3
⊙ Kius Extra Brut Rosato '13	♟	5
○ Capolemole Bianco '15	♟♟	2*
○ Capolemole Bianco '14	♟♟	2*
● Dithyrambus '10	♟♟	5
○ Kius Brut '13	♟♟	3
○ Moro '14	♟♟	3*
○ Moro '13	♟♟	3*
● Tufaliccio '15	♟♟	2*

Casale del Giglio

LOC. LE FERRIERE
S.DA CISTERNA-NETTUNO KM 13
04100 LATINA
TEL. +39 0692902530
www.casaledelgiglio.lt

CELLAR SALES
PRE-BOOKED VISITS
ANNUAL PRODUCTION 1,276,600 bottles
HECTARES UNDER VINE 164.00
SUSTAINABLE WINERY

The decision to return to local, native grape
varieties, from Biancolella di Ponza (vinified
on the island itself) to Bellone di Anzio, has
proven a smart one. Indeed, it's led to
outstanding results, with two wines that
alternately assume a leading role for the
winery. This year the Faro della Guardia
2016 returns to prominence, in a wine that
weds elegance, mineral substance and
depth, fusing approachability and rich
nuance. Its Tre Bicchieri is thoroughly
deserved, and the 2016 Antium wasn't
far-off either. Here, the ungrafted Bellone,
cultivated at historic vineyards, gives its best
The wine is still quite closed at the moment,
but it's easy to see how it will evolve.
Classics, such as the 2014 Mater Matuta
and the 2015 Antinoo, have lived up to
expectations, but we'd especially like to
point out their best 2015 Merlot yet. Fleshy
and full-bodied, it heads a range of
monovarietals that are all top-notch.
Well-deserved kudos to Antonio Santarelli
and Paolo Tiefenthaler.

○ Biancolella Faro della Guardia '16	♟♟♟	5
○ Antium Bellone '16	♟♟	4
● Mater Matuta '14	♟♟	7
⊙ Albiola Rosato '16	♟♟	3
○ Antinoo '15	♟♟	5
● Madreselva '14	♟♟	5
● Merlot '15	♟♟	3
○ Petit Manseng '16	♟♟	4
● Petit Verdot '15	♟♟	4
○ Satrico '16	♟♟	3
● Tempranijo '15	♟♟	5
○ Viognier '16	♟♟	3
○ Antium Bellone '15	♟♟♟	4
○ Antium Bellone '14	♟♟♟	4
○ Biancolella Faro della Guardia '13	♟♟♟	5

Casale della Ioria

LOC. LA GLORIA
S.DA PROV.LE 118 ANAGNI-PALIANO
03012 ANAGNI [FR]
TEL. +39 077556031
www.casaledellaioria.com

CELLAR SALES
PRE-BOOKED VISITS
ANNUAL PRODUCTION 65,000 bottles
HECTARES UNDER VINE 38.00
SUSTAINABLE WINERY

Paolo Perinelli is an entrepreneur who always worked to promote Cesanese and the territory of Piglio. Indeed, he's gone well beyond the mere interests of his own winery. And so it is with pleasure that, after a difficult 2014, we can confirm that his Cesanese del Piglio has returned to form. The 2015 Torre del Piano suddenly leapt into our finals, thanks to a nose featuring red fruits and wild berries, accompanied by a non-intrusive spiciness and a palate with the right tannins and fullness. The Cesanese selection is completed by their 2015 Tenuta della Ioria, a wine with good body, and a simpler 2015 Campo Novo (as well as a Brut Charmat still to be fine-tuned). The project to revive the rare Olivella grape is going forward, while the 2016 Passerina Colle Bianco sees slightly excessive citrusy notes. The Extra Dry version is more interesting, thanks to residual sugar that leads to a better nose-palate symmetry.

● Cesanese del Piglio Sup. Torre del Piano Ris. '15	♟♟ 4
● Cesanese del Piglio Sup. Tenuta della Ioria '15	♟♟ 3
⊙ Cesanese Brut	♟ 3
● Cesanese del Piglio Campo Novo '15	♟ 2
● Olivella '13	♟ 2
○ Passerina Colle Bianco '16	♟ 2
○ Passerina Extra Dry	♟ 2
● Cesanese del Piglio Sup. Torre del Piano Ris. '13	♟♟ 4
● Cesanese del Piglio Sup. Torre del Piano Ris. '12	♟♟ 4

Castel de Paolis

VIA VAL DE PAOLIS
00046 GROTTAFERRATA [RM]
TEL. +39 069413648
www.casteldepaolis.com

CELLAR SALES
PRE-BOOKED VISITS
RESTAURANT SERVICE
ANNUAL PRODUCTION 80,000 bottles
HECTARES UNDER VINE 11.00

The idea of realizing a winery in the heart of the Castelli Romani came to Giulio Santarelli in 1985. He may have been a politician, but his heart was in agriculture, and so he enlisted the help of Prof. Attilio Scienza in an effort revive the old, native varieties that had been afflicted by phylloxera. It required long-term experimentation and research, but in the end, drawing on the volcanic terrain of Grottaferrata, an altitude of 270 meters and the nearby Tyrrhenian Sea, the estate of Castel de Paolis was reborn. The whites shine this year. The 2016 Donna Adriana, a blend of Viognier and Malvasia del Lazio, features a fresh and aromatic nose, with notes of white flowers, medlar and melon emerging on the palate. The 2016 Frascati Superiore is rich in citrusy overtones and exhibits good structure. The 2015 Muffa Nobile also proves to be well-made, fresh and balanced. It's a blend of Semillon, with signature hints of dried apricots.

○ Donna Adriana '16	♟♟ 4
○ Frascati Sup. '16	♟♟ 3
○ Frascati Campo Vecchio '16	♟♟ 2
○ Muffa Nobile '15	♟♟ 5
● I Quattro Mori '13	♟ 5
● Campo Vecchio Rosso '14	♙♙ 3
● Campo Vecchio Rosso '12	♙♙ 3
○ Donna Adriana '15	♙♙ 4
○ Donna Adriana '08	♙♙ 4
○ Frascati Campo Vecchio '14	♙♙ 2*
○ Frascati Cannellino '10	♙♙ 3
○ Frascati Sup. '15	♙♙ 3
○ Frascati Sup. '12	♙♙ 3
● I Quattro Mori '11	♙♙ 5
○ Muffa Nobile '11	♙♙ 5

Cincinnato

VIA CORI - CISTERNA, KM 2
04010 CORI [LT]
TEL. +39 069679380
www.cincinnato.it

CELLAR SALES
PRE-BOOKED VISITS
ACCOMMODATION AND RESTAURANT SERVICE
ANNUAL PRODUCTION 90,000 bottles
HECTARES UNDER VINE 268.00
SUSTAINABLE WINERY

When, as is the case at Cincinnato, the quality of Cori's grapes and cultivar are accompanied by clear guidelines (laid out carefully by Nazareno Milita and Carlo Morettini), and these are followed by the vine growers, cooperation can only lead to outstanding results. The excellent value of their selection is commendable. And we should also consider the results they've obtained with Bellone, which offers up its best with the 2015 Pozzodorico. It's an intense and gutsy wine, but the skillful use of mid-sized casks has brought balance and pleasantness. The more approachable interpretation of the 2016 Castore is not far-off, with its intense notes of citron and white fruit, as well as the 2016 Cori Bianco Illirio. Nero Buono, the other local variety, is combined with Montepulciano and Cesanese for the well-structured 2014 Cori Rosso Raverosse. It's also used to make their two monovarietals, the 2014 Ercole and the 2015 Polluce, with more evolved notes of jam. We also enjoyed the 2016 Pantaleo, made with Greco, and the 2015 Arcatura, made with Cesanese.

○ Castore '16	♟♟ 2*
○ Pozzodorico Bellone '15	♟♟ 2*
○ Cori Bianco Illirio '16	♟♟ 2*
● Cori Rosso Raverosse '14	♟♟ 2*
● Arcatura '15	♟ 3
● Ercole Nero Buono '14	♟ 3
● Pantaleo '16	♟ 2
● Pollùce '15	♟ 2
○ Castore '14	♟♟ 2*
○ Cori Bianco Illirio '15	♟♟ 2*
● Cori Rosso Raverosse '13	♟♟ 2*
● Ercole Nero Buono '13	♟♟ 3*
○ Pantaleo '15	♟♟ 2*
○ Pantaleo '14	♟♟ 2*
○ Pozzodorico Bellone '14	♟♟ 2*

Damiano Ciolli

VIA DEL CORSO
00035 OLEVANO ROMANO [RM]
TEL. +39 069563334
www.damianociolli.it

CELLAR SALES
PRE-BOOKED VISITS
ANNUAL PRODUCTION 25,000 bottles
HECTARES UNDER VINE 5.00
SUSTAINABLE WINERY

Since the founding of his winery in 2001, Damiano Ciolli's name has been associated with the DOC zone of Cesanese di Olevano Romano, the area to which his work is entirely dedicated. Indeed, Damiano has reaped the benefits of descending from a line of four generations of vine growers, having inherited his grandfather's property in 1953. Spurred on by the vineyards' quality, he decided to bottle his own wines. The 2013 Cesanese di Olevano Romano Cirsium Riserva has great structure and character and confirms its place at the top of the appellation. The wine offers up aromas of chocolate, spices and black fruit, together with a bold and succulent palate of bottled cherries and cloves. The 2015 Cesanese di Olevano Romano Silene Superiore is lighter and fruity, with a savory rosemary finish.

● Cesanese di Olevano Romano Cirsium Ris. '13	♟♟ 5
● Cesanese di Olevano Romano Sup. Silene '15	♟♟ 3
● Cesanese di Olevano Romano Cirsium '11	♟♟ 5
● Cesanese di Olevano Romano Cirsium Ris. '12	♟♟ 5
● Cesanese di Olevano Romano Sup. Cirsium Ris. '10	♟♟ 5
● Cesanese di Olevano Romano Sup. Silene '14	♟♟ 3
● Cesanese di Olevano Romano Sup. Silene '13	♟♟ 3
● Cesanese di Olevano Romano Sup. Silene '12	♟♟ 3

Antonello Coletti Conti

Via Vittorio Emanuele, 116
03012 Anagni [FR]
Tel. +39 0775728610
www.coletticonti.it

CELLAR SALES
PRE-BOOKED VISITS
ANNUAL PRODUCTION 20,000 bottles
HECTARES UNDER VINE 20.00

Antonello Coletti Conti is a cellarman by trade, though his heart is in vine growing. He shows painstaking care throughout the entire production cycle, following each step personally. It's a philosophy that comes through in his Cesanese del Piglio wines, and has earned him a place among the appellation's leaders, even in those cases, like this year, when there's no stand out. The 2015 Hernicus wasn't far-off. It opens with a range of black fruit, rhubarb and spices, while its concentrated, elegant palate features fine tannins. As in the past, the 2015 Romanico is further behind (we think it would benefit with a later release, but we understand Antonello's needs because he sells out almost en primeur). The selection is completed with the solid 2015 Cosmato, a varietal Cabernet Franc, and the 2016 Arcadia, which is a Manzoni cross, where powerful alcohol is kept at bay by freshness and richness of flavor.

● Cesanese del Piglio Sup. Hernicus '15	♟♟ 3*
○ Arcadia '16	♟♟ 3
● Cesanese del Piglio Sup. Romanico '15	♟♟ 5
● Cosmato '15	♟♟ 5
● Cesanese del Piglio Romanico '11	♟♟♟ 5
● Cesanese del Piglio Romanico '07	♟♟♟ 5
● Cesanese del Piglio Sup. Hernicus '14	♟♟♟ 3*
● Cesanese del Piglio Sup. Hernicus '12	♟♟♟ 3*
○ Arcadia '15	♟♟ 3
● Cesanese del Piglio Romanico '12	♟♟ 5
● Cesanese del Piglio Sup. Hernicus '13	♟♟ 3
● Cesanese del Piglio Sup. Romanico '14	♟♟ 5
● Cesanese del Piglio Sup. Romanico '13	♟♟ 5
● Cosmato '14	♟♟ 5
○ Passerina del Frusinate Hernicus '14	♟♟ 3

★★Falesco Famiglia Cotarella

S.da St.le Cassia Nord km 94,155
01027 Montefiascone [VT]
Tel. +39 07449556
www.falesco.it

CELLAR SALES
PRE-BOOKED VISITS
ACCOMMODATION
ANNUAL PRODUCTION 3,650,000 bottles
HECTARES UNDER VINE 330.00

The success of the Cotarella family, who've already established a place among the area's leading producers, is unstoppable. Founded by brothers Renzo and Riccardo, today the winery is managed by their daughters. The estate is situated on the volcanic terrain that straddles Lazio and Umbria, with a part of their vineyards in an area that benefits from southern Orvieto's favorable hill climate, while their oldest vineyards grow along Lake Bolsena. Tre Bicchieri for the 2015 Montiano, a long and complex monovarietal Merlot, with notes of black fruit, spices and sweet tobacco. The 2014 Marciliano is a Cabernet with good structure. It's very pleasant and succulent, with notes of red peppers and small black fruit. The 2016 Tellus Syrah has a distinctive spicy palate and cherry aroma. Of the whites, we were impressed by the 2016 Vitiano Vermentino San Pietro, which is balsamic and zesty, with hints of white melon. We also enjoyed the 2016 Est!Est!! Est!!! di Montefiascone 'Poggio dei Gelsi', with its tangy and fresh notes of almond and citrus fruit.

● Montiano '15	♟♟♟ 6
● Marciliano '14	♟♟ 7
○ Appunto '16	♟♟ 2
○ Appunto '16	♟♟ 2
○ Est!Est!!Est!!! di Montefiascone Accenno '16	♟♟ 2
○ Est!Est!!Est!!! di Montefiascone Poggio dei Gelsi '16	♟♟ 2*
● Messidoro '16	♟♟ 2
● Tellus Syrah '16	♟♟ 3
● Trentanni '15	♟♟ 4
○ Vitiano San Pietro '16	♟♟ 2*
⊙ Falesco Brut Rosé M. Cl.	♟ 4
○ Ferentano '15	♟ 4
⊙ Soente '16	♟ 4
⊙ Tellus Rosé '16	♟ 2
● Vitiano '16	♟ 2

Fontana Candida

via Fontana Candida, 11
00040 Monte Porzio Catone [RM]
Tel. +39 069401881
www.fontanacandida.it

CELLAR SALES
PRE-BOOKED VISITS
RESTAURANT SERVICE
ANNUAL PRODUCTION 2,500,000 bottles
HECTARES UNDER VINE 97.00

Fontana Candida is one of Lazio's historic producers. Over the years it has come to be synonymous with Frascati, with the area's native grape varieties a cornerstone of their selection. The winery began bottling in 1958, but it was only when Gruppo Italiano Vini entered the scene that Fontana Candida became the high-profile brand that it is today. And it's been thanks to their ability to take advantage of the characteristics of the area's volcanic terrain that they've been able to raise the bar. Frascatis form the core of the winery's production. The 2016 Frascati Superiore Luna Mater Riserva stands out the most. It's a fragrant wine and full of flavor, with notes of citrus fruit, medlars, apricots and a delicate sage finish. The 2016 Frascati Superiore Vigneto Santa Teresa, which is zesty, with notes of lemon and white fruit, is also top-notch. We see across citrus fruit again in the fresh and aromatic 2016 Malvasia Puntinata. The 2016 Frascati Superiore Terre dei Grifi is simple, and yet it maintains a citrusy supporting acidity, as does the 2016 Frascati Secco.

○ Frascati Sup. Luna Mater Ris. '16	♈♈ 3*
○ Frascati Sup. Vign. Santa Teresa '16	♈♈ 2*
○ Frascati Secco '16	♈ 2
○ Frascati Sup. Terre dei Grifi '16	♈ 2
○ Roma Malvasia Puntinata '16	♈ 3
● Siroe '16	♈ 2
○ Frascati Secco '14	♈♈ 2*
○ Frascati Sup. Luna Mater Ris. '15	♈♈ 3*
○ Frascati Sup. Luna Mater Ris. '14	♈♈ 4
○ Frascati Sup. Terre dei Grifi '15	♈♈ 2*
○ Frascati Sup. Terre dei Grifi '14	♈♈ 2*
○ Frascati Sup. Vign. Santa Teresa '15	♈♈ 2*
○ Roma Malvasia Puntinata '15	♈♈ 3
● Siroe '14	♈♈ 3

Antiche Cantine Migliaccio

via Pizzicato
04027 Ponza [LT]
Tel. +39 3392822252
lucianasabino@libero.it

CELLAR SALES
PRE-BOOKED VISITS
ANNUAL PRODUCTION 10,000 bottles
HECTARES UNDER VINE 3.00

Antiche Cantine Migliaccio's three hectares of vineyards, which stretch across the island, are cultivated with the patience of the ancients and modern techniques. Since the year 2000, when they decided to found their winery on Ponza, Emanuele Vittorio and his wife, Luciana Sabino, have managed to find the right balance between local tradition and modern marketing. The vineyards, which are in part ungrafted, feature native Biancolella, Forastera, Guarnaccia, Aglianico and Piedirosso. A herculean effort is needed to cultivate most of Ponza, with its steep tracks winding through the benchlands. But once again, their wines have proved their excellent quality. The 2016 Fieno di Ponza Bianco is a blend of Biancolella and Forastera, with iodine and citrus aromas, while the palate displays grip, freshness and suppleness. The pleasant and clean 2016 Biancolella di Ponza is tangy and flavorful, with good structure. The 2016 Biancolella Rosato is rich, fleshy and slightly vegetal, with aromas of strawberries and magnolia.

○ Biancolella di Ponza '16	♈♈ 5
○ Fieno di Ponza Bianco '16	♈♈ 4
◉ Fieno di Ponza Rosato '16	♈♈ 4
○ Biancolella di Ponza '15	♈♈ 5
○ Biancolella di Ponza '14	♈♈ 5
○ Biancolella di Ponza '13	♈♈ 5
○ Biancolella di Ponza '12	♈♈ 5
○ Biancolella di Ponza '11	♈♈ 3
○ Fieno di Ponza Bianco '15	♈♈ 4
○ Fieno di Ponza Bianco '14	♈♈ 4
● Fieno di Ponza Rosso '13	♈♈ 4

★Sergio Mottura

LOC. POGGIO DELLA COSTA, 1
01020 CIVITELLA D'AGLIANO [VT]
TEL. +39 0761914533
www.motturasergio.it

CELLAR SALES
PRE-BOOKED VISITS
ACCOMMODATION AND RESTAURANT SERVICE
ANNUAL PRODUCTION 97,000 bottles
HECTARES UNDER VINE 37.00
VITICULTURE METHOD Certified Organic

Respect for typicity and the environment, along with proper management of wood and an ability to confer elegance on his wines have, over the years, made Sergio Mottura a symbol of Grechetto. In addition to the grape, he cultivates other native and international varieties along the clay, calanchi slopes of Civitella d'Agliano, from Procanico to Chardonnay, Montepulciano, Syrah and Pinot Nero. Still at the top of their range is the 2016 Grechetto Poggio della Costa. It's full-bodied, tangy and long, with yellow flowers on the nose, which are integrated on the palate by citrus fruit and chestnut honey. The 2015 Latour Civitella is not far behind. It's round, fresh and tangy, with notes of yellow fruit and sweet spices. The 2010 Sergio Mottura Brut is made with Chardonnay grapes, and is undoubtedly the best sparkling wine in the region. It's a creamy and caressing wine, with notes of peach and crusty bread. The 2016 Orvieto Tragugnano is tangy with notes of thyme and grapefruit, while the 2014 Syracide is fresh and fruity.

○ Poggio della Costa '16	♔♔♔ 3*
○ Grechetto Latour a Civitella '15	♔♔ 5
○ Orvieto Tragugnano '16	♔♔ 3
○ Sergio Mottura Brut M. Cl. '10	♔♔ 5
● Syracide '14	♔♔ 4
○ Civitella Rosato '16	♔ 3
● Civitella Rosso '15	♔ 3
● Nenfro '14	♔ 4
○ Orvieto Secco '16	♔ 3
○ Grechetto Latour a Civitella '11	♔♔♔ 4*
○ Grechetto Poggio della Costa '14	♔♔♔ 3*
○ Poggio della Costa '15	♔♔♔ 3*
○ Poggio della Costa '12	♔♔♔ 3*
○ Poggio della Costa '11	♔♔♔ 3*

Principe Pallavicini

VIA ROMA, 121
00030 COLONNA [RM]
TEL. +39 069438816
www.vinipallavicini.com

CELLAR SALES
PRE-BOOKED VISITS
RESTAURANT SERVICE
ANNUAL PRODUCTION 600,000 bottles
HECTARES UNDER VINE 65.00

The history of the winery goes back to the 1600s, when the Pallavicini, a family of noblemen, purchased the estate in the Castelli Romani. It was the beginning of a long history that, in recent years, has taken on an even greater, more ambitious scope, from enlarging the estate to increased attention for the terroir and its native grape varieties. Sigieri Diaz della Vittoria Pallavicini, who's keeping alive the legacy of his mother, Maria Camilla, was also recently welcomed into the management. The estate is divided into two plots, Colonna (dedicated mostly to Frascati) and Cerveteri (where Sangiovese, Syrah and Merlot are grown). The fresh and tasty varietal wine, the 2016 Roma Malvasia Puntinata, completely respects its typicity. In the absence of the Frascati Superiore Poggi Verde, the 2016 Frascati Secco did very well. It's a bit simple, but fresh and citrusy. The Stillato, made with dried Malvasia Puntinata, is also a solid wine, with its notes of dried apricots and cinnamon, while the 2015 Amarasco proves pleasant, with nice fruit.

● Amarasco '15	♔♔ 3
○ Frascati Secco '16	♔♔ 2*
○ Roma Malvasia Puntinata '16	♔♔ 2*
○ Stillato '15	♔♔ 3
● Casa Romana '13	♔ 5
○ Frascati Sup. Poggio Verde '13	♔♔♔ 2*
● Amarasco '14	♔♔ 3
● Amarasco '11	♔♔ 3
● Casa Romana '12	♔♔ 5
○ Frascati '13	♔♔ 2*
○ Frascati Sup. Poggio Verde '15	♔♔ 2*
○ Frascati Sup. Poggio Verde '14	♔♔ 2*
○ Roma Malvasia Puntinata '15	♔♔ 2*
○ Stillato '13	♔♔ 3*
○ Stillato '12	♔♔ 3

Tenuta La Pazzaglia

S.DA DI BAGNOREGIO, 4
01024 CASTIGLIONE IN TEVERINA [VT]
TEL. +39 0761947114
www.tenutalapazzaglia.it

Pietra Pinta

VIA LE PASTINE KM 20,200
04010 CORI [LT]
TEL. +39 069678001
www.pietrapinta.com

CELLAR SALES
PRE-BOOKED VISITS
ACCOMMODATION
ANNUAL PRODUCTION 56,000 bottles
HECTARES UNDER VINE 12.00

CELLAR SALES
PRE-BOOKED VISITS
ACCOMMODATION AND RESTAURANT SERVICE
ANNUAL PRODUCTION 300,000 bottles
HECTARES UNDER VINE 33.00
VITICULTURE METHOD Certified Organic
SUSTAINABLE WINERY

Tenuta La Pazzaglia was born in 1990, in Castiglione (Teverino), a meeting point between Lazio, Umbria and Tuscany. The winery, which is skillfully run by the Verdecchia family, pursues excellence and development of the territory. Agnese and Randolfo's children were the ones who pushed for native grape varieties (as the winery had previously focused on international cultivar), with Pierfrancesco working the vineyards while his sisters, Maria Teresa and Laura, take care of winemaking and managing the cellar. The 2016 Grechetto 109 is vibrant and flavorsome, with notes of fresh citrus fruit combined with notes of fruit and white flowers. The well-made 2016 Corno is a blend of Grechetto, Chardonnay and Pinot Bianco, with a full flavor and notes of white fruit. The tangy 2015 Grechetto Poggio Triale offers up floral and citrusy aromas, with a lovely supporting acidity. The 2016 Orvieto Vignamia is flavorful and fresh.

Situated right at the foot of the hill leading to Cori, the Ferretti family's cellar and agriturism have, for many years, served as a benchmark in the territory. Here you'll find hospitality, food services, oils (in part for cosmetic products) and, most importantly, wine. As with last year, we think the whites have the edge here. This is especially true for those made with international varieties, which seem to have found their right dimension, including the 2016 Sauvignon varietal and the floral 2016 Viognier. However, it's the 2016 Costa Vecchia Bianco that prevails. It's a successful blend of Chardonnay, Sauvignon and Malvasia Puntinata that brings out the best of each variety. Among the reds, the 2013 Colle Amato confirmed its top quality, where the Nero Buono is brought out by long aging. However, this is lacking in the 2015 Nero Buono and its tannins are still a bit rough at the moment. Both the 2015 Shiraz and the 2016 Costa Vecchia Rosso are good, though we have tasted better versions.

○ Grechetto 109 '16	♟♟♟ 3*
○ Il Corno '16	♟♟ 2*
○ Poggio Triale '15	♟♟♟ 3
● Aurelius '15	♟ 2
○ Orvieto Vignamia '16	♟ 2
● Palagio '15	♟ 2
○ Grechetto 109 '15	♟♟ 3
○ Grechetto 109 '14	♟♟ 3
○ Grechetto 109 '13	♟♟ 3*
○ Il Corno '15	♟♟ 2*
○ Il Corno '14	♟♟ 2*
● Montijone '12	♟♟ 3
○ Poggio Triale '14	♟♟ 3*
○ Poggio Triale '12	♟♟ 3
⊙ Rosé Marie '14	♟♟ 2*

● Colle Amato '13	♟♟ 4
○ Costa Vecchia Bianco '16	♟♟ 2*
○ Chardonnay '16	♟ 2
● Costa Vecchia Rosso '16	♟ 2
○ Malvasia Puntinata '16	♟ 2
● Nero Buono '15	♟ 2
○ Sauvignon '16	♟ 2
● Shiraz '15	♟ 2
○ Viognier '16	♟ 2
○ Chardonnay '15	♟♟ 2
● Colle Amato '12	♟♟ 4
○ Costa Vecchia Bianco '14	♟♟ 2
● Costa Vecchia Rosso '13	♟♟ 2
● Nero Buono '13	♟♟ 2
○ Viognier '15	♟♟ 2

Poggio Le Volpi

VIA COLLE PISANO, 27
00078 MONTE PORZIO CATONE [RM]
TEL. +39 069426980
www.poggiolevolpi.it

CELLAR SALES
PRE-BOOKED VISITS
RESTAURANT SERVICE
ANNUAL PRODUCTION 300,000 bottles
HECTARES UNDER VINE 70.00

Research and experimentation, along with a strong dose of passion, were the engine that drove Felice Mergè, a fourth generation viticulturist, to found his winery in 1990s. He went from producing unbottled wine to bottled varieties, then from producing a local niche selection to making wines that are among the most well-known in the territory. Tre Bicchieri for the 2015 Baccarossa, a monovarietal Nero Buono that offers up notes of ripe black fruit and cherries on the nose, which follow through onto the palate with hints of licorice and sweet spices. The 2016 Frascati Superiore Epos Riserva is less glossy than usual but maintains its typicity, with a fresh palate and good body. Blackberries and plums go hand in hand with nutmeg, cinnamon and tobacco to form the 2015 Sesto 21 Syrah's suite of aromas, while the 2014 Roma Edizione Limitata is rich and full-bodied, though still a bit too woody. The pleasant and well-bodied 2016 Venere is a classic blend of Malvasia Puntinata and Trebbiano.

● Baccarossa '15	▼▼▼ 5
● Roma Ed. Limitata '14	▼▼ 5
○ Frascati Sup. Epos Ris. '16	▼▼ 3
● Sesto 21 '15	▼▼ 5
○ Venere '16	▼▼ 3
● Cupido '14	▼ 5
○ Donnaluce '16	▼ 4
● Panta Rei '15	▼ 5
● Baccarossa '13	♈♈♈ 4*
● Baccarossa '11	♈♈♈ 4*
○ Frascati Sup. Epos '13	♈♈♈ 2*
○ Frascati Sup. Epos '11	♈♈♈ 2*
○ Frascati Sup. Epos Ris. '15	♈♈♈ 3*

San Giovenale

LOC. LA MACCHIA
01010 BLERA [VT]
TEL. +39 066877877
www.sangiovenale.it

CELLAR SALES
PRE-BOOKED VISITS
ACCOMMODATION AND RESTAURANT SERVICE
ANNUAL PRODUCTION 7,000 bottles
HECTARES UNDER VINE 10.00
VITICULTURE METHOD Certified Organic
SUSTAINABLE WINERY

Critical decisions, both in the vineyard and in the cellar, have always been one of Tuscia's distinguishing features, from the realization of an entirely sustainable cellar (with garden roofs, ventilated walls and geothermic temperature control) to the choice to plant international grape varieties, starting with Valle del Rodano. Emanuele Pangrazi's intuition has paid off, and he's been able to create a unique personality for his brand. The 2015 Habemus, a blend of Grenache, Syrah and Carignano, impressed us with its intensity, taste, elegance and complexity. We find cherries, blueberries and pepper in a dense and balanced mix, with well-measured tannins and good supporting acidity. The 2014 Habemus Cabernet is virtually on the same level. It's a monovarietal Franc, with great balance, elegant tannins, a complex and appealing character and a winning freshness on the palate, where the key players are its notes of black wild berries and pepper.

● Habemus '15	▼▼▼ 7
● Habemus Cabernet '14	▼▼ 8
● Habemus '14	♈♈♈ 7
● Habemus '13	♈♈ 7
● Habemus '12	♈♈ 7
● Habemus '11	♈♈ 7
● Habemus '10	♈♈ 4
● Habemus Cabernet '13	♈♈ 8

Tenuta di Fiorano

VIA DI FIORANELLO, 19/31
00134 ROMA
TEL. +39 0679340093
www.tenutadifiorano.it

CELLAR SALES
PRE-BOOKED VISITS
RESTAURANT SERVICE
ANNUAL PRODUCTION 18,000 bottles
HECTARES UNDER VINE 6.00

Tenuta di Fiorano's story is a charming one that began in the 1990s when Alessandrojacopo Boncompagni Ludovisi inherited the right to replant the vineyards of his uncle, Alberico. It may only be six hectares but the estate is a small paradise just outside of Rome. The red grapes are the same they once were, Cabernet Sauvignon and Merlot, while, for the whites, Grechetto and Viognier have replaced Malvasia and Semillon. Tre Bicchieri for the 2012 Fiorano Rosso, which once again proves intense and flavorful. Overtones of small black fruit combine with Mediterranean scrub to provide freshness to a palate made racy by great supporting acidity. The 2015 Fioranello Rosso is pleasant, with notes of small black fruit and spices. The 2015 Fiorano Bianco, on the other hand, exhibits structure and complexity and is juicy, fresh, fruity and spicy. The 2016 Fioranello Bianco sees a simpler structure, but great drinkability and a pleasant citrusy finish.

● Fiorano Rosso '12	▼▼▼	7
○ Fiorano Bianco '15	▼▼	5
○ Fioranello Bianco '16	▼▼	3
● Fioranello Rosso '15	▼▼	4
○ Fiorano Bianco '13	▽▽▽	5
○ Fiorano Bianco '10	▽▽▽	5
● Fiorano Rosso '11	▽▽▽	7
○ Fioranello Bianco '15	▽▽	3
○ Fioranello Bianco '14	▽▽	3
● Fioranello Rosso '14	▽▽	4
○ Fiorano Bianco '14	▽▽	5
○ Fiorano Bianco '11	▽▽	4
● Fiorano Rosso '10	▽▽	7
● Fiorano Rosso '09	▽▽	7

Giovanni Terenzi

FRAZ. LA FORMA
VIA FORESE, 13
03010 SERRONE [FR]
TEL. +39 0775594286
www.viniterenzi.com

CELLAR SALES
PRE-BOOKED VISITS
ANNUAL PRODUCTION 150,000 bottles
HECTARES UNDER VINE 12.00

The Terenzi family have Cesanese in their DNA, and have always supported its cultivation, thanks to their vineyards in Piglio and Olevano Romano. This year they introduced a selection of Cesanese del Piglio that is consistent and even, with the Velobra 2015 standing out from the rest (a surprising feat considering that the wine could be considered the 'younger sibling' of the lot, also in terms of price). The nose is characterized by aromas of red fruit and spices. The palate sees the wine grow in intensity and, while it seems a bit rough around the edges at first, it actually exhibits a nice balance between tannins and alcohol. The 2015 Colle Forma follows tradition, while the concentrated and dark 2015 Vajoscuro needs more time in the bottle to achieve the right balance. The 2013 Quercia Rossa, made with 100% Sangiovese, is less interesting than last year. For the whites, the 2016 Passerina Villa Santa was its usual self, and this year it was joined by the more ambitious and interesting 2015 Zerli, a varietal with hints of citrus fruit and a pleasant freshness to it.

● Cesanese del Piglio Velobra '15	▼▼	3*
● Cesanese del Piglio Sup. Colle Forma '15	▼▼	3
● Cesanese del Piglio Vajoscuro Ris. '15	▼▼	4
○ Passerina Villa Santa '16	▼	2
○ Passerina Zerli '15	▼	4
● Quercia Rossa '13	▼	3
● Cesanese del Piglio Sup. Vajoscuro Ris. '13	▽▽	4
● Cesanese del Piglio Sup. Vajoscuro Ris. '12	▽▽	4
● Cesanese di Olevano Romano Colle S. Quirico '13	▽▽	2*
● Quercia Rossa '12	▽▽	3

Trappolini

VIA DEL RIVELLINO, 65
01024 CASTIGLIONE IN TEVERINA [VT]
TEL. +39 0761948381
www.trappolini.com

CELLAR SALES
PRE-BOOKED VISITS
ANNUAL PRODUCTION 150,000 bottles
HECTARES UNDER VINE 30.00

It was Mario Trappolini who set in motion the family's tradition of winemaking when, in the early 1960s, he started selling the unbottled wine that he produced along the border between Lazio and Umbria. His sons, Roberto and Paolo, kept his legacy alive and transformed the winery (maintaining, however, the selection's foundations in native grape varieties). The Grechetto Terrae Volcani 2016 is a multifaceted wine that reaffirms its position at the top of the production line. Almond, yellow fruit, lemon and sweet spices find length on the palate thanks to freshness and trademark delicate tannins. The 2016 Brecceto, made with Grechetto grapes, is a fleshy and glossy wine, with hints of tangerine and saffron. The 2016 Est!Est!!Est!!! di Montefiascone also impressed, with its aromas of medlars and apricots, while the 2015 Sensi proved structured and rich in fruit. The best reds included the 2015 Paterno, with its freshness and overtones of cherries and sweet spices, and the 2015 Cabernet Franc Terrae Volcani, which brings together notes of peppers and licorice.

○ Brecceto '16	♟♟	3*
○ Grechetto Terrae Volcani '16	♟♟	2*
● Cabernet Franc Terrae Volcani '15	♟♟	3
Cenereto '16	♟♟	2*
○ Est!Est!!Est!!! di Montefiascone '16	♟♟	2*
○ Est!Est!!Est!!! di Montefiascone Sensi '15	♟♟	2*
○ Orvieto '16	♟♟	2*
● Paterno '15	♟♟	4
○ Procanico Terrae Volcani '16	♟♟	2*
Canaiolo Nero '15	♟	2
Idea '16	♟	4
○ Grechetto '14	♟♟♟	2*
○ Grechetto '15	♟♟	2*
○ Procanico '14	♟♟	2*

Valle Vermiglia

VIA A. GRAMSCI, 7
00197 ROMA
TEL. +39 3487221073
www.vallevermiglia.it

CELLAR SALES
ANNUAL PRODUCTION 30,000 bottles
HECTARES UNDER VINE 8.00
SUSTAINABLE WINERY

The story of Valle Vermiglia goes back to the 1950s with Pietro Campilli, who chose the name of a railway station along the Rome-Frascati line for his winery. Mario Masini is keeping his legacy alive, choosing, over the past two decades, to give new life to the family business. He's doing it through the production of a Frascati Superiore called Eremo Tuscolano, which is cultivated on volcanic soil at 600 meters above sea level, on the land of the Camaldolese hermitage of Monte Corona. Unlike previous years, this year saw two different vintages of the Frascati Superiore Eremo Tuscolano, the 2015 and the 2016. The former offers up iodine notes on the nose, with hints of citrus fruit and rosemary, while the palate exhibits body, depth and tanginess. But it was the latter that impressed us most. Alongside citrusy and herby notes, we find white-fleshed fruit and, more importantly, it displays better grip and pressure, which give it length and drinkability.

○ Frascati Sup. Eremo Tuscolano '16	♟♟♟	3*
○ Frascati Sup. Eremo Tuscolano '15	♟♟	3*
○ Frascati Sup. Eremo Tuscolano '13	♟♟♟	3*
○ Frascati Sup. Eremo Tuscolano '14	♟♟	3*
○ Frascati Sup. Eremo Tuscolano '12	♟♟	3*

Casa Divina Provvidenza

VIA DEI FRATI, 58
00048 NETTUNO [RM]
TEL. +39 069851366
www.casadivinaprovvidenza.it

CELLAR SALES
PRE-BOOKED VISITS
RESTAURANT SERVICE
ANNUAL PRODUCTION 100,000 bottles
HECTARES UNDER VINE 35.00
SUSTAINABLE WINERY

○ Dositheo Passito '16	♥♥ 3
○ Moscato '16	♥♥ 4
○ Nettuno Cacchione Neroniano '16	♥♥ 2*
● Cesanese '15	♥ 4

Casale Marchese

VIA DI VERMICINO, 68
00044 FRASCATI [RM]
TEL. +39 069408932
www.casalemarchese.it

CELLAR SALES
PRE-BOOKED VISITS
ANNUAL PRODUCTION 150,000 bottles
HECTARES UNDER VINE 40.00

○ Clemens '15	♥ 3
○ Frascati Sup. '16	♥ 2
● Novum '16	♥ 3

Cantina Sociale Cesanese del Piglio

VIA PRENESTINA, KM 42
03010 PIGLIO [FR]
TEL. +39 0775502356
www.cesanesedelpiglio.it

CELLAR SALES
PRE-BOOKED VISITS
ANNUAL PRODUCTION 450,000 bottles
HECTARES UNDER VINE 18.00

● Cesanese del Piglio Sup. De Antiochia '14	♥♥ 2*
● Cesanese del Piglio Cerciole '15	♥ 2
○ Passerina Contrada Elcini '16	♥ 3

Cordeschi

VIA CASSIA KM 137,400
00121 ACQUAPENDENTE [VT]
TEL. +39 3356953547
www.cantinacordeschi.it

CELLAR SALES
PRE-BOOKED VISITS
ANNUAL PRODUCTION 35,000 bottles
HECTARES UNDER VINE 8.50

● Saino '14	♥♥ 3
● Ost '15	♥ 3
○ Palea '16	♥ 2
⊙ Siele '16	♥ 2

Corte dei Papi

LOC. COLLETONNO
03012 ANAGNI [FR]
TEL. +39 0775769271
www.cortedeipapi.it

CELLAR SALES
PRE-BOOKED VISITS
ANNUAL PRODUCTION 40,000 bottles
HECTARES UNDER VINE 25.00

● Cesanese del Piglio Colle Ticchio '16	♥♥ 2*
● Cesanese del Piglio San Magno '15	♥♥ 4
○ Passerina '16	♥♥ 2*

Paolo e Noemia D'Amico

LOC. PALOMBARO
FRAZ. VAIANO
01024 CASTIGLIONE IN TEVERINA [VT]
TEL. +39 0761948034
www.paoloenoemiadamico.it

CELLAR SALES
PRE-BOOKED VISITS
RESTAURANT SERVICE
ANNUAL PRODUCTION 150,000 bottles
HECTARES UNDER VINE 30.00
SUSTAINABLE WINERY

○ Falesia '15	♥ 5
○ Orvieto Noe dei Calanchi '16	♥ 2
● Villa Tirrena '13	♥ 3

Federici

VIA SANTA APOLLARIA VECCHIA, 30
00039 ZAGAROLO [RM]
TEL. +39 0695461022
www.vinifederici.com

CELLAR SALES
PRE-BOOKED VISITS
ANNUAL PRODUCTION 350,000 bottles
HECTARES UNDER VINE 3.00

- ● Ùle Syrah '15 🍷🍷 3
- ○ Isai '16 🍷🍷 3
- ○ Zagarolo Sup. Le Puche '16 🍷🍷 3
- ● Cesanese del Piglio Sapiens '16 🍷 3

Formiconi

LOC. FARINELLA
00021 AFFILE [RM]
TEL. +39 3470934541
www.cantinaformiconi.it

ANNUAL PRODUCTION 7,500 bottles
HECTARES UNDER VINE 1.80

- ● Cesanese di Affile Cisinianum '15 🍷🍷 3*
- ● Cesanese di Affile Capozzano Ris. '15 🍷 4

Alberto Giacobbe

C.DA COLLE SAN GIOVENALE
03018 PALIANO [FR]
TEL. +39 3298738052
www.vinigiacobbe.it

CELLAR SALES
PRE-BOOKED VISITS
ACCOMMODATION
ANNUAL PRODUCTION 25,000 bottles
HECTARES UNDER VINE 10.00

- ● Cesanese del Piglio Sup. Lepanto Ris. '14 🍷🍷 5
- ○ Passerina Maddalena '15 🍷🍷 3
- ● Cesanese di Olevano Romano Sup. Giacobbe '15 🍷 3

Donato Giangirolami

FRAZ. LE FERRIERE
VIA DEL CAVALIERE, 1414
04100 LATINA
TEL. +39 3358394890
www.donatogiangirolami.it

CELLAR SALES
PRE-BOOKED VISITS
ANNUAL PRODUCTION 80,000 bottles
HECTARES UNDER VINE 38.00
VITICULTURE METHOD Certified Organic

- ○ Propizio '16 🍷🍷 2*
- ○ Regius '16 🍷🍷 2*
- ● Pancarpo '14 🍷 3
- ● Prodigo '15 🍷 2

Gotto d'Oro

LOC. FRATTOCCHIE
VIA DEL DIVINO AMORE, 115
00040 MARINO [RM]
TEL. +39 0693022211
www.gottodoro.it

CELLAR SALES
PRE-BOOKED VISITS
ANNUAL PRODUCTION 9,000,000 bottles
HECTARES UNDER VINE 1400.00

- ● Mitreo Mithra '15 🍷🍷 2*
- ● Petit Verdot Vinea Domini '15 🍷 2
- ○ Roma Bianco '15 🍷 2
- ● Roma Rosso '15 🍷 2

Antica Cantina Leonardi

VIA DEL PINO, 12
01027 MONTEFIASCONE [VT]
TEL. +39 0761826028
www.cantinaleonardi.it

CELLAR SALES
PRE-BOOKED VISITS
ACCOMMODATION
ANNUAL PRODUCTION 100,000 bottles
HECTARES UNDER VINE 37.00
VITICULTURE METHOD Certified Organic

- ● Don Carlo '14 🍷🍷 2*
- ○ Est!Est!!Est!!! di Montefiascone Poggio del Cardinale '16 🍷🍷 2*
- ○ Pensiero '16 🍷🍷 2*

Cantine Lupo

FRAZ. CAMPOVERDE
VIA MEDIANA CISTERNA, 27
04011 APRILIA [LT]
TEL. +39 0692902455
www.cantinelupo.com

CELLAR SALES
PRE-BOOKED VISITS
ANNUAL PRODUCTION 100,000 bottles
HECTARES UNDER VINE 18.00

● Perseide '13		▼▼ 5
○ Terra Marique '16		▼▼ 2*
● Luporosso '16		▼ 2
● Primolupo '15		▼ 3

L'Olivella

VIA DI COLLE PISANO, 5
00044 FRASCATI [RM]
TEL. +39 069424527
www.racemo.it

CELLAR SALES
PRE-BOOKED VISITS
ANNUAL PRODUCTION 68,000 bottles
HECTARES UNDER VINE 1.00
VITICULTURE METHOD Certified Organic

○ Frascati Sup. Racemo '16		▼▼ 3
○ Bombino Diverso '16		▼ 2
○ Frascati Sup. Tre Grome Ris. '14		▼ 3
● Pivot '11		▼ 6

Antonella Pacchiarotti

VIA ROMA, 14
01024 GROTTE DI CASTRO [VT]
TEL. +39 0763796852
www.vinipacchiarotti.it

CELLAR SALES
PRE-BOOKED VISITS
ANNUAL PRODUCTION 10,000 bottles
HECTARES UNDER VINE 3.50
SUSTAINABLE WINERY

● Cavarosso '16		▼▼ 3
○ Ramatico '16		▼▼ 3
○ Matèe '16		▼ 3

Petrucca e Vela

LOC. COCE
03010 PIGLIO [FR]
TEL. +39 0775501032
www.cesanese.it

CELLAR SALES
PRE-BOOKED VISITS
ANNUAL PRODUCTION 45,000 bottles
HECTARES UNDER VINE 7.50
SUSTAINABLE WINERY

● Cesanese del Piglio Nerva '15		▼▼ 3
● Cesanese del Piglio Sup. Tellures Ris. '12		▼ 5
● Cifione '14		▼ 3

Proietti

LOC. CAMPO
VIA MAREMMANA SUPERIORE, KM 2,800
00035 OLEVANO ROMANO [RM]
TEL. +39 069563376
www.aziendaagricolaproietti.it

CELLAR SALES
PRE-BOOKED VISITS
ANNUAL PRODUCTION 80,000 bottles
HECTARES UNDER VINE 11.00

● Cesanese di Olevano Romano Tenuta al Campo Ris. '12		▼▼ 2*
● Cesanese di Olevano Romano Tenuta al Campo Sup. '15		▼ 2

Tenuta Ronci di Nepi

VIA RONCI, 2072
01036 NEPI [VT]
TEL. +39 0761555125
www.roncidinepi.it

CELLAR SALES
PRE-BOOKED VISITS
ANNUAL PRODUCTION 100,000 bottles
HECTARES UNDER VINE 17.00

○ Chardonnay Manti '15		▼▼ 4
○ Grechetto '16		▼ 3
○ Oro di Nè '16		▼ 3
● Veste Porpora '15		▼ 3

Le Rose

VIA PONTE TRE ARMI, 25
00045 GENZANO DI ROMA [RM]
TEL. +39 0693709671
www.aziendaagricolalerose.com

CELLAR SALES
PRE-BOOKED VISITS
ANNUAL PRODUCTION 70,000 bottles
HECTARES UNDER VINE 10.00
VITICULTURE METHOD Certified Organic
SUSTAINABLE WINERY

○ la Faiola '16	♥♥ 5
○ Artemisia '16	♥ 4
○ Colle dei Marmi '15	♥ 5

Cantine San Marco

LOC. VERMICINO
VIA DI MOLA CAVONA, 26/28
00044 FRASCATI [RM]
TEL. +39 069409403
www.sanmarcofrascati.it

CELLAR SALES
PRE-BOOKED VISITS
ANNUAL PRODUCTION 1,500,000 bottles
HECTARES UNDER VINE 32.00

● Solo Shiraz '15	♥♥ 3
○ Bellone De Notari '16	♥ 2
● Cesanese De Notari '15	♥ 2
● Roma Rosso Romae '14	♥ 2

Sant'Andrea

LOC. BORGO VODICE
VIA RENIBBIO, 1720
04019 TERRACINA [LT]
TEL. +39 0773755028
www.cantinasantandrea.it

CELLAR SALES
PRE-BOOKED VISITS
ANNUAL PRODUCTION 1,000,000 bottles
HECTARES UNDER VINE 85.00

● Circeo Rosso Riflessl '16	♥♥ 2*
○ Oppidum Brut '16	♥♥ 2*
○ Circeo Bianco Riflessi '16	♥ 2

Tenuta Sant'Isidoro

LOC. PORTACCIA
01016 TARQUINIA [VT]
TEL. +39 0766869716
www.santisidoro.net

CELLAR SALES
PRE-BOOKED VISITS
ANNUAL PRODUCTION 65,000 bottles
HECTARES UNDER VINE 57.00

● Soremidio '13	♥♥ 4
● Corithus '15	♥ 2
○ Forca di Palma '16	♥ 2
○ Soraluisa '16	♥ 3

Stefanoni

LOC. ZEPPONAMI
VIA STEFANONI, 48
01027 MONTEFIASCONE [VT]
TEL. +39 0761825651
www.cantinastefanoni.it

CELLAR SALES
PRE-BOOKED VISITS
ANNUAL PRODUCTION 100,000 bottles
HECTARES UNDER VINE 10.00

○ Aleatico Colle de' Poggeri '16	♥♥ 2*
○ Est!Est!!Est!!! di Montefiascone Cl. Foltone '16	♥ 2
○ Moscato Colle de' Poggeri '16	♥ 2

Tenuta Le Quinte

VIA DELLE MARMORELLE, 71
00040 MONTECOMPATRI [RM]
TEL. +39 069438756
www.tenutalequinte.it

CELLAR SALES
PRE-BOOKED VISITS
ANNUAL PRODUCTION 250,000 bottles
HECTARES UNDER VINE 20.00

● Primula Lucis '15	♥♥ 2*
● Rasa di Marmorata '15	♥♥ 2*
● Onicorosso '15	♥ 2
● Syrah Nasyr '15	♥ 4

Terra delle Ginestre

S.DA ST.LE 630 AUSONIA, 59
04020 SPIGNO SATURNIA [LT]
TEL. +39 3495617153
www.terradelleginestre.it

CELLAR SALES
PRE-BOOKED VISITS
ANNUAL PRODUCTION 15,000 bottles
HECTARES UNDER VINE 4.00

● Il Generale '15	🍷🍷	3
○ Lentisco '15	🍷🍷	3

Tre Botti

S.DA DELLA POGGETTA, 9
01024 CASTIGLIONE IN TEVERINA [VT]
TEL. +39 07611986704
www.trebotti.it

CELLAR SALES
PRE-BOOKED VISITS
ACCOMMODATION
ANNUAL PRODUCTION 45,000 bottles
HECTARES UNDER VINE 10.00
VITICULTURE METHOD Certified Organic
SUSTAINABLE WINERY

⊙ 3Brosé '16	🍷🍷	2*
● Bludom Passito '16	🍷	3
● Castiglionero '15	🍷	2
○ Orvieto Sup. Incanthus '16	🍷	2

Villa Caviciana

LOC. TOJENA CAVICIANA
01025 GROTTE DI CASTRO [VT]
TEL. +39 0763798212
www.villacaviciana.com

CELLAR SALES
PRE-BOOKED VISITS
ANNUAL PRODUCTION 25,000 bottles
HECTARES UNDER VINE 16.00
VITICULTURE METHOD Certified Biodynamic

● Letizia '14	🍷🍷	6
● Eleonora '15	🍷	4
● Faustina '14	🍷	7
⊙ Tadzio '16	🍷	3

Villa Gianna

LOC. BORGO SAN DONATO
S.DA MAREMMANA
04010 SABAUDIA [LT]
TEL. +39 0773250034
www.villagianna.it

PRE-BOOKED VISITS
ACCOMMODATION
ANNUAL PRODUCTION 1,000,000 bottles
HECTARES UNDER VINE 45.00
SUSTAINABLE WINERY

● Barriano '14	🍷🍷	2*
○ Circeo Bianco Innato '16	🍷🍷	2*
○ Circeo Bianco Nobilvite '16	🍷	2
● Vigne del Borgo Cabernet Sauvignon '16	🍷	2

Villa Simone

VIA FRASCATI COLONNA, 29
00078 MONTE PORZIO CATONE [RM]
TEL. +39 069449717
www.villasimone.it

CELLAR SALES
PRE-BOOKED VISITS
ANNUAL PRODUCTION 200,000 bottles
HECTARES UNDER VINE 21.00
SUSTAINABLE WINERY

○ Frascati Sup. Vign. Filonardi '16	🍷🍷	3
○ Frascati Sup. Villa dei Preti '16	🍷🍷	3
● Cesanese del Piglio '15	🍷	3
● Ferro e Seta '13	🍷	5

Cantine Volpetti

VIA NETTUNENSE, 21
00040 ARICCIA [RM]
TEL. +39 069342000
www.cantinevolpetti.it

CELLAR SALES
PRE-BOOKED VISITS
ANNUAL PRODUCTION 450,000 bottles
HECTARES UNDER VINE 40.00

● Sangiovese Le Piantate '14	🍷🍷	2*
● Cesanese Le Piantate '15	🍷	2
○ Frascati Sup. Le Piantate '15	🍷	2
○ Malvasia del Lazio '16	🍷	3

ABRUZZO

The days when Abruzzo felt like a footnote to our national conversation about winemaking excellence seem like a distant memory. To be clear, a large share of its grapes are still used for bulk wine bottled outside the region, but its reputation and identity are getting stronger by the year, as are its future prospects. Many experts and wine lovers know how good things can get here (especially when it comes to protecting your wallet). And we're not just talking about the region's basic wines, the same holds for those versions that offer more in terms of expressive and gastronomic versatility. There really is something for everyone: Apennine and Mediterranean wines, traditional and modern. There are wines made with classic methods or more artisanal ones, like spontaneous fermentation, maceration with skin contact (including whites), aging in concrete or terra-cotta, and everything in between. And its multitude of interpretations are reflected by the wineries themselves. There are both historic producers and emerging producers, small artisans and brands with production volumes in the millions. And of course we shouldn't forget the role (social before commercial) of Abruzzo's numerous cooperative wineries, which have consistently produced high quality selections. Nor should we overlook that significant slice of producers who are following the 'naturale' movement, and not just in terms of viticulture, but also by adhering to principles of energy conservation and sustainability. It's a philosophic polyphony that turned up serious results during the last round of tasting. In fact, among the list of those recognized, we see the region's territories more or less equally represented, thanks to a series of favorable seasons. 2013 was a good one for long living Montepulcianos, with Santa Maria d'Orni's Ursonia del Feuduccio debuting in the Tre Bicchieri club. Then there's the 2015-2016 Trebbiano and Pecorino whites, which see Feudo Antico's superb 2015 Casadonna earning top-honors for the first time. But the real corker in this edition is Cerasuolo, which delivered on a scale possibly never seen before. Also known as the reddest of the rosés, it gave rise to Montori's 2016 Fonte Cupa, a wine that earned the family the first Tre Bicchieri of its glorious history.

Agriverde

LOC. CALDARI
VIA STORTINI, 32A
66026 ORTONA [CH]
TEL. +39 0859032101
www.agriverde.it

CELLAR SALES
PRE-BOOKED VISITS
RESTAURANT SERVICE
ANNUAL PRODUCTION 900,000 bottles
HECTARES UNDER VINE 65.00
VITICULTURE METHOD Certified Organic
SUSTAINABLE WINERY

In 1830 Camillo Di Carlo announced to his father that the family, one of the oldest winemakers in Abruzzo, had exported its first wine. Giannicola inherited this legacy in the 1980s, and it was he who oversaw the conversion of the family's vineyards to organic. And so the estate, which includes plots in Caldari, Ortona, Rogatti, Frisa and Crecchio, experienced a veritable rebirth. From its vineyards to the architecture of its cellar, its relais and spa, Agriverde stands as benchmark for its environmentally friendly philosophy (and, naturally, for its multivariate selection of wines made with Montepulciano, Pecorino, Trebbiano and Passerina). Their wines are organized into different lines: Eikos, Piano di Maggio, Riseis, Solàrea and Natum Biovegan. The strength of their selection makes itself known once again, with some seven wines rated over Due bicchieri. One of these was the Riseis Pecorino 2016, a wine of distinctive graininess. Then there's the threesome of Montepulcianos: Piane di Maggio 2016 (an earthy and essential wine), the Eikos 2015 (very spicy), and the Solàrea 2013 (more mature and austere).

⊙ Cerasuolo d'Abruzzo Solàrea '16	🍷🍷	3
● Montepulciano d'Abruzzo Eikos '15	🍷🍷	3
● Montepulciano d'Abruzzo Piane di Maggio '16	🍷🍷	2*
● Montepulciano d'Abruzzo Solàrea '13	🍷🍷	4
○ Passerina Riseis '16	🍷🍷	3
○ Pecorino Eikos '16	🍷🍷	3
○ Pecorino Riseis '16	🍷🍷	3
⊙ Cerasuolo d'Abruzzo Natum '16	🍷	2
○ Trebbiano d'Abruzzo Piane di Maggio '16	🍷	2
● Montepulciano d'Abruzzo Plateo '04	🍷🍷🍷	6
● Montepulciano d'Abruzzo Plateo '01	🍷🍷🍷	6
● Montepulciano d'Abruzzo Plateo '00	🍷🍷🍷	6
● Montepulciano d'Abruzzo Plateo '98	🍷🍷🍷	5
● Montepulciano d'Abruzzo Solàrea '03	🍷🍷🍷	4

Barone Cornacchia

C.DA TORRI, 19
64010 TORANO NUOVO [TE]
TEL. +39 0861887412
www.baronecornacchia.it

CELLAR SALES
PRE-BOOKED VISITS
ACCOMMODATION
ANNUAL PRODUCTION 250,000 bottles
HECTARES UNDER VINE 50.00
VITICULTURE METHOD Certified Organic

Along with their father, Piero, it's Filippo and Caterina Cornacchia's turn to oversee the prestigious agricultural estates around Fortezza di Civitella. The family later moved to the hunting grounds in the district of Torri di Torano Nuovo, on the Colline Teramane hills, where today their cellar and most of their 50 hectares of vineyards are located. Their estate, which is certificated organic (a change that was sought after by the latest generation), sees the cultivation of Pecorino, Trebbiano and Passerina. These give life to a natural selection of whites, though the producer's Montepulcianos are their most ambitious wines, with some nine versions. Among these is the Vizzarro 2013. With a tertiary profile that features topsoil and tobacco, it manages to maintain its thickness through its austere palate. The class of 2016 also shines, from the Trebbiano, with its honey and mimosa flavors, to the Pecorino Villa Torri, which is all ginger and tubers, with a felicitous combination of sweetness and vigor. The Cerasuolo also performed superbly.

⊙ Cerasuolo d'Abruzzo Sup. '16	🍷🍷	2*
○ Controguerra Pecorino Villa Torri '16	🍷🍷	2*
● Montepulciano d'Abruzzo Colline Teramane Vizzarro '13	🍷🍷	5
○ Trebbiano d'Abruzzo Sup. '16	🍷🍷	2*
● Montepulciano d'Abruzzo Bio '15	🍷	2
⊙ Cerasuolo d'Abruzzo Sup. '15	🍷🍷	2*
○ Controguerra Passerina Villa Torri '15	🍷🍷	2*
○ Controguerra Pecorino Villa Torri '15	🍷🍷	2*
● Montepulciano d'Abruzzo Colline Teramane Vizzarro '12	🍷🍷	5
● Montepulciano d'Abruzzo Poggio Varano '12	🍷🍷	3
● Montepulciano d'Abruzzo Poggio Varano - Antico Feudo '13	🍷🍷	3
● Montepulciano d'Abruzzo V. Le Coste '12	🍷🍷	3*

Nestore Bosco

C.DA CASALI, 147
65010 NOCCIANO [PE]
TEL. +39 085847345
www.nestorebosco.com

CELLAR SALES
PRE-BOOKED VISITS
ANNUAL PRODUCTION 600,000 bottles
HECTARES UNDER VINE 75.00

Cavalier Bosco's wines are divided into five lines: Eclipse, Storica, Classica, Donna Bosco and Le Riserve. Today, the winery, which takes its name from the man who founded it in the late 1800s, is being run by Giovanni. Along with his children, Nestore and Stefania, he manages more than 70 hectares of vineyards on the Colli Pescaresi hills. Most of these are concentrated in Casali di Nocciano, where his picturesque bottle cave is also situated. And it's here that the winery ages its most important Montepulciano reds, which are interpreted in a variety of ways and skillfully crafted for lengthy aging. Their rosés and Pecorino, Passerina and Trebbiano whites, on the other hand, are characterized by a more approachable style. All that was missing was the cherry on the cake for one of the Bosco family's best performances of all time. Summer fruit, ginger, black pepper ... The Cerasuolo Superiore 2016 offers up a classic profile that's well-sustained by a full-flavored backbone. A complementary style can be found in the Montepulciano Donna Bosco 2015 and R 2014, both of which shine.

Cerasuolo d'Abruzzo Sup. '16	♟♟ 3*
Montepulciano d'Abruzzo Donna Bosco '15	♟♟ 3
Montepulciano d'Abruzzo R '14	♟♟ 3
Pecorino Donna Bosco '16	♟♟ 2*
Montepulciano d'Abruzzo '14	♟ 2
Montepulciano d'Abruzzo Don Bosco Ris. '13	♟ 4
Montepulciano d'Abruzzo Pan Ris. '13	♟ 4
Pecorino '16	♟ 3
Rosato Donna Bosco '16	♟ 2
Trebbiano d'Abruzzo Sup. '16	♟ 3
Cerasuolo d'Abruzzo Sup. '15	♟♟ 3
Montepulciano d'Abruzzo Donna Bosco '14	♟♟ 3
Montepulciano d'Abruzzo Nestore Bosco '13	♟♟ 4

Castorani

C.DA ORATORIO
VIA CASTORANI, 5
65020 AI ANNO [PE]
TEL. +39 3466355635
www.castorani.it

CELLAR SALES
PRE-BOOKED VISITS
ANNUAL PRODUCTION 1,000,000 bottles
HECTARES UNDER VINE 72.00
VITICULTURE METHOD Certified Organic

Raffaele Castorani founded this winery back in 1793. Then it was owned by the illustrious professor Antonio Casulli, before being taken over by a group of partners and friends, including the former racing driver, Jarno Trulls. In just a few years they've transformed it into one of the most important producers in the region. It all starts with their more than 70 hectares of organically cultivated vineyards on the hills around Alanno. The grapes are then transformed into a rich selection that highlights the attributes of Abruzzo's principal varieties. Coste delle Plaie, Le Paranze, Majolica, Podere Castorani, Cadetto, Jarno, Rocco, Paparazzi - there's a wine for every taste and wallet. Yet another superb performance for Castorani with its rustic mountain profile of white fruit and flowering meadows. Pecorino Amorino 2016 delivers for its purity and vigor, while the Montepulciano Cadetto 2015 comes through for the typicity of its sooty hints. But, once again, the star of the show is their Montepulciano Amorino 2013.

● Montepulciano d'Abruzzo Amorino '13	♟♟♟ 3*
○ Abruzzo Pecorino Sup. Amorino '16	♟♟ 3*
● Montepulciano d'Abruzzo Cadetto '15	♟♟ 2*
● Montepulciano d'Abruzzo Podere Castorani Ris. '13	♟♟ 5
○ Trebbiano d'Abruzzo Coste delle Plaie '16	♟♟ 3
○ Trebbiano d'Abruzzo Majolica '16	♟♟ 1*
○ Trebbiano d'Abruzzo Podere Castorani '15	♟♟ 3
⊙ Cerasuolo d'Abruzzo Costa delle Plaie '16	♟ 3
○ Jarno Bianco '14	♟ 5
● Rocco Rosso '14	♟ 4
○ Trebbiano d'Abruzzo Cadetto '16	♟ 2
● Montepulciano d'Abruzzo Amorino '12	♟♟♟ 3*
● Montepulciano d'Abruzzo Amorino '10	♟♟♟ 3*

★Luigi Cataldi Madonna

LOC. PIANO
67025 OFENA [AQ]
TEL. +39 0862954252
www.cataldimadonna.com

CELLAR SALES
PRE-BOOKED VISITS
ANNUAL PRODUCTION 240,000 bottles
HECTARES UNDER VINE 31.00
SUSTAINABLE WINERY

The area of Ofena is one of the most productive in Aquila. Since World War II it has been a national leader in terms of production volume. And yet the Cataldi Madonna family found itself practically alone in Alto Tirino's viticulture sector when it began bottling in 1975 (after more than 50 years in agriculture). Luigi (accompanied by his daughter, Giulia) has further established the family's presence. Their talent for interpreting wines is inscribed in their entire selection (which is based on Montepulciano, Pecorino and Trebbiano grapes). Their wines are designed to evolve over time, but can be appreciated for their zestful vigor and gastronomic versatility even when young. We find precisely these characteristics in their Piè delle Vigne 2015, the 'reddest' of the Cerasuolos in terms of aromatic stratification (blueberry, orange and topsoil) as well as a close-knit, yet dynamic weave, with delicious iodine touches in the finish. But the Montepulciano Tonì 2013, which goes all in on spices and woodland herbs, had a big day as well.

⊙ Cerasuolo d'Abruzzo Piè delle Vigne '15	♔♔♔ 3*
● Montepulciano d'Abruzzo Tonì '13	♔♔ 6
● Montepulciano d'Abruzzo Malandrino '15	♔♔ 3
○ Pecorino Giulia '16	♔♔ 2*
⊙ Cataldino '16	♔ 2
⊙ Cerasuolo d'Abruzzo '16	♔ 2
○ Trebbiano d'Abruzzo '16	♔ 2
● Montepulciano d'Abruzzo Malandrino '13	♔♔♔ 3*
● Montepulciano d'Abruzzo Malandrino '12	♔♔♔ 3*
● Montepulciano d'Abruzzo Tonì '07	♔♔♔ 5
○ Pecorino '11	♔♔♔ 5
○ Pecorino '10	♔♔♔ 5
○ Pecorino Frontone '13	♔♔♔ 5

Centorame

FRAZ. CASOLO DI ATRI
VIA DELLE FORNACI, 15
64030 ATRI [TE]
TEL. +39 0858709115
www.centorame.it

CELLAR SALES
PRE-BOOKED VISITS
ANNUAL PRODUCTION 100,000 bottles
HECTARES UNDER VINE 12.00
SUSTAINABLE WINERY

The more than 10 hectares of vineyards managed by Lamberto Vannucci (and family) are concentrated in the heart of the Calanchi Nature Reserve. Here, among the ominous clay hills eroded by water and time and just a few kilometers from the Adriatic, we find Casale d'Atri (Teramo). Such pedoclimatic particularities are brought out in Centorame's sunny and earthy selection of wines made with Montepulciano, Trebbiano, Pecorino and Passerina grapes. These are divided into various lines according to their enological makeup: San Michele, Scuderie Ducali and Castellum Vetus. In recent vintages, they've been joined by experiments without added sulphur that go under the name Liberamente. The Montepulciano San Michele 2015 showed the best direction in this series of tastings, unfolding warmly and flavorfully across an austere palate. With its black fruit, plowed earth, undergrowth and spiciness, goût de terroir is an understatement here. The caressing and supple Pecorino Tuapina 2016 had an outstanding day as well.

● Montepulciano d'Abruzzo San Michele '15	♔♔
○ Tuapina Pecorino '16	♔♔
⊙ Cerasuolo d'Abruzzo San Michele '16	♔
● Montepulciano d'Abruzzo Liberamente '16	♔
● Montepulciano d'Abruzzo Scuderie Ducali '15	♔
○ Scuderie Ducali Pecorino '16	♔
○ Trebbiano d'Abruzzo Castellum Vetus '15	♔
○ Trebbiano d'Abruzzo San Michele '16	♔
⊙ Cerasuolo d'Abruzzo San Michele '15	♔♔
● Montepulciano d'Abruzzo San Michele '11	♔♔
● Montepulciano d'Abruzzo San Michele '10	♔♔
● Montepulciano d'Abruzzo San Michele '09	♔♔
● Montepulciano d'Abruzzo Scuderie Ducali '14	♔♔
○ Trebbiano d'Abruzzo San Michele '15	♔♔

Cirelli

LOC. TRECIMINIERE
VIA COLLE SAN GIOVANNI, 1
64032 ATRI [TE]
TEL. +39 0858700106
www.agricolacirelli.com

CELLAR SALES
PRE-BOOKED VISITS
ACCOMMODATION AND RESTAURANT SERVICE
ANNUAL PRODUCTION 26,000 bottles
HECTARES UNDER VINE 5.00
VITICULTURE METHOD Certified Organic

Francesco Cirelli needed fewer than 15 years to establish himself as one of Abruzzo's most promising vine growers. He brings his strong advocacy of the new 'naturale' movement to his management of five hectares of vineyards in Treciminiere di Atri, a part of the Colline Teramane that's famous for its majestic 'calanchi' (clay hills). Montepulciano, Cerasuolo and Trebbiano are offered in two lines. A colored amphora on the label means the wine was worked in terra-cotta while the screw caps are used for their Collina Biologica organic wines. In both cases, spontaneous fermentation and a style that is, in many ways, could be called 'jazzy' make for wines that prefer freedom of expression and flavor to formal structure. It's a framework that proves useful for capturing a Montepulciano 2016 that's compressed in its fruit and biting tannins, but still endowed with structure. The Cerasuolo of the same year is easier to read (also from La Collina Biologica): orange and ginger balance the occasional trace of fermentation. A dry, vertical mouth, shows no signs of any stray bitterness.

○ Cerasuolo d'Abruzzo La Collina Biologica '16	🏆🏆 2*
● Montepulciano d'Abruzzo La Collina Biologica '16	🏆🏆 2*
○ Pecorino La Collina Biologica '16	🏆 3
○ Trebbiano d'Abruzzo Amphora '16	🏆 5
○ Trebbiano d'Abruzzo La Collina Biologica '16	🏆 2
○ Cerasuolo d'Abruzzo Amphora '15	🏆🏆 5
○ Cerasuolo d'Abruzzo La Collina Biologica '15	🏆🏆 2*
● Montepulciano d'Abruzzo '14	🏆🏆 2*
○ Montepulciano d'Abruzzo Cerasuolo Amphora '14	🏆🏆 5
● Montepulciano d'Abruzzo La Collina Biologica '15	🏆🏆 2*
○ Trebbiano d'Abruzzo '15	🏆🏆 2*
○ Trebbiano d'Abruzzo Amphora '14	🏆🏆 5

Codice Citra

C.DA CUCULLO
66026 ORTONA [CH]
TEL. +39 0859031342
www.citra.it

CELLAR SALES
PRE-BOOKED VISITS
ANNUAL PRODUCTION 18,000,000 bottles
HECTARES UNDER VINE 6000.00

It's not just production volumes that make Codice Citra a veritable giant in Abruzzo's wine sector (6000 hectares of vineyards managed by 3000 growers with more than 18 million bottles of wine produced annually). Indeed, for some time, nine of the most important cooperative wineries in Chieti have been held together by a common vision: privileging the human dimension before production, in part through continued initiatives. One example was a contest for amateur chefs working for the cooperatives, whose recipes are gathered and available on the winery's blog, thus promoting the gastronomic attributes of the entire selection of wines (made with Montepulciano, Trebbiano, Pecorino and Passerina). Year after year, the selection continues to further establish itself, as demonstrated by the pair of Ferzos that made it to the finals. The Pecorino 2016 is accurate and vivacious, though somewhat latent by aromas that can be traced back to yeast. The Cerasuolo of the same year is even springier on the nose and balanced on the palate.

○ Abruzzo Pecorino Sup. Ferzo '16	🏆🏆 2*
○ Cerasuolo d'Abruzzo Sup. Ferzo '16	🏆🏆 3*
● Montepulciano d'Abruzzo Caroso Ris. '11	🏆🏆 4
● Montepulciano d'Abruzzo Ferzo '15	🏆🏆 3
● Montepulciano d'Abruzzo Laus Vitae Ris. '10	🏆 5
○ Abruzzo Pecorino Sup. Ferzo '15	🏆🏆 2*
○ La Volpe all'Uva Pecorino '12	🏆🏆 3*
● Montepulciano d'Abruzzo Aulicus '12	🏆🏆 3*
⊙ Montepulciano d'Abruzzo Cerasuolo Omen '14	🏆🏆 3
⊙ Montepulciano d'Abruzzo Cerasuolo Palio '14	🏆🏆 2*
● Montepulciano d'Abruzzo Palio '12	🏆🏆 2*
○ Pecorino Palio '14	🏆🏆 2*
○ Trebbiano d'Abruzzo Palio '14	🏆🏆 2*

Collefrisio

LOC. PIANE DI MAGGIO
66030 FRISA [CH]
TEL. +39 0859039074
www.collefrisio.it

CELLAR SALES
PRE-BOOKED VISITS
ANNUAL PRODUCTION 500,000 bottles
HECTARES UNDER VINE 50.00
VITICULTURE METHOD Certified Organic
SUSTAINABLE WINERY

Amedeo De Luca and Antonio Patricelli's
partnership at Collefrisio gets stronger by
the vintage. The winery, which comprises 50
hectares of vineyards divided into three
principal estates, pays homage to the
tradition of wine production here in Frisa, a
hamlet of the Colline Teatine. Mostly
Montepulciano and Trebbiano are grown on
the estates of Valle del Moro and Morrecine,
which face the sea. The slopes of Giuliano
Teatino experience the influence of the
Majella mountain and Venne river to a
greater degree, making them better suited
to the cultivation of Pecorino and other white
varieties. It's a patchwork of soil profiles and
ampelography that are brought together in a
multifaceted selection of wines. Even if it's
been reorganized, Collefrisio's selection
managed to get our attention in the last
round of tasting. Thanks must be given,
especially, to their Montepulciano 2015.
Rather classic in its notes of black pepper,
forest plants and mushrooms, the wine
reconveys these through a palate made
rigorous by its tannins. The Morrecine of the
same vintage is more estery.

● Montepulciano d'Abruzzo '15	▼▼ 2*
● Montepulciano d'Abruzzo Morrecine '15	▼ 2
● Montepulciano d'Abruzzo '14	▼▼ 2*
● Montepulciano d'Abruzzo '11	▼▼ 2*
⊙ Montepulciano d'Abruzzo Cerasuolo '14	▼▼ 2*
● Montepulciano d'Abruzzo Collefrisio di Collefrisio '08	▼▼ 5
● Montepulciano d'Abruzzo Morrecine '13	▼▼ 2*
● Montepulciano d'Abruzzo Morrecine '12	▼▼ 2*
● Montepulciano d'Abruzzo Morrecine '09	▼▼ 2*
● Montepulciano d'Abruzzo Morrecine '08	▼▼ 2*
● Montepulciano d'Abruzzo Vignaquadra '12	▼▼ 3
● Montepulciano d'Abruzzo Zero '11	▼▼ 2*
○ Pecorino Vignaquadra '14	▼▼ 2*
○ Trebbiano d'Abruzzo Filarè '15	▼▼ 2*
○ Trebbiano d'Abruzzo Vignaquadra '11	▼▼ 3*

Contesa

LOC. CAPARRONE
S.DA DELLE VIGNE, 28
65010 COLLECORVINO [PE]
TEL. +39 0858205078
www.contesa.it

CELLAR SALES
PRE-BOOKED VISITS
RESTAURANT SERVICE
ANNUAL PRODUCTION 260,000 bottles
HECTARES UNDER VINE 42.00
SUSTAINABLE WINERY

Two disagreements led to the founding of
Rocco Pasetti's winery: a land dispute that
involved his grandfather, Antonio, in the
early 1900s, and a family argument in 2000
that incited him to start his own business.
Situated in Collecorvino, in the sub zone of
Terre dei Vestini, the winery oversees most
of the 40 hectares of vineyards here (from a
point where, at 250 meters above sea level,
the Adriatic is visible). Traditional, local
grape varieties are cultivated on almost all
of the plots, giving life to a selection that
knows no weak spots. Fruity substance and
an effortless palate come together in their
early-drinking selection, like their Vigna
Corvino, as well as their more ambitious
lines like their Contesa and Antica Persia.
Among the new releases, the 2016 whites
deserve a special place. The Trebbiano's
initial aromas are a bit more latent, a quality
that can be traced back to its yeasts, but
the overall taste structure proves solid and
spirited. The Pecorino presents a similar
profile, playing with primary aromas and a
certain fruity sweetness that guides the
palate.

○ Abruzzo Pecorino '16	▼▼ 2
○ Trebbiano d'Abruzzo '16	▼▼ 2
⊙ Cerasuolo d'Abruzzo '16	▼ 2
● Montepulciano d'Abruzzo '15	▼ 2
● Montepulciano d'Abruzzo V. Corvino '16	▼ 2
● Montepulciano d'Abruzzo Ris. '08	▼▼▼ 3
● Montepulciano d'Abruzzo '14	▼▼ 3
● Montepulciano d'Abruzzo '12	▼▼ 3
● Montepulciano d'Abruzzo Ris. '10	▼▼ 4
● Montepulciano d'Abruzzo Ris. '09	▼▼ 4
● Montepulciano d'Abruzzo V. Corvino '15	▼▼ 2
○ Passerina Vigna Corvino '14	▼▼ 2
○ Pecorino '14	▼▼ 3

Nicoletta De Fermo

C.DA CORDANO
65014 LORETO APRUTINO [PE]
TEL. +39 0858289136
www.defermo.it

CELLAR SALES
PRE-BOOKED VISITS
ANNUAL PRODUCTION 26,000 bottles
HECTARES UNDER VINE 17.00
VITICULTURE METHOD Certified Biodynamic
SUSTAINABLE WINERY

The winery managed by Nicoletta De
Fermo, along with her husband, Stefano
Papetti Ceroni, was officially formed in
2009. There's no doubt that the producer
has since made a contribution to how the
area of Loreto Aprutino, one of Abruzzo's
truly great crus, is being interpeted. For the
moment, a part of their grapes are still sold
to third parties, but the potential for growth
is decidedly high (if we consider the some
17 hectares of Montepulciano, Pecorino
and Chardonnay grapes here). Worked with
spontaneous fermentation and slow aging
in steel and concrete, their wines have an
unmistakable character, almost wild and
often on that ephemeral line that separates
naturalness and anarchy of expression.
Such a style, which is in many ways
uncompromising, comes out in the most
recent tastings. If the Montepulciano
Concrete 2016 and Prologo 2015 give
little in terms of openness and softness,
the Pecorino Don Carlino 2016 balances
its wild, citrus backbone with a
commendable, 'Apennine' clarity of lime,
field herbs and flint.

○ Abruzzo Pecorino Don Carlino '16		♀♀ 4
● Montepulciano d'Abruzzo Concrete '16		♀ 4
● Montepulciano d'Abruzzo Prologo '15		♀ 6
⊙ Montepulciano d'Abruzzo Cerasuolo		
Le Cince '14		♀♀♀ 4*
● Montepulciano d'Abruzzo Prologo '12		♀♀♀ 5
○ Abruzzo Pecorino Sup. Don Carlino '15		♀♀ 4
⊙ Cerasuolo d'Abruzzo Sup. Le Cince '15		♀♀ 4
○ Don Carlino Pecorino '14		♀♀ 4
○ Launegild '13		♀♀ 5
○ Launegild Chardonnay '14		♀♀ 5
⊙ Montepulciano d'Abruzzo Cerasuolo		
Le Cince '12		♀♀ 4
● Montepulciano d'Abruzzo Concrete '15		♀♀ 4
● Montepulciano d'Abruzzo Prologo '13		♀♀ 5
● Montepulciano d'Abruzzo Prologo '11		♀♀ 5
● Montepulciano d'Abruzzo Prologo '10		♀♀ 2*

Tenuta I Fauri

S.DA CORTA, 9
66100 CHIETI
TEL. +39 0871332627
www.tenutaifauri.it

CELLAR SALES
PRE-BOOKED VISITS
ANNUAL PRODUCTION 150,000 bottles
HECTARES UNDER VINE 35.00

Tenuta I Fauri's 35 hectares of vineyards,
opposite Majella and in front of the sea,
unfold along the Colline Teatine. The winery,
which got its start in 1979, is managed
today by Domenico Di Camillo, along with his
children, Luigi and Valentina. I Fauri is
among those wineries representing the 'new
direction' in Abruzzo, one pushing for a more
artisanal approach that includes
spontaneous fermentation, aging in concrete
and the use of native grape varieties.
Montepulciano, Cerasuolo and Trebbiano
make up their Baldovino line (the family's
historic nickname), while their Ottobre Rosso
is comprised of their other Pecorino and
Passerina whites, as well as their sparkling
and semi-sparkling wines. The Trebbiano
Baldovino 2016 and Montepulciano Ottobre
Rosso 2016 didn't disappoint. The former is
characterized by petals, grapefruit and
nectarines, the latter by flavoursome,
close-woven black cherry and pepper. The
Cerasuolo Baldovino 2016 is even broader
and more complete, with varietal notes and
delicately salty energy guiding the palate.

⊙ Cerasuolo d'Abruzzo Baldovino '16		♀♀ 2*
● Montepulciano d'Abruzzo		
Ottobre Rosso '16		♀♀ 2*
○ Trebbiano d'Abruzzo Baldovino '16		♀♀ 2*
○ Abruzzo Pecorino '16		♀ 2
○ Abruzzo Pecorino '14		♀♀♀ 2*
○ Abruzzo Pecorino '13		♀♀♀ 2*
○ Abruzzo Pecorino '12		♀♀ 2*
⊙ Cerasuolo d'Abruzzo Baldovino '15		♀♀ 2*
● Montepulciano d'Abruzzo Baldovino '15		♀♀ 2*
● Montepulciano d'Abruzzo Baldovino '14		♀♀ 2*
● Montepulciano d'Abruzzo		
Ottobre Rosso '15		♀♀ 2*
● Montepulciano d'Abruzzo		
Ottobre Rosso '14		♀♀ 2*
○ Trebbiano d'Abruzzo Baldovino '15		♀♀ 2*
○ Trebbiano d'Abruzzo Baldovino '14		♀♀ 2*

Feudo Antico

via Crocevecchia, 101
66010 Tollo [CH]
Tel. +39 0871969128
www.feudoantico.it

CELLAR SALES
ANNUAL PRODUCTION 80,000 bottles
HECTARES UNDER VINE 20.00
VITICULTURE METHOD Certified Organic

Feudo Antico still hasn't celebrated its 10th birthday, but it's already singled itself out as being among the region's top producers. The winery is a small jewel, with its 20 hectares and 50-some-odd members, among Abruzzo's many cooperative wineries, and it's all thanks to a relatively small-scale business model. In addition to its vineyards in Tullum, we can add a plot hosted by the Tenuta Casadonna in Castel di Sangro (home to the world-famous chef, Niko Romito), which gives life to a magnificent mountain Pecorino (limited edition) produced with spontaneous fermentation and aged in steel. It's just one of a strong selection that sees aging in steel and concrete for Montepulciano, Cerasuolo and Pecorino wines. Feudo Antico gets its first Tre Bicchieri. Their Pecorino Casadonna 2015 is one of the best Italian whites we tasted this year: flowers, herbs and citrus trace an aromatic rainbow, amplified by an electric palate thanks to its rocky, mineral persistence. The Biologico 2016 version is also first-rate.

○ Pecorino Casadonna '15	▼▼▼ 7
○ Tullum Pecorino Biologico '16	▼▼ 3*
⊙ Rosato Biologico '16	▼▼ 2*
● Tullum Rosso Biologico '15	▼▼ 3
○ Tullum Pecorino '16	▼ 3
● Tullum Rosso Ris. '13	▼ 5
○ Pecorino Casadonna '14	▽▽ 7
○ Tullum Bianco '13	▽▽ 3
○ Tullum Pecorino '14	▽▽ 3*
○ Tullum Pecorino '12	▽▽ 3*
○ Tullum Pecorino Biologico '15	▽▽ 3
● Tullum Rosso '11	▽▽ 3

Il Feuduccio di Santa Maria D'Orni

loc. Feuduccio
66036 Orsogna [CH]
Tel. +39 0871891646
www.ilfeuduccio.it

CELLAR SALES
PRE-BOOKED VISITS
ANNUAL PRODUCTION 150,000 bottles
HECTARES UNDER VINE 50.00

Gaetano Lamaletto came home after working for 40 years in Venezuela so as to hatch one of Abruzzo's most inspiring new entries (in this edition). Flanked by his daughter, Laura, and son-in-law, Paolo, along with their four children, they took over the property of Feudo di Santa Maria d'Orni (from which the winery got its name). Their lovely underground cellar is found here, in Teatino, among the hills of Orsogna overlooking the Adriatic and shielded by the Majella. Divided into five levels, this veritable tunnel set in the rocks serves as the center of production for a multivariate selection that draws on Pecorino, Passerina and Montepulciano. The Lamaletto family make a splash in this year's guide with their first Tre Bicchieri. It's an en plein tied to their superb Montepulciano Ursonia 2013. The initial blood-rich touches hold nothing back from the original sequence of blackcurrant, malt, chili and forest herbs, elongated by an elegant wake and velvety tannic weave.

● Montepulciano d'Abruzzo Ursonia '13	▼▼▼ 4*
○ Pecorino '16	▼▼ 2*
⊙ Cerasuolo d'Abruzzo '16	▼ 2
○ Fonte Venna Pecorino '16	▼ 2
● Montepulciano d'Abruzzo '14	▼ 3
● Montepulciano d'Abruzzo Fonte Venna '15	▼ 2
○ Pecorino Yare '15	▼ 5

★Dino Illuminati

c.da San Biagio, 18
64010 Controguerra [TE]
Tel. +39 0861808008
www.illuminativini.it

CELLAR SALES
PRE-BOOKED VISITS
ANNUAL PRODUCTION 1,150,000 bottles
HECTARES UNDER VINE 130.00

The 130 hectares of vineyards belonging to the Illuminati, true patriarchs of viticulture and winemaking in the region, are situated entirely in the areas of Montepulciano d'Abruzzo Colline Teramane and Controguerra. The winery got its start in the late 1800s, under Nicola. But the breakthrough came in the 1960s, when the decorated citizen, Dino, decided to start bottling his own wines and implementing winemaking techniques that were innovative for the area. For some time now, he's been flanked by his children, Lorenzo, Stefano and Anna, who've helped to further reinforce their selection. Wines are differentiated according to the origin of their grapes and production approach, with their classic reds 'de garde' still leading the way. Such stylistic versatility was particularly pronounced during the most recent tastings. The Montepulciano Riparosso 2016 goes all in on intensity and sweetness of fruit, sustained by a vigorous tannic framework. The Cerasuolo Sitàra 2016, on the other hand, proves longer-limbed and earthier in its taste profile.

● Montepulciano d'Abruzzo Riparosso '16	♥♥ 2*
☉ Cerasuolo d'Abruzzo Sitàra '16	♥♥ 2*
○ Controguerra Bianco Costalupo '16	♥♥ 2*
○ Controguerra Bianco Daniele '15	♥ 4
○ Controguerra Bianco Pligia '16	♥ 2
○ Controguerra Pecorino '16	♥ 2
● Montepulciano d'Abruzzo Spiano '16	♥ 2
● Montepulciano d'Abruzzo Colline Teramane Pieluni Ris. '10	♥♥♥ 6
● Montepulciano d'Abruzzo Colline Teramane Zanna Ris. '11	♥♥♥ 5
● Montepulciano d'Abruzzo Colline Teramane Zanna Ris. '10	♥♥♥ 5
● Montepulciano d'Abruzzo Colline Teramane Zanna Ris. '08	♥♥♥ 4*

Lepore

c.da Civita, 29
64010 Colonnella [TE]
Tel. +39 0861/0860
www.vinilepore.it

CELLAR SALES
PRE-BOOKED VISITS
ANNUAL PRODUCTION 330,000 bottles
HECTARES UNDER VINE 43.00

With more than 250 hectares of vineyards, the district of Colonnella is one of Teramo's viticultural capitals. It's an area strongly influenced by the Adriatic and has proved ideal for Montepulciano, Cerasuolo, Trebbiano and Passerina. When cultivated here, such varieties offer up their classic expression, at once lustrous and lively, characteristics that correspond perfectly to the Lepore family's selection. They've been working their 40 hectares of terrain for more than two decades, and yet, in recent vintages, they've managed to push their standards even higher. In terms of price, their selection is affordable (to say the least), both their newer wines and their Re and Luigi Lepore Riserva lines. Thanks to the brilliant performance of its Trebbiano 2016, Lepore has deservedly earned itself a place among Abruzzo's top wine producers,. A suite of summer fruit, touches of grape skin and musk, the wine moves decisively and spiritedly through the mid palate, proving rich in iodinenuance. Their Montepulciano 2015 also did well, offering up light fruit and bouquet garni.

○ Trebbiano d'Abruzzo '16	♥♥ 2*
● Montepulciano d'Abruzzo '15	♥♥ 2*
● Montepulciano d'Abruzzo Colline Teramane Luigi Lepore Ris. '12	♥ 4
● Montepulciano d'Abruzzo '14	♥♥ 2*
● Montepulciano d'Abruzzo '09	♥♥ 2*
● Montepulciano d'Abruzzo '07	♥♥ 2*
● Montepulciano d'Abruzzo Colline Teramane Re '12	♥♥ 3

★★Masciarelli

VIA GAMBERALE, 1
66010 SAN MARTINO SULLA MARRUCINA [CH]
TEL. +39 087185241
www.masciarelli.it

CELLAR SALES
PRE-BOOKED VISITS
ACCOMMODATION
ANNUAL PRODUCTION 2,500,000 bottles
HECTARES UNDER VINE 300.00
SUSTAINABLE WINERY

In 1981, Gianni Masciarelli gave the official 'go ahead' for his winemaking project, one that was fated, in a short time, to revolutionize wine in Abruzzo. His wife, Marina, can testify to the fact, after her 30 years at the producer. Their daughter, Miriam, is also on board full-time, representing a shot of new life at the winery. The effect seems to have been positive, especially on the Gianni Masciarelli line, which pursues a decadent, contemporary style, while their Marina Cvetic wines (Castello di Semivicoli and Villa Gemma) boast a more international touch. It's a complete selection that draws on both native and non-native grape varieties, from 300 hectares of vineyards spread across some 13 municipalities in the region. The most recent tastings confirm Masciarelli's particular feel for Cerasuolo. Their Villa Gemma, a wine that is enticing without being excessively sugary, brings together intensity of fruit and balsamic vigor, developing tangibly with a good nose to palate follow through. Excellent performances for their whole selection of wines.

⊙ Cerasuolo d'Abruzzo Villa Gemma '16	▼▼ 3*
○ Abruzzo Pecorino Castello di Semivicoli '16	▼▼ 3
⊙ Cerasuolo d'Abruzzo Gianni Masciarelli '16	▼▼ 2*
● Montepulciano d'Abruzzo Colline Teramane Marina Cvetic Iskra '14	▼▼ 5
● Montepulciano d'Abruzzo Gianni Masciarelli '15	▼▼ 2*
○ Trebbiano d'Abruzzo Gianni Masciarelli '16	▼▼ 2*
⊙ Cerasuolo d'Abruzzo Villa Gemma '15	▽▽▽ 3*
● Montepulciano d'Abruzzo Marina Cvetic '13	▽▽▽ 4*
● Montepulciano d'Abruzzo Marina Cvetic '11	▽▽▽ 4*
● Montepulciano d'Abruzzo Marina Cvetic '10	▽▽▽ 4*

Camillo Montori

LOC. PIANE TRONTO, 80
64010 CONTROGUERRA [TE]
TEL. +39 0861809900
www.montorivini.it

CELLAR SALES
PRE-BOOKED VISITS
ACCOMMODATION AND RESTAURANT SERVICE
ANNUAL PRODUCTION 600,000 bottles
HECTARES UNDER VINE 50.00

The Montory family's historic winery is found practically at the border between Abruzzo and Marche, among the Controguerra hills that overlook the Adriatic Sea. Camillo was the one, in the 1960s and 70s, to make the decisive push for the brand. Today, it's recognized especially for its Fonte Cupa line of wines (which serves alongside their Casa Montori and Trend lines), which continue to stand out for their consistence and vigor, making for decidedly classic interpretations of Abruzzo's principal types of wine. Behind everything lies an estate of 50 hectares, more than half of which are dedicated to Montepulciano. Trebbiano, Pecorino, Passerina and other international varieties complete the puzzle. The rediscovery of Abruzzo's Cerasuolo includes proudly traditional interpretations, like the Fonte Cupa 2016. Crisp fruit, top soil, exotic spices keep together a red's volume and tannic austerity with the vertical, marine reactivity of the Mediterranean's best rosés.

⊙ Cerasuolo d'Abruzzo Fonte Cupa '16	▼▼▼ 2*
○ Pecorino Fonte Cupa '16	▼▼ 3
● Montepulciano d'Abruzzo Fonte Cupa '12	▼ 2
○ Trebbiano d'Abruzzo Fonte Cupa '16	▼ 2
⊙ Cerasuolo d'Abruzzo Fonte Cupa '15	▽▽ 2*
⊙ Montepulciano d'Abruzzo Cerasuolo Fonte Cupa '14	▽▽ 2*
● Montepulciano d'Abruzzo Colline Teramane Casa Montori '11	▽▽ 2*
● Montepulciano d'Abruzzo Colline Teramane Fonte Cupa Ris. '08	▽▽ 5
○ Pecorino Fonte Cupa '14	▽▽ 3
○ Pecorino Fonte Cupa '13	▽▽ 3*
○ Pecorino Fonte Cupa '12	▽▽ 3*
○ Trebbiano d'Abruzzo Fonte Cupa '12	▽▽ 2*

Cantine Mucci

C.DA VALLONE DI NANNI, 65
66020 TORINO DI SANGRO [CH]
TEL. +39 0873913366
www.cantinemucci.com

CELLAR SALES
PRE-BOOKED VISITS
ANNUAL PRODUCTION 250,000 bottles
HECTARES UNDER VINE 24.00
SUSTAINABLE WINERY

The Mucci family's background in wine production goes back to the late 1800s. Back then, it was Luigi. Today, it's Aurelia and Valentino (with the help of their father, Nicola) taking care of the family vineyards, situated in Teatino, along the hills of Torino di Sangro. Montepulciano, Trebbiano, Pecotrino and Falanghina are divided into various plots, with Sangiovese, Cabernet Sauvignon and Merlot getting a smaller share. Their selection, which features all of Abruzzo's classic wines, is organized into various lines (Cantico, Santo Stefano and Valentino Mucci). Their wines may be traditional in style, but they certainly aren't outdated, showing consistent energy of fruit and spirit. This year, we find them in the main section of the guide thanks, primarily, to the top-notch performance of their Trebbiano Valentino Mucci 2016. This was absolutely one of the best of a difficult vintage. The wine is generous and multiform from the first impact of orange candy, rosemary and bread crust, stimulated on the palate by a welcome, delicately salty sève.

○ Trebbiano d'Abruzzo Valentino Mucci '16	▼▼ 2*
● Montepulciano d'Abruzzo '16	▼ 2
● Montepulciano d'Abruzzo Santo Stefano '16	▼ 3
○ Pecorino P '16	▼ 2
● Montepulciano d'Abruzzo Santo Stefano '11	♙♙ 3
● Montepulciano d'Abruzzo Santo Stefano '10	♙♙ 3
● Montepulciano d'Abruzzo Santo Stefano '09	♙♙ 3
● Montepulciano d'Abruzzo Valentino '13	♙♙ 2*
○ Pecorino Valentino '15	♙♙ 2*
○ Trebbiano d'Abruzzo Valentino '10	♙♙ 2*

Fattoria Nicodemi

C.DA VENIGLIO
64024 NOTARESCO [TE]
TEL. +39 085895493
www.nicodemi.com

CELLAR SALES
PRE-BOOKED VISITS
ANNUAL PRODUCTION 200,000 bottles
HECTARES UNDER VINE 30.00
VITICULTURE METHOD Certified Organic

Bruno Nicodemi deserves credit for having built one of Teramo's most inspiring wineries. In the 1960s, he left Rome (and his former professional life) to reinvent himself as a producer in Notaresco. His children, Elena and Alessandro, followed suit. It was a choice they almost had to make, considering the opportunity they had in a contiguous plot of 30 hectares, situated just a few kilometers from the Adriatic but also shielded, climatically, by Gran Sasso. Cultivated according to organic principles, the estate gives rise to a consistently strong selection of wines, focusing exclusively on Montepulciano, Cerasuolo and Trebbiano. These are divided into two lines (Le Murate and Nortàri), joined by a common close-woven and bright character. The Nicodemi family's reds are always a benchmark for the Colline Teramane, as their outstanding Le Murate 2015 reminds us. This time, however, it was the Trebbiano Superiore Notàri 2015 leading the way, with its summery and yet delicate touch, faithfully reconveyed in a palate without overpowering citrus, but still flavorsome and balanced.

○ Trebbiano d'Abruzzo Sup. Notàri '15	▼▼▼ 3*
● Montepulciano d'Abruzzo Colline Teramane Le Murate '15	▼▼ 3
● Montepulciano d'Abruzzo Colline Teramane Notàri '15	▼ 4
○ Trebbiano d'Abruzzo Le Murate '16	▼ 2
● Montepulciano d'Abruzzo Colline Teramane Neromoro Ris. '09	♙♙♙ 5
● Montepulciano d'Abruzzo Colline Teramane Neromoro Ris. '03	♙♙♙ 5
● Montepulciano d'Abruzzo Colline Teramane Neromoro Ris. '11	♙♙ 5
● Montepulciano d'Abruzzo Colline Teramane Notàri '12	♙♙ 3*
● Montepulciano d'Abruzzo Colline Teramane Notàri '11	♙♙ 3*
● Montepulciano d'Abruzzo Colline Teramane Notàri '10	♙♙ 3*

Orlandi Contucci Ponno

LOC. PIANA DEGLI ULIVI, 1
64026 ROSETO DEGLI ABRUZZI [TE]
TEL. +39 0858944049
www.orlandicontucciponno.com

CELLAR SALES
PRE-BOOKED VISITS
ANNUAL PRODUCTION 185,000 bottles
HECTARES UNDER VINE 31.00

In 2007, Orlandi Contucci Ponno was taken over by the Gussalli Beretta agricultural group. For more than 50 years, the winery has worked along the hills of Roseto deli Abruzzi, with an estate that, today, comprises some 30 hectares. Here, in Teramo, in the valley of the Romano river, the sea is just a few kilometers away and the presence of Gran Sasso regulates local temperatures. Such influences have a notable effect on the expression of the various Montepulciano, Cerasuolo and Trebbiano wines produced here (in addition to a group of wines made with non-native varieties). It's a mixed and eclectic selection, also in terms of winemaking, with different approaches adopted for different plots and in terms of aging. Only the bomber was missing from a squad that was, undoubtedly, up to the task. It's enough to think of the synergic duo of their Trebbiano Colle della Corte 2016 and Montepulciano Colline Teramane Riserva 2013. The former, somewhere between pear and pennyroyal, is more casual, while the latter, with its tight-knit tannins, is more serious and grounded.

● Montepulciano d'Abruzzo Colline Teramane Ris. '13	♟♟ 5	
○ Trebbiano d'Abruzzo Sup. Colle della Corte '16	♟♟ 2*	
● Montepulciano d'Abruzzo Rubiolo '16	♟♟ 2*	
○ Abruzzo Pecorino '16	♟ 3	
● Montepulciano d'Abruzzo Colline Teramane La Regia Specula '14	♟ 3	
⊙ Cerasuolo d'Abruzzo Vermiglio '15	♟♟ 2*	
● Montepulciano d'Abruzzo Colline Teramane La Regia Specula '13	♟♟ 3	
● Montepulciano d'Abruzzo Colline Teramane Podere La Regia Specula '12	♟♟ 3	
● Montepulciano d'Abruzzo Rubiolo '15	♟♟ 2*	
○ Trebbiano d'Abruzzo Sup. Colle della Corte Gusalli Beretta '15	♟♟ 2*	

Pasetti

C.DA PRETARO
VIA SAN PAOLO, 21
66023 FRANCAVILLA AL MARE [CH]
TEL. +39 08561875
www.pasettivini.it

CELLAR SALES
PRE-BOOKED VISITS
ACCOMMODATION AND RESTAURANT SERVICE
ANNUAL PRODUCTION 600,000 bottles
HECTARES UNDER VINE 70.00

Francesca Rachele works in administration, while Massimo takes care of exports. Davide is the winemaker. This is the current generation at Pasetti headquarters. The three young siblings gradually started working alongside their parents, Mimmo and Laura. They were the ones to inherit the legacy of Franco, who'd founded the winery in the 1960s. The cellar is located in Francavilla al Mare, on the coast. But the estate's agricultural core is high in the hills, comprising territories in Pescosansonesco, Castiglione a Casauria and Capestrano, in the heart of the Gran Sasso National Park. Their stylish, meaty selection of wines, made with Montepulciano, Trebbiano, Pecorino, Passerina and Moscatello grapes, reflects the choice to cultivate this particular terrain. Such qualities can be found in their two 2015, delayed-release whites. The Trebbiano Madonnella displays a lovely, spring suite of flowers and pollen, though the progression is a bit lacking in supporting acidity. The most interesting aspect of the Pecorino Colle Civetta is its aromas, offering up blackberry, burnt grain and rosolio.

○ Abruzzo Pecorino Colle Civetta '15	♟♟ 3
○ Trebbiano d'Abruzzo Madonnella '15	♟♟ 5
⊙ Testarossa Rosato '16	♟ 2
○ Abruzzo Pecorino '15	♟♟ 2*
○ Abruzzo Pecorino '14	♟♟ 2*
○ Abruzzo Pecorino Colle Civetta '14	♟♟ 3
● Montepulciano d'Abruzzo '12	♟♟ 2*
● Montepulciano d'Abruzzo '11	♟♟ 2*
● Montepulciano d'Abruzzo '10	♟♟ 2*
⊙ Montepulciano d'Abruzzo Cerasuolo V. Capestrano '12	♟♟ 2*
● Montepulciano d'Abruzzo Testarossa '11	♟♟ 4
● Montepulciano d'Abruzzo Testarossa '10	♟♟ 4
● Montepulciano d'Abruzzo Testarossa '08	♟♟ 4
○ Trebbiano d'Abruzzo Zarachè '14	♟♟ 2*
○ Trebbiano d'Abruzzo Zarachè '13	♟♟ 2*

Emidio Pepe

VIA CHIESI, 10
64010 TORANO NUOVO [TE]
TEL. +39 0861856493
www.emidiopepe.com

CELLAR SALES
PRE-BOOKED VISITS
ACCOMMODATION AND RESTAURANT SERVICE
ANNUAL PRODUCTION 80,000 bottles
HECTARES UNDER VINE 15.00
VITICULTURE METHOD Certified Biodynamic
SUSTAINABLE WINERY

Emidio Pepe (class of 1932) is one of the
most beloved figures in Abruzzo's wine
scene. His history of producing officially
began in the 1960s, though his father and
grandfather were already making renowned
Montepulciano and Trebbiano from their
vineyards in Torano Nuovo (on the Colline
Teramane that border Marche). Helped by
his wife, Rosa, and later by his daughters,
Sofia and Daniela, today Emidio is a symbol
of the 'naturale' movement in Europe. His
15 hectares of land is cultivated according
to organic and biodynamic principles, with
an approach in the cellar that features
spontaneous fermentation, no clarifying or
filtration, and lengthy aging (in concrete and
in the bottles). And this explains why their
wines are so extreme in terms of nose and
palate, yet unmistakable at the same time.
More than ever, such instructions are
necessary for getting at Pepe's most recent
creations. The Trebbiano 2015's hued patina
prepares us for a wine that is decidedly wild,
with timbres of cider, green hazelnut, and
exotic spices, all faithfully conveyed through
a compressed, willful palate.

○ Trebbiano d'Abruzzo '15	▼▼ 5
● Montepulciano d'Abruzzo '98	▼▼▼ 8
● Montepulciano d'Abruzzo '13	▼▼ 6
● Montepulciano d'Abruzzo '12	▼▼ 6
● Montepulciano d'Abruzzo '11	▼▼ 6
● Montepulciano d'Abruzzo '10	▼▼ 6
● Montepulciano d'Abruzzo '09	▼▼ 5
● Montepulciano d'Abruzzo '08	▼▼ 5
● Montepulciano d'Abruzzo '07	▼▼ 5
○ Trebbiano d'Abruzzo '14	▼▼ 5
○ Trebbiano d'Abruzzo '13	▼▼ 5
○ Trebbiano d'Abruzzo '11	▼▼ 5
○ Trebbiano d'Abruzzo '10	▼▼ 6
○ Trebbiano d'Abruzzo '09	▼▼ 5
○ Trebbiano d'Abruzzo '08	▼▼ 5

San Giacomo

C.DA NOVELLA, 51
66020 ROCCA SAN GIOVANNI [CH]
TEL. +39 0872620504
www.cantinasangiacomo.it

CELLAR SALES
PRE-BOOKED VISITS
ANNUAL PRODUCTION 20,000 bottles
HECTARES UNDER VINE 300.00
VITICULTURE METHOD Certified Organic

The well-received revival of Abruzzo's wine
owes much to the work of the numerous
cooperative wineries that have managed to
unite noteworthy production volumes with
quality and consistency. Such is the case
with San Giacomo, historic producer from
the province of Chieti, which comprises 200
members and 300 hectares of vineyards,
spread throughout Rocca San Giovanni (and
surrounding districts) and Costa dei
Trabocchi. It's landed in the main section of
IW thanks to a spectacular series of
Montepulciano, Cerasuolo, Trebbiano and
Pecorino wines, which, in the Casino Murri
and Casino Murri 14 lines, seem to pursue
greater mineral backbone, while maintaining
the light and blissful character of their
base versions. Teamwork beats individual
quality. But in this case those wines with the
Casino Murri 14 label deservedly take on
the role of leader. The Pecorino 2016 brings
together exotic delicacy with vertical
support, while the Montepulciano 2015
is grounded in a coherent palate, despite
aromas of brandied fruit.

⊙ Cerasuolo d'Abruzzo Casino Murri '16	▼▼ 2*
● Montepulciano d'Abruzzo '15	▼▼ 1*
● Montepulciano d'Abruzzo Casino Murri '15	▼▼ 2*
● Montepulciano d'Abruzzo Casino Murri 14 '15	▼▼ 2*
○ Pecorino Casino Murri '16	▼▼ 2*
○ Pecorino Casino Murri 14 '16	▼▼ 2*
⊙ Cerasuolo d'Abruzzo '16	▼ 1*
○ Pecorino '16	▼ 1*
○ Trebbiano d'Abruzzo '16	▼ 1*
● Montepulciano d'Abruzzo '13	▼▼ 1*
● Montepulciano d'Abruzzo Casino Murri '14	▼▼ 2*
○ Pecorino '14	▼▼ 1*
○ Pecorino Casino Murri '15	▼▼ 2*

San Lorenzo Vini

C.DA PLAVIGNANO, 2
64035 CASTILENTI [TE]
TEL. +39 0861999325
www.sanlorenzovini.com

CELLAR SALES
PRE-BOOKED VISITS
ANNUAL PRODUCTION 800,000 bottles
HECTARES UNDER VINE 150.00

San Lorenzo holds many top spots. It's one of the oldest producers in Abruzzo (it was founded in the late 1800s), and has been a leading player since it began bottling its own wines in the 1950s. It's also the largest family estate in Teramo. Its 150 hectares of vineyards occupy three ridges lying halfway between Gran Sasso and the Adriatic coast, on the border with Pescara. And, most importantly, it's among the best wineries in the region in terms of consistent quality, stylistic variety and value of the entire selection (which is managed today by brothers Gianluca and Fabrizio Galasso, along with their uncle, Gianfranco Barbone). There are still many arrows in San Lorenzo's quiver. With their freestyle and reactive profile, the Trebbiano 2016 and Montepulciano 2015 (from the Casabianca Fermentazione Spontanea line), deserve attention. The Pecorino and Rosato 2016, as well the creamy Montepulciano Sirio 2015, deliver with a more conventional style.

○ Abruzzo Pecorino Il Pecorino '16	♥♥	2*
● Montepulciano d'Abruzzo Casabianca Fermentazione Spontanea '15	♥♥	2*
● Montepulciano d'Abruzzo Sirio '15	♥♥	1*
⊙ Rosato '16	♥♥	2*
○ Trebbiano d'Abruzzo Casabianca Fermentazione Spontanea '16	♥♥	2*
● Montepulciano d'Abruzzo Antàres '15	♥	2
● Montepulciano d'Abruzzo Colline Teramane Oinos '13	♥	4
○ Trebbiano d'Abruzzo Sirio '16	♥	1*
● Montepulciano d'Abruzzo Casabianca '13	♀♀	2*
● Montepulciano d'Abruzzo Casabianca '12	♀♀	2*
● Montepulciano d'Abruzzo Colline Teramane Escol Ris. '10	♀♀	5
● Montepulciano d'Abruzzo Sirio '14	♀♀	1*

Tenuta Terraviva

VIA DEL LAGO, 19
64081 TORTORETO [TE]
TEL. +39 0861786056
www.tenutaterraviva.it

CELLAR SALES
PRE-BOOKED VISITS
ANNUAL PRODUCTION 77,000 bottles
HECTARES UNDER VINE 18.00
VITICULTURE METHOD Certified Organic

Situated on the Colline Teramane (in Tortoreto), Tenuta Terraviva spans around 20 hectares of vineyards. The estate is cultivated according to organic principles, an effort that has come to the forefront in recent seasons thanks to the work of Pina Marano and Pietro Topi. The pair are openly inspired by old, artisanal craft, adopting a minimalist production approach in the cellar. Their interpretations of Abruzzo's traditional wines are decidedly original, far removed from sugary shortcuts, both their base versions and their more ambitious selections, like their Trebbiano Mario's, Pecorino 'Ekwo, Passerina 12.1, Cerasuolo Giusi, il Montepulciano Luì, or Solobianco blend. They didn't repeat last year's superb performance, but Tenuta Terraviva's selection still affirmed that it's among the most titillating of the bunch. We were most impressed with the Pecorino 'Ekwo 2016, a clearly marine wine, aggressive even in its share of citrus and iodine, yet capable of unfolding progressively.

○ Abruzzo Pecorino 'Ekwo '16	♥♥	3*
⊙ Cerasuolo d'Abruzzo Giusi '16	♥♥	2*
○ Trebbiano d'Abruzzo Mario's 43 '15	♥♥	3
○ Abruzzo Passerina 12.1 '16	♥	3
● Montepulciano d'Abruzzo Colline Teramane Terraviva '15	♥	2
● Montepulciano d'Abruzzo Luì '13	♀♀♀	3*
○ Abruzzo Pecorino 'Ekwo '15	♀♀	3*
⊙ Cerasuolo d'Abruzzo Giusi '15	♀♀	2*
● Montepulciano d'Abruzzo '13	♀♀	2*
● Montepulciano d'Abruzzo Luì '12	♀♀	3*
● Montepulciano d'Abruzzo Luì '11	♀♀	3*
● Montepulciano d'Abruzzo Luì Terraviva '10	♀♀	2*
● Montepulciano d'Abruzzo Terraviva '13	♀♀	2*
○ Trebbiano d'Abruzzo '14	♀♀	2*
○ Trebbiano d'Abruzzo Mario's 42 '14	♀♀	3

Tiberio

C. DA LA VOTA
65020 CUGNOLI [PE]
TEL. +39 0858576744
www.tiberio.it

CELLAR SALES
PRE-BOOKED VISITS
ANNUAL PRODUCTION 90,000 bottles
HECTARES UNDER VINE 30.00

Riccardo Tiberio's winery got its start in the 1990s, when he purchased a contiguous, 30-hectare plot of land in Cugnoli, on the Colline Pescaresi hills. Situated at 350 meters above sea level, on calcareous soil, his vineyards are influenced by the nearby Adriatic, Majella massif and Gran Sasso mountain. The winery has further established itself thanks to the work of Riccardo's children, Antonio and Cristiana, the authors of mouthfilling, spry wines tied deeply to the unique climate patterns of their vineyards. Tests with international grape varieties have been put aside. Today, the old pergolas of Trebbiano and Montepulciano are accompanied by new Guyot plots and Pecorino. Theirs is a selection without weak spots, thanks to a purest approach to winemaking. It's precisely the compactness of the selection that you appreciate, starting with the synergic duo of Trebbiano 2016 and Montepulciano 2015, who share a similarly dry and spirited common style. But once again it's the Pecorino that singles itself out, with a 2016 version with particularly reserved aromas and graceful taste.

○ Pecorino '16	♛♛♛	3*
● Montepulciano d'Abruzzo '15	♛♛	2*
○ Trebbiano d'Abruzzo '16	♛♛	2*
☉ Cerasuolo d'Abruzzo '16	♛	2
● Montepulciano d'Abruzzo '13	♛♛♛	2*
○ Pecorino '15	♛♛♛	3*
○ Pecorino '13	♛♛♛	3*
○ Pecorino '12	♛♛♛	3*
○ Pecorino '11	♛♛♛	3*
○ Pecorino '10	♛♛♛	3
● Montepulciano d'Abruzzo '14	♛♛	2*
● Montepulciano d'Abruzzo '12	♛♛	2*
☉ Montepulciano d'Abruzzo Cerasuolo '14	♛♛	2*
○ Pecorino '14	♛♛	3*
○ Pecorino FS '14	♛♛	3*
○ Trebbiano d'Abruzzo Fonte Canale '13	♛♛	2*

Cantina Tollo

VIA GARIBALDI, 68
66010 TOLLO [CH]
TFI . +39 087196251
www.cantinatollo.it

CELLAR SALES
ANNUAL PRODUCTION 13,000,000 bottles
HECTARES UNDER VINE 3200.00

Take a production volume of more than 10 million bottles annually, combine it with a balanced selection, stylistically differentiated into various lines and make it competitive (to say the least) in terms of price. Can it be done? Absolutely. Ask Cantina Tolla, a veritable giant in Abruzzo wine production, with its more than 3000 hectares of vineyards managed by some 822 member-growers, some of which are certified organic. We can't think of many other European cooperatives capable of performing so consistently across their entire selection, which features wines made with Montepulciano, Trebbiano, Pecorino, Passerina, Cococciola and Chardonnay, without forgetting their sparkling wines. For the third year in a row, it's the Montepulciano Mo Riserva that brings out the best of Tollo's gifts. Blackberry, black cherry, burnt embers … the 2013 version brings together various sensibilities, thanks to a caressing, modern style. We see such versatility of expression in their Pecorino 2016, as well.

● Montepulciano d'Abruzzo Mo Ris. '13	♛♛♛	3*
○ Pecorino '16	♛♛	3*
○ Trebbiano d'Abruzzo Biologico '16	♛♛	2*
☉ Cerasuolo d'Abruzzo Hedòs '16	♛	3
● Montepulciano d'Abruzzo Biologico '16	♛	2
● Montepulciano d'Abruzzo Cagiòlo Ris. '13	♛	5
● Montepulciano d'Abruzzo Cagiòlo Ris. '09	♛♛♛	4*
● Montepulciano d'Abruzzo Mo Ris. '12	♛♛♛	2*
● Montepulciano d'Abruzzo Mo Ris. '11	♛♛♛	2*
○ Trebbiano d'Abruzzo C'Incanta '11	♛♛♛	4*
○ Trebbiano d'Abruzzo C'Incanta '10	♛♛♛	4*
● Montepulciano d'Abruzzo Aldiano Ris. '08	♛♛	2*
● Montepulciano d'Abruzzo Biologico '15	♛♛	2*
● Montepulciano d'Abruzzo Cagiòlo Ris. '11	♛♛	5
● Montepulciano d'Abruzzo Cagiòlo Ris. '10	♛♛	4

Torre dei Beati

C.DA POGGIORAGONE, 56
65014 LORETO APRUTINO [PE]
TEL. +39 0854916069
www.torredeibeati.it

CELLAR SALES
PRE-BOOKED VISITS
ANNUAL PRODUCTION 100,000 bottles
HECTARES UNDER VINE 20.00
VITICULTURE METHOD Certified Organic
SUSTAINABLE WINERY

The Torre dei Beati represents the tower of salvation in a celebrated 15th century painting on display in Loreto Aprutino. It's an icon that Adriana Galasso and Fausto Albanese adopted for their winery, which they founded in 1999. An organic approach and artisanal sensibility define their wines, with their Montepulciano, Cerasuolo, Trebbiano and Pecorinos among the region's higher echelons for some time now. The colored labels indicate perfectly the joyful and spontaneous expressivity which their 20 hectares of vineyards on the Colline Pescaresi hills give rise to. These are situated at 300 meters above sea level, and experience the dizzying temperature ranges made possible by nearby Gran Sasso. Torre dei Beati puts forward a pair of shining Pecorinos this year. The name itself is auspicious, Giocheremo con i Fiori 2016 ('we'll play with flowers'). From the outset, the wine shows a multivariate, spring suite, which is supported by the palate's glyceric grace and delicately salty vigor. The Bianchi Grilli per la Testa 2015 is even deeper and more multifaceted.

○ Abruzzo Pecorino Bianchi Grilli per la Testa '15	♟♟ 4
○ Abruzzo Pecorino Giocheremo con i Fiori '16	♟♟ 3*
☉ Cerasuolo d'Abruzzo Rosa-ae '16	♟♟ 2*
● Montepulciano d'Abruzzo Cocciapazza '14	♟♟ 5
● Montepulciano d'Abruzzo '14	♟ 2
● Montepulciano d'Abruzzo Mazzamurello '14	♟ 5
○ Trebbiano d'Abruzzo Bianchi Grilli per la Testa '15	♟ 3
● Montepulciano d'Abruzzo Cocciapazza '11	♟♟♟ 4*
○ Trebbiano d'Abruzzo Bianchi Grilli per la Testa '14	♟♟♟ 4*

La Valentina

VIA TORRETTA, 52
65010 SPOLTORE [PE]
TEL. +39 0854478158
www.lavalentina.it

CELLAR SALES
PRE-BOOKED VISITS
ANNUAL PRODUCTION 350,000 bottles
HECTARES UNDER VINE 40.00
VITICULTURE METHOD Certified Organic
SUSTAINABLE WINERY

Despite their more than 20 years of experience, La Valentina manages to maintain a young and dynamic face. The producer, in the hands of Sabatino, Roberto and Andrea Di Properzio since 1994, was among the first to make issues like environmental sustainability central to their production philosophy. Their estate has grown and come to comprise 40 hectares, spread along of the Colline Pescaresi hills, from the slopes of the Majella all the way to the coast. Spoltore, Alanno, Civitella, Scafa, San Valentino, varying altitudes and climate patterns are rendered consistently by their Terroir and Classica selections of wine (Montepulciano, Cerasuolo, Trebbiano, Pecorino and Fiano). As usual, each of the La Valentina wines we tasted performed well. This includes wines from their basic line, like their Montepulciano 2015, a wine that's generous in its share of spices and woodland aromas, with a balanced, compact finish that features hints of roots and bitter herbs. There's also their Pecorino 2016, a wine of more summery taste, with aromas of mountain air.

○ Pecorino '16	♟♟ 2*
☉ Cerasuolo d'Abruzzo '16	♟♟ 2*
● Montepulciano d'Abruzzo '15	♟♟ 2*
● Montepulciano d'Abruzzo Spelt Ris. '13	♟♟ 4
● Montepulciano d'Abruzzo Terre dei Vestini Bellovedere Ris. '13	♟♟ 6
○ Trebbiano d'Abruzzo Spelt '16	♟♟ 3
● Montepulciano d'Abruzzo Binomio Ris. '13	♟ 5
○ Trebbiano d'Abruzzo '16	♟ 2
● Montepulciano d'Abruzzo Bellovedere '05	♟♟♟ 6
● Montepulciano d'Abruzzo Spelt '08	♟♟♟ 3*
● Montepulciano d'Abruzzo Spelt '07	♟♟♟ 3
● Montepulciano d'Abruzzo Spelt '05	♟♟♟ 3
● Montepulciano d'Abruzzo Spelt Ris. '11	♟♟♟ 4*
● Montepulciano d'Abruzzo Spelt Ris. '10	♟♟♟ 3*

★★★Valentini

VIA DEL BAIO, 2
65014 LORETO APRUTINO [PE]
TEL. +39 0858291138

ANNUAL PRODUCTION 20,000 bottles
HECTARES UNDER VINE 70.00

The Valentini family's roots in Loreto Aprutino seem to go back to the dawn of time itself. Francesco Paolo currently leads the winery, which continues to make history, thanks to its distinct artisanal approach to agriculture here in Abruzzo. Just think that of their 70 hectares of vineyards, only a small part of their grapes actually end up in the bottle (with delivery of their bulk wine a veritable local ritual). And so, only the best, and only when the vintage allows for it, for the extraordinarily long-lived Montepulciano, Cerasuolo and Trebbiano wines adorned with the totem-like, yellow label. And precisely on the issue of evolution, their Trebbiano 2013 turned in a memorable performance. The wine needs some time to free up the purity of its nose, which is more northern than previous tastings, while the palate shows a spirit and length that are explosive from the outset. The Cerasuolo 2016 proved itself original for its touches of humus and broad beans.

○ Trebbiano d'Abruzzo '13	🍷🍷🍷	8
☉ Cerasuolo d'Abruzzo '16	🍷🍷	7
● Montepulciano d'Abruzzo '12	🍷🍷🍷	8
● Montepulciano d'Abruzzo '06	🍷🍷🍷	8
☉ Montepulciano d'Abruzzo Cerasuolo '09	🍷🍷🍷	6
☉ Montepulciano d'Abruzzo Cerasuolo '08	🍷🍷🍷	6
☉ Montepulciano d'Abruzzo Cerasuolo '06	🍷🍷🍷	6
○ Trebbiano d'Abruzzo '12	🍷🍷🍷	6
○ Trebbiano d'Abruzzo '11	🍷🍷🍷	6
○ Trebbiano d'Abruzzo '10	🍷🍷🍷	6
○ Trebbiano d'Abruzzo '09	🍷🍷🍷	6
○ Trebbiano d'Abruzzo '08	🍷🍷🍷	6
○ Trebbiano d'Abruzzo '07	🍷🍷🍷	6
○ Trebbiano d'Abruzzo '05	🍷🍷🍷	6

★Valle Reale

LOC. SAN CALISTO
65026 POPOLI [PE]
TEL. +39 0859871039
www.vallereale.it

CELLAR SALES
PRE-BOOKED VISITS
ANNUAL PRODUCTION 250,000 bottles
HECTARES UNDER VINE 46.00
VITICULTURE METHOD Certified Organic
SUSTAINABLE WINERY

'Vine growers in the parks' is the caption chosen by the Pizzolo family to describe the spirit of their winery, Valle Reale. After all, the heart of the winery is situated on the border between Pescara and Aquila, right where Gran Sasso, Majella and Sirente-Velino parks meet. Their 50 hectares of certified organic terrain give rise to one of the most inspiring selections in the region. From Montepulciano to Trebbiano, their wines are interpreted with a contemporary touch, starting with plot-based winemaking and spontaneous fermentation. Popoli, San Calisto, Sant'Eusanio, Capestrano, Vigna del Convento are the crus called on to explore the lively richness of flavor already present in the base versions. Their two 2015 Trebbianos once again proved to be the perfect couple. Vigneto di Popoli offers up marine shrubs and smokey fragrances, unfolding generously. Vigna del Convento di Capestrano's multidimensional palate adds citrus vitality and rocky, mineral depth. It's a wine worthy of Tre Bicchieri.

○ Trebbiano d'Abruzzo		
V. del Convento di Capestrano '15	🍷🍷🍷	6
● Montepulciano d'Abruzzo		
Vign. di Sant'Eusanio '15	🍷🍷	3*
○ Trebbiano d'Abruzzo Vign. di Popoli '15	🍷🍷	5
● Montepulciano d'Abruzzo '16	🍷🍷	3
○ Trebbiano d'Abruzzo '16	🍷🍷	3
☉ Cerasuolo d'Abruzzo '16	🍷	3
○ Trebbiano d'Abruzzo		
V. del Convento di Capestrano '14	🍷🍷🍷	5
○ Trebbiano d'Abruzzo		
V. di Capestrano '13	🍷🍷🍷	5
○ Trebbiano d'Abruzzo		
V. di Capestrano '12	🍷🍷🍷	5
○ Trebbiano d'Abruzzo		
V. di Capestrano '11	🍷🍷🍷	5
○ Trebbiano d'Abruzzo		
V. di Capestrano '10	🍷🍷🍷	5

★Villa Medoro

C.DA MEDORO
64030 ATRI [TE]
TEL. +39 0858708139
www.villamedoro.it

CELLAR SALES
PRE-BOOKED VISITS
ACCOMMODATION
ANNUAL PRODUCTION 300,000 bottles
HECTARES UNDER VINE 100.00

And so the second 20-year cycle in Villa Medoro's production history comes to a close (after the semi-experimental cycle that concluded when, in 1997, they began bottling their own wines). The name derives from the district of Atri, which hosts the winery (in the Colline Teramane). Here, the Morricone family are working, managing to stay in step with the times, as demonstrated by their variegated selection of innovative wines. 100 hectares of land (including the recently purchased Tenuta Fontanelle and Fonte Corvo) give rise to Montepulciano, Cerasuolo, Trebbiano, Pecorino, Passerina and Montonico. From their base to their select lines, both whites and reds, their wines deliver, in particular their Montepulciano reds. Black fruit, cocoa, roots ... their Rosso del Duca 2015 unfolds pervasively and compact on the palate, with close-knit tannins. The base wine of the same year, which is similar in terms of aroma, actually outperforms its teammate for its gourmand profile, which certainly isn't lacking in strength or flavor.

● Montepulciano d'Abruzzo '15		♟♟ 2*
● Montepulciano d'Abruzzo Rosso del Duca '15		♟♟ 3
○ Trebbiano d'Abruzzo '16		♟ 2
○ Trebbiano d'Abruzzo Chimera '16		♟ 2
● Montepulciano d'Abruzzo '08		♟♟♟ 2*
● Montepulciano d'Abruzzo '06		♟♟♟ 2*
● Montepulciano d'Abruzzo Colline Teramane Adrano '10		♟♟♟ 4*
● Montepulciano d'Abruzzo Colline Teramane Adrano '09		♟♟♟ 4*
● Montepulciano d'Abruzzo Colline Teramane Adrano '08		♟♟♟ 2*
● Montepulciano d'Abruzzo Colline Teramane Adrano '06		♟♟♟ 4*

Ciccio Zaccagnini

C.DA POZZO
65020 BOLOGNANO [PE]
TEL. +39 0858880195
www.cantinazaccagnini.it

CELLAR SALES
PRE-BOOKED VISITS
ANNUAL PRODUCTION 1,500,000 bottles
HECTARES UNDER VINE 300.00

Bolognano is one of the main hubs of Abruzzo's wine scene, and a lot of this has to do with the Zaccagnini family's decades of work. After the passing of founder, Ciccio, his son, Marcello, took over the reins of the winery (with the help of his enologist cousin, Concezio Marulli). First, they set out to shore up the terrain, about 300 hectares of land on the Colline Pescaresi, an area that is, in many ways, on the borderland between sea and mountain (from the point of view of pedoclimate). And then there was the work of further bolstering a varied array of affordable wines. Pecorino, Trebbiano, Cerasuolo and Montepulciano are interpreted through a variety of techniques, including experimentations with sparkling wines and no added sulfites. Zaccagnini's current selection stands out for its overall consistency and points of excellence. Faithful to its mature, potent Montepulciano character, the Chronicon 2014 offers up dark aromas of licorice and embers. The Cerasuolo Myosotis 2016, rather, conveys joviality and pleasantness.

○ Cerasuolo d'Abruzzo Myosotis '16		♟♟♟ 3*
● Montepulciano d'Abruzzo Chronicon '14		♟♟ 3*
○ Abruzzo Pecorino Yamada '16		♟♟ 3
● Montepulciano d'Abruzzo Cuvée dell'Abate '15		♟♟ 2*
○ Abruzzo Bianco San Clemente '15		♟ 4
○ Abruzzo Il Vino dal Tralcetto Bianco di Ciccio '16		♟ 2
○ Abruzzo Pecorino La Cuvée dell'Abate '16		♟ 2
● Montepulciano d'Abruzzo Il Vino dal Tralcetto '15		♟ 2
● Montepulciano d'Abruzzo Chronicon '13		♟♟♟ 3*
● Montepulciano d'Abruzzo S. Clemente Ris. '12		♟♟♟ 5
● Montepulciano d'Abruzzo S. Clemente Ris. '11		♟♟♟ 5

Agricosimo

VIA SANTA LUCIA, 11
66010 VILLAMAGNA [CH]
TEL. +39 0871407063
www.agricosimo.it

ANNUAL PRODUCTION 100,000 bottles
HECTARES UNDER VINE 13.00

● Montepulciano d'Abruzzo Scine '15		🏆🏆 2*
○ Natura e Passione Pecorino '16		🏆🏆 3
● Montepulciano d'Abruzzo Vi '15		🏆 3

Ausonia

C.DA NOCELLA
64032 ATRI [TE]
TEL. +39 0859071026
www.ausoniawines.com

ANNUAL PRODUCTION 35,000 bottles
HECTARES UNDER VINE 11.50

○ Abruzzo Pecorino Machaon '15		🏆🏆 3
○ Trebbiano d'Abruzzo Apollo '15		🏆🏆 3
● Montepulciano d'Abruzzo Colline Teramane Apollo '15		🏆 3

Tenute Barone di Valforte

C.DA PIOMBA, 11
64028 SILVI MARINA [TE]
TEL. +39 0859353432
www.baronedivalforte.it

CELLAR SALES
PRE-BOOKED VISITS
ANNUAL PRODUCTION 280,000 bottles
HECTARES UNDER VINE 50.00

☉ Cerasuolo d'Abruzzo Valforte Rosé '16		🏆 2
● Montepulciano d'Abruzzo Colline Teramane Colle Sale '15		🏆 3
○ Pecorino '16		🏆 2

Bove

VIA ROMA, 216
67051 AVEZZANO [AQ]
TEL. +39 086333133
info@cantinebove.it

CELLAR SALES
PRE-BOOKED VISITS
ANNUAL PRODUCTION 1,200,000 bottles
HECTARES UNDER VINE 60.00

● Montepulciano d'Abruzzo Angeli '14		🏆🏆 2*
○ Safari Pecorino '16		🏆🏆 2*
● Montepulciano d'Abruzzo Poggio d'Albe '15		🏆 2
○ Trebbiano d'Abruzzo Poggio d'Albe '16		🏆 2

CantinArte

V.LO L'AQUILA, 18
66100 CHIETI
TEL. +39 0871575427
www.cantinarte.com

CELLAR SALES
PRE-BOOKED VISITS
RESTAURANT SERVICE
ANNUAL PRODUCTION 12,000 bottles
HECTARES UNDER VINE 6.00
VITICULTURE METHOD Certified Organic
SUSTAINABLE WINERY

○ Abruzzo Pecorino Colori '16		🏆🏆 4
● Montepulciano d'Abruzzo Ode '15		🏆 3

Casalbordino

C.DA TERMINE, 38
66021 CASALBORDINO [CH]
TEL. +39 0873918107
www.vinicasalbordino.com

CELLAR SALES
PRE-BOOKED VISITS
ANNUAL PRODUCTION 6,000,000 bottles
HECTARES UNDER VINE 1400.00

● Montepulciano d'Abruzzo Castel Verdino Ris. '13		🏆🏆 2*
● Montepulciano d'Abruzzo Villa Adami '14		🏆🏆 1*
● Montepulciano d'Abruzzo Terre Sabelli '15		🏆 1*

Cerulli Spinozzi

s.da st.le 150 del Vomano km 17,600
64020 Canzano [TE]
Tel. +39 086157193
www.cerullispinozzi.it

CELLAR SALES
PRE-BOOKED VISITS
ACCOMMODATION
ANNUAL PRODUCTION 200,000 bottles
HECTARES UNDER VINE 53.00

○ Trebbiano d'Abruzzo Almorano '16		♟♟ 2*
● Montepulciano d'Abruzzo '16		♟ 2
● Montepulciano d'Abruzzo Colline Teramane Torre Migliori '12		♟ 3

Col del Mondo

c.da Campotino, 35c
65010 Collecorvino [PE]
Tel. +39 0858207831
www.coldelmondo.com

CELLAR SALES
PRE-BOOKED VISITS
ANNUAL PRODUCTION 80,000 bottles
HECTARES UNDER VINE 12.00

● Montepulciano d'Abruzzo Terre dei Vestini '13		♟♟ 3
◐ Cerasuolo d'Abruzzo '16		♟ 2
● Montepulciano d'Abruzzo Sunnae '16		♟ 2

Antonio Costantini

s.da Migliori, 20
65013 Città Sant'Angelo [PE]
Tel. +39 0859699169
www.costantinivini.it

CELLAR SALES
PRE-BOOKED VISITS
ACCOMMODATION AND RESTAURANT SERVICE
ANNUAL PRODUCTION 450,000 bottles
HECTARES UNDER VINE 60.00

○ Trebbiano d'Abruzzo '16		♟♟ 2*
○ Abruzzo Pecorino '16		♟ 3
● Montepulciano d'Abruzzo Febe '16		♟ 2
○ Trebbiano d'Abruzzo Febe '16		♟ 2

De Angelis Corvi

c.da Pignotto
64010 Controguerra [TE]
Tel. +39 086189475
www.deangeliscorvi.it

CELLAR SALES
PRE-BOOKED VISITS
ANNUAL PRODUCTION 40,000 bottles
HECTARES UNDER VINE 12.00
VITICULTURE METHOD Certified Organic
SUSTAINABLE WINERY

◐ Cerasuolo d'Abruzzo Sup. '16		♟♟ 2*
● Montepulciano d'Abruzzo Fonte Raviliano '14		♟ 3

Fontefico

via Difenza, 38
66054 Vasto [CH]
Tel. +39 3284113619
www.fontefico.it

CELLAR SALES
PRE-BOOKED VISITS
RESTAURANT SERVICE
ANNUAL PRODUCTION 35,000 bottles
HECTARES UNDER VINE 15.00
VITICULTURE METHOD Certified Organic
SUSTAINABLE WINERY

○ Abruzzo Pecorino Sup. La Canaglia '16		♟♟ 2*
● Montepulciano d'Abruzzo Cocca di Casa '14		♟♟ 3
○ Trebbiano d'Abruzzo Sup. Portarispetto '15		♟♟ 2*

Cantina Frentana

via Perazza, 32
66020 Rocca San Giovanni [CH]
Tel. +39 087260152
www.cantinafrentana.it

CELLAR SALES
PRE-BOOKED VISITS
ACCOMMODATION
ANNUAL PRODUCTION 800,000 bottles
HECTARES UNDER VINE 22.00

● Montepulciano d'Abruzzo Panarda Ris. '14		♟♟ 2
● Montepulciano d'Abruzzo Torre Vinaria '15		♟♟ 2
○ Pecorino '16		♟♟ 2

Gentile

VIA DEL GIARDINO, 7
67025 OFENA [AQ]
TEL. +39 0862956618
www.gentilevini.it

CELLAR SALES
PRE-BOOKED VISITS
ANNUAL PRODUCTION 90,000 bottles
HECTARES UNDER VINE 12.00

● Montepulciano d'Abruzzo V. V. '13	♥♥ 4
⊙ Cerasuolo d'Abruzzo Particella 604 '16	♥ 2

Marchesi De' Cordano

C.DA CORDANO, 43
65014 LORETO APRUTINO [PE]
TEL. +39 0858289526
www.cordano.it

CELLAR SALES
PRE-BOOKED VISITS
ANNUAL PRODUCTION 180,000 bottles
HECTARES UNDER VINE 50.00
VITICULTURE METHOD Certified Organic
SUSTAINABLE WINERY

● Montepulciano d'Abruzzo Trinità Ris. '12	♥♥ 4
⊙ Cerasuolo Puntarosa '16	♥ 2
○ Cococciola Brilla '16	♥ 3
○ Pecorino Diamine '16	♥ 3

Tommaso Olivastri

VIA QUERCIA DEL CORVO, 37
66038 SAN VITO CHIETINO [CH]
TEL. +39 087261543
www.viniolivastri.com

CELLAR SALES
PRE-BOOKED VISITS
ANNUAL PRODUCTION 50,000 bottles
HECTARES UNDER VINE 15.00

Montepulciano d'Abruzzo La Grondaia '13	♥♥ 2*
● Montepulciano d'Abruzzo La Carrata '12	♥ 4
● Trebbiano d'Abruzzo Santa Clara '16	♥ 2

Praesidium

VIA GIOVANNUCCI, 24
67030 PREZZA [AQ]
TEL. +39 086445103
www.vinipraesidium.it

CELLAR SALES
PRE-BOOKED VISITS
ANNUAL PRODUCTION 26,000 bottles
HECTARES UNDER VINE 5.50

● Montepulciano d'Abruzzo Ris. '12	♥♥ 5

La Quercia

C.DA COLLE CROCE
64020 MORRO D'ORO [TE]
TEL. +39 0858959110
www.vinilaquercia.it

CELLAR SALES
PRE-BOOKED VISITS
ANNUAL PRODUCTION 200,000 bottles
HECTARES UNDER VINE 46.50
SUSTAINABLE WINERY

Montepulciano d'Abruzzo '14	♥♥ 2*
Cerasuolo d'Abruzzo Peladi '16	♥ 1*
Montepulciano d'Abruzzo Peladi '16	♥ 1*

Strappelli

VIA TORRI, 16
64010 TORANO NUOVO [TE]
TEL. +39 0861887402
www.cantinastrappelli.it

CELLAR SALES
PRE-BOOKED VISITS
ANNUAL PRODUCTION 65,000 bottles
HECTARES UNDER VINE 10.00
VITICULTURE METHOD Certified Organic

○ Soprano Pecorino '16	♥♥ 2*
⊙ Cerasuolo d'Abruzzo '16	♥ 2
● Montepulciano d'Abruzzo Colline Teramane Colle Trà '13	♥ 4

Terra d'Aligi - Spinelli

LOC. PIAZZANO
VIA PIANA LA FARA, 90
66041 ATESSA [CH]
TEL. +39 0872897916
www.terradaligi.it

CELLAR SALES
PRE-BOOKED VISITS
ANNUAL PRODUCTION 550,000 bottles
HECTARES UNDER VINE 50.00

● Montepulciano d'Abruzzo '15	❦❦ 2*
● Montepulciano d'Abruzzo Tolos Ris. '12	❦❦ 5
○ Cococciola '16	❦ 2
○ Zite Pecorino '16	❦ 2

Terzini

VIA ROMA, 52
65028 TOCCO DA CASAURIA [PE]
TEL. +39 0859158147
www.cantinaterzini.it

CELLAR SALES
PRE-BOOKED VISITS
ANNUAL PRODUCTION 200,000 bottles
HECTARES UNDER VINE 22.00

○ Abruzzo Pecorino '16	❦❦ 3
○ Trebbiano d'Abruzzo '16	❦❦ 3

Tenuta Ulisse

VIA SAN POLO, 40
66014 CRECCHIO [CH]
TEL. +39 0871942007
www.tenutaulisse.it

CELLAR SALES
PRE-BOOKED VISITS
ANNUAL PRODUCTION 550,000 bottles
HECTARES UNDER VINE 75.00

☉ Cerasuolo d'Abruzzo '16	❦ 3
○ Trebbiano d'Abruzzo '16	❦ 3

Valle Martello

C.DA VALLE MARTELLO, 10
66010 VILLAMAGNA [CH]
TEL. +39 0871300330
www.vallemartello.it

CELLAR SALES
PRE-BOOKED VISITS
ACCOMMODATION
ANNUAL PRODUCTION 120,000 bottles
HECTARES UNDER VINE 40.00
SUSTAINABLE WINERY

○ Brado Pecorino '16	❦❦ 2
● Montepulciano d'Abruzzo Prima Terra '12	❦❦ 4
● Montepulciano d'Abruzzo '15	❦ 2
○ Trebbiano d'Abruzzo '16	❦ 2

Valori

VIA TORQUATO AL SALINELLO, 8
64027 SANT'OMERO [TE]
TEL. +39 087185241
www.vinivalori.it

PRE-BOOKED VISITS
ANNUAL PRODUCTION 150,000 bottles
HECTARES UNDER VINE 26.00
VITICULTURE METHOD Certified Organic
SUSTAINABLE WINERY

○ Abruzzo Pecorino '16	❦❦ 2*
☉ Cerasuolo d'Abruzzo '16	❦ 2
○ Trebbiano d'Abruzzo '16	❦ 2

Vigneti Radica

VIA PIANA MOZZONE, 4
66010 TOLLO [CH]
TEL. +39 0871962227
www.vignetiradica.it

CELLAR SALES
PRE-BOOKED VISITS
ACCOMMODATION
ANNUAL PRODUCTION 80,000 bottles
HECTARES UNDER VINE 14.00
SUSTAINABLE WINERY

● Montepulciano d'Abruzzo '15	❦❦
○ Pecorino '16	❦❦
○ Trebbiano d'Abruzzo '16	❦❦
○ Tullum Pecorino '16	❦

MOLISE

'No news is good news'. The old adage seems to perfectly capture Molise's wine industry, as expressed during the last round of tasting. For at least five years, the same wineries have been at the forefront, and it's clear that if you're looking for a headline with every test, Molise isn't exactly ground zero. On the other hand, the limited turnover can be read as a sign of consolidation. That is, the best wineries are leading the way, while behind them a small team of consistent and competitive producers follow (especially when it comes to price). Among the former, we find authentic and inspiring leaders like the Dorante Di Majo family, once again the only winery in the region to receive Tre Bicchieri (with its 2014 Aglianico Contado Riserva). Then there are producers like Borgo di Colloredo, Claudio Cipressi or Tenimenti Grieco, whose multifaceted selections remind us of the inherently pioneering nature of the area. In fact, independent of its individual successes, the region is primarily characterized by its incredible mosaic of pedoclimatic conditions, geographies and production approaches. And part of the territory's charm also derives from the way it draws on the surrounding regions (Abruzzo, Sannio Beneventano, inner-Lazio, Foggiano) while maintaining its own identity, albeit one that's difficult to pinpoint. Central and southern Italy meet in Molise's Montepulciano and Aglianico reds, with Tintilia's role as a versatile native grape getting stronger by the vintage. But we shouldn't overlook the expressivity of the whites being produced in the region's Adriatic and Apennine zones, where international grapes (primarily Sauvignon and Chardonnay) are accompanied by Falanghina, Greco, Trebbiano and Malvasia. Nor should we neglect its rosés, possibly the category that's grown the most in recent seasons. These are perfect for the wine bar or an array of gastronomic pairings. And that's pretty good, considering the region's limitations. Molise wine country exists, does it ever, and we're convinced that that the time is ripe for it to emerge.

Borgo di Colloredo

LOC. NUOVA CLITERNIA
VIA COLLOREDO, 15
86042 CAMPOMARINO [CB]
TEL. +39 087557453
www.borgodicolloredo.com

CELLAR SALES
PRE-BOOKED VISITS
ACCOMMODATION AND RESTAURANT SERVICE
ANNUAL PRODUCTION 200,000 bottles
HECTARES UNDER VINE 70.00
SUSTAINABLE WINERY

With the purchase of almost 100 hectares
of terrain in Campomarino (near the coast
of Molise), brothers Enrico and Pasquale Di
Giulio took the work begun by their father,
Silvio, to a new level. He started in the
1960s, but it was in the 1990s that a cellar
was built and the Borgo di Colloredo brand
was created (the name comes from an old
farmstead later converted into a church by
the titled D'Avalos D'Aragona family). Their
production lines include Tenute di Giulio,
which focus on native grape varieties in the
Biferno Gironia (white, rosé and red), Nobili
Vitigni (Aglianico and Greco), Classici
(Montepulciano and Falanghina) and Terre
deli Osci (Sangiovese and Malvasia). Two
wines with very different styles lead the
combative troupe under the Di Giulio
brothers' command. The 2016 Gironia is a
classic summer rosé that features a crisp
nose and tidy palate. It's one of the best in
the region. The 2013 Molise Rosso is more
reserved aromatically, but ripe tannins
enhance the palate.

⊙ Biferno Rosato Gironia '16	♈♈ 3	
● Molise Rosso '13	♈♈ 2*	
○ Biferno Bianco Gironia '16	♈ 3	
○ Greco '16	♈ 2	
● Aglianico '10	♈♈♈ 3*	
● Aglianico '13	♈♈ 3	
○ Biferno Bianco Gironia '14	♈♈ 3	
○ Biferno Bianco Gironia '13	♈♈ 2*	
○ Biferno Bianco Gironia '12	♈♈ 2*	
○ Biferno Rosato Gironia '15	♈♈ 2*	
● Biferno Rosso Gironia Ris. '08	♈♈ 4	
○ Molise Falanghina '12	♈♈ 2*	
● Molise Montepulciano '10	♈♈ 2*	
● Molise Rosso '12	♈♈ 2*	
● Molise Rosso '09	♈♈ 2*	

Claudio Cipressi

C.DA MONTAGNA, 11B
86030 SAN FELICE DEL MOLISE [CB]
TEL. +39 3351244859
www.claudiocipressi.it

CELLAR SALES
PRE-BOOKED VISITS
ACCOMMODATION
ANNUAL PRODUCTION 40,000 bottles
HECTARES UNDER VINE 16.00
VITICULTURE METHOD Certified Organic
SUSTAINABLE WINERY

The address says (almost) everything you
need to know about the orographic and
pedoclimatic context of Claudio Cipressi's
winery: Montagna di San Felice del Molise.
Situated in the hills of Campobasso, the
estate spans 16 hectares of certified
organic vineyards, featuring the region's
traditional grape varieties. For the whites
Falanghina and Trebbiano, for the reds
Montepulciano and, especially, Tintilia,
which is used as a monovarietal in the
selections 66 and Macchiarossa, as well
as in the rosè, Collequinto, and in the
field blend, Macchianera. From the
beginning, their wines have stood out for
their concrete, dry style, divorced from
dogmatic production choices. This time
it's the 2012 Macchianera that stands ou
among Claudio Cipressi's rich selection
of wines. It exhibits a gentle but modern
profile, with well-defined aromas of bottle
cherries, cloves and chocolate that
anticipate a rather warm and round palat
The 2016 Falanghina Voira also proved
quite good.

● Molise Rosso Macchianera '12	♈
● Molise Tintilia 66 '16	♈
● Molise Tintilia Macchiarossa '13	♈
○ Voira Falanghina '16	♈
○ Falanghina Voira '13	♈♈
● Molise Rosso Mekan '11	♈♈
● Molise Tintilia 66 '11	♈♈
● Molise Tintilia Macchiarossa '12	♈♈
● Molise Tintilia Macchiarossa '11	♈♈
● Molise Tintilia Settevigne '14	♈♈
● Molise Tintilia Settevigne '13	♈♈
○ Molise Trebbiano Le Scoste '13	♈♈

★Di Majo Norante

FRAZ. NUOVA CLITERNIA
A COLLE SAVINO, 6
86042 CAMPOMARINO [CB]
TEL. +39 087557208
www.dimajonorante.com

CELLAR SALES
PRE-BOOKED VISITS
ANNUAL PRODUCTION 800,000 bottles
HECTARES UNDER VINE 125.00
VITICULTURE METHOD Certified Organic

From Malvasia to Trebbiano, Montepulciano, Sangiovese, Bombino, Falanghina, Greco, Aglianico, Prugnolo, Tintilia and Moscato Reale, an extraordinary range of grapes makes up Di Majo Norante's polychromatic selection of wines. It all starts with the more than 120 hectares of vineyards managed through biocompatible protocols. Most of the terrain is concentrated around Campomarino, in an area where, in the past, the Marquis Santa Cristina once had had their estate. Today, Alesso is managing things, having inherited from his father, Luigi, a legacy that goes all the way back to the early 1800s. Their approach has, over the years, continually stayed in step with the times thanks to clear-minded openness to innovation. Once again, we find a symbiotic couple in the finals. The 2016 Falanghina, with its fresh fruit, medicinal herbs and full-bodied, pleasantly acidulous palate, is simply one of the best whites ever produced in Molise. The savory and precise '14 Aglianico Contado Riserva is also outstanding. Tre Bicchieri.

Molise Aglianico Contado Ris. '14	🏆🏆🏆 3*
Molise Falanghina '16	🏆🏆 2*
Biferno Rosso Ramitello '14	🏆 3
Sangiovese '16	🏆 2
Molise Aglianico Biorganic '11	🏆🏆🏆 2*
Molise Aglianico Contado '03	🏆🏆🏆 2*
Molise Aglianico Contado Ris. '10	🏆🏆🏆 3*
Molise Aglianico Contado Ris. '09	🏆🏆🏆 2*
Molise Aglianico Contado Ris. '07	🏆🏆🏆 2*
Molise Don Luigi '05	🏆🏆🏆 5
Molise Don Luigi Ris. '08	🏆🏆🏆 5
Molise Don Luigi Ris. '06	🏆🏆🏆 5
Molise Rosso Don Luigi Ris. '12	🏆🏆🏆 5
Molise Rosso Don Luigi Ris. '11	🏆🏆🏆 5
Molise Tintilia '13	🏆🏆🏆 3*

Tenimenti Grieco

C.DA DIFENSOLA
86045 PORTOCANNONE [CB]
TEL. +39 0875590032
www.tenimentigrieco.it

CELLAR SALES
PRE-BOOKED VISITS
ANNUAL PRODUCTION 700,000 bottles
HECTARES UNDER VINE 85.00

Tenimenti Grieco's more than 80 hectares of vineyards grow along the slopes of Portocannone, a historic area for viticulture in Molise that looks out on the Adriatic. Led by four partners, it quickly emerged as one of the strongest and most dynamic operations in the region. It's all thanks to a variegated selection realized with both traditional and international grape varieties. Falanghina, Montepulciano, Tintilia, but also Sauvignon, Pinot Bianco, Chardonnay, Cabernet, Merlot and Syrah are interpreted with a focus on brilliance of fruit and drinkability, with their numerous lines highlighting various nuances and timbres. Once again, we get a sense of the chemistry between Tenimenti Grieco and Tintilia, which the winemaker interprets as an early drinker. The 2016 200 Metri is a nice demonstration, with its slim-bodied and balanced palate. If possible, the 2015 Passo alle Tremiti Rosso proves even more complete, calling up aromas of strawberries and topsoil, and coming through pervasive and expansive on the palate.

● Molise Rosso Passo alle Tremiti '15	🏆🏆 3*
● Lenda Aglianico '15	🏆🏆 5
● Molise Tintilia 200 Metri '16	🏆🏆 2*
⊙ Biferno Rosato Bosco Delle Guardie '15	🏆 3
○ Molise Falanghina Passo alle Tremiti '16	🏆 3
⊙ Molise Rosato Passo alle Tremiti '16	🏆 3
● Biferno Bosco delle Guardie '14	🏆🏆 3
● Molise Monterosso '13	🏆🏆 2*
⊙ Molise Rosato Passo alle Tremiti '15	🏆🏆 3
⊙ Molise Rosato Passo alle Tremiti '14	🏆🏆 2*
● Molise Rosso Podere di Sot '08	🏆🏆 2*
● Molise Tintilia '14	🏆🏆 2*
● Molise Tintilia 200 Metri '15	🏆🏆 2*
● Molise Tintilia Cupaia '13	🏆🏆 3
● Triassi '13	🏆🏆 5

Angelo D'Uva

C.DA MONTE ALTINO, 23A
86035 LARINO [CB]
TEL. +39 0874822320
www.cantineduva.com

CELLAR SALES
PRE-BOOKED VISITS
ACCOMMODATION AND RESTAURANT SERVICE
ANNUAL PRODUCTION 70,000 bottles
HECTARES UNDER VINE 20.00
SUSTAINABLE WINERY

● Molise Rosso Console Vibio Ris. '11	♟♟ 3
○ Biferno Bianco Kantharos '16	♟ 2
○ Keres Falanghina '16	♟ 2
● Molise Tintilia Lagena '14	♟ 3

Cantine Salvatore

C.DA VIGNE
86049 URURI [CB]
TEL. +39 0874830656
www.cantinesalvatore.it

CELLAR SALES
PRE-BOOKED VISITS
ANNUAL PRODUCTION 80,000 bottles
HECTARES UNDER VINE 20.00
SUSTAINABLE WINERY

⊙ Rosis '16	♟♟
○ Molise Falanghina Nysias '16	♟
● Molise Rosso Biberius '14	♟

Cantina Sociale San Zenone

C.DA PASTINI
86036 MONTENERO DI BISACCIA [CB]
TEL. +39 087596576
www.cantinasanzenone.it

CELLAR SALES
PRE-BOOKED VISITS
ANNUAL PRODUCTION 100,000 bottles
HECTARES UNDER VINE 300.00
VITICULTURE METHOD Certified Organic

● Molise Tintilia '14	♟♟ 3

Terresacre

C.DA MONTEBELLO
86036 MONTENERO DI BISACCIA [CB]
TEL. +39 0875960191
www.terresacre.net

CELLAR SALES
PRE-BOOKED VISITS
ACCOMMODATION AND RESTAURANT SERVI
ANNUAL PRODUCTION 100,000 bottles
HECTARES UNDER VINE 35.00

○ Molise Falanghina Oravera '15	♟
● Molise Tintilia '16	♟
● Molise Tintilia '15	♟
○ Molise Trebbiano Orovite '16	♟

CAMPANIA

Campania's wine is capable of taking your breath away; it can make you laugh and then cry just a few moments later. It's a marvelous mix of native cultivar and authentic winemakers, producers of impressive whites and mediocre reds, or vice versa. Here, certainties can become doubts. And so it is that, after 700 samples tasted, we find ourselves with more questions than answers. A year as excellent as 2016 for Fiano di Avellino made for wines that won't need much of anything to age supremely well, and a Falanghina del Sanrio whose balsamic hints are somehow subtler and yet more vibrant than usual. All told, we can't say that overall quality is on an upward trend (with 15% of the region's wines not meeting the minimum requirements). There are still too many cases of the overuse of sulphites, and some of the red appellations are raising flags. Taurasi seems to be finding it difficult to emerge from the dangerous tunnel in which it finds itself, the idea of force and concentration at any cost, with wood that seems to get worse by the season, and powdery, crumbly sensations on the palate. Of course, a market that shuns their wines is partially to blame, but the idea of drinkability isn't optional - it's a necessary step. Some Campi Taurasini are showing signs of going in this direction, and we were delighted to discover a series of irreverent, delectable Piedirossos. The message from the region's Tre Bicchieris is clear: Campania is white wine country. And what whites! While tasting, we heard more than one 'wow!', such that the 2016 Fiano di Avellino Quintramara gets 'White of the Year'. Four new wineries land in the highest rankings: Mustilli, the 'inventors' of Falanghina, are at the top with a signature Piedirosso that's both deep and succulent. Donnachiara hits the mark with a rich and complete Greco di Tufo. Cantine di Marzo, after 370 years in the business, delivers big time with a Greco di Tufo that does what it should: appetize. Finally, Pasquale Mitrano di Casebianche's pure and assertive Fric, a happy-go-lucky sparkler for drinking and enjoying with friends, proves to be more than a wine - it's a way of life.

Agnanum

VIA VICINALE ABBANDONATA AGLI ASTRONI, 3
80125 NAPOLI
TEL. +39 3385315272
www.agnanum.it

CELLAR SALES
PRE-BOOKED VISITS
ANNUAL PRODUCTION 25,000 bottles
HECTARES UNDER VINE 7.50

This winery in a fairy-tale setting began making wine in 1960 when Gennaro Moccia planted a vineyard with Falanghina and Piedirosso in the volcanic hills of the Astroni nature reserve. Today, Raffaele draws on the terrain to produce intense, scintillating wines, rich in flavor and vitality, features common to the phosphorous, magnesium and potassium-rich soil here. Raffaele is the guardian of a unique environment here just outside of Naples. It's a place that definitely deserves a visit. The 2016 Piedirosso is a delightful, fragrant and irresistible wine, offering up aromas of small black and red fruits, medicinal herbs and a peppery profile. The palate is fragrant, invigorating and succulent, with a clear and well-paced unfolding of balsamic notes and Mediterranean overtones. A delicately bitter and spicy finish adds length. It's a Tre Bicchieri through and through. The 2015 Falanghina Vigna del Pino features a characteristic touch of resin and aromas of yellow flowers. It's creamy, slow-paced and charming.

● Campi Flegrei Piedirosso '16	▼▼▼ 4*
○ Campi Flegrei Falanghina V. del Pino '15	▼▼ 3
● Campi Flegrei Piedirosso V. delle Volpi '15	▼▼ 4
○ Campi Flegrei Falanghina '16	▼ 3
● Campi Flegrei Piedirosso '15	▼▼▼ 4*
○ Campi Flegrei Falanghina V. del Pino '15	♈♈ 3*
○ Campi Flegrei Falanghina V. del Pino '14	♈♈ 3
● Campi Flegrei Piedirosso '13	♈♈ 3*
● Campi Flegrei Piedirosso V. delle Volpi '12	♈♈ 5
● Campi Flegrei Piedirosso V. delle Volpi '14	♈♈ 4

Alois

LOC. AUDELINO
VIA RAGAZZANO
81040 PONTELATONE [CE]
TEL. +39 0823876710
www.vinialois.it

CELLAR SALES
PRE-BOOKED VISITS
ANNUAL PRODUCTION 300,000 bottles
HECTARES UNDER VINE 36.00
SUSTAINABLE WINERY

The Alois family has always specialized in fine fabrics but through the years they have doubled up the family business to include wine production. Two brothers, Michele and Massimo, manage the producer, while Carmine Valentino helps out with winemaking. Alois is driving Monti Caiatini toward new frontiers thanks to some charming expressions of Pallagrello Bianco and Nero, Casavecchia Falanghina and Aglianico. The Donna Paolina brand in Irpinia completes the range. Alois once again earn a Tre Bicchieri. The 2015 Caiatì is a Pallagrello Bianco of rare aromatic intensity, with a profile that's altogether mature, full and vigorous. The nose offers up vibrant aromas of curry plant and citrus fruit, while the mouth proves solid, fresh, powerful and gradual. It gracefully softens with notes of white pepper and minerals, which add flavor and pace. The 2015 Settimo and the 2013 Trebulanum are dynamic and juicy; the 2016 Falanghina Caulino features delightful freshness and aromas of green tea.

○ Caiatì '15	▼▼
● Aglianico Donna Paolina '16	▼
○ Caulino '16	▼
○ Falanghina Donna Paolina '16	▼
● Settimo '15	▼
● Trebulanum Casavecchia '13	▼
● Campole '15	
○ Greco di Tufo Donna Paolina '16	
● Taurasi Donna Paolina '12	
○ Caiatì '14	♈♈
○ Pallagrello Bianco Caiatì Morrone '13	♈♈
● Trebulanum '10	♈♈
○ Pallagrello Bianco Caiatì '13	♈
● Trebulanum Re Ferdinando '11	♈

antine Astroni

SARTANIA, 48
)126 NAPOLI
L. +39 0815884182
ww.cantineastroni.com

ELLAR SALES
RE-BOOKED VISITS
ESTAURANT SERVICE
NNUAL PRODUCTION 330,000 bottles
ECTARES UNDER VINE 25.00
TICULTURE METHOD Certified Organic
JSTAINABLE WINERY

rraced vineyards cling to the outer slopes
the Astroni crater in this harsh, striking
ndscape within the volcanic Phlegraean
elds. The husband-and-wife team,
erardo Vernazzaro and Emanuela Russo,
unded the winery here in 1999. An oasis
biodiversity where rain falls on layers of
pilli and ash, it produces authentic wines
th an inspired natural eloquence that's
mmon to the Vigna Astroni and Vigna
peratrice crus. Another two plots -- Vigna
maldoli and Vigna Iossa --complete the
nge. The 2016 Piedirosso Colle
tondella offers up pleasant and airy
omas, with free and light red fruit and a
eting, relaxed, very pure and pleasant
late. The final flowery echo of violets and
ses makes it even more enticing. The
)12 Strione, a Falanghina macerated on
e skins, has an original profile, with its
omas of hazelnut and fennel, and a firm
nnic grip that's well-supported by dark
d intense minerality.

Campi Flegrei Piedirosso Colle Rotondella '16	🍷🍷 3
Strione '12	🍷🍷 4
Campi Flegrei Falanghina Colle Imperatrice '16	🍷 2
Campi Flegrei Falanghina V. Astroni '14	🍷 3
Campi Flegrei Falanghina Colle Imperatrice '15	🍷🍷 2*
Campi Flegrei Falanghina V. Astroni '14	🍷🍷 3
Campi Flegrei Falanghina V. Astroni '13	🍷🍷 3
Campi Flegrei Piedirosso Colle Rotondella '15	🍷🍷 3*
Strione '10	🍷🍷 4

I Cacciagalli

LOC. CAIANELLO
FRAZ. AORIVOLA
VIA TEANO, 3
81059 TEANO [CE]
TEL. +39 0823875216
www.icacciagalli.it

CELLAR SALES
PRE-BOOKED VISITS
ACCOMMODATION
ANNUAL PRODUCTION 20,000 bottles
HECTARES UNDER VINE 9.00
VITICULTURE METHOD Certified Organic

Mario Basco and Diana Iannaccone's work is
going forward at a cracking pace and they're
producing some of the most original wines in
the region in terms of style and aromatic
definition. These wines are made using
biodynamic viticulture, amphorae, concrete,
and large barrels. Cacciagalli wines have a
distinctive grip and freshness, and do a good
job representing the slopes of this extinct
Roccamonica volcano in Caserta. It's worth
noting the opening of Bistrot 26 on the
estate, where local dishes are matched with
a selection to satisfy all wine lovers. The
2015 Sphaeranera is in great form. This
Pallagrello Nero is well-paced and refreshing
with a touch of smoke and particularly juicy
fruit. The palate proves vibrant and vigorous,
thanks to a pervasive minerality: it centers
on nuances of pepper with a long, fragrant
finish, and a rustic note that makes you want
to come back for more. The 2015 Phos, an
Aglianico fermented in amphorae with an
irreverent spicy sprint and driving tannins,
also proves lively. The Falanghina Aorivola is
improving, it's particularly ripe wine that's
rich in juice

● Sphaeranera '15	🍷🍷 4
○ Aorivola '16	🍷🍷 3
● Phos '15	🍷🍷 4
● Lucno '15	🍷 4
● Mille '16	🍷 3
○ Zagreo '15	🍷🍷🍷 4*
○ Aorivola '13	🍷🍷 4
● Basco '10	🍷🍷 3
● Lucno '13	🍷🍷 4
● Masseria Cacciagalli '11	🍷🍷 4
● Mille '15	🍷🍷 3
● Phos '13	🍷🍷 4
● Sphaeranera '13	🍷🍷 4
○ Zagreo '14	🍷🍷 4
○ Zagreo '14	🍷🍷 4
○ Zagreo '13	🍷🍷 4

Antonio Caggiano

C.DA SALA
83030 TAURASI [AV]
TEL. +39 082774723
www.cantinecaggiano.it

CELLAR SALES
PRE-BOOKED VISITS
RESTAURANT SERVICE
ANNUAL PRODUCTION 155,000 bottles
HECTARES UNDER VINE 25.00

Antonio Caggiano is the backbone of Irpinia winemaking. His passion for photography and travel drove him to create one of the most beautiful cellars in the region. It is made entirely from local stone with arches and vaulted ceilings housing barriques and bottles. Today his son Giuseppe (Pino to his friends) plays a fundamental role in running the winery. As well as Fiano di Avellino and Greco di Tufo, their historic Vigna Macchia dei Goti deserves a mention. It's a wine made with grapes cultivated on one of the most powerful and long-lived crus in the Taurasi appellation. Their overall selection is quite solid. If the 2013 Taurasi Vigna Macchia dei Goti is still behind development-wise (though it possesses rich extraction and remarkable acidity), the 2015 Taurì is already a delight to drink. It offers up tasty red fruit, aromas of orange peel and a racy and rigid palate; it's a style worth following. The 2016 Devon is also quite good, with its generous aromas and biting salty finish, just as we'd expect from a vintage Greco di Tufo.

● Irpinia Aglianico Taurì '15	♥♥	3*
● Taurasi V. Macchia dei Goti '13	♥♥	6
○ Fiano di Avellino Béchar '16	♥♥	3
○ Greco di Tufo Devon '16	♥♥	3
○ Mel	♥♥	5
○ Fiagre '16	♥	3
● Irpinia Campi Taurasini Salae Domini '15	♥	5
○ Fiano di Avellino Béchar '13	♥♥♥	3*
● Taurasi V. Macchia dei Goti '08	♥♥♥	5
● Taurasi V. Macchia dei Goti '04	♥♥♥	5
● Taurasi V. Macchia dei Goti '99	♥♥♥	5
○ Fiano di Avellino Béchar '14	♥♥	3*
● Taurasi V. Macchia dei Goti '12	♥♥	5

Casa Setaro

LOC. PARCO NAZIONALE DEL VESUVIO
VIA BOSCO DEL MONACO, 34
80040 TRECASE [NA]
TEL. +39 0818628956
www.casasetaro.it

PRE-BOOKED VISITS
RESTAURANT SERVICE
ANNUAL PRODUCTION 50,000 bottles
HECTARES UNDER VINE 10.00

The small Trecase winery on the slopes of Vesuvius, run by Massimo and Mariarosar Setaro, has made its debut among the guide's major players. Their vineyards are located on two slopes of the Vesuvius national park. The highest is Alto Torrione, where the vines are Guyot-trained and sand and lapilli soil allows them to remain ungrafted. The other is further down in Bosco del Monaco, where the old vineyard are grown with the Vesuvian Pergola system. The estate makes seven wines, a from ungrafted native vines. The Capretto variety is particularly worthy of praise. The 2016 Falanghina Campanelle exhibits a persistent and driving palate, with juicy notes of apricot and pencil lead, a smoky pace and a balanced, flavorful finish. The 2013 Caprettone Brut is a fun wine, lining up aromas of latex, bread and ripe citrus fruit. The mouth is assertive, with hints of bitter almonds, a slight tannic note and a warm, tangy finish that's pleasantly rustic

○ Caprettone Brut M. Cl. '13	♥♥	
○ Falanghina Campanelle '16	♥♥	
● Vesuvio Lacryma Christi Rosso Don Vincenzo '13	♥	
● Vesuvio Lacryma Christi Rosso Munazei '16	♥	
● Aglianico Tauro '12	♥♥	
○ Caprettone Brut M. Cl. '13	♥♥	
○ Falanghina Campanelle '16	♥♥	
● Terramatta '13	♥♥	

Casebianche

c.da Case Bianche, 8
84076 Torchiara [SA]
Tel. +39 0974843244
www.casebianche.eu

CELLAR SALES
PRE-BOOKED VISITS
ANNUAL PRODUCTION 35,000 bottles
HECTARES UNDER VINE 5.50
VITICULTURE METHOD Certified Organic
SUSTAINABLE WINERY

Betty Iuorio and Pasquale Mitrano's Cilento winery has made its debut with a deluge of assertive, second fermentation wines. Architects by profession, they made a life choice when they moved to Torchiara to live among fig trees, olive groves and well-tended vineyards. The clay-rich, stony soil is situated between Monte Stella, the Aquasanta stream and the splendid Cilento sea. Here they produce powerful, expressive wines, employing organic management and with minimal frills in the cellar. And the use of sulfites can be kept to a minimum thanks to healthy grapes. In the glass, their wines offer up vitality and drinkability. Their latest creation, the Pashkà, is an equal blend of Barbera and Aglianico made using bottle fermentation. The Fric is a contemporary interpretation of Aglianico. The 2016 proves to be a delight of floral fragrances, crisp fruit, watermelon and blood oranges, with an extravagant rustic and yeasty note, and a tannic, astute finish. The palate is pleasant, with its sparkle setting the pace. The 2016 La Matta offers up tasty overtones of ripe apple and freshly-cut grass.

Il Fric '16	♟♟♟ 3*
Cilento Rosso Dellemore '15	♟♟ 3
La Matta Dosaggio Zero '16	♟♟ 3
Pashkà '16	♟♟ 3
Iscadoro Bianco '16	♟ 3
Cilento Fiano Cumalè '12	♟♟ 2*
Cilento Rosso Dellemore '12	♟♟ 2*
Il Fric '15	♟♟ 3
La Matta Dosaggio Zero '15	♟♟ 3*
La Matta Dosaggio Zero '14	♟♟ 3
La Matta Dosaggio Zero '12	♟♟ 3

Cautiero

c.da Arbusti
82030 Frasso Telesino [BN]
Tel. +39 3387640641
www.cautiero.it

CELLAR SALES
ACCOMMODATION
ANNUAL PRODUCTION 18,000 bottles
HECTARES UNDER VINE 4.00
VITICULTURE METHOD Certified Organic

The formation of Fulvio Cautiero and Imma Cropano's estate is one of the loveliest winemaking stories in Campania. They left their respective jobs in 2002 and set up a large-scale project to develop abandoned land inside the Taburno Regional Park. Using only native varieties, and employing organic farming techniques and alternative energy sources (solar power), the specialty of the house is Falanghina. Here, Cautiero has undoubtedly established one of the most important benchmarks for aromatic precision, expressive lightness and grip. A less-solid performance than what we've become accustomed to. The Falanghina Fois is always tops, though the 2016 is a bit behind development-wise. It features bright green highlights and faintly macerated notes that give way to green tea, aniseed and sage. The mouth is tangy and juicy, with good grip. The only shame is the touch of alcohol that slips out at the finish.

○ Falanghina del Sannio Fois '16	♟♟ 2*
● Sannio Aglianico Fois '14	♟ 2
○ Falanghina del Sannio Fois '13	♟♟♟ 2*
○ Erba Bianca '15	♟♟ 2*
○ Erba Bianca '14	♟♟ 2*
○ Falanghina del Sannio Fois '15	♟♟ 2*
○ Falanghina del Sannio Fois '14	♟♟ 2*
● Piedirosso '13	♟♟ 2*
● Sannio Aglianico Donna Candida '10	♟♟ 4
● Sannio Aglianico Fois '13	♟♟ 2*
● Sannio Aglianico Fois '12	♟♟ 2*
○ Sannio Falanghina Fois '12	♟♟ 2*
○ Sannio Falanghina Fois '11	♟♟ 2*
○ Sannio Greco Trois '15	♟♟ 2*
○ Sannio Greco Trois '14	♟♟ 2*
○ Sannio Greco Trois '13	♟♟ 2*

Tenuta Cavalier Pepe

VIA SANTA VARA
83050 SANT'ANGELO ALL'ESCA [AV]
TEL. +39 082773766
www.tenutapepe.it

CELLAR SALES
PRE-BOOKED VISITS
ACCOMMODATION AND RESTAURANT SERVICE
ANNUAL PRODUCTION 380,000 bottles
HECTARES UNDER VINE 60.00
SUSTAINABLE WINERY

Angelo Pepe is most certainly an entrepreneur devoted to good eating and drinking. In just a few years he has planned the future of his family by setting up a winery and accommodation facility. Today, Pepe wines are sold all over Italy and abroad and include the most famous appellations in Irpinia. Their 50 hectares of vineyards are located in Sant'Angelo all'Esca, Montefusco, Torrioni and Luogosano. Angelo has passed on his expertise, along with the business, to his daughter Milena. Since completing her studies and work experience abroad, she has been the real driving force behind winemaking. The 2012 Taurasi Opera Mia is still clenched and bridled, but still quite well-made. It offers up full notes of Mediterranean scrub and a rich and gradual palate. It remains invigorating and fresh right up to its balsamic finish. Of the whites, the 2015 Greco di Tufo Grancare stands out, with its multifaceted and dynamic aromas of citron and almond. It a long, close-knit wine. The Nestor, a mature and glycerin-rich wine, also did well, exhibiting pace and good supporting acidity.

○ Fiano di Avellino Refiano '16	🍷🍷	3
○ Greco di Tufo Grancare '15	🍷🍷	5
○ Greco di Tufo Nestor '16	🍷🍷	3
● Taurasi Opera Mia '12	🍷🍷	5
○ Fiano di Avellino Brancato '15	🍷	5
○ Irpinia Falanghina Lila '16	🍷	2
● Taurasi La Loggia del Cavaliere Ris. '11	🍷	7
○ Fiano di Avellino Refiano '15	🍷🍷	3
○ Fiano di Avellino Refiano '14	🍷🍷	3
○ Fiano di Avellino Refiano '13	🍷🍷	3
○ Greco di Tufo Nestor '15	🍷🍷	3
● Irpinia Aglianico Terra del Varo '11	🍷🍷	2*
● Taurasi Opera Mia '11	🍷🍷	5
● Taurasi Opera Mia '10	🍷🍷	5

Cenatiempo Vini d'Ischia

VIA BALDASSARRE COSSA, 84
80077 ISCHIA [NA]
TEL. +39 081981107
www.vinicenatiempo.it

CELLAR SALES
PRE-BOOKED VISITS
ANNUAL PRODUCTION 70,000 bottles
HECTARES UNDER VINE 4.00

Confirmation has arrived for this family-run Ischian winery, founded in 1945 by Francesco Cenatiempo. The seventeenth-century cellar is dug out of the Kalimera hill and here they work with the native varieties of the island, especially Biancolella, Forastera and Piedirosso. Their wines exhibit a skilled hand, combining tradition and drinkability with levels of sulfur dioxide that are clearly below the regional average. The whites in particular are always among the most focused and expressive in this endearing corner of the region. The 2016 Forastera just missed out on the big one. This exquisitely marine white proves relaxed and musky, with its aromas of basil and ocean. It's fuller than it is linear, excellently timed, with a slightly more mature and tannic finish that harkens back to the palate. The 2016 Biancolella sees subtler and airier aromas of citron and broom, proving sunny and graceful. The Biancolella Kalimera from the same vintage is richer, more mature and delicately salty, with notes of tropical fruit.

○ Ischia Forastera '16	🍷🍷	4
○ Ischia Biancolella '16	🍷🍷	3
○ Ischia Biancolella Kalimera '16	🍷🍷	4
● Ischia Per' 'e Palummo '16	🍷	3
○ Ischia Biancolella '15	🍷🍷	3
○ Ischia Biancolella '13	🍷🍷	2
○ Ischia Biancolella Kalimera '14	🍷🍷	4
○ Ischia Biancolella Kalimera '13	🍷🍷	4
○ Ischia Forastera '15	🍷🍷	4
● Ischia Per' 'e Palummo '14	🍷🍷	3

Colli di Castelfranci

C.DA BRAUDIANO
83040 CASTELFRANCI [AV]
TEL. +39 082772392
www.collidicastelfranci.com

CELLAR SALES
PRE-BOOKED VISITS
ACCOMMODATION AND RESTAURANT SERVICE
ANNUAL PRODUCTION 150,000 bottles
HECTARES UNDER VINE 25.00

Luciano Gregorio and Gerardo Colucci's winery has fought its way back to a place among the big names. Greco and Fiano are worked in steel while the reds display a skillful use of wood. The yields are much lower than the regional average, and the distribution of the vineyards is out of the ordinary with some plots in the Upper Calore Valley reaching an altitude of 700 meters. As a result, ripening cycles are slower and acidity levels are often high. The 2010 Taurasi Alta Valle Riserva was undoubtedly one of the best we tasted. Its mature and pervasive nose offers up finely-toasted notes while the palate comes through powerful and succulent (though without showing off). It unfolds gradually and deeply, softening into notes of black fruit, balsamic and eastern spices. It also proved excellent in its tannic extraction. Another red keeps it company, the 2014 Aglianico Vadantico, with its intense aromas and a succulent, expansive palate. The 2016 Fiano di Avellino Pendino, with its solid structure, and the 2016 Greco di Tufo Grotte are also well-made.

● Taurasi Alta Valle Ris. '10	♟♟ 7
○ Fiano di Avellino Pendino '16	♟♟ 3
● Irpinia Campi Taurasini Vadantico '14	♟♟ 3
○ Greco di Tufo Grotte '16	♟ 3
○ Sannio Falanghina Gines '16	♟ 2
○ Fiano di Avellino Pendino '16	♟♟ 3
○ Fiano di Avellino Pendino '14	♟♟ 2*
○ Greco di Tufo Grotte '15	♟♟ 2*
○ Greco di Tufo Grotte '14	♟♟ 2*
○ Greco di Tufo Grotte '13	♟♟ 3
○ Irpinia Aglianico Rosato Crote '14	♟♟ 3
● Irpinia Campi Taurasini Vadantico '10	♟♟ 3
○ Irpinia Greco Vallicelli '13	♟♟ 4
○ Irpinia Greco Vallicelli '11	♟♟ 4
● Taurasi Alta Valle '10	♟♟ 5
● Taurasi Alta Valle Ris. '09	♟♟ 7

★Colli di Lapio

VIA ARIANIELLO, 47
83030 LAPIO [AV]
TEL. +39 0825982184
www.collidilapio.it

CELLAR SALES
PRE-BOOKED VISITS
ANNUAL PRODUCTION 6,000 bottles
HECTARES UNDER VINE 8.00

Lapio is one of the few municipalities that can boast a double appellation, Taurasi and Fiano di Avellino. Fiano, the white gold of Avellino, is the key player at Clelia Romano's winery. Here she is supported by her husband, Angelo, and two children who tend to the agricultural side of things. Every year they produce some of the wine's most aromatic interpretations, thanks to an extraordinary depth of taste made possible by tangy verve and bright acidity. These are southern Italian wines with a northern style, due partly to the altitude of the vineyards (over 500 meters) between Arianello and Stazzone. During tasting, the Fiano di Avellino got a 'wow' from our panel. The 2016 is a real gem, a white that starts off slowly, then unfolds with a particularly airy and glossy aromatic profile characterized by aniseed, elderflower, citron and ginger. The palate seems to have a third phase, where it reveals a scintillating taste surge that fires up a balsamic freshness and flavor, making for a wine that lengthens and expands overwhelmingly. There's a marked difference with the two other wines put forward.

○ Fiano di Avellino '16	♟♟♟ 4*
○ Greco di Tufo Alexandros '16	♟ 3
● Taurasi Andrea '12	♟ 5
○ Fiano di Avellino '15	♟♟♟ 4*
○ Fiano di Avellino '14	♟♟♟ 4*
○ Fiano di Avellino '13	♟♟♟ 4*
○ Fiano di Avellino '10	♟♟♟ 4
○ Fiano di Avellino '09	♟♟♟ 4
○ Fiano di Avellino '08	♟♟♟ 4*
○ Fiano di Avellino '07	♟♟♟ 4
○ Fiano di Avellino '05	♟♟♟ 4
○ Fiano di Avellino '04	♟♟♟ 4
○ Fiano di Avellino '12	♟♟ 4
○ Fiano di Avellino '11	♟♟ 4
● Taurasi V. Andrea '05	♟♟ 5

Michele Contrada

C.DA TAVERNA, 31
83040 CANDIDA [AV]
TEL. +39 0825988434
www.vinicontrada.it

CELLAR SALES
PRE-BOOKED VISITS
ANNUAL PRODUCTION 60,000 bottles
HECTARES UNDER VINE 10.00

Like many families in Irpinia, the Contradas worked as vine growers for years before deciding to set up their own winery in Candida, in 2003. They wanted to show the wine world their skilled work on the land, coupled with their extensive knowledge of the vines. Gerardo Contrada heads the winery and farms the land with techniques that reduce the impact on the environment in order to protect the local landscape and preserve traditions. Contrada make several different wines: Taurasi, Fiano di Avellino and Greco di Tufo, as well as various IGT and DOC wines. In Candida, Fiano grapes find a particular richness of taste and minerality; the Aglianico, on the other hand, is made with grapes cultivated in both Candida and Castelfranci. The 2015 Greco di Tufo is pleasantly rustic and approachable, with aromas of aniseed and almonds. In the mouth, it proves generous and juicy, with grassy and musky hints and a very citrusy finish. The 2013 Irpinia Aglianico offers up aromas of cherries and mulberries, a well-sustained palate, integrated tannins and a finish that fades into a nice floral note.

○ Greco di Tufo '15	♟♟ 3*
● Irpinia Aglianico '13	♟♟ 2*
○ Fiano di Avellino Selvecorte '12	♟♟♟ 3*
○ Fiano di Avellino '15	♟♟ 3*
○ Fiano di Avellino '12	♟♟ 3*
○ Fiano di Avellino Selvecorte '13	♟♟ 3*
○ Fiano di Avellino Selvecorte '11	♟♟ 3*
○ Greco di Tufo '12	♟♟ 3
○ Greco di Tufo Gaudioso '13	♟♟ 2*
○ Greco di Tufo Gaudioso '12	♟♟ 3
○ Irpinia Coda di Volpe Taberna '11	♟♟ 2*
● Taurasi '11	♟♟ 5
● Taurasi Hirpus '08	♟♟ 5

Contrade di Taurasi

VIA MUNICIPIO, 41
83030 TAURASI [AV]
TEL. +39 082774483
www.cantinelonardo.it

CELLAR SALES
PRE-BOOKED VISITS
ANNUAL PRODUCTION 18,000 bottles
HECTARES UNDER VINE 5.00
VITICULTURE METHOD Certified Organic

Since 1998, the Lonardo family have been working hard to please Taurasi lovers. They have raised the bar of the appellation by creating different versions of traditional wines, but with a modern style. They use measured extraction to bring out the attributes of the various exposures and soil types, so that their sunny and energetic Coste cru contrasts with the darker and shadier Vigne d'Alto. In addition to the historic plots in Taurasi, some vineyards have been planted with a local variety known as Greco Musc', a delightfully Mediterranean leaning white. The 2015 Grecomusc' particularly impressed us for its relaxed and silent gait, its musky tone and fine, almost ethery aromas that range from white melon to sage. The palate is embellished, fresh and deep, with a lingering, final marine note. Definitely a Tre Bicchieri. The 2012 Taurasi Coste also made it to the finals. It calls up aromas of ripe peaches and black tea, while the palate proves close-knit, with racy tannins. A very well-made wine.

○ Grecomusc' '15	♟♟♟ 5
● Taurasi Coste '12	♟♟ 8
● Taurasi '12	♟♟ 6
○ Grecomusc' Burlesque '15	♟ 5
○ Grecomusc' '12	♟♟♟ 4*
○ Grecomusc' '10	♟♟♟ 4*
● Taurasi '10	♟♟♟ 6
● Taurasi '04	♟♟♟ 6
● Taurasi Coste '11	♟♟♟ 8
● Taurasi Coste '08	♟♟♟ 7
○ Grecomusc' '14	♟♟ 5
○ Grecomusc' Burlesque '14	♟♟ 5
● Taurasi '11	♟♟ 6
● Taurasi Vigne d'Alto '11	♟♟ 8

★Marisa Cuomo

VIA G. B. LAMA, 16/18
84010 FURORE [SA]
TEL. +39 089830348
www.marisacuomo.com

CELLAR SALES
PRE-BOOKED VISITS
RESTAURANT SERVICE
ANNUAL PRODUCTION 109,000 bottles
HECTARES UNDER VINE 18.00

At Marisa Cuomo's winery you can taste the sea and wine in the air. It's a producer that has made the Amalfi Coast famous all over the world. Here in Furore, the vineyards cling to the hills sweeping down towards the rocks and small terraces held up with dry stone walls. The vines sink their roots deep into the rich calcareous rock. Marisa, her husband, Andrea Ferraioli, and their children, Dora and Raffaele, run the twenty hectares of vineyards without applying weedkillers. The varieties are all native: Ripoli, Fenile and Ginestra for the whites, Piedirosso and Sciscinoso for the reds. The Fiorduva has proven that it's a timeless classic. The 2016 offers up an intertwining of charming and showy aromas, from white melon to citrus, white pepper and a hint of saffron. The endless finish leads us to Mediterranean herbs. The wood is perfectly measured and well-integrated with acidity lengthening the wine. The reds are on the up. The 2014 Furore Rosso Riserva is very impressive, multifaceted and complete, as rarely before. The 2016 Ravello Bianco is also quite good.

○ Costa d'Amalfi Furore Bianco Fiorduva '16	♥♥♥ 7
● Costa d'Amalfi Furore Rosso Ris. '14	♥♥ 6
○ Costa d'Amalfi Furore Bianco '16	♥♥ 4
● Costa d'Amalfi Furore Rosso '16	♥♥ 3
○ Costa d'Amalfi Ravello Bianco '16	♥♥ 3
● Costa d'Amalfi Ravello Rosso Ris. '14	♥ 5
⊙ Costa d'Amalfi Rosato '16	♥ 4
○ Costa d'Amalfi Furore Bianco '15	♥♥♥ 4*
○ Costa d'Amalfi Furore Bianco '10	♥♥♥ 4
○ Costa d'Amalfi Furore Bianco Fiorduva '14	♥♥♥ 7
○ Costa d'Amalfi Furore Bianco Fiorduva '10	♥♥♥ 6

D'Ambra Vini d'Ischia

FRAZ. PANZA
VIA MARIO D'AMBRA, 16
80077 FORIO [NA]
TEL. +39 081907210
www.dambravini.com

CELLAR SALES
PRE-BOOKED VISITS
ANNUAL PRODUCTION 450,000 bottles
HECTARES UNDER VINE 14.00

This is without doubt the most important and oldest winery on the island. Founded in 1888 by Francesco D'Ambra, who was the first to understand the potential of growing vines here, it is run today by the fourth generation. Marina manages the commercial side of things, Sara follows winemaking, and both are aided by their father, Andrea. They grow only native varieties: Biancolella, Forastera (both fermented in steel to enhance their marine profile) and Per 'e' Palummo. Their Biancolella cru gives rise to the first white wine in Campania to be awarded Tre Bicchieri. Once again, it's the troupe of whites that impressed us the most, although in some cases we noted quite high levels of sulfur dioxide. The 2016 Biancolella Tenuta Frassitelli offers up marine and iodine notes, a floral attack, good acidity and a finish that's still rather dry. It needs some more time in the bottle. The 2016 Ischia Bianco is spot-on, lightweight and aromatically intense, with notes of basil and thyme, and a fresh, juicy and citrusy palate. The 2016 Forastera proves to be an assertive wine.

○ Ischia Bianco '16	♥♥ 2*
○ Ischia Biancolella '16	♥♥ 3
○ Ischia Biancolella Tenuta Frassitelli '16	♥♥ 4
○ Ischia Forastera '16	♥♥ 3
○ Gocce d'Ambra Passito	♥ 5
● Ischia Per'e Palummo La Vigna dei Mille Anni '14	♥ 5
● Ischia Rosso Dedicato a Mario D'Ambra '14	♥ 4
○ Ischia Biancolella Tenuta Frassitelli '12	♥♥♥ 3*
○ Ischia Biancolella Tenuta Frassitelli '90	♥♥♥ 3*
○ Ischia Biancolella Tenuta Frassitelli '15	♥♥ 4
● Ischia Per'e Palummo La Vigna dei Mille Anni '13	♥♥ 5

Cantine Di Marzo

VIA GAETANO DI MARZO, 2
83010 TUFO [AV]
TEL. +39 0825998022
www.cantinedimarzo.it

CELLAR SALES
PRE-BOOKED VISITS
ANNUAL PRODUCTION 150,000 bottles
HECTARES UNDER VINE 23.00

Their first Tre Bicchieri seals the history of a winery with over 370 years behind it. A visit to the seventeenth-century cellar dug out of volcanic tuff gives you an idea of the legacy the Di Somma family relaunched in 2009. There are 23 hectares of property for three lines of wines made with Greco, Fiano and Aglianico grapes: Stemma, Palazzo and Gamma Premium. Additionally, the Metodo Classico Anni Venti sparkling wine, also from Greco grapes, has proven its merit over the years. The gold goes to the 2016 Greco di Tufo, a wine that manages to unfold perfectly right from the first drop, with ripe, succulent fruit giving way to a laser-like savoriness that delights the palate. The 2016 selection Colle Serrone, with its slower aromatic development, austere elegance and a light, flavorsome, long finish, also delivered.

○ Greco di Tufo '16	♟♟♟ 2*
○ Greco di Tufo Colle Serrone '16	♟♟ 3*
○ Greco di Tufo Brut M. Cl. Anni Venti	♟ 4
○ Fiano di Avellino Donatus '13	♟♟ 3*
○ Fiano di Avellino Donatus '12	♟♟ 3
○ Greco di Tufo '15	♟♟ 2*
○ Greco di Tufo Franciscus '11	♟♟ 3
○ Greco di Tufo Scipio '11	♟♟ 4
○ Greco di Tufo Somnium Scipionis '13	♟♟ 5
○ Greco di Tufo Somnium Scipionis '12	♟♟ 5
● Taurasi Albertus '10	♟♟ 5

Di Meo

C.DA COCCOVONI, 1
83050 SALZA IRPINA [AV]
TEL. +39 0825981419
www.dimeo.it

CELLAR SALES
PRE-BOOKED VISITS
RESTAURANT SERVICE
ANNUAL PRODUCTION 450,000 bottles
HECTARES UNDER VINE 30.00
SUSTAINABLE WINERY

Roberto and Generoso Di Meo's cellar is housed in a picturesque eighteenth-century farmhouse, built on the hunting lodge of the Caracciolos, a local noble family. This is Salza Irpina, land of Fiano di Avellino, where vineyards grow at at 550 meters above sea level on calcareous-clay soil mixed with silt. The Greco di Tufo vineyards are in Santa Paolina and Tufo, while their powerful and long-aged Taurasi wines are made from grapes grown in Montemarano at 650 meters. Di Meo was one of the first wineries to experiment with the longevity of Irpinian whites, which they release onto the market as late as 10-15 years after the vintage, to good effect. The 2007 Greco di Tufo Vittoria is close-knit even in color, and its rocky, musky temperament confers the palate with good pace. The wine features a nice, delicate touch that precedes its long finish. But it's the 2012 Fiano di Avellino Alessandra that once again earns a Tre Bicchieri. It's a generous, slightly sulfurous wine with an incredible breadth of aromas and depth of taste: an all-round white, with a classy and precise finish.

○ Fiano di Avellino Alessandra '12	♟♟♟ 3*
○ Greco di Tufo Vittoria '07	♟♟ 4
○ Coda di Volpe C '16	♟♟ 2*
○ Fiano di Avellino F '16	♟ 3
● Isso Aglianico '15	♟ 2
● Taurasi Ris. '06	♟♟♟ 5
○ Fiano di Avellino Colle dei Cerri '10	♟♟ 4
○ Fiano di Avellino F '15	♟♟ 3*
○ Fiano di Avellino F '12	♟♟ 3
○ Fiano di Avellino F Sel. Alessandra '11	♟♟ 3
○ Greco di Tufo G '07	♟♟ 3
● Taurasi Sel. Hamilton Ris. '08	♟♟ 7
● Taurasi V. Olmo Ris. '10	♟♟ 5
● Taurasi V. Olmo Ris. '08	♟♟ 5

Donnachiara

LOC. PIETRACUPA
VIA STAZIONE
83030 MONTEFALCIONE [AV]
TEL. +39 0825977135
www.donnachiara.com

CELLAR SALES
PRE-BOOKED VISITS
ACCOMMODATION
ANNUAL PRODUCTION 200,000 bottles
HECTARES UNDER VINE 27.00

The Petitto family winery, one of the most dynamic and lively in the crowded Irpinian district, is full steam ahead. At the forefront is Ilaria (Umberto and Chiara's daughter), supported by Riccardo Cotarella in winemaking. Their wines have a particularly rich style. The reds are dense and age in small casks, while the whites seem to gain in precision year after year, even as their wines take on a more powerful structure. It's the 2016 Greco di Tufo that comes through, bringing the winery its first Tre Bicchieri. It's an approachable and aromatic white, with juicy yellow fruit, followed by hints of citron and a creamy palate, with a flavor lengthened by notes of aniseed and mint. The 2012 Taurasi Riserva exhibits a structure marked by notes of orange peel and small red fruit. The palate confirms its good driving flavor, held back nicely by tight-knit and slightly green tannins.

○ Greco di Tufo '16	♟♟♟	3*
● Taurasi Ris. '12	♟♟	7
○ Fiano di Avellino '16	♟	3
● Irpinia Aglianico '14	♟	3
● Taurasi '13	♟	5
○ Falanghina '15	♟♟	2*
○ Falanghina '14	♟♟	2*
○ Falanghina del Beneventano '13	♟♟	2*
○ Fiano di Avellino '13	♟♟	3
○ Fiano di Avellino '12	♟♟	3
○ Greco di Tufo '15	♟♟	3
○ Greco di Tufo '14	♟♟	2*
○ Greco di Tufo '12	♟♟	3
○ Irpinia Coda di Volpe '15	♟♟	3
○ Irpinia Coda di Volpe '14	♟♟	2*

I Favati

P.ZZA DI DONATO
83020 CESINALI [AV]
TEL. +39 0825666898
www.cantineifavati.it

CELLAR SALES
PRE-BOOKED VISITS
ANNUAL PRODUCTION 80,000 bottles
HECTARES UNDER VINE 16.00

Favati is situated in Cesinali, the southernmost part of the valley carved out by the river Sabato. It's run by Rosanna Petrozziello and her husband, Giancarlo, as well as his brother, Piersabino Favati. Over the years, they have built up one of the best wineries in the area, thanks to their deep, territorial and elegant wines. The Fiano Pietramara is made with grapes cultivated on the vineyard of the same name in Atripalda, while the plot of Greco is located in Montefusco. To complete the range there are two reds made with Aglianico, which are more extracted and concentrated than the whites. The 2016 Fiano di Avellino Pietramara is a volatile, volcanic and intensely smoky wine, with nuanced and subtle aromas of wheat and straw. The palate proves racy with good pace and a clear-cut, classy final crescendo. It's not just Tre Bicchieri, it's our 'White of the Year'. The 2016 Greco di Tufo Terrantica made it to the finals, offering up taut and scintillating aromas of citrus peel, ginger and fresh almonds, and a delicately salty palate that features a lovely texture of aniseed and catmint at the finish.

○ Fiano di Avellino Pietramara '16	♟♟♟	3*
○ Greco di Tufo Terrantica '16	♟♟	2*
● Taurasi Terzo Tratto Ris. '11	♟	5
○ Fiano di Avellino Pietramara '15	♟♟♟	3*
○ Fiano di Avellino Pietramara '13	♟♟♟	3*
○ Fiano di Avellino Pietramara '12	♟♟♟	3*
○ Fiano di Avellino Pietramara '14	♟♟	3*
○ Fiano di Avellino Pietramara Et. Bianca '13	♟♟	5
○ Greco di Tufo Terrantica '14	♟♟	2*
○ Greco di Tufo Terrantica '13	♟♟	3*
● Taurasi Terzo Tratto '09	♟♟	5
● Taurasi Terzo Tratto Et. Bianca '08	♟♟	7
● Taurasi Terzo Tratto Et. Bianca Ris. '10	♟♟	7

Benito Ferrara

Fraz. San Paolo, 14a
83010 Tufo [AV]
Tel. +39 0825998194
www.benitoferrara.it

CELLAR SALES
PRE-BOOKED VISITS
ANNUAL PRODUCTION 55,000 bottles
HECTARES UNDER VINE 13.00

Gabriella Ferrara's vineyards fall under the district of San Paolo in the municipality of Tufo (everyone is familiar with the excellent Greco made here). The winery moved quickly into the limelight under Benito Ferrara, head of family. He immediately grasped the potential of the territory, seizing quickly on the idea of making monovarietal Aglianico and Greco wines. Today, Benito's daughter Gabriella carries on the winemaking tradition at 500 meters above sea level on sulfur-colored soil that's, rich in clay and stones, with her famous top-notch Cru, Greco Vigna Cicogna. The Greco di Tufo Vigna Cicogna made it to the finals. In recent years it has become softer, but is just as appealing as the ones we have seen in the past. The 2016 is elegant and supple, with a sweet and ripe fruit that is backed up by an unbridled minerality, for a deep finish between spices, herbs and resinous overtones. The 2016 Greco di Tufo Terra d'Uva also put in a good performance. It's full, tangy and balanced, with an invigorating finish of aniseed and mint.

○ Greco di Tufo V. Cicogna '16	♀♀ 4	
○ Greco di Tufo Terra d'Uva '16	♀♀ 4	
○ Fiano d'Avellino Sequenzha '15	♀ 4	
● Irpinia Aglianico Quattro Confini '15	♀ 3	
○ Greco di Tufo V. Cicogna '15	♀♀♀ 4*	
○ Greco di Tufo V. Cicogna '14	♀♀♀ 4*	
○ Greco di Tufo V. Cicogna '13	♀♀♀ 5	
○ Fiano di Avellino '13	♀♀ 4	
○ Greco di Tufo '13	♀♀ 4	
○ Greco di Tufo '12	♀♀ 3*	
○ Greco di Tufo '09	♀♀ 3	
○ Greco di Tufo '08	♀♀ 3	
○ Greco di Tufo V. Cicogna '04	♀♀ 4	
● Taurasi V. Quattro Confini '08	♀♀ 5	

★★Feudi di San Gregorio

loc. Cerza Grossa
83050 Sorbo Serpico [AV]
Tel. +39 0825986683
www.feudi.it

CELLAR SALES
PRE-BOOKED VISITS
RESTAURANT SERVICE
ANNUAL PRODUCTION 3,500,000 bottles
HECTARES UNDER VINE 250.00
VITICULTURE METHOD Certified Organic

Business is expanding for this renowned cellar in Sorbo Serpico. At the end of 2016, the Campo alle Comete winery in Bolgheri became part of Antonio Capaldo's group. The change in style and the closer bond with the territory are apparent in the glass. They began making a sparkling wine, Dubl, 13 years ago, and this year they have added a rosé to the Esse range. When you visit the cellar, plan to stop in for a meal at the winery's Marannà restaurant. The 2013 Taurasi combines power and precision. It features succulent aromas of small red fruit, a racy and rigid palate, with cossetting tannins and a pure and lingering finish. It earned a Tre Bicchieri effortlessly. The 2016 Fiano di Avellino Pietracalda also made it to the finals, with its signature note of dried fruit and pollen. The palate proves tangy and balanced, with a herby finish. The 2014 Pàtrimo is worth noting, it's decidedly finer and more contemporary in style, and the Dubl Esse also impressed.

● Taurasi '13	♀♀♀ 5	
○ Fiano di Avellino Pietracalda '16	♀♀ 4	
○ Dubl Esse	♀♀ 5	
○ Falanghina del Sannio Serrociclo '16	♀♀ 3	
● Pàtrimo '14	♀♀ 8	
● Taurasi Piano di Montevergine Ris. '12	♀♀ 6	
○ Greco di Tufo Cutizzi '16	♀ 4	
● Irpinia Aglianico Serpico '13	♀ 7	
○ Irpinia Bianco Campanaro '15	♀ 5	
○ Fiano di Avellino Pietracalda '09	♀♀♀ 3	
○ Greco di Tufo Cutizzi '12	♀♀♀ 3*	
○ Greco di Tufo Cutizzi '10	♀♀♀ 3	
● Taurasi Piano di Montevergine Ris. '07	♀♀♀ 6	

Fontanavecchia

VIA FONTANAVECCHIA, 7
82030 TORRECUSO [BN]
TEL. +39 0824876275
www.fontanavecchia.info

CELLAR SALES
PRE-BOOKED VISITS
ACCOMMODATION AND RESTAURANT SERVICE
ANNUAL PRODUCTION 175,000 bottles
HECTARES UNDER VINE 20.00

As a wine producer and president of the
Consorzio Tutela Vini Sannio, Libero Rillo Is
quite a busy man. His winery on the slopes
of Mount Taburno spans 20 hectares of
vineyards (plus some rented plots). Over
the years they've made some of the best
wines in the area. Falanghina, two different
versions of it, takes center stage. One is
made in steel, the other is a Facetus
selection featuring late harvest grapes with
minimal partial-aging in wood (and sold
only after long bottle maturation). Likewise
for the reds, which are put on the market
only after several years in the bottle. The
2016 Falanghina del Sannio is certainly
one of the best we tested. It speaks to the
nature of the vintage, with a subtle and
lingering range of aromas from green tea to
mountain herbs. The palate is supple, and
almost ethery, with a very precise finish of
aniseed and mint. It's going to age quite
well. The 2012 Falanghina Facetus
Vendemmia Tardiva also delivered. The
wine is still very compact and plays on
smoky hints and balsamic freshness.

○ Falanghina del Sannio Taburno '16	♟♟♟	3*
○ Falanghina del Sannio Facetus V. T. '12	♟♟	3*
○ Sannio Greco '16	♟♟	3
◉ Aglianico del Taburno Rosato '16	♟	3
● Orazio '11	♟	5
○ Falanghina del Sannio Taburno '15	♟♟♟	2*
○ Falanghina del Sannio Taburno '14	♟♟♟	2*
○ Falanghina del Sannio Taburno '13	♟♟♟	2*
○ Falanghina del Sannio Taburno '12	♟♟♟	2*
● Aglianico del Taburno '11	♟♟	3
● Aglianico del Taburno '09	♟♟	3
● Aglianico del Taburno V. Cataratte '09	♟♟	5
● Aglianico del Taburno V. Cataratte Ris. '08	♟♟	4
○ Sannio Fiano '13	♟♟	2*
● Sannio Rosso '15	♟♟	2*

Fonzone

LOC. SCORZAGALLINE
83052 PATERNOPOLI [AV]
TEL. +39 08271730100
www.fonzone.it

CELLAR SALES
PRE-BOOKED VISITS
ANNUAL PRODUCTION 57,000 bottles
HECTARES UNDER VINE 22.00
SUSTAINABLE WINERY

Fonzone is one of the most serious and
elaborate operations in Irpinia. It began in
Paternopoli in 2005, when Lorenzo
Fonzone Caccese decided to apply his skills
as a surgeon to the world of wine. The
cellar employs cutting-edge technology and
the vineyards are run with environmentally-
sustainable methods. Vincenzo Mercurio
looks after the winemaking, and the whites
stand out for their aromatic finesse and
unfolding flavors. Except for Fiano Sequoia,
a late harvest wine aged in wood, they are
all vinified in steel. Tre Bicchieri have
returned to Fonzone thanks to a Fiano di
Avellino that still has plenty of life in it. The
2016 gets off to a slow start but finishes in
glory. The palate sees a snappy driving
acidity, clean flavors and a particularly fresh
and lingering finish. The 2014 Irpinia
Aglianico also had a good day, with its
approachable notes of orange, pepper and
black fruit. Its racy palate, tasty fruit and
well-orchestrated wood are rare for the
appellation.

○ Fiano di Avellino '16	♟♟♟	3*
○ Greco di Tufo '16	♟♟	3
● Irpina Aglianico '14	♟♟	3
● Irpinia Campi Taurasini '14	♟	3
○ Greco di Tufo '13	♟♟♟	3*
● Aglianico '12	♟♟	3
○ Fiano di Avellino '14	♟♟	3
○ Fiano di Avellino '13	♟♟	3*
○ Fiano di Avellino '12	♟♟	3
○ Greco di Tufo '14	♟♟	3*
○ Greco di Tufo '12	♟♟	2*
● Irpinia Campi Taurasini '10	♟♟	3
○ Irpinia Fiano Sequoia '13	♟♟	5
● Taurasi Scorzagalline Ris. '10	♟♟	5

La Fortezza

LOC. TORA II, 20
82030 TORRECUSO [BN]
TEL. +39 0824886155
www.lafortezzasrl.it

CELLAR SALES
PRE-BOOKED VISITS
ANNUAL PRODUCTION 300,000 bottles
HECTARES UNDER VINE 50.00

Enzo Rillo is a successful businessman who has worked in different sectors including textiles, road safety and hi-tech services. Never one to balk at challenges, he selected the Torrecuso and Samnium areas for his estate and bought a 30-hectare vineyard on the eastern slope of the Taburno Camposauro regional park. By renting a further twenty hectares he's able to produce a complete range of wines made with local grape varieties. Aglianico, Falanghina and Greco di Tufo are made into two lines of wines: the Classica, which features solid, traditional wines, and Noi Beviamo Con La Testa, which offers a simpler and more approachable selection. The 2010 Aglianico del Taburno Riserva is a well-rounded wine. It stands out for its balsamic and spicy multifaceted profile and fruit. Its great tannic extraction is backed by acidity and a fine and lingering encore of small red berries. The 2016 Sannio Greco is meaty, with aromas of basil and sage, a succulent structure and biting finish. The 2016 Falanghina is also well-made.

● Aglianico del Taburno Ris. '10	�␣♛ 4
○ Sannio Greco '16	♛♛ 2*
○ Falanghina Brut Maleventum	♛ 3
○ Falanghina del Sannio Taburno '16	♛ 2
○ Sannio Fiano '16	♛ 2
● Aglianico del Taburno '12	♛♛ 3
● Aglianico del Taburno Ris. '07	♛♛ 4
● Aglianico Noi Beviamo con la Testa '11	♛♛ 3
○ Beneventano Falanghina '14	♛♛ 2*
○ Falanghina del Sannio Taburno '15	♛♛ 2*
○ Falanghina del Sannio Taburno '14	♛♛ 2*
○ Sannio Fiano '15	♛♛ 2*
○ Sannio Fiano '13	♛♛ 2*
○ Sannio Greco '15	♛♛ 2*

★Galardi

FRAZ. SAN CARLO
S.DA PROV.LE SESSA-MIGNANO
81037 SESSA AURUNCA [CE]
TEL. +39 08231440003
www.terradilavoro.com

CELLAR SALES
PRE-BOOKED VISITS
ANNUAL PRODUCTION 30,000 bottles
HECTARES UNDER VINE 10.00
VITICULTURE METHOD Certified Organic

Fontana Galardi is a small estate located in San Carlo di Sessa Aurunca at an altitude of 400 meters, on top of a cool hill surrounded by olive groves and chestnut and oak woods. The soil is volcanic and alluvial, deep, with high levels of limestone and schist. This is where one of the most famous blends of Aglianico and Piedirosso in Campania is produced. The result is a benchmark in regional winemaking, owing to the work of Luisa Murena, Arturo Celentano, Francesco and Dora Catello, supported by Riccardo Cotarella for the winemaking. The Terra di Lavoro is a rich, Mediterranean wine with character and the slopes of the Roccamonfina volcano make for a truly unique aromatic profile. The 2015 is very spicy, with ripe and succulent fruit. The palate proves weighty, savory and lingering, with a. background that features coffee and pepper. It's a wine that brings together power, extraction and a certain sunniness.

● Terra di Lavoro '15	♛♛ 7
● Terra di Lavoro '13	♛♛♛ 7
● Terra di Lavoro '11	♛♛♛ 7
● Terra di Lavoro '10	♛♛♛ 7
● Terra di Lavoro '09	♛♛♛ 7
● Terra di Lavoro '08	♛♛♛ 7
● Terra di Lavoro '07	♛♛♛ 7
● Terra di Lavoro '06	♛♛♛ 7
● Terra di Lavoro '05	♛♛♛ 7
● Terra di Lavoro '04	♛♛♛ 7
● Terra di Lavoro '03	♛♛♛ 6
● Terra di Lavoro '02	♛♛♛ 6
● Terra di Lavoro '01	♛♛ 6
● Terra di Lavoro '00	♛♛ 6

La Guardiense

c.da Santa Lucia, 104/106
82034 Guardia Sanframondi [BN]
Tel. +39 0824864034
www.laguardiense.it

CELLAR SALES
PRE-BOOKED VISITS
RESTAURANT SERVICE
ANNUAL PRODUCTION 3,700,000 bottles
HECTARES UNDER VINE 1500.00

Guardiense is one of the most dynamic cooperatives in southern Italy, undergirded by 57 years of winemaking history, 1000 members, and 1500 hectares of vineyards. Six hundred of these are planted with Falanghina, the core of their activity. It is made into different versions, all of them vinified in steel to enhance its character. Many of the processes in the cellar are carried out under the watchful eye of Riccardo Cotarella, including sulfite-free wines and the 1000 project. Yields are kept particularly low to increase the quality of a wide range of wines. Divided into four lines, Aglianico is the second most important variety. The 2016 Falanghina del Sannio Janare Senete exhibits a classic profile, with an original and close-focused smoky note, aromas of Mediterranean scrub and yellow peaches, plus a marked tanginess on the palate. Its acidity is well-integrated and leads to an assertive finish. The Falanghina del Sannio Janare, from the same vintage, is fresh and minty, slightly more lacking in thrust and softer in the mouth.

○ Falanghina del Sannio Janare Senete '16	▼▼▼	2*
○ Falanghina del Sannio Janare '16	▼▼	2*
● Sannio Aglianico Cantari Le Janare Ris. '13	▼▼	3
● Sannio Aglianico Lucchero '15	▼▼	3
○ Sannio Fiano Colle di Tilio Janare '16	▼	3
○ Falanghina del Sannio Janare '15	▽▽▽	2*
○ Falanghina del Sannio Janare '14	▽▽▽	2*
○ Falanghina del Sannio Janare '13	▽▽▽	2*
○ Falanghina del Sannio Calvese '13	▽▽	2*
○ Sannio Falanghina Le Janare Senete '12	▽▽	2*
○ Sannio Fiano Janare '14	▽▽	2*
● Sannio Guardia Sanframondi Janare Ris. '13	▽▽	2*
● Sannio Guardiolo Aglianico '11	▽▽	2*
● Sannio Piedirosso Janare '12	▽▽	2*

Salvatore Martusciello

via Spinelli, 4
80010 Quarto [NA]
Tel. +39 0818766123
www.salvatoremartusciello.it

ANNUAL PRODUCTION 87,000 bottles
HECTARES UNDER VINE 2.00

Salvatore Martusciello's winery is full steam ahead, putting the experience he gained over the years at Grotta del Sole to excellent use. He deserves full credit for preserving and relaunching some of the more traditional wines of Campi Flegrei, Agro Aversano and the Sorrento Peninsula with a style that is becoming more contemporary. Their wines have character and are enjoying success on international markets. The selection of wines in this edition is more than solid. The outstanding Lettere Ottouve offers up airy aromas of Mediterranean scrub and black olives. It's juicy and fresh, well-supported by tannins and acidity, with a savory and smoky finish. The Gragnano sees softer fruit, simple hints of redcurrants and wild cherries, with a long and intense notes of violets. The 2016 Piedirosso Settevulcani exhibits a warm and fruity nature and a very original earthy, root-like profile. The last wine is the Asprinio d'Aversa Trentapioli, which is the best tasted in its category. It's as biting as we would expect, as well as vigorous and flavorful. It's a real wild card.

○ Asprinio d'Aversa Trentapioli Brut	▼▼	2*
● Penisola Sorrentina Lettere Ottouve '16	▼▼	3
● Campi Flegrei Piedirosso Settevulcani '16	▼	3
● Penisola Sorrentina Gragnano Ottouve '16	▼	3
● Campi Flegrei Piedirosso Settevulcani '15	▽▽	3
● Penisola Sorrentina Lettere Ottouve '15	▽▽	3

★★Montevetrano

LOC. NIDO
FRAZ. CAMPIGLIANO
VIA MONTEVETRANO, 3
84099 SAN CIPRIANO PICENTINO [SA]
TEL. +39 089882285
www.montevetrano.it

CELLAR SALES
PRE-BOOKED VISITS
ACCOMMODATION
ANNUAL PRODUCTION 76,000 bottles
HECTARES UNDER VINE 5.00

With 20 Tre Bicchieri awards (the first in 1991), Montevetrano is undoubtedly one of the best-known Campanian reds in Italy, and one of the most-consumed southern Italian wines in the world. Over the years, they've managed to combine an international vision with good territorial winemaking. The results speak for themselves. Silvia Imparato, an educated and refined lady of Italian wine, leads the way by consistently making the right decisions. In recent years new wines have come to accompany the Montevetrano, a blend of Aglianico, Cabernet and Merlot. Core, a monovarietal Aglianico, is one of them, as is the Core Bianco, a wine made with Fiano and Greco that's new to our guide. The 2015 Montevetrano is a wine with a mature and expressive Mediterranean texture, alternating a spicy profile with a fresh balsamic and minty side. It offers up aromas of juniper, cigar and redcurrants; on the palate it proves close-knit, with a sweet tannic texture and a still slightly bridled toastiness. We find grassy hints and dark, juicy fruit in the 2015 Core Rosso.

● Montevetrano '15	♟♟ 7
○ Core Bianco '16	♟ 4
● Core Rosso '15	♟ 4
● Montevetrano '14	♟♟♟ 7
● Montevetrano '12	♟♟♟ 7
● Montevetrano '11	♟♟♟ 7
● Montevetrano '10	♟♟♟ 7
● Montevetrano '09	♟♟♟ 7
● Montevetrano '08	♟♟♟ 7
● Montevetrano '07	♟♟♟ 7
● Montevetrano '06	♟♟♟ 7
● Montevetrano '05	♟♟♟ 7
● Montevetrano '04	♟♟♟ 7
● Montevetrano '03	♟♟♟ 7
● Montevetrano '02	♟♟♟ 7
● Montevetrano '01	♟♟♟ 7

Mustilli

VIA CAUDINA, 10
82019 SANT'AGATA DE' GOTI [BN]
TEL. +39 0823718142
www.mustilli.com

CELLAR SALES
PRE-BOOKED VISITS
ACCOMMODATION AND RESTAURANT SERVICE
ANNUAL PRODUCTION 150,000 bottles
HECTARES UNDER VINE 21.00

The first Falanghina sold by the Mustilli family dates back to 1979 and is preserved in the old underground cellars of the Rainone Palace. Here, Leonardo Mustilli, who created the Sant'Agata dei Goti appellation, makes wines from the most successful white grape in Samnium. Many producers are following his example. Today the winery is run by his daughters, Paola and Anna Chiara, overseeing sales, and the vineyards and cellar, respectively. Fortunato Sebastiano takes care of winemaking. A scintillating overall performance and the winery's first Tre Bicchieri. The 2015 Piedirosso Artus is a real gem of dark juiciness and pencil lead, with a meaty, savory and well-timed palate. The 2015 Falanghina Vigna Segreta, a rugged and complex wine, with an elegant and musky pace, aromas of white melon, medicinal herbs, scents of iodine and delicate smoke that make an impression. The 2016 Piedirosso is good to drink, though we find it hard to say whether it's more gutsy than tasty.

● Sannio Sant'Agata dei Goti Piedirosso Artus '15	♟♟♟ 4*
○ Falangina del Sannio Sant'Agata dei Goti V. Segreta '15	♟♟ 4
● Sannio Sant'Agata dei Goti Piedirosso '16	♟♟ 3*
○ Falanghina del Sannio Sant'Agata dei Goti '16	♟♟ 3
● Sannio Aglianico '15	♟ 3
○ Sannio Sant'Agata dei Goti Greco '16	♟ 3
○ Falanghina del Sannio Sant'Agata dei Goti '15	♟♟ 3*
○ Falanghina del Sannio Sant'Agata dei Goti '14	♟♟ 2*
● Sannio Aglianico '12	♟♟ 4
● Sannio Piedirosso '15	♟♟ 3
○ Sannio Sant'Agata dei Goti Greco '15	♟♟ 3
○ Sannio Sant'Agata dei Goti Greco '14	♟♟ 2*

Nanni Copè

VIA TUFO, 3
81041 VITULAZIO [CE]
TEL. +39 330879815
www.nannicope.it

CELLAR SALES
PRE-BOOKED VISITS
ANNUAL PRODUCTION 7,500 bottles
HECTARES UNDER VINE 3.50
SUSTAINABLE WINERY

Giovanni is the owner of the winery. Giovanni is the agronomist. And the winemaker? Giovanni. Nanni Copè is Giovanni Ascione and Giovanni Ascione is Nanni Copè. The cellar is an unparalleled one-man shop that sums up all the personality and stubbornness of one man. Giovanni previously worked as manager of a French winery and as a wine journalist. Since 2007 he has been working as an artisan producer. In his garage-cum-cellar, he handles extraordinary raw materials from the sandstone area of Caiazzo. In his backyard vineyard, Pallagrello and a handful of rows of Aglianico and Casavecchia peacefully co-exist. For the moment he makes only one wine, aged in mid-sized casks. The generous and fortunate vintage helped the 2015 Sabbie di Sopra il Bosco pull off a memorable performance. Its fruit proves pure and fleshy, with redcurrants and black mulberries, intense smoky and sometimes sulfurous notes. The palate is particularly generous and spirited, with overtones of pencil lead, a fruity encore, a truly amazing flavor and an assertive finish. A Tre Bicchieri without the slightest hesitation.

● Sabbie di Sopra il Bosco '15	▼▼▼ 5
● Sabbie di Sopra il Bosco '14	♥♥♥ 5
● Sabbie di Sopra il Bosco '12	♥♥♥ 5
● Sabbie di Sopra il Bosco '11	♥♥♥ 5
● Sabbie di Sopra il Bosco '10	♥♥♥ 5
● Sabbie di Sopra il Bosco '09	♥♥♥ 5
● Sabbie di Sopra il Bosco '13	♥♥ 5
● Sabbie di Sopra il Bosco '08	♥♥ 5

Perillo

C.DA VALLE, 19
83040 CASTELFRANCI [AV]
TEL. +39 082772252
cantinaperillo@libero.it

CELLAR SALES
PRE-BOOKED VISITS
ANNUAL PRODUCTION 20,000 bottles
HECTARES UNDER VINE 5.00

No tasting of Taurasi can be considered complete without sampling Perillo winery's flagship wine. Michele works in some of the most beautiful vineyards in the appellation, located between Contrada Baiano, Montemarano and Contrada Valle. The soil is rich in stones, sometimes with tuff and limestone. Some of the vines on this deep terrain are over 80 years old, and slow aging brings marvelous character, flavor, concentration and energy to the glass. Carmine Valento has supported Michele in the winemaking ever since the first vintage. The 2008 Taurasi did quite well, but we might have expected a bit more, given the great vintage. It opens a bit slow and edgy, with notes of rain-soaked earth, sweet tobacco and coffee. The mouth sees the usual savory change in pace and bright acidity, but it just can't manage the same level as the best versions and the palate proves reined in by its toastier notes.

● Taurasi '08	♥♥ 6
● Taurasi '07	♥♥♥ 6
● Taurasi '05	♥♥♥ 4
● Taurasi Ris. '06	♥♥♥ 6
● Aglianico '04	♥♥ 3
○ Coda di Volpe '07	♥♥ 3
● Irpinia Campi Taurasini '07	♥♥ 4
● Irpinia Campi Taurasini '06	♥♥ 4
○ Irpinia Coda di Volpe '12	♥♥ 3
○ Irpinia Coda di Volpe '09	♥♥ 3
● Taurasi '06	♥♥ 4
● Taurasi '04	♥♥ 4*
● Taurasi Ris. '07	♥♥ 6
● Taurasi Ris. '05	♥♥ 5
● Taurasi Ris. '04	♥♥ 5

Ciro Picariello

VIA MARRONI, 18/A
83010 SUMMONTE [AV]
TEL. +39 082533848
www.ciropicariello.it

CELLAR SALES
PRE-BOOKED VISITS
ANNUAL PRODUCTION 55,000 bottles
HECTARES UNDER VINE 15.00
SUSTAINABLE WINERY

Ciro Picariello is an artisan of the Fiano grape variety and manages to bring out the best of the Irpinia region in his wines. With his wife Rita Guerriero, he produces bottles of Fiano di Avellino with exciting territorial purity, year in, year out. All of the character and grip of the Montefredane and Summonte vineyards is summed up in the glass. In addition to the basic Fiano di Avellino, he produces the Ciro 960, a wine made with grapes cultivated on a single plot in Summonte and aged for one year in the bottle. The character of his Fiano vineyards is discernible also in his Metodo Classico sparkling wine. The 2015 Fiano di Avellino is a more nuanced version, which reflects the rather warm and generous vintage. Its fruit proves ripe and fleshy, with an intense and lingering smoky imprint. The mouth is powerful, with moderately marked alcohol that doesn't hold back its long and juicy finish. The 2013 Fiano di Avellino Ciro 906 was remarkable when re-tasted, very dynamic, with a virtually never-ending finish.

○ Fiano di Avellino '15	♟♟ 4	
○ Fiano di Avellino '14	♟♟♟ 4*	
○ Fiano di Avellino '10	♟♟♟ 3*	
○ Fiano di Avellino '08	♟♟♟ 3*	
○ Brut Contadino	♟♟ 4	
○ Fiano di Avellino '13	♟♟ 4	
○ Fiano di Avellino '11	♟♟ 3*	
○ Fiano di Avellino '09	♟♟ 3	
○ Fiano di Avellino '07	♟♟ 3*	
○ Fiano di Avellino '06	♟♟ 3*	
○ Fiano di Avellino '05	♟♟ 3*	
○ Fiano di Avellino Ciro 906 '13	♟♟ 4	
○ Fiano di Avellino Ciro 906 '12	♟♟ 4	

La Pietra di Tommasone

VIA PROV.LE FANGO, 98
80076 LACCO AMENO [NA]
TEL. +39 0813330330
www.tommasonevini.it

CELLAR SALES
PRE-BOOKED VISITS
ANNUAL PRODUCTION 100,000 bottles
HECTARES UNDER VINE 11.00

Antonio Monti and his daughter Lucia's work is going full tilt. She is the winemaker at the Lacco Ameno cellar on the northern slope of Ischia. Their grapes are cultivated on small plots of land spread out over eight estates (a total of 11 hectares). Altitudes range from 250 to 450 meters at Sant'Angelo in the municipality of Serrara Fontana, and the varieties cover the complete range of grapes grown on the island. Their white wines exhibit full stylistic maturity and potential and are offered at excellent prices. The 2016 Pithecusa Bianco is a blend of Biancolella and Fiano, with bright citrusy overtones, minty aromas and a well-defined and precise finish. The 2016 Rosamonti, made with Aglianico, combines crisp and tasty fruit with notes of Mediterranean scrub and features a finish full of character. Lastly, the 2016 Ischia Biancolella is firm and close-knit, opening tentatively then diving in assertively with notes of flint and pollen.

○ Ischia Biancolella '16	♟♟ 2	
○ Ischia Biancolella V. dei Preti '16	♟♟ 4	
○ Pithecusa Bianco '16	♟♟ 3	
● Rosamonti '16	♟♟ 2*	
○ Ischia Bianco Terradei '16	♟ 2	
○ Epomeo Bianco '15	♟♟ 3	
○ Epomeo Bianco '13	♟♟ 3	
● Epomeo Rosso '11	♟♟ 3	
○ Ischia Biancolella '15	♟♟ 2	
○ Ischia Biancolella '14	♟♟ 2*	
○ Ischia Biancolella V. dei Preti '15	♟♟ 4	
● Ischia Per' 'e Palummo '13	♟♟ 3	
○ Pithecusa Bianco '15	♟♟ 3	

★Pietracupa

C.DA VADIAPERTI, 17
83030 MONTEFREDANE [AV]
TEL. +39 0825607418
pietracupa@email.it

CELLAR SALES
PRE-BOOKED VISITS
ANNUAL PRODUCTION 50,000 bottles
HECTARES UNDER VINE 7.50

Nobody in Irpinia has such a feel for a vintage and can extract its DNA with such surgical precision as Sabino Loffredo. A dramatic personality and sports instructor, he bottles some of the best wines in the country each year. The ease with which he hops between appellations is fascinating. He manages to enhance the best features of the two foremost wine-producing areas in Avellino. His whites have an uncommon balsamic nuance and acidity, while the reds maintain verve and signature elegant tannins. The 2016 Greco and Fiano are a couple of racy, sharpish wines with an assertive length of taste. The Greco is less ready than usual. It starts out slightly undefined but then unfolds into an amazing, savory and pungent palate, enveloped by flavor and grip. The Fiano is incredibly close-knit and subtle, with pure notes of aniseed and white melon. It undergoes a phenomenal change of pace in the mouth, while its finish is ruffled by a slight hint of tannins that makes it even deeper and punchier.

○ Greco di Tufo '16	▼▼▼	3*
○ Fiano di Avellino '16	▼▼	3*
● Taurasi '12	▼▼	5
○ Cupo '10	♀♀♀	5
○ Cupo '08	♀♀♀	5
○ Fiano di Avellino '13	♀♀♀	3*
○ Fiano di Avellino '12	♀♀♀	3*
○ Greco di Tufo '15	♀♀♀	3*
○ Greco di Tufo '14	♀♀♀	3*
○ Greco di Tufo '10	♀♀♀	3*
● Taurasi '10	♀♀♀	5
○ Fiano di Avellino '15	♀♀	3*
○ Fiano di Avellino '14	♀♀	3*
● Taurasi '09	♀♀	5

Regina Viarum

LOC. FALCIANO DEL MASSICO
VIA VELLARIA
81030 FALCIANO DEL MASSICO [CE]
TEL. +39 0823931299
www.reginaviarum.it

CELLAR SALES
PRE-BOOKED VISITS
ANNUAL PRODUCTION 19,000 bottles
HECTARES UNDER VINE 5.00
VITICULTURE METHOD Certified Organic
SUSTAINABLE WINERY

The Appian Way is a wine route. You don't have to be a history buff to understand the importance of this queen of consular roads, which connected Rome and Benevento, passing through the Ager Falernus on the slopes of Monte Massico. Not just wine was transported, but also culture and information. We are pleased to be able to count the Falciano del Massico winery among the guide's big names this year. Established in 2005, in recent years it has demonstrated an impressive consistency. Their small estate, which also features a lovely garden, gives rise to just a few bottles of wine of excellent value. The delightful 2014 Falerno del Massico Primitivo Zero has reached our finals for the first time. It offers up pure and crisp fruit, calling up aromas of red oranges and pencil lead. The palate gradually lengthens with an appealing final nuance of flowers and pepper. The 2012 Vigna Barone also made a very good impression. It features darker aromas and a deep, complex, juicy and dynamic mouth.

● Falerno del Massico Zero5 '14	▼▼	3*
● Falerno del Massico V. Barone '12	▼▼	5
● Falerno del Massico Barone '10	♀♀	5
● Falerno del Massico Zero5 '13	♀♀	3
● Falerno del Massico Zero5 '11	♀♀	3
● Falerno del Massico Zero5 '10	♀♀	3

Fattoria La Rivolta

C.DA RIVOLTA
82030 TORRECUSO [BN]
TEL. +39 0824872921
www.fattorialarivolta.com

CELLAR SALES
PRE-BOOKED VISITS
ACCOMMODATION
ANNUAL PRODUCTION 180,000 bottles
HECTARES UNDER VINE 29.00
VITICULTURE METHOD Certified Organic

The Cotroneo family is at the helm of this dynamic winery in Torrecuso, the pulsing heart of Samnium vinegrowing. Their 29 hectares of vineyards have been under organic management for over twenty years and are dedicated to the area's principal varieties. The winery has an easily recognizable style and character. Their whites are fresh and intense, while the reds (three Aglianico del Taburno wines are on the market) prove more extracted, with fruitiness contrasting acidity. The overall performance was particularly solid. The 2016 Falanghina del Sannio Taburno exhibits a spunky, expansive character, with a fine suite of aromas, a good iodine profile and particularly crisp fruit. The finish is long, fresh and relaxed. A real Tre Bicchieri. The new 2015 Simbiosi, made with Aglianico and Piedirosso, also made it to the finals. The fruit's full and fleshy and the mouth turns out well, ending in a spicy crescendo. The rest of their selection also prove to be in good form.

○ Falanghina del Sannio Taburno '16	♟♟♟	2*
● Simbiosi '15	♟♟	3*
● Aglianico del Taburno '15	♟♟	3
● Sannio Taburno Piedirosso '16	♟♟	3
⊙ Aglianico del Taburno Rosato Mongolfiere a San Bruno '16	♟	3
○ Sannio Taburno Coda di Volpe '16	♟	2
○ Sannio Taburno Fiano '16	♟	3
○ Sogno di Rivolta '15	♟	3
● Aglianico del Taburno '10	♟♟♟	3*
● Aglianico del Taburno Terra di Rivolta Ris. '08	♟♟♟	5
● Aglianico del Taburno '13	♟♟	3*
○ Sannio Taburno Fiano '15	♟♟	3

Rocca del Principe

VIA ARIANIELLO, 9
83030 LAPIO [AV]
TEL. +39 08251728013
www.roccadelprincipe.it

CELLAR SALES
PRE-BOOKED VISITS
ANNUAL PRODUCTION 30,000 bottles
HECTARES UNDER VINE 6.50

As Ercole Zarella, his wife Aurelia Fabrizio, and his brother-in-law Antonio are well aware, Lapio could be considered one of the best crus for Fiano d'Avellino. In 2004 they decided to start vinifying the grapes from their vineyards, such that, today, Rocca del Principe is one of the best-known wineries in the area. They have a vineyard on the slopes of the Arianello hill, the highest land in the area where the air is cooler, harvest comes slightly later, and its volcanic soil is rich in pumice. There is a new wine this year, Tognano, made with a select part of the vineyard where the oldest vines grow. Indeed, it is a cru within a cru. The 2015 Fiano di Avellino is a wine with a double nature, combining a full, sunny and mature side with a crisp and driving profile. Fragrances of green tea, citrus fruit and ginger are followed by a suite of intense, long aromas. The Tognano first-release, which features a subtler and purer expression, also delivered.

○ Fiano di Avellino '15	♟♟	3*
○ Fiano di Avellino Tognano '14	♟♟	3*
○ Fiano di Avellino '14	♟♟♟	3*
○ Fiano di Avellino '13	♟♟♟	3*
○ Fiano di Avellino '12	♟♟♟	3*
○ Fiano di Avellino '10	♟♟♟	3*
○ Fiano di Avellino '08	♟♟♟	2*
○ Fiano di Avellino '07	♟♟♟	2*
○ Fiano di Avellino '11	♟♟	3*
● Irpinia Aglianico '11	♟♟	3*
● Taurasi Master Domini '07	♟♟	5
● Taurasi Mater Domini '09	♟♟	5
● Taurasi Mater Domini '08	♟♟	5
● Taurasi Ris. '10	♟♟	5

Ettore Sammarco

VIA CIVITA, 9
84010 RAVELLO [SA]
TEL +39 089872774
www.ettoresammarco.it

CELLAR SALES
PRE-BOOKED VISITS
ANNUAL PRODUCTION 66,000 bottles
HECTARES UNDER VINE 13.00

Ravello is a magnificent town on the Amalfi Coast situated an altitude of over 300 meters. The wines made here smell of the sea and Mediterranean scrub. Ettore Sammarco, now eighty years old, has been the undisputed boss of local vinegrowing since 1962 when he founded the winery bearing his name. Today his son Bartolo looks after winemaking and the small plots of land. The best is Grotta Piana, their highest vineyard, located on Monte Brusara at 500 meters above sea level. The soil here is clay, dolomitic limestone rock and lapilli. Here they grow the Ginestra, Falanghina and Biancolella varieties. The 2016 Ravello Bianco got the best score of this year's very solid set of wines. Its aromatic approachability sees lively notes of citron and orange blossom, which grow on the palate with freshness and remarkable verve (with a pleasant minty note just showing through). The 2016 Ravello Bianco Vigna Grotta Piana possesses a different character, offering up delicately toasted notes.

○ Costa d'Amalfi Ravello Bianco '16	♟♟ 4
○ Costa d'Amalfi Ravello Bianco V. Grotta Piana '16	♟♟ 4
● Costa d'Amalfi Ravello Rosso Selva delle Monache Ris. '13	♟♟ 5
○ Costa d'Amalfi Bianco Terre Saracene '16	♟ 3
● Costa d'Amalfi Ravello Rosso Selva delle Monache '16	♟ 3
○ Costa d'Amalfi Rosato Terre Saracene '16	♟ 3
○ Costa d'Amalfi Ravello Bianco V. Grotta Piana '15	♟♟♟ 4*
● Costa d'Amalfi Ravello Rosso Selva delle Monache '15	♟♟ 3
● Costa d'Amalfi Ravello Rosso Selva delle Monache Ris. '12	♟♟ 5

Tenuta San Francesco

FRAZ. CORSANO
VIA SOFILCIANO, 18
84010 TRAMONTI [SA]
TEL. +39 089876748
www.vinitenutasanfrancesco.com

CELLAR SALES
PRE-BOOKED VISITS
ACCOMMODATION
ANNUAL PRODUCTION 40,000 bottles
HECTARES UNDER VINE 10.00

Tramonti is one of the most interesting subzones of the Amalfi Coast. It's a unique setting with ungrafted vines planted on old terraces. This is where it all began for three families (Bove, D'Avino and Giordano), who realized the potential of this part of Campania and decided to make wines from local native varieties. Their austere and powerful reds like È Iss or Quattrospine are made with Tintore, Piedirosso and Aglianico, while Falanghina, Pepella and Ginestra grapes go into their Per Eva selection. The 2013 Iss is an unforgettable red, intense and deep, with a tone that's both earthy and minty at the same time. The palate is particularly punchy and vigorous despite its bold structure, with savory traces and a finish with root-like aromas. The 2015 Per Eva is mature and juicy, with an extravagant finish calling up fennel and pepper. It a wine that proves creamy, long and well-sustained. The 2014 Tramonti Rosso offers up pleasant grassy hints and balsamic strength.

○ Costa d'Amalfi Tramonti Bianco Per Eva '15	♟♟ 4
● Costa d'Amalfi Tramonti Rosso '14	♟♟ 3
● E' Iss '13	♟♟ 5
⊙ Costa d'Amalfi Rosato '16	♟ 2
○ Costa d'Amalfi Tramonti Bianco '16	♟ 2
○ Costa d'Amalfi Bianco Per Eva '13	♟♟♟ 4*
○ Costa d'Amalfi Bianco Per Eva '14	♟♟ 4
○ Costa d'Amalfi Bianco Per Eva '12	♟♟ 4
○ Costa d'Amalfi Tramonti Bianco '15	♟♟ 2*
○ Costa d'Amalfi Tramonti Bianco '14	♟♟ 2*
⊙ Costa d'Amalfi Tramonti Rosato '14	♟♟ 2*
● Costa d'Amalfi Tramonti Rosso Quattrospine Ris. '12	♟♟ 5
● Costa d'Amalfi Tramonti Rosso Quattrospine Ris. '11	♟♟ 5
● E' Iss '12	♟♟ 5

San Giovanni

C.DA TRESINO
84048 CASTELLABATE [SA]
TEL. +39 0974965136
www.agricolasangiovanni.it

CELLAR SALES
PRE-BOOKED VISITS
ACCOMMODATION
ANNUAL PRODUCTION 20,000 bottles
HECTARES UNDER VINE 4.00

Punto Tresino is one of the first places that comes to mind when we think of a nature retreat, far from the hustle and bustle of everyday life. Here at the Cilento Nature Reserve, with its sea and Mediterranean air, it's like being in a southern Italian postcard. Indeed, it's not hard to see why Mario and Ida Corrado decided to set up their winery here 15 years ago. Their wines have a marked marine and sunny character. This year sees a new entry, the Fiano selection. After aging at length in the bottle, the wine is finally ready. The troupe of whites put forward this year demonstrates the high profile of their selection. The 2016 Paestum is a yellow wine, with aromas of broom and citrus fruit. Its rich palate features hints of herbs (especially oregano) and a slightly astringent finish with some character. The 2015 Auresu is charming and deep, with resinous notes, acacia and honey. On the palate it proves rich, as a wine from a warm and marine land should be. The 2016 Tresinus, with its aromatic suite calling up orange blossom honey and iodine, also made a good impression.

○ Aureus '15	♈♈	5
○ Paestum '16	♈♈	3*
○ Tresinus '16	♈♈	4
○ Fiano Tresinus '12	♈♈♈	3*
○ Paestum '15	♈♈♈	2*
● Castellabate '11	♈♈	3
○ Fiano Tresinus '15	♈♈	3
○ Fiano Tresinus '14	♈♈	3
● Ficonera '14	♈♈	5
● Ficonera '11	♈♈	5
○ Paestum Bianco '14	♈♈	2*

San Salvatore 1988

VIA DIONISIO
84050 GIUNGANO [SA]
TEL. +39 08281990900
www.sansalvatore1988.it

CELLAR SALES
ACCOMMODATION AND RESTAURANT SERVICE
ANNUAL PRODUCTION 160,000 bottles
HECTARES UNDER VINE 23.00
VITICULTURE METHOD Certified Biodynamic
SUSTAINABLE WINERY

Growth and continuity are watchwords for Giuseppe Pagano, the man behind this Cilento winery. Firmly established on primary international markets as a result of his complete and diverse farming business, he produces rich buffalo mozzarella, oil, cereals and vegetables, as well as wine. And if that's not enough, he also runs a restaurant where local women share recipes. His wine production is biodynamic with solar panels used to reduce environmental impact, and his wide selection is marked by a fruity intensity. The Pian di Stio and Gillo Dorfles are they winery's flagship products. Overall, their wines gave a less-lively performance than usual. In any case, the Trentenare has confirmed its role as a flagship. It's a free and easy Fiano with good drinkability, playing on notes of crisp white fruit and Mediterranean herbs. The mouth features juice and a clean finish. The 2016 Pian di Stio is still very young and is dominated by hints of green apple, while the 2013 Pino di Stio Rosso is made with Pinot Nero and features a racy body with good savory energy.

○ Trentenare '16	♈♈♈	3*
● Ceraso '16	♈♈	3
● Omaggio a Gillo Dorfles '14	♈♈	6
○ Pian di Stio '16	♈♈	4
● Pino di Stio Rosso '13	♈♈	4
○ Falanghina '16	♈	3
○ Fiano Senza Solfiti '16	♈	3
○ Greco '16	♈	3
⊙ Joi Brut Rosé '14	♈	5
● Jungano '15	♈	3
○ Pian di Stio '14	♈♈♈	4
○ Pian di Stio '13	♈♈♈	4*
○ Pian di Stio '12	♈♈♈	3
○ Trentenare '15	♈♈♈	3

Sanpaolo
di Claudio Quarta Vignaiolo

C.DA SAN PAOLO
VIA AUFIERI, 25
83010 TORRIONI [AV]
TEL. +39 0832704398
www.claudioquarta.it

CELLAR SALES
PRE-BOOKED VISITS
ACCOMMODATION
ANNUAL PRODUCTION 115,000 bottles
HECTARES UNDER VINE 22.00

Claudio Quarta and his daughter Alessandra are deeply committed to quality viticulture in the south of Italy. They own two wineries in Apulia and another, San Paolo, in Torrioni (province of Avellino). Their focus is on research and experimentation so as to enhance native varieties, along with social responsibility and protection of the landscape. Their San Paolo vineyards span 22 hectares, with 10 around the winery. Their Greco grapes are cultivated in Tufo, Fiano grapes in Lapio, and Aglianico in Paternopoli. The remaining 12 hectares in Pietrelcina, Benevento, are planted with Falanghina. Once again the Greco di Tufo Selezione Claudio Quarta nabbed the highest score of they year. The 2016 attacks with notes of peach and almond, while on the palate it proves compact and vigorous, with good driving acidity and complexity. It grows, if you wait for it in the glass. The 2016 Falanghina is spot-on and quite enjoyable, flowing across the palate with crisp notes of freshly-cut grass and lemon rind.

○ Falanghina '16	♟♟	2*
○ Greco di Tufo Claudio Quarta '16	♟♟	6
○ Fiano di Avellino '16	♟	3
○ Greco di Tufo '16	♟	3
○ Greco di Tufo Claudio Quarta '13	♟♟♟	6
○ Greco di Tufo Claudio Quarta '12	♟♟♟	6
○ Falanghina '15	♟♟	2*
○ Falanghina '13	♟♟	2*
○ Fiano di Avellino '15	♟♟	2*
○ Fiano di Avellino '13	♟♟	2*
○ Greco di Tufo '13	♟♟	2*
○ Greco di Tufo Claudio Quarta '15	♟♟	6
● Taurasi Ris. '10	♟♟	5
● Taurasi Ris. '09	♟♟	5

Tenuta Sarno 1860

C.DA SERRONI, 4B
83100 AVELLINO
TEL. +39 082526161
www.tenutasarno1860.it

ANNUAL PRODUCTION 15,000 bottles
HECTARES UNDER VINE 6.00

Maura Sarno is not lacking in enthusiasm or determination, and from the beginning she knew she wanted to focus on Fiano di Avellino at her winery. When Maura inherited this family-owned land in Candida, she planted it all with Fiano. It wasn't easy, but she was convinced the calcareous-clay soil could someday produce satisfying and dynamic whites. And in a remarkable short time, she achieved astonishing results. Last year, with the help of winemaker Vincenzo Mercurio, she also made a sparkling Fiano. The Fiano di Maura Sarno has proven its high quality. The 2016 is an all-round white, with scents of chamomile and hazelnut, a sure pace and a full, mature palate. It features a lively basic tanginess, and comes through juicy on the palate, with a good citrusy energy that leads to a linear, precise and well-orchestrated finish.

○ Fiano di Avellino '16	♟♟	4
○ Fiano di Avellino '15	♟♟♟	4*
○ Fiano di Avellino '14	♟♟	3*
○ Fiano di Avellino '13	♟♟	3*
○ Fiano di Avellino '12	♟♟	3*
○ Fiano di Avellino '11	♟♟	3
○ Fiano di Avellino '10	♟♟	3*
○ Sarno 1860 Pas Dosé '15	♟♟	4

Lorenzo Nifo Sarrapochiello

VIA PIANA, 62
82030 PONTE [BN]
TEL. +39 0824876450
www.nifo.eu

CELLAR SALES
PRE-BOOKED VISITS
ANNUAL PRODUCTION 70,000 bottles
HECTARES UNDER VINE 16.00
VITICULTURE METHOD Certified Organic

Lorenzo Nifo Sarrapochiello's winery is making its debut among our guide's major players. He is an enthusiastic vine grower in Ponte, on the slopes of Monte Pèntime, and has recently adopted organic viticulture techniques. He grows Aglianico, Fiano, Greco and, above all, Falanghina. Lorenzo's Falanghina has become a well-defined model. With a style that goes beyond the usual fruit-acidity combination, it offers up a complex sense and lively pace, even in the case of rich extract. The exemplary 2016 Falanghina del Sannio Taburno has reached our finals. It features bright green highlights and aromas of aniseed, catmint and white melon. On the palate it proves well-sustained, rich and dynamic with a refined repertoire of fine spices and a lively finish. The reds put forward prove their ability to balance structure and generous extraction, especially the 2015 Sannio Taburno Rosso, which is succulent, fragrant and savory.

○ Falanghina del Sannio Taburno '16	♚♚ 2*
● Aglianico del Taburno '13	♚♚ 2*
● Aglianico del Taburno D'Erasmo Ris. '11	♚♚ 5
● Sannio Taburno Rosso '15	♚♚ 2*
○ Sannio Taburno Fiano '16	♚ 2
○ Sannio Taburno Greco '16	♚ 2
● Aglianico del Taburno D'Erasmo Ris. '09	♚♚ 4
○ Sannio Fiano '15	♚♚ 2*
○ Sannio Fiano '14	♚♚ 2*
● Sannio Taburno Aglianico '12	♚♚ 2*
○ Sannio Taburno Falanghina '13	♚♚ 2*
○ Sannio Taburno Greco G '13	♚♚ 2*

Sclavia

LOC. MARIANELLO
VIA CASE SPARSE
81040 LIBERI [CE]
TEL. +39 3357406773
www.sclavla.com

CELLAR SALES
PRE-BOOKED VISITS
ANNUAL PRODUCTION 50,000 bottles
HECTARES UNDER VINE 13.00
VITICULTURE METHOD Certified Organic
SUSTAINABLE WINERY

Sclavia is a young winery with a serious and complex project that is constantly evolving. The result is to win a place among the big names in our publication. Here in Marianello, in the municipality of Liberi sui Monti Trebulani, the area is at last enjoying success and renewed interest. Andrea Granito, who is also an osteopath, works with certified organic grapes from his 13 hectares of vineyards. His far-reaching and innovative ideas, which are aimed at drawing attention to this corner of the territory, prove inspiring. His Calù, a Palagrello Bianco with character, once again makes it to the finals. The 2016 version offers up aromas of citron and melon. It's rich and dynamic at the same time, with minty fragrances and an intriguing spicy nuance. The 2015 Don Ferdinando is more succulent and glyceric. It's made with Pallagrello Bianco, while the 2014 Liberi is a spirited and powerful Casavecchia that needs more time in the bottle. The Pallarè is an elegant dried-grape wine with bright aromas and a mouth that's well-sustained by acidity.

○ Calù '16	♚♚ 3
○ Don Ferdinando '15	♚♚ 5
● Liberi '14	♚♚ 5
○ Pallarè '15	♚♚ 5
○ Calù '15	♚♚ 3
● Granito '12	♚♚ 3
● Liberi '12	♚♚ 5

La Sibilla

FRAZ. BAIA
VIA OTTAVIANO AUGUSTO, 19
80070 BACOLI [NA]
TEL. +39 0818688778
www.sibillavini.com

CELLAR SALES
PRE-BOOKED VISITS
ANNUAL PRODUCTION 70,000 bottles
HECTARES UNDER VINE 9.50

Vincenzo De Meo is at the helm of this
small winery set in a landscape with unique
soil and climate in the Baia hills, part of the
Phlegraean Fields. Breezes drift up from the
Bay of Naples and caress the vineyards
planted on volcanic soil characterized by
lapilli and ash. These conditions enable the
vines to survive ungrafted and Vincenzo
exploits this fact to great advantage while
eschewing winemaking frills. Both their
basic and their select lines form a range of
forthright, clean and pure wines that do a
good job representing the territory. A
splendid version of the Cruna deLago has
brought a Tre Bicchieri back to Bacoli. The
2015 offers up an appealing smoky
undertone, with shimmering aromas of
medicinal herbs, oregano and a light buttery
note. The mouth is creamy and assertive,
with an almost spicy, savory and lingering
atmosphere. The 2016 Piedirosso, with its
dry and racy flowers and spices, also put in
a good performance. The 2016 Falanghina
possesses an iodine, musky character.

Luigi Tecce

C.DA TRINITÀ, 6
83052 PATERNOPOLI [AV]
TEL. +39 3492957565
ltecce@libero.it

PRE-BOOKED VISITS
ANNUAL PRODUCTION 10,000 bottles
HECTARES UNDER VINE 5.00

Luigi Tecce is a shy, sincere and determined
vigneron. He is as peculiar and unique as
his original wines, which vary from vintage
to vintage. There is more chance than
technique in his Taurasi Poliphemo or his
Irpinia Campi Taurasi Satyricon, both made
with Aglianico grapes. His meticulously-
tended vineyards are located on the two
hills of Paternopoli and Castelfranci, where
the harvest is carried out by hand and yields
are very low. Weedkillers or other chemical
products are never used here, only copper
and sulfur. Their wine is made in amphorae,
mid-sized casks or chestnut-wood barrels.
The 2014 Satyricon bewitched the regional
panel. It's a wine that stimulates the
appetite and opens the stomach. It tastes of
grilled meat, offering up an earthy
atmosphere of black tea and pepper, with
dark fruit that gradually increases in flavor.
The mouth proves lively, salty and direct (we
won't hide the fact that we actually drank it
during the tasting). We're confidently
waiting for the 2013 Taurasi Poliphemo.

Campi Flegrei Falanghina Cruna deLago '15	▼▼▼ 4*
Campi Flegrei Falanghina '16	▼▼ 3
Campi Flegrei Piedirosso '16	▼▼ 4
Campi Flegrei Piedirosso V. Madre '14	▼ 4
Campi Flegrei Falanghina '13	▽▽▽ 2*
Campi Flegrei Falanghina '15	▽▽ 2*
Campi Flegrei Falanghina '14	▽▽ 3
Campi Flegrei Falanghina Cruna deLago '14	▽▽ 4
Campi Flegrei Falanghina Cruna deLago '13	▽▽ 4
Campi Flegrei Piedirosso '15	▽▽ 3
Campi Flegrei Piedirosso '14	▽▽ 4

● Irpinia Campi Taurasini Satyricon '14	▼▼ 4
● Taurasi Poliphemo '13	▼▼ 6
● Taurasi Poliphemo '08	▽▽▽ 6
● Taurasi Poliphemo '07	▽▽▽ 6
● Irpinia Campi Taurasini Satyricon '13	▽▽ 4
● Irpinia Campi Taurasini Satyricon '12	▽▽ 5
● Irpinia Campi Taurasini Satyricon '10	▽▽ 5
● Irpinia Campi Taurasini Satyricon '09	▽▽ 4
● Taurasi Poliphemo '12	▽▽ 6
● Taurasi Poliphemo '11	▽▽ 6
● Taurasi Poliphemo '10	▽▽ 6
● Taurasi Poliphemo '09	▽▽ 7
● Taurasi Poliphemo '06	▽▽ 6
● Taurasi Poliphemo '05	▽▽ 6

Terre del Principe

LOC. CASTEL CAMPAGNANO
P.ZZA MUNICIPIO 4
81010 CASTEL CAMPAGNANO [CE]
TEL. +39 0823867126
www.terredelprincipe.com

CELLAR SALES
PRE-BOOKED VISITS
ANNUAL PRODUCTION 50,000 bottles
HECTARES UNDER VINE 11.00
VITICULTURE METHOD Certified Organic
SUSTAINABLE WINERY

Peppe Mancini and Manuela Piancastrelli
deserve credit for their efforts to protect and
spread Pallagrello (white and red) and
Casavecchia varieties. On sandstone soil in
the Caiatini hills between the Taburno and
Matese Massifs, the couple run their eleven
hectares of vineyards with organic
management out of deep respect for the
environment. The Caiatini varieties have a
natural tendency towards concentration,
which is enhanced with long ripening in the
vineyard, and the use of small wooden
casks in the cellar. Their reward is
successful winemaking in a modern style.
The 2014 Centomoggia, made with
Casavecchia, reached our finals. It's a
particularly dense and powerful wine,
intensely peppery, with ripe redcurrants. The
mouth is tannic, still reined in, but with good
verve and energy. The 2014 Piancastelli is
remarkable. It's a blend of Pallagrello Nero
and Casavecchia with a Mediterranean
character. It features aromas of
Mediterranean scrub and juniper, with ripe
and sunny wild fruit.

● Piancastelli '14	♈♈ 6
● Casavecchia Centomoggia '14	♈♈ 3
○ Le Sèrole '15	♈ 5
● Ambruco Pallagrello Nero '10	♈♈♈ 5
● Centomoggia '11	♈♈♈ 5
● Centomoggia '08	♈♈♈ 5
● Centomoggia '07	♈♈♈ 5
○ Le Sèrole Pallagrello Bianco '13	♈♈♈ 5
● Ambruco '13	♈♈ 5
● Centomoggia '13	♈♈ 5
○ Le Sèrole '14	♈♈ 5
○ Pallagrello Bianco Fontanavigna '14	♈♈ 3
● Piancastelli '13	♈♈ 6
☉ Roseto del Volturno '14	♈♈ 3

Terre Stregate

LOC. SANTA LUCIA
VIA MUNICIPIO, 105
82034 GUARDIA SANFRAMONDI [BN]
TEL. +39 0824817857
www.terrestregate.it

CELLAR SALES
PRE-BOOKED VISITS
ANNUAL PRODUCTION 100,000 bottles
HECTARES UNDER VINE 22.00
SUSTAINABLE WINERY

Terre Stregate is looking to reach an
international level. In recent years it
made a commitment to focus on
Falanghina producing four different
versions. We have Filomena Iacobucci, an
enthusiastic ambassador for the Samnium
region, to. thank, as well as her brother
Carlo who works in the cellar alongside
their father, Armando. Together they run
their 22 hectares of vineyards, which give
rise to whites defined by their aromatic
richness and fresh acidity, and reds that
feature power and concentration. The
2016 Falanghina del Sannio Svelato
needs a good dose of aeration in order to
reach its full potential. It plays on a
different style, proving more generous and
succulent than the category's more classic
repertoire, with notes of tropical and citrus
fruit following through onto a rich palate
that's well-sustained at the finish. The
2015 Sannio Aglianico Manent sees good
tannic extraction and quality fruit.

○ Falanghina del Sannio Svelato '16	♈♈♈
○ Falanghina Caracara '15	♈♈
● Sannio Aglianico Manent '15	♈♈
○ Falanghina Trama '16	♈
○ Sannio Fiano Genius Loci '16	♈
○ Sannio Greco Aurora '16	♈
○ Falanghina del Sannio Svelato '15	♈♈♈
○ Falanghina del Sannio Svelato '14	♈♈♈
○ Falanghina del Sannio Svelato '13	♈♈♈
○ Falanghina del Sannio Svelato Sur Lies '13	♈♈
○ Falanghina Trama '15	♈♈
● Sannio Aglianico Manent '14	♈♈
● Sannio Aglianico Manent '13	♈♈
○ Sannio Fiano Genius Loci '14	♈♈

Terredora Di Paolo

VIA SERRA
83030 MONTEFUSCO [AV]
TEL. +39 0825968215
www.terredora.com

CELLAR SALES
PRE-BOOKED VISITS
ACCOMMODATION
ANNUAL PRODUCTION 800,000 bottles
HECTARES UNDER VINE 200.00

The vast vineyards of Terredora Di Paolo's
winery include 180 owned hectares and
70 rented ones. The estate is the result of
decisions made in the past by Antonio and
Walter Mastroberardino and it's now being
improved and relaunched by the next
generation, Paolo and Daniela. Their
vineyards are situated among some of the
most famous sites for Irpinian wines:
Lapio for Fiano, Montefusco and Santa
Paolina for Greco and Pietradefusi for
Taurasi. Their Falanghina is cultivated at
Gesualdo, their latest acquisition. Their
top-of-the-range wines are identified by
the CampoRe line (from the great Lapio
cru). Two wines grabbed top marks. The
2010 Taurasi Pago dei Fusi is precise,
austere, compact and deep with notes of
black tea, olives and well-managed spices.
In the mouth it proves long and balanced.
The 2016 Fiano di Avellino is well-paced
and supple, with a profile of delicately
smoky notes calling up herbs, including
thyme and basil. It's a subtle and
well-sustained wine with a relaxed finish.
A fine drink.

Fiano di Avellino '16	♟♟	3
Taurasi Pago dei Fusi '10	♟♟	5
Coda di Volpe '16	♟	3
Fiano di Avellino Campore '13	♟	5
Greco di Tufo Loggia della Serra '16	♟	3
Greco di Tufo Terre degli Angeli '16	♟	4
Taurasi Fatica Contadina '08	♟♟♟	5
Falanghina '14	♟♟	4
Fiano di Avellino Campore '12	♟♟	5
Fiano di Avellino Terredora Di Paolo '15	♟♟	3
Greco di Tufo Loggia della Serra '15	♟♟	3
Irpinia Falanghina '14	♟♟	4
Irpinia Aglianico Il Principio '09	♟♟	4
Lacryma Christi del Vesuvio Bianco '14	♟♟	4

Cantine Tora

VIA TORA II
82030 TORRECUSO [BN]
TEL. +39 0824872406
www.cantinetora.it

CELLAR SALES
PRE-BOOKED VISITS
ANNUAL PRODUCTION 55,000 bottles
HECTARES UNDER VINE 10.00

The Torrecuso winery is making its debut
in this part of our guide. Established in
2004 by Vincenzo Rillo in the wake of a
long family tradition, he now works with
the support of his brothers, Giampiero and
Francesco. They have wisely chosen to use
only the two main Samnium varieties:
Aglianico and Falanghina. The result is a
range of wines divided into different styles,
and marked by a spirit of continual
research under the winemaking
supervision of Angelo Valentino. We
particularly appreciated the jovial style of
their reds, which play on a racier approach
compared to others in the appellation. The
2013 Aglianico del Taburno made it to our
finals. It's an invigorating wine in its
aromas of blackberries and pencil lead,
with creamy driving tannins and a fresh
and savory finish. Close-knit and toastier is
the 2012 Aglianico del Taburno Spartivento
Riserva, with its aromas of Mediterranean
scrub and pepper, a dynamic grip,
backbone and a finish of exotic spices.

● Aglianico del Taburno '13	♟♟	3*
● Aglianico del Taburno Spartivento Ris. '12	♟♟	3
○ Falanghina del Sannio Kissos '16	♟♟	3
○ Cambio Luna '14	♟	3
○ Falanghina Centore '16	♟	2
○ Falanghina del Sannio Kissos '12	♟	3
● Taburno Aglianico '08	♟♟	3
● Taburno Aglianico Ris. Lysios '08	♟♟	4
○ Taburno Falanghina Kissòs '13	♟♟	2*

Torre a Oriente

LOC. MERCURI I, 19
82030 TORRECUSO [BN]
TEL. +39 0824874376
www.torreaoriente.eu

CELLAR SALES
PRE-BOOKED VISITS
ACCOMMODATION AND RESTAURANT SERVICE
ANNUAL PRODUCTION 40,000 bottles
HECTARES UNDER VINE 10.00
SUSTAINABLE WINERY

Patrizia Iannucci and Girogio Gentilcore
own a model winery. They work with
reverent respect for the environment, using
organic management, strict selections and
limited yields. Their 10 hectares of
vineyards give rise to solid artisan wines.
Their flagship is the Falanghina Biancuzita,
which is released only after two years in
the bottle (minimum). It is also worth noting
their world-famous olive oil (made with the
Ortece variety), which was voted
best-value-for-the-money in our latest
guide on the subject. The 2015 Falanghina
Biancuzita made it to our finals, but still
needs more time in the bottle. Ripe aromas
of tropical fruit are the prelude to an
intense mouth that's full-bodied but not
dull, with remarkable depth of taste. The
2016 Falanghina del Sannio Taburno
Siriana is already lively, with driving aromas
of green tea and ginger.

○ Falanghina del Sannio Biancuzita '15	♥♥ 3*
○ Falanghina del Sannio Taburno Siriana '16	♥♥ 2*
● Aglianico del Taburno Don Curzetto '14	♥ 5
● Aglianico del Taburno U' Barone '12	♥ 3
○ Falanghina del Sannio Biancuzita '14	♀♀♀ 3*
○ Falanghina del Sannio Biancuzita '12	♀♀♀ 3*
● Aglianico del Taburno U' Barone '08	♀♀ 3
○ Falanghina del Sannio Biancuzita '11	♀♀ 2*
○ Falanghina del Sannio Taburno Siriana '14	♀♀ 2*
○ Gioconda '13	♀♀ 2*
● Janico '10	♀♀ 2*
● Sannio Aglianico Janico '10	♀♀ 2*
○ Sannio Falanghina Biancuzita '08	♀♀ 2*
● Taburno Aglianico U' Barone '07	♀♀ 3

Villa Diamante

VIA TOPPOLE, 16
83030 MONTEFREDANE [AV]
TEL. +39 0825670014
villadiamante1996@gmail.com

CELLAR SALES
PRE-BOOKED VISITS
ANNUAL PRODUCTION 10,000 bottles
HECTARES UNDER VINE 4.50

The Montefredane hill treats us to some of
the most original, intense and unpredictab
whites in Italian winemaking. Fiano is the
main grape here and its cultivated on two
Fiano di Avellino crus. One is Vigna della
Congregazione, which calls up hints of wil
grass and exhibits a tangy character. The
other is Clos d'Haut, from the upper
Montefredane area, which produces smok
wines with a touch of peat. For many wine
enthusiasts, this is the stuff of dreams.
Antoine Gaeta's extraordinary work is
carried on today by his wife, Diamante
Renna, aided by seasoned winemaker
Vincenzo Mercurio. Only one wine was
presented this year but it's a real gem. The
2016 Fiano di Avellino Vigna La
Congregazione is a white with a pure light
and marvelous clean, fresh hints that are
enticing (to say the least). Notes of meado
herbs, orange peel and ginger anticipate a
palate with an overwhelming tangy sprint.
offers up a delicate smoky tone and prove
more measured than other versions. It's a
seemingly endless and charming wine. The
finish is precise, lively and complex.

○ Fiano di Avellino V. della Congregazione '16	♥♥♥
○ Fiano di Avellino Clos d'Haut '13	♀♀♀
○ Fiano di Avellino V. della Congregazione '15	♀♀♀
○ Fiano di Avellino V. della Congregazione '10	♀♀♀
○ Fiano di Avellino V. della Congregazione '08	♀♀♀
○ Fiano di Avellino Vigna della Congregazione '06	♀♀♀
○ Fiano di Avellino Vigna della Congregazione '04	♀♀♀
○ Fiano di Avellino Clos d'Haut '15	♀♀
○ Fiano di Avellino V. della Congregazione '13	♀♀
○ Fiano di Avellino V. della Congregazione '11	♀♀

★Villa Matilde

S.DA ST.LE DOMITIANA, 18
81030 CELLOLE [CE]
TEL. +39 0823932088
www.villamatilde.it

CELLAR SALES
PRE-BOOKED VISITS
ACCOMMODATION AND RESTAURANT SERVICE
ANNUAL PRODUCTION 700,000 bottles
HECTARES UNDER VINE 130.00
SUSTAINABLE WINERY

Two thousand years ago, the Romans drank, almost a liter of wine a day. They were well aware of how suitable Falerno was for vine growing and classified it as one of the best crus in the empire due to its unique volcanic soil. This legacy was relaunched first by Francesco Avallone, then continued by his children Salvatore and Maria Ida with help from winemaker Riccardo Cotarella. Starting with Falerno del Massico, they gradually expanded their selection with the estates of Tenuta Rocca dei Leoni and Altavilla. The result is a vast and complete range of wines. The 2016 Greco di Tufo deserves its place in the finals. It's a wine with marked intensity and aromas ranging from floral notes to white fruit. The mouth is well-structured, dry and driving, with a sure and rich unfolding of flavor. The 2014 Vigna Caracci is a mature and charming wine. It offers up toasty notes of hazelnut and bay leaf amidst intense fruit and well-managed wood. The 2016 Falanghina Rocca dei Leoni proves quite pleasant, with its aromas of freshly-cut grass, aniseed and mint. It's a pleasure to drink.

○ Greco di Tufo '16	♈♈ 3*
○ Falanghina Rocca dei Leoni '16	♈♈ 2*
○ Falerno del Massico V. Caracci '14	♈♈ 4
○ Falanghina '16	♈ 3
○ Falerno del Massico Bianco '16	♈ 3
○ Fiano di Avellino Tenute di Altavilla '16	♈ 3
○ Mata Rosé	♈ 4
● Stregamora '16	♈ 2
○ Terre Cerasa '16	♈ 2
○ Falerno del Massico Bianco V. Caracci '08	♈♈♈ 3
● Falerno del Massico Camarato '05	♈♈♈ 6
● Falerno del Massico Camarato '04	♈♈♈ 5
● Falerno del Massico Rosso V. Camarato Ris. '10	♈♈ 7
○ Greco di Tufo Tenute di Altavilla '15	♈♈ 3*

Villa Raiano

LOC. SAN MICHELE DI SERINO
VIA BOSCO SATRANO, 1
83020 SERINO [AV]
TEL. +39 0825595663
www.villaraiano.com

CELLAR SALES
PRE-BOOKED VISITS
ANNUAL PRODUCTION 300,000 bottles
HECTARES UNDER VINE 22.00
VITICULTURE METHOD Certified Organic

In just a few years, it went from being an oil-producing farm in the town of Raiano, in the municipality of Serino, to a first-rate winery in Irpinia. The winery was founded in 2009 in a unique setting of chestnut trees and vineyards, near the river Sabato. Sabino and Simone Basso, along with Paolo Sibillo, run 20 hectares of vineyards under certified organic management on a few outstanding plots of land. The entire production chain is scrupulously followed by Irpinian winemaker, Fortunato Sebastiano. There are two lines of wines: Classica and Vigne. A scintillating overall performance was led by the 2015 Fiano di Avellino, with its exhilarating traction, flavor and grip. It's a deep and layered wine, creamy and gradual, with a refreshing and bright finish. A real Tre Bicchieri. The 2015 Greco di Tufo Contrada Marotta features a more pervasive pace that's well-timed in its musky notes. The 2016 Fiano di Avellino performed very well and is a best buy.

○ Fiano di Avellino Alimata '15	♈♈♈ 4*
○ Greco di Tufo Contrada Marotta '15	♈♈ 4
○ Fiano di Avellino '16	♈♈ 3
○ Fiano di Avellino Ventidue '15	♈♈ 4
○ Greco di Tufo '16	♈♈ 3
● Irpinia Campi Taurasini '13	♈♈ 3
● Taurasi '13	♈ 5
○ Fiano di Avellino 22 '13	♈♈♈ 4*
○ Fiano di Avellino Alimata '10	♈♈♈ 4
○ Fiano di Avellino '15	♈♈ 3
○ Fiano di Avellino Alimata '14	♈♈ 4
○ Greco di Tufo '15	♈♈ 3
○ Greco di Tufo Contrada Marotta '14	♈♈ 4
● Taurasi '11	♈♈ 5

Abbazia di Crapolla

LOC. AVIGLIANO
VIA SAN FILIPPO, 2
80069 VICO EQUENSE [NA]
TEL. +39 3383517280
www.abbaziadicrapolla.it

ANNUAL PRODUCTION 12,000 bottles
HECTARES UNDER VINE 2.00

○ Sireo '15		🍷🍷 5
● Sabato '15		🍷🍷 5

Aia dei Colombi

C.DA SAPENZIE
82034 GUARDIA SANFRAMONDI [BN]
TEL. +39 0824817139
www.aladelcolombi.it

CELLAR SALES
PRE-BOOKED VISITS
ANNUAL PRODUCTION 60,000 bottles
HECTARES UNDER VINE 10.00

○ Falanghina del Sannio Guardia Sanframondi V. Suprema '15		🍷🍷 2*
○ Sannio Fiano Guardia Sanframondi '16		🍷🍷 2*

Amarano

C.DA TORRE, 32
83040 MONTEMARANO [AV]
TEL. +39 082763351
www.amarano.it

CELLAR SALES
PRE-BOOKED VISITS
ANNUAL PRODUCTION 20,000 bottles
HECTARES UNDER VINE 7.00

○ Fiano di Avellino Dulcinea '16		🍷🍷 3
○ Irpinia Coda di Volpe Lucinda '16		🍷🍷 3

Antica Hirpinia

C.DA LENZE, 10
83030 TAURASI [AV]
TEL. +39 082774730
www.annodomini1590.it

CELLAR SALES
PRE-BOOKED VISITS
RESTAURANT SERVICE
ANNUAL PRODUCTION 600,000 bottles
HECTARES UNDER VINE 200.00

○ Fiano di Avellino '16		🍷🍷 3
○ Irpinia Coda di Volpe '16		🍷🍷 2*
○ Irpinia Falanghina '16		🍷 2
● Taurasi '10		🍷 5

Antico Castello

C.DA POPPANO, 11BIS
83050 SAN MANGO SUL CALORE [AV]
TEL. +39 3408062830
www.anticocastello.com

CELLAR SALES
PRE-BOOKED VISITS
ACCOMMODATION AND RESTAURANT SERVICE
ANNUAL PRODUCTION 50,000 bottles
HECTARES UNDER VINE 10.00
SUSTAINABLE WINERY

● Irpinia Aglianico Magis '13		🍷🍷 3
● Taurasi '11		🍷🍷 4

Giuseppe Apicella

FRAZ. CAPITIGNANO
VIA CASTELLO SANTA MARIA, 1
84010 TRAMONTI [SA]
TEL. +39 089876075
www.giuseppeapicella.it

CELLAR SALES
PRE-BOOKED VISITS
ANNUAL PRODUCTION 60,000 bottles
HECTARES UNDER VINE 7.00
VITICULTURE METHOD Certified Organic

○ Costa d'Amalfi Tramonti Rosato '16		🍷🍷 3
● Costa d'Amalfi Tramonti Rosso a' Scippata Ris. '12		🍷🍷 5
● Piedirosso '16		🍷🍷 2*

Bambinuto

VIA CERRO
83030 SANTA PAOLINA [AV]
TEL. +39 0825964634
www.cantinabambinuto.com

PRE-BOOKED VISITS
ANNUAL PRODUCTION 25,000 bottles
HECTARES UNDER VINE 6.00

○ Greco di Tufo '15	🍷🍷 2*

Stefania Barbot

S.DA G. IANNACCONE, 6
83100 AVELLINO
TEL. +39 3357295133
www.comuninelvino.it

ANNUAL PRODUCTION 15,000 bottles
HECTARES UNDER VINE 3.00

● Taurasi Fren '13	🍷🍷 5
● Irpinia Campi Taurasini Ion '14	🍷 4

Cantine Barone

VIA GIARDINO, 2
84070 RUTINO [SA]
TEL. +39 0974830463
www.cantinebarone.it

CELLAR SALES
PRE-BOOKED VISITS
ACCOMMODATION
ANNUAL PRODUCTION 100,000 bottles
HECTARES UNDER VINE 12.00
VITICULTURE METHOD Certified Organic

● Cilento Aglianico Miles '13	🍷🍷 5
● Cilento Aglianico Pietralena '15	🍷🍷 3
○ Cilento Fiano Una Mattina '16	🍷🍷 2*
○ Marsia Bianco '16	🍷 1*

Boccella

VIA SANT'EUSTACHIO
83040 CASTELFRANCI [AV]
TEL. +39 082772574
www.boccellavini.it

CELLAR SALES
PRE-BOOKED VISITS
ANNUAL PRODUCTION 10,000 bottles
HECTARES UNDER VINE 5.00
VITICULTURE METHOD Certified Organic

● Irpinia Campi Taurasini Rasott '14	🍷🍷 3
● Taurasi Sant'Eustachio Ris. '07	🍷🍷 5

Borgodangelo

S.DA PROV.LE 52 KM 10
83050 SANT'ANGELO ALL'ESCA [AV]
TEL. +39 082773027
www.borgodangelo.it

CELLAR SALES
PRE-BOOKED VISITS
RESTAURANT SERVICE
ANNUAL PRODUCTION 30,000 bottles
HECTARES UNDER VINE 8.50
SUSTAINABLE WINERY

○ Fiano di Avellino '16	🍷🍷 2*
○ Irpinia Rosato '16	🍷🍷 2*
● Taurasi '11	🍷🍷 4

Vitivinicola Anna Bosco

FRAZ. SAN TOMMASO, 34
82037 CASTELVENERE [BN]
TEL. +39 0824940483
vitivinicolaannabosco@gmail.com

CELLAR SALES
PRE-BOOKED VISITS
ANNUAL PRODUCTION 10,000 bottles
HECTARES UNDER VINE 3.00
SUSTAINABLE WINERY

○ Parito's '16	🍷🍷 3
● Don Bosco '15	🍷 4

Bosco de' Medici

VIA ANTONIO SEGNI, 43
80045 POMPEI [NA]
TEL. +39 0818506463
www.boscodemedici.com

ANNUAL PRODUCTION 15,000 bottles
HECTARES UNDER VINE 8.00

○ Pompeii Bianco '15	♟♟ 3*
● Lacryma Christi del Vesuvio Rosso Lavarubra '15	♟♟ 3

Cantina del Barone

VIA NOCELLETO, 21
83020 CESINALI [AV]
TEL. +39 0825666751
www.cantinadelbarone.it

CELLAR SALES
PRE-BOOKED VISITS
ANNUAL PRODUCTION 30,000 bottles
HECTARES UNDER VINE 2.50

○ Particella 928 '15	♟♟ 3*
○ Paone '15	♟ 3

Cantina del Taburno

VIA SALA, 16
82030 FOGLIANISE [BN]
TEL. +39 0824871338
www.cantinadeltaburno.it

CELLAR SALES
PRE-BOOKED VISITS
ANNUAL PRODUCTION 1,000,000 bottles
HECTARES UNDER VINE 600.00

● Aglianico del Taburno Delius '13	♟♟ 4
○ Falanghina del Sannio Taburno '16	♟♟ 2*

Cantine dell'Angelo

VIA SANTA LUCIA, 32
83010 TUFO [AV]
TEL. +39 3384512965
www.cantinedellangelo.com

CELLAR SALES
PRE-BOOKED VISITS
ANNUAL PRODUCTION 18,000 bottles
HECTARES UNDER VINE 5.00

○ Greco di Tufo Torrefavale '15	♟♟ 3
○ Greco di Tufo Miniere '15	♟ 3

Capolino Perlingieri

VIA MARRAIOLI, 58
82037 CASTELVENERE [BN]
TEL. +39 0824971541
www.capolinoperlingieri.com

CELLAR SALES
PRE-BOOKED VISITS
ANNUAL PRODUCTION 25,000 bottles
HECTARES UNDER VINE 13.00
VITICULTURE METHOD Certified Organic
SUSTAINABLE WINERY

○ Falanghina del Sannio Preta '16	♟♟ 2*
○ Sannio Fiano Nembo '16	♟ 3
○ Sannio Greco Vento '15	♟ 2
⊙ Sannio Vignarosa '16	♟ 2

Tenuta Caprarizzo

PUNTA LICOSA
84048 CASTELLABATE [SA]
TEL. +39 3409062468
www.caprarizzo.it

PRE-BOOKED VISITS
ANNUAL PRODUCTION 15,000 bottles
HECTARES UNDER VINE 2.00

○ La Bella Greco '16	♟♟ 2*
○ Il Caprarizzo	♟ 2

Tenute Casoli

VIA ROMA, 28
83040 CANDIDA [AV]
TEL. +39 3402958099
www.tenutecasoli.it

CELLAR SALES
PRE-BOOKED VISITS
ACCOMMODATION AND RESTAURANT SERVICE
ANNUAL PRODUCTION 65,000 bottles
HECTARES UNDER VINE 13.00

○ Fiano di Avellino Kryos '16	♥♥ 3*
○ Greco di Tufo Le Crete '16	♥♥ 3
● Taurasi Armonia '12	♥♥ 6

Castelle

S.DA NAZIONALE SANNITICA, 48
82037 CASTELVENERE [BN]
TEL. +39 0824940232
www.castelle.it

ANNUAL PRODUCTION 50,000 bottles
HECTARES UNDER VINE 4.00

○ Falanghina del Sannio '16	♥♥ 2*
○ Falanghina del Sannio Kidonia V. T. '15	♥♥ 3
● Sannio Aglianico Propileo Ris. '12	♥♥ 4
○ Sannio Fiano '13	♥♥ 2*

Contrada Salandra

FRAZ. COSTE DI CUMA
VIA TRE PICCIONI, 40
80078 POZZUOLI [NA]
TEL. +39 0815265258
www.dolciqualita.com

CELLAR SALES
PRE-BOOKED VISITS
ANNUAL PRODUCTION 1,800 bottles
HECTARES UNDER VINE 4.70

○ Campi Flegrei Falanghina '15	♥♥ 2*
● Campi Flegrei Piedirosso '14	♥♥ 3

D'Antiche Terre

C.DA LO PIANO
83030 MANOCALZATI [AV]
TEL. +39 0825675358
www.danticheterre.it

CELLAR SALES
PRE-BOOKED VISITS
ACCOMMODATION AND RESTAURANT SERVICE
ANNUAL PRODUCTION 420,000 bottles
HECTARES UNDER VINE 40.00
SUSTAINABLE WINERY

○ Irpinia Coda di Volpe '16	♥♥ 2*
○ Greco di Tufo '16	♥ 3

Viticoltori De Conciliis

LOC. QUERCE, 1
84060 PRIGNANO CILENTO [SA]
TEL. +39 0974831090
www.viticoltorideconciliis.it

CELLAR SALES
PRE-BOOKED VISITS
ANNUAL PRODUCTION 200,000 bottles
HECTARES UNDER VINE 21.00
VITICULTURE METHOD Certified Organic
SUSTAINABLE WINERY

● Naima '09	♥♥ 6
● Bacioilcielo Rosso '16	♥♥ 2*
● Diciotto Supercampano '15	♥♥ 3
● Aglianico Zero Supercampano '12	♥ 3

De Falco Vini

VIA FIGLIOLA, 91
80040 SAN SEBASTIANO AL VESUVIO [NA]
TEL. +39 0817713755
www.defalco.it

CELLAR SALES
PRE-BOOKED VISITS
ANNUAL PRODUCTION 350,000 bottles
HECTARES UNDER VINE 8.00

○ Falanghina '16	♥♥ 2*
● Aglianico '15	♥ 2

Di Prisco

C.DA ROTOLE, 27
83040 FONTANAROSA [AV]
TEL. +39 0825475738
www.cantinadiprisco.lt

CELLAR SALES
PRE-BOOKED VISITS
ANNUAL PRODUCTION 100,000 bottles
HECTARES UNDER VINE 10.00

○ Irpinia Fiano V. Rotole '15	♀♀ 3
● Taurasi '12	♀ 5

Farro

LOC. FUSARO
VIA VIRGILIO, 16/24
80070 BACOLI [NA]
TEL. I 39 0818545555
www.cantinefarro.it

CELLAR SALES
PRE-BOOKED VISITS
ANNUAL PRODUCTION 207,000 bottles
HECTARES UNDER VINE 20.00

○ Campi Flegrei Falanghina '16	♀♀ 2*
○ Campi Flegrei Falanghina Le Cigliate '15	♀♀ 4

Cantine Federiciane Monteleone

FRAZ. SAN ROCCO
VIA ANTICA CONSOLARE CAMPANA, 34
80016 MARANO DI NAPOLI [NA]
TEL. 0815765294
www.federiciane.it

CELLAR SALES
PRE-BOOKED VISITS
ANNUAL PRODUCTION 200,000 bottles
HECTARES UNDER VINE 15.00

● Penisola Sorrentina Lettere '16	♀♀ 2*
● Penisola Sorrentina Gragnano '16	♀ 2

Filadoro

C.DA CERRETO, 19
83030 LAPIO [AV]
TEL. +39 0825982536
www.filadoro.it

CELLAR SALES
PRE-BOOKED VISITS
ANNUAL PRODUCTION 40,000 bottles
HECTARES UNDER VINE 6.00

○ Fiano di Avellino '16	♀♀ 3
○ Greco di Tufo '16	♀ 3
● Irpinia Aglianico '12	♀ 3

Fiorentino

C.DA BARBASSANO
83052 PATERNOPOLI [AV]
TEL. +39 3473474869310

CELLAR SALES
PRE-BOOKED VISITS
ANNUAL PRODUCTION 12,000 bottles
HECTARES UNDER VINE 7.00
SUSTAINABLE WINERY

● Taurasi '12	♀♀ 5
● Irpinia Aglianico Celsì '12	♀♀ 3
⊙ Irpinia Rosato Flavia '14	♀ 3

Fontana Reale

C.DA SAN GIOVANNI A CAPRARA
82100 BENEVENTO
TEL. +39 0824776109
www.fontanareale.com

CELLAR SALES
PRE-BOOKED VISITS
ANNUAL PRODUCTION 50,000 bottles
HECTARES UNDER VINE 15.00
VITICULTURE METHOD Certified Organic

● Aglianico '15	♀♀ 3
○ Falanghina del Sannio '16	♀♀ 3
○ Sannio Aglianico Brut '12	♀♀ 5

Raffaele Guastaferro

VIA A. GRAMSCI
83030 TAURASI [AV]
TEL. +39 3341551543
www.guastaferro.it

CELLAR SALES
ANNUAL PRODUCTION 10,000 bottles
HECTARES UNDER VINE 7.00

● Taurasi Primum '10	♟♟ 4
○ Greco di Tufo Cardinale '16	♟♟ 3
● Taurasi Primum Ris. '11	♟ 7

Historia Antiqua

VIA VARIANTE EST S.DA ST.LE 7BIS, 75
83030 MANOCALZATI [AV]
TEL. +39 0825675240
www.historiaantiqua.it

CELLAR SALES
PRE-BOOKED VISITS
ANNUAL PRODUCTION 90,000 bottles
HECTARES UNDER VINE 30.00

○ Greco Di Tufo '16	♟♟ 3
● Taurasi '12	♟♟ 6

Lunarossa

VIA V. FORTUNATO P.I.P. LOTTO 10
84095 GIFFONI VALLE PIANA [SA]
TEL. +39 0898021016
www.viniepassione.it

CELLAR SALES
PRE-BOOKED VISITS
ANNUAL PRODUCTION 50,000 bottles
HECTARES UNDER VINE 4.50

○ Quartara '14	♟♟ 5
● Camporeale Aglianico '16	♟ 2
⊙ Costacielo Rosato '16	♟ 3

Macchie Santa Maria

VIA CAPONI
83038 MONTEMILETTO [AV]
TEL. +39 0825963476
www.macchiesantamaria.it

○ Greco di Tufo Triarii '16	♟♟ 3
● Taurasi Evocatus Ris. '11	♟♟ 5

Masseria Felicia

FRAZ. CARANO
LOC. SAN TERENZANO
81037 SESSA AURUNCA [CE]
TEL. +39 0823935095
www.masseriafelicia.it

CELLAR SALES
PRE-BOOKED VISITS
ANNUAL PRODUCTION 25,000 bottles
HECTARES UNDER VINE 5.00

● Falerno del Massico Rosso Et. Bronzo Ris. '13	♟♟ 5
● Ioposso '14	♟ 2

Masseria Frattasi

VIA TORRE VARONI, 15
82016 MONTESARCHIO [BN]
TEL. +39 0823797879
www.masseriafrattasi.it

CELLAR SALES
PRE-BOOKED VISITS
ANNUAL PRODUCTION 150,000 bottles
HECTARES UNDER VINE 10.00
VITICULTURE METHOD Certified Biodynamic

○ Falanghina del Sannio Taburno Bonea '16	♟♟ 3
○ Nymphis Sacrae Coda di Volpe '16	♟ 3

★Mastroberardino

VIA MANFREDI, 75/81
83042 ATRIPALDA [AV]
TEL. +39 0825614111
www.mastroberardino.com

CELLAR SALES
PRE-BOOKED VISITS
ACCOMMODATION AND RESTAURANT SERVICE
ANNUAL PRODUCTION 2,000,000 bottles
HECTARES UNDER VINE 300.00
SUSTAINABLE WINERY

● Taurasi Radici Ris. '11	♟♟	5

Salvatore Molettieri

C.DA MUSANNI, 19B
83040 MONTEMARANO [AV]
TEL. +39 082763722
www.salvatoremolettieri.com

CELLAR SALES
PRE-BOOKED VISITS
ANNUAL PRODUCTION 65,000 bottles
HECTARES UNDER VINE 13.00

○ Fiano di Avellino Apianum '15	♟♟	3
● Irpinia Aglianico Cinque Querce '13	♟♟	3
● Irpinia Aglianico O'Calice Rosso '14	♟	3

Montesole

LOC. SERRA DI MONTEFUSCO
VIA SERRA
83030 MONTEFUSCO [AV]
TEL. +39 0825963972
www.montesole.it

PRE-BOOKED VISITS
ANNUAL PRODUCTION 1,200,000 bottles
HECTARES UNDER VINE 120.00

○ Greco di Tufo V. Breccia '16	♟♟	4
○ Falanghina del Sannio V. Zampino '16	♟	3
○ Fiano di Avellino V. Acquaviva '16	♟	4
● Taurasi Ris. '10	♟	4

Cantine Olivella

VIA ZAZZERA, 14
80048 SANT'ANASTASIA [NA]
TEL. +39 0815311388
www.cantineolivella.com

CELLAR SALES
PRE-BOOKED VISITS
ANNUAL PRODUCTION 80,000 bottles
HECTARES UNDER VINE 12.00

○ Catalanesca Kata '16	♟♟	3
○ Lacryma Christi del Vesuvio Bianco Emblema '16	♟♟	3

Fattoria Pagano

S.DA PROV.LE PER FALCIANO
81030 CARINOLA [CE]
TEL. +39 3895475419
www.fattoriapagano.it

CELLAR SALES
PRE-BOOKED VISITS
ANNUAL PRODUCTION 55,000 bottles
HECTARES UNDER VINE 10.00
SUSTAINABLE WINERY

○ Anima V. T. '16	♟♟	3
● Falerno del Massico Rosso Gaurasi '11	♟♟	3
○ Falerno del Massico Bianco Fabula '16	♟	3

Raffaele Palma

LOC. SAN VITO
VIA ARSENALE, 8
84010 MAIORI [SA]
TEL. +39 3357601858
www.raffaelepalma.it

CELLAR SALES
ANNUAL PRODUCTION 20,000 bottles
HECTARES UNDER VINE 6.00
VITICULTURE METHOD Certified Organic
SUSTAINABLE WINERY

○ Costa d'Amalfi Bianco Puntacroce '16	♟♟	6
⊙ Costa d'Amalfi Rosato Salicerchi '15	♟	6

Pietratorcia

FRAZ. CUOTTO
VIA PROVINCIALE PANZA, 309
80075 FORIO [NA]
TEL. +39 081908206
www.pietratorcia.it

CELLAR SALES
PRE-BOOKED VISITS
ANNUAL PRODUCTION 130,000 bottles
HECTARES UNDER VINE 8.00

● Ischia Rosso Tenuta Janno Piro '15	♟♟	3
○ Ischia Bianco Sup. Tenuta Cuotto '16	♟	3
○ Ischia Biancolella '16	♟	3

Scala Fenicia

VIA FENICIA, 15
80073 ANACAPRI [NA]
TEL. +39 0818389403
www.scalafenicia.com

○ Capri Bianco '16	♟♟	5

Sorrentino

VIA RIO, 26
80042 BOSCOTRECASE [NA]
TEL. +39 0818584963
www.sorrentinovini.com

CELLAR SALES
PRE-BOOKED VISITS
ACCOMMODATION AND RESTAURANT SERVICE
ANNUAL PRODUCTION 250,000 bottles
HECTARES UNDER VINE 30.00
VITICULTURE METHOD Certified Organic

○ Lacryma Christi del Vesuvio Bianco '16	♟♟	2*
● Lacryma Christi del Vesuvio Rosso V. Lapillo '15	♟♟	2*
● Don Paolo '15	♟	4

Andrea Reale

B.GO DI GETE
VIA CARDAMONE, 75
84010 TRAMONTI [SA]
TEL. +39 089856144
www.aziendaagricolareale.it

CELLAR SALES
PRE-BOOKED VISITS
ACCOMMODATION AND RESTAURANT SERVICE
ANNUAL PRODUCTION 12,500 bottles
HECTARES UNDER VINE 2.50
VITICULTURE METHOD Certified Organic

○ Costa d'Amalfi Tramonti Rosato Getis '16	♟♟	4
○ Costa d'Amalfi Tramonti Bianco Aliseo '16	♟♟	4
● Costa d'Amalfi Tramonti Rosso Cardamone '15	♟♟	4

Tenuta Scuotto

C.DA CAMPOMARINO, 2/3
83030 LAPIO [AV]
TEL. +39 08251851965
www.tenutascuotto.it

CELLAR SALES
PRE-BOOKED VISITS
ANNUAL PRODUCTION 40,000 bottles
HECTARES UNDER VINE 3.00

○ Greco di Tufo '16	♟♟	3*
○ Falanghina '16	♟♟	3
○ Fiano di Avellino '16	♟♟	2*

Torricino

LOC. TORRICINO, 5
VIA NAZIONALE
83010 TUFO [AV]
TEL. +39 0825998119
www.torricino.it

CELLAR SALES
PRE-BOOKED VISITS
ANNUAL PRODUCTION 40,000 bottles
HECTARES UNDER VINE 6.00
VITICULTURE METHOD Certified Organic
SUSTAINABLE WINERY

○ Fiano di Avellino '15	♟♟	3*

Traerte

C.DA VADIAPERTI
83030 MONTEFREDANE [AV]
TEL. +39 0825607270
info@traerte.it

CELLAR SALES
PRE-BOOKED VISITS
ANNUAL PRODUCTION 81,000 bottles
HECTARES UNDER VINE 6.00

○ Fiano di Avellino Aipierti '16	♟♟ 5	
○ Irpinia Coda di Volpe Torama '16	♟♟ 5	
○ Fiano di Avellino '16	♟ 3	
○ Greco di Tufo Tornante '16	♟ 5	

VentitréFilari

VIA PIANTE, 43
83030 MONTEFREDANE [AV]
TEL. +39 0825672482
www.ventitrefilari.com

ANNUAL PRODUCTION 3,500 bottles
HECTARES UNDER VINE 1.00
SUSTAINABLE WINERY

○ Fiano di Avellino Ventitréfilari Numero Primo '15	♟♟ 4

Vestini Campagnano

VIA COSTA DELL'AIA, 9
81044 CONCA DELLA CAMPANIA [CE]
TEL. +39 0823679087
www.vestinicampagnano.it

CELLAR SALES
PRE-BOOKED VISITS
ANNUAL PRODUCTION 80,000 bottles
HECTARES UNDER VINE 7.00
VITICULTURE METHOD Certified Organic

○ Pallagrello Bianco Le Ortole '16	♟♟ 4
● Casavecchia di Pontelatone Ris. '13	♟ 5
● Kajanero '16	♟ 2
○ Pallagrello Bianco '16	♟ 3

Vigne Guadagno

VIA TAGLIAMENTO, 237
83100 AVELLINO
TEL. +39 08251686379
www.vigneguadagno.it

CELLAR SALES
PRE-BOOKED VISITS
ANNUAL PRODUCTION 47,000 bottles
HECTARES UNDER VINE 10.00

○ Fiano di Avellino '15	♟♟ 3
○ Irpinia Falanghina '16	♟♟ 3
● Taurasi '11	♟ 5

Vitis Aurunca

VIA TORQUATO TASSO
80029 SANT'ANTIMO [NA]
TEL. +39 0815051657
www.vitisaurunca.com

ANNUAL PRODUCTION 20,000 bottles
HECTARES UNDER VINE 7.90

○ Falerno del Massico Bianco Agnese '16	♟♟ 3
● Falerno del Massico Primitivo Mariella '14	♟♟ 3

Votino

VIA FIZZO, 14
82013 BONEA [BN]
TEL. +39 0824834762
www.aziendavotino.com

CELLAR SALES
PRE-BOOKED VISITS
ANNUAL PRODUCTION 100,000 bottles
HECTARES UNDER VINE 5.00
SUSTAINABLE WINERY

● Aglianico del Taburno Furius '14	♟♟ 2*
○ Falanghina del Sannio Taburno Cocceius '16	♟♟ 2*

BASILICATA

This year's round of tasting demonstrated that Basilicata, one of Italy's most beautiful regions, is coming into its own in terms of winemaking. We've always loved its works of art, its immense landscapes and its natural beauty, and for as long as anyone can remember, we've nurtured an intense and frank relationship with its vine growers. Lucania has always been one of Southern Italy's most promising areas, and we're not only talking about its most celebrated terroir, Vulture. More than 2500 years ago, this territory hosted the third center of grape domestication. Back when the first waves of Greeks colonizers arrived, they already found grapes being grown. They brought their own knowledge to cultivation, and so the fruit spread from the south to north, by land and by sea. Finally, today, we see that what were once just promises have come to fruition in a rich array of excellent wines. This year, in fact, some five wines earned Tre Bicchieri. We were particularly struck by a rosé that gave rise to some 15 wines all worthy of serious attention. Of course, the lead role is solidly in the hands of Aglianico del Vulture, which seems to have found new life with the DOCG, but we shouldn't overlook the encouraging signs coming from Matera, the next European Capital of Culture. If we also consider the spirit of cooperation that's spreading among producers and appellations, a phenomenon that the Enoteca Regionale Lucana is encouraging, our hopes for the future get that much brighter. Italy's great enological groups are noticing, and investing more and more in the region, affirming Aglianico del Vulture's appeal, among others. And the experience of its producers can only uplift this little-big region of winemaking, whose success must also be attributed to its viticultural artisans. But it's time for new challenges more structured producers, as well as experience with international markets, can only further encourage the territory's many up-and-coming wineries. And there are more than a few...

Basilisco

LOC. BARILE
VIA DELLE CANTINE, 20
85022 BARILE [PZ]
TEL. +39 0972771033
www.basiliscovini.it

CELLAR SALES
PRE-BOOKED VISITS
ACCOMMODATION
ANNUAL PRODUCTION 55,000 bottles
HECTARES UNDER VINE 25.00
VITICULTURE METHOD Certified Organic
SUSTAINABLE WINERY

Basilisco represents another side of Aglianico, and, in particular, Vulture's version of the grape. It's an effort that took hold in 2011, when Feudi di San Gregorio purchased the winery once owned by Michele Cutolo. Bolstered by a beautiful cellar, carved out of old lava rock, and a 25-hectare estate that comprises historic crus, like Macarico and Gelosia, in just a short time, the winery has managed to become efficient and successful. Credit's also due to Viviana Malafarina. The producer's face and soul, she personally manages the cellar, with the expert support of their vineyard manager, Pierpaolo Sirch. Once again, Basilisco has earned our highest award with an excellent Aglianico Superiore, the 2013 Cruà. It's a wine that certainly possesses structure, but it's also one of the most elegant Aglianicos we've tasted in recent years. It proves complex, well-orchestrated, close-focused and incredibly long. The Fontanelle selection of the same vintage is right up there as well, with its intriguing balsamic hints.

● Aglianico del Vulture Sup. Cruà '13	🍷🍷🍷 5
● Aglianico del Vulture Sup. Fontanelle '13	🍷🍷 5
● Aglianico del Vulture Teodosio '14	🍷🍷 3
○ Sophia '16	🍷 3
● Aglianico del Vulture Basilisco '09	🍷🍷🍷 5
● Aglianico del Vulture Basilisco '08	🍷🍷🍷 5
● Aglianico del Vulture Basilisco '07	🍷🍷🍷 5
● Aglianico del Vulture Basilisco '06	🍷🍷🍷 5
● Aglianico del Vulture Basilisco '04	🍷🍷🍷 5
● Aglianico del Vulture Basilisco '01	🍷🍷🍷 5

Cantine del Notaio

VIA ROMA, 159
85028 RIONERO IN VULTURE [PZ]
TEL. +39 0972723689
www.cantinedelnotaio.com

CELLAR SALES
PRE-BOOKED VISITS
RESTAURANT SERVICE
ANNUAL PRODUCTION 450,000 bottles
HECTARES UNDER VINE 38.00

Cantine del Notaio got its start in 1998, thanks to the agronomist, Gerardo Giuratrabocchetti, who took up the challenge to work with and promote Aglianico. Today, the winery boasts 38 hectares of vineyards in the municipalities of Rionero, Barile, Ripacandida, Maschito and Ginestra, areas renowned for the production of Aglianico del Vulture. The peculiarities of the terrain, and their pedoclimatic exposure allow the grape to ripen perfectly (as it is among the latest to get harvested). The wines (whose names are inspired by the notary profession) are made in Rionero, in their new, modern facility, and age in the historic, 17th-century tuff grottos made by Franciscan monks. Repertorio's continuity confirms its status as their flagship wine, as well as one of the most representative in the appellation. The 2015 vintage notched up another Tre Bicchieri for the wine due to its great expressive precision, which brings the richness of its fruit to the forefront without sacrificing texture. The 2015 Macarì, a balanced wine rich in fine-grained tannins, also delivered.

● Aglianico del Vulture Il Repertorio '15	🍷🍷🍷 4*
● Aglianico del Vulture Macarì '15	🍷🍷 3*
● Aglianico del Vulture Il Sigillo '12	🍷🍷 6
● Aglianico del Vulture Macarico '14	🍷🍷 3
● L'Atto '16	🍷🍷 3
○ L'Autentica '15	🍷🍷 5
● Il Protesto '16	🍷 3
○ La Postilla	🍷 3
⊙ La Raccolta '16	🍷 3
● Aglianico del Vulture Il Repertorio '14	🍷🍷🍷 4*
● Aglianico del Vulture Il Repertorio '13	🍷🍷🍷 4*
● Aglianico del Vulture Il Repertorio '12	🍷🍷🍷 4*
● Aglianico del Vulture La Firma '10	🍷🍷🍷 6
● Aglianico del Vulture La Firma '00	🍷🍷🍷 5

Eubea

S.DA PROV.LE 8
85020 RIPACANDIDA [PZ]
TEL. +39 3284312789
www.agricolaeubea.com

CELLAR SALES
PRE-BOOKED VISITS
ANNUAL PRODUCTION 50,000 bottles
HECTARES UNDER VINE 16.00
VITICULTURE METHOD Certified Organic

The name pays homage to the
Mediterranean island of Eubea. It's
significant because the island once hosted
those great navigators who, with Ionic
colonization, brought Aglianico to southern
Italy. Today, Eugenia Sasso is at the helm of
this inspiring winery, founded in 1997. She
inherited her enthusiasm for wine from her
father, Francesco, a well-known figure in
Basilicata's viticulture scene, and a mentor
for Aglianico del Vulture. Their 16 hectares
of vineyards, situated in Barile and
Ripacandida, span volcanic terrain with a
high capacity for drainage, and that enjoy a
singular microclimate, making for wines
that are complex and concentrated, but
also polished and highly drinkable. This
year we thought the Covo dei Briganti
Aglianico was Eugenia's most intriguing
wine. The 2015 vintage exhibits a
slim-bodied and finely-tuned style, a nice
fruity character and subtle depth, with a
tempting palate backed up by a touch of
tartness and smooth tannins. The Ròinos is
richer and deeper, but less impressive. It
still needs time to find the right balance.

● Aglianico del Vulture Covo dei Briganti '15	🍷🍷 3
● Aglianico del Vulture Ròinos '15	🍷 5
● Aglianico del Vulture Ròinos '01	🍷🍷🍷 8
● Aglianico del Vulture Covo dei Briganti '13	🍷🍷 3*
● Aglianico del Vulture Covo dei Briganti '12	🍷🍷 3
● Aglianico del Vulture Covo dei Briganti '09	🍷🍷 3
● Aglianico del Vulture Eubearosso '09	🍷🍷 2*
● Aglianico del Vulture Ròinos '13	🍷🍷 5
● Aglianico del Vulture Ròinos '12	🍷🍷 5
● Aglianico del Vulture Roinos '11	🍷🍷 5
⊙ La Vie en Rose M. Cl. '12	🍷🍷 2*

★Elena Fucci

C.DA SOLAGNA DEL TITOLO
85022 BARILE [PZ]
TEL. +39 3204879945
www.elenafuccivini.com

CELLAR SALES
PRE-BOOKED VISITS
ANNUAL PRODUCTION 25,000 bottles
HECTARES UNDER VINE 6.70
SUSTAINABLE WINERY

Elena Fucci's winery reflects principles of
bioarchitecture, the use of low energy
consumption technology and reduced
carbon emissions. Their new cellar stands
shoulder-to-shoulder with some of the
most high-profile sustainable facilities
being built. Here, in Solagna del Titolo
(Barile), the volcanic terrain gives rise to the
producer's only wine, Aglianico del Vulture
Titolo. Elena, owner and winemaker, is
flanked by her father, Salvatore, and
husband, Andrea, who look after the
vineyards and oversee every stage of
production. The result is a superior red that
does an excellent job representing the
unique terroir of Vulture. The 2015 vintage
has made for an excellent version of the
Titolo, one of the most representative wines
in the appellation. Elena has managed to
tame Aglianico's powerful structure and
transform it into an elegant, deep red. The
wine proves rich fragrances of fruit, oak
and spices, which give way to a charming
palate and lengthy aromatic persistence.
Tre Bicchieri once again.

● Aglianico del Vulture Titolo '15	🍷🍷🍷 6
● Aglianico del Vulture Titolo '14	🍷🍷🍷 6
● Aglianico del Vulture Titolo '13	🍷🍷🍷 6
● Aglianico del Vulture Titolo '12	🍷🍷🍷 5
● Aglianico del Vulture Titolo '11	🍷🍷🍷 5
● Aglianico del Vulture Titolo '10	🍷🍷🍷 5
● Aglianico del Vulture Titolo '09	🍷🍷🍷 5
● Aglianico del Vulture Titolo '08	🍷🍷🍷 6
● Aglianico del Vulture Titolo '07	🍷🍷🍷 6
● Aglianico del Vulture Titolo '06	🍷🍷🍷 5
● Aglianico del Vulture Titolo '05	🍷🍷🍷 5
● Aglianico del Vulture Titolo '02	🍷🍷🍷 5
● Aglianico del Vulture Titolo '04	🍷🍷 5
● Aglianico del Vulture Titolo '03	🍷🍷 5

Grifalco della Lucania

LOC. PIAN DI CAMERA
85029 VENOSA [PZ]
TEL. +39 097231002
grifalcodellalucania@email.it

CELLAR SALES
PRE-BOOKED VISITS
ANNUAL PRODUCTION 65,000 bottles
HECTARES UNDER VINE 15.00
VITICULTURE METHOD Certified Organic
SUSTAINABLE WINERY

Fabrizio and Cecilia Piccin's background in winemaking began in Tuscany (Montepulciano, to be precise), when Sangiovese, not Aglianico, was being interpreted in various versions. The breakthrough came in 2003, when the Piccins purchased various vineyards in Ginestra, Maschito, Rapolla and Venosa, founding a winery dedicated to Aglianico del Vulture. But their team was bound to grow - enter Lorenzo, one of their three children, who, after studying enology in Alba (and getting experience in a few cellars), brought his enthusiasm and skill back to the family winery. Another son, Andrea, is also on board, working at the commercial end of things. The 2015 Aglianico Gricos presented for tasting received unanimous consensus and made it into our finals. It's an elegant and expansive red, with intact fruit. It's only missing that touch of overall balance needed for top marks. The Grifalco of the same vintage also proved first-rate.

● Aglianico del Vulture Gricos '15	♟♟ 3*
● Aglianico del Vulture Grifalco '15	♟♟ 4
● Aglianico del Vulture Daginestra '12	♟ 5
● Aglianico del Vulture Damaschito '13	♟ 4
● Aglianico del Vulture Gricos '14	♟♟♟ 3*
● Aglianico del Vulture Daginestra '11	♟♟ 5
● Aglianico del Vulture Damaschito '12	♟♟ 4
● Aglianico del Vulture Gricos '13	♟♟ 3*
● Aglianico del Vulture Gricos '12	♟♟ 2*
● Aglianico del Vulture Gricos '11	♟♟ 2*
● Aglianico del Vulture Grifalco '14	♟♟ 4
● Aglianico del Vulture Grifalco '13	♟♟ 4
● Aglianico del Vulture Grifalco '12	♟♟ 3*

Martino

VIA LA VISTA, 2A
85028 RIONERO IN VULTURE [PZ]
TEL. +39 0972721422
www.martinovini.com

CELLAR SALES
PRE-BOOKED VISITS
ANNUAL PRODUCTION 250,000 bottles
HECTARES UNDER VINE 50.00

The Martino family's extensive background in wine started in the late 1980s, and established itself with Donato Martino (the father of the current owner, Armando). He was the one who started bottling wines under his own brand. Today, the winery is among the oldest and most solid of Basilicata. It comprises 50 hectares of vineyards along the volcanic hills of Rionero. Their production facility relies on modern systems and an uold underground cellar with a system of caves for aging their wines. Armando is flanked by the young and tireless Carolin Martino, who's also president of the Consorzio dell'Aglianico del Vulture. We particularly enjoyed the 2014 Aglianico del Vulture. It's an elegant and fresh wine, rich in notes of red fruit, cranberries and Morello cherries. In the mouth it proves savory and caressing, with smooth tannins. Though its structure isn't particularly bold, it wins you over with the balance, cleanness, and pleasantness of its palate. A long finish of sweet almonds and walnuts seals the deal.

● Aglianico del Vulture '14	♟♟ 3
● Aglianico del Vulture Sup. '12	♟♟ 7
○ I Sassi Greco '16	♟♟ 4
● Aglianico del Vulture Sup. Ris. '11	♟ 7
○ Sincerità '16	♟ 4
● Aglianico del Vulture '13	♟♟ 2
● Aglianico del Vulture '12	♟♟ 2
● Aglianico del Vulture '11	♟♟ 2
● Aglianico del Vulture Bel Poggio '10	♟♟ 2
● Aglianico del Vulture Bel Poggio '09	♟♟ 2
● Aglianico del Vulture Oraziano '10	♟♟ 5
● Aglianico del Vulture Oraziano '09	♟♟ 5
● Aglianico del Vulture Pretoriano '10	♟♟ 5
● Aglianico del Vulture Pretoriano '09	♟♟ 5

enuta Parco dei Monaci

a Parco dei Monaci
100 Matera
. +39 0835259546
w.tenutaparcodeimonaci.it

E-BOOKED VISITS
COMMODATION
NNUAL PRODUCTION 20,000 bottles
CTARES UNDER VINE 5.00

sa Padula and Matteo Trabacca both
me from families with historic ties to
culture. Together, they founded one of the
st interesting wineries in the area. Today,
co dei Monaci is a beautiful estate,
ated just five kilometers from Matera, 'the
y of Stones' and equipped with a modern
lar. It's overlooked by an ominous, fortified
nge, once the property of the Benedictine
bey of Montescaglioso. For centuries, the
k, stony terrain of Parco della Murgia,
ch is also underpinned by a layer of tuff,
proved ideal for cultivating grapes and
es. Starting in the 18th century,
nedictine monks cultivated Primitivo here.
appreciated the 2014 Matera Moro
ccasassi for its rich, fruity aromas calling
Morello cherries and brambles, its spicy
es and well balanced oaky hints. The
5 Matera Primitivo Monacello is
verful, caressing and soft, with a palate
de pleasant by a balanced touch of
ness. The 2016 Matera Rosato Rosa per
npre also proved solid.

Matera Moro Spaccasassi '14	⚏⚏ 5
Matera Primitivo Monacello '15	⚏⚏ 4
Matera Rosato Rosa per Sempre '16	⚏ 3
Matera Moro Spaccasassi '13	⚏⚏ 6
Matera Moro Spaccasassi '11	⚏⚏ 6
Matera Primitivo Monacello '14	⚏⚏ 5
Matera Primitivo Monacello '11	⚏⚏ 5

Paternoster

c.da Valle del Titolo
85022 Barile [PZ]
Tel. +39 0972770224
Ronchetto

CELLAR SALES
PRE-BOOKED VISITS
ANNUAL PRODUCTION 150,000 bottles
HECTARES UNDER VINE 20.00
VITICULTURE METHOD Certified Organic

Paternoster's long history is characterized by
persistence, determination and passion for
the land. It goes back to 1925, with Anselmo
Paternoster, and established itself with his
son, Vito. Today, the winery has seen a
change of management, with the entrance of
the Tommasi group, a large, Venetian outfit
that operates in the sector. Both Vito
Paternoster and his winemaker, Fabio
Mecca, share the same goal: bolster the
brand on Italian and international markets,
while stimulating production through
expansion of the vineyards and greater
sustainability. Today, the estate comprises 20
hectares spread throughout various districts
of Barile, which give rise to the prestigious
selections of wines, Don Anselmo and
Rotondo. Both of Patenoster's flagship wines
made it to our tasting finals. Once again, the
skillful 2013 Don Anselmo earns a Tre
Bicchieri. It's a complex, deep, soft and
balanced wine with a great future ahead of it.

● Aglianico del Vulture Don Anselmo '13	⚏⚏⚏ 6
● Aglianico del Vulture Rotondo '13	⚏⚏ 5
● Aglianico del Vulture Giuv Organic '15	⚏⚏ 2*
● Aglianico del Vulture Synthesi '15	⚏⚏ 3
○ Assensi Extra Brut	⚏ 3
○ Vulcanico Falanghina '16	⚏ 3
● Aglianico del Vulture Don Anselmo '09	⚏⚏⚏ 6
● Aglianico del Vulture Don Anselmo '94	⚏⚏⚏ 6
● Aglianico del Vulture Don Anselmo Ris. '05	⚏⚏⚏ 6
● Aglianico del Vulture Rotondo '11	⚏⚏⚏ 5
● Aglianico del Vulture Rotondo '01	⚏⚏⚏ 5
● Aglianico del Vulture Rotondo '00	⚏⚏⚏ 5

Re Manfredi
Cantina Terre degli Svevi

LOC. PIAN DI CAMERA
85029 VENOSA [PZ]
TEL. +39 097231263
www.cantineremanfredi.it

CELLAR SALES
PRE-BOOKED VISITS
RESTAURANT SERVICE
ANNUAL PRODUCTION 230,000 bottles
HECTARES UNDER VINE 120.00

The entrepreneurial skills of the Gruppo
Italiano Vini allowed Paolo Montrone's
winery to position itself as a benchmark for
Vulture's wine culture. With vines as old as
40 years, Vigneto Serpara, in Maschito
represents the producer's historic vineyard,
and gives rise to their only cru wine. The
rest of their 120 hectares can be found in
Venosa and other wine districts, where
white grapes like aromatic Traminer and
Müller Thurgau are cultivated. All their wines
have one thing in common: they tend
towards softness and balance, which
smooths out the tannic strength of Aglianico
del Vulture. Once again, the 2013 Separa
takes home a Tre Bicchieri. It's a deep,
velvety, well-orchestrated wine, rich in
notes of ripe fruit, with very fine tannins, a
good balance of acidity and length. The
2015 Taglio del Tralcio, made from grapes
that are left to partially dry on the vine,
also impressed.

Terra dei Re

VIA MONTICCHIO KM 2,700
85028 RIONERO IN VULTURE [PZ]
TEL. +39 0972725116
www.terradeire.com

CELLAR SALES
PRE-BOOKED VISITS
ACCOMMODATION AND RESTAURANT SERVI
ANNUAL PRODUCTION 70,000 bottles
HECTARES UNDER VINE 11.00
SUSTAINABLE WINERY

Two families and one mission: become on
of the region's leading wine producers. In
just a short time, the Leone and Rabasco
families have managed to identify their
production style, develop technologically,
and position their products on markets tha
recognize powerful, concentrated, rounde
wines like Aglianico del Vulture. The cellar,
modern facility that's currently being
renovated, is headquartered in Rionero in
Vulture, built on underground levels, volca
caves that assure the perfect maturation
and aging of their wines. Their certified
organic vineyards span Barile, Rionero, M
and Rapolla, in extremely well-suited
districts like Piano di Carro, Colignelli, Cala
delle Brecce and Querce di Annibale. Of th
three Aglianicos we tasted, our favorite wa
the 2012 Divinus. It features a close-knit
palate with elegant tannins, indicating goc
integration of oak. It finishes with very lon
fragrances of ripe cherries.

● Aglianico del Vulture Sup. Serpara '12	▼▼▼ 5
● Aglianico del Vulture Taglio del Tralcio '15	▼▼ 3*
○ Re Manfredi Bianco '16	▼ 4
● Aglianico del Vulture Re Manfredi '13	▼▼▼ 6
● Aglianico del Vulture Re Manfredi '11	▼▼▼ 4*
● Aglianico del Vulture Re Manfredi '10	▼▼▼ 4*
● Aglianico del Vulture Re Manfredi '05	▼▼▼ 4
● Aglianico del Vulture Re Manfredi '99	▼▼▼ 4*
● Aglianico del Vulture Serpara '10	▼▼▼ 5
● Aglianico del Vulture Vign. Serpara '03	▼▼▼ 4*
● Aglianico del Vulture Re Manfredi '12	▼▼ 4
● Aglianico del Vulture Serpara '11	▼▼ 5
● Aglianico del Vulture Taglio del Tralcio '13	▼▼ 3*
○ Re Manfredi Bianco '14	▼▼ 3

● Aglianico del Vulture Sup. Divinus '12	▼▼
● Aglianico del Vulture Nocte '14	▼▼
● Aglianico del Vulture Vultur '14	▼▼
○ Claris Malvasia '16	▼
● Aglianico del Vulture Divinus '05	▼▼
● Aglianico del Vulture Nocte '13	▼▼
● Aglianico del Vulture Nocte '10	▼▼
● Aglianico del Vulture Nocte '04	▼▼
● Aglianico del Vulture Vultur '13	▼▼
● Aglianico del Vulture Vultur '06	▼▼
● Pacus '06	▼▼
● Vulcano 800 '15	▼▼

Cantina di Venosa

LOC. VIGNALI
VIA APPIA
85029 VENOSA [PZ]
TEL. +39 097236702
www.cantinadivenosa.it

CELLAR SALES
PRE-BOOKED VISITS
ANNUAL PRODUCTION 800,000 bottles
HECTARES UNDER VINE 800.00
SUSTAINABLE WINERY

This important co-operative winery got its start in 1947, thanks to the efforts of 27 vine growers who sought to promote the Aglianico del Vulture DOC zone in the territory of Venosa (the most densely planted municipality in the region). Today, they've come to count 400 members among their ranks, and, through hard work and excellent products, they've demonstrated the economic importance of a large co-operative for the appellation. They currently have 800 hectares at their disposal, spread throughout Venosa, Ripacandida, Maschito and Ginestra, where their best grapes are cultivated, destined for their top-end wines, including Carato Venusio, an intense and velvety Aglianico del Vulture. As the latest Carato Venusio is still aging, it was down to the 2013 Gesualdo da Venosa to uphold the prestige of the winery. It's a rich Aglianico, aged in new wood, with structure, character and a soft tannic component. The 2016 Dry Muscat is as aromatic and enticing as ever.

● Aglianico del Vulture Gesualdo da Venosa '13	♈♈ 5
○ Terre di Orazio Dry Muscat '16	♈♈ 3
● Aglianico del Vulture Baliaggio '15	♈ 2
● Aglianico del Vulture Verbo '15	♈ 3
○ Verbo Malvasia '16	♈ 3
○ Verbo Rosato '16	♈ 3
● Aglianico del Vulture Bali '13	♈♈ 2*
● Aglianico del Vulture Carato Venusio '12	♈♈ 6
● Aglianico del Vulture Gesualdo da Venosa '11	♈♈ 5
● Aglianico del Vulture Terre di Orazio '13	♈♈ 4
● Aglianico del Vulture Terre di Orazio '12	♈♈ 3*
● Aglianico del Vulture Vignali '13	♈♈ 2*
○ Terre di Orazio Dry Muscat '15	♈♈ 2*

Vigneti del Vulture

C.DA PIPOLI
85011 ACERENZA [PZ]
TEL. +39 0971749363
www.vignetidelvulture.it

PRE-BOOKED VISITS
ANNUAL PRODUCTION 100,000 bottles
HECTARES UNDER VINE 56.00

Vigneti del Vulture is part of the Farnese Vini di Ortona group, which comprises a number of quality producers. They recently purchased, facilities previously owned by the co-operative Acerenza, thus creating a site for the production and management of their wines, which are made with grapes purchased from local growers. It's an already important operation, both for quality and production volumes, that's aiming to become an international benchmark for Vulture. The 2015 Aglianico del Vulture Pipoli Zero is made without added sulfites. This year, the wine impressed less than usual, but we very much appreciated the 2013 Piano del Cerro. It features a lovely, dark ruby-red color and an intriguing bouquet of violets, black fruit and Mediterranean herbs. The palate opens assertively, with character, balance, fruit, smooth tannins and remarkable overall harmony. The close-focused and fruity 2015 Aglianico del Vulture Pipoli and the 2016 Moscato Sensuale, a delicately sparkling, aromatic, sweet and gratifying wine, also delivered.

● Aglianico del Vulture Piano del Cerro '13	♈♈ 5
● Aglianico del Vulture Pipoli '15	♈♈ 2*
● Aglianico del Vulture Pipoli Zero '15	♈♈ 2*
○ Moscato Sensuale '16	♈♈ 2*
○ Pipoli Greco Fiano '16	♈ 2
⊙ Pipoli Rosato '16	♈ 2
● Aglianico del Vulture Piano del Cerro '09	♈♈ 5
● Aglianico del Vulture Piano del Cerro Ris. '08	♈♈ 3
● Aglianico del Vulture Pipoli '12	♈♈ 2*
● Aglianico del Vulture Pipoli Zero '14	♈♈ 2*
● Aglianico del Vulture Pipoli Zero '12	♈♈ 2*

600 Grotte

C.DA SAN PASQUALE
85032 CHIAROMONTE [PZ]
TEL. +39 0973642278
www.600grotte.it

CELLAR SALES
ANNUAL PRODUCTION 15,000 bottles
HECTARES UNDER VINE 5.33
SUSTAINABLE WINERY

● Recepit '14	▼▼ 3
⊙ Recepit '16	▼ 3
● Recepit EL '13	▼ 3

Biscegia

C.DA FINOCCHIARO
85024 LAVELLO [PZ]
TEL. +39 0972877033
www.vinibiscegia.it

CELLAR SALES
PRE-BOOKED VISITS
RESTAURANT SERVICE
ANNUAL PRODUCTION 250,000 bottles
HECTARES UNDER VINE 45.00

● Aglianico del Vulture Sup. Gudarrà '12	▼ 5
● Aglianico del Vulture Gudarrà '14	▼ 4
○ Bosco delle Rose Chardonnay '16	▼ 4

Carbone

VIA NITTI, 48
85025 MELFI [PZ]
TEL. +39 3482338900
www.carbonevini.it

CELLAR SALES
PRE-BOOKED VISITS
ANNUAL PRODUCTION 30,000 bottles
HECTARES UNDER VINE 18.00
VITICULTURE METHOD Certified Organic

● Aglianico del Vulture 400 Some '14	▼▼ 4
● Aglianico del Vulture Stupor Mundi '14	▼ 5

Donata Maria Cervino

C.DA MARCHESE
85036 ROCCANOVA [PZ]
TEL. +39 0973833243
cervinovini@libero.it

CELLAR SALES
PRE-BOOKED VISITS
ANNUAL PRODUCTION 40,000 bottles
HECTARES UNDER VINE 8.00

● Grottino di Roccanova Marchese Rosso '14	▼▼ 3

Consorzio Viticoltori Associati del Vulture

S.DA ST.LE 93
85022 BARILE [PZ]
TEL. +39 0972770386
www.coviv.it

CELLAR SALES
PRE-BOOKED VISITS
ANNUAL PRODUCTION 130,000 bottles
HECTARES UNDER VINE 100.00

● Aglianico del Vulture Vetusto '11	▼▼ 7

Cantine Di Palma Strapellum

C.DA SCAVONE
85028 RIONERO IN VULTURE [PZ]
TEL. +39 3286629077
www.cantinestrapellum.com

CELLAR SALES
PRE-BOOKED VISITS
ANNUAL PRODUCTION 120,000 bottles
HECTARES UNDER VINE 27.70

● Aglianico del Vulture Tenute Piano Regio '13	▼▼ 3
⊙ Cuvée Rosé Brut	▼ 2
○ Il Nibbio Bianco '15	▼ 3

Donato D'Angelo di Filomena Ruppi

, Padre Pio, 10
5028 Rionero in Vulture [PZ]
L. +39 0972724602
ww.agrida.it

ELLAR SALES
RE-BOOKED VISITS
NNUAL PRODUCTION 80,000 bottles
ECTARES UNDER VINE 20.00

Aglianico del Vulture	
Donato D'Angelo '14	♈♈ 3*
Balconara '13	♈ 4

Iacovazzo

via Saragat, 42
75100 Matera
Tel. +39 3286696466
www.tenute-iacovazzo.com

ANNUAL PRODUCTION 35,000 bottles
HECTARES UNDER VINE 5.00

○ Alba Chiara '16	♈ 2
○ Alba Rosa dei Sassi '16	♈ 2
● Nettare d'Uva '15	♈ 2
● Primatem '15	♈ 3

Michele Laluce

Roma, 21
020 Ginestra [PZ]
. +39 0972646145
ww.vinilaluce.com

ELLAR SALES
RE-BOOKED VISITS
NNUAL PRODUCTION 40,000 bottles
ECTARES UNDER VINE 7.00
USTAINABLE WINERY

Aglianico del Vulture S'Adatt '13	♈ 2
Morbino Bianco '16	♈ 3

Tenuta Marino

c.da Piano delle Rose
75027 San Giorgio Lucano [MT]
Tel. +39 0835815978
www.tenutamarino.it

CELLAR SALES
PRE-BOOKED VISITS
ANNUAL PRODUCTION 100,000 bottles
HECTARES UNDER VINE 26.00
VITICULTURE METHOD Certified Organic

● Terra Aspra Bio '14	♈♈ 3
● Matera Primitivo Terra Aspra '11	♈ 4

Vigne Mastrodomenico

Nazionale per Rapolla, 87
022 Barile [PZ]
+39 0972770108
w.vignemastrodomenico.com

LLAR SALES
E-BOOKED VISITS
NUAL PRODUCTION 25,000 bottles
CTARES UNDER VINE 8.00
ICULTURE METHOD Certified Organic
USTAINABLE WINERY

Aglianico del Vulture	
Anniversary Likos '09	♈♈ 5

Musto Carmelitano

via Pietro Nenni, 23
85020 Maschito [PZ]
Tel. +39 097233312
www.mustocarmelitano.it

CELLAR SALES
PRE-BOOKED VISITS
ACCOMMODATION AND RESTAURANT SERVICE
ANNUAL PRODUCTION 20,000 bottles
HECTARES UNDER VINE 14.00
VITICULTURE METHOD Certified Organic

● Aglianico del Vulture Pian del Moro '13	♈♈ 4
● Aglianico del Vulture '15	♈ 6
○ Dhjetë	♈ 3

Ofanto - Tenuta I Gelsi

FRAZ. MONTICCHIO BAGNI
C.DA PADULI
85028 RIONERO IN VULTURE [PZ]
TEL. +39 0972080289
www.tenutaigelsi.com

CELLAR SALES
PRE-BOOKED VISITS
ANNUAL PRODUCTION 60,000 bottles
HECTARES UNDER VINE 10.00
SUSTAINABLE WINERY

● Aglianico del Vulture '13	🏆🏆 4
● Aglianico del Vulture Sup. '11	🏆🏆 5
● Aglianico del Vulture '12	🏆 4

Quarta Generazione

C.DA MACARICO
85022 BARILE [PZ]
TEL. +39 3342039805
www.quartagenerazione.com

ANNUAL PRODUCTION 20,000 bottles
HECTARES UNDER VINE 3.00
VITICULTURE METHOD Certified Organic

● Aglianico del Vulture '13	🏆🏆

Regio Cantina

LOC. PIANO REGIO
85029 VENOSA [PZ]
TEL. +39 057754011
www.tenutepiccini.it

CELLAR SALES
PRE-BOOKED VISITS
ANNUAL PRODUCTION 100,000 bottles
HECTARES UNDER VINE 15.00

● Aglianico del Vulture Donpà '14	🏆🏆 3
● Aglianico del Vulture Genesi '14	🏆🏆 2*

San Martino

C.DA SAN MARTINO
85023 FORENZA [PZ]
TEL. +39 097231002
lorenzo.sanmartino@email.it

CELLAR SALES
PRE-BOOKED VISITS
ANNUAL PRODUCTION 25,000 bottles
HECTARES UNDER VINE 4.00
VITICULTURE METHOD Certified Organic

● Aglianico del Volture Arberesko '15	🏆🏆
● Aglianico del Volture Siir '15	🏆

Taverna

C.DA TAVERNA, 15
75020 NOVA SIRI [MT]
TEL. +39 0835877083
www.aataverna.com

CELLAR SALES
PRE-BOOKED VISITS
ACCOMMODATION AND RESTAURANT SERVICE
ANNUAL PRODUCTION 50,000 bottles
HECTARES UNDER VINE 19.00

○ Matera Greco San Basile '16	🏆🏆 3
● Matera I Sassi '15	🏆🏆 3
☉ Primitivo Rosato Maddalena '16	🏆 2

Troilo

VIA A. DIAZ, 43
85029 VENOSA [PZ]
TEL. +39 097236900
www.troilo.it

○ Gilda Moscato Dolce '16	🏆🏆
● Aglianico del Volture Leukanos '12	🏆
○ Gilda Bianco '16	🏆

PUGLIA

We find Apulia continuing to move in the same direction as previous years, with growth and consistent high-quality defining the region's wine industry. Just 10 years ago, this would have been difficult to imagine; the only explanation is the realization that the region possesses cultivar, vineyards and territories that are truly unique, both nationally and globally. Primitivo is, by now, Apulia's most important variety, and not only in its historic territories of Gioa del Colle and Manduria. Gioa del Colle has been building on its success year after year, thanks to a strong and tight consortium that's focusing on quality. As far as Manduria goes, it's worth pointing out that some of the territory's most important producers have decided to propose their wines outside of the appellation (going back years, in some cases, others more recently) as a reaction to regulations that frankly appear to be a bit dubious. If on the one hand we're delighted to see a number of producers achieving national recognition, on the other we're a bit surprised that there isn't more emerging talent. The Tre Bicchieri awarded are almost all for already-noted wineries, starting with Gioia del Colle's Primitivo and Nicola Chiaromonte's Contrada Barbatto, Polvanera's 17 Vigneto Montevella, Tre Pini's Riserva and Coppi's Senatore. We should also add the return of Viglione's Marpione. In terms of Salice Salentino, the cooperative Due Palme and Leone de Castris confirm their roles as benchmarks for the area, with their Riscrve Selvarossa and Per Lui. It's the same situation in Castel Del Monte, where Francesco Liantonio's winery, Torrevento, has become a model, in particular with their Riserva Vigna Pedale, and not just for the appellation, but for all reds made with Troia. In terms of Primitivo di Manduria, its history is brought out in the Pinfarosa Zinfandel, just as passion and technique are with the Vespa family's Raccontami. Tenuta Rubino once again delivers with the Oltremé, keeping the native grape Susmaniello in the limelight (a cultivar that the Rubino family have worked hard to revive), while Paolo Leo and Carvinea are recognized for wines that are seeing their first awards: a Negramaro and a Primitivo. We close by mentioning once more the odious fashion of extremely heavy bottles. The use of bottles whose weight well surpasses one kilo for 750 ml of wine seems completely out of place. And it's a truly incoherent choice for those producers who profess to follow sustainable methods and carry out organic or biodynamic cultivation.

Giuseppe Attanasio

VIA PER ORIA, 13
74024 MANDURIA [TA]
TEL. +39 0999737121
www.primitivo-attanasio.com

ANNUAL PRODUCTION 11,000 bottles
HECTARES UNDER VINE 6.00

The Attanasio family winery has been among the most well-known in Primitivo di Manduria for some years now. Since 2000, the producer has been making its own wines with grapes cultivated on its estate in Manduria (according to Apulia's ancient, head-training system). Here, in the tuffaceous calcareous soil, only one grape is grown, Primitivo. Their selection features common local wines as well as a rosé. Their 2013 Primitivo di Manduria has hints of prunes, Mediterranean scrub and pencil lead. It's long with good mouthfeel, but it's missing some grip. Their 2013 Primitivo di Manduria Dolce Naturale is also excellent, with fragrances of sour cherry jam and gingerbread. The 2012 Primitivo di Manduria Dolce Naturale has less traction than the 2013 version, though it is well made, as is the 2016 Primitivo Rosato, a full-flavored, flowery wine. We were less impressed with the 2011 Primitivo di Manduria Riserva, which was a bit too evolved in its notes of bottled cherries and fire-cured tobacco.

● Primitivo di Manduria '13	♟♟ 5
● Primitivo di Manduria Dolce Naturale '13	♟♟ 5
● Primitivo di Manduria Dolce Naturale '12	♟♟ 5
⊙ Primitivo Rosato '16	♟♟ 3
● Primitivo di Manduria Ris. '11	♟ 6
● Primitivo di Manduria '07	♟♟ 4
● Primitivo di Manduria Dolce Naturale 15,5° '06	♟♟ 5
● Primitivo di Manduria Dolce Naturale 15° '07	♟♟ 5

Cantele

S.DA PROV.LE SALICE SALENTINO-SAN DONACI KM 35,600
73010 GUAGNANO [LE]
TEL. +39 0832705010
www.cantele.it

CELLAR SALES
PRE-BOOKED VISITS
ANNUAL PRODUCTION 16,000,000 bottles
HECTARES UNDER VINE 200.00

The Cantele family's winery is among the most well-known in the region. Founded in 1979, today the winery is managed by the dynamic foursome of cousins Gianni, Paolo, Umberto and Luisa. The family estate comprises 50 hectares of vineyards, spanning Guagnano, Montemesola and San Pietro Vernotico, with an additional 150 hectares also managed. Mostly native grape varieties are cultivated in the predominantly 'red earth' type of soil here. These give life to a selection of well-crafted wines of notable typicity. Once again, Salice Salentino Rosso Riserva is their flagship wine of the year. Despite the difficult vintage, the 2014 version offers up aromas of ripe, dark fruit and pencil lead, followed by a hint of spice. The palate is relaxed, displaying freshness and good staying power. The 2016 Alticelli Fiano and 2015 Teresa Manara Chardonnay Sedici September are also both well made. The former offers up fragrances of sage and jasmine, with a full-flavored, plucky finish, while the latter is generous in its vanilla and spice aromas, as well as its late-harvest palate.

● Salice Salentino Rosso Ris. '14	♟♟ 2
○ Teresa Manara Chardonnay Sedici Settembre '15	♟♟ 4
○ Alticelli Fiano '16	♟ 2
○ Le Passanti Fiano Passito '11	♟ 5
⊙ Negroamaro Rosato '16	♟ 2
● Primitivo '15	♟ 2
⊙ Rohesia '16	♟ 3
○ Verdeca '16	♟ 2
● Amativo '07	♟♟♟ 4
● Amativo '03	♟♟♟ 3
● Salice Salentino Rosso Ris. '09	♟♟♟ 2
● Amativo '14	♟♟ 4
● Amativo '13	♟♟ 4
● Amativo '12	♟♟ 4
● Amativo '11	♟♟ 4
● Primitivo '11	♟♟ 2

Cantine San Marzano

VIA REGINA MARGHERITA, 149
74020 SAN MARZANO DI SAN GIUSEPPE [TA]
TEL. +39 0999574181
www.cantinesanmarzano.com

CELLAR SALES
ANNUAL PRODUCTION 10,000,000 bottles
HECTARES UNDER VINE 1500.00

Cantine San Marzano is made up of 1200 member-growers, who cultivate 1500 hectares of vineyards and contribute to the production of some 25 different wines. Such numbers define this large co-operative winery. Their grapes come from vineyards around San Marzano, Sava and Francavilla Fontana. Here the soil is, for the most part, residual 'red-earth'. Iron oxides prevail, with a rocky surface underpinned by a calcium-rich substrate. The estate also features a sizable presence of head-trained vines, some of which are over 50-years-old. Even with the 2014 vintage, the Primitivo di Manduria Sessantanni is their preeminent wine. Made with grapes from old, head-trained vines, it offers up aromas of blackberry jam, with a soft, corpulent palate. The rest of the selection also proved strong, with special mentions for the 2016 Tramari (an aromatic, flowery rosé Primitivo that's both close-focused and fruity), the 2016 Primitivo di Manduria Talò (pervasive and rich in body), and the 2014 Primitivo di Manduria Anniversary 62 Riserva (which features fragrances of sweet spice).

● Primitivo di Manduria Sessantanni '14	♟♟	5
○ Edda '16	♟♟	4
● Primitivo di Manduria Anniversario 62 Ris. '14	♟♟	6
● Primitivo di Manduria Talò '16	♟♟	3
⊙ Tramari '16	♟♟	3
● Malvasia Nera Talò '16	♟	3
● Negroamaro F '14	♟	5
● Primitivo di Manduria Talò '13	♟♟♟	3*
● Malvasia Nera Talò '15	♟♟	3*
● Negroamaro Talò '15	♟♟	3
● Primitivo di Manduria Anniversario 62 Ris. '13	♟♟	5
● Primitivo di Manduria Sessantanni '13	♟♟	5
● Primitivo di Manduria Sessantanni '11	♟♟	5
● Primitivo di Manduria Talò '12	♟♟	3*

Carvinea

LOC. PEZZA D'ARENA
VIA PER SERRANOVA
72012 CAROVIGNO [BR]
TEL. +39 0805862345
www.carvinea.com

CELLAR SALES
PRE-BOOKED VISITS
ACCOMMODATION AND RESTAURANT SERVICE
ANNUAL PRODUCTION 35,000 bottles
HECTARES UNDER VINE 12.00
VITICULTURE METHOD Certified Organic

15 years have passed since Beppe di Maria decided to start a new chapter in his life, acquiring the 16th century-esque manor farm of Pezza d'Arena, Carovigno, just a stone's throw from the splendid Torre Guaceto reserve. Here, on his 12 hectares of tuffaceos calcareous terrain, Beppe grows Montepulciano, Aglianico, Petit Verdot, Primitivo, Negroamaro, Ottavianello and Fiano, thus giving life to a well-crafted selection of pleasant, fruity wines. Their 2015 Primitivo gets Tre Bicchieri. The nose offers up hints of pepper and extremely ripe dark fruit, while vegetal, spicy fragrances emerge from the palate. These give way to a finish that is pervasive, intense and concentrated. Other standouts include the 2015 Otto, a mature and Mediterranean wine, the 2015 Negroamaro, which is rich and full-bodied, and 2016 Merula Rosa, a flowery Montepulciano rosé with good grip.

● Primitivo '15	♟♟♟	5
⊙ Merula Rosa '16	♟♟	2*
● Negroamaro '15	♟♟	5
● Otto '15	♟♟	4
⊙ Brut Rosé M. Cl. '12	♟	5
● Frauma '08	♟♟♟	4
● Merula '11	♟♟♟	3*
● Negroamaro '14	♟♟♟	5
● Negroamaro '13	♟♟♟	5
● Negroamaro '11	♟♟♟	3*
● Sierma '09	♟♟♟	5
● Otto '14	♟♟	4
● Primitivo '14	♟♟	5
● Primitivo '13	♟♟	5
● Sierma '12	♟♟	5

Castello Monaci

VIA CASE SPARSE
73015 SALICE SALENTINO [LE]
TEL. +39 0831665700
www.castellomonaci.it

CELLAR SALES
PRE-BOOKED VISITS
RESTAURANT SERVICE
ANNUAL PRODUCTION 1,800,000 bottles
HECTARES UNDER VINE 150.00

The Memmo family continues to manage Castello Monaco, a gorgeous estate just outside Salice Salentino that's owned by the Gruppo Italiano Vini. The estate comprises some 150 hectares of vineyards where mostly native grape varieties are grown. The soil here is characterized by two strata: the clay surface (running about one meter deep) and another, deeper tuffaceous layer, making it perfect for dealing with problems relating to droughts. The winery offers more than twenty wines subdivided into three lines: Castello Monaci, Feudo Monaci and Mirus. Castello Monaci's wines put in a good, overall performance, confirming the producer's solidity and reliability. Their 2014 Salice Salentino Aiace Riserva offers up aromas of spices, followed by a palate of delicious fruit (even if the use of wood has left its mark). The 2016 Pilùna is a fresh, plucky Primitivo. The 2016 Acante is a particularly well-formed Fiano, with Mediterranean fragrances, and the 2016 Kreos, a rosé made with Negroamaro grapes, is particularly pleasant. The 2015 Artas, however, proved beneath our expectations.

○ Acante '16	♥♥ 2*
⊙ Kreos '16	♥♥ 2*
● Pilùna '16	♥♥ 2*
● Salice Salentino Aiace Ris. '14	♥♥ 3
● Artas '15	♥ 5
● Maru '16	♥ 2
○ Petraluce '16	♥ 2
● Salice Salentino Rosso Liante '16	♥ 2
● Artas '07	♥♥♥ 5
● Artas '06	♥♥♥ 4
● Artas '05	♥♥♥ 4*
● Artas '04	♥♥♥ 3*
● Artas '13	♥♥ 5
● Artas '12	♥♥ 5
● Salice Salentino Aiace Ris. '13	♥♥ 3*
● Salice Salentino Aiace Ris. '10	♥♥ 3*

Giancarlo Ceci

C.DA SANT'AGOSTINO
76123 ANDRIA [BT]
TEL. +39 0883565220
www.agrinatura.net

ANNUAL PRODUCTION 350,000 bottles
HECTARES UNDER VINE 60.00
VITICULTURE METHOD Certified Biodynamic
SUSTAINABLE WINERY

Giancarlo Ceci represents the eighth generation of family to manage this sizable estate. 60 of its 200 hectares are vineyards, situated only 20 kilometers from the sea (in Andria and Castle del Monte) at an altitude of 250 meters above sea level. Since 1988 they have been certified organic and, since 2011, biodynamic as well. Ceci is among Apulia's largest producers, but it's commitment to sustainability is evident, with renewable energy providing 100% of its production needs. The 2016 Castle del Monte Rosso (made without added sulfites) offers up aromas of blackberry, with vegetal hints, a fresh, fruity palate, and a succulent, full-flavored finish. The pleasant, well-developed 2015 Parco Marano Nero di Troia, on the other hand, features balsamic and notes of rhubarb. The 2016 Castel del Monte Rosso Parco Grande is rich in fruit and well supported by acidity, while the 2016 Castle del Monte Bombino Nero Rosato Parchitello exhibits notes of flowers and small berries.

● Castel del Monte Rosso Almagia '16	♥♥ 2*
⊙ Castel del Monte Bombino Nero Rosato Parchitello '16	♥♥ 2*
● Castel del Monte Rosso Parco Grande '16	♥♥ 2*
● Parco Marano Nero di Troia '15	♥♥ 3
○ Apnea Brut '15	♥ 3
○ Castel del Monte Bombino Bianco Panascio '16	♥ 2
○ Castel del Monte Chardonnay Chiusolillo '16	♥ 2
⊙ Castel del Monte Rosato Parco Petrullo '16	♥ 2
○ Moscato di Trani Dolce Rosalia '16	♥ 4
● Castel del Monte Nero di Troia Felice Ceci Ris. '12	♥♥ 3*
● Castel del Monte Rosso Almagia '14	♥♥ 2*
○ Moscato di Trani Dolce Rosalia '15	♥♥ 3

Tenute Chiaromonte

.GO ANNUNZIATA
'0021 ACQUAVIVA DELLE FONTI [BA]
EL. +39 080768156
www.tenutechiaromonte.com

CELLAR SALES
PRE-BOOKED VISITS
ANNUAL PRODUCTION 120,000 bottles
HECTARES UNDER VINE 42.00

Over the last few years, Nicola Chiaromonte's winery has become a true benchmark among Apulia's wine producers. his estate includes more than 10 hectares of head-trained Primitivo that range from 60 to more than 100 years old. Thanks to Paolo Montanaro, who recently joined the winery, 0 more hectares are being cultivated, an area whose center will feature a new cellar. l the vineyards are situated in Gioia del olle, at an altitude of more than 300 eters, on calcareous, mineral-rich terrain, ith a slight top-layer of red-earth clay. he Gioia del Colle Primitivo Muro ant'Angelo Contrada Barbatto affirms its osition at the top of the winery's selection, en with the 2014 vintage: Mediterranean crub, dark fruit, spices and flowery hints rm part of a profile rich in matière, yet ll-flavored, long and fresh. A rounder, fuller ne, with good grip, 2012 Gioia del Colle imitivo Riserva performed just as well, as d the fruity 2015 Gioia del Colle Primitivo uro Sant'Angelo.

Gioia del Colle Primitivo	
Muro Sant'Angelo Contrada Barbatto '14	▼▼▼ 5
Gioia del Colle Primitivo	
Muro Sant'Angelo '15	▼▼ 4
Gioia del Colle Primitivo Ris. '12	▼▼ 8
Kimìa Fiano '16	▼▼ 3
Kimìa Rosato '16	▼▼ 3
Primitivo '15	▼▼ 2*
Elè '15	▼ 3
Nigredo '15	▼ 5
Gioia del Colle Primitivo	
Muro Sant'Angelo Contrada Barbatto '13	♈♈♈ 5
Gioia del Colle Primitivo	
Muro Sant'Angelo Contrada Barbatto '12	♈♈♈ 5
Gioia del Colle Primitivo	
Muro Sant'Angelo Contrada Barbatto '11	♈♈♈ 5

Coppi

S.DA PROV.LE TURI – GIOIA DEL COLLE
70010 TURI [BA]
TEL. +39 0808915049
www.vinicoppi.it

CELLAR SALES
PRE-BOOKED VISITS
RESTAURANT SERVICE
ANNUAL PRODUCTION 900,000 bottles
HECTARES UNDER VINE 100.00
VITICULTURE METHOD Certified Organic

Founded in the 1960s by Antonio Coppi, this historic winery has, in recent years, been literally transformed by his children, Lisia, Miriam and Doni. Half of its vineyards, situated in Turi and Gioia del Colle (Marchesato), are composed of head-trained vines and feature local grape varieties. Primitivo, the area's most important grape, takes center stage, but Negroamaro, Aleatico, Malvasia Nera, Malvasia Bianca and Falanghina are also cultivated. Tre Bicchieri go to the 2011 Gioia del Colle Primitivo Senatore, a wine with aromas of blackberry, blueberry and black olive tapenade, and a palate that comes through consistent, generous and long. The 2015 Don Antonio Primitivo also proved well-crafted, full-flavored, grippy and fresh with notes of red fruit on the nose. Their 2016 Pellirosso Negroamaro and 2012 Aleatico both deserve special mentions as well, with the former displaying velvety tannins and good mouthfeel, while the second features balanced sweetness and a finish of licorice and black damson.

● Gioia del Colle Primitivo Senatore '11	▼▼▼ 5
● Don Antonio Primitivo '15	▼▼ 3
● Pellirosso Negroamaro '16	▼▼ 2*
● Vinaccero Aleatico '12	▼▼ 3
⊙ Bollicinechérì Extra Dry Rosé '16	▼ 3
○ Corè '16	▼ 2
○ Guiscardo '16	▼ 3
● Sannace Malvasia Nera '15	▼ 3
● Gioia del Colle Primitivo Senatore '10	♈♈♈ 3*
● Gioia del Colle Primitivo Senatore '08	♈♈ 3
● Negroamaro Pellirosso '12	♈♈ 2*
● Primitivo '08	♈♈ 1*
● Primitivo Don Antonio '13	♈♈ 3
● Primitivo Siniscalco '14	♈♈ 3

★Cantine Due Palme

VIA SAN MARCO, 130
72020 CELLINO SAN MARCO [BR]
TEL. +39 0831617865
www.cantineduepalme.it

CELLAR SALES
PRE-BOOKED VISITS
ACCOMMODATION AND RESTAURANT SERVICE
ANNUAL PRODUCTION 10,000,000 bottles
HECTARES UNDER VINE 2500.00

La Cantine Due Palme, a co-operative winery founded by Angelo Maci in 1989, is made up of more than 1000 members operating on 2500 hectares of vineyards throughout the provinces of Brindisi, Taranto and Lecce. 90% of the grapes grown are red, principally native varieties, with a notable presence of head-trained vines. The many wines offered (25 in all) are technically well-crafted, in a style that seeks to balance tradition and a more modern approach. The Salice Salentino Rosso Selvarossa Riserva once again proves itself a well-crafted wine. The 2014 offers up aromas of prunes and black damson, while the palate displays notable body and structure. The 2016 Primitivo di Manduria San Gaetano, on the other hand, is a fresh, spicy, easy-drinking wine, making it one of the appellation's stronger representatives, while the 2015 Seraia Malvasia Nera has notes of blackcurrant and raspberries on the nose, with a palate rich in fruit and spice.

Tenute Eméra di Claudio Quarta Vignaiolo

FRAZ. MARINA DI LIZZANO
C.DA PORVICA
74123 LIZZANO [TA]
TEL. +39 0832704398
www.claudioquarta.it

CELLAR SALES
PRE-BOOKED VISITS
ACCOMMODATION
ANNUAL PRODUCTION 550,000 bottles
HECTARES UNDER VINE 50.00
SUSTAINABLE WINERY

Claudio Quarta, accompanied by his daughter, Alessandra, is carrying on in his 'second life' as a vine grower, which began in Apulia in 2005 with Tenute Eméra, an estate with vineyards in Manduria and Lizzano. In 2012, Emèra was joined by Cantina Moros, an estate with just over a hectare of vineyards in Guagnano. Their vineyards mostly grow in tuffaceous calcareous soil, enriched by a layer of detritus and clay. Both native and international grape varieties are cultivated Claudio Quarta put in an overall good performance. Even without a breakthrough wine, the selection proved itself well-crafted. The 2016 Lizzano Negroamaro Superiore, Anima di Negroamaro features dark fruit and sweet spices on the nose, while the palate has structure and body. The 2016 Fiano Amure is fresh and fruity, while the 2015 Sud del Sud (a blend of 35% Primitivo and 35% Negroamaro, with Cabernet Sauvignon, Petit Verdot and Syrah displays significant aromatic accuracy.

● Salice Salentino Rosso Selvarossa Ris. '14	♟♟♟ 4*
● Primitivo di Manduria San Gaetano '16	♟♟ 2*
● Seraia Malvasia Nera '15	♟♟ 2*
○ Anthea Falanghina '16	♟ 2
● Canonico Negroamaro '15	♟ 2
⊙ Corerosa Gold Edition '16	♟ 3
⊙ Melarosa Rosé Extra Dry	♟ 2
○ Selvabianca '16	♟ 3
● Salice Salentino Rosso Selvarossa Ris. '13	♟♟♟ 4*
● Salice Salentino Rosso Selvarossa Ris. '12	♟♟♟ 4*
● Salice Salentino Rosso Selvarossa Ris. '11	♟♟♟ 4*
● Salice Salentino Rosso Selvarossa Ris. '10	♟♟♟ 4*

○ Amure '16	♟
● Lizzano Negroamaro Sup. Anima di Negroamaro '16	♟
● Sud del Sud '15	♟
● Lizzano Negroamaro Sup. Anima di Negroamaro '15	♟
● Primitivo di Manduria Anima di Primitivo '15	♟
⊙ Rose '16	♟
● Lizzano Negroamaro Sup. '14	♟♟
● Lizzano Negroamaro Sup. Anima di Negroamaro '13	♟♟
● Primitivo di Manduria Oro di Eméra '14	♟♟
● Salice Salentino Rosso Moros Ris. '13	♟♟
● Salice Salentino Rosso Moros Ris. '12	♟♟
● Sud del Sud '14	♟♟

Felline

VIA SANTO STASI PRIMO, 42B
74024 MANDURIA [TA]
TEL. +39 0999711660
www.agricolafelline.it

CELLAR SALES
PRE-BOOKED VISITS
ANNUAL PRODUCTION 1,000,000 bottles
HECTARES UNDER VINE 120.00
VITICULTURE METHOD Certified Organic
SUSTAINABLE WINERY

Gregory Petrucci is, without a doubt, a leader in Apulia's vine and wine sector. For more than 20 years, he's worked to protect Salento, through the revival and promotion of its historic head-trained vineyards. He's also rediscovering his region's winemaking tradition through the wines themselves, which are defined by their fruity freshness and closely-focused aromas. Different types of soil support the cultivation of their (exclusively) native grape varieties, from the more sandy soil near the sea to a more rocky typology, from red earth to black. The winery's classic Primitivo di Manduria Sinfarosa Zinfadel returns to center stage. The 2015 exhibits hints of blueberry and pomegranate, while the palate is fresh and succulent, rich in fruit and dynamic. Their series of vintages are also well-crafted; standouts include Susumaniello Sum Torre Guaceto (a full-flavored, supple wine), l'Anarkos, (fruity with good staying power), and Primitivo di Manduria (which is soft and easy to drink).

● Primitivo di Manduria Sinfarosa Zinfandel '15	▼▼▼ 3*
● Anarkos '16	▼▼ 2*
● Negriccio Torre Guaceto '16	▼▼ 2*
● Nero di Troia Trullari '16	▼▼ 2*
● Pietraluna Torre Guaceto '16	▼▼ 2*
● Primitivo di Manduria '16	▼▼ 3
● Sum Torre Guaceto '16	▼▼ 4
● Alberello '16	▼ 2
○ Fiano '16	▼ 2
● Malvasia Nera '15	▼ 2
● Primitivo di Manduria Giravolta '16	▼ 3
● Primitivo di Manduria '15	▼▼▼ 3*
● Primitivo di Manduria Archidamo '12	▼▼▼ 2*
● Primitivo di Manduria Archidamo '09	▼▼▼ 3*
● Vigna del Feudo '97	▼▼▼ 4*

Gianfranco Fino

VIA PIAVE, 12
74028 SAVA [TA]
TEL. +39 0997773970
www.gianfrancofino.it

PRE-BOOKED VISITS
ANNUAL PRODUCTION 20,000 bottles
HECTARES UNDER VINE 20.00
SUSTAINABLE WINERY

Gianfranco and Simona Fino are one of the most famous couples in the winemaking industry (and not only in Apulia). They founded their winery in 2004, on less than one and a half hectares of land, yet managed to create a model Primitivo in their Es. Today their estate comprises 12 hectares in Manduria and Sava, all old head-trained vines, some of which go back 90 years. According to the vintage, the 'red clay' and calcareous soil here gives rise to Es, as well as other wines like the Negroamaro Jo, the sweet Es + Sole and the 'Metodo Classico' sparkling wine, Simona Natale. The only wine presented this year was the 2015 Es. It's no longer a DOC Primitivo di Manduria, but the wine affirms its place as among the highest-ranked Primitivos. Intense and concentrated on the nose, it offers up hints of figs, coffee and spices, while the palate exhibits great mouthfeel, but balance as well. The finish is brilliant. Fresh and driven, it features notes of black cherry and small, red fruit.

● Es '15	▼▼ 7
● Primitivo di Manduria Es '12	▼▼▼ 7
● Primitivo di Manduria Es '11	▼▼▼ 7
● Primitivo di Manduria Es '10	▼▼▼ 6
● Primitivo di Manduria Es '09	▼▼▼ 6
● Primitivo di Manduria Es '08	▼▼▼ 6
● Primitivo di Manduria Es '07	▼▼▼ 6
● Primitivo di Manduria Es '06	▼▼▼ 5
● Jo '08	▼▼ 6
● Jo '07	▼▼ 6
● Jo '06	▼▼ 5
● Primitivo di Manduria Dolce Naturale Es + Sole '12	▼▼ 7
● Primitivo di Manduria Es '14	▼▼ 7
● Primitivo di Manduria Es '13	▼▼ 7
● Primitivo di Manduria Es '05	▼▼ 5

Tenute Girolamo

VIA NOCI, 314
74015 MARTINA FRANCA [TA]
TEL. +39 0804402088
www.tenutegirolamo.it

CELLAR SALES
PRE-BOOKED VISITS
ANNUAL PRODUCTION 400,000 bottles
HECTARES UNDER VINE 50.00

Founded in 2010, Tenute Girolamo has, in fewer than 10 years, established itself as one of the most interesting wineries in the area. Their eight hectares of vineyards are situated in Valle d'Itria, at altitudes ranging from 350 to 400 meters, where the soil is a mix of calcareous clay and 'red earth'. The major local grape varieties are cultivated as well as well-known international ones. A blend made of equal parts Primitivo and Negroamaro, 2013 Conte Giangirolamo features intense aromas of prunes and tar, followed by good mouthfeel and texture in the palate and a long finish. The 2015 Monte dei Cocci Primitivo Vendemmia Tardiva is a charming wine, rich in ripe fruit, but still fresh, with good pressure and grip. The 2016 Monte dei Cocci Verdeca is flowery, citrusy and pleasant, while the 2015 Monte dei Cocci Negroamaro is balanced, with fragrances of red berries. Their 2016 La Voliera Primitivo, a plucky wine, offers up notes of blueberry.

● Conte Giangirolamo '13	♛♛ 6
● Monte dei Cocci Negroamaro '15	♛♛ 4
● Monte dei Cocci Primitivo V. T. '15	♛♛ 3
○ Monte dei Cocci Verdeca '16	♛♛ 4
● Primitivo La Voliera '16	♛♛ 3
○ Fiano La Voliera '16	♛ 3
● Monte Tre Carlini '13	♛ 5
● Conte Giangirolamo '12	♛♛ 6
● Conte Giangirolamo '10	♛♛ 4
● Monte dei Cocci Negroamaro '13	♛♛ 4
● Monte dei Cocci Negroamaro '12	♛♛ 4
● Pétrakos '08	♛♛ 3
● Pizzo Rosso '11	♛♛ 2*
● Pizzo Rosso '09	♛♛ 2*
● Primitivo '09	♛♛ 2*

Cantine Paolo Leo

VIA TUTURANO, 21
72025 SAN DONACI [BR]
TEL. +39 0831635073
www.paololeo.it

CELLAR SALES
PRE-BOOKED VISITS
ACCOMMODATION
ANNUAL PRODUCTION 1,300,000 bottles
HECTARES UNDER VINE 35.00

For generations, the Leo family has worked in winemaking, but it's Paolo who's given the decisive push, thanks to his effort to modernize both the vineyards and the cellar. Primitivo and Negroamaro are the leading varieties in their wide selection, which comprises some 43 wines. Their vineyards are located in San Donaci, where the terrain is tuffaceous calcareous, and feature head-trained vines that are, in some cases, more than 40 years old. This year, we were truly impressed with the 2015 Orfeo Negroamaro. Intense aromas of dark fruit and spices give way to a consistent, fruity, long palate with good mouthfeel and fullness. The 2015 Primitivo di Manduria Passo del Cardinale also proved well-made. A pleasant and easy drinking wine, it offers up hints of blackcurrant and wild strawberries. The 2016 Alture Minutolo is fresh and citrusy, with pleasant hints of aromatic herbs.

● Orfeo Negroamaro '15	♛♛♛ 4*
○ Alture Minutolo '16	♛♛ 3
● Primitivo di Manduria Passo del Cardinale '15	♛♛ 3
● Salice Salentino Ris. '11	♛ 4
● Primitivo di Manduria Passo del Cardinale '14	♛♛♛ 3*
● Fiore di Vigna '14	♛♛ 5
● Fiore di Vigna '13	♛♛ 4
● Fiore di Vigna '12	♛♛ 4
● Fiore di Vigna '10	♛♛ 4
● Negramante '13	♛♛ 3
● Orfeo '13	♛♛ 4
● Orfeo '11	♛♛ 4
● Taccorosso '13	♛♛ 3*

★Leone de Castris

VIA SENATORE DE CASTRIS, 26
73015 SALICE SALENTINU [LE]
TEL. +39 0832731112
www.leonedecastris.com

PRE-BOOKED VISITS
ANNUAL PRODUCTION 2,500,000 bottles
HECTARES UNDER VINE 250.00
SUSTAINABLE WINERY

Theirs is a centuries-old story. Leone de Castris was founded in 1665 by the Count of Lemos. The first bottles go back to 1925 and, in 1943, they created the Five Roses, the first rosé bottled in Italy. Indeed, their 42 wines are enough to prove their importance for Apulia. 70% of their vineyards, which are located throughout Salice Salentino, Campi and Guagnano, are head-trained systems. The winery's classics don't disappoint. Their 2016 Salice Salentino Rosso Per Lui Riserva features aromas of quinine and dark fruit. It's a rich wine, with hints of spices and wood, with good flow to the finish. This year, the 2016 Five Roses 73° Anniversario returns to the top of the region. A rosé made with Negroamaro, it's a fresh, flowery wine with notes of Mediterranean shrub and a full-flavored, succulent finish. The rest of the selection is also well-crafted, in particular the various other versions of the Five Roses line.

Masseria Li Veli

S.DA PROV.LE CELLINO-CAMPI, KM 1
72020 CELLINO SAN MARCO [BR]
TEL. +39 0831618259
www.liveli.it

CELLAR SALES
PRE-BOOKED VISITS
ANNUAL PRODUCTION 350,000 bottles
HECTARES UNDER VINE 33.00

Almost twenty years have passed since the Falvo family started making wine in Apulia, with the acquisition and renovation of 'Masseria Li Veli' in 1999. Their vineyards, situated on primarily red earth and sandy soil, are 85% Apulia head-trained, cultivated according to the ancient septunx planting pattern (made up of six vines in a hexagon with one plant in the center). The varieties grown are almost exclusively native, with the exception of a small portion of Cabernet Sauvignon. The 2010 Aleatico Passito finds itself among Apulia's best sweet wines. Aromas of blackberry jam and hints of chocolate are followed by a plate of great density and fullness, but one that also exhibits good freshness and staying power. The 2016 MLV is also well-crafted. This blend of Negroamaro and Cabernet Sauvignon features fragrances of very ripe dark fruit, as well as hints of tar and licorice on the nose, with a long, balsamic palate and a full, tannic finish.

● Salice Salentino Rosso Per Lui Ris. '15	▼▼▼	6
○ Five Roses 73° Anniversario '16	▼▼	3*
○ Five Roses '16	▼▼	3
○ Salice Salentino Brut M.Cl. Five Roses	▼▼	4
● Villa Santera '16	▼▼	3
● Aleikos '16	▼	3
○ Angiò Fiano '16	▼	3
○ Elo Veni '16	▼	2
● Messapia Verdeca '16	▼	2
● Salice Salentino Rosso Donna Lisa Ris. '14	▼	5
● Salice Salentino Rosso 50° Vendemmia Ris. '14	▽▽▽	3*
● Salice Salentino Rosso Per Lui Ris. '13	▽▽▽	6
● Salice Salentino Rosso Per Lui Ris. '12	▽▽▽	6
● Salice Salentino Rosso Ris. '10	▽▽▽	3*

● Aleatico Passito '10	▼▼	8
● MLV '15	▼▼	5
● Askos Susumaniello '16	▼▼	4
○ Askos Verdeca '16	▼▼	4
● Salice Salentino Pezzo Morgana Ris. '15	▼▼	4
● Askos Primitivo '15	▼	4
○ Fiano '16	▼	2
⊙ Primerose '16	▼	2
● Masseria Li Veli '10	▽▽▽	5
● Aleatico Passito '09	▽▽	6
● MLV '13	▽▽	5
● MLV '12	▽▽	5
● MLV '11	▽▽	5
● Salice Salentino Rosso Pezzo Morgana Ris. '14	▽▽	4
● Susumaniello Askos '15	▽▽	3

Masca del Tacco

VIA TRIPOLI, 5/7
72020 ERCHIE [BR]
TEL. +39 0831759786
www.mascadeltacco.it

ANNUAL PRODUCTION 80,000 bottles
HECTARES UNDER VINE 50.00

It was 2010 when Felice Mergè, owner of
Lazio's Poggio Le Volpi, decided to invest
in Apulia. He purchased various plots
around the region, focusing on some of its
most important DOC zones, from
Primitivo di Manduria (where cultivation is
devoted exclusively to head-trained
Primitivo vines older than 50 years), to
Salice Salentino, to Erchie (in Brindisi,
where the cellar is located). Mostly native
grape varieties are cultivated. In addition to
Primitivo, Negroamaro, Susumaniello and
Fiano get special attention. This year,
Masca del Tacco presented an excellent
2015 Primitivo di Manduria Lu Rappaio.
Aromas of damson, blackberry and licorice
give way to a full-flavored, close-woven
palate that's rich in fruit, with a finish that
is succulent and pleasant. The 2013 Salice
Salentino Rosso Lu Ceppu Riserva also
performed well. Hints of dark fruit,
pomegranate and wood are followed by a
full-bodied, fruity palate with hints of
sweet spices.

● Primitivo di Manduria Lu Rappaio '15	♥♥	4
● Primitivo di Manduria Li Filitti Ris. '11	♥♥	4
○ L'Uetta '16	♥	3
● Salice Salentino Lu Ceppu Ris. '13	♥	4
● Primitivo di Manduria Li Filitti Ris. '12	♀♥	4

Morella

VIA PER UGGIANO, 147
74024 MANDURIA [TA]
TEL. +39 0999791482
www.morellavini.com

CELLAR SALES
PRE-BOOKED VISITS
ANNUAL PRODUCTION 26,000 bottles
HECTARES UNDER VINE 20.00
VITICULTURE METHOD Certified Biodynamic

Lisa Gilbee and Gaetano Morella created a
winery that has, in terms of continuity and
consistence, firmly established itself as a
regional leader. Their estate, which is
entirely situated in the area of Manduria,
features vines as old as 100 years. Here,
in the 'red earth' soil common to the area,
mostly Primitivo is cultivated, with smaller
quantities of Neogroamaro, Fiano and
some international varieties. Lisa and
Gaetano seek to best express the territory
by limiting yields in the vineyards and
adopting a minimalist, non-invasive
production approach. Old Vines Primitivo
affirms its outstanding quality, even during
the difficult 2014 vintage. The nose
features dark fruit, Mediterranean shrubs
and pencil lead, while the palate exhibits
freshness and staying power. It's not a
particularly full-bodied wine, but it certainl
possesses significant close-focus and
aromatic accuracy. The 2016 Fiano
Mezzogiorno, a juicy, plucky wine, is
pleasant in its notes of white fruits and
citrus, while the 2014 Primitivo Malbek
hits the mark, but may be a bit simple.

● Old Vines Primitivo '14	♥♥	
○ Mezzogiorno '16	♥♥	
● Primitivo Malbek '14	♥	
● Primitivo La Signora '10	♥♥♥	
● Primitivo La Signora '07	♥♥♥	
● Primitivo Old Vines '09	♥♥♥	
● Primitivo Old Vines '08	♥♥♥	
● Primitivo Old Vines '07	♥♥♥	
● Negroamaro Primitivo Terre Rosse '12	♀♥	
● Old Vines Primitivo '13	♀♥	
● Old Vines Primitivo '10	♀♥	
● Primitivo La Signora '13	♀♥	
● Primitivo La Signora '11	♀♥	
● Primitivo Malbek '11	♀♥	
● Primitivo Negroamaro '10	♀♥	
● Primitivo Old Vines '11	♀♥	

Palamà

VIA A. DIAZ, 6
73020 CUTROFIANO [LE]
TEL. +39 0836542865
www.vinicolapalama.com

CELLAR SALES
PRE-BOOKED VISITS
ACCOMMODATION AND RESTAURANT SERVICE
ANNUAL PRODUCTION 200,000 bottles
HECTARES UNDER VINE 15.00

For some years now, the Palamà family have been among Apulia's elite producers. Their success is the result of the care and passion they show for their work (both in the vineyard and in the cellar) and an approach defined by a focus on the authenticity and typicity of their wines. The estate comprises terrain in Cutrofiano and Matino, where the soil is somewhat compact. Exclusively native grape varieties are cultivated, mostly reds, from Negroamaro to Primitivo, Malvasia Nera and Aleatico. This year, we were particularly impressed with the 2015 Primitivo Mavro, with its intense fragrances of wild berries, its long, well-structured, texture-rich palate and its full, fruity finish. The Metiusco line also proved well-made, in particular the 2016 Rosato, a fresh, plucky wine made with Negroamaro grapes that's consistently among the best of its kind. The 2016 Rosso also stood out, a blend of Negroamaro, Primitivo and Malvasia Nera that's fruity and close-focused, as did the 2015 Rosso Passito, a pleasant, balanced wine.

● Mavro '15	♟♟ 3*
● Metiusco Oro Rosso Passito '15	♟♟ 3
○ Metiusco Rosato '16	♟♟ 2*
● Metiusco Rosso '16	♟♟ 2*
● Albarossa Primitivo '16	♟ 2
● D'Arcangelo '15	♟ 3
○ Metiusco Bianco '16	♟ 2
● Salice Salentino Rosso Albarossa '15	♟ 2
● 75 Vendemmie '11	♟♟♟ 4*
● 75 Vendemmie '15	♟♟ 4
● 75 Vendemmie '12	♟♟ 4
● Mavro '13	♟♟ 3*
● Mavro '12	♟♟ 3*
● Mavro '09	♟♟ 3*
● Salice Salentino Rosso Albarossa '13	♟♟ 1*

Polvanera

S.DA VICINALE LAMIE MARCHESANA, 601
70023 GIOIA DEL COLLE [BA]
TEL. +39 080758900
www.cantinepolvanera.it

CELLAR SALES
RESTAURANT SERVICE
ANNUAL PRODUCTION 300,000 bottles
HECTARES UNDER VINE 90.00
VITICULTURE METHOD Certified Organic

In 2003, Filippo Cassano decided to follow in the family's footsteps. He purchased and renovated an old manor farm in Acquaviva Delle Fonti, creating a charming, modern cellar, carved out of rock, and founding Cantine Polvanera. Their vineyards grow at 300 meters, on karst terrain in Gioia del Colle and Acquaviva Delle Fonti. The systems used include Guyot, cordon-trained and spur-pruned, and head-trained. Primitivo is the most cultivated variety. La Polvanera is a benchmark for the entire region, even for a difficult vintage like 2014. Their 2017 Gioia del Colle Primitivo Montevella features hints of dark fruit and cherry, coffee and chocolate, while the palate exhibits body, structure, staying-power and freshness. The 2016 Gioia del Colle Primitivo, Vigneto San Benedetto, is spicier, with notes of aromatic herbs, while their 2014 Gioia del Colle Primitivo, Vigneto Marchesana, proves fresh, fruity and long, with a plucky, dynamic finish.

● Gioia del Colle Primitivo 17 Vign. Montevella '14	♟♟♟ 6
● Gioia del Colle Primitivo 14 Vign. Marchesana '14	♟♟ 3*
● Gioia del Colle Primitivo 16 Vign. San Benedetto '14	♟♟ 5
○ Polvanera Bianco '15	♟♟ 3
⊙ Rosato '16	♟ 2
● Gioia del Colle Primitivo 17 '13	♟♟♟ 5
● Gioia del Colle Primitivo 17 '10	♟♟♟ 5
● Gioia del Colle Primitivo 17 '09	♟♟♟ 5
● Gioia del Colle Primitivo 17 Vign. Montevella '12	♟♟♟ 6
● Gioia del Colle Primitivo 17 Vign. Montevella '11	♟♟♟ 6

Rivera

S.DA PROV.LE 231 KM 60,500
76123 ANDRIA [BT]
TEL. +39 0883569510
www.rivera.it

CELLAR SALES
PRE-BOOKED VISITS
ANNUAL PRODUCTION 1,200,000 bottles
HECTARES UNDER VINE 75.00

The De Corato family's winery, La Rivera, has been one of Apulia's most important producers for some time. Their vineyards are divided into different plots, situated at altitudes ranging from 200 to 350 meters. The cooler air here leads to grapes with higher acidity, making for plucky, fresh wines that are technically well-crafted. Castel del Monte Rosso Il Facone Riserva is one of the producer's classic wines. The 2012 version of this blend (made with 70% Troia and other traditional grapes) opens with aromas of tanned leather and spices, followed by dark fruit and pepper. The palate is fresh, fruity and full-flavored, with notes of black cherry. The 2012 Castel del Monte Nero di Troia Puer Apuliae Riserva showed good body and length, going all in on balsamic and chocolate; a good performance for this wine, as well as the rest of their selection.

● Castel del Monte Rosso Il Falcone Ris. '12	♟♟ 4
○ Castel del Monte Bianco Fedora '16	♟♟ 2*
◉ Castel del Monte Bombino Nero Pungirosa '16	♟♟ 2*
● Castel del Monte Nero di Troia Puer Apuliae Ris. '12	♟♟ 5
○ Moscato di Trani Piani di Tufara '16	♟♟ 2*
○ Castel del Monte Bombino Marese '16	♟ 2
○ Castel del Monte Chardonnay Preludio n°1 '16	♟ 2
● Castel del Monte Nero di Troia Violante '15	♟ 2
● Castel del Monte Rosso Rupicolo '15	♟ 2
○ Scariazzo '16	♟ 2
● Castel del Monte Nero di Troia Puer Apuliae '04	♟♟♟ 6

★Tenute Rubino

VIA E. FERMI, 50
72100 BRINDISI
TEL. +39 0831571955
www.tenuterubino.com

CELLAR SALES
PRE-BOOKED VISITS
ANNUAL PRODUCTION 1,200,000 bottles
HECTARES UNDER VINE 200.00

The Rubino family estate spans four areas, running from the Adriatic coast to the inland province of Brindisi. Jaddico, which is closer to the sea, hosts the oldest vineyards (more than 75 years). Here, Susumaniello is grown, the variety that best defines the winery. Also near the cost is Marmorelle, which features younger vineyards, while more inland we find Uggio, whose 125 hectares make it the largest plot, and Punta Aquila, which is completely dedicated to the cultivation of Primitivo. Once again, the wines that stand out from the Rubino family's selection are made with Susumaniello. Their 2016 Oltremé offers up fragrances of wild berry and vanilla, with a full, long palate rich in fruit and marked by hints of pepper, while the 2015 Torre Testa Susumaniello, a wine that features notes of dark, ripe fruit, is more complex but less taut and brilliant. The 2015 Visellio, a fresh, full, fruity Primitivo also put in a good performance, as did the 2016 Giancòla, a pleasant, varietal Malvasia Bianca.

● Oltremé '16	♟♟♟ 4*
● Visellio '15	♟♟ 6
○ Giancòla '16	♟♟ 5
● Torre Testa Susumaniello '15	♟♟ 8
● Marmorelle Rosso '15	♟ 3
● Punta Aquila '15	♟ 4
◉ Saturnino '16	♟ 4
○ Torre Testa Rosé '16	♟ 5
● Oltremé Susumaniello '15	♟♟♟ 4*
● Primitivo Visellio '01	♟♟♟ 3*
● Torre Testa '13	♟♟♟ 6
● Torre Testa '12	♟♟♟ 6
● Torre Testa '11	♟♟♟ 6
● Torre Testa '11	♟♟♟ 6
● Torre Testa '02	♟♟♟ 5
● Torre Testa '01	♟♟♟ 5
● Visellio '10	♟♟♟ 4*

Schola Sarmenti

VIA GENERALE CANTORE, 37
73048 NARDÒ [LE]
TEL. +39 0833567247
www.scholasarmenti.it

CELLAR SALES
PRE-BOOKED VISITS
ANNUAL PRODUCTION 240,000 bottles
HECTARES UNDER VINE 41.00
VITICULTURE METHOD Certified Organic

Schola Sarmenti is one of Nardò's strongest supporters of the importance of Apulia's old, head-trained producers. In fact, 85% of their vineyards use the head-trained system, and see the cultivation of local grape varieties (particularly Negroamaro, Primitivo, Fiano and Malvasia Nera). In addition to their traditional local wines, they produce wines inspired by a new style of Primitivo, one that features great intensity and richness of alcohol, but also freshness and drinkability. An overall good performance for Schola Sarmenti. Their 2014 Nardò Rosso Nerìo Riserva offers up aromas of incense and dark fruit, followed by a well-bodied, balsamic palate, with a finish that, despite some wood, comes through long and fruity. The 2016 Nardò Rosato Òpra is full-flavored and fresh, with notes of cherry and pomegranate, while the 2015 Diciotto, a close-knit, complex wine, is held back by its perceptibly high alcohol content and a lack of dynamism. The 2016 Fiano exhibits the right grip and staying power.

● Antièri Susumaniello '15	♛♛ 3
● Diciotto '15	♛♛ 8
○ Fiano '16	♛♛ 3
⊙ Nardò Rosato Opra '16	♛♛ 2*
● Nardò Rosso Nerìo Ris. '14	♛♛ 3
● Cubardi '14	♛ 4
● Cubardi '11	♛♛ 3
● Cubardi '10	♛♛ 3
● Diciotto '13	♛♛ 8
● Diciotto '12	♛♛ 7
● Nardò Nerìo Ris. '10	♛♛ 3
● Nardò Nerìo Ris. '09	♛♛ 3
● Nardò Rosso Roccamora '14	♛♛ 2*
● Nardò Rosso Roccamora '13	♛♛ 2*
● Nauna '14	♛♛ 5

Cantine Soloperto

S.DA ST.LE 7
74024 MANDURIA [TA]
TEL. +39 0999794286
www.soloperto.it

CELLAR SALES
PRE-BOOKED VISITS
ANNUAL PRODUCTION 1,500,000 bottles
HECTARES UNDER VINE 50.00

Soloperto (Est. 1967), is number one on Primitivo di Manduria's roster of producers. Indeed, the winery is, at the moment, one of the most important of the area and the DOC zone. Their vineyards, which grow in both red and brown soils, feature various hectares of Apulia's old, head-trained vines, such as the century-old plot in Bagnolo or the 40-something plot in the districts of Spina and Schiavoni. Their wide range of wines features Primitivo, interpreted in a variety of ways, all of which display a decidedly traditional character. Consistency and quality define the selection proposed this year. The 2014 Primitivo di Manduria Patriarca offers up aromas of dark fruit, with hints of spices and Mediterranean shrub, while the pleasant, fresh palate gives way to a full finish. Their 2015 Primitivo di Manduria Etichetta Nera is rich in flavor and pulp, while the 2016 Primitivo di Manduria is approachable and fruity.

● Primitivo di Manduria '16	♛♛ 1*
● Primitivo di Manduria Et. Nera '15	♛♛ 2*
● Primitivo di Manduria Patriarca '14	♛♛ 4
● Primitivo di Manduria Ceralacca '15	♛ 3
● Primitivo di Manduria Rubinum 17 '15	♛ 2
⊙ Rosato '16	♛ 2
● Primitivo di Manduria '15	♛♛ 1*
● Primitivo di Manduria Centofuochi Tenuta Bagnolo '12	♛♛ 4
● Primitivo di Manduria Mono '11	♛♛ 3
● Primitivo di Manduria Patriarca '13	♛♛ 4
● Primitivo di Manduria Rubinum Et. Rossa '14	♛♛ 2*
● Vecchio Ceppo Primitivo '15	♛♛ 2*

★Tormaresca

LOC. TOFANO
C.DA TORRE D'ISOLA
76013 MINERVINO MURGE [BT]
TEL. +39 0883692631
www.tormaresca.it

CELLAR SALES
PRE-BOOKED VISITS
ACCOMMODATION
ANNUAL PRODUCTION 3,000,000 bottles
HECTARES UNDER VINE 380.00
VITICULTURE METHOD Certified Organic
SUSTAINABLE WINERY

The Antinori family's winery turns 20 this
year. Divided into two large estates, each
with its own facilities and cellar, Tormaresca
offers modern wines that are pleasant and
technically well-crafted, made from both
native and international grape varieties.
Tenuta Bocca di Lupo is located in
Minervino Murge, in Alta Murgia, within the
Castle del Monte DOC zone, while Masseria
Maime is in San Pietro Vernotico, in Alto
Salento. And this year, it was the former,
especially, that made an impression. The
2013 Castel del Monte Aglianico Bocca di
Lupo is intense on the nose, with aromas of
undergrowth, quinine and spices. Despite
its marked tannins, the palate is full, long
and complex, with an austere finish
featuring hints of pencil lead. The balanced,
creamy 2015 Castel del Monte Chardonnay
Pietrabianca is also well-crafted, as is the
2015 Castel del Monte Rosso Trentangeli, a
wine that goes all in on fruit.

● Castel del Monte Aglianico Bocca di Lupo '13	♟♟ 5
○ Castel del Monte Chardonnay Pietrabianca '15	♟♟ 4
● Castel del Monte Rosso Trentangeli '15	♟♟ 3
○ Chardonnay '16	♟ 2
○ Roycello '16	♟ 3
● Torcicoda '15	♟ 4
● Castel del Monte Rosso Trentangeli '11	♟♟♟ 3*
● Masseria Maime '12	♟♟♟ 5
● Masseria Maime '08	♟♟♟ 5
● Masseria Maime '07	♟♟♟ 4
● Torcicoda '11	♟♟♟ 4*
● Torcicoda '10	♟♟♟ 3*
● Torcicoda '09	♟♟♟ 3

★Torrevento

S.DA PROV.LE 234 KM 10,600
70033 CORATO [BA]
TEL. +39 0808980923
www.torrevento.it

CELLAR SALES
ACCOMMODATION AND RESTAURANT SERVICE
ANNUAL PRODUCTION 2,500,000 bottles
HECTARES UNDER VINE 450.00
SUSTAINABLE WINERY

Torrevento is a leader in the Castle del
Monte DOC zone. The winery, who've
adopted an approach centered on
sustainability, have two areas at their
disposal. They have vineyards in the Rurale
della Murgia Park, where their main facility
is also located and where varieties like
Nero di Troia and Aglianico are grown in
rocky, calcareous karst soil. They depend
on their vineyards in Valle d'Itria and in
Salento for their whites, and for wines
based on Negroamaro and Primitivo. The
2014 Castel del Monte Vigna Pedale
Riserva returns to form. The nose is
characterized by fragrances of tobacco,
spices, dark fruit and forest floor, while the
palate is elegant, easy and full-flavored
with good expansion. At the top of the
appellation we also find their 2015 Castel
del Monte Nero di Troia Ottagono Riserva, a
long and full wine with notes of
Mediterranean shrub and turmeric. The rest
of their selection also proved first-rate.

● Castel del Monte Rosso V. Pedale Ris. '14	♟♟♟ 3*
● Castel del Monte Nero di Troia Ottagono Ris. '15	♟♟ 5
● Kebir '14	♟♟ 5
● Matervitae Negroamaro '16	♟♟ 2*
● Primitivo di Manduria Ghenos '16	♟♟ 3
● Torre del Falco '15	♟♟ 2*
● Castel del Monte Bombino Nero Veritas '16	♟ 2
● Matervitae Primitivo '16	♟ 2
● Passione Reale Appassimento '16	♟ 2
● Salice Salentino Rosso Sine Nomine Ris. '14	♟ 3
● Castel del Monte Nero di Troia Ottagono Ris. '14	♟♟♟ 5

Cantine Tre Pini

VIA VECCHIA PER ALTAMURA S.DA PROV.LE 79 KM 16
70020 CASSANO DELLE MURGE [BA]
TEL. +39 080764911
www.cantinetrepini.com

CELLAR SALES
PRE-BOOKED VISITS
ACCOMMODATION AND RESTAURANT SERVICE
ANNUAL PRODUCTION 30,000 bottles
HECTARES UNDER VINE 7.00
VITICULTURE METHOD Certified Organic

Since 1988, the Pantamura family have managed an agrotourism on their estate in the Alta Murgia Park. In 2012, however, they started producing and bottling their own wines, with results that were particularly positive. The vineyards are found throughout Casson delle Murge and Acquaviva delle Fonti, at altitudes ranging from 400 to 450 meters. Here, only two varieties are grown, Primitivo and Malvasia Bianca, in the rocky, karst terrain that's common throughout the area. Gioia del Colle Primitivo Riserva put in a superb performance, with the 2014 earning a Tre Bicchieri. This fresh and full wine, with notes of Mediterranean shrub, autumn leaves and red fruit closes with a long, full-flavored, plucky finish. The rest of the selection also did well. We particularly liked the 2016 Primitivo Crae, a tasty, pleasant wine, and the 2016 Ventifile Rosé, made with Bombino Nero grapes. A flavorsome, flowery wine, it was one of the best rosés we tasted this year.

Gioia del Colle Primitivo Ris. '14	♟♟♟ 5
Crae Primitivo '16	♟♟ 2*
Donna Johanna '16	♟♟ 2*
Trullo di Carnevale '15	♟♟ 2*
Ventifile '16	♟♟ 2*
Gioia del Colle Primitivo Ris. '13	♟♟♟ 4*
Gioia del Colle Primitivo '11	♟♟ 4
Gioia del Colle Primitivo Piscina delle Monache '13	♟♟ 3
Gioia del Colle Primitivo Piscina delle Monache '12	♟♟ 3*
Gioia del Colle Primitivo Ris. '12	♟♟ 4
Trullo di Carnevale '14	♟♟ 2*

Agricola Vallone

VIA XXV LUGLIO, 7
73100 LECCE
TEL. +39 0832308041
www.agricolevallone.it

PRE-BOOKED VISITS
ANNUAL PRODUCTION 424,000 bottles
HECTARES UNDER VINE 161.00
VITICULTURE METHOD Certified Organic
SUSTAINABLE WINERY

Management of this historic winery, founded in 1934, has passed from sisters Vittoria and Maria Teresa to the next generation of the Vallone family, Francesco. The entire estate is made up of three plots: Flaminio, an area in the Brindisi DOC zone where the cellar is found; Iore, in San Pancrazio Salentino, where their most famous wine, Graticciaia, comes from; and Castelserranova, in Carovigno, which hosts their drying loft. The Graticciaia is considered by many a benchmark for winemaking in Apulia. The 2013 affirms its stylistic makeup, with ripe cherry, tobacco and walnut skin on the nose and a relaxed, soft palate without any tannic roughness. The 2013 Castelserranova blend (70% Negroamaro and Susumaniello) may not have the structure, but it flows nicely, featuring good fruit and a plucky finish. The 2016 Tenuta Serranova, a fresh, citrusy Fiano, also proved well-crafted.

● Graticciaia '13	♟♟ 7
● Castelserranova '13	♟♟ 4
○ Tenuta Serranova '16	♟♟ 3
● Susumaniello '16	♟ 2
● Graticciaia '03	♟♟♟ 6
● Graticciaia '01	♟♟♟ 6
● Brindisi Rosato V. Flaminio '13	♟♟ 2*
⊙ Brindisi Rosato V. Flaminio '11	♟♟ 2*
● Brindisi Rosso V. Flaminio '10	♟♟ 2*
● Brindisi Rosso V. Flaminio Ris. '12	♟♟ 3
● Brindisi Rosso V. Flaminio Rls. '09	♟♟ 3
● Graticciaia '12	♟♟ 7
● Graticciaia '10	♟♟ 7
○ Salento Corte Valesio '12	♟♟ 2*
● Vigna Castello '11	♟♟ 5

Vecchia Torre

VIA MARCHE, 1
73045 LEVERANO [LE]
TEL. +39 0832925053
www.cantinavecchiatorre.it

CELLAR SALES
PRE-BOOKED VISITS
ANNUAL PRODUCTION 3,000,000 bottles
HECTARES UNDER VINE 1800.00

This cooperative winery is an integral part of Leverano's history of wine production. When it got its start in 1959, it had just 50 members. Today, they cultivate almost 2000 hectares, with more than 1300 member-growers contributing. Most of the vineyards are situated right in Leverano, with a large presence of old, head-trained vines. Mostly red, native grape varieties are grown (Negroamaro, Primitivo, Malvasia Nera di Lecce), in addition to a small quantity of international ones, making for wines that are both modern and traditionally styled. Once again, this year saw a series of consistent and well-crafted wines. The 2014 A Passo Lento, a well-structured wine made with semi-dried Negroamaro and Syrah grapes, features aromas of dried figs, but manages to stay fresh and balanced. Their 2015 Malvasia Nera is characterized by energy and wild berries. The 2016 Leverano Rosato is full and flowery, while the 2015 Salice Salentino Rosso exhibits structure, as well as notes of prune jam. Finally, the 2016 Vermentino is a full-flavored, pleasant wine.

● A Passo Lento '14	♥♥ 2*
⊙ Leverano Rosato '16	♥♥ 2*
● Malvasia Nera '15	♥♥ 2*
● Salice Salentino Rosso '15	♥♥ 2*
○ Vermentino '16	♥♥ 2*
● Arneide '14	♥ 3
● Leverano Rosso '15	♥ 2
● Primitivo '15	♥ 2
● Primitivo Barocco Reale '13	♥ 3
● Salice Salentino Rosso Ris. '13	♥ 2
● 50° Anniversario '13	♥♥ 3
● 50° Anniversario '12	♥♥ 3*
● Arneide '11	♥♥ 3
● Leverano Rosso '13	♥♥ 2*
● Negroamaro '14	♥♥ 2*
● Salice Salentino Rosso '13	♥♥ 2*

Vespa
Vignaioli per Passione

C.DA RENI
VIA MANDURIA - AVETRANA KM 3
74024 MANDURIA [TA]
TEL. +39 0637514609
www.vespavignaioli.it

CELLAR SALES
ANNUAL PRODUCTION 165,000 bottles
HECTARES UNDER VINE 30.00
SUSTAINABLE WINERY

In 2014 Bruno Vespa, along with his sons Alessandro and Federico, decided to jump into the wine industry, with the help of winemaker, Riccardo Cotarella. They took the next step in 2015, purchasing the farm manor Li Reni, three kilometers from Manduria. Mostly Primitivo is grown in the clay and clay-sand soil common to these parts, though Fiano, Negroamaro and Aleatico are also cultivated. The Primitivo di Manduria Raccontami received Tre Bicchieri in its 2015 version as well. Featuring spicy tones, with hints of figs and dark fruit, it shows good mouthfeel and balance. A soft, pervasive wine, its finish is characterized by length and notable freshness. The 2016 Primitivo di Manduria Il Rosso dei Vespa, on the other hand, is plucky and approachable in its notes of fresh, red fruit. All the other wines presented also hit the mark.

● Primitivo di Manduria Raccontami '15	♥♥♥ 5
● Primitivo di Manduria Il Rosso dei Vespa '16	♥♥ 3
⊙ Flarò '16	♥ 2
○ Il Bianco dei Vespa '16	♥ 2
● Il Bruno dei Vespa '16	♥ 2
● Primitivo di Manduria Raccontami '14	♥♥♥ 5
● Primitivo di Manduria Raccontami '13	♥♥♥ 5
⊙ Brut Rosé M. Cl. Noi Tre '11	♥♥ 5
● Il Bruno dei Vespa '14	♥♥ 4
● Il Bruno dei Vespa '13	♥♥ 4
● Il Rosso dei Vespa '15	♥♥ 3
● Primitivo di Manduria Raccontami '12	♥♥ 5

Tenuta Viglione

S.DA PROV.LE 140 KM 4,100
70029 SANTERAMO IN COLLE [BA]
TEL. +39 0802123661
www.tenutaviglione.it

CELLAR SALES
PRE-BOOKED VISITS
ACCOMMODATION AND RESTAURANT SERVICE
ANNUAL PRODUCTION 400,000 bottles
HECTARES UNDER VINE 60.00
VITICULTURE METHOD Certified Organic

With his Tenuta Viglione, Giovanni Zullo
has, in just a few years, managed to
become a leading figure in Apulia's vine
growing/winemaking scene. His vineyards
are situated in Murgia Barese at about 450
meters above sea level, at the highest
point in the Gioia del Colle DOC zone. The
soil here is a characterized by thin layers
of mixed 'red earth', calcareous and silica
rock, and gives rise to wines defined by
their typicity, as well as freshness. The
2013 version of their Gioia del Colle
Primitivo Marpione Riserva gets a Tre
Bicchieri, earning itself a place among this
guide's top wines. Aromas of dark fruit,
Mediterranean shrub and smoky notes are
followed by a truly pleasant, full-flavored,
fresh palate and a long, taut finish. The
2016 Negroamaro is also well-crafted,
with fragrances of ripe, dark fruit that are
well-supported by grip. The full and
pleasant 2016 Nisia Rosato, made with
Primitivo grapes, is equally good, as is the
2016 Melia, an approachable wine made
with Nero di Troia that features crisp fruit.

● Gioia del Colle Primitivo Marpione Ris. '13	♟♟♟	3*
● Melia '16	♟♟	2*
● Negroamaro '16	♟♟	2*
⊙ Nisia Rosato '16	♟♟	2*
● Gioia del Colle Primitivo '15	♟	2
● Johe '15	♟	2
● Gioia del Colle Primitivo Marpione Ris. '11	♟♟♟	3*
● Gioia del Colle Primitivo Marpione Ris. '10	♟♟♟	3*
● Gioia del Colle Primitivo '12	♟♟	2*
● Gioia del Colle Primitivo Marpione Ris. '12	♟♟	3*
● Johe '13	♟♟	2*
● Johe '12	♟♟	2*

★Conti Zecca

VIA CESAREA
73045 LEVERANO [LE]
TEL. +39 0832925613
www.contizecca.it

CELLAR SALES
PRE-BOOKED VISITS
ANNUAL PRODUCTION 2,800,000 bottles
HECTARES UNDER VINE 320.00
SUSTAINABLE WINERY

The winery may have been founded in
1935, but the Conti Zecca family have
been cultivating their land in Leverano
since 1580. Divided into three plots,
Saraceno (in Leverano), Donna Marzia (in
Cantalupi) and Santo Stefano (in Salice
Salentino), Conti Zecca offer a wide range
of wines (almost 30) using mostly native
grapes. Their style is modern, technically
well-crafted, fresh and rich in fruit. And
once again, Conti Zecca's wines put in a
performance characterized by solidity and
consistence. The 2013 Nero holds its top
spot even if it doesn't manage to reach the
heights of a few years ago - an abundance
of fruit, but woody sensations as well,
make for a palate with good pulp and
structure. The 2016 Cantalupi Vermentino
is fresh, pleasant and approachable, with
notes of Mediterranean shrub and citrus.
The 2016 Cantalupi Primitivo, a fluent and
flavorsome wine, goes all in on fruit, while
the 2016 Venus, a rosé made with
Negroamaro, is among the best of its kind
for grip, flavor and pleasantness.

● Cantalupi Primitivo '16	♟♟	2*
○ Cantalupi Vermentino '16	♟♟	2*
● Nero '13	♟♟	6
⊙ Venus '16	♟♟	3
○ Calavento '16	♟	3
● Cantalupi Negroamaro '16	♟	2
⊙ Cantalupi Rosato '16	♟	2
● Rifugio '15	♟	3
● Salice Salentino Cantalupi Ris. '14	♟	3
● Nero '09	♟♟♟	5
● Nero '08	♟♟♟	5
● Nero '07	♟♟♟	5
● Nero '06	♟♟♟	5
● Nero '03	♟♟♟	5
● Nero '02	♟♟♟	5
● Nero '01	♟♟♟	5

A Mano

VIA SAN GIOVANNI, 41
70015 NOCI [BA]
TEL. +39 0803434872
www.amanowine.it

PRE-BOOKED VISITS
ANNUAL PRODUCTION 235,000 bottles
HECTARES UNDER VINE

● Imprint of Mark Shannon '15	♈♈ 2*
● Negroamaro '16	♈♈ 2*
● Primitivo '16	♈ 2
⊙ Rosato '16	♈ 2

Cantina Albea

VIA DUE MACELLI, 8
70011 ALBEROBELLO [BA]
TEL. +39 0804323548
www.albeavini.com

CELLAR SALES
PRE-BOOKED VISITS
ANNUAL PRODUCTION 380,000 bottles
HECTARES UNDER VINE 40.00

○ Locorotondo Il Selva '16	♈ 2
● Lui '15	♈ 5
● Petranera '15	♈ 3
● Sol '14	♈ 3

Masseria Altemura

S.DA PROV.LE 69 MESAGNE
72028 TORRE SANTA SUSANNA [BR]
TEL. +39 0831740485
www.masseriaaltemura.it

CELLAR SALES
PRE-BOOKED VISITS
ACCOMMODATION
ANNUAL PRODUCTION 400,000 bottles
HECTARES UNDER VINE 150.00

● Aglianico '15	♈♈ 3
○ Fiano '16	♈ 3
● Negroamaro '15	♈ 3
● Primitivo di Manduria Altemura '15	♈ 5

Amastuola

VIA APPIA KM 632,200
74016 MASSAFRA [TA]
TEL. +39 0998805668
www.amastuola.it

CELLAR SALES
PRE-BOOKED VISITS
ACCOMMODATION AND RESTAURANT SERVICE
ANNUAL PRODUCTION 360,000 bottles
HECTARES UNDER VINE 101.00
VITICULTURE METHOD Certified Organic

● Lamarossa '14	♈♈ 2*
● Vignatorta '13	♈♈ 2*
○ Fiano - Malvasia '16	♈ 3

Donato Angiuli

FRAZ. MONTRONE
VIA PRINCIPE UMBERTO, 27
70010 ADELFIA [BA]
TEL. +39 0804597130
www.angiulidonato.com

CELLAR SALES
PRE-BOOKED VISITS
ANNUAL PRODUCTION 20,000 bottles
HECTARES UNDER VINE 6.00

⊙ Maccone Rosato '16	♈♈ 6
● Maccone Rosso 17°	♈♈ 8
○ Moscato '16	♈ 1*
● Nero di Troia '15	♈ 4

Apollonio

VIA SAN PIETRO IN LAMA, 7
73047 MONTERONI DI LECCE [LE]
TEL. +39 0832327182
www.apolloniovini.it

CELLAR SALES
PRE-BOOKED VISITS
ANNUAL PRODUCTION 1,500,000 bottles
HECTARES UNDER VINE 20.00

● Copertino Rosso Mani del Sud '14	♈♈ 3
● Salice Salentino Rosso Mani del Sud '13	♈♈ 3
⊙ Elfo Rosato '16	♈ 2
○ Salice Salentino Bianco Mani del Sud '16	♈ 3

Bonsegna

via A. Volta, 17
73048 Nardò [LF]
Tel. +39 0833561483
www.vinibonsegna.it

CELLAR SALES
PRE-BOOKED VISITS
ANNUAL PRODUCTION 100,000 bottles
HECTARES UNDER VINE 20.00

● Nardò Rosso Danze della Contessa '15	🍷🍷 2*
● Primo '14	🍷🍷 4
● Nardò Rosso Danze della Contessa Barriccato '14	🍷 3

I Buongiorno

c.so Vittorio Emanuele II, 71
72012 Carovigno [BR]
Tel. +39 0831996286
www.ibuongiorno.com

ANNUAL PRODUCTION 50,000 bottles
HECTARES UNDER VINE 10.00

○ Fiano '16	🍷🍷 2*
● Negramaro '15	🍷🍷 2*
● Nicolaus '14	🍷🍷 3
● Primitivo '15	🍷 3

Calosm

via Pietro Siciliani, 8
73058 Tuglie [LE]
Tel. +39 0833598051
www.calosm.it

CELLAR SALES
PRE-BOOKED VISITS
ANNUAL PRODUCTION 85,000 bottles
HECTARES UNDER VINE 22.00

● Primitivo di Manduria Iacco '15	🍷🍷 4
● Primitivo Doxi Valentino '16	🍷🍷 1*
○ Ionia '16	🍷 2
● Tisciano '15	🍷 2

Campa

via Palestro 22
74020 Torricella [TA]
Tel. +39 3383940636
www.erminiocampa.it

CELLAR SALES
ANNUAL PRODUCTION 30,000 bottles
HECTARES UNDER VINE 22.00

● Primitivo di Manduria Li Cameli '15	🍷🍷 5
● Primitivo di Manduria Li Janni '15	🍷🍷 4

Francesco Cannito

.da Parco Bizzarro
0025 Grumo Appula [BA]
Tel. +39 080623529
www.agricolacannito.it

CELLAR SALES
PRE-BOOKED VISITS
ANNUAL PRODUCTION 60,000 bottles
HECTARES UNDER VINE 14.00
VITICULTURE METHOD Certified Organic
SUSTAINABLE WINERY

● Gioia del Colle Primitivo Drùmon Ris. '12	🍷🍷 8
● Gioia del Colle Primitivo Drùmon S '13	🍷🍷 6
● Drùmon F '16	🍷 5
● Gioia del Colle Primitivo Drùmon '13	🍷 5

Castel di Salve

fraz. Depressa
via Salvemini, 30
73026 Tricase [LE]
Tel. +39 0833771041
www.casteldisalve.com

CELLAR SALES
PRE-BOOKED VISITS
ACCOMMODATION
ANNUAL PRODUCTION 170,000 bottles
HECTARES UNDER VINE 41.00

● Cento su Cento Primitivo '14	🍷🍷 5
⊙ Santimedici Rosato '16	🍷🍷 2*
● Cento su Cento '12	🍷 5

Tenuta Coppadoro

S.DA PROV.LE 35 SAN SEVERO - LESINA KM 5,850
71016 SAN SEVERO [FG]
TEL. +39 0882223174
www.tenutacoppadoro.it

CELLAR SALES
PRE-BOOKED VISITS
ANNUAL PRODUCTION 360,000 bottles
HECTARES UNDER VINE 120.00

○ Diomede '16	♟♟ 2*
○ Ratino '16	♟♟ 2*
● Impavido '14	♟ 6
● Radicosa '13	♟ 5

d'Aprì

VIA ZANNOTTI, 30
71016 SAN SEVERO [FG]
TEL. +39 0882227643
www.daprì.it

CELLAR SALES
PRE-BOOKED VISITS
RESTAURANT SERVICE
ANNUAL PRODUCTION 70,000 bottles
HECTARES UNDER VINE 6.00

○ d'Aprì Gran Cuvée XXI Secolo '09	♟♟ 6
○ d'Aprì Pas Dosé	♟♟ 4
○ d'Aprì Nobile Brut Ris. '13	♟ 5

De Falco

VIA MILANO, 25
73051 NOVOLI [LE]
TEL. +39 0832711597
www.cantinedefalco.it

CELLAR SALES
PRE-BOOKED VISITS
ACCOMMODATION
ANNUAL PRODUCTION 300,000 bottles
HECTARES UNDER VINE 20.00

● Salice Salentino Rosso Falco Nero Ris. '14	♟♟ 3
● Negroamaro '16	♟ 1*
● Salice Salentino Negroamaro Salore '14	♟ 2
● Squinzano Rosso Serre di Sant' Elia '15	♟ 2

Ferri

VIA BARI, 347
70010 VALENZANO [BA]
TEL. +39 0804671753
www.cantineferri.it

CELLAR SALES
PRE-BOOKED VISITS
ANNUAL PRODUCTION 40,000 bottles
HECTARES UNDER VINE 5.00

● Ad Mira '12	♟♟ 5
● Duo Rosso '14	♟♟ 2*
● L'Ebrius '14	♟ 2
● Purpureus '12	♟ 3

Feudi di Guagnano

VIA CELLINO, 3
73010 GUAGNANO [LE]
TEL. +39 0832705422
www.feudiguagnano.com

CELLAR SALES
PRE-BOOKED VISITS
ANNUAL PRODUCTION 200,000 bottles
HECTARES UNDER VINE 15.00

● Le Camarde '15	♟♟ 2*
● Salice Salentino Rosso Cupone Ris. '13	♟♟ 2*
● Nero di Velluto '13	♟ 4
● Pietrafinita '14	♟ 4

Vito Donato Giuliani

VIA GIOIA CANALE, 18
70010 TURI [BA]
TEL. +39 0808915335
www.vitivinicolagiuliani.com

ANNUAL PRODUCTION 100,000 bottles
HECTARES UNDER VINE 40.00

● Gioia del Colle Primitivo Lavarossa '14	♟♟ 3
○ Chiancaia '16	♟ 3

Hiso Telaray
Libera Terra Puglia
VICO DEI CANTELMO, 1
72023 MESAGNE [BR]
TEL. +39 0831775981
www.hisotelaray.it

CELLAR SALES
ANNUAL PRODUCTION 120,000 bottles
HECTARES UNDER VINE 27.00
VITICULTURE METHOD Certified Organic
SUSTAINABLE WINERY

⊙ Emmedielle '16	🍷🍷 2*
● Primitivo Antò '15	🍷🍷 3
● Renata Fonte '14	🍷 3

Cantine Imperatore
VIA MARCONI, 36
70010 ADELFIA [BA]
TEL. I 39 0804594041
www.cantineimperatore.com

CELLAR SALES
PRE-BOOKED VISITS
ANNUAL PRODUCTION 20,000 bottles
HECTARES UNDER VINE 5.00

● Gioia del Colle Primitivo Sonya '15	🍷🍷 2*
● Gioia del Colle Primitivo Vincenzo Latorre Ris. '11	🍷🍷 5
⊙ Schietto '16	🍷 2

Alberto Longo
C.DA PADULECCHIA
S.DA PROV.LE 5 LUCERA-PIETRAMONTECORVINO KM 4
71036 LUCERA [FG]
TEL. +39 0881539057
www.albertolongo.it

CELLAR SALES
PRE-BOOKED VISITS
ACCOMMODATION AND RESTAURANT SERVICE
ANNUAL PRODUCTION 150,000 bottles
HECTARES UNDER VINE 35.00

⊙ Donnadele '16	🍷🍷 3
○ Le Fossette '16	🍷🍷 3
● Cacc'e Mmitte di Lucera '14	🍷 3

Menhir
VIA SCARCIGLIA, 18
73027 MINERVINO DI LECCE [LE]
TEL. +39 0836818199
www.cantinemenhir.com

CELLAR SALES
PRE-BOOKED VISITS
RESTAURANT SERVICE
ANNUAL PRODUCTION 520,000 bottles
HECTARES UNDER VINE 18.00

○ Pass-0 '16	🍷🍷 3
⊙ Pietra Rosato '16	🍷🍷 3
● Primitivo di Manduria '16	🍷🍷 2*
● Pietra Susumaniello '16	🍷 3

Mocavero
VIA MALLACCA ZUMMARI
73010 ARNESANO [LE]
TEL. +39 0832327194
www.mocaverovini.it

CELLAR SALES
PRE-BOOKED VISITS
RESTAURANT SERVICE
ANNUAL PRODUCTION 600,000 bottles
HECTARES UNDER VINE 65.00

● Salice Salentino Rosso '15	🍷🍷 3
● Salice Salentino Rosso Puteus Ris. '13	🍷🍷 3
● Sire Negroamaro '16	🍷🍷 3
● Santufili '11	🍷 6

Mottura Vini del Salento
P.ZZA MELICA, 4
73058 TUGLIE [LE]
TEL. +39 0833596601
www.motturavini.it

PRE-BOOKED VISITS
ANNUAL PRODUCTION 2,500,000 bottles
HECTARES UNDER VINE 200.00

● Primitivo di Manduria Le Pitre '15	🍷🍷 6
● Negroamaro del Salento '15	🍷 5
● Primitivo '15	🍷 3
● Primitivo di Manduria Villa Mottura '16	🍷 3

Cantine Paradiso

VIA MANFREDONIA, 39
71042 CERIGNOLA [FG]
TEL. +39 0885428720
www.cantineparadiso.it

ANNUAL PRODUCTION 140,000 bottles
HECTARES UNDER VINE 16.00

● Posta Piana Negroamaro '15	▼▼ 3
● Posta Piana Nero di Troia '15	▼▼ 3
● 1954 '15	▼ 4
● Sant' Andrea Primitivo '16	▼ 2

Pietraventosa

C.DA PARCO LARGO
S.DA VIC.LE LATTA LATTA
70023 GIOIA DEL COLLE [BA]
TEL. +39 3355730274
www.pietraventosa.it

ANNUAL PRODUCTION 20,000 bottles
HECTARES UNDER VINE 5.40
VITICULTURE METHOD Certified Organic
SUSTAINABLE WINERY

⊙ EstRosa '16	▼▼ 3
● Ossimoro '13	▼▼ 3
● Volere Volare '15	▼▼ 2*

Plantamura

VIA V. BODINI, 9A
70023 GIOIA DEL COLLE [BA]
TEL. +39 3474711027
www.viniplantamura.it

CELLAR SALES
PRE-BOOKED VISITS
ANNUAL PRODUCTION 45,000 bottles
HECTARES UNDER VINE 8.00
VITICULTURE METHOD Certified Organic
SUSTAINABLE WINERY

● Gioia del Colle Primitivo Parco Largo '16	▼▼ 3

Podere 29

LOC. BORGO TRESSANTI
FRAZ. CERIGNOLA
S.DA PROV.LE 544
76016 CERIGNOLA [FG]
TEL. +39 3471917291
www.podere29.it

CELLAR SALES
ACCOMMODATION
ANNUAL PRODUCTION 60,000 bottles
HECTARES UNDER VINE 10.00

● Gelso d'Oro '15	▼▼ 5
● Gelso Nero '16	▼▼ 2*
○ Gelso Bianco '16	▼ 3
⊙ Gelso Rosa '16	▼ 2

Produttori Vini Manduria

VIA FABIO MASSIMO, 19
74024 MANDURIA [TA]
TEL. +39 0999735332
www.cpvini.com

CELLAR SALES
PRE-BOOKED VISITS
ANNUAL PRODUCTION 900,000 bottles
HECTARES UNDER VINE 900.00
SUSTAINABLE WINERY

● Primitivo di Manduria Dolce Naturale Madrigale '14	▼▼ 3
● Primitivo di Manduria Elegia Ris. '13	▼▼ 4
● Primitivo di Manduria Lirica '15	▼▼ 2*

Rasciatano

FRAZ. RASCIATANO
S.DA ST.LE 93 KM 13
76121 BARLETTA
TEL. +39 0883510999
www.rasciatano.com

CELLAR SALES
PRE-BOOKED VISITS
ANNUAL PRODUCTION 90,000 bottles
HECTARES UNDER VINE 18.00

● Tenute Nero di Troia '16	▼▼ 3
○ Malvasia Bianca '16	▼ 2
○ Tenute Chardonnay '16	▼ 2
● Tenute Primitivo '16	▼ 3

Vigneti Reale

VIA REALE, 55
73100 LECCE
TEL. +39 0832248433
www.vignetireale.it

PRE-BOOKED VISITS
ACCOMMODATION AND RESTAURANT SERVICE
ANNUAL PRODUCTION 130,000 bottles
HECTARES UNDER VINE 85.00
SUSTAINABLE WINERY

● Norie '15		♟♟ 2*
● Rudiae '15		♟♟ 3
○ Malvasia Bianca '16		♟ 2
● Malvasia Nera '16		♟ 2

Risveglio Agricolo

C.DA TORRE MOZZA
72100 BRINDISI
TEL. +39 0831519948
www.cantinerisveglio.it

CELLAR SALES
PRE-BOOKED VISITS
ANNUAL PRODUCTION 100,000 bottles
HECTARES UNDER VINE 44.00

● 72100 '15		♟♟ 2*
● Susù '15		♟♟ 8
● Buccianera '15		♟ 2
● Pecora Nera '15		♟ 7

Rosa del Golfo

VIA GARIBALDI, 18
73011 ALEZIO [LE]
TEL. +39 0833281045
www.rosadelgolfo.com

CELLAR SALES
PRE-BOOKED VISITS
ANNUAL PRODUCTION 300,000 bottles
HECTARES UNDER VINE 40.00

○ Bolina '16		♟♟ 2*
○ Brut Rosé M. Cl.		♟♟ 4
○ Negroamaro Rosato '16		♟♟ 3
● Portulano '14		♟♟ 2*

Cantina Sociale Sampietrana

VIA MARE, 38
72027 SAN PIETRO VERNOTICO [BR]
TEL. +39 0831671120
www.cantinasampietrana.com

CELLAR SALES
PRE-BOOKED VISITS
ANNUAL PRODUCTION 1,500,000 bottles
HECTARES UNDER VINE 140.00

● Brindisi Since 1952 Ris. '14		♟♟ 2*
● Salice Salentino V. delle Monache Ris. '14		♟♟ 4
● Iussum '14		♟ 4
● Settebraccia '14		♟ 3

Conte Spagnoletti Zeuli

RAZ. SAN DOMENICO
DA PROV.LE 231 KM 60,000
70031 ANDRIA [BT]
TEL. +39 0883569511
www.contespagnolettizeuli.it

CELLAR SALES
PRE-BOOKED VISITS
ANNUAL PRODUCTION 400,000 bottles
HECTARES UNDER VINE 120.00

Castel del Monte Rosso '16		♟♟ 4
Castel del Monte Rosso V. Grande '14		♟♟ 2*
Castel del Monte Rosso Terrarossa Ris. '13		♟ 4
● Jody '16		♟ 2

Spelonga

VIA MENOLA
71047 STORNARA [FG]
TEL. +39 0885431048
www.cantinespelonga.com

CELLAR SALES
PRE-BOOKED VISITS
ANNUAL PRODUCTION 50,000 bottles
HECTARES UNDER VINE 15.00

● Nero di Troia '16		♟♟ 3
● Primitivo '15		♟♟ 3
○ Extrema '16		♟ 3
⊙ Marilina Rosé '16		♟ 2

Masseria Surani

LOC. SURANI
74024 MANDURIA [TA]
TEL. +39 0457701266
www.masseriasurani.it

ANNUAL PRODUCTION 10,000 bottles
HECTARES UNDER VINE 1.00

○ Arthemis '16	♟♟	3
● Heracles '15	♟♟	4
● Primitivo di Manduria Dionysos '12	♟♟	4

Cosimo Taurino

S.DA ST.LE 365 KM 1,400
73010 GUAGNANO [LE]
TEL. +39 0832706490
www.taurinovini.it

CELLAR SALES
PRE-BOOKED VISITS
ANNUAL PRODUCTION 900,000 bottles
HECTARES UNDER VINE 90.00

● Notarpanaro '12	♟♟	3*
● 7° Ceppo '16	♟	3
● Patriglione '12	♟	8
● Salice Salentino Rosso Ris. '12	♟	2

Varvaglione

C.DA SANTA LUCIA
74020 LEPORANO [TA]
TEL. +39 0995315370
www.varvaglione.com

CELLAR SALES
PRE-BOOKED VISITS
ACCOMMODATION
ANNUAL PRODUCTION 3,000,000 bottles
HECTARES UNDER VINE 155.00
SUSTAINABLE WINERY

● Primitivo di Manduria Papale Oro '15	♟♟	5
● Collezionee Privata Cosimo Varvaglione Old Vines '14	♟	6

Tagaro

C.DA MONTETESSA, 63
70010 LOCOROTONDO [BA]
TEL. +39 0802042313
www.tagaro.it

ANNUAL PRODUCTION 120,000 bottles
HECTARES UNDER VINE 15.00

● Cinquenoci '15	♟♟	3
● Seicaselle '15	♟♟	3

Teanum

VIA CROCE SANTA, 48
71016 SAN SEVERO [FG]
TEL. +39 0882336332
www.teanum.it

CELLAR SALES
PRE-BOOKED VISITS
RESTAURANT SERVICE
ANNUAL PRODUCTION 1,500,000 bottles
HECTARES UNDER VINE 190.00

● Òtre Negroamaro Fish '16	♟♟	4
● Òtre Aglianico '14	♟	3
⊙ San Severo Rosato Favùgnë '16	♟	3
● San Severo Rosso Favùgnë '16	♟	3

Vetrere

FRAZ. VETRERE
S.DA PROV.LE 80 MONTEIASI - MONTEMESOLA KM 16
74123 TARANTO
TEL. +39 3402977870
www.vetrere.it

CELLAR SALES
PRE-BOOKED VISITS
ACCOMMODATION
ANNUAL PRODUCTION 150,000 bottles
HECTARES UNDER VINE 37.00

● Barone Pazzo '14	♟♟	4
● Livruni '15	♟♟	3
○ Crè '16	♟	3
⊙ Taranta '16	♟	3

CALABRIA

After decades of sleepy complacency, Calabria's wine industry is finally taking off. It's all thanks to the region's many small producers, who, armed with passion and skill, are carving out a place for themselves in the sector. Some 42 wineries made it into Italian Wines this year, and we really can't think of a time that the region has been so well represented. But the numbers don't reflect how quickly the quality of its wines is improving. Four wines got golds this year. And there could have been more, considering how close so many came. It's also worth noting how many wineries are practicing (or converting to) organic cultivation, and that all of the four wineries awarded this year practice sustainable agriculture (certifiably in some cases and, in the case of Ceraudo, biodynamic). Two new wineries are getting a Tre Bicchieri for the first time. Saracena's Roberto and Maurizio Bisconte made a wine that is a monument to complexity and balance with their 2014 Mastro Terenzio. Indeed, three producers from Saracena made it to the finals, and we're sure that Professor Luigi Viola will be happy to know that his two decades of work in supporting the territory have paid off. The second Tre Bicchieri goes to the Spiriti Ebbri, who also received the award for 'Emerging Winery of the Year'. And it was an unforgettable debut for Pierpaolo Greco, Damiano Mele and Michele Scrivano, the three young men leading Spezzano Piccolo, who charmed the tasting panel with their 2015 Pecorello Neostòs. There was good news from Cosenza and even Reggio Calabria this year, while Cirò continues to play a central role, thanks primarily to the work of Nicodemo Librandi, who helped set in motion a decades-long virtuous cycle that's helped propel the entire region.

'A Vita

FRAZ. CIRÒ MARINA
S.DA ST.LE 106 KM 279,800
88811 CROTONE
TEL. +39 3290732473
www.avitavini.it

CELLAR SALES
PRE-BOOKED VISITS
ANNUAL PRODUCTION 15,000 bottles
HECTARES UNDER VINE 8.00

Francesco and Laura De Franco could be
considered pioneers in Cirò. From the
beginning they ran their vineyards with
deep respect for the environment using
organic management, limiting the use of
sulfur and copper, cover cropping, and
working the soil. They are convinced this is
the only way to preserve biodiversity and
natural soil fertility. And there are no
shortcuts in the cellar, either. Fermentation
is natural, with native yeasts. They use an
absolute minimum of sulfur dioxide and
add no enzymes to obtain wines that reflect
the territory and enhance the
characteristics of the Gaglioppo and Greco
grapes, the only varieties grown The
austere 2013 Cirò Riserva made it to our
finals. It features a full and elegant aroma
profile that starts out balsamic and then
gives way to fragrances of red fruit,
medicinal herbs and a mineral trace of
iodine. The mouth proves well-orchestrated
and savory, with good, intact fruit and
tannins that are still exuberant.

● Cirò Rosso Cl. Sup. Ris. '13	♟♟ 4
☉ Cirò Rosato '16	♟♟ 2*
● Cirò Rosso Cl. Sup. '14	♟♟ 2*
● Cirò Rosso Cl. Sup. Ris. '11	♟♟ 4
☉ Cirò Rosato '14	♟♟ 2*
● Cirò Rosso Cl. '12	♟♟ 2*
● Cirò Rosso Cl. '09	♟♟ 3*
● Cirò Rosso Cl. Ris. '11	♟♟ 4
● Cirò Rosso Cl. Ris. '10	♟♟ 4
● Cirò Rosso Cl. Sup. '09	♟♟ 3*

Roberto Ceraudo

LOC. MARINA DI STRONGOLI
C.DA DATTILO
88815 CROTONE
TEL. +39 0962865613
www.dattilo.it

CELLAR SALES
PRE-BOOKED VISITS
ACCOMMODATION AND RESTAURANT SERVICE
ANNUAL PRODUCTION 70,000 bottles
HECTARES UNDER VINE 20.00
VITICULTURE METHOD Certified Organic

The Dattilo estate is a small paradise just a
stone's throw from Strongoli. As you enter
the gates you find yourself in an ethereal
atmosphere of bygone days. It's an old rural
town with a little church in the center,
surrounded by vineyards and olive groves
that are tended like a garden. This is
Roberto Ceraudo's realm. He was one of the
first Calabrian producers to enthusiastically
embrace organic farming 20 years ago and
he continues to use biodynamics today.
Roberto's daughter Caterina works in the
cellar. Putting her degree in enology from
Milan to good use, she has created a range
of glossy, aromatically complex and thrilling
wines. The 2016 Grisara thoroughly
deserves its Tre Bicchieri. Aromas of star
anise, medicinal herbs and exotic fruit give
way to a tangy palate rich in fruit. The
2014 Gaglioppo Dattilo offers up clear
aromas of red fruit, Mediterranean scrub,
cardamom and rowan. In the mouth it
proves solid with good balance between
fruit and its lovely tannic weave.

○ Grisara '16	♟♟♟ 4*
● Dattilo '14	♟♟ 4
○ Grisara '15	♟♟♟ 4*
○ Grisara '14	♟♟♟ 3*
○ Grisara '13	♟♟♟ 3*
○ Grisara '12	♟♟♟ 3*
● Dattilo '13	♟♟ 4
● Doro Bè '10	♟♟ 3
☉ Grayasusi Et. Argento '15	♟♟ 5
☉ Grayasusi Et. Rame '15	♟♟ 5
○ Imyr '15	♟♟ 5
○ Petelia '15	♟♟ 3
● Petraro '12	♟♟ 5

Feudo dei Sanseverino

VIA VITTORIO EMANUELE, 108/110
87010 SARACENA [CS]
TEL. +39 098121461
www.feudodeisanseverino.it

CELLAR SALES
PRE-BOOKED VISITS
ANNUAL PRODUCTION 20,000 bottles
HECTARES UNDER VINE 6.00
VITICULTURE METHOD Certified Organic
SUSTAINABLE WINERY

It gives us great pleasure to award a Tre Bicchieri to Maurizio and Roberto Bisconte. We see it as an important sign for a small territory like Saracena where until about 15 years ago, there were no structured wineries and few producers making Moscato Passito for personal consumption. To get an idea of how much this small territory has grown, there are now about 10 wineries, and, significantly, three of its Saracena wines made it to the regional finals this year. Production may be low, but its quality is impressive. The 2014 Moscato Passito Mastro Terenzio is a blend of Guarnaccia, Malvasia and Moscato. The nose proves full and lingering, with aromas ranging from dried fruit to quince, mint, sage and candied citrus fruit. The mouth comes through silky, surprisingly fresh and generous, with an unending finish.

iGreco

LOC. SALICE
C.DA GUARDAPIEDI
87062 CARIATI [CS]
TEL. +39 0983969441
www.igreco.it

CELLAR SALES
PRE-BOOKED VISITS
ACCOMMODATION AND RESTAURANT SERVICE
ANNUAL PRODUCTION 250,000 bottles
HECTARES UNDER VINE 80.00
SUSTAINABLE WINERY

The farm of the seven Greco brothers -- 1500 hectares of which are olive groves -- is one of the largest private farms in Italy. The Grecos were already famous for producing high-quality oil when just over a decade ago they decided to try their hand at winemaking. They planted about 80 hectares of vineyards in the best areas of Cariati, which is where their primary premises and cellar are located. Their wines are modern and completely new interpretations of native Calabrian grape varieties. The style is elegant and original and enhances the freshness of the fruit, aiming more toward drinkability than power. Once again, the 2015 Masino has earned Tre Bicchieri. This is an intriguing wine with spicy and balsamic overtones of black berries, dog rose and green tea. The palate proves well-orchestrated with freshness, lovely fleshy fruit and elegant tannins making for great drinkability.

○ Terre di Cosenza Pollino Moscato Passito Mastro Terenzio '14	▼▼▼ 5
○ Terre di Cosenza Pollino Rosato Rosa Lacrima Nera '15	▼▼ 3
● Lacrima Nera '13	♀♀ 3
○ Mastro Terenzio '12	♀♀ 5
○ Mastro Terenzio '11	♀♀ 5
○ Mastro Terenzio '10	♀♀ 5
○ Mastro Terenzio '09	♀♀ 5
○ Mastro Terenzio '08	♀♀ 5
○ Mastro Terenzio '07	♀♀ 5
○ Moscato Passito al Governo di Saracena '09	♀♀ 5
○ Moscato Passito al Governo di Saracena '07	♀♀ 5
○ Moscato Passito Mastro Terenzio '13	♀♀ 5

● Masino '15	▼▼▼ 5
● Catà '15	▼▼ 3
⊙ Savù '16	▼▼ 3
○ Filù '16	▼ 3
● Masino '14	♀♀♀ 5
● Masino '12	♀♀♀ 5
● Masino '11	♀♀♀ 5
● Masino '10	♀♀♀ 5
● Catà '14	♀♀ 3
● Catà '13	♀♀ 3
● Catà '11	♀♀ 2*
⊙ Gaglioppo Gran Cuvée Rosé '11	♀♀ 4
● Masino '13	♀♀ 5

Ippolito 1845

VIA TIRONE, 118
88811 CIRÒ MARINA [KR]
TEL. +39 096231106
www.ippolito1845.it

CELLAR SALES
PRE-BOOKED VISITS
ANNUAL PRODUCTION 1,000,000 bottles
HECTARES UNDER VINE 100.00

The history of the Ippolito family has
intertwined with local winemaking for
centuries. Vincenzo Ippolito founded what is
now the oldest winery in Cirò back in 1845.
Since then 173 years have gone by and
today there is another Vincenzo Ippolito at
the helm. He shares his responsibilities
with his brother Gianluca. These two young
and enthusiastic vinegrowers look to the
future with a proud history behind them. In
only a few years they have managed to
revolutionize the family winery and improve
it by leaps and bounds, thanks to a modern
style with a constant eye on tradition. The
2016 Pecorello did extremely well and
displays great complexity on the nose. The
palate proves tangy and balanced, with
length made possible by fresh acidity. The
160 Anni is elegant and fresh, despite part
of its grapes being dried. On the nose it
proves complex and Mediterranean, while
the mouth comes through fruity and
dynamic.

○ Pecorello '16	🍷🍷 2*
● 160 Anni '14	🍷🍷 5
● Calabrise '16	🍷🍷 2*
● Cirò Rosso Cl. Sup. Colli del Mancuso Ris. '14	🍷🍷 3
● Cirò Rosso Cl. Sup. Liber Pater '15	🍷🍷 2*
● Cirò Rosso Cl. Sup. Ripe del Falco Ris. '07	🍷🍷 5
⊙ Pescanera Rosé '16	🍷🍷 2*
○ Cirò Bianco Res Dei '16	🍷 2
● 160 Anni '13	🍷🍷 5
○ Cirò Bianco Res Dei '15	🍷🍷 2*
● Cirò Rosso Cl. Sup. Ripe del Falco Ris. '06	🍷🍷 5
● I Mori '14	🍷🍷 2*

Tenuta Iuzzolini

LOC. FRASSÀ
88811 CIRÒ MARINA [KR]
TEL. +39 0962373893
www.tenutaiuzzolini.it

CELLAR SALES
PRE-BOOKED VISITS
ANNUAL PRODUCTION 1,000,000 bottles
HECTARES UNDER VINE 100.00

Thanks to a mix of experience and
entrepreneurial skill, Francesco Iuzzolini
has brought his winery back to its former
glory. The conditions were already there:
40 hectares of vineyards in the best areas
of Cirò, a large cellar modernized and
equipped with the most advanced
winemaking technology, and most
importantly, the experience of the Iuzzolini
family, which has been making wine here
for generations. Their wines are modern in
style without compromising the qualities
of Cirò's native grapes. This year the
2015 Artino proves outstanding. It's a
blend of Gaglioppo and Magliocco that's
intense on the nose, rich in fruit and
supported by an extremely fresh acidity.
The 2015 Muranera, a new blend of
Gaglioppo, Magliocco, Merlot and Cabernet
also did quite well. It's balanced and
complex on the nose, while the palate
proves caressing and rich in silky tannins.
The 2016 Gaglioppo Belfresco, a fresh and
supple wine, features a pleasant palate,
and aromas of wild berries and spices.

● Artino '15	🍷🍷 3
● Belfresco '16	🍷🍷 3
● Muranera '15	🍷🍷 4
○ Prima Fila '16	🍷🍷 3
○ Donna Giovanna '16	🍷 5
⊙ Lumare '16	🍷 3
○ Madre Goccia '16	🍷 3
● Principe Spinelli '16	🍷 3
● Artino '14	🍷🍷 3
● Belfresco '10	🍷🍷 3
● Cirò Rosso Cl. Maradea '11	🍷🍷 3
○ Donna Giovanna '14	🍷🍷 5
⊙ Lumare '15	🍷🍷 3
○ Prima Fila '15	🍷🍷 3
● Principe Spinelli '14	🍷🍷 3

Cantine Lento

VIA DEL PROGRESSO, 1
88040 AMATO [CZ]
TEL. +39 096828028
www.cantinelento.it

CELLAR SALES
PRE-BOOKED VISITS
ANNUAL PRODUCTION 500,000 bottles
HECTARES UNDER VINE 70.00

In recent decades, Lento have completely revolutionized their winery, tripling the vineyards and building a large modern cellar better suited to the standard of their current wines. After a few twists and turns they have finally found the right path to improving production: some prudent investments and a wise decision to focus on native varieties. The lower yields and more measured use of wood are reflected in a range of easy-drinking wines offering a good balance between fruit and acidity. They're lacking that standout that's capable of bringing a winning surge, but their new direction in the cellar is clearly discernible in their flagship wines. The 2013 Magliocco almost made it to the finals. It does a nice job of combining fruit, tannins and acidity. The 2016 Contessa Emburga is a complex, fresh and pleasantly tangy blend of Chardonnay and Malvasia.

★Librandi

LOC. SAN GENNARO
S.DA ST.LE JONICA 106
88811 CIRÒ MARINA [KR]
TEL. +39 096231518
www.librandi.it

CELLAR SALES
PRE-BOOKED VISITS
ANNUAL PRODUCTION 2,200,000 bottles
HECTARES UNDER VINE 232.00

For years Librandi mulled a major expansion of its vineyard before finally taking the plunge. Beginning in 1993, with the first massal selection of Gaglioppo, the first experimental vineyards were planted in 2000. It was a long and difficult task, carried out with collaboration from the best Italian experts. Initial results came in 2016 with the first harvest of four selected clones of Gaglioppo, and the outcome was positive. Once again, our tasters agreed this winery shows great promise. The elegant and pervasive 2015 Gravello is a blend of Gaglioppo and Cabernet Sauvignon that never ceases to amaze. It plays more on finesse and balance than muscle and extraction. The 2015 Cirò Riserva Duca Sanfelice is summery and Mediterranean, very worthy of its territory.

Contessa Emburga '16	♥♥ 3
Lamezia Rosso Salvatore Lento Ris. '13	♥♥ 4
Magliocco '13	♥♥ 5
Dragone Bianco '16	♥ 3
Dragone Rosato '16	♥ 3
Dragone Rosso '15	♥ 3
Federico II '13	♥ 4
Lamezia Greco '16	♥ 3
Federico II '12	♀♀ 4
Federico II '11	♀♀ 4
Federico II '10	♀♀ 4
Lamezia Greco '15	♀♀ 3
Lamezia Greco '13	♀♀ 3
Magliocco '12	♀♀ 5
Magliocco '11	♀♀ 5

● Cirò Rosso Cl. Sup. Duca Sanfelice Ris. '15	♥♥ 3*
● Gravello '15	♥♥ 5
○ Cirò Bianco '16	♥♥ 2*
● Cirò Rosso Cl. '16	♥♥ 3
○ Critone '16	♥♥ 2*
○ Efeso '16	♥♥ 4
● Magno Megonio '15	♥♥ 4
☉ Terre Lontane '16	♥♥ 2*
○ Cirò Rosato '16	♥ 2
○ Melissa Bianco Asylia '16	♥ 2
● Cirò Rosso Cl. Sup. Duca Sanfelice Ris. '11	♀♀♀ 3*
● Gravello '14	♀♀♀ 5
● Gravello '10	♀♀♀ 5
● Magno Megonio '13	♀♀♀ 4*
● Magno Megonio '12	♀♀♀ 4*

Santa Venere

LOC. TENUTA VOLTA GRANDE
S.DA PROV.LE 04 KM 10,00
88813 CIRÒ [KR]
TEL. +39 096238519
www.santavenere.com

CELLAR SALES
PRE-BOOKED VISITS
ANNUAL PRODUCTION 125,000 bottles
HECTARES UNDER VINE 25.00
VITICULTURE METHOD Certified Organic

Giuseppe Scala's well-rounded farm produces quality wine and oil, as well as breeding cattle and thoroughbred horses. It was one of the first in Calabria to adopt organic farming and has recently been working to convert the entire farm to biodynamics. They have started an interesting and profitable experiment on two ancient native Calabrian varieties, Guardavalle and Marsigliana Nera. The wines made with these grapes have turned out to be original and reliable. Similar to the rest of their wines, they offer an elegant, modern style that leaves little room for superfluous displays of strength. The 2014 Riserva Federico Scala is made with Gaglioppo and displays perfectly ripe fruit combined with a wide range of floral and spicy notes. Its elegant and well-orchestrated mouth features round and fleshy fruit supported by tight-knit, silky tannins and good acidity. Its finish proves long and gratifying.

● Cirò Rosso Federico Scala Ris. '14	▼▼ 5
○ Cirò Bianco '16	▼▼ 2*
○ Vescovado '16	▼▼ 3
● Vurgadà '15	▼▼ 4
⊙ Cirò Rosato '16	▼ 2
● Cirò Rosso Cl. '16	▼ 2
⊙ Scassabarile '16	▼ 3
● Speziale '16	▼ 3
○ Cirò Bianco '15	♈ 2*
⊙ Cirò Rosato '15	♈ 2*
● Cirò Rosso Cl. '15	♈ 2*
● Cirò Rosso Cl. '13	♈ 2*
○ Vescovado '15	♈ 3
○ Vescovado '14	♈ 3
● Vurgadà '14	♈ 4

Serracavallo

C.DA SERRACAVALLO
87043 BISIGNANO [CS]
TEL. +39 098421144
www.viniserracavallo.it

CELLAR SALES
PRE-BOOKED VISITS
RESTAURANT SERVICE
ANNUAL PRODUCTION 80,000 bottles
HECTARES UNDER VINE 32.00
VITICULTURE METHOD Certified Organic

A few years ago, Demetrio Stancati found himself in the difficult position of having to choose between a career as a doctor and running the family estate. Finding himself at the stage where he could no longer do both, he hung up his white coat and rushe headlong into a new adventure. He started by building a modern cellar and replanting nearly all of the vineyards with native varieties. His Serracavallo wines seek out the generous, Mediterranean character of the Magliocco and Pecorello varieties. To great loss, these native grapes with impressive sensory potential aren't more recognized outside of the region. Our tasting confirms last year's momentum, and this year we're seeing the whites involved as well. The 2013 Vigna Savuco Riserva made it to our finals. It's a wine made with Magliocco grapes whose nose proves rich in fruit and balsamic hints. The mouth is powerful and exhibits a good balance between structure and acidity.

● Terre di Cosenza Colline del Crati Magliocco V. Savuco Ris. '13	▼▼
○ Petramola '16	▼▼
⊙ Terre di Cosenza Filì '16	▼▼
● Terre di Cosenza Quattro lustri '16	▼▼
● Terre di Cosenza Sette Chiese '16	▼▼
● Terre di Cosenza Terraccia '14	▼▼
○ Besidiae '16	▼
⊙ Terre di Cosenza Valle dei Crati Don Filì '16	▼
○ Besidiae '15	♈
⊙ Terraccia '12	♈
● Terre di Cosenza Sette Chiese '15	♈
● Vigna Savuco '12	♈
● Vigna Savuco '11	♈
● Vigna Savuco '10	♈

Spiriti Ebbri

VIA ROMA, 96
87050 SPEZZANO PICCOLO [CS]
TEL. +39 0984408992
www.spiritiebbri.com

CELLAR SALES
PRE-BOOKED VISITS
ANNUAL PRODUCTION 20,000 bottles
HECTARES UNDER VINE 2.50

In 2004, Pierpaolo Greco, Damiano Mele and Michele Scrivano put together a modest plan to produce a wine they could drink with family and friends. But as happens so often in cases like these the desire to prove oneself took over, and in 2011 the three put their wines on the market. Ever present, their Bohemian spirit prevailed when it came to choosing a name for the winery: Spiriti Ebbri. And remaining faithful to their philosophy they make the wines without using chemical products, additives or selected yeasts. All the wines presented were excellent, and the group earned themselves the award for 'Emerging Winery of the Year'. Their 2016 Pecorello Neostòs received a thoroughly-deserved Tre Bicchieri. Vibrant and fruity aromas are marked by hints of saffron and fresher overtones of Mediterranean scrub, while the palate proves intense, dynamic and deep.

○ Neostòs Bianco '16	♈♈♈	4*
● Neostòs Rosso '15	♈♈	4
● Appianum Rosso La Vigna di Alberto '15	♈♈	5
○ Cotidie Neostòs Bianco '16	♈♈	3
⊙ Neostòs Rosato '16	♈♈	4
● Cotidie Neostòs Rosso '15	♈	3

Luigi Viola

VIA ROMA, 18
87010 SARACENA [CS]
TEL. +39 0981349099
www.cantineviola.it

CELLAR SALES
PRE-BOOKED VISITS
ANNUAL PRODUCTION 15,000 bottles
HECTARES UNDER VINE 3.00
VITICULTURE METHOD Certified Organic

Fortunately, the world of Italian wine still provides treats for us, like the story of the hard-headed school teacher, Luigi Viola. For more than 20 years he labored to recover Moscato di Saracena wine, a relic of ancient and glorious history that left only traces in some yellowing pages of a local newspaper. Over this time Viola's Moscato slowly gained fame among the great Italian meditation wines, even becoming a Slow Food Presidium. Currently there are about a dozen producers, guaranteeing its legacy and indeed it now awaits DOC recognition. And by the way, it has set in motion a virtuous circle that has brought wine tourism and employment to Saracena. Hats off to Luigi. The 2016 Moscato Passito just missed out on a gold. A generous bouquet sees fragrances of white chocolate, dried figs, herbs and quince. The palate comes through large and fleshy, but well-supported by vibrant acidity. The 2015 Bianco Margherita, a blend of Guarnaccia and Mantonico, proves to be a complex, tangy and long wine.

○ Moscato Passito '16	♈♈	6
○ Bianco Margherita '15	♈♈	3
● Rosso Viola '14	♈	3
○ Moscato Passito '14	♈♈♈	6
○ Moscato Passito '13	♈♈♈	6
○ Moscato Passito '12	♈♈♈	6
○ Moscato Passito '11	♈♈♈	6
○ Moscato Passito '10	♈♈♈	6
○ Moscato Passito '09	♈♈♈	6
○ Moscato Passito '08	♈♈♈	6
○ Moscato Passito '07	♈♈♈	6
○ Moscato Passito '15	♈♈	6

Sergio Arcuri

VIA ROMA VICO PRIMO
88811 CIRÒ MARINA [KR]
TEL. +39 3280250255
www.sergioarcuri.it

CELLAR SALES
PRE-BOOKED VISITS
ANNUAL PRODUCTION 15,000 bottles
HECTARES UNDER VINE 3.68
VITICULTURE METHOD Certified Organic

● Cirò Rosso Cl. Sup. Aris '14	♟♟ 6
☉ Il Marinetto '16	♟♟ 3

Giuseppe Calabrese

VIA SANTA MARIA MADDALENA, 258
87010 SARACENA [CS]
TEL. +39 3406023820
www.giuseppe-calabrese.it

CELLAR SALES
ANNUAL PRODUCTION 4,000 bottles
HECTARES UNDER VINE 3.00

○ Moscato di Saracena Peppina '15	♟♟ 3*
○ Daipastini '16	♟♟ 2*
● Terre di Cosenza Magliocco '15	♟ 3

Cataldo Calabretta

VIA MANDORLETO, 47
88811 CIRÒ MARINA [KR]
TEL. +39 3923418219
www.cataldocalabretta.it

PRE-BOOKED VISITS
ANNUAL PRODUCTION 30,000 bottles
HECTARES UNDER VINE 13.50
VITICULTURE METHOD Certified Organic
SUSTAINABLE WINERY

○ Cirò Bianco '16	♟♟ 3
☉ Cirò Rosato '16	♟♟ 3
☉ Alicante Rosato '16	♟ 3
● Cirò Rosso Cl. '15	♟ 2

Caparra & Siciliani

BIVIO S.DA ST.LE 106
88811 CIRÒ MARINA [KR]
TEL. +39 0962373319
www.caparraesiciliani.com

CELLAR SALES
PRE-BOOKED VISITS
ANNUAL PRODUCTION 800,000 bottles
HECTARES UNDER VINE 180.00
VITICULTURE METHOD Certified Organic

● Mastro Giurato '14	♟♟ 3
● Cirò Rosso Cl. Sup. Ris. '14	♟ 2
● Cirò Rosso Cl. Sup. Volvito Ris. '14	♟ 2
● Cirò Solagi '15	♟ 2

Capoano

C.DA CERAMIDIO
88072 CIRÒ MARINA [KR]
TEL. +39 096235801
www.capoano.it

CELLAR SALES
ANNUAL PRODUCTION 100,000 bottles
HECTARES UNDER VINE 20.00

● Cirò Rosso Cl. Sup. Don Raffaele Ris. '14	♟♟ 5
● Cirò Rosso Cl. Sup. Neruda '15	♟♟ 3
○ Cirò Bianco '16	♟ 2
● Cirò Rosso Cl. '15	♟ 2

Casa Comerci

LOC. BADIA DI NICOTERA
C.DA COMERCI, 6
89844 NICOTERA [VV]
TEL. +39 09631976077
www.casacomerci.it

CELLAR SALES
PRE-BOOKED VISITS
ANNUAL PRODUCTION 45,000 bottles
HECTARES UNDER VINE 15.00
VITICULTURE METHOD Certified Organic

○ Libìci '12	♟♟ 3*
○ Rèfulu '13	♟ 2

Chimento

C.DA GALLICE - VESCOVADO
87043 BISIGNANO [CS]
TEL. +39 3358258627
www.cantinechimento.it

CELLAR SALES
PRE-BOOKED VISITS
ACCOMMODATION AND RESTAURANT SERVICE
ANNUAL PRODUCTION 40,000 bottles
HECTARES UNDER VINE 7.00

● Luigi Quattordici '14	🍷🍷 6
☉ Gallice '16	🍷 3
● Vescovado '14	🍷 4
● Vitulia '14	🍷 5

Cote di Franze

LOC. PIANA DI FRANZE
88811 CIRÒ MARINA [KR]
TEL. +39 3926911606
www.cotedifranze.it

CELLAR SALES
PRE-BOOKED VISITS
ANNUAL PRODUCTION 18,000 bottles
HECTARES UNDER VINE 9.00
VITICULTURE METHOD Certified Organic

● Cirò Rosso Cl. Sup. Ris. '13	🍷🍷 3
○ Kum'è '16	🍷🍷 2*
○ Cirò Bianco '16	🍷 2

De Mare

VIA SAFFO
88811 CIRÒ MARINA [KR]
TEL. +39 3393768853
www.cantinedemare.it

ANNUAL PRODUCTION 90,000 bottles
HECTARES UNDER VINE 28.00

● Cirò Rosso Cl. Sup. Tempo Reale Ris. '14	🍷🍷 3
○ Camelia '16	🍷 2
○ Cirò Bianco '16	🍷 2
○ Cirò Rosato Prima Luce '16	🍷 2

Cantina Enotria

LOC. SAN GENNARO
S.DA ST.LE JONICA, 106
88811 CIRÒ MARINA [KR]
TEL. +39 0962371181
www.cantinaenotria.com

CELLAR SALES
PRE-BOOKED VISITS
ANNUAL PRODUCTION 1,000,000 bottles
HECTARES UNDER VINE 170.00

☉ Cirò Rosato '16	🍷🍷 2*
○ Cirò Bianco '16	🍷 2
○ Novantuno '16	🍷 3

Ferrocinto

FRAZ. VIGNE
C.DA FERROCINTO
87012 CASTROVILLARI [CS]
TEL. +39 0981415122
www.ferrocinto.it

CELLAR SALES
PRE-BOOKED VISITS
ANNUAL PRODUCTION 700,000 bottles
HECTARES UNDER VINE 45.00
VITICULTURE METHOD Certified Organic

● Dovì Brut Rosé '14	🍷🍷 5
Terre di Cosenza Pollino	
Magliocco 24 Ris. '14	🍷🍷 4
Terre di Cosenza Pollino Bianco '16	🍷 4

Malena

LOC. PETRARO
S.DA ST.LE JONICA 106
88811 CIRÒ MARINA [KR]
TEL. +39 096231758
www.malena.it

CELLAR SALES
PRE-BOOKED VISITS
ANNUAL PRODUCTION 220,000 bottles
HECTARES UNDER VINE 16.00

☉ Bacco Rosato '16	🍷🍷 2*
☉ Cirò Rosato '16	🍷🍷 2*
● Cirò Rosso Cl. Sup.	
Pian della Corte Ris. '14	🍷🍷 3

Poderi Marini

LOC. SANT'AGATA
87069 SAN DEMETRIO CORONE [CS]
TEL. +39 36835250283683525028
www.poderimarini.it

CELLAR SALES
PRE-BOOKED VISITS
ANNUAL PRODUCTION 50,000 bottles
HECTARES UNDER VINE 7.00
VITICULTURE METHOD Certified Organic

● Elaphe '15	♟♟ 4
○ Koronè Bianco '16	♟♟ 2*
⊙ Koronè Rosato '16	♟ 2
● Koronè Rosso '15	♟ 2

Marrelli Wines

LOC. SANT'ANDREA
VIA DELL'ERICA, 28
88841 ISOLA DI CAPO RIZZUTO [KR]
TEL. +39 0962930276
www.marrelliwines.it

CELLAR SALES
PRE-BOOKED VISITS
ACCOMMODATION AND RESTAURANT SERVICE
ANNUAL PRODUCTION 50,000 bottles
HECTARES UNDER VINE 15.00

○ Miscello di Ripe '16	♟♟ 4
⊙ S. Anna di Isola Capo Rizzuto Bizantino Rosato '16	♟♟ 2*
● Lakinio '15	♟ 4

Masseria Falvo 1727

LOC. GARGA
87010 SARACENA [CS]
TEL. +39 098138127
www.masseriafalvo.com

CELLAR SALES
ANNUAL PRODUCTION 80,000 bottles
HECTARES UNDER VINE 26.00
VITICULTURE METHOD Certified Organic

○ Donna Filomena '16	♟♟ 3
○ Guarnaccia '15	♟♟ 2*
○ Hjur Passito '11	♟ 2
○ Terre di Cosenza Pollino Ris. '14	♟ 2

G.B. Odoardi

C.DA CAMPODORATO, 35
88047 NOCERA TERINESE [CZ]
TEL. +39 098429961
www.cantineodoardi.it

CELLAR SALES
ANNUAL PRODUCTION 120,000 bottles
HECTARES UNDER VINE 45.00

● Terra Damia '14	♟♟ 3
○ Terra Damia '16	♟ 2

Tenute Pacelli

FRAZ. PAUCIURI
C.DA ROSE
87010 MALVITO [CS]
TEL. +39 09841634348
www.tenutepacelli.it

CELLAR SALES
PRE-BOOKED VISITS
ACCOMMODATION
ANNUAL PRODUCTION 15,000 bottles
HECTARES UNDER VINE 9.00
VITICULTURE METHOD Certified Organic
SUSTAINABLE WINERY

● Terra Rossa '16	♟♟ 3
⊙ Terra Rosa '16	♟ 2

La Pizzuta del Principe

LOC. PIZZUTA
88816 STRONGOLI [KR]
TEL. +39 096288252
www.lapizzutadelprincipe.it

CELLAR SALES
PRE-BOOKED VISITS
ACCOMMODATION AND RESTAURANT SERVIC
ANNUAL PRODUCTION 80,000 bottles
HECTARES UNDER VINE 13.00

○ Molarella '16	♟♟
● Anno Quinto '09	♟
● Jacca Ventu '15	♟
○ Melissa Bianco Santa Focà '16	♟

Fattoria San Francesco

Loc. Quattromani
88813 Cirò [KR]
Tel. +39 096232228
www.fattoriasanfrancesco.it

CELLAR SALES
PRE-BOOKED VISITS
ANNUAL PRODUCTION 224,000 bottles
HECTARES UNDER VINE 40.00

⊙ Cirò Rosato '16	♀♀ 2*
● Cirò Rosso Cl. '15	♀♀ 2*
● Vigna Corta '15	♀♀ 3
○ Cirò Bianco '16	♀ 2

Senatore Vini

Loc. San Lorenzo
88811 Cirò Marina [KR]
Tel. +39 096232350
www.senatorevini.com

CELLAR SALES
PRE-BOOKED VISITS
ANNUAL PRODUCTION 280,000 bottles
HECTARES UNDER VINE 30.00
SUSTAINABLE WINERY

⊙ Cirò Rosato Puntalice '16	♀♀ 3
● Unico Senator '10	♀♀ 7
○ Eukè '16	♀ 3
● Nerello '12	♀ 4

Statti

C.da Lenti
88046 Lamezia Terme [CZ]
Tel. +39 0968456138
www.statti.com

CELLAR SALES
PRE-BOOKED VISITS
RESTAURANT SERVICE
ANNUAL PRODUCTION 300,000 bottles
HECTARES UNDER VINE 100.00

● Arvino '15	♀♀ 2*
○ Greco '16	♀♀ 2*
● Lamezia Batasarro Ris. '15	♀♀ 4
● Gaglioppo '16	♀ 2

Tenuta del Travale

Loc. Travale, 13
87050 Rovito [CS]
Tel. +39 3937150240
www.tenutadeltravale.it

CELLAR SALES
PRE-BOOKED VISITS
ANNUAL PRODUCTION 14,000 bottles
HECTARES UNDER VINE 2.00
SUSTAINABLE WINERY

● Eleuteria '14	♀♀ 6

Terre del Gufo - Muzzillo

C.da Albo San Martino, 22a
87100 Cosenza
Tel. +39 0984780364
www.terredelgufo.it

CELLAR SALES
PRE-BOOKED VISITS
ANNUAL PRODUCTION 25,500 bottles
HECTARES UNDER VINE 3.00

○ Terre di Cosenza Chiaroscuro '16	♀♀ 2*
Terre di Cosenza Portapiana '15	♀♀ 4
● Timpamara '15	♀♀ 5
Kaulos '16	♀ 3

Terre di Balbia

C.da Montino
87042 Altomonte [CS]
Tel. +39 098435359
www.terredibalbia.it

CELLAR SALES
PRE-BOOKED VISITS
ANNUAL PRODUCTION 10,270 bottles
HECTARES UNDER VINE 8.00

● Fervore '15	♀♀ 5
⊙ Ligrezza '16	♀♀ 4
● Blandus '15	♀ 5

Terre Grecaniche

VIA A. FERRARO, 1
89038 PALIZZI [RC]
TEL. +39 0965769703
www.terregrecaniche.it

CELLAR SALES
PRE-BOOKED VISITS
ACCOMMODATION AND RESTAURANT SERVICE
ANNUAL PRODUCTION 20,000 bottles
HECTARES UNDER VINE
VITICULTURE METHOD Certified Organic

● Aranghia Rosso '14	♟♟ 3
● Aranghia Bariccato '14	♟ 3
○ Calanchi '16	♟ 3
⊙ Damusa '16	♟ 3

Tenuta Terre Nobili

LOC. CARIGLIALTO
87046 MONTALTO UFFUGO [CS]
TEL. +39 0984934005
www.tenutaterrenobili.it

CELLAR SALES
PRE-BOOKED VISITS
ACCOMMODATION
ANNUAL PRODUCTION 80,000 bottles
HECTARES UNDER VINE 15.00
VITICULTURE METHOD Certified Organic

● Alarico '16	♟♟ 3
● Ipazia '16	♟♟ 6
○ Santa Chiara '16	♟♟ 2*
⊙ Donn'Eleonò '16	♟ 2

Tramontana

LOC. GALLICO MARINA
VIA CASA SAVOIA, 156
89139 REGGIO CALABRIA
TEL. +39 0965370067
www.vinitramontana.it

CELLAR SALES
PRE-BOOKED VISITS
ANNUAL PRODUCTION 200,000 bottles
HECTARES UNDER VINE 41.00

● 1890 '14	♟♟ 5
○ 5 Generazioni '16	♟♟ 2*
○ Duemiladodici '16	♟ 3
● Pellaro '15	♟ 2

Vulcano Wine

VIA INDIPENDENZA, 11
88811 CIRÒ MARINA [KR]
TEL. +39 096235381
www.vulcanowine.com

ANNUAL PRODUCTION 250,000 bottles
HECTARES UNDER VINE 4.00

○ Cirò Bianco Capo a Frutto '16	♟♟ 2*
● Cirò Rosso Cl. Cordòne '16	♟ 3

Cantine Zagarella

VIA ROMA, 2
89121 REGGIO CALABRIA
TEL. +39 0965679521
www.aziendazagarella.it

ANNUAL PRODUCTION 45,000 bottles
HECTARES UNDER VINE 9.00

○ Alfieri Bianco '16	♟ 2
● Alfieri Rosso '15	♟ 2
● Terragrande '14	♟ 2

Zito

LOC. PUNTA ALICE
VIA SCALARETTO
88811 CIRÒ MARINA [KR]
TEL. +39 096231853
www.zito.it

CELLAR SALES
PRE-BOOKED VISITS
ANNUAL PRODUCTION 800,000 bottles
HECTARES UNDER VINE 80.00

○ Cirò Bianco Nosside '15	♟♟ 2*
⊙ Cirò Rosato Imerio '16	♟♟ 2*
● Cirò Rosso Cl. Sup. Casale Difesa Difesa Piana '15	♟♟ 2*

SICILY

With some 22 awards, Sicily has confirmed that it's one of Italy's work horses when it comes to wine. The region has never been in such good form, offering a multifaceted, captivating array of wines. It's a region that can stand shoulder-to-shoulder with the world's most prestigious terroir, with its stylistically well-crafted wines, thanks to forward-thinking agronomic choices made years ago, which see native grape varieties, especially, benefitting. And this also testifies to the enological skill of the region's producers, as well as the entrepreneurs who've been driving the region's success. Another aspect that deserve's mention is the progress being made by Sicily's cooperative wineries, which have taken a new direction more focused on technique. It's bringing deserved critical success and, in general, excellent performance on both national and international markets. Credit is due to increasingly professional management, made up increasingly well-trained (and experienced) winemakers and sales directors. Their wines are achieving wider market shares and the results benefit thousands of families who depend on the land. Of course, this should take nothing from the region's wine families, from its small and medium-sized producers who have served as the core artificers of the Sicilian renaissance over the past two decades, and are moving full-speed-ahead. In our opinion, its no coincidence that so many wineries have embraced the DOC Sicilia appellation, which, as of 2017, applied to 30 million bottles of wine (in 2012, there were fewer than 500,000)! The regional system of viticulture is solid by now, bolstering the image of its products and contributing to the island's status as a veritable international brand. Looking more closely, we see the Etna phenomenon hitting its stride, with some nine wines receiving honors this year (including Etna DOC, Sicilia DOC and IGT), confirming this extraordinary territory's value. Finally, we'd like to make note of this year's newcomers to the club of Italian winemaking excellence. Alessandro di Camporeale, an inspiring family-run winery, gave us the excellent 2016 Catarratto Vigna di Mandranova. Etna's Tornatore delivered with their delectable 2015 Etna Rosso. And, last but not least, Nino Caravaglio gave rise to the extraordinary 2016 Malvasia delle Lipari Passito. This last is a great wine, for us the 'Sweet Wine of the Year'.

Abbazia Santa Anastasia

C.DA SANTA ANASTASIA
90013 CASTELBUONO [PA]
TEL. +39 0921671959
www.abbaziasantanastasia.com

CELLAR SALES
PRE-BOOKED VISITS
ACCOMMODATION AND RESTAURANT SERVICE
ANNUAL PRODUCTION 400,000 bottles
HECTARES UNDER VINE 67.50
VITICULTURE METHOD Certified Organic
SUSTAINABLE WINERY

In 1982, Franco Lena purchased a 300-hectare hill estate immersed in the Maquis shrubland. Thanks to the engineer's passion, this center of culture, which has hosted Theatine and Benedictine monks since the 12th century, has been revived. Today, the ancient monastery is an elegant, country relais, with gorgeous vineyards that span almost 70 hectares. The particular characteristics of the terroir, and the owner's heightened sensitivity to the environment, have given rise to a high-quality selection of wines that represent both organic and biodynamic agriculture. The 2013 Litra has confirmed its class. This austere and elegant Cabernet Sauvignon, vibrant ruby red in color, offers up hints of black cherry jam, cloves, mint and walnut skin. The mouth proves silky, cosseting and very gratifying. The citrusy 2013 Grecanico Terre di Anastasia Brut and the very pleasant 2014 Passomaggio, made with Nero d'Avola, Merlot and Cabernet Sauvignon, were also in the spotlight.

● Litra '13	▼▼	7
● Passomaggio '14	▼▼	3
● Sens(i)nverso Nero d'Avola '14	▼▼	4
○ Terre di Anastasia Brut '13	▼▼	6
○ Grillo '16	▼	2
● Nero d'Avola '16	▼	2
○ Sens(i)nverso Chardonnay '15	▼	4
○ Sinestesia '16	▼	4
● Litra '04	♀♀♀	6
● Litra '01	♀♀♀	7
● Montenero '04	♀♀♀	4
● Montenero '13	♀♀	4
● Passomaggio '13	♀♀	3
○ Q 1000 M. Cl. '13	♀♀	5

Alessandro di Camporeale

C.DA MANDRANOVA
90043 CAMPOREALE [PA]
TEL. +39 092437038
www.alessandrodicamporeale.it

CELLAR SALES
PRE-BOOKED VISITS
ANNUAL PRODUCTION 180,000 bottles
HECTARES UNDER VINE 35.00
VITICULTURE METHOD Certified Organic

A territory (Camporeale and the hills surrounding the Mandranova plains) and a family (the Alessandros, whose viticultural roots in the territory go back four generations). These are the basis for a winery founded in 2000 by the Natale brothers, Nino and Rosolino. Along with their children, they oversee every stage of production, from the certified organic cultivation of their vineyards, to winemaking, to wine-tourism efforts and the international sales of the wines themselves (which spans 15 countries). Their recent commitment to Mt. Etna has been bolstered by the acquisition of new vineyards in Castiglione di Sicilia. The Sicilian 2016 Vigna di Mandranova, made with grapes from the Cataratto cru, has won hands down. It offers up perfectly-focused, deep and elegant notes of medlar, citrus fruit and spices. The mouth opens fresh and tangy, with a wonderful textured pulp and a long, well-defined finish. The 2015 Syrah Kaid also made it to the finals, with its close-focused fruit, its stylish and graceful palate, and its nice balsamic encore.

○ Sicilia Catarratto V. di Mandranova '16	▼▼▼	4*
● Sicilia Syrah Kaid '15	▼▼	3*
● Kaid V. T. '16	▼▼	5
○ Sicilia Catarratto Benedè '16	▼▼	2*
○ Sicilia Grillo V. di Mandranova '16	▼▼	3
● Sicilia Nero d'Avola Donnatà '16	▼▼	2*
○ Sicilia Sauvignon Blanc Kaid '16	▼▼	3
● Kaid '13	♀♀	3*
● Kaid V. T. '15	♀♀	5
● Kaid V. T. '14	♀♀	5
○ Sicilia Catarratto Benedè '15	♀♀	2*
○ Sicilia Catarratto V. di Mandranova '15	♀♀	4
● Sicilia DonnaTà '14	♀♀	2*
● Sicilia Syrah Kaid '14	♀♀	3*

Assuli

C.DA CARCITELLA
91026 MAZARA DEL VALLO [TP]
TEL. +39 0923546706
www.assuli.it

CELLAR SALES
ANNUAL PRODUCTION 100,000 bottles
HECTARES UNDER VINE 100.00

Roberto Caruso's ties to the territory of
Sicilia Occidentale go back to the work of
his father, an esteemed entrepreneur and
decorated citizen who worked in marble
extraction (and owned vineyards). Two years
ago, the winery took on its current form,
with the family vineyards coming to span
100 hectares, divided into four plots: Besi
(in Castelvetrano), Fontanabianca (in Salemi,
at 52 hectares this is also the largest),
Conca (Calatafimi-Segesta) and Carcitella
(Mazara del Vallo). The last of these also
serves as the site of a lovely cellar, which is
adorned with Sicilian pearl marble, the
stone discovered and promoted by
Roberto's father, Giacomo. The 2015 Astolfo
premiers with a Tre Bicchieri. It's a Grillo
partly aged in barriques sur lies. Focused
and intense aromas make a full return in
exceptionally concentrated fruit, with a clear,
long finish. The 2016 Lorlando is back in
the finals. This Nero d'Avola is deep and
elegant close-focused notes of cherry,
balsamic and green capers. The mouth
comes through lively, round and lingering.

Astolfo '15	♛♛♛ 4*
Sicilia Nero d'Avola Lorlando '16	♛♛ 3*
Besi '14	♛♛ 5
Donna Angelica '15	♛♛ 3
Fiordiligi '16	♛♛ 2*
Carinda '16	♛ 2
Ruggiero '16	♛ 2
Lorlando '15	♛♛♛ 2*
Lorlando '14	♛♛♛ 2*
Baltasàr '12	♛♛ 5
Carinda '15	♛♛ 2*
Fiordiligi '15	♛♛ 2*
Melkior '12	♛♛ 4
Ruggiero '15	♛♛ 2*

Baglio del Cristo di Campobello

C.DA FAVAROTTA
S.DA ST.LE 123 KM 19,200
92023 CAMPOBELLO DI LICATA [AG]
TEL. +39 0922 877709
www.cristodicampobello.it

PRE-BOOKED VISITS
ANNUAL PRODUCTION 300,000 bottles
HECTARES UNDER VINE 30.00

The Bonetta family's 50 hectare estate,
which includes 30 hectares of vineyards, is
situated in the hills at an altitude of 350
meters. Here, the chalky, calcareous soil is
constantly caressed by the salty breeze of
the nearby coast. The winery, which is
among Sicily's leaders in terms of quality,
also benefits from the dedication and skill
of its owners. With pride, they work to
represent the territory's agricultural
traditions, and Sicilian identity, in part by
bringing these together with a modern,
forward-thinking vision (as evidenced by
their wise decision to renovate the historic,
Sicilian wine baglio). The 2016 Adènzia
Bianco has leapt into the finals. This
successful blend of Inzolia and Grillo proved
to be a hit thanks to its great finesse and
well-defined fragrances of damsons, white
peaches and almonds, supported by a
vibrant mineral background. The palate is
elegant and impressive. The spicy and racy
Lusirà, made with Syrah, the traditionally
styled Nero d'Avola Lu Patri and the fruity
Chardonnay Laudàri (all from the 2015
vintage) are all excellent,.

○ Sicilia Bianco Adènzia '16	♛♛ 3*
● C'D'C' Rosso Cristo di Campobello '16	♛♛ 2*
○ Sicilia Chardonnay Laudàri '15	♛♛ 4
○ Sicilia Grillo Lalùci '16	♛♛ 3
● Sicilia Nero d'Avola Lu Patri '15	♛♛ 5
● Sicilia Syrah Lusirà '15	♛♛ 5
○ C'D'C' Bianco Cristo di Campobello '16	♛ 2
⊙ C'D'C' Cristo di Campobello Rosato '16	♛ 2
● Lu Patri '09	♛♛♛ 5
○ C'D'C' Cristo di Campobello Bianco '15	♛♛ 2*
⊙ C'D'C' Cristo di Campobello Rosato '15	♛♛ 2*
○ Sicilia Bianco Adènzia '15	♛♛ 3
○ Sicilia Chardonnay Laudàri '13	♛♛ 4
● Sicilia Rosso Adènzia '14	♛♛ 3*

Baglio di Pianetto

LOC. PIANETTO
VIA FRANCIA
90030 SANTA CRISTINA GELA [PA]
TEL. +39 0918570002
www.bagliodipianetto.it

CELLAR SALES
PRE-BOOKED VISITS
ACCOMMODATION AND RESTAURANT SERVICE
ANNUAL PRODUCTION 550,000 bottles
HECTARES UNDER VINE 104.00
SUSTAINABLE WINERY

In 1997, Count Paolo Marzotto's love for Sicily took shape among the high hills of Santa Cristina Gela (near Palermo), where he transformed a historic wine baglio into a charming and cozy agritourism. In addition to this estate, Baglio di Pianetto manages vineyards in the district of Baroni (in Pachino), in the southernmost part of Sicily. In both cases, a sensitivity to sustainability brought about a complete conversion to organic of their more than 100 hectares of vineyards. Since 2017, that commitment has also shown in the cellar, with the introduction of a number of 'natural' wines made with native yeasts and without added sulfites. The 2014 Shymer, a blend of Syrah and Merlot, is back with Tre Bicchieri. It's a full-bodied, elegant and intense wine, with subtle balsamic hints and a plush, round and lingering palate. The new and pleasant 2014 Syraco from the Tenuta Baroni is fully ripe, with hints of spice and small red fruit. In the mouth it features great grip and roundness. The 2013 Moscato Ra'is is delicately aromatic and appealing.

● Shymer '14	▼▼▼ 2*
○ Moscato di Noto Ra'is '13	▼▼ 5
○ Sicilia Timeo '16	▼▼ 3
● Syraco '14	▼▼ 3
● Carduni '13	▼ 5
○ Sicilia Bianco Ficiligno '16	▼ 4
○ Sicilia Ginolfo '16	▼ 4
● Ramione '04	▽▽▽ 3*
● Shymer '13	▽▽▽ 2*
● Sicilia Rosso Ramione '13	▽▽▽ 3*
● Carduni '12	▽▽ 5
○ Moscato di Noto Ra'is Essenza '12	▽▽ 5
● Salici '12	▽▽ 4
● Sicilia Ramione '14	▽▽ 4

Barone di Villagrande

VIA DEL BOSCO, 25
95025 MILO [CT]
TEL. +39 0957082175
www.villagrande.it

CELLAR SALES
PRE-BOOKED VISITS
ACCOMMODATION AND RESTAURANT SERVICE
ANNUAL PRODUCTION 180,000 bottles
HECTARES UNDER VINE 19.00
VITICULTURE METHOD Certified Organic

Baroni di Villagrande's story is a long and lovely one. It starts in the late 17th century, when the Nicolosi Asmundo family moved to Etna and began farming (their success was such that, a few decades later, Emperor Carlo VI conferred on them the title of Baron). Since then, some 10 generations have passed and today it's Marco Nicolosi, and his wife, Barbara, who lead this inspiring family business. The couple deserve credit for modernizing the cellar, redesigning their label and realizing a charming wine resort. Under Marco's attentive technical direction (he graduated in enology), the wines have finally found the right direction. They are elegant and well-crafted, fully expressing the attributes of the grapes and territory of Etna. In the spotlight is the 2013 Etna Rossa Contrada Villagrande. The wine ages for a long period in chestnut barrels and features fragrances of flowers, minerals and small red fruit. It's tannic and austere on the palate, with a nice fruity encore.

● Etna Rosso Contrada Villagrande '13	▼▼ 6
○ Etna Bianco Sup. Contrada Villagrande '13	▼▼ 6
⊙ Etna Rosato '16	▼▼ 3
● Etna Rosso '15	▼▼ 3
○ Malvasia delle Lipari '13	▼▼ 5
○ Etna Bianco Sup. '16	▼ 2
⊙ Salina Bianco '16	▼ 3
○ Etna Bianco Legno di Conzo Sup. '08	▽▽ 6
○ Etna Bianco Sup. '13	▽▽ 2
○ Etna Bianco Sup. '12	▽▽ 4
● Etna Rosso '12	▽▽ 3
● Etna Rosso '11	▽▽ 4
● Fiore di Villagrande '12	▽▽ 4
○ Fiore di Villagrande '11	▽▽ 4

Tenuta Bastonaca

C.DA BASTONACA
97019 VITTORIA [RG]
TEL. +39 0932686480
www.tenutabastonaca.it

CELLAR SALES
ACCOMMODATION
ANNUAL PRODUCTION 40,000 bottles
HECTARES UNDER VINE 10.00
SUSTAINABLE WINERY

There's good news for this commendable winery. Owners Silvana Raniolo and Giovanni Calcaterra purchased more terrain in Vittoria, bringing the estate to a total of 15 hectares (ten of which are vineyards and five of which are olive groves). Moreover, the new land is on Etna, in the district of Solicchiata (Castiglione di Sicilia), a small plot of fewer than two hectares that includes 50-year-old Nerello Mascalese, Cappuccio and Carricante vines. The winery has a vision of agriculture that could be called 'natural', adopting a system of exclusively non-irrigated, head-trained vines. As of the 2017 vintage, they will be certified organic. The 2015 Cerasuolo di Vittoria almost made it into the finals. It's a wine that features great personality. Vibrant overtones of mulberries, bilberries and violets are laced with notes of chocolate, pencil lead and licorice. In the mouth it proves fresh, elegant and lingering, with pleasant and polished tannins. Their two new wines also delivered. The balsamic 2015 Sud is made with Nero d'Avola, Grenache and Tannat, and the 2014 Etna Rosso features elegance and typicity.

● Cerasuolo di Vittoria '15	♟♟ 3
● Etna Rosso '14	♟♟ 4
● Frappato '16	♟♟ 3
○ Grillo '16	♟♟ 3
● Nero d'Avola '16	♟♟ 3
● Sud '15	♟♟ 5
● Cerasuolo di Vittoria '14	♟♟ 3
● Frappato '15	♟♟ 3
○ Grillo '15	♟♟ 3
● Nero d'Avola '15	♟♟ 3

★Benanti

VIA GIUSEPPE GARIBALDI, 361
95029 VIAGRANDE [CT]
TEL. +39 095/893399
www.benanti.it

CELLAR SALES
PRE-BOOKED VISITS
RESTAURANT SERVICE
ANNUAL PRODUCTION 160,000 bottles
HECTARES UNDER VINE 28.00
SUSTAINABLE WINERY

Stirred by his family's background in vine growing and winemaking, Giuseppe Benanti has been investing, since the late 1980s, time and resources into supporting Etna's native grape varieties. This required demanding study of the various districts, exposures and positions, as well as identifying the proper models and traditional methods. If, today, Etna is experiencing a revival, it's thanks to this brilliant, decorated citizen and his sons, Antonio and Salvino. The intriguing 2015 Etna Rosso is a pale garnet wine with orange glints. It opens with elegant and charming hints of blackcurrants, yellow peaches and blueberries, embellished with notes of wilted violets, cinnamon, pepper, peppermint and pencil lead. The intense and traditionally styled 2013 Sierra della Contessa and the mineral and lively 2016 Etna Bianco are also top-notch.

● Etna Rosso '15	♟♟ 3*
○ Etna Bianco '16	♟♟ 4
● Etna Rosso Serra della Contessa '13	♟♟ 7
● Il Monovitigno Nerello Mascalese '14	♟♟ 5
○ Etna Bianco Sup. Pietramarina '13	♟ 5
● Etna Rosso Rovittello '13	♟ 5
● Il Monovitigno Nerello Cappuccio '15	♟ 5
○ Etna Bianco Sup. Pietramarina '09	♟♟♟ 5
○ Etna Bianco Sup. Pietramarina '04	♟♟♟ 6
● Etna Rosso Serra della Contessa '06	♟♟♟ 7
● Etna Rosso Serra della Contessa '04	♟♟♟ 7
● Il Drappo '04	♟♟♟ 5
● Etna Rosso '14	♟♟ 4
● Etna Rosso Nerello Mascalese '13	♟♟ 5

Bonavita

LOC. FARO SUPERIORE
C.DA CORSO
98158 MESSINA
TEL. +39 3471754683
www.bonavitafaro.com

PRE-BOOKED VISITS
ANNUAL PRODUCTION 10,000 bottles
HECTARES UNDER VINE 2.50

In 1977, when the Faro DOC zone was established, Giovanni Scarfone still hadn't been born. Even so, his grandfather worked a hectare of land in Faro Superiore. 25 years later he gave it to his recently-graduated grandson, a decision that allowed Giovanni the satisfaction of bottling the first Bonavita wine. Not a lot has changed since then, Giovanni continues to work with the same enthusiasm and passion that drove him in his first days. Over time, his wines have gained in definition and prestige, without losing that 'backyard wine' aura that has allowed them to stand out since the first vintage. The 2015 Faro is as impressive and true to character as ever. This elegant and austere wine offers up distinctive aromas of red fruit jam, spices and Mediterranean forest floor. The palate exhibits a lovely fruity and mineral structure, supported by a vibrant tannic texture that's still unbridled. The 2016 Rosato is pleasantly rustic, with iodine on the nose. It's fresh, long and flowing on the palate.

● Faro '15	♀♀	5
☉ Rosato '16	♀♀	2*
● Faro '14	♀♀	5
● Faro '13	♀♀	5
● Faro '12	♀♀	5
● Faro '11	♀♀	5
● Faro '10	♀♀	5
● Faro '09	♀♀	5
● Faro '08	♀♀	5
☉ Rosato '15	♀♀	2*
☉ Rosato '14	♀♀	2*
☉ Rosato '13	♀♀	2*
☉ Rosato '12	♀♀	2*
☉ Rosato '09	♀♀	2*

Tenute Bosco

S.DA PROV.LE 64 SOLICCHIATA
95012 CASTIGLIONE DI SICILIA [CT]
TEL. +39 0957658856
www.tenutebosco.com

CELLAR SALES
PRE-BOOKED VISITS
ANNUAL PRODUCTION 50,000 bottles
HECTARES UNDER VINE 10.00
VITICULTURE METHOD Certified Organic

Years ago, the volcano cast a spell on Sofia and Concetto Bosco. Since then, a crescendo of passion has led to the revival of the two areas of land that make up the estate, as well as the construction of a charming, modern cellar in lava that integrates perfectly with the setting. Their 10 hectares of vineyards (four of which are revered, pre-phylloxera, head-trained vines) are situated in the municipality of Castiglione di Sicilia, on the north face of Etna, at 700 meters above sea level, and comprises territories in the districts of Piano dei Daini (in Solicchiata) and Santo Spirito (in Passpisciaro). A thoroughly-deserved finals for the 2014 Etna Rosso Vigna Vico. It offers up an elegant bouquet of wilted red roses, black cherries, saffron, Saturn peach, licorice and slate, while the palate proves vibrant, juicy and very lingering. The complex and deep 2015 Etna Rosso Piano dei Daini and its twin, the 2016 Etna Bianco are also outstanding, with the latter featuring extreme finesse, close-focused fruit and wonderful drinkability.

● Etna Rosso Vigna Vico '14	♀♀	8
○ Etna Bianco Piano dei Daini '16	♀♀	5
☉ Etna Rosato Piano dei Daini '16	♀♀	5
● Etna Rosso Piano dei Daini '15	♀♀	5

aravaglio

. MALFA SALINA
NAZIONALE, 33
050 MALFA [ME]
. +39 3398115953
avagliovini@virgilio.it

ELLAR SALES
E-BOOKED VISITS
NUAL PRODUCTION 50,000 bottles
CTARES UNDER VINE 12.00
TICULTURE METHOD Certified Organic
STAINABLE WINERY

ho Caravaglio is a true vine grower, a man
ose personality is both sunny and
losive. After studying agronomy, he
mpletely dedicated himself to producing
lvasia. In 1992, he started with a hectare
vineyards, planted by his parent's house,
d since then he hasn't stopped. He now
nages 12 hectares, scattered throughout
island in 40 different plots. From the
ginning, he's shown extreme care for the
vironment and the fragile, Aeolian
crosystems here, choosing to adopt organic
tivation methods. Indeed, he went so far as
receive organic certification from an outside
hority, before it was even offered in Italy. In
dition to earning top-honors, their
ectable 2016 Malvasia Passito wins our
veet Wine of the Year' award: a passito
d-grape wine with complex aromas of
ndied citrus fruit, apricots, peaches,
dicinal herbs and lavender all set on an
ine background. In the mouth, it's a
asterpiece of balance between sweet fruit
d a fresh crisp acidity that makes it
remely pleasant to drink, even with a
ory dish like sea urchin bruschetta.

Malvasia delle Lipari Passito '16	♈♈♈ 5	
nfatata '16	♈♈ 3	
Malvasia '16	♈♈ 5	
lero du Munti '16	♈♈ 4	
cchio di Terra '16	♈♈ 3	
nfatata '15	♈♈ 3	
nfatata '14	♈♈ 3	
nfatata '13	♈♈ 3	
Malvasia delle Lipari Passito '14	♈♈ 5	
Malvasia delle Lipari Passito '13	♈♈ 5	
Malvasia delle Lipari Passito '12	♈♈ 5	
lero du Munti '14	♈♈ 4	
cchio di Terra '15	♈♈ 3	
alina Bianco '13	♈♈ 3	

Le Casematte

LOC. FARO SUPERIORE
C.DA CORSO
98163 MESSINA
TEL. +39 0906409427
www.lecasematte.it

CELLAR SALES
ANNUAL PRODUCTION 30,000 bottles
HECTARES UNDER VINE 11.00
VITICULTURE METHOD Certified Organic
SUSTAINABLE WINERY

The small DOC zone of Faro is experiencing a
moment of glory thanks to the passionate
producers who believed in it. Gianfranco
Sabbatino, an accountant, and the footballer
Andrea Barzagli, are among those that helped
lead the way, dedicating resources and
showing commitment to the area. The winery
is situated in a singular territory, on the high
hills that overlook the Straight of Messina. The
land is arduous, windy and steep, and gets its
name from the three World War II era
casemates (a kind of military fort) that were
built here. It's an inspiring winery that pursues
what could be defined a decidedly artisanal
style. Tre Bicchieri for the 2015 Faro, a wine
made with Nerello Mascalese, Cappuccio,
Nero d'Avola and Nocera. It thrilled the
commission with its deep and complex
nuances calling up of black cherries,
redcurrants, violets, chocolate and tobacco.
It's a very elegant wine, with tight-knit tannins
and an incredible mouthfeel. Almost on the
same level is the charming 2015 Peloro
Rosso, made with Nerello Mascalese and
Nocera.

● Faro '15	♈♈♈ 5	
● Peloro Rosso '15	♈♈ 2*	
○ Peloro Bianco '16	♈♈ 3	
⊙ Rosematte Nerello Mascalese '16	♈♈ 3	
● Faro '14	♈♈♈ 5	
● Faro '13	♈♈♈ 5	
● Figliodiennenne '12	♈♈ 2*	
○ Peloro Bianco '15	♈♈ 3	
○ Peloro Bianco '14	♈♈ 3	
● Peloro Rosso '14	♈♈ 2*	
● Peloro Rosso '13	♈♈ 2*	
⊙ Rosematte '14	♈♈ 3	
⊙ Rosematte '13	♈♈ 3	
⊙ Rosematte Nerello Mascalese '15	♈♈ 3	

Terra Costantino

VIA GARIBALDI, 417
95029 VIAGRANDE [CT]
TEL. +39 095434288
www.terracostantino.it

CELLAR SALES
PRE-BOOKED VISITS
ANNUAL PRODUCTION 40,000 bottles
HECTARES UNDER VINE 7.00
VITICULTURE METHOD Certified Organic

The father-son team of Dino and Fabio
Costantino are joined together by a common
passion for viticulture. Their winery is
situated in Blandano, on the south side of
Etna, in the municipality of Viagrande, one
of the oldest and best-suited areas for vine
growing in the foothills of this moody
volcano. At between 550 and 650 meters
above sea level, the estate offers a view of
the Ionian sea, but most importantly it
receives its benefits. And during winter, it's
also protected from the cold northern winds
by the volcano at its back. Exclusively native
grape varieties are grown on their seven
hectares of certified organic vineyards. The
2014 Etna Rosso Contrada Blandano is
very much in line with the surrounding
territory. It's a mineral, savory, almost earthy
wine that's rich in fruit on the palate.The
2014 Etna Bianco Contrada Blandano is
also very pleasant. It's iodine, floral and
fresh, and plays well with the balance
between fruit and tanginess in the mouth.

○ Etna Bianco Contrada Blandano '14	♀♀ 5
☉ Etna Rosato De Aetna '16	♀♀ 3
● Etna Rosso Contrada Blandano '14	♀♀ 5
● Etna Rosso De Aetna '15	♀ 3
○ Etna Bianco De Aetna '15	♀ 3
○ Etna Bianco Blandano '13	♀♀ 5
☉ Etna Rosato De Aetna '14	♀♀ 3
● Etna Rosso De Aetna '14	♀♀ 3
● Etna Rosso De Aetna '13	♀♀ 3

Cottanera

LOC. IANNAZZO
S.DA PROV.LE 89
95030 CASTIGLIONE DI SICILIA [CT]
TEL. +39 0942963601
www.cottanera.it

CELLAR SALES
PRE-BOOKED VISITS
ANNUAL PRODUCTION 350,000 bottles
HECTARES UNDER VINE 65.00

With the rehabilitation of an ancient,
amphitheater-shaped vineyard just by the
cellar, the Cambria family now has 65
hectares at its disposal (60 of which are
Nerello and Carricante). Thus Cottanera
has grown into one of the largest estates
on Etna. At the same time, they work on
individual plots, so as to be able (in a few
years) to bottle and label all their wines
according to their district of origin.
Cambria's wines are polished and
technically exemplary, but territory and
cultivar are increasingly central concerns.
Tre Bicchieri for the 2013 Etna Riserva
Zottorinoto, an elegant and complex wine.
It's a noble expression of the terroir which,
if interpreted well, as it is here, makes for
wines with incredible finesse and
personality. The 2014 Etna Feudo di Mezzo
is excellent, with rich and complex aromas
on the nose and lovely fruit supported by
savory acidity that lengthens an unending,
fresh finish.

● Etna Rosso Zottorinoto Ris. '13	♀♀♀
○ Etna Bianco Calderara '15	♀♀
● Etna Rosso Feudo di Mezzo '14	♀♀
○ Barbazzale Bianco '16	♀♀
○ Etna Bianco '16	♀♀
☉ Etna Rosato '16	♀♀
● Etna Rosso Barbazzale '16	♀♀
● Etna Rosso Diciassettesalme '15	♀♀
● Sicilia Sole di Sesta '14	♀♀
○ Etna Bianco '11	♀♀♀
● Etna Rosso '11	♀♀♀
● Etna Rosso Zottorinoto Ris. '12	♀♀♀
● Etna Rosso Zottorinoto Ris. '11	♀♀♀

★★Cusumano

C.DA SAN CARLO
S.DA ST.LE 113 KM 307
90047 PARTINICO [PA]
TEL. +39 0918908713
www.cusumano.it

CELLAR SALES
PRE-BOOKED VISITS
ANNUAL PRODUCTION 2,500,000 bottles
HECTARES UNDER VINE 520.00
SUSTAINABLE WINERY

For some time now, Alberto and Diego Cusumano's inspiring winery has been a Sicilian icon. It all started in the first years of the new millennium, when the two producers chose to draw on ancient family traditions and found Cusumano. Their wines come from different plots, from Ficuzza to Etna, Butera and Pachino, expressing the different terroir and grapes (both native and international) in a modern way. They've been rewarded for their innovative, contemporary approach and commitment to quality by success in major international markets. Once again, the magnificent 2016 Alta Mora Bianco has earned the gold. It offers up sophisticated aromas of peach and slate, while on the mouth it proves vibrant, long and pleasant with strong personality. Of the wines from Butera, the complex and deep 2015 Nero d'Avola Sàgana stands out. It's a wine that's true to character, balsamic and fruity with great structure. The rest of their selection also proved top-notch.

Etna Bianco Alta Mora '16	▼▼▼	4*
Etna Rosso Guardiola Alta Mora '14	▼▼	7
Sicilia Noà '15	▼▼	4
Sicilia Sàgana '15	▼▼	4
Angimbè Tenuta Ficuzza '16	▼▼	3
Benuara Tenuta Presti e Pegni '16	▼▼	3
Etna Rosso Alta Mora '15	▼▼	4
Etna Rosso Feudo di Mezzo Alta Mora '14	▼▼	6
Moscato dello Zucco '11	▼▼	5
Sicilia Jalé '15	▼▼	4
Etna Bianco Alta Mora '14	♀♀♀	3*
Moscato dello Zucco '10	♀♀♀	5
Sàgana '12	♀♀♀	4*
Sicilia Noà '13	♀♀♀	4*

★Donnafugata

VIA S. LIPARI, 18
91025 MARSALA [TP]
TEL. +39 0923724200
www.donnafugata.it

CELLAR SALES
PRE-BOOKED VISITS
ANNUAL PRODUCTION 2,240,000 bottles
HECTARES UNDER VINE 338.00
SUSTAINABLE WINERY

Giacomo Rallo's legacy is in the capable hands of his sons, Antonio and Josè. Along with their mother, Gabriella, they continue to keep alive the success of a winery that has represented the best of Sicilian vine growing and winemaking culture for 35 years. The historic facilities in Marsala are the heart of operations. Inaugurated in 2008, they feature a spectacular underground barrique cellar. The other winemaking facilities and vineyards are in Contessa Entellina (270 hectares) and Pantelleria (68). They recently added 18 hectares in Acate, where Donnafugata kicked off the year with Bell'Assai 2016, a lively Frappato in the Vittoria appellation. The enchanting 2015 Ben Ryé has once again earned a Tre Bicchieri. The nose sees incredible expressiveness, with intense and focused notes of peach, apricot and lavender honey, plus a distinctive mineral finesse. Its sweetness is kept in check by a pulp with incredible density and seemingly endless length. Lastly, the 2012 Mille e una Notte proves to be an intense and firmly-structured wine.

○ Passito di Pantelleria Ben Ryé '15	▼▼▼	7
● Mille e una Notte '12	▼▼	7
● Cerasuolo di Vittoria Bell'Assai '16	▼▼	3
○ Sicilia Contessa Entellina Chiarandà '14	▼▼	5
○ Sicilia Contessa Entellina La Fuga '16	▼▼	3
● Sicilia Nero d'Avola Sherazade '16	▼▼	3
○ Sicilia V. di Gabri '15	▼▼	3
○ Sicilia Zibibbo Lighea '16	▼▼	3
● Tancredi '13	▼▼	5
○ Sicilia Grillo SurSur '16	▼	3
● Sicilia Rosso Angheli '14	▼	4
○ Passito di Pantelleria Ben Ryé '14	♀♀♀	7
○ Passito di Pantelleria Ben Ryé '12	♀♀♀	7
○ Passito di Pantelleria Ben Ryé '11	♀♀♀	7
● Tancredi '11	♀♀♀	5

Duca di Salaparuta

VIA NAZIONALE
S.DA ST.LE 113
90014 CASTELDACCIA [PA]
TEL. +39 091945201
www.duca.it

PRE-BOOKED VISITS
ANNUAL PRODUCTION 9,000,000 bottles
HECTARES UNDER VINE 155.00

Two icons of Sicilian wine, two great parallel paths met thanks to the decision by ILLVA group (owner of Florio) to acquire Corvo in 2001 (a producer that was previously managed by the region of Sicily). The Florio brand encompasses Marsala and their high-quality sweet wines, while Corvo includes their mid-range wines, as well as Duca di Salaparuta (their most prestigious line). Great care goes into their hospitality services at their gorgeous Marsala facility and the historic cellars of Cordo di Casteldaccia (which, as of spring 2017, were completely renovated). The winery's two brands put in a memorable performance this year: the Duca Enrico reached the finals and 2013 saw a return to the finesse, complexity, character and solidity of fruit that characterize the wine's best vintages. The 2006 Targa 1840 features an impressive sensory impact, great elegance and length, while the 2014 Passito di Pantelleria, with its close-focused notes of lavender and dried apricot, proves rich and invigorating in the mouth.

● Duca Enrico '13	♟♟	8
○ Marsala Sup. Semisecco Targa 1840 Ris. Florio '06	♟♟	4
○ Passito di Pantelleria Florio '14	♟♟	6
○ Bianca di Valguarnera '15	♟♟	6
● Calanica Frappato Syrah '15	♟♟	3
○ Calanica Grillo Viognier '16	♟♟	3
● Corvo Irmana '15	♟♟	3
○ Marsala Sup. Ambra Secco Vecchio Florio '13	♟♟	2*
○ Morsi di Luce Florio '13	♟♟	2*
● Passo delle Mule Suor Marchesa '14	♟♟	2*
● Vajasindi Làvico Nerello Mascalese '13	♟♟	5
● Vajasindi Nawàri '14	♟♟	5
● Duca Enrico '03	♟♟♟	6
● Duca Enrico '01	♟♟♟	6

Cantine Europa

S.DA ST.LE 115, KM 42,400
91020 PETROSINO [TP]
TEL. +39 0923961866
www.sibilianavini.it

CELLAR SALES
PRE-BOOKED VISITS
ANNUAL PRODUCTION 2,000,000 bottles
HECTARES UNDER VINE 6300.00

Cantine Europa represents one of Sicily's most important and dynamic co-operatives. Spread throughout the provinces of Agrigento, Palermo and Trapani, the winery is bolstered by its 2100 members and 6300 hectares of terrain. Mostly traditional varieties are cultivated, but well-suited international grapes are also grown. Since 2000, the producer has been led by Eugenio Galfano, a notary with a passion for agriculture. Recently Europa, the first and only co-operative in western Sicily, landed in Etna as well, founding Due Sorbi with a local partner. Their wines gave a brilliant performance this year, starting with the 2016 Roceno, a pleasant, fragrant and easy-drinking Frappato. The two wines from their Eughenès line also impressed: the fruity, plush and elegant 2016 Perricone, and the stylish, mature, deep and balsamic 2016 Nero d'Avola. The 2016 Roceno is right up there, a grassy Grillo with great depth, as is the 2016 Eughenès Grillo Zibibbo.

● Frappato Roceno '16	♟♟	1
○ Grillo Roceno '16	♟♟	2
○ Grillo Zibibbo Eughenès '16	♟♟	2
● Nero d'Avola Sensale '16	♟♟	1
● Sicilia Nero d'Avola Eughenès '16	♟♟	2
● Sicilia Perricone Eughenès '16	♟♟	2
● Sicilia Syrah Nero d'Avola Eughenès '16	♟♟	2
○ Grillo Sensale '16	♟	2
○ Grillo Zibibbo Eughenès '15	♀♀	2
● Nero d'Avola Capofeto '15	♀♀	1
○ Sicilia Grillo Eughenès '15	♀♀	2

Tenuta di Fessina

C.DA ROVITTELLO
VIA NAZIONALE, 22 S.DA ST.LE 120
95012 CASTIGLIONE DI SICILIA [CT]
TEL. +39 3458346477
www.tenutadifessina.com

CELLAR SALES
PRE-BOOKED VISITS
ANNUAL PRODUCTION 70,000 bottles
HECTARES UNDER VINE 13.00
SUSTAINABLE WINERY

Fessina is a happy and deep love story between Silvia Maestrelli (a Tuscan and citizen of the world) and the infinite beauty of Etna. It was a love that struck suddenly, during her travels, but it crystallized in 2007 with the purchase of certain plots of land, as well as an old palmento and baglio (traditional Sicilian winemaking facilities, both of which are now renovated). And, having optimized its small, modern production space, it's also in a position to offer four suites and four rooms as accommodations for the public. Today, this inspiring producer is among the most well-known and esteemed for the personality of its wines. A 2015 with great personality reached our finals: the Nerello Cappuccio Laeneo combines sophisticated nuances of black fruit, wilted violets and flint with an incredible taste texture. Then the refreshing balsamic and smoky notes emerge. Two 2016 whites are also in the spotlight, the tangy and mineral Etna Bianco Erse and the Etna Bianco 'A Puddara, a citrusy, fine and elegant wine.

Laeneo Nerello Cappuccio '15	♟♟ 3*
Etna Bianco A' Puddara '16	♟♟ 5
Etna Bianco Erse '16	♟♟ 4
Etna Rosato Erse '16	♟♟ 4
Etna Bianco A' Puddara '13	♟♟♟ 5
Etna Bianco A' Puddara '12	♟♟♟ 5
Etna Bianco A' Puddara '11	♟♟♟ 5
Etna Bianco A' Puddara '10	♟♟♟ 5
Etna Bianco A' Puddara '09	♟♟♟ 5
Etna Rosso Musmeci '07	♟♟♟ 6
Etna Bianco A' Puddara '14	♟♟ 5
Etna Bianco Erse '15	♟♟ 4
Etna Rosso Erse '15	♟♟ 4

Feudi del Pisciotto

C.DA PISCIOTTO
93015 NISCEMI [CL]
TEL. +39 09331930280
www.castellare.it

CELLAR SALES
PRE-BOOKED VISITS
ACCOMMODATION
ANNUAL PRODUCTION 200,000 bottles
HECTARES UNDER VINE 45.00

After lengthy, detailed renovations, Paolo Panerai has returned the palmento of Feudo del Pisciotto to its original splendor. Today, the large manner house in Siracusa boasts an elegant wine relais, a restaurant and a tasting room (for the producer's wines). Year after year, the technical staff, led by Alessandro Cellai, manages to outdo itself in terms of finding the right balance between terroir and grape, making for original, intense and concentrated wines that, during the hottest vintages, leave little to chance. The 2015 Cerasuolo di Vittoria Giambattista Valli Paris earned Tre Bicchieri. It won over the judges with its typicity, which is expressed on the nose with hints of red fruits, violets and a well-defined mineral note. On the palate, it proves austere and rich in fruit at the same time, with a refined tannic texture and fresh, lively acidity. The 2015 Passito Gianfranco Ferrè, made with Traminer and Semillon, also proved outstanding. It's a complex wine, certainly not cloying.

● Cerasuolo di Vittoria Giambattista Valli Paris '15	♟♟♟ 6
○ Gianfranco Ferrè '15	♟♟ 5
● Nero d'Avola Versace '15	♟♟ 4
● Cabernet Sauvignon Missoni '15	♟♟ 4
● Frappato Carolina Marengo Kisa '15	♟♟ 4
● L'Eterno '15	♟♟ 7
● Merlot Valentino '15	♟♟ 4
○ Tirsat Gurra di Mare '15	♟♟ 4
○ Chardonnay Alberta Ferretti '15	♟ 4
○ Grillo Kisa '16	♟ 4
● Cerasuolo di Vittoria Giambattista Valli Paris '12	♟♟♟ 6
● Cerasuolo di Vittoria Giambattista Valli Paris '11	♟♟♟ 6
● Frappato Carolina Marengo '11	♟♟♟ 4*
● Nero d'Avola Versace '12	♟♟♟ 4*

Feudo Maccari

C.DA MACCARI
S.DA PROV.LE PACHINO-NOTO KM 13,500
96017 NOTO [SR]
TEL. +39 0931596894
www.feudomaccari.it

CELLAR SALES
PRE-BOOKED VISITS
ANNUAL PRODUCTION 167,000 bottles
HECTARES UNDER VINE 50.00
SUSTAINABLE WINERY

Antonio Moretti loves Sicily so much that, if it weren't for constant business travels on behalf of his holding company, he would live here (he just bought a beautiful estate on Mt. Etna). And, if with Saia, his Nero d'Avola brought him great satisfaction, now he's focusing on Grillo, with the intention of making a white wine of great character. After detailed study of clones and a host of trial runs in the cellar, the first results have been more than positive. Thus, year after year, Family and Friends gains in complexity and prestige. Tre Bicchieri for the formidable 2015 Nero d'Avola Saia, a Mediterranean wine with trademark fragrances of topsoil and black fruit. Balsamic, herbaceous and mineral notes complete a well-rounded and lingering profile. In the mouth, it proves well-structured, elegant and succulent, spruced up by good tannins and fresh acidity. The 2015 Syrah Maharis is warm and caressing, with a juicy and gratifying finish.

● Sicilia Saia '15	♥♥♥	4*
○ Family and Friends '16	♥♥	5
● Sicilia Maharis '15	♥♥	5
○ Grillo '16	♥♥	2*
○ Sultana '14	♥♥	5
● Saia '14	♥♥♥	4*
● Saia '13	♥♥♥	4*
● Saia '12	♥♥♥	4*
● Saia '11	♥♥♥	4*
● Saia '10	♥♥♥	4*
● Saia '08	♥♥♥	4*
○ Family and Friends '15	♥♥	5
● Sicilia Mahâris '13	♥♥	5
● Sicilia Syrah Mahâris '14	♥♥	5

Feudo Montoni

C.DA MONTONI VECCHI
92022 CAMMARATA [AG]
TEL. +39 091513106
www.feudomontoni.it

CELLAR SALES
PRE-BOOKED VISITS
ANNUAL PRODUCTION 205,000 bottles
HECTARES UNDER VINE 30.00
VITICULTURE METHOD Certified Organic
SUSTAINABLE WINERY

Dated 1469, today Feudo Montoni's singularly beautiful baglio serves as the producer's beating heart, as well as representing the history of the area's high aristocracy. The Sireci bought the estate in the late 1800s, having been attracted to the terrain's particular characteristics and the wide range of temperatures between day and night, both of which make for for unique grapes (olives and grains are also cultivated here). In recent years, Fabio Sireci, the winery's passionate, curious and determined leader, has brought out their characteristics and potential, making Montoni's selection a must for those who love 'tailored' wines, that is, multifaceted wines of strong character. The entire selection is improving in terms of sensory quality and definition. At the forefront is the elegant 2013 Nero d'Avola Vrucara, a wine with a strong personality that combines richness of fruit and fresh taste. The balsamic 2015 Perricone is on the same level, as is the delicate and elegant 2016 Nerello Mascalese Rosa di Adele, a juicy and lively rosé that's hard to forget.

○ Passito Bianco	♥♥	5
⊙ Sicilia Nerello Mascalese Rose di Adele '16	♥♥	2
● Sicilia Nero d'Avola V. Lagnusa '15	♥♥	4
● Sicilia Nero d'Avola Vrucara '13	♥♥	4
● Sicilia Perricone V. del Core '15	♥	3
○ Sicilia Catarratto V. del Masso '16	♥	2
○ Sicilia Grillo V. della Timpa '16	♥	3
○ Sicilia Inzolia dei Fornelli '16	♥	3
● Nero d'Avola Vrucara '12	♀♀	5
○ Sicilia Grillo V. della Timpa '15	♀♀	3
○ Sicilia Grillo V. della Timpa '14	♀♀	3
○ Sicilia Inzolia dei Fornelli '15	♀♀	3
● Sicilia Nero d'Avola V. Lagnusa '14	♀♀	4
● Sicilia Perricone V. del Core '14	♀♀	3

Feudo Principi di Butera

C.DA DELIELLA
93011 BUTERA [CL]
TEL. +39 0934347726
www.feudobutera.it

CELLAR SALES
PRE-BOOKED VISITS
ANNUAL PRODUCTION 800,000 bottles
HECTARES UNDER VINE 180.00
SUSTAINABLE WINERY

The ancient Feudo (renovated with loving care by the Zonin family) overlooks 350 hectares of countryside in the provinces of Agrigento and Caltanissetta, not far from the sea of Gela. Just over half of the terrain is actually cultivated, in an area that features calcareous soil, wide temperature ranges and sea winds. These factors contribute to the character and polish of the producer's wines. 2017 saw the birth of Deroluce, an 'Italian method' wine made with Nero d'Avola fermented without skin contact. The young, skilled agronomist and winemaker, Antonio Paolo Froio, oversees management of the vineyards and cellar. The 2015 Syrah was a complete surprise, winning Tre Bicchieri with its elegant nose of small red fruit embellished by balsamic and spicy nuances. In the mouth it's a dynamic wine that's rich in fruit, and it finishes with impeccable length. The 2015 Symposio, a blend of Cabernet Sauvignon, Merlot and Petit Verdot, also made it to the finals. It exhibits good fruitiness, elegant green notes, and proves racy with an assertive texture.

Sicilia Syrah '15	🏆🏆🏆 3*
Symposio '15	🏆🏆 5
Sicilia Brut Neroluce	🏆🏆 3
Sicilia Cabernet Sauvignon '15	🏆🏆 3
Sicilia Nero d'Avola '15	🏆🏆 3
Sicilia Chardonnay '16	🏆 3
Sicilia Insolia Serò '16	🏆 4
Sicilia Nero d'Avola Deliella '15	🏆 6
Cabernet Sauvignon '00	🏆🏆🏆 5
Deliella '12	🏆🏆🏆 6
Deliella '05	🏆🏆🏆 6
Deliella '02	🏆🏆🏆 7
Deliella '00	🏆🏆🏆 6
Sicilia Deliella '13	🏆🏆🏆 6

Cantine Fina

C.DA BAUSA
91025 MARSALA [TP]
TEL. +39 0923733070
www.cantinefina.it

CELLAR SALES
PRE-BOOKED VISITS
ACCOMMODATION
ANNUAL PRODUCTION 350,000 bottles
HECTARES UNDER VINE 180.00
VITICULTURE METHOD Certified Organic

The Moorish baglio that hosts the Fina family's cellar is situated in Bausa, high atop a hill looking out over the nearby sea of Stagnone. The winery starting bottling in 2005, with the technical aspects overseen by founder, Bruno Fina, and his son, Sergio (while his other children, Marco and Federica, handle public relations and reception). The vineyards are spread throughout western Sicily, at altitudes ranging from 150 to 700 meters above sea level. The highest ridges host international, white varieties like Traminer, Sauvignon Blanc and Viognier. Over the years, we have learnt to appreciate Fina's white wines. Now we're spoilt for choice between these and her reds. How to choose between the fresh grapefruit and Mediterranean herbs of the 2016 Taif (made with Zibibbo), and the intense fruit, balsamic notes and liveliness of the 2014 Caro Maestro (a blend of Cabernet Sauvignon, Merlot and Petit Verdot)? The rest of the selection also did well.

● Caro Maestro '14	🏆🏆 5
○ Chardonnay '15	🏆🏆 3
○ Kebrilla Grillo '16	🏆🏆 2*
○ Kikè Traminer Aromatico '16	🏆🏆 3
● Perricone '16	🏆🏆 3
○ Taif '16	🏆🏆 3
○ Kebrilla '13	🏆🏆 2*
○ Kikè '15	🏆🏆 3
○ Kike '14	🏆🏆 3
● Perricone '15	🏆🏆 3
○ Sauvignon Blanc '15	🏆🏆 3
○ Sauvignon Blanc '14	🏆🏆 3

★Firriato

LOC. PACECO
VIA VIA TRAPANI, 4
91027 PACECO [TP]
TEL. +39 0923526766
www.firriato.it

CELLAR SALES
PRE-BOOKED VISITS
ANNUAL PRODUCTION 6,000,000 bottles
HECTARES UNDER VINE 320.00
VITICULTURE METHOD Certified Organic

Three territories (Trapani, Etna and Favignana), six estates, a crescendo of success, two brilliant visionaries that have left their mark on the history of current Sicilian wine culture … Salvatore and Vinzia di Gaetano continue to produce surprising wines, bringing together high production volumes and values such as a commitment to quality, love for the expressive capacities of each terroir, and respect for the environment through organic farming. The second generation, represented by Firriato, Irene and her husband, Federico Lombardo di Monte lato, are now active in managing the family business. Nero d'Avola, Perricone, Frappato and Nerello Cappuccio are the key players in the magical blend of native grapes that is the 2014 Quater Vitis, a Tre Bicchieri award-winner. It offers up elegant and complex fruity, spicy and balsamic aromas, with a silky and bold structure. The 2013 Coturnie, delicately complex on the nose and sensational in the mouth, also made it to the finals, as did the 2014 Passulé, an aromatic and sensual wine.

● Quater Vitis Rosso '14	▼▼▼ 4*
● Etna Rosso Cavanera Rovo delle Coturnie '13	▼▼ 6
○ Favinia Passulé '14	▼▼ 6
● Camelot '13	▼▼ 5
○ Etna Bianco Cavanera Ripa di Scorciavacca '15	▼▼ 6
○ Etna Bianco Santagostino Baglio Soria '16	▼▼ 4
○ Quater Vitis Bianco '16	▼▼ 4
● Ribeca '15	▼▼ 6
○ Sicilia Catarratto Caeles '16	▼▼ 3
● Sicilia Nero d'Avola Caeles '14	▼▼ 3
○ Favinia La Muciara '14	▽▽▽ 5
● Harmonium '13	▽▽▽ 5
● Santagostino Rosso Baglio Soria '12	▽▽▽ 4*
● Santagostino Rosso Baglio Soria '11	▽▽▽ 4*

Graci

LOC. PASSOPISCIARO
C.DA FEUDO DI MEZZO
95012 CASTIGLIONE DI SICILIA [CT]
TEL. +39 3487016773
www.graci.eu

CELLAR SALES
PRE-BOOKED VISITS
ANNUAL PRODUCTION 65,000 bottles
HECTARES UNDER VINE 18.00
VITICULTURE METHOD Certified Organic

In addition to a joint venture with Angelo Gaja (which will operate independent of the family), in 2017, Alberto Graci pulled off another stunner, purchasing the gorgeous, historic villa that once belonged to the family of Catania's Ettore Maiorana, a physicist. The estate features some 10 hectares of vineyards (currently being replanted) and, more importantly, a 19th century villa with a still operational palmento. Alberto's wines, which are polished but never over-the-top, are always respectful of terroir. Once again, this year, they've distinguished themselves for the close-focused expressiveness of the principal variety used. Two wines in the finals narrowly missed getting a gold. The rest of the selection's excellent performance testifies to the high level of quality reached in just a few years. The very elegant 2015 Etna Rosso Feudo di Mezzo is balsamic and mineral on the nose, racy and rich in pulp on the palate. The 2016 Etna Bianco is very refined, with fresh, mineral and citrusy fragrances.

○ Etna Bianco '16	▼▼
● Etna Rosso Feudo di Mezzo '15	▼▼
⊙ Etna Rosato '16	▼▼
● Etna Rosso Arcurìa '15	▼▼
○ Etna Bianco '10	▽▽▽
○ Etna Bianco Arcurìa '11	▽▽▽
○ Etna Bianco Quota 600 '10	▽▽▽
● Etna Rosso Arcurìa '13	▽▽▽
● Etna Rosso Arcurìa '12	▽▽▽
○ Etna Bianco '14	▽▽
○ Etna Bianco Arcuria '12	▽▽
● Etna Rosso Arcurìa '14	▽▽
● Etna Rosso Feudo di Mezzo '14	▽▽
● Etna Rosso Quota 600 '11	▽▽

Hauner

LOC. SANTA MARIA
VIA G.GRILLO, 61
98123 MESSINA
TEL. +39 0906413029
www.hauner.it

CELLAR SALES
PRE-BOOKED VISITS
ANNUAL PRODUCTION 80,000 bottles
HECTARES UNDER VINE 18.00

When, in the early 1960s, Carlo Hauner came to Salina as a tourist, Malvasia delle Lipari was practically extinct. Phylloxera and the gradual disuse of the countryside had relegated this precious sweet wine to a thing of the past, a faded memory in a page of Dumas or Maupassant, and nothing more. Hauner, an artist from Brescia, adopted the Aeolian islands as his new home, and with a scholar's loving care, he managed to revive a set of viticultural traditions that are as difficult as they are rewarding. His commitment continues, thanks to the work of his heir, Carlo Junior. In the finals once again is the thrilling 2014 Riserva di Malvasia Passito Carlo Hauner. It offers up an extremely complex, intense and seductive nose, with close-focused notes of dried figs, dates and an elegant iodine minerality. In the mouth it proves dense and round, with great sweetness well-balanced across its long structure. The 2016 Iancura is a very good Aeolian expression of the Malvasia and Inzolia blend.

Malvasia delle Lipari Passito Carlo Hauner Ris. '14	🍷🍷	8
Hierà Rosso '15	🍷🍷	3
Iancura '16	🍷🍷	2*
Malvasia delle Lipari Passito '15	🍷🍷	5
Salina Bianco '16	🍷🍷	2*
Hierà Rosato '16	🍷	3
Rosso Antonello '13	🍷	4
Salina Rosso '15	🍷	2
Malvasia delle Lipari Naturale '85	🍷🍷🍷	8
Malvasia delle Lipari Ris. '11	🍷🍷🍷	8
Malvasia delle Lipari Ris. '10	🍷🍷🍷	8
Hierà '14	🍷🍷	3
Malvasia delle Lipari Passito Carlo Hauner Ris. '13	🍷🍷	8
Salina Rosso '14	🍷🍷	2*

Cantine Mothia

VIA GIOVANNI FALCONE, 22
91025 MARSALA [TP]
TEL. +39 0923737295
www.cantine-mothia.com

CELLAR SALES
PRE-BOOKED VISITS
ANNUAL PRODUCTION 100,000 bottles
HECTARES UNDER VINE 25.00

The Bonomo family has operated in the wine industry for more than 50 years. For 20 of these, they've had an early 20th century baglio as their headquarters. For decades, the site was used for making wine from grapes cultivated on the island of Mozia and the surrounding area. The territory has, in large part, remained the same, with vineyards beaten by winds coming in off the Tyrrhenian coast that faces the Egadi and Stagnone. The barrique cellar houses Marsala, and the precious stocks of 40-plus-year-old Grillo, which constitutes one of the producer's crown jewels, the eternal Stella Fenicia. The 2016 Passito di Zibibbo Mulsum offers up fully defined aromas of apricot and candied orange peel, while the palate proves to be a smooth balance between sweetness and freshness, as well as long. The 2016 Vela Latina is a blend of Grillo and Damaschino, with notes of herbs, grapefruit and tangy fruit. The two 2016 Mosaikon also put in good performances. The Grillo is fleshy with elegant aromas, while the Nero d'Avola is fruity and pleasantly green.

○ Marsala Sup. Dolce Garibaldi The Thousand	🍷🍷	2*
○ Marsala Sup. Secco The Thousand	🍷🍷	2*
○ Mosaikon Grillo '16	🍷🍷	2*
● Mosaikon Nero d'Avola '16	🍷🍷	2*
○ Mulsum Passito di Zibibbo '16	🍷🍷	4
○ Vela Latina Grillo Damaschino '16	🍷🍷	2*
● Hammon '15	🍷	2
● Hammon '06	🍷🍷	2
● Mosaikon '15	🍷🍷	2*
● Mosaikon '05	🍷🍷	2*
○ Mulsum '08	🍷🍷	4
○ Mulsum V. T. '06	🍷🍷	4
● Nero d'Avola '12	🍷🍷	3

Cantine Nicosia

VIA LUIGI CAPUANA, 65
95039 TRECASTAGNI [CT]
TEL. +39 0957806767
www.cantinenicosia.it

CELLAR SALES
PRE-BOOKED VISITS
RESTAURANT SERVICE
ANNUAL PRODUCTION 1,800,000 bottles
HECTARES UNDER VINE 240.00
VITICULTURE METHOD Certified Organic
SUSTAINABLE WINERY

The Nicosia family has been tied to the
world of wine for more than 120 years, but
credit for the founding of the actual winery
must be given to its current owner,
Carmelo. He was the one who bought and
renovated the vineyards that host the large
cellar, which is also equipped with a lovely
hospitality space. He is flanked by his two
sons, Francesco and Graziano, while the
technical aspects of winemaking are
entrusted to enologist Maria Carella. The
vineyards on Etna are below Monte Gorna,
reaching 700 meters above sea level, but
they also have a notable plot of land in
Vittoria (in the district of Bonincontro). The
2016 Etna Bianco Fondo Filara earns a
gold. It offers up an intriguing nose of citrus
fruit and fine balsamic notes of wood resin.
The mouth opens with full, crisp fruit and
proves ample, long and clear at the end.
Accompanying it into the finals is the
2016 Frappato Fondo Filara, a wonderful
liquid expression of the southeastern half of
the estate, with fragrant and jovial aromas
and a fresh, lively mouth.

○ Etna Bianco Fondo Filara Contrada Monte Gorna '16	♥♥♥ 4*
● Sicilia Frappato Fondo Filara '16	♥♥ 3*
● Cerasuolo di Vittoria Cl. Fondo Filara '15	♥♥ 4
● Cerasuolo di Vittoria Hybla '16	♥♥ 2*
○ Etna Bianco Vign. Monte Gorna '13	♥♥ 6
● Etna Rosso Fondo Filara '15	♥♥ 4
● Etna Rosso Monte Gorna Ris. '11	♥♥ 6
● Nero d'Avola Sosta Tre Santi '11	♥♥ 5
● Nero d'Avola Sosta Tre Santi '10	♥♥♥ 5
○ Etna Bianco Contrada Monte Gorna '12	♥♥ 6
○ Etna Bianco Fondo Filara '15	♥♥ 4
● Etna Rosso Fondo Filara '13	♥♥ 4
● Sicilia Nerello Mascalese Fondo Filara '14	♥♥ 3

Occhipinti

S.DA PROV.LE 68 VITTORIA-PEDALINO KM 3,3
97019 VITTORIA [RG]
TEL. +39 09321865519
www.agricolaocchipinti.it

CELLAR SALES
PRE-BOOKED VISITS
ANNUAL PRODUCTION 130,000 bottles
HECTARES UNDER VINE 22.00
VITICULTURE METHOD Certified Organic
SUSTAINABLE WINERY

A lot of time has passed since Arianna, who
still hadn't received her degree in enology,
managed to convince her parents to entrust
her with just over a hectare of vineyards in
Fossa di Lupo, just next to the family's
centuries-old palmento. Driven by passion,
the student transformed the plot into a
veritable force of nature, as overwhelming
and exuberant as the wines it gave rise to.
And so it was that in just a few years,
Arianna took off, making her name one of
the most recognized and loved brands for
wine lovers around the world. It's a
transition vintage for Arianna and, while the
wines tasted showed personality and did a
nice job representing the territory, they still
found it hard to express their best. The
2014 Nero d'Avola Siccagno stalls a bit too
long on overripe aromas before giving way
to fresher herbaceous hints. The palate is
savory and marked by a nice fruity encore.
The 2016 SP 68 is a pleasant white wine
made with Moscato and Albanello.

● Il Frappato '15	♥♥ 6
● Siccagno '14	♥♥ 6
○ SP 68 Bianco '16	♥♥ 3
● SP 68 Rosso '16	♥ 3
● Il Frappato '12	♥♥♥ 5
● Il Frappato '11	♥♥♥ 5
● SP 68 Rosso '15	♥♥♥ 3
● Il Frappato '14	♥♥ 6
● Il Frappato '13	♥♥ 6
● Siccagno '13	♥♥ 6
● Siccagno '12	♥♥ 6
● Siccagno '11	♥♥ 5
○ SP 68 Bianco '14	♥♥ 3
● SP 68 Rosso '14	♥♥ 3

Tenute Orestiadi

V.LE SANTA NINFA
91024 GIBELLINA [TP]
TEL. +39 092469124
www.tenuteorestiadi.it

PRE-BOOKED VISITS
ANNUAL PRODUCTION 1,200,000 bottles
HECTARES UNDER VINE 120.00
VITICULTURE METHOD Certified Organic
SUSTAINABLE WINERY

Tenute Orestiadi is situated in the Valle del
Belice, primarily in an area straddling
Gibellina Vecchia, Mazara del Vallo and
Segesta, at altitudes ranging from 150 to
500 meters above sea level. Their vision
includes a desire to promote Sicilian grape
varieties, especially, in the name of quality
and in a way that best reflects their
potential. Their name evokes their fruitful
partnership with Fondazione Orestiadi (a
partnership whose roots go back to the
winery's beginnings), one of the most
well-respected cultural and artistic
institutions in the Mediterranean. The
2012 Ludovico, made with Nero d'Avola
and a dash of Cabernet Sauvignon, just
missed out on getting the highest honors.
Is magnificent, fresh fragrances of
blueberries and plums are spruced up with
a hint of capers, myrtle and juniper berries,
while the mouth features delightfully soft
and smooth tannins. The exquisite and
fruity 2015 Perricone is also top-quality, as
is the jovial and lively 2015 Frappato, with
its very pleasant mulberry overtones. The
rest of selection also proved sound.

Ludovico '12	▼▼ 4
Frappato '15	▼▼ 3
Molino a Vento Nerello Mascalese '16	▼▼ 2*
Molino a Vento Nero d'Avola '16	▼▼ 2*
Perricone '15	▼▼ 3
Zibibbo Pacènzia '16	▼ 3
Ludovico '11	♀♀ 5
Ludovico '10	♀♀ 5
Marchese Montefusco Nero d'Avola '13	♀♀ 3
Molino a Vento Nerello Mascalese '13	♀♀ 1*
Molino a Vento Nero d'Avola '15	♀♀ 2*
Molino a Vento Nero d'Avola '14	♀♀ 2*
Perricone '14	♀♀ 3

★Palari

LOC. SANTO STEFANO BRIGA
C.DA BARNA
98137 MESSINA
TEL. +39 090630194
www.palari.it

ANNUAL PRODUCTION 50,000 bottles
HECTARES UNDER VINE 7.00

Elegance is Salvatore Geraci's defining trait.
It's a quality that the architect and 'bon
vivant' (in the best sense of the term)
shares with his Faro, a wine that's both a
family legacy and a real gamble
(considering that in the 1980s it was on the
verge of total oblivion). Along with his
brother, Giampiero, he's revived cultivation
of the Nerello Mascalese, Nocera and Nero
d'Avola bush vines planted on his seven
hectares of steep hills along the Straight of
Messina. He's also transformed some of
the rooms in his ancestral villa into a
winemaking cellar. And so it is that his 'vine
de garage' has, in just a short time,
become legendary. It's actually happened:
the Rosso del Soprano, a second-label
wine and Palari's classy wingman, has
pipped its superior to the post. The 2015
vintage sees richly complex aromas of jam,
sweet spices, leather and tobacco following
through onto a memorably elegant palate.
Thus the wine surpasses the 2013 Faro,
despite the latter's intense bouquet and
very pleasant texture.

● Rosso del Soprano '15	▼▼▼ 4*
● Faro Palari '13	▼▼ 6
● Faro Palari '12	♀♀♀ 6
● Faro Palari '11	♀♀♀ 6
● Faro Palari '09	♀♀♀ 6
● Faro Palari '08	♀♀♀ 6
● Faro Palari '07	♀♀♀ 6
● Faro Palari '06	♀♀♀ 6
● Faro Palari '05	♀♀♀ 6*
● Faro Palari '04	♀♀♀ 7
● Faro Palari '03	♀♀♀ 6
● Faro Palari '02	♀♀♀ 6
● Rosso del Soprano '11	♀♀♀ 4*
● Rosso del Soprano '10	♀♀♀ 4*
● Rosso del Soprano '07	♀♀♀ 4

Passopisciaro

LOC. PASSOPISCIARO
C.DA GUARDIOLA
95030 CASTIGLIONE DI SICILIA [CT]
TEL. +39 0578267110
www.vinifranchetti.com

CELLAR SALES
ANNUAL PRODUCTION 75,000 bottles
HECTARES UNDER VINE 26.00

Andrea Franchetti's commitment and
passion has brought certain districts,
veritable crus, to light on Mt. Etna. These
vineyards, which are capable, in their
uniqueness, of giving rise to wines of
exceptional character and finesse, can be
found on the southern side of the volcano,
divided into small plots 500 meters apart,
from the highest, Rampante (at higher than
1000 meters), to the lowest,
Chiappemacine (at 550). The Nerello
Mascalese vines cultivated here are
anywhere from 70 to 100 years old. At
Guardiola there are international varieties
as well: Chardonnay, Petit Verdot and
Cesanese d'Affile. Tre Bicchieri for the
thrilling 2015 Sciaranuova. It offers up very
graceful and subtle balsamic notes of red
fruit and spices, which follow through onto
a seductively soft and long palate. The
2015 Guardiola also made it into our finals,
with more direct fruity aromas, elegant
mineral and animal notes and impeccable
texture. The 2015 Chiappemacine is
intense and pleasant, with lovely peach
jam overtones.

● Contrada Sciaranuova '15	♈♈♈ 6
● Contrada Guardiola '15	♈♈♈ 6
● Contrada Chiappemacine '15	♈♈ 6
● Contrada Porcaria '15	♈♈ 7
○ Passobianco '15	♈♈ 5
● Passorosso '15	♈♈ 5
● Contrada Rampante '15	♈ 6
● Contrada G '11	♈♈♈ 8
● Contrada P '10	♈♈♈ 7
● Contrada P '09	♈♈♈ 7
● Passopisciaro '04	♈♈♈ 5
● Contrada C '13	♈♈ 6
● Contrada P '13	♈♈ 7
● Contrada R '13	♈♈ 6
● Contrada S '13	♈♈ 6

Carlo Pellegrino

VIA DEL FANTE, 39
91025 MARSALA [TP]
TEL. +39 0923719911
www.carlopellegrino.it

CELLAR SALES
PRE-BOOKED VISITS
ANNUAL PRODUCTION 6,900,000 bottles
HECTARES UNDER VINE 150.00
SUSTAINABLE WINERY

In 1880, the notary Paolo Pellegrino, an
enthusiast of agriculture, founded a winery
that would leave its mark on the history of
Sicilian winemaking. These were the golden
years, years of success and expansion, of
commitment and dedication, that saw the
producer from Marsala go from being a
small, family-run business to a veritable
benchmark on the island, all under the
hallmark of quality. Today, the winery, which
has successfully wed its experience with
the changing needs of the modern world,
sees Pietro Alagna and Benedetto Renda a
the helm. The 2015 Passito di Pantelleria
Nes is a classy wine that flew into the
finals. It offers up captivating notes of
apricot, candied pear, dates and custard,
combined with refreshing hints of aniseed,
lavender and citron peel. Charming and
vibrant in the mouth, it elegantly caresses
the palate. The Marsala Superiore Rubino
Dolce is quite pleasant and racy, while the
rest of the wines also proved to be of very
high quality.

● Marsala Sup. Rubino Dolce	♈♈
○ Passito di Pantelleria Nes '15	♈♈
○ Gibelè '16	♈♈
○ Kelbi '16	♈♈
● Gazzerotta '14	♈
○ Marsala Sup. Ambra Semisecco Ris. '85	♈♈♈
○ Passito di Pantelleria Nes '09	♈♈♈
● Tripudium Rosso Duca di Castelmonte '13	♈♈♈
● Tripudium Rosso Duca di Castelmonte '09	♈♈♈
○ Duca di Castelmonte Gibelè '12	♈♈
○ Marsala Vergine Ris. '00	♈♈
○ Passito di Pantelleria Nes '12	♈♈
○ Passito di Pantelleria Nes Duca di Castelmonte '14	♈♈

Pietradolce

FRAZ. SOLICCHIATA
C.DA RAMPANTE
95012 CASTIGLIONE DI SICILIA [CT]
TEL. +39 3484037792
www.pietradolce.it

ANNUAL PRODUCTION 28,000 bottles
HECTARES UNDER VINE 13.00

Founded in 2005 by Mario and Michele
Faro, in just a short time Pietradolce has
become a benchmark on Etna and a cult
figure among wine lovers. It's all thanks to
the dedication and passion of these two
brothers, who revived their vineyards of
exclusively native grapes (in part
pre-phylloxera) and chose to a adopt a
model in which tradition and the utmost
respect for the territory are core principles.
Their fantastic, underground cellar, made of
lava covered with earth and aromatic herbs,
is a tangible manifestation of this vision.
The Vigna Barbagalli has stepped onto the
podium once again. The sensational 2014
edition has reached its highest level ever.
Notes of blueberries and Morello cherries
combine with wisteria, violets, cinchona and
pencil lead. The mouth proves invigorating,
its tannins are marvelously cosseting, with
a lavish palate. The rest of their selection is
also excellent, starting with the polished
2016 Etna Bianco.

● Etna Rosso V. Barbagalli '14	♟♟♟	8
○ Etna Bianco '16	♟♟	4
○ Etna Bianco Archineri '16	♟♟	6
⊙ Etna Rosato Pietradolce '16	♟♟	3
● Etna Rosso Archineri '15	♟♟	6
● Etna Rosso Contrada Rampante '15	♟♟	6
● Etna Rosso Pietradolce '16	♟♟	4
● Etna Rosso Archineri '10	♟♟♟	5
● Etna Rosso V. Barbagalli '13	♟♟♟	8
● Etna Rosso V. Barbagalli '12	♟♟♟	8
● Etna Rosso V. Barbagalli '11	♟♟♟	8
● Etna Rosso V. Barbagalli '10	♟♟♟	8
● Etna Rosso Archineri '14	♟♟	6
● Etna Rosso Archineri '13	♟♟	5

★★Planeta

C.DA DISPENSA
92013 MENFI [AG]
TEL. +39 091327965
www.planeta.it

PRE-BOOKED VISITS
ACCOMMODATION AND RESTAURANT SERVICE
ANNUAL PRODUCTION 2,400,000 bottles
HECTARES UNDER VINE 372.00
SUSTAINABLE WINERY

Planeta represents a breakthrough in the
way we view Sicilian business: the central
role of quality, attention to issues such as
the environment, cultural tradition, art,
promoting and protecting the appellations…
These are just some of the values that
made the winery led by Francesca, Alessio
and Santi into a model of development
capable of inspiring the entire sector. From
their cellar and vineyards of Ulmo (on Lake
Arancio), their estate has grown to include
the plots of la Dispensa (in Menfi), Dorilli (in
Vittoria), Buonivini (in Noto), Feudo di Mezzo
(on Mt. Etna) and La Baronia (in Capo
Milazzo). The 2016 Etna Bianco has
grabbed a Tre Bicchieri by pulling out a
range of aromas with exceptional
cleanness and clarity. We find white peach,
medlar and citrus fruit all intact in a fresh
and tangy mouthfeel. The premier of the
very pleasant 2015 Nocera, a wine with
incredible character, saw it reach our finals,
as did the 2013 Syrah Maroccoli, a more
mature and complex wine with solid fruit
and a nice balsamic encore.

○ Etna Bianco '16	♟♟♟	3*
● Maroccoli Syrah '13	♟♟	4
● Sicilia Nocera '15	♟♟	3*
● Cerasuolo di Vittoria '15	♟♟	3
● Cerasuolo di Vittoria Cl. Dorilli '15	♟♟	3
● Mamertino '15	♟♟	4
○ Menfi Fiano Cometa '16	♟♟	5
● Noto Santa Cecilia '14	♟♟	5
○ Riesling Eruzione 1614 '15	♟♟	4
● Vittoria Frappato '12	♟♟	3
● Cerasuolo di Vittoria Cl. Dorilli '14	♟♟♟	3*
● Cerasuolo di Vittoria Cl. Dorilli '13	♟♟♟	3*
● Cerasuolo di Vittoria Cl. Dorilli '12	♟♟♟	3*
○ Chardonnay '10	♟♟♟	5
● Noto Santa Cecilia '10	♟♟♟	5

Poggio di Bortolone

FRAZ. ROCCAZZO
VIA BORTOLONE, 19
97010 CHIARAMONTE GULFI [RG]
TEL. +39 0932921161
www.poggiodibortolone.it

CELLAR SALES
PRE-BOOKED VISITS
ACCOMMODATION AND RESTAURANT SERVICE
ANNUAL PRODUCTION 80,000 bottles
HECTARES UNDER VINE 15.00
SUSTAINABLE WINERY

Pierluigi Cosenza's wines are polished, summery and never overloaded, marked by their commendable quality and consistency. The winemaker has, over time, managed the difficult task of credibly giving voice to the two souls that struggle within Sicily's vine growing and winemaking culture. His Vittoria Cerasuolos, not mistakenly, are considered icons of the tradition by those who love wines that faithfully reflect territory and cultivar. At the same time, Pierluigi has also successfully used international varieties to produce wines capable of representing this corner of Sicily with lightness and originality. Due to a misprint, the 2014 vintage of the Pigi was erroneously reviewed last year. The 2013 Cerasuolo di Vittoria Il Para Para is a precise wine of rare finesse, almost etheric, with an accomplished expression of its terroir. It proves austere with a sophisticated complexity. The rest of the selection us also quite good, starting with the deep and elegant 2014 Contessa Costanza.

● Cerasuolo di Vittoria Il Para Para '13	♟♟ 4
● Addamanera '16	♟♟ 3
● Cerasuolo di Vittoria Cl. Contessa Costanza '14	♟♟ 3
● Cerasuolo di Vittoria Cl. Poggio di Bortolone '14	♟♟ 3
● Petit Verdò '16	♟♟ 3
● Sicilia Rosso Pigi '14	♟♟ 5
● Vittoria Frappato '16	♟♟ 3
● Cerasuolo di Vittoria V. Para Para '05	♟♟♟ 4
● Cerasuolo di Vittoria V. Para Para '02	♟♟♟ 4*
● Addamanera '14	♟♟ 2*
● Cerasuolo di Vittoria Cl. Poggio di Bortolone '13	♟♟ 3*
● Cerasuolo di Vittoria Il Para Para '12	♟♟ 4
● Petit Verdò '14	♟♟ 3
● Vittoria Frappato '15	♟♟ 2*

Rallo

VIA VINCENZO FLORIO, 2
91025 MARSALA [TP]
TEL. +39 0923721633
www.cantinerallo.it

CELLAR SALES
PRE-BOOKED VISITS
ANNUAL PRODUCTION 420,000 bottles
HECTARES UNDER VINE 110.00
VITICULTURE METHOD Certified Organic

Andrea Vesco has always taken pains to respect the environment and protect biodiversity. He started by converting his more than 100 hectares of vineyards to organic, a decision that, five years ago, seemed like the inevitable next step for his winery. The results of this long and demanding work, which required a major overhaul, are visible to everyone and, more importantly, they're reflected in the final product. Indeed, in recent years, this historic producer's wines have delivered more and more for their elegance, complexity and consistency over time. Once again, from a remarkable selection of wines, the whites come out on top. Tre Bicchieri for the 2016 Bianco Maggiore, a Grillo with well-defined and intense aromas of medlar, almond and citrus fruit. The palate is very fresh with inviting drinkability. The 2016 Zibibbo Al Quasar also made it into the finals, with its elegant herbaceous and citrusy fragrances. It's a vibrant, aromatic and long wine that's rich in pulp.

○ Sicilia Bianco Maggiore '16	♟♟♟ 3*
○ Al Qasar Zibibbo '16	♟♟ 3*
○ Sicilia Evrò '16	♟♟ 3
● Sicilia Il Manto '15	♟♟ 3
● Sicilia La Clarissa '15	♟♟ 2*
● La Zisa '13	♟ 2
○ Alcamo Beleda '15	♟♟♟ 4*
○ Alcamo Beleda '13	♟♟♟ 2*
○ Bianco Maggiore '12	♟♟♟ 3*
○ Sicilia Bianco Maggiore '14	♟♟♟ 3*
○ Al Qasar Zibibbo '15	♟♟ 3*
○ Alcamo Beleda '14	♟♟ 2*
● Sicilia Il Principe '14	♟♟ 2*

Tenute Rapitalà

C.DA RAPITALÀ
90043 CAMPOREALE [PA]
TEL. +39 092437233
www.rapitala.it

CELLAR SALES
PRE-BOOKED VISITS
ANNUAL PRODUCTION 2,600,000 bottles
HECTARES UNDER VINE 175.00

The Gruppo Italiano Vini's historic winery, Camporeale, is a truly formidable operation, with some 175 hectares of vineyards on some of the best-suited terrain in all of Sicily. The producer is bolstered by excellent agronomic management of its vast estate, as well as successful preventative measures, such as careful trimming and low yields. Along with the daily supervision of the vineyards (during the pre-harvest period), these factors assure that their grapes are sufficiently ripe and healthy when they arrive. Such qualities are reflected in their well-crafted, polished wines, representing the perfect mix of territory and cultivar. The 2014 Syrah Solinero is back in the finals, offering up fine balsamic and spicy hints and expanding harmoniously with good grip in the mouth. The 2015 Chardonnay Grand Cru Hugues Bernard de la Gatinais features measured wood and remarkable balance. Its well-defined aromas are floral and fruity, while the palate comes through invigorating and long.

● Solinero '14	▼▼ 5
○ Bouquet '16	▼▼ 3
○ Conte Hugues Bernard de la Gatinais Grand Cru '15	▼▼ 4
● Sicilia Alto Nero d'Avola '15	▼▼ 3
● Sicilia Nuhar '15	▼▼ 3
○ Alcamo Cielo d'Alcamo '13	▼ 5
○ Alcamo Cl. V. Casalj '16	▼ 3
○ Sicilia Grillo '16	▼ 2
○ Conte Hugues Bernard de la Gatinais Grand Cru '10	▽▽▽ 4*
○ Hugonis '01	▽▽▽ 6
● Solinero '03	▽▽▽ 5
○ Conte Hugues Bernard de la Gatinais Grand Cru '14	▽▽ 4
○ Sicilia Grillo '15	▽▽ 2*
○ Solinero '13	▽▽ 5

Riofavara

LOC. VAL DI NOTO
C.DA FAVARA
S.DA PROV.LE 49 ISPICA-PACHINO
97014 ISPICA [RG]
TEL. +39 0932705130
www.riofavara.it

CELLAR SALES
PRE-BOOKED VISITS
ACCOMMODATION
ANNUAL PRODUCTION 70,000 bottles
HECTARES UNDER VINE 27.00
VITICULTURE METHOD Certified Organic
SUSTAINABLE WINERY

This has been a year of transition for Massimo Padova, who, last year, completely shook up the technical staff at Riofavara. He now counts on the enological support of Graziana Grassini and agronomic expertise of Professor Lucio Brancadoro. But the news doesn't end here. Massimo planted 11 more hectares of vineyards (mostly head-trained) on a hill near the cellar, thus bringing the total estate to 27 hectares. The change of direction is already evident in their whites and early-drinking reds, which have made significant gains in terms of freshness and elegance. In the spotlight is the 2015 Nero d'Avola MDCXCIII. On the nose, it offers up fine hints of mulberries and medicinal herbs. In the mouth, there's a lovely nuance of smoked salt, in support of a solid fruity base, with rich and lively tannins. The 2016 Moscato Noto Notissimo offers up aromas of lavender, apricots and candied citrus fruit. It's fresh, with a nice balance between sugar and acidity.

○ Marzaiolo '16	▼▼ 3
○ Moscato di Noto Mizzica '16	▼▼ 3
○ Moscato di Noto Notissimo '16	▼▼ 3
● Sicilia MDCXCIII '15	▼▼ 5
● Eloro Nero d'Avola Spaccaforno '14	▼ 4
● Eloro Sciavè '14	▼ 5
● San Basilio '15	▼ 3
● Eloro Nero d'Avola Sciavè '12	▽▽ 5
● Eloro Nero d'Avola Spaccaforno '13	▽▽ 4
● Eloro Nero d'Avola Spaccaforno '12	▽▽ 3
○ Marzaiolo '15	▽▽ 3
○ Marzaiolo '14	▽▽ 3
○ Moscato di Noto Mizzica '15	▽▽ 3
● S. Basilio '13	▽▽ 2*

Girolamo Russo

LOC. PASSOPISCIARO
VIA REGINA MARGHERITA, 78
95012 CASTIGLIONE DI SICILIA [CT]
TEL. +39 328384024/
www.girolamorusso.it

CELLAR SALES
PRE-BOOKED VISITS
ANNUAL PRODUCTION 65,000 bottles
HECTARES UNDER VINE 15.00
VITICULTURE METHOD Certified Organic

On the one hand, there's a beauty worthy of Apollo and on the other, there's the Dionysian, sensuality of the vineyards set at the foot of Mt. Etna, beneath Hephaestus's smithery. These are two apparently contrasting worlds, but in reality there's a point of contact, which Giuseppe Russo knows well. Coming from a background in music and literature, he's taken on the legacy of his father, Giacomo, and applied his sensibility and dedication to the family vineyards. Situated in Passopisciaro and Randazzo, their decades-old bush vines are cultivated organically. The challenge between the two finalists, two Etna Rosso, saw the 2015 'A Rina come out on top thanks to a bit of expressive pizzazz. It offers up fragrances of pomegranate and a balsamic finesse, with a sensational velvety and lingering texture. It just beat out the more austere but equally complex 2015 Feudo, which features charming notes of iron filings and spices, with a character of great volume and class. The 2016 Etna Rosato exhibits exemplary elegance and drinkability.

● Etna Rosso 'A Rina '15	♛♛♛	4*
● Etna Rosso Feudo '15	♛♛	6
⊙ Etna Rosato '16	♛♛	4
● Etna Rosso Feudo di Mezzo '15	♛♛	6
● Etna Rosso San Lorenzo '15	♛♛	6
● Etna Rosso 'A Rina '12	♛♛♛	3*
● Etna Rosso Feudo '11	♛♛♛	5
● Etna Rosso Feudo '10	♛♛♛	5
● Etna Rosso Feudo '07	♛♛♛	5
● Etna Rosso San Lorenzo '14	♛♛♛	6
● Etna Rosso San Lorenzo '13	♛♛♛	5
● Etna Rosso San Lorenzo '09	♛♛♛	5

Emanuele Scammacca del Murgo

VIA ZAFFERANA, 13
95010 SANTA VENERINA [CT]
TEL. +39 095950520
www.murgo.it

CELLAR SALES
PRE-BOOKED VISITS
ACCOMMODATION AND RESTAURANT SERVICE
ANNUAL PRODUCTION 230,000 bottles
HECTARES UNDER VINE 35.00

This charming story of a territory and a close-knit family goes back to 1860. It was Emanuele Scammacca, the esteemed ambassador and visionary, who, in 1981, began converting the old plots of land into modern farmsteads. He had the capable support of his many children, who manage things today. The strategy was, and is, clear: bring out the best of Etna's local cultivar, and its various districts, without neglecting some of the French grapes that have grown on the volcano since the 19th century. Their preeminent selection of sparkling wines was pioneered by the producer itself. The 2015 Etna Bianco San Michele flew into the finals with its elegant notes of grapefruit, white damsons, tangerine blossom, sage and thyme. It's supple, multifaceted and charming on the palate, with an invigorating freshness and delicate background of rose quartz. All their other wines are in form, from the intense 2014 Murgo Brut, to the elegant and soft 2014 Tenuta San Michele Pinot Nero.

○ Etna Bianco Tenuta San Michele '15	♛♛	5
○ Murgo Brut '14	♛♛	3
⊙ Murgo Brut Rosé '14	♛♛	4
● Tenuta San Michele Pinot Nero '14	♛♛	3
⊙ Etna Rosato '15	♛	2
⊙ Lapilli Rosso '15	♛	2
○ Arbiato '13	♕♕	4
○ Etna Bianco '15	♕♕	2
○ Etna Bianco '13	♕♕	2
● Etna Rosso Tenuta San Michele '14	♕♕	2
● Etna Rosso Tenuta San Michele '12	♕♕	2
⊙ Murgo Brut Rosé '12	♕♕	4
○ Murgo Extra Brut '09	♕♕	5
● Tenuta San Michele Pinot Nero '12	♕♕	3

Cantine Settesoli

S.DA ST.I F 115
92013 MENFI [AG]
TEL. +39 092577111
www.cantinesettesoli.it

CELLAR SALES
PRE-BOOKED VISITS
ANNUAL PRODUCTION 20,000,000 bottles
HECTARES UNDER VINE 6000.00

The wines of Settesoli, one of the largest co-operative wineries in Europe, are a classic example of how large production figures and quality can come together without compromising terroir or the grape varieties used. In recent years, this dynamic operation's tried and true team of experts has worked especially hard at identifying the best clones for Menfi's various types of terrain. To get an idea of how long and complicated a process this was, consider that the co-operative's 2500 members represent 6000 hectares of land. Tre Bicchieri for the 2016 Cavadiserpe, a blend of Merlot and Alicante Bouschet. It's a close-knit and concentrated wine, plush and charming, with elegant and pleasant aromas of grass and small red fruit. The 2015 Nero d'Avola Chartago gave a great performance. It's meaty and long in the mouth, while on the nose it offers up ripe notes of plums and mulberries, cut through by fresh hints of Mediterranean herbs.

★★Tasca d'Almerita

C.DA REGALEALI
90129 SCLAFANI BAGNI [PA]
TEL. +39 0916459711
www.tascadalmerita.it

CELLAR SALES
PRE-BOOKED VISITS
ACCOMMODATION AND RESTAURANT SERVICE
ANNUAL PRODUCTION 3,253,000 bottles
HECTARES UNDER VINE 388.00

The Tasca d'Almerita family have been producing wines for more than 200 years. Count Giuseppe created Regaleali, a lush garden in central Sicily, so as to afford them the right visibility. It was a forward-thinking initiative that's received extraordinary success, and has served as a model for growth for the entire sector. Under Lucio and his sons, Alberto and Giuseppe, the producer has enlarged its presence to include the territories of Capofaro (in Salina), Mozia, Valle dello Jato (with management of Sallier de la Tour) and Tascante (Etna), which, as of 2016 also hosts its cellar. Once again, Tre Bicchieri for Etna, this time with the 2014 Nerello Mascalese Tascante. It's complex and elegant on the nose, while in the mouth it reveals great character and length. The 2014 Cabernet Sauvignon is also in the finals. It's mature, balsamic, focused and pleasantly tannic. The 2010 Extra Brut Contessa Franca offers up creamy and elegant notes of tropical fruit. The rest the of their selection also proved excellent.

● Mandrarossa Cavadiserpe '16	♥♥♥	3*
● Mandrarossa Bonera '16	♥♥	3
● Mandrarossa Timperosse '16	♥♥	3
● Sicilia Mandrarossa Cartagho '15	♥♥	3
○ Sicilia Mandrarossa Urra di Mare '16	♥♥	2*
● Sicilia Seligo Rosso '16	♥♥	2*
○ Mandrarossa Santannella '16	♥	3
○ Sicilia Mandrarossa Costadune '16	♥	2
● Cartagho Mandrarossa '09	♥♥♥	3*
● Cartagho Mandrarossa '08	♥♥♥	3*
● Cartagho Mandrarossa '06	♥♥♥	3*
● Sicilia Mandrarossa Cartagho '14	♥♥♥	3*
● Timperosse Mandrarossa '14	♥♥♥	3*
● Mandrarossa Timperosse '15	♥♥	3

○ Sicilia Nerello Mascalese Tascante '14	♥♥♥	5
● Contea di Sclafani Cabernet Sauvignon '14	♥♥	5
○ Contea di Sclafani Almerita Extra Brut Contessa Franca '10	♥♥	6
○ Contea di Sclafani Chardonnay '15	♥♥	5
● Contea di Sclafani Rosso del Conte '13	♥♥	6
○ Diamante d'Almerita '15	♥♥	5
○ Leone d'Almerita '16	♥♥	3
○ Sicilia Grillo Cavallo delle Fate '16	♥♥	3
○ Sicilia Grillo Tasca d'Almerita Whitaker '16	♥♥	3
○ Tenuta Capofaro Malvasia '16	♥♥	5
● Contea di Sclafani Riserva del Conte '10	♥♥♥	7
● Contea di Sclafani Rosso del Conte '10	♥♥♥	6
○ Sicilia Carricante Buonora Tascante '15	♥♥♥	3*

★Tenuta delle Terre Nere

C.DA CALDERARA
95036 RANDAZZO [CT]
TEL. +39 095924002
www.tenutaterrenere.com

CELLAR SALES
PRE-BOOKED VISITS
ANNUAL PRODUCTION 200,000 bottles
HECTARES UNDER VINE 30.00
VITICULTURE METHOD Certified Organic

Marco de Grazia's estate comprises 30 hectares in four separate districts, at altitudes ranging from 600 meters (in Calderara Sottana) and over 1000 (in Guardiola) - a kind of mosaic of a dozen small vineyards, that go back 50 to 100 years. Since 2002, the grapes have been patiently harvested and fermented separately, making for wines that not only interpret the terroir (and difficult Nerello grape) perfectly, but display that extra something in terms of originality and polish. And this is why they've managed to find a place among Italy's top wines. Among the limited selection of wines sent by De Grazia this year, the traditionally styled 2015 Etna Rosso Calderara Sottana stands out, with its intense bouquet of ripe fruit marked by fresher balsamic, close-knit and lingering overtones. The 2015 Etna Bianco Santo Spirito is also in the finals. It's elegant and appealing on the nose, while in the mouth it proves lively and zesty, with a long finish in which tanginess and fruit find their balance.

○ Etna Bianco Santo Spirito '15	♼♼ 6
● Etna Rosso Calderara Sottana '15	♼♼ 6
○ Etna Bianco Calderara Sottana '15	♼♼ 6
● Etna Rosso Santo Spirito '15	♼♼ 6
● Etna Rosso Calderara Sottana '13	♼♼♼ 6
● Etna Rosso Prephilloxera La V. di Don Peppino '07	♼♼♼ 8
● Etna Rosso Prephilloxera La V. di Don Peppino '06	♼♼♼ 8
● Etna Rosso Prephylloxera La V. di Don Peppino '14	♼♼♼ 8
● Etna Rosso Santo Spirito '12	♼♼♼ 6
● Etna Rosso Santo Spirito '11	♼♼♼ 6
● Etna Rosso Santo Spirito '10	♼♼♼ 6
● Etna Rosso Santo Spirito '08	♼♼♼ 6

Terrazze dell'Etna

C.DA BOCCA D'ORZO
95036 RANDAZZO [CT]
TEL. +39 0916236343
www.terrazzedelletna.it

CELLAR SALES
PRE-BOOKED VISITS
ANNUAL PRODUCTION 120,000 bottles
HECTARES UNDER VINE 38.00

The Bevilacqua family's inspiring winery is situated in one of Etna's best-suited areas for viticulture, on the north face of the volcano, in the district of Bocca d'Orzo (not far from the medieval hamlet of Randazzo). The estate includes a large, modern cellar. Here all their wines are made, including their featured Metodo Classico sparklers and their Etna reds. Even if certification was only requested recently, for more than five years the entire estate has been managed according to organic and sustainable principles of agriculture. Their flagship red, the Cirneco, is a no-show this year because it has to age in the cellar. And so it's up to their two sparkling wines to keep this lovely winery's flag flying. The very pleasant 2014 Cuvée Brut, made with Chardonnay, offers up delicate scents of bergamot orange and yellow flowers, and proves elegant and fruity on the palate. The fragrant and long 2014 Rosé Brut, made with Nerello Mascalese and Pinot Nero, is also a top-quality wine.

○ Ciuri '16	♼♼ 3
○ Cuvée Brut '14	♼♼ 5
○ Cuvée Brut 50 Mesi '12	♼♼ 5
● Etna Rosso Carusu '15	♼♼ 4
⊙ Rosé Brut '14	♼♼ 5
● Etna Rosso Cirneco '09	♼♼♼ 6
● Etna Rosso Cirneco '08	♼♼♼ 5
○ Ciuri '15	♼♼ 3
○ Ciuri '14	♼♼ 3
○ Cuvée Brut '13	♼♼ 5
○ Cuvée Brut '12	♼♼ 5
● Etna Rosso Carusu '14	♼♼ 4
● Etna Rosso Cirneco '12	♼♼ 6
⊙ Rosé Brut '13	♼♼ 5
⊙ Rosé Brut '12	♼♼ 5

Girolamo Tola & C.

VIA GIACOMO MATEOTTI, 2
90047 PARTINICO [PA]
TEL. +39 0918781591
www.vinitola.it

ANNUAL PRODUCTION 180,000 bottles
HECTARES UNDER VINE 55.00

Four generations have dedicated themselves to this down-home estate, an operation that focuses on international markets. Their success is the result of wines of distinct, recognizable character, that manifestly express the terroir and varieties cultivated. The two large estates, which span more than 50 hectares, are situated in the districts of Bosco Falconeria, Giambascio and Grassuri Airoldi, in the province of Palermo. At an altitude of over 400 meters, the gentle hills here are often subject to North African scirocco winds and the cool breeze of the nearby sea. The winery's entire selection exhibits even greater quality and definition. The intensely fruity and mature 2016 Nero d'Avola is in great form, as is the traditionally styled and deep 2014 Nero d'Avola Black Label and the pleasant Terrarossa Nero d'Avola Tenuta Grassuri, a wine with great drinkability. The 2016 Catarratto is close-focused, with fragrances of peach, mint and rosemary on the nose, and a fresh, racy palate. The lively and tangy 2016 Catarratto Insolia exhibits similar qualities.

○ Catarratto '16	♟♟ 2*
○ Catarratto Insolia '16	♟♟ 2*
● Nero d'Avola '16	♟♟ 3
● Nero d'Avola Black Label '14	♟♟ 3
● Nero D'Avola e Merlot '13	♟♟ 3
○ Terrarossa Grillo '16	♟♟ 3
● Terrarossa Nero d'Avola Tenuta Grassuri '16	♟♟ 3
○ Chardonnay Inzolia '16	♟ 2
○ Grillo '16	♟ 3
○ Grillo '13	♟♟ 3
Nero d'Avola '15	♟♟ 3
● Nero d'Avola '14	♟♟ 3

Tornatore

FRAZ. VERZELLA
VIA PIETRAMARINA, 8A
95012 CASTIGLIONE DI SICILIA [CT]
TEL. +39 3339195793
www.tornatorewine.com

CELLAR SALES
PRE-BOOKED VISITS
ANNUAL PRODUCTION 120,000 bottles
HECTARES UNDER VINE 45.00

As a young man, during harvest, Francesco Tornatore loved to visit his grandfather's 18th century palmento and six hectares of vineyards on Etna, in the district of Trimarchisa. And so it was that, some years ago, he took up the family tradition (which, in reality, had never stopped), planting almost 50 hectares of vineyards, exclusively Nerello and Carricante, and building a modern cellar. Tornatore is still deeply tied to his family memories and, from the first vintages, he's sought to bring out the bond between the cultivar and the territory of Etna, producing well-crafted and authentic wines. The 2015 Etna Rosso thoroughly deserves its Tre Bicchieri. It possesses astonishing precision, elegance and pleasant drinkability. Its very fine aromas of mulberries, peach and tobacco marry well with its mineral tone and smoky hints (which are characteristic of Etna's wines). In the mouth it proves austere, marked by a fresh fruity encore and a long, gratifying finish. The 2016 Etna Bianco is also excellent, overflowing on the nose, lively and gutsy on the palate.

○ Etna Rosso '15	♟♟♟ 4*
○ Etna Bianco '16	♟♟ 4
○ Etna Bianco Pietrarizzo '16	♟♟ 5
⊙ Etna Rosato '16	♟♟ 4
● Etna Rosso Pietrarizzo '15	♟♟ 5
● Etna Rosso Trimarchisa '14	♟♟ 6

Valle dell'Acate

C.DA BIDINI
97011 ACATE [RG]
TEL. +39 0932874166
www.valledellacate.com

CELLAR SALES
PRE-BOOKED VISITS
ANNUAL PRODUCTION 400,000 bottles
HECTARES UNDER VINE 100.00
VITICULTURE METHOD Certified Organic
SUSTAINABLE WINERY

This inspiring estate of more than 100 hectares goes back to the 1800s. Spread out in the large valley that lies at the foot of Acate, shaped by the Dirillo river, the area is lined with traditional, local rock walls. Today the winery is led by Gaetana Jacono and Francesco Ferreri, representing the two proprietary families. Here history and modern times interweave, symbolically represented by the centuries-old palmento and modern cellar. The entire selection of wines (made with both local and international grape varieties) stands out for its high-quality and character. The 2014 Cerasuolo di Vittoria Classico made it to the finals. It's a weighty and lustrous wine with charming close-focused hints of bottled cherries, rose petals and herbs. The mouth proves succulent and invigorating with great elegance. The stylish and captivating 2014 Il Moro (made with Nero d'Avola), with its notes of ripe black fruit and fat tannins, proved to be in top form, as did the vigorous 2014 Tané (Nero d'Avola and Syrah).

● Cerasuolo di Vittoria Cl. '14	♥♥ 4
● Sicilia Il Moro '14	♥♥ 3
● Tané '14	♥♥ 6
○ Zagra '16	♥♥ 3
● Vittoria Il Frappato '16	♥ 3
● Cerasuolo di Vittoria Cl. '13	♥♥ 4
● Cerasuolo di Vittoria Cl. '12	♥♥ 3*
● Il Moro '11	♥♥ 3
● Rusciano '11	♥♥ 4
○ Sicilia Bidis '13	♥♥ 4
● Sicilia Il Moro '13	♥♥ 3
● Sicilia Il Moro '12	♥♥ 3
● Sicilia Rusciano '13	♥♥ 4
● Vittoria Frappato Il Frappato '15	♥♥ 3*
● Vittoria Il Frappato '14	♥♥ 3

Zisola

C.DA ZISOLA
96017 NOTO [SR]
TEL. +39 057773571
www.mazzei.it

CELLAR SALES
PRE-BOOKED VISITS
ANNUAL PRODUCTION 120,000 bottles
HECTARES UNDER VINE 21.00
SUSTAINABLE WINERY

The Marquis Mazzei were among the first families to invest in Sicily, purchasing the beautiful estate of Zisola, just a stone's throw from Noto. The base spans some 50 hectares in an area of calcareous, bone-rich soil that's particularly well-suited to the cultivation of Nero d'Avola. And, as called for by tradition, all 21 hectares of vineyards are head-trained vines. Their wines stand out for their fruit and, especially in their Nero d'Avola, for the local, mineral nuances that define the terroir of this corner of Sicily. The 2015 Syrah Achilles, a lively, elegant wine with pleasantly perky tannins, had a great debut thanks to its lovely nose of small red fruit, spices and herbs. The 2014 Doppiozeta is an intriguing Nero d'Avola with elegant aromas of brambles and violets. It's a dry, harmonious wine marked by a saline, mineral note and hints of iodine, as well as good depth.

● Achilles '15	♥♥ 4
● Noto Doppiozeta '14	♥♥ 6
● Noto Effe Emme '14	♥♥ 6
● Noto Zisola '15	♥ 4
● Sicilia Azisa '16	♥ 3
● Effe Emme '13	♥♥ 6
● Effe Emme '12	♥♥ 7
● Noto Doppiozeta '11	♥♥ 6
● Noto Zisola '14	♥♥ 4
● Noto Zisola Doppiozeta '13	♥♥ 6
● Noto Zisola Doppiozeta '12	♥♥ 7
○ Sicilia Azisa '15	♥♥ 3
● Sicilia Zisola '13	♥♥ 4
○ Sicilia Zisola Azisa '14	♥♥ 4

Ampelon

C.DA CALDERARA
95036 RANDAZZO [CT]
TEL. +39 3203298657
www.viniampelon.it

CELLAR SALES
ANNUAL PRODUCTION 50,000 bottles
HECTARES UNDER VINE 7.00
SUSTAINABLE WINERY

● Etna Rosso Le Caldere '13	♟♟ 3	
○ Etna Bianco Ampelon '15	♟ 3	
● Etna Rosso Passo alle Sciare '14	♟ 3	

Antichi Vinai 1877

LOC. PASSOPISCIARO
VIA CASTIGLIONE, 49
95030 CASTIGLIONE DI SICILIA [CT]
TEL. +39 0942983232
www.antichivinai.it

CELLAR SALES
PRE-BOOKED VISITS
ACCOMMODATION
ANNUAL PRODUCTION 300,000 bottles
HECTARES UNDER VINE 59.00

● Etna Koiné Ris. '12	♟♟ 5	
● Il Mascalese '16	♟♟ 4	
○ Etna Bianco Petralava '16	♟ 5	
● Etna Rosso Petralava '16	♟ 5	

Avide - Vigneti & Cantine

C.DA MASTRELLA, 346
97013 COMISO [RG]
TEL. +39 0932967456
www.avide.it

CELLAR SALES
PRE-BOOKED VISITS
ANNUAL PRODUCTION 250,000 bottles
HECTARES UNDER VINE 68.00

○ Nutaru Brut M. Cl.	♟♟ 5	
○ Riflessi di Sole '14	♟♟ 4	
○ Maria Stella '16	♟ 4	
○ Nutaru M. Cl. Rosé	♟ 5	

Baglio Oro

C.DA PERINO, 235
91025 MARSALA [TP]
TEL. +39 0923967744
www.bagliooro.it

CELLAR SALES
PRE-BOOKED VISITS
ANNUAL PRODUCTION 80,000 bottles
HECTARES UNDER VINE 100.00

● Donsar '15	♟♟ 2*	
● Sicilia Guardiani di Ceppineri '15	♟♟ 2*	
○ Sicilia Guardiani di Aralto '16	♟ 2	
○ Sicilia Guardiani di Ceppibianchi '16	♟ 2	

Barraco

C.DA FONTANELLE, 252
91025 MARSALA [TP]
TEL. +39 3292073935
vinibarraco@libero.it

CELLAR SALES
PRE-BOOKED VISITS
ANNUAL PRODUCTION 15,000 bottles
HECTARES UNDER VINE 10.00

○ Grillo '15	♟♟ 3	
● Nero d'Avola '14	♟♟ 4	

Biscaris

VIA MARESCIALLO GIUDICE, 52
97011 ACATE [RG]
TEL. +39 0932990762
www.biscaris.it

CELLAR SALES
ANNUAL PRODUCTION 50,000 bottles
HECTARES UNDER VINE 10.00
VITICULTURE METHOD Certified Biodynamic

● Frappato Barunieddu '16	♟♟ 2*	
● Nero d'Avola Cavalieri '16	♟♟ 2*	
● Cerasuolo di Vittoria Pricipuzzu '16	♟ 3	
○ U' Duca '16	♟ 2	

Calcagno

FRAZ. PASSOPISCIARO
VIA REGINA MARGHERITA, 153
95012 CASTIGLIONE DI SICILIA [CT]
TEL. +39 3387772780
www.vinicalcagno.it

CELLAR SALES
PRE-BOOKED VISITS
ANNUAL PRODUCTION 13,000 bottles
HECTARES UNDER VINE 3.00

⊙ Etna Rosato Arcuria '16	♥♥	3
● Etna Rosso Arcuria '14	♥♥	4
● Etna Rosso Feudo di Mezzo '14	♥	4

Paolo Calì

C.DA SALMÉ
VIA DEL FRAPPATO, 100
97019 VITTORIA [RG]
TEL. +39 0932510082
vinicali.weebly.com

CELLAR SALES
PRE-BOOKED VISITS
ANNUAL PRODUCTION 90,000 bottles
HECTARES UNDER VINE 15.00

● Cerasuolo di Vittoria Cl. Forfice '13	♥♥	6
⊙ Osa! Frappato Rosato '16	♥♥	4
● Vittoria Frappato Mandragola '16	♥♥	3
● Cerasuolo di Vittoria Cl. Manene '15	♥	4

Cantina Viticoltori Associati Canicattì

C.DA AQUILATA
92024 CANICATTÌ [AG]
TEL. +39 0922829371
www.cvacanicatti.it

CELLAR SALES
PRE-BOOKED VISITS
ANNUAL PRODUCTION 900,000 bottles
HECTARES UNDER VINE 1000.00

● Scialo '14	♥♥	3
● Sicilia Aynat '13	♥♥	5
● Sicilia Centouno '14	♥♥	2*
⊙ Delicio '16	♥	2

Caruso & Minini

VIA SALEMI, 3
91025 MARSALA [TP]
TEL. +39 0923982356
www.carusoeminini.it

CELLAR SALES
PRE-BOOKED VISITS
ANNUAL PRODUCTION 1,200,000 bottles
HECTARES UNDER VINE 120.00
VITICULTURE METHOD Certified Organic
SUSTAINABLE WINERY

● Nino '09	♥♥	6
● Delia Nivolelli Cutaja Ris. '14	♥♥	3
● Sicilia Nero d'Avola Naturalmente Bio '16	♥♥	3
○ Sicilia Grillo Timpune '16	♥	3

Casa di Grazia

S.DA PROV.LE 51 KM 3
93012 GELA [CL]
TEL. +39 0933919465
www.casadigrazia.com

CELLAR SALES
ANNUAL PRODUCTION 50,000 bottles
HECTARES UNDER VINE 30.00

○ Sicilia Adorè '16	♥♥	4
○ Sicilia Zahara '16	♥♥	4
● Cerasuolo di Vittoria 1607 Victorya '15	♥	4
⊙ Euphorya Rosato Brut	♥	4

Case Alte

LOC. MACELLAROTTO
VIA PISCIOTTA, 27
90043 CAMPOREALE [PA]
TEL. +39 3297130750
www.casealte.it

ACCOMMODATION
ANNUAL PRODUCTION 12,000 bottles
HECTARES UNDER VINE 8.00
VITICULTURE METHOD Certified Organic

○ Sicilia 12 Filari '16	♥♥	3
● Sicilia 16 Filari '15	♥♥	3
○ Sicilia 4 Filari '16	♥♥	3

Tenuta di Castellaro

FRAZ. QUATTROPANI
VIA CAOLINO
98055 LIPARI [ME]
TEL. +39 035233337
www.tenutadicastellaro.it

CELLAR SALES
PRE-BOOKED VISITS
ANNUAL PRODUCTION 25,000 bottles
HECTARES UNDER VINE
VITICULTURE METHOD Certified Organic

○ Biancopomice '16	♥♥ 5
○ Malvasia delle Lipari Passito '15	♥♥ 6
● Nero Ossidiana '13	♥♥ 5

Centopassi

VIA PORTA PALERMO, 132
90048 SAN GIUSEPPE JATO [PA]
TEL. +39 0918577655
www.centopassisicilia.it

CELLAR SALES
PRE-BOOKED VISITS
ACCOMMODATION AND RESTAURANT SERVICE
ANNUAL PRODUCTION 450,000 bottles
HECTARES UNDER VINE 94.00
VITICULTURE METHOD Certified Organic
SUSTAINABLE WINERY

○ Sicilia Giato Grillo Catarratto '16	♥♥ 2*
● Sicilia Giato Nero d'Avola Perricone '16	♥♥ 2*
● Cimento di Perricone '15	♥ 3
● Pietre a Purtedda da Ginestra '14	♥ 5

Colomba Bianca

VIA GIOVANNI FALCONE, 72
91026 MAZARA DEL VALLO [TP]
TEL. +39 0923942747
www.cantinecolombabianca.it

ANNUAL PRODUCTION 2,000,000 bottles
HECTARES UNDER VINE 7,700.00

● Sicilia Nero d'Avola Vitese '16	♥♥ 2*
● Sicilia Rosso Colomba Bianca '15	♥♥ 3
○ Sicilia Zibibbo Vitese '16	♥♥ 2*
● Sicilia Syrah Vitese '16	♥ 2

Cantine Colosi

LOC. PACE DEL MELA
FRAZ. GIAMMORO
98042 MESSINA
TEL. +39 0909385549
www.cantinecolosi.it

PRE-BOOKED VISITS
ANNUAL PRODUCTION 100,000 bottles
HECTARES UNDER VINE 10.00

○ Cariddi Bianco '16	♥♥ 1*
● Nero D'Avola '16	♥♥ 2*
○ Passito '12	♥♥ 3
○ Malvasia delle Lipari Passito '13	♥ 5

Cossentino

VIA PRINCIPE UMBERTO, 241
90047 PARTINICO [PA]
TEL. +39 0918782569
www.cossentino.it

CELLAR SALES
PRE-BOOKED VISITS
ANNUAL PRODUCTION 70,000 bottles
HECTARES UNDER VINE 17.00
VITICULTURE METHOD Certified Organic

● Muscarò '15	♥♥ 5
● Syrah '14	♥♥ 3
○ Gadi Cattarratto '16	♥ 2
● Nero d'Avola '14	♥ 4

Coste Ghirlanda

LOC. PIANA DI GHIRLANDA
91017 PANTELLERIA [TP]
TEL. +39 3333913695
www.costeghirlanda.it

CELLAR SALES
PRE-BOOKED VISITS
RESTAURANT SERVICE
ANNUAL PRODUCTION 25,000 bottles
HECTARES UNDER VINE 11.00

○ Silenzio '15	♥♥ 6
○ Jardinu '15	♥♥ 5

Curatolo Arini

LOC. BAGLIO CURATOLO ARINI
VIA VITO CURATOLO ARINI, 5
91025 MARSALA [TP]
TEL. +39 0923989400
www.curatoloarini.com

ANNUAL PRODUCTION 2,000,000 bottles
HECTARES UNDER VINE 100.00

○ Grillo '16	🍷🍷 3
○ Zibibbo '16	🍷🍷 6
○ Marsala Sup. Dolce 5 Anni	🍷 4
● Nero d'Avola '15	🍷 6

Curtaz

C.DA PURGATORIO
95033 BIANCAVILLA [CT]
TEL. +39 3480115329
www.federicocurtaz.it

ANNUAL PRODUCTION 18,000 bottles
HECTARES UNDER VINE 8.00

○ Etna Bianco Gamma '15	🍷🍷 5
● Sicilia Nero d'Avola Ananke '15	🍷🍷 4

Curto

LOC. CONTRADA SULLA
S.DA ST.LE 115 ISPICA - ROSOLINI KM 358
97014 ISPICA [RG]
TEL. +39 0932950161
www.curto.it

CELLAR SALES
PRE-BOOKED VISITS
ANNUAL PRODUCTION 70,000 bottles
HECTARES UNDER VINE 30.00

⊙ Eloro Nero d'Avola Eos '16	🍷🍷 2*
● Eloro Nero d'Avola Fontanelle '12	🍷🍷 4
● Eloro Nero d'Avola '14	🍷 2
○ Poiano '16	🍷 2

Di Giovanna

C.DA SAN GIACOMO
92017 SAMBUCA DI SICILIA [AG]
TEL. +39 09251955675
www.di-giovanna.com

CELLAR SALES
PRE-BOOKED VISITS
ANNUAL PRODUCTION 250,000 bottles
HECTARES UNDER VINE 56.00
VITICULTURE METHOD Certified Organic

● Gerbino Rosso '15	🍷🍷 2*
● Nero d'Avola Vurria... '15	🍷🍷 4
○ Gerbino Bianco '16	🍷 2
○ Helios Bianco '16	🍷 3

Gaspare Di Prima

LOC. SAMBUCA DI SICILIA
VIA G. GUASTO, 27
92017 SAMBUCA DI SICILIA [AG]
TEL. +39 0925941201
www.diprimavini.it

CELLAR SALES
PRE-BOOKED VISITS
ANNUAL PRODUCTION 50,000 bottles
HECTARES UNDER VINE 38.00
VITICULTURE METHOD Certified Organic

● Sicilia Nero d'Avola Gibilmoro '15	🍷🍷 3
● Syrah '15	🍷🍷 5
○ Pepita Bianco '16	🍷 2

Feudo Disisa

FRAZ. GRISÌ
C.DA DISISA
90046 MONREALE [PA]
TEL. +39 0919127109
www.vinidisisa.it

CELLAR SALES
PRE-BOOKED VISITS
ANNUAL PRODUCTION 150,000 bottles
HECTARES UNDER VINE 150.00
VITICULTURE METHOD Certified Organic

● Monreale Nero d'Avola Vuarìa '12	🍷🍷 4
○ Sicilia Catarratto Lu Bancu '16	🍷🍷 2*
○ Sicilia Grillo '16	🍷🍷 3
● Roano Syrah '11	🍷 4

Cantine Ermes

C.DA SALINELLA
91029 SANTA NINFA [TP]
TEL. +39 092467153
www.cantineermes.it

CELLAR SALES
PRE-BOOKED VISITS
ANNUAL PRODUCTION 3,000,000 bottles
HECTARES UNDER VINE 5000.00
VITICULTURE METHOD Certified Organic
SUSTAINABLE WINERY

● Vento di Mare Bio Nero d'Avola Cabernet '16	♥♥ 2*
● Vento di Mare Nerello Mascalese '16	♥♥ 2*
● Vento di Mare Nero d'Avola '16	♥♥ 2*

Ferreri

C.DA SALINELLA
91029 SANTA NINFA [TP]
TEL. +39 092461871
www.ferrerivini.it

CELLAR SALES
PRE-BOOKED VISITS
ANNUAL PRODUCTION 70,000 bottles
HECTARES UNDER VINE 30.00

● Nero d'Avola '16	♥♥ 2*
● Pignatello '16	♥♥ 2*
○ Grillo '16	♥ 3
○ Zibibbo '16	♥ 3

Feudo di Santa Tresa

S.DA COM.LE MARANGIO, 35
97019 VITTORIA [RG]
TEL. +39 09321846555
www.santatresa.com

PRE-BOOKED VISITS
ANNUAL PRODUCTION 250,000 bottles
HECTARES UNDER VINE 39.00
VITICULTURE METHOD Certified Organic

● Nivuro '15	♥♥ 2*
○ Rina Ianca '16	♥♥ 2*
● Avulisi '14	♥ 4
● Frappato '16	♥ 2

Fazio Wines

FRAZ. FULGATORE
VIA CAPITAN RIZZO, 39
91010 ERICE [TP]
TEL. +39 0923811700
www.faziowines.com

ANNUAL PRODUCTION 750,000 bottles
HECTARES UNDER VINE 100.00
SUSTAINABLE WINERY

○ Erice Catarratto Calebianche '16	♥♥ 3
● Nerello Mascalese '16	♥♥ 2*
○ Sicilia Bianco Brusìo '16	♥♥ 2*
○ Erice Grillo Aegades '16	♥ 3

Feudo Arancio

C.DA PORTELLA MISILBESI
92017 SAMBUCA DI SICILIA [AG]
TEL. +39 0925579000
www.feudoarancio.it

CELLAR SALES
PRE-BOOKED VISITS
ACCOMMODATION
ANNUAL PRODUCTION 6,000,000 bottles
HECTARES UNDER VINE 750.00
SUSTAINABLE WINERY

○ Barone d'Albius '15	♥♥ 5
● Barone d'Albius '13	♥♥ 5
● Sicilia Nero d'Avola '16	♥♥ 5
○ Sicilia Inzolia '16	♥ 3

Feudo Ramaddini

FRAZ. MARZAMEMI
C.DA LETTIERA
96018 PACHINO [SR]
TEL. +39 09311847100
www.feudoramaddini.com

CELLAR SALES
PRE-BOOKED VISITS
RESTAURANT SERVICE
ANNUAL PRODUCTION 90,000 bottles
HECTARES UNDER VINE 20.00

● Noto Nero d'Avola Patrono '13	♥♥ 5
○ Sicilia Passito di Noto Al Hamen '14	♥♥ 4
○ Quattroventi '16	♥ 4
● Sicilia Nero d'Avola Note Nere '15	♥ 2

Foderà

c.da Giardinello, 154
91025 Marsala [TP]
Tel. +39 0923712776
vignafodera@libero.it

CELLAR SALES
PRE-BOOKED VISITS
ANNUAL PRODUCTION 10,000 bottles
HECTARES UNDER VINE 2.45

○ Grillo '13	♀♀ 5
● Tardivo Merlot '10	♀♀ 5
○ Grillo Brut '14	♀ 7

Fondo Antico

fraz. Rilievo
via Fiorame, 54a
91100 Trapani
Tel. +39 0923864339
www.fondoantico.it

CELLAR SALES
PRE-BOOKED VISITS
ANNUAL PRODUCTION 350,000 bottles
HECTARES UNDER VINE 80.00

○ Bello Mio '16	♀♀ 2*
● Per Te '16	♀♀ 3
○ Sicilia Grillo Parlante '16	♀♀ 2*
☉ Sicilia Aprile '16	♀ 2

Giasira

c.da Ritillini
96019 Rosolini [SR]
Tel. +39 0931501700
www.lagiasira.it

CELLAR SALES
PRE-BOOKED VISITS
ANNUAL PRODUCTION 30,000 bottles
HECTARES UNDER VINE 7.00
VITICULTURE METHOD Certified Organic

○ Giasira Grillo '16	♀♀ 3
● Giasira Rosso Isabella '15	♀♀ 3
○ Giasira Bianco '16	♀ 3
● Giasira Rosso '15	♀ 2

Tenuta Gorghi Tondi

c.da San Nicola
91026 Mazara del Vallo [TP]
Tel. +39 0923719741
www.gorghitondi.com

CELLAR SALES
PRE-BOOKED VISITS
ACCOMMODATION AND RESTAURANT SERVICE
ANNUAL PRODUCTION 1,300,000 bottles
HECTARES UNDER VINE 130.00
VITICULTURE METHOD Certified Organic

○ Sicilia Grillo Kheirè '16	♀♀ 4
● Sicilia Syrah Segreante '15	♀♀ 4
○ Sicilia Zibibbo Rajah '16	♀♀ 4
○ Grillo d'Oro Passito '14	♀ 7

Gulfi

c.da Patria
97012 Chiaramonte Gulfi [RG]
Tel. +39 0932921654
www.gulfi.it

CELLAR SALES
PRE-BOOKED VISITS
ACCOMMODATION AND RESTAURANT SERVICE
ANNUAL PRODUCTION 280,000 bottles
HECTARES UNDER VINE 70.00
VITICULTURE METHOD Certified Organic

● Neromàccarj '12	♀♀ 6
○ Sicilia Carjcanti '14	♀♀ 5
● Nerobufaleffj '12	♀ 6
● Nerojbleo '13	♀ 3

Hibiscus

c.da Tramontana
90010 Ustica [PA]
Tel. +39 0918449543
www.agriturismohibiscus.com

CELLAR SALES
PRE-BOOKED VISITS
ACCOMMODATION
ANNUAL PRODUCTION 10,000 bottles
HECTARES UNDER VINE 3.00

○ L'Isola Bianco '16	♀♀ 2*
○ Zhabib Passito '16	♀♀ 4
○ Grotta dell'Oro '16	♀ 2
○ Onde di Sole '16	♀ 4

Intorcia

VIA MAZARA, 10
91025 MARSALA [TP]
TEL. +39 0923999133
www.Intorcia.it

○ Grillo Perpetuo '16	♟♟ 7
○ Marsala Sup. Ambra Semisecco Tino 5 Ris. '94	♟♟ 6
○ Marsala Vergine Tino 1 Ris. '80	♟♟ 8

Tenute Lombardo

C.DA CUSATINO S.DA ST.LE 122, KM 50
93017 SAN CATALDO [CL]
TEL. +39 09341935148
www.tenutelombardo.it

ANNUAL PRODUCTION 70,000 bottles
HECTARES UNDER VINE 25.00

○ Sicilia Catarratto Bianco d'Altura '16	♟♟ 2*
● Sicilia Nero d'Avola Passadinero V.T. '12	♟♟ 5
○ Sua Altezza 650 Brut	♟♟ 3
● Sicilia Nero d'Avola Nero d'Altura '14	♟ 2

Marchesi di San Giuliano

C.DA SAN GIULIANO
96010 VILLASMUNDO
TEL. +39 0931959022
www.vinimarchesidisangiuliano.it

● Belluzza '13	♟♟ 4
⊙ Rosé '16	♟♟ 3
● Il Pastore '14	♟ 4
● San Giuliano '12	♟ 5

Lisciandrello

VIA CASE NUOVE, 31
90048 SAN GIUSEPPE JATO [PA]
TEL. +39 3395917618
www.aziendalisciandrello.com

ANNUAL PRODUCTION 30,000 bottles
HECTARES UNDER VINE 6.00

○ Chardonnay '15	♟♟ 3
● Nerello Mascalese '15	♟♟ 3
○ Perpetuo di Manfredi	♟♟ 4
○ Cataratto '15	♟ 3

Maggiovini

VIA FILIPPO BONETTI, 35
97019 VITTORIA [RG]
TEL. +39 0932984771
www.maggiovini.com

CELLAR SALES
PRE-BOOKED VISITS
ACCOMMODATION
ANNUAL PRODUCTION 250,000 bottles
HECTARES UNDER VINE 45.00
VITICULTURE METHOD Certified Organic
SUSTAINABLE WINERY

● Cerasuolo di Vittoria Cl. V. di Pettineo '14	♟♟ 2*
● Vittoria Frappato V. di Pettineo '16	♟♟ 3
○ Sicilia Grillo V. di Pettineo '16	♟ 3
● Vittoria Nero D'Avola V. di Pettineo '15	♟ 3

Masseria del Feudo

C.DA GROTTAROSSA
93100 CALTANISSETTA
TEL. +39 0934569719
www.masseriadelfeudo.it

CELLAR SALES
PRE-BOOKED VISITS
ACCOMMODATION
ANNUAL PRODUCTION 100,000 bottles
HECTARES UNDER VINE 12.00
VITICULTURE METHOD Certified Organic

○ Sicilia Haermosa '15	♟♟ 3
● Sicilia Nero d'Avola '16	♟♟ 2*
● Sicilia Nero d'Avola Ris. '14	♟♟ 5
● Sicilia Rosso delle Rose '15	♟ 3

Cantina Modica di San Giovanni

C.DA BUFALEFI
96017 NOTO [SR]
TFL. +39 09311805181
www.vinidinoto.it

CELLAR SALES
PRE-BOOKED VISITS
RESTAURANT SERVICE
ANNUAL PRODUCTION 80,000 bottles
HECTARES UNDER VINE 40.00
SUSTAINABLE WINERY

● Eloro Nero d'Avola Filinona '12	♟♟ 2*
☉ Mamma Draja '16	♟♟ 2*
○ Moscato di Noto Dolcenoto '16	♟♟ 3
● Dolcenero	♟ 5

Morgante

C.DA RACALMARE
92020 GROTTE [AG]
TEL. +39 0922945579
www.morgantevini.it

CELLAR SALES
ANNUAL PRODUCTION 300,000 bottles
HECTARES UNDER VINE 37.00

● Sicilia Don Antonio '15	♟♟ 6
● Sicilia Nero d'Avola '15	♟♟ 2*
○ Bianco di Morgante '16	♟ 3

Tenute dei Paladini

VIA PALESTRO, 23
91025 MARSALA [TP]
TEL. +39 3463513366
www.tenutedeipaladini.com

ANNUAL PRODUCTION 40,000 bottles
HECTARES UNDER VINE 45.00

○ Catarratto Chardonnay Palatium '16	♟♟ 3
○ Emà '16	♟♟ 3
○ Grillo Palatium '16	♟♟ 3
● Nero d'Avola Palatium '16	♟ 3

Palmento Costanzo

LOC. PASSOPISCIARO
C.DA SANTO SPIRITO
95012 CASTIGLIONE DI SICILIA [CT]
TEL. +39 0942983239
www.palmentocostanzo.com

CELLAR SALES
PRE-BOOKED VISITS
RESTAURANT SERVICE
ANNUAL PRODUCTION 75,000 bottles
HECTARES UNDER VINE 14.00
VITICULTURE METHOD Certified Organic
SUSTAINABLE WINERY

● Etna Rosso Mofete '14	♟♟ 3*
○ Etna Bianco Mofete '16	♟♟ 3
● Etna Rosso Nero di Sei '13	♟♟ 5
○ Etna Bianco Vulcano '16	♟ 3

Principe di Corleone Pollara

C.DA MALVELLO
90046 MONREALE [PA]
TEL. +39 0918462922
www.principedicorleone.it

CELLAR SALES
PRE-BOOKED VISITS
ACCOMMODATION AND RESTAURANT SERVICE
ANNUAL PRODUCTION 1,000,000 bottles
HECTARES UNDER VINE 160.00

○ Chardonnay Catarratto '16	♟♟ 3
● Sicilia Quattro Canti Merlot Cabernet '14	♟♟ 4
● Syrah '16	♟♟ 2*
● Syrah Ridente '16	♟♟ 2*

Pupillo

C.DA LA TARGIA
96100 SIRACUSA
TEL. +39 0931494029
www.pupillowines.com

CELLAR SALES
PRE-BOOKED VISITS
ANNUAL PRODUCTION 35,000 bottles
HECTARES UNDER VINE 20.00

○ Moscato di Siracusa Pollio '16	♟♟ 5
○ Moscato di Siracusa Solacium '14	♟♟ 4
○ Sicilia Targetta '16	♟ 2
○ Siracusa Cyane '16	♟ 3

Quignones

VIA VITTORIO EMANUELE, 62
92027 LICATA [AG]
TEL. +39 0922773744
www.quignones.it

CELLAR SALES
PRE-BOOKED VISITS
ANNUAL PRODUCTION 90,000 bottles
HECTARES UNDER VINE 28.00

○ Castel San Giacomo Insolia Chardonnay '16	♟♟ 2*
○ Largasia Insolia Chardonnay '16	♟♟ 3
⊙ Fimmina Rosato di Nero d'Avola '16	♟ 2

Feudo Rudinì

C.DA CAMPOREALE
96018 PACHINO [SR]
TEL. +39 0931595333
www.vinirudini.it

PRE-BOOKED VISITS
ANNUAL PRODUCTION 300,000 bottles
HECTARES UNDER VINE 24.00

● Decauville '16	♟♟ 4
○ Moscato di Noto Baroque '16	♟♟ 3
● Campanile '16	♟ 4
● Eloro Pachino Saro '14	♟ 3

Cantine Russo

LOC. CRASÀ
FRAZ. SOLICCHIATA
VIA CORVO
95014 CASTIGLIONE DI SICILIA [CT]
TEL. +39 0942986271
www.cantinerusso.eu

CELLAR SALES
PRE-BOOKED VISITS
ANNUAL PRODUCTION 190,000 bottles
HECTARES UNDER VINE 15.00

○ Etna Bianco Rampante Contrada Crasà '16	♟♟ 3
● Etna Rosso Contrada Crasà '14	♟♟ 3
○ Mon Pit Brut '14	♟ 5

Sallier de la Tour

C.DA PERNICE
90144 MONREALE [PA]
TEL. +39 0916459711
www.tascadalmerita.it

PRE-BOOKED VISITS
ANNUAL PRODUCTION 250,000 bottles
HECTARES UNDER VINE 41.00

● Monreale Syrah La Monaca '15	♟♟ 5
○ Sicilia Grillo '16	♟♟ 2*
● Sicilia Syrah '15	♟♟ 2*
○ Sicilia Inzolia '16	♟ 2

Solidea

C.DA KADDIUGGIA
91017 PANTELLERIA [TP]
TEL. +39 0923913016
www.solideavini.it

ANNUAL PRODUCTION 12,000 bottles
HECTARES UNDER VINE 1.80

○ Ilios '16	♟♟ 3
○ Moscato di Pantelleria '16	♟♟ 4
○ Passito di Pantelleria '16	♟♟ 5

Terra Mazar

C.DA CARCITELLA
91026 MAZARA DEL VALLO [TP]
TEL. +39 0923546706
www.terramazar.it

○ Grillo '16	♟♟ 2*
● Nero d'Avola '16	♟♟ 2*

Terre di Giurfo

VIA PALESTRO, 536
97019 VITTORIA [RG]
TEL. +39 0957221551
www.terredigiurfo.it

CELLAR SALES
PRE-BOOKED VISITS
ANNUAL PRODUCTION 100,000 bottles
HECTARES UNDER VINE 40.00

● Sicilia Nero d'Avola Kuntàri '15	♛♛ 3
● Vittoria Frappato Belsito '16	♛♛ 2*
● Cerasuolo di Vittoria Maskarìa '13	♛ 3
● Sicilia Syrah Ronna '15	♛ 2

Terre di Shemir

LOC. GUARRATO
91100 TRAPANI
TEL. +39 0923865323
www.terredishemir.com

CELLAR SALES
PRE-BOOKED VISITS
ANNUAL PRODUCTION 40,000 bottles
HECTARES UNDER VINE 9.00

○ Erede Grillo '16	♛♛ 3
○ Fedire Grillo Zibibbo '16	♛♛ 3
● Paradiso di Lara '16	♛♛ 3
● Ennaro Rosso '16	♛ 2

Todaro

C.DA FEOTTO
90048 SAN GIUSEPPE JATO [PA]
TEL. +39 3461056393
www.todarowinery.com

PRE-BOOKED VISITS
ANNUAL PRODUCTION 80,000 bottles
HECTARES UNDER VINE 25.00
VITICULTURE METHOD Certified Organic

● Grappoli di Feotto Perricone '14	♛♛ 5
○ Grappoli Persi Catarratto '16	♛♛ 5
● Shadir Nero d'Avola '15	♛♛ 3
● 4 Elementa '14	♛ 4

Torre Favara

VIA CANNADA, 1
93013 MAZZARINO [CL]
TEL. +39 0934384064
www.torrefavara.com

CELLAR SALES
PRE-BOOKED VISITS
ACCOMMODATION
ANNUAL PRODUCTION 50,600 bottles
HECTARES UNDER VINE 10.00

○ Pian del Grigno '16	♛♛ 2*
● Torre Favara '13	♛♛ 2*
○ Trenta Filari '16	♛♛ 2*
○ Conca del Principe '16	♛ 2

Vaccaro

C.DA COMUNE
91020 SALAPARUTA [TP]
TEL. +39 092475151
www.vinivaccaro.it

CELLAR SALES
ANNUAL PRODUCTION 800,000 bottles
HECTARES UNDER VINE 40.00
VITICULTURE METHOD Certified Organic
SUSTAINABLE WINERY

○ Luna Grillo '16	♛♛ 1*
● Salaparuta Rosso Sofè '15	♛♛ 3
● Salaparuta Rosso Zoe '15	♛♛ 4
○ Catarratto Zibibbo '15	♛ 2

Vivera

LOC. MARTINELLA
S.DA PROV.LE 59 IV
95015 LINGUAGLOSSA [CT]
TEL. +39 095643837
www.vivera.it

CELLAR SALES
PRE-BOOKED VISITS
ANNUAL PRODUCTION 120,000 bottles
HECTARES UNDER VINE 30.00
VITICULTURE METHOD Certified Organic

○ A'mami '14	♛♛ 4
○ Altrove '16	♛♛ 2*
○ Etna Bianco Salisire '12	♛ 3
○ Etna Rosato di Martinella '16	♛ 4

SARDINIA

Sardinia's wines continue to grow in quantity, but especially in quality. First off, we should point out that this year saw a record number of wineries participate (about 100), with 600 wines tasted in all. It's the result of a regional phenomenon that began some years ago. Many young aspirants decided to take up agriculture and winemaking (and this can only be considered positive), and at the same time, some vine growers who were formerly supplying cooperatives decided to go into business for themselves. And then there's the question of quality. Indeed, much of the progress made is due to the fact that many of these new wineries are choosing to produce wines with a territorial focus and that respect traditional cultivar. It's true that modern techniques are employed, but these are never invasive and never compromise typicity. The results are clear if you look at how many wines made it into our guide, regardless of their ranking, and the number of wines that we can whole-heartedly recommend. Moreover, it's important to note that recent vintages were quite hot, though not excessively, and the quality of the grapes in many parts of the island has proved excellent. We've got our eyes on a number of territories, with Gallura surprising us for its reds (its whites have been solid for years), Usini standing out for its Vermentino and Cagnulari, then central Sardinia with Oristano, Mandrolisai, Barbagia and Ogliastra (these last two especially for their Cannonaus). In the south, Serdinia proves to be excellent wine country with some four wineries making it into the guide, while Sulcis continues to prove rock solid. Four Vermentinos and four Cannonaus earned golds, thus affirming their status as the island's two most prestigious cultivar. Cherchi's Tuvaoes and Costarenas's Masone Mannu made headlines, while both Siddura and Pala put in excellent performances as well. Among those whites not made with Vermentino, Sella & Mosca's unique Cuvée di Torbato impressed the most. The Cannonaus awarded arrive from various areas, starting with Mamoiada ('red wine country), then Gallura and Serdinia in the south. Cantina Giba is once again a leader when it comes to Sulcis reds made with Carignano. We conclude by mentioning two 'meditation wines' that are extremely different in terms of variety, territory and production, but joined together by their excellence: Santadi's Latinia and Oristano Jughissa's Vernaccia, both among the best versions yet.

★★Argiolas

VIA ROMA, 28/30
09040 SERDIANA [CA]
TEL. +39 070740606
www.argiolas.it

CELLAR SALES
PRE-BOOKED VISITS
ANNUAL PRODUCTION 2,200,000 bottles
HECTARES UNDER VINE 230.00

This solid winery in Serdiana continues to broaden their range. There are two new DOC Carignano reds from Sulcis, which aim to highlight both the appellation and the native grapes used in their wines. Despite the number of bottles produced, and exporting to the five continents, it remains one of the largest private wineries in Sardinia. Today it is Franco and Pepetto's children (Valentina, Francesca and Antonio) who carry on the good work and spirit of this family-run winery. The Senes, a Cannonau di Sardegna Riserva in its second vintage, has proven that it's in a league of its own. The 2013 offers up aromas of roses, redcurrants and Mediterranean scrub, while its complex palate proves elegant and subtle, but slim-bodied and dynamic as well. It's a deep and savory wine, that once again earns a Tre Bicchieri. The Turriga and Antonio Argiolas 100, two iconic wines that represent the old Cannonau vineyards on the island, also performed quite well.

Capichera

S.S. ARZACHENA-SANT'ANTONIO, KM 4
07021 ARZACHENA [OT]
TEL. +39 078980612
www.capichera.it

CELLAR SALES
PRE-BOOKED VISITS
ANNUAL PRODUCTION 250,000 bottles
HECTARES UNDER VINE 50.00
SUSTAINABLE WINERY

This large brand is well known both in Sardinia and abroad. Production is just below 250,000 bottles and its techniques underline the artisan nature of its winemaking, a bedrock of Capichera's wines. From the beginning, the Ragnedda brothers' courage and determination have enabled this white wine to break through national boundaries. The entire range of northern Sardinian wines is known for its high quality. From their whites made with Vermentino, to their reds from Carignano and Syrah, these are territorial wines with superior aging potential. A great white and a red were tops in the tasting. The first is the Vign'Angena, a Vermentino di Gallura with great tanginess and complex notes of yellow flowers, herbs and almonds. The second, made with Carignano grapes, is a deep and caressing red with good structure. The rest of the range also impressed, thanks to whites with excellent aging potential.

● Cannonau di Sardegna Senes Ris. '13	♙♙♙	5
● Antonio Argiolas 100 '13	♙♙	6
● Turriga '13	♙♙	8
● Carignano del Sulcis Is Solinas Ris. '14	♙♙	4
○ Cerdeña '13	♙♙	7
● Korem '14	♙♙	5
☉ Serralori Rosato '16	♙♙	2*
○ Vermentino di Sardegna Merì '16	♙♙	3
● Cannonau di Sardegna Costera '15	♙	3
● Monica di Sardegna Perdera '15	♙	3
○ Nasco di Cagliari Is Selis '16	♙	3
○ Nuragus di Cagliari S'Elegas '16	♙	2
○ Vermentino di Sardegna Costamolino '16	♙	3
○ Vermentino di Sardegna Is Argiolas '16	♙	3

● Mantenghja '11	♙♙	8
○ Vermentino di Gallura Vigna'Ngena '16	♙♙	5
● Albori di Lampata '12	♙♙	8
● Assajé '13	♙♙	6
○ Capichera '15	♙♙	6
○ Santigaini '12	♙♙	8
☉ També '16	♙	4
○ Vermentino di Sardegna Lintori '16	♙	3
○ Capichera '14	♙♙♙	6
○ Capichera '13	♙♙♙	6
○ Capichera '12	♙♙♙	6
○ Capichera '11	♙♙♙	6
○ Capichera '10	♙♙♙	5
○ Vermentino di Gallura Vigna'Ngena '10	♙♙♙	5
○ Vermentino di Gallura Vigna'Ngena '09	♙♙♙	5

Giovanni Maria Cherchi

LOC. SA PALA E SA CHESSA
07049 USINI [SS]
TEL. +39 079380273
www.vinicolacherchi.it

CELLAR SALES
PRE-BOOKED VISITS
ANNUAL PRODUCTION 170,000 bottles
HECTARES UNDER VINE 30.00

Usini is a small village in the vast Logudoro wine region where Giovanni Maria Cherchi founded his winery in the 1970s. Today his children, Salvatore and Grazia, are at the helm and are following their father's teachings, using native grapes from Vermentino to Cagnulari, a traditional local red variety that Cherchi has relaunched. In recent years they have been experimenting with different wine types, including a Metodo Classico sparkling wine, a dried-grape wine from Vermentino and a cuvée of three different vintages of Tuvaoes. Named Trenta Vendemmie, this was produced to celebrate the thirty vintages of the winery's iconic white wine. The 2016 Tuvaoes proved tops in the tasting. On the strength of a good vintage, the Vermentino del Nord Sardegna exhibited surprising finesse and elegance, bolstered by its aromas of white flowers, good tanginess and plenty of freshness. It's a memorable wine that has earned a Tre Bicchieri. The Billia and the 2015 Cagnulari also made a good impression.

○ Vermentino di Sardegna Tuvaoes '16	♛♛♛ 3*
● Cagnulari '15	♛♛ 3
○ Vermentino di Sardegna Billia '16	♛♛ 2*
● Cannonau di Sardegna '15	♛ 3
● Luzzana '15	♛ 4
● Soberanu '13	♛ 8
○ Vermentino di Sardegna Filighe Brut	♛ 3
○ Vermentino di Sardegna Tuvaoes '88	♛♛♛ 4*
● Cagnulari '14	♛♛ 3
● Cagnulari Billia '15	♛♛ 3
● Cannonau di Sardegna '14	♛♛ 3
● Luzzana '14	♛♛ 4
○ Vermentino di Sardegna Tuvaoes '15	♛♛ 3
○ Vermentino di Sardegna Tuvaoes '14	♛♛ 3

Chessa

VIA SAN GIORGIO
07049 USINI [SS]
TEL. +39 3283747069
www.cantinechessa.it

CELLAR SALES
PRE-BOOKED VISITS
ANNUAL PRODUCTION 43,000 bottles
HECTARES UNDER VINE 15.00

This small winery run by Giovanna Chessa produces wines from traditional local varieties. Blessed with wide temperature ranges (freshness is never lacking in their wines), sea breezes and soil rich in limestone and clay, Usini is a wonderful area for growing Vermentino and Cagnulari grapes, Their wines express the best features of the region and include one white, two reds (the Cagnulari is a perennial winner) and a dessert wine made with overripe grapes, all with outstanding finesse and drinkability. A white and a red stood out in our tastings. The Mattariga is a Vermentino di Sardegna with surprising notes of medlars and meadow flowers. It's tangy and fresh, with a good finish that plays on a slightly bitter note. The Cagnulari affirms that it's a great territorial, Mediterranean red. The rest of the selection also proved well-made.

● Cagnulari '15	♛♛ 3
○ Vermentino di Sardegna Mattariga '16	♛♛ 3
○ Kentàles	♛ 5
● Cagnulari '14	♛♛ 3
● Cagnulari '13	♛♛ 3
● Cagnulari '12	♛♛ 3
● Cagnulari '11	♛♛ 3
● Lugherra '12	♛♛ 5
● Lugherra '10	♛♛ 5
○ Vermentino di Sardegna Mattariga '15	♛♛ 3
○ Vermentino di Sardegna Mattariga '14	♛♛ 3
○ Vermentino di Sardegna Mattariga '13	♛♛ 3
○ Vermentino di Sardegna Mattariga '12	♛♛ 3

Attilio Contini

VIA GENOVA, 48/50
09072 CABRAS [OR]
TEL. +39 0783290806
www.vinicontini.it

CELLAR SALES
PRE-BOOKED VISITS
ANNUAL PRODUCTION 800,000 bottles
HECTARES UNDER VINE 70.00
VITICULTURE METHOD Certified Organic
SUSTAINABLE WINERY

Contini is iconic of Oristano and indeed the whole of Sardinia. It owes its fame to its signature Vernaccia di Oristano, a wine with a long history and tradition. Contini's production is huge. In addition to the Vernaccia, they make Nieddera (a wine made with local native varieties) and Cannonau. Grapes for their Vermentino are cultivated in central and northeastern Sardinia and are used to produce a Vermentino di Gallura. There are also different types of Vernaccia, including a dry sparkling wine, a Vermentino and 25-year-old Riservas. While waiting for the latest vintage of the Riserva di Vernaccia, we once again had the chance to enjoy the Antico Gregori. It's a non-vintage wine, made with the solera method, that's already been awarded in this publication. The 'Inu, a Cannonau Riserva with great complexity and typicity, also delivered this year. Most of the range of wines are quite good, starting with the younger versions of Vernaccia.

● Cannonau di Sardegna 'Inu Ris. '13	🍷🍷 4
○ Vernaccia di Oristano Antico Gregori	🍷🍷 8
● Cannonau di Sardegna Tonaghe '16	🍷🍷 2*
● Nieddera Malu Entu '16	🍷🍷 3
○ Vermentino di Sardegna Mamaioa '16	🍷🍷 2*
○ Vermentino di Sardegna Pariglia '16	🍷🍷 2*
○ Vernaccia di Oristano Componidori '06	🍷🍷 3
○ Vernaccia di Oristano Flor '04	🍷🍷 3
● Cannonau di Sardegna Mamaioa '15	🍷 4
○ I Giganti - Quarant'anni '14	🍷 5
○ Karmis '16	🍷 3
○ Vermentino di Gallura Elibaria '16	🍷 3
○ Vermentino di Sardegna Tyrsos '16	🍷 2
● Barrile '13	🍷🍷🍷 7
● Barrile '11	🍷🍷🍷 6

Cantine di Dolianova

LOC. SANT'ESU
S.S. 387 KM 17,150
09041 DOLIANOVA [CA]
TEL. +39 070744101
www.cantinedidolianova.it

CELLAR SALES
PRE-BOOKED VISITS
ANNUAL PRODUCTION 4,000,000 bottles
HECTARES UNDER VINE 1200.00

Dolianova is one of the largest wine cooperatives on the island and a benchmark for many vinegrowers in the Parteolla region. In recent years the average quality has risen sharply and they have gone from making simple wines to more complex, authentic ones comparable to the best on the island. Recently their range has undergone a change and the new look highlights an improvement in quality, producing excellent results. Focusing mainly on monovarietals, this year sees the debut of the Montesicci, a dry Nasco di Cagliari, and the Terrisicci, made with Barbera Sarda grapes. The reds dominated during our tasting sessions. The 2013 Terresicci, a wine made with Barbera Sarda grapes, is excellent, exhibiting great character and structure. The Falconaro, a Mediterranean and full-flavored red mad with native varieties, also delivered. Lastly, the 2015 Anzenas, a traditional Cannonau di Sardegna, is supple and easy to drink.

● Cannonau di Sardegna Anzenas '15	🍷🍷 2*
● Falconaro '12	🍷🍷 3
● Terresicci '13	🍷🍷 5
● Cannonau di Sardegna Blasio Ris. '12	🍷 3
● Monica di Sardegna Arenada '15	🍷 2
○ Nasco di Cagliari Montesicci '16	🍷 3
○ Nuragus di Cagliari Perlas '16	🍷 2
⊙ Sibiola Rosé '16	🍷 2
○ Vermentino di Sardegna Naeli '16	🍷 2
○ Vermentino di Sardegna Prendas '16	🍷 2
● Falconaro '11	🍷🍷🍷 3*
● Cannonau di Sardegna Blasio Ris. '11	🍷🍷 3
● Terresicci '11	🍷🍷 5

Cantina Dorgali

VIA PIEMONTE, 11
08022 DORGALI [NU]
TEL. +39 078496143
www.cantinadorgali.com

CELLAR SALES
PRE-BOOKED VISITS
ANNUAL PRODUCTION 1,500,000 bottles
HECTARES UNDER VINE 600.00
SUSTAINABLE WINERY

East coast Cannonau is the key player at Dorgali. A wine cooperative since the 1950s, it encompasses hundreds of hectares owned by its growers. Its wines are made with the best local bush-trained vineyards, some of which are very old, and their range is huge. Cannonau is made into different wines, including a simple version fermented in steel, aged versions, and some "Riserva" or "Classico" wines from the Barbagia and Ogliastra subregions. There are also whites made with Vermentino grapes and rosé sparkling wines made with Cannonau. The D53 has proved to be a great Cannonau di Sardegna Classico. It offers up aromas of blackberry, cherry and a nice dose of spices. The palate is fresh, not particularly long, but still savory and elegant. The Hortos is made with Cannonau and Syrah, it's a peppery and full-bodied wine. The Isalle, a vintage Cannonau, proves very fresh, fragrant and easy to drink.

● Cannonau di Sardegna Cl. D53 '14	♟♟ 4
● Cannonau di Sardegna V. di Isalle '15	♟♟ 2*
● Cannonau di Sardegna Viniola Ris. '14	♟♟ 4
● Hortos '12	♟♟ 6
○ Vermentino di Sardegna Calaluna '16	♟ 2
○ Vermentino di Sardegna Filine '16	♟ 2
● Cannonau di Sardegna Cl. D53 '13	♟♟♟ 4*
● Cannonau di Sardegna Cl. D53 '12	♟♟♟ 4*
● Cannonau di Sardegna Viniola Ris. '10	♟♟♟ 4*
● Cannonau di Sardegna Viniola Ris. '07	♟♟♟ 3*
● Cannonau di Sardegna Viniola Ris. '06	♟♟♟ 3*
● Hortos '08	♟♟♟ 6
● Cannonau di Sardegna Viniola Ris. '13	♟♟ 4
● Noriolo '13	♟♟ 4

Fradiles

LOC. CRECCHERÌ
08030 ATZARA [NU]
TEL. +39 3331761683
www.fradiles.it

CELLAR SALES
PRE-BOOKED VISITS
ANNUAL PRODUCTION 25,000 bottles
HECTARES UNDER VINE 14.00
SUSTAINABLE WINERY

Fradiles is a small artisan winery in the heart of the Mandrolisai appellation. It is run by the vigneron Paolo Savoldo, who is managing to bring a breath of optimism to the area with his stubbornness and good wines. He is developing production of Cannonau, Bovale and Monica varieties. Several other wineries have now started focusing on this area, one of the most beautiful on the island. Vine growing is done on high ground, with very old bush-trained vines, some ungrafted, on weathered granite. In addition to their various versions of Mandrolisai, Fradiles also produce a very good monovarietal Bovale. This year, the wine that stands out from the crowd is the Fradiles. It's a young Mandrolisai with a juicy mouthfeel. It's a dynamic wine, but always close-knit, both in its tannins and body. Aromas of dark fruit feature an added touch of spices and an earthy finish. The Bagadiu, made with Bovale grapes, and the Antiogu, another Mandrolisai with more structure and body, also put in strong performances.

● Mandrolisai Fradiles '15	♟♟ 3*
● Bagadiu Bovale '15	♟♟ 3
● Mandrolisai Sup. Antiogu '13	♟♟ 5
● Mandrolisai Sup. Istentu '13	♟♟ 8
● Mandrolisai Azzàra '15	♟ 2
● Mandrolisai Sup. Antiogu '11	♟♟♟ 5
● Bagadiu '13	♟♟ 4
● Mandrolisai Azzara '13	♟♟ 2*
● Mandrolisai Azzarra '14	♟♟ 2*
● Mandrolisai Fradiles '14	♟♟ 3
● Mandrolisai Fradiles '13	♟♟ 3
● Mandrolisai Fradiles '12	♟♟ 4
● Mandrolisai Sup. Istentu '12	♟♟ 8

Giuseppe Gabbas

VIA TRIESTE, 59
08100 NUORO
TEL. +39 078433745
www.gabbas.it

CELLAR SALES
PRE-BOOKED VISITS
ANNUAL PRODUCTION 70,000 bottles
HECTARES UNDER VINE 20.00

20 hectares of vineyards and 5 wines (4 reds and a white). These are the numbers that define Giuseppe Gabbas's winery, one of the most interesting in Sardinia. His is an artisanal selection in which the vineyard figures prominently (Gabbas is a topnotch vine grower) in terms of what comes through in the glass. All their reds are made with Cannonau, and are subdivided into categories according to vineyard and vinification method. The Lillové is a vintage made without the use of wood, while Dule and Arbòre are aged in barrique. There's also a passito dried grape wine (made with Cannonau) and the Manzanile, Vermentino di Sardegna. Although no reds managed to get a gold, the winery headed by Giuseppe Gabbas has proved it truly is one of the most impressive on the island, especially when it comes to Cannonau. The Dule is a great Sardinian red, with aromas of myrtle, forest floor, spices and small fruits, and a mouth that's savory and balanced. The 2014 is just a bit less deep and complex than in previous years. The rest of their selection also proved excellent.

● Cannonau di Sardegna Cl. Dule '14	♥♥	4
● Cannonau di Sardegna Cl. Arbòre '14	♥♥	4
● Cannonau di Sardegna Lillové '16	♥♥	2*
○ Vermentino di Sardegna Manzanile '16	♥	3
● Cannonau di Sardegna Cl. Dule '13	♥♥♥	4*
● Cannonau di Sardegna Cl. Dule '12	♥♥♥	4*
● Cannonau di Sardegna Cl. Dule '11	♥♥♥	4*
● Cannonau di Sardegna Dule Ris. '10	♥♥♥	4*
● Cannonau di Sardegna Dule Ris. '09	♥♥♥	3*
● Cannonau di Sardegna Dule Ris. '08	♥♥♥	3*
● Cannonau di Sardegna Dule Ris. '07	♥♥♥	3*
● Cannonau di Sardegna Dule Ris. '06	♥♥♥	3*
● Cannonau di Sardegna Dule Ris. '05	♥♥♥	3*

Cantina Gallura

VIA VAL DI COSSU, 9
07029 TEMPIO PAUSANIA
TEL. +39 079631241
www.cantinagallura.com

CELLAR SALES
PRE-BOOKED VISITS
ANNUAL PRODUCTION 1,300,000 bottles
HECTARES UNDER VINE 350.00

Of the many cooperatives that stand out for their high-quality, we must include Gallura di Tempio, a winery run by winemaker Dino Addis. The cooperative produces a large number of wines, dominated by a reasonably priced Vermentino di Gallura. For some years the co-op has been working especially with their best-positioned vineyards with the aim of improving quality. In addition to still whites, the winery makes sparkling wines (from Vermentino grapes), a Moscato di Tempio Spumante, and several reds from traditional varieties grown in Gallura. Without a doubt, the white wines have turned in the best performance here. At the top is their Canayli Vendemmia Tardiva, a rich and tangy wine with great complexity on the nose and a long, caressing finish. We also enjoyed the Piras, another Vermentino di Gallura that impresses for its vibrancy and grip.

○ Vermentino di Gallura Canayli V. T. '16	♥♥	4
⊙ Campos '16	♥♥	2*
○ Vermentino di Gallura Gemellae '16	♥♥	2*
○ Vermentino di Gallura Piras '16	♥♥	2*
○ Vermentino di Gallura Sup. Canayli '16	♥♥	2*
● Karana '16	♥	2
○ Vermentino di Gallura Mavriana '16	♥	2
○ Vermentino di Gallura Canayli V. T. '14	♥♥♥	4
○ Vermentino di Gallura Sup. Genesi '10	♥♥♥	5
○ Vermentino di Gallura Sup. Genesi '08	♥♥♥	5
○ Vermentino di Gallura Canayli V. T. '15	♥♥	4
○ Vermentino di Gallura Sup. Canayli '15	♥♥	2

Cantina Giba

VIA PRINCIPE DI PIEMONTE, 16
09010 GIBA [CI]
TEL. +39 0781689718
www.cantinagiba.it

CELLAR SALES
ANNUAL PRODUCTION 100,000 bottles
HECTARES UNDER VINE 15.00

Today, Giba is named after the village where it is located but fifteen years ago it was known as 6Mura. It makes four wines, a fresh vintage wine, one from the old bush-trained vineyards, a still rosé, and a Metodo Classico sparkling rosé. Both rosés are new this year. Located in the heart of Sulcis, this is where the Carignano variety reigns. The winery brings out the best attributes of the territory and seeks to reflect the vintage (the climate is always hot here) and soil in their wines. Their wines are captivating, full of character and easy to drink. Any slight imperfection is a sign of authenticity. The whole of the Sulcis territory is contained in the 2012 6Mura, a superior Carignano with notes of Mediterranean scrub and red fruit. It's mature, warm and caressing, but always dynamic on the palate, thanks to its exemplary richness of flavor. An enthusiastic Tre Bicchieri. The vintage Carignano did quite well, proving fresh and juicy, while the 2016 Vermentino 6Mura is a traditional and captivating wine.

● Carignano del Sulcis 6Mura '12	♈♈♈ 5
● Carignano del Sulcis Giba '16	♈♈ 2*
○ Vermentino di Sardegna 6Mura '16	♈♈ 4
⊙ Carignano del Sulcis Giba Rosato '16	♈ 2
○ Vermentino di Sardegna '16	♈ 4
● Carignano del Sulcis 6Mura '11	♈♈♈ 5
● Carignano del Sulcis 6Mura '10	♈♈♈ 5
● Carignano del Sulcis 6Mura '09	♈♈♈ 5
● Carignano del Sulcis 6Mura '11	♈♈ 5
○ Vermentino di Sardegna 6Mura '15	♈♈ 4

Antichi Poderi Jerzu

VIA UMBERTO I, 1
08044 JERZU [OG]
TEL. +39 078270028
www.jerzuantichipoderi.it

CELLAR SALES
PRE-BOOKED VISITS
ANNUAL PRODUCTION 1,500,000 bottles
HECTARES UNDER VINE 750.00

There are three subzones of Cannonau di Sardegna on the island. One of these is Jerzu, a town in Ogliastra, where the Antichi Podere cooperative was founded. It includes 750 hectares and produces over one and a half million bottles. Several years ago, zoning was carried out to identify the best soil and exposures for growing Cannonau. Since then, quality has improved by leaps and bounds, and the individual wines express the best features of the local area. The range also includes some whites made with Vermentino and a Monica di Sardegna wine. It was an open-ended vintage for the winery in Ogliastra. We thought their best was the 2014 Chuèrra. It's rustic but offers up charming notes of forest floor, bark and leather, and exhibits a nice overall structure. The Lucean le Stelle is a well-made Vermentino, while the Bantù is a simple vintage Cannonau with great drinkability. The Josto Miglior, another Riserva di Jerzu, was a bit subdued.

● Cannonau di Sardegna Chuèrra Ris. '14	♈♈ 5
○ Vermentino di Sardegna Lucean le Stelle '16	♈♈ 3
● Cannonau di Sardegna Bantu '16	♈ 2
● Cannonau di Sardegna Josto Miglior Ris. '14	♈ 5
● Monica di Sardegna Camalda '16	♈ 2
○ Vermentino di Sardegna Telavè '16	♈ 2
● Cannonau di Sardegna Josto Miglior Ris. '05	♈♈♈ 4
● Radames '01	♈♈♈ 5
● Cannonau di Sardegna Bantu '15	♈♈ 2*

Andrea Ledda

VIA MUSIO, 13
07043 BONNANARO [SS]
TEL. +39 079845060
www.vitivinicolaledda.com

CELLAR SALES
PRE-BOOKED VISITS
ANNUAL PRODUCTION 25,000 bottles
HECTARES UNDER VINE 24.00

Ledda is one of the most interesting
wineries to have sprung up as of late. It was
founded a few years ago by businessman
Andrea Ledda and includes three different
estates: one in Bonnanaro, on Monte Santu
where the winery is based, one in Gallura,
and one at the top of an extinct volcano.
This last estate, called Pelao, has been
planted at over 700 meters above sea level.
The purchase of the Tenuta Matteu in
Gallura (a historic Vermentino vineyard and
one of the most beautiful in Gallura)
completes the work started by the founder.
The winery now boasts a property of
about 24 hectares of vineyards. The three
main wines from their three different
estates put in excellent performances. The
2016 Vermentino di Gallura from the Tenuta
Matteu offers up aromas of citrus fruit and
herbs, while in the mouth it flows long and
deep, and features nice acidic vigor. Cerasa
is an excellent Cannonau di Sardegna with
great drinkability. The Vermentino, made
with grapes cultivated at Tenuta Pelao, is an
unusual and fine wine with great acidity. It
will age effortlessly.

○ Vermentino di Gallura Soliànu Tenuta Matteu '16	♟♟ 5
● Cannonau di Sardegna Cerasa Tenuta Monte Santu '14	♟♟ 6
○ Vermentino di Sardegna Azzesu Tenuta del Vulcano Pelao '15	♟♟ 7
● Cannonau di Sardegna Mogano '13	♟♟ 4
● Cannonau di Sardegna Mogano '11	♟♟ 4
● Ebano '12	♟♟ 4
● Ebano '11	♟♟ 4
○ Vermentino di Sardegna Acero '15	♟♟ 3
○ Vermentino di Sardegna Acero '14	♟♟ 3
○ Vermentino di Sardegna Acero '13	♟♟ 3

Alberto Loi

S.S. 125 KM 124,1
08040 CARDEDU [OG]
TEL. +39 070240866
www.albertoloi.it

CELLAR SALES
PRE-BOOKED VISITS
ACCOMMODATION
ANNUAL PRODUCTION 250,000 bottles
HECTARES UNDER VINE 53.00

The estate of this historic winemaking
family, Loi, has helped promote Cannonau
in eastern Sardinia. Their wines come under
the subzone Jerzu, and winemaking is
traditional, with long maceration and long
aging in old and new barrels. Heritage in the
vineyards is remarkable, with a combination
of old vines and bush-training creating the
ideal microclimate for Cannonau. The result
can be seen in the glass - their wines have
character with few imperfections. It should
be noted some Riservas and selections
cannot be fully appreciated until years after
the harvest. The three Riserva di Cannonau
di Sardegna wines have all proved spot-on,
strongly marked by typicity and terroir. The
2014 Cardedo is impressive, full of ripe red
fruit. In the mouth it proves savory with silky
tannins. The 2012 Loi Corona is a bit jaded
and creamy, but exhibits great charm. The
2013 Alberto Loi is full, well-structured and
warm. The rest of their selection also proves
well-made.

● Cannonau di Sardegna Cardedo Ris. '14	♟♟ 3
● Cannonau di Sardegna Jerzu Alberto Loi Ris. '13	♟♟ 3
● Cannonau di Sardegna Jerzu Loi Corona Ris. '12	♟♟ 5
● Cannonau di Sardegna Sa Mola '15	♟ 2
○ Leila '14	♟ 4
● Monica di Sardegna Nibaru '16	♟ 2
● Cannonau di Sardegna Jerzu Alberto Loi Ris. '12	♟♟ 3
● Cannonau di Sardegna Jerzu Sa Mola '14	♟♟ 2*
● Tuvara '13	♟♟ 5

Masone Mannu

LOC. SU CANALE
S.DA ST.LE 199 KM 48
07020 MONTI [SS]
TEL. +39 078947140
www.masonemannu.com

CELLAR SALES
PRE-BOOKED VISITS
ANNUAL PRODUCTION 100,000 bottles
HECTARES UNDER VINE 19.00

A few years ago there was a change of ownership and this winery is now run by a foreign company. It has not, however, affected the path to quality on which this Gallura winery was established. The meticulous work in the vineyards (beautiful plots in the best northeastern areas) together with the microclimate form a solid foundation for clean and elegant wines displaying the grapes' trademark aromas and great longevity. There are 19 hectares, set among olive groves and cork oaks. As well as Vermentino di Gallura, they make some interesting reds and rosés from traditional varieties. It was a great vintage for Masone Mannu's still wines. The Costarenas is one of the best Vermentino di Galluras: it's tangy and fresh, complex and long, with fine and lingering notes of curry plant and citrus fruit. A Tre Bicchieri goes to the 2016. The Petrizza is simple but still quite nice, while their best red proves to be the Zòjosu, an extremely fresh and full-flavored Cannonau di Sardegna.

○ Vermentino di Gallura Sup. Costarenas '16	🍷🍷🍷 3*
● Cannonau di Sardegna Zòjosu '15	🍷🍷 3*
○ Vermentino di Gallura Petrizza '16	🍷🍷 3
● Zurria '15	🍷🍷 3
● Entu '14	🍷 5
⊙ Zeluiu '16	🍷 3
● Cannonau di Sardegna Zòjosu '14	🏆🏆 3
● Entu '13	🏆🏆 5
○ Vermentino di Gallura Petrizza '15	🏆🏆 3
○ Vermentino di Gallura Petrizza '14	🏆🏆 3
○ Vermentino di Gallura Sup. Costarenas '15	🏆🏆 3*

Mesa

LOC. SU BARONI
09010 SANT'ANNA ARRESI [CA]
TEL. +39 0781965057
www.cantinamesa.it

CELLAR SALES
PRE-BOOKED VISITS
ANNUAL PRODUCTION 750,000 bottles
HECTARES UNDER VINE 70.00

Mesa is a modern and efficient winery that was set up a few years ago by the famous publicist Gavino Sanna, when he decided to gamble on the Sulcis area for making wine. In recent years the quality has increased significantly, both for Carignano del Sulcis and a few whites made with Vermentino. Their wines are technically well-made, clean and with fine aromas. There exists a distinctive selection of reds from old vineyards with ungrafted vines on sandy soil, while the winery's whites use traditional grapes bought from the best areas on the island. Some of their wines show a remarkable aging capacity. The two Riserva di Carignanos proved to be a surprise during our tastings, and both made it to the finals. The 2014 Gavino is close-knit, full-bodied, austere and caressing, with complex aromas of ripe red fruit and sometimes earthy notes. The Buio Buio is more elegant and subtle, with its aromas of Mediterranean scrub and marked richness of flavor. As for the whites, we found the Opale to be an excellent Vermentino.

● Carignano del Sulcis Buio Buio Ris. '14	🍷🍷 5
● Carignano del Sulcis Gavino Ris. '14	🍷🍷 5
● Brace Cagnulari '15	🍷🍷 4
● Brama Syrah '15	🍷🍷 4
○ Vermentino di Sardegna Opale '16	🍷🍷 4
● Carignano del Sulcis Buio '16	🍷 3
● Malombra '13	🍷 6
○ Opale Dopo '16	🍷 5
○ Vermentino di Sardegna Giunco '16	🍷 3
● Buio Buio '10	🏆🏆🏆 4*
● Carignano del Sulcis Buio Buio Ris. '13	🏆🏆🏆 5
● Carignano del Sulcis Buio Buio Ris. '12	🏆🏆🏆 5

Cantina di Mogoro
Il Nuraghe

s.s. 131 km 62
09095 Mogoro [OR]
Tel. +39 0783990285
www.cantinadimogoro.it

CELLAR SALES
PRE-BOOKED VISITS
ANNUAL PRODUCTION 850,000 bottles
HECTARES UNDER VINE 480.00

Il Nuraghe is a cooperative in Campidano working in Mogoro, a small town that gives its name to the Semidano di Mogoro appellation. The focus has always been on Semidano, a unique native variety that is found only in this area. The other local grape is Bovale, which produces full-bodied, dense reds. The Semidano is used to make several wines, including a Charmat method sparkling wine and Puisteris, an important long-lived white that is released onto the market three years after the harvest. Bovale produces different types of wines (some vintage, others aged in wood) depending on the age of the vineyards and the soil. The Puisteris confirms that it's a great Sardinian white for aging. The 2015 offers up aromas of citrus fruit, white fruit, Mediterranean herbs and a nice touch of flowers. The palate proves subtle and fresh, very tangy, dry and deep. The best reds are made with Bovale: the Terralba Cavaliere Sardo is in a league of its own.

○ Semidano di Mogoro Sup. Puistèris '15	♟♟	4
● Terralba Bovale Cavaliere Sardo '14	♟♟	2*
● Monica di Sardegna San Bernardino '15	♟	2
○ Nuragus di Cagliari Ajò '16	♟	2
○ Vermentino di Sardegna Don Giovanni '16	♟	2
○ Semidano di Mogoro Sup. Puistèris '10	♟♟♟	4*
○ Mora Bianca '15	♟♟	1*
● Sardegna Terralba '13	♟♟	3
● Sardegna Terralba Bovale Cavaliere Sardo Ris. '13	♟♟	3
● Sardegna Terralba Bovale Tiernu '14	♟♟	3
○ Semidano di Mogoro Sup. Puistèris '13	♟♟	4

Giovanni Montisci

via Asiago, 7b
08024 Mamoiada [NU]
Tel. +39 0784569021
www.barrosu.it

CELLAR SALES
PRE-BOOKED VISITS
ANNUAL PRODUCTION 6,000 bottles
HECTARES UNDER VINE 2.00

They only produce a few thousand bottles and own fewer than three hectares of vineyards in Mamoiada, one of the best areas for Cannonau. These old vineyards are bush-trained and guarantee low yields and grapes with concentrated sugars and extract. Their altitude (700 meters) makes for fresh and balsamic wines. In the cellar the winemaking is simple and traditional to ensure territorial wines with character. Few wines are produced each year: Barosu and the Riserva Franzisca (from the hundred-year-old vineyard), as well as a rosé and Modestu, which is a dry Moscato. The great 2014 vintage turned out to be ideal for the Cannonau cultivated on the estate's oldest vineyard. The Barrosu Riserva Franzisca offers up stunning aromas of myrtle, spices, blackberries and forest floor. The mouth proves dense but exhibits plenty of finesse, elegance and richness of flavor. Tre Bicchieri. The 2015 Barrosu is simple but extremely well-made. The Rosato (a rosé from Cannonau grapes) and the 2016 Modestu (a dry white from Moscato grapes) are both unusual and charming.

● Cannonau di Sardegna Barrosu Franzisca Ris. '14	♟♟♟	6
● Cannonau di Sardegna Barrosu '15	♟♟	6
○ Modestu '16	♟♟	6
○ Rosato '16	♟♟	2*
● Cannonau di Sardegna Barrosu Franzisca Ris. '11	♟♟♟	6
● Cannonau di Sardegna Franzisca Ris. '13	♟♟	6
● Cannonau di Sardegna Barrosu Ris. '11	♟♟	6
● Cannonau di Sardegna Franzisca Ris. '12	♟♟	6

Mura

LOC. AZZANIDÒ, 1
07020 LOIRI PORTO SAN PAOLO [OT]
TEL. +39 078941070
www.vinimura.lt

CELLAR SALES
PRE-BOOKED VISITS
RESTAURANT SERVICE
ANNUAL PRODUCTION 50,000 bottles
HECTARES UNDER VINE 12.00

Mura is a small estate spanning 12 hectares and run by a brother and sister team, Marianna (winemaker) and Salvatore (sales). Their wines are a true expression of Gallura, with a distinctive richness of flavor and freshness, and it is always interesting to taste past vintages. The Vermentino di Gallura is the most-produced wine, followed by fresh, easy-drinking reds. The granite subsoil reveals itself in the aromas and ensures character and authenticity in these wines. The 2016 vintage saw Mura's wines once again living up to expectations. This year, however, the best proved to be a red, the Cannonau di Sardegna Cortes. It's a wine that offers up aromas of blackberries and roses, with its pleasant mouthfeel emerging on the palate. As for the whites, the Cheremi is a Vermentino di Gallura that astonished us for its finesse, both in terms of aromas and taste, featuring notes of medlars and almonds, and a vibrant, deep palate.

● Cannonau di Sardegna Cortes '16	♔♔ 3
○ Vermentino di Gallura Cheremi '16	♔♔ 3
○ Vermentino di Gallura Sup. Sienda '16	♔♔ 3
○ Vermentino di Sardegna Prisma '16	♔ 2
○ Vermentino di Gallura Sup. Sienda '13	♔♔♔ 3*
● Cannonau di Sardegna Cortes '14	♔♔ 3
● Cannonau di Sardegna Cortes '14	♔♔ 3
○ Vermentino di Gallura Cheremi '15	♔♔ 3
○ Vermentino di Gallura Cheremi '14	♔♔ 3
○ Vermentino di Gallura Sienda '15	♔♔ 4
○ Vermentino di Gallura Sup. Sienda '14	♔♔ 3*
○ Vermentino di Gallura Sup. Sienda Il Decennio '13	♔♔ 3

Pala

VIA VERDI, 7
09040 SERDIANA [CA]
TEL. +39 070740284
www.pala.it

CELLAR SALES
PRE-BOOKED VISITS
ANNUAL PRODUCTION 490,000 bottles
HECTARES UNDER VINE 98.00

Mario Pala and his family have done an incredible job in recent years. Their wine quality has increased appreciably as have their sales, and the Pala brand is now well-known in many countries of the world. Everything is based on the vineyards located mostly in Serdiana, and the old ungrafted vineyards planted on sandy soil in Oristano. Grapes from the latter are used to produce a monovarietal Bovale. They produce a wide range with spot-on prices, drinkability, and aromatic finesse. The 2016 Stellato is a captivating territorial Vermentino di Sardegna that has once again earned a Tre Bicchieri. The wine's tanginess, combined with freshness, distinguishes its deep and clean palate, while its nose sees aromas of white fruit joined by overtones of flowers, herbs and iodine. The S'Arai is also tops. It's a complex and structured blend of traditional grapes. Lastly, the monovarietals of the I Fiori line also proved quite good.

○ Vermentino di Sardegna Stellato '16	♔♔♔ 4*
● S'Arai '13	♔♔ 5
● Cannonau di Sardegna I Fiori '16	♔♔ 3
○ Entemari '15	♔♔ 5
○ Nuragus di Cagliari I Fiori '16	♔♔ 2*
○ Vermentino di Sardegna I Fiori '16	♔♔ 3
⊙ Chiaro di Stelle '16	♔ 3
● Essentija '14	♔ 3
● Monica di Sardegna I Fiori '16	♔ 3
○ Silenzi Bianco '16	♔ 2
● Silenzi Rosso '16	♔ 2
● Siyr '14	♔ 3

Cantina Pedres

ZONA IND. SETTORE 7
07026 OLBIA
TEL. +39 0789595075
www.cantinapedres.it

CELLAR SALES
PRE-BOOKED VISITS
ANNUAL PRODUCTION 290,000 bottles
HECTARES UNDER VINE 40.00

Antonella Mancini is the young heir of a great family of vinegrowers. Today she runs Pedres near Olbia with great determination and support from her husband, their winemaker. They own forty hectares of vineyards situated in the best areas of Gallura and produce about 300,000 bottles. Excellent exposures, wide temperature ranges and granite subsoil ensure fresh and linear wines that are fine and elegant. They aim more for depth of taste than richness. In addition to Vermentino di Gallura, the winery produces some interesting Charmat method sparkling wines (both dry and sweet from Moscato di Tempio grapes) and reds from traditional varieties. Once again, the Thilibas did quite well. It's a Vermentino di Gallura Superiore that plays on a fresh and tangy linear palate. This is the first year we've tasted the 2016 Sangusta, which also proved excellent. While waiting for the new vintages of Cannonau, we found the Muros very interesting. It's a blend of Cabernet Sauvignon, Merlot and Syrah.

○ Vermentino di Gallura Sangusta '16	▼▼	3
○ Vermentino di Gallura Sup. Thilibas '16	▼▼	4
● Muros '15	▼	4
○ Vermentino di Gallura Brino '16	▼	3
○ Vermentino di Gallura Sup. Thilibas '10	▽▽▽	3*
○ Vermentino di Gallura Sup. Thilibas '09	▽▽▽	3*
● Cannonau di Sardegna Cerasio '15	▽▽	4
● Cannonau di Sardegna Sulitài '14	▽▽	3
○ Vermentino di Gallura Brino '15	▽▽	3
○ Vermentino di Gallura Sup. Thilibas '15	▽▽	4

Agricola Punica

LOC. BARRUA
09010 SANTADI [CI]
TEL. +39 0781941012
www.agripunica.it

PRE-BOOKED VISITS
ANNUAL PRODUCTION 300,000 bottles
HECTARES UNDER VINE 70.00

Agricola Punica is a winery in Sulcis that was established by winemaker Giacomo Tachis, who became familiar with the area when he worked as a consultant for the Cantina di Santadi. Founded in the early 2000s with Santadi and the Tenuta San Guido in Bolgheri, they make three wines: two reds and a white. The varieties grown are the ever-present Carignano (added to the international varieties Cabernet Sauvignon, Merlot and Syrah) and Vermentino, which is blended with Sauvignon. Their wines are impeccably made, fine and elegant. However, as international wines, they are less inclined to express the features of the territory. We tasted an excellent version of the Barrua. The 2014 offers up notes of Mediterranean scrub, forest floor, bark and spices, while the mouth is savory and velvety and only slightly clenched at the finish, but just as impressive. The Montessu once again proves tasty. This is a simple version with great drinkability. We also found the Samas, made with Vermentino and Sauvignon, to be well-crafted.

● Barrua '14	▼▼	6
● Montessu '15	▼▼	4
○ Samas '16	▼	3
● Barrua '12	▽▽▽	6
● Barrua '10	▽▽▽	6
● Barrua '07	▽▽▽	6
● Barrua '05	▽▽▽	5
● Barrua '13	▽▽	6
● Barrua '11	▽▽	6
● Montessu '14	▽▽	4
● Montessu '13	▽▽	4
● Montessu '12	▽▽	4

Santa Maria La Palma

FRAZ. SANTA MARIA LA PALMA
07041 ALGHERO [SS]
TEL. +39 079999008
www.santamarialapalma.it

CELLAR SALES
PRE-BOOKED VISITS
ANNUAL PRODUCTION 4,000,000 bottles
HECTARES UNDER VINE 650.00

This large cooperative in Alghero gets its name from the area where the cellar and some of the vinegrowers are located. Good quality at a reasonable price is the aim here. Some wines, especially Vermentino di Sardegna Aragosta, are good examples of well-made and pleasant drinking wines. Recently, however, they have raised the bar for quality by selecting the best vineyards to produce more complex wines. In addition to the traditional Sardinian varieties (including Cagnulari, a native grape from eastern Alghero) there are international varieties, Sauvignon, Chardonnay and Cabernet, which have been grown in Alghero for decades. Their entire selection is strong, with a few wines standing out, in particular one white and one red. The 2015 Cagnulari reveals notes of bark, forest floor and leather, while in the mouth the wine proves caressing and soft, with clear ripe tannins. The 2016 Triulas is a monovarietal Chardonnay, with overtones of ripe yellow fruit and a gratifying palate.

● Alghero Cagnulari '15	♟♟ 3
○ Alghero Chardonnay Triulas '16	♟♟ 3
● Cannonau di Sardegna Valmell '16	♟♟ 2*
○ Alghero Sauvignon Estiu '16	♟ 4
● Cannonau di Sardegna Le Bombarde '16	♟ 2
● Cannonau di Sardegna R Ris. '13	♟ 4
● Monica di Sardegna Sup. '15	♟ 2
○ Vermentino di Sardegna Aragosta '16	♟ 2
○ Vermentino di Sardegna Blu '16	♟ 2
○ Vermentino di Sardegna I Papiri '16	♟ 3
● Cannonau di Sardegna Ris. '14	♟♟ 3
○ Vermentino di Sardegna I Papiri '15	♟♟ 3

★Cantina di Santadi

VIA CAGLIARI, 78
09010 SANTADI [CI]
TEL. +39 0781950127
www.cantinadisantadi.it

CELLAR SALES
PRE-BOOKED VISITS
ANNUAL PRODUCTION 1,740,000 bottles
HECTARES UNDER VINE 603.00

The Santadi estate deserves credit for improving vine growing in Sulcis and boosting the quality of wines on the island. It began in the 1970s when the president of the cooperative, Antonello Pilloni (he still holds the position) took a gamble on this area and Carignano del Sulcis. His focus was on quality, starting in the vineyard with the vinegrowers who brought their grapes to the cooperative. Today, the result is high-profile internationally known wines like Terre Brune, Rocca Rubia and Latinia. A strongpoint of the cooperative is the old vineyards, many of which are over a hundred years old and ungrafted on sandy soil. Without detracting from their Carignano del Sulcis (in addition to the excellent 2013 Terre Brune, we tasted an exemplary Rocca Rubia), this year we were astonished by the Latinia. It's a passito dried-grape wine made with Nasco grapes from the valleys of Porto Pino whose racy palate sees sweetness perfectly balanced by tanginess and acidity. Tre Bicchieri.

○ Latinia '11	♟♟♟ 5
● Carignano del Sulcis Sup. Terre Brune '13	♟♟ 7
● Carignano del Sulcis Grotta Rossa '15	♟♟ 2*
● Carignano del Sulcis Rocca Rubia Ris. '14	♟♟ 4
● Shardana '12	♟♟ 5
● Araja '15	♟ 3
● Cannonau di Sardegna Noras '14	♟ 4
⊙ Carignano del Sulcis Rosato Tre Torri '16	♟ 2
● Monica di Sardegna Antigua '16	♟ 2
○ Nuragus di Cagliari Pedraia '16	♟ 2
○ Vermentino di Sardegna Cala Silente '16	♟ 3
○ Villa di Chiesa '15	♟ 5

Sardus Pater

VIA RINASCITA, 46
09017 SANT'ANTIOCO [CI]
TEL. +39 0781800274
www.cantinesarduspater.com

CELLAR SALES
PRE-BOOKED VISITS
ANNUAL PRODUCTION 600,000 bottles
HECTARES UNDER VINE 295.00

Many claim the most beautiful Carignano
vineyards are on Sant'Antioco, an island
joined to Sardinia by an artificial strip of
land. The Sardus Pater cooperative was
set up in the 1950s by a few vinegrowers,
and today it remains a symbol of local
viticulture. Here they produce several
different Carignano del Sulcis wines,
including a Superiore (made with old
ungrafted vines grown on sandy soil) as
well as the Riserva and vintage wines. The
range is completed with sweet wines from
traditional grapes, a few whites and a
Metodo Classico Vermentino. The
Carignano del Sulcis Is Arenas is a
2015 Riserva that features a satisfying
close-knit texture, subtle and ripe tannins
and a nose that offers up aromas of myrtle
and plum. We also enjoyed the Nur and Is
Solus, two simpler Carignano wines that
impress for their juicy mouthfeel and
savory finish. The most convincing among
the whites proved to be the Terre Fenicie.

● Carignano del Sulcis Is Arenas Ris. '15	▼▼ 4
● Carignano del Sulcis Is Solus '16	▼▼ 2*
● Carignano del Sulcis Nur '15	▼▼ 3
○ Vermentino di Sardegna Terre Fenicie '16	▼▼ 2*
⊙ Carignano del Sulcis Horus Rosato '16	▼ 3
● Carignano del Sulcis Sup. Arruga '14	▼ 6
○ Vermentino di Sardegna Lugore '16	▼ 3
● Carignano del Sulcis Arenas Ris. '05	▼▼▼ 3*
● Carignano del Sulcis Is Arenas Ris. '09	▼▼▼ 4*
● Carignano del Sulcis Is Arenas Ris. '08	▼▼▼ 4*
● Carignano del Sulcis Is Arenas Ris. '07	▼▼▼ 3*
● Carignano del Sulcis Is Arenas Ris. '06	▼▼▼ 3*
● Carignano del Sulcis Sup. Arruga '09	▼▼▼ 6
● Carignano del Sulcis Sup. Arruga '07	▼▼▼ 5

Giuseppe Sedilesu

VIA VITTORIO EMANUELE II, 64
08024 MAMOIADA [NU]
TEL. +39 078456791
www.giuseppesedilesu.com

CELLAR SALES
PRE-BOOKED VISITS
ANNUAL PRODUCTION 120,000 bottles
HECTARES UNDER VINE 17.00

Improvement of Mamoiada and its wines is
down largely to the Sedilesu winery. Over
the years they have brought authentic and
sincere Mamoiada wines to market. More
importantly, Francesco Sedilesu has
encouraged several small producers to
focus on making local wines. Cannonau is
the key player here though its many
versions are distinct as they come from
vineyards with different ages, altitudes and
exposures. It's worth mentioning a white
made with Granazza di Mamoiada grapes,
an unusual variety grown only in certain
areas of Barbagia. The latest vintage, 2015,
impresses for its aromas of ripe yellow fruit,
sweet spices and nuts. But the gold goes to
the 2015 Mamuthone, a Cannonau di
Mamoiada with fruity, almost grapey notes
on the nose, and a fresh, dynamic palate
made succulent by its silky tannins and
acidity. It all makes for a deep, flavorsome
wine worthy of its Tre Bicchieri.

● Cannonau di Sardegna Mamuthone '15	▼▼▼ 3*
○ Perda Pintà '15	▼▼ 5
● Cannonau di Sardegna Sartiu '16	▼ 3
● Cannonau di Sardegna Mamuthone '12	▼▼▼ 3*
● Cannonau di Sardegna Mamuthone '11	▼▼▼ 3*
● Cannonau di Sardegna Mamuthone '08	▼▼▼ 3*
○ Perda Pintà '09	▼▼▼ 4
○ Perda Pintà '07	▼▼▼ 5
● Cannonau di Sardegna Mamuthone '14	▼▼ 3*
● Cannonau di Sardegna Sartiu '12	▼▼ 3
○ Perda Pintà '14	▼▼ 5

★★Tenute Sella & Mosca

LOC. I PIANI
07041 ALGHERO [SS]
TEL. +39 079997700
www.sellaemosca.com

CELLAR SALES
PRE-BOOKED VISITS
ANNUAL PRODUCTION 6,700,000 bottles
HECTARES UNDER VINE 541.00

The Franciacorta Moretti family's takeover of the winery has not in the least affected their plans. Their aim was and is to identify the best vineyards on the island and create a complete range of wines that takes advantage of the entire region. Production stands at an impressive 7 million bottles, originating from the largest contiguous set of vineyards in Europe. The quality is impeccable, as is the price and positioning on world markets. There are several wines worth noting: Marchese di Villamarina (flagship of the range), various Torbato, and Vermentino from vineyards in Gallura and Carignano from grapes grown in Sulcis. The Marchese di Villamarina and the Cuvée 161 are both at the top. The latter, in its 2016, proves to be one of the best ever, stepping up for a gold. The nose offers up notes of pear, curry plant and chamomile, while the palate sees a faint presence of grape skins and a close-knit, captivating texture. Tre Bicchieri.

○ Alghero Torbato Terre Bianche Cuvée 161 '16	♛♛♛ 3*
● Alghero Rosso Marchese di Villamarina '13	♛♛ 6
○ Vermentino di Gallura Sup. Monteoro '16	♛♛ 3*
● Alghero Tanca Farrà '14	♛♛ 4
● Cannonau di Sardegna Dimonios Ris. '13	♛♛ 3
○ Alghero Rosato '16	♛ 2
● Carignano del Sulcis Terre Rare Ris. '14	♛ 3
● Alghero Marchese di Villamarina '09	♛♛♛ 6
● Alghero Rosso Marchese di Villamarina '08	♛♛♛ 6
○ Alghero Torbato Terre Bianche Cuvée 161 '15	♛♛♛ 4*
○ Vermentino di Gallura Sup. Monteoro '14	♛♛♛ 3*

Siddùra

LOC. SIDDURA
07020 LUOGOSANTO [OT]
TEL. +39 0796513027
www.siddura.com

CELLAR SALES
PRE-BOOKED VISITS
ACCOMMODATION AND RESTAURANT SERVICE
ANNUAL PRODUCTION 200,000 bottles
HECTARES UNDER VINE 37.00
SUSTAINABLE WINERY

Siddura is set in Luogosanto, a beautiful landscape where vineyards, Mediterranean scrub and oak trees live in harmony, creating a sense of peace and tranquility. The winery was founded a few years ago and from the start it aimed at high quality through obsessive care of the vineyards and advanced winemaking techniques. The result is precise, clean and balanced wines. Vermentino di Gallura is made with local white grapes, while other varieties are bought from the best areas outside the island's northeast. This year there is a new dried-grape wine from Moscato grapes to add to the range. The Maìa is a 2015 Vermentino di Gallura deliberately released a year later and is without a doubt the best of the lot. It offers up aromas of aniseed and fresh almonds combined with overtones of white flowers and tropical fruit. The mouth is fresh, very lingering and clean. Tre Bicchieri. As for the reds, the 2014 Tiros is outstanding, while the 2015 Nùali is an extremely well-crafted passito dried-grape wine (made with Moscato grapes).

○ Vermentino di Gallura Sup. Maìa '15	♛♛♛ 5
● Cannonau di Sardegna Fòla '15	♛♛ 5
○ Moscato di Sardegna Passito Nùali '15	♛♛ 5
● Tiros '14	♛♛ 6
● Bàcco '15	♛ 5
● Èrema '15	♛ 3
○ Vermentino di Gallura Sup. Maìa '14	♛♛♛ 4*
● Bàcco Cagnulari '14	♛♛ 5
● Cannonau di Sardegna Fòla '14	♛♛ 5
● Èrema '14	♛♛ 3
● Èrema '13	♛♛ 3
○ Vermentino di Gallura Spèra '15	♛♛ 3
○ Vermentino di Gallura Sup. Maìa '13	♛♛ 5

Tenute Soletta

LOC. SIGNOR'ANNA
07040 CODRONGIANOS [SS]
TEL. +39 079435067
www.tenutesoletta.it

CELLAR SALES
PRE-BOOKED VISITS
ACCOMMODATION AND RESTAURANT SERVICE
ANNUAL PRODUCTION 100,000 bottles
HECTARES UNDER VINE 15.00
VITICULTURE METHOD Certified Organic
SUSTAINABLE WINERY

Umberto Soletta runs the family winery with passion and skill. It is situated in Codrongianos, a small, traditional rural town in the Logudoro region, which is particularly suited to vinegrowing. Structure, complexity and concentration are the main features of their wines. This is especially true for the Cannonau reds, which have great aging potential, but can be difficult to drink and lacking in suppleness when young. The international-style whites are impressive. They are mainly made with Vermentino grapes, with the addition of international varieties. This year is full of ups and downs for Soletta. We thought the Sardo was the best. It's a close-knit and full-bodied Cannonau di Sardegna with hints of resin and ripe red fruit. The Riserva Corona Majore exhibits good complexity and structure, despite a palate clenched by a slightly mouth-drying finish. The rest of the selection also proves well-made. Their wines get better by the year, proof that they're on the right track.

● Cannonau di Sardegna Corona Majore Ris. '12	♟♟ 4
● Cannonau di Sardegna Sardo '13	♟♟ 3
● Keramos '11	♟ 5
○ Kyanos '15	♟ 4
○ Vermentino di Sardegna Chimera '16	♟ 4
○ Vermentino di Sardegna Sardo '16	♟ 3
● Cannonau di Sardegna Keramos Ris. '07	♟♟♟ 5
● Cannonau di Sardegna Keramos Ris. '04	♟♟♟ 4
● Cannonau di Sardegna Corona Majore '12	♀♀ 4
● Cannonau di Sardegna Corona Majore Ris. '11	♀♀ 3
○ Vermentino di Sardegna Chimera '15	♀♀ 4
○ Vermentino di Sardegna Chimera '14	♀♀ 4

Su Entu

S.DA PROV.LE KM 1,800
09025 SANLURI [CA]
TEL. +39 07093571200
www.cantinesuentu.com

CELLAR SALES
PRE-BOOKED VISITS
ANNUAL PRODUCTION 30,000 bottles
HECTARES UNDER VINE 32.00

Su Entu is owned by Sanluri entrepreneur, Salvatore Pilloni, who took a gamble on the Marmilla area, formerly a cradle of wheat and vines. He runs the winery with the help of his daughters, who deal with sales and marketing. The modern cellar was built with respect for the landscape, and dominates the vineyards. The vineyards are young so it is still early to expect much complexity at this stage, but some wines are already impressive. The range includes Cannonau and Vermentinto (both still and sparkling), as well as other local grapes used to produce the Marmilla IGT. We particularly enjoyed their Bovale, a 2015 red with bold notes of red fruit, licorice, pepper and leather. The mouth proves close-knit, with sharp tannins, and a vibrancy made possible by freshness and savoriness. The 2016 Vermentino di Sardegna and the Mediterraneo, a blend of traditional grapes, also proved outstanding.

● Bovale '15	♟♟ 3*
● Mediterraneo '15	♟♟ 3
○ Vermentino di Sardegna '16	♟♟ 3
○ Aromatico '16	♟ 3
● Cannonau di Sardegna '15	♟ 3
○ Vermentino di Sardegna + '14	♟ 4
○ Aromatico '15	♀♀ 3
● Bovale '14	♀♀ 3
● Bovale '13	♀♀ 3*
● Cannonau di Sardegna '13	♀♀ 3
● Mediterraneo '14	♀♀ 3*
○ Passito '14	♀♀ 5

Vigne Surrau

S.DA PROV.LE ARZACHENA - PORTO CERVO
07021 ARZACHENA [OT]
TEL. +39 078982933
www.vignesurrau.it

CELLAR SALES
PRE-BOOKED VISITS
ANNUAL PRODUCTION 300,000 bottles
HECTARES UNDER VINE 50.00
SUSTAINABLE WINERY

Surrau, in Arzachena, is one of the most interesting new wineries to come onto the scene in recent years. The cellar is a great example of modern architecture. It is perfectly functional for winemaking and includes a reception area ideal for tastings, cultural events and exhibitions. The first harvests focused on great Galluran reds, but the quality of Vermentino di Gallura is emerging. The result is a high-level range of wines, including two Metodo Classico sparkling wines (one from Vermentino and a rosé from Cannonau) which are made in neighboring rooms to where the original winemaking cellar was built. It was an excellent vintage for Surrau. Many of their wines impressed, starting with the Cannonau Riserva which shows how good Gallura is for reds. The 2014 Sincaru offers up aromas of cherries and roses, while the mouth proves elegant, silky and deep. Tre Bicchieri. The Sciala, which is savory, fresh and very lingering, is also outstanding. The rest of their selection proved strong, as well.

● Cannonau di Sardegna Sincaru Ris. '14	♛♛♛ 5
○ Vermentino di Gallura Sup. Sciala '16	♛♛ 5
● Cannonau di Sardegna Sincaru '15	♛♛ 5
● Surrau '15	♛♛ 4
○ Vermentino di Gallura Brut '13	♛♛ 5
○ Vermentino di Gallura Sup. Sciala V.T. '15	♛♛ 5
☉ Brut Rosé '13	♛ 5
○ Vermentino di Gallura Branu '16	♛ 3
● Surrau '09	♛♛♛ 4*
○ Vermentino di Gallura Sup. Sciala '15	♛♛♛ 5
○ Vermentino di Gallura Sup. Sciala '14	♛♛♛ 5
○ Vermentino di Gallura Sup. Sciala '13	♛♛♛ 5
○ Vermentino di Gallura Sup. Sciala '12	♛♛♛ 5

Cantina Sociale della Vernaccia

LOC. RIMEDIO
VIA ORISTANO, 6A
09170 ORISTANO
TEL. +39 078333383
www.vinovernaccia.com

CELLAR SALES
PRE-BOOKED VISITS
ANNUAL PRODUCTION 260,000 bottles
HECTARES UNDER VINE 120.00

The Cantina della Vernaccia (previously known as Cantina del Rimedio) is a small benchmark wine cooperative producing Vernaccia di Oristano and other still wines made with native varieties. In recent years the quality of their wines has increased by leaps and bounds, thanks to work done with the local vinegrowers aimed at raising the quality of the grapes delivered to the cellar. So far there have been excellent results with both the old Riserva di Vernaccia and their young and vintage wines, all of which are very much in demand with consumers. They have presented a textbook range of wines this year. At the top is their most iconic wine, a Vernaccia di Oristano with great complexity and character. The 2008 Jughissa features explosive aromas of nuts, spices, dried fruit and wilted flowers. The mouth is dry, very tangy and long with a charming, fresh unfolding of flavor. Tre Bicchieri. The reds also delivered, starting with their Nieddera Montiprama.

○ Vernaccia di Oristano Sup. Jughissa '08	♛♛♛ 3*
● Cannonau di Sardegna Maiomone '15	♛♛ 2*
● Montiprama Nieddera '14	♛♛ 2*
● Cannonau di Sardegna Corash Ris. '14	♛ 3
○ Terresinis '16	♛ 2
○ Vermentino di Sardegna Is Arutas '16	♛ 2
● Cannonau di Sardegna Corash Ris. '12	♛♛ 3
● Nieddera Montiprama '13	♛♛ 1*
○ Terresinis '14	♛♛ 2*
○ Vernaccia di Oristano Jughissa '07	♛♛ 3

Angelo Angioi

LOC. COLORAS
09079 TRESNURAGHES [OR]
TEL. +39 3409357227
saltodicoloras@gmail.com

CELLAR SALES
PRE-BOOKED VISITS
ANNUAL PRODUCTION 5,000 bottles
HECTARES UNDER VINE 2.80

○ Malvasia di Bosa Dolce Salto di Coloras '15	♟♟ 4
○ Phoenix '16	♟♟ 5
○ Vermentino di Sardegna Filicario '16	♟ 2

Tenuta Asinara

LOC. MARRITZA
GOLFO DELL'ASINARA
07037 SORSO [SS]
TEL. +39 0793402017
www.tenutaasinara.com

CELLAR SALES
PRE-BOOKED VISITS
ANNUAL PRODUCTION 70,000 bottles
HECTARES UNDER VINE 19.00

● Cannonau di Sardegna Indolente '15	♟♟ 2*
● Herculis '12	♟♟ 4
○ Cayenna '13	♟ 4
○ Vermentino di Sardegna Indolente '16	♟ 2

Atha Ruja Poderi

LOC. PRADONOS
08022 DORGALI [NU]
TEL. +39 3478693936
www.atharuja.com

CELLAR SALES
PRE-BOOKED VISITS
ANNUAL PRODUCTION 25,000 bottles
HECTARES UNDER VINE 5.00

● Cannonau di Sardegna Kuentu Ris. '12	♟♟ 5
● Muristellu '12	♟♟ 6
● Cannonau di Sardegna '13	♟ 3
● Tuluj '11	♟ 5

Audarya

S.DA ST.LE 466 KM 10,100
09040 SERDIANA [CA]
TEL. +39 070740437
www.audarya.it

CELLAR SALES
PRE-BOOKED VISITS
ANNUAL PRODUCTION 50,000 bottles
HECTARES UNDER VINE 35.00

● Cannonau di Sardegna '15	♟♟ 2*
● Monica di Sardegna '16	♟♟ 2*
○ Vermentino di Sardegna Camminera '16	♟♟ 2*
● Nuracada '15	♟ 4

Cantina Berritta

VIA KENNEDY, 108
08022 DORGALI [NU]
TEL. +39 078495372
www.cantinaberritta.it

CELLAR SALES
PRE-BOOKED VISITS
ANNUAL PRODUCTION 22,000 bottles
HECTARES UNDER VINE 11.00
SUSTAINABLE WINERY

● Cannonau di Sardegna Thurcalesu '15	♟♟ 4
● Cannonau di Sardegna Monte Tundu '14	♟ 5
● Cannonau di Sardegna Nostranu '15	♟ 3
○ Panzale '15	♟ 4

Cantina di Calasetta

VIA ROMA, 134
09011 CALASETTA [CI]
TEL. +39 078188413
www.cantinadicalasetta.it

CELLAR SALES
PRE-BOOKED VISITS
ANNUAL PRODUCTION 100,000 bottles
HECTARES UNDER VINE 300.00

● Carignano del Sulcis Piede Franco '16	♟♟ 2*
● Carignano del Sulcis Tupei '15	♟♟ 2*
● Carignano del Sulcis Àina Ris. '14	♟ 4
○ Vermentino di Sardegna Cala di Seta '16	♟ 2

Cantina delle Vigne Piero Mancini

loc. Cala Saccaia
via Madagascar, 17
07026 Olbia
tel. +39 078950717
www.pieromancini.it

CELLAR SALES
PRE-BOOKED VISITS
ANNUAL PRODUCTION 1,500,000 bottles
HECTARES UNDER VINE 100.00

Cannonau di Sardegna Falcale '15	🍷🍷 2*
Vermentino di Gallura Cucaione '16	🍷🍷 2*
Vermentino di Gallura Sup. Mancini Primo '16	🍷 4

Carboni

via Umberto 163
08036 Ortueri [NU]
tel. +39 078466213
www.vinicarboni.it

● Balente '14	🍷🍷 3
○ Galante	🍷🍷 4
○ Helios '16	🍷 3
● Mandrolisai Sup. Balente '13	🍷 3

Cantina Castiadas

loc. Olia Speciosa
09040 Castiadas [CA]
tel. +39 0709949004
www.cantinacastiadas.com

CELLAR SALES
PRE-BOOKED VISITS
ANNUAL PRODUCTION 120,000 bottles
HECTARES UNDER VINE 150.00

Cannonau di Sardegna Capo Ferrato Rei '15	🍷🍷 2*
Cannonau di Sardegna Capo Ferrato Ris. '13	🍷🍷 4
Vermentino di Sardegna Notteri '16	🍷 3

Colle Nivera

via Veneto, 14
08100 Nuoro
tel. +39 0784294037
www.collenivera.com

CELLAR SALES
PRE-BOOKED VISITS
ANNUAL PRODUCTION 60,000 bottles
HECTARES UNDER VINE 15.00

● Cannonau di Sardegna '13	🍷🍷 4
○ Vermentino di Gallura Sup. Sintesi '16	🍷 3

Ferruccio Deiana

loc. Su Leunaxi
Gialeto, 7
09040 Settimo San Pietro [CA]
tel. +39 070749117
www.ferrucciodeiana.it

CELLAR SALES
PRE-BOOKED VISITS
ANNUAL PRODUCTION 520,000 bottles
HECTARES UNDER VINE 94.00

Ajana '14	🍷🍷 6
Cannonau di Sardegna Sileno Ris. '14	🍷🍷 4
Cannonau di Sardegna Sileno '15	🍷 3
Vermentino di Sardegna Arvali '16	🍷 3

Tenute Delogu

s.da st.le Sassari-Fertilia 291 - km 22
07100 Sassari
tel. +39 3452862861
www.tenutedelogu.com

○ Vermentino di Sardegna Die '15	🍷🍷 2*
● Cannonau di Sardegna Ego '13	🍷🍷 2*
● Geo '12	🍷🍷 2*
● Ide '14	🍷 2

Vigne Deriu

LOC. SIGNORANNA
07040 CODRONGIANOS [SS]
TEL. +39 079435101
www.vignederiu.it

CELLAR SALES
PRE-BOOKED VISITS
ANNUAL PRODUCTION 35,000 bottles
HECTARES UNDER VINE 6.00

● Cannonau di Sardegna '15	🍷🍷 3
● Cannonau di Sardegna Sàbbiu Ris. '13	🍷🍷 3
● Tiu Filippu '13	🍷 5
○ Vermentino di Sardegna '16	🍷 3

Luca Gungui

C.SO VITTORIO EMANUELE, 21
08024 MAMOIADA [NU]
TEL. +39 3473320735
cantinagungui@tiscali.it

ANNUAL PRODUCTION 3,437 bottles
HECTARES UNDER VINE 2.30

● Cannonau di Sardegna Berteru '16	🍷🍷 6
● Cannonau di Sardegna Berteru Ris. '15	🍷🍷 8

Tenuta l'Ariosa

LOC. PREDDA NIEDDA SUD
S.DA 15
07100 SASSARI
TEL. +39 079261905
www.lariosa.it

ANNUAL PRODUCTION 40,000 bottles
HECTARES UNDER VINE 9.00

● Cannonau di Sardegna Assolo '15	🍷🍷 3
○ Vermentino di Sardegna Arenu '16	🍷🍷 3
○ Vermentino di Sardegna Galatea '16	🍷 3

Antonella Ledà d'Ittiri

FRAZ. FERTILIA
LOC. ARENOSU, 23
07100 ALGHERO [SS]
TEL. +39 079999263
www.margallo.it

CELLAR SALES
PRE-BOOKED VISITS
ANNUAL PRODUCTION 18,000 bottles
HECTARES UNDER VINE 5.50
SUSTAINABLE WINERY

● Ginjol '16	🍷🍷
● Cigala Cagnulari '16	🍷
● Margallò '16	🍷
○ Vermentino di Sardegna Vi Marì '16	🍷

Li Duni

LOC. LI PARISI
07030 BADESI [OT]
TEL. +39 0799144480
www.cantinaliduni.com

CELLAR SALES
PRE-BOOKED VISITS
ANNUAL PRODUCTION 40,000 bottles
HECTARES UNDER VINE 25.00

● Tajanu '12	🍷🍷 4
● Nalboni '15	🍷 2

Pietro Lilliu

VIA SARDEGNA, 13
09020 USSARAMANNA [VS]
TEL. +39 3407591144
www.cantinalilliu.it

CELLAR SALES
PRE-BOOKED VISITS
ANNUAL PRODUCTION 20,000 bottles
HECTARES UNDER VINE 4.00
SUSTAINABLE WINERY

● Biazzu '14	🍷🍷
○ Malvasia di Cagliari Mendula '12	🍷🍷

Nuraghe Crabioni

LOC. LU CRABIONI
07037 SORSO [SS]
TEL. +39 3468292457
www.nuraghecrabioni.com

CELLAR SALES
PRE-BOOKED VISITS
ANNUAL PRODUCTION 60,000 bottles
HECTARES UNDER VINE 35.00
SUSTAINABLE WINERY

● Cannonau di Sardegna '15	♟♟	3
○ Sussinku '16	♟	3
○ Vermentino di Sardegna '16	♟	3
○ Vermentino di Sardegna Kanimari '16	♟	3

Olianas

LOC. PORRUDDU
08030 GERGEI [CA]
TEL. +39 0558300411
www.olianas.it

CELLAR SALES
PRE-BOOKED VISITS
ANNUAL PRODUCTION 120,000 bottles
HECTARES UNDER VINE 19.00
VITICULTURE METHOD Certified Organic
SUSTAINABLE WINERY

● Cannonau di Sardegna '16	♟♟	3
● Cannonau di Sardegna Ris. '14	♟♟	4
○ Vermentino di Sardegna '16	♟	3

Cantina Cooperativa di Oliena

VIA NUORO, 112
08025 OLIENA [NU]
TEL. +39 0784287509
www.cantinasocialeoliena.it

ANNUAL PRODUCTION 300,000 bottles
HECTARES UNDER VINE 180.00

● Cannonau di Sardegna Cl. Nepente di Oliena Irilai '13	♟♟	2*
● Cannonau di Sardegna Nepente di Oliena '15	♟♟	2*

Cantine di Orgosolo

VIA ILOLE
08027 ORGOSOLO [NU]
TEL. +39 0784403096
www.cantinediorgosolo.it

CELLAR SALES
PRE-BOOKED VISITS
RESTAURANT SERVICE
ANNUAL PRODUCTION 17,000 bottles
HECTARES UNDER VINE 16.00
VITICULTURE METHOD Certified Organic

● Cannonau di Sardegna Neale '15	♟♟	3
● Cannonau di Sardegna Urùlu '15	♟	4

Orro

VIA G. VERDI
09070 TRAMATZA [OR]
TEL. +39 3477526617
www.famigliaorro.it

CELLAR SALES
PRE-BOOKED VISITS
ACCOMMODATION
ANNUAL PRODUCTION 15,000 bottles
HECTARES UNDER VINE 5.00

○ Vernaccia di Oristano '10	♟♟	5
● Don Aldo '14	♟	2
○ Tzinnigas '16	♟	2

Poderi Parpinello

LOC. JANNA DE MARE S.DA ST.LE 291
07100 SASSARI
TEL. +39 3465915194
www.poderiparpinello.it

ANNUAL PRODUCTION 110,000 bottles
HECTARES UNDER VINE 20.00

● Cannonau di Sardegna Ris. '14	♟♟	4
○ Vermentino di Sardegna Sassantaquattro '16	♟♟	4
● Cagnulari '15	♟	4

Giuliana Puligheddu

P.ZZA COLLEGIO, 5
08025 OLIENA [NU]
TEL. +39 0784287734
www.agricolapuligheddu.it

CELLAR SALES
PRE-BOOKED VISITS
ANNUAL PRODUCTION 5,000 bottles
HECTARES UNDER VINE 3.00
VITICULTURE METHOD Certified Organic
SUSTAINABLE WINERY

● Cannonau di Sardegna Cupanera '15	🍷🍷 5

Pusole

LOC. PERDA 'E CUBA
08040 LOTZORAI [OG]
TEL. +39 3334047219
roberto.pusole@gmail.com

CELLAR SALES
PRE-BOOKED VISITS
ACCOMMODATION
ANNUAL PRODUCTION 10,000 bottles
HECTARES UNDER VINE 7.50
SUSTAINABLE WINERY

● Cannonau di Sardegna Cl. Sa Scala '14	🍷🍷 3*
● Cannonau di Sardegna '16	🍷🍷 3
○ Karammare '16	🍷 3
○ Vermentino di Sardegna '16	🍷 5

Quartomoro di Sardegna

VIA DINO POLI, 31
09092 ARBOREA [OR]
TEL. +39 3467643522
www.quartomoro.it

CELLAR SALES
PRE-BOOKED VISITS
ANNUAL PRODUCTION 35,000 bottles
HECTARES UNDER VINE 2.50

○ Vermentino di Sardegna VRM Memorie di Vite '14	🍷🍷 4
● BVL Memorie di Vite '15	🍷🍷 4
○ Vermentino di Sardegna Orriu '14	🍷🍷 3

Tenute Rossini

S.DA ST.LE 127 SETTENTRIONALE SARDA, 4
07030 LAERRU [SS]
TEL. +39 3405363814

ANNUAL PRODUCTION 14,000 bottles
HECTARES UNDER VINE 3.00

● Rosso Rossini '15	🍷🍷 3
● Uttìu '15	🍷🍷 3
● Cannonau di Sardegna Rolù '15	🍷 3

Agricola Soi

VIA CUCCHESI, 1
08030 NURAGUS [CA]
TEL. +39 0782818262
www.agricolasoi.it

CELLAR SALES
PRE-BOOKED VISITS
ANNUAL PRODUCTION 12,000 bottles
HECTARES UNDER VINE 4.00

● Cannonau di Sardegna '13	🍷🍷 3
● Lun '14	🍷 3

Gianluca Strano

LOC. S'OREGHINA
07022 BERCHIDDA [OT]
TEL. +39 3403654871

ANNUAL PRODUCTION 10,000 bottles
HECTARES UNDER VINE 1.30

○ Vermentino di Gallura Strano '16	🍷🍷 3

Cantina Tani

loc. Conca Sa Raighina, 2
07020 Monti [SS]
Tel. +39 3386432055
www.cantinatani.it

CELLAR SALES
PRE-BOOKED VISITS
ACCOMMODATION AND RESTAURANT SERVICE
ANNUAL PRODUCTION 65,000 bottles
HECTARES UNDER VINE 15.00

● Cannonau di Sardegna Donosu '16	🍷🍷 3
○ Vermentino di Gallura Sup. Taerra '16	🍷🍷 3
● Serranu '14	🍷 4
○ Vermentino di Gallura Meoru '16	🍷 3

Cantina Tondini

loc. San Leonardo
07023 Calangianus [OT]
Tel. +39 079661359
www.cantinatondini.it

CELLAR SALES
PRE-BOOKED VISITS
ANNUAL PRODUCTION 80,000 bottles
HECTARES UNDER VINE 25.00

○ Vermentino di Gallura Karagnanj '16	🍷🍷 3
○ Vermentino di Gallura Sup. Katala '15	🍷🍷 4
Siddaju '13	🍷 5

Cantina del Vermentino

via San Paolo, 2
07020 Monti [SS]
Tel. +39 078944012
www.vermentinomonti.it

CELLAR SALES
PRE-BOOKED VISITS
ANNUAL PRODUCTION 2,000,000 bottles
HECTARES UNDER VINE 500.00

Cannonau di Sardegna Tamara '15	🍷🍷 3
Vermentino di Gallura Aghilóia Oro '16	🍷🍷 3
Vermentino di Gallura Funtanaliras Oro '16	🍷 3
Vermentino di Gallura S'Éleme Oro '16	🍷 2

Tenute Gregu

loc. Giuncheddu
07023 Calangianus [OT]
Tel. +39 3480364383
www.tenutegregu.com

ANNUAL PRODUCTION 50,000 bottles
HECTARES UNDER VINE 30,00

○ Vermentino di Gallura Sup. Selenu '15	🍷🍷 3
○ Vermentino di Gallura Rias '16	🍷 3

Cantina Trexenta

v.le Piemonte, 40
09040 Senorbì [CA]
Tel. +39 0709808863
www.cantinatrexenta.it

CELLAR SALES
PRE-BOOKED VISITS
ANNUAL PRODUCTION 1,000,000 bottles
HECTARES UNDER VINE 350.00

● Cannonau di Sardegna Goimajor '15	🍷🍷 2*
● Cannonau di Sardegna Tanca su Conti Ris. '14	🍷🍷 4
● Monica di Sardegna Tancas '14	🍷 2

Vigne Rada

fraz. Monte Pedrosu
reg. Guardia Grande, 12
07041 Alghero [SS]
Tel. +39 3274259136
wwww.vignerada.com

ANNUAL PRODUCTION 28,000 bottles
HECTARES UNDER VINE 7.00

● Cannonau di Sardegna Riviera '15	🍷🍷 5
○ Vermentino di Sardegna Stria '16	🍷 5

INDEXES
wineries in alphabetical order
wineries by region

WINERIES IN ALPHABETICAL ORDER

Bambinuto	853	Bindella	560
Bandini - Villa Pomona	557	La Bioca	179
Banfi Piemonte	43	Biondi Santi - Tenuta Il Greppo	561
Erik Banti	687	BioVio	200
Baracchi	557	Biscaris	933
Barbacarlo - Lino Maga	259	Bisceglia	868
Barbaglia	44	Bisci	715
Le Barbaterre	517	Tenuta di Biserno	688
Cantina Sociale Barbera dei Sei Castelli	178	Bisi	223
Barberani	757	Bisol	350
Osvaldo Barberis	44	Bisson	212
Fattoria dei Barbi	558	Tenuta di Blasig	506
Barboglio De Gaioncelli	259	Blason	506
Stefania Barbot	853	Blazic	507
Baricci	558	Bocale	758
Barollo	348	Boccadigabbia	716
Tenuta Baron Di Pauli	307	Boccadoro	260
Baron Widmann	338	Boccella	853
Cantine Barone	853	Enzo Boglietti	49
Barone Cornacchia	798	Bolla	350
Barone de Cles	287	Bolognani	301
Tenute Barone di Valforte	815	Cantina Bolzano	308
Barone di Villagrande	910	Bonaldi - Cascina del Bosco	260
Barone Pizzini	220	Samuele Heydi Bonanini	200
Barone Ricasoli	559	Bonavita	912
Barraco	933	Bondi - Cascina Banaia	49
Fattoria di Basciano	687	Cantine Bondonor	212
Basile	559	Bonfadini	260
Basilisco	862	Marco Bonfante	179
Bastianich	437	Gilberto Boniperti	50
Tenuta Bastonaca	911	Castello Bonomi	224
Batasiolo	45	Bonotto delle Tezze	427
Fabrizio Battaglino	178	Bonsegna	889
Battaglio	178	Tenuta Bonzara	544
Le Battistelle	348	Tenuta Borgo Conventi	507
Bava	45	Borgo dei Posseri	288
Bea - Merenda con Corvi	178	Borgo delle Oche	438
Beato Bartolomeo da Breganze	426	Borgo di Colloredo	820
Pietro Beconcini	560	Borgo La Gallinaccia	260
Lorenzo Begali	349	Borgo Magredo	507
Bel Colle	46	Borgo Maragliano	50
Belisario	715	Borgo Paglianetto	716
Tenuta Bellafonte	757	Borgo Salcetino	561
Bellaveder	287	Borgo San Daniele	438
Bellavista	221	Borgo Savaian	439
Antonio Bellicoso	178	Borgo Stajnbech	351
Bellussi Spumanti	427	Borgodangelo	853
Tenuta Beltrame	437	F.lli Serio & Battista Borgogno	179
Benanti	911	Giacomo Borgogno & Figli	51
Benedetti & Grigi	777	Borgoluce	351
Bera	46	Borin Vini & Vigne	352
Cinzia Bergaglio	47	Boroli	51
Nicola Bergaglio	47	Il Borro	562
Cantina Sociale Bergamasca	259	F.lli Bortolin	427
Bergamini	427	Bortolomiol	352
Bergmannhof	338	Cav. Emiro Bortolusso	439
F.lli Berlucchi	221	Carlo Boscaini	353
Guido Berlucchi & C.	222	La Boscaiola	260
Berretta	688	Poderi Boscarelli	562
Cantina Berritta	960	Francesco Boschis	52
Berry and Berry	212	Agostino Bosco	52
Bersano	48	Nestore Bosco	799
Cantina Bersi Serlini	222	Tenute Bosco	912
Guido Berta	48	Vitivinicola Anna Bosco	853
Bertagna	260	Bosco de' Medici	854
Stefano Berti	518	Rosco del Merlo	353
Le Bertille	688	Bosco Longhino	261
Bessererhof - Otmar Mair	307	Bosio	224
F.lli Bettini	223	Bossi Fedrigotti	288
BiancaVigna	349	Bove	815
Bianchi	282	Giacomo Boveri	179
Maria Donata Bianchi	199	Luigi Boveri	53
Tenuta di Bibbiano	688	Gianfranco Bovio	53
Bigi	777	Alfredo Bracco	507

WINERIES BY REGION